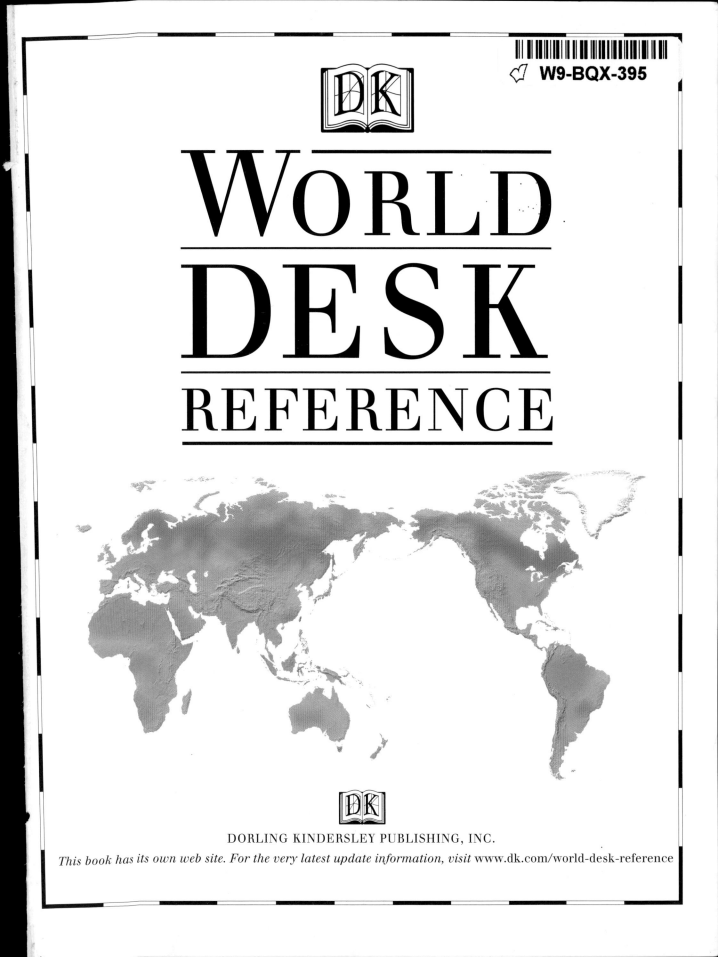

W9-BQX-395

WORLD
DESK
REFERENCE

DORLING KINDERSLEY PUBLISHING, INC.

This book has its own web site. For the very latest update information, visit www.dk.com/world-desk-reference

A DORLING KINDERSLEY PUBLISHING BOOK
www.dk.com

FOR THE THIRD EDITION

EDITOR-IN-CHIEF
Andrew Heritage

SENIOR MANAGING ART EDITOR
Philip Lord

PROJECT EDITOR
Wim Jenkins

PROJECT DESIGNERS
David Douglas, Carol Ann Davis

EDITORIAL UPDATE FOR THIRD EDITION
Cambridge International Reference on Current Affairs (CIRCA)

ADDITIONAL DESIGN ASSISTANCE
Nicola Liddiard, Tony Cutting

READERS
Ailsa Heritage, Lisa Thomas

CARTOGRAPHERS
Tom Coulson, Alka Ranger, Dale Buckton, John Plumer

ADDITIONAL EDITORIAL ASSISTANCE
Zoe Ellinson, Sophie Park, Jo Russ, Sam Atkinson

PICTURE RESEARCH
Louise Thomas

DATABASE MANAGER
Simon Lewis

INDEX GAZETTEER
Julia Lynch

DATABASE
Sophie Park, Jo Russ

PRODUCTION
Gavin Bradshaw

SYSTEMS COORDINATOR
Phil Rowles

CTP PRINTING
Graficas Estella, Spain

DORLING KINDERSLEY CARTOGRAPHY

EDITORIAL DIRECTION
Andrew Heritage

ART DIRECTOR
Chez Picthall

PROJECT CARTOGRAPHERS
Caroline Bowie, Ruth Duxbury,
James Mills-Hicks, John Plumer, Julie Turner

MANAGING EDITOR
Ian Castello-Cortes

MANAGING ART EDITOR
Philip Lord

CARTOGRAPHERS
James Anderson, Roger Bullen, Tony Chambers,
Jan Clark, Martin Darlison, Claire Ellam, Julia Lunn,
Michael Martin, Peter Winfield, Claudine Zante

PROJECT EDITORS
Debra Clapson, Catherine Day, Jo Edwards, Jane Oliver

PROJECT DESIGNERS
Martin Biddulph, Scott David,
Yahya El-Droubie, Karen Gregory

EDITORS
Alastair Dougall, Ailsa Heritage, Nicholas Kynaston,
Susan Turner, Chris Whitwell, Elizabeth Wyse

DESIGNERS
Rhonda Fisher, Nicola Liddiard,
Katy Wall

PICTURE RESEARCH
Alison McKittrick, Sarah Moule, Christine Rista

ADDITIONAL EDITORIAL ASSISTANCE
Louise Keane, Caroline Lucas, Laura Porter,
Crispian Martin St. Valery, Sally Wood, Ulrike Fritz-Weltz

ADDITIONAL DESIGN ASSISTANCE
Paul Bayliss, Carol Ann Davis,
Adam Dobney, Kenny Laurenson,
Paul Williams

DATABASE MANAGER
Simon Lewis

INDEX GAZETTEER
Margaret Hynes, Barbara Nash,
Jayne Parsons, Janet Smy

READERS
Jane Bruton, Reg Grant, Ann Kramer, Lesley Riley

Published in the United States
by Dorling Kindersley Publishing Inc.
95 Madison Avenue, New York, New York 10016

Previously published as the World Reference Atlas

First American Edition 1994
10 9 8 7 6 5 4
Second Edition 1996. Revised 1998 Third Edition (revised) 2000.

A catalog record is available from the Library of Congress

ISBN: 0-7894-4894-7

FOREWORD

T HIS ATLAS is presented to the public in the full knowledge that the world is in a state of continual flux. Political fashions and personalities come and go, while the ebb and flow of peoples and ideas across the face of the planet create constant shifts in the cultural landscape. All the material assembled for this Atlas has been researched from the most up-to-date and authoritative sources; our team of consultants and contributors, designers, editors and cartographers have endeavoured not only to explain the meaning of this material, to place it in a useful and clear context, but also to present it in a way which has a lasting value and relevance, regardless of the turmoil of daily events. This Third Edition has been completely revised and updated, to reflect the global changes of the past few years, and to include the latest statistical data, many additional fields of information, and over sixty new photographs.

The publishers would like to thank the many consultants and contributors whose diligence, perseverance and attention to detail made this book possible.

GENERAL CONSULTANTS
Anthony Goldstone, Senior Editor Asia-Pacific, *The Economist* Intelligence Unit, London
Professor Jack Spence, Director of Studies, The Royal Institute of International Affairs, London

REGIONAL CONSULTANTS

ASIA
Anthony Goldstone, London

USA
Michael Elliot, Diplomatic Editor, *Newsweek*, Washington DC

AFRICA
James Hammill, Lecturer in African Politics,
University of Leicester
Kaye Whiteman, Editor-in-Chief,
West Africa Magazine, London

EUROPE
John Ardagh, London
Rory Clarke, Senior Editor Europe,
The Economist Intelligence Unit, London
Charles Powell, Centre for European Studies,
St Antony's College, Oxford

RUSSIA AND CIS
Martin McCauley, Senior Lecturer, School of Slavonic
and East European Studies, University of London

MIDDLE EAST
John Whelan, Ex Editor-in-Chief, *Middle East Economic Digest*

CENTRAL AND SOUTH AMERICA
Nick Caistor, Producer, Latin American Section,
BBC World Service

PACIFIC
Jim Boutilier, Professor in History,
Royal Roads Military College, Victoria, Canada

CARIBBEAN
Canute James, *The Financial Times*, Kingston, Jamaica

CONTRIBUTORS

Janice Bell, School of Slavonic and East European Studies, University of London
Gerry Bourke, Asia Correspondent, *The Guardian*, Islamabad
Vincent Cable, Director, International Economics Programme
P K Clark, MA, Former Chief Map Research Officer, Ministry of Defence
Ken Davies, Senior Editor, *The Economist* Intelligence Unit, London
Roger Dunn, Analyst, Control Risks Group, London
Aidan Foster-Carter, Senior Lecturer in Sociology, University of Leeds
Professor Murray Forsyth, Centre for Federal Studies, University of Leicester
Natasha Franklin, School of Slavonic and East European Studies, London
Adam Hannestad, *Blomberg Business News*, Copenhagen
Peter Holden, *The Economist* Research Department, London
Tim Jones, Knight Ritter, Brussels
Angella Johnstone, Home Affairs Correspondent, *The Guardian,* London
Oliver Keserü, International Chamber of Commerce, Paris
Robert Macdonald, *The Economist* Intelligence Unit
William Mader, Former Europe Bureau Chief, *Time Magazine*, Washington DC
Professor Brian Matthews, Institute of Commonwealth Studies, London
Nick Middleton, Oriel College, Oxford
Professor Mya Maung, Department of Finance, Boston College, Massachusetts
Judith Nordby, Leeds University
Simon Orme, London
Professor Richard Overy, Department of History, King's College, London
Steve Percy, East Asia Service, BBC World Service

Douglas Rimmer, Honorary Senior Research Fellow,
Centre for West African Studies, University of Birmingham
Donna Rispoli, Linacre College, Oxford
Ian Rodger, *The Financial Times*, Zürich
The Royal Institute of International Affairs, London
Struan Simpson, St. James Research, London
Julie Smith, Brasenose College, Oxford
Elizabeth Spencer, London
Michiel Van Kuyen, Erasmus University, Rotterdam
Steven Whitefield, Pembroke College, Oxford
Georgina Wilde, Regional Director, Asia-Pacific,
The Economist Intelligence Unit, London
H P Willmott, Visiting Professor,
Dept. of Military Strategy & Operations,
The National War College, Washington DC
Andrew Wilson, Sydney Sussex College, Cambridge
Tom Wingfield, *Reuters*, Bangkok
The World Conservation Monitoring Centre, Cambridge

Database research for Third Edition:
Cambridge International Reference on Current Affairs (CIRCA)
Roger East, Rosemary Payne, Catherine Jagger,
Carolyn Postgate,Philippa Youngman

CONTENTS

1
WORLD FACTFILE

2
THE NATIONS
OF THE WORLD

OVERSEAS TERRITORIES & DEPENDENCIES

3

INDEX ~ GAZETTEER

> ── END PAPERS ──
> KEY TO SYMBOLS, ICONS AND
> ABBREVIATIONS USED IN THE ATLAS

KEY TO CHARTS AND ICONS

ICONS AND TREND INDICATORS vary. Not all variations are shown in the key below, but where they do occur the symbols have been "stacked".

COUNTRY PROFILES

1952 Date of country's independence, or formation.

CLIMATE

Indication of the climatic types and zones found in each country.

Statistics are given for the national capital. They represent maximum summer and minimum winter averages.

Average daily temperature — Rainfall
°C/°F / cm/in

TRANSPORTATION

Indicates on which side of the road vehicles are driven in each country.

The country's principal international airport with annual passenger numbers.

Total size of national merchant or cargo fleet.

THE TRANSPORTATION NETWORK
National communications infrastructure given in kilometres and miles.

Extent of national paved road network

Extent of motorways, freeways or major national highways

Extent of commercial rail network

Extent of inland waterways navigable by commercial craft

TOURISM

The ratio of foreign visitors to population.

Number of visitors per year, including business travellers.

Indicators showing trend in recent visitor numbers (up/level/down).

Uruguay 33%	
Chile 15%	
Brazil 13%	
Paraguay 8%	
USA 7%	
Other 24%	

% of total arrivals

The state of each nation's tourism is explained, with reasons given when there is no significant tourist industry. The chart shows the percentage of total visitors by country of origin.

PEOPLE

An easy indication of the population density in each country (high/medium/low).

Main languages spoken, in descending order of importance.

Population density. This is an average over the whole country.

The pie chart proportions show the religious affiliations of those who profess a belief.

This pie chart illustrates the ethnic origin of the country's population.

88% **12%**

This graph represents the proportion of the population living in urban areas (grey) and rural areas (green).

Female	Age	Male
1%	81–100	0.5%
6.5%	61–80	5.1%
10.3%	41–60	10%
14.1%	21–40	14.1%
18.9%	0–20	19.5%

% of population by age group

This chart shows the breakdown of the population by age groupings, providing an interesting insight into the country's demography.

POLITICS

Indicates the existence of full multiparty, democratic elections.

Dates of last and next legislative elections for Upper (U.) and Lower (L.) Houses.

Name of head of state. In many cases this is a nominal position and does not indicate that this is the country's most powerful person.

A graphic representation of the political make-up of the country's government, based on each party's showing at the last election. Where there are two houses, the most important elected body is shown first.

Chamber of Deputies 257 seats
10% Frepaso
53% PJ — 27% UCR — 10% Other

PJ = Justicialist Party (Peronists) UCR = Radical Civic Union
Frepaso = National Solidarity Front MPF = Fueguino Popular Movement MPN = Neuquino Popular Movement
Other = Movement for Dignity and Independence (Modin) and Union of the Democratic Centre (UCeD)

Senate 72 seats
54% PJ — 25% UCR — 3% MPF — 3% MPN — 15% Others

WORLD AFFAIRS

Indication of membership of the UN (United Nations), and date of entry.

Comm Abbreviations indicate membership of international organizations.

Non-membership of additional international organizations.

AID

Indication as to which countries are aid givers (donors), or aid recipients.

The amount of net international aid given or received is shown in US$. Undisclosed military aid is not included.

Symbols indicate whether aid payments or receipts are rising, level or declining.

DEFENSE

An indication of the status of conscription and mandatory military service.

The defense budget, the country's annual expenditure (in US$) on arms and military personnel.

Symbols indicate if the trend in defense spending is rising, level or declining.

THE ARMED FORCES
Icons represent the main branches of the national armed forces.

Army: equipment and personnel

Navy: equipment and personnel

Airforce: equipment and personnel

Nuclear capability: armaments

ECONOMICS

An indication of the average rate of inflation per annum, over the past decade.

Gross National Product (GNP) – the total value of goods and services produced by a country.

Exchange rates against the US$ over the last year. Some currencies are too volatile for a useful figure to be given.

1847 Date when the country's current borders were established.

Aug 2 National Day

GB Vehicle registration plate

+3 Time zone(s) of country (hours plus or minus from GMT)

+44 International telephone Dialling Code

.de Internet country identifying code

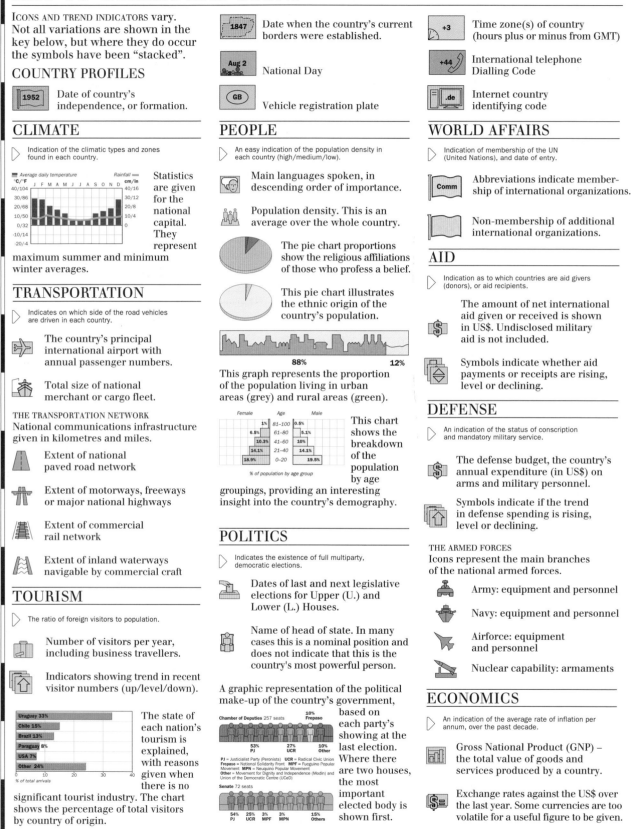

❏ World GNP Ranking	24th
❏ GNP per Capita	$24,388
❏ Balance of Payments	$2.2bn
❏ Inflation	5.6%
❏ Unemployment	10.6%

The score cards are intended to give a broad picture of the country's economy. Gross National Product (GNP), unlike GDP, includes income from investments and businesses held abroad. Balance of payments is the difference between a country's payments to and receipts from abroad.

This graph shows year-on-year variations in GDP and consumer prices.

This pie chart gives a broad picture of the country's principal import trading partners.

This pie chart gives a broad picture of the country's principal export trading partners.

RESOURCES

 Indicates the power output of the combined national electricity generating sources (in Kilowatts).

 Oil produced in barrels per day (b/d). Refining capacity, oil reserves and other fossil fuels are given where applicable.

Estimated livestock resources.

Main mineral reserves are listed in descending order of economic importance.

Fish catch per year (where fishing is a major industry).

Hydro 42% (28.1bn kwh)	
Combustion 46% (30.7bn kwh)	
Nuclear 12% (8.3bn kwh)	
Other 0%	

0   20   40   60   80   100

% of total generation by type

Percentages of the different energy sources used for the generation of electricity are represented graphically ("Combustion" indicates the burning of fossil fuels, wood etc.). An account of the country's resource base is given in the text.

ENVIRONMENT

▷ Indication of the the involvement of Green parties (environmentally-led political parties), in national government.

Percentage of land which is protected or conserved by law. Protection is often only theoretical.

Environmental Consumption Pressure Index – based on a WWF report (high/medium/low).

ENVIRONMENTAL TREATIES
National signatory to international environmental treaties.

Ramsar: (wetlands)
 Montreal Protocol: (CFC emissions)

CITES: (endangered species)
CBD: (biological diversity)

Basel: (hazardous wastes)
Kyoto: (greenhouse gases)

MEDIA

▷ Indicates the average rates of television ownership across the country.

Low, or no political censorship exists in national media.

Partial political censorship exists in national media.

Total political censorship exists in national media.

PUBLISHING AND BROADCAST MEDIA
National broadcast and print media, by size and ownership.

Main national newspapers

Television stations: state-owned/independent

Radio: state-owned/ independent

CRIME

▷ An Indication of the status of capital punishment and the death penalty; either used, or not used.

Prison population statistics

 Symbols show general trend in crime figures.

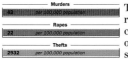

This section records official crime figures only. Reported statistics are normally lower than the actual figures.

CHRONOLOGY

Beginning at a significant date in the recent history of the country, the outline chronology continues through to the present day, and highlights key dates and turning points.

EDUCATION

▷ Displays the age at which children are legally required to attend school until.

Literacy rate. UNESCO defines as literate anyone who can read and write a short statement.

The number of students in tertiary education, with the percentage enrolment among 20–24-year-olds.

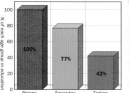

This graph shows the percentages of each age group in education. Primary is up to age 11; secondary is age 11–16/18; tertiary is expressed as a percentage of 20–24-year-olds.

HEALTH

▷ An indication of the existence of health services and benefits provided by the state.

Ratio of doctors per head of population is given as a national average.

Major causes of death are listed.

SPENDING

▷ Indicates the trend in GNP per capita over the previous decade – either showing an increase, or stability (no increase).

Levels of car ownership (per 1,000 head of population)

Rates of telephone connectivity (per 1,000 head of population)

Defense 1.7%	
Education 4.5%	
Health 2.5%	

0   5   10   15   20   25
Defense, Health, Education spending as % of GDP

Percentage of the country's GDP that is spent on defense, education and health.

WORLD RANKING

Schooling, educational attainment and human development rankings are based on the UN Human Development Index (which covers 174 countries).

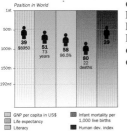

SOURCES OF STATISTICAL DATA USED IN THIS BOOK

Airports Council International

Amnesty International

Automobile Association (AA)

Cambridge International Reference on Current Affairs (CIRCA)

Commonwealth Secretariat:
Small States Economic Review and Basic Statistics

Convention on International Trade in Endangered Species (CITES)

Dorling Kindersley

Europa World Yearbook

European Bank for Reconstruction and Development (EBRD)

Financial Times

Fischer Weltalmanach

Food and Agriculture Organization (FAO)

International Atomic Energy Agency (IAEA)

International Institute for Strategic Studies (IISS):
The Military Balance

International Labor Organization (ILO):
World Labor Report

International Monetary Fund (IMF):
Balance of Payments Statistics Yearbook,
Direction of Trade Statistics Yearbook, Government

Financial Statistics Yearbook,
International Financial Statistics,
World Economic Outlook

International Road Federation

International Union for Conservation of Nature (IUCN)

International Union of Railways

INTERPOL International Crime Statistics

Lloyd's Register of Shipping

Organization for Economic Cooperation Development (OECD):
Economic surveys

OECD Development Assistance Committee (DAC):
Development Cooperation

Organization of Petroleum Exporting Countries (OPEC)

Royal Automobile Club (RAC)

United Nations Demographic Yearbook

United Nations Energy Statistics Yearbook

United Nations Industrial Commodity Statistics Yearbook

United Nations International Trade Statistics Yearbook

United Nations Statistical Yearbook

United Nations Statistical Yearbook of Asia and the Pacific

United Nations Children's Fund (UNICEF)

United Nations Development Programme (UNDP):
Human Development Report

United Nations Educational, Scientific and Cultural Organization (UNESCO): Statistical Yearbook

United Nations Environment Programme (UNEP)

United Nations Population Fund (UNFPA):
The State of World Population

United States Central Intelligence Agency (CIA)

World Bank: World Development Indicators,
World Development Report, World Bank Atlas

World Conservation Monitoring Centre (WCMC):
Biodiversity Data Sourcebook

World Health Organization (WHO)

World Tourist Organization (WTO)

Worldwide Fund for Nature (WWF)

1

WORLD FACTFILE

THE PHYSICAL WORLD

THE EARTH'S SURFACE IS constantly being transformed: it is uplifted, folded and faulted by tectonic forces; weathered and eroded by wind, water and ice. Sometimes change is dramatic, the spectacular results of earthquakes or floods. More often it is a slow process lasting millions of years. A physical map of the world represents a snapshot of the ever-evolving architecture of the Earth. This terrain map shows the whole surface of the Earth, both above and below the sea. The size of the Earth can be measured in different ways. When taken from the Equator, the diameter of the Earth measures 12,756 km; when taken from pole to pole, the diameter measures 12,714 km. Two–thirds of the Earth's surface is covered by oceans. The landscape of the ocean floor, like the surface of the land, has been shaped by movements of the Earth's crust over millions of years to form volcanic mountain ranges, deep trenches, basins and plateaux. Ocean currents constantly redistribute warm and cold water around the world. The largest ocean in the world is the Pacific, which covers an area of over 181 million square kilometres.

GEOGRAPHICAL REGION

ice		cold desert	
tundra		tropical grassland	
needleleaf forest		tropical rainforest	
broadleaf forest		mountain	
cultivated land		submarine regions	
hot desert			

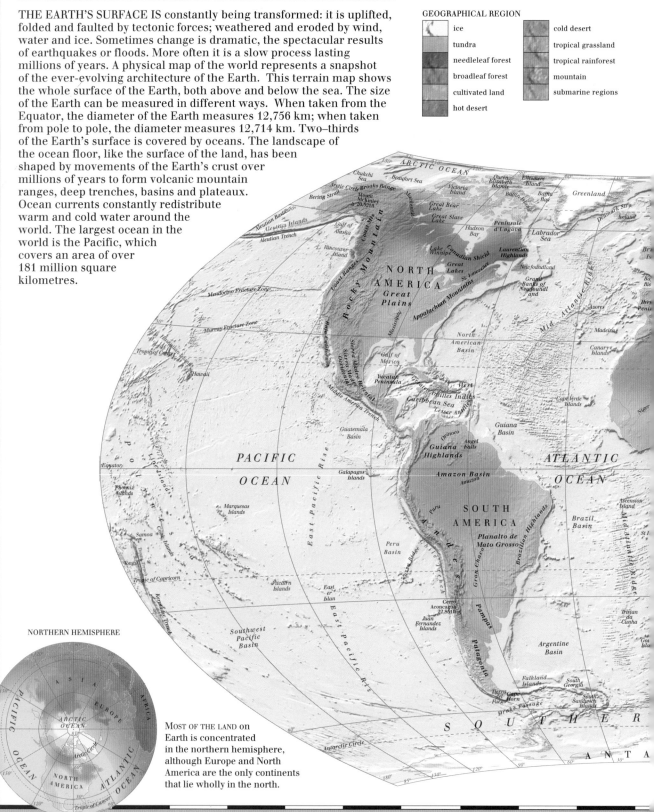

NORTHERN HEMISPHERE

MOST OF THE LAND on Earth is concentrated in the northern hemisphere, although Europe and North America are the only continents that lie wholly in the north.

THE DYNAMIC EARTH

THE EARTH'S CRUST is made up of eight major (and several minor) rigid continental and oceanic tectonic plates, which constantly move relative to one another. It is this movement which causes volcanic eruptions, earthquakes and sometimes tsunamis along the plate boundaries. The largest volcanoes formed by this process are Aconcagua in Argentina at 6,959m, (22,831 ft), and Kilimanjaro in Tanzania at 5,895m (19,450 ft), both of which are now extinct. Plate tectonics are responsible for the formation of the Himalayas – which were created by two colliding plates – and the Hawaiian Islands, created by the Pacific plate's movement over a hot spot of magma.

PHYSICAL WORLD FACTFILE

HIGHEST MOUNTAINS
1 Everest	8,848 m	(29,028 ft)
2 K2	8,611 m	(28,251 ft)
3 Kangchenjunga I	8,590 m	(28,169 ft)
4 Makalu I	8,463 m	(27,766 ft)
5 Cho Oyu	8,201 m	(26,906 ft)

LONGEST RIVERS
1 Nile	6,695 km	(4,160 mi)
2 Amazon	6,516 km	(4,048 mi)
3 Yangtze	6,380 km	(3,964 mi)
4 Mississippi /Missouri	6,019 km	(3,740 mi)
5 Ob'-Irtysh	5,570 km	(3,461 mi)

LARGEST DESERTS
1 Sahara	9,065,000 km²	(3,263,400 mi²)
2 Australian	3,750,000 km²	(1,350,000 mi²)
3 Gobi	1,295,000 km²	(466,200 mi²)
4 Arabian	750,000 km²	(270,000 mi²)
5 Sonoran	311,000 km²	(111,960 mi²)

OCEANS DOMINATE the southern hemisphere. Australia and Antarctica are the only continental landmasses that lie entirely in the south.

SOUTHERN HEMISPHERE

THE POLITICAL WORLD

THERE ARE 192 INDEPENDENT COUNTRIES in the world. With the exception of Antarctica, where territorial claims have been deferred by international treaty, every land area of the Earth's surface either belongs to, or is claimed by, one country or another. Some 60 overseas dependent territories remain, administered variously by France, Australia, Denmark, New Zealand, Norway, the UK, the USA and the Netherlands. In 1950 there were only 82 independent states in the world. Over the last half–century, national self–determination has been a riving force for many states with a history of colonialism and oppression. As more borders are created, the number of international disputes increases. In many cases, where the impetus towards independence has been religious or ethnic, disputes with minority groups have

also caused violent internal conflict. Many newly–formed states have moved peacefully towards independence, successfully establishing democracy. Dictatorship by military regime or individual despot is often the result of the internal power struggles whcih characterize the early stages in the lives of new nations.

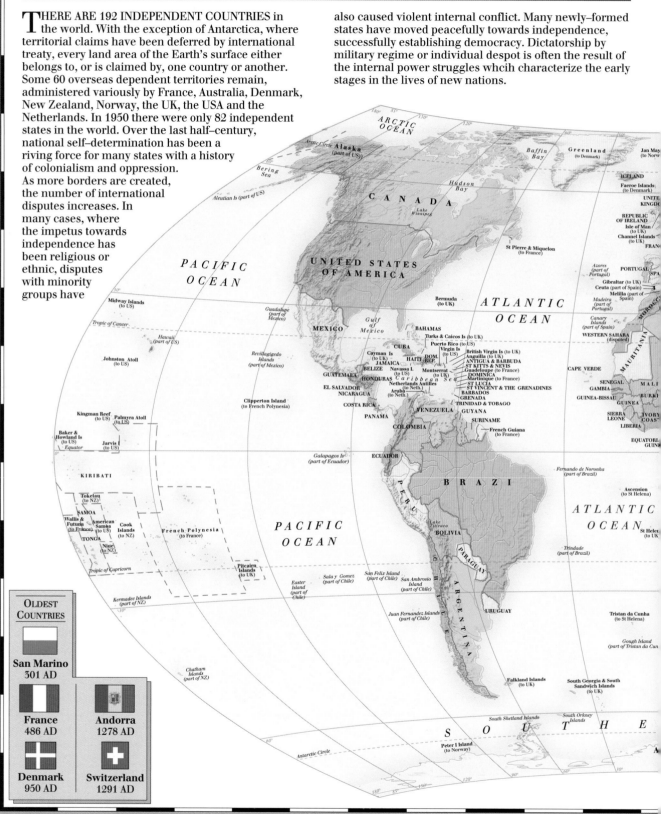

OLDEST
COUNTRIES

San Marino
301 AD

France
486 AD

Andorra
1278 AD

Denmark
950 AD

Switzerland
1291 AD

KEY

————	Full borders
··········	Disputed borders
– – – – –	Undefined borders
— — —	Extent of dependent island territories
— — —	Extent of country boundaries for island territories
Tristan da Cunha (to St Helena)	Dependent territory with self-government
Gough Island (part of Tristan da Cunha)	Territory without self-government (the state it belongs to is given in brackets)

INTERNATIONAL BORDERS

THERE ARE THREE main types of boundary between states. Full borders represent internationally recognised territorial boundaries. Undefined borders exist where no fixed boundary has been demarcated. A disputed border is where a *de facto* territorial boundary exists, which is not agreed upon or is subject to arbitration. Disputed borders exist throughout the world, including the borders between India and Pakistan, between the UK and Ireland, and within Israel.

POLITICAL FACTFILE

COUNTRIES WITH THE MOST LAND BORDERS

1 **China** *14*: (Afghanistan, Bhutan, Myanmar, India, Kazakhstan, Kyrgystan, Laos, Mongolia, Nepal, North Korea, Pakistan, Russian Federation,Tajikistan, Vietnam)

Russian Federation *14*: (Azerbaijan, Belarus, China, Estonia, Finland, Georgia, Kazakhstan, Latvia, Lithuania, Mongolia, North Korea, Norway, Poland, Ukraine)

2 **Brazil** *10*: (Argentina, Bolivia, Colombia, French Guiana, Guyana, Paraguay, Peru, Suriname, Uruguay, Venezuela)

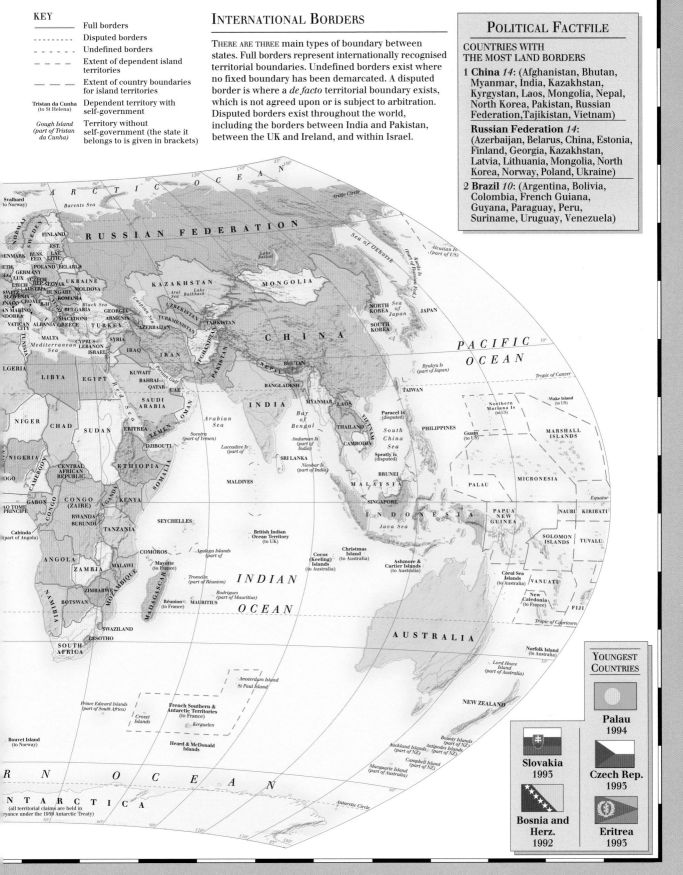

YOUNGEST COUNTRIES

Palau 1994

Slovakia 1993

Czech Rep. 1993

Bosnia and Herz. 1992

Eritrea 1993

MARS

- ⊝ *Diameter: 6,786 km*
- ⬤ *Mass: 642 m million million tons*
- ○ *Temperature: -137 to 37oC*
- ◑ *Distance from Sun: 228 million km*
- ◐ *Length of year: 1.88 years*
- ⊖ *Surface gravity: 1 kg = 0.38 kg*

EARTH

- ⊝ *Diameter: 12,756 km*
- ⬤ *Mass: 5,976 m million million tons*
- ○ *Temperature: -70 to 55°C*
- ◑ *Distance from Sun: 150 million km*
- ◐ *Length of year: 365.25 days*
- ⊖ *Surface gravity: 1kg = 1 kg*

THE EARTH

GASES SUCH AS CARBON dioxide are known as "greenhouse gases" because they allow shortwave solar radiation to enter the Earth's atmosphere, but help to stop longwave radiation from escaping. This traps heat, raising the Earth's temperature. An excess of these gases helps trap more heat and can lead to global warming.

Incoming shortwave solar radiation

Greenhouse gases prevent the escape of longwave radiation

Deflectec longwave radiation emitted by the Earth heats the atmosphere

VENUS

- ⊝ *Diameter: 12,102 km*
- ⬤ *Mass: 4,870 m million million tons*
- ○ *Temperature: 457°C*
- ◑ *Distance from Sun: 108 million km*
- ◐ *Length of year: 224.7 days*
- ⊖ *Surface gravity: 1 kg = 0.88 kg*

MERCURY

- ⊝ *Diameter: 4,878 km*
- ⬤ *Mass: 330 m million million tons*
- ○ *Temperature: -173 to 427°C*
- ◑ *Distance from Sun: 58 million km*
- ◐ *Length of year: 87.97 days*
- ⊖ *Surface gravity: 1 kg = 0.38 kg*

THE SOLAR SYSTEM

THE SOLAR SYSTEM CONSISTS of the nine major planets, their moons, the asteroids and the comets that orbit around the Sun. The Sun itself is composed of 70% hydrogen and 30% helium, and at its core nuclear fusion reactions turning hydrogen into helium produce the heat and light which make life possible on Earth. Of the planets, the inner four (Mercury, Venus, Earth and Mars) are termed terrestrial, whilst the next four (Jupiter, Saturn, Uranus and Neptune) are termed gas giants. Pluto, at the edge of the solar system, is much smaller, and made of rock. The largest natural satellite in the Solar System is Ganymede (5,262 km in diameter), which orbits around Jupiter, the largest planet. Halley's comet is the brightest comet when seen from Earth, and orbits the Sun once every 76 years. The largest asteroid is named Ceres (940 km in diameter), which is found in the large asteroid belt between Mars and Jupiter. The planet Earth is unique within the solar system (and possibly the universe), being the only planet capable of sustaining life.

JUPITER

- ⊝ *Diameter: 142,984 km*
- ⬤ *Mass: 1,900,000,000 million million million tons*
- ○ *Temperature: -153°C*
- ◑ *Distance from Sun: 778 million km*
- ◐ *Length of year: 11.86 years*
- ⊖ *Surface gravity: 1 kg = 2.53 kg*

SATURN

- **Diameter:** 120,660 km
- **Mass:** 570,000 m million million tons
- **Temperature:** -185°C
- **Distance from Sun:** 1,427 million km
- **Length of year:** 29.46 years
- **Surface gravity:** 1 kg = 1.07 kg

URANUS

- **Diameter:** 51,118 km
- **Mass:** 102,000 m million million tons
- **Temperature:** -214°C
- **Distance from Sun:** 2,870 million km
- **Length of year:** 84.01 years
- **Surface gravity:** 1 kg = 0.92 kg

MOON AND TIDES

TIDES ARE CREATED by the pull of the Sun and the Moon's gravity on the surface of the oceans. Waves are formed by wind blowing over the surface of the oceans. The highest tides occur when the Earth, the Moon and the Sun are aligned (*below left*). The lowest tides are experienced when the Sun and Moon align at right angles to one another (*below right*).

NEAR SIDE OF THE MOON

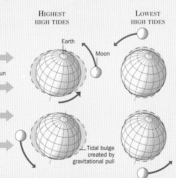

FAR SIDE OF THE MOON

HIGHEST HIGH TIDES   LOWEST HIGH TIDES

Earth

Moon

Sun

Tidal bulge created by gravitational pull

NEPTUNE

- **Diameter:** 49,528 km
- **Mass:** 13 m million million tons
- **Temperature:** -225°C
- **Distance from Sun:** 4,497 million km
- **Length of year:** 164.79 days
- **Surface gravity:** 1 kg = 1.18 kg

PLUTO

- **Diameter:** 2,300 km
- **Mass:** 13 m million million tons
- **Temperature:** -236°C
- **Distance from Sun:** 5,900 million km
- **Length of year:** 248.54 years
- **Surface gravity:** 1 kg = 0.30 kg

Timeline of Space Exploration

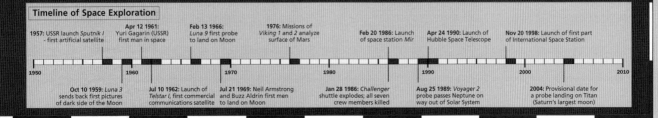

1957: USSR launch *Sputnik I* - first artificial satellite

Apr 12 1961: Yuri Gagarin (USSR) first man in space

Feb 13 1966: *Luna 9* first probe to land on Moon

1976: Missions of *Viking 1* and *2* analyze surface of Mars

Feb 20 1986: Launch of space station *Mir*

Apr 24 1990: Launch of Hubble Space Telescope

Nov 20 1998: Launch of first part of International Space Station

1950   1960   1970   1980   1990   2000   2010

Oct 10 1959: *Luna 3* sends back first pictures of dark side of the Moon

Jul 10 1962: Launch of *Telstar I*, first commercial communications satellite

Jul 21 1969: Neil Armstrong and Buzz Aldrin first men to land on Moon

Jan 28 1986: *Challenger* shuttle explodes; all seven crew members killed

Aug 25 1989: *Voyager 2* probe passes Neptune on way out of Solar System

2004: Provisional date for a probe landing on Titan (Saturn's largest moon)

THE CLIMATE

THE EARTH'S CLIMACTIC TYPES consist of stable patterns of weather conditions averaged out over a long period of time. Different climates are categorized according to particular combinations of temperature and humidity. By contrast, weather consists of short-term fluctuations in wind, temperature and humidity conditions. Different climates are determined by latitude, altitude, the prevailing wind and circulation of ocean currents. Longer-term changes in climate, such as global warming or the onset of ice ages, are punctuated by shorter–term events which comprise the day-to-day weather of a region, such as frontal depressions, hurricanes and blizzards.

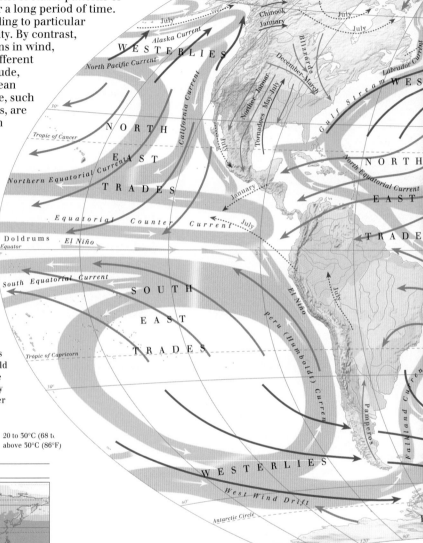

CLIMATE ZONES

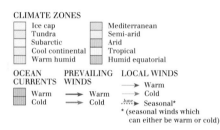

Ice cap
Tundra
Subarctic
Cool continental
Warm humid

Mediterranean
Semi-arid
Arid
Tropical
Humid equatorial

OCEAN CURRENTS

Warm
Cold

PREVAILING WINDS

→ Warm
→ Cold

LOCAL WINDS

→ Warm
→ Cold
→ Seasonal*
* (seasonal winds which can either be warm or cold)

TEMPERATURE

THE WORLD CAN BE DIVIDED into three major climactic zones, stretching like large belts across the latitudes: the tropics which are warm, the cold polar regions, and the temperate zones which lie between them. Temperature is also controlled by altitude: mountainous regions are typically colder than those at sea level.

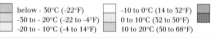

below - 30°C (-22°F)
-30 to -20°C (-22 to -4°F)
-20 to - 10°C (-4 to 14°F)

-10 to 0°C (14 to 32°F)
0 to 10°C (32 to 50°F)
10 to 20°C (50 to 68°F)

20 to 30°C (68 to
above 30°C (86°F)

AVERAGE JULY TEMPERATURE

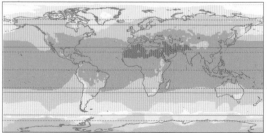

AVERAGE JANUARY TEMPERATURE

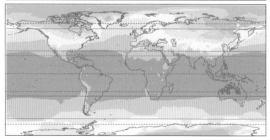

AVERAGE JULY RAINFALL

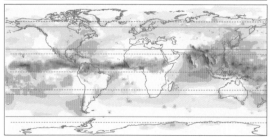

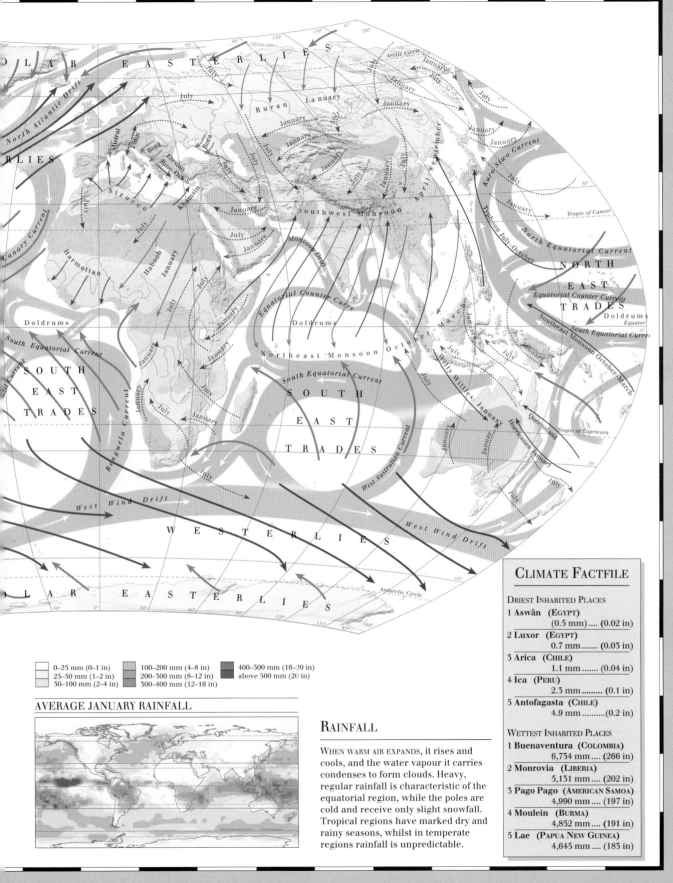

0–25 mm (0–1 in)
25–50 mm (1–2 in)
50–100 mm (2–4 in)
100–200 mm (4–8 in)
200–300 mm (8–12 in)
300–400 mm (12–16 in)
400–500 mm (16–20 in)
above 500 mm (20 in)

AVERAGE JANUARY RAINFALL

RAINFALL

WHEN WARM AIR EXPANDS, it rises and cools, and the water vapour it carries condenses to form clouds. Heavy, regular rainfall is characteristic of the equatorial region, while the poles are cold and receive only slight snowfall. Tropical regions have marked dry and rainy seasons, whilst in temperate regions rainfall is unpredictable.

CLIMATE FACTFILE

DRIEST INHABITED PLACES

1 **Aswân** (EGYPT)
(0.5 mm) .... (0.02 in)

2 **Luxor** (EGYPT)
0.7 mm .... (0.05 in)

3 **Arica** (CHILE)
1.1 mm .... (0.04 in)

4 **Ica** (PERU)
2.5 mm .... (0.1 in)

5 **Antofagasta** (CHILE)
4.9 mm ....(0.2 in)

WETTEST INHABITED PLACES

1 **Buenaventura** (COLOMBIA)
6,734 mm .... (266 in)

2 **Monrovia** (LIBERIA)
5,151 mm .... (202 in)

3 **Pago Pago** (AMERICAN SAMOA)
4,990 mm .... (197 in)

4 **Moulein** (BURMA)
4,852 mm .... (191 in)

5 **Lae** (PAPUA NEW GUINEA)
4,645 mm .... (183 in)

THE ENVIRONMENT

THE EARTH CAN BE DIVIDED into a series of biogeographical regions, or biomes – ecological communities where certain species of plant and animal co-exist within particular climatic conditions. Within these broad classifications, other factors affect the local distribution of species in each biome, such as soil richness, altitude and human activities such as urbanization, intensive agriculture and deforestation. Apart from the polar ice caps, there are few areas which have not been colonized by animals or plants over the course of the Earth's history. Because of all animals reliance on plants for survival, plants are known as primary producers, and the availability of nutrients and temperature of an area is defined as its primary productivity, which affects the quantity and type of animals which are able to live there, although cold and aridity restrict the quantity of life.

BIODIVERSITY

THE NUMBER OF PLANT AND ANIMAL SPECIES, and the range of genetic diversity within the populations of each species, make up the Earth's biodiversity. The plants and animals which are endemic to a region – that is, those which are found nowhere else in the world – are also important in determining levels of biodiversity. Human settlement and intervention have encroached on many areas of the world once rich in endemic plant and animal species. Increasing internatioonal efforts are being made to monitor and conserve the biodiversity of the Earth's remaining wild places.

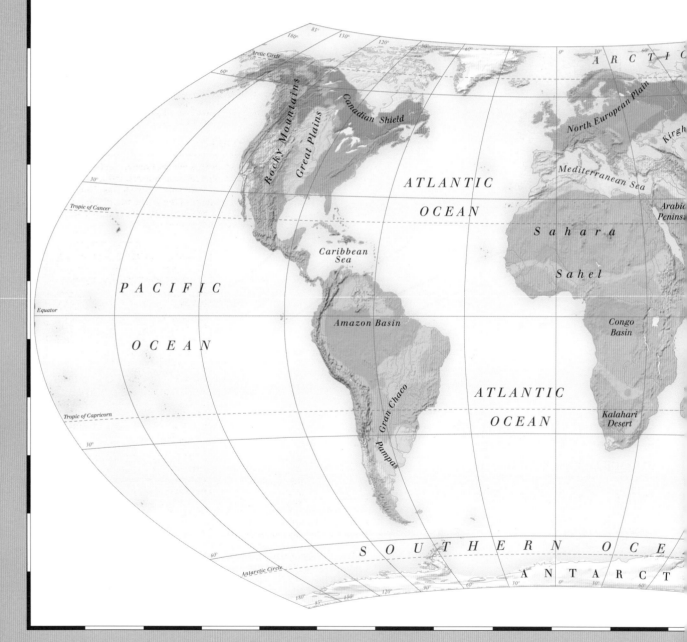

ANIMALS

Number of animal species per country

More than 2000	400–699	0–99
1000–1999	200–399	Data not available
700–999	100–199	

ANIMAL ADAPTION

THE DEGREE OF AN ANIMALS ADAPTABILITY to different climates and conditions is extremely important in ensuring its success as a species. Many animals, particularly the largest mammals, are becoming restricted to ever-smaller regions as human development and modern agricultural practices reduce their natural habitats. In contrast, humans have been responsible – both deliberately and accidentally – for the spread of some of the world's most successful species. Many of these introduced species are now more numerous than the indigenous animal populations.

PLANTS

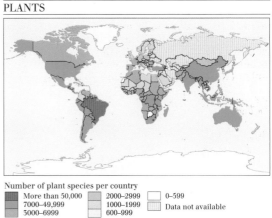

Number of plant species per country

More than 50,000	2000–2999	0–599
7000–49,999	1000–1999	Data not available
3000–6999	600–999	

PLANT ADAPTION

ENVIRONMENTAL CONDITIONS, such as climate, soil type and the competition with other organisms, influence the development of plants into distinctive forms. Similar conditions in different parts of the world create similar adaptions in the plants, which may then be modified by other, local, factors specific to the region.

BIOME TYPES

- Mountains
- Polar regions
- Tundra
- Tropical rain forests
- Dry woodlands
- Savanna
- Temperate grasslands
- Mediterranean
- Coniferous forests
- Temperate rain forests
- Broadleaf forests
- Cold deserts
- Hot deserts
- Wetlands

ENVIRONMENT FACTFILE

LARGEST PROTECTED AREAS

Ecuador	43%
Venezuela	36%
Denmark	32%
Norway	31%
Austria	28%

HIGHEST ANNUAL DEFORESTATION

Brazil	50,000 km²	(19,300 mi²)
Indonesia	12,000 km²	(4,600 mi²)
Burma	8,000 km²	(3,00 mi²)
Mexico	7,000 km²	(2,700 mi²)
Colombia	6,500 km²	(2,500 mi²)

IDENTIFIED SPECIES

Micro-organisms	5,800
Invertebrates	1,021,000
Plants	322,500
Fish	19,100
Reptiles & amphibians	12,000
Mammals	4,000

ENDANGERED SPECIES

Mammals	484
Birds	403
Reptiles	100
Amphibians	49
Fish	291
Invertebrates	763

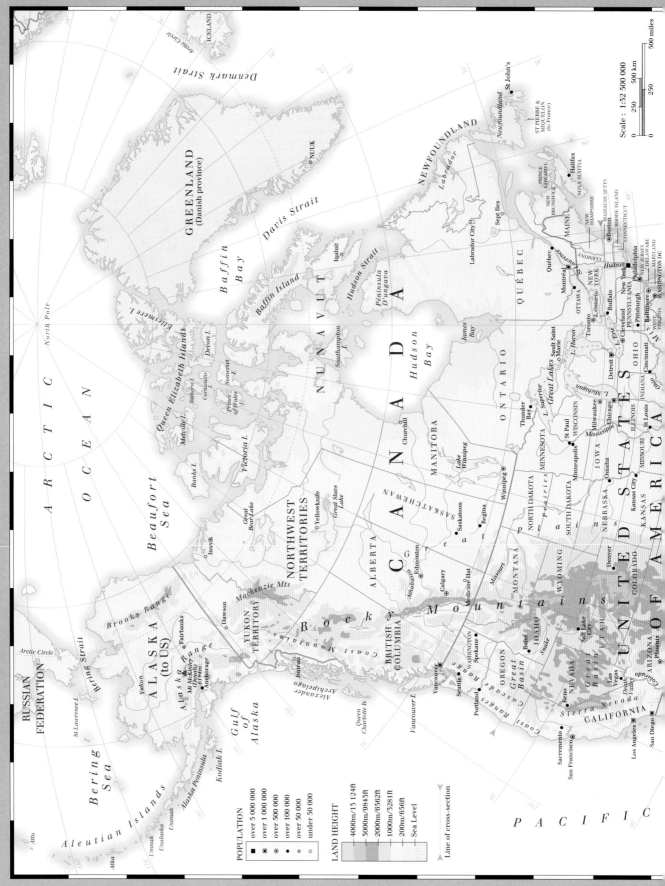

Scale : 1:32 500 000

500 miles

500 km

250

250

ICELAND

Arctic Circle

Denmark Strait

GREENLAND
(Danish province)

Baffin Bay

Davis Strait

NUUK

Baffin Island

NEWFOUNDLAND

St John's

Newfoundland

ST PIERRE & MIQUELON
(to France)

Halifax

PRINCE EDWARD I.

NOVA SCOTIA

NEW BRUNSWICK

NEWFOUNDLAND

Labrador

North Pole

Ellesmere I.

Queen Elizabeth Islands

Devon I.

Cornwallis I.

Bathurst I.

Melville I.

Somerset I.

Prince of Wales I.

NUNAVUT

Southampton I.

Hudson Strait

Peninsula D'ungava

Iqaluit

Sept Iles

MAINE

Boston

VERMONT

NEW HAMPSHIRE

MASSACHUSETTS

RHODE ISLAND

CONNECTICUT

QUÉBEC

Labrador City

St Lawrence

Québec

Montréal

OTTAWA

L. Ontario

Toronto

New York

Buffalo

NEW YORK

Hudson

Philadelphia

NEW JERSEY

DELAWARE

MARYLAND

WASHINGTON DC

WEST VIRGINIA

PENNSYLVANIA

Baltimore

Pittsburgh

ARCTIC OCEAN

Beaufort Sea

Banks I.

Victoria I.

Great Bear Lake

Great Slave Lake

Yellowknife

NORTHWEST TERRITORIES

CANADA

James Bay

Hudson Bay

Churchill

ONTARIO

Thunder Bay

L. Superior

L. Michigan

Great Lakes

Sault Saint Marie

L. Huron

L. Erie

Cleveland

Detroit

OHIO

Cincinnati

INDIANA

MANITOBA

SASKATCHEWAN

ALBERTA

Lake Winnipeg

Winnipeg

St Paul

Minneapolis

Milwaukee

Chicago

WISCONSIN

MINNESOTA

IOWA

ILLINOIS

Mississippi

St Louis

MISSOURI

Saskatoon

Regina

NORTH DAKOTA

SOUTH DAKOTA

NEBRASKA

KANSAS

Omaha

Kansas City

P r a i r i e s

P l a i n s

RUSSIAN FEDERATION

St Lawrence I.

Bering Strait

Arctic Circle

Brooks Range

ALASKA
(to US)

Fairbanks

Yukon

Anchorage

Mt McKinley (Denali)

Alaska Range

Dawson

YUKON TERRITORY

Mackenzie Mts

Rocky Mountains

Coast Mountains

BRITISH COLUMBIA

Edmonton

Athabasca

Calgary

Medicine Hat

MONTANA

WYOMING

Missouri

Denver

COLORADO

UNITED STATES OF AMERICA

Bering Sea

Aleutian Islands

Attu

Umnak

Unalaska

Atka

Unimak

Alaska Peninsula

Kodiak I.

Gulf of Alaska

Alexander Archipelago

Queen Charlotte Is

Vancouver I.

Juneau

Vancouver

Seattle

Portland

WASHINGTON

Spokane

OREGON

Cascade Range

Coast Ranges

IDAHO

Boise

Snake

Great Basin

NEVADA

Reno

Las Vegas

Sierra Nevada

Death Valley

UTAH

Salt Lake City

Great Salt Lake

ARIZONA

Phoenix

Colorado

CALIFORNIA

Sacramento

San Francisco

Los Angeles

San Diego

PACIFIC

POPULATION

over 5 000 000
over 1 000 000
over 500 000
over 100 000
over 50 000
under 50 000

LAND HEIGHT

4000m/13 124ft
3000m/9845ft
2000m/6562ft
1000m/3281ft
200m/656ft
Sea Level

Line of cross-section

NORTH AMERICA

NORTH AMERICA'S climate is as varied as its topography: much of Canada is snowbound or clothed in forest, its sparse population congregating along the US border. Along the continent's western flank are the spectacular Rocky Mountains. To the east lie the older, wooded Appalachians. Between these are the Great Plains – grazed by herds of livestock or sown with cereals. These plains were once home to tribes of native Americans, supplanted by incoming white settlers. America's population and industry are concentrated in the temperate northeast, while the drier south and west are rural and thinly populated. North America is rich in minerals and oil. Mexico is the world's largest Spanish-speaking nation. Central America and the Caribbean contain some 30 countries and numerous small islands. The climate is tropical and prone to storms, the landscape mountainous and volcanic.

CONTINENTAL FACTS

PHYSICAL FEATURES

- LARGEST LAKE: Lake Superior, Canada/USA 83,270 km² (32,140 mi²)
- LONGEST RIVER: Mississippi-Missouri, USA 6,019 km (5,740 miles)
- HIGHEST POINT: Mt McKinley (Denali), Alaska, USA 6,194 m (20,322 ft)
- LOWEST POINT: Death Valley, California, USA 86 m (282 ft) below sea level

POLITICAL FEATURES

- TOTAL POPULATION: 437.2 million
- LARGEST CITY WITH POPULATION: Mexico City, Mexico 18 million
- COUNTRY WITH HIGHEST POPULATION DENSITY: Barbados 612 people/km² (1,584 people/mi²)
- LARGEST COUNTRY: Canada 9,220,970 sq km (3,560,217 square miles)
- SMALLEST COUNTRY: Grenada 340 km² (151 mi²)

CROSS-SECTION THROUGH NORTH AMERICA: 43°N, 126°W–65°W

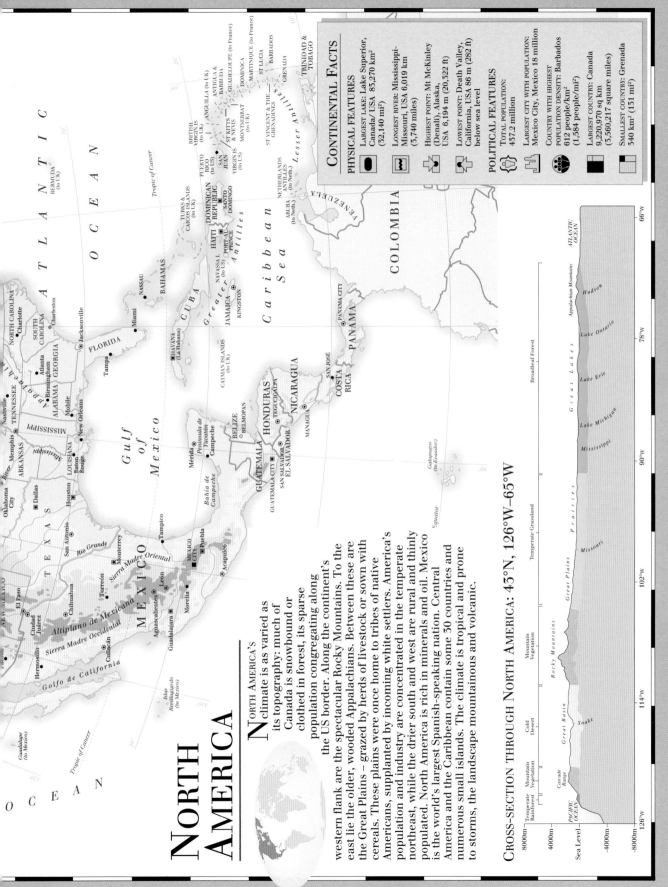

SOUTH AMERICA

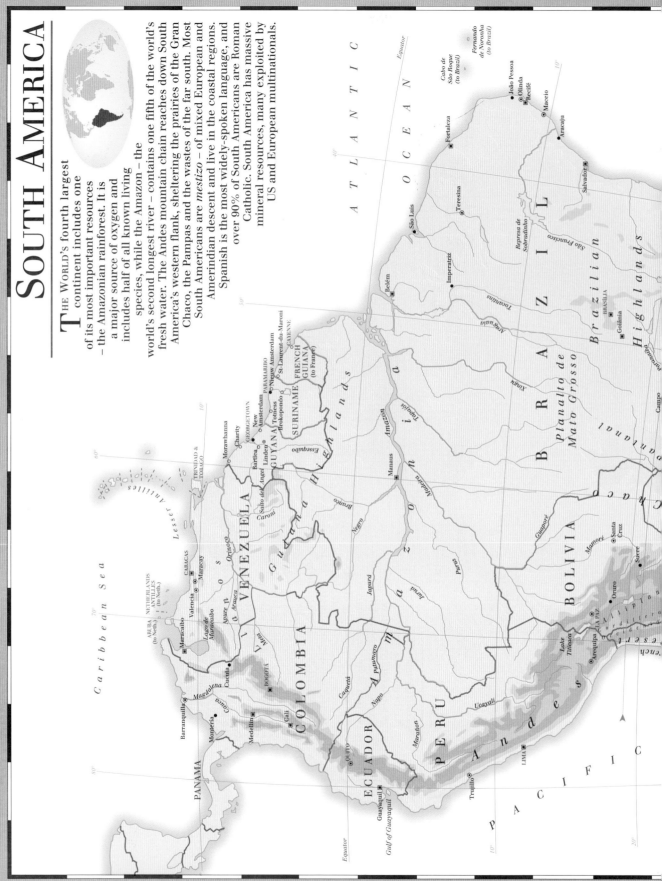

THE WORLD'S fourth largest continent includes one of its most important resources – the Amazonian rainforest. It is a major source of oxygen and includes half of all known living species, while the Amazon – the world's second longest river – contains one fifth of the world's fresh water. The Andes mountain chain reaches down South America's western flank, sheltering the prairies of the Gran Chaco, the Pampas and the wastes of the far south. Most South Americans are *mestizo* – of mixed European and Amerindian descent and live in the coastal regions. Spanish is the most widely-spoken language, and over 90% of South Americans are Roman Catholic. South America has massive mineral resources, many exploited by US and European multinationals.

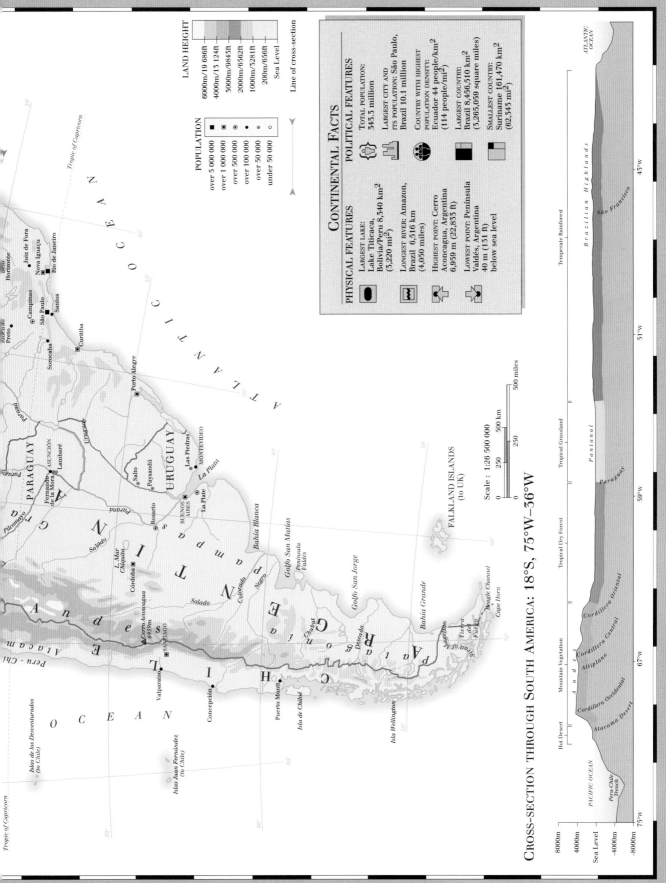

CROSS-SECTION THROUGH SOUTH AMERICA: 18°S, 75°W–36°W

LAND HEIGHT

- 6000m/19 686ft
- 4000m/13 124ft
- 3000m/9845ft
- 2000m/6562ft
- 1000m/3281ft
- 200m/656ft
- Sea Level

Line of cross-section

POPULATION

- over 5 000 000
- over 1 000 000
- over 500 000
- over 100 000
- over 50 000
- under 50 000

CONTINENTAL FACTS

PHYSICAL FEATURES

LARGEST LAKE:
Lake Titicaca,
Bolivia/Peru 8,340 km^2
(3,220 mi^2)

LONGEST RIVER: Amazon,
Brazil 6,516 km
(4,050 miles)

HIGHEST POINT: Cerro
Aconcagua, Argentina
6,959 m (22,835 ft)

LOWEST POINT: Península
Valdés, Argentina
40 m (151 ft)
below sea level

POLITICAL FEATURES

TOTAL POPULATION:
345.3 million

LARGEST CITY AND
ITS POPULATION: São Paulo,
Brazil 10.1 million

COUNTRY WITH HIGHEST
POPULATION DENSITY:
Ecuador 44 people/km^2
(114 people/mi^2)

LARGEST COUNTRY:
Brazil 8,456,510 km^2
(3,265,059 square miles)

SMALLEST COUNTRY:
Suriname 161,470 km^2
(62,345 mi^2)

Scale : 1:26 500 000

0   250   500 km
0   250   500 miles

GREENLAND
(Danish province)

JAN MAYEN
(to Norway)

Denmark Strait

Akureyri
REYKJAVÍK • ICELAND

Norwegian Sea

FAEROE IS
(to Denmark)

Shetland Is

Orkney Is

Outer
Hebrides

Edinburgh

Belfast

North Sea

REPUBLIC
OF
IRELAND
DUBLIN

ISLE OF MAN
(to UK)

UNITED

Manchester

KINGDOM

Cork
Birmingham

NETHERLA

Cardiff
LONDON

AMSTERDAM
Rotterdam

BRUSSELS
BELGI

English Channel

GUERNSEY (to UK)
JERSEY (to UK)

PARIS

Seine

Nantes
Loire

FRANCE

Genè

EUROPE

THE SMALLEST CONTINENT AFTER AUSTRALIA, Europe
has a wide variety of climates and landscapes.
The tundra of the far north gives way to a cool,
wet, heavily-forested region. The North European
Plain is well-drained, fertile and rich in oil, coal
and natural gas. The shores of the Mediterranean are
generally warm, dry and hilly, ideal for cultivating olives,
citrus fruits and grapes. A great curve of mountain ranges, including the
Pyrenees, Alps and Carpathians, divides north from south. To the east, the
rolling plains of European Russia and the Ukraine, clothed in coniferous
forests or ploughed for wheat, run up to the Ural Mountains. Europeans are
mainly Christian – Catholic or Protestant – and speak a variety of languages,
most of which spring from Latin (Romance), Germanic or Slavic roots.

*Bay of
Biscay*

A Coruña

Bordeaux

Massif
Central

Rhône

Toulouse

Pyrenees

ANDORRA

Marseille

Porto

PORTUGAL

Zaragoza

Barcelona

Ebro

SPAIN

MADRID

Menorc

Valencia

Mallorca
Palma

LISBON

Tagus

Eivissa

Balearic Is

Sevilla

Málaga

M e

POPULATION

- ■ over 5 000 000
- ▣ over 1 000 000
- ◉ over 500 000
- • over 100 000
- ◎ over 50 000
- ○ under 50 000

LAND HEIGHT

3000m/9843ft
2000m/6562ft
1000m/3281ft
200m/656ft
Sea Level

Azores
(to Portugal)

ATLANTIC OCEAN

Line of cross-section

Scale : 1:22 500 000

0   250   500 km

0   250   500 miles

GIBRALTAR
(to UK)
Ceuta (to Spain)

Melilla (to Spain)

MOROCCO

ALGERI

CROSS-SECTION THROUGH EUROPE: 46°N, 5°W–48°E

	Broadleaf Forest	Mountain Vegetation	Broadleaf Forest	Mountain Vegetation	Broadleaf Forest	Temperate Grassland	Cold Desert

8000m

4000m

Sea Level

-4000m

-8000m

ATLANTIC
OCEAN

Rhône

Alps

Alföld

Danube

Carpathian
Mountains

Carpații
Occidentali

Black
Sea

Crimea

Sea of
Azov

CASPIAN
SEA

Volga Delta

0°   11°E   22°E   33°E   44°E

CONTINENTAL FACTS

PHYSICAL FEATURES

- **LARGEST LAKE:** Ladoga, European Russia 18,390 km² (7,100 mi²)
- **LONGEST RIVER:** Volga, European Russia 3,688 km (2,290 miles)
- **HIGHEST POINT:** El' brus, Caucasus Mts, European Russia 5,642 m (18,510 ft)
- **LOWEST POINT:** Volga Delta, Caspian Sea, European Russia 28 m (92 ft) below sea level

POLITICAL FEATURES

- **TOTAL POPULATION:** 678.2 million
- **COUNTRY WITH HIGHEST POPULATION DENSITY:** Monaco 16,410 people/km² (42,503 people/mi²)
- **LARGEST CITY AND ITS POPULATION:** Moscow, European Russia 9 million
- **LARGEST COUNTRY:** European Russia 3,955,818 km² (1,527,341 mi²)
- **SMALLEST COUNTRY:** Vatican City, Italy 0.44 km² (0.17 mi²)

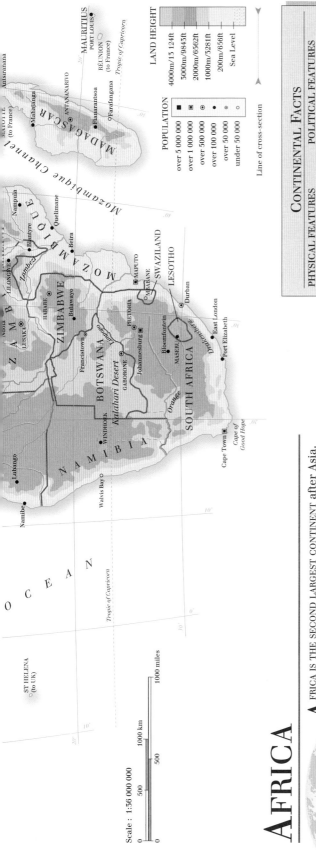

PORT LOUIS
MAURITIUS
RÉUNION
(to France)
Tropic of Capricorn

MAYOTTE
(to France)
Mahajanga
ANTANANARIVO
Fianarantsoa
Farafangana
MADAGASCAR
Antsiranana

Mozambique Channel

ST HELENA
(to UK)

O C E A N

Scale : 1:56 000 000

| 0 | 500 | 1000 km |
| 0 | 500 | 1000 miles |

LAND HEIGHT

	4000m/13 124ft
	3000m/9845ft
	2000m/6562ft
	1000m/3281ft
	200m/656ft
	Sea Level

POPULATION

■	over 5 000 000
▣	over 1 000 000
◉	over 500 000
●	over 100 000
◌	over 50 000
○	under 50 000

Line of cross-section

CONTINENTAL FACTS

PHYSICAL FEATURES

LARGEST LAKE: Lake Victoria 68,880 sq km (26,560 square miles)

LONGEST RIVER: Nile, Uganda/ Sudan/ Egypt 6695 km (4160 miles)

HIGHEST POINT: Kilimanjaro, Tanzania 5895 m (19,341 ft)

LOWEST POINT: Lac' Assal, Djibouti 156 m (512 ft) below sea level

POLITICAL FEATURES

TOTAL POPULATION: 697.5 million

LARGEST CITY AND POPULATION: Cairo, Egypt, 6.4 million

COUNTRY WITH HIGHEST POPULATION DENSITY: Mauritius 595 people per sq km

LARGEST COUNTRY: Sudan 2,576,000 sq km (917,374 square miles)

SMALLEST COUNTRY: Seychelles 270 sq km (104 square miles)

AFRICA

AFRICA IS THE SECOND LARGEST CONTINENT after Asia. It is dominated by the Sahara in the north and the Great Rift Valley in the east. The Mediterranean climate of the extreme north and south enables cultivation of grapes and other fruit. A belt of tropical rainforest lies along the Equator, while Africa's great tropical grasslands provide grazing for herds of wild animals and domestic livestock. A narrow strip of Egypt is watered by the world's longest river, the Nile, which sustained prehistoric communities. The centre and south of the continent are rich in minerals. Almost one tenth of the world's population lives in Africa – a wide variety of peoples with their own distinctive languages and cultures. Although Islam and Christianity are widespread, many Africans adhere to their own local customs and religious beliefs.

CROSS-SECTION THROUGH AFRICA 7°N, 15°W–55°E

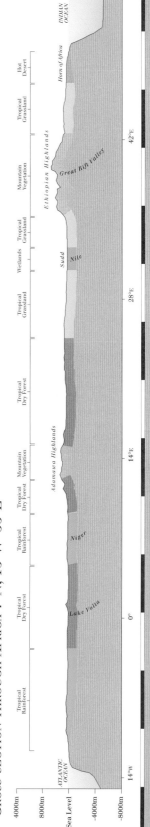

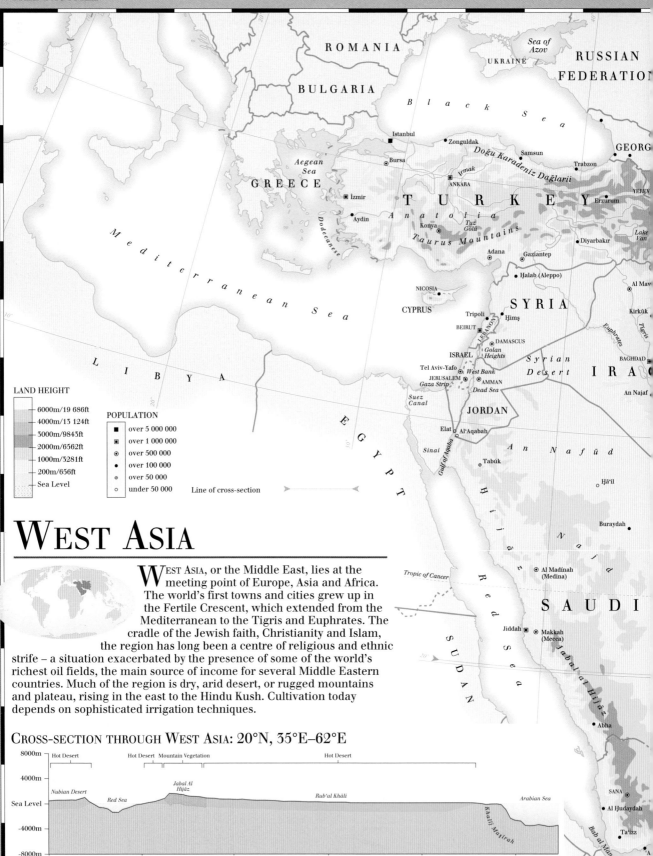

LAND HEIGHT

- 6000m/19 686ft
- 4000m/13 124ft
- 3000m/9843ft
- 2000m/6562ft
- 1000m/3281ft
- 200m/656ft
- Sea Level

POPULATION

- ■ over 5 000 000
- ▣ over 1 000 000
- ◉ over 500 000
- • over 100 000
- ◦ over 50 000
- ○ under 50 000

Line of cross-section

WEST ASIA

WEST ASIA, or the Middle East, lies at the meeting point of Europe, Asia and Africa. The world's first towns and cities grew up in the Fertile Crescent, which extended from the Mediterranean to the Tigris and Euphrates. The cradle of the Jewish faith, Christianity and Islam, the region has long been a centre of religious and ethnic strife – a situation exacerbated by the presence of some of the world's richest oil fields, the main source of income for several Middle Eastern countries. Much of the region is dry, arid desert, or rugged mountains and plateau, rising in the east to the Hindu Kush. Cultivation today depends on sophisticated irrigation techniques.

CROSS-SECTION THROUGH WEST ASIA: 20°N, 35°E–62°E

KAZAKHSTAN

Aral Sea

Kyzyl Kum

⊙ BISHKEK   Karakol
                    Ozero Issyk-Kul'

Kirghiz Range   Naryn

UZBEKISTAN

Dashkhovuz ·   · Urgench

Ozero Aydarkul'

TASHKENT ⊙   KYRGYZSTAN   *Tien Shan*

Namangan ·   · Osh   CHINA

Khudzhand ·

Karakumy   Samarkand ·

Khudzhand

Amu   Karshi ·   TAJIKISTAN

⊙ DUSHANBE   *Pamirs*

Gäncä ·
AZERBAIJAN
⊡ BAKU   Krasnovodsk ·   TURKMENISTAN   Chardzhev ·   Kulyab ·   Khorog ·   *Karakoram Range*
RMENIA   Nebitdag ·   *Amu*   Kurgan-Tyube ·   K2 ▲ 8611m   *Indus*

· Länkäran   *Khrebet Kopetdag*   ASHGABAT ⊡   Mazär-e-Sharif ·
· Tabriz   · Mary   Baghlän ⊙

Caspian Sea

Daryächeh-ye rmiyeh   · Rasht   · Gorgän

TEHRAN ⊡   Mashhad ·

· Hamadän   · Qom

Reshteh-ye Kuhhä ye Alborz

Hindu Kush

Jaläläbäd ·   Peshäwar ·   ⊡ ISLAMABAD
KÄBUL ⊙   Räwalpindi ·

HERÄT ·   AFGHANISTAN   Gujränwäla ·
· Bäkhtarän   IRAN   *Chenab*   ⊡ Lahore

Dasht-e-Kavir   *Plateau of Iran*   ⊡ Faisaläbäd

· Esfahän   *Hämün-e Säberi*   Kandahär ·

· Ahväz   *Zagros Mountains*   · Multän
Al Başrah
· Äbädän   · Kermän   Zähedän ⊙   Quetta ·   *Thar Desert*
· Shiräz   *Helmand*   PAKISTAN

KUWAIT ·
KUWAIT CITY ·   *Persian Gulf*   Sukkur ·   INDIA

BAHRAIN   Bandar-e 'Abbäs ·

MANAMA ·   *Strait of Hormuz*   Dubai · · Sharjah   *Indus*   Hyderäbäd ·
⊡ RIYADH   DOHA ·   Suhär ·
· Al Hufüf   QATAR   ABU DHABI ·   *Gulf of Oman*   Karächi ·   *Tropic of Cancer*
· Ḩaraḍ   UNITED ARAB   MUSCAT ·
                EMIRATES   Ar Rustäq ·   Nazwä ·   *Arabian Sea*
RABIA   Şür ·

Rub' al Khäli   OMAN

Khalīj Maşīrah

YEMEN   Şalälah ·

Hadhramaut   *INDIAN OCEAN*

· Al Mukallä

f Aden   *Socotra (to Yemen)*

CONTINENTAL FACTS

PHYSICAL FEATURES

LARGEST LAKE: Caspian Sea 371,000 km² (143,205 mi²)

LONGEST RIVER: Euphrates, Syria/ Iraq 2,815 km (1750 miles)

HIGHEST POINT: K2, Kashmir, India/ Pakistan 8611m (28,252 ft)

LOWEST POINT: Dead Sea, Israel/Jordan 392 m (1,286 ft) below sea level

POLITICAL FEATURES

TOTAL POPULATION: 401.3 million

LARGEST CITY AND ITS POPULATION: Istanbul, Turkey 6.5 million

COUNTRY WITH HIGHEST POPULATION DENSITY: Bahrain 874 people/km² (2,262 people/mi²)

LARGEST COUNTRY: Saudi Arabia 2,149,690 km² (830,001 mi²)

SMALLEST COUNTRY: Bahrain 680 km² (263 mi²)

CONTINENTAL FACTS

PHYSICAL FEATURES

LARGEST LAKE: Aral Sea, Asiatic Russia 66,500 km² (25,700 mi²)

LONGEST RIVER: Chang Jiang (Yangtze), China 6,380 km (3,965 miles)

HIGHEST POINT: Xixabangma Feng, China 8,012 m (26,286 ft)

LOWEST POINT: Turpan Hami (Turfan Basin), China 154 m (505 ft) below sea level

POLITICAL FEATURES

TOTAL POPULATION: 1,432 million

LARGEST CITY AND ITS POPULATION: Tokyo, Japan 18.1 million

COUNTRY WITH HIGHEST POPULATION DENSITY: Taiwan 666 people/km² (1,724 people/mi²)

LARGEST COUNTRY: Asiatic Russia 13,119,582 km² (5,065,471 mi²)

SMALLEST COUNTRY: Taiwan 32,260 km² (12,455 mi²)

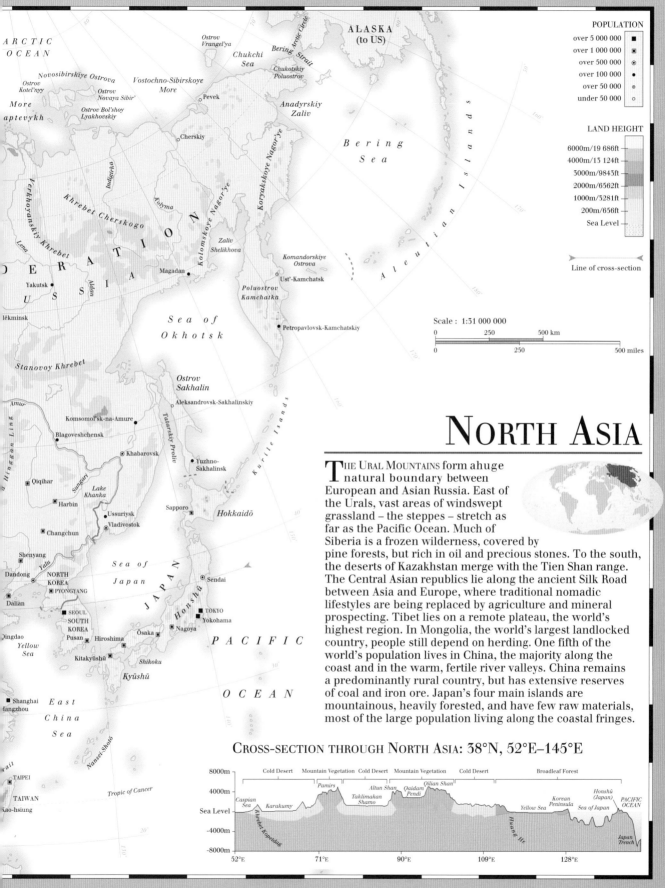

over 5 000 000
over 1 000 000
over 500 000
over 100 000
over 50 000
under 50 000

LAND HEIGHT

6000m/19 686ft
4000m/13 124ft
3000m/9843ft
2000m/6562ft
1000m/3281ft
200m/656ft
Sea Level

Line of cross-section

Scale : 1:31 000 000

0   250   500 km

0   250   500 miles

NORTH ASIA

THE URAL MOUNTAINS form a huge
natural boundary between
European and Asian Russia. East of
the Urals, vast areas of windswept
grassland – the steppes – stretch as
far as the Pacific Ocean. Much of
Siberia is a frozen wilderness, covered by
pine forests, but rich in oil and precious stones. To the south,
the deserts of Kazakhstan merge with the Tien Shan range.
The Central Asian republics lie along the ancient Silk Road
between Asia and Europe, where traditional nomadic
lifestyles are being replaced by agriculture and mineral
prospecting. Tibet lies on a remote plateau, the world's
highest region. In Mongolia, the world's largest landlocked
country, people still depend on herding. One fifth of the
world's population lives in China, the majority along the
coast and in the warm, fertile river valleys. China remains
a predominantly rural country, but has extensive reserves
of coal and iron ore. Japan's four main islands are
mountainous, heavily forested, and have few raw materials,
most of the large population living along the coastal fringes.

CROSS-SECTION THROUGH NORTH ASIA: 38°N, 52°E–145°E

SOUTH ASIA

DOMINATED IN THE NORTH by the Himalayas, the highest mountain range in the world, India is isolated from the rest of Asia, forming a densely populated subcontinent. Its climate and topography range from the mountains of Kashmir in the north to coral beaches in the south. It is the birthplace of Hinduism, Buddhism and Sikhism. Much of mainland Southeast Asia is mountainous and forested, the people living in the river valleys and fertile coastal plains. Tropical rainforests, rich in species, cover much of the region. Indonesia forms a huge arc of some 13,000 volcanic islands. The Philippines, the region's only Christian country, comprises over 7000 mountainous islands.

CROSS-SECTION THROUGH SOUTH ASIA: 28°N, 60°E–124°E

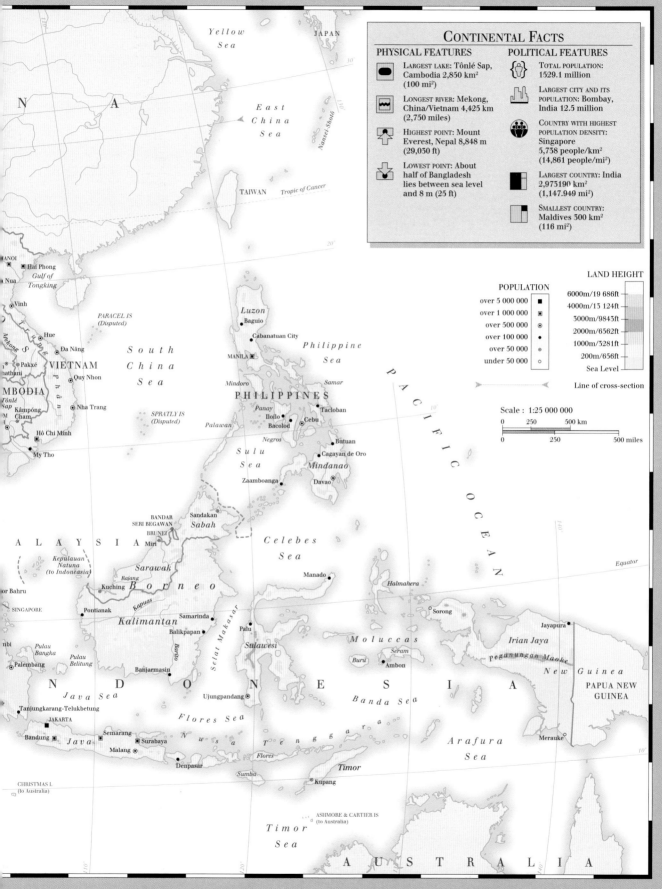

CONTINENTAL FACTS

PHYSICAL FEATURES

LARGEST LAKE: Tônlé Sap, Cambodia 2,850 km² (100 mi²)

LONGEST RIVER: Mekong, China/Vietnam 4,425 km (2,750 miles)

HIGHEST POINT: Mount Everest, Nepal 8,848 m (29,030 ft)

LOWEST POINT: About half of Bangladesh lies between sea level and 8 m (25 ft)

POLITICAL FEATURES

TOTAL POPULATION: 1529.1 million

LARGEST CITY AND ITS POPULATION: Bombay, India 12.5 million

COUNTRY WITH HIGHEST POPULATION DENSITY: Singapore 5,738 people/km² (14,861 people/mi²)

LARGEST COUNTRY: India 2,973190 km² (1,147.949 mi²)

SMALLEST COUNTRY: Maldives 300 km² (116 mi²)

POPULATION

over 5 000 000
over 1 000 000
over 500 000
over 100 000
over 50 000
under 50 000

LAND HEIGHT

6000m/19 686ft
4000m/13 124ft
3000m/9843ft
2000m/6562ft
1000m/3281ft
200m/656ft
Sea Level

Line of cross-section

Scale : 1:25 000 000

0   250   500 km

0   250   500 miles

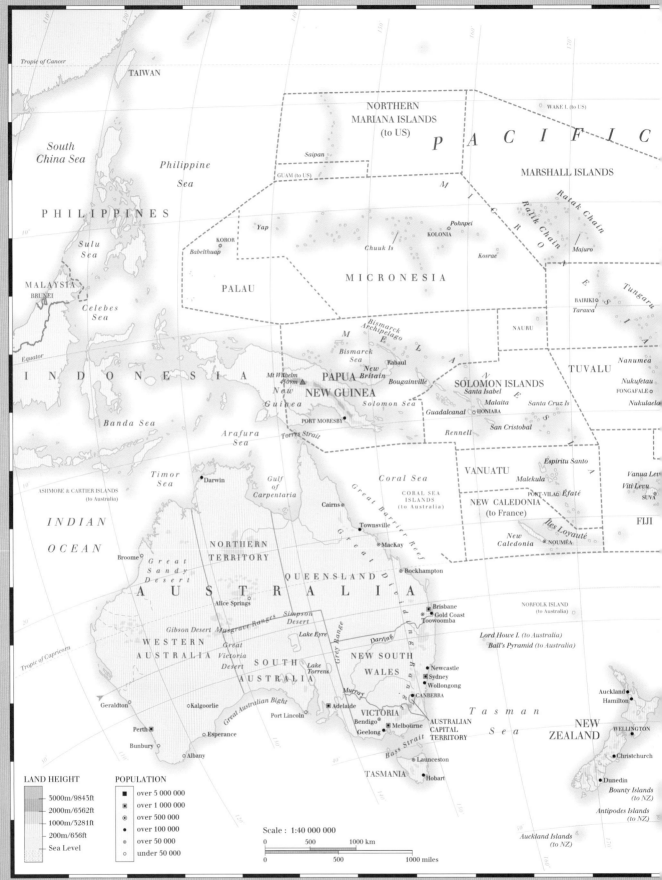

Tropic of Cancer

TAIWAN

South China Sea

Philippine Sea

PHILIPPINES

Sulu Sea

MALAYSIA

BRUNEI

Celebes Sea

NORTHERN MARIANA ISLANDS (to US)

WAKE I. (to US)

P A C I F I C

Saipan

GUAM (to US)

MARSHALL ISLANDS

Ratak Chain

Ratik Chain

M

I

C

R

O

KOROR

Babelthuap

Yap

Pohnpei

KOLONIA

Chuuk Is

Kosrae

PALAU

M I C R O N E S I A

BAIRIKI

Tarawa

Tungaru

E

S

I

A

NAURU

TUVALU

Nanumea

Nukufetau

FONGAFALE

Nukulaelae

10°

Equator

INDONESIA

Bismarck Archipelago

M

E

L

A

Mt Wilhelm 4509m ▲

PAPUA

New Guinea

NEW GUINEA

Bismarck Sea

Rabaul

New Britain

Bougainville

SOLOMON ISLANDS

Santa Isabel

Malaita

HONIARA

Santa Cruz Is

N

E

S

I

A

PORT MORESBY

Solomon Sea

Guadalcanal

San Cristobal

Rennell

VANUATU

Espiritu Santo

Malekula

PORT-VILA *Éfaté*

Vanua Lev

Viti Levu

SUVA

FIJI

Arafura Sea

Torres Strait

Timor Sea

●Darwin

Gulf of Carpentaria

Coral Sea

CORAL SEA ISLANDS (to Australia)

NEW CALEDONIA (to France)

Îles Loyauté

NOUMÉA

New Caledonia

ASHMORE & CARTIER ISLANDS (to Australia)

INDIAN OCEAN

Cairns●

●Townsville

Great Barrier Reef

Broome○

NORTHERN TERRITORY

Great Sandy Desert

●MacKay

●Rockhampton

Great Dividing Range

A U S T R A L I A

QUEENSLAND

Alice Springs○

Gibson Desert

Musgrave Ranges

Simpson Desert

NORFOLK ISLAND (to Australia)

Tropic of Capricorn

WESTERN AUSTRALIA

Great Victoria Desert

Lake Eyre

SOUTH AUSTRALIA

Lake Torrens

NEW SOUTH WALES

Darling

■Brisbane

⊙ Gold Coast

Toowoomba

Lord Howe I. (to Australia)

Ball's Pyramid (to Australia)

20°

Geraldton○

Kalgoorlie○

Great Australian Bight

Port Lincoln○

●Adelaide

Murray

●Newcastle

●Sydney

●Wollongong

●CANBERRA

AUSTRALIAN CAPITAL TERRITORY

Auckland●

Hamilton●

Perth■

Esperance○

VICTORIA

Bendigo○

Geelong○

●Melbourne

Tasman Sea

NEW ZEALAND

WELLINGTON

Bunbury○

Albany○

Bass Strait

●Launceston

TASMANIA

●Hobart

Christchurch●

Dunedin●

Bounty Islands (to NZ)

Antipodes Islands (to NZ)

Auckland Islands (to NZ)

LAND HEIGHT	
	3000m/9843ft
	2000m/6562ft
	1000m/3281ft
	200m/656ft
	Sea Level

POPULATION	
■	over 5 000 000
▣	over 1 000 000
⊙	over 500 000
●	over 100 000
⊙	over 50 000
○	under 50 000

Scale : 1:40 000 000

0   500   1000 km

0   500   1000 miles

AUSTRALASIA & OCEANIA

OCEANIA EMBRACES THE WORLD'S smallest such as New Zealand, Papua New Guinea and Fiji, and the myriad volcanic and coral islands scattered across the Pacific Ocean, consisting of three main groups, Micronesia, Melanesia and Polynesia. Australia, flat and dry, is sparsely populated, most people living along the coastal lowlands, especially in the southeast. The continent's first settlers, the Aboriginal peoples, retain some of their original lands in the interior, but later European and Asian settlers form most of the population. Owing to its isolation from other continents, Australia's flora and fauna have evolved many unique species. The continent is rich in minerals, such as gold, uranium and iron ore, which are the basis of Australia's prosperity. Mountainous Papua New Guinea is covered in tropical rainforest, while New Zealand is temperate, rugged and volcanic in the north. The peoples of Oceania colonized the Pacific by AD1500, and the many insular farming and fishing communities have developed distinctive cultures, the Maoris of New Zealand being among the most notable.

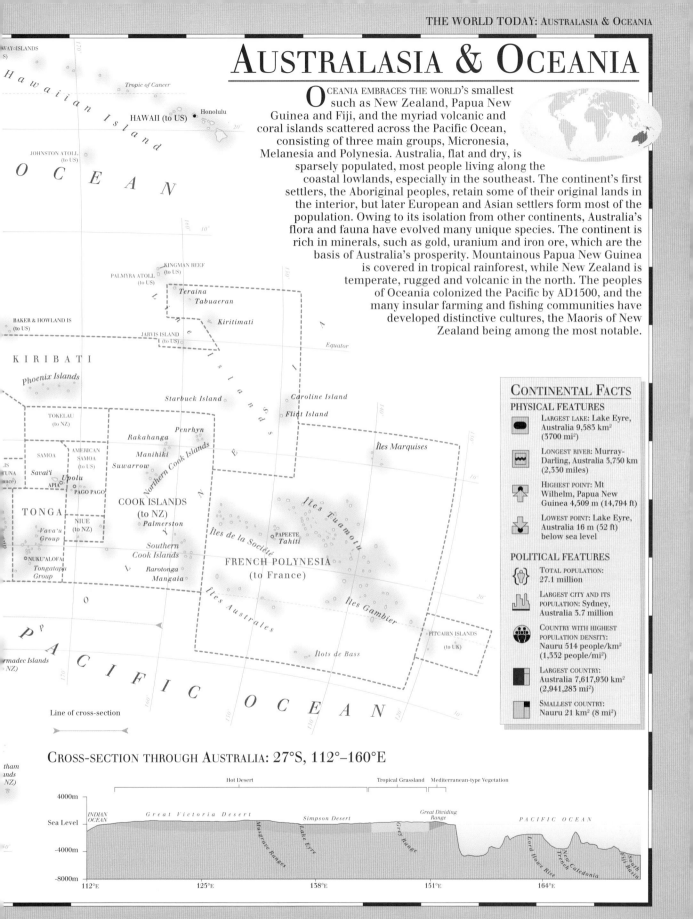

CONTINENTAL FACTS

PHYSICAL FEATURES

LARGEST LAKE: Lake Eyre, Australia 9,583 km² (3700 mi²)

LONGEST RIVER: Murray-Darling, Australia 5,750 km (2,330 miles)

HIGHEST POINT: Mt Wilhelm, Papua New Guinea 4,509 m (14,794 ft)

LOWEST POINT: Lake Eyre, Australia 16 m (52 ft) below sea level

POLITICAL FEATURES

TOTAL POPULATION: 27.1 million

LARGEST CITY AND ITS POPULATION: Sydney, Australia 3.7 million

COUNTRY WITH HIGHEST POPULATION DENSITY: Nauru 514 people/km² (1,332 people/mi²)

LARGEST COUNTRY: Australia 7,617,930 km² (2,941,283 mi²)

SMALLEST COUNTRY: Nauru 21 km² (8 mi²)

CROSS-SECTION THROUGH AUSTRALIA: 27°S, 112°–160°E

CHRONOLOGY OF WORLD HISTORY

THIS TABLE PRESENTS A SUMMARY of the world's crucial historical events, from the first evidence of settlement and agriculture until the year 1997 CE. Each of the six columns is shaded a different colour, with each colour representing a particular continent. Reading across the columns, one can follow the development of cultures across the major landmasses of the world. By reading downwards, each continent's particular cultural history can be seen, from its first steps towards civilization, through periods of migration, empire, and revolution, to its involvement in the global wars and political diplomacy of the late 20th Century.

NORTH AMERICA

- ❑ **15,000 BCE** Evidence of human settlement in North America
- ❑ **7000 BCE** Beginnings of semi-permanent settlement in North America
- ❑ **5000 BCE** Earliest cultivation of maize in Central America
- ❑ **800 BCE** Maya spread northwards into Yucatan peninsula
- ❑ **c.300 CE** Start of classic Maya civilization in Yucatan
- ❑ **900 CE** Toltecs rise to power as Maya sites collapse
- ❑ **c.1000** Vikings colonize Greenland and discover America (Vinland)
- ❑ **1200** Aztecs enter Valley of Mexico
- ❑ **1325** Tenochtitlan founded by the Aztecs
- ❑ **1492** Columbus reaches America
- ❑ **c.1500** Inuit peoples found throughout Arctic region
- ❑ **1502** Introduction of African slaves to the Caribbean
- ❑ **c.1510** African slaves to America
- ❑ **1519** Cortes begins conquest of Aztec Empire
- ❑ **1607** First permanent English settlement in North America (Jamestown, Virginia)
- ❑ **1608** French colonists found Quebec
- ❑ **1620** Puritans on the Mayflower land in New England
- ❑ **1773** Boston Tea Party
- ❑ **1776** American Declaration of Independence
- ❑ **1789** George Washington becomes first President of US
- ❑ **1791** Revolution in Haiti
- ❑ **1803** Louisiana Purchase nearly doubles size of US
- ❑ **1810** Revolution in Mexico
- ❑ **1819** US purchases Florida from Spain
- ❑ **1821** Mexico gains independence
- ❑ **1828** Federalist/Centralist wars in Mexico (to 1859)
- ❑ **1845** Texas annexed by US
- ❑ **1846** US-Mexican War (to 1848)
- ❑ **1848** California Gold Rush

SOUTH AMERICA

- ❑ **c.20,000 BCE** First settlers arrive
- ❑ **c.11,000 BCE** Evidence of settlement at Monte Verde in present-day Chile
- ❑ **c.4500 BCE** Evidence of agriculture in south-central Andes
- ❑ **3000 BCE** Large village settlements begin to appear
- ❑ **c.2500 BCE** Masonry building and temple architecture in the Andes
- ❑ **2000 BCE** Earliest ceramics and large-scale cultivation of maize in Peru
- ❑ **c.1800 BCE** Ceremonial centre of La Florida built in Peru
- ❑ **c.450 CE** Nazca culture flourishing; lines and giant figures drawn in desert
- ❑ **700 CE** Emergence of Chimu on north coast of Peru
- ❑ **c.1200** Incas enter and settle in Andean valley near Cuzco
- ❑ **1438** Incas rise to power and establish empire
- ❑ **1475** Chimu conquered by Incas
- ❑ **1494** Treaty of Tordesillas divides western hemisphere between Spain and Portugal
- ❑ **1498** Columbus anchors off coast near Trinidad
- ❑ **1500** Cabral sights Brazilian coast
- ❑ **1502** First expedition sent from Portugal to exploit coast of Brazil
- ❑ **1525** Civil war in Inca Empire
- ❑ **1532** Pizarro begins the defeat of the Incas (to 1540)
- ❑ **1562** War and disease kill much of Indian population of Brazil (to 1563)
- ❑ **1568** French occupy north Maranhao
- ❑ **1630** Dutch establish New Holland, covering much of northern Brazil
- ❑ **1654** Portuguese regain control of Brazil
- ❑ **1663** Brazil becomes Viceroyalty
- ❑ **1695** Gold discovered in Brazil
- ❑ **1739** Viceroyalty of New Granada established to defend Caribbean coast
- ❑ **1750** Treaty of Madrid defines boundary between Spanish colonies and Brazil

EUROPE

- ❑ **c.6500 BCE** Farms develop in the area around Greece and the Aegean
- ❑ **c.2000 BCE** Building of Stonehenge
- ❑ Minoan civilisation begins in Crete
- ❑ **c.753 BCE** Foundation of Rome
- ❑ **c.750 BCE** Beginnings of the Greek city states
- ❑ **510 BCE** Foundation of Roman Republic
- ❑ **431 BCE** Outbreak of Peloponnesian War between Sparta and Athens
- ❑ **218 BCE** The Carthaginians invade Italy under the command of Hannibal
- ❑ **49 BCE** Julius Caesar conquers Gaul
- ❑ **27 BCE** Roman Republic collapses; birth of Roman Empire
- ❑ **43 CE** Roman invasion of Britain
- ❑ **238 CE** Goths begin to invade the borders of the Roman Empire
- ❑ **350** Constantinople becomes the new capital of the Roman Empire
- ❑ **410** Invasion and pillage of Rome by the Visigoths
- ❑ **486** Founding of the Frankish kingdom
- ❑ **711** Spain invaded by Muslims
- ❑ **793** Viking raids across Europe
- ❑ **800** Charlemagne becomes first Holy Roman Emperor
- ❑ **1066** Norman conquest of England
- ❑ **1236** Russia invaded by the Mongols
- ❑ **1337** Onset of the Hundred Years War
- ❑ **1453** Byzantine Empire collapses as Ottoman Turks capture Constantinople
- ❑ **1478** Ivan III first tsar of Russia
- ❑ **c.1500** Italian Renaissance
- ❑ **1521** Beginning of Protestant Reformation
- ❑ **1534** Henry VIII of England breaks with Rome
- ❑ **1588** Spanish Armada defeated by the English
- ❑ **1618** Thirty Years War
- ❑ **1642** English Civil War (until 1649)
- ❑ **1756** Onset of the Seven Years War
- ❑ **1789** French Revolution

AFRICA

- ❏ **20,000** BCE Terracotta figurines from Algeria
- ❏ **9000** BCE Village settlement in central Africa
- ❏ **3100** BCE King Narmer unifies Upper and Lower Egypt and becomes first pharaoh
- ❏ **c.2650** BCE Start of great pyramid building in Egypt
- ❏ **2040** BCE Middle Kingdom in Egypt
- ❏ **1350** BCE Pharaoh Akhenaton introduces sun worship in Egypt
- ❏ **1085** BCE End of New Kingdom Egypt
- ❏ **814** BCE Foundation of Phoenician colony of Carthage
- ❏ **332** BCE Alexander the Great conquers Egypt
- ❏ **255** BCE Roman invasion of Africa ends in defeat
- ❏ **146** BCE Rome conquers Carthage
- ❏ **31** BCE Cleopatra's death marks end of Ptolemaic dynasty in Egypt
- ❏ **c.600** CE Kingdom of Ghana founded
- ❏ **1067** CE Almoravids destroy Kingdom of Ghana
- ❏ **c.1300** Emergence of empire of Benin (Nigeria)
- ❏ **1390** Formation of the Kingdom of Kongo
- ❏ **1441** Portuguese export slaves from Atlantic coast to Europe
- ❏ **1498** Vasco da Gama rounds Cape of Good Hope
- ❏ **1502** First slaves taken to the New World
- ❏ **1570** Establishment of Portuguese colony of Angola
- ❏ **1652** Dutch establish colony at Cape of Good Hope
- ❏ **1787** Establishment of Sierra Leone for freed slaves in Africa
- ❏ **1795** British capture Cape of Good Hope from the Dutch
- ❏ **1798** Occupation of Egypt by Napoleon
- ❏ **1816** Shaka leads expansion of Zulu
- ❏ **1822** Freed black slaves found colony of Liberia
- ❏ **1830** French invasion of Algeria
- ❏ **1836** Start of Boer Great Trek
- ❏ **1838** Newly arrived Boer settlers resist attack by Zulus
- ❏ **1848** Boers found the Orange Free State
- ❏ **1853** Livingstone discovers Victoria Falls

ASIA AND THE MIDDLE EAST

- ❏ **c.8550** BCE Foundation of Jericho, first walled town in the world
- ❏ **c.3000** BCE Growth of Sumerian culture in Mesopotamia
- ❏ **c.3500** BCE Foundation of earliest Chinese city, Liang-ch'eng chen
- ❏ Invention of the wheel in Mesopotamia
- ❏ **c.1750** BCE Foundation of Babylonian Empire under Hammurabi
- ❏ **c.1200** BCE Exodus of the Jews from Egypt to Palestine
- ❏ **c.1100** BCE Phoenician civilisation spreads throughout the Mediterranean
- ❏ **c.660** BCE Japanese Empire founded by Jimmu
- ❏ **550** BCE Persian Empire founded
- ❏ **334** BCE Alexander the Great invades Asia Minor
- ❏ **332** BCE Foundation of the Mauryan Empire in India
- ❏ **202** BCE Han Dynasty begins in China
- ❏ **c.112** BCE "Silk Road" links China to the West
- ❏ **c.30** BCE Crucifixion of Jesus of Nazereth; beginnings of Christianity
- ❏ **200** CE End of Han Dynasty in China
- ❏ **320** Foundation of Gupta Empire in Northern India
- ❏ **c.350** Huns invade Persia and India
- ❏ **624** China united by the Tang Dynasty
- ❏ **1044** Foundation of Burma
- ❏ **1096** First crusade
- ❏ **1185** Japan is ruled by Minamoto shoguns
- ❏ **1206** Mongols begin to conquer Asia under Genghis Khan
- ❏ **c.1220** Foundation of the first kingdom in Thailand
- ❏ **1258** Baghdad sacked by Mongols
- ❏ **1264** Yuan Dynasty founded in China by Kublai Kahn
- ❏ **1275** Marco Polo arrives in China
- ❏ **1333** Civil war in Japan following the collapse of the Minamoto shogunate
- ❏ **1349** Singapore founded by Chinese
- ❏ **1368** Beginning of the Ming dynasty in China
- ❏ **1392** Korea proclaims independence
- ❏ **1498** Vasco de Gama completes the first European voyage to India
- ❏ **1609** Beginning of Tokuawa shogunate in Japan
- ❏ **1619** The Dutch found Batavia (later Jakarta) in the East Indies

AUSTRALASIA AND OCEANIA

- ❏ **18,000** BCE Fraser Cave on southern tip of Tasmania occupied
- ❏ **c.10,000** BCE Land bridge connecting Australia and Tasmania starts to disappear
- ❏ **10,000** BCE First human-like figures in Australian rock art
- ❏ **c.8000–6000** BCE Rising sea level covers New Guinea land bridge
- ❏ **c.6000** BCE Migrations from Southeast Asia give rise to Austronesian culture
- ❏ **c.4000** BCE Austronesians reach southwestern Pacific islands
- ❏ **c.1000** BCE Emergence of archaic Polynesian society in Fiji, Tonga and Samoa
- ❏ **c.500** CE Easter Island settled
- ❏ **1000** CE Almost all Pacific islands inhabited
- ❏ **1520** Magellan enters the Pacific
- ❏ **1526** Jorge de Meneses first European to sight New Guinea
- ❏ **1606** Torres sails through strait that bears his name; proves New Guinea is an island
- ❏ **1642** Tasman, searching for a southern continent, finds Tasmania and New Zealand
- ❏ **1688** Dampier first Englishman to visit Australia
- ❏ **1768** Cook's first voyage
- ❏ **1773** Cook crosses Antarctic Circle and circumnavigates continent (to 1775)
- ❏ **1779** Cook killed in Hawaii on third voyage
- ❏ **1788** First penal settlement established at Port Jackson (Sydney)
- ❏ **1802** Flinders circumnavigates Australia (to 1803)
- ❏ **1818** Start of Maori 'Musket Wars' in New Zealand
- ❏ **1819** Bellingshausen's expedition sights Antarctica
- ❏ **1823** Weddell sails into Weddell Sea
- ❏ **1829** Britain annexes western third of Australian continent
- ❏ **1850** A mere 200 foreigners, mostly British, permanently resident in New Zealand
- ❏ **1840** Treaty of Waitangi grants sovereignty over New Zealand to the British
- ❏ **1841** New Zealand becomes a separate Crown Colony
- ❏ **1845** Northern War (to 1846)

see pages 68-69 for CHRONOLOGY 1998-1999

NORTH AMERICA (CONTINUED)

- ❏ **1861** US Civil War (to 1865)
- ❏ **1863** Emancipation Proclamation
- ❏ **1865** Lee surrenders to Grant at Appomattox
- ❏ Assassination of President Lincoln
- ❏ Slavery abolished in US
- ❏ **1867** US purchases Alaska from Russia for $50 million
- ❏ Dominion of Canada established
- ❏ **1869** 15th Amendment gives vote to freed slaves in US
- ❏ **1871** Start of Apache Wars
- ❏ **1876** Battle of Little Big Horn: Sioux warriors kill 250 US soldiers
- ❏ **1890** Massacre at Wounded Knee
- ❏ **1896** Klondike Gold Rush
- ❏ **1898** Spanish-American War
- ❏ **1899** Cession of Cuba and Puerto Rico to US by Spain
- ❏ **1910** Mexican Revolution begins
- ❏ **1914** Panama Canal opens
- ❏ **1921** US restricts immigration
- ❏ **1929** Wall Street Crash precipitates world Depression
- ❏ **1933** President Roosevelt introduces New Deal
- ❏ **1940s** Race riots in Harlem, Los Angeles, Detroit and Chicago
- ❏ **1941** US enters war against Germany and Japan
- ❏ **1945** End of Second World War
- ❏ **1949** Formation of NATO
- ❏ Cold War begins
- ❏ **1950** Korean War (to 1953)
- ❏ Start of US involvement in Vietnam
- ❏ **1959** Cuban Revolution
- ❏ **1962** Cuban Missile Crisis
- ❏ **1963** Martin Luther King leads march on Washington
- ❏ Assassination of President Kennedy
- ❏ **1964** US Congress approves war with Vietnam
- ❏ **1968** Assassination of Martin Luther King sparks riots in 124 US cities
- ❏ **1969** US lands first man on the moon
- ❏ **1973** US withdraws from Vietnam
- ❏ **1974** President Nixon resigns over Watergate scandal
- ❏ **1979** Civil war in Nicaragua (to 1990)
- ❏ Civil war in El Salvador (to 1992)
- ❏ **1987** INF treaty between US and USSR; phased limitation of intermediate-range land-based nuclear weapons
- ❏ **1990** US sends troops to The Gulf in response to Iraq's invasion of Kuwait
- ❏ **1991** UN-brokered peace ends 10-year civil war in El Salvador

SOUTH AMERICA (CONTINUED)

- ❏ **1811** Bolivar starts fight to liberate Venezuela
- ❏ Paraguay independent
- ❏ **1817** San Martin wins a decisive victory over the Spanish and liberates Chile
- ❏ **1821** Peru independent
- ❏ **1822** Brazil independent
- ❏ **1823** Slavery abolished in Chile
- ❏ **1825** Bolivia independent
- ❏ **1828** Uruguay independent
- ❏ **1830** Ecuador, Colombia and Venezuela (formerly Great Colombia) become separate states
- ❏ **1851** Slavery abolished in Colombia
- ❏ **1853** Slavery abolished in Ecuador, Argentina and Uruguay
- ❏ **1854** Slavery abolished in Bolivia and Venezuela
- ❏ **1864** Paraguayan War: Brazil, Argentina and Uruguay defeat Paraguay
- ❏ **1870** Slavery abolished in Paraguay
- ❏ **1888** Slavery abolished in Brazil
- ❏ **1900** Major Italian migration to Argentina
- ❏ **1930** Military revolution in Brazil
- ❏ **1932** Chaco War between Bolivia and Paraguay (to 1935); Paraguay defeats Bolivia
- ❏ **1937** "New State" in Brazil launched by Vargas
- ❏ **1946** Peron comes to power in Argentina
- ❏ **1955** Argentinian leader Peron ousted by military coup. Remains out of power until 1973
- ❏ **1968** Tupamaros urban guerrilla group founded in Uruguay
- ❏ Military junta takes over Peru
- ❏ **1970** Allende elected President of Chile
- ❏ **1973** US backs coup against elected government in Chile; Allende assassinated
- ❏ **1974** Brutal dictatorship of Pinochet in Chile
- ❏ **1976** 15,000 political subversives killed during "Dirty War" by right-wing death squads in Argentina
- ❏ **1980s** Return to democracy for many countries
- ❏ **1982** Falklands War between Argentina and UK
- ❏ **1983** Democracy restored in Argentina
- ❏ **1985** Democracy restored in Brazil and Uruguay
- ❏ **1989** Democracy restored in Chile

EUROPE (CONTINUED)

- ❏ **1792** Proclamation of the French Republic
- ❏ **1804** Napoleon becomes Emperor of France
- ❏ **1805** Britain defeats France and Spain at Trafalgar
- ❏ **1812** Russia invaded by Napoleon
- ❏ **1815** Battle of Waterloo; Napoleon defeated
- ❏ **1845** Beginning of Irish Potato Famine
- ❏ **1854** Crimean War (to 1856)
- ❏ **1870** Franco-Prussian War
- ❏ **1913** Outbreak of the First World War (to 1918)
- ❏ **1917** Russian Revolution leads to the foundation of the first socialist state
- ❏ **1933** Nazi revolution begins in Germany as Hitler is proclaimed Chancellor
- ❏ **1936** Spanish Civil War (to 1939)
- ❏ **1939** Germany invades Poland; Britain and France declare war on Germany
- ❏ **1940** Germany invades Norway, Denmark, Belgium, the Netherlands and France
- ❏ **1941** Germany declares war on US, and attempts to invade Russia
- ❏ **1944** Britain and US land in Normandy; Russians advance into Eastern Europe
- ❏ **1945** Defeat of Germany and death of Hitler
- ❏ **1949** Formation of NATO
- ❏ **1955** Signing of the Warsaw Pact by eight East European nations
- ❏ **1957** Construction of the European Economic Community
- ❏ **1961** Building of the Berlin Wall
- ❏ Yuri Gagarin becomes first man in space
- ❏ **1969** Beginning of the Troubles in Northern Ireland
- ❏ **1975** End of dictatorship in Spain with the death of General Franco
- ❏ **1986** Explosion at Chernobyl nuclear power reactor
- ❏ Launch of Mir Space Station
- ❏ **1989** Boris Yeltsin becomes first democratically elected leader of the USSR
- ❏ Berlin Wall demolished
- ❏ **1990** Unification of East and West Germany
- ❏ **1991** The Soviet Union is split up into its component countries
- ❏ The Yugoslavian regions of Slovenia and Croatia claim their independence
- ❏ **1992** Beginning of civil war in Bosnia-Herzegovina

AFRICA (CONTINUED)

❑ **1869** Opening of Suez Canal

❑ **1875** Stanley confirms Nile source as Ripon Falls

❑ **1879** British defeat Zulus in Zulu War

❑ **1881** French occupy Tunisia

❑ **1882** Britain occupies Egypt

❑ **1883** France begins conquest of Madagascar

❑ **1889** Cecil Rhodes' British South Africa Company begins colonization of Rhodesia

❑ **1894** Britain occupies Uganda

❑ **1899** Start of Second Anglo-Boer War

❑ **1902** Boers forced to surrender

❑ **1908** Belgium takes over Congo Free State

❑ **1910** Formation of Union of South Africa

❑ **1911** Italian conquest of Libya

❑ **1935** Italian invasion of Ethiopia

❑ **1942** British halt German advance at El Alamein

❑ **1948** National Party wins power in South Africa

❑ **1956** UK fails to block Egypt's nationalization of Suez Canal

❑ **1960** Outbreak of civil war in Belgian Congo
❑ Fifteen African countries gain independence

❑ **1962** Algeria gains independence

❑ **1963** Northern Rhodesia and Nyasaland granted independence
❑ Foundation of Organization of African Unity (OAU)

❑ **1964** Black leader, Nelson Mandela, sentenced to life imprisonment in South Africa

❑ **1965** Rhodesia declares independence

❑ **1974** Emperor Haile Selassie of Ethiopia deposed

❑ **1975** Angola and Mozambique gain independence; civil wars ensue

❑ **1980** Black majority rule established in Zimbabwe (Rhodesia)

❑ **1981** President Sadat of Egypt assassinated

❑ **1984** Eritrean civil war causes widespread famine (to 1985)

❑ **1987** Famine in Ethiopia

❑ **1990** Mandela released: apartheid begins to be dismantled
❑ Namibia becomes independent

❑ **1994** South Africa holds first multiracial election; Nelson Mandela wins presidency
❑ Massacre of 500,000 Tutsis by Hutu in Rwanda

ASIA AND THE MIDDLE EAST (CONTINUED)

❑ **1747** Foundation of Afghanistan

❑ **1842** Britain annexes Hong Kong

❑ **1854** Japan begins trade with the US

❑ **1868** End of Tokugawa shogunate in Japan

❑ **1877** Queen Victoria is proclaimed Empress of India

❑ **1911** Chinese Revolution

❑ **1917** "Balfour Declaration" promises the Jews a home in Palestine

❑ **1922** The last Ottoman sultan is deposed; Turkey proclaimed a republic

❑ **1926** Chiang Kai-shek reunifies China

❑ **1932** Kingdom of Saudi Arabia founded

❑ **1941** Japan attacks the US at Pearl Harbour

❑ **1945** US drops atom bombs on the Japanese cities of Hiroshima and Nagasaki; Japanese forces surrender

❑ **1946** Beginning of civil war in China

❑ **1947** India and Pakistan proclaim their independence

❑ **1948** Burma and Ceylon proclaim their independence
❑ Establishment of the state of Israel

❑ **1949** Communists win civil war in China; People's Republic proclaimed
❑ Indonesia proclaims its independence

❑ **1950** Korean War (until 1953)

❑ **1954** Laos, Cambodia and Vietnam proclaim their independence

❑ **1959** China occupies Tibet
❑ Beginning of war between North and South Vietnam (until 1975)

❑ **1965** Cultural Revolution in China (until 1969)

❑ **1971** East Pakistan (later Bangladesh) claims independence

❑ **1973** US withdraws from Vietnam

❑ **1975** Civil war in Lebanon
❑ Laos, Cambodia and Vietnam become communist
❑ Foundation of Islamic Republic in Iran
❑ Vietnam invades Cambodia; expulsion of the Khmer Rouge

❑ **1980** Iran/Iraq War (until 1988)

❑ **1982** Invasion of Lebanon by Israel (until 1985)

❑ **1986** Ferdinand Marcos deposed in the Philippines

❑ **1989** Massacre of Tiananmen Square, Peking

❑ **1990** Invasion of Kuwait by Iraq

❑ **1991** Gulf War
❑ Beginning of Middle East peace talks

❑ **1997** Britain returns Hong Kong to China

AUSTRALASIA AND OCEANIA (CONTINUED)

❑ **c.1850** Migrant workers from China, Japan and the Philippines start arriving in Hawaii

❑ **1851** Gold discovered in New South Wales

❑ **1858** King Movement demands Maori state and opposes further land sales

❑ **1860** European settlers outnumber Maoris in New Zealand

❑ **1861** Gold discovered in New Zealand

❑ **1862** Second Maori War

❑ **1864** First French convict settlers in New Caledonia

❑ **1865** 1,000 Chinese brought to Tahiti to work cotton plantation (to 1866)

❑ **1869** Last convict ship arrives in Australia

❑ **1870** Maori resistance crushed
❑ Germans start to buy up large tracts of Western Samoa

❑ **1874** Indian sugar-cane workers arrive in Fiji

❑ **1888** Chile starts colonization of Easter Island

❑ **1890** Gold discovered in Western Australia
❑ Western Australia last state to be granted self-government

❑ **1898** US annexes Hawaii and seizes Guam from Spain

❑ **1901** Australia becomes self-governing federation within British Empire

❑ **1912** Amundsen's expedition reaches South Pole

❑ **1914** Over 60,000 Australian troops lose lives in First World War (to 1918)

❑ **1930s** Australia hit hard by global Depression

❑ **1942** Australia under threat of invasion as Japanese bomb Darwin

❑ **1946** US begins nuclear tests at Eniwetok and Bikini atolls in Micronesia

❑ **1948** White immigration, especially from UK, becomes post-war policy

❑ **1966** France begins testing nuclear bombs in Tuamotu Islands

❑ **1972** Labour government challenges paternalistic attitude of UK to Australia

❑ **1975** Restrictions imposed on immigration

❑ **1985** South Pacific Forum declares nuclear-free Pacific; US and France reject this

❑ **1988** Bicentennial celebrations in Australia occasion Aboriginal protests

❑ **1996** France halts nuclear testing in the Pacific

THE FORMATION OF THE MODERN WORLD

THE WORLD AS WE KNOW IT today, like all of the species that inhabit it, is the product of many thousands of years of evolution. The political and cultural map of the globe bears the hallmark of many varied courses of human development the world over. Nevertheless, much of the modern human geography of the planet can be traced to developments in the relatively recent past. The following pages chart the rise and fall of the various states and empires of the early modern and modern ages. Beginning with the first great achievement of European exploration, the discovery of the Americas in 1492, the maps show the way in which various European and Asian powers expanded their cultural and political influence and control down to the present day. This process left indelible cultural imprints in the form of language, religion, education and systems of government on every part of the planet.

MAJOR MIGRATIONS SINCE 1500

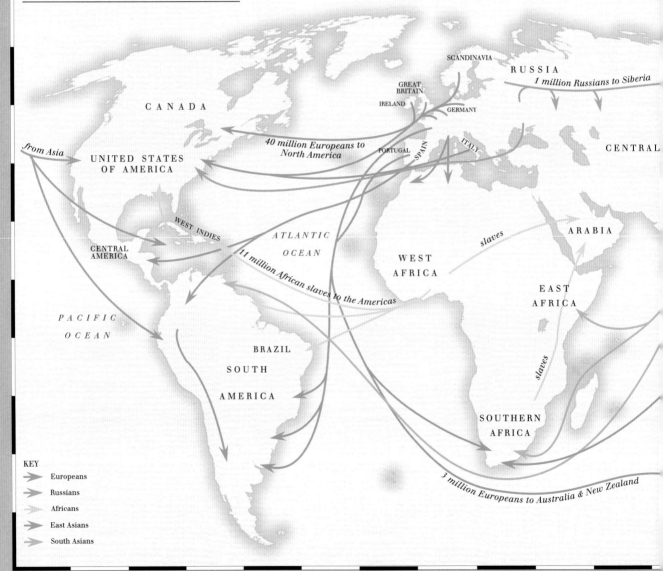

KEY

- Europeans
- Russians
- Africans
- East Asians
- South Asians

LANGUAGES OF THE WORLD

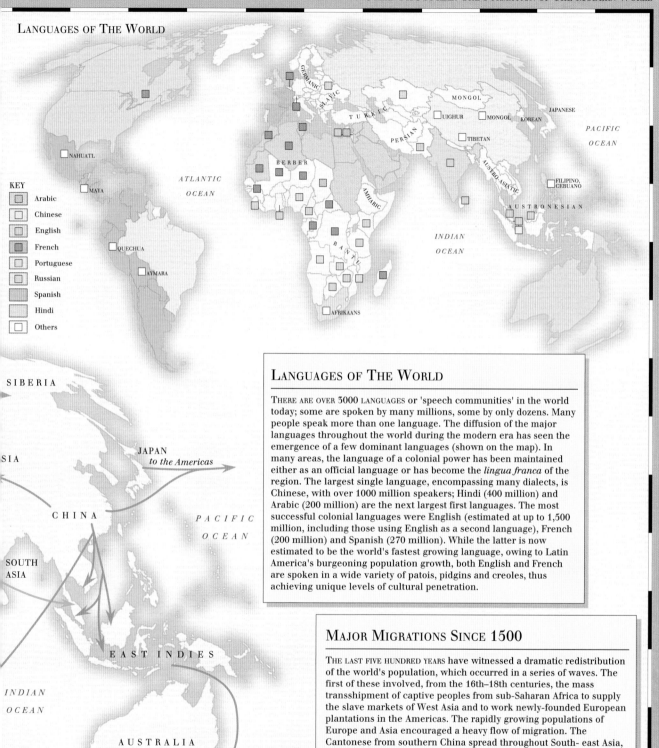

KEY
- Arabic
- Chinese
- English
- French
- Portuguese
- Russian
- Spanish
- Hindi
- Others

LANGUAGES OF THE WORLD

THERE ARE OVER 3000 LANGUAGES or 'speech communities' in the world today; some are spoken by many millions, some by only dozens. Many people speak more than one language. The diffusion of the major languages throughout the world during the modern era has seen the emergence of a few dominant languages (shown on the map). In many areas, the language of a colonial power has been maintained either as an official language or has become the *lingua franca* of the region. The largest single language, encompassing many dialects, is Chinese, with over 1000 million speakers; Hindi (400 million) and Arabic (200 million) are the next largest first languages. The most successful colonial languages were English (estimated at up to 1,500 million, including those using English as a second language), French (200 million) and Spanish (270 million). While the latter is now estimated to be the world's fastest growing language, owing to Latin America's burgeoning population growth, both English and French are spoken in a wide variety of patois, pidgins and creoles, thus achieving unique levels of cultural penetration.

MAJOR MIGRATIONS SINCE 1500

THE LAST FIVE HUNDRED YEARS have witnessed a dramatic redistribution of the world's population, which occurred in a series of waves. The first of these involved, from the 16th–18th centuries, the mass transshipment of captive peoples from sub-Saharan Africa to supply the slave markets of West Asia and to work newly-founded European plantations in the Americas. The rapidly growing populations of Europe and Asia encouraged a heavy flow of migration. The Cantonese from southern China spread throughout South- east Asia, while from the 16th century millions of Europeans emigrated to the 'New Worlds' of the Americas and, later, Australasia. This European diaspora reached a peak at the end of the 19th century. Then, as the colonial empires coalesced in the early years of the 20th century, there was a final wave of global movement within them, when South and East Asians migrated to fill labour markets and exploit opportunities in Africa and the Americas. While homogenous societies have developed in North America and Australia, many diverse ethnic communities remain scattered across the world.

THE WORLD IN 1492

WHEN CHRISTOPHER COLUMBUS sailed west from Europe, seeking a quicker route to Asia, he launched a process of discovery that was eventually to bring the disparate regions of the world into closer contact, to form the global map we know today. The largest political entity in the world at that time was the Chinese Ming empire. Culturally, the Islamic faith had forged a bond of religious unity which extended in a broad swathe from Southeast Asia to the Atlantic coast of North Africa. Europe was a mêlée of rival monarchies; sub-Saharan Africa a patchwork of trading kingdoms; the Americas, a separate world of rich tribal cultures, with empires established only in Central America and the central Andes.

GLOBAL STATES AND TERRITORIES

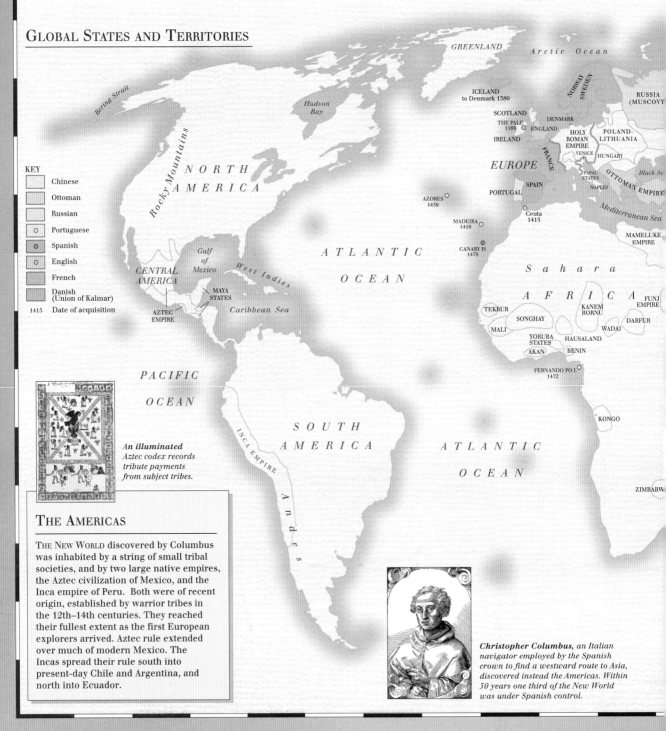

KEY

☐	Chinese
☐	Ottoman
☐	Russian
○	Portuguese
◉	Spanish
○	English
☐	French
☐	Danish (Union of Kalmar)
1415	Date of acquisition

GREENLAND

Arctic Ocean

Bering Strait

ICELAND
to Denmark 1380

NORWAY
SWEDEN

RUSSIA
(MUSCOVY

SCOTLAND
THE PALE
1169
IRELAND

DENMARK
ENGLAND

HOLY
ROMAN
EMPIRE

POLAND-
LITHUANIA

VENICE
HUNGARY

Hudson Bay

Rocky Mountains

NORTH
AMERICA

EUROPE

FRANCE

PAPAL
STATES

OTTOMAN EMPIRE

Black Se

SPAIN

NAPLES

PORTUGAL

AZORES
1459

Mediterranean Sea

Ceuta
1415

MADEIRA
1418

*ATLANTIC
OCEAN*

CANARY IS
1478

MAMELUKE
EMPIRE

Sahara

Gulf
of
Mexico

West Indies

CENTRAL
AMERICA

MAYA
STATES

Caribbean Sea

AZTEC
EMPIRE

AFRICA

TEKRUR

SONGHAY

MALI

YORUBA
STATES

AKAN

KANEM
BORNU

WADAI

HAUSALAND

BENIN

FUNJ
EMPIRE

DARFUR

FERNANDO PO 1
1472

*PACIFIC
OCEAN*

INCA EMPIRE

Andes

SOUTH
AMERICA

*ATLANTIC
OCEAN*

KONGO

ZIMBABW

An illuminated Aztec codex records tribute payments from subject tribes.

THE AMERICAS

THE NEW WORLD discovered by Columbus was inhabited by a string of small tribal societies, and by two large native empires, the Aztec civilization of Mexico, and the Inca empire of Peru. Both were of recent origin, established by warrior tribes in the 12th–14th centuries. They reached their fullest extent as the first European explorers arrived. Aztec rule extended over much of modern Mexico. The Incas spread their rule south into present-day Chile and Argentina, and north into Ecuador.

Christopher Columbus, an Italian navigator employed by the Spanish crown to find a westward route to Asia, discovered instead the Americas. Within 50 years one third of the New World was under Spanish control.

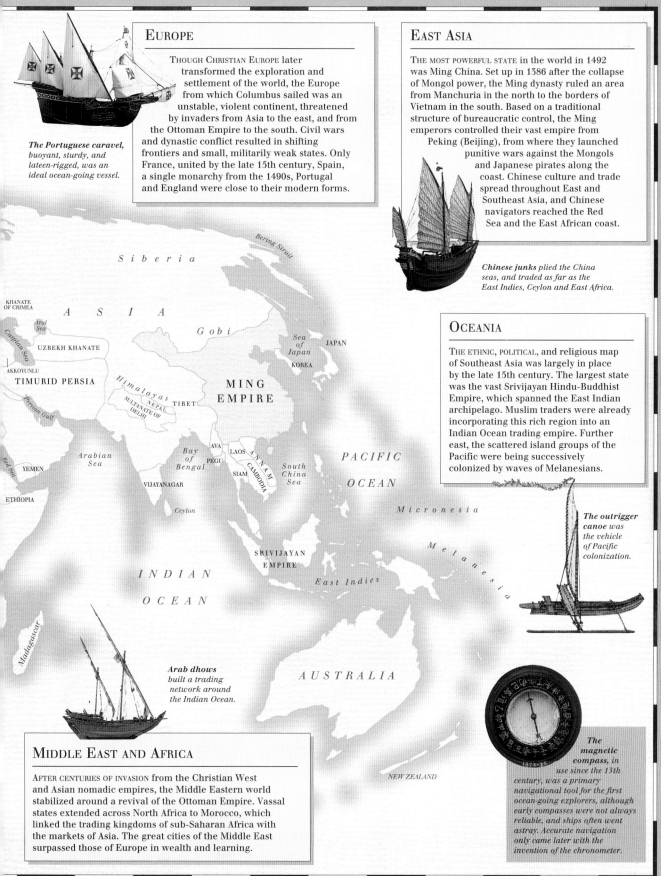

EUROPE

THOUGH CHRISTIAN EUROPE later transformed the exploration and settlement of the world, the Europe from which Columbus sailed was an unstable, violent continent, threatened by invaders from Asia to the east, and from the Ottoman Empire to the south. Civil wars and dynastic conflict resulted in shifting frontiers and small, militarily weak states. Only France, united by the late 15th century, Spain, a single monarchy from the 1490s, Portugal and England were close to their modern forms.

The Portuguese caravel, buoyant, sturdy, and lateen-rigged, was an ideal ocean-going vessel.

EAST ASIA

THE MOST POWERFUL STATE in the world in 1492 was Ming China. Set up in 1386 after the collapse of Mongol power, the Ming dynasty ruled an area from Manchuria in the north to the borders of Vietnam in the south. Based on a traditional structure of bureaucratic control, the Ming emperors controlled their vast empire from Peking (Beijing), from where they launched punitive wars against the Mongols and Japanese pirates along the coast. Chinese culture and trade spread throughout East and Southeast Asia, and Chinese navigators reached the Red Sea and the East African coast.

Chinese junks plied the China seas, and traded as far as the East Indies, Ceylon and East Africa.

OCEANIA

THE ETHNIC, POLITICAL, and religious map of Southeast Asia was largely in place by the late 15th century. The largest state was the vast Srivijayan Hindu-Buddhist Empire, which spanned the East Indian archipelago. Muslim traders were already incorporating this rich region into an Indian Ocean trading empire. Further east, the scattered island groups of the Pacific were being successively colonized by waves of Melanesians.

The outrigger canoe was the vehicle of Pacific colonization.

Arab dhows built a trading network around the Indian Ocean.

MIDDLE EAST AND AFRICA

AFTER CENTURIES OF INVASION from the Christian West and Asian nomadic empires, the Middle Eastern world stabilized around a revival of the Ottoman Empire. Vassal states extended across North Africa to Morocco, which linked the trading kingdoms of sub-Saharan Africa with the markets of Asia. The great cities of the Middle East surpassed those of Europe in wealth and learning.

The magnetic compass, in use since the 13th century, was a primary navigational tool for the first ocean-going explorers, although early compasses were not always reliable, and ships often went astray. Accurate navigation only came later with the invention of the chronometer.

Map labels

Bering Strait
Siberia
KHANATE OF CRIMEA
Aral Sea
Caspian Sea
ASIA
Gobi
Sea of Japan
JAPAN
KOREA
UZBEK KHANATE
AKKOYUNLU
TIMURID PERSIA
Persian Gulf
Himalayas
NEPAL
SULTANATE OF DELHI
TIBET
MING EMPIRE
Red Sea
Arabian Sea
YEMEN
AVA
LAOS
PEGU
ANNAM
SIAM
CAMBODIA
South China Sea
PACIFIC OCEAN
Bay of Bengal
ETHIOPIA
VIJAYANAGAR
Ceylon
Micronesia
Melanesia
INDIAN OCEAN
SRIVIJAYAN EMPIRE
East Indies
Madagascar
AUSTRALIA
NEW ZEALAND
1878-25

THE AGE OF DISCOVERY: 1492-1648

THE FIRST STATE to take advantage of the new age of exploration was Spain. By the middle of the 16th century, under the Emperor Charles V, Spain was established as the foremost European colonial power, and one of the richest and most powerful kingdoms in Europe. Spanish rule was extended over the whole of Central America, much of South America, Florida and the Caribbean; in Asia, Spanish rule was established in the Philippines. Spain led the way in establishing European settler colonies overseas. By the middle of the 17th century, British, Dutch and French colonists began to challenge Spanish dominance in the Americas and East Asia, while pirates around the world plundered Spain's wealthy merchant convoys.

GLOBAL STATES AND TERRITORIES

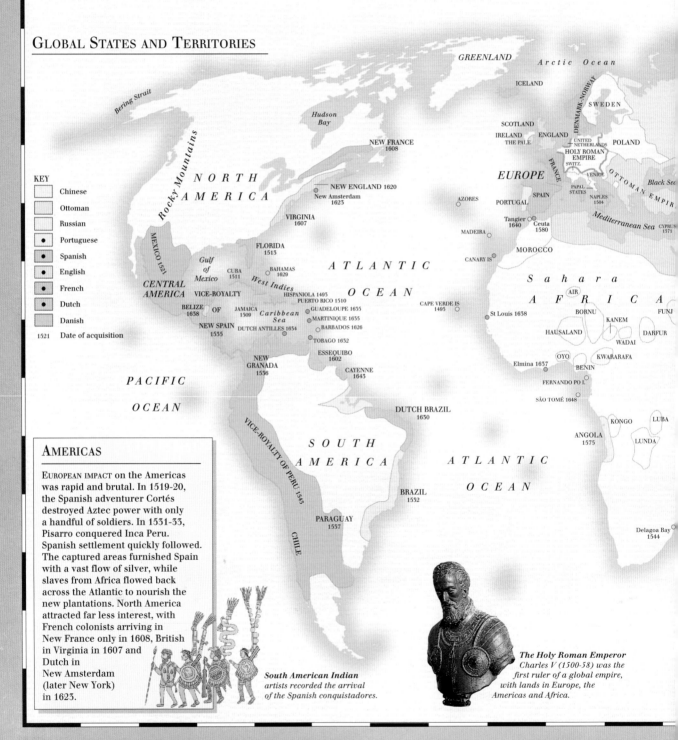

KEY

	Chinese
	Ottoman
	Russian
●	Portuguese
●	Spanish
●	English
●	French
●	Dutch
	Danish
1521	Date of acquisition

AMERICAS

EUROPEAN IMPACT on the Americas was rapid and brutal. In 1519-20, the Spanish adventurer Cortés destroyed Aztec power with only a handful of soldiers. In 1531-33, Pisarro conquered Inca Peru. Spanish settlement quickly followed. The captured areas furnished Spain with a vast flow of silver, while slaves from Africa flowed back across the Atlantic to nourish the new plantations. North America attracted far less interest, with French colonists arriving in New France only in 1608, British in Virginia in 1607 and Dutch in New Amsterdam (later New York) in 1623.

South American Indian artists recorded the arrival of the Spanish conquistadores.

The Holy Roman Emperor *Charles V (1500-58) was the first ruler of a global empire, with lands in Europe, the Americas and Africa.*

EUROPE

FOR MORE THAN A CENTURY after Martin Luther inspired the Protestant Reformation in the 1520s, Europe was torn by religious wars. Scandinavia, England and Scotland adopted the new church but elsewhere bitter civil conflicts led to the prolonged warfare and persecution known as the Thirty Years' War. This ended in 1648; it destroyed wide areas of Central Europe and decimated the German population, but resulted in a religious settlement which carried down to the 20th century. The Dutch Republic and northern Germany became Protestant while southern Germany, Poland and southwest Europe remained Catholic.

Printing, using movable type, was a key development in the dissemination of ideas, knowledge and commerce in early modern Europe.

ASIA

IN 1480, THE SMALL PRINCIPALITY OF MUSCOVY (Moscow) threw off Mongol control, and proceeded to expand Muscovite power over the whole of the area from the Arctic Ocean to the Caspian Sea. In the 1550s, the conquest of Kazan brought Russian power to the Urals, and over the next century it spread across Siberia reaching the Pacific coast by 1649. Much of the area remained uninhabited, but to the south this new empire jostled uneasily with a string of Central Asian Muslim khanates, and with the newly-established Manchurian Ch'ing dynasty, which wrested control of China from the Ming in 1644.

European navigators and surveyors produced accurate maps and charts of their voyages.

The Indian Mughal ruler Shahjahan (1592-1648), builder of the Taj Mahal.

SOUTH ASIA AND OCEANIA

THE PORTUGUESE and the Spanish were the first European powers to open trade with the powerful Asian states of Mughal India and Ch'ing China, the Spanish opening trans-Pacific routes between Central America, the Philippines and China. But the establishment of the Dutch and British East India companies in the early 17th century announced the advent of two new maritime powers.

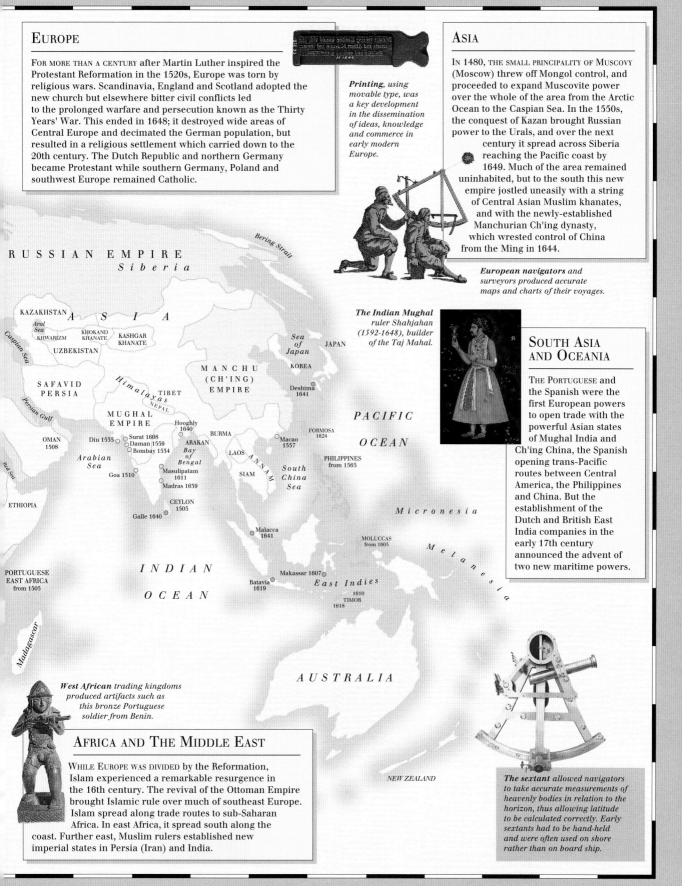

West African trading kingdoms produced artifacts such as this bronze Portuguese soldier from Benin.

AFRICA AND THE MIDDLE EAST

WHILE EUROPE WAS DIVIDED by the Reformation, Islam experienced a remarkable resurgence in the 16th century. The revival of the Ottoman Empire brought Islamic rule over much of southeast Europe. Islam spread along trade routes to sub-Saharan Africa. In east Africa, it spread south along the coast. Further east, Muslim rulers established new imperial states in Persia (Iran) and India.

The sextant allowed navigators to take accurate measurements of heavenly bodies in relation to the horizon, thus allowing latitude to be calculated correctly. Early sextants had to be hand-held and were often used on shore rather than on board ship.

Map labels

RUSSIAN EMPIRE
Siberia
Bering Strait
KAZAKHSTAN
Aral Sea
KHWARIZM
KHOKAND KHANATE
UZBEKISTAN
KASHGAR KHANATE
A S I A
Caspian Sea
SAFAVID PERSIA
Persian Gulf
Himalayas
TIBET
NEPAL
MUGHAL EMPIRE
MANCHU (CH'ING) EMPIRE
Sea of Japan
JAPAN
KOREA
Deshima 1641
OMAN 1508
Diu 1555
Daman 1559
Surat 1608
Bombay 1554
Hooghly 1640
ARAKAN
BURMA
Macao 1557
FORMOSA 1624
Arabian Sea
Goa 1510
Bay of Bengal
Masulipatam 1611
Madras 1639
LAOS
ANNAM
SIAM
South China Sea
PHILIPPINES from 1565
PACIFIC OCEAN
Red Sea
ETHIOPIA
CEYLON 1505
Galle 1640
Micronesia
Malacca 1641
MOLUCCAS from 1605
Melanesia
PORTUGUESE EAST AFRICA from 1505
INDIAN OCEAN
Makassar 1607
Batavia 1619
East Indies
1610
TIMOR 1618
South China Sea
Madagascar
AUSTRALIA
NEW ZEALAND

THE AGE OF EXPANSION: 1648-1789

THE YEARS FROM the middle of the 17th century to the end of the 18th century saw a massive consolidation of European discovery and exploration, which took the form of colonial settlement and political expansion. This period also witnessed the beginning of a sharp rise in European population and in its economic strength, accompanied by rapid developments in the arts and sciences. All these factors powered European expansion – a process that would bring European culture to every part of the globe, gradually filling in the world map, and bringing it into often fatal contact with less robust indigenous cultures. By the last quarter of the 18th century, with Europe poised on the brink of political turmoil, only Africa and Australasia remained largely unmolested by European attentions.

GLOBAL STATES AND TERRITORIES

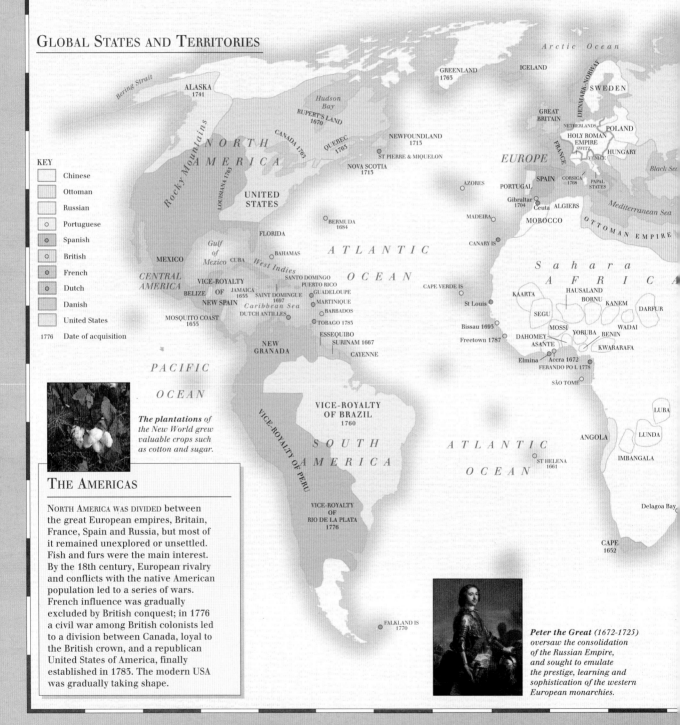

KEY

	Chinese
	Ottoman
	Russian
○	Portuguese
◉	Spanish
◉	British
◉	French
◉	Dutch
	Danish
	United States
1776	Date of acquisition

The plantations of the New World grew valuable crops such as cotton and sugar.

THE AMERICAS

NORTH AMERICA WAS DIVIDED between the great European empires, Britain, France, Spain and Russia, but most of it remained unexplored or unsettled. Fish and furs were the main interest. By the 18th century, European rivalry and conflicts with the native American population led to a series of wars. French influence was gradually excluded by British conquest; in 1776 a civil war among British colonists led to a division between Canada, loyal to the British crown, and a republican United States of America, finally established in 1783. The modern USA was gradually taking shape.

Peter the Great (1672-1725) oversaw the consolidation of the Russian Empire, and sought to emulate the prestige, learning and sophistication of the western European monarchies.

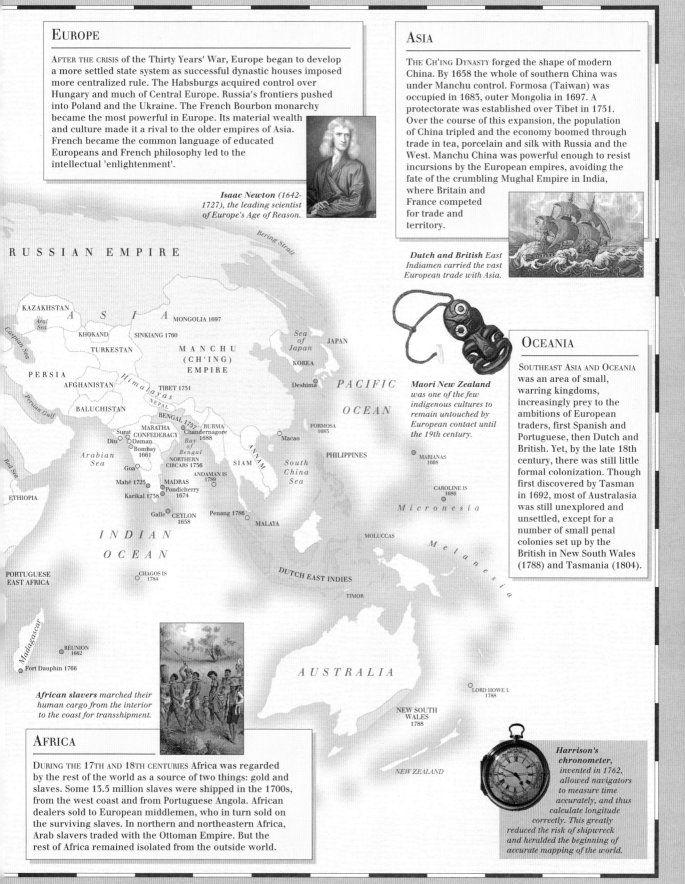

EUROPE

AFTER THE CRISIS of the Thirty Years' War, Europe began to develop a more settled state system as successful dynastic houses imposed more centralized rule. The Habsburgs acquired control over Hungary and much of Central Europe. Russia's frontiers pushed into Poland and the Ukraine. The French Bourbon monarchy became the most powerful in Europe. Its material wealth and culture made it a rival to the older empires of Asia. French became the common language of educated Europeans and French philosophy led to the intellectual 'enlightenment'.

Isaac Newton (1642-1727), the leading scientist of Europe's Age of Reason.

ASIA

THE CH'ING DYNASTY forged the shape of modern China. By 1658 the whole of southern China was under Manchu control. Formosa (Taiwan) was occupied in 1683, outer Mongolia in 1697. A protectorate was established over Tibet in 1751. Over the course of this expansion, the population of China tripled and the economy boomed through trade in tea, porcelain and silk with Russia and the West. Manchu China was powerful enough to resist incursions by the European empires, avoiding the fate of the crumbling Mughal Empire in India, where Britain and France competed for trade and territory.

Dutch and British East Indiamen carried the vast European trade with Asia.

Maori New Zealand was one of the few indigenous cultures to remain untouched by European contact until the 19th century.

OCEANIA

SOUTHEAST ASIA AND OCEANIA was an area of small, warring kingdoms, increasingly prey to the ambitions of European traders, first Spanish and Portuguese, then Dutch and British. Yet, by the late 18th century, there was still little formal colonization. Though first discovered by Tasman in 1692, most of Australasia was still unexplored and unsettled, except for a number of small penal colonies set up by the British in New South Wales (1788) and Tasmania (1804).

African slavers marched their human cargo from the interior to the coast for transshipment.

AFRICA

DURING THE 17TH AND 18TH CENTURIES Africa was regarded by the rest of the world as a source of two things: gold and slaves. Some 13.5 million slaves were shipped in the 1700s, from the west coast and from Portuguese Angola. African dealers sold to European middlemen, who in turn sold on the surviving slaves. In northern and northeastern Africa, Arab slavers traded with the Ottoman Empire. But the rest of Africa remained isolated from the outside world.

Harrison's chronometer, invented in 1762, allowed navigators to measure time accurately, and thus calculate longitude correctly. This greatly reduced the risk of shipwreck and heralded the beginning of accurate mapping of the world.

Map labels:

RUSSIAN EMPIRE
KAZAKHSTAN
Aral Sea
Caspian Sea
A S I A
KHOKAND
SINKIANG 1760
MONGOLIA 1697
TURKESTAN
MANCHU (CH'ING) EMPIRE
Sea of Japan
JAPAN
KOREA
Bering Strait
PERSIA
AFGHANISTAN
Himalayas
TIBET 1751
NEPAL
Deshima
PACIFIC OCEAN
BALUCHISTAN
Persian Gulf
BENGAL 1757
BURMA
MARATHA CONFEDERACY
Chandernagore 1688
Surat
Diu
Daman
Bombay 1661
Bay of Bengal
Macao
FORMOSA 1683
South China Sea
PHILIPPINES
ANNAM
SIAM
Arabian Sea
Goa
NORTHERN CIRCARS 1756
Mahé 1725
MADRAS
ANDAMAN IS 1789
MARIANAS 1668
Karikal 1758
Pondicherry 1674
Red Sea
ETHIOPIA
Galle
CEYLON 1658
Penang 1786
MALAYA
CAROLINE IS 1686
Micronesia
INDIAN OCEAN
MOLUCCAS
Melanesia
PORTUGUESE EAST AFRICA
CHAGOS IS 1784
DUTCH EAST INDIES
TIMOR
Madagascar
RÉUNION 1662
Fort Dauphin 1766
AUSTRALIA
LORD HOWE I. 1788
NEW SOUTH WALES 1788
NEW ZEALAND

THE AGE OF REVOLUTION: 1789-1830

IN 1789 ROYAL POWER was shattered by the French Revolution. The collapse of the most powerful monarchy in Europe reverberated worldwide. The revolutions in France and America ushered in the idea of the modern nation state, and of popular representative government. Revolutionary outbreaks occurred elsewhere in Europe, and overseas colonies in Latin America won their independence. At the same time, an industrial revolution was taking place in Europe, transforming the old trading economy into a manufacturing base which would require a global supply of raw materials and a global market to fuel it. The revolutionary years thus marked the beginning of the modern political and economic world order.

GLOBAL STATES AND TERRITORIES

KEY

	Chinese
	Ottoman
	Russian
○	Portuguese
◉	Spanish
○	British
◉	French
◉	Dutch
	Danish
	United States

1790 — Date of acquisition
[1820] — Date of independence

THE AMERICAS

THE FLEDGLING UNITED STATES OF AMERICA began to expand rapidly, purchasing the Midwest territories from France in 1803, and taking Florida from Spain in 1819. Revolutionary fervour both here and in Europe weakened the control of France, Spain and Portugal throughout Latin America. From 1810 there followed 20 years of violent revolt, with native armies fighting their European masters and each other. The new states were prey to political violence and instability, but they never again came under European rule.

Simón Bolívar (1783-1830), led armies of liberation in Peru, Bolivia, and Venezuela.

Napoleon Bonaparte (1769-1821) began his career as a French Revolutionary commander. By 1804 he had become emperor of much of mainland Europe.

EUROPE

UNDER THE REVOLUTIONARY GENERAL, Napoleon Bonaparte, France conquered a large part of Europe and destroyed the old feudal order. Napoleon helped to shape the new nation states that emerged in 19th-century Europe – Belgium, Italy and Germany. He gave much of Europe its modern legal code and systems of education and local government.

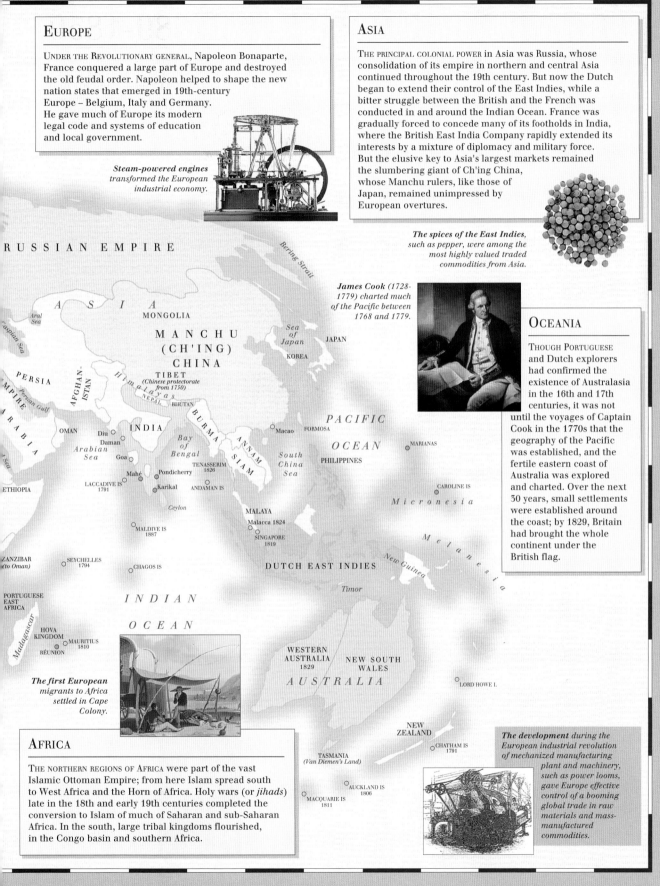

Steam-powered engines transformed the European industrial economy.

ASIA

THE PRINCIPAL COLONIAL POWER in Asia was Russia, whose consolidation of its empire in northern and central Asia continued throughout the 19th century. But now the Dutch began to extend their control of the East Indies, while a bitter struggle between the British and the French was conducted in and around the Indian Ocean. France was gradually forced to concede many of its footholds in India, where the British East India Company rapidly extended its interests by a mixture of diplomacy and military force. But the elusive key to Asia's largest markets remained the slumbering giant of Ch'ing China, whose Manchu rulers, like those of Japan, remained unimpressed by European overtures.

The spices of the East Indies, such as pepper, were among the most highly valued traded commodities from Asia.

James Cook (1728-1779) charted much of the Pacific between 1768 and 1779.

OCEANIA

THOUGH PORTUGUESE and Dutch explorers had confirmed the existence of Australasia in the 16th and 17th centuries, it was not until the voyages of Captain Cook in the 1770s that the geography of the Pacific was established, and the fertile eastern coast of Australia was explored and charted. Over the next 30 years, small settlements were established around the coast; by 1829, Britain had brought the whole continent under the British flag.

RUSSIAN EMPIRE

Bering Strait

A S I A
MONGOLIA

MANCHU
(CH'ING)
CHINA

TIBET
(Chinese protectorate from 1750)

Aral Sea

Caspian Sea

PERSIA

AFGHAN-ISTAN

Himalayas

NEPAL
BHUTAN

BURMA

INDIA

Bay of Bengal

SIAM

ANNAM

Sea of Japan

JAPAN
KOREA

Macao
FORMOSA

PACIFIC
OCEAN

MARIANAS

South China Sea

PHILIPPINES

Micronesia

CAROLINE IS

OMAN

Diu
Daman

Goa

Arabian Sea

Mahé
Pondicherry

Karikal

TENASSERIM
1826

ANDAMAN IS

LACCADIVE IS
1791

Ceylon

MALAYA

Malacca 1824

SINGAPORE
1819

Melanesia

New Guinea

MALDIVE IS
1887

DUTCH EAST INDIES

ETHIOPIA

ZANZIBAR
(to Oman)

SEYCHELLES
1794

CHAGOS IS

Timor

INDIAN

OCEAN

PORTUGUESE
EAST
AFRICA

HOVA
KINGDOM

Madagascar

MAURITIUS
1810

RÉUNION

WESTERN
AUSTRALIA
1829

NEW SOUTH
WALES

A U S T R A L I A

LORD HOWE I.

The first European migrants to Africa settled in Cape Colony.

NEW
ZEALAND

CHATHAM IS
1791

AFRICA

THE NORTHERN REGIONS OF AFRICA were part of the vast Islamic Ottoman Empire; from here Islam spread south to West Africa and the Horn of Africa. Holy wars (or *jihads*) late in the 18th and early 19th centuries completed the conversion to Islam of much of Saharan and sub-Saharan Africa. In the south, large tribal kingdoms flourished, in the Congo basin and southern Africa.

TASMANIA
(Van Diemen's Land)

AUCKLAND IS
1806

MACQUARIE IS
1811

The development during the European industrial revolution of mechanized manufacturing plant and machinery, such as power looms, gave Europe effective control of a booming global trade in raw materials and mass-manufactured commodities.

THE AGE OF EMPIRE: 1830-1914

THE NINETEENTH CENTURY was dominated by the spread of modern industry and transport, and the expansion of European trade and influence worldwide. Industry made Europe rich and powerful; its capital cities were monuments to the self-confidence of the new European age. Railways and steam ships revolutionized communications, bringing a stream of industrial goods, technical know-how, and European settlers across America, Africa and Asia. Modern industry and weapons brought Europe to the summit of global influence. In these developments lay the origins of the division of the world into rich and poor regions; a developed, prosperous north, an under-developed, dependent south.

GLOBAL STATES AND TERRITORIES

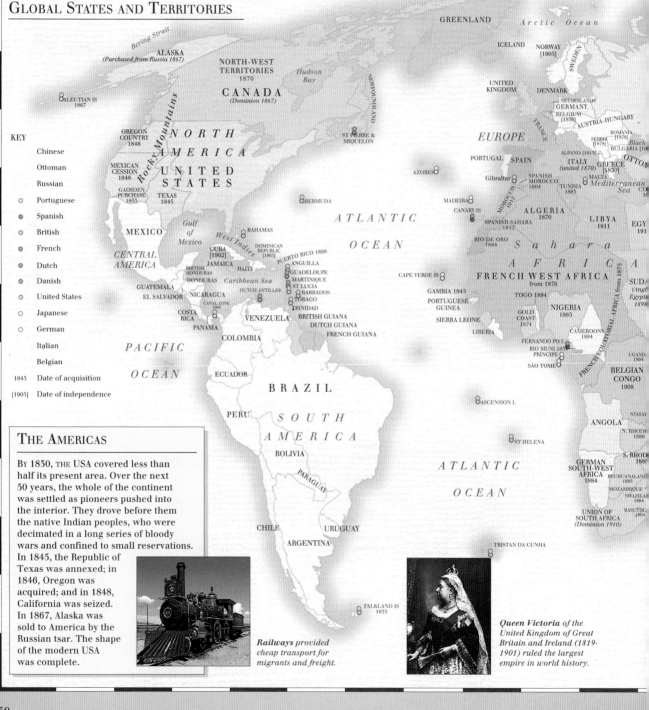

KEY

- Chinese
- Ottoman
- Russian
- ○ Portuguese
- ◉ Spanish
- ○ British
- ◉ French
- ◉ Dutch
- ◉ Danish
- ○ United States
- ○ Japanese
- ○ German
- Italian
- Belgian
- 1845 Date of acquisition
- [1905] Date of independence

THE AMERICAS

By 1830, THE USA covered less than half its present area. Over the next 50 years, the whole of the continent was settled as pioneers pushed into the interior. They drove before them the native Indian peoples, who were decimated in a long series of bloody wars and confined to small reservations. In 1845, the Republic of Texas was annexed; in 1846, Oregon was acquired; and in 1848, California was seized. In 1867, Alaska was sold to America by the Russian tsar. The shape of the modern USA was complete.

Railways provided cheap transport for migrants and freight.

Queen Victoria of the United Kingdom of Great Britain and Ireland (1819-1901) ruled the largest empire in world history.

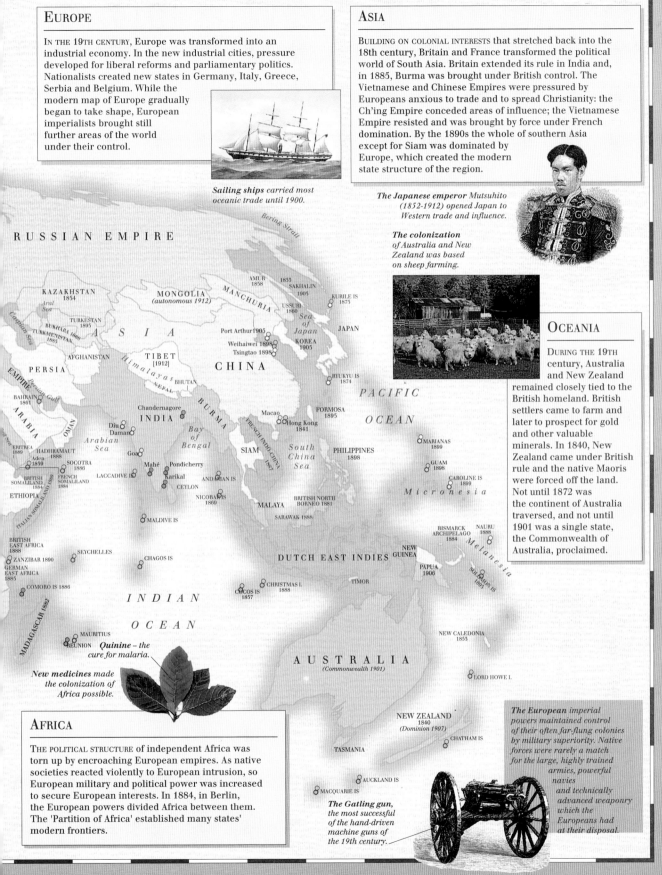

EUROPE

IN THE 19TH CENTURY, Europe was transformed into an industrial economy. In the new industrial cities, pressure developed for liberal reforms and parliamentary politics. Nationalists created new states in Germany, Italy, Greece, Serbia and Belgium. While the modern map of Europe gradually began to take shape, European imperialists brought still further areas of the world under their control.

Sailing ships carried most oceanic trade until 1900.

ASIA

BUILDING ON COLONIAL INTERESTS that stretched back into the 18th century, Britain and France transformed the political world of South Asia. Britain extended its rule in India and, in 1885, Burma was brought under British control. The Vietnamese and Chinese Empires were pressured by Europeans anxious to trade and to spread Christianity: the Ch'ing Empire conceded areas of influence; the Vietnamese Empire resisted and was brought by force under French domination. By the 1890s the whole of southern Asia except for Siam was dominated by Europe, which created the modern state structure of the region.

The Japanese emperor Mutsuhito (1852-1912) opened Japan to Western trade and influence.

The colonization of Australia and New Zealand was based on sheep farming.

OCEANIA

DURING THE 19TH century, Australia and New Zealand remained closely tied to the British homeland. British settlers came to farm and later to prospect for gold and other valuable minerals. In 1840, New Zealand came under British rule and the native Maoris were forced off the land. Not until 1872 was the continent of Australia traversed, and not until 1901 was a single state, the Commonwealth of Australia, proclaimed.

Quinine – the cure for malaria.

New medicines made the colonization of Africa possible.

AFRICA

THE POLITICAL STRUCTURE of independent Africa was torn up by encroaching European empires. As native societies reacted violently to European intrusion, so European military and political power was increased to secure European interests. In 1884, in Berlin, the European powers divided Africa between them. The 'Partition of Africa' established many states' modern frontiers.

The European imperial powers maintained control of their often far-flung colonies by military superiority. Native forces were rarely a match for the large, highly trained armies, powerful navies and technically advanced weaponry which the Europeans had at their disposal.

The Gatling gun, the most successful of the hand-driven machine guns of the 19th century.

THE AGE OF GLOBAL WAR: 1914-45

IN 1914, IMPERIAL AND MILITARY rivalry in Europe provoked the first of two world wars, the largest and most destructive wars in human history. At the end of the first war, in 1918, the old international order was dead. The Russian Empire collapsed in revolution and was transformed by a communist minority into the Soviet Union. The German, Habsburg and Ottoman empires were dismembered. A fragile peace ensued but the old equilibrium was gone. The rise of strident nationalism in Germany, Japan and Italy destroyed the peace once again in 1939. The second war cost the lives of 50 million people and ravaged Europe and Asia. At its end, in 1945, the USA and the Soviet Union had emerged as the new superpowers.

GLOBAL STATES AND TERRITORIES

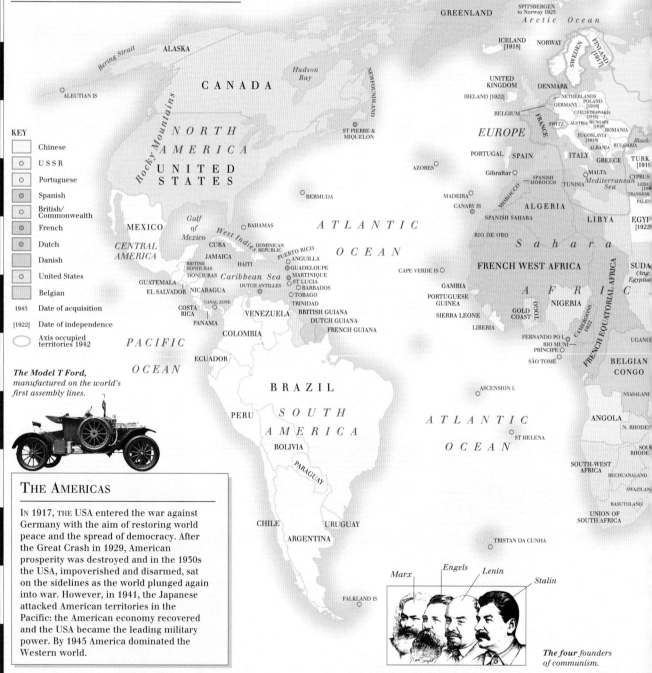

KEY

- Chinese
- USSR
- Portuguese
- Spanish
- British/Commonwealth
- French
- Dutch
- Danish
- United States
- Belgian
- 1945 Date of acquisition
- [1922] Date of independence
- Axis occupied territories 1942

The Model T Ford, manufactured on the world's first assembly lines.

THE AMERICAS

IN 1917, THE USA entered the war against Germany with the aim of restoring world peace and the spread of democracy. After the Great Crash in 1929, American prosperity was destroyed and in the 1930s the USA, impoverished and disarmed, sat on the sidelines as the world plunged again into war. However, in 1941, the Japanese attacked American territories in the Pacific: the American economy recovered and the USA became the leading military power. By 1945 America dominated the Western world.

Marx *Engels* *Lenin* *Stalin*

The four founders of communism.

EUROPE

BOTH WORLD WARS had their origins in Europe. In 1914 Britain, France and Russia combined to defeat Germany, with US help. In 1918 new nation states were established in Eastern Europe. But, by 1939, revived German nationalism started a second world war; much of Western Europe came under a German 'New Order' until the Soviet Union, Britain and the USA developed sufficient military strength to reconquer Europe and defeat Germany.

World War II was decided by mechanical and industrial superiority.

ASIA

THE COLLAPSE OF THE CHINESE EMPIRE in 1911, followed in 1917 by the disappearance of the Russian Empire, produced instability across Asia. Full-scale war broke out between Japan and China in 1937, with Japan trying to conquer China. The Soviet Union was the victim of German aggression from 1941. Both Japan and Germany were held at bay by communist forces which eventually succeeded in imposing stable politics on Asia. By 1945, the Soviet Union had reconquered its lost territories and dominated Eastern Europe. In China, communist armies filled the vacuum left by the Japanese defeat.

Mahatma Gandhi (1868-1948) led India to independence through peaceful non-co-operation and protest.

OCEANIA

FOR THE ONLY TIME in its history, Australia was faced with the very real prospect of invasion. In the Second World War, Japanese armies reached the island of New Guinea, and bombed towns in northern Australia. Japanese submarines attacked Sydney harbour. The Battle of the Coral Sea, in May 1942, saved Australia, but it took almost three years to clear Japanese forces from the South Pacific, where they hung on grimly to the rich oil and mineral resources they had captured.

Japan promoted itself as the liberator of Asia from the chains of European colonialism.

Haile Selassie (1892-1975), ruler of Ethiopia, the only independent empire in Africa.

MIDDLE EAST

IN 1918, THE TURKISH EMPIRE disappeared after 400 years of Ottoman rule. The modern map of North Africa and the Middle East was carved out of its ruins by the victors of the First World War. After the Second World War, the foundation was laid for a new state of Israel, following the genocide of Europe's Jews by Nazi Germany. This led to conflict between native Arabs and Jewish migrants.

The conquest of the air was the most important technological achievement of the period. It added a devastating dimension to warfare, in the form of bombing, while transforming civil transport.

A German Zeppelin airship of the 1930s.

THE MODERN AGE: 1945-PRESENT DAY

THE WARTIME ALLIANCE between the USA and the Soviet Union turned sour in efforts to reconstruct Europe and the Far East. The world became divided into two hostile camps; liberal-capitalism on the one hand, communism on the other. The two sides fought a 'Cold War', each trying to contain and subvert the other. The main conflicts of the war occurred over small issues – Korea (1950-53), Cuba (1962), Vietnam (1954-75). Larger wars were avoided because of the nuclear deterrent. With the crumbling of communist power in Russia and Eastern Europe, the stalemate of the Cold War was replaced by a less stable international order, dominated by economic uncertainty and revived nationalism.

GLOBAL STATES AND TERRITORIES

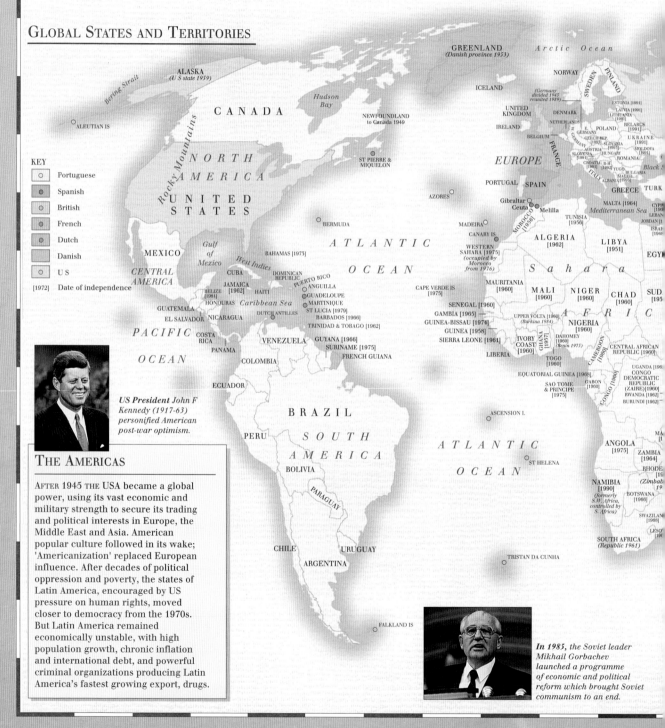

US President John F Kennedy (1917-63) personified American post-war optimism.

In 1985, the Soviet leader Mikhail Gorbachev launched a programme of economic and political reform which brought Soviet communism to an end.

KEY

○	Portuguese
◉	Spanish
○	British
◉	French
◉	Dutch
	Danish
○	U S

[1972] Date of independence

THE AMERICAS

AFTER 1945 THE USA became a global power, using its vast economic and military strength to secure its trading and political interests in Europe, the Middle East and Asia. American popular culture followed in its wake; 'Americanization' replaced European influence. After decades of political oppression and poverty, the states of Latin America, encouraged by US pressure on human rights, moved closer to democracy from the 1970s. But Latin America remained economically unstable, with high population growth, chronic inflation and international debt, and powerful criminal organizations producing Latin America's fastest growing export, drugs.

The Berlin Wall, symbol of the Cold War division of Europe, was demolished in 1989.

EUROPE

IN 1945, EUROPE LAY IN RUINS, but during the next 30 years, Western Europe experienced a long economic boom, restoring widespread prosperity and political stability. It progressed towards economic and political unity under the EC. In Eastern Europe development was overshadowed by Soviet communism until its collapse. As democracies many new nations now face an uncertain future.

ASIA

IN SOUTHERN ASIA, popular nationalist movements came to power in India, Burma, Malaya and Indonesia; in China and Indo-China, power passed to native communist movements whose roots went back to the 1920s. After 1949, China under Mao Zedong became, with its vast population and large military forces, a second communist superpower. But the success story of modern Asia has been Japan. Defeated in 1945, its economy and cities laid waste by bombing, Japan began a programme of economic rebuilding with American aid. By the 1980s Japan had emerged as one of the world's largest manufacturing economies.

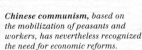

Chinese communism, based on the mobilization of peasants and workers, has nevertheless recognized the need for economic reforms.

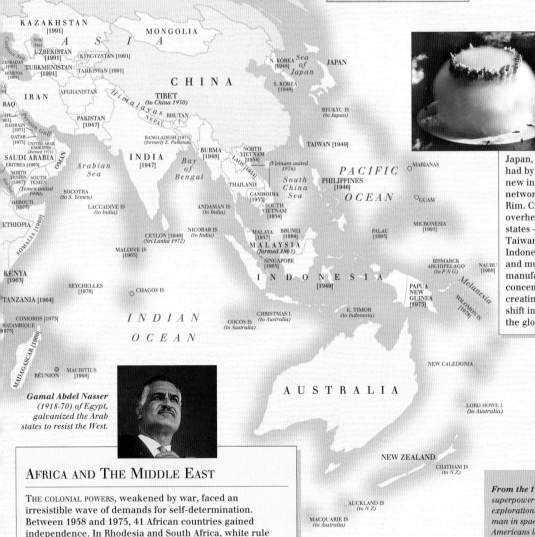

RUSSIAN FEDERATION

KAZAKHSTAN [1991]

MONGOLIA

ASIA

Aral Sea

UZBEKISTAN [1991]
ZERBAIJAN [1991]
TURKMENISTAN [1991]   KYRGYZSTAN [1991]
ARMENIA [1991]   TAJIKISTAN [1991]

Caspian Sea

CHINA

N. KOREA [1948]   Sea of Japan   JAPAN

S. KOREA [1948]

IRAN   AFGHANISTAN
RAQ   Himalayas   TIBET (to China 1950)
                                    BHUTAN
ATE [1961]   PAKISTAN [1947]   NEPAL
BAHRAIN [1971]
QATAR [1971]   UNITED ARAB EMIRATES (formed 1971)
SAUDI ARABIA   BANGLADESH [1971] (formerly E. Pakistan)
ERITREA [1995]   BURMA [1948]   NORTH VIETNAM [1954]
NORTH YEMEN [1967]   SOUTH YEMEN   Arabian Sea   INDIA [1947]   Bay of Bengal   LAOS [1954]   (Vietnam united 1976)

RYUKYU IS (to Japan)

TAIWAN [1949]

PACIFIC   MARIANAS

A treaty banning the testing of nuclear bombs in the Pacific was signed in 1986.

OCEANIA

THE POST-WAR economies of Japan, USA and Australia had by the 1990s created a new industrial and trading network around the Pacific Rim. Cheap labour and low overheads drew younger states – South Korea, Taiwan, Singapore, Indonesia – into the system and much of the world's manufacturing is now concentrated there, creating a consequent shift in the balance of the global economy.

(Yemen united 1990)   SOCOTRA (to S. Yemen)
DJIBOUTI [1977]   THAILAND   South China Sea   PHILIPPINES [1946]   OCEAN   GUAM
ETHIOPIA   LACCADIVE IS (to India)   CAMBODIA [1953]
                           ANDAMAN IS (to India)   SOUTH VIETNAM [1954]
                 CEYLON [1948] (Sri Lanka 1972)   NICOBAR IS (to India)   MALAYA [1957]   BRUNEI [1984]   PALAU [1995]   MICRONESIA [1991]
                 MALDIVE IS [1965]   MALAYSIA (formed 1963)
KENYA [1965]   SINGAPORE [1965]   BISMARCK ARCHIPELAGO (to PNG)   NAURU [1968]
          SEYCHELLES [1976]   CHAGOS IS   INDONESIA [1949]   PAPUA NEW GUINEA [1975]   Melanesia
TANZANIA [1964]   SOLOMON IS [1978]
COMOROS [1975]   INDIAN   CHRISTMAS I. (to Australia)   E. TIMOR (to Indonesia)
OZAMBIQUE 975]   OCEAN   COCOS IS (to Australia)

MAURITIUS [1968]
MADAGASCAR [1960]   RÉUNION   AUSTRALIA   NEW CALEDONIA

LORD HOWE I. (to Australia)

Gamal Abdel Nasser (1918-70) of Egypt, galvanized the Arab states to resist the West.

NEW ZEALAND   CHATHAM IS (to N Z)

AFRICA AND THE MIDDLE EAST

THE COLONIAL POWERS, weakened by war, faced an irresistible wave of demands for self-determination. Between 1958 and 1975, 41 African countries gained independence. In Rhodesia and South Africa, white rule survived independence. In North Africa and throughout the Middle East a new form of anti-imperialism emerged in the 1970s in the form of Islamic fundamentalism.

AUCKLAND IS (to N Z)
MACQUARIE IS (to Australia)

From the 1950s to the 1970s, superpower rivalry focused on space exploration. The Soviets put the first man in space in 1961, and the Americans landed on the moon in 1969. Since then both manned and unmanned missions have become almost everyday events.

POPULATION

THE WORLD'S POPULATION is projected to reach some 10 billion by the year 2025. The global distribution of this rapidly growing population is very uneven, and is dictated by climate, terrain and natural and economic resources. The great majority of the Earth's people live in coastal zones, and along river valleys. Deserts cover over 20% of the Earth's surface, but support less than 5% of the world's population. By the end of the year 2000, it is estimated that over half of the world's population will live in cities – most of them in Asia – as a result of mass migration from rural areas in search of jobs. Improvements in food supply and advances in medicine have both played a major role in the remarkable growth in global population, which has increased five-fold over the last 150 years. Better nutrition, together with higher standards of public health and sanitation, have led to increased longevity and higher birth rates. Current estimates, however, are that nearly 800 million people, almost all in the developing countries, do not have enough food to meet their basic nutritional needs.

POPULATION DENSITY
(People/mi²)

- Below 3
- 3–13
- 13–29
- 30–51
- 52–130
- 131–260
- 261–520
- Above 520

INFANT MORTALITY

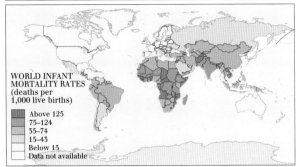

WORLD INFANT
MORTALITY RATES
(deaths per
1,000 live births)

- Above 125
- 75–124
- 35–74
- 15–43
- Below 15
- Data not available

INFANT MORTALITY

INFANT MORTALITY RATES are highest in Africa, South America and south Asia, where poverty and disease are rife, and where the standards of healthcare are not as high as in North America or Europe. The country with the highest infant mortality rate is Sierra Leone, where the recent civil war has devastated communities.

LIFE EXPECTANCY

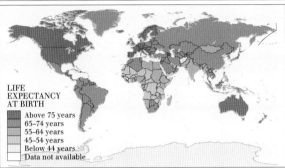

LIFE
EXPECTANCY
AT BIRTH

- Above 75 years
- 65–74 years
- 55–64 years
- 45–54 years
- Below 44 years
- Data not available

LIFE EXPECTANCY

LIFE EXPECTANCY IS also poorest in Africa, for similar reasons to those noted above. In western Europe and North America, life expectancy is increasing at such a rate that each successive generation may expect to live longer than the last. In the developed world, people can now expect to live twice as long as they did a century ago.

Arctic Circle

Beijing
Tokyo
Shanghai
Delhi
Calcutta
Bombay

Tropic of Cancer

Equator

Tropic of Capricorn

Sydney
Melbourne

Antarctic Circle

POPULATION FACTFILE

LARGEST COUNTRIES

1 Russian Federation
17,075,400 km² (6,529,863 mi²)

2 China
9,326,410 km² (3,599,994 mi²)

3 Canada
9,220,970 km² (3,559,924 mi²)

SMALLEST COUNTRIES

1 Vatican City 0.44 km² (0.17 mi²)

2 Monaco 0.95 km² (0.75 mi²)

3 Nauru 21 km² (8.2 mi²)

MOST DENSELY POPULATED COUNTRIES

1 Monaco 15,897 people/km² (41,333 people/mi²)

2 Singapore 5,738 people/km² (14,918 people/mi²)

3 Vatican City 2,273 people/km² (5,882 people/mi²)

MOST SPARSELY POPULATED COUNTRIES

1 Australia 2 people/km² (5 people/mi²)

2 Mauritania 2 people/km² (5 people/mi²)

3 Mongolia 2 people/km² (5 people/mi²)

WORLD ECONOMY

T HE WEALTHY COUNTRIES of the developed world, with
their aggressive, market-led economies and their access
to productive new technologies and international markets,
dominate the world economic system. At the other
extreme, many of the countries of the developing
world are locked in a cycle of national debt, rising
populations and unemployment. The state-
managed economies of the former communist
bloc began to be dismantled during the 1990s,
and China is emerging as a major economic
power following decades of isolation. Since
the late 1980s, technological advances
have enabled transactions between
financial centres to occur at even
greater speed, and new markets
have sprung up throughout
the world.

**BALANCE OF TRADE
(MILLIONS US $)**

over 30,000
10,000–29,000
1000–9999   Surplus
0-999
0–999
1000-9999
10,000–29,999   Deficit
below 30,000
data unavailable

DIRECT INVESTMENT
from USA
from Europe
from Japan

**COUNTRIES RELIANT
ON A SINGLE EXPORT**
bananas
coffee
oil/petroleum
copper

INTERNATIONAL TRADE

WORLD TRADE ACTS as a stimulus to national
economies, encouraging growth. Over the last
three decades, as heavy industries have declined,
services – banking, insurance, tourism, airlines, and
shipping – have taken an increasingly large share of
the world trade. Manufactured articles now account
for nearly two–thirds of world trade; raw materials
and food make up less than a quarter of the total.

**LOCATION OF
MAJOR STOCKMARKETS**
● Major stock markets

INTERNATIONAL TRADE

London
New York
Tokyo

WORLD ECONOMIES	
HIGHEST GNP PER CAPITA	
1 Luxembourg	$45,560
2 Liechenstein	$40,000
3 Japan	$38,160
4 Norway	$36,100
5 Denmark	$34,890
LOWEST GNP PER CAPITA	
1 Somalia	$100
2 Ethiopia and Congo (Zaire)	$110
3 Burundi and Mozambique	$140
4 Sierra Leone	$160
5 Niger and Paraguay	$200

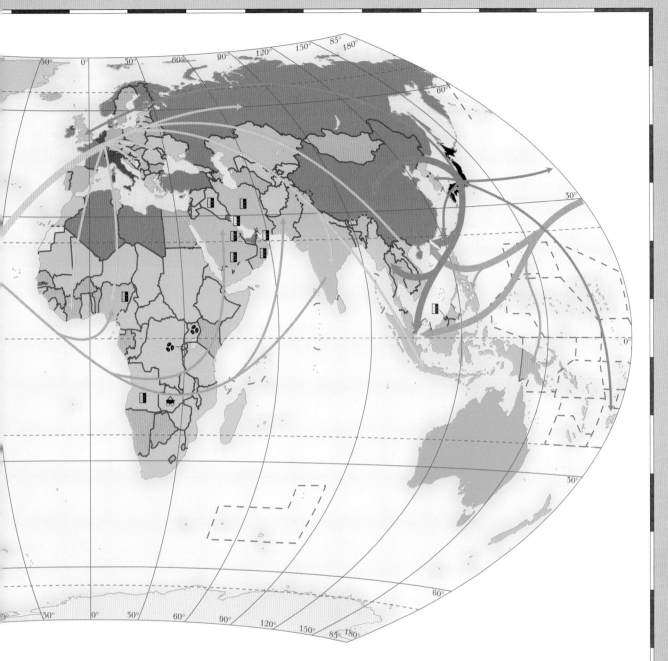

TRADE BLOCS

INTERNATIONAL TRADE BLOCS are formed when groups of countries, often already enjoying close military and political ties, join together to offer mutually preferential terms of trade for both imports and exports. Increasingly, global trade is dominated by three main blocs: the EU, NAFTA, and ASEAN. They are supplanting older trade blocs such as the Commonwealth, a legacy of colonialism.

TRADE BLOCS

TRADE BLOCS

EU	NAFTA	ASEAN	LAIA
CACM	SADC	ECOWAS	CEEAC

WORLD ECONOMY

THE PATTERN OF THE GLOBAL economy frequently relates to an underlying equation: the relationship between population and available resources. Japan, for example, had a much "bigger" economy than the former Soviet Union, India or Latin America as a whole. Such imbalances usually occur because countries differ enormously in their living standards, the education and skills of their work forces, the productivity of their agriculture, and in the value of their markets. A country's economic performance can be evaluated by calculating its Gross National Product (GNP). This is the total value of both the goods, and the services (including so-called "invisible exports" – financial services, tourism, etc.) that it produces. During the last three decades the most rapidly growing sector of world trade is services – banking, insurance, tourism, consultancy, accountancy, films, music and other cultural services, airlines and shipping. Services account for 21% of world trade, almost equivalent to the volume of trade in food and raw materials.

COMPARATIVE WORLD WEALTH

A global assessment of the Gross Domestic Product (GDP) by nation reveals great disparities. The developed world, with only a quarter of the world's population, has 80% of the world's manufacturing income. Civil war, conflict and political instability further undermine the economy of many of the world's poorest nations.

Mass–market tourism *is now an all-important source of revenue in many countries.*

AVERAGE GDP
PER CAPITA (IN $US)
- Above 5,000
- 2,000–5,000
- 600–2,000
- Below 600
- Data unavailable

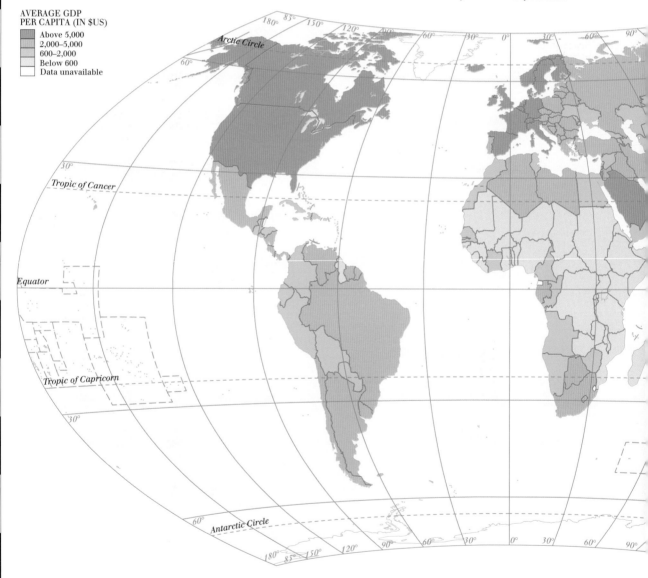

INTERNATIONAL DEBT

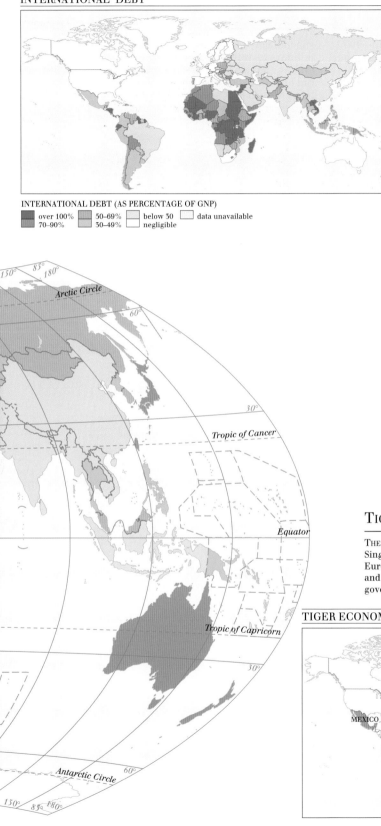

INTERNATIONAL DEBT (AS PERCENTAGE OF GNP)

- over 100%
- 70–90%
- 50–69%
- 30–49%
- below 30
- negligible
- data unavailable

INTERNATIONAL DEBT

FOREIGN INVESTMENT in the developing world during the 1970s led to a global financial crisis in the 1980s, when many countries were unable to meet their debt repayments. The International Monetary Fund (IMF) was forced to reschedule the debts and, in some cases, write them off completely.

WORLD'S 20 LARGEST CORPORATIONS

1	General Motors (USA)	$168,369
2	Ford Motor Company (USA)	$146,991
3	Mitsui (Japan)	$144,942
4	Mitsubishi (Japan)	$140,203
5	Itochu (Japan)	$135,542
6	Royal Dutch/Shell Group (UK/Neth.)	$128,174
7	Marubeni (Japan)	$124,026
8	Exxon (USA)	$119,434
9	Sumitomo (Japan)	$119,281
10	Toyota Motor Company (Japan)	$108,702
11	Wal-Mart Stores (USA)	$106,147
12	General Electric (USA)	$79,179
13	Nissho Iwai(Japan)	$78,921
14	Nippon Telegraph and Telephone (Japan)	$78,320
15	INTL. Business Machines (USA)	$75,947
16	Hitachi (Japan)	$75,669
17	AT&T (USA)	$74,525
18	Nippon Life Insurance (Japan)	$72,575
19	Mobil (USA)	$72,267
20	Daimler Benz (Germany)	$71,589

TIGER ECONOMIES

THE ECONOMIC "TIGERS" of the Pacific rim – Taiwan, Singapore, and South Korea – have grown faster than Europe and the USA over the last decade. Their export– and service–led economies have benefited from stable government, low labour costs, and foreign investment.

TIGER ECONOMIES

GLOBAL TOURISM

TOURISM IS THE WORLD'S biggest industry. In 1995 there were 567 million tourists worldwide; this number is expected to rise to 937 million by 2010. With improved transport, cheaper flights and increased leisure time, many of the countries of the developing world are rapidly becoming tourist meccas. Since the 1960s, mass tourism has become increasingly specialized, encompassing sporting and adventure holidays as well as ecological tours. Although the tourist industry employs 127 million people worldwide, the benefits of tourism are not always felt at a local level, where jobs are often low paid and menial. Unregulated growth of tourism is causing both environmental and social damage.

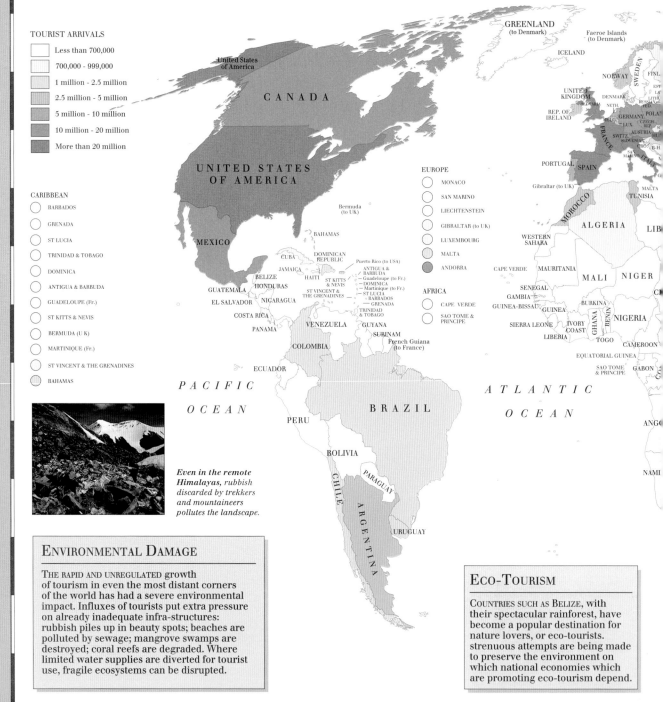

TOURIST ARRIVALS

- Less than 700,000
- 700,000 - 999,000
- 1 million - 2.5 million
- 2.5 million - 5 million
- 5 million - 10 million
- 10 million - 20 million
- More than 20 million

CARIBBEAN
- BARBADOS
- GRENADA
- ST LUCIA
- TRINIDAD & TOBAGO
- DOMINICA
- ANTIGUA & BARBUDA
- GUADELOUPE (Fr.)
- ST KITTS & NEVIS
- BERMUDA (U K)
- MARTINIQUE (Fr.)
- ST VINCENT & THE GRENADINES
- BAHAMAS

EUROPE
- MONACO
- SAN MARINO
- LIECHTENSTEIN
- GIBRALTAR (to UK)
- LUXEMBOURG
- MALTA
- ANDORRA

AFRICA
- CAPE VERDE
- SAO TOME & PRINCIPE

Even in the remote Himalayas, rubbish discarded by trekkers and mountaineers pollutes the landscape.

ENVIRONMENTAL DAMAGE

THE RAPID AND UNREGULATED growth of tourism in even the most distant corners of the world has had a severe environmental impact. Influxes of tourists put extra pressure on already inadequate infra-structures: rubbish piles up in beauty spots; beaches are polluted by sewage; mangrove swamps are destroyed; coral reefs are degraded. Where limited water supplies are diverted for tourist use, fragile ecosystems can be disrupted.

ECO-TOURISM

COUNTRIES SUCH AS BELIZE, with their spectacular rainforest, have become a popular destination for nature lovers, or eco-tourists. strenuous attempts are being made to preserve the environment on which national economies which are promoting eco-tourism depend.

The beautiful island of Phuket, Thailand, is being overtaken by tourist developments.

A TOURIST PARADISE?

THE MOST REMOTE CORNERS of the world are now being penetrated by tourists in their quest for the exotic. In many parts of the developing world, tourism can be described as a form of "neo-colonialism"; hotels and beaches are owned by multinational companies, and most of the profits are taken outside the country. Tourism frequently alienates local people from their own land, and has a negative impact on the local culture and environment.

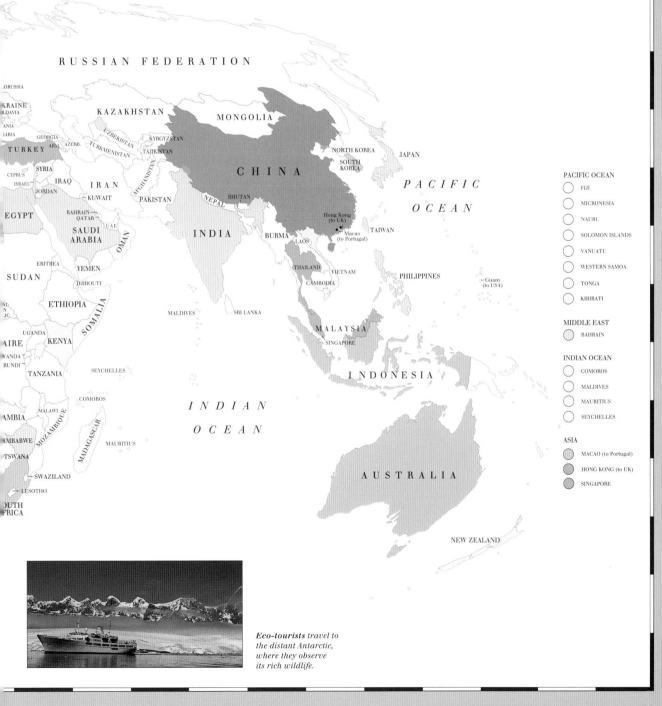

PACIFIC OCEAN
- FIJI
- MICRONESIA
- NAURU
- SOLOMON ISLANDS
- VANUATU
- WESTERN SAMOA
- TONGA
- KIRIBATI

MIDDLE EAST
- BAHRAIN

INDIAN OCEAN
- COMOROS
- MALDIVES
- MAURITIUS
- SEYCHELLES

ASIA
- MACAO (to Portugal)
- HONG KONG (to UK)
- SINGAPORE

Eco-tourists travel to the distant Antarctic, where they observe its rich wildlife.

GLOBAL SECURITY

THE POST–COLD WAR PERIOD has produced a range of threats to the principle states of the international community. Ethnic conflict within states, mass migration and environmental hazards provide examples of new insecurities with potential for conflict of a very different sort from its Cold War counterpart. The spectacle of Yugoslavia's collapse into warring factions and the breakup of the Soviet Union were the most dramatic examples of the decline of the state as a source of security for its citizens and as a pillar of world order. Today, while orthodox diplomacy still has its place, recognition of the inability of the state to cope alone makes multilateral solutions imperative. Western governments are reluctant to intervene in conflict in the developing world fearing the prospect of becoming entangled in a protracted war. The 15 members of the UN Security Council often have difficulty reaching a unilateral decision and taking decisive action swiftly enough. In recent conflicts in Somalia, Yugoslavia and Rwanda, UN peacekeeping forces became embroiled in the bloodshed. However, in the recent troubles in Iraq, it was the UN which advised against military action.

EL SALVADOR

THE CIVIL WAR ended in 1991 with a UN-brokered peace agreement.

NORTHERN IRELAND

SECTARIAN CONFLICT CONTINUED throughout the 1990's. In 1995 the IRA and other republican paramilitary groups agreed to a cease-fire, which lasted for 17 months. In 1998, the Good Friday Peace Agreement was signed by the political parties of Northern Ireland as well as the governments of the UK and Ireland, supported by the US.

ERITREA AND ETHIOPIA

THE ERITREAN PEOPLE'S LIBERATION Front, a rebel force, began fighting for the Eritrea's independence from Ethiopia in 1961. Eritrea effectively seceded in 1991, and formally proclaimed its independence in 1993.

RWANDA

CIVIL WAR IN RWANDA led to mass genocide in 1994, as 500,000 Tutsis were massacred by Hutu supporters of the old regime. A UN war crimes tribunal was set up to deal with the perpetrators.

DISPUTED TERRITORIES AND BORDERS
- Countries involved in active territorial or border disputes
- Disputed borders
- Undefined borders
- Disputed territories

Map labels: ICELAND, Rockall, UNITED KINGDOM, Northern Ireland, REP. OF IRELAND, Gibraltar, Ceuta, SPAIN, MOROCCO, WESTERN SAHARA, GHANA, TOGO, CUBA, Guantanamo Bay, BELIZE, GUATEMALA, EL SALVADOR, NICARAGUA, VENEZUELA, GUYANA, SURINAM, French Guiana, COLOMBIA, ECUADOR, PERU, BRAZIL, BOLIVIA, CHILE, ARGENTINA, URUGUAY, Falkland Islands

Warfare in the Twentieth Century

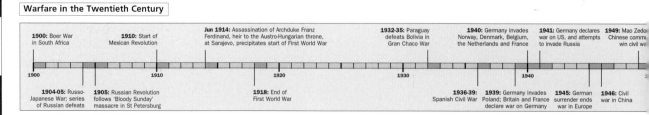

1900: Boer War in South Africa

1910: Start of Mexican Revolution

Jun 1914: Assassination of Archduke Franz Ferdinand, heir to the Austro-Hungarian throne, at Sarajevo, precipitates start of First World War

1932-35: Paraguay defeats Bolivia in Gran Chaco War

1940: Germany invades Norway, Denmark, Belgium, the Netherlands and France

1941: Germany declares war on US, and attempts to invade Russia

1949: Mao Zedong Chinese commu win civil wa

1904-05: Russo-Japanese War; series of Russian defeats

1905: Russian Revolution follows 'Bloody Sunday' massacre in St Petersburg

1918: End of First World War

1936-39: Spanish Civil War

1939: Germany invades Poland; Britain and France declare war on Germany

1945: German surrender ends war in Europe

1946: Civil war in China

1900 1910 1920 1930 1940

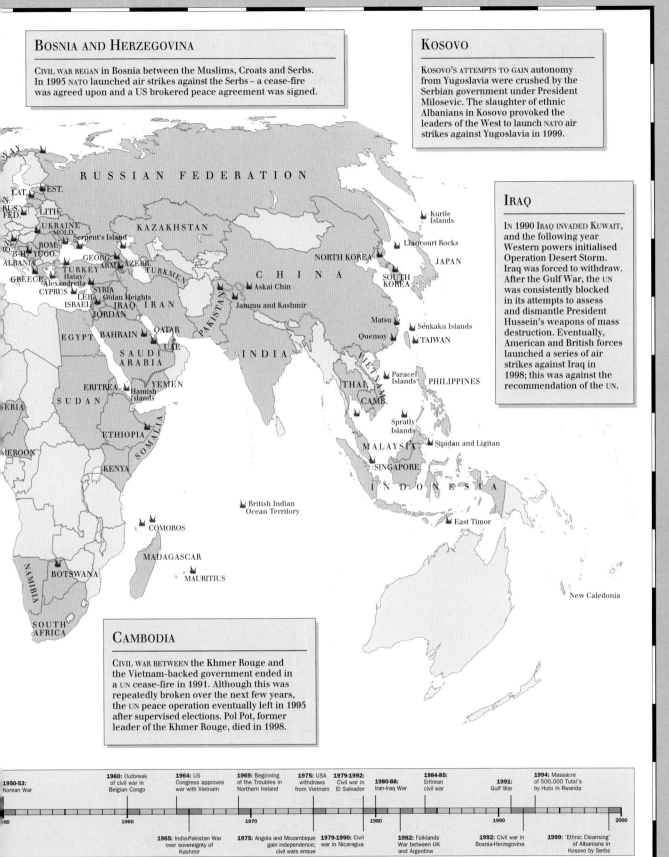

BOSNIA AND HERZEGOVINA

CIVIL WAR BEGAN in Bosnia between the Muslims, Croats and Serbs. In 1995 NATO launched air strikes against the Serbs – a cease-fire was agreed upon and a US brokered peace agreement was signed.

KOSOVO

KOSOVO'S ATTEMPTS TO GAIN autonomy from Yugoslavia were crushed by the Serbian government under President Milosevic. The slaughter of ethnic Albanians in Kosovo provoked the leaders of the West to launch NATO air strikes against Yugoslavia in 1999.

IRAQ

IN 1990 IRAQ INVADED KUWAIT, and the following year Western powers initialised Operation Desert Storm. Iraq was forced to withdraw. After the Gulf War, the UN was consistently blocked in its attempts to assess and dismantle President Hussein's weapons of mass destruction. Eventually, American and British forces launched a series of air strikes against Iraq in 1998; this was against the recommendation of the UN.

CAMBODIA

CIVIL WAR BETWEEN the Khmer Rouge and the Vietnam-backed government ended in a UN cease-fire in 1991. Although this was repeatedly broken over the next few years, the UN peace operation eventually left in 1995 after supervised elections. Pol Pot, former leader of the Khmer Rouge, died in 1998.

Map labels:
RUSSIAN FEDERATION · KAZAKHSTAN · CHINA · NORTH KOREA · SOUTH KOREA · JAPAN · Kurile Islands · Liancourt Rocks · Matsu · Quemoy · Senkaku Islands · TAIWAN · NAY · EST · LAT · N.RUS.FED. · LITH · UKRAINE · MOLD. · Serpent's Island · ROM. · B-H · YUGO. · ALBANIA · GREECE · TURKEY · Hatay · Alexandretta · CYPRUS · SYRIA · GEORG. · ARM · AZERB. · TURKMEN · Golan Heights · ISRAEL · LEBA · JORDAN · IRAQ · IRAN · Askai Chin · Jammu and Kashmir · EGYPT · BAHRAIN · QATAR · UAE · SAUDI ARABIA · PAKISTAN · INDIA · VIETNAM · Paracel Islands · PHILIPPINES · THAI. · CAMB. · Spratly Islands · Sipidan and Ligitan · MALAYSIA · SINGAPORE · INDONESIA · East Timor · ERITREA · YEMEN · Hamish Islands · SUDAN · ETHIOPIA · SOMALIA · KENYA · CAMEROON · ERIA · British Indian Ocean Territory · COMOROS · MADAGASCAR · MAURITIUS · NAMIBIA · BOTSWANA · SOUTH AFRICA · New Caledonia

Timeline:
1950-53: Korean War
1960: Outbreak of civil war in Belgian Congo
1964: US Congress approves war with Vietnam
1965: India-Pakistan War over sovereignty of Kashmir
1969: Beginning of the Troubles in Northern Ireland
1975: USA withdraws from Vietnam
1975: Angola and Mozambique gain independence; civil wars ensue
1979-1992: Civil war in El Salvador
1979-1990: Civil war in Nicaragua
1980-88: Iran-Iraq War
1982: Falklands War between UK and Argentina
1984-85: Eritrean civil war
1991: Gulf War
1992: Civil war in Bosnia-Herzegovina
1994: Massacre of 500,000 Tutsi's by Huto in Rwanda
1999: 'Ethnic Cleansing' of Albanians in Kosovo by Serbs

1950 · 1960 · 1970 · 1980 · 1990 · 2000

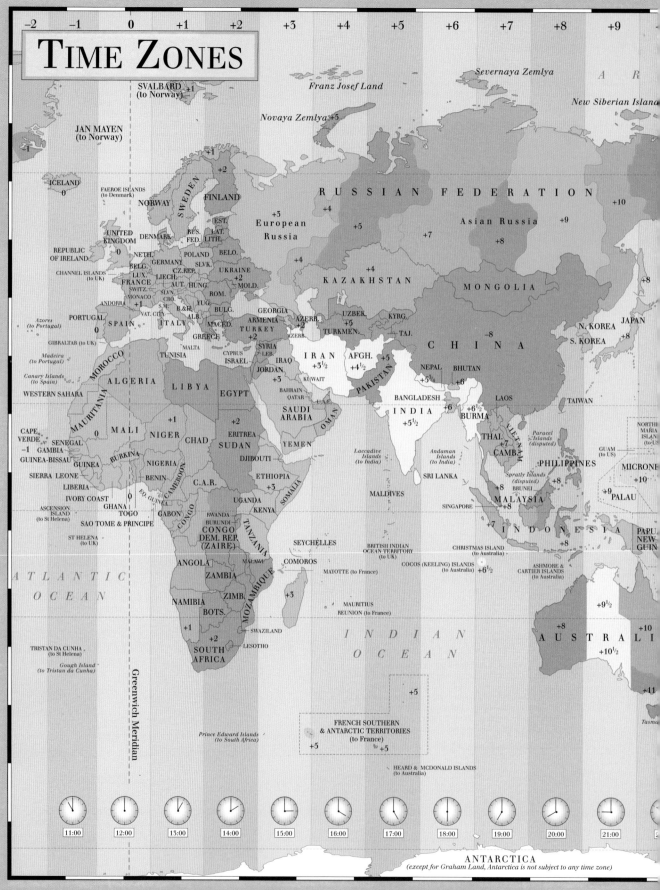

TIME ZONES

+11 +12 –12 –11 –10 –9 –8 –7 –6 –5 –4 –3 –2

International Dateline

ARCTIC OCEAN

Queen Elizabeth Islands

–4

GREENLAND
(to Denmark)

Baffin Island

–3

–1

Arctic Circle

–9

Alaska
(to US)

–8

–7

C A N A D A

–4

–5

–3½ *Newfoundland*

–3

ST PIERRE
& MIQUELON
(to France)

+12

–10

–6

UNITED STATES
OF AMERICA

ATLANTIC

OCEAN

P A C I F I C

O C E A N

MIDWAY ISLANDS
(to US)
–11

BERMUDA
(to UK)

PUERTO RICO (to US)
BRITISH VIRGIN ISLANDS (to UK)
VIRGIN ISLANDS (to US)
ANGUILLA (to UK)
ST KITTS & NEVIS   *Tropic of Cancer*

–10

WAKE ISLAND
(to US)

Hawaii
(to US)

TURKS & CAICOS ISLANDS
(to UK)

CAYMAN ISLANDS
(to UK)

DOM. REP.

BAHAMAS

CUBA

HONDURAS

BELIZE

JAMAICA

–5

ANTIGUA & BARBUDA
MONTSERRAT (to UK)
GUADELOUPE (to France)
DOMINICA
MARTINIQUE (to France)
ST LUCIA
BARBADOS
ST VINCENT & THE GRENADINES
GRENADA
TRINIDAD & TOBAGO

RSHALL
ANDS

–10

JOHNSTON ATOLL (to US)

–10

KINGMAN REEF (to US)
PALMYRA ATOLL (to US)

+12

WALLIS & FUTUNA
(to France)

BAKER &
HOWLAND
ISLANDS (to US)

–10

NAVASSA I.
(to US)

ARUBA
(to Neth.)

HAITI
NETH. ANT.
(to Neth.)

–4

GUATEMALA
EL SALVADOR
NICARAGUA
COSTA RICA

PANAMA

VENEZUELA

COLOMBIA

FRENCH GUIANA
(to France)

Equator

1

AURU

–11

JARVIS ISLAND
(to US)

–10

KIRIBATI

Galápagos Islands
(to Ecuador)

ECUADOR

GUYANA
SURINAM

Clipperton Island
(to France)

B R A Z I L

LOMON
ANDS

TUVALU

TOKELAU
(to NZ)

COOK
ISLANDS
(to NZ)
–10

Iles Marquises

–9½

P
E
R
U

–5

–4

–3

VANUATU

FRENCH POLYNESIA
(to France)

BOLIVIA

1

NEW
ALEDONIA
to France)

FIJI

–10

TONGA

NIUE (to NZ)

SAMOA   AMERICAN SAMOA
(to US)

–8½

PITCAIRN
ISLANDS
(to UK)

PARAGUAY *Tropic of Capricorn*

SEA ISLANDS
Australia)

–11½

NORFOLK ISLAND
(to Australia)

Kermadec Island
(to NZ)

–6

Easter Island
(to Chile)

San Félix Island
(to Chile)

San Ambrosio Island
(to Chile)

CHILE

URUGUAY

A
R
G
E
N
T
I
N
A

–4

)½

NEW
ZEALAND

+12

Chatham Island
(to NZ)

+12¾

P A C I F I C

O C E A N

Juan Fernandez Island
(to Chile)

–3

Bounty Island
(to NZ)

Campbell Island
(to NZ)

Macquarie Island (to Australia)

FALKLAND ISLANDS
(to UK)

CHILE –3

–4

–2

23:00 24:00 01:00 02:00 03:00 04:00 05:00 06:00 07:00 08:00 09:00 10:00

Antarctic Circle

ANTARCTICA
Graham Land

–3

CHRONOLOGY 1998–1999

THE WHOLE OF 1998 and the early half of 1999 has been a time in which the focus of the world's eyes has been firmly set on the private lives of the world's most public figures. President Clinton faced impeachment over his affair with a White House aide; Boris Yeltsin was the target of widespread medical speculation. Yet the public affairs of these powerful figures has also been under scrutiny, especially in relation to such terrible events as the crises in Iraq and Kosovo, civil wars in Sierra Leone, Colombia, and the Democratic Republic of Congo, and the border disputes between India and Pakistan, Eritrea and Ethiopia.

NORTH AMERICA

❏ **1st April 1998** The sexual harassment case filed by Paula Jones against President Clinton is dismissed after a four-year battle.

❏ **3rd January 1999** The Mars Polar Lander blasts off to search for evidence of ice or water on Mars, a necessary ingredient for the possibility of life on Mars.

❏ **16th January 1999** Impeachment trial of President Clinton begins – the American President is accused of committing perjury concerning his relationship with White House aide Monica Lewinsky.

❏ **12th February 1999** Clinton cleared of all charges at his impeachment trial, and is free to continue as the US President until the end of his term.

❏ **1st March 1999** Ottawa treaty banning the use, production and stockpiling of landmines comes into effect. Major producers, such as the United States, China and Russia are once more requested to sign.

❏ **20th April 1999** 16 pupils massacred at Columbine high school, Colorado, by two teenagers.

❏ **4th May 1999** Tornadoes tear across the American Midwest causing many to lose their homes.

❏ **16th July 1999** John F Kennedy JR and his wife Carolyn die in a plane crash 20 miles from Martha's Vineyard, where the couple were to attend a family wedding.

CENTRAL AND SOUTH AMERICA

❏ **2nd January 1998** The opposition party in Guyana calls for a fresh vote after accusations of fraud follow the results of December's general elections.

❏ **26th April 1998** Human rights campaigner Bishop Juan Gerardi is murdered in Guatemala.

❏ **7th May 1998** Flooding in southern Paraguay causes over 75,000 people to leave their homes.

❏ **16th October 1998** Former leader of Chile, General Augusto Pinochet, is arrested in London, following a request for his extradition to Spain for the murder of Spanish nationals during his reign.

❏ **8th January 1999** The Colombian government and left-wing rebels begin the first peace negotiations in six years of civil war.

❏ **29th March 1999** The president of Paraguay, Raul Cubas, resigns to avoid impeachment proceedings against him. He is later granted political asylum in neighbouring Brazil.

❏ **30th July 1999** The US closes down its last large military base in Panama, in accordance with an agreement to remove all US troops and hand over control of the Panama Canal by the end of the year.

EUROPE

❏ **10th April 1998** Good Friday Peace Agreement arrived upon by the political parties of Northern Ireland and the governments of Ireland and Great Britain.

❏ **30th May 1998** A computer malfunction, the last of a series of catastrophes plaguing the Russian space station, Mir, almost causes the death of the three cosmonauts on board.

❏ **15th August 1998** Town of Omagh in Northern Ireland bombed by the Real IRA (a splinter group of the IRA) – 29 people are killed.

❏ **15th September 1998** The new Northern Ireland Assembly meets in Belfast for the first time, to discuss the recent Omagh bombing.

❏ **2nd October 1998** The UN Security Council condemns the massacres of ethnic Albanians in Kosovo.

❏ **22nd November 1998** After a long period of deteriorating health, President Yeltsin of Russia is admitted to a Moscow hospital with pneumonia.

❏ **1st January 1999** Stock markets worldwide begin trading in the new European single currency, the Euro.

❏ **19th February 1999** President Clinton warns Serbia that NATO is ready to attack if peace talks on Kosovo fail.

❏ **3rd March 1999** Kosovo refugees flee into neighbouring Macedonia.

❏ **17th March 1999** Moscow postpones a summit meeting of the leaders of former Soviet states due to the poor health of the Russian leader, Boris Yeltsin.

❏ **21st March 1999** The crew of the Breitling Orbiter 3 hot-air balloon cross the finish line of their record-breaking round the world trip in northern Mauritania.

❏ **24th March 1999** Launch of first NATO air strikes against Yugoslavia and Slobodan Milosevic.

❏ **17th, 24th, 30th April 1999** The communities of Brixton, Brick Lane and Soho are the victims of a campaign of nail bombings targeting minority groups in London.

❏ **6th May 1999** The people of Scotland and Wales elect their own Scottish parliament and Welsh assembly for the first time.

❏ **7th May 1999** The Chinese embassy in Belgrade, Yugoslavia, is destroyed by mistake by NATO forces; the Chinese government demands reparations, and warns that the matter is not ended.

❏ **25th June 1999** The EU decides upon stricter measures to control the production of genetically modified foods.

❏ **11th August 1999** The last total solar eclipse of the millennium crosses over the Atlantic, England, Western Europe, the Middle East and the Indian sub-continent.

❏ **17th August 1999** Earthquake hits western Turkey causing widespread destruction – over 12,000 people are killed.

AFRICA

❑ **13th May 1998** Eritrea calls for international mediation to help settle its border dispute with Ethiopia.

❑ **22nd July 1998** 215 villagers are killed in Angola, and the government blames the attack on the rebel movement UNITA. The UN, fearing a renewed outbreak of civil war, sends an envoy to mediate between the two groups.

❑ **5th February 1999** Nelson Mandela gives his last official address as President of South Africa, following his decision to step down after five years in power.

❑ **1st March 1999** Eight kidnapped Western tourists are killed in Uganda by their terrorist captors during a rescue operation launched by Ugandan soldiers.

❑ **1st March 1999** The former military leader of Nigeria, General Olusegun Obasanjo, wins the country's first democratic presidential election.

❑ **4th March 1999** Mediation begins in Freetown between rebel leader Foday Sankoh and Sierra Leone's religious leaders, in the hope of constructing an agreement between the government and the rebels.

❑ **9th April 1999** President Ibrahim Mainassara of Niger is assassinated by members of his own guard.

❑ **29th June 1999** Talks of a ceasefire to the civil war in the Democratic Republic of Congo begin to finalize in the Zambian capital Lusaka.

❑ **7th July 1999** A peace agreement is signed in Togo by the President of Sierra Leone and the rebel leader Foday Sankoh.

❑ **23rd July 1999** King Hassan II of Morocco, a key player in the Middle Eastern peace process, dies of a heart attack.

❑ **10th August 1999** All remaining hostages being held by Sierra Leone rebels are released.

WEST ASIA/MIDDLE EAST

❑ **13th January 1998** Iraq blocks a UN weapons inspection, claiming that the leader of the predominantly American team is a US spy.

❑ **6th February 1998** An earthquake in Afghanistan kills around 4,000 people and destroys 30 villages.

❑ **17th April 1998** UN inspectors admit that they cannot prove that Iraq has destroyed its weapons of mass destruction, and claims Iraq is withholding information about its germ warfare programme.

❑ **31st October 1998** Iraq refuses to cooperate with UN forces attempting to disarm the country's weapons of mass destruction.

❑ **16th December 1998** American and British air forces begin a campaign of air strikes against the Iraqi capital Baghdad, after UN negotiations with Saddam Hussein fail.

❑ **28th December 1998** Four tourists (three Britons and an Australian) are killed in Yemen by their terrorist kidnappers. The tragedy occurs during an ambush set up by Yemeni security forces.

❑ **29th June 1999** Abdullan Ocalan, the Kurdish rebel leader, is sentenced to death in Turkey.

❑ **11th August 1999** The last total solar eclipse of the millennium crosses over the Middle East and the Indian sub-continent.

NORTH ASIA

❑ **10th January 1998** An earthquake measuring 6.2 on the Richter scale hits the Hebei Province in northern China; in the town of Zhangbei, 90% of the buildings suffer some form of damage.

❑ **20th June 1998** Financial officials from around the world meet in Tokyo to discuss Japan's deepening economic crisis.

❑ **10th January 1999** President Nursultan Nazarbayev wins Kazakhstan's first presidential elections to have a choice of candidates.

❑ **26th February 1999** China vetoes a UN resolution that proposes an enlarged peacekeeping force in Macedonia, due to that country's recognition of Taiwan.

❑ **1st August 1999** Beginning of the severe typhoons which swept across the whole of East Asia, killing hundreds of people and leaving many more homeless.

SOUTH ASIA

❑ **25th January 1998** Members of the Sri Lankan rebel group LTTE stage a suicide bombing at a Buddhist shrine, killing 13 people.

❑ **16th April 1998** Pol Pot, the former leader of the Khmer Rouge and the man responsible for Cambodia's killing fields during the 1970s, is reported dead.

❑ **12th May 1998** Demonstrations turn into riots in the city of Jakarta when six students are killed by security forces.

❑ **21st May 1998** President Suharto of Indonesia resigns over the current economic and political crisis.

❑ **26th May 1999** India launches air strikes against the region of Kashmir on its northern border to drove out Pakistan-backed military forces.

❑ **12th July 1999** India suspends its air strikes in the region of Kashmir as Pakistani infiltrating forces withdraw.

❑ **1st August 1999** Beginning of the severe typhoons which swept across the whole of East Asia, killing hundreds of people and leaving many more homeless.

❑ **11th August 1999** The last total solar eclipse of the millennium crosses over the Indian sub-continent.

❑ **3rd September 1999** Following a positive vote for independence in East Timor from Indonesian rule, militia gangs destroyed the capital, killing thousands and forcing the population to flee. By October, a UN peacekeeping force was in place.

AUSTRALIA AND OCEANIA

❑ **1st January 1998** Papua New Guinea experiences drought; aid workers fear half a million people will starve.

❑ **14th February 1998** A political convention in Canberra, Australia, decides to call for a referendum on the issue of replacing the head of state, Queen Elizabeth II, with an elected president. The referendum is set for November 1999.

❑ **20th February 1998** Beginning of a month-long electrical power failure in the city of Auckland, New Zealand.

❑ **17th July 1998** Papua New Guinea is struck by a tsunami, which devastates an area containing over 12,000 inhabitants.

❑ **20th June 1999** The Australian government unveils plans to set up a giant marine park within its Antarctic territory. The park is to protect colonies of seals and birds indigenous to the region.

INTERNATIONAL ORGANISATIONS

THIS LISTING GIVES the full names of all international organizations referred to, often by acronym, in the Atlas. (Political parties are to be found under the Politics heading within each national entry). The full names are followed by the date of the establishment or foundation, an indication of membership were appropriate and a summary of the organisation's aims and functions.

ACC
Arab Cooperation Council
established 1989
members – Egypt, Iraq, Jordan, Yemen
Promotes Arab economic cooperation

ACP
African, Caribbean and Pacific Countries
established 1976
members – 71 developing countries
Preferential economic and aid relationship with the EU under the Lomè Convention

ACS
Association of Caribbean States
established 1994
members – 24 Caribbean countries
Promotes economic, scientific and cultural cooperation in the region

ADB
Asian Development Bank
established 1966
members – 41 Asian-Pacific countries and territories, 16 non-regional countries
Encourages regional development

AfDB
African Development Bank
established 1964
members – 53 African countries, 24 non-African countries
Encourages African economic and social development

AFESD
Arab Fund for Economic and Social Development
established 1968
members – 21 Arab countries (including Palestine)
Promotes social and economic development in Arab states

AL
League of Arab States (Arab League)
established 1945
members – 22 Arab countries (including Palestine)
Forum to promote Arab cooperation on social, political and military issues

ALADI
Latin American Integration Association
established 1960
members – 12 South American countries
Promotes trade and regional integration

AmCC
Amazonian Cooperation Council
established 1978
members – Bolivia, Brazil, Colombia, Ecuador, Guyana, Peru, Suriname, Venezuela
Promotes the harmonious development of the Amazon region

AMF
Arab Monetary Fund
established 1977
members – 19 Arab countries (including Palestine)
Promotes monetary and economic cooperation

AMU
Arab Maghreb Union
established 1989
members – Algeria, Libya, Mauritania, Morocco, Tunisia
Promotes integration and economic cooperation among North African Arab states

ANZUS
Australia-New Zealand-United States Security Treaty
established 1951
members – Australia, New Zealand, United States
Trilateral security agreement. Security relations between the USA and New Zealand were suspended in 1984 over the issue of US nuclear-powered or potentially nuclear-armed naval vessels visiting New Zealand ports. High-level contacts between the USA and New Zealand were resumed in 1994

AP
Andean Pact (Acuerdo de Cartegena) also known as Andean Community
established 1969
members – Bolivia, Colombia, Ecuador, Peru, Venezuela
Promotes development through integration

APEC
Asia-Pacific Economic Cooperation
established 1989
members – 20 Pacific Rim countries and Hong Kong
Promotes regional economic cooperation

ASEAN
Association of Southeast Asian Nations
established 1967
members – Brunei, Burma, Cambodia, Indonesia, Laos, Malaysia, Philippines, Singapore, Thailand, Vietnam
Promotes economic, social and cultural cooperation

BADEA
Arab Bank for Economic Development in Africa
established 1973
members – 18 Arab countries (including Palestine)
Established as an agency of the Arab League to promote economic development in Africa

BDEAC
Central African States Development Bank
established 1975
members – Cameroon, Central African Republic, Chad, Congo, Equatorial Guinea, France, Gabon, Germany, Kuwait
Furthers economic development

BENELUX
Benelux Economic Union
established 1960
members – Belgium, Luxembourg, Netherlands
Develops economic ties between member countries

BOAD
West African Development Bank
established 1973
members – Benin, Burkina, Guinea-Bissau, Ivory Coast, Mali, Niger, Senegal, Togo
Promotes economic development and integration in West Africa

BSEC
Black Sea Economic Cooperation Group
established 1992
members – Albania, Armenia, Azerbaijan, Bulgaria, Georgia, Greece, Moldova, Romania, Russia, Turkey, Ukraine
Furthers regional stability through economic cooperation

CACM
Central American Common Market
established 1960
members – Costa Rica, El Salvador, Guatemala, Honduras, Nicaragua
Now a subsystem of SICA. Furthers economic ties between members; one of its institutions is the BCIE - Central American Bank for Economic Integration

CAEU
Council of Arab Economic Unity
established 1957
members – 12 Arab countries (including Palestine)
Encourages economic integration

CARICOM
Caribbean Community and Common Market
established 1973
members – 14 Caribbean countries and Montserrat
Fosters economic ties in the Caribbean

CBS
Council of the Baltic Sea States
established 1992
members – Denmark, Estonia, Finland, Germany, Iceland, Latvia, Lithuania, Norway, Poland, Russia, Sweden
Promotes cooperation among Baltic Sea states

CDB
Caribbean Development Bank
established 1969
members – 20 Caribbean countries and dependencies, 7 non-Caribbean countries
Promotes regional development

CE
Council of Europe
established 1949
members – 41 European countries
Promotes unity and quality of life in Europe

CEEAC
Economic Community of Central African States
established 1983
members – 10 Central African countries
Promotes regional cooperation, and aims to establish a Central African common market

CEFTA
Central European Free Trade Agreement
established 1992
members – Bulgaria, Czech Republic, Hungary, Poland, Romania, Slovakia, Slovenia
Promotes trade and cooperation

CEI
Central European Initiative
established 1989
members – 16 Eastern and Central European countries: Albania, Austria, Belarus, Bosnia & Herzegovina, Bulgaria, Croatia, Czech Republic, Hungary, Italy, Macedonia, Moldova, Poland, Romania, Slovakia, Slovenia, Ukraine
Evolved from the Hexagonal Group; promotes economic and political cooperation, within the OSCE

CEMAC
Economic and Monetary Community of Central Africa
established 1994
members – Cameroon, Central African Republic, Chad, Congo, Equatorial Guinea, Gabon
Aims to promote subregional integration, by economic and monetary union (replaced UDEAC)

CEPGL
Economic Community of the Great Lakes Countries
established 1976
members – Burundi, Congo (Zaire), Rwanda
Promotes regional economic cooperation

CERN
European Organization for Nuclear Research
established 1954
members – 19 European countries
Provides for collaboration in nuclear research for peaceful purposes

CILSS
Permanent Interstate Committee for Drought Control in the Sahel
established 1973
members – 9 African countries in the Sahel region
Promotes prevention of drought and crop failure in the region

CIS
Commonwealth of Independent States
established 1991
members – Armenia, Azerbaijan, Belarus, Georgia, Kazakhstan, Kyrgyzstan, Moldova, Russia, Tajikistan, Turkmenistan, Ukraine, Uzbekistan
Promotes interstate relationships among former republics of the Soviet Union

COMESA
Common Market for Eastern and Southern Africa
established 1993
members – 21 African countries
Promotes economic development and cooperation (replaced PTA)

Comm
Commonwealth
established 1931
members – 53 countries (including Nigeria, which was readmitted in 1999; and Fiji, readmitted in 1997). Members are chiefly former members of the British Empire. In addition Tuvalu has special status and does not attend Heads of Government meetings.
Develops relationships and contacts between members

CP
Colombo Plan
established 1950
members – Four donor countries: Australia, Japan, New Zealand, USA (donors) and 20 Asia-Pacific countries
Encourages economic and social development in Asia-Pacific region

Damascus Declaration
established 1991
members – Bahrain, Egypt, Kuwait, Oman, Qatar, Saudi Arabia, Syria, United Arab Emirates
A loose association, formed after the Gulf War, which aims to secure the stability of the region

EAPC
Euro-Atlantic Partnership Council
established 1991
members – 36 countries (members of NATO and former members of Warsaw Pact)
Forum for cooperation on political and security issues (successor to the NACC, North Atlantic Cooperation Council)

EBRD
European Bank for Reconstruction and Development
established 1991
members – 58 countries
Helps transition of former communist European states to market economies

ECO
Economic Cooperation Organization
established 1985
members – Afghanistan, Azerbaijan, Iran, Kazakhstan, Kyrgyzstan, Pakistan, Tajikistan, Turkey, Turkmenistan, Uzbekistan
Aims at cooperation in economic, social and cultural affairs

ECOWAS
Economic Community of West African States
established 1975
members – 16 West African countries
Promotes regional economic cooperation

EEA
European Economic Area
established 1994
members – The 15 members of the EU, and Iceland, Liechtenstein and Norway
Aims to include EFTA members in the EU single market

EFTA
European Free Trade Association
established 1960
members – Iceland, Liechtenstein, Norway, Switzerland
Promotes economic cooperation

ESA
European Space Agency
established 1973
members – 14 European countries Promotes cooperation in space research for peaceful purposes

EU
European Union
established 1992
members – 15 European countries
Aims to integrate the economies of member states and promote cooperation and coordination of policies

Francophone
Francophone states
established Not applicable
members – Francophone summits are attended by France and its external territories, plus over twenty African countries, and other countries such as Vietnam and Canada, with a French colonial connection or a French-speaking minority.
A loose grouping of French-speaking countries

FZ
Franc zone
established Not applicable
members – France (including overseas departments and territories), Monaco, and 15 African states
Aims to form monetary union among countries whose currencies are linked to the French franc

G3
Group of 3
established 1987
members – Colombia, Mexico, Venezuela
Aims to remove trade restrictions

G5
Group of 5
established Not applicable
members – Finance ministers of France, Germany, Japan, UK, USA
Meet informally to establish agenda of G7

G7
Group of 7
established 1975
members – The seven major industrialized countries: Canada, France, Germany, Italy, Japan, UK, USA
Summit meetings of the seven major industrialized countries, originally for economic purposes, but more recently for political purposes as well

G8
Group of 8
established 1994
members – Members of the G7 (Canada, France, Germany, Italy, Japan, UK, USA) and Russia
To include Russia in discussions of the G7 on international affairs

G10
Group of 10
established 1962
members – 11 members: G7 members, plus Belgium, the Netherlands, Sweden and Switzerland
Ministers meet to discuss monetary issues

G15
Group of 15
established 1989
members – 15 developing countries
Meets annually to further cooperation among developing countries

G24
Group of 24
established Not applicable
members – The 24 countries within the IMF which represent the interests of developing countries
Not applicable

GCC
Gulf Cooperation Council
established 1981
members – Bahrain, Kuwait, Oman, Qatar, Saudi Arabia, UAE
Promotes cooperation in economic, political and social affairs

Geplacea
Latin American and Caribbean Sugar Exporting Countries
established 1974
members – 23 countries
A forum for consultation on the production and sale of sugar

IAEA
International Atomic Energy Agency
established 1957
members – 129 countries
Promotes and monitors peaceful use of atomic energy

IBRD
International Bank for Reconstruction and Development (also known as the World Bank)
established 1945
members – 181 countries
UN agency providing economic development loans

ICRC
International Committee of the Red Cross
established 1863
members – Up to 25 Swiss nationals form the international committee. Red Cross or Red Crescent societies exist in 175 countries
Coordinates all international humanitarian activities of the International Red Cross and Red Crescent Movement, giving legal and practical assistance to the victims of wars and disasters. It works through national committees of Red Cross or Red Crescent societies

IGAD
Intergovernmental Authority on Development
established 1996
members – Djibouti, Eritrea, Ethiopia, Kenya, Somalia, Sudan, Uganda
Promotes cooperation on food security, infrastructure and other development issues (supersedes IGADD, founded 1986, to promote cooperation on drought-related matters)

IMF
International Monetary Fund
established 1945
members – 182 countries.
The voting rights of Congo, Dem. Rep. (Zaire) and Sudan are currently suspended.
Promotes international monetary co-operation, the balanced growth of trade and exchange rate stability; provides credit resources to members experiencing balance-of-trade difficulties.

IOC
Indian Ocean Commission
established 1982
members – Comoros, France (representing Rèunion), Madagascar, Mauritius, Seychelles
Promotes regional cooperation

IsDB
Islamic Development Bank
established 1975
members – 52 countries (including Palestine)
Promotes economic development on Islamic principles among Muslim communities (agency of the OIC)

IWC
International Whaling Commission
established 1946
members – 40 countries
Reviews conduct of whaling throughout world; coordinates and funds whale research

LCBC
Lake Chad Basin Commission
established 1964
members – Cameroon, Central African Republic, Chad, Niger, Nigeria
Encourages economic and environmental development in Lake Chad region

LUSOPHONE
Lusophone states
established Not applicable
members – Portugal, Brazil, and five Portuguese-speaking African countries - Angola, Cape Verde, Guinea-Bissau, Mozambique, Sao Tome & Principe
A loose grouping of Portugese-speaking countries

Mekong River Commission
established 1995
members – Cambodia, Laos, Thailand, Vietnam
Accord on the sustainable development of Mekong River basin (replacing the 1958 interim Mekong Secretariat)

MERCOSUR
Southern Common Market
established 1991
members – Argentina, Brazil, Paraguay, Uruguay;
Promotes economic integration, free trade and common external tariffs

MRU
Mano River Union
established 1973
members – Guinea, Liberia, Sierra Leone
Aims to create customs and economic union in order to promote development

NAFTA
North American Free Trade Agreement
established 1994
members – Canada, Mexico, USA
Free-trade zone

NAM
Non-Aligned Movement
established 1961
members – 113 countries (including Palestine)
Fosters political and military cooperation away from traditional Eastern or Western blocs

NATO
North Atlantic Treaty Organization
established 1949
members – 19 countries
Promotes mutual defense cooperation. Since January 1994, NATO's Partnerships for Peace program has provided a loose framework for cooperation with former members of the Warsaw Pact and the ex-Soviet republics. A historic Founding Act signed between Russia and NATO in May 1997 allowed for the organization's eastward expansion, under which the Czech Republic, Hungary and Poland were the first three countries to join.

NC
Nordic Council
established 1952
members – Denmark, Finland, Iceland, Norway, Sweden
Promotes cultural and environmental cooperation in Scandinavia

Not UN
Not a member of the UN
established Not applicable
members – Not applicable

OAPEC
Organization of Arab Petroleum Exporting Countries
established 1968
members – 10 Arab countries: Algeria, Bahrain, Egypt, Iraq, Kuwait, Libya, Qatar, Saudi Arabia, Syria, UAE
Aims to promote the interests of member countries and increase cooperation in the petroleum industry

OAS
Organization of American States
established 1948
members – 34 American countries
Promotes security, economic and social development in the Americas

OAU
Organization of African Unity
established 1963
members – 52 African countries
Promotes unity and cooperation in Africa

OECD
Organization for Economic Cooperation and Development
established 1961
members – 29 industrialised democracies
Forum for coordinating economic policies among industrialized countries

OECS
Organization of Eastern Caribbean States
established 1981
members – 7 Caribbean countries and dependencies: Antigua & Barbuda, Dominica, Grenada, Montserrat, St. Kitts & Nevis, St. Lucia, St. Vincent & the Grenadines
Promotes political, economic and defense cooperation

OIC
Organization of the Islamic Conference
established 1971
members – 55 Islamic countries (including Palestine)
Furthers Islamic solidarity and cooperation

OMVG
Gambia River Development Organization
established 1978
members – Gambia, Guinea, Guinea-Bissau, Senegal
Promotes integrated development of the Gambia River basin

OPANAL
Agency for the Prohibition of Nuclear Weapons in Latin America and the Caribbean
established 1969
members – 29 countries
Aims to ensure compliance with the Treaty of Tlatelolco (banning nuclear weapons from South America and the Caribbean)

OPEC
Organization of the Petroleum Exporting Countries
established 1960
members – 11 oil producers: Algeria, Indonesia, Iran, Iraq, Kuwait, Libya, Nigeria, Qatar, Saudi Arabia, United Arab Emirates, Venezuela
Aims to coordinate oil policies to ensure fair and stable prices

OSCE
Organization for Security and Cooperation in Europe
established 1972
members – 54 countries (excluding Yugoslavia, suspended since 1992)
Aims to strengthen democracy and human rights, and settle disputes peacefully (formerly CSCE; renamed 1994)

Partnerships for Peace (PFP)
see NATO
established Not applicable
members – 24 members: Eastern European and former Soviet countries, Sweden and Malta
see NATO

PC
Pacific Community (formerly South Pacific Commission)
established 1948
members – 27 countries and territories
A forum for dialogue between Pacific countries and powers administering Pacific territories

RG
Rio Group
established 1987
members – Argentina, Bolivia, Brazil, Chile, Colombia, Ecuador, Mexico, Panama, Paraguay, Peru, Uruguay, Venezuela
Forum for Latin American issues (evolved from Contadora Group, established 1948)

SAARC
South Asian Association for Regional Cooperation
established 1985
members – Bangladesh, Bhutan, India, Maldives, Nepal, Pakistan, Sri Lanka
Encourages economic, social and cultural cooperation

SACU
Southern African Customs Union
established 1969
members – 5 southern African countries: Botswana, Lesotho, Namibia, South Africa, Swaziland
Promotes cooperation in trade and customs matters among Southern African states

SADC
Southern African Development Community
established 1992
members – 14 southern African countries
Promotes economic integration

San Josè Group
established 1988
members – Costa Rica, El Salvador, Guatemala, Honduras, Nicaragua, Panama
A 'complementary, voluntary and gradual' economic union

SELA
Latin American Economic System
established 1975
members – 28 countries
Promotes economic and social development through regional cooperation

SICA
Central American Integration System
established 1991
members – 6 countries: Costa Rica, El Salvador, Guatemala, Honduras, Nicaragua, Panama
Coordinates the political, economic, social and environmental integration of the region

SPF
South Pacific Forum
established 1971
members – 16 countries and self-governing territories
Develops regional political cooperation

UEMOA
West African Economic and Monetary Union
established 1994
members – 8 West African countries
Aims for convergence of monetary policies and economic union

UN
United Nations
established 1945
members – 188 countries; permanent members of the Security Council – China, France, Russia, UK, USA
Aims to maintain international peace and security and to promote cooperation over economic, social, cultural and humanitarian problems.
Agencies include the regional commissions of the UN's Economic and Social Council: ECA (Economic Commission for Africa - established 1958); ECE (Economic Commission for Europe – established 1947); ECLAC (Economic Commission for Latin America and the Caribbean – established 1948); ESCAP (Economic and Social Commission for Asia and the Pacific - established 1947); ESCWA (Economic and Social Commission for Western Asia – established 1973). Other bodies of the UN, in which most members participate, include UNICEF (the UN Children's Fund); UNCTAD (the UN Conference on Trade and Development); UNDP (the UN Development Programme); UNHCR (the UN High Commissioner for Refugees); UNFPA (the UN Population Fund); IDA (the International Development Association);
The following sovereign states do not belong to the UN: Switzerland, Taiwan, Tuvalu, and Vatican City. Yugoslavia was a member under communism. Its constituent republics (Bosnia & Herzegovina, Croatia, Former Yugoslav Republic of Macedonia and Slovenia) have all become members of the UN as they gained independence. The Republic of Yugoslavia (Serbia and Montenegro) was suspended from membership in 1992, in the expectation that it would apply to fill the seat of the former Yugoslavia, but it still participates in the work of UN agencies

WEU
Western European Union
established 1955
members – 10 countries
A forum for European military cooperation

WTO
World Trade Organization
established 1995
members – 134 countries (including Hong Kong and Macao)
Aims to liberalize trade through multilateral trade agreements (as the successor to gatt (the General Agreement on Tariffs and Trade)

2

THE NATIONS
OF THE
WORLD

THE NATIONS OF THE WORLD
• AFGHANISTAN ~ ZIMBABWE
OVERSEAS TERRITORIES & DEPENDENCIES

A

AFGHANISTAN

ASIA
Asia
Turkmenistan Uzb. Tajikistan
China
AFGHANISTAN
Iran
Pakistan

OFFICIAL NAME: Islamic State of Afghanistan CAPITAL: Kābul
POPULATION: 23.4 million CURRENCY: Afghani OFFICIAL LANGUAGES: Persian and Pashtu

1919 | 1919 | Aug 19 | AFG | +4.5 | +93 | .af

LANDLOCKED IN central Asia, Afghanistan is surrounded by Iran, Pakistan, China, Tajikistan, Turkmenistan and Uzbekistan. Approximately three-quarters of its territory is inaccessible terrain.Although agriculture is the main economic activity, less than two-thirds of farmland is cultivated after the country was torn by open armed conflict for two decades. After defeating the former communist regime in 1992 Islamic *mujahideen* groups achieved a fragile power-sharing agreement, but in 1996 the *talibaan*, a hard-line Islamic "student" militia, seized power and imposed a strict Islamic regime.

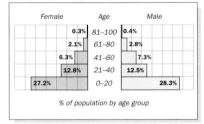
The Band-i-Amir River, in the Hindu Kush. Afghanistan is mountainous and arid. Many Afghans are nomadic sheep farmers.

CLIMATE
▷ Mountain/cold desert

WEATHER CHART

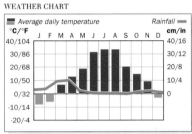

Afghanistan has a harsh continental climate; the severity of winter is accentuated by high altitudes. It has the widest temperature range in the world, with lows of -50°C and highs of 53°C.

TRANSPORTATION
▷ Drive on right

Kābul International | Has no fleet

THE TRANSPORTATION NETWORK

2,800 km (1,740 miles)	None
25 km (16 miles)	1,200 km (746 miles)

The repair and reconstruction of war-damaged roads and the provision of a minimum of facilities to allow air traffic to function safely are the present priorities. Road rebuilding is usually carried out by local communities. However, neighboring Pakistan has undertaken to rebuild a number of key routes, including the Kābul–Torkam link, which will benefit its own trade with central Asia.

Securing key supply routes was a crucial factor in intra-*mujahideen* feuding and remains vital to the *talibaan* in their efforts to secure control over the whole country, as well as to anti-*talibaan* forces still active, especially in the north. Much of Afghanistan's outlying territory is sown with land mines.

TOURISM
▷ Visitors : population 1:5850

4,000 visitors | No change 1995–1997

MAIN TOURIST ARRIVALS

Afghanistan does not publish tourism figures by country of origin

% of total arrivals
0 10 20 30 40 50 60

Afghanistan is a war zone. There are few visitors, while UN and aid agency personnel have been withdrawn because of government restrictions on their activities. Few hotels are open in Kābul and travel is extremely dangerous. *Air Ariana*, the Afghan national airline, no longer flies from Kābul, but from Dushanbe in neighboring Tajikistan.

The lack of a formal economy means that Afghanistan gets few visits from businessmen, and any expatriates who were previously in Kābul have left.

PEOPLE
▷ Pop. density low

Persian, Pashtu, Dari, Uzbek, Turkmen | 36/km² (93/mi²)

THE URBAN/RURAL POPULATION SPLIT

20% 80%

RELIGIOUS PERSUASION

Other 1%
Shi'a Muslim 15%
Sunni Muslim 84%

ETHNIC MAKEUP

Other 3% Uzbek 5%
Hazara 19%
Pashto 52%
Tajik 21%

Ethnic Pashtuns form a majority of the population in Afghanistan and constitute its traditional rulers; the main minorities are Tajiks, Hazaras, and Uzbeks. These ethnic divisions have largely, though not exclusively, determined intra-*mujahideen* feuding since 1992. The predominantly Pashtun *talibaan*, who took power in 1996, wrested control from a Tajik–Uzbek alliance. Sectarian differences between Sunnis and Shi'as have become acute under the *talibaan* regime, which is accused of encouraging discrimination against Shi'as.

Some two million of the country's population were killed as a result of the 1979–1989 war, which followed invasion by the Soviet Union. As many again were maimed. A further six million were forced to flee to neighboring Pakistan and Iran; most have not yet been able to return.

Women in Afghanistan enjoy few rights under the rigid Islamic regime sanctioned by the *talibaan*. They have to observe a rigid dress code, have no access to education and health care, and are strictly banned from seeking any kind of public employment.

POPULATION AGE BREAKDOWN

Female	Age	Male
0.3%	81–100	0.4%
2.1%	61–80	2.8%
6.3%	41–60	7.3%
12.8%	21–40	12.5%
27.2%	0–20	28.3%

% of population by age group

POLITICS   ▷ No multiparty elections

1988/Uncertain   Leader of the Talibaan
Mohammad Omar

AT THE LAST ELECTION

House of Representatives

Following the downfall of Najibullah's regime in April 1992, both houses were dissolved and an interim *mujahideen* legislature formed.

Senate

The *talibaan* government faces opposition from the Northern Alliance, and has discussed power-sharing.

MAIN POLITICAL ISSUES
Elections
According to the 7 March 1993 Islamabad peace accord, elections were to be held by the end of the year. However, they are still awaited.

Control of Kābul
Kābul remains under the control of the *talibaan*, who captured the city in 1996. An opposition alliance headed by Burhanuddin Rabbani of the *Jamiat-i-Islami* has failed to reverse the position.

PROFILE
The political system had virtually collapsed in Afghanistan prior to the *talibaan* takeover. Rival *mujahideen* factions had been in control since April 1992, when President Najibullah, who had remained in office after the withdrawal of Soviet forces in 1989, was forced to step down.

In March 1993 *mujahideen* leaders agreed to a framework for an interim government, pending elections. In January 1994 the agreement collapsed amid differences between opposing factions in government. Fighting escalated with the involvement in early 1995 of the *talibaan*, who eventually laid siege to Kābul. In September 1996 they ousted the government of President Burhanuddin Rabbani and imposed a strict Islamic regime.

By mid-1998 the *talibaan* had extended their control over most northern regions. A UN-sponsored power-sharing arrangement with the Northern Alliance was accepted by the *talibaan* in March 1999 but fighting had resumed by July.

Burhanuddin Rabbani, president from 1992 until 1996.

WORLD AFFAIRS   ▷ Joined UN in 1946

| CP | ECO | IBRD | NAM | OIC |

The *talibaan* government is not represented at the UN and is recognized only by Pakistan, Saudi Arabia and the United Arab Emirates. A key obstacle to wider recognition is its alleged support for a Saudi businessman, Osama bin Laden, operating from Afghanistan, who has been held responsible for terrorist attacks against Western targets abroad. Of all its neighbors, land-locked Afghanistan relies most heavily on Pakistan for overland transit and port facilities. CIS troops are stationed in Tajikistan to curb the movements of Islamic militants and weapons from Afghanistan, which has also taken in refugees opposed to the neo-communist Tajik government.

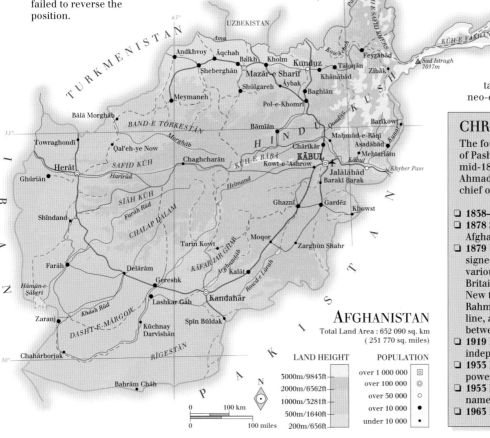

AFGHANISTAN
Total Land Area : 652 090 sq. km
(251 770 sq. miles)

LAND HEIGHT		POPULATION	
3000m/9843ft		over 1 000 000	▣
2000m/6562ft		over 100 000	◉
1000m/3281ft		over 50 000	○
500m/1640ft		over 10 000	●
200m/656ft		under 10 000	·

0   100 km
0   100 miles

CHRONOLOGY
The foundations of an Afghan state of Pashtun peoples were laid in the mid-18th century, when Durrani Ahmad Shah became paramount chief of the Abdali Pashtun peoples.

❑ **1838–1842** First Anglo-Afghan war.
❑ **1878** Second British invasion of Afghan territory.
❑ **1879** Under Treaty of Gandmak signed with Amir Yaqub Ali Khan, various Afghan areas annexed by Britain. Yaqub Ali Khan later exiled. New treaty signed with Amir Abdul Rahman, establishing the Durand line, a contentious boundary between Afghanistan and Pakistan.
❑ **1919** Declaration of Afghan independence.
❑ **1933** Mohammad Zahir Shar takes power.
❑ **1953** Mohammad Daud Khan is named prime minister.
❑ **1963** Daud resigns after king rejects

CHRONOLOGY *continued*

his proposals for democratic reforms.

❑ **1965** Elections held, but monarchy retains power. Marxist Party of Afghanistan (PDPA) formed and banned. PDPA splits into the *Parcham* and *Khalq* factions.

❑ **1973** Daud mounts a successful coup, abolishes monarchy and declares republic. *Mujahideen* rebellion begins. Thousands of refugees flee into Pakistan.

❑ **1978** Opposition to Daud from PDPA culminates in *Saur* revolution. Revolutionary Council under Mohammad Taraki takes power. Daud assassinated.

❑ **1979** Taraki ousted. Hafizullah Amin takes power. Amin killed in December coup backed by USSR. 80,000 Soviet Army troops invade Afghanistan. *Mujahideen* rebellion stepped up into full-scale guerrilla war, with US backing.

❑ **1980** Babrak Karmal, leader of *Parcham* PDPA, installed as head of Marxist regime.

❑ **1986** Najibullah replaces Karmal as head of government.

❑ **1989** Soviet Army withdraws. *Mujahideen* control limited to rural areas. Najibullah remains in power.

❑ **1992** Najibullah hands over power to *mujahideen* factions. Pakistan stops arming its *mujahideen* groups.

❑ **1993** *Mujahideen* agree on formation of government.

❑ **1994** Power struggle between Rabbani and Hekmatyar rekindles civil war.

❑ **1995** Anti-government *talibaan* militia advance toward Kabul.

❑ **1996** *Talibaan* take power, execute Najibullah, and impose strict Islamic regime.

❑ **1998** May, earthquake in northern regions kills thousands; August, *talibaan* take Mazar i Sharif from opposition Northern Alliance.

❑ **1999** March, *talibaan* agree to share power with opposition Northern Alliance under a UN-sponsored plan, but fighting continues.

AID ▷ Recipient

$279m (receipts) ⬆ Up 22% 1996–1997

The UN is the main source of official aid in the form of humanitarian assistance. However, there is tension between foreign aid agencies and the *talibaan* authorities over female education and health care. Working conditions for aid personnel are extremely hazardous because of the lack of a secure environment.

DEFENSE ▷ Compulsory military service

$209m (estimate) ⬆ Up 1% in 1997

Foreign Islamic groups active in Afghanistan encourage arms imports.

AFGHAN ARMED FORCES

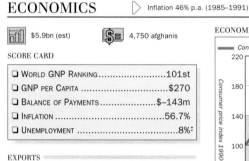

No data	No data
None	None
No data	No data
None	

In 1991, the US–Russian agreement to suspend military supplies to rival Afghan groups marked the end of the superpowers' active involvement in Afghanistan. The Kābul communists, in particular, had been almost totally dependent on Moscow for arms, even after the Soviet withdrawal in 1989. In practice, Afghanistan has no formal defense arrangements, although there is a substantial covert arms trade which has expanded with the activity of Islamic militants from abroad. The bulk of these arms originate in eastern Europe and the former Soviet Union. The *talibaan* militia were greatly strengthened by weapons captured in their rapid advance across most of Afghanistan in 1996.

Afghanistan still has hundreds of the 1,000 *Stinger* missiles which were given by the USA to the *mujahideen* in the 1980s. The USA is now worried that they may be used against civilian airliners, and offered $100,000 each to buy them back. To date, however, none has been returned.

ECONOMICS ▷ Inflation 46% p.a. (1985–1991)

$5.9bn (est) 4,750 afghanis

SCORE CARD

❑ WORLD GNP RANKING........................101st
❑ GNP PER CAPITA $270
❑ BALANCE OF PAYMENTS...................$–143m
❑ INFLATION 56.7%
❑ UNEMPLOYMENT 8%:

EXPORTS

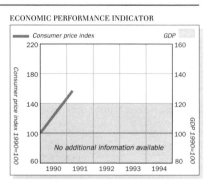

Germany 6%
France 7%
USA 7%
Benelux 9%
Other 51%
Pakistan 20%

IMPORTS

Russia 4%
India 5%
China 7%
Japan 18%
Other 47%
Singapore 19%

STRENGTHS
Very few, apart from illicit opium trade. Agriculture, still the largest sector, accounts for approximately half of GDP.

WEAKNESSES
Protracted fighting since the Soviet invasion of 1979 has devastated the economy. Agriculture and industry are in ruins. Communication links were even further damaged by earthquakes in the north in 1998.

PROFILE
Following ten years of war between the Soviet-backed Kabul government and *mujahideen* rebels and subsequent

ECONOMIC PERFORMANCE INDICATOR

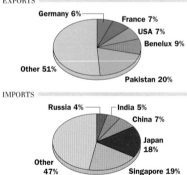

Consumer price index
GDP
No additional information available
1990 1991 1992 1993 1994

mujahideen in-fighting, Afghanistan is one of the poorest and least developed countries in the world. Estimates suggest that $4 billion is needed to rebuild the country and that 80% of its infrastructure has been destroyed. Agricultural activity has fallen back from pre-1979 levels; many farmers have turned back to growing poppies for opium production. The *talibaan* have declared opium production to be anti-Islamic and are urging farmers to plant other crops, under a program funded by the UN.

Mujahideen *guerrillas, members of just one of the many factions vying for power in Afghanistan, prepare to launch a rocket attack.*

RESOURCES

▷ Electric power 494,000 kw

1,300 tonnes

Not an oil producer and has no refineries

14.3m sheep, 1.5m cattle, 2.2m goats, 300,000 horses

Natural gas, salt, coal, copper, lapis lazuli, barytes, talc

ELECTRICITY GENERATION

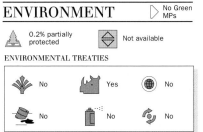

| Hydro 67% (0.4bn kwh) |
| Combustion 33% (0.2bn kwh) |
| Nuclear 0% |
| Other 0% |

0 20 40 60 80 100

% of total generation by type

Natural gas and coal are Afghanistan's most important strategic resources. Restoring the power generation system, which has suffered widespread deterioration and destruction, is a government priority. The construction of dams on the Kunar and Laghman rivers is being considered. Coal production has fallen from pre-war levels and mines are also in urgent need of rehabilitation. Western technology is needed to rebuild the gas industry.

AFGHANISTAN : LAND USE

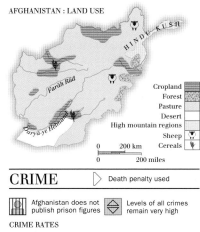

Cropland
Forest
Pasture
Desert
High mountain regions
Sheep
Cereals

0   200 km
0   200 miles

ENVIRONMENT

▷ No Green MPs

0.2% partially protected

Not available

ENVIRONMENTAL TREATIES

No   Yes   No
No   No   No

Environmental priorities are low given Afghanistan's anarchic civil war conditions. However, the country's relative lack of industry, even in Kābul, means that industrial pollution is minimal. The biggest problem facing Afghanistan is land mines: over ten million have been laid, and the UN estimates that it will take 100 years to make the country safe for civilians.

MEDIA

▷ TV ownership low

⊠ Daily newspaper circulation 6 per 1,000 people

PUBLISHING AND BROADCAST MEDIA

	There are 12 daily newspapers, including *Anis*, *Hewad* and the *Kābul New Times*
	1 state-owned service, closed down since 1996
	1 state-owned service, *the voice of Shari'a*

Most of the *mujahideen* factions run their own newspapers and radio stations, which follow the party line and denigrate rivals. Television is banned, as are video cassette recorders and satellite dishes. The BBC, which broadcasts in Pashtu and Dari, is more popular than Radio Free Afghanistan, especially for its soap operas, which convey information on welfare issues.

CRIME

▷ Death penalty used

Afghanistan does not publish prison figures

Levels of all crimes remain very high

CRIME RATES

No statistics for murders, rapes, and thefts are published due to the war situation

Fear of looting in Kābul stifled economic activity prior to the *talibaan* takeover. Gun law operates widely; Herāt, once an exception, also experienced violence after falling to *talibaan* forces.

EDUCATION

▷ School leaving age: 13

32%   12,800 students

The literacy rate for women in Afghanistan is the lowest in the world.

THE EDUCATION SYSTEM

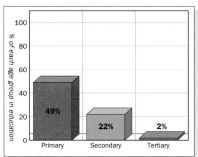

% of age each age group in education

49% Primary   22% Secondary   2% Tertiary

The education system is effectively male-only and based on rigid Islamic precepts, dictated by the *talibaan*. All education for women is banned, including private education. Kābul University has been closed since the fall of the Najibullah regime in 1992.

HEALTH

▷ No welfare state health benefits

1 per 7,358 people

Infectious, parasitic, respiratory, and digestive diseases

Under the *talibaan* regime the majority of women in Afghanistan are denied access to health care.

The health service has collapsed completely and almost all medical professionals have left the country.

Infant and maternal mortality rates are among the highest in the world, and life expectancy the lowest, at 44 years. Parasitic diseases and infections are a particular problem. The UN has organized a well-water chlorination program, following an outbreak of cholera in Kābul.

The admission of women to hospital is strongly discouraged, as is the use of female medical staff.

SPENDING

▷ GDP/cap. increase

CONSUMPTION AND SPENDING

No data   No data

| Defense 12.5% |
| Education   No data |
| Health 1.6% |

0   5   10   15   20   25

Defense, Health, Education spending as % of GDP

The vast majority of Afghans live in conditions of extreme poverty. Afghanistan does not have the resources to feed its people at present. This situation is likely to be exacerbated by the return of refugees from neighboring Pakistan and Iran – and is likely to be heavily dependent on outside assistance for its rehabilitation. However, a number of *mujahideen* leaders have accumulated large personal fortunes during the war. These derive in part from the substantial foreign aid that was once available and, in some cases, from the lucrative trafficking of opium.

WORLD RANKING

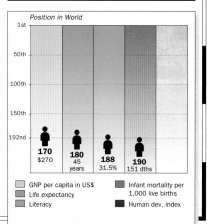

Position in World

1st
50th
100th
150th
192nd

170 $270
180 45 years
188 31.5%
190 151 dths

GNP per capita in US$
Life expectancy
Literacy

Infant mortality per 1,000 live births
Human dev. index

A

ALBANIA

OFFICIAL NAME: Republic of Albania CAPITAL: Tiranë
POPULATION: 3.4 million CURRENCY: Lek OFFICIAL LANGUAGE: Albanian

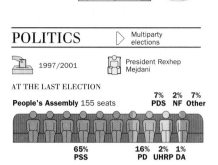

EUROPE

LYING AT THE southeastern end of the Adriatic Sea, opposite the heel of Italy, Albania is a mountainous country. It won *de facto* independence from Turkey in 1912, becoming a one-party communist state in 1944. Multiparty elections were held in 1991, but economic collapse provoked uprisings in 1997, which were only stabilized by OSCE troops. The flood of ethnic Albanian refugees from Kosovo in 1999 have strained Albania severely.

CLIMATE ▷ Mediterranean/ continental

WEATHER CHART

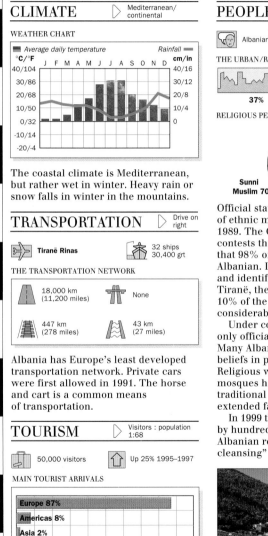

The coastal climate is Mediterranean, but rather wet in winter. Heavy rain or snow falls in winter in the mountains.

TRANSPORTATION ▷ Drive on right

✈ **Tiranë Rinas** 🚢 32 ships 30,400 grt

THE TRANSPORTATION NETWORK

🛣 18,000 km (11,200 miles)		🛤 None	
🚉 447 km (278 miles)		〰 43 km (27 miles)	

Albania has Europe's least developed transportation network. Private cars were first allowed in 1991. The horse and cart is a common means of transportation.

TOURISM ▷ Visitors : population 1:68

🧳 50,000 visitors ⬆ Up 25% 1995–1997

MAIN TOURIST ARRIVALS

Europe 87%	
Americas 8%	
Asia 2%	
Other 3%	

0 10 20 30 40 50 60 70 80 90 100
% of total arrivals

Tourism in the communist era was limited to small organized groups. The war in Kosovo has stalled plans to exploit Albania's scenic beauty.

PEOPLE ▷ Pop. density medium

👤 Albanian, Greek 👥 124/km² (321/mi²)

THE URBAN/RURAL POPULATION SPLIT

37% 63%

RELIGIOUS PERSUASION

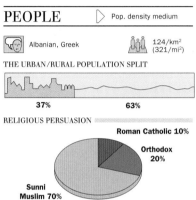

Roman Catholic 10%
Orthodox 20%
Sunni Muslim 70%

Official statistics admitted the existence of ethnic minorities in Albania only in 1989. The Greek minority strongly contests these statistics, which state that 98% of the population are Albanian. Located mainly in the south and identifying with Athens rather than Tiranë, the Greeks claim to make up 10% of the population. They suffer considerable discrimination.

Under communism, Albania was the only officially atheist state in the world. Many Albanians maintained their beliefs in private – 70% are Muslim. Religious worship is now permitted and mosques have reopened. Society is traditional and male-dominated. The extended family remains strong.

In 1999 the country was overwhelmed by hundreds of thousands of ethnic Albanian refugees fleeing the "ethnic cleansing" in neighboring Kosovo.

City of a thousand windows. Berat was preserved as a museum city while a new town was built further down the valley.

POLITICS ▷ Multiparty elections

🗳 1997/2001 President Rexhep Mejdani

AT THE LAST ELECTION

People's Assembly 155 seats

65% PSS 16% PD 2% UHRP 1% DA 7% PDS 2% NF 7% Other

PSS = Socialist Party of Albania **PD** = Democratic Party
PDS = Social Democratic Party **UHRP** = Union for Human Rights Party **NF** = National Front **DA** = Democratic Alliance

Albania was dominated for more than 40 years by communist ruler Enver Hoxha, who died in 1985. Then party reformers gradually gained the upper hand. An exodus of Albanians in 1991 finally persuaded Ramiz Alia, Enver Hoxha's successor, to call multiparty elections. The resulting center-right, PD-led coalition, however, failed to create a Western-style liberal state.

Early 1997 saw a desperate rush into "pyramid" savings schemes, but these collapsed, prompting a rebellion in the south. Forced to resign, the government was replaced by a coalition led by the socialist PSS, victors in elections in mid-1997. Sali Berisha was replaced as president by Rexhep Mejdani. Instability was compounded by conflict between ethnic Albanians and Serbs in the neighboring Serbian province of Kosovo, and the resulting refugee crisis.

WORLD AFFAIRS ▷ Joined UN in 1955

BSEC CE OSCE OIC PfP

The fate of the predominantly ethnic Albanian region of Kosovo in Serbia has dominated foreign policy in recent years. An autonomous province in former Yugoslavia, Kosovo was forcibly integrated into Serbia, one of the Yugoslavian republics, in 1989. Serb persecution of Albanians in Kosovo eventually prompted NATO to begin bombing Yugoslavia in 1999.

AID ▷ Recipient

💲 $155m (receipts) ⬇ Down 30% 1996–1997

After 1991 the West became the main source of aid. Food aid was stepped up in 1997, when anarchy swept the country after the collapse of the pyramid selling scheme, and again in 1999 as hundreds of thousands of ethnic Albanians fled the fighting in neighboring Kosovo.

DEFENSE
▷ Compulsory military service

💲 $94m   ⬇ Down 9% in 1997

The armed forces reestablished officer ranks in 1991. Military service of 18 months is mandatory. The crisis in Kosovo, in neighboring Yugoslavia, prompted Albania in 1999 to make its airspace available to NATO.

ECONOMICS
▷ Inflation 29.4% p.a. (1985–1996)

📊 $2.5bn   💲 146.00–139.95 lekë

SCORE CARD

❏ WORLD GNP RANKING	131st
❏ GNP PER CAPITA	$760
❏ BALANCE OF PAYMENTS	$–272m
❏ INFLATION	33.2%
❏ UNEMPLOYMENT	14%

STRENGTHS
Few. Oil and gas reserves. Growth in farm output more than offset by effects of instability in Kosovo.

WEAKNESSES
Rudimentary infrastructure. Instability discourages investment. Pyramid financial schemes wiped out savings.

EXPORTS

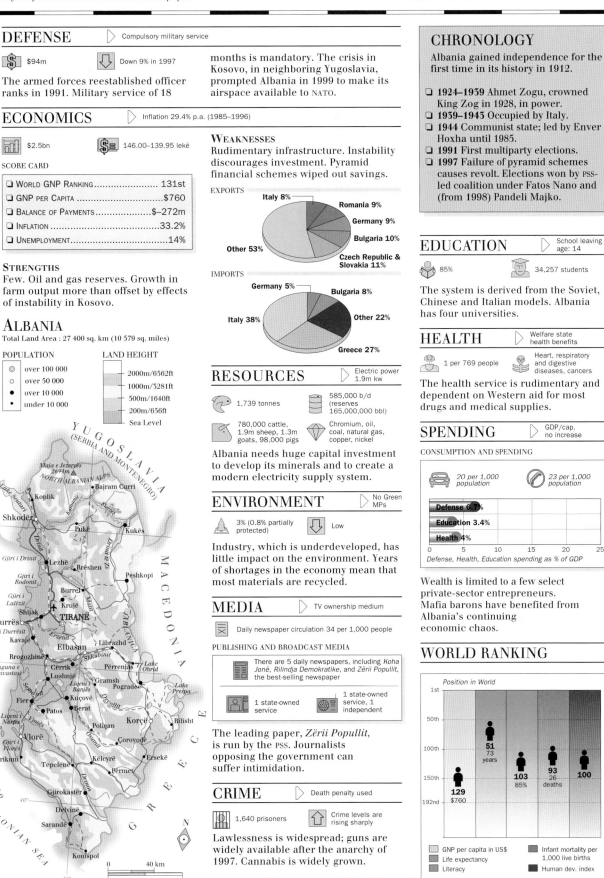

Italy 8%
Romania 9%
Germany 9%
Bulgaria 10%
Czech Republic & Slovakia 11%
Other 53%

IMPORTS

Germany 5%
Bulgaria 8%
Other 22%
Italy 38%
Greece 27%

RESOURCES
▷ Electric power 1.9m kw

🐟 1,739 tonnes   🛢 585,000 b/d (reserves 165,000,000 bbl)

780,000 cattle, 1.9m sheep, 1.3m goats, 98,000 pigs   💎 Chromium, oil, coal, natural gas, copper, nickel

Albania needs huge capital investment to develop its minerals and to create a modern electricity supply system.

ENVIRONMENT
▷ No Green MPs

🌲 3% (0.8% partially protected)   ⬇ Low

Industry, which is underdeveloped, has little impact on the environment. Years of shortages in the economy mean that most materials are recycled.

MEDIA
▷ TV ownership medium

🗞 Daily newspaper circulation 34 per 1,000 people

PUBLISHING AND BROADCAST MEDIA

There are 5 daily newspapers, including *Koha Jonë*, *Rilindja Demokratike*, and *Zëri i Popullit*, the best-selling newspaper

1 state-owned service   1 state-owned service, 1 independent

The leading paper, *Zërii Popullit*, is run by the PSS. Journalists opposing the government can suffer intimidation.

CRIME
▷ Death penalty used

🔒 1,640 prisoners   ⬆ Crime levels are rising sharply

Lawlessness is widespread; guns are widely available after the anarchy of 1997. Cannabis is widely grown.

ALBANIA
Total Land Area : 27 400 sq. km (10 579 sq. miles)

POPULATION
- ◎ over 100 000
- ○ over 50 000
- ● over 10 000
- ∙ under 10 000

LAND HEIGHT
- 2000m/6562ft
- 1000m/3281ft
- 500m/1640ft
- 200m/656ft
- Sea Level

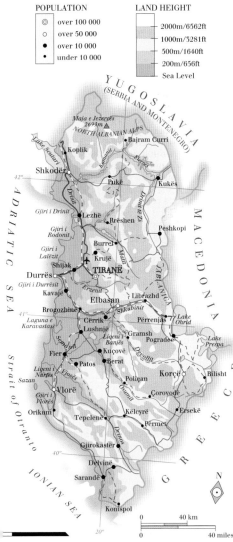

CHRONOLOGY
Albania gained independence for the first time in its history in 1912.

- ❏ **1924–1939** Ahmet Zogu, crowned King Zog in 1928, in power.
- ❏ **1939–1943** Occupied by Italy.
- ❏ **1944** Communist state; led by Enver Hoxha until 1985.
- ❏ **1991** First multiparty elections.
- ❏ **1997** Failure of pyramid schemes causes revolt. Elections won by PSS-led coalition under Fatos Nano and (from 1998) Pandeli Majko.

EDUCATION
▷ School leaving age: 14

👤 85%   🎓 34,257 students

The system is derived from the Soviet, Chinese and Italian models. Albania has four universities.

HEALTH
▷ Welfare state health benefits

1 per 769 people   Heart, respiratory and digestive diseases, cancers

The health service is rudimentary and dependent on Western aid for most drugs and medical supplies.

SPENDING
▷ GDP/cap. no increase

CONSUMPTION AND SPENDING

🚗 20 per 1,000 population   📞 23 per 1,000 population

Defense 6.7%
Education 3.4%
Health 4%

0   5   10   15   20   25
Defense, Health, Education spending as % of GDP

Wealth is limited to a few select private-sector entrepreneurs. Mafia barons have benefited from Albania's continuing economic chaos.

WORLD RANKING

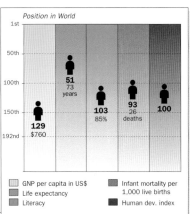

Position in World

1st
50th
100th
150th
192nd

129 $760
51 73 years
103 85%
93 26 deaths
100

- ▢ GNP per capita in US$
- ▢ Life expectancy
- ▢ Literacy
- ▪ Infant mortality per 1,000 live births
- ▪ Human dev. index

A

ALGERIA

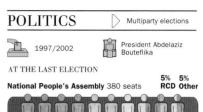

NORTH AFRICA

OFFICIAL NAME: Democratic and Popular Republic of Algeria **CAPITAL:** Algiers
POPULATION: 27.9 million **CURRENCY:** Algerian dinar **OFFICIAL LANGUAGE:** Arabic

| 1962 | 1962 | Nov 1 | DZ | +1 | +213 | .dz |

AFRICA'S SECOND LARGEST COUNTRY, Algeria
shares borders with Morocco, Mauritania, Mali,
Niger, Libya, and Tunisia. Algeria won independence
from France in 1962. Today, the military-dominated government has faced
sustained and bloody opposition to its attempts to create a civilian structure of
government while excluding militant Islamists from power. Algeria has
one of the youngest populations, and highest birthrates, in north Africa.

CLIMATE
▷ Hot desert/ Mediterranean

WEATHER CHART

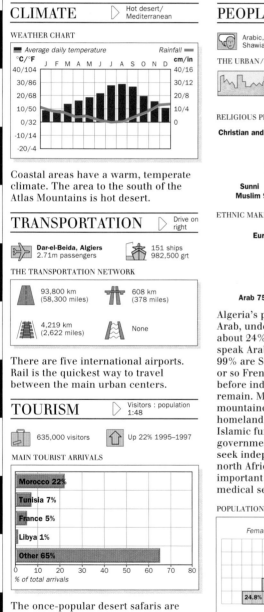

Coastal areas have a warm, temperate
climate. The area to the south of the
Atlas Mountains is hot desert.

TRANSPORTATION
▷ Drive on right

| Dar-el-Beida, Algiers 2.71m passengers | 151 ships 982,500 grt |

THE TRANSPORTATION NETWORK

| 93,800 km (58,300 miles) | 608 km (378 miles) |
| 4,219 km (2,622 miles) | None |

There are five international airports.
Rail is the quickest way to travel
between the main urban centers.

TOURISM
▷ Visitors : population 1:48

| 635,000 visitors | Up 22% 1995–1997 |

MAIN TOURIST ARRIVALS

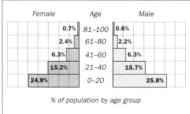

Morocco 22%
Tunisia 7%
France 5%
Libya 1%
Other 65%
0 10 20 30 40 50 60 70 80
% of total arrivals

The once-popular desert safaris are
now rare. Tourists are a target for
militant Islamic groups.

PEOPLE
▷ Pop. density low

| Arabic, Berber (Kabyle, Shawia, Tamashek), French | 13/km² (33/mi²) |

THE URBAN/RURAL POPULATION SPLIT

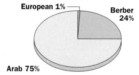

56%   44%

RELIGIOUS PERSUASION

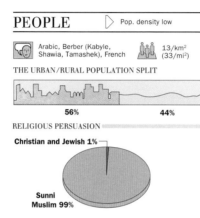

Christian and Jewish 1%
Sunni Muslim 99%

ETHNIC MAKEUP

European 1%
Berber 24%
Arab 75%

Algeria's population is predominantly
Arab, under 30 years of age and urban;
about 24% are Berber. More than 85%
speak Arabic, the official language, and
99% are Sunni Muslim. Of the million
or so French who settled in Algeria
before independence, only about 6,000
remain. Most Berbers consider the
mountainous Kabylia region their
homeland. If the struggle between
Islamic fundamentalists and the
government intensifies, Kabylia may
seek independence. As in the rest of
north Africa, the mosque is an
important provider of social and
medical services.

POPULATION AGE BREAKDOWN

Female		Age		Male
	0.7%	81–100	0.6%	
	2.4%	61–80	2.2%	
	6.3%	41–60	6.3%	
	15.2%	21–40	15.7%	
24.8%		0–20		25.8%

% of population by age group

POLITICS
▷ Multiparty elections

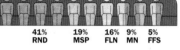

1997/2002   President Abdelaziz Bouteflika

AT THE LAST ELECTION

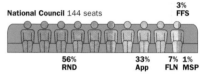

National People's Assembly 380 seats   5% RCD   5% Other

41% RND   19% MSP   16% FLN   9% MN   5% FFS

RND = National Democratic Rally **MSP** = Movement for a
Peaceful Society **FLN** = National Liberation Front
MN = Ennahda Movement **RCD** = Rally of Culture and
Democracy **FFS** = Front of Socialist Forces **App** = Appointed
Other = Workers' Party, Progressive Republican Party, Union
for Democracy and Liberty, Social Liberal Party, Independents

National Council 144 seats   3% FFS

56% RND   33% App   7% FLN   1% MSP

96 seats are elected, 48 are appointed by the President.

Military rule ended in 1994. Elections
were held in June 1997, but Abdelaziz
Bouteflika's presidential election victory
in 1999 was marred by the withdrawal
of all other candidates.

MAIN POLITICAL ISSUES
Islamic fundamentalism
Algeria has been scarred by political
violence since 1992, as Islamic militants
struggle to establish a theocracy. Its
foremost proponent, the Islamic
Salvation Front (FIS) won elections in
1991, but was prevented from taking
power by a military clampdown,
unleashing violence spearheaded by the
extremist Armed Islamic Group (GIA).

The market economy
The FIS's strong showing in the 1991
polls was in part due to popular reaction
against austerity measures, and
economic reforms. After a brief
suspension following the army takeover
in 1992, the liberalization program was
revived under pressure from the IMF and
the World Bank.

PROFILE
Until 1988, Algeria was a Soviet-style
regime. The aging ruling elite adopted
privatization policies, strongly opposed
by Islamic fundamentalists, who were
prevented from taking power by the
army. President Zeroual's RND claimed
victory in elections in 1997. Since 1992
tens of thousands of people have been
killed in a terrorist campaign by Islamic
militants and state counter-terrorist
action. Hopes for peace rose as Bouteflika
succeeded Zeroual as president in 1999.

WORLD AFFAIRS ▷ Joined UN in 1962

| AL | AMU | OIC | NAM | OPEC |

Algeria's struggle for independence from France lasted from 1954 until 1962. Throughout the 1960s and 1970s, Algeria's success in rejecting a colonial power made it a champion for the developing world. It had a leading voice within the UN, the Arab League and the Organization for African Unity. However, relations with the West remained essentially stable. Algeria was increasingly seen by the diplomatic community as a useful bridge between the West and Iran.

In 1981, Algerian diplomats helped to secure the release of US hostages held in Tehran during the last days of President Carter's term of office. Algeria also attempted to act in a mediating role during the 1980–1988 Iran–Iraq War.

Algeria's influence overseas has diminished as the country has become increasingly unstable politically. A victory for the Islamic fundamentalist FIS would greatly encourage Islamic militants in neighboring Morocco and Tunisia, and further undermine Egypt's embattled government. France fears the spill-over of terrorism and has been shocked by the killings, especially those of seven French priests and of the French Roman Catholic bishop of Oran.

European governments are anxious to help stabilize the regime to avoid refugees seeking entry into France, Spain, and Italy.

AID ▷ Recipient

$248m (receipts) Down 22% 1996–1997

As a major oil producer, Algeria receives only small quantities of aid. During the 1980s, its economy became dependent on eastern European manufactures, which were swapped for oil. The collapse of this trade in the 1990s led Algeria to turn to the West for loans. Oil revenues encouraged the West to offer export credits, which in turn helped fortify the regime against criticism of its hard-line methods against Islamic opponents. The IMF has provided loans to help Algeria meet payments on its debt, on condition that it move toward a market-orientated economy.

ALGERIA

Total Land Area :
2 381 740 sq. km
(919 590 sq. miles)

POPULATION
over 500 000 ◉
over 100 000 ◎
over 50 000 ○
over 10 000 ●

LAND HEIGHT
2000m/6562ft
1000m/3281ft
500m/1640ft
200m/656ft
Sea Level

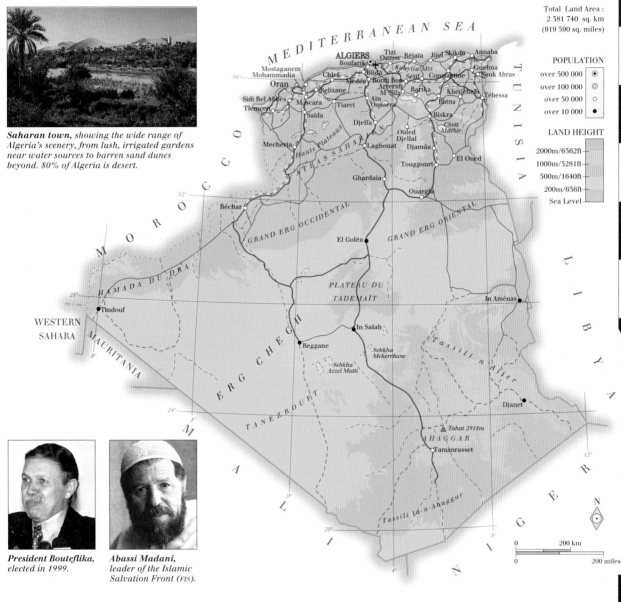

Saharan town, showing the wide range of Algeria's scenery, from lush, irrigated gardens near water sources to barren sand dunes beyond. 80% of Algeria is desert.

President Bouteflika,
elected in 1999.

Abassi Madani,
leader of the Islamic
Salvation Front (FIS).

CHRONOLOGY

The conquest of Algeria by France began in 1830. By 1900, French settlers occupied most of the best land. In 1954, war was declared on the colonial administration by the National Liberation Front (FLN).

❑ **1962** Cease-fire agreed, followed by independence as Algerian republic.

❑ **1965** Military junta topples government of Ahmed Ben Bella. Revolutionary council set up.

❑ **1966** Judiciary "Algerianized." Tribunals try "economic crimes."

❑ **1971** Oil industry nationalized. Boumedienne continues with land reform, a national health service and "socialist" management.

❑ **1976** National Charter establishes a socialist state.

❑ **1979** Bendjedid Chadli sworn in as president.

❑ **1980** Ben Bella released after 15 years' detention. Agreement signed with France, whereby latter gives incentives for return home of 800,000 Algerian immigrants.

❑ **1981** Algeria helps to negotiate release of hostages from US embassy in Tehran, Iran.

❑ **1985** Two most popular Kabyle (Berber) singers given three-year jail sentences for opposing regime.

❑ **1987** Government introduces limited economic liberalization. Cooperation agreement with Soviet Union.

❑ **1988** Anti-FLN violence; state of emergency. Algeria negotiates release of Kuwaiti hostages from aircraft; Shi'a hijackers escape.

❑ **1989** Constitutional reforms, which diminish power of FLN. New political parties include Islamic Salvation Front (FIS). AMU established.

❑ **1990** Political exiles permitted to return. FIS wins municipal elections.

❑ **1991** FIS leaders Abassi Madani and Ali Belhadj arrested. FIS wins large majority in National Assembly.

❑ **1992** Bendjedid overthrown by military. Second round of elections scrapped. President Boudiaf assassinated. Madani and Belhadj given 12 years in jail.

❑ **1994** Political violence led by Armed Islamic Group (GIA).

❑ **1996** Murders continue, including those of Catholic clergy and GIA leader.

❑ **1997** Legislative elections give Zeroual's RND dominance in new National Assembly. Madani released from jail but debarred from active politics. August, hundreds die in a single weekend, the bloodiest yet in six years of civil strife.

❑ **1999** Boycott by other presidential candidates ensures election of Abdelaziz Bouteflika.

DEFENSE

▷ Compulsory military service

💲 $2.1bn   ⬆ Up 16% in 1997

The National Liberation Army (NLA), equipped with Russian weapons, is the dominant power in politics. There are fears that parts of the army will forge an alliance with Muslim militants. The extreme rebel Armed Islamic Group, which has split from the FIS, is led by former army officers. However, the military are also suspected of taking part in reprisal killings of Islamic fundamentalist supporters.

ALGERIAN ARMED FORCES

🪖	890 main battle tanks (275 T–54/–55, 330 T–62, 285 T–72)	105,000 personnel
🚢	2 submarines, 3 frigates, and 19 patrol boats	7,000 personnel
✈	181 combat aircraft (10 Su-24, 40 MiG-23BN, 10 MiG-25, 30 MiG-23B/E)	10,000 personnel
🚀	None	

ECONOMICS

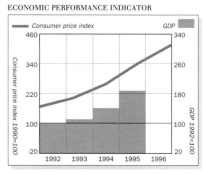

▷ Inflation 21% p.a. (1985–1996)

📊 $43.9bn   💹 58.52–60.75 dinars

SCORE CARD

❑ WORLD GNP RANKING	52nd
❑ GNP PER CAPITA	$1,500
❑ BALANCE OF PAYMENTS	$2.4bn
❑ INFLATION	21.6%
❑ UNEMPLOYMENT	26%

EXPORTS

Netherlands 6%
Other 33%
Spain 10%
France 14%
USA 17%
Italy 20%

IMPORTS

Brazil 5%
Spain 7%
USA 9%
Italy 9%
Other 42%
France 28%

STRENGTHS

Oil and gas. Recent collaboration with Western oil companies should see improvements in productivity. Natural gas is supplied to Europe.

WEAKNESSES

Oil revenues have not recovered from the 1986 collapse in world prices, despite a rise in late 1996. Political turmoil threatens many new projects and has led to an exodus of European and other expatriate workers important to the economy. Lack of skilled labor coupled with high unemployment. Limited agriculture. Shortages of basic foodstuffs. A thriving black market.

PROFILE

Under the pro-Soviet National Liberation Front, the Algerian economy was dominated by centralized socialist planning. After the economic collapse of the Soviet Union in the late 1980s Algeria began moving toward a market economy. However, these reforms were frozen following the military takeover

ECONOMIC PERFORMANCE INDICATOR

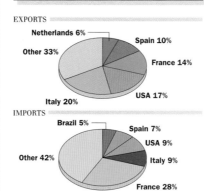

in 1992, although many have since been resumed under pressure from the IMF and the World Bank. The majority of the economy's most productive sectors remain under state control.

Only in the oil industry has private investment been encouraged. A number of Western oil companies have signed exploration contracts with Algiers since it has accepted more competitive production-sharing agreements. However, Western investment levels are likely to remain small as long as the political situation is unstable. Algeria is now importing more than half its grain, and long food lines are routine in the capital.

ALGERIA : MAJOR BUSINESSES

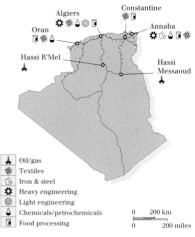

Algiers
Constantine
Oran
Annaba
Hassi R'Mel
Hassi Messaoud

⚓ Oil/gas
❋ Textiles
▨ Iron & steel
✿ Heavy engineering
⚙ Light engineering
🝊 Chemicals/petrochemicals
▤ Food processing

0   200 km
0   200 miles

A

RESOURCES

Electric power 6.0m kw

106,246 tonnes

822,000 b/d
(reserves
9,200,000,000 bbl)

16.8m sheep, 3.1m
goats, 1.2m cattle,
210,000 asses

Oil, natural gas, iron,
phosphates, lead, zinc,
silver, copper, tungsten

ELECTRICITY GENERATION

Hydro 1% (0.1bn kwh)	
Combustion 99% (19.5bn kwh)	
Nuclear 0%	
Other 0%	

0   20   40   60   80   100

% of total generation by type

Crude oil and natural gas, Algeria's
main resources, were first produced in
the 1950s. Algeria also has diverse
minerals, including iron ore, zinc,
silver, copper ore and phosphates.
In the 1960s and 1970s, Algeria sought
to become a manufacturing country,
with investments in building materials,
refined products, and steel; none of
these sectors is competitive on world
markets. Although agriculture employs
one-quarter of Algeria's workforce,
its importance to the economy is
diminishing. State forests cover some
2% of Algeria's land. Most are
brushwood, but some areas include
cork oak trees, Aleppo pine, evergreen
oak, and cedar. Algeria has a large
fishing fleet. Sardines, anchovies, tuna
fish, and shellfish are the major species
caught commercially.

ENVIRONMENT

No Green
MPs

3% (0.1% partially
protected)

Not available

ENVIRONMENTAL TREATIES

Yes   Yes   Yes

Yes   Yes   No

Since most of Algeria is desert or
semidesert, over 90% of the population
is forced to live on the remaining
20% of land. The desert is moving
northward. Vegetation has been
stripped for use as firewood and animal
fodder, leaving fragile soils exposed
which then require expensive specialist
care to conserve them. Water
purification techniques are below
standard and rivers are being
increasingly contaminated by untreated
sewage, industrial effluent, and wastes
from petroleum refining.

MEDIA

TV ownership medium

Daily newspaper circulation 38 per 1,000 people

PUBLISHING AND BROADCAST MEDIA

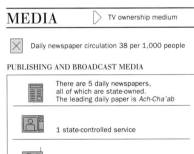

There are 5 daily newspapers,
all of which are state-owned.
The leading daily paper is *Ach-Cha'ab*

1 state-controlled service

4 state-controlled networks

Newspapers, TV and radio are state-
controlled and permit no criticism of
government actions. TV is broadcast in
Arabic, French, and Kabyle (Berber),
received by about 2 million sets. The
five daily newspapers have a combined
circulation of 1.3 million. However,
distribution is limited outside the main
cities.

CRIME

Death penalty used

Algeria does not
publish prison figures

Crime levels rising
sharply

CRIME RATES

Murders
1   per 100,000 population

Rapes
1   per 100,000 population

Thefts
236   per 100,000 population

Thousands have been killed by
radical Islamists since 1992. Human
rights groups accuse pro-government
death squads of brutal reprisal
killings and of persecuting suspected
Islamic militants.

EDUCATION

School leaving
age: 15

60%

347,410 students

Over three quarters of the country's
school-age population receive
a formal education.

THE EDUCATION SYSTEM

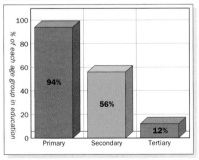

% of each age group in education

100
80
60
40
20
0

94%   56%   12%

Primary   Secondary   Tertiary

The literacy rate is rising. Since 1973,
the curriculum has been Arabized and
the teaching of French has been
restricted. Ten universities and seven
polytechnics provide higher education
to about 350,000 students. New
legislation in 1996 enforced the use
of Arabic in public life.

ALGERIA : LAND USE

Forest
Pasture
Cropland
Desert
Sheep
Potatoes
Dates

SAHARA

0   200 km
0   200 miles

HEALTH

State welfare
health benefits

1 per 1,250 people

Respiratory, heart and
cerebrovascular
diseases, malaria

Primary health care is rudimentary
outside main cities. Despite this,
in 1997 the infant mortality rate,
at 3.2% of live births, was below the
north African average of 4.9%.
Average life expectancy was put at
69 years in 1997, and as such was
just above the average for the
region of 67 years.

SPENDING

GDP/cap decrease

CONSUMPTION AND SPENDING

25 per 1,000
population

48 per 1,000
population

Defense 4.6%
Education 5.2%
Health 5.4%

0   5   10   15   20   25
Defense, Health, Education spending as % of GDP

There is great disparity in
wealth between the political elite
and the rest of the population.
Those connected to the military
are the wealthiest. Most Algerians
have had to contend with soaring
prices for basic necessities.

WORLD RANKING

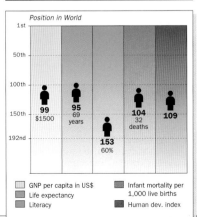

Position in World

1st
50th
100th
150th
192nd

99
$1500

95
69
years

153
60%

104
32
deaths

109

GNP per capita in US$
Life expectancy
Literacy

Infant mortality per
1,000 live births
Human dev. index

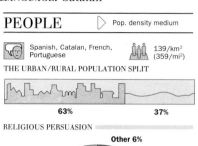

EUROPE

ANDORRA

OFFICIAL NAME: Principality of Andorra **CAPITAL:** Andorra la Vella
POPULATION: 65,000 **CURRENCY:** French franc and Spanish peseta **OFFICIAL LANGUAGE:** Catalan

| 1278 | 1278 | Sept 8 | AD | +1 | +376 | .ad |

A TINY, LANDLOCKED principality between France and Spain, Andorra lies high in the eastern Pyrenees. From the 13th century, French and Spanish co-princes (today the President of France and the Bishop of Urgell) have governed Andorra. In December 1993, the principality held its first full elections. Andorra's spectacular scenery, alpine climate and duty-free shopping have made tourism, especially skiing, its main source of income.

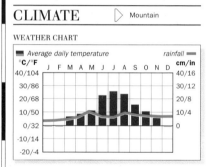

Andorra's outstanding mountain scenery attracts 500,000 skiers a year.

CLIMATE ▷ Mountain

WEATHER CHART

Springs are cool and wet; summers are dry and warm. Snowfalls in December and January provide snow for good skiing up to March. Andorra's climate supports an abundance of wild flowers.

TRANSPORTATION ▷ Drive on right

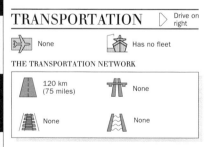

✈ None   🚢 Has no fleet

THE TRANSPORTATION NETWORK

120 km (75 miles)   None
None   None

The road from France to Spain climbs to 2,704 m (8,875 feet) through one of the most dramatic mountain passes in Europe. During the summer months, the sheer number of day-trippers often brings traffic to a standstill around Andorra la Vella.

TOURISM ▷ Visitors : population 123:1

8m visitors   Down 33% 1995-1997

MAIN TOURIST ARRIVALS

France	43%
Spain	41%
Italy	4%
Other	12%

% of total arrivals

Most tourists visit Andorra to ski or shop. However, the traditional trade in day-trippers from France and Spain, coming to shop in the many tax-free designer-label boutiques, is threatened by EU regulations seeking to end Andorra's beneficial tax regime. Five ski resorts receive over 500,000 visitors a year. In summer they cater for mountain hikers; Andorra's wild flowers attract many, but there is also much for the birdwatcher to see. Hunting of wild boar is popular, and the goat-like chamois can be hunted under special license.

PEOPLE ▷ Pop. density medium

Spanish, Catalan, French, Portuguese   139/km² (359/mi²)

THE URBAN/RURAL POPULATION SPLIT

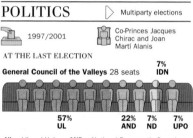

63%   37%

RELIGIOUS PERSUASION

Other 6%
Roman Catholic 94%

Immigration is strictly monitored and restricted by quota to French and Spanish nationals intending to work in Andorra. Divorce is illegal.

POLITICS ▷ Multiparty elections

1997/2001   Co-Princes Jacques Chirac and Joan Martí Alanis

AT THE LAST ELECTION

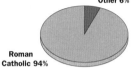

General Council of the Valleys 28 seats   7% IDN

| 57% UL | 22% AND | 7% ND | 7% UPO |

UL = Liberal Union **AND** = National Democratic Grouping
ND = New Democracy **IDN** = National Democratic Initiative
UPO = Unio del Poble d'Ordino

14 members are elected on a national list and 14 are elected in 7 dual-member parishes.

Until recently, Andorra was a semifeudal state. In 1993, a referendum approved measures legalizing political parties and the right to strike, and altered relations with the co-princes. The ruling Liberal Union, led by Marc Forné, was returned to power in elections in February 1997.

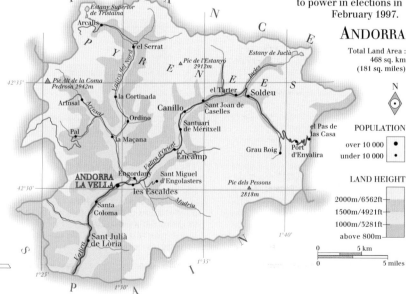

ANDORRA

Total Land Area : 468 sq. km (181 sq. miles)

POPULATION
over 10 000 ●
under 10 000 •

LAND HEIGHT
2000m/6562ft
1500m/4921ft
1000m/3281ft
above 800m

0   5 km
0   5 miles

A

WORLD AFFAIRS

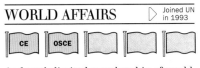

▷ Joined UN in 1993

Andorra's limited membership of world bodies reflects its ambiguous status; it is still not recognized by some countries. In 1991 it joined the EU customs union, applying its external tariff and trade policy. It joined the UN in 1993.

AID

▷ Not applicable

 Andorra has no aid receipts or donations　　Not applicable

The principality of Andorra neither receives nor provides aid, and has no plans to do so.

DEFENSE

▷ No compulsory military service

Andorra has no defense budget　　Not applicable

Andorra has no defense budget; protection is provided by France and Spain. The French intervention of 1933 was the last military action on Andorran soil.

ECONOMICS

▷ Not available

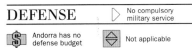 $1bn　　6.02–5.59 French Fr (152.42–141.70 Spanish pesetas)

SCORE CARD

❑ WORLD GNP RANKING 155th
❑ GNP PER CAPITA $15,600
❑ BALANCE OF PAYMENTS ......Included in Spanish total
❑ INFLATION ....Not applicable
❑ UNEMPLOYMENT ....Low unemployment

STRENGTHS

Tourism is the basis of the economy. Strict banking secrecy laws make Andorra an important tax haven; low consumer taxes have also encouraged a healthy luxury retail sector. Farming: cereals, potatoes and tobacco are the major products.

WEAKNESSES

France and Spain effectively decide economic policy. There is a dependence on imported food and raw materials.

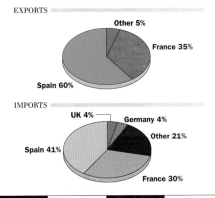

EXPORTS
Other 5%
France 35%
Spain 60%

IMPORTS
UK 4%
Germany 4%
Other 21%
Spain 41%
France 30%

RESOURCES

▷ Not available

None

2,402 sheep, 1,524 cattle, 1,084 horses, 480 goats

Not an oil producer and has no refineries

None

Water is a major resource, hydropower providing most domestic energy needs. However, Andorra has to import twice as much electricity as it produces, and there are plans to increase capacity. A third of the country is designated forest.

ENVIRONMENT

▷ No Green MPs

None　　Not available

Twelve million tourists a year have inevitably had an adverse impact over time on a country of 65,000 people. Concern is growing, at the moment chiefly among NGOs, about the scarring of Andorra's alpine landscape by hotel and ski developments, as well as about the future of its unique mountain flora. Hunting, notably of the Pyrenean chamois and the wild boar, is still a significant tourist attraction. However, restrictions are gradually being introduced to preserve certain animal species.

MEDIA

▷ TV ownership medium

Daily newspaper circulation 58 per 1,000 people

PUBLISHING AND BROADCAST MEDIA

There are 3 daily newspapers, *Diari d'Andorra*, *El Periòdic* and *Poble Andorra*

1 independent service　　2 independent services

Andorra receives most Spanish and French TV broadcasts. A private TV company in Spain broadcasts one hour a day of programs designed specifically for Andorra.

CRIME

▷ Death penalty not used

Andorra does not publish prison figures　　Down 54% from 1992–1996

Tourists are natural targets for thieves, most of whom are not Andorran. Thefts of expensive cars for resale in France and Spain are on the increase. Andorra has two criminal courts – the *Tribunals de Corts*.

EDUCATION

▷ School leaving age: 16

99%　　1,659 students

There are 18 schools in Andorra, most of which teach in Spanish and French. Instruction in Catalan is available, but only in the elementary schools and one secondary school.

CHRONOLOGY

Since 1278, Andorra has been autonomous, ruled by French and Spanish co-princes.

❑ **1970** Women get the vote.
❑ **1982** First constitution enshrines popular sovereignty.
❑ **1983** General Council votes in favor of income tax.
❑ **1984** Government resigns over attempt to introduce indirect taxes.
❑ **1991** EC customs union comes into effect.
❑ **1992** Political demonstrations demanding constitutional reform. Government resigns.
❑ **1993** Referendum approves new constitution. General election.
❑ **1994** Government falls; replaced by center-right UL cabinet, which is reelected in 1997.

HEALTH

▷ Welfare state health benefits

1 per 555 people　　Heart and cerebrovascular diseases

Andorra has one public and one private hospital. Hot springs at les Escaldes are popular with rheumatism sufferers.

SPENDING

▷ GDP/cap no increase

CONSUMPTION AND SPENDING

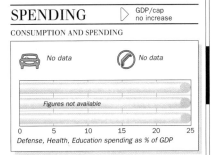

No data　　No data

Figures not available

0　　5　　10　　15　　20　　25
Defense, Health, Education spending as % of GDP

Hotel owners are the wealthiest group of citizens in Andorran society; many choose to live across the border in Spain.

WORLD RANKING

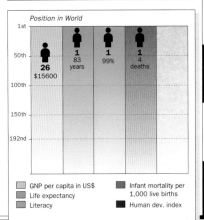

Position in World
1st
50th
100th
150th
192nd

26 $15600
1 83 years
1 99%
1 4 deaths

GNP per capita in US$　　Infant mortality per 1,000 live births
Life expectancy　　Human dev. index
Literacy

A

ANGOLA

OFFICIAL NAME: Republic of Angola   CAPITAL: Luanda
POPULATION: 12 million   CURRENCY: Readjusted kwanza   OFFICIAL LANGUAGE: Portuguese

1975	1975	Nov 11	ANG	+1	+244	.ao

SOUTHERN AFRICA

AN OIL-RICH COUNTRY in southwest Africa, Angola has suffered almost permanent civil war since 1975, when the colonial power, Portugal, left. For many years the West supported UNITA against the Soviet-backed MPLA government. The 1994 UN-backed Lusaka Protocol led to a putative government of national unity, but hopes for peace faded by 1998 as fighting was renewed.

CLIMATE
▷ Tropical/steppe

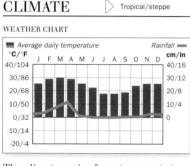

WEATHER CHART

The climate varies from temperate to tropical. Rainfall decreases from north to south. The Benguela Current makes the coast unusually cool and dry.

TRANSPORTATION
▷ Drive on right

Luanda International
766,077 passengers

109 ships
68,031 grt

THE TRANSPORTATION NETWORK

7,955 km (4,943 miles) according to most recent figures. Much has been destroyed during civil war.

2,952 km (1,834 miles) according to most recent figures. Much has been destroyed during civil war.

The war has destroyed Angola's transportation infrastructure, severely restricted the movement of goods and people, and devastated port traffic. UN peacekeepers have struggled to clear mines and repair and reopen roads, bridges and railroads. Both warring parties agreed to remove unauthorized checkpoints, but they still fought for control of Kuito airport and bridges in Bie Province. In early 1999 UNITA launched many road ambushes in central Angola.

TOURISM
▷ Visitors : population 1:1,500

8,000 visitors

No change
1995–1997

Most overseas visitors are Western journalists, or employees of the big oil multinationals in Cabinda. Angola, a disease-ridden war zone, where since October 1992 hundreds of thousands of people have died, attracts no tourists.

PEOPLE
▷ Pop. density medium

Portuguese, Umbundu, Kimbundu, Kikongo

10/km²
(25/mi²)

THE URBAN/RURAL POPULATION SPLIT

32%   68%

ETHNIC MAKEUP

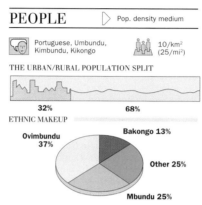

Ovimbundu 37%
Bakongo 13%
Other 25%
Mbundu 25%

UNITA has cast itself as the sole representative of the predominantly rural-dwelling Ovimbundu, in order to attack the mainly urban-based, largely Kimbundu or mixed race (Portuguese–African) MPLA. Religion has revived since the MPLA abandoned its Marxist tenets in the 1980s. Some 20% of the population are internal refugees.

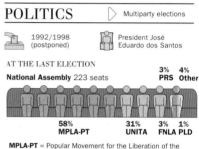

Angola's capital, Luanda. Founded in 1575 by the Portuguese, it became a transshipment point for slaves en route to Brazil.

POLITICS
▷ Multiparty elections

1992/1998
(postponed)

President José
Eduardo dos Santos

AT THE LAST ELECTION

National Assembly 223 seats

3% PRS   4% Other

58% MPLA-PT   31% UNITA   3% FNLA   1% PLD

MPLA-PT = Popular Movement for the Liberation of the Angola-Workers' Party   UNITA = National Union for the Total Independence of Angola   PRS = Social Renovated Party
FNLA = Angolan National Liberation Front
PLD = Social Liberal Democratic Party

Three seats (not filled) represents Angolans abroad.

Angola is dominated by two groups, the MPLA and UNITA. In power since 1975, the MPLA abandoned Marxist rule in 1991 and won Angola's first multiparty elections in 1992. Jonas Savimbi's defeated UNITA responded by reopening the civil war. The rivals signed a peace protocol in Zambia in November 1994, leading to the formation of a government of national unity (GURN) under President José Eduardo dos Santos. UNITA ministers joined GURN in 1997, but were expelled in 1998 as fighting increased. A new MPLA-dominated government was sworn in in 1999.

ANGOLA

Total Land Area :
1 124 670 sq. km
(434 255 sq. miles)

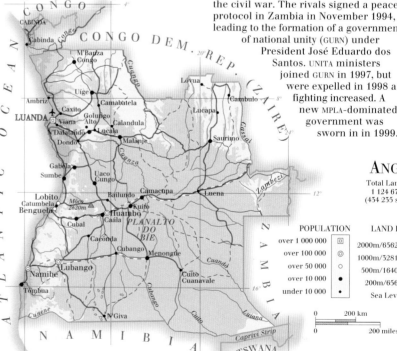

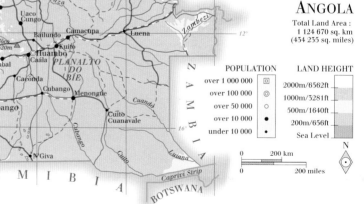

POPULATION

over 1 000 000
over 100 000
over 50 000
over 10 000
under 10 000

LAND HEIGHT

2000m/6562ft
1000m/3281ft
500m/1640ft
200m/656ft
Sea Level

0   200 km
0   200 miles

N

WORLD AFFAIRS

▷ Joined UN in 1976

Angola was a key Cold War frontier in the 1980s. Soviet advisers and Cuban troops supported the MPLA; South Africa and the USA backed UNITA forces. Since 1992, however, UNITA has lost international support, while the MPLA government gained US recognition. Post-apartheid South Africa joined the USA, Russia, and Portugal as guarantors of Angola's peace process after 1994. Regionally, MPLA troops help prop up the government of Congo.

AID

▷ Recipient

💲 $436m (receipts)   ⬇ Down 20% 1996–1997

The World Bank, the EU, the USA, Japan, and Norway in 1995 pledged $1 billion in aid to rebuild the shattered economy.

DEFENSE

▷ No compulsory military service

💲 $658m   ⬆ Up 45% in 1997

Plans to integrate UNITA troops into a national army collapsed when the rebels refused to be confined. In 1998 full-scale fighting erupted as 30,000 UNITA troops wrested control of 68 areas; by 1999 fighting spread to Kuito, Malanje, and Huambo. Meanwhile government soldiers' pay was increased and in the south "youngsters" were conscripted.

ECONOMICS

▷ Inflation 297% p.a. (1985–1996)

$3bn   257,128.00 readjusted kwanza

SCORE CARD

❏ WORLD GNP RANKING	126th
❏ GNP PER CAPITA	$260
❏ BALANCE OF PAYMENTS	$3.3bn
❏ INFLATION	111.2%
❏ UNEMPLOYMENT	50%

STRENGTHS
Oil earns important foreign exchange, but plans for advanced offshore drilling threatened by falling price. Some of the richest mineral deposits in Africa.

WEAKNESSES
Civil war. Destruction of infrastructure. Lack of skilled manpower. Corruption and cronyism sap resources.

EXPORTS

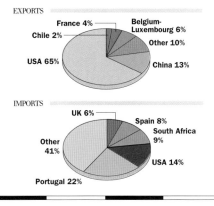

France 4%
Chile 2%
USA 65%
Belgium-Luxembourg 6%
Other 10%
China 13%

IMPORTS

UK 6%
Spain 8%
South Africa 9%
Other 41%
USA 14%
Portugal 22%

RESOURCES

▷ Electric power 617,000 kw

93,847 tonnes   521,300 b/d
3.5m cattle, 810,000 pigs, 245,000 sheep   Oil, diamonds, iron, copper, lead, zinc, gold, manganese

New deep-water oilfields have been found. The hugely rich alluvial diamond deposits are mainly in UNITA areas.

ENVIRONMENT

▷ No Green MPs

🔺 7% (1% partially protected)   Not available

The 1990 drought threatened mass famine. UNITA has been accused of wide-scale ivory poaching.

MEDIA

▷ TV ownership medium

❌ Daily newspaper circulation 12 per 1,000 people.

PUBLISHING AND BROADCAST MEDIA

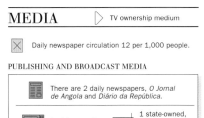
There are 2 daily newspapers, *O Jornal de Angola* and *Diário da República*.

1 state-owned service   1 state-owned, 1 independent service

Foreign journalists have been arrested. UN officials accuse the MPLA of spreading "hostile war propaganda."

CRIME

▷ Death penalty not used

Angola does not publish prison figures   Down 70% from 1992–1996

Murder, theft, corruption, and diamond smuggling are commonplace. Rural areas are effectively controlled by gangs. Both the MPLA and UNITA have poor human rights records. Global companies assist UNITA in sanctions-busting.

EDUCATION

▷ School leaving age: 15

45%   6,331 students

The system has all but collapsed; the government is concentrating funds on educating scholarship students abroad.

CHRONOLOGY

The Portuguese first established coastal forts in 1482.

- ❏ **1956** MPLA founded.
- ❏ **1975** Independence from Portugal. Civil war between Soviet- and Cuban-backed MPLA and US- and South African-backed UNITA.
- ❏ **1979** José Eduardo dos Santos (MPLA) becomes president.
- ❏ **1991** UN-brokered peace.
- ❏ **1992** MPLA election victory provokes UNITA to resume fighting.
- ❏ **1994** Lusaka peace agreement.
- ❏ **1998** Civil war re-erupts.
- ❏ **1999** UN withdraws Angolan mission.

HEALTH

▷ No welfare state health benefits

1 per 14,300 people   Malaria, diarrheal and respiratory diseases, severe malnutrition

By January 1999 the health system was barely able to cope with some 500,000 famine victims and war wounded and the threat of epidemics. Angola has a very high infant mortality rate, and the greatest number of amputees (caused by exploding mines) in the world.

SPENDING

▷ GDP/cap. increase

CONSUMPTION AND SPENDING

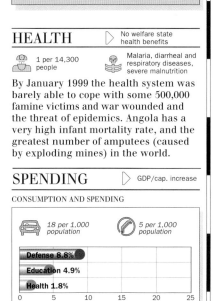

18 per 1,000 population   5 per 1,000 population

Defense 8.8%
Education 4.9%
Health 1.8%

Defense, Health, Education spending as % of GDP

State officials enjoy luxuries, such as access to cars and certain consumer goods, while others struggle to survive. The MPLA accuses its own generals of illicit diamond mining.

WORLD RANKING

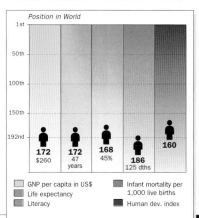

Position in World

172 $260
172 47 years
168 45%
186 125 dths
160

❏ GNP per capita in US$
❏ Life expectancy
❏ Literacy
❏ Infant mortality per 1,000 live births
❏ Human dev. index

A

ANTARCTICA

OFFICIAL NAME: Antarctica **CAPITAL:** None
POPULATION: None **CURRENCY:** None **OFFICIAL LANGUAGE:** None

| 1961 | 1961 | n/a | n/a | n/a | n/a | .aq |

T HE FIFTH-LARGEST CONTINENT, Antarctica is almost entirely covered by ice over 2,000 m (6,560 feet) thick. The area sustains a varied wildlife, including seals, whales, and penguins. The Antarctic Treaty, signed in 1959 and enforced in 1961, provides for international governance of Antarctica. To gain Consultative Status, countries have to set up a program of scientific research in the continent. Following a 1994 international agreement, a whale sanctuary was established in Antarctica.

PEOPLE
▷ Not applicable

English, Spanish, French, Norwegian, Chinese, Polish, Russian, German, Japanese

Not applicable

ETHNIC MAKEUP

Antarctica has a transient population of Americans, English, French, Norwegians, Argentinians, Chileans, Chinese, Russians, Poles and Japanese. Most are involved in research. Few stay more than two years.

Antarctica has no indigenous population. The people who live in the continent are scientists and logistical staff working at the 40 permanent, and as many as 100 temporary, research stations. Most stations are too far apart for direct contact between different nationalities. A few Chilean settler families are resident on King George Island.

CLIMATE
▷ Freezing

WEATHER CHART

Antarctica is the windiest as well as the coldest continent. Powerful winds create a narrow storm belt around the continent, which brings cloud, fog, and severe blizzards. Icebergs, which tend to be slab-shaped, barricade more than 90% of the coastline. Antarctica contains over 80% of the world's fresh water in the form of ice. The blood of polar fish contains antifreeze agents.

TOURISM
▷ Not applicable

9,400 visitors

Up 11% in 1995

Tourism is mainly by cruise ship to the Antarctic Peninsula, Ross Sea and the sub-Antarctic islands. In 1983, the Chileans began flights to King George Island, where an 80-bed hotel has been built. Main attractions are the wildlife, skiing, and visits to scientific stations and historic huts. The growth of tourism has disrupted scientific programs and official regulation of tourism is now essential.

TRANSPORTATION
▷ Not applicable

Airstrips to some stations

Has no fleet

Ships are the main mode of transportation to Antarctica. They are also used for marine research projects. Air traffic from Chile is growing, and France and the UK are building new airstrips. Most planes have to be equipped with skis.

ANTARCTICA
Total Land Area : 13 900 000 sq. km (5 566 790 sq. miles)

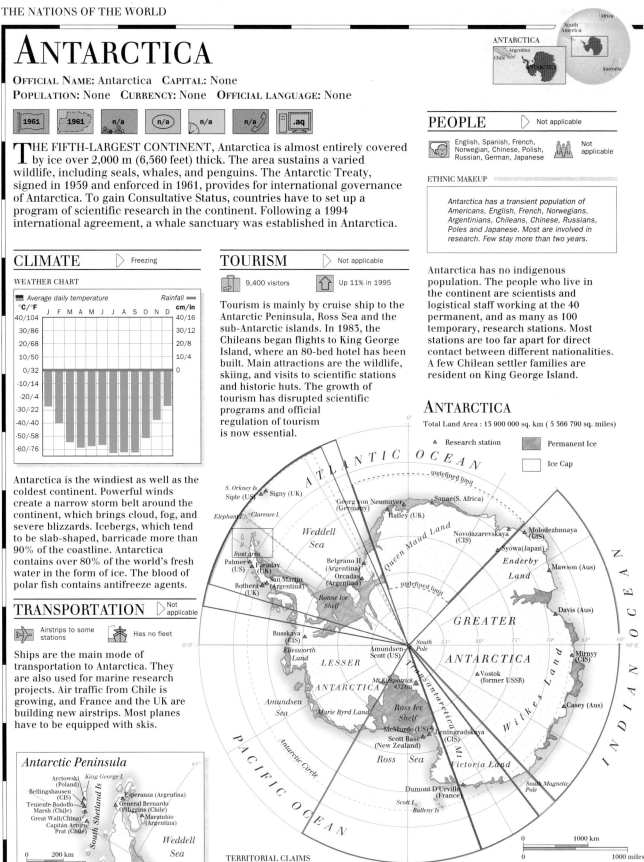

A

Neumayer Channel, Antarctica. *Many states are pressing for the whole of Antarctica to be protected as an international park.*

POLITICS ▷ Not applicable

Not applicable	Consultative Parties to Antarctic Treaty

NO LEGISLATIVE OR ADVISORY BODIES

The Antarctic Treaty of 1959 was signed by 12 nations and acceded to by 26. Consultative meetings are held annually to discuss scientific, environmental and political matters.

There are 30 parties to the Antarctic Treaty and 14 nations with observer status. There are territorial claims by Australia, France, New Zealand and Norway, and overlapping claims in the Antarctic Peninsula by Argentina, Chile and the UK. Other states do not recognize these claims.

Of main concern is the adoption of a wide range of environmental protection measures. Proposals include the monitoring of all scientific activities and also the prosecution of any country if it was demonstrated that its research would lead to detrimental global change.

WORLD AFFAIRS ▷ Non member

Rivalries exist between nations wishing to preserve Antarctica as a world park and those pursuing territorial claims.

AID ▷ Recipient

Each country's research is government-funded	Subject to individual government budgets

Scientific programs in the Antarctic are almost entirely funded by government agencies in the home countries. Some funding is sometimes provided by scientific institutions and universities.

DEFENSE ▷ Not applicable

No defence force	Not applicable

Under the Antarctic Treaty, Antarctica can be used only for peaceful purposes. Any military personnel present perform purely scientific or logistical roles.

ECONOMICS ▷ Not applicable

Not applicable	Antarctica has no currency

Research is government-funded and therefore subject to cuts. The exploitation of marine stocks provides no income to Antarctica.

RESOURCES ▷ Not applicable

Included in national fish catch totals	Not an oil producer and has no refineries
None	Mineral extraction is banned

Antarctica's main resources are its marine stocks, including fin fish, seals and whales. A campaign by environmental groups, supported by Australia and France, to ban mining and declare Antarctica a world park was rewarded in 1991 with an agreement to impose a 50-year ban on mining, and in 1994 by the approval of a whale sanctuary. Prospects for energy sources alternative to fossil fuels, such as solar power and wind generators, are being explored.

ENVIRONMENT ▷ Not applicable

Most of Antarctica is protected	Not available

Antarctica is one of the Earth's last great wildernesses. Its layer of ice, 4,000 m (13,000 feet) thick in places, has formed over thousands of years. Its ecosystem is so fragile that a footprint will leave its mark for years. Several species are unique to the continent, including king penguins. Ecological concerns include overfishing, particularly of krill, cod and squid; the disintegration of ice shelves in the Antarctic Peninsula; and the depletion of the ozone layer over Antarctica, which may adversely affect phytoplankton, the foundation of the food chain for marine life. In 1994, the IWC agreed to a French proposal to create an Antarctic whale sanctuary which, with the Indian Ocean sanctuary, protects the feeding grounds of 90% of the world's whales.

MEDIA ▷ Not applicable

	There are no daily newspapers produced in Antarctica. Any papers would have to be brought in from the home countries

A few bases publish newssheets for local consumption. Local radio stations are found at some of the larger bases.

CRIME ▷ Not applicable

There are no prisons in Antarctica	Crime is negligible

Crime is negligible. Each person in Antarctica is subject to their national laws. Occasional petty theft from stations is linked to visits from tourists.

CHRONOLOGY

The Russian explorer, Thaddeus von Bellingshausen, was the first to sight Antarctica, in 1820. The South Pole was first reached by the Norwegian, Roald Amundsen, in December 1911.

- ❑ **1912** Scott leads UK expedition. All perish on return journey.
- ❑ **1957–1958** Scientific exploration of Antarctica launched by International Geophysical Year.
- ❑ **1959** Antarctic Treaty signed by 12 countries. Territorial claims frozen.
- ❑ **1978** Convention limiting seal hunting comes into force.
- ❑ **1994** Establishment of Antarctic whale sanctuary.
- ❑ **1998** Agreement on 50-year ban on mineral extraction comes into force.

EDUCATION ▷ Not applicable

100%	None

Schoolhouses exist on the Chilean base, Villa Las Estrellas, and the Argentinean base, Esperanza. Teaching is geared to the relevant national system. Some researchers' studies contribute to higher degrees. Antarctic-based research has resulted in a number of scientific breakthroughs, including the discovery of ozone depletion.

HEALTH ▷ Not applicable

1 medical officer per station	Deaths are extremely rare in Antarctica

There is no central health system. Each station has its own medical officer who treats mostly minor complaints. The incidence of disease is rare, as all personnel are medically screened. The problems usually associated with polar conditions, such as frostbite and snow blindness, are very rare. Serious illness cannot be treated locally, and patients have to be evacuated.

SPENDING ▷ Not applicable

Wealth disparities reflect the different levels of base funding. US bases are the best-funded; the future of ex-USSR bases is in doubt. Most stations have a TV and video recorder. Telephone systems operate only within stations. PCs are supplied for scientific research. There are no cars.

WORLD RANKING

The UN Human Development Index conditions are not applicable to Antarctica.

A

ANTIGUA & BARBUDA

OFFICIAL NAME: Antigua and Barbuda CAPITAL: St John's
POPULATION: 66,000 CURRENCY: Eastern Caribbean dollar OFFICIAL LANGUAGE: English

LOCATED BETWEEN THE Atlantic and the Caribbean, Antigua, one of the Leeward Islands, was in turn a Spanish, French, and British colony. British influence is still strong, and most clearly revealed in the Antiguans' passion for cricket. Antigua has two remote dependencies: Barbuda, 50 km (30 miles) to the northeast, sporting a magnificent beach; and Redonda, 40 km (25 miles) southwest, an uninhabited rock with its own king.

CLIMATE
▷ Tropical oceanic

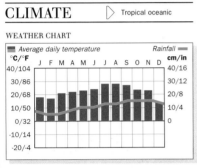

Antigua is less humid than other Caribbean islands. Year-round trade winds moderate the heat.

TRANSPORTATION
▷ Drive on left

V C Bird International, St. John's
727,292 passengers

516 ships
2.21m grt

THE TRANSPORTATION NETWORK

| 384 km (239 miles) | None |
| 77 km (48 miles) | None |

A EC$61 million airport expansion is proceeding, as is road resurfacing in St. John's. Recently 140 km (90 miles) of roads have been improved.

TOURISM
▷ Visitors : population 3.5:1

231,000 visitors

Up 16% 1995–1997

MAIN TOURIST ARRIVALS

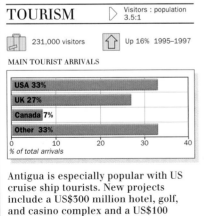

USA 33%
UK 27%
Canada 7%
Other 33%
% of total arrivals

Antigua is especially popular with US cruise ship tourists. New projects include a US$300 million hotel, golf, and casino complex and a US$100 million shopping, entertainment, and hotel center near the airport.

PEOPLE
▷ Pop. density medium

English, English patois

150/km² (389/mi²)

THE URBAN/RURAL POPULATION SPLIT

36%   64%

RELIGIOUS PERSUASION

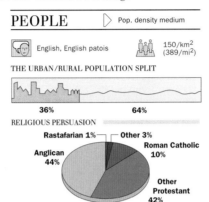

Rastafarian 1%   Other 3%
Anglican 44%   Roman Catholic 10%
Other Protestant 42%

Most of Antigua's population is descended from Africans, brought over between the 16th and 19th centuries. There are, in addition, a few Europeans and South Asians. Racial tensions are few. Life is based around the extended family. Since the 1960s, the status of women has risen as a result of their greater access to education, and many are now entering the legal, financial and medical professions. By Caribbean standards wealth disparities are small.

ANTIGUA & BARBUDA
Total Land Area : 440 sq. km (170 sq. miles)

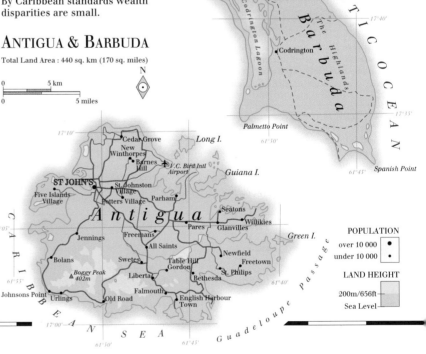

POLITICS
▷ Multiparty elections

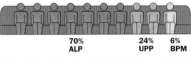

L. House 1999/2004
U. House 1999/2004

HM Queen Elizabeth II

AT THE LAST ELECTION

House of Representatives 17 seats

70% ALP   24% UPP   6% BPM

ALP = Antigua Labour Party UPP = United Progressive Party
BPM =Barbuda People's Movement

Senate 17 seats

11 members chosen by the prime minister, 4 by the leader of the opposition, 1 by the governor general and 1 by the Barbuda Council.

Antigua's multiparty democracy has been dominated for the past 36 years by the Bird family. Vere Bird Sr., veteran prime minister and ALP leader, retired in 1994 and a battle between his two sons to succeed him was won by Lester Bird; Vere Jr. had in 1990 been removed from public office, accused of involvement in gun-running. Lester Bird won the 1994 general election and led the ALP to its sixth consecutive term in March 1999.

POPULATION
over 10 000 ●
under 10 000 ·
LAND HEIGHT
200m/656ft
Sea Level

WORLD AFFAIRS

▷ Joined UN in 1981

Antigua has tended to back US policy in the region, supporting both the US invasion of Grenada in 1983 and economic sanctions against Cuba.

AID

▷ Recipient

💲 $4m (receipts)   ⬇ Down 67% 1996–1997

Donors include the USA, the UK, France, Kuwait, Japan and the EU. In 1998 the opposition accused the Bird regime of the partisan distribution of hurricane relief for electoral gain.

DEFENSE

▷ No compulsory military service

💲 $3m   ⬇ Down 33% in 1997

The government denied reports in 1998 that sophisticated weaponry was imported privately from the US for the 517-strong security force. Two military bases are leased to the USA.

ECONOMICS

▷ Not available

📊 $489m   💲 2.70 East Caribbean dollars

SCORE CARD

❑ WORLD GNP RANKING	166th
❑ GNP PER CAPITA	$7,380
❑ BALANCE OF PAYMENTS	$–40m
❑ INFLATION	1.2%
❑ UNEMPLOYMENT	10%

STRENGTHS

Tourism and construction of tourist hotels and infrastructure. Financial and communications services linked to off-shore financial sector.

WEAKNESSES

Very little diversification makes Antigua vulnerable to downturns in the world tourism market. Evidence of off-shore money laundering harms the country's reputation.

EXPORTS

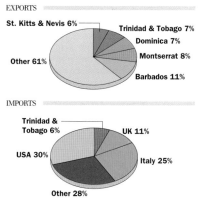

St. Kitts & Nevis 6%
Trinidad & Tobago 7%
Dominica 7%
Montserrat 8%
Other 61%
Barbados 11%

IMPORTS

Trinidad & Tobago 6%
UK 11%
USA 30%
Italy 25%
Other 28%

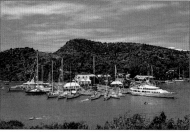

Nelson's Dockyard. *Luxury yachts fitted with 20th-century, state-of-the-art gadgetry contrast with the 18th-century St John's harbor.*

RESOURCES

▷ Electric power 26,000 kw

🐟 470 tonnes   🛢 Not an oil producer

🐄 16,000 cattle, 12,000 sheep, 12,000 goats   💎 None

Antigua has no strategic or commodity resources and has to import almost all its energy requirements.

ENVIRONMENT

▷ No Green MPs

🔺 9%   ⬍ Not available

Uncontrolled sewage disposal from beachfront hotels causes problems. Untreated hotel effluent has also killed valuable inshore fish stocks in swamps. In addition, Antigua's mangrove systems are threatened by poorly planned hotel development.

MEDIA

▷ TV ownership hgh

✉ Daily newspaper circulation 90 per 1,000 people

PUBLISHING AND BROADCAST MEDIA

There is 1 daily newspaper, the *Observer*. The leading paper is the weekly *Outlet*

1 state-owned, 1 independent service

1 state-owned, 3 independent services

Arson was blamed for the destruction of printing equipment of the opposition *Outlet* weekly in 1998. There is an official TV and radio station and there are also private outlets, one US-sourced.

CRIME

▷ Death penalty used

🏛 Antigua and Barbuda does not publish prison figures   ⬇ Down 2% from 1992–1996

Murder is rare. Rape, armed robbery and burglary are main concerns, as is off-shore money laundering.

EDUCATION

▷ School leaving age: 16

📚 95%   🎓 631 students

Education is based on the former British selective 11-plus system. Students go on to the University of the West Indies, or to study in the UK or the USA.

HEALTH

▷ Welfare state health benefits

👥 1 per 1,316 people   ♥ Heart and respiratory diseases, cancers

By Caribbean standards, the health system is efficient, with easy access to the state-run clinics and hospitals. A new hospital was being built in 1999.

SPENDING

▷ GDP/cap. no increase

CONSUMPTION AND SPENDING

🚗 No data   💿 308 per 1,000 population

Defense 0.5%		
Education No data		
Health No data		

0   5   10   15   20   25
Defense, Health, Education spending as % of GDP

Wealthy Antiguans are involved in the country's thriving tourist industry, and some allegedly in money laundering. Unemployment is low and average per capita income is among the highest in CARICOM.

WORLD RANKING

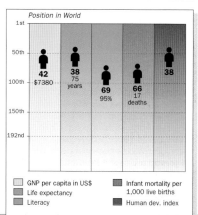

Position in World
1st
50th
100th
150th
192nd

42 $7380
38 75 years
69 95%
66 17 deaths
38

❑ GNP per capita in US$
❑ Life expectancy
❑ Literacy
❑ Infant mortality per 1,000 live births
❑ Human dev. index

A

ARGENTINA

SOUTH AMERICA

OFFICIAL NAME: Argentine Republic   CAPITAL: Buenos Aires
POPULATION: 36.1 million   CURRENCY: Argentine peso   OFFICIAL LANGUAGE: Spanish

| 1816 | 1816 | May 25 | RA | -3 | +54 | .ar |

OCCUPYING MOST OF THE southern half of South America, Argentina extends 3,460 km (2,150 miles) from Bolivia to Cape Horn. The Andes mountains in the west run north-south, forming a natural border with Chile. To the east they slope down to the fertile central pampas, the region known as Entre Ríos. Agriculture, especially beef, wheat, and fruit, and energy resources are Argentina's main sources of wealth. Politics in Argentina has been characterized in the past by periods of military rule. In 1983, however, Argentina returned to multiparty democracy.

Herding cattle in the northeast, near Corrientes. Beef, Argentina's first source of wealth, remains a major export.

CLIMATE

▷ Mountain/steppe/ subtropical

WEATHER CHART

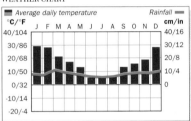

The northeast is near-tropical. The Andes are semiarid in the north and snowy in the south. The western lowlands are desert, while the pampas have a mild climate with heavy summer rains.

TRANSPORTATION

▷ Drive on right

Ezeiza Intl, Buenos Aires
2.6m passengers

513 ships
579,400 grt

THE TRANSPORTATION NETWORK

| 61,440 km (38,177 miles) | 378 km (235 miles) |
| 34,059 km (21,163 miles) | 11,000 km (6,835 miles) |

Argentina has an extensive transportation network but further investment of up to $35 billion is needed by 2000 to bring infrastructure up to international standards. The national airline, *Aerolineas Argentinas* was privatized in 1990 and the operation of 37 airports is now in private hands. Since privatization, the use of the railroad, one of the largest in the world, has increased markedly, mostly for freight, but the Buenos Aires subway and commuter lines are expanding. Some 10,000 km (6,000 miles) of the road network is privatized, but a road building program is currently halted. The six main terminals in the port of Buenos Aires are privately run.

TOURISM

▷ Visitors : population 1:7.9

4.5m visitors

Up 11% 1995–1997

MAIN TOURIST ARRIVALS

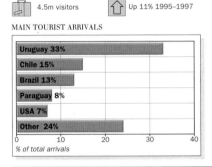

Uruguay 33%
Chile 15%
Brazil 13%
Paraguay 8%
USA 7%
Other 24%

% of total arrivals

Although tourism is a significant export earner, Argentina is still on the fringe of the world tourism market, since 80% of foreign visitors come from adjoining countries, attracted mainly by the city life of Buenos Aires and by the ski resorts. The resort of Mar del Plata on the coast and the ski stations in the Córdoba highlands have become mass tourism destinations. Other major attractions are the Iguazú National Park and Antarctic cruises, starting from the port of Ushuaia on Tierra del Fuego.

PEOPLE

▷ Pop. density low

Spanish, Italian, Amerindian languages

13/km² (34/mi²)

THE URBAN/RURAL POPULATION SPLIT

88%   12%

RELIGIOUS PERSUASION

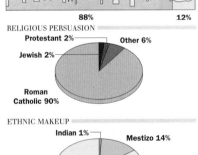

Protestant 2%
Other 6%
Jewish 2%
Roman Catholic 90%

ETHNIC MAKEUP

Indian 1%
Mestizo 14%
European 85%

Most Argentineans of European descent are from recent 20th-century migrations; over one-third are of Italian origin. Indigenous peoples are now a minority, living mainly in Andean regions or in the *Gran Chaco*. Other important communities are Lebanese, Syrians, Armenians, Japanese and Koreans. More than 85% of

POPULATION AGE BREAKDOWN

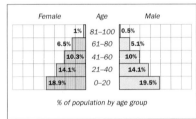

Female	Age	Male
1%	81–100	0.5%
6.5%	61–80	5.1%
10.3%	41–60	10%
14.1%	21–40	14.1%
18.9%	0–20	19.5%

% of population by age group

Argentineans are urban dwellers, with 40% living in the capital, Buenos Aires. In general, there is little ethnic tension.

Catholicism and the extended family remain strong in Argentina. In addition, the family forms the basis of many successful businesses.

Women have a higher profile than in most Latin American countries. Argentinean women were enfranchised before their French counterparts received the vote. Today, many enter the professions and rise to positions of influence in service businesses such as the media. The exception is politics. Eva Perón, who inspired the musical *Evita*, did help to push women into a more active political role in the 1940s and 1950s, but this trend was reversed under military rule.

POLITICS

 Multiparty elections

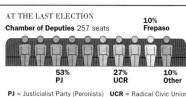

L. House 1997/1999
U. House 1997/1999

President Carlos
Saúl Menem

Argentina is a multiparty democracy; the president is head of state.

MAIN POLITICAL ISSUES
Legacy of Menem years
President Menem's vigorous free market policies rid Argentina of hyperinflation and attracted foreign investment. However, this success has led to a pervasive sense of exclusion among the majority. His opponents highlight social issues but have been unable to articulate a clear alternative to the government's economic strategy.

President Menem was reelected in 1995 after instigating a constitutional amendment to allow him to stand again. His increasing use of vetoes and decrees to secure his policies has provoked widespread resentment. Congress reluctantly approved his request for emergency powers in February 1996 to carry out a "second reform of the state."

"Dollarization" of the economy
President Menem in 1999 announced a highly controversial long-term plan aimed at "dollarizing" the economy, which would eliminate currency risk by doing away with the peso and replacing it with the US dollar.

The military and justice
Menem pardoned officers accused of human rights abuses under military rule (1976–1983). In 1995 the Chiefs of Staff publicly admitted responsibility for past abuses.

ARGENTINA

Total Land Area : 2 756 690 sq. km
(1 056 636 sq. miles)

POPULATION

over 1 000 000	⊡
over 500 000	◉
over 100 000	◎
over 50 000	○
over 10 000	●

LAND HEIGHT

4000m/13124ft	
2000m/6562ft	
1000m/3281ft	
200m/656ft	
Sea Level	

0   200 km
0   200 miles

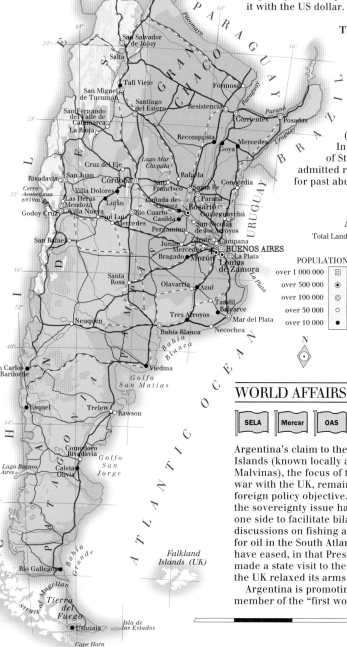

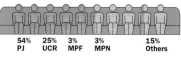

AT THE LAST ELECTION

Chamber of Deputies 257 seats

10% Frepaso

53% PJ	27% UCR	10% Other

PJ = Justicialist Party (Peronists)   UCR = Radical Civic Union
Frepaso = National Solidarity Front   MPF = Fueguino Popular Movement   MPN = Neuquino Popular Movement
Other = Movement for Dignity and Independence (Modin) and Union of the Democratic Centre (UCeD)

Senate 72 seats

54% PJ	25% UCR	3% MPF	3% MPN	15% Others

PROFILE
The Peronists have dominated politics since the 1940s. The party was founded on mass working-class and left-wing intellectual support inimical to the military, which promoted its own interests and that of the right, and mounted coups in 1955, 1966 and 1976. The UCR has tended to stay in opposition, except when the electorate wishes to register a protest vote, as in 1983. President Menem won elections in 1989 on a populist platform but quickly steered the Peronists to the right. He was reelected in 1995, but Peronist reverses in the 1997 legislative elections boosted the prospects of the UCR–FREPASO alliance.

Carlos Menem,
Justicialist Party (Peronist) leader; president since 1989.

Domingo Cavallo,
finance minister until 1996, who initiated radical privatization.

WORLD AFFAIRS

 Joined UN in 1945

SELA	Mercsr	OAS	RG	G15

Argentina's claim to the Falkland Islands (known locally as Islas Malvinas), the focus of the 1982 war with the UK, remains an important foreign policy objective. However, the sovereignty issue has been set to one side to facilitate bilateral discussions on fishing and prospecting for oil in the South Atlantic. Relations have eased, in that President Menem made a state visit to the UK in 1998 and the UK relaxed its arms embargo.

Argentina is promoting itself as a member of the "first world." It has withdrawn from the NAM and plans to apply for membership of the OECD. It also feels that a strengthened MERCOSUR trade grouping, which links Argentina with Brazil, Uruguay, and Paraguay, will increase its ability to negotiate trade accords with NAFTA, whose signatories are Mexico, Canada, and the USA, and with the EU.

The deployment of Argentinean armed forces in a series of UN actions has assisted the government's pro-Western stance. Argentina also has a track record of supporting the USA in the UN but recently they have been divided on several issues, particularly Argentina's patents law.

AID
 ▷ Recipient

$ $222m (receipts) ⬇ Down 20% 1996–1997

Receipts, other than restructured loan arrangements with international bodies, are modest. The latest IMF loan was agreed in 1998.

CHRONOLOGY

The Spanish first established settlements in the Andean foothills in 1543. The indigenous peoples, who had stopped any Inca advance into their territory, also prevented the Spaniards from settling in the east until the 1590s.

❑ **1816** United Provinces of Río de la Plata declare independence; 70 years of civil war follow.
❑ **1835–1852** Dictatorship of Juan Manuel Rosas.
❑ **1853** Federal system set up.
❑ **1857** Europeans start settling the pampas; 6 million by 1930. Most land held by oligarchy of 200 families.
❑ **1877** First refrigerated ship starts frozen beef trade to Europe.
❑ **1878–1883** War against the pampas Indians almost exterminates them.
❑ **1916** Hipólito Yrigoyen wins first democratic presidential elections.
❑ **1930** Military coup.
❑ **1943** New military coup. Gen. Juan Perón organizes trade unions.
❑ **1946** Perón elected president, with military and labor backing.
❑ **1952** Eva Perón, charismatic wife of Juan Perón, dies of leukemia.
❑ **1955** Military coup ousts Perón. Inflation, strikes, unemployment.
❑ **1973** Perón returns from exile in Madrid and is reelected president.
❑ **1974** Perón dies; succeeded by his third wife "Isabelita", who is unable to exercise control.
❑ **1976** Military junta seizes power. Political parties are banned. Brutal repression during Dirty War sees "disappearance" of over 10,000 "left-wing suspects."
❑ **1981** Gen. Galtieri president.
❑ **1982** Galtieri orders invasion of Falkland Islands. UK retakes them.
❑ **1983** Prohuman rights candidate Raúl Alfonsín (UCR) becomes president in free multiparty elections. Hyperinflation.
❑ **1989–1992** Carlos Menem (Peronist) wins presidency; inflation down to 18%.
❑ **1995** Menem reelected. Economy enters recession.
❑ **1996** Resignation in mid-year of powerful Economy Minister Domingo Cavallo; labor protests.
❑ **1997** Peronist reverses in mid-term polls; UCR wins mayorship of Buenos Aires.

DEFENSE
▷ Compulsory military service

$ $4.7bn ⬆ Up 1% in 1997

Despite the military's fall from power in 1983, its influence remains strong. President Menem's amnesty to officers

ARGENTINIAN ARMED FORCES

🚙	230 main battle tanks (TAM)	41,000 personnel
🚢	3 submarines, 6 destroyers, 7 frigates, 14 patrol boats	20,000 personnel
✈	200 combat aircraft (7 *Mirage* 5P, 22 *Dagger Nesher*, 45 IA58A)	12,000 personnel
🚀	None	

found guilty of human rights abuses during the military dictatorship was condemned by human rights groups who were not placated by the military's admissions of guilt in 1995. The repeal of the amnesty laws in 1998 was not to apply retroactively.

An armed forces modernization law in 1998 authorizes the military to analyze, at an international level, the development of a defense system within the framework of the MERCOSUR trade area (Brazil, Argentina, Uruguay, Paraguay). The armed forces have been deployed in a series of UN engagements, and Argentina is a signatory of the Nuclear Non-Proliferation Treaty.

ECONOMICS
▷ Inflation 162.9% p.a. (1985–1996)

📊 $319.3bn 💲 0.99 Argentine pesos

SCORE CARD

❑ WORLD GNP RANKING	17th
❑ GNP PER CAPITA	$8,950
❑ BALANCE OF PAYMENTS	$–10.1bn
❑ INFLATION	0.5%
❑ UNEMPLOYMENT	14%

EXPORTS

Netherlands 3%
China 3%
Chile 7%
USA 8%
Other 48%
Brazil 31%

IMPORTS

France 5%
Germany 5%
Italy 6%
USA 20%
Other 41%
Brazil 23%

ECONOMIC PERFORMANCE INDICATOR

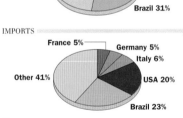

— Consumer price index   ▨ GDP

(Consumer price index 1990=100 / GDP 1993=100; years 1993–1997)

PROFILE
Hyperinflation in the 1980s was reversed under President Menem, who privatized state assets and introduced austerity measures and a new stable currency, pegged to the US dollar, to restore economic order and attract investment. This allowed Argentina to recover rapidly from the deep recession in 1995 due to the Mexican peso crisis and to avoid the worst effects of the 1998/99 financial crisis in Brazil.

STRENGTHS
Rich and varied agricultural base; powerful agribusiness (mainly beef, wheat, fruit, and wine) and a wealth of energy resources. Sound financial system and currency stability – due to the durability of pegging the peso to the dollar backed by foreign exchange – offer some protection from regional instability; good credit lines, including IMF extended fund facility; negligible inflation. Manageable deficits.

WEAKNESSES
Still a relatively closed economy; exposure to renewed crisis in Brazil, the major export market, and vulnerability to tightening of international liquidity or a collapse in US markets; high foreign debt servicing commitment; high unemployment and risk of unrest.

ARGENTINA : MAJOR BUSINESSES

Salta
San Salvador de Jujuy
Corrientes
Córdoba
Santa Fé
Mendoza
Buenos Aires
Viedma

Wine
Textiles
Agribusiness
Metals
Oranges
Tobacco
Vehicle assembly
Light engineering
Cattle/Meat packing
Heavy engineering

0   400 km
0   400 miles   * significant multinational ownership

RESOURCES

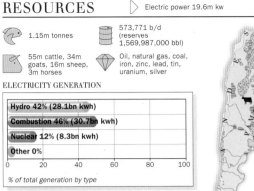

Electric power 19.6m kw

1.15m tonnes

573,771 b/d (reserves 1,569,987,000 bbl)

55m cattle, 34m goats, 16m sheep, 3m horses

Oil, natural gas, coal, iron, zinc, lead, tin, uranium, silver

ELECTRICITY GENERATION

Hydro 42% (28.1bn kwh)
Combustion 46% (30.7bn kwh)
Nuclear 12% (8.3bn kwh)
Other 0%

% of total generation by type

Only one-third of Argentina has been properly surveyed for oil and other mineral resources. Important known

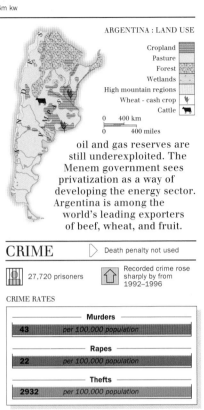

ARGENTINA : LAND USE

Cropland
Pasture
Forest
Wetlands
High mountain regions
Wheat - cash crop
Cattle

0 400 km
0 400 miles

oil and gas reserves are still underexploited. The Menem government sees privatization as a way of developing the energy sector. Argentina is among the world's leading exporters of beef, wheat, and fruit.

ENVIRONMENT

No Green MPs

2% (2% partially protected)

Medium

ENVIRONMENTAL TREATIES

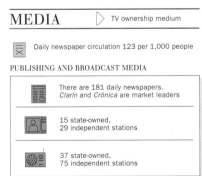

Yes Yes Yes
Yes Yes Yes

Environmental protection has been given a low priority. Legislation is weak and largely ignored by the states which retain a good deal of autonomy and can pass their own laws to suit their circumstances. All political parties also shy away from the level of public spending needed to tackle major social and environmental problems and a corrupt judiciary has meant poor enforcement of existing laws. Key problems are hazardous waste, urban water and air quality, pesticide contamination due to agribusiness, deforestation and illegal hunting.

MEDIA

TV ownership medium

Daily newspaper circulation 123 per 1,000 people

PUBLISHING AND BROADCAST MEDIA

There are 181 daily newspapers. *Clarín* and *Crónica* are market leaders

15 state-owned, 29 independent stations

37 state-owned, 75 independent stations

The press was liberated under the UCR (1983–1989). Many journalists were killed in the late 1970s for expressing their political beliefs. The government has been relentlessly harried by the media over corruption. The 1997 murder of a photo journalist caused a storm of protest.

CRIME

Death penalty not used

27,720 prisoners

Recorded crime rose sharply by from 1992–1996

CRIME RATES

Murders
43 *per 100,000 population*

Rapes
22 *per 100,000 population*

Thefts
2932 *per 100,000 population*

Buenos Aires remains one of the safest cities in Latin America. However, a government-declared war on crime has led to public protests about police practices. In 1998, 47 of the city's 52 police chiefs were replaced.

EDUCATION

School leaving age: 14

96.5%

1.07m students

Argentina's literacy rate is among the region's highest.

THE EDUCATION SYSTEM

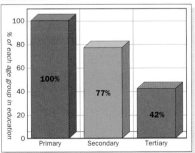

% of each age group in education

100% Primary
77% Secondary
42% Tertiary

Schooling is effectively a mix of the French and US systems. Absenteeism is high in rural areas. Underfunding is a problem. Argentina has a strong tertiary sector, with most students attending free state universities.

HEALTH

Welfare state health benefits

1 per 370 people

Heart diseases, cancers, accidents

Argentina has more doctors per capita than the USA.

Years of austerity, however, have seriously undermined health care across the country, especially in the interior where the states are cash-starved. Doctors charge, but most Argentineans are covered by insurance policies. High-tech equipment is concentrated in private Buenos Aires hospitals. A Workers' Health Plan system, introduced by the Menem government, is nominally intended to improve care for the poor.

SPENDING

No GNP/cap. increase

CONSUMPTION AND SPENDING

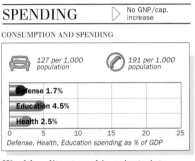

127 per 1,000 population

191 per 1,000 population

Defense 1.7%
Education 4.5%
Health 2.5%

Defense, Health, Education spending as % of GDP

Wealthy elites travel in private jets to their *estancias* (country estates), vacation in Europe and the USA, and play polo and rugby. Argentina is a major market for designer labels.

However, middle-income groups have been squeezed after years of free market reforms and many complain of a lack of a "feel-good factor." Most new jobs for lower income groups are precarious and low-paid. Many are employed in temporary government job creation schemes which in 1998 paid only a meagre $200 a month, when a "basic basket" of essential goods cost $1,200 a month.

Food raids on supermarkets by the poor occurred in 1998/99.

WORLD RANKING

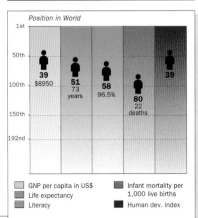

Position in World

1st
50th
100th
150th
192nd

39 $8950
51 73 years
58 96.5%
80 22 deaths
39

GNP per capita in US$
Life expectancy
Literacy
Infant mortality per 1,000 live births
Human dev. index

ARMENIA

OFFICIAL NAME: Republic of Armenia   CAPITAL: Yerevan
POPULATION: 3.6 million   CURRENCY: Dram   OFFICIAL LANGUAGE: Armenian

| 1991 | 1991 | Sept 21 | ARM | +4 | +374 | .am |

LANDLOCKED IN THE Lesser Caucasus Mountains, Armenia is the smallest of the former USSR's republics and was the first to adopt Christianity as its state religion. It is bordered by Muslim states to the south, east and west. Keen to develop links with the CIS, Armenia has kept to a path of radical economic reform, including privatization. The confrontation with Azerbaijan over the enclave of Nagorno Karabakh has dominated national life since 1988.

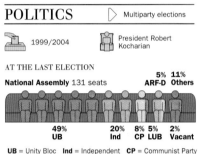

Landscape near Yerevan. Armenia's very dry climate results in expanses of semi-desert. Its famous vineyards flourish in sheltered areas.

CLIMATE ▷ Mountain

WEATHER CHART

| Average daily temperature | Rainfall |

Armenia has a continental climate, with little rainfall in the lowlands. Winters can be very cold.

TRANSPORTATION ▷ Drive on right

🛬 Yerevan Intl   ⚓ Has no fleet

THE TRANSPORTATION NETWORK

| 5,300 miles (8,600 km) | None |
| 490 miles (789 km) | None |

Public transportation has been badly hit by the war-induced fuel crisis, and the main road to Georgia is cut because it crosses Azerbaijani territory. The vital Aras bridge to Iran reopened in 1992.

TOURISM ▷ Not available

Very few, due to war with Azerbaijan   Similar levels from year to year

MAIN TOURIST ARRIVALS

Armenia does not publish tourism figures by country of origin

% of total arrivals

War has discouraged visitors. Ancient churches and the cellar vaults of the cognac-producing regions are Armenia's chief attractions.

PEOPLE ▷ Pop. density medium

Armenian, Russian   121/km² (313/mi²)

THE URBAN/RURAL POPULATION SPLIT

69%   31%

ETHNIC MAKEUP

Other 2%   Azeri 3%
Russian 2%
Armenian 93%

Minority nationalities are well integrated in Armenia. There are strong contacts with the many Armenian emigrants, numbering nine million in the USA, France, and Syria. Conflict with Azerbaijan has forced 350,000 Armenians in Azerbaijan to return to Armenia and 190,000 Azeris in Armenia to return to Azerbaijan.

POLITICS ▷ Multiparty elections

1999/2004   President Robert Kocharian

AT THE LAST ELECTION

National Assembly 131 seats

5% 11%
ARF-D Others

49% UB   20% Ind   8% CP   5% LUB   2% Vacant

UB = Unity Bloc   Ind = Independent   CP = Communist Party
ARF-D = Armenian Revolutionary Federation-Dashnaktsutyun
LUB = Law and Unity Bloc

Armenia became an independent multiparty democracy in 1991. The first parliamentary elections in July 1995 were won by the Republican Bloc dominated by the Pan-Armenian National Movement. A new constitution approved by referendum at the same time set up a presidential republic, and in 1996 President Ter-Petrossian was reelected for a further five-year term. The war with Azerbaijan, over the issue of whether the Armenian enclave of Nagorno Karabakh inside Azerbaijan should become part of Armenia, has simmered in the background since a 1994 cease-fire. Ter-Petrossian unexpectedly resigned in 1998 after parliament opposed his softer line in search of peace. Robert Kocharian, a former governor of Nagorno Karabakh, was elected in his place in March 1998.

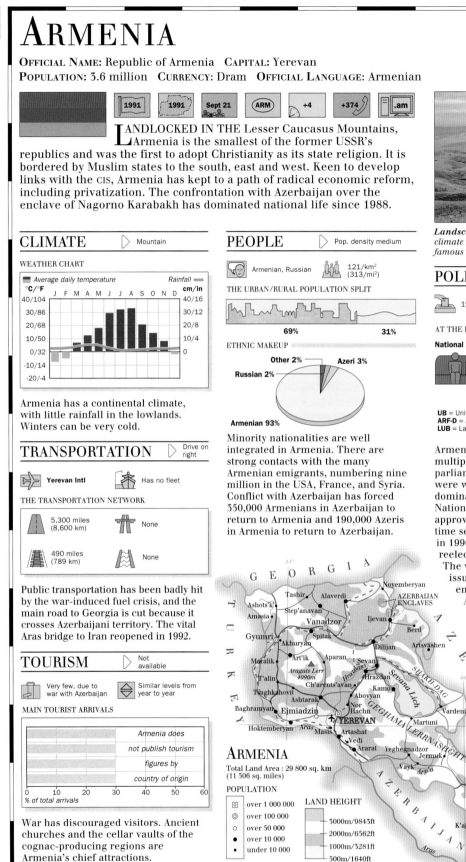

ARMENIA

Total Land Area : 29 800 sq. km
(11 506 sq. miles)

POPULATION
- ▣ over 1 000 000
- ◉ over 100 000
- ○ over 50 000
- ● over 10 000
- • under 10 000

LAND HEIGHT
- 3000m/9843ft
- 2000m/6562ft
- 1000m/3281ft
- 500m/1640ft

A

WORLD AFFAIRS
Joined UN in 1992

Armenia may have come out on top in the fighting in Nagorno Karabakh, but rivalry with Azerbaijan is damaging diplomatically. Azeri and Turkish trade embargoes have been in place since 1988. Moscow is less pro-Armenian since Azerbaijan rejoined the CIS. Work began on a gas pipeline between Iran and Armenia in 1998.

AID
Recipient

$168m (receipts) · Down 43% 1996–1997

Most funds have come from Armenians living abroad, including a $200 million pledge made in 1998 by the US billionaire Kirk Kerkorian.

DEFENSE
Compulsory military service

$138m · Up 26% in 1997

Successes in the fighting over Nagorno Karabakh have increased the profile and autonomy of the 52,000-strong army. In 1993 it ignored President Ter-Petrossian's peace overtures and mounted a further offensive. A cease-fire has broadly held since 1994 as peace talks continue.

ECONOMICS
Inflation 1,293% p.a. (1994–1997)

$2.1bn · 499.87–509.38 dram

SCORE CARD

❑ WORLD GNP RANKING	137th
❑ GNP PER CAPITA	$560
❑ BALANCE OF PAYMENTS	$–303m
❑ INFLATION	13.9%
❑ UNEMPLOYMENT	9%

STRENGTHS
Strong ties with Armenian emigrants. Major deposits of rare metals, as yet unexploited. Well-developed machine-building and manufacturing – includes textiles and bottling of mineral water.

WEAKNESSES
Dependent on imported energy, raw materials and semi-finished goods. High inflation and unemployment. Widespread corruption.

EXPORTS

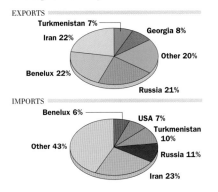

Turkmenistan 7%
Iran 22%
Benelux 22%
Georgia 8%
Other 20%
Russia 21%

IMPORTS

Benelux 6%
Other 43%
USA 7%
Turkmenistan 10%
Russia 11%
Iran 23%

Electric power 3.6m kw

RESOURCES

4,000 tonnes · Minimal oil production

3m poultry, 550,000 sheep, 505,000 cattle · Coal, oil, natural gas, rare metals

Armenia has negligible energy resources, but viable deposits of rare metals have been found. Fruit and vegetables are grown in fertile lowlands, and grains in hills. Wine and brandy are valuable products. Agriculture accounted for 44% of GDP in 1995.

ENVIRONMENT
No Green MPs

7% · Not available

The Medzamor nuclear power station was declared unsafe after the 1988 earthquake. It may be reactivated owing to the energy crisis, despite opposition from environmental groups. HEP generation near Lake Sevan has seriously lowered the lake's water level.

MEDIA
TV ownership medium

Daily newspaper circulation 23 per 1,000 people

PUBLISHING AND BROADCAST MEDIA

There are 11 daily newspapers, including *Ankakhutiun, Azg, Hayastan,* and *Hayastani Hanrapetutyun*

1 state-controlled service · 1 state-controlled service

There are many independent journals and newspapers, but government control of the paper industry gives it an effective censorship weapon.

CRIME
Death penalty used

Armenia does not publish prison figures · Down 24% from 1992–1996

Reforms to the legal system introduced in 1999 included the replacement of the Supreme Court by an Appeals Court. Assassinations of political figures are common.

EDUCATION
School leaving age: 17

99% · 35,517 students

The education system, previously conforming to that of the USSR, now emphasizes Armenian history and culture; 12% of the population have received higher education.

CHRONOLOGY
Armenia lost its autonomy in the 14th century. In 1639, Turkey took the west and Persia the east; Persia ceded its part to Russia in 1828.

- ❑ **1877–1878** Massacre of Armenians during Russo-Turkish war.
- ❑ **1915** Ottomans exile 1.75 million Turkish Armenians; most die.
- ❑ **1917–1918** Russian Armenia's anti-Bolshevik alliance with Georgia and Azerbaijan.
- ❑ **1920** Independence.
- ❑ **1922** Becomes a Soviet republic.
- ❑ **1988** Earthquake kills 25,000.
- ❑ **1990** Declares Nagorno Karabakh (in Azerbaijan) part of Armenia.
- ❑ **1991** Independence from USSR.
- ❑ **1995** First parliamentary elections.
- ❑ **1998** Kocharian elected president.

HEALTH
No welfare state health benefits

1 per 298 people · Circulatory diseases, cancers, accidents, violence

Hospitals suffer from the erratic electricity supply. Poor sewerage and other services have led to a rise in hepatitis, tuberculosis and cholera.

SPENDING
GDP/cap. increase

CONSUMPTION AND SPENDING

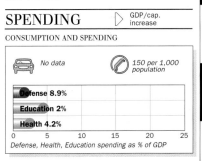

No data · 150 per 1,000 population

Defense 8.9%
Education 2%
Health 4.2%

Defense, Health, Education spending as % of GDP

The richest Armenian people are those living away from Armenia itself, such as in the USA and France. The many refugees from Baku are the poorest.

WORLD RANKING

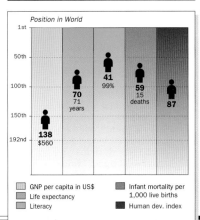

Position in World

138 $560
70 71 years
41 99%
59 15 deaths
87

☐ GNP per capita in US$
☐ Life expectancy
☐ Literacy
☐ Infant mortality per 1,000 live births
☐ Human dev. index

A

AUSTRALASIA

Asia
Pacific Ocean

Indonesia | Papua New Guinea
AUSTRALIA
New Zealand

Australia

AUSTRALIA

OFFICIAL NAME: Commonwealth of Australia **CAPITAL:** Canberra
POPULATION: 18.5 million **CURRENCY:** Australian dollar **OFFICIAL LANGUAGE:** English

| 1901 | 1901 | Jan 26 | AUS | +10 | +61 | .au |

THE WORLD'S SIXTH-LARGEST COUNTRY, Australia is an island continent located between the Indian and Pacific oceans. Its six states and two territories have a variety of landscapes, including tropical rain forests, the deserts of the arid "red center," snow-capped mountains, rolling tracts of pastoral land and magnificent beaches. Famous natural features include Uluru (Ayers Rock) and the Great Barrier Reef. Most Australians live on the coast; all the state capitals, including Sydney, host of the 2000 Olympics, are coastal cities. Only Canberra, the national capital, lies inland. The strip down the length of the eastern seaboard is the country's richest and most populous area.

Uluru (Ayers Rock), Northern Territory.
The renaming of Ayers Rock reflects growing
Aboriginal influence in Australia.

CLIMATE ▷ Hot desert/steppe/ tropical/Mediterranean

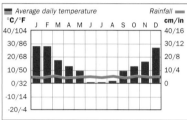

WEATHER CHART

The interior, west, and south are arid or semiarid and very hot in summer; central desert temperatures can reach 50°C (122°F). The north, around Darwin and Cape York Peninsula, is hot all year and humid during the summer monsoon. Only the east and southeast, within 400 km (250 miles) of the coast, and the southwest, around Perth, are temperate. Most Australians live in these areas.

TRANSPORTATION ▷ Drive on left

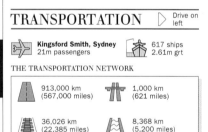

Kingsford Smith, Sydney
21m passengers

617 ships
2.61m grt

THE TRANSPORTATION NETWORK

913,000 km (567,000 miles)		1,000 km (621 miles)	
36,026 km (22,385 miles)		8,368 km (5,200 miles)	

Air transport is well developed and vital to Australia's sparsely populated center and west. Sydney suffers from air congestion; a third runway was added to Kingsford Smith airport in 1994, but a planned Sydney West airport remains controversial. A high-speed train linking Sydney and Canberra is due in 2003. Most long-distance freight in Australia travels in massive trucks, known as "road trains." Improvements in urban transport are a priority, and gained impetus in Sydney in the run-up to the 2000 Olympic Games.

TOURISM ▷ Visitors : population 1:4.3

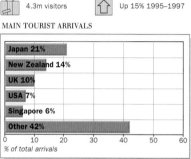

4.3m visitors

Up 15% 1995–1997

MAIN TOURIST ARRIVALS

Japan 21%	
New Zealand 14%	
UK 10%	
USA 7%	
Singapore 6%	
Other 42%	

% of total arrivals

Tourism is now Australia's largest single foreign exchange earner. Faster, cheaper air travel and highly successful government marketing campaigns, both on a national and a state level, draw tourists in increasing numbers. The focus was on drawing tourists from nearby Asian countries during the 1990s. This left the Australian tourism industry vulnerable after the Asian financial crisis of 1997. The Japanese form the largest single group of visitors to Australia, while many tourists also come from Europe, North America and New Zealand. American tourists tend to spend more than other nationalities.

The country's attractions include wildlife, swimming, and surfing off Pacific and Indian Ocean beaches, skin diving along the Great Barrier Reef and skiing in the Australian Alps. Aboriginal culture and the town of Alice Springs are among the outback's attractions. The far north has tropical resorts, the northwest, pearl fishing. Vineyards in the south and southeast attract many visitors, as do the cultural life of Melbourne and Sydney and the arts festivals held in state capitals. Sydney's popularity has also increased in the run-up to the 2000 Sydney Olympic Games.

The mid-1980s saw a phenomenal boom; tourist arrivals rose almost 200% in five years. Growth slowed during the 1990s and arrivals fell at the end of the decade. The rush in the 1980s to invest has left many hotels struggling, especially at the luxury end of the market.

AUSTRALIA

Total Land Area : 7 617 930 sq. km (2 941 283 sq. miles)

POPULATION

- ▣ over 1 000 000
- ◉ over 100 000
- ○ over 50 000
- ● over 10 000
- • under 10 000

LAND HEIGHT

- 1000m/3281ft
- 500m/1640ft
- 200m/656ft
- Sea Level
- -200m/-656ft

PEOPLE

▷ Pop. density low

English, Greek, Italian, Vietnamese, Aboriginal languages

2/km²
(6/mi²)

THE URBAN/RURAL POPULATION SPLIT

85%   15%

The first settlers arrived in Australia at least 40,000 years ago. Today, Aborigines, today make up approximately 1% of the population. European settlement began in 1788 and was dominated by British and Irish immigrants – some of whom were convicts – until the gold rushes of the 1850s. Immigrants of other nationalities – including many Chinese – arrived to prospect for gold, then settled in the cities, especially Melbourne and Sydney. When the new federal government was installed in 1901, one of its first acts was to prevent further Chinese immigration. The act set out the "White Australia" policy, which conditioned attitudes to immigration for almost 70 years.

A massive immigration drive after the Second World War brought many more British settlers to Australia in the 1950s. Further government initiatives to "populate or perish" saw the arrival of large numbers of Italians and Greeks.

From the late 1960s, the "White Australia" policy was progressively wound down. It was officially ended during the 1972–1975 Whitlam administration. Ever since, up to 50% of immigrants each year have come from Asia, transforming Australia from an almost exclusively European enclave into a multicultural society, in which immigrant groups are encouraged to maintain connections with their own cultures and languages.

Aborigines, the exception in an otherwise integrated society, number around 250,000. Economically and socially marginalized, they face considerable discrimination. Until the mid-1960s, they were denied the vote and full social benefits. Their land had been occupied as *terra nullius* – belonging to no one. Since the 1970s, Aborigines have made a more organized stand on land and civil rights. Native title to land was recognised in 1993, although controversies continue over the extent of its application. Civil rights campaigns have moved on from the initial phase of anti-racist protests to demand greater equality in areas such as health, housing and education. Alcoholism is a pervasive problem both in towns and rural areas

Aborigines in urban areas may be relatively better housed but face particular problems in asserting their cultural identity.

During the 1950s and 1960s, Catholic–Protestant differences were sufficient to cause a rift in the ALP.

A subsequent policy encouraging mixed denomination schooling, coupled with a decline in religious observance, has by now largely neutralized the issue.

RELIGIOUS PERSUASION

Roman Catholic 26%
Other Protestant 6%
United Church 8%
Non-religious 13%
Anglican 24%
Other 23%

ETHNIC MAKEUP

Aboriginal and Other 1%
Asian 4%
European 95%

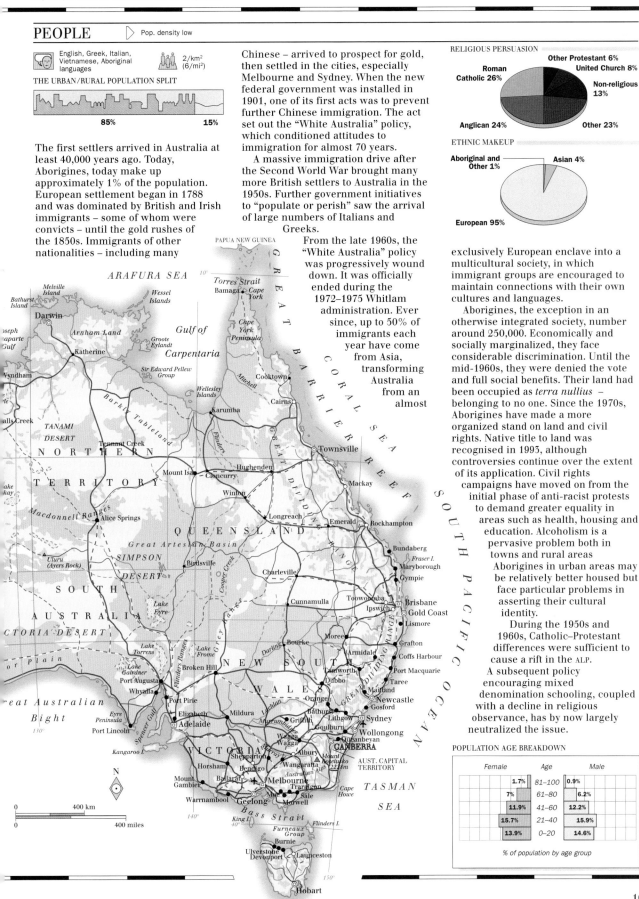

POPULATION AGE BREAKDOWN

Female	Age	Male
1.7%	81–100	0.9%
7%	61–80	6.2%
11.9%	41–60	12.2%
15.7%	21–40	15.9%
13.9%	0–20	14.6%

% of population by age group

CHRONOLOGY

Dutch, Portuguese, French and – decisively – British incursions throughout the 17th and 18th centuries signaled the end of 40,000 years of Aboriginal occupancy. Governor Arthur Philip raised the Union Jack at Sydney Cove on January 26, 1788.

❑ **1901** Inauguration of the Commonwealth of Australia.
❑ **1915** Australian troops suffer heavy casualties at Gallipoli.
❑ **1929** Industrial upheaval and financial collapse: "The Great Depression."
❑ **1939** Prime Minister Menzies announces that Australia will follow Britain into war with Germany.
❑ **1942** Fall of Singapore to Japanese army. Japanese invasion of Australia seems imminent. Government turns to USA for help.
❑ **1950** Australian troops committed to UN–US Korean War against North Korean communists.
❑ **1962** Menzies government commits Australian aid to war in Vietnam.
❑ **1966** Adopts decimal currency.
❑ **1972** Whitlam government elected. Aid to South Vietnam ceases.
❑ **1975** Whitlam government dismissed by Governor-General Sir John Kerr. Malcolm Fraser forms coalition government.
❑ **1983** Bob Hawke becomes prime minister at the head of an ALP government.
❑ **1985** Corporate boom followed by deepening recession.
❑ **1992** Paul Keating defeats Hawke in vote and becomes prime minister; announces "Turning toward Asia" policy. High Court's "Mabo Judgment" recognizes Aboriginal land rights.
❑ **1993** Against most predictions, Keating's ALP government reelected. Native Title Act provides compensation for Aboriginal rights extinguished by existing land title.
❑ **1996** Defeat of Keating government. Liberal John Howard becomes Prime Minister.
❑ **1996** Shooting of 35 people by gunman in Tasmania prompts tightening of gun control laws.
❑ **1996** First death under Northern Territory's controversial euthanasia legislation. Legislation later overruled at federal level.
❑ **1998** October, Howard's Liberal and National coalition retains power with reduced majority after general election. Fears of right-wing One Nation party breakthrough prove unfounded. Constitutional Convention chooses republican model for 1999 referendum.

POLITICS

▷ Multiparty elections

L. House 1998/2001
U. House 1998/2001

HM Queen Elizabeth II

AT THE LAST ELECTION

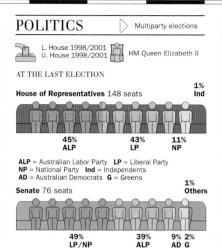

House of Representatives 148 seats

| 45% ALP | 43% LP | 11% NP | 1% Ind |

ALP = Australian Labor Party   **LP** = Liberal Party
NP = National Party   **Ind** = Independents
AD = Australian Democrats   **G** = Greens

Senate 76 seats

| 49% LP/NP | 39% ALP | 9% AD | 2% G | 1% Others |

12 seats in the Senate are apportioned to each of the country's constituent states and two each to the Northern Territory and the Australian Capital Territory.

Australia is a parliamentary democracy on the British model. There are six state governments, all but one (Queensland) bicameral. The Northern Territory became self-governing in 1978.

MAIN POLITICAL ISSUES
Aboriginal rights
Land rights, the subject of controversial recent court judgments and legislation (see overleaf), remain a key underlying issue. The right-wing fringe One Nation party has also sought to mobilize resentment against Aborigines over welfare dependence and alleged areas of positive discrimination.

In 1999 the government agreed to apologize officially over the "stolen generations" of Aborigine children, removed from their families to be brought up by white parents. An inquiry had been set up in 1995 and the 1997 report *Bringing them Home* focused attention on this scandal, the result of government policies on integration which had continued until the 1960s.

Unemployment
The rise in unemployment to around 10% in the early 1990s was expected to sink Prime Minister Keating's ALP government; it survived in 1993 thanks to a skillful campaign, but was swept out of office three years later. For most Australians, unemployment remains a central concern. A short-lived economic boom had ended by 1998, and there are fresh fears about the depth of possible recession. Commentators pointed to unemployment as a big factor in the rise of Pauline Hanson's right-wing, anti-immigrant One Nation party, although her initial breakthrough in Queensland was not sustained in the October 1998 general election.

The Republic
Despite international press coverage,

Vineyards in South Australia. Wine-making has been one of Australia's greatest agricultural success stories in recent years

the republican issue is not of major importance to most Australians. The former ALP government played down the debate in order to avoid inflaming monarchist groups. In his 1996 oath of office, Prime Minister John Howard swore allegiance to Queen Elizabeth II, but not her successors. His government's Constitutional Convention of February 1998 brought together a wide range of people, chosen by popular election, to debate the issue. Various models, including the popular election of the head of state, were rejected in favor of a model giving the power of selection to a two-thirds majority of parliament, put to the people in a 1999 referendum.

PROFILE
The ALP and the Liberal and National parties have dominated Australian politics since 1945. The Liberal and National parties, politically to the right, work together in coalition and broadly represent big business and agricultural interests. The ALP gained some of this support in the 1980s, adopting free-market policies and blurring the differences between parties, but 13 years of ALP rule ended in 1996. A Liberal-National coalition took office after that election, holding on with a much reduced majority in the 1998 poll.

Paul Keating, resigned as ALP leader after his 1996 election defeat.

John Howard, leader of the LP, was elected prime minister in 1996.

Aden Ridgeway, Aboriginal senator.

WORLD AFFAIRS

Joined UN
in 1945

APEC · SPF · Comm · OECD · SPC

Australia's international focus has shifted from Europe and the USA toward Asia. Geopolitically it is in an ambiguous position. Having lost its place as a major trading partner for the UK when the latter joined the then EEC Australia has found that it is still regarded as a European outsider by the Asian nations with which it wishes to foster closer links. Australia has taken practical steps to redefine its role. It was the main backer of the 1989 Asia Pacific Economic Cooperation forum (APEC), an attempt to create a multilateral regional trading bloc, similar to the EU and NAFTA. After a faltering start, APEC began to get results. It was the first group to have China, Taiwan, and Hong Kong sitting around the same table. The USA was a strong supporter, seeing APEC as a means of promoting free-market economics in Asia. Australia's ambition is for APEC to become the leading association in the region. However, the move towards market liberalization slowed following the 1997 Asian financial crisis.

Relations with the USA are tense on questions of trade. Australia objects to subsidized US wheat undercutting its own in Asia, particularly in the key Chinese market. It now sees the EU and the USA as its main competitors in booming southeast Asian economies.

However, on security issues Australia still supports the West. Against much public opposition, it sent troops to the 1991 Gulf War. Its commitment to the Pacific region also remains strong. The end of the Cold War, however, has meant that this is now expressed in terms of development aid rather than defense arrangements.

Within the Pacific region, fishing is a major issue. There have been a number of minor skirmishes with Indonesian and Japanese long-line fishing boats. Australia objects to this form of fishing, which kills large numbers of dolphins, and employs antisubmarine patrols to regulate the industry.

AID

Donor

US$953m
(donations)

Not applicable

Australia spends less than 1% of its GNP on aid programs. Most is spent in the Asia–Pacific region. Particular areas of focus are those of nongovernmental organizations and HIV/AIDS programs. The recipient by far of the greatest amount is Papua New Guinea, where Australian companies such as Broken Hill Proprietary have major mining operations.

DEFENSE

No compulsory military service

US$8.5bn

Down 3% in 1997

AUSTRALIAN ARMED FORCES

🚜	71 main battle tanks (*Leopard* 1A3)	25,400 personnel
🚢	4 submarines, 8 frigates, 3 destroyers and 15 patrol boats	14,300 personnel
✈	126 combat aircraft (17 F–111C, 15 F–111G, 52 F/A–18B)	17,700 personnel
	None	

Strategic ties with the USA remain an important element of defense policy. Australia has defense arrangements with the Philippines, Brunei, and Thailand among others.

Expenditure is designed to keep Australia self-reliant in defense and to encourage the participation of industry. Updating military equipment and exploiting information technologies are priorities.

ECONOMICS

Inflation 3.9% p.a.(1985–1996)

US$382.7bn

1.53–1.63 Australian dollars

SCORE CARD

❑ WORLD GNP RANKING	14th
❑ GNP PER CAPITA	US$20,650
❑ BALANCE OF PAYMENTS	US$–12.9bn
❑ INFLATION	0.3%
❑ UNEMPLOYMENT	9%

EXPORTS

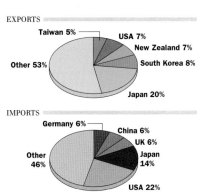

Taiwan 5% · USA 7% · New Zealand 7% · South Korea 8% · Other 53% · Japan 20%

IMPORTS

Germany 6% · China 6% · UK 6% · Other 46% · Japan 14% · USA 22%

STRENGTHS
Efficient agricultural and mining industries. Vast mineral deposits. Highly profitable tourist industry with huge untapped potential. Australia has a good record regarding both growth and inflation.

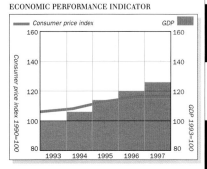

ECONOMIC PERFORMANCE INDICATOR

Consumer price index — GDP

WEAKNESSES
May suffer from EU and NAFTA protectionist policies. Political and financial instability in export markets in southeast Asia affects exports. Competition from Asian economies with lower wage rates and poorer working conditions. Balance of payments deficit. Unemployment likely to remain high.

PROFILE
Australia's companies concentrated during the 1990s on the Asian market, which grew to account for 60% of Australia's trade. They were hit hard when the 1997 Asian financial crisis tipped rapid regional growth into recession. Japan remains Australia's most important trading partner.

In order to compete in Asia, the economy has been undergoing massive structural adjustment. The Howard government, like its ALP predecessor before 1996, has been dismantling the tariffs that had made Australia one of the most heavily protected economies within the OECD. Higher unemployment and the collapse of many businesses

AUSTRALIA : MAJOR BUSINESSES

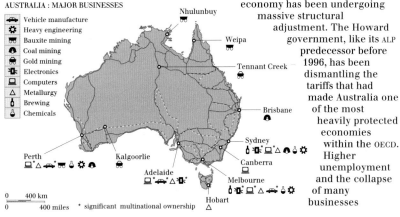

- 🚗 Vehicle manufacture
- ⚙ Heavy engineering
- Bauxite mining
- Coal mining
- Gold mining
- Electronics
- 💻 Computers
- △ Metallurgy
- Brewing
- Chemicals

Nhulunbuy · Weipa · Tennant Creek · Brisbane · Sydney · Canberra · Melbourne · Hobart · Perth · Kalgoorlie · Adelaide

0   400 km
0   400 miles   * significant multinational ownership △

RESESOURCES ▷ Electric power 37.9m kw

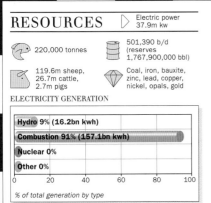

220,000 tonnes

501,390 b/d (reserves 1,767,900,000 bbl)

119.6m sheep, 26.7m cattle, 2.7m pigs

Coal, iron, bauxite, zinc, lead, copper, nickel, opals, gold

ELECTRICITY GENERATION

Hydro 9% (16.2bn kwh)	
Combustion 91% (157.1bn kwh)	
Nuclear 0%	
Other 0%	

0   20   40   60   80   100

% of total generation by type

Australia has one of the world's most important mining industries. It is a world leader in exports of coal, iron ore, gold, bauxite, and copper. Minerals account for a tenth of Australia's GDP and over half of its merchandise export earnings. Since the first discoveries of coal in 1798, mineral production in Australia has risen every year; in the decade to 1992 it doubled. Growth slowed but continued during the 1990s: many new projects are planned. The share of minerals of the total economy is expected to continue growing, but, having benefited from Australia's location close to the markets of southeast Asia, it was left vulnerable following the regional crisis of 1997.

While minerals underpin much of Australia's wealth, there is growing concern at the environmental cost of extraction. There is also ongoing uncertainty over the possibility of Aboriginal claims to land holding valuable minerals. The 1992 "Mabo Judgment" recognized Aboriginal land rights predating European settlement. The 1993 Native Title Act confirmed these rights and in 1996 the High Court's historic "Wik decision" enabled claims to be made over land which was subject to a "pastoral" lease. But legislation passed in 1998 cut back Aborigines' rights to make such claims.

AUSTRALIA : LAND USE

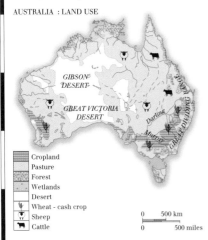

GIBSON DESERT

GREAT VICTORIA DESERT

Darling

Murray

GREAT DIVIDING RANGE

	Cropland
	Pasture
	Forest
	Wetlands
	Desert
↓	Wheat - cash crop
⛖	Sheep
🐂	Cattle

0   500 km
0   500 miles

Green Island, on the Great Barrier Reef Marine Park in the far north of Queensland, stretches 1,995 km (1,240 miles) down the coast.

ENVIRONMENT ▷ Green MPs

7% (2% partially protected)

High

ENVIRONMENTAL TREATIES

Yes		Yes		Yes	
Yes		Yes		Yes	

Australia's voters are among the most environmentally conscious in the world, but its government has strongly resisted any commitment to cutting "greenhouse gas" emissions to help limit global warming. The 1997 Kyoto climate change conference agreed to allow Australia to increase greenhouse emissions by up to 8% until 2010, whereas most industrialized countries had to commit to cuts.

Green issues are dominated by the Australian Conservation Foundation (ACF) and the more radical Greenpeace. The ACF has concentrated on developing industry links and cooperative programs.

MEDIA ▷ TV ownership high

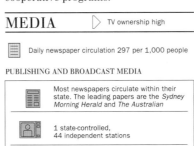

Daily newspaper circulation 297 per 1,000 people

PUBLISHING AND BROADCAST MEDIA

	Most newspapers circulate within their state. The leading papers are the *Sydney Morning Herald* and *The Australian*
	1 state-controlled, 44 independent stations
	6 state-controlled, 166 independent services

The Australian press is firmly in the grip of press "barons" such as Rupert Murdoch and Kerry Packer, although cross-media rules prevent the ownership of newspapers and TV channels in the same city. Public-sector broadcasting remains dominated by the politically neutral Australian Broadcasting Corporation (ABC), which receives complaints about its coverage from both main parties.

CRIME ▷ Death penalty not used

12,557 prisoners

Significant increase in all types of crime

CRIME RATES

Murders	
4	per 100,000 population

Rapes	
not available	

Thefts	
5776	per 100,000 population

Each state has its own police force and court system. The High Court and Family Court both have national jurisdiction. Since the 1970s, the legal system has been placing greater emphasis on individual rights. The disproportionate number of Aboriginal deaths in custody is of concern.

Crime is on the increase. Narcotics-related offenses are rising, and Australia is active in drug control throughout southeast Asia. Gun control laws were strengthened after a gunman killed 35 people in Port Arthur in 1996. In 1997 the Wood inquiry uncovered widespread police corruption in New South Wales and led to major reforms.

EDUCATION ▷ School leaving age : 15

99%

1m students

Education in Australia is a state responsibility, except in Canberra.

THE EDUCATION SYSTEM

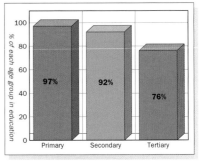

% of each age group in education

100
80
60
40
20
0

Primary 97%   Secondary 92%   Tertiary 76%

State education departments run the government schools and set the policies for educational practice and standards for all schools. (Canberra is funded by the federal government.) Non-government schools, run by religious and other groups, exist in all states. Special provision is made for inaccessible outback areas, with recent moves to bring new technologies to the bush. Schooling is compulsory from age five–six to age 15–16 in all states. After their final year at school, students sit for the Higher School Certificate. Universities are independent of state control and are funded by the federal government.

ABORIGINAL RIGHTS

CENTRAL TO THE ABORIGINAL cultural and spiritual framework is the relationship with tribal lands. Their land rights campaign, like their civil rights campaign, began gathering momentum in the 1960s, when Aborigines were first included in the census and won the right to vote. Now a key political issue, it has far-reaching implications for Australia's national identity, for the country's most disadvantaged people and for powerful mining and farming interests.

BACKGROUND
In the 40,000 years before European settlement, Aboriginal peoples ranged widely over their land. The indigenous population was then greatly reduced by exposure to disease and by conflict. Settlers acquired land without reference to any pre-existing rights of tribal peoples, based on the legal doctrine that before 1788 the land was *terra nullius* - belonging to no-one. Those Aborigines still living a traditional lifestyle were largely confined to reserves.

Land rights campaigns achieved an initial breakthrough when land councils were set up, first in the Northern Territory in 1976, then in other states, notably South Australia. These provided a structure for holding freehold title to land in trust for its tribal inhabitants. The land councils could administer land acquired or handed over from former reserves, but in the absence of a uniform national land rights policy, conservative states such as Queensland – which has the largest Aboriginal population – were able to resist moves to consolidate Aborigine ownership. Particular flashpoints arose when mining companies were granted concessions to exploit sites considered sacred by the Aborigines.

Native dancers from Kuranda, *northern Queensland, perform a traditional dance in front of protesters marching for increased Aboriginal land rights.*

An Aboriginal elder *surveys his native land in Western Australia.*

NATIVE TITLE ACTS IN THE 1990S
The first nationwide Native Title Act was introduced by the ALP federal government in 1993, recognizing the new situation created by a crucial 1992 court ruling. The so-called Mabo judgment, in a case brought by a Torres Strait islander against the Queensland government, established that rights to land ownership did indeed exist in common law based on native title. This effectively reversed the old concept of *terra nullius* and legally recognized the pre-1788 Aboriginal occupancy of the continent.

The 1993 law specified that native title existed for all Crown land, whether held by federal or by state government, where it had not specifically been extinguished. Tribunals were set up in all states to decide on the eligibility of native title claims, against powerful resistance from mining companies especially in Western Australia. Unexpectedly, a court case brought by the Wik people of the Cape York peninsula in northern Queensland took the matter further. The December 1996 Wik ruling said that native title still coexisted with the rights of farmers who had long leases from the Crown on huge tracts of grazing land, granted earlier in the century. Changes of use on such land (to allow mining, cash crops and tourist developments) would therefore require consultation with Aborigines.

The government, by now a Liberal-National coalition, responded with a ten-point plan to protect the leaseholders. Its own Native Title Bill, tightly restricting Aborigine claims, split the country and was twice blocked in the Senate, but eventually passed in July 1998. Campaigners, meanwhile, continue court battles against mining developments on sensitive Aboriginal sites.

HEALTH

▷ Welfare state health benefits

🧍 1 per 455 people

💀 Heart, cerebrovascular and respiratory diseases, cancers

Australia's extensive public health service has standards as high as any in the world. Hospital waiting lists are short. Outback areas are serviced by the efficient Royal Flying Doctor Service. While vigilance continues in the areas of hygiene, nutrition and general living standards, health authorities have targeted Aboriginal health, heart disease, injury prevention, personal fitness, and the prevention of cancers – particularly lung, cervical, breast and skin cancers – as current priorities. Incentives to encourage private health insurance, introduced during the 1990s, sparked fears over public health funding and quality.

SPENDING

▷ GDP/cap. no increase

CONSUMPTION AND SPENDING

🚗 485 per 1,000 population

📞 505 per 1,000 population

Defense	2.2%
Education	5.6%
Health	8.6%

0   5   10   15   20   25
Defense, Health, Education spending as % of GDP

Australians enjoy a reasonable equality of wealth distribution. A large proportion of Australian families own two cars and have relatively high disposable incomes. A benign climate helps most people to live comfortably. However, high unemployment during the 1990s recession has widened the gap between the country's rich and poor, and Australia has slipped down the world standard of living list in recent years. The incidence of homelessness, critical poverty and child neglect due to poverty has increased slightly.

WORLD RANKING

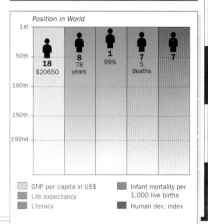

Position in World

	GNP per capita in US$		Infant mortality per 1,000 live births
	Life expectancy		
	Literacy		Human dev. index

18 – $20650
8 – 78 years
1 – 99%
7 – 5 deaths
7

A

AUSTRIA

EUROPE

OFFICIAL NAME: Republic of Austria   **CAPITAL:** Vienna
POPULATION: 8.2 million   **CURRENCY:** Austrian schilling   **OFFICIAL LANGUAGE:** German

| 1918 | 1919 | Oct 26 | A | +1 | +43 | .at |

LYING IN THE HEART OF EUROPE, Austria is dominated by the Alps in the west of the country, while fertile plains make up its eastern half. Created in 1918, after the collapse of the Habsburg empire, Austria was absorbed into Hitler's Germany in 1938, regaining independence in 1955 after the departure of the last Soviet troops from the Allied Occupation Force. Its economy encompasses successful high-tech sectors, a tourist industry which attracts wealthier visitors, and a strong agricultural base. Joining the EU in 1995, in 1999 it was one of 11 EU states to introduce the euro.

TOURISM

Visitors : population 2.1:1

16.6m visitors   Down 3% 1995–1997

MAIN TOURIST ARRIVALS

Germany	58%
Netherlands	7%
Italy	5%
Switzerland	4%
France	3%
Other	23%

% of total arrivals (0 to 60)

CLIMATE

Mountain/continental

WEATHER CHART

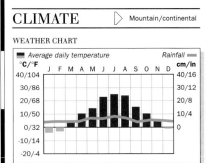

Austria has a temperate continental climate. Alpine areas experience colder temperatures and higher precipitation.

TRANSPORTATION

Drive on right

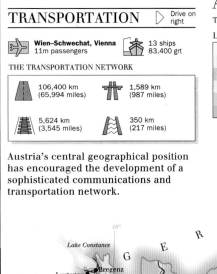

Wien–Schwechat, Vienna
11m passengers

13 ships
83,400 grt

THE TRANSPORTATION NETWORK

106,400 km (65,994 miles)	1,589 km (987 miles)
5,624 km (3,545 miles)	350 km (217 miles)

Austria's central geographical position has encouraged the development of a sophisticated communications and transportation network.

The Tirol is situated in the heart of Austria's Alps. It is the most mountainous region of all and attracts both winter and summer visitors.

Well-developed Alpine skiing and winter sports resorts account for almost one-third of the country's total tourist earnings. Many resorts, such as St. Anton and Kitzbühel, cater for the top end of the market. In the summer season, which peaks in July and August, tourists visit the scenic Tirol and the lakes around Bad Ischl. Vienna and Salzburg, the country's second city, are major attractions. The latter is internationally famous for its summer music festival and as the birthplace of Mozart. However, visitor numbers have fallen in recent years, as have earnings.

AUSTRIA

Total Land Area : 82 730 sq. km (31 942 sq. miles)

LAND HEIGHT

- 3000m/9843ft
- 2000m/6562ft
- 1000m/3281ft
- 500m/1640ft
- 200m/656ft
- Sea Level

POPULATION

- over 1 000 000
- over 500 000
- over 100 000
- over 50 000
- over 10 000

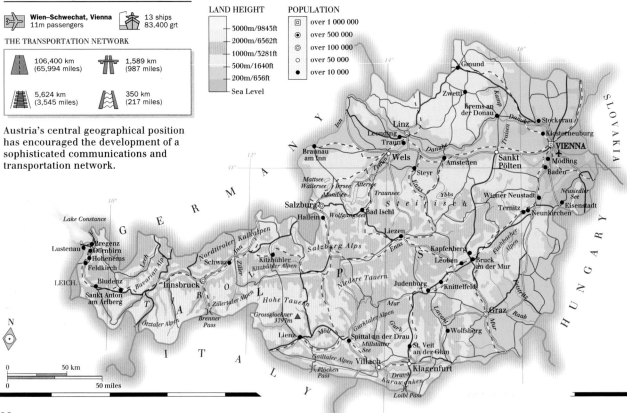

PEOPLE
▷ Pop. density medium

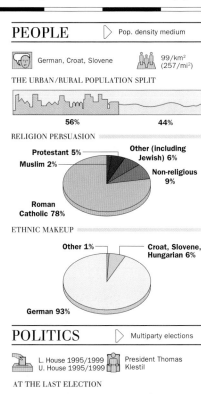

German, Croat, Slovene — 99/km² (257/mi²)

THE URBAN/RURAL POPULATION SPLIT — 56% / 44%

RELIGION PERSUASION — Protestant 5%, Muslim 2%, Other (including Jewish) 6%, Non-religious 9%, Roman Catholic 78%

ETHNIC MAKEUP — Other 1%, Croat, Slovene, Hungarian 6%, German 93%

Austrian society is homogeneous. Almost all Austrians are German speakers. However, Austrians like to consider themselves ethnically distinct from Germans. Minorities are few; there are some ethnic Slovenes, Croats and Hungarians in the south and east, as well as some Romany communities. These minorities have been supplemented by large numbers of immigrants from eastern Europe and refugees from the conflict in former Yugoslavia. The result has been a perceptible increase in ethnic tension, particularly as the downturn in the economy has led some Austrians to claim that migrants are taking jobs from the local population.

The nuclear family is the norm in Austria. It is common for both parents to work. While gender equality is enshrined in the constitution, in practice society is still strongly patriarchal. Compared with the rest of Europe, few women enter politics.

Young Austrians tend to live in their parental home until they marry. This reflects the long time taken to complete university degrees, for which students do not receive maintenance grants. Austrians marry at a younger age than the European average. Nominally a Catholic country, Austria has a less conservative society than some German states.

POPULATION AGE BREAKDOWN

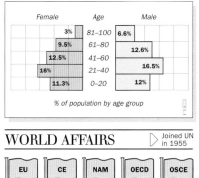

Female	Age	Male
3%	81–100	6.6%
9.5%	61–80	12.6%
12.5%	41–60	16.5%
16%	21–40	
11.3%	0–20	12%

% of population by age group

POLITICS
▷ Multiparty elections

L. House 1995/1999
U. House 1995/1999
President Thomas Klestil

AT THE LAST ELECTION

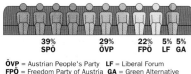

National Council 183 seats

39% SPÖ — 29% ÖVP — 22% FPÖ — 5% LF — 5% GA

ÖVP = Austrian People's Party   LF = Liberal Forum
FPÖ = Freedom Party of Austria   GA = Green Alternative
SPÖ = Social Democratic Party of Austria

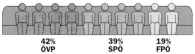

Federal Council 64 seats

42% ÖVP — 39% SPÖ — 19% FPÖ

Austria is a federal, multiparty democracy. The chancellor (premier) holds real executive power. Federal Chancellor Franz Vranitzky stood down in January 1997 after more than ten years as chancellor, and was succeeded by Viktor Klima.

MAIN POLITICAL ISSUES
EU integration
Austria's population was divided over entry into the EU, although a significant 66.4% of voters supported membership in a 1995 referendum. Austrians have benefited from lower food prices and greater consumer choice, but there are fears that membership is eroding national identity and independence, and that further expansion eastwards could bring an influx of cheap Czech, Hungarian, and Slovene labor. The farming lobby remains apprehensive that EU agricultural policy could endanger their livelihood.

Economic recovery
Recession in the early 1990s led to a period of slow growth and to rising unemployment. Since then, however, exports to eastern Europe and especially to Germany – the latter accounts for 35% of total exports – have recovered, prompting an increase in domestic demand. Tight fiscal policies have also been instituted to enable the country to meet the Maastricht economic convergence criteria for economic and monetary union.

PROFILE
A coalition headed by the SPÖ , with the ÖVP as the junior partner, has governed Austria since the 1950s. The left-of-center consensus has at times shown signs of strain, as the ÖVP is losing many of its working-class voters to the right-wing FPÖ. One main reason is the perception that immigrant labor is taking jobs from Austrians. The FPÖ's anti-EU stance has also attracted support.

Local government is run by the nine provincial assemblies. Vienna is dominated by the SPÖ.

Dr. Thomas Klestil, the ÖVP candidate, became Austria's president in 1992.

Viktor Klima succeeded Franz Vranitzky as chancellor in 1997.

WORLD AFFAIRS
▷ Joined UN in 1955

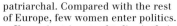

EU — CE — NAM — OECD — OSCE

While Austria wants to be seen as independent of German influence, it cannot avoid the fact that Germany is its main trading partner and the most powerful state in the region. Relations with Germany are therefore a major concern, although there is a conscious policy to create a diplomatic distance from it. Austria is keen to maintain its direct line to Washington. The fact that Austria supplies much of the US army's small arms helps to cement this relationship.

The Austrian government supports the early entry to the EU of east European states. Its geopolitical position gives it considerable influence, and exports to the region trebled in the 1990s. Austria is a neutral state and its forces may not serve abroad. Since Austria joined the EU, this neutrality has begun to be questioned, although in 1998 the SPÖ ruled out membership of NATO. Austria implemented fully the Schengen Convention from April 1998, abolishing border controls with other participating countries in the EU.

AID
▷ Donor

$544m (donations) — Not applicable

New projects are now assessed for their impact on the environment and on gender issues. Austria is a major donor of aid to eastern Europe. Poland is the largest recipient of official aid and Bosnia & Herzegovina the second. A major exporter to former Yugoslavia before the war, Austria has a key role in its reconstruction.

CHRONOLOGY

Austria came under the control of the Habsburgs in 1273. In 1867, the Dual Monarchy of Austria–Hungary was formed under Habsburg rule. Defeat in the First World War led to the breakup of the Habsburg empire in 1918.

❏ **1918** Republic of Austria formed.
❏ **1934** Chancellor Dollfuss dismisses parliament and starts imprisoning Social Democrats, communists and National Socialist Party (NAZI) members. NAZIs attempt coup.
❏ **1938** The Anschluss – Austria forcibly incorporated into Germany by Hitler.
❏ **1945** Austria occupied by Soviet, British, US and French forces. Elections result in People's Party (ÖVP) and Socialist Party (SPÖ) coalition; remains in power for most of the postwar period.
❏ **1950** Attempted coup by Communist Party fails. Marshall aid helps economic recovery. USSR resists calls from France, USA, and UK for independent Austria.
❏ **1955** Soviet troops withdrawn. USSR recognizes Austria as a neutral sovereign state.
❏ **1971** SPÖ government formed under Chancellor Bruno Kreisky who dominates Austrian politics for 13 years.
❏ **1983** Socialists and the Freedom Party (FPÖ) form a coalition government under Fred Sinowatz.
❏ **1986** Dr. Kurt Waldheim, former UN secretary-general, elected president, despite war crimes allegations. Franz Vranitzky replaces Sinowatz as federal chancellor. Nationalist Jörg Haider succeeds more moderate Norbert Steger as FPÖ leader, prompting the SPÖ to pull out of the government. Elections produce stalemate. Return to "grand coalition" between SPÖ and ÖVP.
❏ **1990** ÖVP loses 17 seats in parliamentary elections.
❏ **1992** Thomas Klestil (ÖVP) elected president, replacing Waldheim. Elections confirm some traditional ÖVP supporters defecting to FPÖ.
❏ **1995** Austria joins EU. Elections after coalition disagreement over budget; SPÖ and ÖVP increase representation; "grand coalition" re-forms in early 1996.
❏ **1997** Vranitzky resigns and is replaced by Viktor Klima.
❏ **1998** Klestil reelected President. FPÖ regional deputy absconds to Brazil after running up debts of US$1.5 million.
❏ **1999** Haider's FPÖ wins 42% of votes in Carinthia regional poll.

DEFENSE

 Compulsory military service

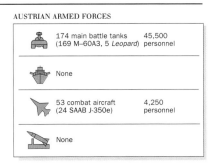

$1.8bn   Down 16% in 1997

AUSTRIAN ARMED FORCES

174 main battle tanks (169 M–60A3, 5 *Leopard*)	45,500 personnel	
None		
53 combat aircraft (24 SAAB J-350e)	4,250 personnel	
None		

Under the 1955 State Treaty, which granted Austria its full independence, the country is neutral, although it has participated in NATO's Partnerships for Peace program since February 1995.

Despite the small size of its own forces, the Austrian arms industry is strong and meets most of the hardware needs of its army. It also exports arms to the USA and other countries.

ECONOMICS

Inflation 2.9% p.a. (1985–1996)

$225.4bn   12.65–11.72 Austrian schillings

SCORE CARD

❏ WORLD GNP RANKING 22nd
❏ GNP PER CAPITA $27,920
❏ BALANCE OF PAYMENTS ....$–3,865m
❏ INFLATION 1.3%
❏ UNEMPLOYMENT 7%

ECONOMIC PERFORMANCE INDICATOR

EXPORTS

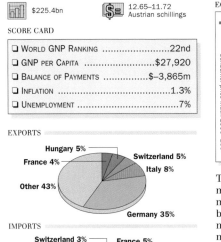

Hungary 5%
France 4%
Switzerland 5%
Italy 8%
Other 43%
Germany 35%

IMPORTS

Switzerland 3%
France 5%
USA 5%
Italy 8%
Germany 42%
Other 37%

STRENGTHS

Large manufacturing base. Strong chemical and petrochemical industries. Electrical engineering sector, textiles and wood processing industries. Highly skilled labor force. Tourism is an important foreign currency earner.

WEAKNESSES

Lacks natural resources. Reliant on imported raw materials, particularly oil and gas. Process of introducing greater competition and deregulation has been slow.

PROFILE

Austria's industrial and high-tech sector is highly developed and contributes over 25% to GDP. Some services, notably tourism, are highly sophisticated and profitable, although tourism receipts have been down in recent years. A recession in the early 1990s was reversed by a rapid increase in exports to eastern Europe and Germany and by increased domestic demand.

There have been benefits from EU membership since 1995. Prices for many products, particularly food and books, have fallen. The Austrian labor market has also seen an influx of migrant labor more willing to accept flexible working arrangements and lower wages. Foreign investment has increased, as more multinationals locate their headquarters for east European operations in Austria. A far-reaching fiscal stabilization program instituted after accession enabled Austria to meet the economic convergence criteria necessary for it to join the final stage of economic and monetary union from January 1999.

AUSTRIA : MAJOR BUSINESSES

❋ Textiles
⚗ Chemicals
△ Metallurgy
🔌 Electronics
🛠 Iron & steel
✒ Pharmaceuticals
⚙ Light engineering
✿ Heavy engineering

0   100 km
0   100 miles

RESOURCES

▷ Electric power 39.7m kw

🐟 4,458 tonnes

🛢 23,700 b/d
(reserves
93,200,000 bbl)

🐷 3.7m pigs,
2.2m cattle,
384,000 sheep

💎 Iron, coal, magnesite,
zinc, lead

ELECTRICITY GENERATION

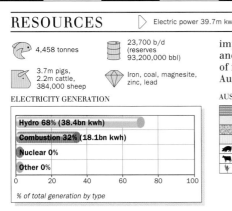

Hydro 68% (38.4bn kwh)	
Combustion 32% (18.1bn kwh)	
Nuclear 0%	
Other 0%	

0   20   40   60   80   100

% of total generation by type

Austria has few resources. It lacks significant oil, coal, and gas deposits and has to import over $3.6 billion-worth of energy every year. Russia is a key energy supplier and gas is provided via pipelines running through the Czech and Slovak republics. Oil is imported up the Danube. Russia and Germany are the major suppliers of iron ore and raw steel for Austria's industry.

ENVIRONMENT

▷ Green MPs

🔺 28% (24% partially
protected)

◇ Medium

ENVIRONMENTAL TREATIES

Yes	Yes	Yes
Yes	Yes	Yes

Environmental awareness is high. Domestic waste has to be separated for recycling, with heavy fines for those failing to observe regulations. Car emissions are increasingly controlled; drivers use lead-free gasoline.

The safety of nuclear reactors in Slovakia and Slovenia is a major concern.

MEDIA

▷ TV ownership high

📋 Daily newspaper circulation 294 per 1,000 people

PUBLISHING AND BROADCAST MEDIA

📰	There are 17 daily newspapers, including the leading *Die Presse*. The *Wiener Zeitung* is the world's oldest daily paper
📺	2 state-owned services
📻	1 state-owned service

TV and radio are more tightly controlled than the press and are operated by *Österreichischer Rundfunk* (ÖRF), under a politically appointed general director. Cable TV is licensed by ÖRF to prevent it taking viewers from existing stations. A satellite program run jointly with German and Swiss TV provides German-language programs to counterbalance those available in English and French.

AUSTRIA : LAND USE

Cropland	
Pasture	
Forest	
High mountain regions	
🐷 Pigs	
🐄 Cattle	
Wheat	

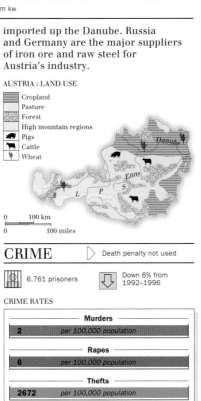

0   100 km
0   100 miles

CRIME

▷ Death penalty not used

⚖ 6,761 prisoners

⬇ Down 6% from
1992–1996

CRIME RATES

Murders	
2	per 100,000 population

Rapes	
6	per 100,000 population

Thefts	
2672	per 100,000 population

Austria's crime rate is below Europe's average. However, the number of burglaries is rising. The arrival of the Russian mafia in Vienna has led to an increase in money laundering.

EDUCATION

▷ School leaving
age: 15

🎓 99%

👨‍🎓 238,981 students

Of total government expenditure 7.7% is spent on education.

THE EDUCATION SYSTEM

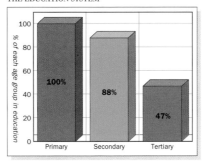

% of each age group in education

Primary 100%   Secondary 88%   Tertiary 47%

Children are streamed into two types of school according to their ability. Those in a *Gymnasium* (11–18) are entitled to enter university, but children in a *Hauptschule* (11–15) are not. The universities are oversubscribed, with students taking six years or more to finish their first degrees.

HEALTH

▷ Welfare state
health benefits

👨‍⚕ 1 per 385 people

💀 Heart and
cerebrovascular
diseases, cancers

Austria has relatively high levels of spending on health, with 11.2% of total government expenditure being spent on it. However, private spending on health is increasing and accounts for 32.9% of the total, the highest proportion of any EU state, as patients increasingly choose to use the private health sector to avoid waiting lists for operations.

SPENDING

▷ GDP/cap.
no increase

CONSUMPTION AND SPENDING

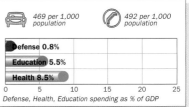

🚗 469 per 1,000
population

💿 492 per 1,000
population

Defense 0.8%	
Education 5.5%	
Health 8.5%	

0   5   10   15   20   25

Defense, Health, Education spending as % of GDP

Despite having had a left-of-center government for most of the last four decades, Austria has retained many of its traditional social divisions. Inherited wealth is still respected above earned wealth, and social mobility is somewhat less than in neighboring Germany. Austrians have the highest savings rate of any country in the OECD. Relatively few Austrians own stocks and shares, and only limited amounts are invested in property. Austria is the only EU country which allows anonymous savings accounts, a system argued to encourage money laundering and insider dealing. Government bonds offer low rates of interest and the property market is weak; many people, particularly in Vienna, tend to rent rather than buy their apartments. The poorest group are the refugees from the various ongoing conflicts in the former Yugoslavia.

WORLD RANKING

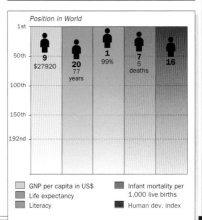

Position in World

9 $27920	20 77 years	1 99%	7 5 deaths	16

1st · 50th · 100th · 150th · 192nd

GNP per capita in US$	Infant mortality per 1,000 live births
Life expectancy	
Literacy	Human dev. index

A

AZERBAIJAN

OFFICIAL NAME: Republic of Azerbaijan **CAPITAL:** Baku
POPULATION: 7.7 million **CURRENCY:** Manat **OFFICIAL LANGUAGE:** Azerbaijani

| 1991 | 1991 | May 28 | AZ | +5 | +994 | .az |

SITUATED ON THE WESTERN COAST of the Caspian Sea, Azerbaijan was the first Soviet republic to declare independence, in 1991. The issue of the disputed enclave of Nagorno Karabakh, which Armenia seeks to annex, led to full-scale war in 1993 and has since dominated Azeri life. The war, with 200,000–250,000 refugees and twice as many internally displaced, has added to the problems of the troubled economy. Its oil wealth, however, gives it long-term potential.

Landscape typical of the Lesser Caucasus mountains near Qazax in the extreme northwest of Azerbaijan.

CLIMATE

▷ Mountain/steppe

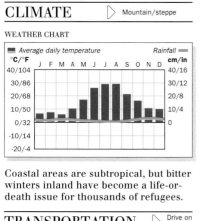

WEATHER CHART

Coastal areas are subtropical, but bitter winters inland have become a life-or-death issue for thousands of refugees.

TRANSPORTATION

▷ Drive on right

✈ **Baku**

288 Ships
632,700 grt

THE TRANSPORTATION NETWORK

| 48,700 km (30,100 miles) | None |
| 2,117 km (1,315 miles) | None |

Improving links with Iran and Turkey to the south, rather than with Moscow, is the focus of transportation spending.

TOURISM

▷ Visitors : population 1:52

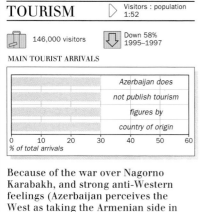

146,000 visitors

Down 58% 1995–1997

MAIN TOURIST ARRIVALS

Azerbaijan does not publish tourism figures by country of origin

% of total arrivals

Because of the war over Nagorno Karabakh, and strong anti-Western feelings (Azerbaijan perceives the West as taking the Armenian side in the conflict), there are few visitors, most of them on business.

PEOPLE

▷ Pop. density medium

Azerbaijani, Russian

89/km² (230/mi²)

THE URBAN/RURAL POPULATION SPLIT

56%   44%

ETHNIC MAKEUP

Other 3%
Russian 5%
Daghestani 3%
Armenian 6%
Azeri 83%

At the last census, held in 1989, Azeris made up 83% of the population. Today the proportion is even greater – thousands of Armenians, Jews and Russians have left as a result of rising Azeri nationalism. Racial hostility against those who remain is increasing.

Women, once prominent in the ruling party, have lost their political status and their general status is declining.

The once effective social security system is under great strain.

POLITICS

▷ Multiparty elections

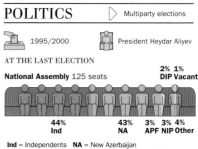

1995/2000

President Heydar Aliyev

AT THE LAST ELECTION

National Assembly 125 seats

2% 1%
DIP Vacant

44% Ind   43% NA   3% APF   3% NIP   4% Other

Ind = Independents **NA** = New Azerbaijan
APF = Azerbaijani Popular Front **NIP** = National Independence (Istiklal) **DIP** = Democratic Independence Party

The 1988 decision of Nagorno Karabakh's Armenian-dominated council to unite with Armenia led in 1993 to war with Armenia, which gained control over 20% of Azeri territory. A 1994 cease-fire has yet to result in a peace accord. In 1995 New Azerbaijan (NA) won a majority in the first legislative poll since independence. NA supports septuagenarian President Heydar Aliyev, first elected in 1993 and reelected in 1998.

AZERBAIJAN

Total Land Area : 86 600 sq. km (33 436 sq. miles)

POPULATION

▣	over 1 000 000
◎	over 100 000
○	over 50 000
●	over 10 000
•	under 10 000

LAND HEIGHT

4000m/13 124ft
3000m/9843ft
2000m/6562ft
1000m/3281ft
500m/1640ft
200m/656ft
Sea Level

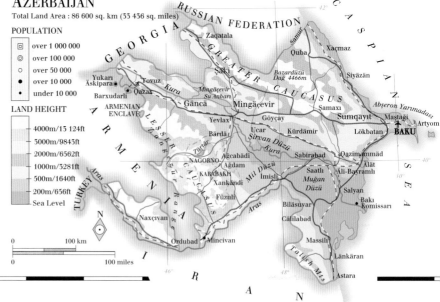

A

WORLD AFFAIRS

> Joined UN in 1992

| CIS | ECO | EAPC | OIC | OSCE |

Azerbaijan has developed contacts with the West as a source of investment and as a counterweight to neighboring Russia and Iran (with a large Azeri population). All are interested in exploiting Azeri oil fields in the Caspian Sea. Turkey – with its common history, language, religion and culture – is a natural ally.

AID

> Recipient

$182m (receipts)   Up 72% 1996–1997

Development aid to Azerbaijan has soared from $22 million in 1993 to $182 million in 1997.

DEFENSE

> Compulsory military service

$146m   Up 10% in 1997

The 72,150-strong Azeri army has performed badly in the war with Armenia. Russia withdrew the last of its 62,000 troops in 1993.

ECONOMICS

> Inflation 1,029% p.a.(1992–1995)

$3.9bn   3,950 manat

SCORE CARD

❏ WORLD GNP RANKING	118th
❏ GNP PER CAPITA	$510
❏ BALANCE OF PAYMENTS	$169m
❏ INFLATION	3.7%
❏ UNEMPLOYMENT	1%

STRENGTHS
Exploitation of extensive oil and natural gas reserves starting to come on stream. Iron, copper, lead and salt deposits. Cotton and silkworms.

WEAKNESSES
Antiquated Soviet-era industry needs modernization. Poor infrastructure and corruption threaten development. The fallout from the war in Nagorno Karabakh still drains state resources.

EXPORTS

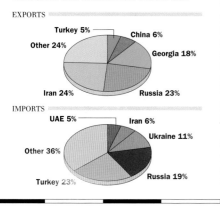

Turkey 5%   China 6%
Other 24%
Georgia 18%
Iran 24%   Russia 23%

IMPORTS

UAE 5%   Iran 6%
Ukraine 11%
Other 36%
Russia 19%
Turkey 23%

RESOURCES

> Electric power 5.2m kw

9,800 tonnes

5.9m sheep, 1.8m cattle, 371,000 goats

185,000 b/d (reserves 1,300,000,000 bbl)

Iron, bauxite, copper, lead, zinc, limestone, salt, oil, gas

The USSR did little to modernize Azerbaijan's oil fields, preferring to concentrate on Siberia, but an international consortium led by BP Amoco is now investing extensively in production.

ENVIRONMENT

> No Green MPs

6%   Not available

Under the Soviet regime there was relatively unchecked oil pollution into the Caspian Sea and an overuse of pesticides in agriculture. Azeris are now far more conscious of the need to protect their environment.

MEDIA

> TV ownership medium

Daily newspaper circulation 28 per 1,000 people

PUBLISHING AND BROADCAST MEDIA

There are 6 daily newspapers, including *Bakinskii Rabochii*, *Khalg Gazeti* and *Hayat*

1 state-controlled service   1 state-controlled service

A 1998 presidential decree abolished censorship, but journalists protest at continued restrictions.

CRIME

> Death penalty not used

Azerbaijan does not publish prison figures   Down 24% from 1992–1996

The judicial system returned to political control in 1993. Levels of crime outside Nagorno Karabakh are relatively low, but in the enclave there are reports of human rights abuses by the armed forces and of criminality in organized camps for the displaced.

EDUCATION

> School leaving age: 17

96%   115,116 students

The return to power of NA is expected to reverse communist control over education policy, which has been particularly noticeable in the teaching of history. Baku, the main university, specializes in Oriental studies.

HEALTH

> Welfare state health benefits

1 per 257 people   Heart, cerebrovascular and respiratory diseases, cancers

The already basic health system has effectively collapsed as a result of the war. Tuberculosis is a major problem.

CHRONOLOGY

Under consecutive Persian, Ottoman, and Russian influence, Azerbaijan, one of the world's major oil producers in 1900, attained independence in 1917.

- ❏ **1920** Red Army invades. Soviet republic established.
- ❏ **1922** Incorporated in Transcaucasian Soviet Federative Socialist Republic (TSFSR).
- ❏ **1930** Forced collectivization of agriculture.
- ❏ **1936** TSFSR disbanded; Azerbaijan a full union republic (ASSR).
- ❏ **1945** Attempted annexation of Azeri region of Iran.
- ❏ **1985** Gorbachev tackles corruption in CPA.
- ❏ **1988** Nagorno Karabakh seeks unification with Armenia.
- ❏ **1990** Nagorno Karabakh attempts secession. Soviet troops move in.
- ❏ **1991** Independence from Moscow.
- ❏ **1993** War with Armenia over Nagorno Karabakh.
- ❏ **1994** Declaration of cease-fire.
- ❏ **1995** Elections: NA gains power.
- ❏ **1998** Aliyev is reelected president.

SPENDING

> GDP/cap. increase

CONSUMPTION AND SPENDING

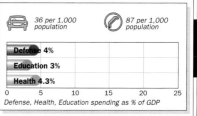

36 per 1,000 population   87 per 1,000 population

Defense 4%
Education 3%
Health 4.3%

0   5   10   15   20   25
Defense, Health, Education spending as % of GDP

New oil revenues are threatening to create a nouveau riche elite without reaching the 60% of Azerbaijan's people currently living in poverty.

WORLD RANKING

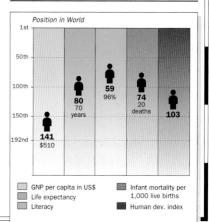

Position in World

1st
50th
100th
150th
192nd

80 70 years
59 96%
74 20 deaths
103
141 $510

▢ GNP per capita in US$		▢ Infant mortality per 1,000 live births
▢ Life expectancy		
▢ Literacy		▢ Human dev. index

BAHAMAS

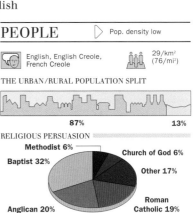

CARIBBEAN

North America

OFFICIAL NAME: The Commonwealth of the Bahamas   CAPITAL: Nassau
POPULATION: 293,000   CURRENCY: Bahamian dollar   OFFICIAL LANGUAGE: English

B

| 1973 | 1973 | July 10 | BS | -5 | +1242 | .bs |

LOCATED OFF THE FLORIDA coast in the western Atlantic, the Bahamas comprises an archipelago of some 700 islands and 2,400 cays, of which 30 are inhabited. One of the first transatlantic tourist destinations, the Bahamas today is also a major offshore financial center. It has one of the world's largest open-registry fleets, but only 0.2% of the total tonnage is owned by Bahamian nationals.

CLIMATE   ▷ Tropical oceanic

WEATHER CHART

Average daily temperature · Rainfall

The whole of the Bahamas chain has a typically subtropical climate with consistently mild winters. Hurricanes may occur from July to December.

TRANSPORTATION   ▷ Drive on left

Freeport International
1.23m passengers

914 ships
25,500 grt

THE TRANSPORTATION NETWORK

| 1,350 km (839 miles) | None |
| None | None |

Getting around 700 islands spread over 260,000 square km (100,386 square miles) is difficult. A catamaran service links Nassau and Miami.

TOURISM   ▷ Visitors : population 5.4:1

1.59m visitors   Up 2% 1995–1997

MAIN TOURIST ARRIVALS

USA 83%	
Canada 7%	
UK 2%	
Other 8%	
0 10 20 30 40 50 60 70 80 90 100
% of total arrivals

Casinos and beaches are major attractions. There are special casino charter flights from the USA. The Bahamas is also one of the Caribbean's major cruise ship destinations. An extra 3,000 hotel rooms will be available by 2000, but there are fears that supply could outpace demand.

PEOPLE   ▷ Pop. density low

English, English Creole, French Creole

29/km² (76/mi²)

THE URBAN/RURAL POPULATION SPLIT

87%   13%

RELIGIOUS PERSUASION

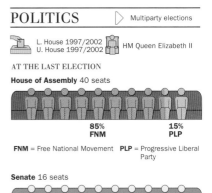

Methodist 6%
Church of God 6%
Baptist 32%
Other 17%
Anglican 20%
Roman Catholic 19%

Africans first arrived as slaves in the 16th century; their descendants constitute most of the population, alongside a rich white minority. The nuclear family is the norm, although absentee fathers are fairly common, especially in outlying fishing communities. More women are now entering the professions.

POLITICS   ▷ Multiparty elections

L. House 1997/2002
U. House 1997/2002

HM Queen Elizabeth II

AT THE LAST ELECTION

House of Assembly 40 seats

85%
FNM

15%
PLP

FNM = Free National Movement   **PLP** = Progressive Liberal Party

Senate 16 seats

The members of the Senate are appointed. 9 are chosen by the prime minister, 4 by the leader of the opposition and 3 by the prime minister after consultation with the leader of the opposition.

The 1992 election defeat of Lynden Pindling, following drug-related corruption allegations, ended 25 years of continuous rule by his PLP. Pindling was instrumental in steering the Bahamas to independence, ending the domination of the white elite in Bahamian politics and bringing blacks into the political process for the first time. Prime minister Hubert Ingraham has concentrated on tightening up ministerial accountability, and in October 1995 introduced legislation to counter money laundering. Economic successes ensured his reelection in 1997. He faced protests in 1999 over government plans to privatize telecommunications.

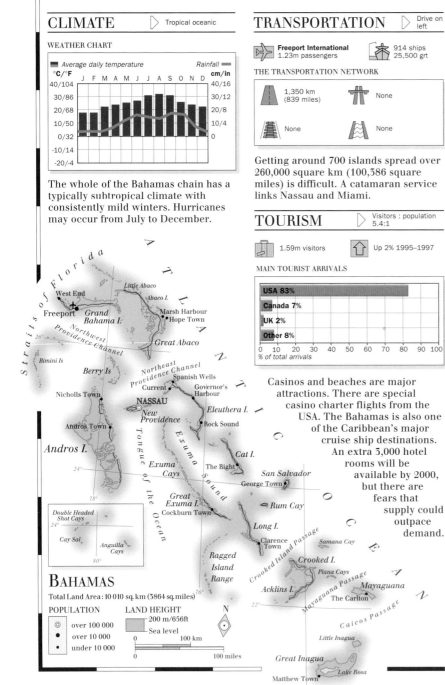

BAHAMAS

Total Land Area: 10 010 sq. km (3864 sq.miles)

POPULATION
◎ over 100 000
● over 10 000
· under 10 000

LAND HEIGHT
200 m/656ft
Sea level

0   100 km
0   100 miles

B

WORLD AFFAIRS

> Joined UN in 1973

| ACS | Caricom | Comm | NAM | OAS |

Repatriating unauthorized immigrants to Haiti and Cuba is a major issue, as are relations with the USA, which considers the islands a money-laundering risk and a center for the transshipment of drugs.

AID

> Recipient

US$3m (receipts) — Up in 1996–1997

Aid is modest. The IDB and the USA provide soft development loans. China in 1998 loaned Nassau $17 million for a convention and theatre complex.

DEFENSE

> No compulsory military service

US$22m — No change in 1997

The UK is the main trainer of and supplier for the 900-strong defense force and coastguard. Intercepting narcotics and Haitian and Cuban refugees are its main activities.

ECONOMICS

> Inflation 4.2% p.a.(1985–1996)

US$3.3bn — 1.00 Bahamian dollar

SCORE CARD

❑ WORLD GNP RANKING	124th
❑ GNP PER CAPITA	US$11,940
❑ BALANCE OF PAYMENTS	US$–462m
❑ INFLATION	0.5%
❑ UNEMPLOYMENT	10%

STRENGTHS

Major international financial services sector, including banking, insurance and business trade center. Major tourism and cruise ship destination. Growing container port. International ship registration.

WEAKNESSES

Growing competition in financial services and tourism from the rest of the Caribbean.

EXPORTS

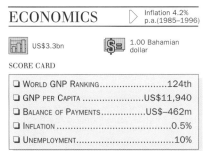

Denmark 6%
Spain 8%
Other 33%
UK 13%
Norway 15%
USA 25%

IMPORTS

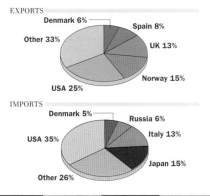

Denmark 5%
Russia 6%
USA 35%
Italy 13%
Japan 15%
Other 26%

Archetypal island paradise. *Its natural beauty attracts more than five tourists per inhabitant to the Bahamas every year.*

RESOURCES

> Electric power 401,000 kw

9,638 tonnes — Not an oil producer

2m chickens, 6,150 sheep, 5,000 pigs, 15,750 goats — Salt, aragonite

The Bahamas has no strategic resources. A 13.5mw electricity generating plant was opened in 1998.

ENVIRONMENT

> No Green MPs

Not available — Not available

As in other Caribbean states, hotel overdevelopment is a major cause for concern. Environmental groups have also pointed out the potential for accidents posed by the Bahamas' enormous oil storage depots.

MEDIA

> TV ownership medium

Daily newspaper circulation 100 per 1,000 people

PUBLISHING AND BROADCAST MEDIA

There are 3 daily newspapers, the *Nassau Guardian*, the *Tribune* and the *Freeport News*

1 limited state-owned service — 1 state-owned and 3 independent licensed services

The state-owned TV channel faces very stiff competition from Florida-based US broadcasters.

CRIME

> Death penalty used

3,789 prisoners — Up 8% in 1990

Two convicted murderers were hanged in 1998. Illegal weapons are readily available. Violent crime ranges from narcotics-related activity to serious vandalism. Two women tourists were murdered in 1998.

EDUCATION

> School leaving age: 14

96% — 5,305 students

Education follows the former British 11-plus selective system, the pattern in the Caribbean. Students go to the University of the West Indies or to the USA.

HEALTH

> Welfare state health benefits

1 per 709 people — Obstetric causes, heart diseases, cancers, crime, accidents

The Bahamian health service combines state and private systems. Access to care in the outlying islands is difficult, relying on unscheduled inter-island or privately owned boats.

SPENDING

> GDP/cap. no increase

CONSUMPTION AND SPENDING

58 per 1,000 population — 283 per 1,000 population

Defense 0.6%		
Education 3.6%		
Health 3.5%		

0 — 5 — 10 — 15 — 20 — 25
Defense, Health, Education spending as % of GDP

There are marked wealth disparities between the urban professionals who work in the thriving financial sector, and the poor fishermen from the outlying islands. Cuban and Haitian refugees, who have no legal status, are the poorest group.

WORLD RANKING

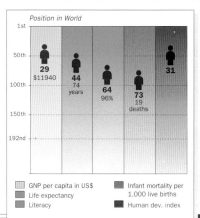

Position in World

1st
50th
100th
150th
192nd

29 $11940
44 74 years
64 96%
73 19 deaths
31

GNP per capita in US$
Life expectancy
Literacy
Infant mortality per 1,000 live births
Human dev. index

B

BAHRAIN

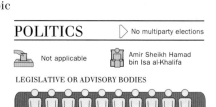

OFFICIAL NAME: State of Bahrain CAPITAL: Manama
POPULATION: 594,000 CURRENCY: Bahrain dinar OFFICIAL LANGUAGE: Arabic

1971 1971 Dec 16 BRN +3 +973 .bh

BAHRAIN IS AN ARCHIPELAGO of 33 islands situated between the Qatar peninsula and the Saudi Arabian mainland. Only three of the islands are inhabited. Bahrain Island is connected to Saudi Arabia's eastern province by a road causeway opened in 1986. Bahrain was the first Gulf emirate to export oil; its reserves are now almost depleted. Services such as offshore banking, insurance and tourism are major employment sectors for skilled Bahrainis.

POLITICS
No multiparty elections

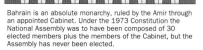

Not applicable

Amir Sheikh Hamad bin Isa al-Khalifa

LEGISLATIVE OR ADVISORY BODIES

Bahrain is an absolute monarchy, ruled by the Amir through an appointed Cabinet. Under the 1973 Constitution the National Assembly was to have been composed of 30 elected members plus the members of the Cabinet, but the Assembly has never been elected.

CLIMATE
Hot desert

WEATHER CHART

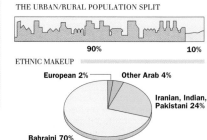

Temperatures soar to 40°C (104°F) in June–September. In December–March the weather is pleasantly warm.

TRANSPORTATION
Drive on right

Bahrain International, Muharraq
3.43m passengers

88 ships
193,600 grt

THE TRANSPORTATION NETWORK

2,160 km (1,342 miles)	None
None	None

Saudi Arabia paid for a 25-km (16-mile) causeway linking it with Bahrain; the four-lane road was completed in 1986.

TOURISM
Visitors : population 3.1:1

1.8m visitors

Tourist levels down 26% during 1995–1997

MAIN TOURIST ARRIVALS

Saudi Arabia 67%
India 5%
Kuwait 4%
Other 24%

0 10 20 30 40 50 60 70 80
% of total arrivals

Bahrain's liberal lifestyle and the opening of the causeway in 1986 has led to a boom in visitors from neighboring Gulf states. Bahrain has a modern airport and is a business convention center.

PEOPLE
Pop. density high

Arabic

874/km²
(2,262/mi²)

THE URBAN/RURAL POPULATION SPLIT

90% 10%

ETHNIC MAKEUP

European 2% Other Arab 4%
Iranian, Indian, Pakistani 24%
Bahraini 70%

The key division in Bahrain is between Sunni and Shi'a Muslims, representing approximately 30% and 70% of the population respectively. The ruling class is Sunni and they hold the best jobs in business and the bureaucracy. Shi'a Muslims tend to do menial work and have a lower standard of living. The most impoverished Shi'a Muslims tend to be of Persian descent.

Bahrain has a smaller expatriate population than many other Arab countries. The ruling al-Khalifa family has responded to declining oil reserves by diversifying the economy to provide service industry jobs for Bahrainis.

Bahrain is the most liberal of the Gulf states. Alcohol is freely available. Women have access to education and are not obliged to wear the veil. Arranged marriages, however, remain common.

The Grand Mosque, Manama. It is the largest building in Bahrain and can accommodate 7000 people.

The al-Khalifa family has dominated Bahraini politics since 1783. Politics is effectively autocratic, and political dissent is not tolerated. An attempt at representative government in 1973 was suspended in 1975 on the grounds that it provoked instability. Since 1993 the Amir has been advised by an appointed Consultative Council.

Bahrain is one of the few Gulf states with political prisoners. Opponents of the regime – usually Shi'a fundamentalists – are frequently exiled and have their passports cancelled. They are backed by Iran, which has encouraged the spread of radical Shi'ism in Bahrain. Radio broadcasts from Tehran also reach Bahrain. In 1996 the government announced that it had foiled an Iranian-backed coup.

The current Amir, Sheikh Hamad bin Isa al-Khalifa, succeeded to the throne in March 1999 and supports the policy of economic liberalization initiated by his late father, Sheikh Isa bin Salman al-Khalifa. The pace of political reform is cautious despite mounting pressure from pro-democracy campaigners and Shi'a activists.

WORLD AFFAIRS
Joined UN in 1971

AL Damasc GCC OIC OAPEC

Bahrain espouses an independent foreign policy. It maintains good relations with the UK and the USA, the main guarantor of its security, but is keen to restore relations with Iraq. Despite its liberal regime, Bahrain maintains good relations with Saudi Arabia. There is tension with Iran and a territorial dispute with Qatar.

AID
Recipient

$84m (receipts)

Up 4% 1996–1997

Bahrain receives low levels of aid, but takes the lion's share of the offshore oil field shared with Saudi Arabia, effectively a subsidy from the latter.

DEFENSE ▷ No compulsory military service

💲 $364m   ⬆ Up 25% in 1997

The emirate's strong defense force includes a small but well-equipped air force. Bahrain has traditionally maintained close relations with the USA. US air bases on Bahrain were used in the 1990–1991 Gulf War. The small navy is hard-pressed to patrol the 33-island archipelago.

ECONOMICS ▷ Inflation 0.3% p.a. (1985–1996)

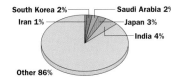 $5.1bn   0.38 Bahrain dinars

SCORE CARD

❏ WORLD GNP RANKING	104th
❏ GNP PER CAPITA	$7,800
❏ BALANCE OF PAYMENTS	$557m
❏ INFLATION	-0.2%
❏ UNEMPLOYMENT	6%

STRENGTHS
Oil. Arab world's major offshore banking sector. Lack of restrictions encourages inward investment. Tourism.

WEAKNESSES
Depleted oil reserves and insufficient diversification could lead to future drop in currently high living standards. High levels of government borrowing.

EXPORTS

South Korea 2%   Saudi Arabia 2%
Iran 1%   Japan 3%
India 4%
Other 86%

IMPORTS

Germany 3%   Japan 4%
UK 6%
USA 9%
Saudi Arabia 41%
Other 37%

RESOURCES ▷ Electric power 1.1m kw

🐟 9,400 tonnes   🛢 39,600 b/d (reserves 69,584,000 bbl)

16,000 goats, 17,000 sheep, 13,000 cattle   💎 Oil, natural gas

Bahrain remains dependent on its oil and gas production. Production of crude oil has declined sharply since the 1970s, and there are fears that reserves may run out by 2010. As oil has declined, so gas has assumed greater importance. Most is used to supply local industries, particularly the aluminum plant which was established in 1972.

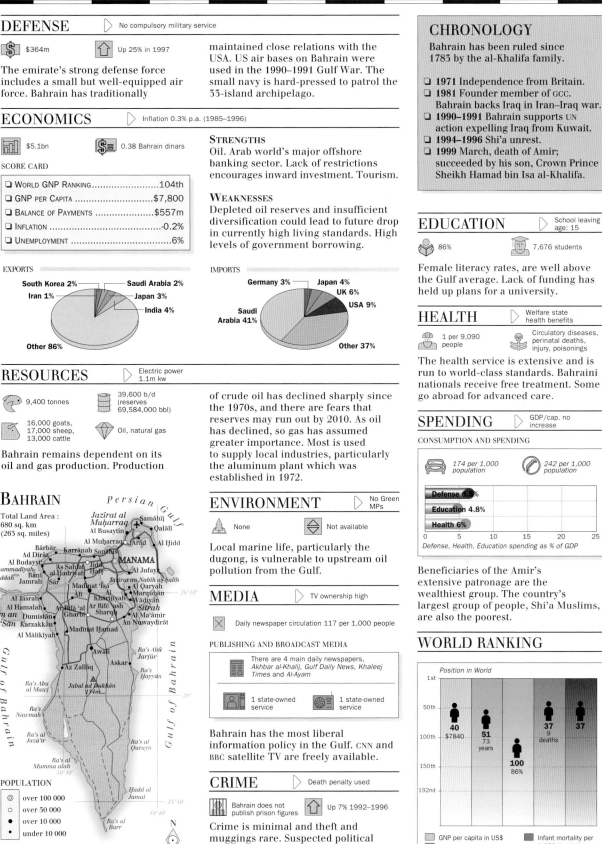

BAHRAIN

Total Land Area : 680 sq. km (263 sq. miles)

Persian Gulf

Jazīrat al Muḥarraq — Samāhīj
Al Busaytīn — Qalālī
Al Muḥarraq — Arād — Al Ḥidd
Bārbār — Karrānah — Sanābis
Al Dirāz
Al Budayyi — As Sahlah — Jidd Ḥafṣ — ⊙ MANAMA
Al Muḥammadīyah — Bānī — al Ḥadīyah
Jiddah — Jamrah — Sār — Jazīrat an Nabīh aṣ Ṣālih
Madīnat 'Īsā — Al Qaryah
Al Jasrah — 'Alī — Al — Marqūbān
Al Ḥamalah — Al Rifā' al Gharbī — Ar Rifā' ash Sharqī — *Sitrah*
mainland [di Arabia] — Dumistān — Al Ma'āmīr
Umm an Na'Sān — Karzakkān — An Nuwaydirāt
Al Mālikīyah — Madīnat Ḥamad
'Awali
Gulf of Bahrain
Ra's Abū Jarjūr
Az Zallāq — Askar — Ra's Ḥayyān
Jabal ad Dukhān (134m)
Ra's Abu al Mawj
Ra's Nawmah
Ra's al Jazā'ir
Ra's al Qurayn
Ra's al Mumma alah 50°30'
Hadd al Jamal
Ra's al Barr
N

POPULATION
◎ over 100 000
○ over 50 000
● over 10 000
• under 10 000

LAND HEIGHT
100m/328ft
Sea Level

0 — 10 km
0 — 10 miles

ENVIRONMENT ▷ No Green MPs

⚠ None   ⬍ Not available

Local marine life, particularly the dugong, is vulnerable to upstream oil pollution from the Gulf.

MEDIA ▷ TV ownership high

⊠ Daily newspaper circulation 117 per 1,000 people

PUBLISHING AND BROADCAST MEDIA

There are 4 main daily newspapers, *Akhbar al-Khalij, Gulf Daily News, Khaleej Times* and *Al-Ayam*

1 state-owned service   1 state-owned service

Bahrain has the most liberal information policy in the Gulf. CNN and BBC satellite TV are freely available.

CRIME ▷ Death penalty used

Bahrain does not publish prison figures   ⬆ Up 7% 1992–1996

Crime is minimal and theft and muggings rare. Suspected political dissidents are monitored by the police.

CHRONOLOGY
Bahrain has been ruled since 1783 by the al-Khalifa family.

❏ **1971** Independence from Britain.
❏ **1981** Founder member of GCC. Bahrain backs Iraq in Iran–Iraq war.
❏ **1990–1991** Bahrain supports UN action expelling Iraq from Kuwait.
❏ **1994–1996** Shi'a unrest.
❏ **1999** March, death of Amir; succeeded by his son, Crown Prince Sheikh Hamad bin Isa al-Khalifa.

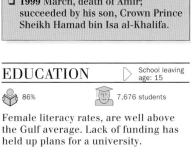

EDUCATION ▷ School leaving age: 15

👤 86%   🎓 7,676 students

Female literacy rates, are well above the Gulf average. Lack of funding has held up plans for a university.

HEALTH ▷ Welfare state health benefits

1 per 9,090 people   Circulatory diseases, perinatal deaths, injury, poisonings

The health service is extensive and is run to world-class standards. Bahraini nationals receive free treatment. Some go abroad for advanced care.

SPENDING ▷ GDP/cap. no increase

CONSUMPTION AND SPENDING

🚗 174 per 1,000 population   📞 242 per 1,000 population

Defense 6.5%
Education 4.8%
Health 6%

0   5   10   15   20   25
Defense, Health, Education spending as % of GDP

Beneficiaries of the Amir's extensive patronage are the wealthiest group. The country's largest group of people, Shi'a Muslims, are also the poorest.

WORLD RANKING

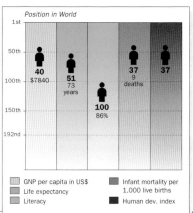

Position in World

1st
50th
100th
150th
192nd

40 $7840
51 73 years
100 86%
37 9 deaths
37

❏ GNP per capita in US$ ❏ Infant mortality per 1,000 live births
❏ Life expectancy ❏ Human dev. index
❏ Literacy

B

BANGLADESH

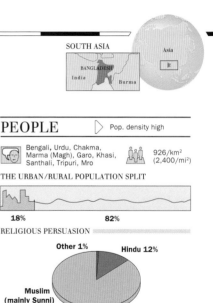

SOUTH ASIA

OFFICIAL NAME: People's Republic of Bangladesh   CAPITAL: Dhaka
POPULATION: 124 million   CURRENCY: Taka   OFFICIAL LANGUAGE: Bengali

| 1971 | 1971 | March 26 | BD | +6 | +880 | .bd |

BANGLADESH LIES AT the north of the Bay of Bengal and shares borders with India and Burma. Most of the country is composed of fertile alluvial plains; the north and northeast are mountainous, as is the Chittagong region. Since its secession from Pakistan in 1971, Bangladesh has had a troubled history of political instability, with periods of emergency rule. Effective democracy was restored in 1991. Bangladesh's major economic sectors are jute production, textiles, and agriculture. Its climate can wreak havoc – in 1991 a massive cyclone killed more than 140,000 people.

CLIMATE   Tropical/subtropical

WEATHER CHART

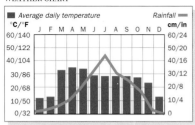

During the monsoon, the water level normally rises 6 m (20 feet) above sea level, flooding two-thirds of the country. The floods are made much worse when the Ganges, Jamuna and Meghna rivers, which converge in a huge delta in Bangladesh, are swollen by the melting of the Himalayan snows and heavy rain, in India. Cyclones regularly build up in the Bay of Bengal, with sometimes devastating effect on the flat coastal region.

TRANSPORTATION   Drive on left

Zia International, Dhaka
1.19m passengers

314 ships
419,200 grt

THE TRANSPORTATION NETWORK

3,840 km (2,386 miles)	None
2,706 km (1,681 miles)	8,433 km (5,240 miles)

Most transportation in Bangladesh is by water, although government transportation policy is now concentrating on developing road and rail links. The Bangabandhu bridge across the Jamuna River, which bisects Bangladesh from north to south, was inaugurated in June 1998; the $500-million project suffered numerous delays. Bangladesh's two major ports, Mungla and Chittagong, are being upgraded to take advanced container ships.

Begum Khaleda Zia, prime minister from 1991 until 1996.

Sheikh Hasina Wajed, Awami League leader and prime minister.

TOURISM   Visitors : population 1:673

184,000 visitors   Up 18% 1995–1997

MAIN TOURIST ARRIVALS

India 34%	
UK 12%	
Pakistan 10%	
USA 7%	
Japan 4%	
Other 33%	

% of total arrivals

Tourist earnings and numbers have started to rise in the late 1990s. Most visitors are Indian businessmen or Bangladeshis who live overseas returning to see their relatives. The Mogul architecture in Dhaka and the Pala dynasty (7th–10th centuries) city of Sonargaon are major attractions.

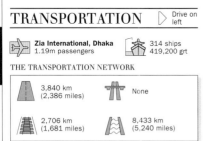

Traders on the Meghna River, which flows into the Padma. Bangladesh's flood-plains are among the most fertile in the world.

PEOPLE   Pop. density high

Bengali, Urdu, Chakma, Marma (Magh), Garo, Khasi, Santhali, Tripuri, Mro

926/km² (2,400/mi²)

THE URBAN/RURAL POPULATION SPLIT

18%   82%

RELIGIOUS PERSUASION

Other 1%
Hindu 12%
Muslim (mainly Sunni) 87%

ETHNIC MAKEUP

Other 2%
Bengali 98%

Bangladesh is one of the most densely populated countries in the world, despite the fact that more than 80% of the population is rural. As in India, there is considerable Muslim-Hindu tension; the destruction of the Ayodhya mosque in northern India in 1992 triggered violence in Bangladesh. The most significant ethnic conflict until recently involved Buddhist tribes – the Chakma – in the Chittagong Hill Tracts who since 1974 had waged a guerrilla campaign for greater autonomy. Thousands of Muslim refugees from Burma who had fled to southern Bangladesh have been repatriated under a settlement reached in 1993.

Although more than 50% of Bangladeshis, rural and urban, still live below the poverty line, there has been an improvement in living standards over the past decade.

The textile trade, by providing an independent income, has been one factor in the growing emancipation of Bangladeshi women. They are now included in official employment statistics and are the main customers of the most successful rural bank. Women lead both government and opposition.

POPULATION AGE BREAKDOWN

Female	Age	Male
2.5%	Over 60	3%
8%	41–60	9.6%
16.1%	21–40	15.4%
21.9%	0–20	23.5%

% of population by age group

POLITICS

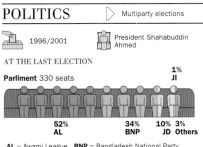

> Multiparty elections

1996/2001

President Shahabuddin Ahmed

AT THE LAST ELECTION

Parliment 330 seats

1% JI

52% AL — 34% BNP — 10% JD — 3% Others

AL = Awami League **BNP** = Bangladesh National Party
JD = Jatiya Dal **JI** = Jamaat-e-Islami

Elections held in February 1996 were boycotted by opposition parties. 30 seats are reserved for women, of which 27 are held by the Awami League.

Bangladesh returned to multiparty democracy in 1991, following a period of military rule.

MAIN POLITICAL ISSUES
The state sector
Bangladesh is coming under increasing pressure from multilateral lending institutions, which account for the vast majority of the country's capital inflows, to cut costs in the state sector. Simultaneously, state-sector workers are demanding wage increases in line with inflation.

Autonomy for Chittagong Hill Tracts
Buddhist Mongol groups – the Chakma – continue to voice demands for greater autonomy, although the low-level guerrilla war they have waged since 1974, has been contained. Many Chakmas fear persecution by Bengali Muslim settlers despite a peace treaty signed in 1997 which provides for local autonomy, amnesty and the return of refugees from India.

PROFILE
Between 1975 and 1990 the military was in power in Bangladesh. The overthrow of President Ershad in 1990 saw a return to multiparty politics; the army remains poised, however, to intervene in the event of a breakdown in law and order. Bangladesh's first woman prime minister, Begum Khaleda Zia, head of the BNP, was elected in February 1991. A change from a presidential to a prime-ministerial system of government followed. The Awami League, which steered Bangladesh to independence in 1971, mounted a sustained campaign against her regime. Sheikh Hasina Wajed, the Awami League's leader, became prime minister after her party won the largest number of seats in a rerun general election in June 1996. Politics remains highly volatile, characterized by party splits, boycotts of parliament and personal animosities.

BANGLADESH

Total Land Area : 133 910 sq. km (51 703 sq. miles)

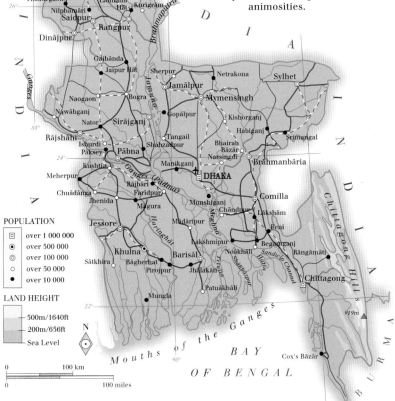

POPULATION

- ▣ over 1 000 000
- ◉ over 500 000
- ◎ over 100 000
- ○ over 50 000
- ● over 10 000

LAND HEIGHT

- 500m/1640ft
- 200m/656ft
- Sea Level

0 ___ 100 km

0 ___ 100 miles

WORLD AFFAIRS

> Joined UN in 1974

Comm | NAM | OIC | SAARC | WTO

B

Priority goes to a good relationship with the West, the main source of essential aid. Relations with Pakistan have slowly improved. Pakistan agreed in 1991 to the repatriation of 250,000 pro-Pakistani Bihari Muslims, in Bangladeshi refugee camps since 1971. Relations with India are improving; the adverse effects of the construction of the Farakka Dam on the Ganges, which deprived Bangladesh of irrigation water, have been alleviated by a 30-year agreement signed in 1996 guaranteeing the right of both parties to share the Ganges water. Relations eased further with the 1997 Chittagong Hill Tracts treaty; India had been accused of fomenting the insurgency.

AID

> Recipient

$1bn (receipts)

Down 20% 1996– 1997

Aid disbursements to Bangladesh each year are over 1,000 times greater than the annual value of foreign investment in the country. Aid also finances the bulk of state capital spending. The Bangladesh Development Aid Consortium meets annually to discuss aid spending under the auspices of the World Bank. One result of the level of aid is that Bangladesh has fallen into one of the traps of an aid-dependent economy: the large middle class has a vested interest in perpetuating a system which provides its members with lucrative contracts and access to external resources.

CHRONOLOGY

British rule in India began in Bengal (now Bangladesh), when Robert Clive, army head of the East India Company, defeated the ruler of Bengal at Plassey in 1765.

- ❏ **1905** Muslims persuade British rulers to partition state of Bengal, to create a Muslim-dominated East Bengal.
- ❏ **1906** Muslim League established in Dhaka.
- ❏ **1912** Partition of 1905 reversed.
- ❏ **1947** British withdrawal from India. Partition plans establish a largely Muslim state of East (present-day Bangladesh) and West Pakistan, separated by 1,600 km (1,000 miles) of Indian, and largely Hindu, territory. The capital of the new, bisected state established at Islamabad in West Pakistan.
- ❏ **1949** Awami League founded to campaign for autonomy from West Pakistan.

CHRONOLOGY *continued*

- ❑ **1968** General Yahya Khan heads government in Islamabad.
- ❑ **1970** Elections give Awami League, under Sheikh Mujibur Rahman, clear majority. Rioting and guerrilla warfare following Yahya Khan's refusal to convene assembly. The year ends with the worst recorded storms in Bangladesh's history – between 200,000 and 500,000 dead.
- ❑ **1971** Civil war, as Sheikh Mujibur and Awami League declare unilateral independence. Ten million Bangladeshis flee to India. Pakistani troops defeated in 12 days by Mukhti Bahini – the Bengal Liberation Army.
- ❑ **1972** Sheikh Mujibur prime minister. Nationalization of key industries, including jute and textiles. Bangladesh achieves international recognition and joins Commonwealth. Pakistan withdraws in protest.
- ❑ **1974** Severe floods damage rice crop.
- ❑ **1975** Sheikh Mujibur assassinated. Military coups end with General Zia Rahman taking power. Institution of single-party state.
- ❑ **1976** Banning of trade union federations.
- ❑ **1977** General Zia assumes presidency. Islam adopted as first principle of the constitution.
- ❑ **1981** General Zia assassinated.
- ❑ **1982** General Ershad takes over.
- ❑ **1983** Democratic elections restored by Ershad. Ershad assumes presidency.
- ❑ **1986** Elections again affected by intimidation and violence. Awami League and BNP fail to unseat Ershad.
- ❑ **1987** Ershad announces state of emergency.
- ❑ **1988** Islam becomes constitutional state religion.
- ❑ **1990** Ershad resigns following demonstrations.
- ❑ **1991** Elections won by BNP. Khaleda Zia becomes prime minister. Ershad imprisoned. Role of the president reduced to ceremonial functions. Floods kill 150,000 people.
- ❑ **1994** Author Taslima Nasreen, who is accused of blasphemy, escapes to Sweden.
- ❑ **1996** General election, boycotted by opposition parties, return BNP to power.
- ❑ **1996** Opposition parties reject February poll result and force fresh elections. Sheikh Hasina Wajed of the Awami League takes power.

DEFENSE

▷ No compulsory military service

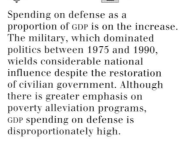

💲 $593m ⬆ Up 8% in 1997

Spending on defense as a proportion of GDP is on the increase. The military, which dominated politics between 1975 and 1990, wields considerable national influence despite the restoration of civilian government. Although there is greater emphasis on poverty alleviation programs, GDP spending on defense is disproportionately high.

BANGLADESHI ARMED FORCES

🚗	140 main battle tanks (T-59/-69, T-55/-54)	101,000 personnel
🚢	4 frigates and 41 patrol boats	10,500 personnel
✈	49 combat aircraft ((12 A-5, 11 F-6, 14 F-7M, 4 FT-7B)	9,500 personnel
🚀	None	

ECONOMICS

▷ Inflation 6.1% p.a. (1985–1996)

📊 $44.1bn 💲 45.45–48.50 taka

SCORE CARD

❑ WORLD GNP RANKING	51st
❑ GNP PER CAPITA	$360
❑ BALANCE OF PAYMENTS	$-286m
❑ INFLATION	5.7%
❑ UNEMPLOYMENT	35%

EXPORTS

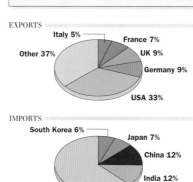

Italy 5%
France 7%
Other 37%
UK 9%
Germany 9%
USA 33%

IMPORTS

South Korea 6%
Japan 7%
China 12%
India 12%
Other 63%

STRENGTHS

Jute is the major industry: Bangladesh accounts for 80% of world jute fiber exports. Low wages ensure a competitive and expanding textile industry, which constitutes one-third of the small manufacturing sector.

WEAKNESSES

Vunerability of the agricultural sector, employing a majority of Bangladeshis, to the violent and unpredictable climate.

PROFILE

Government ministers like to portray Bangladesh as an emerging NIC, but its economy is still overwhelmingly dependent on agriculture and large aid inflows. Agriculture, which provides the major export, jute, is productive; Bangladesh's soils, fed by the Ganges, Jamuna and Meghna rivers, are highly fertile. However, the effects of the weather can be devastating, frequently destroying a whole year's crop. Agricultural wages are among the lowest in the world.

ECONOMIC PERFORMANCE INDICATOR

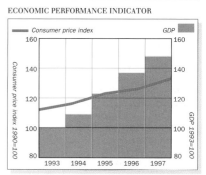

— Consumer price index   GDP

The state sector, which owns large, inefficient and massively loss-making companies (such as the Bangladesh Jute Mills Corporation), is in difficulty. The World Bank, the source of most aid to the country, wants loss-making concerns to cut their workforces or close down.

Textiles and garments are currently the healthiest sectors. Economic zones (Export Processing Zones) with special concessions have attracted foreign investment as well as helped to promote a small indigenous electronics industry. Bangladesh receives generous textile import quotas from the EU and NAFTA, but its economy is so weak that it fails to reach them.

BANGLADESH : MAJOR BUSINESSES

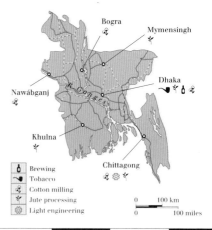

🍺	Brewing
	Tobacco
🌿	Cotton milling
	Jute processing
⚙	Light engineering

0   100 km
0   100 miles

RESOURCES

▷ Electric power 3.3m kw

1.2m tonnes

600 b/d
refines 31,200 b/d

23.4m cattle,
1.2m sheep,
33.5m goats

Salt, oil, natural gas,
limestone

Bangladesh is the world's major jute producer, accounting for 80% of world jute fiber exports and about 50% of world jute manufactures exports.

Bangladesh holds world-class gas reserves. Natural gas from the Bay of Bengal, exploited by the state-owned Bangladesh Oil, Gas and Minerals

ELECTRICITY GENERATION

Hydro 3% (0.3bn kwh)

Combustion 97% (11.3bn kwh)

Nuclear 0%

Other 0%

| 0 | 20 | 40 | 60 | 80 | 100 |

% of total generation by type

Corporation, came on stream in 1988. Gas reserves are estimated at as much as 200 years.

BANGLADESH : LAND USE

Cropland
Wetlands
Forest
Rice
Jute - cash crop

R. Jamuna

R. Ganges

Mouths of the Ganges

| 0 | 100 km |
| 0 | 100 miles |

ENVIRONMENT

▷ No Green MPs

1% (0.7% partially protected)

Low

Bangladesh's climate, which is prone to devastating floods and cyclones, results in huge death tolls and substantial damage to crops. Bangladesh is too poor to finance environmental initiatives.

ENVIRONMENTAL TREATIES

Yes	Yes	Yes
Yes	Yes	No

HEALTH

▷ Welfare state health benefits

1 per 5,000 people

Parasitic, diarrheal and communicable diseases

More resources are needed to boost health care in rural areas. Although primary health care in rural areas has improved over the last decade, Bangladesh's health problems remain severe and are exacerbated by a shortage of medical staff and facilities. The priority given to birth control programs has helped to reduce the population growth rate by more than 20% over the last 15 years.

MEDIA

▷ TV ownership low

Daily newspaper circulation 9 per 1,000 people

PUBLISHING AND BROADCAST MEDIA

	There are 37 daily newspapers. *Dainik Ittefaq*, *Dainik Inquilab* and *Dainik Janakantha* have the highest circulation
	1 state-controlled service
	1 state-controlled service

Press freedom, which emerged after the fall of President Ershad in 1990, has been gradually eroded under successive civilian governments. Of the daily newspapers, the ten English-language titles appeal mainly to the urban elite. Among political weeklies, the most respected is *Holiday* (originally a travel magazine). The vast majority – over 70% – of TV programs are produced locally; about one-third of these are in black and white.

SPENDING

▷ GDP/cap. no increase

CONSUMPTION AND SPENDING

0 per 1,000 population

3 per 1,000 population

Defense 1.9%

Education 2.3%

Health 1.4%

| 0 | 5 | 10 | 15 | 20 | 25 |

Defense, Health, Education spending as % of GDP

Average incomes in Bangladesh remain very low, but wealth disparities are not quite as marked as in India or Pakistan. State officials tend to be among the better-off.

CRIME

▷ Death penalty used

44,111 prisoners

Up 20% 1991-1996

CRIME RATES

Murders

3 per 100,000 population

Rapes

0.5 per 100,000 population

Thefts

13 per 100,000 population

Rising levels of political and religious violence have led to the enforcement of ant-terrorism legislation, containing provisions for summary justice and heavy penalties, including death. There has been a recent sharp rise in crimes against women, including murder, rape, abduction and acid attacks. Deaths in Bangladeshi prisons are common, and in addition the human rights record of the army, especially that of the paramilitary Bangladesh Rifles, has been questioned by Amnesty International.

EDUCATION

▷ School leaving age: 10

40%

434,309 students

Adult literacy, currently estimated at 40%, is notably low by world standards.

THE EDUCATION SYSTEM

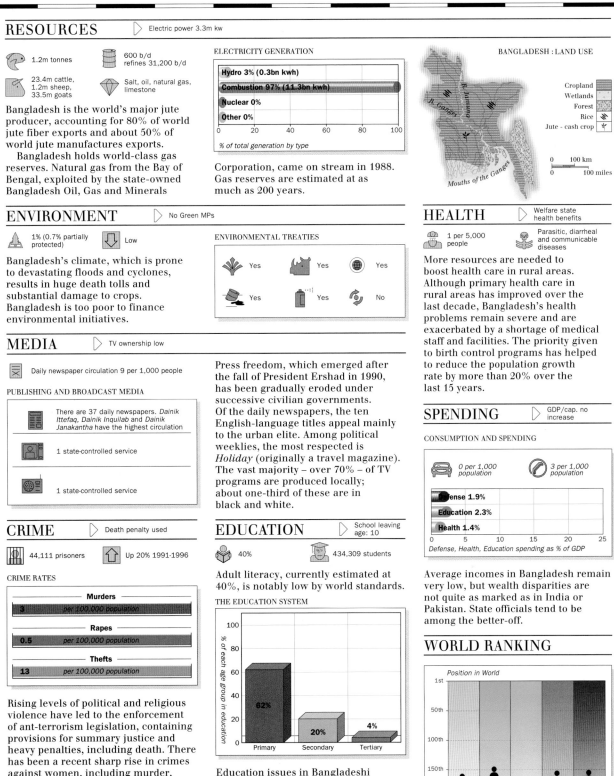

62%	20%	4%
Primary	Secondary	Tertiary

% of each age group in education

Education issues in Bangladeshi society have been poorly addressed, although successive governments have promised to raise literacy levels by increasing expenditure. The country's seven universities are frequently beset by outbreaks of political violence.

WORLD RANKING

Position in World

| 1st | 50th | 100th | 150th | 192nd |

| 156 | 144 | 176 | 151 | 150 |
| $360 | 58 years | 40% | 75 deaths | |

GNP per capita in US$

Life expectancy

Literacy

Infant mortality per 1,000 live births

Human dev. index

BARBADOS

CARIBBEAN

OFFICIAL NAME: Barbados   **CAPITAL:** Bridgetown
POPULATION: 263,000   **CURRENCY:** Barbados dollar   **OFFICIAL LANGUAGE:** English

B

1966	1966	Nov 30	BDS	-4	+1246	.bb

SITUATED TO THE NORTHEAST of Trinidad, Barbados is the most easterly of the West Indian Windward Islands. In the 16th century, the Portuguese became the first Europeans to reach the island, then inhabited by Arawak Indians. However, Barbados was not colonized until the 1620s, when British settlers arrived. Popularly referred to by its neighbors as "little England," Barbados now seeks to forge a new national identity for itself.

CLIMATE   ▷ Tropical oceanic

WEATHER CHART

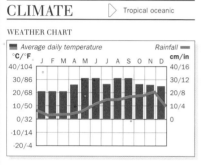

Barbados has a moderate tropical climate and is sunnier and drier than its more mountainous Caribbean neighbors. Hurricanes may occur in the rainy season.

TRANSPORTATION   ▷ Drive on left

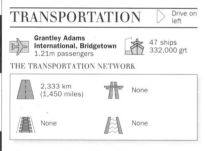

Grantley Adams International, Bridgetown
1.21m passengers

47 ships
332,000 grt

THE TRANSPORTATION NETWORK

2,333 km (1,450 miles)	None
None	None

The expansion of the airport was postponed in 1999 due to budgetary constraints. However, piers at Bridgetown's port have been upgraded with foreign aid, as have the island's paved roads. There are bus routes over most of the island.

House of Assembly, Trafalgar Square, Bridgetown. Barbados's parliament, the third oldest in the Commonwealth, dates from 1639.

TOURISM   ▷ Visitors : population 1.8:1

472,000 visitors   Up 9% 1995-1997

MAIN TOURIST ARRIVALS

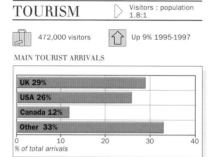

A surge in tourism in 1998 followed record figures in 1997. Visitors come mainly from North America and Europe, periodically boosted by UK cricket fans for test series.

PEOPLE   ▷ Pop. density high

Bajan (Barbadian English), English

612/km² (1,584/mi²)

THE URBAN/RURAL POPULATION SPLIT

47%   53%

RELIGIOUS PERSUASION

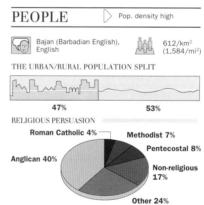

Roman Catholic 4%
Methodist 7%
Pentecostal 8%
Anglican 40%
Non-religious 17%
Other 24%

Most Bajans are the descendants of Africans brought to the island between the 16th and 19th centuries; there are also small groups of South Asians and Europeans, mainly expatriate Britons, many of whom take up residence on retirement. There is some latent tension between the white community, which controls most of the economy, and the majority black population, although this rarely spills over into violence. Increasing social mobility has allowed many black Bajans to move into the professions and the civil service. Barbados enjoys a higher standard of living than most Caribbean countries.

POLITICS   ▷ Multiparty elections

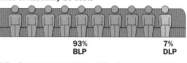

L. House 1999/2004
U. House 1999/2004
HM Queen Elizabeth II

AT THE LAST ELECTION

House of Assembly 28 seats

93% BLP   7% DLP

BLP = Barbados Labour Party   DLP = Democratic Labour Party

Senate 21 seats

The members of the Senate are appointed. Twelve are chosen by the prime minister, 2 by the leader of the opposition and 7 independents by the governor-general.

Barbados is a multiparty democracy. A primarily European, affluent elite, finances the parties and has an indirect influence on government policy. The BLP swept to power in 1994 and won by a landslide in 1999. Owen Arthur, BLP leader and prime minister, prioritizes economic growth and international competitiveness. He has pledged to transform Barbados into a republic, while remaining a member of the Commonwealth.

WORLD AFFAIRS   ▷ Joined UN in 1966

ACS	Comm	Caricom	NAM	OAS

Barbados seeks to be a republic within the Commonwealth. It opposes US sanctions on EU banana imports.

AID   ▷ Recipient

US$3m (receipts)   Down 40% 1996-1997

Most aid comes from the USA, the EU, and the UK, mainly in the form of development project loans and balance of payments support.

DEFENSE   ▷ No compulsory military service

US$14m   No change in 1997

The 1,000-strong Barbadian army and the constabulary benefit from financial support and training from the US and UK governments, which also supply equipment. The country is the headquarters of the Regional Security System, established in 1982 by the Windward and Leeward Islands, a body which acts as a multinational security force for its members.

ECONOMICS

Inflation 3.4% p.a. (1985–1996)

$1.7bn

2.01 Barbados dollars

SCORE CARD

- ❏ WORLD GNP RANKING.........................145th
- ❏ GNP PER CAPITA ....US$6,560
- ❏ BALANCE OF PAYMENTS ....US$7m
- ❏ INFLATION 7.7%
- ❏ UNEMPLOYMENT.................................16%

STRENGTHS

Well-developed tourism based on climate and accessibility. Sugar industries. Information processing and financial services are important new growth sectors.

WEAKNESSES

Narrow economic base, vulnerable to downturns in tourism, failures of sugar harvest and the sector's dependency on loans and secure markets. Relatively high manufacturing costs.

EXPORTS

Venezuela 6% — Trinidad & Tobago 7%
Other 48%
Jamaica 7%
USA 15%
UK 17%

IMPORTS

Canada 4% — Japan 7%
UK 8%
USA 45%
Trinidad & Tobago 9%
Other 27%

BARBADOS

Total Land Area : 430 sq. km (166 sq. miles)

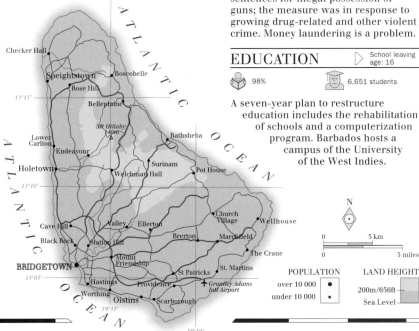

RESOURCES

Electric power 140,000 kw

3.300 tonnes

1246 b/d (reserves 5,892,000 bbl)

3.4m chickens, 41,000 sheep, 30,000 pigs

Oil, natural gas

Barbados has few strategic resources. The domestic petroleum industry provides about one-third of the country's energy requirements.

ENVIRONMENT

No Green MPs

Not available

Not available

Oil slicks created by waste dumped from passing ships are polluting the encircling reef and adversely affecting the life cycle of the flying fish, Barbados's main fish stock.

MEDIA

TV ownership high

Daily newspaper circulation 202 per 1,000 people

PUBLISHING AND BROADCAST MEDIA

There are 2 daily newspapers, the *Barbados Advocate* and the *Nation*

1 state-owned service

1 state-owned, 2 independent services

There is no political interference in the media in Barbados. The two daily newspapers are privately owned, as are two of the radio stations.

CRIME

Death penalty used

260 prisoners

Up 10% in 1991

A firearms amnesty announced in 1998 proposes heavy fines and prison sentences for illegal possession of guns; the measure was in response to growing drug-related and other violent crime. Money laundering is a problem.

EDUCATION

School leaving age: 16

98%

6,651 students

A seven-year plan to restructure education includes the rehabilitation of schools and a computerization program. Barbados hosts a campus of the University of the West Indies.

CHRONOLOGY

Colonized by the British in 1627, Barbados grew rich in the 18th century from sugar produced using slave labor.

- ❏ **1951** Universal adult suffrage introduced.
- ❏ **1961** Full internal self-government.
- ❏ **1966** Full independence from Britain.
- ❏ **1983** Supports and provides a base for the US invasion of Grenada.
- ❏ **1994–1999** The BLP wins two general elections.

HEALTH

Welfare state health benefits

1 per 885 people

Heart and cerebrovascular diseases, cancers

The health system is based on subsidized government-run clinics and hospitals, supplemented by more expensive private clinics and private doctors. Facilities are within easy reach of all Bajans.

SPENDING

GDP/cap.no increase

CONSUMPTION AND SPENDING

44 per 1,000 population

345 per 1,000 population

Defense 0.6%
Education 7.2%
Health 3.9%

0   5   10   15   20   25
Defense, Health, Education spending as % of GDP

A significant disparity exists between most Bajans and a small affluent group, usually of European origin, which owns and controls business and industry, and parades status symbols such as yachts. In 1998, Prime Minister Arthur stated that "abject poverty" existed in the country.

WORLD RANKING

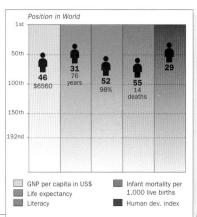

Position in World

1st
50th
100th — 46 ($6560), 31 (76 years), 52 (98%), 55 (14 deaths), 29
150th
192nd

- ◻ GNP per capita in US$
- ◻ Life expectancy
- ◻ Literacy
- ◻ Infant mortality per 1,000 live births
- ◻ Human dev. index

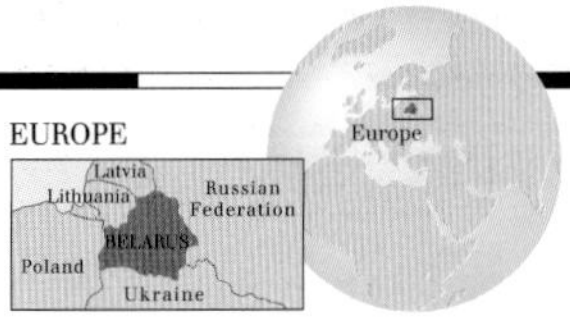

BELARUS (BELORUSSIA)

OFFICIAL NAME: Republic of Belarus **CAPITAL:** Minsk **POPULATION:** 10.3 million
CURRENCY: Belorussian rouble **OFFICIAL LANGUAGE:** Belorussian and Russian

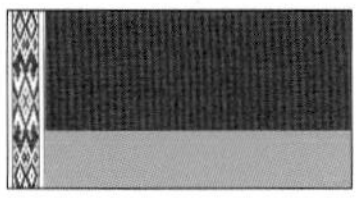

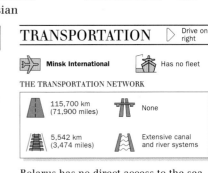

EUROPE

| 1991 | 1991 | July 3 | SU | +2 | +375 | .by |

FORMERLY KNOWN AS White Russia, Belarus is bordered by Lithuania and Latvia in the northwest, Ukraine in the south, and Poland and Russia in the west and east. The landlocked country, which reluctantly became independent of Moscow in 1991, has few resources other than agriculture. The Chornobyl' nuclear disaster in neighboring Ukraine in 1986 has had profound and lasting effects on the environment. The health of Belorussians has suffered severely and many areas are still contaminated.

TRANSPORTATION

▷ Drive on right

✈ **Minsk International**   🚢 Has no fleet

THE TRANSPORTATION NETWORK

| 🛣 115,700 km (71,900 miles) | None |
| �railway 5,542 km (3,474 miles) | Extensive canal and river systems |

Belarus has no direct access to the sea, but is close to the Baltic ports. Railroad communications are good.

TOURISM

▷ Visitors : population 1:41

🧳 250,000 visitors   ⇕ No significant change from year to year

MAIN OVERSEAS ARRIVALS

Russ Fed 48%	
Poland 13%	
Germany 5%	
UK 4%	
USA 3%	
Other 27%	

0   10   20   30   40   50   60
% of total arrivals

Belarus has fewer tourists than its Slav and Baltic neighbors. Many of its historic buildings were destroyed during World War II. Minsk was completely flattened, and is now characterized by Stalinist and high-rise buildings. There are few assets on which to build a tourist industry.

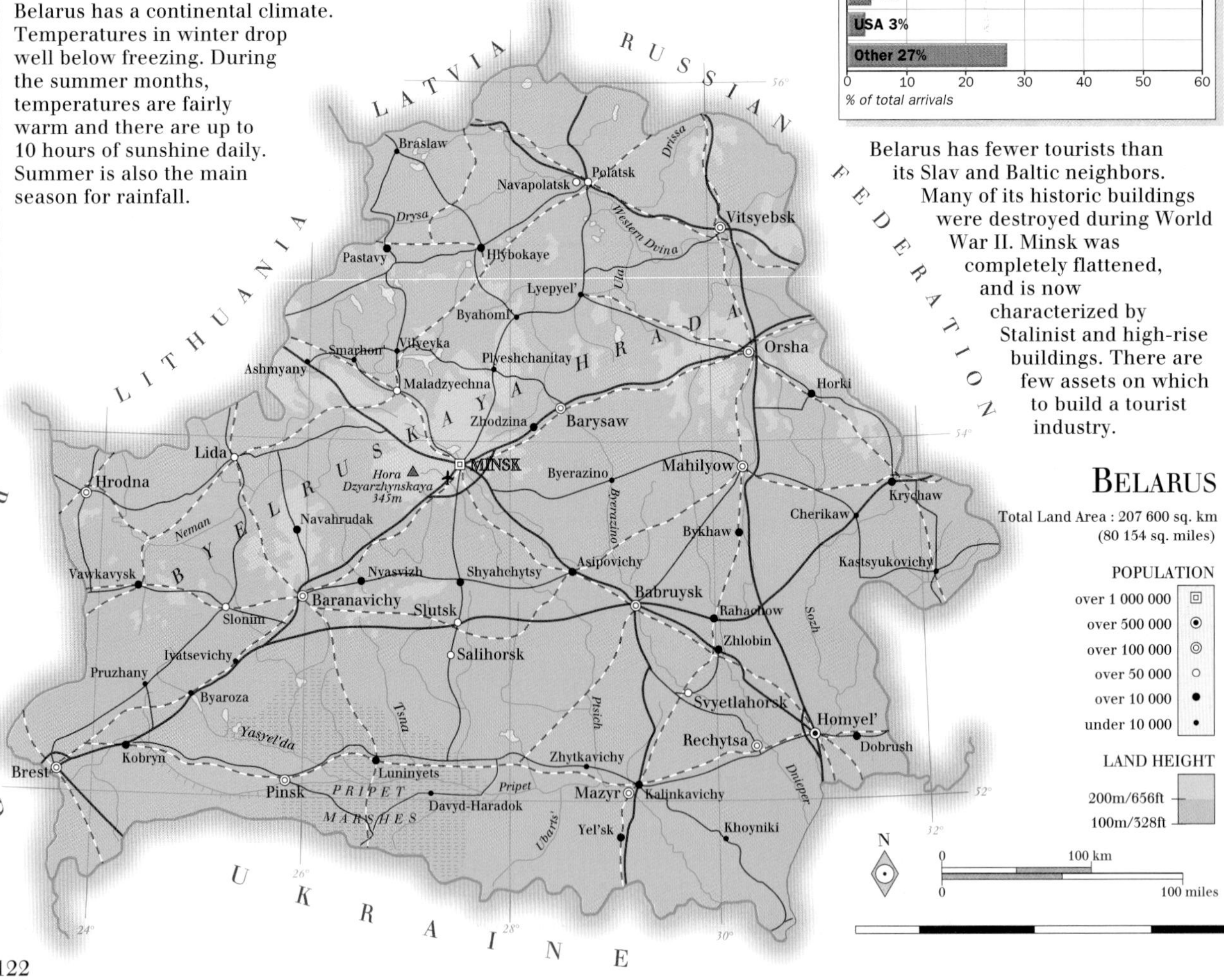

CLIMATE

▷ Continental

WEATHER CHART

■ Average daily temperature   Rainfall ■
°C/°F   cm/in
40/104   40/16
30/86   30/12
20/68   20/8
10/50   10/4
0/32   0
-10/14
-20/-4
        J F M A M J J A S O N D

Belarus has a continental climate. Temperatures in winter drop well below freezing. During the summer months, temperatures are fairly warm and there are up to 10 hours of sunshine daily. Summer is also the main season for rainfall.

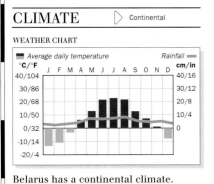

Much of southern Belarus is marshy and sparsely populated. It includes the vast Pripet Marshes and the Dnieper lowlands.

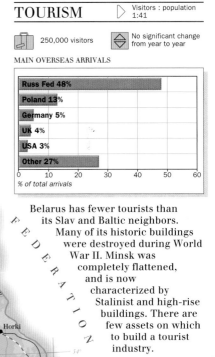

BELARUS

Total Land Area : 207 600 sq. km
(80 154 sq. miles)

POPULATION

over 1 000 000	▣
over 500 000	◉
over 100 000	◎
over 50 000	○
over 10 000	●
under 10 000	•

LAND HEIGHT

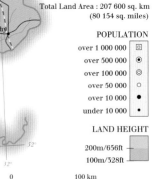

200m/656ft
100m/328ft

N

0   100 km
0   100 miles

B

PEOPLE

▷ Pop.density medium

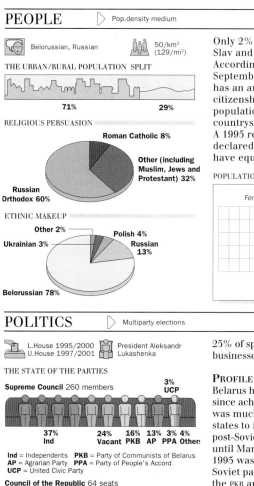

Belorussian, Russian

50/km²
(129/mi²)

THE URBAN/RURAL POPULATION SPLIT

71% 29%

RELIGIOUS PERSUASION

- Roman Catholic 8%
- Other (including Muslim, Jews and Protestant) 32%
- Russian Orthodox 60%

ETHNIC MAKEUP

- Other 2%
- Polish 4%
- Ukrainian 3%
- Russian 13%
- Belorussian 78%

Only 2% of the population is non-Slav and there is little ethnic tension. According to a law passed in late September 1992, the entire population has an automatic right to Belorussian citizenship. Only 11% of the population, most of whom live in the countryside, are fluent in Belorussian. A 1995 referendum and 1998 legislation declared that Belorussian and Russian have equal status.

POPULATION AGE BREAKDOWN

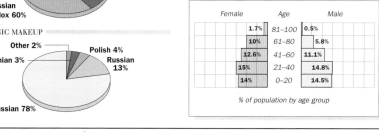

Female	Age	Male
1.7%	81–100	0.5%
10%	61–80	5.8%
12.6%	41–60	11.1%
15%	21–40	14.8%
14%	0–20	14.5%

% of population by age group

POLITICS

▷ Multiparty elections

L.House 1995/2000
U.House 1997/2001

President Aleksandr Lukashenka

THE STATE OF THE PARTIES

Supreme Council 260 members

3% UCP

37% Ind	24% Vacant	16% PKB	13% AP	3% PPA	4% Others

Ind = Independents **PKB** = Party of Communists of Belarus
AP = Agrarian Party **PPA** = Party of People's Accord
UCP = United Civic Party

Council of the Republic 64 seats

The Council of the Republic is indirectly elected

Under the 1994 constitution, amended in 1996, Belarus has a bicameral legislature.

MAIN POLITICAL ISSUES
Relationship with Russia

In April 1994 Belarus and Russia signed an accord to establish monetary union, and Aleksandr Lukashenka has, since his election as president in July 1994, sought ever closer relations with Russia. A union treaty, forming the Community of Sovereign Republics (CSR), was concluded in April 1996 and amplified a year later with pledges of future "voluntary unification."

The environment

The 1986 Chornobyl' nuclear disaster still casts a shadow over life in Belarus. The effects of the accident are still being revealed in high incidences of leukemia and cancers. Much of Belarus's land and farm produce is still tainted with fallout radiation. The cleanup operation is slow and laborious and will take decades. It is a major drain on finances, accounting for

25% of spending. A "Chornobyl' tax" on businesses is still levied.

PROFILE

Belarus has struggled to find an identity since achieving independence in 1991. It was much the slowest of the ex-Soviet states to implement political reform. A post-Soviet constitution was not adopted until March 1994, and only at the end of 1995 was the first fully fledged post-Soviet parliament elected, dominated by the PKB and its ally, the AP. There is no strong pluralist culture to check authoritarian moves by the president.

In a surprise victory, Aleksandr Lukashenka was elected as Belarus's first president in 1994, replacing the ex-communist Mechislau Grib as head of state. Since then Lukashenka has made clear his commitment to union with Russia. A referendum in November 1996 approved a new constitution significantly strengthening his powers and lengthening his term of office. Pro-Lukashenka deputies then voted to replace the Supreme Council with a new House of Representatives which has not, however, been recognized by international bodies such as the OSCE.

President Aleksandr Lukashenka seeks closer ties with the Russian Federation.

Chairman Stanislau Shushkevich, ousted in a vote of no-confidence in 1993.

WORLD AFFAIRS

▷ Joined UN in 1945

CE | CIS | IAEA | NACC | OSCE

Relations with Russia are paramount. Numerous bilateral agreements were signed after independence in 1991. Ties have been strengthened further by the pro-Russian president Aleksandr Lukashenka, although many in Russia are opposed to closer links with Belarus, believing that it represents a drain on Moscow's resources for little strategic gain.

Belarus's isolation was increased in mid-1998 when Lukashenka ordered the eviction of many diplomats from their official residences, an action which prompted the USA, the EU, and others to withdraw their ambassadors from Minsk.

AID

▷ Recipient

$43m (receipts)

Down 42% 1996–1997

Although both the World Bank and the IMF provided loans for Belarus in the early 1990s, the lack of structural reforms since Lukashenka's administration came to power in 1994 has meant that further aid has been stalled. However, economic problems eventually prompted the government to reopen talks with both bodies at the end of the decade.

The EU has extended some credits to Belarus to assist in the conversion of the defense industry to nonmilitary production. Belarus still requires aid to combat the effects of radiation pollution in the wake of the Chernobyl nuclear accident of 1986. Some help has been provided through the UK's Know-How Fund.

CHRONOLOGY

After forming part of medieval Kievan Rus, Belarus experienced rule by three of its neighbors – Poland, Lithuania, and Russia – before incorporation into the USSR.

❏ **1918** Belorussian Bolsheviks stage coup. Independence as Belorussian Soviet Socialist Republic.
❏ **1919** Invaded by Poland.
❏ **1920** Minsk retaken by Red Army. Eastern Belorussia reestablished as Soviet Socialist Republic (BSSR).
❏ **1921** Treaty of Riga – Western Belorussia incorporated into Poland.
❏ **1922** BSSR merges with Russian Federation to form USSR.
❏ **1929** Stalin implements collectivization of agriculture.
❏ **1959** Western Belorussia reincorporated into USSR when Soviet Red Army invades Poland. ▷

CHRONOLOGY *continued*

- ❏ **1941–1944** Belorussia occupied by Germany during World War II.
- ❏ **1945** Belorussia with Ukraine and USSR a founding member of UN.
- ❏ **1965** K. T. Mazurau, leader of Communist Party of Belorussia (PKB), becomes first deputy chair of USSR Council of Ministers.
- ❏ **1986** Accident at Chornobyl' nuclear power plant in Ukraine. Belorussia affected by 70% of plant's radioactive fallout.
- ❏ **1988** Archaeologist Zianon Pazniak reveals evidence of mass executions (over 300,000) by Soviet military between 1937 and 1941 in Kurapaty wood near Minsk. Popular outrage fuels formation of nationalist Belorussian Popular Front (BPF), with Pazniak as president. PKB authorities crush demonstration.
- ❏ **1989** Belorussian adopted as republic's official language.
- ❏ **1990** PKB prevents BPF participating in March elections to Supreme Soviet. BPF members join other opposition groups in Belorussian Democratic Bloc (BDB). BDB wins 25% of seats. July, PKB bows to opposition pressure and issues Declaration of the State Sovereignty of BSSR.
- ❏ **1991** March, 83% referendum vote to preserve union with USSR. April, strikes against PKB's economic policies. August, independence declared. Republic of Belarus adopted as official name. Stanislau Shushkevich elected chair of Supreme Soviet. December, Belarus, Russia, and Ukraine establish CIS.
- ❏ **1992** Supreme Soviet announces that Soviet nuclear weapons must be cleared from Belarus by 1999. Help promised from USA.
- ❏ **1993** Belorussian parliament ratifies START-I and nuclear nonproliferation treaties.
- ❏ **1994** Shushkevich replaced as chair of Supreme Soviet by pro-Russian former communist, Mechislau Grib. New presidential constitution approved. Surprise presidential election victory for Aleksandr Lukashenka over conservative prime minister Vyacheslav Kebich. Monetary union (reentry into ruble zone) agreed with Russia.
- ❏ **1995** First fully fledged post-Soviet parliament elected.
- ❏ **1996** Union treaty with Russia. Referendum approves constitutional changes strengthening Lukashenka's powers.
- ❏ **1997** Belarus and Russia ratify union treaty and Charter.
- ❏ **1998** Western ambassadors withdrawn over eviction from embassies.

DEFENSE

▷ Compulsory military service

💲 $381m   ⬇ Down 25% in 1997

Exports of conventional weapons were worth US$190 million in 1996.

BELARUS ARMED FORCES

1,778 main battle tanks (T–72, T–55, T–62)	43,000 personnel
None	
276 combat aircraft (129 Su–24, 82 Mig–29, 26 Su–27, 27 Mig–23)	22,700 personnel
None	

Under ex-chairman Shushkevich, Belarus adopted a policy of neutrality. By 1993 all tactical nuclear weapons were removed, as were strategic nuclear weapons by 1996. It is committed to destroying conventional arms under the 1990 Conventional Forces in Europe (CFE) Treaty.

In 1995 Belarus joined NATO's Partnerships for Peace program, but Lukashenka has not developed ties further, preferring to establish stronger military links with Moscow. Belarus now bears some of the costs of Russian troops stationed on its territory. The 1996 union treaty with Russia envisaged increased military cooperation and a shared military infrastructure.

ECONOMICS

▷ Inflation 867% p.a. (1992–1997)

📊 $22.1bn   💲 41,998–219,000 Belorussian roubles

SCORE CARD

- ❏ WORLD GNP RANKING.........................61st
- ❏ GNP PER CAPITA $2,150
- ❏ BALANCE OF PAYMENTS....................$–788m
- ❏ INFLATION 63.9%
- ❏ UNEMPLOYMENT............................ ....3%

ECONOMIC PERFORMANCE INDICATOR

EXPORTS

Germany 3% — Poland 3%
Ukraine 6%
Lithuania 2%
Other 21%
Russia 65%

IMPORTS

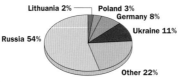

Lithuania 2% — Poland 3%
Germany 8%
Russia 54%
Ukraine 11%
Other 22%

STRENGTHS

Low unemployment of around 3% combined with high social stability. Increases in both industrial production and GDP in recent years. Potential of forestry and agriculture.

WEAKNESSES

Decision not to pursue economic restructuring; support for outmoded businesses. High inflation. Few natural resources. Dependence on Russia for energy. Cleanup costs of Chornobyl' drain finances.

PROFILE

After 1991, Belarus adopted a slower pace of economic reform than other ex-Soviet states. Chairman Shushkevich's attempts to move more quickly to a market economy were thwarted by the largely conservative parliament. Upon election in 1994 Lukashenka suspended privatization moves, resuming them only half-heartedly in 1995. Traditional industries continued to receive big subsidies, as the government printed money to increase production and reported 10% growth in 1997. However, this provoked a currency crisis in 1998, along with rampant inflation and rationing of subsidized cheap foods to prevent illegal exports.

BELARUS : MAJOR BUSINESSES

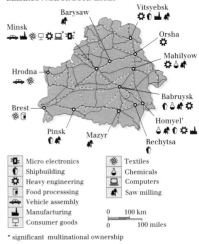

🔲 Micro electronics		🔥 Textiles
⚙ Shipbuilding		⚗ Chemicals
⚙ Heavy engineering		💻 Computers
▢ Food processsing		🔨 Saw milling
🚗 Vehicle assembly		
⚙ Manufacturing		
▢ Consumer goods		

0   100 km
0   100 miles

* significant multinational ownership

B

RESOURCES

Electric power
7.4m kw

5,100 tonnes

40,100 b/d

4.8m cattle,
3.7m pigs,
127,000 sheep

Natural gas, coal,
rock salt

ELECTRICITY GENERATION

Hydro 0%

Combustion 100% (24.8bn kwh)

Nuclear 0%

Other 0%

0   20   40   60   80   100

% of total generation by type

Belarus has no significant strategic
resources and is heavily dependent
on the Russian Federation for fuel
and energy supplies. Small quantities
of oil and natural gas exist close to
the Polish border.

BELARUS : LAND USE

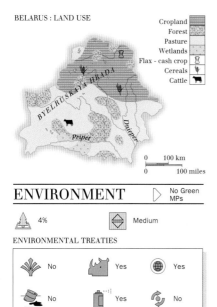

Cropland
Forest
Pasture
Wetlands
Flax - cash crop
Cereals
Cattle

0   100 km
0   100 miles

ENVIRONMENT

No Green
MPs

4%

Medium

ENVIRONMENTAL TREATIES

No   Yes   Yes

No   Yes   No

In 1986 a massive leak from Ukraine's
Chornobyl' nuclear reactor sent a huge
cloud of radiation into Belarus; 70% of
the fallout fell on 40% of the country,
including the capital Minsk; 2.3 million
people were immediately affected. The
government at the time kept the leak
secret. Farmland, forests, and water
were all contaminated, including
underwater streams feeding rivers in
eastern Poland.

Cases of leukemia and cancer are
continuing to increase. Some areas
in the fallout zone are still being
farmed; unscrupulous dealers are
suspected of selling meat meant for
destruction. A cleanup program is
under way, swallowing 25% of
government finances each year.
Belarus is seeking substantial Western
aid to cope with the problem.

MEDIA

TV ownership high

Daily newspaper circulation 174 per 1,000 people

PUBLISHING AND BROADCAST MEDIA

There are 8 daily newspapers, published
in Russian. Weekly newspapers are
published in Belorussian

1 state-controlled service;
there are a number of small
independent stations

1 state-controlled service;
someindependent stations

The media are under government
control. There is no independent TV and
those critical of the government face
constant harassment.

CRIME

Death penalty used

52,033 prisoners

Rising

CRIME RATES

Murders
Not available

Rapes
Not available

Thefts
Not available

As elsewhere in the former Soviet
Union, economic hardship and a
breakdown in law and order have
resulted in a significant rise in crime
both serious and petty. The prison
population of 60,000 is housed in
facilities designed for 40,000. Belarus
has become a transshipment point for
illegal narcotics, while locally produced
opium supplies the internal market.

EDUCATION

School leaving
age: 15

99%

328,750 students

Of total government expenditure just
over 17% is spent on education.

THE EDUCATION SYSTEM

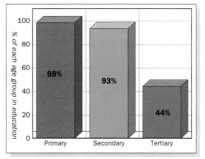

Russian is the main language of
instruction. Belorussian-language
school closures over the last five years
have resulted in a 60% drop in pupils
starting their education in Belorussian.
Universities are of a fairly high standard.

HEALTH

Welfare state health
benefits

1 per 244 people

Heart attacks,
cancers, accidents,
violence

Belarus's good health service was
placed under enormous strain after the
Chornobyl' nuclear disaster. The
number of cancer and leukemia cases
is currently 10,000 above the previous
annual average. More wards and
specialist units have had to be built.
Many Belorussian doctors are being
trained in the latest bone-marrow
techniques in Europe and the USA.

In 1998 more than 2,000 people in
Belarus were HIV-positive, over half
of whom lived in Svetlahorsk in
the Homel region.

SPENDING

GDP/cap. no increase

CONSUMPTION AND SPENDING

110 per 1,000
population

227 per 1,000
population

Defense 2.9%

Education 5.6%

Health 3.2%

0   5   10   15   20   25
Defense, Health, Education spending as % of GDP

The deteriorating economic situation
has resulted in an overall drop in living
standards. Rampant inflation
particularly affects people on fixed
incomes. Wealth is concentrated
among a small, communist elite
opposed to market mechanisms. Now
they have the upper hand, they have
strengthened their grip on the state's
resources. Thus far Belarus has not
seen the expansion of entrepreneurial
activity found in Poland or Russia.
Continued subsidies on foodstuffs have
resulted in prices 200–300% lower
than in Russia and Ukraine, spawning
widespread smuggling across
the border and the introduction of
food rationing in 1998.

WORLD RANKING

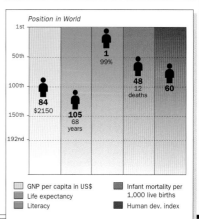

Position in World

1st

50th

1
99%

100th

84
$2150

48
12
deaths

60

105
68
years

150th

192nd

GNP per capita in US$

Life expectancy

Literacy

Infant mortality per
1,000 live births

Human dev. index

B

BELGIUM

OFFICIAL NAME: Kingdom of Belgium **CAPITAL:** Brussels
POPULATION: 10.2 million **CURRENCY:** Belgian franc **OFFICIAL LANGUAGE:** Flemish, French, and German

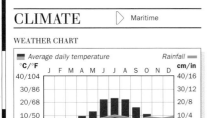

| 1830 | 1919 | July 21 | B | +1 | +32 | .be |

LOCATED BETWEEN GERMANY, France, and the Netherlands, Belgium has a short coastline on the North Sea. The south includes the forested Ardennes region, while the north is criss-crossed by canals. Belgium has been fought over many times in its history; it was occupied by Germany in both world wars. Long-standing tensions have existed between the majority Flemish and minority French-speakers since the 1830s. These have been somewhat defused by Belgium's move to a federal structure and the national consensus on the benefits of EU membership.

CLIMATE ▷ Maritime

WEATHER CHART

Belgium has a typical maritime climate and is influenced by the Gulf Stream. Temperatures are mild with heavy cloud cover and much rain. The west coast climate can be disrupted by widely fluctuating weather conditions, caused by cyclonic disturbances. Summers tend to be short.

TRANSPORTATION ▷ Drive on right

Zaventem International, Brussels
18m passengers

25 ships
115,800 grt

THE TRANSPORTATION NETWORK

| 333,300 km (207,100 miles) | 1,665 km (1,035 miles) |
| 3,422 km (2,126 miles) | 1,951 km (1,212 miles) |

Belgium can be crossed within four hours by car or train, and access to France, Germany, the Netherlands and beyond is easy. Belgium's expressway network is extensive and so well lit that, along with the Great Wall of China, it is the most distinctive sight from orbit. Although the railroad system has been reduced since 1970, it is still one of the world's densest networks. Using high-speed TGV lines, it is possible to reach Paris from Brussels in 1 hour 20 minutes and London via the Channel Tunnel in 2 hours 40 minutes. Antwerp, an old Hanseatic city, is Europe's second-largest port.

TOURISM ▷ Visitors : population 1:1.7

5.9m visitors

Up 13% 1995–1997

MAIN TOURIST ARRIVALS

| France 16% |
| Netherlands 15% |
| UK 15% |
| Germany 14% |
| USA 6% |
| Other 34% |

% of total arrivals

Belgium's main attractions are its historic cities and museums of Flemish art. Bruges, the capital of west Flanders, is often called the "Venice of the North." With unspoiled Renaissance architecture and a complex canal system, it has become a favored destination for British weekend visitors and Japanese honeymooners. In Brussels, the famous "Grand Place," a cluster of Gothic, Renaissance and Baroque buildings in a cobbled square, survived bombing during World War II. Much of the rest of the old city center, however, was destroyed. Belgium has 15 resorts on its 62-km (38-mile) coastline, with a single tramline running its entire length. Forests in the Ardennes to the south attract hikers.

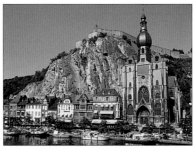

The Ardennes, in the southeast, are famous for their forests, cuisine and lakes. Rivers, such as the Meuse and Semois, dissect the region.

PEOPLE ▷ Pop. density high

Flemish, French, German, Dutch

311/km² (805/mi²)

THE URBAN/RURAL POPULATION SPLIT

97%   3%

RELIGIOUS PERSUASION

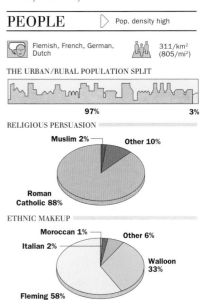

Muslim 2%
Other 10%
Roman Catholic 88%

ETHNIC MAKEUP

Moroccan 1%
Italian 2%
Other 6%
Walloon 33%
Fleming 58%

Belgian history has been marked by the divisions between its Flemish and French-speaking communities. Flemish speakers, who are a majority, are concentrated in Flanders. Wallonia is French-speaking and Brussels is 85% francophone. French-speakers were in the ascendancy for many years, since they controlled the profitable coal and steel industries in Wallonia. Their greater economic wealth was reinforced by a constitution which gave them political control. Tensions between Walloons and Flemings occasionally erupted into violence. However, in the past two decades, the position of the two communities has been reversed. Wallonia's industries have declined and Flanders is now the wealthier region. To contain tensions, Belgium began to change in 1980 from the most centralist to the most federal state in Europe; both communities now have their own governments and control most of their own affairs.

Belgium has a sizeable immigrant population. Women gained the vote in 1948. They account for 40% of the workforce and 19% of administrators.

POPULATION AGE BREAKDOWN

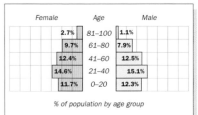

Female	Age	Male
2.7%	81–100	1.1%
9.7%	61–80	7.9%
12.4%	41–60	12.5%
14.6%	21–40	15.1%
11.7%	0–20	12.3%

% of population by age group

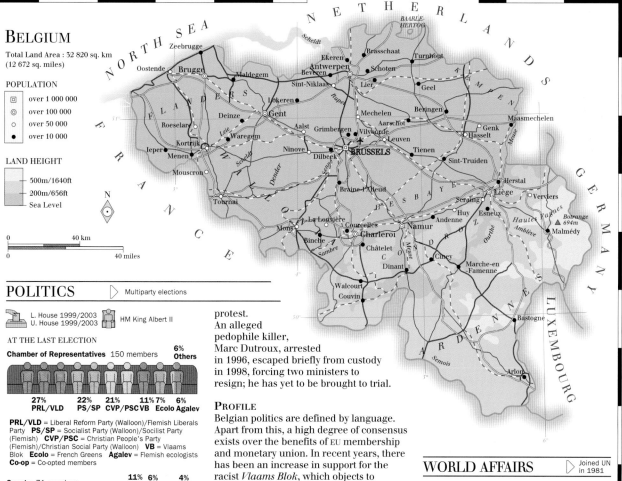

BELGIUM

Total Land Area : 32 820 sq. km
(12 672 sq. miles)

POPULATION

▣	over 1 000 000
◉	over 100 000
○	over 50 000
●	over 10 000

LAND HEIGHT

500m/1640ft
200m/656ft
Sea Level

N

0		40 km
0		40 miles

POLITICS ▷ Multiparty elections

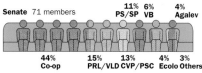

L. House 1999/2003
U. House 1999/2003

HM King Albert II

AT THE LAST ELECTION

Chamber of Representatives 150 members

27% PRL/VLD	22% PS/SP	21% CVP/PSC	11% VB	7% Ecolo	6% Agalev	6% Others

PRL/VLD = Liberal Reform Party (Walloon)/Flemish Liberals Party **PS/SP** = Socialist Party (Walloon)/Socilist Party (Flemish) **CVP/PSC** = Christian People's Party (Flemish)/Christian Social Party (Walloon) **VB** = Vlaams Blok **Ecolo** = French Greens **Agalev** = Flemish ecologists **Co-op** = Co-opted members

Senate 71 members

44% Co-op	15% PRL/VLD	13% CVP/PSC	11% PS/SP	6% VB	4% Ecolo	4% Agalev	3% Others

The Senate has 40 directly elected members and 31 co-opted members.

Until 1970, Belgium was a unitary state. Tensions between language groups led to four waves of federalist reforms from 1980, which culminated in the St. Michel Accords of 1993, confirming the state as a federal monarchy.

MAIN POLITICAL ISSUES
Language
Tensions between the two language groups are receding. However, the divisions remain strong. Each community has a Socialist Party (the PS in Wallonia, the SP in Flanders), and the Liberals are split into the francophone PRL and Flemish VLD. Under the premiership of Jean-Luc Dehaene, the four parties have worked in an uneasy coalition.

Handling of pedophile case
Apparent police incompetence, cover-ups and corruption in combating pedophile rings has provoked public anger and protest.
An alleged pedophile killer, Marc Dutroux, arrested in 1996, escaped briefly from custody in 1998, forcing two ministers to resign; he has yet to be brought to trial.

PROFILE
Belgian politics are defined by language. Apart from this, a high degree of consensus exists over the benefits of EU membership and monetary union. In recent years, there has been an increase in support for the racist *Vlaams Blok*, which objects to Belgium's Turkish and Moroccan minorities. *Vlaams Blok* secured 27.6% of Antwerp's vote in 1995.

The St. Michel Accords of 1993 gave the three regional governments, Flanders, Wallonia, and Brussels, significant powers under a federal government. Most of the population sees this as the best system to cope with the country's diversities.

Public disillusionment with the government, a centrist coalition of the four Socialist and Christian Democrat parties, accompanied the uncovering of corruption and murder by government members, the incompetent handling of the Dutroux affair, and, most recently, a political scandal over contaminated animal feed. It culminated in the government's 1999 electoral defeat

King Albert II, *who succeeded his father King Baudouin who died in 1993.*

Jean-Luc Dehaene, *premier until 1999, led the Christian People's Party (CVP).*

WORLD AFFAIRS ▷ Joined UN in 1981

Benelux	CE	EU	OECD	NATO

Belgium's key concern is its role in the EU. It is a keen supporter of economic and monetary union. As a frequent victim of wars between France and Germany, Belgium sees the EU as a guarantor of western European peace. It is also perceived as an important foundation for Belgium's own federalist structure, without which many fear that Belgium could split into two.

Belgium has little in the way of an independent foreign policy, but does frequently contribute troops to UN operations. Belgian soldiers have served in Bosnia and Somalia in recent years and a number were killed in Rwanda in 1994 during ethnic violence.

AID ▷ Donor

$808m (donations)   Not applicable

In 1997, overseas development aid was about 0.31% of GNP. Aid focuses on education and agricultural projects in Africa. The major beneficiaries are the former colonies of Rwanda and Democratic Republic of Congo. Bolivia is also an aid recipient.

CHRONOLOGY

Formerly ruled by the French dukes of Burgundy, Belgium became a Habsburg possession in 1477. It passed to the Austrian Habsburgs in 1700. Napoleon ended Austrian rule of the Low Countries in 1797.

❏ **1814–1815** Congress of Vienna; European powers decide to merge Belgium with the Netherlands under King William I of Orange.

❏ **1830** Revolt against Dutch; declaration of independence.

❏ **1831** European powers place Leopold Saxe Coburg as king.

❏ **1865** Leopold II crowned king.

❏ **1885** Berlin Conference gives Leopold Congo basin as colony.

❏ **1914** German armies invade. Leopold II declares war on Germany. Germans occupy Belgium until 1918.

❏ **1921** Belgo-Luxembourg Economic Union formed. Belgian and Luxembourg currencies locked.

❏ **1932** Flemish language accorded equal official status with French.

❏ **1936** Belgium declares neutrality.

❏ **1940** Leopold III capitulates to Hitler. Belgium occupied until 1944.

❏ **1948** Customs union with Netherlands and Luxembourg (BENELUX).

❏ **1950** King wins referendum but rumors over his wartime collaboration persist. Abdicates in favor of his son, Baudouin.

❏ **1957** Signs Treaty of Rome as one of six founding members of EEC.

❏ **1992** Christian-Democrat–Socialist government led by Jean-Luc Dehaene takes over federal government.

❏ **1993** Culmination of reforms creating federal state. Greater powers for regions and city governments. Death of Baudouin. Succeeded by Albert II.

❏ **1995** Allegations of corruption and murder involving French-speaking PS force resignations of Walloon premier, federal deputy premier, and Willy Claes as NATO secretary-general.

❏ **1995** General election returns Dehaene administration to power.

❏ **1996** Accusations of incompetence, even collusion, of authorities, amid fears about pedophile rings.

❏ **1998** Claes and 11 others found guilty of bribery.

❏ **1999** January, Belgium among first 11 EU member countries to introduce euro. June, government defeat in elections following contaminated animal feed scandal.

DEFENSE

▷ No compulsory military service

💲 $3.8bn   ⬇ Down 13% in 1997

Exports of conventional weapons were worth $110 million in 1996.

BELGIAN ARMED FORCES

🪖	155 main battle tanks (132 *Leopard* 1A5, 23 *Leopard* 1A1)	28,250 personnel
🚢	3 frigates	2,600 personnel
✈	100 combat aircraft (F–16A, F–16B)	11,600 personnel
🚀	None	

At 1.6% of GDP in 1997, Belgium spends less on defense than the NATO average of 2.2%, although NATO headquarters are based in Brussels. In 1994, as part of Belgium's program to reduce government debt, all three military services were targeted for cuts. The government abolished conscription and cut troop levels. The defense budget was frozen for five years.

Spending on paratroopers and transport planes has increased, however. The aim is to allow Belgian forces to fulfill their role in NATO's new rapid reaction forces. It will also make Belgian forces more useful to the UN's worldwide operations.

ECONOMICS

▷ Inflation 2.9% p.a. (1985–1996)

📊 $272bn   💲 37.05–34.35 Belgian francs

SCORE CARD

❏ WORLD GNP RANKING...........................19th
❏ GNP PER CAPITA $26,730
❏ BALANCE OF PAYMENTS.......................$14bn
❏ INFLATION 1.6%
❏ UNEMPLOYMENT.................................13%

EXPORTS

Italy 5%
UK 10%
Other 38%
Netherlands 12%
France 16%
Germany 19%

IMPORTS

USA 7%
UK 9%
Other 36%
France 13%
Netherlands 17%
Germany 18%

ECONOMIC PERFORMANCE INDICATOR

— Consumer price index   GDP ▨

Consumer price index 1990=100 / *GDP 1993=100* — chart for 1993, 1994, 1995, 1996, 1997 (scale 80–160)

PROFILE

Recession and rising unemployment in the early 1990s prompted the introduction of work-sharing schemes, benefit reforms, and a 1998 two-year, sectorally differentiated pay accord. Unemployment has now begun to fall. Progress in reducing Belgium's massive public debt allowed the country to join the euro from 1999, but it remains almost double the EU target of 60% of GDP.

STRENGTHS

One of world's most efficient producers of metal products and textiles. Flanders is a world leader in new high-tech industries. Successful chemicals industry. Highly educated and motivated multilingual workforce: estimates suggest productivity is 20% above that of Germany. Location makes Belgium an attractive location for US multinationals. Good sea outlets and access to Rhine inland waterway from Antwerp and Ghent.

WEAKNESSES

Public debt of 116% of GDP, well over the EU target of 60%. High long-term and low-skill joblessness with sharp local variations. Large numbers of workers retire early, resulting in high state pension bill. Larger bureaucracy than European average.

BELGIUM : MAJOR BUSINESSES

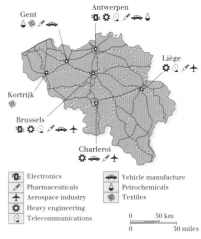

Gent
Antwerpen
Liège
Kortrijk
Brussels
Charleroi

Symbol	Business	Symbol	Business
🔲	Electronics	🚗	Vehicle manufacture
✒	Pharmaceuticals	⚗	Petrochemicals
✈	Aerospace industry	❋	Textiles
✿	Heavy engineering		
◷	Telecommunications		

0   50 km
0   50 miles

RESOURCES

▷ Electric power 14.9m kw

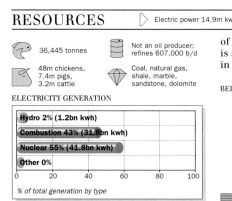

36,445 tonnes

Not an oil producer; refines 607,000 b/d

48m chickens, 7.4m pigs, 3.2m cattle

Coal, natural gas, shale, marble, sandstone, dolomite

ELECTRICITY GENERATION

Hydro 2% (1.2bn kwh)	
Combustion 43% (31.8bn kwh)	
Nuclear 55% (41.8bn kwh)	
Other 0%	

| 0 | 20 | 40 | 60 | 80 | 100 |

% of total generation by type

Belgium has few natural resources and depends largely on the export of goods and services. The once-rich coal mines of Wallonia are almost depleted. There is some deciduous and conifer forestry in the Ardennes region.

BELGIUM : LAND USE

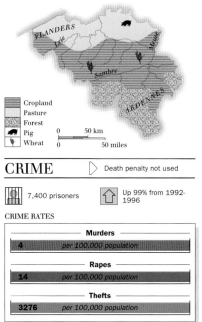

Cropland
Pasture
Forest
Pig
Wheat

0 50 km
0 50 miles

ENVIRONMENT

▷ Green MPs

2.5%

High

ENVIRONMENTAL TREATIES

Yes		Yes		Yes	
Yes		Yes		Yes	

The regional government of Flanders is concerned about the pollution of its groundwater supplies through acid rain, heavy metals, fertilizers and pesticides. It is operating an environmental management plan to meet prescribed standards. Wallonia has initiated strict laws to prevent the illegal tipping of waste, and is also governing air quality and emissions. The population's growing awareness of environmental issues is reflected in the rise of the two Green Parties.

MEDIA

▷ TV ownership high

Daily newspaper circulation 160 per 1,000 people

PUBLISHING AND BROADCAST MEDIA

	There are 30 daily newspapers published in French, Flemish and German
	3 state-owned, 3 independent services
	3 state-owned, numerous independent

Newspapers tend to be regional and divided by language. Circulation is low, with the most widely read newspaper having a circulation of only 370,000. Over 80% of Belgians have cable TV, receiving as many as 30 channels from all over Europe. Commercial TV only began in 1989, with the Flemish station VTM showing imported English-language programs and game shows.

CRIME

▷ Death penalty not used

7,400 prisoners

Up 99% from 1992-1996

CRIME RATES

Murders
4   per 100,000 population

Rapes
14   per 100,000 population

Thefts
3276   per 100,000 population

The establishment has been shaken by alleged incompetence in the investigation of a pedophile ring led by Marc Dutroux, who was arrested in 1996 but has yet to be brought to trial.

EDUCATION

▷ School leaving age: 18

99%

352,630 students

Of total government expenditure just over 10% is spent on education.

THE EDUCATION SYSTEM

% of each age group in education

Primary	Secondary	Tertiary
98%	99%	54%

Since 1959 parents have been able to choose between secular and religious schooling. Since 1989 the system has been administered by the governments of the two main language groups. Education in Flanders is in Dutch, while Wallonia teaches in French. All universities are split by language.

HEALTH

▷ Welfare state health benefits

1 per 270 people

Heart and respiratory diseases, cancers, accidents

Of total government expenditure just over 12% is spent on health.

The quality of health care in Belgium is among the best in the world. Belgium is a world leader in fertility treatment and heart and lung transplants. Treatment is not free, but Belgians hold insurance enabling them to claim up to 75% of their costs. Car accidents are second only to heart disease and cancer as a cause of death; 62,000 accidents resulted in personal injury in 1990.

In 1997, there were more than 10,000 registered AIDS patients.

SPENDING

▷ GDP/cap. increase

CONSUMPTION AND SPENDING

433 per 1,000 population

468 per 1,000 population

Defense 1.6%	
Education 5.7%	
Health 8.1%	

| 0 | 5 | 10 | 15 | 20 | 25 |

Defense, Health, Education spending as % of GDP

Despite high levels of state debt and failing traditional industries, Belgium is one of Europe's richest countries. At $26,400, GDP per capita is lower than for Germany but higher than for Italy or the UK. This masks considerable regional differences. In Flanders, a proliferation of high-tech businesses results in an unemployment rate of just 8%, while in Wallonia 17% are out of work. The presence of highly paid EU and international bank employees has made Brussels a distinctly wealthy and prosperous city. Recession in the early 1990s prompted Belgians to save some 20% of their income, but savings have fallen since then to 15% in 1998, as consumer confidence has recovered.

WORLD RANKING

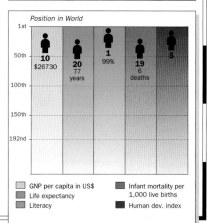

Position in World

1st
50th
100th
150th
192nd

| 10 $26730 | 20 77 years | 1 99% | 19 6 deaths | 5 |

GNP per capita in US$
Life expectancy
Literacy

Infant mortality per 1,000 live births
Human dev. index

BELIZE

OFFICIAL NAME: Belize   **CAPITAL:** Belmopan
POPULATION: 200,000   **CURRENCY:** Belizean dollar   **OFFICIAL LANGUAGE:** English

| 1981 | 1981 | Sept 21 | BH | -6 | +501 | .bz |

FORMERLY CALLED BRITISH HONDURAS, Belize was the last Central American country to gain its independence, in 1981. It lies on the eastern shore of the Yucatan peninsula and shares a border with Mexico along the River Hondo. Belize is Central America's least populous country, and almost one-half of its land area is still forested. Its swampy coastal plains are protected from flooding by the world's second-largest barrier reef.

Small fishing village near Belize City. More than 500 tonnes of Caribbean spiny lobster, the main inshore species, are caught every year.

CLIMATE

▷ Tropical equatorial

WEATHER CHART

■ Average daily temperature   Rainfall ■

Conditions are hot and humid throughout the year. Coastal regions are affected by hurricanes.

TRANSPORTATION

▷ Drive on right

Philip S W Goldson, Belize City
272,000 passengers

27 ships
430,00 grt

THE TRANSPORTATION NETWORK

| 1,419 km (882 miles) | None |
| None | 825 km (513 miles) |

A $16 million IDB loan in 1998 is for highway and feeder road improvements. A new terminal and runway extension have been completed at the international airport near Belize City.

TOURISM

▷ Visitors : population 1:1.4

146,000 visitors

Down 59% in 1997

MAIN TOURIST ARRIVALS

Guatemala 38%	
USA 29%	
Mexico 13%	
Other 20%	

% of total arrivals

Very significant natural resources, Mayan ruins and nature reserves. Ecotourism is strongly promoted.

PEOPLE

▷ Pop. density low

English Creole, Spanish, English, Maya, Garifuna (Carib)

9/km² (23/mi²)

THE URBAN/RURAL POPULATION SPLIT

47%   53%

ETHNIC MAKEUP

- Other 4%
- Asian Indian 4%
- Garifuna 7%
- Maya 11%
- Creole 30%
- Mestizo 44%

Some 40% of people trace part of their roots to Africans brought over in the 17th century; the rest are composed of Maya groups, black Caribs (Garifuna), and immigrants from Mexico, Guatemala, the Middle East, India, and south Asia. Communities of Swiss-descended Mennonites exist.

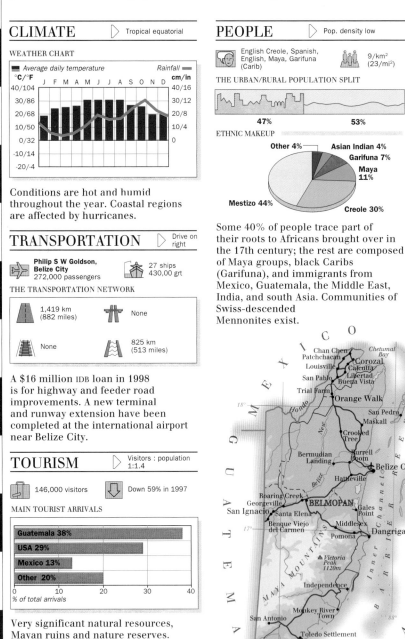

POLITICS

▷ Multiparty elections

L. House 1998/2003
U. House 1998/2003

HM Queen Elizabeth II

AT THE LAST ELECTION

House of Representatives 29 members

90% PUP   10% UDP

PUP = People's United Party
UDP = United Democratic Party

Senate 8 members

The members of the Senate are appointed by the governor-general.

The desire for independence dominated politics until the 1980s. The PUP, under George Price, negotiated this with the British in 1981. During the 1984–1989 UDP administration, maintaining a pro-US line and fears of communism in the region were the main concerns. In the absence of any major ideological or policy distinctions, the UDP lost power to the PUP in 1989, winning it back in 1993; the pendulum swung back to the PUP again in 1998. Growth, job creation, "economic citizenship" for foreigners, and border tension with Guatemala remain key issues, as does political reform.

BELIZE

Total Land Area : 22 800 sq. km (8803 sq. miles)

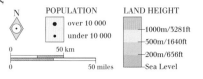

POPULATION
● over 10 000
• under 10 000

LAND HEIGHT
1000m/3281ft
500m/1640ft
200m/656ft
Sea Level

B

WORLD AFFAIRS

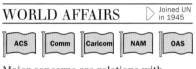

▷ Joined UN in 1945

Major concerns are relations with Guatemala and the right of the London-based Privy Council to grant stays of execution in murder cases.

AID

▷ Recipient

💲 US$14m (receipts)   ⬇ Down 22% 1996–1997

In 1999 the IDB, the Commonwealth Development Corporation, the European Investment Bank and the CDB invested in citrus farms. Belize is one of the highest per capita recipients of US aid.

DEFENSE

▷ No compulsory military service

💲 US$16m   ⬆ Up 7% in 1997

The 1,000-strong Belize Defense Force includes two female platoons and is trained by the UK, the USA and Canada. As a result of Guatemala dropping its territorial claim, the UK withdrew its military garrison in 1994.

ECONOMICS

▷ Inflation 4% p.a. (1985–1996)

📊 US$614m   💲 2.00 Belizean dollars

SCORE CARD

❏ WORLD GNP RANKING	162nd
❏ GNP PER CAPITA	US$2,670
❏ BALANCE OF PAYMENTS	US$–40m
❏ INFLATION	1%
❏ UNEMPLOYMENT	13%

STRENGTHS
Sugar, textile manufacture, citrus fruits, bananas, cocoa, forestry and considerable tourist potential. Sustainable public debt; fair access to concessionary foreign finance.

WEAKNESSES
Narrow export base dependent on preferential market access; reliance on imports of processed foods. Poor fiscal management in recent years.

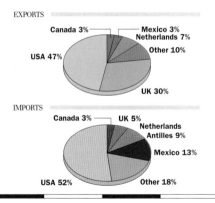

EXPORTS

Canada 3% Mexico 3% Netherlands 7% Other 10% USA 47% UK 30%

IMPORTS

Canada 3% UK 5% Netherlands Antilles 9% Mexico 13% USA 52% Other 18%

RESOURCES

▷ Electric power 23,000 kw

🐟 2,179 tonnes   🛢 Not an oil producer

60,000 cattle, 23,000 pigs, 5,000 horses, 4,400 mules   💎 None

Exploration for oil and gas, largely by US companies, is currently under way in the Corozal basin region.

ENVIRONMENT

▷ No Green MPs

🔺 5% partially protected   ⬍ Not available

Ecotourism and uncontrolled logging threaten tropical forests and wildlife habitats. Mahogany was listed internationally as endangered in 1995, meaning that exports and transshipments all require a certificate of origin.

MEDIA

▷ TV ownership medium

📄 There are no daily newspapers

PUBLISHING AND BROADCAST MEDIA

📰	There are no daily newspapers. The leading papers are the weekly *Belize Times*, the *People's Pulse* and the *Reporter*
📺	1 state-owned and 8 independent services
📻	1 state-owned and 4 independent services

Belize has not suffered the degree of press interference experienced in neighboring states, but successive governments have remained sensitive to even minor criticisms. The two radio stations of the public Broadcasting Corporation of Belize were sold in 1998 to two local stations, but the government has retained ownership of the broadcasting transmitters. Two newspapers support the UDP and one the PUP; one newspaper is independent.

CRIME

▷ Death penalty used

🔳 89 prisoners   ⬆ Increase in gun-related crime

Belize is a major transit point to the USA for cocaine, despite being decertified in 1997 for its anti-narcotics efforts. Drug-related crime is high. Armed robberies by criminal gangs based in neighboring Guatemala are a concern. Police brutality and corruption provoked an official investigation of the force in 1999.

EDUCATION

▷ School leaving age: 14

75%   🎓 9,457 students

Belize's schools are administered by its three main religious denominations: Roman Catholics, Anglicans and Methodists. University College of Belize maintains close links with the University of Michigan, USA.

HEALTH

▷ No welfare state health benefits

👤 1 per 2,128 people   ☠ Respiratory, heart and cerebrovascular diseases

Around 75% of Belizeans have access to government health services, which include seven hospitals and numerous mobile clinics. Sanitation and water supplies have been improved; most homes in Belmopan now have both.

SPENDING

▷ GDP/cap. no increase

CONSUMPTION AND SPENDING

🚗 20 per 1,000 population   📞 134 per 1,000 population

Defense	2.6%
Education	6.1%
Health	2.2%

Defense, Health, Education spending as % of GDP

The European Development Fund granted Bz$3.5 million in 1999 for the reduction of rural poverty. Narcotics trading remains a source of wealth.

WORLD RANKING

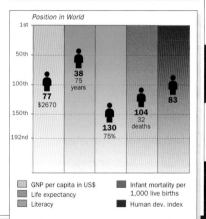

Position in World

	GNP per capita in US$	Life expectancy	Infant mortality per 1,000 live births	Literacy	Human dev. index
	77 $2670	38 75 years	130 75%	104 32 deaths	83

GNP per capita in US$ Life expectancy Literacy Infant mortality per 1,000 live births Human dev. index

BENIN

B

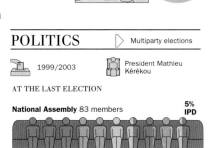

WEST AFRICA

OFFICIAL NAME: Republic of Benin   **CAPITAL:** Porto-Novo
POPULATION: 5.9 million   **CURRENCY:** CFA franc   **OFFICIAL LANGUAGE:** French

| 1960 | 1960 | Nov 30 | DY | +1 | +229 | .bj |

BENIN STRETCHES NORTH from the West African coast, with a 100-km (62-mile) shoreline on the Bight of Benin. Formerly the kingdom of Dahomey, Benin became a French protectorate and then a part of colonial French West Africa. It gained independence in 1960. In 1990, Benin became a pioneer of African multipartyism, ending 17 years of one-party Marxist-Leninist rule. Benin's economy is based on a well-diversified agricultural sector.

CLIMATE

▷ Tropical wet & dry

WEATHER CHART

■ Average daily temperature   Rainfall ■

°C/°F   J F M A M J J A S O N D   cm/in
40/104 .... 40/16
30/86 .... 30/12
20/68 .... 20/8
10/50 .... 10/4
0/32 0
-10/14
-20/-4

There are two rainy seasons. The hot, dusty *harmattan* wind characterizes the December to February dry season.

TRANSPORTATION

▷ Drive on right

Cotonou Cadjehoun
321,741 passengers

8 ships
1,200 grt

THE TRANSPORTATION NETWORK

| 16,000 km (9,900 miles) | None |
| 579 km (360 miles) | None |

The joint Benin–Niger railroad runs only as far as Parakou. The Cotonou to Porto Novo line reopened in 1999.

TOURISM

▷ Visitors : population 1:39

150,000 visitors

Up 9% 1995–1997

MAIN TOURIST ARRIVALS

Europe 56%	
Africa 42%	
North America 1%	
Other 1%	

0 10 20 30 40 50 60
% of total arrivals

Tourism is not well developed, although there are plans to develop package tourism. There is some safari tourism in the north, particularly in the Atakora Mountains. Benin is popular as a weekend break for visitors to Nigeria.

PEOPLE

▷ Pop. density medium

Fon, Bariba, Yoruba, Adja, Houeda, Somba, French

53/km²
(138/mi²)

THE URBAN/RURAL POPULATION SPLIT

31%   69%

RELIGIOUS PERSUASION

Christian 15%
Muslim 15%
Indigenous beliefs 70%

Benin is politically dominated by the southern Fon people. There is some north-south tension, partly because the south is more developed, and partly reflecting a Muslim-Christian divide. Women hold positions of power in the retail trade.

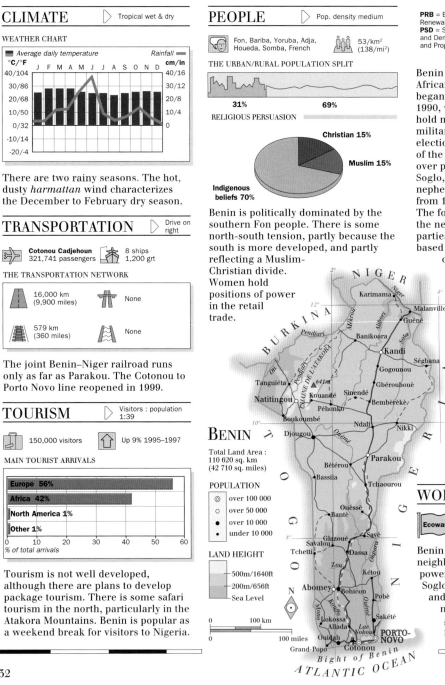

BENIN

Total Land Area :
110 620 sq. km
(42 710 sq. miles)

POPULATION
◎ over 100 000
○ over 50 000
● over 10 000
• under 10 000

LAND HEIGHT
500m/1640ft
200m/656ft
Sea Level

0 ——— 100 km
0 ——— 100 miles

POLITICS

▷ Multiparty elections

1999/2003

President Mathieu Kérékou

AT THE LAST ELECTION

National Assembly 83 members
5% IPD

33% PRB   19% Other   13% PRD   12% FARD   11% PSD   7% MADEP

PRB = Benin Renaissance Party   **PRD** = Party of Democratic Renewal   **FARD** = Action Front for Renewal and Development   **PSD** = Social Democrat Party   **IPD** = Impetus for Progress and Democracy   **MADEP** = African Movement for Democracy and Progress   **Other** = Other opposition Parties

Benin has been at the forefront of African democratization. This process began at the National Conference of 1990, when General Kérékou agreed to hold multiparty elections after years of military one-party rule. Following elections in 1991, Kérékou was the first of the African one-party leaders to hand over power peacefully. Nicéphore Soglo, a former World Bank official and nephew of General Soglo, who ruled from 1965 to 1967, became president. The former ruling party won no seats in the new parliament. The main political parties in Benin tend to be regionally based and depend on the leadership of locally influential individuals.

Politics in Benin is characterized by constantly changing alliances. Soglo did not have an automatic majority in parliament, and was forced to include opposition members in his government. The main issue became the effect on the economy of Soglo's World Bank-style deregulation. He was defeated in March 1996 in a controversial election which brought Kérékou back to power as president. Opposition parties gained a one-seat majority in the March 1999 legislative elections.

WORLD AFFAIRS

▷ Joined UN in 1960

| Ecowas | OAU | OIC | FZ | UEMOA |

Benin is largely dominated by its giant neighbor, Nigeria, by far the most powerful state in the region. President Soglo was a recent chairman of Ecowas and supports regional integration with neighboring countries. Continuing good relations with France, the main source of aid, is critical.

AID

▷ Recipient

$225m (receipts) ⬇ Down 23% 1996-1997

Benin's poverty is such that the maintenance of aid is at the top of the political agenda. France, the main protector of Benin's independence since 1960, is the major aid donor. Other donors include the World Bank and the IMF, the EU, Germany, Belgium, the Netherlands, Spain, and the USA. Almost all development finance comes from aid, and some has been used to finance debt-servicing. There is the usual problem of finding suitable projects, although Benin has a large, well-educated (if top-heavy) civil service, making implementation easier than in many parts of Africa.

DEFENSE

▷ Compulsory military service

$27m ⬍ No change in 1997

The 4,500-strong army is actively involved in the attempt to curb smuggling on the border with Nigeria. In 1989 the army was employed internally against rioters.

ECONOMICS

▷ Inflation 5.6% p.a. (1985–1996)

$2.2bn   601.60–558.62 CFA francs

SCORE CARD

❑ WORLD GNP RANKING	133rd
❑ GNP PER CAPITA	$380
❑ BALANCE OF PAYMENTS	$36m
❑ INFLATION	3.5%
❑ UNEMPLOYMENT	Widespread underemployment

STRENGTHS
Agriculture-based economy, with good product diversification. Long-overdue devaluation of CFA franc in January 1994 made exports more competitive.

WEAKNESSES
Large-scale smuggling. Power failures caused by drought brought major economic problems in 1998, and resultant slowdown in GDP growth. Top-heavy civil service.

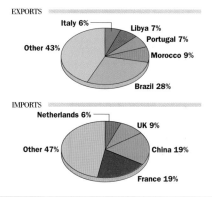

EXPORTS

Italy 6%
Libya 7%
Portugal 7%
Morocco 9%
Other 43%
Brazil 28%

IMPORTS

Netherlands 6%
UK 9%
China 19%
Other 47%
France 19%

Flat landscape near Cotonou, characteristic of Benin's coastal region. Numerous lagoons lie behind its short, 100-km coastline.

RESOURCES

▷ Electric power 15,000 kw

44,500 tonnes

5975 b/d (reserves 19,900,000 bbl)

1.4m cattle, 1m goats, 605,000 sheep

Oil, limestone, marble, gold

Since 1988 most electricity – which previously had to be imported from Ghana – has been generated by the Nangbeto Dam on the River Mono.

ENVIRONMENT

▷ No Green MPs

🌲 7%   ⬇ Low

Desertification in the north is the major problem. Benin has been used in the past as a dumping ground for toxic waste.

MEDIA

▷ TV ownership medium

Daily newspaper circulation 2 per 1,000 people

PUBLISHING AND BROADCAST MEDIA

There is 1 daily newspaper, *Ehuzu*

1 state-owned service, 1 independent

1 state-owned service, 3 independent

Benin has 65 newspapers and periodicals. There are both state-run and privately-owned radio and TV stations.

CRIME

▷ Death penalty used

Benin does not publish prison figures ⬇ Down 26% 1992–1996

There has been a serious upsurge in armed crime since 1995, despite the reintroduction of the death penalty. Smuggling is a major problem, along the border with Nigeria.

EDUCATION

▷ School leaving age: 11

34%   🎓 14,055 students

More is spent on education than on defense, and this is reinforced by Benin's active intellectual community, the "Latin Quarter of Africa." The university at Abomey-Calavi is rated highly in medicine and law.

HEALTH

▷ No welfare state health benefits

1 per 10,000 people

Communicable and diarrheal diseases, malaria

Outside major towns, health services are scarce. It is forecast that one million people will die of AIDS in Benin by 2030.

SPENDING

▷ GDP/cap. increase

CONSUMPTION AND SPENDING

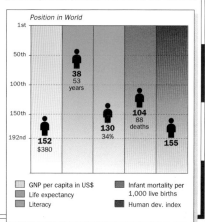

7 per 1,000 population

6 per 1,000 population

Defense 1.3%
Education 3.1%
Health 1.5%

0   5   10   15   20   25
Defense, Health, Education spending as % of GDP

Substantial differences in wealth reflect the strongly hierarchical nature of society, especially in the south. French cars are considered to be status symbols.

WORLD RANKING

Position in World

1st
50th
100th
150th
192nd

38
53 years

152
$380

130
34%

104
88 deaths

155

❑ GNP per capita in US$
❑ Life expectancy
❑ Literacy
❑ Infant mortality per 1,000 live births
❑ Human dev. index

BHUTAN

B

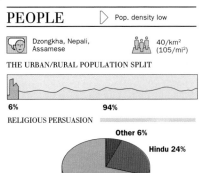

OFFICIAL NAME: Kingdom of Bhutan **CAPITAL:** Thimphu
POPULATION: 1.9 million **CURRENCY:** Ngultrum **OFFICIAL LANGUAGE:** Dzongkha

| 1656 | 1865 | Dec 17 | BHT | +6 | +975 | .bt |

PERCHED IN THE HIMALAYAS between India and China, Bhutan is 70% forested. The land rises from the low, tropical southern strip, through the fertile central valleys, to the high Himalayas, inhabited by seminomadic yak herders. Formally a Buddhist state where power is shared by the king and government, Bhutan began modernizing in the 1960s, but has chosen to do so gradually and remains largely closed to the outside world.

CLIMATE ▷ Mountain

WEATHER CHART

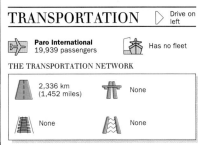

The south is tropical, the north alpine, cold and harsh. The central valleys are warmer in the east than in the west. The summer monsoon affects all parts.

TRANSPORTATION ▷ Drive on left

✈ **Paro International** 19,939 passengers   ⚓ Has no fleet

THE TRANSPORTATION NETWORK

| 🛣 2,336 km (1,452 miles) | 🛤 None |
| 🚆 None | ⛴ None |

The main surfaced road runs east–west across central Bhutan. Two others run south into India. Only the national airline, *Druk Air*, flies into Bhutan.

TOURISM ▷ Visitors : population 1:380

🧳 5,000 visitors   ⬆ Up 25% in 1997

MAIN TOURIST ARRIVALS

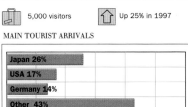

Tourism is restricted to protect Bhutan's culture and natural environment; entry has been easier since the industry was privatized in 1991. Most monasteries are closed to tourists. In 1998 fire damaged the famous Taktsang monastery.

Less than 10% of Bhutan is arable, but its fertility allows almost any crop to grow. The diversity of wild plant species inspired its old name: Southern Valleys of the Medicinal Herbs.

PEOPLE ▷ Pop. density low

Dzongkha, Nepali, Assamese   40/km² (105/mi²)

THE URBAN/RURAL POPULATION SPLIT

6%   94%

RELIGIOUS PERSUASION

Other 6%
Hindu 24%
Mahayana Buddhism 70%

The majority of the population, the Drukpa peoples, originated from Tibet and are devoutly Buddhist. The Hindu minority is made up of Nepalese who settled in the south from 1910 to 1950. Bhutan has 20 languages. Dzongkha, the language of western Bhutan, native to just 16% of the people, was made the official language in 1988. Many southerners have been deported as illegal immigrants, creating acute ethnic tension.

POLITICS ▷ No multiparty elections

Not applicable   HM *Druk Gyalpo* (Dragon King) Jigme Singye Wangchuck

LEGISLATIVE OR ADVISORY BODIES

National Assembly 150 members

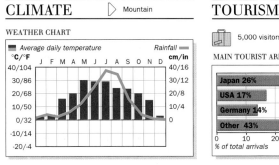

There are no legal political parties; members are elected individually to the National Assembly, to advise the King, who rules as an absolute monarch.

The modernization of Bhutan's absolute monarchy began in 1961. Under further changes proposed in 1998, the king relinquished his right to appoint the government in favour of a cabinet elected by the National Assembly. The National Assembly was also empowered to pass a vote of no confidence against the king. The proposals came in response to a pro-democracy movement fueled by ethnic Nepalese opposed to the Drukpa-dominated political system.

BHUTAN

Total Land Area : 47 000 sq. km (18 147 sq. miles)

LAND HEIGHT

- 6000m/19686ft
- 4000m/13124ft
- 2000m/6562ft
- 1000m/3281ft
- 500m/1640ft
- 200m/656ft
- 160m/252ft

POPULATION

- ● over 10 000
- • under 10 000

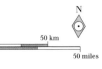

WORLD AFFAIRS
▷ Joined UN in 1971

Bhutan's closest links are with India. Relations with China are cordial and negotiations to settle the China–Bhutan border have progressed smoothly since 1984. There is tension with Nepal over Bhutan's treatment of its ethnic Nepalese minority and the influx of Bhutanese refugees into Nepal.

AID
▷ Recipient

💲 $70m (receipts) ⬇ Down 13% 1996–1997

Bhutan relies on foreign aid for about half of its annual budget. The largest single donor is India.

DEFENSE
▷ No compulsory military service

💲 Small army; India effectively guarantees security ⬇ Little change

Bhutan's army is under the king's command and trained by Indian military instructors. India provides *de facto* military protection and is obliged to defend Bhutan against attack.

ECONOMICS
▷ Inflation 9.3% p.a. (1985–1996)

📊 $315m 💲 39.21–42.50 ngultrum

SCORE CARD

❏ WORLD GNP RANKING	172nd
❏ GNP PER CAPITA	$430
❏ BALANCE OF PAYMENTS	$9m
❏ INFLATION	8.8%
❏ UNEMPLOYMENT	Low rate

STRENGTHS
New development of cash crops for Asian markets (cardamoms, apples, oranges, apricots). Hardwoods in south, especially teak, but exploitation so far tightly controlled. Large hydroelectric potential.

WEAKNESSES
Dependence on Indian workers for many public-sector jobs from road-building to teaching. Majority of the population dependent on agriculture. Cultivated land is extremely restricted because of steep mountain slopes. Very little industry. Few mineral resources.

EXPORTS

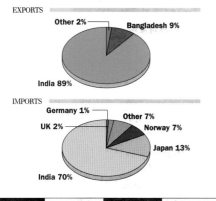

Other 2%
Bangladesh 9%
India 89%

IMPORTS

Germany 1%
Other 7%
UK 2%
Norway 7%
Japan 13%
India 70%

RESOURCES
▷ Electric power 361,000 kw

🐟 340 tonnes 🛢 Not an oil producer and has no refineries

🐖 75,000 pigs, 435,000 cattle, 59,000 sheep 💎 Talc, gypsum, coal, limestone, slate, dolomite

Bhutan's forests remain largely intact and logging is severely controlled. Hydroelectric potential is considerable, but few dams have been built. Power is sold to India from the Chhukha Dam, bringing in substantial foreign earnings.

ENVIRONMENT
▷ No Green MPs

⚠ 18% partially protected ⬇ Not available

Bhutan's forests stabilize the steep mountainsides and supply the bulk of it fuel needs. Road-building, which began in the 1960s, is the biggest cause of deforestation, which has led to topsoil erosion. The high northern pastures are at risk from overgrazing by yaks. Traditional Buddhist values instilling respect for nature and forbidding the killing of animals are still observed.

MEDIA
▷ TV ownership banned

✗ There are no daily newspapers

PUBLISHING AND BROADCAST MEDIA

📰 There are no daily newspapers. *Kuensel* is published weekly by the government in Dzongkha, English and Nepali

No TV service 📡 1 state-owned service

Bhutan has never had a TV service. TV is banned on the grounds that it would dilute Bhutanese values.

CRIME
▷ Death penalty not used

Bhutan does not publish prison figures ⬇ Little variation from year to year

There is little violent crime and levels of theft are low. In 1991, *Driglam namzha*, an ancient code of conduct including the requirement to wear traditional dress, was revived, with fines or imprisonment for non-compliance.

EDUCATION
▷ Not available

🎓 44% 👤 2,055 students

Education is free, but not compulsory. A very small minority of children attend secondary school. There are no universities.

CHRONOLOGY
The Drukpa, originally from Tibet, united Bhutan in 1656. In 1865 the Drukpa lost the Duars Strip to British India.

- ❏ **1907** Monarchy established.
- ❏ **1949** Independence from British India.
- ❏ **1953** National Assembly inaugurated.
- ❏ **1968** King forms first cabinet.
- ❏ **1971** Joins UN.
- ❏ **1990** Ethnic Nepalese launch campaign for minority rights.
- ❏ **1998** King proposes to reform government.

HEALTH
▷ Welfare state health benefits

👥 1 per 5,825 people ☠ Diarrheal, respiratory diseases, tuberculosis, malaria, infant deaths

Free clinics and Thimphu's hospital provide basic health care. Progress is being made in child immunization, and monks have recently been persuaded to teach hygiene. Infant mortality is high. Bhutanese, Tibetan and Chinese traditional medicines are widely practised.

SPENDING
▷ GDP/cap. no increase

CONSUMPTION AND SPENDING

🚗 10 per 1,000 population ☎ 6 per 1,000 population

Defense	No data
Education	No data
Health	4.2%

0   5   10   15   20   25
Defense, Health, Education spending as % of GDP

Most of Bhutan's people are chronically poor, although starvation is virtually unknown. There is a small middle class of public employees and storekeepers.

WORLD RANKING

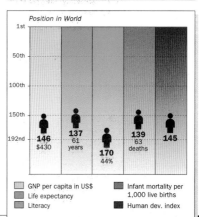

Position in World

1st
50th
100th
150th
192nd

146 — $430
137 — 61 years
170 — 44%
139 — 63 deaths
145

- ❏ GNP per capita in US$
- ❏ Life expectancy
- ❏ Literacy
- ❏ Infant mortality per 1,000 live births
- ❏ Human dev. index

BOLIVIA

B

OFFICIAL NAME: Republic of Bolivia **CAPITAL:** Sucre (official); La Paz (administrative)
POPULATION: 8 million **CURRENCY:** Boliviano **OFFICIAL LANGUAGES:** Spanish, Quechua and Aymará

SOUTH AMERICA

1825 | 1883 | Aug 6 | BOL | -4 | +591 | .bo

BOLIVIA LIES LANDLOCKED high in central South America. Over half of the population lives on the *altiplano*, the windswept plateau between two ranges of the Andes, 3,500 m (11,500 feet) above sea level. La Paz, the highest capital in the world, has spawned a neighboring large twin, El Alto. Bolivia has the world's highest golf course, ski run and football stadium. The eastern lowland regions are tropical and underdeveloped but are rapidly being colonized. Bolivia remains the poorest nation in South America.

TOURISM

> Visitors : population 1:21

375,000 visitors | Up 7% 1995–1997

MAIN TOURIST ARRIVALS

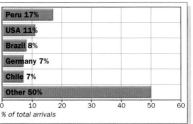

Peru 17%	
USA 11%	
Brazil 8%	
Germany 7%	
Chile 7%	
Other 50%	

% of total arrivals (scale 0 to 60)

CLIMATE

> Tropical/mountain

WEATHER CHART

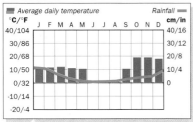

Average daily temperature | Rainfall
°C/°F   J F M A M J J A S O N D   cm/in
40/104 ... 40/16
30/86 ... 30/12
20/68 ... 20/8
10/50 ... 10/4
0/32 ... 0
-10/14
-20/-4

Copacabana on the shores of Lake Titicaca. It lies on a large headland owned by Bolivia on the Peruvian side of the lake.

Foreign tourists are drawn by the traditional festivals, especially carnivals in February or March, the variety of Bolivia's scenery, and its Spanish colonial architecture. Major attractions are the Silver Mountain at Potosí, and Lake Titicaca, the highest navigable lake in the world, covering an area of 8,970 square km (3,463 square miles). Recent political stability has encouraged some growth in tourism, but potential is limited, however, by Bolivia's isolation, the rugged, inaccessible terrain, and the limited infrastructure.

The Andean *altiplano* has an extreme tropical highland climate, with winter night frosts. Annual rainfall in the west is only 25 cm (10 inches). Most rain falls in summer in the hot eastern lowlands.

TRANSPORTATION

> Drive on right

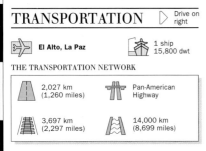

El Alto, La Paz | 1 ship 15,800 dwt

THE TRANSPORTATION NETWORK

2,027 km (1,260 miles)		Pan-American Highway	
3,697 km (2,297 miles)		14,000 km (8,699 miles)	

Obtaining more port access to the Pacific coast for landlocked Bolivia is important. Only 4% of roads are paved. The national railroad was privatized in 1996. Domestic airlines are generally reliable.

***Potato harvest** on the* altiplano.
The government is encouraging migration to the more fertile lands in the east.

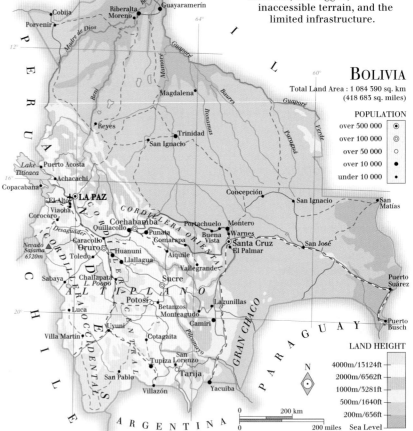

BOLIVIA

Total Land Area : 1 084 390 sq. km (418 683 sq. miles)

POPULATION

over 500 000	⊙
over 100 000	◎
over 50 000	○
over 10 000	●
under 10 000	·

LAND HEIGHT

4000m/13124ft
2000m/6562ft
1000m/3281ft
500m/1640ft
200m/656ft
Sea Level

B

PEOPLE

▷ Pop. density low

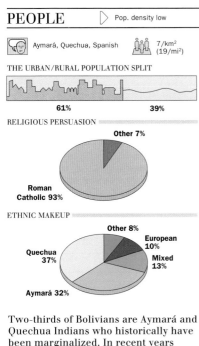

Aymará, Quechua, Spanish

7/km²
(19/mi²)

THE URBAN/RURAL POPULATION SPLIT

61% **39%**

RELIGIOUS PERSUASION

Other 7%

Roman Catholic 93%

ETHNIC MAKEUP

Other 8%

European 10%

Quechua 37%

Mixed 13%

Aymará 32%

Two-thirds of Bolivians are Aymará and Quechua Indians who historically have been marginalized. In recent years however they have played a more active role in politics by supporting new populist parties. Wealthy city elites, dating back to Spanish colonial rule, retain great influence but new entrepreneurs with political ambitions have appeared. Most Bolivians are subsistence farmers, miners, small traders or artisans earning low incomes. There are some 130,000 lowland Indians in western regions. Government schemes, unplanned colonization and the collapse of tin mining have led to large-scale migration from the Andes to lowland eastern regions during the last few decades.

Family life tends to be close-knit; Indians practice Roman Catholicism mixed with their own traditions and culture. Women have low status.

POPULATION AGE BREAKDOWN

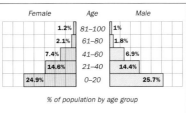

Female		Age	Male	
	1.2%	81–100	1%	
	2.1%	61–80	1.8%	
	7.4%	41–60		6.9%
	14.6%	21–40	14.4%	
24.9%		0–20		25.7%

% of population by age group

POLITICS

▷ Multiparty elections

L. House 1997/2002
U. House 1997/2002

President Hugo
Banzer Suárez

AT THE LAST ELECTION

Chamber of Deputies 130 members

7% Others

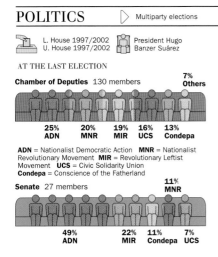

| 25% ADN | 20% MNR | 19% MIR | 16% UCS | 13% Condepa |

ADN = Nationalist Democratic Action **MNR** = Nationalist Revolutionary Movement **MIR** = Revolutionary Leftist Movement **UCS** = Civic Solidarity Union **Condepa** = Conscience of the Fatherland

Senate 27 members

11% MNR

| 49% ADN | 22% MIR | 11% Condepa | 7% UCS |

Bolivia is a multiparty democracy.

MAIN POLITICAL ISSUES
Political stability
The Banzer government is an uneasy "mega-coalition" of parties who are jockeying for position in advance of the 2002 presidential elections. None will want to be associated with unpopular policies as polling approaches, so divisions will occur.

Cocaine
Poor farmers, denied alternatives, are opposed to the government's forced eradication of coca crops to ensure more US aid. Their leaders warn that serious domestic conflict will occur unless troops are withdrawn from coca growing regions. The government aims to eradicate 35,000 hectares by 2002 when its term ends.

PROFILE
Between independence from Spain in 1825 and the early 1980s, Bolivia experienced, on average, more than one armed coup a year, punctuated by a national revolution in 1952 which delivered important reforms. The fragmented and drug-tainted military finally stepped down in 1982, but full elections were delayed until 1985.

The military retains influence but has played out its political role and more populist parties have emerged to challenge traditional politics, although not the drift to free-market economic development. The pattern of politics remains one of parties competing for power in unstable coalitions. Nepotism remains rife, and narcotics, whose profits underpin the economy, are frequently implicated in political corruption scandals. The main trade union federation COB was the traditional focus of opposition, but this role has passed to coca growers and other popular groups.

The right-wing MNR was defeated in the 1997 elections, but the coalition government under President Banzer, a former dictator, has continued with its economic austerity policies.

WORLD AFFAIRS

▷ Joined UN in 1945

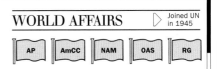

| AP | AmCC | NAM | OAS | RG |

Bolivia's main foreign policy concern is agreeing improved access to the Pacific with Peru and Chile. Relations with the USA are complicated. The USA is Bolivia's main source of aid but this was made conditional on Bolivia taking measures to destroy the cocaine producing and trafficking industry, itself a major buttress of the Bolivian economy, and has put the country over a barrel. The eradication of coca plantations, involving military and police attacks on poor coca plant growers, keeps US aid flowing, but Bolivia, lacking market alternatives, is still a major world producer of refined cocaine.

Bolivia is an associate member of the South American common market MERCOSUR with its neighbors Brazil, Argentina, Paraguay, and Uruguay. As the most isolated and poorest economy in South America, it would be the major beneficiary of a tariff-free zone in the Andean region.

President Hugo Banzer Suárez was elected to power in June 1997.

Gonzalo Sánchez de Lozada, MNR leader and president from 1993 until 1997.

CHRONOLOGY

The Aymará civilization was conquered by the Incas in the late 1400s. Fifty years later, the Incas were defeated by the *conquistadores* and Upper Peru, as it became, was governed by Spain from Lima.

❏ **1545** Cerro Rico, the Silver Mountain, discovered at Potosí. Provides Spain with vast wealth.

❏ **1776** Upper Peru becomes part of Viceroyalty of Río de la Plata centered on Buenos Aires.

❏ **1809** Simón Bolívar inspires first revolutionary uprisings in Latin America at Chuquisaca (Sucre), La Paz and Cochabamba, but they fail.

❏ **1824** Spaniards suffer final defeat by Bolívar's general, José de Sucre.

❏ **1825** Independence.

❏ **1836–1839** Union with Peru fails under presidency of Andrés de Santa Cruz. Internal disorder ensues as wealthy local *caudillos* vie for power.

B

CHRONOLOGY *continued*

- ❑ **1864–1871** Mariano Melgarejo's ruthless rule. Three Indian revolts at seizure of ancestral lands.
- ❑ **1879–1883** War of the Pacific, won by Chile. Bolivia left landlocked.
- ❑ **1880–1950** Period of stable governments. Exports from revived mining industry bring prosperity.
- ❑ **1903** Acre province ceded to Brazil.
- ❑ **1914** Republican Party founded.
- ❑ **1920** Indian rebellion.
- ❑ **1923** Miners bloodily suppressed.
- ❑ **1932–1935** Chaco War with Paraguay. Bolivia loses three-quarters of Chaco. Rise of radicalism and labor movement.
- ❑ **1951** Víctor Paz Estenssoro of MNR elected president. Military coup.
- ❑ **1952** Revolution. Paz Estenssoro and MNR brought back. Land reforms improve Indians' status. Education reforms, universal suffrage, tin mines nationalized.
- ❑ **1964** Military takes over in coup.
- ❑ **1967** Che Guevara killed while trying to mobilize Bolivian workers.
- ❑ **1969-1979** Military regimes rule with increasing severity. 1979 coup fails. Interim civilian rule.
- ❑ **1980** Military takes over again.
- ❑ **1982** President-elect Dr. Siles Zuazo finally heads leftist civilian MIR government. Inflation 24,000%.
- ❑ **1985** Paz Estenssoro's MNR wins elections. Austerity measures. Annual inflation down to 20%.
- ❑ **1986** Tin market collapses. 21,000 miners sacked.
- ❑ **1989** MIR takes power after close-run elections. President Paz Zamora makes pact with 1970s dictator Gen. Hugo Banzer, leader of ADN.
- ❑ **1990** 1.6 m hectares (4 m acres) of rainforest recognized as Indian territory.
- ❑ **1993** MNR voted back to power.
- ❑ **1995** Seven-month state of siege declared by government.
- ❑ **1997** Former president Hugo Banzer of ADN wins most votes in June presidential elections.
- ❑ **1999** Opposition demands inquiry into Banzer's role in regional military repression in 1970s.

AID ▷ Recipient

 $717m (receipts)　　Down 16% 1996–1997

Most aid comes from the USA and depends on progress in coca crop eradication. Smaller amounts come from western European countries. Poor rural areas get project aid from western NGOs, charities and religious organizations. The World Bank, supported by the IADB, granted US$706 million in nominal debt-relief aid in 1998.

DEFENSE ▷ Compulsory military service

 $155m　　　　Down 3% in 1997

The military has not actively interfered in politics for nearly two decades.

BOLIVIAN ARMED FORCES

36 light tanks (36 SK–105 *Kuerassier*)	25,000 personnel
17 patrol boats	4,500 personnel
33 combat aircraft (6 AT–33N)	4,000 personnel
None	

However, it is frequently used to quell internal dissent. The army is the main focus of defense spending, with weaponry bought almost entirely from the USA. The Bolivian navy consists mainly of gunboats on Lake Titicaca, which borders Peru, and on the Pilcomayo River. The army has worked with US forces against the cocaine business, although its integrity is questioned due to its past associations with narcotics trafficking. The main ambition of the military, apart from protecting its own interests and privileges, is the unrealizable aim of recapturing territory that would allow Bolivia access to the Pacific. Military service lasts for one year.

ECONOMICS ▷ Inflation 24.2% p.a. (1985–1996)

7.6bn　　　　5.35–5.65 bolivianos

SCORE CARD

- ❑ WORLD GNP RANKING 91st
- ❑ GNP PER CAPITA $970
- ❑ BALANCE OF PAYMENTS...................$–715m
- ❑ INFLATION 4.7%
- ❑ UNEMPLOYMENT................................10%

EXPORTS

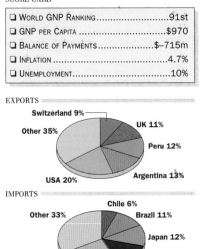

Switzerland 9%
Other 35%
UK 11%
Peru 12%
Argentina 13%
USA 20%

IMPORTS

Chile 6%
Other 33%
Brazil 11%
Japan 12%
Argentina 15%
USA 23%

STRENGTHS
Mineral riches: gold, silver, zinc, lead, tin. Newly discovered oil and natural gas deposits attracting foreign investment.

WEAKNESSES
Raw materials vulnerable to fluctuating world prices. Lack of processed or manufactured exports. High unemployment. Lack of integration between economic sectors and regions. Poor infrastructure.

PROFILE
Traditionally, the state used earnings from the publicly owned state mining sector to control the economy. Years of deep recession in the 1980s, accompanied by accelerating inflation and a collapsing currency, saw the introduction of severe, IMF-approved,

ECONOMIC PERFORMANCE INDICATOR

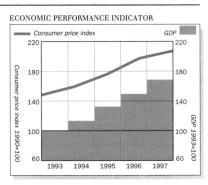

Consumer price index　　GDP

austerity policies. These, along with the introduction of a new currency and tax reform, succeeded in curbing inflation, reducing public spending and restoring international loans but at the price of great social unrest. Growth was restored in the 1990s and a controversial "capitalization" program was launched which allowed for the 50/50 sell-off of shares in all six state companies on attractive terms to investors and employees. Narcotic revenues remain important for the economy.

BOLIVIA : MAJOR BUSINESSES

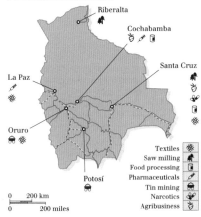

Riberalta
Cochabamba
Santa Cruz
La Paz
Oruro
Potosí

Textiles		
Saw milling		
Food processing		
Pharmaceuticals		
Tin mining		
Narcotics		
Agribusiness		

0　200 km
0　200 miles

B

RESOURCES

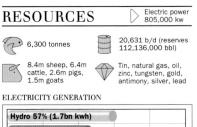

▷ Electric power 805,000 kw

6,300 tonnes

20,631 b/d (reserves 112,136,000 bbl)

8.4m sheep, 6.4m cattle, 2.6m pigs, 1.5m goats

Tin, natural gas, oil, zinc, tungsten, gold, antimony, silver, lead

ELECTRICITY GENERATION

Hydro 57% (1.7bn kwh)

Combustion 43% (1.2bn kwh)

Nuclear 0%

Other 0%

0	20	40	60	80	100

% of total generation by type

Bolivia is the world's largest tin producer. The government is allowing foreign companies to prospect for more oil, and to increase sales of natural gas to Brazil and Argentina.

BOLIVIA : LAND USE

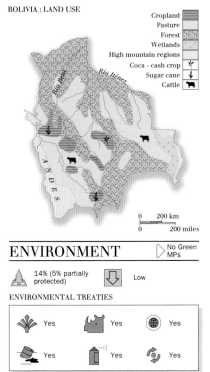

Cropland
Pasture
Forest
Wetlands
High mountain regions
Coca - cash crop
Sugar cane
Cattle

0	200 km
0	200 miles

ENVIRONMENT

▷ No Green MPs

14% (5% partially protected)

Low

ENVIRONMENTAL TREATIES

Yes	Yes	Yes
Yes	Yes	Yes

Deforestation is Bolivia's major ecological problem. Land clearances are running at 200,000 hectares (495,000 acres) a year; this is one of the world's highest annual depletion rates. Much of the cleared land is turned over to cattle ranching or the growing of coca. Pesticide and fertilizer overuse in the coca business is a concern. The industry is effectively uncontrolled and rivers in Amazonia have high pollution levels.

Pollution problems are compounded by waste chemicals used in minerals industries. Mercury, used in the extraction of silver, has been found in dangerous quantities in river systems.

MEDIA

▷ TV ownership medium

Daily newspaper circulation 55 per 1,000 people

PUBLISHING AND BROADCAST MEDIA

There are 18 daily newspapers, including the best-selling *Presencia*, *El Diario* and *La Razón*

1 state-owned with 9 stations, 36 independent

1 state-owned service, 145 independent

Bolivia has strict defamation laws and considerable self censorship. One of many TV stations is university-run, broadcasting mainly educational programs.

CRIME

▷ Death penalty not used

Bolivia does not publish prison figures

Crime is rising in narcotics-trafficking centers

CRIME RATES

Murders
Not Available

Rapes
Not Available

Thefts
Not Available

Violent crime is centered on narcotics-trafficking towns in the eastern lowlands, particularly Santa Cruz. Main cities are much safer for tourists, and have lower crime rates than cities in neighboring Peru. The police and army have a long history of mistreating poor farmers.

EDUCATION

▷ School leaving age: 14

84%

109,503 students

IMF targets for increased school attendance are being met.

THE EDUCATION SYSTEM

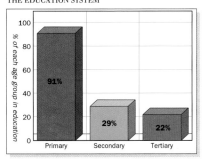

	Primary	Secondary	Tertiary
% of each age group in education	91%	29%	22%

Education, based on a combination of the French and US systems, is seriously underfunded. Although the majority of people speak indigenous languages, most teaching is in Spanish. Bolivia has one of the lowest literacy rates in South America. Reform and multilateral aid have recently led to improvement.

HEALTH

▷ No welfare state health benefits

1 per 2,500 people

Influenza, tuberculosis, other communicable diseases, malaria

Bolivia has one of the lowest numbers of doctors per capita in the whole of Latin America.

Only half the children under one year are immunized, and diseases that are easily preventable by vaccination are a major cause of death. Approximately half of the population of Bolivia has safe drinking water. Rural areas are barely served by medical services. Meeting IMF targets for the care of expectant mothers led to debt relief in 1998.

SPENDING

▷ GDP/cap. increase

CONSUMPTION AND SPENDING

29 per 1,000 population

69 per 1,000 population

Defense 2%

Education 6.6%

Health 2.4%

0	5	10	15	20	25

Defense, Health, Education spending as % of GDP

Havoc created by economic reforms has further widened the huge gap between the rich and poor. Generally, the indigenous population who form the rural poor are the worst off. The Andean highlands suffer from grinding poverty that has hardly changed in generations. Migrants to more prosperous eastern regions have faired better, but skewed land ownership remains a big problem. Poor housing, and lack of utilities and regular income is common to urban poverty.

The IMF in 1998 stated that the government needed to speed up its poverty reduction program and agreed a debt reduction package under its Heavily Indebted Poor Countries Initiative.

WORLD RANKING

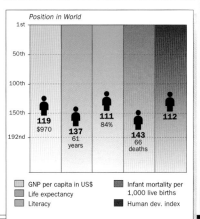

Position in World

1st				
50th				
100th				
150th	119 $970	137 61 years	111 84%	143 66 deaths	112
192nd				

☐ GNP per capita in US$	☐ Infant mortality per 1,000 live births
☐ Life expectancy	
☐ Literacy	☐ Human dev. index

BOSNIA & HERZEGOVINA

B

OFFICIAL NAME: The Republic of Bosnia and Herzegovina **CAPITAL:** Sarajevo
POPULATION: 4 million **CURRENCY:** Maraka **OFFICIAL LANGUAGE:** Serbo-Croat

1992 | 1992 | March 1 | BIH | +1 | +387 | .ba

BOSNIA IS A MOUNTAINOUS country with a few miles of coast on the Adriatic, bordered by Croatia, Serbia and Montenegro. Between 1943 and 1990, the Yugoslavian regime prevented conflict between Muslims, Croats, and Serbs, but with the dissolution of Yugoslavia, the ethnic populations fought over Bosnia. Around 250,000 died, more than two million were displaced and many historic cities destroyed before a settlement was achieved under the 1995 Dayton peace accord.

CLIMATE

▷ Continental

WEATHER CHART

■ Average daily temperature   Rainfall ▬
°C/°F   J F M A M J J A S O N D   cm/in
40/104 .... 40/16
30/86 .... 30/12
20/68 .... 20/8
10/50 .... 10/4
0/32 0
-10/14 ....
-20/-4 ....

Bosnia has a continental climate with warm summers and bitterly cold winters, often with snow.

TRANSPORTATION

▷ Drive on right

✈ **Sarajevo Intl**
276,048 passengers

⛴ Has no fleet

THE TRANSPORTATION NETWORK

| 🛣 21,800 km (13,546 miles) | ⌖ None |
| 🛤 539 km (335 miles) | ⌖ None |

War has severely damaged the transportation network, resulting in wrecked bridges, roads, and railroads. De-mining and reconstruction are now reopening routes. Sarajevo remains the hub of communications networks.

TOURISM

▷ Visitors : population 1:40

🧳 100,000 visitors

⬆ Tourism is gradually increasing

MAIN TOURIST ARRIVALS

	Bosnia & Herzegovina
	does not publish
	tourism figures by
	country of origin
0 10 20 30 40 50 60	
% of total arrivals	

Despite the 1984 Winter Olympics being held in Sarajevo, Bosnia did not develop a tourist infrastructure.

PEOPLE

▷ Pop. density medium

👤 Serbo-Croat

👥 78/km² (203/mi²)

THE URBAN/RURAL POPULATION SPLIT

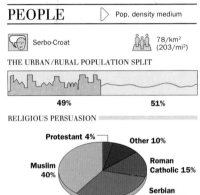

49%   **51%**

RELIGIOUS PERSUASION

Protestant 4%
Other 10%
Muslim 40%
Roman Catholic 15%
Serbian Orthodox 31%

Before the war, the population was 44% ethnic Bosnian (mostly Muslim), 31% Serb, 17% Croat, while 8% described themselves as Yugoslav or of other ethnicity. Intermarriage was common and ethnic violence rare. Society was largely secular and materialistic. Civil war and "ethnic cleansing" displaced some 60% of the population. Only a small proportion have now returned to their former homes.

BOSNIA & HERZEGOVINA

Total Land Area : 51 130 sq. km
(19 741 sq. miles)

POPULATION
◉ over 100 000
○ over 50 000
● over 10 000
• under 10 000

LAND HEIGHT
2000m/6562ft
1000m/3281ft
500m/1640ft
200m/656ft
Sea Level

N

0 ___ 50 km
0 ___ 50 miles

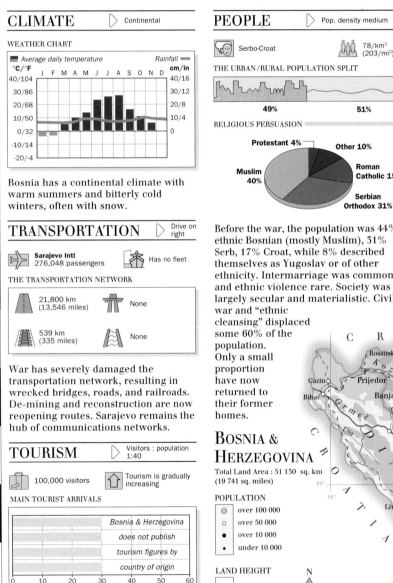

POLITICS

▷ Multiparty elections

L. House 1998/2000
U. House 1998/2000

Chair of the presidency
Zivko Radisic

AT THE LAST ELECTION

Assembly of Union 42 members

9% SDS   5% SDB

40% CSDB   14% HDZ   10% SL   10% SDP   7% Others   5% SRS

CSDB = Coalition for a Single and Democratic Bosnia
HDZ = Croatian Democratic Union **SL** = The Sloga Coalition
SDP = Social Democratic Party **SDS** = Serb Democratic Party **SDB** = Social Democrats of Bosnia **SRS** = Serb Radical Party

House of Peoples 15 members

10 members are appointed from the Federation of Bosnia-Herzegovina and 5 from the Republika Srpska.

The Bosnian state as it emerged after the 1992–1995 war is composed of two separate entities: some 51% of the territory is controlled by a Muslim-Croat Federation and the remaining 49% by the Serbs. Hence, there are currently three distinct political structures in Bosnia: the Republic, with a rotating three-member collective presidency acting as head of state, an Assembly of Union, and a government headed by two co-premiers; the Federation, with a president, parliament and government; and the Republika Srpska (RS), likewise with a president, a People's Assembly and a government.

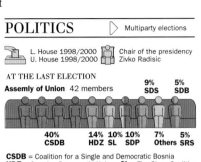

B

WORLD AFFAIRS
▷ Joined UN in 1992

CEI | NAM | OSCE | OIC | IAEA

The 1995 peace accord provided for a 60,000-strong, NATO-led Implementation Force (IFOR) in Bosnia. This was replaced in 1996 by a smaller Stabilization Force (SFOR).

AID
▷ Recipient

$ $863m (receipts)   ⬆ Up 6% 1996-1997

Humanitarian aid has been crucial. Aid receipts averaged $875 million yearly in 1995–1997. Donor countries pledged a further $1.2 billion in mid-1998. Reconstruction projects focus on housing, infrastructure, and job creation, as well as creating the foundations of a market economy.

DEFENSE
▷ Compulsory military service

$ $327m   ⬆ Up 30% in 1997

The merger of Bosnian and Croat forces under the Dayton peace accord was completed in 1997, creating an armed force of 45,000. From 1998 the NATO-led Stabilization Force (SFOR) numbered some 33,000 troops.

ECONOMICS
▷ Not available

$800m   1.86 maraka

SCORE CARD

- WORLD GNP RANKING.......................160th
- GNP PER CAPITA $288
- BALANCE OF PAYMENTS....................$–134m
- INFLATION ....Not available
- UNEMPLOYMENT.................................50%

STRENGTHS

Before 1991, five of former Yugoslavia's largest companies were located in Bosnia. Retail outlets were mostly privately operated and there was a sizeable small-business sector. The country has the potential to become a thriving market economy, with a solid manufacturing base.

WEAKNESSES

War damage of $20-$40 billion. 1997 GDP still half that of 1990. Unemployment 50%. Economic recovery slower in Republika Srpska than in Federation.

EXPORTS/IMPORTS

Bosnia & Herzegovina has no significant exports.
Most imports are in the form of UN aid and arms from the international market.
Oil imports are probably from the Middle East

RESOURCES
▷ Electric power 2.4m kw

2,500 tonnes   Not an oil producer

275,600 sheep, 260,000 cattle, 70,000 pigs   Coal, lignite, iron, bauxite, cement

Bosnia's land is not well suited to agriculture, but has mineral deposits, forests and hydroelectric potential.

ENVIRONMENT
▷ No Green MPs

🔺 1%   Not available

Apart from war damage, Bosnia faces the effects of industrial pollution incurred during the communist regime.

MEDIA
▷ TV ownership low

Daily newspaper circulation 146 per 1,000 people

PUBLISHING AND BROADCAST MEDIA

There are 3 daily newspapers. *Oslobodjenje (Liberation)* was published daily throughout the war

Several local independent services   Several independent services

The three nationalist parties control most broadcasting, which is regulated by the Independent Media Commission. The OSCE criticized two radio stations for bias in the 1998 elections.

CRIME
▷ Death penalty not used

Bosnia does not publish prison figures   ⬆ Rising

All sides in the war, but especially the Serbs, have been accused of war crimes. "Ethnic cleansing," whereby entire populations were forced to evacuate their homes to avoid murder, rape and torture, was common. As of mid-1999 the war crimes tribunal in The Hague had and found eight people guilty of war crimes and publicly indicted 84.

EDUCATION
▷ School leaving age: 15

93%   40,000 students

The conflict has resulted in ethnic bias and segregation in education, but a new curriculum is being developed.

The Muslim town of Mostar. *Its 16th-century bridge at a strategic river crossing and much of the old town have been destroyed by war.*

CHRONOLOGY

In 1945 Bosnia Herzegovina became one of Yugoslavia's six republics.

- ❑ **1990** Nationalists defeat communists in multiparty elections. PDA leader Alija Izetbegovic president.
- ❑ **1991** Parliament announces republican sovereignty.
- ❑ **1992** EC and USA recognize Bosnia. Serbs announce "Serbian Republic." Civil war. UN troops guard aid convoys.
- ❑ **1995** NATO air strikes on Serbs; US-brokered Dayton peace accord.
- ❑ **1996** NATO-led implementation of peace accord. First international war crimes trial since 1945 opens in The Hague. Bosnian elections held under Dayton accord.
- ❑ **1998** Elections: less support for nationalist parties.

HEALTH
▷ No welfare state health benefits

1 per 1,667 people   Cholera and diphtheria epidemics, violence, deaths from war-stress

War strained the service severely and many died for lack of basic treatment. Reconstruction is now under way.

SPENDING
▷ GDP/cap. no increase

CONSUMPTION AND SPENDING

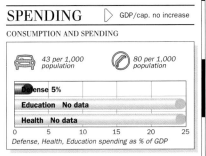

43 per 1,000 population   80 per 1,000 population

Defense 5%
Education No data
Health No data

0   5   10   15   20   25

Defense, Health, Education spending as % of GDP

With some 60% of the country's prewar population displaced, housing, jobs, and reintegration are key challenges. Profiteering and extortion persist.

WORLD RANKING

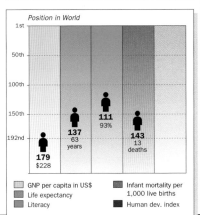

Position in World

1st
50th
100th
150th
192nd

179 $228
137 63 years
111 93%
143 13 deaths

- ☐ GNP per capita in US$
- ☐ Life expectancy
- ☐ Literacy
- ☐ Infant mortality per 1,000 live births
- ☐ Human dev. index

BOTSWANA

SOUTHERN AFRICA · Africa

OFFICIAL NAME: Republic of Botswana   CAPITAL: Gaborone
POPULATION: 1.6 million   CURRENCY: Pula   OFFICIAL LANGUAGE: English

| 1966 | 1966 | Sept 30 | RB | +2 | +267 | .bw |

ARID AND LANDLOCKED, Botswana's central plateau separates the populous eastern grasslands from the Kalahari desert and swamps of the Okavango delta in the west. Botswana is a multiparty democracy, but the Botswana Democratic Party has won every election since independence. Diamonds provide Botswana with a prosperous economy, but rain is an even more precious resource, honored in the name of the currency, the pula.

The Okavango Delta. Plans to draw water from the delta for irrigation were shelved in 1991 in the interests of wildlife conservation.

CLIMATE — Steppe/hot desert

WEATHER CHART

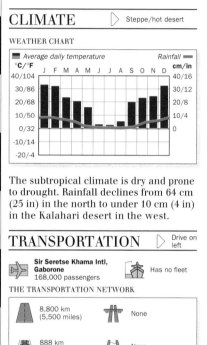

The subtropical climate is dry and prone to drought. Rainfall declines from 64 cm (25 in) in the north to under 10 cm (4 in) in the Kalahari desert in the west.

TRANSPORTATION — Drive on left

Sir Seretse Khama Intl, Gaborone
168,000 passengers

Has no fleet

THE TRANSPORTATION NETWORK

| 8,800 km (5,500 miles) | None |
| 888 km (552 miles) | None |

The opening of the trans-Kalahari road to Namibia in 1998 has reduced Botswana's dependence on South African ports. Upgrading existing rail and road networks are priorities.

TOURISM — Visitors : population 1:2.2

728,000 visitors   Up 7% 1995–1997

MAIN TOURIST ARRIVALS

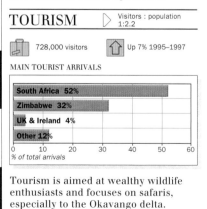

South Africa 52%
Zimbabwe 32%
UK & Ireland 4%
Other 12%

0 10 20 30 40 50 60
% of total arrivals

Tourism is aimed at wealthy wildlife enthusiasts and focuses on safaris, especially to the Okavango delta.

PEOPLE — Pop. density low

Tswana, English, Shona, San, Khoikhoi, Ndebele

3/km² (7/mi)²

THE URBAN/RURAL POPULATION SPLIT

28%   73%

ETHNIC MAKEUP

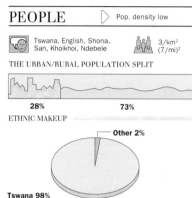

Other 2%

Tswana 98%

Botswana's stability reflects its ethnic homogeneity and the power of traditional authorities, notably the village *kgotla*, or parliament. Almost the whole population is Tswana, with the Bamangwato forming the largest Tswana group. Botswana's first inhabitants, the San (sometimes called Bushmen), have been marginalized. Whites continue to dominate the professions.

POLITICS — Multiparty elections

1994/1999   President Festus Mogae

AT THE LAST ELECTION

National Assembly 40 members

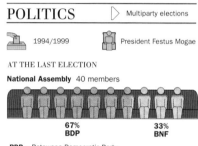

67% BDP   33% BNF

BDP = Botswana Democratic Party
BNF = Botswana National Front

Although Botswana is formally a multiparty democracy, it has been ruled by the BDP since independence in 1966. In 1994, however, economic problems, corruption scandals and steadily increasing urbanization led to the mainly town-based BNF gaining seats from the BDP, which nevertheless retained its absolute parliamentary majority. Since power transferred smoothly from President Masire to Festus Mogae in 1998, the BNF has split in two and electoral apathy has grown.

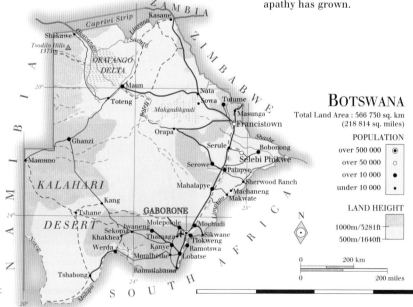

BOTSWANA

Total Land Area : 566 730 sq. km
(218 814 sq. miles)

POPULATION

over 500 000 ⊙
over 50 000 ○
over 10 000 ●
under 10 000 ·

LAND HEIGHT

1000m/3281ft
500m/1640ft

0   200 km
0   200 miles

WORLD AFFAIRS

▷ Joined UN in 1966

| Comm | NAM | OAU | SADC | WTO |

Botswana has strongly backed a politically and economically stable post-apartheid South Africa, and in 1994 appointed its first ambassador to Pretoria since 1966. Potential South African domination of the SADC is another fear. Traditionally pro-Western in orientation, Botswana cherishes its relations with the UK and the USA.

AID

▷ Recipient

$125m (receipts)   ⬆ Up 54% 1996–1997

Botswana's political and economic record has made it a favored aid recipient, notably from the EU, the UK, the USA and the World Bank. Some 90% of EU aid goes to projects which try to balance wildlife needs with rural development. Transport is also an aid target.

DEFENSE

▷ No compulsory military service

$241m   ⬆ Up 3% in 1997

Relatively large sums are still spent on defense and armed police, despite reduced regional tensions following political change in South Africa.

ECONOMICS

▷ Inflation 12.1% p.a. (1985–1996)

$5.1bn   3.81–4.45 pula

SCORE CARD

- ❏ WORLD GNP RANKING.......................105th
- ❏ GNP PER CAPITA $3,310
- ❏ BALANCE OF PAYMENTS $609m
- ❏ INFLATION 9.3%
- ❏ UNEMPLOYMENT ....22%.

STRENGTHS

Diamonds: world's third-largest producer. Strong growth in 1980s, though since reduced. Prudent economic management, large financial reserves and exchange control liberalization. Strong exports of assembly-produced vehicles, copper, nickel, beef.

WEAKNESSES

Overdependence on diamonds (80% of export earnings). Weak agriculture. Small population and water shortages add to diversification problems. Impact of beef industry on environment. High transportation costs to coast. Estimated 22% unemployment.

EXPORTS

Other 3%
Other Europe 4%
Other Africa 5%
UK 3%
SACU 85%

IMPORTS

UK 3%
Zimbabwe 6%
South Korea 7%
Other 11%
SACU 73%

RESOURCES

▷ Not available

2,000 tonnes

Not an oil producer and has no refineries

2.3m cattle, 1.8m goats, 240,000 sheep

Diamonds, copper, coal, nickel, soda ash, gold

Diamonds are mined by the 50% state-owned Debswana. Large coal deposits are the basis of power grid expansion. Water is Botswana's scarcest resource.

ENVIRONMENT

▷ No Green MPs

19% (2% partially protected)   ⬇ Low

Botswana is trying to reduce conflict between rural development and the environment by helping communities to earn a living from wildlife protection.

MEDIA

▷ TV ownership low

Daily newspaper circulation 27 per 1,000 people

PUBLISHING AND BROADCAST MEDIA

There is 1 daily newspaper, *Dikgang Tsa Gompieno*, published by the government

1 limited service

2 state-owned, some commercial services

The government bias of radio and the one daily paper is offset in the many weekly and other journals. The 20,000 TVs also receive South African stations.

CRIME

▷ Death penalty used

Botswana does not publish prison figures   ⬇ Down 11% from 1992–1996

President Mogae warned of a "crime wave" in 1999. Official corruption and diamond smuggling stay major concerns. Human rights are generally respected.

EDUCATION

▷ Not available

74%   8,850 students

Under the National Service Scheme, instituted in 1982, school-leavers work for a year in government departments and/or parastatal institutions.

CHRONOLOGY

From 1600, Tswana migrations slowly displaced San people. In 1895, at local request, the UK set up the Bechuanaland Protectorate to preempt annexation by South Africa.

- ❏ **1965** BDP, led by Sir Seretse Khama, wins first general election and all subsequent general elections.
- ❏ **1966** Independence declared.
- ❏ **1980** Vice President Quett (later Ketumile) Masire succeeds the late Sir Seretse as president.
- ❏ **1985–1986** South African raids.
- ❏ **1992–1993** Strikes and corruption scandals prompt resignations of senior BDP figures.
- ❏ **1994** BDP support eroded in election.
- ❏ **1998** Vice-President Festus Mogae succeeds Masire as president.

HEALTH

▷ Welfare state health benefits

1 per 5,000 people   Tuberculosis, heart diseases, pneumonia

Primary health care remains a priority. The scourge of AIDS is particularly alarming, with one in four adult Bostwanans thought to be HIV positive.

SPENDING

▷ GDP/cap. no increase

CONSUMPTION AND SPENDING

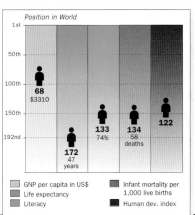

15 per 1,000 population   56 per 1,000 population

Defense 6.%
Education 9.6%
Health 3.2%

0   5   10   15   20   25

Defense, Health, Education spending as % of GDP

At $3,310, GNP per capita is among Africa's highest, but most people are poor. Inequality is increasing and wealth belongs to the urban elite.

WORLD RANKING

Position in World

1st
50th
100th
150th
192nd

68 $3310
172 47 years
133 74%
134 58 deaths
122

- ❏ GNP per capita in US$
- ❏ Life expectancy
- ❏ Literacy
- ❏ Infant mortality per 1,000 live births
- ❏ Human dev. index

BRAZIL

B

OFFICIAL NAME: Federative Republic of Brazil **CAPITAL:** Brasília
POPULATION: 165.2 million **CURRENCY:** Real **OFFICIAL LANGUAGE:** Portuguese

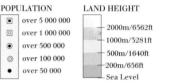

SOUTH AMERICA

| 1822 | 1889 | Sept 7 | BR | -3 | +55 | .br |

THE LARGEST COUNTRY in South America, Brazil became independent of Portugal in 1822. Today, it is renowned as the site of the world's largest tropical rainforest, the threat to which led to the UN's first international environment conference, held in Rio de Janeiro in 1992. Covering one-third of Brazil's total land area, the rainforest grows around the massive Amazon River and its delta. Apart from the basin of the River Plate to the south, the rest of the country consists of highlands. The mountainous north is part forested and part desert. Brazil is the world's leading coffee producer and also has rich reserves of gold, diamonds, oil and iron ore. Cattle-ranching is an expanding industry. The city of São Paulo is the world's third biggest conurbation, with 17 million inhabitants.

BRAZIL

Total Land Area : 8 456 510 sq. km
(3 265 059 sq. miles)

POPULATION

- over 5 000 000
- over 1 000 000
- over 500 000
- over 100 000
- over 50 000

LAND HEIGHT

- 2000m/6562ft
- 1000m/3281ft
- 500m/1640ft
- 200m/656ft
- Sea Level

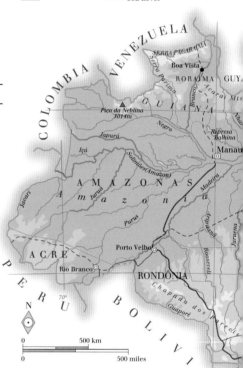

CLIMATE

▷ Tropical equatorial/ wet & dry/ subtropical/ steppe

WEATHER CHART

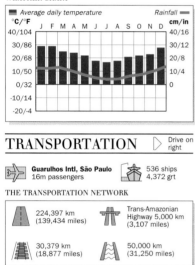

Brazil's share of the Amazon basin, occupying half of the country, has a model tropical, equatorial climate. The 150–200 cm (59–79 inches) of rain are spread throughout the year, although some periods are rather wetter than others according to region. Temperatures are high, with almost no seasonal variation, but scarcely ever rise above 38°C (100°F).

The Brazilian plateau, occupying most of the rest of the country, has far greater temperature ranges. Rain falls mainly between October and April. However, the northeast, the least productive region of Brazil, is very dry and in recent years has been suffering from severe drought, which has compounded its problems. The southern states have hot summers and cool winters, when frost may

TRANSPORTATION

▷ Drive on right

Guarulhos Intl, São Paulo
16m passengers

536 ships
4,372 grt

THE TRANSPORTATION NETWORK

| 224,397 km (139,434 miles) | Trans-Amazonian Highway 5,000 km (3,107 miles) |
| 30,379 km (18,877 miles) | 50,000 km (31,250 miles) |

Investment in integrated mass urban transport is poor, as are the railroads. Almost everyone travels by bus or car. Roads are clogged near cities and poor outside. Competition from air and water transport is growing.

Parati, in Rio state, was one of Brazil's major gold exporting ports in the 17th century. Its colonial architecture is well preserved.

TOURISM

▷ Visitors:population 1:55

3m visitors

Up 58% 1995-1997

MAIN TOURIST ARRIVALS

| Argentina 43% |
| Uruguay 9% |
| USA 8% |
| Paraguay 5% |
| Germany 5% |
| Other 30% |

% of total arrivals

Brazil is under-performing in tourism, with revenues equivalent to 2.5% of GDP in 1996, compared with a world average of around 10%.

Such attractions as 2,000 km (1,200 miles) of good Atlantic beaches, the Amazon river basin, the Pantanal – the vast wetland region in the west – and world famous carnivals are offset by the limited availability of medium-to-low-cost travel and budget hotels, which deters domestic and foreign travelers.

In the virtual absence of low-cost charter flights domestic air travel is expensive. This is blamed on high airport charges and inertia in the Brazil's aviation department which is controlled by the air force.

Average overnight hotel rates are higher than in Europe and the USA and the quality of service is generally poor. Basic infrastructure, such as sanitation and water supply, is also deficient. In 1996, the Caribbean attracted some 19 million foreign visitors and earned upward of US$23 billion. The same year, only some 1.8 million foreign tourists visited the whole of Brazil.

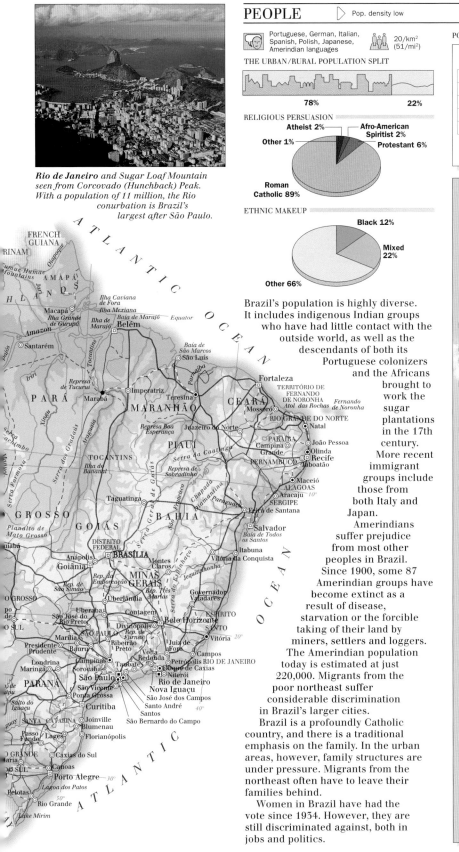

Rio de Janeiro and Sugar Loaf Mountain seen from Corcovado (Hunchback) Peak. With a population of 11 million, the Rio conurbation is Brazil's largest after São Paulo.

PEOPLE

▷ Pop. density low

Portuguese, German, Italian, Spanish, Polish, Japanese, Amerindian languages

20/km² (51/mi²)

THE URBAN/RURAL POPULATION SPLIT

78% 22%

RELIGIOUS PERSUASION

- Atheist 2%
- Afro-American Spiritist 2%
- Other 1%
- Protestant 6%
- Roman Catholic 89%

ETHNIC MAKEUP

- Black 12%
- Mixed 22%
- Other 66%

POPULATION AGE BREAKDOWN

Female		Age	Male	
	0.4%	81–100	0.3%	
	3.6%	61–80	3%	
	9.1%	41–60	8.4%	
17.1%		21–40		16.7%
20.5%		0–20		21%

% of population by age group

Brazil's population is highly diverse. It includes indigenous Indian groups who have had little contact with the outside world, as well as the descendants of both its Portuguese colonizers and the Africans brought to work the sugar plantations in the 17th century.

More recent immigrant groups include those from both Italy and Japan. Amerindians suffer prejudice from most other peoples in Brazil. Since 1900, some 87 Amerindian groups have become extinct as a result of disease, starvation or the forcible taking of their land by miners, settlers and loggers. The Amerindian population today is estimated at just 220,000. Migrants from the poor northeast suffer considerable discrimination in Brazil's larger cities.

Brazil is a profoundly Catholic country, and there is a traditional emphasis on the family. In the urban areas, however, family structures are under pressure. Migrants from the northeast often have to leave their families behind.

Women in Brazil have had the vote since 1934. However, they are still discriminated against, both in jobs and politics.

CHRONOLOGY

The first Portuguese, Pedro Alvares Cabral, arrived in Brazil in 1500. By the time Spain took control of the region, in 1580, it was a thriving colony drawing its wealth from sugar plantations in the northeast, worked by imported Africans, or Amerindians captured from further and further inland.

- ❑ **1637–1654** Dutch control sugar-growing areas.
- ❑ **1763** Rio becomes capital.
- ❑ **1788** *Inconfidência* rebellion, led by Tiradentes, fails.
- ❑ **1807** French invade Portugal. King João VI flees to Brazil with British naval escort. In return, Brazil's ports opened to foreign trade.
- ❑ **1821** King returns to Portugal. Son Pedro made regent of Brazil.
- ❑ **1822** Pedro I declares independence and is made Emperor of Brazil.
- ❑ **1828** Brazil loses Uruguay.
- ❑ **1831** Military revolt after war with Argentina (1825–1828). Emperor abdicates. Five-year-old son succeeds him as Pedro II.
- ❑ **1835–1845** Rio Grande secedes.
- ❑ **1865–1870** Brazil wins war of Triple Alliance with Argentina and Uruguay against Paraguay.
- ❑ **1888** Pedro II abolishes slavery; landowners and military turn against him.
- ❑ **1889** First Republic established. Emperor goes into exile in Paris. Increasing prosperity as result of international demand for coffee.
- ❑ **1891** Federal constitution established.
- ❑ **1914–1918** First World War hits coffee exports.
- ❑ **1920s** Working class and intellectual movements call for end to oligarchic rule.
- ❑ **1930** Coffee prices collapse. Revolt led by Dr. Getúlio Vargas, the "Father of the Poor," who becomes president. Fast industrial growth.
- ❑ **1937** Vargas's position as benevolent dictator formalized in "New State," based on fascist model.
- ❑ **1942** Declares war on Germany. ⇨

CHRONOLOGY *continued*

- ❏ **1945** Vargas forced out by military.
- ❏ **1951** Vargas reelected as leader of Labor Party.
- ❏ **1954** USA opposes Vargas's socialist policies, including plans to double minimum wage. The right, backed by the military, demand his resignation. Commits suicide.
- ❏ **1956–1960** President Juscelino Kubitschek, backed by Brazilian Workers' Party (PTB), attracts foreign investment for new industries, especially from USA.
- ❏ **1960–1961** Conservative Jânio da Silva Quadros president. Tries to break dependence on US trade.
- ❏ **1961** Brasília, built in three years, becomes new capital. PTB leader, João Goulart, elected president.
- ❏ **1961–1964** President's powers briefly curtailed as right wing reacts to presidential policies.
- ❏ **1964** Bloodless military coup under army chief Gen. Castelo Branco.
- ❏ **1965** Branco assumes dictatorship; bans existing political parties, but creates two official new ones. He is followed by a succession of military rulers. Fast-track economic development, the Brazilian Miracle, is counterbalanced by ruthless suppression of left-wing activists.
- ❏ **1974** World oil crisis marks end of economic boom. Brazil's foreign debt now largest in world.
- ❏ **1979** More political parties allowed.
- ❏ **1980** Huge migrations into Rondônia state begin.
- ❏ **1985** Civilian senator Tancredo Neves wins presidential elections at head of new liberal alliance, but dies before taking office. Illiterate adults get the vote.
- ❏ **1987** Gold found on Yanomani lands in Roraima state; illegal diggers rush in by the thousand.
- ❏ **1988** New constitution promises massive social spending but fails to address land reform. Chico Mendes, rubber-tappers' union leader and environmentalist, murdered.
- ❏ **1989** Brazil's first environmental protection plan drawn up. Yearly inflation reaches 1000%. Fernando Collor de Mello wins first fully democratic presidential elections.
- ❏ **1990** Sweeping economic measures. New currency.
- ❏ **1992** Earth Summit in Rio. Collor resigns: impeached for corruption.
- ❏ **1994–1995** Plan Real ends hyperinflation. Congress resists constitutional reforms, but passes key privatizations of state monopolies.
- ❏ **1998–1999** Fernando Henrique Cardoso, in power since 1995, re-elected president. Real devalued in economic crisis.

POLITICS

▷ Multiparty elections

L. House 1998/2002
U. House 1998/2002

President Fernando
Henrique Cardoso

AT THE LAST ELECTION

Chamber of Deputies 513 members

21% PFL	20% PT	19% PSDB	16% PMDB	12% PPB	6% PTB	6% Other

PFL = Liberal Front Party   **PT** = PT-leftist coalition
PSDB = Brazilian Social Democratic Party   **PMDB** = Brazilian Democratic Movement Party   **PPB** = Brazilian Progressive Party   **PTB** = Brazilian Labor Party

Federal Senate 81 members

33% PMDB	23% PFL	20% PSDB	16% PT	7% PPB	1% PTB

The PT-Leftist coalition includes the Workers' Party (PT), the Democratic Labor Party (PDT) and the Brazilian Socialist Party (PSB). Others includes the Popular Socialist Party (PPS).

President Fernando Cardoso, who took office in January 1995.

Former president Itamar Franco, whose government introduced the real.

Brazil is a democratic federal republic with 27 regional parliaments and a national congress. In 1993, Brazilians voted to retain directly elected presidents.

MAIN POLITICAL ISSUES
Reducing the fiscal deficit
The reduction of the fiscal deficit has been a key objective of President Cardoso, but one which he has found hard to achieve. Since his re-election in 1998 pressure for cutting spending has increased with the economic crisis.

Redrafting the constitution
The government seeks to reform the 1988 constitution which has proved unworkable. The state cannot cover its social welfare commitments, while local governments, designed to check federal power, duplicate functions at high overall cost. Reformists want provisions to curb tax evasion, and were successful in 1995 in ending state monopolies and allowing foreign investment in telecommunications, oil, mining and shipping. Another target is electoral reform to curb the increasing involvement of small parties in government. President Cardoso secured an amendment in 1997 enabling him to stand for, and win, a further term from January 1999.

Political stability
The more obstacles Brazilian politicians present to Cardoso's reforms, the more nervous Brazil's international sponsors are likely to become. Plans to reduce tax revenues passed on to states could lead to a stand-off between federal and state governments and delay reform of the country's archaic tax structure.

PROFILE
Military rule between 1964 and 1985 led to gross human rights abuses, particularly against Amazon Indians,

Luís Ignacio da Silva, "Lula," former leader of the left-wing Workers' Party.

and economic mismanagement, which left Brazil with a legacy of huge debts and inefficient state industries.

Brazil's young democracy is characterized by a weak party system, centered around personalities rather than parties. Parties do not have set ideological programs, but form shaky coalitions and engage in horsetrading to get legislation through Congress. The preponderance of small parties and corruption adds to the problems. Former President Collor de Mello was impeached in 1992 on fraud charges.

Dissatisfaction with the center-right provided a boost for the left, led by the influential Luís da Silva, when he came second to Collor de Mello in the 1989 presidential elections. His coming in second place to Cardoso in 1994 and again in 1998, however, revealed there to be a lack of fresh ideas and direction in his Workers' Party. Faced with recession and the expected return of double-digit inflation, the feeling in the Congress and country was that Cardoso, the father of the Real anti-inflation plan, is better equipped to deal with the economic crisis than anybody else.

Coffee plantation, São Paulo state. Coffee was introduced into Brazil in the early 18th century. It is declining in importance and now accounts for less than 4% of export revenues.

WORLD AFFAIRS

▷ Joined UN in 1945

AmCC | G24 | Mercosr | OAS | RG

Brazil plays a leading role with Argentina, Paraguay, and Uruguay in MERCOSUR, the South American common market, whose confidence and influence is growing. By virtue of this, and as the largest economy in Latin America, it is playing a pivotal role in ongoing negotiations with the USA on the nature of the proposed Free Trade Area for the Americas. A possible free trade accord between MERCOSUR and the EU will further boost Brazil's leadership position in the region.

Brazil is campaigning for a permanent seat in an enlarged UN Security Council and wants to maintain even-handedness in its international relations.

The 1998/99 financial crisis underlined the importance of Brazil's stability for the global economy.

AID

▷ Recipient

$487m (receipts) | ⬆ Up 19% 1996–1997

Recent main aid donors are the EU, the World Bank, and Japan for environmental, basic sanitation, road building and antipoverty projects. As well as official aid, much comes from NGOs, mainly for environmental and housing projects.

DEFENSE

▷ Compulsory military service

$13.9bn | ⬇ Down 3% in 1997

Moves are on to transfer the responsibilities of the war ministries to a new Defense Ministry.

BRAZILIAN ARMED FORCES

🚜	60 main battle tanks (*Leopard*)	195,000 personnel
🚢	6 submarines, 2 destroyers, 18 frigates, 36 patrol boats	68,250 personnel
✈	278 combat aircraft (58 AT-26, 46 F-5E/B/F)	50,000 personnel
✈	None	

Although it withdrew from direct participation in government in 1985, the military retains a strong political presence and controls the far north for security reasons. Brazil has a large arms industry.

The government signed the Nuclear Non-Proliferation and Comprehensive Nuclear Test Ban treaties in 1998 and states that it has no intention of using its nuclear energy capacity for military purposes or for the manufacture of nuclear bombs.

ECONOMICS

▷ Inflation 12.1% p.a. (1985–1996)

📊 $784bn | 💵 1.11–1.21 real

SCORE CARD

❏ WORLD GNP RANKING	8th
❏ GNP PER CAPITA	$4,790
❏ BALANCE OF PAYMENTS	$–33.8bn
❏ INFLATION	6.9%
❏ UNEMPLOYMENT	7%

EXPORTS

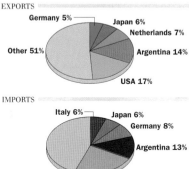

Germany 5% | Japan 6% | Netherlands 7% | Argentina 14% | USA 17% | Other 51%

IMPORTS

Italy 6% | Japan 6% | Germany 8% | Argentina 13% | USA 23% | Other 44%

STRENGTHS

Local industry is well developed, making Brazil dominant in the region. Immense natural resources: the world's largest producer of coffee, second largest producer of soya beans and one of the largest sugar and orange juice exporters. Large deposits of gold, silver and iron. One of world's most important steel producers.

WEAKNESSES

Chaotic finances of the states threatening economic stability. Foreign investment deterred by bribes and fines linked to conducting business. Preferences given to national businesses in the sale of state companies. Vulnerability to commodity price fluctuations. Political instability.

PROFILE

Brazil has one of the world's major economies, but also one of the hardest to manage. During the 1960s and 1970s, GDP expanded by an average of 11% a year. The economy underwent major diversification and industrialization, and today Brazil is a significant producer of cars and computers. However, profligate spending during this period resulted in a debt burden which dominated economic affairs in the 1980s.

Economic reform, initiated in 1990, enabled Brazil to reschedule its debts, but a steep recession followed in 1990–1992. The launching of the new currency, the real, in 1994 was the fifth attempt at monetary stabilization since 1986. It contributed to the dramatic reduction of inflation from around 50% a month in 1994 to less than 5% a year

ECONOMIC PERFORMANCE INDICATOR

by 1997. Economic growth in 1994 boosted regional confidence and facilitated the launch of MERCOSUR, the common market with neighboring Argentina, Paraguay, and Uruguay. In 1995, a fractious Congress blocked reforms of the tax and social security system, but finally agreed to end state monopolies in such sectors as telecommunications and oil, thereby reviving the government's privatization program. The economy grew strongly during 1996 and 1997, but was threatened by an international crisis of investor confidence in 1998. A US$41.5 billion rescue package was arranged with the IMF. Foreign exchange reserves had to be used in support of the currency, which gave way in January 1999 and was devalued after strong speculative pressure. Facing the worst recession on record, the government opted to use tight monetary policy to limit the inflationary impact of the devaluation while simultaneously tackling the budget deficit in a bid to win back investor confidence and renewed capital flows. However rising inflation, debt default, mounting opposition to austerity and further major reforms, especially tax reform, remain real risks.

BRAZIL : MAJOR BUSINESSES

🏦	Banking
🖥	Computers
📖	Publishing
🔌	Electronics
🌲	Saw milling
↓	Sugarcane refining
🚗	Vehicle assembly
☕	Coffee processing

0   1000 km
0   1000 miles

* significant multinational ownership

B

RESOURCES

▷ Electric power 59.0m kw

🐟 850,000 tonnes

🛢 630,732 b/d (reserves 3,030,000,000 bbl)

🐄 161m cattle, 31.4m pigs, 12.6m goats 18.3m sheep

💎 Iron, manganese, coal, bauxite, nickel, oil, tin, silver, diamonds, gold

ELECTRICITY GENERATION

Hydro 92% (253.8bn kwh)
Combustion 7% (19bn kwh)
Nuclear 1% (2.5bn kwh)
Other 0%

| 0 | 20 | 40 | 60 | 80 | 100 |

% of total generation by type

Nuclear power has been dogged by controversy and high costs, but the construction of the Angra-2 nuclear power station was approved in 1996 to complement Angra-1. A plant to supply both with uranium pellets and powder, which were previously imported, was opened in 1999. Hydropower has been more successful, accounting about 90% of electricity generation. Construction of a 3,000-km (1,800-mile) pipeline to transport gas from Bolivia to Brazil's industrial south is finished. Producing ethanol from sugar represents an attempt to reduce gasoline imports, and the welcoming of foreign companies in the areas of exploration and production is set to increase oil and natural gas reserves.

BRAZIL : LAND USE

▦ Cropland
▨ Forest
☐ Pasture
🐄 Cattle
☕ Coffee – cash crop
🍊 Oranges

| 0 | 1000 km |
| 0 | 1000 miles |

Equatorial vegetation near Manaus in the center of Amazonas state. The brown waters of the Rio Solimões and the black waters of the Rio Negro meet near Manaus.

ENVIRONMENT

▷ No Green MPs

🔺 4% (1% partially protected)

⬇ Low

ENVIRONMENTAL TREATIES

🌱 Yes
🦏 Yes
🌐 Yes
🛢 Yes
🔋 Yes
♻ Yes

Federal agencies charged with protecting the Amazon rainforest are underfunded, understaffed, and accused of corruption.

The forest contains an estimated 90% of all the world's plants and animals but the demands of agriculture are leading to its destruction at a rate of between 15,000 and 20,000 sq km (5,700 – 7,700 sq miles) a year. As a result of such massive clearances, usually for cattle pasture and logging, vital genetic diversity is being lost.

Other serious problems are opencast bauxite mines which pollute rivers and threaten the livelihoods of indigenous Amerindians. In the cities, widespread industrial pollution and untreated sewage continue to be major problems.

MEDIA

▷ TV ownership high

📰 Daily newspaper circulation 40 per 1,000 people

PUBLISHING AND BROADCAST MEDIA

There are 380 daily newspapers. The leading newspapers include *A Folha de São Paulo*, *O Día* and *O Globo*

19 state-owned, 218 independent stations

1 state-owned, 2,000 independent services

Although there is now no official censorship, TV and radio operating licenses are awarded as political favors, and state advertising is so extensive that it cannot fail to influence editorial policy. Media ownership is also highly concentrated. The Globo group, Brazil's only nationwide broadcasting company, was able to exclude the left from news reports and debates during the 1989 presidential elections, thus helping to secure the victory of Collor de Mello.

CRIME

▷ No death penalty

🚪 87,053 prisoners

⬆ The rate is sharply up. More street children are being murdered

CRIME RATES

| **Murders** | |
| 10 | per 100,000 population |

| **Rapes** | |
| 6 | per 100,000 population |

| **Thefts** | |
| 74 | per 100,000 population |

Crime levels are among the world's highest, especially in cities, with armed robbery and narcotics-related crime uppermost. Badly paid police are frequently accused of extortion and violence against and murder of citizens. Death squads, thought to be linked to the police, have targeted street children in major cities. A combination of atrocious conditions and overcrowding mean that violent disturbances in prisons are common.

In the countryside, violent land disputes are also common. Landless squatters and indigenous peoples, in theory with a guaranteed right to their land, have been wounded and murdered in the process of being driven off land by gunmen funded by large landowners.

In Roraima state, the discovery of large gold deposits has led to the homelands of Brazil's largest tribe, the Yanomami, being invaded by thousands of gun-toting prospectors, *garimpeiros*.

EDUCATION

▷ School leaving age: 14

🎓 84%

👨‍🎓 1.71m students

Average time spent at school is less than in other Latin American countries.

THE EDUCATION SYSTEM

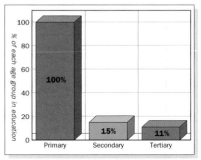

% of each age group in education

| Primary | Secondary | Tertiary |
| 100% | 15% | 11% |

The portion of GDP spent on education is comparable to that of European countries but misapplied, so that basic primary education remains weak while many children of wealthy families receive excellent tuition at free public universities. Of Brazil's 95 universities, 55 are administered by the state.

The illiteracy level around 15%, and nearly 3 million children do not attend school at all, especially those living in the northeast and Amazonia, and the urban poor, including street children.

Education follows the French system with a *bachillerato* (*baccalauréat*) at the end of secondary schooling.

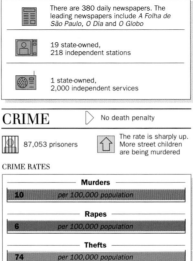

EXPLOITATION VERSUS PROTECTION IN AMAZONIA

THE VAST AMAZON RIVER basin, extending across northern Brazil, contains one of the world's last great remaining virgin rainforests. Road-building projects, especially the construction of the Tranzamazonian and Perimetral North highways to link with the Panamerican Highway, mean that it no longer enjoys the protection of inaccessibility. Since 1970, when it was still 99% intact, more than 550,000 sq km (over 210,000 sq miles) of Amazonia, some 15% of the total, has been deforested. In the late 1990s, deforestation was still running at between 15,000 and 20,000 sq km a year.

DAMAGE TO RAINFOREST

Some of the damage is done by mining, particularly for gold, and the associated pollution of soil and water. Land clearance for ranching may also occur wherever the forest is opened up to exploitation by the building of access roads. It is logging, however, which poses the greatest threat. Amazonian tropical hardwoods are particularly attractive to the timber industry now that the forests of south-east Asia and central Africa are becoming so seriously depleted. A score of foreign-owned multinational companies dominate the timber export business, and some 2,500 logging companies and sawmills operate in the Brazilian Amazon. Brazilian mahogany is now protected by a moratorium on exploitation, but illegal logging is widespread; the government estimates that it accounts for 80% of all timber being extracted from the Amazon today.

ENVIRONMENTAL CONSEQUENCES

The rainforest typically has poor and shallow soil. Its ecology depends on the recycling of minerals in the leaf litter on the forest floor. In a damp environment, the leaf litter is broken down rapidly by soil animals. Once exposed by the loss of tree cover, however, it dries out rapidly and can easily be washed away when the next rain comes. The forest cannot regenerate growth where substantial areas have been cleared. The deforestation has far-reaching implications. Forests act as "carbon sinks", fixing carbon dioxide produced by the burning of fuel, and thus helping to counteract the build-up of the "greenhouse gases" linked with global warming. Amazonia is also immensely rich in native plant and animal species, a genetic pool of incalculable potential value, for example in medicine or agriculture. This biodiversity, including much as yet undiscovered by the international scientific community, is dependent on proper protection of rainforest habitat.

INDIGENOUS PEOPLES

The gradual colonization of the Amazon region has brought violence and devastating epidemics of disease to its indigenous peoples, along with loss of lands, forced removal, confinement to reservations and destruction of their lifestyle and culture. Although many have suffered extinction in the last half century, there remain nearly 200 distinct known forest-dwelling indigenous peoples. Under the 1988 constitution, forest peoples have the right to inhabit their ancestral lands, but not legal ownership over it. In 1991, land along the Venezuela border inhabited by the Yanomami, one of the largest and best-known hunter-gatherer groups, was designated an indigenous park by Presidential decree. However, the National Indian Foundation (FUNAI), a government agency responsible for the demarcation of indigenous reserves, came under heavy criticism internationally in the 1990s for failing to give them adequate protection.

HEALTH

▷ Welfare state health benefits

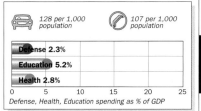

1 per 714 people | Heart diseases, cancers, accidents, violence

Health care will suffer from austerity measures lopping US$7 billion off public spending in 1999.

The federal health system is bankrupt. Fewer than 20% of hospitals are state-run and these are underfunded and need modernization. Private care is very expensive. The World Bank has criticized the under-financing of preventive health care. On average, only 15% of the health budget is allocated to child health, immunization and other preventive programs. Malaria is widespread in Amazonia, mainly in settler towns. Leprosy and parasitic skin infections are common, again often affecting settlers.

SPENDING

▷ GDP/cap. no increase

CONSUMPTION AND SPENDING

128 per 1,000 population | 107 per 1,000 population

Defense 2.3%		
Education 5.2%		
Health 2.8%		

0 5 10 15 20 25
Defense, Health, Education spending as % of GDP

Brazil's income distribution is among the most skewed in the world. Inter-American Development Bank figures in 1999 show that the wealthiest 10% of the country's population take half of the income and the poorest 50% only 10%. The UN classifies over 50% of the population as living in poverty. Governments have failed to tackle the problem of homelessness and street children in Rio, São Paulo, and other large cities. An estimated one to five million families remain landless, while nearly 80% of the country's farmland is owned by 10% of landowners.

WORLD RANKING

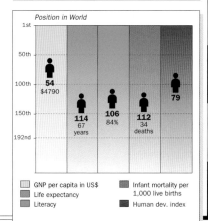

Position in World

1st
50th
100th
150th
192nd

54 $4790
114 67 years
106 84%
112 34 deaths
79

☐ GNP per capita in US$
☐ Life expectancy
☐ Literacy
☐ Infant mortality per 1,000 live births
☐ Human dev. index

BRUNEI

OFFICIAL NAME: The Sultanate of Brunei   **CAPITAL:** Bandar Seri Begawan
POPULATION: 313,000   **CURRENCY:** Brunei dollar   **OFFICIAL LANGUAGE:** Malay

Asia

SOUTHEAST ASIA

| 1984 | 1984 | Feb 23 | BRU | +8 | +673 | .bn |

LYING ON THE NORTHWESTERN coast of the island of Borneo, Brunei is divided in two by a strip of the surrounding Malaysian state of Sarawak. The interior is mostly rain forest. Independent from the UK since 1984, Brunei is ruled by decree of the Sultan. It is undergoing increasing Islamicization. Oil and gas reserves have brought one of the world's highest standards of living.

CLIMATE ▷ Tropical equatorial

WEATHER CHART

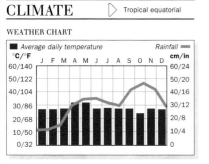

■ Average daily temperature   Rainfall ■

Just 480 km (300 miles) north of the equator, Brunei has a six-month rainy season with extremely high humidity.

TRANSPORTATION ▷ Drive on left

Brunei International, Bandar Seri Begawan

97 ships
365,000 grt

THE TRANSPORTATION NETWORK

1,296 km (805 miles)		None	
19 km (12 miles)		209 km (130 miles)	

Interest-free loans for civil servants, subsidized gasoline and limited public transport account for the high rates of car ownership.

TOURISM ▷ Visitors : population 2.7:1

636,000 visitors

Up 8% in 1994

MAIN TOURIST ARRIVALS

Malaysia 85%	
Singapore 4%	
Indonesia 2%	
Other 9%	

% of total arrivals

Although keen to protect Bruneians from Western influence, the government wants to develop quality tourism as part of its diversification program. Promoted as the "Gateway to Borneo," Brunei's rain forests could be developed for ecotourism. A former attraction was the Churchill Museum, founded by the late Sultan. This has now been superseded by the Museum of Royal Regalia.

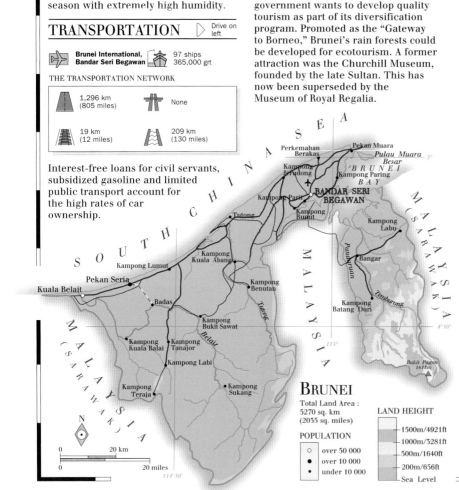

BRUNEI

Total Land Area :
5270 sq. km
(2035 sq. miles)

POPULATION

○ over 50 000
● over 10 000
• under 10 000

LAND HEIGHT

1500m/4921ft
1000m/3281ft
500m/1640ft
200m/656ft
Sea Level

PEOPLE ▷ Pop. density medium

Malay, English, Chinese

59/km²
(154/mi²)

THE URBAN/RURAL POPULATION SPLIT

70%   30%

ETHNIC MAKEUP

Indigenous 6%
Other 11%
Chinese 16%
Malay 67%

Malays benefit from positive discrimination; many in the Chinese community are either stateless or hold British protected person passports. Among indigenous groups, the Murut and Dusuns are favored over the Ibans. Women, less restricted than in some Muslim states, are obliged to wear headscarves but not the veil. Many hold influential posts in the civil service.

POLITICS ▷ No multiparty elections

Not applicable

HM Sultan Haji Sir Hassannal Bolkiah Mu'izzadin Waddaulah

LEGISLATIVE OR ADVISORY BODIES

Council of Cabinet Ministers

Brunei is an absolute monarchy; the Sultan consults four Advisory Councils: Religious Council, Privy Council, Council of Cabinet Ministers and Council of Succession, which he appoints. Political parties have been banned since 1988.

Since a failed rebellion in 1962, a state of emergency has been in force and the Sultan has ruled by decree. Hopes for democracy were dashed when political parties were banned in 1988. In 1990, "Malay Muslim Monarchy" was introduced, promoting Islamic values as the state ideology. This further alienated the large Chinese and expatriate communities. Power is closely tied to the royal family. One of the Sultan's brothers holds the foreign affairs portfolio; the Sultan himself looks after defense and finance.

WORLD AFFAIRS ▷ Joined UN in 1984

| APEC | ASEAN | Comm | OIC | WTO |

Brunei claims part of the Spratly Islands. Political exiles opposed to the government and based in Malaysia are a main concern. Relations with the UK, the ex-colonial power, are good.

The magnificent Omar Ali Saifuddin mosque is surrounded by an artificial lagoon.

AID ▷ Donor

💲 $2.1bn (donations)   ⇕ Not applicable

Aid spending is largely *ad hoc*. It has included donations to the Contras in Nicaragua, the Bosnian Muslims and the homeless of New York.

DEFENSE ▷ No compulsory military service

💲 US$353m   ⬆ Up 3% in 1997

As well as being head of the 5,000-strong armed forces, the Sultan has a personal bodyguard of 2,000 UK-trained Gurkhas. The UK and Singapore are close defense allies.

ECONOMICS ▷ Not available

📊 US$3.9bn   💲 1.69–1.65 Brunei dollars

SCORE CARD

❑ WORLD GNP RANKING	116th
❑ GNP PER CAPITA	$14,240
❑ BALANCE OF PAYMENTS	$2,999m
❑ INFLATION	1.7%
❑ UNEMPLOYMENT	5%

STRENGTHS
Twenty-five years of known oil reserves; 40 years of gas. Earnings from massive overseas investments, mainly in the USA and Europe, now exceed oil and gas revenues.

WEAKNESSES
Single-product economy. Failure of diversification programs could lead to problems in the future.

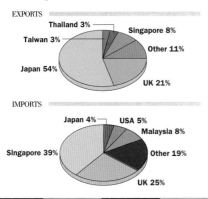

EXPORTS

Thailand 3% — Singapore 8%
Taiwan 3% — Other 11%
Japan 54%
UK 21%

IMPORTS

Japan 4% — USA 5%
Malaysia 8%
Singapore 39% — Other 19%
UK 25%

RESOURCES ▷ Electric power 473,000 kw

🐟 4,822 tonnes   🛢 159,718 b/d (reserves 1,350,000,000 bbl)

🐷 4,500 pigs, 2,200 cattle, 4,700 goats, 3m chickens   💎 Oil, natural gas

Oil and gas are the major resources. Energy policy now focuses on regulating output in order to conserve stocks, since reserves are of relatively limited duration.

ENVIRONMENT ▷ No Green MPs

🔺 5% partially protected   ⇕ Not available

The Forest Strategic Plan aims to protect Brunei's forests (which account for 80% of its land area), but has yet to make specific areas of responsibility clear. The result is that rain forest is still under threat. Brunei's mangrove swamps, the largest on Borneo, remain unprotected.

MEDIA ▷ TV ownership medium

❌ Daily newspaper circulation 69 per 1,000 people

PUBLISHING AND BROADCAST MEDIA

There is 1 newspaper, the daily *Borneo Bulletin*

1 state-owned service   1 state-owned service

The state effectively controls all media. Brunei TV has recently increased its religious programming.

CRIME ▷ Death penalty not used

🔒 312 prisoners   ⬆ Up 132% from 1992–1996

Crime levels are low. Most crime involves petty theft or is linked to alcohol and narcotics (both banned). A stolen car often makes TV news headlines. The state of emergency gives the government the power to detain without charge or trial for indefinitely renewable two-year periods.

EDUCATION ▷ School leaving age: 16

📖 90%   👨‍🎓 1,606 students

Free schooling is available to all the population, with the exception of stateless Chinese, who do not qualify. The University of Brunei Darussalam is undergoing Islamicization.

HEALTH ▷ Welfare state health benefits

🏥 1 per 1,133 people   ☠ Heart diseases, cancers

The health service is free, although for major surgery Bruneians tend to travel to Singapore.

CHRONOLOGY

Under British control since 1841, Brunei became a formal British Protectorate in 1888.

- ❑ **1929** Oil extraction begins.
- ❑ **1959** First constitution enshrines Islam as state religion. Internal self-government.
- ❑ **1962** Pro-democracy rebellion. Declaration of state of emergency.
- ❑ **1984** Independence from Britain. Brunei joins ASEAN.
- ❑ **1990** Ideology of "Malay Muslim Monarchy" introduced.
- ❑ **1991** Imports of alcohol banned.
- ❑ **1992** Joins Non-Aligned Movement.
- ❑ **1998** Sultan's son, Prince Al-Muhtadee Billah, made crown prince.

SPENDING ▷ GDP/cap. no increase

CONSUMPTION AND SPENDING

🚗 167 per 1,000 population   📞 240 per 1,000 population

Defense 6.7%
Education No data
Health 2.2%

0   5   10   15   20   25
Defense, Health, Education spending as % of GDP

The wealthy in Brunei are those closest to the Sultan, the world's richest man according to *Forbes* magazine. A high general standard of living keeps discontent to a minimum. Promotion within the civil service and universal education allow some social mobility among Malays. Bruneians are major consumers of high-tech hi-fi and video equipment, designer-label watches and Western designer clothes. Telephone lines, however, are difficult to install.

WORLD RANKING

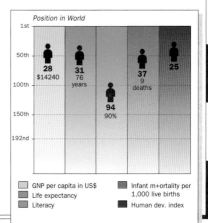

Position in World
1st
50th — 28 $14240 | 31 76 years | | 37 9 deaths | 25
100th — | | 94 90% | |
150th —
192nd

☐ GNP per capita in US$ ☐ Infant m+ortality per
☐ Life expectancy   1,000 live births
☐ Literacy   ☐ Human dev. index

BULGARIA

B

OFFICIAL NAME: Republic of Bulgaria   CAPITAL: Sofia
POPULATION: 8.4 million   CURRENCY: Lev   OFFICIAL LANGUAGE: Bulgarian

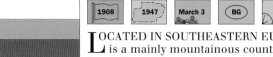

| 1908 | 1947 | March 3 | BG | +2 | +359 | .bg |

LOCATED IN SOUTHEASTERN EUROPE, Bulgaria is a mainly mountainous country. The River Danube forms the northern border, while the popular resorts of the Black Sea lie to the east. The most populated areas are around Sofia in the west, Plovdiv in the south, and along the Danube plain. Bulgaria was ruled by the Turks from 1396 until 1878. In 1908 it became an independent kingdom, and was under communist rule from 1947 to 1989, the last 35 of those years under Todor Zhivkov. The 1990s brought political instability as the country adjusted to democracy and economic reconstruction.

Rila Monastery in the Rila Mountains. It is famous for its 1,200 National Revival Period frescoes dating from the mid-19th century.

CLIMATE
▷ Mediterranean/continental

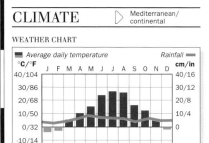

WEATHER CHART

■ Average daily temperature   Rainfall ■

The central valley and the lowlands have warm summers and cold, snowy winters, but hot or cold winds from Russia can bring spells of more extreme weather. The hotter summers on the Black Sea coast have encouraged the growth of tourist resorts. Snow may lie on the high mountain peaks until June.

TRANSPORTATION
▷ Drive on right

Sofia International
1.3m passengers

187 ships
1.1m grt

THE TRANSPORTATION NETWORK

| 37,300 km (23,200 miles) | 266 km (165 miles) |
| 4,292 km (2,667 miles) | 470 km (292 miles) |

At the crossroads between Europe and Asia, Bulgarian railroads and expressways were underfunded under Zhivkov (when north–south routes were deliberately left undeveloped) and in the economic uncertainty of the 1990s. Funding for modernizing key routes is now in place. Ferries are used for most cross-Danube traffic. In 1998 talks continued with Romania on building a second bridge across the river.

TOURISM
▷ Visitors : population 1:3.1

2.7m visitors

Down 35% 1995–1997

MAIN TOURIST ARRIVALS

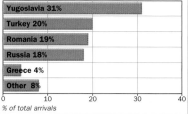

Yugoslavia 31%	
Turkey 20%	
Romania 19%	
Russia 18%	
Greece 4%	
Other 8%	

% of total arrivals

Under communism, the tourist industry catered for the east European mass-market. Western tourists now include Greeks, Germans, and British visitors. Attracted by low prices for ski resorts and beach holidays, they still account for only 5% of visitors. Bulgaria is now privatizing the industry and seeking more upmarket visitors by stressing its heritage. In 1997 the fall in visitor numbers and earnings of the mid-1990s was reduced.

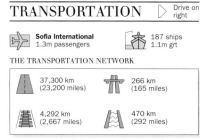

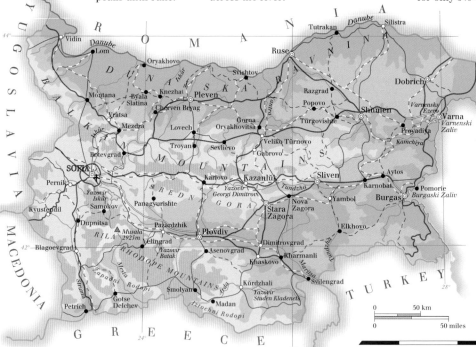

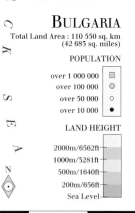

BULGARIA
Total Land Area : 110 550 sq. km (42 685 sq. miles)

POPULATION

over 1 000 000	▣
over 100 000	◎
over 50 000	○
over 10 000	●

LAND HEIGHT

2000m/6562ft	
1000m/3281ft	
500m/1640ft	
200m/656ft	
Sea Level	

B

PEOPLE ▷ Pop. density medium

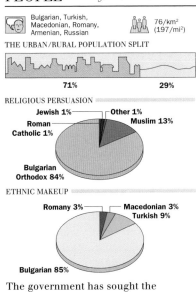

Bulgarian, Turkish, Macedonian, Romany, Armenian, Russian

76/km² (197/mi²)

THE URBAN/RURAL POPULATION SPLIT

71%   29%

RELIGIOUS PERSUASION

Jewish 1% — Other 1%
Roman Catholic 1% — Muslim 13%
Bulgarian Orthodox 84%

ETHNIC MAKEUP

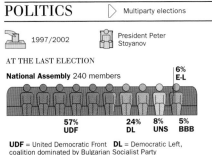

Romany 3% — Macedonian 3%
Turkish 9%
Bulgarian 85%

The government has sought the assimilation of separate ethnic groups, thereby suppressing cultural identities. During the 1970s, Bulgarian Muslims, or *Pomaks*, were forced to change Muslim names to Bulgarian ones. Bulgarian Turks were particularly targeted in the 1980s. Linguistic and religious freedom was granted in 1989, but 300,000 ethnic Turks, or 40%, still left for Turkey. Their farming skills have traditionally been important to agriculture. Recent privatizations have left many Turks landless and have provoked new emigration. The Turkish party, the MRF, which once held the balance of power in parliament, saw electoral support fall in 1994 and 1997.

Macedonians and Romanies each account for 3% of the population. The latter minority has no protection and suffers discrimination at all levels.

Women, especially Turkish women, have equal rights in theory, but society remains patriarchal.

POPULATION AGE BREAKDOWN

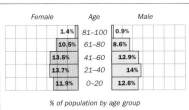

Female		Age	Male	
	1.4%	81–100	0.9%	
	10.5%	61–80	8.6%	
	13.5%	41–60	12.9%	
	13.7%	21–40	14%	
	11.9%	0–20	12.6%	

% of population by age group

WORLD AFFAIRS ▷ Joined UN in 1955

BSEC   CE   IBRD   CEFTA   OSCE

Despite the pro-Western orientation of the current UDF government, Bulgaria has had to accept that it is not one of the front rank applicants for EU and NATO membership. It has sent peacekeepers to Cambodia and has conscientiously adhered to UN sanctions against former Yugoslavia, despite the costs of lost trade. Trade with former Soviet countries continues to supply important raw materials and spare parts. Good relations with Turkey are as important now as they were under communism.

AID ▷ Recipient

$206m   Up 21% 1996–1997

IMF, World Bank, EU and EBRD loans are mainly for infrastructure improvements. In 1993, IMF agreements were suspended because of a growing budget deficit. The financial crisis and collapse of the lev in mid-1996 stalled talks with the IMF on a new loan, but one of $864 million was finally approved in late 1998.

POLITICS ▷ Multiparty elections

1997/2002   President Peter Stoyanov

AT THE LAST ELECTION

National Assembly 240 members

6% E-L

57% UDF   24% DL   8% UNS   5% BBB

UDF = United Democratic Front   **DL** = Democratic Left, coalition dominated by Bulgarian Socialist Party
UNS = Union of National Salvation   **E-L** = Euro-Left
BBB = Bulgarian Business Bloc

Bulgaria is a multiparty democracy.

MAIN POLITICAL ISSUES
Unstable alternation of power
Since its move to democracy in 1990, Bulgaria has suffered from successive weak governments, each brought down by no-confidence votes. In October 1992, the UDF, a broad anti-communist alliance, fell from office and was replaced by a nonparty government supported by BSP votes. An early general election in December 1994 gave the BSP an outright majority. In November 1996, however, the opposition UDF candidate, Peter Stoyanov, was elected president. BSP prime minister Zhan Videnov, blamed for his party's defeat, resigned; after early elections in April 1997 Ivan Kostov (UDF) became prime minister.

Political trials
Former communist officials are now finally being prosecuted for abuses under the former regime. Ex-autocrat Zhivkov, sentenced to seven years' imprisonment in 1992, was released from house arrest in 1997 and died in 1998. The government has now decided to allow access to pre-1989 State Security archives, after blocking access for a time, for fear that such a move would prove to be destabilizing.

PROFILE
Bulgaria is one of several Eastern European countries in which former communists returned to power. The BSP, representing former communists, won the 1994 general election, and thereafter resisted political and economic change. The result was one of the slowest privatization programs in eastern Europe, with the old communist web of patronage still intact, until the new government in 1997 launched free market reforms backed by the IMF.

Zhelyu Zhelev, a founder-member of the UDF, and president 1990–97.

Peter Stoyanov of the UDF, became president in 1996

CHRONOLOGY
Bulgaria was part of the Ottoman empire for five centuries until its independence in 1908. Under King Ferdinand, it sided with Germany during World War I, and subsequently lost valuable territory to Greece and Serbia. Under King Boris, Bulgaria once again sided with Germany in World War II.

❑ **1943** King Boris dies.
❑ **1944** Allies firebomb Sofia. Soviet army invades. Anti-fascist Fatherland Front coalition, including Agrarian Party and Bulgarian Communist Party (BCP), takes power in bloodless coup. Kimon Georgiev prime minister.
❑ **1946** September, referendum abolishes monarchy. Republic proclaimed. October, general election results in BCP majority.
❑ **1947** Prime Minister Georgi Dmitrov discredits Agrarian Party leader Nikola Petkov. Petkov arrested and sentenced to death. International recognition of Dmitrov government. Soviet-style constitution adopted; one-party state established. Country renamed People's Republic of Bulgaria. Nationalization of economy begins.
❑ **1949** Dmitrov dies, succeeded as prime minister by Vasil Kolarov.
❑ **1950** Kolarov dies. "Little Stalin" Vulko Chervenkov replaces him ▷

B

CHRONOLOGY *continued*

and begins BCP purge and collectivization.

❑ **1953** Stalin dies; Chervenkov's power begins to wane.

❑ **1954** Chervenkov yields power to Todor Zhivkov. Zhivkov sets out to make Bulgaria an inseparable part of the Soviet Union.

❑ **1955–1960** Zhivkov exonerates victims of Chervenkov's purges.

❑ **1965** Plot to overthrow Zhivkov discovered by Soviet agents.

❑ **1968** Bulgarian troops aid Soviet army in invasion of Czechoslovakia.

❑ **1971** New constitution. Zhivkov becomes president of State Council and resigns as premier.

❑ **1978** Purge of BCP: 30,000 members expelled.

❑ **1984** Turkish minority forced to take Slavic names.

❑ **1989** June–August, exodus of 300,000 Bulgarian Turks. November, Zhivkov ousted as BCP leader and head of state. Replaced by Petur Mladenov. Mass protest in Sofia for democratic reform. December, Union of Democratic Forces (UDF) formed.

❑ **1990** Economic collapse. January, National Assembly votes to divest BCP of constitutional role as leading political party. Zhivkov arrested. April, BCP changes name to Bulgarian Socialist Party (BSP). June, election produces no overall result. August, Zhelyu Zhelev, UDF leader, becomes president. BSP in government. Country renamed Republic of Bulgaria; communist symbols (grain sheaves and red star) removed from national flag.

❑ **1991** February, price controls abolished; steep price rises. July, new constitution adopted. October, UDF wins elections.

❑ **1992** Continued political and social unrest. October, UDF resigns after losing vote of confidence. December, Movement for Rights and Freedoms (MRF) forms government. Lyuben Berov prime minister. Zhivkov convicted of corruption and human rights abuses.

❑ **1993** Ambitious privatization program begins. Berov survives no-confidence vote tabled by UDF.

❑ **1994** Elections return BSP to power.

❑ **1995** BSP leader, Zhan Videnov, heads coalition government.

❑ **1996** Financial crisis and collapse of lev. Presidential elections won by opposition UDF candidate, Peter Stoyanov; Videnov resigns as prime minister.

❑ **1997** General election won by UDF, whose leader Ivan Kostov becomes prime minister.

DEFENSE
▷ Compulsory military service

💲 $339m   ⬇ Down 10% in 1997

Defense spending fell from 14% of GDP in 1985 to 3.4% in 1997.

BULGARIAN ARMED FORCES

🪖	1,475 main battle tanks (1,042 T-55, 433 T-72)	50,400 personnel
🚢	2 submarines, 1 frigate and 25 patrol boats	6,100 personnel
✈	217 combat aircraft (39 Su-25, 157 Mig-21/23/29)	19,300 personnel
🚀	None	

Cuts in defense spending and moves to reorganize the army have caused disaffection in officer ranks. The defense priority is to ensure that Bulgaria, which retains a large arms industry, can maintain national security without its former Soviet backing. In 1994 it joined NATO's Partnerships for Peace program, and in 1997 the new UDF government announced it would seek full NATO membership – a move opposed by the former communists. In 1999 the Kosovo crisis prompted Bulgaria to make its airspace available to NATO. In March 1999 the government approved plans to reduce the size of the army from 85,000 to 45,000 in five years.

ECONOMICS
▷ Inflation 46.1% p.a. (1985–1996)

📊 $9.75bn   💱 1,785.00–1,665.90 lev

SCORE CARD

❑ WORLD GNP RANKING	82nd
❑ GNP PER CAPITA	$1,170
❑ BALANCE OF PAYMENTS	$444m
❑ INFLATION	1,082.3%
❑ UNEMPLOYMENT	14%

EXPORTS

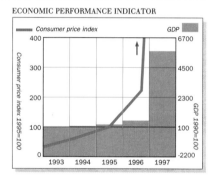

Russia 8%
Greece 9%
Germany 9%
Turkey 10%
Italy 12%
Other 52%

IMPORTS

France 4%
Greece 5%
Italy 8%
Germany 12%
Russia 27%
Other 44%

ECONOMIC PERFORMANCE INDICATOR

Consumer price index   GDP

[Graph: Consumer price index 1995=100 and GDP 1990=100, years 1993–1997]

STRENGTHS
Coal and natural gas. Good agricultural production, especially grapes for well-developed wine industry, and tobacco. Strong expertise in computer software.

WEAKNESSES
Outdated infrastructure and equipment, and outstanding debt throughout industry. Slow pace of privatization and structural reform.

PROFILE
Restructuring the economy is linked to privatization – a process delayed for political and technical reasons. A financial crisis in 1996 triggered the collapse of the national currency, the lev. Private and foreign investment is still negligible, despite laws that since 1992 have allowed foreign firms to own companies outright. Trade has shifted

toward the EU, which accounts for an increasing share of foreign trade. While trade with the former Soviet Union has fallen sharply, better economic relations are envisaged with Russia and Ukraine. The current UDF government has followed IMF advice, with free market reforms, backed by foreign loans, successfully bringing inflation under control and reversing two years of negative growth to achieve growth of 4-5% in 1998.

BULGARIA : MAJOR BUSINESSES

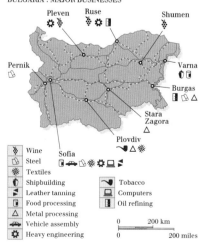

Pleven Ruse Shumen
Pernik
Varna
Burgas
Stara Zagora
Plovdiv
Sofia

🌿 Wine
◇ Steel
❋ Textiles
⚓ Shipbuilding
✂ Leather tanning
🗄 Food processing
△ Metal processing
🚗 Vehicle assembly
⚙ Heavy engineering
🍃 Tobacco
🖥 Computers
🛢 Oil refining

0   200 km
0   200 miles

B

RESOURCES

Electric power 12.1 kw

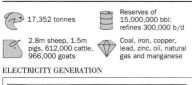

17,352 tonnes

Reserves of 15,000,000 bbl: refines 300,000 b/d

2.8m sheep, 1.5m pigs, 612,000 cattle, 966,000 goats

Coal, iron, copper, lead, zinc, oil, natural gas and manganese

ELECTRICITY GENERATION

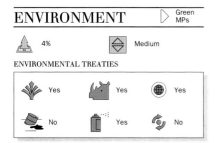

- Hydro 6% (2.3bn kwh)
- Combustion 53% (22.2bn kwh)
- Nuclear 41% (17.2bn kwh)
- Other 0%

0   20   40   60   80   100

% of total generation by type

Bulgaria has modest oil reserves and rather larger ones of coal and natural gas, but still has to import about 70% of its primary energy needs, much of it from the CIS. Unreliable supplies in the past led to frequent winter power cuts. These have largely disappeared, since reduced production in heavy industry and improved domestic supply have lowered import demand. Bulgaria is partly reliant on nuclear power. Two of the four reactors at Kozloduy were upgraded after criticisms over safety measures, and in 1995 the government authorized the restart of the plant. The first generator at the Chaira Dam came into service in 1993. In addition to mining other minerals, Bulgaria has the northern hemisphere's largest manganese mine.

ENVIRONMENT

Green MPs

4%

Medium

ENVIRONMENTAL TREATIES

Yes   Yes   Yes

No   Yes   No

Environmental degradation led to the foundation of the party *Ecoglasnost* in 1989. It circulated information on pollution and nuclear waste dump locations, and brought polluters to court. In 1995, the Kozloduy nuclear plant was restarted, despite concerns for its poor safety standards. Cleaning up the pollution from heating plants fueled by lignite and from mining and smelting works are key challenges. NATO bombing of Serbian chemical and oil refineries on the Danube in 1999 has led to downriver pollution in Bulgaria.

MEDIA

TV ownership high

Daily newspaper circulation 253 per 1,000 people

PUBLISHING AND BROADCAST MEDIA

There are 17 daily newspapers, including *Demokratsiya*, *Duma*, *Zemya* and *Trud*

1 state-owned service, 1 commercial

1 state-owned service, 9 independent

Although liberalized in 1989, media freedom is under pressure from the BSP-led coalition not to present government policies in an unfavorable light. No paper is completely independent, as each is linked to a party or interest. In 1998 the president vetoed a bill which aimed to liberalize the media further.

CRIME

Death penalty not used

9,684 prisoners

Up 4% from 1992-1996

CRIME RATES

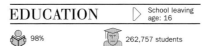

Murders
9   per 100,000 population

Rapes
9   per 100,000 population

Thefts
1812   per 100,000 population

In the 1990s Bulgaria became a key drug trafficking route to western Europe. Some 10,000 young women have been drawn into prostitution in the West. Counterfeiting, protection rackets, and similar activities are increasing. Violations of minority rights are a sensitive political issue.

EDUCATION

School leaving age: 16

98%

262,757 students

Of total government expenditure in 1996, 7% was spent on education.

THE EDUCATION SYSTEM

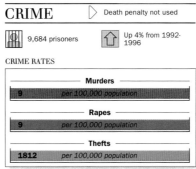

% of each age group in education

- Primary 99%
- Secondary 77%
- Tertiary 41%

Bulgaria has changed its educational system from a Soviet-inspired to a European-style model. Teaching standards are lowest in the rural and Turkish communities.

BULGARIA : LAND USE

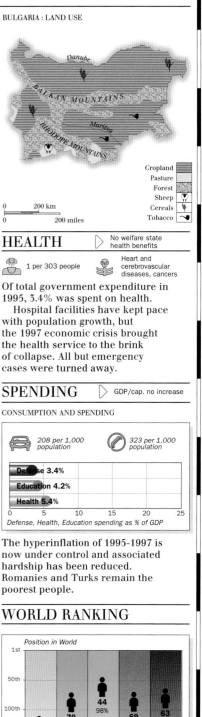

Danube

BALKAN MOUNTAINS

Maritsa

RHODOPE MOUNTAINS

0   200 km
0   200 miles

- Cropland
- Pasture
- Forest
- Sheep
- Cereals
- Tobacco

HEALTH

No welfare state health benefits

1 per 303 people

Heart and cerebrovascular diseases, cancers

Of total government expenditure in 1995, 3.4% was spent on health.

Hospital facilities have kept pace with population growth, but the 1997 economic crisis brought the health service to the brink of collapse. All but emergency cases were turned away.

SPENDING

GDP/cap. no increase

CONSUMPTION AND SPENDING

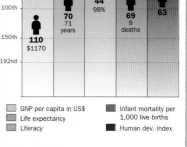

208 per 1,000 population

323 per 1,000 population

- Defense 3.4%
- Education 4.2%
- Health 5.4%

0   5   10   15   20   25
Defense, Health, Education spending as % of GDP

The hyperinflation of 1995-1997 is now under control and associated hardship has been reduced. Romanies and Turks remain the poorest people.

WORLD RANKING

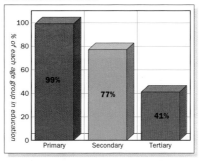

Position in World

1st
50th
100th
150th
192nd

- 110 $1170
- 70 71 years
- 44 98%
- 69 9 deaths
- 63

- GNP per capita in US$
- Life expectancy
- Literacy
- Infant mortality per 1,000 live births
- Human dev. index

BURKINA

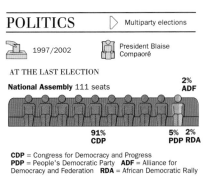

B

OFFICIAL NAME: Burkina Faso CAPITAL: Ouagadougou
POPULATION: 11.4 million CURRENCY: CFA franc OFFICIAL LANGUAGE: French

| 1960 | 1960 | Dec 11 | BF | 0 | +226 | .bf |

LANDLOCKED IN WEST AFRICA, Burkina (formerly Upper Volta) gained independence from France in 1960. The majority of Burkina lies in the arid fringe of the Sahara known as the Sahel. Ruled by military dictators for much of its post-independence history, Burkina became a multiparty state in 1991. However, much power still rests with President Blaise Compaoré. Burkina's economy remains largely based on agriculture.

CLIMATE ▷ Tropical/steppe

WEATHER CHART
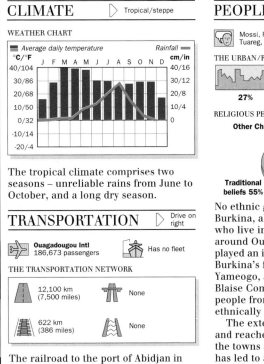
Average daily temperature   Rainfall

The tropical climate comprises two seasons – unreliable rains from June to October, and a long dry season.

TRANSPORTATION ▷ Drive on right

Ouagadougou Intl
186,673 passengers   Has no fleet

THE TRANSPORTATION NETWORK

| 12,100 km (7,500 miles) | None |
| 622 km (386 miles) | None |

The railroad to the port of Abidjan in the Ivory Coast provides the main commercial route to the sea. Roads through Benin, Togo, and Ghana provide alternative access.

TOURISM ▷ Visitors : population 1:82

138,000 visitors   Down 9% in 1997

MAIN TOURIST ARRIVALS

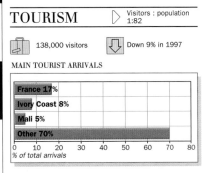

France 17%
Ivory Coast 8%
Mali 5%
Other 70%
0 10 20 30 40 50 60 70 80
% of total arrivals

Some potential exists for safari tourism, and the cities offer an attractive mix of colonial and African architecture. Big game hunting is allowed in some areas.

PEOPLE ▷ Pop. density low

Mossi, Fulani, French, Tuareg, Dyula, Songhai   42/km² (108/mi²)

THE URBAN/RURAL POPULATION SPLIT

27%   73%

RELIGIOUS PERSUASION

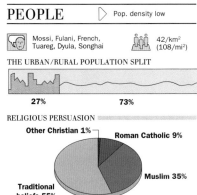

Other Christian 1%
Roman Catholic 9%
Muslim 35%
Traditional beliefs 55%

No ethnic group is dominant in Burkina, although the Mossi people who live in the area of their old empire around Ouagadougou have always played an important role in government. Burkina's first president, Maurice Yameogo, and the present leader, Blaise Compaoré, are both Mossi. The people from the west are much more ethnically mixed.

The extended family is important and reaches from the villages into the towns and cities. Extreme poverty has led to a strong sense of egalitarianism within society. The absence of women in public life belies their real power and influence, particularly within the traditional framework of the extended family. However, most women are still denied access to education and senior professional positions.

***Camel plowing.** Burkina's poor soils and frequent droughts lead many young men to emigrate seasonally in search of work.*

POLITICS ▷ Multiparty elections

1997/2002   President Blaise Compaoré

AT THE LAST ELECTION

National Assembly 111 seats

2% ADF
91% CDP
5% PDP 2% RDA

CDP = Congress for Democracy and Progress
PDP = People's Democratic Party **ADF** = Alliance for Democracy and Federation **RDA** = African Democratic Rally

Chamber of Representatives 178 members

Members of the House of Representatives are appointed or indirectly elected on a nonparty basis by provincial councils and various communities.

A multiparty democracy in theory, Burkina is still dominated in practice by former military dictator Blaise Compaoré, and the army remains influential behind the scenes. Compaoré has been in power since the assassination in 1987 of Capt. Thomas Sankara, his former superior. Several of Compaoré's close military colleagues have been murdered. His grip on power appears to be solid, and he was reelected president in 1997 with almost 91% of the vote. Most opposition leaders still live in exile, and real opposition within Burkina remains underground.

Disaffection with the regime has been growing however. The CDP and the government came under unexpected pressure in 1998 after public opinion was outraged by the assassination of a popular newspaper editor, Norbert Zongo, in which leading figures were implicated.

WORLD AFFAIRS ▷ Joined UN in 1960

| CILSS | Ecowas | OAU | OIC | FZ |

Burkina's landlocked position means that good relations with countries to the south are a major foreign policy concern. Compaoré's relationship with other Ecowas states was damaged by his support for rebellion in Liberia.

AID ▷ Recipient

$370m (receipts)   Down 11% 1996–1997

External aid, mostly from France and the EU, is important to Burkina's economy. The large number of NGOs has caused organizational problems; there is often difficulty in finding suitable projects for all the prospective donors.

BURKINA

Total Land Area : 273 800 sq. km
(105 714 sq. miles)

POPULATION

◎ over 100 000
○ over 50 000
● over 10 000
· under 10 000

LAND HEIGHT

500m/1640ft
200m/656ft
Sea Level

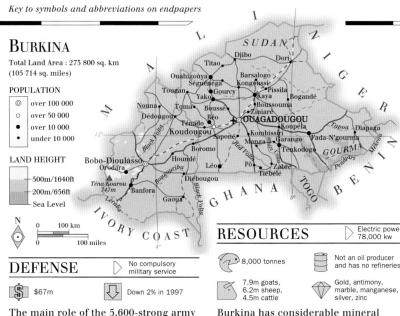

DEFENSE

▷ No compulsory military service

💲 $67m

⬇ Down 2% in 1997

The main role of the 5,600-strong army has been maintaining internal security. Burkina is reliant on France for most equipment and training.

ECONOMICS

▷ Inflation 3.3% p.a. (1985–1996)

📊 $2.6bn

💲 601.60–558.62 CFA francs

SCORE CARD

❏ WORLD GNP RANKING	130th
❏ GNP PER CAPITA	$250
❏ BALANCE OF PAYMENTS	$15m
❏ INFLATION	2.3%
❏ UNEMPLOYMENT	Not available

STRENGTHS

Remittances from plantation workers in Ghana and the Ivory Coast. Strongly improved economic management. Low debt burden. Ability to attract foreign aid. Cotton growing. Gold production is set for a major expansion.

WEAKNESSES

Landlocked. Few economically viable natural resources. Donors' fears over political instability. Food crop fluctuations. Prone to drought. Migrants' remittances have halved to about $80 million since 1988.

EXPORTS

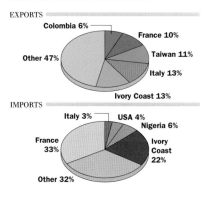

Colombia 6%
France 10%
Other 47%
Taiwan 11%
Italy 13%
Ivory Coast 13%

IMPORTS

Italy 3%　USA 4%
Nigeria 6%
France 33%
Ivory Coast 22%
Other 32%

RESOURCES

▷ Electric power 78,000 kw

🐟 8,000 tonnes

🛢 Not an oil producer and has no refineries

🐐 7.9m goats, 6.2m sheep, 4.5m cattle

💎 Gold, antimony, marble, manganese, silver, zinc

Burkina has considerable mineral wealth, including large manganese and silver deposits. However, the only metal ore being exploited is gold. Three hydroelectric dams will reduce dependence on thermal energy.

ENVIRONMENT

▷ No Green MPs

⚠ 11% (8% partially protected)

⬇ Low

Like other countries on the southern rim of the Sahara, desertification is the major ecological issue. The rate of tree cutting for fuel is on the increase.

MEDIA

▷ TV ownership low

📰 Daily newspaper circulation 1 per 1,000 people

PUBLISHING AND BROADCAST MEDIA

There are 4 daily newspapers, *Sidwaya*, *Le Pays*, *Le Journal de Soir* and *Observateur Paalga*

1 state-owned service

1 state-owned, 2 independent services

Limited press freedom since 1991 has seen the growth of a number of small independent newspapers funded by opposition groups.

CRIME

▷ Death penalty used

Burkina does not publish prison figures

⬆ General crime levels are rising

Crime levels have traditionally been low. However, the urbanization of society and the increase in political violence have seen levels increase.

EDUCATION

▷ School leaving age: 14

📖 21%

🎓 8,911 students

Education is based on the French system. Recently, practical subjects have received more emphasis.

CHRONOLOGY

Ruled by Mossi kings from the 16th century, Burkina became an outpost of the French empire in the late 19th century. It was renamed Upper Volta at independence in 1960.

❏ **1966** Military coup led by Lt.-Col. Sangoulé Lamizana.
❏ **1980** Lamizana ousted, Col. Saye Zerbo becomes president.
❏ **1982** Capt. Thomas Sankara takes power. People's Salvation Council (PSC) begins radical reforms.
❏ **1984** Renamed Burkina Faso.
❏ **1987** PSC reforms cause dissent. Sankara assassinated, Capt. Blaise Compaoré takes power.
❏ **1991** New constitution. Compaoré elected president.
❏ **1994** 50% devaluation of CFA franc.
❏ **1997** CDP landslide election victory.

HEALTH

▷ No wealth state health benefits

👤 1 per 57,300 people

💀 Malaria, diarrheal and respiratory diseases

The focus of the country's health spending is on primary health care and vaccination.

SPENDING

▷ GDP/cap. increase

CONSUMPTION AND SPENDING

🚗 4 per 1,000 population

📞 3 per 1,000 population

Defense 2.2%	
Education 3.6%	
Health 0.6%	

0　5　10　15　20　25
Defense, Health, Education spending as % of GDP

Burkina is a country of extreme, almost universal poverty. Displays of wealth are rare and ownership of electrical items like VCRS are limited to a small elite.

WORLD RANKING

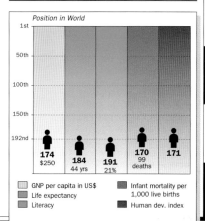

Position in World

1st
50th
100th
150th
192nd

174 $250
184 44 yrs
191 21%
170 99 deaths
171

☐ GNP per capita in US$
☐ Life expectancy
☐ Literacy
■ Infant mortality per 1,000 live births
■ Human dev. index

B

BURMA (MYANMAR)

OFFICIAL NAME: Union of Myanmar   CAPITAL: Rangoon (Yangon)
POPULATION: 47.6 million   CURRENCY: Kyat   OFFICIAL LANGUAGE: Burmese (Myanmar)

| 1948 | 1948 | Jan 4 | BUR | +6.5 | +95 | .mm |

FORMING THE EASTERN SHORES of the Bay of Bengal and the Andaman Sea in southeast Asia, Burma is mountainous in the north, while the once-forested, fertile Irrawaddy basin occupies most of the country. Burma gained independence from British colonial control in 1948 and has recently suffered widespread political repression and ethnic conflict. In 1990, the National League for Democracy (NLD) gained a majority in free elections but was prevented from taking power by the military. Rich in natural resources, which include fisheries and teak forests, Burma's economy remains mostly agricultural.

Transporting timber on the Irrawaddy River near Mandalay. Burma once had the world's largest reserves of teak.

CLIMATE   ▷ Tropical/mountain

WEATHER CHART

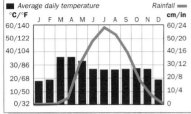

The tropical climate has three seasons: the wet season, when rainfall in the Irrawaddy delta and Tenasserim region can reach 500 cm (197 in); summer, when northern Burma experiences 50°C (122°F) and 100% humidity; and winter, when it is rarely cooler than 15°C (59°F) except in the northern mountains.

TRANSPORTATION   ▷ Drive on right

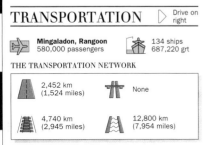

Mingaladon, Rangoon
580,000 passengers

134 ships
687,220 grt

THE TRANSPORTATION NETWORK

| 2,452 km (1,524 miles) | None |
| 4,740 km (2,945 miles) | 12,800 km (7,954 miles) |

Most current construction projects are linked to the booming China–Burma border trade, the majority of which was legalized in 1989. Old bridges and roads (including the famous Burma, Ledo and Silk Roads, all key routes into China) are being renewed and new ones built with Chinese aid. Although it will be easier to distribute key products, including opium, the motives for their construction are military as well as commercial. The state has recently relaxed its monopoly of transport: since 1988, private bus companies have been given licenses to operate. Air and rail routes, however, remain under government control.

TOURISM   ▷ Visitors : population 1:257

185,000 visitors

Up 58% 1995-1997

MAIN TOURIST ARRIVALS

| Europe 32% |
| Thailand 13% |
| Japan 9% |
| USA 8% |
| Other Asia 22% |
| Other 16% |

% of total arrivals

From 1962 until 1988, tourists were limited to one-week stays. Burma has recently adopted an open-door policy, designed to attract foreign exchange. Old hotels are now being renovated and new ones built in joint ventures with private companies. Much of the finance comes from Japan, Singapore and South Korea. China is also helping to build an international airport at Mandalay. There were widespread claims that the junta had used forced labor to restore historic landmarks before "visit Burma" year in 1996.

PEOPLE   ▷ Pop. density medium

Burmese, Karen, Shan, Chin, Kachin, Mon, Palaung, Wa

72/km² (187/mi²)

THE URBAN/RURAL POPULATION SPLIT

26%   74%

RELIGIOUS PERSUASION

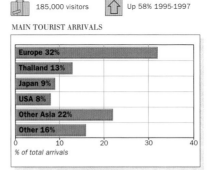

Hindu 1%   Muslim 4%
Other 2%   Christian 6%
Buddhist 87%

ETHNIC MAKEUP

Rakhine 4%   Karen 6%
Shan 9%
Other 13%
Burman (Bamah) 68%

Burma suffers from considerable ethnic tension between the Burman majority and the smaller ethnic groups. At independence, the Shans, Karens, Kachins, Mons, Karennis and Chins all demanded their own state within a federation but were refused by the central government. All groups kept their demands alive with guerrilla activity against the state; in 1988 they united in common cause against the military dictatorship, but almost all factions had signed peace treaties with the junta by early 1996.

A savage history, mainly of Burman repression of smaller groups, still plays a large part in the mistrust felt by the minorities for the Burman. Each group maintains a distinct cultural identity. While the Burman claim racial purity, in fact many of them are of mixed blood or ethnically Chinese.

Family life in Burma is still based around the extended family. Women have a prominent role, with access to education. Many run or own businesses in their own right. However, top jobs in government are still held almost exclusively by men.

POPULATION AGE BREAKDOWN

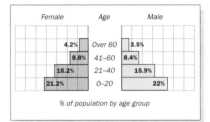

Female	Age	Male
4.2%	Over 60	3.5%
8.8%	41–60	8.4%
16.2%	21–40	15.9%
21.2%	0–20	22%

% of population by age group

POLITICS

▷ No multiparty elections

1990/suspended   Chairman Than Shwe

AT THE LAST ELECTION

Constituent Assembly 485 members

2% NUP   1% MNDF   1% NDP

81% NLD

5% SNLD   2% RDL   8% Others

SNLD = Shan National League for Democracy
MNDF = Mon National Democratic Front
NLD = National League for Democracy
RDL = Rakhine Democracy League
NUP = National Unity Party
NDP = National Democratic Party for Human Rights

A Constituent Assembly, responsible for the drafting of a new constitution and with no legislative power, was elected in 1990, but prevented from convening by the SLORC.

Burma is ruled by the military-backed SPDC, formerly the SLORC, under the leadership of Gen. Than Shwe.

MAIN POLITICAL ISSUES

Restoring democracy
The military rules Burma with little regard to human rights. Opposition is not tolerated and torture and killings are commonplace. Most of the ethnic rebel groups have agreed cease-fire terms with the regime. The focal point of opposition is Aung San Suu Kyi. Although she was freed temporarily from house arrest in 1995, the junta is wary of entering into official dialogue with her.

Refugees
One million refugees, dislocated by events since 1988 to Burma's border regions, are in need of rehabilitation. They include Rohingya Muslims who were repatriated from Bangladesh.

PROFILE
The military seized power in 1988 at the height of mass protests calling for the restoration of democracy. Soon afterwards the State Law and Order Restoration Council (SLORC) was formed. Elections held in 1990 were won by the NLD. However, the SLORC refused to relinquish

Aung San Suu Kyi, figurehead of the pro-democracy movement.

General Ne Win, Burma's leader 1964–1988.

BURMA

Total Land Area : 657 540 sq. km (253 876 sq. miles)

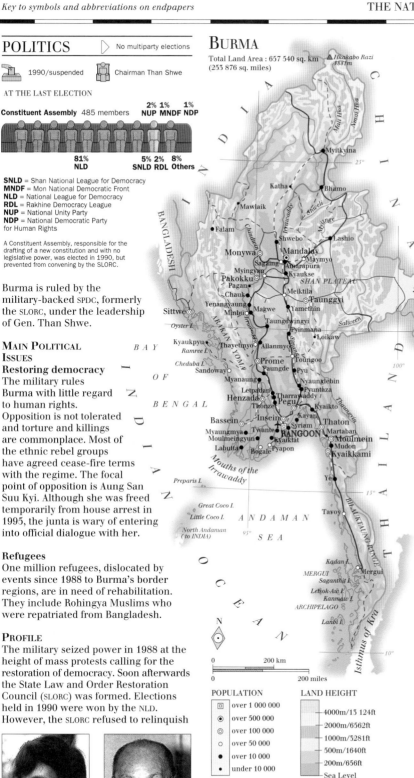

POPULATION

⊡ over 1 000 000
◉ over 500 000
◎ over 100 000
○ over 50 000
● over 10 000
· under 10 000

LAND HEIGHT

4000m/13 124ft
2000m/6562ft
1000m/3281ft
500m/1640ft
200m/656ft
Sea Level

power and suppressed the prodemocracy opposition. The replacement of the SLORC by a State Peace and Development Council (SPDC) in 1997 has brought no major changes. The ethnic rebellion which had been raging for decades in border regions has been quelled.

WORLD AFFAIRS

▷ Joined UN in 1948

CP   IAEA   ASEAN   NAM   WTO

Burma's key relationship is with China, which backs the SPDC military regime and is a major supplier of weapons to the Burmese army. The relationship allows China access to the Indian Ocean and gives it influence over a regime dependent on its support. While Burma's neighbors fear that the arrangement could destabilize the whole of the Asia–Pacific region, many favour a policy of "constructive engagement" with the SPDC. In July 1997 Burma became a member of ASEAN, despite concerns about its human rights record. Western members of the UN and the EU have strongly condemned human rights violations in Burma and threatened to impose economic sanctions in response to the regime's policies. In practice, however, the West maintains an ambiguous position. Economic ties are expanding, particularly between SPDC-owned state enterprises and Western multinationals with an interest in the profitable Burmese offshore oil and gas drilling sectors.

CHRONOLOGY

From the 11th century, Burma's many ethnic groups came under the rule of three Tibeto–Burman dynasties, interspersed with periods of rule by the Mongols and the Mon. The Third Dynasty came into conflict with the British in India, sparking the Anglo–Burmese Wars of 1824, 1852 and 1885.

- ❑ **1886** Burma becomes a province of British India.
- ❑ **1930–1931** Economic depression triggers unrest.
- ❑ **1937** Separation from India.
- ❑ **1942** Japan invades.
- ❑ **1945** Anti-fascist People's Freedom League (AFPFL) led by Aung San, helps Allies reoccupy country.
- ❑ **1947** UK agrees to Burmese independence. Aung San wins elections, but is assassinated.
- ❑ **1948** Independence under new prime minister, U Nu, who initiates socialist policies. Revolts by ethnic separatists and communists, notably Karen liberation struggle.
- ❑ **1958** Ruling AFPFL splits into two. Shan liberation struggle begins.
- ❑ **1960** U Nu's faction wins elections.
- ❑ **1961** Kachin rebellion begins. ➪

B

CHRONOLOGY *continued*

- ❏ **1962** Gen. Ne Win stages military coup. "New Order" policy of "Buddhist Socialism" – isolation from outside world. Mining and other industries nationalized. Free trade prohibited.
- ❏ **1964** Socialist Program Party declared sole legal party.
- ❏ **1976** Social unrest. Attempted military coup. Ethnic liberation groups gain control of 40% of country.
- ❏ **1982** Non-indigenous people barred from public office.
- ❏ **1988** Thousands die in student riots. Ne Win resigns. Martial law. Aung San Suu Kyi, daughter of Aung San, ex-premier U Nu, and others found NLD to form alternative government. Gen. Saw Maung leads military coup. SLORC takes power. Ethnic resistance groups form Democratic Alliance of Burma.
- ❏ **1989** Army arrests NLD leaders and steps up anti-rebel activity. Official name Union of Burma introduced.
- ❏ **1990** Elections permitted. NLD landslide. SLORC, however, remains in power. More NLD leaders arrested.
- ❏ **1991** Aung San Suu Kyi, under house arrest, awarded Nobel Peace Prize. NLD expels her as a result of SLORC pressure. Many parties deregistered.
- ❏ **1992** Gen. Than Shwe takes over as SLORC leader.
- ❏ **1995** Aung San Suu Kyi released from house arrest.
- ❏ **1996** Demonstrations against approval of Burma's membership of ASEAN.
- ❏ **1997** Ruling SLORC renamed State Peace and Development Council (SPDC).
- ❏ **1998** NLD sets deadline for convening of parliament; junta refuses.
- ❏ **1999** Aung San Suu Kyi rejects conditions set by SPDC to visit her husband, Michael Aris, who dies of cancer in the UK.

AID ▷ Recipient

 $45m (receipts)   Down 20% 1996–1997

In 1988, Western countries, the World Bank and certain UN agencies such as the UNDP halted bilateral aid. The UN has, however, continued funding some development projects through its Drug Control Program and the World Health Organization. The largest bilateral donor is China. Since 1997 the USA has tightened economic sanctions in order to force the regime to negotiate with the NLD.

DEFENSE ▷ No compulsory military service

$2.2bn   ⬆ Up 8% in 1997

Burma's growing military capability is used mainly for internal purposes.

BURMESE ARMED FORCES

126 main battle tanks (26 *Comet*, 80 *PRC Type 69ii*, 20 *PRC Type 80*)	352,000 personnel	
65 patrol boats	15,800 personnel	
121 combat aircraft (30 F-7, 6 FT-7, 36 A-5M)	9000 personnel	
None		

The SPDC has steadily obtained modern weapons and military technology from around the world, primarily from China but also from France, Germany, Sweden and the former Yugoslavia. Since 1989, China alone has delivered over $1 billion worth of arms to Burma, including tanks and jet fighters.

The army has suppressed most ethnic insurgent campaigns by utilizing its military superiority and cutting numerous deals with rebel leaders. In early 1996 troops took control of the headquarters of the notorious Shan "drug warlord" Khun Sa in what was widely seen as a "negotiated takeover."

ECONOMICS ▷ Inflation 24.6% p.a. (1985–1996)

$73.9bn   6.25 kyats

SCORE CARD

- ❏ WORLD GNP RANKING 41st
- ❏ GNP PER CAPITA $1,500
- ❏ BALANCE OF PAYMENTS....................$–114m
- ❏ INFLATION 29.7%
- ❏ UNEMPLOYMENT ...Widespread underemployment

ECONOMIC PERFORMANCE INDICATOR

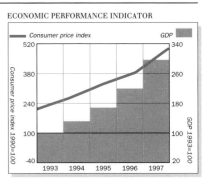

Since 1989, the SPDC's open-door market-economy policy has brought a flood of foreign investment in oil and gas (by Western companies) and in forestry, tourism and mining (by Asian companies). The recent boom in trade with China has turned less developed Upper Burma into a thriving business center. A drug-eradication program has been initiated in the northeastern border states, which account for about 60% of the world's heroin, by encouraging farmers to grow food crops instead of poppy. Few plans exist for the manufacturing sector, however, and dependence on imports continues.

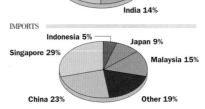

EXPORTS

- China 6%
- Japan 8%
- USA 10%
- Singapore 13%
- India 14%
- Other 49%

IMPORTS

- Indonesia 5%
- Japan 9%
- Singapore 29%
- Malaysia 15%
- China 23%
- Other 19%

STRENGTHS

Very rich in natural resources: fertile soil, rich fisheries, timber including diminishing teak reserves, gems, offshore natural gas and oil.

WEAKNESSES

Shortage of skilled labor, managers and technicians. Rudimentary financial systems and institutions. Nationwide black market. Huge external debt. Dependence on imported manufactures.

PROFILE

Burma's economy is agriculture-based and functions mainly on a cash and barter system. Its key industries are controlled by military-run state enterprises. Every aspect of economic life is permeated by a black market, on which prices are rocketing – a reaction to official price controls.

BURMA : MAJOR BUSINESSES

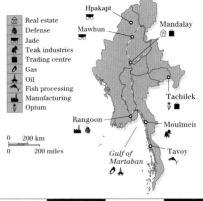

- 🏛 Real estate
- Defense
- Jade
- Teak industries
- Trading centre
- Gas
- Oil
- Fish processing
- Manufacturing
- Opium

Hpakapt
Mawhun
Mandalay
Tachilek
Rangoon
Moulmein
Tavoy
Gulf of Martaban

0   200 km
0   200 miles

B

RESOURCES
▷ Electric power 1.3m kw

🐟 872,965 tonnes 　　🛢 15,037 b/d

🐄 10.5m cattle, 3.5m pigs, 1.3m goats 　　💎 Oil, natural gas, tin, antimony, zinc, copper, tungsten, lead, coal

ELECTRICITY GENERATION

Hydro 40% (1.5bn kwh)	
Combustion 60% (2.2bn kwh)	
Nuclear 0%	
Other 0%	

0　20　40　60　80　100

% of total generation by type

Burma is the world's largest teak exporter. It is also a producer of pearls, rubies and other gems. Foreign capital is funding exploration for natural gas and oil in the Tenasserim peninsula. However, Burma suffers from energy shortages.

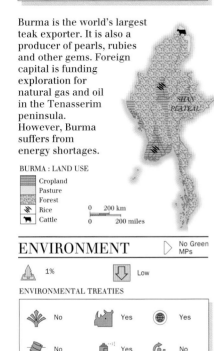

SHAN PLATEAU

BURMA : LAND USE

▨	Cropland
▨	Pasture
▨	Forest
⚒	Rice
🐂	Cattle

0　200 km
0　200 miles

ENVIRONMENT
▷ No Green MPs

🔺 1% 　　⬇ Low

ENVIRONMENTAL TREATIES

🌿	No	🦏	Yes	🌐	Yes
	No	🧴	Yes	♻	No

Deforestation is a major problem and has increased since the 1988 coup. Chinese companies have been given unrestricted logging concessions.

MEDIA
▷ TV ownership low

⊠ Daily newspaper circulation 10 per 1,000 people

PUBLISHING AND BROADCAST MEDIA

📰	There are 5 daily newspapers, including *Myanma Alin* and *New Light of Myanmar*
📺	1 state-controlled service
📻	1 state-controlled service

Political dissent of any kind is a criminal offense. An underground pro-democracy press produces anti-government material.

CRIME
▷ Death penalty used

🏛 Burma does not publish prison figures 　　⬆ Up 12% from 1992–1996

CRIME RATES

Murders	
3	per 100,000 population

Rapes	
2	per 100,000 population

Thefts	
35	per 100,000 population

Levels of robbery, murder, bribery, corruption, embezzlement and black marketing are high, compared with similar totalitarian regimes. The state is guilty of illegal activity. The UN reports regularly on human rights abuses against civilians, and the murder of innocent civilians including children, women, Buddhist monks, students, minorities and political dissidents.

There is a nominal civilian judicial system in Burma, but in practice all judges and lawyers are appointed by the junta and all legal functions executed by the SPDC. The most common charge is that of sedition against the state or the army under the 1975 "Law to Protect the State from Destructionists." Among the SPDC's frequent arbitrary "notices" is the Order 2/88 prohibiting assemblies of more than five persons. Most detainees have no legal rights of representation and are either jailed, used as forced labor or put under house arrest without public trial. Amnesty International is banned.

EDUCATION
▷ School leaving age: 10

📖 83.6% 　　🎓 245,317 students

Political instability has disrupted education and led to the exodus of teachers.

THE EDUCATION SYSTEM

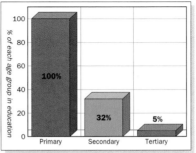

% of each age group in education — Primary 100%, Secondary 32%, Tertiary 5%

The education system provides ten years of schooling. Ethnic-language schools are discouraged. There are two universities and several training institutes. Political instability has contributed to a shortage of teachers, many of whom have left or are in jail.

HEALTH
▷ Welfare state health benefits

👥 1 per 10,000 people 　　☠ Malaria, fevers, heart and diarrheal diseases

Leprosy, although it affects relatively few people compared with other diseases, has a higher prevalence in Burma than in the rest of Asia. There has been an increase in the incidence of malaria in the last few years.

The spread of AIDS poses an additional strain on the health system. The growing number of cases is largely due to migrant prostitution across the Thai-Burmese border.

SPENDING
▷ GDP/cap. no increase

CONSUMPTION AND SPENDING

🚗 2.6 per 1,000 population 　　☎ 5 per 1,000 population

Defense 7.7%	
Education 1.3%	
Health 0.8%	

0　5　10　15　20　25

Defense, Health, Education spending as % of GDP

The state monopoly of the production and distribution of goods by rationing under General Ne Win's administration led to an increase in corruption and the rise of a nationwide black market, with huge disparities between official and unofficial prices. Only the military elite and their supporters could afford to live well. The situation has not changed significantly since 1988. Giant military enterprises grouped under a Defense Services holding company, whose capital amounts to 10% of GDP, now reap wealth and distribute privileges for a minority. Nevertheless, traditional social and economic mobility still exists. Climbing the socio-economic ladder is mainly a matter of loyalty to the military. Dissidents forced out of their jobs and hill tribes are the poorest groups.

WORLD RANKING

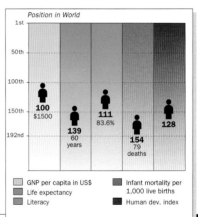

Position in World

100 $1500 · 139 60 years · 111 83.6% · 154 79 deaths · 128

▨ GNP per capita in US$	▨ Infant mortality per 1,000 live births
▨ Life expectancy	
▨ Literacy	▨ Human dev. index

BURUNDI

OFFICIAL NAME: Republic of Burundi **CAPITAL:** Bujumbura
POPULATION: 6.6 million **CURRENCY:** Burundi franc **OFFICIAL LANGUAGE:** French and Kirundi

| 1962 | 1962 | July 1 | RU | +2 | +257 | .bi |

LANDLOCKED BURUNDI lies just south of the equator on the Nile–Congo watershed. Lake Tanganyika forms part of its border with Congo (former Zaire). Tension between the Hutu majority and the dominant Tutsi minority remains the main factor in politics. The current political unrest dates from the assassination of the first-ever Hutu president in a coup by the Tutsi-dominated army in October 1993, which sparked terrible violence.

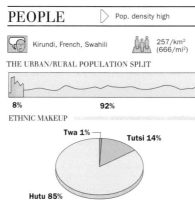

Pig farming and fish ponds. The majority of Burundi's population depends on subsistence farming.

CLIMATE

▷ Tropical wet & dry

WEATHER CHART

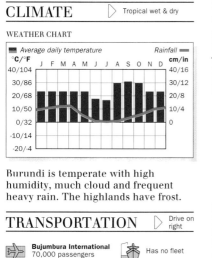

■ Average daily temperature   Rainfall ▬
°C/°F   cm/in
J F M A M J J A S O N D

Burundi is temperate with high humidity, much cloud and frequent heavy rain. The highlands have frost.

TRANSPORTATION

▷ Drive on right

✈ **Bujumbura International** 70,000 passengers

🚢 Has no fleet

THE TRANSPORTATION NETWORK

| 🛣 14,480 km (9,000 miles) | 🛤 None |
| 🚉 None | ⚓ Lake Tanganyika |

The dense road network has been rehabilitated. There are plans to build a railroad linking Burundi with Rwanda, Uganda, and Tanzania.

TOURISM

▷ Visitors : population 1:600

🧳 11,000 visitors

⬇ Down 39% 1995-1997

MAIN TOURIST ARRIVALS

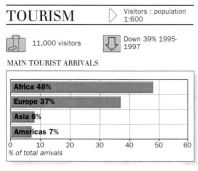

| Africa 48% |
| Europe 37% |
| Asia 8% |
| Americas 7% |

0 10 20 30 40 50 60
% of total arrivals

A lack of basic infrastructure and violent political strife deter tourists. The industry has limited potential, since Burundi lacks its neighbors' spectacular scenery and game parks.

PEOPLE

▷ Pop. density high

Kirundi, French, Swahili

257/km² (666/mi²)

THE URBAN/RURAL POPULATION SPLIT

8%   92%

ETHNIC MAKEUP

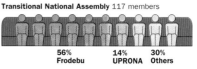

Twa 1%
Tutsi 14%
Hutu 85%

Burundi's history has been marked by violent conflict between the majority Hutu and the Tutsi, formerly the political elite, who still control the army. Large-scale massacres have occurred repeatedly over the past two decades. Hundreds of thousands of people, mostly Hutu, have been killed in political and ethnic conflict since October 1993. The Twa pygmies do not suffer similar repression. Most Burundians are subsistence farmers; the vast majority are Roman Catholic.

POLITICS

▷ No multiparty elections

1998/uncertain

President Pierre Buyoya

AT THE LAST ELECTION

Transitional National Assembly 117 members

56% Frodebu   14% UPRONA   30% Others

Frodebu = Front for Democracy in Burundi
UPRONA = Union pour le progrès national

The Transitional National Assembly, inaugurated in July 1998, consisted of the members of the previous Assembly (or their replacements from the same party) single members of parties not formerly represented, and members of "civil society".

From 1966, the Tutsi-dominated UPRONA was the only legal party. Tutsi dominated the civil service, judiciary and army. In 1990, President Buyoya, a Tutsi, began integrating Hutu into political life. Opposition parties were legalized and in 1993, Burundi's first free elections were won by Melchior Ndadaye, a Hutu and leader of Frodebu. Tutsi fears of Hutu dominance led to a coup and his assassination. Hundreds of thousands of Hutu were killed by the army or fled to neighboring countries. In 1994, Burundi's new president and his Rwandan counterpart died in an air crash. The country plunged into civil war, with the Tutsi-dominated army constantly clashing with Hutu militias. In mid-1996 Maj. Buyoya returned to power in a military coup. Despite efforts to regain international acceptance, an economic boycott by neighboring countries has seriously damaged economic life.

BURUNDI

Total Land Area : 25 650 sq. km
(9 903 sq. miles)

LAND HEIGHT

2000m/6562ft
1000m/3281ft
500m/1640ft

POPULATION

◎ over 100 000
○ over 50 000
● over 10 000
• under 10 000

0 50 km
0 50 miles

B

WORLD AFFAIRS
Joined UN in 1962

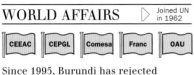

Since 1995, Burundi has rejected proposed UN/OAU military intervention to prevent further bloodshed.

AID
Recipient

$119m (receipts) — Down 42% 1996–1997

The flight of hundreds of thousands since 1993 has disrupted agriculture, and large numbers of people remain dependent on UN food aid.

DEFENSE
No compulsory military service

$60m — Up 16% in 1997

The 18,500-strong army is run by Tutsi. President Ndadaye's attempt to bring Hutu into officer ranks was a major factor behind the October 1993 coup. The army seized power again in 1996, and a state of virtual civil war continues between it and rebel Hutu militia.

ECONOMICS
Inflation 6.6% p.a. (1985–1996)

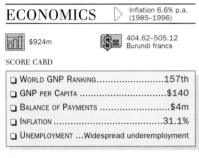

$924m — 404.62–505.12 Burundi francs

SCORE CARD

- World GNP Ranking........................157th
- GNP per Capita $140
- Balance of Payments $4m
- Inflation 31.1%
- Unemployment ...Widespread underemployment

STRENGTHS
Small quantities of gold and tungsten. Potential of massive nickel reserves and oil in Lake Tanganyika.

WEAKNESSES
Harsh regional sanctions since 1996 coup. Overwhelmingly agricultural economy (91% of labor force) under pressure from high birth rate. Little prospect of political stability.

EXPORTS

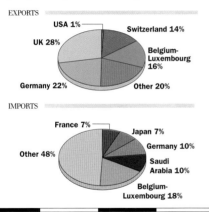

IMPORTS

RESOURCES
Electric power 43,000kw

22,000 tonnes — Not an oil producer and has no refineries

900,000 goats, 346,000 cattle, 320,000 sheep — Gold, tungsten, nickel, vanadium, uranium

Burundi has around 5% of the world's nickel reserves. Extraction, however, is not economically viable. There are also deposits of gold and vanadium. Surveys in the 1980s detected oil reserves below Lake Tanganyika, but production has yet to begin. Burundi imports gasoline from Iran and electricity from Congo, Dem. Rep. (Zaire). New HEP plants at Mugera and Rwegura are intended to meet most domestic electricity requirements.

ENVIRONMENT
No Green MPs

6% — Low

Only 2% of Burundi is forest and even this is now under pressure from one of Africa's highest birth rates. Burundi suffers from the problems associated with deforestation, particularly soil erosion. Some soils are also being exhausted from overuse. Several tree-planting programs have been introduced. UNESCO is also running ecological education initiatives at village level, aimed at women farmers.

MEDIA
TV ownership low

Daily newspaper circulation 3 per 1,000 people

PUBLISHING AND BROADCAST MEDIA

There is 1 daily newspaper, Le Renouveau du Burundi, published by the government.

1 state-controlled service — 1 state-owned, 1 independent service

Pro-Hutu/anti-Tutsi radio stations have been broadcasting since 1994. An EU-funded station promoting peace was launched in 1996.

CRIME
Death penalty used

Burundi does not publish prison figures — Down 53% in 1990

Burundi has an appalling human rights record. There have been frequent massacres of Hutu by the army. The worst pogroms occurred in 1972, 1988, 1993, and 1994.

EDUCATION
School leaving age: 13

45% — 4,256 students

Elementary schooling begins at seven, and is compulsory, though further schooling is not. There are 67 elementary school children per teacher. There is one university.

CHRONOLOGY
From the 16th century, Burundi (formerly Urundi) was ruled by the minority Tutsi with the majority Hutu as their serfs. Merged with Rwanda, Burundi was controlled by Germany from 1884 and by Belgium from 1919.

- **1946** UN trust territory.
- **1959** Split from Rwanda.
- **1961** Elections won by UPRONA.
- **1962** Independence.
- **1966** Army coup. Monarchy overthrown.
- **1972** 150,000 Hutu massacred.
- **1993** June, first free elections. October, army coup; president assassinated. Violence continues.
- **1996** Military coup restores Maj. Pierre Buyoya to power.

HEALTH
No welfare state health benfits

1 per 3,326 people — Communicable infections, parasitic diseases

2.1 million people have no access to health services. Only 7% of woman use contraception; on average, each women has seven children. 62% of people lack access to safe drinking water.

SPENDING
GDP/cap. no increase

CONSUMPTION AND SPENDING

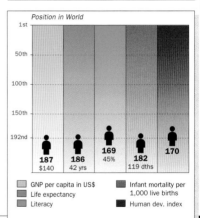

3 per 1,000 population — 3 per 1,000 population

Defense 5.7% / Education 2.8% / Health 0.8%

Defense, Health, Education spending as % of GDP

Wealth is concentrated within the Tutsi political and business elite. Most of Burundi's people live a subsistence existence.

WORLD RANKING

Position in World

187 $140 / 186 42 yrs / 169 45% / 182 119 dths / 170

GNP per capita in US$ / Life expectancy / Literacy / Infant mortality per 1,000 live births / Human dev. index

CAMBODIA

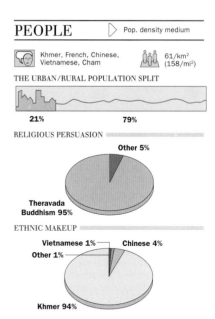

OFFICIAL NAME: Kingdom of Cambodia **CAPITAL:** Phnom Penh
POPULATION: 10.8 million **CURRENCY:** Riel **OFFICIAL LANGUAGE:** Khmer

| 1953 | 1953 | Jan 9 | K | +7 | +855 | .kh |

LOCATED IN THE INDOCHINESE PENINSULA in southeast Asia, Cambodia has a coastline on the Gulf of Thailand and shares borders with Thailand, Laos and Vietnam. Its main topographical feature is the Tonle Sap, or Great Lake, which drains into the Mekong River. Over three-quarters of Cambodia is forested, with mangroves lining the coast. Rice is the principal crop. Cambodia has emerged from two decades of civil war and invasion from Vietnam. The UN's biggest-ever peacekeeping operation resulted in free elections in 1993.

CLIMATE ▷ Tropical monsoon

WEATHER CHART

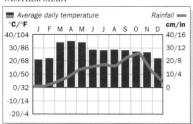

Cambodia has a more varied climate than neighboring Vietnam. Low-lying regions have moderate rainfall and the most consistent yearly temperatures. The wettest areas are the hillsides facing the Gulf of Thailand. The dry season lasts from December to April and is characterized by high temperatures and an average eight hours of sunshine a day. During the rainy season, Cambodia experiences high humidity and sultry heat. From May to September, winds are southeasterly, while from October to April they are north or northeasterly.

TRANSPORTATION ▷ Drive on right

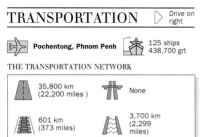

| | Pochentong, Phnom Penh | | 125 ships 438,700 grt |

THE TRANSPORTATION NETWORK

| | 35,800 km (22,200 miles) | | None |
| | 601 km (373 miles) | | 3,700 km (2,299 miles) |

The civil war led to a near-collapse of Cambodia's road and rail system. Some parts of the network are still subject to attack by Khmer Rouge bandits. International aid is now being used to rehabilitate key routes, such as Highways 3 and 5, and to rebuild the Chroy Changba Bridge out of Phnom Penh. The bicycle and the rickshaw are the main forms of urban transport.

Angkor Wat stands in the ruins of the ancient city of Angkor, once the capital of the Khmer empire. It is now one of Cambodia's leading tourist attractions.

TOURISM ▷ Visitors : population 1:49

219,000   Down 1% 1995–1997

MAIN TOURIST ARRIVALS

	% of total arrivals
USA	79%
UK	4%
Japan	3%
France	3%
Germany	2%
Other	9%

Cambodia, the center of the Khmer empire between 800 and 1400 A.D., has some of the most impressive temples in southeast Asia. The most famous is at Angkor Wat, near Siemreab, which is being made safe for tourists after the Khmer Rouge relinquished control of the area in mid-1998. In 1994 three Western tourists were murdered by the Khmer Rouge in southern Cambodia.

Once the political situation is stabilized, Cambodia could have considerable tourism potential. In recent years it has attracted some of the more adventurous independent travelers.

PEOPLE ▷ Pop. density medium

Khmer, French, Chinese, Vietnamese, Cham   61/km² (158/mi²)

THE URBAN/RURAL POPULATION SPLIT

21%   79%

RELIGIOUS PERSUASION

Other 5%
Theravada Buddhism 95%

ETHNIC MAKEUP

Vietnamese 1% — Chinese 4%
Other 1%
Khmer 94%

Cambodian society underwent one of the 20th century's most horrific programs of social transformation between 1975 and 1979 under Pol Pot's Khmer Rouge regime. Over one million Cambodians, or one in eight, died from warfare, starvation, overwork or execution. Half a million more went into exile in Thailand. The Pol Pot regime's reforms led to the scrapping of money, possessions and hierarchy. Only peasants, soldiers of the revolution and some industrial workers were allowed to retain their pre-revolution status. Boys and girls of 13 and 14 were taken from their homes, indoctrinated in the tenets of revolution and allowed to kill those perceived to be guilty of bourgeois crimes. Violence at all levels was sanctioned in the name of revolution. Pol Pot's regime ended with the Vietnamese invasion of 1979. Most professionals who had survived emigrated. The effects of revolution and subsequent civil war are still felt and reflected in the world's highest rate of orphans and widows.

POPULATION AGE BREAKDOWN

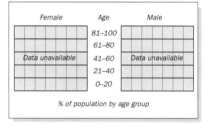

Female	Age	Male
	81–100	
	61–80	
Data unavailable	41–60	Data unavailable
	21–40	
	0–20	

% of population by age group

C

C

POLITICS

 Multiparty elections

 L. House 1998/2003   King Norodom
U. House 1998/2003   Sihanouk

AT THE LAST ELECTION

National Assembly 122 members

| 53% | 35% | 12% |
| CPP | Funcinpec | SRP |

CPP = Cambodian People's Party
Funcinpec = United National Front for an Independent Neutral Peaceful and Cooperative Cambodia
SRP = Sam Rainsy Party

Senate 61 members

| 53% | 35% | 12% |
| CPP | Funcinpec | SRP |

The membership of the Senate, first established in March 1999 is determined in proportion to the results of the 1988 legislative elections.

Elections under UN supervision in 1993 led to a fragile coalition which was destroyed by renewed power struggles.

MAIN POLITICAL ISSUE
Royalist-CPP rivalry

Power struggles between the Funcinpec and the CPP came to a head with CPP leader Hun Sen's mid-1997 coup which ended their coalition arrangement. In November 1998 the two parties agreed to form a new coalition government that broke the deadlock arising from the inconclusive results of legislative elections held in July that year.

PROFILE

In 1975, the US-installed government was overthrown by the Maoist Khmer Rouge under Pol Pot. Pol Pot was ousted following the Vietnamese invasion in 1979. In exile, Cambodia's three main factions – the Khmer Rouge, the Sihanoukists and the Khmer People's National Liberation Front (KPNLF) – united against the Vietnamese-backed regime in Pnom Penh led by Heng Samrin and Hun Sen. The exile coalition, backed by the west and by China, won UN recognition as the government of Democratic Kampuchea.

In 1989 Vietnam withdrew from Cambodia, paving the way for UN-supervised elections in 1993 which were won by the royalist Funcinpec. However, the Khmer Rouge refused to join a coalition government of national reconciliation which included Hun Sen. It resumed armed resistance but surrendered in June 1998, weakened by mass defections and the death of Pol Pot.

The strife-torn coalition held together until July 1997, when CPP leader Hun Sen ousted his co-prime minister Prince Ranariddh. A year later the CPP failed to win a sufficient majority in parliamentary elections, forcing it into a new coalition agreement with Funcinpec in November 1998.

Pol Pot (Saloth Sar): former Khmer Rouge leader who died in 1998.

King Norodom Sihanouk, the pivotal figure in Cambodian society and politics.

WORLD AFFAIRS

 Joined UN in 1955

| Asean | IAEA | IBRD | Mek Riv | NAM |

During the civil war that followed the Vietnamese invasion of 1979, the Phnom Penh government (along with Vietnam) was reduced to an international pariah. It was recognized by few countries outside the Soviet bloc, and its seat at the UN was allotted to a resistance coalition which included the Khmer Rouge.

Although Cambodia's 1993 constitution aims to make the country a non-aligned "island of peace," a neutral foreign policy has been difficult to pursue. The USA opposes any participation in government by the Khmer Rouge; China, on the other hand, favours the group's political rehabilitation.

Cambodia's relations with Vietnam continue to be problematic, fueled in part by the historic animosity between the two countries. Membership of ASEAN, the Association of South East Asian Nations, which had been on hold pending the consolidation of full democratic government in Cambodia, was confirmed in April 1999.

AID

▷ Recipient

$372m (receipts)   Down 18% 1996–1997

Aid is crucial to Cambodia's economy, since it provides the bulk of government revenues. However, widespread corruption and recent political instability have prompted some international donors to withhold their assistance.

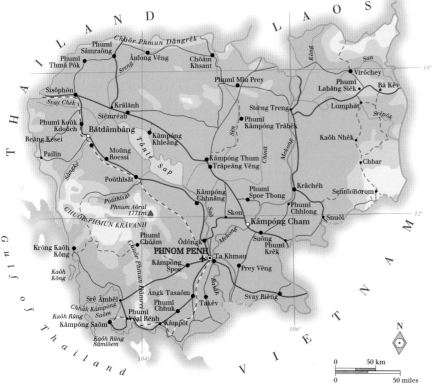

CAMBODIA

Total Land Area : 176 520 sq. km (68 154 sq. miles)

POPULATION

- ⊙ over 500 000
- ○ over 50 000
- ● over 10 000
- • under 10 000

LAND HEIGHT

- 1000m/3281ft
- 500m/1640ft
- 200m/656ft
- Sea Level

N

C

CHRONOLOGY

A former French protectorate, Cambodia gained independence in 1953 as a constitutional monarchy with Norodom Sihanouk as king.

❑ **1955** Sihanouk abdicates to pursue political career.
❑ **1970** Right-wing coup led by Prime Minister Lon Nol deposes Sihanouk. Exiled Sihanouk forms Royal Government of National Union of Cambodia (GRUNC), backed by once hostile communist Khmer Rouge. Lon Nol proclaims Khmer Republic.
❑ **1974** GRUNC forces capture Phnom Penh. Prince Sihanouk head of state, Khmer Rouge assumes power. Hundreds of thousands die during reform program.
❑ **1976** Country renamed Democratic Kampuchea (DK). Elections. Sihanouk resigns; GRUNC dissolved. Khieu Samphan head of state; Pol Pot prime minister.
❑ **1978** Vietnam invades, supported by Cambodian communists opposed to Pol Pot.
❑ **1979** Vietnamese capture Phnom Penh. Khmer Rouge ousted by Kampuchean People's Revolutionary Party (KPRP), led by Pen Sovan. Khmer Rouge starts guerrilla war. Pol Pot held responsible for three million deaths and sentenced to death in absence. Vietnamese and DK forces begin conflict on Thai border.
❑ **1982** Government-in-exile including Khmer Rouge and Khmer People's National Liberation Front, headed by Prince Sihanouk, is recognized by UN.
❑ **1989** Withdrawal of Vietnamese troops.
❑ **1990** UN Security Council approves plan for UN-monitored cease-fire and elections.
❑ **1991** Signing of Paris peace accords. Sihanouk reinstated as head of state of Cambodia.
❑ **1993** UN-supervised elections won by royalist Funcinpec.
❑ **1994** Khmer Rouge refuses to join peace process.
❑ **1995** Former finance minister Sam Rangsi forms opposition party.
❑ **1996** Leading Khmer Rouge member Ieng Sary defects from the rebel group.
❑ **1997** Joint prime minister Hun Sen mounts coup against royalist co-premier Prince Ranariddh.
❑ **1998** April, death of Pol Pot; July, Hun Sen claims victory in parliamentary elections; November, Hun Sen heads coalition government including Funcinpec.

DEFENSE

▷ No compulsory military service

$254m   Up 39% in 1997

The surrender of the Khmer Rouge has made possible unified national forces.

CAMBODIAN ARMED FORCES

🔲	100 main battle tanks (T-54, T-55)	90,000 personnel
🔲	33 patrol boats (2 Sov *Turya* PFI)	2,000 personnel
🔲	20 combat aircraft (MiG-21	2,000 personnel
🔲	None	

The final surrender of Khmer Rouge forces in mid-1998 and the disintegration of remaining pockets of Khmer resistance later that year, have improved the prospects of consolidating a unified national army.

The three main armies are the CPP's Cambodian People's Armed Forces, Funcinpec's Armée Nationale Sihanoukiste, and the KPNLF's Khmer People's National Liberation Armed Forces. The coalition government's defense priority is to unify their command structures, currently under the control of diverse parties.

Although well equipped, the soldiers are poorly paid and have suffered from disease. Morale is low and vulnerable to political tension as was demonstrated in the aftermath of Hun Sen's July 1997 coup, which intensified rivalry between the CPP and Funcinpec.

ECONOMICS

▷ Inflation 4.8% p.a. (1995–1997)

$3.2bn   3,452.00–3,870.00 riel

SCORE CARD

❑ WORLD GNP RANKING 125th
❑ GNP PER CAPITA $300
❑ BALANCE OF PAYMENTS ....$–210m
❑ INFLATION 8%
❑ UNEMPLOYMENT ....Widespread

ECONOMIC PERFORMANCE INDICATOR

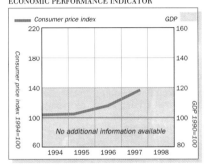

Consumer price index — — —   GDP

No additional information available

EXPORTS

China 7%
Singapore 12%
Vietnam 25%
USA 14%
Thailand 21%
Other 21%

IMPORTS

Japan 8%
Vietnam 10%
Other 43%
Singapore 10%
Switzerland 12%
Thailand 18%

STRENGTHS

Currently very few as economy needs time and investment to recover from civil war. Considerable potential: it could achieve self-sufficiency in rice. Gems, especially sapphires. Possible offshore oil wealth. Timber trade to Thailand exploited illegally.

WEAKNESSES

Tiny tax base makes economic reform hard to implement. Dependence on overseas aid; corruption at most levels of government limits its effectiveness. Loss of skilled workers as a result of Khmer Rouge anti-bourgeois atrocities in the 1970s.

PROFILE

Cambodia's economy was devastated during the Pol Pot years. The Vietnamese attempted some reconstruction based on central planning, then switched to policies encouraging the private sector. The presence of the UN encouraged some limited development.

CAMBODIA : MAJOR BUSINESSES

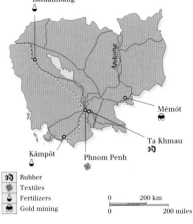

Bătdâmbâng
Mémót
Ta Khmau
Kâmpôt
Phnom Penh

Rubber
Textiles
Fertilizers
Gold mining

0   200 km
0   200 miles

RESOURCES

▷ Electric power 35,000 kw

112,510 tonnes

Not an oil producer

2.9m cattle, 2.2m pigs, 22,000 horses

Salt, phosphates

Tropical rain forest timber, particularly teak and rosewood, is Cambodia's most important resource. Most forests are located in the north and west.

ELECTRICITY GENERATION

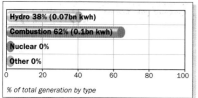

Hydro 38% (0.07bn kwh)
Combustion 62% (0.1bn kwh)
Nuclear 0%
Other 0%

0   20   40   60   80   100

% of total generation by type

CAMBODIA : LAND USE

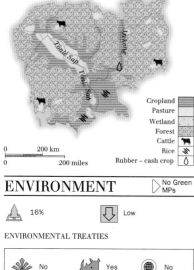

Cropland
Pasture
Wetland
Forest
Cattle
Rice
Rubber – cash crop

0   200 km
0   200 miles

ENVIRONMENT

▷ No Green MPs

16%

Low

ENVIRONMENTAL TREATIES

No   Yes   No
No   No   No

Deforestation is one of the most serious problems. Timber, one of Cambodia's most valuable assets, was sold in huge quantities by all the warring factions to finance their war efforts. According to the UN, in 1992 alone more than 250,000 hectares (620,000 acres) of forest were cleared. This provided over one million cubic meters (35 million cubic feet) of timber. A moratorium on logging was declared at the end of 1992 but largely ignored. Tropical hardwoods extracted illegally from Cambodia find lucrative outlets through Thailand in particular. The environmental consequences – topsoil erosion and increased risk of flooding – are enormous and will hold back Cambodia's reconstruction.

MEDIA

▷ TV ownership medium

There are no daily newspapers

A 1995 press law provides for possible imprisonment for publishing material deemed to affect national security and political instability. The government used it to prosecute at least seven newspapers within its first year for defamation and disinformation.

CRIME

▷ Death penalty not used

2,490 prisoners

Civilian crime rates are now fairly stable

CRIME RATES

Detailed crime figures are not available.

The UN-sponsored peace process followed by elections in 1993 led to a dramatic drop in crime in Cambodia. However, since the July 1997 coup Phnom Penh has witnessed an increase in violent crime owing to the spread of illegally owned firearms. Until the surrender of the Khmer Rouge in 1998, areas under its command, especially in the west around Pailin and Battambang, were particularly dangerous. Banditry was rife and policing virtually non-existent.

There are allegations that Cambodia is becoming Asia's new "narco-state." It is claimed that in recent years there has been a proliferation of narcotics trading, money laundering and illegal banking operations.

EDUCATION

▷ School leaving age: 12

66%

10,019 students

Spending on education ensures that 80% of children attend primary school.

THE EDUCATION SYSTEM

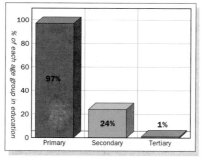

97%   24%   1%
Primary   Secondary   Tertiary

Only 5,000 of Cambodia's 20,000 teachers survived the Pol Pot period. The Vietnamese-installed government trained or retrained about 40,000.

PUBLISHING AND BROADCAST MEDIA

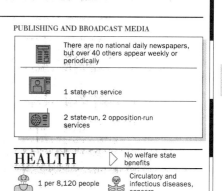

There are no national daily newspapers, but over 40 others appear weekly or periodically

1 state-run service

2 state-run, 2 opposition-run services

HEALTH

▷ No welfare state benefits

1 per 8,120 people

Circulatory and infectious diseases, cancers

Additional resources are needed to restore the devastated health service.

The Cambodian health system was effectively destroyed by the Khmer Rouge's period in power. Only 50 doctors survived the Pol Pot period. In the immediate aftermath of the Vietnamese invasion, Cambodia's health indicators were among the worst in the world. AIDS is widespread, even affecting children in rural areas. Conditions have since improved; however, infant mortality remains high, and malaria and cholera continue to be endemic.

SPENDING

▷ GDP/cap. no increase

CONSUMPTION AND SPENDING

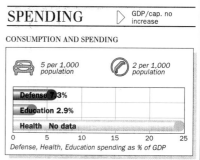

5 per 1,000 population   2 per 1,000 population

Defense 3.3%
Education 2.9%
Health No data

0   5   10   15   20   25
Defense, Health, Education spending as % of GDP

The opening up of the country's economy has slowly led to an influx of capital. The benefits of these new investments, however, are limited to those in positions in power.

WORLD RANKING

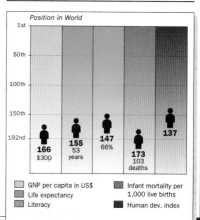

Position in World
1st
50th
100th
150th
192nd

166 $300
155 53 years
147 66%
173 103 deaths
137

GNP per capita in US$
Life expectancy
Literacy
Infant mortality per 1,000 live births
Human dev. index

CAMEROON

WEST AFRICA

OFFICIAL NAME: Republic of Cameroon   CAPITAL: Yaoundé
POPULATION: 14.3 million   CURRENCY: CFA franc   OFFICIAL LANGUAGES: French and English

| 1960 | 1961 | May 20 | CAM | +1 | +237 | .cm |

LOCATED ON THE CENTRAL WEST AFRICAN coast, over half of Cameroon is forested, with equatorial rainforest to the south, and evergreen forest and wooded savanna north of the Sanaga river. Most cities are located in the south, although there are densely populated areas around Mount Cameroon, a dormant volcano. For 30 years Cameroon was effectively a one-party state. Democratic elections in 1992 returned the former ruling party to power.

Savanna landscape below Mindif Pic in Cameroon's far north. From here, the land slopes down to the hot, arid Lake Chad basin.

CLIMATE   ▷ Tropical equatorial

WEATHER CHART

Climate varies from the equatorial south, with 500 cm of rain a year, to the drought-beset Sahelian north.

TRANSPORTATION   ▷ Drive on right

Douala International
436,000 passengers

48 ships
11,400 grt

THE TRANSPORTATION NETWORK

| 29,400 km (18,375 miles) | Trans-African Highway |
| 1,006 km (629 miles) | 2,090 km (1,306 miles) |

Major projects are the east–west Trans-African Highway and realigning the Douala–Nkongsamba railroad.

TOURISM   ▷ Visitors : population 1:140

102,000 visitors

Up 20% 1995–1997

MAIN TOURIST ARRIVALS

France 36%				
Africa 27%				
Germany 6%				
Other 31%				
0	10	20	30	40

% of total arrivals

In 1989, the first tourism minister was appointed to boost the still small industry. Some package tours visit the northern game parks. A new airport near Yaoundé will replace the present one. There are beach hotels near Kribi.

PEOPLE   ▷ Pop. density low

Fang, Bulu, Yaoundé, Duala, Mbum, Fulani, Pidgin English, French, English

31/km² (80/mi²)

THE URBAN/RURAL POPULATION SPLIT

45%   55%

RELIGIOUS PERSUASION

Roman Catholic 35%
Protestant 18%
Muslim 22%
Traditional beliefs 25%

Cameroon is ethnically diverse – there are 230 groups, although no single group is dominant. The largest is the Bamileke of the center southwest, but this group has never held political power. When President Ahidjo, a northern Fulani, retired, he was replaced by Paul Biya of the southeastern Bulu-Beti group. The north–south enmity which affects many other west African states is also present in Cameroon, albeit diminished by the great diversity of peoples. There is tension between the French- and English-speaking peoples, with sections of the latter demanding autonomy.

POLITICS   ▷ Multiparty elections

1997/2002   President Paul Biya

AT THE LAST ELECTION

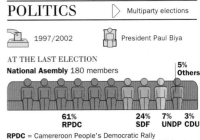

National Asembly 180 members
5% Others

61% RPDC   24% SDF   7% UNDP   3% CDU

RPDC = Cameroon People's Democratic Rally
SDF = Social Democratic Front   UNDP = National Union for Democracy and Progress   CDU = Cameroon Democratic Union

A senate is to be created under the 1995 constitution.

President Biya's RDPC narrowly won control of the new parliament in multiparty elections in 1992, which were boycotted by the main opposition SDF. The SDF candidate John Fru Ndi also disputed Biya's claim of victory in a presidential election that year. In elections in May 1997 the RDPC's apparent landslide victory was condemned by the opposition as the product of intimidation and fraud, as was Biya's reelection as president that October.

CAMEROON

Total Land Area :
465 400 sq. km
(179 691 sq. miles)

POPULATION
over 1 000 000
over 500 000
over 100 000
over 50 000
over 10 000
under 10 000

LAND HEIGHT
2000m/6562ft
1000m/3281ft
500m/1640ft
200m/656ft
Sea Level

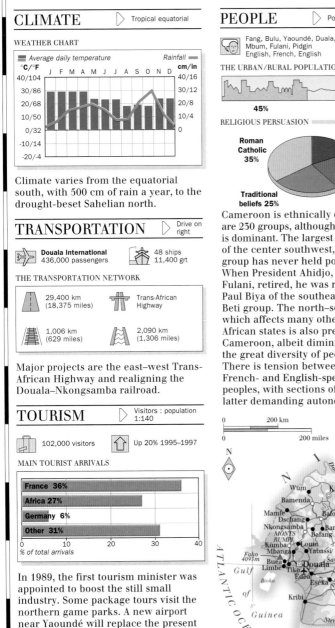

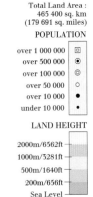

C

WORLD AFFAIRS

 Joined UN in 1960

| BDEAC | Comm | OIC | LCBC | FZ |

Cameroon's most important relationship continues to be with France, although the country has attempted to diversify its international links, joining the Commonwealth in 1995. A longstanding territorial dispute with Nigeria concerns sovereignty over the Bakassi peninsula, where there were clashes in 1996 and 1998.

AID

Recipient

$501m (receipts)   Up 21% 1996–1997

France is by far the most important donor, even having twice paid Cameroon's back debts to the IMF to prevent its being blacklisted. Lack of funding has forced many development projects to be abandoned. Despite poor economic performance, relations with the IMF are improving.

DEFENSE

No compulsory military service

$240m   Up 6% in 1997

The 11,500-strong army has been active in supporting the regime and maintaining order in the face of pro-democratic protests since before independence. Military equipment and training come mainly from France. There is also a 9,000-member paramilitary gendarmerie.

ECONOMICS

Inflation 3.1% p.a. (1985–1996)

$8.6bn   601.60–558.62 CFA francs

SCORE CARD

❑ WORLD GNP RANKING	86th
❑ GNP PER CAPITA	$620
❑ BALANCE OF PAYMENTS	$90m
❑ INFLATION	4.4%
❑ UNEMPLOYMENT	25%

STRENGTHS
French and US companies exploit moderate oil reserves. Very diversified agriculture (timber, cocoa, coffee, bananas). Food self-sufficiency. Strong informal sector. Private sector in fairly good state. Electricity is 95% HEP.

WEAKNESSES
Massive fuel smuggling from Nigeria affects refinery profits. Inflated civil service. Growing national debt owing to failure to adjust to fall in oil revenues.

EXPORTS
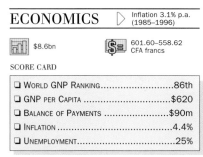
Germany 5%
Netherlands 5%
France 13%
Other 40%
Spain 16%
Italy 21%

IMPORTS
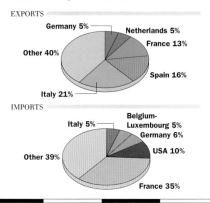
Italy 5%
Belgium-Luxembourg 5%
Germany 6%
Other 39%
USA 10%
France 35%

RESOURCES

Electric power. 620,000 kw

63,947 tonnes
140,710 b/d (reserves 400,000,000 bbl)
5.9m cattle, 3.8m sheep, 3.8m goats, 1.4m pigs
Oil, coal, tin, natural gas, bauxite, iron, uranium, gold

New oil discoveries may bolster declining extraction rates. In spite of large bauxite deposits, much is imported for the Edea smelter, which takes 50% of national electricity output.

ENVIRONMENT

No Green MPs

4% (2% partially protected)   Low

The 1999 Yaoundé Declaration should help to protect some of Cameroon's 22 million hectares of forest, threatened by commercial logging.

MEDIA

TV ownership medium

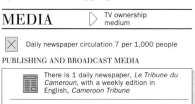
Daily newspaper circulation 7 per 1,000 people

PUBLISHING AND BROADCAST MEDIA

There is 1 daily newspaper, *Le Tribune du Cameroun*, with a weekly edition in English, *Cameroon Tribune*

1 state-owned service   1 state-owned service

There are frequent allegations of censorship and violence against journalists. English-language media are generally more outspoken.

CRIME

Death penalty used

Cameroon does not publish prison figures   Down 79% from 1992–1996

Armed robbery and burglary in Douala and Yaoundé are rising fast. The police are known to use torture.

EDUCATION

School leaving age: 12

72%   33,177 students

The French-speaking majority has failed in its attempt to take over the bilingual system. In 1991, two new single-language universities were created.

CHRONOLOGY

One of the great trading emporia of west Africa, Cameroon was divided between the French and British in 1919, after 30 years of German rule.

- ❑ **1955** Revolt; French kill 10,000.
- ❑ **1960** French sector independent.
- ❑ **1961** British southern sector votes to join Cameroon; north joins Nigeria. Federal system ended in 1972.
- ❑ **1966** One-party state.
- ❑ **1982** Ahidjo dies. Paul Biya succeeds as president.
- ❑ **1983–1984** Coup attempts. Heavy casualties; 50 plotters executed.
- ❑ **1990** Demonstrations and strikes; declaration of multiparty state.
- ❑ **1992** Multiparty elections.
- ❑ **1997** President and ruling RDPC returned in disputed elections.

C

HEALTH

No welfare state benefits

1 per 10,000 people   Malaria, diarrheal and respiratory diseases

A sharp fall in government provision means that more people are using the private health sector or traditional practitioners.

SPENDING

GDP/cap. no increase

CONSUMPTION AND SPENDING

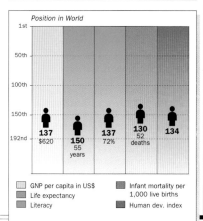
7 per 1,000 population
5 per 1,000 population
Defense 2.9%
Education 2.9%
Health 1%
0   5   10   15   20   25
Defense, Health, Education spending as % of GDP

Cameroon's unevenly distributed wealth declined after the end of oil boom. However there are very few wealthy people.

WORLD RANKING

Position in World

137 $620	150 55 years	137 72%	130 52 deaths	134

☐ GNP per capita in US$ ☐ Infant mortality per 1,000 live births
☐ Life expectancy   ☐ Human dev. index
☐ Literacy

169

CANADA

OFFICIAL NAME: Canada **CAPITAL:** Ottawa **POPULATION:** 30.2 million
CURRENCY: Canadian dollar **OFFICIAL LANGUAGES:** English and French

C

1867	1949	July 1	CDN	-3.5 to -8	+1	.ca

CANADA IS THE WORLD'S third-largest country, stretching north to Cape Colombia on Ellesmere Island, south to Lake Erie, and across five time zones from the Pacific seaboard to Newfoundland. The interior lowlands around Hudson Bay make up 80% of Canada's land area and include the vast Canadian Shield, with the plains of Saskatchewan and Manitoba and the Rocky Mountains to the west. The St. Lawrence, Yukon, Mackenzie and Fraser rivers are among the world's 40 largest. The St. Lawrence river and Great Lakes lowlands are the most populous areas. An Inuit homeland, Nunavut, was created in 1999 covering nearly a quarter of Canada's land area, formerly the eastern part of Northwest Territories. French-speaking Québec's relationship with the rest of Canada has been a key constitutional issue.

CANADA

Total Land Area : 9 220 970 sq. km (3 560 217 sq. miles)

POPULATION
- ⊡ over 1 000 000
- ⊙ over 500 000
- ◎ over 100 000
- ○ over 50 000
- ● over 10 000
- • under 10 000

LAND HEIGHT
- 3000m/9843ft
- 2000m/6562ft
- 1000m/3281ft
- 500m/1640ft
- 200m/656ft
- Sea Level

CLIMATE ▷ Continental/subarctic/mountain

WEATHER CHART

Canada's climate ranges from polar and subpolar in the north, to cool in the south. Winters in the interior are colder and longer than on the coast, with temperatures well below freezing and deep snow; summers are hotter. The Pacific coast around Vancouver has the warmest winters; temperatures rarely fall below zero.

TRANSPORTATION ▷ Drive on right

Lester B Pearson International, Toronto
27m passengers

852 ships
2.53m grt

THE TRANSPORTATION NETWORK

912,000 km (567,000 miles)	Trans-Canada Highway 24,459 km (15,198 miles)
14,098 km (8,760 miles)	3,769 km (2,342 miles)

Canada's size means the emergence of a national economy has depended on the development of an efficient system of transportation. The Trans-Canada Highway and two transcontinental rail systems are the focus of road and rail networks reaching into the far north. Air services are well developed and expanding. However, easy access to the cheap water transport of the Great Lakes–Saint Lawrence Seaway system has helped Ontario and Québec retain their dominance of the economy.

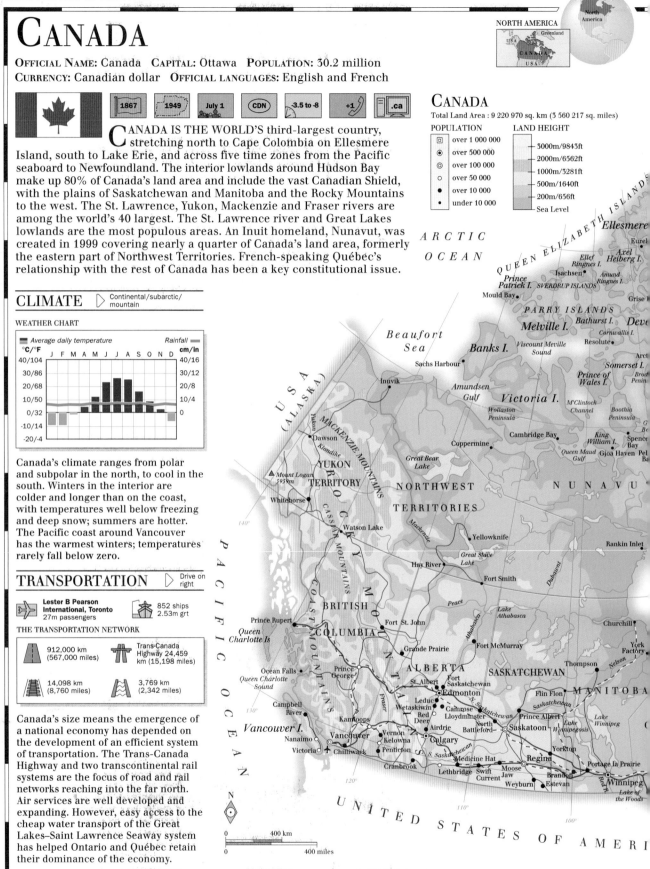

C

TOURISM

▷ Visitors : population 1:1.7

🧳 17.6m visitors   ⬆ Up 54% 1995–1997

MAIN TOURIST ARRIVALS

USA 79%	
UK 4%	
Japan 3%	
France 3%	
Germany 2%	
Other 9%	

0 10 20 30 40 50 60 70 80
% of total arrivals

The majority of tourists come from the USA, often on short visits. Efforts to attract more European visitors emphasize Canada's unpolluted natural beauty. Prince Edward Island, the setting for the *Anne of Green Gables* novels, draws many tourists from Japan, where they are extremely popular.

PEOPLE

▷ Pop. density low

🗣 English, French, Chinese, Italian, German, Ukrainian, Portuguese, Inuktitut, Cree

👥 3/km² 8/mi²

THE URBAN/RURAL POPULATION SPLIT

77%   23%

RELIGIOUS PERSUASION

Non-religious 12%
Roman Catholic 47%
Protestant 41%

ETHNIC MAKEUP

Other 7%
Indigenous Iindian and Innuit 4%
Other European 20%
British origin 44%
French origin 25%

Relations between French-speaking Québécois and the English-speaking majority in Canada have been the dominant issue of the past 30 years. The Québécois wish to preserve their culture and language from further Anglicization, and support for separatist parties has increased, mainly because of the failure of Canada's other provinces to deal with Québec's demand to be recognized as a "distinct society." Québec's controversial 1974 language law made French the province's official language.

More than 65% of the population still lives in the 5% of Canada taken up by the Great Lakes–St. Lawrence lowlands.

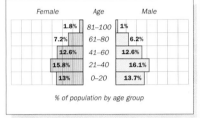

A dude ranch in British Columbia.
Many tourists are attracted by Canada's wide choice of outdoor pursuits.

POPULATION AGE BREAKDOWN

Female	Age	Male
1.8%	81–100	1%
7.2%	61–80	6.2%
12.6%	41–60	12.6%
15.8%	21–40	16.1%
13%	0–20	13.7%

% of population by age group

However, Canada's ethnic mix has changed significantly in the past 20 years due to a move from a restrictive immigration policy to one which welcomes those with money or skills. Significant numbers of Asians have moved to Canada. The government promotes a policy which encourages each group to maintain its own culture. Canada is now officially a "Mosaic of communities."

The largest element of the indigenous population is the 800,000 people of native Indian descent, known in Canada as first nations. There are also 213,000 Métis (French-Indians) and an Inuit population of some 50,000 in the north. In 1992 the Inuit successfully settled their long-standing land claim, and in 1999 the Nunavut area, with only 25,000 mainly Inuit inhabitants, gained the status of a territory, the first part of Canada to be governed by indigenous Canadians in modern history. A Supreme Court land rights ruling in 1997, establishing the principle of "aboriginal title," opened the way for the return of ancestral lands claimed by native Indian nations, and in 1998 the federal government formally apologized for their past mistreatment.

Canada has a long tradition of state welfare more akin to Scandinavia than the USA. Unemployment provision and health care, supported by high taxes, are still generous, despite recent cutbacks. The government has sought to end inequalities. Measures include the "pay-equity" laws which aim to specify pay rates for jobs done mainly by women – such as nurses – equivalent to similar skill jobs for men. Women are well represented at most levels of business and government.

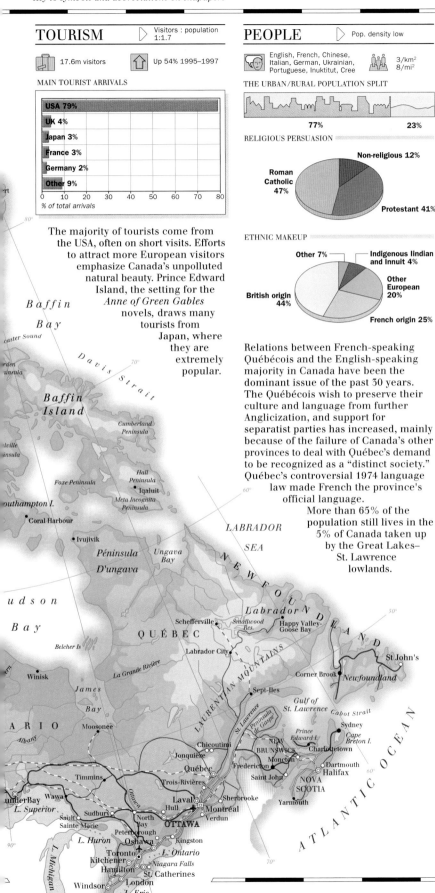

C

CHRONOLOGY

Peopled for centuries by indigenous Inuits and Indians, Canada began to experience extensive European settlement following the landing of the English expedition led by John Cabot in 1497 and the French landing of Jacques Cartier in 1554.

❑ **1754** French and Indian War between Britain and France. France forced to relinquish St. Lawrence and Québec settlements to Britain.

❑ **1774** Act of Québec recognizes Roman Catholicism, French language, culture, and traditions.

❑ **1775–1783** American War of Independence. Canada becomes refuge for loyalists to British Crown.

❑ **1867** Nova Scotia, New Brunswick and Canada united under British North America Act, creating first Confederation.

❑ **1885** Transcontinental railroad completed.

❑ **1897** Klondike gold rush begins.

❑ **1914–1918** Canadian troops fight in World War I.

❑ **1939–1945** Canadian troops fight in World War II.

❑ **1949** Founder member of NATO. Newfoundland joins Confederation.

❑ **1968** Liberal Party under Pierre Trudeau in power. Parti Québécois (PQ) formed to demand complete separation from federal government.

❑ **1970s** Québec secessionist movement grows, accompanied by terrorist attacks.

❑ **1976** PQ wins Québec elections. French made official language in Québec.

❑ **1980** Separation of Québec rejected at referendum. Trudeau prime minister again.

❑ **1982** UK transfers all powers relating to Canada in British law.

❑ **1984** Trudeau resigns. Elections won by Brian Mulroney and Conservatives.

❑ **1987** Meech Lake Accord.

❑ **1989** Canadian–USA Free Trade Agreement.

❑ **1992** Charlottetown Agreement rejected at referendum. Canada, Mexico, and USA finalize terms for NAFTA.

❑ **1993** Crushing election defeat of PCP, rise of regional parties.

❑ **1994** PQ regains power in Québec.

❑ **1994** NAFTA takes effect.

❑ **1995** Narrow "no" vote in Québec sovereignty referendum. Dispute with EU (led by Spain) over overfishing of Canada's waters.

❑ **1997** June, regional considerations again dominate federal election; Liberals retain power based on support in Ontario.

❑ **1998** PQ narrowly holds power in Québec.

❑ **1999** PCP holds power in Ontario, promising tax cuts.

POLITICS

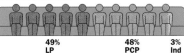

AT THE LAST ELECTION

House of Commons 301 members

| 52% LP | 19% RP | 14% BQ | 7% NDP | 1% Ind | 7% PCP |

LP = Liberal Party **RP** = Reform Party **BQ** = Bloc Québécois
NDP = New Democratic Party **PCP** = Progressive Conservative Party **Ind** = Independent

Senate 104 members

| 49% LP | 48% PCP | 3% Ind |

Senators are appointed for life by the governor-general in Council, to a usual maximum of 104; the prime minister may appoint an extra 8 senators.

Canada is a federal multiparty democracy.

MAIN POLITICAL ISSUES
The unity of the state

Opposition to federal government is not confined to Québec – the 1997 federal elections confirmed growing support for greater autonomy for Canada's western provinces – but Canada has agonized over separatist tendencies in francophone Québec almost since the foundation of the state. Constitutional proposals, to recognize Québec as a distinct society within the Canadian Federation and grant additional powers to other federal provinces, either failed to gain ratification or were rejected by voters both in Québec and at federal level. Despite losing two referendums on separatism, the Parti Québécois (PQ) advocates yet another poll, but its narrow 1998 provincial election win made the demand less pressing. In early 1999, all the provinces except Québec signed a Social Union agreement with the federal government defining their respective rights and obligations on health and social policy spending.

North American integration

The negotiation of a North American Free Trade Agreement (NAFTA) dominated the late 1980s. Now fully implemented, NAFTA has produced a trade boom, especially for Ontario. However, Canadians have problems competing for foreign investment with the USA, and with Mexico where labor costs are lower. The LP federal government propounds a "third way," retaining social welfare systems rather than embracing sharp tax cuts for the sake of competitiveness as the PCP and RP propose. Canadian workers have been forced to accept more flexible US working practices,

Niagara Falls is situated between Lakes Erie and Ontario on the Canada–US border. Horseshoe Falls, in Canada, are 49m (160 ft) high and 790 m (2,591 ft) across.

but most Canadians oppose such ideas as a currency union and ever closer integration with the USA.

PROFILE

Until recently, Canadian politics was dominated by three main parties. The PCP and LP had few ideological differences. The NDP advocated greater government intervention. Only the PCP and LP had held office.

The 1993 elections brought a major political shift – the eclipse of the PCP following the resignation of its leader Brian Mulroney, a landslide LP victory, and the emergence of the populist RP in the western provinces. The trend away from mainstream politics, towards parties representing strong regional interests, was confirmed in the June 1997 elections. The LP retained power thanks to strong support in Ontario, while the populist RP, representing the interests of western provinces, overtook the Bloc Québécois (BQ, the party espousing the separatist cause at federal level), to establish itself as the official opposition.

Lucien Bouchard, the separatist premier of Québec

Brian Mulroney resigned as PCP leader in 1993.

Jean Chrétien, prime minister since 1993

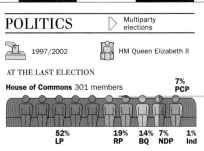

C

WORLD AFFAIRS ▷ Joined UN in 1945

Canada's most important relationship is with the USA, its main trading partner. There are tensions, however. Specific disputes include those over environmental matters, such as fears of pollution damage from the oil pipeline between Alaska and the rest of the USA, and the long-running issue of restricting air pollution from US border plants causing acid rain damage to Canadian forests. A fisheries dispute over Pacific salmon, involving both stock sharing and conservation, marred relations between 1997 and 1999. More contentious still were US efforts to maintain its trade embargo against Cuba by taking measures against Canadian (and other foreign) companies investing there.

Canada led the world in campaigning to outlaw anti-personnel landmines worldwide. A treaty to ban their production, export, and use was opened formally for signature in Ottawa in 1997.

AID ▷ Donor

 US$2.2bn (donations) ⬦ Not applicable

Canada's aid budget was one of the first areas of government spending to be earmarked for cuts in the 1990s. NGOS supported by the Canadian International Development Agency (CIDA) felt the impact of these reductions. Most Canadians support aid, however, and in 1998 the budget earmarked significant extra funding.

Aid now aims to provide know-how skills, rather than funding for large-scale development projects. CIDA has pioneered a theme-based approach, stressing human rights, basic needs, gender issues and good governance. Poland and then Egypt were the biggest recipients in 1997. The regional focus of aid has gradually shifted away from Africa, and toward the Indian subcontinent.

DEFENSE ▷ No compulsory military service

$7.8bn ⬇ Down 10% in 1997

Canada cooperates closely with the USA on North American defense issues.

CANADIAN ARMED FORCES

🚜	114 main battle tanks (*Leopard* C–1)	20,900 personnel
🚢	12 frigates, 3 submarines, 4 destroyers, and 14 patrol boats	9,000 personnel
✈	140 combat aircraft (122 CF–18)	15,000 personnel
🚀	None	

As in other NATO states, defense spending has been cut back since the end of the Cold War. Many Canadians would like to see it cut even further. Canada withdrew its forces stationed in Europe in 1992. The focus of defense planning is now the creation of rapid reaction forces. Canadian troops have served in many UN peacekeeping operations, most recently in former Yugoslavia. Their involvement in Somalia, ending in 1993, was tarnished by a scandal over torture, murder, racist attitudes, and indiscipline.

ECONOMICS ▷ Inflation 2.7% p.a (1985–1996)

US$595 bn 1.431–1.536 Canadian dollars

SCORE CARD

❏ WORLD GNP RANKING	9th
❏ GNP PER CAPITA	US$19,640
❏ BALANCE OF PAYMENTS	US$–9.3bn
❏ INFLATION	1.6%
❏ UNEMPLOYMENT	9%

EXPORTS

South Korea 1% UK 1%
Germany 1% Japan 3%
Other 10%
USA 84%

IMPORTS

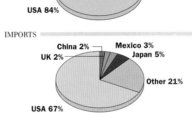

China 2% Mexico 3%
UK 2% Japan 5%
Other 21%
USA 67%

STRENGTHS

A rich resource base. Provides exports, raw materials for manufacturing sector, and massive cheap energy, notably HEP; also large oil and gas reserves. Forestry and agriculture contribute 3% of GDP, mining 4%. Successful manufacturing sector contributes 17% of GDP, notably forestry products, transport equipment, chemicals. Free access to huge US and Mexican markets through NAFTA. Strong recovery and growth since mid-1990s.

WEAKNESSES

Problems of competitiveness: higher taxes, more regulations, lower productivity relative to NAFTA; other threats from globalization. Uncertainty over long-term future and cohesion of Federation dents business confidence. Federal and provincial budget deficits still high.

CANADA : MAJOR BUSINESSES

✈	Aerospace industry		
🚗	Vehicle manufacture	🔌	Electronics
🌲	Timber industries	⚙	Engineering
📖	Pulp & paper	△	Chemicals
🥫	Food processing	△	Metallurgy
🐟	Fish processing	△	Oil & gas

ECONOMIC PERFORMANCE INDICATOR

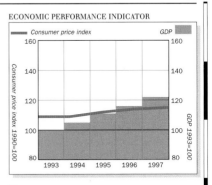

― Consumer price index   GDP

PROFILE

Canada's enormous resource base has delivered one of the OECD's highest standards of living since 1945. After the mid-1980s, however, its manufactured exports faced increasing competition, while prices for its primary exports fell. From 1980 to 1988, real growth averaged 3.5% a year. After 1989, it stagnated, while budget deficits rose, forcing restructuring at both federal and provincial levels. Many of Canada's welfare programs were cut back; the defense budget was sharply reduced. Inflation fell from 5.6% in 1991 to 0.2% in one year and remains low. Growth resumed after 1993 and strengthened towards the end of the decade. Canada's membership of NAFTA has meant that its firms have had to become more competitive to maintain exports. Most have been successful, but better productivity and a shift to high tech has left unemployment at over 8%.

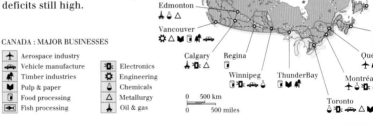

Edmonton	▲ ⬧ △	St John's	
Vancouver	⚙ △ 📖 🌲 🚗	Halifax	🐟
Calgary	▲ 🔌 △	Québec	✈ 🌲 📖 △
Regina	🥫	Winnipeg	🥫🔌 🚗 ⚙
ThunderBay	🥫 🌲	Montréal	✈ ▲ 🔌 🚗 △
Toronto	⬧ 🔌 🚗 △ 📖		

0   500 km
0   500 miles

C

RESOURCES   ▷ Electric power 113.3m kw

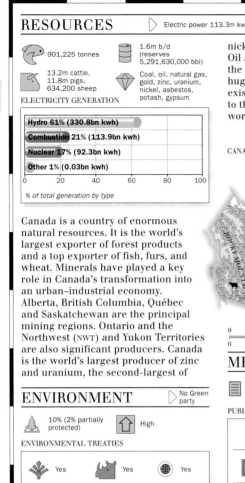

901,225 tonnes

13.2m cattle,
11.8m pigs,
634,200 sheep

1.6m b/d
(reserves
5,291,630,000 bbl)

Coal, oil, natural gas,
gold, zinc, uranium,
nickel, asbestos,
potash, gypsum

ELECTRICITY GENERATION

% of total generation by type					
Hydro 61% (330.8bn kwh)					
Combustion 21% (113.9bn kwh)					
Nuclear 17% (92.3bn kwh)					
Other 1% (0.03bn kwh)					
0	20	40	60	80	100

Canada is a country of enormous natural resources. It is the world's largest exporter of forest products and a top exporter of fish, furs, and wheat. Minerals have played a key role in Canada's transformation into an urban–industrial economy. Alberta, British Columbia, Québec and Saskatchewan are the principal mining regions. Ontario and the Northwest (NWT) and Yukon Territories are also significant producers. Canada is the world's largest producer of zinc and uranium, the second-largest of nickel, asbestos, potash, and gypsum. Oil and gas are exploited in Alberta, off the Atlantic coast, and in the NWT – huge additional reserves are thought to exist in the high Arctic. Most exports go to the USA. Canada is also one of the world's top hydroelectricity producers.

CANADA : LAND USE

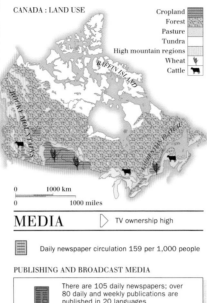

Cropland
Forest
Pasture
Tundra
High mountain regions
Wheat
Cattle

0   1000 km
0   1000 miles

ENVIRONMENT   ▷ No Green party

10% (2% partially protected)

High

ENVIRONMENTAL TREATIES

Yes   Yes   Yes

Yes   Yes   Yes

With a population of only some 30 million living in the world's second-largest country, Canada is justly renowned for vast tracts of wild countryside untroubled by industrial pollution or pollution caused by intensive farming methods. A major issue for conservationists is the battle to stop the logging of virgin forest in northern Ontario and on the west coast. Notable successes were achieved in 1998 and 1999 in pressuring timber companies to adopt more sustainable policies in areas of unique biodiversity.

Canada has tighter pollution controls than neighboring USA. Its rate of carbon dioxide emissions per person, although falling, is still relatively high; it has accepted a target of cutting total emissions by 6% by 2010. Production of hazardous waste is also higher than the European average.

In 1987, Montreal was the site of the international agreement to phase out CFC use to limit damage to the ozone layer. Canada had already followed the US lead in 1978 by banning the use of CFCs for aerosols.

MEDIA   ▷ TV ownership high

Daily newspaper circulation 159 per 1,000 people

PUBLISHING AND BROADCAST MEDIA

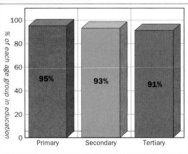

There are 105 daily newspapers; over 80 daily and weekly publications are published in 20 languages

1 publicly-owned, many independent services

1 publicly-owned, also independent services

The public Canadian Broadcasting Corporation (CBC) runs two national TV channels, in English and French. Local cable services are widespread. Canadian TV is renowned for its news and sports coverage. *La Presse* is the leading French-language daily and the *Toronto Globe and Mail* the leading serious newspaper in English; a new national newspaper, the *National Post*, was launched in 1998. Most papers are regional.

Autumn in the tundra *in northern Canada. Trees such as the black spruce are subject to the effects of acid rain originating in the USA's northern industrial regions.*

CRIME   ▷ Death penalty not used

33,882 prisoners

Down 32% from 1991–1996

CRIME RATES

Murders	
5	per 100,000 population

Rapes	
132	per 100,000 population

Thefts	
4857	per 100,000 population

Crime rates in Canada are much lower than in the USA. Canadians ascribe this to their far tighter gun control laws, which have been further tightened in the 1990s. Newfoundland police, the last force in North America to carry guns, began doing so routinely in mid-1998. There have been careful efforts to maintain the inner cities as crime-free zones. The ghetto problems of US inner cities have largely been avoided. However, Canada does have a rising narcotics problem and youth crime is also growing.

EDUCATION   ▷ School leaving age: 16

99%

1.8m students

Education is a responsibility of the provinces and is accorded high priority.

THE EDUCATION SYSTEM

% of each age group in education			
100	Primary 95%	Secondary 93%	Tertiary 91%

The period of free compulsory school attendance varies, but is a minimum of nine years. The prime medium of instruction is English in all provinces except francophone Québec. In several other provinces, French-speaking students are entitled to be taught in French. Multicultural education also helps maintain the cultural identity of immigrant groups.

Canada has 76 universities and some 200 other higher education institutions. Three-quarters of high school graduates go on to some form of higher education – the highest proportion in the industrialized world. The emphasis on education is also reflected in the fact that Canada's education expenditure as a percentage of GDP is among the world's highest.

── QUÉBEC'S DISTINCT SOCIETY AND SEPARATISM ──

QUÉBEC IS CANADA'S largest province, with an area of 1,667,926 sq km (594,860 sq miles). Its population, 7.3 million at the 1996 census, includes over 5 million of Canada's 6.1 million French Canadians, most of whom are Catholics. The province's capital is Québec City. Its main commercial centre, Montréal, has suffered a decline in prestige compared with Toronto, the main city of neighboring Ontario, which is overwhelmingly English-speaking. Québec has massive hydro-electric power resources and vast areas of forest, and its principal industries include timber, pulp and paper, and mining, particularly for iron ore. These economic interests have ensured that environmental protection legislation is relatively lax, and have also brought conflict with those seeking to protect First Nation lands from devastation by logging and massive dam schemes.

Conquered by the British in the 18th century, the Québecois retained the French civil code under the 1774 Quebec Act, but French Canadians only gradually recovered minority language rights suppressed after an unsuccessful rebellion in the 1850s. A so-called "quiet revolution" began in the 1960s, based initially on militant trade unionism. This brought far-reaching changes in the social, economic and political balance in Québec. The wage gap closed, and francophones now slightly out-earn anglophones, partly because many of the best-educated anglophones tend to leave the province. Francophone-owned businesses were built up through the "Quebec Inc" project. The anglophone dominance in government and the civil service was reversed, and higher education opportunities for francophones expanded. Québec now has four French-language and three

French shop signs above the streets of Québec City.

English-language universities. Francophone militancy was also channelled into party politics, fuelled by resentment at a harsh security clampdown against the guerrilla Québec Liberation Front in the early 1970s. The Parti Québécois PQ, which unexpectedly gained control of the provincial Assembly in 1976, moved on two main fronts. A French language charter, Bill 101, was enacted almost immediately. French became not only the official language but compulsory in government and on signs on public display. Non-francophones protested, and the Canadian Supreme Court eventually ruled in 1988 that part of the language charter violated their human rights, but the provincial government managed to keep these rules in force on a "temporary" basis.

The PQ's other - even more explosive - initiative was sovereignty for Québec. After defeat in a referendum in 1980, the idea seemed a spent force. Québec separatism revived in the 1990s, however, amid long-running disputes about the Canadian constitution, after the rejection of both the Meech Lake Accord and the Charlottetown Agreement, successive attempts to resolve provincial-federal relationships. The PQ returned to power in Québec in 1994 promising a second referendum. The vote was held in October 1995, proposing sovereignty in association with Canada. Although 60% of Québec's francophone majority voted in favour, it was defeated by the narrowest of margins, essentially because non-francophones opposed it. The PQ promised to try yet again, but backed off after its majority fell sharply in the 1998 provincial elections.

Bilingual street signs in Québec have now largely been replaced by French-only signs.

HEALTH

▷ Welfare state health benefits

👤 1 per 455 people

☠ Heart and respiratory diseases, cancers, accidents

The comprehensive state health service is funded from national insurance.

A continuing increase in costs is the consequence of an aging population and the spread of more sophisticated and expensive treatments. There is popular backing for retaining the present healthcare system, and this has encouraged the government to bolster it with extra funding, after a period of cuts inspired by efforts to reduce the budget deficit. About 25% of Canadians use private health facilities.

SPENDING

▷ GDP/cap. no increase

CONSUMPTION AND SPENDING

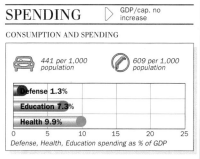

🚗 441 per 1,000 population

📞 609 per 1,000 population

Defense 1.3%	
Education 7.3%	
Health 9.9%	

0   5   10   15   20   25
Defense, Health, Education spending as % of GDP

Despite strains caused by recession during the early 1990s – including a rise in unemployment to just under 10% – life for most Canadians remains very good.

The UN ranks Canada as one of the best countries in the world in which to live. In its overall assessment of human development indicators such as income, education, and life expectancy, Canada consistently comes first.

However, disadvantaged groups do exist, in particular among indigenous Canadians. Unemployment, poor housing, and mortality rates for Indians and Inuit are well above those for other Canadians; the Inuit suicide rate is three times higher. Those who live on reserves are the poorest group.

WORLD RANKING

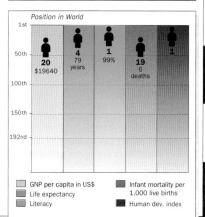

Position in World

20 $19640	4 79 years	1 99%	19 6 deaths	1

□ GNP per capita in US$
□ Life expectancy
□ Literacy
■ Infant mortality per 1,000 live births
■ Human dev. index

C

CAPE VERDE

OFFICIAL NAME: Republic of Cape Verde   **CAPITAL:** Praia
POPULATION: 417,000   **CURRENCY:** Cape Verde escudo   **OFFICIAL LANGUAGE:** Portuguese

C

WEST AFRICA

THE CAPE VERDE ARCHIPELAGO off the west coast of Africa became independent from Portugal in 1975. Most of the islands are mountainous and volcanic; the low-lying islands of Sal, Boa Vista and Maio have agricultural potential, though they are prone to debilitating droughts. Around 50% of the population lives on São Tiago. Following a period of single-party socialist rule, Cape Verde held its first multiparty elections in 1991.

CLIMATE   ▷ Tropical oceanic

WEATHER CHART

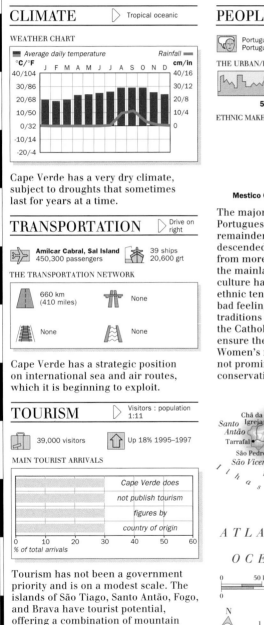

Cape Verde has a very dry climate, subject to droughts that sometimes last for years at a time.

TRANSPORTATION   ▷ Drive on right

✈ **Amílcar Cabral, Sal Island**
450,300 passengers

⚓ 39 ships
20,600 grt

THE TRANSPORTATION NETWORK

660 km (410 miles)		None	
None		None	

Cape Verde has a strategic position on international sea and air routes, which it is beginning to exploit.

TOURISM   ▷ Visitors : population 1:11

🧳 39,000 visitors   📈 Up 18% 1995–1997

MAIN TOURIST ARRIVALS

Cape Verde does
not publish tourism
figures by
country of origin

0   10   20   30   40   50   60
% of total arrivals

Tourism has not been a government priority and is on a modest scale. The islands of São Tiago, Santo Antão, Fogo, and Brava have tourist potential, offering a combination of mountain scenery and extensive beaches.

PEOPLE   ▷ Pop. density medium

Portuguese Creole, Portuguese   103/km² (268/mi²)

THE URBAN/RURAL POPULATION SPLIT

54%   **46%**

ETHNIC MAKEUP

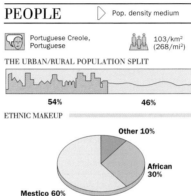

Other 10%

African 30%

Mestiço 60%

The majority of the population is Portuguese–African *mestiço*; the remainder is largely African, descended either from slaves or from more recent immigrants from the mainland. The Creolization of the culture has led to a relative lack of ethnic tension, though there is some bad feeling between islands. African traditions of the extended family and the Catholic Church have helped to ensure the vitality of family life. Women's role in public affairs is not prominent, in part due to the conservative Catholic influence.

POLITICS   ▷ Multiparty elections

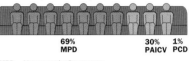

1995/2000   President António Mascarenhas Monteiro

AT THE LAST ELECTION

National People's Assembly 72 members

69%
MPD   **30%**
PAICV   **1%**
PCD

MPD = Movement for Democracy
PAICV = African Party for the Independence of Cape Verde
PCD = Democratic Convergence Party

Cape Verde experienced a peaceful transition to multipartyism in 1991, when elections brought the MPD to power. Although there had previously been a decade of single-party rule under the PAICV, it had in fact operated a liberal system in which opposition and dissent were tolerated. The large number of Cape Verdeans living and working abroad also played an important part in effecting the transition to multiparty politics.

The MPD won an absolute majority in the December 1995 legislative elections, President António Mascarenhas Monteiro being reelected in February 1996. The main issue for the government, apart from that of preserving political consensus, is that of economic survival, particularly in periods of drought.

WORLD AFFAIRS   ▷ Joined UN in 1975

CILSS   Ecowas   Lusoph   NAM   OAU

Cape Verde aims to diversify its international contacts in order to secure aid, while maintaining good relations with the former colonial power, Portugal, although it is not a major donor. Within the region, Cape Verde seeks to restore normal relations with Guinea-Bissau, after withdrawing from proposed union in 1980, and is developing contacts with other mainland states, such as Senegal.

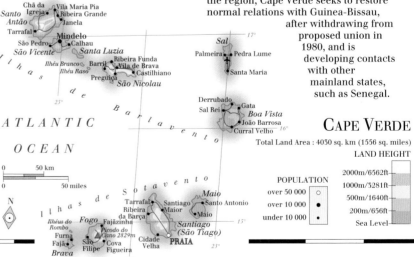

ATLANTIC OCEAN

Chã da Igreja   Vila Maria Pia
Santo Antão   Ribeira Grande
Tarrafal   Janela
São Pedro   Mindelo   Calhau
São Vicente   Santa Luzia
Ilhéu Branco   Barril   Ribeira Funda
Ilhéu Raso   Vila de Brava
Preguiça   Castilhiano
São Nicolau
Sal
Palmeira   Pedra Lume
Santa Maria
Derrubado
Sal Rei   Gata
Boa Vista
João Barrosa
Curral Velho

Tarrafal   Santiago   Maio
Ribeira   Maior   Santo Antonio
da Barça   Maio
Ilhéus do Rombo   Fogo   Fajãzinha   Santiago (São Tiago)
Furna   Picodo do Cano 2829m   Cidade   PRAIA
Fajã   São Filipe   Cova   Velha
Brava   Figueira

CAPE VERDE

Total Land Area : 4030 sq. km (1556 sq. miles)

LAND HEIGHT

2000m/6562ft
1000m/3281ft
500m/1640ft
200m/656ft
Sea Level

POPULATION
over 50 000   ○
over 10 000   ●
under 10 000   ●

C

AID

▷ Recipient

$110m (receipts)   Down 8% 1996–1997

The most important donor is the EU, which has provided substantial food aid in the wake of recent droughts, as well as funding aid programs. The World Bank is also a major source, as are the Netherlands, Sweden, Germany, France, and Italy. Aid finances almost all development in Cape Verde, which is one of the least industrialized countries in the world.

DEFENSE
▷ Compulsory military service

$4m   No change in 1997

After independence, small armed forces were established, now consisting of a 1,000-strong army, a small air force and a naval coastguard. They have never been called upon to play a political role; their main duties are to protect territorial waters against illegal fishing and to curb smuggling.

ECONOMICS
▷ Not available

$436m   95.31–94.52 Cape Verde escudos

SCORE CARD

❏ WORLD GNP RANKING	169th
❏ GNP PER CAPITA	$1,090
❏ BALANCE OF PAYMENTS	$–30m
❏ INFLATION	6.5%
❏ UNEMPLOYMENT	26%

STRENGTHS
Strategic geographical position, off the westernmost tip of Africa, close to the mid-Atlantic where Africa is nearest to Latin America. This has military and economic advantages, including shipping maintenance and air travel. Low debt-servicing costs.

WEAKNESSES
Permanent threat of drought and water supply problems, despite desalination plants. Lack of agricultural land and dependency on food aid. Difficulties of communications between islands.

EXPORTS

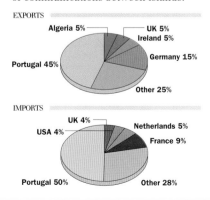

Algeria 5%
UK 5%
Ireland 5%
Germany 15%
Portugal 45%
Other 25%

IMPORTS

UK 4%
USA 4%
Netherlands 5%
France 9%
Portugal 50%
Other 28%

Portuguese colonial-style architecture on Fogo, one of the larger islands. The volcano in its centre is the highest point in Cape Verde.

RESOURCES
▷ Electric power 7,000 kw

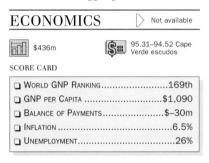

7,081 tonnes   Not an oil producer; refines 15,000 b/d

636,000 pigs
110,000 goats,
22,000 cattle   Salt, pozzolana

Cape Verde has no known strategic resources. With no oil and no possibility of hydroelectric power, it depends on imported petroleum for energy. However, experimental projects have been carried out to investigate the potential of windmills, wave power, and biogas.

ENVIRONMENT
▷ No Green MPs

None   Not available

Cape Verde has recently suffered several years of persistent drought, which has affected food production and reduced livestock herds. It is a very active member of CILSS, which struggles against drought in the Sahel region. Environmental initiatives include reforestation, soil conservation and a water resources program.

MEDIA
▷ TV ownership low

There are no daily newspapers

PUBLISHING AND BROADCAST MEDIA

There are no daily newspapers. Independent publications suffer from financial pressures

1 state-controlled service   1 state-controlled service

The government publishes three weeklies, but there are no daily newspapers. An experimental TV station was forced to close down in the late 1980s, but French assistance has enabled both TV and radio to start broadcasting again.

CRIME
▷ Death penalty not used

Cape Verde does not publish prison figures   Little change from year to year

Crime is not a serious problem, even in urban centers, though smuggling is fairly widespread.

CHRONOLOGY
Cape Verde was a Portuguese colony from 1462 until 1975, and was ruled jointly with Guinea-Bissau.

- ❏ **1961** Joint struggle for independence of Cape Verde and Guinea-Bissau begins.
- ❏ **1974** Guinea-Bissau independent.
- ❏ **1975** Independence.
- ❏ **1981** New constitution formalizes final split from Guinea-Bissau.
- ❏ **1991** MPD wins first multiparty election; returned to power in 1995.

EDUCATION
▷ School leaving age: 13

71%   Not available

At independence, education became a priority after years of neglect; 80% of children now attend elementary school.

HEALTH
▷ No welfare state health benefits

1 per 3,448 people   Heart disease, tuberculosis, typhoid and accidents

Health care has improved since the colonial period, but there are still fewer than 150 doctors.

SPENDING
▷ GDP/cap. no increase

CONSUMPTION AND SPENDING

4 per 1,000 population   57 per 1,000 population

Defense 1.7%
Education 4.2%
Health No data

0   5   10   15   20   25
Defense, Health, Education spending as % of GDP

90% of the country's population is engaged in primary productions. In comparison, the small business class in the capital, Praia, is well-off.

WORLD RANKING

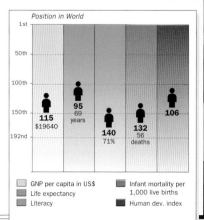

Position in World

1st
50th
100th
150th
192nd

115 $19640
95 69 years
140 71%
132 56 deaths
106

GNP per capita in US$
Life expectancy
Literacy
Infant mortality per 1,000 live births
Human dev. index

CENTRAL AFRICAN REPUBLIC

CENTRAL AFRICA

OFFICIAL NAME: Central African Republic **CAPITAL:** Bangui
POPULATION: 3.5 million **CURRENCY:** CFA franc **OFFICIAL LANGUAGE:** French

1960 | 1960 | Dec 1 | RCA | +1 | +236 | .cf

LANDLOCKED AT THE WESTERN end of the Sahel, the Central African Republic (CAR) is a low plateau stretching north from one of Africa's great rivers, the Ubangi, which forms its border with Congo, Dem. Rep. (Zaire). Most of the people live in the equatorial, rainforested south; the arid north sustains less than 2% of the population. "Emperor" Bokassa's eccentric rule from 1965 to 1979 was followed by military dictatorship. Democracy was restored in 1993.

CLIMATE
▷ Tropical equatorial

WEATHER CHART

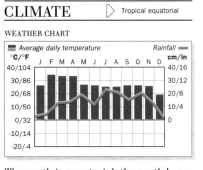

The south is equatorial, the north has a savanna-type climate, and the far north lies within the Sahel.

TRANSPORTATION
▷ Drive on right

Mpoko, Bangui
56,804 passengers | Has no fleet

THE TRANSPORTATION NETWORK

520 km (323 miles)	Trans-African Highway
None	800 km (497 miles)

The CAR has a limited transportation system, depending on the river link to Brazzaville, Congo, and rail from there to Pointe-Noire and Congo river ports.

TOURISM
▷ Visitors : population 1:159

22,000 visitors | Up 340% 1995–1997

MAIN TOURIST ARRIVALS

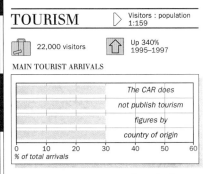

The CAR does not publish tourism figures by country of origin

% of total arrivals

Tourist promotion is small-scale, but since 1979 there has been a modest increase in national park safaris. A new runway in Bangui will permit air charters, chiefly from France.

PEOPLE
▷ Pop. density low

Sango, Banda, Gbaya, French | 6/km² (15/mi²)

THE URBAN/RURAL POPULATION SPLIT

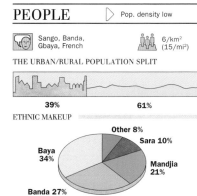

39% | 61%

ETHNIC MAKEUP

Other 8%
Sara 10%
Baya 34%
Mandjia 21%
Banda 27%

Although the Baya and the Banda are the largest ethnic groups, the *lingua franca* is Sango. This is spoken by the southern riverine minorities, who provided the political leaders from independence (Presidents Dacko and Kolingba and "Emperor" Bokassa). President Patasse is from the interior. Resentment against the river peoples occasionally flares up, but ethnic diversity minimizes polarization. Women, as in other non-Muslim African countries, have considerable power. Elizabeth Domitien was prime minister in 1975–1976 and Ruth Rolland ran for president in 1993.

POLITICS
▷ Multiparty elections

1998/2003 | President Ange-Félix Patasse

AT THE LAST ELECTION

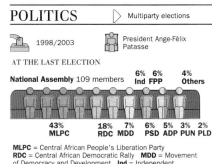

National Assembly 109 members
6% Ind | 6% FPP | 4% Others
43% MLPC | 18% RDC | 7% MDD | 6% PSD | 5% ADP | 3% PUN | 2% PLD

MLPC = Central African People's Liberation Party
RDC = Central African Democratic Rally MDD = Movement of Democracy and Development Ind = Independent
PSD = Social Democratic Party FPP = Patriotic Front for Progress ADP = Alliance for Democracy and Progress
PUN = National Unity Party PLD = Liberal Democratic Party

Democratic elections in 1993 ended four years of General Kolingba's single-party rule, heralding the arrival of

WORLD AFFAIRS
▷ Joined UN in 1960

BDEAC | CEMAC | FZ | LCBC | OAU

Apart from keeping up the momentum of its improving political image in international life, the CAR is anxious to continue good relations with France, whose financial help will be needed for some time, and with Cameroon and Congo, which offer its main outlets to the sea. Insulating itself from the problems of its neighbors, notably Congo, Dem. Rep. (Zaire), is a priority.

AID
▷ Recipient

$92m (receipts) | Down 45% 1996–1997

Almost all the CAR's development projects are funded from external aid. France, as the former colonial power, provides two-thirds of the total. EU countries (notably Belgium, Italy, and Germany), Japan and, since 1989, the USA and Israel, are major donors. The CAR also receives assistance from the IMF and the World Bank.

DEFENSE
▷ Compulsory military service

$39m | Up 28% in 1997

The 2,500-strong army is a heavy drain on the budget, and is well equipped, mostly with French hardware. France provides important military assistance, French officers fill senior army posts, and in addition there is a garrison of 1,300 French troops; in 1996 these intervened to quell an army rebellion.

Ange-Félix Patasse as president. Patasse was Bokassa's prime minister during the 1970s, but was jailed for dissent and subsequently went into exile in Paris. His party, the MLPC, remained the most important in the new parliament after the 1998 elections, but depended on the continuing support of opposition parties to maintain a workable coalition. A French-led multinational force kept the peace from February 1997, after several months of army mutinies including an incident with rebel troops in Bangui, when two French soldiers were killed. The French force was replaced by a UN force of 1,400 troops under the banner of UNMICAR in April 1998.

CENTRAL AFRICAN REPUBLIC

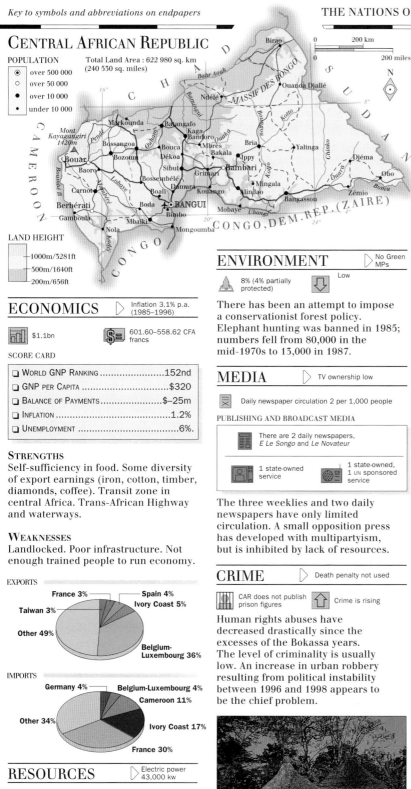

POPULATION

- ⊙ over 500 000
- ○ over 50 000
- ● over 10 000
- • under 10 000

Total Land Area : 622 980 sq. km
(240 550 sq. miles)

LAND HEIGHT

- 1000m/3281ft
- 500m/1640ft
- 200m/656ft

CHRONOLOGY

The French established the colony of Ubangi-Chari in 1905 and gave it autonomy as the CAR in 1958.

- ❏ **1960** Independence under David Dacko; one-party state.
- ❏ **1965** Coup by Jean-Bédel Bokassa.
- ❏ **1977** Bokassa crowned "Emperor."
- ❏ **1979** French help reinstate Dacko.
- ❏ **1981** Gen. Kolingba ousts Dacko.
- ❏ **1993** First multiparty elections.
- ❏ **1996** Government of national unity formed following army rebellion.

ECONOMICS

▷ Inflation 3.1% p.a. (1985–1996)

$1.1bn   601.60–558.62 CFA francs

SCORE CARD

- ❏ WORLD GNP RANKING 152nd
- ❏ GNP PER CAPITA $320
- ❏ BALANCE OF PAYMENTS......................$–25m
- ❏ INFLATION 1.2%
- ❏ UNEMPLOYMENT ....6%.

STRENGTHS

Self-sufficiency in food. Some diversity of export earnings (iron, cotton, timber, diamonds, coffee). Transit zone in central Africa. Trans-African Highway and waterways.

WEAKNESSES

Landlocked. Poor infrastructure. Not enough trained people to run economy.

EXPORTS

- France 3%
- Spain 4%
- Ivory Coast 5%
- Taiwan 3%
- Other 49%
- Belgium-Luxembourg 36%

IMPORTS

- Germany 4%
- Belgium-Luxembourg 4%
- Cameroon 11%
- Other 34%
- Ivory Coast 17%
- France 30%

RESOURCES

▷ Electric power 43,000 kw

- 13,300 tonnes
- Not an oil producer and has no refineries
- 3m cattle, 2.3m goats, 622,100 pigs
- Diamonds, gold, uranium, iron, copper, manganese

With timber, cotton is one of the few major exports, but mineral resources are of potential importance.

ENVIRONMENT

▷ No Green MPs

8% (4% partially protected)   Low

There has been an attempt to impose a conservationist forest policy. Elephant hunting was banned in 1985; numbers fell from 80,000 in the mid-1970s to 13,000 in 1987.

MEDIA

▷ TV ownership low

Daily newspaper circulation 2 per 1,000 people

PUBLISHING AND BROADCAST MEDIA

There are 2 daily newspapers, *E Le Songo* and *Le Novateur*

1 state-owned service   1 state-owned, 1 UN sponsored service

The three weeklies and two daily newspapers have only limited circulation. A small opposition press has developed with multipartyism, but is inhibited by lack of resources.

CRIME

▷ Death penalty not used

CAR does not publish prison figures   Crime is rising

Human rights abuses have decreased drastically since the excesses of the Bokassa years. The level of criminality is usually low. An increase in urban robbery resulting from political instability between 1996 and 1998 appears to be the chief problem.

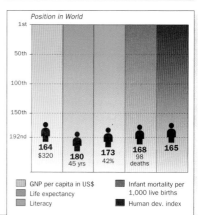

***Baskets of cotton,** Meme village. Cotton is one of the Central African Republic's most significant export crops.*

EDUCATION

▷ School leaving age: 14

42%   3,684 students

Schooling, on the French model, is compulsory, but in practice is only received by 68% of 6–14 year olds.

HEALTH

▷ No welfare state benefits

1 per 5,000 people   Communicable and parasitic diseases, malnutrition

Colonial neglect and post-colonial maladministration have resulted in a poorly developed health system.

SPENDING

▷ GDP/cap. no increase

CONSUMPTION AND SPENDING

No data   3 per 1,000 population

- Defense 4%
- Education 2.8%
- Health 1.3%

Defense, Health, Education spending as % of GDP

There is a small politico-military elite in the Central African Republic, which only arose after colonial days. For this small elite, Paris is the choice destination and style leader.

WORLD RANKING

Position in World

164 $320	180 45 yrs	173 42%	168 98 deaths	165

- □ GNP per capita in US$
- □ Life expectancy
- □ Literacy
- ■ Infant mortality per 1,000 live births
- ■ Human dev. index

CHAD

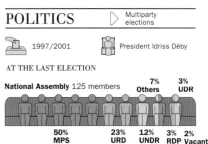

OFFICIAL NAME: Republic of Chad **CAPITAL:** N'Djamena **POPULATION:** 6.9 million
CURRENCY: CFA franc **OFFICIAL LANGUAGES:** Arabic and French

C

1960	1960	Aug 11	TCH	+1	+235	.td

LANDLOCKED IN NORTH central Africa, Chad has had a turbulent history since independence from France in 1960. Intermittent periods of civil war, involving French and Libyan troops, followed a military coup in 1975. In 1990, following a coup, a transitional government commenced the move to multipartyism, now enshrined in a new constitution. The discovery of large oil reserves could eventually have a dramatic impact on the economy. The tropical, cotton-producing south is the most populous region.

CLIMATE ▷ Hot desert/steppe

WEATHER CHART

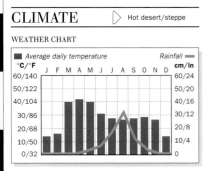

There are three distinct zones: the tropical south, the central semiarid Sahelian belt and the desert north.

TRANSPORTATION ▷ Drive on right

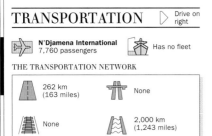

N'Djamena International 7,760 passengers | Has no fleet

THE TRANSPORTATION NETWORK

| 262 km (163 miles) | None |
| None | 2,000 km (1,243 miles) |

Chad has a limited transportation infrastructure. The nearest rail links are in Nigeria and Cameroon.

TOURISM ▷ Visitors : population 1:862

8,000 visitors | Down 53% 1995–1997

MAIN TOURIST ARRIVALS

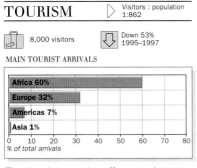

Africa 60%
Europe 32%
Americas 7%
Asia 1%

% of total arrivals

Tourism is now virtually nonexistent. The national parks and game reserves are the main potential attractions. The prehistoric rock painting of the Tibesti plateau and the Muslim cities of central Chad attract the adventurous.

Watering hole at Oum Hadjer, a village on the Batha watercourse in central Chad, 90 miles east of Ati.

PEOPLE ▷ Pop. density low

French, Sara, Arabic, Maba | 5/km² (14/mi²)

THE URBAN/RURAL POPULATION SPLIT

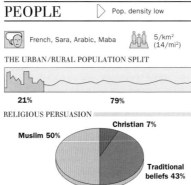

21% 79%

RELIGIOUS PERSUASION

Muslim 50%
Christian 7%
Traditional beliefs 43%

About half the population, mainly the Sara-speaking and related peoples, is concentrated in the south in one-fifth of the national territory. Most of the rest are located in the central sultanates. The northern third of Chad has a population of only 100,000 people, mainly nomadic Muslim Toubou.

CHAD

Total Land Area : 1 259 200 sq. km (486 177 sq. miles)

POPULATION
- ◉ over 500 000
- ◎ over 100 000
- ○ over 50 000
- ● over 10 000
- • under 10 000

LAND HEIGHT
- 3000m/9843ft
- 2000m/6562ft
- 1000m/3281ft
- 500m/1640ft
- 200m/656ft
- 100m/328ft

0 200 km
0 200 miles

POLITICS ▷ Multiparty elections

1997/2001 | President Idriss Déby

AT THE LAST ELECTION

National Assembly 125 members

| 50% MPS | 23% URD | 12% UNDR | 3% RDP | 2% Vacant | 7% Others | 3% UDR |

MPS = Patriotic Salvation Movement **URD** = Union for Renewal and Democracy **UNDR** = National Union for Renewal and Democracy **RDP** = Rally for Democracy and Progress **UDR** = Union for Democracy and the Republic **Others** = Party for Liberty and Development, Action for Unity and Socialism, Front of the Forces of Action for the Republic

Idriss Déby overthrew President Hissène Habré after an invasion from Sudan in 1990. He legalized political parties in 1992 for the first time since the early 1960s. Eventually, the transitional process led to a successful referendum in 1996 on a new constitution based on the French model. President Déby was elected in July 1996. His ruling MPS won 63 parliamentary seats in the 1997 elections, just achieving an overall majority. Despite government attempts to restore peace, in 1999 a rebellion broke out in the north among the nomadic Toubou people.

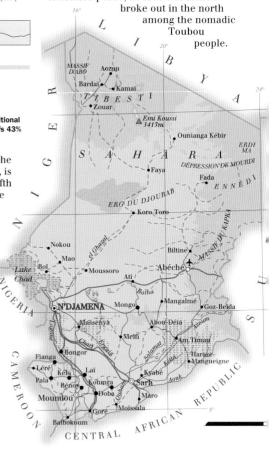

C

WORLD AFFAIRS

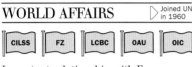

Joined UN in 1960

CILSS | FZ | LCBC | OAU | OIC

Important relationship with France. Libya formerly occupied northern Chad, claiming the uranium-rich Aozou area.

AID

Recipient

$225m (receipts) — Down 26% 1996–1997

France is by far the major donor. Other sources include Libya, the EU, the USA, the IMF, and Arab funds, especially OPEC. Without assistance to cover civil servants' pay over recent years, the administration would have collapsed.

DEFENSE

Compulsory military service

$43m — Up 8% in 1997

On seizing power, Déby swelled the existing army with irregulars. This policy has now been reversed and the army reduced to 25,000, including former rebels. France provides military aid and personnel.

ECONOMICS

Inflation 4% p.a. (1985–1996)

$1.6bn — 601.60–558.62 CFA francs

SCORE CARD

❑ WORLD GNP RANKING	147th
❑ GNP PER CAPITA	$230
❑ BALANCE OF PAYMENTS	$–38m
❑ INFLATION	5.7%
❑ UNEMPLOYMENT	Widespread underemployment

STRENGTHS
Revenues from recent discovery of large oil deposits could transform Chad's poor financial position. Cotton industry; potential for other agriculture in south. Strategic trading location in heart of Africa.

WEAKNESSES
Underdevelopment and poverty. Lack of transport infrastructure. Political instability. Frequent droughts.

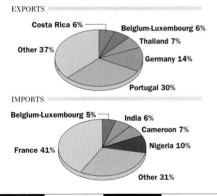

EXPORTS

Costa Rica 6% — Belgium-Luxembourg 6%
Thailand 7%
Other 37%
Germany 14%
Portugal 30%

IMPORTS

Belgium-Luxembourg 5%
India 6%
Cameroon 7%
France 41%
Nigeria 10%
Other 31%

RESOURCES

Electric power 29,000 kw

 90,000 tonnes — Reserves currently unexploited

5.6m cattle, 5m goats, 2.4m sheep — Natron, uranium, oil, kaolin, soda, rock salt

A consortium of ESSO, Shell and ELF has discovered large oil reserves in the south, mostly near Doba, which could make Chad a major African producer. Natron, found north of Lake Chad, is the only mineral currently exploited. There is uranium in the Aozou strip.

ENVIRONMENT

No Green MPs

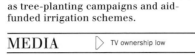 9% — No data

The worst environmental crisis in recent years was the drought of 1983, which coincided with intensified fighting, and decimated livestock. President Déby's government has made protection of the environment a priority, with anti-desertification measures such as tree-planting campaigns and aid-funded irrigation schemes.

MEDIA

TV ownership low

Daily newspaper circulation 0.3 per 1,000 people

PUBLISHING AND BROADCAST MEDIA

There is 1 daily newspaper, *Info-Tchad*, a daily bulletin produced by the government news agency

1 state-controlled service — 1 state-controlled service

Broadcasting is controlled by the government, which sometimes allows the airing of opposition views. There are a few independent publications, of which the best known is the weekly *N'Djamena-Hebdo*.

CRIME

Death penalty used

Chad does not publish prison figures — Crime is rising

The recent easy availability of weapons in the sub-region has meant that local minor disputes often now lead to gun battles. Armed robbery, smuggling, and vandalism are widespread. In several areas, the activities of disaffected former rebels threaten security.

EDUCATION

School leaving age: 12

 50% — 3,446 students

Education is based on the French model, although there are Koranic schools in the north. Recently, World Bank aid has been directed at elementary schooling. The literacy rate is among the lowest in Africa.

CHRONOLOGY

France extended its domination over the area now known as Chad after ousting the last Arab ruler in 1900.

- ❑ **1960** Independence. One-party state.
- ❑ **1966** Libyan-backed insurgency.
- ❑ **1973** Libyans seize Aozou strip.
- ❑ **1975** Coup by Gen. Malloum.
- ❑ **1979–1982** North–south civil war.
- ❑ **1980** Goukouni Oueddei in power.
- ❑ **1982** Hissène Habré (northerner) defeats Goukouni.
- ❑ **1990** Idriss Déby overthrows Habré.
- ❑ **1994** Libya relinquishes Aozou strip.
- ❑ **1996** National cease-fire; new constitution; presidential election won by incumbent Idriss Déby.
- ❑ **1997** Déby's MPS largest party in new parliament.
- ❑ **1999** Rebellion in north.

HEALTH

Welfare state health benefits

1 per 16,667 people — Diarrheal, parasitic, and communicable diseases

There are few city hospitals and fewer than 300 smaller health centers; half are run by religious groups or charities.

SPENDING

GDP/cap. increase

CONSUMPTION AND SPENDING

2 per 1,000 population — 1 per 1,000 population

Defense	4.1%
Education	2.2%
Health	0.5%

0 — 5 — 10 — 15 — 20 — 25
Defense, Health, Education spending as % of GDP

Poverty is almost universal; the middle class is very small. There are very few wealthy individuals. President Hissène Habré looted the treasury when he was overthrown in 1990.

WORLD RANKING

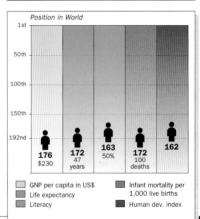

Position in World

1st
50th
100th
150th
192nd

176 $230
172 47 years
163 50%
172 100 deaths
162

❑ GNP per capita in US$
❑ Life expectancy
❑ Literacy
❑ Infant mortality per 1,000 live births
❑ Human dev. index

CHILE

OFFICIAL NAME: Republic of Chile **CAPITAL:** Santiago
POPULATION: 14.8 million **CURRENCY:** Chilean peso **OFFICIAL LANGUAGE:** Spanish

SOUTH AMERICA

| 1818 | 1883 | Sept 18 | RCH | -4 | +56 | .cl |

CHILE EXTENDS IN A NARROW RIBBON 4,350 km (2,700 miles) down the Pacific coast of South America. The plains of the central pampa lie between a coastal range and the Andes; most of the population lives in the fertile heartland around Santiago. Glaciers are a prominent feature of the southern Andes, as are fjords, lakes, and deep sea channels. In 1989, Chile returned to elected civilian rule, following a popular rejection of the Pinochet dictatorship. A recent collapse in copper prices, along with weaker export markets, has interrupted the high growth of the last decade.

General Pinochet, a dictatorial president rejected by popular referendum in 1989.

President Eduardo Frei. He took office following elections in 1993.

CLIMATE

▷ Desert/mountain/maritime

WEATHER CHART

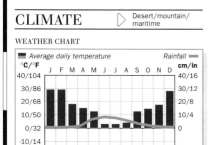

Chile has an immensely varied climate. The north, which includes the world's driest desert, the Atacama, is frequently cloudy and cool for its latitude. The central regions have an almost Mediterranean climate, with changeable winters and hot, dry summers. The higher reaches of the Andes have a typically alpine climate, with glaciers and year-round snow. The south is the wettest region.

TRANSPORTATION

▷ Drive on right

Comodoro Arturo Merino Benítez, Santiago
1.95m passengers

469 ships
722,000 grt

THE TRANSPORTATION NETWORK

| 79,300 km (49,300 miles) | Pan-American highway 3,455 km (2,146 miles) |
| 2,710 km (1,684 miles) | 725 km (450 miles) |

Chile's unusual shape, 4,350 km (2,700 miles) long and nowhere more than 180 km (110 miles) wide, makes air travel indispensable. Internal air routes are well developed; some, including flights to the Juan Fernández Islands, are served by air taxis. Sections of the Pan-American Highway, Chile's only arterial road running from the Peruvian border, via Santiago, to Puerto Montt, are being upgraded. The railroad is being privatized and modernized, as are ports. Santiago is notorious for its severe congestion.

TOURISM

▷ Visitors : population 1:9

1.7m visitors

Up 10% 1995–1997

MAIN TOURIST ARRIVALS

| Argentina 55% |
| Peru 11% |
| USA 6% |
| Bolivia 5% |
| Brazil 3% |
| Other 20% |

0 10 20 30 40 50 60
% of total arrivals

The Pinochet years saw a dramatic decline in tourists from the USA and western Europe. The number of visitors from neighboring Latin American states remained fairly constant; South Americans with a closer knowledge of Chile's political culture were aware that much of the violence was state-directed and aimed at Chileans, not tourists. Since 1988, tourists have returned and Chile has been making more of its stunning Andean scenery, its immensely long coastline and a number of exceptional sites, including Chuquicamata, the world's largest copper mine, the Elqui Valley wine-growing region, and the spectacular glaciers and fjords of southern Chile. Easter Island in the Pacific is another major attraction.

Peaks in the Paine range, southern Chile. Fjords, glaciers and myriad islands typify Chile's very wet, wild and stormy south.

PEOPLE

▷ Pop. density low

Spanish, Amerindian languages

20/km² (51/mi²)

THE URBAN/RURAL POPULATION SPLIT

84% 16%

RELIGIOUS PERSUASION

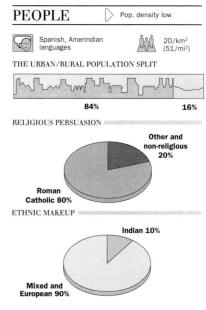

Other and non-religious 20%

Roman Catholic 80%

ETHNIC MAKEUP

Indian 10%

Mixed and European 90%

Chile is highly urbanized, with 84% of the population living in towns and one-third in Santiago. Most people are of mixed Spanish–Indian descent. Some 80,000 Mapuche Indians live around Temuco in the south, some 20,000 Aymara are in the northern Chilean Andes and 2,000 Rapa Nui live on Easter Island. Immigration has been far less than in Brazil or Argentina.

Rapid urbanization has led to large slums on the outskirts of Santiago.

Over 25% of working women are employed in domestic service.

POPULATION AGE BREAKDOWN

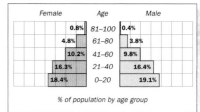

Female	Age	Male
0.8%	81–100	0.4%
4.8%	61–80	3.8%
10.2%	41–60	9.8%
16.3%	21–40	16.4%
18.4%	0–20	19.1%

% of population by age group

Juan Fernández Is

I. Alejandro Selkirk
San Juan Bautista
I. Robinson Crusoe

0   100 km
0   100 miles

Easter I.

Terevaka
Hanga Roa

0   10 km
0   10 miles

CHILE

Total Land Area :
748 800 sq. km
(289 112 sq. miles)

POPULATION

over 1 000 000
over 100 000
over 50 000
over 10 000
under 10 000

LAND HEIGHT

4000m/13124ft
2000m/6562ft
1000m/3281ft
200m/656ft
Sea Level

0   300 km
0   300 miles

POLITICS   ▷ Multiparty elections

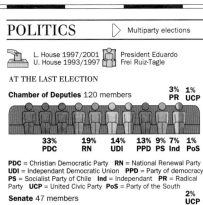

L. House 1997/2001
U. House 1993/1997

President Eduardo
Frei Ruiz-Tagle

AT THE LAST ELECTION

Chamber of Deputies 120 members

| 33% PDC | 19% RN | 14% UDI | 13% PPD | 9% PS | 7% Ind | 3% PR | 1% PoS | 1% UCP |

PDC = Christian Democratic Party   RN = National Renewal Party
UDI = Independant Democratic Union   PPD = Party of democracy
PS = Socialist Party of Chile   Ind = Independant   PR = Radical
Party   UCP = United Civic Party   PoS = Party of the South

Senate 47 members

| 30% PDC | 17% Appointed | 15% RN | 11% Ind | 11% UDI | 9% PS | 5% PPD | 2% UCP |

The Senate has 38 elected members, and 8 appointed
Senators. In addition, former president Pinochet is a
senator-for-life.

After 16 years of military rule under
Pinochet, Chile returned to multiparty
democracy in 1989.

MAIN POLITICAL ISSUES

Pinochet factor and democracy
The detention in the UK of Gen.
Pinochet, pending a decision on his
extradition to Spain on human rights
charges, has complicated the political
picture. His right-wing supporters have
exploited it for their political
advantage, but the consensus view is
that the delicate military–civilian
balance will hold and Chile's transition
to democracy will continue.

Human rights abuse trials
The right-wing-dominated Senate has
frustrated efforts to accelerate justice
for crimes under the military
dictatorship. The ongoing campaign by
plaintiffs and supporters to press for
the reopening of hundreds of pending
cases is resisted by the army.

PROFILE

The 1973 coup by Gen. Augusto
Pinochet overthrew the reformist
socialist government of President
Salvador Allende.

   Allende's nationalization of the
largely US-owned copper mines led the
CIA – which had a specific budget to
overthrow him – to back Pinochet's
coup which resulted in Allende's death,
most probably by suicide, during the
attack on the presidential palace.
Subsequently, thousands of Chileans
were killed by the military,
an estimated 3,000 people
"disappeared," and 80,000 political
prisoners were taken.
Pinochet's politics of a strong nation
state drew on the example of Franco's
Spain and was hostile to Chile's
democratic traditions. His economic
policy reversed Allende's, and was one
of the first experiments in the free-

market Chicago School of monetarism
which was later to be influential in the
West, particularly in the UK under
Margaret Thatcher.

   Pinochet's regime had considerable
support – particularly among Chile's
business and middle classes, which
prospered. Opposition, which was
brutally suppressed by the DINA secret
police, came most visibly from the
Church – an embarrassment to
Pinochet, who saw himself as a
champion of Catholicism – and from
the urban poor. Left-wing guerrillas
were also sporadically active.

   In 1988, Pinochet sought a popular
mandate to remain in power. To his
surprise, in a referendum in which
93% of the population voted, a clear
majority opted for democracy. Pinochet
stepped down, but remained head of the
army. Patricio Aylwin won presidential
elections held in 1989, heading
Concertación, a center-left coalition
dominated by the PDC and PS parties.

   Under Aylwin, politics became more
stable, in part the result of a cross-party
consensus on economic policy.
Continued growth and some
progressive social measures attracted
the support of the trade unions.

   Concertación's free-market and
social policies continued under
Eduardo Frei, who was elected
president in 1993.

   Pinochet retired as army chief in
1998 and heated disagreements over
his entry to the Congress as a senator-
for-life split Concertación on broadly
left and right lines. Disagreements over
Pinochet's subsequent detention in
Europe on human rights charges
further complicated the picture as the
PDC and PS contested presidential
primaries in the run-up to the
December 1999 elections. Both parties
claimed to be the guarantors of peace
and democracy for the future. The
right-wing opposition also began to
downplay their past links with Pinochet
to broaden their electoral appeal.

CHRONOLOGY

The Spanish first attempted the
conquest of Chile against the fierce
indigenous Araucanian people in
1535. Santiago was founded in 1541.
Chile was subject to Spanish rule
until independence in 1818.

❑ **1817–1818** Bernardo O'Higgins
leads the republican Army of the
Andes in victories against royalist
forces at the battles of Chacabuco
and Maipú.

❑ **1879–1883** War of the Pacific with
Bolivia and Peru. Chile gains
valuable nitrate regions. ⇨

C

CHRONOLOGY *continued*

- ❏ **1891–1924** Parliamentary republic ends with growing political chaos.
- ❏ **1936–1946** Communist, Radical and Socialist parties form influential Popular Front coalition.
- ❏ **1943** Chile backs USA in World War II.
- ❏ **1946–1964** Right-wing Chilean presidents follow US McCarthy policy and marginalize left.
- ❏ **1964–1970** Social reforms of PDC government alienate right.
- ❏ **1970** Salvador Allende elected. Reforms provoke strong reaction from right.
- ❏ **1973** Allende dies in military coup. Brutal dictatorship of Gen. Pinochet continuing as president.
- ❏ **1988** Referendum votes "no" to Pinochet staying in power.
- ❏ **1989** Democracy peacefully restored; Pinochet steps down after Aylwin election victory.
- ❏ **1998–1999** Pinochet detained in UK pending extradition to Spain on human rights charges.

WORLD AFFAIRS

▷ Joined UN in 1945

APEC | G15 | NAM | OAS | RG

Chile's most important relationship remains with its main trading partner, the USA, which supplies its critical copper industry. The relationship has not always been easy. During Allende's presidency, the USA actively worked against the government, fearing that the spread of socialism would threaten its investments in Chile and the rest of Latin America. Pinochet's human rights record eventually became embarrassing. Relations are now good.

In territorial disputes with Argentina, Chile was awarded 12 islands in the Beagle Channel in 1984 with Vatican mediation. The dispute threatened war in 1978. A 1998 agreement settled the last pending bilateral dispute over the Patagonian ice cap. Border disputes continue with Bolivia and Peru.

In 1999, in response to Pinochet's detention in the UK and planned extradition to Spain to stand trial on charges of human rights abuses, Chile argued that this amounted to an infringement of its sovereignty and the jurisdiction of its courts.

AID

▷ Recipient

💲 $136m (receipts) | ⬇ Down 33% 1996–1997

The majority of aid is in the form of debts rescheduled by the World Bank at the instigation of the USA.

DEFENSE

▷ Compulsory military service

💲 $2.1bn | ⬆ Up 6% in 1997

The military receives 10% of the export sales of Codelco, the state copper giant,

CHILEAN ARMED FORCES

🚗	130 main battle tanks (100 M-4A3, 19 AMX-30)	51,000 personnel
⚓	4 submarines, 5 destroyers, 4 frigates, 28 patrol boats	30,000 personnel
✈	92 combat aircraft (16 F-5, 21 *Mirage*)	13,500 personnel
🚀	None	

as part of its large budget. It enjoyed preferential treatment under Pinochet. The 1973 coup reflected the military's cohesive command structure rather than any right-wing ideological conviction. Pinochet exercised enormous influence in his position as commander-in-chief, but during his period in office worked with civilian rather than military advisers. The army's considerable influence is demonstrated by the failure of civilian governments since 1990 to press human rights charges over atrocities committed during the Pinochet years. Anger within the army at Pinochet's detention in Europe has yet to upset the delicate military–civilian balance.

ECONOMICS

▷ Inflation 16% p.a. (1985–1996)

📊 $70.5bn | 💲 438.50–473.25 Chilean pesos

SCORE CARD

❏ WORLD GNP RANKING	43rd
❏ GNP PER CAPITA	$4,820
❏ BALANCE OF PAYMENTS	$–4,062m
❏ INFLATION	6.1%
❏ UNEMPLOYMENT	6%

EXPORTS

Brazil 6%
South Korea 6%
UK 6%
Japan 16%
USA 15%
Other 51%

IMPORTS

Japan 6%
Mexico 6%
Brazil 7%
Argentina 10%
USA 23%
Other 48%

STRENGTHS

World's largest copper producer. Fresh fruit exports. Strong investment inflows have kept the economy growing at 7% to 8% over the last decade. Highest credit rating due to fiscal and monetary stability and highly liquid financial system. Development of non-traditional industries such as fresh and prepared fish, and wine.

WEAKNESSES

Dependence on USA as single largest trading partner. Prolonged weakness in Asian export markets. Vulnerability of copper revenues to low world market prices. Rising unemployment.

PROFILE

Chile's economy has been a battleground for competing ideologies. Under Allende, socialist policies

ECONOMIC PERFORMANCE INDICATOR

— Consumer price index   GDP ▒

Consumer price index 1990=100 (left axis 60–220)
GDP 1993=100 (right axis 60–220)
1993 1994 1995 1996 1997

brought huge corporations into the state sector. The Pinochet dictatorship then introduced radical monetarist policies. Drastic cutting of the state sector and the selling-off of state enterprises at below market value led to large profits for investors and speculators. Tough economic measures, irrespective of the social consequences, reduced Chile's inflation rate from 400% to 15%.

The Aylwin and Frei regimes continued with neo-liberal policies, but some 30 companies, including the large Codelco copper company, remain in the state sector. Recent poor copper prices have highlighted the need for more diversification.

CHILE : MAJOR BUSINESSES

- ⚑ Oil
- 🛢 Oil refining
- ⛏ Copper mining
- 🏭 Manufacturing
- 💉 Pharmaceuticals
- ✿ Heavy engineering
- 🐟 Fish processing
- 🌾 Agribusiness

Iquique
Chuquicamata
Vina del Mar
Santiago
Teniente
Talcahuano
Concepción
Punta Arenas
Straits of Magellan

0   500 km
0   300 miles

C

RESOURCES

▷ Electric power
6m kw

7.6m tonnes

14,697 b/d
(reserves
300,000,000 bbl)

3.8m sheep, 3.8m
cattle, 1.8m pigs,
740,000 goats

Coal, copper,
gold, silver, iron,
molybdenum, iodine

ELECTRICITY GENERATION

Hydro 62% (18.4bn kwh)	
Combustion 38% (11.4bn kwh)	
Nuclear 0%	
Other 0%	

0　20　40　60　80　100

% of total generation by type

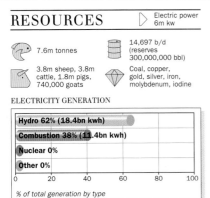

Chile is the world's largest producer of copper, which accounts for some 40% of export revenues. There are important deposits of lithium, molybdenum and especially of gold. Chile also has reserves of natural gas, oil, and coal, and plenty of hydroelectric potential. It also leads the world in fishmeal production and has a flourishing wine industry.

CHILE : LAND USE

Cropland
Pasture
Forest
Desert
High mountain regions
Wheat
Fruits - cash crop
Sheep

0　300 km
0　300 miles

ENVIRONMENT

▷ No Green
MPs

19% (7% partially
protected)

High

ENVIRONMENTAL TREATIES

Yes	Yes	Yes
Yes	Yes	Yes

Environmental concerns do not rank highly on the political agenda. Pinochet's constitution enshrined the right to live in a pollution-free environment, but bad smogs still cover Santiago, due in part to diesel fumes from the city's 14,500 buses. The chief concern is logging in the south by Japanese and other foreign companies. The huge growth of the salmon industry, which fences off sea lakes, is resulting in dolphins losing their natural habitats.

MEDIA

▷ TV ownership
medium

Daily newspaper circulation 99 per 1,000 people

PUBLISHING AND BROADCAST MEDIA

There are 52 daily newspapers, including *El Mercurio*, *Las Ultimas Noticias* and the best-selling *La Tercera*

1 state-owned, many independent services

1 state-owned, 400 independent stations

The media were brutally controlled by Pinochet; journalists "disappeared" in the early years of the regime. They are now relatively free, but journalists can still be tried under military justice for slander or abuse of the armed forces.

CRIME

▷ Death penalty used

2,176 prisoners

Up 16% from 1992–1996

CRIME RATES

Murders	
4	per 100,000 population

Rapes	
11	per 100,000 population

Thefts	
448	per 100,000 population

The judiciary is still not independent and is not pursuing the human rights cases from the Pinochet regime, in spite of the discovery, between 1991 and 1998, of mass graves of victims of the DINA (secret police). Mapuche leaders were among the "disappeared."

EDUCATION

▷ School leaving
age: 13

95%

367,094 students

Recent sustained economic growth has meant increased education spending.

THE EDUCATION SYSTEM

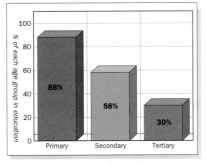

% of each age group in education

100
80
60
40
20
0

88%　Primary
58%　Secondary
30%　Tertiary

Many new private universities now operate for profit and offer vocational courses. Environmental issues and human rights now appear on school curricula.

HEALTH

▷ Welfare state
health benefits

1 per 909 people

Heart diseases, cancers, crime

Sustained growth in recent years has seen increased public spending on health. The public health service covers 80% of people, but is mostly concentrated in urban areas. Rich people have private care. Infant mortality fell from 33 per thousand in 1980 to 11 per thousand in 1997.

SPENDING

▷ GDP/cap.
no increase

CONSUMPTION AND SPENDING

71 per 1,000
population

180 per 1,000
population

Defense 2.8%	
Education 2.9%	
Health 3.4%	

0　5　10　15　20　25

Defense, Health, Education spending as % of GDP

Chile's traditionally large middle class did well under Pinochet and the economic policies of the Chicago School. The wealthiest sections benefited considerably from the sale of state assets at 40% to 50% of their true market value. Five years into the regime, wealth had become highly concentrated, with just nine economic conglomerates controlling the assets of the country's top 250 businesses, 82% of banking and 64% of all financial loans. The regime's artificially high domestic interest rates enabled those with access to international finance to earn an estimated $800 million between 1977 and 1980, simply by borrowing abroad and lending at home. These groups have retained their position. The poor, by contrast, are over 15% worse off than in 1970, with an estimated four million living just above the UN poverty line and one million below it.

WORLD RANKING

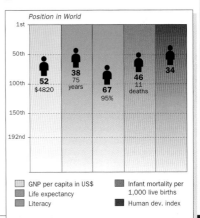

Position in World

1st
50th
100th
150th
192nd

52	38	67	46	34
$4820	75 years	95%	11 deaths	

GNP per capita in US$
Life expectancy
Literacy
Infant mortality per 1,000 live births
Human dev. index

CHINA

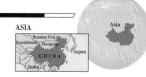

OFFICIAL NAME: People's Republic of China   CAPITAL: Beijing
POPULATION: 1.3 billion   CURRENCY: Yuan   OFFICIAL LANGUAGE: Mandarin

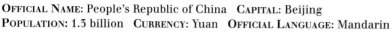

C OVERING A VAST AREA of eastern Asia, China is
bordered by 14 countries; to the east it has a long
Pacific coastline. Two-thirds of China is uplands. The
southwestern mountains include the Tibetan Plateau; in the northwest, the
Tien Shan Mountains separate the Tarim and Dzungarian basins. The low-
lying east is home to two-thirds of the population. China was dominated by
Mao Zedong from the founding of the Communist People's Republic in 1949
until his death in 1976. Despite the major disasters of the 1950s Great
Leap Forward and the 1960s Cultural Revolution, it became an industrial
and nuclear power. Today, China is rapidly developing a market-
orientated economy, but political liberalization is not on the agenda. The
current leadership remains set on enforcing single-party rule, as were
veterans such as "elder statesman" Deng Xiaoping, who died in 1997.

Li River, Guangxi, China's most beautiful
region. Its spectacular scenery has encouraged
large-scale tourist development.

CLIMATE

▷ Mountain/tropical/
continental/steppe

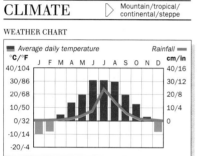

China is divided into two main climatic
regions. The north and west are
semiarid or arid, with extreme
temperature variations. The south and
southeast are warmer and more humid,
with year-round rainfall.

Winter temperatures vary with
latitude and are warmest on the
subtropical southeast coast, where they
average about 16°C (60°F). Summer
temperatures are more uniform, rising
above 21°C (70°F) throughout China; on
the southeast coast, the July average is
about 30°C (86°F). In the north and
west, temperate summers contrast with
harsh winters. In northern Manchuria,
rivers freeze for five months and
temperatures can fall to -25°C (-13°F).
In the deserts of Xinjiang province,
temperatures range from -11°C (12°F)
in winter to 33°C (91°F) in summer.

Summer and autumn are China's
wettest seasons. Winds from the Pacific
during the summer monsoon bring
rains to most of the country. The south
and east also have wet winters, but
elsewhere the winter monsoon brings
cold, dry air from Siberia.

Floods are frequent and sometimes
catastrophic, as in 1998. Droughts can
be even more devastating; that of
1959–1962 contributed to a famine
which killed millions.

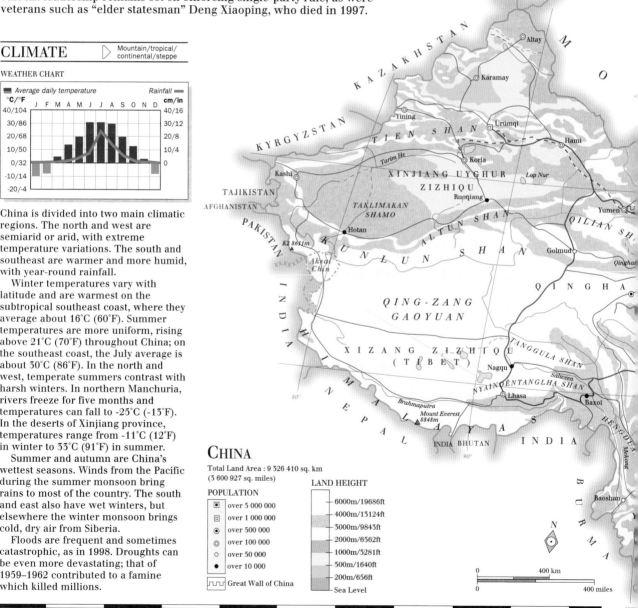

CHINA

Total Land Area : 9 326 410 sq. km
(3 600 927 sq. miles)

POPULATION

- ▣ over 5 000 000
- ⊡ over 1 000 000
- ◉ over 500 000
- ◎ over 100 000
- ○ over 50 000
- ● over 10 000

〰 Great Wall of China

LAND HEIGHT

- 6000m/19686ft
- 4000m/13124ft
- 3000m/9843ft
- 2000m/6562ft
- 1000m/3281ft
- 500m/1640ft
- 200m/656ft
- Sea Level

0   400 km
0   400 miles

TOURISM

▷ Visitors : population
1:52

🧳 23.7m visitors   ⬆ Up 9% 1994–1997

MAIN TOURIST ARRIVALS

	% of total arrivals
Japan 22%	
USA 9%	
Russia 8%	
South Korea 7%	
Mongolia 6%	
Other 48%	

% of total arrivals

Most of China is now open to visitors, and there have been some moves to allow tourists into Tibet, although access to Xinjiang in western China, and other areas, is sometimes impossible. The Great Wall, the Forbidden City in Beijing and the terra-cotta warriors at Xi'an remain among the top attractions.

The easing of restrictions since the 1980s has led to the rapid growth of all kinds of tourism, from luxury tours to budget packages and backpacking. Hong Kong is a major entry point.

TRANSPORTATION

▷ Drive on right

✈ **Chek Lap Kok, Hong Kong**
28m passengers

⚓ 3,175 ships
16.3m grt

THE TRANSPORTATION NETWORK

🛣 1.53m km (948,460 miles)	🛤 3,422 km (2,126 miles)
🚂 59,566 km (37,013 miles)	〰 109,192 km (68,245 miles)

Roads and railroads have been extended since 1949 to provide a basic national network. The transportation system is now being modernized and expanded to support the push for economic growth. Additions to the railroad system – all provinces but Tibet are connected to the system – have been concentrated in the west in the recent past. In the east, railroads are still badly congested. The Ninth Five-Year Plan (1996–2000) provides for 8,100 km (5,000 miles) of new railroad.

Container shipping is growing by some 30% annually. Hong Kong has the best natural harbor and is the busiest container port in the world, while Shanghai handled one-third of all Chinese container traffic before the reversion of Hong Kong to Chinese rule in 1997. The inland waterway system, once in a state of disrepair, is being upgraded. Water transport now accounts for about 33% of internal freight. The Yangtze River (Chang Jiang) is navigable by ships of over 1,000 tonnes for more than 1,000 km (620 miles) from the coast, and this is planned to receive a major boost from the Three Gorges dam project.

Many small airlines have sprung up since the state monopoly ended in 1988. Air transportation is growing rapidly, like private car ownership, as wealth increases. The bicycle is still the main mode of personal transportation.

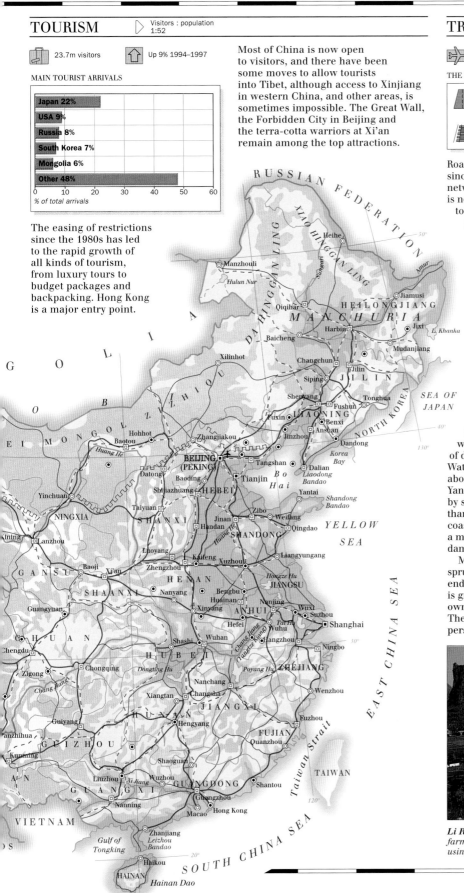

Li River Valley. *Irrigation helps Chinese farmers to feed 20% of the world's people, using only 7% of the world's farmland.*

C

C

PEOPLE ▷ Pop. density medium

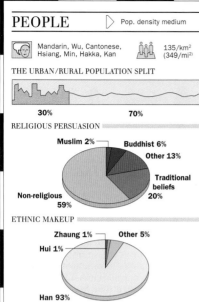

Mandarin, Wu, Cantonese, Hsiang, Min, Hakka, Kan

135/km² (349/mi²)

THE URBAN/RURAL POPULATION SPLIT

30%   70%

RELIGIOUS PERSUASION

Muslim 2%   Buddhist 6%
Other 13%
Traditional beliefs 20%
Non-religious 59%

ETHNIC MAKEUP

Zhaung 1%   Other 5%
Hui 1%
Han 93%

About 93% of China's population of 1.2 billion are Han Chinese. The remaining 92 million belong to one of 55 minority nationalities, or recognized ethnic groups. The minorities have disproportionate political significance because many, such as the Mongolians, Tibetans, or Muslim Uygurs in Xinjiang, live in strategic border areas.

The policy of resettling Han Chinese in remote regions is deeply resented and has led to uprisings in Xinjiang and Tibet, all ruthlessly suppressed. Han Chinese are now a majority in Xinjiang and Nei Mongol Zizhiqu. Tibet, however, has considerable international support over calls for greater political and cultural autonomy.

The government has relaxed family planning controls for minorities, after some small groups were brought near to extinction by the one-child policy adopted in 1979. Most Han Chinese still face strict controls. Even so, by 2025 the population will be nearly 1.5 billion.

Chinese society is patriarchal in practice, and generations tend to live together. However, economic change is breaking down the social controls of the Mao era. Divorce and unemployment are rising; materialism has replaced the puritanism of the past. A resurgence of religious belief is another response to the uncertainties of life in today's China.

POPULATION AGE BREAKDOWN

Female	Age	Male
0.6%	81–100	0.3%
5%	61–80	4.7%
10.6%	41–60	10.9%
17.4%	21–40	17.5%
15.7%	0–20	17.4%

% of population by age group

POLITICS ▷ No multiparty elections

1998/2003   President Jiang Zemin

AT THE LAST ELECTION

National People's Congress 2979 members

The Communist Party of China (CCP) is the only permitted party

China is a single-party state, dominated by the CCP, with 52 million members. The National People's Congress, indirectly elected every five years, is theoretically the supreme organ of state power. It appoints the president and executive State Council, headed by the prime minister. The real focus of power, however, is the 22-member politburo of the CCP and, in particular, its standing committee of seven.

MAIN POLITICAL ISSUES
Economic change and CCP authority
Since the death of Mao Zedong in 1976, China has begun economic reform, while seeking to secure the dominance of the CCP and avoid political upheaval. The "great helmsman" for two decades was Deng Xiaoping, even after he had relinquished all official posts, until his death in 1997. Advocating a fast-track move to a "socialist market economy," Deng and his followers looked to South Korea and Taiwan, as achieving high growth without political reform. At the 1997 party congress the reformers led by Jiang Zemin, by now both head of state and party leader, took the opportunity to realign formal party policy with their desire to privatize large areas of state-run industry. Economic reform remains a real threat to the CCP's central authority. The 22 provinces, particularly those in the southeast, are acting increasingly independently of Beijing. At a popular level, there is growing rural discontent over widening wealth differentials.

Conservatives versus reformers
Conservatives within the CCP, while recognizing a need for economic change, wanted it to be slower and more tightly controlled by the center.

Nanjing Donglu (Nanking Road), in central Shanghai, is one of China's most famous shopping streets. A magnet for foreign investment, Shanghai is China's largest city.

The pro democracy protests of 1989, culminating in the Tiananmen Square massacre, enabled the conservatives under premier Li Peng to gain the upper hand for a while. Deng moved to restore the balance and his longevity shifted the advantage toward his heir apparent, President Jiang Zemin. Jiang has gone on to strengthen his own power base and international stature, while premier Zhu Rongji spearheads the economic reform and anti-corruption campaigns, but former premier Li Peng, since 1998 president of the parliament, still commands support among conservatives within the state and party leadership.

PROFILE
The death in February 1997 of Deng Xiaoping marked in effect the passing of the dominance of the "Immortals" – those who took part with Mao Zedong in the 1934–1935 Long March. Deng, the architect of China's economic reforms, had worked hard forming alliances to promote his reformist ideas and followers. The foremost of these, Jiang Zemin, has consolidated his position as president and CCP general secretary since Deng's death. The profound economic changes under way, transferring much of the state economic system into private ownership, are a challenge to the CCP's ability to monopolize power, but the party has not allowed political opposition to surface.

Deng Xiaoping was China's paramount leader until his death in 1997.

Jiang Zemin, CCP leader and China's president since Deng resigned the post.

Li Peng, president of the National People's Congress.

Zhu Rongji, premier, reformer, and a protégé of Deng Xiaoping.

C

WORLD AFFAIRS

 Joined UN in 1945

The push for economic modernization, and concerns about regional stability, dominate Chinese foreign policy. Investment, technology, and trade considerations outweigh ideology.

Despite continuing human rights concerns, relations with the West have recovered since the 1989 Tiananmen Square massacre. Relations with the UK were dominated by Hong Kong until it

was handed back to China in mid-1997. Unconditional renewal of China's Most Favored Nation (MFN) trading status with the USA from 1996 improved Sino-US relations, culminating in US President Clinton's mid-1998 visit. China, like Russia, opposed NATO's use of force against Yugoslavia in 1999, when the accidental bombing of China's embassy in Belgrade provoked a serious crisis.

China now has significant trade and military contacts with Russia. Relations with Vietnam have been normalized.

While seeking to restrain North Korea, China has developed links with South Korea and with Japan, despite historic animosities.

Taiwan remains a thorny issue. Beijing strongly opposes anything that would perpetuate the division of China or imply Taiwanese statehood. Chinese military exercises off Taiwan in 1996 coincided with the first direct presidential elections held there, and periodic displays of bellicosity disrupt cross-strait cooperation.

AID

▷ Recipient

$2bn (receipts)

Down 22% 1996–1997

In the 1970s aid was an important part of China's diplomacy, going mostly to Africa, but other communist and southeast Asian states were also recipients. Aid flows outward have almost ceased since the late 1970s, as the economic reform process has turned China itself into a major aid recipient. Japan is the biggest bilateral donor, but the potential of the Chinese market means most developed states provide aid. A significant proportion of funding is used to finance high-tech imports. The 1989 Tiananmen Square massacre led to a temporary suspension of aid disbursements by the West.

DEFENSE

▷ Compulsory military service

$36.6bn

Up 2% in 1997

The People's Liberation Army (PLA) is closely linked with the ruling CCP.

CHINESE ARMED FORCES

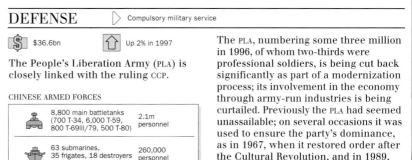

🛡	8,800 main battletanks (700 T-34, 6,000 T-59, 800 T-69III/79, 500 T-80)	2.1m personnel
🚢	63 submarines, 35 frigates, 18 destroyers & 747 patrol boats	260,000 personnel
✈	3,566 combat aircraft (400 Q-5, 1,800 J-6/-B/- D/-E, 500 J-7)	470,000 personnel
🚀	ICBM (7 CSS-4, 10 CSS-3) IRBM (38 CSS-2, 8 CSS-5) SLBM (12 CSS-N-3) SRBM (4DF-15, DF-11)	

The PLA, numbering some three million in 1996, of whom two-thirds were professional soldiers, is being cut back significantly as part of a modernization process; its involvement in the economy through army-run industries is being curtailed. Previously the PLA had seemed unassailable; on several occasions it was used to ensure the party's dominance, as in 1967, when it restored order after the Cultural Revolution, and in 1989, when it fired on civilians in Tiananmen Square to suppress prodemocracy protests. It is also used to suppress dissent in Tibet. China has extended its nuclear weapons capability to include the neutron bomb. It is a significant arms exporter.

ECONOMICS

▷ Inflation 9.2% p.a. (1986–1996)

$1,055bn

8.28 yuan

SCORE CARD

❏ WORLD GNP RANKING	7th
❏ GNP PER CAPITA	$860
❏ BALANCE OF PAYMENTS	$29.7bn
❏ INFLATION	2.3%
❏ UNEMPLOYMENT	3% (official)

STRENGTHS

Domestic market of over 1.2 billion. Self-sufficiency in food. Mineral reserves. Increasingly diversified industrial sector. Low wage costs. Rapid and sustained growth since 1980s. Growing exports. Hong Kong as financial center.

ECONOMIC PERFORMANCE INDICATOR

Consumer price index — GDP

Consumer price index 1990=100 / GDP 1993=100
220, 180, 140, 100, 60
1993 1994 1995 1996 1997

EXPORTS

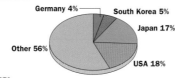

Germany 4%, South Korea 5%, Japan 17%, Other 56%, USA 18%

IMPORTS

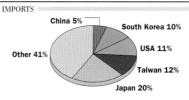

China 5%, South Korea 10%, USA 11%, Taiwan 12%, Japan 20%, Other 41%

WEAKNESSES

Massive underemployment, rising unemployment and migration to cities. Unevenly distributed resources. Poor transport system. Massive task of privatizing debt-ridden state sector.

CHINA : MAJOR BUSINESSES

🛢	Oil
✳	Textiles
🧪	Chemicals
💻	Computers
⚡	Electronics
🔩	Iron & steel
✿	Engineering
📺	Consumer goods
☢	Research & development

* significant multinational ownership

PROFILE

China's shift to a market-oriented economy has steamed ahead since the 1980s, notably in the south, where liberalization has gone furthest. Growth had to be curbed on several occasions to control inflation. The Ninth Five-Year Plan (1996–2000) aimed at intensive rather than extensive growth, with the government retaining strict controls.

The 1997 party congress gave a major boost to privatizing much of the huge state-owned sector. Pledges not to devalue the renminbi helped retain foreign investment during the crisis of confidence in emerging markets through to early 1999. Slackening domestic demand, however, made China less attractive to investors.

C

MINORITIES IN THE AUTONOMOUS REGIONS

AUTONOMOUS REGIONS OF CHINA

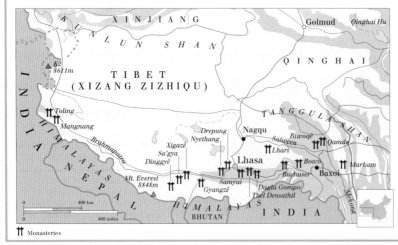

CHINA'S CONSTITUTION STATES that "regional autonomy is practised in areas where people of minority nationalities live in compact communities". The Manchu, Miao, Yi and many others among the 55 recognised ethnic minorities are not regarded as meeting this criterion, but there are five areas which do officially have the status of autonomous region or Zizhiqu. The two most westerly such regions, sparsely populated Tibet and the home of the Uyghur people in Xinjiang are both in particularly sensitive border areas and opposition to Chinese rule there has been suppressed.

TIBET

The vast mountainous region of Tibet has China's lowest population density, at only two inhabitants per sq km, spread across an area of 1,220,000 sq km, with its capital at Lhasa. Tibetans were officially recorded as making up 95% of its total population of 2.2 million at the 1990 census, and Han Chinese, whose immigration has aroused strong local resentment, as under 4%, although another census in 1993 gave a total population figure of nearly 3 million.

Tibet was part of the Manchu empire from the 18th century until 1911, but exercised full control over most of its affairs under the feudal rule of the Dalai Lama, spiritual head of Tibetan Buddhism. The forces of the People's Republic of China invaded Tibet in 1950 and ruthlessly crushed the 1959 independence uprising. The Dalai Lama fled to India amid an exodus of refugees and established a government in exile, but has recently come close to accepting Chinese rule in an effort to win greater real self-government and cultural freedom for the Tibetan people. In 1965 Tibet was made a region of China, known as Xizang Zizhiqu. Opponents of Chinese rule were imprisoned or executed and many Buddhist monasteries destroyed. Clashes between nationalists and Chinese troops in 1987 led to a renewed clampdown. In 1988, in an apparently more conciliatory spirit, the Chinese government accepted Tibetan as a "major official language".

In 1995, there was further tension when the Chinese authorities detained a young boy whom Tibetan Buddhists had recognised as the latest incarnation of their second-ranking spiritual leader, the Panchen Lama. The Chinese government named its own candidate to this office instead, which Tibetans regarded as an unwarranted interference in their religious life. The offence was compounded when China in June 1999 reportedly initiated a search for the next Dalai Lama.

XINJIANG UYGHUR

Consisting largely of desert and bordering on Kyrgyzstan and Kazakhstan, the Xinjiang Uyghur Zizhiqu has a total area of 1,647,000 sq km, or nearly 18% of China's total land mass. Han Chinese are narrowly in the

*The **Kumbum** dagoba at the Palkhor Tschöde monastery, Gyangze (Chiang-tzu), Tibet. At the tip of this 15th century structure is a Buddhist chapel.*

majority in its population of 15.4 million, the total number of (mainly Muslim) Uyghurs being only 7.2 million. Dissent has been firmly suppressed, and restrictions imposed on travelling to Xinjiang in recent years. The regional capital, Ürümqi, is an industrial city noted for iron, steel, oil and chemicals.

INNER MONGOLIA

Inner Mongolia or Nei Mongol Zizhiqu occupies most of the area in northern China along the long land border with Mongolia (i.e. Outer Mongolia, as seen from the Chinese perspective). Han Chinese are the majority in a total population of 21.1 million, of whom 4.8 million, or less than a quarter, are ethnic Mongolian.

NINGXIA HUI

The smallest of all the autonomous regions, Ningxia Hui Zizhiqu occupies an area of only 170 sq km, just south of Nei Mongol Zizhiqu. Its capital is at Yinchuan. The population was 4.7 million at the 1990 census. Many of the Hui people, who number some 8.6 million in all, live outside the region.

GUANGXI ZHUANG

This autonomous region, unlike the others, lies close to China's booming economic heartland, in the south between Guangdong province and the border with Vietnam. Although relatively small, (220 sq km), it has a population density of 192 per sq km and, with a total of 42.5 million inhabitants at the 1990 census, has by far the largest population. The capital is at Nanning. The Zhuang people, although China's largest ethnic minority, still number only 15.5 million in all, and thus are substantially in the minority in the region.

SPECIAL ECONOMIC ZONES, OPEN CITIES AND SPECIAL ADMINISTRATIVE REGIONS

ECONOMIC REFORMS FIRST INSTITUTED by Deng Xiaoping in 1978 began opening China to foreign business. This has spread from a small number of zones operating under special tax regimes, to other cities all along the coastal belt and inland, and has fuelled an extraordinary urban investment boom.

Special Economic Zones (SEZs)   Special Administrative Regions (SARs)

SPECIAL ECONOMIC ZONES
The creation of five Special Economic Zones (SEZs) on the south coast was a major early milestone. Shenzhen, the trail-blazer for the concept, was established in 1980, adjoining Kowloon in Hong Kong. Also in Guangdong province are Zhuhai, adjoining Macao, and Shantou further east, while Xiamen SEZ is in Fujian province opposite Taiwan. These locations reflect the aim of attracting investment from t he 30 million Chinese abroad, especially in Hong Kong and Taiwan, whose ancestral homes were in Guangdong and Fujian. The fifth and least dynamic of the SEZs comprises the southern island province of Hainan.

FOREIGN INVESTMENT
Foreign direct investment reached over $45 billion in 1998, more than any other country except the USA. The inflow then began falling, for the first time for a decade. Most investment goes into the Open Coastal Belt, based on 14 cities, from Dalian in the north to Zhanjiang and Beihai in the south, which were picked in the mid-1980s for the dual role of "windows", opening to the outside world, and "radiators", spreading the development of an export-oriented economy.

Among the most successful development areas is the great port of Shanghai, where the stock exchange reopened in 1990. Investors in the city's Pudong New Zone enjoy more preferential conditions than in the SEZs, including the right to sell goods and financial services. Pudong has attracted a string of major foreign companies keen to establish a foothold in the potentially massive Chinese market, including General Motors, NEC, Sharp Hitachi, Siemens, Unilever, BASF and Pilkington. Pudong also forms the "dragon head" for a chain of open cities, extending up the Yangtze river valley, where foreign investment has been encouraged since 1990. Since 1992 China has also designated a new set of open cities, this time in areas around its land borders, adjoining Russia, Mongolia, Kazakhstan, Burma and Vietnam, to develop infrastructure and promote trade and the growth of export-oriented industries.

INDUSTRIAL GROWTH IN GUANGDONG
Guangdong province, with Guangzhou and Shenzhen at its heart, promises to become Asia's largest industrial region. One in ten of the world's top 500 multinational companies has invested in the Guangzhou Economic and Technical Development District (GET). Shenzhen, meanwhile, has become China's richest city, and the first to start selling state-owned flats freehold. It is being revamped as the science and technology city of the future, complete with parks, pedestrian precincts, civic amenities and a sophisticated communications infrastructure, although its original incentive package of tax concessions for investors is being phased out.

HONG KONG AND MACAO SARS
The success of Shenzhen contrasts with recession-hit Hong Kong in the two years since its reversion to Chinese sovereignty in mid-1997. As a British colony, Hong Kong flourished through its textile industry, subsequently expanding into electronics, but was above all a trade and financial services centre. This role is preserved under its status as a Special Administrative Region (SAR). Hong Kong's population is estimated at 6.69 million, in an area of only 1,095 sq km. Its Basic Law guarantees a high level of autonomy for 50 years under the "one country, two systems" formula, and GDP per capita in 1998 stood at some $22,200, even after that year's 5% negative economic growth. Its government, however, under Chinese-appointed chief executive Tung Chee-hwa, has been increasingly at odds with the Legislative Council since the opposition Democratic Party gained ground at elections in May 1998. English and Chinese are both official languages, and the freely convertible Hong Kong dollar remains as the SAR's currency.

China's other SAR, Macao, ceased to be a Portuguese colony at midnight on 19-20 December 1999. Macao too has free port status, its own currency, the *pataca*, two official languages (Portuguese and Chinese), a partly-elective Legislative Assembly, and a guarantee under its Basic Law that the "one country, two systems" formula will apply for 50 years. Macao's area of only 21.45 sq km was due to increase by 20% on completion of the Nam Van lakes project. The population of 414,128 at the 1996 census, including over 100,000 with Portuguese nationality, had a per capita GDP of $7,330 but the economy, based on tourism and gambling, has recently been in decline.

Hong Kong's return to Chinese soverignty after 157 years of British rule, took place at midnight on 30th June, 1997.

C

CHRONOLOGY

China has the world's oldest continuous civilization. Its recorded history begins 4,000 years ago with the Shang dynasty, founded in the north in 1766 B.C. Succeeding dynasties expanded China's boundaries; it reached its greatest extent under the Manchu (Qing) dynasty in the 18th century. Chinese isolationism frustrated Europe's attempts to expand into the empire until the 19th century, when China had fallen behind the industrializing West. For the previous 3,000 years, it had been one of the world's most advanced nations.

❑ **1859–1860** Opium Wars with Britain. China defeated; forced to open ports to foreigners.
❑ **1850–1873** Internal rebellions against Manchu empire.
❑ **1895** Defeat by Japan in war over Korean peninsula.
❑ **1900** Boxer Rebellion to expel all foreigners suppressed.
❑ **1911** Manchu empire overthrown by nationalists led by Sun Yat-sen. Republic of China declared.
❑ **1912** Sun Yat-sen creates National People's Party (Guomindang).
❑ **1916** Nationalists factionalize. Sun Yat-sen sets up government in Guangdong. Rest of China under control of rival warlords.
❑ **1921** CCP founded in Shanghai.
❑ **1923** CCP joins Soviet-backed Guomindang to fight warlords.
❑ **1925** Sun Yat-sen dies; Chiang Kai-shek becomes Guomindang leader.
❑ **1927** Chiang turns on CCP. CCP leaders, including Mao Zedong, escape to rural south.
❑ **1930–1934** Mao formulates strategy of peasant-led revolution.
❑ **1931** Japan invades Manchuria.
❑ **1934** Chiang forces CCP out of its southern bases. Start of 12,000 km (7,450 miles) Long March.
❑ **1935** Long March ends. Mao becomes CCP leader.
❑ **1936** Chiang agrees to joint offensive with CCP against Japan.
❑ **1937–1945** War against Japan: CCP Red Army in north, Guomindang in south. Japan defeated.
❑ **1945–1949** War between Red Army and Guomindang. US-backed Guomindang retreats to Taiwan.
❑ **1949** 1 October, Mao proclaims People's Republic of China.
❑ **1950** Invasion of Tibet. Mutual assistance treaty with USSR.
❑ **1950–1958** Land reform; culminates in setting up of communes. First five-year plan (1953–1958) fails.
❑ **1958** "Great Leap Forward" to boost production fails; contributes to millions of deaths during ⇨

RESOURCES ▷ Electric power 204.1m kw

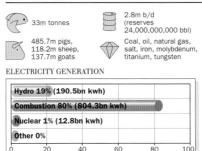

🐟 33m tonnes

🛢 2.8m b/d (reserves 24,000,000,000 bbl)

🐖 485.7m pigs, 118.2m sheep, 137.7m goats

💎 Coal, oil, natural gas, salt, iron, molybdenum, titanium, tungsten

ELECTRICITY GENERATION

Hydro 19% (190.5bn kwh)
Combustion 80% (804.3bn kwh)
Nuclear 1% (12.8bn kwh)
Other 0%

0   20   40   60   80   100

% of total generation by type

China dominates the world market in molybdenum, titanium and tungsten; it has the world's largest deposits of these and a dozen more minerals, and commercial deposits of most others.

China is the world's largest coal producer, with reserves of about 800 billion tonnes, mainly in the Shaanxi and Sichuan basins. Annual output, over 1.3 billion tonnes, used mainly for power generation, far exceeds current demand and many mines face closure.

Power generation, which previously lagged well behind demand, expanded rapidly to create overcapacity by the late 1990s. Nuclear power capacity in 1998 was just over 2,000 MW from three reactors, with major expansion to

50,000 MW planned by 2020. The world's largest hydropower plant, the "Three Gorges" scheme on the Yangtze river, is scheduled for completion in 2009, but faces sustained controversy over its proposed benefits, costs, and environmental consequences.

Crude oil production in 1997 was a record 160 million tonnes. Hopes for the future now center on enormous reserves in the Tarim basin in the far west. Gas production was 22.7 billion cubic m (800 billion cubic feet) in 1997.

CHINA : LAND USE

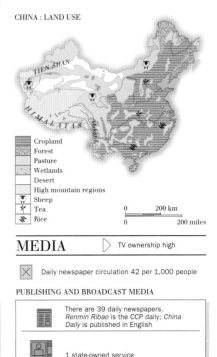

TIEN SHAN
HIMALAYAS
Mekong

Cropland
Forest
Pasture
Wetlands
Desert
High mountain regions
▼ Sheep
⚘ Tea
※ Rice

0   200 km
0   200 miles

ENVIRONMENT ▷ No Green MPs

🌲 6%

⬇ Low

ENVIRONMENTAL TREATIES

🌿 Yes   🦏 Yes   🌐 Yes
🛢 Yes   🧴 Yes   ♻ Yes

Climate and geology mean that natural disasters are quite frequent in China. However, their impact is often made worse by human actions. The economic policies of the 1950s turned drought into a devastating famine, while poor building standards helped push the death toll in the 1976 Tangshan earthquake to over 500,000.

Economic growth is the priority of China's leaders. Industrial pollution and environmental degradation, already widespread, are increasing. However, the environment is a growing concern among educated Chinese, while by the late 1990s the government was less suspicious of Western pressure for environmental controls, and taking steps to respond in particular to acute problems of urban air pollution and water quality . The unsuccessful 1992 campaign to stop the Three Gorges hydroelectric scheme was revived with growing open criticism in the late 1990s.

MEDIA ▷ TV ownership high

⊠ Daily newspaper circulation 42 per 1,000 people

PUBLISHING AND BROADCAST MEDIA

📰 There are 39 daily newspapers. *Renmin Ribao* is the CCP daily; *China Daily* is published in English

👤 1 state-owned service

📻 2 state-owned services

China's more open, market-orientated economy has allowed increasing access to nonofficial sources of information. TV ownership is rising with living standards, and the growing number of satellite-dish owners can choose what to view, while internet access makes central control even more difficult.

In 1996, controls were imposed on electronic financial news services and access to the Internet. The printed media remain on a tight rein. Papers considered undesirable have their licenses removed in periodic clean-ups. The circulations of the main CCP organ, *Renmin Ribao* (*People's Daily*) and the trade union *Workers' Daily* still exceed two million, but their ideological influence is much diminished. Beijing and the provinces have their own dailies.

CHRONOLOGY *continued*

1959–1961 famine. Mao resigns as CCP chair; succeeded by Liu Shaoqi.

- **1960** Sino-Soviet split.
- **1961–1965** More pragmatic economic approach led by Liu and Deng Xiaoping.
- **1966** Cultural Revolution initiated by Mao to restore his supreme power. Youthful Red Guards encouraged to attack all authority. Mao rules with Military Commission under Lin Biao and State Council under premier Zhou Enlai.
- **1967** Army intervenes to restore order amid countrywide chaos. Liu and Deng purged from party.
- **1969** Mao regains chair of CCP. Lin Biao designated his successor, but quickly attacked by Mao.
- **1971** Lin dies in plane crash.
- **1972** US President Nixon visits. More open foreign policy initiated by Zhou Enlai.
- **1973** Mao's wife Jiang Qing, Zhang Chunquio and other "Gang of Four" members elected to CCP politburo. Deng Xiaoping rehabilitated.
- **1976** January, death of Zhou Enlai. April, mass demonstration supporting Zhou and moderates. Mao strips Deng of posts, confirms Hua Guo Feng as premier. September, Mao dies. October, Gang of Four arrested.
- **1977** Deng regains party posts, begins to extend power base.
- **1978** Decade of economic modernization launched. Open door policy to foreign investment; farmers allowed to farm for profit.
- **1980** Deng emerges as China's paramount leader. Economic reform gathers pace, but hopes for political change suppressed.
- **1983–1984** Conservative elderly leaders attempt to slow pace of economic reform. Several then forced to leave politburo.
- **1984** Industrial reforms announced; less successful than earlier agricultural changes.
- **1989** Prodemocracy demonstrations in Tiananmen Square crushed by army; between 1,000 and 5,000 dead. Beijing under martial law.
- **1992–1995** Trials of prodemocracy activists continue. Plans for market economy accelerated.
- **1993** Jiang Zemin president.
- **1997** February, Deng Xiaoping dies at 92. July, UK hands back Hong Kong. September, five-yearly party congress confirms Jiang Zemin's leadership and reformist policies.
- **1998** Conservative Li Peng moves to presidency of parliament.
- **1999** China develops neutron bomb. Friction over Taiwanese claim of statehood.

CRIME

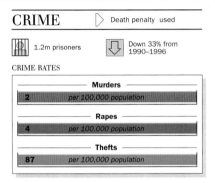

▷ Death penalty used

1.2m prisoners   Down 33% from 1990–1996

CRIME RATES

Murders — 2 per 100,000 population

Rapes — 4 per 100,000 population

Thefts — 87 per 100,000 population

China's legal system is a mix of custom and statute, and has a local reputation for arbitrariness. Economic reform and the breakdown of former social controls have been paralleled by a rise in corruption and violent crime. Many new economic crimes have been made capital offenses and the death penalty is used extensively in anti-crime drives.

China has a poor human rights record and still holds many political prisoners, although a number of detainees have been released since the clampdown on dissent in 1989. The Tiananmen Square massacre that year temporarily brought human rights to the fore in China's relations with the USA and the EU.

EDUCATION

▷ School leaving age: 15

84%   5.8m students

The government has set a target of nine years of education for all.

THE EDUCATION SYSTEM

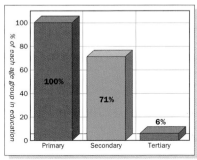

% of each age group in education

- Primary: 100%
- Secondary: 71%
- Tertiary: 6%

Despite the expansion of education since 1949, illiteracy and semiliteracy are still quite widespread. In part, this is due to the Cultural Revolution, when all authority was challenged, leaving a generation with little education. It also reflects lower rural attendance and attitudes to women, a quarter of whom are still illiterate. Attendance fell when fees were introduced in the 1980s, but now nearly 90% of those of secondary school age are in school – some of them catching up with primary education. Higher education, also fee-paying, attracts only some 6% of 20–24-year-olds. Today, selection is based on academic rather than political criteria.

HEALTH

▷ Welfare state health benefits

1 per 629 people   Cardiovascular and diarrheal diseases, cancers, tuberculosis

Economic changes threaten China's extensive primary health care network. Combining traditional and Western medicine, it used to extend to the remotest regions. The system of universal state employment was accompanied by a free health system, and the Chinese enjoyed a life expectancy on a par with many richer nations. Following the change to a market-oriented economy, however, a gaping divide exists between city and rural provision, fees for treatment are rising, and fewer people are employed by the state and treated free.

SPENDING

▷ GDP/cap. no increase

CONSUMPTION AND SPENDING

3 per 1,000 population   56 per 1,000 population

- Defense 5.7%
- Education 2.3%
- Health 2.1%

Defense, Health, Education spending as % of GDP

Economic change has led to improved living standards, seen in the growing demand for consumer goods, but also widening wealth disparities. The burgeoning small-business class and employees of companies with foreign investment have benefited most. They mainly live in the east, especially the southeast, which is home to a number of millionaires. The main losers are the 150 million "surplus" agricultural workers, many of whom have migrated to the cities in search of jobs. The majority of Chinese are still farmers. They initially benefited from reform, but their living standards are now threatened by rising production costs.

WORLD RANKING

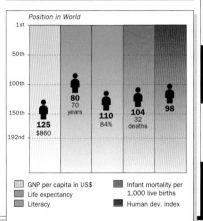

Position in World

- GNP per capita in US$: 125 — $860
- Life expectancy: 80 — 70 years
- Literacy: 110 — 84%
- Infant mortality per 1,000 live births: 104 — 32 deaths
- Human dev. index: 98

C

COLOMBIA

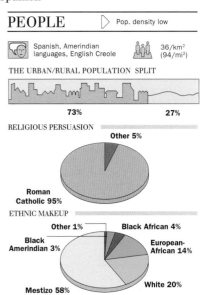

SOUTH AMERICA

OFFICIAL NAME: Republic of Colombia **CAPITAL:** Bogotá
POPULATION: 37.7 million **CURRENCY:** Colombian peso **OFFICIAL LANGUAGE:** Spanish

| 1819 | 1903 | July 20 | CO | -5 | +57 | .co |

L YING IN NORTHWEST SOUTH AMERICA, Colombia has coastlines on both the Caribbean and the Pacific. The east of the country is densely forested and sparsely populated, and separated from the western coastal plains by the Andes mountains. The Andes divide into three ranges (*cordilleras*) in Colombia. The eastern range is divided from the two western ranges by the densely populated Magdalena river valley. The Colombian lowlands are very wet, hot and fertile, supporting two harvests and allowing many crops to be planted at any time of year. A multiparty democracy since 1957, Colombia is noted for its coffee, emeralds, gold and narcotics-trafficking.

CLIMATE

▷ Tropical/mountain

WEATHER CHART

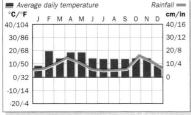

Most of Colombia is wet and the hot Pacific coastal areas receive up to 500 cm (200 inches) of rain a year. The Caribbean coast is a little drier. The Andes have three climatic regions: the *tierra caliente* (hot lowlands), *tierra templada* (temperate uplands), and *tierra fría* (cold highlands); the last has year-round springlike conditions such as those found in Bogotá. The equatorial east has two wet seasons.

TRANSPORTATION

▷ Drive on right

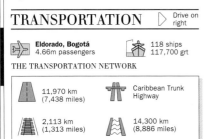

Eldorado, Bogotá
4.66m passengers

118 ships
117,700 grt

THE TRANSPORTATION NETWORK

| 11,970 km (7,438 miles) | Caribbean Trunk Highway |
| 2,113 km (1,313 miles) | 14,300 km (8,886 miles) |

Roads in the north are in reasonable condition. Those in the south and east tend to be rutted and badly affected by the frequent rains. The civil war means roads are frequently blocked by the guerrillas and the military. Most of the railroad is closed.

Rivers are an important means of transport in Colombia; the Magdalena, Orinoco, Atrato and Amazon river systems are all extensively navigable. Plans exist to connect Colombia to the Pan-American Highway.

TOURISM

▷ Visitors : population 1:32

1.2m visitors

Down 9% 1995–1997

MAIN TOURIST ARRIVALS

| Venezuela 55% |
| Ecuador 15% |
| USA 11% |
| Canada 3% |
| Costa Rica 1% |
| Other 15% |

% of total arrivals

Tourism in Colombia is largely limited to the beaches of the Caribbean coast. Cartagena, Barranquilla and Santa Marta are the main resorts. Cartagena has also been developed as a major Latin American conference center.

The expansion of tourism has been limited by Colombia's political instability and the prevalence of narcotics-related crime. The well-publicized activities of the drugs cartels in Medellín and Cali, and instances of kidnappings, particularly in Bogotá, are major deterrents.

Limited infrastructure makes many regions of Colombia, particularly Amazonia to the east of the Andes, almost inaccessible. The Pacific coast is also barely exploited.

Simón Bolívar and Cristóbal Colón, twin peaks with a height of over 19,030 feet in the heart of the Colombian Andes.

PEOPLE

▷ Pop. density low

Spanish, Amerindian languages, English Creole

36/km² (94/mi²)

THE URBAN/RURAL POPULATION SPLIT

73% 27%

RELIGIOUS PERSUASION

Other 5%
Roman Catholic 95%

ETHNIC MAKEUP

Other 1%
Black Amerindian 3%
Black African 4%
European-African 14%
Mestizo 58%
White 20%

The majority of Colombians are people of mixed blood. An estimated 450,000 indigenous Amerindians are largely concentrated in the southwest and Amazonia, although some communities are scattered throughout the country. A small black population lives along both coasts, and especially in Chocó, Colombia's poorest region. Blacks are the most unrepresented group.

Some progress has been made in giving Amerindians a greater political voice. In 1991, constitutional reforms reserved two seats in the Senate for indigenous representatives, and Amerindian pressure groups are increasingly active. Harassment by landowners and narcotics traffickers continues in Amazonia, and very few investigations into suspected human rights violations against Amerindians have led to prosecutions.

Women in Colombia have a higher profile than in much of the rest of Latin America. Many are prominent in the professions, though few reach the top in politics. The traditional extended Catholic family is still the norm. Regional identity is strong.

POPULATION AGE BREAKDOWN

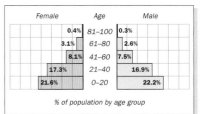

Female	Age	Male
0.4%	81–100	0.3%
3.1%	61–80	2.6%
8.1%	41–60	7.5%
17.3%	21–40	16.9%
21.6%	0–20	22.2%

% of population by age group

C

POLITICS ▷ Multiparty elections

L. House 1998/2002
U. House 1998/2002

President Andres
Pastrana Arango

Colombia is a presidential democracy.
Presidents may not serve two
consecutive terms.

MAIN POLITICAL ISSUES
Peace process
President Pastrana has announced
a "national accord" to keep up the
momentum for a negotiated end to the
guerrilla war and to discuss reforms
However, a resurgence in fighting
underlines the pressure his government
is under from different sides. The Armed
Revolutionary Force of Colombia (FARC),
the largest guerrilla group, and the
National Liberation Army (ELN) are
suspicious of the government's intent as
it continues to prosecute the war against
them. Right-wing paramilitaries and
the army favor a military solution.
Persuading all sides to agree on
compromise proposals to preserve
the ailing peace process will be
difficult. Meanwhile
whole areas of the
country remain
ungovernable.

AT THE LAST ELECTION
House of Representatives 161 members

61% PL	**32%** PSC	**7%** Others

PL= Liberal Party **PSC** = Social Conservative Party
Ind = Independents **Reps** = Representatives of the
indigenous (indian) communities

Senate 102 members

57% PL	**27%** PSC	**13%** Ind **3%** Reps

Two special representatives of the indigenous (Indian)
communities are appointed to the Senate, and one is
elected.

Relations with the USA
Coca cultivation increased by 28%
last year; the US is assisting the anti-
drugs program but lack of progress
could sour bilateral relations.

PROFILE
The PSC and the PL have
shared power for the past
40-odd years. Both have
faithful followers
despite few ideological
differences. Official
corruption both high and
low, and the persistent
violence associated with drugs
cartels, guerrillas, paramilitaries
and the military, have seriously
weakened public confidence in
government and the state,
and have deterred
foreign investors.

*Andres Pastrana
Arango, elected
president in 1998.*

*Pablo Escobar, ex-
leader of Medellín
drugs cartel, gunned
down in 1993.*

WORLD AFFAIRS ▷ Joined UN in 1945

ACS	AP	AmCC	OAS	RG

Relations with the USA, the major
market for its exports and also
Colombia's main source of aid, have
been strained in recent years. The USA
has intervened directly to attack the
narcotics business in Colombia,
making its elimination a condition of
aid. Rapprochement with the Pastrana
government led to the December 1998
military accord entailing further US
training, equipment and intelligence in
the war against narcotics production.
However, the boundary between this
aim and the targeting of guerrilla
groups is increasingly blurred and
complicates the peace process.

Recent agreements with Venezuela,
Colombia's traditional enemy, cover
cooperation in the fight against drug-
trafficking and crime in border areas.

AID ▷ Recipient

$274m (receipts)　　Down 9% 1996–1997

Critics say that US military aid
contributed to the fight against
narcotics is also used against left-wing
guerrillas. An IDB investment fund aids
the peace process.

CHRONOLOGY

In 1525, Spain began the conquest of
Colombia, which became its chief
source of gold.

❏ **1819** Simón Bolívar defeats Spanish
at Boyacá. Republic of Gran
Colombia formed with Venezuela,
Ecuador, and Panama.
❏ **1830** Venezuela and Ecuador split
away during revolts and civil wars.
❏ **1849** Centralist Conservative and
federalist Liberal parties
established.
❏ **1861–1886** Liberals hold monopoly
on power.
❏ **1886–1930** Conservative rule.
❏ **1899–1903** Liberal "War of 1,000
Days" revolt fails; 120,000 die. ▷

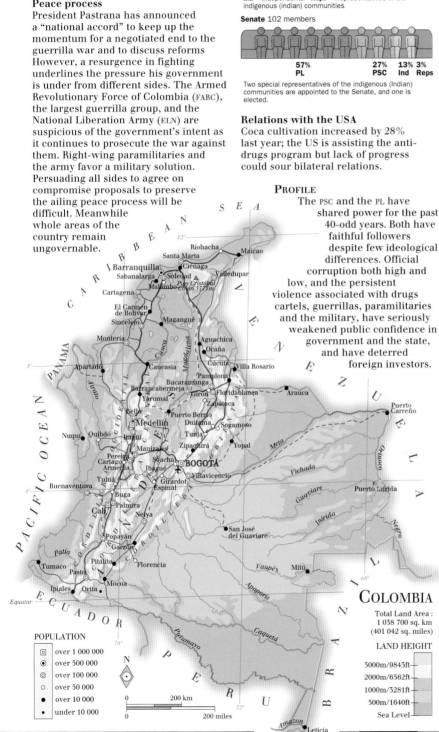

COLOMBIA

Total Land Area :
1 038 700 sq. km
(401 042 sq. miles)

POPULATION

▣	over 1 000 000
◉	over 500 000
◎	over 100 000
○	over 50 000
●	over 10 000
•	under 10 000

N

0　　200 km
0　　200 miles

LAND HEIGHT

3000m/9843ft
2000m/6562ft
1000m/3281ft
500m/1640ft
Sea Level

C

CHRONOLOGY *continued*

- ❏ **1903** Panama secedes, but is not recognized by Colombia until 1921.
- ❏ **1930** Liberal President Olaya Herrera elected by coalition in first peaceful change of power.
- ❏ **1946** Conservatives take over.
- ❏ **1948** Shooting of Liberal mayor of Bogotá and riot known as *El Bogotazo* spark civil war, *La Violencia*, to 1957; 300,000 killed.
- ❏ **1953–1957** Military dictatorship of Rojas Pinilla.
- ❏ **1958** Conservatives and Liberals agree to alternate government in a National Front until 1974. Other parties banned.
- ❏ **1965** Left-wing guerrilla National Liberation Army and Maoist Popular Liberation Army founded.
- ❏ **1966** Pro-Soviet FARC guerrilla group formed.
- ❏ **1968** Constitutional reform allows new parties, but two-party parity continues. Guerrilla groups proliferate from now on.
- ❏ **1971** M-19 emerges as armed left-wing guerrilla group.
- ❏ **1984** Minister of Justice assassinated for attempting to enforce anti-drugs campaign.
- ❏ **1985** M-19 guerrillas blast way into Ministry of Justice; 11 judges and 90 others killed. Patriotic Union (UP) party formed.
- ❏ **1986** Liberal Virgilio Barco Vargas wins presidential elections, so ending power-sharing. UP wins ten seats in parliament. Right-wing paramilitary start murder campaign against UP politicians. Violence perpetrated by both left-wing groups and death squads run by drugs cartels continues.
- ❏ **1989** M-19 reaches peace agreement with government, including the granting of a full pardon. Becomes legal party.
- ❏ **1990** UP and Liberal presidential candidates murdered during general election. Liberal César Gaviria elected on anti-drugs platform.
- ❏ **1991** New constitution legalizes divorce and prohibits extradition of Colombian nationals. Indigenous peoples' democratic rights guaranteed, but territorial claims not addressed.
- ❏ **1992–1993** Medellín drugs cartel leader, Pablo Escobar, captured, escapes and shot dead by police.
- ❏ **1995–1996** President Samper charged with and cleared of receiving Cali cartel drug funds for elections.
- ❏ **1998** Andres Pastrana Arango elected to succeed Samper.
- ❏ **1999** Earthquake: thousands of people killed or injured.

DEFENSE

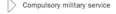 ▷ Compulsory military service

💲 $3.1bn   ⬆ Up 27% in 1997

The military is powerful but rarely intervenes directly in politics. Human

COLOMBIAN ARMED FORCES

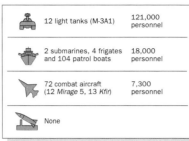

🚙	12 light tanks (M-3A1)	121,000 personnel
🚢	2 submarines, 4 frigates and 104 patrol boats	18,000 personnel
✈	72 combat aircraft (12 *Mirage* 5, 13 *Kfir*)	7,300 personnel
🚀	None	

rights groups accuse the armed forces and their paramilitary allies of gross and systematic abuses, involving torture and murder, in their fight against guerrilla groups and the production of narcotics. The military is suspicious of peace moves and wants a significant strengthening of its capability in the wake of recent serious setbacks at the hands of guerrillas. The government reorganized the high command in 1998 in a bid to strengthen the peace process, and cut the military budget after drastic fiscal adjustments.

Colombia participates in the joint Latin American Defense Force. Most arms, and training is supplied by the USA.

ECONOMICS

▷ Inflation 24.6% p.a. (1985–1996)

📊 $87.1bn   💲 1,296.65–1,547.50 Colombian pesos

SCORE CARD

❏ WORLD GNP RANKING	39th
❏ GNP PER CAPITA	$2,180
❏ BALANCE OF PAYMENTS	$–5,682m
❏ INFLATION	18.5%
❏ UNEMPLOYMENT	12%

EXPORTS

Peru 3% / Ecuador 4% / Germany 7% / Venezuela 8% / Other 40% / USA 38%

IMPORTS

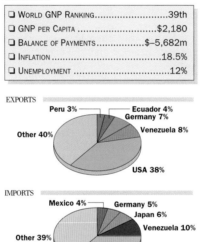

Mexico 4% / Germany 5% / Japan 6% / Venezuela 10% / Other 39% / USA 36%

ECONOMIC PERFORMANCE INDICATOR

— Consumer price index   GDP ▨

Consumer price index 1990=100 / GDP 1992=100

1992 1993 1994 1995 1996

STRENGTHS

Substantial oil and coal deposits plus well-developed hydroelectric power makes Colombia almost self-sufficient in energy. Healthy and diversified export sector – especially coffee and coal. Light manufactures. Worldwide market for cocaine.

WEAKNESSES

Narcotics-related violence, corruption and political instability discourages foreign investors. Domestic industry uncompetitive owing to protection. High unemployment. Coffee and oil subject to world price fluctuations.

PROFILE

Of all the Latin American economies, Colombia's is probably the closest to the US model. The state has traditionally played a relatively minor

role and Colombia has a successful private export sector. A program of privatization has reduced the state's involvement further.

Regional disparities remain marked. Most wealth is centered in the Bogotá, Medellín, and Cali regions, while rural areas are largely underdeveloped. The main obstacle to growth is the instability caused by the narcotics business and the protracted civil war. Given stability and investment, Colombia's potential for growth would be considerable.

COLOMBIA : MAJOR BUSINESSES

Pulp and paper
Narcotics
Steel
Chemicals
Vehicle assembly
Food processing
Textiles
Oil

Barranquilla
Medellín
Cali
Bogotá
Ibagué
Orito

0   200 km
0   200 miles

* significant multinational ownership

C

RESOURCES

▷ Electric power 10.8m kw

167,080 tonnes

444,508 b/d (reserves 1,935,200 bbl)

28.3m cattle, 2.5m pigs, 2.5m horses, 2.4m sheep

Oil, natural gas, coal, nickel, emeralds, gold

ELECTRICITY GENERATION

Hydro 76% (34.2bn kwh)	
Combustion 24% (11bn kwh)	
Nuclear 0%	
Other 0%	

0   20   40   60   80   100

% of total generation by type

Colombia has substantial oil reserves and is increasing investment to boost production. Coal and gas are important, and it is a major producer of gold, platinum, silver and emeralds.

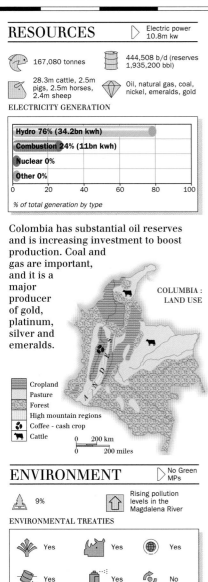

COLUMBIA : LAND USE

Cropland
Pasture
Forest
High mountain regions
Coffee - cash crop
Cattle

0   200 km
0   200 miles

ENVIRONMENT

▷ No Green MPs

9%

Rising pollution levels in the Magdalena River

ENVIRONMENTAL TREATIES

Yes   Yes   Yes
Yes   Yes   No

Cattle-ranching, logging, and coca growing and spraying cause soil degradation and loss of bird habitat.

MEDIA

▷ TV ownership medium

Daily newspaper circulation 49 per 1,000 people

PUBLISHING AND BROADCAST MEDIA

	There are 37 daily newspapers. *El Tiempo* and *El Espectador* have the largest circulation
	1 state-owned, 2 independent services
	31 state-owned, 558 independent stations

The independent press is small. Journalists have been murdered by paramilitaries and held by guerrillas.

CRIME

▷ Death penalty not used

32,549 prisoners

Down 9% from 1991–1996

CRIME RATES

Murders	
59	*per 100,000 population*

Rapes	
3	*per 100,000 population*

Thefts	
118	*per 100,000 population*

Colombia is one of the most violent societies in the world. According to official figures, 194 massacres occurred in 1998, with a total of 1,231 civilian victims. Right-wing paramilitaries were blamed for just under half of the killings, the guerrillas for 21% and the security forces for 8%.

EDUCATION

▷ School leaving age: 12

 91%   644,188 students

Resources available to public education have been reduced due to budget cuts.

THE EDUCATION SYSTEM

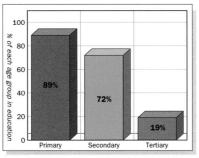

Education is free and compulsory, and is a mix of French and US models, with a *baccalauréat* exam taken at the end of secondary school. Provision in rural areas is poor and absenteeism high. Where provided, public and university education is generally of a high standard, but the rich send their children to private schools and universities in the USA.

HEALTH

▷ Welfare state health benefits

1 per 1,111 people

Cancers, violence, heart diseases, accidents

Budget cuts have reduced health spending. Private care is growing.

Only 16% of Colombians benefit from any social security system, rather fewer than in most neighboring states. Rural areas have little health provision, since most doctors work in the larger cities. A polio vaccination campaign has largely eradicated the virus, except in coastal regions.

NGOs suggest that some 1.5 million Colombians have been uprooted over the past decade as a result of political violence. Homicide is the main cause of death among young men in cities; overall it is the most common cause of death after cancer. Most of the violence is narcotics-related, and Cali and Medellín are the most dangerous cities. The army and police have been accused of participating in the trade. The frequent occurrences of urban armed robbery makes residents extremely security conscious. Wealthier Colombians tend to employ several security guards.

A relatively new phenomenon is that of "social cleansing" – the murder of street children and beggars by armed gangs. Some gangs in Bogotá have been funded by local businesses.

SPENDING

▷ GDP/cap. no increase

CONSUMPTION AND SPENDING

19 per 1,000 population

148 per 1,000 population

Defense 4%	
Education 3.5%	
Health 1.8%	

0   5   10   15   20   25

Defense, Health, Education spending as % of GDP

There is little social mobility in Colombia; the historically wealthy Spanish families are still dominant in political and business life, but the entry of drug-related money has created new layers of wealth in cities and among landowners. The wealthy go to the USA for medical treatment and educate their children overseas. The rural poor are mostly landless. The inhabitants of the sprawling shanty towns of Cali, Barranquilla, Cartagena and Buenaventura are the poorest groups in Colombian society.

WORLD RANKING

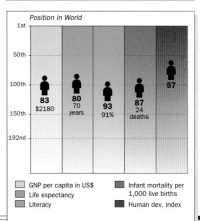

Position in World

1st
50th
100th
150th
192nd

83 $2180
80 70 years
93 91%
87 24 deaths
57

GNP per capita in US$
Life expectancy
Literacy
Infant mortality per 1,000 live births
Human dev. index

COMOROS

OFFICIAL NAME: Federal Islamic Republic of the Comoros **CAPITAL:** Moroni
POPULATION: 672,000   **CURRENCY:** Comoros franc   **OFFICIAL LANGUAGES:** Arabic and French

THE ARCHIPELAGO REPUBLIC of the Comoros lies off the east African coast, between Mozambique and Madagascar. It consists of three main islands and a number of islets. Most of the population are subsistence farmers. In 1975, the Comoros Islands, except for Mayotte, became independent of France. Since then instability has plagued this poor region, with several coups, counter-coups and repeated attempts at secession by smaller islands.

Moroni, the capital, on Njazidja. The Comoros islands are highly fertile and heavily forested. Many are ringed by coral reefs.

CLIMATE
▷ Tropical oceanic

WEATHER CHART

Average daily temperature — Rainfall

The islands are tropical; it is hot and humid on the coasts and cooler higher up, notably on Mount Kartala.

TRANSPORTATION
▷ Drive on right

Moroni-Hahaya, Njazidja   3 ships 2,959 grt

THE TRANSPORTATION NETWORK

638 km (396 miles)	None
None	None

Recent projects have included development of the port at Moroni and upgrading the international airport.

TOURISM
▷ Visitors : population 1:25

26,000 visitors   Up 13% 1995–1997

MAIN TOURIST ARRIVALS

France 51%	
South Africa 24%	
Germany 9%	
Other 16%	

% of total arrivals

In 1988, Sun International of South Africa joined a major project to build four hotels designed to attract 12,000 visitors a year from South Africa, France, and Italy. Mauritius and the Seychelles provide tough competition.

PEOPLE
▷ Pop. density high

Arabic, Comoran, French   301/km² (780/mi²)

THE URBAN/RURAL POPULATION SPLIT
31%   69%

RELIGIOUS PERSUASION

Other 1% — Roman Catholic 1%

Muslim (mainly Sunni) 98%

The Comoros has absorbed Polynesians, Africans, Indonesians, Persians, and Arabs over time. European and Indian immigrants have added to the melting pot. However, some communities retain their individual character; Mwali, for instance, is still primarily African. Ethnic tension is rare, partly owing to the unifying force of Islam, the predominant religion. A more potent divisive factor is regionalism, especially on Anjouan.

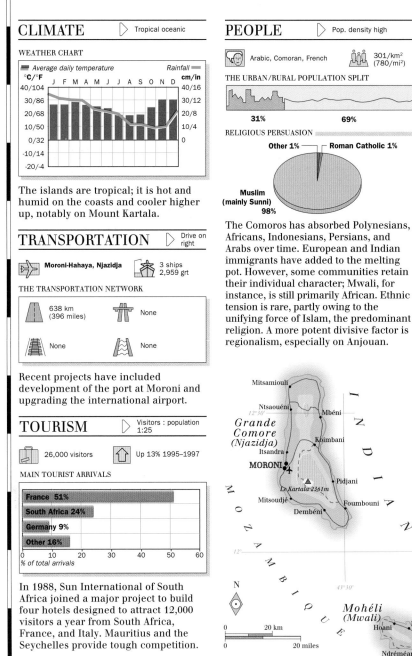

POLITICS
▷ No multiparty elections

1996/2000   President Col. Assoumani Azzali

AT THE LAST ELECTION

Federal Assembly 43 members

2% Ind

91% RND   5% FNJ   2% VA

RND = Rassemblement national pour la Developpement
FNJ = Front National pour la justice **VA** = Votes anulled
Ind = Independent

The Senate was abolished under the 1996 constitution.

Attempted coups in 1990, 1991, 1992, and 1995 undermined the transition to democracy. In 1996 Mohamed Taki Abdoulkarim was elected president and matters seemed to have improved – until Anjouan declared itself "independent" in August 1997; fighting there soon led to unrest on Mohéli and Grande Comore itself. Taki died in 1998, and Tajiddine Ben Said Massonde became interim president. Renewed violence in April 1999 provided Col. Assoumani Azzali with the pretext to overthrow Massonde and become the Comoros' latest president.

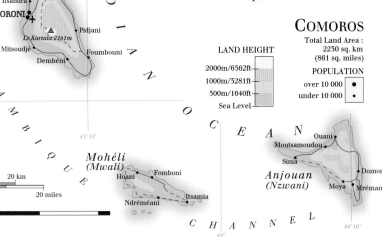

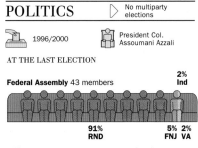

COMOROS

Total Land Area : 2250 sq. km (861 sq. miles)

POPULATION
over 10 000 ●
under 10 000 ⊡

LAND HEIGHT
2000m/6562ft
1000m/3281ft
500m/1640ft
Sea Level

C

WORLD AFFAIRS ▷ Joined UN in 1975

France remains the Comoros' main benefactor, although economic ties with South Africa have strengthened in recent years – a by-product of sanctions-busting during the days of apartheid. An OAU assessment team visited strife-torn Anjouan in February 1999, but it was evacuated after fighting intensified.

AID ▷ Recipient

$28m (receipts) — Down 30% 1996–1997

Foreign aid, mainly from France, the EU, the World Bank and the IMF, accounts for over 40% of GDP. Because of its Islamic links, the Comoros also gets aid from some Arab states and OPEC. In 1998 major donors attacked the government for spending more than 70% on "political superstructure."

DEFENSE ▷ No compulsory military service

$3m (estimated) — No significant change

The small presidential guard is the mainstay of the military. In December 1998 Mauritius was asked for military aid after clashes on Anjouan.

ECONOMICS ▷ Inflation 4% p.a. (1985–1996)

$209m — 445.80–417.23 Comoros francs

SCORE CARD

❏ WORLD GNP RANKING	181st
❏ GNP PER CAPITA	$400
❏ BALANCE OF PAYMENTS	$–19m
❏ INFLATION	1%
❏ UNEMPLOYMENT	20%

STRENGTHS
Vanilla, ylang-ylang and cloves main cash crops. Tourism is a potential growth area.

WEAKNESSES
Underdevelopment of agriculture; subsistence-level farming. Over 50% of food requirements imported. Lack of basic infrastructure. Allegations of financial mismanagement. Strikes in early 1998.

EXPORTS

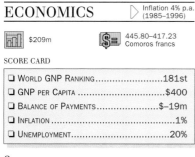

France 45%
USA 18%
Germany 18%
Other 19%

IMPORTS

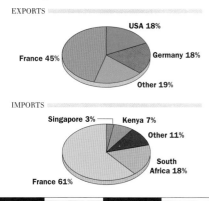

Singapore 3%
Kenya 7%
Other 11%
South Africa 18%
France 61%

RESOURCES ▷ Electric power 5,000 kw

13,200 tonnes — Not an oil producer

128,000 goats, 50,000 cattle, 20,000 sheep — None

There are few strategic resources. An HEP plant is under construction on Nzwani, but most fuel for energy is still imported. Fishing remains a neglected source of future growth.

ENVIRONMENT ▷ No Green MPs

None — No data

The environment is not a major priority in the Comoros; natural disasters, such as the volcanic eruption in 1977 which left 20,000 homeless, are of more immediate concern. The government is promoting tourism and recognizes the long-term commercial value of imposing environmental controls on new developments.

MEDIA ▷ TV ownership low

There are no daily newspapers

PUBLISHING AND BROADCAST MEDIA

There are no daily newspapers. There are 2 weekly newspapers, the state-owned *Al Watany* and the independent *L'Archipel*

No TV service — 1 state-controlled service

France promises to fund the islands' first TV station. In May 1998 police seized an independent radio station critical of the government.

CRIME ▷ Death penalty used

The Comoros does not publish prison figures — The general trend is up

Civil unrest by youths in May 1998 led to police curfews and roadblocks in Moroni. Lawlessness between rival militias escalated throughout the year on Anjouan.

EDUCATION ▷ School leaving age: 16

55% — 348 students

The education system does not extend beyond secondary level. Schools are equipped to teach only basic literacy, hygiene, and agricultural techniques. Pupil-teacher ratios are high.

CHRONOLOGY

Matrilinear sultanates ruled the Comoros until shortly before becoming a French protectorate and then in 1912 a colony.

- ❏ **1961** Internal self-government.
- ❏ **1975** Independence.
- ❏ **1978** Mercenaries restore Abdallah to power.
- ❏ **1989** Abdallah assassinated.
- ❏ **1990** Djohar elected president.
- ❏ **1992** Chaotic first multi-party polls.
- ❏ **1995** Djohar relinquishes power.
- ❏ **1996** Taki elected president.
- ❏ **1997** Anjouan separatists repulse government troops.
- ❏ **1998** Massonde succeeds Taki as president.
- ❏ **1999** Anjouan militias clash; OAU autonomy plan rejected; Col. Azzali overthrows Massonde.

HEALTH ▷ No welfare state health benefits

1 per 10,000 people — Malaria, infectious intestinal and bacterial diseases

Health care is rudimentary, other than two maternity clinics and 30 recently renovated health centers.

SPENDING ▷ GDP/cap. increase

CONSUMPTION AND SPENDING

14 per 1,000 population — 9 per 1,000 population

Defense	No data
Education	3.9%
Health	3.3%

0   5   10   15   20   25
Defense, Health, Education spending as % of GDP

Wealth is concentrated among the elite; most people live close to the poverty line. Unpaid government workers went on strike in May 1998.

WORLD RANKING

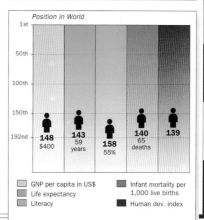

Position in World

1st — 50th — 100th — 150th — 192nd

148 $400
143 59 years
158 55%
140 65 deaths
139

- ▪ GNP per capita in US$
- ▪ Life expectancy
- ▪ Literacy
- ▪ Infant mortality per 1,000 live births
- ▪ Human dev. index

CONGO

OFFICIAL NAME: The Republic of the Congo **CAPITAL:** Brazzaville
POPULATION: 2.8 million **CURRENCY:** CFA franc **OFFICIAL LANGUAGE:** French

WEST AFRICA

| 1960 | 1960 | Aug 15 | RCB | +1 | +242 | .CG |

STRADDLING THE EQUATOR in west central Africa, the Congo achieved independence from France in 1960, soon falling under a Marxist-Leninist form of government which discouraged much foreign investment. Multiparty democracy was achieved in 1991, but has been overtaken since by years of feuding and violence.

CLIMATE ▷ Tropical equatorial

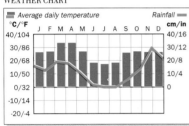
WEATHER CHART

In most years there are two wet seasons and two dry seasons. Rainfall is heaviest in the coastal regions south of the equator.

TRANSPORTATION ▷ Drive on right

✈ **Brazzaville International**   🚢 21 ships / 6,700 grt

THE TRANSPORTATION NETWORK

| 7,400 km (4,600 miles) | None |
| 706 km (439 miles) | 4,385 km (2,725 miles) |

Congo aims to maintain its entrepôt position linking the Central African Republic, Chad, and Cameroon with the Atlantic coast. The Congo Ocean Railroad runs from Brazzaville to the major port of Pointe-Noire.

TOURISM ▷ Visitors : Population 1:147

19,000 visitors   Down 32% 1995–1997

MAIN TOURIST ARRIVALS

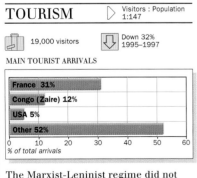

| France 31% |
| Congo (Zaire) 12% |
| USA 5% |
| Other 52% |

% of total arrivals

The Marxist-Leninist regime did not seek to develop tourism, and visitors, mostly on safaris and business-related trips, are still rare.

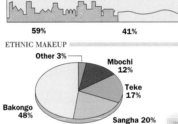

The Loufoulakari Falls, near Brazzaville. Swamps and mangroves border many of the rivers in the Congo's northern region.

PEOPLE ▷ Pop. density low

Kongo, Teke, Lingala, French   8/km² (21/mi²)

THE URBAN/RURAL POPULATION SPLIT

59%   41%

ETHNIC MAKEUP

Other 3%
Mbochi 12%
Teke 17%
Sangha 20%
Bakongo 48%

Congo is one of the most tribally conscious countries in Africa. The main tensions are between the Bakongo, who live in the north, and the Mbochi, who are concentrated in the more prosperous south.
Since the 1950s, women have achieved considerable emancipation.

POLITICS ▷ No multiparty elections

L. House 1993/2000 President Denis
U. House 1995/2000 Sassou-Nguesso

AT THE LAST ELECTION

National Assembly 125 members
12% PCT
5% RDD
38% UPADS
22% MCDDI
13% Others
8% RDPS
2% FDU

UPADS = Pan-African Union for Social Democracy
MCDDI = Congolese Movement for Democracy and Integral Development **RDPS** = Rally for Democratic and Social Progress **PCT** = Congolese Labour Party
Others = Liberation Movement **RDD** = Rally for Democracy and Development **FDU** = Union of Democratic Forces

Senate 60 members

Elections to the Senate are indirect, with one-third of members elected every two years. The Senate is dominated by UPADS.

Lissouba and his UPADS party won elections in 1992–1993, but the results were disputed by opposition parties. Thousands died in fighting in mid-1997 in Brazzaville, as former Marxist dictator Sassou-Nguesso challenged Lissouba, seizing power that October; fighting and instability have continued.

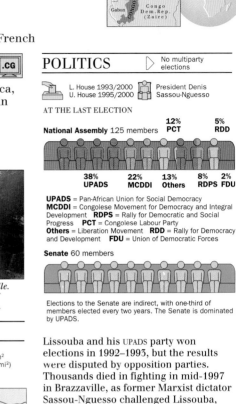

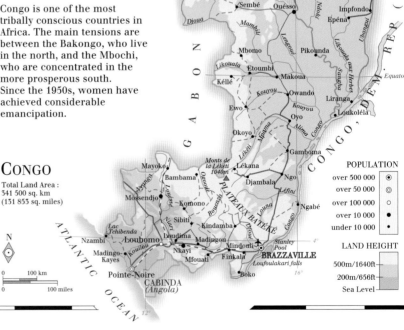

CONGO

Total Land Area :
341 500 sq. km
(131 853 sq. miles)

POPULATION
- over 500 000 ◉
- over 50 000 ◎
- over 100 000 ○
- over 10 000 ●
- under 10 000 ·

LAND HEIGHT
- 500m/1640ft
- 200m/656ft
- Sea Level

WORLD AFFAIRS Joined UN in 1960

| BDEAC | CEMAC | FZ | NAM | OAU |

Carefully balancing relations with France and the USA is a priority, since both seek to extend their stakes in the oil industry; nevertheless relations with old Eastern bloc allies remain strong. Congo has been susceptible in recent years to political instability and wars in the neighboring Democratic Republic of Congo (Zaire) and Angola.

AID ▷ Recipient

$268m (receipts)   Down 38% 1996–1997

Before 1990, the USSR, Cuba, and China were the major donors. Most aid now comes from France. High levels of 1970s debt mean that, despite its oil, Congo remains dependent on aid.

DEFENSE ▷ No compulsory military service

$74m   Up 33% in 1997

The militias of the various political forces were being integrated into the 8,000-strong army, until fighting broke out again between them in mid-1997. The air force is small, but well equipped with 20 MiG-17s and 12 MiG-21s.

ECONOMICS ▷ Inflation 2.1% p.a. (1985–1996)

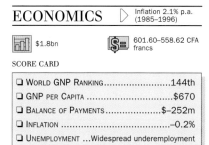

$1.8bn   601.60–558.62 CFA francs

SCORE CARD

❑ WORLD GNP RANKING	144th
❑ GNP PER CAPITA	$670
❑ BALANCE OF PAYMENTS	$–252m
❑ INFLATION	–0.2%
❑ UNEMPLOYMENT	Widespread underemployment

STRENGTHS

Oil has increased in importance, now providing 90% of export revenues compared with 5% in 1970. Significant timber supplies. Skilled and well-trained workforce helps sustain substantial industrial base in the capital and Pointe-Noire.

WEAKNESSES

$4 billion debt by late 1980s. Top-heavy bureaucracy. Overdependence on oil. Political instability.

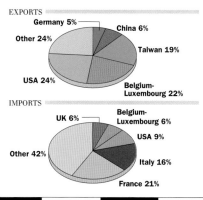

EXPORTS
Germany 5%
China 6%
Other 24%
Taiwan 19%
USA 24%
Belgium-Luxembourg 22%

IMPORTS
Belgium-Luxembourg 6%
UK 6%
USA 9%
Other 42%
Italy 16%
France 21%

RESOURCES ▷ Electric power 118,000 kw

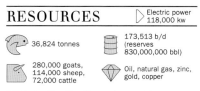

36,824 tonnes   173,513 b/d (reserves 830,000,000 bbl)

280,000 goats, 114,000 sheep, 72,000 cattle   Oil, natural gas, zinc, gold, copper

Oil is by far the Congo's most important resource. Natural gas reserves have yet to be exploited; the oil industry currently flares excess gas. Bauxite and iron ore reserves are not large enough to be profitably mined and phosphate production was abandoned in 1977. Chinese aid has helped build two hydroelectric dams, on the Bouenza and Djoué rivers. A third is currently being built on the Léfini at Imboulou.

ENVIRONMENT ▷ No Green MPs

5%   Low

The 1999 Yaoundé Declaration should help control exploitation of tropical timber. Congo has also been used in the past as a dumping ground for dangerous toxic waste from the West.

MEDIA ▷ TV ownership low

Daily newspaper circulation 8 per 1,000 people

PUBLISHING AND BROADCAST MEDIA

There are 6 daily newspapers, including *Mweti* and *Aujourd'hui*

1 state-controlled service   1 state-controlled service

Two dailies, two weeklies, and national television and radio stations, are all state-owned. During World War II, Radio Brazzaville was vital to de Gaulle's forces.

CRIME ▷ Death penalty not used

Congo does not publish prison figures   The general trend is up

Smuggling remains a major problem. Instability in neighboring countries and the ready availability of guns have increased violent crime.

EDUCATION ▷ School leaving age: 16

77%   13,806 students

Originally pioneered by French Catholic missions, schools are still subject to inspection from Paris.

CHRONOLOGY

The kingdoms of Teke and Loango were incorporated as the Middle Congo (part of French Equatorial Africa) between 1880 and 1883.

- ❑ **1960** Independence. Former priest Fulbert Youlou president.
- ❑ **1964** Marxist-Leninist National Revolution Movement (MNR) becomes sole legal party.
- ❑ **1977** President Ngoumbi assassinated. Yhompi-Opango head of state.
- ❑ **1979** Col. Denis Sassou-Nguesso president.
- ❑ **1992** Elections; Pascal Lissouba president.
- ❑ **1993** Elections: Lissouba's UPADS party gains majority.
- ❑ **1997** Lissouba ousted by forces backing former president Sassou-Nguesso, who returns to power.

C

HEALTH ▷ Welfare state health benefits

1 per 3,333 people   Diarrheal, parasitic and respiratory diseases, malaria

The health service, established by French military doctors at the turn of the century, is considered effective.

SPENDING ▷ GDP/cap. no increase

CONSUMPTION AND SPENDING

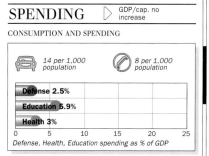

14 per 1,000 population   8 per 1,000 population

Defense 2.5%
Education 5.9%
Health 3%

Defense, Health, Education spending as % of GDP

Wealth generated from oil extraction has sustained an active and confident middle class. French label products are seen as status symbols.

WORLD RANKING

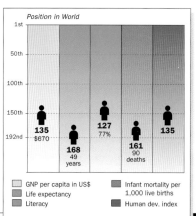

Position in World
1st
50th
100th
150th
192nd

135 $670
168 49 years
127 77%
161 90 deaths
135

❑ GNP per capita in US$
❑ Life expectancy
❑ Literacy
❑ Infant mortality per 1,000 live births
❑ Human dev. index

CONGO, DEM. REP. (ZAIRE)

OFFICIAL NAME: Democratic Republic of the Congo   **CAPITAL:** Kinshasa
POPULATION: 49.2 million   **CURRENCY:** Congolese franc   **OFFICIAL LANGUAGE:** French

CENTRAL AFRICA

| 1960 | 1960 | Nov 24 | ZRE | +1 | +243 | .zr |

LYING IN EAST CENTRAL AFRICA, the Democratic Republic of the Congo (Zaire) is one of Africa's largest countries. The rainforested basin of the Congo river occupies 60% of the land area. Formerly the Belgian Congo, it became independent in 1960, civil war breaking out immediately. The notoriously corrupt General Mobutu took power in 1965, naming the country Zaire. His rule collapsed in the face of an insurgency led by Laurent-Désiré Kabila in May 1997. A rebellion launched in August 1998 plunged the country (now renamed Congo Democratic Republic) into renewed chaos.

The Congo River is navigable for 1,357km (848 miles) and provides one of the most convenient ways of traveling in the country.

CLIMATE
▷ Tropical equatorial/ wet & dry

WEATHER CHART

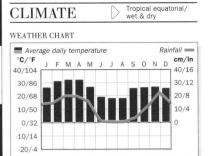

The climate is tropical and humid. Temperatures average 25°C (77°F) and vary little through the year. Annual rainfall is around 150–200 cm (59–79 inches); mountainous areas are wetter. The equator passes through the north of the country, causing marked regional variations. To its south, well-differentiated wet and dry seasons are October–May and June–September respectively. North of the equator, a short dry season lasts from December to February; the rest of the year is wet.

TRANSPORTATION
▷ Drive on right

N'Djili, Kinshasa
525,000 passengers

27 ships
15,000 grt

THE TRANSPORTATION NETWORK

157,000 km (98,125 miles)	None
3,641 km (2,276 miles)	14,500 km (9,063 miles)

The Congo river and its many tributaries provide the main means of communication. The size of the country and the fact that most of it is covered by dense rainforest have severely limited the development of road and rail networks. Many forest settlements are inaccessible except by air. Road maintenance, always poor, has virtually ceased outside the main towns since 1990, isolating even more settlements away from the main rivers.

TOURISM
▷ Not available

Not available   Not available

MAIN TOURIST ARRIVALS

Congo 64%	
France 5%	
Belgium 3%	
USA 2%	
Italy 1%	
Other 25%	

% of total arrivals

Political turmoil and widespread anarchy since early 1997 ensure that the country remains off the itinerary for most travelers. In normal times, tourist attractions consist mainly of scenery and wildlife, but there are few facilities for tourists even in the capital. The Congo, 16 km (10 miles) wide in places, is Africa's longest river after the Nile. Visitors were formerly also attracted by the vibrant music of Kinshasa's many bands. The once-large number of business visitors has also collapsed as a consequence of the chronic instability of the 1990s.

PEOPLE
▷ Pop. density low

Kiswahili, Tshiluba, Kikongo, Lingala, French

22/km² (56/mi²)

THE URBAN/RURAL POPULATION SPLIT

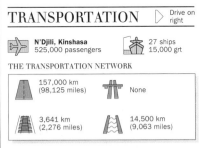

29%   71%

RELIGIOUS PERSUASION

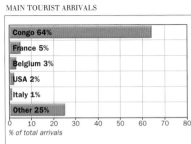

Protestant 13%
Traditional beliefs 50%
Roman Catholic 37%

ETHNIC MAKEUP

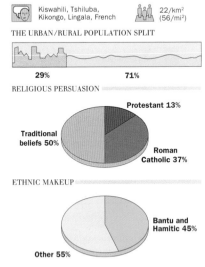

Bantu and Hamitic 45%
Other 55%

The Shaba mining area and major urban centers are densely populated, while the rainforests have a density of fewer than three people per sq km, mostly subsisting on the margins of the cash economy. There is great ethnic diversity, with more than 12 main groups and around 190 smaller ones. The majority are of Bantu origin, but there are also large Hamitic and Nilotic populations, mainly in the north and northeast. The original inhabitants, the forest Pygmies, today form a tiny and marginalized group.

Ethnic tensions inherited from the colonial period were contained under Mobutu until the 1990s, although ethnic violence in Shaba, Kivu, and Kasai provinces in 1993 cost many thousands of lives, and a Hutu refugee influx from Rwanda the following year provoked serious tension among Tutsis in eastern areas; wide-scale revenge killings soon became commonplace. Regarded by Mobutu as foreigners, the Tutsis provided the backbone of the 1996–1997 insurgency that overthrew him, subsequently turning against Kabila also.

POPULATION AGE BREAKDOWN

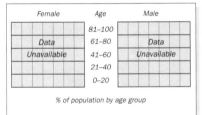

Female	Age	Male
	81–100	
Data	61–80	Data
Unavailable	41–60	Unavailable
	21–40	
	0–20	

% of population by age group

CONGO, DEMOCRATIC REPUBLIC (ZAIRE)

Total Land Area : 2 267 600 sq. km
(875 520 sq. miles)

POPULATION

▣	over 1 000 000
◉	over 500 000
◎	over 100 000
○	over 50 000
●	over 10 000
·	under 10 000

LAND HEIGHT

2000m/6562ft
1000m/3281ft
500m/1640ft
200m/656ft
Sea Level

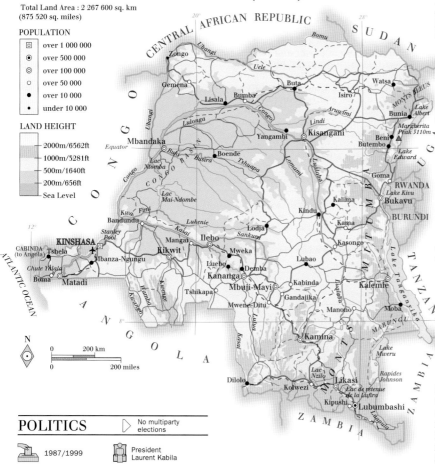

WORLD AFFAIRS

▷ Joined UN 1960

CEPGL	Comesa	Franc	G24	OAU

For almost 25 years, Mobutu's anti-communism made his regime one of the leading African allies of the West, and of the USA and France in particular, although he still managed to maintain close ties with several communist states. Western economic and military aid played a critical role in sustaining his regime. Relations with African countries were more problematic, complicated by Mobutu's support for the UNITA rebels in Angola, and for Morocco's annexation of Western Sahara.

Western attitudes changed from the late 1980s, and increasingly Mobutu was regarded as an embarrassment. Western donors stopped all but humanitarian aid from 1990. Despite diplomatic efforts by France, which feared a further loss of its prestige in central Africa following the Rwandan genocide in 1994, Mobutu was abandoned by the West as Kabila's rebels closed in on Kinshasa, forcing him to flee into exile in May 1997.

For the people of the Democratic Republic of Congo, worse was to come, as Kabila's former supporters in the east turned on him, launching a savage rebellion in August 1998, backed by Rwanda and Uganda. There were frantic inter-African efforts, led by South Africa and Zambia, to arrange a peace settlement during 1998 and 1999. Angola, Zimbabwe, Namibia, Chad, and Sudan were all nonetheless drawn into the conflict on Kabila's side, in what developed into one of the most serious civil wars in post-independence Africa.

AID

▷ Recipient

$168m (receipts)   ⬆ Up 1% 1996–1997

The Mobutu regime's importance to the West during the Cold War brought it aid revenues on a large scale. Between 1970 and 1989, it received $8.3 billion in economic aid – including $1.1 billion from the USA and $6.9 billion from other OECD states – as well as large-scale military assistance. Changing political priorities led the USA to act on long-deferred problems of human rights abuses and misappropriation of aid by Mobutu. In 1990, it suspended all but humanitarian aid; most other donors quickly followed suit, and the IMF declared the government "non-cooperative" over its $10 billion foreign debt. In the postwar era and inheriting this legacy, the country will need massive aid for reconstruction.

POLITICS

▷ No multiparty elections

1987/1999   President Laurent Kabila

AT THE LAST ELECTION

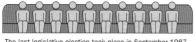

The last legislative election took place in September 1987 when candidates were chosen from Mobutu's Popular Movement for the revolution.

President Laurent-Désiré Kabila came to power in May 1997.

MAIN POLITICAL ISSUES
Securing peace and democracy
Promises of multiparty democracy from 1990 onward were largely subverted as Mobutu clung to power. Following Mobutu's overthrow in May 1997 by rebel forces loyal to Kabila, who was sworn in as president that month, a transition to democracy proved just as elusive. Elections promised for April 1999 did not take place as fighting continued. Instead, Kabila dissolved the Alliance of Democratic Forces for the Liberation of Congo (AFDL) which had brought him to power, accusing its leadership of corruption.

PROFILE
Hoping to satisfy leaders of other powerful groups which had opposed

Laurent Kabila, *who took power in 1997.*

Mobutu, *the ousted dictator, held power from 1965–1997.*

Mobutu, Kabila included members of the Union for Democracy and Social Progress (UDPS) led by the former prime minister, Etienne Tshisekedi, in his ruling coalition, but his dissolution of parliament and scrapping of the constitution fueled concern about his commitment to pluralist democracy, despite his promises. In May 1998, Kabila established the Constituent and Legislative Assembly, in place of a legislature. He reshuffled his cabinet frequently but, crucially, failed to satisfy the political hopes of his ethnic Tutsi supporters, whose armed rebellion against him in August 1998 plunged the country into civil chaos.

CHRONOLOGY

The modern Congo was the site of the Kongo and other powerful African kingdoms and a focus of the slave trade. Belgium's King Leopold II claimed most of the Congo basin after 1876 as his personal possession.

❏ **1885** Brutal colonization of Congo Free State (CFS) as King Leopold's private fief.
❏ **1908** Belgium takes over CFS after international outcry.
❏ **1960** Independence of Republic of Congo. Katanga (Shaba) province secedes. UN intervenes.
❏ **1963** Katanga secession collapses.
❏ **1965** Gen. Joseph-Désiré Mobutu seizes power.
❏ **1970** Mobutu elected president; makes his Popular Revolutionary Movement (MPR) sole legal party.
❏ **1971** Country renamed Zaire.
❏ **1977–1978** Two invasions by former Katanga separatists repulsed with Western help.
❏ **1982** Opposition parties set up Union for Democracy and Social Progress (UDPS).
❏ **1986–1990** Growing unrest; foreign criticism of human rights abuses.
❏ **1990** Belgium suspends aid after security forces kill pro-democracy demonstrators. Mobutu announces transition to multiparty rule. UDPS legalized.
❏ **1991** UDPS leader Etienne Tshisekedi heads short-lived "crisis government" formed by Mobutu.
❏ **1992–1993** Rival governments claim legitimacy: opposition backs Tshisekedi premiership and elects High Council of the Republic (HCR), while Mobutu dismisses Tshisekedi and reconvenes National Assembly.
❏ **1994** Combined HCR-Transitional Parliament established, elects Kengo wa Dondo as prime minister.
❏ **1995** Regime demands international assistance to support million Rwandan Hutu refugees.
❏ **1996** Major insurgency launched in east by Alliance of Democratic Forces for the Liberation of the Congo (AFDL), which unites various rebel groups, including Laurent Kabila's Popular Revolutionary Party (PRP), with disaffected ethnic Tutsi Banyamalunge.
❏ **1997** AFDL forces led by Kabila sweep south and west. Mobutu flees. Kabila takes power. Death of Mobutu in exile.
❏ **1998** Banyamalunge join Kabila's opponents and launch rebellion in east, backed by Rwanda and Uganda. Southern African states, fearing general destabilization of region, give military backing to Kabila.

DEFENSE

▷ No compulsory military service

💲 $308m   ⬆ Up 81% in 1997

The military played a key role in keeping Mobutu in power and was responsible for widespread human rights abuses. His Israeli-trained presidential guard was the elite force. Ordinary troops, poorly equipped and poorly paid, were notorious for rioting, looting, and extortion, but offered no real resistance when Kabila's insurgents swept the country in 1996–1997, many switching sides repeatedly since.

CONGOLESE (ZAIREAN) ARMED FORCES

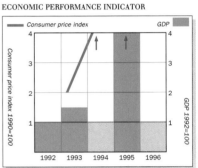

🚜	60 main battle tanks (40 PRC Type-62, 20 PRC Type-59)	50,000 personnel
🚤	7 patrol boats	90 personnel
✈	None	None
🚀	None	

ECONOMICS

▷ Inflation 636.4% p.a. (1985–1996)

📊 $5.2bn   💲 137,500 Congolese franc

SCORE CARD

❏ WORLD GNP RANKING	103rd
❏ GNP PER CAPITA	$110
❏ BALANCE OF PAYMENTS	$–643m
❏ INFLATION	175.5%
❏ UNEMPLOYMENT	Very high

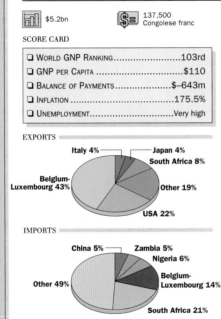

EXPORTS

Italy 4%
Japan 4%
South Africa 8%
Belgium-Luxembourg 43%
Other 19%
USA 22%

IMPORTS

China 5%
Zambia 5%
Nigeria 6%
Other 49%
Belgium-Luxembourg 14%
South Africa 21%

STRENGTHS
Rich resource base. Minerals – notably copper, cobalt, diamonds – provide 85% of export earnings. Energy: oil; possibly Africa's largest hydropower potential. Rich soil; much unutilized arable land. Trade surplus in normal years.

WEAKNESSES
Legacy of 25 years of mismanagement and corruption: $10 billion foreign debt; withdrawal of crucial foreign aid; inadequate, disintegrating social and transportation infrastructures; lack of food self-sufficiency. Political instability. Hyperinflation. Loss of export income. Withdrawal of foreign investment.

PROFILE
By the mid-1990s political instability, systematic corruption, and long-term mismanagement had brought a potentially leading African economy to a state of collapse. Real GDP was falling by 10% or more each year.

ECONOMIC PERFORMANCE INDICATOR

— Consumer price index   GDP

Consumer price index 1990=100 / GDP 1992=100

1992 1993 1994 1995 1996

The budget ran record deficits, and inflation ran virtually out of control from 1994 onwards. Many mines have been closed and most other industry halted. Strikes and riots over plummeting living standards hastened the flight of foreign capital. Subsistence farming and petty trade keep most people going. Even if political stability is restored, the immediate outlook is grim. Resumption of essential large-scale aid and debt relief will depend on reforms and paying off arrears to international creditors. The Kabila regime, despite its Marxist background, claims to want an effective free-market economy.

CONGO, DEM. REP. (ZAIRE) : MAJOR BUSINESSES

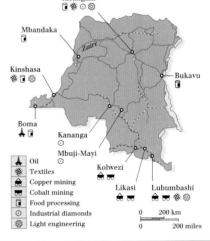

Kisangani
Mbandaka
Kinshasa
Bukavu
Boma
Kananga
Mbuji-Mayi
Kolwezi
Likasi   Lubumbashi

🛢 Oil
🏭 Textiles
⛏ Copper mining
⛏ Cobalt mining
🏢 Food processing
⊙ Industrial diamonds
⚙ Light engineering

0   200 km
0   200 miles

RESURCES

▷ Electric power 3.2m kw

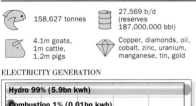

158,627 tonnes

27,569 b/d (reserves 187,000,000 bbl)

4.1m goats, 1m cattle, 1.2m pigs

Copper, diamonds, oil, cobalt, zinc, uranium, manganese, tin, gold

ELECTRICITY GENERATION

Hydro 99% (5.9bn kwh)				
Combustion 1% (0.01bn kwh)				
Nuclear 0%				
Other 0%				
0	20	40	60	80 100

% of total generation by type

What should be a prosperous country, with its rich resources, is instead one of the world's poorest states, exploited and mismanaged by its rulers for decades and damaged further by instability since 1990. In the 1980s, the country was the world's largest cobalt exporter and second-largest industrial diamond exporter. Since 1990, copper and cobalt output has collapsed and diamond smuggling is booming. There are oil reserves, but the main energy wealth lies in HEP potential, which could supply much of Africa if fully exploited. Lack of maintenance has, instead, shut down many turbines and most urban areas face power cuts. Despite rich soils and the fact that 80% of people are involved in farming, the country is not even self-sufficient in food.

CONGO, DEM. REP. (ZAIRE) : LAND USE

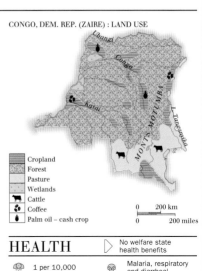

Cropland
Forest
Pasture
Wetlands
Cattle
Coffee
Palm oil – cash crop

0   200 km
0   200 miles

ENVIRONMENT

▷ No Green MPs

5%

Low

ENVIRONMENTAL TREATIES

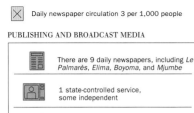

Yes   Yes   Yes

Yes   Yes   No

Rainforests cover over 60% of the country, representing almost 6% of the world's and 50% of Africa's remaining woodlands. They are home to important populations of several endangered species, including gorillas. The poor transportation network has so far prevented large-scale commercial exploitation of timber, but clearance for fuelwood is a problem. The collapse since 1990 of many urban refuse and sewage disposal systems has led to major health and pollution problems.

CRIME

▷ Death penalty used

Congo, Dem. Rep. does not publish prison figures

Violence and crime have risen rapidly since 1990

CRIME RATES

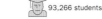

All types of crime are on the increase

Political crisis and economic collapse exacerbate long-standing problems of corruption and human rights abuses. Violence and crime of all kinds are on the increase, and in war zones most law and order has broken down. Mobutu's lawless army was widely feared, and death squads were blamed for "disappearances" and murders. Ethnic violence, suppressed after 1965, resurfaced in the 1990s, particularly in the south.

HEALTH

▷ No welfare state health benefits

1 per 10,000 people

Malaria, respiratory and diarrheal diseases

State services in the Democratic Republic of Congo, which have long been underfunded, have now virtually collapsed. Disease and death rates are rising, especially in rural areas. As of December 1997, close to one million people were estimated to be infected with the HIV/AIDS virus.

SPENDING

▷ GDP/cap. no increase

CONSUMPTION AND SPENDING

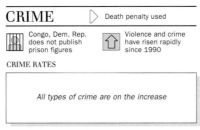

17 per 1,000 population

1 per 1,000 population

Defense 3.3%				
Education 1%				
Health 0.8%				
0	5	10	15	20 25

Defense, Health, Education spending as % of GDP

Mobutu disappeared into exile as one of the world's richest men, worth an estimated $4 billion. Most of his former subjects still live in poverty, exacerbated by civil war.

MEDIA

▷ TV ownership low

Daily newspaper circulation 3 per 1,000 people

PUBLISHING AND BROADCAST MEDIA

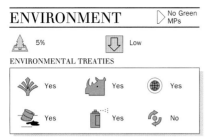

There are 9 daily newspapers, including *Le Palmarès*, *Elima*, *Boyoma*, and *Mjumbe*

1 state-controlled service, some independent

2 state-controlled services, some independent

In contrast to the broadcast media, the press is privately owned. Coverage of opposition politics widened after 1990, but press criticism of Mobutu or the security forces remained muted. One newspaper's Kinshasa offices were burnt down in 1993 after it published a strongly anti-Mobutu article. The post-Mobutu regime has been accused of similarly dictatorial tendencies.

EDUCATION

▷ Not available

77%

93,266 students

About 70% of schooling is now provided by the Catholic Church.

THE EDUCATION SYSTEM

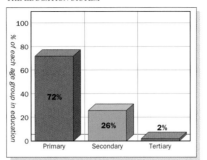

% of each age group in education

100
80
60
40   72%
20   26%
0   2%
Primary Secondary Tertiary

Just over 58% of primary age and 37% of secondary age children were at school in 1997. State provision, as with health care, is patchy and has faced sharp budget cuts since 1980.

WORLD RANKING

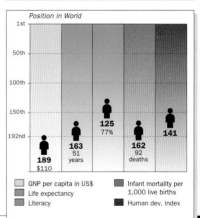

Position in World

1st
50th
100th
150th
192nd

189
$110

163
51 years

125
77%

162
92 deaths

141

GNP per capita in US$
Life expectancy
Literacy

Infant mortality per 1,000 live births
Human dev. index

COSTA RICA

OFFICIAL NAME: The Republic of Costa Rica   **CAPITAL:** San José
POPULATION: 3.7 million   **CURRENCY:** Costa Rican colón   **OFFICIAL LANGUAGE:** Spanish

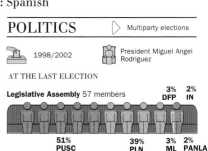

CENTRAL AMERICA

| 1838 | 1838 | Sept 15 | CR | -6 | +506 | | .cr |

LOCATED IN CENTRAL AMERICA, Costa Rica was under Spanish rule until 1821 and gained full independence in 1838. From 1948 until the end of the 1980s, it was the most developed welfare state in Central America. Costa Rica is nominally a multiparty democracy, but in practice two parties dominate. Its constitution is unique in that it contains a clause which forbids the formation of a national army; its own was abolished in 1949.

CLIMATE
▷ Tropical wet & dry

WEATHER CHART

The Atlantic coast has heavy rainfall, while the Pacific coast is much drier. The central uplands are temperate.

TRANSPORTATION
▷ Drive on right

Juan Santamaría, San José
988,000 passengers

14 ships
5,900 grt

THE TRANSPORTATION NETWORK

| 5,814 km (3,613 miles) | Pan-American Highway 663 km (412 miles) |
| 400 km (249 miles) | 730 km (454 miles) |

Privately financed improvements in 1999 include the upgrading of nine major roads and the international airport.

TOURISM
▷ Visitors : population 1:4.5

811,000 visitors   ⬆ Up 2% 1995–1997

MAIN TOURIST ARRIVALS

USA 35%	
Nicaragua 14%	
Panama 7%	
Other 44%	

% of total arrivals: 0 10 20 30 40 50 60

Tourism grew strongly in 1998 supported by a $4 million government publicity campaign. There is to be foreign and domestic investment of $1 billion over 14 years in the Papagayo complex in Guanacaste.

PEOPLE
▷ Pop. density medium

Spanish, English Creole, Bribri, Cabecar

72/km² (188/mi²)

THE URBAN/RURAL POPULATION SPLIT

50%   50%

RELIGIOUS PERSUASION

Other (including Protestant) 24%

Roman Catholic 76%

The majority of the population is *mestizo* of Spanish origin. One-third of people in the Puerto Limón area are black and often English-speaking. There are only about 5,000 indigenous Indians.

POLITICS
▷ Multiparty elections

1998/2002   President Miguel Angel Rodriguez

AT THE LAST ELECTION

Legislative Assembly 57 members

3% DFP   2% IN

51% PUSC   39% PLN   3% ML   2% PANLA

PUSC = Social Christian Unity Party   **PLN** = National Liberation Party   **ML** = Liberty Movement
DFP = Democratic Force Party   **IN** = National Integration
PANLA = National Action Workers' Party of Alajuela

Politics has been long dominated by the PUSC and PLN, both of which have close ties to major banana and coffee families. Historically the USA has exercised a very powerful influence on politics. The PLN held power from 1982 until 1990, when President Rafael Calderón pursued austerity policies. In 1994, José María Figueres of the PLN won the presidency promising reforms, but soon came under pressure from international financial organizations to reduce the budget deficit. He reached a consensus with the PUSC on harsh structural adjustment measures which made him highly unpopular. In the 1998 election the pendulum swung back to the PUSC. President Miguel Angel Rodriguez in 1999 launched a three-year plan to reduce inflation and poverty, create thousands of jobs and stimulate foreign investment in state companies.

WORLD AFFAIRS
▷ Joined UN in 1945

| ACS | Geplac | NAM | OAS | San José |

Trade ties with the USA and the protection of export prices for coffee and bananas are priorities. Trade ties are also being cemented with Mexico, and Trinidad and Tobago. Tensions exist with Nicaragua over the mutual border and illegal immigrants.

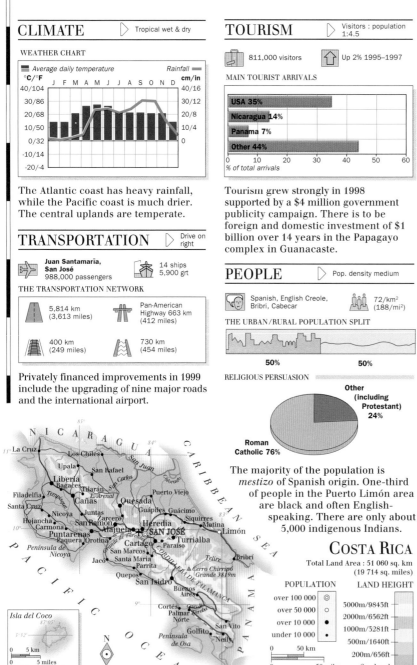

COSTA RICA

Total Land Area : 51 060 sq. km
(19 714 sq. miles)

POPULATION

over 100 000 ◎
over 50 000 ○
over 10 000 ●
under 10 000 ·

LAND HEIGHT

3000m/9843ft
2000m/6562ft
1000m/3281ft
500m/1640ft
200m/656ft
Sea level

0 — 50 km
0 — 50 miles

Pineapple plantation near Buenos Aires, crossed by the Pan-American Highway which runs for 663 km (414 miles) through Costa Rica.

C

C

AID
▷ Recipient

💲 Not applicable | ⇕ Loan repayments exceeded aid received in 1997

During the 1980s Costa Rica received large amounts of US aid designed to maintain it as a useful base against left-wing insurgencies in neighboring El Salvador, Guatemala, and Nicaragua. Peace in the region has seen a sharp decline in such aid, especially given the country's relatively high per capita income. The IDB suspended a $150 million loan in 1999.

DEFENSE
▷ No compulsory military service

💲 $59m | ⇧ Up 12% in 1997

Costa Rica emerged from the 1948 civil war as a neutral, demilitarized modern state. A 7,500-strong Civil Guard is complemented by a largely military-trained police force. Spending on security has long been the lowest in the region. Lack of a common command structure hinders the influence of the security forces but also renders them less accountable to public control. Right-wing paramilitary groups are known to exist.

ECONOMICS
▷ Inflation 17.8% p.a. (1985–1996)

📊 $9.3bn | 💲 243.65–271.42 colones

SCORE CARD

❏ WORLD GNP RANKING	85th
❏ GNP PER CAPITA	$2,680
❏ BALANCE OF PAYMENTS	$–254m
❏ INFLATION	13.2%
❏ UNEMPLOYMENT	6%

EXPORTS

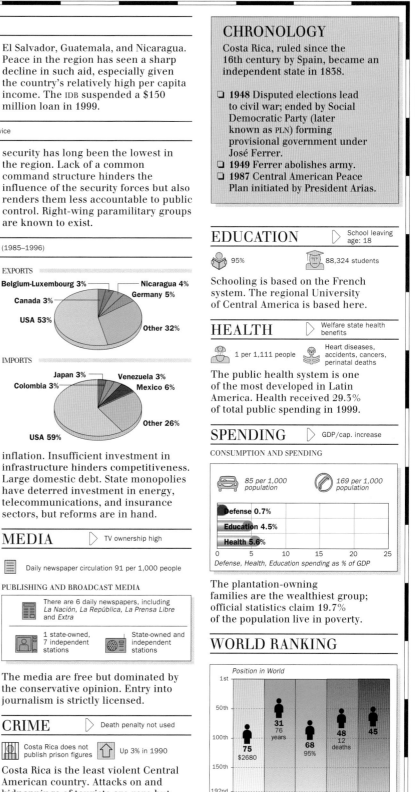

Nicaragua 4%
Germany 5%
Belgium-Luxembourg 3%
Canada 3%
USA 53%
Other 32%

IMPORTS

Japan 3%
Venezuela 3%
Colombia 3%
Mexico 6%
Other 26%
USA 59%

STRENGTHS
Major coffee, beef, and banana exports. Expanding tourism also fueling construction. Strong inward investment. Favorable WTO ruling on banana access to EU market.

WEAKNESSES
Coffee, beef, and bananas vulnerable to falling international prices. Dependence on imported oil. History of high inflation. Insufficient investment in infrastructure hinders competitiveness. Large domestic debt. State monopolies have deterred investment in energy, telecommunications, and insurance sectors, but reforms are in hand.

RESOURCES
▷ Electric power 1.2m kw

27,928 tonnes | Not an oil producer; refines 15,000 b/d

1.5m cattle, 280,000 pigs, 115,000 horses | Gold, bauxite, silver, manganese, mercury

Costa Rica has large bauxite deposits at Boruca – aluminum smelting is an important industry. Small quantities of gold, silver, manganese, and mercury are also mined. Self-sufficiency in energy is being pursued through the development of hydroelectric power. Forests cover 34% of the country.

ENVIRONMENT
▷ No Green MPs

△ 14% (3% partially protected) | ⇕ Medium

Despite good environmental regulation, reckless economic development has contributed to extensive deforestation. Pasture land now covers some 45% of the territory and pesticide abuse by agribusiness has poisoned rivers and threatened species. Urban sprawl has degraded the fertile central valley.

MEDIA
▷ TV ownership high

▤ Daily newspaper circulation 91 per 1,000 people

PUBLISHING AND BROADCAST MEDIA

There are 6 daily newspapers, including *La Nación, La República, La Prensa Libre* and *Extra*

1 state-owned, 7 independent stations | State-owned and independent stations

The media are free but dominated by the conservative opinion. Entry into journalism is strictly licensed.

CRIME
▷ Death penalty not used

 Costa Rica does not publish prison figures | ⇧ Up 3% in 1990

Costa Rica is the least violent Central American country. Attacks on and kidnappings of tourists are rare but have dented its image. Drug cartels use the country to transfer cocaine to the USA and Europe. Police show hostility toward immigrants from neighboring countries.

CHRONOLOGY
Costa Rica, ruled since the 16th century by Spain, became an independent state in 1838.

❏ **1948** Disputed elections lead to civil war; ended by Social Democratic Party (later known as PLN) forming provisional government under José Ferrer.
❏ **1949** Ferrer abolishes army.
❏ **1987** Central American Peace Plan initiated by President Arias.

EDUCATION
▷ School leaving age: 18

📖 95% | 🎓 88,324 students

Schooling is based on the French system. The regional University of Central America is based here.

HEALTH
▷ Welfare state health benefits

👤 1 per 1,111 people | ☠ Heart diseases, accidents, cancers, perinatal deaths

The public health system is one of the most developed in Latin America. Health received 29.3% of total public spending in 1999.

SPENDING
▷ GDP/cap. increase

CONSUMPTION AND SPENDING

🚗 85 per 1,000 population | ☎ 169 per 1,000 population

Defense 0.7%
Education 4.5%
Health 5.6%

0   5   10   15   20   25
Defense, Health, Education spending as % of GDP

The plantation-owning families are the wealthiest group; official statistics claim 19.7% of the population live in poverty.

WORLD RANKING

Position in World

1st
50th
100th
150th
192nd

75 $2680 | 31 76 years | 68 95% | 48 12 deaths | 45

▢ GNP per capita in US$
▢ Life expectancy
▢ Literacy
▢ Infant mortality per 1,000 live births
▢ Human dev. index

CROATIA

OFFICIAL NAME: Republic of Croatia   **CAPITAL:** Zagreb
POPULATION: 4.5 million   **CURRENCY:** Kuna   **OFFICIAL LANGUAGE:** Croatian

C

EUROPE

LOCATED TO THE SOUTH OF SLOVENIA and west of Serbia, Croatia includes the historic regions of Istra, Dalmatia and Slavonia. Its Adriatic coastline is vital for tourism and shipping. After the dissolution of former Yugoslavia, Croatia had to defend its own territory and was involved in the Bosnian war. Military offensives in 1995 ended Serb control over several enclaves, while Eastern Slavonia was administered by the UN until its return to Croatia in January 1998.

CLIMATE
▷ Mediterranean/continental

WEATHER CHART

Northern Croatia has a temperate continental climate. Its Adriatic coast has a Mediterranean climate.

TRANSPORTATION
▷ Drive on right

Pleso International, Zagreb
1.1m passengers

245 ships
871,000 grt

THE TRANSPORTATION NETWORK

27,800 km (17,300 miles)

318 km (195 miles)

2,726 km (1,694 miles)

785 km (488 miles)

Communications in Western Slavonia and Krajina were affected by Croatian military operations which retook the regions in 1995. In 1998 an accord was reached with Bosnia allowing the latter to use the port of Ploce on the Adriatic.

TOURISM
▷ Visitors : population 1:1.2

3.8m visitors

Up 65% 1994–1997

MAIN TOURIST ARRIVALS

Germany 24%
Italy 23%
UK 10%
Other 43%

0   10   20   30   40   50   60
% of total arrivals

Tourism earnings had returned to 60% of pre-war levels until the crisis in nearby Kosovo again deterred visitors.

PEOPLE
▷ Pop. density medium

Croat

80/km² (206/mi²)

THE URBAN/RURAL POPULATION SPLIT

64%   36%

RELIGIOUS PERSUASION

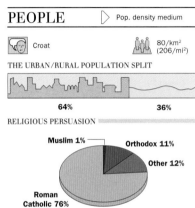

Muslim 1%   Orthodox 11%
Other 12%
Roman Catholic 76%

Before the war Croats made up nearly 80% of the population, Serbs 12%. In 1991, the Serbs, alienated by Croatian nationalism, proclaimed the Republic of Serbian Krajina, made up of the areas where they formed a majority, notably in Krajina, Western and Eastern Slavonia. In May and August 1995 Croatian forces retook Western Slavonia and Krajina. The Croatian government and rebel Croatian Serb leaders agreed in November 1995 that the UN should administer Eastern Slavonia until its full reintegration into Croatia in January 1998.

POLITICS
▷ Multiparty elections

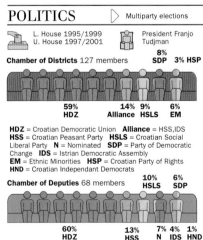

L. House 1995/1999
U. House 1997/2001

President Franjo Tudjman

Chamber of Districts 127 members

8% SDP   3% HSP

59% HDZ   14% Alliance   9% HSLS   6% EM

HDZ = Croatian Democratic Union **Alliance** = HSS,IDS
HSS = Croatian Peasant Party **HSLS** = Croatian Social
Liberal Party **N** = Nominated **SDP** = Party of Democratic
Change **IDS** = Istrian Democratic Assembly
EM = Ethnic Minorities **HSP** = Croatian Party of Rights
HND = Croatian Independant Democrats

Chamber of Deputies 68 members

10% HSLS   6% SDP

60% HDZ   13% HSS   7% N   4% IDS   1% HND

WORLD AFFAIRS
▷ Joined UN in 1992

CE   IAEA   IBRD   NAM   OSCE

The December 1995 Bosnian peace agreement was widely recognized as a major foreign policy success for president Franjo Tudjman. Croatia's major concern was then to complete implementation of a November 1995 agreement, signed with rebel Croatian Serbs, providing for the reintegration of mainly Serb-populated Eastern Slavonia into Croatia. Tudjman made it clear that this was a precondition for normalization of relations between Croatia and Yugoslavia, which followed in August 1996. Croatia maintains close relations with Germany.

AID
▷ Recipient

$44m

Down 67% 1996–1997

EU states have spent nearly $1 billion on reconstruction in Croatia since 1991. There were 600,000 displaced people in 1992 and by end-1997 Croatia still hosted 250,000 Bosnian refugees, 70% of whom had settled there.

DEFENSE
▷ Compulsory military service

$1.1bn

Down 13% in 1997

Croatia's defense forces number 50,000 in the army and some 3,000 each in the navy and air force. The Croat Defense Association (HOS) also has 10,000 soldiers in Bosnia, who remain in place under the 1995 peace accord. The army successfully recaptured Serb-held Western Slavonia and Krajina in 1995.

After the breakup of Yugoslavia, the Croatian independence movement was led by the right-wing Croatian Democratic Union (HDZ) under Franjo Tudjman. Multiparty elections in 1995 consolidated the HDZ's and Tudjman's hold on power. He was reelected to the presidency in 1997, but his government suffered isolation internationally because of its authoritarian nationalist stance and its supposed lukewarm support for the 1995 Bosnian peace accord. Concerns center on the lack of a clear successor to the seriously ill Tudjman within the HDZ government, which is mired in corruption and spying scandals, while the opposition is divided.

C

ECONOMICS

▷ Inflation 386% p.a. (1986–1997)

 $19.3bn   6.32–6.24 kuna

SCORE CARD

- ❏ WORLD GNP RANKING...........................69th
- ❏ GNP PER CAPITA $4,060
- ❏ BALANCE OF PAYMENTS.................$–2,435m
- ❏ INFLATION 4.1%
- ❏ UNEMPLOYMENT...................................16%

STRENGTHS

Currency stabilization and control of hyperinflation achieved in 1993. Growth of over 6% in 1994–1997.

WEAKNESSES

War damage estimated at $50 billion. Slow privatization. Isolation from progress in other transition countries.

EXPORTS/IMPORTS

Before the conflict, Croatia's main trading partners were the former Yugoslavian republics, Italy and Germany.

Dubrovnik, Dalmatia. *This historic city on the Adriatic coast was shelled and besieged by the Yugoslav federal army in 1991.*

RESOURCES

▷ Electric power 3.6m kw

19,160 tonnes   38,436 b/d

10m poultry, 1.2m pigs, 443,000 cattle   Coal, bauxite, iron, oil, china clay, natural gas

Croatia generates 40% of its energy needs from thermal and 60% from hydroelectric sources. It has few minerals, although it does have oil and gas fields. The rich fishing grounds of the Adriatic are a major resource.

ENVIRONMENT

▷ No Green MPs

🌲 7%   ⬇ Low

Croatia was the first Yugoslav republic to create reserves in order to protect endangered and unique wetlands.

MEDIA

▷ TV ownership high

✉ Daily newspaper circulation 114 per 1,000 people

PUBLISHING AND BROADCAST MEDIA

There are 10 daily newspapers, published locally, including *Vercenji List* in Zagreb and *Slobodna Dalmacija* in Split

1 state-controlled service   1 state-controlled service

All three national TV channels are state-owned and controlled. Concerns persist about media freedoms.

CRIME

▷ Death penalty not used

2,572 prisoners   Crime has risen since independence

The regime has shown little enthusiasm for prosecuting members of the former Croat militia in Bosnia, the HOS, suspected of involvement in "ethnic cleansing."

CHRONOLOGY

In 1945–1991 Croatia was a constituent republic of the Yugoslav federation.

- ❏ **1991** Croatian independence. Rebel Croatian Serb republic proclaimed.
- ❏ **1995** Croats retake Krajina and Western Slavonia from rebel Serbs; Tudjman signs Bosnian peace accord.
- ❏ **1997** Tudjman reelected president.
- ❏ **1998** Eastern Slavonia reintegrated.

EDUCATION

▷ School leaving age: 15

👤 98%   🎓 85,752 students

Croatia has a well-developed education system. It has four universities, at Zagreb, Rijeka, Osijek, and Split.

HEALTH

▷ Welfare state health benefits

1 per 500 people   Cerebrovascular and heart diseases, cancers

Most Croats are covered by a health insurance scheme. However, coping with refugees and war casualties puts an extra strain on already scarce funds.

SPENDING

▷ GDP/cap. no increase

CONSUMPTION AND SPENDING

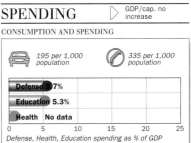 195 per 1,000 population   335 per 1,000 population

Defense	9.7%	
Education	5.3%	
Health	No data	

Defense, Health, Education spending as % of GDP

0   5   10   15   20   25

Wage rises in the mid-1990s led to a spending boom, but Westernized expectations cannot always be met, and many find it difficult to meet basic needs.

WORLD RANKING

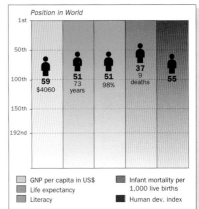

Position in World

1st					
50th					
100th	**59** $4060	**51** 73 years	**51** 98%	**37** 9 deaths	**55**
150th					
192nd					

- ⬜ GNP per capita in US$
- ⬜ Life expectancy
- ⬜ Literacy
- ⬛ Infant mortality per 1,000 live births
- ⬛ Human dev. index

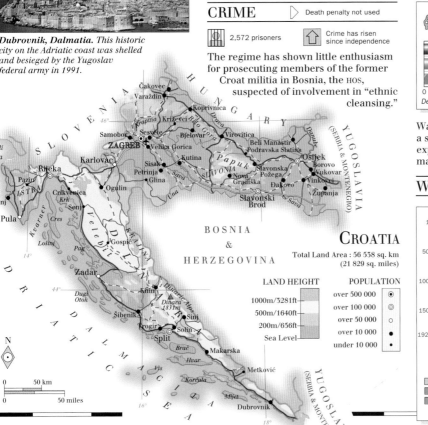

CROATIA

Total Land Area : 56 538 sq. km (21 829 sq. miles)

LAND HEIGHT

- 1000m/3281ft
- 500m/1640ft
- 200m/656ft
- Sea Level

POPULATION

- ⊙ over 500 000
- ◎ over 100 000
- ○ over 50 000
- • over 10 000
- · under 10 000

0   50 km

0   50 miles

BOSNIA & HERZEGOVINA

CUBA

OFFICIAL NAME: Republic of Cuba   **CAPITAL:** Havana
POPULATION: 11.1 million   **CURRENCY:** Cuban peso   **OFFICIAL LANGUAGE:** Spanish

1902 | 1902 | Jan 1 | C | -5 | +53 | .cu

THE CARIBBEAN'S LARGEST ISLAND, Cuba has cultivated lowlands lying between three mountainous areas. The fertile soil supports the sugar cane, rice, and coffee plantations. Sugar, the country's major export, suffers from underinvestment, low yields and fluctuating world prices. A former Spanish colony, Cuba is the one of the few remaining communist states. Veteran president Fidel Castro is still very much in control. Cuba is still subject to US economic sanctions, but the USA currently sees Cuba as less of a threat than it did in the Cold War. In 1962, Soviet nuclear missiles on the island brought the two superpowers close to war.

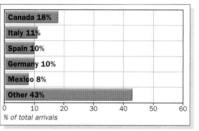

Valle de Viñales, Pinar del Río province.
Cuba's undulating countryside is ideal for growing the main export crop, sugar.

CLIMATE
▷ Tropical oceanic

WEATHER CHART

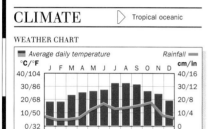

■ Average daily temperature   Rainfall ■
°C/°F   J F M A M J J A S O N D   cm/in
40/104 — 40/16
30/86 — 30/12
20/68 — 20/8
10/50 — 10/4
0/32 — 0
-10/14
-20/-4

Cuba's subtropical climate is hot all year round and very hot in the summer. Rainfall is heaviest in the mountains, which receive up to 250 cm (98 inches) a year. Generally, the north is wetter than the south; the Guantánamo area receives only 20 cm (8 inches) of rainfall annually. In winter, the west is affected sometimes by cold air from the USA, but only for a day or two at a time.

TRANSPORTATION
▷ Drive on right

José Martí, Havana
1.2m passengers

148 ships
203,000 grt

THE TRANSPORTATION NETWORK

14,478 km
(8,996 miles)

627 km
(390 miles)

12,580 km
(7,817 miles)

240 km
(149 miles)

Public transportation has been extremely cheap in Cuba, although fuel shortages have made it increasingly erratic and unreliable. Cubans rely mostly on traditional black bicycles, imported by the thousand from China. Havana owes much of its charm to the number of 45-year-old Chevrolets and Oldsmobiles still being driven around. This is another result of sanctions, but it keeps the many inventive local spare-parts workshops in business.

TOURISM
▷ Visitors : population 1:9.6

1.2m visitors

Up 56% 1995–1997

MAIN TOURIST ARRIVALS

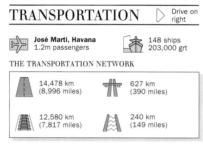

Canada 18%
Italy 11%
Spain 10%
Germany 10%
Mexico 8%
Other 43%

% of total arrivals
0   10   20   30   40   50   60

Cuba is among the Caribbean's most popular holiday destinations, and tourism has supplanted sugar as the most important motor of the economy and largest generator of foreign exchange. Arrivals are officially expected to reach two million in 2000, rising to over five million by 2010. Most visitors come from Europe and Canada. The government seeks to promote family tourism by cracking down on prostitutes who target Havana's main hotels.

GULF OF MEXICO

Straits of Florida

Archipiélago de los Colorados

HAVANA (La Habana)   Guanabo
Mariel   Guanabacoa
Marianao   Matanzas   Varadero
Guanajay   Cárdenas
Artemisa   Jovellanos
San Cristóbal   Perico   Colón
Minas de Matahambre   Hanábana
Consolación del Sur
Pinar del Río
La Fé

Golfo de Batabanó

C. San Antonio

Yucatan Channel

Isla de la Juventud   Nueva Gerona
Santa Fé

Archipiélago de los Canarreos

Cayo Largo

Archipiélago de Sabana
Sagua la Grande   Cifuentes
Santo Domingo   Caibarién
Santa Clara   Chambas   Morón
Placetas   Cayo Romano
Cienfuegos   Cabaiguán   Taguasco
Juragua   Sancti Spíritus
Condado   Ciego de Ávila   Esmeralda
Céspedes   Nuevitas
Florida   Camagüey
Vertientes   Puerto Padre   Jesús Menéndez
Crucero Contramaestre   Guáimaro   Las Tunas
Santa Cruz del Sur   Holg
Golfo de Guacanayabo   Bayamo   guaní
Niquero   Manzanillo   Palma Soriano San
Bartolomé Masó   SIERRA MAESTRA   Santi de Cu
Pico Turquino 1994 m

Archipiélago de Sabana

Archipiélago de Camagüey
Cayo Sabinal

ATLANTIC OCEAN

Archipiélago de los Jardines de la Reina

CARIBBEAN SEA

Guanabo, 25 km east of Havana, is a low-key holiday resort favoured by Cubans. The most modern cars in Cuba are imported, along with computers, in exchange for sugar in a special trading deal with Japan.

CUBA

Total Land Area : 110 860 sq. km
(42 803 sq. miles)

POPULATION
◙ over 1 000 000
◉ over 500 000
◎ over 100 000
○ over 50 000
● over 10 000
· under 10 000

LAND HEIGHT
1000m/3281ft
500m/1640ft
200m/656ft
Sea Level

N

0   50 km
0   50 miles

PEOPLE
▷ Pop. density medium

Spanish   100/km² (259/mi²)

THE URBAN/RURAL POPULATION SPLIT

76%   24%

RELIGIOUS PERSUASION

Protestant 1%
Atheist 6%
Other 4%
Non-religious 49%
Roman Catholic 40%

ETHNIC MAKEUP

Black 12%
European-African 22%
White 66%

Ethnic tension in Cuba is minimal. About 70% of Cubans are of Spanish descent, mainly from the early settlers, but also from the more recent influx of exiles from Franco's Spain. The black population is descended from the slaves and migrants from neighboring states, in particular Jamaica.

Living standards in Cuba have fallen dramatically since the late 1980s collapse of the east European communist bloc, previously its main trading partner, and rationing for most basic foodstuffs was subsequently introduced. The "dollarization" of the economy in recent years has led to great divisions between those who survive on pesos and the more than 50% of the population who have access to dollars. The number of those trying to leave, legally or otherwise, has increased markedly since the early 1990s. An increasing number of women are playing prominent roles in politics, the professions, and the armed forces. Child-care facilities are widespread.

POPULATION AGE BREAKDOWN

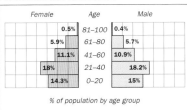

Female		Age	Male	
	0.5%	81–100	0.4%	
	5.9%	61–80	5.7%	
	11.1%	41–60	10.9%	
18%		21–40	18.2%	
14.3%		0–20	15%	

% of population by age group

WORLD AFFAIRS
▷ Joined UN in 1945

ACS   IAEA   SELA   NAM   OAS

Since the 1962 stand-off, when Cuba accepted Russian missiles targeted at US cities, Cuba has been considered a danger by the USA. The end of aid from Moscow after 1991, following the collapse of the USSR, and the US trade blockade increased Cuba's economic isolation despite routine votes in the UN condemning sanctions. The USA, via the 1996 Helms-Burton Act, tightened the embargo by threatening sanctions on international companies trading and investing in Cuba. Sanctions were modified in 1999 to permit more flights, direct mail and US citizens to send money to Cuban relatives. The government argues, however, that such concessions have destabilizing goals.

Pope John Paul's visit in January 1998 created an international opening for Cuba, but recent concerns about the treatment of dissidents risk damaging diplomatic and economic ties with such supportive countries as Canada. Cuba accused Spain of interference in its internal affairs in 1996, but bilateral relations were normalized in 1998.

POLITICS
▷ No multiparty elections

1998/2003   President Fidel Castro Ruz

AT THE LAST ELECTION

National Assembly of People's Power 601 members

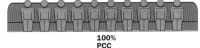

100% PCC

PCC = Cuban Communist Party

Fidel Castro has led Cuba since 1959 and was the founder of the one-party communist system, formalized in the 1976 constitution.

MAIN POLITICAL ISSUES
The succession
The aging Fidel Castro remains securely in place but his succession is a major issue. Some observers predict that a younger, collective and reform-minded leadership would normalize relations with the USA and steer Cuba towards Western-style democracy.

Others warn that Castro's departure could lead to a power vacuum, vulnerable to social unrest, and internal divisions between reformers and communist hard-liners.

Democracy
The trial in 1999 of four

moderate dissidents was part of a tough clampdown on internal opposition. This has reduced hopes for the type of opening seen in the economic sphere and threatens diplomatic and economic ties. It offers the USA justification for its continuing trade embargo.

PROFILE
The 1959 popular revolution, led by Castro, toppled the corrupt Batista dictatorship and launched a far-reaching program of social, economic, and political reforms.

Today the revolution seems under siege in the wake of the collapse of the Soviet Union and tightened trade sanctions by the USA. Supporters still see Cuba as living proof of the triumph of socialist development over adversity but critics view Castro's regime as an intolerant dictatorship.

Raúl Castro, brother of Fidel and the Minister of Defence.

Fidel Castro, Cuba's leader since 1959. The USA is keen to oust his regime.

AID
▷ Recipient

$67m (receipts)   Down 1% 1996–1997

Annual Soviet aid of over $5 billion ended in 1991. Spain, France, and UNICEF have also provided Cuba with aid, and an agreement in 1998 with Japan rescheduled debt over 20 years.

CHRONOLOGY
Originally inhabited by the Arawak people, Cuba was claimed by Columbus for Spain in 1492. Development of the sugar industry from the 18th century, using imported slave labor, made Cuba the world's third-largest producer by 1860.

❑ **1868** End of the slave trade.
❑ **1868–1878** Ten Years' War for independence from Spain.
❑ **1895** Second war of independence. Thousands die in Spanish concentration camps.
❑ **1898** In support of Cuban rebels USA declares war on Spain to protect strong American financial interests in Cuba.
❑ **1899** USA takes Cuba and installs military interim government.
❑ **1901** USA is granted intervention rights and military bases, including Guantánamo Bay naval base.

C

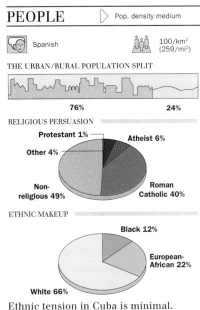
Moa
Baracoa
El Salvador
Guantánamo
GUANTANAMO BAY (to US)
Windward Passage

C

CHRONOLOGY *continued*

- ❏ **1902** Tomás Estrada Palma takes over as first Cuban president. USA leaves Cuba, but intervenes in 1906–1909 and 1919–1924.
- ❏ **1909** Liberal presidency of José Miguel Gómez. Economy prospers; US investment in tourism, gambling and sugar.
- ❏ **1925–1933** Dictatorship of President Gerardo Machado.
- ❏ **1933** Years of guerrilla activity end in revolution. Sergeant Fulgencio Batista takes over and leads military dictatorship.
- ❏ **1955** Fidel Castro exiled after two years' imprisonment for subversion.
- ❏ **1956–1958** Castro returns to lead a guerrilla war in the Sierra Maestra.
- ❏ **1959** Batista flees. Castro takes over; his brother, Raúl, is deputy; Che Guevara third in rank. Wholesale nationalizations; Cuba reorganized on Soviet model.
- ❏ **1961** USA breaks off relations. US-backed, anti-Castro Cubans attempt invasion at Bay of Pigs. Fail. Cuba declares itself Marxist–Leninist.
- ❏ **1962** US economic and political blockade. Missile crisis: May, Khrushchev agrees to defend Cuba; October 14, US spy planes see nuclear missile on site; October 22, Kennedy orders seizure of weapons on Soviet ships in "quarantine zone." USA prepares for war; October 28, Khrushchev orders return of weapons; November 20, USA lifts "quarantine."
- ❏ **1965** Che Guevara resigns. One-party state formalized.
- ❏ **1972** Cuba joins COMECON.
- ❏ **1976** New socialist constitution. Cuban troops in Angola until 1991.
- ❏ **1977** Sends troops to Ethiopia.
- ❏ **1980** 125,000 Cubans, including "undesirables," flee to USA.
- ❏ **1982** USA tightens sanctions and bans flights and tourism to Cuba.
- ❏ **1983** US invasion of Grenada. Cuba involved in clashes with US forces.
- ❏ **1984** Agreement with USA on Cuban emigration and repatriation of "undesirables" is short-lived.
- ❏ **1986** Soviet-style *glasnost* rejected.
- ❏ **1988** UN's second veto of US attempt to accuse Cuba of human rights violations. Diplomatic relations established with EC.
- ❏ **1989** Senior military executed for arms and narcotics smuggling.
- ❏ **1991** Preferential trade agreement with USSR ends. Severe rationing.
- ❏ **1994–1995** Economic reforms.
- ❏ **1996** US Helms-Burton Act tightens sanctions.
- ❏ **1998** Visit of Pope John Paul II.
- ❏ **1999** 40th anniversary of the revolution; leading moderate dissidents put on trial.

DEFENSE

 Compulsory military service

💲 $720m   ⬆ Up 1% in 1997

The military is well represented in the Politburo and the Council of Ministers.

CUBAN ARMED FORCES

🚜	1500 main battle tanks (T-34, T-54/T-55, T-62)	38,000 personnel
🚢	1 submarine, 2 frigates and 5 patrol boats	5,000 personnel
✈	130 combat aircraft (MiG 21/23/29); also 13 SAM missiles	10,000 personnel
	None	

From 1959 to the 1980s, Cuba's efficient military was one of the achievements of the revolution. Under Castro's brother Raúl, it succeeded in repelling the US-sponsored Bay of Pigs invasion in 1961, and saw effective action in Africa in the 1970s, preventing South Africa from taking control of Angola and Somalia from occupying the Ogaden region. Today, with communist regimes collapsed around the world, it has lost much of its prestige. Russia is still the main source of arms. A siege mentality associated with the US economic embargo keeps the military on the alert for perceived internal and external threats.

ECONOMICS

 Not available

📊 $18.3bn   💲 23.00 Cuban pesos

SCORE CARD

- ❏ WORLD GNP RANKING 72nd
- ❏ GNP PER CAPITA $1,650
- ❏ BALANCE OF PAYMENTS ....In deficit
- ❏ INFLATION...High
- ❏ UNEMPLOYMENT 8%

ECONOMIC PERFORMANCE INDICATOR

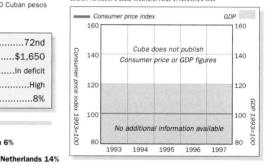

Consumer price index   GDP

Cuba does not publish Consumer price or GDP figures

No additional information available

was reimposed in 1986 after a brief flirtation with market opening. The collapse of the USSR meant the loss of some $5 billion in annual aid and led to a deep recession in the early 1990s.

A cautious adoption of some capitalist-style reforms in the mid-1990s, including the free use of the US dollar, stimulated the growth of a dollarized sector centered on tourism, which has attracted strong foreign investment. Tourism has replaced sugar as the motor of the economy and benefits some 160,000 self-employed and small businesses. Foreign companies are also involved in joint ventures in banking and the oil and gas sectors. There is a very large informal sector.

EXPORTS

Japan 6%   Spain 6%   Netherlands 14%   Canada 15%   Russia 17%   Other 42%

IMPORTS

China 7%   France 9%   Canada 10%   Russia 12%   Spain 20%   Other 42%

STRENGTHS

Buoyant tourism attracts strong foreign investment. Major exporter of sugar and nickel. Premium Cuban cigars. Strengthening banking sector.

WEAKNESSES

US trade embargo denies Cuba a major market and investment capital. Acute shortage of hard currency. Vulnerability of sugar and nickel to world price fluctuations. Difficult terms of trade and weak legal framework deters investment. Infrastructure is deficient. Shortages of fuel, fertilizers, spare parts and other inputs.

PROFILE

For a period after 1959, the state-controlled economy oscillated between concentration on sugar and stabs at industrialization. Total state control

CUBA : MAJOR BUSINESSES

Havana   Matahambre   Cardenas Bay   Ciego de Avila   Cienfuegos   Pinar del Rio   Isla de la Juventud   Santiago de Cuba

- 🛢 Oil refining
- 🏭 Manufacturing
- ↓ Sugar cane refining
- 💉 Pharmaceuticals
- Nickel mining
- Citrus fruits
- Cigars
- Oil

0   100 km
0   100 miles

RESOURCES Electric power 4.0m kw

108,701 tonnes

4.7m cattle,
1.5m pigs,
620,000 horses

18,766 b/d
(reserves
100,000,000 bbl)

Iron, nickel, cobalt,
chromite, gold,
manganese, oil

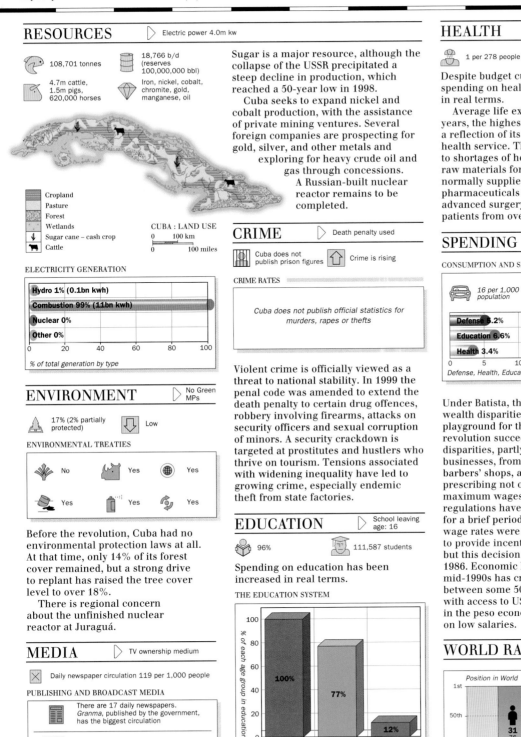

Cropland
Pasture
Forest
Wetlands
↓ Sugar cane – cash crop
🐄 Cattle

CUBA : LAND USE
0   100 km
0   100 miles

Sugar is a major resource, although the collapse of the USSR precipitated a steep decline in production, which reached a 50-year low in 1998.

Cuba seeks to expand nickel and cobalt production, with the assistance of private mining ventures. Several foreign companies are prospecting for gold, silver, and other metals and exploring for heavy crude oil and gas through concessions.

A Russian-built nuclear reactor remains to be completed.

ELECTRICITY GENERATION

Hydro 1% (0.1bn kwh)
Combustion 99% (11bn kwh)
Nuclear 0%
Other 0%

0   20   40   60   80   100
% of total generation by type

ENVIRONMENT ▷ No Green MPs

17% (2% partially protected)   Low

ENVIRONMENTAL TREATIES

No   Yes   Yes

Yes   Yes   Yes

Before the revolution, Cuba had no environmental protection laws at all. At that time, only 14% of its forest cover remained, but a strong drive to replant has raised the tree cover level to over 18%.

There is regional concern about the unfinished nuclear reactor at Juraguá.

MEDIA ▷ TV ownership medium

⊠ Daily newspaper circulation 119 per 1,000 people

PUBLISHING AND BROADCAST MEDIA

There are 17 daily newspapers. *Granma*, published by the government, has the biggest circulation

1 state-owned service

1 state-owned service

There is a catch-all anti-crime law which restricts and penalizes investigative reporting by independent journalists judged to be assisting US policy against Cuba.

CRIME ▷ Death penalty used

Cuba does not publish prison figures   ⬆ Crime is rising

CRIME RATES

Cuba does not publish official statistics for murders, rapes or thefts

Violent crime is officially viewed as a threat to national stability. In 1999 the penal code was amended to extend the death penalty to certain drug offences, robbery involving firearms, attacks on security officers and sexual corruption of minors. A security crackdown is targeted at prostitutes and hustlers who thrive on tourism. Tensions associated with widening inequality have led to growing crime, especially endemic theft from state factories.

EDUCATION ▷ School leaving age: 16

96%   111,587 students

Spending on education has been increased in real terms.

THE EDUCATION SYSTEM

100 ┤
 80 ┤
 60 ┤
 40 ┤ 100%
 20 ┤   77%
  0 ┤   12%
     Primary Secondary Tertiary

% of each age group in education

Education in Cuba combines academic with manual work, in line with Marxist-Leninist principles. The high priority given to education under Castro, which is reflected in the high literacy rate, is now being promoted to attract foreign investment in high-tech industries, particularly biotechnology.

HEALTH ▷ Welfare state health benefits

1 per 278 people   Heart disease, cancers, nutritional disorders

Despite budget cuts in recent years, spending on health has been increased in real terms.

Average life expectancy in Cuba is 76 years, the highest in Latin America, and a reflection of its efficient, countrywide health service. The US blockade has led to shortages of hospital equipment and raw materials for drugs. The latter are normally supplied by Havana's sizable pharmaceuticals industry. Cuba's advanced surgery techniques attract patients from overseas.

SPENDING ▷ GDP/cap. no increase

CONSUMPTION AND SPENDING

16 per 1,000 population   34 per 1,000 population

Defense 5.2%
Education 6.6%
Health 3.4%

0   5   10   15   20   25
Defense, Health, Education spending as % of GDP

Under Batista, there were huge wealth disparities and Cuba was a playground for the rich. The 1959 revolution succeeded in reducing the disparities, partly by taking over all businesses, from oil companies to barbers' shops, and partly by prescribing not only minimum but also maximum wages. Economic regulations have varied since then; for a brief period in 1985, different wage rates were allowed in an attempt to provide incentives for hard workers, but this decision was reversed in 1986. Economic liberalization in the mid-1990s has created a large gulf between some 50% of the population with access to US dollars and those in the peso economy subsisting on low salaries.

WORLD RANKING

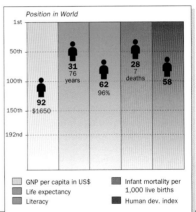

Position in World

1st
50th
100th
150th
192nd

92
$1650

31
76 years

62
96%

28
7 deaths

58

GNP per capita in US$
Life expectancy
Literacy

Infant mortality per 1,000 live births
Human dev. index

CYPRUS

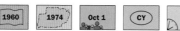

OFFICIAL NAME: Republic of Cyprus **CAPITAL:** Nicosia **POPULATION:** 766,000
CURRENCY: Cyprus pound (Turkish lira) **OFFICIAL LANGUAGES:** Greek and Turkish

EUROPE Europe

| 1960 | 1974 | Oct 1 | CY | +2 | +357 | .cy |

THE ISLAND OF CYPRUS, which rises from a central plateau to a high point at Mount Olympus, lies south of Turkey in the eastern Mediterranean. Cyprus was partitioned in 1974, following an invasion by Turkish troops. The south of the island is the Greek Cypriot Republic of Cyprus (Cyprus); the self-proclaimed Turkish Republic of Northern Cyprus (TRNC) is recognized only by Turkey.

CLIMATE ▷ Mediterranean

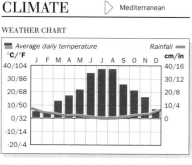

The climate is typically Mediterranean: summers are hot and dry and winters mild, though there is mountain snow.

TRANSPORTATION ▷ Drive on left

🛬 **Larnaka** 4.04m passengers

⚓ 1,650 ships 23.65m grt

THE TRANSPORTATION NETWORK

| 5,781 km (3,592 miles) | 178 km (111 miles) |
| None | None |

Travel between the two zones is impeded. The south regards the airport at Ercan as an illegal point of entry.

TOURISM ▷ Visitors : population 2.7:1

🧳 2.1m visitors

⬇ Down 2% 1995–1997

MAIN TOURIST ARRIVALS

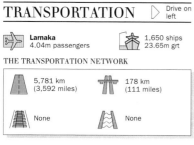

| UK 47% |
| Germany 8% |
| Switzerland 5% |
| Other 40% |

0 10 20 30 40 50 60
% of total arrivals

There are now over two million visitors a year to Cyprus, which is popular with tourists from the former Soviet bloc. Tourism expanded rapidly in the 1980s and more recently in the north. Ecotourism is promoted on the Akamas peninsula in the north.

PEOPLE ▷ Pop. density medium

👤 Greek, Turkish

👥 84/km² (218/mi²)

THE URBAN/RURAL POPULATION SPLIT

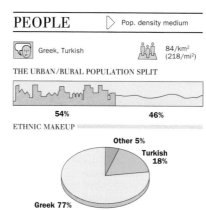

54% 46%

ETHNIC MAKEUP

Other 5%
Turkish 18%
Greek 77%

Cyprus's Greek majority, who make up 77% of the population, are Christian. The 18% Turkish minority are Muslim. Some are the descendants of Turks who settled on the island from the 16th century, under the rule of the Ottoman Empire. Turkish Cypriots have been isolated following the 1974 partitioning, since when they have been officially recognized only by Turkey, which has resettled thousands of mainland Turks on the island. Both communities have suffered great upheavals: in 1974, 200,000 Greek Cypriots were forced to flee to the south, while 65,000 Turkish Cypriots fled in the other direction. Wage levels are on average three times higher in the south, where east European contract labor is brought in to staff the hotel industry. Unemployment levels in the north, meanwhile, are rising.

The 2nd-century theater at the ruined city of Curium, 14 km (19 miles) west of Limassol. Curium was a flourishing Mycenaean colony before 1100 BCE.

POLITICS ▷ Multiparty elections

1996/2001 Cyprus
1998/2003 TRNC

President Glafcos Clerides (Cyprus) President Rauf Denktash (TRNC)

AT THE LAST ELECTION

House of Representatives 80 members

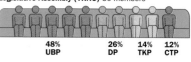

3% KED

30% TC 25% DISY 24% AKEL 12% DIKO 6% EDEK

UBP = National Unity Party **DP** = Democratic Party
TKP = Social Welfare Party **CTP** = Republican Turkish Party
TC = Reserved for Turkish Cypriots **DISY** = Democratic Rally **AKEL** = Progressive Party of the Working People
DIKO = Democratic Party **EDEK** = Socialist Party of Cyprus
KED = Movement of Free Democrats

The 24 seats reserved for Turkish Cypriots have not been occupied since 1964.

Legislative Assembly (TRNC) 50 members

48% UBP 26% DP 14% TKP 12% CTP

The UN-backed proposal of a two-zoned federation for Cyprus is supported by Greek and Turkish governments, eager to solve the dispute. Under this plan, each community would have its own territory but share a number of government functions. TRNC president Rauf Denktash, mindful of the Greek Cypriots' repression of the Turks prior to 1974, is unwilling to accept plans that do not ensure full sovereignty and equality for Turks. Greek Cypriots fear the plan would lead to domination of their affairs by the Turkish minority, able to veto government decisions.

WORLD AFFAIRS ▷ Joined UN in 1960

| CE | Comm | IBRD | NAM | OSCE |

The presence of 1,250 UN troops since 1974, staffing the "Green Line" (only the Middle East and Kashmir have longer-standing peacekeeping forces), costs $45 million a year. Only Turkey recognizes the TRNC. Cyprus applied to join the EU in 1990 and formal negotiations opened in March 1998.

AID ▷ Recipient

💲 $49m (receipts) (Cyprus)

⬆ Up 63% 1996–1997 (Cyprus)

Cyprus receives aid from international agencies, as well as from the EU and individual countries such as the UK. The TRNC is dependent on aid from Turkey of more than $60 million a year.

CYPRUS

Total Land Area :
9251 sq. km
(3572 sq. miles)

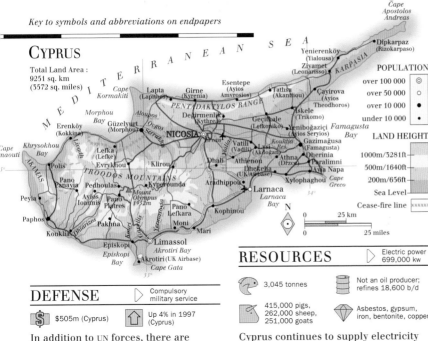

POPULATION

over 100 000	◎
over 50 000	○
over 10 000	●
under 10 000	•

LAND HEIGHT

1000m/3281ft
500m/1640ft
200m/656ft
Sea Level

Cease-fire line ✕✕✕✕✕

0 ___ 25 km
0 ___ 25 miles

DEFENSE

▷ Compulsory military service

💲 $505m (Cyprus)

⬆ Up 4% in 1997 (Cyprus)

In addition to UN forces, there are Greek Cypriot, Turkish Cypriot, Greek, and Turkish troops posted along the buffer zone that divides the island. Both the 10,000-strong Greek Cypriot and 4,500-strong Turkish Cypriot armies rely heavily on conscripts.

ECONOMICS

▷ Inflation 3.8% p.a. (1986–1997)

📊 $7.5bn (Cyprus)

💲 0.53–0.50 Cyprus £

SCORE CARD

❑ WORLD GNP RANKING	92nd
❑ GNP PER CAPITA	$9,400
❑ BALANCE OF PAYMENTS	$–213m
❑ INFLATION	3.6%
❑ UNEMPLOYMENT	3%

STRENGTHS

Tourism: accounts for 20% of GDP. Manufacturing sector and provision of services to Middle Eastern countries.

WEAKNESSES

Tourism damaged by Gulf crisis and "Green Line" tensions. Lack of foreign investment in TRNC. Collapse of Asil Nadir's business empire – employer of 12% of Turkish Cypriots.

EXPORTS

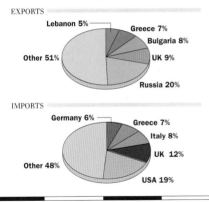

Lebanon 5%
Greece 7%
Bulgaria 8%
Other 51%
UK 9%
Russia 20%

IMPORTS

Germany 6%
Greece 7%
Italy 8%
Other 48%
UK 12%
USA 19%

RESOURCES

▷ Electric power 699,000 kw

 3,045 tonnes

Not an oil producer; refines 18,600 b/d

415,000 pigs, 262,000 sheep, 251,000 goats

Asbestos, gypsum, iron, bentonite, copper

Cyprus continues to supply electricity to TRNC, although it has not been paid for this. An oil refinery has been built by the Greek Cypriot government, BP Amoco, Mobil, and a local company. Water is a scarce resource.

ENVIRONMENT

▷ No green MPs

🔺 0.2% partially protected

Not available

Protection from the threat of development by landholders, including the Orthodox Church, of the 155 square kilometers (60 square miles) of the Akamas peninsula is a major project. This new national park has an unusual variety of wildlife, and contains the bay where the rare green turtle breeds.

MEDIA

▷ TV ownership high

Daily newspaper circulation 111 per 1,000 people

PUBLISHING AND BROADCAST MEDIA

There are 9 daily newspapers. The largest is *Fileleftheros* and others include *Charavgi*, *Simerini* and *Alithia*

1 state-controlled, 1 independent service

1 state-controlled, 9 independent stations

Cyprus's press is lively and tends to be highly politicized. The radio and TV services for British troops based in Cyprus are also popular.

CRIME

▷ Death penalty not used

202 prisoners

⬆ Up 6% from 1992–1996

Crime, including ethnic violence, is not a major problem. Palestinian-linked terrorism has declined. The rape and killing of a Danish tourist by three British soldiers caused outrage, and led Cypriots to question the UK military presence.

CHRONOLOGY

Cyprus came, in turn, under the domination of Egypt, Greece, the Byzantines, the Ottomans and the UK.

- ❑ **1960** Independence from UK.
- ❑ **1963** Turkish Cypriots abandon parliament.
- ❑ **1974** President Makarios deposed by Greek military junta. Turkey invades. Partition.
- ❑ **1983** Self-proclamation of TRNC.
- ❑ **1998** Talks on EU membership start.

EDUCATION

▷ School leaving age: 15

📖 96%

🎓 9,982 students

Education is free and compulsory up to the age of 15. Many Greek Cypriots go to university abroad.

HEALTH

▷ Welfare state health benefits

1 per 433 people

Heart diseases, accidents, cancers

Health care is more advanced in the south; sophisticated surgery is carried out at Lefkosia General Hospital.

SPENDING

▷ GDP/cap. no increase

CONSUMPTION AND SPENDING

🚗 334 per 1,000 population

📞 474 per 1,000 population

Defense 5.8%	
Education 4.4%	
Health 4.2%	

0   5   10   15   20   25

Defense, Health, Education spending as % of GDP

The average income per capita in the southern part of Cyprus is higher than in Greece and Portugal, but slightly lower than that in Spain.

WORLD RANKING

Position in World

1st
50th
100th
150th
192nd

37 — $9400
8 — 78 years
62 — 96%
35 — 8 deaths
26

⬛ GNP per capita in US$	⬛ Infant mortality per 1,000 live births
⬛ Life expectancy	
⬛ Literacy	⬛ Human dev. index

CZECH REPUBLIC

OFFICIAL NAME: Czech Republic **CAPITAL:** Prague
POPULATION: 10.2 million **CURRENCY:** Czech koruna **OFFICIAL LANGUAGE:** Czech

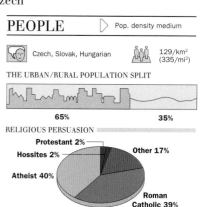

EUROPE

1993	1993	Oct 28	CZ	+1	+420	.cz

LANDLOCKED IN EASTERN Europe, the Czech Republic comprises Bohemia and Moravia and was formerly part of Czechoslovakia. In 1989, Czechoslovakia's "Velvet Revolution" led to the fall of the communist regime. Free elections followed in 1990. In 1993, the Czech Republic and Slovakia peacefully dissolved their federal union to become two independent states.

CLIMATE ▷ Continental

WEATHER CHART

- Average daily temperature
- Rainfall

The Czech climate is more moderate than that of Slovakia, though easterly winds bring low temperatures in winter.

TRANSPORTATION ▷ Drive on right

Ruzyné, Prague
4.6m passengers

18 ships
228,000 grt

THE TRANSPORTATION NETWORK

55,100 km (34,200 miles)	423 km (263 miles)
9,430 km (5,860 miles)	303 km (188 miles)

New rail links and expressways to Germany are being built. Skoda and Volkswagen have formed a joint venture.

TOURISM ▷ Visitors : population 1.7:1

17m visitors

Up 9% 1995–1997

MAIN TOURIST ARRIVALS

- Germany 43%
- Austria 8%
- Italy 7%
- Other 42%

% of total arrivals

Revenues from the expansion of tourism are an invaluable source of foreign earnings for the Czech economy. In 1995, 15,500,000 tourists, mainly Germans, visited the country, revenues from tourism reaching $2.6 billion in that year. Prague, which rivals Paris as the most beautiful capital in Europe, is visited by most tourists. Skiing in the Carpathian Mountains and the many spa towns are the other main attractions.

CZECH REPUBLIC

Total Land Area : 78 864 sq. km (30 449 sq. miles)

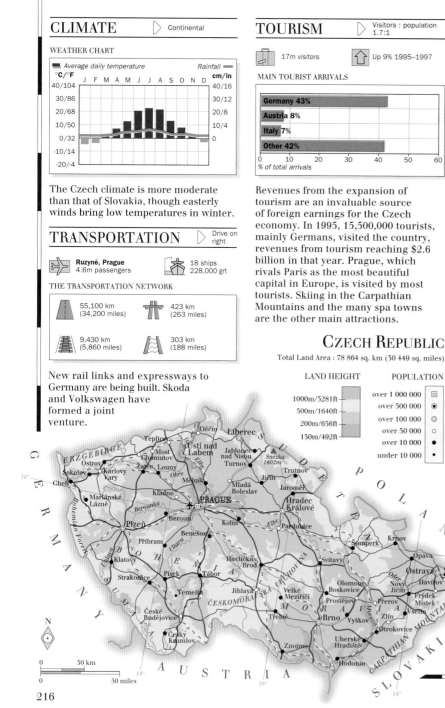

LAND HEIGHT	
1000m/3281ft	
500m/1640ft	
200m/656ft	
150m/492ft	

POPULATION	
over 1 000 000	
over 500 000	
over 100 000	
over 50 000	
over 10 000	
under 10 000	

PEOPLE ▷ Pop. density medium

Czech, Slovak, Hungarian

129/km²
(335/mi²)

THE URBAN/RURAL POPULATION SPLIT

65% 35%

RELIGIOUS PERSUASION

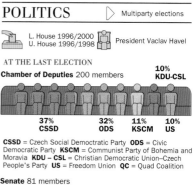

- Protestant 2%
- Hossites 2%
- Atheist 40%
- Other 17%
- Roman Catholic 39%

Czechs make up over 80% of the population, while the next largest group is of Moravians. Some 300,000 Slovaks were left in the country after partition, but dual citizenship is now permitted. Ethnic tensions are few, but Romanian immigrants face discrimination. A new commercial elite is emerging alongside ex-communist entrepreneurs. Divorce rates are high.

POLITICS ▷ Multiparty elections

L. House 1996/2000
U. House 1996/1998

President Vaclav Havel

AT THE LAST ELECTION

Chamber of Deputies 200 members

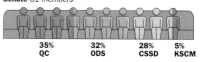

37% CSSD	32% ODS	11% KSCM	10% US	10% KDU-CSL

CSSD = Czech Social Democratic Party **ODS** = Civic Democratic Party **KSCM** = Communist Party of Bohemia and Moravia **KDU–CSL** = Christian Democratic Union–Czech People's Party **US** = Freedom Union **QC** = Quad Coalition

Senate 81 members

35% QC	32% ODS	28% CSSD	5% KSCM

The Quad Coalition comprises the Christian Democratic Union Czech People's Party (KDU-CSL), the Freedom Union (US), the Civic Democratic Alliance (ODA), and the Democratic Union (DEU).

In 1990, Civic Forum won free elections and dissident playwright Vaclav Havel became president. By 1991, Civic Forum had split and Vaclav Klaus's ODS was the dominant party. It continued with privatization and economic reforms, but lost its overall majority in the 1996 elections. Klaus resigned in 1997 amid a scandal over party funding and was replaced by Josef Tosovsky. Milos Zeman formed a new social democrat-led government after elections in June 1998.

C

WORLD AFFAIRS ▷ Joined UN in 1993

In March 1998 the Czech Republic was one of six countries to begin formal negotiations on EU membership.

In May 1998 it was invited, with Hungary and Poland, to join NATO. Good relations with Germany are a priority. A 1997 joint declaration resolved the issue of property restitution for Germans expelled in 1945.

AID ▷ Recipient

$ 107m (receipts) Down 12% 1996–1997

Aid, totaling $122 million in 1996, is crucial for modernizing infrastructure such as telecommunications.

DEFENSE ▷ Compulsory military service

$ $987m Down 19% in 1997

The split with Slovakia left an army too large and expensive for the new Czech state. In 1994, plans to cut the military by 20,000 were approved. Professional soldiers with a communist past were the first to go. Czech armaments exports were worth $183 million in 1997, making it the world's 12th-largest exporter.

ECONOMICS ▷ Inflation 11.5% p.a. (1985–1996)

$54bn 34.67–30.03 Czech koruny

SCORE CARD

❏ World GNP Ranking	48th
❏ GNP per Capita	$5,240
❏ Balance of Payments	$–3.2bn
❏ Inflation	8.4%
❏ Unemployment	5%

STRENGTHS
Skilled industrial labor force. Good industrial base. Speed of privatization of state industries. Attractive to German investors. Draw of Prague for tourists.

WEAKNESSES
Lack of diversification in sectors likely to attract overseas investment. Limited restructuring. Rising unemployment. Currency crisis and inflation were serious threats to stability in 1997.

EXPORTS
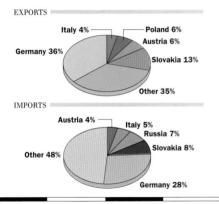
Italy 4% / Poland 6% / Austria 6% / Germany 36% / Slovakia 13% / Other 35%

IMPORTS
Austria 4% / Italy 5% / Russia 7% / Slovakia 8% / Other 48% / Germany 28%

RESOURCES ▷ Electric power 13.9m kw

24,000 tonnes 1,644 b/d

4m pigs, 1.7m cattle, 94,000 sheep Oil, natural gas, copper, lead, zinc, coal

Copper, lead, zinc, and coal are the chief resources. The government is aiming to phase out the worst-polluting coal-fired power stations. Opposition to a planned 2,000mw Soviet-designed nuclear power station at Temelin has delayed its completion.

ENVIRONMENT ▷ No Green MPs

16% Medium

Pollution from the power, chemical and cement industries and the new Temelin nuclear plant are key concerns.

MEDIA ▷ TV ownership high

Daily newspaper circulation 256 per 1,000 people

PUBLISHING AND BROADCAST MEDIA

There are 21 daily newspapers. *Mladá Fronta Dnes* has the largest circulation

2 state-owned, 2 independent services 1 state owned, 60 independent services

Czech media have grown rapidly and the press has flourished. A freedom of information act was passed in 1999.

CRIME ▷ Death penalty not used

19,508 prisoners Crime is rising

While narcotics trading is illegal, possession is not. In 1998, 130 people were found guilty of racist crimes.

EDUCATION ▷ School leaving age: 15

99% 191,604 students

Schooling has reverted to the pre-1945 system. Charles University in Prague was founded in the 13th century.

HEALTH ▷ No welfare state health benefits

1 per 345 people Cancers, heart and cerebrovascular diseases, accidents

Health care expenditure as a share of GDP has increased by 30% since 1990. Wealthy Czechs travel to Germany for complex operations.

The Vltava River in Prague. Over 15 million tourists, mainly from Europe and the USA, now visit Prague each year.

CHRONOLOGY

The Republic of Czechoslovakia (until then part of the Austro-Hungarian empire) was established in 1918; it was invaded by Hitler in 1939.

- ❏ **1968** "Prague Spring." Invasion by Warsaw Pact countries.
- ❏ **1989** "Velvet Revolution."
- ❏ **1990** Free legislative elections; Vaclav Havel president.
- ❏ **1993** Division into Czech Republic and Slovakia.
- ❏ **1998** Invited to join NATO; EU membership negotiations start.

SPENDING ▷ GDP/cap. no increase

CONSUMPTION AND SPENDING

344 per 1,000 population 318 per 1,000 population

Defense 2.2% / Education 6.1% / Health 5.9%
Defense, Health, Education spending as % of GDP

A new entrepreneurial class has emerged since the "Velvet Revolution" in 1989. Almost all Czechs have shares in privatized enterprises.

WORLD RANKING

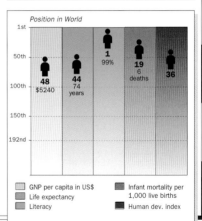
Position in World
48 $5240 / 44 74 years / 1 99% / 19 6 deaths / 36

GNP per capita in US$ / Life expectancy / Literacy / Infant mortality per 1,000 live births / Human dev. index

DENMARK

OFFICIAL NAME: Kingdom of Denmark **CAPITAL:** Copenhagen
POPULATION: 5.3 million **CURRENCY:** Danish krone **OFFICIAL LANGUAGE:** Danish

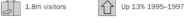

EUROPE

| 950 | 1920 | April 16 | DK | +1 | +45 | .dk |

THE MOST SOUTHERLY COUNTRY in Scandanavia, Denmark occupies the Jutland peninsula, the islands of Sjælland, Fyn, Lolland and Falster, and more than 400 smaller islands. Its terrain is among the flattest in the world. The Faeroe Islands and Greenland in the North Atlantic are self-governing associated territories. Politically, Denmark is stable, despite a preponderance of minority governments since 1945. It possesses a long liberal tradition and was one of the first countries to establish a welfare system, in the 1930s.

TOURISM

Visitors : population 1:2.9

1.8m visitors

Up 13% 1995–1997

MAIN TOURIST ARRIVALS

Germany 47%
Sweden 7%
Norway 4%
Netherlands 3%
UK 1%
Other 38%
% of total arrivals

Denmark is a popular destination for Scandinavian, German, and Dutch tourists. The principal attractions are Copenhagen – with its Tivoli Gardens and fine 18th-century architecture – Legoland, the countryside, and seaside resorts. Greenland attracts wildlife tourists.

CLIMATE

Maritime

WEATHER CHART

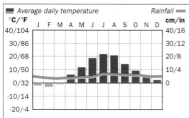

Denmark's temperate, damp climate is one of the keys to its agricultural success. The Faeroes are windy, foggy and cool. Greenland's climate ranges north–south from arctic to sub-arctic.

TRANSPORTATION

Drive on right

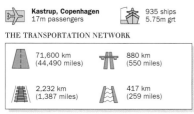

Kastrup, Copenhagen
17m passengers

935 ships
5.75m grt

THE TRANSPORTATION NETWORK

| 71,600 km (44,490 miles) | 880 km (550 miles) |
| 2,232 km (1,387 miles) | 417 km (259 miles) |

There is an extensive, well-integrated transportation network of bus, rail and ferry services. State-owned companies predominate, although privatization of some ferry and rail services have been mooted. Denmark wishes to reduce significant state transport subsidies. A few private companies operate in the Faeroes and Greenland with state support.

Major new construction projects focus on bridge and tunnel links, such as the Storebælt project connecting the islands of Fyn and Sjælland. A 16-km (10-mile) Øresund road and rail link by bridge and tunnel connecting Copenhagen and Malmö in Sweden is expected to open in 1999. Copenhagen's new Metro light railway system is also nearly completed.

The island of Fyn, like the rest of Denmark, is flat and depends on coastal defences to prevent flooding by the sea.

DENMARK

Total Land Area : 43 070 sq. km
(16 629 sq. miles)

POPULATION

over 1 000 000
over 100 000
over 10 000
under 10 000

LAND HEIGHT

175m/574ft
Sea Level
Ferry link

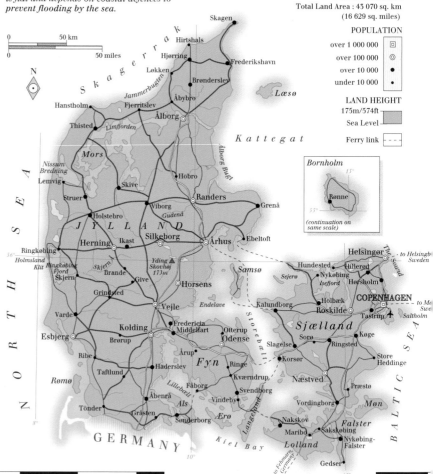

D

D

PEEOPLE ▷ Pop. density medium

Danish | 125/km² (324/mi²)

THE URBAN/RURAL POPULATION SPLIT

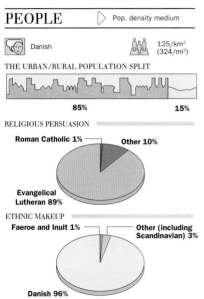

85%   15%

RELIGIOUS PERSUASION

Roman Catholic 1% — Other 10%
Evangelical Lutheran 89%

ETHNIC MAKEUP

Faeroe and Inuit 1% — Other (including Scandinavian) 3%
Danish 96%

Danish society is homogeneous. Out of a population of 5.3 million, just 200,000 are foreign citizens, mainly from other Scandinavian or EU states. The most visible minority groups are the Inuit, Greenland's indigenous inhabitants, and the Turkish community. Rising unemployment has engendered some ethnic tension, although racially motivated attacks are still rare.

Denmark has undergone profound social changes over the last 20 years. The role of women has been transformed. Helped by Denmark's extensive social and educational provision, 76% of women now work in part-time or full-time jobs. Denmark provides the best state child support in Europe. Almost 50% of children under two and 67% of three- to six-year-olds are in day nurseries, compared with under 30% in the 1970s.

Less than half the population lives in a nuclear family, partly due to the high divorce rate. Marriage is also becoming less common; almost 40% of children are brought up by unmarried couples or single parents. Cohabiting couples now have the same legal rights as those who are married. In 1990, Denmark became the first country to allow registered partnerships between homosexual couples, effectively granting them the same legal married status as heterosexuals.

POPULATION AGE BREAKDOWN

Female	Age	Male
2.6%	81–100	1.3%
8.6%	61–80	7.2%
13.4%	41–60	13.7%
14.5%	21–40	15.2%
11.5%	0–20	12%

% of population by age group

POLITICS ▷ Multiparty elections

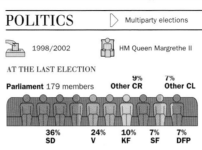

1998/2002 | HM Queen Margrethe II

AT THE LAST ELECTION

Parliament 179 members

Other CR 9%   Other CL 7%

36% SD   24% V   10% KF   7% SF   7% DFP

SD = Social Democrats   **V** = Liberal Party
KF = Conservative People's Party   **Other CR** = Other Centre Right   **SF** = Socialist People's Party   **Other CL** = Other Centre Left   **DFP** = Danish People's Party
Greenland and the Faeroe Islands send 4 members to the Folketing.

Denmark is a constitutional monarchy and a multiparty democracy. The associated territories of Greenland and the Faeroe Islands have home rule.

MAIN POLITICAL ISSUES
Relations with the EU
In recent years, Denmark's left-of-center parties have been suspicious of further EU integration, as was shown by the stir caused by ratification of the Maastricht Treaty in 1992. Approved by parliament, it was rejected in a referendum. Voters objected to the proposed monetary union, common defense force and local election voting rights for European citizens living in Denmark. Later that year an EU summit agreed to allow Denmark to opt out of monetary union, defense and European citizenship. A new referendum in 1993 finally approved the Treaty. Denmark did not introduce the euro in 1999, but a 1998 referendum did approve the Amsterdam Treaty (successor to the Maastricht Treaty).

Immigration
In what many saw as a vindication of Danish liberal traditions, the then Prime Minister Poul Schlüter was

Poul Nyrup Rasmussen, prime minister and SD leader.

Queen Margrethe, who succeeded to the throne in 1972.

forced to resign in 1993 over the "Tamilgate" affair. A judicial inquiry ruled that he had falsely denied in parliament that immigration officials were hindering the entry of the families of Tamil workers resident in Denmark. The position and integration into society of immigrants and refugees, who account for only 4.5% of the population, continues to be a controversial issue. The new far-right, anti-immigrant Danish People's Party won 13 seats in the March 1998 general election.

PROFILE
Denmark's intricate proportional electoral system ensures that parliament truly reflects voters' wishes, but also tends to lead to minority governments. SD governments were predominant until 1982. A decade of Conservative–Liberal rule followed. In 1993, the SD regained power, at the head of a center-left coalition. Although the coalition lost ground in the 1994 elections, it continued to lead a minority government coalition, with the prime minister Poul Nyrup Rasmussen narrowly winning a fresh term of office in the March 1998 general election. Policy differences between the two main political groups are few.

WORLD AFFAIRS ▷ Joined UN in 1945

CE | EU | NATO | OECD | OSCE

Relations with the rest of Europe are the major foreign policy concern, notably the issue of a common defense policy and monetary union. Denmark did not introduce the euro from January 1999, but the krone is pegged to the euro and economic policies follow those of the 11 participating states. Promoting economic ties with Norway, Sweden, and Finland is a priority, as are improved links with former Eastern bloc states, especially those on the Baltic – not least to assist pollution reduction, a serious concern. The country is also strongly committed to Third-World development, especially in Africa.

CHRONOLOGY
Founded in the 10th century, Denmark is Europe's oldest monarchy. It was the dominant Baltic power until the 17th century, when it was eclipsed by Sweden.

❑ **1815** Denmark forced to cede Norway to Swedish rule.
❑ **1849** First democratic constitution.
❑ **1864** Denmark forced to cede provinces of Schleswig and Holstein after losing war with Prussia.
❑ **1914–1918** Denmark neutral in World War I.
❑ **1915** Universal adult suffrage introduced. Rise of SD.
❑ **1920** Northern Schleswig votes to return to Danish rule.
❑ **1929** First full SD government ▷

D

CHRONOLOGY *continued*

takes power under Thorvald Stauning.

- ❑ **1930s** Implementation of advanced social welfare legislation and other liberal reforms under SD.
- ❑ **1939** Outbreak of World War II; Denmark reaffirms neutrality.
- ❑ **1940** Nazi occupation. National coalition government formed.
- ❑ **1943** Danish Resistance successes lead Nazis to take full control.
- ❑ **1944** Iceland declares independence from Denmark.
- ❑ **1945** Denmark recognizes Icelandic independence. After defeat of Nazi Germany, SD leads postwar coalition governments.
- ❑ **1948** Faeroe Islands granted home rule.
- ❑ **1952** Founder member of Nordic Council.
- ❑ **1953** Constitution reformed; single-chamber, proportionally elected parliament created.
- ❑ **1959** Denmark joins the European Free Trade Association(EFTA).
- ❑ **1973** Denmark joins EC.
- ❑ **1979** Greenland granted home rule.
- ❑ **1975–1982** SD's Anker Jorgensen heads series of coalitions; elections in 1977, 1979 and 1981. Final coalition collapses over economic policy differences.
- ❑ **1982** Poul Schlüter first Conservative prime minister since 1894.
- ❑ **1992** Referendum rejects Maastricht Treaty on European Union.
- ❑ **1993** Schlüter resigns over "Tamilgate" scandal. Center-left government led by Poul Nyrup Rasmussen. Danish voters ratify revised Maastricht Treaty. Result greeted with demonstrations.
- ❑ **1994** General election; SD-led minority coalition under Rasmussen returned to power.
- ❑ **1998** General election narrowly reelects Rasmussen.

AID

 Donor

💲 $1.6bn (donations) ⬔ Not applicable

In GNP terms, Denmark is one of the world's leading aid donors, since 1992 contributing an annual average of 1%. It supports both economic and social development projects and policy reforms. Aid is an important political issue; the current debate is over its use as a tool to promote democracy.

Denmark provides aid to Asia and Latin America, but its closest ties are with Africa. Tanzania is the largest single aid recipient. Denmark has also provided considerable support to the other southern African SADC states.

DEFENSE

 Compulsory military service

💲 $2.8bn   ⬇ Down 11% in 1997

Denmark was neutral until 1945. Apart from NATO commitments, defense has a low priority; spending is currently less than 2% of GDP (NATO average 2.2%). Denmark provides troops for the NATO-led forces in former Yugoslavia and observers for other UN peacekeeping operations. One-quarter of its 32,100 armed forces are conscripts. Denmark has observer status at the WEU.

DANISH ARMED FORCES

337 main battle tanks (230 *Leopard* 1A5, 54 *Centurion*, 53 M-41DK1)	22,900 personnel
5 submarines, 3 frigates and 41 patrol boats	3,700 personnel
69 combat aircraft (F-16A/B)	5,500 personnel
None	

ECONOMICS

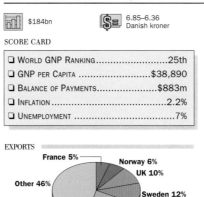 Inflation 3.1% p.a. (1985–1996)

📊 $184bn   💲 6.85–6.36 Danish kroner

SCORE CARD

- ❑ WORLD GNP RANKING.........................25th
- ❑ GNP PER CAPITA $38,890
- ❑ BALANCE OF PAYMENTS.....................$883m
- ❑ INFLATION 2.2%
- ❑ UNEMPLOYMENT 7%

EXPORTS

France 5%
Norway 6%
UK 10%
Other 46%
Sweden 12%
Germany 21%

IMPORTS

France 6%
UK 8%
Netherlands 8%
Other 44%
Sweden 13%
Germany 21%

STRENGTHS

Low inflation. Unemployment halved in four years to 7% (1998). 1995–1998 GDP growth of 3%. Large gas and oil reserves. Strong high-tech, high-profit manufacturing sector. Skilled workforce.

WEAKNESSES

Heavy tax burden. Weakening competitiveness and growing current-account deficit. Strong krone harms exports. Frequent changes of minority governments.

PROFILE

Denmark's mix of a large state sector and a private sector has been successful. At $33,230, GDP per capita is one of the highest among the OECD countries.

A new minority conservative coalition in the 1980s introduced major policy changes. A stable exchange rate policy and tighter budget controls aimed to reduce inflation and reverse the balance-of-payments deficit. Real GNP per capita grew by 2.1% a year in

ECONOMIC PERFORMANCE INDICATOR

Consumer price index   GDP

1981–1991. The balance of payments went into surplus and inflation fell to 2%. After 1991, recession in Europe led to slower growth. An economic upturn since 1993, when a center-left coalition came to power, was first led by private consumption and then buoyed by increased exports and investment.

Voters have refused to accept European monetary union. Denmark did not therefore introduce the euro from January 1999. However, it met the economic convergence criteria, the krone is pegged to the euro, and economic policies follow those of the 11 EU participating states.

DENMARK : MAJOR BUSINESSES

Hirtshals 🐟
Ålborg 🐖⚙
Århus 🐖⚙
Copenhagen 🔧⚗⚙🍾🧪⚗🏢⚙
Esbjerg 🐟⚓
Korsar 🐖⚙
Fredericia 🧵🐖
Odense 🐖⚙

🧪 Oil & gas
🍾 Brewing
🧵 Textiles
⚗ Chemicals
🐖 Agribusiness
🔧 Electronics
⚓ Transport services
⚙ Light engineering
🏢 Trading center
🐟 Fish processing

0   100 km
0   100 miles

RESOURCES
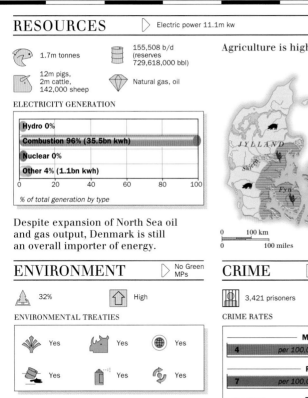

▷ Electric power 11.1m kw

1.7m tonnes

12m pigs,
2m cattle,
142,000 sheep

155,508 b/d
(reserves
729,618,000 bbl)

Natural gas, oil

ELECTRICITY GENERATION

Hydro 0%

Combustion 96% (35.5bn kwh)

Nuclear 0%

Other 4% (1.1bn kwh)

| 0 | 20 | 40 | 60 | 80 | 100 |

% of total generation by type

Despite expansion of North Sea oil
and gas output, Denmark is still
an overall importer of energy.

ENVIRONMENT
▷ No Green MPs

32%　　　　　High

ENVIRONMENTAL TREATIES

Yes　　　Yes　　　Yes

Yes　　　Yes　　　Yes

Popular and governmental concern for
the environment has resulted in many
regulations, including those aimed at
reducing ozone-destroying emissions
and water pollution, among the strictest
in Europe. Fears that they may be
eroded have led to ambivalence toward
the EU. In 1993, Denmark persuaded
the EU to locate its new Environmental
Agency in Copenhagen. It hopes to
extend its own standards to the rest of
Europe and met a year early its 2000
target of recycling 54% of all waste.

MEDIA
▷ TV ownership high

Daily newspaper circulation 311 per 1,000 people

PUBLISHING AND BROADCAST MEDIA

There are 37 daily newspapers, including
BT, Politiken, Ekstra Bladet and
Berlingske Tidende

1 state-owned, 50
independent local services

1 state-owned, 300
independent services

The media has a long history of
political independence, and objectivity
is prized. Most of the press has a
political viewpoint, but expression of
this is largely limited to editorials.
The tone of both TV and the press is
serious; Denmark does not have a
scandal-mongering tabloid press as
found in the USA, the UK and Germany.
Invasion of privacy laws are strict.

Agriculture is highly efficient.
Denmark is the
world's biggest
exporter of
pork.

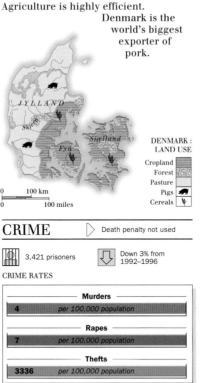

| 0 | 100 km |
| 0 | 100 miles |

DENMARK :
LAND USE

Cropland
Forest
Pasture
Pigs
Cereals

CRIME
▷ Death penalty not used

3,421 prisoners

Down 3% from
1992–1996

CRIME RATES

Murders
4 — per 100,000 population

Rapes
7 — per 100,000 population

Thefts
3336 — per 100,000 population

The main concern is that Mafia-style
organized crime could be imported
from eastern Europe. Computer
hacking, drug-trafficking and rival
motor cycle gangs are also problems.

EDUCATION
▷ School leaving age: 16

99%　　　　166,545 students

Of total government expenditure more
than 12% is spent on education.

THE EDUCATION SYSTEM
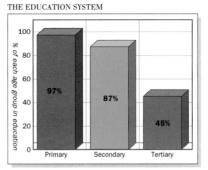

% of each age group in education

Primary 97%
Secondary 87%
Tertiary 45%

The average educational level is
high, in part reflecting the need for
a skilled workforce. Formal
schooling begins at age seven and is
mandatory for nine years. However,
most children receive pre-school
education and over 90% of pupils
go on at the age of 16 to further
academic or vocational training.

HEALTH
▷ Welfare state health benefits

1 per 345 people

Heart diseases,
cancers, accidents

Denmark was one of the first countries
to introduce a state social welfare
system. The national health service,
which still provides free treatment for
almost everything,
is the main reason for Denmark's
high taxation rate. Of total government
expenditure, some 9% is spent
on health, but any attempts to reduce
expenditure will meet with strong
opposition. Repeated surveys show
that most Danes prefer their system
to those which are based on private
health insurance.

SPENDING
▷ GDP/cap. no increase

CONSUMPTION AND SPENDING
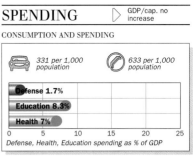

331 per 1,000
population

633 per 1,000
population

Defense 1.7%
Education 8.3%
Health 7%

| 0 | 5 | 10 | 15 | 20 | 25 |

Defense, Health, Education spending as % of GDP

Most Danes are comfortably off.
Income distribution is more even
than in many Western countries and
social mobility is high. Free higher
education means that access to the
professions is more a question of
ability than wealth or connections.
Many top industrialists have made
their fortunes within the last
30 years, but Denmark is still one
of the world's most egalitarian
societies. The generous social
security system means that Danes
suffer little from social deprivation.
Rasmussen's government has
created more kindergarten places
and increased time off for those
with young children. Refugees
and recent immigrants are most the
disadvantaged.

WORLD RANKING
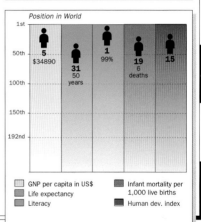

Position in World

1st
50th
100th
150th
192nd

5
$34890

31
50
years

1
99%

19
6
deaths

15

GNP per capita in US$
Life expectancy
Literacy

Infant mortality per
1,000 live births
Human dev. index

See also OVERSEAS TERRITORIES *p.640*　221

D

DJIBOUTI

EAST AFRICA

OFFICIAL NAME: Republic of Djibouti   CAPITAL: Djibouti
POPULATION: 652,000   CURRENCY: Djibouti franc   OFFICIAL LANGUAGES: Arabic and French

| 1977 | 1977 | June 27 | DJI | +3 | +253 | .dj |

A CITY STATE WITH a desert hinterland, Djibouti lies in northeast Africa on the strait linking the Red Sea and the Indian Ocean. Known from 1967 as the French Territory of the Afars and Issas, Djibouti became independent in 1977. Its economy relies on the port, the railroad to Addis Ababa, and French aid. A guerrilla war which erupted in 1991 as a result of tension between the Issas in the south and the Afars in the north has largely been resolved.

CLIMATE
▷ Hot desert

WEATHER CHART

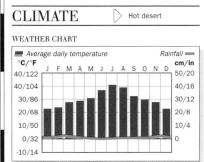

Despite extremely low rainfall, the monsoon season is characterized by very humid conditions. Even locals find the June to August heat hard to bear.

TRANSPORTATION
▷ Drive on right

Ambouli Intl, Djibouti

2 ships
4,800 grt

THE TRANSPORTATION NETWORK

281 km (175 miles)		None	
106 km (66 miles)		None	

Djibouti's port, created by the French in the 19th century and now a modern container facility, is its key asset. The railroad to Addis Ababa is landlocked Ethiopia's vital link to the sea.

TOURISM
▷ Visitors : population 1·34

19,000 visitors

Down 10%
1995–1997

MAIN TOURIST ARRIVALS

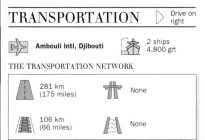

Djibouti does
not publish tourism
figures by
country of origin

0   10   20   30   40
% of total arrivals

Most visitors are passing through on their way to Ethiopia, or coming to see relatives working in the port.

Nomadic Djiboutian village, close to Balho near the Ethiopian border.

PEOPLE
▷ Pop. density low

Somali, Afar, French, Arabic

28/km²
(73/mi²)

THE URBAN/RURAL POPULATION SPLIT

83%   17%

ETHNIC MAKEUP

Other 5%
Afar 35%
Issa 60%

The main ethnic groups are the Afars and Issas; tension between these groups developed into a guerrilla war in 1991. The population was swelled in 1992 by 20,000 Somali refugees. The rural people are mostly nomadic.

POPULATION
◎ over 100 000
• under 10 000

LAND HEIGHT
1000m/3281ft
500m/1640ft
200m/656ft
Sea Level
-200m/656ft

POLITICS
▷ Multiparty elections

1997/2002

President Ismael
Omar Guelleh

AT THE LAST ELECTION

Chamber of Deputies 65 members

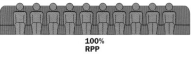

100%
RPP

RPP = Popular Rally for Progress (in alliance with **FRUD** – Front for the Restoration of Unity and Democracy).

From independence in 1977 until April 1999, when he retired, politics was dominated by President Hassan Gouled Aptidon, an Issa, backed by France. Afar fears of Issa domination erupted in 1991, when the Afar guerrilla group FRUD took control of much of the country. The French intervened militarily to keep Gouled in power, but forced him to hold elections in 1992, won by the RPP. The FRUD became a legal political party following a 1996 peace agreement. An alliance of the RPP and FRUD won the elections in 1997. Presidential elections in April 1999 were won by Ismael Omar Guelleh, a former close aide of Gouled, amid opposition claims of electoral fraud.

DJIBOUTI

Total Land Area : 25 180 sq. km
(8950 sq. miles)

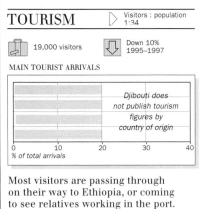

WORLD AFFAIRS

Joined UN in 1977

France, whose military presence is important to security and the local economy, is pressing for greater democratization. Djibouti, Ethiopia, and Eritrea seek to contain secessionist militancy among their Afar communities.

AID

Recipient

$87m (receipts)   Down 10% 1996–1997

France is the major donor, effectively financing one-third of government expenditure. Djibouti has also received aid from Saudi Arabia and Kuwait.

DEFENSE

No compulsory military service

$20m   Down 5% in 1997

The size of the armed forces is a state secret, but is estimated at 9,600 personnel; former FRUD guerrillas were integrated into the army. There is a 3,900-strong French garrison.

ECONOMICS

Not available

$448m   177.72 Djibouti francs

SCORE CARD

- ❏ WORLD GNP RANKING........................167th
- ❏ GNP PER CAPITA $750
- ❏ BALANCE OF PAYMENTS......................$–23m
- ❏ INFLATION 2.6%
- ❏ UNEMPLOYMENT..................................50%

STRENGTHS

Free port in key Red Sea location; large profits from 1991 Gulf War and from 1992 US and UN intervention in Somalia. Development as container transshipment port continuing.

WEAKNESSES

Dependence on French aid and garrison. Civil war has delayed planned Saudi investment. Other ports on Red Sea now providing stiff competition.

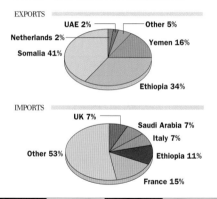

EXPORTS
UAE 2% / Other 5%
Netherlands 2% / Yemen 16%
Somalia 41% / Ethiopia 34%

IMPORTS
UK 7% / Saudi Arabia 7%
Italy 7%
Other 53% / Ethiopia 11%
France 15%

RESOURCES

Electric power 85,000 kw

350 tonnes   Not an oil producer

507,000 goats, 470,000 sheep, 190,000 cattle   Gypsum, mica, amethyst, sulfur

The few mineral resources are scarcely exploited. Geothermal energy is being developed and natural gas has recently been found. The war has delayed attempts to develop underground water supplies for agriculture.

ENVIRONMENT

No Green MPs

None   not available

The concentration of business around Djibouti port means the inland desert areas are not threatened. Ecological issues are not a national concern.

MEDIA

TV ownership low

There are no daily newspapers

PUBLISHING AND BROADCAST MEDIA

There are no daily newspapers. The only weekly, *La Nation de Djibouti*, is published by the government

1 state-controlled service   1 state-controlled service

Djibouti is a member of the Arab Satellite Communications Organization. It has two terrestrial stations for radio, TV and telecommunications.

CRIME

Death penalty not used

Djibouti does not publish prison figures   Down 64% from 1992–1996

The government has accused FRUD of atrocities, but its own human rights record has been criticized by Amnesty International. Prostitution and drug smuggling are rife. Livestock smuggling across the Red Sea is a problem.

EDUCATION

School leaving age: 12

49%   161 students

Schooling is mostly in French, although there has been a growing emphasis on Islamic teaching, particularly as Saudi Arabia has declared an interest in providing aid for education. Djibouti has no university.

HEALTH

Welfare state health benefits

1 per 5,000 people   Respiratory and heart diseases

AIDS is a growing problem in Djibouti port, with its large prostitute population. Estimates suggested 3,500 HIV-positive cases in 1992, as against government figures of 1,600. Small French-financed hospitals cater for the urban elite.

CHRONOLOGY

The French made Djibouti, formerly the Islamic state of Adal, the capital of French Somaliland in 1896.

- ❏ **1917** Railroad from Addis Ababa reaches Djibouti port.
- ❏ **1977** Independence.
- ❏ **1981** One-party state declared.
- ❏ **1989** Violence erupts between Afar and Issa groups.
- ❏ **1991** FRUD launches armed insurrection.
- ❏ **1994** Peace agreement with FRUD.
- ❏ **1999** Ismael Omar Guelleh becomes president.

D

SPENDING

GDP/cap. no increase

CONSUMPTION AND SPENDING

11 per 1,000 population   13 per 1,000 population

Defense 5%
Education 3.8%
Health No data

0   5   10   15   20   25
Defense, Health, Education spending as % of GDP

As in many African states, wealth in Djibouti is concentrated among those closest to government. Djiboutians working in the port also do well, although much port labor is expatriate. The war has had little effect on port life, as it is almost completely isolated from the rest of the country. The nomads of the interior are the poorest social group.

Trade in the mild narcotic *qat*, grown in Ethiopia and shipped through Djibouti, is highly lucrative. The state is now taking its share of the profits, granting export licenses to only a few favored traders. In Djibouti, as in Yemen and Somalia, *qat* chewing is an age-old, if expensive, social ritual.

WORLD RANKING

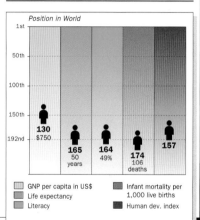

Position in World
1st
50th
100th
150th
192nd
130 $750
165 50 years
164 49%
174 106 deaths
157

GNP per capita in US$ / Infant mortality per 1,000 live births
Life expectancy
Literacy / Human dev. index

DOMINICA

OFFICIAL NAME: Commonwealth of Dominica   **CAPITAL:** Roseau
POPULATION: 74,000   **CURRENCY:** East Caribbean dollar   **OFFICIAL LANGUAGE:** English

1978   1978   Nov 3   WD   -4   +1767   .dm

Dominica is renowned as the Caribbean island that resisted European colonization until the 18th century, when it was controlled first by the French then, from 1759, by the British. Known as the "Nature Island" due to its spectacular, lush, and abundant flora and fauna, which are protected by extensive national parks, Dominica is the most mountainous of the Lesser Antilles. Located between Guadeloupe and Martinique in the West Indian Windward Islands group, its volcanic origin has given it very fertile soils and the second-largest boiling lake in the world.

CLIMATE   ▷ Tropical oceanic

WEATHER CHART

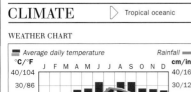

Part of the Windward Islands group in the eastern Caribbean, Dominica is subject to constant trade winds. The rainy season is in the summer, and tropical depressions and hurricanes are likely between June and November. Short, thundery showers in the late afternoon and evening are common all year round.

TRANSPORTATION   ▷ Drive on left

Canefield, Roseau
108,179 passengers

8 ships
2,522 grt

THE TRANSPORTATION NETWORK

500 km (311 miles)	None
None	None

Two airports take only small propeller aircraft, but a new, larger one is planned. Roads need upgrading.

TOURISM   ▷ Visitors : population 1:1.1

65,000 visitors

Up 8% 1995–1997

MAIN TOURIST ARRIVALS

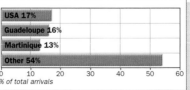

USA 17%
Guadeloupe 16%
Martinique 13%
Other 54%

0   10   20   30   40   50   60
% of total arrivals

The lack of an airport able to take commercial jetliners (visitors arrive on connecting flights from Barbados or Antigua) has made Dominica less accessible to mass-market tourism than its neighbors. Ecotourism is growing, with visitors coming to view the national parks with their rare indigenous birds, hot springs, and sulfur pools.

PEOPLE   ▷ Pop. density medium

French Creole, English   99/km² (256/mi²)

THE URBAN/RURAL POPULATION SPLIT

69%   31%

RELIGIOUS PERSUASION

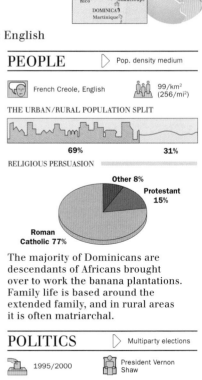

Other 8%
Protestant 15%
Roman Catholic 77%

The majority of Dominicans are descendants of Africans brought over to work the banana plantations. Family life is based around the extended family, and in rural areas it is often matriarchal.

POLITICS   ▷ Multiparty elections

1995/2000   President Vernon Shaw

AT THE LAST ELECTION

House of Assembly 30 members

52% DUWP   24% DPL   24% DFP

DUWP = Dominica United Workers' Party   **DPL** = Dominica Labour Party   **DFP** = Dominica Freedom Party

Dominica's electoral system is based on the British model. Politicians tend to come from the professional classes – usually young lawyers and doctors. Occasionally the larger farmers, who provide most party funding, stand for elections. The center-left DUWP, led by Edison James, narrowly won the 1995 elections, ending 15 consecutive years of rule by the right-wing DFP. However, Vernon Shaw, elected president by the House of Assembly in October 1998, had been a member of the previous DFP administration. The main political issue is that of continued preferential banana exports to the EU.

WORLD AFFAIRS   ▷ Joined UN in 1978

ACS   Comm   Caricom   OAS   OECS

Preferential access to the EU for Caribbean bananas, crucial for Dominica's economy, is the dominant issue. This access is opposed by the USA, which obtained a WTO ruling in its favor in 1999.

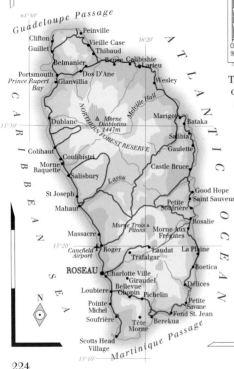

DOMINICA

Total Land Area : 750 sq. km (290 sq. miles)

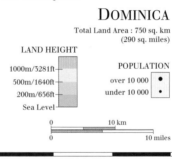

LAND HEIGHT

1000m/3281ft
500m/1640ft
200m/656ft
Sea Level

POPULATION
over 10 000 ●
under 10 000 ●

0   10 km
0   10 miles

Inshore fishing boats, *which mostly supply the domestic market, on a typical Dominican beach.*

AID

▷ Recipient

$ US$14m (receipts)   Down 67% 1996–1997

The European Development Fund allocated ECU 6.5 million in 1998 for ecotourism; Japan and Taiwan gave aid for firefighting and education.

DEFENSE

▷ No compulsory military service

$ Dominican Defense Force officially disbanded in 1981   Not applicable

Dominica has no armed forces, but it does participate in the US-sponsored Regional Security System.

ECONOMICS

▷ Inflation 4.5% p.a. (1985–1996)

US$225m   2.70 East Caribbean dollars

SCORE CARD

❏ WORLD GNP RANKING	179th
❏ GNP PER CAPITA	US$3,040
❏ BALANCE OF PAYMENTS	US$-40m
❏ INFLATION	2.4%
❏ UNEMPLOYMENT	15%

STRENGTHS
Bananas, though this sector is now threatened. Off-shore business center and "economic citizenship" scheme. Growing services sector.

WEAKNESSES
Dependence on preferential access to US and EU markets for its banana crop. Low productivity in public sector. Poor infrastructure hinders development.

EXPORTS

USA 5%
Guadeloupe 6%
Italy 6%
Jamaica 11%
UK 56%
Other 16%

IMPORTS

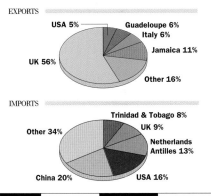

Trinidad & Tobago 8%
UK 9%
Other 34%
Netherlands Antilles 13%
China 20%
USA 16%

RESOURCES

▷ Electric power 8,000 kw

842 tonnes   Not an oil producer

13,400 goats, 10,000 cattle, 8,000 sheep, 5,000 pigs   None

Dominica has no natural resources and has to import almost all its energy. The development of hydroelectric power at Morne Trois Pitons has been proposed.

ENVIRONMENT

▷ No Green MPs

9%   Not applicable

The expansion of agriculture and timber harvesting is threatening Dominica's rain forest; already there is more land under cultivation than planned by the government. The current promotion of ecotourism poses a threat, as do increased tourist arrivals with the expected completion of a new airport capable of handling jets. Two species of parrot – the *Amazonia imperialis* and the Red Necked – are threatened, despite conservation orders. Turtles living on coral reefs off the island will soon be protected.

MEDIA

▷ TV ownership medium

There are no daily newspapers

PUBLISHING AND BROADCAST MEDIA

There are no daily newspapers. The dominant newspaper is the bi-weekly *New Chronicle*, which takes a centre-left editorial stance

No TV service   1 state-owned, 1 independent station

Local franchises, offering cable TV with selected US networks, serve one-third of the island. Broadcasts from other Caribbean states can also be received. There are four newspapers.

CRIME

▷ Death penalty used

Dominica does not publish prison figures   Recorded crime rose sharply from 1992–1996

Dominica has a lower crime rate than most of its Caribbean neighbors. Burglary and armed robbery are the major concerns; murders are rare. Justice is based on British common law and administered by the Eastern Caribbean Supreme Court, which is based in St. Lucia.

EDUCATION

▷ School leaving age: 15

94%   484 students

Education is based on the British system, and retains the selective 11-plus exam for entrance to high school. Students go on to the University of the West Indies or, increasingly, to colleges in the USA and the UK.

HEALTH

▷ Welfare state health benefits

1 per 2,174 people   Heart and respiratory diseases, cancers

There are 44 health centers, but difficult communications hamper emergency hospital access for people living in the interior.

SPENDING

▷ GDP/cap. no increase

CONSUMPTION AND SPENDING

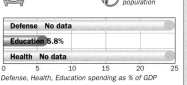

No data   241 per 1,000 population

Defense	No data	
Education	5.8%	
Health	No data	

0   5   10   15   20   25
Defense, Health, Education spending as % of GDP

Wealth disparities are not as marked as on the larger Caribbean islands, but the alleviation of poverty in Dominica was highlighted in the 1998 budget – and included increased economic benefits and help for the country's pensioners.

WORLD RANKING

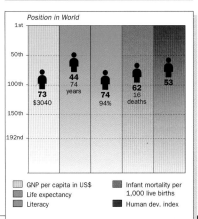

Position in World

1st
50th
100th
150th
192nd

73 $3040
44 74 years
74 94%
62 16 deaths
53

GNP per capita in US$
Life expectancy
Literacy
Infant mortality per 1,000 live births
Human dev. index

DOMINICAN REPUBLIC

OFFICIAL NAME: Dominican Republic   **CAPITAL:** Santo Domingo
POPULATION: 8.2 million   **CURRENCY:** Dominican Republic peso   **OFFICIAL LANGUAGE:** Spanish

1865	1865	Feb 27	DOM	-4	+1809	.do

THE LARGEST TOURIST destination in the Caribbean, the Dominican Republic lies 970 km (600 miles) southeast of Florida. Once ruled by Spain, it occupies the eastern two-thirds of the island of Hispaniola and boasts both the highest point (Pico Duarte, 3,175 m – 10,417 feet) and the lowest point (Lake Enriquillo, 44 m – 144 feet – below sea level) in the West Indies. Spanish-speaking, it seeks closer ties with the anglophone Caribbean.

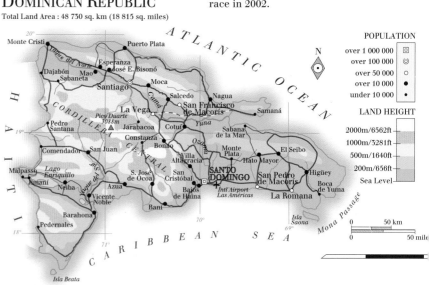

View south from Pico Duarte along the fertile banks of the Río Yaque del Norte.

CLIMATE ▷ Tropical equatorial/ oceanic

WEATHER CHART

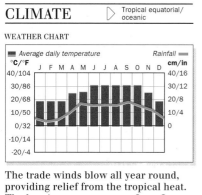

The trade winds blow all year round, providing relief from the tropical heat. The hurricane season runs from June until November.

TRANSPORTATION ▷ Drive on right

🛩 **Aeropuerto Intl de las Américas, Santo Domingo**
2.47m passengers

🚢 25 ships
11,300 grt

THE TRANSPORTATION NETWORK

🛣 5,800 km (3,604 miles)	🛣 None	
🚂 1,600 km (994 miles)	⛰ None	

Urban and rural transportation is poor; railroads are mainly for transporting sugar cane and ores. An international consortium in 1999 won a 30-year concession to operate four airports.

TOURISM ▷ Visitors : population 1:3.7

🧳 2.2m visitors   ⬆ Up 17% 1995–1997

MAIN TOURIST ARRIVALS

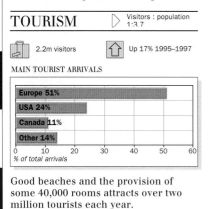

| Europe 51% |
| USA 24% |
| Canada 11% |
| Other 14% |

0 10 20 30 40 50 60
% of total arrivals

Good beaches and the provision of some 40,000 rooms attracts over two million tourists each year.

PEOPLE ▷ Pop. density medium

Spanish, French Creole   169/km² (439/mi²)

THE URBAN/RURAL POPULATION SPLIT

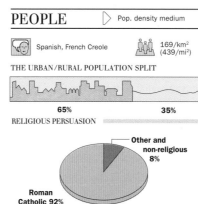

65%   35%

RELIGIOUS PERSUASION

Other and non-religious 8%

Roman Catholic 92%

The white population, primarily the descendants of Spanish settlers, still owns most of the land. The mixed race majority – about 73% – controls much of the republic's commerce, and forms the bulk of the professional middle classes. Blacks, the descendants of Africans, are mainly small-scale farmers and often the victims of latent racism, especially in business. Women in the black community work the farms; in the white and mixed race communities women are starting to appear in the professions.

DOMINICAN REPUBLIC

Total Land Area : 48 750 sq. km (18 815 sq. miles)

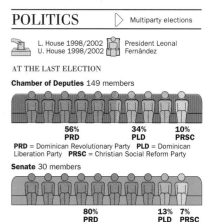

POLITICS ▷ Multiparty elections

L. House 1998/2002   President Leonal
U. House 1998/2002   Fernández

AT THE LAST ELECTION

Chamber of Deputies 149 members

56%   34%   10%
PRD   **PLD**   **PRSC**

PRD = Dominican Revolutionary Party   **PLD** = Dominican Liberation Party   **PRSC** = Christian Social Reform Party

Senate 30 members

80%   13% 7%
PRD   **PLD** **PRSC**

Joaquín Balaguer of the PRSC, a political patriarch since the 1960s and representative of the white elite and the military, achieved a bogus victory in a 1994 poll. He was forced to agree to fresh elections in 1996 which were narrowly won by Leonel Fernández of the more moderate PLD. The PRSC and PLD later joined forces against the opposition center-left PRD, which won control of the Congress in 1998. The PRD wants a fair presidential race in 2002.

WORLD AFFAIRS

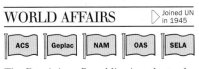 Joined UN in 1945

The Dominican Republic signed a trade pact with Caricom in 1998 and favors a "strategic alliance" between the Caribbean and Central America. Relations with Haiti are important.

AID

Recipient

$76m (receipts)   Down 28% 1996–1997

Multilateral and bilateral aid of some $235 million was granted in 1998 to repair severe hurricane damage.

DEFENSE

No compulsory military service

$120m   Up 4% in 1997

The military has economic and political interests and holds the defense portfolio. It focuses on illegal immigration from Haiti. The main arms supplier is the USA.

ECONOMICS

Inflation 20.5% p.a. (1985–1996)

$14.1bn   14.72–15.80 Dominican Republic pesos

SCORE CARD

- ❏ WORLD GNP RANKING.............................76th
- ❏ GNP PER CAPITA $1,750
- ❏ BALANCE OF PAYMENTS......................$–110m
- ❏ INFLATION...8.3%
- ❏ UNEMPLOYMENT 16%

STRENGTHS

Sustained tourism growth. Mining – mainly of nickel and gold – and sugar are major sectors. Hand-made cigars – biggest sellers in USA. Large hidden economy based on transshipment of narcotics to USA.

WEAKNESSES

Major sectors severely affected by fluctuating world prices and cutbacks in US import quotas. Failure to diversify, stalled privatizations and poor credit worthiness are problems.

EXPORTS

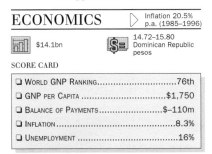

Haiti 1%   Belgium-Luxembourg 2%
USA 10%
Other 86%

IMPORTS

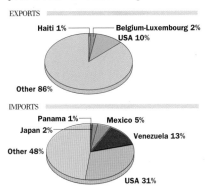

Panama 1%   Mexico 5%
Japan 2%   Venezuela 13%
Other 48%
USA 31%

RESOURCES

Electric power 1.5m kw

28,183 tonnes   Not an oil producer

2.5m cattle, 960,000 pigs, 570,000 goats, 135,000 sheep   Ferro-nickel, bauxite, copper, gold, silver

The government has invested $450 million in two new dams to produce hydroelectric power, but power cuts are frequent. Attempts at oil prospecting have not been successful. Under the terms of the San José Agreement, almost two million tonnes of oil are bought annually from Mexico and Venezuela on preferential terms. Venezuela wants to increase the quota.

ENVIRONMENT

No Green MPs

25% (10% partially protected)   Low

The government is lax about enforcing existing laws protecting diminishing forests. Legislation is often conflicting: a 1931 hunting law effectively nullifies recent wildlife protection measures.

MEDIA

TV ownership medium

Daily newspaper circulation 52 per 1,000 people

PUBLISHING AND BROADCAST MEDIA

There are 12 daily newspapers, including *Listín Diario, Ultima Hora, El Nacional de Ahora* and *El Caribe*

1 state-owned, 6 independent stations   9 state-owned, 100 independent stations

Television broadcasts from both Mexico and the USA can easily be received in the Dominican Republic.

CRIME

Death penalty not used

Dominican Republic does not publish prison figures   Rape down 70% between 1985 and 1988

Drug-trafficking and arms smuggling are linked to high levels of violent crime. Cartels increasingly use the Dominican Republic as a transshipment point to the USA.

EDUCATION

School leaving age: 14

83%   176,995 students

State schools are badly underfunded. The state university of Santo Domingo was in financial crisis in 1999. The rich send their children to study in the USA or Spain.

HEALTH

Welfare state health benefits

1 per 909 people   Heart attacks, infectious and parasitic diseases

Wealthy Dominicans fly to Cuba and the USA for treatment. The poor rely on a rudimentary public service. In 1998 three new hospitals were planned.

The 1697 Franco-Spanish partition of Hispaniola left Spain with the eastern two-thirds of the island, today the Dominican Republic.

- ❏ **1865** Independence from Spain.
- ❏ **1930–1961** Gen. Molina dictator.
- ❏ **1965** Civil war. US intervention.
- ❏ **1966–1978** Balaguer president.
- ❏ **1986** Balaguer reelected .
- ❏ **1994–1995** Balaguer reelection and austerity lead to unrest.
- ❏ **1996** Centrist Leonel Fernández narrowly elected president.
- ❏ **1998** PRD landslide election victory; major hurricane damage.

SPENDING

GDP/cap. increase

CONSUMPTION AND SPENDING

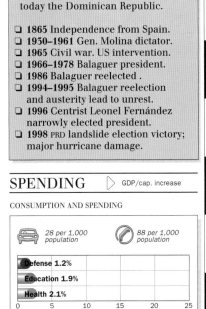

28 per 1,000 population   88 per 1,000 population

Defense 1.2%
Education 1.9%
Health 2.1%

0   5   10   15   20   25
Defense, Health, Education spending as % of GDP

Great disparities exist between the country's rich and poor. The government in 1998 announced a seven-year plan to relieve poverty and reduce the level of malnutrition currently affecting an estimated 2.24 million people. Black Dominicans remain at the bottom of the social ladder, accounting for the major proportion of small farmers and unemployed. Haitian immigrants are poorly paid, badly treated and deported at short notice. Mixed races have shown most upward mobility in recent years, but the old Spanish families remain the wealthiest and retain their grip on valuable estates.

WORLD RANKING

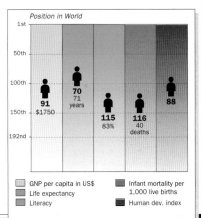

Position in World

1st
50th
100th
150th
192nd

70
71 years

91
$1750

115
83%

116
40 deaths

88

- ☐ GNP per capita in US$
- ☐ Life expectancy
- ☐ Literacy
- ☐ Infant mortality per 1,000 live births
- ☐ Human dev. index

ECUADOR

OFFICIAL NAME: Republic of Ecuador **CAPITAL:** Quito
POPULATION: 12.2 million **CURRENCY:** Sucre **OFFICIAL LANGUAGE:** Spanish

E

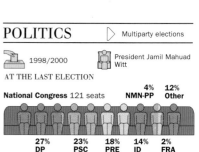

SOUTH AMERICA

| 1830 | 1941 | Aug 10 | EC | -5 | +593 | .ec |

ONCE PART OF THE INCA heartland, Ecuador lies on the western coast of South America. It was ruled by Spain from 1533, when the last Inca emperor was executed, until independence in 1830. Most Ecuadorians live either in the lowland Costa region or in the Andean Sierra. The Amazonian Indians are now successfully pressing for their land rights to be recognized. Oil exports have boosted the economy, but these dived from 1998 onwards.

CLIMATE ▷ Tropical/mountain

WEATHER CHART

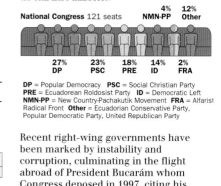

Climate varies from hot equatorial in the Amazon forests, to dry heat in the south and "perpetual spring" in Quito.

TRANSPORTATION ▷ Drive on right

Mariscal Sucre, Quito
1.71m passengers

154 ships
145,000 grt

THE TRANSPORTATION NETWORK

| 6,129 km (3,808 miles) | Pan-American Highway |
| 956 km (594 miles) | 1,500 km (932 miles) |

The road network and railroad is grossly underfunded. El Niño in 1998 devastated coastal infrastructure.

TOURISM ▷ Visitors : population 1:23

525,000 visitors

Up 19% 1995–1997

MAIN TOURIST ARRIVALS

Colombia 33%	
USA 19%	
Peru 13%	
Other 35%	

0   10   20   30   40
% of total arrivals

Tourism is growing. Quito, once the capital of the Inca empire, has had many of its Spanish imperial buildings, including 86 churches, restored. Access to the Galapagos Islands is restricted to 40,000 visitors a year.

PEOPLE ▷ Pop. density low

Spanish, Quechua, other
Amerindian languages

44/km²
(114/mi²)

THE URBAN/RURAL POPULATION SPLIT

58%   42%

RELIGIOUS PERSUASION

Protestant, Jewish and Other 7%

Roman Catholic 93%

Over half of the population is of Indian-Spanish extraction (*mestizo*). Black communities exist on the coast. The Indians, who make up about 25% of the population, are pressing for Ecuador to be described as a plurinational state, where different communities of Indians are recognized as distinct nationalities. The result is a strong and largely unified Indian movement which is at the forefront of social protests.

POLITICS ▷ Multiparty elections

1998/2000

President Jamil Mahuad Witt

AT THE LAST ELECTION

National Congress 121 seats

4% NMN-PP   12% Other

27% DP   23% PSC   18% PRE   14% ID   2% FRA

DP = Popular Democracy PSC = Social Christian Party
PRE = Ecuadorean Roldosist Party ID = Democratic Left
NMN-PP = New Country-Pachakutik Movement FRA = Alfarist Radical Front Other = Ecuadorian Conservative Party, Popular Democratic Party, United Republican Party

Recent right-wing governments have been marked by instability and corruption, culminating in the flight abroad of President Bucarám whom Congress deposed in 1997, citing his mental incapacity. Fresh elections failed to bring consensus. A new majority alliance of seven political parties and independents formed in March 1999 has had an uphill task in pushing through severe austerity measures which have met with widespread protests.

WORLD AFFAIRS ▷ Joined UN in 1945

| AP | AmCC | NAM | OAS | RG |

Access to US and EU markets for bananas and oil prices are major concerns. A border peace accord was finally signed with Peru in 1998.

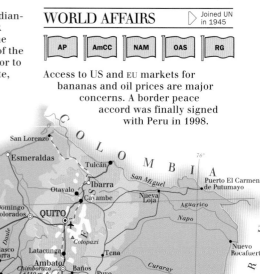

ECUADOR

Total Land Area : 276 840 sq. km
(106 888 sq. miles)

POPULATION

▣	over 1 000 000
◉	over 500 000
◎	over 100 000
○	over 50 000
●	over 10 000
•	under 10 000

LAND HEIGHT

4000m/13124ft
2000m/6562ft
500m/1640ft
Sea Level

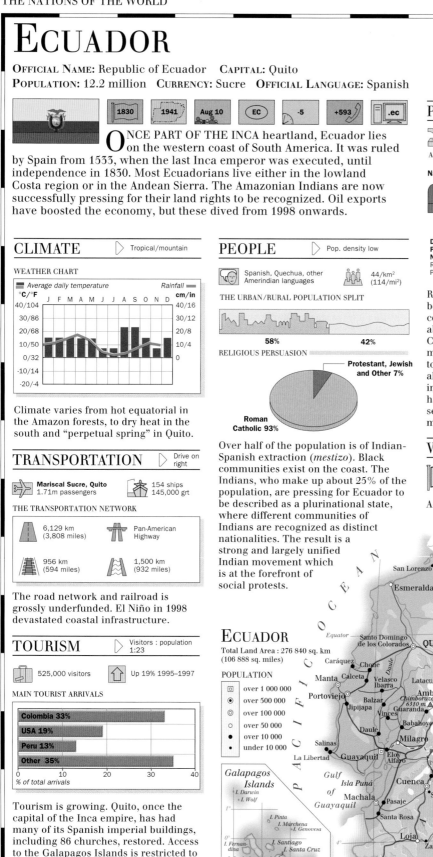

Quito is the highest capital in the world after La Paz in Bolivia. It lies in an Andean valley, lined by 30 volcanoes.

AID
 Recipient

$172m (receipts)   Down 34% 1996–1997

Aid from the USA, the EU, and the World Bank alleviates the heavy foreign debt burden. The Galapagos receive generous grants from UNESCO.

DEFENSE
Compulsory military service

$692m   Up 13% in 1997

Since a brief period of military rule in the mid-1970s, the army has not been directly involved in politics. It accepted grudgingly a peace accord with Peru in 1998 settling a border dispute.

ECONOMICS
Inflation 40.2% p.a. (1985–1996)

$19bn   4,417.50–6,830.00 sucres (official rate)

SCORE CARD
- ❏ WORLD GNP RANKING..........................71st
- ❏ GNP PER CAPITA $1,570
- ❏ BALANCE OF PAYMENTS....................$–743m
- ❏ INFLATION 30.6%
- ❏ UNEMPLOYMENT 9%

STRENGTHS
Net oil exporter. World's biggest banana producer. Fishing industry. Speeding up electricity privatization.

WEAKNESSES
Poor land productivity and infrastructure. Weak banks. Highest regional inflation. Energy crises.

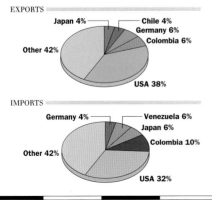

EXPORTS

Japan 4%   Chile 4%
Germany 6%
Colombia 6%
Other 42%
USA 38%

IMPORTS

Germany 4%   Venezuela 6%
Japan 6%
Colombia 10%
Other 42%
USA 32%

RESOURCES
 Electric power 2.5m kw

591,560 tonnes

335,957 b/d (reserves 1,599,793 bbl)

5.3m cattle, 2.8m pigs, 2.1m sheep, 520,000 horses

Oil, natural gas, gold, silver, copper, zinc

The government is encouraging faster oil exploration and higher output. Ecuador left OPEC in 1992. Overfishing is threatening mackerel and squid stocks.

ENVIRONMENT
No Green MPs

43%   Low

Oil drilling in new areas of Amazonia threatens indigenous tribes. In the Galapagos Islands, legal and illegal tourism has upset the islands' delicate ecosystems; the land iguana has become sterile and black coral is being stolen in quantity for souvenirs. Growing urban pollution from traffic and industrial waste is a problem, especially in the port of Guayaquil.

MEDIA
TV ownership high

Daily newspaper circulation 70 per 1,000 people

PUBLISHING AND BROADCAST MEDIA

There are 29 daily newspapers. The most popular are *El Universo* and *El Comercio*

7 independent networks

1 state-owned, 300 independent stations

Ecuador's press is largely independent and free of censorship. It is highly regionalized, based either in the Quito region or around Guayaquil on the coast. The latter is also a center for commercial radio stations.

CRIME
Death penalty not used

Ecuador does not publish prison figures

Up 82% from 1992–1996

Right-wing paramilitaries were blamed for the murders of a trade union leader in November 1998 and a left-wing congressman in February 1999. The paramilitaries are rumored to be supported by Colombians. Left-wing urban guerrillas are also reported. Unprecedented numbers of citizens are applying for arms permits and the illegal arms trade is thriving.

EDUCATION
School leaving age: 15

91%   206,541 students

Some 20% of Ecuadorians in the relevant age group receive higher education at 16 universities. Secondary schools are badly underfunded. Programs have been launched to combat high levels of adult illiteracy in the countryside.

CHRONOLOGY
Alternating republican and military governments ruled Ecuador from independence in 1830 to 1978.

- ❏ **1941–1942** Successful Peruvian invasion of mineral-rich province.
- ❏ **1948–1960** Prosperity from bananas.
- ❏ **1972** Oil production starts.
- ❏ **1979** Return to democracy.
- ❏ **1983** Crisis as oil prices fall.
- ❏ **1992** Indians granted title to 1 million ha (2.5 million acres) in Amazonia.
- ❏ **1997** Abdalá Bucarám Ortíz is deposed as president.
- ❏ **1998–99** Jamil Mahuad of DP wins elections; forms new majority alliance.

E

HEALTH
Welfare state health benefits

1 per 667 people   malnutrition, Intestinal infectious diseases, pneumonia, accidents

Health care is seriously underfunded. Severe budget cuts mean that improvement will depend on more outside aid. Some services exist in poor urban districts but are still unavailable in many rural areas.

SPENDING
GDP/cap. no increase

CONSUMPTION AND SPENDING

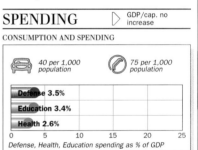
40 per 1,000 population   75 per 1,000 population

Defense 3.5%
Education 3.4%
Health 2.6%

0   5   10   15   20   25
Defense, Health, Education spending as % of GDP

During the 1980s, average income per capita dropped by just over 7%. An estimated 60% of the population live in poverty.

WORLD RANKING

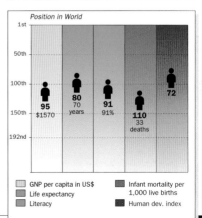

Position in World

1st
50th
100th
95 $1570
80 70 years
91 91%
110 33 deaths
72
150th
192nd

- GNP per capita in US$
- Life expectancy
- Literacy
- Infant mortality per 1,000 live births
- Human dev. index

EGYPT

OFFICIAL NAME: Arab Republic of Egypt **CAPITAL:** Cairo
POPULATION: 65.7 million **CURRENCY:** Egyptian pound **OFFICIAL LANGUAGE:** Arabic

OCCUPYING THE NORTHEAST corner of Africa, Egypt is bisected by the highly fertile Nile valley separating the arid western desert from the smaller semiarid eastern desert. Egypt's 1979 peace treaty with Israel brought security, the return of the Sinai and large injections of US aid. Its essentially pro-Western military-backed regime is now being challenged by an increasingly influential Islamic fundamentalist movement.

18th-Dynasty Temple of Queen Hatshepsut dating from the Middle Kingdom, c 1480 BCE. It is at Deir el-Bahri on the west bank of the Nile opposite Thebes, Egypt's capital at the time.

CLIMATE
▷ Hot desert/ Mediterranean

WEATHER CHART

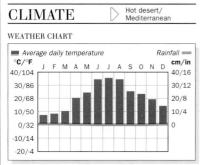

Summers are very hot, especially in the south, but winters are cooler. The only significant rain falls in winter along the Mediterranean coast.

TRANSPORTATION
▷ Drive on right

✈ **Cairo International**
7.11m passengers

🚢 378 ships
1,288 grt

THE TRANSPORTATION NETWORK

🛣	59,900 km (37,200 miles)	🛤	None
🚂	4,976 km (3,092 miles)	⚓	Suez Canal 195km (121 miles)

Egypt's cities are linked by adequate roads, but railroads are the main transport arteries. The Suez Canal is a vital international shipping lane. Cairo's metro opened in 1987.

TOURISM
▷ Visitors : population 1:18

🧳 3.7m visitors

⬆ Up 27% 1995–1997

MAIN TOURIST ARRIVALS

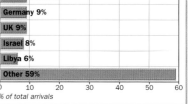

Saudi Arabia	9%
Germany	9%
UK	9%
Israel	8%
Libya	6%
Other	59%

% of total arrivals

Egypt's wealth of antiquities from its ancient civilizations have made it a key tourist destination since the 1880s. Today, it also offers Nile cruises and some of the world's best sub-aqua diving, notably at the coral reefs near Hurghada on the Red Sea.

In the 1990s, however, the industry went into sharp decline when Islamic fundamentalists, whose aim was to pressure the government into moving the state more towards Islam, began attacking Western tourists; in an attack in Luxor in 1997, 58 tourists were killed. The result was a sharp decline in the number of visitors and a major dent in foreign exchange earnings; the business convention trade was particularly affected.

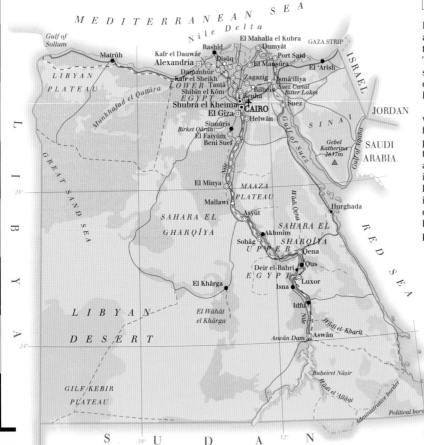

EGYPT

Total Land Area : 995 450 sq. km
(384 545 sq. miles)

POPULATION

over 5 000 000	⊡
over 1 000 000	▣
over 500 000	◉
over 100 000	◎
over 50 000	○
over 10 000	●
under 10 000	·

LAND HEIGHT

2000m/6562ft
1000m/3281ft
500m/1640ft
200m/656ft
Sea Level
-200m/-656ft

0 ___ 200 km
0 ___ 200 miles

E

PEOPLE ▷ Pop. density medium

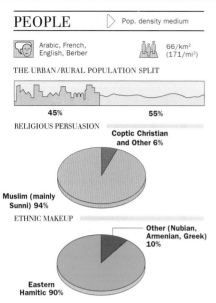

Arabic, French, English, Berber

66/km²
(171/mi²)

THE URBAN/RURAL POPULATION SPLIT

45%   55%

RELIGIOUS PERSUASION

Coptic Christian
and Other 6%

Muslim (mainly
Sunni) 94%

ETHNIC MAKEUP

Other (Nubian,
Armenian, Greek)
10%

Eastern
Hamitic 90%

Egypt has a long tradition of ethnic and religious tolerance. Most Egyptians speak Arabic, though many also have French or English as a second language. There are Berber-speaking communities in the western oases. Small colonies of Greeks and Armenians live in the larger towns. Islam is the dominant religion, followed by Coptic Christianity. While many Jews left Egypt after the creation of Israel in 1948, a small Jewish community remains in Cairo.

Cairo is Africa's most populous city, and a key social question in Egypt is the high birth rate. Aware of the demands this makes on the country's resources, economy, and social services, in 1985 the government set up the National Population Council, which made birth control readily available. Since then, the birth rate has dropped by 10%, but Egypt's population is still growing fast, projected to reach 95.8 million by 2025. The growing influence of Islamic fundamentalists, who are opposed to contraception, could see the rate accelerate once more.

Egyptian women have traditionally been among the most liberated in the Arab world, playing a full part in the education system, politics, and the economy. The steady rise of Islamic fundamentalism, however, threatens their position, particularly in rural areas.

POPULATION AGE BREAKDOWN

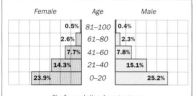

Female		Age	Male	
	0.5%	81–100	0.4%	
	2.6%	61–80	2.3%	
	7.7%	41–60	7.8%	
	14.3%	21–40	15.1%	
	23.9%	0–20	25.2%	

% of population by age group

POLITICS ▷ Multiparty elections

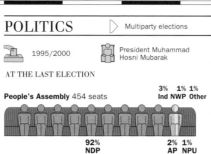

1995/2000

President Muhammad
Hosni Mubarak

AT THE LAST ELECTION

People's Assembly 454 seats

3% 1% 1%
Ind NWP Other

92%
NDP

2% 1%
AP NPU

NDP = National Democratic Party   **Ind** = Independents
NWP = New Wafd Party   **NPU** = National Progressive
Unionist Party   **AP =** Appointed by Head of State

Egypt is a multiparty system in theory. In practice, the ruling NDP, backed by the military, runs a one-party state.

MAIN POLITICAL ISSUES
Islamic fundamentalism

The NDP government is engaged in a struggle against Islamic terrorist groups seeking to turn Egypt into a Muslim theocracy along Iranian lines. Extremists have been responsible for attacks on police and tourists. The Gamaat Islamiya, which advocates a more radical program of Islamic reform than the comparatively moderate Muslim Brotherhood, announced in 1999 that it was giving up the armed struggle. The fundamentalist message, with promises of improved conditions, has proved attractive to both urban and rural poor. Mosques are often the main providers of education and health services that parallel the state's. The government uses draconian measures to counter the terrorist threat, while allowing religious organizations to pursue their social programs.

The state of emergency

The ruling NDP in 1994 extended the national state of emergency in force since the assassination of President Sadat by Islamic terrorists in 1981. Emergency laws have been invoked to justify the ban on religious parties, especially the Muslim Brotherhood. In the last general election, held in 1995, opposition parties accused the NDP of using existing laws to ensure its electoral success. Human rights groups claim that emergency powers are routinely applied to silence the NDP's political opponents.

Hosni Mubarak, president since the assassination of Anwar Sadat in 1981.

Kemal Ahmed al-Ganzuri, who became prime minister in 1996.

PROFILE

Egypt has been politically stable since World War II. Since the death of President Nasser in 1970, it has had just four presidents. Although Anwar Sadat was assassinated in 1981, he was immediately replaced by a man in the same mould, President Hosni Mubarak, who has been in power ever since. The NDP retains a tight grip on the political process through its use of the state of emergency. It has close links with the military (both Sadat and Mubarak were fighter pilots) and with Egypt's massive bureaucracy.

Under Nasser, Egypt promoted Arab socialism, influenced by the Soviet model. Since Sadat, the economy has been liberalized and private enterprise encouraged. However, no parallel liberalization has occurred in politics – one reason for the growing success of Islamic fundamentalists.

WORLD AFFAIRS ▷ Joined UN in 1945

| AL | Damasc | OAPEC | OAU | OIC |

Following the 1979 peace treaty with Israel, Egypt developed closer relations with the USA. Its political and military support for the US-led reaction to Iraq's invasion of Kuwait in 1990 was critical to the success of Operation Desert Storm in 1991. Egypt received massive economic reward from Saudi Arabia for its participation.

Relations are tense with Iran, which actively supports the Islamic groups operating against the NDP government, and describes Egypt as a corrupt state under US influence. Egypt is concerned that the international sanctions imposed on Iraq are simply allowing Iran to extend its power in the Middle East. President Mubarak now advocates a diplomatic solution and has opposed recent US-led air strikes against Iraq, as well as against supposed terrorist targets in Sudan and Afghanistan.

Egypt's diplomatic service is the Arab world's largest, and many Egyptians, such as former UN Secretary-General Boutros Boutros Ghali, serve on international bodies. Cairo hosts the headquarters of the Arab League, and the first Arab summit for four years took place there in mid-1996.

AID ▷ Recipient

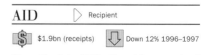

$1.9bn (receipts)   Down 12% 1996–1997

Since the late 1970s, Egypt has received massive levels of US military aid. In 1996–1997 it also received more official US aid than anywhere except Israel, and was equal top for total aid from OECD countries.

E

E

CHRONOLOGY

The centuries-old Ottoman occupation of Egypt ended in 1914, when the country came under British rule. It became fully independent in 1936. Army officers led by Lt.-Col. Nasser seized power in 1952.

- ❏ **1953** Political parties dissolved, monarchy abolished. Republic proclaimed with Gen. Neguib as president.
- ❏ **1954** Nasser deposes Neguib to become president.
- ❏ **1956** Suez Crisis. British troops withdraw from Canal. Nasser orders nationalization of Suez Canal Company to raise revenue for Aswan Dam. Israeli, British, and French forces invade, but withdraw after pressure from UN and USA.
- ❏ **1957** Suez Canal reopens after UN salvage fleet clears blockade.
- ❏ **1958** Egypt merges with Syria as United Arab Republic.
- ❏ **1960** Soviets begin work on the Aswan Dam.
- ❏ **1961** Syria breaks away from union with Egypt.
- ❏ **1967** Six Day War with Israel results in loss of Sinai.
- ❏ **1970** Nasser dies of heart attack. Succeeded by Anwar Sadat.
- ❏ **1971** Readopts the name Egypt. Islam becomes state religion.
- ❏ **1972** Soviet military advisers dismissed from Egypt.
- ❏ **1974–1975** USA brokers partial Israeli withdrawal from Sinai.
- ❏ **1977** Sadat visits Jerusalem for first-ever meeting with Israeli prime minister.
- ❏ **1978** Camp David accords brokered by US, signed by Egypt and Israel.
- ❏ **1979** Egypt and Israel sign peace treaty, alienating most Arab states.
- ❏ **1981** Sadat assassinated by Islamic extremists. Succeeded by Hosni Mubarak.
- ❏ **1982** Last Israeli troops leave Sinai.
- ❏ **1986** President Mubarak meets Israeli Prime Minister Shimon Peres to discuss Middle East peace.
- ❏ **1988** Novelist Naguib Mahfuz wins Nobel Prize for Literature.
- ❏ **1989** After 12-year rift, Egypt and Syria resume diplomatic relations.
- ❏ **1990** Egypt participates in UN operation to liberate Kuwait.
- ❏ **1991** Damascus Declaration provides for a defense pact among Egypt, Syria and GCC countries against Iraq.
- ❏ **1994–1998** Islamic extremists carry out terrorism campaign; government steps up counter-measures.
- ❏ **1999** Banned Gamaat Islamiya ends campaign to overthrow government.

DEFENSE

▷ Compulsory military service

💲 $2.7bn   ⬦ No change in 1997

Egypt's armed forces are the largest in the Arab world.

EGYPTIAN ARMED FORCES

🛡	3,700 main battle tanks (840 T-54/55, 500 T-62, 1,700 M-60)	320,000 personnel
	4 submarines, 1 destroyer, 8 frigates and 42 patrol boats	20,000 personnel
✈	585 combat aircraft (42 *Alpha Jet*, 44 PRC J-6, 29 F-4E)	30,000 personnel
	None	

Egyptian troops are battle-hardened from successive wars with Israel and from participation in Operation Desert Storm to liberate Kuwait in 1991. Over 500,000 reservists augment the regular troops.

After the 1978 Camp David accords with Israel, Egypt stopped buying Soviet weapons and aircraft, turning instead to Western suppliers. Cooperation with the USA has reaped dividends in the form of more sophisticated defense equipment and improved training. Egypt has a small arms industry and sells light weapons, notably a version of the AK-47 assault rifle, to other developing countries.

ECONOMICS

▷ Inflation 14.8% p.a. (1985–1996)

📊 $72.1bn   💲 3.40–3.41 Egyptian pounds

SCORE CARD

- ❏ WORLD GNP RANKING 42nd
- ❏ GNP PER CAPITA $1,200
- ❏ BALANCE OF PAYMENTS ....$–711m
- ❏ INFLATION 4.6%
- ❏ UNEMPLOYMENT 9%

EXPORTS

Netherlands 7%
Germany 7%
Israel 8%
Italy 11%
Other 56%
USA 11%

IMPORTS

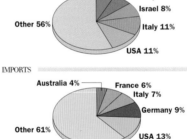

Australia 4%
France 6%
Italy 7%
Germany 9%
Other 61%
USA 13%

STRENGTHS

Oil and gas revenues. Tourist industry. Remittances from Egyptians working overseas. Suez Canal tolls. Agricultural produce, especially cotton. Light industry and manufacturing.

WEAKNESSES

Reduction in remittances from Egyptians working overseas owing to Gulf States' recession. Dependence on imported technology. High birth rate.

PROFILE

Under President Nasser, Egypt followed an economic policy inspired by the Soviet model. Rigid and highly centralized, it gave Egypt one of the largest public sectors of all developing countries. Economic restrictions were first relaxed in 1974. President Sadat's open-door policy allowed joint ventures

ECONOMIC PERFORMANCE INDICATOR

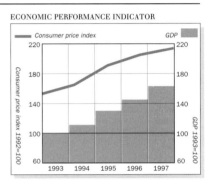

— Consumer price index   ▢ GDP

with foreign partners for the first time, although the business classes were the only ones to profit. Most Egyptians suffered from new austerity measures.

Under President Mubarak, economic reform has quickened and policies are more sensitive to the high levels of unemployment and poverty. Priorities now are to reduce import dependence by encouraging manufacturing, and to sustain economic growth to keep up with the increase in population.

EGYPT : MAJOR BUSINESSES

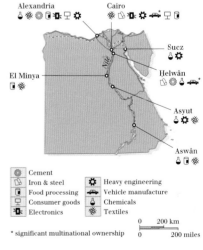

Alexandria
Cairo
Suez
El Minya
Helwân
Asyut
Aswân

Nile

Cement	Heavy engineering
Iron & steel	Vehicle manufacture
Food processing	Chemicals
Consumer goods	Textiles
Electronics	

0   200 km
0   200 miles

* significant multinational ownership

E

RESOURCES

▷ Electric power 16.0m kw

309,576 tonnes

860,000b/d (reserves 3,900,000,000 bbl)

4.3m sheep, 3.2m goats, 3m cattle, 45,000 horses

Natural gas, oil, phosphates, manganese, uranium

ELECTRICITY GENERATION

Hydro 22% (10.8bn kwh)

Combustion 78% (3.8bn kwh)

Nuclear 0%

Other 0%

% of total generation by type

Oil and gas are Egypt's most valuable resources. Most of the oil comes from its western desert, the Red Sea, Sinai, and Upper Egypt. Oil multinationals are involved in new explorations, but Egypt is not as profitable a source as more competitive oil-rich countries, such as Algeria and Yemen; 55% of Egypt's oil production is consumed locally.

Most electricity is derived from hydroelectric power and coal. The massive Aswan Dam provides the bulk of hydroelectricity. Built between 1960 and 1970, the dam has a generating capacity of 10 billion kwh. By 1974, revenue from it had covered construction costs.

EGYPT : LAND USE

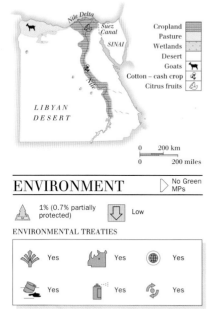

Cropland
Pasture
Wetlands
Desert
Goats
Cotton – cash crop
Citrus fruits

0   200 km
0   200 miles

ENVIRONMENT

▷ No Green MPs

1% (0.7% partially protected)

Low

ENVIRONMENTAL TREATIES

Yes		Yes		Yes	
Yes		Yes		Yes	

Egypt suffers from a chronic lack of water. The Nile, the only perennial source, is increasingly saline because of its much reduced flow due to irrigation and the Aswan Dam. The main cities suffer heavy industrial pollution, and environmental controls are few. In Cairo, a new sewerage system has improved sanitary conditions.

MEDIA

▷ TV ownership medium

Daily newspaper circulation 38 per 1,000 people

Pressure from Islamists has resulted in the media allocating more airtime to Islamic sermons. Press legislation introduced in 1995 imposed draconian penalties for defamation and publishing false information. Severe restrictions were imposed in 1998 after criticism of the government's security clampdown.

CRIME

▷ Death penalty used

Egypt does not publish prison figures

Up 11% in 1991

CRIME RATES

Murders

2 per 100,000 population

Rapes

0 per 100,000 population

Thefts

60 per 100,000 population

Terrorist attacks have tarnished Egypt's reputation as a law-abiding country; street crime and muggings were previously rare. Intercommunity violence – particularly attacks by Muslims on Christians and vice versa – has become more common, as have attacks on Western tourists by Islamic extremists. Human rights groups have criticized the police for abusing current emergency laws resulting in the routine torture and death in police custody of scores of political prisoners.

EDUCATION

▷ School leaving age: 14

 53%

 850,051 students

A small majority of men but a minority of women are literate.

THE EDUCATION SYSTEM

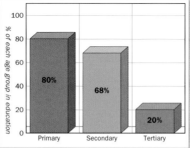

% of each age group in education

- Primary 80%
- Secondary 68%
- Tertiary 20%

Education, which is free, is compulsory in theory until 14 years of age. However, although most Egyptians attend elementary school to the age of 11, not many complete secondary education. Egyptian university education is widely respected in the Arab world.

PUBLISHING AND BROADCAST MEDIA

There are 17 daily papers. Those with the highest circulation are the prestigious, serious *Al Ahram* and the more popular *Al Akhbar*

1 state-owned service

1 state-owned, 1 independent service

HEALTH

▷ Welfare state health benefits

1 per 556 people

Digestive, respiratory and heart diseases, perinatal deaths

Health care is rudimentary – there is only one hospital bed for every 500 people. Patient–doctor ratios are among the lowest in the Arab world. Islamic medical centers based on the mosque organization are spreading and replacing the state system. Female circumcision was banned in public hospitals in 1996; fundamentalists challenged this move in the courts.

SPENDING

▷ GDP/cap. no increase

CONSUMPTION AND SPENDING

23 per 1,000 population

56 per 1,000 population

Defense 4.3%

Education 5.6%

Health 1%

Defense, Health, Education spending as % of GDP

Wealth disparities are highly marked in Egypt. The largely urban Coptic Christian community is the group with the country's highest standard of living. Most Egyptians remain subsistence farmers with low incomes. The return of many unemployed workers from the Gulf states has further depressed conditions in the countryside.

WORLD RANKING

Position in World

- 1st
- 50th
- 100th
- 150th
- 192nd

- 107 $1200
- 122 66 years
- 162 53%
- 128 51 deaths
- 120

GNP per capita in US$
Life expectancy
Literacy

Infant mortality per 1,000 live births
Human dev. index

EL SALVADOR

OFFICIAL NAME: Republic of El Salvador **CAPITAL:** San Salvador
POPULATION: 6.1 million **CURRENCY:** Salvadorean Colón **OFFICIAL LANGUAGE:** Spanish

T HE SMALLEST AND MOST densely populated
Central American republic, El Salvador won full
independence in 1841. Located on the Pacific coast, it lies within a
seismic zone. Between 1979 and 1991, El Salvador was ravaged by
a civil war between US-backed right-wing governments and left-wing
FMLN guerrillas. Since the UN-brokered peace agreement, the country
has been concentrating on rebuilding its shattered economy.

E

CLIMATE ▷ Tropical wet & dry

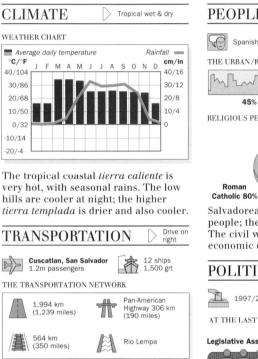

WEATHER CHART

The tropical coastal *tierra caliente* is
very hot, with seasonal rains. The low
hills are cooler at night; the higher
tierra templada is drier and also cooler.

TRANSPORTATION ▷ Drive on right

Cuscatlan, San Salvador
1.2m passengers
12 ships
1,500 grt

THE TRANSPORTATION NETWORK

1,994 km (1,239 miles)		Pan-American Highway 306 km (190 miles)
564 km (350 miles)		Rio Lempa

Roads are poor in rural areas, as is
60% of railroad track. San Salvador's
international airport and the port
of Cutuco are being improved.

TOURISM ▷ Visitors : population 1:16

385,000 visitors
Up 64% 1995–1997

MAIN TOURIST ARRIVALS

USA 32%
Guatemala 19%
Honduras 10%
Other 39%

% of total arrivals

Peace has brought visitors back to the
unspoiled beach resorts. However, high
prices for rooms and air travel, along
with crime, hinders tourist expansion.

PEOPLE ▷ Pop. density high

Spanish
294/km² (763/mi²)

THE URBAN/RURAL POPULATION SPLIT

45%   55%

RELIGIOUS PERSUASION

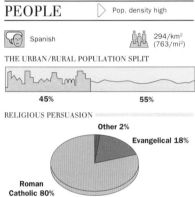

Other 2%
Evangelical 18%
Roman Catholic 80%

Salvadoreans are largely a *mestizo*
people; there are few ethnic tensions.
The civil war was fought over gross
economic disparities, which still exist.

POLITICS ▷ Multiparty elections

1997/2000
President Francisco Flores

AT THE LAST ELECTION

Legislative Assembly 84 seats

4% PRSC   5% Other

33% ARENA   32% FMLN   13% PCN   11% PDC   2% CD

ARENA = Nationalist Republican Alliance
FMLN = Farabundo Marti National Liberation Front
PCN = National Conciliation Party **PDC** = Christian
Democratic Party **PRSC** = Social Christian Renewal Party
CD = Democratic Convergence **Others** = Liberal Democratic
Party, Democratic Movement, Unity Movement

El Salvador was traditionally dominated
by the centrist PDC and right-wing ARENA.
The latter, representing the interests of
powerful agribusiness, faced increased
opposition from the leftist FMLN former
guerrillas who won 25% of the vote in
1994, and in the 1997 elections won
the mayorship of San Salvador and
half the state capitals. However the
FMLN, split between center-left
pragmatists and hardliners, came a
poor second in the 1999 presidential
election to ARENA's Francisco Flores,
who promised income redistribution
and a reduction in poverty.

*View over the capital, San Salvador. It lies
in a depression in the southern and higher of
El Salvador's two mountain ranges, which is
punctuated by more than 20 volcanoes.*

WORLD AFFAIRS ▷ Joined UN in 1945

ACS   Geplac   NAM   OAS   San José

During the 1980s, El Salvador suffered
international pariah status because
of the abuses of human rights
by military death squads. El Salvador's
attempt at the UN to defend its record
failed. Today the country cooperates
with its neighbors in pressing the
USA on such key issues as trade and
immigration, and, in 1999, for aid
in the aftermath of Hurricane
Mitch. It is also involved, with
Guatemala and Honduras, in
protracted negotiations of a free
trade agreement with Mexico.

AID ▷ Recipient

$294m (receipts)
Down 7% 1996–1997

Post-civil war aid focused on efforts to
secure peace and achieve national
reconciliation by funding rebuilding
and refugee resettlement programs.
The emphasis has now shifted
to support for growth. The extended
IMF standby agreement in 1998
emphasized fiscal and monetary
tightness. The World Bank, the IDB,
and Japan have recently provided
specific project loans.

DEFENSE ▷ Compulsory military service

$176m
Up 22% in 1997

Between 1979 and 1991, the US-backed
military fought an unrestricted
war against the FMLN. Human rights
were effectively suspended and
governments that opposed the military
overthrown. Under 1992 peace
accords, the military agreed to
withdraw from politics and internal
security matters but it remains a potent
force capable of intervention.

CENTRAL AMERICA
Guatemala   Honduras
EL SALVADOR
North America

E

ECONOMICS

▷ Inflation 14.6% p.a. (1985–1996)

📊 $10.7bn   💲 8.76–8.74 colónes

SCORE CARD

- ❏ WORLD GNP RANKING............................78th
- ❏ GNP PER CAPITA $1,810
- ❏ BALANCE OF PAYMENTS $96m
- ❏ INFLATION 4.5%
- ❏ UNEMPLOYMENT 8%

STRENGTHS

Coffee. Offshore assembly *maquila* industry. Substantial family remittances from USA.

WEAKNESSES

Exports uncompetitive and dependent on US and Central American markets. Overvalued currency. High tax evasion and unemployment. Low savings.

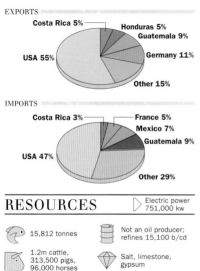

EXPORTS

Costa Rica 5%
Honduras 5%
Guatemala 9%
Germany 11%
USA 55%
Other 15%

IMPORTS

Costa Rica 3%
France 5%
Mexico 7%
Guatemala 9%
USA 47%
Other 29%

RESOURCES

▷ Electric power 751,000 kw

🐚 15,812 tonnes   🛢 Not an oil producer; refines 15,100 b/cd

🐄 1.2m cattle, 313,500 pigs, 96,000 horses   💎 Salt, limestone, gypsum

No significant resources. Several volcanoes facilitate abundant and relatively cheap geothermal energy.

ENVIRONMENT

▷ No Green MPs

🔺 1% (0.2% partially protected)   ⬇ Low

Most of the rain forest has been cut down for agriculture, leading to topsoil erosion and desertification. Pesticide poisoning of land is a major problem.

MEDIA

▷ TV ownership medium

📠 Daily newspaper circulation 48 per 1,000 people

PUBLISHING AND BROADCAST MEDIA

There are 5 daily newspapers. *El Diario de Hoy* has the highest circulation

2 state-owned, 9 independent stations

1 state-owned, 65 independent stations

The media is owned by powerful groups, such as the Dutriz family. Intimidation and self-censorship exist.

CRIME

▷ Death penalty not used

🔒 El Salvador does not publish prison figures   ⬇ Falling since 1991, but still high by regional standards

A weak and corrupt judiciary and national police have been unable to stem a postwar crime wave, including 8,281 murders in 1997. Death squads have reappeared. Readily available arms and uncompleted elements of the peace accords, particularly land transfers, have increased violence.

EDUCATION

▷ School leaving age: 14

👤 77%   👨‍🎓 112,004 students

Education is based on the US system and is limited in rural areas. During the civil war, state universities were closed by the military and replaced by private universities which continue to thrive despite their low standards. A 1995 reform bill tried to address the negative impact of deregulation.

CHRONOLOGY

El Salvador was Spanish until 1821. Part of the United Provinces of Central America until 1838, it became fully independent in 1841.

- ❏ **1932** Army crushes popular insurrection led by Farabundo Martí.
- ❏ **1944–1979** Army rules through PCN.
- ❏ **1979** Reformist officers overthrow PCN government. Fail to curb rising army-backed political violence.
- ❏ **1981** Leftist FMLN launches civil war.
- ❏ **1991** UN-brokered peace. FMLN recognized as a political party.
- ❏ **1997** FMLN makes up ground in elections; leftist Hector Silva wins mayoralty of San Salvador.
- ❏ **1999** ARENA easily defeats FMLN in presidential elections.

HEALTH

▷ Welfare state health benefits

👩‍⚕️ 1 per 1,429 people   ☠ Accidents, violence, circulatory diseases, infections

Health spending, almost halved during the civil war, has been slow to recover. The wealthy go to the USA for surgery.

SPENDING

▷ GDP/cap. no increase

CONSUMPTION AND SPENDING

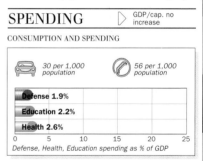

🚗 30 per 1,000 population   ☎ 56 per 1,000 population

Defense **1.9%**
Education **2.2%**
Health **2.6%**

0   5   10   15   20   25
Defense, Health, Education spending as % of GDP

El Salvador has considerable wealth disparities – with 20% of the population owning 70% of national wealth. Land distribution remains highly skewed, and some 1.7 million people live in poverty.

WORLD RANKING

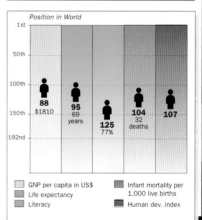

Position in World

1st
50th
100th
150th
192nd

88 $1810
95 69 years
125 77%
104 32 deaths
107

▢ GNP per capita in US$
▢ Life expectancy
▢ Literacy
▢ Infant mortality per 1,000 live births
▢ Human dev. index

EL SALVADOR

Total Land Area : 20 720 sq. km (8000 sq. miles)

POPULATION
- over 500 000 ◉
- over 100 000 ◎
- over 50 000 ○
- over 10 000 ●
- under 10 000 ·

LAND HEIGHT
- 2000m/6562ft
- 1000m/3281ft
- 500m/1640ft
- 200m/656ft
- Sea Level

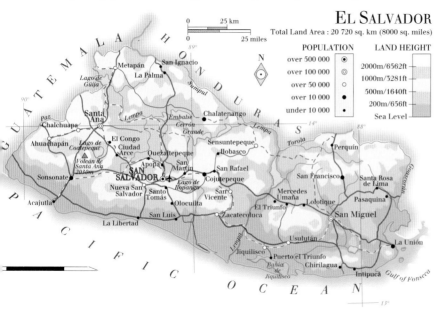

EQUATORIAL GUINEA

OFFICIAL NAME: Republic of Equatorial Guinea **CAPITAL:** Malabo
POPULATION: 430,000 **CURRENCY:** CFA franc **OFFICIAL LANGUAGE:** Spanish

WEST AFRICA

| 1968 | 1968 | Oct 12 | GQ | +1 | +240 | .gq |

COMPRISING FIVE ISLANDS and the territory of Río Muni on the west coast of Africa, Equatorial Guinea lies just north of the equator. Mangrove swamps border the mainland coast. The republic gained its independence in 1968 after 190 years of Spanish rule. Multipartyism was accepted in 1991, but observers questioned the fairness of the subsequent general elections.

E

CLIMATE ▷ Tropical equatorial

WEATHER CHART

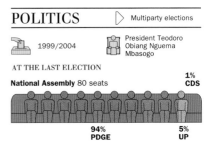

■ Average daily temperature   Rainfall ▬

The island of Bioko is extremely wet and humid, with an annual rainfall of 200 cm (79 inches), while the mainland is only marginally drier and cooler.

TRANSPORTATION ▷ Drive on right

✈ Malabo   🚢 2 ships 35,000 grt

THE TRANSPORTATION NETWORK

| 🛣 508 km (316 miles) | 🛤 None |
| 🚉 None | ⛴ None |

Apart from once- or twice-weekly *Iberia* flights, all air links are through neighboring countries. The Chinese financed the Ncue–Mongomo Highway project in the 1980s.

TOURISM ▷ Not applicable

🧳 Tourism receipts totalled $2m in 1997   △▽ Numbers are increasing slowly

MAIN TOURIST ARRIVALS

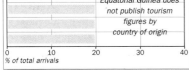

Equatorial Guinea does not publish tourism figures by country of origin

% of total arrivals

Equatorial Guinea is for the adventurous, independent tourist only, despite the potential attraction of Malabo's spectacular scenery and beaches.

PEOPLE ▷ Pop. density low

👤 Spanish, Fang, Bubi   👥 15/km² (40/mi²)

THE URBAN/RURAL POPULATION SPLIT

42%   58%

RELIGIOUS PERSUASION

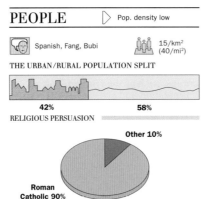

Other 10%
Roman Catholic 90%

The mainland has a majority of Fang, a people who also inhabit Cameroon and northern Gabon. Bioko is populated by a majority of Bubi and a minority of Creoles, known as *Fernandinos*. The Macías dictatorship consolidated the power of the Fang, especially the Mongomo clan, from which both Macías and his successor Obiang come. The extended family is strong and maintained its solidarity despite disruptive social pressure during the Macías dictatorship.

EQUATORIAL GUINEA

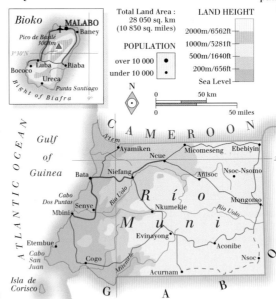

Total Land Area : 28 050 sq. km (10 850 sq. miles)

POPULATION
over 10 000 ●
under 10 000 ·

LAND HEIGHT
2000m/6562ft
1000m/3281ft
500m/1640ft
200m/656ft
Sea Level

0   50 km
0   50 miles

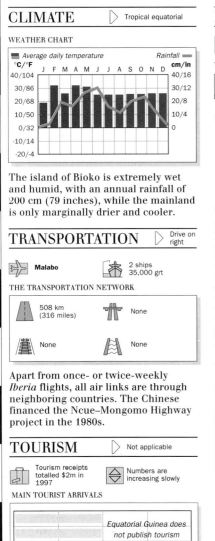

Bioko, formerly Fernando Po. *Although the volcanic land is very fertile, cocoa production fell by 90% during the Macías years.*

POLITICS ▷ Multiparty elections

🗳 1999/2004   👥 President Teodoro Obiang Nguema Mbasogo

AT THE LAST ELECTION

National Assembly 80 seats   1% CDS

94% PDGE   5% UP

PDGE = Equatorial Guinea Democratic Party **UP** = Popular Union **CDS** = Convergence for Social Democracy

Despite officially being a multiparty state since 1991, some of the several exiled political parties have not yet found it safe to return – opposition leaders who publicize themselves tend to be arrested. The ruling PDGE was set up in 1987 by Teodoro Obiang Nguema Mbasogo, nephew of the dictator Francisco Macías Nguema, whom he overthrew in 1979. It replaced Macías' National Workers' Party (PUNT). The PDGE benefits from heavy government patronage, receiving 3% of all salaries.

The movement towards multipartyism – which was initiated in 1988 following the first elections for 20 years – has been marked by instability. The 1993 parliamentary elections were boycotted by the main opposition parties, while the presidential poll in 1996 in which Obiang was the only candidate was declared farcical by foreign observers. The 1999 legislative elections were won easily by the PDGE, but denounced by the opposition.

WORLD AFFAIRS

 Joined UN in 1968

After a period of extreme isolation under the Macías dictatorship, Equatorial Guinea sought to rebuild links, especially its relationship with Spain, the former colonial power and traditionally a haven for political dissenters. However, the international community remains wary of the Obiang regime. Joining the Franc Zone in 1988 did not bring the expected benefits. Spain is suspicious of French commercial ambitions in the country.

AID

▷ Recipient

$24m (receipts)   Down 23% 1996–1997

Equatorial Guinea is poorly developed and therefore heavily dependent on aid. Inefficiency, corruption, and a shortage of skilled people hinder the planning and implemetation of projects, and the government's political record threatens funding. France, Italy, Spain, the World Bank, and Arab funds are all important sources of aid. An IMF program was suspended in 1997 after the government failed to implement reforms.

DEFENSE

▷ No compulsory military service

$5m   Up 150% in 1997

The main concern for the military and paramilitary force is internal security. Morocco has provided a 360-strong presidential guard since the early 1980s to guarantee Obiang's security. Nigeria, Cameroon, and Gabon have interests in maintaining the autonomy of the Malabo and Río Muni regions.

ECONOMICS

▷ Inflation 6.1% p.a. (1985–1996)

$444m   601.60–588.62 CFA francs

SCORE CARD

❑ WORLD GNP RANKING	168th
❑ GNP PER CAPITA	$1,060
❑ BALANCE OF PAYMENTS	$–344m
❑ INFLATION	3%
❑ UNEMPLOYMENT	6%

STRENGTHS

Fertile soils. Timber. Cocoa and coffee. Extensive territorial waters offer potential for fisheries. Strengthening economy as oil and gas reserves are exploited.

WEAKNESSES

Lasting effects of economic regression under the Macías dictatorship. Maladministration and ideological

RESOURCES

▷ Electric power 5,000 kw

3,380 tonnes   Reserves of 3,600,000 bbl

36,000 sheep, 8,100 goats, 4,800 cattle   Oil, natural gas, gold

There are estimated to be ten years of oil and gas reserves at current production levels, with 2.5 million tonnes produced in 1997. Bata is served by a 3.2mw hydropower station built by the Chinese in 1983.

ENVIRONMENT

▷ No Green MPs

None   Not available

The government has failed to take any serious measures to stop timber companies depleting the rainforest.

MEDIA

▷ TV ownership low

 Daily newspaper circulation 5 per 1,000 people

PUBLISHING AND BROADCAST MEDIA

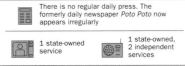

There is no regular daily press. The formerly daily newspaper *Poto Poto* now appears irregularly

1 state-owned service   1 state-owned, 2 independent services

There has been very little sign of press liberalization, despite the adoption of multipartyism. Political parties produce a few tracts and broadsheets.

CRIME

▷ Death penalty used

Equatorial Guinea does not publish prison figures   No measurable change from year to year

Levels of recorded crime are relatively low, although much does not get reported. Many human rights abuses still occur.

EXPORTS

- Germany 4%
- Other 8%
- USA 11%
- Spain 33%
- Japan 17%
- China 27%

IMPORTS

- Cameroon 8%
- UK 10%
- USA 28%
- Spain 15%
- Other 23%
- France 16%

attacks on the educated have restricted growth; under Macías, cocoa production slumped by 90%. Government complains that oil exploitation contracts favor the companies.

CHRONOLOGY

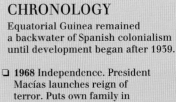

Equatorial Guinea remained a backwater of Spanish colonialism until development began after 1939.

- ❑ **1968** Independence. President Macías launches reign of terror. Puts own family in all top jobs.
- ❑ **1972** Attempt to stop mass exodus: people forbidden to leave country.
- ❑ **1979** Coup puts nephew in power with Spanish approval.
- ❑ **1991** Multiparty constitution.

E

EDUCATION

▷ School leaving age: 11

80%   578 students

Education declined in the Macías years, when attendance rates fell from 90% to 55%. Although declared the state's first priority, funding is poor.

HEALTH

▷ No welfare state health benefits

1 per 4,762 people   Diarrheal and respiratory diseases, malaria

Life expectancy has risen from 37 years in 1960 to 50 years in 1997. There are 21 doctors per 100,000 people.

SPENDING

▷ GDP/cap. no increase

CONSUMPTION AND SPENDING

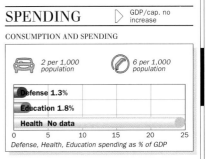

2 per 1,000 population   6 per 1,000 population

Defense	1.3%
Education	1.8%
Health	No data

Defense, Health, Education spending as % of GDP

What wealth exists in Equatorial Guinea, tends to be concentrated in the ruling clan. There is also a relic of Spanish plutocracy.

WORLD RANKING

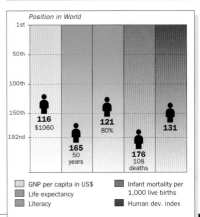

Position in World

- 116 $1060
- 165 50 years
- 121 80%
- 176 108 deaths
- 131

❑ GNP per capita in US$
❑ Life expectancy
❑ Literacy
❑ Infant mortality per 1,000 live births
❑ Human dev. index

ERITREA

EAST AFRICA

OFFICIAL NAME: State of Eritrea **CAPITAL:** Asmara
POPULATION: 3.5 million **CURRENCY:** Nakfa **OFFICIAL LANGUAGES:** Tigrinya and Arabic

E

| 1993 | 1993 | May 24 | ER | +3 | +291 | .er |

L YING ON THE SHORES of the Red Sea, Eritrea's landscape is dominated by rugged mountains, bush, and the Danakil desert. Annexed by Ethiopia in 1962, it seceded in 1991, after a destructive and bloody 30-year war for independence. Like its southern neighbor, Eritrea is prone to recurring droughts, and the constant threat of famine. A border war with Ethiopia began in 1998, with very heavy losses on both sides.

CLIMATE
▷ Hot desert/mountain

WEATHER CHART

Eritrea's harvest is dependent on mid-year rainfall in the highlands. Lowland temperatures may exceed 50°C (122°F).

TRANSPORTATION
▷ Drive on right

Yohannes IV, Asmara
125,363 passengers

6 ships
6,777 grt

THE TRANSPORTATION NETWORK

| 807 km (501 miles) | None |
| 117 km 73 miles | None |

All systems require massive investment. Massawa and Assab ports have potential as transit points for Ethiopia.

TOURISM
▷ Visitors : population 1:7.1

492,000 visitors

Not available

MAIN TOURIST ARRIVALS

Eritrea does not publish tourism figures by country of origin

0 10 20 30 40
% of total arrivals

There is very little tourism, but considerable long-term potential, especially along the Red Sea coast, where underwater attractions draw ecotourists, and in the spectacular Danakil depression. Guides are essential.

PEOPLE
▷ Pop. density low

Tigrinya, Tigre, Afar, Arabic, Bilen, Kunama, Nara, Saho, Hadareb

37/km² (97/mi²)

THE URBAN/RURAL POPULATION SPLIT

17% 83%

RELIGIOUS PERSUASION

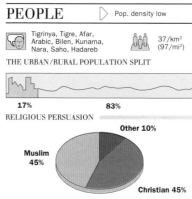

Other 10%
Muslim 45%
Christian 45%

Tigrinya-speakers, mainly Orthodox Christians, form the largest of Eritrea's nine main ethnic groups. A strong sense of nationhood has been forged by the 30-year struggle for independence. Women played an important role in the war. From 1973, 30,000 fought alongside men, some in positions of command. The nomadic peoples of the Danakil desert remain fiercely independent. Over 80% of people are subsistence farmers.

ERITREA

Total Land Area : 93 680 sq. km (36 170 sq. miles)

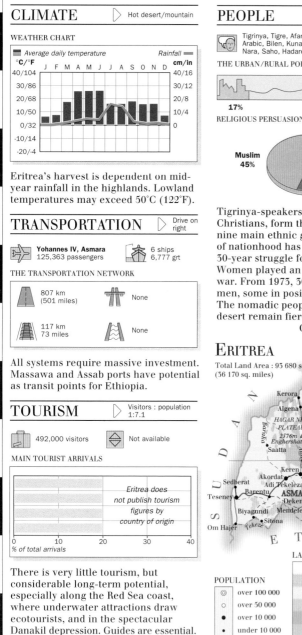

LAND HEIGHT

2000m/6562ft
1000m/3281ft
500m/1640ft
200m/656ft
Sea Level
-200m/-656ft

POPULATION
◎ over 100 000
○ over 50 000
● over 10 000
• under 10 000

0 100 km
0 100 miles

N

POLITICS
▷ No multiparty elections

Elections not yet held

President Issaias Afewerki

AT THE LAST ELECTION

National Assembly 150 seats

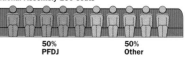

50% PFDJ
50% Other

PFDJ = People's Front for Democracy and Justice (formerly the Eritrean People's Liberation Front)

National Assembly comprises 75 PFDJ central committee members and 75 directly elected members, including 11 seats reserved for women. Elections expected in 1997 under the new Constitution have not yet taken place.

Formerly an Italian colony, Eritrea came under a temporary British mandate in 1941, until in 1952 the UN passed the mandate to Ethiopia under a federal arrangement. The long secessionist struggle began in 1961, after Ethiopia annexed Eritrea. The Eritrean People's Liberation Front (EPLF) finally drove out Ethiopian troops in 1991. A referendum in 1993 endorsed independence.

Until multiparty elections are held, the country is being run by a core of EPLF (now the People's Front for Democracy and Justice (PFDJ)) leaders who conducted the military campaign. A new constitution, adopted in May 1997, forbids parties based on religious or ethnic affiliations.

WORLD AFFAIRS
▷ Joined UN in 1993

| Comesa | iBRD | IGAD | NAM | OAU |

Eritrea's secession was significant, as the first major redrawing of the borders established by Africa's colonizers. The OAU feared that other secessionist movements would be encouraged by Eritrea's success. For Eritrea, the main concern is attracting Western and Arab aid. Relations with Ethiopia's new government, which also fought the Mengistu regime, were good until a border conflict erupted in 1998. Eritrea has resolved other territorial disputes, with Yemen and with Sudan.

AID

$123m (receipts)   Down 22% 1996–1997

Eritrea's economy is almost entirely aid-dependent. Food aid, on which 75% of the population survive, is the most pressing need given the vulnerability of the country to famine. The UN has frequently provided food aid. Western donors have been less generous with aid for the $2 billion reconstruction costs. Compared with Somalia, the country's aid receipts are tiny.

DEFENSE

Compulsory military service

$65m   Up 7% in 1997

The size of Eritrea's standing army, still about 55,000-strong (of whom about one-third are women), is out of all proportion to what the country can afford. Until the renewed outbreak of hostilities with Ethiopia, troops were being reintegrated into the national economy on "food for work" schemes.

ECONOMICS

Not available

$852m   7.55 nafka

SCORE CARD

❏ WORLD GNP RANKING.........................158th
❏ GNP PER CAPITA $230
❏ BALANCE OF PAYMENTS $12m
❏ INFLATION 9.3%
❏ UNEMPLOYMENT ......Widespread underemployment

STRENGTHS
Strategically important position on Red Sea. Potential for mining and oil industries. Government commitment to reducing dependence on food aid. Potential for Red Sea tourism. Resourceful, hard-working population.

WEAKNESSES
Lack of basic information and equipment. Coherent economic policy still being formulated. Not an aid priority for Western donors. Legacy of disruption and destruction from civil war. Port of Massawa heavily bombed. Most of population living at subsistence level. Susceptibility to drought and famine. Expense of repatriating and supporting the 750,000 who fled abroad as refugees and have now returned.

EXPORTS/IMPORTS

Eritrea does not yet publish export or import figures

RESOURCES

Electricity supply is prone to surges

3,826 tonnes   Not an oil producer; oil refinery at Assab

1.3m cattle, 1.5m sheep, 1.4m goats   Copper, potash, gold, iron, silver, zinc, oil, silica, granite, marble

Eritrea has substantial copper reserves, and lesser ones of silver, zinc, and gold. High-quality silica, granite and marble deposits could be exploited. Onshore and offshore oil deposits are believed to exist, but exploration work is at an early stage. There is geothermal power generating potential.

ENVIRONMENT

No Green MPs

5%   Not available

Deforestation and soil erosion are major problems. The Ethiopian army uprooted trees to destroy the cover they provided for Eritrean soldiers. Since 1991, 22 million seedlings have been grown in a replanting scheme. The Red Sea coast is a conservation priority.

MEDIA

TV ownership low

Daily newspaper circulation figures not available

PUBLISHING AND BROADCAST MEDIA

New Eritrea, owned by the PFDJ, is published every 3 days in English, Tigrinya and Arabic

1 state-controlled service   1 state-controlled service

The media is largely controlled by the PFDJ who run both the radio and TV services. Independent newspapers are not encouraged.

CRIME

Death penalty used

 Eritrea does not publish prison figures   Crime levels remain low

Crime has not been a problem since independence. The judiciary and police answer to the PFDJ. There are a number of political prisoners.

EDUCATION

School leaving age: 13

25%   3,096 students

Very few schools functioned during the war. There is one university. In an attempt to reduce potential ethnic tension, all children above the age of 11 are being taught in English.

HEALTH

No welfare state health benefits

1 per 5,000 people   Malaria. Potential risk of famine

The risk of famine overrides normal health concerns. Eritreans built their own hospitals during the independence struggle. Health provision is basic.

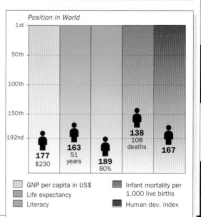

Seasonal river beds carry rain from the Ethiopian highlands into Eritrea, providing essential irrigation for agriculture.

CHRONOLOGY

British military rule replaced Italian colonial authority in 1941.

❏ **1952** Eritrea absorbed by Ethiopia.
❏ **1961** Beginning of armed struggle.
❏ **1987** EPLF refuses offer of autonomy; fighting intensifies.
❏ **1991** EPLF takes control of Asmara.
❏ **1993** Formal independence.
❏ **1997** Elections in six regions. Nakfa replaces Ethiopian birr as currency.
❏ **1998–1999** Border war with Ethiopia.

SPENDING

GDP/cap. no increase

CONSUMPTION AND SPENDING

2 per 1,000 population   6 per 1,000 population

Defense 8.3%
Education 1.8%
Health No data

0   5   10   15   20   25
Defense, Health, Education spending as % of GDP

Over 80% of the country's population are subsistence farmers. A few of the refugees who fled to Arab and Western countries have built up some personal savings.

WORLD RANKING

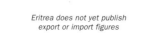

Position in World

1st
50th
100th
150th
192nd

177 $230
163 51 years
189 80%
138 108 deaths
167

❏ GNP per capita in US$ ❏ Infant mortality per 1,000 live births
❏ Life expectancy
❏ Literacy   ❏ Human dev. index

E

ESTONIA

OFFICIAL NAME: Republic of Estonia **CAPITAL:** Tallinn
POPULATION: 1.4 million **CURRENCY:** Kroon **OFFICIAL LANGUAGE:** Estonian

E

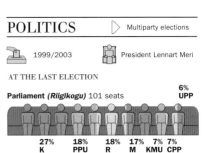

EUROPE

| 1991 | 1991 | Feb 24 | EST | +2 | +372 | .ee |

TRADITIONALLY THE MOST Western-orientated of the Baltic states, Estonia is bordered by Latvia and the Russian Federation. Its terrain is flat, boggy and partly wooded, and includes more than 1,500 islands. Estonia formally regained its independence as a multiparty democracy in 1991. In contrast to the peoples of the other Baltic states, Latvia and Lithuania, Estonians are Finno-Ugric and their language is similar to Finnish.

CLIMATE ▷ Continental

WEATHER CHART

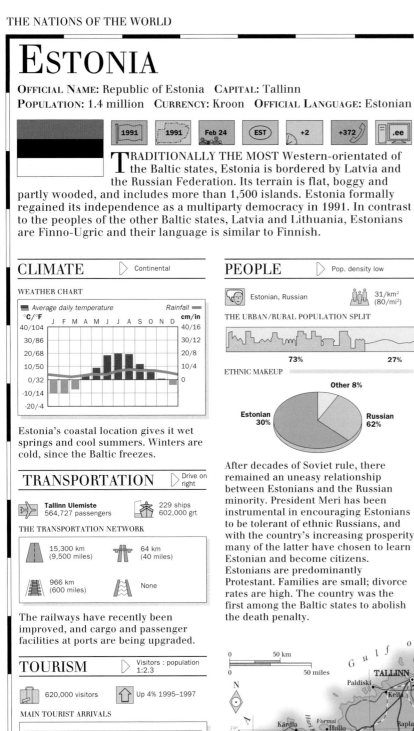

Estonia's coastal location gives it wet springs and cool summers. Winters are cold, since the Baltic freezes.

TRANSPORTATION ▷ Drive on right

| ✈ **Tallinn Ulemiste** 564,727 passengers | ⚓ 229 ships 602,000 grt |

THE TRANSPORTATION NETWORK

| 15,300 km (9,500 miles) | 64 km (40 miles) |
| 966 km (600 miles) | None |

The railways have recently been improved, and cargo and passenger facilities at ports are being upgraded.

TOURISM ▷ Visitors : population 1:2.3

620,000 visitors ⬆ Up 4% 1995–1997

MAIN TOURIST ARRIVALS

Estonia does not publish tourism figures by country of origin

% of total arrivals

Estonia is particularly popular among Finns and Germans. Tallinn's medieval center is a major attraction, and there is growing interest in nature tours. A new yacht basin is being developed in Tallinn city port.

PEOPLE ▷ Pop. density low

Estonian, Russian 👥 31/km² (80/mi²)

THE URBAN/RURAL POPULATION SPLIT

73%   27%

ETHNIC MAKEUP

Other 8%
Estonian 30%
Russian 62%

After decades of Soviet rule, there remained an uneasy relationship between Estonians and the Russian minority. President Meri has been instrumental in encouraging Estonians to be tolerant of ethnic Russians, and with the country's increasing prosperity many of the latter have chosen to learn Estonian and become citizens. Estonians are predominantly Protestant. Families are small; divorce rates are high. The country was the first among the Baltic states to abolish the death penalty.

POLITICS ▷ Multiparty elections

1999/2003   President Lennart Meri

AT THE LAST ELECTION

Parliament (Riigikogu) 101 seats

6% UPP
27% K 18% PPU 18% R 17% M 7% KMU 7% CPP

K = Centre Party **PPU** = Pro Patria Union **R** = Reform Party **M** = Moderates **KMU** = Coalition Party **CPP** = Rural People's Party **UPP** = United People's Party

Coalition government has been the norm since the end of communist rule. In elections on March 7, 1999, the Centre Party of Edgar Savisaar won the most seats, on a platform of a graduated income tax to help overcome wealth disparities. However, Mart Laar, who had been prime minister in 1992–1995, became prime minister in a center-right coalition of the PPU, Reform, and Moderate parties. Laar's government committed itself to pursuing free-market reforms. There was no place for outgoing prime minister Mart Siiman, despite his successes over the previous two years in guiding the country towards prosperity.

ESTONIA

Total Land Area : 45 125 sq. km (17 423 sq. miles)

LAND HEIGHT

200m/565ft
Sea Level

POPULATION

◉	over 500 000
◎	over 100 000
○	over 50 000
●	over 10 000
•	under 10 000

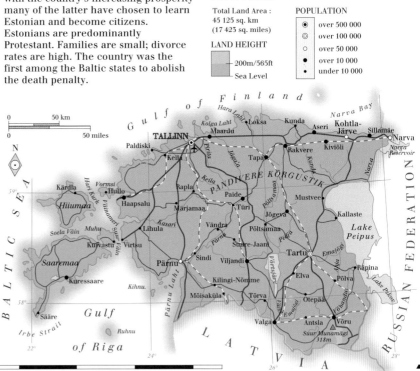

WORLD AFFAIRS

 Joined UN in 1991

Estonia has accepted the *de facto* border with Russia, having effectively ceded territory during the Soviet period. Estonia's trade with the West has been growing following the EU's invitation to begin membership negotiations. Ties with Nordic countries have been particularly emphasized. The USA has promised support for the Baltic states' applications to join NATO.

AID

Recipient

$65m — Up 5% 1996–1997

Finland, Sweden, Germany, the EU and the IMF have provided aid, particularly for infrastructure projects.

DEFENSE

Compulsory military service

$119m — Up 8% in 1997

Estonia is developing a closer relationship with NATO under the Partnership for Peace program. Initial US opposition to full membership of NATO has now been changed to support for the Baltic states' entry into the organization.

ECONOMICS

Inflation 58% p.a. (1985–1996)

$4.9bn — 14.37–13.34 kroons

SCORE CARD

- ❏ WORLD GNP RANKING.......................107th
- ❏ GNP PER CAPITA $3,360
- ❏ BALANCE OF PAYMENTS...................$–562m
- ❏ INFLATION 11.2%
- ❏ UNEMPLOYMENT 2%

STRENGTHS

Improved productivity and strong currency. Simple tax regime. Exports growing. More advantage being taken of natural resources, including timber.

WEAKNESSES

Poor raw materials base. Dependence on imported energy supplies. High inflation. Weak transport infrastructure, but improving.

EXPORTS

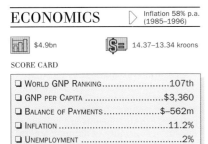

Russia 8%
UK 8%
Germany 9%
Finland 14%
Sweden 16%
Other 45%

IMPORTS

UK 3%
Germany 10%
Sweden 10%
Russia 14%
Finland 31%
Other 32%

RESOURCES

Electric power 3.3m kw

132,343 tonnes

3m poultry, 312,000 cattle, 329,000 pigs

Oil figures not published

Oil shale, coal, peat, phosphorite

The chief resources are oil shale and phosphorite. Timber is now processed to make paper, rather than exported raw.

ENVIRONMENT

No Green MPs

12% — High

Use of oil shale for energy is a major source of pollution. Danger remains of radioactive leaks from former Soviet bases. Improvements have been made to water supply and sewage treatment.

MEDIA

TV ownership high

Daily newspaper circulation 173 per 1,000 people

PUBLISHING AND BROADCAST MEDIA

There are 15 daily newspapers. The main daily newspapers are *Eesti Ekspress*, *Eesti Päevaleht* and *Postimees*

1 state-owned, 4 independent services

1 state-owned service

The media are mostly pro-government. The number of Russian-language programs is declining. Estonians have been able to receive Finnish satellite TV for some years.

CRIME

Death penalty not used

4,034 prisoners — Down 13% from 1992–1996

Robbery and narcotics are the main crime problems. Generally, however, crime levels are still relatively low.

EDUCATION

School leaving age: 16

99% — 43,468 students

Education is becoming increasingly Westernized. Six higher-education establishments have 25,000 students.

HEALTH

Welfare state health benefits

1 per 323 people

Heart diseases, cancers, accidents, violence

The health system, improved since the collapse of communism, is better than that of most former Soviet republics.

The Russian Orthodox convent of Pühtitsa at Kuremäe in Estonia's marshy north. Most of the population is Evangelical Lutheran.

CHRONOLOGY

After Swedish and then Russian rule, Estonia briefly enjoyed independence from 1921 until its incorporation into the Soviet Union in 1940.

- ❏ **1991** Unilateral declaration of independence.
- ❏ **1992** Multiparty elections; center-right coalition government.
- ❏ **1996** President Lennart Meri wins second term of office.
- ❏ **1997** EU agrees to open membership negotiations.
- ❏ **1999** Elections; new center-right government.

SPENDING

GDP/cap. no increase

CONSUMPTION AND SPENDING

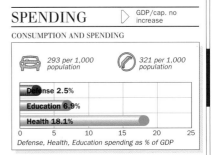

293 per 1,000 population

321 per 1,000 population

Defense 2.5%
Education 6.9%
Health 18.1%

Defense, Health, Education spending as % of GDP

Ongoing market reforms have led to an overall increase in prosperity, although a large gap has opened between rich and poor.

WORLD RANKING

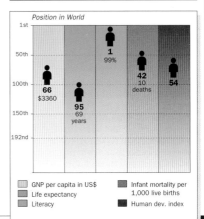

Position in World

66 — $3360
95 — 69 years
1 — 99%
42 — 10 deaths
54

GNP per capita in US$
Life expectancy
Literacy
Infant mortality per 1,000 live births
Human dev. index

E

ETHIOPIA

OFFICIAL NAME: Federal Democratic Republic of Ethiopia **CAPITAL:** Addis Ababa
POPULATION: 62.1 million **CURRENCY:** Ethiopian birr **OFFICIAL LANGUAGE:** Amharic

LOCATED IN NORTHEAST AFRICA, the mountainous former empire of Ethiopia is the cradle of an ancient civilization, which adopted Orthodox Christianity in the fourth century. It has been landlocked since 1993, when Eritrea, its coastal province on the Red Sea, gained its independence. Ethiopia is mountainous except for the desert lowlands in the northeast and southeast, and is subject to devastating droughts and famines. Civil war began in the 1960s and ended in 1991 with the defeat of the Stalinist military dictatorship that had ruled since 1974. Since 1995, a free-market, multiparty democracy has been established, with substantial regional autonomy. A bitter border war with Eritrea began in 1998.

CLIMATE ▷ Mountain/steppe

WEATHER CHART

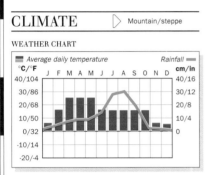

In general, the climate is moderate, except in the lowlands of the Danakil Desert and the Ogaden, which are hot all year round and can suffer severe drought. The highlands are temperate, with night frost in the mountains. The single rainy season in the west brings twice as much rain as do the two wet seasons in the east. During these cloudy periods, thunderstorms occur almost daily.

TRANSPORTATION ▷ Drive on right

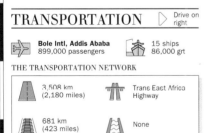

Bole Intl, Addis Ababa
899,000 passengers

15 ships
86,000 grt

THE TRANSPORTATION NETWORK

3,508 km (2,180 miles)		Trans East Africa Highway	
681 km (423 miles)		None	

The single railroad linking Addis Ababa with Djibouti has grown in strategic importance due to the conflict with Eritrea. Ethiopia's main access to the sea by road has been through the Red Sea ports of Assab and Massawa, now part of an independent Eritrea. Inland, pack mules and donkeys are widely used. Ethiopian Airlines has good services to much of Africa, and to European and US cities.

TOURISM ▷ Visitors : population 1:540

115,000 visitors   Up 13% 1995–1997

MAIN TOURIST ARRIVALS

Africa 28%	
Other Europe 22%	
USA 6%	
Italy 6%	
UK 5%	
Other 33%	

% of total arrivals

Despite Ethiopia's unique attractions, tourism is on a small scale, although since 1991 there has been a moderate increase in the number of visitors, mostly on organized tours. Several new hotels are being built. The Gonder castles, Lake Tana, the Rift Valley lakes, and the Blue Nile gorge, with its spectacular scenery, are popular destinations, but guides are essential. Ancient churches and cities such as Aksum, the royal capital of the first Ethiopian kingdom, are now accessible. There are five national parks.

***Lalibela** lies 120 km northwest of Desë in Ethiopia's plateau region, and is typical of the small settlements found across the high mountainous plateau.*

PEOPLE ▷ Pop. density medium

Amharic, Tigrinya, Galla, Sidamo, Somali, English, Arabic

56/km²
(146/mi²)

THE URBAN/RURAL POPULATION SPLIT

13%   87%

RELIGIOUS PERSUASION

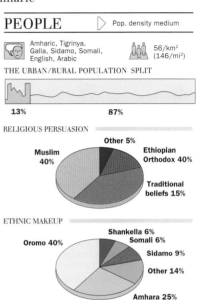

- Ethiopian Orthodox 40%
- Muslim 40%
- Traditional beliefs 15%
- Other 5%

ETHNIC MAKEUP

- Oromo 40%
- Amhara 25%
- Other 14%
- Sidamo 9%
- Somali 6%
- Shankella 6%

There are 76 nationalities in Ethiopia speaking 286 languages. Oromos (or Gallas) form the largest group. Tigreans are fewer than 5%.

Civil war was sparked by fighting between different ethnic groups, but they later united in opposition to the Mengistu regime and its centralist policies. Ethnic tensions are still near the surface, in spite of the new federal structure, and there have been reports of boundary disputes in several regions. The Oromos withdrew from the Tigrean-dominated government in 1992. Hostility to the government has also been voiced by disaffected Amharas, who had been dominant for several centuries, and by the Orthodox Church. The aspirations of ethnic Somalis in the southeast are another source of tension.

No discrimination is shown toward the many small minorities. Most of the small Jewish population was evacuated to Israel in 1991 and the rest began leaving in mid-1999. The participation of women in rural organizations is increasing, reflecting the key role women played in the war.

POPULATION AGE BREAKDOWN

Female	Age	Male
0%	81–100	0%
2.4%	61–80	2.3%
6.4%	41–60	5.9%
11.8%	21–40	11.6%
29.2%	0–20	30.4%

% of population by age group

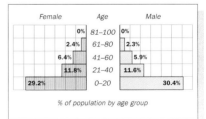

EAST AFRICA

E

ETHIOPIA

Total Land Area :
1 101 000 sq. km
(425 096 sq. miles)

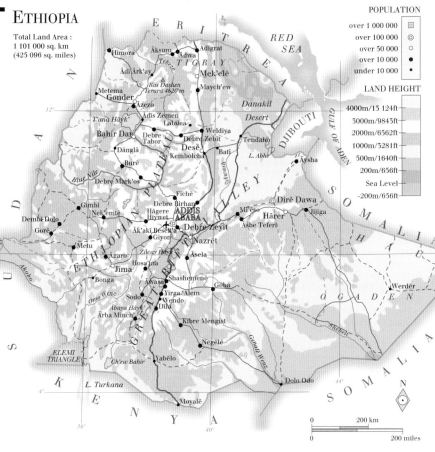

POPULATION

over 1 000 000	▣
over 100 000	◎
over 50 000	○
over 10 000	●
under 10 000	•

LAND HEIGHT

4000m/13 124ft	
3000m/9843ft	
2000m/6562ft	
1000m/3281ft	
500m/1640ft	
200m/656ft	
Sea Level	
-200m/656ft	

0 — 200 km
0 — 200 miles

WORLD AFFAIRS

▷ Joined UN in 1945

Comesa   G24   IGAD   NAM   OAU

Landlocked Ethiopia maintained cordial relations with Eritrea, ensuring continued access to the Red Sea, until in 1998 a border dispute escalated into armed conflict. Relations with Eritrea are likely to remain critical until the major issue of access to the ports of Massawa and Assab is resolved.

Addis Ababa is the headquarters of the OAU and of the UN Economic Commission for Africa. Ethiopia is active in regional diplomacy, including attempts at brokering peace in Somalia, although tension with Somali factions during 1998 and 1999 has escalated into direct Ethiopian armed intervention.

There is a history of tension with Sudan, which has accused Ethiopia of supporting southern rebels since the 1960s. Ethiopia in turn suspected Khartoum of helping Eritrean secessionists. However, the government's official policy is one of non-interference. Links with other African states, as with the USA, the main bilateral donor, and with the EU and Israel, have been strengthened.

E

POLITICS

▷ Multiparty elections

L. House 1995/2000
U. House 1995/2000

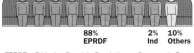

President
Negaso Gidada

AT THE LAST ELECTION

Council of People's Representatives 550 seats

88%	2%	10%
EPRDF	Ind	Others

EPRDF = Ethiopian People's Revolutionary Democratic Front
Ind = Independents

Federal Council 117 seats

The Federal Council is elected on a nonparty basis.

The transitional period, following the collapse of the Mengistu dictatorship in 1991, ended in 1995 with multiparty elections.

MAIN POLITICAL ISSUE
Ethnic representation
The 1994 constitution established a nine-state federation. It grants the states considerable autonomy, including the right of secession, as Eritrea did in 1993. The Ethiopian People's Revolutionary Democratic Front (EPRDF) government believes that this is the best way to prevent secessionist conflict and to maintain a sense of national unity.

The ruling coalition is ideologically dominated by Tigrean politicians.

PROFILE
The current government, elected in 1995, is the successor to that set up in 1991 by the EPRDF, the strongest of the liberation groups that fought Mengistu's Marxist regime and chiefly responsible for winning the civil war. Prime Minister Meles Zenawi is the leader of the Tigrean People's Liberation Front, the largest group within the EPRDF. There is growing opposition to the dominance of Tigreans by the Oromos and Amharas. The nine states are largely governed by elected governments dominated by local liberation movements, which helped to overthrow the Mengistu regime.

Prime Minister Meles Zenawi, *leader of the EPRDF, which ousted the Mengistu regime.*

Mengistu Haile Mariam, *who ran Ethiopia on Soviet lines from 1977–1991.*

CHRONOLOGY

After repelling a devastating Muslim invasion in 1525, Ethiopia developed as an isolated empire until Egyptian and Sudanese incursions in the 1850s led to its renewed political power under Emperor Teodros. His successor, Menelik II, doubled the empire southward and eastward.

❑ **1896** Italian invasion of Tigre defeated. Europeans recognize Ethiopia's independence.
❑ **1913** Menelik II dies.
❑ **1916** His son, Lij Iyasu, deposed for his conversion to Islam and proposed alliance with Turkey. Menelik's daughter, Zauditu, becomes empress with Ras Tafari as regent.
❑ **1923** Joins League of Nations.
❑ **1930** Zauditu dies. Ras Tafari crowned Emperor Haile Selassie.
❑ **1936** Italians occupy Ethiopia. League of Nations fails to react.
❑ **1941** British oust Italians and restore Haile Selassie, who sets up a constitution, parliament and cabinet, but retains personal power and the feudal system.
❑ **1952** Eritrea, ruled by Italy until 1941, then under British mandate, federated to Ethiopia. ⇨

E

CHRONOLOGY *continued*

- ❏ **1962** Unitary state created; Eritrea fully absorbed.
- ❏ **1972–1974** Famine kills 200,000.
- ❏ **1974** Strikes and army mutinies at Haile Selassie's autocratic rule and country's economic decline. Dergue (Military Committee) stages coup.
- ❏ **1975** Becomes socialist state: nationalizations, worker cooperatives, and health reforms.
- ❏ **1977** Col. Mengistu Haile Mariam takes over. Somali invasion of Ogaden defeated with Soviet and Cuban help.
- ❏ **1978–1979** Thousands of political opponents killed or imprisoned.
- ❏ **1984** Workers' Party of Ethiopia (WPE) set up on Soviet model. Live Aid concert raises funds to relieve famine caused by war and three years' drought. One million die.
- ❏ **1986** Eritrean rebels now control the whole northeastern coast.
- ❏ **1987** People's Democratic Republic of Ethiopia declared with Mengistu as president. New serious drought.
- ❏ **1988** Eritrean and Tigrean People's Liberation Fronts (EPLF and TPLF) begin new offensives. Mengistu's budget is for "Everything to the War Front." Ethiopia agrees not to interfere in Somali factional fighting and resumes diplomatic relations severed in 1977.
- ❏ **1989** Military coup attempt fails. TPLF in control of most of Tigre. TPLF and Ethiopian People's Revolutionary Movement form alliance – EPRDF.
- ❏ **1990** WPE renamed Ethiopian Democratic Unity Party and opened to non-Marxists. Moves toward market economy begin. Distribution of food aid for victims of new famine hampered by both government and rebel forces.
- ❏ **1991** Mengistu flees country in face of big advances by EPRDF and EPLF. EPRDF enters Addis Ababa and sets up provisional government, dividing country into 14 semiautonomous regions and promising representation for all ethnic groups. However, fighting continues between the mainly Tigrean EPRDF troops and various opposing groups. EPLF enters Asmara, the Eritrean capital, and sets up government.
- ❏ **1993** Eritrean independence recognized.
- ❏ **1995** Transitional rule ends with multiparty democratic elections and establishment of a new nine-state federation. EPRDF, with landslide victory, forms first democratic government.
- ❏ **1998–1999** Border war with Eritrea.

AID ▷ Recipient

💲 $637m (receipts) | ⬇ Down 25% 1996–1997

The World Food Program and the EU are the largest sources of assistance, while the USA has taken over from Italy and the former Soviet Union as the major bilateral donor. Aid per capita is low by regional standards.

However, long-term development assistance and balance of payments support look set to continue their recent growth. Aid is now playing an increasingly important part in the economy. The emphasis is shifting from food aid toward credit for infrastructure development.

DEFENSE ▷ No compulsory military service

💲 $139m | ⬆ Up 10% in 1997

Ethiopia is one of Africa's most heavily militarized states, a substantial standing army being boosted by conscription at times of crisis. Heavy losses have been sustained in recent fighting with Eritrea. The government is trying to get control of the many ethnic and clan-based militias. Much of the Mengistu regime's $6 billion arms debt to the former USSR is unpaid.

ETHIOPIAN ARMED FORCES

🚂	350 main battle tanks (T-54/55, T-62)	100,000
🚢	Has no navy	None
✈	63 combat aircraft	Included under army
	None	

ECONOMICS ▷ Inflation 5% p.a. (1985–1996)

📊 $6.5bn | 💲 6.70–6.99 Ethiopian birr

SCORE CARD

- ❏ WORLD GNP RANKING............................99th
- ❏ GNP PER CAPITA $110
- ❏ BALANCE OF PAYMENTS.....................$–39m
- ❏ INFLATION 3.7%
- ❏ UNEMPLOYMENT.......Widespread underemployment

ECONOMIC PERFORMANCE INDICATOR

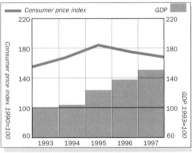

EXPORTS

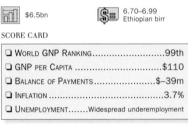

France 5%, Italy 9%, Japan 11%, Other 40%, USA 12%, Germany 21%

IMPORTS

UK 7%, Germany 7%, Japan 8%, Other 58%, USA 10%, Italy 10%

STRENGTHS

Peace and greater flows of economic aid. Dismantling of total state control. Coffee production.

WEAKNESSES

Overwhelming dependence on agriculture – engages 75% of population, accounts for 80% of exports. Periodic serious droughts. War-damaged infrastructure. Massive displacement of population by war and drought. Small industrial base. Lack of skilled workers. Legacy of Mengistu regime's disastrous experiment in a centrally planned economy.

PROFILE

Since the end of the civil war, Ethiopia, one of the world's poorest countries, has begun moving toward a market economy by encouraging foreign investment and reforming land tenure. Economic decline was reversed in 1993 as agricultural and industrial output grew. The latter was fueled by the purchase of parts and raw materials funded by foreign aid.

ETHIOPIA : MAJOR BUSINESSES

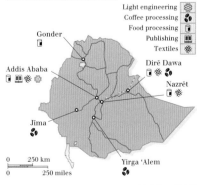

Light engineering, Coffee processing, Food processing, Publishing, Textiles

Gonder, Addis Ababa, Dirē Dawa, Nazrēt, Jima, Yirga 'Alem

0   250 km
0   250 miles

E

RESURCES

▷ Electric power 464,000 kw

🐟 6,380 tonnes

🛢 Not an oil producer; refines 18,000 b/d

30m cattle, 22m sheep, 17m goats, 2.7m horses

💎 Oil, gold, platinum, copper, potash, iron, natural gas

ELECTRICITY GENERATION

| Hydro 87% (1.2bn kwh) |
| Combustion 8% (0.1bn kwh) |
| Nuclear 0% |
| Other 5% (0.07bn kwh) |

0   20   40   60   80   100

% of total generation by type

Manpower and financial constraints have prevented a systematic survey of mineral resources. At present, mining contributes less than 1% of GDP. Ethiopia has great potential for hydroelectric power which, in the long run, could offset a domestic reliance on fuel wood and also slow massive deforestation and soil erosion. Current exploration for oil and gas has revealed reserves in the Ogaden, but exploitation has not begun. When Eritrea seceded in 1993, Ethiopia lost other substantial oil reserves and many oil concessions.

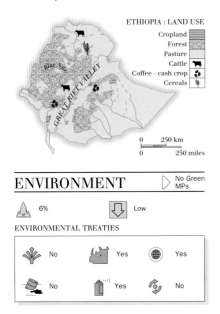

ETHIOPIA : LAND USE

Cropland
Forest
Pasture
🐄 Cattle
Coffee - cash crop
Cereals

0   250 km
0   250 miles

ENVIRONMENT

▷ No Green MPs

🔺 6%

⬇ Low

ENVIRONMENTAL TREATIES

| 🌿 No | 🦏 Yes | 🌐 Yes |
| No | Yes | No |

Deforestation for fuel wood and the resultant rapid soil erosion, particularly in the highlands, are serious problems. Forest cover has fallen from 40% in 1900 to only 2% today. Shortage of wood means that dung is increasingly being used for fuel, its yearly fertilizer value put at $123 million, enough to increase annual grain harvests by up to 1.5 million tonnes. Local projects include terracing hillsides to prevent soil and water run-off – 36,000 km (22,370 miles) of terraces were built in Tigray in 1992.

MEDIA

▷ TV ownership low

❎ Daily newspaper circulation 2 per 1,000 people

The government remains uneasy about the post-Mengistu independent press, which has become prolific and critical, although circulation is small. Legal action has been taken to silence several publications. All main newspapers and broadcasting stations are government-owned and operated.

PUBLISHING AND BROADCAST MEDIA

📰	There are 4 daily newspapers, including *Addis Zemen* and *Ethiopian Herald* published by the government
📺	1 state-owned service
📻	1 state-owned, 3 independent services

CRIME

▷ Death penalty used

🔲 13,585 prisoners

⬡ Murder rate remains high

CRIME RATES

Murders
16 — per 100,000 population

Rapes
1 — per 100,000 population

Thefts
65 — per 100,000 population

A number of human rights abuses by the transitional government have been documented by the independent Ethiopian Human Rights Council. These include detention without trial, "disappearances," and extrajudicial killings. There is some concern over indiscipline among EPRDF forces, who provide a de facto police force in many regions. In many rural areas, the state system has yet to replace traditional forms of justice.

EDUCATION

▷ School leaving age: 13

👤 35%

🎓 35,027 students

Education was severely disrupted during the civil war.

THE EDUCATION SYSTEM

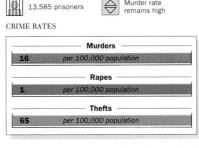

% of each age group in education

100
80
60
40
20
0

37% Primary
11% Secondary
1% Tertiary

Secondary education is in English and Amharic. Addis Ababa University has been a center of political activity, usually anti-EPRDF, and is subject to periodic closures and the sacking of leading academics.

HEALTH

▷ No welfare state health benefits

👥 1 per 25,000 people

☠ Diarrheal and respiratory diseases, tuberculosis, malaria

Only about half of the population lives within 12 km (7 miles) of a health unit. Hospital building, distribution of resources to rural areas, outpatient visits, and referrals are all very slow. Skin and eye diseases are common. Mission hospitals are of a reasonably high standard. The use of traditional remedies is widespread.

SPENDING

▷ Not available

CONSUMPTION AND SPENDING

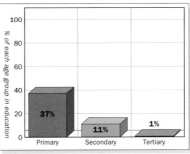

🚗 1 per 1,000 population

🍽 3 per 1,000 population

| Defense 2.1% |
| Education 4.7% |
| Health 0.7% |

0   5   10   15   20   25

Defense, Health, Education spending as % of GDP

Most Ethiopians are extremely poor – many of the country's wealthier families having fled into exile in recent years. Ethiopian Christian culture places more value on maintaining traditional social structures than on individual ambition. Subsistence life and a reliance on traditional agriculture remain the normal expectation.

WORLD RANKING

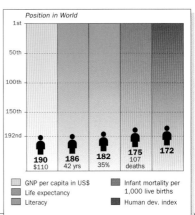

Position in World

1st
50th
100th
150th
192nd

190 $110
186 42 yrs
182 35%
175 107 deaths
172

☐ GNP per capita in US$
☐ Life expectancy
☐ Literacy
☐ Infant mortality per 1,000 live births
☐ Human dev. index

FIJI

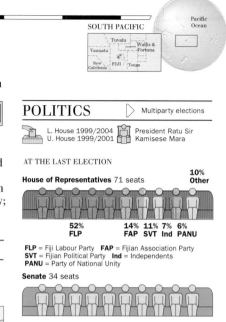

SOUTH PACIFIC

Pacific Ocean

Tuvalu
Wallis & Fortuna
Vanuatu
New Caledonia | FIJI | Tonga

OFFICIAL NAME: Republic of Fiji **CAPITAL:** Suva
POPULATION: 822,000 **CURRENCY:** Fiji dollar **OFFICIAL LANGUAGE:** English

| 1970 | 1970 | Oct 10 | FJI | +12 | +679 | .fj |

FIJI IS A VOLCANIC ARCHIPELAGO in the southern Pacific Ocean, comprising two large islands and 880 islets. From 1874 to 1970, Fiji was a British colony. The British introduced Indian workers; by 1946 Indo-Fijians outnumbered the ethnic Fijian population. In 1987, the democratically elected government was overthrown by ethnic Fijians. After the coups, thousands of Indo-Fijians left the country; the 1997 census showed ethnic Fijians again in the majority, but a discriminatory constitution has now been replaced.

CLIMATE ▷ Tropical oceanic

WEATHER CHART

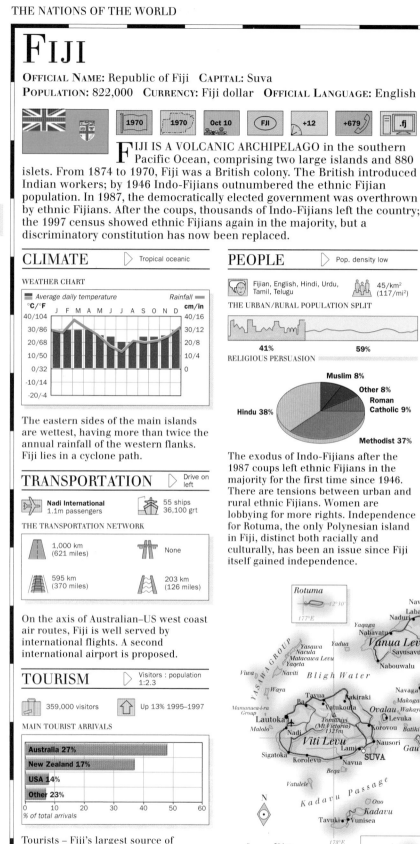

Average daily temperature   Rainfall

The eastern sides of the main islands are wettest, having more than twice the annual rainfall of the western flanks. Fiji lies in a cyclone path.

TRANSPORTATION ▷ Drive on left

Nadi International
1.1m passengers

55 ships
36,100 grt

THE TRANSPORTATION NETWORK

| 1,000 km (621 miles) | None |
| 595 km (370 miles) | 203 km (126 miles) |

On the axis of Australian–US west coast air routes, Fiji is well served by international flights. A second international airport is proposed.

TOURISM ▷ Visitors : population 1:2.3

359,000 visitors   Up 13% 1995–1997

MAIN TOURIST ARRIVALS

Australia 27%
New Zealand 17%
USA 14%
Other 23%

0 10 20 30 40 50 60
% of total arrivals

Tourists – Fiji's largest source of foreign exchange – have returned, after a 76% drop in numbers following the 1987 coups.

PEOPLE ▷ Pop. density low

Fijian, English, Hindi, Urdu, Tamil, Telugu

45/km² (117/mi²)

THE URBAN/RURAL POPULATION SPLIT

41%   59%

RELIGIOUS PERSUASION

Muslim 8%
Other 8%
Roman Catholic 9%
Hindu 38%
Methodist 37%

The exodus of Indo-Fijians after the 1987 coups left ethnic Fijians in the majority for the first time since 1946. There are tensions between urban and rural ethnic Fijians. Women are lobbying for more rights. Independence for Rotuma, the only Polynesian island in Fiji, distinct both racially and culturally, has been an issue since Fiji itself gained independence.

POLITICS ▷ Multiparty elections

L. House 1999/2004
U. House 1999/2001

President Ratu Sir Kamisese Mara

AT THE LAST ELECTION

House of Representatives 71 seats

10% Other

52% FLP   14% FAP   11% SVT   7% Ind   6% PANU

FLP = Fiji Labour Party **FAP** = Fijian Association Party
SVT = Fijian Political Party   **Ind** = Independents
PANU = Party of National Unity

Senate 34 seats

The Senate is appointed by the President of the Republic

The 1987 coups, justified as defending ethnic Fijian land rights, were a move by Fijian chiefs to secure their power, threatened by the growing Indo-Fijian urban class and Westernized younger ethnic Fijians. The 1990 constitution enshrining ethnic Fijian supremacy was replaced by a more internationally acceptable one in 1997. The Indo-Fijian Mahendra Chaudry became prime minister after the 1999 election victory of the mainly Indo-Fijian FLP.

FIJI

Total Land Area : 18 270 sq. km (7054 sq. miles)

POPULATION

over 50 000 ○
over 10 000 ●
under 10 000 ●

LAND HEIGHT

1000m/3281ft
500m/1640ft
Sea Level

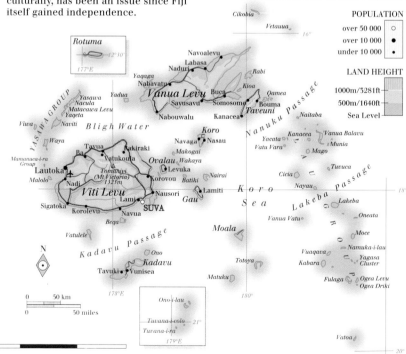

WORLD AFFAIRS

Joined UN in 1970

| ACP | CP | Comm | SPC | SPF |

Fiji is still working to repair its international reputation, damaged by discrimination. Expelled from the Commonwealth, it was readmitted in 1997 after adopting a new constitution.

AID

Recipient

US$44m (receipts)

Down 2% 1996–1997

Fiji is one of the world's highest per capita aid recipients. Australia, Japan, and the EU are the main donors.

DEFENSE

No compulsory military service

US$48m

Down 2% in 1997

Of the almost entirely ethnic Fijian, 3,800-strong military, significant numbers are assigned to UN duties and have served in Lebanon and Egypt.

ECONOMICS

Inflation 4.7% p.a. (1985–1996)

US$2bn

1.54–1.98 Fiji dollars

SCORE CARD

❏ WORLD GNP RANKING	139th
❏ GNP PER CAPITA	US$2,460
❏ BALANCE OF PAYMENTS	US$10m
❏ INFLATION	3.4%
❏ UNEMPLOYMENT	6%

STRENGTHS

Relatively well-diversified economy, with a growing tourist industry. Location on Pacific air routes an impetus to tourism; the many regional and international organizations located in Suva also bring benefits.

WEAKNESSES

Migration of many Indo-Fijian professionals; sugar crops vulnerable to drought. Major exports – sugar, copra and gold – subject to large fluctuations in world prices.

EXPORTS

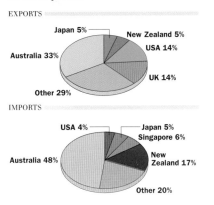

Japan 5%
New Zealand 5%
USA 14%
Australia 33%
UK 14%
Other 29%

IMPORTS

USA 4%
Japan 5%
Singapore 6%
Australia 48%
New Zealand 17%
Other 20%

Cane field on the west side of Viti Levu, between Nadi and Lautoka. Sugar accounts for about one-third of Fiji's exports.

RESOURCES

Electric power 200,000 kw

34,577 tonnes

Not an oil producer

360,000 cattle, 220,000 goats, 145,000 pigs

Gold, silver

The varied terrain allows diversified agriculture. There are gold and other minerals. The Monasavu hydroelectric station meets 95% of electricity needs.

ENVIRONMENT

No green MPs

0.3%

Not available

The government is environmentally aware; Fiji is downwind of French Pacific nuclear test sites. Tourism is damaging coral reefs. Fertilizers are overused.

MEDIA

TV ownership low

Daily newspaper circulation 50 per 1,000 people

PUBLISHING AND BROADCAST MEDIA

There are 2 English-language dailies, the *Fiji Times* and the *Daily Post*. *Nai Lalakai* and *Shanti Dut* are the Fijian and Indian weeklies

1 state-owned service

5 state-controlled, 2 independent stations

The 1995 revisions to the Official Secrets Act and 1998 Emergency Powers Bill are of concern, as is the government's 1999 purchase of 45% ownership of the *Daily Post*.

CRIME

Death penalty not used

961 prisoners

Up 9% in 1992

Theft and drink-related violence top the crime list. Fiji also has one of the world's highest *crime passionel* rates.

EDUCATION

Scool leaving age: 15

92%

7,908 students

Education, originally modeled on the British system, is now mostly run by local committees and is increasingly racially segregated. Attendance, though high, is not compulsory.

CHRONOLOGY

The British decision to import Indian sugar workers between 1879 and 1916, many of whom settled, dramatically changed Fijian society.

- ❏ **1970** Independence from Britain.
- ❏ **1987** Indo-Fijian coalition wins power. Rabuka's coups secure rule for minority ethnic Fijians. Ejected from Commonwealth.
- ❏ **1989** Mass Indo-Fijian emigration.
- ❏ **1990** Constitution discriminating against Indo-Fijians introduced.
- ❏ **1992** Rabuka wins general election.
- ❏ **1997** Fiji rejoins Commonwealth with new constitution.
- ❏ **1999** General election won by FLP. First Indo-Fijian prime minister.

F

HEALTH

Welfare state health benefits

1 per 1,784 people

Cerebrovascular and heart diseases, cancers, accidents

There are fears that Fiji will be unable to afford the drugs needed for AIDS patients. Fiji is free of almost all tropical diseases, including malaria.

SPENDING

GDP/cap. increase

CONSUMPTION AND SPENDING

59 per 1,000 population

84 per 1,000 population

Defense	2.6%
Education	5.4%
Health	No data

0   5   10   15   20   25
Defense, Health, Education spending as % of GDP

Ostentatious displays of wealth are rare in Fiji; prestige is derived from the family and from landholdings. The professional middle class, while still dominated by Indo-Fijians, is becoming more mixed.

WORLD RANKING

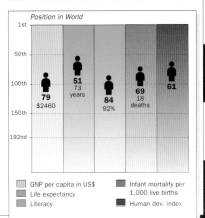

Position in World

79 $2460
51 73 years
84 92%
69 18 deaths
61

GNP per capita in US$
Life expectancy
Literacy
Infant mortality per 1,000 live births
Human dev. index

FINLAND

OFFICIAL NAME: Republic of Finland **CAPITAL:** Helsinki
POPULATION: 5.2 million **CURRENCY:** Markka **OFFICIAL LANGUAGES:** Finnish and Swedish

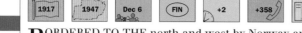

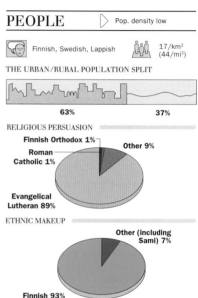

EUROPE

BORDERED TO THE north and west by Norway and Sweden, and to the east by Russia, Finland is a low-lying country of forests and 187,888 lakes. Politics are based on consensus, and it has been stable despite successive short-lived coalitions. Russia annexed Finland in 1809, ruling it until 1917, and subsequently Finland accepted a close relationship with the Soviet Union as the price of maintaining its independence. It joined the European Union in 1995 and, despite popular suspicion of Brussels bureaucracy, Finland was among the 11 EU states to introduce the euro from 1999.

CLIMATE

▷ Subarctic/continental

WEATHER CHART

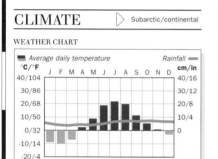

North of the Arctic Circle the climate is extreme. Temperatures fall to –30°C (–22°F) in the six-month winter and rise to 27°C (81°F) during the 73 days of summer midnight sun. In the south, summers are mild and short, winters are cold.

TRANSPORTATION

▷ Drive on right

Helsinki-Vantaa, 9.37m passengers

277 ships 1.56m grt

THE TRANSPORTATION NETWORK

77,800 km (48,300 miles)	431 km (268 miles)
5,865 km (3,644 miles)	17,190 km (10,744 miles)

Finland has a well-integrated transportation system. The railroad connects with the Swedish and Russian networks. There are frequent air services to most neighboring states and links with Baltic states are being expanded. Internal air travel is important, particularly north of the Arctic Circle.

With 187,888 lakes and a major river network, Finland has Europe's largest inland waterway system. It still carries freight, but is now used mainly for recreation. Finland's international ports handle around 70 million tonnes a year. Kotka is the chief export port, while Helsinki, with five specialized harbors, handles most imports.

TOURISM

▷ Visitors : population 1:2.8

1.8m visitors

Up 20% 1995–1997

MAIN TOURIST ARRIVALS

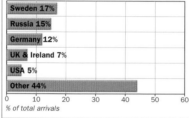

% of total arrivals

The scenery of the southern lakes and the vast forests of its Arctic north are Finland's main attractions. Helsinki is an important cultural center and hosts an annual arts festival. Its opera house has an international reputation and the capital has many first-class restaurants. Most tourists try a sauna, a Finnish invention, and the local vodka, which is reputedly among the world's finest.

Visitors come mostly from other Nordic countries, particularly neighboring Sweden, and from Germany. Since 1990, the number of visitors from the Baltic states and Russia has risen and Finland is also attracting more British tourists.

A summer's night at Kilpisjärvi, 'The Way of the Four Winds', which lies at the point where Finland, Sweden and Norway meet.

PEOPLE

▷ Pop. density low

Finnish, Swedish, Lappish

17/km² (44/mi²)

THE URBAN/RURAL POPULATION SPLIT

63%   37%

RELIGIOUS PERSUASION

Finnish Orthodox 1%
Roman Catholic 1%
Other 9%
Evangelical Lutheran 89%

ETHNIC MAKEUP

Other (including Sami) 7%
Finnish 93%

Most Finns are of Scandinavian–Baltic extraction. Finnish belongs to the small Finno-Ugric linguistic group and is a legacy of the country's earliest invaders from Asia. Although they were later ousted by the ancestors of today's Finns, their language was retained. Lappish, also a Finno-Ugric language, is spoken by the small Sami (Lapp) population, who live above the Arctic Circle. Around 6% of the population live in the Åland Islands in the southwest and speak Swedish.

More than 50% of Finns live in the five southernmost districts around Helsinki. Families tend to be close-knit, although divorce rates are high. The sauna is an integral part of everyday life; there are 1.5 million saunas among five million Finns.

Finnish women have a long tradition of political and economic participation. They were the first women in Europe to get the vote, in 1906, and the first in the world who were entitled to stand for seats in parliament. Almost 50% of women now work outside the home and one-third of the cabinet is female.

POPULATION AGE BREAKDOWN

Female	Age	Male
2.3%	81–100	0.9%
9.2%	61–80	6.7%
13.9%	41–60	14.2%
13.5%	21–40	14%
12.4%	0–20	12.9%

% of population by age group

POLITICS

 ▷ Multiparty elections

1999/2003　　President Martti Ahtisaari

Finland's constitution combines parliamentary government with a strong presidency. The external territory of the Åland Islands has internal self-government.

MAIN POLITICAL ISSUES
EU membership
Finland joined the EU in 1995. The small but influential farming community was hostile to membership. Others feared that public spending cuts, in particular welfare cuts, would be required to meet the economic convergence criteria for

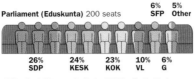

AT THE LAST ELECTION

Parliament (Eduskunta) 200 seats

6% SFP　5% Other

26% SDP　24% KESK　23% KOK　10% VL　6% G

SDP = Social Democratic Party　**KESK** = Centre Party
KOK = National Coalition Party　**VL** = Left Wing Alliance
G = Greens　**SFP** = Swedish People's Party
Others includes the Finnish Christian League (SKL)

membership. The government of Prime Minister Paavo Lipponen nevertheless pushed ahead determinedly and succeeded in meeting these criteria; Finland was among the 11 EU countries to introduce the euro from January 1999.

Unemployment
SDP candidate Martti Ahtisaari won the 1994 presidential election; the policies of the conservative coalition then in power had resulted in record unemployment levels and welfare cuts. After the 1995 general election an SDP-led coalition continued many of the previous government's austerity policies. Unemployment has since successfully been reduced, to 12.7% in 1997.

PROFILE
Proportional representation has led to government by coalition, usually dominated by the SDP or KESK. The emphasis on consensus has favored stability but resulted in slow decision-making. The current "rainbow" coalition includes five parties from across the political spectrum.

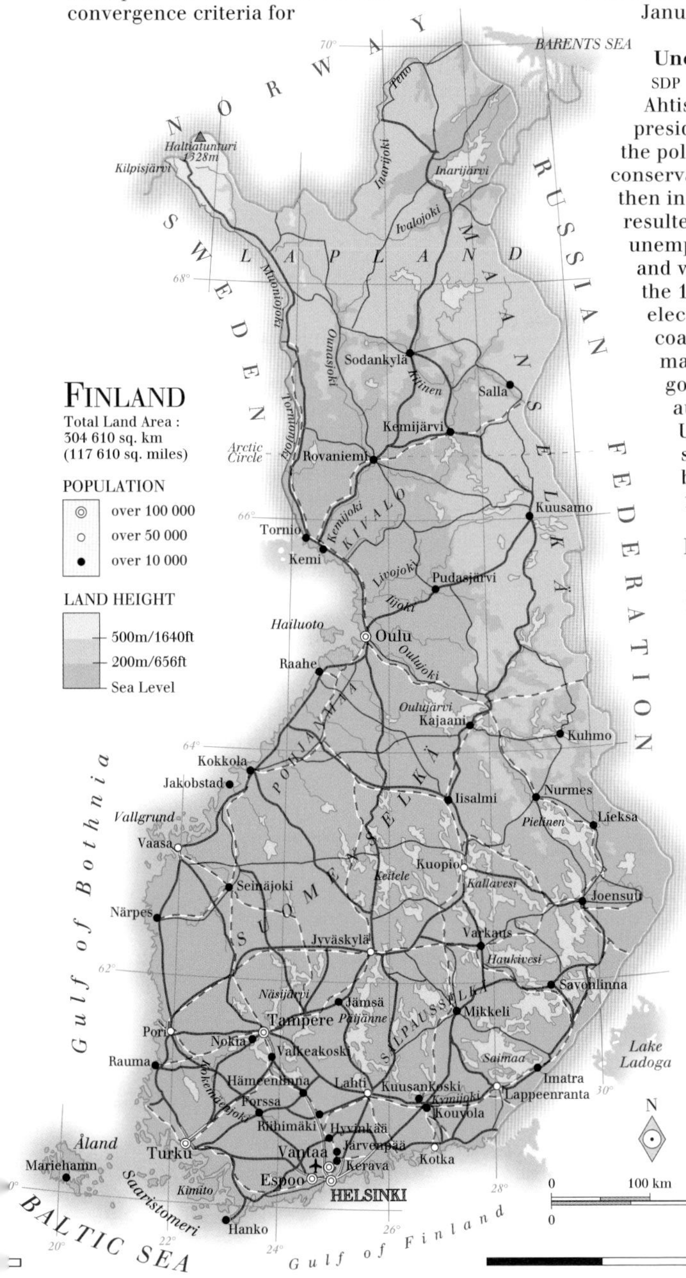

President Martti Ahtisaari, *who won the 1994 presidential election.*

Prime Minister, Paavo Lipponen, *leader of the SDP-led coalition.*

F

WORLD AFFAIRS
▷ Joined UN in 1955

CE　EU　OECD　OSCE　PfP

After carefully balancing its relations with the Soviet Union and the West during the Cold War, Finland has now decided that its national interest lies within western Europe. In addition to joining the EU, it has observer status at the WEU. However, acknowledging historical and geographical realities, the government is also keen to maintain a special relationship with Russia.

AID
▷ Donor

$379m (donations)　Not applicable

Finland allocated an average of 0.33% of GNP to aid in 1995–1997 (less than the UN target of 0.7%). The main recipients are China, Bosnia–Herzegovina and southern Africa.

CHRONOLOGY

Finland's history has been closely linked with the competing interests of Sweden and Russia.

❑ **1523** Treaty of Pähkinäsaari. Finland part of Swedish Kingdom.
❑ **1809** Treaty of Fredrikhamn, Sweden cedes Finland to Russia. Finland becomes a Grand Duchy enjoying considerable autonomy.
❑ **1812** Helsinki becomes capital.
❑ **1863** Finnish becomes an official language alongside Swedish.
❑ **1865** Grand Duchy acquires its own monetary system.
❑ **1879** Conscription law lays the foundation for a Finnish army.
❑ **1899** Tsar Nicholas II begins process of Russification. Labor Party founded.
❑ **1900** Gradual imposition of Russian as the official language begins.
❑ **1901** Finnish army disbanded, Finns ordered into Russian units. Disobedience campaign prevents men being drafted into the army. ▷

FINLAND

Total Land Area :
304 610 sq. km
(117 610 sq. miles)

POPULATION
◎ over 100 000
○ over 50 000
● over 10 000

LAND HEIGHT
500m/1640ft
200m/656ft
Sea Level

[Map of Finland showing cities including Helsinki, Tampere, Turku, Oulu, Rovaniemi, Vaasa, and geographic features including Gulf of Bothnia, Baltic Sea, Gulf of Finland, Barents Sea, and neighboring Norway, Sweden, and Russian Federation]

0　100 km
0　100 miles

F

CHRONOLOGY *continued*

- ❑ **1903** Labor Party becomes SDP.
- ❑ **1905** National strike forces restoration of 1899 status quo.
- ❑ **1906** Parliamentary reform. Universal suffrage introduced.
- ❑ **1910** Responsibility for important legislation passed to Russian *Duma*.
- ❑ **1917** Russian revolution allows Finland to declare independence.
- ❑ **1918** Civil war between Bolsheviks and right-wing government. Gen. Mannerheim leads government to victory at Battle of Tampere.
- ❑ **1919** Finland becomes republic. Kaarlo Ståhlberg elected president with wide political powers.
- ❑ **1920** Treaty of Tartu: Soviet Union recognizes Finland's borders.
- ❑ **1921** London Convention. Åland Islands become part of Finland.
- ❑ **1939** August, Hitler–Stalin non-aggression pact gives USSR a free hand in Finland. November, Soviet invasion; strong Finnish resistance in ensuing Winter War.
- ❑ **1940** Treaty of Moscow. Finland cedes one-tenth of national territory.
- ❑ **1941** Finnish troops join Germany in its invasion of USSR.
- ❑ **1944** June, Red Army invades. August, President Ryti resigns. September, Finland, led by Marshal Mannerheim, signs armistice.
- ❑ **1946** President Mannerheim resigns, Juho Paasikivi president.
- ❑ **1948** Signs friendship treaty with USSR. Agrees to resist any attack on USSR made through Finland by Germany or its allies.
- ❑ **1952** Payment of $570 million in war reparations completed.
- ❑ **1956** Uhro Kekkonen, leader of the Agrarian Party, becomes president.
- ❑ **1956–1991** A series of coalition governments involving SDP and Agrarians, renamed KESK in 1965, hold power.
- ❑ **1981** President Kekkonen resigns.
- ❑ **1982** Mauno Koivisto president.
- ❑ **1989** USSR recognizes Finnish neutrality for first time.
- ❑ **1991** Non-SDP government elected. Austerity measures.
- ❑ **1992** January, signs ten-year agreement with Russia which, for first time since World War II, involves no military agreement.
- ❑ **1994** SDP candidate Martti Ahtisaari elected president in show of electoral dissatisfaction with conservative government.
- ❑ **1995** Finland joins EU. General election returns SDP-led coalition under Paavo Lipponen.
- ❑ **1999** Finland among first 11 countries to introduce euro. General election returns Lipponen's coalition to power.

DEFENSE

 Compulsory military service

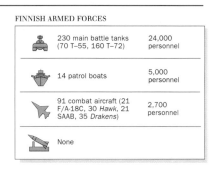

💲 $2bn   ⬇ Down 14% in 1997

Finland is a neutral country. Its armed forces are 31,700-strong, with 500,000 active reservists and 3,400 border guards. Russia's instability has reinforced concern about border security, the main defense issue. Finland participates in NATO's Partnerships for Peace program and has WEU observer status. Defense spending was $1,956 million in 1997 (or 1.7% of GDP).

FINNISH ARMED FORCES

🚜	230 main battle tanks (70 T–55, 160 T–72)	24,000 personnel
🚢	14 patrol boats	5,000 personnel
✈	91 combat aircraft (21 F/A-18C, 30 Hawk, 21 SAAB, 35 Drakens)	2,700 personnel
	None	

ECONOMICS

 Inflation 3.6% p.a. (1985–1996)

📊 $127.4bn   💲 5.45–5.06 markkaa

SCORE CARD

- ❑ WORLD GNP RANKING...........................31st
- ❑ GNP PER CAPITA $24,790
- ❑ BALANCE OF PAYMENTS $6bn
- ❑ INFLATION 1.2%
- ❑ UNEMPLOYMENT...................................13%

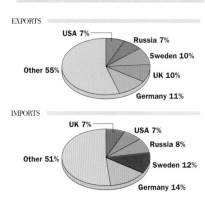

EXPORTS

USA 7% — Russia 7% — Sweden 10% — UK 10% — Germany 11% — Other 55%

IMPORTS

UK 7% — USA 7% — Russia 8% — Sweden 12% — Germany 14% — Other 51%

STRENGTHS

Industry export- and quality-oriented. Large high-tech sector. World leader in pulp and paper. Exports quick to recover from recession. Low inflation, now less than 2% a year. Improved foreign investment incentives. Gateway to Russian and Baltic economies.

WEAKNESSES

Severe recession in 1991–1993 after decade of record growth; real GDP declined 15% but has recovered to grow by nearly 5% per annum in 1994–1998. Danger of economy overheating. High level of public and foreign debt. Joblessness of 20% in 1993, falling to 12.7% in 1997. Small domestic market. Peripheral position in Europe.

PROFILE

Finland is a wealthy market economy, despite the worst recession in 60 years in the early 1990s. The boom years of the 1980s, when GDP grew by almost 4% a year, came to an abrupt end in 1990. The collapse of the former Soviet

ECONOMIC PERFORMANCE INDICATOR

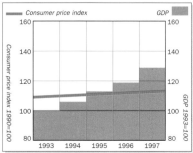

Consumer price index — GDP

Union, which had taken 28% of Finland's exports, was largely responsible for the downturn. Russia took only 5% of Finland's exports in 1995. A rapid rise in unemployment and business failures pushed up government spending. The floating of the markka in 1992 and austerity measures, including welfare benefit cuts, higher taxes and wage restraints, improved competitiveness. Unemployment is now falling as the construction and retail sectors have picked up, although there is a risk of the economy overheating. Finland was one of the 11 EU countries to introduce the euro in January 1999.

FINLAND : MAJOR BUSINESSES

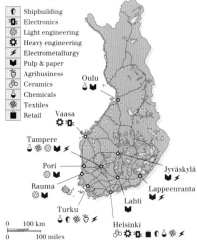

- 🚢 Shipbuilding
- ⚡ Electronics
- ⚙ Light engineering
- ✿ Heavy engineering
- ⚡ Electrometallurgy
- 🍃 Pulp & paper
- 🐂 Agribusiness
- ⚭ Ceramics
- 🧪 Chemicals
- ✳ Textiles
- ■ Retail

RESOURCES
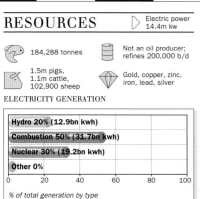

▷ Electric power 14.4m kw

184,288 tonnes

Not an oil producer; refines 200,000 b/d

1.5m pigs, 1.1m cattle, 102,900 sheep

Gold, copper, zinc, iron, lead, silver

ELECTRICITY GENERATION

Hydro 20% (12.9bn kwh)
Combustion 50% (31.7bn kwh)
Nuclear 30% (19.2bn kwh)
Other 0%

% of total generation by type

Finland's trees are its prime natural resource. Commercial forests cover 65% of the land, and wood products account for 40% of exports. Finland has no oil, but has significant hydroelectric resources. Industry's high energy demands are met chiefly by thermal and nuclear power. A fifth nuclear power station is planned. Oil import costs have risen since 1990, when the collapse of the USSR ended a 42-year agreement on the exchange of Finnish manufactures for Soviet oil.

FINLAND : LAND USE

Cropland
Forest
Pasture
Y Reindeer
Barley

0   100 km
0   100 miles

ENVIRONMENT

▷ Green MPs

6%   High

ENVIRONMENTAL TREATIES

Yes   Yes   Yes
Yes   Yes   Yes

Finland has strict laws on industrial emissions. Energy efficiency is a priority; over 40% of homes are connected to district heating systems. Growing public concern about nuclear safety has led to opposition to the planned fifth nuclear plant and to proposals for the greater use of waste materials in energy generation. The government is funding nuclear safety programs in Russia. Rising levels of pollution in the Baltic are of concern.

MEDIA

▷ TV ownership high

Daily newspaper circulation 455 per 1,000 people

PUBLISHING AND BROADCAST MEDIA

There are 56 daily papers. The most important are *Helsingin Sanomat, Ilta-Sanomat, Turun Sanomat, Aamulehti, Kaleva*

1 state-owned, 3 independent services

4 state-owned, 4 independent services

Nine out of ten adult Finns read a daily paper, the world's fifth-highest per capita ratio. Regional papers dominate; the only national is the independent *Helsingin Sanomat*. There is no censorship, but the press shows restraint in criticizing the government.

CRIME

▷ Death penalty not used

3,018 prisoners

Down 10% from 1992–1996

CRIME RATES

Murders
1 per 100,000 population

Rapes
6 per 100,000 population

Thefts
2601 per 100,000 population

The jump in unemployment, from 3.5% in 1990 to 20% in 1993, was one cause of rising crime. There is concern about links with organized crime in Russia.

EDUCATION

▷ Scool leaving age: 16

99%   213.995 students

Of total government expenditure almost 12% is spent on education.

THE EDUCATION SYSTEM

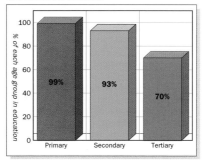

Primary 99%, Secondary 93%, Tertiary 70%
% of each age group in education

Compulsory education lasts from seven to 16 years of age. Almost all children receive preschool education and go on to three years of upper secondary education. Tough examinations mean that only 35% of entrants qualify to attend one of the 20 universities.

HEALTH

▷ Welfare state health benefits

1 per 370 people

Cerebrovascular and heart diseases, cancers, suicides

Of total government expenditure nearly 15% is spent on Finland's well-developed health system. Every Finn is legally guaranteed access to a local health center staffed by up to four doctors, as well as nurses and a midwife. National health insurance covers most non-hospital medical costs; hospital fees are moderate. Private spending on health represents only 19.1% of total spending on health.

F

SPENDING

▷ GDP/cap. no increase

CONSUMPTION AND SPENDING

379 per 1,000 population
556 per 1,000 population

Defense 1.7%
Education 7.6%
Health 8.9%

Defense, Health, Education spending as % of GDP

Income disparities are more marked in Finland than in the rest of Scandinavia. However, the economic boom and labor shortages of the 1980s led to a sharp rise in all living standards. Personal consumption reached Swedish levels, and many families were able to take two vacations a year. Social security benefits were extended. Since the recession began in 1990, however, this improvement has been reversed. Wealth disparities have widened and expenditure cuts led to lower social security benefits for the jobless. Those in work have had to accept lower pay rises and higher taxes. Average real disposable income has dropped by more than 7% since 1991, but the situation is now improving. Estonian immigrants form the poorest group.

WORLD RANKING

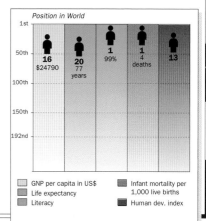

Position in World

16 $24790
20 77 years
1 99%
1 4 deaths
13

GNP per capita in US$
Life expectancy
Literacy
Infant mortality per 1,000 live births
Human dev. index

FRANCE

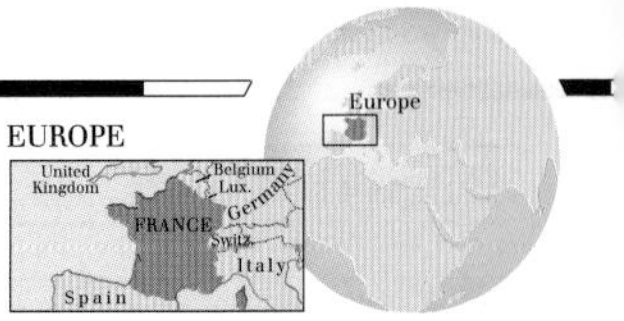

OFFICIAL NAME: The French Republic   **CAPITAL:** Paris
POPULATION: 58.7 million   **CURRENCY:** Franc   **OFFICIAL LANGUAGE:** French

| 486 | 1919 | July 14 | F | +1 | +33 | .fr |

EUROPE

S TRADDLING WESTERN EUROPE from the English
Channel to the Mediterranean, France was Europe's
first modern republic and possessed a colonial empire
second only to Britain's. Today, it is one of the world's major industrial
powers and its fourth largest exporter. Industry is the leading economic
sector, but the agricultural lobby remains powerful – French farmers are
willing to mount the barricades in defense of their interests. Today,
France's focus is very much toward Europe. Together with Germany it
was a founder member of the European Economic Community, and
following a referendum in 1992, France endorsed the Maastricht Treaty
on European Union. Paris, the French capital, is generally considered one
of the world's most beautiful cities. It has been home to some of the 20th
century's most influential artists, writers and filmmakers.

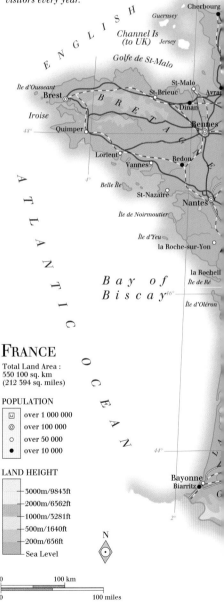

Le Plessis-Bourré, Loire Valley. The region
is famous for its many chateaux,
which attract thousands of
visitors every year.

CLIMATE ▷ Maritime/Mediterranean/ mountain/continental

WEATHER CHART

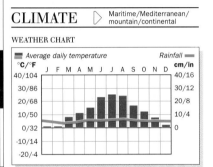

France has, in broad terms, three
climates – continental, maritime and
Mediterranean. The northwest, in
particular Brittany, is mild but damp.
The east has hot summers and stormy
winters. Summers in the south are dry
and hot, and forest fires are common.

TRANSPORTATION ▷ Drive on right

✈ **Charles de Gaulle, Paris**
39m passengers

⚓ 4.12m grt

THE TRANSPORTATION NETWORK

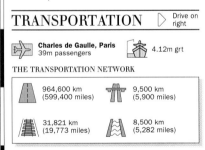

964,600 km
(599,400 miles)

9,500 km
(5,900 miles)

31,821 km
(19,773 miles)

8,500 km
(5,282 miles)

Pioneers of aviation and cobuilders
of Concorde, the French also led the
world in high-speed train technology.
The first TGV (*train à grande vitesse*)
line, from Paris to Lyon, was opened
in 1983, and TGV lines have since been
built to Belgium, Italy, Spain, and the
Channel Tunnel. There is a very well
developed road traffic system,
and France is a major center for
commercial airline traffic, thanks
to its economic significance and
the importance of tourism.

TOURISM ▷ Visitors:population 1.1:1

🧳 66.9m visitors   ⬆ Up 11% in 1997

MAIN TOURIST ARRIVALS

UK & Ireland 19%
Germany 17%
Belgium & Luxembourg 11%
Netherlands 9%
Italy 9%
Other 35%

% of total arrivals

France is the world's leading tourist
destination, with well over 60 million
visitors a year. It tops the list for the
Germans, the British, the Italians,
and the Dutch. Most French people
also prefer to take vacations in their
own country, although many do visit
Spain and Italy.

Paris is the most visited European
city. Its attractions include the Eiffel
Tower, Nôtre Dame cathedral, the
Pompidou Centre and the Louvre, the
world's largest and most popular
museum. Disneyland Paris has
established itself as another crowd-
puller, having first gone into profit in
1995 with over 10 million visitors.

Other destinations throughout the
country attract tourists for a wide
variety of reasons: wine, its historic
sites, its architecture, and the high
quality of its seaside, skiing and hiking,
and sailing destinations. Modern
tourism was all but invented on the
Côte d'Azur, when crowned heads and
grandees flocked to fashionable resorts
such as Nice at the end of the 19th
century. Today, Cannes hosts the
world's leading film festival, and has
a growing business convention trade.

FRANCE

Total Land Area :
550 100 sq. km
(212 394 sq. miles)

POPULATION

⊡ over 1 000 000
◎ over 100 000
○ over 50 000
● over 10 000

LAND HEIGHT

3000m/9843ft
2000m/6562ft
1000m/3281ft
500m/1640ft
200m/656ft
Sea Level

0   100 km
0   100 miles

(map labels: Cherbourg, Guernsey, Channel Is (to UK), Jersey, ENGLISH, Golfe de St-Malo, St-Malo, Île d'Ousseant, Brest, Iroise, BRETAGNE, St-Brieuc, Dinan, Avran, Quimper, Rennes, Lorient, Redon, Vannes, Belle Île, St-Nazaire, Nantes, Île de Noirmoutier, Île d'Yeu, la Roche-sur-Yon, ATLANTIC OCEAN, Bay of Biscay, la Rochell, Île de Ré, Île d'Oléron, Bayonne, Biarritz)

F

PEDGE ▷ Pop. density medium

French, Provençal, German, Breton, Catalan, Basque

107/km²
(276/mi²)

Although there is a strong national identity and the French language has traditionally been promoted as a unifying force, France has long incorporated the traditions of Bretons,

THE URBAN/RURAL POPULATION SPLIT

73%   **27%**

POPULATION AGE BREAKDOWN

Female		Age	Male	
	2.7%	81–100	1.2%	
	8.7%	61–80	7%	
	11.8%	41–60	11.8%	
15%		21–40	15%	
13.1%		0–20	13.7%	

% of population by age group

Flemings, Alsatians, Basques, Occitans in Provence, Catalans, and Corsicans. In 1998 improved state recognition of their minority languages was proposed. There are nearly five million foreign-born residents, 25% of whom are now naturalized citizens, and a sizable French-born population of immigrant parentage. The Jewish community numbers over 700,000.

RELIGIOUS PERSUASION

Buddhist 1%   Protestant 2%
Jewish 1%   Muslim 8%

Roman Catholic 88%

ETHNIC MAKEUP

Other 1%   German 2%
           North African 6%
Breton 1%

French 90%

Despite France's liberal traditions, high unemployment led to a rise in intolerance, exploited politically since the 1980s by the racist National Front (FN). Black migrants from France's present-day overseas departments are full French citizens, but Africans without proper papers have been targeted for deportation. Large antiracist rallies have countered FN propaganda, however, and youth solidarity among "black, blanc, beur" ("black, white, Arab") was boosted by the 1998 World Cup football success of France's multiracial team.

There are sizable Protestant, Jewish, and Muslim minorities, but Roman Catholicism remains dominant, albeit with waning influence. Abortion and birth control were legalized in the 1970s, and couples now commonly live together before marriage. Some two million unmarried couples of two or more years' standing, including gay couples, gained legal status under 1998 legislation recognizing the civil solidarity pact.

Women did not get the vote until 1945, and are still under-represented in parliament, although there has been a woman premier and women took five senior cabinet posts in the incoming Socialist-led government in June 1997.

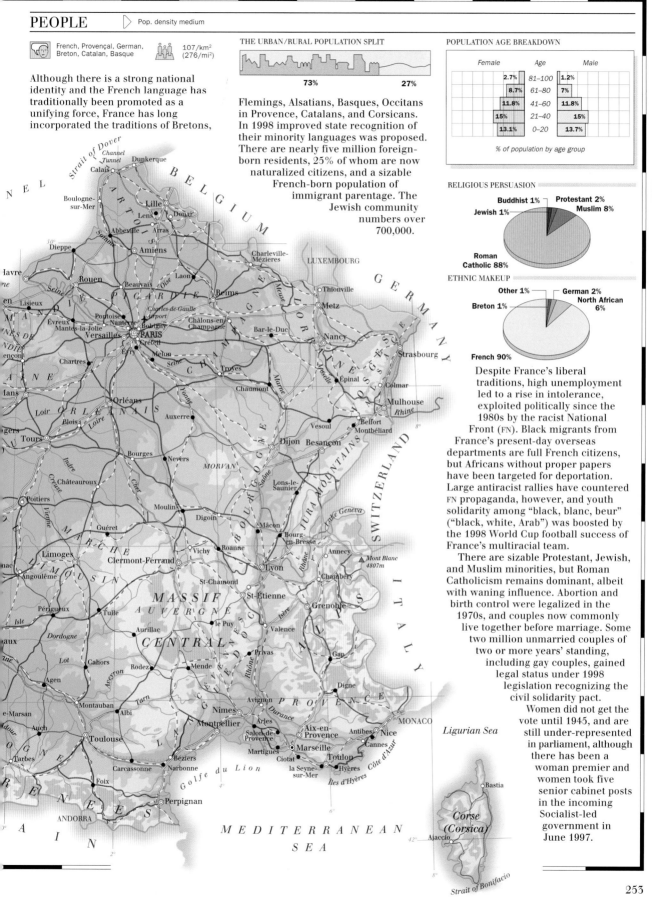

F

253

F

CHRONOLOGY

The French Revolution of 1789 overthrew a monarchy that had lasted for more than 1,300 years. It ushered in a period of alternating republicanism, Napoleonic imperialism and monarchism. In 1870 the founding of the Third Republic established France firmly in the republican tradition.

- ❏ **1914–1918** 1.4 million Frenchmen killed in World War I.
- ❏ **1918–1939** Economic recession and political instability; 44 governments and 20 prime ministers.
- ❏ **1940** Capitulation to Germany. Puppet Vichy regime. General de Gaulle leads "Free French" abroad.
- ❏ **1944** Liberation of France.
- ❏ **1946–1958** Fourth Republic. Political instability: 26 governments. Nationalizations. France takes leading role in EEC formation.
- ❏ **1958** Fifth Republic. De Gaulle becomes president with strong executive powers.
- ❏ **1960** Most French colonies gain independence.
- ❏ **1962** Algerian independence after bitter war with France.
- ❏ **1966** France withdraws from NATO military command.
- ❏ **1968** General strike and riots over education policy and low wages. National Assembly dissolved; Gaullist victory in June elections.
- ❏ **1969** De Gaulle resigns after defeat in referendum on regional reform; replaced by Georges Pompidou.
- ❏ **1981** PS victory in elections; François Mitterrand president.
- ❏ **1983–1986** Left-wing coalition changes course over handling economic recession, governs without PCF support.
- ❏ **1986** *Cohabitation* between socialist president and new right-wing government led by Jacques Chirac. Privatization program introduced.
- ❏ **1988** Mitterrand wins second term. PS-led coalition returns.
- ❏ **1993** Center-right under Edouard Balladur wins elections. Second period of *cohabitation*.
- ❏ **1995** Jacques Chirac wins presidential election.
- ❏ **1995–1996** Controversial series of Pacific nuclear tests.
- ❏ **1996** Unpopular austerity measures to prepare economy for European monetary union.
- ❏ **1997** Voters reject center-right in parliamentary elections called early by Chirac. PS-led government takes office in reversed *cohabitation*. Lionel Jospin prime minister.
- ❏ **1998–1999** Extensive privatization program.
- ❏ **1999** France introduces euro.

POLITICS ▷ Multiparty elections

U. House 1998/2001
L. House 1997/2002

President Jacques Chirac

AT THE LAST ELECTION

National Assembly 577 seats

43% PS	24% RPR	19% UDF	6% PCF	2% VR	5% VL	1% Green

PS = Socialist Party **RPR** = Rally for the Republic
UDF = Union for French Democracy **PCF** = Communist Party of France **VL** = Various Left **VR** = Various Right
UC = Centrist Union **RDSE** = European Democratic and Social Rally **RCC** = Republicans, Communists and Citizens

Senate 321 seats

31% RPR	24% PS	16% UC	15% Rep	5% RCC	7% RDSE	2% Ind

France is a multiparty democracy. The president has strong executive powers, but rules in tandem with a prime minister and government chosen by the Assemblée Nationale. The two are elected separately and serve, respectively, seven-and five-year terms. This can result in periods of *cohabitation*, when the president and Assemblée are of opposite political persuasions. Presidents tend to look after foreign policy and defense issues, while the government focuses on domestic and economic policy.

MAIN POLITICAL ISSUES
The presidential system
The presidency has had to adapt to *cohabitation*, first between a Socialist president and right-wing governments in 1986–1988 and 1993–1995, and, since June 1997, between the Gaullist President Chirac and a socialist government. Many argue that presidential and legislative terms should run concurrently and for the same duration.

Racism and "exclusion"
With unemployment rates high, the racist FN has profited from blaming immigrants. Legislation on immigration has been tightened. There is concern too about inner city deprivation and violence. "Exclusion" of the unemployed and homeless is widely recognized as socially divisive. Resenting economic austerity policies, the electorate in 1997 chose a government which promised greater social concern, but realignment of the defeated right-wing parties opened the possibility of more mainstream acceptance of the FN.

Costs of European integration
Before German reunification in 1990, there was little argument in France against European integration. In the early 1990s, opposition grew amid fears of the increased German power and of losing French sovereignty and identity. Austerity measures to prepare for European monetary union brought out huge protest demonstrations. Now part of the euro single currency, the French look for benefits in terms of stability and economic growth. The most strident voice opposing EU integration is the FN.

PROFILE
Two decades of right-of-center government, under de Gaulle, Pompidou, and Giscard d'Estaing, ended in 1981 with the united left victory. François Mitterrand became president and a PS-led government nationalized many of France's most famous businesses, while local government was decentralized. However, the failure of its reflationary policy forced the PS to change course, adopting monetarist policies instead. Tainted by scandal and loss of direction, the PS suffered a crushing electoral defeat in 1993 and lost the presidency in 1995 to the right-of-center Gaullist, Jacques Chirac. PS party leader Lionel Jospin, however, brought his party back to head a government two years later, having reached preelection agreements with other left-wing groups. By 1999, Chirac's popularity had fallen as his *cohabitation* with the Jospin government grew increasingly difficult.

The far left has declined since 1945, when the PCF had 25% of the vote, but the racist FN has built up support of some 15%. It won only one seat in the 1997 elections, but it had a disproportionate political impact. Formerly treated as a pariah, the FN convinced some in both the existing right-of-center groupings to explore a realignment. Complex party splits left mainstream factions still refusing any dealing with the FN.

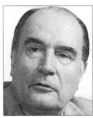

François Mitterrand, the former president who died in 1996.

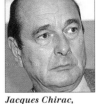

Jacques Chirac, elected president of France in 1995.

Lionel Jospin, who became prime minister in 1997.

WORLD AFFAIRS

> Joined UN in 1945

French foreign policy has followed two, apparently contradictory, strands since World War II – maintenance of a strongly independent line and furtherance of French interests within a united Europe. France's leading role within the EU was a way of combining the two strands, but after 1989 the weight of a reunited Germany within Europe created something of a backlash against European integration on the French nationalist right. This swelled the minority "no" vote in the 1992 Maastricht referendum almost to the point of rejecting the Treaty on European Union. However, the Franco-German thrust toward greater European integration remains the keystone of French foreign policy. France also supported broadening of the EU to include Scandinavia as well as further enlargement to the east.

France also seeks to offset US dominance in both foreign affairs and culture. It left NATO's military command in 1966, maintained an independent nuclear deterrent (which it insisted on testing in the Pacific in 1995–1996 despite a wave of international criticism), and sought a role in the post-Cold War world as a counterweight to US influence in the Middle East and Africa.

AID

> Donor

$6.35bn (donations)

Not applicable

France is one of the world's major aid donors. Its motives are not simply commercial; it also wishes to maintain the influence of the French language, particularly in west Africa, which has been the main aid recipient. *Médecins sans Frontières* reflects a long French tradition of NGO aid agencies.

DEFENSE

> No compulsory military service

$41.5bn

Down 13% in 1997

Traditionally independent on defense, France increasingly supports European integration.

FRENCH ARMED FORCES

1210 main battle tanks (1071 AMX-30, 139 *Leclerc*)	203,200 personnel	
1 carrier, 14 submarines, 1 cruiser, 4 destroyers and 35 frigates	63,300 personnel	
505 combat aircraft (*Mirage F-1B/1C/1CR/ Jaguar, Alpha Jet*)	781,000 personnel	
64 SLBM in 4 SSBN		

ECONOMICS

> Inflation 2.6% p.a. (1985-1996)

$1,542bn

5.59 francs

SCORE CARD

❏ WORLD GNP RANKING	4th
❏ GNP PER CAPITA	$26,300
❏ BALANCE OF PAYMENTS	$39.5bn
❏ INFLATION	1.2%
❏ UNEMPLOYMENT	12%

EXPORTS

Spain 8%
Belgium-Luxembourg 8%
Italy 9%
UK 10%
Other 49%
Germany 16%

IMPORTS

Belgium-Luxembourg 8%
UK 8%
USA 9%
Other 49%
Italy 10%
Germany 16%

STRENGTHS

Engineering, reflected in the TGV and nuclear industries. Specializations such as cars and telecommunications. Defense sector a major exporter, with Mirage jets and Exocet missiles, but sales falling in 1990s. Pharmaceutical and chemical industries. Strong technocratic traditions: unlike in USA or UK, top graduates are attracted into engineering. Luxury goods: world leader in cosmetics, perfumes, and quality wines. Europe's leading agricultural producer.

WEAKNESSES

High unemployment, over 11% in 1999 despite improving economy. High tax and social charges and labor costs. Losing its positions in traditional industries such as iron and steel, metallurgy and textiles. Some major

A founder member of NATO, France left its military command structure in 1966, in opposition to US domination. It maintained an independent nuclear deterrent through the Cold War, but in the 1990s has had rapprochement with NATO. Participation with Germany in the Eurocorps is partly symbolic of reconciliation, as well as an expression of the need for an EU defense structure.

The influence of the army, once very strong, is now much diminished. The government in mid-1996 began phasing out compulsory military service.

France has one of the world's largest and most export-oriented defense industries, producing tanks, jet fighter aircraft, and missiles.

ECONOMIC PERFORMANCE INDICATOR

Consumer price index
GDP

high-tech industries, such as telecommunications, run partly to further national pride, rather than on a strictly commercial basis.

PROFILE

Initially slow to industrialize, protectionist France started competing in world markets and modernizing its industry in the 1950s and 1960s. Integration in western Europe, starting with the coal and steel industry in the 1950s, placed France at the heart of the EU. It was one of the 11 EU countries to introduce the euro in 1999. One of the world's top exporters, its foreign trade balance runs a healthy surplus. France has a long tradition of state involvement in running the economy. Nationalization of key industries began in the late 1930s, with a fresh burst in 1981–83, but has now been reversed. Right-of-center governments in 1986–87 and 1993–96, and the socialists in office since 1997, have pursued privatization with vigor, reaching deep into the defense industry, telecommunications, aviation, insurance, and banking. France is the EU's largest agricultural producer and its farmers are a powerful political lobby.

FRANCE : MAJOR BUSINESSES

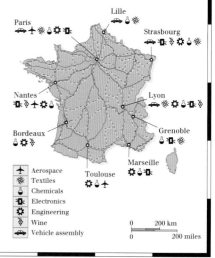

Lille
Paris
Strasbourg
Nantes
Lyon
Bordeaux
Grenoble
Marseille
Toulouse

✈ Aerospace
✺ Textiles
⌂ Chemicals
⬛ Electronics
✿ Engineering
⚲ Wine
🚗 Vehicle assembly

0   200 km
0   200 miles

F

F

RESOURCES

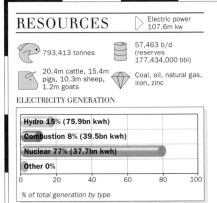

▷ Electric power
107.6m kw

793,413 tonnes

57,463 b/d
(reserves
177,434,000 bbl)

20.4m cattle, 15.4m
pigs, 10.3m sheep,
1.2m goats

Coal, oil, natural gas,
iron, zinc

ELECTRICITY GENERATION

Hydro 15% (75.9bn kwh)					
Combustion 8% (39.5bn kwh)					
Nuclear 77% (37.7bn kwh)					
Other 0%					
0	20	40	60	80	100

% of total generation by type

France is the world's most committed user of nuclear energy, which provides over three-quarters of its electricity requirements. The policy reflects a desire for national energy self-sufficiency. Coal, once plentiful in the north and Lorraine, is now mostly exhausted, as are the gas fields off the southwest coast.

FRANCE : LAND USE

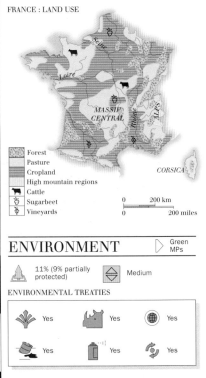

Forest
Pasture
Cropland
High mountain regions
Cattle
Sugarbeet
Vineyards

CORSICA

0   200 km
0   200 miles

ENVIRONMENT

▷ Green MPs

11% (9% partially protected)

Medium

ENVIRONMENTAL TREATIES

Yes	Yes	Yes
Yes	Yes	Yes

"Green" consciousness has risen with a series of campaigns against major infrastructure projects. Air pollution has become a major issue, especially in Paris. The Seine has been cleaned up, the size of buildings on the south coast restricted, and state backing for big projects (*gigantisme*) called into question. Nuclear power's importance, however, puts the environmentalist lobby in perspective. Nuclear weapons tests in the Pacific in 1995–1996 aroused strong international opposition.

THE IMPACT OF MODERN TRANSPORTATION

WHILE THE FRENCH REGIONS retain distinctive characteristics, the country's modern transport and telecommunications network, with Paris at its hub, has brought the main provincial cities within much easier access of the capital. It also helps France play a central role in European business.

THE AUTOROUTE NETWORK
The toll-charging autoroute freeways, with a speed limit of 130 km per hour, now reach almost every corner of the map except the Cherbourg peninsula and Brittany in the north-west. They have relieved the previous generation of town-to-town highways of much of their former traffic congestion, but have also encouraged the upsurge in trans-European heavy freight vehicle movement, carrying through traffic to and from Spain, Italy, Switzerland, Germany, the Benelux countries and the Channel ports. There has been much controversy about the environmental impact of several as yet uncompleted cross-country links, notably the E11 route south from Clermont-Ferrand to join the Mediterranean network.

FRENCH LEADERSHIP IN HIGH SPEED TRAINS
French pride in leading-edge engineering, and a capacity for ambitious centralized planning and state-backed investment, has been apparent in its high speed train system, the *train à grande vitesse* (TGV). Overtaken only by the Japanese "bullet train" as the fastest in passenger service, the TGV can run at sustained speeds of over 300 km/h (186 mph). It has hit domestic airline traffic hard on some of the prime routes, by offering a combination of comfort and shorter door-to-door journey times in many instances. During the 1990s some double-decker trains have been introduced, to help meet high demand for seats, and a new generation of TGV trains was unveiled by the engineers Alstom in 1998-1999.

The first element of the project was the TGV south-east. Construction began in 1975 and the Paris-Lyon section came into service in 1983, with subsequent extensions southwards and plans to reach both Montpellier and Marseilles. By the end of the 1980s a western route from Paris, initially to Le Mans, was also in service.

FRANCE : ROAD AND RAIL

Autoroute
TGV route
Other rail

The northern Paris- Lille route opened in 1993 with extensions to Brussels and to Calais and the Channel Tunnel.

EXTENDING THE TRAIN NETWORK
The existing TGV lines, which use mainly modernized but also some purpose-built track, are a highly profitable part of the French rail network. Seeing the likely economic benefits, many towns have lobbied hard to be include. The next planned line, however, from Paris east to Strasbourg, has faced more opposition as well as escalating cost estimates. Construction began in early 1999, aiming for completion in six to seven years. To make money, this line will need to provoke a big shift in existing travelling habits. The French government's commitment is also in part a strategic political decision, designed to reinforce Strasbourg's role "at the heart of European integration".

A link via Tours to Bordeaux is intended to be part of the next stage of expansion, along with the completion of links to Turin, from Montpellier to Barcelona, and via Strasbourg to Stuttgart and Frankfurt and thus into the German high-speed ICE train network.

Modern office blocks
in Montpellier, a city whose new dynamic image owes much to its transport links and investment in communications technology.

MEDIA

▷ TV ownership high

▦ Daily newspaper circulation 218 per 1,000 people

PUBLISHING AND BROADCAST MEDIA

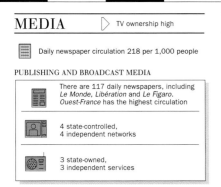

There are 117 daily newspapers, including *Le Monde, Libération* and *Le Figaro. Ouest-France* has the highest circulation

4 state-controlled, 4 independent networks

3 state-owned, 3 independent services

TV and radio were freed from direct state influence in the 1980s. TF1, the primary TV network, is now privately owned and financed by advertising revenue. France 2 is still owned by the state but is now fairly autonomous. Commercial channels have multiplied with the growth of satellite and cable. The TV service is weak, with many bought-in US soaps. The once innovative Minitel electronic communications system is widely used but has inhibited development of internet activity.

The prestigious *Le Monde* and rival national newspapers compete amid dwindling circulations. Regional newspapers are strong.

EDUCATION

▷ School leaving age : 16

📖 99%   🎓 2.1m students

Teaching is highly centralized with a state-set curriculum and final exam.

THE EDUCATION SYSTEM

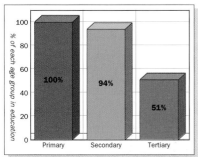

% of each age group in education
- Primary: 100%
- Secondary: 94%
- Tertiary: 51%

Despite some relaxation of the system brought about by the student riots of 1968, the education ministry organizes the curriculum, sets examinations, including the *baccalauréat* which determines university entrance, and decides staffing issues. Most schools have little autonomy. Catholic Church schools, which take most of the 17% of privately educated children (but are not fee paying and receive large state subsidies), are the exception. However, despite relative independence, they still have to follow the national curriculum.

The focus in teaching remains the acquisition of a broad range of knowledge; classes are highly

CRIME

▷ No death penalty

🏛 53,697 prisoners   ⬇ Down 8% from 1992–1996

CRIME RATES

Murders
4 per 100,000 population

Rapes
12 per 100,000 population

Thefts
4017 per 100,000 population

Criminal justice is based on inquisitorial rather than adversarial principles. The *juge d'instruction*, with considerable powers in examining witnesses and assessing evidence, is arguably the most important figure. The press are not restricted by *sub judice* rules in reporting trials and can speak freely of suspects. Political corruption cases attract much attention.

Public concern about rising petty crime and violence helped the right – with a law and order platform – return to power in 1993. The current socialist government, despite its greater concern with social problems, has not changed the emphasis on tough policing.

disciplined. French children tend to be better informed than their counterparts in other western European countries.

France has over 70 universities (13 in Paris) and higher education bodies with 1.2 million students. Entry is not competitive, but based on passing the secondary-level exam, the *baccalauréat*. Most students attend their local university. The universities have not been given the funds or staff to cope with the huge increase in student numbers in recent years. The 150 *Grandes Écoles* are outside the university system and have just a few hundred carefully selected students each. The most influential tertiary institutions, they open the door to the top civil service and professional jobs.

Massif Central, Auvergne. *The Massif's lonely granite plateaus and extinct volcanoes are France's oldest rock formations.*

HEALTH

▷ Welfare state health benefits

🧑 1 per 357 people   🫀 Accidents, heart and cerebrovascular diseases, cancers

Under the French national health system, patients pay for treatment, and get the majority of the cost reimbursed by an insurance company paid by the social services. A major and fiercely contested cost-cutting reform plan was pushed through in the mid-1990s which effectively reduced health benefit levels. The French consume more medicines per capita than any other nation. However, although health awareness has risen in recent years, a 1992 law banning smoking in public places is widely ignored, alcoholism remains a problem, and cirrhosis of the liver is not uncommon as a cause of death.

SPENDING

▷ GDP/cap. no increase

CONSUMPTION AND SPENDING

🚗 442 per 1,000 population   ☎ 575 per 1,000 population

Defense 3%
Education 5.9%
Health 9.1%

0 5 10 15 20 25
Defense, Health, Education spending as % of GDP

Wealth and income disparities in France are higher than in most OECD countries. The Socialists narrowed the wealth gap a little during the 1980s with the introduction of the legal minimum wage (*le* SMIC). Most tax is indirect – a result of a long French tradition of income-tax evasion – which hits the poor and rich equally.

France has a fairly rigid class structure, although social mobility is increasing. The wealthy citizens favor expensive French, German, or British cars, and take exotic vacations to the Himalayas, the Andes and Polynesia.

WORLD RANKING

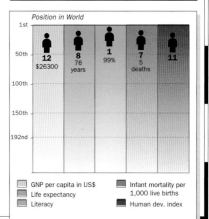

Position in World

12 $26300	8 76 years	1 99%	7 5 deaths	11

▦ GNP per capita in US$
▦ Life expectancy
▦ Literacy
▦ Infant mortality per 1,000 live births
■ Human dev. index

F

GABON

OFFICIAL NAME: The Gabonese Republic   **CAPITAL:** Libreville
POPULATION: 1.2 million   **CURRENCY:** CFA franc   **OFFICIAL LANGUAGE:** French

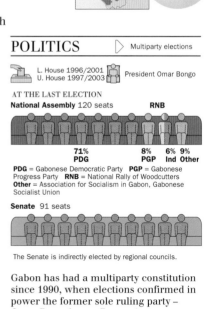

WEST AFRICA

| 1960 | 1960 | Aug 17 | G | +1 | +241 | .ga |

AN EQUATORIAL COUNTRY on the west coast of
Africa, Gabon's major economic activity is oil. Only
a small area of Gabon is cultivated and more than two-
thirds constitute one of the world's finest virgin rainforests. Gabon
became independent of France in 1960. A single-party state from 1968,
it returned to multiparty democracy in 1990. Gabon's population is small
and the government is encouraging its increase.

G

CLIMATE
▷ Tropical equatorial

WEATHER CHART

- ■ Average daily temperature   Rainfall ▬

°C/°F   J F M A M J J A S O N D   cm/in
40/104   40/16
30/86   30/12
20/68   20/8
10/50   10/4
0/32   0
-10/14
-20/-4

Gabon's climate is heavily equatorial,
with very little distinction between
seasons. The cold Benguela current
lowers coastal temperatures.

TRANSPORTATION
▷ Drive on right

✈ **Léon M'Ba, Libreville**
871,000 passengers

🚢 7 ships
37,000 grt

THE TRANSPORTATION NETWORK

🛣 4,900 km (3,000 miles)	🛤 None		
🚆 814 km (506 miles)	⚓ 1,600 km (994 miles)		

The Trans-Gabon Railroad from Owendo
port near Libreville to Massoukou, is
the key transportation link. Air
transportation is well developed, and
most big companies have airstrips.

TOURISM
▷ Visitors : population 1:8.8

🧳 137,000 visitors   ⬆ Up 31% 1995–1997

MAIN TOURIST ARRIVALS

Europe 75%	
Africa 13%	
Americas 6%	
Other 6%	

0 10 20 30 40 50 60 70 80 90 100
% of total arrivals

Despite Libreville's many hotels,
Gabon has little tourism, in part a
reflection of its lack of good beaches.

PEOPLE
▷ Pop. density low

Fang, French, Punu, Sira,
Nzebi, Mpongwe

5/km²
(12/mi²)

THE URBAN/RURAL POPULATION SPLIT

50%   50%

ETHNIC MAKEUP

- French 2%
- European and other African 9%
- Fang 35%
- Eshira 25%
- Other Bantu 29%

The largest ethnic group in Gabon is
the Fang, who live mainly in the north,
but they have yet to gain control of
government. President Omar Bongo,
from a subgroup of the minority Bateke
in the southeast, has artfully united the
common interests of other ethnic
groups to keep the Fang from power.
The Myene group around Port-Gentil
consider themselves to be the aristocrats
of Gabonese society owing to their
long-standing ex-colonial contacts.
Oil wealth has led to the
growth of a distinct
bourgeoisie.

POLITICS
▷ Multiparty elections

L. House 1996/2001
U. House 1997/2003

President Omar Bongo

AT THE LAST ELECTION

National Assembly 120 seats

RNB

71% PDG   8% PGP   6% Ind   9% Other

PDG = Gabonese Democratic Party   **PGP** = Gabonese
Progress Party   **RNB** = National Rally of Woodcutters
Other = Association for Socialism in Gabon, Gabonese
Socialist Union

Senate 91 seats

The Senate is indirectly elected by regional councils.

Gabon has had a multiparty constitution
since 1990, when elections confirmed in
power the former sole ruling party –
Omar Bongo's PDG. Bongo, in power
since 1967, was reelected president in
1993, in a poll whose fairness was widely
disputed. In parliamentary elections in
December 1996 the PDG again won a
majority. Bongo was reelected president
in 1998, this time for a seven-year term.
Jean-François Ntoutoume-Emane was
appointed prime minister, replacing
Paulin Obame-Nguema in January 1999.

WORLD AFFAIRS
▷ Joined UN in 1960

| FZ | G24 | OAU | OIC | OPEC |

Gabon still maintains close links with
France, although US companies are also
making inroads into Gabon's oil-rich
economy. In regional terms, Gabon
remains influential in
francophone Africa, although
relations further afield,
particularly with OPEC
(Gabon was chair in 1995),
are also important.

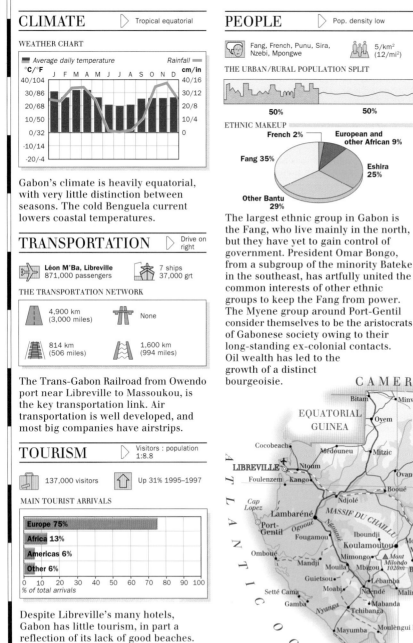

GABON

Total Land Area :
257 670 sq. km
(99 486 sq. miles)

POPULATION

over 100 000	◎
over 10 000	●
under 10 000	·

LAND HEIGHT

500m/1640ft
200m/656ft
Sea Level

0   100 km
0   100 miles

AID

▷ Recipient

💲 $40m (receipts)   ⬇ Down 69% 1996-1997

France is by far the major aid donor, providing two-thirds of total receipts. For a middle-income country with one of the highest GNPs per capita in the developing world, Gabon has benefited from considerable aid. Its indebtedness is the result of excessive borrowing encouraged by Western banks in the 1970s. Much aid goes to servicing this debt.

DEFENSE
▷ No compulsory military service

💲 $115m   ⬆ Up 1% in 1997

President Bongo's background in the military is reflected in Gabon's large defense budget and prestige weaponry, which includes French *Mirage* jets.

Even the presidential guard has its own squadron of 12 aircraft. France guarantees Gabon's security and keeps a 600-strong garrison in Libreville; this last intervened in 1964 to suppress an attempted coup.

ECONOMICS
▷ Inflation 3.8% p.a. (1985–1996)

📊 $4.8bn   💲 601.60–558.62 CFA francs

SCORE CARD

❏ WORLD GNP RANKING	110th
❏ GNP PER CAPITA	$4,120
❏ BALANCE OF PAYMENTS	$100m
❏ INFLATION	4%
❏ UNEMPLOYMENT	14%

STRENGTHS
Oil and a relatively small population give Gabon a high per capita GNP. Other abundant resources – including some of the world's best tropical hardwoods – are just beginning to be tapped.

WEAKNESSES
Large debt burden incurred in the 1970s. Continuing dependence on French technical assistance.

EXPORTS

Japan 3%   France 8%
Bahamas 1%   China 9%
Other 10%
USA 69%

IMPORTS

Belgium-Luxembourg 4%   UK 4%
Netherlands 5%
USA 8%
Other 40%
France 39%

RESOURCES
▷ Electric power 310,00 kw

🐟 45,180 tonnes   🛢 341,000 b/d (reserves 730,000,000 bbl)

🐑 173,000 sheep, 208,000 pigs, 86,000 goats   💎 Oil, manganese, uranium, gold, iron, natural gas

Oil is the major export earner. Gabon also has large deposits of uranium and over 100 years' reserves of manganese. The unexploited iron ore deposits at Bélinga are the world's largest.

ENVIRONMENT
▷ No Green MPs

🔺 3%   ⬇ Low

The Trans-Gabon Railroad has sliced through one of the world's finest virgin rainforests and has opened the interior to indiscriminate exploitation of rare woods such as oleoirme. Gabon abandoned plans for nuclear power following the 1986 Chernobyl disaster.

MEDIA
▷ TV ownership medium

✉ Daily newspaper circulation 30 per 1,000 people

PUBLISHING AND BROADCAST MEDIA

There are 2 daily newspapers, *L'Union* and *Gabon-Matin*

1 state-owned, 2 independent services   2 state-owned, 3 independent services

The media have become much more diverse since 1990 and Gabon now has an opposition press and *La Griffe*, a satirical weekly. *L'Union*, the state paper, carries occasional contributions from Omar Bongo, the president.

CRIME
▷ Death penalty used

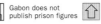 Gabon does not publish prison figures   ⬆ Recorded crime rose sharply from 1992-1996

Urban crime rates (Gabon is one of Africa's most urbanized nations) have been growing. Gabon's human rights record has improved in recent years.

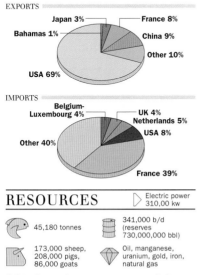
Albert Schweitzer Hospital, Lambaréné, on *the lower Ogooué River. Schweitzer won a Nobel Prize for his pioneering work in Africa.*

CHRONOLOGY
Gabon became a French colony in 1886, administered as part of French Equatorial Africa.

- ❏ **1960** Independence. Léon M'ba president.
- ❏ **1964** Military coup. French intervene to reinstate M'ba.
- ❏ **1967** Albert-Bernard (later Omar) Bongo president.
- ❏ **1968** Single-party state instituted.
- ❏ **1990** Multiparty democracy.
- ❏ **1998** Bongo reelected president.

EDUCATION

▷ School leaving age: 16

👤 66%   🎓 4,655 students

Education follows the French system. Libreville University, founded in the 1970s, now has over 4,000 students.

HEALTH
▷ No welfare state health benefits

👷 1 per 2,000 people   ☠ Heart and diarrheal diseases, pneumonia, accidents

Oil revenues have allowed substantial investment in the health service, which is now among the best in Africa.

SPENDING
▷ GDP/cap. no increase

CONSUMPTION AND SPENDING

🚗 22 per 1,000 population   ⭕ 33 per 1,000 population

Defense 1.9%
Education 2.8%
Health 3.2%

0   5   10   15   20   25
Defense, Health, Education spending as % of GDP

Oil wealth has led to the growth of an affluent bourgeoisie class. Menial and low-income jobs are done by immigrant workers.

WORLD RANKING
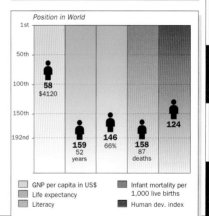

Position in World

1st
50th
100th   **58** $4120
150th
192nd   **159** 52 years   **146** 66%   **158** 87 deaths   **124**

- GNP per capita in US$
- Life expectancy
- Literacy
- Infant mortality per 1,000 live births
- Human dev. index

G

GAMBIA

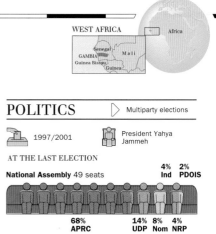

WEST AFRICA

OFFICIAL NAME: Republic of The Gambia   **CAPITAL:** Banjul
POPULATION: 1.9 million   **CURRENCY:** Dalasi   **OFFICIAL LANGUAGE:** English

| 1965 | 1965 | Feb 18 | WAG | 0 | +220 | .gm |

A NARROW COUNTRY on the western coast of Africa, The Gambia had been renowned as a stable democracy until an army coup in 1994. Agriculture accounts for 65% of GDP, yet more Gambians are leaving rural areas for the towns, where average incomes are four times higher. Its position as a semi-enclave within Senegal seems likely to endure following the failure of an experiment in federation in the 1980s.

G

CLIMATE   ▷ Tropical wet & dry

WEATHER CHART

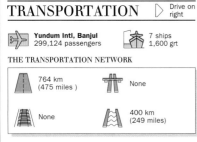

The subtropical and sunny dry season is punctuated by intermittent hot *harmattan* winds.

TRANSPORTATION   ▷ Drive on right

Yundum Intl, Banjul
299,124 passengers

7 ships
1,600 grt

THE TRANSPORTATION NETWORK

| 764 km (475 miles) | None |
| None | 400 km (249 miles) |

The river Gambia carries more traffic than the roads – ships of up to 3,000 tonnes can reach Georgetown. Yundum airport was upgraded by NASA in 1989 for US space shuttle emergency landings.

TOURISM   ▷ Visitors : population 1:15

80,000 visitors

Up 78% 1995–1997

MAIN TOURIST ARRIVALS

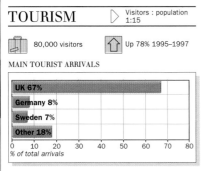

| UK 67% |
| Germany 8% |
| Sweden 7% |
| Other 18% |

% of total arrivals

A successful tourist industry offers sunshine, beaches, and resort hotel life. Most visitors are Europeans escaping winter, including many single women.

PEOPLE   ▷ Pop. density medium

Mandinka, Fulani, Wolof, Diola, Soninke, English

119/km² (309/mi²)

THE URBAN/RURAL POPULATION SPLIT

26%   74%

ETHNIC MAKEUP

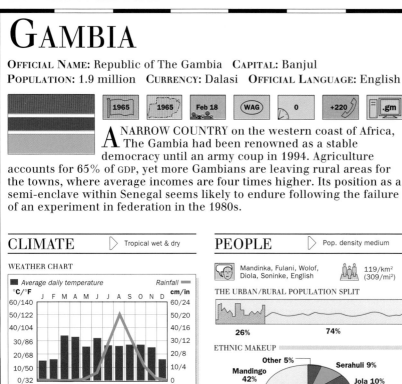

Other 5%
Serahuli 9%
Mandingo 42%
Jola 10%
Wolof 16%
Fulani 18%

Until the 1994 coup, led by Lt.-Col. Yahya Jammeh, the 1962–1994 government of President Sir Dawda Jawara had tried to offset minority resentment of the Mandinka's domination of politics, distributing political offices fairly according to ethnic origins. Jammeh, a fervent Muslim, is from the minority Jola (or Diola) community, numerous across the border in Senegal, where they are active in a local rebellion. About 85% of Gambians follow Islam, although there is no official state religion. There is a yearly influx of migrants, who come from Senegal, Guinea, and Mali to trade in groundnuts. The Gambia is still a very poor country, with 80% of the labor force engaged in agriculture. Women are active as traders in an otherwise male-dominated society.

Fishing village. *Overfishing in the waters off the Gambia and Senegal, mainly by distant nations, is a growing problem.*

POLITICS   ▷ Multiparty elections

1997/2001

President Yahya Jammeh

AT THE LAST ELECTION

National Assembly 49 seats

4% Ind   2% PDOIS

68% APRC   14% UDP   8% Nom   4% NRP

APRC = Alliance for Patriotic Reorientation and Construction
UDP = United Democratic Party   **Nom** = Nominated
NRP = National Reconciliation Party   **PDOIS** = People's Democratic Organization for Independence and Socialism

The PPP (People's Progressive Party) was in government from 1962 until 1994, for most of which time The Gambia was one of Africa's few multiparty democracies. Since the 1994 coup, the party and the three main opposition parties at the time have been banned.

During the army's coup, Sir Dawda Jawara took refuge aboard a visiting US warship, and went into exile in Britain. The coup's leaders claimed that it had been initiated in a bid to end corruption and pledged to preserve democracy. A new government was swiftly announced, in which several portfolios went to civil servants who had served in the Jawara administration. The coup drew no active response from the potentially influential Senegal or Nigeria. Military leader Yahya Jammeh was elected president in controversial elections in September 1996, and the following January his APRC won the majority of seats in a parliamentary election.

WORLD AFFAIRS   ▷ Joined UN in 1965

| CILSS | Comm | Ecowas | OAU | OIC |

President Jammeh has vigorously cultivated new partnerships following strong Commonwealth and Western criticism of his coup in 1994. Also, close ties have been cultivated with Nigeria as a counterweight to Senegal, with which relations have sometimes been strained since the collapse in 1989 of the confederation.

AID   ▷ Recipient

$40m (receipts)

Up 5% 1996–1997

Western aid flows, suspended after the 1994 coup, have largely resumed. The World Bank, the IMF, the AfDB, the UK, the USA, Japan, Libya, Egypt, the Gulf states, Cuba, and Taiwan are all significant donors.

GAMBIA

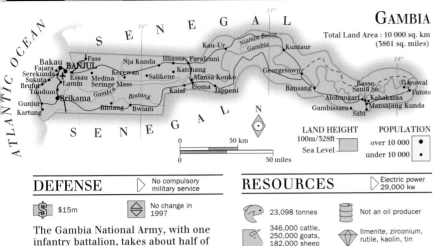

Total Land Area : 10 000 sq. km
(3861 sq. miles)

LAND HEIGHT
100m/328ft
Sea Level

POPULATION
- over 10 000 ●
- under 10 000 ·

0   50 km
0   50 miles

G

DEFENSE
▷ No compulsory military service

💲 $15m   ⬍ No change in 1997

The Gambia National Army, with one infantry battalion, takes about half of the defense budget; the rest finances the 600-strong gendarmerie. Most arms are bought from the UK, although supplies are now increasingly coming from Nigeria too. A defense pact with Senegal collapsed with the federation in 1989.

ECONOMICS
▷ Inflation 11% p.a. (1985–1996)

📊 $407m   💲 10.07–11.18 dalasi

SCORE CARD
- ❏ WORLD GNP RANKING.........................170th
- ❏ GNP PER CAPITA $340
- ❏ BALANCE OF PAYMENTS.......................$-24m
- ❏ INFLATION 2.8%
- ❏ UNEMPLOYMENT.....Widespread underemployment

STRENGTHS
Low tariffs make The Gambia a focus of regional trade. Natural deep-water harbor at Banjul, one of the finest on the west African coast. Well-managed economy, favorably viewed by donors.

WEAKNESSES
Small size of country, and hence small size of market, sometimes inhibits investment. Smuggling, which deprives government of significant revenues. Lack of resources and little diversification in agriculture.

EXPORTS

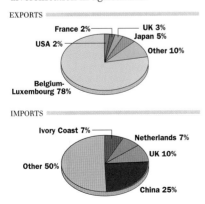

France 2%
UK 3%
Japan 5%
USA 2%
Other 10%
Belgium-Luxembourg 78%

IMPORTS

Ivory Coast 7%
Netherlands 7%
UK 10%
Other 50%
China 25%

RESOURCES
▷ Electric power 29,000 kw

🐟 23,098 tonnes   🛢 Not an oil producer

🐄 346,000 cattle, 250,000 goats, 182,000 sheep   💎 Ilmenite, zirconium, rutile, kaolin, tin

The Gambia river is one of Africa's few good waterways, but it is underused since it is separated from its natural hinterland by the Gambia–Senegal border. Irrigation is at present provided by a single dam; plans for further dams for power generation have met with opposition. Oil deposits are believed to exist offshore.

ENVIRONMENT
▷ No Green MPs

🔺 2%   ⬇ Low

The impact of tourism on the country's environment and overfishing in Gambian waters are major concerns.

MEDIA
▷ TV ownership low

✖ Daily newspaper circulation 2 per 1,000 people

PUBLISHING AND BROADCAST MEDIA

There is 1 daily newspaper, *The Daily Observer*

1 state-owned service

1 state-owned, 2 independent services

Journalists and newspaper proprietors have suffered low-level harassment since the 1994 coup, and a popular private radio station has been closed down.

CRIME
▷ Death penalty used

The Gambia does not publish prison figures   General crime levels are rising

Crime levels are relatively low in what is a peaceful society compared with many other states in the region.

EDUCATION
▷ Not available

👤 33%   🎓 1,591 students

The literacy rate is low for the level of school enrollment – 75% in primary and 20% in secondary schools. A university was established in 1998.

CHRONOLOGY

Mandinka traders brought Islam in the 13th century and were the main influence until the 18th century. The 1700s and 1800s saw colonial rivalry between Britain and France.

- ❏ **1888** British possession.
- ❏ **1959** Dawda Jawara founds PPP.
- ❏ **1962** Jawara prime minister.
- ❏ **1965** Independence.
- ❏ **1970** Republic; Jawara president.
- ❏ **1981** Senegalese troops help crush army coup attempt.
- ❏ **1982–1989** Federation with Senegal.
- ❏ **1994** Jawara ousted in army coup.
- ❏ **1996** Yahya Jammeh wins presidential election.

HEALTH
▷ No welfare state health benefits

👥 1 per 5,000 people   ☠ Malaria, tuberculosis, parasitic diseases

Most people have access to basic medicines, but these are no longer free. Advanced medical care in the public sector is limited. An influx of Cuban doctors has helped extend services.

SPENDING
▷ GDP/cap. increase

CONSUMPTION AND SPENDING

🚗 8 per 1,000 population   ☎ 21 per 1,000 population

- Defense 3.7%
- Education 5.5%
- Health 1.6%

0   5   10   15   20   25
Defense, Health, Education spending as % of GDP

Public service and the professions have created wealth and some people are now comfortably off, although great wealth is not a feature of Gambian life. Unemployed young men in Banjul are regarded as the underclass.

WORLD RANKING

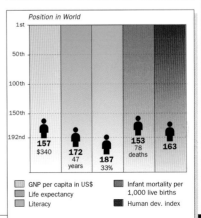

Position in World

1st
50th
100th
150th
192nd

- 157 $340
- 172 47 years
- 187 33%
- 153 78 deaths
- 163

- ▢ GNP per capita in US$
- ▢ Life expectancy
- ▢ Literacy
- ▢ Infant mortality per 1,000 live births
- ▢ Human dev. index

GEORGIA

OFFICIAL NAME: Republic of Georgia **CAPITAL:** Tbilisi
POPULATION: 5.4 million **CURRENCY:** Lari **OFFICIAL LANGUAGE:** Georgian

EUROPE

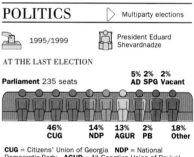

| 1991 | 1991 | May 26 | GE | +4 | +995 | .ge |

G

SITUATED ON THE EASTERN coast of the Black Sea, Georgia is largely mountainous. Its coastline stretches from Abkhazia in the north to Ajaria in the south. Georgia was one of the first republics to demand independence from Moscow, but has been plagued over recent years by civil war and ethnic disputes in Abkhazia and South Ossetia. The birthplace of Stalin, Georgia is primarily agricultural and is famous for its wine.

CLIMATE

▷ Mountain/subtropical

WEATHER CHART

Average daily temperature · Rainfall

°C/°F / cm/in

Georgia's climate is continental inland and subtropical along the coast, where grapes, citrus fruit and tea are grown.

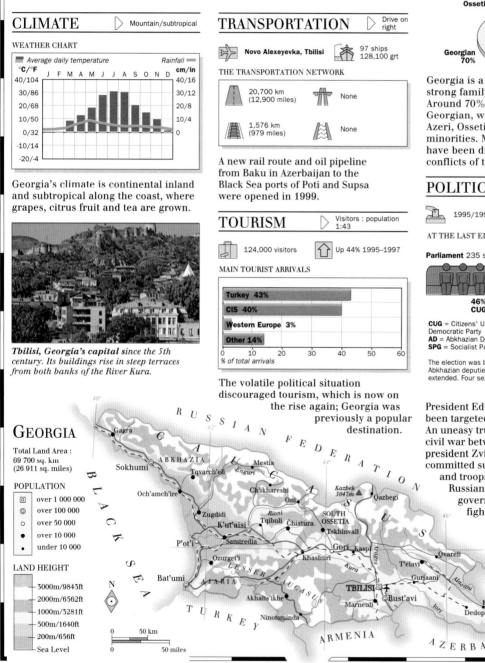

Tbilisi, Georgia's capital since the 5th century. Its buildings rise in steep terraces from both banks of the River Kura.

TRANSPORTATION

▷ Drive on right

✈ Novo Alexeyevka, Tbilisi
🚢 97 ships 128,100 grt

THE TRANSPORTATION NETWORK

🛣	20,700 km (12,900 miles)		None
🚉	1,576 km (979 miles)		None

A new rail route and oil pipeline from Baku in Azerbaijan to the Black Sea ports of Poti and Supsa were opened in 1999.

TOURISM

▷ Visitors : population 1:43

🧳 124,000 visitors
↑ Up 44% 1995–1997

MAIN TOURIST ARRIVALS

Turkey 43%	
CIS 40%	
Western Europe 3%	
Other 14%	

% of total arrivals

The volatile political situation discouraged tourism, which is now on the rise again; Georgia was previously a popular destination.

PEOPLE

▷ Pop. density medium

👤 Georgian, Russian
👥 77/km² (201/mi²)

THE URBAN/RURAL POPULATION SPLIT

58%   42%

ETHNIC MAKEUP

Ossetian 3%
Azeri 6%
Russian 6%
Other 7%
Armenian 8%
Georgian 70%

Georgia is a paternalistic society, with strong family and cultural traditions. Around 70% of the population is Georgian, with Armenian, Russian, Azeri, Ossetian, Greek, and Abkhaz minorities. More than 300,000 people have been displaced by the internal conflicts of the 1990s.

POLITICS

▷ Multiparty elections

🏛 1995/1999
👤 President Eduard Shevardnadze

AT THE LAST ELECTION

Parliament 235 seats

| 46% CUG | 14% NDP | 13% AGUR | 2% PB | 5% AD | 2% SPG | 2% Vacant | 18% Other |

CUG = Citizens' Union of Georgia **NDP** = National Democratic Party **AGUR** = All Georgian Union of Revival **AD** = Abkhazian Deputies **PB** = Progess bloc **SPG** = Socialist Party of Georgia

The election was boycotted in Abkhazia: the mandates of 12 Abkhazian deputies elected to the previous session were extended. Four seats remained vacant.

President Eduard Shevardnadze has been targeted in assassination attempts. An uneasy truce followed the 1990–1993 civil war between the supporters of ex-president Zviad Gamsakhurdia, who committed suicide at the end of 1993, and troops loyal to the government. Russian military intervention on the government's side brought the fighting to an end.

In Abkhazia, a civil war flared up as ethnic Abkhazians attempted to secede from Georgia. Ethnic Georgians were expelled from the region and fighting flares up sporadically.

GEORGIA

Total Land Area :
69 700 sq. km
(26 911 sq. miles)

POPULATION
▣ over 1 000 000
◉ over 100 000
○ over 50 000
● over 10 000
• under 10 000

LAND HEIGHT
3000m/9843ft
2000m/6562ft
1000m/3281ft
500m/1640ft
200m/656ft
Sea Level

0 — 50 km
0 — 50 miles

RUSSIAN FEDERATION

CAUCASUS

Gagra
Sokhumi
ABKHAZIA
Tqvarch'eli
Och'amch'ire
Zugdidi
P'ot'i
Samtredia
K'ut'aisi
Ozurget'i
Bat'umi
AJARIA
Akhalts'ikhe
Ninotsminda

Mestia
Enguri
Ch'ikhareshi
Oni
Rioni
Tqibuli Chiatura
Tskhinvali
SOUTH OSSETIA
Gori Kaspi
Khashuri
LESSER CAUCASUS

Kazbek 5047m
Qazbegi
Kura
T'elavi
Gurjaani
Alazani
Qvareli
K'vemo K'edi
Dedoplistsqaro

TBILISI
Marneuli Rust'avi
Iori

BLACK SEA

TURKEY

ARMENIA

AZERBAIJAN

WORLD AFFAIRS

▷ Joined UN in 1992

Georgia joined the CIS in 1993, to secure Russian support against Gamsakhurdia, and the Council of Europe in 1999.

AID

▷ Recipient

💲 $246m (receipts)   ⬇ Down 23% 1996–1997

Georgia received US$318 million in aid in 1996 (accounting for 7% of GNP) and US$246 million in 1997.

DEFENSE

▷ Compulsory military service

💲 $109m   ⬇ Down 1% in 1997

Georgia's military strength has been boosted by the 9,200 Russian troops based in the country since it joined the CIS in 1993. The Abkhazian conflict now dominates the agenda for the Georgian army. Training for the government security forces is provided by the CIA.

ECONOMICS

▷ Not available

 $4.7bn   💲 Not available

SCORE CARD

❑ WORLD GNP RANKING	111th
❑ GNP PER CAPITA	$860
❑ BALANCE OF PAYMENT	$–278m
❑ INFLATION	7.1%
❑ UNEMPLOYMENT	3%

STRENGTHS

Gateway to the West for Azeri oil through pipelines across Georgia to Black Sea ports. 1996 IMF loan. Strong economic growth after 1993–1994 near-collapse. Hyperinflation brought under control.

WEAKNESSES

War damage and severance of links with other ex-Soviet republics. Large black economy and influential Mafia. Drought and currency crisis in 1998.

EXPORTS

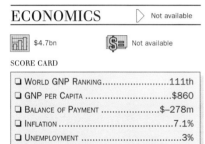

Switzerland 6%
Armenia 8%
Other 32%
Azerbaijan 11%
Turkey 13%
Russia 30%

IMPORTS

Ukraine 6%
Turkey 12%
Other 43%
Azerbaijan 12%
USA 13%
Russia 13%

RESOURCES

▷ Electric power 4.6m kw

3,156 tonnes

2,005 b/d

14m poultry, 1m cattle, 543,000 sheep, 330,000 pigs

Manganese, coal, oil, natural gas, zinc, cobalt, vanadium

Known oil reserves are as yet undeveloped. Georgia is dependent on Russia for much of its energy supply, although a new US–Georgian oil refinery was opened in eastern Georgia in 1998. Cobalt and vanadium are mined but only in small quantities. Georgia is a predominantly agricultural country, and food processing and wine production are the major industries.

ENVIRONMENT

▷ Green MPs

🌲 3%   ⬇ Low

Radiation from materials left by departing Russian soldiers is a growing problem, as is Black Sea pollution and protection of upland pastures.

MEDIA

▷ TV ownership high

 Daily newspaper circulation figures not available

PUBLISHING AND BROADCAST MEDIA

There are 11 daily newspapers, some published in Georgian. These include *Rezonansi* and *Vestnik Gruzii*

1 state-controlled service

1 state-controlled service

There is little press freedom since the media survive on government subsidies. All TV broadcasting is controlled by the state.

CRIME

▷ Death penalty not used

Georgia does not publish prison figures

Levels of all crime, especially organized crime, are rising

Organized crime under the control of Mafia-style groups has flourished since independence in 1991. The judicial system currently favors Shevardnadze and his supporters.

EDUCATION

▷ School leaving age: 14

👤 99%   🎓 163,345 students

Since independence education has stressed Georgian language and history. All levels of education are seriously underfunded. Tbilisi University was formerly of a high standard.

HEALTH

▷ Welfare state health benefits

👤 1 per 238 people

Circulatory and respiratory diseases, cancers, accidents

The health system was limited under the Soviet Union. Internal strife and a lack of resources have prevented any recent investment.

CHRONOLOGY

A Russian protectorate from 1763, Georgia was absorbed into the Russian empire in 1801. It was established as an independent state under a Menshevik socialist government in 1918.

- ❑ **1879** Stalin born in Gori.
- ❑ **1920** Recognized as an independent state by Soviet Russia.
- ❑ **1921** Soviet Red Army invades. Effectively part of USSR.
- ❑ **1922** Incorporated into Transcaucasian Soviet Federative Socialist Republic (TSFSR).
- ❑ **1956** TSFSR dissolved.
- ❑ **1989** Pro-independence riots in Tbilisi put down by Soviet troops.
- ❑ **1990** Declares sovereignty.
- ❑ **1991** Independence. Zviad Gamsakhurdia elected president.
- ❑ **1992** Gamsakhurdia flees Tbilisi. Shevardnadze elected chair of Supreme Soviet and State Council.
- ❑ **1995** Shevardnadze narrowly survives an assassination attempt; subsequently elected president.
- ❑ **1999** Opening of oil pipeline from Caspian to Black Sea.

G

SPENDING

▷ GDP/cap. no increase

CONSUMPTION AND SPENDING

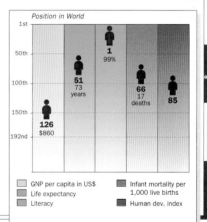

🚗 79 per 1,000 population   114 per 1,000 population

Defense 2.9%
Education 5.2%
Health 4.5%

0   5   10   15   20   25
Defense, Health, Education spending as % of GDP

The majority of the country's people live in poverty, with a small wealthy and extravagant elite. Wages and welfare are often in arrears.

WORLD RANKING

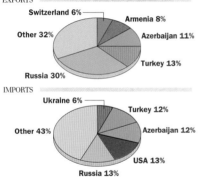

Position in World

1st
50th
100th
150th
192nd

1
99%

51
73 years

66
17 deaths

85

126
$860

❑ GNP per capita in US$
❑ Life expectancy
❑ Literacy

❑ Infant mortality per 1,000 live births
❑ Human dev. index

GERMANY

OFFICIAL NAME: Federal Republic of Germany **CAPITAL:** Berlin
POPULATION: 82.4 million **CURRENCY:** Deutsche Mark **OFFICIAL LANGUAGE:** German

| 1871 | 1990 | Oct 3 | D | +1 | +49 | .de |

WITH COASTLINES on both the Baltic and North Seas, Germany is bordered by nine states. There are plains and rolling hills in the north and more mountainous terrain in the south. The most populous country in Europe after Russia, Germany is also its foremost industrial power and, after the USA, the world's second-biggest exporter. United by 1871, it was divided after the defeat of the Nazi regime in 1945. The western part became a free-market democracy aligned with the West, the east a communist-ruled state in the Soviet bloc. The collapse of the East German regime in 1989 paved the way for reunification in 1990. Tensions created by the wealth differences between east and west were exacerbated by a lengthy economic recession and rising unemployment. Many Germans, proud of the strength of the mark, are concerned that European monetary union will damage stability.

CLIMATE ▷ Continental/Maritime

WEATHER CHART

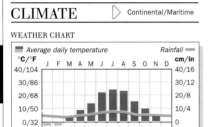

Germany has a broad climatic range. The upper Rhine Valley is very mild and suitable for wine-making. The Bavarian Alps, the Harz Mountains and the Black Forest are by contrast cold, with heavy falls of snow in winter.

TRANSPORTATION ▷ Drive on right

Frankfurt/Main International
43m passengers

1,125 ships
6.95m grt

THE TRANSPORTATION NETWORK

633,000 km
(393,300 miles)

11,190 km
(6,950 miles)

38,450 km
(23,890 miles)

7,400 km
(4,598 miles)

Germany virtually invented the modern highway with the first *Autobahnen* in the 1930s. These have since become Europe's most elaborate highway network. There are generally no tolls or speed limits, despite environmentalist protests. The efficient railroad system has been restructured as a first step towards privatization. Germany's high-speed ICE railroad opened its main north–south routes in 1991 and has expanded greatly since then. A technologically advanced MAGLEV train service is planned.

TOURISM ▷ Visitors:population 1:5.2

15.8m visitors   Up 7% 1995–1997

MAIN TOURIST ARRIVALS

	% of total arrivals
Netherlands 13%	
USA 12%	
UK 10%	
Italy 6%	
Switzerland 6%	
Other 53%	

Northerly beaches and a colder climate make Germany less of a tourist draw than France or Italy. Skiing in the Bavarian Alps, the historic castles of the Rhine Valley, the Black Forest and, for visitors, Germany's excellent beer are all major attractions. Before 1989 Berlin attracted many tourists with its rich cultural life and the Wall separating capitalist West and communist East. Now capital of the reunified Germany, it has a huge reconstruction program and a dynamic and vibrant atmosphere.

The Stillach Valley, Allgäu Alps, Bayern *(Bavaria). Germany's forests, which are found mainly in its mountain regions, are suffering badly from the effects of acid rain.*

GERMANY

Total Land Area : 349 520 sq. km
(134 910 sq. miles)

POPULATION

over 1 000 000
over 500 000
over 100 000
over 10 000

LAND HEIGHT

2000m/6562ft
1000m/3281ft
500m/1640ft
200m/656ft
Sea Level

PEPLE

▷ Pop. density high

German

236/km²
(611/mi²)

THE URBAN/RURAL POPULATION SPLIT

87%   13%

RELIGIOUS PERSUASION

Muslim 2%
Protestant 36%
Other 27%
Roman Catholic 35%

ETHNIC MAKEUP

Turkish 2%   Other European 3%
Other 3%
German 92%

The majority of German-speakers live in Germany itself, although Austria and the greater part of Switzerland are German-speaking, as are parts of eastern France. Germans share a common language, but they speak it in a variety of dialects, reflecting a strong sense of regionalism. The north is still largely Protestant, while the south and southwest, particularly Bayern (Bavaria), have strong Catholic traditions.

A large immigrant population, now some seven million people, provided much of the labor on which the former West Germany's economic recovery was built. Legislation in 1999 improved the rights of these *Gastarbeiter* (guest workers) to take full German nationality, but they still do not have equal rights. The two million Turks are the largest single group.

Germany's once liberal asylum laws were tightened in 1993 in response to domestic tension over the huge influx of ethnic Germans and "economic" refugees from Russia and eastern Europe after the collapse of communism. Unemployment and disappointed expectations, particularly among young Germans, has helped extreme right-wing parties win a significant but still limited following. Germany has since taken in more refugees from the war in

former Yugoslavia than all other Western countries put together.

Family ties in Germany are little different from those in the USA or the UK. Millions of couples live together in common-law arrangements, and since this is frowned on by the Catholic Church, it is largely in rural districts in Bayern (Bavaria) that traditional habits are still observed. The birth rate is one of Europe's lowest, and the population would be falling were it not for the influx of immigrants since the 1950s.

Women have full rights under the law and play a bigger role in politics than in most other European countries. In 1998, 30% of *Bundestag* (Federal Assembly) members were women. They are less well represented in top jobs in business and industry, however. Germany has a tradition of strong feminism. Abortion remains a charged issue. Women in former East Germany had wanted to keep their right to abortion on demand, but the constitutional court, after strong Catholic lobbying, overruled the relatively liberal 1992 compromise for the whole country. Under a law finally passed in mid-1995, women can get abortions (but only after counseling) within three months of conception.

Germans retain relatively formal social habits, with clear distinctions drawn between acquaintances and good friends. The formal *Sie* rather than the more familiar *du* is the normal form of address.

G

POPULATION AGE BREAKDOWN

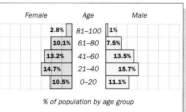

Female	Age	Male
2.8%	81–100	1%
10.1%	61–80	7.5%
13.2%	41–60	13.5%
14.7%	21–40	15.7%
10.5%	0–20	11.1%

% of population by age group

CHRONOLOGY

German unification in the 19th century brought together a mosaic of states with a common linguistic but varied political heritage.

❏ **1815** German Confederation under nominal Austrian leadership.
❏ **1834** Zollverein Customs Union of 18 states, including Prussia.
❏ **1862** Otto von Bismarck appointed Prussian chancellor.
❏ **1864–1870** Prussia defeats Danes, Austrians and French; north German states under Prussian control.
❏ **1871** Southern states join Prussian-led unified German Empire under Wilhelm I.
❏ **1870s** Rapid industrialization.
❏ **1890** Kaiser Wilhelm II accedes with aspirations for German world role. Bismarck sacked.
❏ **1914–1918** World War I.
❏ **1918** Germany signs armistice; Weimar Republic created.
❏ **1919** Treaty of Versailles: colonies lost and payment of reparations. Rhineland demilitarized. ⇨

G

*The **Messeturm**, Frankfurt, the tallest office building in Europe. Frankfurt is Germany's financial services center and home to many of its leading companies.*

POLITICS

 Multiparty elections

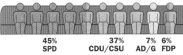 1998/2002 | President Johannes Rau

AT THE LAST ELECTION

Federal Assembly 669 seats

45% SPD | 37% CDU/CSU | 7% AD/G | 6% FDP | 5% PDS

SPD = Social Democratic Party of Germany
CDU/CSU = Christian Democratic Union/ Christian Social Union **AD/G** = Alliance 90/ Greens **FDP** = Free Democratic Party **PDS** = Party of Democratic Socialism

Federal Council 69 seats

Each of the 16 states (Länder) is represented by between 3 and 6 members in the Bundesrat, who are appointed after the elections in each Land.

Germany is a federal democratic republic of 16 states, or *Länder*. The government is led by the federal chancellor, elected by the *Bundestag* (Federal Assembly). The president's role is largely ceremonial. The 1948 "Basic Law" of West Germany became the 1990 federal constitution after reunification.

MAIN POLITICAL ISSUES
Reunification
The overwhelming majority of Germans supported reunification in 1990, but the general rejoicing which greeted the fall of the Berlin Wall in 1989 quickly soured as the true costs of the changes became clear. Unemployment in the east rose to 30% with the collapse of inefficient industries, and the "solidarity surcharge" on income tax became a semi-permanent feature, although in 1996 the government promised to reduce it by degrees. Over DM1,000 billion has now been spent on reconstruction.

The economy and unemployment
Germans, used to constant growth since the 1950s, were shocked by recession in 1991, doubly painful because it coincided with the enormous costs of reunification. A recovery faltered in 1995, as the government reined in public spending to meet targets for European monetary union; these austerity policies were maintained in succeeding years despite unrest and an unprecedented rise in unemployment.

Nationalism
Increasing unemployment has led to anti-immigrant attacks and support for far-right parties. Some Germans fear that foreigners are taking "their" jobs. Foreign workers, particularly Turks, and asylum seekers have been subject to shocking attacks. The problem of racism, even if no worse than in many other European states, is more sensitive, given Germany's history.

PROFILE
Germany's politics are now strongly democratic and essentially stable, with a long tradition of federative association. Before unification in 1871, Germany was a mass of separate principalities, kingdoms and city states, a tradition in many ways maintained by Bismarck in his unification constitution. The 1933–1945 Nazi period, during which the federal system was abolished, was very much a hiatus. The Allies reestablished the federal system in West Germany in 1949; in the east, the *Länder* were restored after reunification in 1990. In many ways, the *Länder* are at the heart of German political life. Each *Land* has its own elected parliament and largely controls its own finances. In addition German cities have larger budgets than their European counterparts and city mayors wield considerable power. By general consensus the system delivers efficient and commercially astute government.

Nationally, the conservative CDU dominated parliament in 1949–1966 and then headed a "grand coalition" with the social democratic SPD until 1969. An SPD-led coalition with the liberal FDP, with Willy Brandt and Helmut Schmidt as chancellors, held power for the next 13 years. A conservative government then held power again until in September 1998 the electorate chose moderate SPD leader Gerhard Schröder in a vote for change, instead of approving yet another term for long-serving Chancellor Helmut Kohl. In practice, at least on domestic policy, there have been few major differences between coalitions. All parties support the social market economy on which German prosperity was built.

Helmut Kohl, long-serving chancellor until 1998.

Gerhard Schröder, elected chancellor in place of Kohl in 1998.

Oskar Lafontaine, left-wing SPD leader who resigned in 1999.

WORLD AFFAIRS ▷ Joined UN in 1973

Before reunification, Germany played only a modest part in international politics. The focus of West Germany was integration in Western Europe (creating what is now the EU) and a more

flexible *Ostpolitik* – to improve relations with the Soviet bloc, with 400,000 troops stationed in East Germany.

Since 1990, the emphasis has changed: a united Germany is starting to voice a foreign policy reflecting its position as the most powerful country in Europe. On the world stage, this has

raised the possibility of Germany becoming a permanent member of the UN Security Council. The united Germany's focus has inevitably shifted more of its attention eastward. It is the biggest investor in all the ex-COMECON economies, bringing the region once again under German influence.

AID ▷ Donor

$ $5.9bn (donations) ⇕ Not applicable

Unlike the USA, the UK and France, Germany's aid programs are not directly motivated by its desire for political influence in the world's poorer regions. Most are multilateral, although there is also a strong tradition of direct aid. Much comes directly from church organizations such as the Protestant *Brot für die Welt*. Many German volunteers and missionaries work overseas on aid programs.

DEFENSE ▷ Compulsory military service

$ $33bn ⬇ Down 17% in 1997

The German army is Europe's largest. US and UK troops in western Germany are being withdrawn. The constitutional court ruled in 1994 that army units could take part in collective defense activities abroad. Germany participated in the 1999 NATO bombing of Serbia – its first active military action abroad since 1945. Weapons exports totaled US$1,464 million in 1996.

GERMAN ARMED FORCES

🛡	2,716 main battle tanks (888 *Leopard* 1A1,A3,A4,A5, 1,828 *Leopard* 2)	230,600 personnel
🚢	14 submarines, 3 destroyers, 12 frigates and 30 patrol boats	26,700 personnel
✈	451 combat aircraft (152 F-4, 276 *Tornado*, 23 MiG-29)	76,200 personnel
	None	

G

ECONOMICS ▷ Inflation 3% p.a. (1985–1996)

📊 $2,320bn 💲 1.79–1.67 Deutsche Marks

SCORE CARD

❏ WORLD GNP RANKING	3rd
❏ GNP PER CAPITA	$28,280
❏ BALANCE OF PAYMENTS	$–1.2bn
❏ INFLATION	1.8%
❏ UNEMPLOYMENT	13%

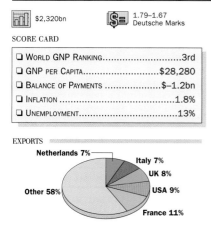

EXPORTS
- Netherlands 7%
- Italy 7%
- UK 8%
- USA 9%
- France 11%
- Other 58%

IMPORTS
- UK 7%
- USA 8%
- Italy 8%
- Netherlands 8%
- France 10%
- Other 59%

ECONOMIC PERFORMANCE INDICATOR

Consumer price index / GDP
(Consumer price index 1991=100; GDP 1993=100)
1993, 1994, 1995, 1996, 1997

obligations with an aging population. Competition from efficient, low-wage Asian economies. Relatively few small firms, a short working week, and poorly developed service sector.

PROFILE
West Germany's remarkable postwar recovery, to become the world's third-strongest economy, was based on the concept of a social market economy, under which the state provided welfare and ensured workers' rights, while the economy was largely in private hands. Major banks and businesses are privately owned, except for the partly state-owned Volkswagen. The state privatization agency, the Treuhand, had completed by the mid-1990s its mandate to sell off former East German state concerns. Rebuilding the east remains one of the greatest challenges for Germany.

The government of Helmut Kohl had convinced a somewhat skeptical public of the case for completing European monetary union, and the euro was introduced from January 1999, beside the DM.

GERMANY : MAJOR BUSINESSES

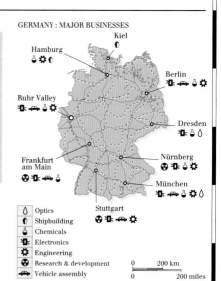

- Kiel
- Hamburg
- Berlin
- Ruhr Valley
- Dresden
- Frankfurt am Main
- Nürnberg
- München
- Stuttgart

◊	Optics
○	Shipbuilding
△	Chemicals
▣	Electronics
✿	Engineering
☢	Research & development
🚗	Vehicle assembly

0 200 km
0 200 miles

The SPD-led government elected in 1998 has staked its reputation on its success in tackling unemployment, which peaked at 11.5% in 1997, and in maintaining growth.

The reconstruction of Potsdamer Platz,
Berlin, following the re-unification of East and West Germany and the fall of the Berlin Wall.

STRENGTHS
Europe's major industrial power and, until now, most successful economy. Efficient industry benefits from low-inflation environment. Workers and managers live up to their reputation for hard work, thoroughness, and discipline. Strongest sectors are cars, heavy engineering, electronics and chemicals; all have massive export success.

WEAKNESSES
Underestimation of the costs of updating highly inefficient eastern German economy. High wages and social security costs; pension

RESOURCES ▷ Electric power 115.4m kw

298,017 tonnes

65,744 b/d (reserves 449,814,000 bbl)

25m pigs, 15.2m cattle, 2.3m sheep, 680,000 horses

Coal, oil, natural gas, copper, salt, potash, tin, nickel

ELECTRICITY GENERATION

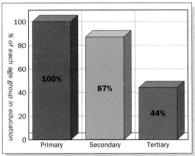

- Hydro 4% (24.2bn kwh)
- Combustion 67% (356.2bn kwh)
- Nuclear 29% (154.1bn kwh)
- Other 0%

% of total generation by type

Germany has relatively few natural resources, importing over 50% of its energy needs. Coal, the basis of its industrialization, now accounts for only 14% of energy, compared with over 50% 30 years ago. Unlike France, the former West Germany did not invest heavily in nuclear power; the 1986 accident at Chernobyl in Ukraine strengthened the antinuclear lobby's case. In the east, the Soviet-built stations have been shut down and the "red–green" coalition elected in 1998 has pledged to phase out nuclear power (which provides over 30% of electricity). Renewable resources account for 2% of total energy supplies.

ENVIRONMENT ▷ Green MPs

27%

Medium

ENVIRONMENTAL TREATIES

Yes   Yes   Yes
Yes   Yes   Yes

Germans are among the world's most environmentally conscious people. Led by the Green Party, which emerged as a powerful political force in the 1980s, environmental campaigns have influenced the policies of all major parties. At national level, the Greens are a significant force in the *Bundestag*; they joined the SPD-led federal government coalition in 1998, and are strongly represented in *Land* parliaments and local councils.

Germany has some of the strictest pollution controls in the world, adding extra costs to businesses and forcing them to become even more efficient. Germans recycle 47% of their waste paper, reprocess 70% of their used tires and sort 75% of their glass according to color, to aid recycling.

Apart from the nuclear debate, which has been vigorously fought and won by the Greens, the main concern is Germany's forests. Acid rain from car fumes and industrial pollution was suspected to be killing trees in all parts of the country. Official estimates in 1986 suggesting that up to 50% of trees were sick or dying led to Germany becoming the first European country to insist that new cars be fitted with catalytic converters. The east had the highest per capita rate of sulfur emissions in the world, but these have been reduced by the closure of industrial plants and the elimination of the noxious Trabant cars.

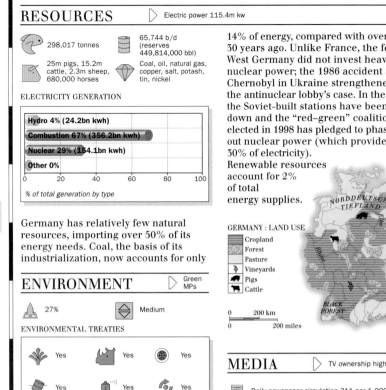

GERMANY : LAND USE

- Cropland
- Forest
- Pasture
- Vineyards
- Pigs
- Cattle

NORDDEUTSCHES TIEFLAND

BLACK FOREST

0   200 km
0   200 miles

MEDIA ▷ TV ownership high

Daily newspaper circulation 311 per 1,000 people

PUBLISHING AND BROADCAST MEDIA

There are 375 daily newspapers, including the *Frankfurter Allgemeine Zeitung*, the *Süddeutsche Zeitung* and *Die Welt*

3 state-controlled, 2 independent networks

13 state-controlled networks

TV is supervised by the political parties to ensure a balance of views. The public channels, ARD and ZDF, have recently faced more competition from satellite and cable TV. Media conglomerates such as Kirch and Bertelsmann have expanded abroad. Newspapers are mostly regional and serious. An exception is *Bild Zeitung*, the right-wing, sensationalist tabloid, which sells 4.5 million copies daily.

Neuschwanstein Castle, Bayern (Bavaria), one of Germany's major tourist attractions. It was built for the eccentric King Ludwig II.

EDUCATION ▷ School leaving age : 18

99%

2.1m students

Of total government expenditure 9.4% is spent on education.

THE EDUCATION SYSTEM

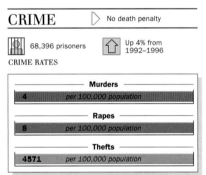

% of each age group in education

- Primary 100%
- Secondary 87%
- Tertiary 44%

Education in Germany is run by the *Länder*. They coordinate teaching policies, but have autonomy within their borders. The German approach to education stresses academic and vocational achievement. Sporting or cultural activities tend to be organized informally.

Those who wish to go to university attend the upper-secondary *Gymnasien* to prepare for the *Abitur* exam. Since this was made easier, resources have been strained as thousands more have decided to go to university. They take an average of seven years to complete their diploma. New legislation has now added shorter bachelor's and master's degrees as in other countries. Research is done as much by major companies as by the universities.

CRIME ▷ No death penalty

68,396 prisoners

Up 4% from 1992–1996

CRIME RATES

Murders
4 *per 100,000 population*

Rapes
8 *per 100,000 population*

Thefts
4571 *per 100,000 population*

Crime rates in Germany are lower than in most other European countries. This is largely the result of a genuine respect for the law, coupled with a strong police force. Recently, however, rising unemployment has led to an increase in petty theft and a wave of violence, notably against immigrants.

German politicians, once with an enviably clean reputation, have suffered several corruption scandals. Civil service corruption remains rare. People convicted under environmental laws can face ten-year jail sentences.

G

—BERLIN, REUNIFICATION AND CENTRAL EUROPE—

THE SO-CALLED "BONN REPUBLIC" created in West Germany in the postwar period ended symbolically in September 1999. Bonn could justifiably claim to have been home for some 50 years to Germany's only enduringly successful parliamentary democracy. The decision to move the capital to Berlin, however, symbolizing German unity, was enshrined in the 1990 unification treaty only months after the fall of the Berlin Wall in November 1989. It took time to confirm that both government and parliament would be transferred – the lower house of parliament, the *Bundestag*, only voted to move in 1994 – but five years after that vote, in the same month that federal Chancellor Schröder moved into his office in Berlin, the *Bundestag* held its first full session there.

The dramatic glass interior of the new Reichstag building in Berlin.

PROSPECTS FOR BERLIN

The parliament's new home is the former *Reichstag* building, impressively redesigned by British architect Sir Norman Foster. Topped with a transparent dome and lit up at night from within, it epitomises the emphasis on architectural and engineering achievements in modern Berlin. New government, commercial and tourist facilities have brought a lengthy construction boom in Berlin, which is Germany's largest city with a population of some 3.5 million. The proliferation of cultural and artistic activity has also contributed to a strong sense of excitement, boosting the city's image with the international media and public. Berlin nevertheless faces many problems, including an unemployment rate well above the national average and the need to revitalize its declining industrial base. The outward movement of business and population, from central urban areas to surrounding regions, has been an established trend for decades in major western German cities, but is now happening much more rapidly in Berlin, whose western half was for years an enclave within East Germany. The city has a long way to go in attracting major companies to make their headquarters there; only 12 of the largest German companies are located in Berlin compared with over 40 each in Hamburg, Munich and Frankfurt.

COSTLY REUNIFICATION

The costs of reconstruction of the former East Germany far outweighed initial expectations. Achievements stand out in telecommunications and rail transport, but most infrastructure in the east is still well below the standard of the west, despite subsidies amounting to the transfer of some 7% of West German GDP per year for a decade. Unemployment is higher, labor productivity lower and living conditions less attractive to the majority of Germans.

GERMANY'S NEW CENTRE OF GRAVITY

The transfer of the capital reinforces the shift in Germany's centre of gravity brought about by reunification. Coinciding with the collapse of communism across the whole former Soviet bloc, came a revival of interest in Germany's role in central Europe or *Mitteleuropa*. In the former communist countries German economic influence is now particularly strong. West Germany was firmly anchored in Western Europe, in economic terms by the European Economic Community (now the European Union), and in a political-military sense by its membership of the NATO alliance. The imminent eastward expansion of the EU, however, suggests the emergence of France-Germany-Poland as a new and powerful axis in the Europe of the 21st century.

Unemployed Germans demonstrate for the right to work.

HEALTH

▷ Welfare state health benefits

👤 1 per 303 people　　☠ Heart and cerebro-vascular diseases, cancers, accidents

The German social security system, first pioneered by Bismarck, is one of the most comprehensive in the world. Health insurance is compulsory, and employer and employee contributions are high. Although most hospitals are run by the *Länder*, some are still owned by Germany's wealthy churches. Of total health spending 28.2% is now private.

Germans are increasingly health-conscious, paying great attention to diet. Nearly a million people go on cures every year to the country's 200-plus spas. In the east, the incidence of lung diseases caused by pollution is higher.

SPENDING

▷ GDP/cap. no increase

CONSUMPTION AND SPENDING

🚗 500 per 1,000 population　　⬭ 550 per 1,000 population

Defense 1.6%		
Education 4.7%		
Health 9.1%		

Defense, Health, Education spending as % of GDP (scale 0, 5, 10, 15, 20, 25)

The effects of the Nazi period, which discredited many of Germany's ruling class, and the destruction of the property of millions of families in the war, account for the relatively classless nature of German society. Status is now more closely linked to wealth than to birth. In the west, disparities are less than in most of Europe; workers are generally well paid and social security is generous. East German wages, however, are still pegged below western rates, and there are a disproportionate number of unemployed living on welfare benefit.

WORLD RANKING

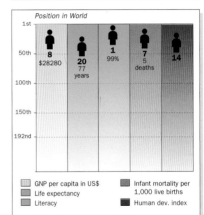

Position in World (1st, 50th, 100th, 150th, 192nd)

8 $28280	20 77 years	1 99%	7 5 deaths	14

☐ GNP per capita in US$
☐ Life expectancy
☐ Literacy
☐ Infant mortality per 1,000 live births
■ Human dev. index

G

GHANA

OFFICIAL NAME: Republic of Ghana **CAPITAL:** Accra
POPULATION: 18.9 million **CURRENCY:** Cedi **OFFICIAL LANGUAGE:** English

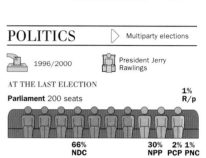

WEST AFRICA

Africa

| 1957 | 1957 | March 6 | GH | 0 | +233 | .gh |

THE HEARTLAND OF THE ancient Ashanti kingdom, modern Ghana is a union of the former British colony of the Gold Coast and the British-administered part of the UN Trust Territory of Togoland. Ghana gained independence in 1957, the first British colony to do so. Its recent history has been one of intermittent military rule; the embracing of multiparty democracy in 1992 confirmed former military leader Jerry Rawlings in power.

CLIMATE
▷ Tropical wet & dry/ equatorial

WEATHER CHART

■ Average daily temperature   Rainfall ■

Southern Ghana has two rainy seasons: from April to July and September to November. The drier north has just one, from April to September.

TRANSPORTATION
▷ Drive on right

Kotoka Intl, Accra
467,000 passengers

206 ships
129,700 grt

THE TRANSPORTATION NETWORK

| 7,300 km (4,536 miles) | 30 km (19 miles) |
| 947 km (588 miles) | 168 km (104 miles) |

In 1983, work began to restore Ghana's roads, which had fallen into disrepair in the 1960s and 1970s; the network is now improving.

TOURISM
▷ Visitors : population 1:58

325,000 visitors

Up 14% 1995–1997

MAIN TOURIST ARRIVALS

Nigeria	14%
UK	9%
USA	7%
Other	70%

% of total arrivals

Tourism is still small-scale; most visitors come from the rest of Africa, the UK, and the USA. Good beaches and old coastal forts are major attractions.

PEOPLE
▷ Pop. density medium

Twi, Fanti, Ewe, Ga, Adangbe, Gurma, Dagomba (Dagbani)

82/km² (213/mi²)

THE URBAN/RURAL POPULATION SPLIT

36%   64%

RELIGIOUS PERSUASION

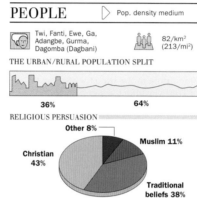

Other 8%
Muslim 11%
Christian 43%
Traditional beliefs 38%

Ghana contains various cultural-linguistic groups. The largest is the Akan, who include the Ashanti and Fanti peoples. Other important groups are the Mole-Dagbani in the north, Ga-Adangbe around Accra, and Ewe in the southeast. There are few tribal tensions. Family ties are strong.

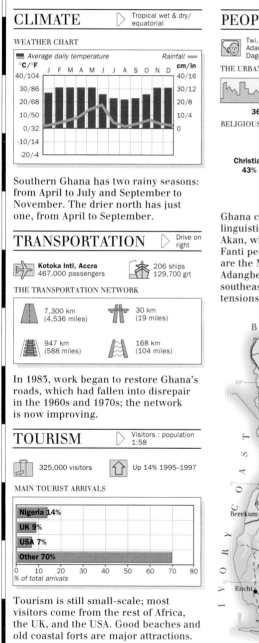

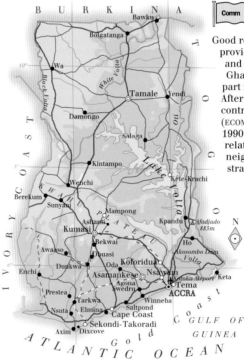

POLITICS
▷ Multiparty elections

1996/2000

President Jerry Rawlings

AT THE LAST ELECTION

Parliament 200 seats

1% R/p

66% NDC   30% NPP   2% PCP   1% PNC

NDC = National Democratic Congress **NPP** = New Patriotic Party **PCP** = People's Convention Party **PNC** = People's National Convention **R/p** = Result pending

Ghana's return to multiparty rule in 1992 marked the effective legitimization of the military government of Jerry Rawlings. An air force flight-lieutenant of Ewe–Scottish descent and one of the great survivors of African politics, Rawlings staged coups in 1979 and 1981, and led the 1981–1992 Provisional National Defense Council (PNDC) military government. As the NDC candidate in the 1992 presidential election, Rawlings won 58% of the vote. Opposition parties claimed malpractice and boycotted parliamentary elections, which the NDC won easily, the following month. Since 1992 political dissent has been accepted, but elections in December 1996 gave Rawlings a further presidential term and renewed his NDC's majority in the parliament.

WORLD AFFAIRS
▷ Joined UN in 1957

| Comm | Ecowas | G24 | IAEA | OAU |

Good relations with the West, which provides the bulk of Ghana's military and development aid, are a priority. Ghana has played a significant part in UN peacekeeping operations. After Nigeria, it was the main contributor to the Ecowas forces (ECOMOG) in war-torn Liberia from 1990 to 1997. Ghana maintains good relations with its French-speaking neighbors, despite periods of strain with Togo.

GHANA

Total Land Area :
258 540 sq. km (92 100 sq. miles)

LAND HEIGHT	POPULATION
500m/1640ft	over 500 000 ◉
200m/656ft	over 100 000 ◎
Sea Level	over 50 000 ○
	over 10 000 ●
	under 10 000 •

0   100 km
0   100 miles

G

AID

> Recipient

$493m (receipts) — Down 25% 1996–1997

A largely successful economic recovery program backed by World Bank and IMF aid began in 1983. Between 1984 and 1989, Ghana received $3.5 billion, the third-largest recipient of World Bank aid after India and China, and inflows continue to rise.

DEFENSE

> No compulsory military service

$134m — Up 9% in 1997

In 1966, 1972, 1979, and 1981, the military mounted successful coups, and there have also been several unsuccessful coup attempts. Outside Ghana, the 5,000-strong army has been deployed mainly in UN and Ecowas operations. Ghana's navy is small, with four patrol boats. The air force has 17 combat aircraft.

ECONOMICS

> Inflation 31.3% p.a. (1985–1996)

$7bn — 2,260–2,340 cedis

SCORE CARD

- ❏ WORLD GNP RANKING...........................95th
- ❏ GNP PER CAPITA $390
- ❏ BALANCE OF PAYMENTS....................$–541m
- ❏ INFLATION 27.9%
- ❏ UNEMPLOYMENT...................................20%

STRENGTHS
Since 1983, economic recovery policies have raised GNP 5% a year. Cocoa exports account for 15% of the world total. Since 1996, Ashanti Goldfields Co Ltd has expanded into a multinational active in 12 African countries. Ghana's gold production was 50,000 kg in 1996.

WEAKNESSES
High budget deficits and debt repayments; the cedi was devalued in 1983 and has since tended to float downward. Foreign investors generally invest solely in gold mining. Very high inflation levels.

EXPORTS
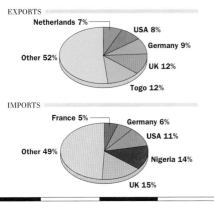
Netherlands 7% — USA 8% — Germany 9% — UK 12% — Togo 12% — Other 52%

IMPORTS
France 5% — Germany 6% — USA 11% — Nigeria 14% — UK 15% — Other 49%

Dixcove harbor, close to Ghana's most southerly cape. The majority of Ghanaians lead a traditional subsistence existence.

RESOURCES

> Electric power 1.2m kw

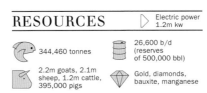

344,460 tonnes — 26,600 b/d (reserves of 500,000 bbl)

2.2m goats, 2.1m sheep, 1.2m cattle, 395,000 pigs — Gold, diamonds, bauxite, manganese

Gold production has expanded strongly since the mid-1980s; by 1993, gold was the major export. Diamonds, bauxite, and manganese are also exported. Hydropower from the Volta Dam is exported to Togo and Benin, but is hit by periodic droughts.

ENVIRONMENT

> No Green MPs

5% — Low

Cutting of wood for fuel, timber, and farming has destroyed 70% of forests. Mining devastation is now being tackled under a World Bank project.

MEDIA

> TV ownership medium

Daily newspaper circulation 14 per 1,000 people

PUBLISHING AND BROADCAST MEDIA

There are 4 daily newspapers, including the *Ghanaian Times,* and the *Daily Graphic*

1 state-controlled service — 1 state-controlled service

New independent weeklies reflect the increase in private press ownership. Radio and TV tend to follow government reporting guidelines.

CRIME

> Death penalty used

Ghana does not publish prison figures — Up 8% from 1990–1996

The judiciary has little independence and the government often resorts to ad hoc "people's tribunals." Corruption is now less of a problem.

EDUCATION

> School leaving age: 14

66% — 9,609 students

All sectors of the education system are oversubscribed. There are a few high-quality boarding schools and four universities.

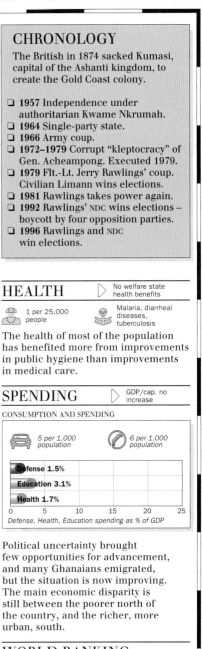

CHRONOLOGY

The British in 1874 sacked Kumasi, capital of the Ashanti kingdom, to create the Gold Coast colony.

- ❏ **1957** Independence under authoritarian Kwame Nkrumah.
- ❏ **1964** Single-party state.
- ❏ **1966** Army coup.
- ❏ **1972–1979** Corrupt "kleptocracy" of Gen. Acheampong. Executed 1979.
- ❏ **1979** Flt.-Lt. Jerry Rawlings' coup. Civilian Limann wins elections.
- ❏ **1981** Rawlings takes power again.
- ❏ **1992** Rawlings' NDC wins elections – boycott by four opposition parties.
- ❏ **1996** Rawlings and NDC win elections.

G

HEALTH

> No welfare state health benefits

1 per 25,000 people — Malaria, diarrheal diseases, tuberculosis

The health of most of the population has benefited more from improvements in public hygiene than improvements in medical care.

SPENDING

> GDP/cap. no increase

CONSUMPTION AND SPENDING

5 per 1,000 population — 6 per 1,000 population

Defense 1.5%
Education 3.1%
Health 1.7%

0   5   10   15   20   25
Defense, Health, Education spending as % of GDP

Political uncertainty brought few opportunities for advancement, and many Ghanaians emigrated, but the situation is now improving. The main economic disparity is still between the poorer north of the country, and the richer, more urban, south.

WORLD RANKING

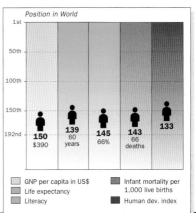

Position in World

150 $390	**139** 60 years	**145** 66%	**143** 66 deaths	**133**

- ☐ GNP per capita in US$
- ☐ Life expectancy
- ☐ Literacy
- ■ Infant mortality per 1,000 live births
- ■ Human dev. index

GREECE

OFFICIAL NAME: Hellenic Republic **CAPITAL:** Athens
POPULATION: 10.6 million **CURRENCY:** Drachma **OFFICIAL LANGUAGE:** Greek

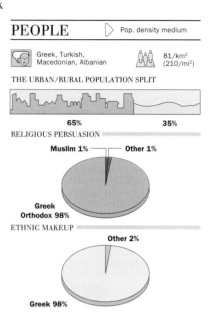

EUROPE

| 1829 | 1947 | March 25 | GR | +2 | +30 | .gr |

THE SOUTHERNMOST COUNTRY of the Balkans, Greece is surrounded by the Aegean, Ionian and Cretan seas. Its mainly mountainous territory includes more than 2,000 islands. Only one-third of the land is cultivated. Greece has a strong seafaring tradition and some of the world's biggest ship-owners. Greece is rich in minerals, including chromium, which is rare. Greek concern about the potential claim of the Former Yugoslav Republic of Macedonia (FYRM) over the Greek province of Macedonia has recently been overshadowed by the revival of ancient Greek territorial disputes with Turkey.

CLIMATE   ▷ Mediterranean

WEATHER CHART

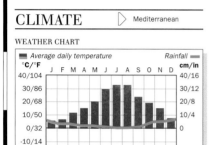

■ *Average daily temperature*   Rainfall ■

The climate varies from region to region. The northwest is alpine, while parts of Crete border on the subtropical. The large central plain experiences high summer temperatures. Water is a problem, since many rivers have been diverted underground by earthquakes.

TRANSPORTATION   ▷ Drive on right

✈ **Athinai, Athens**
6.3m passengers

🚢 1,987 ships
25.7m grt

THE TRANSPORTATION NETWORK

| 29,400 km (18,300 miles) | 420 km (260 miles) |
| 2,503 km (1,555 miles) | Corinth Canal |

The easiest and cheapest method of transportation between the islands and the mainland is by boat or Russian-built hovercraft. Greece has 444 ports, of which 123 are large enough to handle passenger or freight traffic. A major new airport at Spata, 20 km east of Athens, is to open in 2001 with a capacity of 16 million passengers a year. Greece has a good, if increasingly congested, road network. Two expressway routes are nearing completion, with the help of EU funds, as is the upgrading of the Athens metro. An inter-urban bus system and fleet of air-conditioned tourist Pullmans offer an extensive service. Piraeus is the country's main port.

TOURISM   ▷ Visitors : population 1:1.1

🧳 10.2m visitors   ⬆ Up 1% 1995–1997

MAIN TOURIST ARRIVALS

| Germany 21% |
| UK 18% |
| Italy 5% |
| France 5% |
| Netherlands 5% |
| Other 46% |

% of total arrivals

Tourism is a mainstay of the Greek economy, contributing some 15% to GDP, and a major source of foreign exchange. Until recently, the state gave grants for hotel development and many third-grade hotels were built, especially on Crete and Rhodes. Smaller islands also tried to encourage tourism, but few have sufficient water supplies or sandy beaches. Visitor numbers fell in the mid-1990s as people chose cheaper vacations elsewhere. The break-up of former Yugoslavia deterred visitors, as has the 1999 war in Kosovo. The tourist industry is now promoting year-round activity holidays and conference tourism. The 2004 Olympics, to be held in Athens, are a stimulus to upgrade the city's facilities.

The theater at Dodona. *Classical sites such as this amphitheater in northwestern Greece, have helped to make tourism one of Greece's most important industries.*

PEOPLE   ▷ Pop. density medium

Greek, Turkish, Macedonian, Albanian

81/km² (210/mi²)

THE URBAN/RURAL POPULATION SPLIT

65%   35%

RELIGIOUS PERSUASION

Muslim 1%   Other 1%
Greek Orthodox 98%

ETHNIC MAKEUP

Other 2%
Greek 98%

The Greeks were for many centuries a largely agrarian and seafaring nation. The German occupation during World War II, and the civil war that followed, destroyed much of the fabric of rural life and there was rapid urbanization after the 1950s. There was also extensive emigration in the 1950s and 1960s to northern Europe, Australia, the USA, Canada and southern Africa. However, many people returned to Greece in the 1980s, putting pressure on the labor market. The socialist PASOK governments of 1981–1989 spent large sums, mostly from EU sources, on developing the infrastructure and business life of the rural regions with a view to halting emigration to the cities. The policy was mostly successful, but a majority still lives in or near the capital, Athens, and Thessaloníki in the north.

Some 98% of the population belong to the Greek Orthodox Church. Civil marriage and divorce only became legal in 1982. There are minorities of Muslims, Catholics, and Jews, as well as more recently more than 300,000 Albanian immigrants.

POPULATION AGE BREAKDOWN

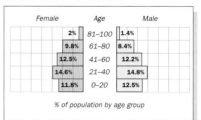

Female	Age	Male
2%	81–100	1.4%
9.8%	61–80	8.4%
12.5%	41–60	12.2%
14.6%	21–40	14.8%
11.8%	0–20	12.5%

% of population by age group

POLITICS

 Multiparty elections

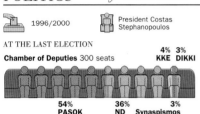 1996/2000

President Costas Stephanopoulos

AT THE LAST ELECTION

Chamber of Deputies 300 seats

4% **KKE** 3% **DIKKI**

54% **PASOK** 36% **ND** 3% **Synaspismos**

PASOK = Pan-Hellenic Sociialist Movement **ND** = New Democracy **KKE** = Communist Party of Greece **Synaspismos** = Left Coaltion **DIKKI** = Deomcratic Renewal Movement

Greece is a multiparty democracy. A military government was in power between 1967 and 1974.

MAIN POLITICAL ISSUES

European monetary union
The chief priority of the socialist government of Kostas Simitis is to meet the economic convergence criteria needed to introduce the euro. Greece, the poorest member of the EU, now looks set to do so, but the austerity measures and crackdown on tax evasion have led to widespread protests and industrial unrest.

Relations with Macedonia
In 1995, Greece finally recognized the sovereignty of the Former Yugoslav Republic of Macedonia. Tensions in Macedonia following the 1999 influx of refugees from Kosovo increased Greek regional security concerns.

Albanian refugees
Thousands of Albanians of Greek descent entered Greece illegally after 1990. Willing to work for very low wages, they swelled Greece's thriving black economy. Eventually a 1998 legalization program resulted in the registration of 375,000 Albanians.

PROFILE
The 1993 elections returned PASOK to power, when economic realities forced it to continue with the policies of the preceding ND government. In April 1996 Andreas Papandreou resigned as prime minister,

Kostas Simitis, *prime minister since January 1996.*

Andreas Papandreou, *former leader of* PASOK *1981–1989, 1993–1996.*

dying two months later. His successor Kostas Simitis led PASOK to a general election victory in September 1996.

WORLD AFFAIRS

Joined UN in 1945

EU NATO OECD OSCE CE

Throughout the Cold War, Greece was closely allied to the West, but there are sympathies with Russians and Serbs, who also have an Orthodox heritage. Greece withdrew from NATO's military command in 1974 in protest at its failure to prevent the Turkish invasion of Cyprus. It has since rejoined under an agreement to negotiate with Turkey new command and control accords over the Aegean, but these remain unresolved. The current priority is acceding to European monetary union.

AID

Donor

$152 (donations)

Not applicable

Greek overseas development assistance represented 0.13% of GNP in 1995, the lowest level in western Europe. However, Greek companies are increasingly seeking to invest in the potentially large Balkan market. Greece is a large net receiver of regional development assistance from the EU. In particular, it is a major beneficiary of the EU's structural and cohesion funds. The allocation of cohesion funds for Greece are estimated to amount to around $3.5 billion over the 1994–1999 period. Some of the money has been used to reverse the decline of northeast Greece – the EU's least developed region.

G

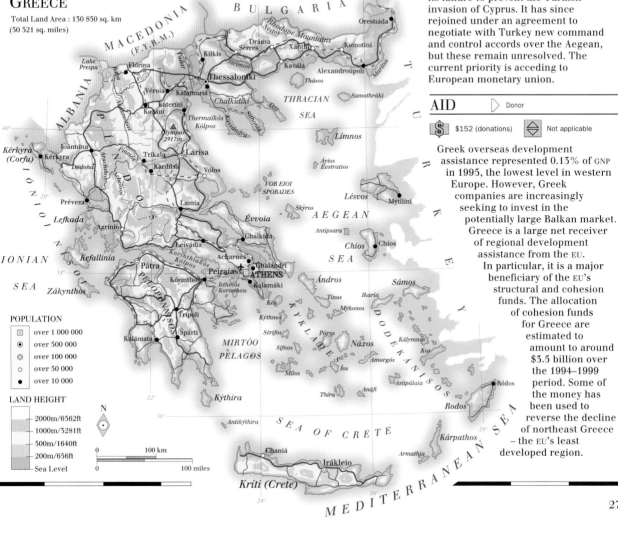

GREECE

Total Land Area : 130 850 sq. km (50 521 sq. miles)

POPULATION

▣ over 1 000 000
◉ over 500 000
◎ over 100 000
○ over 50 000
● over 10 000

LAND HEIGHT

2000m/6562ft
1000m/3281ft
500m/1640ft
200m/656ft
Sea Level

N

0   100 km
0   100 miles

G

CHRONOLOGY

Greece was occupied by Nazi Germany between 1941 and 1944. After liberation by the Allies, communists and royalists fought a five-year civil war. This ended with communist defeat, and King Paul became the constitutional monarch.

- ❏ **1964** King Paul dies. Succeeded by son, King Constantine.
- ❏ **1967** Military coup. King in exile. Colonel Papadopoulos premier.
- ❏ **1973** Greece declared a republic, with Papadopoulos as president. Papadopoulos overthrown in military coup. Lt.-Gen. Ghizikis becomes president with Adamantios Androutsopoulos as prime minister.
- ❏ **1974** Greece leaves NATO in protest at Turkish occupation of northern Cyprus. "Colonels' regime" falls. Constantinos Karamanlis becomes premier and his ND party wins subsequent elections.
- ❏ **1975** Konstantinos Tsatsou becomes president.
- ❏ **1977** Elections: ND reelected.
- ❏ **1980** Karamanlis president. Georgios Rallis prime minister. Greece rejoins NATO.
- ❏ **1981** PASOK wins elections. Andreas Papandreou first-ever socialist premier. Greek joins EC.
- ❏ **1985** Proposals to limit power of president. Karamanlis resigns. Christos Sartzetakis president. Greece and Albania reopen borders, closed since 1940.
- ❏ **1985–1989** Civil unrest caused by economic austerity program.
- ❏ **1988** Cabinet implicated in financial scandal. Leading members resign.
- ❏ **1989** Defense agreement with USA. After inconclusive elections, Left coalition forms government. Charilaos Florakis president. ND join Left coalition in government. Further election inconclusive. All-party coalition.
- ❏ **1990** Coalition government collapses. ND wins elections. Mitsotakis prime minister; Karamanlis president.
- ❏ **1990–1992** Strikes against economic reform.
- ❏ **1992** EC persuaded to withhold recognition of Republic of Macedonia (FYRM).
- ❏ **1993** PASOK wins general election, Andreas Papandreou premier.
- ❏ **1995** Kostas Stephanopoulos elected president; recognition of Macedonian sovereignty.
- ❏ **1996** Andreas Papandreou resigns as prime minister; succeeded by Kostas Simitis.
- ❏ **1997–1998** Protest at austerity measures, but progress made towards introduction of euro.

DEFENSE

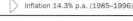 Compulsory military service

💲 $5.6bn   ⬇ Down 3% in 1997

Greece spends a higher percentage of GDP on defense than any other NATO country. Its main concern is the perceived threat from Turkey. In the late 1990s tensions concerned sovereignty over islands in the Dodecanese and the stationing of Greek S-300 anti-aircraft missiles on Cyprus (eventually sited in Crete). The armed forces number 168,500, with 291,000 reservists.

GREEK ARMED FORCES

🛡	1,735 main battle tanks (714 M-48, 669 M-60, 352 *Leopard*)	116,000 personnel
🚢	7 submarines, 4 destroyers, 12 frigates and 42 patrol boats	19,500 personnel
✈	402 combat aircraft (A-7, F-5, F-4E, F-16, *Mirage* F-1, *Mirage* 2000)	33,000 personnel
	None	

ECONOMICS

Inflation 14.3% p.a. (1985–1996)

📊 $122.4bn   💲 283.71–280.05 drachmas

SCORE CARD

- ❏ WORLD GNP RANKING 32nd
- ❏ GNP PER CAPITA $11,640
- ❏ BALANCE OF PAYMENTS.....................$4.9bn
- ❏ INFLATION 5.5%
- ❏ UNEMPLOYMENT...................................10%

ECONOMIC PERFORMANCE INDICATOR

EXPORTS

France 5%, USA 5%, UK 6%, Italy 14%, Germany 18%, Other 52%

IMPORTS

UK 6%, Netherlands 7%, France 9%, Germany 14%, Italy 18%, Other 46%

STRENGTHS

One of the major tourist destinations in Europe. Efficient agricultural exporter. Shipping: the world's largest beneficially owned fleet.

WEAKNESSES

High levels of public debt. High interest rates and bureaucratic banking system discourage private initiative. Large, often poorly managed public sector. Black economy accounts for 30%–50% of GDP.

PROFILE

Greece took longer than most other European countries to recover from World War II. It was not until the 1960s that any substantial investment occurred. The Colonels' dictatorship curbed inflationary pressures by the introduction of a wage freeze. When civilian government was restored in 1974, a spate of high wage settlements and the oil price shocks of 1973 and 1979 drove inflation to above 20%, a level at which it hovered for some

years. In 1982–1986, Greece's largest companies made substantial losses. A modest return to profitability followed the socialists' austerity program of 1986–1987.

The only one of the 12 EU countries seeking to introduce the euro in 1999 which failed to meet the economic convergence criteria, Greece has since brought the budget deficit and inflation under control, although public-sector debt remains high. The drachma joined the exchange rate mechanism in 1998.

GREECE : MAJOR BUSINESSES

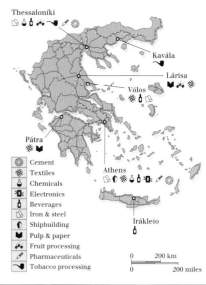

🔘 Cement
✳ Textiles
🍶 Chemicals
🔌 Electronics
🍶 Beverages
🏷 Iron & steel
⚓ Shipbuilding
📑 Pulp & paper
🍇 Fruit processing
💉 Pharmaceuticals
🍃 Tobacco processing

0   200 km
0   200 miles

RESOURCES

⊳ Electric power 8.9m kw

198,217 tonnes

13,092 b/d (reserves 41,000,000 bbl)

9.5m sheep, 5.9m goats, 938,000 pigs, 580,000 cattle

Coal, iron, bauxite, marble, nickel, magnesite, chromium

ELECTRICITY GENERATION

Hydro 9% (3.8bn kwh)	
Combustion 91% (37.7bn kwh)	
Nuclear 0%	
Other 0%	

0 20 40 60 80 100

% of total generation by type

Greece has an oil and gas field off the coast of Thasos island. Reserves may be available in its eastern waters, ownership of which is contested by Turkey. Coal, iron and other mining contributes less than 2% to GDP. Greece is a leading producer of marble.

ENVIRONMENT

⊳ No Green MPs

2% (0.2% partially protected)

Medium

ENVIRONMENTAL TREATIES

Yes Yes Yes

Yes Yes Yes

Local fishing interests have formed a successful anti-pollution organization, HELMEPA. Smog in Athens is irritating to the eyes and throat and highly damaging to ancient monuments: the Parthenon in Athens has suffered more erosion in the last two decades than in the previous 2,000 years. Forest fires regularly cause havoc, damaging flora and fauna.

MEDIA

⊳ TV ownership high

Daily newspaper circulation 153 per 1,000 people

PUBLISHING AND BROADCAST MEDIA

	There are 156 daily newspapers. *Eleftheros Typos* has the highest circulation figures
	3 state-owned, 17 independent services
	1 state-owned, 1 independent service

The state had a monopoly on radio and TV until 1990. Commercial broadcasting has made politicians far more answerable to the electorate than ever before. It has also had a cultural impact, with the import of more foreign, particularly US, programming. In 1998 there were 17 private TV networks, as well as pirate stations.

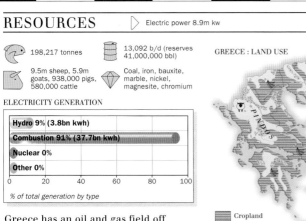

GREECE : LAND USE

RHODOPE MTS

PINDUS

AEGEAN ISLANDS

	Cropland
	Forest
	Pasture
	High mountain regions
	Sheep
	Fruit

0 100 km
0 100 miles

CRIME

⊳ Death penalty not used

5,897 prisoners

Up 3% in 1992

CRIME RATES

Murders	
3	per 100,000 population

Rapes	
2	per 100,000 population

Thefts	
791	per 100,000 population

An influx of migrants has seen an increase in violent crime. The terrorist group November 17 has assassinated more than 20 people. There is corruption in the police force.

EDUCATION

⊳ School leaving age: 15

97%

329,185 students

Of total government expenditure 7% is spent on education.

THE EDUCATION SYSTEM

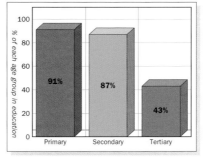

% of each age group in education

100
80
60
40
20
0

91% Primary
87% Secondary
43% Tertiary

Teachers are poorly paid and qualifications are low. University places are limited and many students go abroad for tertiary education. Technical courses, funded by the EU, have increased since the 1990s.

HEALTH

⊳ Welfare state health benefits

1 per 250 people

Accidents, heart and cerebrovascular diseases, cancers

The socialists (PASOK) introduced a National Health Service and a national pharmaceuticals industry. In the early 1990s ND tried to upgrade private medicine and incorporate its activities with those in state hospitals. Greece now has the second-highest number of doctors per head of population in the EU, but primary care is poor, as is that in state hospitals, which are short of nurses. Many Greeks needing major surgery go abroad, to Germany, Switzerland, or the UK, for treatment. Of total government expenditure just over 12% is spent on health.

G

SPENDING

⊳ GDP/cap. no increase

CONSUMPTION AND SPENDING

223 per 1,000 population

516 per 1,000 population

Defense 4.6%	
Education 3.7%	
Health 4.8%	

0 5 10 15 20 25

Defense, Health, Education spending as % of GDP

Greek society changed dramatically in the postwar period. Previously, Greece was a largely isolated agricultural community – rapid urbanization during the 1950s led to many former agricultural workers making fortunes. Many grabbed opportunities presented by the shipping industry. Among these were the prominent Niarchos and Onassis families.

The advent of the republic in 1973 reflected social changes which had occurred since the war. New wealth and success became more admired than aristocratic birth or prestige. Greece is now a socially mobile society. Living standards have improved throughout society since the 1950s.

WORLD RANKING

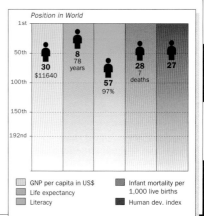

Position in World

1st
50th
100th
150th
192nd

30 $11640
8 78 years
57 97%
28 7 deaths
27

GNP per capita in US$		Infant mortality per 1,000 live births	
Life expectancy			
Literacy		Human dev. index	

GRENADA

OFFICIAL NAME: Grenada   **CAPITAL:** St George's
POPULATION: 98,600   **CURRENCY:** East Caribbean dollar   **OFFICIAL LANGUAGE:** English

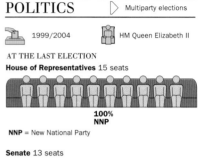

CARIBBEAN

| 1974 | 1974 | Feb 7 | WG | -4 | +473 | .gd |

THE MOST SOUTHERLY of the Windward Islands, Grenada also includes the islands of Carriacou and Petite Martinique. It is the world's second-largest nutmeg producer. Grenada became a focus of attention in 1983 when the USA, with token backing from several Caribbean states, mounted an invasion to sever its growing links with Castro's Cuba. Grenada is one of the seven members of the Organization of Eastern Caribbean States (OECS).

CLIMATE   ▷ Tropical oceanic

WEATHER CHART

■ Average daily temperature   Rainfall ▬

Rainfall totals 150 cm (59 inches) on the coast, and twice that in the mountains. Hurricanes occur in the rainy season.

TRANSPORTATION   ▷ Drive on left

🛬 **Point Salines, St George's**
206,000 passengers

🚢 5 ships
887 grt

THE TRANSPORTATION NETWORK

| 580 km (360 miles) | None |
| None | None |

Roads in the interior are poor. The airport is being expanded and a new cruise ship port is planned.

TOURISM   ▷ Visitors : population 1.1:1

🧳 110,000 visitors   ⬆ Up 2% 1995-1997

MAIN TOURIST ARRIVALS

| USA 28% |
| UK 16% |
| Trinidad & Tobago 7% |
| Other 49% |

% of total arrivals

Tourism has developed since the completion of the international airport in 1984. The tourism promotion budget was doubled to EC $8.5 million in 1998 in a bid to attract more stay-over and cruise ship visitors.

PEOPLE   ▷ Pop. density high

English, English Creole   290/km² (751/mi²)

THE URBAN/RURAL POPULATION SPLIT

37%   63%

RELIGIOUS PERSUASION

Other 15%
Anglican 17%
Roman Catholic 68%

Most Grenadians are descendants of Africans, brought over to work sugar plantations in the 16th to 19th centuries. Intermarriage between this group and the small numbers of Europeans and indigenous Indians has meant that there is little racial tension. As in other Caribbean states, extended families with absentee fathers are not uncommon.

GRENADA

Total Land Area : 340 sq. km (131 sq. miles)

POPULATION
● over 10 000
● under 10 000

LAND HEIGHT
500m/1640ft
200m/656ft
Sea Level

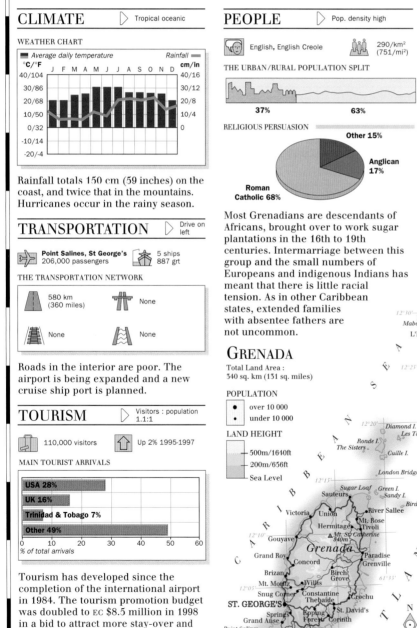

POLITICS   ▷ Multiparty elections

1999/2004   HM Queen Elizabeth II

AT THE LAST ELECTION

House of Representatives 15 seats

100% NNP

NNP = New National Party

Senate 13 seats

The members of the Senate are appointed by the prime minister and the leader of the opposition

The past 25 years have seen Grenada move from a position of political isolation toward integration with the rest of the region. The late Sir Eric Gairy, when prime minister, was as well known for his eccentric requests to the UN Security Council – he once asked it to investigate UFOs on the island – as for his intimidation of political opponents by means of organized gangs. Gairy was overthrown in 1979 by armed militants of the New Jewel Movement led by Maurice Bishop, a charismatic socialist who in turn was deposed and executed by former allies in 1983. This coup was the pretext for the US invasion, whose primary motive was to end the perceived Cuban influence in Grenada. A new government was elected in 1984, and the USA provided large amounts of aid. Politics has since been center-right, and ideologically there is little to choose between the four main parties, the latest elected being the NNP, led by Keith Mitchell. Having been elected in June 1995, it achieved victory over a divided opposition in an early general election held in January 1999, taking all 15 seats. Mitchell promised "explosive" growth and lower unemployment.

WORLD AFFAIRS
Joined UN in 1974

Priorities are the relations with the rest of the Windward Islands group, preferential access to the EU for banana exports and strategies with Indonesia aimed at steadying world nutmeg prices. Since 1983, it has supported US policy in the Caribbean.

AID
Recipient

US$8m (receipts) — Down 27% 1996–1997

The main aid sources are the UK, the EU, the USA, Japan, and Taiwan. Cuba, before the 1983 invasion, helped build the airport at Point Salines.

DEFENSE
No compulsory military service

Minimal receipts — Defense spending is falling

The People's Revolutionary Army, created by Maurice Bishop in the wake of his 1979 coup, was replaced in 1983 by a paramilitary defense unit trained by the USA and the UK.

ECONOMICS
Inflation 1.9% p.a. (1987–1997)

US$300m — 2.70 East Caribbean dollars

SCORE CARD

❑ World GNP Ranking	174th
❑ GNP per Capita	US$3,140
❑ Balance of Payments	US$–58m
❑ Inflation	1.2%
❑ Unemployment	20%

STRENGTHS
Second-largest producer of nutmeg after Indonesia. Important sectors are tourism, bananas, construction and financial services.

WEAKNESSES
Weak tax base, lack of diversification. Poor infrastructure. Low labor productivity. Large avoidance of custom duties. Smuggling.

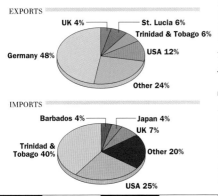

EXPORTS — UK 4%, St. Lucia 6%, Trinidad & Tobago 6%, USA 12%, Germany 48%, Other 24%

IMPORTS — Barbados 4%, Japan 4%, UK 7%, Trinidad & Tobago 40%, Other 20%, USA 25%

RESOURCES
Electric power 9,000 kw

1,577 tonnes — Not an oil producer

13,000 sheep, 5,300 pigs, 7,000 goats, 4,400 cattle — None

Grenada has no strategic resources and has to import most of its energy. Its major asset is the nutmeg industry, which accounts for almost one-quarter of total world production.

ENVIRONMENT
No Green MPs

None — Not available

Ecotourism threatens some key environmental sites, including a remnant of rain forest. Resort projects have caused serious beach erosion, in turn requiring costly coastal defenses. An environmental levy on visitors is opposed by cruise companies.

MEDIA
TV ownership high

There are no daily newspapers

PUBLISHING AND BROADCAST MEDIA

There are no daily newspapers. The *Grenadian Voice* and the *Grenada Guardian* are published weekly

1 partly state-owned service — 1 state-owned, 2 independent stations

The press, which is privately owned, and privately owned radio are largely free from overt political interference.

CRIME
Death penalty used

Grenada does not publish prison figures — Up sharply from 1989–1996

The doubling of poverty over the last decade as well as high unemployment are associated with a rise in the crime rate. Narcotics-trafficking in particular is a growing problem.

EDUCATION
School leaving age: 16

96% — 535 students

Education follows the former British selective 11-plus system. Many students go on to the University of the West Indies, or to college in the USA.

HEALTH
Welfare state health benefits

1 per 2,000 people — Heart diseases, cancers, nutritional disorders

After Maurice Bishop took power in 1979, Cuban physicians provided a basic health care system. Treatment in subsidized state hospitals now matches the Caribbean average. A new Cuban-designed hospital was planned to start construction in 1999.

St George's Harbour. *The newest hotel developments are on the beaches to the south of the capital.*

G

CHRONOLOGY

A French colony from 1650, Grenada was captured by the British in 1762.

- ❑ **1951** Universal suffrage introduced.
- ❑ **1967–1974** Internal self-government. Full independence from UK.
- ❑ **1979** Coup. Maurice Bishop prime minister. Growing links with Cuba.
- ❑ **1983–1984** US invasion establishes pro-US administration.
- ❑ **1999** NNP reelected, taking all 15 seats in parliament.

SPENDING
GDP/cap. no increase

CONSUMPTION AND SPENDING

No data — 255 per 1,000 population

Defense – No data	
Education – No data	
Health – No data	

0 5 10 15 20 25
Defense, Health, Education spending as % of GDP

Wealth disparities in Grenada are less marked than in most other Caribbean states, but poverty is growing. The wealthiest groups are those that control the nutmeg trade.

WORLD RANKING

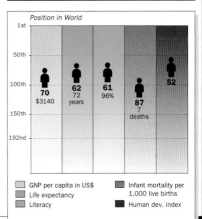

Position in World

70 $3140 | 62 72 years | 61 96% | 87 7 deaths | 52

- GNP per capita in US$
- Life expectancy
- Literacy
- Infant mortality per 1,000 live births
- Human dev. index

GUATEMALA

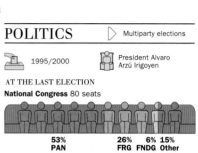

CENTRAL AMERICA

North America

OFFICIAL NAME: Republic of Guatemala **CAPITAL:** Guatemala City
POPULATION: 11.6 million **CURRENCY:** Quetzal **OFFICIAL LANGUAGE:** Spanish

| 1838 | 1838 | Sept 15 | GCA | -6 | +502 | .gt |

LARGEST AND MOST POPULOUS of the states of the
Central American isthmus, Guatemala was home
to the ancient Maya civilization. Its fertile Pacific and Caribbean coastal
lowlands give way to the highlands which dominate the country.
Independent since 1838, Guatemala's history since 1954 has been one
of military rule. Civilian rule returned in 1986, but 90% of people still
live below the poverty line.

G

CLIMATE
▷ Tropical equatorial/ wet & dry

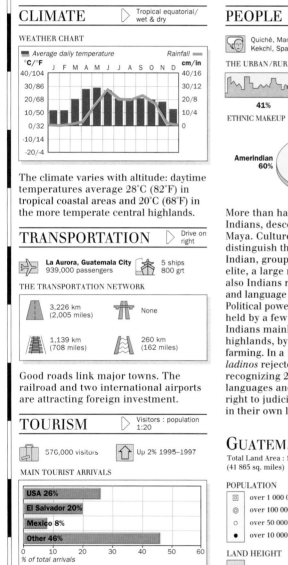

WEATHER CHART

Average daily temperature Rainfall
°C/°F J F M A M J J A S O N D cm/in

The climate varies with altitude: daytime
temperatures average 28°C (82°F) in
tropical coastal areas and 20°C (68°F) in
the more temperate central highlands.

TRANSPORTATION
▷ Drive on right

La Aurora, Guatemala City
939,000 passengers

5 ships
800 grt

THE TRANSPORTATION NETWORK

| 3,226 km (2,005 miles) | None |
| 1,139 km (708 miles) | 260 km (162 miles) |

Good roads link major towns. The
railroad and two international airports
are attracting foreign investment.

TOURISM
▷ Visitors : population 1:20

576,000 visitors

Up 2% 1995–1997

MAIN TOURIST ARRIVALS

USA 26%					
El Salvador 20%					
Mexico 8%					
Other 46%					
0	10	20	30	40	50	60

% of total arrivals

Tourism rapidly revived after the
military excesses in the 1980s, but
adverse reports on human rights and
attacks on tourists tarnished its image.
Maya ruins are the top attractions.

PEOPLE
▷ Pop. density medium

Quiché, Mam, Cakchiquel, Kekchí, Spanish

107/km² (277/mi²)

THE URBAN/RURAL POPULATION SPLIT

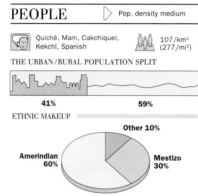

41%   59%

ETHNIC MAKEUP

Other 10%
Amerindian 60%
Mestizo 30%

More than half of Guatemalans are
Indians, descendants of the original
Maya. Culture and language
distinguish them from *ladino*, non-
Indian, groups. *Ladinos* include a white
elite, a large mixed race group, and
also Indians rejecting traditional dress
and language to avoid discrimination.
Political power and 65% of land is
held by a few *ladino* families.
Indians mainly live in the
highlands, by subsistence
farming. In a 1999 plebiscite,
ladinos rejected reforms
recognizing 23 Indian
languages and the Indians'
right to judicial hearings
in their own languages.

GUATEMALA

Total Land Area : 108 430 sq. km
(41 865 sq. miles)

POPULATION

▢ over 1 000 000
◎ over 100 000
○ over 50 000
● over 10 000

LAND HEIGHT

3000m/9843ft
2000m/6562ft
1000m/3281ft
500m/1640ft
200m/656ft
Sea Level

POLITICS
▷ Multiparty elections

1995/2000

President Alvaro Arzú Irigoyen

AT THE LAST ELECTION

National Congress 80 seats

| 53% PAN | | 26% FRG | 6% FNDG | 15% Other |

PAN = National Advancement Party **FRG** = Guatemalan
Republican Front **FNDG** = Guatemalan Democratic Front

In 1954, the military, with US backing,
toppled a reformist democratic
government and suppressed all
opposition. Its 32-year rule was based
on the violent suppression of all
opposition. Death-squad murders and
scorched-earth campaigns against
highland Indians from 1979 to 1984
led to the suspension of US aid but not
of covert CIA support. World criticism
and the wishes of moderate army
factions helped bring back civilian
rule in 1986. The shaky transition to
democracy survived an attempted
"self-coup" by President Serrano in
1993. President Arzú, inaugurated in
January 1996, promised national
reconciliation and concluded a peace
agreement with the URNG guerrillas,
ending the 36-year civil war which
had claimed some 200,000 lives, most
of them innocent civilians.

WORLD AFFAIRS

▷ Joined UN in 1945

Relations with the USA and regional trade ties are priorities. In 1991 Guatemala formally dropped its claim to neighboring Belize.

AID
▷ Recipient

$302m (receipts)   ⬆ Up 40% 1996–1997

In 1998 the government agreed the disbursement of the remaining $926 million of the $1.9 billion pledged by the international donors for postwar reconstruction. 8.4 million quetzales were loaned in hurricane relief.

DEFENSE
▷ Compulsory military service

$182m   ⬇ Down 19% in 1997

A damning "truth commission" report in 1999 found the armed forces and their allies guilty of 93% of human rights violations during the civil war. The army remains largely unreformed and a potent sociopolitical force.

ECONOMICS
▷ Inflation 17.4% p.a. (1985–1996)

$16.6bn   6.20–6.71 quetzales

SCORE CARD

- ❏ WORLD GNP RANKING...........................74th
- ❏ GNP PER CAPITA $1,580
- ❏ BALANCE OF PAYMENTS...................$–624m
- ❏ INFLATION 9.2%
- ❏ UNEMPLOYMENT 5%

STRENGTHS
Coffee, sugar, bananas, beef, cardamom top exports. Privatizations boosting foreign investor confidence.

WEAKNESSES
Traditional exports vulnerable to world price shifts. Shaky financial system. Inequalities in land and wealth limit domestic market. Tax evasion.

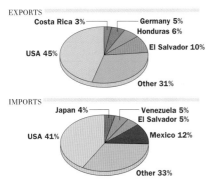

EXPORTS
- Costa Rica 3%
- Germany 5%
- Honduras 6%
- El Salvador 10%
- USA 45%
- Other 31%

IMPORTS
- Japan 4%
- Venezuela 5%
- El Salvador 5%
- USA 41%
- Mexico 12%
- Other 33%

North Acropolis, Tikal, Petén. *One of the largest lowland Maya cities, Tikal was virtually abandoned by about 900CE.*

RESOURCES
▷ Electric power 766,000 kw

11,074 tonnes   6,135 b/d (reserves of 27,000,000 bbl)

2.3m cattle, 825,600 pigs, 551,000 sheep   Oil, antimony, lead, tungsten, nickel, copper

Agriculture provides 25% of GDP and about 70% of export earnings. World's largest producer of cardamom. Guatemala's civil war hindered the exploitation of oil reserves and hydroelectric potential.

ENVIRONMENT
▷ No Green MPs

17% (0.5% partially protected)   ⬇ Low

Forest cover has been halved to 35% since 1954 due to intensive a griculture. Excessive use of pesticides, many banned in the USA, threaten health. In Guatemala City especially, pollution and waste are serious problems.

MEDIA
▷ TV ownership medium

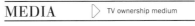
Daily newspaper circulation 31 per 1,000 people

PUBLISHING AND BROADCAST MEDIA

There are 7 daily newspapers, including *Prensa Libre, Siglo Veintiuno, El Gráfico* and the state *Diario de Centroamerica*

1 state-owned, 5 independent stations   5 state-owned, 80 independent stations

Powerful families control newspapers and TV channels. There is less military, government or private-sector control over radio stations.

CRIME
▷ Death penalty used

Guatemala does not publish prison figures   ⬆ All types of crime are increasing

Criminal violence is one of the biggest threats to human rights: 3,196 people were recorded murdered in 1998.

EDUCATION
▷ School leaving age: 14

67%   80,228 students

Education is a privilege. An illiteracy rate of nearly 50% makes Guatemala one of the worst educated countries in Latin America.

CHRONOLOGY

Site of the Maya civilization, Guatemala declared independence from Spain in 1821. It became fully independent in 1838.

- ❏ **1954** US-backed coup topples reformist government.
- ❏ **1966–1984** Counterinsurgency war; highlands "pacification."
- ❏ **1986–1993** Return of civilian rule; President Serrano elected. Flees country after abortive "self-coup."
- ❏ **1996** President Arzú elected; peace deal with URNG guerrillas.
- ❏ **1998** Bishop Juan Gerardi, human rights campaigner, murdered.
- ❏ **1999** UN-backed "truth commission" blames military for most human rights abuses in civil war.

G

HEALTH
▷ Welfare state health benefits

1 per 3,333 people   Heart disease, violence, tuberculosis

Mortality and malnutrition rates are the highest, while health spending is the lowest, in the region. Main causes of death are gastrointestinal and other infections directly linked to poverty.

SPENDING
▷ GDP/cap. no increase

CONSUMPTION AND SPENDING

10 per 1,000 population   41 per 1,000 population

Defense 1.5%
Education 1.7%
Health 2.1%

0   5   10   15   20   25
Defense, Health, Education spending as % of GDP

Poverty has risen since 1980: 90% of the country's population now live below the poverty line. The richest 20% control some 58% of the national wealth.

WORLD RANKING

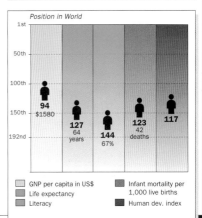
Position in World

1st
50th
100th
150th
192nd

94 $1580
127 64 years
144 67%
123 42 deaths
117

- ☐ GNP per capita in US$
- ☐ Life expectancy
- ☐ Literacy
- ☐ Infant mortality per 1,000 live births
- ☐ Human dev. index

GUINEA

OFFICIAL NAME: Republic of Guinea **CAPITAL:** Conakry
POPULATION: 7.7 million **CURRENCY:** Guinea franc **OFFICIAL LANGUAGE:** French

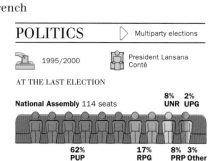

WEST AFRICA

| 1958 | 1958 | Oct 2 | RG | 0 | +224 | .gn |

GUINEA LIES ON the western coast of Africa. Central densely forested or savanna highlands slope down to coastal plains and swamps in the west and to the semidesert of the north. Military rule, established in 1984, ended with legislative elections in 1995; however, the results were disputed.

CLIMATE ▷ Tropical monsoon

WEATHER CHART

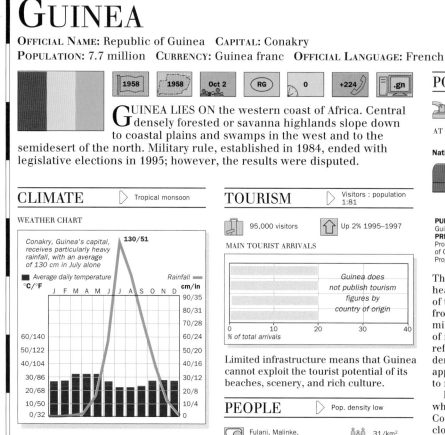

Conakry, Guinea's capital, receives particularly heavy rainfall, with an average of 130 cm in July alone

130/51

■ Average daily temperature Rainfall ━━

Guinea's climate is similar to that of Sierra Leone; the rainy season lasts from April to September.

TRANSPORTATION ▷ Drive on right

Conakry-Gbessia
287,835 passengers   30 ships
                      9,000 grt

THE TRANSPORTATION NETWORK

4,490 km (2,790 miles)		None
1,045 km (649 miles)		1,295 km (805 miles)

Major roads and rail lines are being rebuilt with World Bank and French aid. Much of the rail network is exclusively for the use of the bauxite industry.

A small mosque in Conakry. Muslims make up 85% of the population; 8% are Christian. The remainder follow traditional beliefs.

TOURISM ▷ Visitors : population 1:81

95,000 visitors   Up 2% 1995–1997

MAIN TOURIST ARRIVALS

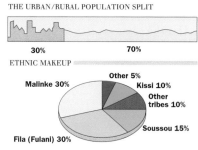

Guinea does not publish tourism figures by country of origin

% of total arrivals

Limited infrastructure means that Guinea cannot exploit the tourist potential of its beaches, scenery, and rich culture.

PEOPLE ▷ Pop. density low

Fulani, Malinke, Soussou, French   31/km² (81/mi²)

THE URBAN/RURAL POPULATION SPLIT

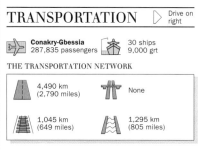

30%   70%

ETHNIC MAKEUP

Malinke 30%
Fila (Fulani) 30%
Other 5%
Kissi 10%
Other tribes 10%
Soussou 15%

Guinea's population of nearly eight million people consists of a number of ethnic groups. Since 1984, and the death of the Marxist dictator Sekou Touré, traditional rivalries have reemerged. The largest ethnic group, the Malinke, lost the power they held under Sekou Touré, and have suffered reprisals. Today, the coastal peoples, including the Soussou, are dominant, benefiting from renewed rivalry between the two major groups – Malinke and Fulani, the latter based in the highland region of Fouta Jallon.

Daily life in Guinea revolves around the extended family, which survived the climate of suspicion generated by paid informers under Sekou Touré. Women acquired influence within his Marxist party, but a Muslim revival since 1984 has reversed this trend.

POLITICS ▷ Multiparty elections

1995/2000   President Lansana Conté

AT THE LAST ELECTION

National Assembly 114 seats

8% UNR   2% UPG
62% PUP   17% RPG   8% PRP   3% Other

PUP = Party of Unity and Progress **RPG** = Rally of the Guinean People **UNR** = Union for the New Republic **PRP** = Party of Renewal and Progress **UPG** = Union for the Prosperity of Guinea **Other** = Djama Party, Democratic Party of Guinea, African Democratic Rally, National Union for Progress

The death in 1984 of Sekou Touré, who headed the Marxist single-party regime of the Guinea Democratic Party (PDG) from 1958, opened the way for the military to intervene, with promises of multiparty elections. In 1990, a referendum overwhelmingly approved democratic changes, but the military appointed a Transitional Committee to run the country.

Elections were finally held in 1993, when the incumbent, Gen. Lansana Conté, won with 52% of the votes. His closest rival, the Malinke leader Alpha Condé, who had been in exile until 1992, received 20% of the votes. The result was contested by opposition parties, which alleged that the elections had been rigged, and serious violence broke out. A disputed victory for Conté's Party of Unity and Progress (PUP) in the 1995 legislative elections was followed by a further win for Conté in the December 1998 presidential election.

WORLD AFFAIRS ▷ Joined UN in 1958

| Ecowas | Franc | OAU | OIC | OMVG |

Guinea contributed troops to Ecowas peacekeeping forces in the subregion throughout the 1990s. A growing concern is balancing the interests of its two major aid donors, France and the USA.

AID ▷ Recipient

$382m (receipts)   Up 29% 1996–1997

In 1969, the World Bank funded the Boké bauxite project, then one of its most ambitious projects. Since 1986, Western aid has grown, to finance over 85% of all development projects. The 1997–2000 World Bank/IMF structural reform program foresees annual growth of 5%.

G

GUINEA

Total Land Area :
245 860 sq. km
(94 926 sq. miles)

POPULATION

- ⊙ over 500 000
- ○ over 50 000
- ● over 10 000
- • under 10 000

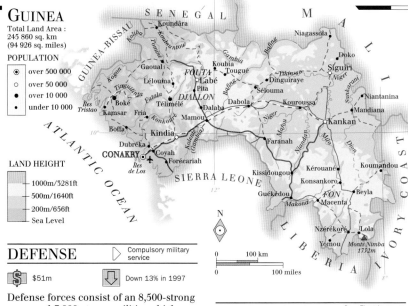

LAND HEIGHT

- 1000m/3281ft
- 500m/1640ft
- 200m/656ft
- Sea Level

DEFENSE

▷ Compulsory military service

$51m

Down 13% in 1997

Defense forces consist of an 8,500-strong army and 7,000-strong militia, which have been partly merged since the 1984 coup. China, North Korea, and the Eastern bloc used to be the main arms procurement markets. Most weaponry is now supplied by France and the USA.

ECONOMICS

▷ Not available

$3.8bn

1,135.50–1,267.50 Guinea francs

SCORE CARD

- ❏ WORLD GNP RANKING 119th
- ❏ GNP PER CAPITA $550
- ❏ BALANCE OF PAYMENTS ....$–91m
- ❏ INFLATION 1.9%
- ❏ UNEMPLOYMENT ....Widespread underemployment

STRENGTHS

Natural resources including bauxite, gold, diamonds. Major iron ore deposits at Mount Nimba. Good soil and climate give high cash-crop yields and the prospect of food self-sufficiency. Relatively low inflation.

WEAKNESSES

Legacy of maladministration from Touré years. Poor infrastructure. 1990–1997 Liberian civil war set back major joint projects.

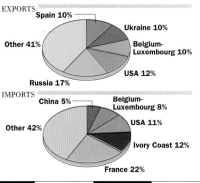

EXPORTS

- Spain 10%
- Ukraine 10%
- Belgium-Luxembourg 10%
- Other 41%
- USA 12%
- Russia 17%

IMPORTS

- China 5%
- Belgium-Luxembourg 8%
- Other 42%
- USA 11%
- Ivory Coast 12%
- France 22%

0   100 km
0   100 miles

RESOURCES

▷ Electric power 176,000 kw

68,764 tonnes

Not an oil producer

2.3m cattle, 669,000 sheep, 53,000 pigs

Bauxite, diamonds, gold, iron

Bauxite accounts for over 90% of export earnings. Guinea, with 30% of known world reserves, is the world's largest producer after Australia. Demand for electricity for bauxite processing is high. Gold production has grown steadily since 1995.

ENVIRONMENT

▷ No Green MPs

1%

Low

Uncontrolled deforestation, particularly of rainforest areas, is the major long-term problem.

MEDIA

▷ TV ownership low

There are no daily newspapers

PUBLISHING AND BROADCAST MEDIA

There is 1 daily newspaper, *Fonike*

1 state-owned service

1 state-owned service

Guinea's limited broadcast media are state-owned. There has been a relaxation in censorship. *Horoya*, the main newspaper, is a weekly.

CRIME

▷ Death penalty not used

Guinea does not publish prison figures

Up 20% in 1992

The state's human rights record has not improved since 1984, and there has been an increase in political violence. Diamond smuggling is commonplace.

CHRONOLOGY

France colonized Guinea in 1890, strongly opposed by the Fulani Muslim empire of Fouta Djallon.

- ❏ **1958** Full independence under Sekou Touré.
- ❏ **1984** Sekou Touré dies. Army coup.
- ❏ **1993** Disputed presidential elections.
- ❏ **1995** Multiparty legislative elections.
- ❏ **1998** Conté reelected president.

EDUCATION

▷ School leaving age: 13

38%

8,151 students

French was readopted as the main teaching language in 1984, after Touré's Marxist-inspired experiments.

HEALTH

▷ No welfare state health benefits

1 per 5,000 people

Malaria, diarrheal and respiratory diseases, tuberculosis

Health provision is very poor, reflected in an infant mortality rate of 120 per 1,000 live births and an average life expectancy of 47 years.

SPENDING

▷ GDP/cap. no increase

CONSUMPTION AND SPENDING

2 per 1,000 population

3 per 1,000 population

- Defense 1.6%
- Education 2.4%
- Health 1%

0   5   10   15   20   25
Defense, Health, Education spending as % of GDP

Private enterprise has brought with it a new business class and Guinea now has some wealthy exiles, but much of the country remains poor and underdeveloped, and GNP is below $600 per head.

WORLD RANKING

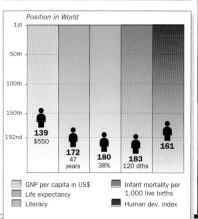

Position in World

1st
50th
100th
150th
192nd

- 139 $550
- 172 47 years
- 180 38%
- 183 120 dths
- 161

- GNP per capita in US$
- Life expectancy
- Literacy
- Infant mortality per 1,000 live births
- Human dev. index

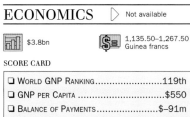

GUINEA-BISSAU

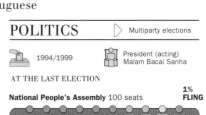

OFFICIAL NAME: Republic of Guinea-Bissau **CAPITAL:** Bissau
POPULATION: 1.1 million **CURRENCY:** Guinea peso **OFFICIAL LANGUAGE:** Portuguese

| 1974 | 1974 | Sept 24 | GNB | 0 | +245 | .gw |

LYING ON AFRICA'S west coast, impoverished Guinea-
Bissau, a former Portuguese territory, is bordered
by Senegal to the north and Guinea to the south and east. Apart from
savanna highlands in the northeast, the country is low-lying. The ruling
PAIGC initiated change to multiparty democracy in 1990, and elections were
held in 1994. After a turbulent period of army rebellion in 1998 followed
by a peace agreement, the military seized power in May 1998.

CLIMATE ▷ Tropical monsoon

WEATHER CHART

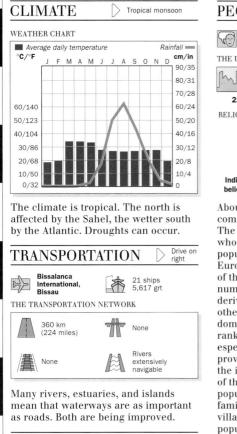

■ Average daily temperature   Rainfall ▬

The climate is tropical. The north is
affected by the Sahel, the wetter south
by the Atlantic. Droughts can occur.

TRANSPORTATION ▷ Drive on right

Bissalanca International, Bissau

21 ships
5,617 grt

THE TRANSPORTATION NETWORK

360 km (224 miles)		None
None		Rivers extensively navigable

Many rivers, estuaries, and islands
mean that waterways are as important
as roads. Both are being improved.

TOURISM ▷ Not available

A small number of visitors

No significant change from year to year

MAIN TOURIST ARRIVALS

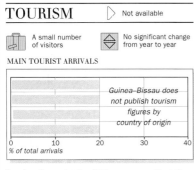

Guinea–Bissau does
not publish tourism
figures by
country of origin

0   10   20   30   40
% of total arrivals

Lack of tourist facilities means that the
country remains a destination for only
the most independent of travelers.

PEOPLE ▷ Pop. density low

Portuguese Creole, Balante,
Fulani, Malinke, Portuguese

39/km²
(101/mi²)

THE URBAN/RURAL POPULATION SPLIT

22%   78%

RELIGIOUS PERSUASION

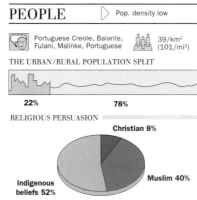

Christian 8%

Indigenous
beliefs 52%

Muslim 40%

About 98% of Guinea-Bissau's people
come from indigenous ethnic groups.
The largest is the southern Balante,
who form almost one-third of the
population. Mixed-race *mestiço* and
European minorities make up just 2%
of the population. Although small in
number, the *mestiços* – many of whom
derive from Cape Verde, Portugal's
other former west African colony – still
dominate the bureaucracy and the top
ranks of the PAIGC. Resentment at this,
especially among the Balante, who
provided most of the PAIGC troops in
the independence war, was one cause
of the 1980 coup. The majority of the
population live and work on small
family farms, grouped in self-contained
villages. The bulk of the urban
population live in the capital, Bissau.

POLITICS ▷ Multiparty elections

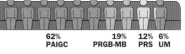

1994/1999

President (acting)
Malam Bacai Sanha

AT THE LAST ELECTION

National People's Assembly 100 seats

1% FLING

62% PAIGC   19% PRGB-MB   12% PRS   6% UM

PAIGC = African Party for the Independence of Guinea and
Cape Verde **PRGB-MB** = Guinea-Bissau Resistance
Party–Bafata Movement **PRS** = Party for Social Revolution
UM = Union for Change **FLING** = Front for the Struggle for
Guinea-Bissau's National Independence

Guinea-Bissau was ruled by the PAIGC
from independence in 1974. The party
was declared winner in multiparty
elections in 1994, but the opposition
disputed the result. A period of
instability led to an army rebellion in
June 1998 and eight months of fighting
between loyalists of President Vieira
and the army chief, General Ansumane
Mane, displacing about half the
population. Peace was restored by
ECOWAS troops and a national unity
government formed, but this was
overthrown by the army in May 1999.
Mane, the coup leader, promised that
elections would take place before the
end of 1999. Meanwhile the Assembly's
speaker became acting president.

WORLD AFFAIRS ▷ Joined UN in 1974

| Ecowas | Lusoph | Franc | OAU | OIC |

Senegalese and Guinean troops
intervened in mid-1998 at
the request of President Vieira,
to suppress a revolt led by the
army chief, a Gambian. Resultant
subregional tensions appear to
have been settled, thanks to
Ecowas mediation.

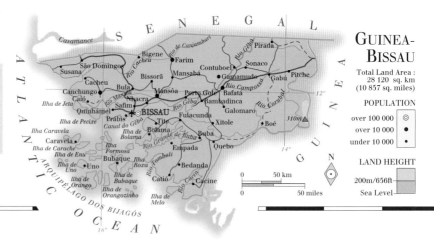

GUINEA-BISSAU

Total Land Area :
28 120 sq. km
(10 857 sq. miles)

POPULATION

over 100 000 ◎
over 10 000 ●
under 10 000 ·

LAND HEIGHT

200m/656ft
Sea Level

G

AID

▷ Recipient

[$] $125m (receipts)   ⬇ Down 31% 1996–1997

Portugal is Guinea-Bissau's largest aid donor. Balance of payments support is critical to the economy. Export earnings rarely top $20 million and import and debt service costs are over $100 million. Despite the freezing of donor support in 1991 because of Guinea-Bissau's World Bank arrears, the government pushed ahead with economic reforms begun in the mid-1980s. Aid levels rose in 1990–1996, but fell in 1997. The infrastructure, education, and health care are the main targets of project aid.

DEFENSE

▷ Compulsory military service

[$] $8m   ⬇ Down 13% in 1997

Resentment among the Balante troops at lack of promotion and the predominance of *mestiços* in the senior ranks was a cause of the 1980 coup. An army rebellion in 1998 was ended by an Ecowas force, but the army then seized power in May 1999.

ECONOMICS

▷ Inflation 62.5% p.a. (1985-1996)

[chart] $264m   [$] 601.60–558.62 Guinea pesos

SCORE CARD

❑ WORLD GNP RANKING........................176th
❑ GNP PER CAPITA $230
❑ BALANCE OF PAYMENTS.....................$–26m
❑ INFLATION 49.1%
❑ UNEMPLOYMENT....Widespread underemployment

STRENGTHS
Presently minimal, but good fisheries and timber potential. Offshore oil potential.

WEAKNESSES
Lack of sufficiency in rice staple. Few exports, mainly cashew nuts, groundnuts. Minimal industry. Lack of entrepreneurial business class. High illiteracy. Poor state economic management.

EXPORTS

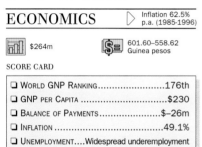

Portugal 4%
Thailand 4%
Other 10%
India 59%
Italy 10%
Singapore 13%

IMPORTS

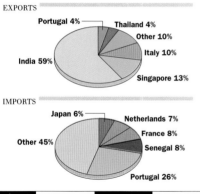

Japan 6%
Netherlands 7%
France 8%
Senegal 8%
Other 45%
Portugal 26%

Bafatá, the chief town *in central Guinea-Bissau. It lies on the Gêba River and is also an important inland port.*

RESOURCES

▷ Electric power 11,000 kw

[fish] 6,329 tonnes   [barrel] Not an oil producer

[livestock] 510,000 cattle, 335,000 pigs, 275,000 sheep   [gem] Bauxite, phosphate

Fish and timber are the main natural resources; local exploitation is only 10% of the sustainable levels of 250,000 tonnes and 100,000 tonnes a year. Considerable hydropower potential is also underexploited.

ENVIRONMENT

▷ No Green MPs

[icon] None   ⬇ Low

Drought and locust plagues are serious natural hazards. A small population and minimal industry mean there are few serious environmental problems.

MEDIA

▷ TV ownership low

[icon] Daily newspaper circulation 6 per 1,000 people

PUBLISHING AND BROADCAST MEDIA

[icon] There are 2 daily newspapers, *Voz da Guiné* and *Nô Printcha*, published by the government

[icon] 1 state-owned service   [icon] 1 state-owned service

Only one newspaper, *Baguerra*, and one magazine, *Expresso-Bissau*, are independently owned. Portugal helps to fund the TV service, started in 1989.

CRIME

▷ Death penalty used

[icon] Guinea-Bissau does not publish prison figures   ⬆ Up 66% in 1992

The death penalty was abolished in 1993. Reform of the legal system is in progress to make it more independent of the PAIGC. The government has been criticized for human rights abuses.

EDUCATION

▷ School leaving age: 13

[icon] 34%   [icon] 404 students

Around 65% of children receive rudimentary education. Guinea-Bissau has no university.

CHRONOLOGY

The Portuguese explored the area in the 15th century. The colony of Portuguese Guinea was established in 1879. A war of independence began in the 1960s, led by the PAIGC.

❑ **1974** Independence. PAIGC led by Luis Cabral takes power.
❑ **1980** Coup. João Vieira replaces Cabral.
❑ **1990** Vieira accepts principle of multiparty politics.
❑ **1994** PAIGC multiparty election win.
❑ **1998** Army rebellion. ECOWAS intervention.
❑ **1999** Transitional government formed. Army seizes power.

G

HEALTH

▷ No welfare state health benefits

[icon] 1 per 5,556 people   [icon] Parasitic, diarrheal and communicable diseases, malaria

Guinea-Bissau's health statistics are among the world's worst, due partly to the minimal medical facilities. Average life expectancy is just 45 years; infant mortality is 130 per 1,000 live births; the maternal death rate is high.

SPENDING

▷ GDP/cap. no increase

CONSUMPTION AND SPENDING

[car] 6 per 1,000 population   [phone] 7 per 1,000 population

Defense 2.6%		
Education No data		
Health 1.3%		

0   5   10   15   20   25
Defense, Health, Education spending as % of GDP

Living conditions for the majority of Guinea-Bissau's people are extremely poor; over 70% of the population are unable to meet their basic needs. The tiny elite is mainly *mestiço*.

WORLD RANKING

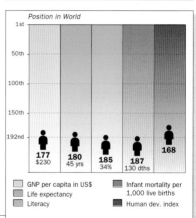

Position in World

1st
50th
100th
150th
192nd

177 $230
180 45 yrs
185 34%
187 130 dths
168

GNP per capita in US$
Life expectancy
Literacy
Infant mortality per 1,000 live births
Human dev. index

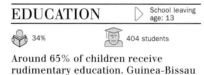

GUYANA

OFFICIAL NAME: Co-operative Republic of Guyana **CAPITAL:** Georgetown
POPULATION: 856,000 **CURRENCY:** Guyana dollar **OFFICIAL LANGUAGE:** English

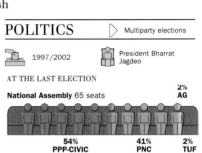

SOUTH AMERICA

| 1966 | 1966 | Feb 23 | GUY | -4 | +592 | .gy |

GUYANA LIES ON the northeast coast of South America, bordered by Venezuela, Brazil, and Suriname. Dense interior rainforest covers some 85% of its territory but this is diminishing at a worrying rate as a result of logging. Independence from Britain came in 1966. Exports of sugar, bauxite, rice, gold, and timber sustain the economy. The vast majority of Guyana's population lives on the narrow coastal plain partially reclaimed from the sea.

G

CLIMATE
▷ Tropical equatorial

WEATHER CHART

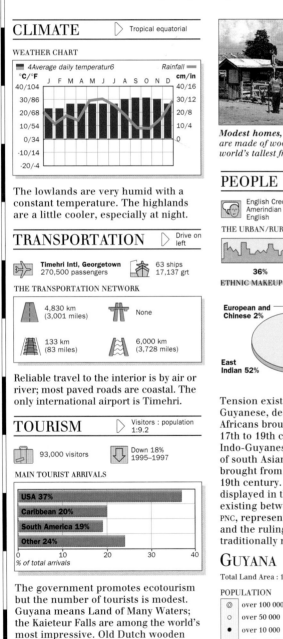

The lowlands are very humid with a constant temperature. The highlands are a little cooler, especially at night.

TRANSPORTATION
▷ Drive on left

✈ **Timehri Intl, Georgetown**
270,500 passengers

⚓ 63 ships
17,137 grt

THE TRANSPORTATION NETWORK

| 🛣 4,830 km (3,001 miles) | None |
| 🚂 133 km (83 miles) | ⚓ 6,000 km (3,728 miles) |

Reliable travel to the interior is by air or river; most paved roads are coastal. The only international airport is Timehri.

TOURISM
▷ Visitors : population 1:9.2

🧳 93,000 visitors

⬇ Down 18% 1995–1997

MAIN TOURIST ARRIVALS

| USA 37% |
| Caribbean 20% |
| South America 19% |
| Other 24% |

% of total arrivals
0 10 20 30 40

The government promotes ecotourism but the number of tourists is modest. Guyana means Land of Many Waters; the Kaieteur Falls are among the world's most impressive. Old Dutch wooden architecture characterizes Georgetown.

Modest homes, Georgetown. Most buildings are made of wood. The cathedral is one of the world's tallest freestanding wooden buildings.

PEOPLE
▷ Pop. density low

👤 English Creole, Hindi, Tamil, Amerindian languages, English

👥 4/km² (11/mi²)

THE URBAN/RURAL POPULATION SPLIT

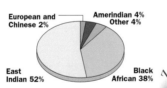

36% 64%

ETHNIC MAKEUP

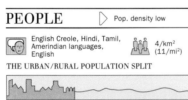

European and Chinese 2%
Amerindian 4%
Other 4%
East Indian 52%
Black African 38%

Tension exists between Afro-Guyanese, descended from Africans brought over in the 17th to 19th centuries, and Indo-Guyanese, descendants of south Asian laborers brought from India in the 19th century. This is currently displayed in the hostility existing between the opposition PNC, representing Afro-Guyanese and the ruling PPP/CIVIC, traditionally representing Indians.

POLITICS
▷ Multiparty elections

1997/2002

President Bharrat Jagdeo

AT THE LAST ELECTION

National Assembly 65 seats

2% AG

54% PPP-CIVIC   41% PNC   2% TUF

PPP-CIVIC = People's Progressive Party–CIVIC
PNC = People's National Congress **AG** = Alliance for Guyana
TUF = The United Force **RR** = Regional Representatives

The 29-year rule of the PNC was pro-Afro-Guyanese. This was reversed with the success of the Indian-dominated PPP in the 1992 elections, widely seen as the first fair poll since independence. PPP/CIVIC leader Cheddi Jagan, a Marxist before adopting free-market beliefs, died in office in March 1997. The presidential election victory of his widow Janet was rejected by the PNC, causing a political crisis. A CARICOM-brokered peace led to a review commission, asked in 1999 to draft a new constitution. Janet Jagan resigned on health grounds later in 1999.

GUYANA

Total Land Area : 196 850 sq. km (76 004 sq. miles)

POPULATION
◎ over 100 000
○ over 50 000
● over 10 000
• under 10 000

LAND HEIGHT
1000m/3281ft
500m/1640ft
200m/656ft
Sea Level

WORLD AFFAIRS

▷ Joined UN in 1966

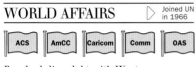

Rescheduling debt with Western creditor states is paramount. Also important are the long-standing border dispute with Venezuela and closer integration with the Caribbean.

AID

▷ Recipient

US$272m (receipts)   ⬆ Up 89% 1996–1997

Most aid comes from the USA, the EU and the UK. Aid in 1998 covered public health projects, business development and protection of the rainforest.

DEFENSE

▷ No compulsory military service

US$7m   No change in 1997

The security forces, which include a 1,400-strong army, benefit from financial support and training provided by the US and UK governments.

ECONOMICS

▷ Inflation 14.4% p.a. 1983–1992

US$677m   142.80–151.80 Guyana dollars

SCORE CARD

❏ WORLD GNP RANKING	162nd
❏ GNP PER CAPITA	US$800
❏ BALANCE OF PAYMENTS	US$–135m
❏ INFLATION	3.6%
❏ UNEMPLOYMENT	12%

STRENGTHS

Gold, rice, sugar, bauxite, diamond, and timber production. Ecotourism potential. Debt reduction plan agreed with multilateral agencies.

WEAKNESSES

High per capita foreign debt. Political instability dents investor confidence. Currency vulnerable to exchange rate pressure. Main exports vulnerable to lower international commodity prices and fluctuations. Weak manufacturing base.

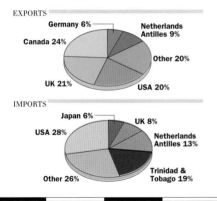

EXPORTS

Germany 6%
Canada 24%
Netherlands Antilles 9%
Other 20%
UK 21%
USA 20%

IMPORTS

Japan 6%
USA 28%
UK 8%
Netherlands Antilles 13%
Other 26%
Trinidad & Tobago 19%

RESOURCES

▷ Electric power 114,000 kw

45,000 tonnes

220,000 cattle, 130,000 sheep, 79,000 goats

Not an oil producer

Bauxite, gold, diamonds, gemstones, oil, manganese, uranium

Gold, bauxite, and timber are important resources. Offshore and onshore prospecting for oil has not reduced the need for petroleum imports for electricity generation. There are plans for hydroelectric power plants on the many rivers.

ENVIRONMENT

▷ No Green MPs

0.05%   Not available

Disrepair of the 18th-century sea defense system threatens the urbanized coastline which lies below sea level. Commercial logging threatens the rainforest. Pollution of rivers because of gold and diamond mining is a serious problem.

MEDIA

▷ TV ownership low

Daily newspaper circulation 50 per 1,000 people

PUBLISHING AND BROADCAST MEDIA

There are 2 daily newspapers. The *Guyana Chronicle* is published by the government

1 state-owned, 2 independent services

1 state-owned service

The main parties run periodicals and there are several independent ones. There are a state-controlled TV and radio station.

CRIME

▷ Death penalty used

Guyana does not publish prison figures   ⬆ Rising

The police are strongly criticized for corruption and ineffectiveness in the face of rising urban crime. Serious violence between PNC and PPP/CIVIC supporters erupted in 1998 and 1999.

EDUCATION

▷ School leaving age: 14

98%   7,680 students

Education is based on the British system. Entry to high schools is by 11-plus examination. Guyana has a state-financed university, although many students go to the USA or the UK.

HEALTH

▷ Welfare state health benefits

1 per 303 people   Heart diseases, violence, accidents, cancers

Around 95% of the population have access to Guyana's mainly state-run health service. The referral system is relatively good.

CHRONOLOGY

During the 17th and 18th centuries, the Dutch founded three colonies, Essequibo, Demerara, and Berbice, in the region. In 1814, these came under British control, and were later combined to form the colony of British Guiana.

❏ **1953** First universal elections won by PPP under Cheddi Jagan; parliament later suspended by UK.
❏ **1964** PNC dominates ruling coalition.
❏ **1966** Independence from UK.
❏ **1973** PPP boycotts parliament, accusing PNC of electoral fraud.
❏ **1985–1992** PNC founder Forbes Burnham dies; succeeded by Desmond Hoyte. Fair elections won by PPP/CIVIC. Jagan president.
❏ **1997–1998** Jagan dies in office; PNC rejects his widow Janet's election victory. Political crisis.
❏ **1999** Constitutional review.

SPENDING

▷ GDP/cap. no increase

CONSUMPTION AND SPENDING

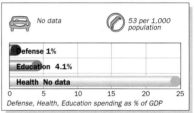

No data   53 per 1,000 population

Defense 1%
Education 4.1%
Health No data

Defense, Health, Education spending as % of GDP

Significant urban and rural poverty has forced the government to make provision in the country's budget for poverty alleviation. Public-sector redundancies have exacerbated the problem. The poorest group are the Amerindians, who rely upon subsistence farming. A few very affluent urban families derive their wealth from business and farming.

WORLD RANKING

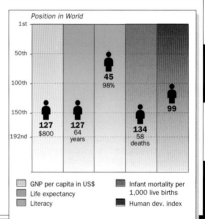

Position in World

1st
50th
100th
150th
192nd

45 — 98%
127 — $800
127 — 64 years
134 — 58 deaths
99

GNP per capita in US$
Life expectancy
Literacy
Infant mortality per 1,000 live births
Human dev. index

HAITI

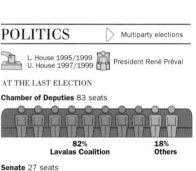

CARIBBEAN

North America

OFFICIAL NAME: Republic of Haiti **CAPITAL:** Port-au-Prince **POPULATION:** 7.5 million
CURRENCY: Gourde **OFFICIAL LANGUAGES:** French and French Creole

| 1804 | 1844 | Jan 1 | RH | -5 | +509 | | .ht |

HAITI OCCUPIES the western third of the Caribbean island of Hispaniola. Formerly a Spanish colony, it was the first Caribbean state to achieve independence, in 1804, and has been in a state of political chaos virtually ever since. Democracy did not materialize with the exile of the dictator Jean-Claude Duvalier in 1986. Elections were held in 1990, but by 1991 the military were back in power and were only ousted in 1994 through US intervention.

CLIMATE

▷ Tropical equatorial/oceanic

WEATHER CHART

Average daily temperature | Rainfall
°C/°F | J F M A M J J A S O N D | cm/in
40/104 | | 40/16
30/86 | | 30/12
20/68 | | 20/8
10/50 | | 10/4
0/32 | | 0
-10/14 |
-20/-4 |

Haiti lies mostly in the rain shadow of the central mountains, so is slightly less humid than average for the Caribbean.

TRANSPORTATION

▷ Drive on right

Port-au-Prince
545,000 passengers

7 ships
1,600 grt

THE TRANSPORTATION NETWORK

| 600km (373 miles) | | None |
| None | | 100 km (62 miles) |

Roads, especially in the interior, are poor. Ferries provide the main transportation to the southern peninsula.

TOURISM

▷ Visitors : population 1:49

152,000 visitors

Up 14% 1995–1997

MAIN TOURIST ARRIVALS

USA 73%
Canada 12%
Europe 8%
Other 7%

0 10 20 30 40 50 60 70 80
% of total arrivals

Haiti's location, history and culture provided much of its attraction for tourists in the 1960s and 1970s. Political instability and violence in the 1980s, however, led to the industry's near collapse and it has yet to recover.

PEOPLE

▷ Pop. density high

French Creole, French

272/km²
(705/mi²)

THE URBAN/RURAL POPULATION SPLIT

32% | 68%

RELIGIOUS PERSUASION

Non-religious 1%
Other 3%
Protestant 16%
Roman Catholic 80%

Most Haitians are the descendants of Africans; a few have European roots, primarily French. The majority of the population lives in extreme poverty: Haiti is the poorest country in the Americas, and Port-au-Prince has the worst slums in the Caribbean. Social tensions run high, and focus on class rather than race. In recent years, the combination of political repression and a collapsing economy led many to emigrate illegally to the USA, or across the border to the neighboring Dominican Republic.

HAITI

Total Land Area : 27 560 sq. km
(10 641 sq. miles)

POPULATION
□ over 1 000 000
◎ over 500 000
● over 10 000
• under 10 000

LAND HEIGHT
1000m/3281ft
500m/1640ft
200m/656ft
Sea Level

0   50 km
0   50 miles

N

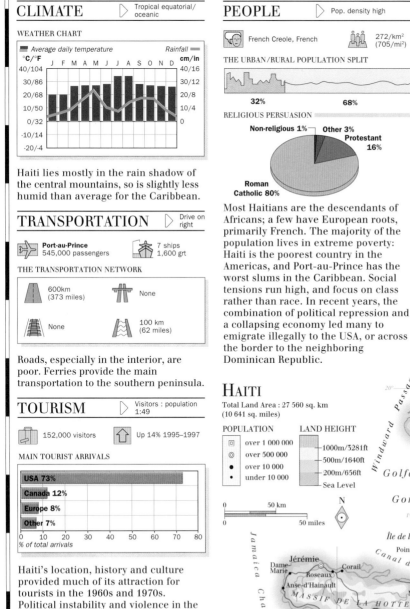

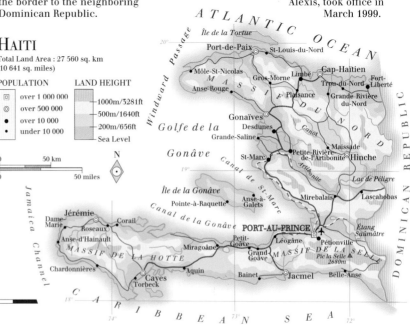

POLITICS

▷ Multiparty elections

L. House 1995/1999
U. House 1997/1999

President René Préval

AT THE LAST ELECTION

Chamber of Deputies 83 seats

82% Lavalas Coalition | 18% Others

Senate 27 seats

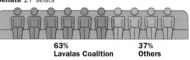

63% Lavalas Coalition | 37% Others

The April 1997 Senate elections were intended to be for nine seats. Only two seats were decided in the first round; in June 1997 the second round was postponed indefinitely.

A wealthy elite, backed by the military, supported the Duvalier dictatorship. After the overthrow of "Baby Doc" Duvalier in 1986, they regularly financed coups. The military last intervened in 1991, following the 1990 election of Jean-Bertrand Aristide, who was exiled by the army and his supporters suppressed. The UN imposed sanctions and the USA intervened militarily, restoring Aristide to office in 1994, primarily to stem the refugee flow. Aristide's Lavalas Party won elections in 1995 and René Préval was made president in 1996. His appointed prime minister Rosny Smarth came under strong US pressure to impose austerity policies, but encountering a backlash he stepped down in 1997. Political deadlock ensued until a new government, headed by prime minister Jacques Edouard Alexis, took office in March 1999.

H

WORLD AFFAIRS
▷ Joined UN in 1945

After years of sanctions, economic links with the outside world have been restored. Illegal immigration to the USA and relations with the Dominican Republic are major issues.

AID
▷ Recipient

 $332m (receipts)   Down 11% 1996–1997

The IMF granted $21 million in emergency aid in 1998 for hurricane damage. The IDB approved loans for water and health and Taiwan granted $60.4 million in aid.

DEFENSE
▷ No compulsory military service

 $99m   Down 5% in 1997

In 1994, the military were ousted and democracy was restored. The armed forces and police were disbanded and an interim public security force of 3,000 formed. A new national police force of some 4,000 personnel was funded and trained by the USA.

ECONOMICS
▷ Inflation 16.6% p.a. (1985–1996)

 $2.9bn   16.77–16.57 gourdes

SCORE CARD

❏ WORLD GNP RANKING	128th
❏ GNP PER CAPITA	$380
❏ BALANCE OF PAYMENTS	$–138m
❏ INFLATION	20.6%
❏ UNEMPLOYMENT	60%

STRENGTHS
Coffee exports. Remittances by Haitians living abroad. US demand for goods assembled in Haiti. Large profits from transshipment of narcotics to USA.

WEAKNESSES
Huge tax avoidance. Foreign investment and promised aid deterred by political instability.

EXPORTS

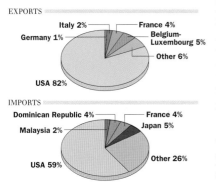

Italy 2%   France 4%
Germany 1%   Belgium-Luxembourg 5%
Other 6%
USA 82%

IMPORTS

Dominican Republic 4%   France 4%
Malaysia 2%   Japan 5%
Other 26%
USA 59%

Haiti: the poorest country in the Americas. In remote villages, most houses are made of earth and have no windows.

RESOURCES
▷ Electric power 153,000 kw

6,000 tonnes   Not an oil producer

1.3m cattle
800,000 pigs
490,000 horses   Marble, limestone, clay, silver, gold, natural asphalt

Haiti has no strategic resources. Under the recent economic sanctions, it had to find unofficial sources of oil; much was imported from Europe.

ENVIRONMENT
▷ No Green MPs

  1%   Low

One-third of soil is seriously eroded, and forest cover is now only 1.5% of the total land area. 4,000 tonnes of toxic waste illegally dumped on the shore near Gonaïves is finally being removed.

MEDIA
▷ TV ownership low

 Daily newspaper circulation 3 per 1,000 people

PUBLISHING AND BROADCAST MEDIA

 There are 4 daily newspapers including *Le Nouvelliste* and *Le Matin*

 1 state-owned service, 4 independent   1 state-owned service, 15 independent

Under the military, the media were largely controlled through intimidation. The transition to democracy has produced a more open press.

CRIME
▷ Death penalty not used

Haiti does not publish prison figures   Crime is rising

Extrajudicial killings, torture, and brutality continue, despite the ending of military dictatorship. Narcotics-trafficking is highly organized. Police are inexperienced and the judicial system is slow and open to corruption.

EDUCATION
▷ School leaving age: 12

 46%   6,288 students

The run-down state education system is based on the French; the *baccalauréat* pass rate in 1998 was only 7% to 8%. The wealthy go abroad.

H

CHRONOLOGY

In 1697, Spain ceded the west of Hispaniola to France. Ex-slave Toussaint l'Ouverture's rebellion in 1791 led to independence in 1804.

- ❏ **1915–1934** US occupation.
- ❏ **1957–1971** François "Papa Doc" Duvalier's brutal dictatorship.
- ❏ **1971–1986** Rule of son Jean-Claude, "Baby Doc," who eventually flees.
- ❏ **1987** Elections abandoned.
- ❏ **1990** Jean-Bertrand Aristide elected; exiled in 1991 coup.
- ❏ **1994–1995** US forces oust military. Aristide reinstated; elections.
- ❏ **1997–1999** Serious political deadlock; new government named.

HEALTH
▷ No welfare state health benefits

1 per 10,000 people   Malaria, other parasitic diseases, tuberculosis

Most Haitians cannot afford health care. In rural areas, help is often sought from voodoo priests.

SPENDING
▷ GDP/cap. increase

CONSUMPTION AND SPENDING

4 per 1,000 population   8 per 1,000 population

Defense 5.2%
Education 1.8%
Health 3.2%

0   5   10   15   20   25
Defense, Health, Education spending as % of GDP

Haiti's rigid class structure maintains extreme disparities of wealth between the mass of the population, who live in slums without running water or proper sanitation, and a few affluent families. According to the United Nations, 80% of Haitians cannot meet their basic daily needs.

WORLD RANKING

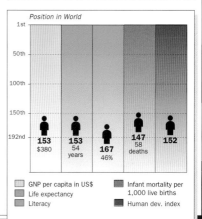

Position in World

153 $380	153 54 years	167 46%	147 58 deaths	152

☐ GNP per capita in US$
☐ Life expectancy
☐ Literacy
☐ Infant mortality per 1,000 live births
☐ Human dev. index

HONDURAS

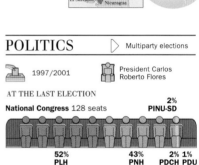

CENTRAL AMERICA

North America

OFFICIAL NAME: Republic of Honduras   **CAPITAL:** Tegucigalpa
POPULATION: 6.1 million   **CURRENCY:** Lempira   **OFFICIAL LANGUAGE:** Spanish

| 1838 | 1838 | Sept 15 | HN | -6 | +504 | .hn |

STRADDLING THE Central American isthmus, Honduras has only a short Pacific coast. Its long Caribbean shoreline includes the virtually uninhabited Mosquito Coast; most of the rest of the country is mountainous. After a succession of military governments it returned to full civilian rule in 1984. In 1998 Honduras was devastated by Hurricane Mitch, which resulted in at least 5,600 people dead and damage estimated at some $3 billion.

CLIMATE

▷ Tropical equatorial

WEATHER CHART

Average daily temperature / Rainfall

Honduras' Caribbean coast is extremely hot. The central highlands are much cooler.

TRANSPORTATION

▷ Drive on right

Toncontín, Tegucigalpa
404,000 passengers

1,339 ships
1.1m grt

THE TRANSPORTATION NETWORK

| 2,543 km (1,580 miles) | None |
| 996 km (619 miles) | 465 km (289 miles) |

In 1998 Hurricane Mitch destroyed roads and bridges across the country; reconstruction will take years.

TOURISM

▷ Visitors : population 1:24

257,000 visitors   Up 20% 1995–1997

MAIN TOURIST ARRIVALS

USA 39%	
El Salvador 14%	
Nicaragua 9%	
Other 38%	

% of total arrivals (0–40)

Hurricane Mitch seriously affected popular resorts on the Atlantic coast and the Bay Islands favored for snorkeling. The remote region inland from the Mosquito Coast and jungle river rafting appeal to ecotourists.

PEOPLE

▷ Pop. density medium

Spanish, Black Carib, English Creole

55/km² (141/mi²)

THE URBAN/RURAL POPULATION SPLIT

44%   56%

ETHNIC MAKEUP

White 1%
Indian 4%
Black African 5%
Mestizo 90%

As in most of Central America, very few pure indigenous groups remain. The estimated 45,000 Miskito Indians, and an English-speaking *garífuna* (black) population on the Caribbean coast united in 1999 to oppose a constitutional amendment allowing foreigners to buy land in coastal areas, traditionally their communal lands. Poverty is the root cause of social tension; whites still have the best opportunities. Rural poverty and strong Roman Catholicism (93% are Roman Catholic) mean that the family is a powerful unifying force. Women's status is low; many work in domestic service.

POLITICS

▷ Multiparty elections

1997/2001

President Carlos Roberto Flores

AT THE LAST ELECTION

National Congress 128 seats

| 52% PLH | 43% PNH | 2% PDCH | 1% PDU | 2% PINU-SD |

PLH = Liberal Party of Honduras PNH = National Party of Honduras PINU-SD = Innovation and Unity Party–Social Democracy PDCH = Honduran Christian Democratic Party PDU = Party of Democratic Unification

The traditional power brokers have been the military, the US embassy and the United Fruit Company, the biggest banana producers in Honduras.

The military held power intermittently from 1956 until 1982, when, under pressure from the US government, it allowed a return to civilian rule. However, during the 1980s, US President Reagan effectively converted the country into a US "aircraft carrier" to counter a perceived communist threat from El Salvador and Nicaragua. Peace in the region then saw a cut in US aid.

The PNH and PLH, with few real ideological differences, have generally alternated in power. Presidents, able to serve only one four-year term, have tended to be weak. The PLH government in 1994 introduced unpopular austerity measures but began reducing the autonomy of the military by abolishing conscription. President Flores, also PLH, elected in 1997, continued this "demilitarization" process by naming a civilian defense minister in 1999.

Reconstruction after Hurricane Mitch in 1998 will be a long-term undertaking.

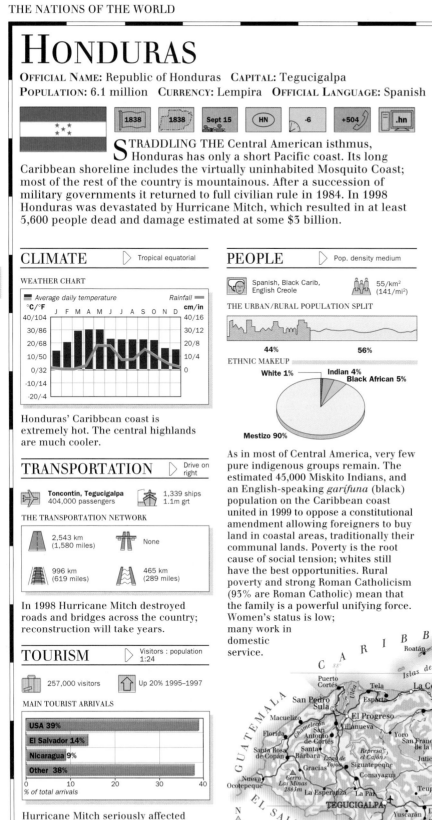

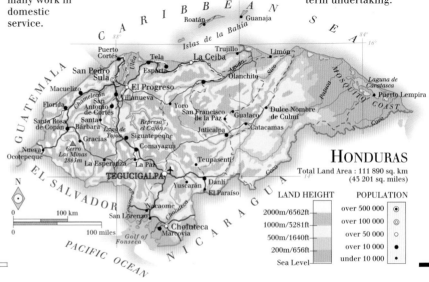

HONDURAS

Total Land Area : 111 890 sq. km (43 201 sq. miles)

LAND HEIGHT	
2000m/6562ft	
1000m/3281ft	
500m/1640ft	
200m/656ft	
Sea Level	

POPULATION	
over 500 000	◉
over 100 000	◎
over 50 000	○
over 10 000	●
under 10 000	●

H

WORLD AFFAIRS

Joined UN in 1945

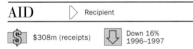

Hurricane aid, trade, immigration issues with the USA, and a free trade agreement with Mexico (jointly with El Salvador and Guatemala), are priorities.

AID

Recipient

$308m (receipts)

Down 16% 1996–1997

Hurricane aid on favorable terms from the IMF and the World Bank amounted to $567 million. Western countries agreed debt relief of $1.2 billion.

DEFENSE

No compulsory military service

$101m

Up 2% in 1997

The first civilian defense minister was appointed in 1999. This completed the "demilitarization" process begun in 1984 with the return to civilian rule. Until 1994 the military operated with virtual impunity.

ECONOMICS

Inflation 14.8% p.a. (1985–1996)

$4.4bn

13.20–13.78 lempiras

SCORE CARD

- ❏ WORLD GNP RANKING........................113th
- ❏ GNP PER CAPITA $740
- ❏ BALANCE OF PAYMENTS....................$–272m
- ❏ INFLATION 20.2%
- ❏ UNEMPLOYMENT 3%

STRENGTHS
Economic boost due to hurricane reconstruction. Hardwoods. Unexploited mineral deposits. Bananas. Flowers, coffee, fruit.

WEAKNESSES
Servicing of foreign debt. Corruption. Weak industrial base. Vulnerability of banana exports. High unemployment and underemployment. Absence of land reform. Overdependence on hydroelectric power.

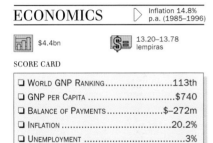

EXPORTS

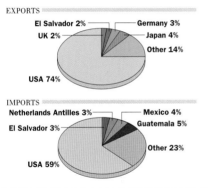

El Salvador 2% — Germany 3%
UK 2% — Japan 4%
— Other 14%
USA 74%

IMPORTS

Netherlands Antilles 3% — Mexico 4%
El Salvador 3% — Guatemala 5%
— Other 23%
USA 59%

Tobacco field. *Tobacco accounts for 1% of export revenues. Honduras' biggest earners are bananas, almost 40%, and coffee, 20%.*

RESOURCES

Electric power 305,000 kw

24,119 tonnes

Not an oil producer; refines 14,000 b/d

1.9m cattle, 700,000 pigs, 175,000 horses

Lead, zinc, silver, gold, copper, iron, tin, coal

Oil reserves are being explored, but not mineral deposits. The hydroelectric supply is erratic.

ENVIRONMENT

No Green MPs

10%

Low

Unregulated timber, cotton and cattle industries, land colonization, and pesticides have led to ecological crisis.

MEDIA

TV ownership medium

Daily newspaper circulation 55 per 1,000 people

PUBLISHING AND BROADCAST MEDIA

There are 7 daily newspapers, including *La Prensa*, *El Heraldo* and *La Tribuna*

6 independent services

1 state-owned, 4 independent services

Self-censorship, dependence on US sources, corruption and intimidation guarantee a largely compliant media.

CRIME

Death penalty not used

Honduras does not publish prison figures

Violence in the cities, especially La Ceiba, is increasing

Drug crime is a major problem. Some 100 youth gangs in Tegucigalpa are blamed for rising violence.

EDUCATION

School leaving age: 12

71%

54,106 students

State-run education follows the US system; the drop-out rate from secondary schools is high.

HEALTH

No welfare state health benefits

1 per 2,500 people

Circulatory, infectious and parasitic diseases, malaria

Only 66% of people have easy access to health services, although most infants receive basic care.

H

CHRONOLOGY

Honduras was a Spanish possession until 1821. In 1823, it joined the United Provinces of Central America with four neighboring nations.

- ❏ **1838** Declares full independence.
- ❏ **1890s** US banana companies set up plantations.
- ❏ **1932–1949** Dictatorship of Gen. Tiburcio Carías Andino of PNH.
- ❏ **1954–1957** Elected PLH president Villeda Morales deposed and reelected.
- ❏ **1963** Military coup.
- ❏ **1969** 13-day Football War with El Salvador sparked by World Cup.
- ❏ **1980–1983** PLH wins elections but Gen. Alvarez holds real power.
- ❏ **1984** Return to democracy.
- ❏ **1988** 12,000 Contra rebels forced out of Nicaragua into Honduras.
- ❏ **1995** Military defies human rights charges.
- ❏ **1998** Hurricane Mitch wreaks havoc across country.
- ❏ **1999** Appointment of first civilian defense minister.

SPENDING

GDP/cap. increase

CONSUMPTION AND SPENDING

13 per 1,000 population

37 per 1,000 population

Defense 2.1%
Education 3.9%
Health 2.9%

0   5   10   15   20   25
Defense, Health, Education spending as % of GDP

The social structure of Honduras is chacterized by great inequalities: 4% of people own 60% of the land. Relief agencies estimate that 85% of people live below the poverty line, compared with 80% before Hurricane Mitch.

WORLD RANKING

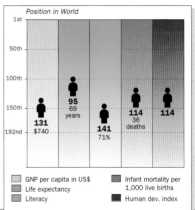

Position in World

1st
50th
100th
150th
192nd

131 $740
95 69 years
141 71%
114 36 deaths
114

- ▢ GNP per capita in US$
- ▢ Life expectancy
- ▢ Literacy
- ▪ Infant mortality per 1,000 live births
- ▪ Human dev. index

HUNGARY

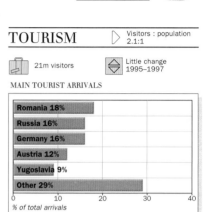

EUROPE

OFFICIAL NAME: Republic of Hungary **CAPITAL:** Budapest
POPULATION: 9.9 million **CURRENCY:** Forint **OFFICIAL LANGUAGE:** Hungarian

1918 | 1947 | Aug 20 | H | +1 | +36 | .hu

LYING AT THE HEART of central Europe, Hungary is landlocked and has borders with seven states. Historically a cosmopolitan cultural center, during its years of market socialism it was more prosperous than the other Eastern Bloc countries. Hungary's economic and political reforms have brought it closer to the EU and NATO membership. It now receives the lion's share of overseas investment in the former COMECON states. Treatment of Hungarian minorities in neighboring Romanian Transylvania, Serbian Vojvodina, and Slovakia is a major foreign policy concern.

TOURISM

▷ Visitors : population 2.1:1

🧳 21m visitors   ⬧ Little change 1995–1997

MAIN TOURIST ARRIVALS

	% of total arrivals
Romania 18%	
Russia 16%	
Germany 16%	
Austria 12%	
Yugoslavia 9%	
Other 29%	

(0, 10, 20, 30, 40)
% of total arrivals

CLIMATE

▷ Continental

WEATHER CHART

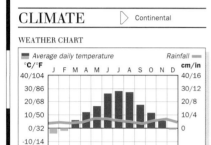

Hungary has a continental climate, with wet springs, late summers, and cold, cloudy winters. There are no great differences of weather and climate within the country. Conditions in summer and winter may, however, differ from one year to the next. The transition between seasons tends to be sudden.

TRANSPORTATION

▷ Drive on right

✈ **Budapest Ferihegy** 3.94m passengers   ⚓ 6 ships 27,000 grt

THE TRANSPORTATION NETWORK

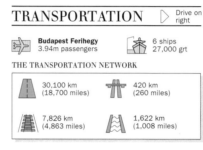

30,100 km (18,700 miles)	420 km (260 miles)
7,826 km (4,863 miles)	1,622 km (1,008 miles)

Freight travels mainly via the rail link from Budapest to the Austrian border. Most foreign investment is located along this corridor. A new Budapest–Vienna expressway has been opened, and three more are under construction with EIB and EBRD funding.

Tourism is an important source of hard currency earnings, and over 20 million visit each year, mostly from eastern Europe, Germany, and Austria. Since 1989, Hungary has invested heavily in tourism. The number of travel agents and hotels has risen dramatically. Lake Balaton is the traditional summer destination. In the capital city, Budapest, the baths, some of which date from the Ottoman period, are among the most popular tourist attractions. Budapest is also promoting itself as an international business convention center.

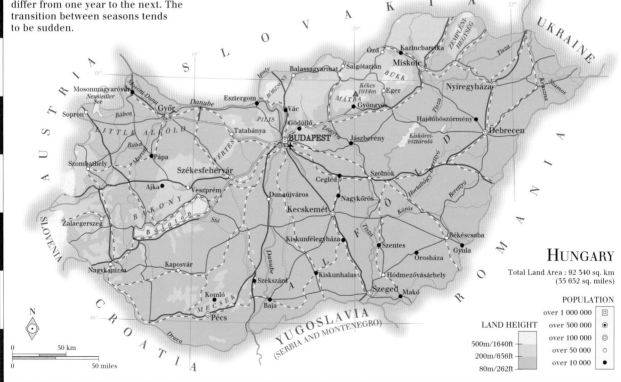

HUNGARY

Total Land Area : 92 540 sq. km (35 652 sq. miles)

POPULATION

over 1 000 000	▣
over 500 000	◉
over 100 000	⊚
over 50 000	○
over 10 000	●

LAND HEIGHT

500m/1640ft
200m/656ft
80m/262ft

H

PEOPLE

▷ Pop. density medium

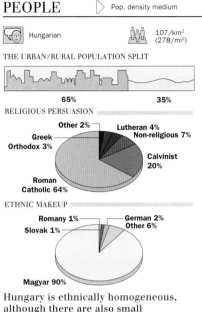

Hungarian

107/km²
(278/mi²)

THE URBAN/RURAL POPULATION SPLIT

65%   35%

RELIGIOUS PERSUASION

Other 2%
Lutheran 4%
Non-religious 7%
Greek Orthodox 3%
Calvinist 20%
Roman Catholic 64%

ETHNIC MAKEUP

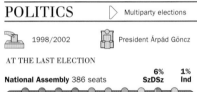

Romany 1%
German 2%
Other 6%
Slovak 1%

Magyar 90%

Hungary is ethnically homogeneous, although there are also small minorities of Germans, Slovaks, Romanies, Serbs, Croats and Romanians. There is little ethnic tension at home, although there is considerable concern about the treatment of Hungarian minorities in neighboring states. In terms of religion, the country is more diversified. The 100,000-strong Jewish community in Hungary is the largest in eastern Europe. Occasional anti-Semitic outbursts, and also discrimination against Romanies, belie generally tolerant attitudes.

Hungary has a severe housing shortage. Most family homes are overcrowded, possibly contributing to the high rate of stress-related health disorders. Since 1989 a new bourgeoisie has benefited from the market economy, but life for the unskilled and unemployed is tougher than under communism. Hungary has the highest suicide rate in the world.

POPULATION AGE BREAKDOWN

Female	Age	Male
1.8%	81–100	0.8%
9.9%	61–80	6.8%
14.2%	41–60	13%
13.6%	21–40	14%
12.5%	0–20	13.4%

% of population by age group

POLITICS

▷ Multiparty elections

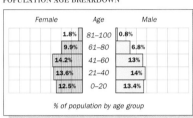

1998/2002

President Árpád Göncz

AT THE LAST ELECTION

National Assembly 386 seats

38% Fidesz-MPP	35% MSzP	12% FKgP	4% MDF	4% MIEP	6% SzDSz	1% Ind

Fidesz-MPP = Young Democrats-Hungarian Civic Party **MSzP** = Hungarian Socialist Party **FKgP** = Independent Smallholders' Party **SzDSz** = Alliance of Free Democrats **MDF** = Hungarian Democrat Forum **MIEP** = Hungarian Justice and Life Party **Ind** = Independents

Hungary has been a multiparty democracy since 1990.

MAIN POLITICAL ISSUES
Social welfare vs. free-market economics
Reforms to assist transition to a market economy have led to strong economic recovery in the Budapest area and the western part of the country. Widening income differentials between young, skilled workers and those in education, health, and other state sectors have provoked protests and strikes.

Hungarian minorities abroad
In 1989–1991, 50,000 Magyars (ethnic Hungarians) living abroad moved to Hungary. Many complained of poor treatment by nationalistic neighboring states, while those already in Hungary are wary of competition for jobs. The 1998–1999 Kosovo crisis led to a new influx of refugees from the predominately Magyar province of Vojvodina in northern Serbia.

PROFILE
MDF leader József Antall, prime minister from 1990, was a symbol of stability in Hungarian politics until his death in 1993. However, party disintegrations and the lack of an economic upturn led to an increase in apathy and disillusionment among voters.

In the 1994 general election, voters rejected the MDF's Christian nationalist stance and voted ex-communists back into power. The victorious MSZP, under Gyula Horn, pledged to work in coalition in order to ease the passage of economic and social reforms through parliament. Four years later it was supplanted by a right-of-center coalition after a narrow defeat in a general election in May 1998.

President Árpád Göncz *was elected in 1990 and is head of the armed forces.*

Gyula Horn, *ex-communist foreign minister and leader of the MSZP.*

The Hungarian parliament *buildings in Budapest, viewed across the Danube from the castle area of the city.*

WORLD AFFAIRS

▷ Joined UN in 1955

CE   CEFTA   NATO   OECD   OSCE

Hungary joined NATO's Partnership for Peace program and gained WEU associate status in 1994. In a 1997 referendum 85% of voters approved NATO membership and in March 1999, with Poland and the Czech Republic, Hungary joined the organization. Joining the EU is a slower process. Hungary has had an association agreement since early 1994. In 1998 it was one of six applicant countries to open formal membership negotiations.

Hungary has a cooperation and friendship treaty with Russia, but relations have been strained by Hungary's open courting of the West. Difficult relations with Slovakia and Romania were eased by friendship treaties concluded in 1995 and 1996.

CHRONOLOGY

The region today occupied by Hungary was first settled by the Finno-Ugrian Magyar peoples from the 8th century. In the 16th and 17th centuries, it came under Austrian domination, lasting until 1867, when Austria–Hungary was formed.

❑ **1918** Hungarian Republic created as successor state to Austria–Hungary.

❑ **1919** Béla Kún leads a short-lived communist government. Romania intervenes militarily and hands power to Admiral Horthy.

❑ **1938–1941** Hungary gains territory from Czechoslovakia, Yugoslavia, and Romania in return for supporting Nazi Germany.

❑ **1941** Hungary drawn into World War II on Axis side when Hitler attacks Soviet Union.

❑ **1944** Nazi Germany preempts Soviet advance on Hungary by invading. Deportation of Hungarian Jews and gypsies to extermination camps begins. Soviet Red Army enters in October. Horthy forced to resign.

➪

H

H

CHRONOLOGY *continued*

- ❏ **1945** Liberated by Red Army. Soviet-formed provisional government installed. Imre Nagy introduces land reform.
- ❏ **1947** Communists emerge as largest party in second postwar election.
- ❏ **1948** Forcible merger of Social Democrats with communists to establish Hungarian Socialist Workers' Party (HSWP) in 1956.
- ❏ **1949** New constitution; formally becomes People's Republic.
- ❏ **1950–1951** First Secretary Rákosi uses authoritarian powers to collectivize agriculture and industrialize the economy.
- ❏ **1953** Imre Nagy, Rákosi's rival, becomes premier and reduces political terror.
- ❏ **1955** Nagy deposed by Rákosi.
- ❏ **1956** Rákosi out. Student demonstrations demanding withdrawal of Soviet troops and Nagy's return become popular uprising. Nagy becomes premier and Kádár First Secretary. Nagy announces Hungary will leave Warsaw Pact. Three days later, Soviet forces suppress protests. About 25,000 killed. Kádár becomes premier.
- ❏ **1958** Nagy executed.
- ❏ **1968** Kádár introduces New Economic Mechanism to bring market elements to socialism.
- ❏ **1986** Police suppress commemoration of 1956 uprising. Democratic opposition demands Kádár resign.
- ❏ **1987** Party reformers establish MDF as a political movement.
- ❏ **1988** Kádár ousted. Protests force suspension of plans for Nagymaros Dam on the Danube.
- ❏ **1989** Parliament votes to allow independent parties. Nagy rehabilitated posthumously and given full state funeral. First opposition candidate since 1947 elected in by-election. Round table talks between HSWP and opposition.
- ❏ **1990** József Antall's MDF wins multiparty elections decisively. Speed of economic reform hotly debated. Árpád Göncz elected president (and reelected 1995).
- ❏ **1991** Warsaw Pact dissolved. Last Soviet troops leave.
- ❏ **1993** Antall dies. Peter Boross elected prime minister.
- ❏ **1994** Hungary joins NATO Partnership for Peace program. MSZP wins general election. Austerity program prompts protests.
- ❏ **1998** EU membership negotiations open. Right-of-center coalition led by Viktor Orban (Fidesz-MPP) takes office after election victory in May.
- ❏ **1999** Joins NATO.

AID

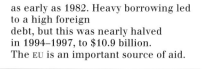

▷ Recipient

$152m (receipts) — Down 18% 1996–1997

Hungary receives net official aid amounting to less than 1% of its GNP. It won substantial World Bank assistance as early as 1982. Heavy borrowing led to a high foreign debt, but this was nearly halved in 1994–1997, to $10.9 billion. The EU is an important source of aid.

DEFENSE

▷ Compulsory military service

$666m — Down 6% in 1997

Real defense spending fell from 7.2% to 1.4% of GDP in 1985–1997. Troop numbers have been more than halved. Conventional arms and the military hierarchy were updated in advance of NATO membership, which took formal effect in March 1999. Almost immediately, Hungary permitted NATO to use its airspace to bomb Serbia, despite concerns for the Hungarian minority living there.

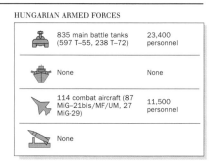

HUNGARIAN ARMED FORCES

835 main battle tanks (597 T–55, 238 T–72)	23,400 personnel	
None	None	
114 combat aircraft (87 MiG–21bis/MF/UM, 27 MiG-29)	11,500 personnel	
None		

ECONOMICS

▷ Inflation 18.9% p.a (1985–1996)

$45.7bn — 204.23–215.30 forint

SCORE CARD

- ❏ WORLD GNP RANKING.........................50th
- ❏ GNP PER CAPITA $4,510
- ❏ BALANCE OF PAYMENTS..................$–982m
- ❏ INFLATION 18.3%
- ❏ UNEMPLOYMENT 9%

EXPORTS

France 4% — Russia 5% — Italy 6% — Austria 11% — Germany 38% — Other 36%

IMPORTS

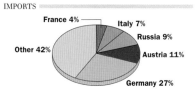

France 4% — Italy 7% — Russia 9% — Other 42% — Austria 11% — Germany 27%

STRENGTHS

Openness to foreign direct investment. Favorable tax regime, streamlined bureaucracy and possibility of fully owned subsidiaries attract international business. Strong export-led growth in late 1990s. High industrial production, especially at new, state-of-the-art factories.

WEAKNESSES

MSZP government's revival of privatization program marred by forced resignation in 1996 of management board of state privatization agency over illegal payments. East–west split as development bypasses rural eastern areas. Widening income differentials.

ECONOMIC PERFORMANCE INDICATOR

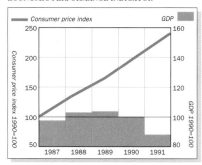

— Consumer price index   GDP ▭

PROFILE

The collapse of COMECON trade caused a reorientation of trade toward western Europe. After several years of difficult transition the economy began to grow again in 1994, when the MSZP came to power. Since then competitiveness has improved and exports increased rapidly to register real GDP growth of nearly 5% in 1998.

HUNGARY : MAJOR BUSINESSES

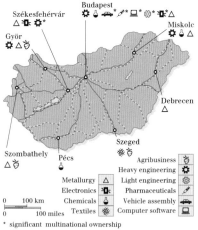

0   100 km
0   100 miles

Agribusiness 🌾
Heavy engineering ✿
Light engineering ✸
Metallurgy △
Electronics ▣
Chemicals 🧪
Textiles ✳
Pharmaceuticals 💉
Vehicle assembly 🚗
Computer software 💻

* significant multinational ownership

RESOURCES

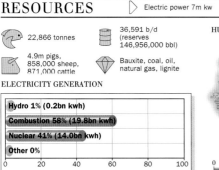

▷ Electric power 7m kw

22,866 tonnes

36,591 b/d (reserves 146,956,000 bbl)

4.9m pigs, 858,000 sheep, 871,000 cattle

Bauxite, coal, oil, natural gas, lignite

ELECTRICITY GENERATION

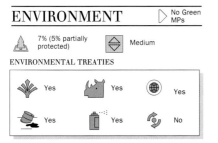

Hydro 1% (0.2bn kwh)

Combustion 58% (19.8bn kwh)

Nuclear 41% (14.0bn kwh)

Other 0%

0   20   40   60   80   100

% of total generation by type

Hungary has bauxite, brown coal, lignite and natural gas reserves. It is dependent for over 40% of its electricity

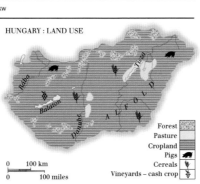

HUNGARY : LAND USE

0   100 km
0   100 miles

Forest
Pasture
Cropland
Pigs
Cereals
Vineyards – cash crop

on nuclear energy from four power units. Fertile farmlands provide grains, sugar beet and potatoes. Wine production is also important.

ENVIRONMENT

▷ No Green MPs

7% (5% partially protected)

Medium

ENVIRONMENTAL TREATIES

Yes   Yes   Yes

Yes   Yes   No

Hungary's oil reserves have a high sulfur content, which exacerbates the already serious air pollution in industrial zones. CO_2 emissions fell by 30% in 1980–1995, but vehicle emissions remain a serious problem.

Hungarian opposition to the Gabcikovo-Nagymaros dam project on the Danube frontier with Slovakia, which would involve extensive destruction of wetlands, has strained relations with Slovakia.

MEDIA

▷ TV ownership high

Daily newspaper circulation 189 per 1,000 people

PUBLISHING AND BROADCAST MEDIA

There are 40 daily newspapers, including *Népszabadság* and *Népszava*

1 state-owned service

1 state-owned, 1 independent service

When official censorship ended in 1988–1989, the number of newspapers and magazines soared. Most are fiercely independent and critical of government policy. TV broadcasting is nominally independent, but in practice the state controls its news coverage. In 1994 the constitutional court declared state interference in the media unlawful. Allegations of interference persist.

CRIME

▷ Death penalty not used

12,455 prisoners

Up 5% 1992–1996

CRIME RATES

Murders
4   *per 100,000 population*

Rapes
4   *per 100,000 population*

Thefts
2768   *per 100,000 population*

Of the 281 homicides in 1997 a growing number were of the elderly for financial gain. Organized crime, money-laundering and smuggling of illegal immigrants are rising.

EDUCATION

▷ School leaving age: 16

99%

194,607 students

In 1995 spending on education was equivalent to 6.6% of GNP.

THE EDUCATION SYSTEM

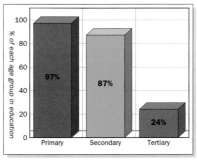

100
80
60
40
20
0

% of each age group in education

97%   87%   24%

Primary   Secondary   Tertiary

Education is free and compulsory from the ages of six to 16. Bilingual schools are being established to provide education in the language of Hungary's ethnic minorities. There are 77 higher education institutions – including 11 universities – from which 32,400 students graduated in 1995.

HEALTH

▷ Welfare state health benefits

1 per 278 people

Accidents, heart and cerebrovascular diseases, cancers

Medical treatment is free of charge to all patients, although there is a 15% charge toward the cost of prescriptions. Spending on the health service has fallen in recent years in real terms, and in 1997 it was equivalent to 6.4% of GDP. The ratio of doctors to patients is high, but there is a shortage of nurses. In order to jump waiting lists or get better care, it is common for patients in the state health system to offer doctors gifts or bribes. The state provides sickness benefit at 75% of wages.

SPENDING

▷ GDP/cap. increase

CONSUMPTION AND SPENDING

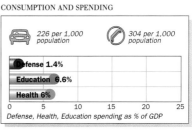

226 per 1,000 population

304 per 1,000 population

Defense 1.4%
Education 6.6%
Health 6%

0   5   10   15   20   25

Defense, Health, Education spending as % of GDP

Hungary enjoys a higher standard of living than other ex-COMECON countries in Eastern Europe. Demand for luxury goods is rising. Access to mobile phones and the internet is higher than in most former Eastern Bloc countries.

Real wages initially fell less than in neighboring transition economies, but fell by 15% in 1995–1997, before rising by 4% in 1998. Hungarians have to work longer hours to pay for basic consumer goods than workers in Western Europe. At around $5,000 a year, GDP per capita is still lower than any EU state but higher than all former Eastern Bloc states except Slovenia. Inequality between those working in the state and private sectors is growing.

WORLD RANKING

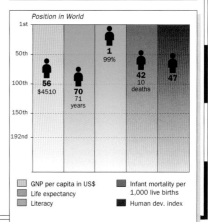

Position in World

1st
50th
100th
150th
192nd

56
$4510

70
71 years

1
99%

42
10 deaths

47

GNP per capita in US$
Life expectancy
Literacy
Infant mortality per 1,000 live births
Human dev. index

H

ICELAND

OFFICIAL NAME: Republic of Iceland **CAPITAL:** Reykjavík
POPULATION: 277,000 **CURRENCY:** New Icelandic króna **OFFICIAL LANGUAGE:** Icelandic

| 1944 | 1944 | June 17 | IS | 0 | +354 | .is |

EUROPE'S WESTERNMOST COUNTRY, Iceland has a strategic location in the north Atlantic, just south of the Arctic Circle. Its position, on the rift where the North American and European continental plates are pulling apart, accounts for its 200 volcanoes and its numerous geysers and solfataras. Previously a Danish possession, Iceland became fully independent in 1944. Most settlements are along the coast, where ports remain ice-free in winter.

POLITICS

▷ Multiparty elections

1999/2003

President Olafur Ragnar Grimsson

AT THE LAST ELECTION

Parliament 63 seats

| 41% IP | 27% ULP | 19% PP | 10% L-GA | 3% LP |

IP = Independence Party **ULP** = United Left Party
PP = Progressive Party **L-GA** = Left–Green Alliance
LP = Liberal Party

From independence Iceland has been ruled by coalitions, but in the 1980s the traditional four-party system began to splinter. After the 1991 election, a new IP/Social Democratic coalition promoted market-led reforms. Arguments over whether or not to join the EU were defused in 1992 with the successful negotiation of the EEA, giving Iceland access to the key EU market.

The coalition collapsed after the 1995 general election, when both parties had lost support, and was replaced by a center-right government led by the IP, with David Oddsson as prime minister. He has successfully built on a recovery under way since 1994 and strengthened his position in the 1999 general election.

CLIMATE

▷ Subarctic

WEATHER CHART

Iceland sits in the Gulf Stream. Winters are consequently mild. Summers are cool, with fine, long sunny days.

PEOPLE

▷ Pop. density low

Icelandic

3/km²
(7/mi²)

THE URBAN/RURAL POPULATION SPLIT

92%   8%

RELIGIOUS PERSUASION

Other Christian 1%   Non-religious 6%
Evangelical Lutheran 93%

Descended from Norwegians and Celts, Icelanders form an ethnically homogeneous society. Almost all follow the Evangelical Lutheran Church. Some 60% of the population live in or near Reykjavík. Living standards are high and there are few social tensions. The main cultural influence is from the USA.

TRANSPORTATION

▷ Drive on right

Keflavík Intl, Reykjavík
557,000 passengers

977 ships
244,812 grt

THE TRANSPORTATION NETWORK

| 2,838 km (1,763 miles) | None |
| None | None |

Icelanders rely entirely on cars, internal airplane and helicopter flights. Most freight moves by sea. The only main road is the island ring road.

TOURISM

▷ Visitors : population 1:1.4

202,000 visitors

Up 6% In 1997

MAIN TOURIST ARRIVALS

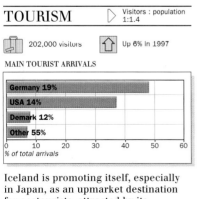

| Germany 19% |
| USA 14% |
| Demark 12% |
| Other 55% |

% of total arrivals

Iceland is promoting itself, especially in Japan, as an upmarket destination for ecotourists, attracted by its spectacular scenery, glaciers, green valleys, fjords and hot springs.

ICELAND

Total Land Area : 100 250 sq. km
(38 707 sq. miles)

POPULATION
○ over 50 000
● over 10 000
• under 10 000

LAND HEIGHT
1000m/3281ft
500m/1640ft
200m/656ft
Sea Level
Ice Cap

WORLD AFFAIRS ▷ Joined UN in 1946

CE | NATO | OECD | OSCE | EEA

Although a member of NATO and EFTA, Iceland has traditionally maintained arm's-length relations with the EU and the USA. In 1992 it left the International Whaling Commission when a commercial whaling ban was continued. The EEA, which includes Iceland, came into being in 1994. Links with other Nordic states are strong.

AID ▷ Donor

💲 $6m (donations)　　⇕ Not applicable

Aid donations are modest, and form a smaller proportion of the budget than in other Scandinavian states.

DEFENSE ▷ No compulsory military service

💲 Coastguard is only military force　　⇕ Not applicable

Iceland, a NATO member and an associate WEU member, has no armed forces. US troops are based at Keflavík.

ECONOMICS ▷ Inflation 11% p.a. (1985–1996)

📊 $7.2bn　　💲 72.37–69.32 New Icelandic króna

SCORE CARD

❏ WORLD GNP RANKING...........................94th
❏ GNP PER CAPITA $26,580
❏ BALANCE OF PAYMENTS.....................$–133m
❏ INFLATION 1.7%
❏ UNEMPLOYMENT 4%

STRENGTHS

High-tech fishing industry with exclusive access to prime fishing grounds. Very cheap geothermal power. Strong economic recovery in late 1990s; low inflation and unemployment.

WEAKNESSES

Dependence on fish for over 70% of export earnings. Large state-owned banking sector limits market flexibility.

EXPORTS

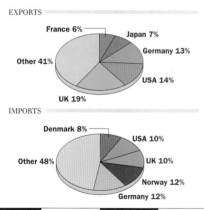

France 6% — Japan 7%
Germany 13%
Other 41%
USA 14%
UK 19%

IMPORTS

Denmark 8% —
USA 10%
Other 48%
UK 10%
Norway 12%
Germany 12%

Lava towers, *near Lake Mÿvatn in northern Iceland – an area of grassy lowlands. Iceland's centre consists of lava desert and glaciers.*

RESOURCES ▷ Electric power 1.1m kw

🐟 1.6m tonnes　　🛢 Not an oil producer

🐑 477,000 sheep, 80,000 horses, 75,000 cattle　　💎 Diatomite

Iceland has virtually no minerals. All energy needs are met by geothermal and hydroelectric sources. It has implemented measures to try to restore its once abundant fish stocks.

ENVIRONMENT ▷ Green MPs

🔺 7% partially protected　　⇕ Not available

Iceland has no nuclear or coal-fired power stations. Pollution levels are low. Believing that minke whales eat valuable cod stocks, Iceland resumed whale hunting in 1992. The 1996 eruption of the Loki volcano under Vatna glacier caused extensive flooding and damage.

MEDIA ▷ TV ownership high

📰 Daily newspaper circulation 535 per 1,000 people

PUBLISHING AND BROADCAST MEDIA

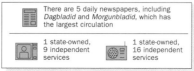

There are 5 daily newspapers, including *Dagbladid* and *Morgunbladid*, which has the largest circulation

1 state-owned, 9 independent services　　1 state-owned, 16 independent services

Iceland is renowned for having one of the highest per capita newspaper circulations in the world.

CRIME ▷ Death penalty not used

⛓ 113 prisoners　　⇕ Crime rates are fairly stable

Crime rates are comparatively low. The rate of alcohol-related murders is higher than the European average.

EDUCATION ▷ School leaving age: 16

🎒 99%　　🎓 7,483 students

Icelanders buy more books per capita than any other nation. Education is state-run; some 40% of school students go on to university at Reykjavík or Akureyri or to colleges in the USA.

CHRONOLOGY

Settled in the 9th century by Norwegians, Iceland was ruled by Denmark in 1380–1944, becoming fully self-governing in 1918.

❏ **1940–1945** Occupied by UK and USA.
❏ **1944** Independence as a republic.
❏ **1949** Founder member of NATO.
❏ **1951** US air base built at Keflavík despite strong local opposition.
❏ **1972–1976** Extends fishing limits to 50 miles; two "cod wars" with UK.
❏ **1975** Sets 200-mile fishing limit.
❏ **1980** Vigdís Finnbogadóttir world's first elected woman head of state.
❏ **1985** Declares nuclear-free status.
❏ **1995** General election: formation of center-right coalition under David Oddsson which is reelected in 1999.

HEALTH ▷ Welfare state health benefits

👥 1 per 333 people　　Heart disease, cancers, accidents

The state health system is free to all Icelanders. Iceland has one of the lowest infant mortality rates and one of the highest longevity rates in the world.

SPENDING ▷ GDP/cap. no increase

CONSUMPTION AND SPENDING

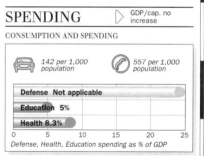

🚗 142 per 1,000 population　　📞 557 per 1,000 population

Defense	Not applicable	
Education	5%	
Health	8.3%	

0　5　10　15　20　25
Defense, Health, Education spending as % of GDP

Wealth distribution is comparatively even and social mobility is high. Domestic heating, generated from the island's extensive geothermal sources, is almost free.

WORLD RANKING

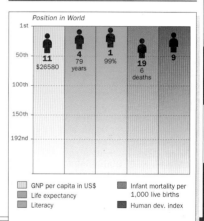

Position in World

1st

50th — 11 $26580 | 4 79 years | 1 99% | 19 6 deaths | 9

100th

150th

192nd

☐ GNP per capita in US$
☐ Life expectancy
☐ Literacy
☐ Infant mortality per 1,000 live births
☐ Human dev. index

INDIA

OFFICIAL NAME: Republic of India **CAPITAL:** New Delhi
POPULATION: 976 million **CURRENCY** Rupee **OFFICIAL LANGUAGES:** Hindi and English

SOUTH ASIA

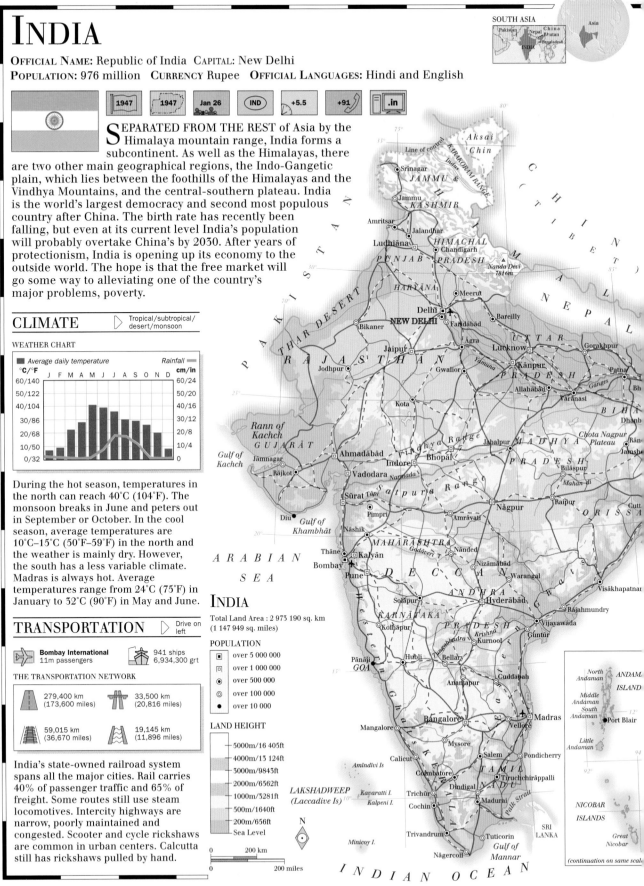

| 1947 | 1947 | Jan 26 | IND | +5.5 | +91 | | .in |

S EPARATED FROM THE REST of Asia by the Himalaya mountain range, India forms a subcontinent. As well as the Himalayas, there are two other main geographical regions, the Indo-Gangetic plain, which lies between the foothills of the Himalayas and the Vindhya Mountains, and the central-southern plateau. India is the world's largest democracy and second most populous country after China. The birth rate has recently been falling, but even at its current level India's population will probably overtake China's by 2030. After years of protectionism, India is opening up its economy to the outside world. The hope is that the free market will go some way to alleviating one of the country's major problems, poverty.

CLIMATE
▷ Tropical/subtropical/ desert/monsoon

WEATHER CHART

Average daily temperature		Rainfall

India's population ranges from 24°C (75°F) in January to 32°C (90°F) in May and June.

During the hot season, temperatures in the north can reach 40°C (104°F). The monsoon breaks in June and peters out in September or October. In the cool season, average temperatures are 10°C–15°C (50°F–59°F) in the north and the weather is mainly dry. However, the south has a less variable climate. Madras is always hot. Average temperatures range from 24°C (75°F) in January to 32°C (90°F) in May and June.

TRANSPORTATION
▷ Drive on left

✈ **Bombay International**
11m passengers

🚢 941 ships
6,934,300 grt

THE TRANSPORTATION NETWORK

279,400 km (173,600 miles)	33,500 km (20,816 miles)
59,015 km (36,670 miles)	19,145 km (11,896 miles)

India's state-owned railroad system spans all the major cities. Rail carries 40% of passenger traffic and 65% of freight. Some routes still use steam locomotives. Intercity highways are narrow, poorly maintained and congested. Scooter and cycle rickshaws are common in urban centers. Calcutta still has rickshaws pulled by hand.

INDIA

Total Land Area : 2 973 190 sq. km
(1 147 949 sq. miles)

POPULATION

■	over 5 000 000
▣	over 1 000 000
◉	over 500 000
◎	over 100 000
●	over 10 000

LAND HEIGHT

5000m/16 405ft
4000m/13 124ft
3000m/9843ft
2000m/6562ft
1000m/3281ft
500m/1640ft
200m/656ft
Sea Level

0   200 km
0   200 miles

A religious festival. Such festivals are a frequent occurrence and form an important part of Hindu culture.

BAY OF
BENGAL

TOURISM ▷ Visitors:population 1:411

🧳 2.4m visitors　　⬆ Up 12% in 1995

MAIN TOURIST ARRIVALS

UK 16%	
Bangladesh 15%	
USA 9%	
Sri Lanka 5%	
Germany 5%	
Other 50%	

% of total arrivals (0 10 20 30 40 50 60)

Tourism is India's sixth-largest foreign exchange earner. There are more luxury hotels, and wildlife and adventure tourism are being promoted. However, India still has only a small share of the world tourism market.

The inauguration in early 1999 of the first tourist bus service to Pakistan is expected to raise tourist revenues.

PEOPLE ▷ Pop. density high

🗣 Hindi, Urdu, Bengali, Marathi, Telugu, Tamil, Bihari, Gujarati, Kanarese

👥 328/km² (850/mi²)

THE URBAN/RURAL POPULATION SPLIT

27%　　　　**73%**

RELIGIOUS PERSUASION

Other 1% — Sikh 2%
Buddhist 1% — Christian 2%
Muslim 11%
Hindu 83%

ETHNIC MAKEUP

Mongoloid and Other 3%
Dravidian 25%
Indo-Aryan 72%

India is the world's second most populous country after China. Despite a major birth control program, the decrease in population growth has been marginal. Nationwide awareness campaigns aim to promote the idea of smaller families. India's planners consider the rise in the population the most significant brake on development. Cultural and religious pressures encourage large families, however, and the extended family is seen as an essential security for old age.

The fertile rice-growing areas of the Gangetic plain and delta are very densely populated. The northern state of Uttar Pradesh has the largest population, followed by neighboring Bihar and the western state of Maharashtra. Maharashtra is also the most urbanized state, with more than half of its people living in towns or cities. Elsewhere, most Indians live in rural areas, although poverty continues to drive many to the swelling cities.

The overwhelming majority of the population are Hindus. Each Hindu belongs to one of thousands of castes and subcastes. Hindus are born into their caste and caste determines whom they marry and their future status and occupation. Various attempts to reform the system have met with violent opposition.

POPULATION AGE BREAKDOWN

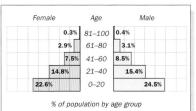

Female	Age	Male
0.3%	81–100	0.4%
2.9%	61–80	3.1%
7.5%	41–60	8.5%
14.8%	21–40	15.4%
22.6%	0–20	24.5%

% of population by age group

CHRONOLOGY

The origins of an Indus valley civilization may be traced back to the third millennium BCE. By the 3rd century BCE, the Mauryan kingdom under Ashoka encompassed most of modern India. Following the Battle of Plassey in 1757, British rule – through the East India Company – was consolidated.

❏ **1885** Formation of Indian National Congress.
❏ **1919** Act of parliament introduces "responsible government."
❏ **1920–1922** Mahatma Gandhi's first civil disobedience campaign.
❏ **1935** Government of India act grants autonomy to provinces.
❏ **1936** First elections under new constitution.
❏ **1942–1943** "Quit India" movement.
❏ **1947** August, independence and partition into India and Pakistan. Jawarhalal Nehru becomes first prime minister.
❏ **1948** Assassination of Mahatma Gandhi. War with Pakistan over Kashmir. India becomes a republic.
❏ **1951–1952** First general election won by Congress party.
❏ **1957** Second elections won by Congress. First elected communist government anywhere installed in Kerala.
❏ **1960** Bombay divided into states of Gujarat and Maharashtra.
❏ **1962** Congress party reelected. Border war with China.
❏ **1964** Death of Nehru. Lal Bahadur Shastri becomes prime minister.
❏ **1965** Second war with Pakistan over Kashmir.
❏ **1966** Shastri dies; Indira Gandhi (daughter of Jawarhalal Nehru) becomes prime minister.
❏ **1969** Congress party splits into two factions, larger of which led by Indira Gandhi.
❏ **1971** Indira Gandhi's Congress party wins elections. Third war with Pakistan over creation of Bangladesh.
❏ **1972** Simla (peace) Agreement signed with Pakistan.
❏ **1974** Explosion of first nuclear device in underground test.
❏ **1975–1977** Imposition of state of emergency.
❏ **1977** Congress loses general election. People's Party (JD) takes power at the center.
❏ **1978** New political group, Congress (Indira) – Congress (I) – formally established.
❏ **1980** Indira Gandhi's C(I) wins general election.
❏ **1984** Indian troops storm Sikh Golden Temple in Amritsar. Assassination of Indira Gandhi ▷

I

CHRONOLOGY *continued*

by Sikh bodyguard; her son Rajiv becomes prime minister. Gas explosion at US-owned Union Carbide Corporation plant in Bhopal kills 2,000 people, becoming the country's worst environmental disaster.

❏ **1985** Peace accords with militant separatists in Assam and Punjab.

❏ **1987** Deployment of Indian peacekeeping force in northern Sri Lanka to combat Tamil Tigers.

❏ **1989** General election setback for C(I), which is implicated in Bofors scandal; National Front forms minority government with BJP support.

❏ **1990** Withdrawal of peacekeeping force from Sri Lanka. BJP leader Lal Advani arrested. No confidence motion in parliament.

❏ **1991** C(I) led by Rajiv Gandhi, Indira's son, ousts minority government. Rajiv Gandhi assassinated. Following a general election, P V Narasimha Rao becomes prime minister at head of a C(I) minority government. Program of economic liberalization is initiated.

❏ **1992** Demolition of the Babri Masjid mosque at Ayodhya by Hindu extremists triggers widespread violence, leaving 1,200 people dead.

❏ **1993** Resurgence of Hindu–Muslim riots. Bomb explosions in Bombay. Border troop agreement with China.

❏ **1994** Rupee made fully convertible. Outbreak of pneumonic plague. C(I) routed in key state elections amid growing allegations of corruption in ruling party.

❏ **1995** C(I) suffers electoral setbacks in further state elections. Punjab Chief Minister is assassinated by Sikh extremists.

❏ **1996** Corruption scandal triggers political crisis. C(I) suffers its worst electoral defeat. The largest party, the Hindu nationalist BJP, fails to win a vote of confidence, and a leftist United Front coalition government takes office instead.

❏ **1997** Successive governments fall as C(I) withdraws support.

❏ **1998** General election; BJP led by Atal Bihari Vajpayee forms coalition government. Sonia Gandhi, widow of Rajiv Gandhi, becomes president of C(I). India detonates nuclear bomb.

❏ **1999** March, Vajpayee travels to Pakistan to inaugurate bus service from India. India and Pakistan agree to issue advance warning of future nuclear tests. April, Government falls following vote of no confidence.

❏ **1999** May-July, confrontation in Kasmir leads to fighting.

❏ **1999** October, general election. BJP-led coalition wins majority.

POLITICS ▷ Multiparty elections

U. House 1998/2000
L. House 1999/2004
President Kocheril
Raman Narayanan

AT THE 1998 ELECTION

House of the People (Lok Sabha) 545 seats

49% BJP	31% C(I)	18% UF	2% Other

BJP = Indian People's Party **C(I)** = Congress (I)
UF = United Front **Nom** = Nominated

Council of the States (Rajya Sabha) 245 seats

39% C(I)	21% Other	17% BJP	8% UF	5% Nom	10% Vacant

233 members are elected to the Rajya Sabha by State Legislative Assemblies, and 12 "distinguished citizens" are nominated by the Head of State; the party figures relate to the composition of the house after the 1998 elections. 25 seats were not filled in the February 1998 election.

India is a multiparty democracy. The *Lok Sabha* (lower house) is directly elected by universal adult suffrage, while the *Rajya Sabha* (upper house) is indirectly elected by the state assemblies. There are 25 self- governing states. Of the seven union territories, Delhi and Pondicherry have their own assemblies.

MAIN POLITICAL ISSUES
Political corruption

Allegations of political corruption have recently dominated Indian politics. In 1989, the C(I) prime minister Rajiv Gandhi was accused of accepting bribes from the Swedish arms company Bofors. The C(I) was also implicated in a financial scandal in 1992. Corruption across the political spectrum resurfaced in 1996, when several C(I) government ministers and the leader of the opposition BJP resigned from office. The issue continues to plague government and politics at the highest level and remains a pressing concern.

Hindu militancy

The right-wing Hindu BJP has emerged as a credible alternative to the C(I). Its first major breakthrough in the 1989 general election was consolidated two years later; with its militant ally, the *Shiv Sena*, it took 123 seats in the union parliament. In 1996 the BJP was elected as the largest party in parliament, despite being tainted by allegations of corruption. Although it failed on that occasion to form a viable administration, its renewed show of strength in the 1998 and 1999 elections enabled it to lead a coalition government.

The free market

The introduction of the free-market economy has been vigorously resisted. Critics contend that free trade will undermine local production, and that participation by foreign companies in India will damage the national economy.

In the mid-1990s governments increased spending on rural development programs to soften the impact of economic liberalization. The BJP-led coalition, although more partial to urban interests, is generally opposed to competition from foreign businesses.

PROFILE

Narasimha Rao, who became leader of the C(I) following the assassination of Rajiv Gandhi and was prime minister in 1991–1996, was only the second leader of India's main party not to be related to the Nehru dynasty. He was also notable for his bold program of economic liberalization which broke with the traditional policies of the C(I), founded in the 1930s as a left-of-center umbrella group fighting for independence.It remains the only party with a localized organizational structure

Allegations of corruption under Rao's regime undermined the party, resulting in heavy electoral defeats in 1996 and 1998. After April 1998 hopes for a political revival rested on C(I) president Sonia Gandhi, who as the widow of former Prime Minister Rajiv Gandhi, restored the influence of the Nehru family over the party.

The main challenge to the C(I) comes from regional parties and the Hindu nationalist BJP. In 1996 regional parties formed the core of a C(I) center-left United Front coalition government which held power until April 1997.

The 1998 general election established the BJP as a significant political force. Headed by A. B. Vajpayee, it emerged with a strong enough mandate to lead a coalition government. Elections held in October 1999 returned the coalition to power with an overall majority.

***P. V. Narasimha Rao,** prime minister from 1991–1996.*

***President K. R. Narayanan,** in office since 1997.*

***A. B. Vajpayee,** BJP leader and prime minister since 1998.*

WORLD AFFAIRS ▷ Joined UN in 1945

| Comm | G15 | G24 | NAM | SAARC |

Delhi's overriding preoccupation in foreign policy is the disputed territory of Kashmir, where rival claims between India and Pakistan have sparked two wars, in 1948 and 1965.

The issue has accelerated the nuclear race between the two countries, which have so far refused to limit their nuclear arsenals. In May 1998 India triggered international condemnation by carrying out nuclear weapons tests, prompting Pakistan to follow suit. The USA imposed sanctions against India in June 1998 for ignoring the ban on nuclear weapons testing. Since then India has declared its intention to sign the CTBT (comprehensive test ban treaty). Relations with Pakistan improved in early 1999 after top-level talks. Clashes in Kashmir then threatened war, but Pakistan backed down.

AID ▷ Recipient

$1.7bn (receipts) | Down 13% 1996-1997

India receives aid but is not dependent on it. Nuclear tests in 1998 led some countries, including the USA, to impose sanctions and suspend aid. Environmentalists recently forced the World Bank to withdraw funding for the Narmada Dam project.

DEFENSE ▷ No compulsory military service

$12.8bn | Up 7% in 1997

The development of nuclear weapons has become important.

INDIAN ARMED FORCES

🛡	3,414 main battle tanks (700 T–55, 1,500 T–72, 1,200 *Vijayanta*)	980,000 personnel
🚢	19 submarines, 1 carrier, 6 destroyers, 18 frigates and 49 patrol boats	55,000 personnel
✈	772 combat aircraft (88 *Jaguar* S(I), MiG–21/23/27/29)	140,000 personnel
	Nuclear capability	

India has the fourth largest army in the world, with a total of 980,000 personnel. In May 1998 it carried out a series of nuclear weapons tests. Included in its arsenal is the *Prithvi* missile. However, replacement of India's outdated foreign weaponry, squeezed by budget cuts, is also likely to be affected by US sanctions imposed in mid-1998, which suspended military assistance. India produces its own *Arjun* battle tank.

ECONOMICS ▷ Inflation 9% p.a. (1985–1996)

📊 $357bn | 💲 30.2–42.50 Indian rupees

SCORE CARD

❏ WORLD GNP RANKING	15th
❏ GNP PER CAPITA	$370
❏ BALANCE OF PAYMENTS	$–3.5bn
❏ INFLATION	7.2%
❏ UNEMPLOYMENT	Widespread underemployment

EXPORTS

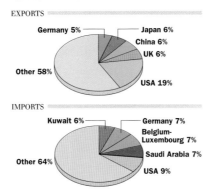

Germany 5% — Japan 6% / China 6% / UK 6% / USA 19% / Other 58%

IMPORTS

Kuwait 6% — Germany 7% / Belgium-Luxembourg 7% / Saudi Arabia 7% / USA 9% / Other 64%

STRENGTHS

Massive home market of over 800 million people. Cheap labor. Some of the workforce possess skills for new high-tech industries such as software programming. Highly efficient textile sector and garment manufacturers. Growing competitiveness on world market, reflected in strong export growth. Competition is encouraging firms to manufacture according to international standards.

There has been a massive rise in foreign direct investment as the economy was opened up to foreign competition after 1991; $3 billion worth of investment was approved by the government in 1993 alone. Large multinationals, such as Coca-Cola and IBM, are returning, despite protests from some opposition groups hostile to the growing presence of foreign businesses in the country.

WEAKNESSES

A large budget deficit dogs the economy. In 1997–1998, the budget deficit reached 6.1% of GDP; estimates for 1998–1999 suggest only a modest fall to 5.6% of GDP. The value of the rupee has declined sharply. Inflation, compounded by a rise in wholesale food prices, stood at over 10% in 1995, and is now running at between 6% and 7%. Poor roads, ports, and telecommunications systems, coupled with power shortages, have all acted as a brake on economic growth. US sanctions imposed in 1998 are also expected to have an adverse effect. Mass unemployment and underemployment: there are tens of millions of urban unemployed.

ECONOMIC PERFORMANCE INDICATOR

Consumer price index / GDP
Consumer price index 1990=100 / GDP 1992=100
1992 1993 1994 1995 1996

PROFILE

The economy is undergoing radical changes. India has converted from a highly protectionist mixed economy, which built the basis of a modern industrial state, to a free-market economy. It is now entering the global marketplace. Wide-ranging reforms, from lowering trade barriers to attracting foreign investment, have been implemented. Despite objections from opposition parties, India ratified the GATT world trade agreement in 1995.

INDIA : MAJOR BUSINESSES

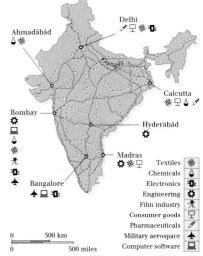

Delhi / Ahmadābād / Calcutta / Bombay / Hyderābād / Madras / Bangalore

Textiles / Chemicals / Electronics / Engineering / Film industry / Consumer goods / Pharmaceuticals / Military aerospace / Computer software

0   500 km
0   500 miles

Hillside monastery in Ladakh, Kashmir, northern India. The Ladakhi Buddhists maintain their traditional farming existence and are known for their friendliness.

I

RESOURCES

 Electric power 93.8m kw

5.3m tonnes

549,109 b/d (reserves 6,049,068,000 bbl)

209m cattle, 121m goats, 56.5m sheep

Iron, diamonds, coal, limestone, zinc, lead

ELECTRICITY GENERATION

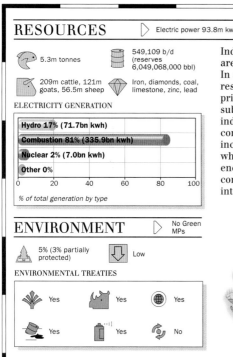

- Hydro 17% (71.7bn kwh)
- Combustion 81% (335.9bn kwh)
- Nuclear 2% (7.0bn kwh)
- Other 0%

% of total generation by type

ENVIRONMENT

 No Green MPs

5% (3% partially protected)

Low

ENVIRONMENTAL TREATIES

Yes	Yes	Yes
Yes	Yes	No

Deforestation is one of India's most pressing environmental problems. Unplanned industrial development and the pressure for more agricultural land have felled once lush tree cover and less than 11% of original forest cover remains. The effect has been a sharp rise in soil erosion, the silting up of dams, and landslides. India experienced its worst environmental accident in 1984, when an explosion at the Union Carbide plant in Bhopal led to an escape of lethal gases. Over 2,000 people died.

MEDIA

TV ownership medium

Daily newspaper circulation 27 per 1,000 people

PUBLISHING AND BROADCAST MEDIA

	There are 3,037 daily newspapers. *The Times of India*, the *Statesman* and the *India Express* publish nationally
	1 state-owned service
	1 state-owned service

Satellite TV is increasingly popular in India. Services range from the BBC World Service to CNN, Hindi language Zee TV and MTV, and one state-run channel. More than seven million households are estimated to have acquired dishes. State-run terrestrial TV has suffered as a result. Critics fear a Western onslaught on Indian values. Recent newspaper launches include the *Asian Age*, which is simultaneously published in London by satellite and claims to be India's first truly international paper.

India's most significant mineral exports are iron ore and cut diamonds. In addition, there are large coal reserves. The steel industry has been privatized. Steel imports are now subject to lower duties, but the industry has so far withstood external competition, and exports have increased. However, production, which consumes up to twice as much energy as that used by some foreign competitors, is inefficient by international standards.

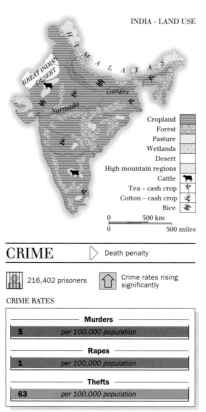

INDIA - LAND USE

- Cropland
- Forest
- Pasture
- Wetlands
- Desert
- High mountain regions
- Cattle
- Tea – cash crop
- Cotton – cash crop
- Rice

0   500 km

0   500 miles

CRIME

Death penalty

216,402 prisoners

Crime rates rising significantly

CRIME RATES

Murders	
5	per 100,000 population

Rapes	
1	per 100,000 population

Thefts	
63	per 100,000 population

Violent crime is on the increase, particularly in the big cities. Theft has risen sharply as consumer spending increases.

Many violent criminal gangs operating in major cities such as Bombay (Mumbai) have made vast profits from smuggling, prostitution, narcotics, protection and extortion rackets, and forcibly taking land from the poor. Bombay's gangs have strong connections with Dubai and the Middle East; they are also said to have contacts among politicians and the police.

In large areas of central India and particularly in the region around Gwalior, *dacoits* still operate. Modeled on the *thugee* gangs of the 19th century, they are outlaws who live by highway robbery and terrorizing small rural communities.

The state is currently unable to meet the country's demand for electricity. Petroleum and coal are the main sources of energy generation although these are imported.

A recent scheme in Maharashtra to increase output by attracting investment from the US-led consortium, Enron, became mired in controversy when the BJP state government temporarily suspended negotiations in response to nationalist groups which were opposed to foreign businesses.

EDUCATION

School leaving age: 14

54%

6.1m students

Half of the adult population is illiterate, significantly affecting development.

THE EDUCATION SYSTEM

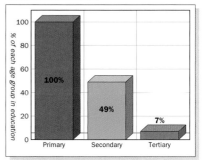

% of each age group in education

- Primary: 100%
- Secondary: 49%
- Tertiary: 7%

There is now a primary school in every village across the subcontinent. However, many children drop out of school to provide supplementary income for their families. There are more than 50 million students at secondary level, and an estimated 10 million graduates from nearly 200 universities.

Women make up almost 10% of those enrolled in higher education, a high percentage for a low-income economy. India has one of the largest pools of science graduates anywhere in the world.

Corn cultivation in terraced fields in central India. In addition to rice, wheat, sorghum, corn, millet and barley are also important cereal crops.

THE SANGH MOVEMENT FOR A HINDU NATIONAL IDENTITY

THE IDEA OF *HINDUTVA*, a specifically Hindu-based national identity, has existed in Indian politics since pre-independence days. For decades, however, its supporters were no more than a minor strand of the opposition to the secularist Congress party, which ruled almost uninterruptedly for four decades. In the late 1980s the rise of the BJP made the divisive concept of *Hindutva* a national issue. When the party led a government coalition after the March 1998 elections, Prime Minister A. B. Vajpayee kept its ideology in the background, but militant elements in the movement still expect the BJP to fulfil their pro-Hindu aims. Especially symbolic for the so-called 'saffron brigade' is the call to build a Hindu temple in place of a Muslim mosque at Ayodhya, Uttar Pradesh, supposed birthplace of the Hindu god Rama. In 1990 the then BJP leader L.K. Advani made the controversial site the focus of his nationwide "pilgrimage", and in 1992 the mosque was destroyed by Hindu activists, setting off communal rioting in which hundreds died.

THE *SANGH* MOVEMENT

The BJP's ideological basis is the *Sangh* movement built around the *Rashtriya Swayamsevak Sangh* (RSS). The RSS, whose name translates as the National Union of Selfless Servants, was first formed in Nagpur in 1925 to recruit men and women as *swayemsevaks*, volunteers dedicated to the creation of a Hindu nation (Hindu *rashtra*). Banned briefly in 1948 over its association with the Hindu extremist assassin of Mahatma Gandhi, the RSS has no clear organizational structure or membership. It has educational and trade union-based arms, and a religious wing in the World Hindu Council (VHP). The main political channel for the *Sangh's* influence is the BJP, although it is also linked with fringe organizations including the *Bajrang Dal*, the group recently blamed for attacks on Christian missionaries in Gujarat.

In March 1999, *Prime Minister A.B. Vajpayee made an historic trip to Pakistan, to inaugurate a new bus service, operating between Pakistan and India.*

The October 1999 general election strengthened the party's position, giving the BJP led coalition the parliamentary majority.

REGIONAL APPEAL

The appeal of *Hindutva* is strongest in the Hindi-speaking heartland, the 'cow belt', centered on Uttar Pradesh and Madhya Pradesh, with Bihar and Orissa to the east, Maharashtra, and Gujarat in the west. While seeking to be inclusive and appeal to all Hindus, the movement is rooted in Brahmin culture, and faces rivalry in some states from parties focusing on combating the oppression of the lowest castes *(dalits)*.

In Maharashtra, the BJP has allied itself with a more extreme local rival Hindu chauvinist party, *Shiv Sena* (the 'army of Shivaji', a 17th century warrior king). *Shiv Sena* leader Bal Thackeray, an open admirer of Adolf Hitler, is the main force in local politics. Thackeray also led the campaign for Bombay's change of name to Mumbai in 1995.

The growth of regional parties in India in general has made coalition-building a feature of government. In practice this has been a major restraint on the BJP's more militant ideologues at the national level. Dependent on so many allies to form a government in 1998, the party under Vajpayee's leadership effectively shelved controversial policies like building the temple at Ayodhya. It now campaigns mainly on its claim to offer good governance, Vajpayee's moderate leadership, and his strong hand at the helm in international affairs.

Young Hindu miltants *on a pilgrimage to Ayodhya in Uttar Pradesh, northern India.*

HEALTH

▷ Welfare state health benefits

👥 1 per 2,500 people

💀 Respiratory, nutritional and diarrheal diseases, malaria

Malnutrition, always a primary cause of ill-health, is extremely common among the poor, and infant mortality is widespread. Much of this is due to preventable diseases such as diarrhea. AIDS has accelerated and HIV infection rates are rising. An unusual outbreak of pneumonic plague in 1994 was estimated to have killed more than 100 people. Health programs are primarily the responsibility of the state governments, but there are various national health projects, including a massive polio eradication program.

SPENDING

▷ GDP/cap. no increase

CONSUMPTION AND SPENDING

🚗 4 per 1,000 population

📞 19 per 1,000 population

Defense 3.3%	
Education 3.5%	
Health 1.3%	

0   5   10   15   20   25

Defense, Health, Education spending as % of GDP

According to the government, 240 million people (30% of the population), mostly in rural areas, were living below the poverty line in the late 1980s. Recent studies dispute whether this figure is rising or falling. Extremes of wealth, particularly with the opening up of the economy, are frequently seen alongside extremes of poverty. The middle classes, who number some 150–200 million, have an exceedingly comfortable lifestyle, with servants and plush housing. Many of the slums in cities such as Bombay and Calcutta have five to nine people living in one room; few slum houses have sanitation. In Bombay alone, over 100,000 people live on the sidewalks.

WORLD RANKING

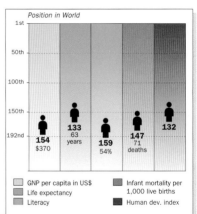

Position in World

1st
50th
100th
150th
192nd

154 $370
133 63 years
159 54%
147 71 deaths
132

- ▢ GNP per capita in US$
- ▢ Life expectancy
- ▢ Literacy
- ▢ Infant mortality per 1,000 live births
- ▢ Human dev. index

INDONESIA

OFFICIAL NAME: Republic of Indonesia   **CAPITAL:** Jakarta
POPULATION: 206.5 million   **CURRENCY:** Rupiah   **OFFICIAL LANGUAGE:** Bahasa Indonesia

| 1949 | 1976 | Aug 17 | RI | +7 | +62 | .id |

The world's largest archipelago, Indonesia's islands stretch 5,000 km (3,100 miles) eastward across the Pacific, from the Malay Peninsula to New Guinea. Sumatra, Java, Kalimantan, Irian Jaya and Sulawesi are mountainous, volcanic, and densely forested. Formerly the Dutch East Indies, Indonesia achieved independence in 1949. Politics has since been dominated by the military. Demands for greater autonomy on outlying islands, and for liberation for East Timor, have been forcefully opposed. This hard-line stance weakened after the fall of Suharto in 1998, but militias ravaged East Timor after its independence vote in 1999.

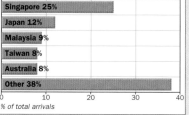

Rice terraces on Bali, *one of Indonesia's 13,677 islands and its most popular tourist destination. Rice is the staple food crop.*

CLIMATE

▷ Tropical equatorial/ monsoon

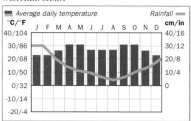

WEATHER CHART

Indonesia's climate is mainly tropical monsoon. Variations relate mainly to differences in latitude and physical structure; hilly areas are cooler overall. Rain falls throughout the year, often in thunderstorms, but there is a relatively dry season from June to September. December–March is the wettest period, except in the Moluccas, which receive the bulk of their rain between June and September. Rainfall averages between 150 and 400 cm (50 and 157 inches) a year.

TRANSPORTATION

▷ Drive on left

Sukarno-Hatta, Jakarta
8.8m passengers

2,383 ships
3.2m grt

THE TRANSPORTATION NETWORK

175,400 km (109,000 miles)	200 km (124 miles)
6,362 km (3,953 miles)	21,579 km (13,409 miles)

With 13,677 islands spread across nearly 5,000 km (3,100 miles) and three time zones, communications are an obvious government priority. Indonesia entered into satellite communications early, and a countrywide, satellite-based telephone system is being installed.

Indonesia's road and shipping infrastructure is also being improved. Ports are being extended and expressway projects include the recently completed Jakarta–Bandung link. The toll roads around Jakarta were contracted to former President Suharto's daughter, Siti.

TOURISM

▷ Visitors : population 1:41

5m visitors

Up 17% 1995–1997

MAIN TOURIST ARRIVALS

Singapore 25%	
Japan 12%	
Malaysia 9%	
Taiwan 8%	
Australia 8%	
Other 38%	

% of total arrivals

Tourism took off during the 1980s. By the mid-1990s the number of tourists had exceeded four million, although political unrest in 1998 and early 1999 discouraged many visitors. Bali, Java and Sumatra are the most popular destinations. The expansion has been encouraged by a major investment in hotels and the opening of Bali to airlines other than the national carrier, *Garuda Indonesia.*

INDONESIA

Total Land Area : 1 811 570 sq. km
(699 447 sq. miles)

LAND HEIGHT

4000m/13 124ft	
3000m/9843ft	
2000m/6562ft	
1000m/3281ft	
500m/1640ft	
Sea Level	

POPULATION

■	over 5 000 000
▣	over 1 000 000
◉	over 500 000
◎	over 100 000
○	over 50 000

PEOPLE

▷ Pop. density medium

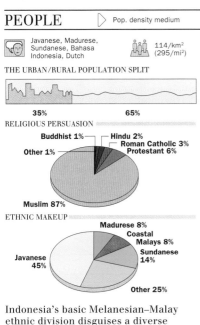

Javanese, Maderese, Sundanese, Bahasa Indonesia, Dutch

114/km² (295/mi²)

THE URBAN/RURAL POPULATION SPLIT

35%   65%

RELIGIOUS PERSUASION

Buddhist 1% — Hindu 2%
Roman Catholic 3%
Other 1% — Protestant 6%

Muslim 87%

ETHNIC MAKEUP

Maderese 8%
Coastal Malays 8%
Sundanese 14%
Javanese 45%
Other 25%

Indonesia's basic Melanesian–Malay ethnic division disguises a diverse society. The national language, Bahasa Indonesia, coexists with at least 250 other spoken languages or dialects. Attempts by the Javanese political elite to suppress local cultures have been vigorously opposed especially by the East Timoreans, the Aceh of northern Sumatra and the Papuans of Irian Jaya. Religious and inter-ethnic hostility is increasing. In 1998 there were fatal clashes between Muslims and Christians on Ambon island. Similar clashes occurred in Kalimantan in early 1999 between indigenous Dayaks and ethnic Maderese immigrants.

Discrimination against ethnic Chinese has encouraged vicious attacks on Chinese businesses as in Jakarta in 1998.

There is sexual equality before the law, and women are able to take an active part in public life.

POPULATION AGE BREAKDOWN

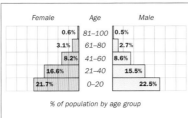

Female	Age	Male
0.6%	81–100	0.5%
3.1%	61–80	2.7%
8.2%	41–60	8.6%
16.6%	21–40	15.5%
21.7%	0–20	22.5%

% of population by age group

POLITICS

▷ Multiparty elections

1999/2004

President Bacharuddin J. Habibie

AT THE LAST ELECTION

House of Representatives 500 seats   7% PAN   8% Other

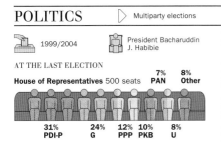

31% PDI-P   24% G   12% PPP   10% PKB   8% U

PDI-P = Indonesian Democratic Party of Struggle **G** = Golkar
PPP = United Development Party **PKB** = National Awaking Part
U = Unelected (army) seats **PAN** = National Mandate Party

People's Consultative Assembly 700 seats

500 members of House of Representatives and 200 further members, including delegates from regional assemblies and representatives of political organizations.

General Suharto ran Indonesia under tight control for over three decades. He was forced to resign in May 1998 amid a wave of protest over economic crisis, deep-seated corruption and the denial of democratic rights. His stop-gap successor until November 1999, his former deputy B. J. Habibie, conceded legislative elections in June 1999 and a referendum on East Timor's future.

PROFILE

Under Suharto, the army was the main source of political power. The dominant political organization was Golkar, a federation of groups representing sectional interests. The only two legal parties – the PPP and the PDI – served as "partners" of government. The mainly Muslim PPP profited in the 1997 elections from government-instigated maneuvers to split the PDI and neutralize the "youth power" appeal of Megawati Sukarnoputri, daughter of the country's first president. Centralist policies fueled secessionism in Aceh (northern Sumatra) and Irian Jaya.

After the fall of Suharto, amid sustained student protests, Megawati's PDI-P won most seats in elections in June 1999. A new president was to be chosen in November by the People's Consultative Assembly. The prospects of a democratic transfer of power remained dependent on the attitude of the army leadership.

General Suharto, *ex-army chief of staff. President 1968–1998.*

Dr. Sukarno, *first president and "Father of Independence."*

WORLD AFFAIRS

▷ Joined UN in 1950

APEC   ASEAN   G15   OIC   OPEC

Indonesia under General Suharto was nonaligned but with a decidedly pro-Western bias.

China remains a major foreign policy concern despite the restoration of diplomatic ties in 1990. Indonesia and Australia signed a ground-breaking security cooperation agreement in late 1995, but in 1999 Australia led the intervention in East Timor.

The post-Suharto government is under pressure from Western governments to improve its human rights record. The East Timor massacres in 1999 severely damaged its international standing.

AID

▷ Recipient

$832m (receipts)   Down 26% 1996–1997

Japan and the World Bank account for the provision of most bilateral and multilateral aid respectively, relied on to cover the current-account deficit. A significant portion has been affected by "leakage," including corruption.

I

EAST TIMOR

The East Timor referendum in August 1999 showed overwhelming support for independence (78.5% in a near 100% turnout). Instead of preparing to implement this result by November, the Indonesian army allowed savage reprisals by militia gangs. Destroying most of the capital, Dili, they drove the whole population into hiding. Thousands died, and many were taken forcibly to camps in West Timor. The UN observer mission and other foreign personnel were evacuated, but in mid-September the UN agreed to send in an Australian-led peacekeeping force.

BACKGROUND

A former Portuguese colony with an area of 14,925 sq. km (5,763 sq. miles), and a population of 850,000, East Timor was invaded by Indonesia in December 1975. Brutally suppressing the left-wing Fretilin independence movement, Indonesia annexed the territory in July 1976. An estimated 100,000 were killed. Fretilin kept up its guerrilla struggle, but its leader Xanana Gusmão was captured in 1992. Violent suppression of protests kept East Timor in the news spotlight, as did the 1996 Nobel Peace Prize award to Bishop Belo and exiled politician José Ramos Horta. Conceding a UN-monitored referendum after Suharto's fall, the Indonesian regime released Gusmão in August 1999.

CHRONOLOGY

On the trade route between India and China, the Indonesian archipelago has long attracted outside interest – Hindu, Buddhist and Islamic, then, from the 16th century, European. The Dutch were victors in the rivalry to exploit its valuable spices. Colonization began in the 17th century on Java. By 1910, the Dutch East Indies encompassed present-day Indonesia, whereas Portugal held East Timor.

❏ **1927** Indonesian National Party formed under Dr. Sukarno.

❏ **1930s** Dutch repression.

❏ **1942–1945** Japanese occupation. Sukarno works with Japanese while promoting independence.

❏ **1945** August, days after Japanese surrender, independence declared.

❏ **1945–1949** Nationalist guerrilla war – interspersed with negotiations.

❏ **1949** Dutch grant independence. United States of Indonesia formed under President Sukarno. Irian Jaya stays Dutch until 1962.

❏ **1950** Federation dissolved. Unitary Republic of Indonesia.

❏ **1950–1959** Sukarno introduces authoritarian "guided democracy," then martial law.

❏ **1965** Communist PKI alliance with military ends. Suharto takes command of army, crushes abortive cup. Up to a million killed in PKI purge. PKI banned.

❏ **1966** Sukarno hands over power to General Suharto.

❏ **1968** Suharto becomes president (reelected every five years to 1998) and reinforces rule by military.

❏ **1971** First elections since 1955 won by government-sponsored Golkar.

❏ **1975** Indonesia invades East Timor; incorporated as Indonesia's 27th province in 1976.

❏ **1984** Muslim protests in Jakarta trigger Islamic movement.

❏ **1985** Fretilin liberation front declares independence of East Timor; military repression.

❏ **1989** Unrest in Java and Sumbawa.

❏ **1991** Indonesian troops massacre pro-independence demonstrators in Dili in East Timor.

❏ **1996** Anti-government demonstrations in Jakarta.

❏ **1997** Economic recession. Smog pollution from forest fires extends into Malaysia and the Philippines.

❏ **1998** Suharto resigns amid unrest. Succeeded by Vice-President B.J. Habibie until November 1999.

❏ **1999** June, elections: opposition led by Megawati Sukarnoputri emerges as winner. August, East Timor referendum backs independence, sets off violent backlash.

DEFENSE

▷ Compulsory military service

$4.8bn   ⬦ No change in 1997

Defense spending is relatively low, despite the prominence of the military.

INDONESIAN ARMED FORCES

🛡	355 light tanks (275 AMX-13, 30 PT-76, 50 *Scorpion*)	235,000 personnel
🚢	2 submarines, 17 frigates, 57 patrol boats	43,000 personnel
✈	91 combat aircraft (20 A-4, 10 F-16, 13 HAWK Mk 53)	21,000 personnel
⚓	None	

Military service is selective and lasts for two years. The constitution enshrines the political role of the military, and it remains the key influence in Indonesia. The recent "civilianization" of political parties, the bureaucracy and state companies has reduced the presence of the military in these areas, if not their influence. "Off-budget funds" often supplement official defense allocations.

Western arms sales are being made increasingly dependent on the improvement of Indonesia's human rights record.

The main defense issues are internal security, East Timor and the perceived Chinese threat.

ECONOMICS

▷ Inflation 8.6% p.a (1985–1996)

$221.5bn   5,495–7,950 rupiahs

SCORE CARD

❏ World GNP Ranking	23rd
❏ GNP per Capita	$1,110
❏ Balance of Payments	$–4.8bn
❏ Inflation	11.6%
❏ Unemployment	15%

EXPORTS

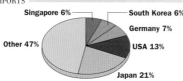

China 5%
South Korea 7%
Singapore 8%
Other 42%
USA 14%
Japan 24%

IMPORTS

Singapore 6%
South Korea 6%
Germany 7%
Other 47%
USA 13%
Japan 21%

ECONOMIC PERFORMANCE INDICATOR

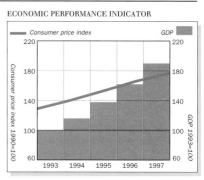

Consumer price index   GDP

(chart: Consumer price index 1990=100 on left axis 60–220; GDP 1993=100 on right axis 60–220; years 1993, 1994, 1995, 1996, 1997)

STRENGTHS

Varied resources, especially oil. Expansion of manufacturing, including high tech. Recent evidence of high growth. Cheap and plentiful labor.

WEAKNESSES

Red tape; corruption. State control of economy. $95 billion debt burden. Continuing economic recession. Collapse of foreign investor confidence.

PROFILE

Under Suharto the economy grew rapidly, fueled largely by oil, until its collapse in 1997–1998. State-owned corporations played a significant role, and the economy enjoyed protection from foreign competition. Non-oil exports, especially manufactures, were diversified, but the debt burden used up a third of export earnings. Government promises to cut red tape and privatize were delayed by the unresolved conflict between advocates of deregulation and "technologists" who favored industrialization over profitability for state concerns. Corruption was rife among members of Suharto's family. As foreign speculators withdrew to escape the economic crisis that hit the region in 1997, neither reform nor retrenchment could stem the tide towards recession.

INDONESIA : MAJOR BUSINESSES

🆗	Rubber
✿	Heavy engineering
◊	Gas
⚗	Chemicals
🌲	Timber industries
⬣	Oil
🛢	Oil refining
⚡	Electronics
🚗	Vehicle assembly
✈	Aerospace industry

* significant multinational ownership

Medan
Balikpapan
Banjarmasin
Kendari
Sorong
Palembang
Jakarta
Bandung
Surabaya
Ujung Pandang

0   500 km
0   500 miles

RESOURCES
▷ Electric power 20.3m kw

4.4m tonnes

1.3m b/d (reserves 5,779,000,000 bbl)

15.2m goats, 12.2m cattle, 8.2m sheep

Oil, natural gas, tin, bauxite, nickel, copper, gold, coal

ELECTRICITY GENERATION

Hydro 15% (10.4bn kwh)

Combustion 82% (56.6bn kwh)

Nuclear 0%

Other 3% (1.8bn kwh)

| 0 | 20 | 40 | 60 | 80 | 100 |

% of total generation by type

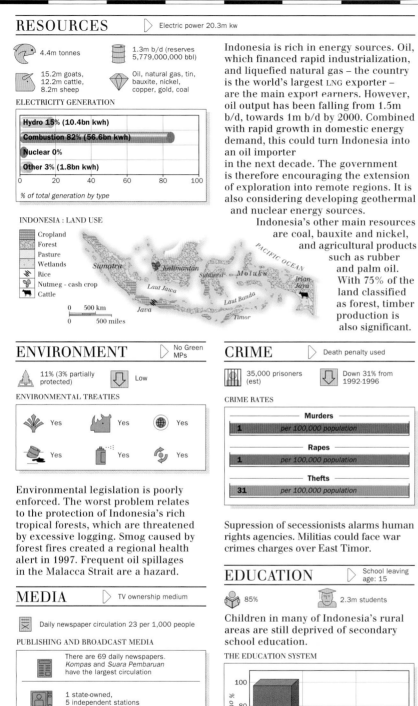

INDONESIA : LAND USE

- Cropland
- Forest
- Pasture
- Wetlands
- Rice
- Nutmeg - cash crop
- Cattle

0　500 km
0　500 miles

Indonesia is rich in energy sources. Oil, which financed rapid industrialization, and liquefied natural gas – the country is the world's largest LNG exporter – are the main export earners. However, oil output has been falling from 1.5m b/d, towards 1m b/d by 2000. Combined with rapid growth in domestic energy demand, this could turn Indonesia into an oil importer in the next decade. The government is therefore encouraging the extension of exploration into remote regions. It is also considering developing geothermal and nuclear energy sources.

Indonesia's other main resources are coal, bauxite and nickel, and agricultural products such as rubber and palm oil. With 75% of the land classified as forest, timber production is also significant.

ENVIRONMENT
▷ No Green MPs

11% (3% partially protected)

Low

ENVIRONMENTAL TREATIES

Yes　Yes　Yes

Yes　Yes　Yes

Environmental legislation is poorly enforced. The worst problem relates to the protection of Indonesia's rich tropical forests, which are threatened by excessive logging. Smog caused by forest fires created a regional health alert in 1997. Frequent oil spillages in the Malacca Strait are a hazard.

MEDIA
▷ TV ownership medium

Daily newspaper circulation 23 per 1,000 people

PUBLISHING AND BROADCAST MEDIA

There are 69 daily newspapers. *Kompas* and *Suara Pembaruan* have the largest circulation

1 state-owned, 5 independent stations

1 state-owned, 1 independent station

A severe press crackdown in 1994 led to a ban on three popular news magazines. One of them, *Detik*, reappeared under the name *Detak* in July 1998, following Suharto's resignation. Since then there has been greater pressure to extend press freedom.

CRIME
▷ Death penalty used

35,000 prisoners (est)

Down 31% from 1992-1996

CRIME RATES

Murders

1 per 100,000 population

Rapes

1 per 100,000 population

Thefts

31 per 100,000 population

Supression of secessionists alarms human rights agencies. Militias could face war crimes charges over East Timor.

EDUCATION
▷ School leaving age: 15

85%

2.3m students

Children in many of Indonesia's rural areas are still deprived of secondary school education.

THE EDUCATION SYSTEM

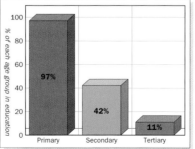

% of each age group in education

Primary 97%
Secondary 42%
Tertiary 11%

Primary education is compulsory. Secondary schooling is expanding, but is still limited in rural areas.

HEALTH
▷ Welfare state health benefits

1 per 6,423 people

Lower respiratory and diarrheal diseases

Significant improvements in health care have raised life expectancy.

Hospitals are relatively few; about half are privately administered. However, the extensive network of clinics, down to village level, means that access to health care is reasonable. As a result, health indicators have improved significantly. The death rate declined from 20 per 1,000 in 1965 to nine per 1,000 in 1990, helping to increase average life expectancy while infant mortality more than halved. East Timorese driven from their homes in the September 1999 violence faced problems of disease and hunger.

SPENDING
▷ GDP/cap. no increase

CONSUMPTION AND SPENDING

13 per 1,000 population

25 per 1,000 population

Defense 2.2%

Education 1.4%

Health 0.7%

| 0 | 5 | 10 | 15 | 20 | 25 |

Defense, Health, Education spending as % of GDP

Despite its oil wealth, rapid industrialization and improvements in agricultural productivity of the past 30 years, Indonesia is still grouped among the low-income economies by the World Bank. Health and education have improved, but many Indonesians live in relative poverty, and those on the peripheral islands, notably Irian Jaya, northern Sumatra and East Timor, live in real poverty. The concentration of wealth in the hands of close associates and relatives of former President Suharto, dominates the political agenda and is currently the subject of an official investigation.

WORLD RANKING

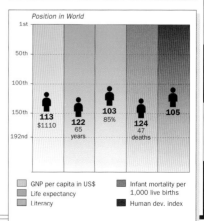

Position in World

1st
50th
100th
150th
192nd

113 $1110
122 65 years
103 85%
124 47 deaths
105

- GNP per capita in US$
- Life expectancy
- Literacy
- Infant mortality per 1,000 live births
- Human dev. index

I

IRAN

OFFICIAL NAME: Islamic Republic of Iran **CAPITAL:** Tehran
POPULATION: 73.1 million **CURRENCY:** Iranian rial **OFFICIAL LANGUAGE:** Farsi

| 1502 | 1990 | Feb 11 | IR | +3.5 | +98 | .ir |

IRAN IS SURROUNDED by powerful neighbors, with republics of the former Soviet Union to the north, Afghanistan and Pakistan to the east, and Iraq and Turkey to the west. The south faces the Persian Gulf and the Gulf of Oman. Since 1979, when a revolution led by Ayatollah Khomeini deposed the Shah, Iran has become the world's largest theocracy and the leading center for militant Shi'a Islam. Iran's active support for Islamic fundamentalist movements has led to strained relations with Central Asian, Middle Eastern and North African nations, as well as the USA and western Europe.

The Reshteh-ye Kuhhā-ye Alborz (Elburz Mountains). Their Caspian Sea slopes are rainy and forested; the southern slopes are dry.

CLIMATE

▷ Mountain/cold desert

WEATHER CHART

■ Average daily temperature   Rainfall ▬

The area bordering the Caspian Sea is Iran's most temperate region. Most of the country has a desert climate.

TRANSPORTATION

▷ Drive on right

Mehrabad International, Tehran
1.16m passengers

417 ships
3,553,000 grt

THE TRANSPORTATION NETWORK

| 76,200 km (47,300 miles) | 470 km (290 miles) |
| 5,995 km (3,725 miles) | 130 km (81 miles) |

Adequate roads link main towns, but rural areas are less well served. Most freight travels by rail. A ferry runs from Bandar-e Abbas to the UAE.

TOURISM

▷ Visitors : population 1:126

580,000 visitors

Up 33% 1995–1997

MAIN TOURIST ARRIVALS

| Russia 34% |
| Pakistan 23% |
| Afghanistan 8% |
| Bahrain 6% |
| Germany 3% |
| Other 26% |

% of total arrivals

Iran's historical heritage, mosques and bazaars formerly attracted sizable numbers of tourists. This flow was cut off by the 1979 revolution, which deterred visitors, especially from the West. In the 1990s, however, there has been a rise in the number of business people visiting Iran. Procedures at Tehran's Mehrabad airport have been simplified and the capital's hotels refurbished. In late 1998 President Khatami's more liberal regime welcomed a delegation of US tourists, despite opposition from conservative groups.

PEOPLE

▷ Pop. density low

Farsi (Persian), Azerbaijani, Gilaki, Mazanderani, Kurdish, Baluchi, Arabic, Turkmen

45/km² (116/mi²)

THE URBAN/RURAL POPULATION SPLIT

59%   41%

RELIGIOUS PERSUASION

Other 1%   Sunni Muslim 4%
Shi'a Muslim 95%

ETHNIC MAKEUP

Arab 2%   Kurd 8%
Other 10%
Persian 50%
Lur and Bakhtiari 10%
Azeri 20%

The population comprises several ethnic groups. The people of the north and center – about half of all Iranians – speak Farsi (Persian), while about a quarter speak related languages, including Kurdish in the west and Baluchi in the southeast. Another quarter of the population speaks Turkic languages, primarily the Azeris in the northwest and the Turkmen in the northeast. Smaller groups, such as the Circassians and Georgians, are found in the northern provinces.

Until the 16th century, much of Iran followed the Sunni interpretation of Islam, but since then the Shi'a sect has been dominant. Religious minorities, accounting for just 1% of the population, include followers of the Bahai faith, who suffer discrimination, Zoroastrians, Christians and Jews. The regime has a remarkably liberal attitude to refugees of the Muslim faith. Nearly three million Afghan refugees were received during the height of the Afghan civil war, although many have since been repatriated. In Khorosan province in the east, refugees account for nearly a quarter of the population; near the Turkish border they constitute half the total population. Many are young, resulting in intense competition with Iranians for jobs and consequent ethnic tensions.

One of the main consequences of the 1979 Islamic revolution was to reverse the policy of female emancipation, introduced during the Shah's rule. The revolution restricted the public role of women and enforced a strict dress code, obliging women to wear the ankle-length *hijab* and keep their heads covered with a scarf. More liberal attitudes have appeared gradually, notably the appointment in 1995 of the first woman minister since the 1979 revolution.

POPULATION AGE BREAKDOWN

Female		Age	Male	
	0.2%	81–100	0.2%	
	2.5%	61–80	3%	
	5.9%	41–60	6.2%	
	14.4%	21–40	14.6%	
26%		0–20		26.9%

% of population by age group

POLITICS
▷ No Multiparty elections

 1996/2000

President Mohammad Khatami

AT THE LAST ELECTION
Consultative Council (Majlis) 270 members

There are no officially recognized political parties.

Iran is a theocracy. An uneasy relationship exists between the mullahs (their leader exercises supreme authority, in theory) and the secular authorities, headed by an elected president.

MAIN POLITICAL ISSUE
Mosque versus secular state
The division of power between the mullahs and the secular state remains ill-defined. This has resulted in a power struggle between the conservative clergy and reformist politicians. In 1996 the right-wing Society for Combatant Clergy lost its

Ayatollah Khamenei, who became spiritual leader after the death of Ayatollah Khomeini.

Mohammad Khatami, reformist president, in office since 1997.

overall majority in parliament, when the newly formed and more liberal Servants of Iran's Construction made substantial electoral gains. The reformist faction was strengthened further in 1997 by the election as president of Mohammad Khatami.

Khatami is committed to modernizing the economy. However, he is opposed by the mullahs, for whom people's adherence to religious values is more important than their material welfare. Student protests demanding more liberal reforms rocked Iran in mid-1999.

PROFILE
Iran's religious revolution was fueled by popular outrage at the corruption, repression, and inequalities of the Shah's regime. Successive Iranian governments have since maintained that the clergy have a religious duty to establish a just social system. The legislature, the executive, and the judiciary may thus, in theory, be overruled by the religious leadership. Rafsanjani's moderate policies were questioned by radical clergymen advocating "permanent revolution." However, the mullahs' failure to address Iran's economic problems have eroded their political standing. Reformists were encouraged by the election of Khatami in 1997, but the clergy remains powerful. A campaign against the reformist mayor of Tehran, Gholamhossein Karbaschi, who was convicted of corruption and jailed in May 1999, sparked off huge student demonstrations.

WORLD AFFAIRS
▷ Joined UN in 1945

ECO   G24   NAM   OIC   OPEC

Following the 1979 revolution, Iran assumed international significance as the voice of militant Shi'a Islam. This was exemplified by the 1989 Salman Rushdie affair, in which Khomeini issued a *fatwa* (edict) (lifted only in 1998) against the novelist, calling for his death for blasphemy. Iran is also accused of backing terrorist activity by Muslim extremists and fostering unrest among Shi'as in other Islamic states. In 1995 the USA took action by imposing sanctions against Iran, reinforcing this in mid-1996 with penalties on foreign companies investing in Iran's energy sector. Under President Khatami, Iran has tried to convey a less confrontational image in international affairs. In 1999 Khatami visited Italy, and became the first Iranian leader since 1979 to be officially welcomed by a Western government. Iran's main security preoccupation is Iraq, which allows *mujahideen* guerrillas to mount attacks on Iran from its territory.

IRAN

Total Land Area : 1 636 000 sq. km
(631 660 sq. miles)

POPULATION
- ▣ over 1 000 000
- ◉ over 500 000
- ◎ over 100 000
- ○ over 50 000

LAND HEIGHT
- 3000m/9843ft
- 2000m/6562ft
- 1000m/3281ft
- 500m/1640ft
- 200m/656ft
- Sea Level

0   200 km

0   200 miles

CHRONOLOGY

Iran (Persia) was ruled by the shahs as an absolute monarchy until 1906, when the first constitution was approved. The Pahlavis took power in 1925 and changed the country's name to Iran in 1935.

- ❏ **1957** SAVAK, Shah's secret police, established to control opposition.
- ❏ **1964** Ayatollah Khomeini exiled to Iraq for criticizing secular state.
- ❏ **1971** Shah celebrates 2,500th anniversary of Persian monarchy.
- ❏ **1975** Agreement with Iraq over Shatt al Arab waterway.
- ❏ **1977** Khomeini's son dies. Anti-Shah demonstrations during mourning.
- ❏ **1978** Riots and strikes. Khomeini settles in Paris.
- ❏ **1979** Shah goes into exile. Ayatollah Khomeini returns and declares an Islamic republic. Students seize 63 hostages at US Embassy in Tehran.
- ❏ **1980** Shah dies in exile. Start of eight-year Iran–Iraq war. Iraq invades, annulling 1975 Shatt al Arab waterway agreement.
- ❏ **1981** US hostages released. Hojatoleslam Ali Khamenei elected president.
- ❏ **1985** Khamenei reelected.
- ❏ **1987** Around 275 Iranian pilgrims killed in riots in Mecca.
- ❏ **1988** USS *Vincennes* shoots down Iranian airliner; 290 killed. Iran–Iraq war ends with UN-arranged cease-fire.
- ❏ **1989** Khomeini issues *fatwa* condemning Salman Rushdie to death for blasphemy in his novel *The Satanic Verses*. Khomeini dies. President Ali Khamenei appointed Supreme Religious Leader. Hashemi Rafsanjani elected president.
- ❏ **1990** Earthquake in northern Iran kills 45,000 people.
- ❏ **1992** *Majlis* elections.
- ❏ **1993** Rafsanjani reelected president.
- ❏ **1995** Imposition of US sanctions.
- ❏ **1996** *Majlis* elections. Society for Combatant Clergy loses ground to the more liberal Servants of Iran's Construction. US penalties for foreign firms investing in Iran's energy sector.
- ❏ **1997** An earthquake south of Mashhad kills 1,500 people. Mohammad Khatami elected president.
- ❏ **1998** Khatami government dissociates itself from *fatwa* against Salman Rushdie.
- ❏ **1999** First nationwide local elections since 1979. President Khatami visits Italy, becoming first Iranian leader to be welcomed by a Western government since 1979.

AID

 ▷ Recipient

💲 $196m (receipts)   ⬆ Up 15% 1996–1997

As an oil exporter, Iran does not qualify for much aid. Hardliners also oppose Western aid. However, Iran receives some UN aid for its millions of mainly Afghan and Iraqi refugees. Concern that Iran supports Muslim terrorism has recently affected aid programs. In 1994, the World Bank suspended loans. US sanctions imposed in 1995 ended bilateral assistance, although European oil companies announced new deals in 1998 and 1999.

DEFENSE

▷ Compulsory military service

💲 $4.7bn   ⬆ Up 38% in 1997

Iran's growing military capability threatens regional peace.

With more than 400,000 men under arms, including the Revolutionary Guard Corps (*Pasdaran*), Iran is regarded by neighboring states as a serious military threat. The testing of medium-range cruise and ballistic missiles in 1998 has increased concern. The *Pasdaran* form one-third of personnel and are also responsible for the enforcement of moral standards set by the mullahs. They were used in mass frontal assaults in the Iran–Iraq war. Clashes with Iraq and the USA have weakened the navy. Two years' military service is compulsory.

IRANIAN ARMED FORCES

🛡	1,400 main battle tanks (T–54/55, Ch T–59, T–62, T–72, *Chieftain* Mk3/5)	350,000 personnel
⚓	3 submarines, 3 frigates, 65 patrol boats	20,600 personnel
✈	307 combat aircraft (60 F–4D/E, 60 F–5E/F, 60 F–14, 30 MiG–29)	45,000 personnel
	None	

ECONOMICS

 ▷ Inflation 23.6% p.a. (1985–1996)

📊 $109bn   💲 3,000 Iranian rials

SCORE CARD

- ❏ WORLD GNP RANKING..........................34th
- ❏ GNP PER CAPITA $1,780
- ❏ BALANCE OF PAYMENTS......................$5.2bn
- ❏ INFLATION 17.2%
- ❏ UNEMPLOYMENT.................................30%

EXPORTS

- Greece 5%
- South Africa 6%
- Italy 6%
- South Korea 6%
- Japan 13%
- Other 64%

IMPORTS

- Argentina 5%
- France 6%
- Italy 6%
- Japan 7%
- Germany 13%
- Other 63%

STRENGTHS

OPEC's second-biggest oil producer. Potential for related industries and increased production of traditional exports: carpets, pistachio nuts and caviar.

WEAKNESSES

Theocratic government restricts contact with West, and access to technology. High unemployment and inflation. Excessive foreign debts. Sharp decline in oil revenues following US sanctions in 1995 and 1996.

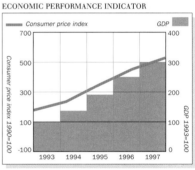

ECONOMIC PERFORMANCE INDICATOR

— Consumer price index   GDP ▨

(Consumer price index 1990=100; GDP 1993=100; years 1993 1994 1995 1996 1997)

PROFILE

Iran has few industries other than oil. The oil sector was hit by US legislation in mid-1996 which imposed penalties on foreign companies investing in Iran's energy sector.

IRAN : MAJOR BUSINESSES

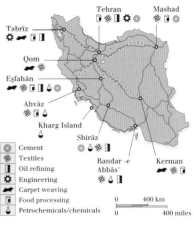

- 🌀 Cement
- Textiles
- Oil refining
- ⚙ Engineering
- Carpet weaving
- Food processing
- Petrochemicals/chemicals

(Cities: Tehran, Mashad, Tabrīz, Qom, Eşfahān, Ahvāz, Kharg Island, Shīrāz, Bandar-e Abbās', Kerman)

0   400 km
0   400 miles

RESOURCES

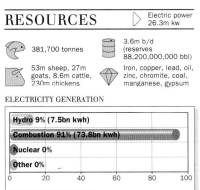

▷ Electric power 26.3m kw

381,700 tonnes

3.6m b/d (reserves 88,200,000,000 bbl)

53m sheep, 27m goats, 8.6m cattle, 230m chickens

Iron, copper, lead, oil, zinc, chromite, coal, manganese, gypsum

ELECTRICITY GENERATION

Hydro 9% (7.5bn kwh)

Combustion 91% (73.8bn kwh)

Nuclear 0%

Other 0%

% of total generation by type

Iran has substantial oil reserves. It also has metal, coal and salt deposits, but these are relatively undeveloped. The agricultural sector is an important part of Iran's economy. Principal crops are wheat, barley, rice, sugar beet, tobacco and pistachio nuts.

Iran was once an opium exporter, but its cultivation and use have since been banned. The vodka industry has also been closed down. Enough wool is produced to supply the carpet weaving industry. Iran has insufficient livestock to supply the domestic meat market and has to import large quantities. The Caspian Sea fisheries are controlled by the state, which sells caviar for export.

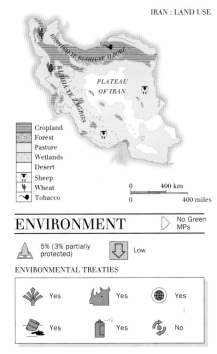

IRAN : LAND USE

- Cropland
- Forest
- Pasture
- Wetlands
- Desert
- Sheep
- Wheat
- Tobacco

PLATEAU OF IRAN

0   400 km
0   400 miles

ENVIRONMENT

▷ No Green MPs

5% (3% partially protected)

▽ Low

ENVIRONMENTAL TREATIES

Yes		Yes		Yes	
Yes		Yes		No	

War damage to southern Iran, especially at Bandar Khomeini, the tanker terminal at Kharg Island and the refinery at Abadan has caused significant environmental harm. Environmental issues are not of concern to the religious leadership.

MEDIA

▷ TV ownership medium

⊠ Daily newspaper circulation 24 per 1,000 people

PUBLISHING AND BROADCAST MEDIA

Five of the 32 daily newspapers are national. *Kayhan* and *Ettela'at*, controlled by the religious authorities, are the leaders

1 state-controlled service

1 state-controlled service

Press freedom under Khatami's regime has been expanded, despite opposition from the mullahs. Radio and TV are state-controlled. Satellite dishes are banned.

CRIME

▷ Death penalty used

Iran does not publish prison figures

Little change from year to year

CRIME RATES

Iran does not publish crime statistics. However, general crime rates are relatively low

Revolutionary guards enforce law and order. More than one hundred offences carry the death sentence. However, moves to extend the death penalty to economic crimes was rejected by the *Majlis* in 1995. Executions, of both men and women, are common for political "crimes." Iran is accused by Western governments of international terrorism by Muslim extremists abroad.

EDUCATION

▷ School leaving age: 11

 73%

579,070 students

Students support President Khatami's reformist agenda.

THE EDUCATION SYSTEM

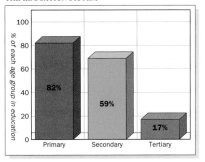

% of each age group in education

- Primary: 82%
- Secondary: 59%
- Tertiary: 17%

Over half the population is literate. Education in state primary schools and universities is free, but a small fee is charged for secondary education. Most schools are single-sex. Students are strong supporters of President Khatami's liberal regime.

HEALTH

▷ Welfare state health benefits

1 per 3,333 people

Heart and respiratory diseases, injuries, neonatal deaths

The high birth rate has forced the introduction of birth control programs.

Although an adequate system of primary health care exists in the cities, conditions in rural areas are basic. The major problem facing the nation's health is the fast-growing population. Under Khomeini, producing children became a political and religious duty. Sterilization and contraception programs are now officially promoted. Growing drug addiction has resulted in rehabilitation programs and anti-drug propaganda.

SPENDING

▷ GDP/cap. no increase

CONSUMPTION AND SPENDING

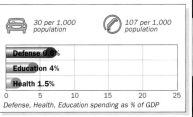

30 per 1,000 population

107 per 1,000 population

- Defense 6.6%
- Education 4%
- Health 1.5%

Defense, Health, Education spending as % of GDP

Since the Khomeini revolution in 1979, living standards have declined markedly. A shortage of foreign exchange has stifled the import of consumer goods. Rationing, brought in during the war with Iraq, is still partly in force, and smuggling from the Arab Gulf states is rife.

Unemployment is high, with few Iranians able to gain access to modern technology such as telephones. Official figures for income per capita do not relate to conditions on the ground. In reality, oil wealth fails to reach the economically deprived.

Private businesses have gradually emerged with the launch in 1994 of the country's first private savings and loans associations.

WORLD RANKING

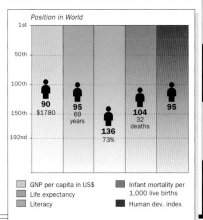

Position in World

- 1st
- 50th
- 100th
- 150th
- 192nd

- 90 $1780
- 95 69 years
- 136 73%
- 104 32 deaths
- 95

- ☐ GNP per capita in US$
- ☐ Life expectancy
- ☐ Literacy
- ☐ Infant mortality per 1,000 live births
- ■ Human dev. index

I

309

IRAQ

OFFICIAL NAME: Republic of Iraq   **CAPITAL:** Baghdad   **POPULATION:** 21.8 million
CURRENCY: Iraqi dinar   **OFFICIAL LANGUAGE:** Arabic

| 1932 | 1991 | July 7 | IRQ | +3 | +964 | .iq |

OIL-RICH IRAQ, divided by the Euphrates and Tigris rivers, shares borders with Iran, Turkey, Syria, Jordan, Saudi Arabia, and Kuwait. The Euphrates valley is fertile, but most of the country is desert or mountains. Iraq was the site of the ancient civilization of Babylon. Today, it encompasses Shi'a Muslim holy shrines. Since the removal of the monarchy in 1958, Iraq has experienced domestic political turmoil and defeat in the 1991 Gulf War. The current regime retains power through repression.

Golden Mosque at Sāmarrā' on the Tigris. Among the extensive remains of its ancient city are those of the Great Mosque built in 847CE.

CLIMATE   ▷ Hot desert/steppe

WEATHER CHART

The weather is dry and rainfall is low and unreliable, except in the northeast. Iraq experiences a wide range of temperatures. The south has a desert climate, with hot, dry summers and mild winters. The summers are also dry in the north, but in mountainous Iranian and Turkish border regions winters can be harsh, with frost and heavy falls of snow. Sudden hot spells are a unique feature of winter in the center and north of the country.

TRANSPORTATION   ▷ Drive on right

Saddam International, Baghdad   102 ships 572,000 grt

THE TRANSPORTATION NETWORK

| 47,400 km (29,500 miles) | 1,264 km (785 miles) |
| 2,799 km (1,739 miles) | 130 km (81 miles) |

Transportation is adequate. The land route to the Gulf states via Kuwait is closed. Ferry services to the UAE operate from Umm Qasr, near Basra.

TOURISM   ▷ Visitors : population 1:63

346,000 visitors   Up 2% 1995–1997

MAIN TOURIST ARRIVALS

Iraq does not publish tourism figures by country of origin

% of total arrivals

The Shi'a holy shrines in the south attract thousands of pilgrims each year. Iraq is effectively closed to Western tourists, who once visited its many archaeological sites. In particular, the ruins of Babylon, and its fabled hanging gardens, were once a major tourist attraction. Westerners also used to journey to the marshlands close to the Shaṭṭ al 'Arab waterway. However, this area of ecological importance is now being drained as part of a campaign to suppress the Marsh Arabs.

IRAQ

Total Land Area : 437 370 sq. km
(168 869 sq. miles)

POPULATION

- over 1 000 000
- over 500 000
- over 100 000
- over 50 000
- over 10 000

LAND HEIGHT

- 3000m/9843ft
- 2000m/6562ft
- 1000m/3281ft
- 500m/1640ft
- 200m/656ft
- Sea Level

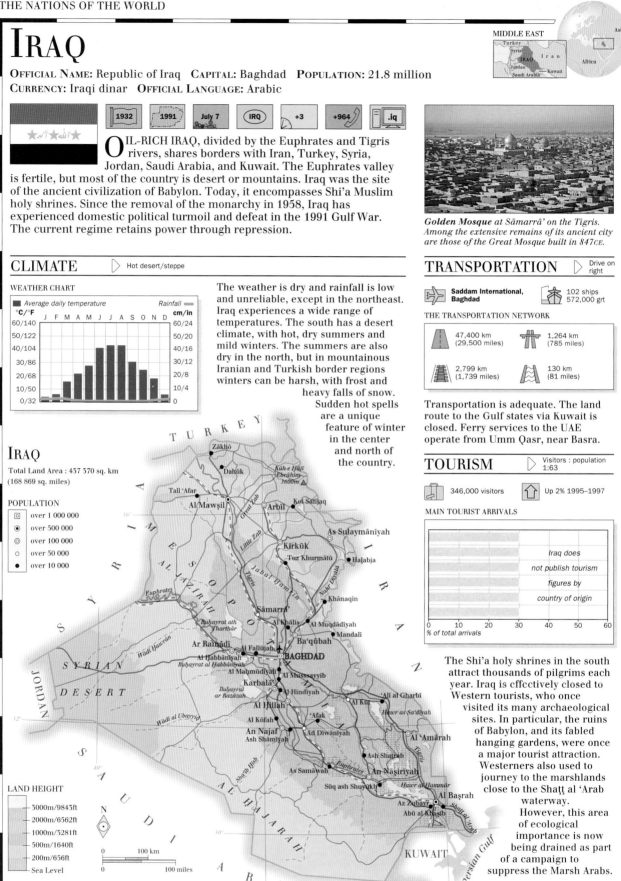

PEOPLE   ▷ Pop. density medium

Arabic, Kurdish, Armenian, Assyrian   50/km² (129/mi²)

THE URBAN/RURAL POPULATION SPLIT

75%   **25%**

RELIGIOUS PERSUASION

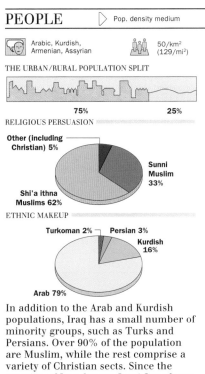

Other (including Christian) 5%

Sunni Muslim 33%

Shi'a ithna Muslims 62%

ETHNIC MAKEUP

Turkoman 2%   Persian 3%

Kurdish 16%

Arab 79%

In addition to the Arab and Kurdish populations, Iraq has a small number of minority groups, such as Turks and Persians. Over 90% of the population are Muslim, while the rest comprise a variety of Christian sects. Since the creation of Israel, most Iraqi Jews have emigrated. The Arab Muslims are divided into Sunni and Shi'a sects. The Shi'a form the largest single religious group; however, Shi'a divines do not have as intimate a connection with the people as they do in Iran and their influence on government is limited.

Since the mid-1970s, many Iraqis have moved, or been forced to move, to the cities, where some 75% of the population now live.

In the marshes of the extreme south, communities of Marsh Arabs survive. In the wake of the 1991 Gulf War, some of these attempted a rebellion against the state, which is now draining the marshes in order to destroy both the people and their culture.

POPULATION AGE BREAKDOWN

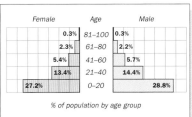

Female	Age	Male
0.3%	81–100	0.3%
2.3%	61–80	2.2%
5.4%	41–60	5.7%
13.4%	21–40	14.4%
27.2%	0–20	28.8%

% of population by age group

WORLD AFFAIRS   ▷ Joined UN in 1945

AL   NAM   OAPEC   OIC   OPEC

In 1990, Saddam Hussein embarked on a grand plan in a bid to show himself to be the undisputed leader of the Arab world: the invasion of Kuwait . His plan was frustrated by the formation of a US-led military coalition, including major Arab states, which inflicted a crushing defeat on Iraq in the Gulf War of 1991.

Iraq was ousted from Kuwait, subjected to heavy sanctions by the UN Security Council, and economically and diplomatically isolated. No major Western state has yet restored diplomatic relations, although economic links have resumed with some countries. Among Arab states, Sudan alone is a close ally. The regime remains obstructive about UN weapons inspection and has demanded the lifting of sanctions. A series of tense standoffs, as recently as late 1998, have led to punitive air strikes by US and UK forces.

Relations with Iran are tense. Iranian opposition groups continue to use Iraq as a base for their operations.

I

POLITICS   ▷ No multiparty elections

1996/2000   President Saddam Hussein

AT THE LAST ELECTION

National Assembly 250 seats

The National Assembly is composed of Ba'athists and their allies.

President Saddam Hussein has dominated Iraqi politics since overthrowing his predecessor in 1979. In theory, the highest state authority rests with the nine-member Revolutionary Command Council, of which Saddam Hussein is the chairman.

MAIN POLITICAL ISSUES
Sanctions
Iraq's invasion of Kuwait in 1990 and its defeat by a US-led international coalition in the 1991 Gulf War, resulted in the imposition of UN sanctions. These remain in force pending Iraq's full compliance with UN Gulf War resolutions. In 1994, Iraq recognized Kuwait but failed to secure an end to sanctions because of its repeated defiance of UN weapons inspection programs. Campaigns for the lifting of sanctions focus on the impact they have on innocent civilians, particularly children. Since 1996 Iraq has been authorized to sell limited quantities of oil under UN supervision for the purchase of humanitarian supplies. Despite the sanctions regime, Iraq pursues a program of reconstruction.

Threats to the regime
There is little unity among opposition groups. The most significant are the Tehran-based Supreme Council for the Islamic Revolution in Iraq and the Iraqi National Congress operating from London. The murder in 1996 of one of Saddam Hussein's senior ministers, a close relative who had defected to Jordan, was a blow to the opposition as well as a further demonstration of the regime's ruthlessness.

The separatist Kurdish minority in the north is divided by factional disputes which triggered a civil war and the intervention of Iraqi troops in 1996. Iraq's enemies are reluctant to endorse Kurdish plans for Iraq's territorial dismemberment.

PROFILE
Iraq's autocratic regime is dominated by President Saddam Hussein and trusted members of his Takriti tribe. The defection to Jordan in 1995 of Saddam Hussein's relative, senior government minister General Hussein Kamil, suggested dissent within the ruling circle. However, Kamil's assassination in 1996 effectively neutralized a potential threat.

Tarek Aziz, *deputy prime minister and mediator between Iraq and the UN.*

Saddam Hussein, *Iraq's dictatorial leader since he seized power in 1979.*

Saddam Hussein has promoted a massive personality cult. In a typical political broadcast, his name is mentioned 30 to 50 times an hour, and his public movements bring streets to a standstill. The regime relies on terror and a ruthless intelligence network. In 1996 it tightened its grip by again winning the country's first legislative elections since 1989.

AID   ▷ Recipient

$281m (receipts)   Down 27% 1996–1997

Before its invasion of Kuwait, Iraq received economic aid from neighboring Gulf states. Under UN sanctions, Iraq is entitled only to humanitarian aid, but there is mounting evidence of covert trade, especially through Jordan and Turkey.

CHRONOLOGY

Iraq became independent in 1932. In 1958, the Hashemite dynasty was overthrown when King Faisal died in a coup led by the military under Brigadier Kassem. He was initially supported by the Iraqi Ba'ath Party.

- ❏ **1961** Start of Kurdish rebellion in northern Iraq. Iraq claims sovereignty over Kuwait on the eve of Kuwait's indepndence.
- ❏ **1963** Kassem overthrown. Colonel Abd as-Salem Mohammad Aref takes power. Kuwait's sovereignty recognized.
- ❏ **1964** Ayatollah Khomeini, future leader of Iran, takes refuge at Najaf in Iraq.
- ❏ **1966** Aref is succeeded by his brother, Abd ar-Rahman.
- ❏ **1968** Ba'athists under Ahmad Hassan Al-Bakr take power.
- ❏ **1970** Revolutionary Command Council agrees manifesto on Kurdish autonomy.
- ❏ **1972** Nationalization of Western-controlled Iraq Petroleum Company.
- ❏ **1978** Iraq and Syria form economic and political union.
- ❏ **1979** Saddam Hussein replaces President al-Bakr.
- ❏ **1980** Outbreak of Iraq-Iran war.
- ❏ **1982** Shi'a leader Mohammed Baqir al-Hakim, exiled in Tehran, forms Supreme Council of the Islamic Revolution in Iraq.
- ❏ **1988** Iraq and Iran agree cease-fire. Iraqi chemical weapons attack on Kurdish village of Halabja.
- ❏ **1990** British journalist Farzad Bazoft hanged for spying. Iraq and Iran restore diplomatic relations. Iraq invades Kuwait. UN imposes trade sanctions.
- ❏ **1991** Gulf War. US-led military coalition defeats Iraq and liberates Kuwait. Iraqi regime suppresses Shi'a rebellion.
- ❏ **1992** Western powers proclaim air exclusion zone over southern Iraq.
- ❏ **1993** Iraqi attempts to recover military equipment from Kuwait provoke Western air attacks.
- ❏ **1994** Iraq recognizes Kuwaiti sovereignty.
- ❏ **1995** Government minister Gen. Hussein Kamil defects to Jordan, and is murdered on his return to Iraq in January 1996.
- ❏ **1996** First legislative elections since 1989 are won by ruling Ba'ath Party. UN supervises limited sales of Iraq oil to purchase humanitarian supplies.
- ❏ **1996** Outbreak of Kurdish civil war.
- ❏ **1998–1999** UN weapons inspection teams refused reentry into Iraq; USA and UK mount punitive air strikes.

DEFENSE   ▷ Compulsory military service

💲 $1.25bn   ⬇ Down 2% in 1997

UN inspection programs have weakened Iraq's military capability.

IRAQI ARMED FORCES

🚜	2,700 main battle tanks (T–54/55, Ch T–59/69, T–62/72, M–77)	375,000 personnel
⚓	2 frigates and 6 patrol boats	2,000 personnel
✈	310 combat aircraft (est) (MiG–21/23/25, Mirage F1EQ)	17,000 personnel
🚀	None	

Iraq's military defeat by the US-led coalition in 1991 led to the destruction of much of Iraq's arsenal. Since then UN Security Council resolutions have required the elimination of the bulk of Iraq's weapons of mass destruction, and inspection teams have sought to enforce this. There is a shortage of high-tech weaponry that could match the kind acquired by Kuwait and Saudi Arabia from US and other Western suppliers since the Gulf War. The army is large, but poorly trained and equipped. The military relies on tanks and aircraft from the former Soviet Union and China. The air force has some French *Mirage* fighters and US helicopters.

ECONOMICS   ▷ Not available

📊 $20bn   💱 0.31 Iraqi dinars

SCORE CARD

❏ WORLD GNP RANKING	65th
❏ GNP PER CAPITA	$950
❏ BALANCE OF PAYMENTS	Not available
❏ INFLATION	45%
❏ UNEMPLOYMENT	Not available

ECONOMIC PERFORMANCE INDICATOR

■ Consumer price index   GDP ▨

No additional information available

(chart: Consumer price index 1990=100, y-axis 60–220; GDP 1990=100, y-axis -50–550; x-axis years 1990 1991 1992 1993 1994)

EXPORTS

Netherlands 7%
Italy 8%
USA 12%
Other 40%
France 16%
Spain 17%

IMPORTS

France 7%
China 8%
Other 33%
Thailand 9%
USA 12%
Australia 31%

STRENGTHS
Second-largest crude oil and natural gas reserves in OPEC. Large labor force.

WEAKNESSES
Severe restrictions on selling oil on the international market; UN sanctions halved Iraq's gross national product. Once-thriving agricultural sector devastated by war.

PROFILE
Before 1990, Iraq was the world's third-largest oil supplier. Under sanctions, oil was produced only for domestic consumption. Limited oil exports under strict UN supervision were resumed for the first time in December 1996.

The denial of Western assistance and the severance of trade following the 1991 Gulf War has stifled Iraq's economy, although the recent resumption of informal economic links with France and Russia may lead to some improvement. Iraq was formerly rich in agriculture, but this was badly affected by the war. The manufacturing industry remains at a standstill, while the state seeks to avert economic catastrophe. The introduction of draconian penalties, including the death sentence, have failed to curb the black market or halt the sharp depreciation in the value of the dinar.

IRAQ : MAJOR BUSINESSES

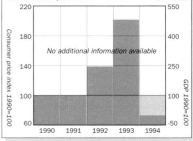

Al Mawşil
Arbil
Kirkūk
Baiji
Tuz Khurmātū
Karbalā'
Khānaqīn
Baghdad
Al Kūfah
Al Başrah
An Nāşirīyah
Az Zubayr

🌀 Cement
✳ Textiles
🧂 Salt mining
🛢 Oil refining
⚒ Iron & steel
🍲 Food processing
⚗ Petrochemicals/fertilizers

0   200 km
0   200 miles

RESURCES

▷ Electric power 9.5m kw

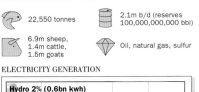

22,550 tonnes

6.9m sheep,
1.4m cattle,
1.5m goats

2.1m b/d (reserves
100,000,000,000 bbl)

Oil, natural gas, sulfur

ELECTRICITY GENERATION

Hydro 2% (0.6bn kwh)	
Combustion 98% (28,4bn kwh)	
Nuclear 0%	
Other 0%	

0   20   40   60   80   100

% of total generation by type

Iraq has huge reserves of oil and gas. The oil industry is controlled by the Iraqi National Oil Company. In 1990,

proven reserves were conservatively estimated at 100,000 million barrels – sufficient for 97 years' production at 1989 levels of 4.5 million b/d.

Total gas reserves, three quarters of which are associated with oil, are estimated at around 2.69 billion cubic meters. Most electricity is generated from oil and gas, although hydro-electric power makes a small contribution.

Before the invasion of Kuwait and subsequent war, Iraq was supplying 80% of the world's trade in dates. Production is now sharply down. Foods are now produced simply for domestic consumption. Iraq has, however, achieved a degree of self-sufficiency in crops such as wheat, rice and sugar.

IRAQ : LAND USE

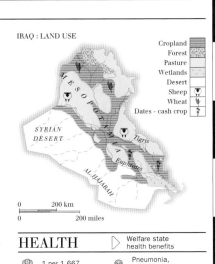

Cropland	
Forest	
Pasture	
Wetlands	
Desert	
Sheep	
Wheat	
Dates - cash crop	

0   200 km
0   200 miles

ENVIRONMENT

▷ No Green MPs

None

Medium

ENVIRONMENTAL TREATIES

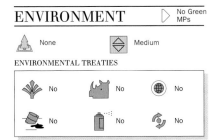

No   No   No

No   No   No

Wars with Iran and with the US-led alliance over the Kuwait occupation led to massive environmental damage. Hundreds of thousands of land mines remain in the Kuwait border regions, posing lethal hazards to farmers, livestock and wild animals. The north has been affected by chemical weapons, used by the regime against the Kurds. In the south, an entire wetland ecosystem is being destroyed by an engineering program aimed at draining the marshes for largely political reasons.

MEDIA

▷ TV ownership medium

 Daily newspaper circulation 20 per 1,000 people

PUBLISHING AND BROADCAST MEDIA

The 4 daily newspapers, including *Ath-Thawra* and the English *Baghdad Observer* are all state owned

1 state-controlled service

1 state-controlled service

The media are strictly controlled, although rebel groups circulate clandestine newspapers. There are very few daily newspapers, one of which, the *Baghdad Observer*, is in English. Saddam Hussein's son, Uday, controls the influential Arabic newspaper, *Babil*, which opposes UN Gulf War resolutions. All foreign journalists are vetted.

CRIME

▷ Death penalty used

Iraq does not publish prison figures

Up 28% in 1992

CRIME RATES

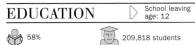

Murders
7   *per 100,000 population*

Rapes
Iraq does not publish rape statistics

Thefts
63   *per 100,000 population*

Iraq was formerly a law-abiding society, but economic collapse has sent crime rates soaring, especially in cities. Theft has been made a capital offense – encouraging thieves to murder in order to escape detection.

EDUCATION

▷ School leaving age: 12

58%

209,818 students

University scientists work with the regime on weapons research programs.

THE EDUCATION SYSTEM

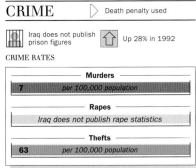

% of each age group in education

100
80
60   76%
40   42%
20   11%
0
Primary   Secondary   Tertiary

Primary and secondary education is free and universal, except in remote rural areas. There are six universities. Academics from Iraq authorized the organized plunder of antiquities and university equipment from Kuwait during the 1990 occupation.

HEALTH

▷ Welfare state health benefits

1 per 1,667 people

Pneumonia, influenza, cancers, heart diseases

UN sanctions have aggravated shortages of medical supplies and equipment.

Deaths among children and the elderly spiraled under the UN embargo. The increase in children born with birth defects since 1991 is attributed to the use of depleted uranium shells in the Gulf War.

SPENDING

▷ GDP/cap. increase

CONSUMPTION AND SPENDING

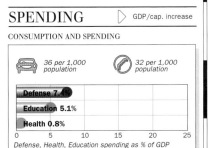

36 per 1,000 population

32 per 1,000 population

Defense 7.4%	
Education 5.1%	
Health 0.8%	

0   5   10   15   20   25
Defense, Health, Education spending as % of GDP

Many middle-class Iraqi citizens and traders have taken advantage of Iraq's open border policy with Jordan to relocate from Baghdad to Jordan's capital, Amman.

WORLD RANKING

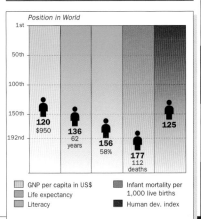

Position in World

1st
50th
100th
150th
192nd

120 $950
136 62 years
156 58%
177 112 deaths
125

GNP per capita in US$
Life expectancy
Literacy
Infant mortality per 1,000 live births
Human dev. index

IRELAND

OFFICIAL NAME: Republic of Ireland **CAPITAL:** Dublin **POPULATION:** 3.6 million
CURRENCY: Punt **OFFICIAL LANGUAGES:** Irish, English

| 1922 | 1922 | March 17 | IRL | 0 | +353 | .ie |

LYING IN THE ATLANTIC OCEAN, off the west coast of Britain, the Irish state occupies about 85% of the island of Ireland. Low coastal mountain ranges surround a central basin with lakes, hills and peat bogs. Centuries of struggle against English colonialism led to the formation of the Irish Free State in 1922 and full sovereignty in 1937. Hopes for the resolution of the Northern Ireland conflict center on the 1998 Good Friday accord, to which Ireland is a party.

CLIMATE ▷ Maritime

WEATHER CHART

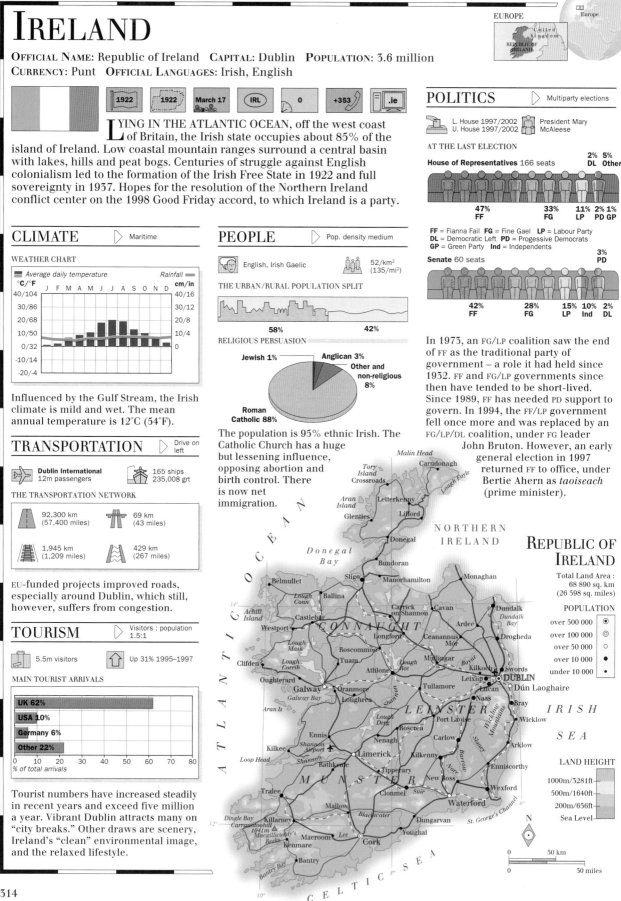

Influenced by the Gulf Stream, the Irish climate is mild and wet. The mean annual temperature is 12°C (54°F).

TRANSPORTATION ▷ Drive on left

Dublin International
12m passengers

165 ships
235,008 grt

THE TRANSPORTATION NETWORK

| 92,300 km (57,400 miles) | 69 km (43 miles) |
| 1,945 km (1,209 miles) | 429 km (267 miles) |

EU-funded projects improved roads, especially around Dublin, which still, however, suffers from congestion.

TOURISM ▷ Visitors : population 1.5:1

5.5m visitors

Up 31% 1995–1997

MAIN TOURIST ARRIVALS

| UK 62% |
| USA 10% |
| Germany 6% |
| Other 22% |

0 10 20 30 40 50 60 70 80
% of total arrivals

Tourist numbers have increased steadily in recent years and exceed five million a year. Vibrant Dublin attracts many on "city breaks." Other draws are scenery, Ireland's "clean" environmental image, and the relaxed lifestyle.

PEOPLE ▷ Pop. density medium

English, Irish Gaelic

52/km² (135/mi²)

THE URBAN/RURAL POPULATION SPLIT

58% 42%

RELIGIOUS PERSUASION

Jewish 1%
Anglican 3%
Other and non-religious 8%
Roman Catholic 88%

The population is 95% ethnic Irish. The Catholic Church has a huge but lessening influence, opposing abortion and birth control. There is now net immigration.

POLITICS ▷ Multiparty elections

L. House 1997/2002
U. House 1997/2002
President Mary McAleese

AT THE LAST ELECTION

House of Representatives 166 seats

47% FF 33% FG 11% LP 2% PD 1% GP 2% DL 5% Other

FF = Fianna Fail **FG** = Fine Gael **LP** = Labour Party
DL = Democratic Left **PD** = Progessive Democrats
GP = Green Party **Ind** = Independents

Senate 60 seats

42% FF 28% FG 15% LP 10% Ind 2% DL 3% PD

In 1973, an FG/LP coalition saw the end of FF as the traditional party of government – a role it had held since 1932. FF and FG/LP governments since then have tended to be short-lived. Since 1989, FF has needed PD support to govern. In 1994, the FF/LP government fell once more and was replaced by an FG/LP/DL coalition, under FG leader John Bruton. However, an early general election in 1997 returned FF to office, under Bertie Ahern as *taoiseach* (prime minister).

REPUBLIC OF IRELAND

Total Land Area :
68 890 sq. km
(26 598 sq. miles)

POPULATION

over 500 000
over 100 000
over 50 000
over 10 000
under 10 000

IRISH SEA

LAND HEIGHT

1000m/3281ft
500m/1640ft
200m/656ft
Sea Level

0   50 km
0   50 miles

WORLD AFFAIRS

▷ Joined UN in 1955

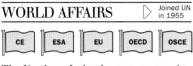

The Northern Ireland peace process is the main issue, prompting considerable contact with the UK as well as the USA.

AID

▷ Donor

$ $187m (donations)   ⇕ Not applicable

Africa is the main recipient of Irish aid, equivalent to 0.31% of GNP in 1997. It is also a big recipient of EU aid.

DEFENSE

▷ No compulsory military service

$ $767m   ⬆ Up 1% in 1997

Ireland is determined to maintain its neutrality, despite EU moves to establish a common European defense policy. It has observer status at the WEU.

ECONOMICS

▷ Inflation 2.6% p.a. (1985–1996)

$65.1bn   0.70–0.67 Punt

SCORE CARD

❏ WORLD GNP RANKING	44th
❏ GNP PER CAPITA	$17,790
❏ BALANCE OF PAYMENTS	$2bn
❏ INFLATION	1.4%
❏ UNEMPLOYMENT	11%

STRENGTHS

One of Europe's fastest-growing economies: real GDP growth was 9% a year in the latter half of the 1990s. Trade surplus. Low inflation. Efficient agriculture and food processing. Expanding high-tech sector; electronics account for 25% of exports. Large recipient of EU infrastructure aid. Highly educated workforce.

WEAKNESSES

Many key sectors owned by overseas multinationals. Danger of economy overheating. Unemployment high, if falling. Housing shortage. Rapid growth now straining infrastructure.

EXPORTS

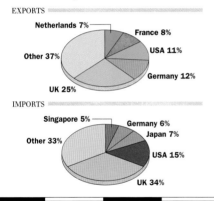

Netherlands 7%
France 8%
Other 37%
USA 11%
Germany 12%
UK 25%

IMPORTS

Singapore 5%
Germany 6%
Japan 7%
Other 33%
USA 15%
UK 34%

RESOURCES

▷ Electric power 4.4m kw

 412,722 tonnes

7.1m cattle, 5.6m sheep, 1.8m pigs

Not an oil producer; refines 56,000 b/d

Lead, zinc, natural gas, silver, coal

Oil has been found off the south coast. Studies suggest that this may be in commercially exploitable quantities.

ENVIRONMENT

▷ Green MPs

⚠ 1%   ⇕ Medium

Main environmental concerns are the overexploitation of peat bogs for fuel and the recent expansion of conifer plantations. While Ireland's levels of forest cover will increase in the next few years, most new planting is of conifers. In 1994 stringent new laws increased pollution controls. A small windpower industry is expanding.

MEDIA

▷ TV ownership high

Daily newspaper circulation 153 per 1,000 people

PUBLISHING AND BROADCAST MEDIA

There are 6 daily newspapers. These include the *Irish Times* and the *Irish Independent*

1 state-owned, 1 independent service

1 state-owned service

Censorship of coverage of Sinn Fein was lifted in 1994. There is wide access to British newspapers, TV and radio.

CRIME

▷ Death penalty not used

2,032 prisoners   ⬆ Up 6% from 1992–1996

Rural Ireland has the EU's lowest crime rate. Growing urban crime and narcotics are a problem in Dublin and Cork.

EDUCATION

▷ School leaving age: 15

99%   128,284 students

The Catholic Church runs many schools. Massively increased education spending has resulted in a skilled workforce.

Clew Bay in County Mayo, on the western coast of Ireland, viewed from the slopes of neighboring Croagh Patrick.

CHRONOLOGY

English colonization, which began in 1167, was reinforced after 1558 by oppressive anti-Catholic legislation and the settlement of Scottish Protestants in the north.

- ❏ **1845–1855** Famine. One million die, 1.5 million emigrate.
- ❏ **1919–1921** Anglo-Irish war after Sinn Fein proclaims independence.
- ❏ **1922** Irish Free State set up.
- ❏ **1949** Ireland becomes a republic.
- ❏ **1973** FG/LP win elections.
- ❏ **1990–1997** Mary Robinson elected Ireland's first woman president.
- ❏ **1992** Resignation of FF *taoiseach* Charles Haughey.
- ❏ **1995** Referendum favors divorce.
- ❏ **1998** Good Friday accord on Northern Ireland.

HEALTH

▷ Welfare state health benefits

1 per 500 people   Heart diseases, cancers, accidents

Free care is means tested. Others pay to visit their doctor and for prescriptions, and there is a modest charge for hospital care.

SPENDING

▷ GDP/cap. no increase

CONSUMPTION AND SPENDING

272 per 1,000 population   411 per 1,000 population

Defense 1%
Education 6.3%
Health 8%

0   5   10   15   20   25
Defense, Health, Education spending as % of GDP

Living standards for those people in full-time employment are rising steadily. Welfare for those who are unemployed is fairly low by OECD standards.

WORLD RANKING

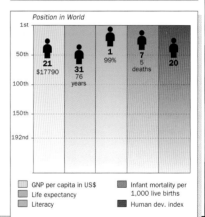

Position in World

1st
50th
21 $17790
31 76 years
1 99%
7 5 deaths
20
100th
150th
192nd

☐ GNP per capita in US$
☐ Life expectancy
☐ Literacy
☐ Infant mortality per 1,000 live births
☐ Human dev. index

I

ISRAEL

OFFICIAL NAME: State of Israel   **CAPITAL:** Jerusalem   **POPULATION:** 5.9 million
CURRENCY: New Israeli shekel   **OFFICIAL LANGUAGE:** Hebrew & Arabic

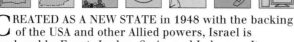

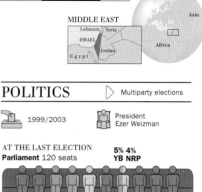

MIDDLE EAST

CREATED AS A NEW STATE in 1948 with the backing of the USA and other Allied powers, Israel is bordered by Egypt, Jordan, Syria, and Lebanon. Its topography varies from the Negev desert in the south to the Dead Sea, the lowest point on the Earth's surface. After wars with its Arab neighbors, Israel unilaterally extended its original boundaries to control the Golan Heights in the north, the West Bank and Gaza Strip (now the subject of a limited autonomy agreement with the Palestinians), and East Jerusalem.

CLIMATE
▷ Hot desert/Mediterranean

WEATHER CHART

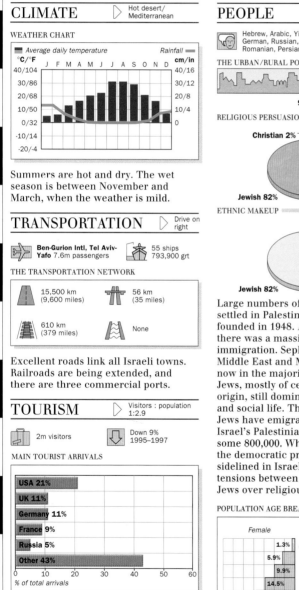

Summers are hot and dry. The wet season is between November and March, when the weather is mild.

TRANSPORTATION
▷ Drive on right

Ben-Gurion Intl, Tel Aviv-Yafo 7.6m passengers

55 ships
793,900 grt

THE TRANSPORTATION NETWORK

15,500 km (9,600 miles)	56 km (35 miles)
610 km (379 miles)	None

Excellent roads link all Israeli towns. Railroads are being extended, and there are three commercial ports.

TOURISM
▷ Visitors : population 1:2.9

2m visitors

Down 9% 1995–1997

MAIN TOURIST ARRIVALS

USA 21%
UK 11%
Germany 11%
France 9%
Russia 5%
Other 43%

% of total arrivals

Jerusalem is the main tourist destination. Terrorist violence has led to a recent fall in tourist numbers.

PEOPLE
▷ Pop. density high

Hebrew, Arabic, Yiddish, German, Russian, Polish, Romanian, Persian

290/km² (752/mi²)

THE URBAN/RURAL POPULATION SPLIT

91%   9%

RELIGIOUS PERSUASION

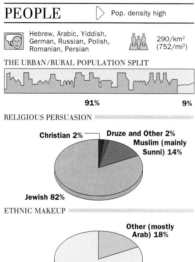

Christian 2%   Druze and Other 2%
Muslim (mainly Sunni) 14%
Jewish 82%

ETHNIC MAKEUP

Other (mostly Arab) 18%
Jewish 82%

Large numbers of Jewish immigrants settled in Palestine before Israel was founded in 1948. After World War II, there was a massive increase in immigration. Sephardic Jews from the Middle East and Mediterranean are now in the majority, but Ashkenazi Jews, mostly of central European origin, still dominate politics, business, and social life. Thousands of Russian Jews have emigrated since 1989. Israel's Palestinian population totals some 800,000. While many take part in the democratic process, they remain sidelined in Israeli life. There are tensions between Orthodox and secular Jews over religious observance.

POPULATION AGE BREAKDOWN

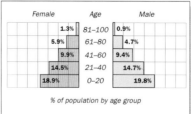

Female	Age	Male
1.3%	81–100	0.9%
5.9%	61–80	4.7%
9.9%	41–60	9.4%
14.5%	21–40	14.7%
18.9%	0–20	19.8%

% of population by age group

POLITICS
▷ Multiparty elections

1999/2003

President Ezer Weizman

AT THE LAST ELECTION
Parliament 120 seats

5% 4%
YB NRP

22% One Isr   16% Likud   14% Shas   8% M   31% Other

One Isr = One Israel (comprises Labor, Gesher and Meymad)
M = Meretz–Democratic Israel   YB = Yisrael Ba'aliya
NRP = National Religious Party
Other includes Hadash, United Torah Judaism, The Third Way, United Arab List, Moledet

Israel is a multiparty democracy. The prime minister and his cabinet wield executive power under the president.

MAIN POLITICAL ISSUES
Peace with the Palestinians
Whether Israel's security should be based on military and police strength, or on "land for peace" deals with Palestinians and neighboring countries, is a central issue. Jewish settlers adamantly oppose returning territory. The Likud government of 1996–1999 lost all momentum toward a final status agreement with Palestinians in the occupied West Bank. Hopes for resuming the peace process were raised when Labor returned to government.

Peace with Syria
Before the 1996 election Shimon Peres had been committed to concluding a peace deal with Syria. Likud opposed Israel's trading the Golan Heights for a Syrian deal. The Labor victory in 1999 put this back on the agenda.

PROFILE
Israeli governments are elected by proportional representation. Since 1996 the prime minister has been elected directly by voters during simultaneous elections to the *Knesset* (parliament). Labour leader Ehud Barak defeated Benjamin Netenyahu, head of the Likud-led government, in May 1999.

Yitzhak Rabin, the prime minister was assassinated in November 1995.

Yasser Arafat, the militant-turned-moderate leader of the PLO.

WORLD AFFAIRS

▷ Joined UN in 1949

EBRD IAEA IBRD WTO

Israel remains technically at war with all Arab states except Egypt and Jordan. Peace in the Middle East depends upon Israel reaching agreement with Syria on the Golan Heights. Israel maintains extremely close relations with the USA.

AID

▷ Recipient

$1.2bn (receipts)   Down 46% 1996–1997

Israel receives massive military and economic aid from the USA. Large ad hoc donations are also received from Jewish NGOs.

ISRAEL

Total Land Area : 20 350 sq. km (7849 sq. miles)

POPULATION

◎ over 100 000
○ over 50 000
● over 10 000

LAND HEIGHT

1000m/3281ft
500m/1640ft
200m/656ft
Sea Level
-200m/-656ft

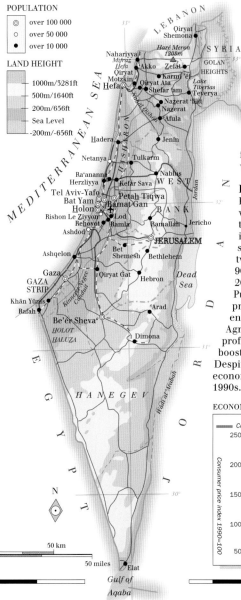

DEFENSE

▷ Compulsory military service

$11.1bn   Down 1% in 1997

The only Middle Eastern country known to possess a nuclear deterrent, Israel has a small regular defense force which can be boosted by nearly 600,000 reservists; it is one of relatively few countries with a substantial number of women in combat roles. The military is equipped with some of the latest US technology, and the firepower of the Israeli armed forces is vastly superior to that of its Arab neighbors.

ISRAELI ARMED FORCES

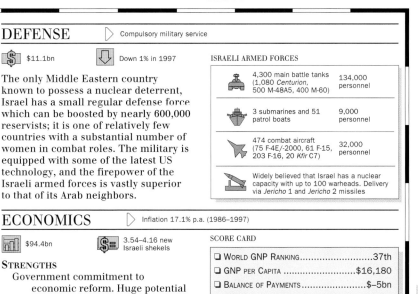

4,300 main battle tanks (1,080 *Centurion*, 500 M-48A5, 400 M-60)	134,000 personnel
3 submarines and 51 patrol boats	9,000 personnel
474 combat aircraft (75 F-4E/-2000, 61 F-15, 203 F-16, 20 *Kfir* C7)	32,000 personnel
Widely believed that Israel has a nuclear capacity with up to 100 warheads. Delivery via *Jericho* 1 and *Jericho* 2 missiles	

ECONOMICS

▷ Inflation 17.1% p.a. (1986–1997)

$94.4bn   3.54–4.16 new Israeli shekels

STRENGTHS

Government commitment to economic reform. Huge potential of agriculture, manufacturing and industrial products. Important banking sector. Prospect of peace in region. Sizable aid from US government and international Jewish organizations.

WEAKNESSES

High unemployment and inflation. Large defense budget. History of regional and internal instability inhibits foreign investment. Little trade with Arab neighbors.

PROFILE

Progress in the peace negotiations with Syria would be a huge boost to the economy. The government is seeking ways to reduce state spending, which accounts for two-thirds of GNP. The state owns 90% of all land and controls over 20% of all industries and services. Public companies are being privatized and there are plans to end restrictive labor practices. Agriculture is highly specialized and profitable. The state is now aiming to boost the service sector.

Despite a world recession, Israel's economy has continued to expand in the 1990s. The engine of this continued

SCORE CARD

- ❏ WORLD GNP RANKING.........................37th
- ❏ GNP PER CAPITA $16,180
- ❏ BALANCE OF PAYMENTS......................$–5bn
- ❏ INFLATION 9%
- ❏ UNEMPLOYMENT 8%

EXPORTS

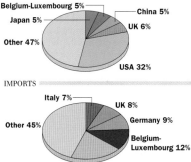

Belgium-Luxembourg 5%   China 5%
Japan 5%   UK 6%
Other 47%
USA 32%

IMPORTS

Italy 7%   UK 8%
Other 45%   Germany 9%
Belgium-Luxembourg 12%
USA 19%

growth has been the mass immigration of Jews, many highly educated, from the former Soviet Union. Although unemployment levels have risen as a result of immigration, new skills and contacts have also helped the Israeli economy toward sustained export-led growth.

ISRAEL : MAJOR BUSINESSES

Hefa
Nazerat
Tel Aviv-Yafo
Ashqelon
Jerusalem
Be'ér Sheva'

❋ Textiles
⚗ Chemicals
💻 Computers
🍴 Food processing
✏ Pharmaceuticals
📺 Consumer goods

0   50 km
0   50 miles

ECONOMIC PERFORMANCE INDICATOR

— Consumer price index   GDP

Consumer price index 1990=100
GDP 1993=100
1993 1994 1995 1996 1997

ISRAEL AND THE PALESTINIANS

THE DISPUTE BETWEEN ISRAEL and the Palestinians – the Arab population of the pre-1948 British mandated territory of Palestine – is central to the region's politics. An exodus of Palestinians followed the creation of the state of Israel, and 300,000 more left territories occupied by Israel in 1967. The Palestine Liberation Organization (PLO) claimed to be their "sole legitimate representative", but only until 1993 did the Palestinians begin getting self-rule in the West Bank and Gaza – inhabited by over 2,000,000 Palestinians and 300,000 Jewish settlers. A timetable in 1999 promised to complete this, and resolve "final status" issues, within a year. Palestinians expect this to entail full statehood.

BACKGROUND
In 1947 the UN approved a plan to partition Palestine, to create separate Jewish and Arab states. This was accepted by the Jewish side but not the Arabs. When the British Mandate ended in May 1948, Arab states invaded Palestine but were pushed back by Israeli forces well beyond the UN partition lines. The 1949 armistices left only East Jerusalem, the West Bank (5900 sq. km.) and the Egyptian-administered coastal Gaza Strip (1000 sq. km) outside Israeli hands. Jordan declared East Jerusalem and the West

Poor slum housing in Gaza.

GAZA STRIP

Bank to be part of its territory, only renouncing this claim formally in 1988.

In the 1967 war, Israel took East Jerusalem, the West Bank and Gaza. Jewish settlers began moving in, regarding these occupied territories as part of the biblical-era Land of Israel. Plans for Palestinian autonomy were part of the 1978 Camp David agreement, but failed to materialize. Diplomatically, there was deadlock. The PLO didn't recognize Israel's right to exist, until 1988, while Israel refused to "negotiate with terrorists".

PALESTINIAN AUTONOMY
Turning away from armed struggle, the PLO in 1993 concluded a historic "land for peace" deal with Israel, the Oslo Accords, reached in secret negotiations in Norway. The two sides formally recognized one another, and Arafat and Israeli Prime Minister Rabin signed a historic Declaration of Principles in Washington in September 1993. Palestinians were to get interim self-rule, initially in Gaza and Jericho, and gradually in the whole West Bank. This meant Palestinian police taking over responsibility for security from the Israeli military, who had struggled since 1998 to end an insurrection led by the radical Islamic organization Hamas. A five-year timetable for "permanent status" negotiations would also tackle the future of Jewish settlements and the Palestinian demand for East Jerusalem as their capital.

GAZA AND JERICHO FIRST
The first step, Palestinian control of Gaza and Jericho, was achieved in May 1994. The Palestinian National Authority (PNA) was established on Palestinian territory, based in Gaza. Arafat – its chairman – made a triumphal return that July.

ELECTIONS
Arafat was a clear winner in elections in January 1996 for the presidency of the 88-member Palestinian Legislative Council, elected at the same time.

DELAYS IN PEACE PROCESS
The "Oslo B" accord put six other West Bank towns under PNA rule in 1995. After repeated delays Israel also relinquished control of Hebron (but not of rural areas) in January 1997. Mutual mistrust and violence, however, threatened to derail the peace process even before it reached the stage of "final status" talks. Arafat risked losing credibility among radical Palestinians. Attacks by rogue Hamas guerrillas, including spectacular suicide bombings, overshadowed Israel's elections in mid-1996. A new right-wing government promised a tougher stance and did little

Area under Palestinian control
■ Israeli settlement
□ Urban areas

WEST BANK

▨ Town under Palestinian control
■ Israeli settlement
□ Other major settlement

0 ____ 25 km
0 ____ 25 miles

N

to restrain the Jewish settlers, who fiercely opposed the whole "land for peace" deal. The peace process effectively stalled, despite international pressure.

BREAKTHROUGH IN 1999
Hopes rose after the change of government at Israel's 1999 elections. Arafat, holding back from making a unilateral declaration of full statehood according to the original five-year Oslo Accord timetable, met new Israeli Prime Minister Ehud Barak in July. Within two months an ambitious timetable was in place for a permanent agreement in the year 2000.

Bethlehem, situated in the troubled West Bank, is just one of the many holy places that remain a principal attraction for visitors.

RESOURCES

Electric power 4.5m kw

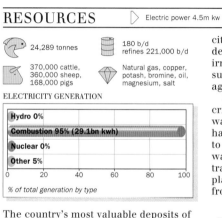

24,289 tonnes

180 b/d
refines 221,000 b/d

370,000 cattle,
360,000 sheep,
168,000 pigs

Natural gas, copper,
potash, bromine, oil,
magnesium, salt

ELECTRICITY GENERATION

Hydro 0%	
Combustion 95% (29.1bn kwh)	
Nuclear 0%	
Other 5%	
0 20 40 60 80 100	

% of total generation by type

The country's most valuable deposits of minerals are potash, bromine (of which Israel is the world's largest exporter), and other salts mined near the Dead Sea. Reserves of copper ore and gold were discovered in 1988. In the coastal plain, mixed farming, vineyards, and citrus groves are plentiful. Former desert areas now have extensive irrigation systems supporting specialized agriculture.

Israel's most critical resource is water. Shortages have forced Israel to purchase water, transported in plastic bags, from Turkey.

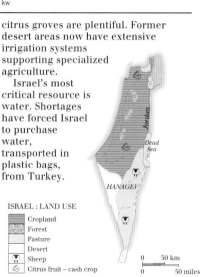

HANAGEV

ISRAEL : LAND USE

Cropland
Forest
Pasture
Desert
Sheep
Citrus fruit – cash crop

0   50 km
0   50 miles

ENVIRONMENT

No Green MPs

15%   Medium

Since 1993–1994, designated Environment Year, the government has aimed to promote recycling schemes, the cleanup of rivers and a healthier urban environment.

ENVIRONMENTAL TREATIES

No		Yes		Yes
No		Yes		No

MEDIA

TV ownership high

Daily newspaper circulation 291 per 1,000 people

PUBLISHING AND BROADCAST MEDIA

There are 34 daily newspapers. The leading papers are the Hebrew *Ha'aretz* and *Davar*, and the English *Jerusalem Post*

1 state-owned, 1 independent service

1 state-owned, 1 independent service

The left-wing press favors the Arab–Israeli peace process. The number of private radio stations is rising.

CRIME

Death penalty not used

43,900 prisoners

Down 3% from 1992–1996

CRIME RATES

| **Murders** | |
| 2 | *per 100,000 population* |

| **Rapes** | |
| 13 | *per 100,000 population* |

| **Thefts** | |
| 2440 | *per 100,000 population* |

Attacks by Arab and Jewish extremists are the most dramatic issue. The army has been accused of abuses.

EDUCATION

School leaving age: 15

95%   198,766 students

A highly educated population has been the engine of Israel's economic growth.

THE EDUCATION SYSTEM

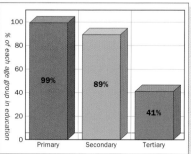

Primary 99%, Secondary 89%, Tertiary 41%
% of each age group in education

Education is free and compulsory for all between five and 15. There are both secular and religious universities. Many students study in the USA.

HEALTH

Welfare state health benefits

1 per 350 people

Heart and cerebrovascular diseases, cancers

The standard of health care is high. Israel has one of the world's highest ratios of doctors per head of population. Primary health care reaches all communities, and Israeli hospitals have pioneered many innovative treatments.

CHRONOLOGY

The creation of Israel in Palestine in 1948 realized the Zionist dream of a Jewish homeland.

❏ **1967** Six Day War; Israel annexes Gaza Strip, Sinai Peninsula, Golan Heights and the West Bank of the Jordan river.
❏ **1973** Egypt and Syria attack Israel.
❏ **1979** Camp David peace with Egypt.
❏ **1982** Israel invades Lebanon.
❏ **1993** Oslo Accords endorse Palestinian autonomy in Gaza Strip and Jericho.
❏ **1995** Palestinian autonomy extended to much of West Bank Prime minister Rabin assassinated: replaced by Peres.
❏ **1996** Palestinian and Israeli elections. Netanyahu (Likud) becomes first directly elected Israeli prime minister. Peace process falters.
❏ **1998** Israel concludes, then stalls on, US-backed Wye Agreement to revive progress on Palestinian autonomy. Yasser Arafat International Airport opens in Gaza Strip.
❏ **1999** Israeli elections: Ehud Barak becomes prime minister, heads Labor-led government.

SPENDING

GDP/cap. no increase

CONSUMPTION AND SPENDING

213 per 1,000 population   450 per 1,000 population

Defense 11.5%	
Education 6.6%	
Health 4.2%	
0 5 10 15 20 25	

Defense, Health, Education spending as % of GDP

Israel's income per head is high, but taxation is heavy. Some Israelis live in kibbutzim and eschew personal material wealth.

WORLD RANKING

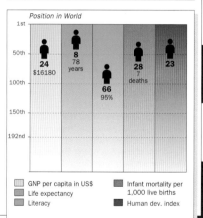

Position in World

24 $16180 | 8 78 years | 66 95% | 28 7 deaths | 23

GNP per capita in US$
Life expectancy
Literacy
Infant mortality per 1,000 live births
Human dev. index

ITALY

OFFICIAL NAME: Italian Republic **CAPITAL:** Rome
POPULATION: 57.2 million **CURRENCY:** Italian lira **OFFICIAL LANGUAGE:** Italian

1870	1947	June 2	I	+1	+39	.it

THE BOOT-SHAPED Italian peninsula stretches 800 km (496 miles) southwards into the Mediterranean, while the Alps form a natural boundary to the north. Italy also includes Sicily, Sardinia and several smaller islands. The south is an area of seismic activity, with two famous volcanoes, Vesuvius and Etna. Rival city-states flourished in Renaissance Italy, a unified country only in Roman times and since 1870. Fascist rule under Mussolini from 1922 ended with Italy's defeat in World War II. The Christian Democrats (CD) then dominated Italy's notoriously short-lived governments for decades, until in the 1990s the established parties and patronage systems were shaken up by corruption investigations. New groupings emerged, with more durable government since 1996 under the center-left "Olive Tree" alliance.

CLIMATE ▷ Mediterranean/mountain

WEATHER CHART

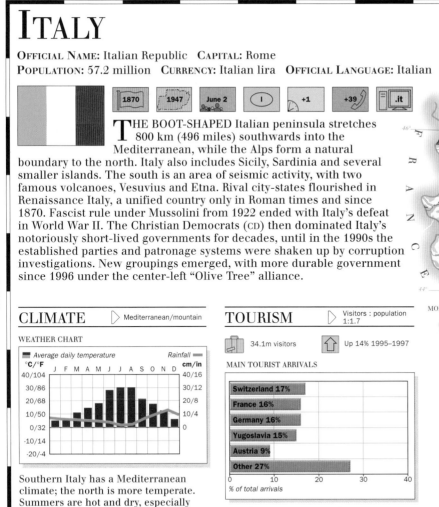

Southern Italy has a Mediterranean climate; the north is more temperate. Summers are hot and dry, especially in the south. Temperatures range from around 24°C (75°F) to over 27°C (81°F) in Sardinia and Sicily. Southern winters are mild; northern ones are cooler and wetter. The mountains usually have heavy snow. The Adriatic coast suffers from cold winds such as the *bora*.

TRANSPORTATION ▷ Drive on right

Leonardo da Vinci (Fiumicino), Rome
25m passengers

1,324 ships
6.2m grt

THE TRANSPORTATION NETWORK

308,400 km (191,600 miles)	8,860 km (5,505 miles)
16,030 km (9,961 miles)	16,030 km (9,961 miles)

Italy's roads, carrying the bulk of its trade, are badly congested. The *autostrada* (expressway) network lacks key links, and serious bottlenecks affect the main north–south artery. Plans to widen the trans-Apennine Bologna–Florence section have been blocked. The planned high speed Naples–Turin train is behind schedule and over budget, the first section unlikely to open before 2002.

TOURISM ▷ Visitors : population 1:1.7

34.1m visitors

Up 14% 1995–1997

MAIN TOURIST ARRIVALS

	% of total arrivals
Switzerland	17%
France	16%
Germany	16%
Yugoslavia	15%
Austria	9%
Other	27%

Italy has been a tourist destination since the 16th century and probably invented the concept. Roman popes consciously aimed to make their city the most beautiful in the world to attract travelers. In the 18th century, Italy was the focus of any Grand Tour. Today, its many unspoiled centers of Renaissance culture continue to make Italy one of the world's major tourism destinations. The industry accounts for 3% of Italy's GDP, and a million people – 5% of the workforce – have jobs in hotels and restaurants.

Most visitors travel to the northern half of the country, to cities such as Rome, Florence, Venice, and Padua. Many are increasingly traveling to the northern lakes. Beach resorts such as Rimini attract a large, youthful crowd in summer. Italy is also growing in popularity as a skiing destination.

Fears have been expressed that tourism may be having a detrimental impact on Italy's environment. The pressure of visitors to Venice, in particular, is such that in summer one-way systems for pedestrians have to be introduced and day-trippers are often turned away.

Tuscan landscape. *Chianti wine is produced in this region, where many northern Europeans own holiday homes.*

ITALY

Total Land Area : 294 060 sq. km
(301 270 sq. miles)

POPULATION

over 1 000 000	⊡
over 500 000	◉
over 100 000	◎
over 50 000	○
over 10 000	●

LAND HEIGHT

5000m/9843ft	
2000m/6562ft	
1000m/3281ft	
500m/1640ft	
200m/656ft	
Sea Level	

PEOPLE

▷ Pop. density medium

Italian, German, French, Rhaeto–Romanic, Sardinian

195/km²
(504/mi²)

THE URBAN/RURAL POPULATION SPLIT

67%   **33%**

RELIGIOUS PERSUASION

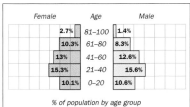

Other and non-religious 17%

Roman Catholic 83%

ETHNIC MAKEUP

Sardinian 2%   Other 4%

Italian 94%

Italy is a remarkably homogenous society. Most Italians are Roman Catholics and Italy has far fewer ethnic minorities than its EU neighbors. Most are fairly recent immigrants from Ethiopia, the Philippines, and Egypt. A sharp rise in illegal immigration in the 1980s and 1990s, from north and west Africa, Turkey, and Albania, generated a right-wing backlash and tighter controls. It became a major election issue in 1993 and a factor in the rise of the federalist

Northern League. Further stringent measures against illegal immigrants were introduced in 1995.

Difficult economic conditions caused many Italians to emigrate in the 1950s and 1960s. There are now five million Italians living abroad. About half live in other EU countries, the rest mainly in the USA, South America and Australia. Most migrants then, as now, are from the poorer south – the *Mezzogiorno*. Within Italy, prejudice still exists in the north against southern Italians.

Italians do not have a strong sense of national identity – except when it comes to sport. State institutions are viewed as inefficient and corrupt. Allegiance is to Europe, the region or the community, above all to the family. The extended family remains Italy's key social and economic support system. Most Italians live at home before marriage. Marriage rates are among the highest in Europe and divorce rates the lowest. However, Catholicism has not stopped Italy having the lowest birth rate and one of the highest abortion rates in the EU.

Italians have long been at the forefront of design. They tend to dress well, their fashion designers also leading the field. The preoccupation with style reflects the traditional importance of *bella figura* – image, cutting a dash – in Italian life as much as the high living standards which most now enjoy.

POPULATION AGE BREAKDOWN

Female	Age	Male
2.7%	81–100	1.4%
10.3%	61–80	8.3%
13%	41–60	12.6%
15.3%	21–40	15.6%
10.1%	0–20	10.6%

% of population by age group

CHRONOLOGY

Previously a collection of independent city states, dukedoms and monarchies, Italy became a unified state in 1870.

❏ **1922** Mussolini asked to form government by king.
❏ **1928** One-party rule by Fascists.
❏ **1929** Lateran Treaties with Vatican recognize sovereignty of Holy See.
❏ **1936–1937** Axis formed with Nazi Germany. Ethiopia conquered.
❏ **1939** Albania annexed.
❏ **1940** Italy enters World War II on German side.
❏ **1943** Invaded by Allies. Mussolini imprisoned by Victor Emmanuel III. Armistice concluded with Allies. Italy declares war on Germany. ⇨

N

0   100 km
0   100 miles

I

POLITICS ▷ Multiparty elections

U. House 1996/2001   President Carlo
L. House 1996/2001   Azeglioi Ciampi

AT THE LAST ELECTION
Chamber of Deputies 630 seats   **1% Other**

45% OTA   **39% AF**   **9% NL** **6% RC**

OTA = Olive Tree Alliance   **AF** = Freedom Alliance (Freedom Alliance   **NL** = Northern League   **RC** = Communist Refoundation   **Nm**=Nominated
Olive Tree Alliance includes Democratic Party of the Left, Italian People's Party, Prodi List, Dini List, Greens; Freedom Alliance includes Christian Democratic Center (DC), Union of the Democratic Center, Forza Italia

Senate 326 seats   **3% RC**

48% OTA   **36% AF**   **9% NL** **3% Nm** **2% Other**

The Senate comprises 315 elected members and several life Senators (11 after the election of 1996).

Italy is a multiparty democracy.

MAIN POLITICAL ISSUES
Corruption
Precipitated by 1992 revelations of illegal party financing in Milan, the *Mani pulite*, "Clean Hands," investigations revealed a network of corruption linking traditional parties and business. They destroyed the old political order. Thousands of people, many of them public figures, were arrested. Several, such as Carlo de Benedetti, head of Olivetti, one of Italy's most prestigious firms, were imprisoned. An enormous backlog of cases included bribery-related charges against former prime minister Silvio Berlusconi, and charges that another former prime minister, Giulio Andreotti, had close links to the Mafia.

Institutional Reform
The center-left alliance elected in 1996

Romano Prodi, prime minister in 1996–1998.

Umberto Bossi, leader of the regionalist Northern League.

Silvio Berlusconi, former prime minister and leader of Forza Italia.

The church of Santa Maria della Salute marks the entrance to Venice. The city state managed to retain its independence until Napoleon Bonaparte's invasion of Italy.

failed to win cross-party support on sweeping constitutional reforms. The right insisted on a French-style strong presidency, whereas the left preferred a stronger role for parliament on the German model. To complete partial electoral reforms in the early 1990s, a 1999 referendum proposed to strengthen the first-past-the -post system further and abolish the 25% of seats still elected by proportional representation. The proposal fell, although few voters opposed it, because the turnout was under 50%.

PROFILE
The discrediting of a whole political class over the corruption issue precipitated a major realignment. An interim government won approval for substantial electoral reforms, moving away from proportional representation, in time for the 1994 elections. A left-wing alliance headed by the PDS, the reformed communists, was kept from power by millionaire businessman Silvio Berlusconi's newly-formed *Forza Italia* in coalition with the secessionist NL and neo-fascist MSI/NA.

This so-called Freedom Alliance collapsed when the NL withdrew in December 1994. A technocratic government, led by Lamberto Dini, lasted until 1996. Fresh elections then resulted in an historic victory for the center-left Olive Tree alliance, whose leader Romano Prodi promised new stability.

Success in qualifying for membership of the single European currency crowned the Prodi government's economic achievements after two years in office. The separatist Northern League (LN) leader Umberto Bossi failed to rouse mass support for his declaration in September 1996 of an independent northern state of "Padania."

Prodi's government eventually fell in October 1998, after the communists again challenged its budget. Massimo D'Alema of the Left Democrats (DS) then took over as prime minister, heading a reshuffled government again drawn from the Olive Tree alliance groups.

WORLD AFFAIRS

▷ Joined UN in 1955

| EU | G7 | NATO | OECD | OSCE |

Italy has remained one of the most committed EU members. Its strategic position has also made it a key member of NATO, whose South European Command is based in Naples. Although basically Atlanticist in foreign policy, Italy nevertheless sometimes sought a mediatory role both with eastern Europe and with other states, notably Iran and Libya in the late 1990s. Dependence on Libya for energy supplies made Italy especially keen to see UN sanctions lifted.

A major concern in the 1990s has been upheaval in Albania and conflict in the former Yugoslavia. The use in 1999 of Italian bases for NATO's air attacks on Yugoslavia in the Kosovo conflict, despite some domestic hostility, confirmed Italy's commitment to the Atlantic Alliance.

AID

▷ Donor

$1.2bn (donations) ⬦ Not applicable

Aid directed at former Yugoslavia and Albania aims to stave off a feared flood of "economic" migrants; Italian military personnel have run relief operations through successive upheavals. The massive Kosovo refugee crisis of 1998–1999 gave a fresh focus to this issue.

DEFENSE

▷ Compulsory military service

$22bn ⬇ Down 9% in 1997

Plans to abolish conscription remain controversial for social policy reasons.

ITALIAN ARMED FORCES

🛡	1,299 main battle tanks (823 *Leopard*, 400 *Centauro* B-1, 76 *Ariete*)	165,600 personnel
🚢	8 submarines, 1 carrier, 1 cruiser, 4 destroyers, 24 frigates, 17 patrol boats	40,000 personnel
✈	253 combat aircraft (77 *Tornado*, 65 F-104 ASA, 6 TF104G, 80AMX)	63,600 personnel
☢	None	

Since the Cold War, conflicts in former Yugoslavia have helped refocus defense priorities. A "New Model Defense" was announced in 1992, and in mid-1999 the government reaffirmed its intention to create a smaller all-professional army by 2005. This army is to play a rapid-intervention role on NATO's southern flank, while the navy fulfils Mediterranean coastal functions rather than retaining ocean-going capabilities. Defense spending remains low, despite pressures to modernize weapons systems.

ECONOMICS

▷ Inflation 6% p.a.(1985–1996)

📊 $1,160bn   💲 1,768–1,649 lire

SCORE CARD

❏ WORLD GNP RANKING	6th
❏ GNP PER CAPITA	$20,170
❏ BALANCE OF PAYMENTS	$33.4bn
❏ INFLATION	2%
❏ UNEMPLOYMENT	12%

EXPORTS

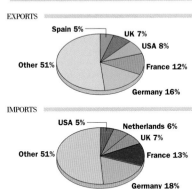

Spain 5%
UK 7%
USA 8%
France 12%
Germany 16%
Other 51%

IMPORTS

USA 5%
Netherlands 6%
UK 7%
France 13%
Germany 18%
Other 51%

STRENGTHS

Highly competitive, innovative small- to medium-size business sector. World leader in industrial and product design, textiles, and household appliances. Several highly innovative firms include Fiat (cars), Montedison (plastics), Olivetti (communications) and Benetton (clothes). Strong tourism and agriculture sectors, prestigious fashion houses.

WEAKNESSES

High public deficit and government debt. Pressure for pension reform. Slow growth. Inefficient public sector undergoing major privatizations. Uneven wealth distribution: northern Italy far richer than the south, which suffers three times more unemployment. Relatively small companies face strong competition in free international market. Heavy dependence on imported energy.

PROFILE

Since World War II, Italy has developed from a mainly agricultural society into a world industrial power. The economy is characterized by a large state sector, a mass of family-owned businesses, relatively high levels of protectionism and strong regional differences. Compared with other G7 economies, Italy also has relatively few multinationals.

The Institute for Industrial Reconstruction (IRI), a state-owned holding company, has been progressively privatizing its electronics, steel, telecommunications, engineering, shipbuilding, transport, and aerospace companies. The National Hydrocarbons Group (ENI), one of the world's top players in the energy and chemicals sectors, has itself been privatized, as has Telecom Italia, but the Treasury still owns the electricity corporation Enel. City, and regional authorities also own utilities, banks, and other businesses.

Family-owned businesses, the backbone of Italy's private sector, include Fiat, whose interests include aero engines, telecommunications, and bioengineering, as well as cars. Similar businesses tend to congregate. This geographical specialization encourages local competition which has translated into national success.

The *Mezzogiorno* remains the exception. State attempts to attract new investment have met with success in areas immediately south of Rome, but elsewhere organized crime has deterred investors and siphoned off state funds. Anger at the misuse of state funds in the south has been a powerful factor in the growth of the Northern League with its demands for autonomy. One-third of Italian tax revenue is generated in Italy's industrial heartland of Milan.

ECONOMIC PERFORMANCE INDICATOR

Consumer price index — GDP
Consumer price index 1990=100
GDP 1993=100
1993 1994 1995 1996 1997

I

ITALY : MAJOR BUSINESSES

Milano
Torino
Venezia
Bologna
Genova
Firenze
Rome
Napoli
Palermo

☀ Textiles
⚗ Chemicals
👕 Garments
🔌 Electronics
💊 Pharmaceuticals
⚙ Light engineering
🛡 Defence industries
🚗 Vehicle manufacture
✈ Aerospace industries

0   200 km
0   200 miles

I

Remains of the Greek theater at Taormina, eastern Sicily. It was rebuilt by the Romans in the 2nd century CE. Today, the theatre is the venue for an annual arts festival.

RESOURCES

▷ Electric power 65.8m kw

609,768 tonnes

89,804 b/d (reserves 746,977,000 bbl)

10.9m sheep, 8.3m pigs, 7.2m cattle, 1.3m goats

Coal, oil, lignite, pyrites, fluorspar, barytes, bauxite

ELECTRICITY GENERATION

Hydro 17% (41.9bn kwh)

Combustion 81% (195.8bn kwh)

Nuclear 0%

Other 2% (3.5bn kwh)

0 — 20 — 40 — 60 — 80 — 100

% of total generation by type

Italy has very few natural resources. It produces just 1% of its oil needs and is highly vulnerable to both fluctuations in world prices and political instability in its north African suppliers. It has reduced its exposure since 1973, when oil accounted for 71% of its needs. Even so, oil still accounts for 56% of energy consumption. Some power is generated from hydro and geothermal sources. Nuclear power was rejected in a 1987 referendum and development has effectively been abandoned. Italy's mineral assets are small and the sector contributes little to national wealth.

ITALY : LAND USE

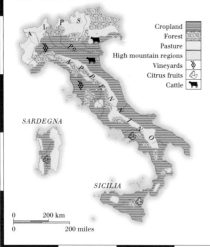

Cropland
Forest
Pasture
High mountain regions
Vineyards
Citrus fruits
Cattle

SARDEGNA

SICILIA

0 — 200 km
0 — 200 miles

ENVIRONMENT

▷ Green MPs

7%

Medium

ENVIRONMENTAL TREATIES

Yes — Yes — Yes
Yes — Yes — Yes

Italy has extensive environmental legislation but, compared with other EU states, has faced problems in enforcing directives. The right-wing government of the mid-1990s was not keen to introduce further environmental measures such as energy taxes and laws on waste recycling, which could restrict business competitiveness. Green party members in government in the Olive Tree alliance from 1996 insisted on a more active environmental stance.

Pollution in cities such as Naples and Rome is a major concern. Bans on traffic for up to seven hours during windless days are not uncommon. Acid rain has also damaged forests; 10% of trees are affected. The hunting of migrant birds, a popular sport in Italy, attracts international criticism. The use in the Ionian Sea of drift nets – up to 30 km (19 miles) long and prone to catching dolphins and turtles as well as fish – has been made illegal under EU law, which prohibits all drift nets over 2.5 km (1.5 miles) long.

MEDIA

▷ TV ownership high

Daily newspaper circulation 104 per 1,000 people

PUBLISHING AND BROADCAST MEDIA

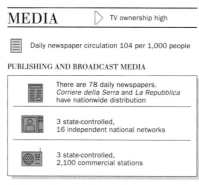

There are 78 daily newspapers. *Corriere della Serra* and *La Repubblica* have nationwide distribution

3 state-controlled, 16 independent national networks

3 state-controlled, 2,100 commercial stations

Italy's media are dominated by a few conglomerates, notably the Fininvest Group owned by Silvio Berlusconi and Carlo de Benedetti's Ferruzzi group. It has traditionally been highly politicized. Until the exposures of the post-1992 corruption investigations brought reform, this was particularly true of the state TV RAI channels. Like the rest of the state sector, they were apportioned between the main parties: RAI 1 to the Christian Democrats, RAI 2 to the Socialists and RAI 3 to the former Communist Party. All the media reflect the Italian love of sport, especially football. *La Gazzetta dello Sport* has one of the largest circulations of the national dailies.

CRIME

▷ Death penalty not used

47,323 prisoners

Up 2% from 1992–1996

CRIME RATES

Murders	
5	per 100,000 population

Rapes	
Italy does not publish rape statistics	

Thefts	
2440	per 100,000 population

Organized crime in the south remains a major problem, but a bureaucracy cleaned up since 1992 has weakened its grip. The Sicilian Mafia, the *Cosa Nostra*, in particular, was hit hard by arrests and trials when former members provided key evidence. A turning point was public revulsion against the killing in 1992 of anti-Mafia magistrate Giovanni Falcone. The *Cosa Nostra* and its counterparts in Naples and Calabria – *Camorra* and *'ndrangheta* – still control wholesale agricultural markets and much of the narcotics trade, bleed businesses of protection money, and manipulate public works contracts.

EDUCATION

▷ School leaving age; 16

98%

1.8m students

Schooling is state-run, apart from a few religious and elite private institutions.

THE EDUCATION SYSTEM

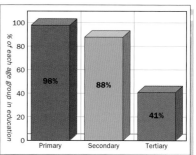

100
80
60
40
20
0

% of each age group in education

Primary 98% — Secondary 88% — Tertiary 41%

The pupil-teacher ratio in Italian schools is one of the best in Europe. In 1993, the minimum school leaving age was raised from 14 to 16 years, bringing Italy into line with the rest of Europe. The drop-out rate in schools - as high as 50% in Sicily - remains a problem, however. Plans to issue educational credits aim to tackle shortcomings in information technology training.

Universities in Italy are oversubscribed. Rome has 180,000 students, only 30% of whom gain a degree. Many Italian educationalists wish to restrict entry. Another concern is the fact that Italy devotes only 1.4% of its GNP to research, compared with a European average of 2.5%.

REGIONALISM AND NORTHERN SEPARATISM

THE ECONOMIC DIVISION of Italy into two, the more dynamic and prosperous north and the impoverished south or Mezzogiorno, is a source of continuing tension. It helps explain why, in a country as homogeneous as Italy in terms of ethnicity, language and religion, there is a strong demand for more devolution of power to the regional level. Moreover, a political party calling for the break-up of the country can gain a significant following – the Northern League (NL). Created in 1991 and built around the earlier Lombard League, the NL won over 10% of the vote at the last general election. It appeals to the economic self-interest of northern Italians, and their resentment at seeing their taxes going to fund substantial subsidies to the poorer south.

***Run-down housing** in the poor, rural area of Calabria in southern Italy.*

REGIONS WITH MORE DYNAMIC ECONOMIES
GDP per capita is almost three times higher in the richest northern areas, like Milan in Lombardy and Bologna in Emilia-Romagna, than in southern areas such as Reggio di Calabria. Emerging from the 1996 recession, the north achieved more rapid growth, creating more new jobs faster. Lombardy and Piedmont attract the lion's share of inward investment. Turin, the capital of Piedmont and home of Fiat, is boosting its industrial image by completing high speed rail links and staging the Winter Olympics in 2006. Some southern areas are trying to attract investment by emphasising that labour is cheaper there, and getting unions to accept lower wages locally in so-called "territorial pacts", but poor infrastructure remains a major obstacle.

PADANIA
The NL invented in the latter part of the 1990s the idea of creating a "Republic of Padania" to secede from the rest of Italy (Rome, its surrounding Lazio region, and the south). The NL leader Umberto Bossi declared Padania's "independence" in a ceremony in September 1996 after a pilgrimage the length of the River Po, the symbolic artery of "Padania", from Piedmont in north-west Italy to the Adriatic south of Venice. Bossi declared that independence was to take effect a year later, supposedly to allow time to negotiate with the Italian government on an agreed separation. Meanwhile the NL set up a self-styled government and parliament, a national guard and a flag. Mantua was described as the capital, but it remained unclear precisely how far its intended territory extended. Usually understood to refer to the nine most northerly regions, as far south as Florence and the rest of Tuscany, it was sometimes defined by the NL as also including the Umbria and Marche regions.

The Italian government refused to take the Padania idea seriously, dismissing it as a publicity stunt. NL leaders were subsequently persuaded, by a series of bad local election results including losing the mayorships of Mantua and Milan, that the time was not right to press forward with their project. Some of its impetus – the desire of northern businesses to be at the centre of European Union integration, not held back by the south – also disappeared when the central government's achievements in economic management unexpectedly allowed Italy to qualify for membership of the European single currency in 1999.

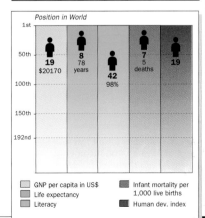

***Shopping center** in Milan, Italy's center of fashion and commerce.*

HEALTH
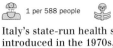
Welfare state health benefits

1 per 588 people

Heart and cerebrovascular diseases, cancers

Italy's state-run health system, introduced in the 1970s, faces spending cuts. Standards of health care vary across the country, as services are run by the regions, but few Italians rate their hospitals very highly. The health system initially provided services free at the point of use, but charges have been levied since 1988 for some dental and prescription costs; patients also have to pay a daily hospital charge and a yearly health fee. AIDS patients are exempt.

SPENDING
GDP/cap. no increase

CONSUMPTION AND SPENDING

533 per 1,000 population

447 per 1,000 population

Defense 1.9%
Education 4.9%
Health 8.3%

Defense, Health, Education spending as % of GDP (0, 5, 10, 15, 20, 25)

Italians, particularly in the north, are today among the world's wealthiest people in terms of disposable income. This is a result not only of growth, but also of the structure of Italian society.

Many Italians have more than one job. The extended families in which most people still live often have access to more than one income. Few people have mortgages, and savings and tax avoidance levels are high.

The main exceptions are in parts of the south. Although inward investment has been attracted to the Bari area, many people still live in poverty in other places, such as Naples and the Calabria region, where investment has been lowest, unemployment is highest and even tourism is underdeveloped.

WORLD RANKING

Position in World

19 $20170	8 78 years	42 98%	7 5 deaths	19

GNP per capita in US$
Life expectancy
Literacy
Infant mortality per 1,000 live births
Human dev. index

IVORY COAST

OFFICIAL NAME: Republic of Côte d'Ivoire   **CAPITAL:** Yamoussoukro
POPULATION: 14.6 million   **CURRENCY:** CFA franc   **OFFICIAL LANGUAGE:** French

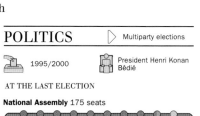
WEST AFRICA

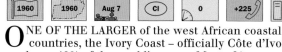
| 1960 | 1960 | Aug 7 | CI | 0 | +225 | .ci |

ONE OF THE LARGER of the west African coastal countries, the Ivory Coast – officially Côte d'Ivoire – produces 40% of the world's cocoa. Most of its population lives along the sandy coastal strip; the forested interior, apart from the capital, is sparsely populated. It is often held up as one of Africa's rare models of political stability and economic success, largely due to the pragmatic policies of the francophile President Houphouët-Boigny, who ruled from independence in 1960 until his death in 1993.

POLITICS

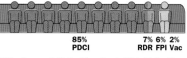 Multiparty elections

1995/2000   President Henri Konan Bédié

AT THE LAST ELECTION

National Assembly 175 seats

85% PDCI	7% 6% 2% RDR FPI Vac

PDCI = Democratic Party of Ivory Coast   **RDR** = Rally of the Republicans   **FPI** = Ivorian Popular Front   **Vac** = Vacant

President Houphouët-Boigny's reluctance to name a successor created years of uncertainty until his death in 1993. Contenders were the then prime minister, Alassane Ouattara, a Muslim northerner, and Henri Konan Bédié, then president of the National Assembly. France's support for Konan Bédié proved decisive, and Ouattara resigned to take a senior IMF appointment, but he remains a potential future presidential candidate. Konan Bédié, an arch-conservative in the mould of his predecessor, has since surrounded himself with loyalists of the highly organized ruling PDCI, while the pro-government media have systematically vilified Ouattara, claiming that he is not of pure Ivorian descent. Konan Bédié has cleverly undermined the already weak opposition parties.

CLIMATE

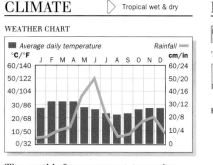 Tropical wet & dry

WEATHER CHART

The south's four seasons – two rainy and two dry – merge in the north into a single wet season with lower rainfall.

TRANSPORTATION

Drive on right

Abidjan–Port-Bouët 1.2m passengers

43 ships 11,400 grt

THE TRANSPORTATION NETWORK

50,400 km (31,300 miles)	None
639 km (397 miles)	980 km (609 miles)

The relatively good transportation system focuses on Abidjan, the premier port of francophone west Africa.

TOURISM

Visitors : population 1:53

274,000 visitors   Up 46% 1995–1997

MAIN TOURIST ARRIVALS

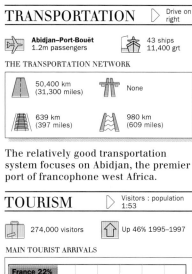

France 22%
USA 7%
Nigeria 6%
Other 65%
% of total arrivals

Ambitious plans for an "African Riviera" east of Abidjan and the opening of a hotel by the French *Club Méditerranée* have helped increase tourism. The giant Roman Catholic basilica at Yamoussoukro is an attraction.

PEOPLE

Pop. density low

Akan, French, Kru, Voltaic   45/km² (119/mi²)

THE URBAN/RURAL POPULATION SPLIT

44%   56%

RELIGIOUS PERSUASION

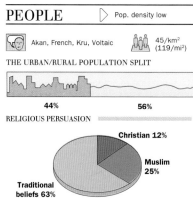

Christian 12%
Muslim 25%
Traditional beliefs 63%

There are more than 60 ethnic groups, the key ones being the Baoulé in the center, the Agri in the east, the Senufo in the north, the Dioula in the northwest and west, the Bété in the center-west and the Dan-Yacouba in the west. Houphouët-Boigny promoted his own group, the Baoulé, who account for 23% of the population. The succession of Konan Bédié, another Baoulé, has annoyed many groups, the Bété in particular.

The extended family is an important force in the shanty towns of Abidjan. Migrants from other west African countries account for up to 40% of the population.

IVORY COAST

Total Land Area : 318 000 sq. km (122 780 sq. miles)

0   100 km
0   100 miles

POPULATION
▣ over 1 000 000
◉ over 100 000
○ over 50 000
● over 10 000
• under 10 000

LAND HEIGHT
1000m/3281ft
500m/1640ft
200m/656ft
Sea Level

I

WORLD AFFAIRS

▷ Joined UN in 1960

The Ivory Coast is preoccupied with instability in other west African states, such as neighboring Liberia. Relations with the main creditors, the World Bank and France, the chief source of private investment and bilateral loans, are a major concern. The country plays an important role in the international cocoa and coffee organizations.

AID

▷ Recipient

$444m (receipts)

Down 54% 1996–1997

France is the largest source of bilateral aid. Structural adjustment loans from the World Bank have been important in easing the acute burden of a debt accumulated as a result of over-inflated oil hopes in the 1970s and early 1980s.

DEFENSE

▷ Compulsory military service

$101m

Up 5% in 1997

France is the main supplier of equipment and trainer of officers for the 6,800-strong army. It also maintains a garrison near Abidjan. There is a large paramilitary gendarmerie.

ECONOMICS

▷ Inflation 3.2% p.a. (1985–1996)

$10.2bn

601.60–558.62 CFA francs

SCORE CARD

❏ WORLD GNP RANKING	81st
❏ GNP PER CAPITA	$710
❏ BALANCE OF PAYMENTS	$35m
❏ INFLATION	5.6%
❏ UNEMPLOYMENT	14%

STRENGTHS

Well developed agricultural sector: major cocoa and coffee producer. Relatively good infrastructure. Expanding oil and gas industries. Healthy foreign investment levels.

WEAKNESSES

Debt burden. Failure to invest enough in education and professional training. Over-dependence on cocoa and coffee, to detriment of other crops.

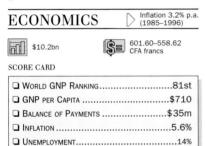

EXPORTS

Italy 6%
Netherlands 6%
USA 7%
Germany 8%
France 17%
Other 56%

IMPORTS

Italy 5%
Belgium-Luxembourg 5%
USA 5%
Nigeria 19%
Other 38%
France 28%

RESOURCES

▷ Electric power 1.2m kw

70,526 tonnes

Reserves of 100,000,000 bbl; refines 6516 b/d

1.3m sheep, 1.3m cattle, 1m goats 271,130 pigs,

Oil, diamonds, cobalt, gold, iron, manganese, nickel

There are substantial offshore oil and gas reserves. Large plantations are generally well managed.

ENVIRONMENT

▷ No Green MPs

6% (0.3% partially protected)

Low

The government imposed a ban on unprocessed timber exports in 1995 to protect Ivorian forests.

MEDIA

▷ TV ownership medium

☒ Daily circulation 16 per 1,000 people

PUBLISHING AND BROADCAST MEDIA

There are 12 daily newspapers, including *Fraternité-Matin* and *Ivoir-Soir*, both published by the government

1 state-owned service

1 state-owned, 4 independent service

Heavy censorship has eased since the early 1990s, but there are still cases of official harassment of the media.

EDUCATION

▷ School leaving age: 13

43%

52,228 students

A high percentage of students fail the *baccalauréat*. As expenditure has been cut, student agitation has grown.

CRIME

▷ Death penalty not used

Ivory Coast does not publish prison figures

Up 32% from 1992–1996

Abidjan has a reputation as the crime capital of west Africa, for which foreign immigrants are often blamed.

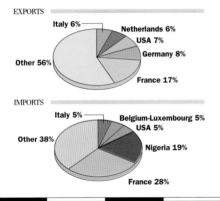

The basilica, Yamoussoukro. *Built in the new capital, Houphouët-Boigny's birthplace, it is modeled on St Peter's, Rome.*

CHRONOLOGY

One of the great trading emporia of West Africa, the Ivory Coast was made a French colony in 1893. By 1918, the French had defeated the Malinke empire and the forest peoples of the interior.

- ❏ **1903–1935** Establishment of plantation economy.
- ❏ **1960** Félix Houphouët-Boigny declares independence.
- ❏ **1970** Oil production starts.
- ❏ **1990** First contested elections: Houphouët-Boigny and PDCI win.
- ❏ **1993** Houphouët-Boigny dies.
- ❏ **1995** Election victories for Konan Bédié and PDCI.
- ❏ **1998** Constitutional changes increase presidential power and apparently bar Ouattara from standing in the 2000 elections.

I

HEALTH

▷ No welfare state benefits

1 per 10,000 people

Malaria, communicable diseases, neonatal deaths

Health care has improved slowly since the 1980s. Incidence of HIV/AIDS is among the highest in Africa.

SPENDING

▷ GDP/cap. no increase

CONSUMPTION AND SPENDING

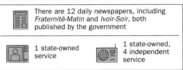

21 per 1,000 population

9 per 1,000 population

Defense 0.9%
Education 5%
Health 1.7%

0   5   10   15   20   25
Defense, Health, Education spending as % of GDP

A large bourgeoisie grew rich in the boom years of the late 1960s and 1970s. Living standards within the cities and urban areas are better than in many African countries.

WORLD RANKING

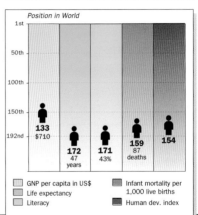

Position in World

1st
50th
100th
150th
192nd

133 $710
172 47 years
171 43%
159 87 deaths
154

❏ GNP per capita in US$
❏ Life expectancy
❏ Literacy

■ Infant mortality per 1,000 live births
■ Human dev. index

JAMAICA

OFFICIAL NAME: Jamaica **CAPITAL:** Kingston
POPULATION: 2.5 million **CURRENCY:** Jamaican dollar **OFFICIAL LANGUAGE:** English

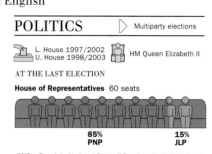
CARIBBEAN

| 1962 | 1962 | Aug 6 | JA | -5 | +1876 | .jm |

FIRST COLONIZED BY THE SPANISH and then, from 1655, by the English, Jamaica is located in the Caribbean, 145 km (90 miles) south of Cuba. It was the first of the Caribbean island nations to become independent from colonial control in the postwar years, and remains an influential force in Caribbean politics. Jamaica is also influential on the world music scene; *reggae* and *ragga* (or dancehall) developed in the tough conditions of Kingston's poor districts.

CLIMATE
▷ Tropical oceanic

WEATHER CHART

Tropical and humid conditions at sea level give way to temperate weather in mountain areas. Rainfall is seasonal, with marked regional variations.

TRANSPORTATION
▷ Drive on left

Donald Sangster International, Kingston
2.6m passengers

12 ships
9,600 grt

THE TRANSPORTATION NETWORK

| 3,000 km (1,864 miles) | None |
| 339 km (211 miles) | None |

Kingston harbor has been expanded and its airport is being improved. Main roads encircle the island. Private buses provide public transportation.

TOURISM
▷ Visitors : population 1:2.1

1.2m visitors   Up 17% 1995–1997

MAIN TOURIST ARRIVALS

- USA 64%
- UK 10%
- Canada 9%
- Other 17%

% of total arrivals

Tourism is the major earner of foreign exchange. Most tourists stay in large, enclosed beach resorts. Social unrest in 1999 damaged the sector.

PEOPLE
▷ Pop. density high

English Creole, English   231/km² (598/mi²)

THE URBAN/RURAL POPULATION SPLIT
54%   46%

RELIGIOUS PERSUASION
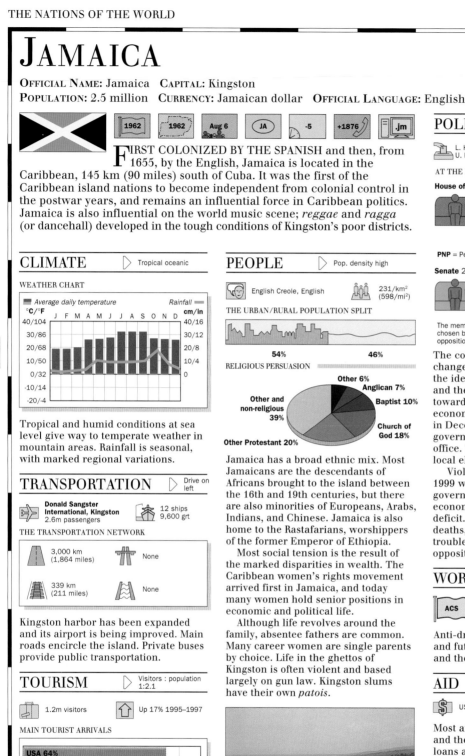
- Other 6%
- Anglican 7%
- Baptist 10%
- Church of God 18%
- Other Protestant 20%
- Other and non-religious 39%

Jamaica has a broad ethnic mix. Most Jamaicans are the descendants of Africans brought to the island between the 16th and 19th centuries, but there are also minorities of Europeans, Arabs, Indians, and Chinese. Jamaica is also home to the Rastafarians, worshippers of the former Emperor of Ethiopia.

Most social tension is the result of the marked disparities in wealth. The Caribbean women's rights movement arrived first in Jamaica, and today many women hold senior positions in economic and political life.

Although life revolves around the family, absentee fathers are common. Many career women are single parents by choice. Life in the ghettos of Kingston is often violent and based largely on gun law. Kingston slums have their own *patois*.

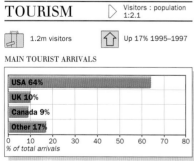
Bauxite mine and terminal, *Runaway Bay. Bauxite – from which aluminum is made – is the main source of foreign income.*

POLITICS
▷ Multiparty elections

L. House 1997/2002
U. House 1998/2003   HM Queen Elizabeth II

AT THE LAST ELECTION

House of Representatives 60 seats
85% PNP   15% JLP

PNP = People's National Party **JLP** = Jamaica Labour Party

Senate 21 seats

The members of the Senate are appointed. 13 members are chosen by the prime minister and 8 by the leader of the opposition.

The country's political complexion changed markedly in the late 1980s, as the ideologies of the once socialist PNP and the conservative JLP converged toward a moderate free-market economic approach. A general election in December 1997 gave the PNP government a third consecutive term in office. The party subsequently swept the local elections in 1998.

Violent disturbances in 1998 and 1999 were in response to the government's attempts to deal with economic recession and a large fiscal deficit. The unrest, which led to several deaths, gave new life to the internally troubled JLP, which identified itself with opposition to fuel tax increases.

WORLD AFFAIRS
▷ Joined UN in 1962

| ACS | Caricom | Geplac | Comm | OAS |

Anti-drugs cooperation with the USA and future relations within Caricom and the Commonwealth predominate.

AID
▷ Recipient

US$71m (receipts)   Up 18% 1996–1997

Most aid comes from the USA, the EU and the UK. It includes both project loans and balance of payments support.

DEFENSE
▷ No compulsory military service

US$29m   Up 4% in 1997

Jamaica's 3,300-strong defense force buys its arms from the USA, but is trained by the UK. Today, the defense force is used against narcotics smugglers and to assist the police to break up unrest, as in 1999.

J

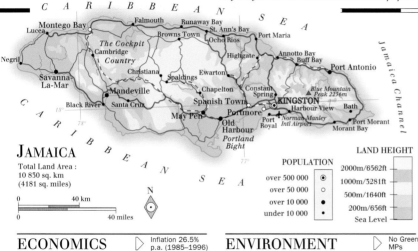

JAMAICA

Total Land Area :
10 850 sq. km
(4181 sq. miles)

POPULATION

over 500 000	◉
over 50 000	○
over 10 000	●
under 10 000	•

LAND HEIGHT

2000m/6562ft	
1000m/3281ft	
500m/1640ft	
200m/656ft	
Sea Level	

CHRONOLOGY

Spain occupied the island in 1510, wiping out the indigenous Arawak population. Britain seized it in 1655.

- ❑ **1958–1961** West Indies Federation.
- ❑ **1962** Independence under JLP.
- ❑ **1972** PNP elected. Reforms fail; street violence begins.
- ❑ **1980** Unpopular IMF austerity measures lead to JLP election win.
- ❑ **1991–1995** PNP returned and austerity continues.
- ❑ **1999** Violent protests over fuel tax increases.

ECONOMICS

▷ Inflation 26.5% p.a. (1985–1996)

🏛 US$4bn

💲 34.75–37.05 Jamaican dollars

SCORE CARD

❑ WORLD GNP RANKING	117th
❑ GNP PER CAPITA	US$1550
❑ BALANCE OF PAYMENTS	US$–376m
❑ INFLATION	9.7%
❑ UNEMPLOYMENT	16%

STRENGTHS

Relatively broadly based economy. Mining and refining of bauxite for aluminum. Tourism attracting US and EU visitors. Agriculture, including sugar, bananas, rum, and coffee. Light manufacturing and data processing for US companies are growing sectors.

WEAKNESSES

Banking and insurance sectors. Financing of sugar production. Stagnant growth. High debt burden.

EXPORTS

Norway 6%
Germany 6%
Canada 10%
USA 39%
UK 11%
Other 28%

IMPORTS

UK 3%
France 5%
Japan 5%
USA 49%
Trinidad & Tobago 8%
Other 30%

RESOURCES

▷ Electric power 1.2m kw

15,943 tonnes

440,000 goats, 400,000 cattle, 180,000 pigs

Not an oil producer; refines 32,000 b/d

Bauxite, marble, gypsum, silica, clay

Jamaica is the world's third-largest producer of bauxite. Sugar and bananas are major exports.

ENVIRONMENT

▷ No Green MPs

None

⬇ Low

Acidic dust which is a by-product from bauxite processing is a major problem, as is urban pollution in Kingston and its bay.

MEDIA

▷ TV ownership high

Daily newspaper circulation 64 per 1,000 people

PUBLISHING AND BROADCAST MEDIA

There are 3 daily newspapers, the *Daily Gleaner*, the *Daily Star* and the *Jamaica Herald*

1 independent service

6 independent services

The government has loosened its hold on broadcasting. The Jamaican press is one of the most influential in the Caribbean.

CRIME

▷ Death penalty used

4,350 prisoners

⬆ Up 13% from 1992–1996

Armed crime is a major problem. Many murders are the result of armed robberies linked to narcotics gangs competing for territory. Much of the world crack trade is still controlled from Jamaica. Large areas of Kingston are ruled by Dons, gang leaders who administer their own violent justice. The armed police are also frequently accused of the arbitrary shooting of suspects.

Although no executions have been carried out since 1988, death sentences continue to be imposed on murderers and drug dealers.

EDUCATION

▷ School leaving age: 12

86%

16,018 students

Education is based on the former British 11-plus selection system. Jamaica hosts the largest of the three campuses of the University of the West Indies.

HEALTH

▷ No welfare state health benefits

1 per 2,000 people

Cerebrovascular and heart diseases, cancers, diabetes

The once-efficient state health service is now seriously underfunded. There are fewer doctors and nurses than in the 1980s, hospitals generally have a shortage of drugs, and there is only rudimentary medical equipment.

SPENDING

▷ GDP/cap. no increase

CONSUMPTION AND SPENDING

41 per 1,000 population

140 per 1,000 population

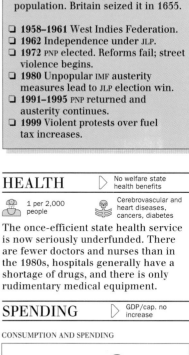

Defense 0.6%
Education 8.2%
Health 2.9%

Defense, Health, Education spending as % of GDP

Wealth disparities are highly marked in Jamaica, although better education has seen an increase in the number of black Jamaicans taking more lucrative, white-collar jobs. The poorest in Jamaica, mostly migrants from the island's rural areas, live in the slums of Kingston.

WORLD RANKING

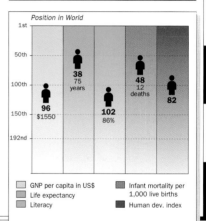

Position in World

- 96 $1550
- 38 75 years
- 102 86%
- 48 12 deaths
- 82

❑ GNP per capita in US$	❑ Infant mortality per 1,000 live births
❑ Life expectancy	❑ Human dev. index
❑ Literacy	

JAPAN

OFFICIAL NAME: Japan **CAPITAL:** Tokyo
POPULATION: 125.9 million **CURRENCY:** Yen **OFFICIAL LANGUAGE:** Japanese

1600 | 1972 | Dec 23 | J | +9 | +81 | .jp

A CONSTITUTIONAL MONARCHY, with an emperor as head of state, Japan lies off the east Asian coast in the north Pacific. It comprises four principal islands and more than 3,000 smaller islands. Sovereignty over the most southerly islands in the Kurile chain is disputed with the Russian Federation. The terrain is mostly mountainous, with fertile coastal plains; over two-thirds is woodland. The Pacific coast is vulnerable to *tsunamis* – tidal waves triggered by submarine earthquakes. Most cities are located by the sea; the Kanto plain around Tokyo, Kawasaki, and Yokohama is the most populous and heavily industrialized. To the north, Hokkaido is the most rural of the main islands. Japan's power in the global economy, with annual trade surpluses exceeding $100 billion and massive overseas investments, has been shaken since the early 1990s by a series of bad debt crises, bankruptcies in the financial sector, and prolonged recession since 1997.

Traditional paddy field in Hokkaido. Rice farming is among the most protected sectors of the Japanese economy.

CLIMATE ▷ Continental/subtropical

WEATHER CHART

■ Average daily temperature   Rainfall ━
°C/°F   J F M A M J J A S O N D   cm/in
40/104 .... 40/16
30/86 .... 30/12
20/68 .... 20/8
10/50 .... 10/4
0/32 0
-10/14
-20/-4

The Sea of Japan has a moderating influence on the climate. Winters are less cold than on the Asian mainland. Japan also has much higher rainfall. Spring is perhaps the most pleasant season, with warm, sunny days but without the sultry, oppressive heat and rainfall of the summer. Recent freak storms and damaging floods have raised concern over global climate change.

TRANSPORTATION ▷ Drive on left

Haneda, Tokyo 51m passengers | 9,310 ships 18.52m grt

THE TRANSPORTATION NETWORK

11.6m km (720,800 miles)	6,070 km (3,772 miles)
20,175 km (12,536 miles)	1,770 km (1,100 miles)

Railroads are the most important means of transport in Japan. The *Shinkansen*, known in the West as the bullet train, is the second fastest in the world. It is renowned as much for its reliability, timed to the second, as for its speed. The Tokyo–Chitose air route is the busiest in the world.

JAPAN

Total Land Area : 376 520 sq. km
(145 374 sq. miles)

POPULATION

▣	over 5 000 000
▣	over 1 000 000
◉	over 500 000
◎	over 100 000
○	over 50 000
●	over 10 000

LAND HEIGHT

1500m/4921ft
1000m/3281ft
500m/1640ft
Sea Level

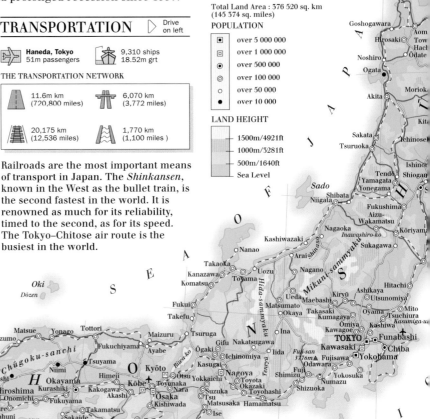

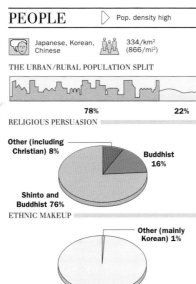

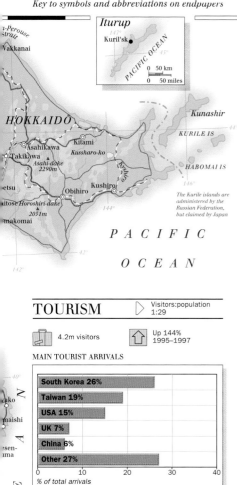

PEOPLE ▷ Pop. density high

Japanese, Korean, Chinese   334/km² (866/mi²)

THE URBAN/RURAL POPULATION SPLIT

78%   22%

RELIGIOUS PERSUASION

- Other (including Christian) 8%
- Buddhist 16%
- Shinto and Buddhist 76%

ETHNIC MAKEUP

- Other (mainly Korean) 1%
- Japanese 99%

The Kurile islands are administered by the Russian Federation, but claimed by Japan

TOURISM ▷ Visitors:population 1:29

🧳 4.2m visitors   ⬆ Up 144% 1995–1997

MAIN TOURIST ARRIVALS

South Korea 26%	
Taiwan 19%	
USA 15%	
UK 7%	
China 6%	
Other 27%	

% of total arrivals

Japan is expensive for foreign tourists, partly because of the yen exchange rate. Most come from South Korea, Taiwan, the USA, the UK, and, increasingly, China. The ancient imperial capital, Kyoto, and the temples and gardens of Nara are popular tourist destinations. Other attractions include the extraordinary variety of energetic high-tech urban living in Tokyo and Osaka. Traditional agricultural life can be found in rural areas such as Tohoku in northern Honshu. Wilderness areas of Hokkaido attract mainly Japanese climbers and hikers.

High Street, Ginza District, Tokyo.
Japan's well-policed cities are among the safest in the world.

Japan is one of the most racially homogeneous societies in the world. Its sense of order is reflected in the phenomenon of the lifetime employer. Many Japanese men define themselves by the company they work for rather than the job they do. An employer's influence stretches even to encouraging and approving marriages.

Women mostly play a traditional role, running the home and supervising the all-important education of their children. They tend to work until the age of 26, when many will marry and continue to work part-time. Some women are, however, beginning to take up long-term careers. More are entering the medical and legal professions. Japan saw its first female party leader – Takako Doi – in 1991.

Social form remains extremely important in Japanese society. Respect for elders and for social and business superiors is strongly ingrained. There is little tradition of generation rebellion, but the youth market is powerful and current fashions place teenagers at their center. Although many may still follow their parents' lifestyles, established attitudes are under challenge. Working for the same company for life and giving up free time to entertaining company clients became harder to justify in the economically turbulent 1990s.

POPULATION AGE BREAKDOWN

Female	Age	Male
2.2%	81–100	1.1%
9.8%	61–80	8.1%
14.5%	41–60	14.4%
13.7%	21–40	14.1%
10.8%	0–20	11.4%

% of population by age group

CHRONOLOGY

Japan's tendency to limit its contacts with the outside world ended in 1853, when a US naval squadron coerced trading concessions from the last of the Tokugawa shoguns.

- **1868** Meiji Restoration; overthrow of Tokugawa regime and restoration of imperial power.
- **1872** Modernization along Western lines. Japan's strong military tradition becomes state-directed.
- **1889** Constitution modeled on Bismarck's Germany adopted.
- **1894–1895** War with China; ends in Japanese victory.
- **1904–1905** War with Russia; ends in Japanese victory. Formosa and Korea annexed.
- **1914** Japan joins World War I on Allied side. Sees limited naval action.
- **1919** Versailles peace conference gives Japan limited territorial gains in the Pacific.
- **1923** Yokohama earthquake kills 140,000.
- **1927** Japan enters period of radical nationalism, and introduces the notion of a "coprosperity sphere" in southeast Asia under Japanese control. Interpreted in the USA as a threat to its Pacific interests.
- **1931** Manchuria invaded, placed under Japanese control and renamed Manchukuo.
- **1937** Japan launches full-scale invasion of China.
- **1938** All political parties placed under one common banner; Japan effectively ruled by militarists.
- **1939** Undeclared border war with Soviet Union results in Japanese defeat.
- **1940** Fall of France in Europe; Japan occupies French Indo-China.
- **1941** USA imposes total trade embargo, including oil, on Japan thereby threatening to stifle its military machine. Japan responds in December by launching attack on US fleet at Pearl Harbor and invading US, British and Dutch possessions in the Pacific.
- **1942** Japan loses decisive naval battle of Midway. Thereafter tide of war turns as Japanese forces are driven back toward their home islands.
- **1945** Huge US bombing campaign culminates in atomic bombing of Hiroshima and Nagasaki. Soviet Union declares war on Japan. Emperor Hirohito surrenders, gives up divine status. Japan placed under US military government with Gen. MacArthur installed as supreme commander of Allied Powers in Japan. ⇨

J

CHRONOLOGY *continued*

- ❑ **1947** New Japanese constitution: modeled on USA's, but retains emperor in ceremonial role.
- ❑ **1950** Korean War. US army contracts lead to quick expansion of Japanese economy.
- ❑ **1952** Treaty of San Francisco. Japan regains independence. Industrial production recovers to 15% above 1936 levels.
- ❑ **1955** Merger of conservative parties to form LDP which governs for next 38 years.
- ❑ **1964** Tokyo Olympics. Bullet train (*Shinkansen*) inaugurated. Japan admitted to OECD.
- ❑ **1973** Oil crisis. Economic growth cut. Government-led economic reassessment decides to concentrate on high-tech industries.
- ❑ **1976** LDP shaken by Lockheed bribery scandal; in subsequent election remains in power but for first time fails to win majority.
- ❑ **1979** Second oil crisis. Growth continues at 6% per year.
- ❑ **1980** Elections: restoration of LDP overall majority.
- ❑ **1982** Honda establishes first car factory in USA.
- ❑ **1988** Japan becomes world's largest aid donor and overseas investor.
- ❑ **1989** Death of Hirohito. Recruit–Cosmos bribery scandal: resignation of Prime Minister Noburo Takeshita; replaced by Sosuke Uno, forced to resign over sexual scandal. Tokyo stock market crash.
- ❑ **1991–1992** LDP torn by factional disputes, further financial scandals and issue of electoral reform.
- ❑ **1993** Reformists split from LDP and create new parties. Elections; LDP loses power. Morihiro Hosokawa becomes prime minister at head of seven-party coalition.
- ❑ **1994** Hosokawa resigns. Withdrawal of Social Democratic Party of Japan (SDPJ) causes collapse of coalition two months later. New three-party coalition includes LDP and SDPJ.
- ❑ **1994** Opposition parties unified by creation of Shinshinto. Far-reaching political and electoral reforms, aimed at eradicating "money politics."
- ❑ **1995** January, Kobe earthquake kills more than 5,000 people.
- ❑ **1996** Elections: Ryutaro Hashimoto forms LDP minority government.
- ❑ **1996** Copper trader Yasuo Yamanaka arrested, accused of incurring losses of US$2.6 billion while acting for Sumitomo Corporation.
- ❑ **1997** Economy enters severe recession.
- ❑ **1998** Crisis over reform of banking and financial system. Keizo Obuchi replaces Hashimoto.

POLITICS   ▷ Multiparty elections

L. House 1996/2000
U. House 1998/2001

Emperor Tsegu no Miya Akihito

AT THE LAST ELECTION

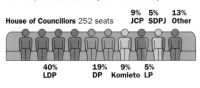

House of Representatives 500 seats

| 48% LDP | 31% Shinshinto | 10% DPJ | 5% JCP | 1% Sakigake | 3% SDPJ | 2% Others |

LDP = Liberal Democratic Party **DPJ** = Democratic Party of Japan **SDPJ** = Social Democratic Party of Japan
JCP = Japan Communist Party **LP** = Liberal Party

House of Councillors 252 seats

| 40% LDP | 19% DP | 9% Komieto | 5% LP | 9% JCP | 5% SDPJ | 13% Other |

Japan is a multiparty democracy. The Emperor has a ceremonial role.

MAIN POLITICAL ISSUES
LDP strength and opposition weakness
Japanese postwar politics was dominated by a system of patronage, linking big business, the bureaucracy, and the ruling LDP, until the 1993 elections. Numerous scandals and public disaffection with the LDP then saw the party briefly ousted from government. Far-reaching electoral reforms adopted in 1994 abolished multimember constituencies, the foundation of the old system of LDP factions and the "money politics" by which they were financed. The unification of opposition groups by Ichiro Ozawa to create the Shinshinto party then promised a realignment towards a two-party system based on center-right parties. Adroit maneuvering, however, restored the LDP's position, bolstered by its hold on the centralized bureaucracy.

Keizo Obuchi, *who became prime minister in 1998.*

Ichiro Ozawa *founder of united opposition party* Shinshinto.

Emperor Akihito. He acceded in 1989 on the death of his father, Hirohito.

The military issue
The Japanese constitution enshrines the principle of pacifism, renouncing war as a sovereign right and "the threat or use of force as a means of settling international disputes." This prohibition is a matter of hot debate within Japan; critics such as Shintaro Ishihara, elected as Tokyo governor in 1999, argue that its economic power should be better reflected in foreign policy and the defense arena.

PROFILE
Morihiro Hosokawa, taking over as the first non-LDP prime minister in 1993, was helped by the fact that he was not associated with the tainted world of Tokyo politics. Four LDP prime ministers had been forced to resign because they were implicated in scandals, or failed to stamp out corruption. Hosokawa too, however, was accused of financial irregularities, and resigned in 1994. His government had nevertheless laid the basis for electoral reform, apologized for Japan's war crimes and had also begun the process of institutional deregulation.

The fragile seven-party coalition collapsed in June 1994 after the withdrawal of the SDPJ, which then joined a coalition with the LDP. In January 1996, LDP leader Ryutaro Hashimoto became prime minister.

In elections in October 1996, principally a contest for the center-right vote, the LDP emerged as the largest party ahead of Shinshinto, formed two years earlier by Ichiro Ozawa as a merger of opposition groups. Eventually Hashimoto formed a minority government, exclusively from within his LDP. This arrangement proved unexpectedly durable, but the economic crisis and a poor LDP performance in upper house elections in July 1998 led to Hashimoto's replacement by Keizo Obuchi. His minority government was strengthened by an agreement with Ozawa, now leader of the Liberal Party.

Ryutaro Hashimoto, *prime minister in 1996–1998.*

WORLD AFFAIRS

Joined UN
in 1956

APEC | G7 | IAEA | WTO | OECD

After years of limiting its role on the world stage to that of a minor power rather than that of one of the world's most powerful economies, Japan is beginning to make its influence felt. Its eventual aim is a seat on the UN's Security Council, which would be commensurate with its economic influence. Tentative moves were made in 1993, with Japanese forces joining UN peacekeepers in Cambodia. The lobby fearing a resurgence of Japanese militarism is still strong, however, and wants to avoid any foreign entanglements. In Asia, Japan remains burdened by the legacy of distrust and bitterness arising from its military expansion and the harsh colonial exploitation of its neighbors in the first half of the 20th century.

AID

Donor

$9.4bn (donations) | Not applicable

Japan's is the world's largest aid donor. Most of the country's official aid goes to Asia and the Pacific, particularly China, Indonesia, and other ASEAN states. Polynesian islands are heavily dependent on Japanese aid to support their islands' main livelihood, fishing.

DEFENSE

No compulsory
military service

$40.9bn | Down 11% in 1997

In the postwar period any military activity in Japan arouses fierce debate.

JAPANESE ARMED FORCES

	1,090 main battle tanks (70 Type-61, 870 Type-74, 150 Type-90)	151,800 personnel
	16 submarines, 9 destroyers, 48 frigates, 6 patrol boats	43,800 personnel
	329 combat aircraft (F-1, F-4EJ, F-15J/DJ)	45,600 personnel
	None	

The defense establishment in Japan has not recovered from the effects of the 1941–1945 war. Involvement even in UN peacekeeping duties, which Japan first undertook in Cambodia in 1993, is hotly contested by pacifists. Japan's Self-Defense Forces, however, have grown quite large. Shots fired in March 1999, to deter an intrusion by two North Korean vessels, fueled fresh debate about the renunciation of military force under the

ECONOMICS

Inflation 1% p.a. (1985–1996)

$4,812.1 bn | 130–112 yen

ECONOMIC PERFORMANCE INDICATOR

SCORE CARD

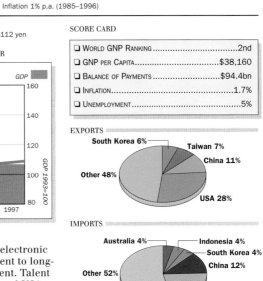

SCORE CARD	
❑ WORLD GNP RANKING	2nd
❑ GNP PER CAPITA	$38,160
❑ BALANCE OF PAYMENTS	$94.4bn
❑ INFLATION	1.7%
❑ UNEMPLOYMENT	5%

EXPORTS

IMPORTS

STRENGTHS

Major producer of high-tech electronic products and cars. Commitment to long-term research and development. Talent for developing ideas from EU and USA. Global spread of business, including plants in EU and USA. Once-revolutionary management and production techniques. *Keiretsu* – vertically integrated families of companies which agree to cooperate – keep non-Japanese companies out of Japanese markets.

WEAKNESSES

Heavy dependence on imported oil. Trade surplus a source of international tension. Financial system in need of reform, burdened by high level of bad debts and lack of transparency.

PROFILE

Continuing recession has brought a serious crisis since 1997.

The Tokyo stock market crash in 1990, and particularly the collapse of the sky-high property market, ended a period of remarkable economic growth. The contraction in demand stemmed the flow of imports – particularly of European luxury products. Industrial production fell by 8% in 1992 and corporate profits were sharply down. However, the overall economy continued to grow, companies did not shed great amounts of labor, and research and development spending went up. The government stepped in with a five-year economic plan of infrastructure spending.

Japan's trade surplus climbed to $100 billion a year by 1993. Pushed to do more to encourage imports, for the sake of relations with the USA and the EU, Japan shifted from concentrating almost totally on export-led growth to stimulating the domestic economy.

Problems in the financial sector remained acute. The collapse of securities firm Yamaichi in November 1997 was followed by more bankruptcies, and even

corporations such as Hitachi reported record losses. Unemployment rose to 5% of the labor force. Searching for a lasting recovery from the worst recession since the war, industry leaders began arguing that Japan needed a fundamental change in thinking. Unable to compete with neighboring Asian countries in terms of low production costs for basic manufacturing, its future would depend on catching up with modern service industries and creating a more knowledge-based economy.

JAPAN : MAJOR BUSINESSES

RESOURCES

 Electric power 227m kw

6.8m tonnes

17,183 b/d (reserves 59,850,000 bbl)

9.8m pigs, 4.7m cattle, 28,500 goats

Limestone, sulfur, coal

ELECTRICITY GENERATION

Hydro 9% (91.3bn kwh)

Combustion 61% (604.2bn kwh)

Nuclear 30% (291.3bn kwh)

Other 0%

% of total generation by type

Japan has few commercially exploitable resources. Production costs make coal extraction uneconomical,

ENVIRONMENT

No Green MPs

7%

High

ENVIRONMENTAL TREATIES

Yes   Yes   Yes

Yes   Yes   Yes

Internationally, Japan has backed moves to set up a global foundation to aid sustainable development in the third world, and also hosted the 1997 international meeting in Kyoto on climate change, but has agreed to cut its emissions of so-called "greenhouse gas" only by a modest 6% by 2010. Japan is criticized for its consumption of tropical timber, overfishing, and whaling – although it contends that minke whales are not threatened.

A deeply embedded respect for nature has echoes in the vigorous grassroots ecological movement. Its impact includes preventing a second runway at Tokyo's Narita airport, and opposing nuclear power expansion and waste processing. In early 1997 Japan suffered its worst oil spill in 20 years when a Russian tanker broke in half along the country's western shoreline.

Datsetsusan National Park, Hokkaido. Japan's northerly island is the least populous of the main group.

and Japan has become the world's largest coal importer. In an attempt to reduce dependence on imported fuels, Japan has developed alternative sources of energy. It is now the world's fourth-biggest generator of nuclear power. However, environmentalists strongly oppose any expansion of this sector.

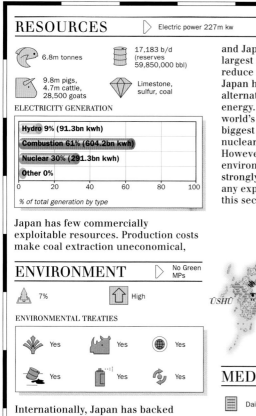

JAPAN : LAND USE

Cropland
Forest
Pasture
Sheep
Fruits
Rice

0   300 km
0   300 miles

MEDIA

TV ownership high

Daily newspaper circulation 580 per 1,000 people

PUBLISHING AND BROADCAST MEDIA

There are 122 daily newspapers. *Asahi Shimbun, Mainichi Shimbun* and *Yomiuri Shimbun* are among the most popular

2 publicly-owned, 126 commercial services

3 publicly-owned, 97 commercial services

The Japanese are among the world's most avid newspaper readers; daily sales exceed 70 million. Most dailies carry serious news and are owned by large media groups who also have TV and cable interests. Weekly newspapers carry more tabloid journalism. The magazine market is huge. Over 36 billion copies of magazines are sold in Japan every year; *Non Non*, a women's magazine, is the best-selling title. In addition, 1.5 billion books are sold annually. Lifestyle magazines, encouraging the Japanese to make more use of their limited leisure time, are a growing sector of the market.

Japan has redefined much of the world's media. It invented the personal stereo and created the huge computer games market. From the early 1990s this market showed exponential growth. Nintendo, a leading games company, became one of the most profitable in Japan. The internet, slow to take off in Japan, had more than 15 million users by 1999.

EDUCATION

School leaving age : 15

99%

3.9m students

The Japanese education system is highly pressurized and competitive.

THE EDUCATION SYSTEM

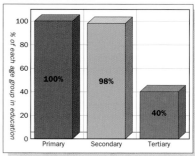

% of each age group in education

100% Primary
98% Secondary
40% Tertiary

One of the key dividing lines in society is between university graduates, who get the coveted white-collar jobs for life, and nongraduates; the latter have difficulty reaching management level.

Competition for university places is intense, and starts with the choice of kindergarten, attended from the age of four. Once at university, students tend to relax – the important thing is getting in. Tokyo, Kyoto, Waseda, and Keio are the most prestigious universities. Their graduates have access to top civil service and business jobs. The system succeeds in producing a uniform, and thoroughly educated, workforce. However, it has also been criticized for not fostering individual responsibility,

CRIME

Death penalty used

46,622 prisoners

Up 3% from 1992–1996

CRIME RATE

Murders	
1	per 100,000 population

Rapes	
1	per 100,000 population

Thefts	
1264	per 100,000 population

Japan has one of the lowest crime rates in the world, in part the result of an efficient police system. Cities are safe, with police kiosks at frequent intervals. However, the crime rate is rising. Young people are now more involved, and drug abuse has become more common.

The major crime problem is fraud and the activities of the *kumi*, organized Mafia-style syndicates whose members are known as *yakuza*. The authorities seek to contain rather than eradicate their activities. *Kumi* are suspected of having connections with the extreme right in Japanese politics.

URBAN STRESS AND GARDENS OF HARMONY

A QUARTER OF JAPAN'S entire population lives in the Tokyo Metropolitan Area, which sprawls south to merge with Kawasaki and Yokohama. The average commuter faces a journey of well over an hour each way, some 30% longer than the typical London commute, between the business centre and high-density housing in outlying areas. Although the city's public transport system rightly enjoys a reputation for efficiency and punctuality, passengers in Tokyo have to put up with serious overcrowding during peak hours. Rail staff may even be employed to help shove them into the carriages, although longer-term measures have been taken recently to lengthen both trains and platforms.

HIGH DENSITY URBAN DEVELOPMENT

People migrated steadily to Tokyo between the 1950s and 1970s. In the 1980s the demand for Tokyo office space was so great that new buildings were crammed into every available piece of land. The property boom then ended abruptly at the end of that decade, migration to Tokyo slowed, and the trend was actually reversed in the 1990s. However, one legacy of the previous build-up is a city where housing is twice as expensive as in the USA as a proportion of average earnings. Apartments tend to be small, and several other features of overcrowded urban living strike the visitor, including the so-called "capsule hotels" providing the bare minimum space for sleeping. Tokyo has few open spaces and parks - just 2.6 sq metres per person, one tenth of that in London and even less in comparison with Washington D.C.'s 46 sq metres. Aware of both the advantages and the disadvantages of city life, most Japanese acknowledge that Tokyo is an extremely crowded physical environment which leaves much to be desired. On the other hand it is relatively safe, offers the convenience

The peaceful surroundings of the Toji-in temple gardens, in Kyoto.

of services available around the clock, and has a rich cultural life.

CALM IN THE TRADITIONAL GARDEN

One respite from urban stress, firmly established in Japanese culture, is to visit a traditional garden. The guiding principle of garden design is the creation of a controlled and harmonious environment, intended to nourish the spirit and allow anxiety to subside, making room for quiet reflection. Among the inspirations behind the Japanese garden is the reverence paid in Shinto animist beliefs to special "spirit places" in the landscape, such as gnarled trees, waterfalls, and islands. Sacred places, created to communicate with the gods, featured sacred stones for the gods from above, and sacred ponds for those from beyond the sea. Complex principles were also brought in by Buddhist monks for creating outdoor spaces along Zen principles, and mirroring a spiritual passage from the noisy city to the inner sanctuary, using the concepts of entry, threshold and enclosure.

The five main styles, with different combinations of water, garden plants, stones, waterfalls, trees, and bridges, are the gardens of the Heian aristocrats, Zen Buddhism gardens arranged with sand and stones such as the famous Ryoanji garden in Kyoto, tea gardens providing the setting for the rituals of the tea ceremony, enclosed Tsubo gardens, and Edo strolling gardens like the Meiji in Tokyo.

High density housing in the Shinjuku district of Tokyo.

HEALTH

▷ Welfare state health benefits

👤 1 per 556 people

💀 Heart and circulatory diseases, cancers, accidents

Contributory national health insurance is based on earnings-related premiums. The government subsidizes care for the elderly and the self-employed.

Japan has a world-class health system, which has delivered the lowest infant mortality rates and one of the highest life expectancy rates in the world. The poorest in society receive free treatment; expensive high-tech hospital facilities can also offer the latest techniques. Japan's rapidly aging population presents a major future funding challenge.

SPENDING

▷ GDP/cap. no increase

CONSUMPTION AND SPENDING

🚗 373 per 1,000 population

🌐 479 per 1,000 population

Defense 1%

Education 3.8%

Health 6.8%

0	5	10	15	20	25

Defense, Health, Education spending as % of GDP

Measured in consumer goods, the Japanese are wealthy; car ownership is only low because city parking is so restricted. Most households have substantial savings, enabling them to withstand economic recession. Despite the recession, the country's wealthiest men became even wealthier in 1998; the top 10 had fortunes averaging US$2.5 billion, three of them being newly rich personal finance tycoons. Tokyo living costs are very high and most who work there live outside the city center, facing a long, cramped commuter journey. Girls and young women who still live in their parents' homes are one group with high disposable income.

WORLD RANKING

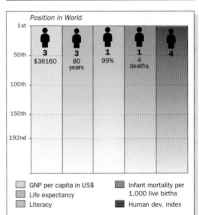

Position in World

3 $38160	3 80 years	1 99%	1 4 deaths	4

☐ GNP per capita in US$
☐ Life expectancy
☐ Literacy

■ Infant mortality per 1,000 live births
■ Human dev. index

J

335

JORDAN

MIDDLE EAST
Asia
Africa
Lebanon Syria Iraq
Israel JORDAN Saudi Arabia
Egypt

OFFICIAL NAME: Hashemite Kingdom of Jordan **CAPITAL:** Amman
POPULATION: 6 million **CURRENCY:** Jordanian dinar **OFFICIAL LANGUAGE:** Arabic

| 1946 | 1967 | May 25 | HKJ | +2 | +962 | .jo |

S HARING BORDERS WITH Iraq, Syria, Israel, and
Saudi Arabia, Jordan has just 26 km (16 miles) of
coastline on the Gulf of Aqaba. Jordanian territory legally includes the
West Bank of the Jordan river and East Jerusalem, but Israel has
occupied these areas since 1967. Jordan ceded its claim to the West Bank
to the PLO in 1988. Phosphates and tourism associated with important
historical sites such as Petra are the mainstays of the economy.

CLIMATE ▷ Hot desert/steppe

WEATHER CHART

Summers are hot and dry, winters cool
and wet. Areas below sea level are very
hot in summer and warm in winter.

TRANSPORTATION ▷ Drive on right

Queen Alia Intl, Amman
2m passengers

7 ships
42,799 grt

THE TRANSPORTATION NETWORK

| 6,600 km (4,100 miles) | | None |
| 293 km (182 miles) | | None |

Adequate roads link main cities. A
railroad links the port of Al Aqabah
with the Syrian capital, Damascus.

TOURISM ▷ Visitors : population 1:5.3

1.1m visitors

Up 5% 1995–1997

MAIN TOURIST ARRIVALS

| Egypt 32% |
| Syria 22% |
| Saudi Arabia 14% |
| Other 32% |

0 10 20 30 40
% of total arrivals

Al Aqabah offers fine beaches, water
sports and subaqua diving, while the
ancient city of Petra attracts visitors
interested in Roman remains. Amman
is developing as a center for Arabic
culture and the arts.

PEOPLE ▷ Pop. density medium

Arabic

67/km²
(175/mi²)

THE URBAN/RURAL POPULATION SPLIT

71% 29%

ETHNIC MAKEUP

Circassian 1% Armenian 1%
Arab 98% (40% Palestinian)

Jordan is a predominantly Muslim
country drawn from Bedouin roots,
with a Christian minority and a large
Palestinian population. The monarchy's
power base lies among the rural tribes,
which also provide the backbone of the
military. National identity is strong.

POLITICS ▷ Multiparty elections

L. House 1997/2001
U. House 1997/2001

HM King Abdullah ibn al-Hussein

AT THE LAST ELECTION

House of Deputies 80 seats

3% AAP

62% Ind
20% IAF
15% Other

Ind = Independents **IAF** = Islamic Action Front
AAP = Al-Ahd Party

Senate 40 seats

The members of the Senate (Majlis Al-Aayan) are appointed
by the King.

King Hussein, in power since 1952,
died in February 1999, to be succeeded
by Abdullah, his eldest son, designated
as crown prince only in January, in
place of Hussein's brother, Hassan.
Abdullah lacks political experience, but
is respected by the army and supported
by Jordan's tribal leaders. His wife,
Queen Rania, is a Palestinian.

Multiparty elections, initiated in
1993, have benefited pro-government
parties which since 1997 have
dominated the House of Deputies.

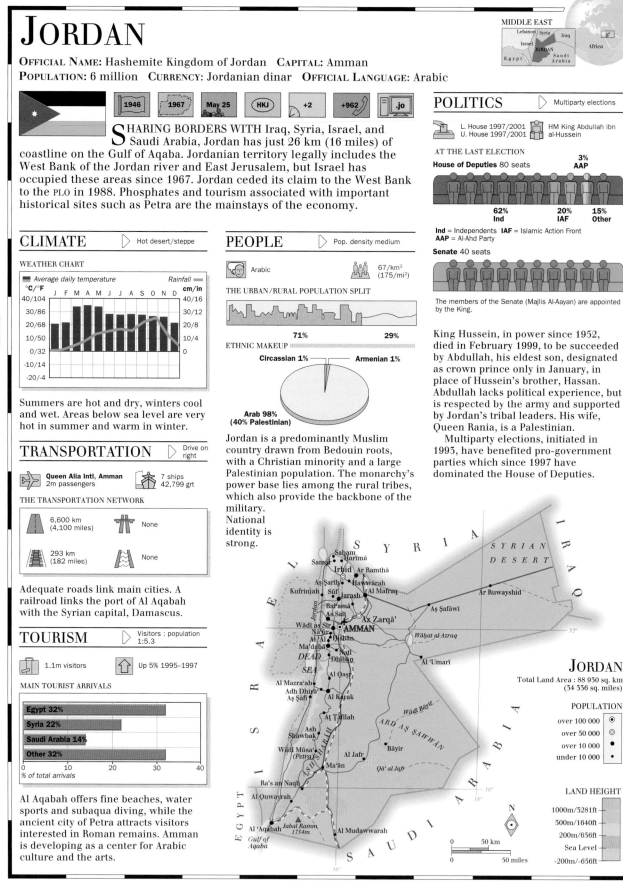

JORDAN

Total Land Area : 88 950 sq. km
(34 336 sq. miles)

POPULATION

over 100 000
over 50 000
over 10 000
under 10 000

LAND HEIGHT

1000m/3281ft
500m/1640ft
200m/656ft
Sea Level
-200m/-656ft

J

WORLD AFFAIRS

▷ Joined UN in 1955

Jordan's position as a key player in Middle East politics is under question, following the death in February 1999 of King Hussein, the region's longest-reigning and internationally respected ruler. Policy toward the newly emerging Palestinian state is uncertain. Relations with the Gulf states and the West, which deteriorated sharply in 1991 over Jordan's refusal to join the anti-Iraq coalition, have improved since Jordan distanced itself from the Iraqi regime in 1995.

AID

▷ Recipient

$462m (receipts)   Down 10% 1996–1997

The Gulf states have pledged to restore aid to Jordan after King Hussein moved to distance himself from Iraq in 1995.

DEFENSE

▷ No compulsory military service

$496m   Up 9% in 1997

Jordanian forces played no part in the 1991 Gulf War. The armed forces are loyal to the monarchy. They have a reputation for thorough training and professionalism. The forces are dependent on Western support for credit in purchasing advanced arms and equipment.

ECONOMICS

▷ Inflation 4.6% p.a. (1985–1996)

$6.8bn   0.71 Jordanian dinars

SCORE CARD

❏ WORLD GNP RANKING..........................96th
❏ GNP PER CAPITA $1,520
❏ BALANCE OF PAYMENTS $29m
❏ INFLATION 3%
❏ UNEMPLOYMENT...................................20%

STRENGTHS
Positive impact of 1994 peace treaty with Israel. Major exporter of phosphates. Skilled work force. Recovery of tourist industry after 1991 Gulf crisis.

WEAKNESSES
Reliant on imports to satisfy energy requirements. Unemployment owing to influx of Jordanians and Palestinians expelled from Kuwait.

EXPORTS

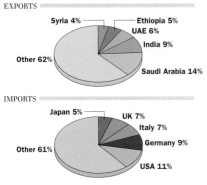

Syria 4%
Ethiopia 5%
UAE 6%
India 9%
Other 62%
Saudi Arabia 14%

IMPORTS

Japan 5%
UK 7%
Italy 7%
Germany 9%
Other 61%
USA 11%

RESOURCES

▷ Electric power 1.1m kw

533 tonnes   60 b/d (reserves 4,000,000 bbl)
23.3m chickens, 2m sheep, 795,000 goats   Oil, phosphates, potash

Oil deposits have been discovered. Phosphates, livestock and crops such as tomatoes, wheat, olives and vegetables are the main resources.

ENVIRONMENT

▷ No Green MPs

3%   Low

Conservation is a government priority. Rare animals are protected, and species that became extinct in the wild in the 1950s are being reintroduced into controlled environments.

MEDIA

▷ TV ownership low

Daily newspaper circulation 45 per 1,000 people

PUBLISHING AND BROADCAST MEDIA

There are 4 daily newspapers, including *Ad-Dustour* and *Ar-Rai*

1 state-controlled service   1 state-controlled service

Radio and TV are controlled by the state. A controversial publications law enacted in 1998 further restricts press freedom.

CRIME

▷ Death penalty used

Jordan does not publish prison figures   Down 65% from 1992–1996

Jordan is largely peaceful. Crime levels are generally low, although theft in urban areas is rising.

EDUCATION

▷ School leaving age: 15

87%   112,959 students

Men and women receive the same education. Jordanian teachers work all over the Middle East.

HEALTH

▷ Welfare state health benefits

1 per 625 people   Heart, digestive and respiratory diseases, accidents, cancers

Health care is subsidized by the government. Hospitals are found throughout the country.

CHRONOLOGY

Jordan, previously the British mandated territory of Transjordan, became independent in 1946.

❏ **1958** Iraq and Jordan end federation.
❏ **1967** Israel seizes West Bank territories.
❏ **1988** Jordan cedes claims to West Bank to PLO.
❏ **1994** Peace treaty with Israel.
❏ **1999** Death of King Hussein, Jordan's ruler since 1952.

The King's Highway, *seen from the castle at Al Karak. This strategic fortress was built by Crusader knights in the 12th century.*

SPENDING

▷ GDP/cap. no increase

CONSUMPTION AND SPENDING

50 per 1,000 population   70 per 1,000 population

Defense 6.4%
Education 6.3%
Health 1.8%

0   5   10   15   20   25
Defense, Health, Education spending as % of GDP

The wealthiest Jordanians are the entrepreneurs, bankers and engineers based in the capital, Amman. Poverty is relatively rare.

WORLD RANKING

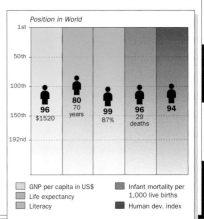

Position in World

1st
50th
100th
150th
192nd

96 $1520   80 70 years   99 87%   96 29 deaths   94

❏ GNP per capita in US$
❏ Life expectancy
❏ Literacy
❏ Infant mortality per 1,000 live births
❏ Human dev. index

J

KAZAKHSTAN

OFFICIAL NAME: Republic of Kazakhstan   **CAPITAL:** Astana
POPULATION: 16.9 million   **CURRENCY:** Tenge   **OFFICIAL LANGUAGE:** Kazakh

ASIA

1991 · 1991 · Oct 25 · CIF · +5/+6 · +7 · .kz

THE SECOND-LARGEST of the former Soviet
republics, Kazakhstan extends almost 2,000 km
(1,240 miles) from the Caspian Sea in the west to the Altai Mountains in
the east, and 1,300 km (806 miles) north to south. It borders Russia to the
north and China to the east. Kazakhstan was the last Soviet republic to
declare its independence, in 1991. In 1994, elections confirmed the
former communist Nursultan Nazarbayev and his supporters in power.
Kazakhstan is mineral-rich and has considerable economic potential.
Many Western companies are seeking to exploit its natural resources.

*The Altai Mountains, eastern Kazakhstan.
Subject to harsh continental winters, the Altai
range is a cold, inhospitable place. Rivers
carry meltwater down onto the vast steppe.*

CLIMATE
▷ Cold desert/steppe

WEATHER CHART

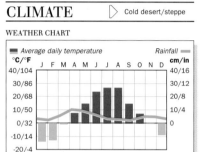
■ *Average daily temperature*   *Rainfall* ▬
°C/°F   cm/in
J F M A M J J A S O N D
40/104   40/16
30/86   30/12
20/68   20/8
10/50   10/4
0/32   0
-10/14
-20/4

Kazakhstan has a continental climate
with large temperature variations:
average January temperatures range
from –18°C (0°F) on the northern Kazakh
steppe to –3°C (27°F) in the deserts
1,300 km (800 miles) south; July
temperatures average 19°C (66°F) and
30°C (86°F) respectively. As the Caspian
Sea never freezes, winters are mildest
on Kazakhstan's southwestern coast.

TRANSPORTATION
▷ Drive on right

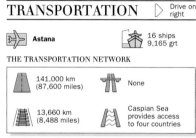
✈ **Astana**   🚢 16 ships 9,165 grt

THE TRANSPORTATION NETWORK

141,000 km (87,600 miles)   None

13,660 km (8,488 miles)   Caspian Sea provides access to four countries

Transportation networks focus
on the north and east, the key
economic areas. Most roads are in
urgent need of repair. The railroads
link into the Russian system and most
international flights go via Moscow,
although there are direct flights to
Germany. A rail link with China was
opened in 1992. Kazakhstan has access
to Caspian Sea ports.

TOURISM
▷ Not available

🏨 Visitors still largely limited to business people   ⬆ Gradually increasing

MAIN TOURIST ARRIVALS

*Kazakhstan does
not publish tourism
figures by
country of origin*

0   10   20   30   40   50   60
% of total arrivals

The number of visitors to Kazakhstan is
increasing; very few, however, come
solely as tourists. The majority are
business travelers, and a dense web of
contacts with foreign companies has
evolved. Of the Central Asian states,
Kazakhstan has cultivated the
closest links with the West.
Most foreign business
people are concentrated
in Almaty.

KAZAKHSTAN

Total Land Area : 2 717 300 sq. km
(1 049 150 sq. miles)

POPULATION

⊙ over 500 000
◎ over 100 000
○ over 50 000
● over 10 000
· under 10 000

LAND HEIGHT

3000m/9843ft
2000m/6562ft
1000m/3281ft
500m/1640ft
200m/656ft
Sea Level
-200m/-656ft

0   200 km
0   200 miles

K

PEEPLE

PEOPLE

▷ Pop. density low

Kazakh, Russian, German, Uigur, Korean

6/km² (16/mi²)

THE URBAN/RURAL POPULATION SPLIT

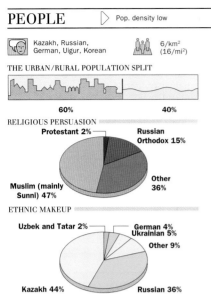

60%   40%

RELIGIOUS PERSUASION

Protestant 2%   Russian Orthodox 15%

Muslim (mainly Sunni) 47%   Other 36%

ETHNIC MAKEUP

Uzbek and Tatar 2%   German 4%
Ukrainian 5%
Other 9%

Kazakh 44%   Russian 36%

POPULATION AGE BREAKDOWN

Female	Age	Male
0.9%	81–100	0.3%
5.4%	61–80	3.3%
10.3%	41–60	9.2%
15.6%	21–40	16%
19.3%	0–20	19.9%

% of population by age group

Kazakhstan's ethnic diversity arose from the forced settlement of Germans, Tatars and Russians during the Soviet era. Russian settlement began in the 19th century, but peaked after 1920. By 1959, ethnic Russians outnumbered Kazakhs. The balance has in recent years been redressed by the immigration of ethnic Kazakhs from neighboring states.

Tension between Kazakhs and ethnic Russians has grown steadily. In 1995, ethnic Russians criticized the country's new constitution for preventing dual citizenship with Russia and refusing to recognize Russian as an official language. Central control over ethnic Russians has been reinforced by shifting the capital to Astana (formerly Akmola) in the north, where the majority of ethnic Russians currently live.

Only a minority of Kazakhs retain their traditional nomadic life. However, commitment to Islam and loyalty to the clan remain strong.

POLITICS

▷ Multiparty elections

L. House 1995/2000
U. House 1995/2000

President Nursultan Nazarbayev

AT THE LAST ELECTION

Assembly 67 seats

10% Other

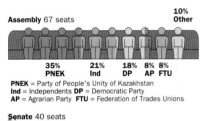

| 35% PNEK | 21% Ind | 18% DP | 8% AP | 8% FTU |

PNEK = Party of People's Unity of Kazakhstan
Ind = Independents **DP** = Democratic Party
AP = Agrarian Party **FTU** = Federation of Trades Unions

Senate 40 seats

Two members elected by each of 20 districts, and 7 nominated by the President.

Legislative authority is vested in the 114-member bicameral Supreme *Kenges* comprising the Assembly and the Senate. The president, who must be fluent in Kazakh, has supreme executive power.

MAIN POLITICAL ISSUE
Presidential powers
The increased powers of President Nazarbayev are the focus of political controversy; his critics accuse him of developing a personality cult. The 1995 constitution strengthened presidential powers, giving Nazarbayev a veto over the decisions of the Constitutional Council. In 1995 Nazarbayev, who was due to face reelection in 1996, also won a referendum which extended his term of office until 2000. However, constitutional amendments approved by the legislature in 1998 forced him to hold a presidential election in January 1999. Although re-elected, Nazarbayev was tarnished by allegations of voting irregularities.

PROFILE
Despite a democratic government, the president enjoys political dominance, and the patronage of the Kazakh clans is still important. Since coming to power in 1989, Nazarbayev has concentrated on market reforms. However, his political credibility was badly shaken in 1994, when allegations of widespread electoral fraud led to the annulment of legislative elections. New elections were held in 1995. Re-elected in 1999, Nazarbayev faces mounting domestic and international criticism of his attempts to expand the scope of presidential powers.

***President Nursultan Nazarbayev**, who steered Kazakhstan to independence.*

***Azekhan Kazhageldin**, prime minister in 1994–1997.*

WORLD AFFAIRS

▷ Joined UN in 1992

CIS   ECO   EAPC   OIC   OSCE

Maintaining close ties with other former Soviet republics is a priority. Relations with Russia, although strained at times by Moscow's concern over Kazakhstan's ethnic Russians, have been cemented by a 25-year cooperation treaty. The question of the rights of Kazakhstan's ethnic German minority has renewed interest in closer relations with Germany.

Kazakhstan's rich mineral resources have generated wider economic links with potential investors from Europe, the USA and Asia. Ties with South Korea grew particularly fast, partly reflecting President Nazarbayev's interest in South Korea's model of economic development. Relations with China remain strained, however, as Beijing has territorial claims to parts of eastern Kazakhstan.

AID

▷ Recipient

$131m (receipts)   Up 6% 1996–1997

Kazakhstan joined the IMF and the World Bank in 1992, and is also a member of the EBRD. Most multilateral and bilateral aid is aimed at supporting economic reform and improving health care, transport and communications. The government is seeking to link the dismantling of nuclear warheads to aid payments from the West.

CHRONOLOGY

Once part of the Mongol Empire, Kazakhstan was absorbed by the Russian Empire in the 19th century. Ethnic Russians began to settle on land used by nomadic Kazakhs. Russian settlement intensified after the 1917 revolution and Kazakhstan was subjected to intensive industrial and agricultural development.

❑ **1916** Rebellion against Russian rule brutally suppressed.
❑ **1917** Russian Revolution inspires civil war in Kazakhstan between Bolsheviks, anti-Bolsheviks and Kazakh nationalists.
❑ **1918** Kazakh nationalists set up autonomous republic.
❑ **1920** Bolsheviks take control. Kirghiz Autonomous Soviet Socialist Republic (ASSR) set up within Russian Soviet Federative Socialist Republic.
❑ **1925** Kirghiz ASSR renamed Kazakh ASSR.
❑ **1936** Kazakhstan becomes full union republic of the USSR as Kazakh SSR. ⇨

K

CHRONOLOGY *continued*

- ❏ **1930s** Stalin's collectivization program leads to increase in Russian settlement and the deaths of an estimated one million Kazakhs.
- ❏ **1941–1945** Large-scale deportations of Germans, Jews, Crimean Tatars and others to Kazakhstan.
- ❏ **1950s** Nuclear test site set up at Semipalatinsk; 500 nuclear explosions follow before testing ends in 1991.
- ❏ **1954–1960** Khrushchev's policy to plow "Virgin Lands" for grain most vigorously followed in Kazakhstan. Russian settlement reaches a peak.
- ❏ **1986** Riots in Almaty after an ethnic Russian, Gennadi Kolbin, appointed head of Kazakhstan Communist Party (CPK) to replace Kazakh, Dinmukhamed Kunyev.
- ❏ **1989** Kolbin replaced by Nursultan Nazarbayev, an ethnic Kazakh and chair of Council of Ministers. Reform of political and administrative system.
- ❏ **1990** CPK wins elections to Supreme Soviet by overwhelming majority. Nazarbayev appointed first president of Kazakhstan. Kazakhstan declares sovereignty.
- ❏ **1991** Kazakhstan votes to preserve USSR as union of sovereign states. USSR authorities hand control of enterprises in Kazakhstan to Kazakh government. CPK ordered to cease activities in official bodies following abortive August coup in Moscow. CPK restructures itself as Socialist Party of Kazakhstan (SPK). Independence of Republic of Kazakhstan declared; joins CIS.
- ❏ **1992** Opposition demonstrations against dominance of reformed communists in Supreme Soviet, now Supreme Kenges. Nationalist groups form Republican Party, *Azat*.
- ❏ **1993** Adoption of new constitution. Introduction of new currency, the tenge.
- ❏ **1994** Legislative elections annulled after proof of widespread voting irregularities.
- ❏ **1995** Adoption of new constitution extending presidential powers; referendum extends Nazarbayev's term until 2000; legislative elections.
- ❏ **1998** Legislature approves constitutional amendments, including the holding of early presidential election.
- ❏ **1999** Nazarbayev reelected president for a new seven-year term.

DEFENSE

▷ Compulsory military service

$503m   ⬇ Down 11% in 1997

A former nuclear power, Kazakhstan is a potential guarantor of regional stability.

KAZAKH ARMED FORCES

🚜	630 main battle tanks (T-72)	40,000 personnel
🚢	10 patrol boats	100 personnel
✈	123 combat aircraft (MiG-23/27/29, Su-24)	15,000 personnel
	None	

Kazakhstan, as the largest of the five former Soviet Central Asian republics, is a potential guarantor of regional peace. Kazakhstan ratified the START-I nuclear reduction treaty in 1992 and the NPT in 1993, but the process of disarmament has been delayed, due mainly to financial problems. In 1993, the USA agreed to grant Kazakhstan $84 million to dismantle its nuclear weapons. In 1995, Kazakhstan announced that all its nuclear weapons had been transferred to Russia or destroyed. Later that year military relations with Russia were sealed with a landmark agreement under which Kazakh and Russian armed forces were to be unified within a year.

ECONOMICS

▷ Inflation 527.3% p.a. (1994–1997)

📊 $21.3bn   💲 76.49–83.93 tenge

SCORE CARD

❏ WORLD GNP RANKING	62nd
❏ GNP PER CAPITA	$1,350
❏ BALANCE OF PAYMENTS	$–954m
❏ INFLATION	17.4%
❏ UNEMPLOYMENT	4%

ECONOMIC PERFORMANCE INDICATOR

> *Consumer prices have risen sharply since 1991. GDP is likely to rise following new foreign investment.*

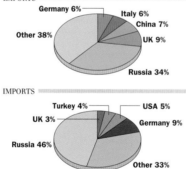

EXPORTS

Germany 6%
Italy 6%
China 7%
UK 9%
Russia 34%
Other 38%

IMPORTS

Turkey 4%
USA 5%
Germany 9%
UK 3%
Russia 46%
Other 33%

STRENGTHS
Vast mineral resources, notably oil and gas. Also bismuth and cadmium, used in electronics industry. Foreign investors attracted by liberal investment laws. Joint oil and gas ventures recently concluded with Western companies. Mass privatization program launched in 1994.

WEAKNESSES
Collapse of former Soviet economic and trading system. Heavy reliance on imported consumer goods. Rapid introduction of the tenge in 1993 increased economic instability and fueled sharp price rises. Inefficient industrial plants.

PROFILE
Under Nazarbayev, Kazakhstan has moved faster than other former Soviet republics to establish a market economy. It was the first to introduce free economic zones, investment incentives and privatization. Prices have been freed, foreign trade largely decontrolled and the tax system reformed. Despite these reforms, growth has been elusive. Unemployment and inflation have risen sharply, due in large part to the impact of the collapse of the wider Soviet economy.

More than $9 billion have already been committed in foreign direct investment, mainly in the energy sector. Outdated equipment and inadequate distribution networks mean that Kazakhstan, surprisingly, has to import a considerable amount of energy, although it is a net exporter of fossil fuel. It hopes to become self-sufficient by 2000.

KAZAKHSTAN : MAJOR BUSINESSES

⚓ Oil	
Steel	
❄ Textiles	
⚗ Chemicals	🗄 Food processing
Oil refining	⚙ Light engineering
⛏ Coal mining	✎ Pharmaceuticals

0   500 km
0   500 miles   * significant multinational ownership

RESOURCES

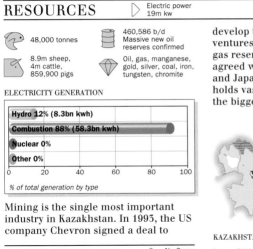

▷ Electric power
19m kw

🐟 48,000 tonnes

🛢 460,586 b/d
Massive new oil
reserves confirmed

🐑 8.9m sheep,
4m cattle,
859,900 pigs

💎 Oil, gas, manganese,
gold, silver, coal, iron,
tungsten, chromite

ELECTRICITY GENERATION

| Hydro 12% (8.3bn kwh) |
| Combustion 88% (58.3bn kwh) |
| Nuclear 0% |
| Other 0% |

0   20   40   60   80   100

% of total generation by type

Mining is the single most important industry in Kazakhstan. In 1993, the US company Chevron signed a deal to develop the huge Tengiz oilfield. Joint ventures to exploit substantial oil and gas reserves in the Caspian Sea were agreed with Russia in 1995, and the USA and Japan in 1998. Kazakhstan also holds vast iron ore reserves and one of the biggest goldfields.

KAZAKHSTAN : LAND USE

0   500 km
0   500 miles

Cropland
Forest
Pasture
Desert
Sheep
Cereals

ENVIRONMENT

▷ No Green MPs

🌲 3%

⬦ Medium

ENVIRONMENTAL TREATIES

| 🌿 No | 🦏 No | 🌐 Yes |
| 🛢 No | 🧴 No | ♻ Yes |

The environmental damage caused by intensive industrial and agricultural development is a major concern. The eastern cities are heavily polluted and farmlands are being eroded. The Aral Sea has been polluted by the overuse of fertilizers and has shrunk by 40% owing to the diversion of rivers for irrigation.

In 1991, environmental pressure groups succeeded in ending 42 years of nuclear testing at Semipalatinsk in the northeast. The green lobby is now pressing for tighter pollution controls.

MEDIA

▷ TV ownership medium

⊠ Daily newspaper circulation 30 per 1,000 people

PUBLISHING AND BROADCAST MEDIA

There are 3 principal daily newspapers and over 400 other registered newspapers

1 state-owned,
2 independent services

1 state-owned service

The state-owned media compete with independent publications and privately owned radio and television stations, some of which are controlled by members of President Nazarbayev's family. All reports pertaining to ethnic minorities are censored. There are more than 400 registered newspapers, of which fewer than half are in Kazakh.

CRIME

▷ Death penalty not used

🔳 Kazakhstan does not publish prison figures

⬆ Crime levels are rising

CRIME RATES

Theft is rising more sharply than other crime.

Organized crime, especially narcotics smuggling, has increased; there is UN help in combating the problem. A two-year moratorium on the death penalty was announced in 1998.

EDUCATION

▷ School leaving age: 17

👤 99%

🎓 419,460 students

Education systems remain based upon the Soviet model.

THE EDUCATION SYSTEM

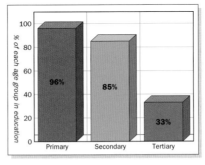

96%   85%   33%

Primary   Secondary   Tertiary

% of each age group in education

Since the adoption of Kazakh as the state language in 1995, teaching in Russian has declined. However, there is a shortage of Kazakh textbooks and Kazakh-speaking teachers to replace the Russian speakers. There are a large number of higher-education institutions and medical schools.

HEALTH

▷ No welfare state benefits

👤 1 per 265 people

Heart attacks, cancers, accidents, violence, tuberculosis

An ill-equipped and poorly funded health system has produced the highest infant mortality rate in Central Asia.

The health system is limited in terms of both facilities and coverage. Rural people have minimal access to clinics. The country's size means that extending coverage and improving the quality of care will be costly. Attempts are therefore being made to attract foreign investment into the health sector. Many doctors have emigrated to Russia.

SPENDING

▷ GDP/cap. increase

CONSUMPTION AND SPENDING

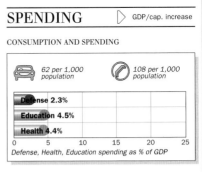

🚗 62 per 1,000 population

☎ 108 per 1,000 population

| Defense 2.3% |
| Education 4.5% |
| Health 4.4% |

0   5   10   15   20   25

Defense, Health, Education spending as % of GDP

Life for the majority of Kazakhs has always been hard, and has grown even more difficult since 1989. Living standards have deteriorated universally, and unemployment has risen as a result of market-oriented reforms within Kazakhstan. The liberalization of the economy also fueled sharp price rises for essential commodities.

The rural population, the poorest group, has been badly affected. The small wealthy elite is made up mainly of former communist officials, many of whom have benefited from privatization, or belong to President Nazarbayev's clan. In 1995, the government banned all foreign currency transactions by Kazakhs.

WORLD RANKING

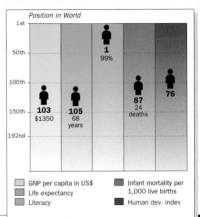

Position in World

1st
50th
100th
150th
192nd

1   99%

103   $1350
105   68 years
87   24 deaths
76

GNP per capita in US$
Life expectancy
Literacy

Infant mortality per 1,000 live births
Human dev. index

K

KENYA

OFFICIAL NAME: Republic of Kenya CAPITAL: Nairobi
POPULATION: 29 million CURRENCY: Kenya shilling OFFICIAL LANGUAGE: Swahili

| 1963 | 1963 | Dec 12 | EAK | +3 | +254 | .ke |

KENYA STRADDLES THE EQUATOR on Africa's east
coast. Its central plateau is bisected by the Great Rift
Valley. The land to the north is desert, while to the east
lies a fertile coastal belt. After independence from Britain in 1963, politics
was dominated by Jomo Kenyatta, who was succeeded in 1978
by President Daniel arap Moi. Moi's divide-and-rule policies have drawn
accusations of favoritism and of fomenting ethnic hatreds. He won
multiparty elections easily in 1992 and 1997, amid accusations of electoral
fraud. The economic mainstays are tourism and agriculture, but high
population growth is a major problem.

*Kenyatta Conference Center, Nairobi. The
modern skyline of the business centre contrasts
sharply with the slums on the city's outskirts.*

CLIMATE

▷ Steppe/mountain/ tropical

WEATHER CHART

Average daily temperature — Rainfall

The coast and Great Rift Valley are hot
and humid, the plateau interior is
temperate and the northeastern desert
hot and dry. Rain generally falls from
April to May and October to November.

TRANSPORTATION

▷ Drive on left

Jomo Kenyatta, Nairobi
1.52m passengers

38 ships
19,800 grt

THE TRANSPORTATION NETWORK

63,800 km (39,600 miles)		None
1,911 km (1,187 miles)		Lake Victoria

Kenya's railroads, ports and main
airport are being upgraded, a reflection
of the importance of tourism and
of Kenya's role as an outlet for
landlocked neighbors.

*Great Rift Valley, Kenya. This huge crack in
the Earth's crust runs from the River Jordan
right through Africa to the Zambezi River.*

TOURISM

▷ Visitors : population 1:41

700,000 visitors

Down 22% 1995–1997

Tourism is vital to the economy and a
key foreign exchange earner. However,
after a boom in package safaris and
beach holidays during the 1980s, visitor
numbers declined during the 1990s.
The main factors were world recession,
reports of instability, the much-
publicized murder of
several tourists
and the 1998
US embassy
bombing.

MAIN TOURIST ARRIVALS

Germany 15%	
UK 15%	
Tanzania 12%	
Uganda 8%	
USA 7%	
Other 43%	

% of total arrivals

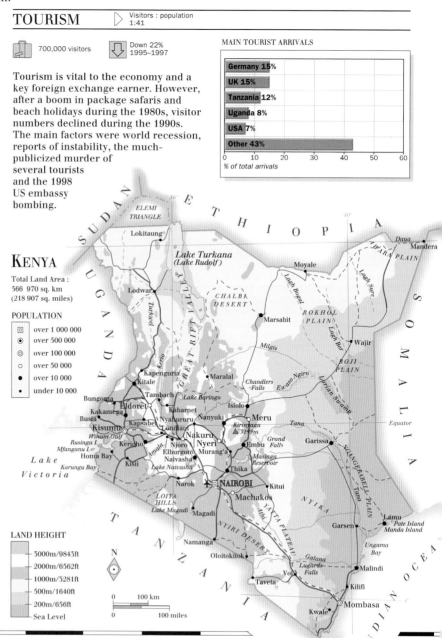

KENYA

Total Land Area : 566 970 sq. km (218 907 sq. miles)

POPULATION

- over 1 000 000
- over 500 000
- over 100 000
- over 50 000
- over 10 000
- under 10 000

LAND HEIGHT

- 5000m/9843ft
- 2000m/6562ft
- 1000m/3281ft
- 500m/1640ft
- 200m/656ft
- Sea Level

0   100 km
0   100 miles

PEOPLE ▷ Pop. density medium

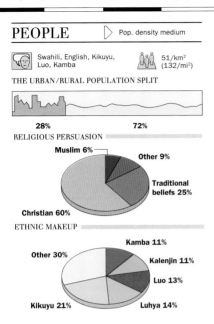

Swahili, English, Kikuyu, Luo, Kamba

51/km² (132/mi²)

THE URBAN/RURAL POPULATION SPLIT

28%   **72%**

RELIGIOUS PERSUASION

Muslim 6%
Other 9%
Traditional beliefs 25%
Christian 60%

ETHNIC MAKEUP

Kamba 11%
Kalenjin 11%
Luo 13%
Other 30%
Kikuyu 21%
Luhya 14%

Kenya's ethnic diversity, with about 70 different groups, reflects its past as a focus of population movements. Asians, Europeans, and Arabs form 1% of the population. The rural majority retains strong clan and extended family links, although these are being weakened by urban migration. Poverty and a high population growth rate are the root causes of the land hunger which has recently been fueling a surge in ethnic violence. Much violence is concentrated in western Kenya, where Kikuyu, formerly the dominant tribe, are the main targets of attacks by Kalenjin, Masai, and Pokor groups. Several hundred thousand Kikuyu are believed to have been displaced from their villages.

POPULATION AGE BREAKDOWN

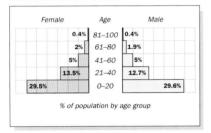

Female	Age	Male
0.4%	81–100	0.4%
2%	61–80	1.9%
5%	41–60	5%
13.5%	21–40	12.7%
29.5%	0–20	29.6%

% of population by age group

WORLD AFFAIRS ▷ Joined UN in 1963

Comm   Comesa   IAEA   IGAD   OAU

Relations with neighboring states and with key Western donors are Kenya's priorities. The US embassy closed temporarily in 1998 after a terrorist bombing caused carnage there. In 1991, human rights concerns were partly responsible for a two-year suspension of aid.

Kenya's border dispute with Sudan over the Elemi Triangle remains unresolved; this arid piece of land has a concentration of Christian refugees fleeing Sudanese government repression.
Kenya is greatly concerned by the situations in neighboring Rwanda, Burundi, and Congo (former Zaire), as well as by conflicts in Sudan, Somalia and Ethiopia.

POLITICS ▷ Multiparty elections

1997/2002   President Daniel arap Moi

AT THE LAST ELECTION

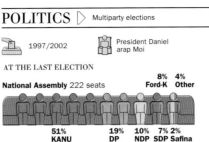

National Assembly 222 seats

8% Ford-K   4% Other

51% KANU   19% DP   10% NDP   7% SDP   2% Safina

KANU = Kenya African National Union   DP = Democratic Party
NDP = National Development Party   FORD-K = Forum for the Restoration of Democracy – Kenya   SDP = Social Democratic Party

Other includes Shirikisho, Forum for the Restoration of Democracy – Asili, Kenya Social Congress

The National Assembly comprises 210 elected members, 12 nominated by the President, and two ex-officio.

Kenya has been led by President Daniel arap Moi since 1978, and became a multiparty democracy in 1992.

MAIN POLITICAL ISSUE
Ethnic violence
The ethnic polarization of political parties in Kenya and rising poverty are fueling ethnic violence. Determined to ensure KANU dominance, President Moi, a Kalenjin, is turning the party into an alliance of smaller ethnic groups opposed to the once dominant Kikuyu. The latter are the largest ethnic group, the main victims of violence, and the main supporters of the opposition. Rift Valley, Nyanga and western provinces – those with most seats in parliament – are focuses of anti-Kikuyu ethnic cleansing.

PROFILE
After 1982, President Moi's efforts to entrench KANU's power provoked demands at home for the introduction of multiparty politics, and condemnation abroad of human rights abuses. Forced in 1992 to concede free elections, Moi helped ensure KANU's victory by curtailing the campaign period. He has been widely accused of manipulating ethnic conflict, part of his strategy to entrench KANU's power. His reelection in December 1997 was marred by widespread allegations of intimidation and electoral fraud.
In July 1999, President Moi appointed paleontologist Richard Leakey, a former political opponent, to head a drive against official corruption.

President Daniel arap Moi, Kenya's leader since 1978.

Mwai Kibaki, opposition leader.

AID ▷ Recipient

$457m (receipts)   Down 25% 1996–1997

Kenya has been a major recipient of aid from donors – such as the UK, Japan, the EU, the World Bank, and the IMF – who are keen to support its free-market approach, despite their concerns about human rights. Little, however, has trickled down to the majority of the population, partly because a high proportion of aid is tied to construction projects and donor-country firms, and partly because of mismanagement and official corruption. In 1996 Western creditor governments decided to link aid disbursements to improvements in human rights.

CHRONOLOGY

From the 10th century, Arab coastal settlers mixed with indigenous peoples in the region. Britain's need for a route to landlocked Uganda led to the formation in 1895 of the British East African Protectorate in the coastal region.

❑ **1900–1918** White settlement.
❑ **1920** Interior becomes British colony.
❑ **1930** Jomo Kenyatta goes to UK; stays 14 years.
❑ **1944** Kenyan African Union (KAU) formed; Kenyatta returns to lead it.
❑ **1952–1956** *Mau Mau*, Kikuyu-led violent campaign to restore African lands. State of emergency; 13,000 people killed.
❑ **1953** KAU banned. Kenyatta jailed.
❑ **1960** State of emergency ends. Tom Mboya and Oginga Odinga form KANU.
❑ **1961** Kenyatta freed; takes up presidency of KANU.
❑ **1963** KANU wins elections. Kenyatta prime minister. Full independence declared.
❑ **1964** Republic of Kenya formed with Kenyatta as president and Odinga as vice president.
❑ **1966** Odinga defects to form Kenya People's Union (KPU). ▷

K

K

CHRONOLOGY *continued*

- ❏ **1969** KANU is sole party to contest elections (also 1974). KANU Sec.-Gen. Tom Mboya assassinated. Unrest. KPU banned and Odinga arrested.
- ❏ **1978** Kenyatta dies. Vice-President Daniel arap Moi succeeds him.
- ❏ **1982** Kenya declared a one-party state. Opposition to Moi. Abortive air force coup. Odinga rearrested.
- ❏ **1983** Election turnout under 50%.
- ❏ **1986** Open "queue-voting" replaces secret ballot in first stage of general elections. Other measures to extend Moi's powers incite opposition.
- ❏ **1987** Government acts to suppress opposition groups. Political arrests and human rights abuses attract overseas criticism.
- ❏ **1988** Moi wins third term and extends his control over judiciary.
- ❏ **1989** Vice-president replaced by finance minister George Saitoti after corruption allegations. Political prisoners freed.
- ❏ **1990** Government implicated in deaths of foreign minister Robert Ouko and Anglican archbishop. Riots. Odinga and others form FORD, outlawed by government.
- ❏ **1991** Arrest of FORD leaders; attempts to stop prodemocracy protests. Donors suspend aid. Moi agrees to introduce multiparty system. Ethnic violence on increase.
- ❏ **1992** FORD splits into factions led by ex-minister Kenneth Matiba and Odinga. Opposition weakness helps Moi win December elections.
- ❏ **1994** Odinga dies.
- ❏ **1997** Moi wins further term in widely criticized elections.

DEFENSE

▷ No compulsory military service

💲 $235m   ⬆ Up 9% in 1997

Destabilization of the northeastern border by the Somali civil war is the main defense issue.

KENYAN ARMED FORCES

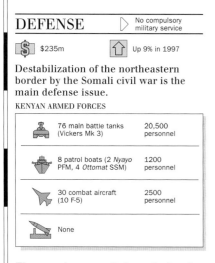

🛡	76 main battle tanks (Vickers Mk 3)	20,500 personnel
🚤	8 patrol boats (2 *Nyayo* PFM, 4 *Ottomat* SSM)	1200 personnel
✈	30 combat aircraft (10 F-5)	2500 personnel
	None	

The army has recently been deployed to suppress tribal fighting in the Rift Valley. The military has historically played no part in politics.

ECONOMICS

▷ Inflation 12.2% p.a. (1985–1996)

📊 $9.7bn   💲 63.05–61.78 Kenya shillings

SCORE CARD

❏ WORLD GNP RANKING	83rd
❏ GNP PER CAPITA	$340
❏ BALANCE OF PAYMENTS	-$454m
❏ INFLATION	12%
❏ UNEMPLOYMENT	35%

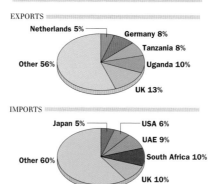

EXPORTS

- Netherlands 5%
- Germany 8%
- Tanzania 8%
- Uganda 10%
- Other 56%
- UK 13%

IMPORTS

- Japan 5%
- USA 6%
- UAE 9%
- South Africa 10%
- Other 60%
- UK 10%

STRENGTHS

Tourism – the largest foreign exchange earner. Broad agricultural base, especially cash crops such as coffee and tea. Largest, most diversified manufacturing sector in East Africa.

WEAKNESSES

Fluctuating world prices for coffee and tea. Corruption. Poor recent GDP growth. High population growth. Land shortage means uneconomical small units. Country's image problem affects tourism.

PROFILE

Kenya has been hailed as an example to the rest of Africa of the benefits of a mainly free-market economy. Government involvement has been relatively limited, and recently further reduced by privatization. Foreign investment has been encouraged, with some success. Tourism has become the leading foreign exchange earner over the past 20 years, despite suffering serious setbacks in the 1990s. Manufacturing now accounts for 21% of GDP, and is the most diversified sector in east Africa, but needs to expand rapidly so as to create more jobs.

Economic growth was good by African standards during the 1980s, averaging over 4% a year. However, it was not good enough to compensate for one of the world's highest population growth rates, approximately 3.5% , although the UN estimates that growth will fall to 2.2% in the early 2000s. For the majority of Kenyans, farming ever-smaller landholdings or earning a living in the informal sector, life has become harsher.

Other problems, including inflation, a heavy debt burden ($7.4 billion in 1997), and growing dependence on balance of payments support had come to a head in the early 1990s, when economic growth gave way to recession. Real GDP growth fell to 0.4% in 1992 and has remained low, typically at 1.2% in 1997. The rise in poverty-linked violence and political unrest hit tourism; earnings fell by 15% in the early 1990s, and although tourist numbers have risen since, the industry has yet to recover fully.

Partly as a response to pressure from donors, including the 1991–1993 freeze on balance of payments support, the government has implemented some economic liberalization measures. These include floating the Kenya shilling, raising interest rates and giving exporters direct access to their hard currency earnings. However, sustained growth is likely to remain elusive until Kenya overcomes two fundamental problems – the official corruption which drains vital resources, including foreign aid, and the poor image which has been affecting its tourist industry.

ECONOMIC PERFORMANCE INDICATOR

KENYA : MAJOR BUSINESSES

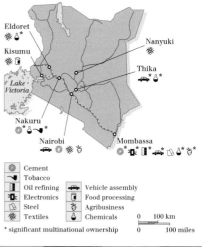

- Eldoret
- Kisumu
- Nanyuki
- Thika
- Lake Victoria
- Nakuru
- Nairobi
- Mombassa

Cement	
Tobacco	
Oil refining	Vehicle assembly
Electronics	Food processing
Steel	Agribusiness
Textiles	Chemicals

0   100 km
0   100 miles
* significant multinational ownership

RESOURCES

Electric power
809,000 kw

193,790 tonnes

Not an oil producer;
refines 90,000 b/d

14.1m cattle,
7.5m goats,
5.7m sheep

Soda ash, fluorspar,
limestone, rubies,
gold, vermiculite

ELECTRICITY GENERATION

Hydro 83% (3.1bn kwh)

Combustion 9% (0.3bn kwh)

Nuclear 0%

Other 8% (0.3bn kwh)

0   20   40   60   80   100

% of total generation by type

Agriculture underpins Kenya's economy and is still the largest sector, accounting for 27% of GDP. Kenya's varied topography means that tropical, subtropical and temperate crops may be grown. Coffee and tea, the main export crops, have been affected by falling world prices. Efforts to reduce dependence on these crops have led to the growth of a successful export-oriented horticultural industry.

Kenya has few mineral resources, and mining accounts for only 0.2% of GDP. Hydroelectric and geothermal sources are being developed to reduce energy imports – currently 70% of total requirements. Oil exploration in the Great Rift Valley and the northeast has revealed deposits in Turkana District.

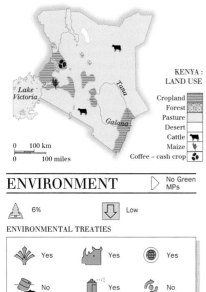

KENYA :
LAND USE

Cropland
Forest
Pasture
Desert
Cattle
Maize
Coffee – cash crop

0   100 km
0   100 miles

ENVIRONMENT

No Green
MPs

6%

Low

ENVIRONMENTAL TREATIES

Yes

Yes

Yes

No

Yes

No

The government recognizes the importance to the tourist industry of wildlife conservation, and recent elephant protection schemes have been a success. However, initiatives to set up national reserves are competing with agriculture for land. The effect of dams on the Tana River is another concern.

MEDIA

TV ownership low

Daily newspaper circulation 9 per 1,000 people

PUBLISHING AND BROADCAST MEDIA

There are 4 daily newspapers. The *Daily Nation* has the largest circulation

2 state-controlled services

1 state-controlled network

Government intolerance of criticism is long-standing and includes plays and novels as well as the media. Ngugi wa Thiongo, Kenya's most famous novelist, was exiled for his criticism of KANU.

CRIME

Death penalty used

Kenya does not publish prison figures

Up 15% in 1992

CRIME RATES

Murders
6   *per 100,000 population*

Rapes
2   *per 100,000 population*

Thefts
84   *per 100,000 population*

Nairobi's high crime levels are spreading countrywide, as a result of worsening poverty, ethnic violence, and rising banditry in the northeast. An increase in the use of guns underlies the rapid increase in violent crime.

EDUCATION

School leaving
age: 14

79%

35,421 students

The education system is loosely based on the British model.

THE EDUCATION SYSTEM

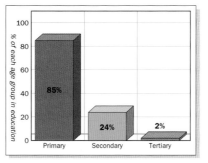

% of each age group in education

100

80

60

85%

40

24%

20

2%

0

Primary   Secondary   Tertiary

Schooling is not compulsory, but free primary education means that 85% of children attend; the drop-out rate at secondary level is high; only about 24% attend. The emphasis is on vocational training in higher education. Education spending represents 7.4% of GNP.

HEALTH

No welfare state
health benefits

1 per 6,667
people

Respiratory and
diarrheal diseases,
malaria

The health system is a mix of state and private facilities, the latter mainly run by charities and missions. The state system has been hit by recession, which has worsened the already limited access of the rural majority. Poverty-related illnesses are increasing, particularly among children and women, and the country has a high incidence of HIV and AIDS. Kenya has 15 doctors and 23 qualified nurses for every 100,000 people.

SPENDING

GDP/cap. no
increase

CONSUMPTION AND SPENDING

10 per 1,000
population

8 per 1,000
population

Defense 2.4%

Education 7.4%

Health 2.7%

0   5   10   15   20   25

Defense, Health, Education spending as % of GDP

Wealth disparities in Kenya are large and growing, exacerbated by land hunger and constant migration to the country's major cities, where jobs are few and existence depends on the informal economy. The slum dwellers of Nairobi's Amarthi Valley are among Africa's poorest, worst-nourished people. Their lives contrast with those of the country's elite – top government officials with access to patronage; white Kenyans, who derive their wealth largely from agricultural estates; and the largely Asian business community. Among these groups, Mercedes and the latest four-wheel-drive cars are popular as status symbols, as are designer-label clothes. Wealthy Kenyans often send their children abroad for higher education.

WORLD RANKING

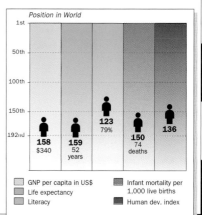

Position in World

1st

50th

100th

150th

192nd

158
$340

159
52
years

123
79%

150
74
deaths

136

GNP per capita in US$

Life expectancy

Literacy

Infant mortality per
1,000 live births

Human dev. index

K

KIRIBATI

OFFICIAL NAME: Republic of Kiribati **CAPITAL:** Bairiki
POPULATION: 78,000 **CURRENCY:** Australian dollar **OFFICIAL LANGUAGE:** English

1979 | 1979 | July 12 | KIR | +12 | +686 | .ki

FORMERLY PART OF THE British colony of the Gilbert and Ellice Islands, the Gilberts became independent in 1979 and adopted the name Kiribati (pronounced Kiribass). British interest in the Gilberts rested solely on the exploitation of the phosphate deposits on Banaba; these ran out in 1980. In 1981, Kiribati won damages (but not the costs of litigation) from the British for decades of phosphate exploitation.

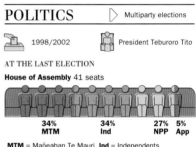

Banreaba Island, Tarawa atoll. None of the atolls is more than 8 m (26 ft)high except Banaba, the main source of phosphates.

CLIMATE
▷ Tropical oceanic

WEATHER CHART

- Average daily temperature
- Rainfall

Kiribati's small land area in the vast Pacific means that it often goes for months without rain. In March 1999, a nationwide drought emergency was declared.

TRANSPORTATION
▷ Drive on right

Bonriki Intl, Tarawa
51,000 passengers (est)   6,400 grt

THE TRANSPORTATION NETWORK

483 km (300 miles)		None	
None		5 km (3 miles)	

Kiribati has a limited air link with Fiji. Small-scale shipping and good satellite communications also keep it in touch with the outside world.

TOURISM
▷ Visitors : population 1:13

6,000 visitors   Up 50% 1995–1997

MAIN TOURIST ARRIVALS

USA 21%	
Australia 13%	
Japan 7%	
Other 59%	

% of total arrivals

Kiritimati, which has a weekly air service to Honolulu, attracts a small but steady stream of visitors.

PEOPLE
▷ Pop. density medium

English, Micronesian dialect   110/km² (284/mi²)

THE URBAN/RURAL POPULATION SPLIT

36%   64%

RELIGIOUS PERSUASION

- Other 8%
- Kiribati Protestant Church 39%
- Roman Catholic 53%

Locals still refer to themselves as Gilbertese. Apart from the inhabitants of Banaba, who employed anthropologists to establish their racial distinction, almost all Gilbertese are Micronesian. Tension with the Banabans is intense, but mostly fueled by the historic value of Banaba's phosphate deposits. Most Gilbertese are poor. Many go to Nauru as guest workers, living in barracks-like conditions, or work as merchant shipping crew. Those who stay at home go through a circular migration from the outlying islands to Tarawa, returning to see relatives. Women play a prominent role, especially on outlying islands, where they run most of the farms.

POLITICS
▷ Multiparty elections

1998/2002   President Teburoro Tito

AT THE LAST ELECTION

House of Assembly 41 seats

34% MTM	34% Ind	27% NPP	5% App

MTM = Mañeaban Te Mauri **Ind** = Independents
NPP = National Progressive Party **App** = Appointed

There are also one appointed and one ex-officio member of the House of Assembly.

The traditional chiefs still effectively rule Kiribati, through a party system on the British model. Victory for the MTM in the 1994 elections ended 15 years of rule by the NPP. The main concern is the economy, which is extremely vulnerable to any fluctuations in world demand for coconuts. The overpopulation of Tarawa is the other major issue. Possible restrictions on travel to the island have been discussed. In part, the problem of migration is caused by the poverty and lack of opportunity on the outer islands. A resettlement program has now begun, aiming to move people out of Tarawa.

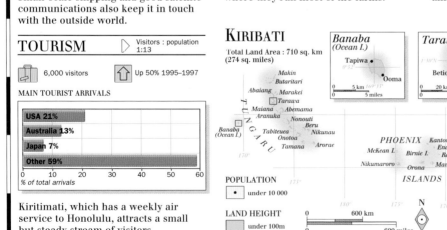

KIRIBATI

Total Land Area : 710 sq. km (274 sq. miles)

POPULATION
- under 10 000

LAND HEIGHT
- under 100m

WORLD AFFAIRS

 Joined UN in 1999

Kiribati has little international significance because of its tiny size and remote location, but is able to make its voice heard regionally through the South Pacific Forum. In 1986, Kiribati was a signatory to a deal between the USA and a number of Pacific Island states that resulted in the USA paying US$60 million in return for access to Pacific fishing grounds. In the Cold War era Kiribati played the USSR off against the USA, extracting a high price for selling fishing leases which allowed boats to spy on US nuclear testing on the neighboring Kwajalein atoll in the Marshall Islands.

AID

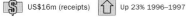 Recipient

US$16m (receipts) Up 23% 1996–1997

Aid is mostly for small infrastructure projects. In March 1999 Kiribati appealed for aid when it declared a nationionwide drought emergency.

DEFENSE

No compulsory military service

Kiribati has no defense budget Not applicable

Australia and New Zealand provide *de facto* protection, with regular antisubmarine patrols.

ECONOMICS

Not available

US$76m 1.53–1.63 Australian dollars

SCORE CARD

- ❏ WORLD GNP RANKING.........................188th
- ❏ GNP PER CAPITA ....US$910
- ❏ BALANCE OF PAYMENTS ....US$1m
- ❏ INFLATION 4%
- ❏ UNEMPLOYMENT 2%

STRENGTHS

Subsistence economy has survived, and there is little need to import food. Coconuts provide some export income: the EU is the biggest market. Fisheries have limited potential.

WEAKNESSES

Lack of resources since Banaba's phosphate deposits ran out. Isolation, and large distances between islands. Heavy dependence on international aid. Almost no economic potential.

EXPORTS

Fiji 4% Australia 5% Denmark 5% Other 7% USA 12% Netherlands 67%

IMPORTS

China 6% New Zealand 8% Japan 9% Other 12% Australia 46% Fiji 19%

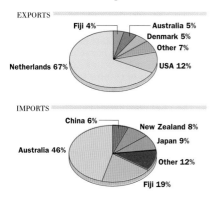

RESOURCES

 Electric power 2,000 kw

25,000 tonnes Not an oil producer

9,500 pigs, 300,000 chickens None

Phosphate deposits on Banaba ran out in 1980. All energy supplies have to be imported. Underwater agriculture is being developed.

ENVIRONMENT

No Green MPs

39% (including marine and semi-protected areas) Not available

Rising sea levels cause serious coastal erosion. Tarawa's protective coral reef which holds important inshore fish stocks in the lagoon, is threatened by untreated effluent. Approaches have been made by international – mainly US – companies seeking to dump industrial waste into the lagoons. A nationwide drought emergency was declared in March 1999.

MEDIA

TV ownership low

 There are no daily newspapers

PUBLISHING AND BROADCAST MEDIA

There are no daily newspapers. There are 2 weekly newspapers, *Atoll Pioneer* and *Te Uekera*

1 independent service 1 independent service

The main sources of news and information on Kiribati are *Pacific Islands Monthly* and *Islands' Business* magazines.

CRIME

Death penalty not used

 91 prisoners Down 46% in 1990

Crime, apart from brawls resulting from drunkenness, is minimal. The judicial system is based on the British model.

EDUCATION

School leaving age: 15

 98% Not applicable

Education is British-inspired and compulsory from six to 15. The best students go on to university in Fiji.

CHRONOLOGY

The British established the phosphate-producing colony of the Gilbert and Ellice Islands in 1892.

- ❏ **1957** First British nuclear tests take place near Kiritimati.
- ❏ **1979** Independence as two states, Kiribati and Tuvalu.
- ❏ **1981** British agree to pay damages for phosphate mining.
- ❏ **1986** Kiribati–US fishing deal.
- ❏ **1994** NPP, in power since independence, loses election.
- ❏ **1999** Nationwide drought emergency declared.

HEALTH

Welfare state health benefits

1 per 1,939 people Heart diseases, diabetes

Most Gilbertese are healthy, thanks to a home-grown diet and free medical care. Those on Tarawa import tinned food because of a lack of agricultural land, and nutrition is becoming a problem.

SPENDING

GDP/cap. no increase

CONSUMPTION AND SPENDING

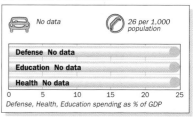

No data 26 per 1,000 population

Defense	No data
Education	No data
Health	No data

0   5   10   15   20   25
Defense, Health, Education spending as % of GDP

Life in Kiribati is modest. Civil servants in the capital, Bairiki, are the country's wealthiest group. There is a handful of cars on Tarawa, and these are confined to the single 29-km (18-mile) stretch of road, from Tarawa to the airport. Most Gilbertese live by subsistence farming and fishing.

WORLD RANKING

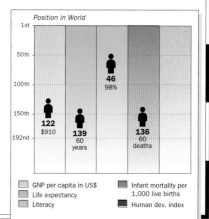

Position in World

1st
50th
100th
150th
192nd

122 $910
139 60 years
46 98%
136 60 deaths

- ☐ GNP per capita in US$
- ☐ Life expectancy
- ☐ Literacy
- ☐ Infant mortality per 1,000 live births
- ☐ Human dev. index

K

Asia

EAST ASIA

China · N. KOREA · S. Korea · JAPAN

NORTH KOREA

OFFICIAL NAME: Democratic People's Republic of Korea   **CAPITAL:** Pyongyang
POPULATION: 23.2 million   **CURRENCY:** North Korean Won   **OFFICIAL LANGUAGE:** Korean

| 1948 | 1953 | Sept 9 | DRK | +9 | +850 | .kp |

NORTH KOREA COMPRISES the northern half of the Korean peninsula and is separated from the capitalist South close to the 38th parallel. Much of the country is mountainous; the Chaeryong and Pyongyang plains in the southwest are the most fertile regions. Established as an independent communist republic in 1948, North Korea remains largely isolated from the outside world. Its economy, starved of development capital, is now facing severe difficulties and a food crisis requiring large-scale international assistance.

CLIMATE ▷ Continental

WEATHER CHART

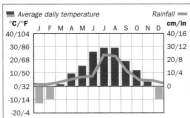

North Korea has a typically continental climate. Winters in the north can be extreme, with several months of snow.

TRANSPORTATION ▷ Drive on right

✈ Sunan, Pyongyang   🚢 182 ships 692,900 grt

THE TRANSPORTATION NETWORK

| 1,861 km (1,156 miles) | 524 km (326 miles) |
| 8,533 km (5,302 miles) | 2,253 km (1,400 miles) |

North Korea relies heavily on the antiquated railroad network built by the Japanese during their occupation. The Pyongyang–Kaesong highway, completed in 1992, is open only to very limited, officially approved traffic.

TOURISM ▷ Visitors : population 1:181

128,000   No change 1995–1997

MAIN TOURIST ARRIVALS

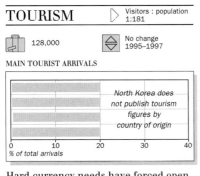

North Korea does not publish tourism figures by country of origin

% of total arrivals

Hard currency needs have forced open tourism. The South Korean Hyundai company is developing Mt. Kumgang.

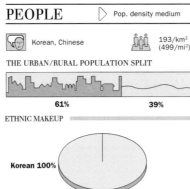

Rice paddy-field. The hot, wet summers are ideal for rice growing. Most farms are run as cooperatives.

PEOPLE ▷ Pop. density medium

Korean, Chinese   193/km² (499/mi²)

THE URBAN/RURAL POPULATION SPLIT

61%   39%

ETHNIC MAKEUP

Korean 100%

North Korea operates a strict "estates" system, by which the population is classed according to three categories: loyal, wavering and hostile. Inclusion in the first category is a prerequisite for advancement. Those deemed hostile – usually Christians and the children of landlords or of Koreans who fled to the South – have barely any rights. People live severely regulated lives. Divorce is nonexistent and extramarital sex highly frowned upon. Women form more than 50% of the workforce, but are also expected to run the home; it is not uncommon for them to rise at 4 a.m., and end their working day at 7 p.m. From an early age, children are looked after by an extensive system of state-run crèches. The privileged lifestyle of the political elite – numbering only about 200,000 – is a source of considerable popular resentment.

POLITICS ▷ No multiparty elections

1998/2002   Eternal President Kim Il Sung

AT THE LAST ELECTION

Supreme People's Assembly 687 seats

100% DFRF

DFRF = Democratic Front for the Reunification of the Fatherland
The Democratic Front for the Reunification of the Fatherland (led by the Workers Party of Korea) was the sole party permitted to take part in the 1998 elections.

The 3 million-strong KWP (Worker's Party of Korea) is the only legal party; membership is essential for individual advancement. Kim Il Sung, the subject of an absurdly lavish personality cult, died in 1994 after almost 50 years as leader. Since then the key question has been how his son and chosen successor, Kim Jong Il, will handle the leadership. Three years passed before the younger Kim was formally installed as head of the party, and he makes few public appearances. He lacks his father's authority, and has yet to seal the succession.

WORLD AFFAIRS ▷ Joined UN in 1991

NAM

The worldwide collapse of communism isolated North Korea by destroying its framework of traditional allies. Although in 1991 it joined the UN, North Korea had a protracted dispute with the IAEA over its refusal to allow inspection of its nuclear industry. In 1994, a deal was signed with the US whereby North Korea froze its nuclear program in return for assistance in replacing its reactors with models less suited to the manufacture of weapons. Despite desultory talks over reunification, North and South Korean forces remain in a state of alert across the border. Clashes betwebb their navies in disputed waters in mid-1999 marred plans to resume talks.

AID ▷ Recipient

$202m (receipts)   Up 370% 1996–1997

Rice harvests were badly damaged by alternate drought and flood in the mid-1990s, precipitating a famine. A massive international aid effort is required to stave off starvation.

K

NORTH KOREA

Total Land Area : 120 410 sq. km (46 490 sq. miles)

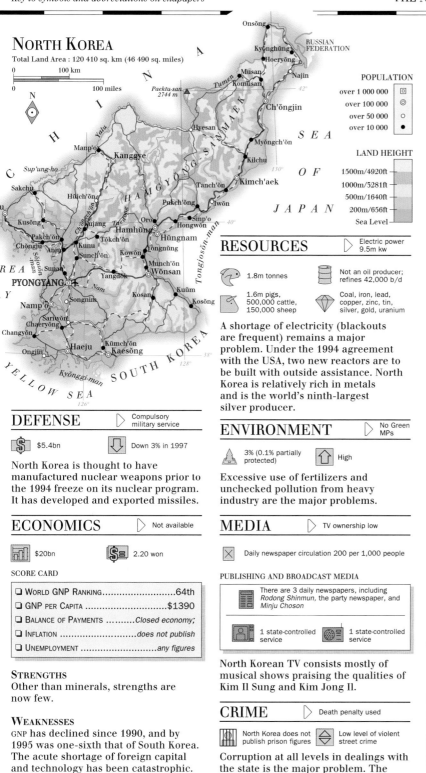

POPULATION

over 1 000 000	▣
over 100 000	◉
over 50 000	○
over 10 000	●

LAND HEIGHT

1500m/4920ft
1000m/3281ft
500m/1640ft
200m/656ft
Sea Level

CHRONOLOGY

The peninsula was divided at the 38th parallel in 1945; North Korea became an independent state in 1948.

❏ **1950–1953** Korean War.
❏ **1994** Withdrawal from IAEA. Kim Il Sung dies.
❏ **1997** Threat of famine worsens. Kim Jong Il declared party leader.
❏ **1998** Kim Il Sung declared Eternal President.

EDUCATION
▷ School leaving age: 15

📖 95%   🎓 390,000 students

North Korea claims to have created over one million "intellectuals." Kim Il Sung, Pyongyang, is the only university.

HEALTH
▷ Welfare state health benefits

👤 1 per 370 people   Heart diseases, cancers, digestive diseases

Life expectancy, raised by free health care, is now threatened by malnutrition and outright starvation.

SPENDING
▷ GDP/cap. no increase

CONSUMPTION AND SPENDING

🚗 No data   💿 49 per 1,000 population

Defense 27%	
Education No data	
Health No data	

0 5 10 15 20 25
Defense, Health, Education spending as % of GDP

An elite group within the KWP lives well, with access to specialist shops and consumer goods such as VCRS, televisions and computers. Both private car and telephone ownership are strictly forbidden.

RESOURCES
▷ Electric power 9.5m kw

🥧 1.8m tonnes

🛢 Not an oil producer; refines 42,000 b/d

🐖 1.6m pigs, 500,000 cattle, 150,000 sheep

💎 Coal, iron, lead, copper, zinc, tin, silver, gold, uranium

A shortage of electricity (blackouts are frequent) remains a major problem. Under the 1994 agreement with the USA, two new reactors are to be built with outside assistance. North Korea is relatively rich in metals and is the world's ninth-largest silver producer.

ENVIRONMENT
▷ No Green MPs

🌲 3% (0.1% partially protected)   ⬆ High

Excessive use of fertilizers and unchecked pollution from heavy industry are the major problems.

MEDIA
▷ TV ownership low

✖ Daily newspaper circulation 200 per 1,000 people

PUBLISHING AND BROADCAST MEDIA

There are 3 daily newspapers, including *Rodong Shinmun*, the party newspaper, and *Minju Choson*

1 state-controlled service   1 state-controlled service

North Korean TV consists mostly of musical shows praising the qualities of Kim Il Sung and Kim Jong Il.

CRIME
▷ Death penalty used

North Korea does not publish prison figures   Low level of violent street crime

Corruption at all levels in dealings with the state is the major problem. The criminal code is weighted to protect the state against "subversion," rather than the rights of the individual. North Korea has a very poor human rights record and there is a *gulag* of more than 100,000 "subversives," where those accused are sent along with their families and where torture is routine.

DEFENSE
▷ Compulsory military service

💲 $5.4bn   ⬇ Down 3% in 1997

North Korea is thought to have manufactured nuclear weapons prior to the 1994 freeze on its nuclear program. It has developed and exported missiles.

ECONOMICS
▷ Not available

📊 $20bn   💲 2.20 won

SCORE CARD

❏ WORLD GNP RANKING.........................64th
❏ GNP PER CAPITA $1390
❏ BALANCE OF PAYMENTS ....*Closed economy;*
❏ INFLATION ....*does not publish*
❏ UNEMPLOYMENT ....*any figures*

STRENGTHS
Other than minerals, strengths are now few.

WEAKNESSES
GNP has declined since 1990, and by 1995 was one-sixth that of South Korea. The acute shortage of foreign capital and technology has been catastrophic.

EXPORTS/IMPORTS

North Korea's main trading partners are Russia, China and Japan

WORLD RANKING

Position in World

1st
50th
100th
150th
192nd

102
$1390

133
63
years

69
95%

132
66
deaths

☐ GNP per capita in US$	☐ Infant mortality per 1,000 live births
☐ Life expectancy	
☐ Literacy	☐ Human dev. index

K

349

SOUTH KOREA

OFFICIAL NAME: Republic of Korea **CAPITAL:** Seoul
POPULATION: 46.1 million **CURRENCY:** Won **OFFICIAL LANGUAGE:** Korean

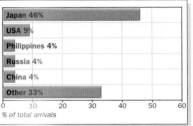

EAST ASIA

 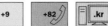

1948 · 1953 · Aug 15 · ROK · +9 · +82 · .kr

SOUTH KOREA OCCUPIES the southern half of the Korean peninsula in East Asia. Over 80% of its terrain is mountainous and two-thirds is forested. Rice is the major agricultural product, grown by over 85% of South Korea's three million farmers. Most of the urban population lives along the coastal plains. Under US sponsorship, South Korea was separated from the communist North after World War II. Although the two states have discussed reunification, the legacy of hostility arising from the 1950–1953 Korean War remains a major obstacle.

CLIMATE ▷ Continental

WEATHER CHART

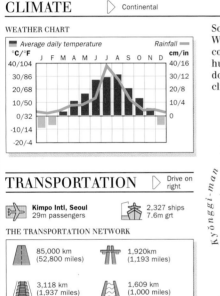

- ■ Average daily temperature
- ▬ Rainfall

South Korea has four distinct seasons. Winters are dry and can be bitterly cold. Summers are hot and humid. The island of Cheju-do has a tropical climate.

TRANSPORTATION ▷ Drive on right

Kimpo Intl, Seoul
29m passengers

2,327 ships
7.6m grt

THE TRANSPORTATION NETWORK

85,000 km (52,800 miles)	1,920km (1,193 miles)
3,118 km (1,937 miles)	1,609 km (1,000 miles)

South Korea has a highly integrated transportation policy. Massive investments have been made in all aspects of communications. A mainly toll-based nationwide motor expressway joins most major urban centers. Air travel has expanded rapidly, bringing forward plans to replace Kimpo International with a new airport. Competition for Korean Air (KAL) has come with the licensing of a second airline, Asiana.

South Korea has perhaps the world's best public transportation system. One timetable integrates all forms of travel, which have a reputation for punctuality. A $14 billion high-speed rail link is being built between Seoul and Pusan. The collapse of a major road bridge in Seoul in 1994, causing the death of 32 people, has raised questions about the quality of some of the country's architecture.

TOURISM ▷ Visitors : population 1:12

3.9m visitors · Up 4% 1995–1997

MAIN TOURIST ARRIVALS

Japan 46%	
USA 9%	
Philippines 4%	
Russia 4%	
China 4%	
Other 33%	

% of total arrivals

Overseas tourism to South Korea has increased ten-fold since 1969. Most visitors are Japanese, who come for the golf and Seoul's nightlife; Cheju-do is a favored honeymoon destination. Whereas visiting relations of US army personnel once made up 13% of all tourists, today Los Angeles-based Korean-Americans make up the greatest proportion of US visitors. However, despite the publicity generated by the 1988 Olympics, and the decision to make 1994 "Visit Korea Year," South Korea is still not seen in the West as a prime tourist destination.

SOUTH KOREA

Total Land Area : 98 750 sq. km
(58 120 sq. miles)

POPULATION

over 5 000 000	▣
over 1 000 000	◉
over 500 000	◉
over 100 000	◎
over 50 000	○
over 10 000	•
under 10 000	•

LAND HEIGHT

1000m/3281ft
500m/1640ft
200m/656ft
Sea Level

K

PEPLE

PEOPLE   ▷ Pop. density medium

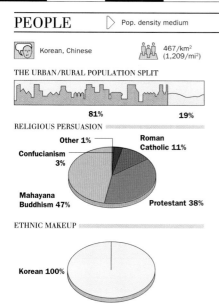

Korean, Chinese

467/km²
(1,209/mi²)

THE URBAN/RURAL POPULATION SPLIT

81%   19%

RELIGIOUS PERSUASION

Other 1%
Roman
Catholic 11%

Confucianism
3%

Mahayana
Buddhism 47%

Protestant 38%

ETHNIC MAKEUP

Korean 100%

South Korea, like the North, is unusual in having been inhabited by one ethnic group for the last 2,000 years. There is a tiny Chinese community, but this is diminishing as most emigrate to Taiwan. One result of economic growth has been an increase in illegal immigrants from the poorer Asian countries, who take menial jobs that Koreans now refuse. Family life is a central and clearly defined part of Korean society. Most Koreans can trace their ancestry back thousands of years. This is significant, since those of the same surname group (rather than the same surname – 60% of Koreans are called Lee, Kim or Park) may not marry. Pressure on housing has led to an increase in nuclear families, as city-center apartments do not have room for the traditional household of three generations. Women play a traditional role in society: it is still not respectable for those who are married to have a job.

POPULATION AGE BREAKDOWN

Female	Age	Male
0.6%	81–100	0.2%
5%	61–80	3.5%
10.6%	41–60	10.8%
18.5%	21–40	19.2%
15.1%	0–20	16.5%

% of population by age group

POLITICS   ▷ Multiparty elections

1996/2000   President Kim Dae Jung

AT THE LAST ELECTION

National Assembly 299 seats

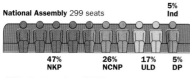

5%
Ind

47%   26%   17%   5%
NKP   NCNP   ULD   DP

NKP = New Korea Party **NCNP** = National Congress for
New Politics **ULD** = United Liberal Democrats
Ind = Independents **DP** = Democratic Party

Officially a democracy, in practice South Korea was ruled by military dictators until 1987. Inaugurated in 1988, the Sixth Republic has been characterized by multiparty democratic politics.

MAIN POLITICAL ISSUES
Corruption
The popular anti-corruption campaign initiated by then president Kim Young Sam (1993–1998) resulted in the death sentence passed on former president Chun Doo Hwan in 1996. Kim himself later faced allegations of corruption.

The economy
Economic performance was one of the world's most impressive until the late 1997 regional crisis resulted in severe financial austerity and retrenchment.

Faction-led parties
South Korea's political parties are highly factionalized and fragmented, and regroup often. Voters have recently demanded unified parties that represent clearer ideological positions.

PROFILE
Politics changed radically in 1987 with the introduction of direct presidential elections, a parliament with enhanced powers and a free press. In 1993, the first nonmilitary leader in 30 years, Kim Young Sam, became president. He established his independence from the military and launched an anti-corruption campaign. Kim's ruling NKP (the former Democratic Liberal Party) lost its overall majority in the 1996 general election, but remained in office. In early 1997 a steel scandal forced the resignation of the new government. Later that year, amid a gathering economic crisis, the opposition leader Kim Dae Jung was elected president with effect from February 1998.

Kim Dae Jung, veteran activist and president since 1998.

Roh Tae-Woo, one of two former presidents amnestied in 1998.

WORLD AFFAIRS   ▷ Joined UN in 1991

APEC   CP   IAEA   OECD   WTO

Since the 1950s, relations with North Korea have been the major concern of foreign policy; they remain unresolved. North Korea has indicated a willingness to consider reunification and, under US pressure, has dismantled its suspected nuclear-weapons program. However, hostility and suspicion continue to characterize the relations between the two Korean states. South Korea is also concerned that the North Korean economy may be about to collapse, thereby seriously increasing the social and economic costs of union. Relations with China, once an important ally of North Korea, have improved. Japan is also a major trading partner, although South Koreans harbor resentment over the 1910–1945 Japanese colonization.

AID   ▷ Donor

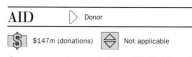

$147m (donations)   Not applicable

Once a massive recipient of US aid, and then of Japanese war reparations, South Korea emerged in the 1970s and 1980s as a major aid donor. However, the economic crisis which first hit South Korea in 1997 forced it to seek financial assistance internationally to salvage key sectors of its threatened economy.

CHRONOLOGY
The Yi dynasty, founded in Seoul in 1392, ruled the kingdom of Korea until 1910. Korea had become a vassal state of China in 1644.

❑ **1860** Korea reacts to French and British occupation of Peking by preventing Western influence; becomes the "Hermit Kingdom."
❑ **1904–1905** Russo-Japanese War. Japan conquers Korea.
❑ **1910** Japan annexes Korea.
❑ **1919** Widespread independence protests violently suppressed.
❑ **1945** US and Soviet armies arrive. Korea split at 38°N. South comes under de facto US rule.
❑ **1948** Republic of South Korea created.
❑ **1950** Hostilities between North and South, each aspiring to rule a united Korea. North invades South, sparking Korean War. USA, with UN backing, enters on South's side; China unofficially assists the North. In 1951 the fighting stabilizes in the vicinity of the 38th parallel.
❑ **1953** Armistice establishes a *de facto* border at the cease-fire line, which lies close to 38th parallel.

⇨

K

CHRONOLOGY *continued*

- ❏ **1960** Syngman Rhee, president since 1948, toppled by revolt.
- ❏ **1961** Military coup leads to Park Chung-Hee's authoritarian junta.
- ❏ **1963** Pressure for civilian government. Park reelected as president (as in 1967 and 1971). Strong manufacturing base and exports drive massive economic development program.
- ❏ **1965** Links restored with Japan.
- ❏ **1966** 45,000 troops engaged in South Vietnam.
- ❏ **1972** Martial law stifles political opposition. New constitution with greater presidential powers.
- ❏ **1979** Park assassinated. Gen. Chun Doo Huan, intelligence chief, leads coup. Kim Young Sam, opposition leader, expelled from parliament.
- ❏ **1980** Army massacre of 200 students and dissidents in Kwangju. Chun chosen as president. Kim Dae Jung and other opposition figures arrested.
- ❏ **1986** Car exports start.
- ❏ **1987** Emergence of prodemocracy movement. Roh Tae-Woo, Chun's chosen successor, elected president.
- ❏ **1988** Inauguration of Sixth Republic: genuine multiparty democracy.
- ❏ **1990** Government party and two opposition parties, including Kim Young Sam's, merge to form DLP.
- ❏ **1991** Joins UN. Reunification discussions with North.
- ❏ **1992** Links with China established.
- ❏ **1993** Kim Young Sam inaugurated as Roh's successor.
- ❏ **1995** DLP renamed NKP. Unprecedented charges of corruption and treason against former presidents Chun and Roh.
- ❏ **1996** Chun sentenced to death for organizing 1979–1980 coup; Roh given 22-year prison term; both amnestied in 1998.
- ❏ **1996** Membership of OECD.
- ❏ **1997** Protests against new labor laws. Cabinet resigns over steel scandal. Economic crisis worsens.
- ❏ **1998** Veteran opposition leader Kim Dae Jung succeeds as president.

Seoul lit up at night. *The city is home to more than 10 million people – one-quarter of South Korea's population. Seoul means "capital*

K

DEFENSE Compulsory military service

💲 $14.7bn   ⬇ Down 10% in 1997

The main defense concern is the North Korean regime.

SOUTH KOREAN ARMED FORCES

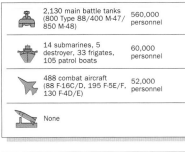

🛡	2,130 main battle tanks (800 Type 88/400 M-47/ 850 M-48)	560,000 personnel
🚢	14 submarines, 5 destroyer, 33 frigates, 105 patrol boats	60,000 personnel
✈	488 combat aircraft (88 F-16C/D, 195 F-5E/F, 130 F-4D/E)	52,000 personnel
	None	

South Korea has fewer troops, tanks, artillery and aircraft than the North, but claims parity through having superior technology and 35,000 US troops permanently based on its territory. However, recent US computer simulations have questioned whether South Korea could resist an invasion by the North's one-million-strong army.

The army's standing and role in national politics were sharply downgraded in the mid-1990s. This was due to a vigorous government campaign to investigate allegations of corruption in the armed forces, especially pertaining to arms procurement, and to inquire into past military involvement in politics.

ECONOMICS Inflation 6% p.a. (1985–1996)

📊 $485.2bn   💱 1,695–1,202 won

SCORE CARD

❏ WORLD GNP RANKING	11th
❏ GNP PER CAPITA	$10,550
❏ BALANCE OF PAYMENTS	$–8.2bn
❏ INFLATION	4.4%
❏ UNEMPLOYMENT	3%

EXPORTS

- Singapore 4%
- Japan 11%
- USA 16%
- China 19%
- Other 50%

IMPORTS

- Germany 4%
- Other 44%
- Saudi Arabia 5%
- China 7%
- Japan 19%
- USA 21%

STRENGTHS
The world's most successful shipbuilder, with 45% of the market. Continuing benefits of highly valued yen –making Korean exports more competitive than Japan's. Strong demand from China for Korean goods, particularly cars.

WEAKNESSES
Financial sector lacking in openness. High level of indebtedness and vulnerability to international capital movements. Increasingly militant workforce since 1997. State sector a burden on the economy. Strong competition from Japan.

PROFILE
South Korea's economic miracle began with centralized planning. Conglomerates known as *chaebol*, such as Samsung, achieved impressive

ECONOMIC PERFORMANCE INDICATOR

Consumer price index — GDP

growth rates in strategic industries such as car manufacture, shipbuilding and electronics. A well-educated workforce and cheap state credit gave a competitive edge. The government then encouraged foreign investment and an emphasis on smaller industries to maintain growth. In 1996 South Korea joined the OECD. However, the 1997 major financial crisis and threat of a debt implosion forced the government to turn to the IMF for a huge credit agreement.

SOUTH KOREA : MAJOR BUSINESSES

Garments	👕
Chemicals	🧪
Electronics	🔌
Iron & steel	
Shipbuilding	⚓
Fish processing	
Vehicle assembly	🚗
Telecommunications	☎

0   50 km
0   50 miles

RESOURCES

▷ Electric power 35.4m kw

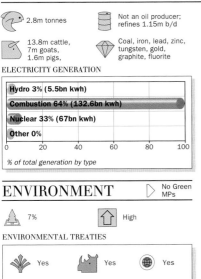

2.8m tonnes

Not an oil producer; refines 1.15m b/d

13.8m cattle, 7m goats, 1.6m pigs,

Coal, iron, lead, zinc, tungsten, gold, graphite, fluorite

ELECTRICITY GENERATION

Hydro 3% (5.5bn kwh)	
Combustion 64% (132.6bn kwh)	
Nuclear 33% (67bn kwh)	
Other 0%	

% of total generation by type

(scale: 0 20 40 60 80 100)

South Korea has few natural resources. It has to import all of its oil and has built a series of nuclear reactors for generating electricity. Under the terms of the 1994 agreement between North Korea and the USA, two South Korean reactors are also to be built in North Korea which, in the event of reunification, will be connected to the national grid.

Agriculture remains a highly protected sector. Plans announced in 1994 to open up the rice market led to massive demonstrations in Seoul.

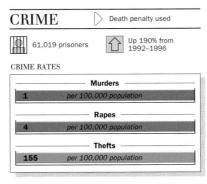

SOUTH KOREA :
LAND USE

- Cropland
- Pasture
- Forest
- Poultry
- Rice
- Cereals

0   50 km
0   50 miles

Cheju-do

ENVIRONMENT

▷ No Green MPs

7%

High

ENVIRONMENTAL TREATIES

Yes		Yes		Yes	
Yes		Yes		Yes	

Environmental groups in southeast Asia have expressed concern at South Korea's fast-track nuclear power program. The country's rapid industrialization has resulted in environmental problems. In September 1998 the government agreed to sign the Kyoto Protocol, which aims to reduce carbon dioxide emissions, indicating its recognition of the problem of air pollution in urban areas, particularly in Seoul. Rivers in rural areas have been polluted by fertilizers and chemicals.

CRIME

▷ Death penalty used

61,019 prisoners

Up 190% from 1992–1996

CRIME RATES

Murders
1 per 100,000 population

Rapes
4 per 100,000 population

Thefts
155 per 100,000 population

The government has begun to treat corruption as a crime. Otherwise, crime rates are relatively low and cases of violent crime uncommon. Since 1987, the internal security forces' operations have been restricted, although left-wing activists are still harassed. Striking workers and student demonstrators are subjected to tear gas and other methods of crowd control.

HEALTH

▷ Welfare state health benefits

1 per 784 people

Tuberculosis, heart and cerebrovascular diseases, cancers

The health service has improved in line with economic growth. Most hospitals are equipped with modern facilities, and many offer advanced treatments comparable with those in the USA and western Europe. Health indicators such as infant mortality and longevity have improved accordingly.

SPENDING

▷ GDP/cap. no increase

CONSUMPTION AND SPENDING

165 per 1,000 population

444 per 1,000 population

Defense 3.3%	
Education 3.7%	
Health 2.7%	

Defense, Health, Education spending as % of GDP

(scale: 0 5 10 15 20 25)

Most South Koreans have benefited from the country's economic growth, but are worse off since the 1997 recession. The Cholla region remains the poorest.

MEDIA

▷ TV ownership high

Daily newspaper circulation 394 per 1,000 people

PUBLISHING AND BROADCAST MEDIA

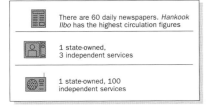

There are 60 daily newspapers. *Hankook Ilbo* has the highest circulation figures

1 state-owned, 3 independent services

1 state-owned, 100 independent services

South Korea's media have been freed of most restrictions since the advent of full multiparty democracy. However, criticisms of the armed forces are still frowned upon, and journalists tend to avoid the subject of the role of the military in society altogether. Caution also has to be exercised in reporting facts about North Korea. In the past, South Korean journalists who have made favorable mention of the communist regime in North Korea have suffered harassment and intimidation.

EDUCATION

▷ School leaving age: 15

97%

2.5m students

A well-educated workforce has been the foundation of South Korea's impressive economic growth.

THE EDUCATION SYSTEM

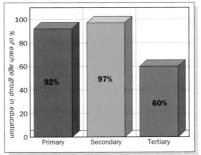

% of each age group in education

Primary	Secondary	Tertiary
92%	97%	60%

South Korea embarked on a concentrated education program in the 1950s. The high priority given to education contributed greatly to South Korea's subsequent economic success. Tertiary enrolment is around 60%, one of the highest rates in the world.

K

WORLD RANKING

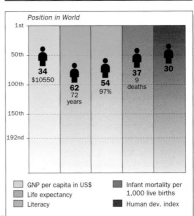

Position in World

1st

50th

100th

150th

192nd

34 $10550	
62 72 years	
54 97%	
37 9 deaths	
30	

- GNP per capita in US$
- Life expectancy
- Literacy
- Infant mortality per 1,000 live births
- Human dev. index

KUWAIT

OFFICIAL NAME: State of Kuwait **CAPITAL:** Kuwait City
POPULATION: 1.8 million **CURRENCY:** Kuwaiti dinar **OFFICIAL LANGUAGE:** Arabic

1961 | **1961** | **Feb 25** | **KWT** | **+3** | **+965** | **.kw**

AT THE NORTHWEST EXTREME of the Persian Gulf, Kuwait is dwarfed by its neighbors Iraq, Iran, and Saudi Arabia. The flat, almost featureless landscape conceals huge oil and gas reserves, which made Kuwait the world's first oil-rich state. In 1990 Iraq invaded, claiming Kuwait as its 19th province. A US-led alliance, under the aegis of the UN, expelled Iraqi forces following a short war in 1991. Since its liberation, Kuwait has built a wall separating its territory from Iraq.

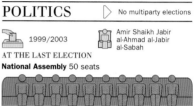

Saffar Towers in the business center of Kuwait City. The postwar cost of rebuilding Kuwait's economy is put at $25 billion.

CLIMATE
▷ Hot desert

WEATHER CHART

Average daily temperature / Rainfall

Summer temperatures can soar to over 40°C (104°F), but winters can be cold, with frost at night.

TRANSPORTATION
▷ Drive on right

Kuwait International, Kuwait City
3.7m passengers

211 ships
2m grt

THE TRANSPORTATION NETWORK

1,512 km (940 miles)	280 km (174 miles)
None	None

Kuwait has a system of radial expressways around the capital and good connecting roads to Saudi Arabia.

TOURISM
▷ Visitors : population 1:51

35,000 visitors

Down 53% 1995–1997

MAIN TOURIST ARRIVALS

Saudi Arabia	29%
Egypt	13%
India	11%
Other	47%

% of total arrivals

Most Western visitors to Kuwait go specifically to see relatives working in the oil industry. The limited tourism from neighboring Arab states, notably Saudi Arabia, has not recovered since the 1990–1991 Gulf War.

PEOPLE
▷ Pop. density medium

Arabic, English

101/km² (262/mi²)

THE URBAN/RURAL POPULATION SPLIT

97% | 3%

ETHNIC MAKEUP

- Kuwaiti 45%
- Iranian 4%
- Other 7%
- South Asian 9%
- Other Arab 35%

Kuwait is a fundamentalist Sunni Muslim society. Women have considerable freedom, and will be allowed to vote from 2003.

Kuwait's oil wealth has drawn in thousands of workers from India, Pakistan and other Arab countries. Before the Iraqi invasion in 1990, Kuwait had the largest Palestinian population in the Arabian peninsula. The PLO's support for Iraq's invasion led to most Palestinians being driven out. After the war, Kuwaitis vowed never again to become a minority in their own country. In 1995, native Kuwaitis only just outnumbered resident foreign nationals.

POLITICS
▷ No multiparty elections

1999/2003

Amir Shaikh Jabir al-Ahmad al-Jabir al-Sabah

AT THE LAST ELECTION

National Assembly 50 seats

100% Ind

The electorate comprises civilian men over 21 years of age whose families have been resident in Kuwait since before 1921. Women are to be enranchised for the general election due in 2003.

In 1992, Kuwait's ruler, Amir Shaikh Jabir, restored the National Assembly and allowed elections. Islamic and independent candidates were elected; some dissidents given cabinet posts to create a new sense of national unity. Progovernment candidates again won a majority of seats in the 1996 and 1999 elections. In 1999 the franchise was extended to women with effect from 2003.

KUWAIT

Total Land Area :
17 820 sq. km
(6880 sq. miles)

POPULATION
- ◎ over 100 000
- ○ over 50 000
- ● over 10 000
- • under 10 000

LAND HEIGHT
- 200m/656ft
- Sea Level

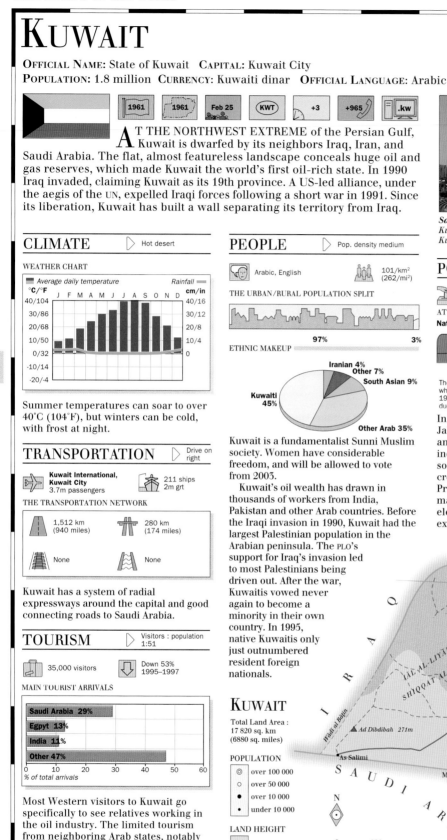

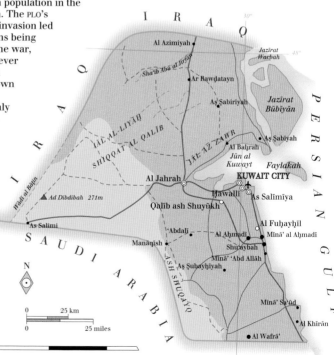

K

WORLD AFFAIRS

 Joined UN in 1963

Kuwait's strategic importance is as a major exporter of crude oil and natural gas. As such, it has always maintained

very close links with the West. Since the war with Iraq, its foreign policy has become even more pro-Western. It therefore depends on its neighbor Saudi Arabia and on Western allies for its future security.

AID

Donor

$371m (donations)   Not applicable

The Kuwait Fund for Arab Economic Development continued to give aid even during the invasion crisis.

DEFENSE

Compulsory military service

$3.6bn   Down 10% in 1997

Kuwait's 11,000-strong, partly volunteer army was easily overrun by vastly superior Iraqi forces in August 1990. Since the liberation, defense pacts have been signed with the USA, the UK, France, and Russia. Kuwait is rearming fast, with weapons purchased from major Western suppliers.

ECONOMICS

Inflation 2.9% p.a. (1985–1996)

$28.9bn   0.31–0.30 Kuwaiti dinars

SCORE CARD

❑ WORLD GNP RANKING	58th
❑ GNP PER CAPITA	$17,390
❑ BALANCE OF PAYMENTS	$7.7bn
❑ INFLATION	0.7%
❑ UNEMPLOYMENT	2%

STRENGTHS

Production of oil and gas has been restored to pre-invasion levels. Large overseas investments.

WEAKNESSES

Economy devastated by Iraqi scorched-earth policy, when oil installations were destroyed. Vulnerability to Iraqi attack deters Western industrial investment. Skilled labor, food and raw materials have to be imported.

EXPORTS

Singapore 8%
Other 28%
South Korea 11%
USA 13%
India 16%
Japan 24%

IMPORTS

Italy 6%
Other 35%
Germany 8%
UK 13%
Japan 15%
USA 23%

RESOURCES

Electric power 7.0m kw

8,700 tonnes

445,000 sheep, 125,000 goats, 21,600 cattle

2.1bn b/d (reserves 96,500,000,000 bbl)

Oil, natural gas, salt

The oil industry is Kuwait's most profitable sector, accounting for over 80% of export earnings. It was badly hit as a result of the Gulf War, when large numbers of oil wells were deliberately fired, but with foreign assistance it was quickly rehabilitated. Kuwait also possesses valuable reserves of natural gas.

ENVIRONMENT

No Green MPs

2%   High

The Iraqi invasion and the subsequent war caused an ecological disaster. Although the effects of this did not prove as grave as some observers first feared, marine life has been damaged and many thousands of hectares of cultivated land have been obliterated. Millions of land mines still litter Kuwait's border areas.

MEDIA

TV ownership high

 Daily newspaper circulation 376 per 1,000 people

PUBLISHING AND BROADCAST MEDIA

There are 8 daily newspapers, including *Al-Qabas* and *As-Seyassah*

1 state-controlled service   1 state-controlled service

Radio and TV are state-controlled, but satellite TV is freely available. Press freedom exists in theory.

CRIME

Death penalty used

500 prisoners   Up 35% from 1992–1996

Isolated acts of terrorism related to the war still occur. There have been reports of human rights abuses.

EDUCATION

School leaving age: 14

80%   28,705 students

Kuwaiti citizens receive free education from nursery to university. Since the liberation, more emphasis has been placed on technology in the curriculum.

CHRONOLOGY

Kuwait traces its independence to 1710, but was under British rule from the late 18th century until 1961. The government denies any historical link with Iraq.

- ❑ **1961** Independence from the UK. Iraq claims Kuwait.
- ❑ **1976** Amir suspends Assembly.
- ❑ **1990** Iraqi invasion.
- ❑ **1991** Liberation following Gulf War.
- ❑ **1992** National Assembly elections.
- ❑ **1999** Islamists and liberals win more seats; women enfranchized from 2003.

HEALTH

Welfare state health benefits

1 per 5,000 people   Heart diseases, accidents, cancers, perinatal deaths

Despite theft of equipment during the Iraqi invasion, Kuwait has restored its Western-standard health care service. Nationals receive free treatment.

SPENDING

GDP/cap. increase

CONSUMPTION AND SPENDING

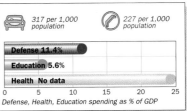

317 per 1,000 population   227 per 1,000 population

Defense 11.4%
Education 5.6%
Health No data

Defense, Health, Education spending as % of GDP

As well as the oil rich elite, most Kuwaitis enjoy high incomes, and the government has repeatedly rescued citizens who have suffered stock market or other financial losses. School and university leavers are guaranteed jobs. Capital is easily transferred abroad and there are effectively no exchange controls.

WORLD RANKING

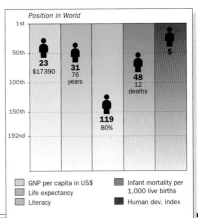

Position in World

23 $17390
31 76 years
48 12 deaths
119 80%
5

GNP per capita in US$
Life expectancy
Literacy

Infant mortality per 1,000 live births
Human dev. index

K

KYRGYZSTAN

OFFICIAL NAME: Kyrgyz Republic   **CAPITAL:** Bishkek
POPULATION: 4.5 million   **CURRENCY:** Som   **OFFICIAL LANGUAGES:** Kyrgyz & Russian

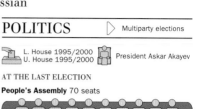

CENTRAL ASIA

1991   1991   Aug 31   KS   +6   +996   .kg

KYRGYZSTAN IS A SMALL and very mountainous state in Central Asia. It is the least urbanized of the former Soviet republics (the rural population is growing faster than the towns) and was among the last to develop its own cultural nationalism. Its moderate government is treading uncertainly between Kyrgyz nationalist pressures and ensuring that the minority Russians are not alienated, since they tend to possess the skills necessary to run a market-based economy.

CLIMATE
▷ Mountain

WEATHER CHART

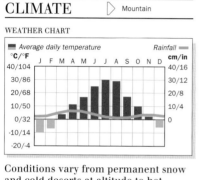

Conditions vary from permanent snow and cold deserts at altitude to hot deserts in low regions. Intermediate slopes and valleys receive some rain.

TRANSPORTATION
▷ Drive on right

✈ Bishkek International   🚢 Has no fleet

THE TRANSPORTATION NETWORK

18,500 km (11,563 miles)		None	
417 km (261 miles)		600 km (373 miles)	

Kyrgyzstan does not have the funds to improve its poor mountain road network.

TOURISM
▷ Visitors : population 1:346

🧳 13,000 visitors   ⬆ Up 8% 1995–1997

MAIN TOURIST ARRIVALS

Kyrgyzstan does not publish tourism figures by country of origin

0   10   20   30   40
% of total arrivals

The tourist industry is undeveloped. Most visitors to Kyrgyzstan are people on business from Turkey and China in search of new contracts, or working on multilateral aid projects.

PEOPLE
▷ Pop. density low

Kyrgyz, Russian   23/km² (59/mi²)

THE URBAN/RURAL POPULATION SPLIT

39%   61%

ETHNIC MAKEUP

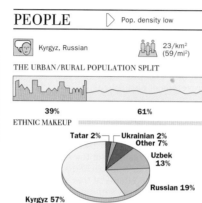

Tatar 2%   Ukrainian 2%
Other 7%
Uzbek 13%
Russian 19%
Kyrgyz 57%

Despite claims to the contrary, Kyrgyzstan suffers from a forceful nationalism similar to that in other ex-Soviet republics. There is considerable tension between the Kyrgyz and other minorities, particularly Uzbeks. The preference given to Kyrgyz in the political system and in particular in the land laws, which exclude all others from full title, has aggravated tensions. The trend in politics is toward greater Islamicization, which is linking religion and race issues more closely and adding pressure on "foreigners," particularly Russians, to leave.

Since 1989 their high birth rate has enabled the Kyrgyz to resume being the main ethnic group, replacing the Russian community which until recently controlled the economy. In 1994, however, the government moved to stem the tide of Russian emigration by declaring Russian an official language.

Loess landscape, Naryn valley. Kyrgyzstan is dominated by the ice-capped Tien Shan Mountains, but valleys are green and fertile.

POLITICS
▷ Multiparty elections

L. House 1995/2000
U. House 1995/2000
President Askar Akayev

AT THE LAST ELECTION

People's Assembly 70 seats

Legislative elections were held for the first time since independence in February 1995. Party affiliations were declared for only 15 of the 105 members elected.

Legislative Assembly 35 seats

Kyrgyzstan has been a keen advocate of political change. In 1991 it was the first Soviet republic to ban the Communist Party, which was eventually revived in 1992 and renamed the Communists of the Republic of Kyrgyzstan.

President Akayev, who has been in power since 1990, has successfully balanced the demands of nationalist Kyrgyz and minorities such as the Uzbeks – involved in ethnic clashes in Osh in 1990. His free-market economic policies, however, have shown few tangible results.

Critics have accused Akayev of fostering a personality cult. In 1995, parliament rejected a proposal for a referendum to extend Akayev's tenure until 2001. Later that year, he was reelected president for a second five-year term, having held the post since 1990. In 1998 the Constitutional Court ruled that Akayev could seek re-election in 2000. Although the 1994 constitution restricts the president to two terms, the Court judged that Akayev's first term had begun in 1995 rather than 1990.

WORLD AFFAIRS
▷ Joined UN in 1992

CIS   ECO   OIC   OSCE   EAPC

Relations with Russia are good, though Kyrgyzstan is working to reduce its dependence on it. Turkey, the second country to establish a mission in Bishkek after the USA, is developing close links aimed at restraining Iranian fundamentalist influence in the region. Relations with Uzbekistan, which supports antidemocratic forces in Kyrgyzstan, are tense.

AID
▷ Recipient

$240m (receipts)   ⬆ Up 3% 1996–1997

The USA and Japan are main donors. By January 1999, Kyrgyzstan had received World Bank credits of $473 million.

K

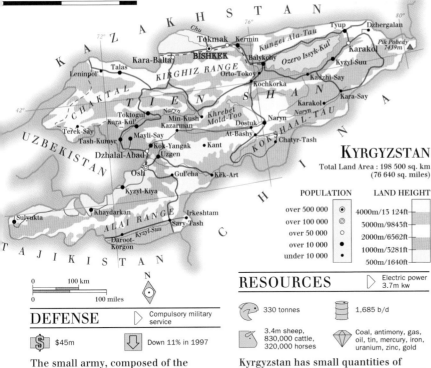

KYRGYZSTAN

Total Land Area : 198 500 sq. km
(76 640 sq. miles)

POPULATION		LAND HEIGHT
over 500 000	◉	4000m/13 124ft
over 100 000	◎	3000m/9843ft
over 50 000	○	2000m/6562ft
over 10 000	•	1000m/3281ft
under 10 000	·	500m/1640ft

DEFENSE

▷ Compulsory military service

💲 $45m

⬇ Down 11% in 1997

The small army, composed of the Kyrgyz remnants of the former CIS force, is weak and not influential in politics. Recruitment to a 7,000-strong National Guard was set up in 1992. Kyrgyzstan looks to its alliance with the CIS, particularly Russia, for its security.

ECONOMICS

▷ Inflation 27.9% p.a. (1996–1997)

📊 $2.2bn

💲 Not available

SCORE CARD

- ❏ WORLD GNP RANKING......................134th
- ❏ GNP PER CAPITA $480
- ❏ BALANCE OF PAYMENTS....................$–139m
- ❏ INFLATION 25.5%
- ❏ UNEMPLOYMENT 4%

STRENGTHS

Agricultural self-sufficiency. Private land ownership since 1998. Mercury and gold exports. Large hydroelectric power potential.

WEAKNESSES

Agriculture-based economy, still dominated by the state and the collective farming mentality. Sharp economic decline since 1991 break-up of USSR, on which it depended totally for trade and supplies. Chronic high inflation.

EXPORTS/IMPORTS

Trade is overwhelmingly with the Russian Federation. A smaller proportion is with other states of the former Soviet Union.

RESOURCES

▷ Electric power 3.7m kw

🐟 330 tonnes

🛢 1,685 b/d

🐑 3.4m sheep, 830,000 cattle, 320,000 horses

💎 Coal, antimony, gas, oil, tin, mercury, iron, uranium, zinc, gold

Kyrgyzstan has small quantities of commercially exploitable coal, oil, and gas, and great hydroelectric power potential. Energy policy, which relies on Western aid and technology, is primarily aimed at developing these further in order to reduce dependence on supplies from Russia, and eventually to achieve self-sufficiency in energy.

ENVIRONMENT

▷ No Green MPs

🌲 4%

⬍ Not available

The major problem is the salination of the soil caused by excessive irrigation of cotton. Kyrgyzstan has a poor record in limiting industrial pollution.

MEDIA

▷ TV ownership low

✉ Daily newspaper circulation 15 per 1,000 people

PUBLISHING AND BROADCAST MEDIA

There are 3 daily newspapers, *Kyrgyz Tuusu*, *Slovo Kyrgyzstana* and *Vechernii Bishkek*.

1 state-owned service

1 state-owned, 1 independent service

TV programming is mostly from Russia. The Kyrgyz press is the most liberal in Central Asia.

CRIME

▷ Death penalty not used

Kyrgyzstan does not publish prison figures

⬆ The crime rate is rising

Violence is fueled by ethnic tension. Economic decline has encouraged the narcotics trade. A two-year death penalty moratorium was announced in 1998.

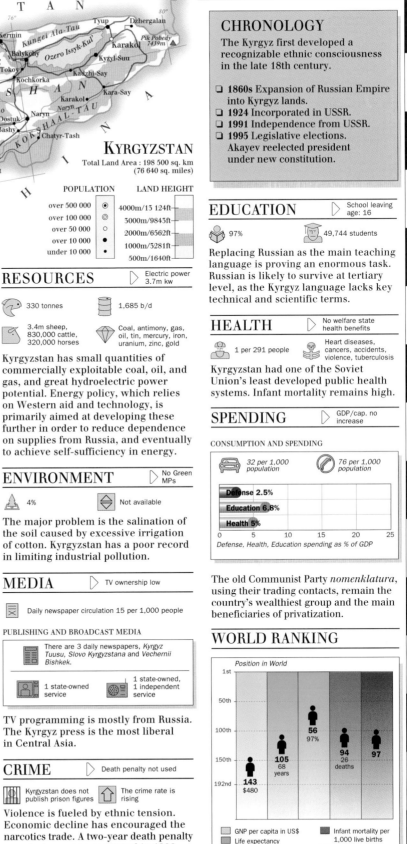

CHRONOLOGY

The Kyrgyz first developed a recognizable ethnic consciousness in the late 18th century.

- ❏ **1860s** Expansion of Russian Empire into Kyrgyz lands.
- ❏ **1924** Incorporated in USSR.
- ❏ **1991** Independence from USSR.
- ❏ **1995** Legislative elections. Akayev reelected president under new constitution.

EDUCATION

▷ School leaving age: 16

📖 97%

🎓 49,744 students

Replacing Russian as the main teaching language is proving an enormous task. Russian is likely to survive at tertiary level, as the Kyrgyz language lacks key technical and scientific terms.

HEALTH

▷ No welfare state health benefits

1 per 291 people

Heart diseases, cancers, accidents, violence, tuberculosis

Kyrgyzstan had one of the Soviet Union's least developed public health systems. Infant mortality remains high.

SPENDING

▷ GDP/cap. no increase

CONSUMPTION AND SPENDING

🚗 32 per 1,000 population

📞 76 per 1,000 population

Defense 2.5%
Education 6.8%
Health 5%

Defense, Health, Education spending as % of GDP

(scale: 0, 5, 10, 15, 20, 25)

The old Communist Party *nomenklatura*, using their trading contacts, remain the country's wealthiest group and the main beneficiaries of privatization.

WORLD RANKING

Position in World

	GNP per capita	Life expectancy	Literacy	Infant mortality	Human dev. index
	143 $480	105 68 years	56 97%	94 26 deaths	97

- GNP per capita in US$
- Life expectancy
- Literacy
- Infant mortality per 1,000 live births
- Human dev. index

K

LAOS

OFFICIAL NAME: Lao People's Democratic Republic
CAPITAL: Vientiane **POPULATION:** 5.4 million **CURRENCY:** New kip **OFFICIAL LANGUAGE:** Lao

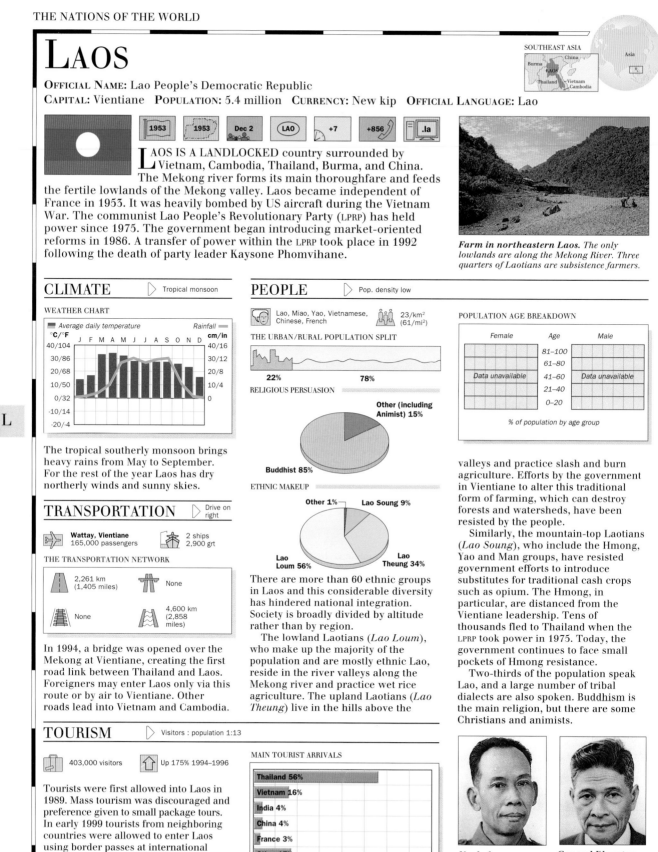

SOUTHEAST ASIA | Asia

| 1953 | 1953 | Dec 2 | LAO | +7 | +856 | .la |

LAOS IS A LANDLOCKED country surrounded by Vietnam, Cambodia, Thailand, Burma, and China. The Mekong river forms its main thoroughfare and feeds the fertile lowlands of the Mekong valley. Laos became independent of France in 1953. It was heavily bombed by US aircraft during the Vietnam War. The communist Lao People's Revolutionary Party (LPRP) has held power since 1975. The government began introducing market-oriented reforms in 1986. A transfer of power within the LPRP took place in 1992 following the death of party leader Kaysone Phomvihane.

Farm in northeastern Laos. *The only lowlands are along the Mekong River. Three quarters of Laotians are subsistence farmers.*

CLIMATE
▷ Tropical monsoon

WEATHER CHART

Average daily temperature | Rainfall

The tropical southerly monsoon brings heavy rains from May to September. For the rest of the year Laos has dry northerly winds and sunny skies.

TRANSPORTATION
▷ Drive on right

Wattay, Vientiane 165,000 passengers | 2 ships 2,900 grt

THE TRANSPORTATION NETWORK

| 2,261 km (1,405 miles) | None |
| None | 4,600 km (2,858 miles) |

In 1994, a bridge was opened over the Mekong at Vientiane, creating the first road link between Thailand and Laos. Foreigners may enter Laos only via this route or by air to Vientiane. Other roads lead into Vietnam and Cambodia.

TOURISM
▷ Visitors : population 1:13

403,000 visitors | Up 175% 1994–1996

Tourists were first allowed into Laos in 1989. Mass tourism was discouraged and preference given to small package tours. In early 1999 tourists from neighboring countries were allowed to enter Laos using border passes at international checkpoints under the guidance of Lao tour companies. Hotels are few, and travel outside Vientiane is difficult.

MAIN TOURIST ARRIVALS

Thailand 56%
Vietnam 16%
India 4%
China 4%
France 3%
Other 17%

% of total arrivals

PEOPLE
▷ Pop. density low

Lao, Miao, Yao, Vietnamese, Chinese, French | 23/km² (61/mi²)

THE URBAN/RURAL POPULATION SPLIT

22%   78%

RELIGIOUS PERSUASION

Other (including Animist) 15%
Buddhist 85%

ETHNIC MAKEUP

Other 1%   Lao Soung 9%
Lao Loum 56%
Lao Theung 34%

There are more than 60 ethnic groups in Laos and this considerable diversity has hindered national integration. Society is broadly divided by altitude rather than by region.

The lowland Laotians (*Lao Loum*), who make up the majority of the population and are mostly ethnic Lao, reside in the river valleys along the Mekong river and practice wet rice agriculture. The upland Laotians (*Lao Theung*) live in the hills above the valleys and practice slash and burn agriculture. Efforts by the government in Vientiane to alter this traditional form of farming, which can destroy forests and watersheds, have been resisted by the people.

Similarly, the mountain-top Laotians (*Lao Soung*), who include the Hmong, Yao and Man groups, have resisted government efforts to introduce substitutes for traditional cash crops such as opium. The Hmong, in particular, are distanced from the Vientiane leadership. Tens of thousands fled to Thailand when the LPRP took power in 1975. Today, the government continues to face small pockets of Hmong resistance.

Two-thirds of the population speak Lao, and a large number of tribal dialects are also spoken. Buddhism is the main religion, but there are some Christians and animists.

POPULATION AGE BREAKDOWN

Female	Age	Male
	81–100	
	61–80	
Data unavailable	41–60	Data unavailable
	21–40	
	0–20	

% of population by age group

Nouhak Phoumsavan, *president from 1992–1998*

General Khamtay Siphandon, *president and head of the LPRP.*

L

POLITICS ▷ No multiparty elections

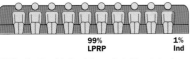

1997/2002   President Khamtay
                     Siphandon

AT THE LAST ELECTION

National Assembly 99 seats

99%   1%
LPRP   Ind

LPRP = Lao People's Revolutionary Party (the sole legal
political party) **Ind** = Independent
Many candidates ran as independents, but all were
effectively approved by the LPRP.

Laos is a communist, one-party state
under the direct control and
administration of the LPRP.

MAIN POLITICAL ISSUES
Political reform
Reforms are currently being introduced
to modernize key state functions. The
country's first written constitution was
adopted in 1991, and a modern legal
infrastructure has been introduced.

The LPRP has begun to relax its total
hold on power. The executive branch of
government appears to be asserting its
authority, although it still relies on the
LPRP for broad guidelines. The legislative
branch is also taking more initiative and
the National Assembly is no longer
simply a rubber stamp for LPRP edicts.

Central control
Tensions continue to be felt between the
communist government in the capital
Vientiane and the rural areas, where the
rank and file of the LPRP and the military
have their roots. There is particular
resistance to central attempts to alter
traditional farming methods.

PROFILE
Laos has been ruled by the same circle
of communist revolutionaries since
1975. They have proved to be one of the
world's most durable and closely knit
hierarchies.

The vacuum left by the death of long-
time LPRP leader, Kaysone Phomvihane,
in 1992 was quickly filled by his
protégés, who show no sign of deviating
from the path he laid down. The
military, the LPRP and the executive
branch remain closely intertwined, with
party chairman General Khamtay
Siphandon becoming the country's
president in February 1998. Despite
limited moves toward political reform,
the LPRP, which is modeled on the
Communist Party of Vietnam,
continues to dominate political
life at every level.

The long-standing
problem of corruption,
sometimes at high levels,
has become a matter of
concern as Laos has
opened to foreign
investors. Economic
reform has not been
accompanied by
political
liberalization.

WORLD AFFAIRS ▷ Joined UN in 1955

ASEAN   CP   IBRD   Mek Riv   NAM

Throughout the 1960s and 1970s,
Vietnam was Laos's most important
ally. In the 1980s the party leadership
began to seek improved relations
particularly with the West, although the
regime still remains firmly under the
influence of Vietnam. Closer ties with
Japan and rapprochement with both
Thailand and with two former enemies,
the USA and France, were secured. The
motivation was mainly the need for
foreign aid.

Following the collapse of
communism in eastern Europe, Laos
turned to its northern neighbor, China,
for ideological support and to
counterbalance the growing influence
of Thailand. At the same time, the
government was careful not to
jeopardize links with Vietnam.

Laos was admitted to full
membership of ASEAN in 1997, having in
1992 acceded to ASEAN's Treaty of Amity
and Concord. This had marked the
beginning of a new relationship with
former adversaries.

L

CHRONOLOGY

In the late 19th century, France
established control over the three
small kingdoms of Champasak,
Louangphrabang and Vientiane.

- ❏ **1893** Franco-Siamese treaty
  establishes French control over all
  territory east of the Mekong.
- ❏ **1899** Creation of a unified Laos
  under the French.
- ❏ **1941** Japanese seize power from
  Vichy French in Indo-China.
- ❏ **1946** French rule resumed.
- ❏ **1950** Lao Patriotic Front, (LPF), set
  up to oppose French rule. Gains
  support of newly formed communist
  Lao People's Party (LPP).
- ❏ **1953** Independence as a
  constitutional monarchy backed by
  France and the USA.
- ❏ **1963** LPF begins armed struggle
  against royal government through
  its armed wing, the Pathet Lao.
- ❏ **1964** US bombing of North
  Vietnamese sanctuaries in Laos;
  later escalated along the Ho Chi
  Minh trail.
- ❏ **1973** LPRP (formerly the LPF) and
  royal government form a coalition
  after withdrawal of US forces from
  Indo-China.
- ❏ **1975** LPRP seizes power, abolishes
  monarchy and proclaims Lao
  People's Democratic Republic.
  Premier Kaysone Phomvihane
  adopts policies for "socialist
  transformation" of economy. ⇨

LAOS

Total Land Area : 230 800 sq. km
(89 112 sq. miles)

POPULATION   LAND HEIGHT

⊚ over 100 000
○ over 50 000   2000m/6562ft
● over 10 000   1000m/3281ft
· under 10 000   500m/1640ft
                             75m/246ft

N

0   100 km
0   100 miles

L

CHRONOLOGY *continued*

- ❏ **1977** The Treaty of Friendship and Cooperation, providing for mutual assistance in national security, signed with Vietnam. Relations with China begin to cool.
- ❏ **1978** Popular unrest and resistance to collectivization. Former king and crown prince are arrested and die in captivity. Almost 50,000 Laotians flee to Thailand.
- ❏ **1979** Softer economic line adopted and the speed of "socialist transformation" slows.
- ❏ **1986** Fourth Party Congress introduces market-oriented reforms.
- ❏ **1988** Brief border war with Thailand. Restoration of diplomatic relations with China.
- ❏ **1989** National elections held. All candidates approved by LPRP. Rapprochement with Thailand.
- ❏ **1990** Counter-offensives against right-wing, largely Hmong, guerrilla bases located in the outer provinces. Most agricultural collectives and state farms disbanded. Arrest of three former government officials for promoting multiparty democracy.
- ❏ **1991** A constitution providing for a National Assembly, confirming the leading role of the LPRP, and enshrining the right of private ownership, is promulgated. Kaysone steps down as prime minister and takes up post of president. Khamtay Siphandon becomes prime minister.
- ❏ **1992** Death of President Kaysone; Khamtay becomes head of the LPRP. Laos accedes to the Treaty of Amity and Concord of the ASEAN countries.
- ❏ **1994** Thailand–Laos bridge opens over Mekong – first direct road link between the two countries.
- ❏ **1995** Former President Souphanouvong – the "Red Prince" – dies.
- ❏ **1997** Laos becomes a member of ASEAN.
- ❏ **1998** Former prime minister Khamtay becomes president.

AID ▷ Recipient

💲 $341m (receipts) ⬆ Up 1% 1996–1997

Laos has one of the highest per capita aid inflows in the developing world. However, severe problems have been encountered in the implementation of aid programs. In the 1980s, Laos was heavily dependent on the USSR and Vietnam for aid. Today, donors include the IMF, the World Bank, the ADB, France, Sweden, Australia, and Japan.

DEFENSE ▷ Compulsory military service

💲 $63m ⬇ Down 21% in 1997

The armed forces are estimated by the West to number almost 30,000 personnel. This total is further swelled by a paramilitary militia. Eighteen months' military service is compulsory for all Laotian males .

The military and the ruling LPRP have close links. Defense forces are being deployed to ensure border security and control the narcotics trade along the Thai border; however, recent allegations of narcotics smuggling across the Lao–Thai border have implicated sections of the army . In 1977, Laos signed a treaty with

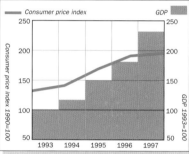

LAOTIAN ARMED FORCES

🛡	30 main battle tanks (T-54/55, I-34/85)	25,000 personnel
⛴	16 patrol boats	600 personnel
✈	26 combat aircraft (20 MiG-21)	3500 personnel
🚀	None	

Vietnam, providing for mutual assistance in the event of a threat to national security.

ECONOMICS ▷ Inflation 22% p.a. (1985–1996)

📊 $1.9bn 💲 4,203.50 new kips

SCORE CARD

❏ WORLD GNP RANKING	142nd
❏ GNP PER CAPITA	$400
❏ BALANCE OF PAYMENTS	$–316m
❏ INFLATION	13%
❏ UNEMPLOYMENT	2%

ECONOMIC PERFORMANCE INDICATOR

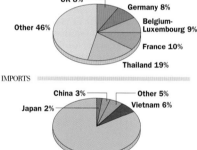

EXPORTS

UK 8%
Germany 8%
Belgium-Luxembourg 9%
Other 46%
France 10%
Thailand 19%

IMPORTS

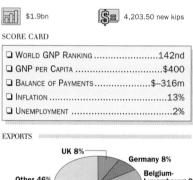

China 3%
Other 5%
Japan 2%
Vietnam 6%
Thailand 83%

STRENGTHS
Rising levels of overseas investment. Potential of garment manufacturing, mining, timber plantations, wood processing, tourism, banking, and aviation. Mineral deposits.

WEAKNESSES
One of the world's 20 least-developed countries. Lack of technical expertise a major constraint to further development. Imbalance in sources of foreign investment – most is Thai. Problems in targeting aid efficiently.

PROFILE
The LPRP introduced market-oriented reforms in 1986. The collapse of the Soviet Union speeded up this process in the early 1990s. Price controls on rice and other crops were removed, and farmers helped to achieve a degree of food self-sufficiency.

The reforms also led to the privatization of a number of state-owned companies, including the national brewery. The national currency, the new kip, was floated, interest rates eased and trade restrictions lifted. Foreign investment was encouraged, Laos being the first country in Indo-China to do this. However, most foreign interest has been confined to the service sector and exploitation of natural resources, such as logging and mining.

In 1998 the economy suffered a sharp setback owing to the financial crisis in southeast Asia. The value of the new kip fell by over 80% against the US dollar, forcing up inflation which was running at about 100% a year.

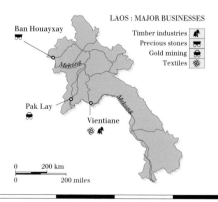

LAOS : MAJOR BUSINESSES

Ban Houayxay

Timber industries
Precious stones
Gold mining
Textiles

Pak Lay

Vientiane

0   200 km
0   200 miles

RESODURCES ▷ Electric power 256,000 kw

 40,400 tonnes

Not an oil producer

1.5m pigs
1.1m cattle,
122,000 goats

Tin, gypsum, iron,
copper, potash, lead,
limestone, antimony

ELECTRICITY GENERATION

Hydro 95% (0.9bn kwh)

Combustion 5% (0.04bn kwh)

Nuclear 0%

Other 0%

0   20   40   60   80   100
% of total generation by type

Laos's most important agricultural resources are timber and coffee. The country is rich in minerals. Important deposits include tin and gypsum (which are exported), iron ore, copper, potash, limestone, antimony, manganese, lead and salt. An increasing number of foreign companies have been awarded concessions to mine for gold and precious stones. Two oil and gas exploration agreements with oil multinationals were also negotiated between 1990 and 1991. Laos's principal source of electricity is hydroelectric power. Surpluses are exported to Thailand.

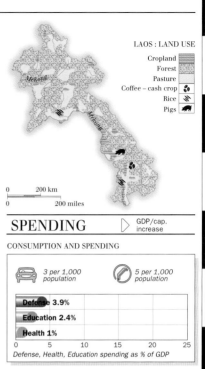

LAOS : LAND USE

Cropland
Forest
Pasture
Coffee – cash crop
Rice
Pigs

0   200 km
0   200 miles

ENVIRONMENT ▷ No Green MPs

None

Low

ENVIRONMENTAL TREATIES

No   No   Yes

No   No   No

Bombing and the use of defoliants in the Vietnam War did serious ecological damage. Slash-and-burn farming and illegal logging are destroying forests.

SPENDING ▷ GDP/cap. increase

CONSUMPTION AND SPENDING

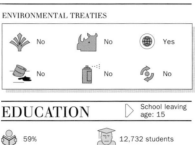

3 per 1,000 population   5 per 1,000 population

Defense 3.9%

Education 2.4%

Health 1%

0   5   10   15   20   25
Defense, Health, Education spending as % of GDP

There are large inequalities of wealth throughout Laos. A rapidly expanding group of Laotian entrepreneurs is profiting from the gradual liberalization of the country's economy. The elite live in French -style villas. Mercedes are not uncommon in the capital and the number of motorcycles has increased significantly in recent years.

Development is unevenly spread around the country. Many in the highlands and mountainous regions lead a subsistence existence, while farmers in the fertile Mekong valley are relatively well-off. Most homes along the Mekong have TV sets which can receive broadcasts from Thai stations. Bribes are a key part of most bureaucrats' incomes.

MEDIA ▷ TV ownership low

Daily newspaper circulation 4 per 1,000 people

PUBLISHING AND BROADCAST MEDIA

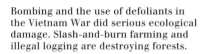

There are 3 daily newspapers, including the government-published *Vientiane Mai*

2 state-owned services

1 state-owned,
1 independent service

Newspapers are owned and controlled by the LPRP. Revelations of corruption by state officials are not uncommon, but criticism of the party and its leaders remains taboo. In 1990, the illegal Radio Station of the Government for the Liberation of the Lao Nation began broadcasting antigovernment propaganda for four hours a day.

EDUCATION ▷ School leaving age: 15

59%   12,732 students

Educational programs are being expanded to combat low literacy rates.

THE EDUCATION SYSTEM

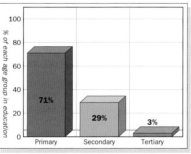

% of each age group in education

100

80

71%

29%

3%

Primary   Secondary   Tertiary

Literacy rates in Laos remain low, at below 50% for women and around 70% for men. However, adult education is currently being expanded and new schools are being built.

CRIME ▷ Death penalty not used

 Laos does not publish prison figures

Rising overall, particularly corruption

CRIME RATES

Most crime is rising. However the trend in mountain regions is hard to establish.

Laos is the world's third-largest opium producer. Since 1990, attempts have been made to combat the production and trafficking of illegal drugs. The USA is providing funds to substitute cash crops for poppies in the mountainous northeastern provinces.

HEALTH ▷ Welfare state health benefits

1 per 5,000 people

Diarrheal, respiratory and parasitic diseases, malaria, influenza

More health education is needed to improve standards of health, particularly outside Vientiane. Poor standards of nutrition and sanitation throughout most of rural Laos are reflected in the standard indicators of health and longevity. Infant mortality remains at about 10% and life expectancy is just over 50 years. Malaria and hemorrhagic fever have continued to increase.

WORLD RANKING

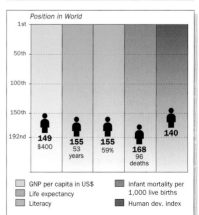

Position in World

1st

50th

100th

150th

192nd

149   155   155   168   140
$400   53 years   59%   96 deaths

GNP per capita in US$
Life expectancy
Literacy

infant mortality per 1,000 live births
Human dev. index

L

LATVIA

OFFICIAL NAME: Republic of Latvia **CAPITAL:** Riga
POPULATION: 2.4 million **CURRENCY:** Lats **OFFICIAL LANGUAGE:** Latvian

| 1991 | 1991 | Nov 18 | LV | +2 | +371 | .lv |

L YING BETWEEN ESTONIA and Lithuania, Latvia is situated on the eastern coast of the Baltic Sea. To the east it borders the Russian Federation and Belarus. The whole country is a low-lying plain, which nowhere rises above 300 meters (975 feet). Latvia's independence was recognized by Moscow in 1991. Defense-related industries and agriculture play an important role in the economy. Only 52% of the population are ethnic Latvians.

CLIMATE

▷ Continental

WEATHER CHART

Average daily temperature Rainfall

°C/°F	J F M A M J J A S O N D	cm/in
40/104		40/16
30/86		30/12
20/68		20/8
10/50		10/4
0/32		0
-10/14		
-20/-4		

Latvia's coastal position means that the climate is temperate, with cold winters and cool summers.

TRANSPORTATION

▷ Drive on right

Riga International
554,854 passengers

233 ships
723,400 grt

THE TRANSPORTATION NETWORK

| 20,400 km (12,750 miles) | None |
| 2,413 km (1,508 miles) | 300 km (186 miles) |

The Via Baltica linking Poland and Finland runs through Latvia. Ventspils port is now the deepest on the Baltic and is ice-free all year. Riga has the busiest container port in the Baltic. The rail system is being improved.

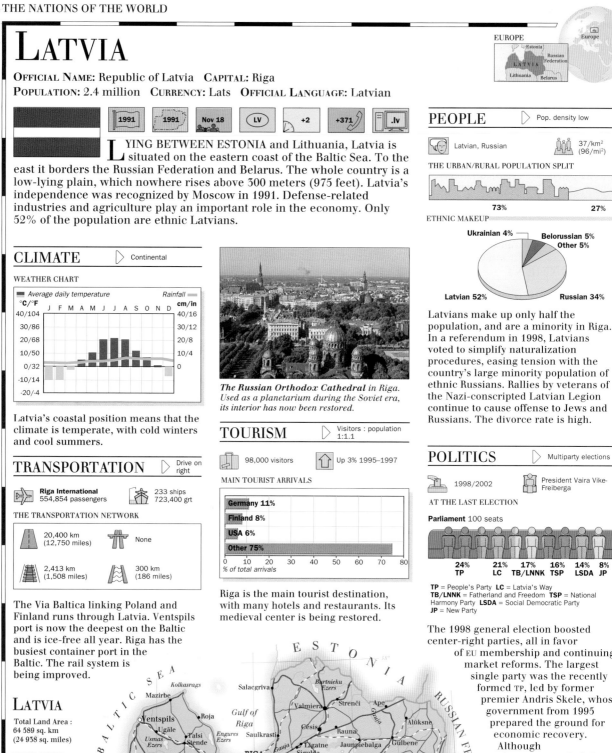

The Russian Orthodox Cathedral in Riga. Used as a planetarium during the Soviet era, its interior has now been restored.

TOURISM

▷ Visitors : population 1:1.1

98,000 visitors Up 3% 1995–1997

MAIN TOURIST ARRIVALS

Germany 11%	
Finland 8%	
USA 6%	
Other 75%	

0 10 20 30 40 50 60 70 80
% of total arrivals

Riga is the main tourist destination, with many hotels and restaurants. Its medieval center is being restored.

PEOPLE

▷ Pop. density low

Latvian, Russian 37/km² (96/mi²)

THE URBAN/RURAL POPULATION SPLIT

73% 27%

ETHNIC MAKEUP

Ukrainian 4% Belorussian 5%
Other 5%
Latvian 52% Russian 34%

Latvians make up only half the population, and are a minority in Riga. In a referendum in 1998, Latvians voted to simplify naturalization procedures, easing tension with the country's large minority population of ethnic Russians. Rallies by veterans of the Nazi-conscripted Latvian Legion continue to cause offense to Jews and Russians. The divorce rate is high.

POLITICS

▷ Multiparty elections

1998/2002 President Vaira Vike-Freiberga

AT THE LAST ELECTION

Parliament 100 seats

| 24% TP | 21% LC | 17% TB/LNNK | 16% TSP | 14% LSDA | 8% JP |

TP = People's Party **LC** = Latvia's Way
TB/LNNK = Fatherland and Freedom **TSP** = National Harmony Party **LSDA** = Social Democratic Party
JP = New Party

The 1998 general election boosted center-right parties, all in favor of EU membership and continuing market reforms. The largest single party was the recently formed TP, led by former premier Andris Skele, whose government from 1995 prepared the ground for economic recovery. Although the TP was excluded from a government formed under Vilis Kristopans of LC, this coalition proved short-lived and the populist Skele returned to power in July 1999.

LATVIA

Total Land Area :
64 589 sq. km
(24 938 sq. miles)

POPULATION

⊙ over 500 000
◎ over 100 000
○ over 50 000
● over 10 000
· under 10 000

LAND HEIGHT

200m/656ft
Sea Level

L

WORLD AFFAIRS

Joined UN in 1991

CE CBSS OSCE EAPC PfP

Having signed an association agreement with the EU in June 1995, Latvia applied for full EU membership,

but was not invited to open negotiations. The country has US backing for entry to NATO. Relations with Russia had been deteriorating until the 1998 referendum vote in favor of easing naturalization procedures.

AID

Recipient

$ 81m (receipts) ⬆ Up 3% 1996-1997

Aid to Latvia comes mainly from the World Bank, the IMF, and the EU. Most goes toward improving the country's infrastructure.

DEFENSE

Compulsory military service

$ $156m ⬆ Up 13% in 1997

Building up the military is a priority, and there is now US backing for entry into NATO. Latvia has been participating in NATO's Partnership for Peace program. In September 1998, Russian forces began to dismantle their last military installation in Latvia, the Skrunda radar station.

ECONOMICS

Inflation 52.2% p.a. (1985–1996)

$6bn 0.59–0.57 lati

SCORE CARD

- ❏ WORLD GNP RANKING......................100th
- ❏ GNP PER CAPITA $2430
- ❏ BALANCE OF PAYMENTS....................$-441m
- ❏ INFLATION 8.4%
- ❏ UNEMPLOYMENT 7%

STRENGTHS

Industrial production improving after slump. Service sector now providing 52% of GDP. Foreign investment rising. Inflation under control.

WEAKNESSES

Lack of raw materials. Farming technically backward after dismantling of collective farms. Dependence on imported oil and natural gas for energy.

EXPORTS

Lithuania 8%
Sweden 8%
Other 35%
Germany 14%
Russia 21%
UK 14%

IMPORTS

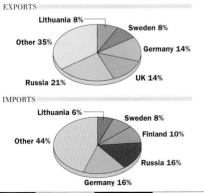

Lithuania 6%
Sweden 8%
Other 44%
Finland 10%
Russia 16%
Germany 16%

RESOURCES

Electric power 2.1m kw

143,024 tonnes Not an oil producer

434,000 cattle, 421,000 pigs, 29,000 sheep Amber, dolomite, gravel, gypsum, limestone, peat, sand

Latvia has limited natural resources and is dependent on imports to meet energy requirements. Deposits of petroleum and natural gas have been located but not exploited. Electricity comes chiefly from Lithuania and Estonia; oil is imported from Russia and Lithuania. Ventspils is being promoted as an oil terminal for CIS states.

ENVIRONMENT

No Green MPs

🌲 13% ⬍ Medium

Peat extraction – Latvia is 5% bog – has damaged the environment. Pollution of the Baltic Sea and general air and water quality are also of concern. Environmental awareness is strong. In the run-up to independence green issues had a high profile.

MEDIA

TV ownership high

Daily newspaper circulation 246 per 1,000 people

PUBLISHING AND BROADCAST MEDIA

There are 241 daily newspapers, including *Diena*, and *Neatkariga Rite Avize*

1 state-owned service, 1 independent 1 state-owned service

The press is now relatively free from state interference. Previously, the media were predominantly in Russian. Since 1991, the state, aiming to broaden the use of the official language, has actively promoted Latvian publications.

CRIME

Death penalty not used

🔒 9,608 prisoners ⬇ Down 35% from 1992–1996

Organized crime is a growing problem, but general crime levels are lower than in other former Soviet states.

EDUCATION

School leaving age: 15

📖 99% 56,187 students

Schools have opened for many minority ethnic groups. More than 50,000 students are in higher education.

CHRONOLOGY

Latvia was dominated by Germany and, briefly, Sweden before Russia completed its conquest in 1795.

- ❏ **1917** Opposes Russian Bolshevik revolution. Declares independence.
- ❏ **1918–1920** Invaded by Bolsheviks in east and Germany in west.
- ❏ **1920** Gains independence.
- ❏ **1944** Incorporated into USSR.
- ❏ **1989** Popular Front (PLF) wins elections and declares independence.
- ❏ **1995** Inconclusive elections. Broad coalition led by Andris Skele of TP
- ❏ **1998** Elections: new LC-led coalition. Naturalization procedure eased, benefiting ethnic Russians.
- ❏ **1999** First woman president. Skele returns as premier.

HEALTH

Welfare state health benefits

1 per 333 people Heart diseases, cancers, accidents, respiratory diseases

The state-run system suffers shortages of medicines and equipment. Some improvements have been made, but it is still seriously underfunded.

SPENDING

GDP/cap. no increase

CONSUMPTION AND SPENDING

175 per 1,000 population 302 per 1,000 population

Defense 4.6%
Education 6.3%
Health No data

0 5 10 15 20 25
Defense, Health, Education spending as % of GDP

The old bureaucracy from the Soviet era has retained its privileged status and contacts, and remains the country's wealthiest group.

WORLD RANKING

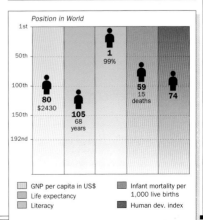

Position in World

1st
50th
100th
150th
192nd

80 $2430
105 68 years
1 99%
59 15 deaths
74

- ❏ GNP per capita in US$
- ❏ Life expectancy
- ❏ Literacy
- ❏ Infant mortality per 1,000 live births
- ❏ Human dev. index

L

LEBANON

OFFICIAL NAME: Republic of Lebanon **CAPITAL:** Beirut
POPULATION: 3.2 million **CURRENCY:** Lebanese pound **OFFICIAL LANGUAGE:** Arabic

MIDDLE EAST

Asia
Africa

Cyprus Syria
LEBANON
Israel Jordan

| 1944 | 1944 | Nov 22 | RL | +2 | +961 | .lb |

L EBANON IS DWARFED BY its two powerful neighbors, Syria and Israel. The country's coastal strip is fertile and the hinterland mountainous. Although in the minority, Maronite Christians have traditionally ruled Lebanon. A civil war between Muslim and Christian factional groups which began in 1975 threatened to lead to the break-up of the state. However, Saudi Arabia brokered a peace agreement in 1989; politics became more stable and reconstruction began.

CLIMATE
▷ Mediterranean/mountain

WEATHER CHART

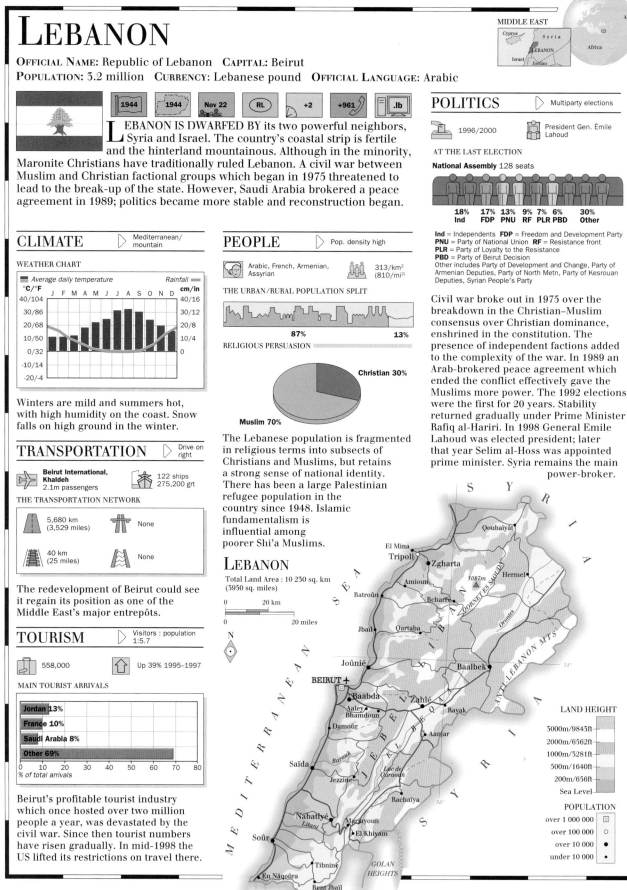

■ Average daily temperature   Rainfall ■

°C/°F   J F M A M J J A S O N D   cm/in
40/104   40/16
30/86   30/12
20/68   20/8
10/50   10/4
0/32   0
-10/14
-20/-4

Winters are mild and summers hot, with high humidity on the coast. Snow falls on high ground in the winter.

TRANSPORTATION
▷ Drive on right

Beirut International, Khaldeh
2.1m passengers

122 ships
275,200 grt

THE TRANSPORTATION NETWORK

| 5,680 km (3,529 miles) | None |
| 40 km (25 miles) | None |

The redevelopment of Beirut could see it regain its position as one of the Middle East's major entrepôts.

TOURISM
▷ Visitors : population 1:5.7

558,000   Up 39% 1995–1997

MAIN TOURIST ARRIVALS

Jordan 13%
France 10%
Saudi Arabia 8%
Other 69%

0 10 20 30 40 50 60 70 80
% of total arrivals

Beirut's profitable tourist industry which once hosted over two million people a year, was devastated by the civil war. Since then tourist numbers have risen gradually. In mid-1998 the US lifted its restrictions on travel there.

PEOPLE
▷ Pop. density high

Arabic, French, Armenian, Assyrian

313/km² (810/mi²)

THE URBAN/RURAL POPULATION SPLIT

87%   13%

RELIGIOUS PERSUASION

Christian 30%

Muslim 70%

The Lebanese population is fragmented in religious terms into subsects of Christians and Muslims, but retains a strong sense of national identity. There has been a large Palestinian refugee population in the country since 1948. Islamic fundamentalism is influential among poorer Shi'a Muslims.

POLITICS
▷ Multiparty elections

1996/2000

President Gen. Émile Lahoud

AT THE LAST ELECTION

National Assembly 128 seats

| 18% Ind | 17% FDP | 13% PNU | 9% RF | 7% PLR | 6% PBD | 30% Other |

Ind = Independents **FDP** = Freedom and Development Party
PNU = Party of National Union **RF** = Resistance front
PLR = Party of Loyalty to the Resistance
PBD = Party of Beirut Decision
Other includes Party of Development and Change, Party of Armenian Deputies, Party of North Metn, Party of Kesrouan Deputies, Syrian People's Party

Civil war broke out in 1975 over the breakdown in the Christian–Muslim consensus over Christian dominance, enshrined in the constitution. The presence of independent factions added to the complexity of the war. In 1989 an Arab-brokered peace agreement which ended the conflict effectively gave the Muslims more power. The 1992 elections were the first for 20 years. Stability returned gradually under Prime Minister Rafiq al-Hariri. In 1998 General Emile Lahoud was elected president; later that year Selim al-Hoss was appointed prime minister. Syria remains the main power-broker.

LEBANON

Total Land Area : 10 230 sq. km
(3950 sq. miles)

0   20 km
0   20 miles

SYRIA
Qoubaïyât
El Mina
Tripoli Zgharta
Amioun 3087m Hermel
Batroûn Bcharré Orontes
Jbaïl Qartaba
Joûnié Baalbek
BEIRUT
Baabda Zahlé
Aaley Rayak
Bhamdoun
Damoûr Aanjar
Saïda Lac de Qaraoun
Jezzine
Rachaïya
Nabatîyé Marjayoun
Litani
Soûr El Khiyam
Tibnine GOLAN HEIGHTS
En Nâqoûra
Bent Jbaïl
ISRAEL

MEDITERRANEAN SEA
JEBEL EL BEQAA
LIBAN
ANTI-LEBANON MTS

LAND HEIGHT
3000m/9843ft
2000m/6562ft
1000m/3281ft
500m/1640ft
200m/656ft
Sea Level

POPULATION
over 1 000 000
over 100 000
over 10 000
under 10 000

L

WORLD AFFAIRS

 Joined UN in 1945

The devastating civil war and 1982 Israeli invasion ended with an Arab solution in 1989, but the Arab–Israeli dispute still threatens peace. The Iranian-backed *Hezbollah* militia clash frequently with Israeli forces in southern Lebanon; over 100 civilians died at a UN base in 1996 in a misdirected Israeli attack. Israel's new government in 1999 planned to withdraw its forces from the so-called "security zone."

AID

Recipient

$239m (receipts)   Up 3% 1996–1997

The government is seeking billions of dollars to rebuild the center of Beirut and restore shattered infrastructure.

DEFENSE

Compulsory military service

$676m   Up 38% in 1997

Under the Taif Agreement, 40,000 Syrian troops are based in Lebanon; its own army has 53,300 troops. In 1999 the new Israeli government proposed removing its forces from the so-called "security zone" in the south, controlled by the Israeli-backed South Lebanon Army. A UN force attempts to police the border with Israel.

ECONOMICS

Inflation 87.4% p.a. (1983–1994)

$13.9bn   1,527–1,513 Lebanese pounds

SCORE CARD

❏ WORLD GNP RANKING	77th
❏ GNP PER CAPITA	$3,350
❏ BALANCE OF PAYMENTS	$–4,809m
❏ INFLATION	8.5%
❏ UNEMPLOYMENT	18%

STRENGTHS
Peace will allow Lebanon to regain its position as an Arab center for banking and services. Potentially a major producer of wine and fruit.

WEAKNESSES
Dependent on imported oil and gas. Infrastructure – especially in Beirut – wrecked by civil war. Agriculture still at 40% of prewar levels. High public debt and inflation.

EXPORTS

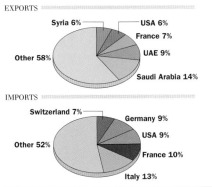

Syria 6%
USA 6%
France 7%
UAE 9%
Saudi Arabia 14%
Other 58%

IMPORTS

Switzerland 7%
Germany 9%
USA 9%
France 10%
Italy 13%
Other 52%

RESOURCES

Electric power 1.2m kw

4,485 tonnes

450,000 goats, 350,000 sheep, 80,000 cattle

Not an oil producer; refines 37,500 b/d

Lignite, iron ore

Wine, cotton, fruit, and vegetables are the main crops. Thermal power stations are fueled by imported petroleum.

ENVIRONMENT

No Green MPs

None   Medium

Rebuilding Beirut's basic infrastructure and ridding the country of mines are the government's priorities.

MEDIA

TV ownership high

Daily newspaper circulation 141 per 1,000 people

PUBLISHING AND BROADCAST MEDIA

There are 15 daily newspapers, including *Al-Anwar*, *An-Nahar*, and its French companion, *L'Orient-Le Jour*

1 state-controlled service   1 state-owned service

Beirut could once again become a center for Arab media. However, in 1994 private TV stations were banned.

CRIME

Death penalty used

Lebanon does not publish prison figures   Crime is sharply down since 1989

The kidnapping of hostages and the breakdown of law during the civil war made Beirut a dangerous city for Western visitors.

Politically motivated violence has recently declined, though the risk of urban terrorism remains. Rural areas untouched by the conflict have low levels of crime.

The Corniche, Beirut, being rebuilt by US consultant engineers and architects in a privately financed scheme.

CHRONOLOGY

Lebanon became independent, after 20 years of French mandate, in 1944.

- ❏ **1975** Civil war erupts.
- ❏ **1982** Israeli invasion.
- ❏ **1989** Taif Agreement ends civil war.
- ❏ **1991** Western hostages released.
- ❏ **1992–1996** General elections; Rafiq al-Hariri prime minister.
- ❏ **1996** Israeli attack kills over 100 civilians at UN base in Qana.
- ❏ **1998** Emile Lahoud elected president.

EDUCATION

Not applicable

84%   81,588 students

Lebanon has one of the highest literacy rates in the Arab world. Education was severely disrupted by the war.

HEALTH

Welfare state health benefits

1 per 526 people   Heart diseases, infectious and parasitic diseases

An adequate system of primary health care exists. Hospital staffing is returning to prewar levels.

SPENDING

GDP/cap. no increase

CONSUMPTION AND SPENDING

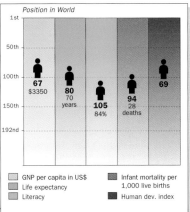

299 per 1,000 population   179 per 1,000 population

Defense 4.5%	
Education 2%	
Health No data	

0   5   10   15   20   25
Defense, Health, Education spending as % of GDP

Average income per capita statistics conceal the fact that a huge gulf exists between Lebanon's poor and a small, massively rich elite.

WORLD RANKING

Position in World
1st
50th
100th
150th
192nd

67 $3350
80 70 years
105 84%
94 28 deaths
69

❏ GNP per capita in US$
❏ Life expectancy
❏ Literacy
■ Infant mortality per 1,000 live births
■ Human dev. index

L

LESOTHO

OFFICIAL NAME: Kingdom of Lesotho **CAPITAL:** Maseru
POPULATION: 2.2 million **CURRENCY:** Loti **OFFICIAL LANGUAGES:** English and Sesotho

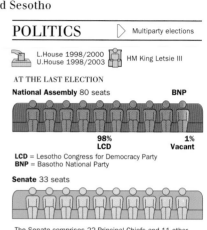

SOUTHERN AFRICA

1966	1966	Oct 4	LS	+2	+266	.ls

A MOUNTAINOUS AND landlocked country entirely surrounded by South Africa, Lesotho is economically dependent on its larger neighbor, which also provides all land transportation links with the outside world. However, Lesotho is beginning to benefit from the export of energy from the recently completed Highlands Water Scheme. Elections in 1993 ended a period of military rule, but South Africa had to intervene militarily when serious political unrest erupted in 1998.

CLIMATE ▷ Mountain

WEATHER CHART

■ *Average daily temperature*   *Rainfall* ▬

Drought is often followed by torrential rain storms. Snow is frequent in the mountains in winter.

TRANSPORTATION ▷ Drive on left

Moshoeshoe Intl, Maseru
43,000 passengers

Has no fleet

THE TRANSPORTATION NETWORK

496 km (799 miles)	None
3 km (2 miles)	None

Lesotho relies on South African road and rail outlets. New roads have been constructed to service the Highlands Water Scheme.

TOURISM ▷ Visitors : population 1:19

112,000 visitors

Up 11% 1995–1997

MAIN TOURIST ARRIVALS

South Africa 96%	
UK 1%	
Botswana 1%	
Other 2%	

0 10 20 30 40 50 60 70 80 90 100
% of total arrivals

Spectacular scenery and watersports on artificially created lakes attract many tourists, mostly South African. US officials warned against visiting Maseru, following political violence in 1998.

PEOPLE ▷ Pop. density medium

English, Sesotho, Zulu

72/km² (188/mi²)

THE URBAN/RURAL POPULATION SPLIT

23%   77%

ETHNIC MAKEUP

European and Asian 3%

Basotho 97%

The overwhelming majority of the population are Basotho, though there are also small minority communities of European, south Asian and Chinese origin. Ethnic homogeneity and a strong sense of national identity have tended to minimize ethnic tension. However, in 1991 rioters attacked south Asian and Chinese storekeepers, whose control of business they resented. The export of male contract labor to South African mines means that women head 72% of households; they also run farming, regarded by Lesotho men as "women's work"

POLITICS ▷ Multiparty elections

L.House 1998/2000
U.House 1998/2003

HM King Letsie III

AT THE LAST ELECTION

National Assembly 80 seats   **BNP**

98%   1%
LCD   **Vacant**

LCD = Lesotho Congress for Democracy Party
BNP = Basotho National Party

Senate 33 seats

The Senate comprises 22 Principal Chiefs and 11 other members named by the King.

The armed forces have been key political players in Lesotho since 1986, when Chief Jonathan's Basotho National Party (BNP) government was deposed in a bloodless military coup. Military rule ended in 1993, and elections resulted in a victory for the BCP. However, the army maintained its precedence in matters of national security. In 1994 King Moshoeshoe II was restored to the throne, his son Letsie III succeeding him in 1996 when he died in a car accident. The BNP lost power in mid-1997, when the prime minister set up his own rival LCD party, which won easily in the 1998 election. Mass protests led to an attempted coup in September 1998, giving rise to South African military intervention. Letsie III was popular, but the government openly muzzled his national broadcasts. In October, South Africa brokered an SADC-approved agreement between the king and Lesotho's 12 parties, to restore democracy.

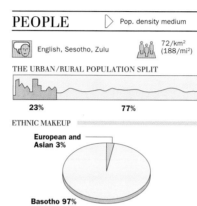

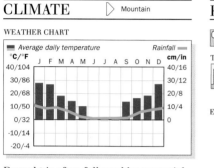

LESOTHO

Total Land Area : 30 350 sq. km
(11 718 sq. miles)

POPULATION

over 100 000	◎
under 10 000	•

LAND HEIGHT

3000m/9843ft
2000m/6562ft
1000m/3281ft

0   50 km
0   50 miles

L

WORLD AFFAIRS ▷ Joined UN in 1966

| Comm | Comesa | NAM | OAU | SADC |

Foreign policy is dominated by the nature of Lesotho's relationship with South Africa. Lesotho currently has duty-free access to the EU for most manufactured goods and preferential access to US and Scandinavian markets.

AID ▷ Recipient

$93m (receipts)　　Down 13% 1996–1997

Aid accounts for 26% of Lesotho's GNP; about half comes from the SACU. Most aid is devoted to making Lesotho self-sufficient in food. In October 1998, World Bank investigators visited Maseru to assess how to alleviate the damage caused by unrest and looting.

DEFENSE ▷ No compulsory military service

$32m　　Down 3% in 1997

The 2,000-strong army could not contain political violence in 1998, and had to call in South African military assistance.

ECONOMICS ▷ Inflation 11.1% p.a. (1985–1996)

$1.4bn　　4.87–5.88 maloti

SCORE CARD

❏ WORLD GNP RANKING	150th
❏ GNP PER CAPITA	$680
❏ BALANCE OF PAYMENTS	$108m
❏ INFLATION	9.3%
❏ UNEMPLOYMENT	50%

STRENGTHS
Educated workforce. Boom in textiles and other manufacturing. Membership of SACU. Highlands Water Scheme major earner and employer.

WEAKNESSES
Economic overdependence on South Africa. Weak agricultural sector. Retail sector suffered badly during 1998 disturbances.

EXPORTS

Taiwan 4% | Other 13% | SACU 83%

IMPORTS

China 3% | Taiwan 5% | Other 8% | SACU 84%

Landscape near Mohales Hoek in Lesotho's lowest lands – over 1300 m (4,260 ft) above sea level. This spiral aloe grows only in Lesotho.

RESOURCES ▷ Not available

40 tonnes　　Not an oil producer and has no refineries

1.1m sheep, 730,000 goats, 580,000 cattle　　Diamonds

The hugely ambitious Highlands Water hydroelectric scheme will supply all of Lesotho's energy requirements, while diverting nearly half of the country's water for use in South Africa. Diamonds are mined in the northeast.

ENVIRONMENT ▷ No Green MPs

1%　　Not available

Land is seriously eroded due to climate and overgrazing. The Highlands Water Scheme has flooded acres of peasant farmland; some fear long-term damage. However, the project's pylons are bird-friendly, and it aims to protect the Maluti mountain minnow in its reservoirs.

MEDIA ▷ TV ownership low

Daily newspaper circulation 7 per 1,000 people

PUBLISHING AND BROADCAST MEDIA

| There are 2 daily newspapers, including *Mphatlatsane. Leselinyana la Lesotho* is a popular religious periodical |

1 state-owned service　　1 state-owned service

Government blocking of the king's radio and TV broadcasts in October 1998 exacerbated the political crisis.

CRIME ▷ Death penalty used

Lesotho does not publish prison figures　　Up 1% in 1992

The 1998 political crisis led to looting, arms theft and violence, although crime levels are generally fairly low.

EDUCATION ▷ School leaving age: 13

82%　　4,614 students

Lesotho has very high school enrolment levels and one of the highest literacy rates in Africa.

CHRONOLOGY

As Basutoland, Lesotho became a British Crown colony in 1884.

- ❏ **1966** Independent kingdom.
- ❏ **1970** Chief Jonathan of BNP annuls elections and bans parties.
- ❏ **1986** Military coup.
- ❏ **1990** King Moshoeshoe exiled.
- ❏ **1993** Free elections; BCP wins.
- ❏ **1994** Return of Moshoeshoe.
- ❏ **1996** Letsie III succeeds to throne.
- ❏ **1998** New LCD wins elections. South African forces intervene following coup attempt. SADC reconcile king and parties, set timetable for restoration of democracy.

HEALTH ▷ Welfare state health benefits

1 per 20,000 people　　Tuberculosis, parasitic diseases, nutritional disorders

Private health organizations and NGOs account for half of all health services. A government-operated flying doctor service covers the highlands. The main endemic disease is tuberculosis. Political conflict in late 1998 ruined whole communities, and led to 35,000 children needing emergency food aid.

L

SPENDING ▷ GDP/cap. increase

CONSUMPTION AND SPENDING

6 per 1,000 population　　10 per 1,000 population

Defense	4.6%
Education	5.9%
Health	1.2%

0　5　10　15　20　25
Defense, Health, Education spending as % of GDP

Social mobility is relatively limited in Lesotho; the ruling elite keeps a tight control on power and wealth. Over 90% of the population live below the poverty line and many are migrant laborers.

WORLD RANKING

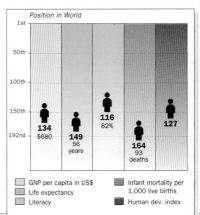

Position in World

1st / 50th / 100th / 150th / 192nd

134 $680 | 149 56 years | 116 82% | 164 93 deaths | 127

- ❏ GNP per capita in US$
- ❏ Life expectancy
- ❏ Literacy
- ■ Infant mortality per 1,000 live births
- ■ Human dev. index

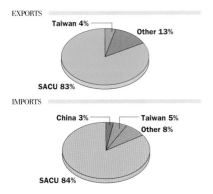

LIBERIA

OFFICIAL NAME: The Republic of Liberia **CAPITAL:** Monrovia
POPULATION: 2.7 million **CURRENCY:** Liberian dollar **OFFICIAL LANGUAGE:** English

WEST AFRICA

| 1847 | 1947 | July 26 | LB | 0 | +231 | .lr |

FOUNDED IN 1847 by freed slaves from the USA, Liberia today is struggling to recover from a civil war which reduced it to anarchy between 1990 and 1996. Facing the Atlantic in equatorial West Africa, most of its coastline is characterized by lagoons and mangrove swamps. Inland, a grassland plateau supports the limited agriculture (just 1% of land is arable). Liberia has the world's largest flag of convenience merchant fleet.

CLIMATE

▷ Tropical equatorial

WEATHER CHART

■ Average daily temperature   100/39   Rainfall ▬
°C/°F   cm/in

Except in the extreme southeast there is only one rainy season, from May to October. Temperatures are consistently high. During the October to March dry season, when the dust-laden *harmattan* wind blows, they rise even higher inland.

TRANSPORTATION

▷ Drive on right

🛬 Roberts Field Intl, Monrovia
🚢 1,684 ships 60m grt

THE TRANSPORTATION NETWORK

| 🛣 2,400 km (1,491 miles) | 🛤 None |
| 🚂 490 km (304 miles) | ⚓ None |

Most roads in Liberia are unpaved. The 490-km (304-mile) railroad was built to transport iron ore and carries little other traffic. Roberts Field airport was built by the USA during World War II.

TOURISM

▷ Not available

🧳 Tourists deterred by civil war
⬦ Not available

MAIN TOURIST ARRIVALS

Liberia does not publish tourism figures by country of origin

% of total arrivals
0   10   20   30   40

As a result of the civil war and continuing insecurity, tourism, never a significant activity in Liberia, is now non-existent.

PEOPLE

▷ Pop. density low

Kpelle, Vai, Bassa, Kru, Grebo, Kissi, Gola, Loma, English
28/km² (73/mi²)

THE URBAN/RURAL POPULATION SPLIT

45%   55%

ETHNIC MAKEUP

Americo-Liberians 5%
Indigenous tribes (16 main groups) 95%

A key distinction has been between Americo-Liberians, the descendants of those freed from slavery (known as "civilized persons"), and the majority indigenous "tribals." The latter were long held in contempt by the Americos, but intermarriage and political assimilation since 1944 have softened attitudes. Intertribal tension is now a more serious problem; it was the main cause of the civil war which erupted in 1990, sending up to 700,000 Liberians into exile in neighboring countries.

POLITICS

▷ Multiparty elections

L. House 1997/2003
U. House 1997/2006
President Charles Taylor

AT THE LAST ELECTION

House of Representatives 64 seats
5% ALCP
76% NPP
11% UP
8% Other

NPP = National Patriotic Party **UP** = Unity Party
ALCP = All Liberia Coalition Party

Senate 26 seats
81% NPP
11% UP
8% ALCP

A long stable period ended in 1980 when army sergeant Samuel Doe seized power. Liberian politics collapsed into a chaotic, bloody, and many-sided conflict after 1990. A peace agreement was reached in 1996 provided for presidential and legislative elections in 1997, won by Charles Taylor and his NPP (formerly the National Patriotic Front of Liberia (NPFL) the predominant armed faction. Some 700,000 refugees began returning, but instability continued as government forces hunted down civil war faction leaders.

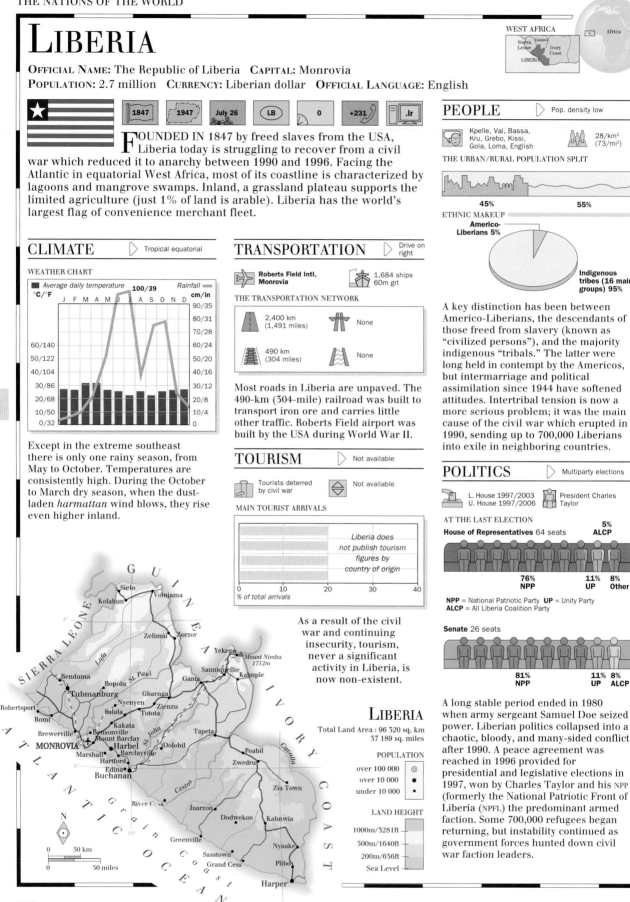

LIBERIA

Total Land Area : 96 520 sq. km
37 189 sq. miles

POPULATION
over 100 000 ◎
over 10 000 ●
under 10 000 ·

LAND HEIGHT
1000m/3281ft
500m/1640ft
200m/656ft
Sea Level

WORLD AFFAIRS

 Joined UN in 1945

ACP | Ecowas | IAEA | NAM | OAU

The USA was the main foreign influence in Liberia until the arrival of ECOMOG (the peacekeeping force of ECOWAS), backed chiefly by Nigeria and Ghana, in 1990. Burkina, Ivory Coast, and Libya were suspected of backing the NPFL. Pressure from ECOWAS brought the UN-led peace process back on track when it foundered, in 1993, 1995, and 1996.

AID

Recipient

 US$95m (receipts) | Down 54% 1996–1997

International development aid was halted in 1986. The USA continued giving aid to the Doe regime until 1990, when all but humanitarian aid ceased.

DEFENSE

No compulsory military service

US$45m | Down 2% in 1997

Peace agreements in 1995 and 1996 provided for the demobilization of the various warring factions and the formation of a single national army.

ECONOMICS

Not available

 US$1.02 bn | 1 Liberian dollar

SCORE CARD

❏ WORLD GNP RANKING........................154th
❏ GNP PER CAPITA ....US$330
❏ BALANCE OF PAYMENTS................US$–145m
❏ INFLATION 9.1%
❏ UNEMPLOYMENT...................................43%

STRENGTHS
Possible revival of operations of the Firestone rubber plantation and huge LAMCO iron ore mine. Tropical timber, but reserves declining.

WEAKNESSES
Little commercial activity, and low confidence. State of anarchy after 1990 led to collapse of economy.

EXPORTS

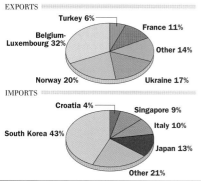
Turkey 6%
France 11%
Belgium-Luxembourg 32%
Other 14%
Norway 20%
Ukraine 17%

IMPORTS

Croatia 4%
Singapore 9%
Italy 10%
South Korea 43%
Japan 13%
Other 21%

Village near Gbarnga. *The Kpelle, the largest of Liberia's 16 indigenous ethnic groups, are concentrated in this part of Liberia.*

RESOURCES

Electric power 332,000 kw

 7,700 tonnes

Not an oil producer; refines 15,000 b/d

 220,000 goats, 210,000 sheep, 120,000 pigs

Iron ore, diamonds, gold, barytes, kyanite, columbite, manganese

Liberia has an estimated billion tonnes of iron ore reserves at Mount Nimba. Even when peaceful conditions return, the current state of world demand would barely justify exploitation.

ENVIRONMENT

No Green MPs

None | Not available

The NPFL and other armed groups cut down tropical forests to finance their armies.

MEDIA

TV ownership low

Daily newspaper circulation 15 per 1,000 people

PUBLISHING AND BROADCAST MEDIA

There are 6 daily newspapers, including the independent *Daily Observer* and *The News*, published by the government

1 partly state-owned service | 2 state-owned, 4 independent services

The Monrovia press has been freer since the fall of Doe, but distribution problems in a state of war lessened the impact of newspapers.

CRIME

Death penalty used

Liberia does not publish prison figures | Crime is rampant. There are no enforcing agencies

Human rights have figured little in Liberian life, and after 1990 they disappeared altogether. The warring factions regularly massacred civilians, press-ganged armies and displaced thousands into seeking refuge in neighboring states.

EDUCATION

School leaving age: 16

38% | 5,095 students

Originally based on the US model, the education system effectively collapsed during the civil war.

CHRONOLOGY

Between 1816 and 1892, 22,000 people liberated from slavery, most from the USA, resettled in Liberia.

❏ **1847** Independent republic.
❏ **1980** Coup. President William Tolbert assassinated by Master Sergeant Samuel Doe.
❏ **1990** Outbreak of civil war.
❏ **1991** Doe assassinated.
❏ **1996** Ruth Perry interim head of state. New peace agreement.
❏ **1997** Charles Taylor elected president.
❏ **1999** Withdrawal of ECOMOG.

HEALTH

No welfare state health benefits

1 per 9,350 people | Communicable, diarrheal, parasitic and heart diseases

Fewer than 12% of people have access to basic health care. The infant mortality rate remains the highest in the world.

SPENDING

GDP/cap. no increase

CONSUMPTION AND SPENDING

41 per 1,000 population | 2 per 1,000 population

Defense 3.9%
Education No data
Health 0.8%

0   5   10   15   20   25
Defense, Health, Education spending as % of GDP

Power and wealth have a very direct connection in Liberia. Both the Americo-Liberian regimes, and the military regime of Samuel Doe who replaced them, saw the state as a source of plunder in the form of well-paid jobs and kick-backs from contracts. The warring factions sought similar power. Most ordinary Liberians live in rural poverty.

WORLD RANKING

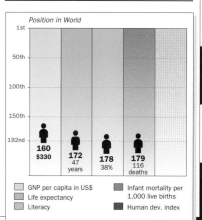
Position in World

1st
50th
100th
150th
192nd

160 $330 | 172 47 years | 178 38% | 179 116 deaths

GNP per capita in US$ | Infant mortality per 1,000 live births
Life expectancy
Literacy | Human dev. index

L

LIBYA

OFFICIAL NAME: The Great Socialist People's Libyan Arab Jamahiriya
CAPITAL: Tripoli **POPULATION:** 6 million **CURRENCY:** Libyan dinar **OFFICIAL LANGUAGE:** Arabic

| 1951 | 1951 | Sept 1 | LAR | +1 | +218 | .ly |

LIBYA IS SITUATED between Egypt and Algeria on the Mediterranean coast of north Africa, with Chad and Niger on its southern borders. Apart from the coastal strip and the mountains in the south, it is desert or semidesert. Libya's strategic position and abundant oil and gas resources made it an important trading partner for European states. Recently it has been politically marginalized by the West for its links with terrorism. However, in 1999 Libya handed over the two men suspected of the 1988 Lockerbie bombing. This resulted in the suspension of UN sanctions.

Roman amphitheatre, Sabrãtah. Libya's impressive Classical heritage testifies to its importance in ancient times.

CLIMATE ▷ Hot desert

WEATHER CHART

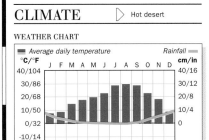

The coastal region has a warm, temperate climate, with mild, wet winters and hot, dry summers.

TRANSPORTATION ▷ Drive on right

| ✈ Tripoli International | 🚢 150 ships 680,500 grt |

THE TRANSPORTATION NETWORK

| 10,800 km (6,711 miles) | None |
| None | None |

The National Coast Road runs 1,825 km (1,135 miles) from the Tunisian to the Egyptian border linking the principal urban centers. Until mid-1999, UN sanctions on international flights meant that the major transit point was through Tunisia.

Al Kufrah Oasis. As 90% of Libya is arid rock and sand, oases provide essential agricultural land, besides being tourist attractions.

TOURISM ▷ Visitors : population 1:63

| 94,000 visitors | Up 88% 1995–1997 |

MAIN TOURIST ARRIVALS

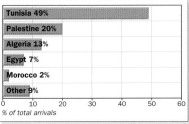

| Tunisia 49% |
| Palestine 20% |
| Algeria 13% |
| Egypt 7% |
| Morocco 2% |
| Other 9% |

% of total arrivals

Libya possesses a rich Roman and Greek heritage, centered on the ancient Roman coastal towns of Labdah (Leptis Magna) and Sabratah near Tripoli, and Shahhat (Cyrene) further east. There are fine beaches at Tripoli, which is also famous for its annual International Fair. Until mid-1999 UN sanctions on air links with Libya effectively closed the country to Western tourists.

PEOPLE ▷ Pop. density low

| Arabic, Tuareg | 3/km² (9/mi²) |

THE URBAN/RURAL POPULATION SPLIT

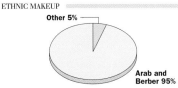

86%   14%

POPULATION AGE BREAKDOWN

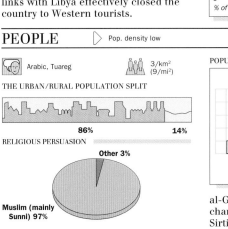

Female	Age	Male
0.3%	81–100	0.3%
1.6%	61–80	1.6%
5.2%	41–60	5.5%
12.1%	21–40	12.8%
29.8%	0–20	30.8%

% of population by age group

RELIGIOUS PERSUASION

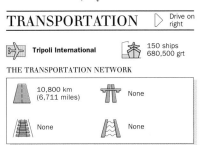

Other 3%

Muslim (mainly Sunni) 97%

ETHNIC MAKEUP

Other 5%

Arab and Berber 95%

95% of Libyans are of Arab and Berber origin, split into many tribal groupings. They were brought together when Libya was created in 1951 by the unification of the three historic Ottoman provinces of Tripolitania, Cyrenaica and the Fazzan. The pro-Western monarchy, set up under King Idris, perpetuated the dominance of Cyrenaican tribes and the Sanusi religious order.

The revolution of 1969 brought to the fore Arab nationalist Colonel Muammar al-Gaddafi, who embodied the character and aspirations of the rural Sirtica tribes from Fazzan: fierce independence, deep Islamic convictions, belief in a communal lifestyle, and hatred for the urban rich. His revolution wiped out private enterprise and the middle classes, banished European settlers and Jews, undermined the function of the religious Muslim establishment and imposed a form of popular democracy through the *jamahiriya* (state of the masses). However, resentment of the regime increased as it became clear that power now lay mainly with the Sirtica tribes, especially Gaddafi's own clan, the Qadhadhfa.

The years since the revolution have seen Libya change from being largely a country of nomads and livestock herders to a society where the great majority are city-dwellers.

L

POLITICS  No multiparty elections

 Not applicable　　Leader of the Revolution
Col Muammar al-Gaddafi

AT THE LAST ELECTION

General People's Congress 750 seats

The constitution makes no provision for direct elections. Last renewal January 1994.

Executive power is exercised by the General People's Committee. The General People's Congress elects the head of state, the Leader of the Revolution.

MAIN POLITICAL ISSUES
Repression
Political dissidents, including Islamist militants, continue to be suppressed and on occasion executed, while the murder of Libyan dissidents abroad, allegedly by government agents, is not unusual. Political parties were banned in 1971, but opposition groups, notably the Libyan Democratic Movement and the National Front for the Salvation of Libya, are active in Egypt and Sudan.

The regime's public image
In the past few years, the regime has made a deliberate effort to improve its international image. Measures have included freeing some political prisoners, allowing exiles to visit the country and permitting foreign travel.

PROFILE
In 1977, a new form of direct democracy was promulgated, through which some 2,000 People's Congresses sought to involve every adult in policy-making. In theory, their wishes are carried out by popular committees. In practice, ultimate control rests with Colonel Gaddafi and his collaborators, many of whom date from the 1969 revolution. In recent years some are believed to have been alienated from the regime. These include Gaddafi's deputy, Major Abdessalem Jalloud, who in 1994 was reportedly marginalized after expressing differences with Gaddafi. In 1995, another of Gaddafi's close associates, Khoueldi Hamidi, a defense commander, was also said to have become disillusioned with Gaddafi. Gaddafi is now believed to rely on members of his own tribal clan.

Colonel Gaddafi,
Libya's leader since 1969, rejects all official titles.

Ex -King Idris
deposed by Colonel Gaddafi in 1969.

WORLD AFFAIRS  Joined UN in 1955

AL　AMU　NAM　OIC　OPEC

Libya's international standing, already compromised by its ill-concealed support for terrorist groups, was finally undermined by allegations of its complicity in the bombing of a US airliner over Lockerbie, Scotland, in 1988. Libya's refusal to hand over for trial two suspects, resulted in 1992 in UN sanctions. These were suspended in 1999, after Libya finally handed the suspects over in April for eventual trial in the Netherlands, under Scottish law. Relations with the UK were restored in 1999 when Libya acknowledged responsibility for the shooting of a policewoman in London in 1984. Regional states have distanced themselves from Libya's opposition to the ongoing Middle East peace process.

L

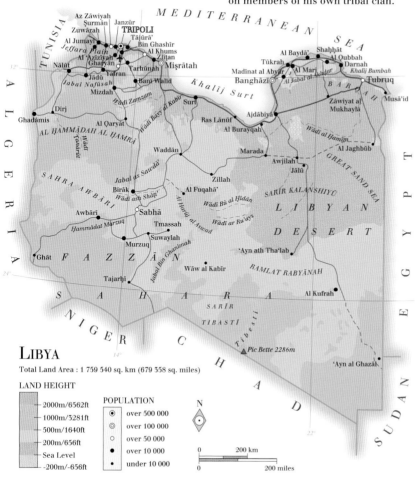

LIBYA

Total Land Area : 1 759 540 sq. km (679 358 sq. miles)

LAND HEIGHT

- 2000m/6562ft
- 1000m/3281ft
- 500m/1640ft
- 200m/656ft
- Sea Level
- -200m/-656ft

POPULATION
- ◉ over 500 000
- ◎ over 100 000
- ○ over 50 000
- ● over 10 000
- · under 10 000

N

0　200 km

0　200 miles

CHRONOLOGY

Italy occupied Libya and expelled the Turks in 1911. Britain and France agreed to a UN plan for an independent monarchy in 1951.

❏ **1969** King Idris deposed in coup by Revolutionary Command Council led by Colonel Gaddafi. Tripoli Charter sets up revolutionary alliance with Egypt and Sudan.
❏ **1970** UK and US military ordered out. Property belonging to Italians and Jews confiscated. Western oil company assets nationalized, a process completed in 1973.
❏ **1973** Libya forms abortive union with Egypt. Gaddafi launches Cultural Revolution. Libya occupies Aozou Strip in Chad.
❏ **1974** Libya forms union of Libya and Tunisia.
❏ **1977** Official name changed to The Great Socialist People's Libyan Arab *Jamahiriya*.
❏ **1979** Members of Revolution Command Council replaced by elected officials. Gaddafi remains Leader of the Revolution. ⇨

CHRONOLOGY *continued*

- ❏ **1981** USA shoots down two Libyan aircraft over Gulf of Sirte.
- ❏ **1984** Gunman at Libyan embassy in London kills British policewoman; UK severs diplomatic relations. Libya signs accord with Morocco for Arab Africa Federation.
- ❏ **1985** Expulsion of 30,000 foreign workers; Tunisia severs diplomatic relations.
- ❏ **1986** US aircraft bomb Libya, killing 101 people and destroying Gaddafi's residence.
- ❏ **1988** Army and police abolished. Bomb causes Pan-Am airliner to explode over Lockerbie, Scotland; allegations of Libyan complicity in planting bomb.
- ❏ **1989** Arab Maghreb Union established with Algeria, Morocco, Mauritania, and Tunisia. Libya and Chad cease-fire in Aozou Strip.
- ❏ **1990** Libya expels Palestinian splinter group led by Abu Abbas.
- ❏ **1991** Opening of first branch of Great Man-Made River project.
- ❏ **1992–1993** UN sanctions imposed as Libya fails to hand over Lockerbie suspects; sanctions made stricter.
- ❏ **1994** Religious leaders obtain right to issue religious decrees (*fatwas*) for first time since 1969. Return of Aozou strip to Chad.
- ❏ **1995** US intelligence report casts doubt on Libyan complicity in Lockerbie bombing. Gaddafi expels an estimated 30,000 Palestinians ordered to go "home" to Palestine; later revokes order.
- ❏ **1999** Lockerbie suspects handed over for trial in Netherlands under Scottish law; UN sanctions lifted. Responsibility for 1984 shooting of London policewoman admitted; relations with UK normalized.

AID
▷ Donor

💲 $9m (receipts)   ⬇ Down 10% 1996–1997

As an oil exporting state, Libya fails to qualify for international aid, despite being a developing country. During the 1970s, Colonel Gaddafi aided several well-established African liberation movements, such as FROLINAT in Chad, and helped dissidents by training them in his Pan-African legion. He has also given finance to the PLO in the Middle East, the IRA in Northern Ireland, the Moros in the southern Philippines, and Basques, Corsicans, and other ethnic causes in Europe. In 1993, Libya granted aid totaling $27 million, despite UN sanctions and a lack of surplus resources.

DEFENSE
▷ Compulsory military service

💲 $1.3m   ⬇ Down 6% in 1997

In 1989, the armed forces were replaced by "the Armed People."

LIBYAN ARMED FORCES

🛡	985 main battle tanks (560 T-54/55, 280 T-62, 145 T-72)	35,000 personnel
⚓	2 submarines, 3 frigates and 33 patrol boats	8,000 personnel
✈	420 combat aircraft (6 Tu-22, 40 MiG-23BN, 15 MiG-23U, 58 *Mirage*)	22,000 personnel
	None	

Attempts to depoliticize the army received a setback following confirmation of an abortive military coup in 1993. The armed forces suffered a blow in 1987 with the loss of thousands of men and equipment worth $1.4 billion in the Chad civil war. The burden of the border war with Chad ended in 1994, when the the Aozou Strip was returned to Chad. UN sanctions have resulted in the concentration of military hardware that is outdated. Despite the suspension of these sanctions in 1999, fresh arms contracts would be too controversial for most potential suppliers.

ECONOMICS
▷ Not available

📊 $29.2bn   💲 0.38–0.45 Libyan dinars

SCORE CARD

- ❏ WORLD GNP RANKING...........................57th
- ❏ GNP PER CAPITA $5,220
- ❏ BALANCE OF PAYMENTS.....................$2.2bn
- ❏ INFLATION 6%
- ❏ UNEMPLOYMENT...................................25%

EXPORTS

France 4% — Turkey 5%
Spain 10%
Italy 41%
Germany 17%
Other 23%

IMPORTS
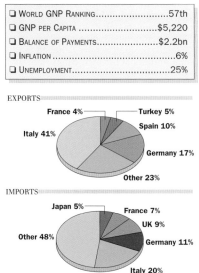

Japan 5% — France 7%
UK 9%
Other 48%
Germany 11%
Italy 20%

ECONOMIC PERFORMANCE INDICATOR

— Consumer price index   GDP ▦

No additional information available

Consumer price index 1983=100

GDP 1983=100

1983 1984 1985 1986 1987

STRENGTHS
Oil and gas production. High investment in downstream industries - petrochemicals, refineries, fertilizers and aluminum smelting.

WEAKNESSES
Single-resource economy subject to oil-market fluctuations. Most food is imported. Reliance on foreign labor. Lack of water for agriculture. History of international unreliability.

PROFILE
Western oil companies had close business ties with Libya until the imposition of UN sanctions over the Lockerbie affair in April 1992. In 1993, Gaddafi called for the program of privatization, authorized by the General People's Congress in late 1992, to be revived but there have been few tangible results. In the 1970s an ambitious program of industrialization was launched.

Gaddafi's most controversial economic project is the Great Man-Made River, intended to bring underground water from the Sahara to the coast. Started in 1984 and engineered by European and Korean companies, this scheme was partially completed in 1996.

LIBYA : MAJOR BUSINESSES

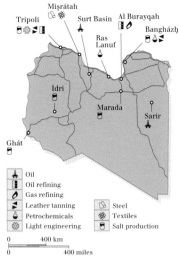

Mişrátah
Tripoli   Surt Basin   Al Burayqah
                          Banghází
                   Ras Lanuf
Idri
            Marada
                          Sarir
Ghát

♠ Oil
🛢 Oil refining
🛢 Gas refining
Leather tanning
Petrochemicals
Light engineering
Steel
Textiles
Salt production

0 ——— 400 km
0 ——— 400 miles

L

RESORCES

Electric power 4.6m kw

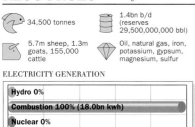

34,500 tonnes

5.7m sheep, 1.3m goats, 155,000 cattle

1.4bn b/d (reserves 29,500,000,000 bbl)

Oil, natural gas, iron, potassium, gypsum, magnesium, sulfur

ELECTRICITY GENERATION

Hydro 0%	
Combustion 100% (18.0bn kwh)	
Nuclear 0%	
Other 0%	

0   20   40   60   80   100

% of total generation by type

With considerable crude oil reserves, Libya is likely to remain an oil exporting country well into the next century. Natural gas potential is more limited but, provided links are developed with other north African states, the future is assured. Libya also has reserves of iron ore, potassium, sulfur, magnesium, and gypsum. With the Great Man-Made River project now partially on stream, the area of irrigated land has been increased, but 90% of Libya is desert. Animal husbandry is the basis of farming, but some cereal crops are grown, as well as dates, olives, and citrus fruits. Cement production is sufficient to meet national demand and relies on local raw materials. Most other manufacturing inputs had to be imported at considerable cost owing to UN sanctions.

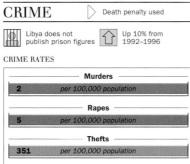

LIBYA : LAND USE

- Cropland
- Pasture
- Desert
- Sheep
- Dates

0   400 km
0   400 miles

ENVIRONMENT

No Green MPs

1% (0.1% partially protected)

Medium

ENVIRONMENTAL TREATIES

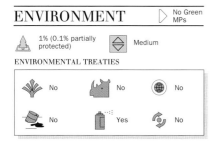

No

No

No

No

Yes

No

The UN Development Program has described Libya as more than 90% "wasteland." Both nature and man have conspired against the environment. Apart from two coastal strips - the Jafara Plain and the Al Jabal al-Akhdar in Cyrenaica - together with the Fazzan Oasis, most of Libya is desert. Much of the irrigated area is saline because of unwise use of naturally occurring water from artesian wells. Seawater has penetrated the water table as far as 20 km (12 miles) inland near Tripoli.

MEDIA

TV ownership medium

Daily newspaper circulation 13 per 1,000 people

PUBLISHING AND BROADCAST MEDIA

There are 4 daily newspapers, including *Al-Fajr al-Jadid*, published by the Jamahiriyah News Agency (JANA)

1 state-controlled service

1 state-controlled service

Libya's press and TV are a mouthpiece for the leadership. The official news agency has voiced criticism of the wealthy elite for living in closed villas sprouting with satellite dishes. The main daily newspaper is published in Arabic and has a circulation of 40,000 readers. The TV station broadcasts mainly in Arabic, with some programs in Italian, French, and English.

CRIME

Death penalty used

Libya does not publish prison figures

Up 10% from 1992–1996

CRIME RATES

Murders	
2	*per 100,000 population*

Rapes	
5	*per 100,000 population*

Thefts	
351	*per 100,000 population*

Policing is often in the hands of gangs appointed by Gaddafi's lieutenants to root out student protesters and other dissidents. Hit squads allegedly operate abroad against Libyan exiles.

EDUCATION

School leaving age: 15

77%

72,899 students

Some one million Libyans receive formal education.

THE EDUCATION SYSTEM

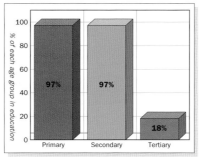

% of each age group in education

100
80
60
40
20
0

97%   97%   18%

Primary   Secondary   Tertiary

Education is compulsory between the ages of six and 15 and rates of attendance are very high; however, it varies in quality and can be basic in rural areas. There are 13 universities, and institutes for vocational training. The literacy rate has improved from 39% in 1970 to 77% in 1995.

HEALTH

Welfare state health benefits

1 per 909 people

Pneumonia, diarrheal diseases, accidents, cancers

An adequate system of primary health care exists except in remote areas, and health services are free. Hospitals lack equipment and UN sanctions until 1999 aggravated the shortage of medical supplies.

SPENDING

GDP/cap. no increase

CONSUMPTION AND SPENDING

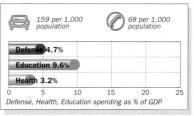

159 per 1,000 population

68 per 1,000 population

Defense 4.7%	
Education 9.6%	
Health 3.2%	

0   5   10   15   20   25

Defense, Health, Education spending as % of GDP

There is widespread poverty in Libya after years of import constraints; UN sanctions in force since 1999 worsened the situation. In 1994, Gaddafi promised to distribute oil earnings to low-income families.

WORLD RANKING

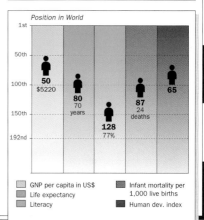

Position in World

1st
50th
100th
150th
192nd

50
$5220

80
70 years

128
77%

87
24 deaths

65

- GNP per capita in US$
- Life expectancy
- Literacy
- Infant mortality per 1,000 live births
- Human dev. index

L

LIECHTENSTEIN

OFFICIAL NAME: Principality of Liechtenstein   **CAPITAL:** Vaduz
POPULATION: 31,000   **CURRENCY:** Swiss franc   **OFFICIAL LANGUAGE:** German

EUROPE

| 1719 | 1719 | Aug 15 | FL | +1 | +4175 | .li |

PERCHED IN THE ALPS between Switzerland and Austria, Liechtenstein is rare among small states in having both a thriving banking sector and a well-diversified manufacturing economy. It is closely allied to Switzerland, which handles its foreign relations and defense. Life in Liechtenstein is stable and conservative. Its banking secrecy laws and low taxes make it home to many overseas trusts, banks, and investment companies.

CLIMATE ▷ Mountain

WEATHER CHART

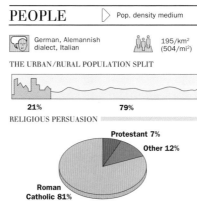

Climate varies with altitude. Excellent skiing conditions are the result of heavy settling snow from December to March. Summers are warm and dry.

TRANSPORTATION ▷ Drive on right

✈ None   ⚓ Has no fleet

THE TRANSPORTATION NETWORK

| 🛣 323 km (201 miles) | ⌁ None |
| 🚂 19 km (12 miles) | 〰 26 km 16 miles |

Public transport in Liechtenstein is mostly by the postal bus network. The single-track railroad has few stops. Zürich, a two-hour drive away, is the nearest airport.

TOURISM ▷ Visitors : population 1.8:1

🧳 57,000 visitors   ⬇ Down 3% 1995–1997

MAIN TOURIST ARRIVALS

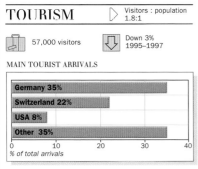

Germany 35%
Switzerland 22%
USA 8%
Other 35%

% of total arrivals

Liechtenstein's alpine scenery attracts skiers in the winter, and climbers and hikers in the summer.

PEOPLE ▷ Pop. density medium

👤 German, Alemannish dialect, Italian   👥 195/km² (504/mi²)

THE URBAN/RURAL POPULATION SPLIT

21%   79%

RELIGIOUS PERSUASION

Protestant 7%
Other 12%
Roman Catholic 81%

Liechtenstein's role as a financial center accounts for the many foreign residents (over 35% of the population), of whom half are Swiss and the rest mostly German. The high standard of living results in few ethnic or social tensions. Family life is highly traditional; women received the vote only in 1984, after much controversy. A proposal the following year that equal rights for women be enshrined in the constitution was rejected in a referendum by a large majority.

POLITICS ▷ Multiparty elections

🗳 1997/2003   👥 Prince Hans-Adam II von und zu Liechtenstein

AT THE LAST ELECTION

Parliament 25 seats

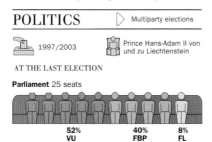

52%   40%   8%
VU   FBP   FL

VU = Fatherland Union **FBP** = Progressive Citizens' Party
FL = Free List

Since 1938 the VU and the FBP have alternated as coalition leaders, except briefly in 1993, till a second election that year resulted in the return of the VU–FBP coalition under Mario Frick, then 28 and Europe's youngest premier. Frick was returned in the 1997 general election. Referenda have increasingly been used to decide policy issues.

WORLD AFFAIRS ▷ Joined UN in 1990

| CE | EEA | IAEA | OSCE | WTO |

Liechtenstein effectively gave up control of its external relations when it signed the 1924 Customs Union Treaty with Switzerland. This requires Swiss approval for any treaty arrangements between Liechtenstein and a third state. The country became a member of the UN only in 1990. It joined EFTA in 1991, and has been a participant in the EEA since 1995. However, Switzerland's rejection of EU membership in a 1992 referendum effectively ended any prospect of Liechtenstein joining the EU in the foreseeable future.

AID ▷ Donor

💲 Donor, but does not publish figures   ⬡ Not applicable

Although overseas aid donations are small and aid issues have little political importance, Liechtenstein has helped to fund shelter and reconstruction projects in former Yugoslavia and local development projects in Bulgaria.

LIECHTENSTEIN

Total Land Area :
160 sq. km
(62 sq. miles)

POPULATION
under 10 000 •

LAND HEIGHT

2000m/6562ft
1500m/4921ft
1000m/3281ft
500m/1640ft
400m/1312ft

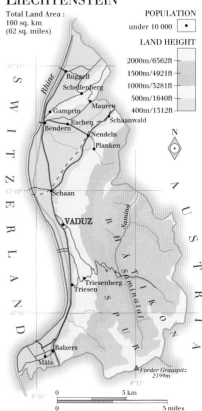

Alpine scenery near Vaduz. The state budget includes 2% allocated to restoring mountain vegetation and coordinating land use.

DEFENSE
▷ No compulsory military service

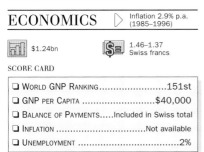

No defense force　Not applicable

There has been no standing army since 1868 and there is only a small police force. *De facto* protection is provided by Switzerland. In theory, any male under 60 is liable for military service during a national emergency, although this law has never been invoked.

ECONOMICS
▷ Inflation 2.9% p.a. (1985–1996)

$1.24bn　1.46–1.37 Swiss francs

SCORE CARD
- ❏ World GNP Ranking........................151st
- ❏ GNP per Capita $40,000
- ❏ Balance of Payments.....Included in Swiss total
- ❏ Inflation ....Not available
- ❏ Unemployment 2%

STRENGTHS
Stability and customs union with Switzerland make Liechtenstein a favored tax haven; its lack of EU membership makes the banking sector less vulnerable to future changes in EU banking laws. The economy is well diversified; chemicals, furniture, coatings for the electro-optical industry, construction services, and precision instruments are all thriving sectors.

WEAKNESSES
Very few. Need to balance integration with other countries with safeguarding economic independence.

EXPORTS

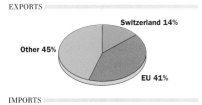

Switzerland 14%
Other 45%
EU 41%

IMPORTS

With a limited domestic market, Liechtenstein's industry is export-oriented. Liechtenstein has a customs union with Switzerland and does not publish separate import figures.

RESOURCES
▷ Not available

None　Not an oil producer and has no refineries
6,000 cattle, 3,000 pigs, 3,000 sheep　None

Liechtenstein has to import 94% of its energy. Almost all of its electricity comes from German power stations.

ENVIRONMENT
▷ Green MPs

38% partially protected　Not available

Protection of Liechtenstein's alpine scenery is sufficiently important for one of the five councilors, or ministers, to be responsible for the environment. As in Switzerland, the greatest worry is the effect of through traffic and high rates of automobile ownership. However, the 1988 experiment in providing free public bus transport proved a failure, as Liechtensteiners remained firmly wedded to their automobiles.

MEDIA
▷ TV ownership high

Daily newspaper circulation 606 per 1,000 people

PUBLISHING AND BROADCAST MEDIA

There are 2 daily newspapers, *Liechtensteiner Vaterland* and *Liechtensteiner Volksblatt*

No TV service　1 radio service

The two newspapers, although free of formal state control, are both run by political parties: the *Vaterland* by the VU; the *Volksblatt* by the FBP. Both have circulations of 8,000–9,500.

CRIME
▷ Death penalty not used

Liechtenstein does not publish prison figures　Crime does not pose any great problems

Crime is a minor problem, a result of the relatively even distribution of wealth and high average living standard. Liechtenstein has also taken great care to protect its tax-haven status by careful regulation of its financial sector. There have been no major scandals, such as the BCCI collapse which tainted the reputation of its main competitor, Luxembourg.

EDUCATION
▷ School leaving age: 16

99%　Not available

Education, modeled on the German system, includes two types of school at secondary level – the grammar-style *Gymnasium* and the *Realschule*. Liechtenstein has no university; students go on to colleges in Austria, Switzerland and Germany, or to business schools in the USA.

CHRONOLOGY
In 1719 Liechtenstein became an independent principality of the Holy Roman Empire.

- ❏ **1919** Switzerland replaces Austria in representing Liechtenstein's interests abroad.
- ❏ **1924** Customs union with Switzerland.
- ❏ **1990** Joins UN.
- ❏ **1995** Joins EEA.
- ❏ **1997** Mario Frick returned for second term leading VU–FBP coalition.

HEALTH
▷ Welfare state health benefits

1 per 948 people　Heart and respiratory diseases, cancers

Although clinics and hospitals are few, the health system provides advanced care. Many Liechtensteiners have private health insurance arrangements, which also give them access to Swiss medical expertise and facilities. Rabies remains a problem.

SPENDING
▷ GDP/cap. no increase

CONSUMPTION AND SPENDING

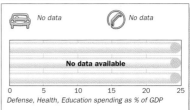

No data　No data
No data available

0　5　10　15　20　25
Defense, Health, Education spending as % of GDP

Most Liechtensteiners have a high standard of living, similar to that of the Swiss. Unlike other tax havens, such as Monaco, it does not attract the jet-set rich, displaying a more conservative prosperity and private deposit accounts are not a key part of its banking business. The state welfare system is generous.

WORLD RANKING

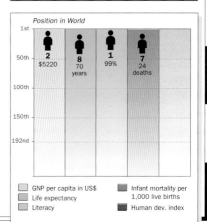

L

LITHUANIA

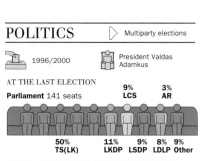

EUROPE

OFFICIAL NAME: Republic of Lithuania   CAPITAL: Vilnius
POPULATION: 3.7 million   CURRENCY: Litas   OFFICIAL LANGUAGE: Lithuanian

1991	1991	Feb 16	LT	+2	+370	.lt

L YING ON THE EASTERN COAST of the Baltic Sea,
Lithuania is bordered by Latvia, Belarus, Poland and
the Kaliningrad area of the Russian Federation. Its
terrain is mostly flat with many lakes, moors and bogs. Now a multiparty
democracy, Lithuania achieved independence from the former USSR in
1991. Industrial production and agriculture are the mainstays of the
economy. Russia finally withdrew all its troops from Lithuania in 1993.

CLIMATE   ▷ Continental

WEATHER CHART

Average daily temperature — Rainfall
°C/°F   cm/in
J F M A M J J A S O N D
40/104 — 40/16
30/86 — 30/12
20/68 — 20/8
10/50 — 10/4
0/32 — 0
-10/14
-20/-4

Lithuania's coastal position moderates
an otherwise continental-type climate.
Summers are cool.

TRANSPORTATION   ▷ Drive on right

Vilnius Intl
462,000 passengers

227 ships
571,500 grt

THE TRANSPORTATION NETWORK

21,100 km (13,188 km)	None
1,998 km (1,249 km)	None

Rail track and signaling are being
improved and roads upgraded. Flights
to the West are increasing.

TOURISM   ▷ Visitors : population 1:13

288,000 visitors

Up 37% 1995–1997

MAIN TOURIST ARRIVALS

Russ Fed 23%	
Germany 25%	
Poland 7%	
Other 55%	

0 10 20 30 40 50 60
% of total arrivals

Tourism has expanded in recent years.
Vilnius is well preserved; its historic
center survived German and Russian
occupation. Trakai, the capital of the
Grand Duchy in the 16th century, is
also popular with visitors.

PEOPLE   ▷ Pop. density medium

Lithuanian, Russian

57/km²
(147/mi²)

THE URBAN/RURAL POPULATION SPLIT

72%   28%

ETHNIC MAKEUP

Belorussian 2%
Other 2%
Polish 7%
Russian 9%
Lithuanian 80%

Relations with ethnic Russians are best
of all the Baltic states, but there are
fewer of them. The mainly Catholic
population has strong historical links
with Poland, although there has been
tension between Lithuanians and Poles
in recent years. Relations with the
Jewish minority remain strained. More
than 90% of non-ethnic Lithuanians
have been granted citizenship.

POLITICS   ▷ Multiparty elections

1996/2000

President Valdas
Adamkus

AT THE LAST ELECTION

Parliament 141 seats

| 50% TS(LK) | 11% LKDP | 9% LSDP | 8% LDLP | 9% Other | 9% LCS | 3% AR |

TS(LK) = Homeland Union (Lithuanian Conservatives)
LKDP = Lithuanian Christian Democratic Party
LCS = Lithuanian Centre Union LSDP = Lithuanian Social
Democratic Party LDLP = Lithuanian Democratic Labour
Party AR = awaiting rerun

The first round of elections were declared invalid
in 4 constituencies.

President Valdas Adamkus was elected
in run-off elections in January 1998,
replacing former communist Algirdas
Brazauskas. A former US citizen who
returned to Lithuania only in 1997,
having fled in 1944, Adamkus achieved
great popularity in the opinion polls,
despite his narrow victory in the
election. A new government was
formed in March 1998. Former mayor
of Vilnius Rolandas Paksas took over as
premier in June 1999 from conservative
nationalist Gediminas Vagnorius.

Lithuania is the most politically
stable of the three Baltic republics,
but the banking crisis of 1995–1996,
and the conduct of the then prime
minister, Adolfas Slezevicius, in
withdrawing savings shortly before
bank operations were suspended,
caused a severe political crisis. In 1998,
former defense minister Audrius
Butkevicius was sentenced to five
years' hard labor for taking a bribe.

LITHUANIA

Total Land Area :
65 200 sq. km
(25 174 sq. miles)

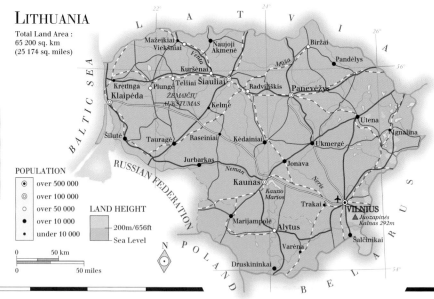

POPULATION
⊙ over 500 000
◎ over 100 000
○ over 50 000
● over 10 000
· under 10 000

LAND HEIGHT

200m/656ft
Sea Level

0   50 km
0   50 miles

WORLD AFFAIRS

Joined UN in 1991

Lithuania has better relations with Russia than the other Baltic states. It aims to join the EU and NATO, and is forming a joint peacekeeping force with Poland.

AID

Recipient

$102m (receipts)   Up 15% 1996-1997

Aid, mostly from the IMF and the EU, is used for infrastructure projects and to promote private enterprise.

DEFENSE

Compulsory military service

$135m   Up 6% in 1997

Lithuania's security is in the hands of its army, the small navy and air force, and a large National Guard formed to patrol its frontiers. Twelve months' military service is compulsory. The USA is now supporting Latvia's entry into NATO.

ECONOMICS

Inflation 111.1% p.a. (1993–1997)

$8.4bn   4.00 litas

SCORE CARD

❑ WORLD GNP RANKING	88th
❑ GNP PER CAPITA	$2,260
❑ BALANCE OF PAYMENTS	$-981m
❑ INFLATION	8.9%
❑ UNEMPLOYMENT	6%

STRENGTHS
Privatization has stimulated economy to some extent. Inflation is under control.

WEAKNESSES
Agriculture in the doldrums following de-collectivization. Exports badly hit by Russian economic crisis. Poor raw materials base. Need to import oil and natural gas from Russia. Difficulty in attracting significant foreign investment.

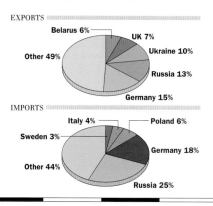

EXPORTS
Belarus 6%
UK 7%
Other 49%
Ukraine 10%
Russia 13%
Germany 15%

IMPORTS
Italy 4%
Poland 6%
Sweden 3%
Germany 18%
Other 44%
Russia 25%

One of Lithuania's 3,000 lakes. The entire country is low-lying. Its coast, fringed by sand dunes and pine forests, is famous for amber.

RESOURCES

Electric power 6.3m kw

56,721 tonnes

Not an oil producer; refines 1,464 b/d

1.1m cattle, 1.2m pigs, 82,000 horses

Sand, gravel, clay, limestone, gypsum

Lithuania has significant reserves of peat and materials used in construction industry. The Ignalina nuclear plant provides more than 80% of the country's electricity. Oil is mostly imported from Russia.

ENVIRONMENT

No Green MPs

10%   Medium

The Ignalina Chernobyl-type nuclear plant continues to cause concern. Leaks have taken place, and there is more chance of leaks in the event of an accident, since the reactors are only partly contained in reinforced concrete.

MEDIA

TV ownership high

Daily newspaper circulation 92 per 1,000 people

PUBLISHING AND BROADCAST MEDIA

There are 2 daily newspapers, *Lietuvos Rytas* and *Respublika*

1 state-owned service, 9 independent

1 state-owned service, 22 independent

The mainstream media, Russian under communism, now publish and broadcast mainly in Lithuanian.

CRIME

Death penalty not used

13,228 prisoners   Up 49% from 1991–1996

Levels of crime are low compared with other parts of the former USSR. Robbery is a growing problem.

EDUCATION

School leaving age: 15

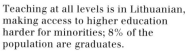

99%   83,645 students

Teaching at all levels is in Lithuanian, making access to higher education harder for minorities; 8% of the population are graduates.

CHRONOLOGY

Russia annexed Lithuania in 1795. The suppression of rebellions in 1831 and 1863 failed to undermine its nationalist movement.

- ❑ **1915** Occupied by German troops.
- ❑ **1918** Independence declared.
- ❑ **1926** Military coup leads to one-party rule.
- ❑ **1941–1944** Nazi occupation.
- ❑ **1940** Annexed by Soviet Union.
- ❑ **1945** Incorporated into USSR.
- ❑ **1991** Achieves full independence.
- ❑ **1992** First multiparty elections.
- ❑ **1993** Russian troops withdraw.
- ❑ **1996** February, prime minister forced from office in banking scandal. November, general election brings to power Homeland Union.
- ❑ **1998** Valdas Adamkus elected president.

HEALTH

No welfare state health benefits

1 per 250 people   Heart diseases, cancers, accidents, tuberculosis

The 1997 reorganization of the health service involves replacing state funding with finance from insurance funds.

SPENDING

GDP/cap. no increase

CONSUMPTION AND SPENDING

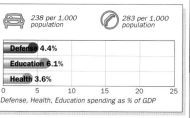

238 per 1,000 population   283 per 1,000 population

Defense 4.4%
Education 6.1%
Health 3.6%

0   5   10   15   20   25
Defense, Health, Education spending as % of GDP

Lithuanians are on average poorer than their neighbors in the other Baltic states. Since 1991 a large gap has opened between the incomes of rich and poor.

WORLD RANKING

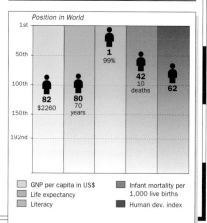

Position in World
1st
50th
100th
150th
192nd

82 $2260
80 70 years
1 99%
42 10 deaths
62

☐ GNP per capita in US$
☐ Life expectancy
☐ Literacy
■ Infant mortality per 1,000 live births
■ Human dev. index

L

LUXEMBOURG

OFFICIAL NAME: Grand Duchy of Luxembourg **CAPITAL:** Luxembourg
POPULATION: 422,000 **CURRENCY:** Luxembourg franc **OFFICIAL LANGUAGES:** French, Letzeburgish and German

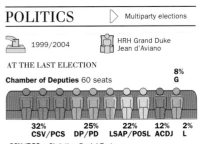

L UXEMBOURG SHARES BORDERS with the industrial regions of Germany, France, and Belgium, and has the highest per capita income in the EU. Making up part of the plateau of the Ardennes, its countryside is undulating and forested. Its prosperity was once based on steel; before World War II it produced more per capita than the USA. Today, it is known as a tax haven and banking center, and as the headquarters of key EU institutions.

L

CLIMATE ▷ Maritime

WEATHER CHART

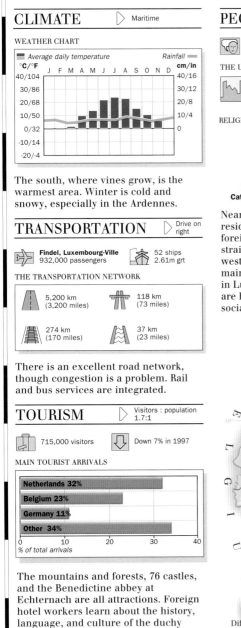

The south, where vines grow, is the warmest area. Winter is cold and snowy, especially in the Ardennes.

TRANSPORTATION ▷ Drive on right

✈ **Findel, Luxembourg-Ville** 932,000 passengers
🚢 52 ships 2.61m grt

THE TRANSPORTATION NETWORK

🛣 5,200 km (3,200 miles)	118 km (73 miles)
🚆 274 km (170 miles)	37 km (23 miles)

There is an excellent road network, though congestion is a problem. Rail and bus services are integrated.

TOURISM ▷ Visitors : population 1.7:1

🧳 715,000 visitors
⬇ Down 7% in 1997

MAIN TOURIST ARRIVALS

Netherlands 32%	
Belgium 23%	
Germany 11%	
Other 34%	

0   10   20   30   40
% of total arrivals

The mountains and forests, 76 castles, and the Benedictine abbey at Echternach are all attractions. Foreign hotel workers learn about the history, language, and culture of the duchy under a government initiative.

PEOPLE ▷ Pop. density medium

Letzeburgish, German, French
163/ km² (423/mi²)

THE URBAN/RURAL POPULATION SPLIT

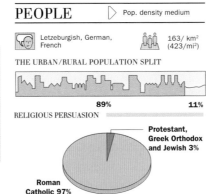

89%   11%

RELIGIOUS PERSUASION

Protestant, Greek Orthodox and Jewish 3%

Roman Catholic 97%

Nearly a third of Luxembourg's residents and half of its workers are foreigners. Integration has been straightforward; most are fellow western Europeans and Catholics, mainly from Italy and Portugal. Life in Luxembourg is comfortable. Salaries are high, unemployment very low, and social tensions few.

POLITICS ▷ Multiparty elections

1999/2004
HRH Grand Duke Jean d'Aviano

AT THE LAST ELECTION

Chamber of Deputies 60 seats

8% G

32% CSV/PCS   25% DP/PD   22% LSAP/POSL   12% ACDJ   2% L

CSV/PCS = Christian Social Party
DP/PD = Democratic Party **LSAP/POSL** = Luxembourg Socialist Workers' Party **ACDJ** = Action Committee for Democracy and Justice **G** = Greens **L** = The Left

Council of State 21 members

The members of the Council of State are appointed for life by the Grand Duke.

Luxembourg's politics have achieved remarkable consensus – characterized by coalitions and long-serving prime ministers. The main issues relate to European integration, especially economic and monetary union.

WORLD AFFAIRS ▷ Joined UN in 1945

Benelux   EU   NATO   OECD   OSCE

Luxembourg has long been the keenest member of the EU. It was during its EU presidency that the Maastricht agreement for closer European union was brokered; Luxembourg was not only the first member state to meet the economic, financial and legal requirements of union under Maastricht, but did so a year early. This commitment reflects the tremendous benefits Luxembourg has gained from EU membership. It is home to both the Secretariat of the European Parliament and the Court of Justice. In 1995, prime minister Jacques Santer left office to become President of the European Commission, but had to resign in 1999 amid allegations of corruption in the Commission.

LUXEMBOURG

Total Land Area : 2585 sq. km (998 sq. miles)

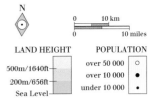

LAND HEIGHT
500m/1640ft
200m/656ft
Sea Level

POPULATION
over 50 000
over 10 000
under 10 000

Charlotte Bridge, Luxembourg.
The modern road system provides excellent communications with the rest of Europe.

AID

▷ Donor

$87m (donations)   ⬦ Not applicable

Aid has been increased substantially and equaled 0.55% of GNP in 1997. Most goes to sub-Saharan Africa.

DEFENSE
▷ No compulsory military service

$129m   ⬇ Down 12% in 1997

Luxembourg's army numbers 800 full-time soldiers. Spending is 0.8% of GDP and has fallen slightly in recent years.

ECONOMICS
▷ Inflation 2.1% p.a (1985–1996)

$18.9bn   37.05–34.35 Luxembourg francs

SCORE CARD

- ❏ WORLD GNP RANKING..........................70th
- ❏ GNP PER CAPITA $45,360
- ❏ BALANCE OF PAYMENTS...Included in Belgian total
- ❏ INFLATION 1.4%
- ❏ UNEMPLOYMENT 4%

STRENGTHS
Site of EU institutions. Banking secrecy and expertise make the capital home to around 1,000 investment funds and 221 banks – more than in any other city in the world.

WEAKNESSES
International service industries account for 65% of GDP, making Luxembourg vulnerable to changing conditions overseas. Downturn in steel market.

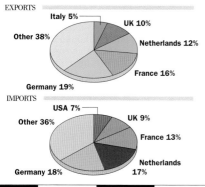

EXPORTS

Italy 5% — UK 10%
Other 38%
Netherlands 12%
France 16%
Germany 19%

IMPORTS

USA 7% — UK 9%
Other 36%
France 13%
Netherlands 17%
Germany 18%

RESOURCES
▷ Electric power 1.3m kw

 Not available   Not an oil producer and has no refineries

Cattle, deer, wild boar, sheep   Iron

Luxembourg can meet few of its own energy needs; it produces only a small amount of hydroelectricity. Arbed is the world's seventh-largest steel producer.

ENVIRONMENT
▷ Green MPs

 None   ⬆ High

Acid rain from European industry has affected 20% of Luxembourg's trees and, in the worst cases, 30% of trees in mature stands. The duchy is a member of an international committee on reducing pollution of the Rhine.

MEDIA
▷ TV ownership high

 Daily newspaper circulation 327 per 1,000 people

PUBLISHING AND BROADCAST MEDIA

There are 5 daily newspapers. The leading newspaper, in terms of both circulation and influence, is the *Luxemburger Wort*

1 independent service   5 independent services

Broadcasting is dominated by RTL (*Radio-Television Luxembourg*), one of the largest media groups in Europe, which exports programs in a variety of languages.

CRIME
▷ Death penalty used

469 prisoners   ⬇ Down 5% from 1992-1996

Luxembourg's stringent banking secrecy rules can provide a cover for both tax evasion and – as in the case of the collapsed BCCI bank, which was registered in Luxembourg – fraud.

EDUCATION
▷ School leaving age: 15

99%   1,415 students

Teaching is mainly in German at primary and French at secondary level. Higher education is limited and many students go to universities in other European countries. Training given by Luxembourg banks is reputed to be the best in Europe.

HEALTH
▷ Welfare state health benefits

1 per 476 people   Heart and cerebrovascular diseases, cancers

There are no private commercial hospitals in Luxembourg; they are run either by the state or by nuns. Patients' fees are refunded from the *Union de caisse de maladie* (state sickness fund).

CHRONOLOGY

Until 1867, Luxembourg was ruled by a succession of neighboring European powers.

- ❏ **1890** Link with Dutch throne ends.
- ❏ **1921** Economic union with Belgium. End of German ties.
- ❏ **1940–1944** German occupation.
- ❏ **1948** 1944 Benelux treaty creating a customs union comes into effect.
- ❏ **1960** Economic Union Treaty comes into effect: internal frontiers removed.
- ❏ **1995** Premier Jacques Santer becomes President of European Commission.
- ❏ **1999** Euro introduced. Santer resigns amid corruption allegations. Socialist losses in general election.

SPENDING
▷ GDP/cap. no increase

CONSUMPTION AND SPENDING

248 per 1,000 population   565 per 1,000 population

Defense 0.8%
Education 4.1%
Health 6.6%

0   5   10   15   20   25
Defense, Health, Education spending as % of GDP

With the highest per capita income in the EU, Luxembourgers enjoy a comfortable lifestyle. Recent strong economic performance has allowed them to benefit both from lower taxes and an increase in spending on social security. Low rates of unemployment have led to the recruitment of foreign workers, mainly from other EU countries such as Portugal and Italy, to take the country's less well-paid jobs. As elsewhere in western Europe, financing the ageing population is likely to be a burden in the future.

WORLD RANKING

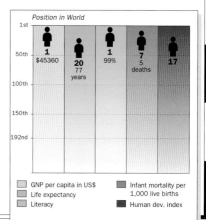

Position in World
1st
50th
100th
150th
192nd

1 $45360
20 77 years
1 99%
7 5 deaths
17

- ▢ GNP per capita in US$
- ▢ Life expectancy
- ▢ Literacy
- ▮ Infant mortality per 1,000 live births
- ▮ Human dev. index

L

MACEDONIA

OFFICIAL NAME: Former Yugoslav Republic of Macedonia **CAPITAL:** Skopje
POPULATION: 2.2 million **CURRENCY:** Macedonian denar **OFFICIAL LANGUAGE:** Macedonian

| 1991 | 1991 | Aug 2 | MK | +1 | +389 | .mk |

THE FORMER YUGOSLAV REPUBLIC of Macedonia (FYRM) is landlocked in southeastern Europe. Despite the signing of an accord in 1995, Greece remains hostile to the FYRM because it suspects that it may try to absorb northern Greece – also called Macedonia – in a "Greater Macedonia." Thousands of NATO troops launched the peacekeeping operation in neighboring Kosovo from Macedonia in 1999.

A fisherman's hut on Lake Dojran, which lies on the border with Greece in southeastern Macedonia and is shared by the two countries.

CLIMATE ▷ Continental

WEATHER CHART

Average daily temperature | Rainfall

°C/°F   J F M A M J J A S O N D   cm/in
40/104   40/16
30/86   30/12
20/68   20/8
10/50   10/4
0/32   0
-10/14
-20/4

The FYRM has a continental climate, with dry autumns and wet springs. Winter snow supports skiing.

TRANSPORTATION ▷ Drive on right

Skopje International
511,703 passengers

Has no fleet

THE TRANSPORTATION NETWORK

| 8,700 km (5,438 miles) | None |
| 699 km (437 miles) | None |

An east–west road and rail route through Macedonia, linking Tirana and Sofia, is being built to avoid Yugoslavia.

TOURISM ▷ Visitors : population 1:15

147,000 visitors | No change in 1995

MAIN TOURIST ARRIVALS

The FYRM does not publish tourism figures by country of origin

0   10   20   30   40
% of total arrivals

Tourism is a traditionally important income source. Lake resorts and skiing in the Sara mountains are among the attractions. Conflict and instability in the region means that visitors are aid workers rather than tourists.

PEOPLE ▷ Pop. density medium

Macedonian, Serbo-Croatian | 86/km² (222/mi²)

THE URBAN/RURAL POPULATION SPLIT

60%   40%

ETHNIC MAKEUP

- Other 2%
- Serb 2%
- Turkish 4%
- Romany 2%
- Albanian 23%
- Macedonian 67%

Around two-thirds of the population are ethnically Slav Macedonians; 23% are Albanian, though Albanians themselves claim to account for 40%. Unlike in nearby Kosovo, Slav Macedonian–Albanian tension was fairly restrained until 1999, when many thousands of ethnic Albanians fled Kosovo, leading to fears that the delicate ethnic balance might be undermined. Macedonians are mostly Eastern Orthodox, but there are a substantial number of Slavic Muslims, whose ancestors converted during the Ottoman occupation. Ethnic Albanians are mostly Muslim.

POLITICS ▷ Multiparty elections

1998/2002 | President Kiro Gligorov

AT THE LAST ELECTION

Assembly of the Republic 120 seats

| 41% VMRO-DPMNE | 22% SDSM | 11% PDP | 11% DA | 3% LDP | 1% SPM | 9% DPA | 1% AR |

VMRO-DPMNE = Democratic Party for Macedonian National Unity **SDSM** = Social Democratic Alliance of Macedonia **PDP** = Party of Democratic Prosperity **DA** = Democratic Alternative **DPA** = Democratic Party of Albanians **LDP** = Liberal Democratic Party **AR** = Romany Alliance **SPM** = Socialist Party of Macedonia

The early 1990s were overshadowed by the dispute with Greece over the state's name. A 1995 accord provided for both states to respect the sovereignty, territorial integrity, and political independence of the other, and confirmed their common existing frontier as an inviolable international border.

Politics fragment along nationalist lines, and are influenced by tensions in neighboring states. Although the Slav Macedonian and Albanian communities have acted with restraint, ethnic tensions remain. Ethnic Albanian parties are pursuing recognition as a constituent nation within the FYRM.

In elections in late 1998 an alliance of right-wing nationalist parties led by Ljubco Georgievski wrested power from former communists, whose leader Kiro Gligorov of the SDSM continued as president.

WORLD AFFAIRS ▷ Joined UN in 1993

| CE | IAEA | IBRD | PfP | OSCE |

Recognition was stalled by Greek objections but a UN-brokered accord was signed in 1995. Its hosting of NATO troops during the Kosovo war in 1999 has placed it firmly in the Western fold.

AID ▷ Recipient

$149m | Up 42% 1996–1997

A $25 million grant from the Soros Foundation has boosted foreign exchange reserves. Official assistance totaled $149 million in 1997; foreign direct investment is limited because of regional security fears.

DEFENSE ▷ Compulsory military service

$132m | Up 9% in 1997

The army is dominated by officers who resigned from the Yugoslav army in 1992. NATO troops, in Macedonia from late 1998, launched operations against Yugoslavia from there in 1999.

M

EUROPE

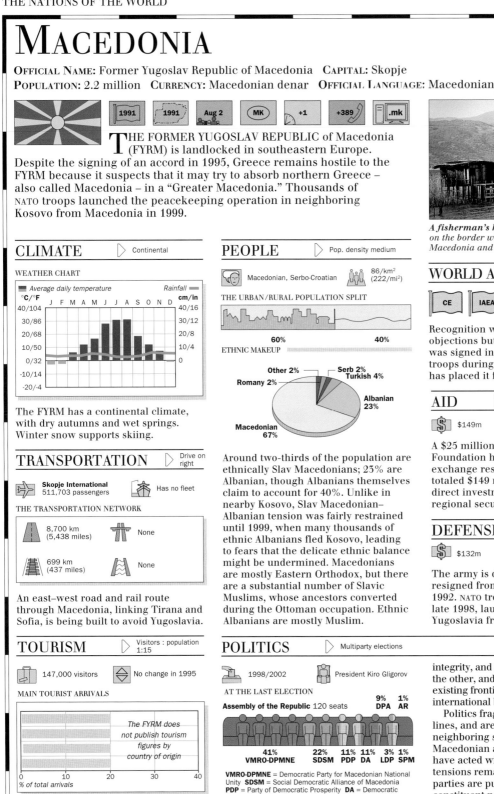

ECONOMICS

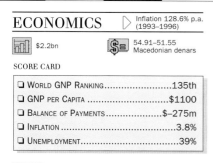

▷ Inflation 128.6% p.a. (1993–1996)

$2.2bn

54.91–51.55 Macedonian denars

SCORE CARD

❑ WORLD GNP RANKING	135th
❑ GNP PER CAPITA	$1100
❑ BALANCE OF PAYMENTS	$–275m
❑ INFLATION	3.8%
❑ UNEMPLOYMENT	39%

EXPORTS

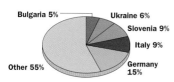

Slovenia 5%
Ukraine 8%
Other 45%
Italy 10%
USA 13%
Germany 19%

IMPORTS

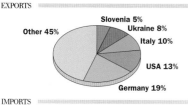

Bulgaria 5%
Ukraine 6%
Slovenia 9%
Italy 9%
Other 55%
Germany 15%

STRENGTHS

Strong growth in private sector. 1996 creation of Skopje stock exchange.

WEAKNESSES

Poorest of former Yugoslav republics. Loss of trade due to Greek embargo in 1994–1996 and embargo on trade with Yugoslavia. Dependence on oil, gas, and machinery imports. Disruption caused by Kosovo conflict.

FORMER YUGOSLAV REPUBLIC OF MACEDONIA

Total Land Area :
25 715 sq. km
(9929 sq. miles)

LAND HEIGHT

2000m/6562ft
1000m/3281ft
500m/1640ft
50m/164ft

POPULATION

⊙ over 500 000
◎ over 100 000
○ over 50 000
● over 10 000
• under 10 000

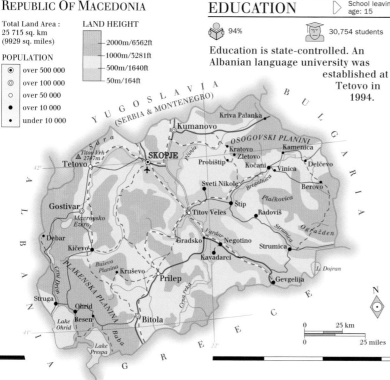

RESOURCES

▷ Electric power 1.5m kw

989 tonnes

Not an oil producer

1.8m sheep,
1.7m pigs,
298,000 cattle,

Coal, copper, bauxite, iron, antimony, chromium, lead, zinc

Electricity plants are fueled by coal. South-facing fertile plains are ideal for early fruit and vegetables for EU market.

ENVIRONMENT

▷ No Green MPs

7%

Low

The 1999 war in Kosovo led to fears of pollution from depleted uranium. During the conflict, birds flew south to Macedonia to nest.

MEDIA

▷ TV ownership high

Daily newspaper circulation 19 per 1,000 people

PUBLISHING AND BROADCAST MEDIA

There are 3 daily newspapers including the government-funded Albanian *Flaka e Vellazerimit* and the Turkish *Birlik*

1 state-owned, 2 independent services

1 state-owned, also independent services

The free and often critical press includes the influential *Nova Makedonija* and *Vecer*.

CRIME

▷ Death penalty not used

Macedonia does not publish prison figures

Illegal labour market increasing rapidly

The local Albanian Mafia controls the illegal trade in cigarettes, narcotics, hard currency, and arms in Skopje.

EDUCATION

▷ School leaving age: 15

94%

30,754 students

Education is state-controlled. An Albanian language university was established at Tetovo in 1994.

CHRONOLOGY

Following the Balkan wars, Macedonia was partitioned between Greece and Serbia in 1912–1913.

❑ **1944** Tito establishes Republic of Macedonia, consolidating national identity, to reduce Bulgarian influence.
❑ **1945** Adoption of standardized Macedonian language.
❑ **1989–1990** Communists concede multiparty elections: won by former communist SKM/PDP (later SDSM).
❑ **1991** Independence declared. EC recognition delayed by Greeks.
❑ **1995** Accord with Greece. President survives assassination attempt.
❑ **1998** SDSM defeated in elections by right-wing VMRO/DPMNE coalition.

HEALTH

▷ Welfare state health benefits

1 per 435 people

Heart and cerebrovascular diseases, cancers

In theory, the state guarantees universal health care, but effective and speedy treatment is increasingly only available in the private sector. Most pharmacies have also been privatized.

SPENDING

▷ GDP/cap. increase

M

CONSUMPTION AND SPENDING

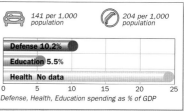

141 per 1,000 population

204 per 1,000 population

Defense 10.2%	
Education 5.5%	
Health No data	

0   5   10   15   20   25
Defense, Health, Education spending as % of GDP

Incomes have fallen almost universally by more than two-thirds since 1990, though smuggling has made a few people rich.

WORLD RANKING

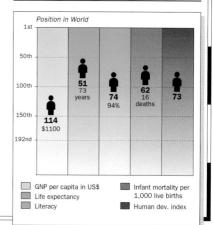

Position in World

1st
50th
100th
150th
192nd

51
73 years

74
94%

62
16 deaths

73

114
$1100

☐ GNP per capita in US$
☐ Life expectancy
☐ Literacy
☐ Infant mortality per 1,000 live births
☐ Human dev. index

MADAGASCAR

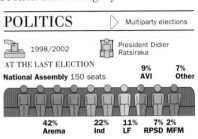

OFFICIAL NAME: Republic of Madagascar   CAPITAL: Antananarivo
POPULATION: 16.3 million   CURRENCY: Malagasy franc   OFFICIAL LANGUAGES: French and Malagasy

| 1960 | 1960 | June 26 | RM | +3 | +261 | .mg |

L YING IN THE INDIAN Ocean, Madagascar is the world's fourth-largest island. Its isolation means that it is home to a host of unique wildlife and plants. To the east, the large central plateau drops precipitously through forested cliffs to the coast. On the west, gentler gradients give way to fertile plains. A former French colony, it became independent in 1960. After 18 years of radical socialism under Didier Ratsiraka, Madagascar became a multiparty democracy. It has become heavily dependent on IMF support as it struggles to rebuild its agriculturally based economy.

CLIMATE
▷ Tropical

WEATHER CHART

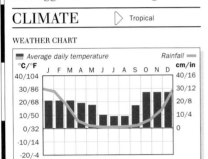

Tropical Madagascar often has cyclones. The coastal lowlands are humid: rainfall averages 200 cm (79 in) in the east, but under 80 cm (31 in) in the southwest. The central plateau is cooler, with 100–150 cm (39–59 inches) of rain a year.

TRANSPORTATION
▷ Drive on right

| Ivato, Antananarivo 611,423 passengers | 99 ships 39,300 grt |

THE TRANSPORTATION NETWORK

| 5,350 km (3,324 miles) | None |
| 1,095 km (680 miles) | 432 km (268 miles) |

An extensive domestic air network – due for privatization – compensates for the fact that many roads are impassable during the rains and the rail network is very limited. Toamasina port handles about 70% of total traffic.

TOURISM
▷ Visitors : population 1:194

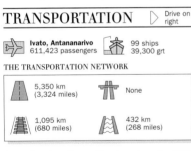

| 84,000 visitors | Up 22% 1995–1997 |

MAIN TOURIST ARRIVALS

| France 31% |
| Germany 20% |
| Switzerland 9% |
| Other 40% |

0   10   20   30   40
% of total arrivals

With 5,000 km (3,100 miles) of tropical beaches and unique flora and fauna, Madagascar has great tourism potential. An important foreign exchange earner, tourism nonetheless remains underdeveloped. Tourist arrivals increased after the marked decline of 1991, thanks partly to restored political stability.

PEOPLE
▷ Pop. density low

| Malagasy, French | 28/km² (73/mi²) |

THE URBAN/RURAL POPULATION SPLIT

27%   73%

RELIGIOUS PERSUASION

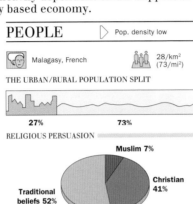

Muslim 7%
Christian 41%
Traditional beliefs 52%

The people of Madagascar, like their language, Malagasy, are essentially Malay–Indonesian in origin. Their ancestors migrated across the Indian Ocean in successive waves from the 1st century. Later migrants from the African mainland intermixed and provided the many African words in Malagasy; Arab traders provided another ingredient. The main ethnic division is between the central plateau and *côtier* peoples. The plateau Merina, of more pronounced Malay extraction, were Madagascar's historic rulers. They remain the social elite – to the resentment of the poorer *côtiers*. President Didier Ratsiraka owes much of his political longevity to the fact that he is a *côtier*. The extended family remains the focus of social life for the rural majority.

POLITICS
▷ Multiparty elections

1998/2002
President Didier Ratsiraka

AT THE LAST ELECTION

National Assembly 150 seats

42% Arema   22% Ind   11% LF   7% RPSD   2% MFM   9% AVI   7% Other

Arema = Avant-garde de la révolution malgache
Ind = Independents   **LF** = Leader (Fanilo)
RPSD = Rally for Socialism and Democracy
MFM = Militant Party for the Development of Madagascar

The Senate, as of late-1999, had yet to be established. Two-thirds of its members are to be elected by an electoral college, the remainder nominated by the president.

In 1993, 18-year *de facto* one-party rule, ended with opposition victory, but former head of state Didier Ratsiraka won presidential elections in 1997. A new constitution in 1998 gave him increased powers over the choice of government members.

MADAGASCAR

Total Land Area : 581 540 sq. km
(224 555 sq. miles)

POPULATION
- ◉ over 500 000
- ◎ over 100 000
- ○ over 50 000
- ● over 10 000
- · under 10 000

LAND HEIGHT
- 2000m/6562ft
- 1000m/3281ft
- 500m/1640ft
- 200m/656ft
- Sea Level

0   200 km
0   200 miles

M

WORLD AFFAIRS ▷ Joined UN in 1960

Once-close ties with Moscow and North Korea waned as Madagascar has cemented relations with its main Western trading partners, especially France and the USA. Since Zafy's demise, cooperation with the IMF has improved too. Regionally, Madagascar has reestablished ties with South Africa and in 1994 joined Comesa.

AID ▷ Recipient

$838m (receipts) — Up 130% 1996–1997

Major donors include France, the EU and the World Bank. In 1999 the IMF pledged assistance for Ratsiraka's bold fiscal and economic reforms.

DEFENSE ▷ Compulsory military service

$37m — Down 3% in 1997

The army, a key political force, aims to maintain a stable, unitary state. In 1992, it acted against federalist *côtiers*.

ECONOMICS ▷ Inflation 20.1% p.a. (1985–1996)

$3.58bn — 5,000–5,220 Malagasy francs

SCORE CARD

- ❏ WORLD GNP RANKING.........................120th
- ❏ GNP PER CAPITA $250
- ❏ BALANCE OF PAYMENTS.....................$–291m
- ❏ INFLATION 4.5%
- ❏ UNEMPLOYMENT... Widespread underemployment

STRENGTHS
Varied agricultural base; vanilla, coffee, and clove exports. Offshore oil and gas. Prawns. Tourism. Literate workforce.

WEAKNESSES
Losing out to cheaper vanilla exporters. Vulnerability to drought. Attempts to cut central controls and budget deficit yet to bear fruit. Not self-sufficient in rice, the food staple.

EXPORTS

UK 6%
Japan 6%
Germany 8%
France 40%
USA 10%
Other 30%

IMPORTS

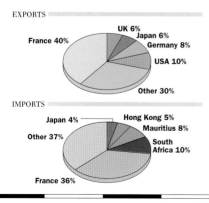

Japan 4%
Hong Kong 5%
Mauritius 8%
Other 37%
South Africa 10%
France 36%

Tôlañaro (also known as Fort Dauphin), a port on the southeast coast. This was the area first settled by the French in the 16th century.

RESOURCES ▷ Electric power 220,000 kw

119,352 tonnes — Not an oil producer; refines 16,350 b/d

10.3m cattle, 1.7m pigs, 1.3m goats — Chromite, graphite, mica, iron, bitumen, gemstones, marble

Madagascar is the world's second-largest vanilla exporter. Rich deposits of high quality sapphires were found in 1998.

ENVIRONMENT ▷ No Green MPs

2% (1% partially protected) — Low

Madagascar's environment is a unique resource; 80% of its plant and many animal species, such as the lemur, are found nowhere else. Aid donations help to combat deforestation and soil erosion.

MEDIA ▷ TV ownership low

 Daily newspaper circulation 4 per 1,000 people

PUBLISHING AND BROADCAST MEDIA

There are 5 daily newspapers, including the *Madagascar Tribune* and *Midi-Madagasikara*

1 state-owned service

1 state-owned, 6 independent services

Even before the return of multiparty democracy in 1993, there was a flourishing opposition press, including the Catholic-sponsored *La Croix*.

CRIME ▷ Death penalty not used

33,280 prisoners — Crime is rising

Urban crime levels are rising, with theft a particular concern. The army faces accusations of abusing human rights and of shooting federalists in 1993.

EDUCATION ▷ School leaving age: 13

47% — 26,715 students

Madagascar boasts one of Africa's highest literacy rates. Universal primary education will soon be based on French, not Malagasy. About 40% of children attend secondary school.

HEALTH ▷ Welfare state health benefits

1 per 10,000 people — Malaria, enteric and respiratory diseases

Private health care was legalized in 1993. State care is free but inadequate. Malaria is at epidemic levels. There are outbreaks of bubonic plague.

SPENDING ▷ GDP/cap. no increase

CONSUMPTION AND SPENDING

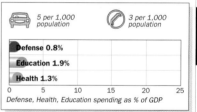

5 per 1,000 population — 3 per 1,000 population

Defense 0.8%
Education 1.9%
Health 1.3%

Defense, Health, Education spending as % of GDP

Most of Madagascar's people are terribly poor, although central plateau dwellers are richer than the *côtier* farmers and fishermen.

WORLD RANKING

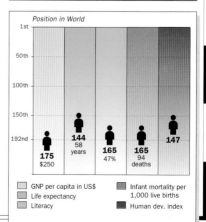

Position in World

| | 175 $250 | 144 58 years | 165 47% | 165 94 deaths | 147 |

GNP per capita in US$
Life expectancy
Literacy
Infant mortality per 1,000 live births
Human dev. index

M

MALAWI

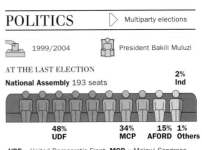

SOUTHERN AFRICA

Africa

OFFICIAL NAME: Republic of Malawi **CAPITAL:** Lilongwe **POPULATION:** 10.4 million
CURRENCY: Malawi kwacha **OFFICIAL LANGUAGE:** English

| 1964 | 1964 | July 6 | MW | +2 | +265 | .mw |

L ANDLOCKED IN SOUTHEAST AFRICA, Malawi borders the Great Rift Valley. One-fifth of the country's area is occupied by Africa's third-largest expanse of water, Lake Malawi. In the 1980s Malawi hosted large numbers of Mozambican refugees, but at some cost to its fragile economy. A former British colony, Malawi moved to democracy in 1994 after three decades of one-party rule under Hastings Banda. Bakili Muluzi was reelected president in June 1999.

M

CLIMATE
▷ Tropical wet & dry

WEATHER CHART

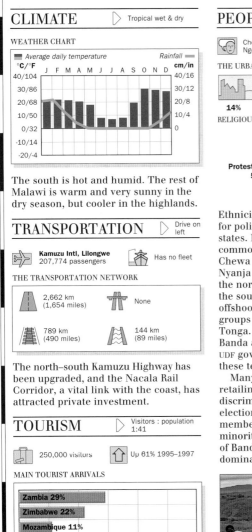

■ Average daily temperature   Rainfall ━━
°C/°F   J F M A M J J A S O N D   cm/in
40/104 ・・・・・・・・・・・・ 40/16
30/86 ・・・・・・・・・・・・ 30/12
20/68 ・・・・・・・・・・・・ 20/8
10/50 ・・・・・・・・・・・・ 10/4
0/32 ・・・・・・・・・・・・ 0
-10/14
-20/-4

The south is hot and humid. The rest of Malawi is warm and very sunny in the dry season, but cooler in the highlands.

TRANSPORTATION
▷ Drive on left

🛫 **Kamuzu Intl, Lilongwe**
207,774 passengers

🚢 Has no fleet

THE TRANSPORTATION NETWORK

| 🛣 2,662 km (1,654 miles) | 🛤 None |
| 🚂 789 km (490 miles) | ⚓ 144 km (89 miles) |

The north–south Kamuzu Highway has been upgraded, and the Nacala Rail Corridor, a vital link with the coast, has attracted private investment.

TOURISM
▷ Visitors : population 1:41

🧳 250,000 visitors

⬆ Up 61% 1995–1997

MAIN TOURIST ARRIVALS

Zambia 29%
Zimbabwe 22%
Mozambique 11%
Other 38%
0 10 20 30 40 50 60
% of total arrivals

Tourist numbers have increased in recent years. The national parks and Lake Malawi's fishing and water sports make tourism the state's most promising area for development.

PEOPLE
▷ Pop. density medium

👤 Chewa, Lomwe, Yao, Ngoni, English

👥 111/km² (286/mi²)

THE URBAN/RURAL POPULATION SPLIT

14%   **86%**

RELIGIOUS PERSUASION

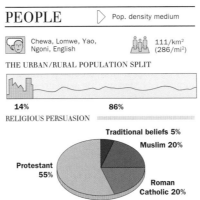

Traditional beliefs 5%
Muslim 20%
Protestant 55%
Roman Catholic 20%

Ethnicity has not been exploited for political ends as in neighboring states. Most Malawians share a common Bantu origin, with the Chewa dominant in the central region, Nyanja in the south, Tumbuka in the north, the mostly Muslim Yao in the southeast, and the Ngoni, a Zulu offshoot, in the lowlands. Other groups include the Chieoka and Tonga. Northerners felt ignored by Banda and his MCP, but the new UDF government has largely reduced these tensions.

Many Muslim Asians work in retailing. They no longer suffer discrimination as before. The election of President Muluzi, a member of Malawi's 15% Muslim minority, arguably signals the failure of Banda's plan to enforce Protestant domination in Malawi.

Fruit and vegetable sellers on the Mozambican border. The south of the country is intensively cultivated.

POLITICS
▷ Multiparty elections

🗳 1999/2004

🪑 President Bakili Muluzi

AT THE LAST ELECTION

National Assembly 193 seats

2% Ind

48% UDF   34% MCP   15% AFORD   1% Others

UDF = United Democratic Front **MCP** = Malawi Congress Party **AFORD** = Alliance for Democracy **Ind** = Independent

Results of the 1999 election were not available in Oct.1999., but it appeared that the UDF were in the lead.

From independence in 1964 Malawi was ruled by the autocratic Hastings Banda. His single-party regime outlawed dissent; torture and imprisonment without trial were common. In 1992 international aid was suspended because of the regime's human rights record. A referendum in 1993 forced Banda to introduce multiparty politics. In 1994 elections saw the mainly southern-based UDF under Bakili Muluzi score a dramatic victory. In simultaneous presidential polls Muluzi resoundingly beat Banda, ending one of the world's longest lasting dictatorships. Muluzi shrewdly recruited several prominent MCP politicians to his team. He vowed to restore personal and religious freedom, liberalize and revive the economy, and improve Malawi's regional standing. Muluzi was narrowly reelected in June 1999; but opposition leader Gwanda Chakuamba contested the results, and violence against Muslims and UDF supporters erupted in the north.

WORLD AFFAIRS
▷ Joined UN in 1964

| Comm | Comesa | NAM | OAU | SADC |

Malawi aims to protect its restored status as a recipient of Western aid. In 1998 Britain pledged to support President Muluzi's fiscal policies and anti-poverty drive. Malawi also wants to preserve ties with South Africa, unbroken since 1967, a unique record in black Africa. One in ten Mozambicans fled to Malawi as refugees in the 1980s.

AID
▷ Recipient

💲 $350m (receipts)

⬇ Down 30% 1996–1997

Nonhumanitarian aid resumed with the advent of democracy, and international donors have pledged $1.2 billion. Malawi manages repayments on its $24 billion external debt. The IMF backs Malawi's anti-inflationary policies.

DEFENSE

▷ No compulsory military service

💲 $23m

⬇ Down 4% in 1997

The new government is confident of the loyalty of the 9,800-strong military. In the last days of Banda rule, the military lost confidence in the ruling party, forcing the pace of democratization. In 1993, it disarmed the Young Pioneers, a militarized section of the MCP.

ECONOMICS

▷ Inflation 25.9% p.a. (1993–1997)

📊 $2.1bn

💱 19.26–45.11 kwacha

SCORE CARD

- ❏ WORLD GNP RANKING........................136th
- ❏ GNP PER CAPITA $210
- ❏ BALANCE OF PAYMENTS....................$–450m
- ❏ INFLATION 37.6%
- ❏ UNEMPLOYMENT...Widespread underemployment

STRENGTHS

Tobacco, earning 76% of foreign exchange. Tea and sugar production. Unexploited bauxite, asbestos, and coal reserves. Much tourist potential.

WEAKNESSES

Agriculture vulnerable to drought and price fluctuations. Only 14% of GDP derived from industry. Small domestic market, few skilled workers. Strain of housing Mozambican refugees.

EXPORTS

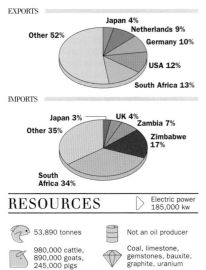

Japan 4%
Netherlands 9%
Other 52%
Germany 10%
USA 12%
South Africa 13%

IMPORTS

Japan 3%
UK 4%
Zambia 7%
Other 35%
Zimbabwe 17%
South Africa 34%

RESOURCES

▷ Electric power 185,000 kw

🐟 53,890 tonnes

🛢 Not an oil producer

🐄 980,000 cattle, 890,000 goats, 245,000 pigs

💎 Coal, limestone, gemstones, bauxite, graphite, uranium

One 215mw hydropower plant on Shire River accounts for nearly 85% of generating capacity, but only 5% of total energy use. Most rely on fuelwood for energy needs. Malawi now encourages privatization, crop diversification, improved irrigation and regional economic integration via the SADC to exploit its naturally limited resources. A deep-seam coal mine currently operates at Rumphi.

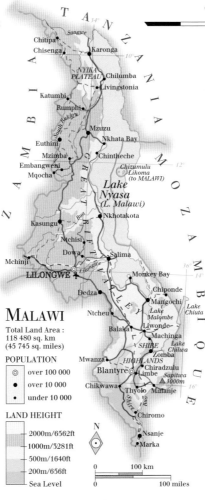

MALAWI

Total Land Area : 118 480 sq. km (45 745 sq. miles)

POPULATION

◎ over 100 000
● over 10 000
• under 10 000

LAND HEIGHT

2000m/6562ft
1000m/3281ft
500m/1640ft
200m/656ft
Sea Level

0 — 100 km
0 — 100 miles

ENVIRONMENT

▷ No Green MPs

🔺 11%

⬇ Low

Drought, devastating agriculture in 1992, eclipses all other problems. Ecological husbandry now attracts tourism.

MEDIA

▷ TV ownership low

📧 Daily newspaper circulation 3 per 1,000 people

PUBLISHING AND BROADCAST MEDIA

There are 5 daily newspapers, including the *Daily Times*

1 state-owned service

1 state-owned service

The first TV company was launched in 1995. In 1998 President Muluzi accused newspapers of "spreading despondency."

CRIME

▷ Death penalty not used

Malawi does not publish prison figures

⬆ Up 10% in 1990

Urban crime is on the increase. The proliferation of weapons, particularly guns, is contributing to an increase in armed robbery.

CHRONOLOGY

After strong Scottish missionary activity, Malawi came under British rule as Nyasaland in 1891.

- ❏ **1964** Independence under Hastings Banda.
- ❏ **1966** One-party state.
- ❏ **1992** Antigovernment riots. Illegal prodemocracy groups unite.
- ❏ **1993** Referendum for multipartyism.
- ❏ **1994** Banda and MCP defeated in multiparty elections.
- ❏ **1999** President Muluzi reelected.

EDUCATION

▷ School leaving age: 14

58%

5,561 students

Primary-level education is widespread, with 73% of boys and 60% of girls attending school regularly.

HEALTH

▷ Welfare state health benefits

1 per 50,000 people

Infectious, parasitic and respiratory diseases

Access to health services is difficult and preventive care is viewed as a priority. Most doctors train abroad.

SPENDING

▷ GDP/cap. increase

CONSUMPTION AND SPENDING

🚗 3 per 1,000 population

📞 4 per 1,000 population

Defense 1.1%
Education 5.7%
Health 0.2%

0   5   10   15   20   25
Defense, Health, Education spending as % of GDP

The ousted MCP elite grew wealthy, allegedly through embezzlement. However, 80% of Malawians remain mired in poverty, surviving on less than $1 a day.

WORLD RANKING

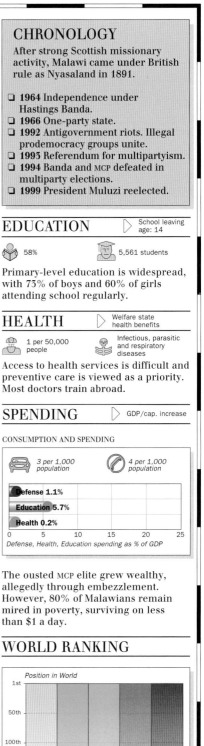

Position in World

1st
50th
100th
150th
192nd

181 — $210
191 — 39 yrs
157 — 58%
188 — 135 dths
159

- GNP per capita in US$
- Infant mortality per 1,000 live births
- Life expectancy
- Literacy
- Human dev. index

MALAYSIA

OFFICIAL NAME: Federation of Malaysia **CAPITAL:** Kuala Lumpur
POPULATION: 21.5 million **CURRENCY:** Ringgit **OFFICIAL LANGUAGES:** English and Malay

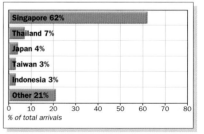

SOUTHEAST ASIA

Asia

| 1963 | 1965 | Aug 31 | MAL | +8 | +60 | .my |

COMPRISING THE THREE separate territories of Malaya, Sarawak and Sabah, Malaysia stretches over 2,000 km (1,240 miles) from Peninsular Malaysia to the northeastern end of the island of Borneo. It shares borders with Thailand, Indonesia, Singapore, and Brunei. A central mountain chain divides Malaya, separating fertile western plains from a narrow eastern coastal belt. Sarawak and Sabah are characterized by swampy coastal plains rising to mountains on the border with Indonesia. Putrajaya just south of Kuala Lumpur is a high-tech new development intended as the future capital.

CLIMATE ▷ Tropical equatorial

WEATHER CHART

The whole of Malaysia has an equatorial climate. The country has rainfall throughout the year; it falls on between 150 and 200 days almost everywhere. However, there are two distinct rainy seasons, when the heaviest rain falls – from March to May and from September to November. Coastal areas are also subject to the alternating southwest and northeast monsoon winds.

Tea plantation in the Cameron Highlands, in central-western Malaya. This region also contains one of Asia's most popular mountain resorts.

TRANSPORTATION ▷ Drive on left

Subang Intl, Kuala Lumpur 15m passengers

755 ships 4.2bn grt

THE TRANSPORTATION NETWORK

64,200 km (39,900 miles)	580 km (360 miles)
1,614 km (1,003 miles)	3,209 km (1,994 miles)

A major north–south highway is being built and in Kuala Lumpur a new mass transit system is being constructed to extend to its outer suburbs. Malaysia's "national car," the Proton, has been a success; since 1985, national car ownership has tripled. Several ports are being updated to reduce Malaysia's current dependence on Singapore.

TOURISM ▷ Visitors : population 1:3.5

6.2m visitors

Down 17% 1995–1997

MAIN TOURIST ARRIVALS

Singapore 62%	
Thailand 7%	
Japan 4%	
Taiwan 3%	
Indonesia 3%	
Other 21%	

% of total arrivals

Malaysia is southeast Asia's major tourist destination, with over six million visitors a year. Most tourists come for the excellent tropical beaches on the east coast, to hike in the Cameron Highlands or to trek in the world's oldest rain forests in Borneo. There has recently been an increase in the international business convention trade.

By 1990, when the government ran the Visit Malaysia Year campaign, tourism had become Malaysia's third-biggest foreign exchange earner. There is still untapped potential for growth. Over half of visitors to Malaysia are short-stay trippers from Singapore, and tourists' spending per day is less than that in Thailand. A second Visit Malaysia Year was launched in 1994, and a third coincided with the holding of the Commonwealth Games in Malaysia in 1998. Hotel capacity has been currently growing at 10% a year and 70 new beach resorts are planned.

MALAYSIA

Total Land Area : 328 550 sq. km (126 853 sq. miles)

POPULATION		LAND HEIGHT	
⊙	over 500 000		2000m/6562ft
◎	over 100 000		1000m/3281ft
○	over 50 000		500m/1640ft
●	over 10 000		200m/656ft
·	under 10 000		Sea Level

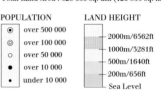

M

PEOGLE

▷ Pop. density medium

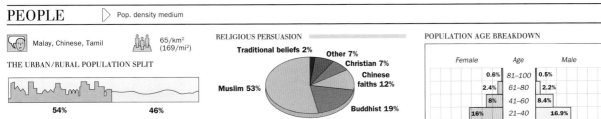

Malay, Chinese, Tamil

65/km²
(169/mi²)

THE URBAN/RURAL POPULATION SPLIT

54%   46%

RELIGIOUS PERSUASION

Traditional beliefs 2%   Other 7%
Muslim 53%   Christian 7%
Chinese faiths 12%
Buddhist 19%

POPULATION AGE BREAKDOWN

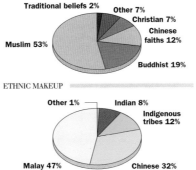

Female		Age	Male	
	0.6%	81–100	0.5%	
	2.4%	61–80	2.2%	
	8%	41–60	8.4%	
16%		21–40		16.9%
21.8%		0–20		23.1%

% of population by age group

ETHNIC MAKEUP

Other 1%   Indian 8%
Indigenous tribes 12%
Malay 47%   Chinese 32%

The key distinction in Malaysian society is between the indigenous Malays, termed the "Bumiputras" (literally, sons of the soil), and the Chinese. The Malays form the largest group, accounting for 47% of the population. However, the smaller Chinese population (32%) has traditionally controlled most business activity. The New Economic Policy (NEP), introduced in the 1970s, was designed to address this imbalance by offering positive opportunities to the Malays through the education system and by making jobs available to them in both the state and private sectors. There are estimated to be more than one million Indonesian and Filipino immigrants in Malaysia, attracted by the country's labor shortages and a dearth of employment in their own countries. In addition, more than 200,000 Vietnamese refugees were offered asylum in Malaysia in the last decade; most have now been resettled, but around 6,000 remain in the country. In an attempt to promote Islamic tradition, Muslim Malay women have been encouraged to wear veils.

POLITICS

▷ Multiparty elections

L. House 1995/2000
U. House 1998/2001

Sultan Salehuddin Abdul Aziz

AT THE LAST ELECTION

House of Representatives 192 seats

5% DAP   4% PAS
84% BN   4% PBS   3% S'46

BN = National Front DAP = Democratic Action Party
PBS = United Sabah Party PAS = Pan-Malaysian Islamic
Party S'46 = Spirit of '46

Senate 69 seats

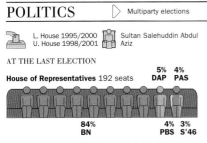

The Senate comprises 26 members indirectly elected by the State Legislative Assemblies, and 43 appointed by the Head of State.

Supreme power rests in theory with the monarch, who acts on the advice of parliament. Opposition parties, while legal, are under tight control.

MAIN POLITICAL ISSUE
Malay superiority

While the current administration of Mahathir Mohamad has declared that it no longer wishes to discriminate positively in favor of Malays, the Chinese community is feeling increasingly isolated. It has accused the government of corruption and uncompetitive practices, declaring that Malays are still favored in the placing of government contracts. In 1993, investment in the domestic economy by indigenous Chinese fell by an estimated 30%. The pro-Malay policy is also expressed in a more restrictive Islamic society, which further alienates the Chinese community.

PROFILE

Malaysia has been dominated by the United Malays National Organization UMNO, part of the ruling BN coalition, since independence in 1947. It controls a huge network of patronage. The already feeble political opposition was weakened further in 1996 with the dissolution of the opposition party, Semangat '46, following its official merger with UMNO.

However, the economic crisis of 1997 and recent expressions of dissent within the ruling coalition have shaken Mahathir's political authority. In September 1998 Anwar Ibrahim, deputy prime minister and once Mahathir's chosen successor, was dismissed after challenging the government's economic policy and calling for political reform. His conviction in April 1999 for corruption and six-year prison sentence sparked riots and led to the formation of the National Justice Party headed by Anwar's wife, Wan Azizah.

WORLD AFFAIRS

▷ Joined UN in 1957

APEC   ASEAN   Comm   G15   OIC

Mahathir sees himself as one of the developing world's leading voices. He maintains a strongly anti-US line in his public speeches and has chastized the West for failing to control currency traders whom he blames for the recent Asian economic crisis. Mahathir's pro-Malay policies cause tensions with Singapore, exacerbated by the latter's dependence on Malaysia for water.

AID

▷ Recipient

$-241m (receipts)

Loan repayments exceeded aid received in 1997

Most Western aid was until recently used for large infrastructure projects. Malaysia also disbursed aid, to Bosnia and Vietnam. However, the southeast Asian economic crisis in 1997–1998 forced Malaysia to seek assistance to support an economic recovery program.

Anwar Ibrahim, *in 1998 controversially dismissed by Mahathir.*

Mahathir Mohamad, *prime minister since 1981.*

M

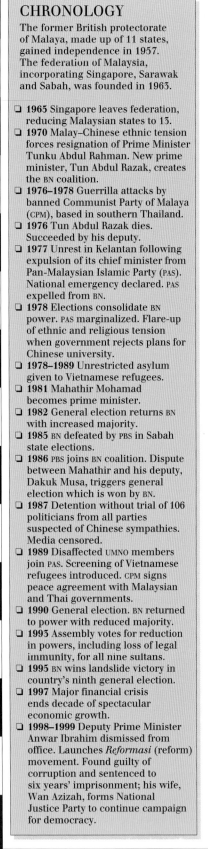

CHRONOLOGY

The former British protectorate of Malaya, made up of 11 states, gained independence in 1957. The federation of Malaysia, incorporating Singapore, Sarawak and Sabah, was founded in 1963.

❏ **1965** Singapore leaves federation, reducing Malaysian states to 13.

❏ **1970** Malay–Chinese ethnic tension forces resignation of Prime Minister Tunku Abdul Rahman. New prime minister, Tun Abdul Razak, creates the BN coalition.

❏ **1976–1978** Guerrilla attacks by banned Communist Party of Malaya (CPM), based in southern Thailand.

❏ **1976** Tun Abdul Razak dies. Succeeded by his deputy.

❏ **1977** Unrest in Kelantan following expulsion of its chief minister from Pan-Malaysian Islamic Party (PAS). National emergency declared. PAS expelled from BN.

❏ **1978** Elections consolidate BN power. PAS marginalized. Flare-up of ethnic and religious tension when government rejects plans for Chinese university.

❏ **1978–1989** Unrestricted asylum given to Vietnamese refugees.

❏ **1981** Mahathir Mohamad becomes prime minister.

❏ **1982** General election returns BN with increased majority.

❏ **1985** BN defeated by PBS in Sabah state elections.

❏ **1986** PBS joins BN coalition. Dispute between Mahathir and his deputy, Dakuk Musa, triggers general election which is won by BN.

❏ **1987** Detention without trial of 106 politicians from all parties suspected of Chinese sympathies. Media censored.

❏ **1989** Disaffected UMNO members join PAS. Screening of Vietnamese refugees introduced. CPM signs peace agreement with Malaysian and Thai governments.

❏ **1990** General election. BN returned to power with reduced majority.

❏ **1993** Assembly votes for reduction in powers, including loss of legal immunity, for all nine sultans.

❏ **1995** BN wins landslide victory in country's ninth general election.

❏ **1997** Major financial crisis ends decade of spectacular economic growth.

❏ **1998–1999** Deputy Prime Minister Anwar Ibrahim dismissed from office. Launches *Reformasi* (reform) movement. Found guilty of corruption and sentenced to six years' imprisonment; his wife, Wan Azizah, forms National Justice Party to continue campaign for democracy.

M

DEFENSE

 No compulsory military service

$3.4bn ⬇ Down 9% in 1997

The military is entirely composed of Malays. Although defense spending currently accounts for less than 4% of

MALAYSIAN ARMED FORCES

26 light tanks (*Scorpion*)	85,000 personnel	
6 frigates and 39 patrol boats	12,500 personnel	
89 combat aircraft (8 HAWK 108, 17 HAWK 208, 11 MB-339, 8 F/A-18D)	12,500 personnel	
None		

GDP, there are plans to raise it to 6%, in line with neighboring Singapore. Malaysia is an important market for Western arms suppliers. However, in 1994 Malaysia signed an agreement to buy Russian MiG-29 fighter aircraft. The deal meant that Malaysia became the first noncommunist state in southeast Asia to operate Russian military equipment. The main defense concerns are Singapore, with its large and highly mechanized army, and more recently, though to a lesser extent, Indonesia. Also important is growing Chinese influence in the South China Sea. Patrolling east and west Malaysia is a key function of the navy, which is large by regional standards.

ECONOMICS

 Inflation 3.2% p.a. (1985–1996)

 $98.2bn   3.89–3.80 ringgits

SCORE CARD

❏ WORLD GNP RANKING	36th
❏ GNP PER CAPITA	$4,530
❏ BALANCE OF PAYMENTS	$–4.8bn
❏ INFLATION	2.7%
❏ UNEMPLOYMENT	3%

EXPORTS

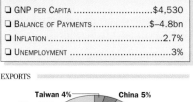

Taiwan 4%
Other 39%
China 5%
Japan 13%
USA 19%
Singapore 20%

IMPORTS

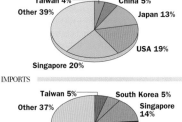

Taiwan 5%
Other 37%
South Korea 5%
Singapore 14%
USA 17%
Japan 22%

STRENGTHS

Electronics: the world's biggest producer of disk drives. Proton car a national and international success. Heavy industries such as steel. Latex and rubber industries.

MALAYSIA : MAJOR BUSINESSES

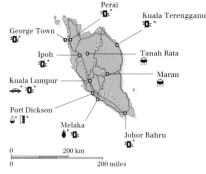

Perai
Kuala Terengganu
George Town
Ipoh
Tanah Rata
Kuala Lumpur
Maran
Port Dickson
Melaka
Johor Bahru

0   200 km
0   200 miles

ECONOMIC PERFORMANCE INDICATOR

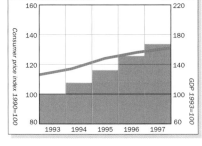

— Consumer price index   GDP

WEAKNESSES

High level of debt. Vulnerability to international capital movements. Shortage of skilled labor. Competition from new NICs.

PROFILE

Growth in the economy took off in 1987, largely state-directed and underpinned by a push for foreign investment and a drive to privatize state assets. For almost a decade, it expanded at an average yearly rate of 8%. However, the severity of the financial crisis of 1997 forced Malaysia to adopt economic austerity measures, readjust to the prospect of much lower growth rates, and to revise its plan for full industrialization, known as "Vision 2020."

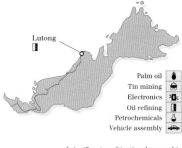

Lutong

Palm oil
Tin mining
Electronics
Oil refining
Petrochemicals
Vehicle assembly

* significant multinational ownership

RESURCES

▷ Electric power 10.6m kw

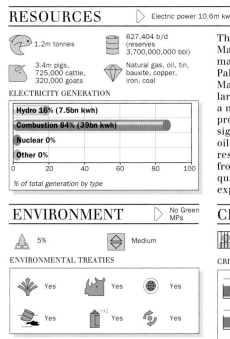

1.2m tonnes

627,404 b/d (reserves 3,700,000,000 bbl)

3.4m pigs, 725,000 cattle, 320,000 goats

Natural gas, oil, tin, bauxite, copper, iron, coal

ELECTRICITY GENERATION

Hydro 16% (7.5bn kwh)	
Combustion 84% (39bn kwh)	
Nuclear 0%	
Other 0%	

0   20   40   60   80   100

% of total generation by type

Thailand has overtaken Malaysia as the world's major rubber producer. Palm oil, of which Malaysia is the world's largest producer, is now a more important export product. Malaysia is a significant exporter of oil and natural gas. Oil reserves are offshore from Sabah and Sarawak. The good quality of the oil means that most is exported, while crude imports are

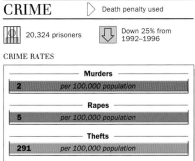

PENINSULAR MALAYSIA

MALAYSIA : LAND USE

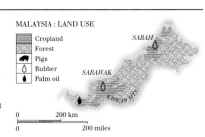

Cropland	
Forest	
Pigs	
Rubber	
Palm oil	

SABAH

SARAWAK

KAPUAS MTS

0   200 km
0   200 miles

refined. Malaysia accounts for nearly half of world timber exports, most of which come from Sarawak.

ENVIRONMENT

▷ No Green MPs

5%

Medium

ENVIRONMENTAL TREATIES

Yes	Yes	Yes
Yes	Yes	Yes

Logging is the overwhelming concern of groups such as Sahabat Alam Malaysia (Friends of the Earth, Malaysia). Unprocessed log exports from Sarawak have risen dramatically. World Bank estimates suggest that trees are being cut down at four times the sustainable rate. Indigenous forest communities are being destroyed and some species of wood such as Ramin are near extinction. In 1992, the state of Sarawak began to take action to diversify the economy; however, the profits from logging are hard to resist.

In September 1997, smog caused by burning forests and scrub in Indonesia created a pollution and health alert across the whole region.

CRIME

▷ Death penalty used

20,324 prisoners

Down 25% from 1992–1996

CRIME RATES

Murders	
2	per 100,000 population

Rapes	
5	per 100,000 population

Thefts	
291	per 100,000 population

The judiciary and the UMNO maintain close links. The death sentence for possession of narcotics is mandatory. Kelantan state has attempted to implement the Islamic penal code, including stoning for adulterers and amputation for thieves.

EDUCATION

▷ School leaving age: 16

86%

191,290 students

The involvement of students in politics is firmly discouraged.

THE EDUCATION SYSTEM

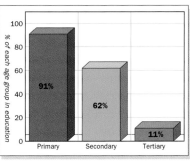

% of each age group in education

100
80
60
40
20
0

91% — Primary
62% — Secondary
11% — Tertiary

Malays are favored above other communities at tertiary level by a quota system which gives them preference for places. The Chinese community has its own schools, although plans for a private Chinese university were vetoed by the government. Many students, particularly the Chinese, complete their studies in the UK or the USA.

HEALTH

▷ Welfare state health benefits

1 per 2,076 people

Heart diseases, cancers

There is growing disparity between modern medical care available in cities and the traditional medicine practiced in rural and outlying areas. Herbal cures and homeopathy are particularly favored by the Chinese community.

SPENDING

▷ GDP/cap. no increase

CONSUMPTION AND SPENDING

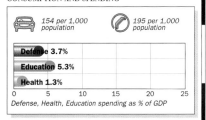

154 per 1,000 population

195 per 1,000 population

Defense 3.7%	
Education 5.3%	
Health 1.3%	

0   5   10   15   20   25

Defense, Health, Education spending as % of GDP

The Chinese remain the wealthiest community in Malaysia. However, following riots in 1970, the UMNO government embarked on a deliberate program of achieving 30% Malay ownership of the corporate sector. Many Malay people earned quick profits from preferential privatization share allocations in the early 1990s.

WORLD RANKING

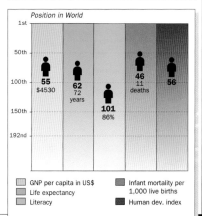

Position in World

1st
50th
100th
150th
192nd

55 $4530	62 72 years	101 86%	46 11 deaths	56

☐ GNP per capita in US$		☐ Infant mortality per 1,000 live births
☐ Life expectancy		
☐ Literacy		☐ Human dev. index

MEDIA

▷ TV ownership medium

⊠ Daily newspaper circulation 163 per 1,000 people

PUBLISHING AND BROADCAST MEDIA

	There are 42 daily newspapers. The most influential are the *New Straits Times*, *Utusan Malaysia* and *Xingzhou*
	3 state-controlled services broadcasting to Peninsular Malaysia, Sarawak and Sabah, 2 independent services
	3 state-controlled services broadcasting to Peninsular Malaysia, Sarawak and Sabah, 1 independent service

Almost all newspapers in Malaysia are controlled by UMNO, the dominant political party. The party owns the *Straits* group, which includes the most influential press. Radio and TV are also strictly controlled, under the 1987 Broadcasting Act, and Western commercials are banned. Singaporean TV can be received in the south.

M

MALDIVES

OFFICIAL NAME: Republic of Maldives **CAPITAL:** Male'
POPULATION: 282,000 **CURRENCY:** Rufiyaa **OFFICIAL LANGUAGE:** Dhivehi

INDIAN OCEAN
MALDIVES / India / Asia / Sri Lanka

| 1965 | 1965 | Jan 7 | MV | +5 | +960 | .mv |

THE MALDIVES IS AN archipelago of 1,190 small coral islands set in the Indian Ocean southwest of Sri Lanka. The islands, none of which rise above 1.8 m (6 feet), are protected by encircling reefs or *faros*. Only 200 are inhabited. Tourism has grown in recent years, though vacation islands are separate from settled islands. In 1998, President Maumoon Abdul Gayoom, who has survived three coup attempts, was elected for a fifth term in office.

CLIMATE

▷ Tropical oceanic

WEATHER CHART

- Average daily temperature
- Rainfall

The Maldives has a tropical climate, with abundant rainfall and high temperatures throughout the year. The northern islands are occasionally affected by violent storms caused by tropical cyclones. Most rain falls in the southern islands, from November to March.

TRANSPORTATION

▷ Drive on left

Male' Intl, Hulule Island
1.5m passengers

10 ships
96,000 grt

THE TRANSPORTATION NETWORK

| 10 km (6 miles) | None |
| None | None |

It is possible to walk across Male' island in 20 minutes. Inter-island travel is mostly by ferry and traditional *dhoni*.

TOURISM

▷ Visitors : population 1.3:1

366,000 visitors

Up 13% 1995–1997

MAIN TOURIST ARRIVALS

- Germany 24%
- Italy 16%
- UK 9%
- Other 51%

% of total arrivals

Tourism is the largest source of foreign exchange, accounting for about 18% of GDP. The first resort was opened in 1972, and hotels financed by local and foreign capital have since been built on uninhabited islands. Some 350,000 tourists visited the Maldives in 1997.

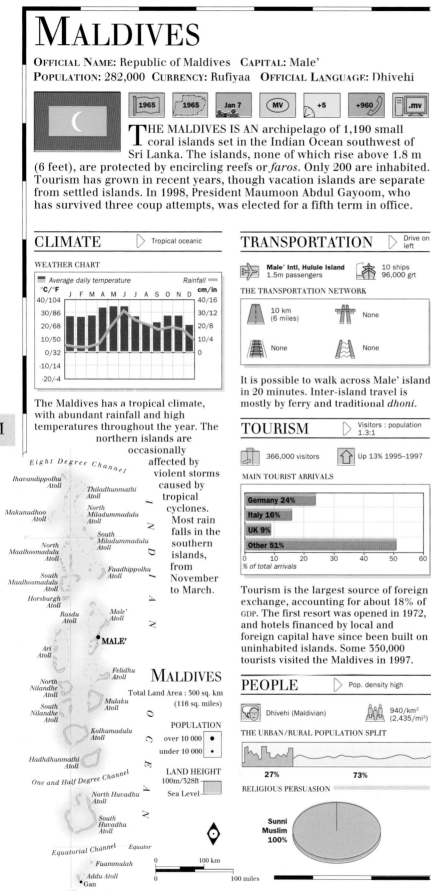

Eight Degree Channel

Ihavandippolhu Atoll
Thiladhunmathi Atoll
Makunudhoo Atoll
North Miladummadulu Atoll
South Miladummadulu Atoll
North Maalhosmadulu Atoll
Faadhippolhu Atoll
South Maalhosmadulu Atoll
Horsburgh Atoll
Rasdu Atoll
Male' Atoll
Ari Atoll
• MALE'
Felidhu Atoll
North Nilandhe Atoll
South Nilandhe Atoll
Mulaku Atoll
Kolhumadulu Atoll
Hadhdhunmathi Atoll

One and Half Degree Channel

North Huvadhu Atoll
South Huvadhu Atoll

Equatorial Channel Equator

Fuammulah
Addu Atoll
• Gan

MALDIVES
Total Land Area : 300 sq. km (116 sq. miles)

POPULATION
over 10 000 ●
under 10 000 ·

LAND HEIGHT
100m/328ft
Sea Level

0 ____ 100 km
0 ____ 100 miles

Traditional Maldivian trading yacht. The 1,190 coral islands are grouped in natural atolls, derived from the Maldivian word 'atolu'.

POLITICS

▷ No multiparty elections

1994/1999

President Maumoon Abdul Gayoom

AT THE LAST ELECTION

Citizens' Assembly 48 seats

There are no political parties. 40 members of the Majlis (Assembly) are elected, and 8 appointed by the President.

Politics in the Maldives is restricted to a small group of influential families. Most were already dominant under the sultanate. Formal parties with ideological objectives are virtually non-existent, politics being organized around family and clan loyalties.

A few figures have dominated politics since independence. Former president Ibrahim Nasir abolished the premiership in 1975 and substantially strengthened the presidency. The main figure now is Maumoon Abdul Gayoom, a wealthy businessman, president since 1978. His brother-in-law, Ilyas Ibrahim, is regarded as his main rival.

Under a new constitution in force since 1998, rival candidates may seek to be parliament's presidential nominee; only one name then goes forward for popular endorsement in a referendum.

PEOPLE

▷ Pop. density high

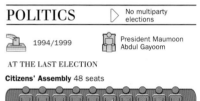

Dhivehi (Maldivian)

940/km² (2,435/mi²)

THE URBAN/RURAL POPULATION SPLIT

27% 73%

RELIGIOUS PERSUASION

Sunni Muslim 100%

It is believed that the islands were inhabited as early as 1500 BCE; Aryan immigrants arrived around 500 BCE. The islands were then discovered by Arab traders. The people, who are all Sunni Muslims, live on only 200 of the 1,190 islands. About 25% of the total population live on the island capital of Male'. It is estimated that 12,000 guest workers from neighboring Sri Lanka and India work in the Maldives. The country's new-found prosperity has seen the emergence of a commercial elite.

M

WORLD AFFAIRS

▷ Joined UN in 1965

The Maldives is a long-standing member of the NAM. The government continues to support it and rejects the criticism that it does not have a role to play in the post-Cold War world. The Maldives' international standing was enhanced in 1990, when it hosted the fifth SAARC summit meeting, held in Male'.

AID

▷ Recipient

$26m (receipts)   Down 21% 1996-1997

Aid has helped to finance the development of port and airport facilities. Japan is the most important bilateral aid donor. In 1991, India, Pakistan, and the USA supplied relief aid to help victims of violent storms which caused damage estimated at $30 million.

DEFENSE

▷ No compulsory military service

Paramilitary police force only   Not applicable

The British military presence ended in 1975, when troops were withdrawn from the staging post on Gan, in the Addu atoll. The Maldives follows a policy of non-alignment, but in 1988 called on India for military assistance to help suppress a coup attempt.

ECONOMICS

▷ Inflation 8.6% p.a. (1985–1996)

$301m   11.77 rufiyaa

SCORE CARD

❑ WORLD GNP RANKING	173rd
❑ GNP PER CAPITA	$1,180
❑ BALANCE OF PAYMENTS	$–16m
❑ INFLATION	7.6%
❑ UNEMPLOYMENT	1%

STRENGTHS

Boom in tourism. Thriving fishing industry, especially tuna. Shipping. Clothing. Coconut production. Economic reforms since 1989 have eased import restrictions and encouraged foreign investment.

WEAKNESSES

Too dependent on fluctuating tourist industry. Growing trade deficit. Skilled labor shortage. Small manufacturing base; cottage industries employ 25% of workforce; little scope for expansion.

EXPORTS

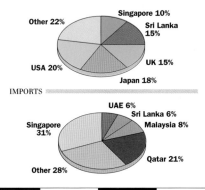

Other 22%
Singapore 10%
Sri Lanka 15%
USA 20%
UK 15%
Japan 18%

IMPORTS

UAE 6%
Sri Lanka 6%
Singapore 31%
Malaysia 8%
Other 28%
Qatar 21%

RESOURCES

▷ Electric power 14,000 kw

105,558 tonnes   Not an oil producer

31,000 cattle, 11,000 sheep, 20,000 goats   None

Natural resources include abundant stocks of fish, particularly tuna. Fishing, still carried out by the traditional pole and line method to help conserve stocks, employs over 20% of the working population. Coconut production is also important. All oil products and virtually all staple foods are imported.

ENVIRONMENT

▷ No Green MPs

None   Not available

Global warming, climate change, and a rise in sea level are believed to threaten to submerge the islands, which have an average height of just 1.5 m (5 feet). A sea wall has been built around the capital island. Other environmental concerns are sewerage, waste disposal, and the mining of coral for building.

MEDIA

▷ TV ownership low

Daily newspaper circulation 18 per 1,000 people

PUBLISHING AND BROADCAST MEDIA

There are 2 daily newspapers, *Haveeru Daily* and *Aafathis*, published in Dhivehi and English

1 state-owned service   1 state-owned service

There is a marked degree of press censorship. In the past, journalists and satirists have been imprisoned. There are only two newspapers.

CRIME

▷ Death penalty not used

The Maldives does not publish prison figures   Up 90% from 1992-1996

The Maldives is a strict Islamic society. Narcotics crimes are heavily punished. Political prisoners are banished to outer islands. The judiciary and the executive are closely linked.

CHRONOLOGY

The Maldives was a British protectorate from 1887 and gained its independence in 1965.

❑ **1932** First written constitution.
❑ **1968** Sultanate abolished; republic declared. Ibrahim Nasir elected as first president.
❑ **1978** Gayoom becomes president.
❑ **1994** Nonparty legislative elections.
❑ **1998** New constitution; Gayoom reelected for fifth five-year term.

EDUCATION

▷ Not available

96%   Not available

Primary education has been improved. Secondary education is less developed in the outer islands; the first school outside Male' was opened in 1992.

HEALTH

▷ Welfare state health benefits

1 per 1,955 people   Infectious and parasitic diseases, tuberculosis

There is a lack of general equipment and facilities. Health care is less developed on the outlying islands.

SPENDING

▷ GDP/cap. increase

CONSUMPTION AND SPENDING

2 per 1,000 population   57 per 1,000 population

Defense	No data
Education	8.4%
Health	5%

0   5   10   15   20   25
Defense, Health, Education spending as % of GDP

Great disparities exist between the people who live in the capital Male', and those who live on the more distant outer islands.

WORLD RANKING

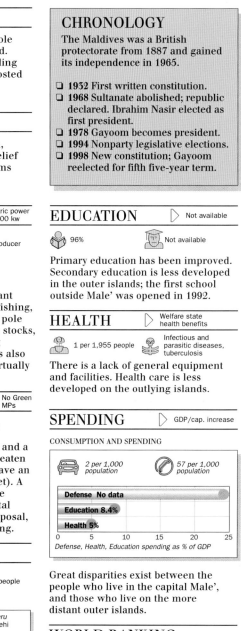

Position in World

109 $1180
122 65 years
65 96%
104 32 deaths
93

❑ GNP per capita in US$
❑ Life expectancy
❑ Literacy
■ Infant mortality per 1,000 live births
■ Human dev. index

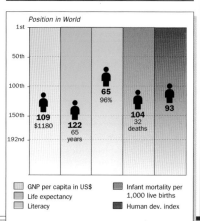

M

MALI

OFFICIAL NAME: Republic of Mali **CAPITAL:** Bamako
POPULATION: 11.8 million **CURRENCY:** CFA franc **OFFICIAL LANGUAGE:** French

| 1960 | 1960 | Sept 22 | RMM | 0 | +223 | .ml |

MALI IS LANDLOCKED in the heart of west Africa. Its mostly flat terrain comprises virtually uninhabited Saharan plains in the north and more fertile savanna land in the south, where most of the population live. The Niger river irrigates the central and southwestern regions. Mali achieved independence in 1960. Multiparty democratic elections under a new constitution, in 1992 and then in 1997, provoked accusations of severe irregularities.

CLIMATE ▷ Hot desert/steppe

WEATHER CHART

Average daily temperature Rainfall
°C/°F   J F M A M J J A S O N D   cm/in
40/104   40/16
30/86   30/12
20/68   20/8
10/50   10/4
0/32   0
-10/14
-20/4

In the south, intensely hot, dry weather precedes the westerly rains. Mali's northern half is almost rainless.

TRANSPORTATION ▷ Drive on right

Bamako-Senou
39,900 passengers

Has no fleet

THE TRANSPORTATION NETWORK

| 15,100 km (9,438 miles) | None |
| 729 km (456 miles) | 1,815 km (1,128 miles) |

Mali is linked by rail with the port of Dakar in Senegal, and by good roads to the port of Abidjan in Ivory Coast.

TOURISM ▷ Visitors : population 1:115

102,000 visitors

Up 137% 1995–1997

MAIN TOURIST ARRIVALS

Mali does not publish tourism figures by country of origin

0   10   20   30   40
% of total arrivals

Tourism is largely safari-oriented, although the historic cities of Djénné, Gao, and Mopti, lying on the banks of the Niger river, also attract visitors. A national domestic airline began operating in 1990.

PEOPLE ▷ Pop. density low

Bambara, Fulani, Senufo, Soninke, French

10/km² (25/mi²)

THE URBAN/RURAL POPULATION SPLIT

27%   73%

RELIGIOUS PERSUASION

Other 1% Christian 1%
Traditional beliefs 18%
Muslim (mainly Sunni) 80%

Mali's most significant ethnic group, the Bambara, is also politically dominant. The Bambara speak the *lingua franca* of the Niger river, which is shared with other groups including the Malinke. Relations between the Bambara–Malinke majority and the Tuareg nomads of the Saharan north are tense and sometimes violent. As elsewhere in Africa, the extended family, often based on the village, is a vital social security system and link between the urban and rural poor. There are a few powerful women in Mali, but, in general, women have little status.

POLITICS ▷ Multiparty elections

1997/2002

President Alpha Oumar Konaré

AT THE LAST ELECTION

National Assembly 147 seats

87% ADEMA   5% PARENA   8% Other

ADEMA = Alliance for Democracy in Mali
PARENA = Party for National Renewal
After the 1997 election, ADEMA held 137 of the 147 seats. There is no information on the remaining 10 seats.

The successful transition to multiparty politics in 1992 followed the overthrow in the previous year of Moussa Traoré, Mali's dictator for 23 years. The army's role was crucial in leading the coup, while Colonel Touré, who acted as interim president, was responsible for a return to civilian rule in less than a year. The change marked Mali's first experience of multipartyism. Maintaining good relations with the Tuaregs, after a peace agreement in 1991, is a key issue. However, the main challenge facing President Alpha Oumar Konaré's government is to alleviate poverty while placating the opposition, which accuses his government of electoral fraud and boycotted the 1997 general election, won by Konaré and his ADEMA party. Konaré's economic austerity measures have met with opposition.

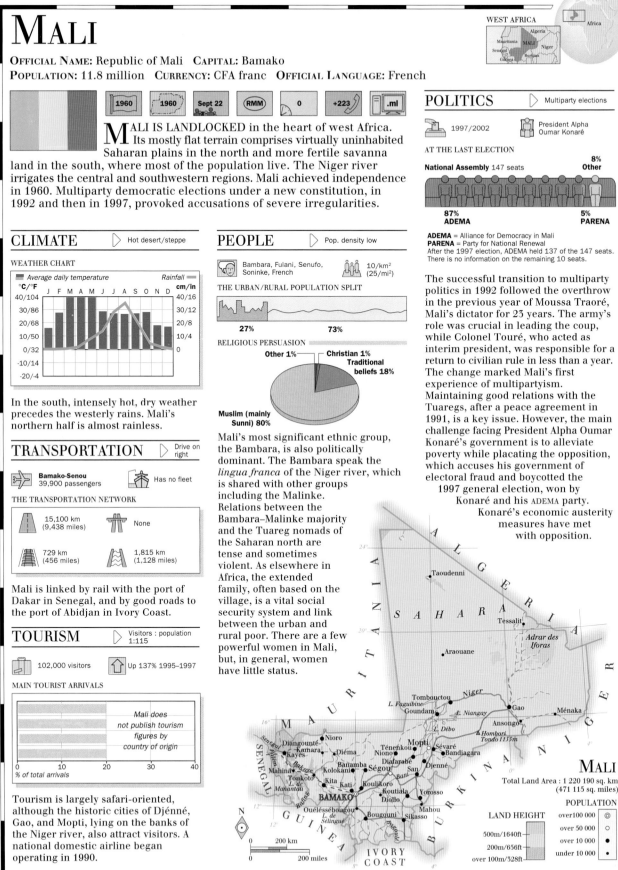

MALI

Total Land Area : 1 220 190 sq. km
(471 115 sq. miles)

LAND HEIGHT

500m/1640ft
200m/656ft
over 100m/328ft

POPULATION

⊚ over 100 000
○ over 50 000
● over 10 000
• under 10 000

WORLD AFFAIRS ▷ Joined UN in 1960

| Ecowas | FZ | OAU | OIC | Franc |

Mali concentrates on maintaining good relations with the Ecowas countries to its south and northern neighbors such as Algeria. Relations with Libya, which is suspected of fomenting Tuareg revolt, are tense. There are good relations with the USA and other Western aid providers.

AID ▷ Recipient

💲 $455m (receipts)   ⬇ Down 10% 1996–1997

Mali is highly dependent on foreign aid, which comes from France, the EU, China, a few Arab states, the USA and international lending institutions.

DEFENSE ▷ Compulsory military service

💲 $43m   ⬆ Up 3% in 1997

Mali's 15,000-strong armed forces have stayed out of politics since the overthrow of President Traoré in 1991.

ECONOMICS ▷ Inflation 4.9% p.a. (1985–1996)

📊 $2.7bn   💲 601.6–558.62 CFA francs

SCORE CARD

❏ WORLD GNP RANKING........................129th
❏ GNP PER CAPITA $260
❏ BALANCE OF PAYMENTS....................$–178m
❏ INFLATION ....-0.4%
❏ UNEMPLOYMENT...Widespread underemployment

STRENGTHS
Producer of high-quality cotton. Irrigation potential from the Niger and Senegal rivers. Rapid expansion of gold production now under way.

WEAKNESSES
Serious poverty and underdevelopment. Landlocked status and vast size of country present considerable communications problems. Drought-prone climate.

EXPORTS

Brazil 5%
China 9%
Taiwan 12%
Thailand 17%
Italy 21%
Other 36%

IMPORTS

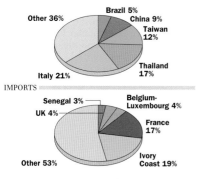

Senegal 3%
Belgium-Luxembourg 4%
UK 4%
France 17%
Ivory Coast 19%
Other 53%

***Village near Bandiagara.** These low, broken hills typical of the east and southeast of Mali are the homeland of the Dogon people.*

RESOURCES ▷ Electric power 87,000 kw

🐟 133,000 tonnes   🛢 Not an oil producer

🐐 8.6m goats, 5.7m cattle, 6m sheep, 650,000 asses   💎 Gold, salt, marble, phosphate, diamonds, tungsten, oil

Gold deposits are now being mined, and prospecting is under way for tungsten, diamonds, and oil. The exploitation of other natural resources is hampered by Mali's poor infrastructure and landlocked situation. Almost all electric power comes from the Selingue dam on the Niger. When the Manantali dam, on the Senegal, comes into operation in 2000, there should be a surplus.

ENVIRONMENT ▷ No Green MPs

🌲 4%   ⬇ Low

The 1983 drought destroyed herds and accelerated desertification and deforestation. The Selingue dam seriously affects the levels of the Niger, even in years of good rainfall.

MEDIA ▷ TV ownership low

📰 Daily newspaper circulation 1 per 1,000 people

PUBLISHING AND BROADCAST MEDIA

There are 3 daily newspapesr, including *L'Essor – La Voix du Peuple*, published by the government

1 state-owned service

1 state-owned, 15 independent services

Even before the coup, previously rigid controls had begun to be relaxed. The militant campaigning by the privately owned press in early 1991 was a significant factor in the overthrow of the Traoré regime.

CRIME ▷ Death penalty used

Mali does not publish prison figures   ⬆ Crime is rising slowly

Crime is not particularly prevalent compared with some other countries in the region, owing to strong family ties and the relative lack of urbanization. In towns, robbery, juvenile delinquency, and smuggling are problems.

CHRONOLOGY

Mali was a major trans-Saharan trading empire. The French colonized the area between 1881 and 1895.

❏ **1960** Independence under anti-French socialist Modibo Keita.
❏ **1968** Coup by Gen. Traoré.
❏ **1990** Prodemocracy demonstrations.
❏ **1991** Traoré arrested.
❏ **1992** Free multiparty elections.
❏ **1997** President Konaré and ADEMA party reelected in disputed polls boycotted by opposition.

EDUCATION ▷ School leaving age: 16

📖 36%   🎓 6,073 students

Education is free and officially compulsory from seven to 16 years of age, but school attendance levels are among the lowest in the world.

HEALTH ▷ No welfare state health benefits

1 per 10,000 people   Malaria, pneumonia, parasitic and diarrheal diseases

Health provision is poor. Infant mortality is 118 per 1,000 live births and average life expectancy 53 years.

SPENDING ▷ GDP/cap. increase

CONSUMPTION AND SPENDING

🚗 3 per 1,000 population   📞 2 per 1,000 population

Defense 1.7%			
Education 2.2%			
Health 1%			
0	5	10	15	20	25

Defense, Health, Education spending as % of GDP

Chronic poverty is widespread. Wealth is limited to a very small elite, although Malians disapprove of flaunted wealth and public ostentation is rare.

WORLD RANKING

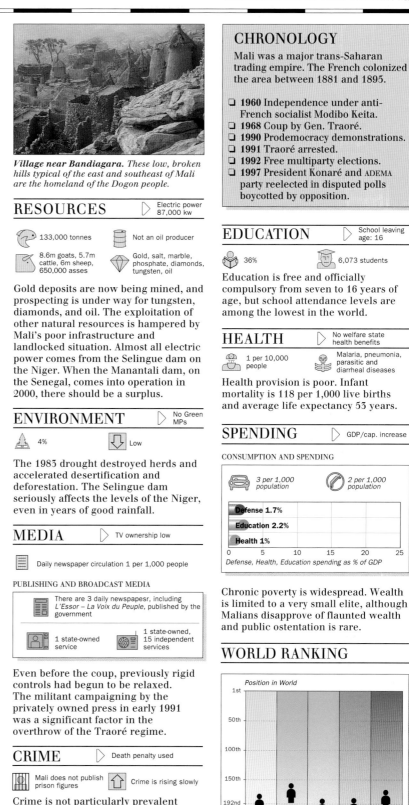

Position in World
1st
50th
100th
150th
192nd

173 $260
155 53 years
181 36%
180 118 dths
166

□ GNP per capita in US$
□ Life expectancy
□ Literacy
■ Infant mortality per 1,000 live births
■ Human dev. index

MALTA

EUROPE

Italy · Greece · MALTA · Tunisia

Europe

OFFICIAL NAME: Republic of Malta **CAPITAL:** Valletta
POPULATION: 374,000 **CURRENCY:** Maltese lira **OFFICIAL LANGUAGES:** English and Maltese

1964 | 1964 | Sept 21 | M | +1 | +356 | .mt

THE MALTESE ARCHIPELAGO is strategically located, lying midway between Europe and north Africa. Controlled throughout its history by successive colonial powers, Malta gained independence from the UK in 1964. The islands are mainly low-lying, with rocky coastlines; only Malta, Gozo, and Kemmuna are inhabited. Tourism is Malta's chief source of income, with an influx of tourists each year of nearly three times the islands' population.

M

CLIMATE ▷ Mediterranean

WEATHER CHART

— Average daily temperature   Rainfall —
°C/°F   cm/in
J F M A M J J A S O N D
40/104 — 40/16
30/86 — 30/12
20/68 — 20/8
10/50 — 10/4
0/32 — 0
-10/14
-20/-4

The climate is very similar to that of Greece, with at least six hours of sunshine a day, even in winter.

TRANSPORTATION ▷ Drive on left

Luqa Intl, Valletta
2.8m passengers

2,966 ships
22.3m grt

THE TRANSPORTATION NETWORK

1,471 km
(914 miles)

None

None

None

Malta Freeport at Marsaxlokk exploits Malta's strategic shipping location in the Mediterranean. In summer, a five-minute helicopter flight from the international airport links the islands of Malta and Gozo. There is a well-developed public transport system, with ferry and hovercraft services and buses on both islands.

Traditionally painted **luzzus** *at St. Julian's harbor. The fish caught are now only for domestic and tourist consumption.*

TOURISM ▷ Visitors : population 2.9:1

1.1m visitors

Down 0.4%
1995–1997

MAIN TOURIST ARRIVALS

UK 45%
Germany 17%
Italy 8%
Other 30%

0 10 20 30 40 50 60
% of total arrivals

Tourism is vital to the economy and accounts for about 25% of the total value of exports of goods and services. In addition to beaches and scenery, the government is promoting the historical attractions of Mdina and Valletta. Development on the quieter island of Gozo is limited to luxury-grade hotels.

PEOPLE ▷ Pop. density high

Maltese, English

1,169/km²
(3,027/mi²)

THE URBAN/RURAL POPULATION SPLIT

89%   11%

RELIGIOUS PERSUASION

Other and non-religious 2%
Roman Catholic 98%

Malta's population has been subject over the centuries to diverse Arabic, Sicilian, Norman, Spanish, English, and Italian influences. Today, many young Maltese go abroad to find work, especially to the USA or Australia; opportunities for them on the islands are few.

The Maltese are staunch Roman Catholics, on a percentage basis more so than virtually any other nation. The remainder are mainly Anglicans, who are included within the diocese of Gibraltar. Divorce is illegal.

POLITICS ▷ Multiparty elections

1998/2003

President Guido de Marco

AT THE LAST ELECTION

House of Representatives 65 seats

54%   46%
NP   MLP

NP = Nationalist Party **MLP** = Malta Labor Party

The Labor leader and prime minister of the 1970s and 1980s, the charismatic Dom Mintoff, championed state control of industry and a strategy of international nonalignment. The Nationalists (NP), coming to power in 1987 under Edward Fenech Adami, retained the nonaligned policy and wrote it into the constitution, but moved away from divisive internal policies. In 1990 they succeeded in sealing a three-way accord between government, unions, and businesses, under which wages are agreed in line with inflation.

While the Nationalists secured reelection in 1992, largely due to a rise in living standards and economic growth, a modernized Labor party returned to power with the narrowest of majorities in 1996. Under Alfred Sant, a leading Maltese writer and Harvard MBA, Labor diluted its traditional links with the unions and "froze" Malta's EU application. However, Fenech Adami's pro-EU NP was unexpectedly returned to power after early elections in 1998.

WORLD AFFAIRS ▷ Joined UN in 1964

CE | Comm | IBRD | NAM | OSCE

Malta applied to join the EU in 1990 and began updating legislation in accordance with EU directives. However, the anti-EU Labour government which came to power in 1996 stalled this process, with the result that Malta was not among the six countries opening membership negotiations with the EU in March 1998. The return of the staunchly pro-EU NP leader Fenech Adami to power in September 1998 has led to a change of policy.

Closer links with Europe are balanced by traditionally strong ties with the Arab world and north Africa. Relations with Libya and the Gaddafi regime – very close under Dom Mintoff in the 1970s – remain good; a co-operation treaty was renewed in 1995. Malta maintains close commercial links with the CIS and China.

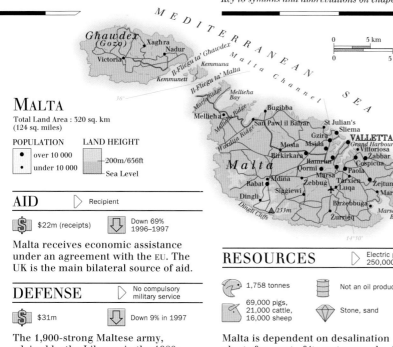

MALTA

Total Land Area : 320 sq. km
(124 sq. miles)

POPULATION LAND HEIGHT
- • over 10 000
- • under 10 000

—200m/656ft
—Sea Level

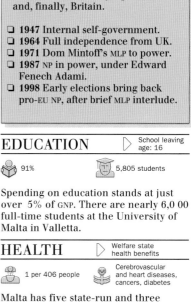

CHRONOLOGY

Malta was dominated in turn by Phoenicians, Carthaginians, Greeks, and Romans, and later ruled by the Arabs, Norman Sicily, Spain, France and, finally, Britain.

- ❏ **1947** Internal self-government.
- ❏ **1964** Full independence from UK.
- ❏ **1971** Dom Mintoff's MLP to power.
- ❏ **1987** NP in power, under Edward Fenech Adami.
- ❏ **1998** Early elections bring back pro-EU NP, after brief MLP interlude.

AID

▷ Recipient

💲 $22m (receipts)   ⬇ Down 69% 1996–1997

Malta receives economic assistance under an agreement with the EU. The UK is the main bilateral source of aid.

DEFENSE

▷ No compulsory military service

💲 $31m   ⬇ Down 9% in 1997

The 1,900-strong Maltese army, advised by the Libyans in the 1980s, now receives training and equipment from Italy, Germany, and the UK.

ECONOMICS

▷ Inflation 2.1% p.a. (1985–1996)

📊 $3.5bn   💲 0.39–0.38 Maltese liri

SCORE CARD

❏ WORLD GNP RANKING	122nd
❏ GNP PER CAPITA	$9,330
❏ BALANCE OF PAYMENTS	$–167m
❏ INFLATION	3.3%
❏ UNEMPLOYMENT	4%

STRENGTHS

Tourism and naval dockyards. Schemes to attract foreign high-tech industry. Malta Freeport container distribution center. Offshore banking. Strategic position between Europe and Africa, on main Mediterranean shipping lines.

WEAKNESSES

Cut-rate competition from Africa and Asia in traditional textile industry. Need to import almost all requirements.

EXPORTS

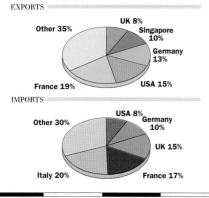

Other 35%   UK 8%   Singapore 10%   Germany 13%   France 19%   USA 15%

IMPORTS

Other 30%   USA 8%   Germany 10%   UK 15%   Italy 20%   France 17%

RESOURCES

▷ Electric power 250,000 kw

🐟 1,758 tonnes   🛢 Not an oil producer

🐖 69,000 pigs, 21,000 cattle, 16,000 sheep   💎 Stone, sand

Malta is dependent on desalination plants for most of its water supply. All oil has to be imported, mostly from Libya. However, there are petroleum reserves, which are under exploration, in Maltese waters.

ENVIRONMENT

▷ No Green MPs

🌲 None   ⬍ Not available

The main environmental concern is linked to the tourist industry. A lack of planning controls in the 1970s was responsible for unsightly beach developments. These are now tightly controlled, particularly on Gozo.

MEDIA

▷ TV ownership low

📰 Daily newspaper circulation 130 per 1,000 people

PUBLISHING AND BROADCAST MEDIA

📄	There are 4 daily newspapers, *In-Nazzjon Taghna*, *L-Orizzont*, *The Times* and *The Malta Independent*
📺	1 state-owned, 1 independent service
📻	1 state-owned, 10 independent services

The Maltese press is largely party politically oriented. Two of the three main press groups are affiliated to the NP or MLP; one is independent.

CRIME

▷ Death penalty not used

🔒 196 prisoners   ⬇ Down 19% from 1992–1996

Crime rates are low compared with those on the European mainland. There has, however, been an increase in narcotics transshipment and associated crimes.

EDUCATION

▷ School leaving age: 16

👤 91%   🎓 5,805 students

Spending on education stands at just over 5% of GNP. There are nearly 6,0 00 full-time students at the University of Malta in Valletta.

HEALTH

▷ Welfare state health benefits

1 per 406 people   Cerebrovascular and heart diseases, cancers, diabetes

Malta has five state-run and three private hospitals. Around 11% of government spending is on health.

SPENDING

▷ GDP/cap. no increase

CONSUMPTION AND SPENDING

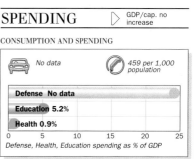

🚗 No data   💿 459 per 1,000 population

Defense No data		
Education 5.2%		
Health 0.9%		

0   5   10   15   20   25
Defense, Health, Education spending as % of GDP

Remittances from Maltese working abroad are an important source of income for many island families.

WORLD RANKING

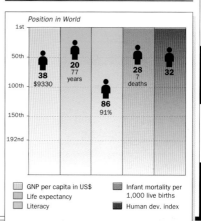

Position in World

38 $9330	**20** 77 years	**86** 91%	**28** 7 deaths	**32**

1st — 50th — 100th — 150th — 192nd

- GNP per capita in US$
- Life expectancy
- Literacy
- Infant mortality per 1,000 live births
- Human dev. index

M

MARSHALL ISLANDS

OFFICIAL NAME: Republic of the Marshall Islands   **CAPITAL:** Delap District
POPULATION: 59,000   **CURRENCY:** US dollar   **OFFICIAL LANGUAGES:** English and Marshallese

| 1986 | 1986 | May 1 | MH | +12 | +692 | .mh |

THE MARSHALL ISLANDS comprise a group of 34 widely scattered atolls in the central Pacific Ocean, formerly under US rule as part of the UN Trust Territory of the Pacific Islands. An agreement which granted internal sovereignty in free association with the US became operational in 1986, and the Trust was formally dissolved in 1990. The economy is almost entirely dependent on US aid and rent for the US missile base on Kwajalein atoll.

Ebeye Island in the Marshalls. *Population pressures have led to the disappearance of most tree and grass cover on the island.*

CLIMATE
▷ Tropical oceanic

WEATHER CHART

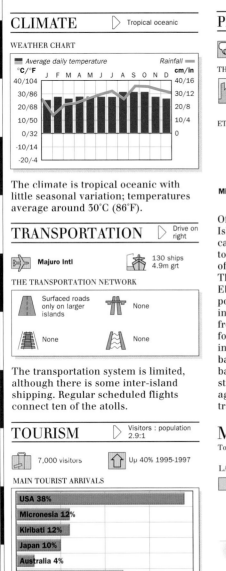

The climate is tropical oceanic with little seasonal variation; temperatures average around 30°C (86°F).

TRANSPORTATION
▷ Drive on right

✈ **Majuro Intl**   130 ships / 4.9m grt

THE TRANSPORTATION NETWORK

| Surfaced roads only on larger islands | None |
| None | None |

The transportation system is limited, although there is some inter-island shipping. Regular scheduled flights connect ten of the atolls.

TOURISM
▷ Visitors : population 2.9:1

🧳 7,000 visitors   ⬆ Up 40% 1995-1997

MAIN TOURIST ARRIVALS

| USA 38% |
| Micronesia 12% |
| Kiribati 12% |
| Japan 10% |
| Australia 4% |
| Other 24% |
| 0   10   20   30   40 |

There are few hotels and tourist amenities – most visitors are American; many are war veterans.

PEOPLE
▷ Pop. density high

Marshallese, English, Japanese, German   327/km² (848/mi²)

THE URBAN/RURAL POPULATION SPLIT

69%   31%

ETHNIC MAKEUP

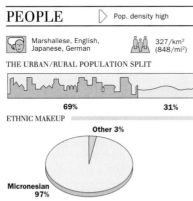

Other 3%
Micronesian 97%

Of the 34 atolls making up the Marshall Islands, 24 are inhabited. Majuro, the capital and commercial center, is home to almost half of the population, many of whom live in its overcrowded slums. The other main center of population is Ebeye, where tensions are high due to poor living conditions. Most of Ebeye's inhabitants were forcibly relocated from Kwajalein in 1947 to make way for a US missile tracking, testing and interception base; many still travel back to Kwajalein daily to work at the base. Life on the outlying islands is still centered around subsistence agriculture and fishing. Society is traditionally matrilineal.

POLITICS
▷ Multiparty elections

1995/1999   President Imata Kabua

AT THE LAST ELECTION

Parliament 33 seats

The 33 members are elected from 25 districts.

Council of Chiefs 12 seats

All 12 members are high chiefs.

Politics is traditionally dominated by chiefs. Amata Kabua, the islands' high chief, was president from the beginning of self-government in 1979 until his death in December 1996. He was succeeded as president in early 1997 by Imata Kabua. There are two main political groupings, the government and the opposition Ralik-Ratak Democratic Party. The main political issue is the islands' continuing inability to achieve financial self-sufficiency; their economy is almost totally dependent on US aid. Discussion has centered recently on a number of projects proposed by foreign states, which could bring in additional revenue. These include a proposal for a plant to generate electricity by burning used tires and a project to use toxic waste to build a causeway on Kwajalein. The likely environmental impact of such projects is an important issue.

MARSHALL ISLANDS

Total Land Area : 181 sq. km (70 sq. miles)

LAND HEIGHT
100m/328ft
Sea Level

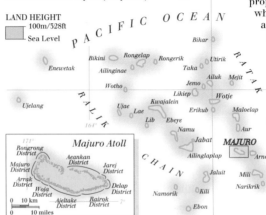

Majuro Atoll

WORLD AFFAIRS

▷ Joined UN in 1991

From 1947, the islands were controlled by the USA as part of the Trust Territory of the Pacific Islands. Under a Compact of Free Association signed in 1982 and operational from 1986, in return for paying $1 billion in aid over 15 years, the USA can use Kwajalein as a missile firing range, and controls foreign and defense policies. Negotiations began in 1999 on the future of the Compact post–2001. Taiwan has become a source of development funding.

AID

▷ Recipient

$63m (receipts) Down 14% 1996–1997

Aid from the USA accounts for around two-thirds of the islands' revenue. Australia and Taiwan also provide some assistance.

DEFENSE

▷ No compulsory military service

USA responsible for defense Not applicable

There is no defense force. All defense is provided by the USA under the Compact of Free Association. The USA does not have offensive weapons sited in the Marshalls, but its navy regularly patrols the region.

ECONOMICS

▷ Not available

$97m 1 dollar

SCORE CARD

❏ World GNP Ranking	185th
❏ GNP per Capita	$1,610
❏ Balance of Payments	$–6m
❏ Inflation	4.8%
❏ Unemployment	16%

STRENGTHS
Aid from the USA, on which the islands are almost totally dependent. Strategic refusal by US to allow them to become impoverished, so that no other foreign power can gain influence. Copra.

WEAKNESSES
Dependence on imports, which are 11 times greater than exports. All fuel has to be imported. Vulnerability to storm damage. Large state sector employing 75% of workers.

EXPORTS/IMPORTS

The Marshall Islands' main trading partners are the USA and Japan.

RESOURCES

▷ Not available

270 tonnes Not an oil producer and has no refineries

Not available Phosphates

There are few known strategic resources. Exploratory tests have revealed some high-grade phosphate deposits, but not in economically viable quantities. Small diesel generators are used for electricity production.

ENVIRONMENT

▷ No Green MPs

None Not available

Between 1946 and 1958, a series of US nuclear military tests rendered Bikini and Enewetak atolls uninhabitable. Enewetak residents were allowed to return in 1980, following some land decontamination, and a 1999 tribunal adopted stringent standards for further decontamination. The USA has now paid out over $101 million to victims of nuclear testing. Nuclear waste imports were banned in 1999. The effects of rising sea levels are a major concern. Erosion affects beaches and soil is being contaminated by brackish water. Desalination plants are used for drinking water.

MEDIA

▷ TV ownership low

 There are no daily newspapers

PUBLISHING AND BROADCAST MEDIA

There are no daily newspapers. The one weekly newspaper, the *Marshall Islands Journal*, is privately owned

2 independent services

1 state-owned, 2 independent services

Radio is the main source of information in the Marshalls. There is also a subscription-only TV service. The US personnel stationed on Kwajalein have their own TV and radio stations.

CRIME

▷ Death penalty not used

The Marshalls do not publish prison figures Little change from year to year

Crime levels are generally low; however, the rate is up on Ebeye. Outlying islands are crime-free.

EDUCATION

▷ School leaving age: 14

91% Not available

Education, compulsory between the ages of six and 14 years, is based on the US model. The number of secondary school graduates exceeds the availability of suitable employment in the Marshall Islands. Many go on to university in the USA.

CHRONOLOGY

After a period under Spanish rule, the Marshall Islands became a German protectorate in 1885; Japan took possession at the start of the First World War. The islands were transferred to US control in 1945.

- ❏ **1946** US nuclear testing begins.
- ❏ **1947** UN Trust Territory of the Pacific established.
- ❏ **1961** Kwajalein becomes US army missile range, the target for ICBMs fired from California.
- ❏ **1979** Constitution approved in referendum. Government set up.
- ❏ **1986** Compact of Free Association with US operational.
- ❏ **1990** Trust terminated by UN security council.
- ❏ **1997** Imata Kabua is elected president after death in office of president Amata Kabua.

HEALTH

▷ No welfare state health benefits

1 per 3,294 people Respiratory, heart and diarrheal diseases

Medical facilities are rudimentary. Complex operations are performed in Hawaii. Levels of malnutrition and Vitamin A deficiency are high.

SPENDING

▷ Not available

CONSUMPTION AND SPENDING

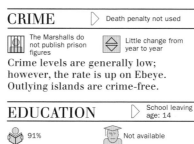

No data No data

No data available

0 5 10 15 20 25
Defense, Health, Education spending as % of GDP

Wealth disparities are small. Very few citizens can afford luxuries such as air conditioning and cars.

WORLD RANKING

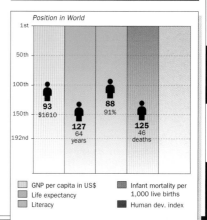

Position in World

1st
50th
100th
150th
192nd

93 $1610

127 64 years

88 91%

125 46 deaths

☐ GNP per capita in US$
☐ Life expectancy
☐ Literacy
☐ Infant mortality per 1,000 live births
■ Human dev. index

M

MAURITANIA

OFFICIAL NAME: Islamic Republic of Mauritania **CAPITAL:** Nouakchott
POPULATION: 2.5 million **CURRENCY:** Ouguiya **OFFICIAL LANGUAGES:** Arabic and French

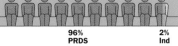

NORTH AFRICA

| 1960 | 1960 | Nov 28 | RIM | 0 | +222 | .mr |

LOCATED IN NORTHWEST AFRICA, Mauritania is a member of both the OAU and the Arab League. Formerly a French colony, the country has taken a strongly Arab direction since 1964; today, it is the Maures who control political life and dominate the minority black population. The Sahara extends across two-thirds of Mauritania's territory; the only productive land is that drained by the Senegal river in the south and southwest.

CLIMATE ▷ Hot desert

WEATHER CHART

■ Average daily temperature	Rainfall ▬
°C/°F J F M A M J J A S O N D	cm/in
40/104	40/16
30/86	30/12
20/68	20/8
10/50	10/4
0/32	0
-10/14	
-20/-4	

The dusty Saharan *harmattan* wind often aggravates the very hot, dry conditions. Some rain falls in the south.

TRANSPORTATION ▷ Drive on right

✈ **Nouakchott**   131 ships / 42,679 grt

THE TRANSPORTATION NETWORK

| 1,710 km (1,063 miles) | None |
| 740 km (460 miles) | River Senegal |

The transportation system is limited and unevenly developed. There are two major roads, but shifting sands mean that they require constant maintenance.

TOURISM ▷ Not available

Not available   Not available

MAIN TOURIST ARRIVALS

Mauritania does not publish tourism figures by country of origin

0 10 20 30 40
% of total arrivals

There are few tourists apart from desert safari enthusiasts. The more mountainous areas are especially dramatic, but access is difficult. Nouakchott has some hotels.

PEOPLE ▷ Pop. density low

Hassaniyah Arabic, Wolof, French   2/km² (6/mi²)

THE URBAN/RURAL POPULATION SPLIT

54%   46%

RELIGIOUS PERSUASION

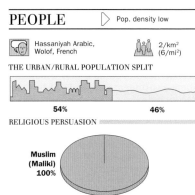

Muslim (Maliki) 100%

The politically dominant Maures make up the majority of the population. The black population is composed of the Havalin, the Senegalese, and the Tukolor, Peulh, and Wolof groups. Ethnic tension centers on the oppression of blacks by Maures. The old black bourgeoisie has now been superseded by a Maurish class; tens of thousands of blacks are estimated to be in slavery. Ethnic tension came to a head in 1989, when 200,000 Maures fled from Senegal. There were attacks on Senegalese in Mauritania and many fled or were deported to refugee camps along the Senegal River. Family solidarity among nomads is particularly strong.

POLITICS ▷ Multiparty elections

L. House 1996/2001   President Moaouia ould
U. House 1998/2000   Sidi Mohammed Taya

AT THE LAST ELECTION

National Assembly 79 seats   1% AC

89% PRDS   10% Ind

PRDS = Democratic and Social Republican Party
Ind = Independents   **AC** = Action for Change

Senate 56 seats   2% AC

96% PRDS   2% Ind

The Senate is indirectly elected.

Mauritania officially adopted multiparty democracy in 1991. However, the 1992 and 1997 presidential elections simply returned to power the incumbent military ruler, Moaouia ould Sidi Mohammed Taya, with around 90% of the vote. Legislative elections have been boycotted by the opposition parties, which accuse the government of fraud. There have been frequent government changes in recent years. The opposition parties are mainly Maure-led, whereas the blacks of the south support exiled parties, such as the Dakar-based liberation group The African Liberation Forces of Mauritania(FLAM).

MAURITANIA

Total Land Area : 1 025 520 sq. km
(395 953 sq. miles)

POPULATION
- ⊙ over 500 000
- ● over 10 000
- · under 10 000

LAND HEIGHT
- 500m/1640ft
- 200m/656ft
- Sea Level

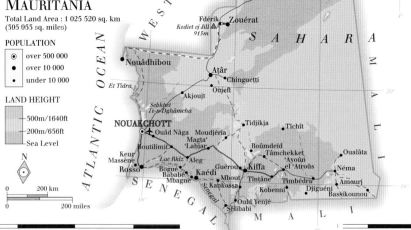

M

WORLD AFFAIRS

Joined UN in 1961

Mauritania has been through periods of tension with all its neighbors, although relations with Senegal have improved since the conflicts of 1989. In seeking to maintain its balance in relations with sub-Saharan Africa and the Arab world it belongs to both Ecowas and the AMU.

AID

Recipient

$250m (receipts) — Down 9% 1996–1997

France, Germany, the IMF, OPEC and Iraq are all donors. Most aid is used for development projects, such as the EU-funded Trans-Mauritanian Highway.

DEFENSE

Compulsory military service

$24m — Down 10% in 1997

The 15,000-strong military is a strain on Mauritania's budget. Troops are used increasingly in public works projects. France is the main arms supplier.

ECONOMICS

Inflation 7% p.a. (1985–1996)

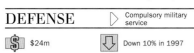

$1.1bn — 166.45–203.75 ouguiyas

SCORE CARD

❏ WORLD GNP RANKING	153rd
❏ GNP PER CAPITA	$440
❏ BALANCE OF PAYMENTS	$22m
❏ INFLATION	4.6%
❏ UNEMPLOYMENT	23%

STRENGTHS

Iron from the Cominor mine at Zouérat. Largest gypsum deposits in the world. Copper, yet to be properly exploited. Offshore fishing among the best in West Africa.

WEAKNESSES

"Debt-distressed," with a debt of nearly $2 billion. Poor land. Drought, locust attacks, fluctuating commodity prices. Very hot, dry desert climate.

EXPORTS

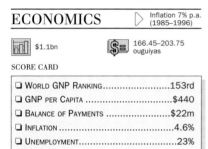

IMPORTS

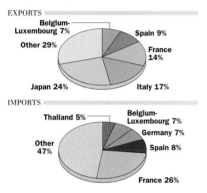

Mauritania's extreme aridity means that only 1% of the land is arable. Two-thirds of the country is part of the Sahara desert; sparse vegetation over the rest supports some livestock.

RESOURCES

Electric power 105,000 kw

90,000 tonnes — Not an oil producer

6.2m sheep, 4.1m goats, 1.3m cattle — Iron, gypsum, copper, gold, phosphates, yttrium

Iron, which in the 1960s brought economic profitability, continues to be exploited, despite low prices on the world market. Mining and fisheries represent 99.7% of exports. Electricity generation expanded by 40% between 1989 and 1996, and further expansion is expected to come from the Manantali dam. Phosphates have been found near the Senegal river.

ENVIRONMENT

No Green MPs

2% (0.2% partially protected) — Low

The chief environmental problem in Mauritania is that of the encroaching Sahara desert, a situation worsened by the droughts of 1973 and 1983, which caused widespread loss of grazing land. The consequent exodus of people away from the land has led to Nouakchott's population increasing from 20,000 in 1960 to almost a million today.

MEDIA

TV ownership medium

Daily newspaper circulation 0.5 per 1,000 people

PUBLISHING AND BROADCAST MEDIA

There are 3 daily newspapers, including *Ach-Chaab*, published by the government

1 state-owned service — 1 state-owned service

The main government papers are *Horizon* (French) and *Ach-Chaab*, in Arabic. Harassment led to the 1998 closure of popular weekly *Mauritanie Nouvelles*.

CRIME

Death penalty used

Mauritania does not publish prison figures — Down 23% from 1992–1996

The main problems are smuggling and robbery. Levels of violence are lower than the west African average.

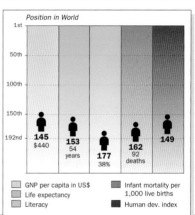

CHRONOLOGY

Once part of the Islamic Almoravid state, Mauritania became a French colony in 1814.

- ❏ **1960** Independence.
- ❏ **1960** One-party state established.
- ❏ **1972** Peace with Polisario in war waged over Western Sahara.
- ❏ **1984** Col. Moaouia ould Taya takes power in bloodless coup.
- ❏ **1992** First multiparty elections.

EDUCATION

School leaving age: 12

38% — 8,496 students

Despite improvements in education, over half of the population is illiterate. Arabic has been compulsory in all schools since 1988.

HEALTH

No welfare state health benefits

1 per 10,000 people — Diarrheal and respiratory diseases, influenza, tuberculosis

Historic regional inequalities persist and the best facilities are in the capital. The overall level of care is on a par with neighboring states.

SPENDING

GDP/cap. no increase

CONSUMPTION AND SPENDING

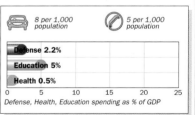

8 per 1,000 population — 5 per 1,000 population

Defense, Health, Education spending as % of GDP

The small ruling Maures elite form the wealthiest sector. Wealthy Maures travel to Mecca to perform the *haj* (Muslim pilgrimage).

WORLD RANKING

Position in World

145 $440	153 54 years	177 38%	162 92 deaths	149

- ☐ GNP per capita in US$
- ☐ Life expectancy
- ☐ Literacy
- ☐ Infant mortality per 1,000 live births
- ☐ Human dev. index

M

MAURITIUS

OFFICIAL NAME: Mauritius **CAPITAL:** Port Louis
POPULATION: 1.2 million **CURRENCY:** Mauritian rupee **OFFICIAL LANGUAGE:** English

| 1968 | 1968 | March 12 | MS | +4 | +230 | .mu |

THE ISLANDS THAT MAKE UP Mauritius lie in the Indian Ocean east of Madagascar. The main island, from which the country takes its name, is of volcanic origin and surrounded by coral reefs. The outer islands, 500 km (311 miles) to the north, are Rodrigues, the Agalega Islands, and the Cargados Carajos Shoals. Mauritius has enjoyed considerable economic success following recent industrial diversification and the expansion of its tourist industry.

CLIMATE ▷ Tropical oceanic

WEATHER CHART

- Average daily temperature
- Rainfall

The climate is subtropical and humid. December to March are the hottest and wettest months. Tropical cyclones are an occasional threat at this time.

TRANSPORTATION ▷ Drive on left

Sir Seewoosagur Ramgoolam Intl
870,000 passengers

50 ships
243,600 grt

THE TRANSPORTATION NETWORK

| 1,703 km (1,058 miles) | 29 km (18 miles) |
| None | None |

Roads are extensive, but often congested. Plans exist for a monorail link between Port Louis and Curepipe.

TOURISM ▷ Visitors : population 1:2.2

536,000 visitors
Up 27% 1995–1997

MAIN TOURIST ARRIVALS

France	27%
Réunion	19%
South Africa	10%
Other	44%

% of total arrivals

Tourism has expanded rapidly in the past decade. Spectacular beaches, water sports, and big game fishing are major attractions. However, many new hotels are usually only half full.

PEOPLE ▷ Pop. density high

French Creole, Hindi, Urdu, Tamil, Chinese, English, French

649/km² (1,680/mi²)

THE URBAN/RURAL POPULATION SPLIT

41%   59%

RELIGIOUS PERSUASION

- Protestant 2%
- Other 3%
- Muslim 17%
- Hindu 52%
- Roman Catholic 26%

The majority of the population descend from indentured Indian laborers brought over in the 19th century. Creoles make up 27% of the population, while 3% are of Chinese origin. The wealthiest group is the small minority of French descent, who control much of business, including the sugar cane industry. Clashes between Hindus, Muslims, and Creoles no longer occur.

POLITICS ▷ Multiparty elections

1995/2000
President Cassam Uteem

AT THE LAST ELECTION

National Assembly 66 seats

88% PTr/MMM
5% OPR
2% H
3% 2% MR PGD

PTr/MMM = Labour Party/Mauritian Militant Movement
OPR = Organization for the People of Rodrigues
MR = Mouvement Rodriguais **H** = Hizbullah
PGD = Gaetan Duval Party

Mauritius became a republic in 1992. Politics are characterized by coalition governments, largely based around personalities. In 1995 a PTR–MMM alliance inflicted a humiliating defeat on prime minister Sir Aneerood Jugnauth who had led the country since 1982. The new prime minister, Navin Ramgoolam, stresses regional integration and economic liberalization to attract much-needed investment.

WORLD AFFAIRS ▷ Joined UN in 1968

| Comm | Comesa | IOC | OAU | SADC |

Mauritius hosted a francophone summit in 1995, and the first OAU human rights conference in 1999. Links with South Africa and India are important. Disputes persist over UK-administered Diego Garcia and French-ruled Tromelin.

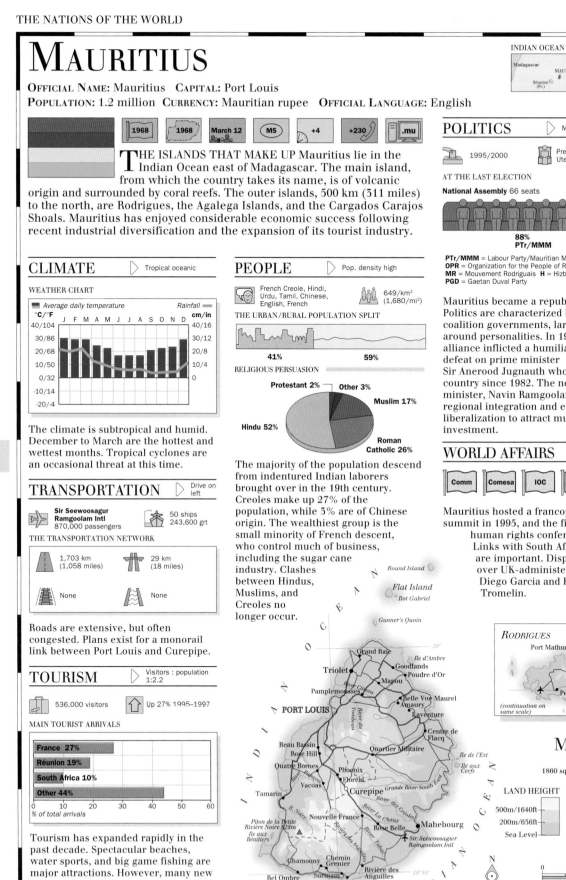

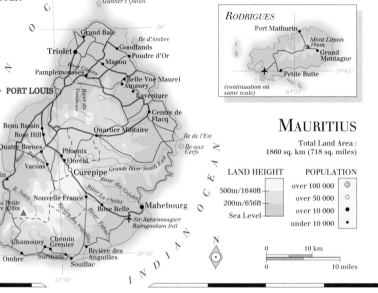

RODRIGUES

Port Mathurin
Mont Limon 396m
Grand Montagne
Petite Butte

(continuation on same scale)

MAURITIUS

Total Land Area : 1860 sq. km (718 sq. miles)

LAND HEIGHT
- 500m/1640ft
- 200m/656ft
- Sea Level

POPULATION
- over 100 000
- over 50 000
- over 10 000
- under 10 000

AID

▷ Recipient

💲 $42m (receipts)   ⬆ Up 110% 1996–1997

Aid is predominantly bilateral, with France and the UK as the main donors. Mauritius also receives aid from Norway, from the EU, under the Lomé Convention, and from other international organizations. The World Bank assisted a five-year conservation program, starting in 1990, and promised $53 million toward transforming Port Louis into a free port.

DEFENSE

▷ No compulsory military service

💲 $87m   ⬇ Down 12% in 1997

Mauritius has no defense forces. There is, however, a special police unit to ensure internal security. Expenditure on policing accounts for 0.5% of total government spending.

ECONOMICS

▷ Inflation 8.4% p.a. (1985–1996)

📊 $4.4bn   💲 22.21–24.73 Mauritian rupees

SCORE CARD

❏ WORLD GNP RANKING	112th
❏ GNP PER CAPITA	$3870
❏ BALANCE OF PAYMENTS	$–115m
❏ INFLATION	6.8%
❏ UNEMPLOYMENT	10%

STRENGTHS
Economic growth averaging 6% a year over last decade. Sugar industry, which accounts for 30% of export earnings. Export Processing Zone (EPZ), especially for clothing manufacture. Tourism – third-largest foreign exchange earner. Highly educated work force, low unemployment. Ongoing development as offshore financial center.

WEAKNESSES
Vulnerability to droughts and fluctuating world sugar price. 75% of food requirements imported. Occasional cyclones mean few crops other than sugar. Remoteness. Lack of strategic resources.

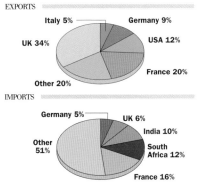

EXPORTS

Italy 5% — Germany 9%
UK 34%
USA 12%
France 20%
Other 20%

IMPORTS

Germany 5% — UK 6%
India 10%
Other 51%
South Africa 12%
France 16%

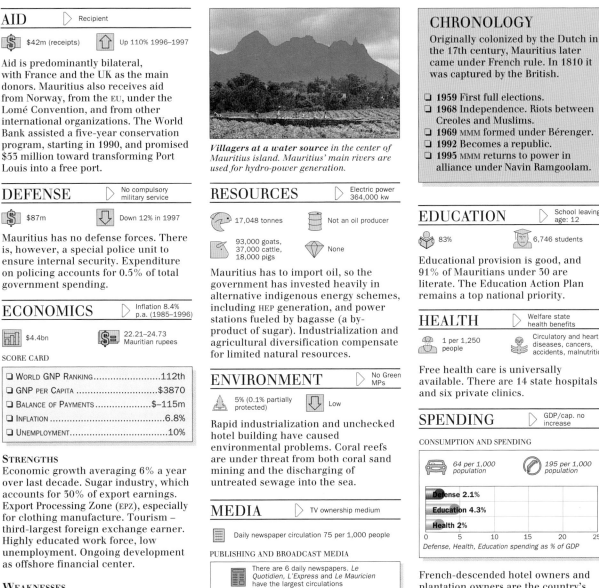

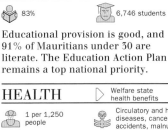

Villagers at a water source in the center of Mauritius island. Mauritius' main rivers are used for hydro-power generation.

RESOURCES

▷ Electric power 364,000 kw

🐟 17,048 tonnes   🛢 Not an oil producer

🐐 93,000 goats, 37,000 cattle, 18,000 pigs   💎 None

Mauritius has to import oil, so the government has invested heavily in alternative indigenous energy schemes, including HEP generation, and power stations fueled by bagasse (a by-product of sugar). Industrialization and agricultural diversification compensate for limited natural resources.

ENVIRONMENT

▷ No Green MPs

⚠ 5% (0.1% partially protected)   ⬇ Low

Rapid industrialization and unchecked hotel building have caused environmental problems. Coral reefs are under threat from both coral sand mining and the discharging of untreated sewage into the sea.

MEDIA

▷ TV ownership medium

📰 Daily newspaper circulation 75 per 1,000 people

PUBLISHING AND BROADCAST MEDIA

📰 There are 6 daily newspapers. *Le Quotidien, L'Express* and *Le Mauricien* have the largest circulations	
👤 1 independent service	📡 1 independent service

Mauritius has an active press, subject to few regulations and with a wide readership. Newspapers are published in English, French, Creole, Hindi, Chinese, and Tamil. However, opposition parties complain that TV and radio broadcasts are consistently biased toward the government.

CRIME

▷ Death penalty not used

🏛 2,145 prisoners   ⬇ Down 25% from 1992–1996

Crime rates on the main island are fairly low. There has been a small increase in thefts and drug smuggling. Outlying islands are virtually crime-free.

CHRONOLOGY

Originally colonized by the Dutch in the 17th century, Mauritius later came under French rule. In 1810 it was captured by the British.

- ❏ **1959** First full elections.
- ❏ **1968** Independence. Riots between Creoles and Muslims.
- ❏ **1969** MMM formed under Bérenger.
- ❏ **1992** Becomes a republic.
- ❏ **1995** MMM returns to power in alliance under Navin Ramgoolam.

EDUCATION

▷ School leaving age: 12

🎓 83%   👨‍🎓 6,746 students

Educational provision is good, and 91% of Mauritians under 30 are literate. The Education Action Plan remains a top national priority.

HEALTH

▷ Welfare state health benefits

👥 1 per 1,250 people   ☠ Circulatory and heart diseases, cancers, accidents, malnutrition

Free health care is universally available. There are 14 state hospitals and six private clinics.

SPENDING

▷ GDP/cap. no increase

CONSUMPTION AND SPENDING

🚗 64 per 1,000 population   ☎ 195 per 1,000 population

Defense 2.1%
Education 4.3%
Health 2%

0   5   10   15   20   25
Defense, Health, Education spending as % of GDP

French-descended hotel owners and plantation owners are the country's wealthiest social group. Government employees are well paid.

WORLD RANKING

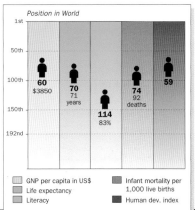

Position in World

1st
50th
100th
150th
192nd

60 $3850
70 71 years
114 83%
74 92 deaths
59

❏ GNP per capita in US$
❏ Life expectancy
❏ Literacy
■ Infant mortality per 1,000 live births
■ Human dev. index

M

MEXICO

OFFICIAL NAME: United States of Mexico **CAPITAL:** Mexico City
POPULATION: 95.8 million **CURRENCY:** Mexican peso **OFFICIAL LANGUAGE:** Spanish

| 1836 | 1848 | Sept 16 | MEX | -6 | +52 | .mx |

INCREASINGLY CONSIDERED a part of North rather than Central America, Mexico straddles the southern end of the continent. Coastal plains along its Pacific and Atlantic seaboards rise into an arid central plateau, which includes the world's biggest conurbation, Mexico City, built on the site of the Aztec capital, Tenochtitlán. Colonized by the Spanish for its silver mines, Mexico achieved independence in 1836. In the "Epic Revolution" of 1910–1920, in which 250,000 died, much of modern Mexico's structure was established. In 1994, Mexico signed the North American Free Trade Agreement (NAFTA).

The cathedral of Santa Prisca at Taxco in Cuernavaca. It was built in Spanish Churriguera style between 1748 and 1758.

CLIMATE
▷ Tropical/mountain/desert

WEATHER CHART

■ Average daily temperature   Rainfall ■
°C/°F   J F M A M J J A S O N D   cm/in
40/104   40/16
30/86   30/12
20/68   20/8
10/50   10/4
0/32   0
-10/14
-20/-4

The plateau and high mountains are warm for much of the year. The Pacific coast has a tropical climate.

TRANSPORTATION
▷ Drive on right

Benito Juárez International, Mexico City
19m passengers

630 ships
1.13m grt

THE TRANSPORTATION NETWORK

| 88,601 km (55,054 miles) | 6,740 km (4,188 miles) |
| 26,445 km (16,432 miles) | 2,900 km (1,802 miles) |

A privately financed $14 billion road network, some 6,000 km (3,730 miles) of toll roads built under the Salinas government, is seriously underused and a commercial failure. The construction of another 6,000 km (3,730 miles) before 2000 has been interrupted. Tolls are being lowered in an effort to attract more traffic. The government has sold off parts of the railroad and intends to privatize airports.

TOURISM
▷ Visitors : population 1:4.9

19.4m visitors   Down 4% 1995-1997

MAIN TOURIST ARRIVALS

USA 93 %
South America 3%
Europe 2%
Canada 1%
Other 1%
0 10 20 30 40 50 60 70 80 90 100
% of total arrivals

Tourism is probably the largest employment sector. Attractions include excellent beach resorts such as Acapulco on the Pacific, and the new resorts of the Peninsula de Yucatán on the Atlantic coast. Aztec and Maya World Heritage archaeological sites are other major draws, as are the many Spanish colonial cities, such as Morelia and Guadalajara, which have remained virtually intact since conquest. The government in 1999 warned that it will not tolerate political activity in Chiapas by foreigners under the guise of tourism. Many have been expelled.

M

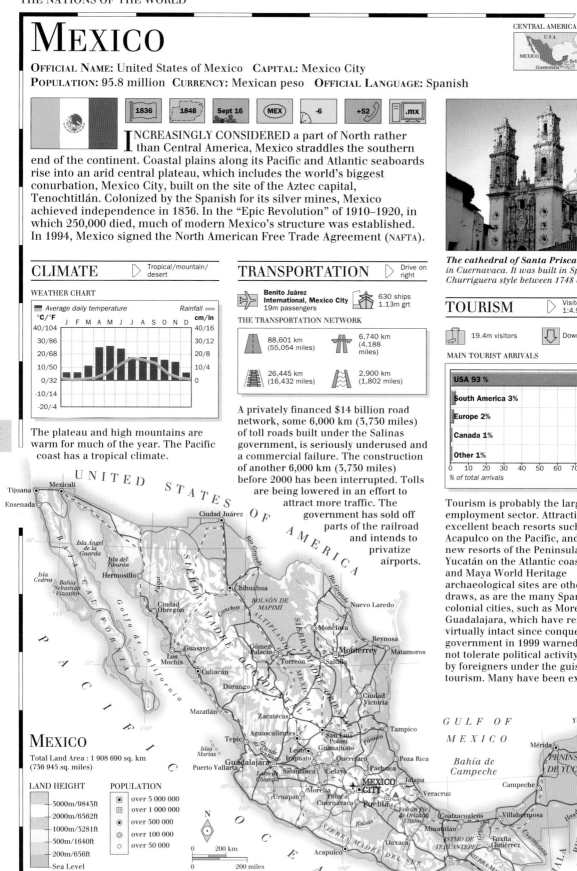

MEXICO

Total Land Area : 1 908 690 sq. km
(736 945 sq. miles)

LAND HEIGHT   POPULATION
3000m/9843ft   ■ over 5 000 000
2000m/6562ft   ▣ over 1 000 000
1000m/3281ft   ◉ over 500 000
500m/1640ft   ◎ over 100 000
200m/656ft   ○ over 50 000
Sea Level

PEOPLE

▷ Pop. density medium

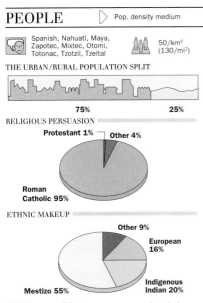

Spanish, Nahuatl, Maya, Zapotec, Mixtec, Otomi, Totonac, Tzotzil, Tzeltal

50/km² (130/mi²)

THE URBAN/RURAL POPULATION SPLIT

75%   25%

RELIGIOUS PERSUASION

Protestant 1%   Other 4%

Roman Catholic 95%

ETHNIC MAKEUP

Other 9%
European 16%
Indigenous Indian 20%
Mestizo 55%

POPULATION AGE BREAKDOWN

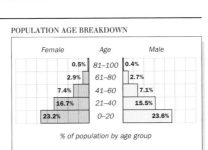

Female	Age	Male
0.5%	81–100	0.4%
2.9%	61–80	2.7%
7.4%	41–60	7.1%
16.7%	21–40	15.5%
23.2%	0–20	23.6%

% of population by age group

While most Mexicans are *mestizo*, it is Mexico's Indian culture which is promoted by the state. This obscures the fact that rural Indians are largely segregated from Hispanic society. This situation dates back to the Spanish colonial period and only recently has it

been seriously challenged. The small black community, which is found concentrated along the eastern coast, is well integrated.

The 1994 Chiapas *Zapatista* (EZLN) guerrilla uprising was on behalf of Indian rights, and in protest against the poverty of landless Indians. In an unofficial EZLN plebiscite in 1999, up to three million Mexicans said that Indians should play an active part in the country's development and that their rights should be recognized in the constitution.

As in much of Latin America, men retain their dominance in business and relatively few women take part in the political process.

POLITICS

▷ Multiparty elections

L. House 1997/2000
U. House 1997/2000

President Ernesto Zedillo Ponce de León

AT THE LAST ELECTION

Federal Chamber of Deputies 500 seats

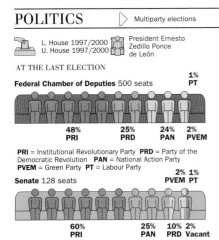

1% PT

48% PRI   25% PRD   24% PAN   2% PVEM

PRI = Institutional Revolutionary Party **PRD** = Party of the Democratic Revolution **PAN** = National Action Party **PVEM** = Green Party **PT** = Labour Party

Senate 128 seats

2% PVEM   1% PT

60% PRI   25% PAN   10% PRD   2% Vacant

Until the 1997 elections, Mexico was a multiparty democracy in name only, the PRI having retained power for decades by tampering with the election process.

MAIN POLITICAL ISSUES
Political stability
The opposition's majority in the lower house of Congress is a boost for multiparty democracy. However, the ruling PRI's reluctance to come to terms with the new balance of power has frequently led to legislative paralysis. The lead-up to the 2000 elections will increase strife within the PRI over the presidential nomination and deepen divisions already visible within the PRD and PAN opposition parties.

Social unrest
The government is criticized for its heavy-handed approach to social unrest in the southern state of Chiapas. EZLN left-wing guerrillas have refused to engage in what they see as a state-controlled peace process and have won international and domestic support for the right of indigenous people to be granted official recognition and fair treatment. Human rights violations are harming the government's credibility.

PROFILE
The PRI dominated Mexico from 1929 onwards, until multiparty agreements to reform the flawed electoral system were eventually concluded after a succession of state elections had demonstrated the strength of both left-wing and conservative opposition. The watershed July 1997 elections effectively ended the PRI's monopoly.

***Ernesto Zedillo Ponce de León,** elected Mexican president in 1994.*

***Sub-commander Marcos,** leader of the Zapatista National Liberation Army.*

WORLD AFFAIRS

▷ Joined UN in 1945

G15   NAFTA   OECD   OAS   RG

The signing of the NAFTA has effectively bound together the economies of Mexico and the USA, and has complicated bilateral relations. Sectors of US business and trade unions are hostile to the agreement, since competitive Mexican imports have undercut some US farmers and manufacturers. Job losses have also occurred in the USA as multinationals have relocated south to benefit from lower Mexican labor rates. Large-scale illegal immigration from Mexico to the USA has led to tougher policing on the border. Another point of friction is the limited success of bilateral law enforcement, which has aided powerful Mexican drug cartels supplying the US market.

Mexico also seeks stronger trade links with MERCOSUR – Brazil, Argentina, Paraguay, and Uruguay – and with the EU. It has recently cooperated with other oil producers to cut world production.

AID

▷ Recipient

$108m (receipts)   Down 63% 1996–1997

Mexico receives modest aid. Some European and US NGOs provide assistance, particularly for literacy campaigns in poorer areas.

CHRONOLOGY

The Aztec kingdom of Montezuma II was defeated the in war with the Spaniard, Hernán Cortés, in 1521. By 1546, the Spaniards had discovered major silver mines at Zacatecas. Mexico, then known as New Spain, became a key part of the Spanish colonial empire.

❏ **1808** Napoleon invades Spain.
❏ **1810** Fr. Miguel Hidalgo leads abortive rising against Spanish.
❏ **1821** Spanish viceroy forced to leave by Agustín de Iturbide.
❏ **1822** Federal Republic established.
❏ **1823** Texas opened to US immigration.
❏ **1829** Spanish military expedition fails to regain control.
❏ **1836** The USA is the first country to recognize Mexico's independence. Spain then follows suit. Texas declares its independence from Mexico.
❏ **1846** War breaks out between Mexico and the USA.
❏ **1848** Loses modern-day New Mexico, Arizona, Nevada, Utah, California and part of Colorado.

M

CHRONOLOGY *continued*

- ❏ **1858–1861** War of Reform won by anticlerical Liberals.
- ❏ **1862** France, Britain and Spain launch military expedition.
- ❏ **1863** French troops capture Mexico City. Maximilian of Austria established as Mexican emperor.
- ❏ **1867** Mexico recaptured by Benito Juárez. Maximilian shot.
- ❏ **1876** Porfirio Díaz president. Period of economic growth; Mexico's rail system built.
- ❏ **1901** First year of oil production.
- ❏ **1910** Start of Epic Revolution provoked by excessive exploitation by foreign companies and desire for land reform.
- ❏ **1911** Díaz overthrown by Francisco Madero. Guerrilla war breaks out in north. Emilio Zapata leads peasant revolt in the south.
- ❏ **1913** Madero deposed and murdered. Civil war claims 250,000 lives.
- ❏ **1917** New constitution limits power of Church. Minerals and subsoil rights reserved for the nation.
- ❏ **1926–1929** *Cristero* rebellion led by militant Catholic priests.
- ❏ **1929** National Revolutionary Party (later PRI) formed; in power ever since.
- ❏ **1934** Gen. Cárdenas president. Land reform accelerated, cooperative farms established, railroads nationalized and US and UK oil companies expelled.
- ❏ **1940s** US war effort helps Mexican economy to grow.
- ❏ **1970** Accelerating population growth reaches 3% a year.
- ❏ **1982** Mexico declares it cannot repay its foreign debt of over $800 billion. IMF insists on economic reforms to reschedule the debt.
- ❏ **1984** Government contravenes constitution by relaxing laws on foreign investment.
- ❏ **1985** Earthquake in Mexico City. Official death toll 7,000. Economic cost estimated at $425 million.
- ❏ **1988** Carlos Salinas de Gortari, minister of planning during the earthquake, elected president.
- ❏ **1990** Privatization program initiated.
- ❏ **1994–1996** Guerrilla rebellion in southern Chiapas state brutally suppressed by army; 100 dead. Mexico joins NAFTA. PRI presidential candidate Luis Colosio murdered. Zedillo replaces him and is elected. Economic crisis.
- ❏ **1997** Watershed elections end PRI's monopoly on power in Congress.
- ❏ **1999** Austerity budget and controversial bail-out of the banking system approved with PAN support.

M

DEFENSE

▷ Compulsory military service

💲 $3.7bn   ⬆ Up 1% in 1997

The Mexican military has, in general, avoided direct interference in politics.

Although large in regional terms, Mexico has no ambitions beyond its borders, and the army acts to defend internal security. Most arms procurement is from the USA and France. In 1994, the role of controlling the border with the USA was passed to the police.

The *Zapatista* rebellion in Chiapas in 1994 elicited a brutal response from the army, which was acting on PRI orders. The increasing militarization of the state ever since has hindered the peace process and has led to the proliferation of paramilitaries, with the tacit blessing of the local PRI, who are blamed by human rights groups for the massacre of Indians.

MEXICAN ARMED FORCES

🪖	No main battle tanks	130,000 personnel
🚢	3 destroyers, 6 frigates, 106 patrol boats	37,000 personnel
✈	125 combat aircraft (8 F–5E)	8,000 personnel
	None	

ECONOMICS

▷ Inflation 41% p.a. (1985–1996)

📊 $348.6bn   💲 8.06–9.89 Mexican pesos

SCORE CARD

❏ WORLD GNP RANKING	16th
❏ GNP PER CAPITA	$3,700
❏ BALANCE OF PAYMENTS	$-7.5bn
❏ INFLATION	20.6%
❏ UNEMPLOYMENT	3%

EXPORTS

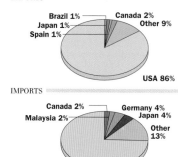

Brazil 1% — Canada 2%
Japan 1% — Other 9%
Spain 1%
USA 86%

IMPORTS

Canada 2% — Germany 4%
Malaysia 2% — Japan 4%
Other 13%
USA 75%

STRENGTHS

One of the world's largest oil producers, with substantial reserves. Extensive mineral resources. Increased foreign investment, diversification of exports and some shielding from international crises due to NAFTA membership. Low wages.

WEAKNESSES

Weak banking system. Vulnerable currency. High unemployment. Political instability. Corruption.

PROFILE

Traditionally the PRI effectively ran the economy. The debt crisis of the 1980s, however, forced a program of privatizations. The 1994 peso crisis necessitated a USA-led $20 billion international bail-out and brought on the worst slump in living memory. The

ECONOMIC PERFORMANCE INDICATOR

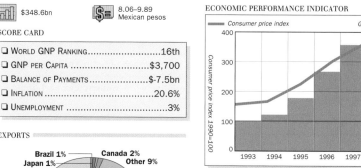

— Consumer price index   GDP (shaded)

Zedillo government launched a tough reform program to achieve a rapid recovery. This was aided by closer economic ties with the USA via NAFTA, but it failed to shield the economy from the worst effects of recent global instability.

Major concerns surround oil – which generates 32% of government revenues – the future of the peso, high inflation, and a weak banking sector. In addition there are doubts about effecting essential social and institutional reforms.

MEXICO : MAJOR BUSINESSES

Food processing 📦	Petrochemicals 🛢
Vehicle assembly 🚗	Oil refining
	Computers 🖥
	Silver mining
	Electronics
	Brewing 🍺
	Textiles

Tijuana, Ciudad Juárez, Monterrey, Reynosa, Tampico, Minatitlán, Durango, Guadalajara, Salamanca, Mexico City

0   400 km
0   400 miles

* significant multinational ownership

RESOURCES
▷ Electric power 44.3m kw

1.4m tonnes

2.79m b/d (reserves 51,298,000,000 bbl)

25.6m cattle, 15.5m pigs, 8.6m goats

Oil, gas, gold, silver, copper, coal, fluorite, mercury, antimony

ELECTRICITY GENERATION

Hydro 19% (29bn kwh)	
Combustion 72% (108.7bn kwh)	
Nuclear 4%	
Other 5%	

% of total generation by type

Mexico is one of the largest oil exporters outside the OPEC cartel. Most oil production comes from offshore drilling platforms in the Gulf of Mexico. The industry was state-owned and state-run by PEMEX, the world's fifth-largest oil company, employing a workforce of 120,000. The decision to privatize

ENVIRONMENT
▷ Green MPs

4% (4% partially protected)

Low

ENVIRONMENTAL TREATIES

Yes	Yes	Yes
Yes	Yes	Yes

The largely unplanned conurbation of Mexico City struggles to accommodate over 20 million inhabitants as the absence of environmental controls contributes to perhaps the world's worst air quality and waste problems. PEMEX stands accused of massive pollution.

Maquiladoras have no effective environmental controls (making them much cheaper than in the USA) and are usually surrounded by slums with no sanitation. The few remaining tropical forests in the southwest are fast disappearing.

MEDIA
▷ TV ownership high

Daily newspaper circulation 97 per 1,000 people

PUBLISHING AND BROADCAST MEDIA

	There are 295 daily newspapers. *Excélsior* is a prominent newspaper both within Mexico and the rest of Latin America
	Many state-owned and independent services
	Many state and independent services

The state retains a tight grip on the media, frequently paying the press to run favorable front page stories.

MEXICO : LAND USE

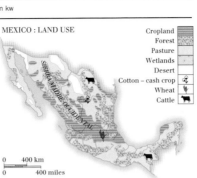

▨	Cropland
	Forest
	Pasture
	Wetlands
	Desert
⚘	Cotton – cash crop
⚘	Wheat
🐄	Cattle

0   400 km
0   400 miles

SIERRA MADRE OCCIDENTAL

petrochemical plants has provoked serious social unrest and further sell-offs, and deregulation remains politically highly sensitive. Despite its oil reserves, Mexico has embarked on a nuclear power program and on projects to modernize the national electricity grid and boost natural gas production.

CRIME
▷ Death penalty not used

Mexico does not publish prison figures

Down 2% in 1987

CRIME RATES

Mexico does not publish murder, theft or rape statistics.

Northern Mexico is a major center for narcotics shipments to the USA. Anti-drugs police are accused by the USA of corruption. Guns are rife and minor incidents may end in shootings. The high crime rate in Mexico City is a major political issue. Reform of the judiciary and of the whole police force are considered top priorities.

EDUCATION
▷ School leaving age: 14

90%

1.5m students

Public education is underfunded and rural provision is poor.

THE EDUCATION SYSTEM

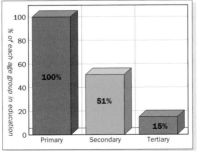

% of each age group in education

- Primary: 100%
- Secondary: 51%
- Tertiary: 15%

The system is a mixture of the French and US models. The public university system is well developed.

HEALTH
▷ Welfare state health benefits

1 per 769 people

Heart diseases, accidents, cancers, violence

Mexico's national health care system is rudimentary and is also seriously underfunded.

Those in employment who pay social security receive slightly better care. Mexico has a good reputation for surgery and dentistry, but this is mostly in the private sector. The rich also go to the USA for treatment.

SPENDING
▷ Not available

CONSUMPTION AND SPENDING

93 per 1,000 population

96 per 1,000 population

Defense 1%	
Education 5.3%	
Health 1.6%	

Defense, Health, Education spending as % of GDP

Mexico has enormous wealth disparities, from a small number of dollar-billionaires, to the 16% of the population who live in extreme poverty. In the past, the wealthy did not generally pay taxes and often benefited from the large state machine. Tax evasion remains a serious problem. There is little social mobility; the old Spanish families retain their hold on institutions.

Rural Indians are probably the most disadvantaged group. In the last decade, poverty has forced them into city slums to work in factories or *maquiladoras* – assembly plants for foreign, usually US, goods – where conditions and pay are poor. Generally, real wages have fallen by 71% in the last ten years. The 1994 Chiapas rebellion was fed by demands for more land and more assistance in farming it. The flow of poor rural migrants to the USA stems from the need to subsidize families at home.

WORLD RANKING

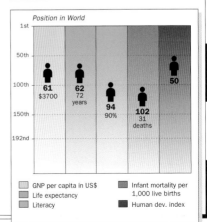

Position in World

- 61 $3700
- 62 72 years
- 94 90%
- 102 31 deaths
- 50

▨ GNP per capita in US$	▨ Infant mortality per 1,000 live births
▨ Life expectancy	
▨ Literacy	▨ Human dev. index

M

MICRONESIA

OFFICIAL NAME: Federated States of Micronesia   **CAPITAL:** Palikir (Pohnpei Island)
POPULATION: 109,000   **CURRENCY:** US dollar   **OFFICIAL LANGUAGE:** English

| 1986 | 1986 | Nov 3 | FSM | +11 | +691 | .fm |

THE FEDERATED STATES of Micronesia (FSM), situated in the Pacific Ocean, encompasses all the Caroline Islands except Palau. It is composed of four main island cluster states: Pohnpei, Kosrae, Chuuk and Yap. The FSM was formerly under US rule as part of the UN Trust Territory of the Pacific Islands. An agreement which granted internal sovereignty in free association with the USA became operational in 1986, and the Trust was formally dissolved in 1990. The islands continue to receive considerable aid from the USA.

CLIMATE
▷ Tropical oceanic

WEATHER CHART

Average daily temperature · Rainfall

The islands are humid and fairly hot all year round, and the daily temperature range is small. Rainfall is abundant.

TRANSPORTATION
▷ Drive on right

✈ **Chuuk**

🚢 19 ships 9,200 grt

THE TRANSPORTATION NETWORK

| 39 km (24 miles) | None |
| None | None |

Flights between Micronesia's main islands are fairly regular, although Pohnpei airport's sinking runways often need repair. Shipping is mainly used for bulk cargoes and copra.

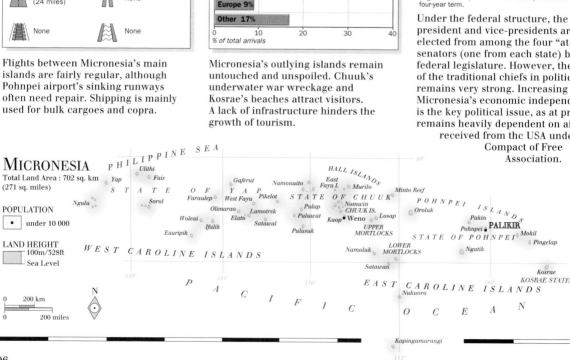

Micronesia, aerial view of rock islands. Like many Pacific states, Micronesia fears rising sea levels as a result of global warming.

TOURISM
▷ Visitors : population 1:5.5

🧳 20,000 visitors
⬆ Up 82% in 1996

MAIN TOURIST ARRIVALS

| Japan 40% |
| USA 34% |
| Europe 9% |
| Other 17% |

% of total arrivals

Micronesia's outlying islands remain untouched and unspoiled. Chuuk's underwater war wreckage and Kosrae's beaches attract visitors. A lack of infrastructure hinders the growth of tourism.

PEOPLE
▷ Pop. density medium

Trukese, Pohnpeian, Mortlockese, Losrean, English

156/km² (403/mi²)

THE URBAN/RURAL POPULATION SPLIT

28%   72%

RELIGIOUS PERSUASION

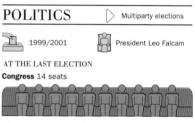

Other 2%
Roman Catholic 50%
Protestant 48%

Increasing numbers of Melanesians, especially Filipino laborers, threaten to swamp the resident Micronesian population. Most islanders live without electricity or running water and many are effectively recipients of US welfare. Society is traditionally matrilineal on most of the islands.

POLITICS
▷ Multiparty elections

1999/2001   President Leo Falcam

AT THE LAST ELECTION

Congress 14 seats

There are no political parties. Congress has 14 members, 10 senators directly elected for a two-year term and four 'at large' senators (one from each state) who are elected for a four-year term.

Under the federal structure, the president and vice-presidents are elected from among the four "at-large" senators (one from each state) by the federal legislature. However, the power of the traditional chiefs in politics remains very strong. Increasing Micronesia's economic independence is the key political issue, as at present it remains heavily dependent on aid received from the USA under the Compact of Free Association.

MICRONESIA

Total Land Area : 702 sq. km (271 sq. miles)

POPULATION
• under 10 000

LAND HEIGHT
100m/328ft
Sea Level

WORLD AFFAIRS

 Joined UN in 1991

Micronesia's most important relationship is with the USA, which administered the islands from 1947 as part of the Trust Territory of the Pacific Islands. Under the Compact of Free Association, the USA has exclusive

control over the FSM's foreign and defense policies. The FSM government is planning a trust fund to support its expenditure after Compact funds from the USA dry up in 2001. Japan is also important, with the Tokyo government providing aid, and the FSM has recently cultivated strong links with China.

AID

Recipient

$96m (receipts) — Down 15% 1996–1997

The USA is the principal donor of aid, which funds hospitals, schools, food stamps and construction projects.

DEFENSE

No compulsory military service

USA responsible for defense — Not applicable

Defense is entirely in the hands of the USA. Airstrips in the FSM were used by the USA in the Vietnam War.

ECONOMICS

Not available

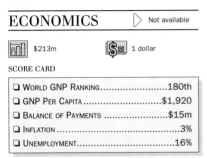
$213m — 1 dollar

SCORE CARD

❑ WORLD GNP RANKING	180th
❑ GNP PER CAPITA	$1,920
❑ BALANCE OF PAYMENTS	$15m
❑ INFLATION	3%
❑ UNEMPLOYMENT	16%

STRENGTHS

Access to US economy, especially for garment manufacture through preferential trading rights. Construction industry is the largest private-sector activity. Tourism, fishing and copra production. US strategic interest in Micronesia, and US budget subsidies.

WEAKNESSES

Dependence on USA for imports, especially for fuel. $30 million debt. Acute shortage of water limits development potential. High levels of underemployment.

EXPORTS

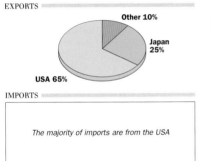

Other 10%
Japan 25%
USA 65%

IMPORTS

The majority of imports are from the USA

RESOURCES

Not applicable

1,555 tonnes — Not an oil producer and has no refineries

Not available — None

The FSM is entirely dependent on external sources for its energy supply. Almost all electricity is produced by small diesel generators. The main resources are copra and valuable fish stocks, especially tuna.

ENVIRONMENT

No Green MPs

None — Not available

The FSM does not face pollution on the scale of that in the neighboring Marshall Islands. However, Chuuk suffers serious droughts; occasionally water rationing has had to be introduced for short periods. In 1992, the US government used naval vessels to transport water from Guam to alleviate a severe water shortage.

MEDIA

TV ownership low

There are no daily newspapers

PUBLISHING AND BROADCAST MEDIA

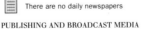

There are no daily newspapers.
The National Union is a popular fortnightly

1 state-owned, 2 independent services — 1 state-owned service

A newspaper editor was not allowed to reenter the FSM in 1997, provoking allegations of government interference.

CRIME

Death penalty not used

Micronesia does not publish prison figures — Little change from year to year

On Chuuk, assault, especially alcohol-related cases, is increasing. The outlying islands are crime-free.

EDUCATION

School leaving age: 14

89% — 1,461 students

Education is compulsory between the ages of six and 14 years. The future of US grants for some students to attend US universities is uncertain.

CHRONOLOGY

The Caroline Islands were first colonized by the Spanish, but sold to Germany in 1899. Having formed an important Japanese base in the Second World War, the islands were transferred to US control in 1945.

- ❑ **1947** UN Trust Territory of the Pacific Islands established.
- ❑ **1979** Becomes independent.
- ❑ **1986** Compact of Free Association with USA operational.
- ❑ **1990** Official termination of trusteeship agreement.
- ❑ **1991** Joins UN.
- ❑ **1995** President Olter reelected.
- ❑ **1997** Jacob Nena formally succeeds Bailey Olter as president after the latter is incapacitated as a result of a stroke.

HEALTH

Welfare state health benefits

1 per 2,311 people — Heart, cerebrovascular and intestinal diseases

Basic health care is accessible to all. Diabetes and drug abuse are growing problems. An increase in imported food has led to dietary problems.

SPENDING

GDP/cap. increase

CONSUMPTION AND SPENDING

No data — No data

No data available

0   5   10   15   20   25
Defense, Health, Education spending as % of GDP

The gap between rich and poor is ever increasing as Miconesia's businessmen and local officials exploit US aid donations.

WORLD RANKING

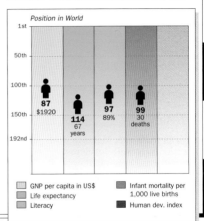

Position in World

1st
50th
100th
150th
192nd

87 $1920
114 67 years
97 89%
99 30 deaths

- ❑ GNP per capita in US$
- ❑ Life expectancy
- ❑ Literacy
- ❑ Infant mortality per 1,000 live births
- ❑ Human dev. index

MOLDOVA

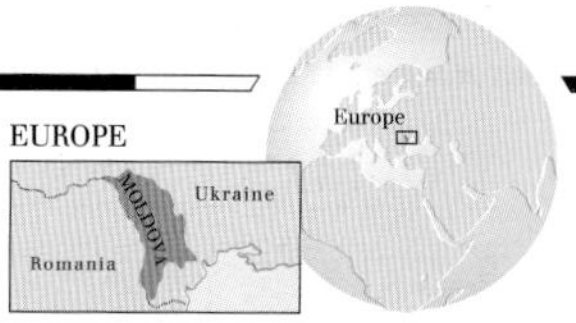
EUROPE
Europe
Ukraine
MOLDOVA
Romania

OFFICIAL NAME: Republic of Moldova **CAPITAL:** Chişinău
POPULATION: 4.5 million **CURRENCY:** Moldovan leu **OFFICIAL LANGUAGE:** Romanian

1991 | 1991 | Aug 27 | MD | +2 | +373 | .md

ONCE A PART OF ROMANIA, Moldova was incorporated into the Soviet Union in 1940. Independence in 1991 brought with it the expectation that Moldova would be reunited with Romania. In a 1994 plebiscite, however, Moldovans voted against the proposal. Moldova, mostly undulating steppe country, is the smallest and most densely populated of the former Soviet republics. Most of its population is engaged in intensive agriculture.

***Agricultural landscape.** Warm summers and even rainfall are ideal for cereal and fruit farming. Moldova is famous for its wine.*

CLIMATE

Continental

WEATHER CHART

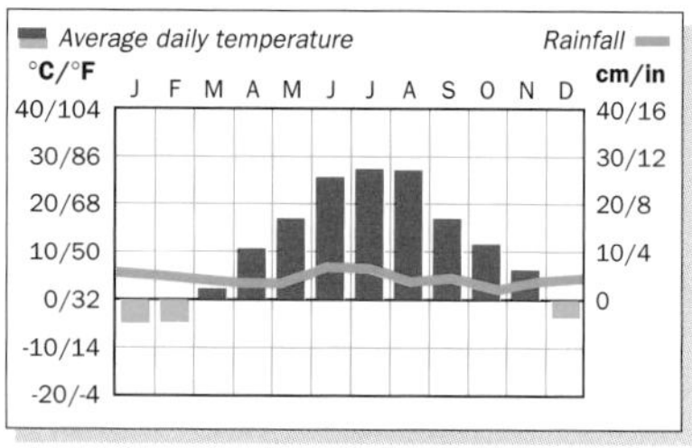
Average daily temperature
Rainfall
°C/°F
cm/in
J F M A M J J A S O N D
40/104
30/86
20/68
10/50
0/32
-10/14
-20/-4
40/16
30/12
20/8
10/4
0

Warm summers, mild winters, and moderate rainfall give Moldova an ideal climate for cultivation.

TRANSPORTATION

Drive on right

Chişinău International — Not available

THE TRANSPORTATION NETWORK

17,100 km (10,686 miles) — None

1,322 km (826 miles) — Mouth of the Danube

The "Transport Corridor Europe–Caucasus–Asia," including a gas pipeline, is planned to cross Moldova.

TOURISM

Visitors : population 1:136

33,000 visitors — Up 50% 1995–1997

MAIN TOURIST ARRIVALS

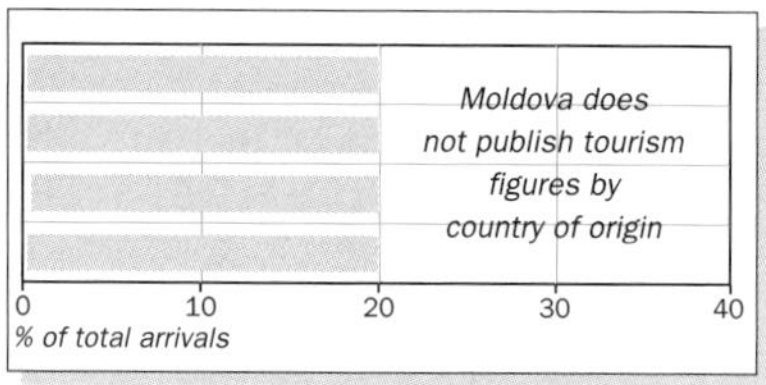
Moldova does not publish tourism figures by country of origin
0
10
20
30
40
% of total arrivals

Few tourists visit Moldova. However, its relatively well-developed infrastructure could allow some expansion of tourism in future. The vineyards and underground wine vault "streets" are the main attractions.

PEOPLE

Pop. density medium

Moldovan, Romanian, Russian — 134/km² (346/mi²)

THE URBAN/RURAL POPULATION SPLIT

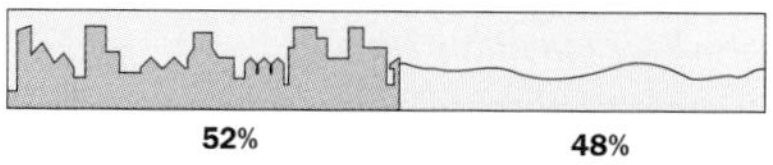
52%
48%

ETHNIC MAKEUP

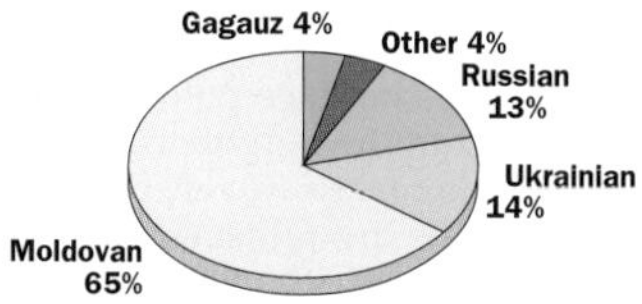
Gagauz 4%
Other 4%
Russian 13%
Ukrainian 14%
Moldovan 65%

Moldovans have the same ethnic grouping as Romanians. The southern Gagauzi (Orthodox Christian Turks), and the population of mixed Russian–Moldovan–Ukrainian parentage on the eastern bank of the Dniester, declared themselves separate republics in 1990.

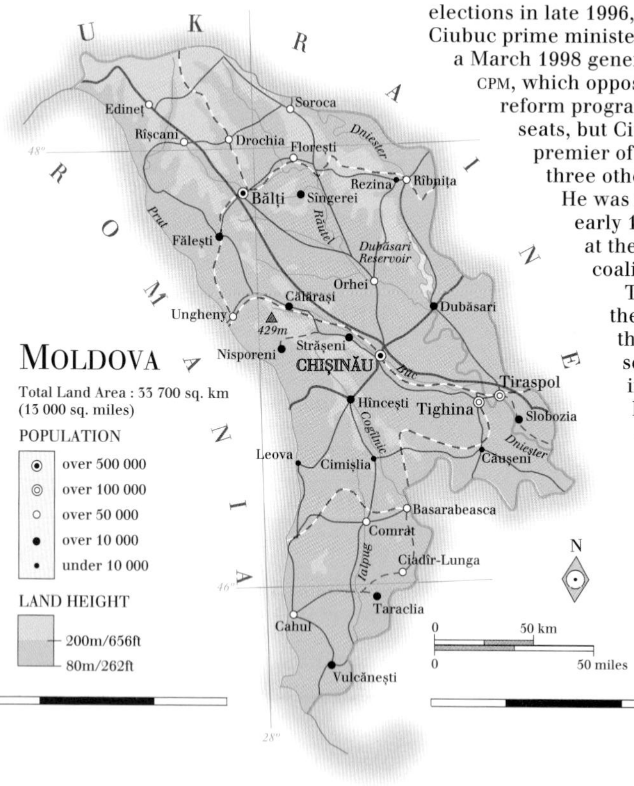
UKRAINE
ROMANIA
Edineţ
Rîşcani
Soroca
Drochia
Floreşti
Dniester
Rezina
Rîbniţa
Bălţi
Sîngerei
Prut
Făleşti
Răutel
Dubăsari Reservoir
Orhei
Călăraşi
Dubăsari
Ungheny
429m
Străşeni
Nisporeni
CHIŞINĂU
Bîc
Tiraspol
Hînceşti
Tighina
Slobozia
Cogîlnic
Leova
Cimişlia
Căuşeni
Dniester
Basarabeasca
Comrat
Ialpug
Ciadîr-Lunga
Taraclia
Cahul
Vulcăneşti
48°
46°
28°
N
0 50 km
0 50 miles
MOLDOVA
Total Land Area : 33 700 sq. km (13 000 sq. miles)
POPULATION
over 500 000
over 100 000
over 50 000
over 10 000
under 10 000
LAND HEIGHT
200m/656ft
80m/262ft

POLITICS

Multiparty elections

1998/2002 — President Petru Lucinschi

AT THE LAST ELECTION

Parliament 101 seats

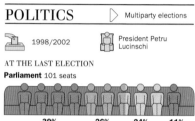

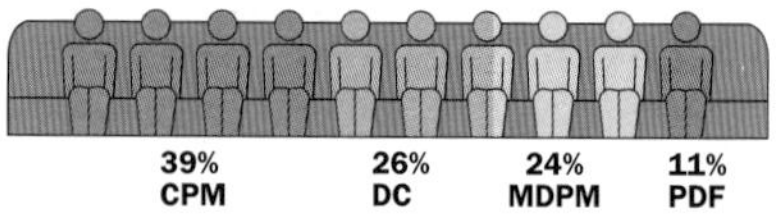
39% CPM
26% DC
24% MDPM
11% PDF

CPM = Moldovan Communist Party **DC** = Democratic Convention **MDPM** = Movement for a Democratic and Prosperous Moldova **PDF** = Party of Democratic Forces

Moldova declared its independence in 1991. In February 1994 multiparty elections the ADP won an absolute majority of seats. The possibility of unification with neighboring Romania was rejected overwhelmingly in a March 1994 national plebiscite.

Petru Lucinschi won presidential elections in late 1996, appointing Ion Ciubuc prime minister in early 1997. In a March 1998 general election the CPM, which opposed Lucinschi's reform program, won most seats, but Ciubuc continued as premier of a coalition of the three other main parties. He was succeeded in early 1999 by Ion Sturza at the head of the same coalition.

Transdniestria (on the eastern bank of the river Dniester) seeks independence and has rejected autonomous status as provided for in the 1994 constitution. The 153,000 Gagauzi minority also aspire to independence.

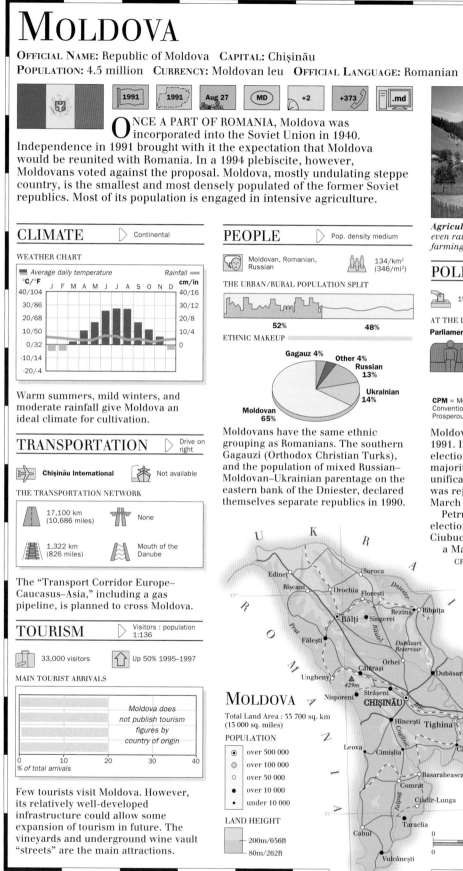

M

WORLD AFFAIRS

 Joined UN in 1992

Ties with countries in the Black Sea Economic Zone, including Romania and Ukraine, are being developed. The creation of a free economic zone at the mouth of the Danube is under discussion. Economic pressure from Russia persuaded Moldova to rejoin the CIS at the end of 1993. Russia still has troops stationed in Moldova.

AID

 Recipient

$63m (receipts) — Up 11% in 1997

IMF and World Bank support, blocked in mid-1997, resumed in early 1999. The EU, Romania, Turkey, and Bulgaria are also important sources of aid.

DEFENSE

Compulsory military service

$53m — Up 86% in 1995

Under a 1999 accord Russian forces in Transdniestria will be withdrawn by end-2005. Plans were also announced to cut army personnel by 30% and reduce military service from 18 to 12 months.

ECONOMICS

Not available

$1.97bn — 4.68–8.43 Moldovan leu

SCORE CARD

❏ WORLD GNP RANKING.........................140th
❏ GNP PER CAPITA $460
❏ BALANCE OF PAYMENTS...................$–268m
❏ INFLATION 11.8%
❏ UNEMPLOYMENT 2%

STRENGTHS
Agriculture – notably wine, tobacco, and cotton – and food processing. Light manufacturing. Low inflation.

WEAKNESSES
Dependent on Russian raw materials and fuel; isolated location; weak transportation network; slow pace of reform; cumbersome bureaucracy; strong black economy. Foreign debt – over 50% of GDP – costs 20% of export earnings to service. Currency crisis in Russia (destination of 65% of exports) in late 1998 provoked economic crisis.

EXPORTS

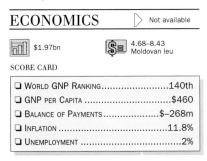

Belarus 4% — Ukraine 6% — USA 7% — Romania 7% — Russia 57% — Other 19%

IMPORTS

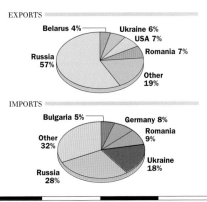

Bulgaria 5% — Germany 8% — Romania 9% — Other 32% — Ukraine 18% — Russia 28%

RESOURCES

Electric power 2.6m kw

700 tonnes — Oil and gas reserves not exploited
12m poultry, 1m sheep, 485,400 cattle — Lignite, phosphate, gypsum, oil, natural gas

Moldova has few mineral resources. It has to import all its fuel requirements and most of its electricity.

ENVIRONMENT

No Green MPs

1% — Low

In 1998 environmentalists opposed the transit of Bulgarian nuclear waste to Russia. Overuse of pesticides on tobacco farms is a problem.

MEDIA

TV ownership high

 Daily newspaper circulation 59 per 1,000 people

PUBLISHING AND BROADCAST MEDIA

There are 4 leading daily newspapers, including the independent *Nezavisimaya Moldova*

1 state-controlled service — 1 state-controlled service

The press was privatized in 1993. The many new publications represent widely differing interest groups.

CRIME

Death penalty not used

10,363 prisoners — Crime levels are rising

Instability in Transdniestria has allowed crime, including smuggling of Russian arms from the area, to spread to neighboring regions. A human kidney smuggling operation was uncovered in 1999.

EDUCATION

School leaving age: 17

98% — 93,759 students

Since 1990 moves have been made to switch from a Soviet to a Romanian (French-inspired) system. Engineering is the largest university faculty.

HEALTH

Welfare state health benefits

1 per 278 people — Circulatory diseases, cancers, accidents

The centralized health service is poor by regional standards, with basic equipment and poorly trained doctors.

SPENDING

GDP/cap. no increase

CONSUMPTION AND SPENDING

39 per 1,000 population — 145 per 1,000 population

Defense 4.4%
Education 6.1%
Health 2.9%

Defense, Health, Education spending as % of GDP

Former communist officials have been well placed to benefit from the advent of capitalism in Moldova, following the collapse of the Soviet Union. Pensions and wages are often months in arrears. In 1998 benefits for low-income families and veterans were scrapped. Ethnic Gagauzi (Orthodox Christian Turks) are the poorest group.

WORLD RANKING

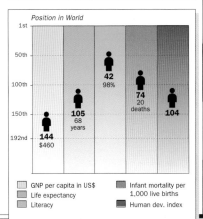

Position in World

144 $460 — 105 68 years — 42 98% — 74 20 deaths — 104

❏ GNP per capita in US$
❏ Life expectancy
❏ Literacy
❏ Infant mortality per 1,000 live births
❏ Human dev. index

M

MONACO

OFFICIAL NAME: Principality of Monaco **CAPITAL:** Monaco
POPULATION: 32,000 **CURRENCY:** French franc **OFFICIAL LANGUAGE:** French

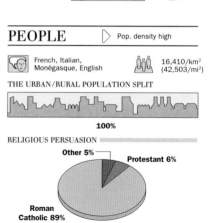

EUROPE

| 1861 | 1861 | Nov 19 | MC | +1 | +377 | .mc |

M ONACO IS A TINY ENCLAVE on the Côte d'Azur in southeastern France. Its destiny changed radically in 1863 when Prince Charles III, after whom Monte Carlo is named, opened the casino. Today, Monaco is a lucrative banking and services center, as well as a tourist destination. Prince Rainier's marriage to film star Grace Kelly, and some astute management of the economy, successfully transformed Monaco into a center for the international jet set. In 1962, the prince's absolute authority was abolished in a new, democratic constitution.

CLIMATE ▷ Mediterranean

WEATHER CHART

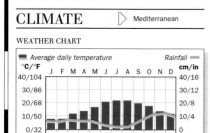

■ *Average daily temperature* *Rainfall* ━━

Summers are hot and dry; days with 12 hours of sunshine are not uncommon. Winters are mild and sunny.

TRANSPORTATION ▷ Drive on right

Héliport de Monaco, Fontvieille
153,000 passengers

8 ships

THE TRANSPORTATION NETWORK

| 50 km (31 miles) | | None |
| 2 km (1 mile) | | None |

A new underground railway station reached by a tunnel from Cap d'Ail on the French side is nearing completion and will add 4 hectares to Monaco's existing 195 hectares. Work on a FFr1.8 billion floating jetty extension on the west side of Condamine port is shortly to begin.

TOURISM ▷ Visitors : population 8.1:1

259,000 visitors

Up 11% 1995–1997

MAIN TOURIST ARRIVALS

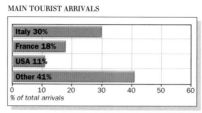

Italy 30%
France 18%
USA 11%
Other 41%

% of total arrivals

A nation of only 32,000 people, Monaco attracts huge numbers of tourists, mainly from France and Italy. Almost all are day-trippers, drawn by the casinos and Monaco's high life. The Grimaldi Forum conference center, due to open in June 2000, seeks to attract more business travelers. Monaco is a favorite destination of the rich, especially Italians, whose numbers have now begun to recover after the 1992 collapse of the lira. Less welcome has been a recent influx of Russian Mafia visitors. Spring offers several major social and sporting events: the Rose Ball (March), the Tennis Open (April) and the Grand Prix (May).

PEOPLE ▷ Pop. density high

French, Italian, Monégasque, English

16,410/km² (42,503/mi²)

THE URBAN/RURAL POPULATION SPLIT

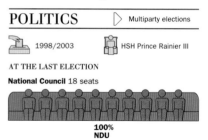

100%

RELIGIOUS PERSUASION

Other 5%
Protestant 6%
Roman Catholic 89%

Less than a fifth of Monaco's residents are Monégasque. Around half are French, the rest Italian, American, British and Belgian. Monégasques enjoy considerable privileges, including housing subsidies to protect them from Monaco's high property prices, and the right of first refusal before a job can be offered to a foreigner. Women have equal status, but only acquired the vote in the constitutional changes of 1962.

POLITICS ▷ Multiparty elections

1998/2003

HSH Prince Rainier III

AT THE LAST ELECTION

National Council 18 seats

100% NDU

NDU = National Democratic Union
There are no formal political parties.

The Grimaldi princes have been hereditary rulers of Monaco for 700 years. Prince Rainier III renounced absolute rule in 1962 but retains considerable power. In National Council elections – based on personalities rather than parties – held in 1998, those returned were members of the National and Democratic Union.

WORLD AFFAIRS ▷ Joined UN in 1993

FZ IAEA OSCE

A key concern is to protect both banking secrecy and the liberal tax regime from EU regulation, though the principality did decide to introduce the euro from January 1999. French citizens have been banned from banking in Monaco since 1962.

M

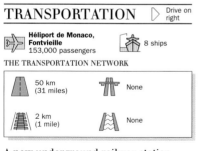

MONACO

Total Land Area : 1.95 sq. km (0.75 sq. miles)

Places of Interest
Parks and Gardens
Grand Prix Circuit

0   500 m
0   656 ft

Monte Carlo with its luxury hotels and yacht harbor. The only space for new development is on land reclaimed from the sea.

AID
▷ Not applicable

 Monaco has no aid receipts or donations | Not applicable

Monaco neither receives nor gives aid, and the issue is not of concern to Monégasques.

DEFENSE
▷ No compulsory military service

France responsible for defense | Not applicable

Monaco has no armed forces and no defense budget. France, as the protecting power, bears responsibility for the defense of the principality.

ECONOMICS
▷ Inflation 3% p.a. (1985–1996)

$4.9bn | 6.02–5.59 French francs

SCORE CARD
❑ WORLD GNP RANKING.......................106th
❑ GNP PER CAPITA $11,000
❑ BALANCE OF PAYMENTS.....Included in French total
❑ INFLATION ....Included in French total
❑ UNEMPLOYMENT 3%

STRENGTHS
Revision of banking secrecy laws, which had made Monaco vulnerable to money laundering, under 1994 accord with France, obliges banks to furnish details of suspicious accounts. Strict banking confidentiality and low taxes still attract billions of dollars of overseas deposits. Strong tourism sector. Assets managed by Monaco banks have increased by 18% a year over the last five years. No formal debt and reserves of over FFr15 billion.

WEAKNESSES
Continuing vulnerability to money laundering and health of French and Italian economies. Dependence on VAT for 55% of revenues. Pressure from EU states to end privileged tax and banking laws. Total dependence on imports because of lack of natural resources.

EXPORTS/IMPORTS

Monaco has a full customs union with France.

RESOURCES
▷ Not applicable

3 tonnes | Not an oil producer and has no refineries
Included within French total | None

Monaco has no strategic resources and imports all its energy from France. It has no agricultural land.

ENVIRONMENT
▷ No Green MPs

None | Not available

Monaco has built the most extensive underground car parking facilities in the world to tackle congestion. The quality of the built environment around the harbor occasionally arouses local passions. Important populations of red coral are under threat from land reclamation and pollution.

MEDIA
▷ TV ownership high

Daily newspaper circulation 250 per 1,000 people

PUBLISHING AND BROADCAST MEDIA

There is 1 daily newspaper. *Nice-Matin*, a regional French newspaper, publishes a Monaco edition

1 independent service | 1 service (part owned by French state)

In addition to its domestic radio and TV, Monaco receives all the mainstream French and Italian channels.

CRIME
▷ Death penalty not used

Monaco does not publish prison figures | Down 13% from 1992–1996

Low crime rates make it safe for the rich to sport their furs and jewelry in public. In late 1998 the appeals court upheld Monaco's first conviction of an individual for money laundering.

EDUCATION
▷ School leaving age: 16

99% | Not available

The education system is essentially the same as that of France, with students studying for the *baccalauréat* exam. Most go on to university in France, but then return to claim good jobs in Monaco. The Catholic Church exerts considerable influence and is still responsible for primary schooling.

HEALTH
▷ Welfare state health benefits

1 per 373 people | Heart and cerebrovascular diseases, cancers

Most medical care is provided by private health insurance. Doctors train in France. The Princess Grace Hospital can serve 60,000 people and thus also caters for patients from outside Monaco.

CHRONOLOGY
In 1297, the Grimaldis established themselves as the principality's hereditary rulers.

❑ **1911** Constitution promulgated.
❑ **1912** Customs union with France.
❑ **1949** Prince Rainier III accedes to throne.
❑ **1962** Constitution rewritten: end of absolute authority of the prince.
❑ **1963** Democratic legislative elections held for first time.
❑ **1982** Princess Grace dies following car accident.

SPENDING
▷ GDP/cap. no increase

CONSUMPTION AND SPENDING

No data | No data

No data available

0   5   10   15   20   25
Defense, Health, Education spending as % of GDP

Monaco's image abroad has changed dramatically since Prince Rainier acceded in 1949. From being considered simply as a gambling spot, it is now ranked as one of the world's most glamorous international jet set destinations. In part, this was the result of Prince Rainier's wedding to Grace Kelly, then a leading Hollywood star, which brought Monaco to the attention of US high society. More important was Rainier's work in turning Monaco into a major tax haven and an up-market resort, by making the most of its Mediterranean coastal location. Today, many tax exiles are resident, among them the Wall Street investment guru Bob Beckman and Luciano Pavarotti.

WORLD RANKING

Position in World

33 $11000 | 8 78 years | 1 99% | 28 7 deaths

GNP per capita in US$ | Infant mortality per 1,000 live births
Life expectancy | Human dev. index
Literacy

M

MONGOLIA

OFFICIAL NAME: Mongolia **CAPITAL:** Ulan Bator **POPULATION:** 2.6 million
CURRENCY: Tughrik (togrog) **OFFICIAL LANGUAGE:** Khalkha Mongol

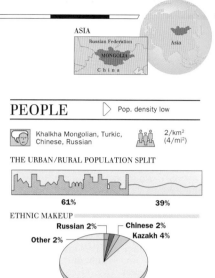

ASIA

| 1924 | 1924 | July 11 | MNG | +8 | +976 | .mn |

LANDLOCKED BETWEEN Russia and China, Mongolia rises from the semiarid Gobi Desert to mountainous steppe. Mongolia was unified by Genghis Khan in 1206 and became part of Manchu China in 1697. Independent in 1924, Mongolia became a communist state, and was officially aligned with the USSR from 1936. In 1990, it became the first Asian nation to abandon communist rule; in 1992 the former communists were voted back into power, only to be defeated by a liberal coalition in 1996.

CLIMATE

▷ Mountain/cold desert/steppe

WEATHER CHART

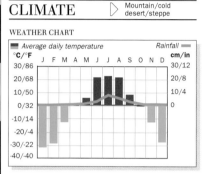

Temperatures vary from –32°C (–26°F) to 41°C (106°F). Sudden cold periods in early spring, known as *zud*, can kill many young livestock.

TRANSPORTATION

▷ Drive on right

Buyant-Ukhaa, Ulan Bator ✈ Has no fleet

THE TRANSPORTATION NETWORK

42,400 km (26,500 miles)	None
1,810 km (1,131 miles)	397 km (247 miles)

The focus of state transportation policy is shifting away from Moscow toward improved links with China and access to a Pacific port facility. Gasoline shortages have meant a large increase in the use of draft-animals.

MONGOLIA

Total Land Area : 1 565 000 sq. km (604 247 sq. miles)

0   400 km

0   400 miles

POPULATION
- ⊙ over 500 000
- ○ over 50 000
- • over 10 000
- • under 10 000

LAND HEIGHT
- 3000m/9843ft
- 2000m/6562ft
- 1000m/3281ft
- above 500m

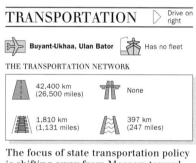

TOURISM

▷ Visitors : population 1:32

🧳 82,000 visitors   ⬇ Down 4% 1995–1997

MAIN TOURIST ARRIVALS

CIS 84%	
China 4%	
Poland 3%	
Other 9%	

0 10 20 30 40 50 60 70 80 90 100
% of total arrivals

Tourism has expanded since the easing of visa restrictions in 1991. Under communism, all travel was arranged through the state agency, *Zhuuichin*, but private companies are now entering the market.

Traditional gers in the Gobi Desert.
Most Mongolians still choose to pursue a nomadic lifestyle, living in felt tents called gers.

PEOPLE

▷ Pop. density low

Khalkha Mongolian, Turkic, Chinese, Russian   2/km² (4/mi²)

THE URBAN/RURAL POPULATION SPLIT

61%   39%

ETHNIC MAKEUP

Russian 2%   Chinese 2%
Other 2%   Kazakh 4%
Mongol 90%

Khalkh Mongols are the dominant ethnic group. The Kazakhs, who live in the northwest and speak a Turkic language, form the largest non-Mongol group. Since the collapse of the USSR, many Kazakhs have been emigrating to Kazakhstan. There is little indigenous ethnic tension, although there is considerable antagonism toward Chinese and Russian minorities.

POLITICS

▷ Multiparty elections

🗳 1996/2000   President Natsagyn Bagabandi

AT THE LAST ELECTION

People's Great Hural 76 seats   1% MUPNT

50% MNDP   33% MPRP   16% SDP

MNDP = Mongolian National Democratic Party
MPRP = Mongolian People's Revolutionary Party
SDP = Social Democratic Party
MUPNT = Mongolian United Party of National Traditions

The end of communism and the advent of democracy in 1990 revolutionized Mongolian politics. However, the shock of economic reform led many Mongolians to look back to the certainties of the communist era. In 1992 the Democrats lost power to the renamed communists (MPRP). Their failure to revive the economy swung the pendulum back in favor of a democratic coalition in 1996. Since 1998 the ruling MNDP-led Democratic Union has been engaged in a fierce power struggle with President Natsagyn Bagabandi of the MPRP who took office in 1997.

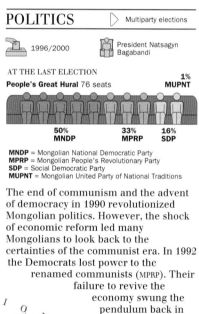

M

WORLD AFFAIRS

 Joined UN in 1961

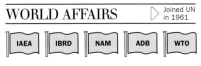

Since 1990, Mongolia has tried to balance China's influence with that of Japan and other east Asian states. Mongolia is seeking to improve economic and political relations with China, but there is a fear of Chinese designs on its sovereignty. Mongolia is trying to ensure its security by joining international organizations.

AID

▷ Recipient

$248m (receipts) ⬆ Up 22% 1996–1997

A large balance of payments deficit makes aid vital. The main donors are the USA and Japan.

DEFENSE

▷ Compulsory military service

$18m ⬆ Up 21% in 1997

The last Soviet forces left in 1992 after the collapse of communism in Russia. The Mongolian forces have been drastically reduced and have barely any equipment. Video surveillance is being used to monitor the Chinese border.

ECONOMICS

▷ Inflation 43% p.a. (1985–1996)

$998m 784.44–863.24 tughriks

SCORE CARD

- ❏ WORLD GNP RANKING.....................156th
- ❏ GNP PER CAPITA $390
- ❏ BALANCE OF PAYMENTS...................$–291m
- ❏ INFLATION 44.6%
- ❏ UNEMPLOYMENT..................................15%

STRENGTHS
Coal and oil, but mostly untapped. Traditional farming economy still strong, supporting population efficiently.

WEAKNESSES
Limited infrastructure. Little manufacturing. April 1996 massive forest fires, devastating countryside.

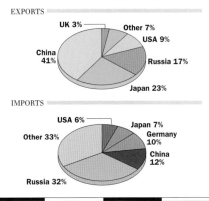

EXPORTS

UK 3% — Other 7%
USA 9%
China 41%
Russia 17%
Japan 23%

IMPORTS

USA 6% — Japan 7%
Other 33% Germany 10%
China 12%
Russia 32%

RESOURCES

▷ Electric power 901,000 kw

231 tonnes

Contracts have recently been signed with oil prospectors

14.2m sheep, 10.2m goats, 2.6m cattle, 2.9m horses

Oil, coal, copper, lead, fluorite, tungsten, tin, gold, uranium

Under communism, Mongolia's vast mineral resources were barely exploited, and prospecting has only recently begun. A uranium-mining joint venture with Russia has been established. Mongolia is rich in oil, with sufficient reserves to meet future domestic needs. In 1999 an oil extraction agreement was signed with China.

ENVIRONMENT

▷ No Green MPs

10% Low

Industrial pollution around Ulan Bator is a concern; prevailing winds carry power station emissions over residential areas and there is a high incidence of chest diseases. The level of pollution in Lake Hövsgöl is also a serious problem.

MEDIA

▷ TV ownership medium

Daily newspaper circulation 27 per 1,000 people

PUBLISHING AND BROADCAST MEDIA

There are 4 daily newspapers, including *Ulaabaatar*, *Önöödör*, and *Ardyn Erh*

1 state-owned, 1 independent service

1 state-owned, 1 independent service

Since 1990, Mongolia's press has enjoyed unlimited freedom; there are no slander or libel laws. Legislation enacted in January 1999 eased remaining curbs on the media. However, the shortage of paper and fuel supplies has restricted the number of publications and their distribution.

CRIME

▷ Death penalty used

Mongolia does not publish prison figures ⬆ Up 110% from 1991-1996

Crime has risen rapidly since 1990, particularly organized crime and muggings by knife gangs. Ulan Bator is the most dangerous area, especially for foreigners; Russians, Chinese, and dollar-carrying US tourists are the main targets.

EDUCATION

▷ School leaving age: 16

84% 44,088 students

Education is modeled on the former Soviet system. The majority of teachers are women on low salaries. Private-sector schools emphasizing Mongol culture are beginning to open.

CHRONOLOGY

In the 17th century, the Manchus took control of Mongolia. It stayed in Chinese hands until 1911.

- ❏ **1911** Mongolia declares independence from China.
- ❏ **1919** China reoccupies Mongolia.
- ❏ **1924** Independent communist state.
- ❏ **1989** Prodemocracy protests; communist election defeat.
- ❏ **1992** Former communists, renamed MPRP, voted back to power.
- ❏ **1996** Democratic Union coalition wins general election.
- ❏ **1997** Natsagyn Bagabandi of MPRP elected president.

HEALTH

▷ Welfare state health benefits

1 per 370 people Heart, parasitic and respiratory diseases

Shortages of drugs and equipment have renewed interest in traditional Mongolian herbal medicine. As well as the state-run system, some Buddhist monasteries provide health care.

SPENDING

▷ GDP/cap. increase

CONSUMPTION AND SPENDING

14 per 1,000 population 37 per 1,000 population

Defense 2%
Education 5.6%
Health No data

0   5   10   15   20   25
Defense, Health, Education spending as % of GDP

Economic liberalization has fueled great disparities in wealth. Those with access to dollars import luxury goods, especially cars, but an estimated one-third of the people live in poverty; the poorest cannot even afford to buy the most basic of foods, such as bread.

WORLD RANKING

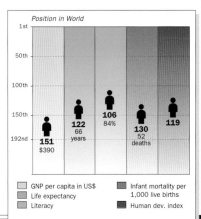

Position in World

1st

50th

100th

150th

192nd

151
$390

122
66 years

106
84%

130
52 deaths

119

- ▢ GNP per capita in US$
- ▢ Life expectancy
- ▢ Literacy
- ▢ Infant mortality per 1,000 live births
- ▢ Human dev. index

M

MOROCCO

OFFICIAL NAME: Kingdom of Morocco   **CAPITAL:** Rabat
POPULATION: 28 million   **CURRENCY:** Moroccan dirham   **OFFICIAL LANGUAGE:** Arabic

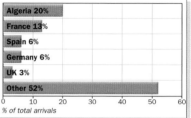

MOROCCO, SITUATED IN northern Africa, is bordered by Algeria and Western Sahara, the future of which is to be determined under a UN-supervised referendum. Its northern regions have a Mediterranean climate, while the south comprises semiarid desert. The late King Hassan's international prestige gave Morocco status out of proportion to its wealth. The main issues concerning the country are the unresolved fate of Western Sahara and the internal threat of Islamic militancy. Tourism, phosphate production, and agriculture are key economic strengths.

TOURISM

⊳ Visitors : population 1:8.9

🧳 3.1m visitors   ⬆ Up 20% 1995–1997

MAIN TOURIST ARRIVALS

	% of total arrivals
Algeria 20%	
France 13%	
Spain 6%	
Germany 6%	
UK 3%	
Other 52%	

0   10   20   30   40   50   60
% of total arrivals

CLIMATE

⊳ Hot desert/mountain/ mediterranean

WEATHER CHART

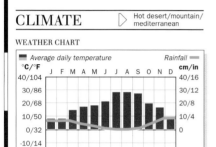

The climate ranges from warm and temperate in the north to semiarid in the south, but temperatures are cooler in the mountains, especially in the high Atlas. During the summer, the effects of the *sirocco* and *chergui*, hot winds from the Sahara, are felt.

TRANSPORTATION

⊳ Drive on right

✈ **Mohammed V, Casablanca**
3.2m passengers

🚢 481 ships
403,400 grt

THE TRANSPORTATION NETWORK

🛣 60,400 km (37,750 km)	🛤 150 km (93 miles)
🚃 1,907 miles (1,185 km)	〰 None

Morocco has six international airports. A highway links Rabat and Casablanca; however, roads tend to peter out in the rural areas. The railroad service is cheap, although its routes are limited.

Tourism is vital to the Moroccan economy. Good beaches abound; Agadir has 300 days of sunshine a year. Fès and Marrakech offer cultural interest, while the Atlas mountains attract walkers, skiers, and cyclists. Desert safaris are offered in the Sahara. Most Western tourists come from France, Germany, and Spain.

M

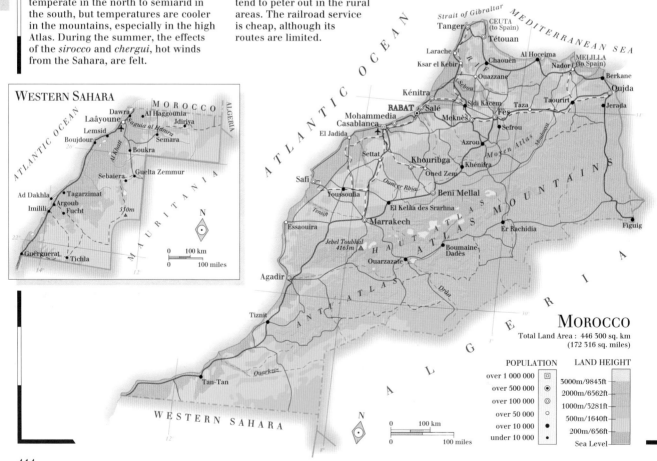

WESTERN SAHARA

MOROCCO

Total Land Area : 446 300 sq. km
(172 316 sq. miles)

POPULATION		LAND HEIGHT	
over 1 000 000	▣	3000m/9843ft	
over 500 000	◉	2000m/6562ft	
over 100 000	◎	1000m/3281ft	
over 50 000	○	500m/1640ft	
over 10 000	●	200m/656ft	
under 10 000	·	Sea Level	

PEOPLE ▷ Pop. density medium

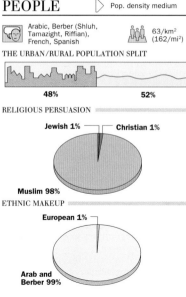

Arabic, Berber (Shluh, Tamazight, Riffian), French, Spanish

63/km² (162/mi²)

THE URBAN/RURAL POPULATION SPLIT

48%　　　　**52%**

RELIGIOUS PERSUASION

Jewish 1% — Christian 1%

Muslim 98%

ETHNIC MAKEUP

European 1%

Arab and Berber 99%

Morocco, the westernmost of the Maghreb states, is the last refuge for descendants of the original Berber inhabitants of northwest Africa. About 35% of Moroccans are Berber-speaking. They live mainly in mountain villages, while the Arab majority inhabit the lowlands. Before independence from France, 450,000 Europeans lived in Morocco; numbers have since greatly diminished. Some 45,000 Jews enjoy religious freedom and full civil rights – a role in society unique among Arab countries. Most people speak Arabic, and French is also spoken in urban areas. Sunni Muslim is the religion of most of the population. The king is the spiritual leader through his position as Commander of the Faithful. The emancipation of women was slow to take root in Morocco, despite advances in education and increasing freedom of social intercourse between the sexes.

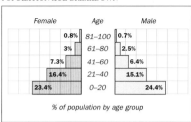

POPULATION AGE BREAKDOWN

Female	Age	Male
0.8%	81–100	0.7%
3%	61–80	2.5%
7.3%	41–60	6.4%
16.4%	21–40	15.1%
23.4%	0–20	24.4%

% of population by age group

The town of Boumaine-Dadès lies in the southern foothills of the Atlas Mountains. The region's outstanding scenery makes it one of Morocco's major tourist attractions.

WORLD AFFAIRS ▷ Joined UN in 1956

AL　AMU　IBRD　NAM　OIC

Morocco's important role in the quest for lasting peace in the Middle East was underlined by Israeli prime minister Yitzhak Rabin's visit to Rabat following the signing in Washington of the 1993 peace accord with the Palestine Liberation Organization. King Hassan's foreign policy was ambiguous, for while he negotiated with Israel he also headed the Jerusalem Committee of the Islamic Conference Organization. Generally more pro-Western than other Arab states, Morocco has also earned respect by protecting its Jewish minority.

International disapproval has focused on Morocco's occupation since 1975 of the former Spanish colony of Western Sahara. Resistance by Polisario Front guerrillas, fighting for an independent Western Sahara, began in 1983 and has continued, despite a UN-brokered peace plan in 1991. In 1994, the UN approved plans for a voter identification process, to lead to a referendum on self-determination. However, continuing disagreements between Morocco and the Polisario Front over voter eligibility have ensured the passing of many referendum deadlines; a new date of March 2000 was agreed at the end of 1998.

Relations with the EU have been strengthened with the signing of an association agreement in late 1995, envisaging free trade in industrial goods within 12 years. However, a fisheries dispute with the EU involving Spanish and Portuguese fishing rights off the Moroccan coast remains to be resolved.

POLITICS ▷ Multiparty elections

U. House 1997/2000
L. House 1997/2001

HM King Mohammed VI

AT THE LAST ELECTION

House of Representatives 325 seats

31% K	31% W	29% C	3% MPCD	1% Other	3% FFD	2% PSD

K = Koutla Bloc W = Wifaq Bloc C = Centre Bloc
MPCD = Constitutional and Democratic Popular Movement
FFD = Democratic Forces Front PSD = Social Democratic Party

Consultative Council 270 seats

Since December 1997 there is an indirectly elected Consultative Council.

Morocco is a constitutional monarchy with a single assembly, to which members are elected every six years.

MAIN POLITICAL ISSUES
The death of King Hassan
The new king, Mohammed VI, is less dominating than his late father, and may wield less power. Most Moroccans accept the need for a strong unifying power – a feature of Hassan's long reign. Mohammed VI, without Hassan's personal association with the occupation of Western Sahara, may be more flexible on that front.

Islamic militancy
The government deals ruthlessly with Islamic militants, although in recent years it has been less repressive regarding human rights. All Islamist groups are banned, while the death sentence is applicable to those defying this law. Fear that Morocco is losing its Islamic identity fuels popular support for Islamic fundamentalism.

PROFILE
During his reign, King Hassan adopted a policy of divide and rule in his relationship with political parties. The constitution allows the majority party in parliament to choose the government, but the king still appoints the prime minister. In 1995, King Hassan chose a new center-right government after the failure of talks with the left-wing opposition. Elections in 1997 again left parliament split between left, center and right; only nine seats went to Islamists. The formation of a socialist-led government was seen as an expression of the growing role of the party system.

Hassan II, who ruled from 1961 until his death in 1999.

King Mohammed VI, who succeeded his father, Hassan II.

AID ▷ Recipient

$462m (receipts)　　Down 29% 1996–1997

Saudi Arabia wrote off $2.7 billion of Moroccan debt after the Gulf War. The World Bank has given help to Morocco, but the country receives little aid.

M

CHRONOLOGY

Independence from France in 1956 was only the first step in ending colonial rule for the oldest kingdom in the Arab world, even though the present Alaoui dynasty has been in power for three centuries.

- ❏ **1956** France recognizes Moroccan independence under Sultan Mohammed Ibn Yousif. Morocco joins UN. Spain renounces control over most of its territories.
- ❏ **1957** Sultan Mohammad king.
- ❏ **1961** Hassan succedes as king.
- ❏ **1967** Morocco backs Arab cause in Six Day War with Israel.
- ❏ **1969** Spain returns enclave of Ifni to Morocco.
- ❏ **1971** Right-wing army officers stage abortive coup.
- ❏ **1972** King Hassan survives assassination attempt.
- ❏ **1975** International Court of Justice grants right of self-determination to Western Saharan people. King Hassan orders Moroccan forces to seize Saharan capital.
- ❏ **1976** Morocco and Mauritania partition Western Sahara.
- ❏ **1979** Mauritania renounces claim to part of Western Sahara, which is added to Morocco's territory.
- ❏ **1984** King Hassan and Colonel Gaddafi of Libya sign Oujda Treaty as first step toward Maghreb union. Morocco withdraws from OAU after criticism of its role in Western Sahara.
- ❏ **1986** Morocco abrogates Oujda Treaty.
- ❏ **1987** Defensive wall around Western Sahara.
- ❏ **1989** Arab Maghreb Union (AMU) creates no-tariff zone between Morocco, Algeria, Tunisia, Libya, and Mauritania.
- ❏ **1990** Morocco condemns Iraq's invasion of Kuwait.
- ❏ **1991** Morocco accepts UN plan for referendum in Western Sahara.
- ❏ **1992** New constitution grants majority party in parliament right to choose the government.
- ❏ **1993** First general election for nine years. After major parties refuse his invitation, king appoints nonparty government.
- ❏ **1994** King Hassan replaces veteran prime minister Karim Lamrani with Abdellatif Filali.
- ❏ **1995** Islamist leader Mohammad Basri returns after 28 years of exile.
- ❏ **1998** Socialists enter government with Abderrahmane el Youssoufi as prime minister.
- ❏ **1999** After expiry of latest Western Sahara referendum deadline, new date set of March 2000. July, death of King Hassan.

DEFENSE

▷ Compulsory military service

💲 $1.4bn   ⬇ Down 3% in 1997

Military service, lasting 18 months, is compulsory.

MOROCCAN ARMED FORCES

🛡	524 main battle tanks (224 M–48A5, 300 M–60 A1/A3)	175,000 personnel
🚢	1 frigate, 27 patrol boats	7,800 personnel
✈	89 combat aircraft (16 F–5E, 14 *Mirage* F-1EH, 15 Mirage F–1CH)	13,500 personnel
⚓	None	

Morocco's long struggle in Western Sahara against Polisario Front guerrillas has given its forces a formidable reputation. Moroccans have also fought as mercenaries in the Gulf.

In the 1980s, sappers constructed a 2,500-km (1,550-mile) defensive wall to cordon off Western Sahara in an attempt to prevent incursions from Polisario guerrillas oparating from bases in Algeria.

Morocco's pro-Western stance has allowed its forces access to sophisticated weapons and training from the West, particularly the USA - unlike neighboring north African states, which are dependent on the former Soviet bloc.

The air force was formed in 1956 and flies US and European aircraft, notably Mirage interceptors. The navy uses Western-supplied ships, but is insignificant in regional terms. There are also a paramilitary gendarmerie and auxiliary force.

Over 4% of national income is spent on defense – a relatively high figure for a developing country.

ECONOMICS

▷ Inflation 5% p.a. (1985–1996)

📊 $34.4bn   💲 9.74–9.25 Moroccan dirhams

SCORE CARD

❏ WORLD GNP RANKING	54th
❏ GNP PER CAPITA	$1,260
❏ BALANCE OF PAYMENTS	$–87m
❏ INFLATION	0.9%
❏ UNEMPLOYMENT	16%

EXPORTS

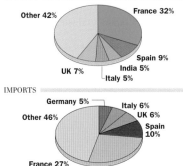

France 32%
Spain 9%
India 5%
Italy 5%
UK 7%
Other 42%

IMPORTS

Germany 5%
Italy 6%
UK 6%
Spain 10%
France 27%
Other 46%

STRENGTHS

Probusiness policies and abundant labor attract foreign investment. Low inflation. Tourist industry, phosphates, and agriculture all have great potential.

WEAKNESSES

High unemployment and population growth. Dirham not fully convertible. Droughts have hit agriculture. Cannabis trade (30% of Europe's supply) complicates closer EU links.

PROFILE

The government's large-scale privatization program, which began in 1992, was designed to attract

ECONOMIC PERFORMANCE INDICATOR

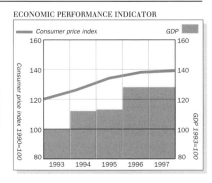

investment, particularly from Europe. Opposition to new, often foreign-based owners and deteriorating working conditions triggered strikes. Severe drought in 1995 made austerity measures necessary. The socialist-led government since 1998 has given social policy a higher priority.

MOROCCO : MAJOR BUSINESSES

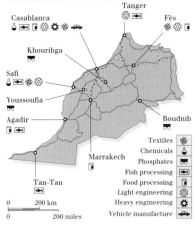

Tanger
Casablanca
Fès
Khouribga
Safi
Youssoufia
Agadir
Boudnib
Marrakech
Tan-Tan

Textiles	🕸
Chemicals	🧪
Phosphates	🏭
Fish processing	🐟
Food processing	🍴
Light engineering	🔧
Heavy engineering	⚙
Vehicle manufacture	🚗

0   200 km
0   200 miles

M

RESOURCES

▷ Electric power 3.8m kw

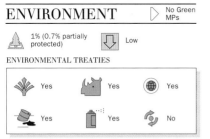

846,200 tonnes

221 b/d
refines 154,600 b/cd

17.6m sheep, 6.2m goats, 2.6m cattle, 950,000 asses

Phosphates, oil, gas, coal, iron, barytes, lead, copper, zinc

ELECTRICITY GENERATION

Hydro 5% (0.6bn kwh)	
Combustion 95% (11bn kwh)	
Nuclear 0%	
Other 0%	

% of total generation by type

Morocco possesses 75% of the world's phosphate reserves. Other minerals include anthracite and iron ore.

ENVIRONMENT

▷ No Green MPs

1% (0.7% partially protected)

⬇ Low

ENVIRONMENTAL TREATIES

Yes   Yes   Yes

Yes   Yes   No

Morocco's wealth of plant and animal life has suffered severely from long periods of drought, most recently in the early 1980s and early 1990s. The unplanned development of tourist resorts is posing a threat to fragile coastal ecosystems.

MEDIA

▷ TV ownership medium

Daily newspaper circulation 26 per 1,000 people

PUBLISHING AND BROADCAST MEDIA

	There are 22 daily newspapers, including *Le Matin du Sahara*, *Rissalat al-Oumma*, *al-Alam* and *L'opinion*
	1 state-owned, 1 independent service
	1 state-owned, 1 independent service

The media are careful to avoid criticism of the monarchy, and the reporting of current affairs tends to be cautious. The sports pages, especially the football reports, are the most dynamic sections of the press – and may also contain implicit criticisms of the establishment. Newspapers are published both in Arabic and French. *L'Economiste* supplies the most authoritative economic information. State-owned TV began transmissions in Arabic and French in 1962. Radio broadcasts are in Arabic, Berber, French, Spanish, and English from Rabat and Tangier.

Forestry is carried out in the mountains. Crops include grain, fruit, peppers, tomatoes, and cut flowers.

MOROCCO : LAND USE

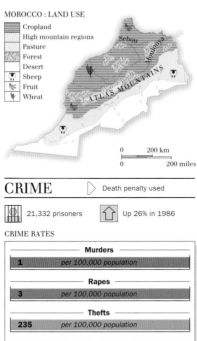

	Cropland
	High mountain regions
	Pasture
	Forest
	Desert
	Sheep
	Fruit
	Wheat

0   200 km
0   200 miles

CRIME

▷ Death penalty used

21,332 prisoners

⬆ Up 26% in 1986

CRIME RATES

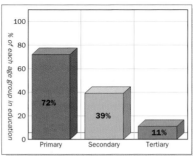

Murders
1   per 100,000 population

Rapes
3   per 100,000 population

Thefts
235   per 100,000 population

Urban crime is increasing, but muggings are rare. There has been relatively little recent civil unrest. Police watch Islamic militant activists. A major antismuggling campaign was undertaken in 1995.

EDUCATION

▷ School leaving age: 16

46%

294,502 students

Education is officially compulsory between the ages of seven and 16 years.

THE EDUCATION SYSTEM

% of each age group in education

Primary **72%**   Secondary **39%**   Tertiary **11%**

Only 14% of Morocco's rural population is literate, as opposed to 50% in the cities. The literacy level and elementary school enrollment rates are well below average for countries with similar living standards. There are 14 universities with a combined total of nearly 300,000 students.

HEALTH

▷ Welfare state health benefits

1 per 2,500 people

Neonatal causes, cerebrovascular and heart diseases

Despite recent progress, child mortality and nutritional standards for the poorest Moroccans remain well below average for countries with a similar standard of living. Outside the cities, primary health care is virtually nonexistent, so that people depend on traditional remedies for illnesses. Government spending on health in 1995 was an estimated 3.6% of total expenditure. All employees contribute to a Social Welfare Fund which among other things operates a system of benefits in the event of illness.

SPENDING

▷ GDP/cap. no increase

CONSUMPTION AND SPENDING

38 per 1,000 population   50 per 1,000 population

Defense 4.2%	
Education 5.6%	
Health 0.9%	

Defense, Health, Education spending as % of GDP

Income per head is considerably lower than in neighboring Algeria and Tunisia. About one in seven Moroccans live below the poverty line – an improvement on the 1985 figure, which was one in five. About 52% of the population live in rural areas and the rural-urban gap in wealth is considerable. A period of drought during the 1990s accelerated rural-urban migration.

Unrest has largely been avoided owing to Morocco's thriving informal sector. Apart from the illegal hashish trade and the smuggling of alcohol and Western goods, this provides jobs in clothes manufacturing, food processing, goods transport, and the hotel and building trades.

WORLD RANKING

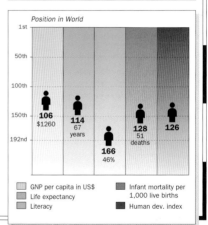

Position in World

1st   50th   100th   150th   192nd

106 $1260   **114** 67 years   **166** 46%   **128** 51 deaths   **126**

GNP per capita in US$	Infant mortality per 1,000 live births
Life expectancy	
Literacy	Human dev. index

M

MOZAMBIQUE

OFFICIAL NAME: Republic of Mozambique   **CAPITAL:** Maputo
POPULATION: 18.7 million   **CURRENCY:** Metical   **OFFICIAL LANGUAGE:** Portuguese

| 1975 | 1975 | June 25 | MOC | +2 | +258 | .mz |

SITUATED ON THE SOUTHEAST African coast, Mozambique is bisected from east to west by the Zambezi River, which is dammed at Cahora Bassa. South of the Zambezi lies a semiarid savanna lowland. The north-central delta provinces around Tete are the most fertile and are home to most of the ethnically diverse population. Following independence in 1975 from Portugal, Mozambique was torn apart by a savage and devastating civil war between the (then Marxist) FRELIMO government and the South African-backed RENAMO. The conflict finally ended in 1992 after UN arbitration. Subsequent multiparty elections returned FRELIMO to government. Massive international aid is devoted to Mozambique's recovery.

CLIMATE ▷ Tropical wet & dry

WEATHER CHART

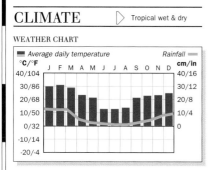

In theory, Mozambique has a rainy and a dry season. However, in the 1980s, frequent failure of the rains contributed to two disastrous famines: in 1982–1984 (when 100,000 died) and in 1986–1987. The coast south of Beira and the highlands adjoining Malawi and Zimbabwe are the wettest areas. The northern coast is dry because the moist trade winds are blocked by Madagascar. The Zambezi valley is the driest region.

TRANSPORTATION ▷ Drive on left

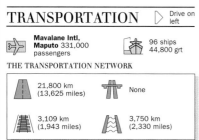

Mavalane Intl, **Maputo** 331,000 passengers

96 ships 44,800 grt

THE TRANSPORTATION NETWORK

21,800 km (13,625 miles)	None	
3,109 km (1,943 miles)	3,750 km (2,330 miles)	

The billion dollar Maputo Corridor, launched in 1995, will reconnect South African industrial centers with the Mozambican coast, and should also facilitate port modernization. The state-owned CFM railway company is cooperating with neighboring states. The national airline is again returning profits. Even so, millions of land mines still hamper access, damaged bridges have yet to be rebuilt, and remote rural communities remain isolated.

Tea picking. *Other important cash crops are cashew nuts, cotton, sugar, copra and citrus fruits. Agriculture employs 85% of workers.*

TOURISM ▷ Not available

Tourism has still not recovered after war

No change due to effects of war

MAIN TOURIST ARRIVALS

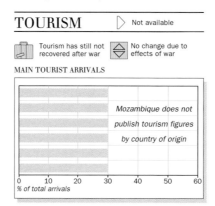

Mozambique does not publish tourism figures by country of origin

In the 1970s the tourist industry drew some 300,000 South Africans and Rhodesians; destroyed by the civil war, it is only slowly being rebuilt. Land mines still render travel outside the capital hazardous, while food shortages, costly international flights, and poor infrastructure are added obstacles.

Given political stability, though, Mozambique could yet exploit its excellent beaches and game reserves, which include the Gorongosa Game Park. There are plans afoot to incorporate reserves into South Africa's much-visited Kruger Park, just across the border. Some foreign hotel groups are once more targeting Maputo as a luxury tourist and conference venue.

PEOPLE ▷ Pop. density low

Makua, Tsonga, Sena, Lomwe, Portuguese

24/km² (62/mi²)

THE URBAN/RURAL POPULATION SPLIT

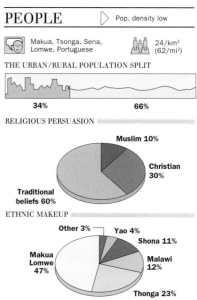

34%   66%

RELIGIOUS PERSUASION

Muslim 10%
Christian 30%
Traditional beliefs 60%

ETHNIC MAKEUP

Other 3%   Yao 4%
Shona 11%
Makua Lomwe 47%
Malawi 12%
Thonga 23%

Mozambique is ethnically diverse, with the large black African majority divided into numerous groups, and tiny minorities of whites, mixed-race groups and Asians. However, the predominant social tensions are regional: RENAMO, strong in the north and central regions, accuses the FRELIMO government of consistently favoring the south. Antiwhite feelings are growing, too, as "Africanists" claim that whites enjoy excessive political influence – incendiary charges in a nation where life expectancy is below 50 years and poverty is endemic.

Mozambican society centers on the extended family. In some provinces, notably Zambezia, Cabo Delgado and Tete, this is matriarchal. Polygamy is fairly widespread among men who can support second wives. FRELIMO pays special attention to women's rights. Many women served in FRELIMO armies, and are now protected by divorce, child-custody and husband-desertion laws. The Mozambican Women's Organization encourages participation in political life.

POPULATION AGE BREAKDOWN

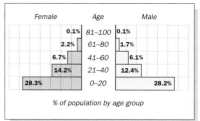

Female	Age	Male
0.1%	81–100	0.1%
2.2%	61–80	1.7%
6.7%	41–60	6.1%
14.2%	21–40	12.4%
28.3%	0–20	28.2%

% of population by age group

M

POLITICS ▷ Multiparty elections

1994/1999

President Joaquim Alberto Chissano

AT THE LAST ELECTION

Assembly of the Republic 250 seats

52% FRELIMO	45% RENAMO	3% UD

FRELIMO = Front for the Liberation of Mozambique
RENAMO = Mozambique National Resistance
UD = Democratic Union

MAIN POLITICAL ISSUES
The move to democracy

In 1993, the UN secured, with difficulty, the $260 million and the 7,500 multinational forces required both to demobilize Mozambique's warring factions and to stage the first democratic elections.

Despite last-minute hitches, elections were held in 1994 which returned FRELIMO to power. However, support for RENAMO was stronger than expected. The former guerrillas won 112 of the 250 seats in the new parliament and in the presidential elections their leader, Afonso Dhlakama, polled 33% of votes cast.

Reconstruction

The government faces an enormous task in rebuilding a country ravaged by civil war, with its toll of 900,000 dead, one million refugees and an estimated 90% of the remaining population living below the poverty line.

Joaquim Chissano, president since 1986, has pushed towards political pluralism.

RENAMO leader, Afonso Dhlakama, has turned from militarism to politics.

PROFILE

Between 1977 and 1990, Mozambique was a one-party state ruled by the Soviet-backed FRELIMO. It had campaigned for independence from Portugal since the 1960s. The then Rhodesia and white South Africa backed anti-Marxist RENAMO rebels, who fought FRELIMO under the guise of seeking democracy.

Changing international realities persuaded FRELIMO to adopt a democratic constitution in 1990. Meanwhile, RENAMO lost its external sponsors. Today little distinguishes the two ideologically. Although FRELIMO is the biggest party in parliament, RENAMO is clearly popular, and demands recognition for its 15 years of struggle. New groups, such as the antiwhite PALMO, COINMO, and UNAMO, have recently emerged; FRELIMO is pushing ahead with plans to decentralize power. But RENAMO's boycott of the 1998 municipal elections rekindled fears for the future of multiparty democracy.

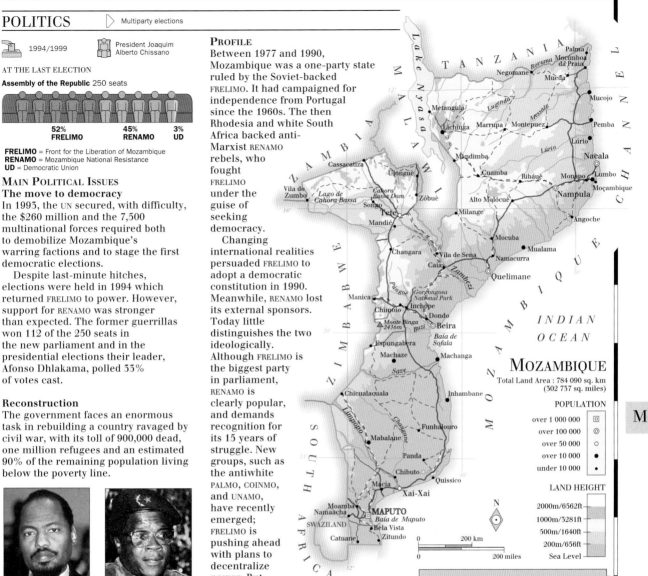

MOZAMBIQUE

Total Land Area : 784 090 sq. km
(302 757 sq. miles)

POPULATION

over 1 000 000	▣
over 100 000	◎
over 50 000	○
over 10 000	●
under 10 000	·

LAND HEIGHT

2000m/6562ft	
1000m/3281ft	
500m/1640ft	
200m/656ft	
Sea Level	

M

WORLD AFFAIRS ▷ Joined UN in 1975

Comm · Lusoph · OAU · OIC · SADC

Mozambique was a key Cold War battleground between Soviet-backed Marxism, and capitalism sponsored by the USA and South Africa. The resultant civil war devastated the country between 1977 and 1992.

In the early 1980s, however, the FRELIMO government's position began to shift as Soviet aid became erratic. Responding to President Samora Machel's overtures, the USA lifted its ban on economic assistance in 1984. Britain agreed to train FRELIMO's forces

in 1987. South Africa continued to support RENAMO until at least 1990, despite its 1984 pledge. Zimbabwean troops helped Mozambique guard the strategically important Beira and Limpopo corridors, but left in 1993.

In 1995, the UN withdrew its 6,000 peacekeepers and a democratic Mozambique joined the Commonwealth, despite having no formal links with the old British Empire. President Chissano became deputy head of the SADC, but regional tensions persisted, with Mozambique accusing South Africans of gun-running, and Swaziland claiming Maputo Province as its own.

CHRONOLOGY

The Portuguese tapped the local trade in slaves, gold, and ivory in the 16th century and made Mozambique a colony in 1752. Large areas were run by private companies until 1929.

❏ **1964** FRELIMO starts war of liberation.

❏ **1975** Independence. Marxist FRELIMO leader Samora Machel is president. Most Portuguese leave, but destroy much transport and machinery.

❏ **1976** Resistance movement RENAMO set up inside Mozambique by Rhodesians.

❏ **1976–1980** Mozambique closes Rhodesian border and supports Zimbabwean freedom fighters. Reprisals by RENAMO.

❏ **1980** South Africa takes over backing of RENAMO. ⇨

CHRONOLOGY *continued*

❑ **1982** Zimbabwean troops arrive to guard Mutare–Beira corridor.
❑ **1984** Nkomati Accord: South Africa agrees to stop support for RENAMO, and Mozambique for ANC. Ineffectual. Fighting continues.
❑ **1986** RENAMO declares war on Zimbabwe. Tanzanian troops support FRELIMO. Machel dies in mysterious air crash in South Africa. Joaquim Chissano replaces him.
❑ **1988** Nkomati Accord reactivated. Mozambicans allowed back to work in South African mines.
❑ **1989** War and malnutrition said to claim 1,000,000 lives. FRELIMO drops Marxism-Leninism.
❑ **1990** Multipartyism and free-market economy in new constitution. RENAMO breaches cease-fire.
❑ **1992** Chissano and RENAMO's leader, Afonso Dhlakama, sign peace agreement.
❑ **1994** Democratic elections return FRELIMO to power.
❑ **1995** Joins Commonwealth; launches economic reforms.
❑ **1998** RENAMO boycotts municipal elections.
❑ **1999** G7 chooses Mozambique as flagship for international debt relief initiative.

AID

 Recipient

$963m (receipts)   Up 4% 1996-1997

Mozambique is the world's second most aid-dependent country. Aid accounts for fully 60% of national earnings, and pays for the food needs of some seven million citizens. In 1999, Mozambique became one of only four countries to receive the G7 debt relief scheme for HIPC nations, which is worth nearly $3 billion. The main donor states are Italy, the UK, the USA, Sweden, Denmark, the Netherlands, Norway and, recently, South Africa. Debts from earlier Soviet aid have been written off.

DEFENSE

Compulsory military service

$72m   Up 13% in 1997

The military's role in society has greatly diminished since 1992.

During the civil war the armed forces swallowed some 40% of state income annually; by 1994 that figure stood at a little over 5%. Military figures, once prominent in the FRELIMO government, have been largely stripped of political influence. The new post-peace, British-trained permanent army was formally inaugurated in August 1994. Truly national in character, and now only some 3–5,000 strong, it consists of both former government and RENAMO troops. A byproduct of reorganization was the demobilization of some 75,000 battle-hardened soldiers. Their severance pay ended in mid-1996, and it has not been easy to retrain them, or reintegrate them into civilian life. Some have turned to banditry.

The war's end also saw the departure of external forces, such as the Zimbabwean troops who once guarded strategic railroads against RENAMO attack, and about 6,000 UN peacekeepers.

MOZAMBICAN ARMED FORCES

80 main battle tanks 100 T-54/55	5,000 personnel
3 patrol boats	100 personnel
No combat aircraft	1,000 personnel
None	

ECONOMICS

Inflation 51% p.a. (1985–1996)

$2.41bn   11,495–12,317 meticals

SCORE CARD

❑ WORLD GNP RANKING 132nd
❑ GNP PER CAPITA $140
❑ BALANCE OF PAYMENTS....................$–359m
❑ INFLATION 5.5%
❑ UNEMPLOYMENT....................................50%

EXPORTS

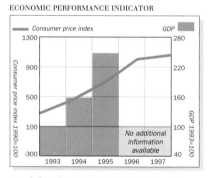

Japan 7%
Portugal 10%
Other 39%
USA 11%
South Africa 13%
Spain 20%

IMPORTS

UAE 4%
USA 4%
Portugal 4%
Zimbabwe 8%
South Africa 51%
Other 29%

ECONOMIC PERFORMANCE INDICATOR

Consumer price index — GDP

Consumer price index 1990=100 / GDP 1993=100

No additional information available

1993 1994 1995 1996 1997

STRENGTHS

Following IMF advice, the government has adopted privatization, exchange rate reforms and trade liberalization, enabling Mozambique to attract aid, increase exports, reduce inflation and maintain a 6% growth rate. Massive rural development programs target agriculture, employing 85% of the workforce. The fisheries industry has great potential. Maputo was modernized in 1989, and improved transport links will help it to service southern Africa's landlocked regions.

WEAKNESSES

Mozambique's economy remains fragile. Overseas aid is essential to prevent at least half the population starving. Over-dependence on foreign donors and companies is another long-term concern. Mozambique is susceptible to drought and cyclones. Destroyed transport links hinder the exploitation of minerals. Skilled workers often choose to work in other countries; their absence has delayed the return to normal economic activity.

PROFILE

Mozambique's enormous problems are further exacerbated by the failure of the socialist model in industry and agriculture. However, with peace assured and buoyed by aid pledges of $780 million, the government in 1995 produced an optimistic plan, based on World Bank recommendations, to eradicate poverty and raise annual GDP growth to 8–9% by 2000.

MOZAMBIQUE : MAJOR BUSINESSES

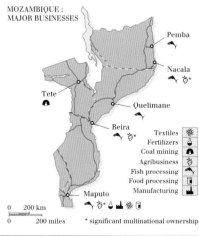

Pemba
Nacala
Tete
Quelimane
Beira
Textiles
Fertilizers
Coal mining
Agribusiness
Fish processing
Food processing
Manufacturing
Maputo

0   200 km
0   200 miles   * significant multinational ownership

RESOURCES

 Electric power 2.4m kw

26,870 tonnes

Not an oil producer and has no refineries

1.3m cattle, 388,000 goats, 176,000 pigs

Coal, iron, tantalite, uranium, gold, diamonds, copper,

ELECTRICITY GENERATION

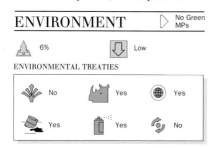

Hydro 9% (0.05bn kwh)

Combustion 91% (0.5bn kwh)

Nuclear 0%

Other 0%

% of total generation by type

Mozambique's mineral reserves of coal, iron, bauxite, uranium, and natural gas are under-exploited, due to poor means of transport. Cotton seems set to overtake cashew nuts as the chief crop. Fishing is a vital sector, with shrimps a lucrative export. Electricity supplies are being restored.

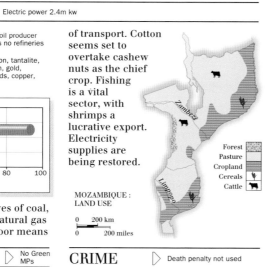

MOZAMBIQUE : LAND USE

Forest
Pasture
Cropland
Cereals
Cattle

0   200 km
0   200 miles

ENVIRONMENT

No Green MPs

6%

Low

ENVIRONMENTAL TREATIES

No

Yes

Yes

Yes

Yes

No

Perennial floods followed by droughts are often devastating. A three-year drought between 1982 and 1984 killed 100,000 and left four million close to starvation. Then in 1984 massive flooding left 50,000 homeless and destroyed harvests. War pushed rural populations towards the cities and coasts, resulting in overcrowding, disease, water pollution, and desertification from abandoned farms. RENAMO slaughtered an estimated 50,000 elephants for ivory to help fund its war effort. However, ecological concerns are still low on the political agenda.

MEDIA

TV ownership low

Daily newspaper circulation 3 per 1,000 people

PUBLISHING AND BROADCAST MEDIA

There are 2 daily newspapers. *Notícias* and *Diário de Moçambique*

1 state-owned service

1 state-owned, 3 independent stations

The press, traditionally a FRELIMO publicity machine, has enjoyed greater freedom since the 1990 constitution and 1994 multiparty elections. In 1999, however, one editor resigned, citing editorial restrictions. With just three TV sets per 1,000 people, the political impact of television is minimal.

CRIME

Death penalty not used

Mozambique does not publish prison figures

Crime levels are rising

CRIME RATES

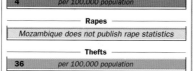

Murders

4   *per 100,000 population*

Rapes

Mozambique does not publish rape statistics

Thefts

36   *per 100,000 population*

Mozambique is awash with weapons. Banditry, often carried out by former soldiers, is endemic. Senior officials are accused of misappropriating food aid and failing to stop drug smuggling.

EDUCATION

School leaving age: 14

41%

7,143 students

Civil war completely disrupted education between 1983 and 1990.

THE EDUCATION SYSTEM

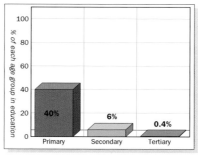

% of each age group in education

40%   6%   0.4%

Primary   Secondary   Tertiary

To safeguard Mozambique's long-term recovery, the government increased education's share of the budget to 18.2% in 1998. Targeting rural areas especially, Maputo hopes that by 2000 at least 86% of children will get an education. Currently, only 6% attend secondary schools.

HEALTH

Welfare state health benefits

1 per 50,000 people

Tuberculosis, gastroenteric infections, pneumonia

Thousands lost limbs from land mines, or suffered other appalling injuries and psychological trauma, during the savage civil war. Happily, since it ended, health services have improved. Preventive medicines and antenatal care are provided free. Doctors serve a mandatory two years in rural areas. Many private clinics have been established since 1987. However, in 1999 cholera, a lingering by-product of war, was reported in Beira, and in Niassa, Cabo Delgado, and Nampula provinces. An estimated one million of the population have AIDS.

SPENDING

GDP/cap. no increase

CONSUMPTION AND SPENDING

0 per 1,000 population

4 per 1,000 population

Defense 3.9%

Education 6.2%

Health 4.4%

0   5   10   15   20   25

Defense, Health, Education spending as % of GDP

Mozambique is one of the world's poorest countries, with GNP per capita estimated at under $150. Over 90% of the population live below the breadline. Measures adopted to attract Western aid have made conditions tougher, raising the price of rice by 600%. The recent export boom has generally bypassed the traditional subsistence farmer. If poverty persists, some fear a backlash by unreconstructed FRELIMO Marxists. Only the higher echelons of FRELIMO, RENAMO and the other political parties acquire luxuries. Free-market reform, however, is gradually increasing access to consumer goods.

WORLD RANKING

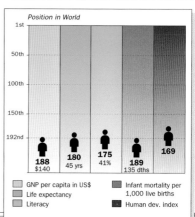

Position in World

1st
50th
100th
150th
192nd

188   180   175   189   169
$140   45 yrs 41%   135 dths

GNP per capita in US$
Life expectancy
Literacy

Infant mortality per 1,000 live births
Human dev. index

M

NAMIBIA

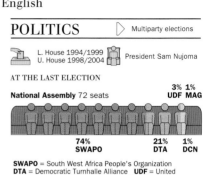

SOUTHERN AFRICA

OFFICIAL NAME: The Republic of Namibia   CAPITAL: Windhoek
POPULATION: 1.7 million   CURRENCY: Namibian dollar   OFFICIAL LANGUAGE: English

| 1990 | 1994 | March 21 | NAM | +2 | +264 | .na |

LOCATED IN SOUTHWESTERN AFRICA, Namibia has an arid coastal strip formed by the Namib Desert. After many years of guerrilla warfare, Namibia achieved independence from South Africa in 1990. Despite the move away from apartheid, Namibia's economy remains reliant on the expertise of the small white population, a legacy of the previously poor education for blacks. Namibia is Africa's fourth-largest minerals producer.

CLIMATE   ▷ Hot desert/steppe

WEATHER CHART

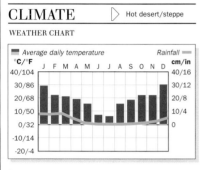

Namibia is almost rainless. The coast is usually shrouded in thick, cold fog unless the hot, very dry *berg* blows.

TRANSPORTATION   ▷ Drive on left

Windhoek Intl
258,373 passengers

114 ships
58,591 grt

THE TRANSPORTATION NETWORK

| 5,010 km (3,113 miles) | None |
| 2,382 km (1,480 miles) | None |

Large-scale industry is well served by road and rail. Plans exist to build a new harbor at Walvis Bay.

TOURISM   ▷ Visitors : population 1:4.1

410,000 visitors   Up 61% in 1997

MAIN TOURIST ARRIVALS

| South Africa 61% |
| Germany 12% |
| Angola 5% |
| Other 22% |

0 10 20 30 40 50 60 70 80
% of total arrivals

Tourists, largely from South Africa, make a very limited contribution to GDP. German tourists Windhoek's German sector. There are plans to limit tourists to 300,000 a year to preserve Namibia's fragile desert ecology.

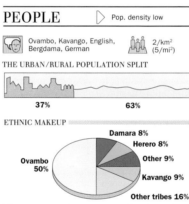

Spitzkoppe, west of Karibib. *Unique scenery such as this is attracting increasing numbers of eco-tourists to Namibia.*

PEOPLE   ▷ Pop. density low

Ovambo, Kavango, English, Bergdama, German   2/km² (5/mi²)

THE URBAN/RURAL POPULATION SPLIT

37%   63%

ETHNIC MAKEUP

Ovambo 50%
Damara 8%
Herero 8%
Other 9%
Kavango 9%
Other tribes 16%

The largest ethnic group, the Ovambo, tend to live in the sparsely populated north of the country. Whites – 60% of whom speak Afrikaans – are concentrated in Windhoek, which is home to a wealthy century-old German community. Namibia's original inhabitants, the San and Khoi (once called Bushmen) now constitute a tiny, marginalized minority.

The ethnic strife predicted in 1990 has not materialized. For the most part, black Namibians, predominantly subsistence farmers, have accepted the greater wealth of the white community. Families are large in Namibia; many black women have six or more children. The constitution supports sexual equality and discriminates in favor of women; few, however, have official jobs or own property.

POLITICS   ▷ Multiparty elections

L. House 1994/1999
U. House 1998/2004   President Sam Nujoma

AT THE LAST ELECTION

National Assembly 72 seats

74% SWAPO   21% DTA   1% DCN   3% UDF   1% MAG

SWAPO = South West Africa People's Organization
DTA = Democratic Turnhalle Alliance   **UDF** = United Democratic Front   **MAG** = Monitor Action Group
DCN = Democratic Coalition of Namibia
Six additional non-voting members may be appointed to the National Assembly by the President.

National Council 26 seats

Two members are elected by each of the 13 Regional Councils to the National Council.

SWAPO guerrillas fought for, and won independence from South Africa in 1990, when Namibia switched from apartheid to a multiparty democracy. SWAPO has since dominated the National Assembly. Its main support comes from the Ovambo community, although its center-left stance also appeals to state employees.

Despite launching programs to create jobs, improve schools and redress poverty, SWAPO has not yet eradicated Namibia's wealth inequalities. Land reform is behind schedule, whites still control most of the economy, and black unemployment remains high. In 1998 a constitutional amendment allowed President Nujoma to run for a third term. SWAPO's main opposition comes from the center-right DTA, a coalition of 11 parties favoring a free-market approach.

WORLD AFFAIRS   ▷ Joined UN in 1990

| Comm | Comesa | NAM | OAU | SADC |

In 1992, South Africa settled its border dispute with Namibia, and in 1994 it relinquished control of Walvis Bay – Namibia's only deep-water port. South Africa has also written off Namibia's earlier debts. Namibian troops are deployed in a monitoring role in conflict-ridden Congo (former Zaire).

AID   ▷ Recipient

US$166m (receipts)   Down 12% 1996-1997

The UN provides most aid; Germany is the main unilateral donor. Around one-third of aid is spent on education.

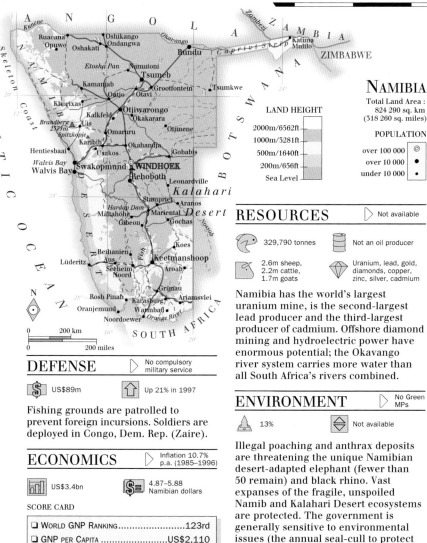

NAMIBIA

Total Land Area :
824 290 sq. km
(318 260 sq. miles)

LAND HEIGHT

2000m/6562ft
1000m/3281ft
500m/1640ft
200m/656ft
Sea Level

POPULATION

over 100 000 ◎
over 10 000 ●
under 10 000 ·

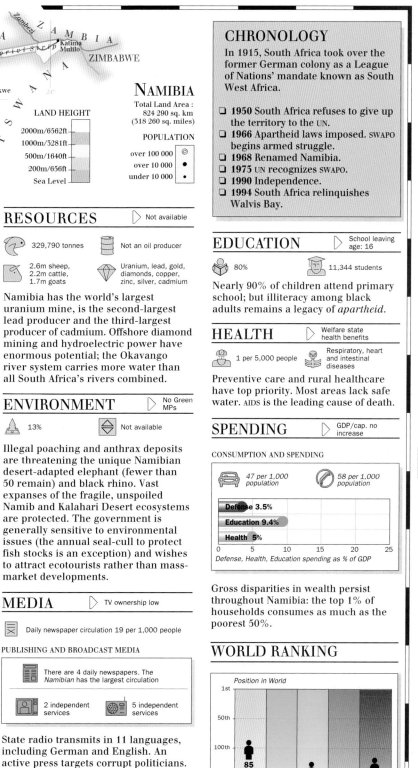

CHRONOLOGY

In 1915, South Africa took over the former German colony as a League of Nations' mandate known as South West Africa.

- ❑ **1950** South Africa refuses to give up the territory to the UN.
- ❑ **1966** Apartheid laws imposed. SWAPO begins armed struggle.
- ❑ **1968** Renamed Namibia.
- ❑ **1973** UN recognizes SWAPO.
- ❑ **1990** Independence.
- ❑ **1994** South Africa relinquishes Walvis Bay.

DEFENSE

▷ No compulsory military service

💲 US$89m

⬆ Up 21% in 1997

Fishing grounds are patrolled to prevent foreign incursions. Soldiers are deployed in Congo, Dem. Rep. (Zaire).

ECONOMICS

▷ Inflation 10.7% p.a. (1985–1996)

US$3.4bn

4.87–5.88 Namibian dollars

SCORE CARD

- ❑ WORLD GNP RANKING........................123rd
- ❑ GNP PER CAPITA ....US$2,110
- ❑ BALANCE OF PAYMENTS ....US$193m
- ❑ INFLATION 8.8%
- ❑ UNEMPLOYMENT...................................30%

STRENGTHS

Varied mineral resources: third-wealthiest country in sub-Saharan Africa. Vibrant stock exchange, export processing zones and tax breaks. Rich fishing grounds. Potential of Walvis Bay as conduit for landlocked neighbors.

WEAKNESSES

Most manufactured goods imported. Sensitivity to fluctuations in mineral prices. Recessionary ripple effect due to currency pegging with South African rand. Lack of skilled labor; high unemployment. Severe drought in 1996.

IMPORTS/EXPORTS

Namibia has yet to publish official trade figures. South Africa remains the major source of imports and destination for exports.

RESOURCES

▷ Not available

329,790 tonnes

Not an oil producer

2.6m sheep, 2.2m cattle, 1.7m goats

Uranium, lead, gold, diamonds, copper, zinc, silver, cadmium

Namibia has the world's largest uranium mine, is the second-largest lead producer and the third-largest producer of cadmium. Offshore diamond mining and hydroelectric power have enormous potential; the Okavango river system carries more water than all South Africa's rivers combined.

ENVIRONMENT

▷ No Green MPs

13%

Not available

Illegal poaching and anthrax deposits are threatening the unique Namibian desert-adapted elephant (fewer than 50 remain) and black rhino. Vast expanses of the fragile, unspoiled Namib and Kalahari Desert ecosystems are protected. The government is generally sensitive to environmental issues (the annual seal-cull to protect fish stocks is an exception) and wishes to attract ecotourists rather than mass-market developments.

MEDIA

▷ TV ownership low

Daily newspaper circulation 19 per 1,000 people

PUBLISHING AND BROADCAST MEDIA

There are 4 daily newspapers. The *Namibian* has the largest circulation

2 independent services

5 independent services

State radio transmits in 11 languages, including German and English. An active press targets corrupt politicians.

CRIME

▷ Death penalty not used

Namibia does not publish prison figures

Crime is rising, particularly in urban areas

Burglary and theft are rising, particularly in urban areas. Ostrich smuggling to the USA is common.

EDUCATION

▷ School leaving age: 16

80%

11,344 students

Nearly 90% of children attend primary school; but illiteracy among black adults remains a legacy of *apartheid*.

HEALTH

▷ Welfare state health benefits

1 per 5,000 people

Respiratory, heart and intestinal diseases

Preventive care and rural healthcare have top priority. Most areas lack safe water. AIDS is the leading cause of death.

SPENDING

▷ GDP/cap. no increase

CONSUMPTION AND SPENDING

47 per 1,000 population

58 per 1,000 population

Defense 3.5%
Education 9.4%
Health 5%

0   5   10   15   20   25
Defense, Health, Education spending as % of GDP

Gross disparities in wealth persist throughout Namibia: the top 1% of households consumes as much as the poorest 50%.

WORLD RANKING

Position in World

1st
50th
100th
150th
192nd

85 $2110

159 52 years

122 80%

140 65 deaths

115

GNP per capita in US$
Life expectancy
Literacy

Infant mortality per 1,000 live births
Human dev. index

N

NAURU

OFFICIAL NAME: The Republic of Nauru   **CAPITAL:** *No official capital*
POPULATION: 11,000   **CURRENCY:** Australian dollar   **OFFICIAL LANGUAGE:** Nauruan

PACIFIC OCEAN

| 1968 | 1968 | Jan 31 | NAU | +12 | +674 | | .nr |

N AURU, THE WORLD'S smallest republic, lies in the
Pacific, 4,000 km (2,480 miles) northeast of Australia.
A former British colony, Nauru was exploited for its phosphate by the UK,
Australia, and New Zealand. After independence in 1968, the phosphates
industry made Nauruan citizens among the wealthiest in the world, but
economic mismanagement and the approaching end of phosphate reserves
left Nauru facing ruin in the late 1990s, prompting economic reform.

CLIMATE ▷ Tropical oceanic

WEATHER CHART

Nauru's tiny size means that rain
clouds often miss the island; at times
years pass without rain.

TRANSPORTATION ▷ Drive on left

✈ **Nauru Island Intl**   🚢 3 ships 1,000 grt

THE TRANSPORTATION NETWORK

| 🛣 16 km (10 miles) | | None |
| 🚃 5 km (3 miles) | | None |

Nauru operates its own airline with a
Boeing 737 piloted by Australians. The
Nauru Steamship Line is Nauru's main
link with the outside world. However,
all external travel is very expensive.
Nauru has no harbor, so ships
loading phosphates have to dock
with engines still running on
huge concrete caissons
floating out at sea. The
single circular road is
often littered with
abandoned cars, such
as Mercedes, as it has
been much cheaper
for Nauruans to
import new vehicles
than to attempt to
repair existing
ones. The number
of car accident
fatalities is one of
the highest in the
South Pacific.

TOURISM ▷ Not available

🧳 Minimal tourist arrivals   ⇕ Little variation from year to year

MAIN TOURIST ARRIVALS

Nauru does not publish tourism figures by country of origin

Even if Nauru had any conventional
tourist attractions, the enormous cost of
getting there would dissuade most
tourists from making the journey. The
main feature of interest on the island is
the bizarre lunar landscape created by
over 80 years of phosphate extraction.
There are no beaches on Nauru and
only a few basic hotels.

NAURU

Total Land Area : 21.2 sq. km (8.2 sq. miles)

LAND HEIGHT
- 200m/565ft
- Sea Level

▢ Urban area
⋯ Phosphate mineworks

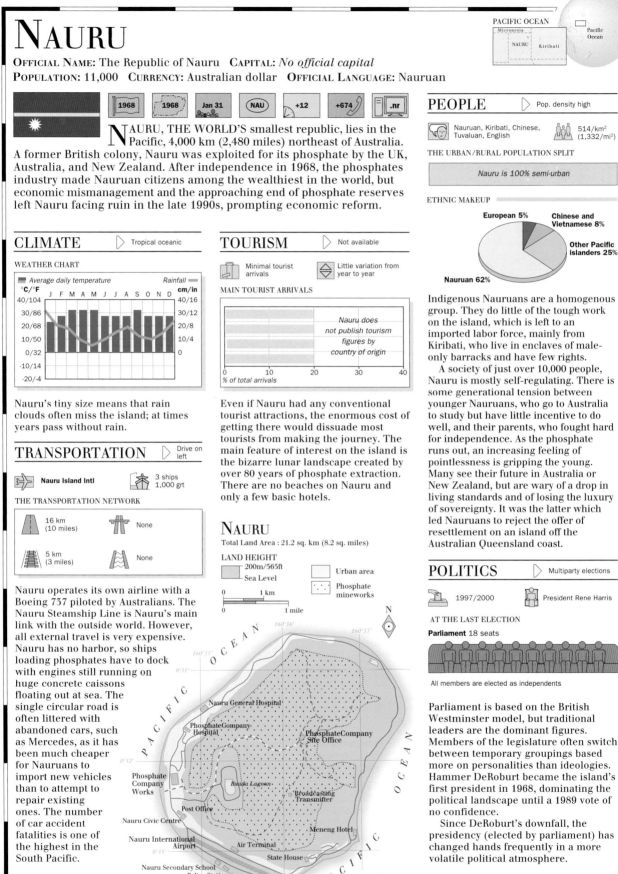

PEOPLE ▷ Pop. density high

Nauruan, Kiribati, Chinese, Tuvaluan, English   514/km² (1,332/mi²)

THE URBAN/RURAL POPULATION SPLIT

Nauru is 100% semi-urban

ETHNIC MAKEUP

- European 5%
- Chinese and Vietnamese 8%
- Other Pacific islanders 25%
- Nauruan 62%

Indigenous Nauruans are a homogenous
group. They do little of the tough work
on the island, which is left to an
imported labor force, mainly from
Kiribati, who live in enclaves of male-
only barracks and have few rights.

A society of just over 10,000 people,
Nauru is mostly self-regulating. There is
some generational tension between
younger Nauruans, who go to Australia
to study but have little incentive to do
well, and their parents, who fought hard
for independence. As the phosphate
runs out, an increasing feeling of
pointlessness is gripping the young.
Many see their future in Australia or
New Zealand, but are wary of a drop in
living standards and of losing the luxury
of sovereignty. It was the latter which
led Nauruans to reject the offer of
resettlement on an island off the
Australian Queensland coast.

POLITICS ▷ Multiparty elections

1997/2000   President Rene Harris

AT THE LAST ELECTION

Parliament 18 seats

All members are elected as independents

Parliament is based on the British
Westminster model, but traditional
leaders are the dominant figures.
Members of the legislature often switch
between temporary groupings based
more on personalities than ideologies.
Hammer DeRoburt became the island's
first president in 1968, dominating the
political landscape until a 1989 vote of
no confidence.

Since DeRoburt's downfall, the
presidency (elected by parliament) has
changed hands frequently in a more
volatile political atmosphere.

N

WORLD AFFAIRS

Joined UN in 1999

| Comm | SPC | SPF | ADB | UN |

The case for compensation for phosphate exploitation brought by Nauru against the UK government was rejected in 1992 after the longest suit in British legal history. However, an Australian settlement in 1993 brought payments eventually totaling A$107 million. Nauru's main concern is participation in the South Pacific Forum and the management of trust funds to support Nauruans when phosphate deposits run out. Nauru joined the UN in 1999. It seeks a voice on environmental issues.

AID

Recipient

US$3m (receipts)　　No change 1996–1997

Nauru is neither an aid recipient nor donor, except as a member of the South Pacific Forum (SPF).

DEFENSE

No compulsory military service

Australia responsible for defense　　Not applicable

Nauru, which faces no outside threats, has no defense force. Australia, under a de facto arrangement, is responsible for the island's security.

ECONOMICS

Not available

US$80m　　1.53–1.63 Australian dollars

SCORE CARD

❑ WORLD GNP RANKING	187th
❑ GNP PER CAPITA	US$7,270
❑ BALANCE OF PAYMENTS	Not available
❑ INFLATION	Low inflation rate
❑ UNEMPLOYMENT	Minimal unemployment

STRENGTHS

Considerable investments in Australian and Hawaiian property and hotels. Possible future as a tax haven.

WEAKNESSES

Phosphate has been virtually exhausted; past mining has left 80% of the island uninhabitable and uncultivable. Nauru, prone to poor investments, faced ruin in the late 1990s, prompting economic reform. Some losses were recouped in 1996 by suing its legal advisers. "Concrete cancer" in the Nauru House flagship skyscraper in Melbourne cost millions of dollars to repair.

IMPORT/EXPORTS

Nauru's only export commodity is phosphates, in which it trades with Australia and New Zealand. Almost all food, drinking water and manufactured goods are imported, mostly from Australia, New Zealand, the UK and Japan.

RESOURCES

Electric power 10,000 kw

400 tonnes　　Not an oil producer

2.1 million sheep 2,800 pigs, 5,000 chickens　　Guano (phosphates)

Since 1888 Nauru has been exploited by the Germans, British, Australians, New Zealanders, and recently by Nauruans themselves, for its valuable phosphate reserves. Extraction has destroyed 80% of the island, and the deposits have been virtually exhausted. Nauru has no other resources. The island is entirely dependent on outside energy supplies and the cost of oil is over 50% higher than the Pacific average, since Nauru does not lie on any shipping routes. Most electricity is produced by small diesel generators.

ENVIRONMENT

No Green MPs

None　　Not available

The main concern is contamination from the former French nuclear test sites in the Pacific: Nauru lies downwind of these. Ecological awareness has been minimal as Nauruans' source of wealth has effectively destroyed their island. A rehabilitation program is planned.

MEDIA

TV ownership low

There are no daily newspapers

PUBLISHING AND BROADCAST MEDIA

There are no daily newspapers. *The Bulletin* is published weekly

1 state-owned service　　1 state-owned service

Nauru has one national TV broadcasting service; some overseas programs are made available on video.

CRIME

Death penalty not used

Nauru does not publish prison figures　　Crime levels are rising slightly

Theft is almost nonexistent. Assaults and dangerous driving as a result of drunkenness are the major problems.

Nauru is almost circular with a single, 16-km ring road. The overcrowded coastal strip is the sole habitable land.

CHRONOLOGY

Colonized by Germany in 1888, from 1919 the island was administered jointly by the UK, Australia, and New Zealand.

- ❑ **1968** Independence.
- ❑ **1970** Gains phosphate control.
- ❑ **1992** Australia agrees compensation for phosphate extraction.

EDUCATION

School leaving age: 16

99%　　Not available

Many Nauruans attend boarding school in Australia from a young age. Few go on to university.

HEALTH

Welfare state health benefits

1 per 700 people　　Tuberculosis, vitamin deficiencies, diabetes

A diet of processed imported foods and widespread obesity are the major problems. One-third of the population suffers from non-insulin-dependent diabetes. Industrial accidents are treated in Australia.

SPENDING

GDP/cap. no increase

CONSUMPTION AND SPENDING

No data　　157 per 1,000 population

Defense	No data
Education	No data
Health	No data

0　　5　　10　　15　　20　　25
Defense, Health, Education spending as % of GDP

Nauru is carrying out a major economic adjustment program, to be funded by the Asian Development Bank. The program should allow Nauru to adjust to the loss of income when the phosphate reserves are exhausted.

WORLD RANKING

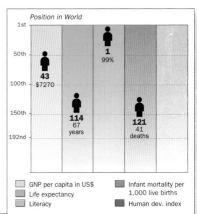

Position in World

1st · 50th · 100th · 150th · 192nd

43 $7270 · 1 99% · 114 67 years · 121 41 deaths

GNP per capita in US$　　Infant mortality per 1,000 live births
Life expectancy　　Human dev. index
Literacy

N

NEPAL

OFFICIAL NAME: Kingdom of Nepal   CAPITAL: Kathmandu
POPULATION: 23.2 million   CURRENCY: Nepalese rupee   OFFICIAL LANGUAGE: Nepali

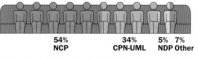

ON THE SHOULDER of the southern Himalayas, Nepal is surrounded by India and China. It is one of the poorest countries in the world, and its largely agricultural economy is heavily dependent on the prompt arrival of the monsoon. New sources of income are now being developed, including hydroelectric power and tourism. In 1991, democratic elections were held for the first time since 1959, marking the end of a period of absolute rule by the king.

CLIMATE
▷ Mountain/subtropical

WEATHER CHART

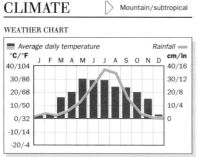

The warm July to October monsoon affects the whole country, causing flooding in the hot Terai plain, but generally decreases northward and westward. The rest of the year is dry, sunny and mild, except in the Himalayas, where valley temperatures in winter may average -10°C (14°F).

TRANSPORTATION
▷ Drive on left

Tribhuvan International, Kathmandu
800,000 passengers

Has no fleet

THE TRANSPORTATION NETWORK

3,436 km (2,135 miles)	None
101km (63 miles)	None

Domestic flights link the main towns. There are paved roads in the south and in the Kathmandu valley; only one runs north to China. Two short stretches of railroad cross into India.

Himalayan harvest. *The steep mountainsides and easily eroded soils mean that most fields are terraced. 90% of Nepalese are farmers.*

TOURISM
▷ Visitors : population 1:55

418,000 visitors

Up 15% 1995–1997

MAIN TOURIST ARRIVALS

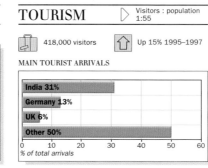

India 31%
Germany 13%
UK 6%
Other 50%
% of total arrivals

A serious conflict exists between the wish to preserve the environment and the desire for tourist revenue. Areas in the northwest were opened up to tourists in 1989, but degradation caused by 72,000 trekkers a year on popular routes forced the government to set up the Annapurna Conservation Project. Fuelwood cutting for tourists is said to have increased deforestation, and hence soil erosion, by 10%.

PEOPLE
▷ Pop. density medium

Nepali, Maithilli, Bhojpuri

170/km² (439/mi²)

THE URBAN/RURAL POPULATION SPLIT

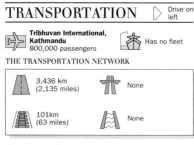

14%   86%

RELIGIOUS PERSUASION

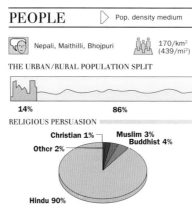

Christian 1%   Muslim 3%
Other 2%   Buddhist 4%

Hindu 90%

There are few tensions among different ethnic groups such as the Sherpas in the north, the inhabitants of the Terai in the south and the Newars of the Kathmandu valley. Hindu women are more restricted than Sherpas and Buddhists. Polygamy is practiced in the hills. Since 1990, thousands of ethnic Nepalese refugees from Bhutan have settled in the country.

POLITICS
▷ Multiparty elections

L. House 1999/2004
U House 1999/2001

HM King Birendra Bir Bikram Shah Deva

AT THE LAST ELECTION

House of Representatives 205 seats

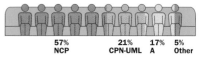

54% NCP   34% CPN-UML   5% 7% NDP Other

NCP = Nepali Congress Party **CPN-UML** = Communist Party of Nepal-United Marxist-Leninist **NDP** = National Democratic Party **A** = Appointed

National Council 60 seats

57% NCP   21% CPN-UML   17% A   5% Other

The end of absolute monarchy and the end of the party-less *panchayat* system in 1990, led to the country's first multiparty elections being held in 1991 which were won by the NCP. In 1994, Nepal had its first communist government, controlled by the Unified Marxist-Leninist Party (UML), which resigned a year later. There followed a series of unstable coalitions. A government was formed by Krishna Prasad Bhattarai after the NCP's general election victory in May 1999.

WORLD AFFAIRS
▷ Joined UN in 1955

CP   IBRD   NAM   SAARC   ADB

Nepal's security relations with India were under review by the pro-Chinese UML government. The NCP government has revived close links with India, on which Nepal depends for its external trade. Relations with Bhutan are strained over the issue of Bhutanese refugees in Nepal.

AID
▷ Recipient

$414m (receipts)

Up 3% 1996–1997

Nepal's strategic position has made it a focus for powerful donors, including the USA, China, India, Japan, and member states of the CIS.

DEFENSE
▷ No compulsory military service

$42m

Up 8% in 1997

The army, 46,000 strong, is small. It has no tanks, combat aircraft or armed helicopters. The limited weaponry comes from the UK and India.

N

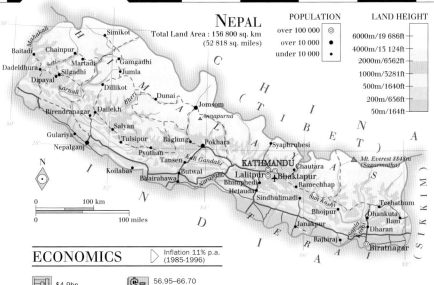

NEPAL

Total Land Area : 136 800 sq. km
(52 818 sq. miles)

POPULATION

over 100 000	◎
over 10 000	●
under 10 000	·

LAND HEIGHT

6000m/19 686ft
4000m/13 124ft
2000m/6562ft
1000m/3281ft
500m/1640ft
200m/656ft
50m/164ft

CHRONOLOGY

The foundations of the Nepalese state were laid in 1769, when King Prithvi Narayan Shah conquered the region.

- ❑ **1816–1923** Establishment of quasi-British protectorate.
- ❑ **1959** First multiparty constitution.
- ❑ **1960** King Mahendra bans political parties and suspends the constitution.
- ❑ **1962** *Panchayat* system launched.
- ❑ **1991** Multiparty elections won by NCP.
- ❑ **1994** Election of first UML communist government.
- ❑ **1995–1997** UML government replaced by NCP, in turn replaced by UML-led coalition.
- ❑ **1998** Ruling coalition splits. NCP forms short-lived government.
- ❑ **1999** NCP election victory: Krishna Prasad Bhattarai prime minister.

ECONOMICS

▷ Inflation 11% p.a. (1985-1996)

$4.9bn

56.95–66.70 Nepalese rupees

SCORE CARD

❑ WORLD GNP RANKING	108th
❑ GNP PER CAPITA	$220
❑ BALANCE OF PAYMENTS	$-418m
❑ INFLATION	2.9%
❑ UNEMPLOYMENT	5%

STRENGTHS

Self-sufficiency in grain most years. Economic liberalization under NCP government. Potential for hydroelectric power generation. Low debt level.

WEAKNESSES

Agricultural dependency: only 10% of GDP from manufacturing. Landlocked status. Low savings rate. Absence of active entrepreneurial class.

EXPORTS

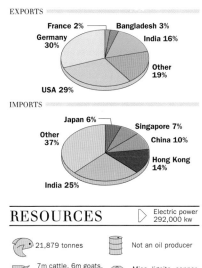

France 2%
Bangladesh 3%
Germany 30%
India 16%
Other 19%
USA 29%

IMPORTS

Japan 6%
Singapore 7%
Other 37%
China 10%
Hong Kong 14%
India 25%

RESOURCES

▷ Electric power 292,000 kw

21,879 tonnes

Not an oil producer

7m cattle, 6m goats, 870,000 sheep, 725,000 pigs

Mica, lignite, copper, cobalt, iron

The Mahakali River project, developed under an agreement signed with India in 1996, will boost hydro-resources.

ENVIRONMENT

▷ No Green MPs

8% (1% partially protected)

Low

Deforestation and soil erosion are serious problems. The native tiger is fast disappearing. In 1995, the World Bank canceled funding for the Arun III hydroelectric project, east of Kathmandu, on environmental grounds.

MEDIA

▷ TV ownership low

Daily newspaper circulation 11 per 1,000 people

PUBLISHING AND BROADCAST MEDIA

There are 29 daily newspapers, including the leading *Gorkhapatra*, *Nepal Hindi Daily* and *Rising Nepal*

1 limited state-owned service

1 state-owned service

The Nepal TV service began broadcasting in 1985, and 18% of the country now receives it. The press is mainly Kathmandu-based with low circulations. The *Sunday Dispatch* is the paper most critical of government.

CRIME

▷ Death penalty not used

Nepal does not publish prison figures

Up 233% from 1992–1996

Petty theft and smuggling are the main problems. The legal provision for detention without trial is used and police suppression of demonstrations is often brutal.

EDUCATION

▷ School leaving age: 11

38%

99,300 students

Over 80% of boys attend school in Nepal, but still only a minority of girls. Nepal's literacy rate is among the lowest in the world.

HEALTH

▷ Welfare state health benefits

1 per 12,500 people

Respiratory and diarrheal diseases, maternal deaths

There are about 100 *dharmi-jhankri* (faith healers) for every health worker. Maternal mortality is high, the result of harmful traditional birth practices; a reeducation program for midwives has been established.

SPENDING

▷ GDP/cap. no increase

CONSUMPTION AND SPENDING

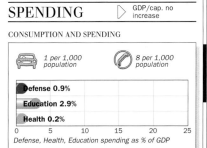

1 per 1,000 population

8 per 1,000 population

Defense 0.9%
Education 2.9%
Health 0.2%

0   5   10   15   20   25
Defense, Health, Education spending as % of GDP

Nepal is one of the poorest countries in the world. Average income per head is only $220 a year.

WORLD RANKING

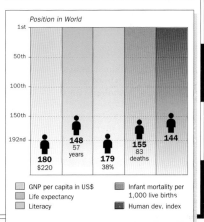

Position in World

1st
50th
100th
150th
192nd

180   $220
148   57 years
179   38%
155   83 deaths
144

▢ GNP per capita in US$	▢ Infant mortality per 1,000 live births
▢ Life expectancy	
▢ Literacy	▢ Human dev. index

N

NETHERLANDS

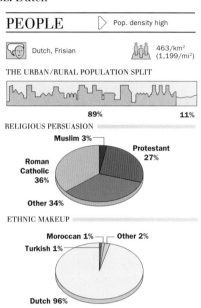

OFFICIAL NAME: Kingdom of the Netherlands **CAPITALS:** Amsterdam, The Hague
POPULATION: 15.7 million **CURRENCY:** Netherlands guilder **OFFICIAL LANGUAGE:** Dutch

THE NETHERLANDS IS LOCATED at the delta of five major rivers in northwest Europe. The few hills in the eastern and southern part of the country fall into a flat coastal area, bordered by the North Sea to the north and west. This is protected by a giant infrastructure of dunes, dikes, and canals, as 27% of the coast is below sea level. The Netherlands became one of the world's first confederative republics after Spain recognized its independence in 1648. Its highly successful economy has a long trading tradition, and Rotterdam, its main port, is also the world's largest.

CLIMATE ▷ Maritime

WEATHER CHART

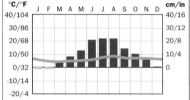

The Netherlands has a temperate climate, which is characterized by mild winters and cool summers. The country's coastal areas have the mildest climate, although northerly gales are fairly frequent, particularly in autumn and winter.

TOURISM ▷ Visitors : population 1:2.4

🧳 6.7m visitors ⬆ Up 2% 1995–1997

MAIN TOURIST ARRIVALS

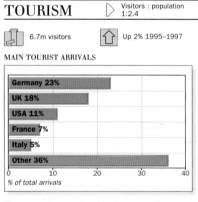

% of total arrivals

Tourism is a major business in the Netherlands. Visitors go mainly to Amsterdam, although cities such as Groningen and Maastricht are growing in popularity. Amsterdam caters for a diverse tourism market. Its world-famous museums include the Rijksmuseum, with its collection of Vermeers and Rembrandts, while its network of canals is popular. Amsterdam is also renowned as the sex capital of Europe; its liberal traditions

TRANSPORTATION ▷ Drive on right

✈ **Schiphol, Amsterdam** 34m passengers   🚢 1,115 ships 4m grt

THE TRANSPORTATION NETWORK

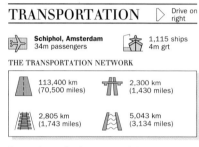

113,400 km (70,500 miles)	2,300 km (1,430 miles)
2,805 km (1,743 miles)	5,043 km (3,134 miles)

Rotterdam, the key transshipment port for northern Europe, is also the world's largest. It handled a record 310.1 million tons in 1997. Schiphol is Europe's fourth-largest passenger airport and third-largest cargo airport, and is one of the air transport hubs of Europe. Amsterdam is now linked by high-speed Thalys train to Brussels and Paris.

and red-light district draw millions every year. In the past decade, the city has also become a center for the European gay community, with celebrations held on 30 April (Queen's Day) and in August (Amsterdam Pride). A thriving club scene and liberal drug laws attract enthusiasts from neighboring countries.

In spring and summer, the tulip fields and North Sea beaches attract large numbers of visitors.

***Windmill at Baambrugge,** near Amsterdam. A century ago there were 10,000 in the country compared with today's 1000. A protective ring of 900 mills kept Amsterdam from flooding.*

PEOPLE ▷ Pop. density high

😊 Dutch, Frisian   👥 463/km² (1,199/mi²)

THE URBAN/RURAL POPULATION SPLIT

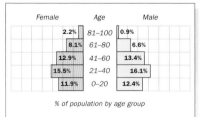

89%   11%

RELIGIOUS PERSUASION

Muslim 3%
Protestant 27%
Roman Catholic 36%
Other 34%

ETHNIC MAKEUP

Moroccan 1% Other 2%
Turkish 1%
Dutch 96%

The Dutch see their country as the most tolerant in Europe and it has a long history of welcoming refugees seeking religious and political asylum. In the 20th century, immigrants from former colonies have settled in the Netherlands and are fully accepted as citizens. They came first from Indonesia and then from the former colonies of Suriname and the Netherlands Antilles. The small Turkish community, however, does not enjoy full citizenship, but has guest worker status as in Germany.

The tradition of tolerance is reflected in liberal attitudes to sexuality. In 1998 gay couples gained rights similar to those of married couples (except for adoption). The government plans to legalize civil marriage for gays.

The state does not try to impose a particular morality on its citizens. Drug taking is seen as a matter of personal choice, as is euthanasia.

Women enjoy equal rights and hold 37% of seats in the Second Chamber, but they are not well represented at boardroom level.

POPULATION AGE BREAKDOWN

Female	Age	Male
2.2%	81–100	0.9%
8.1%	61–80	6.6%
12.9%	41–60	13.4%
15.5%	21–40	16.1%
11.9%	0–20	12.4%

% of population by age group

N

POLITICS ▷ Multiparty elections

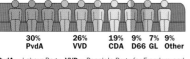

L. House 1998/2002 — HM Queen Beatrix
U. House 1999/2003 — Wilhelmina Armgard

AT THE LAST ELECTION

Second Chamber of the States-General 150 seats

30%	26%	19%	9%	7%	9%
PvdA	VVD	CDA	D66	GL	Other

PvdA = Labour Party **VVD** = People's Party for Freedom and
Democracy **CDA** = Christian Democratic Appeal
D66 = Democrats 66 **GL** = Green Left

First Chamber of the States-General 75 seats

31%	25%	19%	9%	5%	11%
VVD	CDA	PvdA	D66	GL	Other

The First Chamber of the States-General is indirectly elected.

The Netherlands is a constitutional
monarchy. Legislative power is vested
in parliament, and the monarch has
only nominal power.

MAIN POLITICAL ISSUES
The future of social welfare
Despite cutbacks in the
1980s, the Dutch still had one
of Europe's most generous
welfare systems. Most
political parties
accepted that levels
of welfare could not
be maintained
indefinitely. The
debate thus
focuses on how

*Queen Beatrix, who
acceded in 1980 and
rebuilt support for
the Dutch monarchy.*

*Wim Kok, won the
1994 elections and is
the first labour prime
minister since 1977.*

much and in which areas cuts should
be made.

Political refugees
In recent years, a rising number of
people have sought political asylum
in the Netherlands. Increasingly
this has led to concerns over
the costs involved, and worries that
this trend might lead to a rise in
support for extreme right-wing

nationalist parties. Since 1994
asylum laws have been tightened
in the Netherlands, as in
neighboring countries.

Strength of the coalition
Wim Kok's "purple coalition" was
shaken in mid-1997 when it emerged
that foreign minister Hans van Mierlo
(D66) had used diplomatic means
to hinder the arrest of former
Surinamese dictator Desi Bouterse on
drug trafficking charges. In mid-1999
D66 was only persuaded at the eleventh
hour not to leave the coalition after a
bill providing for wider use of
referendums was defeated.

PROFILE
Dutch politics are characterized
by coalitions and a high degree
of consensus. Most Dutch agree
on the social function of government
and readily accept relatively high
taxes and a generous social security
system. Political debate is more a
question of the stress and focus of
policy than of ideology. The CDA has
traditionally led two-party coalition
governments, either with the
left-of-center PvdA or with the right-
wing VVD. However, the PvdA won the
1994 elections, and confirmed its
position four years later with further
electoral success.

WORLD AFFAIRS ▷ Joined UN in 1945

| Benelux | EU | NATO | OECD | OSCE |

EU political and monetary integration
have strong popular support. In 1995,
internal border controls were lifted
under the Schengen Convention.

In 1999 it was one of the 11 EU states
to introduce the euro, while former
minister Wim Duisenberg heads the
European Central Bank. The
International Court of Justice and the
International Criminal Tribunal for
Former Yugoslavia sit in The Hague, as
will the International Criminal Court.

AID ▷ Donor

$2.9bn (donations)   Not applicable

With 0.81% of GNP devoted annually
in 1995–1997 to development aid, the
country is one of the few to exceed
the UN target of 0.7% of GNP. It actively
pursues a policy of linking foreign aid
and human rights. In 1993 it clashed
with Indonesia, a former colony,
which rejected all Dutch aid, accusing
the latter of interfering in its internal
affairs. A recent priority has been
links between development and
conflict management.

NETHERLANDS

Total Land Area :
33 920 sq. km
(13 097 sq. miles)

POPULATION

over 1 000 000 ⊡
over 500 000 ◉
over 100 000 ◎
over 50 000 ○
over 10 000 ●

LAND HEIGHT

100m/328ft
Sea Level
-100m/-328ft

N

0 — 40 km
0 — 40 miles

CHRONOLOGY

Suppression of Protestantism by the ruling Spanish Habsburgs led to the revolt of the Netherlands and the independence of the northern provinces as a republic in 1581.

❏ **1813** Dutch oust French after 30 years of French rule and choose to become a constitutional monarchy.
❏ **1815** United Kingdom of Netherlands formed to include Belgium and Luxembourg.
❏ **1830** Catholic southern provinces secede as Belgium.
❏ **1848** New constitution – ministers to be accountable to parliament.
❏ **1897–1901** Wide-ranging social legislation enacted. Development of strong trade unions.
❏ **1898** Wilhelmina succeeds to throne, ending Luxembourg union, where Salic Law is in force.
❏ **1914–1918** Dutch neutrality respected in World War I.
❏ **1922** Women fully enfranchised.
❏ **1940** Dutch assert neutrality, but Germany invades. Fierce resistance.
❏ **1942** Japan invades Dutch East Indies.
❏ **1944–1945** "Winter of starvation."
❏ **1945** Liberation. International Court of Justice set up in The Hague.
❏ **1946** PvdA formed.
❏ **1946–1958** PvdA leads center-left coalitions with CVP. Marshall Aid from USA speeds reconstruction.
❏ **1948** Juliana becomes queen.
❏ **1949** Joins NATO. Most of East Indies colonies gain independence as Indonesia.
❏ **1957** Founder member of EEC.
❏ **1960** Economic union with Belgium and Luxembourg comes into effect.
❏ **1973** PvdA wins power after 15 years spent mainly in opposition. Center-left coalition.
❏ **1980** Two main opposition Protestant parties unite in CDA. Beatrix becomes queen.
❏ **1977–1981** CDA/VVD coalition.
❏ **1982** PvdA rejects deployment of US cruise missiles in Netherlands. CDA/VVD center-right coalition under Ruud Lubbers.
❏ **1989** VVD refuses to support finance for 20-year National Environment Policy (NEP). Elections. Lubbers forms CDA/PvdA center-left coalition.
❏ **1990** NEP introduced.
❏ **1992** Licensed brothels and euthanasia legalized.
❏ **1994** Elections. Wim Kok of PvdA heads new coalition with VVD and D66.
❏ **1998** Kok strengthens PvdA position in early election.
❏ **1999** Netherlands among 11 EU countries to introduce euro.

DEFENSE

▷ No compulsory military service

💲 $6.9bn ⬇ Down 14% in 1997

Exports of conventional weapons were worth $450 million in 1996.

DUTCH ARMED FORCES

🚜	600 main battle tanks (270 *Leopard* 1A4, 330 *Leopard* 2)	27,000 personnel
🚢	4 submarines, 12 frigates and 4 destroyers	13,800 personnel
✈	170 combat aircraft (F-16A/B)	11,980 personnel
	None	

The Dutch military has undergone major restructuring since the the Cold War to make it a rapidly deployable, more flexible military force as befits a NATO member state. Compulsory military service was abolished in 1996 and personnel cut by 44%, with the number of army divisions reduced from three to two. In 1995, a joint Dutch–German army corps numbering 28,000 was inaugurated. The armed forces' new role was evidenced when it sent troops to take part in the international peace implementation force and then the stabilization force in Bosnia. The Netherlands also has a large defense industry specializing in submarines, weapons systems and aircraft.

ECONOMICS

▷ Inflation 2% p.a. (1985–1996)

📊 $403.1bn 💲 2.03–1.88 guilders

SCORE CARD

❏ WORLD GNP RANKING	12th
❏ GNP PER CAPITA	$25,830
❏ BALANCE OF PAYMENTS	$21.2bn
❏ INFLATION	2.2%
❏ UNEMPLOYMENT	6%

ECONOMIC PERFORMANCE INDICATOR

Consumer price index --- GDP

tech industries such as electronics, telecommunications and chemicals, there is a successful agricultural sector. Productivity rates are high and agricultural produce such as cheese, vegetables, meat, and flowers are significant export earners. Job creation schemes have reduced unemployment to half the EU average, though many people are on sick and disability pay.

EXPORTS

Italy 5% UK 8%
France 10%
Other 39%
Belgium-Luxembourg 12%
Germany 26%

IMPORTS

France 9%
USA 10%
Other 34%
UK 12%
Belgium-Luxembourg 13%
Germany 22%

STRENGTHS

Highly skilled, educated, multilingual work force. Sophisticated infrastructure. Many blue-chip multinationals, including Philips and Shell. Strong consensus between employers and employees. Low inflation. Tradition of high-tech innovation, including development of music cassette and CD.

WEAKNESSES

Costly welfare system, resulting in high taxes and social insurance premiums; one-third of national income spent on social security. High labor costs.

PROFILE

Trade has been central to the success of the economy since the 16th century. Most goods travel through Rotterdam, the world's biggest port. As well as high-

NETHERLANDS : MAJOR BUSINESSES

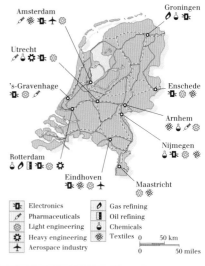

🔌 Electronics	🔥 Gas refining
💉 Pharmaceuticals	🛢 Oil refining
⚙ Light engineering	🧪 Chemicals
✿ Heavy engineering	※ Textiles
✈ Aerospace industry	

0   50 km
0   50 miles

RESOURCES

▷ Electric power 19.0m kw

521,377 tonnes

57,042 b/d (reserves 144,650,000 bbl)

11.4m pigs, 4.3m cattle, 1.7m sheep, 97,000 horses

Natural gas, oil

ELECTRICITY GENERATION

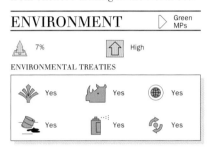

Hydro 0% (0.09bn kwh)

Combustion 95% (76bn kwh)

Nuclear 5% (4bn kwh)

Other 0%

| 0 | 20 | 40 | 60 | 80 | 100 |

% of total generation by type

There are large natural gas reserves in the north. There is some oil production from offshore drilling in the North Sea.

NETHERLANDS : LAND USE

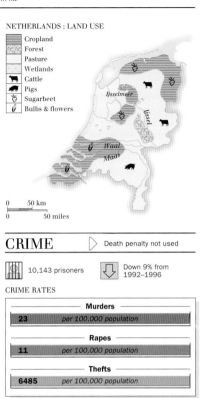

Cropland
Forest
Pasture
Wetlands
Cattle
Pigs
Sugarbeet
Bulbs & flowers

Ijsselmeer

Ijssel

Waal

Maas

| 0 | 50 km |
| 0 | 50 miles |

ENVIRONMENT

▷ Green MPs

7%

High

ENVIRONMENTAL TREATIES

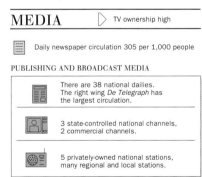

Yes   Yes   Yes

Yes   Yes   Yes

The country has a strong environmental tradition, a legacy in part of living in one of the most densely populated states in the world. NGOs such as Greenpeace are well supported and the Green Party is well represented in parliament.

The Dutch recycle their domestic trash and have a good record of energy conservation. An eco-tax on energy users was introduced in 1996 – the first of its kind in the West, though big businesses are exempt. Government spending on environmental measures equaled nearly 3% of GDP in 1997, more than any other industrialized country. Recent rapid expansion of Schiphol airport raises concerns about air and noise pollution.

MEDIA

▷ TV ownership high

Daily newspaper circulation 305 per 1,000 people

PUBLISHING AND BROADCAST MEDIA

There are 38 national dailies. The right wing *De Telegraph* has the largest circulation.

3 state-controlled national channels, 2 commercial channels.

5 privately-owned national stations, many regional and local stations.

Newspaper circulation is high. While editorially independent, broadcasting is strongly regulated. Dutch law does not recognize a right of reply or a right to protect information sources.

CRIME

▷ Death penalty not used

10,143 prisoners

Down 9% from 1992–1996

CRIME RATES

Murders	
23	per 100,000 population

Rapes	
11	per 100,000 population

Thefts	
6485	per 100,000 population

Liberal drugs laws make the Netherlands a gateway for the narcotics trade. Several politicians have suggested decriminalizing the trade in order to reduce the crime generated by the huge profits from the business. However, such a policy faces opposition from fellow parties to the Schengen Convention.

EDUCATION

▷ School leaving age: 18

99%

491,748 students

Corporate funding plays an important part in university research.

THE EDUCATION SYSTEM

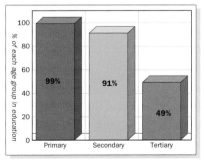

% of each age group in education

	Primary	Secondary	Tertiary
	99%	91%	49%

Public, municipal-run schools attract 35% of pupils and private (mostly religious) schools are attended by 65%. Both types are fully state funded.

HEALTH

▷ Welfare state health benefits

1 per 400 people

Heart and respiratory diseases, cancers

Dutch health care is largely funded by the state, though around 25% of funding comes from private sources. High spending ensures that it is among the best in the world. However, there are fears that the Dutch may have to accept lower standards in future, particularly since the population is aging. Major health problems are similar to those in the rest of western Europe. Incidence of AIDS is higher than in Sweden or the UK but lower than in Switzerland, France, or Spain.

SPENDING

▷ GDP/cap. no increase

CONSUMPTION AND SPENDING

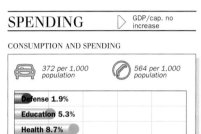

372 per 1,000 population

564 per 1,000 population

Defense 1.9%

Education 5.3%

Health 8.7%

| 0 | 5 | 10 | 15 | 20 | 25 |

Defense, Health, Education spending as % of GDP

The Netherlands is, per capita, one of the richest countries in the world. Oil executives, stock market traders and businessmen are among the wealthiest people. A progressive taxation system and extensive social welfare has resulted in wealth being fairly evenly distributed. There is a small elite who have considerable inherited wealth, but extravagant displays of wealth are rare.

Class does not play a big part in Dutch society. Most citizens would consider themselves to be middle class. Immigrant communities, however, are the exception; they often live on the edges of towns in deprived areas. The poorest are the illegal immigrants.

WORLD RANKING

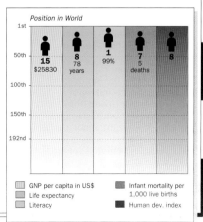

Position in World

15	8	1	7	8
$25830	78 years	99%	5 deaths	

GNP per capita in US$
Life expectancy
Literacy

Infant mortality per 1,000 live births
Human dev. index

NEW ZEALAND

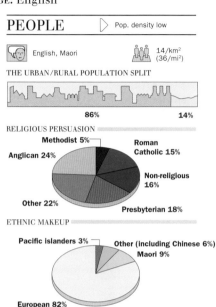

AUSTRALASIA

OFFICIAL NAME: The Dominion of New Zealand **CAPITAL:** Wellington
POPULATION: 3.7 million **CURRENCY:** New Zealand dollar **OFFICIAL LANGUAGE:** English

L YING IN THE SOUTH PACIFIC, 1,600 km (990 miles) southeast of Australia, New Zealand comprises the main North and South Islands, separated by the Cook Strait, and numerous smaller islands. South Island is the more mountainous; North Island contains hot springs and geysers, and the bulk of the population. The political tradition is liberal and egalitarian, and has been dominated by the National and Labor parties. Radical, and often unpopular, reforms since 1984 have restored economic growth, speeded up economic diversification, and strengthened New Zealand's position within the Pacific Rim countries.

CLIMATE
▷ Maritime/subtropical

WEATHER CHART

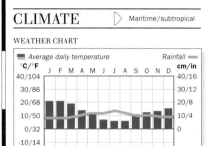

New Zealand's climate is generally temperate and damp, with an average temperature of 12°C (54°F). There are differences between the islands, which extend north–south nearly 2,000 km (1,240 miles). The extreme north is almost subtropical; southern winters are cold. It is windy; Wellington is particularly known for bouts of blustery weather that can last for days.

TRANSPORTATION
▷ Drive on left

✈ **Auckland International**
7.25m passengers

🚢 176 ships
385,733 grt

THE TRANSPORTATION NETWORK

🛣 92,000 km (57,000 miles)	⛩ 10,453 km (6,495 miles)
🚉 3,913 km (2,431 miles)	⚓ 1,609 km (1,000 miles)

Both New Zealand's major islands are well served by transportation services, although the more populous North Island's road and rail network is more extensive than the South's. Air and ferry services complement the land networks and provide links between the North and South Islands, as well as with the numerous smaller islands. Cargo ferry services are particularly important for remote populations in the Ross Dependency. Links with the Cook Islands, Niue and the Tokelau atolls, New Zealand's associated territories, are being improved.

TOURISM
▷ Visitors : population 1:2.3

1.6 million ⬆ Up 15% 1995–1997

MAIN TOURIST ARRIVALS

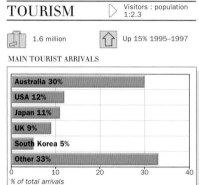

New Zealand's prime attraction is its scenery. Unspoiled and, relative to the country's size, the most varied in the world, it offers mountains, fjords and lakes, glaciers, rain forests, beaches, boiling mud pools, and geysers. Other attractions are the Maori culture, and outdoor activities such as river rafting, fishing, skiing, whale watching and bungee jumping, a local invention.

Tourists come mainly from Australia, the USA, Japan, the UK, and South Korea. Tourism is the largest single foreign-exchange earner, generating NZ\$4 billion yearly and nearly one and a half million visitors. Tourism is growing, although the industry was hit by the 1998 Asian economic crisis which saw Asian tourism drop by 10%.

Mount Egmont, *an extinct volcano, is one of the numerous popular natural attractions of New Zealand's North Island.*

PEOPLE
▷ Pop. density low

English, Maori   14/km² (36/mi²)

THE URBAN/RURAL POPULATION SPLIT

86%   14%

RELIGIOUS PERSUASION

Methodist 5%
Anglican 24%
Roman Catholic 15%
Non-religious 16%
Other 22%
Presbyterian 18%

ETHNIC MAKEUP

Pacific islanders 3%
Other (including Chinese 6%)
Maori 9%
European 82%

New Zealand is a country of migrants. The first settlers were the Maoris, migrating from Polynesia about 1,200 years ago. Today's majority European population consists mainly of descendants of British migrants who settled after 1840. Newer migrants include Asians from Hong Kong and Malaysia, and those who left Fiji after the 1987 coups. There has been a recent immigration program to attract skilled South Americans, Russians, Chinese, and Africans to revitalize the economy.

The Maoris ceded sovereignty to the British by the 1840 Treaty of Waitangi. Some 9% of the population, their living and education standards are generally lower, and unemployment rate higher, than average. Relations with the European majority have been tense in recent years as they campaign for land compensation. A settlement of fishing claims was made in 1992. The crown signed the Waikato Raupato Claims Settlement Act and officially apologized to the Maoris in 1995. Three years later, the Waitangi Tribunal ordered the government to return confiscated land.

POPULATION AGE BREAKDOWN

Female	Age	Male
1.7%	81–100	0.9%
6.8%	61–80	6%
11.7%	41–60	11.5%
15.9%	21–40	15.2%
14.8%	0–20	15.5%

% of population by age group

N

POLITICS ▷ Multiparty elections

🏛 1996/1999　　　👤 HM Queen Elizabeth II

AT THE LAST ELECTION
House of Representatives 120 seats　　　**7% ACT**

37% NP	31% LP	14% NZF	10% All	1% UP

NP = National Party **LP** = Labour Party **NZF** = New Zealand First Party **All** = Alliance **ACT** = ACT New Zealand (Association of Consumers and Taxpayers) **UP** = United Party

James Bolger,
fprime minister from 1990–1997.

Jenny Shipley,
NP leader, and prime minister since 1997.

New Zealand is a single-chamber parliamentary democracy within the Commonwealth. The Cook Islands and Niue are self-governing territories.

MAIN POLITICAL ISSUES
Electoral reform

New Zealand shifted to a system of proportional representation for the 1996 general election. Popular endorsement of this reform in a referendum in 1993 reflected widespread disillusionment with the NP and LP. The new German-style system strengthened the role of smaller parties. As predicted, the first election to use the system produced a coalition government, consisting of the NP and the minority New Zealand First party. But the coalition ended with the 1998 sacking of Deputy Prime Minister NZF leader Winston Peters. The NP formed a minority government and proposed a review of the proportional voting system.

PROFILE

Politics were dominated by the NP and the LP under the first-past-the-post system. Since 1984 the economy has undergone massive reforms. Cuts to the welfare system and privatization of public assets have been unpopular. Jenny Shipley took over NP leadership in late 1997, becoming the country's first woman prime minister. Shipley maintained her leadership by forming a minority government after the coalition split.

WORLD AFFAIRS ▷ Joined UN in 1945

Comm	APEC	OECD	SPF	SPC

Many New Zealanders remain strongly committed to the British crown and the Commonwealth, but the importance of the UK has diminished. The UK's involvement in the EU has forced New Zealand to reorient its trade and foreign policy toward its Pacific Rim neighbors, especially Australia. The 1983 Closer Economic Relationship (CER) treaty freed trade between the two states. Australia is now New Zealand's largest trading partner, strengthened in 1996 by the signing of a mutual recognition agreement. Relations with Asia are growing in importance. The 1998 Asian economic crisis had a significant impact on trade, particularly tourism. Relations with the USA are improving after a low point when New Zealand's antinuclear stance led to its exclusion from the ANZUS pact. Relations with France were strained in 1985 after French agents bombed Greenpeace ship *Rainbow Warrior* in Auckland harbor. Official ties were restored in 1997.

AID ▷ Donor

💲 US$145m (donations)　　　◈ Not applicable

Over half of New Zealand's overseas aid is bilateral. Particular areas of focus are the Pacific states and Pacific-wide organizations. New Zealand is a major supporter of the South Pacific Forum, the University of the South Pacific, and the Pacific Environment Program. It also offers scholarships allowing overseas students to study or train in New Zealand.

N

Chatham Is
Petre Bay　　Chatham I.
Waitangi
Pitt Strait　Pitt I.
(continuation on same scale)

NEW ZEALAND
Total Land Area : 268 670 sq. km
(103 733 sq. miles)

LAND HEIGHT		POPULATION	
2000m/6562ft		over 500 000	⊙
1000m/3281ft		over 100 000	◎
500m/1640ft		over 50 000	○
200m/656ft		over 10 000	•
Sea Level		under 10 000	•

N

0		100 km
0		100 miles

CHRONOLOGY

A former British colony, New Zealand became a dominion in 1907 and fully independent in 1947.

- ❏ **1962** Western Samoa gains independence.
- ❏ **1965** The Cook Islands become self-governing.
- ❏ **1975** Conservative NP wins elections. Economic austerity program introduced by Prime Minister Robert Muldoon.
- ❏ **1976** Immigration cut by over 80%.
- ❏ **1984** LP elected; David Lange prime minister. Auckland harbor headland restored to Maoris.
- ❏ **1985** New Zealand prohibits nuclear vessels from ports and waters. French agents sink Greenpeace ship *Rainbow Warrior* in Auckland harbor.
- ❏ **1986** USA suspends military obligations under ANZUS Treaty.
- ❏ **1987** LP wins elections. Controversial privatization program introduced. Nuclear ban enshrined in legislation.
- ❏ **1989** Cabinet split. Lange resigns. Succeeded by Geoffrey Palmer.
- ❏ **1990** Palmer resigns. LP defeated by NP in elections. James Bolger prime minister.
- ❏ **1991** Widespread protests against spending cuts.
- ❏ **1992** Maoris win South Island fishing rights. Majority vote for electoral reform in referendum.
- ❏ **1993** First French naval ship since 1985 docks. NP returned with single-seat majority in election. Proportional representation introduced by referendum.
- ❏ **1994** Senior-level US contacts restored; agrees not to send nuclear-armed ships to New Zealand ports. Maoris reject government ten-year, NZ$1,000 million land claims settlement.
- ❏ **1995** Waitangi Day celebrations abandoned after Maori protests. Crown apologizes to Maoris and signs Waikato Raupatu Claims Act. UK warship visits resume.
- ❏ **1996** NP forms coalition to preserve overall legislative majority. First general election under new system of proportional representation.
- ❏ **1997** NP forms a coalition government with New Zealand First party. Bolger resigns. Jenny Shipley becomes the country's first woman prime minister.
- ❏ **1998** Shipley sacks leader of NZF party, Winston Peters, as deputy prime minister, and forms minority government when coalition splits. Waitangi Tribunal orders government to return to Maoris NZ$6.1million of confiscated land.

N

DEFENSE

> No compulsory military service

US$901m   Down 17% in 1997

ANZUS, the security pact between Australia, New Zealand and the USA, and the focus of New Zealand's defense policy since 1951, has been strained by New Zealand's refusal since 1984 to allow nuclear warships into its ports. The USA suspended joint military exercises, forcing New Zealand to seek closer links with Australia. Senior-level contacts were resumed in 1994 and the USA announced that it would not send nuclear-armed warships to New Zealand ports. Since then, the UK has also resumed naval visits.

The armed forces number about 10,000 troops with an additional 8,500 reserves. New Zealand's defense strategy centers on protection against low-level economic threats, terrorism, regional security, and peacekeeping.

NEW ZEALAND ARMED FORCES

20 light tanks (*Scorpion*)	4,400 personnel
4 frigates and 4 patrol boats	2,100 personnel
42 combat aircraft (14 A-4K, 5 TA-4K)	3,050 personnel
None	

ECONOMICS

> Inflation 5.2% p.a. (1985–1996)

US$59.5bn   1.72–1.89 New Zealand dollars

SCORE CARD

- ❏ WORLD GNP RANKING..........................47th
- ❏ GNP PER CAPITA ....US$15,830
- ❏ BALANCE OF PAYMENTS................US$–5.2bn
- ❏ INFLATION 1.2%
- ❏ UNEMPLOYMENT 7%

ECONOMIC PERFORMANCE INDICATOR

EXPORTS

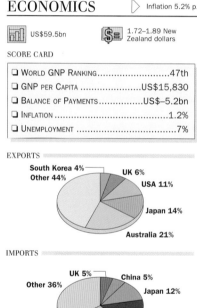

- South Korea 4%
- Other 44%
- UK 6%
- USA 11%
- Japan 14%
- Australia 21%

IMPORTS

- UK 5%
- China 5%
- Other 36%
- Japan 12%
- USA 18%
- Australia 24%

STRENGTHS

Modern agricultural sector; world's biggest exporter of butter and (per capita) of wool. Rapidly expanding tourist sector. Manufacturing with emphasis on high tech. One of world's most open economies. Expanded trade links within Pacific Rim.

WEAKNESSES

One of the highest levels of public debt outside developing world. Continuing reliance on imported manufactured goods and foreign investment.

PROFILE

Since 1984, New Zealand has changed from being one of the most regulated to one of the most open economies in the world. Radical reforms, drastic cuts in social security and related government spending, and deregulation helped to restore growth and cut inflation to minimal levels. Diversification into new markets and products benefited from the regional boom prior to the 1997 Asian crisis. High public debt and poor levels of private investment remain a problem. Recession hit hard in 1998.

NEW ZEALAND : MAJOR BUSINESSES

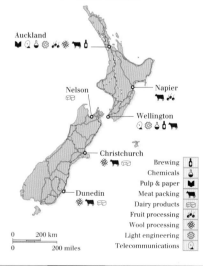

- Auckland
- Nelson
- Napier
- Wellington
- Christchurch
- Dunedin

Brewing	
Chemicals	
Pulp & paper	
Meat packing	
Dairy products	
Fruit processing	
Wool processing	
Light engineering	
Telecommunications	

0   200 km
0   200 miles

RESOURCES

▷ Electric power 7.5m kw

612,223 tonnes

34,546 b/d (reserves 169,670,000 bbl)

47.6m sheep, 8.7m cattle, 227,000 goats, 340,000 pigs

Coal, oil, natural gas, iron, gold, silica sand

ELECTRICITY GENERATION

- Hydro 66% (20bn kwh)
- Thermal 27% (8bn kwh)
- Nuclear 0%
- Other 7% (2bn kwh)

% of total generation by type

New Zealand's rich pastures, a result of even rainfall throughout the year, have traditionally been its key resource. The sheep, wool and dairy products on which the country's wealth was built are still important. Newer export industries include products such as fruit, vegetables, fish, cork, wood, and textile fibers.

New Zealand is well endowed with energy resources. It has coal, oil, natural gas and huge hydroelectric potential.

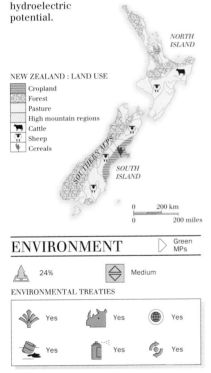

NORTH ISLAND

NEW ZEALAND : LAND USE

- Cropland
- Forest
- Pasture
- High mountain regions
- Cattle
- Sheep
- Cereals

SOUTHERN ALPS

SOUTH ISLAND

0 — 200 km
0 — 200 miles

ENVIRONMENT

▷ Green MPs

24%

Medium

ENVIRONMENTAL TREATIES

Yes	Yes	Yes
Yes	Yes	Yes

New Zealand's isolation, small population and limited industry have helped to keep it one of the world's most pollution-free countries. It has been a leading opponent of French nuclear testing in the Pacific and has banned nuclear vessels from its ports. Ozone depletion over Antarctica, deforestation, and protection of native flora and fauna are major issues.

MEDIA

▷ TV ownership high

Daily newspaper circulation 223 per 1,000 people

PUBLISHING AND BROADCAST MEDIA

There are 23 daily newspapers. The leading newspaper is the *New Zealand Herald*

2 state-owned, 2 independent services

1 state-owned, 22 independent services

The Auckland-based *New Zealand Herald* is the only daily with a national circulation; the others are primarily local papers. TV4 became the fourth free-to-air network in 1998.

CRIME

▷ Death penalty not used

4,553 prisoners

Down 3% from 1992–1996

CRIME RATES

Murders
3 — per 100,000 population

Rapes
35 — per 100,000 population

Thefts
7515 — per 100,000 population

Crime rates in New Zealand's urban areas have increased in recent years. However, overall, the country remains one of the world's safest and most peaceful places in which to live.

EDUCATION

▷ School leaving age:16

99%

162,350 students

Education is compulsory between the ages of six and 16.

THE EDUCATION SYSTEM

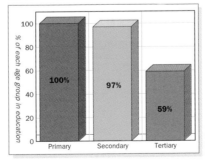

% of each age group in education

- Primary: 100%
- Secondary: 97%
- Tertiary: 59%

Recent plans to decentralize the education system by giving schools direct financial control have been controversial. A new qualification is being introduced for senior secondary students. New Zealand has one of the highest proportions of the population with tertiary qualifications in the OECD.

HEALTH

▷ Welfare state health benefits

1 per 476 people

Heart disease, cancers, accidents

In 1936, New Zealand was the first country to introduce a full welfare state. Government efforts since 1991 to impose UK-style market systems on the health service have been very unpopular. While life expectancy continues to improve, the nation's OECD health ranking is falling. In comparison with other OECD countries New Zealand has high mortality rates for heart disease, respiratory disease, and breast and bowel cancer, and for motor vehicle accidents; the suicide rate is also high.

SPENDING

▷ GDP/cap. no increase

CONSUMPTION AND SPENDING

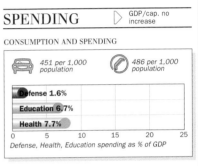

451 per 1,000 population

486 per 1,000 population

- Defense 1.6%
- Education 6.7%
- Health 7.7%

Defense, Health, Education spending as % of GDP

The years since 1984 have been very difficult for New Zealanders, who are used to affluence within a generous welfare state. A rash of economic and social reforms has held back wages, raised unemployment and cut welfare benefits. Even so, average living standards are still high, and a strong egalitarian tradition means that wealth remains fairly evenly distributed.

Quality of life in New Zealand is among the world's best, in terms of access to basic necessities, and a pure, healthy urban and rural environment. Social mobility is fairly high. Wealthier people tend to spend their money on houses close to the water. Yachts are a major status symbol.

WORLD RANKING

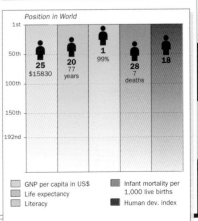

Position in World

- 25 — $15830
- 20 — 77 years
- 1 — 99%
- 28 — 7 deaths
- 18

- GNP per capita in US$
- Life expectancy
- Literacy
- Infant mortality per 1,000 live births
- Human dev. index

N

NICARAGUA

OFFICIAL NAME: Republic of Nicaragua **CAPITAL:** Managua
POPULATION: 4.5 million **CURRENCY:** Córdoba oro **OFFICIAL LANGUAGE:** Spanish

| 1838 | 1838 | Sept 15 | NIC | -6 | +505 | .ni |

BOUNDED BY THE Pacific Ocean to the west and the Caribbean Sea to the east, Nicaragua lies at the heart of Central America. After more than 40 years of dictatorship, the Sandinista revolution in 1978 led to 11 years of civil war, which almost destroyed the economy. The Sandinistas unexpectedly lost elections in 1990. Right-wing parties through the 1990s. The Sandinistas remain the main opposition on the left, despite a party split.

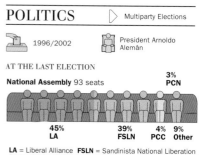

Oil refinery at Bluefields, on the Atlantic coast. Under the Sandinistas, most crude oil came from the former USSR, via Cuba.

CLIMATE

▷ Tropical equatorial/ wet & dry

WEATHER CHART

- Average daily temperature
- Rainfall

The climate is tropical and often violent, as evidenced by Hurricane Mitch in 1998. Earthquakes also occur.

TRANSPORTATION

▷ Drive on right

Augusto C Sandino Intl, Managua
225,725 passengers

27 ships
4,200 grt

THE TRANSPORTATION NETWORK

1,598 km (993 miles)	Pan-American Highway 384 km (239 miles)
none	2,220 km (1,379 miles)

Hurricane Mitch damaged major roads and destroyed 35 key bridges. Reconstruction will take years.

TOURISM

▷ Visitors : population 1:13

350,000 visitors

Up 25% 1995–1997

MAIN TOURIST ARRIVALS

Honduras 26%	
USA 15%	
Costa Rica 15%	
Other 44%	

% of total arrivals

The civil war caused the near-collapse of tourism, and slow recovery has been interrupted by the damage caused by Hurricane Mitch. Foreign direct investment in the sector grew in 1997–1998.

PEOPLE

▷ Pop. density low

Spanish, English Creole, Miskito

38/km² (98/mi²)

THE URBAN/RURAL POPULATION SPLIT

63% 37%

ETHNIC MAKEUP

- Zambos 4%
- Indigenous Indian 5%
- Black 8%
- White 14%
- Mestizo 69%

The Atlantic regions, which in 1987 achieved limited independence, are isolated from the more populous Pacific regions. The indigenous Miskito tribes and the descendants of Africans, brought over by Spanish colonists in the 18th century to work the plantations, are concentrated along the Atlantic coast, where English Creole is widely spoken.

The Sandinista revolution improved the status of women through changes in the legal system and the incorporation of women into means of production and political life. However, poverty and lack of permanent employment have since forced many women into prostitution.

POLITICS

▷ Multiparty Elections

1996/2002

President Arnoldo Alemán

AT THE LAST ELECTION

National Assembly 93 seats

3% PCN

| 45% LA | 39% FSLN | 4% PCC | 9% Other |

LA = Liberal Alliance **FSLN** = Sandinista National Liberation Front **PCC** = Christian Road Party **PCN** = Conservative Party of Nicaragua
The Liberal Alliance coalition includes the Liberal Constitutionalist Party (PLC).

Defeated in the 1990 and 1996 polls by right-wing parties, the FSLN underwent an internal crisis. The Liberal Alliance government of President Arnoldo Alemán, which took office in 1997, promised to unite the country but quickly became unpopular because of its austerity measures and following allegations of corruption. Without a congressional majority because of defections, Alemán now faces renewed protests which the FSLN has backed.

NICARAGUA

Total Land Area : 118 750 sq. km (45 849 sq. miles)

POPULATION

- ⊙ over 500 000
- ◎ over 100 000
- ○ over 50 000
- ● over 10 000
- • under 10 000

LAND HEIGHT

- 1000m/3281ft
- 500m/1640ft
- 200m/656ft
- Sea Level

100 km

100 miles

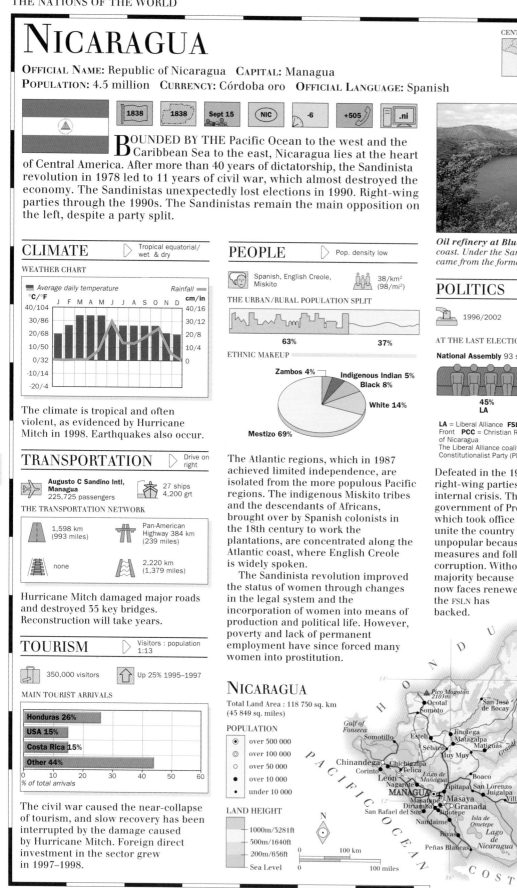

N

WORLD AFFAIRS

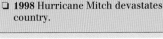 Joined UN in 1945

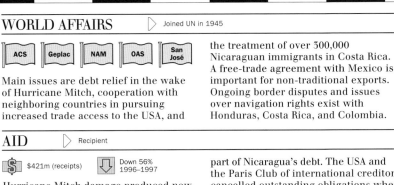
ACS · Geplac · NAM · OAS · San José

Main issues are debt relief in the wake of Hurricane Mitch, cooperation with neighboring countries in pursuing increased trade access to the USA, and the treatment of over 300,000 Nicaraguan immigrants in Costa Rica. A free-trade agreement with Mexico is important for non-traditional exports. Ongoing border disputes and issues over navigation rights exist with Honduras, Costa Rica, and Colombia.

AID

Recipient

$421m (receipts) · Down 56% 1996–1997

Hurricane Mitch damage produced new World Bank and IDB loans. France, Finland, Cuba, and Spain pardoned all or part of Nicaragua's debt. The USA and the Paris Club of international creditors cancelled outstanding obligations when it was included in the IMF-run Highly Indebted Poor Countries initiative.

DEFENSE

Compulsory military service

$36m · Down 3% in 1997

The FSLN forces that overthrew the Somoza regime were the basis of the army, which expanded to some 134,000 troops during the war but was cut to 10,000 by 1995. Senior Sandinistas were among officers retired in 1998. The army is to be involved in more community-based roles focused on the defense of natural resources and the clearance of landmines.

ECONOMICS

Inflation 531% p.a. (1985–1996)

$1.9bn · 9.95–11.12 córdobas oro

SCORE CARD

❏ WORLD GNP RANKING	143rd
❏ GNP PER CAPITA	$410
❏ BALANCE OF PAYMENTS	$–671m
❏ INFLATION	11.6%
❏ UNEMPLOYMENT	13%

STRENGTHS
Coffee, sugar, and grain exports. Foreign aid and public and private reconstruction work after Hurricane Mitch will benefit tourism, energy, services and construction.

WEAKNESSES
$5.9 billion foreign debt. Main exports subject to commodity price fluctuations. High unemployment. Poor infrastructure and energy supply. Lack of investment and diversification. Delays in privatization. Skewed land ownership and protracted disputes over property rights.

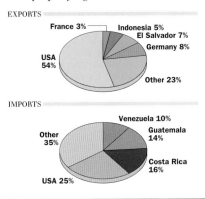

EXPORTS
France 3% · Indonesia 5% · El Salvador 7% · Germany 8% · USA 54% · Other 23%

IMPORTS
Venezuela 10% · Guatemala 14% · Other 35% · Costa Rica 16% · USA 25%

RESOURCES

Electric power 457,000 kw

18,010 tonnes · Not an oil producer; refines 16,000 b/d

1.7m cattle, 400,000 pigs, 245,000 horses · Gold, silver, lead, zinc, copper, tungsten, salt

Nicaragua has small quantities of gold and silver and no oil. New thermal generation projects are planned to overcome traditional energy deficits.

ENVIRONMENT

No Green MPs

8% · Low

Deforestation over large areas and widespread use of pesticides are major problems.

MEDIA

TV ownership medium

Daily newspaper circulation 32 per 1,000 people

PUBLISHING AND BROADCAST MEDIA

There are 4 daily newspapers, *La Prensa* and *El Nuevo Diario*

1 state-owned service · 1 state-owned, 60 independent stations

Since the civil war, radio, TV and newspapers have tended to ally themselves with the government or the opposition; there is little room for independents.

CRIME

Death penalty not used

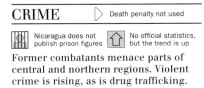

Nicaragua does not publish prison figures · No official statistics, but the trend is up

Former combatants menace parts of central and northern regions. Violent crime is rising, as is drug trafficking.

CHRONOLOGY

Nicaragua became independent in 1838. Guerrilla forces, led by Gen. Sandino, opposed the US marine presence in the early 1930s.

- ❏ **1978–1990** FSLN revolution ends 44-year Somoza dictatorship; civil war between FSLN and US-backed Contras.
- ❏ **1998** Hurricane Mitch devastates country.

EDUCATION

 School leaving age: 12

83% · 50,769 students

The Sandinista "Literacy Crusade" achieved dramatic results in the 1980s, but has long since died away. Student protests in recent years have been for increases in the education budget.

HEALTH

 Welfare state health benefits

1 per 1,429 people · Diarrheal and heart diseases, accidents and tuberculosis

Life expectancy in Nicaragua rose from 50 to 64 years between 1960 and 1988. Real spending on health, however, fell by 71% between 1988 and 1993 and has yet to recover.

SPENDING

GDP/cap. no increase

CONSUMPTION AND SPENDING

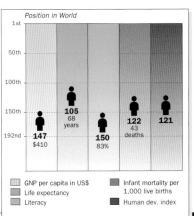

16 per 1,000 population · 29 per 1,000 population

Defense 1.4%
Education 3.6%
Health 6.7%

Defense, Health, Education spending as % of GDP

A UNDP study in 1998 found that 44% of Nicaragua's population survive on the equivalent of less than $1 a day.

WORLD RANKING

Position in World

147 $410 · 105 68 years · 150 83% · 122 43 deaths · 121

- ▢ GNP per capita in US$
- ▢ Life expectancy
- ▢ Literacy
- ▢ Infant mortality per 1,000 live births
- ▢ Human dev. index

N

NIGER

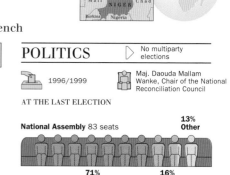

WEST AFRICA

OFFICIAL NAME: Republic of Niger CAPITAL: Niamey
POPULATION: 10.1 million CURRENCY: CFA franc OFFICIAL LANGUAGE: French

| 1960 | 1960 | Dec 18 | RN | +1 | +227 | .ne |

LANDLOCKED IN THE WEST of Africa, Niger is linked to the sea by the Niger river. The northern regions, the area around the Aïr mountains, and particularly the vast uninhabited northeast have Saharan conditions. Niger was ruled by one-party or military regimes until 1992 when a multiparty constitution was introduced, but a much-troubled democratic process was disrupted by military coups in 1996 and 1999.

CLIMATE

Hot desert/steppe

WEATHER CHART

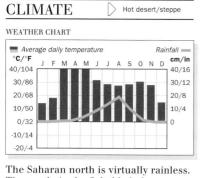

The Saharan north is virtually rainless. The south, in the Sahel belt, has an unreliable rainy season, preceded by a period of extreme daytime heat.

N

TRANSPORTATION

Drive on right

Niamey International
74,319 passengers

Has no fleet

THE TRANSPORTATION NETWORK

| 3,265 km (2,029 miles) | Trans-Sahara Highway 428 km (266 miles) |
| None, but shares administration of Benin's railroad | 300 km (186 miles) |

A very small proportion of Niger's road network is paved. There are international airports at Niamey and Agadez. There is no railroad.

TOURISM

Visitors : population 1:561

18,000 visitors

Up 6% 1995–1997

MAIN TOURIST ARRIVALS

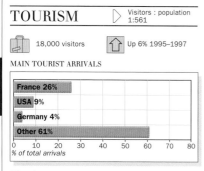

France 26%
USA 9%
Germany 4%
Other 61%

0 10 20 30 40 50 60 70 80
% of total arrivals

The Aïr mountains, southern Hausa cities and Saharan Tuareg culture attract some tourists in spite of Niger's limited infrastructure and its instability.

PEOPLE

Pop. density low

Hausa, Djerma, Fulani, Tuareg, Teda, French

8/km² (21/mi²)

THE URBAN/RURAL POPULATION SPLIT

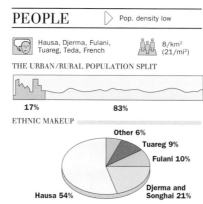

17%   83%

ETHNIC MAKEUP

Other 6%
Tuareg 9%
Fulani 10%
Djerma and Songhai 21%
Hausa 54%

Considerable tensions exist between the Tuaregs in the north and the southern groups. The Tuaregs' sense of alienation from mainstream Niger politics has increased since the 1973 and 1983 droughts, which disrupted the Tuaregs' nomadic way of life. A five-year rebellion by northern Tuaregs ended in 1995 with a peace agreement. In eastern Niger, Toubou and Arab groups have also been in revolt.

A more subtle antagonism exists between the Djerma and Hausa groups. Until recently, the Djerma elite from the southwest dominated politics. Since 1993, however, control has passed to the Hausa majority.

Niger is an overwhelmingly Islamic society. Women have, on the whole, only limited rights and restricted access to education.

Testing boating poles in the market at Ayorou on the River Niger, the country's only major permanent watercourse.

POLITICS

No multiparty elections

1996/1999

Maj. Daouda Mallam Wanke, Chair of the National Reconciliation Council

AT THE LAST ELECTION

National Assembly 83 seats

13% Other

71% UNIRD

16% UNIRD-S

UNIRD = National Union of Independents for Democratic Renewal and its allies UNIRD-S = UNIRD supporters

The death of dictator Seyni Kountché, in 1987, paved the way for prodemocracy demonstrations and eventually led to multiparty elections in 1993. President Mahamane Ousmane's power struggle in 1996, with opponents who had gained control of the Assembly, provoked a military coup. Col. Ibrahim Barre Mainassara promulgated a new constitution and won a presidential election condemned as fraudulent by the opposition. Mainassara was assassinated by his presidential guard in April 1999. The new military leadership drew up yet another constitution, with a formula for power-sharing between president and prime minister, and promised elections by the year's end.

WORLD AFFAIRS

Joined UN in 1960

| CILSS | Ecowas | FZ | OAU | OIC |

Relations with Libya and Algeria have improved since the end of the Tuareg rebellion in 1995. Ecowas members and the OAU condemned the 1999 coup, as did all key donors, led by France. The new military leader launched an intense diplomatic campaign to regain international backing.

AID

Recipient

$341m (receipts)

Up 32% 1996–1997

Almost all development is aid-funded. France is the principal donor, followed by the IMF and Arab funds. Most aid was frozen after the 1999 coup.

DEFENSE

Compulsory military service

$22m

No change in 1997

Niger's armed forces and paramilitary elements total 10,700. Politics has been dominated by the military since 1974.

NIGER

Total Land Area : 1 266 700 sq. km
(489 073 sq. miles)

POPULATION   LAND HEIGHT

- ⊚ over 100 000
- ○ over 50 000
- ● over 10 000
- • under 10 000

- 1000m/3281ft
- 500m/1640ft
- 200m/656ft
- 150m/492ft

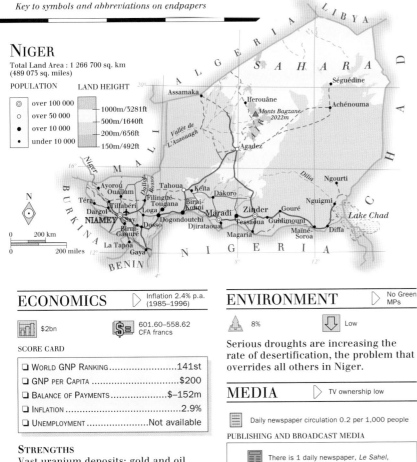

CHRONOLOGY

The powerful Islamic Sokoto Empire dissolved as the French took Niger over between 1883 and 1901.

- ❑ **1960** Independence. Hamani Diori's one-party PPN state.
- ❑ **1968** French open uranium mines.
- ❑ **1973** Drought; 60% of livestock die.
- ❑ **1974** Military coup; parties banned.
- ❑ **1984** New drought; Niger river dries up for first time in history. Uranium boom ends.
- ❑ **1987** Kountché dies. Gen. Saibou eases transition to democracy.
- ❑ **1990** Tuareg rebellion begins.
- ❑ **1993** Democratic elections.
- ❑ **1996** Military coup. Gen. Mainassara tries to legitimize rule through staged elections.
- ❑ **1999** Mainassara assassinated. Military promise early return to civilian rule.

ECONOMICS

▷ Inflation 2.4% p.a. (1985–1996)

$2bn

601.60–558.62 CFA francs

SCORE CARD

- ❑ WORLD GNP RANKING.........................141st
- ❑ GNP PER CAPITA $200
- ❑ BALANCE OF PAYMENTS....................$–152m
- ❑ INFLATION 2.9%
- ❑ UNEMPLOYMENT ....Not available

STRENGTHS

Vast uranium deposits; gold and oil discoveries in late 1990s revived hopes for economic viability.

WEAKNESSES

Aid-dependent. Collapse of uranium prices in 1980s created large debt burden. Only 3% of land is cultivable. Weak infrastructure. Frequent droughts. Political instability.

EXPORTS

- Nigeria 5%
- UK 13%
- USA 30%
- France 15%
- Greece 16%
- Other 21%

IMPORTS

- Belgium-Luxembourg 5%
- USA 5%
- Germany 5%
- Ivory Coast 7%
- France 15%
- Other 63%

RESOURCES

▷ Electric power 63,000 kw

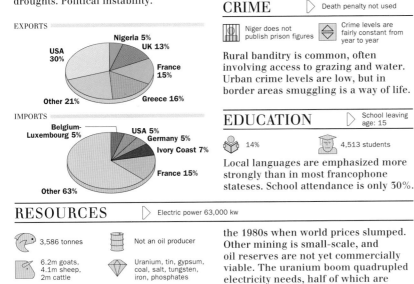

3,586 tonnes

Not an oil producer

6.2m goats, 4.1m sheep, 2m cattle

Uranium, tin, gypsum, coal, salt, tungsten, iron, phosphates

During the 1970s, Niger's uranium mines boomed, but output collapsed in the 1980s when world prices slumped. Other mining is small-scale, and oil reserves are not yet commercially viable. The uranium boom quadrupled electricity needs, half of which are now met by Nigeria's Kainji dam on the Niger river.

ENVIRONMENT

▷ No Green MPs

8%

Low

Serious droughts are increasing the rate of desertification, the problem that overrides all others in Niger.

MEDIA

▷ TV ownership low

Daily newspaper circulation 0.2 per 1,000 people

PUBLISHING AND BROADCAST MEDIA

There is 1 daily newspaper, *Le Sahel*, published by the government

1 state-owned service

1 state-owned, some independent services

The BBC World Service's Hausa programming is more influential than local French short-wave radio.

CRIME

▷ Death penalty not used

Niger does not publish prison figures

Crime levels are fairly constant from year to year

Rural banditry is common, often involving access to grazing and water. Urban crime levels are low, but in border areas smuggling is a way of life.

EDUCATION

▷ School leaving age: 15

14%

4,513 students

Local languages are emphasized more strongly than in most francophone stateses. School attendance is only 30%.

HEALTH

▷ No welfare state health benefits

1 per 33,333 people

Malaria, tuberculosis, meningitis, measles, malnutrition

In spite of progress in rural health care, immunization, malaria control, and child nutrition are still limited.

SPENDING

▷ GDP/cap. no increase

CONSUMPTION AND SPENDING

4 per 1,000 population

2 per 1,000 population

Defense 1.4%

Education 3.1%

Health 0.2%

| 0 | 5 | 10 | 15 | 20 | 25 |

Defense, Health, Education spending as % of GDP

Much of the country's wealth is controlled by a small circle of secretive trading families who evade taxation.

WORLD RANKING

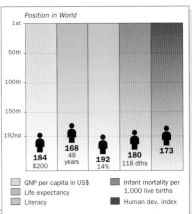

Position in World

- 1st
- 50th
- 100th
- 150th
- 192nd

- **184** $200
- **168** 49 years
- **192** 14%
- **180** 118 dths
- **173**

- ❑ GNP per capita in US$
- ❑ Life expectancy
- ❑ Literacy
- ❑ Infant mortality per 1,000 live births
- ❑ Human dev. index

NIGERIA

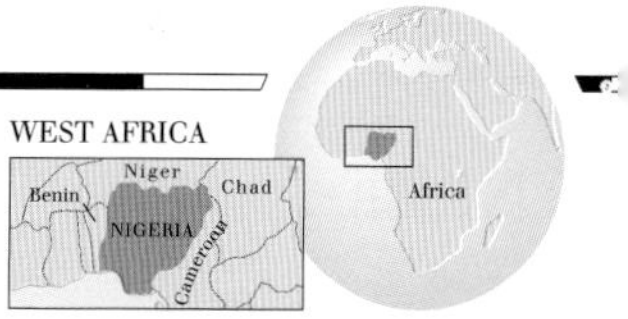

WEST AFRICA

OFFICIAL NAME: Federal Republic of Nigeria **CAPITAL:** Abuja
POPULATION: 122 million **CURRENCY:** Naira **OFFICIAL LANGUAGE:** English

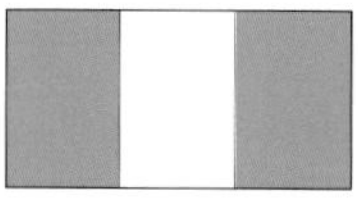

| 1960 | 1961 | Oct 1 | WAN | +1 | +234 | .ng |

AFRICA'S MOST POPULOUS state, Nigeria gained its independence from Britain in 1960. Bordered by Benin, Niger, Chad, and Cameroon, its terrain varies from tropical rain forest and swamps in the south to savanna in the north. Nigeria has been dominated by military governments since 1966. After many delays, a promised return to civilian rule came about in 1999, with the election as president of Olusegun Obasanjo, a former general who had been head of state from 1976 to 1979. Nigeria is OPEC's fourth-largest oil producer, but it has experienced a fall in living standards since the 1970s oil boom.

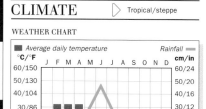
Village beneath Tengele Peak *in Bauchi State. A large proportion of Nigerians live from subsistence agriculture.*

CLIMATE

▷ Tropical/steppe

WEATHER CHART

The south is hot, rainy and humid for most of the year. The arid north experiences only one, uncomfortably humid, rainy season from May to September. Its very hot dry season is marked by the dust-laden *harmattan* wind. The Jos Plateau and the eastern highlands are cooler than the rest of Nigeria. Forcados in the Niger delta gets most rain with 380 cm (150 inches) a year.

TRANSPORTATION

▷ Drive on right

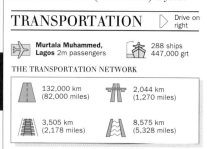

Murtala Muhammed, Lagos 2m passengers	288 ships 447,000 grt

THE TRANSPORTATION NETWORK

132,000 km (82,000 miles)	2,044 km (1,270 miles)
3,505 km (2,178 miles)	8,575 km (5,328 miles)

Nigeria relies almost entirely on road transportation. During the oil-boom years of the 1970s, new long-distance road links and stretches of freeway were built. The country's network of roads is now badly maintained and in urgent need of repair. The road accident rate is among the world's highest and there is severe chronic traffic congestion in Lagos. The railway lines are narrow gauge. Nigerian Airways' international operations have been privatized as a new corporation, Air Nigeria. The internal air market has shrunk since the 1970s.

TOURISM

▷ Visitors : population 1:199

611,000 visitors

Up 215% 1994–1997

Nigeria has attempted to build a tourist industry, but numbers remain low. Year-round tropical temperatures and poor infrastructure have limited its growth. The major deterrent to visitors, however, is crime. Travel can be hazardous, and Lagos has one of the world's highest crime rates.

MAIN TOURIST ARRIVALS

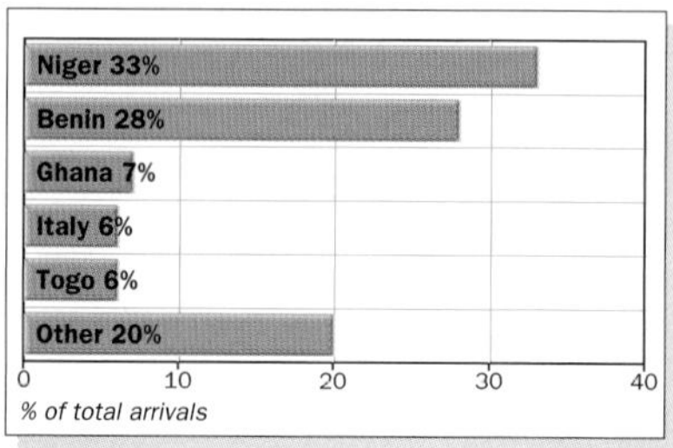

Niger 33%
Benin 28%
Ghana 7%
Italy 6%
Togo 6%
Other 20%

% of total arrivals

NIGERIA

Total Land Area : 910 770 sq. km (351 648 sq. miles)

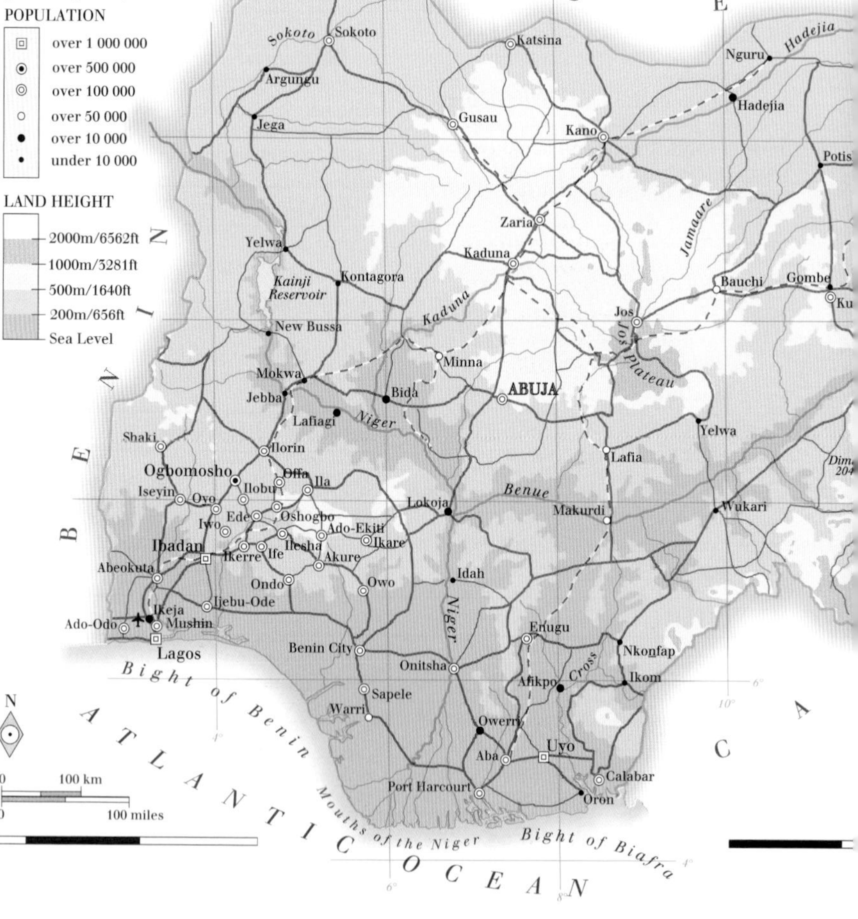

POPULATION
- ⊡ over 1 000 000
- ◉ over 500 000
- ◎ over 100 000
- ○ over 50 000
- ● over 10 000
- • under 10 000

LAND HEIGHT
- 2000m/6562ft
- 1000m/3281ft
- 500m/1640ft
- 200m/656ft
- Sea Level

PEEOPLE ▷ Pop. density medium

Hausa, English Creole, Yoruba, Ibo, English

134/km² (346/mi²)

THE URBAN/RURAL POPULATION SPLIT

39%   61%

RELIGIOUS PERSUASION

Traditional beliefs 10%

Muslim 50%

Christian 40%

ETHNIC MAKEUP

Fulani 11%

Other ethnic groups 29%

Ibo 18%

Yoruba 21%

Hausa 21%

In recent years, Nigeria has largely managed to contain the passions generated by the ethnic, religious, and language differences that characterize its people. There is intense rivalry among the Hausa, Yoruba, and Ibo, the three main ethnic groups, as well as among the 245 smaller ones. Members of one group tend to blame those of another for their problems. Religion is a particular source of tension. Outbreaks of communal violence, particularly in the north, are frequently attributable to clashes between Muslim fundamentalists and Christian proselytizers. Except in the Islamic north, women have traditionally possessed independent economic status. In recent years they have, however, been subjected to some prejudice in professional circles.

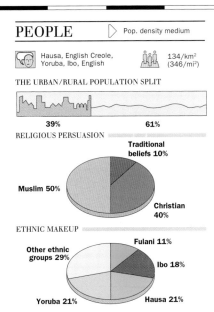

Lake Chad

Damasak Baga

Ngala

aiduguri

POPULATION AGE BREAKDOWN

Female	Age	Male
0.5%	81–100	0.5%
1.9%	61–80	2.2%
5.2%	41–60	6%
15.1%	21–40	13.1%
27.3%	0–20	28.2%

% of population by age group

POLITICS ▷ Multiparty elections

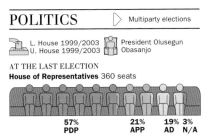

L. House 1999/2003
U. House 1999/2003

President Olusegun Obasanjo

AT THE LAST ELECTION
House of Representatives 360 seats

57% PDP   21% APP   19% AD   3% N/A

PDP = People's Democratic Party **APP** = All People's Party
AD = Alliance for Democracy
N/A = results for the final 12 seats were not available as of Sept 1999

Senate 109 seats

54% PDP   27% APP   18% AD

Since May 1999 Nigeria has a new civilian constitution, after 16 years of military dictatorships. President Olusegun Obasanjo and his People's Democratic Party promise national reconciliation.

MAIN POLITICAL ISSUES
Corruption
International agencies have identified corruption as a major cause of Nigeria's debt levels. Bureaucrats commonly demanded lucrative kickbacks when granting contracts. President Obasanjo has promised to stamp out corruption.

Ethnic tensions
The Obasanjo government faces difficulties in reversing old rivalries among three main tribal communities, the Hausa, Yoruba, and Ibo.

PROFILE
Despite having pledged to restore civilian government General Babangida annulled the results of the 1993 presidential election and imprisoned the presumed winner, Chief Moshood Abiola. Public and international hostility persuaded Babangida to stand down, but his successor, General Abacha, clung to power. Abacha's sudden death in June 1998, followed by the death of Abiola, left General Abdulsalam Aboubakar to usher in civilian rule. Elections in February 1999 were won by Olusegun Obasanjo, a popular general who had been head of state from 1976 to 1979. He assumed office in May 1999.

Olusegun Obasanjo, elected president in 1999.

Gen. Abacha. Head of state from 1993 till his death in 1998.

CHRONOLOGY

Before formal colonization by the British, begun only in 1861, Nigeria was a collection of African states owing their considerable wealth to trans-Saharan and transatlantic trade. During the 18th century the principal commodity was slaves: over 15,000 people were exported annually from the Bight of Benin and another 15,000 from the Bight of Biafra.

❑ **1885** George Goldie's Royal Niger Company given official responsibility for British sphere of influence along Niger and Benue rivers. British armed forces coerce local rulers into accepting British rule.
❑ **1897** West Africa Frontier Force (WAFF) established; subjugation of the north begins.
❑ **1898** The Royal Niger Company's charter revoked.
❑ **1900** British Protectorate of Northern Nigeria established.
❑ **1906** Lagos incorporated into the Protectorate of Southern Nigeria.
❑ **1914** Protectorates of Northern and Southern Nigeria joined to form colony of Nigeria.
❑ **1960** Independence. Nigeria established as a federation.
❑ **1961** Northern part of UK-administered UN Trust Territory of the Cameroons incorporated as part of Nigeria's Northern Region.
❑ **1966** January, first military coup, led by Maj.-Gen. Ironsi. July, counter-coup mounted by group of northern army officers. Ironsi murdered. Thousands of Ibo in Northern Region massacred. Gen. Gowon in control of north and west.
❑ **1967–1970** Civil war. Lt.-Col. Ojukwu calls for secession of oil-rich east under the new name Biafra. Over one million Nigerians die before secessionists defeated by federal forces.
❑ **1970** Gowon in power.
❑ **1975** Gowon toppled in bloodless coup. Brig. Murtala Mohammed takes power.
❑ **1976** Murtala Mohammed murdered in abortive coup.
❑ **1978** Political parties legalized, on condition they represent national, not tribal, interests.
❑ **1979** Elections won by Alhaji Shehu Shagari and National Party of Nigeria (NPN), marking return to civilian government.
❑ **1983** Military coup. Maj.-Gen. Mohammed Buhari heads Supreme Military Council.
❑ **1985** Maj.-Gen. Ibrahim Babangida takes over in bloodless coup, promising a return to democracy. ▷

N

CHRONOLOGY *continued*

- ❑ **1993** August, Babangida annuls presidential election probably won by Moshood Abiola; international protest and strikes. Babangida resigns presidency; military sets up Interim National Government (ING) led by Chief Adegunle Shonekan. November, ING dissolved. Military, under Gen. Sani Abacha, takes over.
- ❑ **1994** Abiola arrested, opposition harassed.
- ❑ **1995** Ban on political parties lifted. Conviction by a military tribunal of former head of state Gen. Olusegun Obasanjo and 39 others for plotting coup. Relations with Commonwealth and individual states breached after execution of Ken Saro-Wiwa and eight other Ogoni activists.
- ❑ **1998** Abacha dies; Abiola dies; Abacha's successor Gen. Abdulsalam Aboubakar announces timetable for restoring civilian rule by May 1999.
- ❑ **1999** Elections for state governors, legislature and president, won by Olusegun Obasanjo, former military head of state.

WORLD AFFAIRS

Joined UN in 1960

Nigerian governments like to regard their country as Africa's leading voice. Nigeria is a keen sponsor of ECOWAS and of the OAU, and has been the main contributor to Ecowas intervention forces. However, the military regime's violations of human rights (most notoriously the execution of Ken Saro-Wiwa and eight other Ogoni activists in 1995) prompted UN condemnation and Nigeria's suspension from the Commonwealth. Membership was only restored after Obasanjo came to power in 1999.

Nigeria was an implacable opponent of *apartheid*, and relations with South Africa were restored only after democratic elections there in 1994. President Obasanjo's government is expected to forge close links with South Africa, the two countries being the continent's leading powers.

AID

Recipient

$202m (receipts)   Up 5% 1996–1997

Nigeria's debt rocketed with the 1981 drop in world oil prices, turning Nigeria from an aid donor into a major receiver of World Bank assistance. However, international assistance was halted after the execution of Ken Saro-Wiwa and others in late 1995.

DEFENSE

No compulsory military service

$1.97bn   Up 3% in 1997

The military in Nigeria suffers from problems caused by corruption. During Babangida's rule (1985–1993), most of the air force's prestige jets were grounded, as money for spare parts was diverted into senior officers' bank accounts. Soldiers' salaries have been steadily declining in real terms in recent years, barrack conditions have deteriorated and morale is low. The military government which took power in 1993 encouraged expectations of improved conditions among the army rank and file, and these expectations will no doubt be a problem for the civilian administration which took over in 1999. Nigerian forces intervened as effective regional peacemakers in civil wars in Liberia (1990–1996) and Sierra Leone (1998–1999).

NIGERIAN ARMED FORCES

	200 main battle tanks (50 T-55, 150 Vickers Mk 3)	62,000 personnel
	1 frigate, 51 patrol boats (2 *Exocet* missiles)	5,500 personnel
	91 combat aircraft (19 *Alpha Jet*, 22 MiG, 15 *Jaguar*)	9,500 personnel
	None	

ECONOMICS

Inflation 34% p.a. (1985–1996)

$33bn   21.89–21.89 naira

SCORE CARD

- ❑ WORLD GNP RANKING..........................55th
- ❑ GNP PER CAPITA $280
- ❑ BALANCE OF PAYMENTS $552m
- ❑ INFLATION 8.2%
- ❑ UNEMPLOYMENT..................................28%

EXPORTS

France 4%
USA 38%
Germany 5%
India 7%
Spain 9%
Other 37%

IMPORTS

Italy 6%
France 7%
UK 11%
Germany 12%
USA 13%
Other 51%

STRENGTHS

One of world's top oil producers at 2.1 million b/d. Vast reserves of natural gas, still only partly exploited. Almost self-sufficient in food. Strong entrepreneurial class. Large domestic market of over 120 million people.

WEAKNESSES

Overdependence since the 1970s on oil, which accounts for 90% of export earnings and 80% of government revenue, and encourages massive state inefficiency. Advantages of a large domestic market mitigated by low per capita purchasing power and high unit transportation costs. Entrepreneurs focus on trade rather than production. Of Nigeria's traditional agricultural exports only cocoa remains. Notorious corruption and maladminstration undermine investors' confidence.

ECONOMIC PERFORMANCE INDICATOR

Consumer price index   GDP

Consumer price index 1990=100

GDP 1990=100

1990 1991 1992 1993 1994

PROFILE

The economy has been characterized by massive government spending and the running-up of debts which could not be serviced after the 1981 oil price fall. Led by the IMF, creditors want major cuts in spending – especially on loss-making public-sector companies – and subsidies. Gasoline subsidies alone are estimated to have cost $2.4 billion a year. Changes are politically fraught. In May 1999 the new government began reviewing recent contracts in an anti-corruption drive.

NIGERIA : MAJOR BUSINESSES

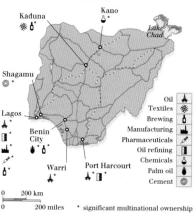

Kaduna
Kano
Lake Chad
Shagamu
Lagos
Benin City
Warri
Port Harcourt

Oil
Textiles
Brewing
Manufacturing
Pharmaceuticals
Oil refining
Chemicals
Palm oil
Cement

0   200 km
0   200 miles   * significant multinational ownership

RESOURCES

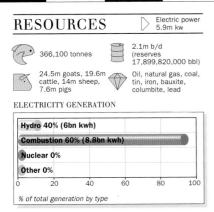

▷ Electric power 5.9m kw

366,100 tonnes

2.1m b/d (reserves 17,899,820,000 bbl)

24.5m goats, 19.6m cattle, 14m sheep, 7.6m pigs

Oil, natural gas, coal, tin, iron, bauxite, columbite, lead

ELECTRICITY GENERATION

	% of total generation by type
Hydro 40% (6bn kwh)	
Combustion 60% (8.8bn kwh)	
Nuclear 0%	
Other 0%	

Oil has been Nigeria's main resource since the 1970s. Government policy is to increase output to 2.5 million b/d. Domestic demand is 300,000 b/d, much of it smuggled to neighboring countries. Nigeria's vast gas deposits are still underexploited. The state retains 60% control of the oil and gas industry. Shell is the main foreign shareholder, but most oil multinationals are represented.

Nigeria has sizable iron ore deposits. These are not yet utilized in the state-run steel industry; imported ore is used instead. Bauxite deposits are also currently under-exploited. There are, however, plans for establishing an aluminum industry. Nigeria also has deposits of coal and tin.

NIGERIA : LAND USE

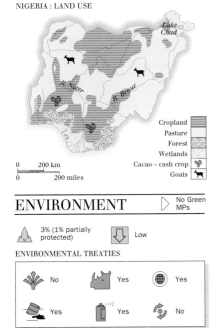

Lake Chad

R. Niger   R. Benue

Cropland	
Pasture	
Forest	
Wetlands	
Cacao – cash crop	
Goats	

0   200 km
0   200 miles

ENVIRONMENT

▷ No Green MPs

3% (1% partially protected)

⬇ Low

ENVIRONMENTAL TREATIES

	No		Yes		Yes
	Yes		Yes		No

Oil industry pollution in the Niger delta is a major local concern, coming to international attention in 1995. Shell has been particularly condemned. Before the discovery of a highly toxic cargo in Lagos in 1988, Nigeria was a dumping ground for European chemical waste.

MEDIA

▷ TV ownership medium

Daily newspaper circulation 24 per 1,000 people

Nigerians are avid newspaper readers and the press is traditionally one of Africa's liveliest. However, under the military regime there was little willingness to tolerate criticism, and some press harassment. There are more than 20 current-affairs periodicals.

CRIME

▷ Death penalty used

Nigeria does not publish prison figures

⬆ Rising

CRIME RATES

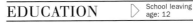

Murders	
94	per 100,000 population

Rapes
Nigeria does not publish rape statistics

Thefts	
1256	per 100,000 population

The military government frequently used ad hoc tribunals for politically sensitive cases. Nigeria has one of the highest crime rates in the world. Murder often accompanies even minor burglaries. Corruption pervades the bureaucracy; the provision of kick-backs to supporters is considered routine rather than a crime. Rich Nigerians live in high-security compounds, equipped with electric fencing and patrolled by armed guards.

EDUCATION

▷ School leaving age: 12

60%

335,824 students

Education has suffered from the massive debt repayment burden.

THE EDUCATION SYSTEM

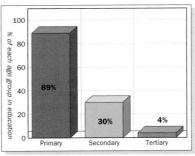

During the oil-boom years, Nigeria concentrated on creating 31 universities with prestigious medical and scientific schools. However, standards in primary education, which has not received the same level of investment, have fallen since the 1970s. About 90% of children attend primary school, but only about 30% receive secondary education.

PUBLISHING AND BROADCAST MEDIA

There are 25 daily newspapers. The *Daily Times*, published by the government has highest circulation

1 state-controlled service, 14 licensed private stations

1 state-controlled service, 1 opposition, 2 independent commercial services

HEALTH

▷ Welfare state health benefits

1 per 5,000 people

Yellow fever, malaria, trachoma, yaws

The health service is concentrated in urban areas and is mostly aimed at richer Nigerians. Modern medical care is not available to those living in rural areas. Health provision, with other public services, has suffered from the crisis in government revenues. In 1997, an estimated 2.3 million Nigerians were HIV/AIDS carriers.

SPENDING

▷ GDP/cap. no increase

CONSUMPTION AND SPENDING

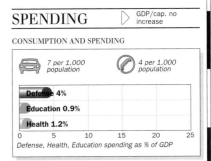

7 per 1,000 population

4 per 1,000 population

Defense 4%	
Education 0.9%	
Health 1.2%	

Defense, Health, Education spending as % of GDP

Nigerians with access to the rich pickings of political office spent on a massive scale during the country's oil boom – on expensive cars such as Maseratis and Mercedes, and on overseas education for their children. Much was financed by government loans. Habits have not changed with the fall in oil revenues: borrowing has simply grown.

WORLD RANKING

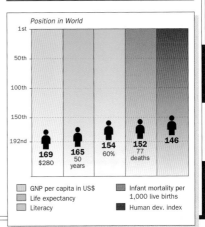

Position in World

169 $280	165 50 years	154 60%	152 77 deaths	146

GNP per capita in US$
Life expectancy
Literacy
Infant mortality per 1,000 live births
Human dev. index

N

NORWAY

OFFICIAL NAME: Kingdom of Norway **CAPITAL:** Oslo **POPULATION:** 4.4 million
CURRENCY: Norwegian krone **OFFICIAL LANGUAGE:** Norwegian

| 1905 | 1905 | May 17 | N | +1 | +47 | .no |

OCCUPYING THE WESTERN PART of Scandinavia, Norway borders Sweden, Finland, and Russia to its east; its western coastline features numerous fjords and islands. Large oil and gas revenues have brought prosperity. Gro Harlem Brundtland became Norway's first woman prime minister in 1981. Despite the Europe-wide recession in the early 1990s, Norway managed to contain unemployment, which peaked at 6% in 1993. The duty of government to create conditions that enable every person to find work is enshrined in the constitution.

The village of Reine on Moskenesøya, 99 mi. inside the Arctic Circle in the Lofoten Islands. It is a popular destination for summer visitors.

CLIMATE ▷ Maritime/subarctic

WEATHER CHART

■ Average daily temperature   Rainfall ■

The whole of Norway's west coast is kept ice-free by the warm Gulf Stream. It receives much more precipitation than the rest of the country; Bergen has a yearly average of 225 cm (89 inches). Norway enjoys the highest mean temperatures in Scandinavia, but in winter the temperature in Oslo can drop to −25°C (−13°F).

NORWAY

Total Land Area : 306 850 sq. km
(118 467 sq. miles)

LAND HEIGHT

2000m/6562ft
1000m/3281ft
500m/1640ft
200m/656ft
Sea Level

POPULATION

◎ over 100 000
○ over 50 000
● over 10 000
• under 10 000

TRANSPORTATION ▷ Drive on right

Fornebu Intl, Oslo
13m passengers

2,227 ships
21.81m grt

THE TRANSPORTATION NETWORK

| 91,300 km (56,700 miles) | 106 km (66 miles) |
| 4,021 km (2,499 miles) | 5,633 km (3,500 miles) |

It has been impossible to extend rail links further than Bodø, inside the Arctic Circle. To reach Lofoten or Narvik and beyond, the most common form of transport is air. Some 5% of the world's total shipping tonnage is controlled by Norway, making it the sixth-largest shipping nation.

The royal palace, Oslo. This is situated near the national theater, at one end of the Karl Johanisgate, the city's main thoroughfare.

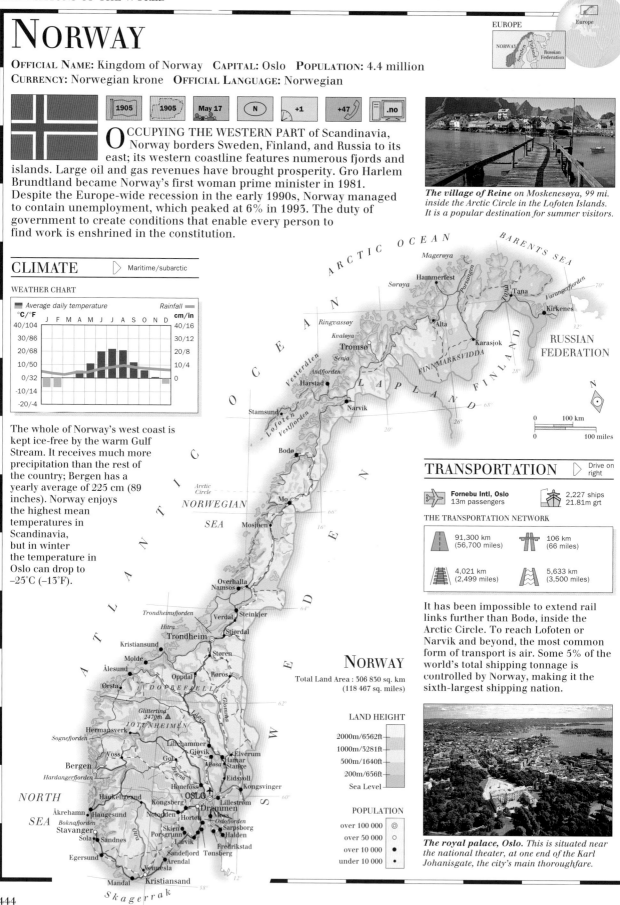

TOURISM

▷ Visitors : population 1:1.6

2.7m visitors

Down 6% 1995–1997

Norway is a popular destination, with visitors from Sweden, Germany, Denmark, the UK, and the USA. Its winter tourism industry is based on skiing and has been boosted by the location of the 1994 Winter Olympics in Lillehammer. Cruising along the fjords is popular with summer visitors. Areas within the Arctic Circle are a particular attraction in June, when tourists go in search of the midnight sun. Oslo has a reputation for good classical music and jazz. However, the strength of the

MAIN TOURIST ARRIVALS

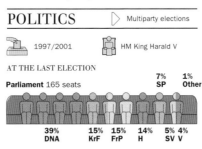

- Germany 6%
- Denmark 5%
- Sweden 5%
- UK 3%
- USA 3%
- Other 78%

% of total arrivals

krone and the high cost of living make Norway expensive.

PEOPLE

▷ Pop. density low

Norwegian (*Bokmål* "book language" and *Nynorsk* "new Norsk"), Lappish

14/km² (37/mi²)

THE URBAN/RURAL POPULATION SPLIT

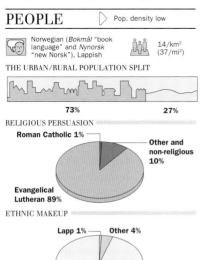

73%   27%

RELIGIOUS PERSUASION

Roman Catholic 1%

Other and non-religious 10%

Evangelical Lutheran 89%

ETHNIC MAKEUP

Lapp 1%   Other 4%

Norwegian 95%

Norway has a minimal immigrant population. In the early 1990s the numbers of asylum seekers increased, especially as a result of the Bosnian conflict. Some refugees have been attacked by right-wing groups but generally they are welcomed.

The family is traditionally close and nuclear. Men are expected to share responsibility for raising children.

Children frequently attend day schools from below the age of two years. Women in Norway enjoy considerable power and freedom. Former premier Brundtland is one of many prominent women in politics. Over half of marriages end in divorce.

POPULATION AGE BREAKDOWN

Female	Age	Male
2.7%	81–100	1.3%
8.6%	61–80	7.2%
12.1%	41–60	12.6%
14.6%	21–40	15.2%
12.5%	0–20	13.2%

% of population by age group

POLITICS

▷ Multiparty elections

1997/2001

HM King Harald V

AT THE LAST ELECTION

Parliament 165 seats

				7% SP	1% Other
39% DNA	15% KrF	15% FrP	14% H	5% SV	4% V

DNA = Norwegian Labour Party **KrF** = Christian Democratic Party **FrP** = Progress Party **H**= Hoeyre (Conservative Party) **SP** = Centre Party **SV** = Socialist Left Party **V** = Venstre (Liberal Party)
The Parliament (Stortinget) is elected as one body but divides itself for most legislative purposes into an upper chamber (Lagting, with 42 members) and a lower chamber (Odelsting, with 123 members).

Norway is a constitutional monarchy, with a king as head of state and an elected parliament.

MAIN POLITICAL ISSUES
Membership of the EU
In a referendum in November 1994, 52% voted against EU membership. Terms for accession had been agreed, and government and industry supported the move, but opponents argued successfully that it would lead to a loss of control of national resources. Membership was rejected once before in 1972; another possible application is a divisive issue.

PROFILE
Political decisions are based on consensus building between the government, parliament and the trade unions. The SP, against joining the EU, more than doubled its representation in 1993 elections, whereas the pro-EU Conservatives slipped badly. The DNA defeat in 1997 opened the way for a center-right coalition led by Kjell Magne Bondevik of the Christian People's Party.

The DNA hold on power from 1990 to 1997, was partly due to the personal standing of Gro Harlem Brundtland, prime minister until she stood down in 1996 to become director-general of the World Health Organization in 1998. While her pro-whaling stance damaged her image abroad, it was popular at home.

WORLD AFFAIRS

▷ Joined UN in 1945

CE   NATO   OECD   OSCE   EEA

A founder member of NATO, Norway continues to provide strong support for the organization. It also became an associate member of the WEU in 1992.

The 1994 referendum decision to reject EU membership means that the European Economic Area (EEA) offers Norway its chief access to the European single market. As a Nordic Council member it is also associated with the Schengen Convention. The question of EU membership is unlikely to be raised again under the current government.

Norway has played peacemaker in a number of major international conflicts, notably in helping to progress toward a resolution of the Palestinian–Israeli conflict.

The government has been unable to control the ecological effects of acid rain, which is destroying its forests, and blames lax pollution controls in the UK, Germany, and Russia. Representatives of 25 European countries and Canada met in Oslo in 1994 and signed a UN protocol on reducing sulfur emissions.

King Harald V, *who succeeded his father King Olaf V in 1991.*

Gro Harlem Brundtland, *prime minister, 1989–1989 and1990–96.*

CHRONOLOGY

Norway gained independence from the Swedish crown in 1905 and elected its own king, Håkon VII.

- ❑ **1935** DNA forms government.
- ❑ **1940–1945** Nazi occupation. Puppet regime led by Vidkun Quisling.
- ❑ **1945** DNA resumes power.
- ❑ **1949** Norway joins NATO.
- ❑ **1957** King Håkon dies. Succeeded by son, Olaf V.
- ❑ **1960** Becomes member of EFTA.
- ❑ **1962** Unsuccessfully applies for EC membership.
- ❑ **1965** DNA electoral defeat by SP coalition led by Per Borten.
- ❑ **1967** Norway makes second bid for EC membership.
- ❑ **1971** Prime minister Per Borten resigns following disclosure of secret negotiations to join EC. DNA government, led by Trygve Bratteli.
- ❑ **1972** EC membership rejected by ➪

N

CHRONOLOGY *continued*

people in referendum by 3% majority. Bratteli resigns. Center coalition government takes power. Lars Korvald prime minister.

❑ **1973** Elections. Bratteli returns to power as prime minister.

❑ **1976** Bratteli succeeded by Odvar Nordli.

❑ **1981** Nordli resigns owing to ill health. Gro Harlem Brundtland becomes first woman prime minister. Elections bring to power Norway's first Conservative Party (H) government for 53 years. Kare Willoch prime minister.

❑ **1983** H forms coalition with SP and KRF.

❑ **1985** Election. Willoch's H–SP–KRF coalition returned. Norway agrees to suspend commercial whaling.

❑ **1986** 100,000 workers demonstrate for better pay and shorter working week. Parliament rejects tax increase on gasoline. Willoch resigns. Brundtland forms minority DNA government. Currency devalued by 12%.

❑ **1989** Brundtland resigns. H–KRF coalition to power. USSR agrees exchange of information after fires on Soviet nuclear submarines off Norwegian coast.

❑ **1990** H–KRF coalition breaks up over closer ties with EU. Brundtland and DNA in power.

❑ **1991** Olaf V dies; succeeded by son, King Harald V.

❑ **1994** EEA into effect. Referendum rejects EU membership.

❑ **1996** Brundtland resigns; Thorbjoern Jagland (also DNA) takes over.

❑ **1997** DNA loses ground in general election; Kjell Magne Bondevik forms center-right coalition.

AID ▷ Donor

 $1bn (donations) Not applicable

Norway has been granting more than the UN development target of 0.7% of GNP in aid every year since 1975. Although Norway's ratio of aid to GNP. declined from 1.17% to 0.85% in 1996, it remains (with Denmark) the highest in the world. The vast majority of Norway's bilateral aid goes to the least developed countries of southeastern Africa, southern Asia and Central America, though Palestine and Bosnia are also important recipients. The Norwegian government also allocates funds to various multilateral assistance programs. The 1999 budget included a debt relief program to help reduce developing country indebtedness.

DEFENSE ▷ Compulsory military service

$3.3bn Down 11% in 1997

Norway spends 2.3% of GDP on defense, mostly on its conscript army. It joined NATO in 1949, unlike Sweden and Finland. The overriding defense issue is the stability of Russia and the security of their common border. Five Russian diplomats were expelled in March 1998 after a double agent revealed that Russia had extensive information on Norwegian defenses and the oil industry.

NORWEGIAN ARMED FORCES

170 main battle tanks (Leopard)	15,200 personnel	
12 submarines, 4 frigates and 22 patrol boats	6,100 personnel	
79 combat aircraft (15 F-A/B, 58 F-16A/B)	6,700 personnel	
None		

ECONOMICS ▷ Inflation 2.9% p.a. (1985–1996)

$159bn 7.37–7.62 Norwegian kroner

SCORE CARD

❑ WORLD GNP RANKING.........................27th
❑ GNP PER CAPITA $36,100
❑ BALANCE OF PAYMENTS.....................$8.1bn
❑ INFLATION 2.6%
❑ UNEMPLOYMENT 4%

ECONOMIC PERFORMANCE INDICATOR

EXPORTS

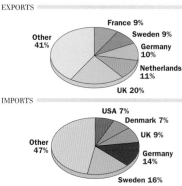

France 9%
Sweden 9%
Germany 10%
Netherlands 11%
UK 20%
Other 41%

IMPORTS

USA 7%
Denmark 7%
UK 9%
Germany 14%
Sweden 16%
Other 47%

STRENGTHS

Western Europe's biggest producer and exporter of oil and natural gas. Mineral reserves. Hydroelectric power satisfies much of country's energy demands, allowing most oil to be exported. Petroleum fund for current profits to provide for future generations. Large merchant shipping fleet. Balance of payments surplus. Low inflation and unemployment compared with rest of Europe.

WEAKNESSES

Overdependence on oil revenue. Small home market and inaccessible geographical location. Harsh climate limits agriculture. Shortage of skilled labor.

PROFILE

The state is interventionist by nature. In 1991, it stepped in to rescue most of the main commercial banks, which had been hit by bad loans. It began returning them to the private sector in 1994. The state also manages the

distribution of offshore oil and gas licenses, maintaining control of over 50% of these through its own company, Statoil.

Norway's immediate future prosperity is guaranteed by its lucrative offshore sector. There is currently a shortage of skilled labor, partly eased by the arrival of workers from other Scandinavian countries, but creating upward pressure on wages. Continuing the strong regional policy of redirecting resources from the more prosperous south to the isolated north is likely to remain a priority, both for social and strategic reasons.

NORWAY : MAJOR BUSINESSES

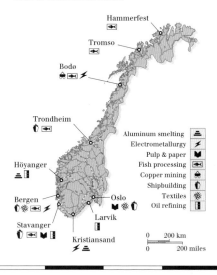

Hammerfest
Tromso
Bodø
Trondheim
Höyanger
Bergen
Oslo
Larvik
Stavanger
Kristiansand

Aluminum smelting
Electrometallurgy
Pulp & paper
Fish processing
Copper mining
Shipbuilding
Textiles
Oil refining

0   200 km
0   200 miles

N

RESOURCES
▷ Electric power 27.7m kw

2.8m tonnes

2.4m sheep, 1m cattle, 770,000 pigs, 63,100 goats

2.1m b/d (reserves 8,805,734,000 bbl)

Oil, natural gas, iron, coal, copper, lead, zinc

ELECTRICITY GENERATION

Hydro 99% (122bn kwh)	
Combustion 1% (0.6bn kwh)	
Nuclear 0%	
Other 0%	

% of total generation by type

Norway is Europe's largest oil producer, with an output of some 2.1 million b/d; it also has sizeable gas reserves. Most of Norway's electricity is produced by hydropower. In summer, the HEP surplus is exported. Fish and forestry are traditionally significant sectors. With agriculture, they account for only 5% of the work force and 2.5% of GDP, but to many Norwegians they are important enough to merit rejection of EU membership. Salmon farms are especially efficient.

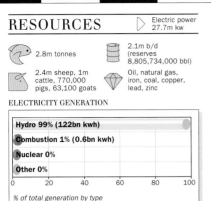

NORWAY : LAND USE

Cropland
Pasture
Forest
High mountain regions
Tundra
Cereals
Sheep

0   200 km
0   200 miles

ENVIRONMENT
▷ No Green MPs

31%

High

ENVIRONMENTAL TREATIES

Yes   Yes   Yes
Yes   Yes   Yes

In 1986 northern Norway suffered radioactive contamination after the Chernobyl nuclear disaster. In 1993, it lifted a ban on fishing minke whales, arguing that the species was not threatened. Norway has introduced a tax on carbon dioxide emissions and was instrumental in securing agreement on the 1997 Kyoto Protocol to reduce greenhouse gas emissions. In 1998 Norway agreed to the dismantling of the controversial Brent Spar oil platform for use as a ferry terminal.

MEDIA
▷ TV ownership high

Daily newspaper circulation 593 per 1,000 people

PUBLISHING AND BROADCAST MEDIA

There are 83 daily newspapers, including *Verdens Gang, T Dagens Nairingsliv, Aftenposten* and *Dagbladet*

1 publicly-owned service, 1 private commercial station

1 publicly-owned service, 1 private commercial station

Norway has the second highest newspaper readership per head in the world, with a total circulation of over two million. *Verdens Gang* is the leading daily with a circulation of 484,000.

CRIME
▷ Death penalty not used

2,398 prisoners

Up 72% from 1992–1996

CRIME RATES

Murders	
3	per 100,000 population

Rapes	
12	per 100,000 population

Thefts	
4499	per 100,000 population

Norway has low levels of crime, even by Scandinavian standards. Violent crime barely exists – the murder rate is a quarter of that of Sweden, and there are considerably fewer assaults and robberies.

EDUCATION
▷ School leaving age: 15

99%

180,383 students

The period of compulsory schooling was increased from nine to ten years

THE EDUCATION SYSTEM

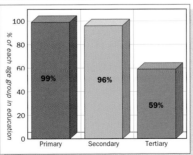

% of each age group in education

Primary 99%   Secondary 96%   Tertiary 59%

from the school year 1997/1998. Most schools are run by municipalities. There are four universities; specialized colleges include the Nordic College of Fisheries. Promotion of continuing education kept youth unemployment down during the early 1990s recession.

HEALTH
▷ Welfare state health benefits

1 per 303 people

Heart and cerebrovascular diseases, cancers

Norway's infant mortality rate is one of the world's lowest and life expectancy at birth one of the highest. Spending on health is no higher than the OECD average, however, and Norway has a third of the number of hospital beds of neighboring Finland.

Telemedicine (online remote audio and image diagnosis) allows remote northern hospitals to obtain specialist consultations without having to send patients to the regional hospital.

Reports in 1998 indicated that hospitals had carried out sterilization experiments on insane and mentally retarded patients in 1974–1994.

SPENDING
▷ GDP/cap. no increase

CONSUMPTION AND SPENDING

399 per 1,000 population

621 per 1,000 population

Defense 2.3%	
Education 8.3%	
Health 8.4%	

0   5   10   15   20   25

Defense, Health, Education spending as % of GDP

In terms of income distribution, the Nordic countries are the most egalitarian in the world. The top 10% of Norway's population owns 21% of its wealth. (In Switzerland the comparable proportion of wealth would be 30%.) Homelessness and social deprivation are very rare. Recent refugees from the Bosnian conflict are the most disadvantaged group.

The discrepancy between men's and women's pay is greater than in either Sweden or Finland, although still well below the European average. Social provision was maintained even through the recession. Benefits are generous.

WORLD RANKING

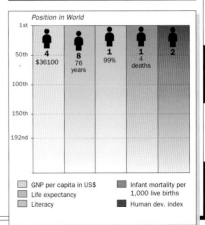

Position in World

1st
50th
100th
150th
192nd

4   8   1   1   2
$36100   76 years   99%   4 deaths

GNP per capita in US$
Life expectancy
Literacy

Infant mortality per 1,000 live births
Human dev. index

N

OMAN

OFFICIAL NAME: Sultanate of Oman **CAPITAL:** Muscat
POPULATION: 2.5 million **CURRENCY:** Omani rial **OFFICIAL LANGUAGE:** Arabic

| 1951 | 1951 | Nov 18 | OM | +4 | +968 | .om |

S HARING BORDERS WITH Yemen, the United Arab
Emirates and Saudi Arabia, Oman occupies a
strategic position at the entrance to the Gulf. It is the least developed of
the Gulf states. The most densely populated areas are the northern coast
and the southern Salalah plain. Oil exports have given Oman modest
prosperity under a paternalistic sultan, who defeated a Marxist-led
insurgency in the 1970s.

CLIMATE

▷ Hot desert

WEATHER CHART

Average daily temperature — Rainfall

The north blisters under temperatures
often above 45°C (113°F) in summer.
The south has a monsoon climate.

TRANSPORTATION

▷ Drive on right

Seeb Intl, Muscat 2.76m passengers — 21 ships 16,000 grt

THE TRANSPORTATION NETWORK

5,900 km (3,666 miles) — None

None — None

There are good roads to neighboring
Gulf states, yet Oman's north–south
road was only completed in 1982.

TOURISM

▷ Visitors : population 1:6.7

375,000 visitors — Up 7% 1995–1997

MAIN TOURIST ARRIVALS

Europe	39%
West Asia	17%
Southeast Asia & Oceania	15%
Other	29%

% of total arrivals

Until the late 1980s, Oman was closed
to all but business or official visitors.
The sultanate's rich cultural heritage,
fine beaches and luxury hotels are
now enjoyed by thousands of Western
visitors a year.

PEOPLE

▷ Pop. density low

Arabic, Baluchi — 12/km² (30/mi²)

THE URBAN/RURAL POPULATION SPLIT

13% — 87%

RELIGIOUS PERSUASION

Other Muslim and Hindu 25%

Ibadhi Muslim 75%

Native Omanis, who include Arab
refugees who fled Zanzibar in the
1960s, make up three-quarters of the
population. Baluchis are the largest
foreign grouping. Expatriates
pose no threat to the regime
and Westerners enjoy
considerable freedom.
Although urban drift has taken
place, most Omanis still live
on the land, especially in the
south. Oman has a number of
distinct minorities; the most
numerous are the Jebalis in
Dhofar – nomadic
herdsmen who speak a
language which resembles
Ethiopian. Many Dhofaris
supported the Marxist-led
insurgents in the 1970s, but
they are now considered
loyal. Most Omanis are
Ibadi Muslims who
follow an
appointed
leader,
called
the
Imam.
Ibadism
is not
opposed to
freedom for
women, and a
few women
enjoy positions
of authority.

POLITICS

▷ No multiparty elections

Not applicable — Sultan Qaboos bin Said

LEGISLATIVE OR ADVISORY BODIES

Consultative Council 82 seats

There are no political parties. The members of the
Consultative Council (Majlis ash-shoura) are appointed by the
Sultan.

Sultan Qaboos is an authoritarian but
paternalistic monarch, whose
dynasty traces its roots to the 18th
century. In addition to being head
of state, he is prime minister and
minister for foreign affairs, defense
and finance. Family members hold
other key posts. The regime faces no
serious challenge, although Qaboos
keeps a careful eye on the religious
right wing. In 1991, he took the
step of
creating the Consultative Council
(*majlis ash-shoura*), which gives a
semblance of democracy. The main
political issues include the planned
privatization of medium-sized
government projects, and the
question of Oman's self-defense
capability.

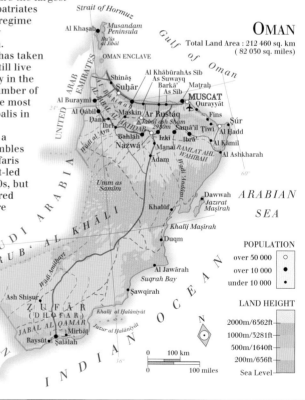

OMAN

Total Land Area : 212 460 sq. km
(82 050 sq. miles)

POPULATION

○ over 50 000
● over 10 000
• under 10 000

LAND HEIGHT

2000m/6562ft
1000m/5281ft
500m/1640ft
200m/656ft
Sea Level

WORLD AFFAIRS

Joined UN in 1971

| AL | AMF | Dam Dec | GCC | OIC |

Sultan Qaboos has built up relatively close relations with Israel in recent years. Oman is firmly pro-Western, but does not subscribe to Western anxieties about the region, maintaining good ties with Iran and calling for an easing of sanctions against Iraq.

A watchtower above an oasis. *Most of Oman is gravelly desert. The only large area of cultivation is the 20-km-wide Al Batinah plain.*

AID

Recipient

$20m (receipts)

Down 68% 1996–1997

Oman is a recipient of World Bank, US and UK overseas assistance. Agencies face difficulty in allocating aid to Oman as it has yet to hold a census. Oman itself donated aid to anticommunist causes in the 1970s.

DEFENSE

No compulsory military service

$1.8bn

Down 8% in 1997

The defense forces and internal security together absorb nearly 50% of government spending. The UK is the main supplier of equipment. During the 1991 Gulf War, Oman provided services and communications to US and UK forces. The army relies on Baluchi mercenaries to maintain full strength.

ECONOMICS

Not available

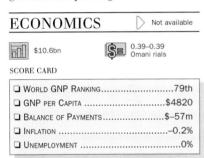

$10.6bn

0.39–0.39 Omani rials

SCORE CARD

❏ WORLD GNP RANKING	79th
❏ GNP PER CAPITA	$4820
❏ BALANCE OF PAYMENTS	$–57m
❏ INFLATION	–0.2%
❏ UNEMPLOYMENT	0%

STRENGTHS

Oil industry, led by Royal Dutch Shell. Oman has benefited from staying out of OPEC and selling oil at spot prices without quotas. Rich waters off the Indian Ocean coast, with potential for sizable fishing industry.

WEAKNESSES

Overdependence on oil (90% of GNP) with less than 20 years' known reserves. Services sector less well-developed than in the United Arab Emirates. Reliance on foreign workers in all sectors of the economy.

EXPORTS

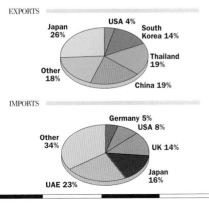

Japan 26%
USA 4%
South Korea 14%
Thailand 19%
China 19%
Other 18%

IMPORTS

Germany 5%
USA 8%
UK 14%
Japan 16%
UAE 23%
Other 34%

RESOURCES

Electric power 1.7m kw

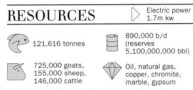

121,616 tonnes

890,000 b/d (reserves 5,100,000,000 bbl)

725,000 goats, 155,000 sheep, 146,000 cattle

Oil, natural gas, copper, chromite, marble, gypsum

Oman's policy of limiting oil production to conserve resources was abandoned in 1993 following a number of exploration successes.

ENVIRONMENT

No Green MPs

16%

Medium

The overpumping of ground water is becoming a pervasive problem; sea water is seeping into coastal aquifers in traditional irrigation areas.

MEDIA

TV ownership high

Daily newspaper circulation 27 per 1,000 people

PUBLISHING AND BROADCAST MEDIA

There are 4 daily newspapers, *Al-'Uman*, its English language companion the *Oman Daily Observer*, *Al-Watan* and the *Times of Oman*

2 state-controlled networks

1 state-controlled service

Nothing critical of the government may be published in Oman. Foreign press is censored for the Omani market.

CRIME

Death penalty used

Oman does not publish prison figures

Crime levels are low

Reckless driving by young Omani males is a problem. A "flying court" serves remote communities.

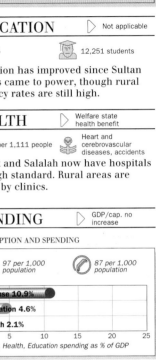

CHRONOLOGY

The present Albusaidi dynasty has ruled in Oman since 1749.

- ❏ **1932** Sultan bin Taimur in power.
- ❏ **1970** Sultan Qaboos bin Said seizes power from his father.
- ❏ **1975** Suppression of Dhofar revolt.
- ❏ **1991** Consultative Council set up.
- ❏ **1997** Sultan Qaboos appoints Consultative Council and newly established Council of State.

EDUCATION

Not applicable

67%

12,251 students

Education has improved since Sultan Qaboos came to power, though rural illiteracy rates are still high.

HEALTH

Welfare state health benefit

1 per 1,111 people

Heart and cerebrovascular diseases, accidents

Muscat and Salalah now have hospitals of a high standard. Rural areas are served by clinics.

SPENDING

GDP/cap. no increase

CONSUMPTION AND SPENDING

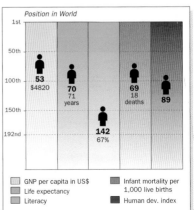

97 per 1,000 population

87 per 1,000 population

Defense 10.9%

Education 4.6%

Health 2.1%

Defense, Health, Education spending as % of GDP

Omanis living in urban areas enjoy the same high living standards as are found in other Gulf states. Among the nation's rich, hunting trips to Pakistan are a popular pastime, and a *khanjar*, a curved dagger, is a status symbol.

WORLD RANKING

Position in World

53 $4820
70 71 years
142 67%
69 18 deaths
89

❏ GNP per capita in US$
❏ Life expectancy
❏ Literacy
❏ Infant mortality per 1,000 live births
❏ Human dev. index

O

PAKISTAN

OFFICIAL NAME: Islamic Republic of Pakistan **CAPITAL:** Islamabad
POPULATION: 147.8 million **CURRENCY:** Pakistani rupee **OFFICIAL LANGUAGE:** Urdu

ONCE A PART OF BRITISH INDIA, Pakistan was created in 1947 in response to the demand for an independent, largely Muslim state. Initially the new country included East Pakistan, present-day Bangladesh, which became independent of Islamabad in 1971. Eastern and southern Pakistan, the flood plain of the Indus river, is highly fertile and produces cotton, the basis of the large textile industry.

Barren landscape in Kachhi, Baluchistan. This area of Pakistan has some of the highest May-to-September temperatures in the world.

CLIMATE

Mountain/steppe/ hot desert

WEATHER CHART

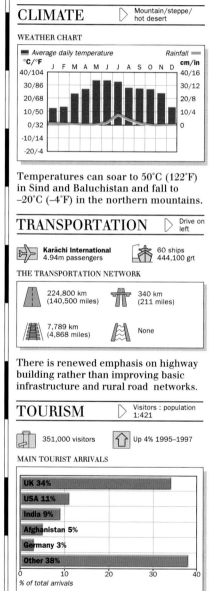

Temperatures can soar to 50°C (122°F) in Sind and Baluchistan and fall to –20°C (–4°F) in the northern mountains.

TRANSPORTATION

Drive on left

Karāchi International 4.94m passengers

60 ships 444,100 grt

THE TRANSPORTATION NETWORK

224,800 km (140,500 miles)	340 km (211 miles)
7,789 km (4,868 miles)	None

There is renewed emphasis on highway building rather than improving basic infrastructure and rural road networks.

TOURISM

Visitors : population 1:421

351,000 visitors

Up 4% 1995–1997

MAIN TOURIST ARRIVALS

UK 34%	
USA 11%	
India 9%	
Afghanistan 5%	
Germany 3%	
Other 38%	

% of total arrivals (0 10 20 30 40)

Relatively few tourists visit Pakistan, despite its rich cultural heritage and unspoiled natural beauty.

PEOPLE

Pop. density medium

Punjabi, Sindhi, Pashto, Urdu, Baluchi, Brahui

192/km² (497/mi²)

THE URBAN/RURAL POPULATION SPLIT

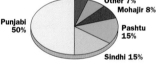

35%   65%

RELIGIOUS PERSUASION

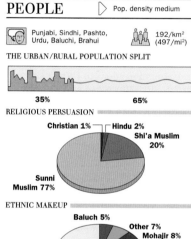

Christian 1%   Hindu 2%
Shi'a Muslim 20%
Sunni Muslim 77%

ETHNIC MAKEUP

Baluch 5%
Other 7%
Mohajir 8%
Punjabi 50%
Pashtu 15%
Sindhi 15%

Punjabis account for over 50% of the population, while Sindhis, Pathans and Baluch are also prominent. *Mohajirs* – Urdu-speaking immigrants from India at the time of partition – predominate in Karāchi and Hyderābād, Sind's main urban centers. Punjabi dominance of the army and bureaucracy, and the central government's distance from the smaller provinces, has spawned many separatist and autonomy movements. Pathans have frequently threatened to establish a homeland with ethnic kinfolk over the border in Afghanistan. Tensions between the Baluch and Pathan refugees from Afghanistan sporadically erupt into violence, as do those between native Sindhis and immigrant *Mohajirs*.

The gap between rich and poor, as exemplified by the "feudal" land-owning class which dominates the ruling elite and their serfs, is considerable. Barring a massive education drive or an even less likely social revolution, it will not close. There is an expanding middle class of small-scale traders and manufacturers.

There has been a marked increase in Islamic militancy, accompanied by

POPULATION AGE BREAKDOWN

Female		Age	Male	
	0.2%	81–100	0.2%	
	2.7%	61–80	2.9%	
	7.4%	41–60	8.1%	
	13.2%	21–40	14.4%	
24.9%		0–20		26%

% of population by age group

growing discrimination against religious minorities. In 1995, a controversial blasphemy law which carries a mandatory death sentence caused international outrage when it was used to convict a Christian child; he was subsequently acquitted.

The extended family is an enduring institution, and ties between its members are strong, reflected in the dynastic and nepotistic nature of the political system. Although some women hold prominent positions, and Benazir Bhutto has twice been prime minister, relatively few are allowed out to work by their religiously conservative menfolk. Pakistan has one of the world's lowest ratios of females to males, implying widespread neglect and some female infanticide. Women's rights groups exist – however, they are mainly urban-based and have made little impact.

POLITICS
▷ Multiparty elections

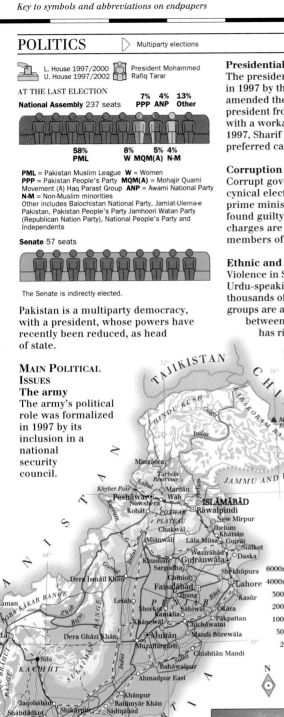

L. House 1997/2000
U. House 1997/2002

President Mohammed Rafiq Tarar

AT THE LAST ELECTION

National Assembly 237 seats

7% PPP   4% ANP   13% Other

58% PML   8% W   5% MQM(A)   4% N-M

PML = Pakistan Muslim League   **W** = Women
PPP = Pakistan People's Party   **MQM(A)** = Mohajir Quami Movement (A) Haq Parast Group   **ANP** = Awami National Party
N-M = Non-Muslim minorities
Other includes Balochistan National Party, Jamiat-Ulema-e Pakistan, Pakistan People's Party Jamhoori Watan Party (Republican Nation Party), National People's Party and Independents

Senate 57 seats

The Senate is indirectly elected.

Pakistan is a multiparty democracy, with a president, whose powers have recently been reduced, as head of state.

MAIN POLITICAL ISSUES
The army
The army's political role was formalized in 1997 by its inclusion in a national security council.

Presidential powers
The president's powers were restricted in 1997 by the Sharif government, which amended the constitution to prevent the president from dismissing a government with a workable majority. In December 1997, Sharif secured the election of his preferred candidate as president.

Corruption
Corrupt governments have produced a cynical electorate. In 1999 former prime minister Benazir Bhutto was found guilty of corruption. Similar charges are pending against some members of the Sharif government.

Ethnic and religious violence
Violence in Sind between Sindhis and Urdu-speaking separatist *Mohajirs* killed thousands of people in the 1990s. Islamic groups are active, and sectarian violence between Sunnis and minority Shi'as has risen since 1994.

PROFILE
Pakistan is a weak democracy – fragile coalitions have had to rule alongside the army and the president. In 1997 the PML, led by Nawaz Sharif, was returned to power with a landslide victory.

Benazir Bhutto, PPP leader and former Prime Minister.

Nawaz Sharif, PMLN leader and Prime Minister.

WORLD AFFAIRS
▷ Joined UN in 1947

Comm   ECO   NAM   OIC   SAARC

Pakistan's major concern is to avoid another war with India over Kashmir. Border fighting flared up in mid-1999. Pakistan backs the separatist movement in the largely Muslim Kashmir, and supports the idea of a plebiscite to allow self-determination. India, which fears losing, opposes it. The USA regards the region as a potential nuclear flashpoint, and in 1990 cut aid to Pakistan, which was suspected of developing nuclear weapons. In May 1998 Pakistan carried out nuclear tests in response to similar tests by India. Missile tests followed in April 1999. The tests provoked international condemnation and the re-imposition of US sanctions which had been partially lifted in 1995. Relations with the USA remain strained over the Sharif government's pro-Islamic policies. China, a traditional ally, continues to provide military assistance.

P

CHRONOLOGY
From the 8th to the 16th centuries, Islamic rule extended to northwest and northeast India. The British East India Company annexed Punjab and Sind in the 1850s. They were ceded to the British Raj in 1857.

❑ **1906** Muslim League founded as the organ of Indian Muslim separatism.
❑ **1947** Partition of India. Muhammad Ali Jinnah becomes the first governor-general of Pakistan, divided by 1,600 km (994 miles) of Indian territory, into East and West Pakistan. Millions displaced by large-scale migration.
❑ **1948** First Indo-Pakistan war over Kashmir.
❑ **1949** Awami League (AL) founded, seeking autonomy for East Pakistan.
❑ **1951** Liaqat Ali Khan, successor to Jinnah, assassinated.
❑ **1956** Constitution establishes Pakistan as an Islamic republic. ▷

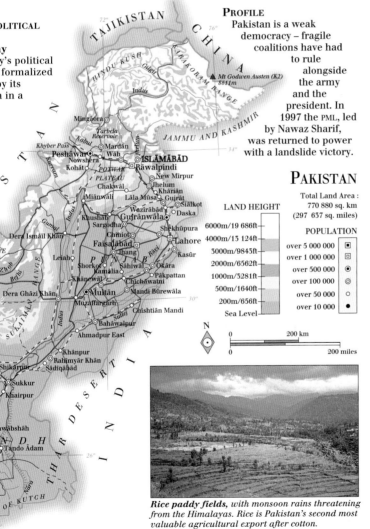

PAKISTAN

LAND HEIGHT

Total Land Area : 770 880 sq. km (297 637 sq. miles)

6000m/19 686ft
4000m/13 124ft
3000m/9843ft
2000m/6562ft
1000m/3281ft
500m/1640ft
200m/656ft
Sea Level

POPULATION
over 5 000 000
over 1 000 000
over 500 000
over 100 000
over 50 000
over 10 000

N

0   200 km
0   200 miles

Rice paddy fields, with monsoon rains threatening from the Himalayas. Rice is Pakistan's second most valuable agricultural export after cotton.

CHRONOLOGY *continued*

- ❏ **1958** Martial law. Gen. Muhammad Ayubb Khan takes over.
- ❏ **1960** Ayubb Khan elected president.
- ❏ **1970** Ayubb Khan resigns. Gen. Agha Yahya Khan takes over. First direct elections are won by AL, but west Pakistani parties reject result. Military crackdown in East Pakistan. War with India over Indian support for East Pakistan.
- ❏ **1971** East Pakistan secedes as Bangladesh. Zulfikar Ali Bhutto, leader of PPP, becomes president.
- ❏ **1972** Simla peace agreement signed with India.
- ❏ **1973** New constitution; Bhutto, now prime minister, initiates "Islamic socialism."
- ❏ **1977** General election. Riots over allegations of vote rigging. Gen. Zia ul-Haq stages military coup.
- ❏ **1979** Bhutto executed.
- ❏ **1986** Bhutto's daughter Benazir returns from exile to lead PPP.
- ❏ **1988** Zia killed in air crash. Bhutto wins general election.
- ❏ **1990** Ethnic violence in Sind. President dismisses Bhutto. Nawaz Sharif becomes premier.
- ❏ **1991** Muslim *sharia* law incorporated in legal code.
- ❏ **1992** Violence between Sindhis and *Mohajirs* escalates in Sind.
- ❏ **1993** President Khan and prime minister Sharif resign simultaneously. General election. Bhutto returns to power.
- ❏ **1996** President dismisses Bhutto government.
- ❏ **1997** PML wins landslide election victory; Sharif prime minister. Constitutional amendment removes president's power to dismiss prime minister.
- ❏ **1998** Nuclear tests.
- ❏ **1999** Bhutto sentenced to five years' imprisonment for corruption. More clashes with India over Kashmir.

AID

▷ Recipient

 $597m (receipts) — Down 32% 1996–1997

Pakistan is heavily dependent on aid, although the government has a long history of misdirecting aid payments. Aid intended for major projects has regularly been used to fund the current account deficit. In mid-1998 the IMF agreed to help Pakistan meet its international debt obligations after the USA and other Western aid donors cut off aid in protest against Pakistan's nuclear tests. The USA subsequently resumed some aid, but Pakistan's economy was badly damaged. Japan and Germany are among other main bilateral donors. Aid is also provided by the World Bank and the ADB.

P

DEFENSE

▷ No compulsory military service

💲 $3.5bn — Down 4% in 1997

Pakistan established itself as a nuclear power after successfully conducting a number of nuclear tests in May 1998. Defense spending ranks high in the government's priorities, although since the mid-1990s debt servicing has overtaken it as the largest single item of expenditure. Nevertheless, defense spending still accounts for about a quarter of all expenditure.

The USA was the most important arms supplier until sanctions were imposed in 1990 and 1998. Pakistan's other main defense procurements are from France, the UK, and China.

The army is politically significant.

In 1997 it assumed a formal role in civilian decision-making when its representatives were included in a national security council.

PAKISTANI ARMED FORCES

🛡	2,120 main battle tanks (15 M-47, 345 M-48A5, 50 T-54/55)	520,000 personnel
⚓	9 submarines, 2 destroyers, 8 frigates, 10 patrol boats	22,000 personnel
✈	410 combat aircraft (56 *Mirage* 5, 49 Q-5)	45,000 personnel
🚀	Capability undisclosed; weapons tested in May 1998	

ECONOMICS

▷ Inflation 9.2% p.a. (1985–1996)

📊 $64.6bn — 44.01–49.02 Pakistani rupees

SCORE CARD

- ❏ WORLD GNP RANKING..........................45th
- ❏ GNP PER CAPITA $500
- ❏ BALANCE OF PAYMENTS...................$–1.8bn
- ❏ INFLATION 11.4%
- ❏ UNEMPLOYMENT 5%

EXPORTS

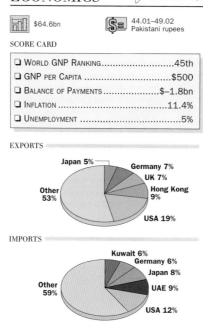

Japan 5%
Germany 7%
UK 7%
Hong Kong 9%
Other 53%
USA 19%

IMPORTS

Kuwait 6%
Germany 6%
Japan 8%
UAE 9%
Other 59%
USA 12%

STRENGTHS

Gas, water, coal, oil. Substantial untapped natural resources. Low labor costs. Potentially huge market. One of the world's leading producers of cotton and a major exporter of rice.

WEAKNESSES

Weather conditions cause fluctuation in annual production and sales of cotton and rice. Inefficient and haphazard government economic policies. Weak and overstretched infrastructure.

PROFILE

Pakistan has yet to show progress in tackling its considerable economic problems. Successive governments have reversed the nationalization policies instituted in the 1970s, but private enterprise has been stifled by the rules of a massive bureaucracy. There is

ECONOMIC PERFORMANCE INDICATOR

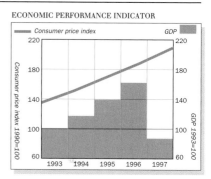

— Consumer price index — GDP

(Consumer price index 1990=100; GDP 1993=100; years 1993–1997)

some foreign investment in previously state-only sectors such as banking, water and other utilities. However, corruption, which was particularly acute under the administration of former prime minister Benazir Bhutto, has undermined economic confidence. The new Sharif government has done little to curb military spending, which remains a rein on development.

Despite Pakistan's considerable economic potential, much of its population lives below the poverty line.

PAKISTAN : MAJOR BUSINESSES

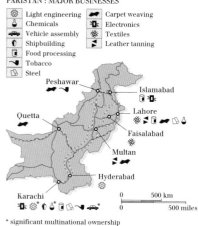

- 🔧 Light engineering
- ⚗ Chemicals
- 🚗 Vehicle assembly
- ⚓ Shipbuilding
- 🍴 Food processing
- Tobacco
- Steel
- Carpet weaving
- Electronics
- Textiles
- Leather tanning

Peshawar
Islamabad
Quetta
Lahore
Faisalabad
Multan
Hyderabad
Karachi

0   500 km
0   500 miles

* significant multinational ownership

RESOURCES

▷ Electric power 14.0m kw

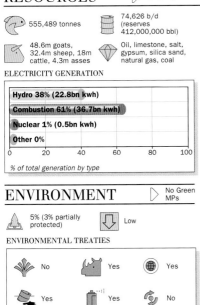

555,489 tonnes

74,626 b/d (reserves 412,000,000 bbl)

48.6m goats, 32.4m sheep, 18m cattle, 4.3m asses

Oil, limestone, salt, gypsum, silica sand, natural gas, coal

ELECTRICITY GENERATION

Hydro 38% (22.8bn kwh)

Combustion 61% (36.7bn kwh)

Nuclear 1% (0.5bn kwh)

Other 0%

| 0 | 20 | 40 | 60 | 80 | 100 |

% of total generation by type

Apart from cotton and rice, Pakistan's major resources are oil, coal, gas, and water. The state hopes that the privatization of the utilities industries will reduce energy imports and shortages – peak electricity demand, for example, exceeds supply by 20%. Steps are being taken to attract more foreign investment in oil and gas exploration, extraction and distribution. Pakistan's current refining capacity of 150,000 b/d cannot meet the present 280,000 b/d demand, let alone the projected future demand.

PAKISTAN : LAND USE

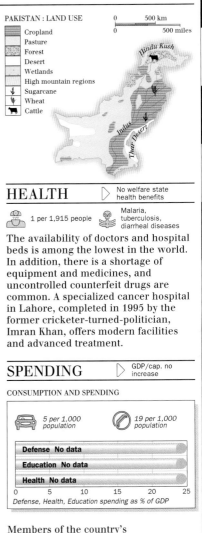

| | 0 | 500 km |
| | 0 | 500 miles |

- Cropland
- Pasture
- Forest
- Desert
- Wetlands
- High mountain regions
- ↓ Sugarcane
- ↓ Wheat
- ☐ Cattle

ENVIRONMENT

▷ No Green MPs

5% (3% partially protected)

Low

ENVIRONMENTAL TREATIES

No	Yes		Yes
Yes	Yes		No

Tough measures are in force to curb illegal logging. Urban pollution affects many cities. Local groups increasingly voice environmental concerns.

MEDIA

▷ TV ownership medium

 Daily newspaper circulation 21 per 1,000 people

PUBLISHING AND BROADCAST MEDIA

There are 264 daily newspapers. The best-selling paper is *Daily Jang*, published in Urdu

2 independent networks

2 state-owned, 1 independent services

State-run radio and TV dominate the mass media. Journalists who challenge official views are routinely harassed.

CRIME

▷ Death penalty used

44,640 prisoners

Crime levels at similarly high levels from year to year

CRIME RATES

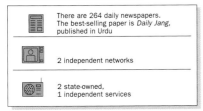

Murders	
78	per 100,000 population

Rapes
Pakistan does not publish rape statistics

Thefts	
18	per 100,000 population

Compared with similar Islamic states, Pakistan has a high incidence of violent crime and narcotics-trafficking. The main causes for concern are corruption

EDUCATION

▷ Not available

41%

954,000 students

Literacy rates in Pakistan are among the lowest in the world.

THE EDUCATION SYSTEM

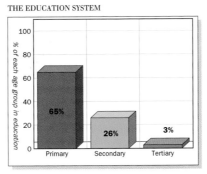

% of each age group in education

- Primary 65%
- Secondary 26%
- Tertiary 3%

The education system is heavily Islamicized, and weighted toward educating males. The great majority of children enrolled in primary schools are boys.

The 23 universities, 99 professional colleges and 675 arts and sciences colleges all have a heavy preponderance of arts students. Wealthy parents frequently choose to send their children abroad for higher education, mainly to colleges in the UK or USA.

and the abuse of women; women are being increasingly reported killed or threatened with death for refusing to accept arranged marriages. Torture and deaths in custody are frequent, as is the rape of women prisoners. The most dangerous area is Sind province, where the Mohajir Quami Movement terrorizes Karachi's residents. Militant sectarian groups are also blamed for a recent rise in crime in Punjab.

Heavily armed *dacoits* (bandits) still hold sway in the interior. Pressure from Islamic parties has forced the government in the North West Frontier Province to replace British-based civil law by the rulings of *sharia* courts.

HEALTH

▷ No welfare state health benefits

1 per 1,915 people

Malaria, tuberculosis, diarrheal diseases

The availability of doctors and hospital beds is among the lowest in the world. In addition, there is a shortage of equipment and medicines, and uncontrolled counterfeit drugs are common. A specialized cancer hospital in Lahore, completed in 1995 by the former cricketer-turned-politician, Imran Khan, offers modern facilities and advanced treatment.

SPENDING

▷ GDP/cap. no increase

CONSUMPTION AND SPENDING

5 per 1,000 population

19 per 1,000 population

Defense	No data
Education	No data
Health	No data

| 0 | 5 | 10 | 15 | 20 | 25 |

Defense, Health, Education spending as % of GDP

Members of the country's bureaucratic and political elite tend to be extremely rich, as are some of the top military. Bonded laborers, often Christians or recent converts to Islam, form the underclass.

WORLD RANKING

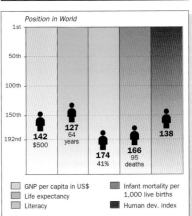

Position in World

- 1st
- 50th
- 100th
- 150th
- 192nd

- 142 $500
- 127 64 years
- 174 41%
- 166 95 deaths
- 138

☐ GNP per capita in US$
☐ Life expectancy
☐ Literacy
■ Infant mortality per 1,000 live births
■ Human dev. index

P

PALAU

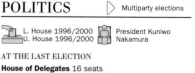

OFFICIAL NAME: Palau   **CAPITAL:** Koror   **POPULATION:** 17,700
CURRENCY: US dollar   **OFFICIAL LANGUAGES:** Palauan and English

1994	1994	Oct 1/2	PAL	+9	+680	.pw

THE REPUBLIC OF PALAU (also known as Belau) is situated in the western Pacific and comprises more than 200 islands in the Caroline Islands archipelago. Formerly a part of the US-administered Trust Territory of the Pacific Islands, Palau became independent in association with the USA in 1994, but continues to be heavily dependent on US aid.

CLIMATE   ▷ Tropical oceanic

WEATHER CHART

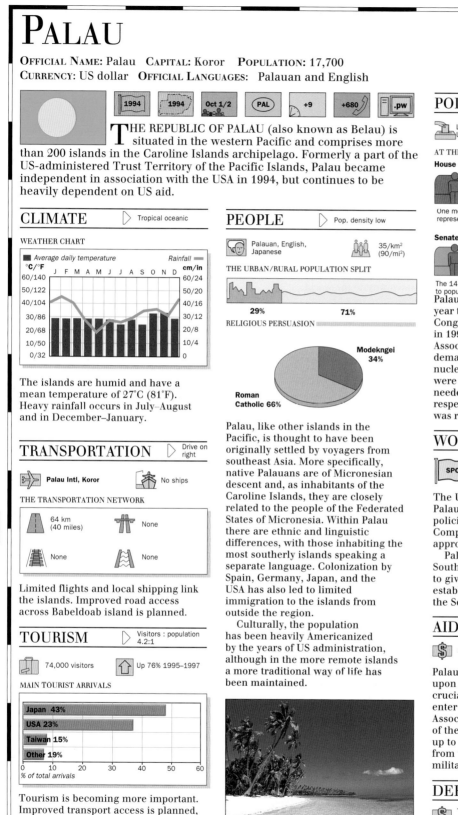

■ Average daily temperature   Rainfall ▬
°C/°F   J F M A M J J A S O N D   cm/in

The islands are humid and have a mean temperature of 27°C (81°F). Heavy rainfall occurs in July–August and in December–January.

TRANSPORTATION   ▷ Drive on right

🛩 Palau Intl, Koror   🚢 No ships

THE TRANSPORTATION NETWORK

64 km (40 miles)	None
None	None

Limited flights and local shipping link the islands. Improved road access across Babeldoab island is planned.

TOURISM   ▷ Visitors : population 4.2:1

🧳 74,000 visitors   ⬆ Up 76% 1995–1997

MAIN TOURIST ARRIVALS

Japan	43%
USA	23%
Taiwan	15%
Other	19%

0   10   20   30   40   50   60
% of total arrivals

Tourism is becoming more important. Improved transport access is planned, amid concerns about impact on traditional culture. Several islands have battle sites from the Pacific War. The outlying islands remain unspoiled.

PEOPLE   ▷ Pop. density low

Palauan, English, Japanese   35/km² (90/mi²)

THE URBAN/RURAL POPULATION SPLIT

29%   71%

RELIGIOUS PERSUASION

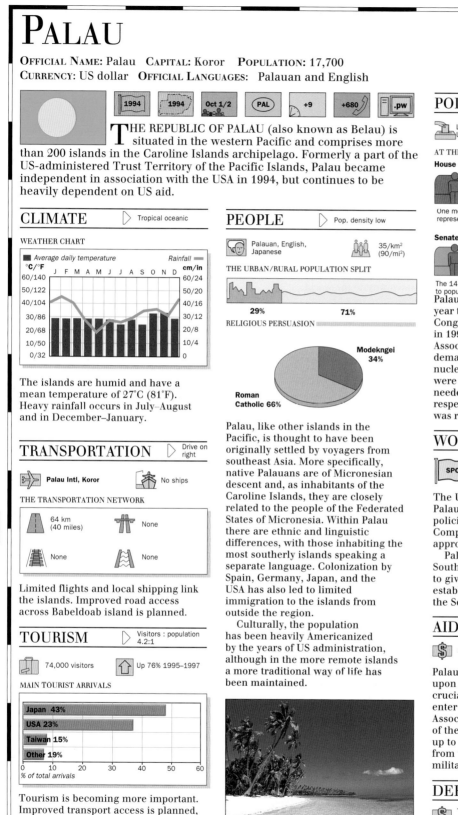

Modekngei 34%
Roman Catholic 66%

Palau, like other islands in the Pacific, is thought to have been originally settled by voyagers from southeast Asia. More specifically, native Palauans are of Micronesian descent and, as inhabitants of the Caroline Islands, they are closely related to the people of the Federated States of Micronesia. Within Palau there are ethnic and linguistic differences, with those inhabiting the most southerly islands speaking a separate language. Colonization by Spain, Germany, Japan, and the USA has also led to limited immigration to the islands from outside the region.

Culturally, the population has been heavily Americanized by the years of US administration, although in the more remote islands a more traditional way of life has been maintained.

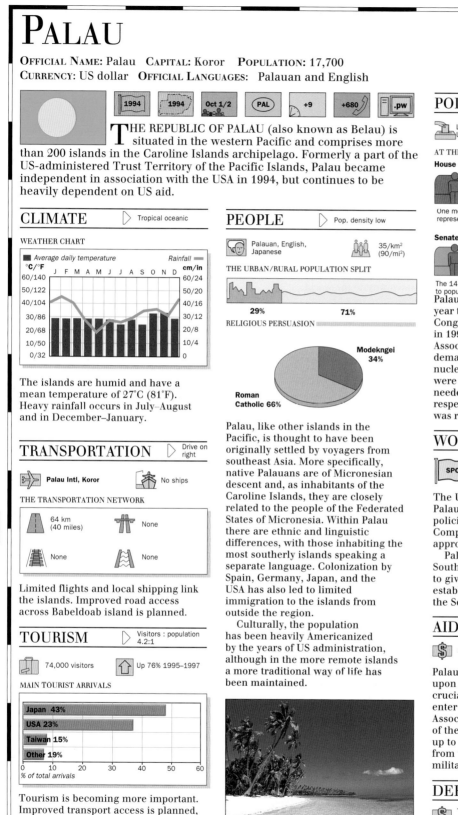

Palau's islands have many idyllic beaches, but tourism remains underdeveloped due to a lack of resources and the country's remoteness.

POLITICS   ▷ Multiparty elections

L. House 1996/2000
U. House 1996/2000
President Kuniwo Nakamura

AT THE LAST ELECTION

House of Delegates 16 seats

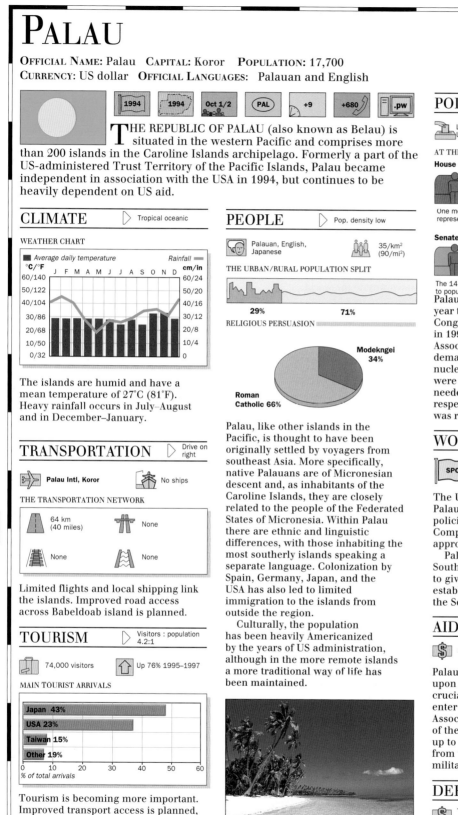

One member is elected to the House of Delegates to represent each of the 16 states.

Senate 14 seats

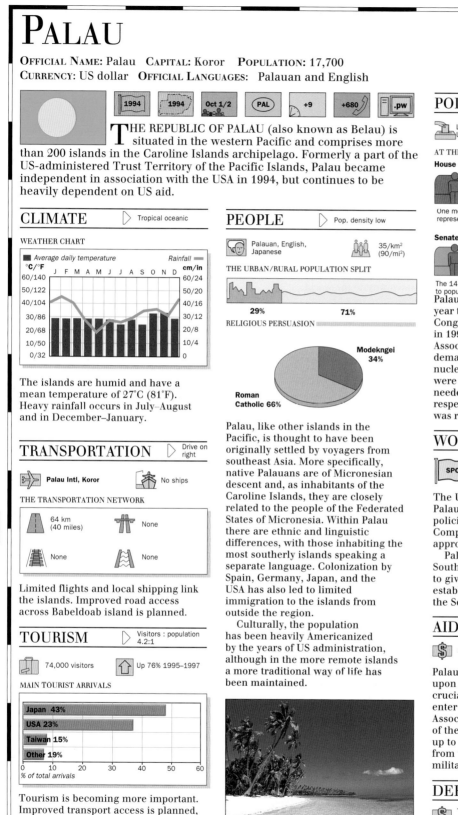

The 14 Senators represent geographical districts, according to population.

Palau has a president elected for a four-year term, and a bicameral National Congress. Palau achieved independence in 1994 under the Compact of Free Association signed in 1982, which initially demanded the transit and storage of nuclear materials. Repeated referendums were held to achieve the 75% approval needed to alter the constitution in this respect. In 1992, the approval required was reduced to a simple majority.

WORLD AFFAIRS   ▷ Joined UN in 1994

SPC	SPF	IBRD		

The USA has exclusive control over Palau's foreign affairs and defense policies under the conditions of the Compact of Free Association finally approved in 1994.

Palau strained its relations with the South Pacific Forum with its bid to give Japan the right to veto the establishment of a whale sanctuary in the South Pacific.

AID   ▷ Recipient

💲 $39m (receipts)   ⬇ Down 37% 1996–1997

Palau's economy is heavily dependent upon the USA. Receipt of aid was a crucial factor in Palau's decision to enter into the 1994 Compact of Free Association with the USA after the end of the UN trusteeship. Palau will receive up to US$700 million over 15 years from the USA in return for furnishing military facilities.

DEFENSE   ▷ No compulsory military service

There are no armed forces   Not applicable

Under the Compact of Free Association, the USA is responsible for Palau's defense.

P

ECONOMICS ▷ Not available

🏛 $82m   💲 1 dollar

SCORE CARD

- ❏ WORLD GNP RANKING.......................186th
- ❏ GNP PER CAPITA $5,000
- ❏ BALANCE OF PAYMENTS.....................$–25m
- ❏ INFLATION.............................Not available
- ❏ UNEMPLOYMENT 7%

STRENGTHS

Access to US economy through preferential trading rights. Tourism, fishing, and copra production. Some minerals (especially gold). Trade agreement with Philippines.

WEAKNESSES

Heavy dependence on US aid. High levels of underemployment. Remote location. Limited resources for education. Aid dependent culture. Few natural resources. Limited but expanding transport infrastructure.

EXPORTS

Palau does not publish export figures by country

IMPORTS

Japan 3%   UK 5%   New Zealand 11%   Australia 41%   Other 40%

RESOURCES ▷ Electric power 62,000 kw

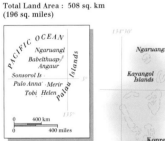

1,300 tonnes   Not an oil producer and has no refineries

Not available   Gold

On some of the 200 islands the soil is highly fertile, although the nature of the terrain of the larger islands makes farming extremely difficult. Some of the islands are densely forested. Palau has copra and some gold deposits. There is also the possibility of exploitation of reserves of minerals on the seabed. It has a small fishing industry, which is considerably underdeveloped.

PALAU

Total Land Area : 508 sq. km
(196 sq. miles)

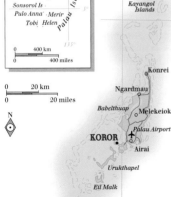

ENVIRONMENT ▷ No Green MPs

🌲 None   ⬍ Environmental issues not paramount

Palau suffers from inadequate facilities for the disposal of solid waste. Sand and coral dredging and illegal fishing practices pose a significant threat to the marine ecosystem. There is also concern about the decimation of fruit bat colonies. Recommendations have been made to ban the commercial export of fruit bats and establish protected areas. Typhoons sometimes cause severe damage to buildings.

MEDIA ▷ TV ownership medium

🗎 There are no daily newspapers

PUBLISHING AND BROADCAST MEDIA

There are no national daily newspapers. *Tia Belau* is published fornightly in English and Palauan.

1 commercial TV station   3 radio stations

The country's TV and radio stations tend to deal in material which is largely derived from the USA.

CRIME ▷ Death penalty not used

Palau does not publish prison figures   ⬍ Little change from year to year

There is a little alcohol-related crime, but much of the country, particularly the outlying islands, is crime-free.

EDUCATION ▷ School leaving age: 14

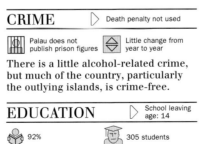 92%   305 students

Education is compulsory between the ages of six and 14. After eight years' compulsory elementary schooling a pupil can enroll in a high school.

CHRONOLOGY

The Caroline Islands were colonized in turn by Spain, Germany and Japan before being transferred to US control in 1945.

- ❏ **1947** UN Trust Territory of the Pacific Islands established.
- ❏ **1982** Palau signs Compact of Free Association with USA.
- ❏ **1993** Compact approved.
- ❏ **1994** Palau becomes independent in free association with the USA on October 1.

HEALTH ▷ No welfare state health benefits

 1 per 83 people   Heart, cerebrovascular and intestinal diseases

Basic health care is available. Many outlying islands do not have easy access to qualified doctors and often rely on nurses or traditional health remedies. Main causes of death are heart, cerebrovascular and intestinal disease.

SPENDING ▷ GDP/cap. no increase

CONSUMPTION AND SPENDING

🚗 No data   ⭕ No data

No data available

0   5   10   15   20   25
Defense, Health, Education spending as % of GDP

The gap between the country's rich and poor is steadily growing, as entrepreneurs and government officials exploit US aid and develop Palau's growing tourist industry. Many Palauans lead a very basic existence.

WORLD RANKING

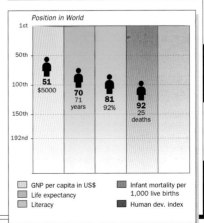

Position in World

1st			
50th			
100th	**51** $5000	**70** 71 years	**81** 92%
150th			**92** 25 deaths
192nd			

- ☐ GNP per capita in US$
- ☐ Life expectancy
- ☐ Literacy
- ☐ Infant mortality per 1,000 live births
- ☐ Human dev. index

P

PANAMA

CENTRAL AMERICA

North America

OFFICIAL NAME: Republic of Panama   CAPITAL: Panama City
POPULATION: 2.8 million   CURRENCY: Balboa   OFFICIAL LANGUAGE: Spanish

| 1903 | 1903 | Nov 3 | PA | -5 | +507 | .pa |

PANAMA IS THE SOUTHERNMOST of the seven countries occupying the isthmus that joins North and South America. The rain forests of the Darien peninsula are some of the wildest areas left in the Americas. Elected governments have held power since the US invasion of 1989. Panama's traditional economic strength is its banking sector. The USA returned control of the Panama Canal Zone to Panama on December 31, 1999.

Cruise liner on the Panama Canal. The canal takes 4,800 km off the otherwise shortest sea route from the east coast of the USA to Japan.

CLIMATE   ▷ Tropical wet & dry

WEATHER CHART

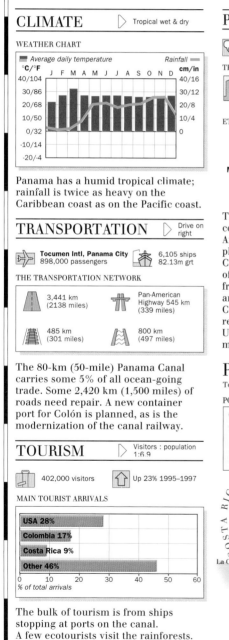

Average daily temperature   Rainfall
°C/°F   cm/in
J F M A M J J A S O N D
40/104 — 40/16
30/86 — 30/12
20/68 — 20/8
10/50 — 10/4
0/32 — 0
-10/14
-20/-4

Panama has a humid tropical climate; rainfall is twice as heavy on the Caribbean coast as on the Pacific coast.

TRANSPORTATION   ▷ Drive on right

Tocumen Intl, Panama City   6,105 ships
898,000 passengers   82.13m grt

THE TRANSPORTATION NETWORK

| 3,441 km (2138 miles) | Pan-American Highway 545 km (339 miles) |
| 485 km (301 miles) | 800 km (497 miles) |

The 80-km (50-mile) Panama Canal carries some 5% of all ocean-going trade. Some 2,420 km (1,500 miles) of roads need repair. A new container port for Colón is planned, as is the modernization of the canal railway.

TOURISM   ▷ Visitors : population 1:6.9

402,000 visitors   Up 23% 1995–1997

MAIN TOURIST ARRIVALS

| USA 28% |
| Colombia 17% |
| Costa Rica 9% |
| Other 46% |

0   10   20   30   40   50   60
% of total arrivals

The bulk of tourism is from ships stopping at ports on the canal. A few ecotourists visit the rainforests.

PEOPLE   ▷ Pop. density low

Spanish, English Creole, Amerindian languages, Chibchan

37/km² (95/mi²)

THE URBAN/RURAL POPULATION SPLIT

53%   47%

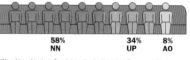

ETHNIC MAKEUP

- Other 2%
- Asian 4%
- Mestizo 60%
- Indigenous Indian 8%
- Black 12%
- White 14%

The northwest coast has a large black community, mostly descended from African immigrants who worked the plantations. The majority speak English Creole rather than Spanish. About 8% of the population are Indians mainly from the Kunas, Guaymies, Chocoes and Ngobe-Buglé tribes. Roman Catholicism and the extended family remain strong, although the canal and US military bases have given society a more cosmopolitan outlook.

PANAMA

Total Land Area : 75 990 sq. km (29 340 sq. miles)

POPULATION
- ◉ over 500 000
- ◎ over 100 000
- ○ over 50 000
- • over 10 000
- · under 10 000

LAND HEIGHT
- 2000m/6562ft
- 1000m/3281ft
- 500m/1640ft
- 200m/656ft
- Sea Level

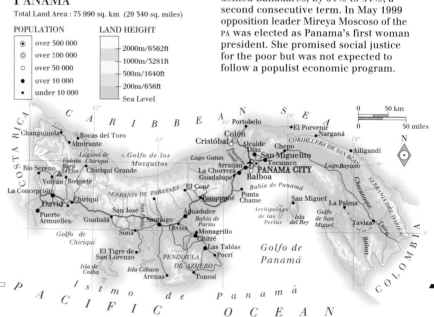

POLITICS   ▷ Multiparty elections

1999/2004   President Mireya Moscoso

AT THE LAST ELECTION

Legislative Assembly 71 seats

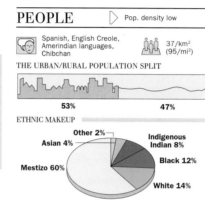

58%   34%   8%
NN   UP   AO

NN = New Nation Coalition (including the Democratic Revolutionary Party – PRD) **UP** = Union for Panama Coalition including the Arnulfisto Party – PA) **AO** = Action for the Opposition

In 1989, the USA invaded Panama and arrested its ruler, General Manuel Noriega, for narcotics smuggling. US forces installed the compliant Endara government, criticized for corruption. The 1994 presidential and legislative elections were won by Ernesto Pérez Balladares and the PRD, Noriega's party, but the new government was largely pro-US and attracted widespread discontent due to its economic reforms. In a 1998 referendum Panamanians denied Balladares, by 64% to 34%, a second consecutive term. In May 1999 opposition leader Mireya Moscoso of the PA was elected as Panama's first woman president. She promised social justice for the poor but was not expected to follow a populist economic program.

P

WORLD AFFAIRS

▷ Joined UN in 1945

The Canal Zone reverted to Panama on 31 December 1999, but the USA wishes to retain 2,000 US troops to oversee a $60 million international anti-drug center in the zone. Panama objects to a continued US military presence, however, and wants any agreement to cover only three to four years, not the 12 years wanted by the USA.

AID

▷ Recipient

💲 $124m (receipts) ⬆ Up 38% 1996–1997

After the overthrow of Noriega in 1989, the USA provided $480 million, but aid has since tapered off.

DEFENSE

▷ No compulsory military service

💲 $114m ⬆ Up 2% in 1997

The National Guard and defense forces were disbanded following the 1989 US invasion and were replaced by the Public Force of police which numbers some 11,800. Panama is allied militarily to the USA, although the US military was to withdraw from the Canal Zone at the end of 1999.

ECONOMICS

▷ Inflation 1.5% p.a. (1985–1996)

📊 $8.4bn 💲 1 balboa

SCORE CARD

❏ WORLD GNP RANKING	92nd
❏ GNP PER CAPITA	$2,670
❏ BALANCE OF PAYMENTS	$–1,209m
❏ INFLATION	1.2%
❏ UNEMPLOYMENT	12.5%

STRENGTHS

Colón Free Trade Zone second-largest in world. Strong banking, financial, insurance and other allied services. Banana, shrimp exports. Merchant shipping payments for sailing under the Panamanian flag.

WEAKNESSES

History of political instability and corruption. Large foreign debt. High unemployment, underemployment. Poor infrastructure.

EXPORTS

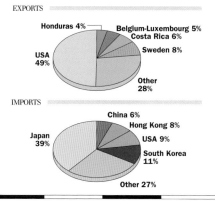

IMPORTS

$60 million international anti-drug center in the zone. Panama objects to a continued US military presence, however, and wants any agreement to cover only three to four years, not the 12 years wanted by the USA.

ENVIRONMENT

▷ No Green MPs

 19% ⬍ Medium

The destruction of rain forests is proceeding at an increasingly rapid rate, resulting in widespread soil erosion. Large numbers of rare bird and animal species are threatened. Sewage from Panama City and Colón is discharged directly into coastal waters, canals and ditches. Stretches of mangrove swamps are cut down to make way for urban development, shrimp farms, and resorts.

RESOURCES

▷ Electric power 957,000 kw

181,781 tonnes

Not an oil producer; refines 100,000 b/d

1.4m cattle, 245,000 pigs, 165,000 horses

Copper, coal, gold, silver, manganese, salt, clay

The Petaquilla area has great copper and gold potential. The government has stepped up hydroelectric production to reduce the country's dependence on oil imports; four state energy plants were privatized in 1999. Tropical hardwoods are being cut down at an alarming rate.

MEDIA

▷ TV ownership medium

 Daily newspaper circulation 62 per 1,000 people

PUBLISHING AND BROADCAST MEDIA

There are 7 daily newspapers, including *La Prensa* and *La Estrella de Panamá*

32 independent stations

1 state-owned, 200 independent stations

A more independent press has flourished since Noriega's overthrow. Radio reaches the greatest number of people.

CRIME

▷ Death penalty not used

Panama does not publish prison figures ⬆ Up 300% between 1989 and 1993

Panama City and Colón have high crime levels. Money laundering, drug-trafficking, and corruption are rife.

EDUCATION

▷ School leaving age: 15

📖 91% 🎓 80,962 students

Schooling is based on the US model. Provision for the urban poor, blacks, and indigenous people is limited.

CHRONOLOGY

On independence from Spain in 1821, Panama was incorporated into Gran Colombia. Panama gained independence from Colombia with US support in 1903.

- ❏ **1903** USA buys concession for Panama Canal.
- ❏ **1914–1939** Canal opens to traffic. US protectorate status ended.
- ❏ **1968–1981** Rule of Col. Torrijos Herrera.
- ❏ **1989** Gen. Noriega, indicted by USA as drug trafficker, annuls elections to retain power. US invasion. Endara made president.
- ❏ **1994** PRD's Ernesto Balladares wins presidential election. PRD largest party in parliament.
- ❏ **1999** PA's Mireya Moscoso elected as first woman president.

HEALTH

▷ Welfare state health benefits

👤 1 per 556 people Heart diseases, cancers, violence, accidents

Primary health care is accessible to some two-thirds of the rural population. The isolation of many villages hinders efforts to improve the system.

SPENDING

▷ GDP/cap. no increase

CONSUMPTION AND SPENDING

🚗 76 per 1,000 population 📞 134 per 1,000 population

Defense 1.3%	
Education 5.2%	
Health No data	

0   5   10   15   20   25
Defense, Health, Education spending as % of GDP

Wealth disparities are large. Over 40% of the population are estimated to live below the poverty line – clustered in the cities rather than in rural areas.

WORLD RANKING

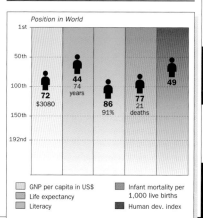

⬜ GNP per capita in US$	⬛ Infant mortality per 1,000 live births
⬜ Life expectancy	
⬜ Literacy	⬛ Human dev. index

P

PAPUA NEW GUINEA

OFFICIAL NAME: The Independent State of Papua New Guinea **CAPITAL:** Port Moresby
POPULATION: 4.6 million **CURRENCY:** Kina **OFFICIAL LANGUAGE:** English

| 1975 | 1975 | Sept 16 | PNG | +10 | +675 | .pg |

THE MOST LINGUISTICALLY diverse country in the world, with approximately 750 languages, Papua New Guinea (PNG) achieved independence from Australia in 1975. The country occupies the eastern end of the island of New Guinea, and several other groups of islands. Much of the country is still isolated and much of the rural population experiences basic living conditions.

CLIMATE
▷ Equatorial monsoon

WEATHER CHART

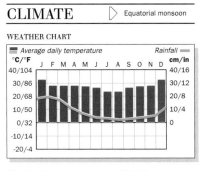

Hot lowlands contrast with Mount Victoria's snow. 1998 was unusually affected by drought and tsunamis.

TRANSPORTATION
▷ Drive on left

🛩 **Jacksons, Port Moresby**
745,000 passengers

🚢 39 ships
57,000 grt

THE TRANSPORTATION NETWORK

640 km (398 miles)	None
None	10,940 km (6,798 miles)

Infrastructure is improving with the construction and upgrading of major link roads and airports.

Papua New Guinea's 600 or so outer islands are mainly high and volcanic, with lush vegetation and fringing coral reefs.

TOURISM
▷ Visitors : population 1 : 69

🧳 66,000 visitors

⬆ Up 61% 1995–1997

MAIN TOURIST ARRIVALS

Australia 42%	
USA 10%	
UK 7%	
Other 41%	

% of total arrivals

Tourism, especially eco-tourism, has great potential, but it is hampered by the high rates of poverty-related violent crime, particularly in urban centers.

PEOPLE
▷ Pop. density low

Pidgin English, Papuan, English, Motu, 750 (est) native languages

10/km² (26/mi²)

THE URBAN/RURAL POPULATION SPLIT

16%   84%

RELIGIOUS PERSUASION

Other 4%
Anglican 5%
Indigenous beliefs 34%
Lutheran 16%
Roman Catholic 22%
Other Protestant 19%

PNG has an extraordinary diversity of peoples, with around 750 different language groups and even more tribes. The key distinction is between the lowlanders, who have frequent contacts with the outside world, and the very isolated highlanders. Great tensions exist between highland tribes; anyone who is not a *wontok* (of one's tribe) is seen as potentially hostile. Vendettas can often last several generations and tribal battles are not infrequent.

POLITICS
▷ Multiparty elections

1997/2002

HM Queen Elizabeth II

AT THE LAST ELECTION

National Parliament 109 seats   6% PAP   16% Other

35% Ind   15% PPP   14% PP PDM   8% PDM   6% NA

Ind = Independent **PPP** = People's Progress Party
PP = Pangu (Papua New Guinea Unity) Pati **PDM** = People's Democratic Movement **PAP** = People's Action Party
NA = National Alliance

PNG's many political parties lack clear ideological foundations. The patronage required to maintain coalition groupings encourages corruption. Issues include land rights and resource exploitation. Strong local traditions as well as communications problems make centralization difficult. Sir Julian Chan, prime minister until 1997, resigned amid outrage over using Western-led mercenaries against insurgents on Bougainville. His successor Bill Skate signed a peace agreement with Bougainville rebels in 1998, but resigned in July 1999 after controversially establishing diplomatic relations with Taiwan.

PAPUA NEW GUINEA

Total Land Area : 452 860 sq. km (174 849 sq. miles)

POPULATION

◎ over 100 000
○ over 50 000
● over 10 000
• under 10 000

LAND HEIGHT

5000m/9843ft
2000m/6562ft
1000m/3281ft
500m/1640ft
200m/656ft
Sea Level

0   200 km
0   200 miles

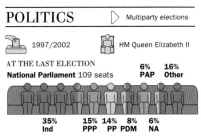

WORLD AFFAIRS

▷ Joined UN in 1975

APEC | Comm | NAM | SPC | SPF

Conflict on the island of Bougainville dominated Papua New Guinea's affairs until the 1998 peace agreement there. A pro-Taiwan policy, in return for aid funding, provoked Chinese anger in 1999.

AID

▷ Recipient

💲 $349m (receipts)   ⬇ Down 9% 1996–1997

Australia, Papua New Guinea's largest donor, plans to phase out cash support for direct project aid.

DEFENSE

▷ No compulsory military service

💲 $63m   ⬇ Down 22% in 1997

Papua New Guinea agreed to withdraw its defense force from Bougainville as part of the 1998 cease-fire agreement.

ECONOMICS

▷ Inflation 5.5% p.a. (1985-1996)

$4.2bn   1.75–2.05 kina

SCORE CARD

❏ WORLD GNP RANKING	115th
❏ GNP PER CAPITA	$930
❏ BALANCE OF PAYMENTS	$313m
❏ INFLATION	3.9%
❏ UNEMPLOYMENT	5%

STRENGTHS
Significant mineral resources particularly copper, gold, nickel, cobalt, oil and natural gas. A proposed gas pipeline between the highlands and Australia is expected to net $219 million a year. Agriculture sustains the population.

WEAKNESSES
Agricultural production and mining were significantly disrupted by the 1998 droughts. Poor transport and banking infrastructures. Political instability. Foreign exploitation of resources.

EXPORTS

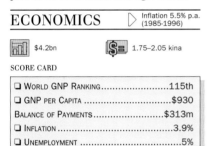

South Korea 4%
UK 5%
Germany 7%
Other 40%
Japan 17%
Australia 27%

IMPORTS

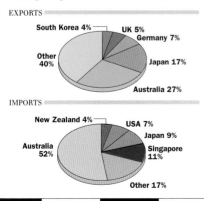

New Zealand 4%
USA 7%
Japan 9%
Australia 52%
Singapore 11%
Other 17%

RESOURCES

▷ Electric power 490,000 kw

26,200 tonnes

1.5m pigs, 86,000 cattle, 6,000 sheep, 1,600 horses

Reserves of 340,000,000 bbl

Copper, gold, silver, natural gas, oil, chromite, cobalt

Papua New Guinea is mineral rich. The Ok Tedi in the Star Mountains is now the most productive copper mine. Porgera gold mine is one of the world's largest. Production at both mines was significantly affected by drought in 1998. Prospecting has revealed extensive oil and natural gas reserves.

ENVIRONMENT

▷ No Green MPs

None   Medium

Deforestation and heavy-metal pollution are major issues. Droughts, affecting 1.2 million people in 1998, were blamed on deforestation. The northwest coastline was devastated in the same year by three tsunamis, killing 2,000 people and leaving homeless thousands more.

MEDIA

▷ TV ownership low

Daily newspaper circulation 15 per 1,000 people

PUBLISHING AND BROADCAST MEDIA

There are 2 daily newspapers, the *Papua New Guinea Post-Courier* and the *Niugini Nius*

2 independent services

1 state-owned, 2 independent services

The National Broadcasting Commission recently announced plans to commercialize in order to raise revenue.

CRIME

▷ Death penalty not used

PNG does not publish prison figures   Up 22% in 1992

Violent crime, by gangs of "Rascals," is common. There is increasing popular pressure for the death penalty.

EDUCATION

▷ Not applicable

74%   13,663 students

Education is not compulsory. Equipment charges and fees have been introduced. Universities are suffering funding cuts.

HEALTH

▷ Welfare state health benefits

1 per 10,000 people   Malaria, pneumonia, diarrheal diseases

The health system has suffered from recent cuts. HIV and tuberculosis co-infections are at crisis level. Life expectancy rates are among the lowest in the Pacific. Access to clean water and sanitation are major issues.

SPENDING

▷ GDP/cap. no increase

CONSUMPTION AND SPENDING

7 per 1,000 population   11 per 1,000 population

Defense 1.2%
Education No data
Health 2.8%

0   5   10   15   20   25
Defense, Health, Education spending as % of GDP

P

There is a growing gap between the country's rich and poor, particularly in urban areas. High unemployment makes crime almost inevitable. The government plans to cut public services, in order to raise revenue for basic infrastructure, education and public health.

WORLD RANKING

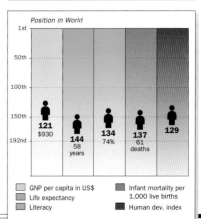

Position in World

1st
50th
100th
150th
192nd

121 $930
144 58 years
134 74%
137 61 deaths
129

GNP per capita in US$
Life expectancy
Literacy
Infant mortality per 1,000 live births
Human dev. index

PARAGUAY

OFFICIAL NAME: Republic of Paraguay **CAPITAL:** Asunción
POPULATION: 5.2 million **CURRENCY:** Guaraní **OFFICIAL LANGUAGE:** Spanish

SOUTH AMERICA

| 1811 | 1938 | May 15 | PY | -4 | +595 | .py |

LANDLOCKED IN SOUTH America and a Spanish possession until 1811, Paraguay won large tracts of land from Bolivia in 1835. From then until the overthrow in 1989 of General Stroessner, South America's longest-surviving dictator, it experienced periods of anarchy and military rule. The Paraguay river divides the eastern hills and fertile plains, where 90% of people live, from the almost uninhabited Chaco in the west. Paraguay's economy is largely agricultural.

CLIMATE ▷ Tropical/subtropical

WEATHER CHART

■ Average daily temperature   Rainfall ▬

Paraguay is subtropical, with all parts experiencing floods and droughts, but the Chaco is generally drier and hotter.

TRANSPORTATION ▷ Drive on right

Silvio Pettirossi Intl, Asunción
320,000 passengers

44 ships
43,600 grt

THE TRANSPORTATION NETWORK

| 2,785 km (1,731 miles) | Pan-American Highway 700 km (435 miles) |
| 441 km (274 miles) | 3,100 km (1,926 miles) |

Foreign investment is needed to upgrade roads. Most passenger rail services have been withdrawn.

TOURISM ▷ Visitors : population 1:13

387,000 visitors

Down 12% 1995–1997

MAIN TOURIST ARRIVALS

| Argentina 33% |
| Brazil 20% |
| Uruguay 8% |
| Other 39% |

% of total arrivals

Tourism numbers are small. Most visitors are cross-border day-trippers from Brazil and Argentina, who flock to Ciudad del Este to buy cheap, mainly Far Eastern, electrical goods. The Chaco attracts ecotourists.

PEOPLE ▷ Pop. density low

Guaraní, Spanish

13/km² (34/mi²)

THE URBAN/RURAL POPULATION SPLIT

53%   47%

ETHNIC MAKEUP

Indigenous Indian 2%   Other 8%
Mestizo 90%

Most Paraguayans are of combined Spanish and native Guaraní origin. The majority are bilingual, although outside the large cities Guaraní is spoken almost exclusively. Many of the rural Indians have been deprived of their ancestral lands. Some 20% of the people are descendants of European immigrants. Japanese, Koreans, and South Africans have arrived more recently.

POLITICS ▷ Multiparty elections

L. House 1998/2003
U. House 1998/2003

President Luis Gonzalez Macchi

AT THE LAST ELECTION

Chamber of Deputies 80 seats

56% ANR-PC   44% DA

ANR-PC = National Republican Association-Colorado Party
DA = Democratic Alliance
The Democratic Alliance is a coalition led by the Authentic Radical Liberal Party (PLRA)

Senate 45 seats

53% ANR-PC   44% DA   3% Other

Splits in the military led to the 1989 coup which ended the 34-year dictatorship of General Stroessner. In 1993, the first free elections in 60 years saw the PC, Stroessner's old ruling party, keep power, and President Wasmosy continued to rely on the military. The party retained power in 1998, despite a serious split over the presidential candidature of former army chief General Lino Oviedo. The assassination in March 1999 of Vice President Luis Argaña, Oviedo's main opponent in the PC, led to social unrest and the resignation of President Raúl Cubas, an Oviedo supporter. A fragile governing coalition was left with urgent problems of governability and a stagnant economy.

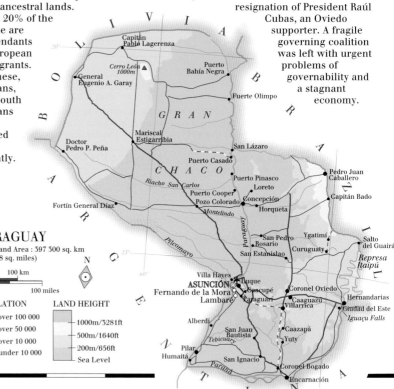

PARAGUAY

Total Land Area : 397 300 sq. km
(153 398 sq. miles)

| 0   100 km |
| 0   100 miles |

POPULATION

◎ over 100 000
○ over 50 000
● over 10 000
• under 10 000

LAND HEIGHT

1000m/3281ft
500m/1640ft
200m/656ft
Sea Level

P

WORLD AFFAIRS

Joined UN in 1945

IBRD | IAEA | OAS | Mercosr | RG

Main aims are fairer integration in the MERCOSUR common market and good relations with the USA.

AID

Recipient

$116m (receipts) — Up 20% 1996–1997

The World Bank gives development aid, the IMF conditional loans. NGO charities run small programs in rural areas.

DEFENSE

Compulsory military service

$134m — No change in 1997

Under Stroessner, the military controlled political and economic life. In 1994–1995 Congress tried to limit its powers but its political and institutional role was endorsed by the actions of President Wasmosy. The pact between the military and the PC, in power since 1947, continues.

ECONOMICS

Inflation 23.2% p.a. (1985–1996)

$10.2bn — 2,250.00–2,839.50 guaraníes

SCORE CARD

❏ WORLD GNP RANKING	80th
❏ GNP PER CAPITA	$200
❏ BALANCE OF PAYMENTS	$-749m
❏ INFLATION	7%
❏ UNEMPLOYMENT	8%

STRENGTHS

Electricity exporter: earnings obtain foreign exchange. Self-sufficiency in wheat and other staple foodstuffs. Cotton, oilseeds, notably soya, exports.

WEAKNESSES

Reliance on agriculture and Brazilian and Argentine markets. No hydrocarbons produced. Weak banking and financial sectors. High unemployment. Political instability deters foreign investment.

EXPORTS

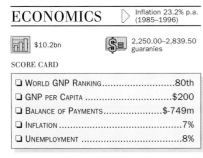

Chile 4%
Japan 7%
Netherlands 8%
Brazil 39%
Other 21%
Argentina 21%

IMPORTS

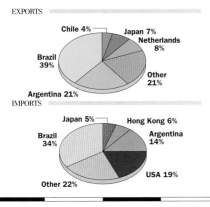

Japan 5%
Hong Kong 6%
Brazil 34%
Argentina 14%
USA 19%
Other 22%

***The Iguaçu Falls**, on the border with Brazil and Argentina, are composed of over 20 cataracts, separated by rocks and tree-covered islands.*

RESOURCES

Electric power 6.5m kw

22,000 tonnes — Not an oil producer; refines 7,500 b/d

9.8m cattle, 2.5m pigs, 387,000 sheep — Gypsum, marble, clay, kaolin, iron, manganese, uranium

The joint Paraguay–Brazil Itaipú hydroelectric dam is the world's largest. The massive Yacyretá dam is operated jointly with Argentina.

ENVIRONMENT

No Green MPs

4% — Low

Apart from the destruction of forests for farming and for dams, a major ecological worry is the smuggling abroad of endangered species.

MEDIA

TV ownership medium

Daily newspaper circulation 43 per 1,000 people

PUBLISHING AND BROADCAST MEDIA

There are 5 daily newspapers, including *ABC Color, El Diario Noticias, Popular* and *Ultima Hora*

4 independent services — 1 state-owned, 10 independent services

The media, historically sponsored by political parties, flourished after the fall of Stroessner, publishing details of corruption and abuses of human rights. The constitution protects the rights of columnists to air their views.

CRIME

Death penalty not used

Paraguay does not publish prison figures — Down 42% from 1992–1996

Paraguay is the contraband capital of Latin America, with trade in everything from cars to cocaine. Jungle airstrips near Brazil provide a route for narcotics.

EDUCATION

School leaving age: 12

92% — 42,302 students

Education is compulsory to the age of 12; only about 28% go on to secondary school. Provision is limited in remote rural areas.

CHRONOLOGY

Paraguay was controlled by Spain from 1536 until 1811.

- ❏ **1864–1870** Loses War of the Triple Alliance against Argentina, Brazil and Uruguay.
- ❏ **1928–1935** Two Chaco Wars against Bolivia; Paraguay wins most of the disputed land.
- ❏ **1954** Gen. Alfredo Stroessner seizes power; repressive military regime.
- ❏ **1989–93** Stroessner deposed by Gen. Andrés Rodríguez; first democratic elections.
- ❏ **1996** Coup attempt by Gen. Lino Oviedo.
- ❏ **1998–99** President Raúl Cubas elected president; resigns after assassination of Vice President Luis María Argaña; Cubas and Oviedo leave the country.

HEALTH

Welfare state health benefits

1 per 3,333 people — Heart disease, cancers, obstetric causes, tuberculosis

Hepatitis, typhoid, dysentery and tuberculosis are endemic and leprosy is common. Medical care is expensive.

SPENDING

GDP/cap. no increase

CONSUMPTION AND SPENDING

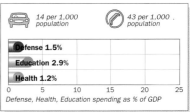

14 per 1,000 population — 43 per 1,000 population

Defense 1.5%
Education 2.9%
Health 1.2%

0   5   10   15   20   25
Defense, Health, Education spending as % of GDP

Income inequality and rural poverty remain. Top military ranks and business and landed elites control much of the country's wealth.

WORLD RANKING

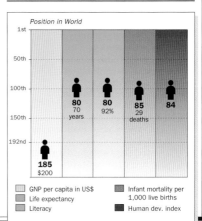

Position in World

1st
50th
100th
150th
192nd

80 — 70 years
80 — 92%
85 — 29 deaths
84
185 — $200

❏ GNP per capita in US$
❏ Life expectancy
❏ Literacy
❏ Infant mortality per 1,000 live births
❏ Human dev. index

P

PERU

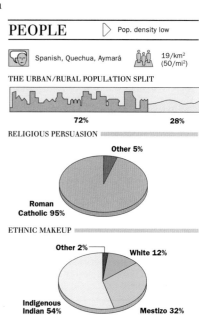
SOUTH AMERICA

OFFICIAL NAME: Republic of Peru   **CAPITAL:** Lima   **POPULATION:** 24.8 million
CURRENCY: Nuevo sol (new sol)   **OFFICIAL LANGUAGES:** Spanish and Quechua

| 1824 | 1941 | July 28 | PE | -5 | +51 | .pe |

LYING JUST SOUTH of the equator, on the Pacific coast of South America, Peru became independent from Spain in 1824. It rises from an arid coastal strip to the Andes, dominated in the south by volcanoes; about half of Peru's population live in mountain regions. Its border with Bolivia to the south runs through Lake Titicaca, the highest navigable lake in the world. In 1995, Peru was involved in a brief border war with Ecuador, its northern neighbor, and the issue was finally settled in 1998.

CLIMATE
Tropical/mountain/desert

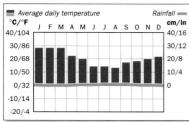
WEATHER CHART

Peru has several distinct climatic regions. The arid or desert coastal region experiences the *garúa*, persistent low cloud and fog, giving Lima cool winters even though it is close to the equator. The temperate slopes of the Andes have large daily temperature ranges and one rainy season, while the tropical Amazon Basin receives year-round rains.

TRANSPORTATION
Drive on right

Jorge Chávez International, Lima
2.57m passengers

695 ships
345,600 grt

THE TRANSPORTATION NETWORK

| 72,800 km (45,500 miles) | Pan-American Highway 2,495 km (1,550 miles) |
| 1,691 km (1,057 miles) | 8,600 km (5,344 miles) |

Peru's infrastructure remains poor, despite substantial improvements to the road network and internal air services. Most roads remain unpaved. Work on a transcontinental highway from Ilo, a free port on the Pacific, via Puerto Suárez in Bolivia, to the port of Santos in Brazil is ongoing. The two rail networks, the Central and Southern, are as yet unconnected. The Lima–La Oroya line is the world's highest stretch of standard-gauge railroad. River transport provides major access to Iquitos in Amazonia. There are more than 130 airstrips.

Spanish colonial church near Urubamba. *The River Urubamba with its deep gorges was known as the Sacred Valley to the Incas.*

TOURISM
Visitors : population 1:39

635,000 visitors

Up 31% 1995–1997

MAIN TOURIST ARRIVALS

	% of total arrivals
USA 22%	
Chile 12%	
Argentina 6%	
Bolivia 3%	
Italy 4%	
Other 53%	

0 10 20 30 40 50 60
% of total arrivals

Tourism, plunged into crisis in the early 1990s by guerrilla activity, crime and cholera fears, is gradually recovering. The heavily indebted industry has been unable to take full advantage of new investment opportunities, but privatization programs have seen the sale of state hotels. Visitors face poor infrastructure and accommodation to see incomparable sites such as the Inca ruins at Machu Picchu in the Andes. Ecotourism to the Amazon is also growing, but environmentalists are concerned about the impact on indigenous people. The pre-Colombian areas cleared in patterns in the desert by the Nazca civilization (known as the Nazca lines), dating from the 2nd century BCE, are another major attraction.

PEOPLE
Pop. density low

Spanish, Quechua, Aymará

19/km² (50/mi²)

THE URBAN/RURAL POPULATION SPLIT

72%   28%

RELIGIOUS PERSUASION

Other 5%
Roman Catholic 95%

ETHNIC MAKEUP

Other 2%
White 12%
Mestizo 32%
Indigenous Indian 54%

The majority of Peruvians are Indian or *mestizo*. The small elite of Spanish descendants retain a strong hold on the economy, power and social standing. A few Chinese and Japanese live in the northern cities.

Previously remote Andean Indians are increasingly informed of developments in Lima and the coastal strip by ethnic radio and relatives in urban centers, which have compensated for problems associated with the marginalization of their native Quechua and Aymará languages in a Spanish-speaking culture. A further 250,000 Amazonian Indians live in the eastern lowlands. Together with the small community of blacks (descendants of plantation workers), they tend to suffer the worst discrimination in towns.

The extended family remains strong. A part of traditional native Indian traditions, its role as a social bond was strengthened by Catholicism. In recent years, economic difficulties have raised its profile as the key social support system for most Peruvians.

POPULATION AGE BREAKDOWN

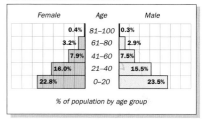

Female	Age	Male
0.4%	81–100	0.3%
3.2%	61–80	2.9%
7.9%	41–60	7.5%
16.0%	21–40	15.5%
22.8%	0–20	23.5%

% of population by age group

P

POLITICS

▷ Multiparty elections

 1995/2000

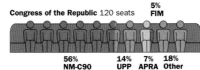 President Alberto Keinya Fujimori

Alberto Fujimori, president since 1990, has increased the power of the presidency.

Former UN Secretary General Pérez de Cuéllar, presidential candidate in 1995.

AT THE LAST ELECTION

Congress of the Republic 120 seats

5% FIM

56% NM-C90 | 14% UPP | 7% APRA | 18% Other

NM-C90 = New Majority–Change 90 **UPP** = Union for Peru
APRA = American Popular Revolutionary Alliance
FIM = Independent Moralizing Front

Peru is nominally a multiparty democracy in which the president holds executive power.

MAIN POLITICAL ISSUES
Democracy and Fujimori's reelection
In 1992, President Fujimori, backed by the army, dismissed Congress, replacing it with an unelected body. He then introduced a new constitution allowing him to run again for election in 1995. Most

Peruvians initially accepted his coup as necessary for strong government and the fight against *Sendero Luminoso* terrorism, but now increasingly oppose his concentration of power and military-backed bid to be reelected in 2000. The opposition sees Fujimori's promises of reform purely as devices to secure his reelection.

Judicial corruption
Widespread corruption in the judiciary has resulted in more than 600 judges and prosecutors being dismissed or detained over the last five years. Many were accused of accepting bribes, some from drug traffickers. The government claims that this proves its resolve to clean up justice, but critics say it is more concerned with keeping the courts under their political thumb by controlling appointments and dismissals.

Growth
After virtual stagnation in 1998, exacerbated by the ruinous effects of El Niño on fishing and agriculture, a new economic team was predicting

strong recovery in 1999. However, growth prospects are expected to remain poor due to weak domestic demand and the predicted continuation of depressed world commodity prices.

PROFILE
President Fujimori ended the long tradition of large parties dominating politics by winning the 1990 presidential elections with a loose coalition. His 1992 "self-coup" dismissed Congress and nearly half the Supreme Court judges. After international protests, a new constitution created a compliant legislature and permitted his reelection in 1995. His defeat of hyperinflation and successful onslaught on the *Sendero Luminoso* guerrillas boosted his popularity, but his public standing has since plummeted as he has tightened his control on government. Few checks on the executive remain as Fujimori's alliance of convenience with the military continues to marginalize the opposition. He intends to stand for a third term in 2000.

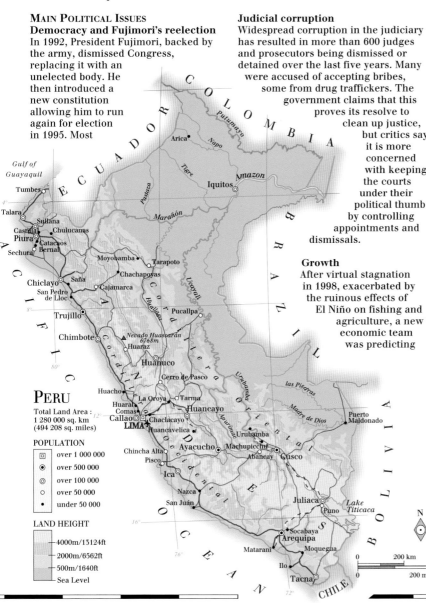

PERU
Total Land Area :
1 280 000 sq. km
(494 208 sq. miles)

POPULATION

⊡ over 1 000 000
◉ over 500 000
◎ over 100 000
○ over 50 000
• under 50 000

LAND HEIGHT

4000m/13124ft
2000m/6562ft
500m/1640ft
Sea Level

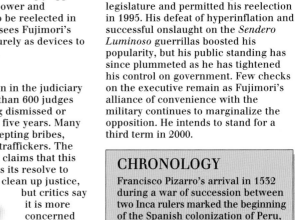

CHRONOLOGY
Francisco Pizarro's arrival in 1532 during a war of succession between two Inca rulers marked the beginning of the Spanish colonization of Peru, and the end of the Inca empire.

❑ **1821** Independence proclaimed in Lima after its capture by the Argentine liberator, José de San Martín, who had just freed Chile.
❑ **1824** Spain suffers final defeats at battles of Junín and Ayacucho by Simón Bolívar and Gen. Sucre, the liberators of Venezuela and Colombia.
❑ **1836–1839** Peru and Bolivia joined in short-lived confederation.
❑ **1866** Peruvian–Spanish War.
❑ **1879–1884** War of the Pacific. Chile defeats Peru and Bolivia. Peru loses territory in south.
❑ **1908** Augusto Leguía y Salcedo's dictatorial rule.
❑ **1919** USA starts financing public works.
❑ **1924** Víctor Raúl Haya de la Torre founds nationalist American Revolutionary Popular Alliance (APRA) in exile in Mexico.
❑ **1930** Leguía ousted. APRA moves to Peru as first political party.
❑ **1931–1945** APRA banned.
❑ **1939–1945** Moderate, pro-US civilian government.
❑ **1948–1956** Gen. Manuel Odría in power. APRA banned again.
❑ **1956–1962** Civilian government.
❑ **1962–1963** Two military coups.
❑ **1963** Election of Fernando.

P

CHRONOLOGY *continued*

Belaúnde Terry. Land reform, but military used to suppress communist-inspired insurgency.

- ❑ **1968** Military junta takes over. Attempts to alleviate poverty. Large-scale nationalizations.
- ❑ **1975–1978** New right-wing junta.
- ❑ **1980** Belaúnde reelected. Popular Action (AP) wins majority. Maoist guerrilla organization, *Sendero Luminoso*(Shining Path), begins armed struggle.
- ❑ **1981** Border war with Ecuador over Cordillera del Cóndor, which a 1942 protocol had given to Peru. Ecuador wants access to Amazon.
- ❑ **1982** Deaths and "disappearances" start to escalate as army cracks down on guerrillas and narcotics.
- ❑ **1985** Electoral win for left-wing APRA under Alán García Pérez.
- ❑ **1987** Peru bankrupt. Plans to nationalize banks blocked by new *Libertad* movement led by writer Mario Vargas Llosa.
- ❑ **1990** More than 3,000 political murders. Alberto Fujimori, an independent, is elected president on anticorruption platform. Severe economic austerity program.
- ❑ **1992–95** Fujimori "self-coup." New constitution. Fujimori reelected.
- ❑ **1996–1997** Left-wing Tupac Amarú guerrillas hold hundreds of people hostage at Japanese ambassador's residence in four-month siege.
- ❑ **1998** Border agreement with Ecuador.

WORLD AFFAIRS ▷ Joined UN in 1945

Development funding depends on gaining backing from multilateral financial institutions. Cooperation with the USA, the main source of aid, extends to the war on cocaine, although Peru remains the world's largest producer of coca. Fujimori stirred up resentment in Colombia when in a speech in Washington in 1999 he called on the whole region to join forces against the threat allegedly posed by Colombian guerrillas.

AID ▷ Recipient

💲 $488m (receipts)   ⬆ Up 19% 1996–1997

The USA mostly aids anti-narcotics work. $1.3 billion in loans from the IADB, the World Bank and Japan are conditional on specific health and educational targets being met and progress on privatizations. State management of aid has been criticized.

DEFENSE ▷ Compulsory military service

💲 $1.3bn   ⬆ Up 13% in 1997

The president exercises unprecedented control over the armed forces.

The military, in power from 1968 to 1980, supported President Fujimori's 1992 "self-coup." It continues to exert a powerful influence in politics and currently controls a quarter of the national territory which remains under a state of emergency, despite the defeat of the *Sendero Luminoso* guerrillas. Fujimori's control over promotions and the National Intelligence Service (SIN) guarantees a loyal armed forces leadership, as does his 1995 amnesty law protecting the military from human rights charges. The 1998 peace accord with Ecuador rankled with sections of the military command. US military advise on anti-drug programs.

PERUVIAN ARMED FORCES

🛡	300 main battle tanks (T-54/T-55)	85,000 personnel
🚢	8 submarines, 2 cruisers 1 destroyer, 4 frigates, 11 patrol boats	25,000 personnel
✈	118 combat aircraft (8 *Canberra*, 28 Su-22, 18 Su-25, 10 *Mirage* 2000P)	15,000 personnel
🚀	None	

ECONOMICS ▷ Inflation 236.6% p.a. (1985–1996)

📊 $63.7bn   💲 2.73–3.16 new soles

SCORE CARD

❑ WORLD GNP RANKING	46th
❑ GNP PER CAPITA	$2,610
❑ BALANCE OF PAYMENTS	$–3.4bn
❑ INFLATION	8.6%
❑ UNEMPLOYMENT	7%

EXPORTS

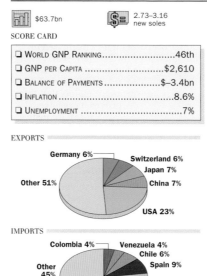

Germany 6%
Switzerland 6%
Japan 7%
China 7%
USA 23%
Other 51%

IMPORTS

Colombia 4%
Venezuela 4%
Chile 6%
Spain 9%
USA 32%
Other 45%

STRENGTHS
Abundant mineral resources, including oil. Rich Pacific fish stocks. Wide climatic variety, allowing diverse and productive agriculture; cotton and coffee are important. Well-developed textile industry.

WEAKNESSES
Over-dependency on metals and commodities whose fluctuating prices undermine trade and investment. Stalled privatization. Corruption and poor infrastructure deterring investment. Weak banks.

PROFILE
Wealth and economic activity in Peru are largely confined to the cities of the coastal plain. The inhabitants of the Andean uplands are subsistence farmers or coca producers. Peru's strict fiscal and monetary policy

ECONOMIC PERFORMANCE INDICATOR

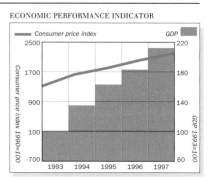

is to continue. In 1999 another three-year loan package was being discussed with the IMF, although some pump-priming of the economy was likely in a pre-election year. Three external shocks – the disruption of fishing by El Niño storms, the Asian economic crises and Russian-provoked turmoil in emerging markets – hit growth hard in 1998, as did depressed world commodity prices. Recovery will be slow. Privatizations are set to be accelerated.

PERU : MAJOR BUSINESSES

Arica
Talara
Sechura
Trujillo
Cerro de Pasco
Lima
Ica
Pucallpa
Arequipa

- 🛢 Oil
- Oil refining
- Textiles
- Mining
- Fish processing
- Food processing
- 🚗 Vehicle assembly

0   400 km
0   400 miles

* significant multinational ownership

RESOURCES

▷ Electric power 3.8m kw

🐟 9.52m tonnes

🛢 124,290 b/d (reserves 380,866,000 bbl)

🐑 13.6m sheep, 4.7m cattle, 2.5m pigs, 2m goats

💎 Oil, coal, lead, zinc, silver, iron, gold, copper

ELECTRICITY GENERATION

Hydro 82% (13.7bn kwh)	
Combustion 18% (2.9bn kwh)	
Nuclear 0%	
Other 0%	

0 20 40 60 80 100

% of total generation by type

Peru is an important exporter of copper and lead. Development of the huge Antamina copper and zinc deposit is under way. The government plans to proceed with the $3 billion Camisea hydrocarbon project, and to explore the full extent of its large oil reserves. The further development of hydroelectric power is a priority.

PERU : LAND USE

▨ Cropland
▨ Pasture
▨ Forest
▨ Desert
▨ High mountain regions
↓ Sugarcane - cash crop
🐑 Sheep

0   400 km
0   400 miles

ENVIRONMENT

▷ No Green MPs

🔺 3%

⬇ Low

ENVIRONMENTAL TREATIES

🌿 Yes	🦏 Yes	🌐 Yes
🛢 Yes	🍶 Yes	♻ Yes

Environmentalists have long been concerned about coastal industrial pollution and the activities of the fishing industry. Over-fishing of anchovies almost resulted in their extinction in the 1970s. Today, attention has switched to the rise in the number of dolphins being caught in drift nets. Unchecked urban and industrial pollution, especially in Lima, is a major problem.

Environmentalists fear that Peru's and the USA's policy of using powerful air-sprayed herbicides to destroy coca crops is adding to river pollution in the Andes, where mining also causes severe environmental problems.

MEDIA

▷ TV ownership medium

✕ Daily newspaper circulation 85 per 1,000 people

PUBLISHING AND BROADCAST MEDIA

📰	There are 74 daily newspapers. These include the conservative *El Comercio* and *Expreso*, and the left-wing *La República*
👤	1 state–owned, 10 independent services
📻	3 state–owned, many independent networks

Media freedom is severely restricted. Journalists and newspaper editors regularly receive death threats.

CRIME

▷ Death penalty not used

🚪 17,368 prisoners

⬆ Up 15% in 1992

CRIME RATES

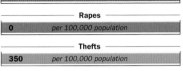

Murders
9 per 100,000 population

Rapes
0 per 100,000 population

Thefts
350 per 100,000 population

Kidnappings, murders, armed robberies, and drug-related crime remain serious problems, especially in Lima. Corruption is deep-seated in the police and security forces. Despite the near-destruction of the left-wing *Sendero Luminoso* guerrillas, main cities frequently have curfews, and those who can afford it protect themselves with high-security homes and armed guards.

EDUCATION

▷ School leaving age: 12

📖 89%

🎓 755,929 students

Provision of state education, especially for the poor, remains a major challenge.

THE EDUCATION SYSTEM

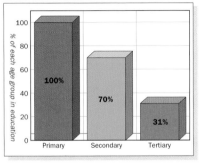

% of each age group in education

- Primary: 100%
- Secondary: 70%
- Tertiary: 31%

Education is based on the US system. Spending has been declining. The state and private university system is accessible to a small minority.

HEALTH

▷ Welfare state health benefits

👥 1 per 1,000 people

☠ Respiratory, heart, infectious and parasitic diseases

Peru's public health system almost collapsed in the 1980s and is poor. In many areas primary care is non-existent. Advanced treatment is available only to private patients in city clinics. Goiter, a thyroid abnormality, is widespread, especially among children in mountain areas. Infant mortality is rising due to social deprivation, diarrheal diseases and tuberculosis. Malaria is again widespread, and cholera reached epidemic proportions in 1994. Thousands of poor women have been forcibly sterilized in the last three years as part of a government program to lower the birth rate.

SPENDING

▷ GDP/cap. no increase

CONSUMPTION AND SPENDING

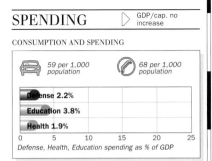

🚗 59 per 1,000 population

📞 68 per 1,000 population

- Defense 2.2%
- Education 3.8%
- Health 1.9%

0 5 10 15 20 25

Defense, Health, Education spending as % of GDP

Most wealth and power in Peru is still retained by old Spanish families. Indigenous peoples remain excluded from both. The rich live in a state of siege; a key status symbol is the number of armed guards and security cameras protecting family property. Overpopulation and rural migration accentuate poverty in Lima where some 2.7 million live in shanty towns, many of them minus such basic utilities as running water and electricity. The UN estimates that over 30% of Peruvians live below the poverty line.

WORLD RANKING

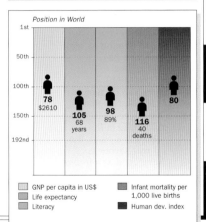

Position in World

1st
50th
100th
150th
192nd

- 78 $2610
- 105 68 years
- 98 89%
- 116 40 deaths
- 80

▨ GNP per capita in US$
▨ Life expectancy
▨ Literacy
▨ Infant mortality per 1,000 live births
▨ Human dev. index

P

PHILIPPINES

SOUTHEAST ASIA

OFFICIAL NAME: Republic of the Philippines   **CAPITAL:** Manila
POPULATION: 72.2 million   **CURRENCY:** Philippine peso   **OFFICIAL LANGUAGES:** Filipino and English

| 1946 | 1946 | June 12 | PP | +8 | +63 | .ph |

Lying in the western Pacific Ocean, the Philippines is the world's second-largest archipelago after Indonesia. It comprises 7,107 islands, of which 4,600 are named and 1,000 inhabited. There are three main island groupings: the Luzon group, the Visayan group, and the Mindanao and Sulu islands. Located on the Pacific "ring of fire," the Philippines is subject to frequent earthquakes and volcanic activity. Since the fall of the Marcos regime in 1986, successive governments have worked hard to bring political stability to the country. However, economic expansion has not been able to keep pace with the Philippines' population growth rate.

Bohol Island has over 1,000 of these famous mounds, also known as "the chocolate hills."

CLIMATE

▷ Tropical monsoon/equatorial

WEATHER CHART

The Philippines is warm and humid all year. The rainy season lasts from June to October. Humidity falls from 85% in September to 71% in March.

TOURISM

▷ Visitors : population 1:32

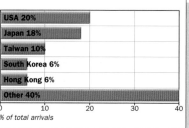

2.2m visitors   Up 38% 1995–1997

MAIN TOURIST ARRIVALS

	% of total arrivals
USA 20%	
Japan 18%	
Taiwan 10%	
South Korea 6%	
Hong Kong 6%	
Other 40%	

Tourism remains a smaller business in the Philippines than in the NICs of southeast Asia. Much of it is based around the sex industry. However, business may suffer as international pressure intensifies to end sex-tourism. The most popular tourist beach resort is the island of Boracay. Palawan, one of the least spoilt, retains most of its tropical rain forest and coral lagoons. The rice terraces of northern Luzon are another attraction.

TRANSPORTATION

▷ Drive on right

Nino Aquino Intl, Pasay City
12m passengers

1,617 ships
9.03m grt

THE TRANSPORTATION NETWORK

26,790 km (16,646 miles)	None
805 km (500 miles)	3,219 km (2,000 miles)

Spending on transportation infrastructure has fallen by over 40% since 1984. As a result, many main roads are in need of repair. Traffic jams in Manila are a major problem and are holding back economic growth. Air travel is the only means of getting around the islands quickly.

In 1992, the state airline, Philippines Airlines, was privatized. Since then, more than $1 billion have been budgeted to buy new aircraft and expand its regional network. Subic Bay, the USA's largest overseas base until 1992, when the US navy left, has a prime location, which the government is now exploiting. On the South China Sea coast, the deep natural harbor is being developed as a free port and enterprise zone. The Taiwanese are the biggest investors in this project.

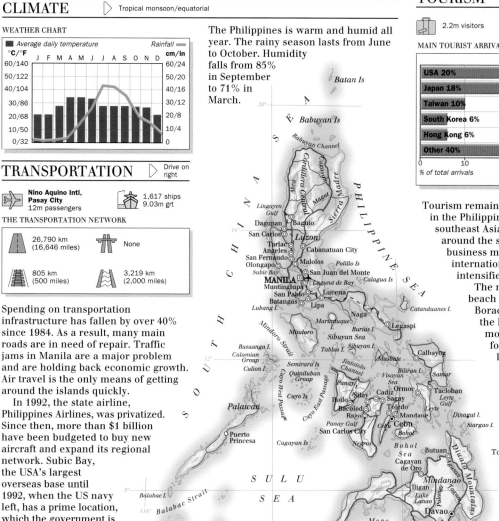

PHILIPPINES

Total Land Area : 300 000 sq. km (777 001 sq. miles)

POPULATION

over 1 000 000	▣
over 500 000	◉
over 100 000	◎

LAND HEIGHT

2000m/6562ft
1000m/3281ft
500m/1640ft
200m/656ft
Sea Level

PEOPLE ▷ Pop. density high

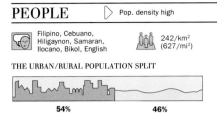

Filipino, Cebuano, Hiligaynon, Samaran, Ilocano, Bikol, English

242/km² (627/mi²)

THE URBAN/RURAL POPULATION SPLIT

54% **46%**

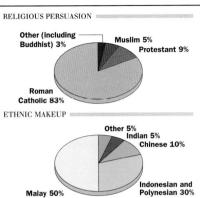

RELIGIOUS PERSUASION

Other (including Buddhist) 3%
Muslim 5%
Protestant 9%
Roman Catholic 83%

ETHNIC MAKEUP

Other 5%
Indian 5%
Chinese 10%
Indonesian and Polynesian 30%
Malay 50%

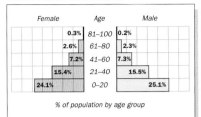

POPULATION AGE BREAKDOWN

Female	Age	Male
0.3%	81–100	0.2%
2.6%	61–80	2.3%
7.2%	41–60	7.3%
15.4%	21–40	15.5%
24.1%	0–20	25.1%

% of population by age group

The Philippines encompasses more than 100 distinct ethnic groups. The majority of Filipinos are of Malay origin, and Christian. Most Christians belong to the Tagalog, Cebuano, Llocan, Longgo, Bicolano, Waray, Pampangueno or Pangasinense ethnic groups. They are concentrated on the main island, Luzon, and are a majority on Mindanao. Most Muslims live on Mindanao, but many are also found in the Sulu archipelago. The Chinese minority, which was well established by 1603, has remained significant in business and trade. More than 120 Chinese schools have ensured that it has retained a distinct identity.

There are also a number of cultural minorities who practice animist religions. They include the Ifugaos, Bontocks, Kalingas, and Ibalois on Luzon, the Manobo and Bukidnon on Mindanao, and the Mangyans on Palawan. Many of these groups speak Malayo-Polynesian dialects. Limited intermarriage with other peoples has meant that groups in the more remote regions have managed to retain their traditional ways of life.

The Philippines is the only Christian state in Asia; over 80% of Filipinos are Roman Catholics and the Church is the dominant cultural force in the country. It opposes state-sponsored family planning programs, which are designed to curb accelerating population growth.

Women have traditionally played a prominent part in Philippine life. Inheritance laws give them equal rights with men. Many go into politics, banking, and business, and in several professional sectors women form a majority.

POLITICS ▷ Multiparty elections

L. House 1998/2001
U. House 1998/2001
President Joseph Estrada

AT THE LAST ELECTION

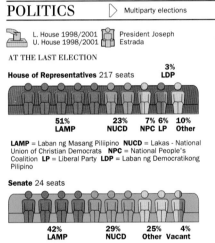

House of Representatives 217 seats

3% LDP

| 51% LAMP | 23% NUCD | 7% NPC | 6% LP | 10% Other |

LAMP = Laban ng Masang Piliipino **NUCD** = Lakas - National Union of Christian Democrats **NPC** = National People's Coalition **LP** = Liberal Party **LDP** = Laban ng Democratikong Pilipino

Senate 24 seats

| 42% LAMP | 29% NUCD | 25% Other | 4% Vacant |

One Senate seat remains vacant.

The Philippines is a multiparty democracy.

MAIN POLITICAL ISSUES
Power cuts
The 1986–1992 Aquino administration neglected investment in power stations. As a result, the Philippines suffers from widespread power cuts, disrupting business and thereby deterring foreign investment in the Philippines. Under the Electric Power Crisis Law of 1993, President Ramos was given extra powers to deal with the problem, exempting new power station projects from planning controls.
Communist and Muslim separatists
Communist and Muslim separatists have been fighting Manila

governments for over 30 years. More than ten thousand armed confrontations with rebels have been recorded by the army during this period. Much of the support for secession has been fueled by the failure of successive governments to curb poverty.

Since 1992, the government has been pursuing a peace process with all armed groups. The most powerful, the communist New People's Army (NPA), is in decline. Once regarded as a heroic army of the oppressed and as an alternative to traditional politics, it has split into factions. The Ramos government signed a peace agreement in 1996 with the Moro National Liberation Front (MNLF), the main organization representing the secessionist Muslim rebels active in Mindanao. Meanwhile, a militant breakaway faction – the Muslim Islamic Liberation Front (MILF) – emerged as a new threat. Its clashes with troops forcing the government to abandon a massive irrigation project.

PROFILE
Democracy was restored to the Philippines in 1986. Ferdinand Marcos, in power since 1965, was shown to have no popular legitimacy as " people power" massed in support of his presidential election opponent Corazon Aquino. She then got crucial support from army units headed by Fidel Ramos and from Marcos's defense minister, Juan Ponce Enrile. When they declared Aquino the true winner of the

Joseph Estrada was elected president in June 1998.

Imelda Marcos, wife of the former dictator Ferdinand Marcos.

1986 elections, the USA decided to withdraw its support for Marcos and his power crumbled. Corazon Aquino's government succeeded in handing over power through fair elections in 1992. Fidel Ramos, the victor, concentrated on achieving stability and economic growth. However, his dependence on loose coalition arrangements in Congress created difficulties for the government's economic liberalization program. Ramos's presidential term ended in 1998, when he was succeeded by a former film star, Joseph Estrada.

WORLD AFFAIRS ▷ Joined UN in 1945

APEC · ASEAN · G24 · NAM · WTO

Regional relationships are paramount. The Philippine state took over US bases in 1992. The US navy resumed port calls and joint exercises in 1999, after a three year suspension, under the Visiting Forces Agreement. Manila has established a claim to the Spratly Islands.

P

CHRONOLOGY

Ceded to the USA by Spain in 1898, the Philippines became self-governing in 1935. After Japanese occupation during World War II, the Philippines became an independent republic in 1946.

- ❑ **1965** Ferdinand Marcos becomes president.
- ❑ **1969–1972** Marcos reelected amid malpractice allegations.
- ❑ **1972** Marcos declares martial law. Opposition leaders arrested, National Assembly suspended, press censored.
- ❑ **1977** Ex-LP leader Benigno Aquino sentenced to death. Criticism forces Marcos to delay execution.
- ❑ **1978** Elections won by Marcos's new party, New Society (KBL). Marcos named president and prime minister.
- ❑ **1980** Aquino allowed to travel to USA for medical treatment.
- ❑ **1981** Martial law ends. Marcos reelected president by referendum.
- ❑ **1983** Benigno Aquino shot dead at Manila airport on return from USA. Inquiry blames military conspiracy.
- ❑ **1986** USA compels presidential election. Result disputed. Army rebels led by Gen. Fidel Ramos, and public demonstrations, bring widow of Benigno Aquino, Corazon, to power. Marcos exiled to USA.
- ❑ **1987** New constitution. Aquino-led coalition wins Congress elections.
- ❑ **1989** Marcos dies in USA.
- ❑ **1990** Imelda Marcos acquitted of fraud charges in USA. Earthquake in Baguio City leaves 1,600 dead.
- ❑ **1991** Mt. Pinatubo erupts. USA leaves Clark Air Base. Imelda Marcos returns.
- ❑ **1992** Gen. Fidel Ramos wins presidential election. LDP secures most seats in parliament. USA withdraws from Subic Bay base.
- ❑ **1996** Peace agreement with Muslim secessionists.
- ❑ **1998** Joseph Estrada elected president.
- ❑ **1999** First execution in 22 years following reinstatement of death penalty.

AID

▷ Recipient

 $689m (receipts)　Down 22% 1996–1997

The Philippines' main bilateral aid donors are the USA and Japan. Large remittances are also received from Filipinos overseas. In 1975, there were 40,000 OCWS (overseas contract workers). By 2000 this is expected to rise to almost one million. Many NGOS operate in the outlying islands.

DEFENSE

▷ No compulsory military service

$1.4bn　　Down 7% in 1997

A strong US military presence until recently has helped maintain defense spending below regional standards.

Subic Bay, vacated by the USA in 1992, was the largest US base outside America; it was used most recently during the 1991 Gulf War. The military retains its political influence. In early 1999 Estrada's government announced its intention to modernize the armed forces.

PHILIPPINE ARMED FORCES

🛡	41 light tanks (*Scorpion*)	74,500 personnel
⚓	1 frigate and 67 patrol boats	25,900 personnel
✈	39 combat aircraft (F-5-A/B	17,400 personnel
🚀	None	

ECONOMICS

▷ Inflation 8.9% p.a. (1985–1996)

$88.4bn　　39.9–38.9 Philippine pesos

SCORE CARD

❑ WORLD GNP RANKING	38th
❑ GNP PER CAPITA	$1,200
❑ BALANCE OF PAYMENTS	$–4.3bn
❑ INFLATION	5.1%
❑ UNEMPLOYMENT	8%

EXPORTS

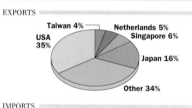

USA 35% | Taiwan 4% | Netherlands 5% | Singapore 6% | Japan 16% | Other 34%

IMPORTS

Other 45% | Taiwan 5% | South Korea 6% | Singapore 7% | USA 17% | Japan 20%

STRENGTHS
Economy now fully open to outside investment. Agricultural productivity rising. Remittances from Filipinos working overseas. Well-equipped ex-US military installations with economic potential, such as Subic Bay.

WEAKNESSES
Power failures limit scope for expansion. Rudimentary infrastructure. Low domestic savings rates make Philippines reliant on foreign finance.

PROFILE
In the 1950s, the Philippines was one of the strongest economies in Asia. Since then, it has fallen behind once much poorer nations such as Thailand, Malaysia, and South Korea. Around 50% of the population live on the poverty line. It is this poverty that has fueled many of the secessionist movements that have threatened the stability of successive governments.

The economy is undergoing slow reform. The Ramos administration

ECONOMIC PERFORMANCE INDICATOR

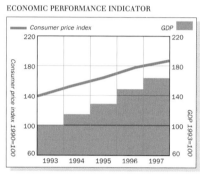

— Consumer price index　　GDP

aimed to emulate the success of other southeast Asian NICs. Backed by the IMF, it deregulated the economy to encourage foreign investment. It also tried to trim the power of some of the large privately run monopolies. The target of raising per capita income to $1,000 was achieved by 1995. Other key goals were to reduce to 30% the proportion of the population affected by poverty, and to raise economic growth to double figures – a target which receded dramatically when the whole region was hit by economic crisis in 1997.

PHILIPPINES : MAJOR BUSINESSES

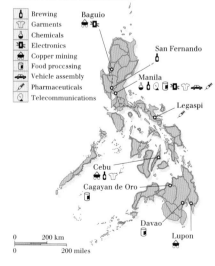

🍺 Brewing
👕 Garments
⚗ Chemicals
⧈ Electronics
⛏ Copper mining
🗃 Food processing
🚗 Vehicle assembly
💉 Pharmaceuticals
📡 Telecommunications

P

RESOURCES

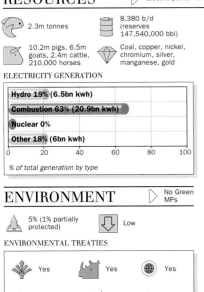

▷ Electric power 7.7m kw

2.3m tonnes

8,380 b/d (reserves 147,540,000 bbl)

10.2m pigs, 6.5m goats, 2.4m cattle, 210,000 horses

Coal, copper, nickel, chromium, silver, manganese, gold

ELECTRICITY GENERATION

Hydro 19% (6.5bn kwh)

Combustion 63% (20.9bn kwh)

Nuclear 0%

Other 18% (6bn kwh)

% of total generation by type

The Philippines is the world's biggest supplier of refractory chrome. Copper is also a significant export. Substantial gold reserves have been mined since 1996. However, more than 90% of mineral potential remains undeveloped. Oil production off Palawan began in 1979. The Philippines is the world's second-biggest user of geothermal power after the USA; almost 25% of electricity on Luzon is provided by this method. In 1989, timber exports were halted, although illegal logging continues to cause deforestation.

ENVIRONMENT

▷ No Green MPs

5% (1% partially protected)

Low

ENVIRONMENTAL TREATIES

Yes Yes Yes

Yes Yes Yes

The environment has become a major issue. Most of the tropical rain forest has been destroyed, except for pockets such as the island of Palawan. Fishermen have dynamited unique coral habitats, and continue to use cyanide and muro-ami techniques to increase the size of their catches.

The government has recognized the costs of environmental damage. Soil run-off is silting rivers and reducing the power generated by hydroelectric dams. Fast-depleting coral habitats reduce tourist attractions. Logging has been banned, but enforcement is difficult; many loggers have their own private armies. In addition, continued use of slash-and-burn farming has aided deforestation.

MEDIA

▷ TV ownership medium

Daily newspaper circulation 82 per 1,000 people

PUBLISHING AND BROADCAST MEDIA

There are 47 daily newspapers. The most influential newspapers are the *Philippine Star* and the *Philippine Daily Globe*

1 state-owned, 6 independent services

31 state-owned, 355 independent stations

The lifting of censorship following Corazon Aquino's election in 1986 led to a burgeoning of the media. As well as the national press, there are more than 250 regional newspapers in local dialects. State TV and radio broadcast in English and Filipino. Four independent television stations serve Metro Manila.

CRIME

▷ Death penalty used

17,843 prisoners

Down 8% in 1990

CRIME RATES

Murders

30 | *per 100,000 population*

Rapes

3 | *per 100,000 population*

Thefts

72 | *per 100,000 population*

The death penalty, abolished in 1987, was reinstated in 1993. In February 1999 a convicted child rapist was the first person to be executed in over 20 years.

EDUCATION

▷ School leaving age: 12

95%

2m students

High literacy rates have not had any effect on reducing widespread poverty.

THE EDUCATION SYSTEM

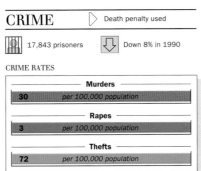

% of each age group in education

- Primary: 100%
- Secondary: 60%
- Tertiary: 30%

The Philippines has one of the highest literacy rates among developing countries. The education system is based on the US model, but characterized by many private schools. Sectarianism in education is common; the Chinese community has its own schools. Most colleges and universities are also run privately. The universities of San Carlos in Cebu city and Santo Tomas in Manila are Spanish colonial foundations, dating from 1595 and 1611 respectively.

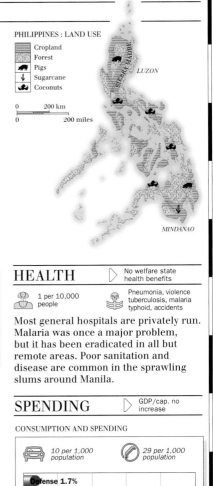

PHILIPPINES : LAND USE

- Cropland
- Forest
- Pigs
- Sugarcane
- Coconuts

LUZON

SIERRA MADRE

MINDANAO

0 — 200 km
0 — 200 miles

HEALTH

▷ No welfare state health benefits

1 per 10,000 people

Pneumonia, violence tuberculosis, malaria typhoid, accidents

Most general hospitals are privately run. Malaria was once a major problem, but it has been eradicated in all but remote areas. Poor sanitation and disease are common in the sprawling slums around Manila.

SPENDING

▷ GDP/cap. no increase

CONSUMPTION AND SPENDING

10 per 1,000 population

29 per 1,000 population

- Defense 1.7%
- Education 2.2%
- Health 1%

Defense, Health, Education spending as % of GDP

Around 50% of Filipinos live on or below the poverty line. Wealth remains highly concentrated in a few select business families, based in the capital, Manila.

WORLD RANKING

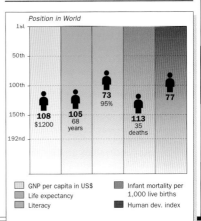

Position in World

- GNP per capita in US$: 108 — $1200
- Life expectancy: 105 — 68 years
- Literacy: 73 — 95%
- Infant mortality per 1,000 live births: 113 — 35 deaths
- Human dev. index: 77

Legend:
- GNP per capita in US$
- Life expectancy
- Literacy
- Infant mortality per 1,000 live births
- Human dev. index

P

POLAND

OFFICIAL NAME: Republic of Poland **CAPITAL:** Warsaw
POPULATION: 38.7 million **CURRENCY:** Zloty **OFFICIAL LANGUAGE:** Polish

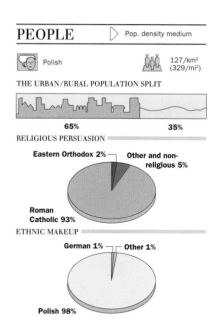

1918 1945 May 3 PL +1 +48 .pl

LOCATED IN THE HEART OF EUROPE, Poland's low-lying plains extend from the Baltic shore in the north to the Tatra Mountains on its southern border with the Czech Republic and Slovakia. Since the fall of the communist regime, Poland has undergone massive social, economic and political change. It has experienced rapid economic growth since the early 1990s and is negotiating to join the EU. It has already been accepted as a member of NATO, and its size and strategic location in central Europe mark it out as a major player in European politics in the future.

CLIMATE ▷ Continental

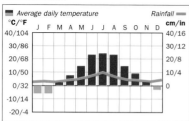

WEATHER CHART

Most of the country experiences a similar climate. Summers are hot, with heavy rainfall often accompanied by thunder. Winters are severe, with snow covering the ground on the southern mountains and for as much as 60–70 days in the east.

TRANSPORTATION ▷ Drive on right

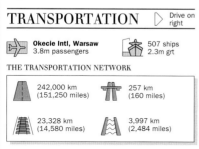

Okecie Intl, Warsaw
3.8m passengers

507 ships
2.3m grt

THE TRANSPORTATION NETWORK

242,000 km (151,250 miles)	257 km (160 miles)
23,328 km (14,580 miles)	3,997 km (2,484 miles)

The state airline LOT is continuing to increase links with Western countries, and is due for privatization. Russian aircraft have all been replaced with Western models. Airports are being upgraded. LOT's charter business is on the increase, as more middle-class Poles holiday abroad.
A 15-year roads expansion program was begun in 1997. New investment in railways will bring "fast tram" systems for cities and long-distance high-speed links.
   Telecommunications are undergoing a restructuring program, involving the privatization of Telekomunikacja Polska and the end of its monopoly on long-distance calls.

The medieval administrative center of Lublin lies in Poland's southeastern agricultural heartland.

TOURISM ▷ Visitor : population 1:1.9

19.5m visitors

Up 2% 1995-1997

MAIN TOURIST ARRIVALS

Germany 64%	
Czech Republic 19%	
Former USSR 13%	
Other 4%	

% of total arrivals

Despite considerable environmental problems, Poland is renowned for its skiing and hiking, especially in the Tatra Mountains. Kraków's medieval core has been preserved, while Toruńlhas restored its historic German Hanseatic buildings.
   Warsaw's historic center has been reconstructed, following the destruction of 80% of it by the German army in 1944. More hotels and restaurants are being opened.
   Poznańlhas exploited its location between Warsaw and Berlin to create an international exhibition and business convention industry.
   The state airline LOT and other carriers have increased their flights from the West to take advantage of the country's tourist potential.

PEOPLE ▷ Pop. density medium

Polish

127/km²
(329/mi²)

THE URBAN/RURAL POPULATION SPLIT

65%   35%

RELIGIOUS PERSUASION

Eastern Orthodox 2%
Other and non-religious 5%
Roman Catholic 93%

ETHNIC MAKEUP

German 1%
Other 1%
Polish 98%

Poland has a strongly Catholic population, with little ethnic diversity. The Church believes that stronger links with the West, especially through joining the EU, will weaken its influence. Abortion is still a major issue, and attempts to liberalize the law in 1996 were overturned by the Constitutional Tribunal.
   Some small ethnic groups have opened schools and cultural and religious centers. Others are becoming more assertive, particularly the Germans in Silesia. Jews are still resentful of past discrimination, and there is some evidence of residual anti-Semitism at a high level. The site of the Auschwitz concentration camp continues to cause conflict between Jews and Catholics.
   Wealth disparities are small, although the growing wealth of the entrepreneurial class is causing tension. The major political parties on left and right agree on continuing economic reform.
   Women are prominent policy makers. Hanna Suchocka was prime minister in 1992–1993.

POPULATION AGE BREAKDOWN

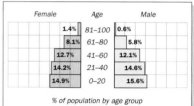

Female	Age	Male
1.4%	81–100	0.6%
8.1%	61–80	5.8%
12.7%	41–60	12.1%
14.2%	21–40	14.6%
14.9%	0–20	15.6%

% of population by age group

P

POLITICS ▷ Multiparty elections

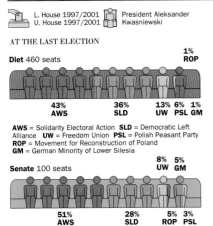

L. House 1997/2001
U. House 1997/2001

President Aleksander
Kwasniewski

AT THE LAST ELECTION

Diet 460 seats

| 43% AWS | 36% SLD | 13% UW | 6% PSL | 1% GM | 1% ROP |

AWS = Solidarity Electoral Action **SLD** = Democratic Left Alliance **UW** = Freedom Union **PSL** = Polish Peasant Party **ROP** = Movement for Reconstruction of Poland **GM** = German Minority of Lower Silesia

Senate 100 seats

| 51% AWS | 28% SLD | 8% UW | 5% GM | 5% ROP | 3% PSL |

Since 1989, Poland has been a multiparty parliamentary democracy.

MAIN POLITICAL ISSUES
Coalition rule
Poland's emerging party system has been hindered by a superfluity of political factions, and sustaining coalitions has proved difficult.

Parties are required to have at least 5% of the vote in order to gain a seat, and 8% to be eligible to join a coalition government.

Church-state relations
Building on the legitimization of its authority in the martial law years, the Catholic Church has been outspoken in its views on social and political policy. Debates over abortion, worship in schools, and values in the media have fueled a heated dialogue over the proper role of the Church. Abortion laws were eased in 1996 until the Constitutional Tribunal ruled that this move was unconstitutional.

PROFILE
From 1993 until 1997, successive governments were formed by the reformed communists of the SLD and the PSL, which pursued a policy of market reforms. Aleksander Kwasniewski, the leader of the SLD, was elected president in 1995.

The 1997 election produced a victory for the electoral alliance AWS, with 201 *Sejm* seats. The SLD won 164. Jerzy Buzek, a member of Solidarity since its formation in 1980, became the new

Former president Lech Walęsa. He was awarded the Nobel Peace Prize in 1983.

President Aleksander Kwasniewski, leader of the SLD, who was elected in 1995.

premier. A right-wing grouping with vocal Catholic and nationalist elements, the AWS nevertheless formed an alliance with the liberal UW.

Local government reform was introduced in July 1998. In subsequent local elections, the AWS won the most seats, but the SLD gained control of more of the provinces.

A threatened split in the government coalition over the issue of controversial health service reforms was averted in early 1999 by the resignation of the health minister.

WORLD AFFAIRS ▷ Joined UN in 1945

| CE | CEFTA | OECD | NATO | OSCE |

Poland has good relations with the Baltic states and the other countries of central Europe. It was admitted to NATO in 1999, and is negotiating to join the EU.

A treaty recognizing the postwar border between the two countries was signed with Germany in 1990. Relations with Belarus deteriorated in February 1998 following the imposition of tighter border controls.

POLAND

Total Land Area : 304 460 sq. km
(117 552 sq. miles)

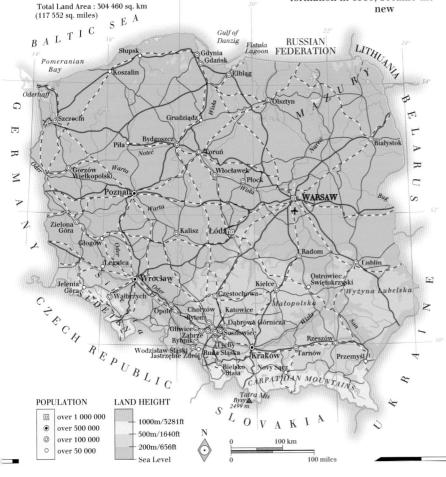

POPULATION
- ⊡ over 1 000 000
- ⊙ over 500 000
- ◎ over 100 000
- ○ over 50 000

LAND HEIGHT
- 1000m/3281ft
- 500m/1640ft
- 200m/656ft
- Sea Level

0 — 100 km
0 — 100 miles

CHRONOLOGY
Poland has Europe's second oldest written constitution. In 1795, it was partitioned between Austria–Hungary, Germany and Russia.

- ❑ **1918** Polish state recreated.
- ❑ **1921** Democratic constitution.
- ❑ **1926–1935** Pilsudski heads military coup. Nine years of authoritarian rule.
- ❑ **1939** Germany invades and divides Poland with Russia.
- ❑ **1941** First concentration camps built on Polish soil.
- ❑ **1944** Warsaw Uprising.
- ❑ **1945** Potsdam and Yalta Conferences set present borders and determine political allegiance to Soviet Union.
- ❑ **1947** Communists manipulate elections to gain power. ⇨

P

CHRONOLOGY *continued*

- ❑ **1956** More than 50 people killed in rioting in Poznań.
- ❑ **1970** Food price increases lead to strikes and riots in the Baltic port cities. Hundreds of people are killed.
- ❑ **1979** Cardinal Karol Wojtyla of Kraków is elected Pope and takes the name of John Paul II.
- ❑ **1980** Strikes force the government to negotiate with the Solidarity union. Resulting Gdańsk Accords grant the right to strike and to form free trade unions.
- ❑ **1981** General Wojciech Jaruzelski becomes prime minister.
- ❑ **1981–1983** Martial law. Solidarity forced into underground existence. Many of its leaders, including Lech Wałeşa, are interned.
- ❑ **1983** Wałeşa awarded Nobel Peace Prize.
- ❑ **1986** Amnesty for political prisoners.
- ❑ **1987** Referendum rejects government austerity program.
- ❑ **1988** Renewed industrial unrest.
- ❑ **1989** PUWP holds talks with Solidarity, which is relegalized. Partially free elections are held. First postwar noncommunist government formed.
- ❑ **1990** Launch of market reforms. Wałeşa elected president.
- ❑ **1991** Free elections lead to fragmented parliament.
- ❑ **1992** Last Russian troops leave.
- ❑ **1993** Reformed communists form coalition government after elections.
- ❑ **1994** Launch of mass privatization.
- ❑ **1995** Leader of reformed communists Aleksander Kwasniewski is elected president.
- ❑ **1996** Historic Gdańsk shipyard is declared bankrupt and closed down.
- ❑ **1997** April, Parliament finally adopts a new postcommunist constitution. September, legislative elections end former communist majority with big swing to Solidarity Election Action coalition. December, EU agrees to open membership negotiations.
- ❑ **1999** Joins NATO.

AID

 Recipient

💲 641m (receipts) ⬇ Down 44% 1996–1997

Poland had half of its foreign debt canceled by the Paris Club in 1994. Following this agreement, foreign investment in the country increased significantly. The IMF, EBRD and EU have all given support to Poland's stabilization and reform program. The country lost some of its EU aid for reconstruction in 1998.

DEFENSE

 Compulsory military service

💲 $3.1bn   ⬇ Down 22% in 1997

Poland joined NATO in March 1999, after working with the organization since 1994 under the Partnership for Peace program.

Poland's standing army is the largest in Europe after Russia's. There are also large paramilitary units, including border guards.

A 15-year program to modernize the armed forces was introduced by the government in 1997.

POLISH ARMED FORCES

🛡	1,727 main battle tanks (839 T-55, 772 T-72)	142,500 personnel
🚢	3 submarines, 1 destroyer, 1 frigate, 33 patrol boats	17,100 personnel
✈	297 combat aircraft (133 MiG-21, 27 MiG-23, 99 Su-22)	55,300 personnel
🚀	None	

ECONOMICS

 Inflation 68% p.a. (1985–1996)

📊 $139bn   💲 3.52–3.51 zlotys

SCORE CARD

❑ WORLD GNP RANKING	29th
❑ GNP PER CAPITA	$3,590
❑ BALANCE OF PAYMENTS	$–5.7bn
❑ INFLATION	15.9%
❑ UNEMPLOYMENT	12%

EXPORTS

UK 4%
Italy 6%
Czech Republic & Slovakia 4%
Netherlands 6%
Other 49%
Germany 31%

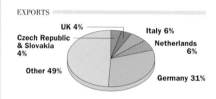

IMPORTS

France 5%
UK 5%
Russia 6%
Italy 10%
Other 50%
Germany 24%

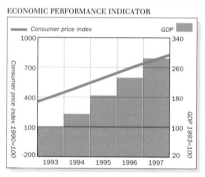

ECONOMIC PERFORMANCE INDICATOR

Consumer price index — GDP

Consumer price index 1990=100
GDP 1993=100
1993 1994 1995 1996 1997

STRENGTHS

Restructuring of loss-making coal industry begun in 1998. Successful privatizations, leading to plans for more, including that of state airline LOT. Modernization, with foreign help, of oil refining and electricity supply industries envisaged.

WEAKNESSES

Agriculture suffers from overmanning and lack of subsidy. Steel, mining, shipbuilding, energy and chemicals industries lack competitiveness.

PROFILE

After deep economic crisis in the 1980s, the new government introduced a plan in 1990 to bring about a swift transition to a market economy. Most prices were freed, trade was opened and the zloty was made convertible. The result was a dramatic rise in economic growth, and more foreign investment was attracted, especially after the cancellation of half of the country's debt by the Paris Club in 1994.

There are still large-scale heavy industrial plants left over from the communist era, but some restructuring of these has taken place. Many state farms have been liquidated, but agricultural efficiency continues to improve only slowly. The 27% of the workforce employed in the agricultural sector produces only 6% of the GDP.

Growth was slowing at the end of the 1990s, but this situation had more to do with the world economic downturn than with Poland's internal problems. Although inflation remained high, it had been brought down considerably during this period.

POLAND : MAJOR BUSINESSES

Gdańsk
Warsaw
Szczecin
Białystok
Poznań
Wrocław
Łódź
Kraków

Iron & steel		Optics	
Coal mining		Vehicle assembly	
Shipbuilding		Pharmaceuticals	
Electronics			
Textiles			
Engineering			
Chemicals			

0   200 km
0   200 miles

RESESOURCES

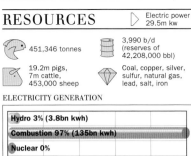

◁ Electric power 29.5m kw

451,346 tonnes

3,990 b/d (reserves of 42,208,000 bbl)

19.2m pigs, 7m cattle, 453,000 sheep

Coal, copper, silver, sulfur, natural gas, lead, salt, iron

ELECTRICITY GENERATION

Hydro 3% (3.8bn kwh)	
Combustion 97% (135bn kwh)	
Nuclear 0%	
Other 0%	

% of total generation by type

Poland has significant quantities of coal, sulfur, copper, natural gas, silver, lead and salt. The country aims to achieve self-sufficiency and eventually to export fuels; plans are in place to privatize the fuel and energy industries. Coal supplies two-thirds of electricity generation. The amounts of copper ores mined are too small to affect world markets.

POLAND : LAND USE

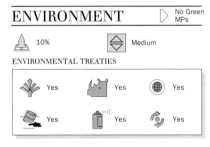

- Cropland
- Pasture
- Forest
- 🐷 Pigs
- 🐄 Cattle
- 🌾 Cereals

0   200 km
0   200 miles

ENVIRONMENT

◁ No Green MPs

🔺 10%   ⬦ Medium

ENVIRONMENTAL TREATIES

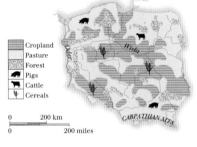

Yes   Yes   Yes
Yes   Yes   Yes

Pollution problems in Poland are serious, but improving. Silesia is still badly affected, but industry there only emits a third of the pollutants it emitted in 1990. Now that much of heavy industry has been cleaned up, and is contracting, there is more concern over small factories, domestic coal fires and the increased use of private cars.

Water pollution is still considerable: only one-third of sewage flowing into the Baltic is treated to standards required by Polish law.

Widespread flooding in southern Poland in 1997 caused 55 deaths and severe damage to property and infrastructure.

MEDIA

◁ TV ownership high

📰 Daily newspaper circulation 113 per 1,000 people

Polish TV is becoming more diverse, with the introduction of new digital cable channels to add to existing public service and commercial channels. *Gazeta Wyborcza*, set up by Solidarity in 1989, is still the leading daily, and its owners are expanding into other media.

CRIME

◁ Death penalty not used

🔳 65,819 prisoners   ⬆ Up 15% from 1992–1996

CRIME RATES

Murders	
3	per 100,000 population

Rapes	
5	per 100,000 population

Thefts	
1387	per 100,000 population

Smuggling is the most significant problem and Warsaw is a main center for this. Expensive cars are transferred eastward to Russia and drugs westward to Berlin. A former police chief was assassinated in Warsaw in June 1998. He had been about to take up an EU liaison post designed to combat organized crime.

EDUCATION

◁ School leaving age: 15

📖 99%   🎓 720,267 students

Education is free and compulsory for eight years from age seven.

THE EDUCATION SYSTEM

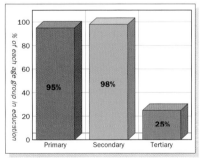

% of each age group in education — Primary 95%, Secondary 98%, Tertiary 25%

A standard curriculum is followed throughout the country. Prior to the collapse of communism, the Soviet model was followed, but now more Western ideas are being introduced. The Catholic Church has been allowed to operate schools since 1989. Most of the almost 140 higher education institutions offer business-related courses. Public spending on education has fallen by a fifth in real terms since 1989.

PUBLISHING AND BROADCAST MEDIA

There are 55 national daily newspapers, including *Gazeta Wyborcza*, *Rzeczpospolita*, *Kurier Polski* and *Zycie Warszawy*

2 national public, 1 private commercial channel

2 independent, 3 commercial services

HEALTH

◁ Welfare state health benefits

👤 1 per 435 people   ☠ Arteriosclerosis, heart disease, cancers, accidents

Reforms were introduced in the health service in 1999, including a "market" system which gives patients the right to choose where to go for treatment. Patients have found the new system confusing, with hospitals and doctors competing for business. Medical care is free for most people, but private health care is increasingly available for those who can afford it.

SPENDING

◁ GDP/cap. no increase

CONSUMPTION AND SPENDING

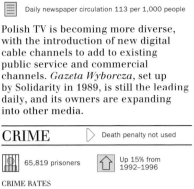

🚗 221 per 1,000 population   📞 194 per 1,000 population

Defense 2.3%	
Education 4.6%	
Health 5.1%	

Defense, Health, Education spending as % of GDP

Market reforms have led to some structural unemployment, and the inevitable hardship that this represents. More restructuring of heavy industry is planned. Pensioners have enjoyed benefits amounting to a higher percentage of GDP than in most other countries, but state cutbacks are making private pensions more necessary.

WORLD RANKING

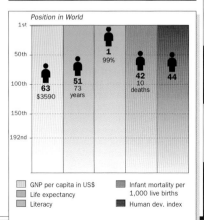

Position in World

- 63 $3590 — GNP per capita in US$
- 51 73 years — Life expectancy
- 1 99% — Literacy
- 42 10 deaths — Infant mortality per 1,000 live births
- 44 — Human dev. index

P

PORTUGAL

EUROPE

OFFICIAL NAME: Republic of Portugal   **CAPITAL:** Lisbon
POPULATION: 9.8 million   **CURRENCY:** Escudo   **OFFICIAL LANGUAGE:** Portuguese

| 1640 | 1640 | June 10 | P | 0 | +351 | .pt |

PORTUGAL, WITH ITS long Atlantic coast, lies on the western side of the Iberian peninsula. The river Tagus divides the more mountainous north from the lower, undulating terrain to the south. In 1974, a bloodless military coup overthrew a long-standing conservative dictatorship. Democratic elections were held in 1975 and the armed forces withdrew from politics thereafter. The 1980s witnessed the implementation of a substantial program of socioeconomic modernization. Membership of the EU since 1986 has helped underpin this process.

Santa Marta de Penanguiao, a small village in the heart of Portugal's wine-producing region, which is centered on the Douro valley.

CLIMATE
▷ Mediterranean/ maritime

WEATHER CHART

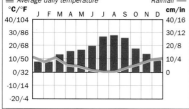

Portugal has a mild, Mediterranean climate, which is moderated by the influence of the Atlantic. Summers are hot and humid, while winters are relatively mild. Inland areas have more variable weather than coastal regions. Rainfall is generally higher in the mountainous north, while the central areas are more temperate. The southern Algarve region is predominantly dry and sunny.

TRANSPORTATION
▷ Drive on right

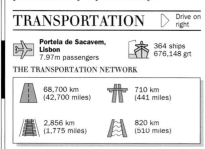

Portela de Sacavem, Lisbon
7.97m passengers

364 ships
676,148 grt

THE TRANSPORTATION NETWORK

| 68,700 km (42,700 miles) | 710 km (441 miles) |
| 2,856 km (1,775 miles) | 820 km (510 miles) |

The Portuguese road system, which was formerly one of the least developed in Europe, has been extensively improved in recent years with grants from the EU. However, road links with Spain remain limited, despite a number of modernization schemes. Increased traffic, poor road construction and dangerous driving mean that Portugal has Europe's highest rate of road deaths. Lisbon, the densely populated capital, now has the new 18-kilometer Vasco da Gama bridge over the river Tagus and a small, efficient metro.

TOURISM
▷ Visitors : population 1:1

10.1m visitors

Up 4% 1995–1997

MAIN TOURIST ARRIVALS

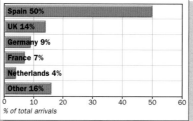

Spain 50%
UK 14%
Germany 9%
France 7%
Netherlands 4%
Other 16%

% of total arrivals

Since the 1960s, Portugal's popularity as a tourist destination has been linked to qualities which reflected its relatively poor economic development, such as low prices and little crime. Substantial economic growth has eroded some of its appeal, but Portugal's 10 million visitors each year remain a major income-earner. The most popular destination is the Algarve, the southernmost province, followed by the western resorts of Figueira da Foz and the Tróia Peninsula. Visitors are also attracted by Portugal's architecture, notably that dating from the Manueline period (1490–1520), and handicrafts, such as ceramics, lace and tapestries. Portugal has some of Europe's finest golf courses.

PORTUGAL

Total Land Area : 91 950 sq. km (35 502 sq. miles)

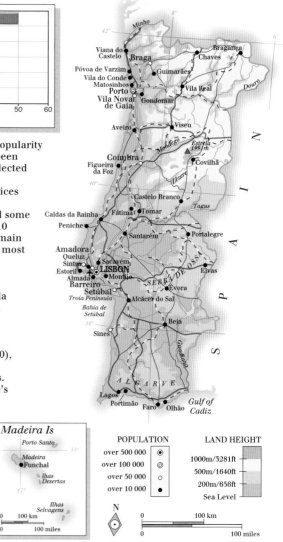

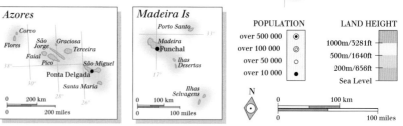

Azores

Madeira Is

POPULATION
over 500 000
over 100 000
over 50 000
over 10 000

LAND HEIGHT
1000m/3281ft
500m/1640ft
200m/656ft
Sea Level

PEOPLE

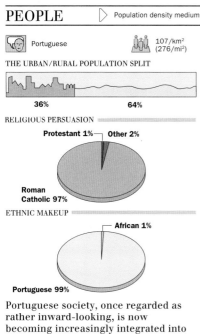

Population density medium

Portuguese   107/km²
(276/mi²)

THE URBAN/RURAL POPULATION SPLIT

36%   **64%**

RELIGIOUS PERSUASION

Protestant 1%   Other 2%

Roman
Catholic 97%

ETHNIC MAKEUP

African 1%

Portuguese 99%

Portuguese society, once regarded as rather inward-looking, is now becoming increasingly integrated into the rest of western Europe. Ethnic and religious tensions are limited. African immigrants, who come mainly from the former colonies, such as Angola, Mozambique and Guinea, have been assimilated with relative ease.

As in other Catholic countries, the Church has now lost some of its social influence, as shown by falling birth rates and more liberal attitudes to abortion and divorce. A 1998 referendum narrowly rejected a new law relaxing the abortion law, but was not binding because of the low turnout. Apart from large urban areas, the north is still devoutly Catholic.

Family ties remain all-important. Women now have greater access to business and media jobs. Overall, democracy and rapid socioeconomic change have tended to produce a more egalitarian society.

POPULATION AGE BREAKDOWN

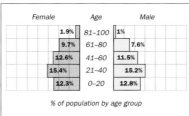

Female	Age	Male
1.9%	81–100	1%
9.7%	61–80	7.6%
12.6%	41–60	11.5%
15.4%	21–40	15.2%
12.3%	0–20	12.8%

% of population by age group

POLITICS

Multiparty elections

 1995/1999

President Jorge
Sampãio

AT THE LAST ELECTION

Assembly of the Republic 230 seats

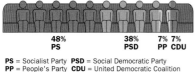

| **48%**
PS | **38%**
PSD | **7%**
PP | **7%**
CDU |

PS = Socialist Party   **PSD** = Social Democratic Party
PP = People's Party   **CDU** = United Democratic Coalition

Portugal is a multiparty democracy.

MAIN POLITICAL ISSUES
Transformation
Portugal has been transformed in recent decades. The consolidation of democracy since the 1974 "carnation revolution" and of EU membership since 1986 has brought Portugal into the European mainstream. This new confidence was shown in 1998 with Expo '98 in Lisbon; in the same year José Saramago was the first Portuguese-language Nobel literature prizewinner. In 1999 Portugal was among the 11 EU countries which first introduced the euro.

Presidential election
The 1995 election also ended a ten-year period in which the presidency and the government had been controlled by opposing parties, encouraging conflict and obstruction. This position was maintained in the presidential election of February 1996 when former PS leader Jorge Sampãio defeated Aníbal Cavaco Silva in the contest to succeed President Mário Soares.

PROFILE
A decade of center-right government was brought to an end by the legislative elections of 1995 when the PSD was ousted from power by the PS. The PS polled almost 44% of the vote and its leader, António Guterres, replaced Cavaco Silva as prime minister at the head of a minority government. Having fought the election on a platform of social reform, within weeks of the PS victory finance minister António Sousa Franco warned that his first priority would be to reduce the budget deficit by cutting public spending. The success of these measures has put the economy on a strong footing and secured popular support for the government.

Dr. Mário Soares, former socialist prime minister, and president 1986–1996.

António Guterres, prime minister since 1995.

WORLD AFFAIRS

Joined UN
in 1955

| EU | CE | NATO | OECD | OSCE |

Since 1986, Portugal's foreign policy has dealt almost exclusively with the consequences of membership of the EU, from which the country has greatly benefited. It is a committed member of NATO, though its relative strategic importance has declined as a result of Spanish membership. Relations with the former African colonies are occasionally turbulent and remain a high priority, as do those with Brazil. Relations with China over the return of Macao to the latter in 1999 are cordial.

AID

Donor

$251m (donations)   Not applicable

Portugal became an aid donor only in the early 1980s. It currently earmarks 0.25% of its GDP for aid to developing countries, more than 60% of it going to former colonies in Africa, especially Mozambique, where Portuguese funding helped rebuild the massive war-damaged Cahora Bassa dam and hydroelectric power station.

CHRONOLOGY

Portugal has existed as a nation state since the 11th century, although it was frequently challenged by Spain. Portugal reached its zenith in the 16th century, after which it entered a period of decline.

❏ **1755** Earthquake destroys Lisbon.
❏ **1793** Joins coalition against revolutionary France.
❏ **1807** France invades; royal family flees to Brazil.
❏ **1808** British troops arrive under Wellington. Start of Peninsular War.
❏ **1810** French leave Portugal.
❏ **1820** Liberal revolution.
❏ **1822** King John VI returns and accepts first Portuguese constitution. His son Dom Pedro declares independence of Brazil.
❏ **1854** Dom Pedro returns to Portugal to end civil war and installs his daughter as Queen Mary II.
❏ **1875–1876** Republican and Socialist parties founded.
❏ **1890** British ultimatum ends land connection between Angola and Mozambique.
❏ **1891** Republican uprising in Porto.
❏ **1908** Assassination of King Carlos I and heir to the throne.
❏ **1910** Abdication of Manuel II and proclamation of the Republic. Church and state separated.
❏ **1916** Portugal joins allied side in World War I. ⇨

P

P

DEFENSE

▷ Compulsory military service

💲 $2.6bn   ⬇ Down 3% in 1997

Portugal, a member of NATO since 1949, has a small but relatively modern navy. The army and air force are less efficient. Mounting opposition to military service is causing strains on these already semiprofessional bodies. The USA, which is the major arms supplier, has a strategic air base in the Azores. In 1997 defense spending represented 2.6% of GDP (NATO average is 2.2%).

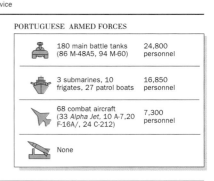

PORTUGUESE ARMED FORCES

🛡	180 main battle tanks (86 M-48A5, 94 M-60)	24,800 personnel
⚓	3 submarines, 10 frigates, 27 patrol boats	16,850 personnel
✈	68 combat aircraft (33 *Alpha Jet*, 10 A-7,20 F-16A/, 24 C-212)	7,300 personnel
	None	

ECONOMICS

▷ Inflation 10.3% p.a. (1985–1996)

📊 $109.5bn   💲 183.85–170.73 escudos

SCORE CARD

- ❏ WORLD GNP RANKING..........................33rd
- ❏ GNP PER CAPITA $11,010
- ❏ BALANCE OF PAYMENTS....................$–1.9bn
- ❏ INFLATION 2.2%
- ❏ UNEMPLOYMENT 7%

EXPORTS

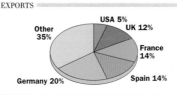

- USA 5%
- UK 12%
- France 14%
- Spain 14%
- Germany 20%
- Other 35%

IMPORTS

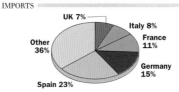

- UK 7%
- Italy 8%
- France 11%
- Germany 15%
- Spain 23%
- Other 36%

STRENGTHS

Relatively low, though rapidly rising, labor costs. Flexible labor market. High rate of domestic and direct foreign investment. Strong banking and tourism sectors. Tourism makes up 6% of GDP, the highest ratio in the EU; potential for further growth. Strong clothing and shoe manufacturing sectors now overtaken by machinery and equipment as chief exports. Fast-track improvement of transportation infrastructure under way. Good deep-water port at Lisbon. Wine, especially port. Tomatoes, citrus fruit, cork, sardines.

WEAKNESSES

Large agricultural sector (5% of GDP, 10% of workforce) is most inefficient in EU. Outdated farming methods, small landholdings, low crop yields. Farm product prices undercut by Spain. High dependence on imported oil.

PROFILE

EU membership in 1986 brought a sharp increase in foreign investment to largely

ECONOMIC PERFORMANCE INDICATOR

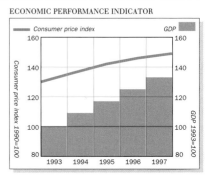

— Consumer price index   ▮ GDP

rural Portugal. Exports rose dramatically until the economy went into recession in 1991, but it began to recover in 1994 and recorded growth of over 3% a year in the second half of the 1990s.

At one time participation in EU monetary union seemed a distant prospect. In the event the socialist government of António Guterres which came to power in 1995 was able to meet the required economic convergence criteria with relative ease. In January 1999 a now confident Portugal was one of the 11 EU countries to introduce the euro, albeit the poorest of them. Portuguese wages are about 70% of the EU average, but unemployment is among the lowest in the EU.

PORTUGAL : MAJOR BUSINESSES

- Steel
- Wine
- Textiles
- Cement
- Ceramics
- Chemicals
- Vehicle manufacture
- Light engineering
- Fish processing
- Shipbuilding

Braga, Matosinhos, Porto, Aveiro, Lisbon, Setúbal, Faro

0   100 km
0   100 miles

RESCOURCES

▷ Electric power 9.4m kw

265,508 tonnes

Not an oil producer; refines 294,000 b/cd

6.3m sheep, 2.4m pigs, 1.3m cattle, 815,000 goats

Coal, limestone, granite, marble, copper, tin

ELECTRICITY GENERATION

Hydro 26% (8.4bn kwh)

Combustion 73.5% (24.7bn kwh)

Nuclear 0%

Other 0.5% (0.05bn kwh)

% of total generation by type

Portugal has been plagued by a lack of natural resources, including water. Mining has historically been important, notably for tungsten, copper and tin. Industry has relied on small coal deposits and large oil imports. The once economically crucial fish catch has been declining in recent years.

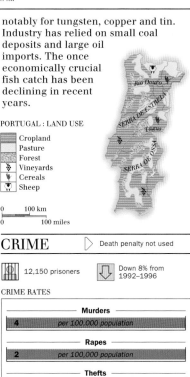

PORTUGAL : LAND USE

Cropland
Pasture
Forest
Vineyards
Cereals
Sheep

0   100 km
0   100 miles

ENVIRONMENT

▷ Green MPs

6%

High

ENVIRONMENTAL TREATIES

Yes   Yes   Yes

Yes   Yes   Yes

The unrestricted development of tourist resorts in the Algarve and the huge investment in new harbor, road and bridge developments are having detrimental effects on natural habitats. EU agricultural grants for projects such as draining meadows, and monoculture afforestation, notably of *Eucalyptus* and *Pinus*, are degrading biodiversity. Much toxic waste is dumped on any available land as few official controls or infill sites exist. New waste management regulations are being planned.

MEDIA

▷ TV ownership high

Daily newspaper circulation 75 per 1,000 people

PUBLISHING AND BROADCAST MEDIA

There are 27 daily newspapers. The most prestigious is the *Diário de Not'cias*, but *Expresso* has a wider circulation

1 state-owned, 2 independent services

1 state-owned, many independent services.

Newspaper circulation figures are among Europe's lowest. Most papers have regional rather than national distribution; radio and TV are therefore the main source of news. In 1992, two independent TV stations began broadcasting, breaking the state's monopoly. By 1997 there were 383,000 subscribers to cable TV services. Most English-language footage is not dubbed.

CRIME

▷ Death penalty not used

12,150 prisoners

Down 8% from 1992–1996

CRIME RATES

Murders

4   *per 100,000 population*

Rapes

2   *per 100,000 population*

Thefts

459   *per 100,000 population*

Compared with most western European countries, Portugal still enjoys a remarkably low crime rate. However, narcotics trafficking and related offenses are rising.

EDUCATION

▷ School leaving age: 15

91%

300,573 students

Portuguese is the seventh most widely spoken language in the world.

THE EDUCATION SYSTEM

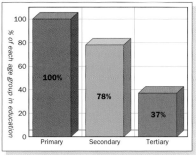

% of each age group in education

100% Primary
78%   Secondary
37%   Tertiary

Free state education is available to all pupils between the ages of three and 15, although the preschool stage up to the age of six is not compulsory. Middle-class parents rely heavily on the private sector. State universities are large and oversubscribed. There are several prestigious private universities.

HEALTH

▷ Welfare state health benefits

1 per 345 people

Heart and cerebrovascular diseases, cancers

Of total government expenditure nearly 10% is spent on health.

Portugal has had a publicly funded, free national health service since 1979. Spending on health has increased markedly in recent years, but the service remains below the EU average. There are strong regional differences in facilities. Larger urban hospitals are modern and well equipped. Private health care schemes are both affordable and good value for money; over 40% of the population use the private system.

SPENDING

▷ GDP/cap. no increase

CONSUMPTION AND SPENDING

288 per 1,000 population

402 per 1,000 population

Defense 2.6%

Education 5.4%

Health 6.2%

0   5   10   15   20   25

Defense, Health, Education spending as % of GDP

Wealth differentials in Portugal are smaller than in most EU countries. After the 1974 "carnation revolution" many wealthy families transferred their assets abroad or left Portugal altogether. The 1976 constitution enshrined socialist goals. Since then governments have introduced limited wealth redistribution measures.

Families owning land with tourist development potential, such as golf courses, have made large profits. Others saw the value of their assets fall when land prices fell dramatically in 1986. By the late 1990s economic growth and low interest rates led to a surge in property purchases. Wages, just over half the EU average in 1986, are now at 70%.

WORLD RANKING

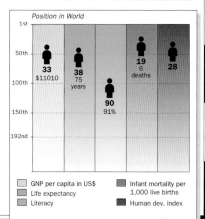

Position in World

1st

50th

33   $11010
38   75 years
19   6 deaths
28

90   91%

100th

150th

192nd

GNP per capita in US$
Life expectancy
Literacy

Infant mortality per 1,000 live births
Human dev. index

P

QATAR

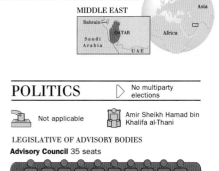

OFFICIAL NAME: State of Qatar   **CAPITAL:** Doha
POPULATION: 600,000   **CURRENCY:** Qatar riyal   **OFFICIAL LANGUAGE:** Arabic

| 1971 | 1971 | Sept 3 | Q | +3 | +974 | .qa |

PROJECTING NORTH FROM the Arabian peninsula into the Persian Gulf, Qatar has land borders with Saudi Arabia and the United Arab Emirates, and a disputed sea border with Bahrain. Most of the country is flat, semi arid desert. Qatar is a founder member of OPEC, and its plentiful oil and natural gas reserves make it one of the wealthiest states in the region. The country enjoys political stability under the rule of the al-Thani clan.

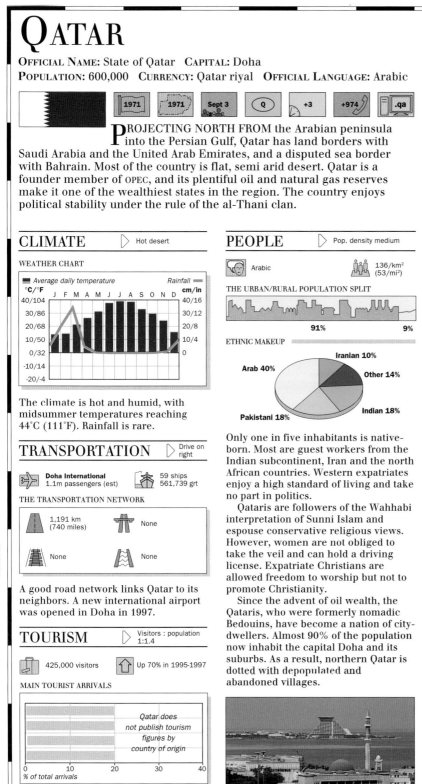

CLIMATE
▷ Hot desert

WEATHER CHART

The climate is hot and humid, with midsummer temperatures reaching 44°C (111°F). Rainfall is rare.

TRANSPORTATION
▷ Drive on right

Doha International 1.1m passengers (est)   59 ships 561,739 grt

THE TRANSPORTATION NETWORK

| 1,191 km (740 miles) | None |
| None | None |

A good road network links Qatar to its neighbors. A new international airport was opened in Doha in 1997.

TOURISM
▷ Visitors : population 1:1.4

425,000 visitors   Up 70% in 1995-1997

MAIN TOURIST ARRIVALS

Qatar does not publish tourism figures by country of origin

% of total arrivals

Qatar attracts several thousand European visitors a year, who enjoy unspoiled beaches, duty-free shopping, modern hotels and the desert hinterland. Alcohol is permitted in five-star hotels for non-Muslims.

PEOPLE
▷ Pop. density medium

Arabic   136/km² (53/mi²)

THE URBAN/RURAL POPULATION SPLIT

91%   9%

ETHNIC MAKEUP

Arab 40%
Iranian 10%
Other 14%
Indian 18%
Pakistani 18%

Only one in five inhabitants is native-born. Most are guest workers from the Indian subcontinent, Iran and the north African countries. Western expatriates enjoy a high standard of living and take no part in politics.

Qataris are followers of the Wahhabi interpretation of Sunni Islam and espouse conservative religious views. However, women are not obliged to take the veil and can hold a driving license. Expatriate Christians are allowed freedom to worship but not to promote Christianity.

Since the advent of oil wealth, the Qataris, who were formerly nomadic Bedouins, have become a nation of city-dwellers. Almost 90% of the population now inhabit the capital Doha and its suburbs. As a result, northern Qatar is dotted with depopulated and abandoned villages.

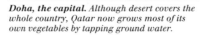

Doha, the capital. *Although desert covers the whole country, Qatar now grows most of its own vegetables by tapping ground water.*

POLITICS
▷ No multiparty elections

Not applicable   Amir Sheikh Hamad bin Khalifa al-Thani

LEGISLATIVE OF ADVISORY BODIES

Advisory Council 35 seats

Qatar is an absolute monarchy and has no legislature. The Amir rules with the assistance of the Council of Ministers and the Advisory Council.

Qatar is a traditional emirate. Its government and religious establishment is dominated by the Amir, Shaikh Hamad, who took power from his father, Shaikh Khalifa, in a bloodless coup in 1995. A failed coup against Hamad in early 1996 was linked with efforts to regain power by Khalifa, now based in the United Arab Emirates. The largely middle-class prodemocracy movement has called for reform of the 35-member Advisory Council. Shaikh Hamad's response was to authorize Qatar's first ever election, to a new municipal council in March 1999, in which all adults, including women, were entitled to vote and stand as candidates.

WORLD AFFAIRS
▷ Joined UN in 1971

| AL | OIC | GCC | OAPEC | OPEC |

Qatar is a founder member of the GCC, but Shaikh Hamad has caused some consternation within its ranks by adopting an independent, and at times belligerent, stance. Hamad boycotted part of the Council's annual summit in 1995 in protest at the appointment of a Saudi official. Relations with Bahrain are strained over a disputed Gulf island. Qatar has responded to the general thaw in Arab relations with Israel by agreeing to supply it with liquefied natural gas (LNG). The Amir is keen to retain strong links with Western states, notably the UK and the USA, but criticized both countries in early 1999 for their daily bombing of Iraq to force its compliance with UN resolutions. Within the quotas set by OPEC, Qatar has supported a moderate oil price.

AID
▷ Recipient

$1m (receipts)   Down 50% 1996–1997

Qatar donated aid generously to developing countries during the 1970s and early 1980s, but in the early 1990's became a net recipient.

Q

Qatar

Total Land Area : 11 000 sq. km
(4247 sq. miles)

POPULATION

over 100 000 ◎
under 10 000 •

| 0 | | 50 km |
| 0 | | 30 miles |

LAND HEIGHT

200m/1640ft

Sea Level

DEFENSE

▷ No compulsory military service

$1.3bn   ⬆ Up 78% in 1997

The estimated 12,000-strong armed forces are too small to play a significant role in Qatari affairs, even in the event of political turmoil. A ten-year defense agreement with the USA provides for joint exercises, the stockpiling of US equipment and US access to bases.

ECONOMICS

▷ Inflation 2.3% p.a. (1985–1996)

$7.4bn   3.64 Qatar riyals

SCORE CARD

❏ World GNP Ranking	93rd
❏ GNP per Capita	$11,600
❏ Balance of Payments	Not available
❏ Inflation	7.4%
❏ Unemployment	Not available

STRENGTHS

Steady supply of crude oil and huge gas reserves, plus related industries. Modern infrastructure.

WEAKNESSES

Dependence on foreign work force. All raw materials and most foods imported. Virtually all water has to be desalinated. Government has large foreign reserves,

---

RESOURCES

▷ Electric power 1.4m kw

4,740 tonnes

661,000 b/d (reserves 3,729,000,000 bbl)

3.9m chickens, 200,000 sheep 172,000 goats

Oil, natural gas

Qatar has the third-smallest reserves of crude oil within OPEC but abundant reserves of gas, including the world's largest nonassociated gas field, known as North Field.

ENVIRONMENT

▷ No Green MPs

None   Not applicable

The desert hinterland supports little plant or animal life. Oil pollution has damaged marine life. On land, game has been hunted out and most native species are extinct in the wild.

MEDIA

▷ TV ownership high

Daily newspaper circulation 161 per 1,000 people

PUBLISHING AND BROADCAST MEDIA

There are 5 daily newspapers, *Ar-Rayah* and its English companion *Gulf Times*, *Al-'Arab* and *Ash-Sharq*

1 state-controlled service   1 state-controlled service

Shaikh Hamad has relaxed censorship of Qatari newspapers. Qatari television is the most independent in the region, and satellite TV channels are freely available.

CRIME

▷ Death penalty not used

6,285 prisoners   ⬆ Up 33% from 1992–1996

Traditional Islamic punishments have deterred crime. However, narcotics trafficking is on the increase. The incidence of street crime is low.

EXPORTS

USA 3%   Thailand 4%   South Korea 12%

Japan 49%

Singapore 12%

Other 20%

IMPORTS

Italy 6%   USA 9%

Other 37%

Japan 10%

France 13%

UK 25%

but new industries depend on cementing agreements with foreign partners. Potential threat to security from Iraq and Iran makes some multinationals wary of investment.

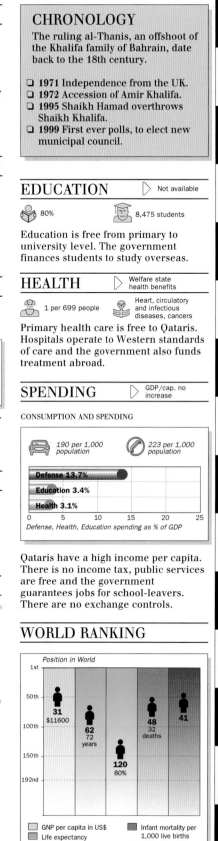

CHRONOLOGY

The ruling al-Thanis, an offshoot of the Khalifa family of Bahrain, date back to the 18th century.

- ❏ **1971** Independence from the UK.
- ❏ **1972** Accession of Amir Khalifa.
- ❏ **1995** Shaikh Hamad overthrows Shaikh Khalifa.
- ❏ **1999** First ever polls, to elect new municipal council.

EDUCATION

▷ Not available

80%   8,475 students

Education is free from primary to university level. The government finances students to study overseas.

HEALTH

▷ Welfare state health benefits

1 per 699 people   Heart, circulatory and infectious diseases, cancers

Primary health care is free to Qataris. Hospitals operate to Western standards of care and the government also funds treatment abroad.

SPENDING

▷ GDP/cap. no increase

CONSUMPTION AND SPENDING

190 per 1,000 population   223 per 1,000 population

Defense 13.7%
Education 3.4%
Health 3.1%

| 0 | 5 | 10 | 15 | 20 | 25 |

Defense, Health, Education spending as % of GDP

Qataris have a high income per capita. There is no income tax, public services are free and the government guarantees jobs for school-leavers. There are no exchange controls.

WORLD RANKING

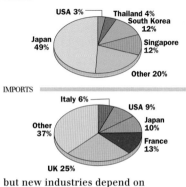

Position in World

1st
50th
100th
150th
192nd

31 — $11600
62 — 72 years
120 — 80%
48 — 32 deaths
41

▢ GNP per capita in US$	▣ Infant mortality per 1,000 live births
▢ Life expectancy	
▢ Literacy	▣ Human dev. index

Q

ROMANIA

OFFICIAL NAME: Romania   **CAPITAL:** Bucharest
POPULATION: 22.6 million   **CURRENCY:** Leu   **OFFICIAL LANGUAGE:** Romanian

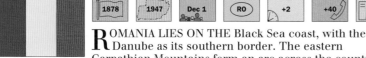

| 1878 | 1947 | Dec 1 | RO | +2 | +40 | .ro |

ROMANIA LIES ON THE Black Sea coast, with the Danube as its southern border. The eastern Carpathian Mountains form an arc across the country, curving around the upland basin of Transylvania. Long dominated by the Ottoman, Russian and Habsburg empires, Romania became an independent monarchy in 1878. After World War II, this was supplanted by a communist People's Republic, headed from 1965 by Nicolae Ceauşescu. A coup in 1989 resulted in his execution and a limited democracy. A liberal democratic coalition more committed to a free-market economy took office in 1996.

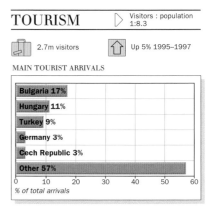

Village in northeastern Romania, in the foothills of the Carpathian Mountains, close to the border with Ukraine. Corn and wheat are Romania's main crops.

CLIMATE

▷ Continental

WEATHER CHART

Average daily temperature   Rainfall
°C/°F   cm/in
J F M A M J J A S O N D
40/104   40/16
30/86   30/12
20/68   20/8
10/50   10/4
0/32   0
-10/14
-20/-4

Romania has a continental climate with two growing seasons. Rainfall is generally moderate, with most falling in spring and early summer. Very heavy spring rains occasionally destroy new crops. Snow is frequent in winter, which can be bitterly cold.

TRANSPORTATION

▷ Drive on right

Bucharest-Otopeni Intl
1.6m passengers

420 ships
2.6m grt

THE TRANSPORTATION NETWORK

| 53,400 km (85,875 miles) | 113 km (70 miles) |
| 11,380 km (7,113 miles) | 1,724 km (1,071 miles) |

Outdated infrastructure is a major obstacle to development. Upgrading of the road network with international funding has focused on the expressway from Bucharest to Hungary. The port of Constanţa is being modernized, and will accommodate a container port and new grain silo.

TOURISM

▷ Visitors : population 1:8.3

2.7m visitors   Up 5% 1995–1997

MAIN TOURIST ARRIVALS

Bulgaria 17%
Hungary 11%
Turkey 9%
Germany 3%
Cech Republic 3%
Other 57%

0   10   20   30   40   50   60
% of total arrivals

The Black Sea, Danube delta and Carpathian Mountains are the primary natural attractions, while Transylvania has a rich historical heritage. However, tourist facilities are generally poor. Under Ceauşescu, the need for foreign currency meant that tourists came before Romanians in accommodation priorities. Today, privatization of property and an acute housing shortage have reduced accommodation available to visitors. By 1992, tourism was no longer a net foreign exchange earner for Romania.

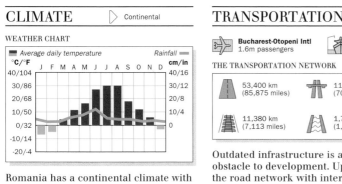

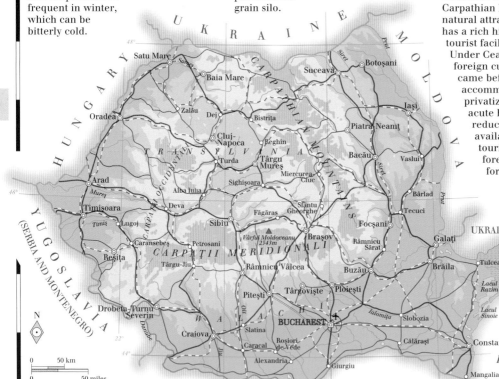

ROMANIA

Total Land Area: 230 340 sq. km
(88 954 sq. miles)

POPULATION

over 1 000 000   ▣
over 100 000   ◉
over 50 000   ○

LAND HEIGHT

2000m/6562ft
1000m/3281ft
500m/1640ft
200m/656ft
Sea Level

R

PEPLE

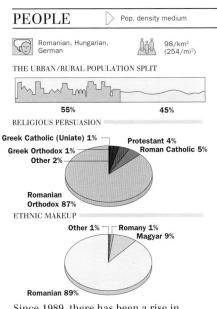

▷ Pop. density medium

Romanian, Hungarian, German

98/km² (254/mi²)

THE URBAN/RURAL POPULATION SPLIT

55%   45%

RELIGIOUS PERSUASION

Greek Catholic (Uniate) 1%
Greek Orthodox 1%
Other 2%
Protestant 4%
Roman Catholic 5%
Romanian Orthodox 87%

ETHNIC MAKEUP

Other 1%   Romany 1%
Magyar 9%
Romanian 89%

Since 1989, there has been a rise in Romanian nationalism, aggravated by the hardships brought by the austerity measures of economic reform. The incidence of ethnic violence has also risen, particularly toward Romanies and Hungarians, but attacks by Romanies on Hungarians have also increased. Ethnic Hungarians form the largest minority group in Romania. They are partly protected by the influence of the Hungarian state, whereas the Romanies do not have any similar support and tend to suffer greater discrimination.

Romania's population is currently decreasing. This is due to rising emigration since 1989, mainly for economic reasons, and to a falling birth rate since the early 1990s. The latter trend is in sharp contrast to the 1980s, when the Ceauşescu regime enforced a "pronatalist" policy, banning abortion and contraception. The government also taxed childless adults and those with fewer than four children, and obliged married women to have monthly fertility examinations. The birth rate rose, but the population as a whole did not rise significantly due to an increase in the mortality rate. Abortion was legalized in 1989; maternal death rates have recently declined. Homosexuality was decriminalized in 1998.

POPULATION AGE BREAKDOWN

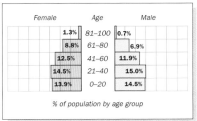

Female	Age	Male
1.3%	81–100	0.7%
8.8%	61–80	6.9%
12.5%	41–60	11.9%
14.5%	21–40	15.0%
13.9%	0–20	14.5%

% of population by age group

WORLD AFFAIRS

▷ Joined UN in 1955

BSEC   CE   EBRD   OSCE   CEFTA

Romania's priority is building closer links with western Europe. In 1993, it signed an association agreement with the EU and in 1995 formally applied for membership, but it was not one of the front-runners with which the EU opened negotiations in 1998. Nor was it among the three former Warsaw Pact countries to join NATO in 1999.

In 1996 Romania signed a treaty of reconciliation and friendship with Hungary, with which relations have long been tense; Romania has resisted the demands of the Hungarian minority in Transylvania for greater autonomy. In 1997 Romania also signed a treaty with Ukraine recognizing its sovereignty over parts of Bessarabia and Bukovina which Romania had ruled in 1919–1940.

AID

▷ Recipient

$197m (receipts)

Down 10% 1996–1997

Aid increased after 1989 to a peak of $276 million in 1995 but has since declined to $197 million in 1997, reflecting uncertainty over the implementation of reform. There is now a danger that Romania will default on IMF and World Bank loans.

POLITICS

▷ Multiparty elections

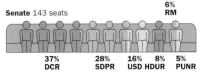

L. House 1996/2000
U. House 1996/2000
President Emil Constantinescu

AT THE LAST ELECTION

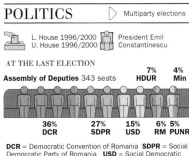

Assembly of Deputies 343 seats

7% HDUR   4% Min

36% DCR   27% SDPR   15% USD   6% RM   5% PUNR

DCR = Democratic Convention of Romania SDPR = Social Democratic Party of Romania USD = Social Democratic Union HDUR = Hungarian Democratic Union of Romania RM = Greater Romania Party PNUR = Party of Romanian National Unity Min = 15 seats reserved for National

Senate 143 seats

6% RM

37% DCR   28% SDPR   16% USD   8% HDUR   5% PUNR

A 1991 referendum approved a new constitution with a multiparty democracy led by a directly elected president.

MAIN POLITICAL ISSUES
Economic performance
Poor performance and lack of a coherent economic policy led to general strikes in 1994 protesting at falling living standards. The center-right coalition in power since 1996 faced protests by miners in early 1999.

Ethnic tensions
Economic difficulties have led to increased ethnic tensions. The far right has made political gains and nationalism is increasingly accepted. In 1993, extreme right elements advocated labor camps for ethnic minorities. Romanies have been victims of violent, racially motivated attacks.

PROFILE
Romania's 1989 "revolution" left an old communist elite in power. Unlike Poland, Hungary, and Czechoslovakia, Romania had no organized group ready to introduce real democracy and with the ability to create a market economy. Democracy was in place on the surface but political intimidation and ballot-rigging were widespread. Only the victory of the center-right in 1996 elections brought more far-reaching renewal.

Many of the state assets privatized under the former Iliescu regime remained in the hands of people tied to the ruling clique. Now in opposition he retains the support of conservative groups, such as miners and rural workers. The coalition in power since 1996 has suffered from divisions and in 1998 prime minister Victor Ciorbea was replaced by Radu Vasile.

Former president
Ion Iliescu succeeded Ceauşescu and was reelected in 1992.

Emil Constantinescu,
president since replacing Nikolae Vacaroiu in 1996.

CHRONOLOGY

Many foreign policy tensions stem from Romania's continually redrawn borders. It retains a Hungarian minority in Transylvania; post-Soviet Moldova opted not to rejoin Romania.

❑ **1859** Unification of Moldova and Wallachia forms basis of future Romania.
❑ **1878** Independence, but at cost of losing Bessarabia to Russia.
❑ **1916–1918** Enters World War I on Allied side. At end of war, gains substantial territory, including Transylvania from Hungary. ⇨

R

CHRONOLOGY *continued*

- ❏ **1924** Communists banned in unstable political arena. Rise of fascist "Iron Guard."
- ❏ **1938** King Carol establishes royal autocracy.
- ❏ **1940** Territory forcibly ceded to Soviet Union, Bulgaria, and Hungary. Iron Guard stages coup. King Carol abdicates in favor of son, Michael. Tripartite Pact with Germany.
- ❏ **1941** Enters war on Axis side, hoping to recover Bessarabia from Soviet Union.
- ❏ **1944** Romania switches sides as Soviet troops reach border.
- ❏ **1945** Soviet-backed regime installed. Romanian Communist Party plays an increasing role.
- ❏ **1946** Romania gains Transylvania but not Bessarabia, which goes to Soviet Union, which also demands huge reparations. Communist-led National Democratic Front wins majority in disputed elections.
- ❏ **1947** King Michael forced to abdicate.
- ❏ **1948–1953** Centrally planned economy put in place.
- ❏ **1953** Leaders of Jewish community prosecuted for Zionism.
- ❏ **1958** Soviet troops withdraw.
- ❏ **1964** Prime Minister Gheorghiu-Dej declares national sovereignty. Proposes joint COMECON planning to lessen Soviet economic control.
- ❏ **1965** Ceauşescu party secretary after death of Gheorghiu-Dej.
- ❏ **1968–1980** Condemns Soviet invasion of Czechoslovakia; successfully courts USA and EC.
- ❏ **1982** Ceauşescu vows to pay off foreign debt.
- ❏ **1989** Demonstrations: many killed by military. Armed forces join with opposition in National Salvation Front (NSF) to form government. Ion Iliescu declared president. Ceauşescu summarily tried and shot.
- ❏ **1990** NSF election victory. Political prisoners freed but many later reinterned.
- ❏ **1991** New constitution, providing for market reform, approved in referendum.
- ❏ **1992** Second free elections. NSF splits into two factions: DNSF and NSF. DNSF forms minority government.
- ❏ **1994** General strike since 1989 demands faster economic reform.
- ❏ **1996** Reconciliation treaty with Hungary. Center right wins elections, breaking with communist past; Emil Constantinescu president.
- ❏ **1997** Treaty recognizes Ukraine's sovereignty over territory Romania ruled in 1919–1940.
- ❏ **1998** Replacement of prime minister Victor Ciorbea by Radu Vasile.

R

DEFENSE

 Compulsory military service

💲 $793m   ⬆ Up 4% in 1997

The military received limited funding under the Ceauşescu regime, and troops were routinely deployed as cheap labor.

Romania was the first country to join NATO's Partnerships for Peace program in 1994. Since 1996 the government has actively sought membership but was not among the first three former Warsaw Pact countries to join the alliance in 1999.

ROMANIAN ARMED FORCES

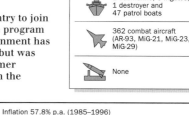

🚜	1,253 main battle tanks (T-34, T-55, T-72, TR-85, TR-580)	111,300 personnel
🚢	1 submarine, 6 frigates, 1 destroyer and 47 patrol boats	22,100 personnel
✈	362 combat aircraft (AR-93, MiG-21, MiG-23, MiG-29)	46,300 personnel
🚀	None	

ECONOMICS

 Inflation 57.8% p.a. (1985–1996)

📊 $31.8bn   💲 8,070–11,000 lei

SCORE CARD

❏ WORLD GNP RANKING	56th
❏ GNP PER CAPITA	$1,410
❏ BALANCE OF PAYMENTS	$–2.3bn
❏ INFLATION	154.8%
❏ UNEMPLOYMENT	7%

ECONOMIC PERFORMANCE INDICATOR

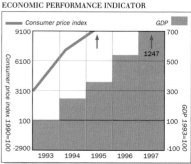

EXPORTS

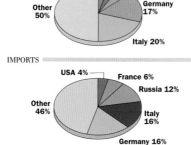

USA 4% — Turkey 4% — France 5% — Germany 17% — Italy 20% — Other 50%

IMPORTS

USA 4% — France 6% — Russia 12% — Italy 16% — Germany 16% — Other 46%

STRENGTHS

Many foreign joint ventures. Tourism potential. Recent fall in inflation.

WEAKNESSES

Slow transition from centrally planned to market economy. Delays in implementing economic reform. Low foreign investment levels. Large bureaucracy.

PROFILE

Romania undertook few economic reforms in the first five years after 1989, compared with other east European states. While all suffered recession in the reform process, Romania's was the most severe. The chemical, petrochemical, metal, transport, and food industries are the priority areas for liberalization and structural overhaul. The reform-oriented government elected in 1996 took tough measures to curb inflation and the budget deficit. Although growth began to recover in the mid-1990s, it fell by 7% each year in 1997 and 1998.

Real wages have fallen since 1989 and only a few are doing well. Since 1991 land reform has restored 72% of farmland to private hands, but it remains severely undermechanized. Agricultural processing is still under state control.

Romania was the first east European country to open its economy to foreign investment, allowing 100% foreign ownership from 1990. The number of joint ventures is the highest in eastern Europe, but most are small-scale. Bureaucracy and doubts about the country's stability have hindered foreign investment. Nearly 4,000 state-owned enterprises had been privatized by late 1997, the majority in 1996–1997.

ROMANIA : MAJOR BUSINESSES

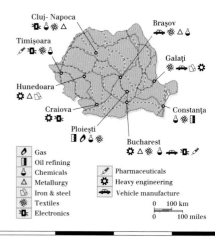

Cluj-Napoca, Braşov, Timişoara, Galaţi, Hunedoara, Craiova, Ploieşti, Constanţa, Bucharest

🜁 Gas
▮ Oil refining
🜔 Chemicals
△ Metallurgy
🜨 Iron & steel
🜊 Textiles
▤ Electronics
⚙ Pharmaceuticals
✿ Heavy engineering
🚗 Vehicle manufacture

0   100 km
0   100 miles

RESOURCES

▷ Electric power 22.3m kw

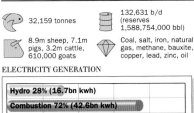

32,159 tonnes

8.9m sheep, 7.1m pigs, 3.2m cattle, 610,000 goats

132,631 b/d (reserves 1,588,754,000 bbl)

Coal, salt, iron, natural gas, methane, bauxite, copper, lead, zinc, oil

ELECTRICITY GENERATION

Hydro 28% (16.7bn kwh)					
Combustion 72% (42.6bn kwh)					
Nuclear 0%					
Other 0%					

0 20 40 60 80 100

% of total generation by type

Romania has oil and gas reserves, but production is insufficient to meet domestic demand. Production from onshore fields fell during the 1980s as reserves were depleted, and oil imports have risen substantially since 1989. Efforts are being concentrated on developing offshore reserves in the Black Sea. Romania has opened up exploration and processing to foreign investors. Deposits of other minerals are small and contribute little to export earnings.

The electricity supply is outdated and has been insufficient to meet national demand for the last 20 years. Price liberalization measures in 1997 doubled energy prices, providing strong incentives to improve poor efficiency. The first nuclear power station was completed in 1997.

ENVIRONMENT

▷ Green MPs

5% (4% partially protected)

⬦ Medium

ENVIRONMENTAL TREATIES

Yes Yes Yes
Yes Yes Yes

The southern region has the most serious pollution problems. Cement plant and power-station emissions have been linked to respiratory diseases. Industrial water pollution is a major problem. NATO bombing of Yugoslavian chemical and oil refineries on the Danube in 1999 has led to downriver pollution in Romania. Nevertheless, nature conservation is beginning to receive more attention. The Danube delta has been identified as a site for a biosphere reserve.

MEDIA

▷ TV ownership medium

Daily newspaper circulation 271 per 1,000 people

PUBLISHING AND BROADCAST MEDIA

There are 106 daily newspapers, including *Evenimentul Zilei; Adevărul, România Liberă, Curierul National* and *Cotidinul*

2 state-controlled, 3 independent services

3 state-controlled, 1 independent service

The number of newspapers rose to 1,600 after 1989, but many are now closing, since rising prices mean that people can no longer afford them. The government reimposed political censorship in 1994 and in practice now also controls the national independent TV service. The first satellite TV channel was launched in 1994, as was the first exclusively Hungarian radio station in 1999.

CRIME

▷ Death penalty not used

45,309 prisoners

Up 124% from 1992–1996

CRIME RATES

Murders
7   per 100,000 population

Rapes
6   per 100,000 population

Thefts
511   per 100,000 population

The black economy is the primary source of income for a third of the population. Levels of tax evasion are estimated to be among the highest in the world.

EDUCATION

▷ School leaving age: 15

98%

411,687 students

Of total government expenditure 13.6% is spent on education.

THE EDUCATION SYSTEM

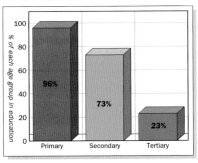

Primary 96%
Secondary 73%
Tertiary 23%

% of each age group in education

School attendance is far below the European average. As university enrolment is no longer restricted, the number of tertiary students has risen rapidly. In 1996, 22.5% of the relevant age group went on to further education, temporarily reducing high unemployment among young adults.

ROMANIA : LAND USE

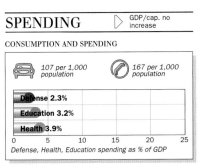

Cropland
Pasture
Forest
Wetlands
Potatoes
Cereals
Sheep

0   100 km
0   100 miles

HEALTH

▷ Welfare state health benefits

1 per 556 people

Heart & cerebrovascular diseases, cancers, tuberculosis

At 70 years, average life expectancy is among the lowest in Europe; in the worst polluted parts of Transylvania it is 61 years. Striking health workers in 1998 warned that the health system was on the verge of collapse. The incidence of tuberculosis is the highest in Europe.

SPENDING

▷ GDP/cap. no increase

CONSUMPTION AND SPENDING

107 per 1,000 population

167 per 1,000 population

Defense 2.3%
Education 3.2%
Health 3.9%

0   5   10   15   20   25

Defense, Health, Education spending as % of GDP

Real incomes have fallen 40% since the fall of the Ceaușescu regime in 1989. Over 90% of people now own their own homes (but overcrowding is a problem) and many have small plots of land. Fewer than 10% of rural homes have running water or sewerage.

WORLD RANKING

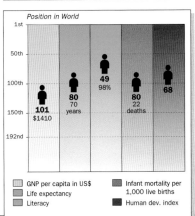

Position in World

1st
50th
100th
150th
192nd

101 $1410
80   70 years
49   98%
80   22 deaths
68

GNP per capita in US$
Life expectancy
Literacy

Infant mortality per 1,000 live births
Human dev. index

R

RUSSIAN FEDERATION

OFFICIAL NAME: Russian Federation **CAPITAL:** Moscow
POPULATION: 147.2 million **CURRENCY:** Rouble **OFFICIAL LANGUAGE:** Russian

| 1991 | 1991 | June 12 | RUS | +2-12 | +7 | .ru |

W ITH A TERRITORY of 17 million square km (6.6 million square miles), Russia is the world's largest state, almost twice as big as either the USA or China. Bounded by the Arctic and Pacific oceans on its northern and eastern coasts, it has land boundaries with 13 countries. With the formal dissolution of the USSR in 1991, Russia became an independent sovereign state. Within the CIS, it maintains a traditionally dominant role in central Asia and Eurasia. Ethnic Russians make up 80% of the population, but there are around 150 smaller ethnic groups, many with their own national territories within Russia's borders. Regionalism and separatism are major political issues. The situation is complicated by the fact that many of these territories are rich in key resources such as oil, gas, gold, and diamonds.

The Kremlin, Moscow. *Rebuilt in 1475 by Ivan the Great, who commissioned architects from Pskov and Italy, it is enclosed by walls 4 km (1.5 miles) long and lies on the Moscow River.*

CLIMATE ▷ Subarctic/continental/mountain/steppe

WEATHER CHART

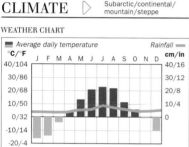

Russia has a cold continental climate, characterized by two widely divergent main seasons. Spring and autumn are very brief periods of transition between warm summers and freezing winters. The country is open to the influences of the Arctic and Atlantic to the north and west. However, mountains to the south and east prevent any warming effects filtering across from the Indian and Pacific oceans. Severe winters affect most regions. Winter temperatures vary surprisingly little from north to south, but fall sharply in eastern regions. The January temperature of −70°C (−94°F) recorded at Verkhoyansk in Siberia is the world record low outside Antarctica.

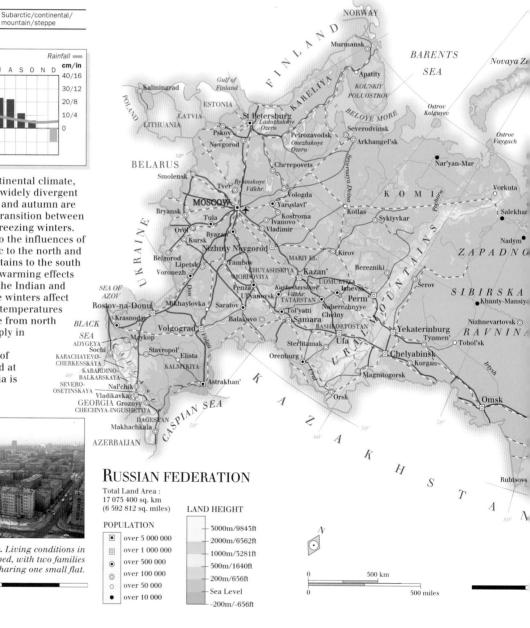

Housing in Moscow. *Living conditions in major cities are cramped, with two families often sharing one small flat.*

RUSSIAN FEDERATION

Total Land Area :
17 075 400 sq. km
(6 592 812 sq. miles)

POPULATION

▣	over 5 000 000
▢	over 1 000 000
◉	over 500 000
◎	over 100 000
○	over 50 000
●	over 10 000

LAND HEIGHT

	3000m/9843ft
	2000m/6562ft
	1000m/3281ft
	500m/1640ft
	200m/656ft
	Sea Level
	−200m/−656ft

TRANSPORTATION

▷ Drive on right

Sheremetyevo, Moscow
4.03m passengers

4,886 ships
13.76m grt

THE TRANSPORTATION NETWORK

963,000 km (601,875 miles)		None	
86,660 km (54,163 miles)		101,000 km (63,125 miles)	

Russia has a comprehensive transportation network. However, since 1991, all systems have seen some decline due to lack of funding. Cities are still served by good trolley and bus systems and Moscow has one of the most impressive subway systems in the world. In rural areas, car ownership is low and the population relies on an extensive bus service. The railroads, which were already declining in the Soviet era, are seriously overburdened, and accidents and delays are increasing. About 20% of the railroad track should be renewed annually owing to frost and other damage; shortage of funds means this is no longer done. Roads are also deteriorating, especially in major cities, but interurban highways are also affected. Crime is growing on railroads – notably the Trans-Siberian – and roads.

Since 1991, many new airlines have been set up as routes are privatized. However, Aeroflot, the previous state monopoly airline, is still the largest. Now called Russian International Airlines on overseas routes, it uses Boeing aircraft on flights from Moscow to London, Paris, Frankfurt, New York, and Tokyo.

Standards on international routes are generally high. However, the safety record of internal routes is declining.

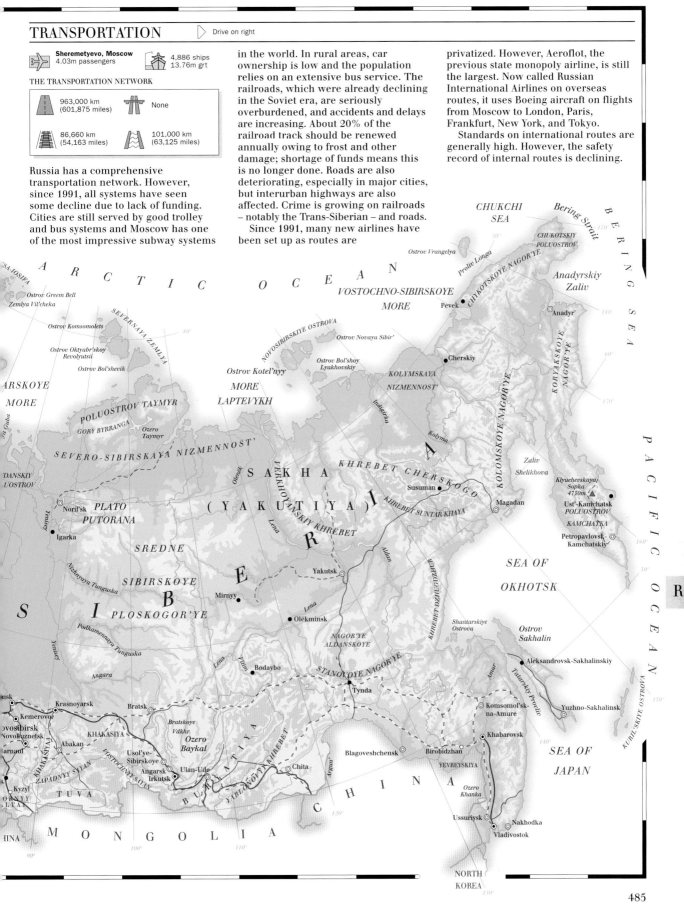

485

TOURISM

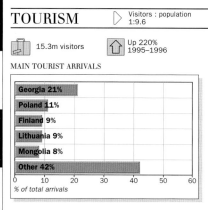

▷ Visitors : population 1:9.6

🧳 15.3m visitors   ⬆ Up 220% 1995–1996

MAIN TOURIST ARRIVALS

- Georgia 21%
- Poland 11%
- Finland 9%
- Lithuania 9%
- Mongolia 8%
- Other 42%

% of total arrivals

The privatization and break-up of *Intourist*, the previous sole tourist agency, has led to a vast expansion of tourism opportunities; each region wants to earn hard currency by attracting rich visitors. By 1998 the total number of tourists per year was nearly 16 million.

At the luxury end of the market, trips from St. Petersburg to Tashkent are now available on former president Brezhnev's official train. Trips down the Volga and visits to medieval monasteries are increasingly popular. Tourists can also experience life in a Russian forest, or fish for salmon in the Kola peninsula. The defense sector now offers flights in MiG jets, or drives in T-84 Russian tanks.

Moscow and St. Petersburg remain favorite destinations, where hotels tend either to cater for the well-off, or to be of a basic standard. The St. Petersburg region is also increasingly explored. Novgorod has many fine churches, and the Pskov area is celebrated as the setting for many of Pushkin's works, including *Eugene Onegin*.

Many parts of Russia remain inaccessible to most tourists. The communist ban on foreigners visiting the Urals has only recently been lifted, but the area still has very few facilities. However, resorts such as Sochi on the Black Sea have experienced a building boom, including the 2,500-room *Dagomys* Acapulco-style hotel complex.

PEOPLE

▷ Pop. density low

👤 Russian   👥 9/km² (22/mi²)

THE URBAN/RURAL POPULATION SPLIT

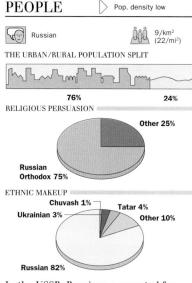

76%   24%

RELIGIOUS PERSUASION

- Russian Orthodox 75%
- Other 25%

ETHNIC MAKEUP

- Russian 82%
- Ukrainian 3%
- Chuvash 1%
- Tatar 4%
- Other 10%

In the USSR, Russians accounted for just over 50% of the population, but in Russia they form the great majority. Significant numbers of Russians still live in some neighboring republics, notably Ukraine and Latvia and those of central Asia. However, a rise in nationalism throughout the former USSR has persuaded many central Asian Russians to return to Russia.

Within Russia there has also been an increase in ethnic tension, especially in the Caucasus. There are 57 nationalities with their own territories within the federation and 95 nationalities without a territory (although these groups make up only 6% of the population).

Social life in Russia has not changed significantly since the demise of communism. However, with the lifting of censorship, there has been a greater expression of sexuality as well as of political and religious views. While there has been some increase in the availability of pornography and in prostitution, this is mostly confined to major urban centers. There has been some revival of both the Russian Orthodox and Muslim faiths. However, church attendance is still below Western levels. One marked change of which Russians speak is the growing importance attached to money. The mutual support systems of extended friendships are now in decline.

The position of women has changed little. Many have suffered from the rise in unemployment, but this reflects the demise of many part-time or badly paid jobs, rather than gender-motivated change. Most Russians have very modest living standards and have been further impoverished by the collapse of the economy in the late 1990s. In early 1999, unemployment was estimated to have reached almost nine million, or 12.4% of the workforce, although only 2.4% were officially registered.

POPULATION AGE BREAKDOWN

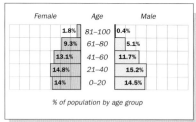

Female	Age	Male
1.8%	81–100	0.4%
9.3%	61–80	5.1%
13.1%	41–60	11.7%
14.8%	21–40	15.2%
14%	0–20	14.5%

% of population by age group

POLITICS

▷ Multiparty elections

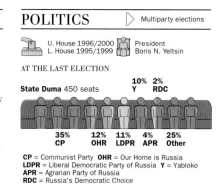

🏛 U. House 1996/2000   L. House 1995/1999   President Boris N. Yeltsin

AT THE LAST ELECTION

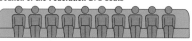

State Duma 450 seats

35% CP   12% OHR   11% LDPR   4% APR   10% Y   2% RDC   25% Other

CP = Communist Party   **OHR** = Our Home is Russia
LDPR = Liberal Democratic Party of Russia   **Y** = Yabloko
APR = Agrarian Party of Russia
RDC = Russia's Democratic Choice

Council of the Federation 178 seats

Each of 89 regions is represented in the Council of the Federation (Soviet Federatsii) by its governor and one other member.

Russia has an elected parliament, and a directly elected president with executive powers.

MAIN POLITICAL ISSUES
Living standards
Russians are disillusioned at the failure of politicians to improve their living standards. The securities which used to underpin life – such as long-term employment, guaranteed housing and a basic diet – have been swept away. Uneven and crisis-prone efforts at transition to a market economy have created much insecurity, even before the 1998 crisis, since when the situation has deteriorated sharply.

Crime
Crime has risen alarmingly since the collapse of communism. Main cities are unsafe after dark. Mafia killings target opponents of organized crime. Bureaucratic corruption is rife – officials demand payment for most services.

PROFILE
The elections of 1995 made the Communist Party the single largest party in the *Duma*, although President Yeltsin had appealed to the electorate not to "allow the forces of the past to seize power again." Yeltsin responded in early 1996 by dropping

President Yeltsin, *set on completing his term, but using his powers erratically.*

Mikhail Gorbachev, *whose restructuring ultimately led to the break-up of the USSR.*

R

POLITICS *continued*

a number of high-profile reformers – including Anatoly Chubais – from his administration, thereby making the government less vulnerable to communist and nationalist criticism. His party was boosted by a much-needed IMF loan secured in March 1996.

Communist Party leader Gennady Zyuganov was Yeltsin's main challenger in the 1996 presidential election. Many commentators felt that Yeltsin could not win while Russian troops were fighting and dying in Chechnya. But for all the communists' advantages of a nostalgic and angry populace and an efficient organization, Yeltsin won by a considerable margin in the second round, having gained the backing of the third-placed candidate General Aleksandr Lebed by his dramatic appointment as national security adviser and secretary of the Security Council.

A peace agreement was signed with Chechen leaders in August, and by the beginning of 1997 Russia completed the withdrawal of its troops.

General Lebed was dismissed from office by Yeltsin in October 1996, at the height of speculation about Yeltsin's health and a power struggle over the succession. Hospitalized twice in 1995 on account of a heart problem, Yeltsin had to undergo major surgery at the end of 1996. Concern about his health remains a key issue in Russian politics which flares up with each new sign of unexplained fatigue or erratic behavior. The return of Chubais as presidential head of staff, then as deputy premier and finance minister, encouraged the proreform lobby, but Chubais, unpopular in the country at large, lost his ministerial portfolio over a scandal in late 1997. Yeltsin took a high risk stance in March 1998 in a confrontation with the *Duma* when he unexpectedly dismissed the whole Council of Ministers and insisted on his authority to impose the young and little-known Sergei Kiriyenko as prime minister in place of long-serving Viktor Chernomyrdin.

Within five months, and facing a major crisis of confidence in the Russian economy, Yeltsin changed tack

Yuri Luzhkov, *charismatic mayor of Moscow.*

Yevgeny Primakov, *strong contender for the succession.*

again and tried to bring back Chernomyrdin. This time he was blocked by the *Duma*, and an acute political crisis developed, until Foreign Minister Yevgeny Primakov was named as a replacement prime minister in a compromise acceptable to the large Communist parliamentary bloc.

Primakov was dismissed in May 1999, to be succeeded by Sergey Stepashin and, only three months later, by Vladimir Putin. The sacking of Primakov was generally interpreted as a move by Yeltsin against a powerful rival, ahead of the presidential elections due in mid-2000. Primakov was later named as leader of a new political movement, Our Fatherland is All Russia, recently formed by regional governors and the charismatic mayor of Moscow, Yuri Luzhkov, to contest the 1999 parliamentary elections.

WORLD AFFAIRS   ▷ Joined UN in 1945

| CE | CIS | IAEA | G8 | OSCE |

Immediately following 1991, Russia displayed little independent initiative in foreign affairs, allying itself closely to the USA. Its weak economy and a need for regular infusions of hard currency put it in no position to antagonize the Western powers and Japan. However, from 1993, Russia set out to develop a more independent foreign policy.

In early 1996, Andrei Kosyrev was replaced as foreign minister by Yevgeny Primakov. Kosyrev had been heavily criticized by nationalists and communists for his relatively soft line on Bosnia. Primakov, regarded as more skeptical of Western intentions toward Russia, adopted a tough line on major issues, including NATO's eastward expansion. He won enough respect for this stance at home to make him an acceptable compromise prime minister in the political crisis of August–September 1998. The NATO bombardment of Yugoslavia the following year, over the Kosovo crisis, pushed Russia's relations with the West to a new low. Russians felt strong kinship with Yugoslavia's Orthodox Christian and slavic Serb population. Some Russian prestige was restored, however, by participation both in diplomatic initiatives and in the eventual peacekeeping operation in Kosovo.

Russia remains the overwhelmingly dominant partner in the CIS. It regards the successor states of the USSR as the "near abroad" and maintains troops in many of them. Belarus openly courts closer integration and even reunion with Russia.

St. Basil's Cathedral, Moscow. *It was comissioned by Tsar Ivan the Terrible and built in 1555-1561. The exterior domes were decorated in the 1670s.*

AID   ▷ Recipient

💲 $718m (receipts)   ⬇ Down 41% 1996–1997

Russia has received billions of dollars in aid from Western countries on several occasions to stave off government payments problems and to promote economic reform. IMF credits of about $16 billion, made available in 1995–1996, were reinforced with further IMF aid in the 1998 crisis rescue package.

DEFENSE   ▷ Compulsory military service

💲 $64bn   ⬇ Down 14% in 1997

Morale in the armed forces has fallen amid recurrent failures to pay wages.

RUSSIAN ARMED FORCES

🛡	15,500 main battle tanks (T-54/-55, T-62, T-64A, T-72, T-80)	420,000 personnel
🚢	98 submarines, 1 carrier, 13 destroyers, 17 cruisers, 13 frigates, 124 patrol boats	180,000 personnel
✈	1,855 combat aircraft (MiG 29, MiG 27, MiG 25, Su-27, Su-24, Su-25)	210,000 personnel
🚀	756 ICBM, 26 SSBN, 100 ABM	

In 1991, Russia inherited armed forces of 2.7 million men, 2.1 million within its borders. Unable to afford such a large army, by 1998 it had more than halved total numbers in the armed forces, and a crisis plan for restructuring envisaged further cuts. Conscription remains – although there are plans to abolish it by 2005 – but draft dodging has increased. Defense budgets have been reduced to the point where outlay on strategic nuclear forces is now limited to barely adequate physical protection of warheads. Early warning and space programs have also been sharply reduced. The navy has been worst affected: the northern and Pacific fleets are inactive and deteriorating fast. There was also difficulty reaching agreement with Ukraine over the Black Sea fleet. The air force suffers from fuel shortages.

R

ECONOMIC CRISIS AND COHESION

THE CRISIS OF CONFIDENCE in the Russian economy in August 1998 put the spotlight on the chronic weakness of central government finances. Collapse was only narrowly averted, with a combination of devaluation and an international rescue package. A year later, corruption in the banking system remained a major barrier to any kind of financial stability. The latest scandals, which emerged from investigation into money laundering and the diversion of foreign loan funds, revealed the labyrinth of links between the central bank, domestic banks, commercial banks operating abroad, organised crime, and powerful figures in Russian political circles.

IMPROVING GOVERNMENT FINANCES
Helped by the 1998 devaluation and its default on domestic debt, and by collecting more tax revenue, the government headed by Yevgeny Primakov (and his successors) started to make real improvements in its own financial position. This at least enabled it to begin catching up on the arrears of payments to civil servants, without as much recourse to the printing of additional money as many economists had feared.

Residents of St. Petersburg queue in the streets for the limited supplies of basic foodstuffs.

POVERTY AND SUBSISTENCE
Russian manufacturers were also better able to compete with imported goods, since imports had become so much more expensive after the devaluation of the rouble. In the course of 1999 Russian-made goods started appearing in shops in Moscow and St Petersburg once again. There were suddenly big increases in supplies of such things as bicycles, refrigerators, washing machines and electric kettles. Middle class Russians

in the cities, who had found ways to survive the August 1998 crisis, were eager buyers of these products.

For the majority of Russians, however, wages and pensions, if they were at least being paid with greater regularity, were still between one and three months late and a long way from keeping pace with inflation. Teachers' wages, for example, had not been increased for five years. The state statistical committee itself calculated that in the first quarter of 1999 almost 38% of Russians were trying to get by on incomes lower than the official subsistence level. The World Bank estimated that 20% would be on incomes of below half the subsistence level by early in the year 2000. Impoverished pensioners can commonly be seen attempting to sell their remaining possessions from makeshift stalls on street corners, at least in cities where there is some prospect of finding people with money to buy them.

VICTIMS OF DISMANTLING THE COMMAND ECONOMY
For many people in the provinces, the dismantling of the old Soviet-style command economy has meant the disappearance of what was often the sole source of employment. Far-flung towns had been built exclusively around a particular heavy industry, such as steel, coal, shipbuilding, machine tools and arms production. Many of these concerns were impossible to privatise, having no market for their output, and thus remained in state hands. Their workers, put on short time or laid off, have been reduced to living on promises, state handouts and barter arrangements.

The disappearance of proper welfare state provision in areas such as health care makes the situation even more catastrophic, and leaves millions with

Heavy industries have declined dramatically since the fall of the Soviet Union, and many factories now lie idle.

Poor maintenance and under-funding has resulted in cracks and leaks along Russia's network of oil pipelines, which not only cost the country economically, but also in the environmental damage caused.

little apparent alternative but to resort to illegal migration. Rates of alcoholism, drug abuse and suicide have all risen. Most hard pressed are people with access to neither work nor land, living with children in small urban settlements. Wherever possible, however, people grow food to make themselves as self-sufficient as possible, and use what they can for barter. Great reliance is also placed on family support networks. The relevance of the formal economy is thereby much reduced, while rents, utility bills and transport are still heavily subsidised. Even when cash does change hands, only 28% of the money spent in shops is being recorded on the cash register, according to a report in November 1998 by the state auditor in charge of tax revenues, who estimated that 40% of all purchases involve the black market in one way or another.

The running down of heavy industry has left some areas with massive environmental damage, among the most notorious instances being the pollution of rivers by toxic waste from the metallurgy industry in the Kola peninsula in the north. Problems of disposal of radioactive wastes affect northern coastal areas in particular, although the worst such legacies of the former Soviet Union, dealing with the effects of the nuclear accident at Chernobyl and the old nuclear test site at Semipalatinsk, have been left respectively to Belarus and Ukraine and to Kazakhstan.

REGIONAL STAKES IN OIL AND GAS
One heavy industry with an apparently brighter economic outlook in 1999 is oil and gas, whose export earnings

R

have been boosted both by the low rouble and by the improvement of prices from their recent low levels. Gazprom, the giant company which monopolises the gas industry, has been the biggest beneficiary. The Russian petroleum industry, however, still suffers from high costs. This is both because of its own inefficiencies, and because of the distance which pipelines have to cover to bring the output of distant fields to market – usually in western Europe.

Some of the republics within the Russian Federation are showing an increasing desire to assert greater control over their mineral resources. In the oil industry in particular, they often believe that they can be managed more profitably at the region level, and resent the outflow of earnings to poorer regions. Regionalism based on dissatisfaction with central economic management began emerging as a key political issue as the 1999-2000 parliamentary and presidential elections approached.

Tatarstan is a case in point. Lying on the Volga some 1,000 km east of Moscow, the republic (alone except for Chechnya) refused in 1992 to sign the treaty between the Russian Federation and its constituent parts. Instead, Tatar president Mintimer Shaimiev negotiated better autonomy terms in a 1994 agreement, whose detailed revenue-sharing provisions were extended for a further five years from 1999. Tatarstan also avoided rushing into privatization in such a manner as to allow former managers to effectively appropriate huge assets. Its continuing control of the republic's oil company, Tatneft, has provided both a source of revenue and a route for foreign borrowing on relatively favourable terms.

New gas pipelines being laid across the frozen expanses of Siberia.

ECONOMICS

▷ Inflation 288.3% p.a. (1993–1997)

$394.9bn

6.00–21.55 roubles (official rate)

SCORE CARD

❏ WORLD GNP RANKING..........................13th
❏ GNP PER CAPITA.............................$2,680
❏ BALANCE OF PAYMENTS.......................$3.3bn
❏ INFLATION 14.6%
❏ UNEMPLOYMENT................................11%

EXPORTS

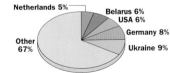

Netherlands 5%
Belarus 6%
USA 6%
Germany 8%
Ukraine 9%
Other 67%

IMPORTS

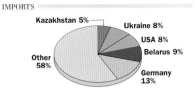

Kazakhstan 5%
Ukraine 8%
USA 8%
Belarus 9%
Germany 13%
Other 58%

STRENGTHS

Huge natural resources; in particular hydrocarbons, precious metals, fuel, timber. Enormous engineering and scientific base. Some dynamic small joint-stock enterprises. Huge potential for oil and natural gas.

WEAKNESSES

Corrupt sale of state enterprises; former managers acquired assets at knock-down prices. Privatized companies asset-stripped. Organized crime syndicates own huge areas of economy. Public disillusionment over "shares for loans" privatization scheme. Many skills developed under communism not relevant in increasingly competitive economy. Inadequate legal infrastructure governing property rights and trading transactions. Russian companies

ECONOMIC PERFORMANCE INDICATOR

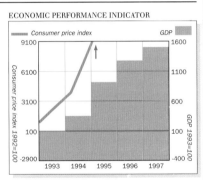

— Consumer price index   ▨ GDP

keep billions of US dollars in Western bank accounts: outflow of capital damages domestic economy. Rampant inflation undermines domestic savings and purchasing power. Crisis of investor confidence in mid-1998 forced sharp devaluation and fresh IMF rescue arrangement.

PROFILE

The collapse of industrial production began with Gorbachev's introduction of market principles to the command economy in the late 1980s. In the mid-1990s, hopes rose when a tight monetary squeeze reduced inflation to the lowest level since reforms began, the budget deficit was reduced and the value of the rouble was successfully defended through the introduction of a currency "corridor." Yeltsin's stabilization program was backed by the international community and the IMF, with loans of over $16 billion.

These achievements were swept away again in the 1998 crisis. Yeltsin oscillated between taking proreform positions and appeasing the hostile public and the communists in parliament. The Primakov government formed in September 1998 restored communist-backed figures to key positions, including the central bank.

R

RUSSIAN FEDERATION : MAJOR BUSINESSES

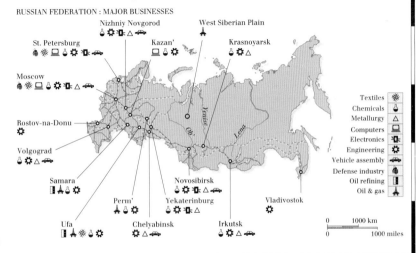

Nizhniy Novgorod
West Siberian Plain
St. Petersburg
Kazan'
Krasnoyarsk
Moscow
Rostov-na-Donu
Volgograd
Samara
Novosibirsk
Perm'
Yekaterinburg
Vladivostok
Ufa
Chelyabinsk
Irkutsk

Yenisei
Ob'
Lena

Textiles
Chemicals
Metallurgy
Computers
Electronics
Engineering
Vehicle assembly
Defense industry
Oil refining
Oil & gas

0   1000 km
0   1000 miles

CHRONOLOGY

The first Russian state (Rus) was in present-day Ukraine. Occupation by the Tatars (1240-1480) left a mark on the Russian language and character. From the 17th century, rule was under the Romanovs.

- ❏ **1904–1905** Russian war against Japan; ends in defeat for Russia.
- ❏ **1905** Revolution.
- ❏ **1909–1914** Rapid economic expansion.
- ❏ **1914** Enters World War I against Germany.
- ❏ **1917** February Revolution; abdication of Nicholas II. October Revolution; Bolsheviks take over with Lenin as leader.
- ❏ **1918** July, Nicholas II and family murdered.
- ❏ **1918-1920** Civil war.
- ❏ **1921** New Economic Policy; retreat from socialism.
- ❏ **1922** USSR established.
- ❏ **1924** Lenin dies. Struggle for leadership eventually won by Stalin.
- ❏ **1928** First Five-Year Plan: forced industrialization and collectivization.
- ❏ **1929** Trotsky banished to Kazakhstan, then deported to Turkey.
- ❏ **1936–1938** Show trials and campaigns against actual and suspected members of opposition. Millions sent to gulags in Siberia and elsewhere. Purges widespread.
- ❏ **1959** Hitler–Stalin pact gives USSR Baltic states, eastern Poland, and Bessarabia.
- ❏ **1941** Germany attacks USSR. Stalin unprepared. December, Battle of Moscow is first German defeat.
- ❏ **1943** February, great Soviet victory at Stalingrad.
- ❏ **1944–1945** Soviet offensive penetrates Balkans.
- ❏ **1945** Germany defeated. Under Yalta and Potsdam agreements eastern and southeastern Europe are Soviet zone of influence.
- ❏ **1947** Cold War begins; Stalin on defensive, fears penetration of Western and capitalist values.
- ❏ **1953** Stalin dies.
- ❏ **1956** Hungarian uprising crushed. Krushchev's "secret speech" attacking Stalin at Party congress.
- ❏ **1957** Krushchev consolidates power. Sputnik launched.
- ❏ **1961** Yuri Gagarin first man in space.
- ❏ **1962** Cuban missile crisis.
- ❏ **1964** Krushchev ousted in coup, replaced by Leonid Brezhnev.
- ❏ **1975** Helsinki Final Act; confirms European frontiers as at end of World War II. Soviets agree human rights are concern of international community.
- ❏ **1979** Invades Afghanistan. Beginning of new Cold War.
- ❏ **1982** Brezhnev dies. ⇨

RESOURCES

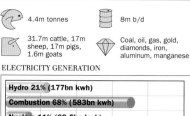

▷ Elecric power 210.9m kw

4.4m tonnes

8m b/d

31.7m cattle, 17m sheep, 17m pigs, 1.6m goats

Coal, oil, gas, gold, diamonds, iron, aluminum, manganese

ELECTRICITY GENERATION

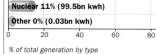

Hydro 21% (177bn kwh)

Combustion 68% (583bn kwh)

Nuclear 11% (99.5bn kwh)

Other 0% (0.03bn kwh)

% of total generation by type

RUSSIAN FEDERATION : LAND USE

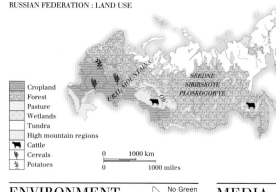

- Cropland
- Forest
- Pasture
- Wetlands
- Tundra
- High mountain regions
- 🐄 Cattle
- Cereals
- Potatoes

0   1000 km
0   1000 miles

Russia is a leading world producer of oil, natural gas, and electricity, among other resources. Confirmed reserves make Russia the world's leading country in terms of hydrocarbons, gold, precious metals, diamonds, and timber.

Unlike some of the other republics of the former Soviet Union, Russia has not opened its resources up to foreign concerns. It does not wish to lose any control to Western multinationals. They are consequently underexploited owing to a lack of investment and technology.

Most of the major resources are also located in national territories such as Tatarstan and Sakha Yakutia in Siberia. The regions' desire for greater autonomy from Moscow has turned the ownership of these resources into a delicate political issue.

ENVIRONMENT

▷ No Green MPs

3%

Medium

ENVIRONMENTAL TREATIES

Yes   Yes   Yes

Yes   Yes   Yes

Awareness of Russia's environmental problems has risen sharply since the demise of communism. However, the resources, political will and know-how to tackle them are still lacking. While Russia now has an active green movement, it did not gain significant support at the 1995 general elections.

Each region has its own particular problems. The north suffers from the effects of nuclear dumping in the Barents Sea. Over 17,000 contaminated containers were dumped there by the Russian navy, including the old nuclear reactor from the icebreaker *Lenin*. Thousands of tons of chemical weapons have been dumped in the Baltic, although their exact location has not been revealed. The river Volga in central Russia is so polluted and diverted by dam-building that many fish species are now extinct. The worst problems are probably in the Urals and the cities of European Russia. Chemical and heavy industrial plants still lack adequate protection. Most do not treat their effluents at all.

MEDIA

▷ TV ownership high

Daily newspaper circulation 105 per 1,000 people

PUBLISHING AND BROADCAST MEDIA

There are 285 daily newspapers, including *Izvestiya*, *Rossiiskaya*, *Komsomolskaya Pravda* and *Trud*

4 state-owned national and regional, several independent channels

3 state-owned networks

Russians are avid newspaper readers. In 1990, daily sales topped 166 million, in a population of 149 million. Since then the economic situation has caused falls in circulation, and many titles have ceased to appear. The old CPSU daily, *Pravda*, suspended publication in 1996. *Argumenty i Fakty*, founded in 1978, is the best-selling weekly, with a three million circulation. Regional and local press, often funded by local government, has grown in importance. Attacks on journalists have increased, with several killings. Some have been prosecuted for alleged violations of military secrets.

State broadcasting was reorganized in 1995. Public Russian Television (ORT) runs two main TV channels. The state-owned RTR follows a pro-Yeltsin line, while TV Tsentr is identified with Moscow mayor Yuri Lyzhkov. News is seen as partisan, but as less biased than formerly. Many Russians with satellite dishes tune in to CNN and other Western channels.

R

CHRONOLOGY *continued*

- **1985** Gorbachev in power. Beginning of *perestroika*, era of new political thinking and the break-up of the USSR. First of three US–USSR summits resulting in arms reduction treaties. Nationality conflicts surface.
- **1988** Law of State Enterprises gives more power to enterprises: inflation and dislocation of economy.
- **1990** Gorbachev becomes Soviet president. First partly freely elected parliament (Supreme Soviet) meets.
- **1991** Boris Yeltsin elected president of Russia. Right-wing attempted coup successfully opposed by Yeltsin and Muscovites. CIS established; demise of USSR.
- **1992** Economic shock therapy.
- **1993** Yeltsin decrees dissolution of Supreme Soviet and uses force to disband parliament. Elections return conservative state *Duma*.
- **1994** Russian military offensive against Chechnya.
- **1995** Communist victory in state *Duma* elections.
- **1996** Yeltsin reelected despite strong Communist challenge. Peace accord ends war in Chechnya. Gen. Lebed dismissed as Secretary of Security Council. Yeltsin undergoes extensive heart surgery.
- **1997** Russian troop withdrawal from Chechnya, where former rebel leader Aslan Maskhadov wins presidential elections.
- **1998** Yeltsin twice changes prime minister in successive political crises which diminish his remaining authority. Economic turmoil forces devaluation of rouble. Severe recession, rampant inflation.
- **1999** March–June, resentment over NATO bombing of Yugoslavia. May, August, Yeltsin names successive new prime ministers. Ousted Primakov becomes presidential candidate for Our Fatherland movement. Conflict with separatist Islamic rebels in Dagestan and Chechnya.

Tundra in Russia's far east. *Russia has some of the largest uninhabited tracts of land in the world.*

CRIME

Death penalty not used

1m prisoners — Up 27% in 1992

CRIME RATES

Murders	
15	per 100,000 population

Rapes	
9	per 100,000 population

Thefts	
1273	per 100,000 population

Crime is now a formidable problem in Russia, and the police cannot keep up with its rise. Reported murders have risen dramatically in recent years.

Most murders are the result of intergang violence. Muggings and street crime in the larger cities are also sharply up. Corruption and Mafia-style activity are also widespread. Protection rackets, prostitution, smuggling, and narcotics are the Russian Mafia's main sources of profit. Russian crime bosses also fund similar activities in western Europe, using banks as fronts. The rise in crime has become a major issue for most Russians, contributing to the popularity of political platforms with a strongly authoritarian element.

EDUCATION

School leaving age:15

99% — 4.5m students

Schooling is free, and compulsory for nine years up to age 15.

THE EDUCATION SYSTEM

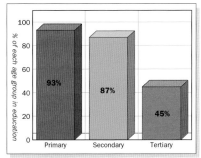
Primary 93%, Secondary 87%, Tertiary 45%

Since the end of communist rule, efforts at revising the presentation of history and other subjects have been hampered by a lack of funds. New private lycées, such as those run by the Orthodox Church, often offer courses in English and in German, which has made a come-back as a key commercial language. Students get some state financial support when in full-time higher education. Some institutions introduced fees in the 1990s. The system is seriously underfunded. Prestigious institutions such as the Academy of Sciences have cut staff and research. Most academics have to rely on extramural earnings.

HEALTH

Welfare state health benefits

1 per 219 people — Heart disease, cancers, accidents, violence, tuberculosis

The health care system is in crisis and medicines are often in short supply. Until 1991, state enterprises provided considerable health care. Employers are now supposed to make payments through the Medical Insurance Fund, but many privatized concerns seek to cut costs. Local authorities lack the resources to take over these responsibilities. Bribing medical staff to obtain treatment is commonplace and there is a lack of pharmaceutical products and drugs. Hospital patients are normally fed by their relatives.

SPENDING

GDP./cap. no increase

CONSUMPTION AND SPENDING

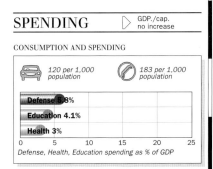
120 per 1,000 population — 183 per 1,000 population
Defense 5.8%, Education 4.1%, Health 3%
Defense, Health, Education spending as % of GDP

Wealth disparities in Russia are increasing rapidly. A small minority of the population made huge profits from the dismantling of the old Soviet command economy. About 10% are thought to have benefited in some way.

Especially in Moscow, a growing number of dollar millionaires flaunt their wealth. The bosses of organized crime are society's wealthiest group. Russia is now the biggest buyer of Rolls Royces, while BMWs, Mercedes and Volvos are relatively common in Moscow and St. Petersburg. A considerable amount of wealth is deposited abroad. There are now thousands of Russian offshore bank accounts; Northern Cyprus is a favorite location.

WORLD RANKING

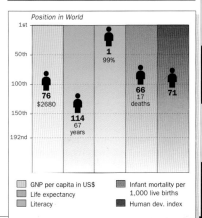
Position in World
76 $2680, 114 67 years, 1 99%, 66 17 deaths, 71
- GNP per capita in US$
- Life expectancy
- Literacy
- Infant mortality per 1,000 live births
- Human dev. index

R

RWANDA

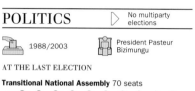

CENTRAL AFRICA

OFFICIAL NAME: Republic of Rwanda   **CAPITAL:** Kigali
POPULATION: 6.5 million   **CURRENCY:** Rwanda franc   **OFFICIAL LANGUAGES:** French and Rwandan

| 1962 | 1962 | July 1 | RWA | +2 | +250 | .rw |

LYING JUST SOUTH OF THE EQUATOR in east central Africa, Rwanda is far from the nearest port. Since independence in 1962, ethnic tensions have dominated politics. In 1994, the violent death of the president led to appalling political and ethnic violence in which some 500,000 Rwandans died. Over half the surviving population were displaced. The perpetrators of the genocide held sway in desperately overcrowded refugee camps in adjacent countries, and greatly complicated the process of eventual repatriation and reintegration.

CLIMATE

▷ Tropical wet & dry

WEATHER CHART

■ Average daily temperature   Rainfall

°C/°F   J F M A M J J A S O N D   cm/in
40/104   40/16
30/86   30/12
20/68   20/8
10/50   10/4
0/32   0
-10/14
-20/-4

Rwanda's climate is tropical, tempered by altitude. Two wet seasons allow for two harvests each year.

TRANSPORTATION

▷ Drive on right

✈ **Kanombe Intl, Kigali**
123,363 passengers

⚓ Has no fleet

THE TRANSPORTATION NETWORK

| 🛣 954 km (593 miles) | 🛤 None |
| None | ⛴ Lake Kivu |

The road network is well developed. The international airport near Kigali was completed in 1986.

TOURISM

▷ Visitors : population 1:6,500

🧳 Aid workers and journalists are the only visitors

◇ No change 1995–1997

MAIN TOURIST ARRIVALS

Rwanda does not publish tourism figures by country of origin

0   10   20   30   40
% of total arrivals

Tourism has effectively ceased as a result of the civil war. When peace is secured, Rwanda may be able to regain its status as a destination for wealthy wildlife enthusiasts. Top attractions are the mountain gorillas and Lake Kivu.

PEOPLE

▷ Pop. density high

Kinyarwanda, French, Kiswahili, English

261/km² (675/mi²)

THE URBAN/RURAL POPULATION SPLIT

6%   94%

ETHNIC MAKEUP

Other (including Twa) 2%   Tutsi 8%

Hutu 90%

The Hutu and Tutsi are the main groups; the Twa pygmies, the original inhabitants, have been marginalized. For over 500 years, the cattle-owning Tutsi were politically dominant, oppressing the land-owning Hutu majority. In 1959, violent revolt led to a reversal of the roles. The two groups have since been waging a spasmodic war. It is estimated that 500,000 were killed in the violence of the mid-1990's, the majority Tutsi victims of Hutu massacres. Under the new government, many Tutsi in exile since 1959 are returning to Rwanda.

POLITICS

▷ No multiparty elections

1988/2003

President Pasteur Bizimungu

AT THE LAST ELECTION

Transitional National Assembly 70 seats

The last legislative election took place in December 1988 when candidates were chosen from the National Republican Movement for Development and Democracy (MRND) list. Polls due in 1999 were postponed until 2003.

After 14 years of one-party rule under the MRND, Rwanda adopted a multiparty system in 1991. A peace accord to end the rebellion launched in 1990 by the Tutsi-dominated Rwandan Patriotic Front (FPR) was signed in 1993. However, the fragile peace process was halted in 1994 by the death of the president in a plane crash. Genocidal violence was unleashed between the predominantly Hutu supporters of the old regime and its mainly, but not exclusively, Tutsi opponents. An estimated 500,000 died and millions fled the conflict, in which the FPR eventually gained control of the country. Hutu have been allocated the key posts in the government, including the presidency. The government's priorities are ensuring the resettlement of the displaced population and bringing the perpetrators of the genocide to justice.

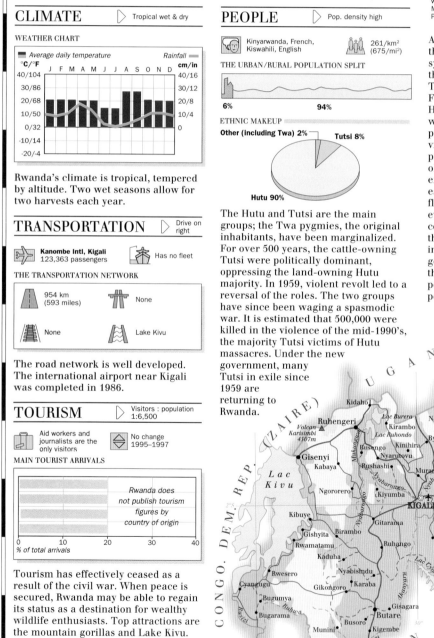

RWANDA

Total Land Area : 24 950 sq. km (9653 sq. miles)

POPULATION
over 100 000   ◎
over 10 000   ●
under 10 000   ·

LAND HEIGHT
3000m/9843ft
2000m/6562ft
1000m/3281ft

0   40 km
0   40 miles

R

WORLD AFFAIRS

 Joined UN in 1962

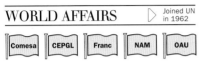

Accused of abandoning Rwanda during 1994, the UN later set up a war crimes tribunal on the genocide. Involvement in conflict in Congo (former Zaire) is bound up with large-scale refugee movements and ethnic massacres.

AID

 Recipient

$592m (receipts)

Down 12% 1996–1997

Large amounts of aid are required, particularly for the agriculture sector severely disrupted by the war. Aid agencies in the refugee camps face the dilemma of assisting the perpetrators of violence and intimidation.

DEFENSE

No compulsory military service

$103m

Up 6% in 1997

The Tutsi-led RPF now dominates the army. Former Hutu militias, regrouped in refugee camps, were forced to return to Rwanda in late 1996/early 1997.

ECONOMICS

 Inflation 11.2% p.a. (1985–1996)

$1.7bn

346.49–320.63 Rwanda francs

SCORE CARD

- WORLD GNP RANKING.........................146th
- GNP PER CAPITA $210
- BALANCE OF PAYMENTS.....................$–93m
- INFLATION 11.5%
- UNEMPLOYMENT.......Few have formal employment

STRENGTHS
Currently none. Assuming stability, Rwanda produces coffee. Possible oil and gas reserves.

WEAKNESSES
Economic activity completely disrupted by the 1994 violence. 1,600-km (1,000-mile) journey to both Kenyan and Tanzanian ports imposes high transportation costs. Few resources.

EXPORTS

USA 4% | Turkey 4% | Pakistan 7% | Germany 21% | Belgium-Luxembourg 36% | Other 28%

IMPORTS
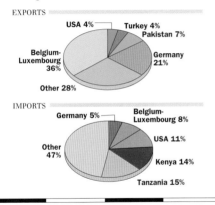

Germany 5% | Belgium-Luxembourg 8% | USA 11% | Kenya 14% | Tanzania 15% | Other 47%

Terraced hillside. *Before the war, Rwanda was the most densely populated country in Africa and its land was intensively cultivated.*

RESOURCES

Electric power 34,000 kw

3,349 tonnes | Not an oil producer
500,000 cattle, 270,000 sheep, 80,000 pigs | Tin, tungsten, gold, columbo-tantalite, methane gas

Gas deposits in Lake Kivu are likely to be explored with Congo (former Zaire). Only 20% of urban homes are on the national power grid.

ENVIRONMENT

No Green MPs

15% | Low

Soil erosion and forest loss are the major environmental problems, the effects of war aside. The tourist industry underpinned the preservation of the mountain gorilla.

MEDIA

TV ownership low

 Daily newspaper circulation 0.1 per 1,000 people

PUBLISHING AND BROADCAST MEDIA

There is 1 daily newspaper. The monthly *Inkingi* and *La Relève* are published in Kinyarwanda and French respectively

1 state-controlled service | 1 state-controlled service

The media have been used as an important propaganda tool by both sides in the political conflict.

CRIME

Death penalty used

Rwanda does not publish prison figures | Down 13% in 1992, before the genocide of 1994

Previously benefiting from a low crime rate, an orgy of violence broke out in 1994, with thousands murdered and raped. Around 47,000 suspects are being held in relation to these crimes.

EDUCATION

School leaving age: 13

63% | 3,389 students

Schools are run by the state and Christian missions. Primary education is officially compulsory, but only 71% of children attended in 1991; just 8% go on to secondary schooling.

CHRONOLOGY

The Hutu majority began to arrive in the 14th century, the warrior Tutsi in the 15th. From 1890, German and then Belgian colonizers acted to reinforce Tutsi dominance.

- **1962** Independence under Hutu-led government.
- **1960s** Tutsi revolt; massacres by Hutu; thousands of Tutsi in exile.
- **1973** Habyarimana seizes power.
- **1993** Peace accord with FPR.
- **1994** April, Habyarimana dies in plane crash. Outbreak of genocidal violence. August, FPR-dominated government takes office.
- **1995** Start of war crimes tribunal.
- **1997** Tens of thousands of Hutu refugees forced to return after being caught up in Congo (Zaire) civil war.

HEALTH

Welfare state health benefits

1 per 40,600 people | Malaria, measles, diarrheal diseases, violence

Rwanda has a network of 34 hospitals and 188 health centers. This should mean that the majority have access to care, although treatment is rarely free.

SPENDING

Not available

CONSUMPTION AND SPENDING

2 per 1,000 population | 3 per 1,000 population

Defense 5.5%
Education 3.8%
Health 0.5%

Defense, Health, Education spending as % of GDP

Wealth is limited to the country's political elite. Most Rwandans are poor farmers; Twa pygmies and refugees are poorer still.

WORLD RANKING

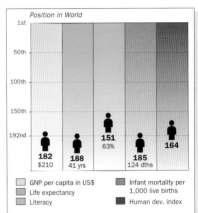

Position in World

182 $210 | 188 41 yrs | 151 63% | 185 124 dths | 164

☐ GNP per capita in US$
☐ Life expectancy
☐ Literacy
☐ Infant mortality per 1,000 live births
☐ Human dev. index

R

ST. KITTS & NEVIS

OFFICIAL NAME: Federation of Saint Christopher and Nevis   **CAPITAL:** Basseterre
POPULATION: 41,000   **CURRENCY:** Eastern Caribbean dollar   **OFFICIAL LANGUAGE:** English

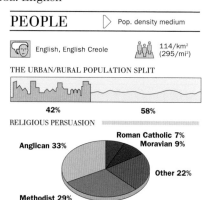

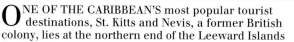

1983   1983   Sept 19   KN   -4   +1869   .kn

ONE OF THE CARIBBEAN'S most popular tourist destinations, St. Kitts and Nevis, a former British colony, lies at the northern end of the Leeward Islands chain. St. Kitts is of volcanic origin; Mount Liamuiga, a dormant volcano with a crater 227 m (745 feet) deep, is the highest point on the island. Nevis, separated from St. Kitts by a channel 3 km (2 miles) wide, is the lusher but less developed of the two islands. In the 18th century, the famed hot and cold springs gained Nevis the title "the Spa of the Caribbean."

CLIMATE   ▷ Tropical oceanic

WEATHER CHART

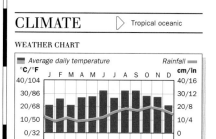

A combination of high temperatures, trade breezes, and moderate rainfall in summer account for St. Kitts' typically Caribbean climate.

TRANSPORTATION   ▷ Drive on left

Golden Rock Intl, Basseterre   1 ship 600 grt

THE TRANSPORTATION NETWORK

| 124 km (77 miles) | None |
| 58 km (36 miles) | None |

Most roads on the islands follow the coast, with just a few crossing through the interior. A new road into the remote southeast peninsula of St Kitts has been completed. The airport on St. Kitts takes large jets; Nevis airport accepts only light aircraft. Regular ferries connect both islands.

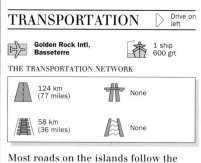

The southeastern peninsula of St. Kitts, looking across to Nevis in the background, on a typical December evening.

TOURISM   ▷ Visitors : population 2:1

83,000 visitors   Down 14% 1995–1997

MAIN TOURIST ARRIVALS

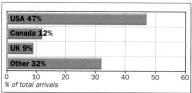

USA 47%
Canada 12%
UK 9%
Other 32%
% of total arrivals

St. Kitts has long targeted the mass US tourist market. Moves to boost tourism include the opening up of the St. Kitts southern peninsula, where work on a new casino, condominiums, a US$50 million hotel and 2,000-seat convention center started in 1998 at Frigate Bay. Most visitors come for sand, sun and the Caribbean mood, although safaris inland to see wildlife and mineral springs have become more popular. On St. Kitts, the old Brimstone Hill fortress has been converted into a museum, as has the Nevis birthplace of Alexander Hamilton, one of the architects of the US constitution.

PEOPLE   ▷ Pop. density medium

English, English Creole   114/km² (295/mi²)

THE URBAN/RURAL POPULATION SPLIT

42%   58%

RELIGIOUS PERSUASION

Anglican 33%
Roman Catholic 7%
Moravian 9%
Other 22%
Methodist 29%

Most of the population is descended from Africans brought over in the 17th century; intermarriage has blurred other racial lines. There was opposition to government plans to grant citizenship to 3,000 Hong Kong business executives in exchange for investment in the islands.

POLITICS   ▷ Multiparty elections

1995/2000   HM Queen Elizabeth II

AT THE LAST ELECTION

National Assembly 11 seats

64% SKLP   18% CCM   9% NRP   9% PAM

SKLP = St. Kitts Labour Party   **CCM** = Concerned Citizens' Movement   **NRP** = Nevis Reformation Party   **PAM** = People's Action Movement
Nevis has its own legislature and executive, the Nevis Island Assembly, which exercises local power.

The center-left SKLP ended 15 years of rule by the right-wing PAM by its victory in the 1995 general election, held three years early. A plan for secession by the government on Nevis was narrowly defeated in a referendum in August 1998.

ST. KITTS & NEVIS

Total Land Area : 360 sq. km (139 sq. miles)

LAND HEIGHT
- 1000m/3281ft
- 500m/1640ft
- 200m/656ft
- Sea Level

POPULATION
- over 10 000
- under 10 000

0   5 km
0   5 miles

N

S

WORLD AFFAIRS

Joined UN in 1983

Preferential access to EU and US markets for sugar is a priority. Hanging was resumed in 1998, when an execution was carried out before there could be an appeal to the London Privy Council.

AID

Recipient

US$7m (receipts)

No change 1996–1997

The IMF in 1999 granted US$2.3 million in emergency financial assistance to support an economic recovery and relief program, following damage by Hurricane Georges. Most aid is from the USA, the EU and the UK.

DEFENSE

No compulsory military service

Army duties undertaken by Volunteer Defense Force

Not applicable

An army existed for six years before it was disbanded to cut government expenditure in 1981. A small paramilitary unit remains within the police; it made a token appearance with US forces during the 1983 invasion of Grenada.

ECONOMICS

Inflation 2.5% p.a. (1985–1996)

US$256m

2.70 Eastern Caribbean dollars

SCORE CARD

❑ WORLD GNP RANKING	177th
❑ GNP PER CAPITA	US$6,260
❑ BALANCE OF PAYMENTS	US$−26m
❑ INFLATION	8.6%
❑ UNEMPLOYMENT	4%

STRENGTHS

Sugar industry, currently UK-managed, with preferential access to US and EU markets. Tourism – source of recent growth – set to expand further.

WEAKNESSES

Dependence on sugar cane industry, itself sensitive to fluctuating world market prices.

EXPORTS

IMPORTS

RESOURCES

Electric power 16,000 kw

220 tonnes

Not an oil producer

8,000 sheep, 14,600 goats, 3,600 cattle, 3000 pigs

None

St. Kitts has no strategic resources. Almost all energy has to be imported, mainly oil from Venezuela and Mexico. Sugar output is insignificant in world terms. New crops, such as Sea Island cotton on Nevis, are being introduced. Offshore fishing has potential.

ENVIRONMENT

No Green MPs

None

Not applicable

Hurricanes are the greatest environmental threat. Hurricane Georges in September 1998 caused damage estimated at US$400 million to sugar crops, housing, and infrastructure. As in the rest of the Caribbean, benefits from encouraging tourism must be set against potential ecological damage. The government has shown sensitivity, with strict preservation orders on the remaining rainforest and on indigenous monkeys.

MEDIA

TV ownership medium

There are no daily newspapers

PUBLISHING AND BROADCAST MEDIA

There are no daily newspapers. The two main weekly newspapers are The Democrat and the Labour Spokesman

1 state-owned station

1 state-owned, 3 independent stations

The government owns a TV and radio station. The funding for two weekly newspapers, *The Democrat* and *The Labour Spokesman*, is provided by the political parties.

CRIME

Death penalty used

St. Kitts does not publish prison figures

Down 7% in 1988

The judicial system is based on British common law. The police are UK-trained. Hanging, not used since 1985, was resumed in 1998 for a convicted murderer before he could appeal to the Judicial Committee of the Privy Council in London. Narcotics-related crimes are rising.

EDUCATION

School leaving age: 17

90%

394 students

Education is based on the former British 11-plus selective system and is mostly state-run. Students attend the regional University of the West Indies, or go on to colleges in the USA and UK.

CHRONOLOGY

A British colony since 1783 and part of the Leeward Islands Federation until 1956, St. Kitts and Nevis achieved independence in 1983.

- ❑ **1932** Pro-independence St. Kitts-Nevis-Anguilla Labour Party formed.
- ❑ **1967** Internal self-government.
- ❑ **1980** Anguilla formally separates from St. Kitts and Nevis.
- ❑ **1983** Independence from UK.
- ❑ **1995** Opposition SKLP wins election.
- ❑ **1998** Nevis referendum narrowly rejects secession.

HEALTH

Welfare state health benefits

1 per 1,124 people

Heart and respiratory diseases, cancers

The government-run health service now provides rudimentary care on both St. Kitts and Nevis. The EU and France provided EC$8 million in 1998 for repairs to the main hospital at Basseterre, which was badly damaged by Hurricane Georges.

SPENDING

GDP/cap. no increase

CONSUMPTION AND SPENDING

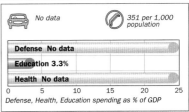

No data

351 per 1,000 population

Defense	No data
Education	3.3%
Health	No data

Defense, Health, Education spending as % of GDP

Native professionals and civil servants have replaced expatriates over the past 20 years. They are now the best-paid group, but there are no great extremes of income. Status symbols include Japanese cars and TV satellite dishes.

S

WORLD RANKING

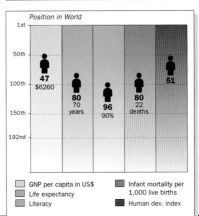

Position in World

47 $6260	80 70 years	96 90%	80 22 deaths	51

- ☐ GNP per capita in US$
- ☐ Life expectancy
- ☐ Literacy
- ☐ Infant mortality per 1,000 live births
- ☐ Human dev. index

ST. LUCIA

OFFICIAL NAME: Saint Lucia   **CAPITAL:** Castries
POPULATION: 142,000   **CURRENCY:** Eastern Caribbean dollar   **OFFICIAL LANGUAGE:** English

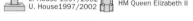

| 1979 | 1979 | Feb 22 | WL | -4 | +1758 | | .lc |

ST. LUCIA IS ONE OF THE MOST BEAUTIFUL islands of the Windward group of the Antilles. The twin Pitons, south of Soufrière, are one of the most striking natural features in the Caribbean. Ruled by the French and the British at different times in its past, St. Lucia retains the character of both. A multiparty democracy, it lives by banana-growing and beach and cruise-ship tourism. Its rainforest makes it a popular ecotourist destination.

CLIMATE   ▷ Tropical oceanic

WEATHER CHART

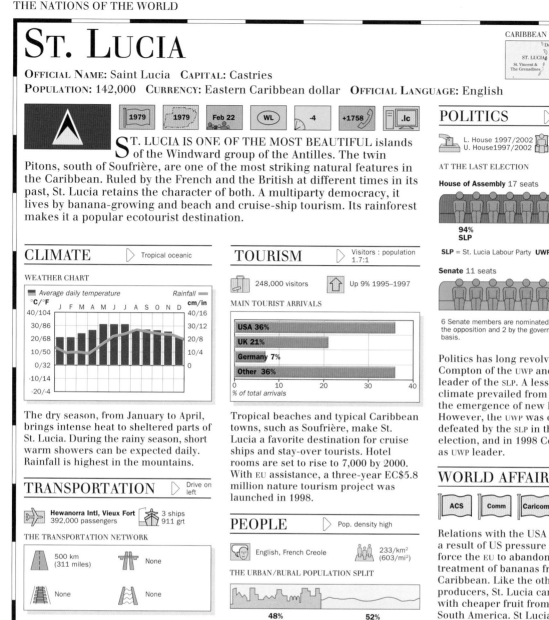

■ Average daily temperature   Rainfall ▬
°C/°F   J F M A M J J A S O N D   cm/in
40/104 ... 40/16
30/86 ... 30/12
20/68 ... 20/8
10/50 ... 10/4
0/32 ... 0
-10/14
-20/-4

The dry season, from January to April, brings intense heat to sheltered parts of St. Lucia. During the rainy season, short warm showers can be expected daily. Rainfall is highest in the mountains.

TRANSPORTATION   ▷ Drive on left

Hewanorra Intl, Vieux Fort
392,000 passengers

3 ships
911 grt

THE TRANSPORTATION NETWORK

| 500 km (311 miles) | | None |
| None | | None |

Roads are confined to the west and southeast coasts. The government ceased to subsidize a direct daily flight from Miami by American Airlines in 1999, but flag carrier Helenair planned to raise direct services in the region.

One of the twin Pitons south of Soufrière, marking the entrance to the Jalousie Plantation harbor.

TOURISM   ▷ Visitors : population 1.7:1

248,000 visitors

Up 9% 1995–1997

MAIN TOURIST ARRIVALS

USA 36%				
UK 21%				
Germany 7%				
Other 36%				

0   10   20   30   40
% of total arrivals

Tropical beaches and typical Caribbean towns, such as Soufrière, make St. Lucia a favorite destination for cruise ships and stay-over tourists. Hotel rooms are set to rise to 7,000 by 2000. With EU assistance, a three-year EC$5.8 million nature tourism project was launched in 1998.

PEOPLE   ▷ Pop. density high

English, French Creole

233/km² (603/mi²)

THE URBAN/RURAL POPULATION SPLIT

48%   52%

RELIGIOUS PERSUASION

Other 10%

Roman Catholic 90%

St. Lucia has a rich, tension-free racial mix of descendants of Africans, Carib Indians and European settlers. Despite relaxed attitudes, family life is central to most St. Lucians, many of whom are practising Roman Catholics. The nuclear family is the norm, but in rural districts, where women run many of the farms, absentee fathers are fairly common. In recent years, women have had greater access to higher education and moved into professions. A bill to permit the occasional use of Creole in parliament was passed in 1998.

POLITICS   ▷ Multiparty elections

L. House 1997/2002
U. House 1997/2002

HM Queen Elizabeth II

AT THE LAST ELECTION

House of Assembly 17 seats

94%
SLP

6%
UWP

SLP = St. Lucia Labour Party   **UWP** = United Workers' Party

Senate 11 seats

6 Senate members are nominated by the government, 3 by the opposition and 2 by the governor-general on a nonparty basis.

Politics has long revolved around John Compton of the UWP and Julian Hunte, leader of the SLP. A less personalized climate prevailed from 1996 with the emergence of new leaders. However, the UWP was overwhelmingly defeated by the SLP in the 1997 general election, and in 1998 Compton returned as UWP leader.

WORLD AFFAIRS   ▷ Joined UN in 1979

| ACS | Comm | Caricom | OECS | OAS |

Relations with the USA are strained as a result of US pressure in the WTO to force the EU to abandon its preferential treatment of bananas from the Caribbean. Like the other Caribbean producers, St. Lucia cannot compete with cheaper fruit from Central and South America. St Lucia supports Japan, an aid donor, in its bid for a permanent seat on the UN Security Council. It participates in discussions for a proposed confederation of Barbados and the seven-country OECS, of which it is a member.

AID   ▷ Recipient

US$24m (receipts)

Down 38% 1996–1997

The USA, the EU, and the UK are main donors. China and Japan granted aid and grant loans in 1998.

DEFENSE   ▷ No compulsory military service

Police force has special service unit for defense purposes

Not applicable

A police force of 500 is supported by a small paramilitary unit. Training is provided by the USA and the UK.

S

St. Lucia

Total Land Area : 620 sq. km (239 sq. miles)

POPULATION

- ●   over 10 000
- •   under 10 000

LAND HEIGHT

- 500m/1640ft
- 200m/656ft
- Sea Level

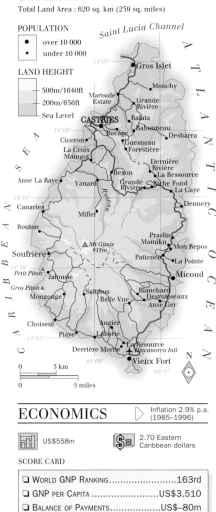

ECONOMICS

▷ Inflation 2.9% p.a. (1985–1996)

US$558m

2.70 Eastern Caribbean dollars

SCORE CARD

- ❏ World GNP Ranking........................163rd
- ❏ GNP per Capita ....US$3,510
- ❏ Balance of Payments.................US$–80m
- ❏ Inflation 6.2%
- ❏ Unemployment.....................................15%

STRENGTHS
Bananas, but preferential access to EU threatened. Tourism, fisheries potential.

WEAKNESSES
Most tourist resorts foreign-owned; profits do not directly benefit St. Lucia.

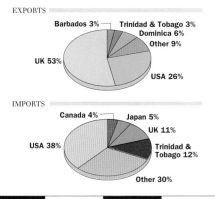

EXPORTS

Barbados 3% | Trinidad & Tobago 3%
Dominica 6%
Other 9%
UK 53%
USA 26%

IMPORTS

Canada 4% | Japan 5%
UK 11%
USA 38%
Trinidad & Tobago 12%
Other 30%

RESOURCES

▷ Electric power 22,000 kw

1,272 tonnes

Not an oil producer

12,500 sheep, 14,700 pigs, 12,500 cattle

None

St. Lucia has no mineral resources and imports most of its energy. Plans exist to develop geothermal energy from the hot springs in the volcanic interior.

ENVIRONMENT

▷ No Green MPs

2% partially protected

Not applicable

St. Lucians are proud of their island and environmental questions arouse fierce debate. In recent years, the greatest controversy has surrounded the decision to allow a luxury hotel development on the ecologically important Jalousie Plantation, which encompasses the extraordinary twin Pitons and includes an important Amerindian archaeological site. The issue illustrates a key problem in St. Lucia, where business pressures to develop tourism can outweigh vital environmental concerns. One notable conservation success has been the St. Lucian parrot. In 1978, there were 150 birds; strict laws against the trade in parrots ensured that by 1992 numbers had risen to 400.

MEDIA

▷ TV ownership medium

There are no daily newspapers

PUBLISHING AND BROADCAST MEDIA

There are no daily newspapers. The *Star* and the *Mirror* are published weekly

2 independent services

1 state-owned, 3 independent services

The privately owned press is free from government intervention. It is possible to receive TV programs from US, Mexican and some Caribbean stations.

CRIME

▷ Death penalty used

1,016 prisoners

Up 17% between 1985 and 1989

Murder is rare, but drug-related deaths are increasing, as is violence in schools. The government in 1998 strengthened the police force to combat rising urban crime.

EDUCATION

▷ School leaving age: 15

82%

2,760 students

Education is based on the British system. St. Lucia has the most Nobel laureates per capita in the world, namely Sir Arthur Lewis (1915–1991, economics) and Derek Walcott (b. 1930, literature).

CHRONOLOGY

In the 17th and 18th centuries, St. Lucia, then an excellent naval raiding base in the Caribbean, was fought over by France and Britain. Ownership alternated before it was finally ceded to Britain in 1814. French influence survives in St. Lucian patois and the local cuisine.

- ❏ **1958** Joins West Indies Federation.
- ❏ **1964** Sugar growing ceases.
- ❏ **1979** Gains independence and joins Commonwealth.
- ❏ **1990** Establishes body with Dominica, Grenada and St. Vincent to discuss forming a Windward Islands Federation.
- ❏ **1997** Hitherto ruling UWP reduced to one seat in general election.
- ❏ **1998** John Compton returns as UWP leader, replacing Vaughan Lewis.

HEALTH

▷ Welfare state health benefits

1 per 2,857 people

Heart and respiratory diseases, cancers

Health care has improved since the 1960s. State hospitals are supplemented by private clinics.

SPENDING

▷ GDP/cap. increase

CONSUMPTION AND SPENDING

16 per 1,000 population

184 per 1,000 population

Defense	No data	
Education	9.9%	
Health	No data	

0   5   10   15   20   25
Defense, Health, Education spending as % of GDP

The island's large-scale banana growers and hotel owners are the richest social group; currently, 19% of St. Lucia's households are considered poor.

WORLD RANKING

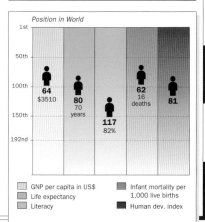

Position in World

- 64 $3510
- 80 70 years
- 117 82%
- 62 16 deaths
- 81

- ☐ GNP per capita in US$
- ☐ Life expectancy
- ☐ Literacy
- ☐ Infant mortality per 1,000 live births
- ☐ Human dev. index

S

ST. VINCENT & THE GRENADINES

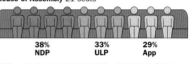

OFFICIAL NAME: Saint Vincent and the Grenadines   CAPITAL: Kingstown
POPULATION: 111,000   CURRENCY: Eastern Caribbean dollar   OFFICIAL LANGUAGE: English

| 1979 | 1979 | Oct 27 | WV | -4 | +1809 | .vc |

AMONG THE MOST ATTRACTIVE of the Windward Islands group, St. Vincent and the Grenadines is renowned as the Caribbean playground of the international jet set. Tourism and bananas are the economic mainstays, and St. Vincent is also the world's largest arrowroot producer. St. Vincent is mostly volcanic; the one remaining active volcano, La Soufrière, last erupted in 1979. The Grenadines are flat, mainly bare coral reefs.

CLIMATE   ▷ Tropical oceanic

WEATHER CHART

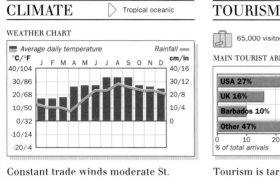

Constant trade winds moderate St. Vincent's tropical climate. Rainfall is heaviest during the summer months. Tropical depressions and hurricanes are likely between June and November.

TRANSPORTATION   ▷ Drive on left

Arnos Vale, Kingstown   1,168 ships 7.1m grt

THE TRANSPORTATION NETWORK

| 484 km (301 miles) | None |
| None | None |

Over EC$50 million was spent on roads between 1991 and 1994. Paved roads encompass most of St. Vincent's coast. Port improvements have been completed in recent years. In 1992, an airport able to take executive jets was completed on Bequia.

Aerial view of Union Island in the Grenadines chain. The government is developing the island as a major yachting centre.

TOURISM   ▷ Visitors : population 1:1.7

65,000 visitors   Up 8% 1995–1997

MAIN TOURIST ARRIVALS

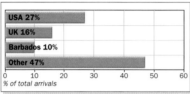

USA 27%
UK 16%
Barbados 10%
Other 47%
% of total arrivals

Tourism is targeted at the jet set and cruise ship rather than the mass-market, and is concentrated on the Grenadines. Mustique attracts Mick Jagger and Princess Margaret among others. Union Island is a playground for the yachting rich, and luxury villas, apartments, golf course, and casino have been built on Canouan. On St. Vincent, Layou is the site of pre-Columbian Amerindian petroglyphs.

PEOPLE   ▷ Pop. density high

English, English Creole   327/km² (846/mi²)

THE URBAN/RURAL POPULATION SPLIT

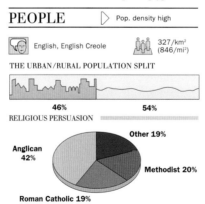

46%   54%

RELIGIOUS PERSUASION

Anglican 42%
Roman Catholic 19%
Methodist 20%
Other 19%

Family life on St. Vincent is heavily influenced by the Anglican Church. Racial tensions are few, and intermarriage has meant that the original communities of descendants of African slaves, Europeans and the few indigenous Carib Indians can no longer be distinguished. Many locals fear that the traditional island way of life is being threatened by the expanding tourist industry.

POLITICS   ▷ Multiparty elections

1998/2003   HM Queen Elizabeth II

AT THE LAST ELECTION

House of Assembly 21 seats

38% NDP   33% ULP   29% App

NDP = New Democratic Party   ULP = Unity Labour Party
App = Six senators are appointed by the Governor-General.

Although prime minister James Mitchell's NDP won a fourth consecutive term in the 1998 general election, it scraped back to power only on a minority vote; the opposition claimed that the election was highly flawed. In 1999 Mitchell advocated a united move by CARICOM to press for a federal presidential system in place of the British monarchy.

ST. VINCENT & THE GRENADINES

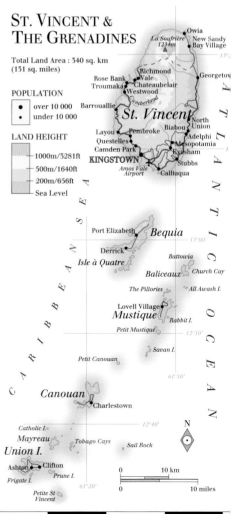

Total Land Area : 340 sq. km (131 sq. miles)

POPULATION
● over 10 000
• under 10 000

LAND HEIGHT
1000m/3281ft
500m/1640ft
200m/656ft
Sea Level

WORLD AFFAIRS ▷ Joined UN in 1980

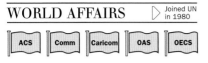

Relations with the USA are strained due to US opposition to the EU's preferential treatment of Caribbean banana imports. St. Vincent supports a united move by CARICOM to promote a presidential system of government in place of the British monarchy.

AID ▷ Recipient

US$6m (receipts) — Down 78% 1996–1997

The EU agreed grant aid of EC$15.5 million in 1998 and the Caribbean Development Bank US$5.1 million in development and housing loans.

DEFENSE ▷ No compulsory military service

US$3m (est.) — No significant change from year to year

St. Vincent has no army. A 500-strong police force, trained by the USA and UK, is part of the Windward and Leeward Islands' Regional Security System.

ECONOMICS ▷ Inflation 3.1% p.a. (1985–1996)

US$272m — 2.70 Eastern Caribbean dollars

SCORE CARD

❏ World GNP Ranking	175th
❏ GNP per Capita	US$2420
❏ Balance of Payments	US$–35m
❏ Inflation	0.4%
❏ Unemployment	40%

Strengths
Bananas, with preferential access to the EU. Great tourist potential. Currency stability. Leading producer of arrowroot starch. Improving infrastructure.

Weaknesses
Little diversification. Vulnerability to US moves to deregulate the world banana market.

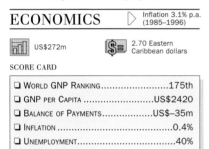

RESOURCES ▷ Electric power 14,000 kw

1,300 tonnes　　Not an oil producer

13,000 sheep, 9,000 pigs, 6,000 cattle　　None

There is a hydroelectric plant on the Cumberland river. Virtually all other energy requirements have to be imported. Some of the Grenadines have no fresh water sources.

ENVIRONMENT ▷ No Green MPs

21% (including marine and semi-protected areas)　　Not available

Hurricanes are the main environmental threat; Hurricane Emily destroyed 70% of the banana crop in 1987. The former inaccessibility of St. Vincent and the Grenadines meant that tourism was a minor environmental threat, and the untouched, idyllic landscape of islands such as Mustique was their attraction. Mustique is reasonably well protected – buildings have been restricted and further development is limited, since fresh water has to be shipped in. On Bequia, the new airport – and increase in visitors – are seen as a mixed blessing. Schemes to develop Canouan have similarly been opposed by locals.

MEDIA ▷ TV ownership medium

Daily newspaper circulation 9 per 1,000 people

PUBLISHING AND BROADCAST MEDIA

There is 1 daily newspaper. The main newspaper is the independent weekly, the *Vincentian*

1 state-owned service　　1 state-owned station

Only one of the four weekly papers is privately owned; the rest are published by political parties. Freedom of the press is written into the constitution.

CRIME ▷ Death penalty used

281 prisoners　　Down 9% in 1990

Rape and robbery are the main local concerns, although on the outlying islands both are very rare. St. Vincent is used for drug transshipment to the USA.

EDUCATION ▷ School leaving age: 15

82%　　677 students

State schools follow the former British 11-plus selective system. There are a few private schools. University students go on to the regional University of the West Indies in Jamaica, although increasing numbers are also studying in the USA and the UK.

HEALTH ▷ Welfare state health benefits

1 per 2,174 people　　Heart and respiratory diseases, cancers

Doctors train at the University of the West Indies. The system is a mixture of state and private hospitals and clinics; facilities are scarcer on the Grenadines.

SPENDING ▷ Not applicable

CONSUMPTION AND SPENDING

No data　　164 per 1,000 population

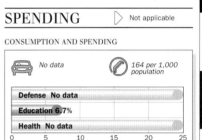

Defense	No data
Education	6.7%
Health	No data

Defense, Health, Education spending as % of GDP

Jet set wealth in the islands coexists with the low wages paid to most local workers. Union Island and Mustique in particular attract the wealthy, who favor jeeps and motor yachts.

WORLD RANKING

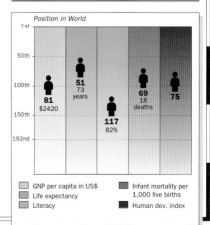

Position in World

- □ GNP per capita in US$
- □ Life expectancy
- □ Literacy
- ■ Infant mortality per 1,000 live births
- ■ Human dev. index

81 $2420 / 51 73 years / 117 82% / 69 18 deaths / 75

S

SAMOA

OFFICIAL NAME: Independent State of Samoa **CAPITAL:** Apia
POPULATION: 170,000 **CURRENCY:** Tala **OFFICIAL LANGUAGES:** Samoan & English

PACIFIC OCEAN

| 1962 | 1962 | June 1 | WS | -11 | +685 | .ws |

S AMOA LIES IN THE HEART of the South Pacific, 2,400 km (1,500 miles) north of New Zealand. Four of its nine volcanic islands are inhabited – Apolima, Manono, Sava'ai (the largest), and Upolu, home to 72% of the population. Rain forests cloak the mountains; vegetable gardens and coconut plantations thrive around the coasts. A German protectorate until 1914, Western Samoa was then administered by New Zealand until independence in 1962.

CLIMATE

▷ Tropical oceanic

WEATHER CHART

The climate is humid and temperatures rarely drop below 25°C (77°F). December to March is the hurricane season.

TRANSPORTATION

▷ Drive on right

Faleolo Apia
191,727 passengers

4 ships
6,200 grt

THE TRANSPORTATION NETWORK

| 375 km (233 miles) | | None |
| None | | None |

Apia port has been improved with Japanese aid. International links are mainly by air. Ferries provide inter-island connections.

TOURISM

▷ Visitors : population 1:2.5

68,000 visitors

Up 36% 1995–1997

MAIN TOURIST ARRIVALS

- American Samoa 37%
- New Zealand 17%
- Australia 11%
- Other 35%

% of total arrivals

Tourism is a rapidly growing industry; it is expected that tourist numbers will exceed the target of 78,000 visitors by the year 2004. Village-based eco-tourism is encouraged.

PEOPLE

▷ Pop. density medium

Samoan, English

60/km² (156/mi²)

THE URBAN/RURAL POPULATION SPLIT

21% 79%

RELIGIOUS PERSUASION

Christian 100%

Ethnic Samoans – around 90% of the population – are the world's second-largest Polynesian group, after the Maoris. The *fa'a Samoa*, Samoan way of life, is communal and formalized. Extended family groups, in which most people live, own 80% of the land, and are not permitted to sell it. Each family is headed by a *matai*, or elected chief, who looks after its political and social interests. Large-scale migration to New Zealand and the USA reflects a lack of jobs and the attractions of Western life. Conflict between the *fa'a Samoa* and modern life is strongest among the young, who have a high suicide rate.

SAMOA

Total Land Area : 2830 sq. km (1093 sq. miles)

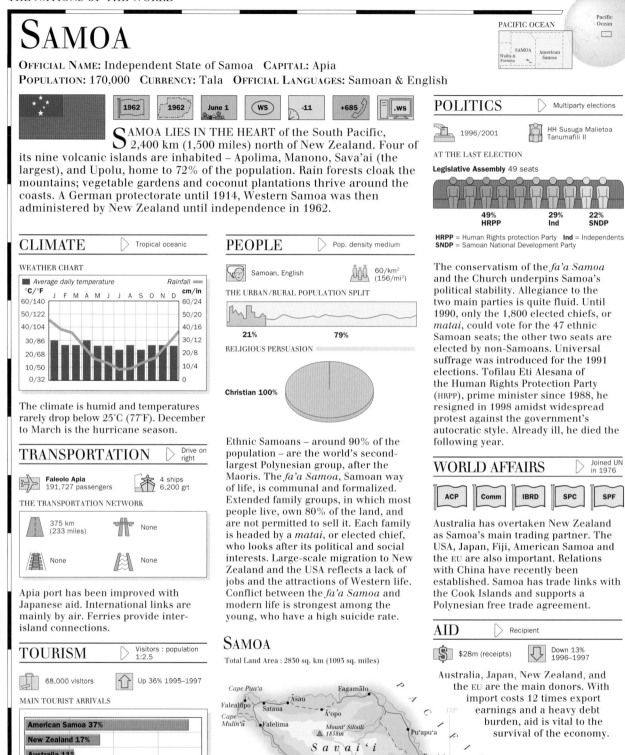

POPULATION
• over 10 000
• under 10 000

LAND HEIGHT
1000m/3281ft
500m/1640ft
200m/656ft
Sea Level

POLITICS

▷ Multiparty elections

1996/2001

HH Susuga Malietoa Tanumafili II

AT THE LAST ELECTION

Legislative Assembly 49 seats

49% HRPP 29% Ind 22% SNDP

HRPP = Human Rights protection Party **Ind** = Independents
SNDP = Samoan National Development Party

The conservatism of the *fa'a Samoa* and the Church underpins Samoa's political stability. Allegiance to the two main parties is quite fluid. Until 1990, only the 1,800 elected chiefs, or *matai*, could vote for the 47 ethnic Samoan seats; the other two seats are elected by non-Samoans. Universal suffrage was introduced for the 1991 elections. Tofilau Eti Alesana of the Human Rights Protection Party (HRPP), prime minister since 1988, he resigned in 1998 amidst widespread protest against the government's autocratic style. Already ill, he died the following year.

WORLD AFFAIRS

▷ Joined UN in 1976

| ACP | Comm | IBRD | SPC | SPF |

Australia has overtaken New Zealand as Samoa's main trading partner. The USA, Japan, Fiji, American Samoa and the EU are also important. Relations with China have recently been established. Samoa has trade links with the Cook Islands and supports a Polynesian free trade agreement.

AID

▷ Recipient

$28m (receipts)

Down 13% 1996–1997

Australia, Japan, New Zealand, and the EU are the main donors. With import costs 12 times export earnings and a heavy debt burden, aid is vital to the survival of the economy.

DEFENSE
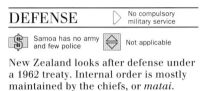

▷ No compulsory military service

💲 Samoa has no army and few police

⬦ Not applicable

New Zealand looks after defense under a 1962 treaty. Internal order is mostly maintained by the chiefs, or *matai*.

ECONOMICS

▷ Inflation 6.2% p.a. (1985–1996)

📊 $199m

💲 2.76–3.02 tala

SCORE CARD

❏ WORLD GNP RANKING 182nd
❏ GNP PER CAPITA $1,140
❏ BALANCE OF PAYMENTS $9m
❏ INFLATION 10.5%
❏ UNEMPLOYMENT................. Underemployment

STRENGTHS
Light manufacturing expanding, attracting foreign, especially Japanese, firms. Tourism growing rapidly with improved infrastructures. Services expanding rapidly since 1989 launch of offshore banking. Tropical agriculture: taro, coconut cream, cocoa, copra are main exports.

WEAKNESSES
Development adversely affected by cyclones. Fluctuating international markets for copra and cocoa. Poor transport facilities. Dependence on aid and expatriate remittances.

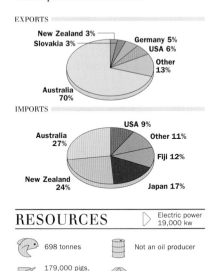

EXPORTS

New Zealand 3%
Slovakia 3%
Germany 5%
USA 6%
Other 13%
Australia 70%

IMPORTS

USA 9%
Australia 27%
Other 11%
Fiji 12%
New Zealand 24%
Japan 17%

RESOURCES

▷ Electric power 19,000 kw

🐟 698 tonnes

🛢 Not an oil producer

🐖 179,000 pigs, 26,000 cattle, 7,000 donkeys

💎 None

With no minerals, Samoa's main resources are its forests and tropical agriculture. The rain forests in lower-lying areas are increasingly exploited for timber. Mahogany and teak plantations are being developed. The volcanic soils, particularly on Upolu, allow a wide range of staple and export crops to be grown. Two-thirds of the population work in agriculture.

***Apia, the capital**, on Upolu, Samoa's second-largest island. It has a central volcanic range of mountains and many rivers.*

ENVIRONMENT

▷ No Green MPs

🔺 None

⬦ Not available

Strict logging regulations have been introduced to halt irreparable damage to the environment; 80% of forests have been replaced by plantations. Overhunting and loss of habitat have endangered rare species of fruit bat and pigeon. Samoa is concerned about its marine resources and has taken a firm stance against driftnet fishing.

MEDIA

▷ TV ownership low

❎ There are no daily newspapers

PUBLISHING AND BROADCAST MEDIA

There are no daily newspapers. The *Samoa Times* and the *Samoa Observer*, are published five times a week

1 state-owned service

1 state-owned, 2 independent services

The government attempted to sue the *Samoa Observer* in mid-1997 for publishing an article criticizing it.

CRIME

▷ Death penalty not used

🔒 Western Samoa does not publish prison figures

⬇ Down 27% in 1992

Alcohol-related violence is a problem at weekends; otherwise, violent crime is almost unknown. Theft is increasing in urban areas.

EDUCATION

▷ Not available

🎓 98%

🎓 562 students

Education is based on the New Zealand system. School attendance is universal and literacy levels high. Samoa's university, established in 1988, has recently been upgraded.

HEALTH

▷ No welfare state health benefits

⚕ 1 per 2,632 people

💀 Heart and cerebrovascular diseases, suicide

The Samoan preference for being big went well with traditional diets. Diabetes and heart disease are rising as people change to Western-style foods.

CHRONOLOGY
Polynesians settled Samoa in about 1000 BCE. Western rivalry after 1830 led to the 1899 division of the islands into German Western and American Eastern Samoa.

❏ **1914** New Zealand occupies Western Samoa.
❏ **1962** Becomes first independent Polynesian nation.
❏ **1990** Cyclone Ofa leaves 10,000 homeless. A year later, Cyclone Val causes worse damage, kills 12.
❏ **1991** HRPP retains power in first election under universal adult suffrage.
❏ **1996** HRPP retains power in elections.
❏ **1997** The country's name is changed from Western Samoa to Samoa.

SPENDING

▷ GDP/cap. no increase

CONSUMPTION AND SPENDING

🚗 No data

💿 46 per 1,000 population

Defense No data				
Education 4.2%				
Health 5.6%				
0	5	10	15	20	25

Defense, Health, Education spending as % of GDP

One of the world's least developed nations according to the UN, Samoa has the lowest wage and highest unemployment rates in Oceania. As a result, emigration is high. Some 60,000 Samoans live in New Zealand, 50,000 in the USA and 10,000 in neighboring American Samoa, where generous US support makes life much easier. Most people depend on subsistence farming and the remittances of relatives for their livelihood. Two-thirds of those with a job work for the government.

S

WORLD RANKING

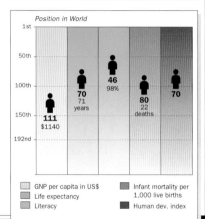

Position in World

1st
50th
100th — 70 / 71 years — 46 / 98% — 80 / 22 deaths — 70
150th — 111 / $1140
192nd

◻ GNP per capita in US$
◻ Life expectancy
◻ Literacy
▨ Infant mortality per 1,000 live births
■ Human dev. index

SAN MARINO

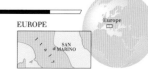

OFFICIAL NAME: Republic of San Marino **CAPITAL:** San Marino
POPULATION: 25,000 **CURRENCY:** Lira **OFFICIAL LANGUAGE:** Italian

| 301 | 301 | Sept 3 | RSM | +1 | +378 | .sm |

PERCHED ON THE SLOPES of Mount Titano in the Italian Appennines, San Marino is, after Nauru, the world's smallest republic. It has maintained its independence since the 4th century. The territory is divided into nine castles, or districts. One third of Sanmarinesi live in the northern town of Serravalle. Today San Marino lives by agriculture, tourism and limited industry. Italy effectively controls most of its affairs.

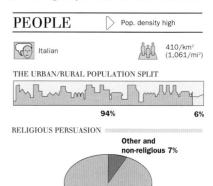

San Marino's second fortress, the Cesta, built in the 13th century, dominates the republic from its highest pinnacle, 755 m above sea level.

CLIMATE
▷ Mediterranean

WEATHER CHART

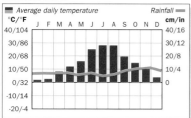

San Marino's Mediterranean climate is moderated by cool sea breezes and its height above sea level. In summer, temperatures can reach 27°C (81°F), while in winter they fall to 7°C (45°F). Rainfall is more common in the winter.

TRANSPORTATION
▷ Drive on right

None   Has no fleet

THE TRANSPORTATION NETWORK

| 237 km (147 miles) | None |
| None | None |

The 24-kilometer (15-mile) highway to Rimini, which has the nearest airport, is San Marino's most important link. Congestion is a major problem, especially during the annual *Mille Miglia* car rally. A funicular railroad climbs the east side of Mount Titano. The railroad to Rimini, closed since 1945, is being rebuilt.

PEOPLE
▷ Pop. density high

Italian   410/km² (1,061/mi²)

THE URBAN/RURAL POPULATION SPLIT

94%   6%

RELIGIOUS PERSUASION

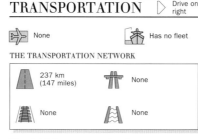

Other and non-religious 7%

Roman Catholic 93%

San Marino citizenship requires 30 years residence, and will no longer be transmissible by marriage under changes planned in 1999. Women gained the vote in 1960, but could not stand for public office until 1973. Twenty thousand San Marino citizens are resident abroad, mainly in Italy.

TOURISM
▷ Visitors : population 21.4:1

535,000 visitors   No change in 1995

MAIN TOURIST ARRIVALS

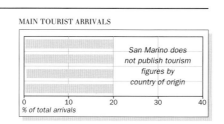

San Marino does not publish tourism figures by country of origin

% of total arrivals

Tourism is the mainstay of San Marino's economy, contributing 60% of government revenue, and employment for 20% of the workforce. Earnings from tourism are equivalent to over 40% of GDP. Half a million visitors annually (and a further 2.5 million day visitors from Italy) come to sample its folklore and museums, and to explore the fortifications of Mount Titano.

The Titano fortresses of *la Rocca*, *la Cesta*, and *Montale*, built during the Middle Ages, command superb views and are the main attractions. Many visitors to San Marino are day-trippers

Religious procession. The official state religion of San Marino is Roman Catholicism, in contrast to Italy, which has no state religion.

from Italy. The republic's tourist industry is boosted by the close proximity of two international airports, at Rimini and Pisa.

Efforts have been made to attract business meetings and conferences with extensive publicity in the Italian media.

The San Marino tourist bureau is also attracting thousands of sports enthusiasts to the republic by hosting a series of top international sporting events. In March, both the Rimini–San Marino marathon and the *Mille Miglia* veteran car meeting are held. May heralds the San Marino Grand Prix, when thousands of Formula One fans descend on the country. June, meanwhile, attracts more motor-racing fans for the World Motocross Championships.

SAN MARINO

Total Land Area : 61 sq. km (24 sq. miles)

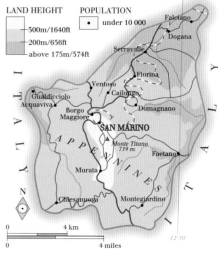

LAND HEIGHT

500m/1640ft
200m/656ft
above 175m/574ft

POPULATION

• under 10 000

Faetano
Dogana
Serravalle
Fiorina
Ventoso
Cailungo
Gualdicciolo
Acquaviva
Borgo Maggiore
Domagnano
SAN MARINO
APPENNINES
Monte Titano 739 m
Faetano
Murata
Chiesanuova
Montegiardino

ITALY

0   4 km
0   4 miles

POLITICS ▷ Multiparty elections

1998/2003 | Captains-Regent Marino Bollini and Giuseppe Arzilli

San Marino is a parliamentary democracy. The party system is parallel to Italy's, with regular coalition governments. The PDCS holds the majority of seats in the Great and General Council and governs in coalition with the PSS. The communists have been in decline since 1957.

WORLD AFFAIRS ▷ Joined UN in 1992

CE | OSCE | | | |

Foreign affairs are effectively decided by Italy, on which San Marino is entirely dependent. In 1992, San Marino acquired a seat at the UN.

AID ▷ Neither

Neither an aid donor nor receiver | Not applicable

San Marino does not receive aid. However, annual subsidies from Italy and free access to the Italian market are essential to the economy.

DEFENSE ▷ No compulsory military service

Combined Voluntary Military Forces | Not applicable

San Marino has a small territorial army and fortification guards. There is no compulsory military service, but males aged 16–55 may be called up in a national emergency.

ECONOMICS ▷ Inflation 5.9% p.a. (1985–1996)

$190m | 1,768.05–1,648.94 Italian lira

SCORE CARD

- ❏ WORLD GNP RANKING........................183rd
- ❏ GNP PER CAPITA $7,830
- ❏ BALANCE OF PAYMENTS $53m
- ❏ INFLATION.............................Not available
- ❏ UNEMPLOYMENT 4%

STRENGTHS
Tourism, providing 60% of government revenue. Light industry, notably mechanical engineering and clothing, with emphasis on sportswear and high-quality prestige lines. Postage stamps.

WEAKNESSES
Need to import all raw materials.

EXPORTS/IMPORTS

Does not publish independent trade statistics; trade movements are included in the Italian totals.

AT THE LAST ELECTION

Great and General Council 60 seats

3% RC

| 42% PDCS | 24% PSS | 18% PPDS | 10% APDS | 3% SR |

PDCS = San Marino Christian Democratic Party **PSS** = San Marino Socialist Party **PPDS** = Progressive Democratic Party **APDS** = Popular Democratic Alliance **RC** = Communist Refoundation **SR** = Socialists for Reform

RESOURCES ▷ Not applicable

None | Not an oil producer and has no refineries

Small numbers of cattle, pigs, sheep and horses | None

San Marino has to import all its energy from Italy. It has no exploitable mineral resources now that the stone quarry on Mount Titano has been exhausted.

ENVIRONMENT ▷ No Green MPs

None | Not applicable

Mount Titano is a unique limestone outcrop in the surrounding Italian plain, and so has a very localized ecosystem.

MEDIA ▷ TV ownership high

Daily newspaper circulation 72 per 1,000 people

PUBLISHING AND BROADCAST MEDIA

There are 3 daily newspapers. Regional Italian newspapers, especially *Il Resto del Carlino*, include coverage of San Marino

1 state-owned service | 1 state-owned, 1 independent service

In 1993, a local TV station, San Marino RTV, began broadcasting. Sanmarinesi can also receive Italian TV.

CRIME ▷ Death penalty not used

San Marino does not publish prison figures | Little change from year to year

San Marino has a low crime rate. Justice is mainly administered in Italy. Until mid-1997 homosexuality was illegal.

EDUCATION ▷ School leaving age: 14

96% | Not applicable

The government spends 13% of the budget on education. Secondary school pupils can go on to Italian universities.

HEALTH ▷ Welfare state health benefits

1 per 375 people | Heart diseases, cancers, accidents

Health care is free and available to all. There is a hospital, but those requiring difficult operations normally go to Rimini for treatment.

CHRONOLOGY

Founded in the 4th century, the Republic of San Marino became one of many medieval Italian city states. It refused to join the unified Italian state created in 1871.

- ❏ **1862** San Marino signs friendship treaty with Italy.
- ❏ **1914–1918** San Marino fights for Italy in World War I.
- ❏ **1940** Supports Axis powers and declares war on the Allies.
- ❏ **1943** Declares neutrality shortly before Italy surrenders.
- ❏ **1960** Women obtain vote.
- ❏ **1978** Coalition of San Marino Communist Party (PCS) and PSS – sole communist-led government in western Europe.
- ❏ **1986** Financial scandals lead to a new PDCS/PCS government.
- ❏ **1988** Joins Council of Europe.
- ❏ **1990** PCS renames itself the Democratic Progress Party (PDP).
- ❏ **1992** Joins UN. Collapse of communism in Europe sees PDCS/PDP alliance replaced by a PDCS/PSS coalition government.
- ❏ **1999** Euro introduced.

SPENDING ▷ GDP/cap. no increase

CONSUMPTION AND SPENDING

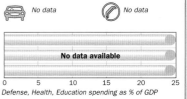

No data | No data

No data available

0   5   10   15   20   25
Defense, Health, Education spending as % of GDP

Living standards are similar to those of northern Italy. The unemployment rate of 4% is below the Italian average rate.

S

WORLD RANKING

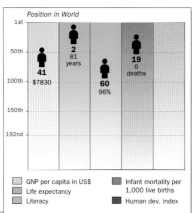

Position in World

41 $7830	2 81 years	60 96%	19 6 deaths

1st — 50th — 100th — 150th — 192nd

- ☐ GNP per capita in US$
- ☐ Life expectancy
- ☐ Literacy
- ☐ Infant mortality per 1,000 live births
- ☐ Human dev. index

SAO TOME & PRINCIPE

OFFICIAL NAME: Democratic Republic of Sao Tome and Principe **CAPITAL:** São Tomé
POPULATION: 131,000 **CURRENCY:** Dobra **OFFICIAL LANGUAGE:** Portuguese

 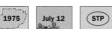

COMPOSED OF the main islands of São Tomé and Príncipe and surrounding islets, the republic of Sao Tome and Principe is situated off the western coast of Africa. In 1975, a classic Marxist single-party regime was established following independence from Portugal, but a referendum in 1990 resulted in a 72% vote in favor of democracy. São Tomé's main concerns are to rebuild relations with Portugal and to seek closer ties with the EU and the USA.

CLIMATE
▷ Tropical equatorial

WEATHER CHART

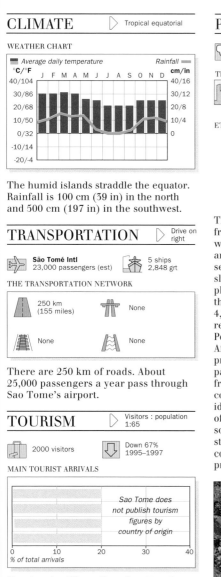

The humid islands straddle the equator. Rainfall is 100 cm (39 in) in the north and 500 cm (197 in) in the southwest.

TRANSPORTATION
▷ Drive on right

São Tomé Intl
23,000 passengers (est)

5 ships
2,848 grt

THE TRANSPORTATION NETWORK

250 km (155 miles)		None	
None		None	

There are 250 km of roads. About 25,000 passengers a year pass through Sao Tome's airport.

TOURISM
▷ Visitors : population 1:65

2000 visitors

Down 67%
1995–1997

MAIN TOURIST ARRIVALS

Sao Tome does not publish tourism figures by country of origin

% of total arrivals

Tourism is still small-scale, attracting wealthy Gabonese and Europeans. Despite recent foreign investment, the islands attract relatively few tourists annually. The first modern hotel opened in 1986.

PEOPLE
▷ Pop. density medium

Portuguese Creole, Portuguese

137/km²
(354/mi²)

THE URBAN/RURAL POPULATION SPLIT

46%   54%

ETHNIC MAKEUP

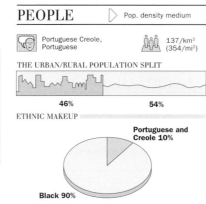

Portuguese and Creole 10%

Black 90%

The population is entirely descended from immigrants, since the islands were uninhabited when the Portuguese arrived in 1470. As the Portuguese settled, they imported Africans as slaves to work the sugar and cocoa plantations. The abolition of slavery in the 19th century, and the departure of 4,000 Portuguese at independence, has resulted in a population which is 10% Portuguese and Creole and 90% black African, although Portuguese culture predominates. Blacks run the political parties. Society is well integrated and free of racial tensions. The main conflicts relate to class or differing ideologies. The extended family still offers the best, if not the only, form of social security. Women have a higher status than in most other African countries; many have attained prominent positions in the professions.

Lush vegetation on São Tomé. *The tropical climate is slightly moderated by the cool Benguela current.*

POLITICS
▷ Multiparty elections

1998/2002

President Miguel Trovoada

AT THE LAST ELECTION

National Assembly 55 seats

56% MLSTP-PSD	29% ADI	15% PCD

MLSTP-PSD = Sao Tome and Principe Liberation Movement – Social Democratic Party **ADI** = Independent Democratic Action **PCD** = Democratic Convergence Party

In 1990, a new multiparty constitution swept away the Marxist single-party state that had existed since independence in 1975. The former leader Pinto da Costa steered the way to multipartyism. Miguel Trovoada returned from 11 years' exile to be reelected as an independent in the 1990 presidential election. The opposition PCD was swept to victory in 1991, and early elections in 1994 saw its return to power as the renamed MLSTP/PSD, which won again in November 1998. Relations between the president and the ruling party are tense and, in December 1998, Trovoada vetoed the first cabinet proposed by Guilherme Posser da Costa, the prime minister. A new cabinet was sworn in in January 1999. The most important pressure groups are the Roman Catholic Church and the trade unions. The main political concerns are to uphold the multiparty system and stimulate growth in the economy.

WORLD AFFAIRS
▷ Joined UN in 1975

| ACP | CEEAC | Lusoph | NAM | OAU |

Sao Tome has achieved rapprochement with Portugal and seeks to maintain links with other former Portuguese colonies, notably Angola. It has always had close ties with Gabon and, while not dropping its ex-communist links, is seeking closer relations with other CEEAC countries, France, and the USA.

AID
▷ Recipient

$33m (receipts)

Down 30%
1996–1997

Sao Tome has one of the highest aid-to-population ratios in Africa. Joining the Lomé convention in the 1970s has meant that Sao Tome has found new sources of aid fairly easily since the demise of communism worldwide. The World Bank and the IMF are the main donors.

S

DEFENSE

No compulsory military service

Defense budget not disclosed

Not applicable

Since independence, the armed forces have figured prominently in national life. They have put down several attempted coups, notably in 1978, after which 2,000 Angolan troops plus Soviet and Cuban advisers were invited in, and in 1988. In 1995, a group of army officers seized temporary control of the country. The national armed forces are believed to number 2,000. With the collapse of the Eastern bloc, Sao Tome now receives military assistance from the West.

ECONOMICS

Not available

$40m

2,390 dobras

SCORE CARD

❏ World GNP Ranking........................189th
❏ GNP per Capita $290
❏ Balance of Payments......................$–2m
❏ Inflation 71.3%
❏ Unemployment 28%

EXPORTS

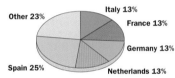

Other 23%
Italy 13%
France 13%
Germany 13%
Spain 25%
Netherlands 13%

Sao Tome & Principe

Total Land Area : 960 sq. km (371 sq. miles)

POPULATION

- ● over 10 000
- • under 10 000

LAND HEIGHT

1000m/3281ft
500m/1640ft
200m/656ft
Sea Level

0   10 km
0   10 miles

Ilha Bombom
Príncipe
1°40'
Santo António
Infante Dom Henrique
Ilha Caroço
1°30'
7°30'
Tinhosa Pequena
Tinhosa Grande
1°20'
(continuation on same scale)
7°30'
6°40'

N
6°30'
0°20'
Ilha das Cabras
SÃO TOMÉ
Santana
Pico de São Tomé 2024m
São Tomé
0°10'
Santa Cruz
Gulf of Guinea
Porto Alegre
Equator
Ilha das Rôlas

RESOURCES

Electric power 6,000 kw

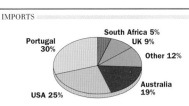

2,800 tonnes

Not an oil producer

4,700 goats, 3,950 cattle, 2,600 sheep

None

São Tomé has no mineral resources, although oil prospecting began in 1990. Almost all energy needs, apart from firewood, are met by oil imported from Angola. São Tomé is very fertile; cocoa estates are finally back to pre-1975 productivity and crop diversification is now a priority. Príncipe has better ports, but its wild scenery makes it more suitable for tourism than farming.

IMPORTS

South Africa 5%
UK 9%
Portugal 30%
Other 12%
Australia 19%
USA 25%

Strengths
Legacy of Portuguese-built infrastructure. Potential for tourism, agricultural and fisheries development. Ability to attract substantial aid.

Weaknesses
Cocoa accounts for 90% of export earnings. Skilful diplomacy has attracted high levels of aid, but mismanagement of these funds has resulted in severe debt. Weak currency.

ENVIRONMENT

No Green MPs

None

Not available

Fish conservation, deforestation for fuelwood, and potential tourism expansion are the major issues.

MEDIA

TV ownership medium

There are no daily newspapers

PUBLISHING AND BROADCAST MEDIA

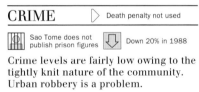

There are no daily newspapers. *Diário da República*, *Notícias* and *Povo* are published weekly by the government

1 state-controlled service

1 state-controlled service

The strict censorship of the Marxist regime has been relaxed since 1988. Radio ownership is high for Africa.

CRIME

Death penalty not used

Sao Tome does not publish prison figures

Down 20% in 1988

Crime levels are fairly low owing to the tightly knit nature of the community. Urban robbery is a problem.

CHRONOLOGY

The entire preindependence history of the islands was as a Portuguese colony exploited by plantation owners.

- ❏ **1972–1973** Strikes by plantation workers.
- ❏ **1975** Independence as Marxist state. Plantations nationalized.
- ❏ **1978** Abortive coup.
- ❏ **1990** New democratic constitution.
- ❏ **1991–1996** Miguel Trovoada elected president; reelected.
- ❏ **1995** Island of Príncipe granted autonomy.

EDUCATION

School leaving age: 14

75%

Not available

Education is compulsory for 7–14-year-olds. All staff at the one technical and three secondary schools are foreigners.

HEALTH

No welfare state health benefits

1 per 3,125 people

Malaria, respiratory and diarrheal diseases

Although health care is not free, Sao Tome has a better system of basic care than other ex-colonial African countries.

SPENDING

GDP/cap. increase

CONSUMPTION AND SPENDING

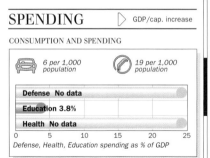

6 per 1,000 population

19 per 1,000 population

Defense No data
Education 3.8%
Health No data

0   5   10   15   20   25
Defense, Health, Education spending as % of GDP

Wealth disparities are not conspicuous. There is a growing business class. Cocoa workers are the country's poorest socio-economic group.

WORLD RANKING

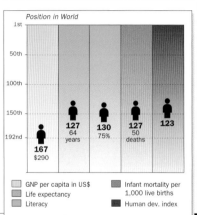

Position in World

1st
50th
100th
150th
192nd

167
$290

127
64 years

130
75%

127
50 deaths

123

GNP per capita in US$
Life expectancy
Literacy

Infant mortality per 1,000 live births
Human dev. index

S

SAUDI ARABIA

OFFICIAL NAME: Kingdom of Saudi Arabia **CAPITAL:** Riyadh
POPULATION: 20.2 million **CURRENCY:** Saudi riyal **OFFICIAL LANGUAGE:** Arabic

 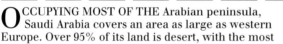

| 1932 | 1935 | Sept 23 | KSA | +3 | +966 | .sa |

OCCUPYING MOST OF THE Arabian peninsula, Saudi Arabia covers an area as large as western Europe. Over 95% of its land is desert, with the most arid part, known as the "Empty Quarter" or Rub al Khali, in the southeast. Saudi Arabia has the world's largest oil and gas reserves and major refining and petrochemicals industries. It includes Islam's holiest cities, Medina and Mecca, visited each year by two million Muslims performing the pilgrimage known as the *haj*. The al-Sa'ud family have been Saudi Arabia's absolutist rulers since 1932.

TOURISM

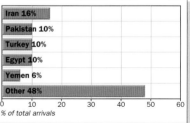

▷ Visitors : population 1:5.6

🧳 3.6m visitors ⬆ Up 75% 1994–1997

MAIN TOURIST ARRIVALS

	% of total arrivals
Iran 16%	
Pakistan 10%	
Turkey 10%	
Egypt 10%	
Yemen 6%	
Other 48%	

(axis: 0 10 20 30 40 50 60)
% of total arrivals

CLIMATE ▷ Hot desert

WEATHER CHART

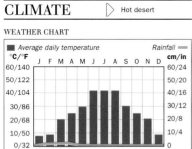

■ Average daily temperature   Rainfall ▬
°C/°F   J F M A M J J A S O N D   cm/in
60/140 / 60/24
50/122 / 50/20
40/104 / 40/16
30/86 / 30/12
20/68 / 20/8
10/50 / 10/4
0/32 / 0

The kingdom's only reliable rainfall is in the southern Asir province, making agriculture viable. The central plateau requires deep artesian wells to water crops. Inland, summer temperatures often soar above 48°C (118°F), but in winter, especially in the northwest, they may fall to freezing point.

SAUDI ARABIA

Total Land Area : 2 149 690 sq. km
(829 995 sq. miles)

POPULATION

- ▣ over 1 000 000
- ◉ over 500 000
- ◎ over 100 000
- ○ over 50 000
- ● over 10 000
- · under 10 000

LAND HEIGHT

- 3000m/9843ft
- 2000m/6562ft
- 1000m/3281ft
- 500m/1640ft
- Sea Level

TRANSPORTATION ▷ Drive on right

✈ **King Abd al-Aziz Intl, Jiddah** 9.8m passengers

🚢 276 ships 1.2m grt

THE TRANSPORTATION NETWORK

| 🛣 91,400 km (57,125 miles) | 🛣 Trans-Arabian Highway |
| 🛤 1,392 km (870 miles) | 〜 None |

Since the advent of oil wealth in the 1970s, a modern transportation infrastructure has been created, linking the main centers of population to the Gulf states, Jordan, and Egypt.

Saudi Arabia discourages foreign tourism. Only Muslim pilgrims, business people and foreign workers are permitted entry. Non-Muslims are banned from the holy cities of Mecca and Medina. Over two million Muslims perform the *haj* (pilgrimage) as a religious obligation in the twelfth month of the Arabic year. Although strict quotas have been imposed, stampedes of pilgrims in 1990 and 1997 killed and injured thousands. The *umra*, or little pilgrimage, has also become popular, since it can be made at any time of year. An estimated $2.5 billion has been spent in recent years on improving *haj* facilities. Jizan on the Red Sea offers excellent scuba diving. The Hejaz railroad and the Nabatean ruins at Medain Salih are of archaeological interest.

Network of modern road junctions spread out across the landscape near Mecca.

S

PEOPLE

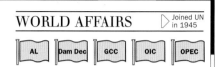

▷ Pop. density low

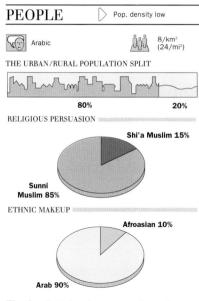

Arabic

8/km²
(24/mi²)

THE URBAN/RURAL POPULATION SPLIT

80% 20%

RELIGIOUS PERSUASION

Shi'a Muslim 15%

Sunni Muslim 85%

ETHNIC MAKEUP

Afroasian 10%

Arab 90%

The Saudis take their name from the ruling al-Sa'ud family. They were united by conquest between 1902 and 1932 by King Abdul Aziz al-Sa'ud, who expelled the Turks.

The vast majority of Saudis are Sunni Muslims who follow the *wahhabi* (puritan) interpretation of Islam and embrace *sharia* (Muslim) law in their daily lives.

The politically dominant Nejadi tribes from the central plateau around Riyadh are Bedouin in origin. The Hejazi tribes from southern and western Saudi Arabia, who have a more cosmopolitan, mercantile background, have largely been displaced from politics. In the eastern province there is a Shi'a minority of some 300,000, many of whom are employed in the oilfields.

Women are obliged to wear the veil, cannot hold a driving license and have no role in public life. They are effectively barred from the workplace except as teachers and nurses.

POPULATION AGE BREAKDOWN

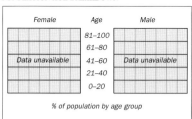

Female	Age	Male
	81–100	
	61–80	
Data unavailable	41–60	Data unavailable
	21–40	
	0–20	

% of population by age group

POLITICS

▷ No multiparty elections

Not applicable

King Fahd ibn Abdul Aziz al-Sa'ud

LEGISLATIVE OR ADVISORY BODIES

Consultative Council 90 seats

Saudi Arabia is an absolute monarchy. The King rules with the assistance of an appointed Council of Ministers.

Saudi Arabia is an absolute monarchy. A 90-man Consultative Council *(majlis ashoura)* is appointed by the king.

MAIN POLITICAL ISSUES
Questioning the ruling family
Following the 1991 Gulf War, a civil rights campaign emerged to challenge the authority of the ruling family, demanding closer adherence to Islamic values. The movement objected to the presence of US troops on Saudi territory and the consequent exposure to "corrupt" Western culture – particular outrage was expressed at the presence of women soldiers. The al-Sa'uds moved swiftly to quash the protest but exiled opponents have continued their activities using fax machines and e-mail.

The succession issue
The question of succession and the possibility of a future power struggle emerged as major issues in early 1996, when King Fahd – suffering the effects of a stroke – formally ceded the management of the kingdom's day-to-day affairs to his half-brother, Crown Prince Abdullah. A few weeks later, Fahd resumed control. It was a move which few doubted had its roots in rivalries which are endemic to the House of Sa'ud.

PROFILE
The royal family rules by carefully manipulating appointments in all sectors of government. Frequent changes of personnel within the armed forces ensure that officers do not build personal followings. All influential cabinet portfolios, apart from those of oil and religious affairs, are held by princes.

Absolutist rule means that domestic politics are virtually nonexistent. The regime retains feudal elements: weekly *majlis*, or councils, are held where citizens can present petitions or grievances to leading members of the royal family. Large cash sums are often dispensed at these meetings.

The legitimacy of the regime is built on its adherence to Islamic values, and the backing of the *ulema* (scholars). It is the stress on Islam that colors Saudi life most. The 5,000-strong *mutawa* (religious police) enforce the five-times-a-day call to prayer, when businesses must close. During Ramadan the *mutawa* are especially active.

WORLD AFFAIRS

▷ Joined UN in 1945

AL | Dam Dec | GCC | OIC | OPEC

Saudi Arabia's strategic importance is derived entirely from its oil reserves and worldwide investments. Relations with the USA are particularly close, and the Saudis remain important institutional investors in the West.

Saudi Arabia's reaction to Iraq's invasion of Kuwait in 1990 demonstrated its determination to maintain the current status quo in the Middle East. It took a leading role in consolidating the Arab coalition against Iraq and gave sanctuary to the Kuwaiti royal family. It also provided military bases to the Western allies and supplied more troops than any other Arab country. However, the continued presence of foreign forces has provoked some hostility; in mid-1996 a bomb attack at a US military complex near Dahran killed 19 US personnel.

Saudi Arabia has been an influential power broker in the civil war in Afghanistan, where its support ensured the success of the *talibaan*.

As the guardian of Mecca, Saudi Arabia has immense importance as the spiritual center for more than one billion Muslims all over the world.

AID

▷ Donor

$235m (donations)

Not applicable

Through the Saudi Fund for Development, the kingdom makes generous loans and grants to other Arab and developing countries, mainly for infrastructure projects. Saudi Arabia promotes Islam through charitable foundations, especially in Africa, Asia and the former Soviet Union. The royal purse also supports scientific and medical research. Since the liberation of Kuwait in 1991, Saudi Arabia has given large sums to countries that supported the US-led alliance, notably Egypt, Syria, Morocco, and Turkey. In addition, the Saudi government substantially reimbursed the USA and the UK for the cost of their expeditionary forces, as well as favoring companies from the allied countries for reconstruction contracts.

S

King Fahd ibn Abdul Aziz *acceded to the Saudi throne in 1982.*

Crown Prince Abdullah ibn Abdul Aziz, *Commander of the National Guard.*

CHRONOLOGY

The unification of Saudi Arabia under King Abdul Aziz (ibn-Sa'ud) was achieved in 1932. The kingdom remains the only country in the world named after its royal family.

- ❏ **1937** Oil reserves discovered near Riyadh.
- ❏ **1939** Ceremonial start of oil production at Az Zahran.
- ❏ **1953** King Sa'ud succeeds on the death of his father Abdul Aziz.
- ❏ **1964** King Sa'ud abdicates in favor of his brother Faisal.
- ❏ **1967** Saudi Arabia joins Jordan and Iraq against Israel during Six Day War.
- ❏ **1969** Air force officers stage abortive coup against King Fahd.
- ❏ **1973** Saudi Arabia imposes oil embargo on Western supporters of Israel.
- ❏ **1975** King Faisal assassinated by a deranged nephew and is succeeded by his brother Khalid.
- ❏ **1979** Muslim fundamentalists led by Juhaiman ibn Seif al-Otaibi seize the Grand Mosque in Mecca and proclaim a *Mahdi* (messiah) on first day of Islamic year 1400.
- ❏ **1981** Formation of Gulf Cooperation Council, with secretariat in Riyadh.
- ❏ **1982** King Fahd succeeds on the death of his brother King Khalid. Promises to create consultative assembly.
- ❏ **1986** Opening of King Fahd Causeway to Bahrain. Sheikh Yamani sacked as oil minister.
- ❏ **1987** Diplomatic relations with Iran deteriorate after 402 people die in riots involving Islamic fundamentalists at Mecca during the *haj* (pilgrimage).
- ❏ **1989** Saudi Arabia signs nonaggression pact with Iraq. Saudi Arabia brokers political settlement to end Lebanese civil war.
- ❏ **1990** Kuwaiti royals seek sanctuary in Taif after Iraqi invasion.
- ❏ **1990–1991** US, UK, French, Egyptian and Syrian forces assemble in Saudi Arabia for Operation Desert Storm. Public executions are halted.
- ❏ **1991** Iraqis seize border town of Al Khafji, but are repulsed by Saudi, US and Qatari forces.
- ❏ **1993** King Fahd appoints 60-man Consultative Assembly.
- ❏ **1996** King Fahd briefly relinquishes control to Crown Prince Abdullah. Bomb attack at US military complex in Dahran kills 19 US citizens.
- ❏ **1997** Expansion of Consultative Council.

DEFENSE

▷ No compulsory military service

💲 $18.2bn   ⬆ Up 3% in 1997

The liberation of Kuwait increased the Saudi armed forces' prestige. Its substantial military contribution to the 1991 Gulf War enhanced its image as a major regional power. Military equipment is purchased mostly from the USA, the UK and France. Weapons systems are advanced and include Patriot missiles and AWACS early warning radar. However, skilled foreign personnel operate many of these: 1,000 US Air Force troops are employed to keep AWACS flying. The air force, the elite branch of the military, was briefly politicized in 1969, when officers attempted a coup. Tribal supporters of the al-Sa'ud regime form the paramilitary National Guard; its commander-in-chief is the crown prince rather than the defense minister.

SAUDI ARABIAN ARMED FORCES

🛡	710 main battle tanks (115 M-1A2, 145 AMX–30, 450 M60A3)	70,000 personnel
🚢	8 frigates, 29 patrol boats	13,500 personnel
✈	432 combat aircraft (56 F–5E, 90 *Tornado* IDS, 24 *Tornado* ADV)	18,000 personnel
🚀	None	

ECONOMICS

▷ Inflation 1.4% p.a. (1985–1996)

📊 $143.4bn   💲 3.75 Saudi riyals

SCORE CARD

❏ WORLD GNP RANKING	287th
❏ GNP PER CAPITA	$7,150
❏ BALANCE OF PAYMENTS	$254m
❏ INFLATION	0.1%
❏ UNEMPLOYMENT	6%

EXPORTS

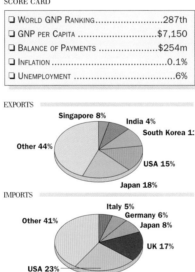

Singapore 8%
India 4%
South Korea 1%
Other 44%
USA 15%
Japan 18%

IMPORTS

Italy 5%
Germany 6%
Japan 8%
Other 41%
UK 17%
USA 23%

ECONOMIC PERFORMANCE INDICATOR

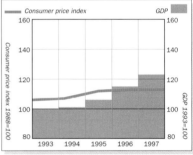

— Consumer price index   ▢ GDP

STRENGTHS

Vast oil and gas reserves. World-class associated industries. Accumulated surpluses and steady current income. Large income from two million annual pilgrims to Mecca.

WEAKNESSES

Lack of skilled workers. Food production requires heavy subsidy. Most consumer items and industrial raw materials imported.

PROFILE

Since the 1970s, strenuous efforts have been made to shift the economy away from its dependence on oil exports and to provide employment for young Saudis. While most investment in oil is from the government, Saudi entrepreneurs have become more involved in secondary industries. Saudi financial markets are poorly developed, however, owing to religious inhibitions about paying or receiving interest. Saudi Aramco, the Middle East's largest employer, controls the national oil industry and has ambitious plans for new exploration. Large sums have been spent on giving Saudi Arabia a US-standard infrastructure, with the aim of providing the basis for a manufacturing economy. The economy, however, remains dependent on foreign workers.

SAUDI ARABIA : MAJOR BUSINESSES

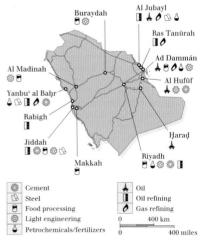

🏭 Cement		⛏ Oil	
Steel		Oil refining	
Food processing		Gas refining	
Light engineering			
Petrochemicals/fertilizers			

0   400 km
0   400 miles

S

RESOURCES

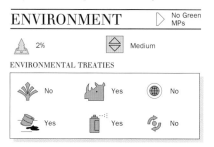

Electric power 20.9m kw

50,782 tonnes

8.25m b/d (reserves 261,200,000,000 bbl)

8m sheep, 4.4m goats, 200,000 cattle

Oil, natural gas, limestone, gypsum, marble, clay, salt

ELECTRICITY GENERATION

Hydro 0%

Combustion 100% (99.8bn kwh)

Nuclear 0%

Other 0%

0   20   40   60   80   100

% of total generation by type

The repository of the world's biggest oil and gas reserves, Saudi Arabia plays a key role in the global economy and is

ENVIRONMENT

No Green MPs

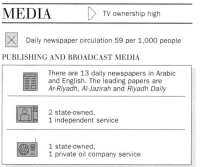

2%

Medium

ENVIRONMENTAL TREATIES

No

Yes

No

Yes

Yes

No

Pollution in the Gulf and Red Sea has threatened some wildlife and their habitats, as have hunters using high-velocity rifles and off-road vehicles. The government has taken steps to confine manufacturing to industrial estates. Environmental legislation is, nevertheless, poorly developed, although planning controls apply in the major cities.

MEDIA

TV ownership high

Daily newspaper circulation 59 per 1,000 people

PUBLISHING AND BROADCAST MEDIA

There are 13 daily newspapers in Arabic and English. The leading papers are *Ar-Riyadh*, *Al-Jazirah* and *Riyadh Daily*

2 state-owned, 1 independent service

1 state-owned, 1 private oil company service

The government imposes total censorship and insists on strict morality in the Saudi press. In 1994, private citizens were banned from owning satellite dishes, reflecting the wish to keep Western broadcasts out of Saudi homes. No allowance is made for Arab satellite broadcasts, recently criticized for covering anti-Islamic issues. *Sharq Al Awsat* (*The Middle East*), published in Saudi Arabia, is a leading Arabic daily. Saudi investors own the influential press agency United Press International.

among the top ten traders of all the world's major industrialized nations.

SAUDI ARABIA : LAND USE

Cropland
Desert
Pasture
Wheat
Dates
Sheep

RUB ' AL KHALI

0   400 km
0   400 miles

CRIME

Death penalty used

Saudi Arabia does not publish prison figures

Up 50% from 1992–1996

CRIME RATES

Murders

1   per 100,000 population

Rapes

1   per 100,000 population

Thefts

84   per 100,000 population

Strict Islamic punishments – stoning for adultery, amputation for stealing, and beheading for murder – are enforced. In 1997 Saudi Arabia acceded to the UN Convention Against Torture.

EDUCATION

Not applicable

73%

273,992 students

Growing numbers of Western-educated Saudis have intensified pressure for social and political change.

THE EDUCATION SYSTEM

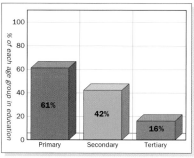

% of each age group in education

100

80

60   61%

40   42%

20   16%

0

Primary   Secondary   Tertiary

In the 1950s, the then Crown Prince Faisal persuaded the religious establishment to give women equal opportunities in education. Much government money has gone into higher education and Islamic universities, though many Saudis still travel abroad to complete their studies.

HEALTH

Welfare state health benefits

1 per 769 people

Diarrheal, respiratory, heart, metabolic and parasitic diseases

In the 1970s, resources were committed to building a network of modern hospitals at the expense of primary health care, which, outside major centers such as Riyadh and Jiddah, remains relatively undeveloped, given Saudi Arabia's huge economic resources. However, large sums have been spent on employing Western expertise. The private sector has also been encouraged. Many Saudis are still sent overseas for treatment, especially for transplant operations, which pose ethical problems for religious leaders.

SPENDING

GDP/cap. increase

CONSUMPTION AND SPENDING

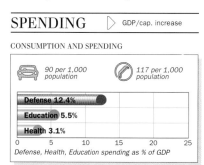

90 per 1,000 population

117 per 1,000 population

Defense 12.4%

Education 5.5%

Health 3.1%

0   5   10   15   20   25

Defense, Health, Education spending as % of GDP

Saudi citizens are among the most prosperous people in the world. The al-Sa'uds have used their wealth to create a cradle-to-grave welfare system. Ownership of TVs, telephones and VCRs is among the region's highest. The distribution of wealth is carefully controlled by the royal family through the *majlis* system: petitioners attend weekly assemblies held by prominent royals and beg favors, which are usually granted. There is no stock market, although shares in public companies are traded privately. Many Saudis refuse to accept interest on deposits with banks, but Islamic banks offer profit-sharing investment schemes as an alternative.

S

WORLD RANKING

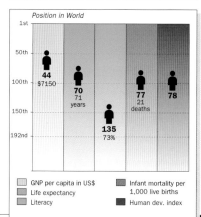

Position in World

1st

50th

100th   44 $7150

70   71 years

77   21 deaths

78

150th

135   73%

192nd

GNP per capita in US$
Life expectancy
Literacy

Infant mortality per 1,000 live births
Human dev. index

SENEGAL

OFFICIAL NAME: Republic of Senegal **CAPITAL:** Dakar
POPULATION: 9 million **CURRENCY:** CFA franc **OFFICIAL LANGUAGE:** French

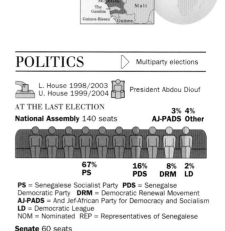
WEST AFRICA

1960 | 1960 | April 4 | SN | +0 | +221 | .sn

S ENEGAL'S CAPITAL, Dakar, lies on the westernmost
cape of Africa. The country is mostly low, with open
savanna and semidesert in the north and thicker
savanna in the south. After independence from France in 1960, Senegal
was ruled until 1981 by President Léopold Senghor, who maintained a
system of virtual single-party rule. He was succeeded by his prime minister,
Abdou Diouf. Senegal became a multiparty democracy in the 1980s.

CLIMATE ▷ Steppe/tropical

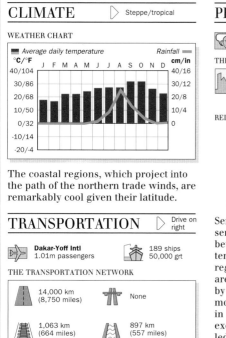

WEATHER CHART

The coastal regions, which project into
the path of the northern trade winds, are
remarkably cool given their latitude.

TRANSPORTATION ▷ Drive on right

Dakar-Yoff Intl
1.01m passengers

189 ships
50,000 grt

THE TRANSPORTATION NETWORK

| 14,000 km (8,750 miles) | None |
| 1,063 km (664 miles) | 897 km (557 miles) |

Dakar is an important west African
port, as well as Senegal serving Guinea,
the hinterland of Mali, and southern
Mauritania. The key rail link to Bamako,
Mali's capital, was built in the 1920s.

TOURISM ▷ Visitors:population 1:30

300,000 visitors

Up 7% 1995–1997

MAIN TOURIST ARRIVALS

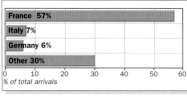

France	57%
Italy	7%
Germany	6%
Other	30%

% of total arrivals

In addition to French package tours to
coastal resorts, tours for African-
Americans to Gorée, an old slave
island, are increasingly popular.

PEOPLE ▷ Pop. density low

Wolof, Fulani, Serer,
Diola, Malinke, Soninke,
Arabic, French

47/km² (121/mi²)

THE URBAN/RURAL POPULATION SPLIT

42%   58%

RELIGIOUS PERSUASION

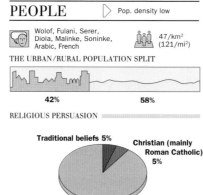

Traditional beliefs 5%
Christian (mainly Roman Catholic) 5%
Muslim 90%

Senegal has a fairly well-developed
sense of nationhood, and intermarriage
between groups has reduced ethnic
tensions. Groups can still be identified
regionally, however. Dakar is a Wolof
area, the Senegal river is dominated
by the Toucouleur, and the Malinke
mostly live in the east and the Diola
in Casamance. The Diola have felt
excluded from politics, and this has
led to a long-running rebellion
in Casamance. A French-influenced
class system is still prevalent and
has become increasingly apparent
in recent years.

POLITICS ▷ Multiparty elections

L. House 1998/2003
U. House 1999/2004
President Abdou Diouf

AT THE LAST ELECTION

National Assembly 140 seats

| | 3% 4% |
| | AJ-PADS Other |

67% PS | 16% PDS | 8% DRM | 2% LD

PS = Senegalese Socialist Party PDS = Senegalse
Democratic Party DRM = Democratic Renewal Movement
AJ-PADS = And Jef-African Party for Democracy and Socialism
LD = Democratic League
NOM = Nominated REP = Representatives of Senegalese

Senate 60 seats

75% PS | 20% Pres | 5% O/s

Three members of the Senate are elected to represent
citizens overseas, 12 are named by the President.

Senegal is a multiparty democracy but
the ruling party has been in power since
the 1950s, and has spread its influence
into throughout the administration. A
constitutional amendment in 1998
ended a restriction preventing the
president from serving more than two
terms. The main issue is the economy,
still recovering from the impact of the
50% CFA franc devaluation in 1994.

WORLD AFFAIRS ▷ Joined UN in 1960

CILSS | Ecowas | FZ | OIC | OMVG

Maintaining good relations with France,
the main ally and aid donor, is pro-
western Senegal's major foreign affairs
concern. Relations with neighboring
Gambia, Mauritania, and Guinea-Bissau
are also a constant preoccupation.
Relations with Mauritania have improved
since tension was caused in 1989
by the expulsion of 200,000
Mauritanians.

SENEGAL

Total Land Area :
192 550 sq. km
(74 336 sq. miles)

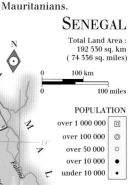

POPULATION

| over 1 000 000 |
| over 100 000 |
| over 50 000 |
| over 10 000 |
| under 10 000 |

LAND HEIGHT

200m/656ft

Sea Level

S

AID
 Recipient

$427m (receipts)　Down 27% 1996–1997

Senegal is one of the highest recipients of aid per capita in Africa, mostly from France, the EU and the World Bank. Aid is used to import 400,000 tonnes of rice annually, but also helps to finance a sizeable civil service, now being cut back. An important structural adjustment program has been in force, backed by the IMF, and was renewed for a further three years in 1998.

DEFENSE
Compulsory military service

$71m　Down 7% in 1997

France maintains an important naval base at Dakar. The army totals 13,350, with a paramilitary force of about 4,000, but the military has never intervened in politics. Senegalese forces took part in Operation Desert Storm in 1991 and intervened in conflicts in Liberia, Rwanda, and the Central African Republic, and to help quell revolts in Gambia and Guinea-Bissau.

ECONOMICS
Inflation 4.4% p.a. (1985–1996)

$4.78bn　601.60–558.62 CFA francs

SCORE CARD
- World GNP Ranking........................109th
- GNP per Capita $540
- Balance of Payments.....................-$58m
- Inflation 1.7%
- Unemployment...Widespread underemployment

Strengths
Skilled industrial workforce in Dakar area. Dakar port linked to interior by good French-built infrastructure. Relatively strong industrial sector.

Weaknesses
Few natural resources exploited. Access to oil potential of Casamance hampered by rebellion and poor transport links. Inadequate diversification. Impact of recent appreciation of French currency.

EXPORTS

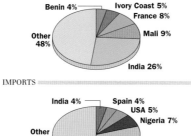

Benin 4%　Ivory Coast 5%
France 8%
Mali 9%
Other 48%
India 26%

IMPORTS

India 4%　Spain 4%
USA 5%
Nigeria 7%
Other 49%
France 31%

RESOURCES
Electric power 231,000 kw

358,677 tonnes　Not an oil producer

4.2m sheep, 3.6m goats, 2.9m cattle　Phosphates, bauxite, salt, natural gas, marble, iron, copper

Senegal's electricity capacity is largely dependent on imported fuel; cheaper supplies are expected to become available soon from the Manantali dam in Mali. Initial explorations suggest oil reserves may exist off Casamance.

ENVIRONMENT
No Green MPs

11% (6% partially protected)　Low

The damming of the Senegal river has caused concern that traditional farming practices, which rely on seasonal floods, may be disrupted. Two major droughts in 1973 and 1983 led to the advance of the Sahara in the west of the country.

MEDIA
TV ownership low

Daily newspaper circulation 5 per 1,000 people

PUBLISHING AND BROADCAST MEDIA

There are 4 daily newspapers, *Le Soleil*, *Wal Fadjiri*, *Sud Quotidien* and *Réveil de l'Afrique Noire*

1 state-owned, 1 private service

1 state-owned, 2 independent services

The independent media flourished with multipartyism. Senegal had the first satirical journal in Africa with the founding of *Le Politicien* in 1978.

CRIME
Death penalty not used

Senegal does not publish prison figures　Little change from year to year

Senegal has comparatively low crime rates, though levels are on the increase in Dakar and the surrounding shanty towns, where gangs are based.

The mosque in Touba, religious capital of the Muslim Mouride sect, which was founded in 1887 in Senegal's groundnut-growing district.

CHRONOLOGY
France colonized Senegal, a major entrepôt from the 15th century, in 1890. Dakar was the capital of French West Africa.

- ❑ **1885** Gambia split off as British enclave within Senegal.
- ❑ **1960** Independence under socialist president Léopold Sédar Senghor.
- ❑ **1966** One-party state.
- ❑ **1976** Three-party system.
- ❑ **1981** Abdou Diouf president. Full multipartyism restored.

EDUCATION
School leaving age: 13

35%　24,081 students

Illiteracy is the major challenge faced by the system. There are universities at Dakar and Saint-Louis.

HEALTH
No welfare state health benefits

1 per 10,000 people　Malaria, diarrheal diseases

Senegal's state health system is rudimentary. Rich Senegalese are well served by private clinics.

SPENDING
GDP/cap. increase

CONSUMPTION AND SPENDING

10 per 1,000 population　13 per 1,000 population

Defense 1.6%
Education 3.6%
Health 2.3%

0　5　10　15　20　25
Defense, Health, Education spending as % of GDP

Senegal's wealth disparities are considerable and poverty is widespread. Those close to the government are the wealthiest group.

S

WORLD RANKING

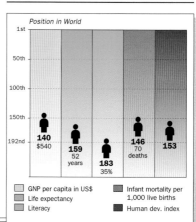

Position in World

1st
50th
100th
150th
192nd

140 $540
159 52 years
183 35%
146 70 deaths
153

- ❑ GNP per capita in US$
- ❑ Life expectancy
- ❑ Literacy
- ❑ Infant mortality per 1,000 live births
- ❑ Human dev. index

SEYCHELLES

OFFICIAL NAME: Republic of the Seychelles **CAPITAL:** Victoria
POPULATION: 75,000 **CURRENCY:** Seychelles rupee **OFFICIAL LANGUAGE:** French Creole

1976	1976	June 18	SY	+4	+248	.sc

THE 115 ISLANDS of the Seychelles, lying in the Indian Ocean, support unique flora and fauna, including the giant tortoise and the world's largest seed, the *coco-de-mer*. Formerly a UK colony and then under one-party rule for 16 years, the Seychelles became a multiparty democracy in 1993. The economy is reliant on tourism.

CLIMATE ▷ Tropical oceanic

WEATHER CHART

The islands have a tropical oceanic climate, with very little variation in temperature.

TRANSPORTATION ▷ Drive on left

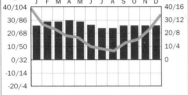

Pointe Larue Intl, Mahé
155,000 passengers

7 ships
3,720 grt

THE TRANSPORTATION NETWORK

219km (136 miles)	None
None	None

Nine islands have airstrips. The public transportation fleet and roads are being renewed. Victoria's deep-sea harbor is one of the best run in the region.

TOURISM ▷ Visitors : population 1.7:1

130,000 visitors

Up 7% 1995–1997

MAIN TOURIST ARRIVALS

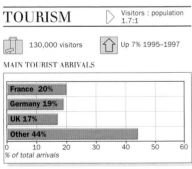

| France 20% |
| Germany 19% |
| UK 17% |
| Other 44% |

% of total arrivals

Tourism has become the mainstay of the economy, and employs 30% of the workforce. New hotels must comply with laws to protect the islands' beauty and unique wildlife. There is substantial foreign investment, but at the same time international competition is growing.

PEOPLE ▷ Pop. density high

French Creole, English, French

279/km² (722/mi²)

THE URBAN/RURAL POPULATION SPLIT

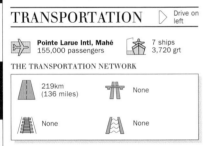

54% 46%

RELIGIOUS PERSUASION

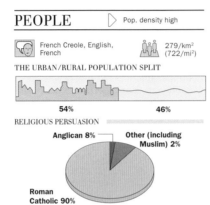

Anglican 8% Other (including Muslim) 2%

Roman Catholic 90%

The Seychelles islands were uninhabited before French settlers arrived in the 1770s. Intermarriage between different ethnic groups has resulted in a markedly homogeneous population. The Creoles are the descendants of the French settlers and of the Africans who were settled on the islands by British administrators. There are small Chinese and Indian minorities. Almost 90% of Seychellois live on Mahé. Population growth has been very low, as about 1,000 people a year have been emigrating. This trend may be reversed as a result of the transition to democracy.

POLITICS ▷ Multiparty elections

1998/2003

President France-Albert René

AT THE LAST ELECTION

National Assembly 34 seats

88% SPPF   9% 3% UO DP

SPPF = Seychelles People's Progressive Front **UO** = United Opposition **DP** = Democratic Party

In 1993, the Seychelles returned to democracy after 16 years of one-party rule under President René, who as prime minister had seized power in a coup soon after independence. Opposition divisions at the 1993 elections, however, allowed René to retain the presidency. His SPPF retained its majority in the 1998 elections; having dramatically changed its former leftist ideology, it has adopted reforms, encouraging privatization. The highlight is a scheme to develop the Seychelles as an International Trading Zone, with free-port facilities and new industry.

WORLD AFFAIRS ▷ Joined UN in 1976

ACP	Comm	IOC	NAM	OAU

The Seychelles is non-aligned, but its strategic location encourages competing world powers to seek its friendship. It claims the Chagos Archipelago from the UK. Trade accords exist with other Indian Ocean states.

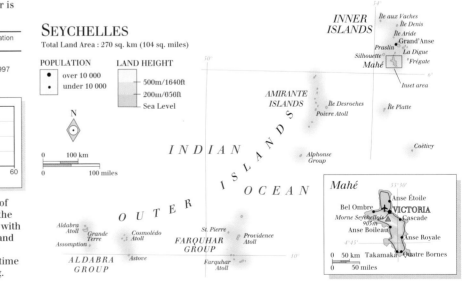

SEYCHELLES

Total Land Area : 270 sq. km (104 sq. miles)

POPULATION
• over 10 000
• under 10 000

LAND HEIGHT
500m/1640ft
200m/656ft
Sea Level

INNER ISLANDS

Île aux Vaches
Île Denis
Île Aride
Grand'Anse
Praslin
La Digue
Silhouette
Mahé
Frégate
Inset area

AMIRANTE ISLANDS
Île Desroches
Poivre Atoll
Île Platte

INDIAN OCEAN

Alphonse Group
Coëtivy

OUTER ISLANDS

Aldabra Atoll
Grande Terre
Assomption
Cosmolédo Atoll
St. Pierre
Providence Atoll
FARQUHAR GROUP
Astove
Farquhar Atoll
ALDABRA GROUP

Mahé
Bel Ombre
Morne Seychellois 905m
Anse Boileau
VICTORIA
Anse Étoile
Cascade
Anse Royale
Takamaka Quatre Bornes

AID

 Recipient

$15m (receipts)   Down 21% 1996–1997

Multilateral agencies, notably the EU and the Arab Development Fund, support development projects. In 1996, $13 million was spent on protecting the environment, improving transport and rehabilitating Victoria Market. Bilateral aid comes mostly from France, the USA, the UK, Australia, and Japan.

DEFENSE

No compulsory military service

$10m   Down 10% in 1997

The Seychelles has a 300-strong army, and a paramilitary guard of 1,500. The latter includes a small coast guard made up of air and sea forces. The army, set up in 1977, was initially trained by Tanzania, and Tanzanian troops were brought in for three years after a coup attempt in 1981. North Korea provided advisers until 1989.

ECONOMICS

Inflation 3.2% p.a. (1985–1996)

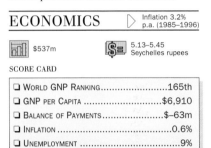

$537m   5.13–5.45 Seychelles rupees

SCORE CARD

❑ WORLD GNP RANKING	165th
❑ GNP PER CAPITA	$6,910
❑ BALANCE OF PAYMENTS	$–63m
❑ INFLATION	0.6%
❑ UNEMPLOYMENT	9%

STRENGTHS

Tourism. Fish exports, especially shrimps and tuna. Profitable re-export trade. International Trading Zone attracting foreign industrial interest. Copra. Cinnamon. Tea.

WEAKNESSES

Growing deficits in early 1990s, caused by drop in tourism following 1991 Gulf War, spending on hosting 1993 Indian Ocean Games, and cost of four recent elections. High debt servicing costs. Reliance on food imports, especially for tourist industry. Copra production declining. Reliance on expatriate labor.

EXPORTS

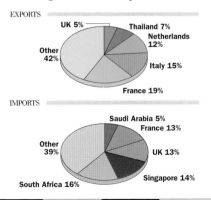

UK 5%   Thailand 7%
Netherlands 12%
Other 42%
Italy 15%
France 19%

IMPORTS

Saudi Arabia 5%
France 13%
Other 39%
UK 13%
Singapore 14%
South Africa 16%

One of the 40 central islands. *These are mostly mountainous, with lush vegetation, and are the only granitic islands in the world.*

RESOURCES

Electric power 28,000 kw

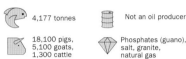

4,177 tonnes   Not an oil producer

18,100 pigs, 5,100 goats, 1,300 cattle   Phosphates (guano), salt, granite, natural gas

There are virtually no mineral resources. All fuel is imported; only three islands have electricity. Offshore discoveries of natural gas have spurred a search for oil. Natural habitat and free trade environment are great assets.

ENVIRONMENT

No Green MPs

95%   Not available

The Seychelles has been praised for its commitment to conservation. It has two natural World Heritage sites. and helped promote the idea of whale sanctuaries

MEDIA

TV ownership medium

Daily newspaper circulation 46 per 1,000 people

PUBLISHING AND BROADCAST MEDIA

There is 1 daily newspaper, the government-owned *Seychelles Nation*

1 state-owned service   1 state-owned service

The state broadcasting company has been reorganized and is now ostensibly free of government control. Private periodicals are now permitted.

CRIME

Death penalty not used

1,060 prisoners   Down 41% from 1992–1996

Violent crime is rare in the Seychelles. The main concern is the increasing rate of petty theft.

EDUCATION

School leaving age: 16

84%   1,682 students

Private schools have operated since 1993. National Youth Service is mandatory for entry to higher education. Some 13% of state expenditure is on education.

CHRONOLOGY

The French claimed the islands in 1756. Franco-British rivalry for control ended when France ceded them to the UK in 1815.

- ❑ **1952** Political parties formed, led by F. A. René (pro-independence) and James Mancham (pro-UK rule).
- ❑ **1965** UK returns Desroches, Aldabra, and Farquhar islands, which are leased to USA to 1976.
- ❑ **1976** Independence. Coalition with Mancham president, René premier. US tracking station set up on Mahé.
- ❑ **1977** René takes over in coup.
- ❑ **1979** One-party socialist state.
- ❑ **1979–1987** Several coup attempts.
- ❑ **1992** Politicians in exile return.
- ❑ **1993** Democratic elections.

HEALTH

Welfare state health benefits

1 per 962 people   Heart and cerebrovascular diseases, cancers

State health care is free. Private medicine is allowed under new social legislation. Life expectancy is over 70 years.

SPENDING

GDP/cap. no increase

CONSUMPTION AND SPENDING

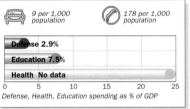

9 per 1,000 population   178 per 1,000 population

Defense 2.9%
Education 7.5%
Health No data

0   5   10   15   20   25
Defense, Health, Education spending as % of GDP

Living standards are the highest among OAU states. There are no slums in the Seychelles, and the state welfare system caters for all.

S

WORLD RANKING

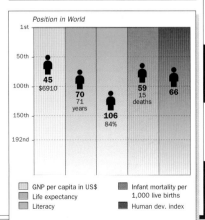

Position in World

1st
50th
100th
150th
192nd

45 $6910
70 71 years
106 84%
59 15 deaths
66

◻ GNP per capita in US$	◼ Infant mortality per 1,000 live births
◻ Life expectancy	
◻ Literacy	◼ Human dev. index

513

SIERRA LEONE

WEST AFRICA

OFFICIAL NAME: Republic of Sierra Leone **CAPITAL:** Freetown
POPULATION: 4.6 million **CURRENCY:** Leone **OFFICIAL LANGUAGE:** English

| 1961 | 1961 | April 27 | WAL | 0 | +232 | .sl |

THE WEST AFRICAN STATE of Sierra Leone was founded by the British in 1787 as a settlement for Africans freed from slavery. The terrain rises from coastal lowlands to mountains in the northeast. A democratic government took office in 1996 against a background of bloody rebellion. Sierra Leone soon plunged into a bloodbath of savage civil war, until a 1999 peace agreement which was greeted by public rejoicing.

CLIMATE

▷ Tropical equatorial/ monsoon

WEATHER CHART

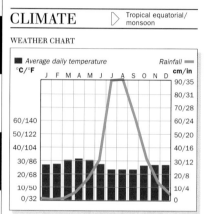

Coastal rainfall can be as high as 500 cm (197 in) a year, making Sierra Leone one of the wettest places in coastal west Africa. Humidity is consistently high – about 80% – during the rainy season. The dusty, northeasterly *harmattan* wind often blows during the hotter dry season from November to April. The northeastern savannas are drier, with 190–250 cm (75–98 in) of rain, but are one of the hottest areas.

TRANSPORTATION

▷ Drive on right

Lungi Intl, Freetown
84,547 passengers

56, ships
19,361 grt

THE TRANSPORTATION NETWORK

| 1,284 km (798 miles) | None |
| 84 km (52 miles) | 800 km (497 miles) |

Little progress has been made in improving Sierra Leone's roads. The 300-km (186-mile) narrow-gauge railroad was abandoned in 1971 as uneconomic, although 84 km (52 miles) of track still runs to the closed iron ore mines at Marampa. Having failed in 1987, Sierra Leone's national airline resumed flights – to Paris only – in 1991. The airport is across the estuary from the capital. The only link between the two is a limited ferry service.

TOURISM

▷ Visitors : population 1:95.8

48,000 visitors

Up 14% in 1997

MAIN TOURIST ARRIVALS

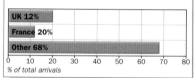

UK 12%
France 20%
Other 68%

% of total arrivals

Sierra Leone has never attracted many tourists, apart from occasional cruise ship calls. Years of civil war have prevented the development of tourism. Among the chief potential attractions are the beaches along the Freetown peninsula, at present virtually undeveloped.

SIERRA LEONE

Total Land Area : 71 620 sq. km (27 652 sq. miles)

POPULATION

◎ over 100 000
● over 10 000
• under 10 000

LAND HEIGHT

1000m/3281ft
500m/1640ft
200m/656ft
Sea Level

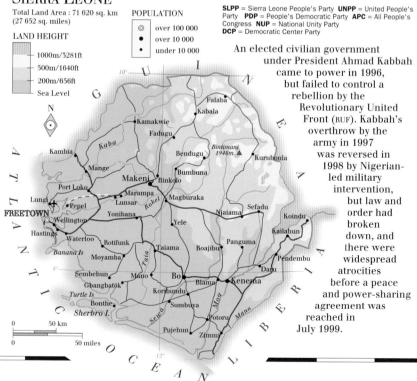

PEOPLE

▷ Pop. density medium

Mende, Temne, Krio, English

64/km² (166/mi²)

THE URBAN/RURAL POPULATION SPLIT

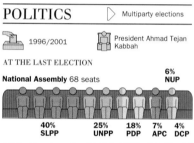

36% 64%

ETHNIC MAKEUP

Kuranko 4%
Limba 8%
Mende 35%
Other 21%
Temne 32%

Freetown was founded as a settlement for freed slaves. Its citizens' British and North American origins account for Sierra Leone's strongly anglicized Creole culture. Hundreds of thousands of people fled to neighboring countries during the civil war.

POLITICS

▷ Multiparty elections

1996/2001

President Ahmad Tejan Kabbah

AT THE LAST ELECTION

National Assembly 68 seats

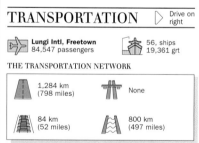

6% NUP

40% SLPP
25% UNPP
18% PDP
7% APC
4% DCP

SLPP = Sierra Leone People's Party **UNPP** = United People's Party **PDP** = People's Democratic Party **APC** = All People's Congress **NUP** = National Unity Party **DCP** = Democratic Center Party

An elected civilian government under President Ahmad Kabbah came to power in 1996, but failed to control a rebellion by the Revolutionary United Front (RUF). Kabbah's overthrow by the army in 1997 was reversed in 1998 by Nigerian-led military intervention, but law and order had broken down, and there were widespread atrocities before a peace and power-sharing agreement was reached in July 1999.

WORLD AFFAIRS

▷ Joined UN in 1961

| Comm | Ecowas | MRU | OAU | OIC |

Concern over instability in Sierra Leone in the 1990s prompted a Nigerian-led Ecowas military intervention.

AID

▷ Recipient

💲 $130m (receipts)

⬇ Down 33% 1996–1997

Sierra Leone has not been able to fulfill the terms of the aid package agreed with the IMF in 1989. Funds have been diverted to cope with the humanitarian needs of refugees from Liberia, internal migrants fleeing the civil war, and the near collapse of public services.

DEFENSE

▷ No compulsory military service

💲 $52m

⬆ Up 11% in 1997

After last intervening in politics in 1968, the army resumed a central role in the 1992 and 1997 coups. It has little credibility, however, as a fighting force.

ECONOMICS

▷ Inflation 58.3% p.a. (1985–1996)

📊 $762m

💲 900.00–1,500.00 leones

SCORE CARD

❑ World GNP Ranking	161st
❑ GNP per Capita	$160
❑ Balance of Payments	$–127m
❑ Inflation	14.9%
❑ Unemployment	Widespread

STRENGTHS
Diamonds, although much of the output is smuggled. Some bauxite and rutile production. National reconciliation and a more dynamic economic approach should encourage flows of aid needed in post-war reconstruction.

WEAKNESSES
Years of instability have affected the most productive areas of the country, including diamond fields.

EXPORTS

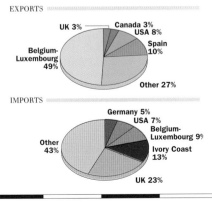

UK 3%
Canada 3%
USA 8%
Spain 10%
Belgium-Luxembourg 49%
Other 27%

IMPORTS

Germany 5%
USA 7%
Belgium-Luxembourg 9%
Ivory Coast 13%
Other 43%
UK 23%

RESOURCES

▷ Electric power 126,000 kw

🐟 62,313 tonnes

🛢 Not an oil producer; refines 10,000 b/d

🐄 400,000 cattle, 350,000 sheep, 190,000 goats

💎 Diamonds, rutile, bauxite, gold, titanium

The large diamond deposits need fresh investment as areas currently being mined become depleted. The southeast is the most fertile region.

ENVIRONMENT

▷ No Green MPs

🔺 1%

⬇ Low

Population pressures and the neglect resulting from years of civil war have depleted the land's productivity.

MEDIA

▷ TV ownership low

❌ Daily newspaper circulation 5 per 1,000 people

PUBLISHING AND BROADCAST MEDIA

There is 1 daily newspaper, the *Daily Mail*, published by the government and numerous periodicals.

1 state-owned service

1 state-owned service

Freetown's Creole population is well served by a broad range of periodicals. President Kabbah's government has promised press freedom.

CRIME

▷ Death penalty used

Sierra Leone does not publish prison figures

⬆ Crime is rising

Widespread instability and the ready availability of weapons led to savage atrocities and mass looting of resources during the civil war, when law and order collapsed. Illegal diamond mining and smuggling are among the most lucrative crimes, in which several government members have been implicated over the years.

EDUCATION

▷ Not available

👤 33%

🎓 4,742 students

Freetown has a long tradition of education, and its university, Fourahbay College, became affiliated with Durham University in the UK in 1876. In recent times, its students have often been active in political dissent. Educational provision has deteriorated with the economic situation over the past decade.

HEALTH

▷ No welfare state health benefits

1 per 14,300 people

Communicable diseases, malaria, malnutrition

Only traditional health care is available outside the capital. Average life expectancy fell by 1997 to 37 years, the lowest in the world.

The main street, Kabala. In 1999, Sierra Leone was bottom of the UN's Human Development Index.

CHRONOLOGY

Freetown was founded in 1787 and became a British colony in 1808; the interior was annexed in 1896.

- ❑ **1961** Independence.
- ❑ **1978** Single-party republic under Siaka Stevens. National bankruptcy.
- ❑ **1991** RUF rebellion starts.
- ❑ **1992** Army coup.
- ❑ **1996** Civilian rule under President Kabbah. Civil war continues.
- ❑ **1997** Army coup.
- ❑ **1998** ECOMOG forces restore Kabbah to power; fighting continues.
- ❑ **1999** Peace and power-sharing deal.

SPENDING

▷ GDP/cap. no increase

CONSUMPTION AND SPENDING

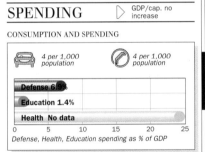

🚗 4 per 1,000 population

⬤ 4 per 1,000 population

Defense 6.9%
Education 1.4%
Health No data

0   5   10   15   20   25
Defense, Health, Education spending as % of GDP

The UN ranked Sierra Leoneans as the world's poorest people in 1999, in terms of quality of life. Wealth is associated with political power.

S

WORLD RANKING

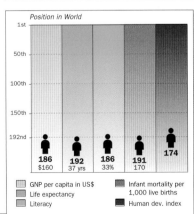

Position in World

1st
50th
100th
150th
192nd

186 $160
192 37 yrs
186 33%
191 170
174

☐ GNP per capita in US$
☐ Life expectancy
☐ Literacy
☐ Infant mortality per 1,000 live births
☐ Human dev. index

SINGAPORE

OFFICIAL NAME: Republic of Singapore **CAPITAL:** Singapore City
POPULATION: 3.5 million **CURRENCY:** Singapore dollar **OFFICIAL LANGUAGES:** Malay, Chinese, Tamil and English

1965 | 1965 | Aug 9 | SGP | +8 | +65 | .sg

AN ISLAND STATE linked to the southernmost tip of the Malay peninsula by a causeway, Singapore was largely uninhabited between the 14th and 18th centuries. In 1819, an official of the British East India Company, Stamford Raffles, recognized the island's strategic position on key trade routes and established Singapore as a trading settlement. Today, Singapore is still one of the most important entrepôts in Asia.

CLIMATE ▷ Tropical equatorial

WEATHER CHART

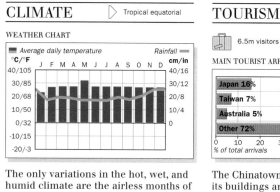

The only variations in the hot, wet, and humid climate are the airless months of September and March, when the trade winds change direction.

TRANSPORTATION ▷ Drive on left

✈ **Changi International**
24m passengers

🚢 1,480 ships
16m grt

THE TRANSPORTATION NETWORK

🛣 3,056 km (1,900 miles)	🛤 148 km (92 miles)		
🚇 26 km (16 miles)	None		

The Mass Rapid Transit System (subway), completed in 1991, is among the world's most efficient. Space for new roads has run out and monthly auctions are held to sell certificates entitling people to buy from a quota of new cars. The massive port at Pasir Panjang is being expanded on reclaimed land.

The financial center. More than a quarter of Singapore's GDP is generated by financial and business services.

TOURISM ▷ Visitors : population 1.9:1

🧳 6.5m visitors

⬆ Up 2% 1995–1997

MAIN TOURIST ARRIVALS

Japan 16%
Taiwan 7%
Australia 5%
Other 72%

0 10 20 30 40 50 60 70 80
% of total arrivals

The Chinatown district is a tourist asset; its buildings are being restored. A Singaporean consortium is involved in developing a tourist resort on Indonesia's Bintan Island, some 45 km (28 miles) across the Strait of Singapore.

PEOPLE ▷ Pop. density high

Chinese, Malay, Tamil, English

5,738/km² (14,861/mi²)

THE URBAN/RURAL POPULATION SPLIT

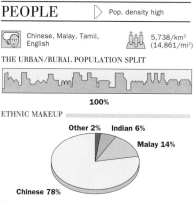

100%

ETHNIC MAKEUP

Other 2% Indian 6%
Malay 14%
Chinese 78%

Singapore is dominated by the Chinese, who make up 78% of the community; the old English-speaking Straits Chinese and newer Mandarin-speakers are now well integrated. Indigenous Malays are generally the poorest group. There is now little overt ethnic tension. There is a significant foreign work force, but quotas and special taxes are imposed on their employers. A labor shortage has forced the government to try to attract scientists from the CIS, eastern Europe and Hong Kong. Society is highly regulated and government campaigns to improve public behavior are frequent.

POLITICS ▷ Multiparty elections

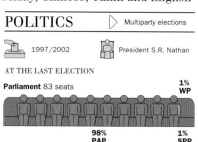

1997/2002

President S.R. Nathan

AT THE LAST ELECTION

Parliament 83 seats

1% WP
98% PAP
1% SPP

PAP = People's Action Party **SPP** = Singapore People's Party
WP = Workers' Party
In addition to the 83 elected members of Parliament, up to three may be nominated from the losers with the most votes.

Singapore is a multiparty democracy, although the ruling PAP effectively controls all parts of the political process and much of the economy. Following a constitutional amendment in 1993, Ong Teng Cheong became the first directly elected president.

The government promotes the development of Singapore as a strong free-market economy, while continuing to place emphasis on social welfare. There are plans to create a national ideology ("shared values") based on Confucian traditions.

The PAP, which has given Singaporeans one of the highest living standards in the world, maintains its grip on power. Although it can no longer rely on the complete support of the Chinese working class, it still regularly wins the overwhelming majority of parliamentary seats.

WORLD AFFAIRS ▷ Joined UN in 1965

APEC | ASEAN | Comm | NAM | WTO

Singapore has established diplomatic relations with China while continuing to maintain close economic ties with Taiwan. After 15 years of talks, in 1995 Singapore and Malaysia finally agreed their territorial water boundary.

AID ▷ Recipient

US$1m (receipts)

Down 93% 1996–1997

Aid is not an important issue in Singapore. The state does not provide aid to any states in southeast Asia.

DEFENSE ▷ Compulsory military service

US$4.1bn

No change in 1997

Despite its small size, Singapore has powerful armed forces. Defense spending is now under 5% of GDP.

S

ECONOMICS

 Inflation 3.1% p.a. (1985–1996)

US$101.8bn

1.69–1.65
Singapore dollars

SCORE CARD

❑ WORLD GNP RANKING	35th
❑ GNP PER CAPITA	US$32,810
❑ BALANCE OF PAYMENTS	US$14.8bn
❑ INFLATION	2%
❑ UNEMPLOYMENT	2%

STRENGTHS

Massive accumulated wealth derived from success as an entrepôt and as center of high-tech industries; over half of total manufacturing production electronic products and components. Huge state enterprises, such as TAMESEK, with over 450 companies, have proved highly flexible in responding to market conditions. World leader in new biotechnologies.

RESOURCES

 Electric power 4.5m kw

13,727 tonnes

Not an oil producer; refines 1.03m b/d

190,000 pigs, 300 goats, 200 cattle

None

Singapore has no strategic resources and has to import almost all the energy and food it needs. Its main resources, on which its wealth as a center of commerce has been built, are its strategic position and its people.

ENVIRONMENT

 No Green MPs

None

High

There is a small green belt around the causeway. Singapore sees itself as a world leader in providing the perfect urban environment. There is no litter, thanks to instant heavy fines; chewing gum is banned by law.

SINGAPORE

Total Land Area : 610 sq. km (236 sq. miles)

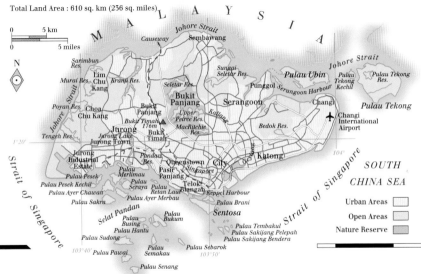

Urban Areas
Open Areas
Nature Reserve

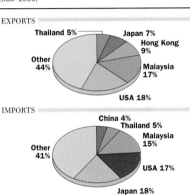

EXPORTS

Thailand 5%
Japan 7%
Hong Kong 9%
Other 44%
Malaysia 17%
USA 18%

IMPORTS

China 4%
Thailand 5%
Malaysia 15%
Other 41%
USA 17%
Japan 18%

WEAKNESSES

Dependence on Malaysia for water. All food and energy imported. Skills shortages, especially engineering. Vulnerable to fluctuations in world electronics market. Lack of land for further development.

MEDIA

 TV ownership high

Daily newspaper circulation 324 per 1,000 people

PUBLISHING AND BROADCAST MEDIA

There are 8 daily newspapers, including the leading *Straits Times* and *Business Times*

2 privately-owned services

2 privately-owned services

The government is very sensitive to any criticism that might reflect badly on Singapore. The successful prosecution of two libel suits against the *International Herald Tribune* in 1995 focused debate on the country's stringent media laws.

CRIME

 Death penalty used

8,500 prisoners

Down 18% from 1992–1996

Crime is limited and punishment can be severe. The Triads are no longer a problem; the main issue is intellectual piracy.

EDUCATION

 Not applicable

91%

92,140 students

Schooling is not compulsory, but attendance is high. Education is seen as the key to a good salary, especially among the Chinese community.

HEALTH

 Welfare state health benefits

1 per 664 people

Heart and cerebrovascular diseases, cancers

Singapore has an efficient modern health system. Incentives exist aimed at preserving the extended family, so that the elderly are cared for at home.

SPENDING

 GDP/cap. no increase

CONSUMPTION AND SPENDING

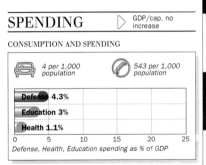

4 per 1,000 population

543 per 1,000 population

Defense 4.3%
Education 3%
Health 1.1%

Defense, Health, Education spending as % of GDP

Consumer durables sell well in Singapore, although apartments are generally not particularly luxurious. Low-wage manufacturing is increasingly done outside Singapore.

S

WORLD RANKING

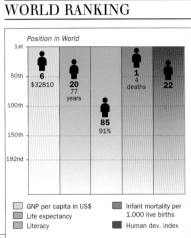

Position in World

6
$32810

20
77 years

85
91%

1
4 deaths

22

❑ GNP per capita in US$
❑ Life expectancy
❑ Literacy
■ Infant mortality per 1,000 live births
■ Human dev. index

SLOVAKIA

OFFICAL NAME: Slovak Republic **CAPITAL:** Bratislava
POPULATION: 5.4 million **CURRENCY:** Koruna **OFFICAL LANGUAGE:** Slovak

EUROPE

SLOVAKIA IS BORDERED by the Czech Republic, Austria, Poland, Hungary, and Ukraine. Southern lowlands contrast with the Carpathian mountain range, which extends along the Polish border. An independent democracy since 1993, Slovakia is the less developed half of the former Czechoslovakia. It is facing difficulties in making its heavy-industry-based economy efficient.

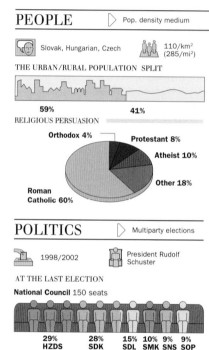

Levoča, in northeastern Slovakia, dates from the 13th century and still retains its medieval street plan and town walls.

CLIMATE ▷ Continental

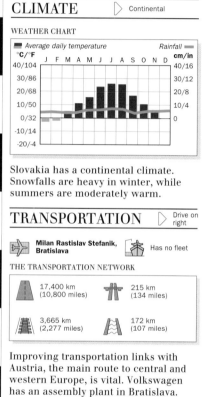

WEATHER CHART

Slovakia has a continental climate. Snowfalls are heavy in winter, while summers are moderately warm.

TRANSPORTATION ▷ Drive on right

Milan Rastislav Stefanik, Bratislava Has no fleet

THE TRANSPORTATION NETWORK

17,400 km (10,800 miles)	215 km (134 miles)
3,665 km (2,277 miles)	172 km (107 miles)

Improving transportation links with Austria, the main route to central and western Europe, is vital. Volkswagen has an assembly plant in Bratislava.

TOURISM ▷ Visitors : population 1:6.7

808,000 visitors Down 3% 1995–1997

MAIN TOURIST ARRIVALS

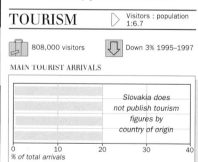

Slovakia does not publish tourism figures by country of origin

% of total arrivals

The Tatra Mountains are popular with skiers, hikers and cavers. Slovakia's nearly one million visitors a year are also attracted to the many thermal-spring health spas. Most of the tourist industry has now been privatized.

PEOPLE ▷ Pop. density medium

Slovak, Hungarian, Czech 110/km² (285/mi²)

THE URBAN/RURAL POPULATION SPLIT

59% 41%

RELIGIOUS PERSUASION

Orthodox 4%
Protestant 8%
Atheist 10%
Other 18%
Roman Catholic 60%

POLITICS ▷ Multiparty elections

1998/2002 President Rudolf Schuster

AT THE LAST ELECTION

National Council 150 seats

29% HZDS	28% SDK	15% SDL	10% SMK	9% SNS	9% SOP

HZDS = Movement for a Democratic Slovak **SDK** = Slovak Democratic Coalition **SDL** = Party of the Democratic Left
SMK = Hungarian Coalition Party **SNS** = Slovak National Party **SOP** = Party of Civic Understanding

The move to independence in 1993 was more a result of Czech than Slovak policies. Václav Klaus, the Czech leader, offered Slovakia continued membership of the federation on Czech terms, or separation. Slovak leader Vladimir Meciar, while apparently favoring greater power within a federation, was tempted by independence as enhancing his power base.

Meciar dominated Slovak politics but clashed repeatedly with President Michal Kovac, both of them members of the HZDS. Meciar lost power to an opposition coalition in elections in September 1998 and in May 1999 came second in Slovakia's first direct presidential elections, which were won by Rudolf Schuster. The Hungarian minority has its own parties, but the Romanies have no official representation.

Slovaks dominate society, but 9% of the population is Hungarian, and there is a large Romany minority which faces discrimination. Tensions between Slovaks and Hungarians, high during the Meciar regime, have lessened since the Party of the Hungarian Coalition joined a new government in 1998. There were 300,000 Slovaks living in the Czech lands in 1993. Dual citizenship is now permitted. Catholicism remains a powerful social force.

WORLD AFFAIRS ▷ Joined UN in 1993

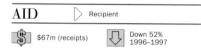

CE	CEFTA	IBRD	EAPC	OSCE

The 1998 change of government reversed the pro-Russian Meciar years. Most Slovaks favor joining the EU. 80% of trade is with the West and the Czech Republic. Relations with Hungary have improved.

AID ▷ Recipient

$67m (receipts) Down 52% 1996–1997

Slovakia received $145 million in overseas aid in 1996 (0.78% of GNP), but in 1997 it fell sharply, to $67 million.

DEFENSE ▷ Compulsory military service

$414m Down 13% in 1997

Slovak armed forces now number 45,450, including 13,600 conscripts. Prime Minister Dzurinda, who took office in late 1998, has reversed Meciar's pro-Russian defense policies.

RESOURCES ▷ Electric power 7.1m kw

2,366 tonnes 1,403 b/d

14m chickens, 1.8m pigs, 803,000 cattle, 417,000 sheep

Coal, lignite, gas, oil, antimony, copper, iron, mercury, zinc

44% of electricity was nuclear-generated, even before the Mochovce nuclear station began operations in 1998.

S

SLOVAKIA

Total Land Area : 49 036 sq. km
(18 953 sq. miles)

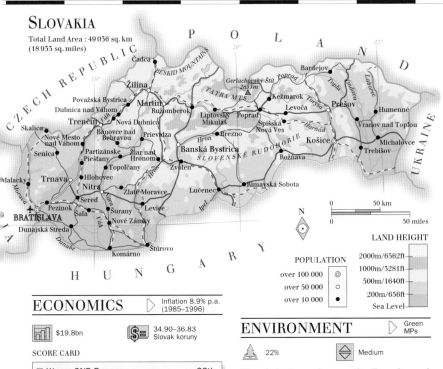

POPULATION
over 100 000
over 50 000
over 10 000

LAND HEIGHT
2000m/6562ft
1000m/3281ft
500m/1640ft
200m/656ft
Sea Level

CHRONOLOGY

Once part of the Austro-Hungarian empire, Slovakia and the Czech Lands formed the Republic of Czechoslovakia in 1918.

- ❏ **1939–1945** Separate Slovak state under pro-Nazi Jozef Tiso.
- ❏ **1945** Prewar state restored.
- ❏ **1947** Communists seize power.
- ❏ **1968** "Prague Spring" ended by Warsaw pact invasion.
- ❏ **1989** "Velvet Revolution."
- ❏ **1990** Free multiparty elections.
- ❏ **1993** Jan 1, separate Slovak and Czech states established.
- ❏ **1994** Vladimir Meciar's HZDS wins clear election victory.
- ❏ **1998** Broad-based opposition coalition wins general election.
- ❏ **1999** Rudolf Schuster defeats Meciar in first direct presidential poll.

ECONOMICS
▷ Inflation 8.9% p.a. (1985–1996)

$19.8bn   34.90–36.83 Slovak koruny

SCORE CARD

❏ WORLD GNP RANKING	66th
❏ GNP PER CAPITA	$3,680
❏ BALANCE OF PAYMENTS	$–1.4bn
❏ INFLATION	6.1%
❏ UNEMPLOYMENT	12%

STRENGTHS

Strong growth since 1994, especially in Bratislava and surrounding area. Tourism potential, particularly skiing in the Tatras. New government since 1998 committed to reform and restructuring of public and private sectors.

WEAKNESSES

Growing current-account deficit of around 10% of GDP. High foreign indebtedness. Dependence on foreign trade makes economy vulnerable to global recession. Heavy industry products have found new markets in the West but sector has failed to restructure sufficiently. Slow growth of small and medium-sized enterprises. Much poorer eastern region.

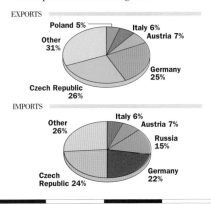

EXPORTS

Poland 5%   Italy 6%   Austria 7%
Other 31%
Germany 25%
Czech Republic 26%

IMPORTS

Italy 6%   Austria 7%
Other 26%
Russia 15%
Germany 22%
Czech Republic 24%

ENVIRONMENT
▷ Green MPs

22%   Medium

The Gabcikovo dam on the Danube and the Mochovce nuclear power station have provoked criticism at home and abroad.

MEDIA
▷ TV ownership high

 Daily newspaper circulation 185 per 1,000 people

PUBLISHING AND BROADCAST MEDIA

There are 19 daily newspapers. *Nový Čas* and *Pravda* have the highest circulation figures

1 state-controlled, 1 independent service   1 state-controlled service

Accusations of political bias of the state-run media under Meciar led to dismissals after the 1998 general election.

CRIME
▷ Death penalty not used

7,979 prisoners   Up 33% in 1993

Organized crime has increased rapidly in recent years. Politically motivated crime has also risen and includes the 1995 abduction of the son of the then President Kovac, and the 1999 murder of a former economics minister, who was accused of embezzlement.

EDUCATION
▷ School leaving age: 15

99%   101,764 students

Schooling now draws on pre-1939 Slovakian traditions but is not adequately resourced, especially in rural areas. There is a modern university in Bratislava.

HEALTH
▷ Welfare state health benefits

1 per 357 people   Cancers, heart and cerebrovascular diseases, accidents

Rising demand and costs are straining the health service severely. Restoring viability is now a government priority.

SPENDING
▷ GDP/cap. no increase

CONSUMPTION AND SPENDING

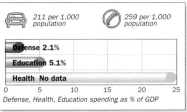

211 per 1,000 population   259 per 1,000 population

Defense 2.1%
Education 5.1%
Health No data

0   5   10   15   20   25
Defense, Health, Education spending as % of GDP

A new elite is increasing demand for Western goods. Rural workers, Romanies and those in the east are the poorest.

WORLD RANKING

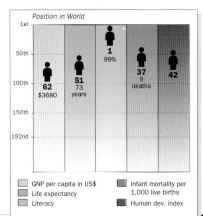

Position in World

1st
50th
100th
150th
192nd

62 $3680
51 73 years
1 99%
37 9 deaths
42

❏ GNP per capita in US$
❏ Life expectancy
❏ Literacy
❏ Infant mortality per 1,000 live births
❏ Human dev. index

S

SLOVENIA

OFFICIAL NAME: Republic of Slovenia **CAPITAL:** Ljubljana
POPULATION: 1.9 million **CURRENCY:** Tolar **OFFICIAL LANGUAGE:** Slovene

EUROPE

| 1991 | 1991 | June 25 | SLO | +1 | +386 | .si |

O F ALL THE FORMER Yugoslav republics, Slovenia has the closest links with western Europe. Located at the northeastern end of the Adriatic Sea, this small, alpine country controls some of Europe's major transit routes. Slovenia's transition to independence in 1991 avoided the violence of the breakup of Yugoslavia. The most prosperous of the former communist European states, it is the only former Yugoslav republic on the "fast track" to EU membership.

CLIMATE ▷ Continental

WEATHER CHART

Average daily temperature — Rainfall
°C/°F / J F M A M J J A S O N D / cm/in
40/104 — 40/16
30/86 — 30/12
20/68 — 20/8
10/50 — 10/4
0/32 — 0
-10/14
-20/-4

Slovenia's interior has a continental climate. Its small coastal region has a mild Mediterranean climate.

TRANSPORTATION ▷ Drive on right

Brnik Intl, Ljubljana
786,721 passengers

2 ships
200 grt

THE TRANSPORTATION NETWORK

| 14,900 km (9,300 miles) | 109 km (68 miles) |
| 1,201 km (746 miles) | None |

Slovenia is strategically situated at some of Europe's major crossroads. In addition, its Adriatic ports provide Austria with its main maritime outlet.

TOURISM ▷ Visitors : population 1:1.3

974,000 visitors

Up 33% 1995–1997

MAIN TOURIST ARRIVALS

Italy 23%
Germany 19%
Austria 15%
Other 43%
0 10 20 30 40 50 60
% of total arrivals

After the upheavals of the early 1990s visitors are returning, attracted by scenic Lake Bled, Trigalev national park, Postojna cave (the world's second largest), the Adriatic, and casinos.

PEOPLE ▷ Pop. density medium

Slovene, Serbo-Croat

94/km² (243/mi²)

THE URBAN/RURAL POPULATION SPLIT

64% 36%

ETHNIC MAKEUP

Bosniak 1% Croat 3%
Serb 2% Other 6%
Slovene 88%

Slovenia is ethnically homogeneous; around 90% are Slovene, with small communities of Italians and Hungarians. The Slovene language is sufficiently different from Serbo-Croat to foster a separate identity from its Yugoslav neighbors. Slovenia has traditionally identified more with the alpine countries to the west than its Balkan neighbors. Access to Italy and Austria during the 1970s and 1980s encouraged a separatist movement. These factors, combined with a well-developed economy, aided Slovenia's relatively peaceful secession from the former Yugoslavia in 1991.

POLITICS ▷ Multiparty elections

L. House 1996/2000
U. House 1997/2002

President Milan Kučan

AT THE LAST ELECTION

National Assembly 90 seats

6% Other

28% LDS 21% SLS 18% SDS 11% SKD 10% ZLSD 6% DeSUS

LDS = Liberal Democracy of Slovenia **SLS** = Slovene People's Party **SDS** = Social Democratic Party of Slovenia **SKD** = Christian Democrats of Slovenia **ZLSD** = United List of Social Democrats **DeSUS** = Democratic Party of Pensioners of Slovenia

National Council 40 seats

22 members are indirectly elected, and 18 are chosen by an electoral college to represent various interests.

Slovenia has been a force for stability in the war-torn former Yugoslavia. Milan Kučan has been president since independence. He was first elected in 1992 and again in 1997. Janez Drnovsek has been prime minister since May 1992. He won reelection later that year and again in November 1996, this time as head of a centrist alliance comprising the two strongest parties – his Liberal Democrats (LDS) and the conservative People's Party (SLS) – and the small Democratic Party of Pensioners. Old pro- or anti-communist divisions are starting to fade. Economic growth is a priority but not at the expense of a strong welfare state. Further privatization and reform are planned to prepare for EU membership.

SLOVENIA

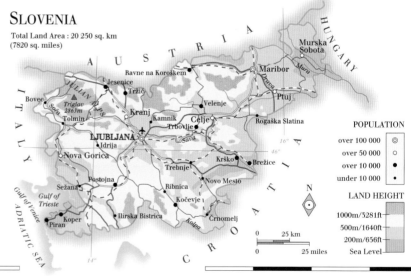

Total Land Area : 20 250 sq. km (7820 sq. miles)

POPULATION

over 100 000 ◎
over 50 000 ○
over 10 000 ●
under 10 000 ·

LAND HEIGHT

1000m/3281ft
500m/1640ft
200m/656ft
Sea Level

S

WORLD AFFAIRS

Joined UN in 1992

| CE | IAEA | OSCE | PfP | WTO |

In November 1998 Slovenia was one of the six countries on the "fast track" to EU membership to begin negotiations with Brussels.

AID

Recipient

$97m (receipts)

Up 18% 1996–1997

Foreign development assistance has increased from a mere $7 million in 1993 to $ 97 million in 1997, assisting the rapid restructuring of the economy.

DEFENSE

Compulsory military service

$310m

Up 29% in 1997

Troops staved off Yugoslav forces after secession in 1991 but Slovenia, with its 9,550-strong army, was not among the three states invited to join NATO in 1997.

ECONOMICS

Inflation 39.9% p.a. (1992–1997)

$19.6bn

168.46–161.83 tolar

SCORE CARD

❏ WORLD GNP RANKING	67th
❏ GNP PER CAPITA	$9,840
❏ BALANCE OF PAYMENTS	$37m
❏ INFLATION	9.1%
❏ UNEMPLOYMENT	7%

EXPORTS

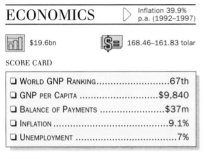

France 6%
Austria 7%
Croatia 10%
Other 33%
Italy 15%
Germany 29%

IMPORTS

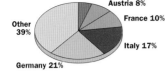

Croatia 5%
Austria 8%
France 10%
Other 39%
Italy 17%
Germany 21%

STRENGTHS
Competitive manufacturing industry. Revoz, Slovenia's largest enterprise, seen by majority-owner Renault as springboard for central and eastern European car market. Competitive port at Koper. Least indebted of central and eastern European states.

WEAKNESSES
Dangers of cronyism following privatization. Capital market controls discourage foreign investment. Slower economic growth rates than other emerging markets.

Lake Bled in the Julian Alps, *which lie astride the Slovenian–Italian border. The lake is a popular tourist destination.*

RESOURCES

Electric power 2.5m kw

3,212 tonnes

40 b/d, refines 14,700 b/d

578,193 pigs, 445,724 cattle, 28,189 sheep

Coal, lignite, lead, zinc, uranium, silver, mercury

Slovenia has come under pressure from Austria to close the nuclear plant at Krško, which provides one-third of Slovenia's power. It has deposits of brown coal and lignite, but they are difficult to extract and of poor quality.

ENVIRONMENT

No Green MPs

6%

Medium

Slovenes were in the vanguard of former Yugoslavia's environmental movement. Protecting the country's alpine ecology is a priority.

MEDIA

TV ownership high

Daily newspaper circulation 206 per 1,000 people

PUBLISHING AND BROADCAST MEDIA

There are 7 daily newspapers. *Dnevnik* is privately owned

1 state-controlled, 3 independent services

1 state-controlled service

The Slovene media actively worked to undermine Yugoslav institutions during the secession crisis, reinforcing the sense of national identity.

CRIME

Death penalty not used

630 prisoners

Down 32% from 1992–1996

Slovenia has traditionally been a transit point for drugs smuggling into western Europe. The trade declined when the UN imposed sanctions on Serbia.

EDUCATION

School leaving age: 15

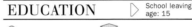

99%

51,009 students

School is compulsory from seven to 15 years, and standards are high. In 1996, there were more than 51,000 students in tertiary education. The university at Ljubljana was founded in 1595.

CHRONOLOGY

Slovenia was part of the Austro-Hungarian empire until 1918. It was the first republic to secede from the Federal Republic of Yugoslavia.

- ❏ **1918** Slovenia joins Yugoslav kingdom.
- ❏ **1949** Tito's break with Moscow.
- ❏ **1989** Parliament confirms right to secede. Calls multiparty elections.
- ❏ **1990** Control over army asserted, referendum approves secession.
- ❏ **1991** Independence declared. Yugoslav federal army attacks held off. EU-brokered cease-fire.
- ❏ **1992** EU recognizes Slovenia. First multiparty elections held. Milan Kučan elected president.
- ❏ **1993** Member of IMF and IBRD.
- ❏ **1997** Kučan reelected.

HEALTH

Welfare state health benefits

1 per 1,449 people

Cerebrovascular and heart diseases, cancers, accidents,

National health care in Slovenia uses health centers and outpatient clinics to increase accessibility for patients.

SPENDING

GDP/cap. no increase

CONSUMPTION AND SPENDING

385 per 1,000 population

364 per 1,000 population

Defense 1.7%
Education 5.8%
Health No data

0	5	10	15	20	25

Defense, Health, Education spending as % of GDP

Slovenia has the highest standard of living of the central and eastern European states, with earnings at 60% of the EU average.

WORLD RANKING

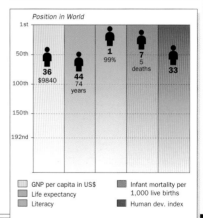

Position in World

1st
50th
36 $9840
44 74 years
1 99%
7 5 deaths
33
100th
150th
192nd

❏ GNP per capita in US$
❏ Life expectancy
❏ Literacy
❏ Infant mortality per 1,000 live births
❏ Human dev. index

S

SOLOMON ISLANDS

OFFICIAL NAME: Solomon Islands **CAPITAL:** Honiara
POPULATION: 417,000 **CURRENCY:** Solomon Islands dollar **OFFICIAL LANGUAGE:** English

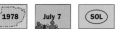

| 1978 | 1978 | July 7 | SOL | +11 | +677 | .sb |

S CATTERED OVER 645,000 square km (245,000 square miles), the Solomons archipelago consists of several hundred islands. Most of the population live on the six largest islands – Guadalcanal, Malaita, New Georgia, Makira, Santa Isabel and Choiseul. The Solomons have been settled since at least 1000 BCE and the Spanish reached the islands in 1568. They gained independence from Britain in 1978. Most of the Solomons are coral reefs. Just 1% of the islands' land area is cultivable.

CLIMATE

▷ Tropical equatorial

WEATHER CHART

- Average daily temperature
- Rainfall

There is little variation in the humid, subtropical climate, but ferocious cyclones can occur in the rainy season.

TRANSPORTATION

▷ Drive on left

Henderson, Honiara
22,000 passengers

2 ships
10,000 grt

THE TRANSPORTATION NETWORK

| 100 km (62 miles) | | None |
| None | | None |

The principal international airport, located 13 km from Honiara, has recently been upgraded. Most airfields are simple grass strips.

Unloading seed coconuts near Munda on New Georgia in the Solomons' southern chain of islands. Coconuts are by far the largest and most commercially important crop.

TOURISM

▷ Visitors : population 1:26

🧳 16,000 visitors   ⬆ Up 33% 1995–1997

MAIN TOURIST ARRIVALS

- Australia 34%
- New Zealand 12%
- Papua New Guinea 8%
- Other 46%

% of total arrivals

More tourists are expected now that Boeing 747 jets can land at the main airport. Guadalcanal, a key battle site of the World War II in the Pacific, has seen a decline in visitors in recent years. Outlying islands cater for visitors wishing to "get away from it all."

PEOPLE

▷ Pop. density low

English, Pidgin English, Melanesian Pidgin

15/km² (39/mi²)

THE URBAN/RURAL POPULATION SPLIT

17%   83%

RELIGIOUS PERSUASION

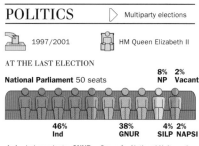

- Church of Melanesia (Anglican) 34%
- Other 9%
- Seventh-day Adventist 10%
- Methodist 11%
- South Seas Evangelical Church 17%
- Roman Catholic 19%

Almost all Solomon Islanders are Melanesian. In 1957, large numbers of Gilbertese were resettled in the Solomons following a hurricane; a few stayed on and today form a small, distinct community. Over 50 dialects are spoken in the Solomons, a state of 417,000 people spread over 1,600 km (1,000 miles). As in other Melanesian island states, villagers are expected to share their wealth with their *wontoks*, or clan. Almost all islanders are nominally Christian. Most also maintain their traditional animist beliefs.

POLITICS

▷ Multiparty elections

1997/2001   HM Queen Elizabeth II

AT THE LAST ELECTION

National Parliament 50 seats

| 46% Ind | 38% GNUR | 4% SILP | 2% NAPSI | 8% NP | 2% Vacant |

Ind = Independents GNUR = Group for National Unity and Reconciliation NP = National Party SILP = Solomon Islands Labor Party NAPSI = National Action Party of the Solomon Islands

The Solomons parliament is based on the Westminster model. Unlike other Pacific states, there is no one class of chiefs which dominates the political process. It is prominent figures in village life – known locally as "big men" – who stand as candidates. Legislators are often in parliament for just one term, since elections tend to result in a large turnover of members. Party arrangements within parliament are fluid and coalitions unstable. Allegations of corruption and poor economic management dominate recent history.

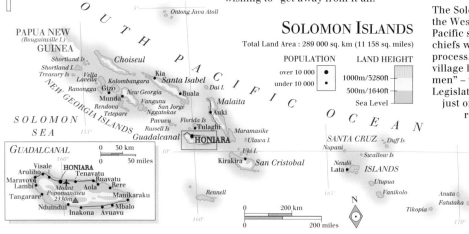

SOLOMON ISLANDS

Total Land Area : 289 000 sq. km (11 158 sq. miles)

POPULATION
- over 10 000 ●
- under 10 000 ·

LAND HEIGHT
- 1000m/3280ft
- 500m/1640ft
- Sea Level

WORLD AFFAIRS
▷ Joined UN in 1978

ACP | Comm | IBRD | SPC | SPF

Relations with neighboring Papua New Guinea (PNG) were strained for many years by the Bougainville conflict, since Honiara supported the Bougainville secessionist movement. But recent changes of government in both countries and advances in the peace process have significantly improved ties.

AID
▷ Recipient

$ US$42m (receipts)   ⬇ Down 2% 1996–1997

In recent years Australia and the EU withdrew aid in protest against the islands' refusal to implement sustainable logging practices. To demonstrate commitment to improving relations, Papua New Guinea recently agreed to grant the Solomon Islands aid worth US$5.7 million a year.

DEFENSE
▷ No compulsory military service

$ Australia responsible for defense   ⬍ Not applicable

The islands receive training and logistical support from Australia and New Zealand. A small national surveillance and reconnaissance force has been established. The Police Field Force has seven fast patrol boats which are used to protect fisheries from Taiwanese and Okinawan poachers.

ECONOMICS
▷ Inflation 10.8% p.a. (1985–1996)

US$350m $ 4.70–4.76 Solomon Islands dollars

SCORE CARD

❑ WORLD GNP RANKING.......................171st
❑ GNP PER CAPITA ....US$870
❑ BALANCE OF PAYMENTS...................US$-28m
❑ INFLATION 8.1%
❑ UNEMPLOYMENT............Some underemployment

EXPORTS

Thailand 3% | Germany 4% | UK 8% | Philippines 9% | Japan 59% | Other 17%

IMPORTS

Malaysia 4% | New Zealand 6% | Japan 11% | Australia 41% | Singapore 16% | Other 22%

STRENGTHS
Survival of subsistence agriculture. Coconuts are major cash crop. Modest diversification of economy into oil palm and cocoa.

WEAKNESSES
Debt almost three times estimated revenue. Copra industry increasingly unproductive. Opposition to overexploitation of timber. Dependence on imported energy. Location away from main sea and air routes.

RESOURCES
▷ Electric power 12,000 kw

53,286 tonnes   Not an oil producer

57,000 pigs, 10,000 cattle, 185,000 chickens   Gold, copper, bauxite, lead, zinc, silver, cobalt, phosphates

Bauxite deposits have been discovered on Rennett Island. In addition, there are traces of gold and copper on Guadalcanal. There is increasing concern over the exploitation of forest and marine resources.

ENVIRONMENT
▷ No Green MPs

None   ⬇ Low

The environmental movement is strong in the Solomon Islands. Depletion of forest and marine resources are a major concern and have given rise to campaigns. In 1998 a new government introduced a sustainable forest harvesting policy.

MEDIA
▷ TV ownership low

There are no daily newspapers

PUBLISHING AND BROADCAST MEDIA

There are no daily newspapers. The *Solomon Star*, *Solomons Toktok*, *Solomons Voice* and *Solomon Nius* are published weekly

No TV service   1 independent service

The one radio station broadcasts in English and Pidgin. Islanders oppose TV, since it would dilute their culture.

CRIME
▷ Death penalty not used

150 prisoners   Crime rate rising

There has been a small increase in crime on Honiara. Most offenses are drink-related.

CHRONOLOGY
Settled since before 1000 B.C. by Melanesian peoples, the Solomons became a British colony in 1893.

❑ **1900** Britain acquires northern Solomons from Germany.
❑ **1943** Occupying Japanese lose control to USA after fierce fighting.
❑ **1978** Independence from UK.
❑ **1997** Legislature enlarged to 50 seats; Bartholomew Ulufa'alu elected prime minister.

EDUCATION
▷ Not available

62%   Not available

Education is modeled on the British system. Tertiary students go to the University of the South Pacific in Fiji.

HEALTH
▷ Welfare state health benefits

1 per 8,719 people   Not available

The main hospital is in Honiara. Known as "Number 9," it was built as a military hospital by the US Army during World War II.

SPENDING
▷ GDP/cap. no increase

CONSUMPTION AND SPENDING

No data   17 per 1,000 population

Defense	No data	
Education	4.2%	
Health	5%	

0   5   10   15   20   25

Defense, Health, Education spending as % of GDP

Solomon Islanders in government jobs are the wealthiest group. Outlying islands are extremely poor.

WORLD RANKING

Position in World

1st | 50th | 100th | 150th | 192nd

62 / 72 years
124 / $870
152 / 62%
85 / 23 deaths
118

GNP per capita in US$
Life expectancy
Literacy
Infant mortality per 1,000 live births
Human dev. index

S

SOMALIA

OFFICIAL NAME: Somali Democratic Republic   **CAPITAL:** Mogadishu
POPULATION: 10.7 million   **CURRENCY:** Somali shilling   **OFFICIAL LANGUAGES:** Somali & Arabic

1960	1960	July 1	SP	+3	+252	.so

OCCUPYING THE HORN of Africa, Italian Somaliland and British Somaliland were united in 1960 to form an independent Somalia. The land is semiarid except in the more fertile south. Years of clan-based civil war have resulted in the collapse of central government, frustrating US and UN intervention initiatives aimed at easing the major reugee crisis and mass starvation.

CLIMATE ▷ Hot desert/steppe

WEATHER CHART

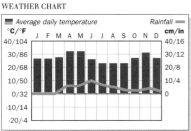

Somalia is very dry. The northern coast is very hot and humid, the eastern less so. The interior has some of the world's highest mean yearly temperatures.

TRANSPORTATION ▷ Drive on left

✈ **Mogadishu International**   🚢 22 ships 13,900 grt

THE TRANSPORTATION NETWORK

6,199 km (3,852 miles)	None
None	None

About 50% of Somalis are nomads for whom the camel is the principal means of transportation. In 1990, the IDA agreed to repair the road network, but by 1999 no work had started on the seven-year project.

TOURISM ▷ Visitors : population 1:1,070

🧳 10,000 visitors   ⬍ No change 1995–1997

MAIN TOURIST ARRIVALS

Somalia does not publish tourism figures by country of origin

0   10   20   30   40
% of total arrivals

Aid workers and foreign journalists are the only visitors. Land mines are a hazard.

Baydhabo market. *Subsistence farming supports most people, despite chaos created by the fighting.*

PEOPLE ▷ Pop. density low

👤 Somali, Arabic, English, Italian   👥 17/km² (44/mi²)

THE URBAN/RURAL POPULATION SPLIT

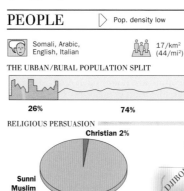

26%   74%

RELIGIOUS PERSUASION

- Christian 2%
- Sunni Muslim 98%

The clan system is at the root of all social, political, and commercial issues in Somalia. Shifting allegiances characterize its structure – a tendency stifled by Siad Barre's dictatorship but revived after his fall in 1991. His undermining of the traditional brokers of justice, the elders, contributed to the present power vacuum, while his persecution of the Issaqs led to Somaliland's declaration of secession in 1991. However, the entire population is ethnic Somali and national identity remains strong, reflected in the widespread opposition to the UN peace-keeping force.

POLITICS ▷ No multiparty elections

🗳 1984/Uncertain   No internationally recognized Head of State

AT THE LAST ELECTION

National Assembly suspended

There has been no prospect of organizing new elections since the overthrow of Siad Barre.

Civil war started in the north in the 1980s and spread as other opposition groups took up arms against the dictator, President Siad Barre, who eventually fled in early 1991.

Subsequent civil war in the south and the self-proclaimed independence of Somaliland in May that year effectively ended the unitary state. Despite the deployment of US-led UN peace-keepers in 1992, the south remained in the grip of warring clan factions and opportunist warlords, and anarchy persisted after the UN withdrawal in 1995. General Aideed, a major protagonist, was killed in 1996. The other principal contender, Ali Mahdi, in early 1997 saw his claim for recognition strengthened when 26 clan factions signed an accord; they agreed to set up a National Salvation Council including him in its nominally collective leadership. Reports of agreement on creating a joint interim government have come to nothing.

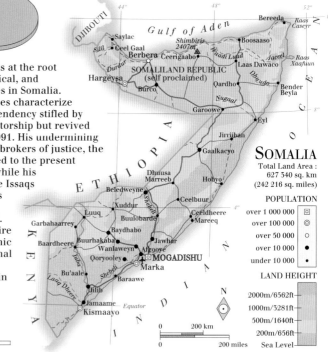

SOMALIA

Total Land Area : 627 340 sq. km (242 216 sq. miles)

POPULATION

over 1 000 000	⊡
over 100 000	◎
over 50 000	○
over 10 000	●
under 10 000	•

LAND HEIGHT

2000m/6562ft	
1000m/3281ft	
500m/1640ft	
200m/656ft	
Sea Level	

WORLD AFFAIRS
 Joined UN in 1960

Following the withdrawal of the controversial UN force, whose success was limited to alleviating starvation, the international community appears to have abandoned Somalia. Self-declared Somaliland is pressing for international recognition, with borders of former British Somaliland. Even though fighting has stopped there, no help other than emergency aid is being provided because the region lacks official status.

AID
 Recipient

$104m (receipts)   Up 14% 1996–1997

Mass starvation among the Somali population in 1991 finally prompted the UN to launch a large-scale humanitarian aid effort. In this the UN was largely effective, averting widescale starvation and restoring food security.

DEFENSE
No compulsory military service

$40m   Down 19% in 1997

Somalia is awash with weapons supplied by both the USA and the former USSR during the Cold War.

ECONOMICS
Not available

$835m   2,620 Somali shillings

SCORE CARD

❏ WORLD GNP RANKING	159th
❏ GNP PER CAPITA	$100
❏ BALANCE OF PAYMENTS	$-157m
❏ INFLATION	81.9%
❏ UNEMPLOYMENT	*Widespread underemployment*

STRENGTHS
Very few. Export of livestock to Arabian peninsula resumed in the north. Inflow of money from Somalis living abroad. Growing market in stolen food aid.

WEAKNESSES
Every commodity, except arms, in extremely short supply. The south has little economic potential. Effects of drought include death of nomads' livestock herds.

EXPORTS

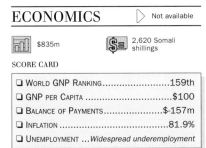

Oman 1%   Other 5%   Yemen 9%
Saudi Arabia 57%   Italy 13%
United Arab Emirates 15%

IMPORTS

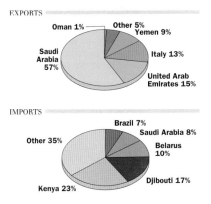

Brazil 7%   Saudi Arabia 8%
Other 35%   Belarus 10%
Djibouti 17%
Kenya 23%

RESOURCES
 Electric power 70,000 kw

15,500 tonnes   Not an oil producer; refines 10,000 b/d
13.5m sheep, 12.5m goats, 5.3m cattle   Salt, tin, zinc, copper, gypsum, manganese, uranium, iron

Commercially exploitable minerals remain untapped. Oil experts are confident of discovering large offshore reserves in the north.

ENVIRONMENT
No Green MPs

0.3% (partially protected)   Low

Human deprivation and starvation caused by the effects of drought and war on land and livestock outweigh all other ecological considerations.

MEDIA
TV ownership low

 Daily newspaper circulation 1 per 1,000 people

PUBLISHING AND BROADCAST MEDIA

There are 2 daily newspapers
1 limited service   Several independent services

There are three radio stations in Mogadishu, one run by Ali Mahdi, one by the Aideed faction, and one by a former ally of Aideed. There are few newspapers as paper is currently in very short supply.

CRIME
 Death penalty used

Somalia does not publish prison figures   Widespread breakdown in law and order since 1991

Armed clan factions (some, in remoter regions, engaged in family feuds rather than the war) and bandits rule large areas. Police forces exist in some cities but, with few resources, dare not risk confrontation with warlords. Muslim *sharia* law, now the *de facto* system, is run in a makeshift fashion by elders.

EDUCATION
School leaving age: 14

24%   15,672 students

The system collapsed during the civil war. There were reports of improvised open-air schools starting up again in urban areas in 1993. Somali has been a written language only since 1972.

CHRONOLOGY
The lands of the Somalis became UK and Italian colonies in the 1880s.

- ❏ **1941–1950** UK rules both areas.
- ❏ **1960** Unification at independence.
- ❏ **1964** Somalia's claim to Ogaden leads to war with Ethiopia.
- ❏ **1969** Gen. Siad Barre seizes power.
- ❏ **1977–1978** Attack on Ethiopia fails.
- ❏ **1981** Guerrilla war begins.
- ❏ **1987** Reconciliation with Ethiopia.
- ❏ **1991** Siad Barre ousted. Civil war and clan chaos. Mass starvation. Somaliland declares secession.
- ❏ **1992** Warlords plunder food aid. US sends in military with UN backing.
- ❏ **1995** UN force withdrawn.
- ❏ **1996** Self-styled "president" Gen. Aideed dies in gun battle.
- ❏ **1997** Factions sign accord.

HEALTH
No welfare state health benefits

1 per 14,300 people   Diarrheal, communicable and parasitic diseases

The state-run system has collapsed entirely. A few very rudimentary facilities are run by foreign workers.

SPENDING
GDP/cap. no increase

CONSUMPTION AND SPENDING

No data   No data

Defense 4.8%
Education No data
Health 0.6%

0   5   10   15   20   25
Defense, Health, Education spending as % of GDP

Bandits and warlords gained rich pickings in the aid-stealing racket. Money sent by relatives living overseas is the main income for some.

S

WORLD RANKING

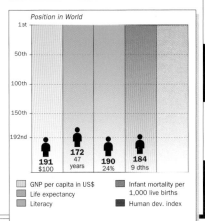

Position in World

1st
50th
100th
150th
192nd

191 $100   172 47 years   190 24%   184 9 dths

❏ GNP per capita in US$ ❏ Infant mortality per 1,000 live births
❏ Life expectancy
❏ Literacy   ❏ Human dev. index

SOUTH AFRICA

SOUTHERN AFRICA

OFFICIAL NAME: Republic of South Africa   **CAPITAL:** Pretoria
POPULATION: 44.3 million   **CURRENCY:** Rand   **OFFICIAL LANGUAGES:** Afrikaans and English

RICH IN NATURAL RESOURCES, South Africa comprises a central plateau, or *veld*, bordered to the south and east by the Drakensberg Mountains. After eight decades of white minority rule, and racial segregation under the apartheid policy since 1948, South Africa held its first multiracial elections in 1994. The revolution in South Africa's politics began in 1990, when black freedom groups were legalized and the dismantling of apartheid began. The African National Congress (ANC), under Nelson Mandela and then his successor Thabo Mbeki, is now the leading political movement.

Nelson Mandela, *who became president of South Africa in April 1994.*

Thabo Mbeki, *elected president in 1999 to succeed Mandela.*

CLIMATE

▷ Desert/subtropical/ Mediterranean

WEATHER CHART

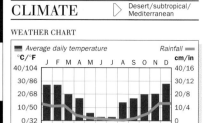

Despite the moderating effects of oceans on three sides, the warm temperate climate is dry; 65% of South Africa has less than 50 cm (20 inches) of rain a year. Drought is a periodic hazard.

TRANSPORTATION

▷ Drive on left

Jan Smuts International, Johannesburg
11m passengers

6 ships
371,000 grt

THE TRANSPORTATION NETWORK

33,800 km (21,000 miles)	1,142km (710 miles)
22,916 km (14,239 miles)	None

Priorities include expanding port capacity and cross-border rail networks such as the Maputo Corridor. Another concern is South Africa's road death rate, one of the world's worst.

Cape Town, *backed by the dramatic mountains of Cape Province.*

TOURISM

▷ Visitors : population 1:8.0

5.53m visitors

Up 23% 1995–1997

MAIN TOURIST ARRIVALS

Lesotho 30%
Zimbabwe 14%
Swaziland 14%
Botswana 10%
Namibia 5%
Other 27%

% of total arrivals

South Africa has huge tourist potential, with attractions ranging from beaches to mountains, from prize-winning vineyards to world renowned wildlife reserves. The enormous Kruger National Park boasts 137 species of mammal and 450 species of bird. Although the number of visitors increased by over 20% between 1994 and 1995, the sector is still recovering from its isolation during the apartheid era. Today, the key constraint on expansion is rising crime. Studies suggest that tourism could create an additional 450,000 jobs by 2005.

PEOPLE

▷ Pop. density low

English, Afrikaans, Zulu, Xhosa, Ndebele, Setswana, Siswati, North Sotho, South Sotho, Tsongo, Venda

36/km² (94/mi²)

THE URBAN/RURAL POPULATION SPLIT

51%   49%

RELIGIOUS PERSUASION

Methodist 6%
Zion Christian Church 5%
Other 53%
Roman Catholic 8%
Dutch Reformed 11%
Other Black Independent 17%

ETHNIC MAKEUP

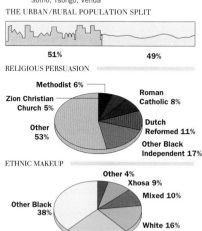

Other 4%
Xhosa 9%
Mixed 10%
White 16%
Zulu 23%
Other Black 38%

Under apartheid, South Africans were divided into racial categories: whites (Afrikaners and English-speakers), and three black groups (Coloreds – people whose descent was deemed mixed; Asians – mainly Indians; and Africans). Each category had different political, economic and social rights, with whites

enjoying the most privileges and Africans the fewest. While blacks now dominate politics, English-speaking whites continue to control the economy.

The extended family has been undermined by regulations forcing men to migrate for work, leaving their wives and children in the rural areas. A small black middle class has developed, but most black South Africans are underemployed.

The expected post-apartheid ethnic conflict failed to materialize, although *Inkatha* has exploited feelings of Zulu identity in its quest for greater political power. However, demands for a white homeland have faded.

Many women are now prominent in public life. The new constitution guarantees equality of the sexes.

POPULATION AGE BREAKDOWN

Female	Age	Male
0.5%	81–100	0.2%
3.2%	61–80	2.5%
8.1%	41–60	8.1%
16%	21–40	16.5%
22.3%	0–20	22.6%

% of population by age group

S

POLITICS   ▷ Multiparty elections

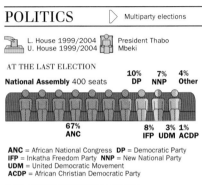

L. House 1999/2004
U. House 1999/2004

President Thabo
Mbeki

AT THE LAST ELECTION

National Assembly 400 seats

| 10% DP | 7% NNP | 4% Other |

| 67% ANC | | 8% IFP | 3% UDM | 1% ACDP |

ANC = African National Congress **DP** = Democratic Party
IFP = Inkatha Freedom Party **NNP** = New National Party
UDM = United Democratic Movement
ACDP = African Christian Democratic Party

National Council of Provinces 90 seats

10 members are elected to the National Council of Provinces
by each of the nine provincial legislatures.

South Africa became a multiracial
democracy following elections in 1994.

MAIN POLITICAL ISSUES
Maintaining unity
In April 1994, South Africa confounded
the proponents of violence and ethnic
division by holding peaceful elections.
The former ruling whites-only NP,
initially part of the ANC-led "unity
government," withdrew in mid-1996.
The ANC, while heeding the aspirations
of the black majority, has
tried to avoid marginalizing
South Africa's minorities.

To deal with the apartheid past, it
inaugurated a Truth and Reconciliation
Commission (TRC). Two years of
hearings culminated in a final report in
1998, which won praise for addressing
wrongdoings on all sides.

Reconstruction and development
The government's costly Reconstruction
and Development Program (RDP) aims
at improving social conditions and
boosting employment. Implementation
is too slow for many blacks, who had
hoped for immediate benefits from
democratic rule, while some members of
the minorities see the RDP's affirmative
action as reverse discrimination.

PROFILE
In the 1994 elections, ending 45 years of
white rule by the NP, the ANC narrowly
missed the two-thirds majority it needed
to govern alone. In 1996, the IFP replaced
the NP as the ANC's coalition partner; a
new liberal Constitution was adopted.
In the 1999 elections the ANC slightly
increased its majority, Thabo Mbeki
succeeded Nelson Mandela as president,
while the DP overtook the strife-ridden
NP in opposition. Mbeki's gratifying
mandate should help him face the
immense challenges of creating
jobs, attracting investors
and healing old
ethnic wounds.

WORLD AFFAIRS   ▷ Joined UN in 1945

| Comm | WTO | NAM | OAU | SADC |

After several decades of political
isolation and economic sanctions,
South Africa has been welcomed back
to the international fold, and rejoined
the UN and the Commonwealth. It now
hopes to attract international investors
and to encourage the return of those
who stopped investing during
the 1980s. Improved relations with
neighboring states and non-aligned
countries are also important. South
Africa joined the SADC and led
continental opinion on Congo (former
Zaire), Angola, and Nigeria. Former
President Mandela often intervened
to help resolve foreign conflicts.
However, some saw his dispatch of
troops to Lesotho in 1998 as bungling,
unwarranted interference. Likewise,
Western powers were wary of
Mandela's loyalty to Libya and Cuba,
who had supported the ANC during the
period of apartheid.

SOUTH AFRICA

Total Land Area : 1 221 040 sq. km
(471 443 sq. miles)

0   200 km

0   200 miles

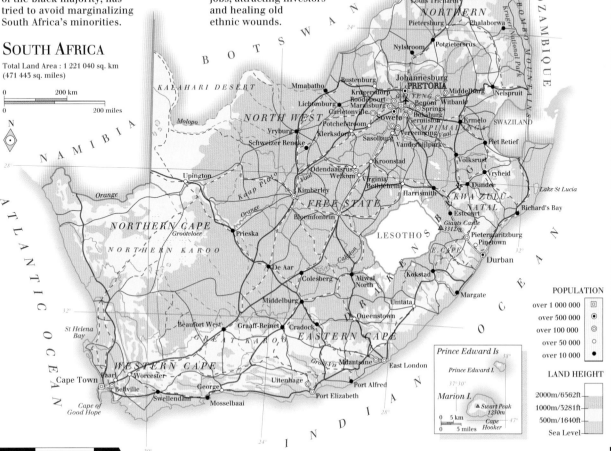

POPULATION

over 1 000 000	⊡
over 500 000	◉
over 100 000	◎
over 50 000	○
over 10 000	●

LAND HEIGHT

| 2000m/6562ft |
| 1000m/3281ft |
| 500m/1640ft |
| Sea Level |

S

AID ▷ Recipient

💲 $497m (receipts) ⬆ Up 38% 1996–1997

South Africa was denied aid during the apartheid years, particularly from the World Bank and the IMF. It now seeks financial assistance for massive reconstruction programs. In 1998 the UK pledged up to 275 million rand annually to fund customs, training, policing, and environmental measures.

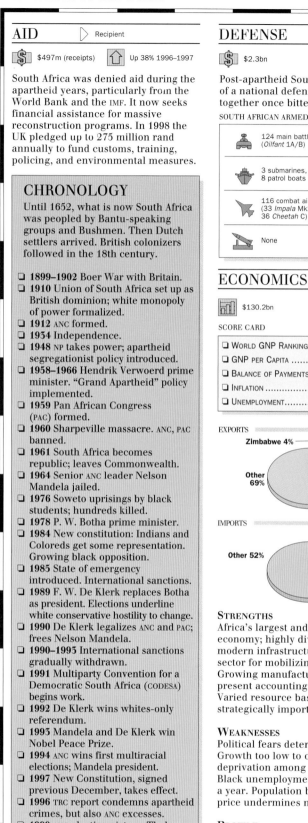

CHRONOLOGY

Until 1652, what is now South Africa was peopled by Bantu-speaking groups and Bushmen. Then Dutch settlers arrived. British colonizers followed in the 18th century.

- ❏ **1899–1902** Boer War with Britain.
- ❏ **1910** Union of South Africa set up as British dominion; white monopoly of power formalized.
- ❏ **1912** ANC formed.
- ❏ **1934** Independence.
- ❏ **1948** NP takes power; apartheid segregationist policy introduced.
- ❏ **1958–1966** Hendrik Verwoerd prime minister. "Grand Apartheid" policy implemented.
- ❏ **1959** Pan African Congress (PAC) formed.
- ❏ **1960** Sharpeville massacre. ANC, PAC banned.
- ❏ **1961** South Africa becomes republic; leaves Commonwealth.
- ❏ **1964** Senior ANC leader Nelson Mandela jailed.
- ❏ **1976** Soweto uprisings by black students; hundreds killed.
- ❏ **1978** P. W. Botha prime minister.
- ❏ **1984** New constitution: Indians and Coloreds get some representation. Growing black opposition.
- ❏ **1985** State of emergency introduced. International sanctions.
- ❏ **1989** F. W. De Klerk replaces Botha as president. Elections underline white conservative hostility to change.
- ❏ **1990** De Klerk legalizes ANC and PAC; frees Nelson Mandela.
- ❏ **1990–1993** International sanctions gradually withdrawn.
- ❏ **1991** Multiparty Convention for a Democratic South Africa (CODESA) begins work.
- ❏ **1992** De Klerk wins whites-only referendum.
- ❏ **1993** Mandela and De Klerk win Nobel Peace Prize.
- ❏ **1994** ANC wins first multiracial elections; Mandela president.
- ❏ **1997** New Constitution, signed previous December, takes effect.
- ❏ **1996** TRC report condemns apartheid crimes, but also ANC excesses.
- ❏ **1999** ANC election victory; Thabo Mbeki succeeds Mandela as president.

DEFENSE ▷ No compulsory military service

💲 $2.3bn ⬇ Down 19% in 1997

Post-apartheid South Africa's creation of a national defense force has fused together once bitter enemies: soldiers

SOUTH AFRICAN ARMED FORCES

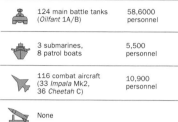

🪖	124 main battle tanks (*Oilfant* 1A/B)	58,6000 personnel
🚢	3 submarines, 8 patrol boats	5,500 personnel
✈	116 combat aircraft (33 *Impala* Mk2, 36 *Cheetah* C)	10,900 personnel
🚀	None	

ECONOMICS ▷ Inflation 12.8% p.a. (1985–1996)

📊 $130.2bn 💲 4.87–5.88 rand

SCORE CARD

- ❏ WORLD GNP RANKING..........................30th
- ❏ GNP PER CAPITA $3,210
- ❏ BALANCE OF PAYMENTS...................$–1.93bn
- ❏ INFLATION 8.5%
- ❏ UNEMPLOYMENT..................................30%

EXPORTS

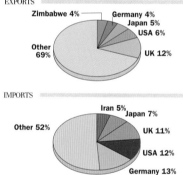

Zimbabwe 4%, Germany 4%, Japan 5%, USA 6%, Other 69%, UK 12%

IMPORTS

Iran 5%, Japan 7%, Other 52%, UK 11%, USA 12%, Germany 13%

STRENGTHS

Africa's largest and most developed economy; highly diversified with modern infrastructure. Strong financial sector for mobilizing investment. Growing manufacturing sector, at present accounting for 23% of GDP. Varied resource base, particularly of strategically important minerals.

WEAKNESSES

Political fears deter foreign investment. Growth too low to overcome deprivation among black majority. Black unemployment growing by 2.5% a year. Population boom. Falling gold price undermines many sectors.

PROFILE

South Africa has a large and diverse private sector, much of it controlled by multinationals. International sanctions

from the old white-run army, and guerrillas from the liberation groups. However, swingeing cuts in defense spending were allegedly hampering the army's ability to defend the nation's borders. Cuts particularly damaged the navy. A 29 billion rand arms procurement program, announced in late 1998 satisfied some critics, but others criticized the government for its "unwise" spending priorities.

In 1998, possibly foreshadowing a leading regional security role, South African troops (controversially) helped quell unrest in neighboring Lesotho. Sanctions encouraged a major arms industry, making South Africa the world's twelfth largest arms exporter.

ECONOMIC PERFORMANCE INDICATOR

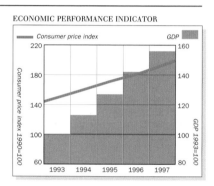

Consumer price index, GDP

forced the government to play a central economic role through state corporations in the 1980s. This is now being reduced in a series of privatizations. The ANC has declared its intention to work with big business in order to revivify the economy and develop the townships.

SOUTH AFRICA : MAJOR BUSINESSES

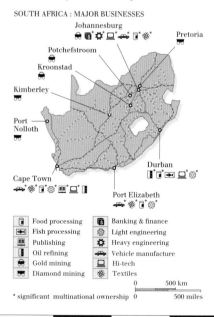

🍴	Food processing	🏦	Banking & finance
🐟	Fish processing	⚙	Light engineering
📖	Publishing	✿	Heavy engineering
🛢	Oil refining	💻	Vehicle manufacture
⛏	Gold mining	🖥	Hi-tech
🚃	Diamond mining	✳	Textiles

0 ———— 500 km
0 ———— 500 miles

* significant multinational ownership

RESOURCES

▷ Electric power 35.9m kw

575,177 tonnes

Not an oil producer; refines 430,500 b/d

30m sheep, 13.8m cattle, 7m goats

Gold, coal, vanadium, vermiciline, diamonds, chromium, manganese

ELECTRICITY GENERATION

Hydro 1% (0.8bn kwh)

Combustion 95% (180bn kwh)

Nuclear 4% (9.6bn kwh)

Other 0%

% of total generation by type

South Africa has some of the continent's richest natural resources, in particular minerals. Its dominance of the world market in gold and diamonds helped it survive sanctions during apartheid. The current output of 600 tonnes of gold a year accounts for 30% of the world total. South Africa is the largest single producer of manganese, chrome ore, vanadium and vermiciline. It also produces uranium and platinum.

In the absence of oil, South Africa has pioneered the transformation of coal into oil; its huge coal reserves are also used to generate 87% of electricity. A priority is to bring electricity to the 80% of black homes without; the government is considering non-grid options.

Agriculture is varied.

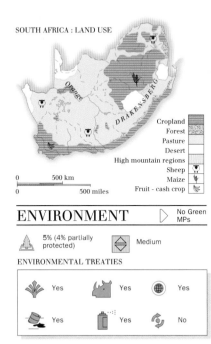

SOUTH AFRICA : LAND USE

Cropland	
Forest	
Pasture	
Desert	
High mountain regions	
Sheep	
Maize	
Fruit - cash crop	

0   500 km
0   500 miles

ENVIRONMENT

▷ No Green MPs

5% (4% partially protected)

Medium

ENVIRONMENTAL TREATIES

	Yes		Yes		Yes
	Yes		Yes		No

Floods and drought are hazards; the main concern is protecting animal species. One 1998 plan envisages conserving forests in former homeland areas. Environmental measures could conflict with economic demands.

MEDIA

▷ TV ownership medium

Daily newspaper circulation 30 per 1,000 people

PUBLISHING AND BROADCAST MEDIA

There are 17 daily newspapers. *The Sowetan, The Star* and *The Citizen* have the highest circulation figures

1 state-owned service

1 state-owned service

The end of censorship has bolstered a press which ranges from far left to extreme right. A 1998 bill to regulate broadcasting faced opposition.

CRIME

▷ Death penalty not used

110,120 prisoners

Rapid rise in violent crime

CRIME RATES

Murders	
129	per 100,000 population

Rapes	
120	per 100,000 population

Thefts	
2929	per 100,000 population

South Africa is a dangerous country: one murder occurs every 29 minutes; armed robberies and muggings are rife. Little of the violence is now said to be political. Vigilanteism is a huge problem in the Cape. The death penalty was abolished in 1997. Since 1998, tough laws have targeted drugs gangs and organized crime.

EDUCATION

▷ School leaving age: 16

84%

617,897 students

Black adults suffer the effects of earlier school boycotts and closures.

THE EDUCATION SYSTEM

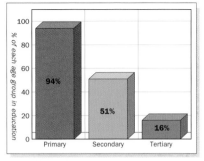

% of each age group in education

- Primary: 94%
- Secondary: 51%
- Tertiary: 16%

In 1999, the new education minister promised to address persistent illiteracy, violence, and unequal resources. Government/NGO cooperation provides worksite training programs and technology in school.

HEALTH

▷ Welfare state health benefits

1 per 1,695 people

Heart, respiratory and diarrheal diseases, cancers, road deaths

Health services were formally desegregated in 1990, but equal access to care is still a distant goal. Statistics on medical provision hide a strong bias toward whites and urban areas, where 80% of doctors work. Poor provision for rural areas may explain why one in five children die before the age of five – a rate considerably higher than the sub-Saharan average. Affordable grassroots initiatives are tackling this problem. However, the incidence of tuberculosis is 60 times higher than in the USA, for example; and AIDS/HIV is spreading alarmingly.

SPENDING

▷ GDP/cap. increase

CONSUMPTION AND SPENDING

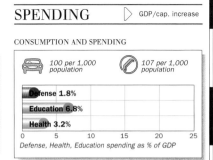

100 per 1,000 population

107 per 1,000 population

- Defense 1.8%
- Education 6.8%
- Health 3.2%

Defense, Health, Education spending as % of GDP

In South Africa, the black majority is the poorest group. Wealth disparities are marked. At the top, the white elite enjoys living standards similar to those of Californians. In contrast, black living conditions are among Africa's poorest. Nearly half of black adults are unemployed. Most lack decent housing, education, and health facilities. In between are the mixed race and Asian communities, who enjoyed more privileges under apartheid's strict racial hierarchy. A small black middle class is growing slowly, with some black-owned firms doing well on the stock market.

S

WORLD RANKING

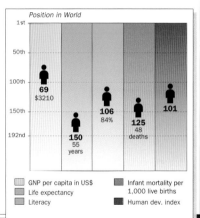

Position in World

- 69 $3210
- 150 55 years
- 106 84%
- 125 48 deaths
- 101

GNP per capita in US$	Infant mortality per 1,000 live births
Life expectancy	Human dev. index
Literacy	

SPAIN

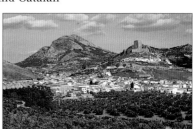
EUROPE

OFFICIAL NAME: Kingdom of Spain **CAPITAL:** Madrid **POPULATION:** 39.8 million
CURRENCY: Spanish Peseta **OFFICIAL LANGUAGES:** Spanish, Galician, Basque and Catalan

| 1492 | 1713 | Oct 12 | E | +1 | +34 | .es |

Situated in Southwest Europe, Spain has a wet Atlantic and a dry Mediterranean coast. It is dominated by a central plateau drained by the Duero, Tagus and Guadiana rivers. After the death of General Franco in 1975, Spain managed a rapid and relatively peaceful transition to democracy under the supervision of King Juan Carlos I. Since joining the EU in 1986, there has been an increasing devolution of power to the regions. For 13 years from 1982 center-left administrations led by Felipe González ruled Spain but the 1996 elections brought the right-of-center Popular Party to power.

Alcaudete, Jaén Province, in the Andalusian mountains between Granada and the River Guadalquivir. The ruined castle is Moorish.

CLIMATE
▷ Mediterranean/maritime/mountain

WEATHER CHART

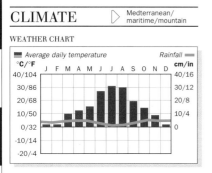

- ▪ Average daily temperature
- Rainfall

The central plateau, or *meseta*, endures an extreme climate. Coastal areas are milder, and wetter in the north than in the south.

TRANSPORTATION
▷ Drive on right

Barajas, Madrid
25m passengers

1,713 ships
1.67m grt

THE TRANSPORTATION NETWORK

341,900 km (212,450 miles)	7,747 km (4,814 miles)
15,903 km (9,882 miles)	1,045 km (649 miles)

Modern communications include the AVE, a high-speed train linking Madrid and Seville. Significant expressway construction is under way in Galicia.

TOURISM
▷ Visitors : population 1.1:1

43.4m visitors

Down 3% 1995–1997

MAIN TOURIST ARRIVALS

- France 22%
- Portugal 17%
- Germany 16
- UK 15%
- Italy 5%
- Other 25%

% of total arrivals

Tourism accounts for some 10% of GDP and employs around 8% of the working population. Spain thrives on the vacation package sector despite marketing strategies to boost additional cultural, historical and environmental tourism. The cut-price vacation sector has benefited from the emerging markets of central and eastern Europe and from political turbulence in potential competitor countries in the Mediterranean. France, Germany, and the UK still account for over 50% of all arrivals.

PEOPLE
▷ Pop. density medium

Spanish, Catalan, Galician, Basque

80/km² (206/mi²)

THE URBAN/RURAL POPULATION SPLIT

76%   24%

RELIGIOUS PERSUASION

- Roman Catholic 96%
- Other 4%

ETHNIC MAKEUP

- Romany 1%
- Galician 6%
- Other 2%
- Basque 2%
- Catalan 17%
- Castilian Spanish 72%

A vigorous ethnic regionalism in Spain, suppressed under Franco, now flourishes. Despite a high-profile terror campaign, ETA separatists fighting for independence remain in a minority in the Basque region. In September 1998 ETA announced a unilateral cease-fire.

Spain today has one of the lowest birth rates in Europe, and the influence of the Catholic Church on personal behavior has declined. However, many traditional aspects of Spanish life remain. While attitudes to sexuality are now relaxed, Church-going remains popular. The divorce rate is extremely low and family ties remain strong; young men live at home until their late 20s.

Economic growth from the 1970s led to a change in the composition of society. Migration from poor rural regions to the coast was associated with the arrival of large numbers of job-seeking immigrants, mainly from Latin America and north Africa. Economic downturn in the 1990s has led to a rise in racial tensions and racism, a pattern echoed in France.

Spanish women are increasingly emancipated and more influential in politics, now making up over 20% of the Spanish Congress.

POPULATION AGE BREAKDOWN

Female	Age	Male
2.3%	81–100	1.2%
9.8%	61–80	8%
11.8%	41–60	11.5%
15.9%	21–40	16.3%
11.3%	0–20	11.9%

% of population by age group

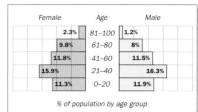

POLITICS ▷ Multiparty elections

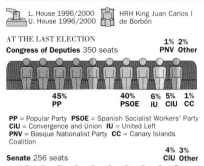

L. House 1996/2000
U. House 1996/2000

HRH King Juan Carlos I
de Borbón

AT THE LAST ELECTION
Congress of Deputies 350 seats

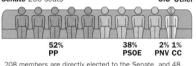

| 45% PP | 40% PSOE | 6% IU | 5% CiU | 1% CC | 1% PNV | 2% Other |

PP = Popular Party **PSOE** = Spanish Socialist Workers' Party
CiU = Convergence and Union **IU** = United Left
PNV = Basque Nationalist Party **CC** = Canary Islands
Coalition

Senate 256 seats

| 52% PP | 38% PSOE | 2% PNV | 1% CC | 4% CiU | 3% Other |

208 members are directly elected to the Senate, and 48 appointed by autonomous communities.

Since 1978, Spain has been a semifederal multiparty parliamentary monarchy. The regions have their own legislative assemblies.

MAIN POLITICAL ISSUES
Increasing regionalism
Spain has 17 autonomous regions, all vying for greater funds or independence from Madrid. Many have bypassed central government to borrow funds on the international money markets and have come close to breaching their legal debt limits. In 1996 the PP government approved a new model of financing for the autonomous regions which gave them new tax revenue raising powers.

Clean government
The PSOE has been discredited by a stream of corruption scandals and allegations that ministers masterminded the undercover shooting and kidnapping of ETA separatists in the 1980s. In 1998 the Supreme Court found the former interior minister and two other top PSOE figures guilty of involvement in the 1983 kidnapping of a French Basque businessman who was mistaken for a wanted ETA member. Each was sentenced to 10 years' imprisonment.

PROFILE
Felipe González's PSOE dominated politics for 13 years until its defeat in 1996 and its replacement by the minority PP government of José María Aznar. Such a long period in power blurred the boundaries between party and state. The *Cortes* (parliament) failed to check executive power, and political disputes were often left to the judiciary. Ideological issues no longer sharply divide the main parties, which hold similar views on economic policy and EU membership. Political corruption has undermined voters' faith in Spain's political system.

King Juan Carlos, who became Head of State on the death of Gen. Franco in 1975.

José María Aznar, who became prime minister in 1996.

WORLD AFFAIRS ▷ Joined UN in 1955

CE | NATO | OECD | OSCE | EU

Spain remains an enthusiastic member of the EU, but has been chary of enlarging the union to include central Europe, which it sees as a threat to its direct financial benefit. Elsewhere, Spain has sponsored an Ibero-American Community of Nations (a Hispanic Commonwealth). Spain is anxious to establish itself as a major international player. In 1995 former Spanish defense minister Javier Solana was appointed NATO Secretary-General; in 1999 he was nominated to head a new EU common foreign and security policy office in Brussels. Spain has contributed troops to the UN peacekeeping force in former Yugoslavia.

CHRONOLOGY
United under Ferdinand and Isabella in 1492, Spain became a dominant force in Europe. A long period of economic and political decline followed, however. By the mid-19th century, Spain lagged behind many other European countries in stability and prosperity.

- ❑ **1874** Constitutional monarchy restored under Alfonso XII.
- ❑ **1879** Spanish Socialist Workers' Party (PSOE) founded.
- ❑ **1881** Trade unions legalized.
- ❑ **1885** Death of Alfonso XII.
- ❑ **1898** Defeat in war with USA results in loss of Cuba, Puerto Rico, and Philippines.
- ❑ **1914–1918** Spain neutral in World War I.
- ❑ **1921** Spanish army routed by Berbers in Spanish Morocco.
- ❑ **1923** Coup by Gen. Primo de Rivera accepted by King Alfonso XIII. Military dictatorship.
- ❑ **1930** Primo de Rivera dismissed by monarchy.
- ❑ **1931** Second Republic proclaimed. Alfonso XIII flees Spain. ➡

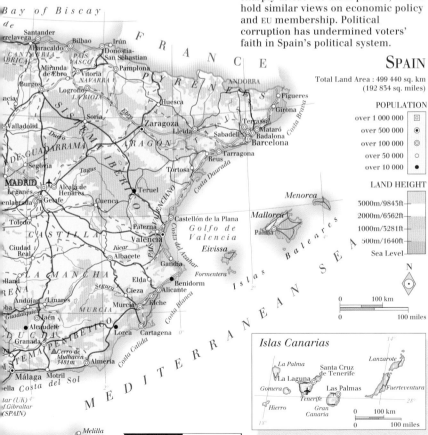

SPAIN
Total Land Area : 499 440 sq. km
(192 854 sq. miles)

POPULATION
over 1 000 000	▣
over 500 000	◉
over 100 000	◎
over 50 000	○
over 10 000	●

LAND HEIGHT
3000m/9843ft
2000m/6562ft
1000m/3281ft
500m/1640ft
Sea Level

0 — 100 km
0 — 100 miles

Islas Canarias
0 — 100 km
0 — 100 miles

S

CHRONOLOGY *continued*

- ❏ **1933** Center-right coalition wins general election.
- ❏ **1934** Asturias uprising quashed by army. Failure of attempt to form Catalan state.
- ❏ **1936** Popular Front wins elections. Right-wing military uprising against Republic. Gen. Franco subsequently appointed leader.
- ❏ **1939** Franco wins civil war which claims 500,000 lives.
- ❏ **1940** Franco meets Hitler, but does not enter World War II.
- ❏ **1946** UN condemns Franco regime.
- ❏ **1948** Spain excluded from Marshall Plan.
- ❏ **1950** UN lifts veto.
- ❏ **1953** Concordat with Vatican. Spain grants USA military bases.
- ❏ **1955** Spain joins UN.
- ❏ **1959** Stabilization Plan is basis for 1960s rapid economic growth.
- ❏ **1962** Franco government applies for eventual membership of EEC.
- ❏ **1969** Gen. Franco names Juan Carlos, grandson of Alfonso XIII, his successor.
- ❏ **1970** Spain signs preferential trade agreement with EEC.
- ❏ **1973** Prime Minister Carrero Blanco assassinated by Basque separatists. Succeeded by Arias Navarro.
- ❏ **1975** Death of Franco. Proclamation of King Juan Carlos I.
- ❏ **1976** King replaces Arias Navarro with Adolfo Suárez.
- ❏ **1977** First democratic elections since 1936 won by Suárez's Democratic Center Union.
- ❏ **1978** New constitution declares Spain a parliamentary monarchy.
- ❏ **1981** Leopoldo Calvo Sotelo replaces Suárez. King foils military coup. Calvo takes Spain into NATO.
- ❏ **1982** Felipe González wins landslide victory for PSOE.
- ❏ **1986** Spain joins EC. González wins referendum to keep Spain in NATO.
- ❏ **1992** Olympic Games held in Barcelona, Expo '92 in Seville.
- ❏ **1996** PSOE loses general election; José María Aznar of PP prime minister.
- ❏ **1998** Former PSOE interior minister and two others found guilty of involvement in Basque kidnappings.
- ❏ **1999** Introduction of euro.

AID ▷ Donor

 $1.2bn (donations) ⬦ Not applicable

Spain has taken steps to increase grant aid after criticism that Spanish aid was of poor quality and tied to the acquisition of goods and services. Aid in 1997 represented 0.23% of GNP.

DEFENSE ▷ Compulsory military service

💲 $7.7bn ⬇ Down 13% in 1997

A substantial, largely state-owned and commercially nonviable defense industry is subsidized for strategic reasons. Exports of conventional weapons were worth $57 million in 1996.

Defense spending has fallen in recent years, to well under 2% of GDP in 1997, the lowest of any NATO country except Luxembourg. National service is due to end in 2001.

SPANISH ARMED FORCES

🛡	725 main battle tanks (209 AMX-30, 164 M-48A5E, 244 M-60, 108 *Leopard*)	127,000 personnel
🚢	1 carrier, 8 submarines 17 frigates and 32 patrol boats	36,950 personnel
✈	193 combat aircraft (83 EF/A-18 A/B, 14 RF-4C, 66 Mirage 78 C-212)	30,000 personnel
	None	

ECONOMICS ▷ Inflation 6.1% p.a. (1985–1996)

📊 $569.6bn 💲 152.42–141.70 pesetas

SCORE CARD

- ❏ WORLD GNP RANKING...........................10th
- ❏ GNP PER CAPITA $14,490
- ❏ BALANCE OF PAYMENTS...................$2.49bn
- ❏ INFLATION 2%
- ❏ UNEMPLOYMENT....................................21%

EXPORTS

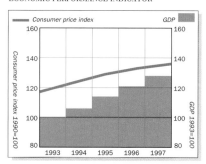

UK 8%
Portugal 9%
Other 42%
Italy 10%
Germany 13%
France 18%

IMPORTS

USA 6%
Other 44%
UK 8%
Italy 9%
Germany 15%
France 17%

STRENGTHS

Spain now has one of the fastest growing OECD economies. The labor force is well qualified, and labor costs are relatively low. Privatization is introducing greater competition into the telecommunications, electricity, gas, and oil refining sectors.

WEAKNESSES

Massive foreign penetration of economy and absence of Spanish multinationals pose long-term problems. Low investment in research and development, a concentration in declining industries and low productivity – notably in agriculture – are major weaknesses. Unemployment has remained persistently high at over 20% since 1993, although it is gradually beginning to fall.

PROFILE

Real convergence with the major European economies seemed possible in 1986–1991 as Spain posted the highest investment-led output growth

ECONOMIC PERFORMANCE INDICATOR

— Consumer price index   GDP ▮

Consumer price index 1990=100 / GDP 1993=100

1993 1994 1995 1996 1997

in the OECD. By 1991, GDP per capita stood at almost 80% of the EC average. In 1992, however, Spain plunged into recession along with its major trading partners. In 1992–1993, three devaluations of the peseta, by a total of 18%, just kept it within the ERM. Economic recovery produced growth of 3% by 1995, including strong domestic demand, and this has since been maintained. Spain succeeded in meeting the convergence criteria necessary for economic and monetary union and was among the 11 EU countries to introduce the euro in 1999.

SPAIN : MAJOR BUSINESSES

La Coruña
Bilbao
Zaragoza
Barcelona
Vigo
Madrid
Huelva
Valencia
Sevilla
Cartagena
Málaga

❋ Textiles
🐄 Agribusiness
⚗ Chemicals
⚓ Shipbuilding
🚗 Vehicle manufacture
⚙ Heavy engineering
⚙ Light engineering
🔲 Fish processing

0   200 km
0   200 miles

* significant multinational ownership

RESOURCES

▷ Electric power 45.8m kw

🐟 1.3m tonnes

🛢 21,514 b/d (reserves 22,518,000 bbl)

🐑 24.5m sheep, 19.3m pigs, 5.8m cattle

💎 Coal, oil, iron, uranium, mercury, fluorite, gypsum

ELECTRICITY GENERATION

Hydro 15% (24.6bn kwh)	
Combustion 52% (86.4bn kwh)	
Nuclear 33% (55.5bn kwh)	
Other 0%	

0　20　40　60　80　100

% of total generation by type

Spain lacks natural resources, especially water, and is heavily dependent on imported oil and gas. Contrary to popular belief, food products, such as fruit and vegetables, constitute less than 15% of its exports. Spain has one of the world's largest fishing fleets, but EU restrictions have limited catches in the 1990s.

SPAIN : LAND USE

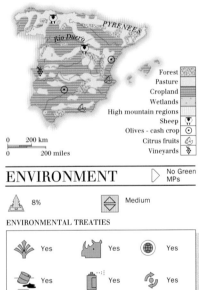

PYRENEES

Rio Duero

Forest	
Pasture	
Cropland	
Wetlands	
High mountain regions	
Sheep	🐑
Olives - cash crop	☉
Citrus fruits	🍊
Vineyards	🍇

0　200 km
0　200 miles

ENVIRONMENT

▷ No Green MPs

🔺 8%

⬍ Medium

ENVIRONMENTAL TREATIES

🌿 Yes　🦏 Yes　🌐 Yes

🛢 Yes　🧴 Yes　♻ Yes

Little attention was paid to environmental matters until very recently, but public opinion is becoming increasingly demanding. The benefits of a national tree planting scheme to reduce soil erosion have been offset by losses from increasingly frequent intentional forest fires. More land has national park status than in any other country in Europe. In 1998 five million cu. m of toxic waste leaked into the Guadiamar river near Seville, polluting farmland and the nearby Coto de Doñana wetlands, Europe's largest bird reserve. A large new dam project is threatening the habitat and hence the survival of Spain's last brown bears.

MEDIA

▷ TV ownership high

📰 Daily newspaper circulation 99 per 1,000 people

PUBLISHING AND BROADCAST MEDIA

📰 There are 87 daily newspapers, including *ABC*, *Ya* and *El País*.

📺 16 state-owned, also independent services

📻 13 state-owned, 350 independent services

Despite the large number of daily newspapers, readership is among the lowest in Europe. Both public and private TV are popular. Radio is of a generally high standard.

CRIME

▷ Death penalty not used

⚖ 40,157 prisoners

⬇ Down 2% from 1992–1996

CRIME RATES

Murders	
2	per 100,000 population

Rapes	
3	per 100,000 population

Thefts	
1869	per 100,000 population

Spain is a major crossroads in the world narcotics trade, and drugs related crime is rising. Rape is increasing (or reported more often), as is property-related crime.

EDUCATION

▷ School leaving age: 16

📖 97%

👨‍🎓 1.6m students

Of total government expenditure 12.6% is spent on education.

THE EDUCATION SYSTEM

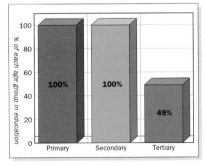

% of each age group in education

Primary	Secondary	Tertiary
100%	100%	49%

Some 35% of all schooling is private. Compulsory secondary education remains a major political priority. Most teaching in oversubscribed universities is lecture-based. Students with parental funding and good English are increasingly completing their education abroad, often in the USA.

HEALTH

▷ Welfare state health benefits

🧑‍⚕️ 1 per 244 people

☠ Heart and circulatory diseases, cancers, accidents

Of total government expenditure 11.8% is spent on health. Public health care is of high quality and readily available, and public hospitals are generally considered to be better than private ones. In spite of very high tobacco and alcohol consumption, Spain has a healthy population, possibly due to its Mediterranean diet. The incidence of AIDS, however, is the highest in Europe and higher than that in the USA.

SPENDING

▷ GDP/cap. no increase

CONSUMPTION AND SPENDING

🚗 389 per 1,000 population

📞 403 per 1,000 population

Defense 1.4%	
Education 5%	
Health 6.5%	

0　5　10　15　20　25
Defense, Health, Education spending as % of GDP

In the late 1980s, it became fashionable in Spain to compete openly, make money and consume. Rapid economic growth at this time greatly enriched the professional and managerial classes. The latter became the best-paid, in real terms, in Europe. Some media celebrities, such as the now disgraced banker Mario Conde of Banesto, rivaled soccer players in popularity. In spite of high taxes, the rich became richer and more ostentatious. Spain quickly became an important market for luxury cars and yachts; a personal bodyguard was also a status symbol in the early 1990s. The recession of the early 1990s changed attitudes, as unemployment rates soared to become the highest in Europe, although they have begun to fall as growth has resumed.

S

WORLD RANKING

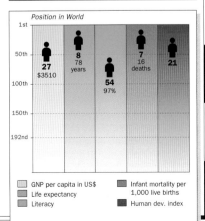

Position in World

1st
50th
100th
150th
192nd

27 $3510
8 78 years
54 97%
7 16 deaths
21

☐ GNP per capita in US$		☐ Infant mortality per 1,000 live births
☐ Life expectancy		
☐ Literacy		☐ Human dev. index

SRI LANKA

OFFICIAL NAME: Democratic Socialist Republic of Sri Lanka   **CAPITAL:** Colombo
POPULATION: 5 million   **CURRENCY:** Sri Lanka rupee   **OFFICIAL LANGUAGE:** Sinhalese

1948   1948   Feb 4   CL   +5.5   +94   .lk

SEPARATED FROM INDIA by the Palk Strait, Sri Lanka comprises one large island and several coral islets to the northwest known as Adam's Bridge. The main island is dominated by rugged central uplands. The fertile plains to the north are criss-crossed by rivers and bordered to the southeast by the Mahaweli Ganga river. Sri Lankan affairs are dominated by the conflict between the government and the Tamils, who are fighting for an independent state.

CLIMATE
Tropical monsoon/ equatorial

WEATHER CHART

■ Average daily temperature   Rainfall ■

The climate is tropical, with afternoon breezes on the coast and cooler air in the highlands. The northeast is driest.

TRANSPORTATION
Drive on left

Katunayake, Colombo
2.37m passengers

32 ships
438,200 grt

THE TRANSPORTATION NETWORK

25,879 km (16,174 miles)	None	
1,509 km (943 miles)	160 km (99 miles)	

Main roads are crowded and slow, but those to resorts are being improved. Air Lanka now flies nonstop to Europe.

TOURISM
Visitors : population 1:50

366,000 visitors   Down 9% 1995–1997

MAIN TOURIST ARRIVALS

Germany 23%	
UK 12%	
India 11%	
Other 54%	

% of total arrivals

Tourism continues despite the northern conflict and setbacks in the mid-1990s, when Colombo was the target of Tamil bomb attacks. Sri Lanka is popular with gay tourists, and has been targeted by Western pedophile rings.

PEOPLE
Pop. density high

Sinhalese, Tamil, Sinhalese-Tamil, English

286/km² (740/mi²)

THE URBAN/RURAL POPULATION SPLIT

22%   78%

ETHNIC MAKEUP

Burgher, Malay and Veddha 1%
Moor 7%
Tamil 18%
Sinhalese 74%

Ethnic tensions between the minority Tamils and majority Sinhalese erupted into civil war in 1983. The Tamils were the minority group favored by the British colonists. When the British left, laws were passed to redress the balance by favoring the Sinhalese. The effect was to make Tamils feel sidelined, and support for secession grew. The conflict also has a religious dimension. Most Sinhalese are Buddhist, while Tamils are mostly Muslim or Hindu.

POLITICS
Multiparty elections

1994/2000

President Chandrika Bandaranaike Kumaratunga

AT THE LAST ELECTION

Parliament 225 seats

47% PA	42% UNP	4% EPDP	2% TULF	1% DPLF	3% SLMC	1% Other

PA = People's Alliance (led by the SLFP = Sri Lankan Freedom Party) **UNP** = United National Party **EPDP** = Eelam People's Democratic Party **SLMC** = Sri Lanka Muslim Congress **TULF** = Tamil United Liberation Front **DPLF** = Democratic People's Liberation Front

The Tamil–Sinhalese conflict colors all political debate. In 1983, civil war erupted between the Liberation Tigers of Tamil Eelam (LTTE or Tamil Tigers) and the government. The LTTE wants an independent state in the north and east. The government is committed to keeping Sri Lanka unified, although it has pursued plans for greater regional autonomy. Attempts at a political settlement with the LTTE came to nothing with the collapse of talks in April 1995. A massive army operation gave the government military ascendancy but not a victory, as a civilian bombing campaign by the LTTE resumed.

SRI LANKA

Total Land Area : 64 740 sq. km (24 996 sq. miles)

POPULATION	
⊙	over 500 000
◎	over 100 000
○	over 50 000
●	over 10 000
•	under 10 000

LAND HEIGHT	
	2000m/6562ft
	1000m/3281ft
	500m/1640ft
	200m/656ft
	Sea Level

0   50 km
0   100 miles

N

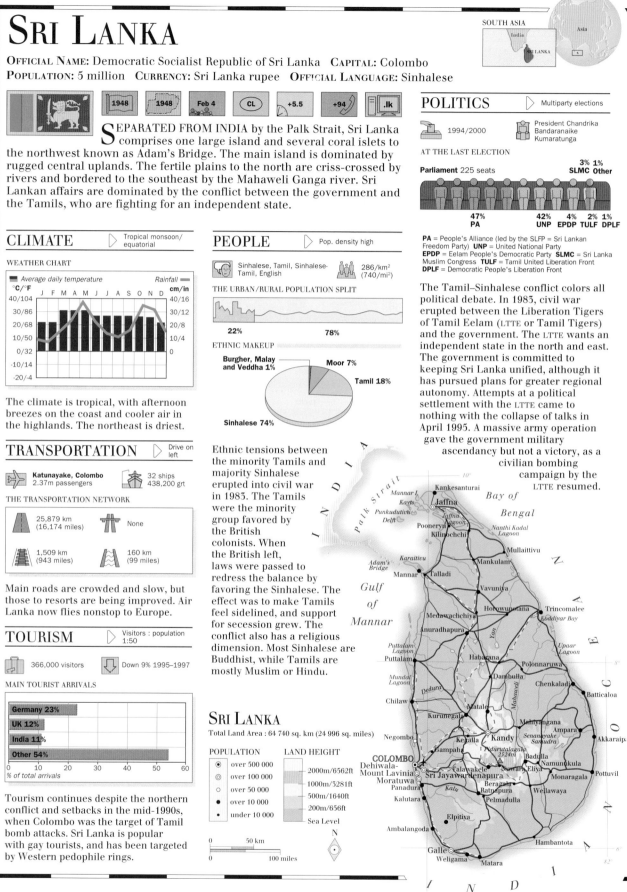

WORLD AFFAIRS

> Joined UN in 1955

Relations with India are paramount. The 1987 Indo-Sri Lankan accords led to Indian troops playing a peacekeeping role. Becoming embroiled in fighting the LTTE, however, they were forced to pull out. LTTE militants were behind the 1992 assassination of former Indian prime minister Rajiv Gandhi.

AID

> Recipient

 $345m (receipts) — Down 30% 1996–1997

The president has responded positively to Western aid donors seeking improvements in Sri Lanka's human rights record.

DEFENSE

> No compulsory military service

 $898m — Up 1% in 1997

Defeating the LTTE is the overwhelming concern. The collapse of peace talks in 1995 prompted the government to seek greater military assistance from abroad.

ECONOMICS

> Inflation 10.9% p.a. (1985–1996)

 $14.8bn — 61.75–68.43 Sri Lanka rupees

SCORE CARD

❏ WORLD GNP RANKING	75th
❏ GNP PER CAPITA	$800
❏ BALANCE OF PAYMENTS	$–388m
❏ INFLATION	9.6%
❏ UNEMPLOYMENT	11%

STRENGTHS

World's largest tea exporter. Export Processing Zones and state privatization programs attracting foreign investment. The left-wing government of President Kumaratunga has continued the sale of state assets.

WEAKNESSES

Civil war is a drain on government funds and deters investors and many tourists.

EXPORTS

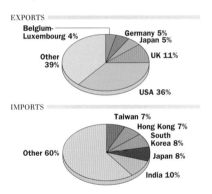

Belgium-Luxembourg 4%
Germany 5%
Japan 5%
Other 39%
UK 11%
USA 36%

IMPORTS

Taiwan 7%
Hong Kong 7%
South Korea 8%
Other 60%
Japan 8%
India 10%

Adam's peak in mountainous central Sri Lanka is a famous religious site with a Buddhist shrine at the summit.

RESOURCES

> Electric power 1.6m kw

 232,500 tonnes — Not an oil producer; refines 50,000 b/d

1.6m cattle, 519,300 goats, 76,300 pigs — Gemstones, graphite, iron, monazite, uranium, ilmenite, clay

Sri Lanka has to import all its oil. Hydropower supplies 75% of electricity; droughts are frequent and supplies can be erratic. Sri Lanka is keen to diversify power sources and is turning to coal-powered generation.

ENVIRONMENT

> No Green MPs

 13% (4% partially protected) — Low

Sri Lanka has successfully promoted national parks. Their development is opposed by the Veddha people who have traditionally occupied such land.

MEDIA

> TV ownership medium

 Daily newspaper circulation 29 per 1,000 people

PUBLISHING AND BROADCAST MEDIA

There are 9 daily newspapers, including the *Daily News*, *Davasa*, *Observer* and *Dinamina*	
2 state-owned, 3 independent services	1 state-owned, 4 independent services

Press censorship was imposed in 1995 to control war reporting by local news agencies. Since 1998 foreign journalists have faced similar restrictions.

CRIME

> Death penalty used

 14,128 prisoners — Up 52% from 1992–1996

Both the army and the LTTE have been accused of human rights abuses. The civil war has claimed tens of thousands of lives since 1983. LTTE members carry cyanide capsules in case of arrest.

EDUCATION

> School leaving age: 15

91% — 63,660 students

Sri Lanka has the highest literacy rate of any developing nation. Many Sri Lankans attend US universities.

CHRONOLOGY

Sri Lanka has been inhabited by the Tamils and Sinhalese since before the 6th century. Named Ceylon under the British Empire, the island became independent in 1948.

- ❏ **1948** Indian Tamil workers stripped of suffrage and citizenship rights.
- ❏ **1956** SLFP wins election: Sinhalese becomes sole national language.
- ❏ **1972** Name changed to Sri Lanka.
- ❏ **1983** Civil war erupts between Tamil LTTE and Sinhalese.
- ❏ **1990** Failed peace talks.
- ❏ **1993** President Premadasa murdered.
- ❏ **1994** Left-wing People's Alliance wins general election. Chandrika Kumaratunga elected president.
- ❏ **1995** Collapse of peace talks.
- ❏ **1996** Nationwide emergency as civil war resumes.

HEALTH

> Welfare state health benefits

1 per 10,000 people — Heart attacks, cancers, pneumonia, strokes

Years of high spending on health have resulted in an accessible, fee-free system. Ayurvedic medicine is popular.

SPENDING

> GDP/cap. increase

CONSUMPTION AND SPENDING

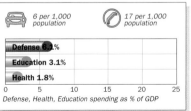

6 per 1,000 population — 17 per 1,000 population

Defense 6.1%
Education 3.1%
Health 1.8%

0 5 10 15 20 25
Defense, Health, Education spending as % of GDP

Economic growth has created a new class of wealthy Sinhalese. Tamil tea workers are the poorest group.

WORLD RANKING

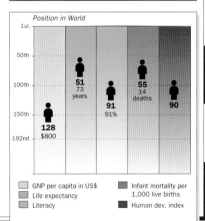

Position in World

1st
50th
100th
150th
192nd

128 $800
51 73 years
91 91%
55 14 deaths
90

▢ GNP per capita in US$	▪ Infant mortality per 1,000 live births
▢ Life expectancy	
▢ Literacy	▪ Human dev. index

S

SUDAN

OFFICIAL NAME: Republic of Sudan **CAPITAL:** Khartoum **POPULATION:** 28.5 million
CURRENCY: Sudanese pound or dinar **OFFICIAL LANGUAGE:** Arabic

EAST AFRICA

| 1956 | 1956 | Jan 1 | SUN | +2 | +249 | .sd |

BORDERED BY THE RED SEA, Sudan is the largest country in Africa. Its landscape changes from desert in the north to lush tropical in the south, with grassy plains and swamps in the center. Tensions between the Arab north and African south have led to two civil wars since independence from British and Egyptian rule in 1956. The second of these conflicts remains unresolved. In 1989, an army coup installed a military Islamic fundamentalist regime.

Camel caravan in the dry north. Periodic drought coupled with war disruption mean that Sudan requires large amounts of food aid.

CLIMATE

Hot desert/steppe/tropical

WEATHER CHART

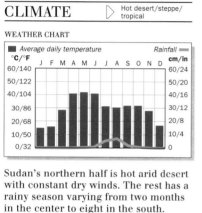

Sudan's northern half is hot arid desert with constant dry winds. The rest has a rainy season varying from two months in the center to eight in the south.

TRANSPORTATION

Drive on right

Khartoum International

7 ships
72,752 grt

THE TRANSPORTATION NETWORK

| 11,900 km (7,438 miles) | None |
| 4,595 km (2,298 miles) | 4,068 km (2,528 miles) |

The Port Sudan–Khartoum railroad and road are Sudan's most important links. There are few other roads, but Iran is financing a Rabak–Malakal highway. Civil war has stopped all Nile shipping.

TOURISM

Visitors : population 1:445

64,000 visitors

Visitor numbers rose in 1997

MAIN TOURIST ARRIVALS

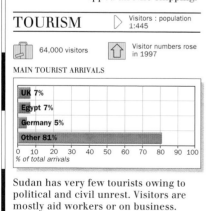

UK 7%
Egypt 7%
Germany 5%
Other 81%
% of total arrivals

Sudan has very few tourists owing to political and civil unrest. Visitors are mostly aid workers or on business.

PEOPLE

Pop. density low

Arabic, Dinka, Nuer, Nubian, Beja, Zande, Bari, Fur, Shilluk, Lotuko

12/km² (31/mi²)

THE URBAN/RURAL POPULATION SPLIT

25%   75%

RELIGIOUS PERSUASION

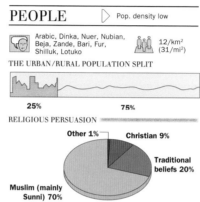

Other 1%
Christian 9%
Traditional beliefs 20%
Muslim (mainly Sunni) 70%

Sudan has a large number of ethnic and linguistic groups. About two million Sudanese are nomads. The major social division, however, is between the Arabized Muslims in the north and the mostly African, largely animist or Christian population in the south. Attempts to impose Arab and Islamic values throughout Sudan have been the root cause of the civil war that has ravaged the south since 1983. However, the rebels have now split into two factions, pitting southern Sudan's small ethnic groups against the Dinka, the south's largest tribe. There are some non-Arab groups in the north and the densely populated Darfur region. Women not wearing Islamic dress can suffer harassment or even public flogging.

SUDAN

Total Land Area : 2 376 000 sq. km (917 374 sq. miles)

0   400 km
0   400 miles

LAND HEIGHT

2000m/6562ft
1000m/3281ft
500m/1640ft
200m/656ft
Sea Level

POPULATION

over 500 000
over 100 000
over 50 000
over 10 000
under 10 000

POLITICS

No multiparty elections

1996/2000

President Omar Hassan Ahmad al-Bashir

AT THE LAST ELECTION

National Assembly 400 seats

Legislative elections were held in 1996 on a nonparty basis: 275 seats of the National Assembly are directly elected, the 125 others are indirectly elected.

The military regime headed by General al-Bashir took over in a coup in 1989. It banned all political parties except the National Islamic Front (NIF). After the nonparty 1996 elections, NIF leader Hassan al-Turabi, Sudan's most influential figure, became president of the National Assembly. A strict policy of Islamicization, including *sharia* law, has been imposed, but is rejected by the non-Muslim southern rebels. Dissent elsewhere has been violently crushed. A new constitution introduced in January 1999 allows "political associations," but not parties.

S

WORLD AFFAIRS

Joined UN in 1956

Sudan's support for Iraq in the Gulf War and suspicion that it sponsors terrorism have led to increasing isolation from the West and the Arab world. Only Iran, Yemen, and Libya maintain friendly relations.

AID

Recipient

$187m (receipts)

Down 19% 1996–1997

Sudan's only substantial bilateral aid comes from Iran. IMF funding ceased in 1990. Sudan depends on food aid.

DEFENSE

Compulsory military service

$418m

Up 2% in 1997

The NIF controls the military and police and has its own paramilitary militia. Sudan's 116,800-strong army is engaged in fighting the two factions of the southern Sudanese People's Liberation Army, numbering up to 100,000 men.

ECONOMICS

Inflation 89.9% p.a. (1988–1993)

$7.92bn

161.29–196.00 Sudanese dinars

SCORE CARD

- ❑ World GNP Ranking...........................90th
- ❑ GNP per Capita $290
- ❑ Balance of Payments....................$–828m
- ❑ Inflation 46.7%
- ❑ Unemployment.................................30%

STRENGTHS

Oil, gas, cotton, gum arabic, sesame, sugar. Some gold mining.

WEAKNESSES

Low industrialization. Lack of foreign exchange for importing energy and spare parts for industry. Drought. Little transportation infrastructure. Huge distances between towns. Exploitation of oil reserves prevented by civil war. Alienation of Arab donors and investors.

EXPORTS

France 5%
Japan 4%
Germany 8%
Italy 13%
Saudi Arabia 21%
Other 49%

IMPORTS

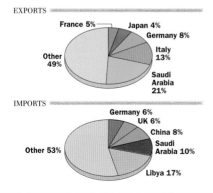

Germany 6%
UK 6%
China 8%
Saudi Arabia 10%
Libya 17%
Other 53%

RESOURCES

Electric power 500,000 kw

45,000 tonnes

Reserves of 300m bbl; refines 21,700 b/d

42.4m sheep, 37.3m goats, 34.6m cattle, 2.9m camels

Oil, gas, gold, copper, gypsum, marble, mica, silver, chromium, zinc

Large oil and gas reserves were found in the south in the 1980s, but civil war has prevented their exploitation. The half-thermal, half-hydroelectric generating capacity is insufficient, and week-long power cuts are frequent. Gold mining has expansion potential.

ENVIRONMENT

No Green MPs

4% (0.3% partially protected)

Low

Flooding from the White Nile into the Sudd, the world's largest swamp and a rich wetland habitat, would have been affected by the Jonglei canal irrigation scheme, halted in 1986.

MEDIA

TV ownership medium

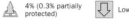

Daily newspaper circulation 27 per 1,000 people

PUBLISHING AND BROADCAST MEDIA

There are 5 daily newspapers, including *Al-Anbaa, Ar-Rai al-Amm* and *Al-Nasr*

1 state-controlled service

1 state-controlled, 1 rebel-controlled service

The media were relatively free from 1985 to 1989, but all are now controlled by the government or the army.

CRIME

Death penalty used

Sudan does not publish prison figures

Up 26% in 1992

Antigovernment dissent is often suppressed by violence, and torture by the security forces is widespread. The UN has condemned Sudan's poor human rights record, most recently in 1996.

EDUCATION

School leaving age: 13

53%

59,824 students

In 1991, measures were introduced to Islamicize education. Primary school children must have two years of Islamic religious instruction, and men wishing to enter university must first serve for a year in the NIF's People's Militia.

HEALTH

Welfare state health benefits

1 per 10,000 people

Infectious and parasitic diseases, malnutrition

As most health funds are tied to urban hospitals, health service standards in rural areas are basic. The civil war has led to an increase in communicable diseases, especially leishmaniasis.

CHRONOLOGY

Northern Sudan was taken by Egypt in 1821, the south by Britain in 1877.

- ❑ **1882** British invade Egypt.
- ❑ **1883** Muslim revolt in Sudan led by Muhammad Ahmed, the Mahdi.
- ❑ **1898** Mahdists defeated. Anglo-Egyptian condominium set up.
- ❑ **1955** Rebellion in south starts 17 years of civil war.
- ❑ **1956** Independence as republic.
- ❑ **1958–1964** Military rule.
- ❑ **1965** Civilian revolution, elections.
- ❑ **1969** Army coup led by Col. Nimeri.
- ❑ **1972** South gets limited autonomy.
- ❑ **1973** Sudanese Socialist Union (former communist) sole party.
- ❑ **1983** Southern rebellion resumes. *Sharia* law imposed.
- ❑ **1984** Devastating drought.
- ❑ **1986** Army coup restores civilian government.
- ❑ **1989** Gen. al-Bashir takes over.
- ❑ **1991** *Sharia* penal code instituted. Sudan backs Iraq in Gulf War.
- ❑ **1996** Bashir wins presidential election. Fundamentalist NIF strengthens position in parliament.
- ❑ **1999** New peace attempt in south.

SPENDING

GDP.cap no increase

CONSUMPTION AND SPENDING

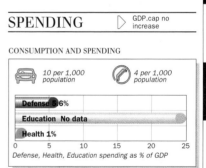

10 per 1,000 population

4 per 1,000 population

Defense 5.6%
Education No data
Health 1%

Defense, Health, Education spending as % of GDP

Wealth is limited to the NIF and southern rebel elites. Most of the population struggles to survive.

S

WORLD RANKING

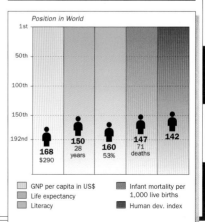

Position in World

168 $290
150 28 years
160 53%
147 71 deaths
142

- ❑ GNP per capita in US$
- ❑ Life expectancy
- ❑ Literacy
- ❑ Infant mortality per 1,000 live births
- ❑ Human dev. index

SURINAME

SOUTH AMERICA

OFFICIAL NAME: Republic of Suriname   **CAPITAL:** Paramaribo
POPULATION: 442,000   **CURRENCY:** Suriname guilder or florin   **OFFICIAL LANGUAGE:** Dutch

| 1975 | 1975 | Nov 25 | SME | -3 | +597 | .sr |

L OCATED ON THE NORTH COAST of South America,
Suriname is bordered by Guyana, French Guiana
and Brazil. The interior is rainforested highlands; most
people live near the coast. In 1975, after almost 300 years of Dutch rule,
Suriname became independent. The Netherlands is still its main aid
supplier, and home to one-third of Surinamese. Multiparty democracy was
restored in 1991, after almost 11 years of military rule.

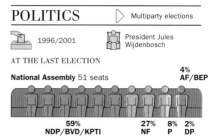

*Congested street in Paramaribo. It boasts
18th and 19th century Dutch architecture and
the Caribbean's largest mosque.*

CLIMATE

▷ Tropical equatorial

WEATHER CHART

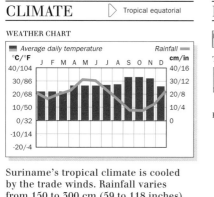

Suriname's tropical climate is cooled
by the trade winds. Rainfall varies
from 150 to 300 cm (59 to 118 inches)
between coast and interior.

TRANSPORTATION

▷ Drive on left

Johann Pengel Intl, Paramaribo
175,000 passengers

19 ships
7,824 grt

THE TRANSPORTATION NETWORK

942 km (585 miles)	None
157 km (98 miles)	1,500 km (932 miles)

The road network runs east–west and
focuses on the coast and its immediate
hinterland. Rivers provide the main
north–south links. The vast interior
relies on water or air transportation.

TOURISM

▷ Visitors : population 1:4.9

90,000 visitors

Up 200% 1994–1997

MAIN TOURIST ARRIVALS

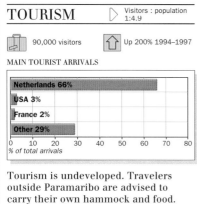

| Netherlands 66% |
| USA 3% |
| France 2% |
| Other 29% |

0   10   20   30   40   50   60   70   80
% of total arrivals

Tourism is undeveloped. Travelers
outside Paramaribo are advised to
carry their own hammock and food.

PEOPLE

▷ Pop. density low

Pidgin English (Taki-Taki),
Dutch, Hindi, Javanese,
Saramacca, Carib

3/km²
(7/mi²)

THE URBAN/RURAL POPULATION SPLIT

50%   **50%**

ETHNIC MAKEUP

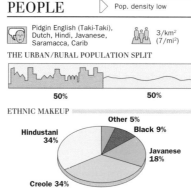

Hindustani 34%
Creole 34%
Javanese 18%
Black 9%
Other 5%

About 250,000 Surinamese, one-third of
the ethnically diverse population, have
emigrated since 1975. Of those still in
Suriname, 90% live near the coast. The
rest live in very scattered rain forest
communities. About 7,000 are native
Amerindians. The remainder are
bosnegers – the descendants of runaway
African slaves. They fought the Creole-
dominated government in the 1980s.
Many Indians and Javanese (from
Indonesia) work in farming.

POLITICS

▷ Multiparty elections

1996/2001

President Jules
Wijdenbosch

AT THE LAST ELECTION

National Assembly 51 seats

4%
AF/BEP

59%
NDP/BVD/KPTI

27%
NF

8%
P

2%
DP

NDP/BVD/KPTI = National Democratic Party/Movement for
Renewal and Change/Party for Unity and Harmony
NF = New Front for Democracy and Development (includes
Suriname National Party, Suriname Labour Party)
P = Pendawalima (Javanese Party)   **AF/BEP** = Alternative
Forum/Brotherhood and Unity in Politics
DP = Democratic Party

A coalition government of traditional
parties representing Creoles, Indians
and Indonesians took power in 1991.
Divisions saw them lose in 1996 to the
NDP, controlled by Desi Bouterse, the
military ruler from 1980 to 1988, who
was behind a 1990 coup. A grand
coalition of employers, unions and
opposition parties demanded the
resignation of President Jules
Wijdenbosch's NDP
government in
1998. In mid-1999
Wijdenbosch
faced another
attempt by
opponents in
the National
Assembly to
replace him. He
held on to office
but promised
fresh elections
by May 2000.

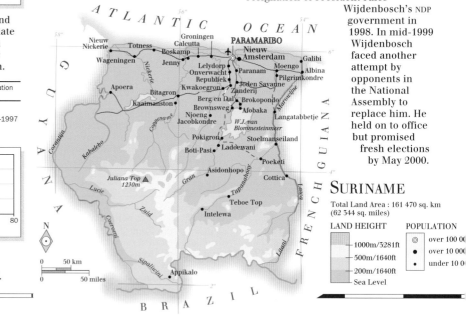

SURINAME

Total Land Area : 161 470 sq. km
(62 344 sq. miles)

LAND HEIGHT

1000m/3281ft
500m/1640ft
200m/1640ft
Sea Level

POPULATION

◎ over 100 000
● over 10 000
• under 10 000

WORLD AFFAIRS

▷ Joined UN in 1975

Relations with the Netherlands and the USA, Suriname's key aid and trading partners, have been weakened over charges of official connivance in drug-trafficking. The Dutch have unsuccessfully demanded former ruler Desi Bouterse's extradition on drugs charges. Greater integration with the Caribbean is a priority.

AID

▷ Recipient

$77m (receipts) — Down 31% 1996–1997

The Netherlands is the largest donor, but deteriorating relations in recent years has seen aid suspended. In 1998 the IDB and European Investment Bank granted loans for agricultural and industrial development.

DEFENSE

▷ No compulsory military service

$15m — Up 7% in 1997

The army was politically dominant in the 1980s under Col. Desi Bouterse, who resigned as army chief in 1992. President Wijdenbosch was his right-hand man. A six-year civil war against *bosneger* rebels ended in 1992.

ECONOMICS

▷ Inflation 77.4% (1985–1996)

$544m — 401 Suriname guilders

SCORE CARD

❑ WORLD GNP RANKING	164th
❑ GNP PER CAPITA	$1,320
❑ BALANCE OF PAYMENTS	$73m
❑ INFLATION	7.1%
❑ UNEMPLOYMENT	11%

STRENGTHS
Bauxite. Gold. Timber potential. Oil. Agricultural exports: rice, bananas, citrus fruits. Shrimp exports.

WEAKNESSES
Overdependence on declining bauxite reserves and on Dutch aid. Weak currency. Severe shortage of foreign exchange. Vulnerability to falls in world commodity prices. Net food importer.

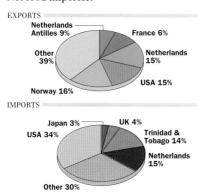

EXPORTS

- Netherlands Antilles 9%
- France 6%
- Other 39%
- Netherlands 15%
- USA 15%
- Norway 16%

IMPORTS

- Japan 3%
- UK 4%
- USA 34%
- Trinidad & Tobago 14%
- Netherlands 15%
- Other 30%

RESOURCES

▷ Electric power 425,000 kw

13,150 tonnes

10,000 b/d (reserves 80,490,000 bbl)

89,000 cattle, 20,000 pigs, 7,400 sheep

Bauxite, iron, manganese, copper, nickel, platinum, gold

Suriname is a major exporter of aluminum and bauxite, but the sector has recently been hit by poor world prices, as has raw gold production. State oil production was 10,000 b/d in 1998, but the sector reported a loss of US$7 million. Exploitation of rainforests has begun. Rice and fruit are the key agricultural products.

ENVIRONMENT

▷ No Green MPs

4% partially protected

Economic growth has precedence over ecological concerns

In 1998 the government declared some 16,000 sq km of rainforest, almost a tenth of the country, a natural reserve barred to logging. The US organization Conservation International gave US$1 million in support.

MEDIA

▷ TV ownership medium

Daily newspaper circulation 116 per 1,000 people

PUBLISHING AND BROADCAST MEDIA

There are 2 daily newspapers, *De Ware Tijd* and *De West*

2 state-owned services

2 state-owned, 8 independent services

There are radio broadcasts in a number of languages. Dutch is used by the daily newspapers and mainly in TV stations.

CRIME

▷ Death penalty not used

Suriname does not publish prison figures

Relatively high crime levels from year to year

Human rights abuses associated with the former military regime have largely ended. Rival armed factions remain in some interior regions. Drug trafficking and money laundering are a problem, as is urban street crime.

EDUCATION

▷ School leaving age: 12

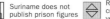

94%

4,319 students

Education is free and includes adult literacy programs. There is a long tradition of higher education, but most graduates now live in the Netherlands.

HEALTH

▷ Welfare state health benefits

1 per 2,500 people

Heart attacks, cancers, malaria, malnutrition

Urban medical facilities are relatively good; Paramaribo has five hospitals. Provision in the interior is basic.

SPENDING

▷ GDP/cap. no increase

CONSUMPTION AND SPENDING

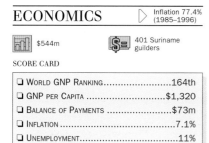

59 per 1,000 population

130 per 1,000 population

- Defense 4.4%
- Education 3.5%
- Health 5.7%

Defense, Health, Education spending as % of GDP

Living standards have fallen since 1982, due to the effects of civil war and aid and loan suspension. Urban Creoles dominate the rich elite. Amerindians and *bosnegers* are the poorest groups.

WORLD RANKING

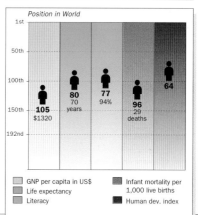

Position in World

- 105 $1320
- 80 70 years
- 77 94%
- 96 29 deaths
- 64

- GNP per capita in US$
- Life expectancy
- Literacy
- Infant mortality per 1,000 live births
- Human dev. index

S

SWAZILAND

OFFICIAL NAME: Kingdom of Swaziland **CAPITAL:** Mbabane
POPULATION: 900,000 **CURRENCY:** Lilangeni **OFFICIAL LANGUAGES:** English and Siswati

1968	1968	Sept 6	S	+1	+46	.sz

THE TINY SOUTHERN AFRICAN kingdom of Swaziland, bordered on three sides by South Africa and to the east by Mozambique, comprises mainly upland plateaus and mountains. Governed by a strong hereditary monarch, Swaziland is a country in which tradition is being challenged by demands for modern multiparty government. King Mswati III, crowned in 1986, has overhauled the electoral process, but has still to legalize party politics.

CLIMATE ▷ Subtropical

WEATHER CHART

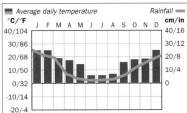

Swaziland is temperate. Temperatures rise and rainfall declines as the land descends eastward, from high to low *veld*. The Low Veld is prone to drought.

TRANSPORTATION ▷ Drive on left

Matsapha, Manzini
93,000 passengers

Has no fleet

THE TRANSPORTATION NETWORK

814 km (506 miles)	None
301 km (187 miles)	None

A sharp rise in road traffic has necessitated road improvements. The railroad, running to Mozambique and South Africa, mainly carries exports.

TOURISM ▷ Visitors : population 1:2.9

322,000 visitors

Up 2% 1995–1997

MAIN TOURIST ARRIVALS

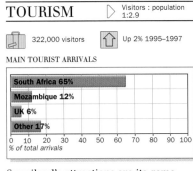

South Africa 65%							
Mozambique 12%							
UK 6%							
Other 17%							

0 10 20 30 40 50 60 70 80 90 100
% of total arrivals

Swaziland's attractions are its game reserves, mountain scenery and, for the South Africans who make up more than 70% of tourists, its casinos.

The outskirts of Mbabane. It lies on the High Veld, where traditional cattle farming has become more difficult owing to overgrazing.

PEOPLE ▷ Pop. density medium

Siswati, English, Zulu

54/km² (140/mi²)

THE URBAN/RURAL POPULATION SPLIT

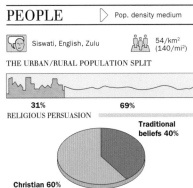

31%   69%

RELIGIOUS PERSUASION

Traditional beliefs 40%
Christian 60%

Over 95% of the population belong to the Swazi ethnic group, making Swaziland one of Africa's most homogeneous states. It is also very conservative, although it is now facing pressure from urban-based modernizers. A powerful monarchy dominates politics. Ancient traditions remain popular. Society is patriarchal and focused around the clan. Chiefs own much "national land," and wield authority through local consultations, called *tindkhundla*. Polygamy is tolerated. Women farm and may vote, but lack economic or political power. The exception is the Queen Mother, the "Great She Elephant," whose power as regent was clear during the interregnum of the mid-1980s.

POLITICS ▷ No multiparty elections

L. House 1998/2003
U. House 1998/2003

HM King Mswati III

AT THE LAST ELECTION

House of Assembly 65 seats

There are no political parties. 10 members of the House of Assembly are appointed by the Head of State.

Senate 30 seats

20 members of the Senate are appointed by the Head of State and 10 elected by the House of Assembly.

Politics is dominated by a strong executive monarchy and rivalries within the ruling Dlamini clan. Royal advisers complement a nominated cabinet. Direct elections were held in 1993, but parties remained banned. Responding to popular pressure, the king in 1996 appointed Sibusiso Dlamini as prime minister and set up a commission to review the political system and draft a new constitution by 2000.

SWAZILAND

Total Land Area : 17 200 sq. km (6641 sq. miles)

POPULATION	LAND HEIGHT
○ over 50 000	1000m/3281ft
● over 10 000	500m/1640ft
• under 10 000	200m/656ft
	Sea Level

S

WORLD AFFAIRS ▷ Joined UN in 1968

Swaziland's membership of the SACU reinforces its traditional economic dependence on South Africa. While welcoming the election of an ANC-led government in Pretoria, King Mswati has expressed concern over their support for Swazi prodemocracy campaigners. Peace in Mozambique has meant the return there of 134,000 Mozambican refugees.

AID ▷ Recipient

$27m (receipts)   Down 13% 1996–1997

Aid helps repair the Swazi balance of payments, and funds the development of the Matsapha industrial estate, roads, and social projects. Donors include Germany, the USA, the UK and the World Bank. EU aid mainly targets "microprojects," such as schools, and supports constitutional reform.

DEFENSE ▷ No compulsory military service

$20m (estimate)   No significant change

The Swaziland Defense Force numbers just 3,000 troops. Although it does not play an overt political role, its loyalty is to the monarch and the status quo.

ECONOMICS ▷ Inflation 11.8% p.a. (1985–1996)

$1.46bn   4.87–5.88 emalangeni

SCORE CARD

❑ WORLD GNP RANKING	149th
❑ GNP PER CAPITA	$1,520
❑ BALANCE OF PAYMENTS	$-49m
❑ INFLATION	9.7%
❑ UNEMPLOYMENT	22%

STRENGTHS
Economy quite diversified and buoyant; grew 4.5% a year during 1980s. Manufacturing 32% of GDP. Investment rules attractive. Sugar 33% of export earnings. Wood pulp. Debt service low: only 3.8% of export earnings in 1993. Renewed regional stability has reduced risk to exports.

WEAKNESSES
Sugar vulnerable to price fluctuations. Dependence on South Africa for jobs, revenue, investment, electricity, imported goods. Small plots of land and lack of land title hinder farm modernization. High population growth.

EXPORTS
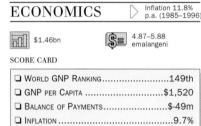

UK 3%
Other 50%
South Africa 47%

IMPORTS
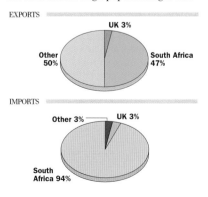

Other 3%   UK 3%
South Africa 94%

welcoming the election of an ANC-led government in Pretoria, King Mswati has expressed concern over their support for Swazi prodemocracy campaigners. Peace in Mozambique has meant the return there of 134,000 Mozambican refugees.

RESOURCES ▷ Not available

148 tonnes   Not an oil producer and has no refineries

650,000 cattle, 435,000 goats, 30,000 pigs   Coal, diamonds, gold, asbestos, cassiterite, iron, tin

Swaziland's main export is sugar cane; wood pulp, coal, and asbestos are also exported. The HEP station at Lupholo-Ezulwim, completed in the 1980s, will reduce energy imports from South Africa.

ENVIRONMENT ▷ No Green MPs

3% (partially protected)   Not available

In 1998 Swaziland, Mozambique, and South Africa began an ecological project on the the world's largest wetlands – the foothills of the Lebombo mountains.

MEDIA ▷ TV ownership low

Daily newspaper circulation 330 per 1,000 people

PUBLISHING AND BROADCAST MEDIA

There are 3 daily newspapers, *The Times of Swaziland, Tikhatsi Temaswati* and the *Swaziland Observer*

1 state-owned service   1 state-owned, 2 independent services

The Times of Swaziland and *Swaziland Observer* are independent. Generally respectful of the monarchy, the press has recently become less subservient.

CRIME ▷ Death penalty used

Swaziland does not publish prison figures   Up 17% in 1992

The crime rate is low but rising. The numbers of illegal weapons brought in by refugees have boosted armed crime.

EDUCATION ▷ School leaving age: 13

78%   5,658 students

Education is compulsory. Parents pay fees at all levels; even so, primary enrolment is about 93%. Drop-out rates at secondary level are high.

HEALTH ▷ No welfare state health benefits

1 per 18,800 people   Diarrheal and respiratory diseases

Health facilities are basic. About one-quarter of the population between 15 and 49 is said to carry HIV/AIDS.

SPENDING ▷ GDP/cap. no increase

CONSUMPTION AND SPENDING

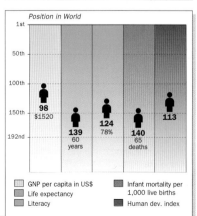

61 per 1,000 population   21 per 1,000 population

Defense	No data	
Education	8.1%	
Health	5.8%	

0   5   10   15   20   25
Defense, Health, Education spending as % of GDP

About 50% of Swazis live below the UN poverty line. The royal Dlamini clan enjoys Western luxuries and travel.

WORLD RANKING

Position in World

1st
50th
100th
150th
192nd

98 $1520
139 60 years
124 78%
140 65 deaths
113

❑ GNP per capita in US$
❑ Life expectancy
❑ Literacy

❑ Infant mortality per 1,000 live births
❑ Human dev. index

S

SWEDEN

OFFICIAL NAME: Kingdom of Sweden **CAPITAL:** Stockholm
POPULATION: 8.9 million **CURRENCY:** Swedish krona **OFFICIAL LANGUAGE:** Swedish

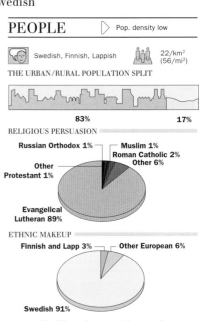

EUROPE

| 1809 | 1905 | June 6 | S | +1 | +46 | .se |

SITUATED ON THE SCANDINAVIAN peninsula, between Norway and Finland, Sweden is a densely forested country with numerous lakes. The north of Sweden falls within the Arctic Circle; much of the south is fertile and widely cultivated. Sweden has one of the most extensive welfare systems in the world, and is among the world's leading proponents of equal rights for women. Its economic strengths include high-tech industries and car production, including Volvo and Saab. It joined the EU in January 1995, along with Finland and Austria but not neighboring Norway.

CLIMATE

▷ Subarctic/continental

WEATHER CHART

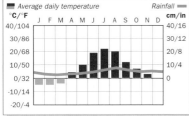

Sweden has a largely continental climate. The Baltic Sea often freezes in winter, making the east coast much colder than the west. Summers are cool everywhere, with temperatures varying surprisingly little between northern and southern regions.

TRANSPORTATION

▷ Drive on right

Arlanda, Stockholm
16m passengers

413 ships
3m grt

THE TRANSPORTATION NETWORK

| 98,100 km (61,000 miles) | 1,330 km (826 miles) |
| 11,168 km (6,939 miles) | 2,052 km (1,275 miles) |

Maintaining and improving transportation links in Europe's fourth-largest country is a key issue. Swedish governments have traditionally spent large sums on infrastructure. Transportation spending is also seen as a way of boosting the economy as a whole. A $20 billion program is financing road, rail and port development. A 16-km (10-mile) Øresund road and rail link by bridge and tunnel connecting Malmö with Copenhagen is due to open in 1999, providing a new road and rail link with Denmark and the rest of Europe. A new rail link between Arlanda airport and Stockholm is also planned. By law, cars must travel with their headlights on at all times.

TOURISM

▷ Visitors : population 1:3.7

2.4m visitors

Increasing

MAIN TOURIST ARRIVALS

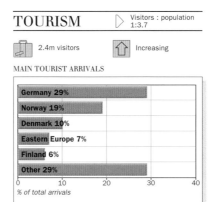

Germany 29%
Norway 19%
Denmark 10%
Eastern Europe 7%
Finland 6%
Other 29%

% of total arrivals

Sweden expanded rapidly as a tourist destination in the 1970s and 1980s. Stockholm, the capital, is renowned for its palaces. The 1970s international success of the pop group Abba boosted its vibrant nightlife. Visitors to the capital are typically young and affluent.

Sweden has fewer lakes than Finland, and lacks Norway's dramatic scenery, but it has many natural attractions. The mountains of the "Midnight Sun" lie north of the Arctic Circle, while the southern coast has many white sandy beaches. The vast tracts of deserted landscape and the simple country communal living also attract visitors, but the cost of travel to Sweden means that most visitors come from other Scandinavian countries or Germany.

A crofter's holding in Dalarna, Central Sweden, an area which is over 50% forested. The timber and paper industries account for almost 20% of Sweden's exports.

PEOPLE

▷ Pop. density low

Swedish, Finnish, Lappish

22/km² (56/mi²)

THE URBAN/RURAL POPULATION SPLIT

83%   17%

RELIGIOUS PERSUASION

Russian Orthodox 1%
Muslim 1%
Roman Catholic 2%
Other 6%
Other Protestant 1%
Evangelical Lutheran 89%

ETHNIC MAKEUP

Finnish and Lapp 3%
Other European 6%
Swedish 91%

As in all of Scandinavia, the nuclear family forms the basis of society. The birth rate is low with, on average, fewer than two children per family. Marriage is declining, and cohabitation outside marriage is common.

Swedish society has an egalitarian tradition. The role of the state is seen as providing conditions allowing each individual to gain economic independence through employment. Sweden's welfare system is one of the most extensive in the world. However, in the early 1990s, recession reduced benefits. Mothers in particular face increasing problems with the closure of childcare facilities. Women make up nearly half the work force, one of the highest proportions in Europe. Over 40% of MPs are women, the highest percentage in the world.

Sweden has generous asylum laws, but immigration is tightly controlled. A 17,000-strong minority of Sami (Lapps) live in northern Sweden. Their traditional way of life is protected.

In 1995 the Evangelical Lutheran church agreed that it should be disestablished from January 2000.

POPULATION AGE BREAKDOWN

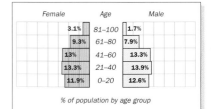

Female	Age	Male
3.1%	81–100	1.7%
9.3%	61–80	7.9%
13%	41–60	13.3%
13.3%	21–40	13.9%
11.9%	0–20	12.6%

% of population by age group

POLITICS ▷ Multiparty elections

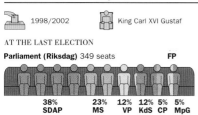

1998/2002   King Carl XVI Gustaf

AT THE LAST ELECTION

Parliament (Riksdag) 349 seats   **FP**

38%	23%	12%	12%	5%	5%
SDAP	MS	VP	KdS	CP	MpG

SDAP = Social Democratic Labour Party MS = Moderate
Party VP = Left Party KdS = Christian Democratic Party
CP = Center Party FP = Liberal Party MpG = Green Party

Sweden is a constitutional monarchy
with an elected parliament under the
leadership of the prime minister.

MAIN POLITICAL ISSUES
EU membership
Sweden joined the EU with Austria and
Finland in 1995 but, like the UK and
Denmark, opted out of introducing the
euro from 1999.

High cost of the welfare state
The cost of the welfare system
contributed to an enormous budget
deficit in 1993. While this has been
brought under control, social
security pressures remain from
continuing high unemployment
and the growing number of
pensioners.

PROFILE
Politics have traditionally
been split between the
monolithic Social
Democrats (SDAP) and
trade unions on the left,
and a host of moderate
center and right-wing
parties. Since the 1930s,
the SDAP has governed
every term, except in
1976–1982 and 1991–

SWEDEN

Total Land Area : 411 620 sq. km
(158 926 sq. miles)

POPULATION
- ▣ over 1 000 000
- ◉ over 100 000
- ○ over 50 000
- ● over 10 000

LAND HEIGHT
- 1000m/3281ft
- 500m/1640ft
- 200m/656ft
- Sea Level

N

0   100 km
0   100 miles

1994. A shift to the right in 1991 was
reversed in the 1994 elections, but the
SDAP failed to gain an absolute majority
of seats. Ingvar Carlsson, SDAP leader,
formed a minority government but
resigned in 1996 and was replaced by
Göran Persson. The SDAP lost ground in
elections in 1998, leaving Persson more
heavily dependent on support from the
Left Party and
the Greens.

Carl XVI Gustaf,
ascended the throne
in 1973. His role is
purely ceremonial.

Göran Persson
became prime
minister in 1996.

WORLD AFFAIRS ▷ Joined UN in 1946

EU	CE	NAM	OECD	OSCE

Sweden's main recent foreign policy
concern has been adjustment to EU
membership, which it achieved in
1995. In 1998 parliament voted to join
the Schengen passport-free zone
linking nine EU states. Since the
collapse of the Soviet Union, Sweden
has altered its traditionally neutral
stance and now has WEU observer
status. This contrasts sharply with
prime minister Olof Palme's period
in office in the 1980s, when Sweden
was a vociferous critic of the USA's
antagonistic policy towards the USSR.
Sweden participates in several UN
peacekeeping operations.

AID ▷ Donor

$1.7bn (donations)   Not applicable

Sweden is one of the few countries to
exceed the UN target of allocating
0.75% of GNP to development aid. Most
bilateral aid goes to African countries.

CHRONOLOGY

Sweden's history has been closely
linked to the control of the Baltic Sea
and its highly profitable trade
routes. Under the house of Vasa,
Sweden became a major power,
controlling much of the Baltic
region. By the 18th century,
however, Sweden's position had
been eroded by its regional rivals,
particularly Russia.

❑ **1814–1815** Congress of Vienna.
Sweden cedes territory to Russia
and Denmark. Period of unbroken
peace begins.
❑ **1865–1866** Minister of Justice Louis
De Greer reforms the Riksdag into a
bicameral parliament.
❑ **1905** Norway gains independence
from Sweden.
❑ **1911** First Liberal government.
❑ **1914** Government resigns over
defense policy.
❑ **1914–1917** Sweden remains ▷

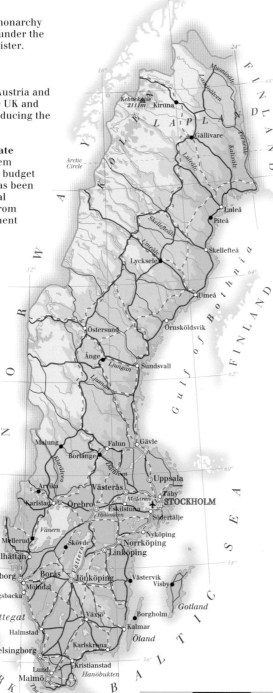

S

CHRONOLOGY *continued*

neutral but supplies Germany. Allied blockade.

- **1917** Food shortages. Conservative government falls. Nils Edén forms Liberal government: limits exports contributing to German war effort.
- **1919** Universal adult suffrage.
- **1921** Finland gains Åland Islands as retribution for Sweden's war role.
- **1932** Severe recession. Social Democrat government under Per Albin Hansson elected.
- **1939–1945** Sweden neutral. Grants transit rights to German forces.
- **1945–1976** Continuing Social Democratic rule under Tage Erlander eschews "Functional Socialism." Establishes Sweden as world's most advanced welfare state, and one of the most affluent.
- **1950** Gustav VI Adolf becomes king.
- **1953** Nordic Council member.
- **1959** Founder member of EFTA.
- **1969** Erlander succeeded by Olof Palme as prime minister.
- **1973** Carl XVI Gustaf on throne.
- **1975** Major constitutional reform. Riksdag becomes unicameral with a three-year term. Role of monarchy reduced to ceremonial functions.
- **1976** SDAP lose power. Nonsocialist coalition led by Thorbjörn Fälldin in government.
- **1978** Fälldin resigns over issue of nuclear power. Ola Ullsten prime minister.
- **1979** Fälldin prime minister again.
- **1982** Elections. SDAP form minority government. Palme prime minister.
- **1986** Palme shot dead. His deputy, Ingvar Carlsson, succeeds him as prime minister. Police fail to find assassin.
- **1990** Carlsson introduces moderate austerity package, cuts government spending, raises indirect taxes.
- **1991** Sweden applies to join EU. SDAP remains largest party in general election but is unable to form government; Carlsson resigns. Carl Bildt, leader of Moderate Party (MS), forms coalition of nonsocialist parties in middle of serious recession.
- **1992** Austerity measures succeed in reducing inflation but SDAP refuses to support further spending cuts.
- **1993** Negotiations for EU membership begin. MS coalition survives vote of no confidence.
- **1994** Terms of EU membership settled. Elections return SDAP to power. Referendum favors joining EU.
- **1995** Joins EU.
- **1996** Carlsson resigns; replaced by Göran Persson.
- **1998** Persson remains in office despite SDAP losses in elections.

S

DEFENSE
▷ Compulsory military service

 $5.5bn   Down 17% in 1997

Exports of conventional weapons were worth $481 million in 1997.

SWEDISH ARMED FORCES

537 main battle tanks (60 *Centurion*, 239 Strv-103B, 160 Strv-121 *Leopard* 2)	35,100 personnel
10 submarines, 27 patrol boats	9,200 personnel
362 combat aircraft (36 SAAB AJ-37, 14 SAAB SK-37, 53 SAAB JAS-39)	8,800 personnel
None	

Sweden maintains a powerful military force. Spending is concentrated on defense, reflecting a traditional need to protect its neutrality. Most weaponry, including Saab fighter jets and Bofor antiaircraft guns, is supplied by its advanced home defense industry.

With the end of the Cold War, strategic priorities have changed. Sweden feels less bound to its neutral stance; it has participated in NATO's Partnerships for Peace program since 1994 and has WEU observer status. In 1999 spending cuts of more than 10% were announced, foreshadowing halving the size of the armed forces, because of the reduced military threat in the Nordic and Baltic region.

ECONOMICS
▷ Inflation 4.9% p.a. (1985–1996)

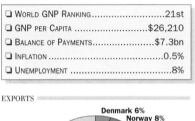 $231.9bn   7.93–8.11 Swedish kronor

SCORE CARD

- ❏ WORLD GNP RANKING..........................21st
- ❏ GNP PER CAPITA $26,210
- ❏ BALANCE OF PAYMENTS.....................$7.3bn
- ❏ INFLATION 0.5%
- ❏ UNEMPLOYMENT 8%

ECONOMIC PERFORMANCE INDICATOR

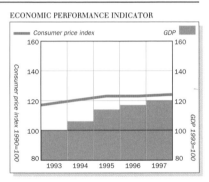

EXPORTS
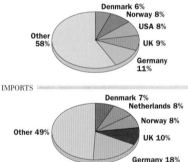

Denmark 6%, Norway 8%, USA 8%, UK 9%, Germany 11%, Other 58%

IMPORTS

Denmark 7%, Netherlands 8%, Norway 8%, UK 10%, Germany 18%, Other 49%

STRENGTHS
Companies of global importance, such as Ericsson, Saab, Volvo, Electrolux and SKF, the world's biggest roller bearing manufacturer. Highly developed and constantly updated infrastructure. Sophisticated technology. Skilled labor force is virtually bilingual in English.

WEAKNESSES
Uncompetitive labor costs, although this is beginning to change slowly. Highest taxation in the OECD, accounting for over 60% of GDP. Peripheral location, raising costs for producers and exporters.

PROFILE
The state plays a significant role in the economy, but tends to restrict its role to services and infrastructure. Sweden's industrial giants have mostly been private-sector companies.

The early 1990s saw a shift in government economic policy. Some elements of postwar consensus on the social role of government were abandoned in favor of measures designed to help business. However, greater growth did not follow, and unemployment and the overall cost of welfare drove up the budget deficit to one of the OECD's highest in 1994. Growth has now resumed and the deficit has been cut back, though unemployment has been above 8% since 1993. Sweden opted not to introduce the euro in 1999.

SWEDEN : MAJOR BUSINESSES

Vehicle manufacture, Telecommunications, Electrometallurgy, Iron ore mining, Electronics, Pulp & paper, Engineering, Chemicals, Textiles

RESOURCES

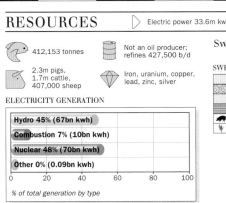

Electric power 33.6m kw

412,153 tonnes

Not an oil producer; refines 427,500 b/d

2.3m pigs, 1.7m cattle, 407,000 sheep

Iron, uranium, copper, lead, zinc, silver

ELECTRICITY GENERATION

Hydro 45% (67bn kwh)

Combustion 7% (10bn kwh)

Nuclear 48% (70bn kwh)

Other 0% (0.09bn kwh)

Sweden is rich in minerals, pig iron, copper, and silver. While mining and quarrying account for only 0.3% of GDP, they underpin other industrial sectors. Despite abundant uranium deposits, making up 15% of global reserves,

ENVIRONMENT

Green MPs

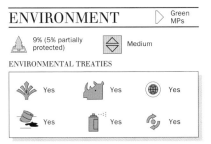

9% (5% partially protected)

Medium

ENVIRONMENTAL TREATIES

Yes · Yes · Yes

Yes · Yes · Yes

Since the Environment Protection Act of 1969, investment in environmental protection measures has totaled 20 billion kronor. Sweden has blamed the considerable acid rain damage to forests and lakes on airborne sulfur dioxide from factories in western Europe. Swedish nuclear reactors are said to be very safe, with filtered venting systems designed to retain 90% of all radioactivity released in the event of a core meltdown.

MEDIA

TV ownership high

Daily newspaper circulation 446 per 1,000 people

PUBLISHING AND BROADCAST MEDIA

There are 94 daily newspapers, including *Expressen, Dagens Nyheter, Aftonbladet* and *Svenska Dagbladet*

2 independent public service channels

4 independent public service stations, 90 private local stations

Press freedom is strongly entrenched, although radical views are rarely expressed. The major dailies' influence is largely confined to Stockholm, since the provinces have their own strong press. Six companies control most of Sweden's magazines. Political parties finance many newspapers.

Sweden decided to abandon nuclear power by the year 2010. In 1997, it decided that to increase use of renewable energy and reduce electricity consumption, it would decommission two of the country's four reactors by 2001.

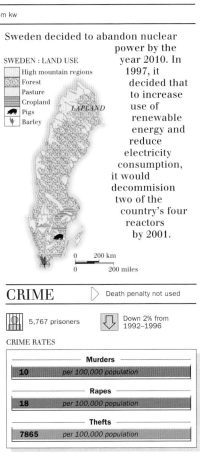

SWEDEN : LAND USE

High mountain regions
Forest
Pasture
Cropland
Pigs
Barley

LAPLAND

0   200 km
0   200 miles

CRIME

Death penalty not used

5,767 prisoners

Down 2% from 1992–1996

CRIME RATES

Murders	
10	per 100,000 population

Rapes	
18	per 100,000 population

Thefts	
7865	per 100,000 population

Crime rates are below the European average, although they are the highest among Scandinavian countries. Assault, rape, and theft are growing problems, especially in the cities.

EDUCATION

School leaving age: 15

99%

261,209 students

Education spending, as a percentage of GDP, is among the OECD's highest.

THE EDUCATION SYSTEM

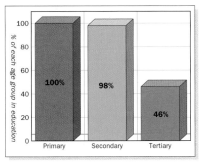

% of each age group in education

Primary 100% · Secondary 98% · Tertiary 46%

Coeducational comprehensive schools are the norm. The higher education system is freely available to most of the population, and many adults return to college to do further courses.

HEALTH

Welfare state health benefits

1 per 333 people

Heart and cerebrovascular diseases, cancers

Sweden's health care system is comprehensive and of a universally high standard. Spending has fallen by an average of 2% in real terms since 1992, but this is expected to return to zero growth in 2000. Savings have been made by increasing outpatient care, closing hospital beds, and cutting jobs. Since 1994 individuals have had the right to choose their own doctor, while doctors and specialists can now set up private practices. In 1999 the government agreed to compensate more than 60,000 people subjected to enforced sterilization in 1935–1975.

SPENDING

GDP/cap. no increase

CONSUMPTION AND SPENDING

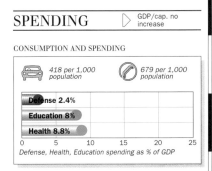

418 per 1,000 population

679 per 1,000 population

Defense 2.4%
Education 8%
Health 8.8%

Defense, Health, Education spending as % of GDP

Sweden has limited income disparities, and Swedish executives are generally paid less than their counterparts in France, Germany, or Italy. Social competition and a sense of hierarchy are limited compared with other European states or the USA. Despite some cuts in services, the welfare system still offers some of the best health, unemployment, and pension provisions in Europe.

Swedes are keen overseas property buyers, particularly of villas in Italy and the south of France. Net overseas per capita investment remains among the highest in the world.

S

WORLD RANKING

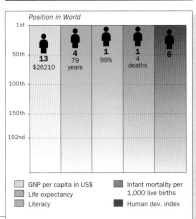

Position in World

1st
50th
100th
150th
192nd

13 $26210
4 79 years
1 99%
1 4 deaths
6

GNP per capita in US$
Life expectancy
Literacy

Infant mortality per 1,000 live births
Human dev. index

SWITZERLAND

OFFICIAL NAME: Swiss Confederation **CAPITAL:** Berne (Bern)
POPULATION: 7.3 million **CURRENCY:** Swiss franc **OFFICIAL LANGUAGES:** French, German and Italian

EUROPE

1291 | 1815 | Aug 1 | CH | +1 | +41 | .ch

SWITZERLAND LIES AT THE center of western Europe geographically, but outside it politically. Sometimes called Europe's water tower, it is the source of western Europe's largest rivers: the Po, the Rhine, the Rhône and the Inn-Danube. Switzerland has built one of the world's most prosperous economies, and has managed to retain its neutral status through every major European conflict since 1815. Whether or not to join in the process of greater European political and economic integration is a central issue.

The Eiger in the Berner Oberland. In 1994, a referendum voted to ban all lorry transit traffic from the Swiss Alps from 2004.

CLIMATE
▷ Mountain/continental

WEATHER CHART

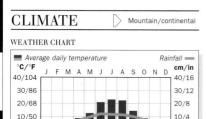

■ Average daily temperature   Rainfall ■
°C/°F   J F M A M J J A S O N D   cm/in
40/104   40/16
30/86   30/12
20/68   20/8
10/50   10/4
0/32   0
-10/14
-20/-4

Temperature and weather vary enormously, as a result of the seasons, the huge variations in altitude, and the country's location in the center of Europe. On the plateau north of the Alps, where most of the population lives, summers are warm and winters dry, cool, and often foggy. South of the Alps, it is warmer and sunnier. Strong southerly winds, or *föhn*, can bring summerlike weather even in winter. Avalanches have been a problem in recent years.

TRANSPORTATION
▷ Drive on right

Kloten, Zürich
19m passengers

20 ships
400,000 grt

THE TRANSPORTATION NETWORK

71,300 km (44,300 miles)	1,594 km (990 miles)
3,184 km (1,978 miles)	1,208 km (751 miles)

Switzerland is a major European freight transit route. Pollution from trucks is a major concern, as is tunnel safety after a major fire in the Mont Blanc tunnel in 1999. The NEAT project, approved in 1992, will provide two new high-speed rail lines linking Basel and Milan, through two 57- and 33-km tunnels, on which trucks will be carried.

TOURISM
▷ Visitors : population 1.5:1

11.1m visitors

Down 4% 1995–1997

MAIN TOURIST ARRIVALS

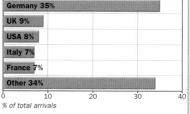

Germany 35%
UK 9%
USA 8%
Italy 7%
France 7%
Other 34%

0   10   20   30   40
% of total arrivals

Tourism is Switzerland's third-largest industry. About 350,000 Swiss earn their living from it, and tourism accounts for over 5% of GDP. The Alps are the main attraction, drawing winter and summer tourists from around the world. However, several factors have led to the recent downturn in the industry: warmer winters have resulted in a shorter skiing season; the rise in value of the Swiss franc has made Switzerland an expensive destination; and Austria is offering tough competition.

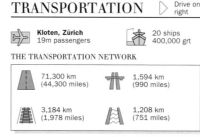

SWITZERLAND

Total Land Area : 39 770 sq. km
(15 355 sq. miles)

POPULATION

over 100 000   ◎
over 50 000   ○
over 10 000   ●

LAND HEIGHT

3000m/9843ft
2000m/6562ft
1000m/3281ft
500m/1640ft
200m/656ft

PEOPLE

▷ Pop. density medium

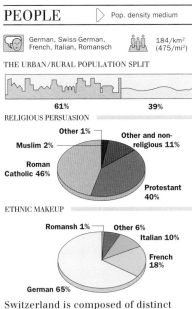

German, Swiss-German, French, Italian, Romansch

184/km² (475/mi²)

THE URBAN/RURAL POPULATION SPLIT

61%   **39%**

RELIGIOUS PERSUASION

Other 1%
Muslim 2%
Roman Catholic 46%
Other and non-religious 11%
Protestant 40%

ETHNIC MAKEUP

Romansh 1%
Other 6%
Italian 10%
French 18%
German 65%

Switzerland is composed of distinct Italian–Swiss, French–Swiss and German–Swiss linguistic groups. About 40,000 in the canton of Grisons speak Romansch. The German–Swiss are in the majority. They are a tightly knit community, with a dialect that is impenetrable to most outsiders. In recent years, the three groups have grown further apart. The French–Swiss, in favor of joining the EU, are opposed by the German–Swiss. In Ticino, originally an Italian–Swiss canton, a political party has emerged to champion Italian–Swiss interests. There has also been a rise in tension between Swiss and guest workers. The fear that Swiss are losing jobs to recent immigrants is commonly expressed. Swiss society retains strong conservative elements. Two half-cantons granted women the vote at regional level only in 1989 and 1990. Marriage rates are high and divorce less common than in most other European states.

POPULATION AGE BREAKDOWN

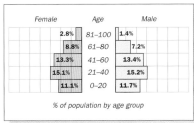

Female	Age	Male
2.8%	81–100	1.4%
8.8%	61–80	7.2%
13.3%	41–60	13.4%
15.1%	21–40	15.2%
11.1%	0–20	11.7%

% of population by age group

POLITICS

▷ Multiparty elections

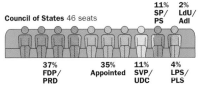

L. House 1995/1999
U. House 1995/1999

President Ruth Dreifuss

AT THE LAST ELECTION

National Council 200 seats

4% GPS/PES   11% Other

27% SP/PS
23% FDP/PRD
17% CVP/PDC
15% SVP/UDC
3% FPS/AP

SP/PS = Social Democratic Party **FDP/PRD** = Radical Democratic Party **CVP/PDC** = Christian Democratic People's Party **SVP/UDC** = Swiss People's Party **FPS/AP** = Freedom Party of Switzerland/Automobile Party **GPS/PES** = Green Party of Switzerland **LPS/PLS** = Liberal Party of Switzerland **LdU/AdI** = Independent Alliance

Council of States 46 seats

11% SP/PS   2% LdU/AdI

37% FDP/PRD
35% Appointed
11% SVP/UDC
4% LPS/PLS

Switzerland is a federal democratic republic with 26 autonomous cantons.

MAIN POLITICAL ISSUES
European integration

Almost all of the country's prominent politicians and business leaders favor joining the EU, but voters remain sharply divided. The Swiss are strongly attached to their decentralized style of government and fear that this would be lost within the EU. There are also fears that in a barrier-free Europe, Switzerland's high standards of living would fall because of a large influx of immigrants.

Swiss banks and Holocaust victims' funds

The banks have faced criticism for failing to help return deposited funds to the relatives of victims of the Nazi Holocaust. In 1997 Swiss banks agreed to establish a Holocaust fund, while the government formed a new Fund for Needy Holocaust Victims. In 1998 the two largest banks agreed a $1.25 billion settlement with 31,500 Holocaust victims and their families in return for agreement that there would be no future claims against Swiss banks or the government.

PROFILE

The same four-party coalition has been in power in Switzerland since 1959. Domestic and foreign policies have changed little. Politics has recently become more contentious, however, with voting patterns becoming more polarized. Divisive issues are those of drugs and of membership of the EU. Both right-wing and green minority parties have recently gained more seats in parliament.

Switzerland's political system is unique in Europe. Important decisions are all made on the results of referenda. A petition of more than 100,000 signatures can force a referendum on any issue.

WORLD AFFAIRS

▷ Not a member of the UN

CE   G10   OECD   OSCE   EEA

The basis of Switzerland's foreign policy remains its neutrality. Geneva has retained its position as a center for many international organizations. The UN has its European headquarters there, and it is also home to the ICRC. The city has often hosted diplomatic negotiations: those for the Camp David accords, START nuclear reduction treaties and attempts to resolve the conflict in former Yugoslavia all took place in Geneva.

Switzerland has chosen not to join the process of closer European integration. It rejected membership of the EEA and voted in a 1992 referendum against joining the EU. Many believe, however, that the case for joining the EU will become overwhelming now that the majority of Switzerland's EFTA partners have joined. Opponents of integration argue that Switzerland's seeming isolation will enhance its role as an international tax haven. In 1998 it agreed a new accord with the EU on matters including trade, transport, research, and free movement of people.

***Ruth Dreifuss**, of the CVP, first woman president, held office in 1999.*

***Adolf Oggi**, of the SP/PS/PDC, president for 2000.*

CHRONOLOGY

The autonomy of the Swiss cantons was curtailed by the Habsburg Empire in the 11th century. In 1291, the three cantons of Unterwalden, Schwyz and Uri set up the Perpetual League to pursue Swiss liberty. Joined by other cantons, they succeeded in 1499 in gaining virtual independence. The Habsburgs retained a titular role.

❑ **1648** Peace of Westphalia ending 30 Years War, in which Switzerland played no active part, recognizes full Swiss independence.
❑ **1798** Invaded by French.
❑ **1815** Congress of Vienna after Napoleon's defeat confirms Swiss independence and establishes its neutrality. Geneva and Valais join Swiss Confederation.

⇨

S

S

CHRONOLOGY *continued*

- ❏ **1848** New constitution – central government given more powers, but cantons' powers guaranteed.
- ❏ **1857** Joined by Neuchâtel.
- ❏ **1864** Henri Dunant founds International Red Cross in Geneva.
- ❏ **1874** Referendum established as important decision-making tool.
- ❏ **1914–1918** Plays humanitarian role in World War I.
- ❏ **1919** Proportional representation ensures future political stability.
- ❏ **1920** Joins League of Nations.
- ❏ **1939–1945** Neutral again. Refuses to join UN in 1945.
- ❏ **1959** Founder-member of EFTA. Present four-party coalition comes to power, taking over FDP/PRD dominance of government.
- ❏ **1967** Right-wing groups make electoral gains, campaigning to restrict entry of foreign workers.
- ❏ **1971** Most women granted right to vote in federal elections.
- ❏ **1984** Parliament approves application for UN membership. Elisabeth Kopp is first woman minister (justice minister).
- ❏ **1986** Referendum opposes joining UN. Immigrant numbers restricted.
- ❏ **1988** Kopp resigns over her alleged violation of secrecy of information laws.
- ❏ **1990** Kopp acquitted. Case revealed Public Prosecutor's office held secret files on 200,000 people. Violent protests. State security laws amended.
- ❏ **1991** Large increase in attacks on asylum-seekers' hostels.
- ❏ **1992** Joins IMF and World Bank. Referendum against joining EEA.
- ❏ **1994** Referendum approves new antiracism law and tighter laws against narcotics traffickers and illegal immigrants.
- ❏ **1995** General election strengthens ruling coalition despite divisions over possible EU membership.
- ❏ **1998** $1.25 billion compensation accord for Holocaust victims whose funds were deposited in Swiss banks.
- ❏ **1999** Ruth Dreifuss become first woman president.

AID

 Donor

💲 $839m ◇ Not applicable

With total disbursements amounting to 0.34% of GNP in 1995, 1996 and 1997 Switzerland ranks above the (OECD) average of 0.22% in 1997 as an aid donor. Good governance and promoting investment are current priorities. The largest recipients are India, Mozambique, Bolivia, and Tanzania.

DEFENSE

 Compulsory military service

💲 $3.84bn ⬇ Down 19% in 1997

1997 defense spending of $3,837 million was equivalent to 1.5% of GDP.

SWISS ARMED FORCES

769 main battle tanks (370 Pz-87 *Leopard* 2, 186 Pz-68, 186 Pz-68/88)	3,000 personnel
None	
171 combat aircraft (89 *Tiger* II/F-5E, 29 *Mirage* IIIS)	300 personnel
None	

Switzerland has one of the largest armed forces in Europe. Military service and further training at intervals is compulsory for males, up to the age of 50. The army is organized so almost 400,000 conscripts can be called up and armed in a few hours; it still uses skis, bicycles and horses to protect the Alps. Bridges and tunnels are mined in accordance with a defense strategy drafted earlier this century. As in the rest of Europe, force numbers are being cut in response to the end of the Cold War. In 1995, legislation allowing civilian service in place of military service was passed. Switzerland is also considering allowing its armed troops to join UN peacekeeping operations.

ECONOMICS

 Inflation 2.8% p.a. (1985–1996)

📊 $305bn 💵 1.46–1.37 Swiss francs

SCORE CARD

- ❏ WORLD GNP RANKING...........................18th
- ❏ GNP PER CAPITA $26,210
- ❏ BALANCE OF PAYMENTS....................$20.5bn
- ❏ INFLATION 0.5%
- ❏ UNEMPLOYMENT 5%

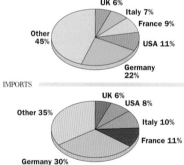

EXPORTS

UK 6%
Italy 7%
France 9%
USA 11%
Germany 22%
Other 45%

IMPORTS

UK 6%
USA 8%
Italy 10%
France 11%
Germany 30%
Other 35%

STRENGTHS

Highly skilled workforce. Reliable service provider. Major machine tool and precision engineering industries. Powerful chemical, pharmaceutical and banking multinationals. Banking secrecy laws attract foreign capital; banking sector contributes 9% of GNP. Ability to innovate to capture mass markets, typified by Swatch watch and proposed Swatch car.

WEAKNESSES

Protected cartels result in many overpriced goods. Highly subsidized agricultural sector.

PROFILE

The Swiss economy is widely diversified, with 61% of GDP coming from services and 26% from industry. The country is home to several large multinational enterprises and has a successful banking sector. It manages around one-third of the world's offshore private wealth. Bank accounts of Nazi Holocaust victims have now been uncovered. In 1997 a Holocaust fund was established, and in 1998 the three largest Swiss banks offered $1.25 billion to settle victims' claims.

ECONOMIC PERFORMANCE INDICATOR

Consumer price index / GDP

SWITZERLAND : MAJOR BUSINESSES

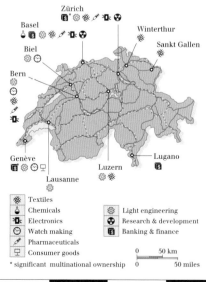

Zürich
Basel
Biel
Bern
Winterthur
Sankt Gallen
Genève
Lausanne
Luzern
Lugano

✳ Textiles	⚙ Light engineering
🧪 Chemicals	☢ Research & development
⚡ Electronics	🏦 Banking & finance
⏱ Watch making	
💉 Pharmaceuticals	
🖥 Consumer goods	0 ___ 50 km
	0 ___ 50 miles

* significant multinational ownership

RESOURCES
▷ Electric power 16.7m kw

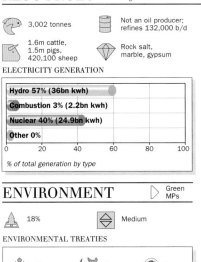

3,002 tonnes

1.6m cattle,
1.5m pigs,
420,100 sheep

Not an oil producer;
refines 132,000 b/d

Rock salt,
marble, gypsum

ELECTRICITY GENERATION

Hydro 57% (36bn kwh)

Combustion 3% (2.2bn kwh)

Nuclear 40% (24.9bn kwh)

Other 0%

| 0 | 20 | 40 | 60 | 80 | 100 |

% of total generation by type

Switzerland is poor in natural resources, having no valuable minerals in commercially exploitable quantities. Over half of its electricity comes from hydropower, while five nuclear plants supply most of the rest. This allows spending on imported oil and coal to be kept to a minimum – they account for less than 4% of the total import bill. The Chernobyl accident inspired large-scale antinuclear-power demonstrations and a sixth plant was canceled. However, a referendum approved continued use of existing plants.

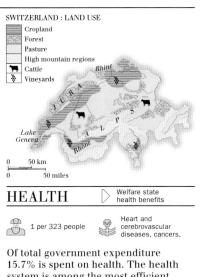

SWITZERLAND : LAND USE

Cropland
Forest
Pasture
High mountain regions
Cattle
Vineyards

| 0 | 50 km |
| 0 | 50 miles |

ENVIRONMENT
▷ Green MPs

18%

Medium

ENVIRONMENTAL TREATIES

Yes   Yes   Yes

Yes   Yes   Yes

The Swiss are among the most environmentally conscious people in the world and are willing to back their convictions with money: the Basel–Milan tunnel plan was approved by referendum, despite the estimated $13.3bn cost. The planners aim to achieve a total ban on truck transit traffic by 2004, although some argue that a ban will not be necessary, since transporting them on trains will cut two hours off the Basel–Milan truck journey.

The Swiss are keen recyclers and taxation is used to encourage this.

MEDIA
▷ TV ownership high

Daily newspaper circulation 330 per 1,000 people

PUBLISHING AND BROADCAST MEDIA

There are 88 daily newspapers. The largest circulations are held by *Tages Anzeiger* and the Zürich-based tabloid *Blick*

3 services broadcasting in German, Romansch, French and Italian

3 services broadcasting in German, Romansch, French and Italian

The Swiss media are organized broadly along regional lines, and reflect the country's linguistic divisions. The German-, Romansch-, French- and Italian-language TV and radio stations tend to focus on the interests of their specific communities. German, Italian, and French satellite TV is widely available. Few newspapers are available throughout the country. *Tribune de Genève* and *Neue Zürcher Zeitung* are exceptions.

CRIME
▷ Death penalty not used

5,655 prisoners

Down 7% from 1992–1996

CRIME RATES

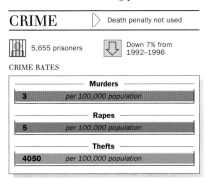

Murders

3   per 100,000 population

Rapes

5   per 100,000 population

Thefts

4050   per 100,000 population

Crime rates are low by international standards. Muggings and burglaries are on the increase and are often related to narcotics. More cases of banking secrecy laws attracting laundered funds are coming to light.

EDUCATION
▷ School leaving age: 16

99%

148,024 students

Of total government expenditure 15.6% is spent on education.

THE EDUCATION SYSTEM

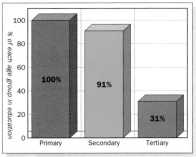

% of each age group in education

100%	91%	31%
Primary	Secondary	Tertiary

Most students after the age of 16 are encouraged to take up vocational studies. Training is thorough and is usually combined with three or four years' apprenticeship in the student's chosen field. The higher education institutions have the funds to attract top European academics. Zürich's Federal Technological Institute has gained an international reputation for its computer programming research.

HEALTH
▷ Welfare state health benefits

1 per 323 people

Heart and cerebrovascular diseases, cancers,

Of total government expenditure 15.7% is spent on health. The health system is among the most efficient and pioneering in the world. Health costs are covered by compulsory insurance schemes.

SPENDING
▷ GDP/cap. no increase

CONSUMPTION AND SPENDING

469 per 1,000 population

661 per 1,000 population

Defense 1.5%

Education 5.5%

Health 8%

| 0 | 5 | 10 | 15 | 20 | 25 |

Defense, Health, Education spending as % of GDP

Foreign "guests workers" do most low-paid and menial jobs. Wages in office jobs are relatively high, although the cost of living is also well above the European average. Many workers choose to live in France and commute across the border. The land market is highly regulated.

WORLD RANKING

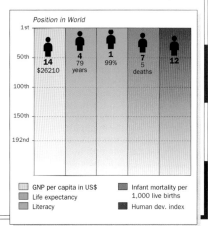

Position in World

1st					
50th	14 $26210	4 79 years	1 99%	7 5 deaths	12
100th					
150th					
192nd					

GNP per capita in US$
Life expectancy
Literacy

Infant mortality per 1,000 live births
Human dev. index

S

SYRIA

OFFICIAL NAME: Syrian Arab Republic CAPITAL: Damascus
POPULATION: 15.3 million CURRENCY: Syrian pound OFFICIAL LANGUAGE: Arabic

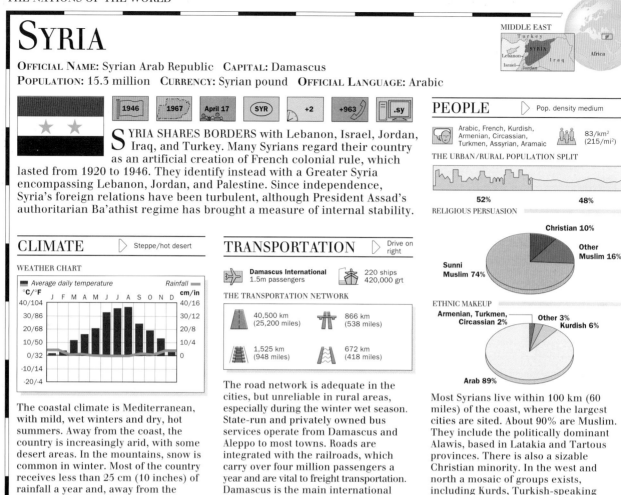

MIDDLE EAST

| 1946 | 1967 | April 17 | SYR | +2 | +963 | .sy |

S YRIA SHARES BORDERS with Lebanon, Israel, Jordan, Iraq, and Turkey. Many Syrians regard their country as an artificial creation of French colonial rule, which lasted from 1920 to 1946. They identify instead with a Greater Syria encompassing Lebanon, Jordan, and Palestine. Since independence, Syria's foreign relations have been turbulent, although President Assad's authoritarian Ba'athist regime has brought a measure of internal stability.

PEOPLE

Pop. density medium

Arabic, French, Kurdish, Armenian, Circassian, Turkmen, Assyrian, Aramaic

83/km²
(215/mi²)

THE URBAN/RURAL POPULATION SPLIT

52%   48%

RELIGIOUS PERSUASION

Sunni Muslim 74%
Christian 10%
Other Muslim 16%

ETHNIC MAKEUP

Arab 89%
Armenian, Turkmen, Circassian 2%
Other 3%
Kurdish 6%

CLIMATE

Steppe/hot desert

WEATHER CHART

Average daily temperature
Rainfall

The coastal climate is Mediterranean, with mild, wet winters and dry, hot summers. Away from the coast, the country is increasingly arid, with some desert areas. In the mountains, snow is common in winter. Most of the country receives less than 25 cm (10 inches) of rainfall a year and, away from the coast, rainfall is very unpredictable.

TRANSPORTATION

Drive on right

Damascus International
1.5m passengers

220 ships
420,000 grt

THE TRANSPORTATION NETWORK

| 40,500 km (25,200 miles) | 866 km (538 miles) |
| 1,525 km (948 miles) | 672 km (418 miles) |

The road network is adequate in the cities, but unreliable in rural areas, especially during the winter wet season. State-run and privately owned bus services operate from Damascus and Aleppo to most towns. Roads are integrated with the railroads, which carry over four million passengers a year and are vital to freight transportation. Damascus is the main international airport and Latakia the main port.

Most Syrians live within 100 km (60 miles) of the coast, where the largest cities are sited. About 90% are Muslim. They include the politically dominant Alawis, based in Latakia and Tartous provinces. There is also a sizable Christian minority. In the west and north a mosaic of groups exists, including Kurds, Turkish-speaking communities and Armenians, the latter based in cities. Damascus, Al Qamishli and Aleppo have small Jewish communities, and there are three villages where Aramaic is spoken. In addition, some 300,000 Palestinian refugees have settled in Syria. Minorities were initially attracted to the ruling Ba'ath Party because of its emphasis on the state over sectarian interests. However, disputes between factions led to the Shi'a Muslim Alawis taking control, fostering resentment among the Sunni Muslim majority.

The emancipation of women, promoted by the Ba'ath regime in the late 1960s, has been carried forward under President Assad. His first woman cabinet minister was appointed in 1976.

TOURISM

Visitors : population 1:18

842,000 visitors

Up 13% 1995–1997

MAIN TOURIST ARRIVALS

Lebanon 33%
Jordan 22%
Iran 14%
Turkey 13%
Other Arabic countries 7%
Other 11%

% of total arrivals

they are now gradually recovering. Syria's main attractions are the antiquities of Damascus – the oldest inhabited city in the world – and Aleppo and Palmyra, with their covered markets (soukhs), mosques, and baths. Syria has a wealth of castles dating back to the Crusades and sites associated with the advent of Islam. In addition, there are as many as 3,500 as yet unexcavated archaeological sites. Syria's Mediterranean coastline has fine beaches, and there are mountain resorts in Latakia.

Years of political turbulence, allegations of human rights abuses committed under the Assad regime and strict, complex travel regulations retarded the development of tourism. However, just before the 1990–1991 Gulf War, Syria began to compete in popularity as a holiday destination with other Middle Eastern states. Modern hotels were built in most main cities and facilities improved to cater for growing numbers of Western visitors. Following the war, tourist numbers dropped sharply, but

The ancient city of Palmyra, in Syria's central region, possesses some of the Middle East's finest Classical monuments.

POPULATION AGE BREAKDOWN

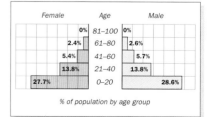

Female		Age	Male	
	0%	81–100	0%	
	2.4%	61–80	2.6%	
	5.4%	41–60	5.7%	
	13.8%	21–40	13.8%	
27.7%		0–20		28.6%

% of population by age group

S

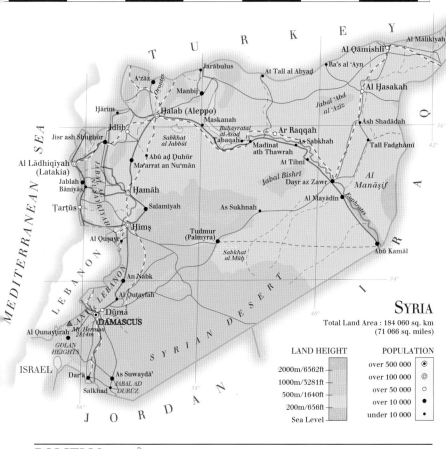

SYRIA

Total Land Area : 184 060 sq. km
(71 066 sq. miles)

LAND HEIGHT		POPULATION	
2000m/6562ft		over 500 000	◉
1000m/3281ft		over 100 000	◎
500m/1640ft		over 50 000	○
200m/656ft		over 10 000	•
Sea Level		under 10 000	·

WORLD AFFAIRS ▷ Joined UN in 1945

Following Egypt's 1979 accord with Israel, Syria sees itself as the major barrier to Israel's regional dominance. Syria has extended its influence over Lebanon (where it has achieved a high degree of control) and radical Palestinian factions, as well as seeking alliances with north African states. The biggest single issue between Syria and Israel remains the Golan Heights, seized by Israel during the Six Day War in 1967. Peace negotiations made little progress, until the Israeli change of government in 1999, on the central issue of security arrangements in the event of an Israeli withdrawal from the Golan Heights.

Syria faced international isolation in the 1980s because of the Assad government's alleged backing of terrorists. It regained a measure of respect in 1990 by securing the release of Western hostages in Lebanon from Shi'a militants. Assad followed up this diplomatic triumph by backing the Western allies in the 1990–1991 Gulf War, contributing troops to liberate Kuwait from Iraqi forces. Syria's involvement in the Gulf War was vital in legitimizing the action in the eyes of the Arab world. Syria emerged as a major ally of the West in containing Iraqi expansionism.

AID ▷ Recipient

$199m (receipts) — Down 12% 1996–1997

Syria has historically received little aid owing to its human rights record and substantial oil income. However, one-off payments totaling $2 billion in 1992 and $1.2 billion in 1993 were received after the Gulf War, mainly from Saudi Arabia and the Gulf states, but with contributions from the West and Japan.

President Assad, who was elected for a fifth term of office in 1999.

Mahmoud az-Zoubi, who became prime minister of Syria in 1990.

POLITICS ▷ No multiparty elections

1998/2002 — President Hafez al-Assad

AT THE LAST ELECTION

People's Assembly 250 seats
67% Ba'ath Party — **33% Other Ba'ath**

Syria is, in practice, a single-party state. Its military-backed leader since 1971 has been President Assad, a lifelong Ba'ath Party militant, dedicated to its campaign for Arab revival. His regime combines Pan-Arabism, nationalism and socialist ideology.

MAIN POLITICAL ISSUES
Human rights
The regime has improved its human rights record in recent years. Many political prisoners have been released, and in 1994 all members of the Jewish minority were granted exit visas to travel abroad. However, the regime is alleged to maintain links with a number of international terrorist groups.

Political pluralism
President Assad is the dominant figure and his military-backed regime, drawn mainly from the Shi'a Alawi minority grouping to which he belongs, keeps a tight hold on power. Promises to permit more political parties, made under international pressure, remain unfulfilled although some political prisoners have been released. He was sworn in for another seven-year term in 1999, but is old and ill, with no clear successor.

PROFILE
The Ba'athist military swept to power in 1963 with a vision of uniting all Arab nations under one Syrian-dominated socialist system. The coup ended the power of city elites and promoted citizens from rural areas. The state became the main employer.

When Assad came to power in 1971, he consolidated the Ba'ath Party as the major political force. Unrest among Islamic militants was crushed, and Assad focused on foreign affairs in a bid to make Syria a major power.

Syria initially found a Ba'athist ally in Iraq, and the two countries embarked on a plan for union in 1978. Relations soon foundered amid mutual charges of interference in each other's internal affairs – to the extent that, alone among Arab countries, Syria backed Iran in the Iran–Iraq War.

S

CHRONOLOGY

Complete independence from France was achieved in 1946. In 1958–1961, Syria merged with Egypt to form the United Arab Republic.

❑ **1963** Ba'athist military junta, the National Council of the Revolutionary Command, seizes power. Maj. Gen. Amin al-Hafez president.
❑ **1966** Hafez is ousted by military coup supported by radical Ba'ath Party members.
❑ **1967** Israel overruns Syrian positions above Lake Tiberias, seizes Golan Heights and occupies Quneitra. Syria boycotts Arab summit and rejects compromise with Israel.
❑ **1970** Hafez al-Assad seizes power in "corrective coup."
❑ **1971** Assad elected president for seven-year term.
❑ **1973** New constitution approved by plebiscite confirming Ba'ath Party as dominant force. War launched with Egypt against Israel to regain territory lost in 1967. Further territory lost to Israel.
❑ **1976** With peacekeeping mandate from Arab League, Syria intervenes militarily to quell fighting in Lebanon.
❑ **1977** Relations broken off with Egypt after President Sadat's visit to Jerusalem.
❑ **1978** National charter signed with Iraq for union. Assad returned for second term.
❑ **1980** Membership of Muslim Brotherhood made capital offense. Treaty of Friendship with USSR.
❑ **1981** Israel formally annexes Golan Heights. Charter with Iraq collapses.
❑ **1982** Islamic extremist uprising in Hama crushed; thousands killed. Israel invades Lebanon; Syrian missiles in Bekaa Valley destroyed.
❑ **1985** Assad reelected president. USA claims Syrian links to airport bombings at Rome and Vienna.
❑ **1986** Syrian complicity alleged in planting of bomb aboard Israeli airliner in London. EU states, with exception of Greece, impose sanctions.
❑ **1989** Diplomatic relations reestablished with Egypt.
❑ **1990** Troops take part in Operation Desert Storm to liberate Kuwait from Iraqi forces. Diplomatic relations with UK restored after Syrian help in freeing Western hostages in Lebanon.
❑ **1991** Damascus Declaration aid and defense pact signed with Egypt, Saudi Arabia, Kuwait, UAE, Qatar, Bahrain, and Oman.
❑ **1992–1999** Assad reconfirmed as president.

DEFENSE

▷ Compulsory military service

💲 $2.2bn   ⬆ Up 5% in 1997

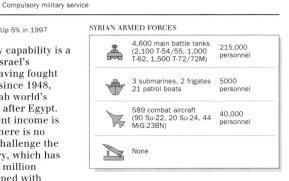

SYRIAN ARMED FORCES

4,600 main battle tanks (2,100 T-54/55, 1,000 T-62, 1,500 T-72/72M)	215,000 personnel
3 submarines, 2 frigates 21 patrol boats	5000 personnel
589 combat aircraft (90 Su-22, 20 Su-24, 44 MiG-23BN)	40,000 personnel
None	

Syria's extensive military capability is a significant deterrent to Israel's territorial expansion – having fought four wars against Israel since 1948, Syria has become the Arab world's strongest military power after Egypt. Nearly 50% of government income is spent on weapons, and there is no political mechanism to challenge the dominance of the military, which has more than a quarter of a million troops. It is mostly equipped with weapons obtained from the former Soviet Union.

During the 1980s, Syrian armed forces fought off a series of Israeli encroachments in the region, and also foiled Israeli attempts to control Lebanon. Syria remains the power Israel fears most.

ECONOMICS

▷ Inflation 15.7% p.a. (1985–1996)

📊 $16.6bn   💲 41.35–45.00 Syrian pounds

SCORE CARD

❑ WORLD GNP RANKING	73rd
❑ GNP PER CAPITA	$1,120
❑ BALANCE OF PAYMENTS	$–564m
❑ INFLATION	1.9%
❑ UNEMPLOYMENT	12%

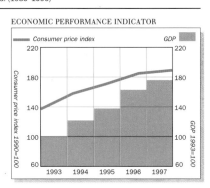

ECONOMIC PERFORMANCE INDICATOR

— Consumer price index   GDP

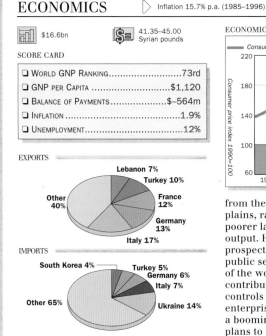

EXPORTS

Lebanon 7%
Turkey 10%
Other 40%
France 12%
Germany 13%
Italy 17%

IMPORTS

South Korea 4%
Turkey 5%
Germany 6%
Italy 7%
Other 65%
Ukraine 14%

STRENGTHS

Exporter of crude oil – production increasing as a result of new oil strikes. Manufacturing base has grown. Thriving agricultural sector.

WEAKNESSES

High defense spending is a major drain on economy. Large black market. High inflation. Economy dominated by inefficient state-run companies. Autocratic regime deters foreign investment. High population growth.

PROFILE

Billions of dollars flowed into the Syrian economy from the USA, Japan, the EU, and Saudi Arabia and other Gulf states following the 1991 Gulf War. This cash injection, along with increased oil revenue, led to rapid growth. Also, a decision to divert water from the river Euphrates toward fertile plains, rather than using it to irrigate poorer land, led to a rise in agricultural output. However, long-term economic prospects remain uncertain. The large public sector, which employs 20% of the workforce, makes little contribution to the economy. State controls have inhibited private enterprise and investment and created a booming black market. Turkey's plans to draw water from the Euphrates threaten farming in Syria.

SYRIA : MAJOR BUSINESSES

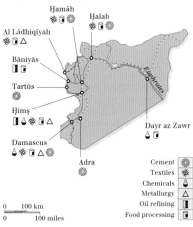

Ḥamāh
Ḥalab
Al Lādhiqīyah
Bāniyās
Tartūs
Ḥimṣ
Dayr az Zawr
Damascus
Adra

	Cement
	Textiles
	Chemicals
	Metallurgy
	Oil refining
	Food processing

0   100 km
0   100 miles

RESOURCES

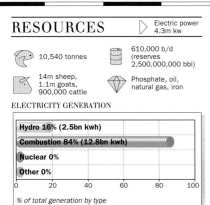

▷ Electric power 4.3m kw

🐟 10,540 tonnes

🛢 610,000 b/d (reserves 2,500,000,000 bbl)

🐑 14m sheep, 1.1m goats, 900,000 cattle

💎 Phosphate, oil, natural gas, iron

ELECTRICITY GENERATION

Hydro 16% (2.5bn kwh)	
Combustion 84% (12.8bn kwh)	
Nuclear 0%	
Other 0%	

0 — 20 — 40 — 60 — 80 — 100

% of total generation by type

Syria has large supplies of oil, mostly good-quality light crude, which was discovered along the Euphrates in the 1980s. Gas was found in substantial quantities near Palmyra. Syria's other important minerals are phosphates and iron ore. The manufacturing base is largely made up of oil-derived industries, including plastics and chemicals, textiles and food products. Cotton is the main cash crop, but fruit and vegetables are also grown. Livestock, especially sheep and goats, supports the rural economy.

SYRIA : LAND USE

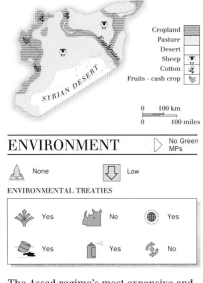

Cropland	
Pasture	
Desert	
Sheep	▼
Cotton	✿
Fruits - cash crop	

0 — 100 km
0 — 100 miles

ENVIRONMENT

▷ No Green MPs

🔺 None

⬇ Low

ENVIRONMENTAL TREATIES

🌿	Yes	🦏	No	🌐	Yes
	Yes		Yes	♻	No

The Assad regime's most expensive and controversial environmental project has been the Euphrates dam, power station and irrigation network at Tabaqah. The dam's vast man-made reservoir, Lake Buhayratal al Asad, engulfed some 300 villages and destroyed 25,000 hectares (62,000 acres) of fertile farm land. Syria's industrial program has on occasion damaged the environment. A giant cement factory, built by former East Germany at Tartus in the mid-1970s, has been responsible for polluting a stretch of Mediterranean coastline.

MEDIA

▷ TV ownership medium

☒ Daily newspaper circulation 20 per 1,000 people

Virtually all daily newspapers, which include the English-language *Syria Times*, are state-owned or have government affiliations. Radio and TV, the news agency SANA, press distribution and advertising companies are also controlled by the regime. There is no freedom of information.

CRIME

▷ Death penalty used

🔲 Syria does not publish prison figures

⬇ Down 1% in 1992

CRIME RATES

Murders	
1	per 100,000 population

Rapes	
1	per 100,000 population

Thefts	
42	per 100,000 population

There is no truly independent judiciary. The powerful security services exercise arbitrary powers of arrest and detention. There are widespread reports of torture in custody. Most politicians overthrown by President Assad in the 1970s have recently been released from prison in Damascus.

EDUCATION

▷ School leaving age: 12

👤 72%

🎓 215,734 students

A universally accessible system of education remains an important objective.

THE EDUCATION SYSTEM

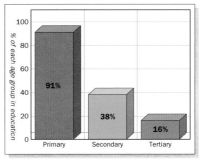

100
80
60
40 — 91%
20 — 38%
0 — 16%
Primary — Secondary — Tertiary

% of each age group in education

A free and compulsory system of primary education for all was a priority of the Ba'ath Party when it came to power. Under Assad, coeducation for boys and girls began in the cities and spread to rural areas. Higher education is provided by seven universities, notably at Damascus, Aleppo, Tishrin and Homs. There are almost 150,000 university students. Education ranks second – though by a considerable margin – to defense in government expenditure.

PUBLISHING AND BROADCAST MEDIA

📰	There are 8 daily newspapers, including *Al-Ba'ath*, *Ath-Thawra* and *Tishrin*
📺	1 state-controlled service
📻	1 state-controlled service

HEALTH

▷ Welfare state health benefits

🧑‍⚕ 1 per 1,250 people

💀 Heart, respiratory, digestive, infectious and parasitic diseases

An adequate system of primary health care has been set up since the Ba'ath Party came to power. Treatment is free for those unable to pay. However, hospitals often lack modern equipment and medical services are in need of further investment. Rural areas, in particular, need assistance to combat the spread of heart, respiratory, and infectious diseases.

SPENDING

▷ GDP/cap. no increase

CONSUMPTION AND SPENDING

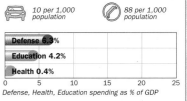

🚗 10 per 1,000 population

📞 88 per 1,000 population

Defense 6.3%	
Education 4.2%	
Health 0.4%	

0 — 5 — 10 — 15 — 20 — 25

Defense, Health, Education spending as % of GDP

Syria is far from the equitable society that early Ba'ath Party thinkers envisioned. The gulf between Syria's rich and poor is widening. Syria's political elite, many of whom live in the West Malki suburb of Damascus, is more numerous and richer than ever before. Palestinian refugees and the urban unemployed make up the poorest groups.

WORLD RANKING

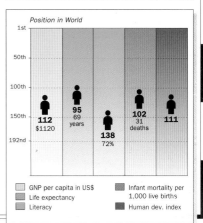

Position in World

1st
50th
100th
150th
192nd

112 $1120
95 69 years
138 72%
102 31 deaths
111

◻	GNP per capita in US$	◻	Infant mortality per 1,000 live births
◻	Life expectancy		
◻	Literacy	◼	Human dev. index

S

TAIWAN

OFFICIAL NAME: Republic of China (Taiwan)   **CAPITAL:** Taipei
POPULATION: 21.5 million   **CURRENCY:** Taiwan dollar   **OFFICIAL LANGUAGE:** Manderin Chinese

SOUTHEAST ASIA · Asia

| 1949 | 1949 | Jan 1 | RC | +8 | +886 | .tw |

THE ISLAND REPUBLIC of Taiwan lies 130 km (80 miles) off the southeast coast of mainland China. Formerly known as Formosa, the Republic of China was established in 1949 by Chiang Kai-Shek's Kuomintang (KMT), expelled from government in Beijing by the communists under Mao Zedong. Beijing still considers Taiwan a renegade province and all but a few, mostly small, countries officially accept Chinese claims of sovereignty. Taiwan island is dominated by a mountain region which runs north to south and covers two-thirds of the island. The lowlands are highly fertile, cultivated mostly with rice, and densely populated. In 1986, Taiwan adopted democracy in place of de facto military rule. The KMT has been in power since 1949.

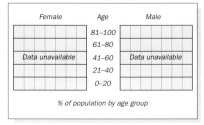

Wen Wu Temple, *on the shores of Sun Moon Lake in the mountains of central Taiwan – a region famous for its many temples.*

CLIMATE ▷ Tropical monsoon

WEATHER CHART

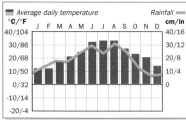

Taiwan has a tropical monsoon climate similar to that of the southern Chinese mainland. Typhoons from the South China Sea between July and September bring the heaviest rains.

TRANSPORTATION ▷ Drive on right

Chiang Kai-Shek Intl, Taoyuan
16m passengers

692 ships
5.93m grt

THE TRANSPORTATION NETWORK

| 19,600 km (12,250 miles) | North–South highway |
| 1,108 km (693 miles) | None |

Taiwan launched several major new transportation infrastructure projects as part of the latest six-year economic plan. Subway and rapid transit systems are being built in Taipei and Kao-hsiung. Several new roads are in progress, including an extension of the north-–south highway to Pingtung. The plan is motivated by the fear that congestion will restrain future growth. Most urban Taiwanese currently ride motor scooters, but transportation planners anticipate a sharp increase in car ownership over the next decade. The bicycle is not as popular in Taiwan as in mainland China. However, Taiwan is the world's biggest bicycle producer, exporting mostly to Europe and the USA.

TOURISM ▷ Visitors : population 1:9.2

2.3m visitors   Up 10% in 1995

MAIN TOURIST ARRIVALS

Japan 38%	
USA 13%	
South Korea 6%	
Thailand 5%	
Philippines 3%	
Other 35%	

% of total arrivals

Taiwan is not a major tourist destination and has only recently begun to target tourists in the USA and Japan. As part of the most recent Six-Year Plan, hotels are being upgraded and tourist facilities at international airports are being improved. The major attraction is the Palace Museum in Taipei, which includes the massive treasure looted by the Nationalists from Beijing. Only 5% can be shown at any one time. Sex tourism is an important business in Taipei, which is second only to Bangkok. Sex establishments masquerade as barber shops.

PEOPLE ▷ Pop. density high

Amoy Chinese, Mandarin Chinese, Hakka Chinese

666/km² (1,724/mi²)

THE URBAN/RURAL POPULATION SPLIT

69%   31%

RELIGIOUS PERSUASION

Other 2%   Christian 5%
Buddhist, Confucian, Taoist 93%

ETHNIC MAKEUP

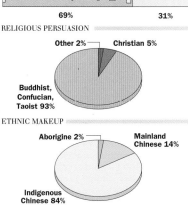

Aborigine 2%   Mainland Chinese 14%
Indigenous Chinese 84%

Most Taiwanese are Han Chinese, descendants of the 1644 migration of the Ming dynasty from mainland China. The 100,000 Nationalists who arrived in 1949 established themselves as a ruling class and monopolized the most prestigious jobs in the civil service.

This caused resentment among the local inhabitants, but as the generation elected on the mainland in 1947 have aged, so local Taiwanese have entered the political process.

There is little ethnic tension in Taiwan, although the indigenous minorities who live in the eastern hills do suffer considerable discrimination.

As in the rest of southeast Asia, the extended family is still important and provides a social security net for the elderly. However, the trend is toward European-style nuclear families, a result partly of housing shortages. Women are not well represented in the political process, but are prominent in business and the civil service.

POPULATION AGE BREAKDOWN

Female	Age	Male
	81–100	
	61–80	
Data unavailable	41–60	Data unavailable
	21–40	
	0–20	

% of population by age group

T

POLITICS ▷ Multiparty elections

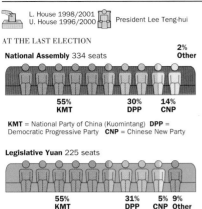

L. House 1998/2001
U. House 1996/2000   President Lee Teng-hui

AT THE LAST ELECTION

National Assembly 334 seats
2% Other

55% KMT   30% DPP   14% CNP

KMT = National Party of China (Kuomintang) **DPP** = Democratic Progressive Party **CNP** = Chinese New Party

Legislative Yuan 225 seats

55% KMT   31% DPP   5% CNP   9% Other

Until 1986, Taiwan was effectively a one-party state. Today, it is a fully functioning multiparty democracy.

MAIN POLITICAL ISSUES
Relations with China
The main opposition DPP advocates independence from China. The ruling KMT, officially committed to

TAIWAN

Total Land Area : 32 260 sq. km (12 456 sq. miles)

POPULATION

▣ over 1 000 000
◉ over 500 000
◎ over 100 000
○ over 50 000
● over 10 000
· under 10 000

LAND HEIGHT

3000m/9843ft
2000m/6562ft
1000m/3281ft
500m/1640ft
200m/656ft
Sea Level

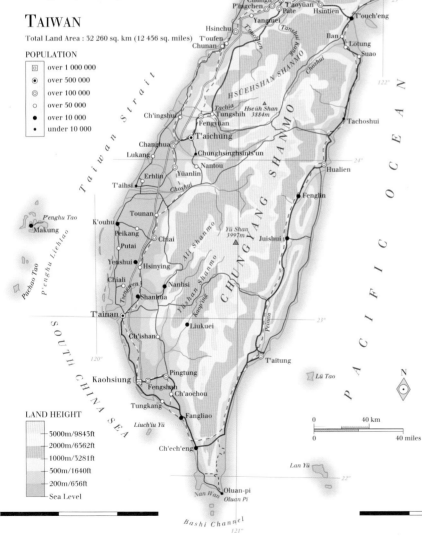

eventual reunification with China, now favors a more flexible arrangement that presupposes the recognition of a separate Taiwanese national identity. The CNP advocates a nonconfrontational stance and reunification with the mainland. China mounted military exercises in 1995 and 1996 ahead of the legislative and presidential elections amd again in July 1999, when president Lee spoke of Taiwan as a separate state. China angrily denounced this "dangerous provocation". Despite this, both depend on each other economically. Taiwan is a major foreign investor in China.

Political stability
In the 1998 legislative elections, the ruling KMT which had posted its worst-ever result in 1995, secured an absolute

Chiang Kai Shek, *who established Taiwan in 1949.*

Lee Teng-hui, *president since 1988, reelected in 1996.*

majority. The proindependence opposition DPP also performed impressively, but the CNP, with its emphasis on reunification with China, won little support. The outcome strengthened the moderate wing of the KMT under President Lee, who has increasingly favored the development of a "new Taiwanese" identity that blurs the ethnic division between native Taiwanese and Chinese from the mainland. The preservation of political and economic stability, however, remains essential as China intensifies its sovereignty claims on Taiwan after the return of Hong Kong in 1997.

PROFILE
Between 1949 and 1986, Chiang Kai-Shek's KMT monopolized political power, ruling by strict martial law. In 1986, General Chiang Ching-Kuo, Chiang Kai-Shek's son and successor, began to move toward democracy, and free multiparty elections were first held that year. In March 1996 Lee Teng-hui was the first president to be directly elected.

WORLD AFFAIRS ▷ Not a member of the UN

APEC   ADB

Countries wanting good relations with China cannot have formal links with Taiwan. China rejects Taiwan's sovereignty claims, regarding it as a renegade province, so Taiwan conducts its overseas relations mainly via trade delegations. It cannot gain representation at the UN; China repeatedly blocks its attempts to do so. The handover to China of Hong Kong by the UK in July 1997 deepened fears that China would intensify pressure on countries to sever links with Taiwan.

Official relations have been problematic with the USA, since its recognition of China in 1972. Taiwan effectively lost its status as a US client state, and US security guarantees to Taiwan have since been ambiguous. A strong US naval presence in early 1996 was merely a symbolic riposte to provocative Chinese military exercises. In practice, however, strong bilateral ties exist with both the USA and Japan.

T

AID ▷ Donor

💲 US$92m (donations) ⬌ Not applicable

Taiwan has a large aid fund, devoted mainly to states which have agreed to maintain formal diplomatic relations. In 1998, for example, more than US$2 million went to seven Central American countries, including Panama, to promote literacy. Central America has become the main focus for its aid-backed diplomatic efforts, but other recipients include the Pacific states of Kiribati, Tuvalu, and Tonga.

CHRONOLOGY

Following the 1949 communist revolution in China, Gen. Chiang Kai-Shek's nationalist KMT party sought refuge in the island province of Taiwan. The KMT saw the revolution as illegal and itself as the sole rightful Chinese government.

❏ **1971** People's Republic of China replaces Taiwan at UN and on UN Security Council.
❏ **1973** Taipei's KMT regime rejects Beijing's offer of secret talks on reunification of China.
❏ **1975** President Chiang Kai-Shek dies. His son Gen. Chiang Ching-Kuo becomes KMT leader. Yen Chia-kan succeeds as president.
❏ **1978** Chiang Ching-Kuo elected president.
❏ **1979** USA severs relations with Taiwan in favor of People's Republic of China.
❏ **1984** President Chiang reelected.
❏ **1986** Political reforms: KMT allows multiparty democracy, ends martial law and permits visits to Chinese mainland for "humanitarian" purposes for first time in 38 years. In 1988, mainland Chinese are allowed to visit Taiwan on same basis.
❏ **1988** Lee Teng-hui president.
❏ **1989** Ruthless suppression by mainland regime of student dissent ends period of rapprochement.
❏ **1990** Lee Teng-hui reelected president. KMT formally ends state of war with People's Republic of China.
❏ **1991** DPP draft constitution for Taiwan independence opposed by ruling KMT and Beijing. KMT reelected with large majority.
❏ **1995–1996** Legislative elections. KMT majority reduced.
❏ **1996** Chinese military exercises off Taiwanese coast. Lee Teng-hui elected president.
❏ **1998** KMT secures absolute majority in elections to upper legislative chamber (Legislative *Yuan*).
❏ **1999** Chinese threats over reference to "separate states" status. September, earthquake hits Taipei – 2,000 killed.

DEFENSE ▷ Compulsory military service

💲 US$13.7bn ⬇ Down 3% in 1997

Taiwan has the fifth-largest army in the world in order to face a possible Chinese invasion, despite official consensus on reunification. Worries about US loyalty have resulted in the purchase of French *Mirage* fighters in addition to US F-16s. In 1996 the AIDC defense research development body acquired a stake in the production of 700 helicopters with the US Sikorsky company.

TAIWANESE ARMED FORCES

🛡	719 main battle tanks (100 M-48A5, 450 M-48H, 169 M-60A3)	240,000 personnel
🚢	4 submarines, 18 destroyers, 18 frigates, 101 patrol boats	68,000 personnel
✈	529 combat aircraft (274 F-5, 100 *Chung-Kuo*, 30 Mirage, 60 F-16A/B)	68,000 personnel
	None	

ECONOMICS ▷ Inflation 5% p.a. (1985–1996)

📊 US$247bn   💲 32.67–32.22 Taiwan dollars

SCORE CARD

❏ WORLD GNP RANKING..........................20th
❏ GNP PER CAPITA ....US$10,320
❏ BALANCE OF PAYMENTS ....US$4.8bn
❏ INFLATION 3%
❏ UNEMPLOYMENT 3%

EXPORTS

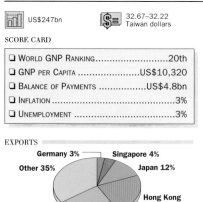

Germany 3% Singapore 4%
Other 35% Japan 12%
Hong Kong 23%
USA 23%

IMPORTS

South Korea 4% Malaysia 4%
Germany 5%
Other 40% USA 20%
Japan 27%

STRENGTHS

Highly educated and ambitious workforce, many US-trained and educated, with an inside knowledge of the US market. Manufacturing economy based on small companies which have proved extremely adaptable to changing market conditions. Track record of capturing major markets. Taiwan was successively the world's biggest TV producer, watch producer, PC producer and track shoe manufacturer. Economy in strong surplus, allowing it to invest in burgeoning southeast Asian economies.

WEAKNESSES

Taiwan's small economic units lack the muscle of Japanese and other Western multinationals; they are consequently unable to follow predatory pricing policies. Weak research and development: economy has no tradition of generating new products or creating new markets. Unresponsive banking system.

ECONOMIC PERFORMANCE INDICATOR

— Consumer price index   GDP (shaded)

Consumer price index 1991=100 (left axis, 80–160)
GDP 1993=100 (right axis, 80–160)
Years: 1993, 1994, 1995, 1996, 1997

PROFILE

One of the world's most successful economies, although double-digit growth is now over, Taiwan emerged relatively unscathed from the financial crisis engulfing most Asian economies in 1997–1998. Competition from underdeveloped countries with low production costs is dictating a difficult transition to service industries. Comprehensive six-year plans reflect a strong element of state direction, while heavy investment abroad includes over 60% of inward investment into China since 1990.

TAIWAN : MAJOR BUSINESSES

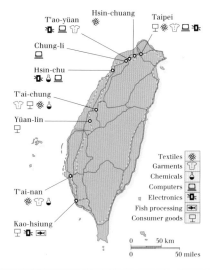

Hsin-chuang
T'ao-yüan
Taipei
Chung-li
Hsin-chu
T'ai-chung
Yüan-lin
T'ai-nan
Kao-hsiung

Textiles
Garments
Chemicals
Computers
Electronics
Fish processing
Consumer goods

0   50 km
0   50 miles

T

RESURCES

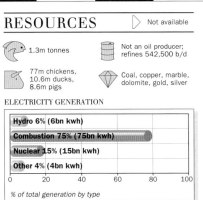

▷ Not available

1.3m tonnes

Not an oil producer;
refines 542,500 b/d

77m chickens,
10.6m ducks,
8.6m pigs

Coal, copper, marble,
dolomite, gold, silver

ELECTRICITY GENERATION

Hydro 6% (6bn kwh)	
Combustion 75% (75bn kwh)	
Nuclear 15% (15bn kwh)	
Other 4% (4bn kwh)	

0 20 40 60 80 100
% of total generation by type

Taiwan has few strategic resources and its minerals industry is not a significant foreign exchange earner. Oil is imported. Taiwan is a major buyer of South African uranium, but heavy reliance on nuclear power is now politically unfeasible due to serious safety and waste disposal problems. Hydroelectric power has been largely exploited and thermal power remains a controversial option. Fishing is highly successful and Taiwan is a major supplier to the huge Japanese market. The fishing fleet is often accused of plundering Atlantic stocks.

TAIWAN : LAND USE

- Cropland
- Forest
- Pasture
- Wetlands
- 🐗 Pigs
- Rice

0   50 km
0   50 miles

ENVIRONMENT

▷ Green MPs

3% partially protected

High

ENVIRONMENTAL TREATIES

No	No	No
No	No	No

The dash for growth meant the absence of city planning or pollution laws. An increasingly aware public now opposes a fourth nuclear power station and is wary of coal-fired thermal power. A 1997 agreement to ship nuclear waste to North Korea was abandoned in 1998. The fishing industry has been criticized for plundering other nations' fishing grounds without regard to stock levels.

MEDIA

▷ TV ownership high

Daily newspaper circulation figures not available

PUBLISHING AND BROADCAST MEDIA

	There are 35 daily newspapers. The independent *Lienho Pao* has the largest circulation
	4 independent commercial services
	78 independent services

The rigid state control which used to exist over the media has been relaxed. Opposition parties now have access to the state media. Before the 1990s, press with simplified Chinese characters was banned, thus excluding all publications from the mainland. Taiwan has a large domestic TV and film industry.

CRIME

▷ Death penalty used

Taiwan does not publish prison figures

Little change from year to year

CRIME RATES

Most Taiwanese are highly conscious of crime. However rates are low by US or European standards.

Since the end of martial law in 1986, most political prisoners have been released. Taiwan does not suffer from organized crime to the extent found in Hong Kong or Japan. Multimedia pirating is a major problem.

EDUCATION

▷ School leaving age: 15

94%

795,547 students

The reform of Taiwan's antiquated education system is a major priority.

THE EDUCATION SYSTEM

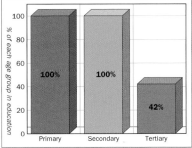

% of each age group in education

- Primary: 100%
- Secondary: 100%
- Tertiary: 42%

The education system is the same as that found on the mainland and inspired by 1922 reforms proposed by Bertrand Russell and John Dewey. The regime is rigid and heavily exam-oriented. Attendance at tertiary level is one of the highest in the world. Many Taiwanese study in the USA.

HEALTH

▷ No welfare state health benefits

1 per 894 people

Cerebrovascular and heart diseases, hypertension

Most health provision in Taiwan is in the private sector. Taiwanese take out elaborate health insurance schemes and it is essential to prove cover before treatment is provided. Health facilities are on a par with the best in the world and Taiwanese enjoy a high life expectancy, similar to that in Sweden or Japan. The incidence of AIDS is in line with the southeast Asian average. An enteroviral epidemic swept Taiwan in 1998, killing scores of babies and affecting thousands of young children.

SPENDING

▷ GDP/cap. increase

CONSUMPTION AND SPENDING

No data   No data

Defense 4.7%	
Education 3.6%	
Health No data	

0   5   10   15   20   25
Defense, Health, Education spending as % of GDP

Until 1987, Taiwan had the largest cash reserves of any country in the world. This reflected the closed nature of its markets and the success of the export economy. Taiwanese have shared in much of this wealth. Inequalities of income distribution are comparatively small, and a high degree of social cohesion has been achieved. In part, this is the result of the land reforms of the 1950s, which gave agricultural workers control of the land while compensating landowners and encouraging them to set up business in the cities. Today, most Taiwanese would describe themselves as middle class. Taiwan is perhaps the most consumerist society on earth; conspicuous consumption is celebrated.

WORLD RANKING

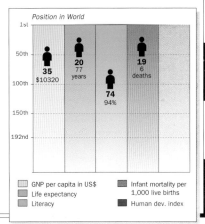

Position in World

- 35 $10320
- 20 77 years
- 74 94%
- 19 6 deaths

GNP per capita in US$	Infant mortality per 1,000 live births
Life expectancy	Human dev. index
Literacy	

T

TAJIKISTAN

OFFICIAL NAME: Republic of Tajikistan **CAPITAL:** Dushanbe
POPULATION: 6.2 million **CURRENCY:** Tajik rouble **OFFICIAL LANGUAGE:** Tajik

CENTRAL ASIA

| 1991 | 1991 | Sept 9 | TJ | +5 | +7 | .tj |

TAJIKISTAN LIES ON the western slopes of the Pamirs in central Asia. The Tajiks' language and traditions are similar to those of Iran rather than those of Turkic Uzbekistan. Tajikistan decided on independence only when neighboring Soviet republics declared theirs in late 1991. Fighting between communist government forces and Islamic rebels, which erupted shortly afterwards, has been contained since 1997 by a tenuous peace agreement.

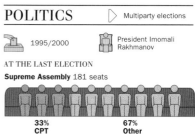
The Varzob Gorge, *north of Dushanbe. Half of the country is over 3000 m above sea level.*

CLIMATE
▷ Mountain

WEATHER CHART

■ *Average daily temperature*   *Rainfall* ■

Chart axes: °C/°F 40/104, 30/86, 20/68, 10/50, 0/32, -10/14, -20/-4; Months J F M A M J J A S O N D; cm/in 40/16, 30/12, 20/8, 10/4, 0

Rainfall is low in the valleys. Winter temperatures can fall below –45°C (–49°F) in mountainous areas.

TRANSPORTATION
▷ Drive on right

✈ **Dushanbe Intl**   ⚓ Has no fleet

THE TRANSPORTATION NETWORK

| 🛣 13,700 km (8,563 miles) | 🛤 None |
| 🚉 547 km (391 miles) | 〰 200 km (124 miles) |

Tajikistan has good cross-border roads and well-maintained airfields, the result of its use as a staging post by Soviet forces during the war in Afghanistan. The best way to visit the mountainous interior is by air.

TOURISM
▷ Not available

🧳 Almost no tourists   ⬦ Little change from year to year

MAIN TOURIST ARRIVALS

Tajikistan does not publish tourism figures by country of origin

0   10   20   30   40
% of total arrivals

The conflict in Tajikistan makes travel almost impossible. Journalists from the West are often attacked.

PEOPLE
▷ Pop. density low

👤 Tajik, Russian   👥 43/km² (112/mi²)

THE URBAN/RURAL POPULATION SPLIT

32%   68%

RELIGIOUS PERSUASION

- Shi'a Muslim 5%
- Other 15%
- Sunni Muslim 80%

The main ethnic conflict in Tajikistan is between the Tajiks and Uzbeks – peoples of Persian and Turkic origin respectively. As in neighboring Uzbekistan, however, Russians are discriminated against and their ranks have thinned from 400,000 in 1989 to less than 200,000. By 1990, the 35,000-strong German minority had left. The struggle between Dushanbe-based communists and the Islamic militants in the central and eastern regions displaced more than 50,000 refugees into Afghanistan, whose own Tajik population numbers over one million. It is estimated that around 20,000 refugees still remain in Afghanistan.

POLITICS
▷ Multiparty elections

1995/2000   President Imomali Rakhmanov

AT THE LAST ELECTION

Supreme Assembly 181 seats

33% CPT   67% Other

CPT = Communist Party of Tajikistan
Genuine opposition was banned at the elections of 1990. Other main parties are the Democratic Party of Tajikistan, the Islamic Renaissance Party (IRP) and Rebirth.

The lull in fighting between government forces and Islamic rebels, aided by a 1997 peace accord, has consolidated the regime of former communists led by President Rakhmanov. His powers were enhanced under a constitution adopted in 1994; in 1995 a third of the deputies returned in elections were communists. In 1998, the pro-Islamic United Tajik Opposition (UTO) joined the government in accordance with the 1997 agreement, which provided for a National Reconciliation Commission and parliamentary elections. However, despite the accord, fighting continues.

TAJIKISTAN

Total Land Area :
145 100 sq. km
(55 251 sq. miles)

POPULATION
- ⊙ over 500 000
- ◎ over 100 000
- ○ over 50 000
- ● over 10 000
- • under 10 000

LAND HEIGHT
- 4000m/13 124ft
- 3000m/9843ft
- 2000m/6562ft
- 1000m/3281ft
- 500m/1640ft
- 200m/656ft

0   100 km
0   100 miles

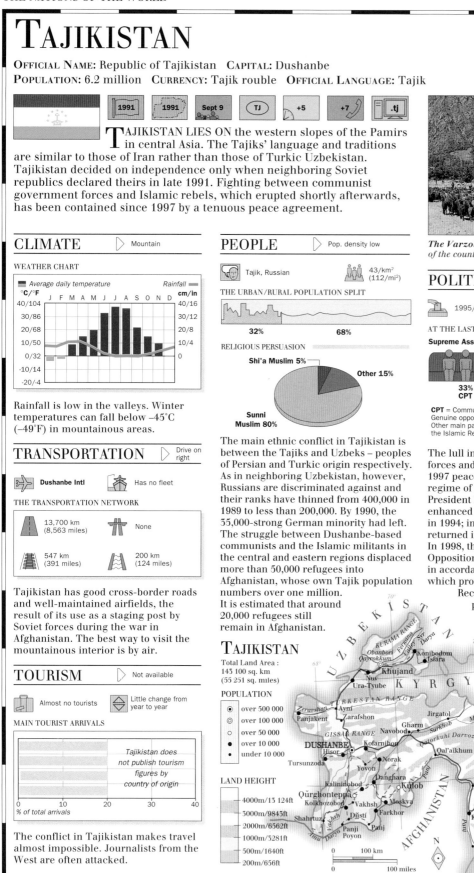

WORLD AFFAIRS

▷ Joined UN in 1992

Tajikistan is heavily dependent on Russia for economic and military assistance. In 1993, Tajikistan was the only central Asian state to submit to Russia's conditions for membership of the rouble zone, thereby ceding considerable control over economic policy to Russia. This was partially reversed with the introduction in 1995 of the Tajik rouble. However, Russia shares the Tajik government's concern to limit the influence of Islamic fundamentalism, and lends military support to further this objective.

AID
▷ Recipient

$101m (receipts)   ⬇ Down 11% 1996–1997

The government in Dushanbe is reliant on Russian and Uzbek military aid in its fight with the Afghan-based rebels.

DEFENSE
▷ Compulsory military service

$132m   ⬆ Up 12% in 1997

The Tajik armed forces are dependent on CIS peacekeeping forces to contain Tajik rebels, who are active in the Gorno Badakhshan region bordering Afghanistan, They are kept at bay by government forces assisted by Russian border guards.

ECONOMICS
▷ Not available

$2bn   Not available

SCORE CARD

- ❏ WORLD GNP RANKING.........................138th
- ❏ GNP PER CAPITA $330
- ❏ BALANCE OF PAYMENTS......................$-116m
- ❏ INFLATION 88%
- ❏ UNEMPLOYMENT 2%

STRENGTHS
Few, although Tajikistan has 14% of known world uranium reserves. Hydroelectric power has considerable potential. Carpet-making.

WEAKNESSES
Formal economy on verge of collapse. Dependence on barter economy. No central planning. Little diversification in agriculture; only 6% of land is arable. Skilled Russians leaving. Production in all sectors in decline.

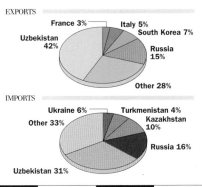

EXPORTS

France 3% | Italy 5%
Uzbekistan 42% | South Korea 7%
| Russia 15%
| Other 28%

IMPORTS

Ukraine 6% | Turkmenistan 4%
Other 33% | Kazakhstan 10%
| Russia 16%
Uzbekistan 31%

RESOURCES
▷ Electric power 4.4m kw

333 tonnes   1284 b/d

1.6m sheep, 1m cattle, 618,000 goats, 50,000 horses   Uranium, gold, iron, coal, lead, mercury, tin

Tajikistan has one key resource – uranium – which accounted for 30% of the USSR's total production before 1990. The end of the nuclear arms race has reduced its value, however. Most of Tajikistan is bare mountain and just 6% of the land can be used for agriculture. Industry is concentrated in the Fergana Valley, close to the Uzbek border.

ENVIRONMENT
▷ No Green MPs

△ 4%   ⬍ Not available

Landslides are a problem which in 1998 caused the country's worst natural disaster in 30 years. Excessive irrigation for cotton production has increased salination of the soil.

MEDIA
▷ TV ownership high

Daily newspaper circulation 20 per 1,000 people

PUBLISHING AND BROADCAST MEDIA

There are 3 daily newspapers published in Tajik, *Djavononi Todjikiston*, *Sadoi mardum* and *Tochikistoni*

1 state-controlled service   1 state-controlled service

Communist control over the media was tightened in early 1994 with the takeover by President Rakhmanov of the press and broadcast media.

CRIME
▷ Death penalty used

Tajikistan does not publish prison figures   Crime has been rising dramatically

Only remote areas escape the violence perpetrated by armed gangs. Drug smuggling along the border with Afghanistan is on the increase.

EDUCATION
▷ School leaving age: 17

99%   108,203 students

The university at Dushanbe has been weakened by the departure of its Russian academics.

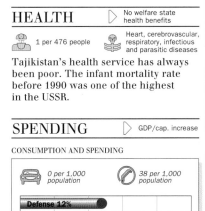

CHRONOLOGY

In the 19th century, Tajikistan was a collection of semi-independent principalities, some under Russian control, others under the influence of the Emirate of Bukhara.

- ❏ **1925** Soviets take over Tajikistan.
- ❏ **1940** Cyrillic script introduced.
- ❏ **1989** Tajik replaces Russian as official language.
- ❏ **1991** Independence from Moscow.
- ❏ **1994** Rakhmanov reelected president.
- ❏ **1995** Legislative elections; Tajik rouble introduced.
- ❏ **1997** Accord with pro-Islamic rebels.
- ❏ **1998** Opposition UTO group joins government.

HEALTH
▷ No welfare state health benefits

1 per 476 people   Heart, cerebrovascular, respiratory, infectious and parasitic diseases

Tajikistan's health service has always been poor. The infant mortality rate before 1990 was one of the highest in the USSR.

SPENDING
▷ GDP/cap. increase

CONSUMPTION AND SPENDING

0 per 1,000 population   38 per 1,000 population

Defense 12%
Education 8.6%
Health 6%

0   5   10   15   20   25
Defense, Health, Education spending as % of GDP

More than 80% of Tajik people live below the UN-defined poverty line. The war has made conditions even harder. The old communist bureaucrats are still the country's wealthiest group.

WORLD RANKING

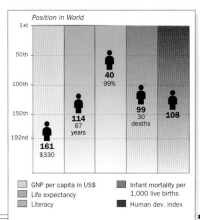

Position in World

1st
50th
100th
150th
192nd

40 — 99%
114 — 67 years
99 — 30 deaths
108
161 — $330

- ❏ GNP per capita in US$
- ❏ Life expectancy
- ❏ Literacy
- ❏ Infant mortality per 1,000 live births
- ❏ Human dev. index

T

TANZANIA

OFFICIAL NAME: United Republic of Tanzania   **CAPITAL:** Dodoma
POPULATION: 32.2 million   **CURRENCY:** Tanzanian shilling   **OFFICIAL LANGUAGES:** English and Swahili

1961 | 1964 | April 26 | EAT | +3 | +255 | .tz

TANZANIA LIES BETWEEN KENYA and Mozambique on the east African coast. Formed by the union of Tanganyika and Zanzibar and other islands, Tanzania comprises a coastal lowland, volcanic highlands and the Great Rift Valley. It includes Mount Kilimanjaro, Africa's highest peak. Tanzania was led by the socialist Julius Nyerere from 1962 until 1985. The Revolutionary Party of Tanzania (CCM) was returned in multiparty elections in 1995.

EAST AFRICA

Arusha National Park. Lying within the Ngurdoto volcanic crater, the park has herds of buffalo, rhinos, elephants and giraffes.

CLIMATE
▷ Tropical/mountain

WEATHER CHART

- ■ Average daily temperature
- Rainfall

The coast and Zanzibar are tropical. The central plateau is semiarid and the highlands are semitemperate.

TRANSPORTATION
▷ Drive on left

Dar es Salaam Intl
453,000 passengers

53 ships
45,200 grt

THE TRANSPORTATION NETWORK

| 34,300 km (21,440 miles) | | None |
| 2,721 km (1,701 miles) | | Lakes Tanganyika, Victoria, Nyasa |

The roads, railroads and ports are being upgraded, notably by a $870 million program to improve 70% of Tanzania's trunk roads.

TOURISM
▷ Visitors : population 1:92

350,000 visitors

Up 19% 1995–1997

MAIN TOURIST ARRIVALS

| Kenya 19% |
| UK 11% |
| USA 8% |
| Other 62% |

% of total arrivals

One-third of Tanzania is national park or game reserve. The Ngorongoro Crater and the Serengeti Plain are top attractions. Tourist numbers have risen sharply since 1990.

PEOPLE
▷ Pop. density low

Swahili, Sukuma, Chagga, Nyamwezi, Hehe, Makonde, Yao, Sandawe, English

36/km² (94/mi²)

THE URBAN/RURAL POPULATION SPLIT

24% | 76%

RELIGIOUS PERSUASION

- Other 4%
- Muslim 33%
- Traditional beliefs 30%
- Christian 33%

For many Tanzanians the family is the focus of traditional rural life. About 99% belong to one of 120 small ethnic Bantu groups. The remaining 1% comprises Arab, Asian, and European minorities. The use of Swahili as a *lingua franca* has helped make ethnic rivalries almost nonexistent.

POLITICS
▷ Multiparty elections

1995/2000

President Benjamin Mkapa

AT THE LAST ELECTION

National Assembly 275 seats

| 77% CCM | 10% CUF | 1% C | 2% Nom | 7% NCCR-M | 2% UDP |

CCM = Revolutionary Party of Tanzania **CUF** = Civic United Front **NCCR-M** = National Convention for Reconstruction and Reform - Mageuzi **C** = Chadema: Chama cha Democrasia na Maendeleo **Nom** = Reserved for the attorney-general and 5 nominations by the Zanzibari government.

Julius Nyerere was the dominant force in Tanzanian politics for 21 years. He founded the ruling party, the CCM, and his philosophy of African socialism guided Tanzania's development. Ali Hassan Mwinyi succeeded Nyerere as president in 1985, introducing a transition to multiparty democracy. Having served two five-year terms, Mwinyi stood down in 1995 when Benjamin Mkapa was elected president. Separatism in Zanzibar is a key issue.

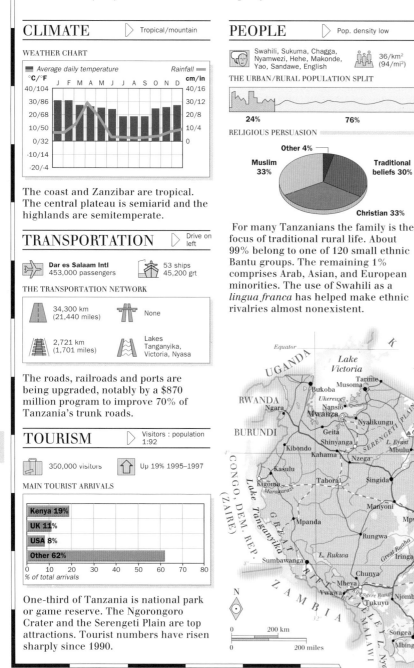

TANZANIA

Total Land Area : 886 040 sq. km (342 100 sq. miles)

POPULATION

- over 1 000 000
- over 100 000
- over 50 000
- over 10 000
- under 10 000

LAND HEIGHT

- 3000m/9843ft
- 2000m/6562ft
- 1000m/3281ft
- 500m/1640ft
- 200m/656ft
- Sea Level

WORLD AFFAIRS

▷ Joined UN in 1961

Tanzania is concerned about the instability of its central African neighbors. It accepted over half a million Rwandan and Burundian refugees in the 1990s, but instigated mass repatriations in 1996. Relations with Uganda and Kenya have warmed since 1985, prompting efforts to revive the East African Community.

AID

▷ Recipient

💲 $963m (receipts)   ⬆ Up 8% 1996–1997

Tanzania is heavily dependent on aid to help offset a severe balance of payments deficit. Most aid is now linked to an IMF-backed economic reform program. Net aid receipts constituted 25% of GNP in 1991, but this had fallen to 13% in 1997.

DEFENSE

▷ Compulsory military service

💲 $123m   ⬆ Up 11% in 1997

Defense accounts for 3.5% of budget spending. The armed forces are closely linked with the ruling CCM. There is an 80,000-strong citizens' reserve force.

ECONOMICS

▷ Inflation 346.8% p.a. (1985–1996)

📊 $6.6bn   💲 618.60–676.08 Tanzanian shillings

SCORE CARD

- ❏ WORLD GNP RANKING..........................97th
- ❏ GNP PER CAPITA $210
- ❏ BALANCE OF PAYMENTS...................$–567m
- ❏ INFLATION 16.1%
- ❏ UNEMPLOYMENT ....unavailable

STRENGTHS

Coffee, cotton, sisal, tea. Cloves from Zanzibar, the world's third-largest producer. Diamonds. State commitment to reforms which have cut inflation and the budget deficit. Rise in inward investment. A return to positive growth.

WEAKNESSES

Growth still too low to increase per capita income. Shortage of foreign exchange. Poor credit and equipment limit agricultural development.

EXPORTS

IMPORTS

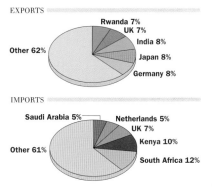

RESOURCES

▷ Electric power 543,000 kw

🐟 360,000 tonnes   🛢 Not an oil producer; refines 17,000 b/d

14.3m cattle, 9.7m goats, 4m sheep   💎 Natural gas, oil, iron, diamonds, gold, salt, phosphates, coal, gypsum, kaolin, tin

Agriculture, including livestock and forestry, is the key economic resource. It accounts for 60% of GDP and 80% of employment and exports. Forests cover 50% of Tanzania. More than 90% of energy demand is met from wood and charcoal. Hydropower provides 70% of electricity and is being expanded. To reduce oil imports, which take 40% of export earnings, Tanzania is starting to exploit offshore gas at Songo Songo. Oil has been discovered off Pemba Island.

ENVIRONMENT

▷ No Green MPs

🌲 16%   ⬇ Low

Demand for fuelwood is a threat to forests. Tourism's demands have to be carefully balanced with those of delicate wildlife environments such as the Ngorongoro Crater and the Serengeti.

MEDIA

▷ TV ownership low

📰 Daily newspaper circulation 4 per 1,000 people

PUBLISHING AND BROADCAST MEDIA

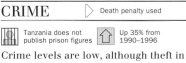

There are 3 daily newspapers, the *Daily News*, *Uhuru* and *Kipanga*

Dar Television and *Television Zanzibar*   1 state-owned, 2 independent services

The daily press is state-owned. There are several privately owned Swahili papers, and independent TV stations.

CRIME

▷ Death penalty used

Tanzania does not publish prison figures   ⬆ Up 35% from 1990–1996

Crime levels are low, although theft in Dar es Salaam has risen. Tanzania's human rights record is good.

EDUCATION

▷ School leaving age: 14

📖 72%   🎓 12,776 students

Primary education is free; secondary students pay fees. In 1997, 47.4% of primary age children received schooling, but the percentage attending secondary school is considerably lower.

CHRONOLOGY

The mainland became the German colony of Tanganyika in 1884. The Sultanate of Zanzibar became a British protectorate in 1890.

- ❏ **1918** Tanganyika British mandate.
- ❏ **1961** Tanganyika independent.
- ❏ **1962** Nyerere becomes president.
- ❏ **1963** Zanzibar independent.
- ❏ **1964** Zanzibar signs union with Tanganyika to form Tanzania.
- ❏ **1977** One-party state. Mainland and Zanzibari parties form CCM.
- ❏ **1985** Nyerere retires. President Mwinyi begins relaxation of Nyerere's socialist policies.
- ❏ **1992** Political parties allowed.
- ❏ **1995** Multiparty elections. Benjamin Mkapa becomes president.
- ❏ **1996** 1,000 die in Lake Victoria ferry disaster.

HEALTH

▷ Welfare state health benefits

🧑 1 per 25,000 people   💀 Diarrheal and respiratory diseases, malaria

Basic care is provided by the state and Christian missions. The AIDS epidemic is causing appalling damage.

SPENDING

▷ GDP/cap. no increase

CONSUMPTION AND SPENDING

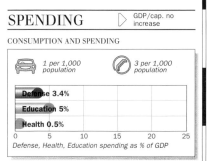

The majority of Tanzanians are impoverished subsistence farmers. The country's wealthy elite is small, composed mainly of Asian and Arab business families.

WORLD RANKING

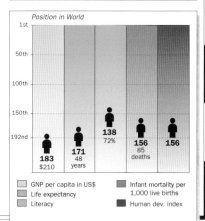

T

THAILAND

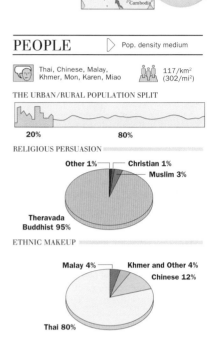

SOUTHEAST ASIA

OFFICIAL NAME: Kingdom of Thailand **CAPITAL:** Bangkok
POPULATION: 59.6 million **CURRENCY:** Baht **OFFICIAL LANGUAGE:** Thai

| 1782 | 1907 | Dec 5 | T | +7 | +66 | .th |

THAILAND LIES IN SOUTHEAST ASIA, between the Indian and Pacific oceans. The north, the western border with Burma, and the long Isthmus of Kra are mountainous. The central plain is the most fertile and densely populated area, while the low northeastern plateau is the poorest region. Thailand has been an independent kingdom for most of its history and, since 1932, a constitutional monarchy with alternating military and civilian governments. Continuing rapid industrialization is resulting in massive congestion in Bangkok and a serious depletion of natural resources.

CLIMATE

Tropical equatorial/monsoon

WEATHER CHART

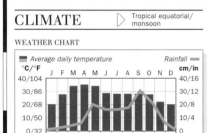

Thailand's tropical monsoon climate has three seasons – a hot sultry period, rains from May to October, and a dry, cooler season from November to March.

TRANSPORTATION

Drive on left

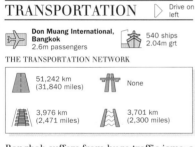

Don Muang International, Bangkok
2.6m passengers

540 ships
2.04m grt

THE TRANSPORTATION NETWORK

51,242 km (31,840 miles)	None	3,976 km (2,471 miles)	3,701 km (2,300 miles)

Bangkok suffers from huge traffic jams; a private funding package for its first mass transit system – an elevated railroad – was approved in 1996. Good US-built roads run to the north and east. The Chao Phraya river carries most freight.

Island in the Andaman Sea. The over-development of Thailand's best-known resorts is pushing tourism into new, remoter locations.

TOURISM

Visitors : population 1:8.2

7.26m visitors

Up 4% 1995–1997

MAIN TOURIST ARRIVALS

Malaysia	15%
Japan	11%
Taiwan	7%
South Korea	6%
Singapore	6%
Other	55%

% of total arrivals

Tourism is an important contributor to the Thai economy. Tourist numbers fell in the early 1990s as a result of both the worldwide recession and local overdevelopment during the 1980s boom. Although the number of arrivals has since recovered, visitors are tending to seek the less developed resorts. Bangkok's hotel occupancy rates are still falling as yet more hotels are built. Pattaya beach resort has seen such uncontrolled development that sea pollution is now a serious problem, while opposition to the intrusion of large numbers of tourists is growing among northern hill tribes.

Although prostitution is illegal, Bangkok and Pattaya are centers for sex tourism, which thrives despite the state's embarrassment at its effect on Thailand's image. Japanese and German men are among the main clients, while Burmese girls are increasingly recruited as prostitutes. Child prostitution is also a major problem.

There has been a boom in golf tourism, especially among the Japanese. The large number of new golf courses which are under construction will make Thailand the largest golf destination in Asia. The vast amounts of water needed to maintain the courses is aggravating Thailand's serious water shortage.

PEOPLE

Pop. density medium

Thai, Chinese, Malay, Khmer, Mon, Karen, Miao

117/km²
(302/mi²)

THE URBAN/RURAL POPULATION SPLIT

20%   80%

RELIGIOUS PERSUASION

Other 1%   Christian 1%
Muslim 3%

Theravada Buddhist 95%

ETHNIC MAKEUP

Malay 4%   Khmer and Other 4%
Chinese 12%

Thai 80%

There is little ethnic tension in Thailand, and Buddhism is a great binding force. The majority of Thais follow Theravada Buddhism, although the reformist Asoke Santi Buddhist sect, which advocates a new moral austerity, is gaining influence. Its principles have been espoused by the Palang Dharma (PD), which seeks to clean up politics.

The far north and northeast are home to about 600,000 hill tribespeople with their own languages, and to permanently settled refugees from Laos, mostly of the Hmong tribal group.

The large Chinese community is the most assimilated in southeast Asia. Sino-Thais are particularly dominant in agricultural marketing. Most of Thailand's one million Muslim Malays live in southern Thailand, bordering Malaysia. They feel stronger affinity with Muslims in Malaysia than with Thai culture, and this has given rise to a secessionist movement.

Women are important in business, but their involvement in national politics is limited.

POPULATION AGE BREAKDOWN

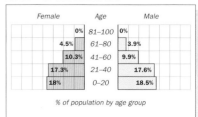

Female	Age	Male
0%	81–100	0%
4.5%	61–80	3.9%
10.3%	41–60	9.9%
17.3%	21–40	17.6%
18%	0–20	18.5%

% of population by age group

POLITICS ▷ Multiparty elections

L. House 1996/2000
U. House 1996/2000

HM King Bhumibol
Adulyadej (Rama IX)

AT THE LAST ELECTION

House of Representatives 393 seats

5% SAP

| 32% NAP | 31% DP | 13% CP | 10% CT | 5% PT | 4% Other |

NAP = New Aspiration Party **DP** = Democrat Party
CP = National Development **CT** = Thai Nation
SAP = Social Action Party **PT** = Prachakorn Thai

Senate 270 seats

The members of the Senate are appointed by the
Head of State.

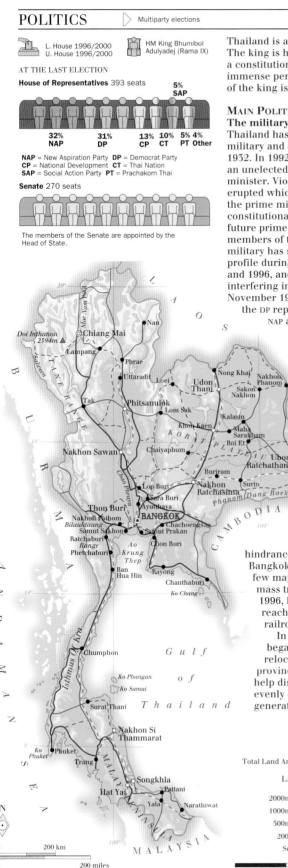

Thailand is a parliamentary democracy.
The king is head of state. Despite being
a constitutional monarch, he has
immense personal prestige. Criticism
of the king is not tolerated.

MAIN POLITICAL ISSUES
The military–democratic cycle

Thailand has been ruled by alternating
military and civilian governments since
1932. In 1992 promilitary parties chose
an unelected army general as prime
minister. Violent demonstrations
erupted which forced the resignation of
the prime minister and precipitated a
constitutional amendment obliging
future prime ministers to be elected
members of the legislature. The
military has since maintained a low
profile during general elections in 1995
and 1996, and refrained from
interfering in government changes as in
November 1997 when Chuan Leekpai of
the DP replaced Gen. Chaovalit of the
NAP as prime minister.

Congestion in Bangkok

A major issue is the
concentration of
industry and
commerce in
the Bangkok
area.
Uncontrolled
development
has left it
with traffic
congestion
which is
among the
world's
worst and
a serious
hindrance to economic activity.
Bangkok is also one of the world's
few major cities not to have a
mass transit system. In early
1996, however, agreement was
reached to finance an elevated
railroad for the city.

In 1993, the government
began offering incentives for
relocating industry to the
provinces. This is also intended to
help distribute wealth more
evenly – up to 60% of GDP is
generated in the Bangkok area.

*HM King Bhumibol
Adulyadej. He stepped
in to resolve the
political crisis in 1992.*

*Chuan Leekpai of
the DP, who became
prime minister
in 1997.*

Water

The national water shortage, caused by
rapid industrialization, is so acute that it
is affecting industrial and farm output.

PROFILE

The Thai political process is highly
personalized and parties seldom have
strong ideologies. Coalitions are often
unstable, while the lack of coordination
between coalition partners is a
recurring problem. A political stalemate
in 1996 was resolved only by calling
a fresh general election, from which
the NAP emerged as the largest party and
its leader Chaovalit Yongchaiyuth as
prime minister. This government fell
in 1997, blamed for mismanaging
the economic crisis. It was replaced
by another coalition under Chuan
Leekpai of the DP.

Though less prominent in the Senate
since 1996, the military are influential
in most political parties. Communists
are no longer a political force. The
main internal threat is from southern
Muslim separatists.

WORLD AFFAIRS ▷ Joined UN in 1946

APEC ASEAN Mek Riv NAM WTO

Thailand has friendly relations with
China and Burma. Many Thai logging
concerns, often run by the military,
have been active in Burma since
Thailand's 1988 domestic logging ban.
Following border disputes, relations
with Laos and Cambodia are improving,
as are those, more tentatively, with the
traditional enemy, Vietnam. Thailand
supported Khmer Rouge guerrilla
resistance to the Vietnamese regime
in Cambodia in the 1980s.

Thailand, Indonesia, and Malaysia
have liberalized trade to promote
development in southern Thailand,
Sumatra, and northern Malaysia –
regions which all are distant from
their respective capitals.

Thailand maintains close relations
with the USA, despite some tension
over intellectual property rights and
minor trade issues, but no longer has
any US military bases on its territory.

THAILAND

Total Land Area : 510 890 sq. km (197 255 sq. miles)

LAND HEIGHT	POPULATION	
2000m/6562ft	over 5 000 000	■
1000m/3281ft	over 1 000 000	▣
500m/1640ft	over 100 000	◉
200m/656ft	over 50 000	○
Sea Level	over 10 000	●

0 200 km
0 200 miles

T

AID ▷ Recipient

💲 $626m (receipts) ⬇ Down 25% 1996-1997

The World Bank and Japan are the largest aid donors. Thailand has imposed a ceiling on foreign borrowing to keep its debt stable.

CHRONOLOGY

Thailand emerged as a kingdom in the 13th century, and by the late 17th century its capital, then Ayutthaya, was the largest city in southeast Asia. In 1767, Burmese invaders destroyed the city. In 1782, the present Chakri dynasty and a new capital, Bangkok, were founded.

❏ **1855** King Mongut signs Bowring trade treaty with British – Thailand never colonized by Europeans.
❏ **1868–1910** King Chulalongkorn westernizes Thailand.
❏ **1925** King Prajadhipok begins absolute rule.
❏ **1932** Bloodless military–civilian coup. Constitutional monarchy.
❏ **1933** Military takes control.
❏ **1941** Japanese invade. Government collaborates. Free-Thai movement aids Allies.
❏ **1944** Pro-Japanese prime minister Phibun voted out of office.
❏ **1945** Exiled King Ananda returns.
❏ **1946** Ananda assassinated. King Bhumibol accedes.
❏ **1947** Military coup. Phibun back.
❏ **1957** Military coup. Constitution abolished.
❏ **1965** Thailand allows USA to use Thai bases in Vietnam War.
❏ **1969** New constitution endorses elected parliament.
❏ **1971** Army suspends constitution.
❏ **1973–1976** Student riots lead to interlude of democracy.
❏ **1976** Military takeover.
❏ **1980–1988** Gen. Prem Tinsulanond appointed prime minister. Partial democracy restored.
❏ **1988** Elections. Gen. Chatichai Choonhaven, right-wing CT leader, named prime minister.
❏ **1991** Military coup. Civilian Anand Panyarachun caretaker premier.
❏ **1992** Elections. Gen. Suchinda named premier. Widespread demonstrations. King forces Suchinda to step down, reinstalls Anand. Moderates win new elections.
❏ **1995** CT wins general election.
❏ **1996** Chaovalit Yongchaiyuth of the NAP becomes prime minister following early general election.
❏ **1997** Financial and economic crisis, tarnishing Thailand's "Asian tiger" image; Chaovalit government falls and Chuan Leekpai of DP becomes prime minister.

DEFENSE ▷ No compulsory military service

💲 $3.25bn ⬇ Down 27% in 1997

Military intervention in politics remains a threat, despite recent moves to reaffirm civilian control over the state.

THAI ARMED FORCES

🛡	277 main battle tanks (150 M–48A5, 77 M–60A)	190,000 personnel
🚢	14 frigates, 87 patrol boats	73,000 personnel
✈	206 combat aircraft (8 F-5A/B, 36 F-16A/B, 35 F-5-E/F)	43,000 personnel
🚀	None	

The military has either ruled Thailand, or played a prominent role in politics, since 1932. Its last intervention was its takeover of power in 1991. In 1996, its role in the appointed Senate – hitherto a military stronghold – was reduced. Retired military figures are, however, prominent in the major political parties.

Since 1986, spending has focused on the navy and air force. China, Germany, and Spain are supplying naval vessels, the UK, the USA, and Russia, aircraft.

The main defense concerns are border disputes with Cambodia, Burma, and Laos; the Muslim secessionist movement in the south; and piracy and fishing disputes in the South China Sea.

ECONOMICS ▷ Inflation 4.8% p.a. (1985–1996)

📊 $165.8bn 💲 48.15–36.34 baht

SCORE CARD

❏ WORLD GNP RANKING	26th
❏ GNP PER CAPITA	$2,740
❏ BALANCE OF PAYMENTS	$–2.9bn
❏ INFLATION	5.6%
❏ UNEMPLOYMENT	1%

EXPORTS

Malaysia 4% | Hong Kong 6% | Singapore 11% | Japan 16% | USA 20% | Other 43%

IMPORTS

Malaysia 4% | Germany 4% | Singapore 4% | USA 12% | Japan 22% | Other 54%

ECONOMIC PERFORMANCE INDICATOR

— Consumer price index   GDP

Consumer price index 1990=100 / GDP 1993=100

1993 1994 1995 1996 1997

STRENGTHS

Success of export-based and import-substituting manufacturing. Rapid economic growth. Natural gas. Tourism. Chief world exporter of rice and rubber.

WEAKNESSES

Concentration of economic activity in Bangkok area, with poor infrastructure. Inadequate water storage facilities affecting agriculture and industry. 60% of population in low-profit farming. Rapid growth of foreign debt.

PROFILE

Until the recent Asian economic crisis, Thailand's economy had grown at over 9% a year since 1988, driven by a rise in manufacturing and huge overseas investments, especially from Japan.

However, as domestic wages rose, Thailand faced stiff competition from cheaper labor in China and Vietnam. Though a big producer of electronics goods, Thailand also lacked a skilled labor force to develop high technology.

In 1997 a crisis of confidence over mounting foreign debt and the sharp depreciation of the baht, made an IMF-led rescue package necessary. Massive retrenchment and stringent austerity measures followed. Economic growth was expected to shrink 3% in 1998–1999.

THAILAND : MAJOR BUSINESSES

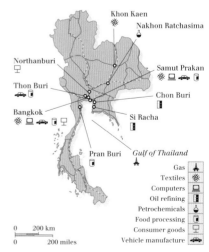

Khon Kaen
Nakhon Ratchasima
Northanburi
Samut Prakan
Thon Buri
Chon Buri
Bangkok
Si Racha
Pran Buri
Gulf of Thailand

Gas	
Textiles	
Computers	
Oil refining	
Petrochemicals	
Food processing	
Consumer goods	
Vehicle manufacture	

0   200 km
0   200 miles

T

RESOURCES

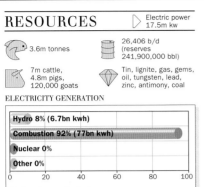

Electric power
17.5m kw

3.6m tonnes

26,406 b/d
(reserves
241,900,000 bbl)

7m cattle,
4.8m pigs,
120,000 goats

Tin, lignite, gas, gems,
oil, tungsten, lead,
zinc, antimony, coal

ELECTRICITY GENERATION

Hydro 8% (6.7bn kwh)	
Combustion 92% (77bn kwh)	
Nuclear 0%	
Other 0%	

0   20   40   60   80   100

% of total generation by type

Thailand has minimal crude oil and has rejected the nuclear option in favor of speeding up development of its large natural gas fields. It also has significant lignite deposits for power generation. World demand for Thailand's tin has declined, but recent gold and copper finds offer new potential. Thailand has valuable gemstone deposits. It is also the world's biggest shrimp producer.

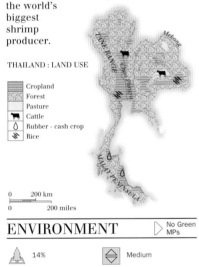

THAILAND : LAND USE

- Cropland
- Forest
- Pasture
- Cattle
- Rubber - cash crop
- Rice

0   200 km
0   200 miles

ENVIRONMENT

No Green
MPs

14%   Medium

ENVIRONMENTAL TREATIES

Yes		Yes		No	
No		Yes		Yes	

Deforestation, especially of the watersheds in the north, has led to the increasing severity of both floods and droughts. Particularly serious flooding in the south resulted in a total logging ban in 1988. Illegal logging continues, however. Reafforestation projects, some criticized for using single quick-growing species, will not solve the national water shortage. There is evidence of growing official concern at pollution levels. The worst polluting factories are being forced to move out of Bangkok and no new factories may use CFCs.

MEDIA

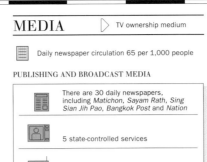

TV ownership medium

Daily newspaper circulation 65 per 1,000 people

PUBLISHING AND BROADCAST MEDIA

There are 30 daily newspapers, including *Matichon, Sayam Rath, Sing Sian Jih Pao, Bangkok Post* and *Nation*

5 state-controlled services

3 state-controlled stations

Newspapers enjoy a high level of freedom in political reporting. Two of the five TV stations are run by the military. A fast expansion of cable-TV networks is planned.

CRIME

Death penalty used

106,676 prisoners

Up 95% from
1992–1996

CRIME RATES

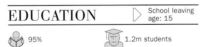

Murders	
7	per 100,000 population

Rapes	
6	per 100,000 population

Thefts	
72	per 100,000 population

Political imprisonment has been almost nonexistent since the early 1980s. There is some police involvement in crime, however, and extrajudicial killings and ill-treatment of prisoners in police detention are quite common.

The king has inspired an opium-substitution crop program. The government has cracked down on music, software and video piracy.

EDUCATION

School leaving
age: 15

95%   1.2m students

A poorly developed education system has led to a shortage of skills required for the expansion of high technology.

THE EDUCATION SYSTEM

100
88% Primary
57% Secondary
20% Tertiary

% of each age group in education

In 1993, the first steps were taken to make schooling compulsory for nine years instead of six.

HEALTH

Welfare state
health benefits

1 per 4,180 people

Heart diseases,
gastroenteritis

High-quality health care is heavily concentrated in Bangkok. Most of the 75% of the population who live in rural areas have access to primary health care. Trained personnel are aided by village health volunteers, monks, teachers, and traditional healers. In 1993, the decision was taken to improve the skills of primary health workers, rather than increase the number of fully trained doctors, as a means to improve rural health care.

The government operates a system whereby the poor can apply annually for a certificate entitling them to free health care. However, estimates suggest that 30% of users can afford to pay.

High-profile family planning programs are slowing population growth, while an effective AIDS prevention campaign has helped reduce the number of new infections. Prostitutes are among those who are benefiting from an extensive sex education program.

SPENDING

GDP/cap. no
increase

CONSUMPTION AND SPENDING

28 per 1,000
population

80 per 1,000
population

Defense 2.1%	
Education 4.2%	
Health 1.1%	

0   5   10   15   20   25
Defense, Health, Education spending as % of GDP

The government is trying to spread the great concentration of people and wealth from Bangkok, out to the provinces. Northeast Thailand in particular is a very poor region. The gap between rich and poor is greater in Thailand than in other industrializing southeast Asian states.

WORLD RANKING

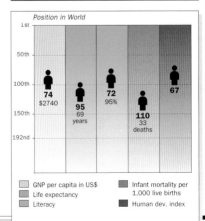

Position in World

1st
50th
100th
150th
192nd

74
$2740

95
69
years

72
95%

110
33
deaths

67

- GNP per capita in US$
- Life expectancy
- Literacy
- Infant mortality per 1,000 live births
- Human dev. index

T

TOGO

OFFICIAL NAME: Togolese Republic   CAPITAL: Lomé
POPULATION: 4.4 million   CURRENCY: CFA franc   OFFICIAL LANGUAGE: French

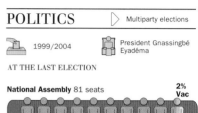

WEST AFRICA

| 1960 | 1960 | April 27 | TG | 0 | +228 | .tg |

TOGO IS SANDWICHED between Ghana and Benin in west Africa. A central forested region is bounded by savanna lands to the north and south. The port of Lomé is an important entrepôt for west African trade. The president, General Gnassingbé Eyadéma, has been in power since 1967.

CLIMATE
▷ Tropical equatorial/ wet & dry

WEATHER CHART

| Average daily temperature | Rainfall |

Togo has a typical Gulf of Guinea climate – very hot and humid on the coast and drier inland.

TRANSPORTATION
▷ Drive on right

Tokoin, Lomé
220,098 passengers

6 ships
1,128 grt

THE TRANSPORTATION NETWORK

| 1,886 km (1,172 miles) | None |
| 537 km (334 miles) | None |

Improving the already good road network and Lomé's port facilities are priorities, given Togo's role as an entrepôt. The only railroad runs from Lomé to Kpalimé.

TOURISM
▷ Visitors : population 1:48

92,000 visitors

Up 67% 1995–1997

MAIN TOURIST ARRIVALS

| France 14% |
| Burkina 13% |
| Benin 8% |
| Other 65% |

0   10   20   30   40   50   60   70   80
% of total arrivals

There is some package tourism, mainly French and German, to coastal tourist villages and hotels built during the expansion program of the 1980s. Tourists have been deterred by the political uncertainty since 1990.

PEOPLE
▷ Pop. density medium

Ewe, Kabye, Gurma, French

81/km²
(210/mi²)

THE URBAN/RURAL POPULATION SPLIT

31%   69%

RELIGIOUS PERSUASION

Muslim 15%
Traditional beliefs 50%
Christian 35%

A bitter divide has existed between north and south since before independence. Most southern resentment is directed toward a minority in the north, the Kabye people from the Kabye plateau, because of their domination of the military. The Kabye and other northerners in turn resent their own underdevelopment in contrast to the high development, especially educationally, of all southerners. The dominant southern group is the Ewe, who make up more than 40% of the population.

As elsewhere in Africa, the extended family is important, and tribalism and nepotism are key factors in everyday life. Some Togolese ethnic groups, such as the Mina, have matriarchal societies. The "Nana Benz," the market-women of Lomé market, who control the retail trade, have considerable private money. Politics, however, remains a male preserve.

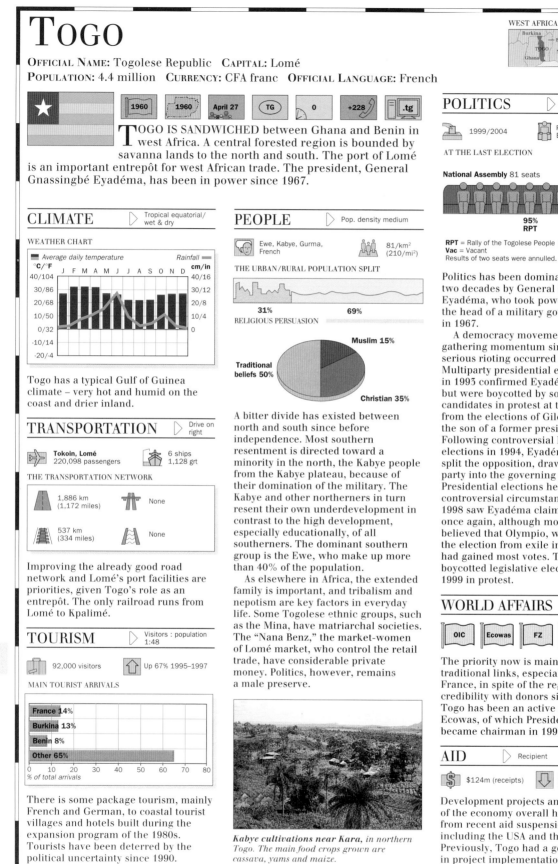

Kabye cultivations near Kara, in northern Togo. The main food crops grown are cassava, yams and maize.

POLITICS
▷ Multiparty elections

1999/2004

President Gnassingbé Eyadéma

AT THE LAST ELECTION

National Assembly 81 seats

2% Vac
95% RPT
3% Ind

RPT = Rally of the Togolese People Ind = Independents
Vac = Vacant
Results of two seats were annulled.

Politics has been dominated for two decades by General Gnassingbé Eyadéma, who took power at the head of a military government in 1967.

A democracy movement has been gathering momentum since 1990, when serious rioting occurred in Lomé. Multiparty presidential elections held in 1993 confirmed Eyadéma in power, but were boycotted by some opposition candidates in protest at the exclusion from the elections of Gilchrist Olympio, the son of a former president. Following controversial legislative elections in 1994, Eyadéma successfully split the opposition, drawing the UTD party into the governing coalition. Presidential elections held in controversial circumstances in 1998 saw Eyadéma claim victory once again, although most observers believed that Olympio, who contested the election from exile in Ghana, had gained most votes. The opposition boycotted legislative elections in 1999 in protest.

WORLD AFFAIRS
▷ Joined UN in 1960

| OIC | Ecowas | FZ | OAU | UEMOA |

The priority now is maintaining traditional links, especially with France, in spite of the regime's loss of credibility with donors since 1990. Togo has been an active member of Ecowas, of which President Eyadéma became chairman in 1998.

AID
▷ Recipient

$124m (receipts)

Down 25% 1996–1997

Development projects and the health of the economy overall have suffered from recent aid suspensions by donors including the USA and the EU. Previously, Togo had a good record in project implementation.

T

Togo

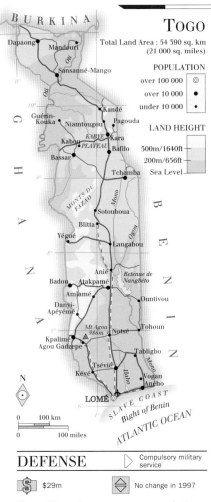

Total Land Area : 54 390 sq. km
(21 000 sq. miles)

POPULATION

over 100 000 ◎
over 10 000 ●
under 10 000 ·

LAND HEIGHT

500m/1640ft
200m/656ft
Sea Level

RESOURCES

▷ Electric power 34,000 kw

🐟 12,222 tonnes

🛢 Not an oil producer

🐖 1.1m goats, 850,000 pigs, 740,000 sheep

💎 Phosphates, iron, chromite, bauxite, marble, dolomite

Phosphates are Togo's most important resource. Oil and gas deposits were found in territorial waters in 1999. The Nangbeto dam, constructed jointly with Benin and opened in 1988, has reduced dependence on Ghana for energy.

ENVIRONMENT

▷ No Green MPs

🏔 8%

⬇ Low

Ecologists have been critical of the transformation of nature reserves into hunting grounds for the military elite. Other problems include coastal erosion around Aneho, and desertification.

MEDIA

▷ TV ownership low

✖ Daily newspaper circulation 4 per 1,000 people

PUBLISHING AND BROADCAST MEDIA

There is 1 daily newspaper, *Togo-Presse*, published by the government	
1 state-owned service	1 state-owned service, 1 independent

Opposition papers now challenge the government daily *Togo-Presse*, despite some official harassment.

CRIME

▷ Death penalty not used

Togo does not publish prison figures

Theft on increase in the capital

Togo is normally relatively peaceable, but urban crime, especially robbery, increased during the 1990s, particularly during periods of political unrest in the capital.

CHRONOLOGY

After colonization by Germany in 1894, Togoland was divided between France and the UK in 1922.

❑ **1960** French sector independent as Togo (UK part joined to Ghana).
❑ **1967** Eyadéma takes power.
❑ **1991–1992** General strike; repression.
❑ **1993** Eyadéma elected president.
❑ **1998** Eyadéma claims victory in disputed election.

EDUCATION

▷ School leaving age: 12

📖 53%

🎓 11,639 students

Schooling is based on the French model. The University of Benin in Lomé has more than 4,000 students.

HEALTH

▷ No welfare state health benefits

👥 1 per 10,000 people

💀 Malaria, diarrheal, infectious and parasitic diseases

Health care suffers from a lack of resources. Over 50% of qualified medical staff are based in Lomé.

SPENDING

▷ GDP/cap. no increase

CONSUMPTION AND SPENDING

🚗 19 per 1,000 population

📞 6 per 1,000 population

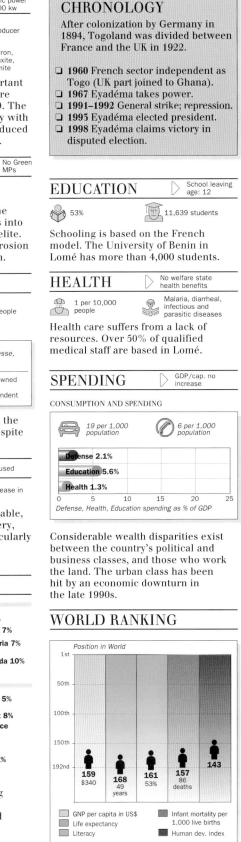

Defense 2.1%
Education 5.6%
Health 1.3%

0   5   10   15   20   25
Defense, Health, Education spending as % of GDP

Considerable wealth disparities exist between the country's political and business classes, and those who work the land. The urban class has been hit by an economic downturn in the late 1990s.

DEFENSE

▷ Compulsory military service

💲 $29m

No change in 1997

The military has an important role in Togo, and spending on defense is high. The army's senior ranks are dominated by loyalists from President Eyadéma's northern Kabré tribe. France guarantees Togo's security through a defense accord, and supplies most military equipment and training.

ECONOMICS

▷ Inflation 5.4% p.a. (1985–1996)

📊 $1.5bn

💲 601.60–558.62 CFA francs

SCORE CARD

❑ World GNP Ranking........................148th
❑ GNP per Capita $340
❑ Balance of Payments.....................$–63m
❑ Inflation 8.3%
❑ Unemployment ....Not available

EXPORTS

South Africa 6%
Taiwan 7%
Brazil 7%
Nigeria 7%
Canada 10%
Other 63%

IMPORTS

China 7%
Hong Kong 5%
Ivory Coast 8%
France 13%
Other 46%
Ghana 21%

Strengths

Efficient civil service. Ideal location for role as entrepôt, based on Lomé port. Proceeds of widespread smuggling. Resourcefulness of entrepreneurs, notably market-women. Phosphate deposits have the world's highest mineral content. Self-sufficient in basic foodstuffs. Diverse range of food crops.

Weaknesses

Political pariah status led to running down of much aid during 1990s. Hydropower generation vulnerable to drought. Low world prices for phosphates.

WORLD RANKING

Position in World

1st
50th
100th
150th
192nd

| 159 $340 | 168 49 years | 161 53% | 157 86 deaths | 143 |

▢ GNP per capita in US$
▢ Life expectancy
▢ Literacy
▢ Infant mortality per 1,000 live births
▢ Human dev. index

T

567

TONGA

OFFICIAL NAME: Kingdom of Tonga **CAPITAL:** Nuku'alofa
POPULATION: 97,000 **CURRENCY:** Pa'anga **OFFICIAL LANGUAGES:** English and Tongan

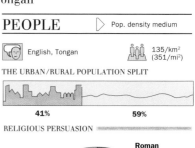

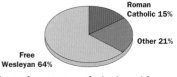

1970	1970	June 4	TO	+13	+676	.to

LOCATED IN THE SOUTH PACIFIC northeast of New Zealand, Tonga is an archipelago of 170 islands. These are divided into three main groups, Vava'u, Ha'apai and Tongatapu. Tonga's easterly islands are generally low and fertile. Those in the west are higher and volcanic in origin. Tonga's economy is based on agriculture, especially coconut, cassava, and passion fruit production. Politics is effectively controlled by the King.

CLIMATE ▷ Tropical oceanic

WEATHER CHART

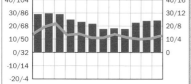

Tonga has a tropical oceanic climate, with year-round temperatures ranging between 20°C (68°F) and 30°C (86°F).

TRANSPORTATION ▷ Drive on left

Fua'amotu International, Tongatapu
67,000 passengers

8 ships
11,400 grt

THE TRANSPORTATION NETWORK

312 km (194 miles)		None
None		None

Nuku'alofa has recently been linked to Fua'amotu Airport in a Japanese-financed project.

TOURISM ▷ Visitors : population 1:3.7

26,000 visitors

Down 10% 1995–1997

MAIN TOURIST ARRIVALS

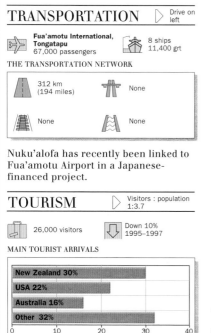

New Zealand 30%
USA 22%
Australia 16%
Other 32%
% of total arrivals

Tonga's main attractions are its tropical beaches. Tourist arrivals, mainly from New Zealand and the USA, have been declining recently. Fears have been expressed that too many visitors may erode traditional Tongan culture.

Mountainous scenery typical of Tonga's westerly islands. Tonga's 170 islands are scattered over a wide expanse of the South Pacific. Only 45 are inhabited.

TONGA

Total Land Area : 720 sq. km (278 sq. miles)

POPULATION
● over 10 000
● under 10 000

LAND HEIGHT
200m/656ft
Sea Level

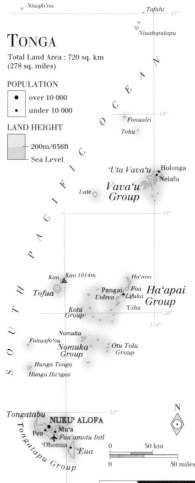

PEOPLE ▷ Pop. density medium

English, Tongan

135/km² (351/mi²)

THE URBAN/RURAL POPULATION SPLIT

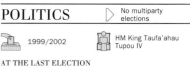

41%   59%

RELIGIOUS PERSUASION

Roman Catholic 15%
Other 21%
Free Wesleyan 64%

Tonga has strong ethnic ties with eastern Fiji and there has traditionally been considerable population movement between the two states. Tongans tend to see themselves as unique among Pacific islanders as they were never fully colonized and retain their monarchy.

Respect for traditional values and institutions remains high. Tongans are strong churchgoers; the Wesleyan, Roman Catholic and Mormon churches are influential and often fund education. A new generation of Western-educated Tongans is querying some traditional attitudes.

POLITICS ▷ No multiparty elections

1999/2002

HM King Taufa'ahau Tupou IV

AT THE LAST ELECTION

Legislative Assembly 30 seats

The Legislative Assembly comprises the King, the 11 members of the Privy Council, 9 directly elected, 9 indirectly elected by nobles.

The main power brokers in Tongan politics are the king, the noble establishment and the landowners. King Taufa'ahau succeeded his mother Queen Salote in 1965, effectively heads his government, frequently exercising kingly powers. The legislative assembly defers to his judgment and the King has taken the initiative in instigating several development projects which have been undertaken without reference to the government.

Younger westernized Tongans are now increasingly questioning the role of the monarchy, and there is a growing movement in support of democratic change. When the current king dies, pressure for reform is likely to accelerate.

T

WORLD AFFAIRS

> Joined UN in 1999

ACP | Comm | SPC | SPF | ADB

Tonga has historically come within New Zealand's sphere of influence. It is a member of the South Pacific Forum; in 1996 it finally acceded to the South Pacific Nuclear-Free Zone Treaty. Tonga has recently broken its ties with Taiwan in return for closer relations with China.

AID

> Recipient

$28m | Down 13% 1996–1997

Aid finances major infrastructure projects; Australia, the USA, New Zealand, the EU, and the ADB are primary donors. Since 1997, Tonga has been fighting to retain its "least developed country" status.

DEFENSE

> No compulsory military service

$2m (est.) | No significant change

Tonga has a small defense force, which includes both regulars and reserves; 5% of the state budget is currently allocated to defense.

ECONOMICS

> Inflation 7.6% p.a. (1985–1996)

$177m | 1.53–1.63 pa'anga

SCORE CARD

❏ WORLD GNP RANKING	184th
❏ GNP PER CAPITA	$1,810
❏ BALANCE OF PAYMENTS	$–6m
❏ INFLATION	2.1%
❏ UNEMPLOYMENT	1%

STRENGTHS
Agriculture contributes largest percentage of GDP. Tourism main source of hard currency earnings.

WEAKNESSES
Off main shipping routes. Heavily dependent on aid. Large importer of food. Many productive Tongans live abroad.

EXPORTS

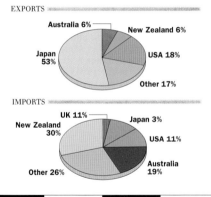

Australia 6% | New Zealand 6%
Japan 53% | USA 18%
Other 17%

IMPORTS

UK 11% | Japan 3%
New Zealand 30% | USA 11%
Other 26% | Australia 19%

RESOURCES

> Electric power 7,000 kw

2,841 tonnes | Not an oil producer

81,000 pigs, 14,000 goats, 11,000 horses | None

Tonga has no strategic or mineral resources. Electricity is generated from imported fuel, which is brought ashore in oil drums, an uneconomic form of delivery. Recent exploration has failed to identify any oil reserves.

ENVIRONMENT

> No Green MPs

None | Low

Tonga does not suffer from serious environmental problems, although it is occasionally afflicted by natural disasters, such as the 1982 typhoon. Commercial activity has made little impact on the environment.

MEDIA

> TV ownership low

Daily newspaper circulation 71 per 1,000 people

PUBLISHING AND BROADCAST MEDIA

There is 1 daily newspaper. Weeklies include the *Conch Shell* and the *Tonga Chronicle*	
1 service relaying US programs	2 independent services

Journalists have been imprisoned for criticizing the government. In 1997 the government forbade any of its employees to speak to the media.

CRIME

> No death penalty used

58 prisoners | Rising levels of theft

Crime rates are generally low, partly due to the strong influence of the family. However, offenses such as breaking and entering have increased with rising unemployment levels among young Tongans.

EDUCATION

> School leaving age: 14

99% | 705 students

Education is based on the Australian and New Zealand models and church participation in schools is high. The 'Atenisi Institute offers university level courses. A few students go on to the University of the South Pacific in Fiji.

HEALTH

> No welfare state health benefits

1 per 2,176 people | Heart, cerebrovascular and diarrheal diseases

Tonga has some modern health care facilities. However, patients have to be flown out to Australia or New Zealand for sophisticated surgery.

CHRONOLOGY

Originally discovered by Polynesians, Tonga was visited by the Dutch in the 17th century and Captain Cook in the 18th. In the latter half of the 19th century, during the reign of King George Tupou I, the islands became a unified state after a period of civil war.

- ❏ **1875** First constitution established by King George Tupou I.
- ❏ **1900** Concern over German regional ambitions leads to signing with UK of Friendship and Protection Treaty.
- ❏ **1918–1965** Reign of Queen Salote Tupou III.
- ❏ **1958** Greater autonomy from UK enshrined in Friendship Treaty.
- ❏ **1965** King Taufa'ahau Tupou IV accedes on his mother's death.
- ❏ **1970** Independence within British Commonwealth.
- ❏ **1988** Treaty signed allowing US nuclear warships right of transit through Tongan waters.
- ❏ **1996–1999** General elections: strong showing by prodemocracy candidates in the minority of seats decided by universal suffrage.

SPENDING

> GDP/cap. no increase

CONSUMPTION AND SPENDING

2 per 1,000 population | 64 per 1,000 population

Defense 1.1% (est.)
Education 4.7%
Health No data

0 | 5 | 10 | 15 | 20 | 25

Defense, Health, Education spending as % of GDP

Tongans rarely indulge in ostentatious displays of wealth. The well-off provide financial support for relatives.

WORLD RANKING

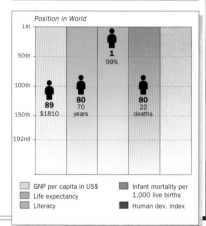

Position in World

1st
50th — 1 (99%)
100th
150th — 89 ($1810) | 80 (70 years) | 80 (22 deaths)
192nd

❏ GNP per capita in US$
❏ Life expectancy
❏ Literacy
❏ Infant mortality per 1,000 live births
❏ Human dev. index

T

TRINIDAD & TOBAGO

OFFICIAL NAME: Republic of Trinidad and Tobago   **CAPITAL:** Port-of-Spain
POPULATION: 1.3 million   **CURRENCY:** Trinidad and Tobago dollar   **OFFICIAL LANGUAGE:** English

| 1962 | 1962 | Aug 31 | TT | +4 | +1868 | .tt |

THE TWO ISLANDS of Trinidad and Tobago are the most southerly of the Caribbean Windward Islands and lie just 15 km (9 miles) off the Venezuelan coast. They gained joint independence from Britain in 1962, and Tobago was given internal autonomy in 1987. The spectacular mountain ranges and large swamps are rich in tropical flora and fauna. Pitch Lake in Trinidad is the world's largest natural reservoir of asphalt.

CLIMATE

▷ Tropical oceanic

WEATHER CHART

Average daily temperature | Rainfall

The islands are a little warmer than others in the Caribbean and escape the hurricanes, which pass by to the north.

TRANSPORTATION

▷ Drive on left

Piarco International, Port-of-Spain
1.58m passengers

51 ships
18,500 dwt

THE TRANSPORTATION NETWORK

| 4,000 km (2,485 miles) | None |
| None | None |

The road network is well developed; there are taxis or minibuses for set routes. National carrier BWIA, in financial trouble in 1998, and Air Caribbean operate Trinidad–Tobago routes.

TOURISM

▷ Visitors : population 1:4

324,000 visitors

Up 20% 1995–1997

MAIN TOURIST ARRIVALS

| USA 37% |
| Canada 13% |
| UK 11% |
| Other 39% |

% of total arrivals

Concentration on oil meant that Trinidad was one of the last Caribbean states to develop tourism. Most is centered on Tobago (said to be the model for the island in Robinson Crusoe), which is famous for its wildlife, particularly butterflies. Work on a Hilton hotel began in 1998.

TRINIDAD & TOBAGO

Total Land Area : 5130 sq. km (1981 sq. miles)

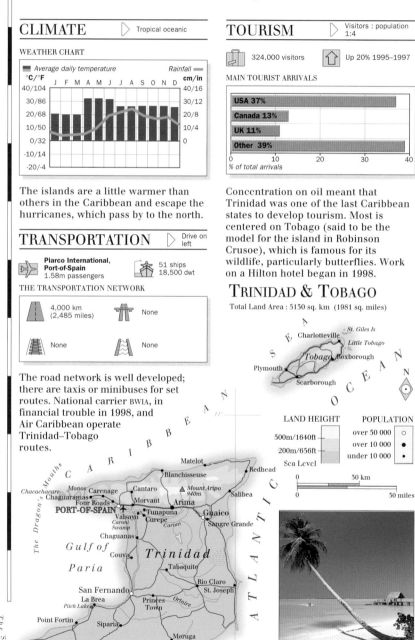

LAND HEIGHT

500m/1640ft
200m/656ft
Sea Level

0   50 km
0   50 miles

POPULATION

over 50 000
over 10 000
under 10 000

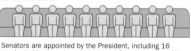

PEOPLE

▷ Pop. density high

English Creole, English, Hindi, French, Spanish

253/km² (656/mi²)

THE URBAN/RURAL POPULATION SPLIT

72%   28%

ETHNIC MAKEUP

White and Chinese 1%
Mixed 19%
Asian 40%
Black 40%

Trinidad's south Asian community is the largest in the Caribbean, and holds on to its Muslim and Hindu inheritance. The open discussion of racial issues in Trinidad goes some way to dissipating latent tensions between black and south Asian Trinidadians.

POLITICS

▷ Multiparty elections

L. House 1995/2000
U. House 1995/2000

President Arthur N. Robinson

AT THE LAST ELECTION

House of Representatives 36 seats

47% PNM   47% UNC   6% NAR

PNM = People's National Movement UNC = United National Congress NAR = National Alliance for Reconstruction

Senate 31 seats

Senators are appointed by the President, including 16 nominated by the prime minister and 6 by the leader of the opposition.

Trinidad has lacked a major political figure since the death of Eric Williams, the autocratic leader of the PNM, who presided over independence in 1962. Decades of increasingly right-wing PNM rule, interrupted in the mid-1980s, saw political fragmentation and the 1990 coup attempt by a Black Muslim sect. The UNC's Basdeo Panday, who led his party to power at the 1995 election, is the first prime minister of south Asian origin. He pledged his coalition government committed to reducing unemployment, crime, and racial discrimination.

Tobago's white sand beaches, verdant landscape and natural anchorages have enabled it to develop a thriving tourist industry.

T

WORLD AFFAIRS

Joined UN in 1962

Trinidad withdrew from the IACHR and the UNHCR in 1998 and 1999 respectively, over appeals against death sentences. There are new trade agreements with Costa Rica, Panama, Dominican Republic and Mexico, and maritime border disputes over fishing and marine oil rights with Venezuela.

AID

Recipient

US$33m (receipts)   Up 94% 1996–1997

Aid is modest: the Caribbean Development Bank has approved a US$34.9 million loan for road repairs.

DEFENSE

No compulsory military service

US$83m   Up 23% in 1997

Defense forces comprise a 2,100-strong army and coastguard. The latter is used to patrol fishing grounds.

ECONOMICS

Inflation 6.2% p.a. (1985–1996)

US$5.6bn   6.20–6.25 Trinidad and Tobago dollars

SCORE CARD

❑ WORLD GNP RANKING	102nd
❑ GNP PER CAPITA	US$4250
❑ BALANCE OF PAYMENTS	US$294m
❑ INFLATION	3.6%
❑ UNEMPLOYMENT	16%

STRENGTHS

Oil, which accounts for 70% of export earnings. Gas increasingly exploited to support new industries. Oil methanol, ammonia, iron and steel exports. Tourism, especially on Tobago.

WEAKNESSES

Insufficiently diversified economy highly sensitive to world oil price movements. High unemployment.

EXPORTS

UK 4%
Guyana 4%
France 6%
Jamaica 9%
USA 43%
Other 34%

IMPORTS

Colombia 6%
UK 6%
Germany 6%
Venezuela 11%
USA 45%
Other 26%

RESOURCES

Electric power 1.2m kw

12,805 tonnes

140,530 b/d (reserves 572,600,000 bbl)

59,000 goats, 39,000 cattle, 28,000 pigs

Oil, natural gas, asphalt, coal, gypsum, iron, fluorspar

Oil and gas are major resources. In 1998 big off-shore gas and oil finds were made, including the largest discovery of crude oil in 25 years.

ENVIRONMENT

No Green MPs

4%   Medium

Spillages from oil tankers threaten coastal conservation areas such as the Caroni Swamp, with its 500 species of butterfly. Forest fires due to periodic drought and traffic-related pollution and congestion are serious concerns.

MEDIA

TV ownership high

Daily newspaper circulation 121 per 1,000 people

PUBLISHING AND BROADCAST MEDIA

There are 4 daily newspapers, including the *Trinidad and Tobago Express* and the *Trinidad Guardian*	
1 state-owned, 1 independent service	1 state-owned, 3 independent services

The government plans to merge its two TV and four radio stations into one entity, saying that it will be free from official control.

CRIME

Death penalty used

2,387 prisoners   Down 1% in 1992

Narcotics-related crime boosts the murder rate. Trinidad works with the USA and the UK to combat drug trafficking and money laundering. The death penalty is implemented.

EDUCATION

School leaving age: 12

98%   7,249 students

Education is based on the former British 11-plus system. Most students go on to the University of the West Indies; Trinidad hosts the St. Augustine campus. However, wealthy Trinidadians go to universities in the USA.

HEALTH

Welfare state health benefits

1 per 1,429 people

Heart disease, cancers, diabetes, accidents, violence

Oil wealth has given Trinidad a better public health service than most Caribbean states, and more private clinics, mainly serving the expatriate community. However, treatment delays are a problem. 98% of the population have safe water.

CHRONOLOGY

Britain seized Trinidad from Spain in 1797 and Tobago from France in 1802. They were unified in 1888.

- ❑ **1956** Eric Williams founds PNM and wins general election: main support from blacks. Indian population supports opposition.
- ❑ **1961** Leaves West Indian Federation (joined 1958).
- ❑ **1962** Independence.
- ❑ **1970** Black Power demonstrations cause brief state of emergency.
- ❑ **1980** Tobago gets own House of Assembly; internal autonomy 1987.
- ❑ **1990–1991** Premier taken hostage in failed fundamentalist coup. PNM returned to power.
- ❑ **1995** UNC's Basdeo Panday becomes first Asian-origin prime minister.
- ❑ **1998–1999** Trinidad withdraws from international human rights bodies over death sentences.

SPENDING

GDP/cap. no increase

CONSUMPTION AND SPENDING

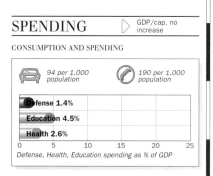

94 per 1,000 population   190 per 1,000 population

Defense 1.4%
Education 4.5%
Health 2.6%

Defense, Health, Education spending as % of GDP

Wealth disparities between the affluent oil-rich business elite, many of whom are expatriate, and farm laborers are particularly marked in Trinidad. Service workers in Tobago's high-value tourism sector are poorly paid. Rural poverty in the interior, particularly among south Asian Trinidadian farmers, is a serious problem.

WORLD RANKING

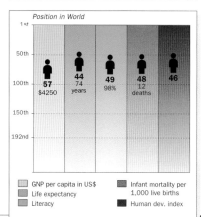

Position in World

| 57 $4250 | 44 74 years | 49 98% | 48 12 deaths | 46 |

GNP per capita in US$
Life expectancy
Literacy
Infant mortality per 1,000 live births
Human dev. index

T

TUNISIA

OFFICIAL NAME: Republic of Tunisia   **CAPITAL:** Tunis
POPULATION: 9.5 million   **CURRENCY:** Tunisian dinar   **OFFICIAL LANGUAGE:** Arabic

1956	1956	March 20	TN	+1	+216	.tn

NORTH AFRICA'S SMALLEST country, Tunisia lies sandwiched between Libya and Algeria. The populous north is mountainous, fertile in places and has a long Mediterranean coastline. The south is largely desert. Habib Bourguiba ruled the country from independence in 1956 until a bloodless coup in 1987. Under President Ben Ali, the government has moved toward multiparty democracy, but faces a challenge from Islamic fundamentalists. Closer ties with the EU, Tunisia's main trading partner, were strengthened through the first Euro-Mediterranean conference held in 1995. Manufacturing and tourism are expanding.

TOURISM

▷ Visitors : population
1:2.2

🧳 4.3m visitors   ⬆ Up 3% 1995–1997

MAIN TOURIST ARRIVALS

Germany 22%	
Algeria 17%	
Libya 14%	
France 13%	
UK 7%	
Other 27%	

% of total arrivals

CLIMATE

▷ Mediterranean/ hot desert

WEATHER CHART

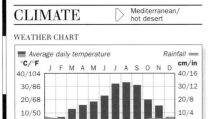

■ *Average daily temperature*   *Rainfall* ■

Tunisia is hot in summer. The north is often wet and windy in winter. The far south is arid. The spring brings the dry, dusty *chili* wind from the Sahara.

TRANSPORTATION

▷ Drive on right

✈ **Tunis-Carthage**
3.46m passengers

⚓ 77 ships
157,900 grt

THE TRANSPORTATION NETWORK

🛣 20,500 km (12,813 miles)		Highway from Tunis to Carthage airport
🚃 1,820 km (1,138 miles)		None

Tunisia has six international airports. A highway from Tunis to Carthage airport opened in 1993. A light metro in Tunis and a rail link from Gafsa to Gabès are being built. The southern third of the country has few roads.

Tourists have flocked to Tunisia since the 1960s, attracted by its winter sunshine, beaches, desert, and Roman remains. One of the Mediterranean's cheapest package destinations, Tunisia attracts almost two million European visitors a year. However, numbers were hit in 1990–1991 by the Gulf War and the fear of attacks by Islamic militants. Tourism employs more than 200,000 people and is a focus of investment. Capacity is set to top 200,000 beds by the year 2000. However, concern about the environmental impact is growing.

PEOPLE

▷ Pop. density medium

👥 Arabic, French

👪 61/km²
(158/mi²)

THE URBAN/RURAL POPULATION SPLIT

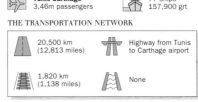

57%   43%

RELIGIOUS PERSUASION

Christian 1% ─┐ ┌─ Jewish 1%

Muslim 98%

ETHNIC MAKEUP

European 1% ─┐ ┌─ Other 1%

Arab and Berber 98%

The population is almost entirely of Arab and Berber descent, although there are Jewish and Christian minorities. Many Tunisians still live in extended family groups, in which three or four generations are represented.

Tunisia has traditionally been one of the most liberal Arab states. The 1956 Personal Statutes Code of President Bourguiba gave women better rights than in any other Arab country. Further legislation has since given women the right to custody of children in divorce cases, made family violence against women punishable by law and helped divorced women to get alimony. Family planning and contraception have been freely available since the early 1960s. Now Tunisia's population grows only minimally each year. Women make up 25% of the total work force and 35% of the industrial work force. Company ownership by women is steadily increasing; politics, however, remains exclusively a male preserve.

These freedoms are threatened by the growth in recent years of Islamic fundamentalism, which also worries the mainly French-speaking political and business elite which desires to strengthen links with Europe.

The Ben Ali regime, although not as repressive as its predecessor, has been criticized for its actions against Islamic activists, in particular the banned *Al-Nahda* party. Amnesty International

has detailed a number of human rights abuses, mainly against female members of *Al-Nahda*.

POPULATION AGE BREAKDOWN

Female	Age	Male
0.5%	81–100	0.5%
3.5%	61–80	3.8%
7.4%	41–60	7.2%
15.9%	21–40	15.8%
22.2%	0–20	23.2%

% of population by age group

Roman remains at the village of La-Kesra *in Tozeur region, a low-lying area of oases in western central Tunisia.*

T

POLITICS ▷ Multiparty elections

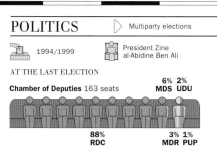

1994/1999

President Zine
al-Abidine Ben Ali

AT THE LAST ELECTION

Chamber of Deputies 163 seats

6% 2%
MDS UDU

88%
RDC

3% 1%
MDR PUP

RDC = Constitutional Democratic Rally **MDS** = Movement of
Social Democrats **MR** = Movement for Renewal
UDU = Unionist Democratic Union **PUP** = Popular Unity Party
144 seats in the Chamber of Deputies are directly elected,
and 19 reserved for parties coming second in national poll
constituencies.

President Ben Ali
*became head of
state in 1987.*

Dr Hamed Karoui
*was appointed prime
minister in 1988.*

Legally a multiparty democracy since 1988, Tunisia is still dominated by the RCD and President Ben Ali.

MAIN POLITICAL ISSUES
Fundamentalism
The RDC has clamped down on Islamic fundamentalists, particularly the outlawed *Al-Nahda*, or Renewal Party. In 1991, 500 *Al-Nahda* members were arrested following a failed coup, thought to be inspired by fundamentalists. Its leader, Rachid Gannouchi, is now in exile.

Human rights
The RDC has been under increasing attack over its human rights record. In 1995, Amnesty International claimed that the torture of detainees had become "common currency." The RDC is committed to promoting women's rights.

PROFILE
President Ben Ali has made efforts to liberalize the political system. The life presidency has been abolished, and political parties and press freedom are encouraged. The 1994 general election aimed at a national coalition against the growing trend of Islamic fundamentalism. However, a complex proportional representation system ensured that there was an overwhelming victory for the RDC, while allowing for a degree of political plurality. Since 1994, there has been evidence of a renewed crackdown against the left-wing opposition.

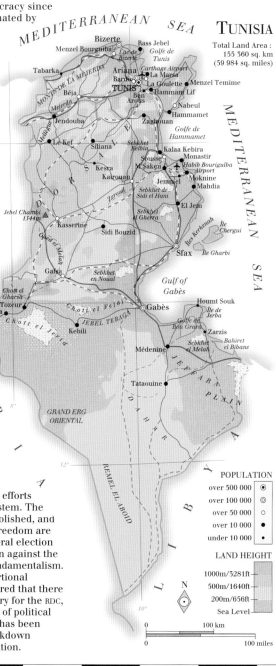

TUNISIA

Total Land Area :
155 360 sq. km
(59 984 sq. miles)

POPULATION

over 500 000 ⊙
over 100 000 ◎
over 50 000 ○
over 10 000 ●
under 10 000 ·

LAND HEIGHT

1000m/3281ft
500m/1640ft
200m/656ft
Sea Level

0 — 100 km

0 — 100 miles

WORLD AFFAIRS ▷ Joined UN in 1956

AL AMU IBRD NAM OIC

A foreign policy priority is to strengthen contacts with the West, which have generally been good because of Tunisia's liberal economic and social policies. Attention is focused on the EU, Tunisia's main export market, with Tunisia playing an important role in the run-up to the first Euro-Mediterranean conference held in 1995.

Tunis was host to the PLO after that organization was expelled from Lebanon. Relations with other Arab states, particularly Kuwait and Saudi Arabia, were soured by Tunisia's support for Iraq in the Gulf War. The government regards the political success of Islamic fundamentalism in neighboring Algeria with concern. Relations with Libya are improving, helped by the fact that Tunisia has been turning a blind eye to sanctions-busters operating through its territory.

CHRONOLOGY

Tunisia has been home to the Zenata Berbers since earliest times and its history is linked to the rise and fall of the Mediterranean-centered empires. Carthage (near present-day Tunis), founded in the 9th century BCE, became the hub of a 1,000-year Phoenician trading empire which linked European and African trading networks. Tunisia was then incorporated into the Roman, Byzantine, Arab, Ottoman, and, finally, French empires.

❑ **1883** La Marsa Treaty makes Tunisia a French protectorate, ending its semi-independence. Bey of Tunis remains monarch.

❑ **1900** Influx of French and Italian settlers.

❑ **1920** Destour (Constitution) Party formed; calls for self-government.

❑ **1935** Habib Bourguiba forms Neo-Destour (New Constitution) Party.

❑ **1943** Defeat of Axis powers by British troops restores French rule.

❑ **1955** Internal autonomy. Bourguiba returns from exile.

❑ **1956** Independence. Bourguiba elected prime minister. Personal Statutes Code gives rights to women. Family planning introduced.

❑ **1957** Bey is deposed. Tunisia becomes republic with Bourguiba as first president.

❑ **1964** Neo-Destour becomes sole legal political party; changes its name to Destour Socialist Party (PSD). Moderate socialist economic program is introduced. ⇨

T

CHRONOLOGY *continued*

- ❏ **1969** Agricultural collectivization program, begun 1964, abandoned.
- ❏ **1974** Bourguiba president for life.
- ❏ **1974–1976** Hundreds imprisoned for belonging to "illegal organizations."
- ❏ **1978** Trade union movement, UGTT, holds 24-hour general strike; more than 50 killed in clashes. UGTT leadership replaced with PSD loyalists.
- ❏ **1980** New prime minister Muhammed Mazli ushers in greater political tolerance.
- ❏ **1981** Elections. Opposition groups allege electoral malpractice.
- ❏ **1984** Widespread riots after food price increases.
- ❏ **1986** Gen. Zine al-Abidine Ben Ali becomes interior minister. Four Muslim fundamentalists sentenced to death.
- ❏ **1987** Fundamentalist leader Rachid Gannouchi arrested. Ben Ali becomes prime minister; takes over presidency after doctors certify Bourguiba senile. PSD becomes RDC.
- ❏ **1988** Most political prisoners released. Constitutional reforms introduce multiparty system and abolish life presidency. Two opposition parties legalized.
- ❏ **1989** Elections: RDC wins all seats, Ben Ali president. Fundamentalists take 13% of vote.
- ❏ **1990** Tunisia backs Iraq over invasion of Kuwait. Clampdown on fundamentalists intensifies.
- ❏ **1991** Abortive coup blamed on *Al-Nahda*; over 500 arrests.
- ❏ **1993** Multiparty agreement on electoral reform.
- ❏ **1994** Presidential and legislative elections. Ben Ali, sole candidate, reelected president. Ruling RDC wins all elected seats; opposition parties gain 19 reserved seats.
- ❏ **1996** Mohammed Moada, leader of opposition MDS, sentenced to 11 years' imprisonment for dealings with foreign agents.

AID ▷ Recipient

💲 $194m (receipts)   ⬆ Up 54% 1996–1997

France is the largest single donor, providing almost a quarter of bilateral aid. Italy, Germany, the World Bank, and the African Development Bank are other important sources of assistance. Oil-rich Arab states, including Saudi Arabia and Kuwait, have suspended their aid programs to Tunisia since 1990 because of its pro-Iraq stance in the Gulf War. Tunisia's total external debt is estimated at some 50% of GNP.

DEFENSE ▷ Compulsory military service

💲 $334m   ⬇ Down 18% in 1997

Despite its small size – 35,000 troops, of whom two-thirds are conscripts – the military is an important political force, armed mainly with US weapons. Officer training is carried out in the USA and France, as well as in Tunisia. Border security with Algeria was tightened in 1995 after Algerian Islamists attacked Tunisian border guards in protest against Tunisian support for Algerian security forces.

TUNISIAN ARMED FORCES

🛡	84 main battle tanks (54 M–60A3, 30 M–60A1)	27,000 personnel
⚓	20 patrol boats	4,500 personnel
✈	44 combat aircraft (15 F–5E/F)	3,500 personnel
	None	

ECONOMICS ▷ Inflation 5.6% p.a. (1985–1996)

📊 $19.4bn   💲 1.15–1.09 dinars

SCORE CARD

- ❏ WORLD GNP RANKING...........................68th
- ❏ GNP PER CAPITA $2,110
- ❏ BALANCE OF PAYMENTS....................$–640m
- ❏ INFLATION 3.7%
- ❏ UNEMPLOYMENT..................................15%

EXPORTS

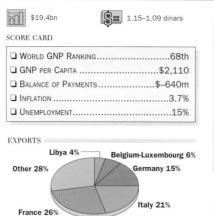

- Libya 4%
- Belgium-Luxembourg 6%
- Germany 15%
- Italy 21%
- France 26%
- Other 28%

IMPORTS

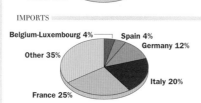

- Belgium-Luxembourg 4%
- Spain 4%
- Germany 12%
- Italy 20%
- France 25%
- Other 35%

STRENGTHS
A well-diversified economy, despite limited resources. Tourism. Oil and gas exports. Manufacturing is expanding. European investment.

WEAKNESSES
Dependence on growth of drought-prone agricultural sector. Growing domestic energy demand on oil and gas resources.

PROFILE
Since it began a process of structural adjustment in 1988, supported by the IMF and the World Bank, Tunisia has become an increasingly open, market-oriented economy. Real GDP growth has averaged 5% since 1987 and rose to 6%–7% in 1995–1996. However, the budget deficit rose to 4% of GDP in 1994, after being reduced to 2% of GDP in 1993. Liberalization measures mean that prices have been freed, most state companies privatized, and import barriers reduced.

ECONOMIC PERFORMANCE INDICATOR

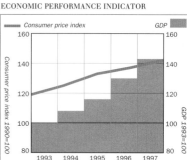

Consumer price index — GDP

(Consumer price index 1990=100; GDP 1993=100; years 1993–1997)

The government has also begun a search for foreign investment. High foreign investment levels are essential if Tunisia is to reach its goal of providing an extra 313,000 jobs for young people by the end of the century, and cut the overall unemployment rate. Another problem is the balance of payments, which relies on fluctuating tourism receipts to offset a trade deficit. The government must also balance growth with better social provisions. Negotiations to increase trading opportunities with the EU, already Tunisia's main trading partner, are under way.

TUNISIA : MAJOR BUSINESSES

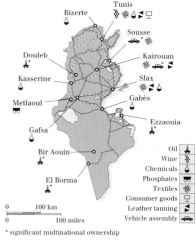

- Tunis
- Bizerte
- Sousse
- Douleb
- Kairouan
- Kasserine
- Sfax
- Metlaoui
- Gabès
- Gafsa
- Ezzaouia
- Bir Aouin
- El Borma

0   100 km
0   100 miles

- Oil
- Wine
- Chemicals
- Phosphates
- Textiles
- Consumer goods
- Leather tanning
- Vehicle assembly

* significant multinational ownership

T

RESOURCES

▷ Electric power 1.7m kw

84,405 tonnes

85,000 b/d (reserves 400,000,000 bbl)

6.6m sheep, 1.3m goats, 770,000 cattle

Phosphates, iron, zinc, lead, salt, oil, gas

ELECTRICITY GENERATION

Hydro 1% (0.03bn kwh)					
Combustion 99% (7.6bn kwh)					
Nuclear 0%					
Other 0%					
0	20	40	60	80	100

% of total generation by type

Tunisia is one of the leading producers of phosphates for fertilizers, mainly from mines near Gafsa. Oil and gas are

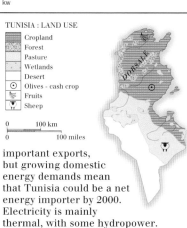

TUNISIA : LAND USE

Cropland
Forest
Pasture
Wetlands
Desert
⊙ Olives - cash crop
Fruits
Sheep

0   100 km
0   100 miles

important exports, but growing domestic energy demands mean that Tunisia could be a net energy importer by 2000. Electricity is mainly thermal, with some hydropower.

ENVIRONMENT

▷ No Green MPs

1%

Low

ENVIRONMENTAL TREATIES

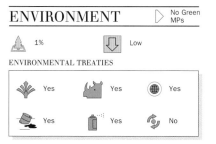

Yes   Yes   Yes

Yes   Yes   No

Desertification is a serious problem in the arid central and southern regions. However, the dominant environmental issue is the rapid expansion of tourism since the 1980s. Large, insensitively designed hotel and resort developments, which do not fit in with the local architecture, are spoiling coastal areas such as the Isle of Jerba and Hammamet (although building height restrictions are applied here). Tourism is also making an impact on the fragile desert ecology of the south.

MEDIA

▷ TV ownership medium

Daily newspaper circulation 111 per 1,000 people

PUBLISHING AND BROADCAST MEDIA

	There are 8 daily newspapers, including *L'Action, al-Amal, La Presse de Tunisie* and *As-Sabah*
	1 state-owned service
	1 state-owned service

Reforms since the late 1980s have in theory increased press freedom in Tunisia, a country traditionally considered a source of liberal ideas in the Arab world. In practice, government restrictions remain. The foreign press is also occasionally banned, as in 1994–1995, but the arrival of satellite TV from Europe has enabled people to receive a wide range of programs.

CRIME

▷ Death penalty used

Tunisia does not publish prison figures

Up 6% from 1992–1996

CRIME RATES

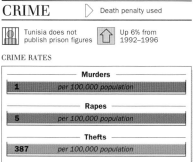

Murders
1   per 100,000 population

Rapes
5   per 100,000 population

Thefts
387   per 100,000 population

Street crime is unusual. However, Tunisia's human rights record has prompted criticism of its maltreatment of political and other detainees. Arbitrary arrests and torture while in police custody, especially of suspected Islamic activists, are routine.

EDUCATION

▷ School leaving age: 16

67%   121,787 students

Education is compulsory for ten years between the ages of six and 16.

THE EDUCATION SYSTEM

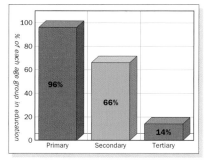

% of each age group in education

96% Primary
66% Secondary
14% Tertiary

Arabic is the first language in schools, but French is also taught, and is used almost exclusively in higher education. There are four universities; a total of more than 120,000 students were enrolled in 1996/1997.

HEALTH

▷ Welfare state health benefits

1 per 1,667 people

Heart and cerebrovascular diseases

Well-developed family planning facilities have almost halved Tunisia's birthrate over the past 30 years. The population growth rate has dropped from 3.2% to 1.9% – the lowest in the region. The mortality rate has been halved, to 6.4 per 1,000 population a year, reflecting the extension of free medical services to over 70% of the population. Services lack sophistication, but an umbrella of primary care facilities covers all but the most isolated rural communities. Regional committees for social security care for the old, needy, and orphaned.

SPENDING

▷ GDP/cap. no increase

CONSUMPTION AND SPENDING

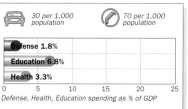

30 per 1,000 population

70 per 1,000 population

Defense 1.8%				
Education 6.8%				
Health 3.3%				
0	5	10	15	20	25

Defense, Health, Education spending as % of GDP

Today 6% of Tunisians are estimated to live in absolute poverty. In 1970, the figure was 30%. The poorest people tend to live in the urban shanty towns, or *bidonvilles*. The Western-oriented elite has links to government or business. Social security covers sickness, old age and maternity, but not unemployment, currently at 15%. The government is concerned that unemployment is encouraging the spread of Islamic fundamentalism. Economic growth is its medium-term solution to the problem. Special projects are being set up in the most deprived urban areas to offset the worst effects of poverty.

WORLD RANKING

T

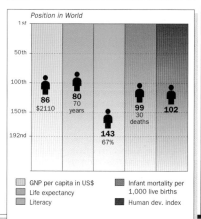

Position in World

1st
50th
100th
150th
192nd

86 $2110
80 70 years
143 67%
99 30 deaths
102

☐ GNP per capita in US$
☐ Life expectancy
☐ Literacy
■ Infant mortality per 1,000 live births
■ Human dev. index

TURKEY

OFFICIAL NAME: Republic of Turkey **CAPITAL:** Ankara
POPULATION: 63.8 million **CURRENCY:** Turkish lira **OFFICIAL LANGUAGE:** Turkish

TURKEY MAINLY IN WEST ASIA, also includes the region of Eastern Thrace in Europe. The entrance to the Black Sea is straddled by Turkey's largest city, Istanbul. Most Turks live in the western half of the country. The eastern and southeastern Anatolia Plateau are Kurdish regions. Turkey's strategic location gives it great influence in the Black Sea, the Mediterranean, and the Middle East. Lying on a major earthquake fault line, many Turkish towns are vunerable to quakes such as the one which hit Izmit in 1999.

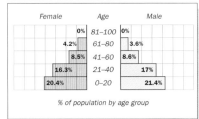

The island of Akdamar, eastern Anatolia.
Surrounded by Lake Van, the island is the site of the 10th-century Church of the Holy Cross.

CLIMATE
▷ Mountain/ Mediterranean

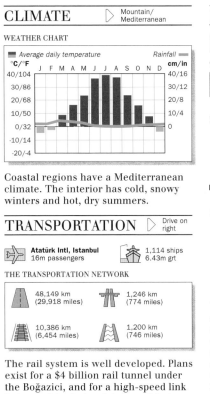

WEATHER CHART

Coastal regions have a Mediterranean climate. The interior has cold, snowy winters and hot, dry summers.

TRANSPORTATION
▷ Drive on right

✈ **Atatürk Intl, Istanbul** 16m passengers

🚢 1,114 ships 6.43m grt

THE TRANSPORTATION NETWORK

48,149 km (29,918 miles)	1,246 km (774 miles)
10,386 km (6,454 miles)	1,200 km (746 miles)

The rail system is well developed. Plans exist for a $4 billion rail tunnel under the Boğazici, and for a high-speed link between Istanbul and Ankara. More highways are planned, including a road bridge across the Dardanelles.

TOURISM
▷ Visitors : population 1:7.1

🧳 9.04m visitors

⬆ Up 28% 1995–1997

Attacks on foreign tourists by Kurdish militants in 1994 discouraged tourists, but they have since returned. In 1997 tourists spent $7 billion. Visitors are attracted by the fine beaches, classical sites, and antiquities from prehistoric, Roman, Byzantine, and Ottoman periods. Istanbul attracts shoppers, especially collectors of antiques and carpets.

MAIN TOURIST ARRIVALS

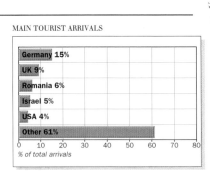

Germany 15%
UK 9%
Romania 6%
Israel 5%
USA 4%
Other 61%

% of total arrivals

PEOPLE
▷ Pop. density medium

Turkish, Kurdish, Arabic, Circassian, Armenian, Greek, Georgian, Ladino

83/km² (215/mi²)

THE URBAN/RURAL POPULATION SPLIT

69% / 31%

RELIGIOUS PERSUASION

Other 1%
Muslim (mainly Sunni) 99%

ETHNIC MAKEUP

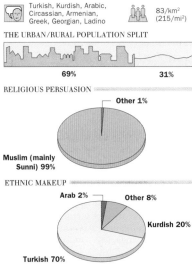

Arab 2%
Other 8%
Kurdish 20%
Turkish 70%

The Turks are racially diverse. Many are the descendants of refugees, often from the Balkans, but a strong sense of national identity is rooted in a shared language and religion. Most are Sunni Muslim, although a Shi'a community is growing fast, including the heterodox Alawite sect. The largest minority are the Kurds, while there are some 500,000 Arabic speakers. While women have equal rights in law, men dominate political and even family life. There is controversy over the right of women to wear Islamic headscarves. Tansu Çiller was Turkey's first woman prime minister, in 1993–1996.

POPULATION AGE BREAKDOWN

Female	Age	Male
0%	81–100	0%
4.2%	61–80	3.6%
8.5%	41–60	8.6%
16.3%	21–40	17%
20.4%	0–20	21.4%

% of population by age group

POLITICS ▷ Multiparty elections

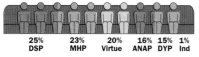

1999/2004   President Süleyman Demirel

AT THE LAST ELECTION

Turkish Grand National Assembly 550 seats

25% DSP	23% MHP	20% Virtue	16% ANAP	15% DYP	1% Ind

DSP = Democratic Left Party **MHP** = Nationalist Action Party
Virtue = Virtue Party **ANAP** = Motherland Party **DYP** = True
Path Party **Ind** = Independents

Under the 1982 constitution, Turkey is a multiparty republic with a national assembly elected every five years. The president serves a seven-year term and appoints the prime minister.

MAIN POLITICAL ISSUES
Islamic fundamentalism
Necmettin Erbakan's 1996–1997 premiership was the first pro-Islamic government since the formation of the republic in 1923. In the 1995 election his RP, backed mainly by the urban poor opposed to Ataturk's secularism, became the largest parliamentary party. The secular parties kept it out of power till mid-1996 when Erbakan formed a coalition with the DYP. Ousted from power in mid-1997, the RP was banned in January 1998. Many RP MPs have now allied with the new Virtue Party (FP).

Kurdish separatism
Thousands have been killed since 1984 in a bitter civil war in southeastern Turkey. The secessionist Kurdistan Workers' Party (PKK) has proclaimed three cease-fires since 1992 and now professes simply to favor recognition of Kurdish rights within Turkey. It suffered a major setback in 1999 when PKK leader Abdullah Ocalan was captured, tried, and in early July sentenced to death.

Human rights
Turkey's human rights record has been subject to intense international criticism. Reforms in 1995 lifted a number of civil liberty restrictions written into the 1982 constitution, but concerns remain over the many disappearances and illegal executions and the treatment of the Kurdish minority.

PROFILE
Apart from the Islamic-secular division, politics are divided more by personalities than ideologies. The military-dominated National Security Council also retains political influence.

Tansu Çiller's DYP represents small businesses. Her coalition with the pro-Islamist RP from mid-1996 was controversial and collapsed in mid-1997, and the RP was banned in 1998. Mesut Yilmaz, leader of ANAP (backed by Istanbul's metropolitan interests), was Prime Minister from mid-1997. He was replaced in early 1999 by Bulent Ecevit of the Democratic Left Party (DSP), after its strong performance in the general election. Ecevit went on to form a right-wing coalition with the Nationalist MHP and ANAP.

Tansu Çiller, DYP leader and first woman prime minister in 1993–1996.

Süleyman Demirel, who became president in 1993.

WORLD AFFAIRS ▷ Joined UN in 1945

CE | NATO | OECD | OIC | OSCE

With the end of the Cold War, Turkey's strategic value as NATO's first Western line of defense against the USSR has diminished, and it now seeks closer ties with neighboring states. In 1992, Turkey joined the Black Sea Economic Cooperation Project, and has tried to mediate in the war between Armenia and Azerbaijan. Turkey lent assistance to the Gulf War allies against Iraq in 1991, and has cordial relations with Arab states. Turkey's pro-Islamic government in 1996–1997, although inept in handling foreign affairs, posed a short-lived threat of upheaval.

Membership of the EU remains problematic. Greece has opposed Ankara's membership because Turkey occupies northern Cyprus, while its human rights record continues to cause concern among other EU members. Trading links with the EU were strengthened, however, with Turkey's entry into the EU customs union in 1995.

AID ▷ Recipient

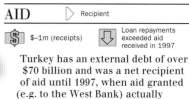

$–1m (receipts)   Loan repayments exceeded aid received in 1997

Turkey has an external debt of over $70 billion and was a net recipient of aid until 1997, when aid granted (e.g. to the West Bank) actually exceeded aid received. The government received over $4 billion in aid from Gulf War allies. In 1994, the USA suspended some aid in protest at Turkish treatment of Kurds.

TURKEY

Total Land Area : 769 630 sq. km(297 154 sq. miles)

LAND HEIGHT	POPULATION
3000m/9843ft	over 5 000 000
2000m/6562ft	over 1 000 000
1000m/3281ft	over 500 000
500m/1640ft	over 100 000
200m/656ft	over 50 000
Sea Level	over 10 000
	under 10 000

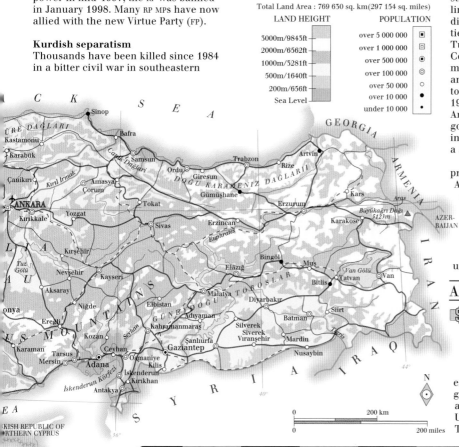

T

577

CHRONOLOGY

Following the collapse of the Ottoman Empire and Turkey's defeat in World War I, nationalist Mustafa Kemal Ataturk deposed the ruling sultan in 1922, declaring Turkey a republic in 1923.

❑ **1924** Religious courts abolished.
❑ **1928** Islam no longer state religion.
❑ **1934** Women given the vote.
❑ **1938** President Ataturk dies. Succeeded by Ismet Inonu.
❑ **1945** Turkey declares war on Germany. Joins postwar UN.
❑ **1952** Joins Council of Europe and NATO.
❑ **1960** Army stages coup against ruling Democratic Party and suspends National Assembly.
❑ **1961** New constitution.
❑ **1963** EEC association agreement.
❑ **1974** Invades northern Cyprus.
❑ **1980** Military coup. Imposition of martial law.
❑ **1982** New constitution.
❑ **1983** General election won by Turgut Özal's ANAP.
❑ **1984** Turkey recognizes "Turkish Republic of Northern Cyprus." Kurdish separatist PKK launches guerrilla war in southeast.
❑ **1987** Applies for EC membership.
❑ **1990** Turkey grants permission to US-led coalition to launch air strikes on Iraq from Turkish bases.
❑ **1991** Elections won by DYP. Süleyman Demirel premier.
❑ **1992** Turkey joins Black Sea alliance.
❑ **1993** Demirel elected president. Çiller becomes DYP leader and heads DYP-SHP coalition. Cease-fire with PKK breaks down and conflict resumes.
❑ **1994** Austerity measures to control economic crisis. Mounting international pressure to improve Turkey's human rights record.
❑ **1995** Major anti-Kurdish offensive. Democratic reforms lower voting age 18. Çiller coalition collapses. Pro-Islamic RP emerges as largest party in general election, but is in minority. Customs union with EU.
❑ **1996** Short-lived center-right DYP-ANAP coalition falls. RP leader Necmettin Erbakan heads first pro-Islamic government since the 1923 creation of secular republic.
❑ **1997** Erbakan's government falls; Yilmaz reappointed prime minister of minority ANAP government.
❑ **1998** January, RP banned; many former RP MPs join Virtue Party (FP). November, Yilmaz resigns amid corruption allegations; replaced by Bulent Ecevit of DSP.
❑ **1999** DSP wins largest share of seats in election; Ecevit returns as premier of right-wing coalition. August, earthquake hits Izmit and kills 14,000

T

DEFENSE ▷ Compulsory military service

💲 $8.11bn   ⬆ Up 6% in 1997

Turkey's armed forces total are the second-largest in NATO.

TURKISH ARMED FORCES

🚜	4,205 main battle tanks (2,876 M-48, 932 M-60, 397 *Leopard*)	525,000 personnel
🚢	16 submarines, 2 destroyers, 19 frigates and 50 patrol boats	51,000 personnel
✈	440 combat aircraft (175 F-16C/D, 87 F-5, 178 F-4E)	63,000 personnel
🚀	None	

The army occasionally intervenes in Turkish politics (e.g. in the 1980 military coup). With 18 months' service compulsory for all males at the age of 20, Turkey is a sizable military power. It spends a higher percentage of GDP (4.2% in 1997) on defense than any other NATO country except Greece. NATO membership gives Turkey easy access to Western arms suppliers, although in 1994 Germany threatened a ban on arms sales, claiming that they were being used to suppress the Kurdish minority. Offensives against Kurdish separatists based in northern Iraq and in Turkey's own southeastern provinces have involved over 50,000 troops and incursions into Iraqi territory.

ECONOMICS ▷ Inflation 65.6% p.a. (1985–1996)

📊 $199.4bn   💲 207,125–315,400 Turkish lira

SCORE CARD

❑ WORLD GNP RANKING..........................24th
❑ GNP PER CAPITA $3,130
❑ BALANCE OF PAYMENTS.................$–2.75bn
❑ INFLATION 85.7%
❑ UNEMPLOYMENT 7%

EXPORTS

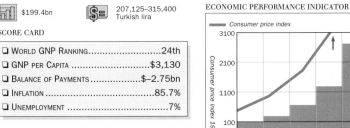

Italy 5%
UK 6%
USA 8%
Russia 8%
Other 53%
Germany 20%

IMPORTS

France 6%
UK 6%
USA 9%
Italy 9%
Other 54%
Germany 16%

STRENGTHS

Liberalized economy has resulted in strong growth in the 1990s. Self-sufficient in agriculture. Textiles, manufacturing and construction sectors competitive on world markets. Tourism industry. Dynamic private sector economy. Skilled labor force. Customs union with EU since 1995 has deepened trade links.

WEAKNESSES

Persistently high inflation. Unsound public finances. Large government bureaucracy. Privatization program only begun in 1994. Influence of organized crime. High cost of civil war with Kurds.

PROFILE

Turkey has one of the oldest and most advanced emerging market economies. In the 1990s it registered strong

ECONOMIC PERFORMANCE INDICATOR

Consumer price index — GDP

growth, but is also the only big market economy to suffer from persistently high inflation. In 1997–1998 the government of Mesut Yilmaz succeeded in reducing inflation, introduced new tax laws to improve tax collection, embarked upon structural reforms, and restarted the stalled privatization program. The 1999 Izmit earthquake caused massive damage to low quality buildings.

TURKEY : MAJOR BUSINESSES

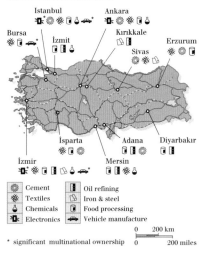

🔲 Cement		🔲 Oil refining	
❋ Textiles		🔲 Iron & steel	
🜂 Chemicals		🔲 Food processing	
⚡ Electronics		🚗 Vehicle manufacture	

0   200 km
0   200 miles

* significant multinational ownership

RESOURCES

▷ Electric power 21m kw

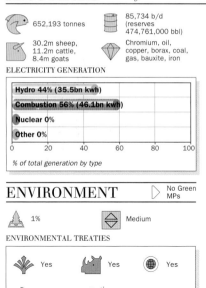

652,193 tonnes

85,734 b/d
(reserves
474,761,000 bbl)

30.2m sheep,
11.2m cattle,
8.4m goats

Chromium, oil,
copper, borax, coal,
gas, bauxite, iron

ELECTRICITY GENERATION

Hydro 44% (35.5bn kwh)

Combustion 56% (46.1bn kwh)

Nuclear 0%

Other 0%

0   20   40   60   80   100

% of total generation by type

Under the Southeastern Anatolian Project (GAP) launched in the mid-1980s, Turkey is building 22 dams on the Tigris and Euphrates rivers to provide irrigation and hydroelectric power. In 1999 controversy focused on the Ilisu dam on the Tigris, which will flood 15 towns and 52 villages. Syria, Iraq, and Jordan have protested that the GAP threatens their water supplies.

Turkey produces oil in Garcan and Raman. Eastern provinces are rich in minerals, such as chromium, of which Turkey is the world's largest producer.

TURKEY : LAND USE

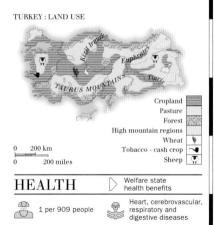

0   200 km
0   200 miles

Cropland
Pasture
Forest
High mountain regions
Wheat
Tobacco - cash crop
Sheep

ENVIRONMENT

▷ No Green MPs

1%

Medium

ENVIRONMENTAL TREATIES

Yes   Yes   Yes

Yes   Yes   No

Turkey's program of dam-building on the Tigris and Euphrates has met with international condemnation, particularly from Syria and Iraq, whose rivers will suffer reduced flow rates as a result. Concern has also been expressed at plans to build a nuclear power plant. Much of the western coast has been spoilt by lack of planning and by uncontrolled tourist developments.

CRIME

▷ Death penalty used

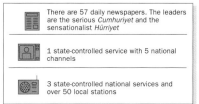 49,895 prisoners

Up 140% from 1992–1996

CRIME RATES

Murders
3   per 100,000 population

Rapes
1   per 100,000 population

Thefts
191   per 100,000 population

Crime levels, especially Mafia and narcotics-related crime, increased in the 1990s. Routine torture of prisoners by the police and deaths in custody cause concern among human rights groups. Kurdish militants continue to attack pipelines and other targets.

HEALTH

▷ Welfare state health benefits

1 per 909 people

Heart, cerebrovascular, respiratory and digestive diseases

Turkey possesses an adequate national system of primary health care. By Western standards, however, hospitals are under-equipped. There are fewer doctors per head than in any western European country.

SPENDING

▷ GDP/cap. no increase

CONSUMPTION AND SPENDING

59 per 1,000 population

250 per 1,000 population

Defense 4.2%

Education 3.4%

Health 1.5%

0   5   10   15   20   25

Defense, Health, Education spending as % of GDP

The economic expansion of the 1980s created a new class of wealthy entrepreneurs. Urban/rural differences in Turkey remain pronounced. High inflation in the 1990s eroded earnings of those on fixed incomes. Many Turks take jobs abroad as *Gastarbeiter* (guest workers) in Germany and the Netherlands.

MEDIA

▷ TV ownership high

Daily newspaper circulation 111 per 1,000 people

PUBLISHING AND BROADCAST MEDIA

There are 57 daily newspapers. The leaders are the serious *Cumhuriyet* and the sensationalist *Hürriyet*

1 state-controlled service with 5 national channels

3 state-controlled national services and over 50 local stations

The Turkish press is diverse, vigorous and largely privately owned. In 1995, the National Assembly amended censorship laws dating back to 1980, to ease restrictions on the propagation of Kurdish rights. A particularly high number of journalists are, however, imprisoned in Turkey. Islam is the dominant religion, but the media are not subject to the moral censorship found in the Gulf states. Almost all Istanbul newspapers are printed in Ankara and Izmir on the same day. Foreign satellite or cable broadcasts are available, as well as the five national channels of the state Turkish Radio and Television Corporation.

EDUCATION

▷ School leaving age: 14

86%   1.17m students

Turkey spent a relatively high 11.2% of its state budget on education

THE EDUCATION SYSTEM

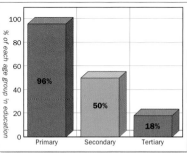

% of each age group in education

96%   Primary
50%   Secondary
18%   Tertiary

in 1996.
After 1923, educational establishments were nationalized. In 1928, an alphabet with Latin characters was introduced. In 1997 compulsory education was extended from five to eight years, raising the age from 11 to 14 for entry into Islamic schools, seen as designed to reduce attendance at such schools. Engineering is usually the strongest

WORLD RANKING

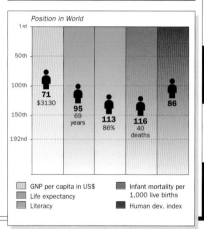

Position in World

1st
50th
100th
150th
192nd

71    $3130
95   69 years
113   86%
116   40 deaths
86

GNP per capita in US$
Life expectancy
Literacy
Infant mortality per 1,000 live births
Human dev. index

T

TURKMENISTAN

CENTRAL ASIA

OFFICIAL NAME: Turkmenistan **CAPITAL:** Ashgabat
POPULATION: 4.3 million **CURRENCY:** Manat **OFFICIAL LANGUAGE:** Turkmen

| 1991 | 1991 | Oct 27/28 | TM | +5 | +993 | .tm |

ORIGINALLY THE POOREST state among the former Soviet republics, Turkmenistan has adjusted better than most to independence, exploiting the market value of its abundant natural gas supplies. A largely Sunni Muslim area, Turkmenistan is part of the former Turkestan, the last expanse of central Asia incorporated into tsarist Russia. Much of life is still based on tribal relationships. Turkmenistan is isolated – telephones are rare and other communications limited.

CLIMATE   ▷ Desert/steppe

WEATHER CHART

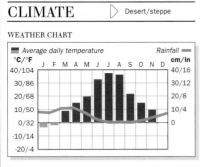

Most of Turkmenistan is arid desert, so that only 2% of the total land area is suitable for agriculture.

TRANSPORTATION   ▷ Drive on right

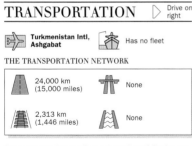

🛫 Turkmenistan Intl, Ashgabat
🚢 Has no fleet

THE TRANSPORTATION NETWORK

| 24,000 km (15,000 miles) | None |
| 2,313 km (1,446 miles) | None |

The upgrading of road and rail links to Tehran have priority. There are plans to modernize Ashgabat airport.

TOURISM   ▷ Visitors : population 1:18

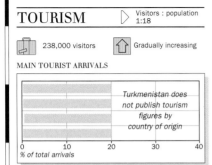

238,000 visitors
⬆ Gradually increasing

MAIN TOURIST ARRIVALS

Turkmenistan does not publish tourism figures by country of origin

% of total arrivals

Most visitors are businessmen attracted by Turkmenistan's stability under President Niyazov. Turkmenistan may become a popular tourist destination in future; traditional Turkmen Muslim monuments are slowly being restored.

Kara Kum Canal zone: salt flats and the Kopetdag mountains on the Iranian border. The Kara Kum is Turkmenistan's largest desert.

PEOPLE   ▷ Pop. density low

Turkmen, Uzbek, Russian
9/km² (23/mi²)

THE URBAN/RURAL POPULATION SPLIT

45%   55%

RELIGIOUS PERSUASION

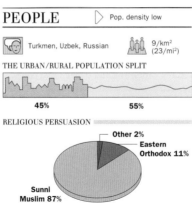

- Other 2%
- Eastern Orthodox 11%
- Sunni Muslim 87%

Before tsarist Russia annexed Turkmenistan in 1884, the Turkmen were a largely nomadic tribal people. The tribal unit remains strong – the largest tribes are the Tekke in the center, the Ersary on the eastern Afghan border and the Yomud in the west. Tribal conflicts among the Turkmen, rather than tensions with the two main minorities – Russians and Uzbeks – are a source of strife. Paradoxically, this has meant that since independence from Moscow there has been less virulent nationalism than in other former Soviet republics. Since 1989, Turkmenistan has been rehabilitating its traditional language and culture, as well as reassessing its history. Islam is again central to the Turkmen, although few make the *haj* (pilgrimage) to Mecca and many continue to maintain a cult of ancestors.

POLITICS   ▷ Multiparty elections

🗳 L. House 1998/2003
U. House 1994/1999
👤 President Saparmurad Niyazov

AT THE LAST ELECTION

Parliament 50 seats

In elections to the Parliament in 1994 the majority of seats were won (unopposed) by members of the ruling Democratic Party of Turkmenistan (the only registered party).

People's Council 110 seats

Comprises 50 elected members, the 50 members of Parliament, 10 appointed regional members and a varying number of ex-officio members.

Officially, Turkmenistan became a multiparty democracy at independence. As in other former Soviet states, however, former Communist Party members, regrouped as the Democratic Party of Turkmenistan, still dominate the political process. The DPT harbors the traditional communist suspicion of Islamic fundamentalism.

President Niyazov has encouraged a personality cult, exemplified by the observance since 1995 of an official holiday to mark his birthday and the unveiling in 1998 of a 12-m high gold-plated statue of himself in the center of Ashgabat. He sustains his popularity through the provision of free electricity and water.

The main concern is to prevent the social and nationalistic conflicts that have blighted other former Soviet republics. Russian continues to be the bureaucratic language.

WORLD AFFAIRS   ▷ Joined UN in 1992

| CIS | ECO | EAPC | OIC | OSCE |

Turkmenistan is concentrating on establishing good relations with Iran and Turkey. It needs investment from both countries, but is wary of Islamic fundamentalism. President Niyazov opposes economic union with the CIS, and has also expressed caution about closer political union with other Turkic-speaking central Asian states.

AID   ▷ Recipient

💲 $11m (receipts)
⬇ Down 54% 1996–1997

Aid is mostly concentrated in the oil and gas industries and comes from Turkey, Iran, Switzerland, and Germany.

T

POPULATION

over 100 000	◎
over 50 000	○
over 10 000	●
under 10 000	●

LAND HEIGHT

1000m/1640ft
500m/1640ft
200m/656ft
Sea Level
-200m/-656ft

TURKMENISTAN

Total Land Area : 488 100 sq. km (188 455 sq. miles)

0   200 km
0   200 miles

N

CHRONOLOGY

The nomadic peoples of western Turkestan came under Russian imperial control from the 1850s.

❏ **1881** Russians found present-day Ashgabat.
❏ **1924** Creation of Turkmenistan.
❏ **1991** Independence from USSR.
❏ **1992** Niyazov reelected president.
❏ **1994** Former communists win elections. Referendum extends to 2002 Niyazov's term of office.

EDUCATION
▷ School leaving age: 17

98%   76,000 students

The Turkmen language and literature (banned until 1987) are now on the syllabus. However, Russian schools still have higher standards.

HEALTH
▷ Welfare state health benefits

1 per 313 people   Cerebrovascular, heart and respiratory diseases

Highly polluted water is a major health hazard; less than 40% of the population have treated mains supply.

SPENDING
▷ GDP/cap. increase

CONSUMPTION AND SPENDING

No data   78 per 1,000 population

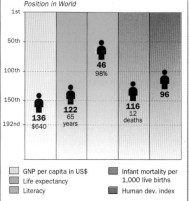

Defense 2.7%
Education 3.9%
Health 5%

0   5   10   15   20   25
Defense, Health, Education spending as % of GDP

DEFENSE
▷ Compulsory military sevice

$107m   Down 25% in 1997

Compared with other regional states, Turkmenistan is reasonably stable. Its army is under joint control with Russia, on which it is dependent for defense.

ECONOMICS
▷ Not available

$2.99bn   Not available

SCORE CARD

❏ WORLD GNP RANKING	127th
❏ GNP PER CAPITA	$640
❏ BALANCE OF PAYMENTS	$–580m
❏ INFLATION	83.7%
❏ UNEMPLOYMENT	2%

STRENGTHS
Cotton and gas, as the USSR's major supplier of cotton, and supplier of 12% of its gas. Hard-currency trading allows real prices to be paid for these commodities. The decision in 1995 to abolish collective farms is encouraging private initiative and enterprise.

WEAKNESSES
Cotton monoculture has forced rising food imports. A thriving black market virtually wiped out the value of the manat in 1995.

EXPORTS/IMPORTS

Most imports and exports are still from and to Russia and other CIS republics. However, Turkmenistan is beginning to establish a wide range of Western contacts.

RESOURCES
▷ Electric power 4.0m kw

9,209 tonnes   94,296 b/d

5.4m sheep, 900,000 cattle, 360,000 goats   Oil, natural gas, potassium, sulfur, sodium sulfate

During the Soviet years most Turkmen agriculture was turned over to cotton – seen by Moscow as a strategic crop.

ENVIRONMENT
▷ No Green MPs

4%   Not available

The building of the Kara Kum canal, hailed as a progressive move by Moscow in 1958, has drained 35% of the Aral Sea's water, leading to an increase in unproductive salinated soil.

MEDIA
▷ TV ownership medium

Daily newspaper circulation figures are not available

PUBLISHING AND BROADCAST MEDIA

There are 2 newspapers, *Neitralnyi Turkmenistan* and *Turkmenistan*, both published in Turkmen

1 state-controlled service   1 state-controlled service

Iranian and Afghan radio stations, beaming in Islamic programs, are popular. TV is only available in cities.

CRIME
▷ Death penalty not used

Turkmenistan does not publish prison figures   Increasing levels of theft

Levels of crime are generally low. A moratorium on the death penalty was announced in January 1999.

The ex-communist bureaucrats are still the richest group. They favor Japanese and Korean luxury goods.

WORLD RANKING

Position in World

1st
50th
100th
150th
192nd

46
98%

136
$640

122
65 years

116
12 deaths

96

▢ GNP per capita in US$	▢ Infant mortality per 1,000 live births
▢ Life expectancy	
▢ Literacy	▢ Human dev. index

T

TUVALU

OFFICIAL NAME: Tuvalu   **CAPITAL:** Fongafale, on Funafuti Atoll   **POPULATION:** 9000
CURRENCIES: Australian dollar, Tuvaluan dollar   **OFFICIAL LANGUAGE:** English

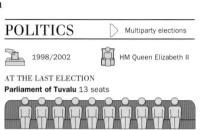

PACIFIC OCEAN

1978 | 1978 | Oct 1 | TUV | +12 | +688 | .tv

ONE OF THE WORLD'S smallest, most isolated states, Tuvalu lies 1,050 km (650 miles) north of Fiji in the central Pacific. A chain of nine coral atolls, it has a land area of just 26 square km (10 square miles). As the Ellice Islands, it was linked to the Gilbert Islands as a British colony until independence in 1978. Politically and socially conservative, Tuvaluans live by subsistence farming and fishing.

CLIMATE ▷ Tropical oceanic

WEATHER CHART

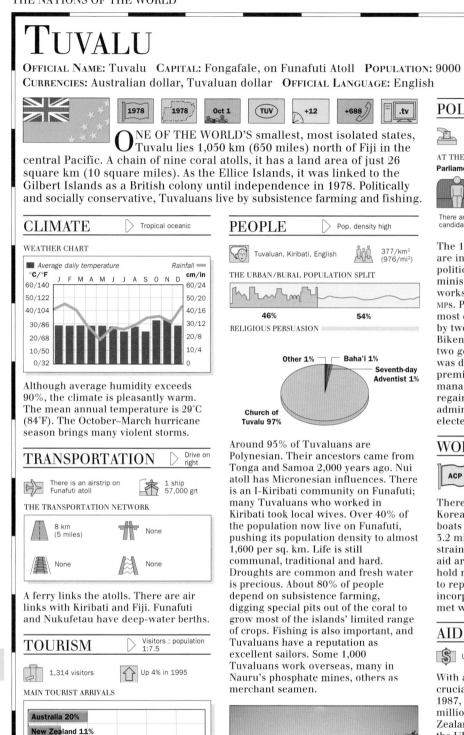

■ Average daily temperature   Rainfall ▬

Although average humidity exceeds 90%, the climate is pleasantly warm. The mean annual temperature is 29°C (84°F). The October–March hurricane season brings many violent storms.

TRANSPORTATION ▷ Drive on right

There is an airstrip on Funafuti atoll

1 ship
57,000 grt

THE TRANSPORTATION NETWORK

8 km
(5 miles)

None

None

None

A ferry links the atolls. There are air links with Kiribati and Fiji. Funafuti and Nukufetau have deep-water berths.

TOURISM ▷ Visitors : population 1:7.5

1,314 visitors

Up 4% in 1995

MAIN TOURIST ARRIVALS

Australia 20%	
New Zealand 11%	
USA 10%	
Other 59%	

% of total arrivals

Unspoiled and lapped by some of the world's warmest waters, these remote coral atolls have few visitors. Tourism plans focus around the recently paved airstrip, and Taiwanese investment in Tuvalu's only hotel, on Funafuti.

PEOPLE ▷ Pop. density high

Tuvaluan, Kiribati, English

377/km²
(976/mi²)

THE URBAN/RURAL POPULATION SPLIT

46%   **54%**

RELIGIOUS PERSUASION

Other 1%   Baha'i 1%
Seventh-day Adventist 1%
Church of Tuvalu 97%

Around 95% of Tuvaluans are Polynesian. Their ancestors came from Tonga and Samoa 2,000 years ago. Nui atoll has Micronesian influences. There is an I-Kiribati community on Funafuti; many Tuvaluans who worked in Kiribati took local wives. Over 40% of the population now live on Funafuti, pushing its population density to almost 1,600 per sq. km. Life is still communal, traditional and hard. Droughts are common and fresh water is precious. About 80% of people depend on subsistence farming, digging special pits out of the coral to grow most of the islands' limited range of crops. Fishing is also important, and Tuvaluans have a reputation as excellent sailors. Some 1,000 Tuvaluans work overseas, many in Nauru's phosphate mines, others as merchant seamen.

Tuvalu's soil is porous, but sufficiently fertile to support coconut palms, pandanus and salt-tolerant plants. Fresh water supply is limited.

POLITICS ▷ Multiparty elections

1998/2002   HM Queen Elizabeth II

AT THE LAST ELECTION
Parliament of Tuvalu 13 seats

There are no political parties. All members are Independent candidates.

The 13 MPs, elected every four years, are independents who work in loose political associations. The prime minister, an MP elected by Parliament, works with a cabinet of up to four other MPs. Politics has been dominated for most of the postindependence period by two men, Tomasi Puapua and Bikenibeu Paeniu. After the second of two general elections in 1993 Paeniu was defeated in a contest for the premiership by Kamuta Laatasi, BP Oil's manager in Tuvalu, but Paeniu regained power in 1996. Day-to-day administration is in the hands of elected councils on each island.

WORLD AFFAIRS ▷ Not a member of the UN

ACP | Comm | SPC | SPF | ADB

There are agreements with Taiwan, Korea, and the USA, allowing their boats to exploit Tuvalu's fish-rich 3.2 million square mile EEZ. Despite strained relations with the UK over aid arrangements, only a minority hold republican sentiments. Moves to replace the original flag, incorporating a Union Jack, were met with mass protests.

AID ▷ Recipient

US$10m (receipts)

No change 1996–1997

With a visible trade deficit, aid is crucial to Tuvalu. Most importantly, in 1987, a trust fund was set up, with A$41 million in grants from Australia, New Zealand and the UK. While support from the UK has reduced, aid from Taiwan and Japan grows. Tuvalu is planning to reduce its reliance on aid through public-sector reform and privatization.

DEFENSE ▷ No compulsory military service

There are no armed forces

Not applicable

Tuvalu has no military. Internal security is the responsibility of the small police force.

T

ECONOMICS ▷ Not available

US$3m

1.53–1.63
Australian dollars

SCORE CARD

❑ WORLD GNP RANKING	190th
❑ GNP PER CAPITA	US$330
❑ BALANCE OF PAYMENTS	Deficit
❑ INFLATION	3.8%
❑ UNEMPLOYMENT	Low

STRENGTHS

Exclusive Economic Zone. Regular income from trust fund. Possible mineral potential. Sustainable subsistence economy. Internet deal earns up to US$175 million a year.

WEAKNESSES

World's smallest economy. Physical

RESOURCES ▷ Not available

400 tonnes

Not an oil producer

27,000 chickens
12,600 pigs

None

Tuvalu's resource potential lies in the waters of its 3.2 million square mile Exclusive Economic Zone (EEZ). Its rich fish stocks are being exploited mainly by foreign boats in return for licensing fees. Hopes of valuable mineral reserves have been raised by the discovery of an undersea mountain in the EEZ. Solar energy is being developed to cut the use of gasoline for power generation. Fuel accounts for about 14% of import costs. The rights to Tuvalu's Internet suffix have been sold to a Canadian TV company for US$175 million a year.

TUVALU

Total Land Area : 26 sq. km (10 sq. miles)

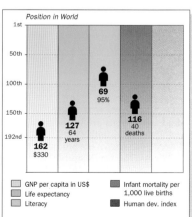

POPULATION

• under 10 000

LAND HEIGHT

100m/328ft

Sea Level

EXPORTS

Tuvalu does not publish export figures by country of destination.

IMPORTS

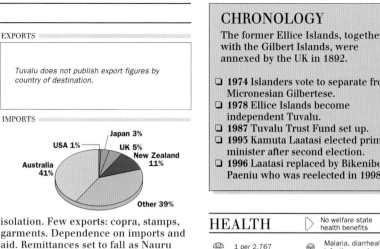

USA 1%
Australia 41%
Japan 3%
UK 5%
New Zealand 11%
Other 39%

isolation. Few exports: copra, stamps, garments. Dependence on imports and aid. Remittances set to fall as Nauru phosphate mines nearly worked out.

ENVIRONMENT ▷ No Green MPs

None

Not available

Efforts to protect the environmentally fragile atolls include reafforestation and solar energy projects. On Funafuti, population pressure is leading to overfishing in the atoll lagoon. The "greenhouse effect" is a major concern, since climate changes attributed to it are blamed for a steep rise in cyclone frequency. Any rise in sea levels induced by global warming would quickly submerge the atolls.

MEDIA ▷ TV ownership low

There are no daily newspapers

PUBLISHING AND BROADCAST MEDIA

There are no daily newspapers. *Sikuleo o Tuvalu* and *Tuvalu Echoes*, in Tuvaluan and English respectively, are published fortnightly

No TV service

1 state-owned service

Two bimonthly papers and a religious monthly, *Te Lama*, are the only publications.

CRIME ▷ Death penalty not used

Tuvalu does not publish prison figures

Little change from year to year

Crime is minimal and the result mainly of alcohol-related violence, particularly at the weekends.

EDUCATION ▷ School leaving age: 14

95%

Not available

Each island has a primary school. A secondary school and a marine training school are based on Funafuti. There are 20 state-funded students at the University of the South Pacific.

HEALTH ▷ No welfare state health benefits

1 per 2,767 people

Malaria, diarrheal, infectious and parasitic diseases

Concerted efforts since independence to improve health care have cut the incidence of communicable diseases. However, infant mortality rates remain high and average life expectancy, at 64 years, is still well below the Pacific mean of 71 years.

SPENDING ▷ GDP/cap. no increase

CONSUMPTION AND SPENDING

No data

13 per 1,000 population

Defense	No data
Education	No data
Health	No data

0   5   10   15   20   25
Defense, Health, Education spending as % of GDP

Although living standards are very low, traditional social support systems mean that extreme poverty is rare. Most people rely on subsistence agriculture and fishing, supplemented by remittances from expatriate Tuvaluans.

WORLD RANKING

Position in World

69
95%

127
64 years

116
40 deaths

162
$330

☐ GNP per capita in US$		☐ Infant mortality per 1,000 live births	
☐ Life expectancy			
☐ Literacy		☐ Human dev. index	

UGANDA

OFFICIAL NAME: Republic of Uganda   **CAPITAL:** Kampala
POPULATION: 21.3 million   **CURRENCY:** New Uganda shilling   **OFFICIAL LANGUAGE:** English

EAST AFRICA

| 1962 | 1962 | Oct 9 | EAU | +3 | +256 | .ug |

AN EAST AFRICAN COUNTRY of fertile upland plateaus and mountains, Uganda has outlets to the sea through Kenya and Tanzania. Its history from independence in 1962 until 1986 was one of ethnic strife. Since 1986, under President Museveni, peace has been restored and steps taken to rebuild the economy and democracy.

Kampala, Uganda's capital. It has 774,000 inhabitants, but only 25,000 of the city's households are supplied with running water.

CLIMATE

▷ Tropical wet & dry

WEATHER CHART

■ *Average daily temperature*   *Rainfall* ■

°C/°F	J F M A M J J A S O N D	cm/in
40/104		40/16
30/86		30/12
20/68		20/8
10/50		10/4
0/32		0
-10/14		
-20/-4		

Altitude and the influence of Lake Victoria moderate Uganda's equatorial climate. Spring is the wettest period.

TRANSPORTATION

▷ Drive on left

✈ **Entebbe International**
446,395 passengers

🚢 2 ships
5,900 dwt

THE TRANSPORTATION NETWORK

| 28,700 km (17,938 miles) | | None |
| 1,250 km (781 km) | | Lake Victoria |

The government is rebuilding the transportation infrastructure with the help of international aid.

TOURISM

▷ Visitors : population 1:93.8

227,000 visitors

⬆ Up 88% 1995–1997

MAIN TOURIST ARRIVALS

Uganda does not publish tourism figures by country of origin

0   10   20   30   40
% of total arrivals

Major attractions are Uganda's lakes and mountains, notably the rugged Ruwenzori range – the Mountains of the Moon. The brutal murder of eight foreign tourists by Rwandan fighters at the Bwindi national park in March 1999 was a severe setback for Uganda's recovery as a tourist destination.

PEOPLE

▷ Pop. density medium

Luganda, Nkole, Chiga, Lango, Acholi, Teso, Lugbara, English

107/km² (276/mi²)

THE URBAN/RURAL POPULATION SPLIT

13%   87%

RELIGIOUS PERSUASION

- Muslim (mainly Sunni) 5%
- Roman Catholic 38%
- Protestant 33%
- Other (including Hindu) 11%
- Traditional beliefs 13%

The predominantly rural population consists of 13 main ethnic groups. Traditional animosities, manipulated by ex-presidents Amin and Obote, underlay the ethnic conflict which has marred Uganda's history. Since 1986, President Museveni has worked hard for reconciliation. In 1993, he allowed the restoration of Uganda's four historical monarchies.

UGANDA

Total Land Area : 199 550 sq. km
(77 046 sq. miles)

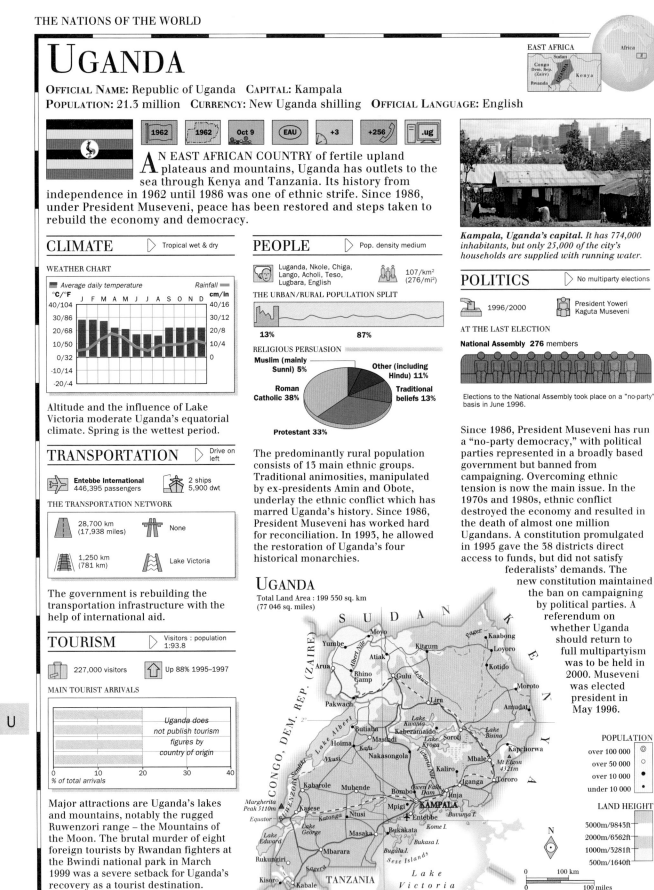

POPULATION

◎	over 100 000
○	over 50 000
●	over 10 000
·	under 10 000

LAND HEIGHT

- 3000m/9843ft
- 2000m/6562ft
- 1000m/3281ft
- 500m/1640ft

0   100 km
0   100 miles

POLITICS

▷ No multiparty elections

1996/2000

President Yoweri Kaguta Museveni

AT THE LAST ELECTION

National Assembly 276 members

Elections to the National Assembly took place on a "no-party" basis in June 1996.

Since 1986, President Museveni has run a "no-party democracy," with political parties represented in a broadly based government but banned from campaigning. Overcoming ethnic tension is now the main issue. In the 1970s and 1980s, ethnic conflict destroyed the economy and resulted in the death of almost one million Ugandans. A constitution promulgated in 1995 gave the 38 districts direct access to funds, but did not satisfy federalists' demands. The new constitution maintained the ban on campaigning by political parties. A referendum on whether Uganda should return to full multipartyism was to be held in 2000. Museveni was elected president in May 1996.

U

WORLD AFFAIRS

 Joined UN in 1962

Relations with Sudan and Congo (former Zaire) are strained. However, Uganda's support for anti-government rebels in both countries seemed to end during 1999. Conflicts in both these countries and in Rwanda have caused a large influx of refugees into Uganda. A revival of the East African Community is being considered with Tanzania and Kenya.

AID

 Recipient

$840m (receipts) — Up 23% 1996–1997

Aid receipts, mainly from the World Bank and the IMF, rose in the late 1980s, encouraged by Uganda's adoption of economic liberalization and private sector investment policies. Aid has focused on balance of payments support and the rehabilitation of the key transport sector.

DEFENSE

 No compulsory military service

$166m — Up 7% in 1997

The pre-1986 army, dominated by northern Acholi and Langi groups, was responsible for many atrocities under Amin. During the 1990s, Uganda was occupied with conflicts in neighboring countries, not least Congo (former Zaire), where it supported anti-government rebels. The army has been active in suppressing internal rebellions.

ECONOMICS

Inflation 60.3% p.a. (1985–1996)

$6.6bn — 1,135.00–1,361.00 new Uganda shillings

SCORE CARD

❑ WORLD GNP RANKING	98th
❑ GNP PER CAPITA	$330
❑ BALANCE OF PAYMENTS	$-388m
❑ INFLATION	7%
❑ UNEMPLOYMENT	Widespread

STRENGTHS

Agriculture. Coffee brings in 93% of export earnings. Potential for more export crops. Road system being repaired. Proinvestment policies.

WEAKNESSES

Lack of skilled people. Instability in the subregion affects confidence. World coffee price fluctuations. High transportation costs.

EXPORTS

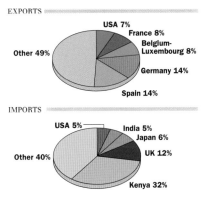

USA 7%
France 8%
Belgium-Luxembourg 8%
Other 49%
Germany 14%
Spain 14%

IMPORTS

USA 5%
India 5%
Japan 6%
Other 40%
UK 12%
Kenya 32%

RESOURCES

Electric power 162,000 kw

208,807 tonnes — Not an oil producer and no refineries

5.4m cattle, 3.6m goats, 2m sheep — Copper, cobalt, tin, apatite, magnetite, tungsten, gold

Mineral resources are varied but barely exploited. Uganda has sizable copper deposits. The mines, closed under Obote, are now being reopened. Gold and cobalt mining are also due to resume and oil exploration is under way. Hydroelectric output is being expanded, notably at Owen Falls, with the aim of replacing 50% of oil imports.

ENVIRONMENT

No Green MPs

10% (4% partially protected) — Low

Uganda's priority is economic reconstruction, but ecological issues are not ignored. Construction of a huge hydroelectric power station at the Murchison Falls was canceled, following strong local environmental objections to the choice of site.

MEDIA

 TV ownership low

Daily newspaper circulation 2 per 1,000 people

PUBLISHING AND BROADCAST MEDIA

There are 5 daily newspapers, including *New Vision*, *The Star*, *Munno* and *Taifa Uganda Empya*

1 state-controlled, 1 independent service — 1 state-controlled, 3 independent services

The 13 daily and weekly papers cover the political and religious spectrum; eight are published in English. Only *New Vision* is government-controlled.

CRIME

Death penalty used

10,080 prisoners — Up 10% from 1992–1996

Crime levels are far lower than in neighboring Kenya, although theft in Kampala is a growing problem. Uganda now has one of the best human rights records in Africa.

EDUCATION

Not applicable

64% — 30,266 students

Education is not compulsory and all schools charge fees. Only 11% of pupils go on to secondary school.

HEALTH

Welfare state health benefits

1 per 25,000 people — Malaria, respiratory and diarrheal diseases, measles

The health system, badly hit by war and the loss of foreign personnel, is slowly being rebuilt. Some 700,000 Ugandans had died of AIDS by 1999.

SPENDING

GDP/cap. no increase

CONSUMPTION AND SPENDING

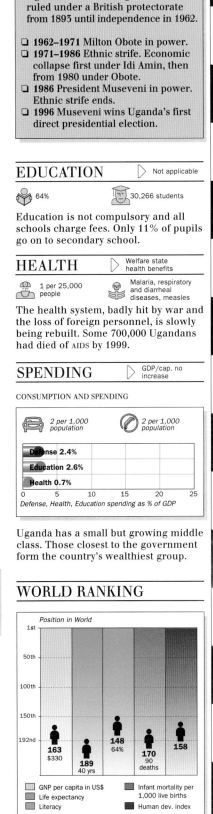

2 per 1,000 population — 2 per 1,000 population

Defense 2.4%
Education 2.6%
Health 0.7%

Defense, Health, Education spending as % of GDP

Uganda has a small but growing middle class. Those closest to the government form the country's wealthiest group.

WORLD RANKING

Position in World

1st
50th
100th
150th
192nd

163 $330
189 40 yrs
148 64%
170 90 deaths
158

❑ GNP per capita in US$
❑ Life expectancy
❑ Literacy
❑ Infant mortality per 1,000 live births
❑ Human dev. index

U

UKRAINE

EUROPE

OFFICIAL NAME: Ukraine   CAPITAL: Kiev
POPULATION: 51.2 million   CURRENCY: Hryvna   OFFICIAL LANGUAGE: Ukrainian

| 1991 | 1991 | Aug 24 | UA | +2 | +380 | .ua |

UKRAINE IS BORDERED by seven states; to the south it lies on the Black Sea and the Sea of Azov. An independent Ukrainian state was established in 1918, but was overrun in the same year by Soviet forces from the east and Polish forces from the west. In 1991, Ukraine again became an independent state. The country has historically been divided between the nationally conscious and Ukrainian-speaking west (which was not under Russian occupation until World War II) and the east, which has a large ethnic Russian population.

View toward the Cathedral of the Assumption in Kharkiv. Many Ukrainian cities are equipped with elaborate trolley networks.

CLIMATE

▷ Continental/steppe

WEATHER CHART

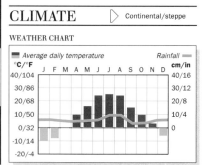

- Average daily temperature   Rainfall
- °C/°F   J F M A M J J A S O N D   cm/in
- 40/104 / 30/12
- 30/86 / 20/8
- 20/68 / 10/4
- 10/50 / 0
- 0/32
- -10/14
- -20/-4

Ukraine has a continental climate, with the exception of the southern coast of Crimea, which has a Mediterranean climate. There are four distinct seasons.

TRANSPORTATION

▷ Drive on right

Boryspiel Intl, Kiev
1.4m passengers

1061 ships
3.8m grt

THE TRANSPORTATION NETWORK

172,800 km (108,000 miles)		None
22,546 km (14,091 miles)		4,400 km (2,734 miles)

There are Soviet-style subways and trolley networks in major cities. The main highway linking Kiev and Lviv and the rail system are to be upgraded. Part of a former submarine port at Sevastopol was opened to commercial shipping in 1998.

TOURISM

▷ Visitors : population 1:62

818,000 visitors   Up 3% 1995-1997

MAIN TOURIST ARRIVALS

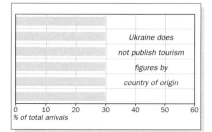

Ukraine does not publish tourism figures by country of origin

0   10   20   30   40   50   60
% of total arrivals

Among potential tourist attractions are warm resort areas in Crimea and the south, and the Carpathian Mountains. The government has maintained a highly regulated system of managing tourism. Because of bureaucratic hurdles, no Western-style international hotel has yet opened in Kiev.

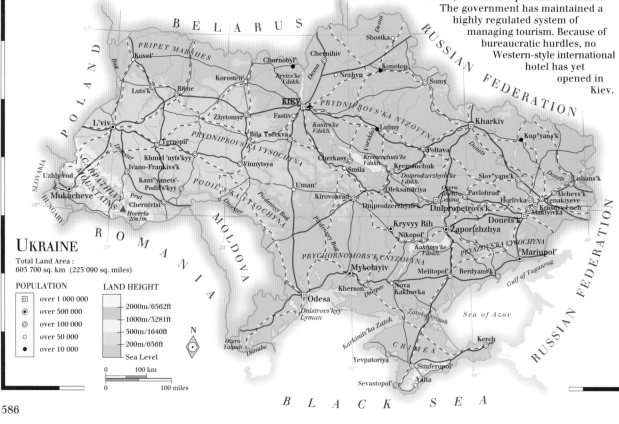

UKRAINE

Total Land Area :
605 700 sq. km (223 090 sq. miles)

POPULATION
- ▣ over 1 000 000
- ◉ over 500 000
- ◎ over 100 000
- ○ over 50 000
- ● over 10 000

LAND HEIGHT
- 2000m/6562ft
- 1000m/3281ft
- 500m/1640ft
- 200m/656ft
- Sea Level

0   100 km
0   100 miles

U

PEOPLE ▷ Pop. density medium

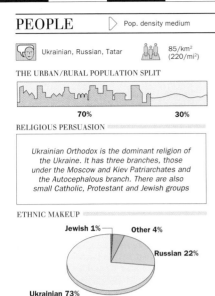

Ukrainian, Russian, Tatar   85/km² (220/mi²)

THE URBAN/RURAL POPULATION SPLIT

70%   **30%**

RELIGIOUS PERSUASION

Ukrainian Orthodox is the dominant religion of the Ukraine. It has three branches, those under the Moscow and Kiev Patriarchates and the Autocephalous branch. There are also small Catholic, Protestant and Jewish groups

ETHNIC MAKEUP

Jewish 1% — Other 4%

Russian 22%

Ukrainian 73%

In the cities and countryside of western Ukraine, Ukrainians make up the vast majority of the population, but in several of the large cities of the east and south, Russians form a majority. The large Russian population there is a legacy of 19th-century industrialization, and of more recent migration in the Soviet era. At independence, most Russians accepted Ukrainian sovereignty, though tensions remain.

In Crimea, Russians, which the Kiev government suspects of separatist tendencies, make up two-thirds of the population. There are tensions with ethnic Ukrainians and Tatars, a Turkic-speaking people. The Tatars were deported *en masse* to the eastern USSR under Stalin in 1944. They have been returning to the Crimea since 1990 and now make up 12% of its population. There is a Romanian-speaking minority in the Odessa region.

POPULATION AGE BREAKDOWN

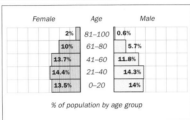

Female	Age	Male
2%	81–100	0.6%
10%	61–80	5.7%
13.7%	41–60	11.8%
14.4%	21–40	14.3%
13.5%	0–20	14%

% of population by age group

Leonid Kuchma, *who became president in 1994.*

Leonid Kravchuk, *president 1991–1994. He tried to postpone democratic elections.*

WORLD AFFAIRS ▷ Joined UN in 1945

BSEC   CE   CIS   IAEA   OSCE

Attitudes to Russia, once the main foreign relations threat, have improved, helped by greater understanding both in Russia and Ukraine of the benefits of close bilateral cooperation. Ties have strengthened since 1994, when Leonid Kuchma was elected president. In 1997 a friendship treaty and in 1998 a 10-year economic cooperation accord were signed.

Ukraine's internal instability and the hostility of some nationalist Russians toward it still remain a source of concern. Ukrainians fear that if the pro-Russian regions in Ukraine demand unification with Russia, it could spark a civil war and encourage Russian intervention. Alternatively, should Russian nationalists seize power in Moscow, they would seek to incorporate Ukraine into Russia. This would be resisted by the USA and some European states which regard Ukraine as a buffer to Russia.

POLITICS ▷ Multiparty elections

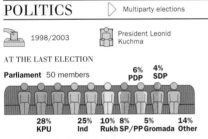

1998/2003   President Leonid Kuchma

AT THE LAST ELECTION

Parliament 50 members   6% PDP   4% SDP

28% KPU	25% Ind	10% Rukh	8% SP/PP	5% Gromada	14% Other

KPU = Communist Party   **Ind** = Independent
Rukh = Ukrainian People's Movement   **SP/PP** = Socialist-Peasants Alliance   **PDP** = People's Democratic Party
SDP = Social Democratic Party
Other includes the Green Party and the Progressive Socialist Party

Ukraine has been a multiparty democracy since 1991.

MAIN POLITICAL ISSUES
Economic reform and corruption
Western and central Ukraine generally favor greater economic reform than do eastern regions, but progress has been slow. Major industries remain state-owned. Corruption and bureaucracy stifle enterprise. In late 1998 former premier Pavlo Lazarenko was arrested in Switzerland on suspicion of embezzling millions of dollars of state funds. He was returned to Ukraine but then detained by US authorities in early 1999, trying to gain entry to the USA.

Relations with Russia
Western Ukrainians vehemently oppose closer Russian ties, but these are favored in eastern Ukraine.

Citizens in the Donetsk region voted in 1994 for closer links with the CIS and to make Russian a joint official language. In Crimea, where ethnic Russians are in the majority, voters have demanded dual Russian–Ukrainian citizenship.

Potential destabilization
The regions challenge Kiev's authority, particularly in Crimea, where ethnic Russians dominate. In 1994, the Crimean parliament declared, but later rescinded, its independence. Kiev has reaffirmed Crimea's status as an autonomous republic. A new Crimean constitution, in which Ukrainian is the state language and Russian the official language, was approved in 1996, but tensions remain. Other regions with large Russian minorities, such as the Donbass, have pressed for greater autonomy.

PROFILE
Leonid Kravchuk was the dominant political figure from 1990 until 1994, when Leonid Kuchma won the presidential elections. Kuchma gained increased powers after 1996 constitutional changes. These are tempered by a vocal parliament, for which multiparty elections were first held in 1994. The strong position of the communists and allied pro-Kuchma groups was confirmed at legislative elections in March 1998.

CHRONOLOGY

In 1240, Kiev was conquered by the Mongols. The Ukrainian Cossacks later came under the domination of Lithuania, Poland, and Russia.

❏ **1918** Independent Ukrainian state after collapse of Russian and Austrian empires. Brest-Litovsk Treaty signed with Germany.
❏ **1919** Red Army invades. Ukrainian Soviet Socialist Republic proclaimed.
❏ **1920** Poland invades. Western Ukraine comes under Polish occupation.
❏ **1922** USSR founded; Ukrainian SSR is one of founder members.
❏ **1922–1930** Cultural revival results from "Ukrainianization" policy adopted by Lenin to pacify national sentiment.

➪

U

❏ **1932–1933** "Ukrainianization" policy reversed. Stalin's government induces famine to eliminate Ukraine as source of opposition; seven million die.

❏ **1939** Soviet Union invades Poland and incorporates ethnic Ukrainian territories of Poland into Ukrainian SSR.

❏ **1941** Germany invades USSR. Seven and a half million Ukrainians die by 1945.

❏ **1942** Nationalists form Ukrainian Insurgent Army, which wages war against both Germans and Soviets.

❏ **1954** Crimea ceded to Ukrainian SSR.

❏ **1972** Widespread arrests of intellectuals and dissidents by Soviet state. Shcherbitsky, a Brezhnevite, replaces moderate reformer Shelest as head of Communist Party of Ukraine (CPU).

❏ **1986** World's worst nuclear disaster takes place at Chernobyl nuclear power station.

❏ **1989** First major coalminers' strike in Donbass. Pro-Gorbachev Ivashko becomes head of CPU.

❏ **1990** Ukrainian parliament declares the Ukrainian SSR a sovereign state. Leonid Kravchuk replaces Ivashko.

❏ **1991** Crimea declared an autonomous republic within Ukrainian SSR. Government declares full independence, conditional on approval by referendum, supported by 90% of voters. CPU banned.

❏ **1993** Major strike in Donbass results in costly settlement, which exacerbates budget deficit and stimulates hyperinflation. CPU reestablished at Donetsk congress.

❏ **1994** Crimea elects Yuri Meshkov as its first president. Leonid Kuchma defeats Kravchuk to become first democratically elected president.

❏ **1996** Hryvna replaces karbovanets as national currency. New constitution comes into force.

❏ **1997** Friendship treaty signed with Russia. Accord on Black Sea fleet.

❏ **1998** 10-year economic cooperation agreement with Russia. CPU secures largest number of seats in general election. Valeri Pustovoitenko, prime minister since mid-1997, continues in office.

❏ **1999** Former premier Lazarenko faces embezzlement charges.

AID

▷ Recipient

$176m (receipts)   Down 54% 1996–1997

Ukraine's strategic importance has enabled it to attract substantial assistance from the USA, the EU and international financial bodies. This has averaged $300 million in 1993–1997.

DEFENSE

▷ Compulsory military service

$1.32bn   Up 3% in 1997

Ukraine exported armaments worth $500 million in 1997.

UKRAINIAN ARMED FORCES

🚜	4,014 main battle tanks (154 T-54/55, 1 T-62, 2,281 T-64, 1,305 T-72)	171,300 personnel
🚢	Black Sea Fleet controlled jointly with Russia	12,500 personnel
✈	768 combat aircraft (MiG-23, MiG-25, MiG-27, MiG-29)	124,400 personnel
🚀	115 ICBMs	

Ukraine is a member of the CIS, but is consolidating its own forces for fear of increasing Russian willingness to intervene in other former Soviet republics. The main focus of defense spending is the modernization of weaponry.

In late 1993, the Ukrainian parliament ratified the START-I nuclear disarmament treaty. In 1994, Ukraine began transferring its nuclear warheads to Russia under the accord and completed this process in mid-1996.

The long-smoldering dispute between Ukraine and Russia over control of the Black Sea fleet was finally resolved in May 1997. Division of the fleet was agreed, Russia was to lease territory for 20 years and paid Ukraine for vessels and equipment. A friendship treaty was also signed. Ukraine joined NATO's Partnership's for Peace in 1994 and signed a security pact with NATO in 1997, when joint maneuvers were also held.

ECONOMICS

▷ Inflation 1,219.8% p.a (1993–1997)

$52.6bn   1.90–4.03 hryvna

SCORE CARD

❏ WORLD GNP RANKING	49th
❏ GNP PER CAPITA	$1,040
❏ BALANCE OF PAYMENTS	$–1,335m
❏ INFLATION	15.9%
❏ UNEMPLOYMENT	1%

ECONOMIC PERFORMANCE INDICATOR

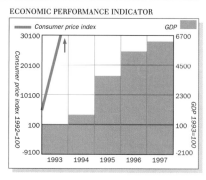

EXPORTS

IMPORTS

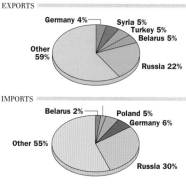

STRENGTHS
Well educated workforce. Good urban transportation infrastructure. Potential for grain and food export. Mineral reserves. Technological potential, especially in aerospace and computers; many research institutes in these areas.

WEAKNESSES
Failure to reform centrally planned economy. High inflation. Weak hryvna. Antireform political elites. Inefficient, subsidized manufacturing industries. Slow privatization. Corruption.

PROFILE
The economy has contracted by over half since 1991. Privatization of large enterprises has barely begun, but some small industries have been privatized. Many small traders have sprung up but bureaucracy stifles private enterprise and investment. Lack of land reform holds back agriculture in the "bread basket" of Europe.

UKRAINE : MAJOR BUSINESSES

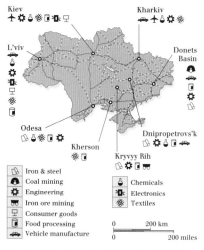

▨ Iron & steel	⚗ Chemicals
● Coal mining	▥ Electronics
✿ Engineering	✳ Textiles
🏭 Iron ore mining	
🖥 Consumer goods	
🍴 Food processing	0 200 km
🚗 Vehicle manufacture	0 200 miles

U

RESOURCES

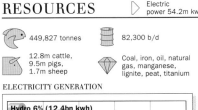

Electric power 54.2m kw

449,827 tonnes

82,300 b/d

12.8m cattle, 9.5m pigs, 1.7m sheep

Coal, iron, oil, natural gas, manganese, lignite, peat, titanium

ELECTRICITY GENERATION

Hydro 6% (12.4bn kwh)

Combustion 66% (128.3bn kwh)

Nuclear 28% (53.3bn kwh)

Other 0%

| 0 | 20 | 40 | 60 | 80 | 100 |

% of total generation by type

Ukraine imports 90% of its oil needs and 80% of its gas (its main source of energy), mostly from Russia. Yet

Ukraine has oil and gas reserves of its own, as well as extensive hydrocarbon reserves. One third of electricity is nuclear generated. Ukraine's most successfully exploited fuel resource is coal. Most coal is mined in the Donbass, around Donetsk and Luhansk.

Ukraine has 5% of global mineral reserves, including the largest titanium reserves, the third-largest deposits of iron ore, and 30% of global manganese ore. There is also mercury, uranium, nickel and some gold. The metal industry accounted for nearly 20% of GDP in 1997 and 28% of exports. The steel industry, which employs 500,000, has now begun to grow again after seven years of decline.

ENVIRONMENT

Green MPs

1%

Medium

ENVIRONMENTAL TREATIES

Yes

Yes

Yes

No

Yes

No

As a result of the Chernobyl nuclear disaster – the world's worst nuclear accident – over three million Ukrainians now live in dangerously radioactive areas and 12% of arable land is contaminated.

The government has resumed nuclear production because of the rising cost of Russian oil imports. In 1996 reactors from Chernobyl were still being used to produce nuclear power, despite being widely regarded as unsafe. Agreements concluded with the G-7 industrialized countries in 1995–1996 commit Ukraine to the closure of the Chernobyl plant by 2000, though this appears unlikely.

Industrial pollution is widespread, especially in the Donbass region.

MEDIA

TV ownership high

Daily newspaper circulation 54 per 1,000 people

PUBLISHING AND BROADCAST MEDIA

There are 44 daily newspapers, including *Holos Ukrainy* which has the highest circulation figures

1 state-controlled, 2 independent stations

1 state-controlled service

A number of independent, mass-circulation newspapers are now published. Local TV stations reflect regional political differences.

CRIME

Death penalty used

203,988 prisoners

Up 52% from 1991–1996

CRIME RATES

Murders

9 *per 100,000 population*

Rapes

3 *per 100,000 population*

Thefts

590 *per 100,000 population*

Crime rates have increased steadily since 1991 because of economic problems and a breakdown in law and order. The police are underfunded and ineffective. Corruption is rampant across the economy. The Mafia is highly influential, as in Russia. In 1999 Anatoliy Onopriyenko was sentenced to death for murdering 52 people.

EDUCATION

School leaving age: 15

99%

1.54m students

Of total government expenditure 15.7% is spent on education.

THE EDUCATION SYSTEM

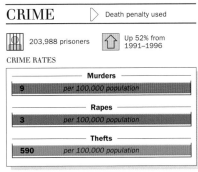

87% Primary

91% Secondary

41% Tertiary

% of each age group in education

In eastern regions, most university teaching is in Russian, in western ones, in Ukrainian. Some schools in the west no longer teach Russian.

UKRAINE : LAND USE

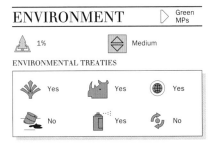

Cropland
Forest
Pasture
Cattle
Wheat - cash crop
Sugar beet

| 0 | 200 km |
| 0 | 200 miles |

HEALTH

Welfare state health benefits

1 per 227 people

Heart disease, cancers, accidents, violence, tuberculosis

Health and health care have declined significantly in the post-Soviet period. A $2 million UN program offers treatment and preventive care for 350,000 people directly affected by the Chernobyl disaster. Over three million people live on radioactively contaminated land.

SPENDING

GDP/cap. no increase

CONSUMPTION AND SPENDING

96 per 1,000 population

186 per 1,000 population

Defense 2.7%

Education 7.7%

Health 3.3%

| 0 | 5 | 10 | 15 | 20 | 25 |

Defense, Health, Education spending as % of GDP

The gap between rich and poor has widened significantly since Ukraine's independence in 1991. Wage arrears are a major problem.

WORLD RANKING

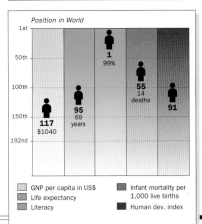

Position in World

1st
50th
100th
150th
192nd

117 $1040

95 69 years

1 99%

55 14 deaths

91

GNP per capita in US$
Life expectancy
Literacy
Infant mortality per 1,000 live births
Human dev. index

U

UNITED ARAB EMIRATES

OFFICIAL NAME: United Arab Emirates **CAPITAL:** Abu Dhabi
POPULATION: 2.4 million **CURRENCY:** UAE dirham **OFFICIAL LANGUAGE:** Arabic

MIDDLE EAST

| 1971 | 1972 | Dec 2 | UAE | +4 | +971 | .ae |

T HE ARAB WORLD'S only working federation, the United Arab Emirates (UAE) shares borders with Oman, Saudi Arabia, and Qatar, as well as a disputed maritime boundary with Iran. The UAE is mostly semiarid desert relieved by occasional oases. The cities, watered by extensive irrigation systems, have lavish greenery. The UAE's economic prosperity once relied on pearls, but it is now a sizable gas and oil exporter, and has a growing services sector.

CLIMATE

▷ Hot desert

WEATHER CHART

Although rainfall is minimal, summers are humid. Sand-laden *shamal* winds often blow in winter and spring.

TRANSPORTATION

▷ Drive on right

| Dubai International | 316 ships |
| 9.7m passengers | 890,00 grt |

THE TRANSPORTATION NETWORK

| 3,000 km (1,864 miles) | None |
| None | None |

The roads are good. Five of the seven emirates have international airports, of which the busiest is Dubai International.

TOURISM

▷ Visitors : population 1:1.3

1.8m visitors

Up 32% 1995-1997

MAIN TOURIST ARRIVALS

About 60% of visitors are from Arab states. The rest come from India, the UK, Iran, Pakistan and the USA.

% of total arrivals

Until the mid-1980s, tourism was minimal. Led by Dubai, the UAE has now launched initiatives to attract visitors during the northern winter for sunshine, heritage, water sports, desert safaris and duty-free shopping.

PEOPLE

▷ Pop. density low

Arabic, Persian, Indian and Pakistani languages, English

29/km² (7/mi²)

THE URBAN/RURAL POPULATION SPLIT

84%   16%

ETHNIC MAKEUP

Other 8%
Emirian 19%
Asian 50%
Other Arab 23%

UAE nationals are largely city dwellers, with Abu Dhabi and Dubai the dominant centers. They are outnumbered by expatriates who flocked to the country in the 1970s during the oil boom; UAE nationals make up one-fifth of the population.

UAE citizens are mostly conservative Sunni Muslims of Bedouin descent. There is a Shi'a community in Dubai with links to Iran. The Western expatriate community is permitted a virtually unrestricted lifestyle. Islamic fundamentalism, however, is a growing force among the young.

Poverty is rare in the UAE. The government remains the biggest employer. Women in theory enjoy equal rights with men.

POLITICS

▷ No multiparty elections

Not applicable

President Shaikh Zayed bin Sultan al-Nahyan

LEGISLATIVE OR ADVISORY BODIES

Federal National Council 40 members

The method of appointment of members of the Federal National Council is determined individually by each of the 7 members of the Federation. There are no political parties.

The UAE's seven emirates – Abu Dhabi, Dubai, Sharjah, Ras al Khaimah, Ajman, Umm al Qaiwain, and Fujairah – are dominated by their ruling families. The main personalities are the ruler of Abu Dhabi, Shaikh Zayed, who holds the UAE presidency, and the four al-Maktoum brothers who control Dubai. The eldest, Shaikh Maktoum al-Maktoum, is ruler of Dubai and vice-president and prime minister of the UAE.

President Zayed has relaunched the advisory Federal National Council in response to criticism of the lack of democracy. The growth of Islamic fundamentalism is also a concern. The freedoms granted to Westerners have aroused some anger but, for economic reasons, are unlikely to be withdrawn.

UNITED ARAB EMIRATES

Total Land Area : 83 600 sq. km (32 278 sq. miles)

POPULATION

◎ over 100 000
• under 10 000

LAND HEIGHT

1000m/3281ft
500m/1640ft
Sea Level

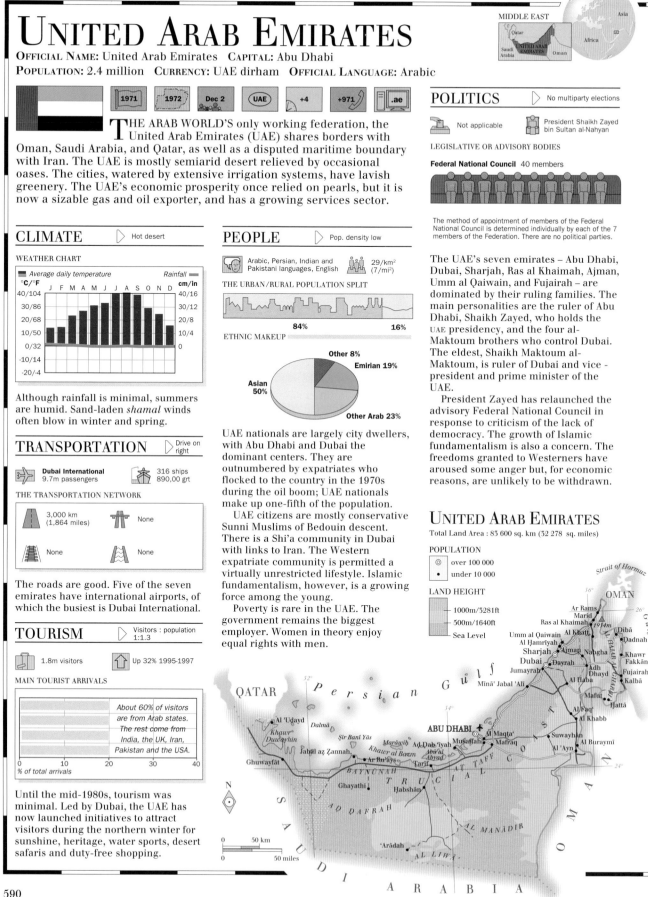

WORLD AFFAIRS  Joined UN in 1971

The UAE is well known as an advocate of moderation within the Arab world. It maintains close links with most OECD economies, especially the UK and the USA. In 1992, conflict flared when Iran seized control of three islands in the Strait of Hormuz. Attempts are being made to settle the dispute through diplomacy.

AID ▷ Donor

💲 $65m (donations)   ⬦ Not applicable

Once a generous donor to developing countries, the UAE's contributions have fluctuated with varying energy prices.

DEFENSE ▷ No compulsory military sevice

💲 $2.4bn   ⬆ Up 15% in 1997

Numbering more than 64,000, the UAE's forces are too small and too scattered among the emirates to be a threat to the traditional rulers. Although they are well equipped, training is limited and personnel are largely drawn from other Arab states and the Indian subcontinent. During the 1991 Gulf crisis, UAE air bases were used by Western forces for strikes against Iraq.

ECONOMICS ▷ Not available

📊 $42.8bn   💲 3.67 UAE dirhams

SCORE CARD

❏ WORLD GNP RANKING	53rd
❏ GNP PER CAPITA	$17,400
❏ BALANCE OF PAYMENTS	$4bn
❏ INFLATION	4.4%
❏ UNEMPLOYMENT	0%

STRENGTHS
Oil and gas reserves are the fourth-biggest in OPEC. Service industries have been developed to support the economy when the wells run dry.

WEAKNESSES
Lack of skilled manpower. Most raw materials and foodstuffs have to be imported. Water resources scarce as ground water is depleted.

EXPORTS

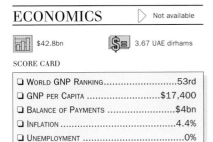

IMPORTS

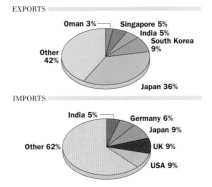

RESOURCES ▷ Electric power 5.4m kw

🐟 105,554 tonnes   🛢 2.3m b/d (reserves 98,100,000,000 bbl)

🐐 1m goats, 385,000 sheep, 76,000 cattle   💎 Oil, natural gas

The UAE is a major exporter of crude oil and natural gas; Abu Dhabi has especially abundant reserves. The largest economic sector is oil production, accounting for almost 90% of export revenue. Mina Jabal Ali in Dubai is the world's largest man-made port, drawing companies from more than 50 countries.

ENVIRONMENT ▷ No Green MPs

🌲 None   ⬆ High

Despite its harsh desert climate, the UAE has a rich variety of plant and animal life; rare species, however, are threatened by hunting.

MEDIA ▷ TV ownership high

✖ Daily newspaper circulation 170 per 1,000 people

PUBLISHING AND BROADCAST MEDIA

There are 7 daily newspapers. The leading Arabic newspaper is *Al-Ittihad. Emirates News* is its English-language counterpart

1 state-owned, 2 independent services

2 state-owned, 1 independent service

Radio and TV are state-run; satellite TV is unrestricted. The privately owned press follows censorship guidelines.

CRIME ▷ Death penalty used

🔒 The UAE does not publish prison figures   ⬆ Up 2% from 1992–1996

Street crime and muggings are rare. However, Dubai has a reputation as a transit point for narcotics.

An oasis village, *inland from Fujairah, now accessible through a well-developed network of new roads.*

EDUCATION ▷ School leaving age: 12

👤 75%   🎓 10,641 students

UAE citizens enjoy free education from nursery to university. The government funds overseas student scholarships.

HEALTH ▷ Welfare state health benefits

👥 1 per 1,250 people   ☠ Circulatory and respiratory diseases, cancers

A high-quality system of primary health care is in place for all UAE citizens, with hospitals able to perform most operations.

SPENDING ▷ GDP/cap. increase

CONSUMPTION AND SPENDING

🚗 82 per 1,000 population   📞 351 per 1,000 population

Defense 5.5%
Education 1.8%
Health 9%

| 0 | 5 | 10 | 15 | 20 | 25 |

Defense, Health, Education spending as % of GDP

UAE nationals have the highest incomes per head in the Arab world. There is no income tax and oil revenues subsidize public services. Government policies encourage entrepreneurs.

WORLD RANKING

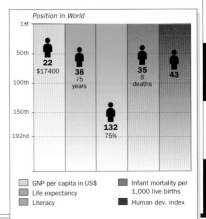

Position in World
1st
50th — 22 $17400, 38 /5 years, 35 8 deaths, 43
100th
150th — 132 75%
192nd

☐ GNP per capita in US$ ☐ Infant mortality per 1,000 live births
☐ Life expectancy   ☐ Human dev. index
☐ Literacy

U

UNITED KINGDOM

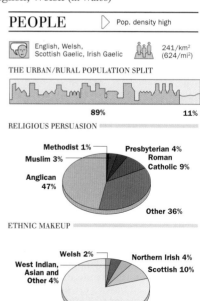

EUROPE

OFFICIAL NAME: United Kingdom of Great Britain and Northern Ireland **CAPITAL:** London
POPULATION: 58.2 million **CURRENCY:** Pound sterling **OFFICIAL LANGUAGES:** English, Welsh (in Wales)

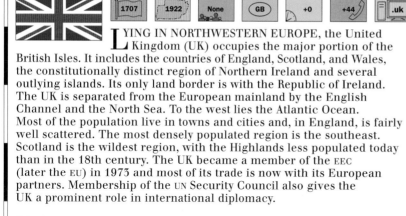

| 1707 | 1922 | None | GB | +0 | +44 | .uk |

LYING IN NORTHWESTERN EUROPE, the United Kingdom (UK) occupies the major portion of the British Isles. It includes the countries of England, Scotland, and Wales, the constitutionally distinct region of Northern Ireland and several outlying islands. Its only land border is with the Republic of Ireland. The UK is separated from the European mainland by the English Channel and the North Sea. To the west lies the Atlantic Ocean. Most of the population live in towns and cities and, in England, is fairly well scattered. The most densely populated region is the southeast. Scotland is the wildest region, with the Highlands less populated today than in the 18th century. The UK became a member of the EEC (later the EU) in 1973 and most of its trade is now with its European partners. Membership of the UN Security Council also gives the UK a prominent role in international diplomacy.

CLIMATE ▷ Maritime

WEATHER CHART

Average daily temperature / Rainfall
°C/°F J F M A M J J A S O N D cm/in
40/104 — 40/16
30/86 — 30/12
20/68 — 20/8
10/50 — 10/4
0/32 — 0
-10/14
-20/-4

The UK has a generally mild, temperate, and highly changeable climate. Rain, regarded as synonymous with Britain's weather, is fairly well distributed throughout the year, but a sequence of unusually dry years has caused sporadic problems of water shortage in some areas. The west is generally wetter than the east, and the south warmer than the north.

TRANSPORTATION ▷ Drive on left

Heathrow, London
61m passengers

1,429 ships
3.87m grt

THE TRANSPORTATION NETWORK

| 372,000 km (231,000 miles) | 3,226 km (2,005 miles) |
| 17,176 km (10,673 miles) | 5,700 km (3,542 miles) |

Britain has an extensive system of expressways, including the world's busiest beltway, the M25. The Labour government elected in 1997 promised a more integrated transportation policy in the face of congestion, pollution, and motorists' resentment of high fuel taxes. A high-speed rail link has yet to be built between London and the Channel Tunnel, which opened in 1994.

TOURISM ▷ Visitors : population 1:2.2

26m visitors

Up 9% 1995–1997

MAIN TOURIST ARRIVALS

| USA 14% |
| France 13% |
| Germany 12% |
| Ireland 8% |
| Netherlands 6% |
| Other 47% |

% of total arrivals (0 10 20 30 40 50 60)

The UK ranks fifth in the world as a tourist destination, and tourism is among the country's most important industries and a growing source of employment. North Americans, French, and Germans are the main visitors, and London, with its art galleries, theaters and historic buildings, remains the major destination. Visitors choosing to bypass the capital may head for the Roman splendors of Bath, the Shakespearean theater of Stratford-upon-Avon, the university city of Oxford, medieval York, or Scotland, where the highlands are a particular attraction.

View of Oxford, with the Clarendon Building and Sheldonian Theatre in the foreground. The 17th-century Sheldonian (right) was one of Sir Christopher Wren's first commissions.

PEOPLE ▷ Pop. density high

English, Welsh, Scottish Gaelic, Irish Gaelic

241/km² (624/mi²)

THE URBAN/RURAL POPULATION SPLIT

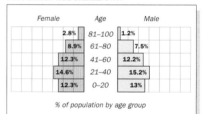

89%   11%

RELIGIOUS PERSUASION

Methodist 1%
Muslim 3%
Anglican 47%
Presbyterian 4%
Roman Catholic 9%
Other 36%

ETHNIC MAKEUP

Welsh 2%
West Indian, Asian and Other 4%
Northern Irish 4%
Scottish 10%
English 80%

The UK ranks 21st in the world for population size, but sixth for density. The Scottish and Welsh nations are recognizably distinct, government has recently become more devolved and Scots retain their own legal, religious and educational systems.

Britain's ethnic minorities account for less than 5% of the total population. Over 50% were born in Britain. Ethnic minority communities are generally found in the inner cities, where they face problems of deprivation and social stress. There is little support for overt racist politics, and progress has been made in tackling racial disadvantage since the 1970s. In key areas such as policing, however, multi-ethnic recruitment has made little progress and prejudices persist.

Marriage is in decline; legislation in 1996 made divorce easier. A third of all births occur outside marriage, compared with 12% in 1980, but most of them to cohabiting couples. Single-parent households account for one-fifth of all families with children under 18.

POPULATION AGE BREAKDOWN

Female	Age	Male
2.8%	81–100	1.2%
8.9%	61–80	7.5%
12.3%	41–60	12.2%
14.6%	21–40	15.2%
12.3%	0–20	13%

% of population by age group

U

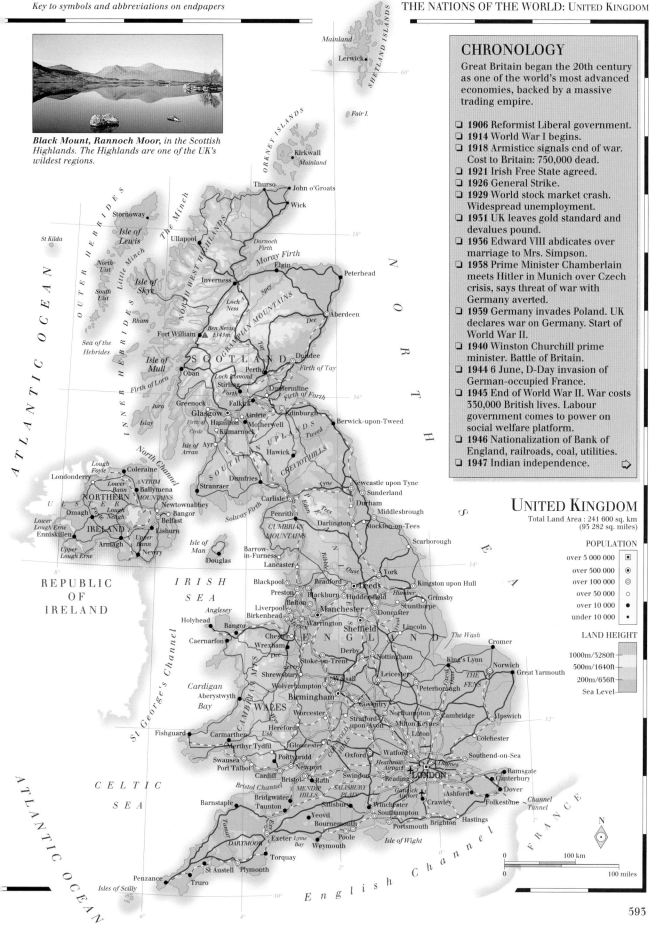

Black Mount, Rannoch Moor, in the Scottish Highlands. The Highlands are one of the UK's wildest regions.

CHRONOLOGY

Great Britain began the 20th century as one of the world's most advanced economies, backed by a massive trading empire.

- ❏ **1906** Reformist Liberal government.
- ❏ **1914** World War I begins.
- ❏ **1918** Armistice signals end of war. Cost to Britain: 750,000 dead.
- ❏ **1921** Irish Free State agreed.
- ❏ **1926** General Strike.
- ❏ **1929** World stock market crash. Widespread unemployment.
- ❏ **1931** UK leaves gold standard and devalues pound.
- ❏ **1936** Edward VIII abdicates over marriage to Mrs. Simpson.
- ❏ **1938** Prime Minister Chamberlain meets Hitler in Munich over Czech crisis, says threat of war with Germany averted.
- ❏ **1939** Germany invades Poland. UK declares war on Germany. Start of World War II.
- ❏ **1940** Winston Churchill prime minister. Battle of Britain.
- ❏ **1944** 6 June, D-Day invasion of German-occupied France.
- ❏ **1945** End of World War II. War costs 330,000 British lives. Labour government comes to power on social welfare platform.
- ❏ **1946** Nationalization of Bank of England, railroads, coal, utilities.
- ❏ **1947** Indian independence. ▷

UNITED KINGDOM

Total Land Area : 241 600 sq. km
(93 282 sq. miles)

POPULATION

over 5 000 000	▣
over 500 000	◉
over 100 000	◎
over 50 000	○
over 10 000	●
under 10 000	·

LAND HEIGHT

1000m/3280ft	
500m/1640ft	
200m/656ft	
Sea Level	

U

ATLANTIC OCEAN

SHETLAND ISLANDS
Mainland
Lerwick
60°

ORKNEY ISLANDS
Fair I.
Kirkwall
Mainland

St Kilda
OUTER HEBRIDES
Stornoway
Isle of Lewis
North Uist
South Uist
Sea of the Hebrides
Rhum
Isle of Skye
Little Minch
The Minch
INNER HEBRIDES

Thurso
John o'Groats
Wick

NORTH WEST HIGHLANDS
Ullapool
Dornoch Firth
58°
Moray Firth
Elgin
Inverness
Peterhead
Loch Ness
Spey
GRAMPIAN MOUNTAINS
Dee
Aberdeen
Ben Nevis ▲ 1343m
Fort William
SCOTLAND
Oban
Isle of Mull
Loch Lomond
Perth
Dundee
Firth of Tay
Stirling
Forth
Dunfermline
Firth of Forth
56°
Jura
Islay
Firth of Lorn
Greenock
Falkirk
Glasgow
Airdrie
Edinburgh
Hamilton
Motherwell
Isle of Arran
Kilmarnock
Ayr
Berwick-upon-Tweed
Tweed
SOUTHERN UPLANDS
Hawick
CHEVIOT HILLS

NORTH SEA

REPUBLIC OF IRELAND

Lough Foyle
Londonderry
Coleraine
Lower Bann
ANTRIM MOUNTAINS
Ballymena
Newtownabbey
ULSTER
Lough Neagh
Bangor
NORTHERN IRELAND
Omagh
Belfast
Lisburn
Lower Lough Erne
Enniskillen
Upper Bann
Armagh
Newry
Upper Lough Erne
8°
Isle of Man
Douglas

North Channel
Dumfries
Stranraer
Tyne
Newcastle upon Tyne
Sunderland
Carlisle
Durham
Eden
Middlesbrough
Solway Firth
Penrith
Darlington
Stockton-on-Tees
CUMBRIAN MOUNTAINS
Tees
Scarborough
Barrow-in-Furness
Ouse
Lancaster
54°
Ribble
York
IRISH SEA
Blackpool
Bradford
Leeds
Kingston upon Hull
Preston
Blackburn
Huddersfield
Humber
Grimsby
Bolton
Manchester
Scunthorpe
Liverpool
Warrington
Doncaster
Birkenhead
Sheffield
Lincoln
Anglesey
Holyhead
Chester
ENGLAND
Trent
The Wash
Cromer
Bangor
Wrexham
Derby
Caernarfon
Dee
Stoke-on-Trent
Nottingham
King's Lynn
Norwich
CAMBRIAN MTS
Shrewsbury
Leicester
THE FENS
Great Yarmouth
Cardigan Bay
Aberystwyth
Walsall
Peterborough
Severn
Wolverhampton
Birmingham
52°
WALES
Wye
Worcester
Coventry
Northampton
Cambridge
Ipswich
Fishguard
Hereford
Stratford-upon-Avon
Milton Keynes
Carmarthen
Usk
Gloucester
Luton
Colchester
Merthyr Tydfil
COTSWOLD HILLS
Oxford
Watford
Pontypridd
Newport
Swindon
Southend-on-Sea
Swansea
Cardiff
Bristol
Reading
LONDON
Thames
Port Talbot
Bath
Ramsgate
Bristol Channel
MENDIP HILLS
SALISBURY PLAIN
Heathrow Airport
Canterbury
CELTIC SEA
Bridgwater
Gatwick Airport
Dover
Barnstaple
Taunton
Salisbury
Winchester
Ashford
Folkestone
Crawley
Channel Tunnel
Yeovil
Southampton
Brighton
Hastings
DARTMOOR
Exe
Bournemouth
Portsmouth
FRANCE
Exeter
Lyme Bay
Poole
Isle of Wight
0°
Weymouth
Torquay
2°
Penzance
St Austell
Plymouth
Truro
Tamar
50°
Isles of Scilly
English Channel
6°
4°

0 100 km
0 100 miles

N

CHRONOLOGY *continued*

- ❏ **1948** National Health Service established.
- ❏ **1949** UK founder member of NATO.
- ❏ **1956** Suez crisis. UK intervenes in Canal Zone. Withdraws under US pressure.
- ❏ **1957** US nuclear missiles accepted on UK soil.
- ❏ **1961** UK application to EC rejected by French President de Gaulle.
- ❏ **1968** Abortion and homosexuality legalized.
- ❏ **1969** British troops sent into Northern Ireland.
- ❏ **1970** Conservatives in power under Edward Heath.
- ❏ **1973** UK joins EC. Oil crisis. Industry on three-day week following strikes by power workers and miners.
- ❏ **1974** Labour government, under Harold Wilson, concedes miners' demands and strikes end. High inflation.
- ❏ **1975** Margaret Thatcher Conservative leader. Referendum ratifies EEC membership. First North Sea oil pipeline in operation.
- ❏ **1979** Start of 18 years of Conservative rule.
- ❏ **1980** Anti-US Cruise missiles protests. Rising unemployment. Inner-city riots.
- ❏ **1981** Conservatives launch privatization program.
- ❏ **1982** Argentina invades Falklands. Islands retaken by UK task force.
- ❏ **1985** Tax-cutting policies.
- ❏ **1986** Financial services market deregularized ("Big Bang").
- ❏ **1990** John Major Conservative leader. UK joins Gulf War.
- ❏ **1992** Conservatives win fourth consecutive election.
- ❏ **1994** Tony Blair Labour leader.
- ❏ **1996** Dunblane primary school massacre, tightening of gun control laws. Public health crisis linking "mad cow" disease (BSE) with fatal Creutzfeldt-Jakob disease (CJD).
- ❏ **1997** May 1, Landslide election victory for Labour. August, Diana, Princess of Wales, killed in car crash in Paris, unleashing wave of emotion and impassioned argument about media hounding of public figures. September, Scottish and Welsh referendums approve creation of own assemblies.
- ❏ **1998–1999** "Good Friday" agreement on political settlement in Northern Ireland, endorsed by referendum but held up by disputes over decommissioning paramilitary weapons.
- ❏ **1999** March–June, involvement in NATO air war with Yugoslavia over Kosovo. May–July, Scottish Parliament and Welsh Assembly elected, inaugurated.

POLITICS

 Multiparty elections

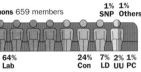 1997/2002   HM Queen Elizabeth II

AT THE LAST ELECTION

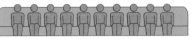

House of Commons 659 members

| 64% Lab | 24% Con | 7% LD | 2% UU | 1% PC | 1% SNP | 1% Others |

Lab = Labour Party **Con** = Conservative Party
LD = Liberal Democrat Party **SNP** = Scottish Nationalist Party **UU** = Ulster Unionist parties (official) Ulster Unionist Party, Democratic Unionist Party, UK Unionist
PC = Plaid Cymru

House of Lords 1200 members

The House of Lords is an unelected body of 772 hereditary, 26 spiritual (bishops) and 402 life peers (including Lords of Appeal – judges), appointed by the Monarch.

The UK is a multiparty democracy. The monarch holds no real power.

MAIN POLITICAL ISSUES

Europe
Labour broadly favors the euro single currency but rules out participation before the next election. In opposition the Conservatives have become increasingly "Eurosceptic," critical of EU erosions of British sovereignty.

Constitutional change
The UK has no formal written constitution, but there have been major changes in its systems of government in the late 1990s. Devolution, in particular, was opposed by the Conservatives at the 1997 elections as a threat to the unity of the UK. A separate Scottish Parliament, with substantially devolved powers, was nevertheless approved by referendum and elected in May 1999, as was a new Welsh Assembly. The long disputed situation in Northern Ireland was the subject of the April 1998 Good Friday agreement, although the implementation of power-sharing was later stalled. Elections in Scotland, Wales, and Northern Ireland, and for the European Parliament, used elements of proportional representation, yet to be introduced for elections to the UK House of Commons at Westminster. The nature of the House of Lords, however, was substantially changed by the abolition of voting rights for all but 92 hereditary peers under proposals agreed in 1999, pending complete overhaul of the second chamber.

The economy
Labour won support by blaming the Conservatives for the length and seriousness of the recession. There is now a broad consensus between the two main parties on economic policy, since Labour no longer believes in renationalizing privatized industries, raising taxes, or boosting social welfare spending. Committed to restraint in public expenditure, it aims to impress business and the electorate by sound management of the economy.

Health
Labour now admits it may take ten years to "turn around" the National Health Service (NHS), having promised to cut waiting lists and improve services in an overhaul which involved moving away from the "internal market" approach.

PROFILE
Margaret Thatcher's 1979 election victory ushered in almost 18 years of Conservative rule, and monetarist and privatization policies. John Major became Prime Minister in 1990 but his government, re-elected in 1992, lost impetus and popularity thereafter. The Labour party won back power in 1997 after Tony Blair moved what he called "New Labour" to the political center.

Margaret Thatcher, prime minister 1979–1990; Conservative Party leader 1975–1990.

John Major, prime minister and Conservative Party leader 1990–1997.

Tony Blair, became Labour Party leader after his predecessor John Smith died suddenly of a heart attack in 1994. Led the Labour Party to a spectacular landslide victory in the 1997 general election.

Canary Wharf, the centerpiece of the London Docklands development.

WORLD AFFAIRS ▷ Joined UN in 1945

The UK, historically a "great power" in world affairs, has a permanent seat on the UN Security Council. It was the third country to achieve nuclear weapons status. A founder member of NATO, it joined the EC only in 1973, and remains suspicious of full European integration. Generally following a pro-US line in the Cold War, in the 1990s it continued to do so, most notably supporting US-led actions against Iraq, beginning with the Gulf War in 1991. In 1999 it was the USA's main partner in NATO's air war to compel Yugoslav forces to pull out of Kosovo.

In 1997 the UK completed the handover of Hong Kong to China, thus relinquishing the most important of its remaining overseas territories.

AID ▷ Donor

$3.4bn (donations)   Not applicable

UK foreign aid fell between 1980 and 1997 to 0.26% of GNP, well below the nominal target 0.7% for industrialized countries. The new Labour government in 1997 promised to end the decline and to focus on aiding the poorest countries and on partnership with non-governmental organizations, building upon a change of emphasis already introduced in 1996, when 85% of bilateral aid was directed at 20 countries in sub-Saharan Africa and south Asia. The new government also abolished the "trade for aid" provision by which much of the aid budget was tied to contracts for British firms.

Prominent UK-based NGOS such as Oxfam now focus not only on emergency assistance but also on encouraging sustainable development.

DEFENSE ▷ No compulsory military service

$35.7bn   Up 1% in 1997

Despite cuts, defense spending is high. Conscription ended in 1960.

BRITISH ARMED FORCES

	545 main battle tanks (426 *Challenger*, 61 *Chieftain*, 58 *Challenger* 2)	113,900 personnel
	3 carriers, 15 submarines 12 destroyers, 23 frigates and 26 patrol boats	44,500 personnel
	450 combat aircraft (248 *Tornado*, 54 *Jaguar*, 69 *Harrier*, 98 Hawk)	52,540 personnel
	48 SLBM in 3 SSBN	

The post-Cold War program implemented in 1993 made significant cuts in army and navy personnel and equipment orders. The UK's independent nuclear deterrent was scaled down. Although troops remained stationed in Northern Ireland, the strategic emphasis turned increasingly to developing military capabilities relevant for rapid reaction. UK forces were prominent in peace-keeping in Bosnia, in NATO action against Yugoslavia in 1999, and in enforcing the Kosovo agreement thereafter.

The UK is a leading arms exporter. Major buyers include Middle Eastern and southeast Asian countries.

ECONOMICS ▷ Inflation 4.5% p.a. (1985–1996)

$1,231bn   0.61–0.60 pounds sterling

SCORE CARD

❏ WORLD GNP RANKING	5th
❏ GNP PER CAPITA	$20,870
❏ BALANCE OF PAYMENTS	$6.8bn
❏ INFLATION	3.1%
❏ UNEMPLOYMENT	6%

EXPORTS

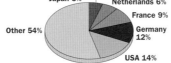

Ireland 5%, Netherlands 7%, France 9%, Germany 11%, USA 13%, Other 55%

IMPORTS

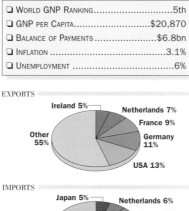

Japan 5%, Netherlands 6%, France 9%, Germany 12%, USA 14%, Other 54%

STRENGTHS

World leader in financial services, pharmaceuticals and defense industries. Strong multinationals such as Glaxo, ICI. Precision engineering and high-tech industries. Energy sector based on North Sea oil and gas production. Innovative in computer software development. Flexible working practices and lower wage rates than in other parts of western Europe. Recent success in controlling former propensity for inflation.

WEAKNESSES

Decline of manufacturing sector since 1970s, particularly heavy industries. Quick-return mentality of many investment decisions does not create environment for sustaining long-term growth. High levels of consumer and government debt. Non-participation in euro single currency threatens former status as EU's largest recipient of inward investment.

PROFILE

Manufacturing is still the largest sector of the UK economy, although its importance has declined as the services and energy have grown. During the 1980s, there was a sharp decline in heavy industries such as steel and engineering, located mostly in the Midlands and the north, while sectors such as financial services expanded rapidly in the south. After sharp recession in 1991, revival was sluggish, with consumer spending hampered by fears of unemployment. In 1996 and 1997 growth was strong, and interest rate cuts then helped prevent another recession, although exporters remained concerned that sterling was overvalued.

ECONOMIC PERFORMANCE INDICATOR

Consumer price index   GDP

UNITED KINGDOM : MAJOR BUSINESSES

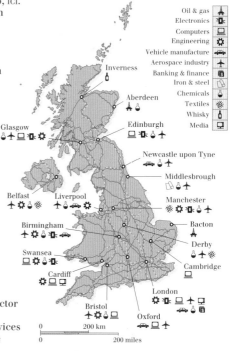

U

RESESOURCES

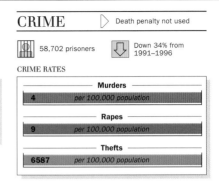

Electric power 70.2m kw

1.01 tonnes

1.8m b/d (reserves 4,143,530,000 bbl)

155m poultry, 44.5m sheep, 11.5m cattle, 8.1m pigs

Coal, oil, limestone, natural gas

ELECTRICITY GENERATION

Hydro 2% (6.8bn kwh)	
Combustion 71% (238.3bn kwh)	
Nuclear 27% (89bn kwh)	
Other 0% (0.3bn kwh)	

0   20   40   60   80   100

% of total generation by type

The UK has the largest energy resources of any EU state, with substantial oil and gas reserves offshore on the continental shelf in the North Sea, and fresh fields in the north Atlantic. Drilled under difficult conditions, North Sea oil is of a high grade. Revenues from taxes on oil companies have been a major contributor to government finances, averaging around $12 billion a year.

Coal reserves are also sizable, but all but a handful of pits have closed, faced with cheap imports and falling demand. Privatization of the electricity industry, and pressure to cut pollution, encouraged the switch from coal to gas-fired power plants, prompting emergency government measures in the late 1990s and efforts to boost the role of "cleaner coal" technology.

The UK produces few other minerals in significant quantities. Cornwall's last tin mines teeter between closure and rescue. Some very small-scale gold mining survives in Wales and Scotland.

UNITED KINGDOM : LAND USE

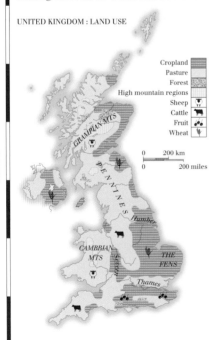

Cropland
Pasture
Forest
High mountain regions
Sheep
Cattle
Fruit
Wheat

0   200 km
0   200 miles

GRAMPIAN MTS
PENNINES
Humber
CAMBRIAN MTS
THE FENS
Thames

ENVIRONMENT

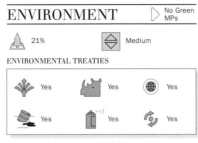

No Green MPs

21%

Medium

ENVIRONMENTAL TREATIES

Yes	Yes	Yes
Yes	Yes	Yes

Apart from destruction of habitat and rural environments by road building and sprawling development, the most important issues are health-related. Urban air pollution from traffic is a major focus, as are water quality and nuclear waste disposal. Food safety issues have gripped the public since BSE ("mad cow" disease) was linked in the mid-1990s with human deaths. Opposition to genetically modified (GM) foods is widespread. There are militant campaigns to stop GM crop trials, in case modified genes contaminate other species.

MEDIA

TV ownership high

Daily newspaper circulation 332 per 1,000 people

PUBLISHING AND BROADCAST MEDIA

	There are 99 daily newspapers, including *The Times, The Daily Telegraph, The Independent* and *The Guardian*
	2 publicly-financed, 3 independent networks
	5 publicly-financed, many independent networks

Newspapers are owned mostly by large media corporations. Many publish Internet editions. Criticized for invasions of privacy, the press presents self-regulation as preferable to legislation. Publication deemed contrary to "national interests" may be banned. Satellite TV and digital terrestrial broadcasting have increased competition for the BBC. The BBC's World Service, despite cutbacks, remains an influential international news source.

The Welsh coal industry *has virtually disappeared. Wales now has the highest percentage of small business start-ups, relative to the population, of any part of the UK.*

CRIME

Death penalty not used

58,702 prisoners

Down 34% from 1991–1996

CRIME RATES

Murders	
4	per 100,000 population

Rapes	
9	per 100,000 population

Thefts	
6587	per 100,000 population

Burglary and car theft have risen sharply since the 1970s. Inner city violence is partly fueled by drug dependency and trafficking. Gun controls were tightened after a shocking massacre at Dunblane primary school in Scotland in 1996. The Labour government since 1997 has retained a "tough on crime" stance, but sentencing policies place the penal system under serious strain.

EDUCATION

School leaving age: 16

99%

1.8m students

State education has been restructured around a national curriculum.

THE EDUCATION SYSTEM

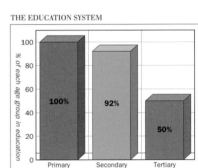

% of each age group in education

100%   Primary
92%   Secondary
50%   Tertiary

The state system is used by 94% of children. Others attend fee-paying private schools, including the traditional elite public schools.

Most state education until the 1960s was based on selectivity, but this two-tier system was gradually replaced by mixed ability comprehensive schools. Education reforms in 1988 introduced a program of required teaching and weakened the role of local education authorities, but few schools exercised the new right to "opt out" for greater administrative autonomy. The post-1997 Labour government has focused on teaching standards and "failing" schools.

Entry to university depends on end-of-school A-level exams. Many colleges were given university status in the 1990s but established centers, particularly Oxford and Cambridge, are the most prestigious and best resourced.

DEVOLUTION IN THE 1990s

THE UNITED KINGDOM dates from 1801 and the Act of Union joining Ireland with Great Britain - partly undone when Ireland (except Northern Ireland) become independent in 1922. The English and Scottish crowns had been united in 1603 (James VI of Scotland becoming James 1 of England), and their parliaments in 1707, also by an Act of Union, although Scotland's legal system remained separate. The principality of Wales had lost its separate status and been joined with England in 1536.

The rise of Welsh and particularly Scottish nationalism prompted an abortive initiative in the 1970s to devolve powers to regional governments. The post-1997 Labour government gave fresh impetus to devolution, created new parliaments in Northern Ireland, Scotland and Wales, and also raised the idea of English regional assemblies.

NORTHERN IRELAND
In Northern Ireland (pop. 1.65 million, area 14,120 km²/ 5,450 mi², capital Belfast) the majority Protestant community dominated a "home rule" parliament at Stormont throughout its 50-year existence, until 1972. After that the troubled province was mainly under direct rule from London, interspersed with attempts to create power-sharing institutions, until the 1998 Good Friday agreement. This created a 108-member Northern Ireland Assembly, elected that June by proportional representation, and a 12-member power-sharing executive. However, implementation of the agreement stalled amid disputes mainly about disarming rival Irish republican and unionist "loyalist" paramilitaries.

The Scottish Parliament building, Edinburgh.

SCOTLAND AND WALES
A Scottish National Party breakthrough in general elections in 1974 was fuelled by the perception that independence could be viable, if Scotland controlled the oil wealth of the North Sea. The UK government offered devolution to both Scotland and Wales (whose nationalist Plaid Cymru party also held seats in the Westminster parliament) but got a lukewarm response in referendums in 1979. The majority in Scotland was insufficient to carry the proposals, while Wales actually voted no. The devolution proposals of 1997, on the other hand, won endorsement both in Scotland and (narrowly) in Wales.

Scotland (pop. 5.13 million, area 78,742 km²/ 30,394 mi², capital Edinburgh) now has a Scottish Parliament of 129 members (MSPs), elected in May 1999. The Scottish Executive, consisting of a First Minister and an 11-member cabinet, is responsible to the parliament. The Parliament's powers cover education policy and taxation – to generate revenue for Scottish expenditure.

In Wales (pop. 2.9 million, area 20,761 km²/ 8,041 mi², capital Cardiff) the 60-member Welsh Assembly was also elected in May 1999. It exercises more limited powers, not including tax-raising, through an eight-member administration headed by a First Secretary.

The extensive upland areas of both Scotland and Wales are used extensively for sheep farming and forestry.

HEALTH
▷ Welfare state health benefits

1 per 667 people   Heart, cerebrovascular and respiratory diseases, cancers

The National Health Service (NHS) offers universal free health care, but financial pressures have led to hospital closures and shortages of facilities. Significant charges are now made in certain areas, except for those on low incomes. Private health care has grown rapidly since the 1970s. Recent crises have focused on food safety, from cases of poisoning to the transmission of fatal brain disease, attributed to eating beef from cattle with "mad cow" disease.

SPENDING
▷ Not available

CONSUMPTION AND SPENDING

371 per 1,000 population   540 per 1,000 population

Defense 2.8%	
Education 5.5%	
Health 6.6%	

0   5   10   15   20   25
Defense, Health, Education spending as % of GDP

Income inequality in the UK is greater than in 1884, when records first began. Much wealth is well hidden, invested in property, on the stock market, and overseas; a series of disastrous losses on the Lloyds insurance market in the early 1990s left some wealthy investors unusually exposed. In the 1980s and early 1990s, the purchasing power of salaries rose sharply while taxation for higher earners was cut, whereas unemployment tripled and the value of state benefits and pensions fell. Labour's 1997 election promises precluded raising income tax, limiting scope for redistributive action. Tax cuts in the 1999 budget left anti-poverty strategies even more dependent on promises of better targeting of welfare benefits.

WORLD RANKING

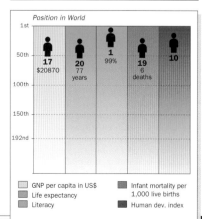

Position in World

1st
50th
100th
150th
192nd

| 17 $20870 | 20 77 years | 1 99% | 19 6 deaths | 10 |

☐ GNP per capita in US$
☐ Life expectancy
☐ Literacy
☐ Infant mortality per 1,000 live births
☐ Human dev. index

U

See also OVERSEAS TERRITORIES *p.640*

UNITED STATES

OFFICIAL NAME: United States of America   **CAPITAL:** Washington, DC
POPULATION: 273.8 million   **CURRENCY:** US dollar   **OFFICIAL LANGUAGE:** English

| 1776 | 1959 | July 4 | USA | -5 to -11 | +1 | - |

THE WORLD'S FOURTH-LARGEST country, the United States is neither overpopulated (like China) nor in the main subject to extremes of climate (like much of Russia and Canada). Its main landmass, bounded by Canada and Mexico, contains 48 of its 50 states. The two others, Alaska at the northwest tip of the Americas and Hawaii in the Pacific, became states in 1959. The USA was not built on ethnic identity but on a concept of nationhood intimately bound up with the 18th century Founding Fathers' ideas of democracy and liberty – still powerful touchstones in both a political and an economic sense. Since the break-up of the former Soviet Union, the USA has held a unique position as the sole truly global superpower.

CLIMATE

Continental/subtropical/mountain/desert/maritime

weather is frequently dramatic, with tornadoes, cyclones, thunderstorms, floods, and droughts. In the 1990s these seem to have become more frequent and serious, due to global climate change.

The Chippendale Block, New York, a notable example of postmodern architecture by the influential US architect Philip Johnson.

Spanning a continent and extending far into the Pacific Ocean, the USA displays a full range of climatic conditions. Mean annual temperatures range from 29°C (84°F) in Florida to –13°C (9°F) in Alaska. Except for New England, Alaska, and the Pacific northwest, summer temperatures are higher than in Europe. Southern summers are humid; in the southwest they are dry. Winters are particularly severe in the western mountains and plains and the Midwest – where the Great Lakes can freeze. The northeast can have heavy snow from November to April. The

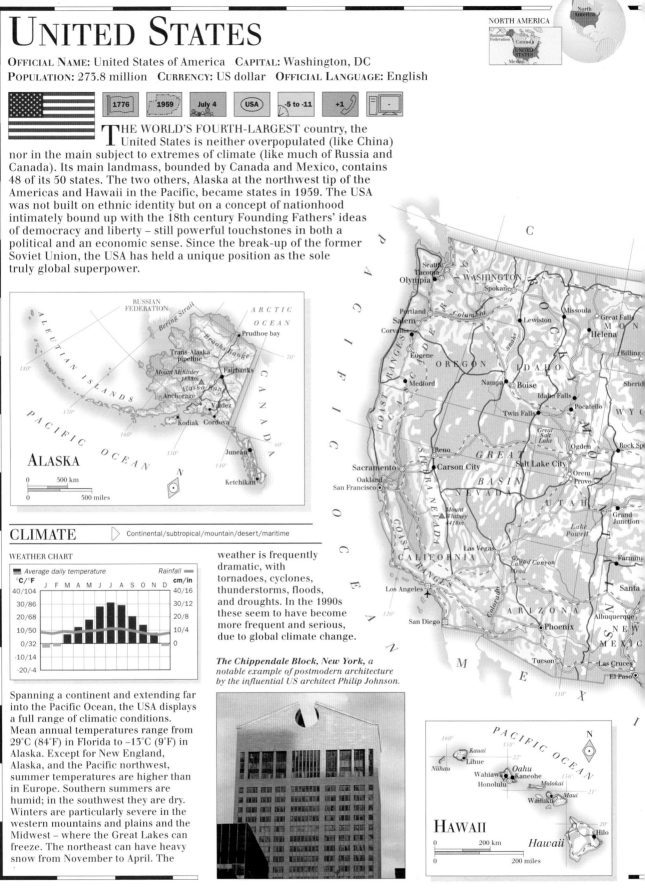

U

TRANSPORTATION

▷ Drive on right

Atlanta, Georgia
7.3m passengers

495 ships
17.5m grt

THE TRANSPORTATION NETWORK

6.24m km (3.9m miles)		84,361 km (52,419 miles)	
235,238 km (147,024 miles)		41,009 km (25,482 miles)	

The Mississippi–Missouri river system provided the USA's first transportation network. Today, the USA has the world's cheapest, most extensive internal air network and a good system of interstate highways. Railroads, comparatively neglected for years, mainly carry freight, although modern high-speed trains are starting to attract passengers back. Americans have been wedded to the car since Henry Ford began mass production 90 years ago. In 1919, Ford sold one million cars; today, there are over 255 million in the USA, making more than half of the world's car journeys. Cheap gasoline underpinned this growth, and cities like Los Angeles have come to depend on the car. With growing air pollution problems, and the long-term prospect of domestic oil supplies running out, the car's role in society needs reviewing.

The Mittens, Monument Valley, Arizona.
These striking natural rock formations are created by erosion of red sandstone. The Valley is home to the Navajo people.

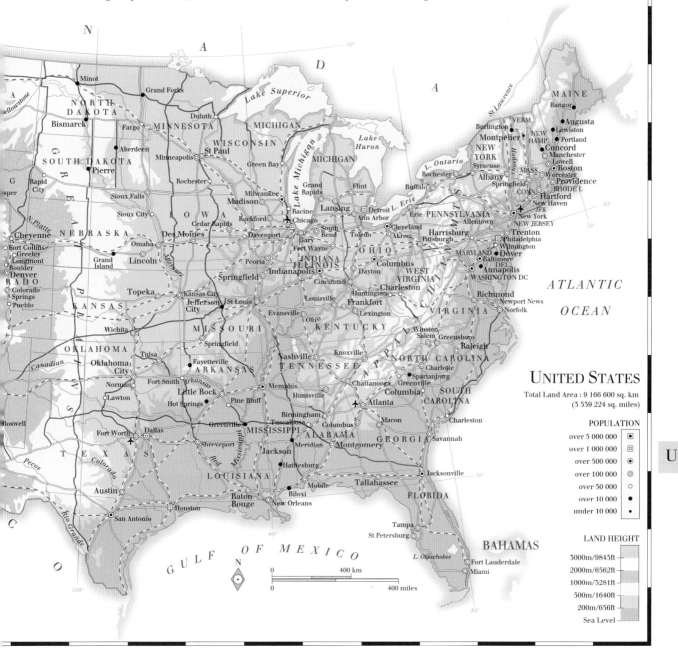

UNITED STATES

Total Land Area : 9 166 600 sq. km
(3 539 224 sq. miles)

POPULATION

over 5 000 000	▣
over 1 000 000	▢
over 500 000	◉
over 100 000	◎
over 50 000	○
over 10 000	●
under 10 000	·

LAND HEIGHT

3000m/9843ft
2000m/6562ft
1000m/3281ft
500m/1640ft
200m/656ft
Sea Level

U

TOURISM ▷ Visitors : population 1:5.7

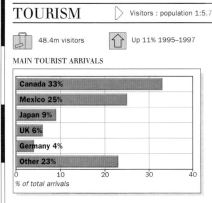

48.4m visitors   Up 11% 1995–1997

MAIN TOURIST ARRIVALS

Canada 33%	
Mexico 25%	
Japan 9%	
UK 6%	
Germany 4%	
Other 23%	

% of total arrivals

Tourism is an important industry, catering to ever-growing demand from both overseas visitors and Americans themselves, and bringing in some $70 billion a year in receipts from foreign tourists. The number of foreign visitors has doubled in the past 15 years, boosted especially by the deregulation of air fares. Domestic tourism has expanded just as rapidly, as real incomes have risen.

Tourism is a major generator of jobs, especially in areas of industrial decline, such as the northeast. All the states have their attractions, however, and most court tourists. Top tourist destinations include Florida's Disney World and Disneyland in California, Niagara Falls, Las Vegas, New York, San Francisco, Los Angeles and Hollywood, the Grand Canyon, New Orleans, Atlantic City, and Washington, DC.

The parks and sites run by the National Parks Service (NPS) have been particular casualties of tourism's rapid expansion; visitor numbers have rocketed in the three decades since 1970. To try and reduce pressure on the most popular areas, there has been a significant expansion of NPS-managed land since the mid-1970s. Even so, Yellowstone Park has a continuing traffic management crisis, bumper to bumper cars plague other high-profile attractions, and those wanting to ride rafts down the Grand Canyon must go on a waiting list for years.

PEOPLE ▷ Pop. density low

English, Spanish, Italian, German, French, Polish, Chinese, Tagalog, Greek   30/km² (77/mi²)

THE URBAN/RURAL POPULATION SPLIT

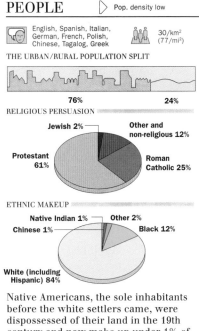

76%   24%

RELIGIOUS PERSUASION

Jewish 2%
Other and non-religious 12%
Protestant 61%
Roman Catholic 25%

ETHNIC MAKEUP

Native Indian 1%   Other 2%
Chinese 1%   Black 12%
White (including Hispanic) 84%

Native Americans, the sole inhabitants before the white settlers came, were dispossessed of their land in the 19th century and now make up under 1% of the total population. Native American reservations conceal some of the country's worst poverty and deprivation.

There is still significant population growth, with some 25 million added to the total number of residents during the 1990s. This is partly due to an immigration boom since the 1960s, which peaked in the late 1980s and early 1990s; there were 1.8 million legal immigrants in 1991 alone, but numbers have fallen to below a million a year since then. The new immigrants are disproportionately drawn from Asia and Latin America. In the 1980s, more than 2 million came from Mexico alone.

Census Bureau projections for the year 2050 suggest that 53% of the population will be white non-Hispanics, and just under 14% black, and nearly 9% Asians; as many as a quarter of the population will be Hispanics. There is already concern about the growth of immigration marginalizing the position of American blacks, who increasingly find they have to compete both politically and economically with the newer immigrants. In some communities, such as Los Angeles, this has been a source of tension which has led to inner-city riots.

Successful entrepreneurs can achieve great wealth, but only one black person – television personality Oprah Winfrey – makes the list of the 400 richest. The 1995 "Million Man March" on Washington DC, organized by militant Muslim leader Louis Farrakhan and his Nation of Islam movement, emphasized values of self-discipline, self-improvement and community in the quest for empowerment among African-Americans.

POPULATION AGE BREAKDOWN

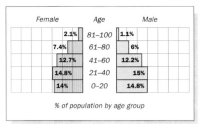

Female	Age	Male
2.1%	81–100	1.1%
7.4%	61–80	6%
12.7%	41–60	12.2%
14.8%	21–40	15%
14%	0–20	14.8%

% of population by age group

POLITICS ▷ Multiparty elections

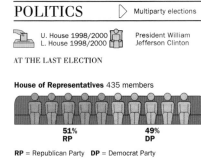

U. House 1998/2000
L. House 1998/2000   President William Jefferson Clinton

AT THE LAST ELECTION

House of Representatives 435 members

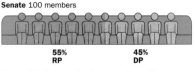

51% RP   49% DP

RP = Republican Party   DP = Democrat Party

Senate 100 members

55% RP   45% DP

Presidential elections take place every 4 years, House elections every 2 years. One third of the senators are elected every 2 years for six-year terms.

The USA has a federal system which means that individual states control many improtabnt issues, including education.

MAIN POLITICAL ISSUES
Crime, race, and poverty
The black community – 60% of those living in poor districts – is particularly severely affected by high urban crime. Both rates of criminality and crime victims are higher in the black community than in any other. Black organizations have backed calls for tighter gun controls, although the prominence of this issue in 1999 was due less to inner-city violence than to a spate of dramatic shootings at high schools.

Efforts are being made to promote regeneration through a combination of new economic opportunities and programs that give poor people more power over their own lives (for example, by self-management of public housing projects). Tough anti-crime policies in cities like New York have had a real impact in reducing the level of violence.

Health
The USA's health care system is based on private insurance; costs are increasing faster than private or public budgets can tolerate, and it gives a patchy service to clients. In addition to the escalation of costs, some one-third of Americans have

President Bill Clinton *re-elected for a second term as president in 1996.*

Madeleine Albright, *first woman Secretary of State.*

U

POLITICS *continued*

no health insurance. President Clinton during his first term of office aimed at a fundamental overhaul of the system, seeking to extend cover to all while forcing employers to bear most of the cost. The plan, for which Hillary Clinton was given prime responsibility, constituted one of the most important legislative proposals for 50 years and had significant public support. However, although Clinton had characterized the legislation as the defining feature of his domestic agenda, it foundered in Congress in the face of resolute opposition from powerful vested interests and Republican opposition.

The Clinton presidency

The Clinton administration, beset by personal, financial, and political scandals, was hamstrung in the latter part of its second term by impeachment proceedings launched in 1998, although Clinton retained remarkably high public opinion ratings. Since the midterm elections in November 1994, there have been Republican majorities in both the House of Representatives and the Senate for the first time in 30 years. Clinton won reelection for a second term in November 1996, but, on top of the problem of containing the damage from the Whitewater financial scandal, he had to deal with the prospect of having to answer sexual harassment charges. By the end of 1998 the House had voted to impeach him, his moral authority fatally compromised by the exposure of the sordid details of an affair with a White House intern. He had laid himself open to the accusation of perverting justice by his attempts to conceal and then deny this affair in the face of relentless investigation by a zealous special prosecutor. There was no real likelihood of a sufficient Senate majority to remove him from office, and the Senate, as expected, acquitted him in early 1999. The scandal, however, discredited and isolated the Clinton presidency, leaving Democratic contenders for the November 2000 election seeking damage limitation strategies to minimize association with him.

PROFILE

In modern times, the Republican Party has dominated the presidency, and the Democratic Party the Congress. The election of Bill Clinton at the end of 1992 was meant to end the resultant "gridlock" between the executive and legislative branches. This proved not to be the case, however, as the complex legislative process and independent power of Congress continued to preclude rapid legislative results. The Republican majority in the House of Representatives, the first for 30 years, was elected in part on the promise of the enactment of a ten-point "Contract with America." However, most of these measures faltered in the Senate, and it was through the special prosecutor's investigations that his Republican opponents were most effective in damaging the Clinton presidency.

The Supreme Court, which has periodically made some of the country's most momentous decisions, currently has a much less salient position in US politics, although recent decisions on euthanasia, censorship, and the internet have again brought it into the public eye.

WORLD AFFAIRS ▷ Joined UN in 1945

The USA has for much of its history been able to choose the extent of its involvement in the affairs of others. For most of the first half of the 20th century it pursued an isolationist policy, becoming only reluctantly involved in World Wars I and II. After 1945, however, it swapped isolationism for involvement. The UN was headquartered in New York, and the USA took its seat on the Security Council. As leader of one side of the struggle between capitalism and communism, the USA helped set up NATO. For the USA, the Cold War was most immediate – and costly – in the Korean and Vietnam Wars. The heavy death toll and shock of defeat in Vietnam kept the USA out of military involvement overseas for over a decade. Instead, it concentrated on diplomacy – with particular success in China and the Middle East – and on supporting the opponents of left-wing regimes in the developing world, in Nicaragua, Cuba, Angola, Afghanistan and elsewhere.

The collapse of the Eastern bloc after 1989 led to renewed debate. As the only remaining superpower, the USA had to determine the scope of its foreign responsibilities in an era when there was no longer a perceived threat to its survival. In the early 1990s, it seemed set to take on the role of world policeman, taking a lead in the interventions in the 1991 Gulf War and in Somalia. A fiasco in Somalia and a lack of clear policy on Bosnia and Haiti, however, showed the USA as still uncertain about such a role. Air strikes on Sudan and Afghanistan in mid-1998, reinforcing a tough stance against anti-US international terrorism, were viewed with particular hostility in the Islamic world. Increasingly isolated in actions against Iraq, the USA again showed its reliance on air power – and aversion to committing ground forces – in the 1999 bombardment of Yugoslavia over the Kosovo crisis.

***Manhattan Island,** bounded by the Hudson and East Rivers. New York's two main clusters of skyscrapers are found in the financial district and in midtown Manhattan.*

AID ▷ Donor

 $6.2bn (donations) ⬦ Not applicable

The USA gives proportionately little foreign aid, and such aid as it does give is perennially held hostage to special pleading in Congress. The lion's share goes to Israel and Egypt, although of late there has been substantial assistance to the countries of the former USSR and eastern Europe.

DEFENSE ▷ No compulsory military service

 $273bn ⬇ Down 2% in 1997

Emphasis has shifted from strategic nuclear deterrence to rapid intervention capabilities built around air power.

AMERICAN ARMED FORCES

7,836 battle tanks (192 M-60A3, 7,644 M-1)	479,400 personnel
84 submarines, 12 carriers, 57 destroyers, 44 frigates and 21 patrol boats	380,600 personnel
2,398 combat aircraft (F-4, F15, F16, A-10A, F-117, OA-10A)	370,300 personnel
432 SLBM in 18 SSBN, 680 ICBM	

The enormous US military–industrial complex dates from the years since 1945. Before then, the armed forces were small in number, poorly equipped and rapidly dismantled at the end of wars. Defense spending has peaked three times since 1945: at the time of the Korean War in the 1950s, during the 1963–1973 Vietnam War, and again in the defense build-up of 1979–1986.

A combination of the end of the Cold War and the need to cut the budget deficit meant spending cuts in the 1990s. In real terms, the defense budget fell to its lowest level since 1945. This had one unanticipated but troubling side effect: the armed forces is the area where blacks have found it easiest to gain top positions; as the military shrinks, so do the opportunities for black American advancement.

U

THE IMPACT OF INFORMATION TECHNOLOGY

THE UNITED STATES has been, and remains, at the forefront of the so-called information revolution. US society is undergoing profound changes as a result of the spread of the personal computer, and connectivity through access to electronic mail (email) and the World Wide Web. The Web is a phenomenon of the 1990s, although the internet on which it is based originated in the 1960s. The Net, developed to allow vital defence communications to be maintained in the event of an attack on a central control site, was first popularized within the academic community as a medium for exchange within and between universities.

ACCESS TO VIRTUAL SPACE

Mass ownership of the motor car and cheap fuel had conditioned the attitudes of previous generations of Americans to distance, and helped determine the pattern of development of the cities and towns in which the majority of them live. Information technology, the concept of "cyberspace" and the availability of instant "virtual" interaction, are now sometimes described as having abolished distance.

High speed connections to the internet are becoming increasingly popular, but for most ordinary individual users the link is by dial-up on an ordinary telephone line to the local number of their internet service provider. One consequence has been an explosion in phone line use, particularly because the recently deregulated telephone industry offers most Americans the chance to pay for their local calls on a single flat rate rather than by the minute. Computer modems can thus be left connected for long periods.

As with the motor car, however, part of society is left out. In 1998, PC ownership stood at some 43 per cent of the population, of whom half were online, connected to the internet. This proportion is still rising fast, and there

Access to the internet remains out of reach to those who cannot afford a personal computer, such as residents of some of the USA's poverty-stricken innner city areas like the Bronx in New York City.

The Microsoft Campus in Redmond, Washington. Microsoft is the world's biggest computer software manufacturer and its founder, Bill Gates, is the USA's richest man.

are frequent proposals for special initiatives to spread access among disadvantaged groups, including such suggestions as giving portable notebook computers to the homeless.

IMPACT ON THE POLITICAL PROCESS

The US administration and Congress now publish huge amounts of information of all kinds via the internet. Citizens can also use the Net interactively to lodge requests and file the returns required of them, amongst other things for income tax purposes. The technology has greatly reinforced the impact of laws ensuring freedom of information, as well as exposing its users to the problems of information overload and a deluge of unsolicited communication. The notion of a "wired" democracy has taken hold to the extent that most politicians have their own web site and many use them extensively to publicise their activities. The presidential election in the year 2000 has been heralded as the first "internet election," just as the campaign in which John F. Kennedy defeated Richard Nixon 40 years previously was regarded as marking the ascendancy of television in the US political process.

SECURITY

Through the 1990s, activists of different kinds made increasing use of the internet to spread their views and maintain contact among their supporters. There are serious security concerns about the use of this tool not only by mainstream political organisations and lobbyists, but by fringe groups, terrorists and the pornography and sex industries. Such concerns underlie the battle about the

use of encryption software to ensure the privacy of electronic communications. The Federal Bureau of Investigation (FBI) and the Central Intelligence Agency (CIA) have fought to ensure that all such software should have a key allowing the security authorities to decipher messages. Unfortunately for them, it is notoriously difficult to prevent the rapid spread of software which is made available on the internet, and impossible to pin down the location of such programs in the usual geographical sense. The policing of a national jurisdiction is compromised by a communications network which recognises no national boundaries. The same is true with computer viruses, which can infect the programs running on computers that come into contact with them and affect the way they function, in some cases very destructively.

Shopping malls are a typical feature of the urban and suburban landscape of the USA. Online "virtual malls" are fast spreading.

COMMERCE

The shopping mall, which has had a major influence in reshaping consumer shopping habits since the 1960s, and the mail order catalog on which many American households rely so heavily for clothes and similar purchases, are now under challenge from the online "virtual mall." The online shopping landscape is only now really taking shape, with many companies having to take a trial and error approach to developing e-commerce. By 1998 only 10% of Americans had made purchases online. However, as many as 40% of retail companies were offering goods for sale online (amounting to 1% of their turnover), and three quarters were either doing so or planning to do so, as were a quarter of all manufacturing companies. It has been predicted that the number of people in the USA who regularly buy necessities such as

U

groceries and related goods online will reach 20 million by 2007.

TRAFFIC

The take-up of e-commerce on this scale would replace at least half of Americans' average 17 monthly shopping trips made to grocery stores and related outlets. It has the added attraction of shielding shoppers from the perceived dangers of being assaulted or robbed when venturing outside their homes. This is an area where the out-of-town shopping mall itself, complete with security guards and closed circuit television monitoring, had hitherto prospered as a more attractive option than shopping downtown.

Information technology is affecting patterns of personal transportation and mobility in other ways too. At one level, online information services and selling techniques make it more convenient and efficient to book airline tickets. At the same time, improvements in communications make it increasingly possible and productive for people to work at home or in decentralised facilities away from company headquarters. So-called "knowledge workers" in particular have had to learn new ways of networking electronically to replace the face-to-face contact of the office environment, and the use of special interest discussion facilities and so-called newsgroups on the internet has mushroomed accordingly. The number of "telecommuters," still only a small fraction of the total US working population, is nevertheless becoming significant in terms of managing peak time commuter traffic. Videoconferencing is beginning to make headway as an alternative to travelling long distances for business meetings, with the active encouragement of some gurus in the environmental lobby.

The rise of the electronic superhighway is changing the way in which US citizens both shop, and work. Home working is set to rise in the next decade, minimizing the need for the daily commute to work.

ECONOMICS

 Inflation 3.2% p.a. (1985–1996)

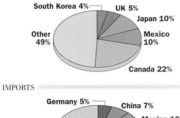 $7,783.1bn   Not applicable

SCORE CARD

❏ WORLD GNP RANKING	1st
❏ GNP PER CAPITA	$29,080
❏ BALANCE OF PAYMENTS	$–166.8bn
❏ INFLATION	2.3%
❏ UNEMPLOYMENT	5%

EXPORTS

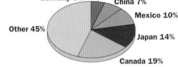

South Korea 4%   UK 5%
Japan 10%
Other 49%   Mexico 10%
Canada 22%

IMPORTS

Germany 5%   China 7%
Mexico 10%
Other 45%   Japan 14%
Canada 19%

STRENGTHS

The world's largest economy. Wealth of natural resources, including energy, raw materials and foods. Strong high-tech base and world-leading research and development. Sophisticated service sector, as well as advanced and competitive manufacturing industry. World-class multinationals such as Ford, GM, Exxon. Global leader in computer software. Entrepreneurial business ethic. High quality of post-graduate education, especially related to application of high-tech to business. Global dominance of US culture a major boost to US manufacturers.

UNITED STATES : MAJOR BUSINESSES

🖳	Computers
⛏	Oil & gas
▯	Oil refining
▣	Electronics
🜹	Chemicals
✿	Engineering
🎬	Film industry
🗑	Food processing
⚓	Defense industry
🏦	Banking & finance
🚗	Vehicle manufacture
🖵	Research & development
✈	Aerospace industry (civil)

Anchorage
Seattle
Denver
Chicago
St Louis
Detroit
New York
Phoenix
Atlanta
Houston
Los Angeles
Dallas
Miami

0   500 km
0   500 miles

ECONOMIC PERFORMANCE INDICATOR

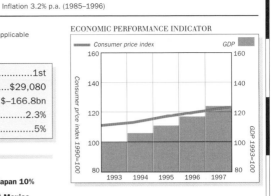

— Consumer price index   GDP

1993 1994 1995 1996 1997

WEAKNESSES

Dramatic fall in manufacturing employment over last 25 years, although manufacturing sector has remained constant as a share of GDP. Postwar economic boom was built on low-skilled, high-waged employment in areas such as car industry. Globalization, problem of job losses to lower-wage economies. Tough competition from Asia and EU, particularly in future leading-edge technologies. Lower savings rate than many competitors. World's largest debtor country.

PROFILE

In 1945, the USA accounted for about 50% of world output; by the 1990s its share was down to about 25%. That is not, as Americans often think, a sign of failure, but a clear indication that the 1940s and 1950s were unusual periods. The current total of 25% is about the same share of the world market that the USA claimed in 1914, when it was already the world's greatest economy.

The USA has become a great exporter, and continues to have both a stable political system and a uniquely strong combination of skilled labor and natural resources.

U

CHRONOLOGY

The original 13 colonies, first established by British settlers on the eastern seaboard in the 17th century, joined to wage a war for independence, 1775–1781, which Britain recognized in 1783. The Constitution of 1787 then established the USA. A century of westward expansion began. Following the victory of the northern states in the 1861–1865 Civil War, slavery was abolished throughout the USA, but native Americans were dispossessed of their land in a series of conflicts.

❏ **1917** Enters World War I.
❏ **1929** New York stock market collapse; economic depression.
❏ **1941** Japanese attack on Pearl Harbor; enters World War II.
❏ **1950–1953** Korean War.
❏ **1954** Supreme Court rules racial segregation in schools is unconstitutional. Blacks, seeking constitutional rights, start campaign of civil disobedience.
❏ **1959** Alaska, Hawaii become states.
❏ **1961** John F. Kennedy president. Promises aid to South Vietnam. US-backed invasion of Cuba defeated at Bay of Pigs.
❏ **1962** Soviet missile bases found on Cuba; threat of nuclear war averted.
❏ **1963** November, Kennedy assassinated. Lyndon Baines Johnson president.
❏ **1964** US involvement in Vietnam stepped up. Civil Rights Act gives blacks constitutional equality.
❏ **1968** Martin Luther King assassinated.
❏ **1969** Republican Richard Nixon takes office as president. Growing public opposition to Vietnam War.
❏ **1972** Nixon reelected. Makes historic visit to China.
❏ **1973** Withdrawal of US troops from Vietnam; 58,000 US troops dead by end of war.
❏ **1974** August, Nixon resigns following "Watergate" scandal over break-in to DP headquarters. Gerald Ford president.
❏ **1976** Democrat Jimmy Carter elected president.
❏ **1978** US-sponsored "Camp David" agreement between Egypt and Israel.
❏ **1979** Seizure of US hostages in Tehran, Iran.
❏ **1980** Ronald Reagan wins elections for Republicans. Adopts tough anticommunist foreign policy.
❏ **1983** Military invasion of Grenada.
❏ **1985** Air strikes against Libyan cities. Relations with USSR improve; first of three summits held.
❏ **1986** Iran–Contra affair revealed.

⇨

RESOURCES

▷ Electric power 764.9m kw

5.6m tonnes

7.3m b/d (reserves 24,682,000,000 bbl)

99.7m cattle, 60.9m pigs, 7.6m sheep, 6.2m horses

Phosphate, gypsum, oil, coal, sulfur, lead, zinc, copper, gold

ELECTRICITY GENERATION

Hydro 9% (308.3bn kwh)	
Combustion 70% (2345.6bn kwh)	
Nuclear 20% (673.4bn kwh)	
Other 1% (18bn kwh)	

0   20   40   60   80   100

% of total generation by type

The USA has an abundance of natural resources, including oil, although the country is a net oil importer. There are massive deposits of coal in the western states – where almost all mining is open-cast – and substantial mineral deposits in the mountains and intramontane basins.

Environmental concerns have prevented the development of new sources of nuclear power since the accident at Three Mile Island in 1979. Environmentalism has also forced the

timber industry to retreat from the Pacific northwest, especially from Washington State. It has moved to the south, where great stands of pine are harvested as if they were fields of wheat. The USA has harnessed hydroelectric power in the past; today, imports of hydropower from Canada are commonplace.

By comparison with western Europe, the USA is not intensively farmed. The huge size of farms in the Midwest and west has allowed both arable and livestock farming to be based on a low-input for low-output model.

UNITED STATES : LAND USE

▦ Cropland		🐄	Cattle
Pasture		🌿	Cotton
Forest		🌾	Cereals
High mountain regions		🌱	Tobacco
Wetland		🍊	Citrus fruits
Desert/tundra			

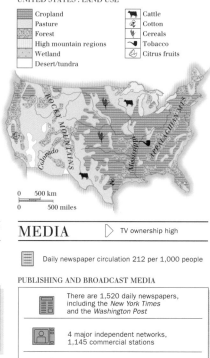

0   500 km
0   500 miles

ENVIRONMENT

▷ No Green MPs

13% (6% partially protected)

High

ENVIRONMENTAL TREATIES

🌿	Yes	🦏	Yes	🌐	No
	No		Yes	♻	Yes

The USA lags behind other Western countries on environmental issues, although environmental teaching is strong in schools. Food packaging is astonishingly wasteful and many automobiles are still "gas-guzzlers," despite laws aimed at cutting vehicle emissions. Genetically modified crops are widely grown. There is strong political opposition to any further regulation of free market activity. Oil companies and heavy fossil fuel users campaigned hard to stop government commitment to cutting down carbon dioxide emissions from fuel burning. The deal signed after the 1997 Kyoto conference, promising a 7% cut in US emissions by 2010, remains highly controversial. The intramontane west is a battleground between those wanting to maintain its beauty and those advocating "wise use" – in practice often giving ranchers and miners free rein.

MEDIA

▷ TV ownership high

Daily newspaper circulation 212 per 1,000 people

PUBLISHING AND BROADCAST MEDIA

📰	There are 1,520 daily newspapers, including the *New York Times* and the *Washington Post*
📺	4 major independent networks, 1,145 commercial stations
📻	7 major networks, 10,313 licensed commercial stations

Mass media as a phenomenon was born in the USA, where the internet, linking millions of users by computer, is the most recent of a series of communication revolutions. No other society has ever had anything quite like American network TV, or moved so easily into the world of multi-channel TV; homes with 50 or more channels are commonplace. Newspapers, however, are having a difficult time. With a few exceptions they are local, and also tend to have very low cover prices and to gain most of their revenue from advertising, a business under increasing threat from cable TV and other outlets. Many firms are exploring multimedia opportunities, investing in providing online news, information and other services.

U

CHRONOLOGY *continued*

- ❏ **1987** Intermediate Nuclear Forces Treaty signed by USA and USSR.
- ❏ **1988** Republican Vice-President George Bush wins presidency.
- ❏ **1989** Panama: US troops overthrow government, arrest ruler General Noriega on drug-trafficking charges.
- ❏ **1991** January–February, Gulf War against Iraq. USA and USSR sign START arms reduction treaty.
- ❏ **1992** Black youths riot in Los Angeles and other cities. Bush–Yeltsin summit agrees further arms reductions. Democrat Bill Clinton defeats Bush in elections.
- ❏ **1994** Legislation to reform health care system defeated in Congress.
- ❏ **1994** Special counsel investigation begins, over Clintons' financial dealings in Arkansas. Sexual harassment charges filed against Clinton by former Arkansas employee. Midterm elections result in Republican majorities in both houses of Congress.
- ❏ **1995** Oklahoma bomb kills more than 160 people in worst ever US terrorist incident. Conflict over budget between Clinton and Congress; temporary closures of government departments.
- ❏ **1996** Bomb kills two in Atlanta during Olympic Games there. President Clinton reelected, defeating Bob Dole.
- ❏ **1997** President Clinton starts second term; Madeleine Albright first woman to head State Department.
- ❏ **1998** Scandal over Clinton's affair with White House intern Monica Lewinsky leads to impeachment proceedings in Congress. August, bombing of US embassies in Kenya, Tanzania; revenge air strikes on Sudan, Afghanistan. December, air strikes against Iran.
- ❏ **1999** February, Clinton acquitted in Senate impeachment trial. April, Columbine High School shootings by two students. March–June, USA leads NATO involvement in Kosovo conflict, bombardment of Yugoslavia.

Bison in Yellowstone National Park.
The park's ecosystem is under severe strain due to the number of visitors it attracts.

CRIME

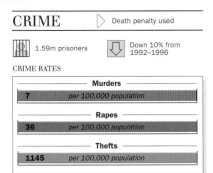

▷ Death penalty used

1.59m prisoners

⬇ Down 10% from 1992–1996

CRIME RATES

Murders	
7	per 100,000 population

Rapes	
36	per 100,000 population

Thefts	
1145	per 100,000 population

Violent crime – especially murder – is much more common than in other developed countries. This is the case even in relatively well-off parts of the country. Incidents of mass shootings have made gun control a major political issue, but a powerful lobby opposes restrictions, basing its arguments on the Constitution and the defense of individual liberties.

The rate of incarceration for narcotics crimes in the USA is much higher than in most Western countries. Capital punishment has made a strong comeback since the 1980s, especially in the south. Texas is the state that carries out most executions; most of the liberal "northern tier" states, by contrast, have abolished the death penalty.

EDUCATION

▷ School leaving age:16

99%

14.3m students

Education in the USA is primarily the responsibility of the state governments.

THE EDUCATION SYSTEM

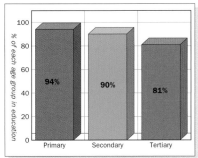

Recent reports critical of standards in US high schools cite problems of discipline and lack of resources in many areas as driving people away from the public education sector. Private education at secondary level continues to develop rapidly. While the number of Catholic private schools has shrunk, more nondenominational fee-paying schools have been founded.

Four out of every five high school students now go on to some form of tertiary college. The leading US universities are recognized internationally as being of world class.

HEALTH

▷ No welfare state health benefits

1 per 400 people

Heart and cerebrovascular diseases, cancers

Reform of the health care system, high on the political agenda, was blocked by Congress in President Clinton's first term.

Health provision is subject to enormous disparities. On one hand, sophisticated techniques are available to those with insurance (typically provided by their employer). The Texas Medical Center, in Houston, the epitome of high-tech medicine, has a budget equivalent to that of some small countries. On the other hand, treatment costs have skyrocketed, and facilities for those dependent on state medical care and aid are woefully underfunded. Preventive health care fails to reach all sections of society, and infant mortality statistics in some parts of the country are at near-African levels.

SPENDING

▷ GDP/cap. no increase

CONSUMPTION AND SPENDING

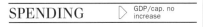
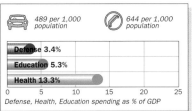

489 per 1,000 population

644 per 1,000 population

Defense 3.4%	
Education 5.3%	
Health 13.3%	

Defense, Health, Education spending as % of GDP

Between 1945 and 1973, all sectors of the population became richer. After that, however, a new pattern emerged, whereby those who finished high school saw their standard of living continue to rise, while those who did not do so saw no improvement. This "education effect" is leading to noticeable class divisions not seen for 50 years, despite the sustained economic boom of the Clinton years.

WORLD RANKING

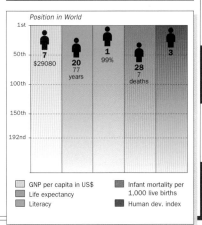

Position in World

- ☐ GNP per capita in US$
- ☐ Life expectancy
- ☐ Literacy
- ◼ Infant mortality per 1,000 live births
- ◼ Human dev. index

See also OVERSEAS TERRITORIES *p.640* 605

U

URUGUAY

SOUTH AMERICA

OFFICIAL NAME: Eastern Republic of Uruguay **CAPITAL:** Montevideo
POPULATION: 3.2 million **CURRENCY:** Uruguayan peso **OFFICIAL LANGUAGE:** Spanish

| 1828 | 1828 | Aug 25 | ROU | -3 | +598 | .uy |

URUGUAY IS SITUATED IN SOUTHEASTERN
South America. Its capital, Montevideo, is an
Atlantic port on the River Plate, lying across the river
from Buenos Aires, Argentina's capital. Uruguay became independent
in 1828, after nearly 150 years of Spanish and Portuguese control.
Decades of liberal government ended in 1973 with a military coup
that was to result in 12 years of dictatorship, during which 400,000
people emigrated. Most have since returned. Almost the entire
low-lying landscape is devoted to the rearing of livestock, especially
cattle and sheep. Uruguay is the world's second-biggest wool
exporter. Tourism and offshore banking now bring in
substantial foreign earnings.

Uruguayan grasslands. *Rich pasture covers
three-quarters of the country, ideal for cattle
and sheep. Animals and animal products
account for over one-third of export earnings.*

CLIMATE
▷ Subtropical

WEATHER CHART

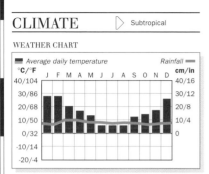

- Average daily temperature
- Rainfall

°C/°F — J F M A M J J A S O N D — cm/in
40/104 ... 40/16
30/86 ... 30/12
20/68 ... 20/8
10/50 ... 10/4
0/32 ... 0
-10/14
-20/-4

Uruguay has one of the most benign
climates in the world. It is uniformly
temperate over the whole country.
Winters are mild, frost is rare and it
never snows. Summers are generally
cool for these latitudes and rarely
tropically hot. The moderate rainfall
tends to fall in heavy showers, leaving
most days sunny.

TRANSPORTATION
▷ Drive on right

Carrasco, Montevideo
1.2m passengers

88 ships
100,100 grt

THE TRANSPORTATION NETWORK

| 52,000 km (32,311 miles) | 8,683 km (5,395 miles) |
| 2,073 km (1,288 miles) | 1,250 km (777 miles) |

Uruguay's transportation plans for the
1990s center on privatization. The
government has sold off its share in the
national bus industry – there are
extensive internal and international
coach and bus services – and has
closed down all passenger railroad
services. In 1998 the Senate gave the
go-ahead for a $1 billion, 45-km road
bridge across the River Plate from
Colonia to Buenos Aires.

TOURISM
▷ Visitors : population 1:1.4

2.3m visitors

Up 12% 1995–1997

MAIN TOURIST ARRIVALS

| Argentina 71% |
| Brazil 7% |
| Chile 1% |
| Other 21% |

0 10 20 30 40 50 60 70 80
% of total arrivals

Major attractions are sandy beaches
near the River Plate estuary. The old
Spanish fortifications of Montevideo
have been destroyed, but the city
retains a colonial atmosphere. Punta
del Este, 138 km (86 miles) east of the
capital, is the major beach resort.
Argentines account for over two-thirds
of visitors.

PEOPLE
▷ Pop. density low

Spanish

18/km² (47/mi²)

THE URBAN/RURAL POPULATION SPLIT

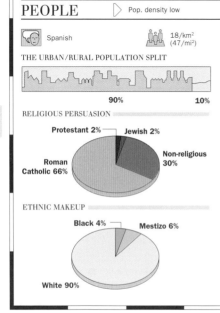

90%   10%

RELIGIOUS PERSUASION

Protestant 2% — Jewish 2%

Roman
Catholic 66%

Non-religious
30%

ETHNIC MAKEUP

Black 4%   Mestizo 6%

White 90%

Most Uruguayans are second- or third-
generation European, mostly of
Spanish or Italian descent. There are
also some *mestizos* and a small
minority of people descended from
Africans or immigrants from Brazil,
who live in or around the capital
Montevideo or near the Brazilian
border. All indigenous Amerindian
groups became integrated in the
mestizo population by the mid-19th
century. More recent immigrants
include Jews, Armenians and Lebanese.
Ethnic tensions are low. The birthrate
is low for Latin America.

The considerable prosperity derived
from cattle ranching allowed Uruguay
to become a welfare state long before
any other Latin American country. In
spite of Uruguay's serious economic
decline since the end of the 1950s,
there is still a sizable, if less
prosperous, middle class. A clear sign
of the country's economic and social
deterioration during the years of
military dictatorship was the
unprecedented growth of shanty towns
around Montevideo.

Although a Roman Catholic country,
Uruguay is liberal in its attitude to
religion of all forms is tolerated.
Divorce is legal. Women are regarded
as equal to men and have the vote.
There is no capital punishment.

POPULATION AGE BREAKDOWN

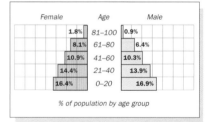

Female	Age	Male
1.8%	81–100	0.9%
8.1%	61–80	6.4%
10.9%	41–60	10.3%
14.4%	21–40	13.9%
16.4%	0–20	16.9%

% of population by age group

U

POLITICS ▷ Multiparty elections

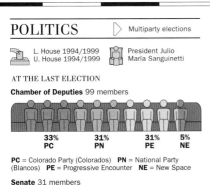

L. House 1994/1999
U. House 1994/1999

President Julio
María Sanguinetti

AT THE LAST ELECTION

Chamber of Deputies 99 members

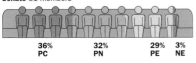

33%	31%	31%	5%
PC	PN	PE	NE

PC = Colorado Party (Colorados) PN = National Party
(Blancos) PE = Progressive Encounter NE = New Space

Senate 31 members

36%	32%	29%	3%
PC	PN	PE	NE

Uruguay is a presidential multiparty
democracy.

MAIN POLITICAL ISSUES
Future of economy

Almost 50% of Uruguay merchandise
exports are to Brazil and Argentina and
these are exposed to recession in both
countries. High public-sector
involvement in the economy, slow
privatization, and a low savings rate are
also concerns.

The aging population

Uruguay's long-established welfare
system is under strain from the
increasing proportion of elderly people
in the population. The emigration of
young workers to Europe and
Argentina is exacerbating the problem.

PROFILE

The elections of 1984 marked
Uruguay's return to democracy. Since
then the main *Colorado* (PC) and *Blanco*
(PN) parties have monopolized power,
either singly or in coalitions, despite
being traditional opponents. The
smaller left-wing Broad Front has been
the effective opposition, frequently
in alliance with trade unions fighting
austerity measures and reform of
the social security system. Despite
the crowded electoral calendar
in 1999, and in-fighting among *Blanco*
factions, there was broad political
consensus on the need for continuing
economic reform.

*Luis Alberto
Lacalle Herrera,
president from
1990–1995.*

*President Julio
María Sanguinetti,
who took office in
March 1995.*

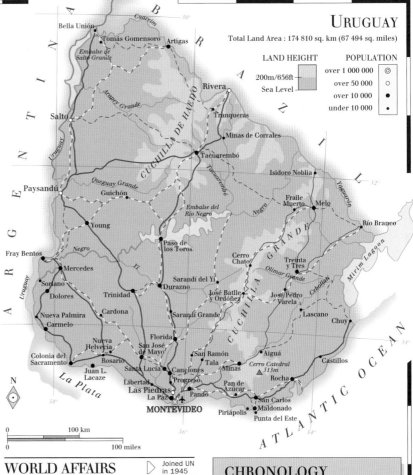

URUGUAY

Total Land Area : 174 810 sq. km (67 494 sq. miles)

LAND HEIGHT		POPULATION	
200m/656ft		over 1 000 000	◎
Sea Level		over 50 000	○
		over 10 000	●
		under 10 000	·

WORLD AFFAIRS ▷ Joined UN in 1945

IAEA Mercsr NAM OAS RG

Uruguay's chief foreign policy aim is
achieving full regional integration,
with Argentina, Brazil, and Paraguay,
in MERCOSUR, the common market of
southern South America. It considers
that its role has been reduced to being
a buffer state between Brazil and
Argentina. Uruguay is part of
a continental defense alliance with
other Latin American countries and
the USA. Ongoing border problems
exist with Brazil. Uruguay allowed
the UK to use its ports during the
Falklands conflict.

Uruguay and the USA have signed a
legal assistance treaty to allow easier
access to the bank accounts of those
suspected of laundering the proceeds
from narcotics trafficking. This has
increasingly been carried out through
Montevideo's liberal banking sector.

AID ▷ Recipient

💲 $57m (receipts)   ⬆ Up 12% 1996–1997

Uruguay received IMF-supported debt
reduction loans in the early 1990s, but
aid remains modest.

CHRONOLOGY

The Spaniards were the first to
colonize the area north of the River
Plate. In 1680, the Portuguese also
founded a colony there, at Colonia
del Sacramento, so starting 150
years of rivalry between the colonial
powers for control of the territory.

❑ **1726** Spaniards found Montevideo.
By end of century, whole country is
divided into large cattle ranches.

❑ **1808** Montevideo declares
independence from Buenos Aires.

❑ **1811** Patriotic rancher and local
caudillo, José Gervasio Artigas,
fends off Brazilian attack.

❑ **1812–1820** Uruguayans, known as
Orientales ("Easterners," from the
eastern side of the River Plate), fight
wars against Argentinian and
Brazilian invaders. Brazil finally
takes Montevideo.

❑ **1827** Gen. Lavalleja defeats
Brazilians with Argentine help.

❑ **1828** Seeing trade benefits that an
independent Uruguay would bring
as a buffer state between Argentina
and Brazil, Britain mediates and
secures Uruguayan independence.

❑ **1836** Start of large-scale European
immigration. ⇨

U

CHRONOLOGY *continued*

- ❏ **1838–1865** La Guerra Grande civil war between *Blancos* (Whites, future conservative party) and *Colorados* (Reds, future liberals).
- ❏ **1865–1870** *Colorado* president, Gen. Venancio Flores, takes Uruguay into War of the Triple Alliance against Paraguay.
- ❏ **1872** Peace under military rule. *Blancos* strong in country, *Colorados* in city.
- ❏ **1890s** Violent strikes by immigrant trade unionists against landed elite enriched by massive European investment in ranching.
- ❏ **1905–1907** Reformist *Colorado*, José Batllé y Ordóñez, president.
- ❏ **1911–1915** Batllé serves second term in office. *Batllismo* creates the only welfare state in Latin America with pensions, social security and free education and health service; also nationalizations, disestablishment of Church, abolition of death penalty.
- ❏ **1933** Military coup. Opposition groups excluded from politics.
- ❏ **1942** President Alfredo Baldomir dismisses government and tries to bring back proper representation.
- ❏ **1939–1945** Neutrality.
- ❏ **1951** New constitution replaces president with nine-member council. Decade of great prosperity follows until world agricultural prices plummet. Sharp drop in foreign investment.
- ❏ **1958** *Blancos* win elections for first time in 93 years.
- ❏ **1962** Tupamaros urban guerrillas founded. Its guerrilla campaign continues until 1973.
- ❏ **1966** Presidency reinstated. *Colorados* back in power.
- ❏ **1967** Jorge Pacheco president. Tries to stifle opposition to tough anti-inflation policies.
- ❏ **1973** Military coup. Promises to encourage foreign investment counteracted by denial of political freedom and brutal repression of the left; 400,000 emigrate.
- ❏ **1974** EEC bans meat imports.
- ❏ **1984** Military agrees to step down. Elections held.
- ❏ **1985** Julio Sanguinetti (*Colorado*) elected president.
- ❏ **1986** Those guilty of human rights abuse granted amnesty.
- ❏ **1988** Drought: one million cattle die.
- ❏ **1989** Referendum endorses amnesty in interests of stability. Elections won by Lacalle Herrera and *Blancos*. Attempt to include *Colorado* ministers fails.
- ❏ **1991** Signs MERCOSUR agreement.
- ❏ **1994–1995** Sanguinetti reelected, forms coalition government.
- ❏ **1995** MERCOSUR membership.

U

DEFENSE

▷ No compulsory military service

💲 $307m | ⬆ Up 8% in 1997

URUGUAYAN ARMED FORCES

🛡	15 main battle tanks (T-55)	17,600 personnel
🚢	3 frigates and 10 patrol boats	5,000 personnel
✈	33 combat aircraft (10 A37B, 6 T-33A)	3,000 personnel
	None	

The defense budget is modest; most equipment is bought from the USA. The military withdrew from power in 1984 and has since respected civilian rule. Four "lodges" operate within the army to promote officers' interests and in 1995 and 1996 some displayed opposition to the government's replacements and promotions within the military hierarchy. A 1986 law virtually blocked investigations into killings, torture and "disappearances" during the dictatorship, but there is still pressure to bring guilty officers to justice. A presidential decree in 1997 granted amnesty to officers punished for political offenses under military rule.

ECONOMICS

▷ Inflation 62.9% p.a. (1985–1996)

📊 $20bn | 💲 9.99–10.78 new Uruguayan pesos

SCORE CARD

- ❏ WORLD GNP RANKING..........................63rd
- ❏ GNP PER CAPITA $6,130
- ❏ BALANCE OF PAYMENTS....................$–321m
- ❏ INFLATION 19.8%
- ❏ UNEMPLOYMENT.................................10%

EXPORTS

Germany 4% — China 5% — USA 6% — Argentina 13% — Brazil 34% — Other 38%

IMPORTS

France 3% — Italy 5% — USA 12% — Argentina 21% — Brazil 22% — Other 37%

STRENGTHS

Substantial earnings from offshore banking. Buoyant tourism. Fertile grasslands. World's second-biggest wool exporter.

WEAKNESSES

Few natural resources. Dependence on Brazil and Argentine markets. Modest industry. State sector.

PROFILE

Traditionally an agricultural economy, three-quarters of the country is rich pasture, supporting livestock. Much of the rest is given over to crops. Farming, which formerly brought great wealth, still employs about 15% of the labor force, accounting for some 19% of GDP. Livestock and animal products, especially meat and wool, account for over one-third of export earnings. Manufacturing, accounting for some

ECONOMIC PERFORMANCE INDICATOR

Consumer price index / GDP

1305

18% of GDP, is farm-based. Tourism has become increasingly important. Most economic activity – and half the population – is concentrated in Montevideo. The Sanguinetti government has tightened public-sector management and increased private-sector participation in previously state-monopolized markets. It has cut its deficit significantly, inflation is at a 50-year low, and borrowing is manageable. However, Uruguay is vulnerable to recession in Brazil and Argentina.

URUGUAY : MAJOR BUSINESSES

Salto
Paysandú
Río Branco
Fray Bentos
Colonia del Sacramento
Durazno
Montevideo

- ⚙ Heavy engineering
- 🔋 Food processing
- 🛢 Oil refining
- 🧵 Wool spinning
- 🐄 Meat packing
- ✂ Leather
- ✳ Textiles

0 100 km
0 100 miles

RESOURCES

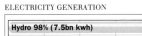
Electric power 2.1m kw

123,382 tonnes

Not an oil producer; refines 28,500 b/d

17.8m sheep, 10.5m cattle, 270,000 horses

Gold, iron, gemstones, copper, zinc, lead, manganese

Most of Uruguay is farmland, much of it given over to cattle and sheep. Rice is the country's only other significant crop on the world market. There are no known oil or natural gas resources. Mineral resources may be considerable, but have not yet been exploited. Small quantities of building materials and jewelry-quality agate and

ELECTRICITY GENERATION

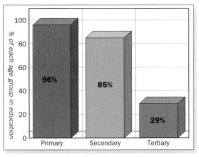

Hydro 98% (7.5bn kwh)

Combustion 2% (0.1bn kwh)

Nuclear 0%

Other 0%

% of total generation by type

amethysts are mined. Hydroelectric power generates most of the electricity. Its export offsets Uruguay's total dependence on imports for its oil needs.

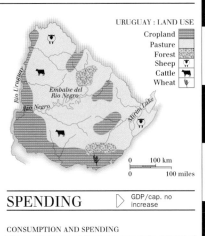

URUGUAY : LAND USE

Cropland
Pasture
Forest
Sheep
Cattle
Wheat

Río Uruguay
Río Negro
Embalse del Río Negro
Mirin Lake

0   100 km
0   100 miles

ENVIRONMENT

No Green MPs

1% (0.1% partially protected)

Medium

ENVIRONMENTAL TREATIES

Yes   Yes   Yes

Yes   Yes   Yes

Pollution of the main Uruguay and River Plate rivers is a concern, as is traffic density in Montevideo.

MEDIA

TV ownership medium

Daily newspaper circulation 296 per 1,000 people

PUBLISHING AND BROADCAST MEDIA

There are 36 daily newspapers, including *El País*, *El Diario* and *La Mañana*

1 state-owned, 3 independent services

2 state-owned, 160 independent stations

The press is relatively free. *El País* supports the *Blancos* (PN), while *La Mañana* backs the *Colorados* (PC).

CRIME

Death penalty not used

1,910 prisoners

Up 29% in 1990

CRIME RATES

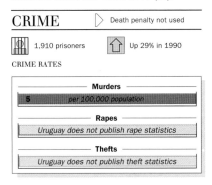

Murders
5   *per 100,000 population*

Rapes
Uruguay does not publish rape statistics

Thefts
Uruguay does not publish theft statistics

Crime levels in Uruguay are low, particularly compared with its neighbors Brazil and Argentina. Domestic theft is the main problem. Bribery is not common.

EDUCATION

School leaving age: 14

98%

79,691 students

Lowering the fiscal deficit has placed constraints on educational spending.

THE EDUCATION SYSTEM

% of each age group in education

Primary 96%
Secondary 85%
Tertiary 29%

Education, inspired by the French *lycée* system, is state-funded up to secondary level (12 years) and compulsory for all children between the ages of six and 14. Comprehensive reform to improve the quality and provision of public education is planned. Both state and private schools follow the same curriculum; private schools are monitored by the government. Facilities are rudimentary in rural areas. Uruguay has two state-funded universities. The children of wealthy Uruguayans tend to complete their studies in the USA.

HEALTH

Welfare state health benefits

1 per 313 people

Cerebrovascular and heart diseases, cancers, accidents

Health spending has recently suffered under government budget cuts and social security reforms.

Most Uruguayans have easy access to health services. Average life expectancy is high. Public services provide for 40% of the population, while the private sector caters for the remaining 60%. Despite opposition, the government has privatized some of the state medical establishments.

SPENDING

GDP/cap. no increase

CONSUMPTION AND SPENDING

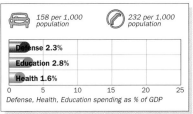

158 per 1,000 population

232 per 1,000 population

Defense 2.3%
Education 2.8%
Health 1.6%

0   5   10   15   20   25

Defense, Health, Education spending as % of GDP

Uruguay possesses the social mobility typical of countries created through decades of large-scale immigration. Many professionals come from modest backgrounds. A 1999 report by the IADB exempts Uruguay (along with Costa Rica and Jamaica) from the regional trend of serious income inequality.

The wealthy tend either to be landowners or are employed in the financial sector. They have traditionally looked toward Europe, rather than the USA, for luxury goods and the latest fashions.

The most deprived sections of Uruguayan society are the urban poor of Montevideo, a large proportion of whom are of mixed African and European descent, and the rural poor, who own little or no land.

WORLD RANKING

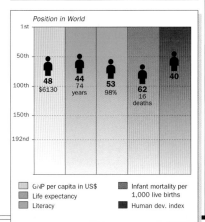

Position in World

1st
50th
100th
150th
192nd

48 $6130
44 74 years
53 98%
62 16 deaths
40

GNP per capita in US$
Life expectancy
Literacy

Infant mortality per 1,000 live births
Human dev. index

U

UZBEKISTAN

OFFICIAL NAME: Republic of Uzbekistan **CAPITAL:** Tashkent
POPULATION: 24.1 million **CURRENCY:** Som **OFFICIAL LANGUAGE:** Uzbek

CENTRAL ASIA
Kazakhstan
Kyrgyzstan
UZBEKISTAN
Turkmenistan Tajikistan
Afghanistan
Asia

| 1991 | 1991 | Sept 1 | UZ | +5 | +7 | .uz |

SHARING THE ARAL SEA coastline with its northern neighbor, Kazakhstan, Uzbekistan has common borders with five countries, including Afghanistan to the south. It is the most populous central Asian republic and has considerable natural resources. Uzbekistan contains the ancient Muslim cities of Samarkand, Bukhara, Khiva, and Tashkent. The dictatorship of President Karimov has prevented the spread of Islamic fundamentalism.

CLIMATE

Desert/mountain

WEATHER CHART

Average daily temperature   Rainfall

°C/°F
40/104
30/86
20/68
10/50
0/32
-10/14
-20/4
J F M A M J J A S O N D

cm/in
40/16
30/12
20/8
10/4
0

Uzbekistan has a harsh continental climate. Summers can be extremely hot and dry. Large areas of the country are desert.

TRANSPORTATION

Drive on right

Tashkent Intl   Has no fleet

THE TRANSPORTATION NETWORK

81,600 km (51,000 miles)	None	
3,461 km (2,163 miles)	1,100 km (688 miles)	

Uzbekistan has a well-developed transportation system. An extensive network of buses serves country areas, while good Soviet-style systems of trolley buses and trolleys operate in the major cities. Road and rail networks have, however, deteriorated since 1991, and are concentrated in the south and east. The national airline is *Uzbek Khavo Yullari* (Uzbekistan Airways).

TOURISM

Not available

Small numbers of tourists   Little change from year to year

MAIN TOURIST ARRIVALS

Uzbekistan does
not publish tourism
figures by
country of origin

0   10   20   30   40   50   60
% of total arrivals

Uzbekistan has considerable tourist potential. Bukhara, once a trading center on the silk route, is famous worldwide for its architecture and carpet-making. It has great religious significance for Muslims, who are encouraged to make at least one pilgrimage to its holy shrines. Bukhara's Kalyan Mosque is famous for its minaret built of unbaked bricks. The city of Samarkand was built in the 14th century by Timur, and contains the monumental gateway of the Shir Dar Madrasa, which vies with India's Taj Mahal as one of the most beautiful buildings in the Islamic world.

UZBEKISTAN

Total Land Area : 447 400 sq. km
(172 741 sq. miles)

LAND HEIGHT	POPULATION
3000m/9843ft	▣ over 1 000 000
2000m/6562ft	◉ over 100 000
1000m/3281ft	○ over 50 000
500m/1640ft	● over 10 000
200m/656ft	
Sea Level	

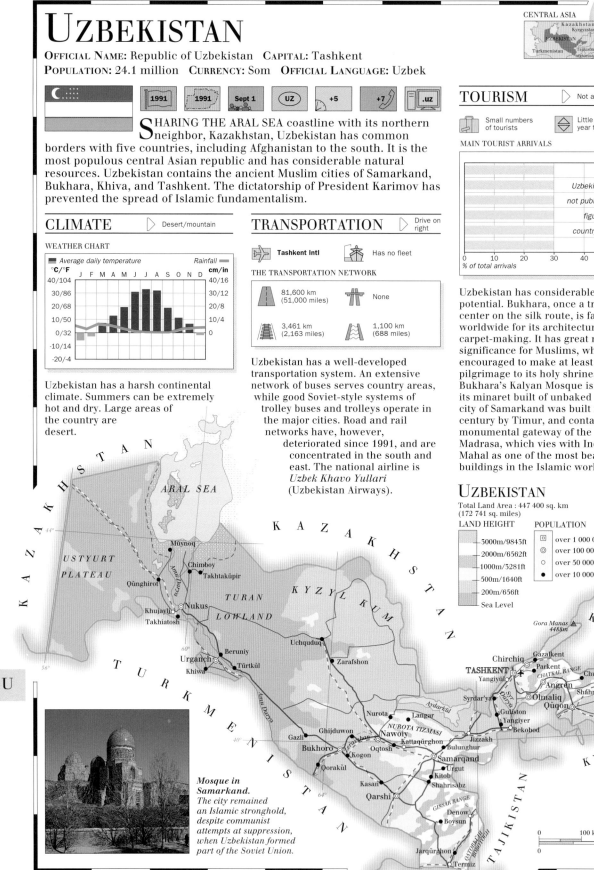

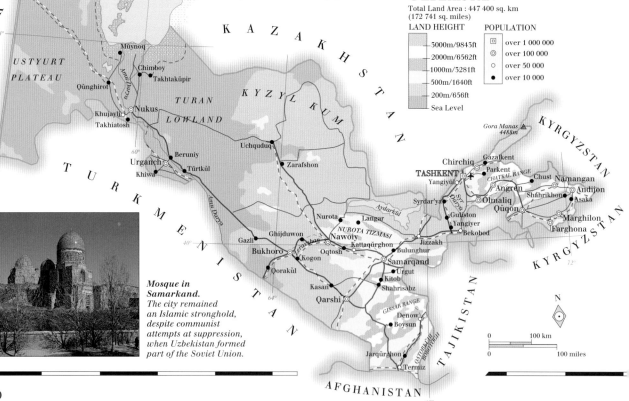

Mosque in Samarkand.
The city remained an Islamic stronghold, despite communist attempts at suppression, when Uzbekistan formed part of the Soviet Union.

0   100 km
0   100 miles

U

PEOPLE

▷ Pop. density medium

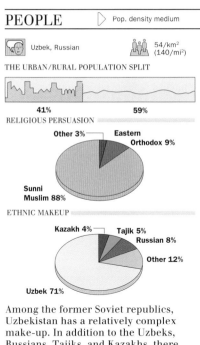

Uzbek, Russian

54/km²
(140/mi²)

THE URBAN/RURAL POPULATION SPLIT

41%   59%

RELIGIOUS PERSUASION

Other 3%   Eastern
            Orthodox 9%

Sunni
Muslim 88%

ETHNIC MAKEUP

Kazakh 4%   Tajik 5%
            Russian 8%
            Other 12%

Uzbek 71%

Among the former Soviet republics, Uzbekistan has a relatively complex make-up. In addition to the Uzbeks, Russians, Tajiks, and Kazakhs, there are small minorities of Tatars and Karakalpaks. The proportion of Russians has been declining since the 1970s, when net emigration of Russians began. Tensions among ethnic groups have the potential to create regional and racial conflict. The authoritarian nature of the Karimov leadership has so far prevented these antagonisms becoming violent. Incidents such as the 1989 and 1990 clashes between Meskhetian Turks and Uzbeks are rare. The removal of the Communist Party's leadership has meant that Uzbek society has reverted to traditional social patterns based on family, religion, clan and region, rather than on membership of the party. Independence has done little to alter the minor role of women in politics. Arranged marriages are still the custom in the countryside.

POPULATION AGE BREAKDOWN

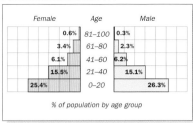

Female	Age	Male
0.6%	81–100	0.3%
3.4%	61–80	2.3%
6.1%	41–60	6.2%
15.5%	21–40	15.1%
25.4%	0–20	26.3%

% of population by age group

POLITICS

▷ Multiparty elections

1994/1999

President Islam
Karimov

AT THE LAST ELECTION

Supreme Assembly 250 members

66% LN	28% PDP	6% FP

LN = Local Nominees **PDP** = People's Democratic Party
FP = Fatherland Progress Party
Approximately 120 of the local council nominees were members of the PDP. The PDP and the FP were the only parties permitted to contest the elections.

Uzbekistan is effectively run by a presidential dictatorship.

MAIN POLITICAL ISSUES
Islamic fundamentalism
The civil war in neighboring Tajikistan has made the Karimov leadership wary of Islamic fundamentalism taking hold in Uzbekistan. The Uzbek constitution stipulates the separation of Islam and the state, and Islam has continued to be carefully kept out of politics.

Regionalism
Uzbekistan's high birth rate is placing pressure on the country's limited agricultural resources. There have been calls for secession from some regions wishing to stop large numbers of people moving from poorer areas. In the Fergana Valley, one of the country's most densely populated regions, there have been a number of violent incidents.

PROFILE
President Islam Karimov's People's Democratic Party of Uzbekistan (PDP) has not been willing to devolve or share power. A constitution adopted in December 1992 appeared to endorse multiparty politics along Western lines. However, Karimov took advantage of greater powers granted to his office by banning a number of opposition parties, including the nationalist *Birlik* (Unity) movement and the Islamic Renaissance Party. The only legal opposition party, *Erk* (Will), was proscribed in 1993, and in 1995 incurred the wrath of the government; as a result, a group of activists received stiff prison sentences after being found guilty of political subversion.

Opposition is now entirely underground. The intimidation and arbitrary imprisonment of political dissidents are common. Karimov has kept the support of the Russian minority by avoiding nationalist rhetoric.

Islam A Karimov,
first elected president
in 1990; his term has
been extended by
referendum until 2000.

WORLD AFFAIRS

▷ Joined UN
in 1992

CIS	ECO	OIC	NAM	OSCE

Unlike neighboring Turkmenistan, Kyrgyzstan, and Tajikistan, Uzbekistan has the resources to follow a relatively independent foreign policy. The Karimov leadership has used this to promote Uzbekistan as the leading central Asian state. It has established itself as the CIS power base in the region, and was a key player in the formation of a central Asian common market (with Kazakhstan and Kyrgyzstan) in 1994. In 1995, Karimov called for a common "Turkestan" republic comprising the five former Soviet central Asian republics, and later that year endorsed plans for a common central Asian defense council.

Relations with Turkey are also developing. While Western companies have difficulty in sealing contracts in Uzbekistan, Turkish companies have been commissioned to build vital installations such as telecommunications.

The crucial relationship, however, remains that with Russia, which has 100,000 troops stationed in the country. In 1994 there was, a bilateral treaty envisaging Uzbekistan's economic integration with Russia. Karimov's antinationalist approach to domestic politics has Russian support.

CHRONOLOGY

Part of the great Mongol empire, present-day Uzbekistan was incorporated into the Russian Empire between 1865 and 1876. Russification of the area was superficial, and it was not until Soviet rule that significant Slav immigration occurred. A further influx of Slavs into Uzbekistan occurred during Stalin's program of forced collectivization.

❏ **1917** Soviet power established in Tashkent.
❏ **1918** Turkestan Autonomous Soviet Socialist Republic (ASSR), incorporating present-day Uzbekistan, proclaimed.
❏ **1923–1941** Language changed four times, from Arabic alphabet to Latin, then based on Iranized Tashkent, and finally replaced by Cyrillic.
❏ **1924** Basmachi rebels who resisted Soviet rule crushed. Uzbek SSR founded (which, until 1929, included Tajik ASSR).
❏ **1925** Anti-Islamic campaign bans schools and closes mosques.
❏ **1936** Karakalpak ASSR (formerly part of the Russian Soviet Federative Socialist Republic) incorporated into the Uzbek SSR. ▷

U

CHRONOLOGY *continued*

- ❏ **1937** Stalin purges Uzbek communist leadership.
- ❏ **1941–1945** Industrial boom.
- ❏ **1959** Sharaf Rashidov becomes first secretary of CPUZ. Retains position until 1983.
- ❏ **1983** Yuri Andropov becomes president in Moscow. His anticorruption purge results in replacement of 40 party secretaries by a new generation of central Asian officials. Uzbekistan's managerial elite now youngest in USSR.
- ❏ **1989** First noncommunist political movement, Unity Party (*Birlik*), formed but not officially registered. June, clashes between Meskhetian Turks and indigenous Uzbek population of Fergana Valley leave more than 100 dead. October, *Birlik* campaign leads to Uzbek being declared the official language.
- ❏ **1990** March, Islam Karimov becomes executive president of new Uzbek Supreme Soviet. Further interethnic fighting in Fergana Valley; 320 killed.
- ❏ **1991** August, independence proclaimed. September, Republic of Uzbekistan adopted as official name. October, Uzbekistan signs treaty establishing economic community with seven other former Soviet republics. November, Communist Party of Uzbekistan restructured as the People's Democratic Party of Uzbekistan (PDPU). Karimov remains its leader. December, Karimov confirmed in post of president. Uzbekistan joins CIS.
- ❏ **1992** Price liberalization provokes student riots in Tashkent. New post-Soviet constitution adopted along Western democratic lines. All religious parties banned. September, Uzbekistan sends troops to Tajikistan to suppress violence and strengthen border controls.
- ❏ **1993** Growing harassment of opposition political parties, *Erk* and *Birlik*.
- ❏ **1994** March, signing of integration treaty with Russia. July, introduction of new currency, the som, which becomes sole legal tender in October.
- ❏ **1995** January, legislative elections won by Karimov's PDP. March, referendum extends Karimov's presidential term until 2000. April, Erk activists receive stiff prison sentences. December, Otkir Sultanov replaces Abdulhashim Mutalov as prime minister.

U

AID

▷ Recipient

$130m (receipts) ⬆ Up 106% 1996–1997

A lack of commitment to economic stabilization and allegations of human rights violations have generally deterred bilateral aid donors. The World Bank is the largest donor, allocating millions of dollars to support economic reform and a range of agricultural, financial, and social projects.

DEFENSE

▷ Compulsory military service

$447m ⬆ Up 1% in 1997

Uzbekistan has a 700-strong National Guard, which generally acts as the personal army of Karimov. Russian troops are still based on Uzbek territory to protect the Russian minority. In 1995, Uzbekistan approved a joint central Asian regional defense council with Kazakhstan and Kyrgyzstan.

President Karimov is a strong advocate of a nuclear-free zone in central Asia.

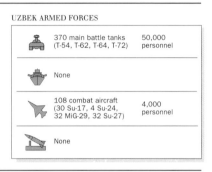

UZBEK ARMED FORCES

🛡	370 main battle tanks (T-54, T-62, T-64, T-72)	50,000 personnel
🚢	None	
✈	108 combat aircraft (30 Su-17, 4 Su-24, 32 MiG-29, 32 Su-27)	4,000 personnel
⚓	None	

ECONOMICS

▷ Not available

$24.2bn 465.00 som

SCORE CARD

- ❏ WORLD GNP RANKING..........................59th
- ❏ GNP PER CAPITA $1,020
- ❏ BALANCE OF PAYMENTS.....................$–53m
- ❏ INFLATION 70.9%
- ❏ UNEMPLOYMENT............Unemployment is rising

ECONOMIC PERFORMANCE INDICATOR

No additional information available

EXPORTS

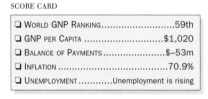

China 4%
Tajikistan 6%
Ukraine 6%
Italy 7%
Other 44%
Russia 32%

IMPORTS

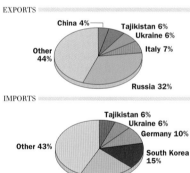

Tajikistan 6%
Ukraine 6%
Germany 10%
South Korea 15%
Other 43%
Russia 20%

Tashkent, which became an industrial area during World War II. Promarket reforms have been slow, despite fresh assistance from the World Bank to raise the efficiency of privatized companies. Rocketing food prices fueled by a 1,500% inflation rate led to rationing in early 1995. The gold sector has attracted investment by US companies. Energy resources are still to be fully exploited.

STRENGTHS

Gold. Well-developed cotton market. Considerable unexploited deposits of oil and natural gas. Current production of natural gas makes significant contribution to electricity generation. Manufacturing tradition includes agricultural machinery and central Asia's only aviation factory.

WEAKNESSES

Dependent on imports for grain, as it produces only 25% of domestic needs. Very limited economic reform. High inflation. Environmentally damaging irrigation scheme for cotton production.

PROFILE

Uzbekistan's economy is predominantly agricultural with the exception of

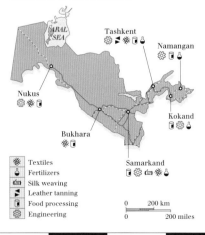

UZBEKISTAN : MAJOR BUSINESSES

Tashkent
Namangan
Nukus
Kokand
Bukhara
Samarkand
ARAL SEA

❄ Textiles
🌡 Fertilizers
🧵 Silk weaving
🔧 Leather tanning
📦 Food processing
⚙ Engineering

0   200 km
0   200 miles

RESOURCES

Electric
power 11.4m kw

6,500 tonnes

110,300 b/d

5.3m cattle,
8m sheep,
800,000 goats

Natural gas, coal, oil,
gold, uranium, copper,
tungsten, aluminum

As well as containing the world's largest single gold mine, at Murantau, Uzbekistan has large deposits of natural gas, petroleum, coal, and uranium. An important oilfield was discovered in 1992 in the Namangan region and production will rise with further investment. Most gas produced is currently used domestically, but gas could also become a strong export.

Cotton is the main focus of agriculture: Uzbekistan is the world's

ELECTRICITY GENERATION

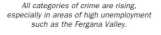

Hydro 15% (7.1bn kwh)
Combustion 85% (40.1bn kwh)
Nuclear 0%
Other 0%

| | | | | | |
|0|20|40|60|80|100|

% of total generation by type

fourth-largest producer. A post-independence decision to diversify was reversed when the value of cotton as a commodity on the world market became clear. Fruit, silk cocoons, and vegetables for Moscow's markets are also of rising importance.

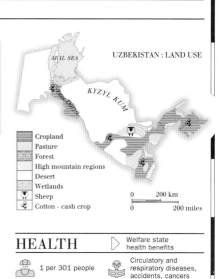

UZBEKISTAN : LAND USE

ARAL SEA

KYZYL KUM

Cropland
Pasture
Forest
High mountain regions
Desert
Wetlands
Sheep
Cotton - cash crop

0   200 km
0   200 miles

ENVIRONMENT

No Green
MPs

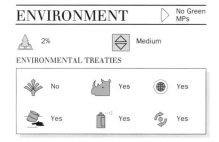

2%

Medium

ENVIRONMENTAL TREATIES

No

Yes

Yes

Yes

Yes

Yes

The irrigation schemes required to sustain Uzbekistan's cotton industry have wreaked considerable environmental damage. Soil salination is now a major problem. The Aral Sea has also been seriously depleted: by 2000 it is expected to have shrunk to an area of only 23,400 sq. km (9,035 square miles), just over one-third of its size in 1974. In 1998 the World Bank approved more than $11 million to save the Aral Sea region. The indiscriminate use of fertilizers and pesticides to raise production has polluted many rivers.

MEDIA

TV ownership high

Daily newspaper circulation 3 per 1,000 people

PUBLISHING AND BROADCAST MEDIA

There are 3 daily newspapers, including the Uzbek *Khaik Suzi* and the Russian *Narodnoye Slovo*

1 state-controlled service

1 state-controlled service broadcasting in several languages

Restrictions on independent publications, designed to encourage the promotion of the personality cult and policies of Karimov, were eased in mid-1998 with the publication of the first private newspaper. However, the opposition press is still closely monitored and the expression of Islamic and nationalist opinion forbidden.

CRIME

Death penalty used

Uzbekistan does not publish prison figures

Crime is rising

CRIME RATES

> *All categories of crime are rising, especially in areas of high unemployment such as the Fergana Valley.*

A decline in living standards has meant a general increase in crime. Many of the rural population grow drug plants, particularly opium poppies, to supplement their falling incomes. Unofficial Islamic courts set up by disaffected young men in the Fergana Valley are an indication of growing Muslim opposition to the government.

EDUCATION

School leaving age: 17

99%

638,200 students

Growing Islamic consciousness has encouraged mosques to rival schools as centers of learning.

THE EDUCATION SYSTEM

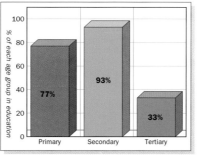

% of each age group in education

100	
80	**77%**
60	**93%**
40	
20	**33%**
0	
	Primary Secondary Tertiary

The system still follows the Soviet model, though some instruction is in Uzbek. In the late 1980s, there were a few ethnic Tajik schools and a university in Samarkand. These were closed down in 1992 as relations deteriorated between Uzbekistan and Tajikistan. Religious education through mosques has become widespread.

HEALTH

Welfare state
health benefits

1 per 301 people

Circulatory and respiratory diseases, accidents, cancers

The health service has been declining since the dissolution of the USSR. Some rural areas are not served by even the most rudimentary of health services. Serious respiratory diseases among cotton growers are increasing. Poor living conditions and inadequate health care have contributed to a sharp rise in cases of tuberculosis.

SPENDING

GDP/cap. no increase

CONSUMPTION AND SPENDING

No data

63 per 1,000 population

Defense 3.9%
Education 9.5%
Health 5.9%

| | | | | |
|0|5|10|15|20|25|

Defense, Health, Education spending as % of GDP

Former communists are still the wealthiest group, since they retain control of the economy. Many rural poor live below the poverty line.

WORLD RANKING

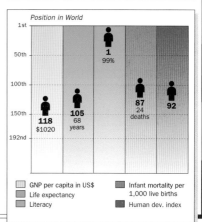

Position in World

Position	
1st	
50th	**1** 99%
100th	
150th	**105** 68 years **87** 24 deaths **92**
192nd	**118** $1020

GNP per capita in US$
Life expectancy
Literacy
Infant mortality per 1,000 live births
Human dev. index

U

VANUATU

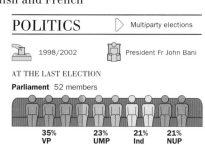
PACIFIC OCEAN

OFFICIAL NAME: Republic of Vanuatu **CAPITAL:** Port-Vila
POPULATION: 200,000 **CURRENCY:** Vatu **OFFICIAL LANGUAGES:** Bislama, English and French

1980 | 1980 | July 30 | VU | +11 | +678 | .vu

AN ARCHIPELAGO strung out over 1,300 km (800 miles) of the South Pacific, Vanuatu lies 1,000 km (620 miles) west of Fiji. Mountainous and volcanic in origin, only 12 of the 82 islands are of significant size – Espiritu Santo and Malekula are the largest. The capital, Port-Vila, is on Éfaté. Formerly the New Hebrides, Vanuatu became independent in 1980. Politics since independence have been democratic but volatile.

CLIMATE

▷ Tropical oceanic

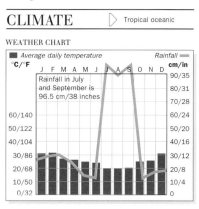
WEATHER CHART

The climate is tropical and hot. Rainfall and temperatures decrease north to south. Cyclones occur November–April.

TRANSPORTATION

▷ Drive on right

Bauerfield, Port-Vila
119 ships 1.7m grt

THE TRANSPORTATION NETWORK

| 250 km (155 miles) | None |
| None | None |

Frequent air and shipping services link the islands. State-owned *Air Vanuatu* flies to Australia and New Zealand.

TOURISM

▷ Visitors : population 1:4.1

49,000 visitors
Up 11% 1995–1997

MAIN TOURIST ARRIVALS

| Australia 54% |
| New Caledonia 13% |
| New Zealand 13% |
| Other 20% |

0 10 20 30 40 50 60
% of total arrivals

Tourism, concentrated on Éfaté, Espiritu Santo and Tanna, is the fastest-growing sector of the economy. Touring smaller islands is starting to occur.

PEOPLE

▷ Pop. density low

Bislama (Melanesian pidgin), English, French
16/km² (42/mi²)

THE URBAN/RURAL POPULATION SPLIT

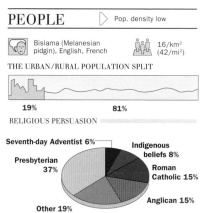
19% 81%

RELIGIOUS PERSUASION

- Seventh-day Adventist 6%
- Presbyterian 37%
- Indigenous beliefs 8%
- Roman Catholic 15%
- Anglican 15%
- Other 19%

Indigenous Melanesians, ni-Vanuatu, comprise 94% of the population. Of Vanuatu's 82 islands, 67 are inhabited, but 80% of people live on 12 main islands. The population is becoming more urbanized as one in eight ni-Vanuatu now lives in Port-Vila. However, 75% of the population still live by subsistence agriculture.

Vanuatu is home to some of the Pacific's most traditional peoples, and local social and religious customs are strong. With 105 indigenous languages, Vanuatu boasts the world's highest per capita density of languages. Bislama pidgin is the lingua franca.

Women have lower social status than men, and bride price is still commonly paid. Many educated women refuse to marry because of loss of property rights. To boost equality, primary schools must now take 50% girls.

Vanuatu's *unspoilt beaches are one of the reasons for the upsurge in the tourist industry.*

POLITICS

▷ Multiparty elections

1998/2002
President Fr John Bani

AT THE LAST ELECTION

Parliament 52 members

| 35% VP | 23% UMP | 21% Ind | 21% NUP |

VP = Vanua'aku Pati **UMP** = Union of Moderate Parties
Ind = Independents **NUP** = National United Party

France and Britain formerly ruled Vanuatu jointly. Political instability in the islands contributed to France's reluctance – not shared by the UK – to grant independence in 1980. The anti-French stance of the Vanua'aku Party (Our Land Party – VP), in power in 1980–1991, was reinforced by French support for the short-lived 1980 secession of Espiritu Santo. Rivalries and splits in the VP culminated in a constitutional crisis in 1988, when President Sokomanu backed a bid to oust Prime Minister Walter Lini. It failed and Fred Timakata became president, but Lini's increasingly autocratic stance led to his 1991 dismissal by the VP.

The opposition francophone UMP won the 1991 elections and formed an anti-VP coalition including the NUP set up by Lini. Despite factional fighting, the coalition was returned in 1995. President Jean-Marie Leye Lenelgau dissolved the parliament in 1997. A new VP-led government based on patching up relations with Lini was formed after the 1998 elections. Lini died the following year.

WORLD AFFAIRS

▷ Joined UN in 1981

ACP | Comm | NAM | SPC | SPF

Vanuatu was the first South Pacific nation to gain full membership of the Non-Aligned Movement. Relations with France have improved since the 1993 bilateral cooperation agreement.

AID

▷ Recipient

$27m (receipts)
Down 13% 1996–1997

Vanuatu is Melanesia's most aid-dependent state. Leading donors are Australia, New Zealand, the UK, Japan, and France. In 1997 Vanuatu asked to be reclassified by the UN under "least developed country" to receive more aid support.

V

DEFENSE

▷ No compulsory military service

 There are no military forces

Not applicable

There is a small paramilitary force. Papua New Guinea troops helped to end the 1980 secessionist movement on Espiritu Santo under a defense agreement signed after independence.

ECONOMICS

▷ Inflation 6.2% p.a. (1985-1996)

$238m

123.96–130.50 vatu

SCORE CARD

❏ WORLD GNP RANKING	178th
❏ GNP PER CAPITA	$1,340
❏ BALANCE OF PAYMENTS	$–19m
❏ INFLATION	2.8%
❏ UNEMPLOYMENT	Low rate

STRENGTHS

Expanding services sector, including tourism and offshore finance. Major economic reforms recently instituted, including the introduction of a 12.5% value added tax and resizing of the public service in return for assistance from the Asian Development Bank.

WEAKNESSES

Large trade and budget deficits. Rate of growth has stagnated in recent years, averaging just over 2%. Dependence on agricultural sector, vulnerable to adverse weather and fluctuating market prices. Shortage of skilled indigenous labor.

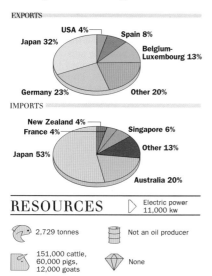

EXPORTS

USA 4%
Japan 32%
Spain 8%
Belgium-Luxembourg 13%
Germany 23%
Other 20%

IMPORTS

New Zealand 4%
France 4%
Singapore 6%
Japan 53%
Other 13%
Australia 20%

RESOURCES

▷ Electric power 11,000 kw

2,729 tonnes

Not an oil producer

151,000 cattle, 60,000 pigs, 12,000 goats

None

Vanuatu's main resources are its arable land – only 17% is utilized – and its forests and waters. These could be exploited by the tourist, timber and fishing industries. New export crops are being explored to offset declining copra and cocoa exports. Beef is of growing importance. Nuclear power development was banned under 1983 legislation.

VANUATU

Total Land Area : 12 190 sq. km
(4707 sq. miles)

POPULATION
over 10 000 ●
under 10 000 ·

LAND HEIGHT

1000m/3281ft
500m/1640ft
200m/656ft
Sea Level

0   100 km
0   100 miles

ENVIRONMENT

▷ No Green MPs

None

Not applicable

Logging is growing, but 75% of the rain forest remains and round log exports are banned. Population growth is high, at 2% a year, but not yet a major problem. A majority of the population does not have access to a potable and reliable water supply.

MEDIA

▷ TV ownership low

There are no daily newspapers

PUBLISHING AND BROADCAST MEDIA

There are no daily newspapers. *Vanuatu Weekly* is published weekly by the government

1 state-owned limited service

1 state-owned service

The *Vanuatu Weekly* appears in three languages. Television Blong Vanuatu broadcasts four hours a day.

CRIME

▷ Death penalty not used

Vanuatu does not publish prison figures

Little change from year to year

Domestic violence apart, Vanuatu is almost crime-free, unlike other Melanesian states.

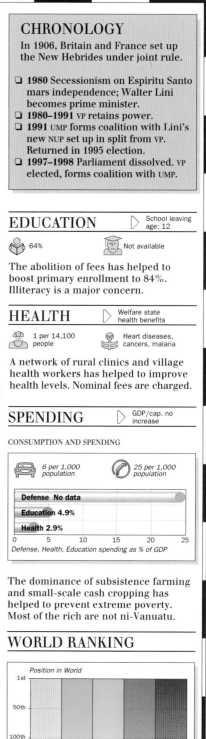

CHRONOLOGY

In 1906, Britain and France set up the New Hebrides under joint rule.

❏ **1980** Secessionism on Espiritu Santo mars independence; Walter Lini becomes prime minister.
❏ **1980–1991** VP retains power.
❏ **1991** UMP forms coalition with Lini's new NUP set up in split from VP. Returned in 1995 election.
❏ **1997–1998** Parliament dissolved. VP elected, forms coalition with UMP.

EDUCATION

▷ School leaving age: 12

64%

Not available

The abolition of fees has helped to boost primary enrollment to 84%. Illiteracy is a major concern.

HEALTH

▷ Welfare state health benefits

1 per 14,100 people

Heart diseases, cancers, malaria

A network of rural clinics and village health workers has helped to improve health levels. Nominal fees are charged.

SPENDING

▷ GDP/cap. no increase

CONSUMPTION AND SPENDING

6 per 1,000 population

25 per 1,000 population

Defense	No data
Education	4.9%
Health	2.9%

0   5   10   15   20   25
Defense, Health, Education spending as % of GDP

The dominance of subsistence farming and small-scale cash cropping has helped to prevent extreme poverty. Most of the rich are not ni-Vanuatu.

WORLD RANKING

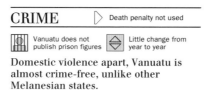

Position in World

1st
50th
100th
150th
192nd

179 $238
114 67 years
148 64%
115 37 deaths
116

GNP per capita in US$
Life expectancy
Literacy
Infant mortality per 1,000 live births
Human dev. index

VATICAN CITY

OFFICIAL NAME: State of the Vatican City **CAPITAL:** Vatican City
POPULATION: 1,000 **CURRENCY:** Lira **OFFICIAL LANGUAGES:** Italian and Latin

| 1929 | 1929 | Oct 22 | V | +1 | +39 | .va |

T HE VATICAN CITY lies close to the Tiber in central Rome and is a fully independent state. It also includes ten other buildings in Rome and the pope's residence at Castel Gandolfo. As the Holy See, it is the seat of the Catholic Church, deriving its income from investments and voluntary contributions known as Peter's Pence.

The buildings and gardens of the Vatican City. St. Peter's Basilica was built from 1506–1626 on the traditional site of St. Peter's tomb.

CLIMATE ▷ Mediterranean

WEATHER CHART

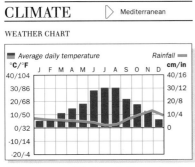

Winters are mild, though November is particularly gray, and summers are hot.

TRANSPORTATION ▷ Drive on right

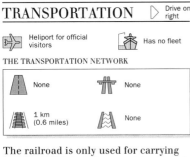

Heliport for official visitors

Has no fleet

THE TRANSPORTATION NETWORK

None   None   1 km (0.6 miles)   None

The railroad is only used for carrying freight. Official visitors are transferred from Rome airport by helicopter.

TOURISM ▷ Not available

The Vatican Museums can accommodate 20,000 visitors daily

Little change from year to year

MAIN TOURIST ARRIVALS

Most visitors come from Italy, Germany, Spain, Central and South America. Numbers from eastern Europe are rising.

% of total arrivals

Almost all tourists who visit Rome visit the Vatican, while others come as pilgrims. Up to 100,000 hear the pope's annual Easter Message in St. Peter's Square. The Vatican's art collections are among the greatest in the world. Years of restoration work on the Sistine Chapel frescoes were completed in 1994.

PEOPLE ▷ Pop. density high

Italian, Latin

2,273/km² (5,886/mi²)

THE URBAN/RURAL POPULATION SPLIT

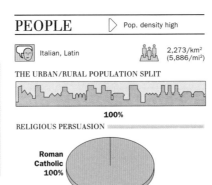

100%

RELIGIOUS PERSUASION

Roman Catholic 100%

The Vatican has about 1,000 permanent inhabitants, including several hundred lay persons, and employs a further 3,400 lay staff. Citizenship can be acquired through stable residence and holding an office or job within the City. A citizen's family can gain residence only by authorization.

The pope is spiritual head of almost 18% of the world's population. The countries with the largest number of Roman Catholics are Brazil, Mexico, Italy, the USA, and the Philippines.

POLITICS ▷ No multiparty elections

On death of reigning Pope

His Holiness Pope John Paul II

LEGISLATIVE OR ADVISORY BODIES

College of Cardinals 120 members

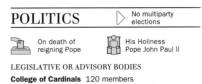

120 Cardinals are eligible to elect a new Pope. There are no political parties.

The Vatican City operates in the manner of an elected monarchy, as the reigning pope has supreme executive, legislative, and judicial powers, and holds office for life. He is elected by 120 members of the College of Cardinals, who vote until one candidate for the position of Supreme Pontiff achieves a two-thirds majority.

The administration of the Vatican City State, of which the pope is temporal head, is conducted by the Pontifical Commission. The Holy See, which is the governing body of the Catholic Church worldwide and of which the pope is spiritual head, is governed by the Roman Curia, the Church's administrative network. It is the Holy See that maintains diplomatic relations abroad. Pope John Paul II, elected in 1978, is the first non-Italian Pope since 1523.

VATICAN CITY

Total Land Area : 0.44 sq. km (0.17 sq. miles)

Main Entrance

Pigna Courtyard

Vatican Museums

Vatican

ROME

Monte Vaticano

Radio Vatican

Gardens

Belvedere Courtyard

Raphael Stanza

Sistine Chapel

Papal apartments

C Papal Heliport

Vatican Railway Station

Saint Peter's Basilica

St Peter's Square

ROME

0   200 metres
0   800 feet

N

WORLD AFFAIRS

 Not a member of the UN

The Vatican maintains a neutral stance in world affairs and has observer status in many international organizations. It has mediated in many conflicts, notably achieving the 1993 peace agreement in Mozambique. Pope John Paul II has traveled more extensively than any other pope to promote peace, overcome religious and racial discrimination, support the rights of minorities, whether foreign or indigenous, and to spread Roman Catholicism. The Holy See now has diplomatic relations with Russia and other former Soviet-bloc countries, and in 1993 the pope reestablished the Catholic Church in previously atheist Albania.

AID

 Donor

Undisclosed   Undisclosed

Aid is donated through the Pope's Charities (such as The Holy Childhood Association, which distributes $15 million a year for children's causes), through funds donated for use at the pope's discretion, and through religious orders acting under papal charter.

DEFENSE

No compulsory military service

Ceremonial Swiss Guard only   Not applicable

The Vatican is strictly neutral territory. Under the 1954 Hague Convention, it is recognized as "a moral, artistic and cultural patrimony worthy of being respected as a treasure for all mankind."

ECONOMICS

Not applicable

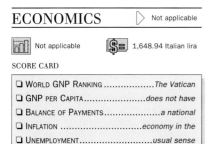

Not applicable   1,648.94 Italian lira

SCORE CARD

- ❏ WORLD GNP RANKING ....*The Vatican*
- ❏ GNP PER CAPITA......................*does not have*
- ❏ BALANCE OF PAYMENTS...................*a national*
- ❏ INFLATION ....*economy in the*
- ❏ UNEMPLOYMENT.........................*usual sense*

STRENGTHS

Istituto per le Opere di Religione has assets of $3–$4 billion. Voluntary contributions from Catholics worldwide (Peter's Pence). Interest on investments. Gold reserves in Fort Knox, USA. Stamp and coin issues. Budgetary deficit of 23 years reversed to modest surplus in 1993.

WEAKNESSES

Losses incurred by Vatican radio and newspaper, cost of foreign papal visits, buildings maintenance and diplomatic missions. Repayment of creditors from Banco Ambrosiano bankruptcy in 1982.

EXPORTS/IMPORTS

The Vatican produces no goods for export. All commodities are imported, mainly from Italy.

RESOURCES

Not applicable

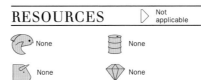

None   None

None   None

The Vatican imports all its energy. It has no farmland as its area is restricted to buildings and their formal gardens.

ENVIRONMENT

No Green MPs

None   Medium

The Vatican is increasingly concerned about the need to balance development and conservation. In 1993, the Pope urged a gathering of scientists to press colleagues worldwide to inform people on the need to protect the environment.

MEDIA

TV ownership medium

 Daily newspaper circulation figures not available

PUBLISHING AND BROADCAST MEDIA

There is one daily newspaper, *L'Osservatore Romano*, which is also published weekly in 5 European languages, and monthly in Polish

1 state-owned service   1 state-owned service

The Vatican produces its own religious TV programs, but has no transmitter. Its radio broadcasts in 37 languages.

CRIME

Death penalty not used

There are no prisons in the Vatican City   Minimal crime levels

The reputation of the 105-strong Swiss Guard was shaken in 1998 when a young guard shot dead his commandant and the latter's wife and then committed suicide. Three Vatican Bank officials were earlier alleged to have been involved in the Banco Ambrosiano affair.

EDUCATION

Not applicable

99%   14,403 students

The university, founded by Gregory XIII, is renowned for its theological and philosophical learning. There are more than 110,000 Catholic primary and secondary schools around the world.

CHRONOLOGY

The Vatican is located in Rome because tradition held that St. Peter was buried on the site of the Church of Constantine, which was pulled down in the Renaissance to make way for the building of St. Peter's Basilica. The Vatican has been the pope's usual residence since 1417, when the pontiffs returned from Avignon in France at the end of the 39 years of Great Schism.

- ❏ **1870** Italy occupies Papal States – 41,500 sq. km (16,000 square miles) in central Italy.
- ❏ **1929** Lateran Treaty – Italy recognizes Vatican City as independent state.
- ❏ **1978** Cardinal Karol Wojtyla pope.
- ❏ **1981–1982** Attempts on pope's life.
- ❏ **1984** Catholicism disestablished as Italian state religion.
- ❏ **1985** Catholic Catechism revised for first time since 1566.
- ❏ **1994–1995** Vatican reiterates opposition to contraception and abortion at UN Population Conference in Cairo and UN Women's Conference in Beijing.
- ❏ **1998** Statement repenting Catholic passivity during Nazi Holocaust.

HEALTH

Welfare state health benefits

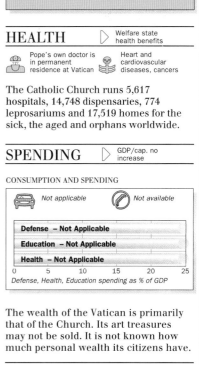

Pope's own doctor is in permanent residence at Vatican   Heart and cardiovascular diseases, cancers

The Catholic Church runs 5,617 hospitals, 14,748 dispensaries, 774 leprosariums and 17,519 homes for the sick, the aged and orphans worldwide.

SPENDING

GDP/cap. no increase

CONSUMPTION AND SPENDING

Not applicable   Not available

Defense	– Not Applicable
Education	– Not Applicable
Health	– Not Applicable

0   5   10   15   20   25
Defense, Health, Education spending as % of GDP

The wealth of the Vatican is primarily that of the Church. Its art treasures may not be sold. It is not known how much personal wealth its citizens have.

WORLD RANKING

The Pope and his Vatican staff enjoy one of the highest standards of living in the world.

V

VENEZUELA

OFFICIAL NAME: Republic of Venezuela **CAPITAL:** Caracas **POPULATION:** 23.2 million
CURRENCY: Bolívar **OFFICIAL LANGUAGES:** Spanish and Amerindian languages

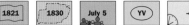

1821 1830 July 5 YV -4 +58 .ve

L OCATED ON THE northern coast of South America, Venezuela's vast central plain is drained by the Orinoco, while the Guiana Highlands dominate the southwest of the country. A Spanish colony until 1811, Venezuela was lauded as Latin America's most stable democracy. Recent political upheavals have, however, led to fears of instability. With one of the largest known oil deposits outside the Middle East, Venezuela still has much of its population living in shanty-town squalor.

Carlos Andrés Pérez, AD leader, who was deposed from the presidency in 1993.

Dr Rafael Caldera Rodríguez, who won the presidency for a second time in 1994.

CLIMATE
▷ Tropical wet & dry/ equatorial

WEATHER CHART

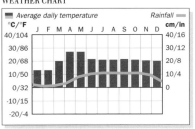

The hot Maracaibo coast is surprisingly dry; the Orinoco *Llanos* are alternately parched or flooded. Uplands are cold.

TRANSPORTATION
▷ Drive on right

Simón Bolívar Intl, Caracas
6.94m passengers

239 ships
697,200 grt

THE TRANSPORTATION NETWORK

29,954 km (18,613 miles)	2,690 km (1,671 miles)
402 km (250 miles)	7,100 km (4,412 miles)

Massive road-building from the 1960s onwards has benefited the oil and aluminum industries.The French-designed Caracas subway was completed in 1995. Work on the Centro–Occidental highway and other major roads is ongoing, as is rail development.

The Orinoco. Its huge Llanos (plains) are grazed by five million cattle, which are herded down close to the river in the dry season.

TOURISM
▷ Visitors : population 1:29

796,000 visitors

Up 33% 1995–1997

MAIN TOURIST ARRIVALS

USA 25%
Italy 9%
Spain 8%
Germany 7%
Netherlands 6%
Other 45%

% of total arrivals

Tourism is still a relatively minor industry in Venezuela, but one with enormous potential. Venezuela has many beaches that are the equal of any Caribbean island's, and a fascinating jungle interior which is a target for ecotourists. For many years, the high value of the bolívar made Venezuela an expensive destination but, after recent devaluations, it has become one of the cheapest in the Caribbean. Privatizing state-run hotels was part of a drive to attract foreign investment.

PEOPLE
▷ Pop. density low

Spanish, Amerindian languages

26/km² (68/mi²)

THE URBAN/RURAL POPULATION SPLIT

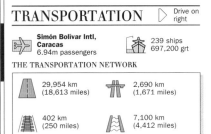

93%   7%

RELIGIOUS PERSUASION

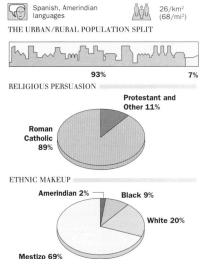

Protestant and Other 11%

Roman Catholic 89%

ETHNIC MAKEUP

Amerindian 2%
Black 9%
White 20%
Mestizo 69%

Venezuela is one of the most highly urbanized societies in Latin America, with most of its population living in cities, mainly in the north. Historically a "melting pot," it has experienced large-scale immigration from Italy, Portugal, Spain, and all over Latin America. There is little of the white Hispanic aristocracy that survives in Colombia and Ecuador. The small number of native Indians, such as the

Yanomami, live in remote regions which are now threatened by illegal settlers. Most of the black population, descended from Africans brought over to work in the cacao industry in the 19th century, live along the Caribbean coast.

Oil wealth has brought comparative prosperity, but life in the *barrios* (shanty towns), which sprawl over the hillsides around Caracas, is one of extreme poverty. Discontent peaked in the food riots of 1989 and 1991, which left scores dead, along with the country's reputation for being a model democracy. The oil boom accelerated change for women, who today find employment in all the professions. Politics, however, remains a largely masculine preserve. Oil wealth also brought Americanization – boxing and baseball are among the most popular sports.

POPULATION AGE BREAKDOWN

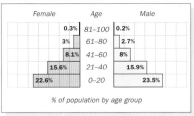

Female	Age	Male
0.3%	81–100	0.2%
3%	61–80	2.7%
8.1%	41–60	8%
15.6%	21–40	15.9%
22.6%	0–20	23.5%

% of population by age group

VENEZUELA

Total Land Area : 882 050 sq. km
(340 560 sq. miles)

POPULATION

▣	over 1 000 000
⊙	over 500 000
◎	over 100 000
○	over 50 000
●	over 10 000

LAND HEIGHT

	3000m/9843ft
	2000m/6562ft
	1000m/3281ft
	500m/1640ft
	Sea Level
-- -	Projected Railway

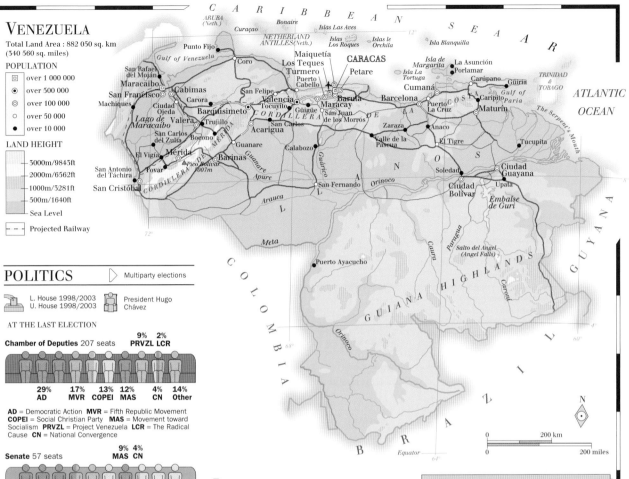

POLITICS   ▷ Multiparty elections

L. House 1998/2003 U. House 1998/2003	President Hugo Chávez

AT THE LAST ELECTION

Chamber of Deputies 207 seats

				9% PRVZL	2% LCR

29% AD	17% MVR	13% COPEI	12% MAS	4% CN	14% Other

AD = Democratic Action **MVR** = Fifth Republic Movement
COPEI = Social Christian Party   **MAS** = Movement toward
Socialism **PRVZL** = Project Venezuela **LCR** = The Radical
Cause **CN** = National Convergence

Senate 57 seats

		9% MAS	4% CN

35% AD	14% MVR	12% COPEI	26% Other

Venezuela is a democracy, holding
multiparty elections.

MAIN POLITICAL ISSUES
Political and judicial reform
President Chávez's fiery rhetoric and
populist stance won him the presidency
in 1998, with strong support among
the poor. He set out to rewrite the
constitution, reform the Congress and
the judiciary and by calling elections
to a new Constituent Assembly. This
body convened in August 1999 and
took over many of the powers of the
existing Congress, provoking protests
from Chávez's opponents who called
it an effective *coup d'état*.

Trimming the state sector
The sharp decline in oil revenues
has produced the highest budget
deficit this century. The left-leaning
Chávez has pledged to reform the
bloated state sector, while advocating
tax reform, but he may be unable to
finance the huge deficit without
recourse to unpopular measures
approved by the IMF.

PROFILE
Official corruption, austerity, rising
poverty and anti-price-rise riots in
Caracas were the backdrop for two coup
attempts in 1992. One of these was led
by Chávez, whose election as president
in 1998 broke the stranglehold on power
of the traditional parties. Economic
recession weighs against radical social
and economic change being delivered.

WORLD AFFAIRS   ▷ Joined UN in 1945

Venezuela has traditionally been seen
as pro-US, since the USA was the
destination of most of its oil exports
and the source of its imports. Although
a pragmatist, President Chávez wants
to steer a more independent line,
especially in relation to Cuba.

Ongoing objectives are support of oil
prices and quotas within OPEC, closer
economic integration with the
Caribbean region and Andean
neighbors, and a free-trade agreement
with MERCOSUR. Oil-sector marketing
and technology cooperation has been
agreed with Brazil.

There are ongoing border disputes
with Colombia and Guyana.

CHRONOLOGY

Venezuela was the first of the Spanish
imperial colonies to repudiate Madrid's
authority under the guidance of the
revolutionary, Simón Bolívar, in 1811.

❑ **1821** Battle of Carabobo finally
overthrows Spanish rule and leads
to consolidation of independence
within Gran Colombia (Venezuela,
Colombia, and Ecuador).

❑ **1830** Gran Colombia collapses. José
Antonio Páez rules Venezuela;
coffee planters effectively in control.

❑ **1870** Guzmán Blanco in power.
Attracts foreign investment to build
rail system.

❑ **1908** Gen. Juan Vicente Gómez
dictator; oversees development of
oil industry.

❑ **1935** Gómez falls from power.
Increasing mass participation in
political process.

❑ **1945** Military coup overthrows
General Isías Medina Angarita.
Rómulo Betancourt of AD takes
power as leader of a civilian–
military junta.

❑ **1948** February, AD wins elections,
with novelist Rómulo Gallegos as
presidential candidate.   ➮

V

CHRONOLOGY *continued*

- ❑ **1948** Gallegos overthrown in military coup. Marcos Pérez Jiménez forms government, with US and military backing.
- ❑ **1958** General strike. Admiral Larrázabal leads military coup deposing Jiménez government.
- ❑ **1958** Free elections. Betancourt, newly returned from exile, wins presidential election as AD candidate. Anticommunist campaign mounted. A few state welfare programs introduced.
- ❑ **1960** Movement of the Revolutionary Left (MIR) splits from AD, begins antigovernment activities.
- ❑ **1961** Venezuela becomes a founder member of OPEC.
- ❑ **1962** Communist-backed guerrilla warfare attempts repetition of Cuban revolution in Venezuela. Fails to gain popular support.
- ❑ **1963** Raúl Leoni (AD) elected president – the first democratic transference of power in Venezuelan history. Antiguerrilla campaign continues.
- ❑ **1966** Unsuccessful coup attempt by supporters of former president, Pérez Jiménez.
- ❑ **1969** Elections. Rafael Caldera Rodríguez of the Social Christian Party (COPEI) becomes president. Continues Leoni policies.
- ❑ **1973** Elections. Oil and steel industries nationalized. World oil crisis. Venezuelan currency peaks in value against the US dollar.
- ❑ **1978** Elections won by COPEI's Luis Herrera Campíns. Disastrous economic programs.
- ❑ **1983** Elections. AD victory under Jaime Lusinchi. Fall in world oil prices leads to unrest and cuts in state welfare.
- ❑ **1988–1989** Carlos Andrés Pérez wins elections for AD. Caracas food riots; 1,500 dead.
- ❑ **1993** Andrés Pérez ousted on charges of corruption.
- ❑ **1994–1995** Caldera Rodríguez reelected. Civil and economic rights temporarily suspended.
- ❑ **1998–1999** Elections. Hugo Chávez's Patriotic Front coalition defeats COPEI-led coalition; Chávez embarks on political reform.
- ❑ **1999 August.** Controversial Constitutional Assembly elected, assumes wide-ranging powers.

AID ▷ Recipient

$28m (receipts)   Down 36% 1996–1997

Aid from the IADB is in support of long-term reform of the social security system.

V

DEFENSE ▷ Compulsory military service

$962m   Up 18% in 1997

President Chávez has named military officers to run key ministries.

Relatively junior officers, opposed to the austerity policies and corruption, staged coup attempts in 1992, one being led by Hugo Chávez, who as president has deployed members of the armed forces as the "spearhead of social development" to improve the economic and social infrastructure.

VENEZUELAN ARMED FORCES

70 main battle tanks (AMX-30)	34,000 personnel
2 submarines, 6 frigates and 6 patrol boats	15,000 personnel
116 combat aircraft (15 CF-5A/B, 7 NF-5A/B, 7 *Mirage*, 23 F-16A/B)	7000 personnel
None	

ECONOMICS ▷ Inflation 42% p.a. (1985–1996)

$79bn   504.30–564.51 bolívares

SCORE CARD

- ❑ WORLD GNP RANKING 40th
- ❑ GNP PER CAPITA $3480
- ❑ BALANCE OF PAYMENTS $6bn
- ❑ INFLATION 50%
- ❑ UNEMPLOYMENT................................10%

EXPORTS

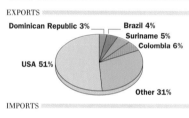

Dominican Republic 3% Brazil 4% Suriname 5% Colombia 6% USA 51% Other 31%

IMPORTS

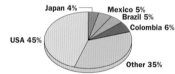

Japan 4% Mexico 5% Brazil 5% Colombia 6% USA 45% Other 35%

STRENGTHS

The largest proven oil deposits outside the Middle East and the CIS. Massive reserves of coal, bauxite, iron and gold and successful development of Orimulsion, new bitumen fuel which has attracted considerable foreign investment. Other new foreign investment in sectors including banking, telecoms, iron and steel. World's most efficient producer of high-grade aluminum. More flexible labor market.

WEAKNESSES

Huge, cumbersome state sector; despite some privatization, large areas of the state sector are still over-manned and inefficient and subject to widespread corruption. Poor public services which, despite Venezuela's wealth during the oil boom years, have been badly maintained. Major infrastructure renewal is now long overdue. Widespread tax evasion. Weak currency.

ECONOMIC PERFORMANCE INDICATOR

Consumer price index   GDP

Consumer price index 1990=100 / GDP 1993=100
1993 1994 1995 1996 1997

PROFILE

Venezuela is an economic paradox. One of the strongest economies in Latin America, its government finances are in crisis due to a culture of non-accountability and politically motivated patronage in state-owned industries and government bureaucracies. To date, privatizations and government cuts have failed to solve the problem. President Chávez has promised to deal with excesses and diversify the economy by lowering dependence on crude oil exports and promoting domestic processing industries. However, these undertakings have received a mixed response from investors who favour more market-oriented reforms.

VENEZUELA : MAJOR BUSINESSES

Valencia Caracas Maracaibo Aragua R. Orinoco Ciudad Bolívar Puerto Ordaz

- ⬥ Oil
- ⬥ Rum
- ⬥ Brewing
- ⬥ Oil refining
- ⬥ Ceramics
- ⬥ Agribusiness
- ⬥ Tobacco
- ⬥ Engineering
- ⬥ Metals
- ⬥ Vehicle assembly

0   200 km
0   200 miles

* significant multinational ownership

RESOURCES

Electric power 20.0m kw

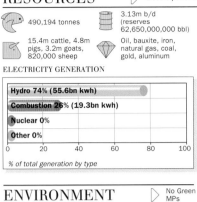

490,194 tonnes

3.13m b/d
(reserves
62,650,000,000 bbl)

15.4m cattle, 4.8m
pigs, 3.2m goats,
820,000 sheep

Oil, bauxite, iron,
natural gas, coal,
gold, aluminum

ELECTRICITY GENERATION

Hydro 74% (55.6bn kwh)	
Combustion 26% (19.3bn kwh)	
Nuclear 0%	
Other 0%	

% of total generation by type

Scale: 0, 20, 40, 60, 80, 100

ENVIRONMENT

No Green MPs

36%   Medium

ENVIRONMENTAL TREATIES

🌿 Yes	🦏 Yes	🌐 Yes			
🎩 Yes	🔋 Yes	♻ No			

Concerns are rain forest destruction, oil pollution of Lake Maracaibo, and illegal gold mining harming soil and lakes.

MEDIA

TV ownership medium

Daily newspaper circulation 206 per 1,000 people

PUBLISHING AND BROADCAST MEDIA

📰	There are 86 daily newspapers. *El Universal* and *El Nacional* are the most prominent
📺	2 state-owned, 6 independent commercial services
📻	13 state-owned, 200 independent commercial stations

Most of the press is independent of the main political parties. Venezuelan soap operas vie with Mexican rivals for dominance.

CRIME

Death penalty not used

32,000 prisoners

Recorded crime remained steady from 1992–1996

CRIME RATES

Murders	
23	per 100,000 population

Rapes	
16	per 100,000 population

Thefts	
173	per 100,000 population

Urban robberies and violence involving young delinquents is a major problem, as is narcotics-related crime. Cattle-smuggling to Colombia is rife.

Venezuela has a remarkable diversity of resources. It has proven oil reserves of 62 billion barrels, vast quantities of coal, iron ore, bauxite and gold, and cheap hydroelectric power. Huge investment programs are currently under way to raise production in all these sectors as well as in oil refining capacity. However, the Chávez government wants to reduce the investment budget of the state oil company, PDVSA, reduce its output and increase its contributions to the exchequer. Such uncertainty could unsettle private investors.

Venezuela has begun exploitation of Orimulsion, a new bitumen-based fuel from the Orinoco; commercially exploitable reserves are estimated at 270 billion barrels. Venezuela's aim to be the world's largest aluminum producer is threatened after failures to privatize the troubled sector.

EDUCATION

School leaving age: 15

92%   550,783 students

The private sector is expanding while the state system is starved of resources.

THE EDUCATION SYSTEM

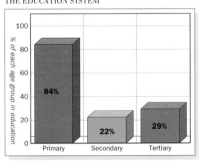

% of each age group in education

Primary: 84%
Secondary: 22%
Tertiary: 29%

State education suffers from a shortage of qualified teachers, and student drop-out rates are high. The standard of education at state universities is low.

HEALTH

Welfare state health benefits

1 per 625 people

Heart diseases, accidents, violence, cancers

Reduced budgets and privatizations mean less care for the poor.

The health service has suffered along with other public services from poor management in the 1970s and severe cuts in the 1980s and 1990s. Hospitals need modernization.

Most health care is concentrated in the towns, and people from indigenous communities often have to travel long distances to receive treatment. Medicines, which have to be paid for, are expensive, and preventable diseases are recurring.

VENEZUELA : LAND USE

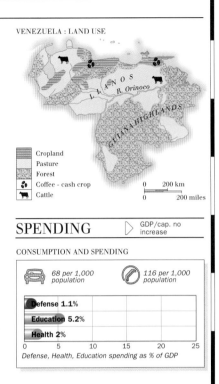

Cropland	
Pasture	
Forest	
🐾 Coffee - cash crop	
🐄 Cattle	

0   200 km
0   200 miles

SPENDING

GDP/cap. no increase

CONSUMPTION AND SPENDING

68 per 1,000 population

116 per 1,000 population

Defense 1.1%	
Education 5.2%	
Health 2%	

Defense, Health, Education spending as % of GDP

Scale: 0, 5, 10, 15, 20, 25

The oil boom years of the 1970s largely benefited the already rich, with middle-income consumers doing well out of government-sponsored social improvements in health and education and subsidised goods, largely at the expense of the poor.

The collapse of world oil prices, economic austerity measures, high inflation and the devaluation of the bolívar in the 1980s and 1990s has squeezed the middle class. In addition, the living standards of working-class households have been seriously eroded. The *Centro de Documentación y Análisis de los Trabajadores* in 1999 put forward the claim that 85% of Venezuelans live in poverty.

WORLD RANKING

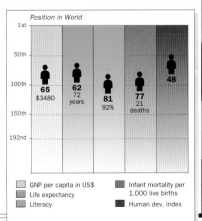

Position in World

1st
50th
100th
150th
192nd

65 — $3480
62 — 72 years
81 — 92%
77 — 21 deaths
48

GNP per capita in US$	Infant mortality per 1,000 live births
Life expectancy	Human dev. index
Literacy	

V

VIETNAM

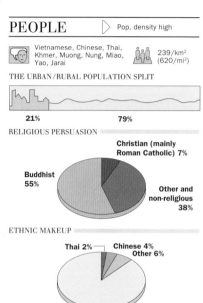
SOUTHEAST ASIA

OFFICIAL NAME: Socialist Republic of Viet–Nam   CAPITAL: Hanoi
POPULATION: 77.9 million   CURRENCY: Dông   OFFICIAL LANGUAGE: Vietnamese

 1954   1976   Sept 2   VN   +7   +84   .vn

LOCATED ON THE EASTERN COAST of the Indochinese peninsula, over half of Vietnam is dominated by the heavily forested mountain range, the Chaîne Annamitique. The most populated areas, which are also the most intensively cultivated, are along the Red and Mekong rivers. Partitioned after the end of World War II, the communist north reunited the country after the world's longest 20th-century conflict, the 1962–1975 Vietnam War. Today, Vietnam is a single-party state ruled by the Communist Party. Since 1986, the regime has followed a liberal economic policy known as *doi moi* (renovation).

CLIMATE   ▷ Tropical monsoon

WEATHER CHART

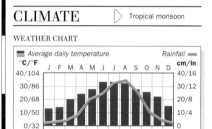

Vietnam has a sharply contrasting climate. The north has cool winters, while the south is tropical with even temperatures all year round. The central provinces are affected by typhoons. The most intensively cultivated areas are the deltas of the Red and Mekong rivers, which are respectively subject to drought and heavy flooding.

TRANSPORTATION   ▷ Drive on right

Tan Son Naht Intl, Ho Chi Minh City | 604 ships 808,000 grt

THE TRANSPORTATION NETWORK

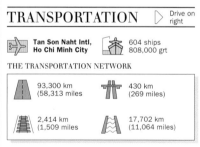

93,300 km (58,313 miles) | 430 km (269 miles)
2,414 km (1,509 miles) | 17,702 km (11,064 miles)

Rebuilding infrastructure destroyed during the war is still the priority. A key project is likely to be the reconstruction of Highway 1, linking Hanoi and Ho Chi Minh City (formerly Saigon). Ports and railroads require rehabilitation, while construction is in progress on two new port facilities, at Vung Tau in the south and Cai Lan in the north. Trains travel slowly in Vietnam, with an average speed of around 15 km/h (9 mph). The journey from Hanoi to Ho Chi Minh City takes three days.

V

TOURISM   ▷ Visitors : populaton 1:45

1.7m visitors | Up 37% 1995–1997

MAIN TOURIST ARRIVALS

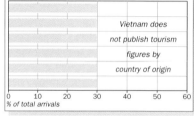

Vietnam does not publish tourism figures by country of origin

% of total arrivals

Russians, eastern Europeans and backpackers from the West made up the bulk of the 400,000 or so tourists Vietnam received each year during the 1980s. Other travelers were either on business, or overseas Vietnamese, *Viet Kie*, visiting relatives.

Since 1990, the government has opened the way to large-scale tourism – a "master plan" was adopted in 1995. Massive investment is now going into hotels, and an official target of three million tourists a year by 2000 was set. Poor infrastructure, however, remains a problem. For the moment, Vietnam's appeal rests on its unspoiled Asian way of life and areas of spectacular natural beauty such as Ha Long Bay on the Red river delta.

Boats moored near Nha Trang. *A network connecting Vietnam's main ports provides an important internal communications link.*

PEOPLE   ▷ Pop. density high

Vietnamese, Chinese, Thai, Khmer, Muong, Nung, Miao, Yao, Jarai | 239/km² (620/mi²)

THE URBAN/RURAL POPULATION SPLIT

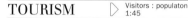

21%   79%

RELIGIOUS PERSUASION

Christian (mainly Roman Catholic) 7%
Buddhist 55%
Other and non-religious 38%

ETHNIC MAKEUP

Thai 2%   Chinese 4%   Other 6%
Vietnamese 88%

Overseas Chinese constitute the largest minority group in Vietnam, and suffered considerable discrimination in the early years of the communist takeover. The Saigon Chinese, with their Taiwanese links, were seen as corrupt bourgeoisie, while the northern Mountain Chinese were suspected as a fifth column for China's ambitions in Vietnam. Other mountain minorities (*Montagnards*), with a history of collaboration with the French and Americans, who continued armed resistance, were also sidelined by the regime in Hanoi. Today, the main source of tension is the resettling of lowlanders in mountain regions, which is putting pressure on limited farming and forest resources.

Women outnumber men, largely because of war deaths. They form a high proportion of the industrial workforce, but have only recently been given greater political representation. The vice-president (Nguyen Thi Banh) is a woman, as is one member of the politburo (Nguyen Thi Xuan My).

Family life is strong and is based on kinship groups within village clans.

POPULATION AGE BREAKDOWN

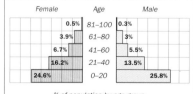

Female	Age	Male
0.5%	81–100	0.3%
3.9%	61–80	3%
6.7%	41–60	5.5%
16.2%	21–40	13.5%
24.6%	0–20	25.8%

% of population by age group

Le Duc Anh,
president 1992–1997.

Vo Van Kiet, now a
senior adviser..

POLITICS

▷ No multiparty elections

1997/2002

President
Tran Duc Luong

AT THE LAST ELECTION

National Assembly 450 members

14%
Other VFF

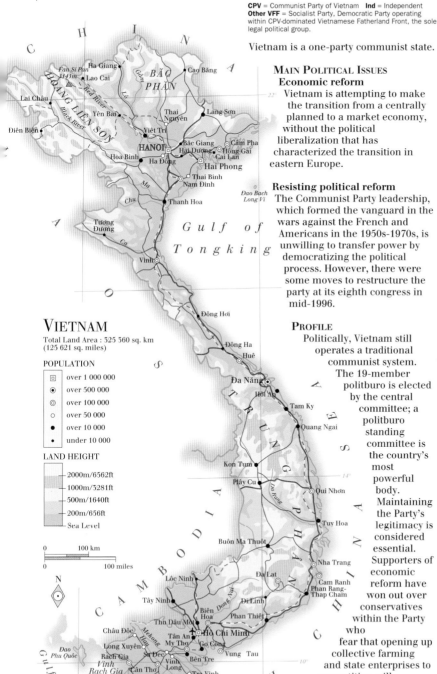

85%
CPV

1%
Ind

CPV = Communist Party of Vietnam **Ind** = Independent
Other VFF = Socialist Party, Democratic Party operating
within CPV-dominated Vietnamese Fatherland Front, the sole
legal political group.

Vietnam is a one-party communist state.

MAIN POLITICAL ISSUES
Economic reform
Vietnam is attempting to make the transition from a centrally planned to a market economy, without the political liberalization that has characterized the transition in eastern Europe.

Resisting political reform
The Communist Party leadership, which formed the vanguard in the wars against the French and Americans in the 1950s-1970s, is unwilling to transfer power by democratizing the political process. However, there were some moves to restructure the party at its eighth congress in mid-1996.

PROFILE
Politically, Vietnam still operates a traditional communist system. The 19-member politburo is elected by the central committee; a politburo standing committee is the country's most powerful body. Maintaining the Party's legitimacy is considered essential. Supporters of economic reform have won out over conservatives within the Party who fear that opening up collective farming and state enterprises to competition will undermine its crucial power base.

WORLD AFFAIRS

▷ Joined UN in 1977

ASEAN IAEA IBRD Mek Riv NAM

Vietnam's economic liberalization has led to improvements in its relationship with the USA. In 1993, Washington finally lifted its aid embargo, allowing the World Bank to start investing in reconstruction and US companies to bid for contracts. Full diplomatic relations were established in mid-1995. The removal of Vietnamese troops from neighboring Cambodia in 1989 improved relations with China, although border disputes remain a source of tension. Recent attacks by Khmer Rouge guerrillas against ethnic Vietnamese citizens in Cambodia have soured Vietnamese–Cambodian relations.

AID

▷ Recipient

$997m (receipts)

Up 8% 1996–1997

The Vietnamese invasion of Cambodia in 1978 halted all aid from China, Japan, and the West, with the exception of the Scandinavian countries. Until the mid-1980s the USSR financed Vietnam's trade deficit. Western aid was resumed in the early 1990s. In 1992 the USA restored humanitarian aid, in 1993 lifting economic restrictions. Aid now provides for almost 90% of all capital expenditure.

CHRONOLOGY
From 1825, the brutal persecution of the Catholic community, originally converted by French priests in the 17th century, gave France the excuse to colonize Cochin-China, Annam and Tonkin, and then merge them with Laos and Cambodia.

❏ **1920** *Quoc ngu* (Roman script) replaces Chinese script.
❏ **1950** Ho Chi Minh founds Indochina Communist Party.
❏ **1940** Japanese invasion.
❏ **1941** Viet Minh resistance founded in exile in China.
❏ **1945** Viet Minh take Saigon and Hanoi. Emperor abdicates. Republic with Ho Chi Minh as president.
❏ **1946** French reenter. First Indo-China War.
❏ **1954** French defeated at Dien Bien Phu. Vietnam divided at 17ºN. USSR supports North; USA arms South.
❏ **1960** Groups opposed to Diem regime in South unite as Viet Cong.
❏ **1961** USA pours in military advisers.
❏ **1964** US Congress approves war.
❏ **1965** Gen. Nguyen Van Thieu takes over military government of South. First US combat troops arrive; in three years they total 500,000 men.
⇨

VIETNAM

Total Land Area : 525 360 sq. km
(125 621 sq. miles)

POPULATION
▣ over 1 000 000
◉ over 500 000
◎ over 100 000
○ over 50 000
● over 10 000
• under 10 000

LAND HEIGHT
2000m/6562ft
1000m/3281ft
500m/1640ft
200m/656ft
Sea Level

0 — 100 km
0 — 100 miles

[Map of Vietnam with locations: Ha Giang, Cao Bang, Lao Cai, Fan Si Pan 3143m, HOANG LIEN SON, BAO PHAN, Lai Chau, Red River, Yen Bai, Thai Nguyen, Lang Son, Dien Bien, Black River, Viet Tri, Hoa Binh, HANOI, Bac Giang, Cam Pha, Hai Duong, Hong Gai, Cai Lan, Ha Dong, Hai Phong, Thai Binh, Nam Dinh, Dao Bach Long Vi, Thanh Hoa, Gulf of Tongking, Tuong Duong, Vinh, Dong Hoi, Dong Ha, Hue, Da Nang, Hoi An, Tam Ky, Quang Ngai, Kon Tum, Plây Cu, Qui Nhon, Tuy Hoa, Buôn Ma Thuot, Nha Trang, Da Lat, Cam Ranh, Phan Rang-Thap Cham, Di Linh, Phan Thiet, Loc Ninh, Tay Ninh, Biên Hoa, Thu Dau Mot, Tân An, Ho Chi Minh, My Tho, Go Cong, Vung Tau, Bên Tre, Vinh Long, Tra Vinh, Châu Doc, Long Xuyên, Rach Gia, Sa Dec, Cân Tho, Soc Trăng, Bac Liêu, Ca Mau, Mekong Delta, Côn Dao, Dao Phu Quôc, Gulf of Thailand, Vinh Rach Gia, CAMBODIA, CHINA, LAOS]

V

623

CHRONOLOGY *continued*

- ❏ **1965–1968** Operation Rolling Thunder – intense bombing of North by South and USA.
- ❏ **1967** Antiwar protests start in USA and elsewhere.
- ❏ **1968** *Tet* (New Year) Offensive – 105 towns attacked simultaneously in South with infiltrated arms. Viet Cong suffer serious losses. Peace talks begin. USA eases bombing and starts withdrawing troops.
- ❏ **1969** Ho Chi Minh dies. War intensifies in spite of talks.
- ❏ **1970** USA begins secret attacks in Laos and Cambodia and new mass bombing of North to try to stop arms reaching Viet Cong.
- ❏ **1972** 11-day Christmas Campaign is heaviest US bombing of war.
- ❏ **1973** Paris Peace Agreements signed, but fighting continues.
- ❏ **1975** Fall of Saigon to combined forces of North and Provisional Revolutionary (Viet Cong) Government of South. Further one million flee after end of war.
- ❏ **1976** Vietnam united as Socialist Republic of Vietnam, with Le Duan continuing to hold the real power as general secretary of Communist Party. Saigon renamed Ho Chi Minh City.
- ❏ **1977** Vietnam begins incursions into Kampuchea (Cambodia).
- ❏ **1978** Thousands of ethnic Chinese flee Vietnam.
- ❏ **1979** Nine-Day War with China. Chinese troops destroy everything for 40 km (25 miles) inside Vietnam. Chinese pushed back. Vietnam ousts Pol Pot in full-scale invasion of Kampuchea and installs friendly regime. "Boat people" (illegal emigrants) now creating crisis of international proportions. At UN conference, Vietnam agrees to allow legal emigration, but exodus continues.
- ❏ **1986** Nguyen Van Linh appointed general secretary. Initiates liberal economic *doi moi* (renovation) policy.
- ❏ **1987** Fighting in Thailand as Vietnam pursues Kampuchean resistance fighters across border.
- ❏ **1989** Troops leave Cambodia.
- ❏ **1991** Open anticommunist dissent made a criminal offense.
- ❏ **1992** Revised constitution allows foreign investment, but essential role of Communist Party is unchanged.
- ❏ **1995** US–Vietnamese relations are normalized.
- ❏ **1996** Eighth Communist Party congress.
- ❏ **1997** Legislative elections. Tran Duc Luong elected president; Phan Van Khai becomes prime minister.

DEFENSE

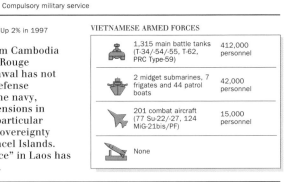

▷ Compulsory military service

💲 $990m   ⬆ Up 2% in 1997

Since the withdrawal from Cambodia in 1989 (only the Khmer Rouge suggests that the withdrawal has not occurred), the focus of defense spending has moved to the navy, a reflection of growing tensions in the South China Sea, in particular over disputed claims to sovereignty over the Spratly and Paracel Islands. Vietnam's "volunteer force" in Laos has also been much reduced.

VIETNAMESE ARMED FORCES

🛡	1,315 main battle tanks (T-34/-54/-55, T-62, PRC Type-59)	412,000 personnel
🚢	2 midget submarines, 7 frigates and 44 patrol boats	42,000 personnel
✈	201 combat aircraft (77 Su-22/-27, 124 MiG-21bis/PF)	15,000 personnel
	None	

ECONOMICS

▷ Inflation 85.4% p.a. (1985–1996)

📊 $24bn   💲 12,292– 13,893 dong

SCORE CARD

- ❏ WORLD GNP RANKING..........................60th
- ❏ GNP PER CAPITA $310
- ❏ BALANCE OF PAYMENTS.................$−1,868m
- ❏ INFLATION 3.2%
- ❏ UNEMPLOYMENT..................................25%

ECONOMIC PERFORMANCE INDICATOR

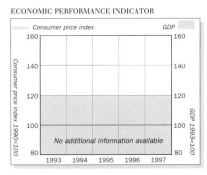

No additional information available

EXPORTS

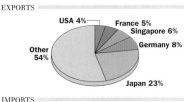

USA 4%   France 5%   Singapore 6%   Germany 8%   Other 54%   Japan 23%

IMPORTS

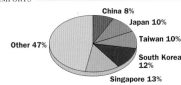

China 8%   Japan 10%   Taiwan 10%   South Korea 12%   Singapore 13%   Other 47%

STRENGTHS

Diverse resource base. Location in east Asia. Much lower labor costs than second-tier NICs such as Malaysia and Thailand.

WEAKNESSES

Weak economic institutions will make transition to a full market economy difficult. Enormous task of reconstruction after war; dependent on aid from the West, Japan, and China.

PROFILE

Vietnam is already being billed by some commentators as the next Asian "tiger." The prospect is still distant, though the potential certainly exists. Mineral resources, located mostly in the north, and a resumption of Western aid to the capital-starved economy, are the foundations on which the adoption of a full market economy will be based. The major concerns are the need to develop the private sector and to maintain inflation at a tolerable level. In the mid-1990s it was running at around

6%, compared with 600% in 1987–1988. The tax net also needs to be widened if government finances are to stabilize.

Even before the collapse of the USSR, there was a widespread acceptance in Vietnam that the centrally planned economy had problems. The encouragement of private enterprise began in 1988. Between 1988 and 1995, foreign investors proposed new projects worth over $16 billion. Most of the money was put into oil and gas, tourism, property, and light industry. Since the early 1990s, the economy has grown by around 8%–9% a year. The government has set a target of doubling Vietnam's GDP in the next decade.

VIETNAM : MAJOR BUSINESSES

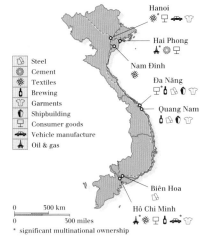

Steel
Cement
Textiles
Brewing
Garments
Shipbuilding
Consumer goods
Vehicle manufacture
Oil & gas

Hanoi
Hai Phong
Nam Đinh
Đa Năng
Quang Nam
Biên Hoa
Hồ Chi Minh

0   500 km
0   500 miles
* significant multinational ownership

V

RESOURCES

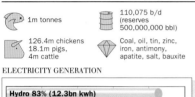

Electric power 4.5m kw

1m tonnes

110,075 b/d (reserves 500,000,000 bbl)

126.4m chickens
18.1m pigs,
4m cattle

Coal, oil, tin, zinc, iron, antimony, apatite, salt, bauxite

ELECTRICITY GENERATION

Hydro 83% (12.3bn kwh)	
Combustion 13% (1.9bn kwh)	
Nuclear 0%	
Other 4% (0.6bn kwh)	

% of total generation by type

Vietnam is the world's third-largest exporter of rice, after Thailand and the USA. Oil production, at around 110,000 b/d, is negligible by world standards, but sufficient to make it Vietnam's biggest export earner. Oil and gas exploitation is undertaken under the auspices of the Oil and Gas Corporation of Vietnam (PetroVietnam) which is involved in joint ventures with oil firms from the USA, Spain and Japan. Other companies engaged in exploration activities are the Australian company BHP, British Gas from the UK and Mobil Oil. Vietnam has unexploited gas reserves in the South China Sea; gas from the only producing field has to be flared off.

Northern Vietnam has a surplus of electricity. A new power line will make this available to the south.

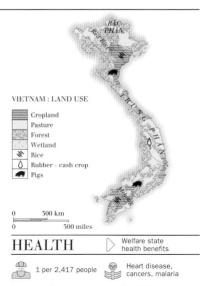

VIETNAM : LAND USE

Cropland
Pasture
Forest
Wetland
Rice
Rubber – cash crop
Pigs

0   300 km
0   300 miles

ENVIRONMENT

No Green MPs

3%

Low

ENVIRONMENTAL TREATIES

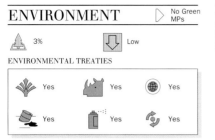

Yes   Yes   Yes
Yes   Yes   Yes

Vietnam is still counting the massive environmental cost of the war; 7 million tonnes of bombs were dropped, and the defoliant chemical Agent Orange was sprayed over more than 1.5 million ha (4.2 million acres). In addition to infrastructure destroyed, 50% of Vietnam's forests were seriously damaged and some 5% destroyed. Continuing deforestation remains a major problem. Each year, an estimated 200,000 ha (494,200 acres) are lost, with resulting soil erosion and flooding.

MEDIA

TV ownership medium

Daily newspaper circulation 4 per 1,000 people

PUBLISHING AND BROADCAST MEDIA

	There are 10 daily newspapers including *Nhan Dan, Quan Doi Nhan Dan, Ha Noi Moi* and *Saigon Giai Phong*
	1 state-owned service with 53 provincial stations
	1 state-owned service with more than 5,000 local stations

Although the media are tightly regulated and all editors have to be Party members, criticism of the authorities is still possible. The weekly *Tuoi Tre* is known for its investigative reporting, and even *Nhan Dan*, the Party newspaper, has been known to expose laxity in the system, especially in the judiciary. The army daily, *Quan Doi Nhan Dan*, is the most hardline paper.

CRIME

Death penalty used

Vietnam does not publish prison figures

Increase in petty theft

CRIME RATES

Rates of murder and rape remain fairly constant. Theft has risen slightly.

The judicial system is based on the Soviet model. The education camps established after liberation have now closed, but religious and political dissidents are still held without trial.

Petty theft from foreigners is a problem in the major cities. There has been a sharp rise in corruption since economic liberalization.

Religious tensions have provoked disturbances. In 1995, a number of high-ranking dissident Buddhists were jailed for "sabotaging religious solidarity."

EDUCATION

School leaving age: 11

92%

297,900 students

A law approved in 1998 encourages private sponsorship of education.

THE EDUCATION SYSTEM

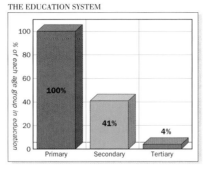

% of each age group in education

Primary 100%   Secondary 41%   Tertiary 4%

State primary education is free, but students pay fees for higher education. Vietnamese universities have a strong liberal arts tradition.

HEALTH

Welfare state health benefits

1 per 2,417 people

Heart disease, cancers, malaria

Vietnam's main medical achievements are the development of a vaccine for hepatitis B, and the extraction of artemisinin (an antimalarial drug) from the indigenous Thanh Hao tree. A campaign has been launched to combat the spread of AIDS, which currently affects 59 of the country's 61 provinces.

SPENDING

GDP/cap. increase

CONSUMPTION AND SPENDING

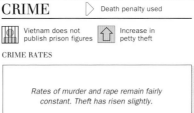

No data

21 per 1,000 population

Defense 4.1%
Education 2.7%
Health 1.1%

Defense, Health, Education spending as % of GDP

The Party remains the route to advancement. Ostentatious displays of wealth are still frowned upon.

WORLD RANKING

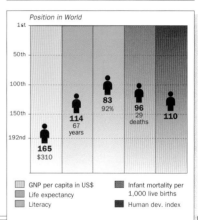

Position in World

165 $310
114 67 years
83 92%
96 29 deaths
110

GNP per capita in US$
Life expectancy
Literacy
Infant mortality per 1,000 live births
Human dev. index

V

YEMEN

MIDDLE EAST

Asia

OFFICIAL NAME: Republic of Yemen   **CAPITAL:** Sana
POPULATION: 16.9 million   **CURRENCY:** Rial (N. Yemen) and dinar (S. Yemen)   **OFFICIAL LANGUAGE:** Arabic

| 1990 | 1990 | May 22 | ADN | +3 | +967 | .ye |

YEMEN IS LOCATED in southern Arabia between Saudi Arabia and Oman. The north is mountainous, with a fertile strip along the Red Sea. The south is largely arid mountains and desert. Yemen was until 1990 two countries, the Yemen Arab Republic in the north and the People's Democratic Republic of Yemen in the south. The north was run by successive military regimes; the poorer south was the Arab world's only Marxist state. Postunification conflict between the two ruling hierarchies, nominally in coalition, led to civil war in 1994 and the ousting of the southern-based former Marxists.

CLIMATE

▷ Hot desert/mountain

WEATHER CHART

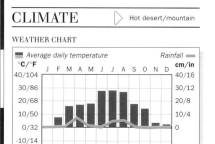

The desert climate is modified by altitude, affecting temperatures by as much as 12°C (54°F). Rainfall increases in northwest and central Yemen.

TRANSPORTATION

▷ Drive on right

🛬 **Sana International**
624,000 passengers

⚓ 42 ships
25,100 grt

THE TRANSPORTATION NETWORK

| 3,000 miles (4,760 km) | None |
| None | None |

Aden's position at the entrance to the Red Sea makes it a key shipping port. The main cities are linked by adequate roads, but many rural areas are inaccessible. Sana and Aden are served by international airlines.

Hilltop village in northern Yemen, showing traditionally decorated, multistorey houses built from mud bricks.

TOURISM

▷ Visitors:population 1:201

🧳 84,000 visitors

⬆ Up 40% in 1995–1997

MAIN TOURIST ARRIVALS

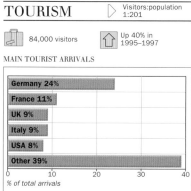

Germany 24%
France 11%
UK 9%
Italy 9%
USA 8%
Other 39%

% of total arrivals

Believed to be the home of the legendary Queen of Sheba, Yemen attracts tourists interested in Arab society, architecture, archaeology, and historical remains. The Romans called Yemen *Arabia Felix* because of its fertile farmlands and dominance in the frankincense trade. Yemen was the second country, after Saudi Arabia, to convert to Islam.

Southern Yemen has been open to Western visitors only since 1990. Its run-down infrastructure and lack of hotels, especially on the coast, have hindered tourism. Sana, a walled medieval city, is the more interesting center for tourists. It has impressive architecture, particularly tall stone and mud brick Arab houses, and the palaces of the former imamate. Despite being over 100 km (62 miles) from the capital, the Marib Dam, built in ancient times, is another major attraction.

German and French tourists were the first to travel to North Yemen during the 1980s. Hopes of a rise in tourism following the end of the 1994 civil war were dashed in 1998 after tribesmen killed four Western tourists.

Tourists are subject to a ban on the consumption of alcohol, except in five-star hotels. Whisky and beer are available on the black market, which operates out of Djibouti.

PEOPLE

▷ Pop. density low

Arabic

32/km² (83/mi²)

THE URBAN/RURAL POPULATION SPLIT

34%   66%

RELIGIOUS PERSUASION

Christian, Hindu and Jewish 3%

Sunni Muslim 42%   Shi'a Muslim 55%

ETHNIC MAKEUP

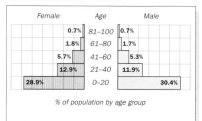

Indian, Somali, European 2%   Afro-Arab 3%

Arab 95%

Yemenis are almost entirely of Arab and Bedouin descent, though there is a small, dwindling, Jewish minority. The majority are Sunni Muslims, of the Shafi sect. In the north, many people have close family in Saudi Arabia. Many Yemenis consider Saudi Arabia's Asir province to be part of Yemen.

Agriculture employs more than half the population. Many Yemenis sought jobs in Saudi Arabia and the Gulf states during the 1970s oil boom. More than one million worked in Saudi Arabia, most as manual laborers and farm hands. Their expulsion, a result of Yemen's support for Iraq's invasion of Kuwait in 1990, has raised unemployment within Yemen.

In rural areas and in the north, Islamic orthodoxy is strong and most women wear the veil. In the south, however, women still claim the freedoms they had under the Marxist regime, especially in urban areas.

Tension continues to exist between the south, led by the cosmopolitan city of Aden, and the more conservative north. Clashes between their former armies escalated into civil war in 1994.

POPULATION AGE BREAKDOWN

Female	Age	Male
0.7%	81–100	0.7%
1.8%	61–80	1.7%
5.7%	41–60	5.3%
12.9%	21–40	11.9%
28.9%	0–20	30.4%

% of population by age group

Y

YEMEN

Total Land Area : 527 970 sq. km
(203 849 sq. miles)

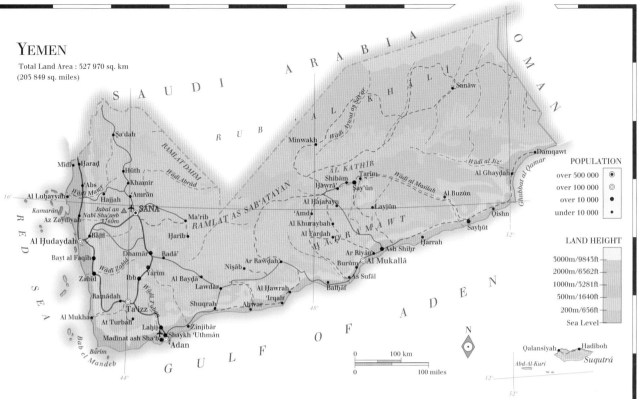

POPULATION

over 500 000 ⊙
over 100 000 ◎
over 10 000 •
under 10 000 ·

LAND HEIGHT

3000m/9843ft
2000m/6562ft
1000m/3281ft
500m/1640ft
200m/656ft
Sea Level

0   100 km
0   100 miles

N

POLITICS ▷ Multiparty elections

🏛 1997/2001   👤 President Ali Abdullah Saleh

AT THE LAST ELECTION

House of Representatives 301 members

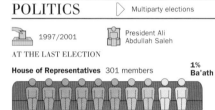

62% GPC	18% Ind	18% YAR	1% NUPO	1% Ba'ath

GPC = General People's Congress **Ind** = Independent
YAR = YAR-al-Islah (Yemeni Alliance for Reform (al-Islah))
NUOP = Nasserite Unionist Popular Organization
Ba'ath = Arab Socialist Ba'ath Party

Yemen is a multiparty democracy. The president retains executive power while the House of Representatives holds legislative power.

MAIN POLITICAL ISSUES
Growing tribal insurgency
President Saleh's regime faces threats from disgruntled southern tribesmen, who are angry at levels of poverty in their oil-rich country. Since 1992, tribesmen have kidnapped more than 100 foreigners, including diplomats and tourists. In 1998 four Western hostages were killed.

Saudi interference
Relations with Saudi Arabia have long been strained by accusations that Riyadh is funding insurgent tribesmen. In early 1995 the two sides signed a memorandum of understanding on border issues, but clashed violently in 1998 over their disputed border.

Militant Islamic groups
The arrest and trial in 1998–1999 of a small group of activists, alleged to have been inspired by Islamic militant leaders based abroad, indicated the government's preoccupation with security. It also complicated relations with the UK, since most of those arrested were British nationals.

PROFILE
The merger of North and South Yemen in 1990 united Yemenis under one ruler for the first time since 1735. In 1994, a civil war erupted, fueling a secessionist movement in the south. The fighting was centered in the south around Aden, the scene of mass evacuations by European workers. By mid-1994, the fighting had subsided and the southern secessionists were crushed. In 1997 elections President Saleh's GPC won an absolute majority.

Ali Abdullah Saleh, former North Yemen president, now leader of the unified Yemen.

Ali Salem al-Baidh, former vice-president, ousted when south resecession failed.

CHRONOLOGY

From the 9th century, the Zaydi dynasty ruled Yemen until their defeat by the Ottoman Turks in 1517. The Turks were expelled by the Zaydi Imams in 1636.

❏ **1839** Britain occupies Aden.
❏ **1918** Yemen secures independence.
❏ **1937** Aden made a Crown Colony, hinterland a Protectorate.
❏ **1962** Army coup. Imam deposed, Yemen Arab Republic (YAR) declared in north.
❏ **1962–1970** Northern civil war between royalists and republicans.
❏ **1963** Aden and Protectorate united to form Federation of South Arabia.
❏ **1967** British troops leave Aden.
❏ **1970** South Yemen renamed People's Democratic Republic of Yemen (PDRY). Republicans victorious in the north.
❏ **1971** Civilian elections in YAR.
❏ **1972** War between YAR and PDRY ends in peace settlement.
❏ **1974** Army coup in YAR.
❏ **1975** Sultan of Oman defeats PDRY-backed revolt in Dhofar province.
❏ **1978** Lt.-Col. Ali Saleh YAR president. Coup in PDRY. Radical Abdalfattah Ismail in power.
❏ **1979** February–March, brief war. October, PDRY signs 20-year treaty with USSR.
❏ **1980** Ismail replaced by moderate Ali Muhammad.

Y

627

CHRONOLOGY *continued*

- ❑ **1982** President of PDRY Ali Muhammad signs peace treaty with Sultan of Oman.
- ❑ **1984** YAR signs 20-year cooperation treaty with USSR.
- ❑ **1986** Coup attempt in PDRY becomes civil war. Rebels take control of Aden, install Haydar Al Attas as president. Presidents of PDRY and YAR meet.
- ❑ **1987** Oil production starts in YAR.
- ❑ **1988** YAR holds elections for consultative council; Muslim brotherhood gains influence.
- ❑ **1989** Unification process speeds up dramatically. June, telephone links established. July, PDRY publishes a program of free-market reforms. November, YAR and PDRY sign unification agreement. December, constitution published.
- ❑ **1990** January, restrictions on travel between YAR and PDRY lifted. May, formal unification amid protests from pro-Islamic groups opposed to secular constitution. Ali Saleh becomes president of Republic of Yemen.
- ❑ **1991** Yemeni guest workers expelled by Saudi Arabia in retaliation for Yemen's position over the Iraqi invasion of Kuwait. Arab states boycott independence celebrations.
- ❑ **1992** Assassinations and political unrest delay elections.
- ❑ **1993** Elections return ruling parties to power.
- ❑ **1994** Southern secessionists defeated in civil war.
- ❑ **1997** President Saleh's GPC wins absolute majority in elections.
- ❑ **1998–1999** Violent border dispute with Saudi Arabia. Group of Western tourists kidnapped, four killed; three members of Islamic Army of Adan (IAA) sentenced to death for their murder.

WORLD AFFAIRS ▷ Joined UN in 1947/67

Yemen's links with the West have not recovered fully after its support for Iraq during the Gulf War, and Yemen is relatively isolated internationally. Relations with Saudi Arabia remain the main specific foreign policy concern.

AID ▷ Recipient

💲 $366m (receipts)   ⬆ Up 41% in 1996–1997

In early 1996, Yemen received some $700 million from the IMF and donor countries in support of its economic reform program.

DEFENSE ▷ Compulsory military service

💲 $403m   ⬆ Up 10% in 1997

A border dispute with Saudi Arabia and the control of insurgent tribesmen are the main security concerns.

Following unification, mutual suspicion slowed the integration of the former North and South defense forces. Sporadic, bitter clashes have taken place, most notably in 1994. Soviet weapons were formerly bought by both governments, although the north also possesses US-made arms.

YEMENI ARMED FORCES

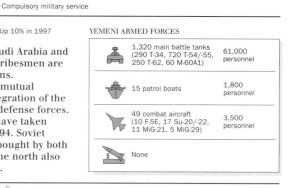

🛡	1,320 main battle tanks (290 T-34, 720 T-54/-55, 250 T-62, 60 M-60A1)	61,000 personnel
⚓	15 patrol boats	1,800 personnel
✈	49 combat aircraft (10 F-5E, 17 Su-20/-22, 11 MiG-21, 5 MiG-29)	3,500 personnel
🚀	None	

ECONOMICS ▷ Not available

📊 $4.4bn   💲 124.00–136.66 Yemeni rials

SCORE CARD

❑ WORLD GNP RANKING	114th
❑ GNP PER CAPITA	$270
❑ BALANCE OF PAYMENTS	$159m
❑ INFLATION	54%
❑ UNEMPLOYMENT	30%

ECONOMIC PERFORMANCE INDICATOR

EXPORTS

Japan 5% Brazil 5% China 31% Thailand 17% Other 23% South Korea 19%

IMPORTS

Brazil 5% France 6% USA 7% Saudi Arabia 8% UAE 9% Other 65%

STRENGTHS

Rising oil production. Salt mining. Deposits of copper, gold, lead, zinc and molybdenum. Industries include oil refining, chemicals, food products.

WEAKNESSES

Political instability deters foreign investment. Well-organized black market undermines tax base. Overall dependence on subsistence agriculture.

PROFILE

Yemen's unification in 1990 was designed to transform the economy. High expectations were placed on the exploitation of large oil and natural gas reserves, discovered in 1984. Exports of oil began in 1987. Plans were also made to encourage industrial investment around the port of Aden. Both these policies for regeneration suffered severe setbacks as a result of the 1990–1991 Gulf War. In addition, the expulsion of over one million Yemeni guest workers from Saudi Arabia imposed a huge burden on the economy and ended the flow of workers' remittances.

Economic crisis forced the government to reduce expenditure and subsidies on certain staple foods. This provoked widespread civil unrest and encouraged many farmers to switch from food crops, such as wheat, to growing the more profitable narcotic plant *qat*. As a result, Yemen has increasingly had to import foodstuffs.

The 1994 civil war had a serious impact on the economy – water systems, oil refineries, and communications centers were destroyed. In 1995, the government began an IMF-backed reform program to stabilize the economy. However, a decision in June 1998 to remove subsidies altogether from staple foods led to violent demonstrations.

YEMEN : MAJOR BUSINESSES

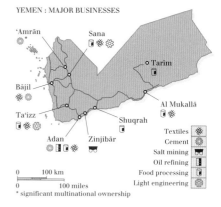

Textiles 🏭
Cement
Salt mining
Oil refining
Food processing
Light engineering ⚙

* significant multinational ownership

RESOURCES
▷ Electric power 810,000 kw

103,740 tonnes

340,000 b/d (reserves 4bn bbl)

4.5m sheep, 4m goats, 1.2m cattle

Oil, natural gas, salt, marble, gypsum

ELECTRICITY GENERATION

ELECTRICITY GENERATION	
Hydro 0%	
Combustion 100% (2bn kwh)	
Nuclear 0%	
Other 0%	

% of total generation by type

0   20   40   60   80   100

There are considerable reserves of oil and gas. Crude oil production and refining based in Aden, is rising but has been held back by Western companies' reluctance to offend Saudi Arabia, whose relations with Yemen are strained. Despite attacks by bandits, exploration is continuing in many areas. Salt is the only other mineral that is commercially exploited at present, and its production continues to grow steadily.

The agricultural sector employs 55% of the working population and accounts for more than 20% of GDP. Cotton is grown as a cash crop. There is also some forestry and hunting for animal skins. Livestock and their products, including dairy produce and hides, are the economic mainstays of the north.

Yemen's rich fishing grounds in the Arabian Sea have been developed. They now provide a major source of earnings, despite poor equipment.

YEMEN : LAND USE

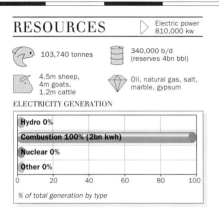

RUB 'AL KHALI

0	100 km	
0	100 miles	

Cropland
Pasture
Desert
Cotton
Grapes
Sheep

ENVIRONMENT
▷ No Green MPs

None

Low

ENVIRONMENTAL TREATIES

	No		Yes		Yes
	Yes		Yes		No

Yemen's low economic development has resulted in large untouched areas of land. However, game animals are under severe threat from hunters.

MEDIA
▷ TV ownership high

Daily newspaper circulation 15 per 1,000 people

PUBLISHING AND BROADCAST MEDIA

There are 3 daily newspapers, including the *Ath-Thawrah, Ar-Rabi' 'Ashar Min Uktubar* and *Al-Jumhuriyah*

1 state-controlled service

1 state-controlled service

CRIME
▷ Death penalty used

Yemen does not publish prison figures

Crime down 51% from 1991–1996

CRIME RATES

Murders	
3	per 100,000 population

Rapes	
0	per 100,000 population

Thefts	
28	per 100,000 population

Political assassinations continue to threaten political stability. There is little formal law enforcement outside the main cities; Western companies risk personnel being kidnapped and equipment stolen by Bedouin raiders. There is a proliferation of illicit weapons. In 1998, an unofficial estimate of the number of firearms was 50 million – three times the population size.

EDUCATION
▷ School leaving age: 15

43%

65,675 students

Unpopular economic policies have encouraged student activism.

THE EDUCATION SYSTEM

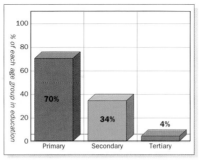

% of each age group in education

- Primary 70%
- Secondary 34%
- Tertiary 4%

Some 80% of the population have no formal classroom education. Schooling barely extends into rural areas. Illiteracy is especially high among women: 74% cannot read or write. Only 13% of students at Yemen's two universities – Sana and Aden – are female. Yemen also has some technical colleges.

Yemen has a long, distinguished tradition of intellectual debate, but the press is poorly developed. The government keeps a tight control on the media and vets the entry of foreign journalists. TV and radio are state-controlled and have a limited range around the principal cities. Satellite TV is not generally available. The ownership of radio and TV receivers is low, with only a small minority of the population owning a television set.

HEALTH
▷ No welfare state health benefits

1 per 10,000 people

Diarrheal diseases, tuberculosis, malaria, bilharzia

The major cities have an adequate primary health care system. Rural areas are less well served. Yemen has only one doctor for every 10,000 people. Health services are under threat from tribal gangs. In 1998 three nuns working as health volunteers at the Dar al-Salam Hospital in the western city of Hudaydah were shot dead by a tribal gunman.

SPENDING
▷ GDP/cap. no increase

CONSUMPTION AND SPENDING

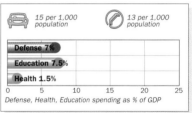

15 per 1,000 population

13 per 1,000 population

- Defense 7%
- Education 7.5%
- Health 1.5%

0   5   10   15   20   25

Defense, Health, Education spending as % of GDP

Most Yemenis suffered a fall in living standards after Saudi Arabia expelled its Yemeni workers. The lack of jobs in other Gulf states has fueled unemployment, estimated at more than 30%. Except for a small elite, the ownership of consumer goods is low.

WORLD RANKING

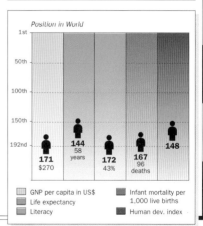

Position in World

1st
50th
100th
150th
192nd

- 171 $270
- 144 58 years
- 172 43%
- 167 96 deaths
- 148

☐ GNP per capita in US$	☐ Infant mortality per 1,000 live births
☐ Life expectancy	
☐ Literacy	☐ Human dev. index

Y

YUGOSLAVIA (SERBIA & MONTENEGRO)

OFFICIAL NAME: Federal Republic of Yugoslavia **CAPITAL:** Belgrade
POPULATION: 10.4 million **CURRENCY:** Dinar **OFFICIAL LANGUAGE:** Serbo-croat

| 1992 | 1992 | Nov 29 | YU | +1 | +381 | | .yu |

THE FEDERAL REPUBLIC of Yugoslavia (FRY) consists of Serbia and the much smaller Montenegro – two of the six elements of former Yugoslavia. The FRY, widely regarded as chiefly responsible for conflicts in the region in the 1990s, was not recognized by most states. UN sanctions were imposed during the Bosnian war in 1992–1995, to be followed by the aerial bombing of Serbia and entry of NATO-led forces in March–June 1999 after "ethnic cleansing" of Kosovo had precipitated an exodus of its ethnic Albanian population. In 1999 Slobodan Milošević, long dominant in Serb politics, was indicted for war crimes.

CLIMATE ▷ Continental

WEATHER CHART

The climate is continental inland and Mediterranean along the Montenegrin coast. Summers are hot and springs rainy. Winters are cold, with heavy snowfalls. In July and August, the average maximum in Belgrade is 28°C (82°F), while in January it is 3°C (37°F).

TRANSPORTATION ▷ Drive on right

Surcin, Belgrade
1.38m passengers

53 ships
432,000 grt

THE TRANSPORTATION NETWORK

| 49,500 km (30,938 miles) | 350 km (217 miles) |
| 4,031 km (2,519 miles) | Danube River is the major waterway |

About one-third of railroads in the FRY are electrified. The rail link to Greece, one of Serbia's main trading links, was closed in 1993–1995 as a result of international sanctions. Bridges and railroad links were targeted by NATO bombing in 1999, while foreign travel effectively ceased and international civilian flights into Belgrade were suspended.

Even before the eruption of the Kosovo conflict in 1998–1999, most foreign travelers chose to take longer routes through neighboring countries, although Yugoslavia issued transit visas relatively freely, and travel on the main Budapest–Sofia highway through Serbia had resumed.

The former Yugoslavia's mountain scenery and beaches attracted over five million tourists a year before 1991.

TOURISM ▷ Visitors : population 1:34

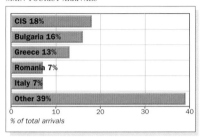

298,000 visitors

Tourism seriously affected by the Kosovo situation

MAIN TOURIST ARRIVALS

	% of total arrivals
CIS 18%	
Bulgaria 16%	
Greece 13%	
Romania 7%	
Italy 7%	
Other 39%	

Serbia has never been a center of tourism. The Montenegrin coast, however, has renowned beaches. The impact of UN sanctions and the conflict over Kosovo meant that foreign tourism ceased. Before 1999 Montenegrin tourism was monopolized by Serbians, particularly by political and criminal elements of the Serbian elite. Hyperinflation and recession kept the average Yugoslav vacationer away.

YUGOSLAVIA
(SERBIA & MONTENEGRO)

Total Land Area : 102 173 sq. km (39 449 sq. miles)

POPULATION

over 1 000 000
over 100 000
over 50 000

LAND HEIGHT

2000m/6562ft
1000m/3281ft
500m/1640ft
200m/656ft
Sea Level

PEOPLE   ▷ Pop. density medium

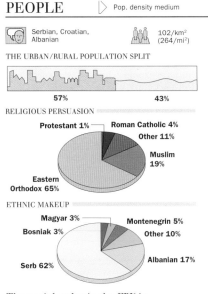

Serbian, Croatian, Albanian   102/km² (264/mi²)

THE URBAN/RURAL POPULATION SPLIT

57%   43%

RELIGIOUS PERSUASION

Protestant 1%   Roman Catholic 4%
Other 11%
Muslim 19%
Eastern Orthodox 65%

ETHNIC MAKEUP

Magyar 3%   Montenegrin 5%
Bosniak 3%   Other 10%
Serb 62%   Albanian 17%

The social order in the FRY is disintegrating. The professional classes have effectively been driven out; at least 100,000 have left since 1991. There has been massive upheaval in Kosovo, where 800,000 ethnic Albanians fled the 1999 conflict. The June 1999 agreement ensured their return and raised the question of the future of the minority Serb population of Kosovo. The absence of a middle class, who might speed a recovery, is strongly felt.

Even before the Kosovo conflict erupted, an estimated two-thirds of the population were living below subsistence level. Many suffer from malnutrition and health problems are aggravated by bitingly cold winters. Apart from the desperate situation of refugees and internally displaced families, unsupported pensioners are faring worst. Real monthly pensions are virtually worthless and there is a depressingly high suicide rate among the old living in cities.

POPULATION AGE BREAKDOWN

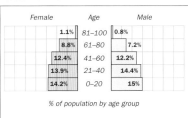

Female	Age	Male
1.1%	81–100	0.8%
8.8%	61–80	7.2%
12.4%	41–60	12.2%
13.9%	21–40	14.4%
14.2%	0–20	15%

% of population by age group

POLITICS   ▷ Multiparty elections

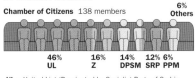

L.House 1998/2000
U.House 1996/2000

Federal President
Slobodan Milošević

AT THE LAST ELECTION

Chamber of Citizens 138 members   6% Others

46% UL	16% Z	14% DPSM	12% SRP	6% PPM

UL = United List (Dominated by Socialist Party of Serbia (SPS) **Z** = Zajedno **DPSM** = Democratic Party of Socialists of Montenegro **SRP** = Serbian Radical Party **PPM** = People's Party of Montenegro

Chamber of Republics 40 members

20 delegates are elected to the Chamber of Republics by each of the two republican assemblies of Serbia and Montenegro.

Serbia and Montenegro each have a unicameral parliament, a president, and send members to the bicameral Federal Assembly.

Main Political Issues
Kosovo
Tensions between separatist tendencies and Serbian repression in its majority Albanian-inhabited province of Kosovo escalated in 1998. Peace talks halted in March 1999, when Yugoslavia refused to sign the Rambouillet accord. NATO bombing was initially defied and repression in Kosovo intensified. By June, the FRY had to agree to withdraw its forces and police, and allow an international force to enable the return of hundreds of thousands of refugees.

Future of Milošević
Indicted as a war criminal and forced to withdraw Serb forces from Kosovo in 1999, Milošević faces isolation abroad and internal opposition. During the Kosovo conflict ranks closed around him, but soon reemerged challenges to his hold on power.

Profile
Milošević has dominated Yugoslav politics, as Serbian president from 1989 and federal president from 1997. Montenegro was less subservient after the 1997 election of Milo Djukanović as its president. The Kosovo conflict, NATO bombing, and the deployment of an international peace force in 1999 profoundly affect the internal political balance within the FRY.

Radoje Kontić, federal prime minister 1993–1998.

Slobodan Milošević, Serbian leader, and since 1997 president of the FRY.

WORLD AFFAIRS   ▷ Joined UN in 1945

G24   IAEA   NAM

The Balkans were left in a state of flux after the 1995 Bosnian peace accord. Mutual recognition paved the way for a formal normalization of relations among the former Yugoslav states. The FRY signed accords with Bosnia, Slovenia, Macedonia, and lastly with Croatia, following the implementation of a 1995 agreement to reintegrate into Croatia Serb-occupied eastern Slavonia. UN sanctions against the FRY were lifted, but a renewed crisis arose over repression in Kosovo. The indictment of Milošević by the International Criminal Tribunal for the former Yugoslavia in 1999 underlined his international pariah status, while NATO hardened its stance over Kosovo. After sustained air strikes, NATO-led forces went in to supervise an autonomy agreement. The conflict had far-reaching implications for relations with the West, neighboring states, and Russia.

AID   ▷ Recipient

$97m (receipts)   Up 39% 1996–1997

Aid, except to Montenegro, is obstructed by Milošević's pariah status. It also depends on FRY compliance with the June 1999 accord on Kosovo, just as aid was conditional on implementation of the 1995 Bosnian peace accord.

CHRONOLOGY

The Serbs were defeated by the Turks at the Battle of Kosovo in 1389. Parts of the region were later ruled by the Austrian Habsburg empire.

❏ **1878** Independence gained by Serbia and Montenegro at Congress of Berlin.
❏ **1918** Joint Kingdom of Serbs, Croats and Slovenes created.
❏ **1929** King Alexander of Serbia assumes absolute powers over state; changes name to Yugoslavia.
❏ **1941** Germans launch surprise attack. Rival resistance groups: Chetniks (Serb royalist) and Partisans (communist, under Tito).
❏ **1945** Federal People's Republic of Yugoslavia founded with Tito as prime minister. Vojvodina and Kosovo provinces gain autonomy within Serbia.
❏ **1948** Tito breaks with Stalin.
❏ **1951** Farmers permitted to sell produce on free market.
❏ **1955** Yugoslav–Soviet detente.   ➪

Y

CHRONOLOGY *continued*

- **1973** Economic cooperation agreement signed with West Germany. Agreement of noninterference signed with Soviet Union. Croat nationalists purged from party leadership and government.
- **1974** New constitution decentralizes government. Vojvodina and Kosovo given autonomy within Serbia.
- **1980** Tito dies. Succeeded by collective presidency.
- **1981** Unrest among Kosovo Albanians; state of emergency.
- **1985** Serbian intellectuals publish memorandum listing Serb grievances within Yugoslavia.
- **1986** Slobodan Milošević becomes leader of Communist (later Socialist) Party in Serbia (SPS).
- **1987** Wage freeze to combat inflation. Banking system crisis.
- **1988** Belgrade protests against economic austerity. Mikulić government brought down over budget failure.
- **1989** Kosovo Albanians protest at presence of Serb police unit; crackdown ends Kosovo's autonomy. King Nicholas I reburied in Montenegro. 600th anniversary of Battle of Kosovo.
- **1990** Milošević and Socialist Party victorious in elections in Serbia. Communists win presidency and dominate assembly in multiparty elections in Montenegro.
- **1992** EC recognizes breakaway republics of Croatia, Slovenia, and Bosnia–Herzegovina. UN sanctions imposed. Ibrahim Rugova elected president of self-declared republic of Kosovo. Vance–Owen plan for Bosnia fails. Milošević defeats premier Milan Panić but is reelected president, but SPS lose absolute majority. Momir Bulatović wins Montenegrin presidency.
- **1993** SPS gains seats in elections. EU initiative in peace talks over Bosnia.
- **1995** Milošević and Croatian and Bosnian Muslim leaders sign Bosnian peace accord.
- **1996** UN sanctions formally lifted.
- **1997** Milošević makes concessions after antigovernment protests; acknowledges malpractice in municipal elections; becomes federal president. Extreme nationalist Serbian Radical Party performs well in elections.
- **1998** Conflict in Kosovo escalates.
- **1999** March, Kosovo talks break down. NATO aerial bombing of FRY. "Ethnic cleansing" precipitates mass exodus. June, FRY agrees to withdrawal of Serbian forces and police from Kosovo, and entry of international force, KFOR.

Y

DEFENSE ▷ Compulsory military service

 $1.5bn   Down 1% in 1997

Real military spending was estimated to be around 8% of GDP in 1997.

SERBIAN ARMED FORCES

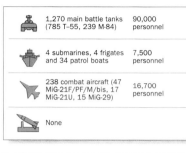

🛡	1,270 main battle tanks (785 T–55, 239 M-84)	90,000 personnel
⚓	4 submarines, 4 frigates and 34 patrol boats	7,500 personnel
✈	238 combat aircraft (47 MiG-21F/PF/M/bis, 17 MiG-21U, 15 MiG-29)	16,700 personnel
🚀	None	

The FRY's military capability was specifically targeted for "degrading" by NATO air strikes in March–June 1999. The impact on anti-aircraft defenses, heavy weaponry, logistics capacity and infrastructure was less severe than first claimed, however. The CIA gave the strength of the Kosovo Liberation Army (KLA) as 17,000, but others estimated double that figure.

The Serbian military played a major role in the conflicts in former Yugoslavia. Traditionally the center of Yugoslav armaments manufacture, Serbia was able to arm itself. The need to create money to pay for domestically produced weapons was a major factor in the crippling hyperinflation of 1993.

ECONOMICS ▷ Not available

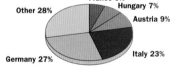 **$9.5bn**   **5.86–9.98 dinars**

SCORE CARD

- ❑ WORLD GNP RANKING 84th
- ❑ GNP PER CAPITA $900
- ❑ BALANCE OF PAYMENTS .... $–161m
- ❑ INFLATION 6,147%
- ❑ UNEMPLOYMENT 26%

EXPORTS

UK 4% Hungary 5%
Italy 38% France 5%
Other 20%
Germany 28%

IMPORTS

France 6%
Other 28% Hungary 7%
Austria 9%
Italy 23%
Germany 27%

STRENGTHS
Brief boom after 1996 lifting of UN sanctions devastated by Kosovo conflict and bombing damage in 1999.

WEAKNESSES
Economic collapse caused by sanctions, Kosovo crisis and 1999 NATO bombing. Blockage of IMF credits and foreign aid even after 1996. Dwindling hard currency reserves. Effects of hyperinflation.

PROFILE
After the transition to a multiparty system, a reformist government began reforms, but the Bosnian war stalled these initiatives. Sanctions stifled trade and decimated both the emerging private and the state sectors. In 1993–1994 hyperinflation pushed the

ECONOMIC PERFORMANCE INDICATOR

The breakup of the former Yugoslavia and the extent of current economic collapse in Serbia and Montenegro mean that consistent economic trends between 1993 and 1997 cannot be established.

economy to virtual collapse, making savings worthless. Currency reform in 1994 achieved brief stabilization. Lack of foreign direct investment persisted, even after 1996, and high inflation loomed again. The FRY estimated damage to the infrastructure by NATO bombing in 1999 at $60 billion and the EBRD estimated reconstruction costs to be $20 billion over three years.

YUGOSLAVIA : MAJOR BUSINESSES

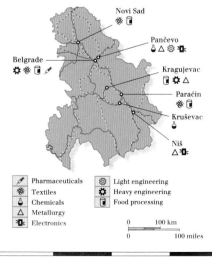

Novi Sad
Pančevo
Belgrade
Kragujevac
Paraćin
Kruševac
Niš

✎ Pharmaceuticals	⚙ Light engineering
❋ Textiles	✿ Heavy engineering
🜪 Chemicals	📦 Food processing
△ Metallurgy	
⚡ Electronics	

0   100 km
0   100 miles

RESOURCES   ▷ Electric power 11.8m kw

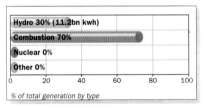

6,926 tonnes

4.2m pigs, 2.4m sheep, 1.9m cattle, 86,000 horses

Some oil production

Coal, bauxite, iron, lead, copper, zinc

ELECTRICITY GENERATION

Hydro 30% (11.2bn kwh)	
Combustion 70%	
Nuclear 0%	
Other 0%	

0   20   40   60   80   100

% of total generation by type

The FRY is self-sufficient in coal and electricity production. Vojvodina caters for one-third of oil needs, but the oil industry was badly hit by the NATO bombing in March–June 1999.

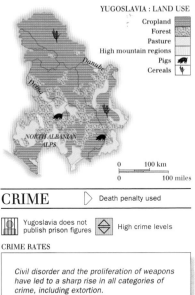

YUGOSLAVIA : LAND USE

- Cropland
- Forest
- Pasture
- High mountain regions
- Pigs
- Cereals

Danube

Drina

NORTH ALBANIAN ALPS

0   100 km
0   100 miles

ENVIRONMENT   ▷ No Green MPs

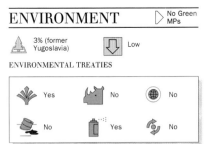

3% (former Yugoslavia)

Low

ENVIRONMENTAL TREATIES

Yes		No		No	
No		Yes		No	

In Serbia, ecological awareness peaked in the late 1980s when the Ecological Forum was active. Opposition in Montenegro to the Tara River dam project caused the dam to be moved upstream from a scenic canyon. NATO bombing of Serbia in 1999 caused extensive pollution of the Danube, and raised fears of contamination from dioxins and depleted uranium.

MEDIA   ▷ TV ownership high

 Daily newspaper circulation 110 per 1,000 people

PUBLISHING AND BROADCAST MEDIA

	There are 18 daily newspapers. *Politika* has the largest circulation
	2 state-controlled, several independent services
	3 state-controlled, several independent services

Public opinion continues to be shaped by the state-regulated broadcast media. Nationalization in 1996 of the private TV station Studio B removed the main outlet for opposition news. Coverage of the Kosovo conflict in 1999 was closely managed and the outcome presented as a victory for the FRY. State control of newsprint supplies was used to put pressure on *Nasa Borba,* the Serbian opposition paper. The official news agency Tanjug was purged in 1991 to eliminate criticism of the regime.

CRIME   ▷ Death penalty used

Yugoslavia does not publish prison figures

High crime levels

CRIME RATES

> Civil disorder and the proliferation of weapons have led to a sharp rise in all categories of crime, including extortion.

An estimated 40% of all economic activity, from currency trading to black market goods, takes place in the illegal market. Formerly on the main east–west smuggling route, Montenegro's drugs trade was disrupted by sanctions and even more so by the 1999 Kosovo conflict. It is feared that the Serbian militia will turn to Mafia-type extortion.

EDUCATION   ▷ School leaving age: 15

93%   172,313 students

Schooling was totally disrupted by the Kosovo conflict in 1999.

THE EDUCATION SYSTEM

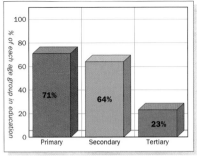

% of each age group in education

Primary	Secondary	Tertiary
71%	64%	23%

The education system is in crisis; a wealthy few go abroad for their education. Literacy rates in Kosovo, where ethnic Albanian schools were closed in 1990, were below the FRY average even before the conflict. To rebuild its education system is vital to reconstruction and reconciliation.

HEALTH   ▷ Welfare state health benefits

1 per 500 people

Heart, cerebrovascular diseases, cancers and accidents

Isolation from former trading partners has affected the quality of the health service, despite the exemption of medicines and medical supplies from sanctions. Most people cannot afford medicines and death rates among infants and the elderly have risen dramatically. Particular controversy surrounded (accidental) NATO bombing of hospitals and civilians in March–June 1999.

SPENDING   ▷ GDP/cap. no increase

CONSUMPTION AND SPENDING

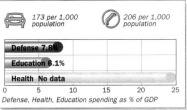

173 per 1,000 population

206 per 1,000 population

Defense 7.8%	
Education 6.1%	
Health No data	

0   5   10   15   20   25
Defense, Health, Education spending as % of GDP

The country as a whole was seriously impoverished by sanctions; real incomes fell dramatically, yet food prices remained higher than in much of western Europe. Bank collapses in 1992 and continuing hyperinflation in 1993–1994 wiped out dinar savings. The lifting of sanctions in 1995–1996 had hardly begun to be reflected in improvements in living conditions when the Kosovo conflict brought further dislocation and hardship in 1999.

Those who have amassed wealth have largely done so by exploiting the chaos of war through the black market. One of the few areas of business expansion in recent years was in exploiting markets for previously imported goods. The few rich bought sanctions-busting goods illegally imported from western Europe.

WORLD RANKING

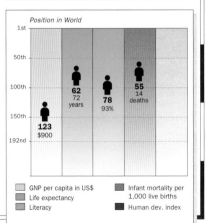

Position in World

1st
50th
100th
150th
192nd

123 $900	
62 72 years	
78 93%	
55 14 deaths	

- GNP per capita in US$
- Life expectancy
- Literacy
- Infant mortality per 1,000 live births
- Human dev. index

Y

ZAMBIA

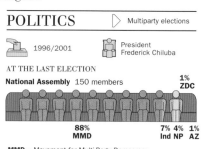

SOUTHERN AFRICA

Africa

OFFICIAL NAME: Republic of Zambia   **CAPITAL:** Lusaka
POPULATION: 8.7 million   **CURRENCY:** Zambian kwacha   **OFFICIAL LANGUAGE:** English

| 1964 | 1964 | Oct 24 | Z | +2 | +260 | .zm |

L YING IN THE HEART of southern Africa, Zambia is a country of upland plateaus, bordered to the south by the Zambezi river. Its economic fortunes are tied to the copper industry. Falling copper prices in the late 1970s, and then the growing inaccessibility of remaining reserves, have led to a severe decline in the economy. In 1991, Zambia achieved a peaceful transition from single-party rule to multiparty democracy.

CLIMATE

Tropical wet & dry

WEATHER CHART

Average daily temperature   Rainfall

Zambia has a tropical climate, with rains from November to April. The southwest is prone to drought.

TRANSPORTATION

Drive on left

Lusaka International
339,944 passengers

Has no fleet

THE TRANSPORTATION NETWORK

| 39,700 km (24,700 miles) | 60 km (37 miles) |
| 1,273 km (791 miles) | 2,250 miles (1,398 miles) |

The poor rail and road networks, in need of urgent rehabilitation, could sabotage economic recovery. Zambian Airways was liquidated in 1994, and private airlines are now in operation.

TOURISM

Visitors : population 1:31

278,000 visitors

Up 60% 1994-1997

MAIN TOURIST ARRIVALS

Zimbabwe 37%
South Africa 11%
UK 8%
Other 44%

% of total arrivals

Wildlife, the Victoria Falls and white-water rafting on the Zambezi are the main tourist attractions. Expansion plans are being hit by funding shortages.

PEOPLE

Pop. density low

Bemba, Nyanja, Tonga, Kaonde, Lunda, Luvale, Lozi, English

12/km² (30/mi²)

THE URBAN/RURAL POPULATION SPLIT

43%   57%

RELIGIOUS PERSUASION

Muslim and Hindu communities 1%

Indigenous beliefs 36%

Christian 63%

Although ethnically heterogeneous, with more than 70 different groups, Zambia has been less affected by ethnic tension than many African states. The largest ethnic group, about 34% of the population, is the Bemba, who live in the northeast and predominate in the central Copperbelt. Other major groups are the southern Tonga people, the eastern Nyanja, and the Lozi, who live to the west.

Zambia is one of Africa's most urbanized countries, with many third and fourth generation town-dwellers in the Copperbelt, the main urban area. Urban life has done little to change the traditionally subordinate role of women in the family and politics. They are, however, increasingly involved in business, and two women hold cabinet posts. The rural population live mainly by subsistence farming.

Victoria Falls, known to Africans as Musi-o-Tunyi (The Smoke That Thunders). Spray from the falls can be seen 30 km away.

POLITICS

Multiparty elections

1996/2001

President
Frederick Chiluba

AT THE LAST ELECTION

National Assembly   150 members

1% ZDC

88% MMD

7% Ind   4% NP   1% AZ

MMD = Movement for Multi-Party Democracy
Ind = Independent   **NP** = National Party
AZ = Agenda for Zambia
ZDC = Zambia Democratic Congress

The 1991 defeat of Kenneth Kaunda and the UNIP in the first multiparty elections for 19 years was the expression of popular discontent with an ailing economy and official corruption. President Frederick Chiluba and the MMD government have since made little economic headway, despite painful reforms. In 1995, Kaunda resumed leadership of the UNIP, but was barred from the presidential elections in 1996. Most opposition parties boycotted the polls, and Chiluba and his MMD were returned to power. Chiluba, once widely respected as a rallying-point for the democratic opposition to Kaunda, is now much criticized for his arbitary and authoritarian rule.

WORLD AFFAIRS

Joined UN in 1964

| Comm | G15 | NAM | OAU | SADC |

Under Kaunda, Zambia led Africa's opposition to apartheid South Africa. The MMD now enjoys close links with Pretoria; but critics warn against dealings with Angola's UNITA rebels.

AID

Recipient

$618m (receipts)

Up 1% 1996–1997

The EU, the World Bank and others once spent nearly $1.5 billion a year to help Zambia diversify its economy, but frustrated by state corruption and draconian policies, donors froze aid in 1997. In 1999, however, the IMF granted Zambia a $349 million three-year loan.

DEFENSE

No compulsory military service

$59m

Down 2% in 1997

Despite the relatively small budget, the 21,600-strong armed forces are well equipped. Security along the Angolan border is a main concern.

Z

ECONOMICS

▷ Inflation 74.4% p.a. (1985–1996)

$3.5bn

1,442.50–2,470.00 Zambian kwacha

SCORE CARD

❏ World GNP Ranking	121st
❏ GNP per Capita	$370
❏ Balance of Payments	$–306m
❏ Inflation	24.8%
❏ Unemployment	22%

STRENGTHS

Potential for self-sufficiency in food. Boom in new export crops, such as cotton and flowers. Minerals, notably copper, cobalt, and coal. Market-oriented reforms; privatizations attract foreign private investors.

WEAKNESSES

Dependence on copper for 90% of export earnings, as its price plummets. Domestic reserves declining. Shortage of finance for restructuring, exacerbated by aid donors' boycott. High inflation, negative growth, and serious drought in 1998. Arable land underutilized. Delays in privatizing state-owned copper consortium.

EXPORTS

France 7%
India 8%
Thailand 9%
Saudi Arabia 10%
Other 55%
Japan 11%

IMPORTS

USA 3%
Saudi Arabia 6%
Zimbabwe 7%
UK 8%
South Africa 48%
Other 28%

ZAMBIA

Total Land Area : 740 720 sq. km (285 992 sq. miles)

POPULATION

- ⊙ over 500 000
- ◎ over 100 000
- ○ over 50 000
- ● over 10 000
- · under 10 000

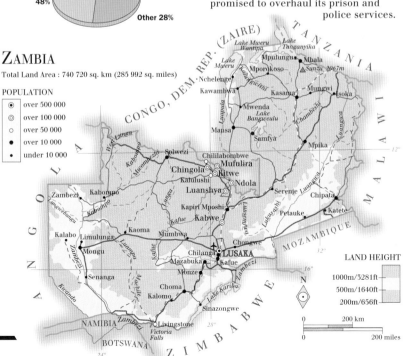

LAND HEIGHT

1000m/3281ft
500m/1640ft
200m/656ft

200 km
200 miles

RESOURCES

▷ Electric power 2.4m kw

66,332 tonnes

3.1m cattle, 600,000 goats, 285,000 pigs

Not an oil producer; refines 23,750 b/d

Copper, cobalt, coal, zinc, lead, gold, emeralds, amethyst

Despite declining reserves, copper is still the key resource; Zambia is the world's sixth-largest producer. It also has rich hydropower potential.

ENVIRONMENT

▷ No Green MPs

9%

Low

Drought is a recurrent hazard. Rhinos are almost extinct as a result of poaching. Revenues from legal hunting are being channeled into villages to encourage support for conservation.

MEDIA

▷ TV ownership medium

Daily newspaper circulation 14 per 1,000 people

PUBLISHING AND BROADCAST MEDIA

There are 3 daily newspapers, including the state-owned *Times of Zambia* and the *Zambia Daily Mail*.

1 state-controlled service

1 state-controlled service

Dailies face competition from privately owned weeklies. After 1996 opposition journalists were accused of treason.

CRIME

▷ Death penalty used

Zambia does not publish prison figures

Up 26% in 1992

Cases of violent crime, burglary, and rape are rising rapidly. In 1998 Zambia promised to overhaul its prison and police services.

CHRONOLOGY

Former Northern Rhodesia was developed by Britain solely for its copper resources. Kenneth Kaunda and the UNIP took power at Zambian independence in 1964.

- ❏ **1972** UNIP one-party government.
- ❏ **1982–1991** Austerity measures and corruption: pressure for democracy.
- ❏ **1991** MMD government elected; Frederick Chiluba defeats Kaunda.
- ❏ **1996** Controversial elections return Chiluba and MMD to power.

EDUCATION

▷ School leaving age: 14

75%

10,489 students

Primary education is compulsory. New fees at secondary level will hit the already low attendance rate of 16%.

HEALTH

▷ No welfare state health benefits

1 per 10,000 people

Respiratory infections, diarrheal diseases, malaria

Austerity measures have resulted in health service cutbacks. HIV/AIDS is a significant and growing problem.

SPENDING

▷ GDP/cap. increase

CONSUMPTION AND SPENDING

17 per 1,000 population

9 per 1,000 population

Defense 1.7%
Education 1.8%
Health 2.2%

0 5 10 15 20 25
Defense, Health, Education spending as % of GDP

Real per capita GDP is now lower than at the time of Zambia's independence in 1964. Some 60% of the country's people lack basic nutrition.

WORLD RANKING

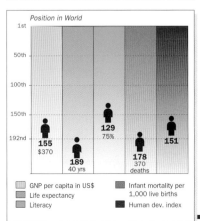

- GNP per capita in US$
- Life expectancy
- Literacy
- Infant mortality per 1,000 live births
- Human dev. index

Z

ZIMBABWE

SOUTHERN AFRICA

Africa

Zambia
ZIMBABWE Mozambique
Botswana
South Africa

OFFICIAL NAME: Republic of Zimbabwe **CAPITAL:** Harare **POPULATION:** 11.9 million
CURRENCY: Zimbabwe dollar **OFFICIAL LANGUAGE:** English

| 1980 | 1980 | April 18 | ZW | +2 | +263 | .ZW |

S ITUATED IN SOUTHERN AFRICA, Zimbabwe is
bordered by South Africa, Botswana, Zambia, and
Mozambique. The upland center is crisscrossed by rivers, which flow
into Lake Kariba and the Zambezi river. The Zambezi possesses
Zimbabwe's most spectacular natural feature, the Victoria Falls.
Formerly the British colony of Southern Rhodesia, the country achieved
independence in 1980 after a struggle between the white minority, led
by the prime minister, Ian Smith, and the black majority, represented
by Robert Mugabe's and Joshua Nkomo's Patriotic Front (PF).

*The Kariba Dam, which has created the vast
Lake Kariba on the Zambezi River, lies on
Zimbabwe's northwest border with Zambia.*

CLIMATE

▷ Tropical wet & dry/ steppe

WEATHER CHART

Average daily temperature / Rainfall
°C/°F J F M A M J J A S O N D cm/in
40/104 — 40/16
30/86 — 30/12
20/68 — 20/8
10/50 — 10/4
0/32 — 0
-10/14
-20/-4

Due to altitude, Zimbabwe is relatively
temperate for a country in the tropics;
humidity is also low. The rainy season
occurs between November and
March. But, with the exception
of the eastern highlands, rainfall
is erratic and drought is common.
Annual rainfall ranges from
140 cm (55 in) in the
eastern highlands to
40 cm (16 in) in the
Limpopo valley.

TRANSPORTATION

▷ Drive on left

🛫 **Harare International**
1.02m passengers

🚢 Has no fleet

THE TRANSPORTATION NETWORK

🛣️ 14,572 km
(9,055 miles)

🛤️ None

🚆 2,759 km
(1,714 miles)

⛴️ Lake Kariba

The number of international air links
is being increased. Zimbabwe's rail
network, among the densest in
sub-Saharan Africa, is being updated.

TOURISM

▷ Visitors : population 1:6.3

🧳 1.9m visitors

↗️ Up 42% 1995–1997

MAIN TOURIST ARRIVALS

South Africa 45%	
Zambia 32%	
Mozambique 6%	
UK & Ireland 4%	
USA & Canada 2%	
Other 11%	

0 10 20 30 40 50 60
% of total arrivals

Tourists visit Zimbabwe for both cultural
and safari vacations. The country's
principal attractions are the Victoria
Falls, the Kariba dam, numerous
national parks, the Great
Zimbabwe ruins near Masvingo,
and World's View in the Matopo
Hills. Increasingly, action
vacations – such as canoeing
trips and white-water rafting
on the Zambezi, or trout
fishing and climbing in the
eastern highlands – are
catered for.
    Zimbabwe is wary of
a glut of mass-market
tourists, as this may
seriously damage the
environment. However,
the lure of foreign exchange
has encouraged the
development of conference
facilities in Harare and
vacation complexes around
Victoria Falls, such as
Elephant Hills. State law
requires 30% local ownership
of tourist ventures, but related
import controls have been
relaxed and prices deregulated.
A two-tier pricing structure
now prevails, allowing locals
to pay less; foreigners must
pay in hard currencies.

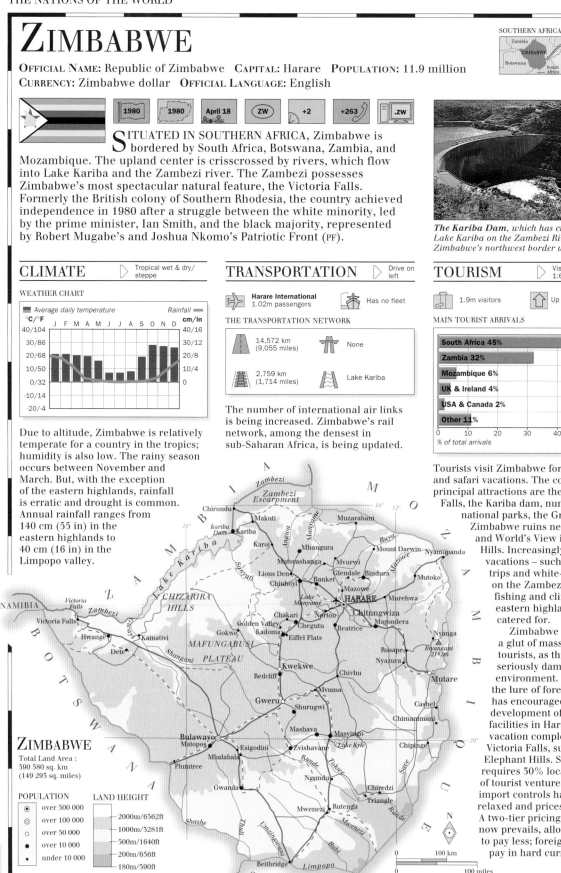

ZIMBABWE

Total Land Area :
390 580 sq. km
(149 293 sq. miles)

POPULATION
◉ over 500 000
◎ over 100 000
○ over 50 000
● over 10 000
• under 10 000

LAND HEIGHT
2000m/6562ft
1000m/3281ft
500m/1640ft
200m/656ft
180m/590ft

100 km
100 miles

PEOPLE ▷ Pop. density low

Shona, Ndebele, English　　31/km² (80/mi²)

THE URBAN/RURAL POPULATION SPLIT

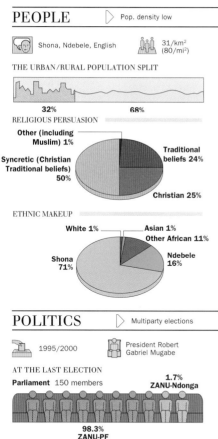

32%　　　68%

RELIGIOUS PERSUASION

- Other (including Muslim) 1%
- Traditional beliefs 24%
- Syncretic (Christian Traditional beliefs) 50%
- Christian 25%

ETHNIC MAKEUP

- White 1%
- Asian 1%
- Other African 11%
- Ndebele 16%
- Shona 71%

POPULATION AGE BREAKDOWN

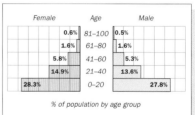

Female		Age	Male	
	0.6%	81–100	0.5%	
	1.6%	61–80	1.6%	
	5.8%	41–60	5.3%	
	14.9%	21–40	13.6%	
28.3%		0–20		27.8%

% of population by age group

There are two main ethnic groups, the Ndebele (popularly known as the Matabele) in the south and the Shona (known as the Mashona) in the north. The Mashona outnumber the Matabele by about four to one. Europeans and Asians comprise 2% of the population. Tension between the Matabele and the Mashona was rife in the 1980s. This was caused by an attempt by President Mugabe's ruling ZANU–PF, linked to the Mashona, to suppress the leading opposition party, the predominantly Matabele Zimbabwe African People's Union (PF–ZAPU). The conflict was most intense in 1983, when the army killed 1,500 Matabele. Tension abated following the Unity Accord of 1987 and the 1990 appointment of ZAPU leader Joshua Nkomo as vice-president.

As a legacy of colonial rule, whites remain generally far more affluent than blacks. This imbalance has been somewhat redressed by government policies to increase black education and white-collar employment.

Families are large, and almost half the population is under 15. Zimbabwean society is traditionally patriarchal. In 1999 a Supreme Court ruling provoked protest by according only "junior male" status to black women, especially those marrying under traditional law.

POLITICS ▷ Multiparty elections

1995/2000　　　President Robert Gabriel Mugabe

AT THE LAST ELECTION

Parliament 150 members

1.7% ZANU-Ndonga

98.3% ZANU-PF

ZANU-PF = Zimbabwe African National Union
ZANU-Ndonga = Zimbabwe African National Union - Ndonga
30 seats are set aside for presidential appointments and traditional chiefs

Zimbabwe is constitutionally a multiparty state; 80% of MPs are elected and serve a five-year term. Every six years, parliament elects the president, who is eligible for reelection.

MAIN POLITICAL ISSUES
Political dominance of ZANU–PF
At independence, the PF was a coalition of ZANU, led by Robert Mugabe, and ZAPU, led by Joshua Nkomo. As ZANU–PF became more powerful, the coalition split and PF–ZAPU supporters resorted to guerrilla activity until 1987, when a unity agreement was signed with Nkomo, later made vice-president. With the main opposition party absorbed, Mugabe, now president, attempted to promulgate a one-party, socialist state. These plans were abandoned in 1991 and other parties have since emerged. But repression continues, and the civil service is closed to non-supporters of the ruling party.

Land redistribution
The Land Acquisition Act of 1992 allows the compulsory purchase of 1,500 white-owned farms, and the resettling there of landless black peasants. Meant to redress the racial wealth disparity, it instead provoked protests and allegations of corruption. While local blacks started seeing it as a populist smokescreen, agricultural investors were scared off. A compromise scheme was mooted in 1998.

PROFILE
The ruling ZANU–PF appears to have lost direction following the collapse of the Eastern bloc and the end of apartheid in South Africa. The influence of Robert Mugabe is waning, but he has no clear successor. The only candidate in the 1996 presidential election, Mugabe won on a small turnout. No other party seems to offer credible opposition. However, since the death of Vice President Joshua Nkomo in 1999, the new ZANU–2000 appears to be gaining ground.

Robert Mugabe, elected prime minister in 1980 and president in 1987.

Simon Muzenda, senior vice-president.

AID ▷ Recipient

US$327m (receipts)　　Down 13% 1996-1997

In 1992 the IMF promised Zimbabwe US$484 million to support its economic and financial reform program; the EU pledged somewhat less. However, as aid intended for small farmers and indigenous enterprises was siphoned off to large industrial projects, bilateral donors, including the UK, France, Germany, Denmark, and the USA, reduced grants by a third between 1994 and 1996. In 1998 the IMF approved US$175 million in standby credit, as Mugabe announced new pledges from Cuba and Libya.

WORLD AFFAIRS ▷ Joined UN in 1980

Comm　G15　NAM　OAU　SADC

Zimbabwe cooperates with its neighbors through the SADC and the Preferential Trade Area for East and South Africa, and has consistently followed a policy of non-alignment. The regime took an activist stance against apartheid; after 1990, when Nelson Mandela was freed, relations with Pretoria improved.

For ideological reasons, and to maintain access to the sea, Zimbabwe supported the socialist Mozambican government against RENAMO guerrillas in 1982, and Mugabe helped to mediate the Mozambican peace accord in 1992. In 1993, he sent troops to Somalia; in 1998 a much larger contingent went to support the president of Congo, Dem. Rep. (Zaire), Laurent Kabila. Mugabe also defied sanctions on Libya, accused the UK of hostile propaganda, and promised to back the Angolan government against UNITA rebels. But the cost of radicalism abroad has been resentment at home.

Z

CHRONOLOGY

In 1953, the UK colony of Southern Rhodesia, with Northern Rhodesia (now Zambia) and Nyasaland (now Malawi), formed the Federation of Rhodesia and Nyasaland.

❑ **1959** Banning of African National Congress (ANC), led by Joshua Nkomo.
❑ **1961** Nkomo forms ZAPU.
❑ **1962** ZAPU banned. Racial segregationist Rhodesian Front (RF) wins elections.
❑ **1963** African nationalists in Northern Rhodesia and Nyasaland demand dissolution of Federation. ZANU, offshoot of ZAPU, formed by Rev. Sithole and Robert Mugabe.
❑ **1964** New RF prime minister Ian Smith rejects British demands for majority rule. ZANU banned.
❑ **1965** May, RF re-elected. November, state of emergency declared (renewed until 1990). Smith makes unilateral declaration of independence. UK imposes economic sanctions. ANC, ZANU, and ZAPU begin guerrilla war.
❑ **1970** Rhodesia declared republic.
❑ **1974** RF regime agrees cease-fire terms with African nationalists.
❑ **1975–1979** Intermittent negotiations between British government, RF, and nationalists to reach settlement.
❑ **1976** ZANU and ZAPU unite as Patriotic Front (PF).
❑ **1977** PF backed by "frontline" African states: Mozambique, Tanzania, Botswana, and Zambia.
❑ **1979** PF rejects settlement drafted by Ian Smith and moderate African nationalists. Eventual agreement on constitution.
❑ **1980** Independence as Zimbabwe. Following violent election campaign, Robert Mugabe becomes prime minister of ZANU-PF/ZAPU-PF coalition. Relations severed with South Africa.
❑ **1985–1984** Unrest in Matabeleland, ZAPU-PF's power base.
❑ **1985** Elections return ZANU-PF, with manifesto to create one-party state. Many ZAPU–PF members arrested.
❑ **1987** June, ZAPU–PF banned. September, provision for white seats in parliament abolished. December, ZANU–PF and ZAPU–PF sign unity agreement (merge in 1989). Mugabe elected president.
❑ **1990** Elections won by ZANU–PF. Mugabe re-elected president.
❑ **1991** Mugabe abandons plan for one-party state.
❑ **1998** Nationwide strikes, student protests and talk of attempted military coup.
❑ **1999** Death of Vice President Joshua Nkomo.

DEFENSE

 No compulsory military service

US$304m   Up 27% in 1997

Reports of an attempted coup in December 1998, although denied by Harare, suggest that President Mugabe may no longer be in control of his armed forces. Even in the early 1980s, some soldiers deserted to fight government forces in the Matabele bush and formed the nucleus of dissidents who plagued the regime until the Unity Accord of 1987.

Zimbabwe receives military aid and training from the UK and South Korea. Although formally non-aligned, Zimbabwe supported the Mozambican regime against RENAMO guerrillas, backed the US-led operation in Somalia in 1992–1995, and in 1998 dispatched 11,000 troops to help President Kabila fight rebels in Congo, Dem. Rep. (Zaire) – a huge drain on the national purse.

ZIMBABWEAN ARMED FORCES

32 main battle tanks (PRC Type-59, PRC Type-69)	35,000 personnel
None	
62 combat aircraft (11 *Hunter*, 11 *Hawk*)	4,000 personnel
None	

ECONOMICS

Inflation 18.7% p.a. (1985–1996)

US$8.2bn   18.45–37.22 Zimbabwe dollars

SCORE CARD

❑ WORLD GNP RANKING..........................89th
❑ GNP PER CAPITA ....US$720
❑ BALANCE OF PAYMENTS.................US$–425m
❑ INFLATION 18.3%
❑ UNEMPLOYMENT..................................45%

ECONOMIC PERFORMANCE INDICATOR

EXPORTS

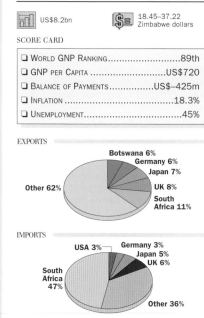

Botswana 6%
Germany 6%
Japan 7%
UK 8%
South Africa 11%
Other 62%

IMPORTS

USA 3%
Germany 3%
Japan 5%
UK 6%
South Africa 47%
Other 36%

STRENGTHS

Most broadly based African economy after South Africa. Sound infrastructure. Good international credit rating, owing to policy of debt-servicing in 1980s. Virtual self-sufficiency in food and energy. Gold, coal, tobacco, horticulture.

WEAKNESSES

Drought has hit agriculture and reduced hydroelectric output. Large budget deficits. High inflation; unemployment almost 50%. Labor unrest, bank collapses, food price riots. Currency halved in value in 1998. Cheap imports damaging local industries.

PROFILE

In the 1980s, the government's commitment to socialist policies was tempered by pragmatism. The main aim was to correct the imbalance between black and white incomes; acquisition of white-owned farms is a perennial issue. In 1991 a five-year structural adjustment program was launched, but a more market-oriented economy has increased unemployment and inflation. Prospects for the mining industry appear bleak: privatization of state copper interests was repeatedly delayed, and collapsing mineral prices have forced the closure of diamond, gold, platinum, and chromium mines.

ZIMBABWE : MAJOR BUSINESSES

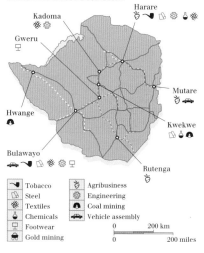

Tobacco	Agribusiness	
Steel	Engineering	
Textiles	Coal mining	
Chemicals	Vehicle assembly	
Footwear		
Gold mining		

0   200 km
0   200 miles

Z

RESURCES

▷ Electric power 2.1m kw

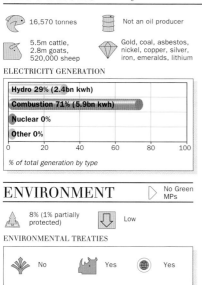

- 16,570 tonnes
- Not an oil producer
- 5.5m cattle, 2.8m goats, 520,000 sheep
- Gold, coal, asbestos, nickel, copper, silver, iron, emeralds, lithium

ELECTRICITY GENERATION

- Hydro 29% (2.4bn kwh)
- Combustion 71% (5.9bn kwh)
- Nuclear 0%
- Other 0%

% of total generation by type

Almost 40% of Zimbabwe's electricity needs are met by hydropower, notably from the Kariba dam, jointly owned with Zambia. The state power company is seeking to maximize capacity. In 1991, the government agreed to build an extension facility at Kariba South, and with Zambia a joint HEP station at Bartoka Gorge. An oil pipeline from Beira, Mozambique, to Mutare is being extended to Harare. Coal mining is expanding at Hwange, where Malaysian investments are helping to exploit deposits of 400 million tonnes.

ZIMBABWE : LAND USE

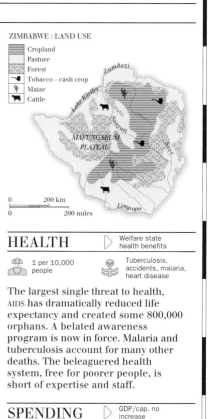

- Cropland
- Pasture
- Forest
- Tobacco - cash crop
- Maize
- Cattle

ENVIRONMENT

▷ No Green MPs

- 8% (1% partially protected)
- Low

ENVIRONMENTAL TREATIES

- No
- Yes
- Yes
- No
- Yes
- No

The 1991–1992 drought left half the population in need of drought relief, and used up 20% of public spending.

In communal areas, the land is suffering from overpopulation and overstocking. Deforestation, soil erosion, and deterioration of wildlife and water resources are widespread.

Measures have been taken to protect the black rhinoceros, including moving animals to safer areas and combating poaching – patrols have killed 150 poachers since 1986. The government also supports a scheme for dehorning rhinos – the horn is the poachers' main target. On the other hand, Zimbabwe argues that elephants no longer require special protection. In 1997 it led the move at the Convention on International Trade in Endangered Species to allow a limited resumption of international trade in ivory.

CRIME

▷ Death penalty used

- 21,000 prisoners
- Up 7% from 1991–1996

CRIME RATES

Murders
11 *per 100,000 population*

Rapes
23 *per 100,000 population*

Thefts
738 *per 100,000 population*

Urban areas have a high incidence of murder and narcotics-related offenses. An ailing economy has encouraged crime in rural areas. The Central Intelligence Organization – the secret service – and increasingly the army itself have drawn international criticism for allegedly abusing human rights.

EDUCATION

▷ School leaving age: 15

- 91%
- 46,673 students

Improving education has been one of ZANU–PF's great successes.

THE EDUCATION SYSTEM

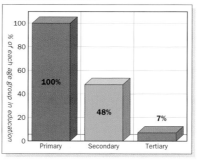

In barely ten years, primary school attendance rose from 820,000 to 2.3 million. Education is compulsory and instruction is in English. Fees were introduced after 1992. The government built two new universities; it encourages vocational training to create a workforce with skills in agriculture, medicine, and engineering.

MEDIA

▷ TV ownership low

- Daily newspaper circulation 18 per 1,000 people

PUBLISHING AND BROADCAST MEDIA

- There are 2 daily newspapers. the *Herald* and the *Chronicle*
- 1 state-controlled service
- 1 state-controlled service

The state has a controlling interest in the two main newspapers; some smaller publications operate independently. In early 1999 the army illegally arrested and reputedly tortured one editor.

HEALTH

▷ Welfare state health benefits

- 1 per 10,000 people
- Tuberculosis, accidents, malaria, heart disease

The largest single threat to health, AIDS has dramatically reduced life expectancy and created some 800,000 orphans. A belated awareness program is now in force. Malaria and tuberculosis account for many other deaths. The beleaguered health system, free for poorer people, is short of expertise and staff.

SPENDING

▷ GDP/cap. no increase

CONSUMPTION AND SPENDING

- 29 per 1,000 population
- 17 per 1,000 population

- Defense 4.7%
- Education 8.5%
- Health 3.2%

Defense, Health, Education spending as % of GDP

Recent currency depreciation, quadrupling of the maize price, and inflation have reduced real wages to 1980 levels.

WORLD RANKING

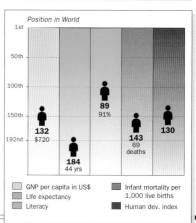

Position in World

- 132 $720
- 184 44 yrs
- 89 91%
- 143 69 deaths
- 130

- GNP per capita in US$
- Life expectancy
- Literacy
- Infant mortality per 1,000 live births
- Human dev. index

Z

639

OVERSEAS TERRITORIES & DEPENDENCIES

DESPITE THE RAPID process of decolonization since 1945 (pages 52-55), roughly 7 million people around the world still live in non-sovereign territories under the protection of the UK, USA, France, Netherlands, Denmark, Norway, Australia or New Zealand. These remnants of former colonial empires may have persisted for economic, strategic or political reasons.

Hong Kong and Macao reverted to Chinese control in the late 1990's. Others await political developments, such as referenda, which will determine their future status. Finally, a large group of territories are considered too small, remote or weak to be able to survive as independent nations.

UNITED KINGDOM

THE UK STILL HAS THE LARGEST number of overseas territories in the world. They are split into Crown colonies, Crown dependencies and dependent territories. The distinction between each is largely constitutional, since most sustain a large degree of local autonomy. Britain generally operates a policy of non-interference. If a territory expresses a constitutional desire for formal independence then it may have it, as long as it can form a viable independent country.

NEW ZEALAND

NEW ZEALAND'S GOVERNMENT has no desire to retain any overseas territories. However, the economic weakness of its dependent territory Tokelau and its freely-associated states, Niue and the Cook Islands, has forced New Zealand to remain responsible for their foreign policy and defense.

French Southern and Antarctic territories are not included in the following section. Any territories which involve an Antarctic claim are not shown.

Map labels:

Svalbard (to Norway)
BARENTS SEA
Jan Mayen (to Norway)
Faeroe Islands (to Denmark)
NORTH SEA
NORWAY
Isle of Man (to UK)
UNITED KINGDOM
DENMARK
BALTIC SEA
NETHERLANDS
Channel Islands: Guernsey and Jersey (to UK)
FRANCE
EUROPE
Gibraltar (to UK)
MEDITERRANEAN SEA
ASIA
SEA OF JAPAN
YELLOW SEA
EAST CHINA SEA
AFRICA
ARABIAN SEA
Paracel Islands (Disputed)
Northern Mariana Islands (to US)
Guam (to US)
SOUTH CHINA SEA
Spratly Islands (Disputed)
British Indian Ocean Territory (to UK)
Cocos (Keeling) Islands (to Australia)
JAVA SEA
Ascension (Administered by St Helena)
Mayotte (to France)
Christmas Island (to Australia)
Ashmore & Cartier Islands (to Australia)
ARAFURA SEA
Coral Islar (to Aus
St Helena (to UK)
ATLANTIC OCEAN
Réunion (to France)
INDIAN OCEAN
AUSTRALIA
Europa (Administered by Réunion)
Bassas da India (Administered by Réunion)
Tristan da Cunha (Administered by St Helena)
Gough Island (Administered by St Helena)
Amsterdam Island
St. Paul Island
French Southern & Antarctic Territories (France)
Crozet Islands
Kerguelen
Bouvet Island (to Norway)
Heard & McDonald Islands (to Australia)

UNITED STATES OF AMERICA

AMERICA'S OVERSEAS TERRITORIES have been seen as strategically useful, if expensive, links with its 'backyards'. The US has, in most cases, given the local population a say in deciding their own status. Thus, three former US-administered UN Trust Territories have been granted full sovereignty. A US Commonwealth territory, such as Puerto Rico has a greater level of independence than that of a US unincorporated or external territory.

OVERSEAS TERRITORIES AND DEPENDENCIES

Australia		Denmark	
New Zealand		Netherlands	
United Kingdom		Norway	
United States		Disputed	
France			

ARCTIC OCEAN

BEAUFORT SEA

Greenland
(to Denmark)

ATLANTIC OCEAN

BERING SEA

NORTH AMERICA

UNITED STATES
OF AMERICA

◦ Midway Islands
(to US)

Johnston Atoll
◦ (to US)

PACIFIC OCEAN

Kingman Reef (to US)

Palmyra Atoll ◦
(to US)

ker & Howland
Islands (to US)

Jarvis Island
(to US)

Clipperton Island
(Administered by
French Polynesia)

Tokelau (to NZ)

s & Futuna
(to France)

Cook Islands
(to NZ)

American Samoa
(to US)

Niue
(to NZ)

French
Polynesia
(to France)

New Caledonia
to France)

◦ Norfolk Island
(to Australia)

Pitcairn Islands
(to UK)

NEW
ZEALAND

St Pierre & Miquelon
(to France)

Bermuda
(to UK) ◦

Gulf of Mexico

Cayman Islands
(to UK) ◦

Navassa Island
(to US)

CARIBBEAN SEA

SOUTH
AMERICA

Turks & Caicos Islands
(to UK)

Puerto Rico
(to US)

British Virgin Islands
(to UK)

Anguilla
◦ (to UK)

Virgin Islands
(to US)

Guadeloupe
(to France)

CARIBBEAN SEA

Netherlands Antilles
(to Neth.)

Montserrat
(to UK)

Aruba
(to Neth.)

Martinique
(to France)

French Guiana
(to France)

Falkland Islands
(to UK)

South Georgia and
South Sandwich Islands
(to UK)

FRANCE

FRENCH *TERRITOIRES D'OUTRE-MER* are considered an indivisible part of the French Republic. As a result, France has developed economic ties, and stressed the advantage of interdependence over independence, with its overseas territories. A distinct hierarchy has been developed. Overseas *départements*, officially part of France, have their own governments. Territorial *collectivités* are administered by a French-appointed commissioner and a locally-elected council, whilst overseas *territoires* have varying degrees of autonomy.

AMERICAN SAMOA

STATUS: Unincorporated territory of the USA **CLAIMED:** 1900
CAPITAL: Pago Pago **POP.:** 60,000 **DENSITY:** 305/km² (790/mi²)

AMERICAN SAMOA CONSISTS of five volcanic islands and two coral atolls in the southern Pacific Ocean. It has a tropical climate with an average annual rainfall of 500 cm (200 inches). Typhoons and tropical storms are common from December to March. *Fa'a Samoa*, meaning the Samoan way of life, still directs Samoan society. The extended family, the *aiga*, forms the base of Samoan life, and chiefs still hold a central role in government. The resident population is still growing even though many young Samoans, attracted by the lifestyle of *fa'a America*, have emigrated to the USA. One-fifth of all tuna consumed in the USA passes through Pago Pago's canneries, which produce 95% of the territory's exports. Recently, the American Samoan government has tried to encourage the development of other light industries and tourism, which has been helped by the designation of a national park to protect a large area of native forest and coral reef.

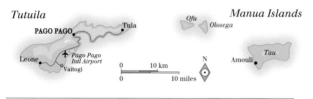

ANGUILLA

STATUS: British dependent territory **CLAIMED:** 1650
CAPITAL: The Valley **POP.:** 10,300 **DENSITY:** 107/km² (277/mi²)

ANGUILLA IS SITUATED in the Caribbean, at the northern end of the Leeward Islands. It has a subtropical climate, the heat and humidity being tempered by trade winds. In 1967, Anguillans refused to follow St. Kitts and Nevis into independence, preferring instead to retain the economic stability that came with dependent status. The People's Progressive Party, renamed the Anguilla National Alliance in 1980, dominated politics until ousted by an opposition coalition in 1994. Chief Minister Hubert Hughes, reelected in 1999, continues a policy of developing the tourist sector and expanding offshore banking. Economic growth has been due largely to tourism. Visitor numbers dropped after the devastating hurricane of 1995, but have since recovered.

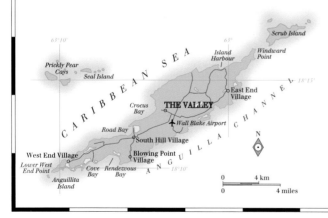

ARUBA

STATUS: Autonomous part of the Netherlands **CLAIMED:** 1643
CAPITAL: Oranjestad **POP.:** 88,000 **DENSITY:** 456/km² (1,181/mi²)

ONE OF THE SMALLEST islands in the Dutch Caribbean, Aruba lies 25 km (16 miles) off the coast of Venezuela. It has a tropical climate moderated by constant trade winds sweeping in from the Atlantic. Formerly part of the Netherlands Antilles, Aruba, the richest of the islands, became a separate dependency of the Netherlands in 1986. Transition to full independence, expected in 1996, was halted in 1994, by agreement between the governments of the Netherlands, Aruba, and the Netherlands Antilles. The Netherlands voiced concern over the island's security and the danger of it becoming a base for narcotics trafficking, and the Aruban government, led by Hendrik Eman, questioned the desirability of full independence, citing high unemployment and economic instability. The economy of Aruba, formerly dependent on oil refining, has diversified since 1986. Tourism and offshore

***Palm Beach, Aruba,** also known as the Turquoise Coast, lies on the western side of the island. The beach stretches for 10 km and is the site of a low-rise beach resort.*

finance have become the most important sectors of the economy, and there are now more than 600,000 visitors annually; nearly 60% of them come from the USA. However, the rapid expansion of tourism has put a considerable strain on Aruba's infrastructure, and some attempt has been made to restrict numbers of visitors. At the same time facilities have been improved to encourage the growth of a data-processing industry.

***Oranjestad,** Aruba's capital, contains many Dutch colonial style buildings. Although first claimed by the Spanish in 1499, Aruba was colonized by the Dutch in the 17th century.*

Cooperation with the USA in the late 1990s has included action against narcotics trafficking in the region, including new legislation to facilitate the extradition of suspected drug traffickers and money launderers, which took effect in 1997. In early 1999 discussion took place on the possibility of US military bases being established in Aruba on the departure of US troops from Panama the following December.

BERMUDA

STATUS: British Crown colony **CLAIMED:** 1612
CAPITAL: Hamilton **POP.**: 60,144 **DENSITY:** 1,135/km² (2,940/mi²)

SITUATED MORE THAN 900 km (558 miles) east of South Carolina, USA, Bermuda consists of a chain of over 150 coral islands. The Gulf Stream, flowing between Bermuda and

America's eastern seaboard, keeps the climate mild and humid. Bermuda is racially mixed; some 60% of the population are of mostly European extraction. Racial tension has declined since the 1960s and 1970s. A more representative electoral system was established after a Royal Commission visited Bermuda in 1978.

From the time of its first general election, held in 1968, Bermuda was ruled for 30 years by the conservative United Bermuda Party (UBP). Its veteran leader, Sir John Swan, resigned as prime minister and party leader in 1995 when voters in a referendum decisively rejected his campaign for independence from the UK. In a general election in November 1998 the UBP, now under the leadership of Pamela Gordon, was decisively defeated by the Progressive Labour Party, led by Jennifer Smith, who said that she had no plans to pursue her party's own pro-independence aspirations. Major issues are social and economic challenges posed by the withdrawal in 1995 of both the US naval base and the British military base, environmental issues, and narcotics trafficking. Bermuda is overwhelmingly a service economy. Lilies are grown for export, but few other agricultural products are grown in sufficient quantity to export, and the island is heavily dependent on food imports.

A tourist and tax haven which attracts more than half a million visitors a year (more than 80% of them from the US), Bermuda recently passed laws to prohibit the introduction of franchised fast-food restaurants. It has one of the highest average per capita incomes in the world. Bermuda is also a leading insurance market and operates one of the world's largest flag-of-convenience shipping fleets.

Bermuda has one of the highest densities of golf courses in the world. Eight courses have now been developed.

BRITISH INDIAN OCEAN TERRITORY

STATUS: British dependent territory **CLAIMED:** 1814
CAPITAL: Diego Garcia **POP.**: 930 **DENSITY:** 16/km² (41/mi²)

THE BRITISH Indian Ocean Territory, or Chagos Islands, lies in the middle of the Indian Ocean. The coral atolls are now uninhabited except for the US–UK military base on Diego Garcia, and the UK has undertaken to cede the islands to Mauritius when they are no longer required for military purposes. In 1999 the Ilois people brought an action against the UK government over their eviction from the Chagos Islands in 1968.

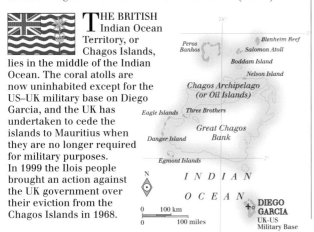

BRITISH VIRGIN ISLANDS

STATUS: British dependent territory **CLAIMED:** 1672
CAPITAL: Road Town **POP.**: 17,896 **DENSITY:** 117/km² (303/mi²)

AN ARCHIPELAGO OF 40 Caribbean islands, 15 of them inhabited, the British Virgin Islands lie at the eastern end of the Greater Antilles. The tropical climate suits tourism, now a major economic activity, but there is concern about its effect on the environment. The offshore finance sector is also important, and has been more tightly regulated since 1990, following scandals involving foreign companies registered in the islands. Veteran Chief Minister Lavity Stoutt, the dominant political figure for three decades, died in 1995.

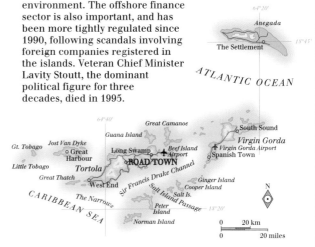

CAYMAN ISLANDS

STATUS: British dependent territory **CLAIMED:** 1670
CAPITAL: George Town **POP.:** 35,000 **DENSITY:** 135/km² (401/mi²)

THE LARGEST OF Britain's remaining territories in the Caribbean, the Cayman Islands are situated nearly 300 km (186 miles) northwest of Jamaica. Convinced that the islands' economic prosperity is directly linked to the stability its dependent territory status gives, the islanders in 1994 revoked amendments to the constitution which would have given them greater autonomy. The absence of tax and foreign-exchange controls makes the islands one of the world's largest offshore financial centers.

However, tourism underpins the economy, providing employment for more than half of the working population.

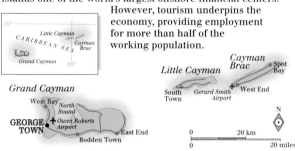

CHRISTMAS ISLAND

STATUS: Australian external territory **CLAIMED:** 1958
CAPITAL: Flying Fish Cove **POP.:** 1,275 **DENSITY:** 9/km² (23/mi²)

SO NAMED because it was sighted on Christmas Day in 1643, the island lies in the Indian Ocean, 300 km (186 miles) south of Java. The population is mostly Malay and Chinese, descended from laborers imported to mine rich phosphate deposits. The mine – closed in 1987 – was reopened in 1990 by a private operator. Tourism, mainly connected with the national park covering most of the island, is growing slowly.

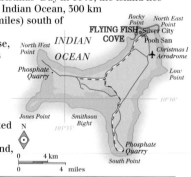

COCOS (KEELING) ISLANDS

STATUS: Australian external territory **CLAIMED:** 1955
CAPITAL: West Island **POP.:** 670 **DENSITY:** 85/km² (220/mi²)

IN ALL, 27 coral atolls make up the Cocos (Keeling) Islands, situated in the Indian Ocean, roughly halfway between Australia and Sri Lanka, and since 1992 part of the Northern Territory electoral district. The inhabited islands are the European-dominated West Island and Home Island, a mainly Cocos Malay community. Coconuts are the sole cash crop.

COOK ISLANDS

STATUS: Territory in free association with New Zealand **CLAIMED:** 19●
CAPITAL: Avarua **POP.:** 20,200 **DENSITY:** 85/km² (220/mi²)

LYING 3,500 KM (2,174 miles) northeast of New Zealand, the Cook Islands are a combination of 24 coral atolls and volcanic islands. The islands achieved self-government in 1965 and have adopted a diverse approach to their economy. As well as tourism and banking, giant clam and pearl farming has been developed, but suffered serious damage from cyclone Martin in 1997.

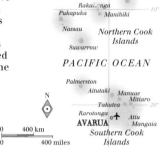

With the suspension of the ANZUS alliance in 1986, the Cook Islands declared their neutrality as doubts grew over New Zealand's ability to defend them.

In 1991, the territory signed a friendship treaty with France covering economic development, trade, and French surveillance of its territorial waters and exclusive economic zone (EEZ). Relations with France deteriorated, however, when the latter went ahead in 1995–1996 with six nuclear-weapons tests in the Pacific, at Mururoa Atoll.

FAEROE ISLANDS

STATUS: Self-governing territory of Denmark **CLAIMED:** 1380
CAPITAL: Tórshavn **POP.:** 43,382 **DENSITY:** 31/km² (80/mi²)

MIDWAY BETWEEN Scotland and Iceland in the north Atlantic, the Faeroe Islands have a moderate climate for their latitude – the result of the warm Gulf Stream current. Home rule since 1948 has given the Faeroese a strong sense of national identity – they voted against joining the EC with Denmark in 1973, but now have favorable terms of trade with most EU members. Fishing is the dominant industry, providing over 90% of exports. In the face of international criticism, the Faeroese have also continued their traditional cull of pilot whales and bottle-nosed dolphins. Sheep farming is important, and there is a small textile industry.

The belief that Denmark's future lies within an integrated Europe has led to an increase in internal pressure for complete independence. In 1998 the government started negotiations for "sovereign nation" status under the Danish monarchy, which would need approval by referendum. However, the islands' economic dependency on Danish subsidies would make independence difficult.

LAND HEIGHT ▢ above Sea Level ▢ 200m/656ft ▢ 500m/1640ft ▢ 1000m/3281ft ▢ 1500m/4572ft ▢ above 2000m/6562ft

FALKLAND ISLANDS

STATUS: British dependent territory CLAIMED: 1832
CAPITAL: Stanley POP.: 2,564 DENSITY: 0.21/km² (0.54/mi²)

SITUATED IN the south Atlantic Ocean, over 12,000 km (7,440 miles) from Britain, the Falkland Islands are influenced by the cold Antarctic current. The main islands of East and West Falkland and the hundreds of outlying islands have a cool, temperate climate with frequent strong winds.

The islands gained international renown with the Argentine invasion, and subsequent British recapture, in 1982. Since then, the British government has invested heavily in a "Fortress Falklands" policy. A new runway and military base were built at Mount Pleasant to house an enlarged garrison. The islanders, for their part, are determined to maintain the political status quo, but in 1999 improving relations led to the restoration of scheduled air connections with Argentina (via Chile). Since the Falklands War, the economy of the islands has prospered. Falklanders invested heavily in schools, roads, and tourism in a fresh drive for a strong identity. By 1987, the Falklands had become financially solvent due to the sale of fishing licenses. However, sales of cheaper, less restrictive licenses by Argentina caused a slump in fishing revenues. Depressed wool prices also began to affect the living standards of the predominantly sheep-farming community. The UK and Argentina reached agreement in 1995 on oil exploration, and the discovery of oil reserves in the Falklands' territorial waters is revolutionizing economic prospects; islanders have indicated willingness to use oil revenues to offset the cost of their defense.

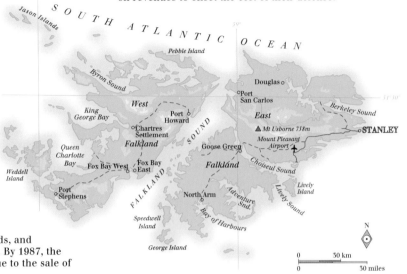

FRENCH GUIANA

STATUS: French overseas department CLAIMED: 1817
CAPITAL: Cayenne POP.: 152,300 DENSITY: 2/km² (5/mi²)

SANDWICHED BETWEEN Brazil and Suriname on the northeast coast of South America, French Guiana is the only remaining colony in South America. A belt of coastal marsh, and an interior of equatorial jungle, combine in a location which was for years notorious for the offshore penal colony, Devil's Island. The rainforest is particularly rich in flora and fauna. It harbors over 400,000 species, including more different kinds of birds than in the whole of Europe.

Concentrated near the coast, the population is ethnically mixed. There are some 5,000 Indians and one of South America's largest group of "bush Negroes," descended from escaped slaves.

Kourou was selected for the launch of the Ariane rocket because of its equatorial site. The town has grown from 800 to 15,000 people.

A campaign for greater autonomy in the late 1970s and early 1980s led to limited decentralization of power to a regional council. The previous grip on local power by the Guianese Socialist Party PSG has been threatened since 1993 by a more unified opposition, but it is still the largest party in the regional council.

During the 1990s the people have become increasingly vocal in their condemnation of the French government's perceived indifference to their country's problems, and there were riots in 1996 and 1997 over the education system. The PSG has accordingly campaigned for greater autonomy. As an overseas *département* of metropolitan France, French Guiana is also a region of the EU, but it is heavily dependent on France for aid, food, and manufactured goods. It has a number of valuable natural resources, including gold, fishing, and forestry, and also has potential for increased tourism, especially eco-tourism, but these are yet to be fully exploited because of a lack of skilled labor and investment and an underdeveloped infrastructure. The European Space Agency (ESA) rocket launch facility for the Ariane rocket at Kourou makes French Guiana strategically important to France.

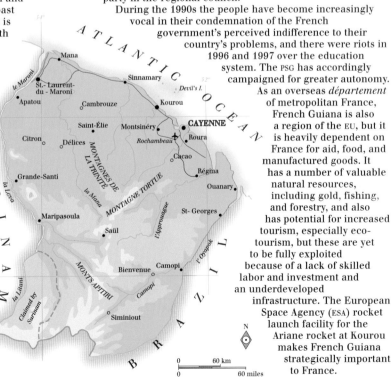

POPULATION ◌ under 5000 ⦿ under 10 000 ● over 10 000 ○ over 50 000 ◉ over 100 000 ☐ Urban areas AIRPORTS ✚ International ✛ Local

FRENCH POLYNESIA

STATUS: French overseas possession **CLAIMED:** 1843
CAPITAL: Papeete **POP.** : 219,521 **DENSITY:** 62/km² (161/mi²)

A SCATTER OF 130 South Pacific islands and coral atolls combine to form French Polynesia, in an area the size of Europe. The average annual temperature varies between 20°C (68°F) and 29°C (84°F), with annual rainfall of over 150 cm (58 in). Nearly 75% of the population live on the main island of Tahiti. The French administration has developed the islands with little regard for local wishes and the Polynesian majority have seen their simple, self-sufficient economy transformed into one dependent on the French military and tourism. In particular, although nuclear testing on Mururoa atoll created many jobs, there was growing opposition to the testing, and a final series of tests, conducted in 1995–1996 despite widespread international protests, provoked local demonstrations which led to riots in Tahiti.

The Polynesian majority has increasingly called for greater autonomy, a reduction in tourism, and a program for rebuilding indigenous trade.

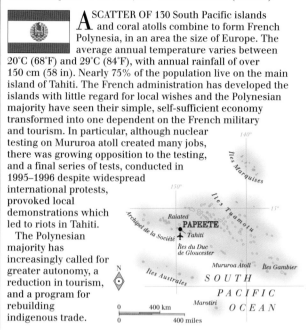

GIBRALTAR

STATUS: British Crown colony **CLAIMED:** 1713
CAPITAL: Gibraltar **POP.** : 27,086 **DENSITY:** 3,869/km² (10,021/mi²)

GUARDING THE western entrance to the Mediterranean, Gibraltar has survived on military and marine revenues. However, as Britain has cut defense spending, so its military presence on the Rock has declined. In response Gibraltarians have developed a vibrant offshore banking industry. Strict antismuggling legislation, in force since 1995, has curbed extensive smuggling from north Africa into Spain. Gibraltar's relationship with Britain and Spain remains contentious. The Social Democrats, under Peter Caruana, favor closer ties with the UK, while Spain continues to press for control over the Rock. The border with Spain is frequently obstructed.

The Rock of Gibraltar. The British built 143 caves, 50 km of roads and as many km of tunnels for defensive purposes.

GREENLAND

STATUS: Self governing territory of Denmark **CLAIMED:** 1380
CAPITAL: Nuuk **POP.** : 56,076 **DENSITY:** 0.03/km² (0.08/mi²)

THE WORLD'S LARGEST island after Australia, Greenland is situated in the north Atlantic and surrounded by seas that are either frozen or cooled by cold Arctic currents. The island has an Arctic climate and much of its land is permanently covered in ice. Granted home rule in 1979, Greenlanders are an independent people – a mix of Inuit and European in origin. Younger islanders are increasingly rejecting the traditional subsistence lifestyle by moving to towns. This move away from self-sufficiency, allied to a decline in the dominant fishing industry, has placed a heavy burden on Greenland's advanced welfare system.

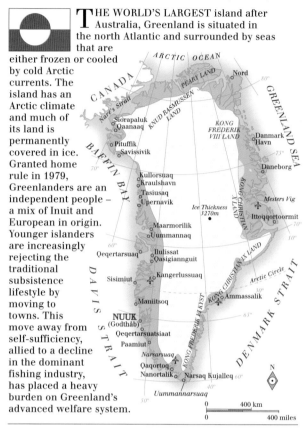

GUADELOUPE

STATUS: French overseas department **CLAIMED:** 1635
CAPITAL: Basse-Terre **POP.** : 419,500 **DENSITY:** 236/km² (611/mi²)

GUADELOUPE lies at the northern end of the Windward Islands in the Caribbean. The movement for independence from France has been pronounced and intermittently violent since the 1960s. The economy is largely based on agriculture and tourism, with sugar, rum, and bananas the main exports, but the islands are dependent on French and EU regional aid. The vulnerability of banana production to hurricanes and world market prices has led the local government to seek to expand sugar production and to develop tourism.

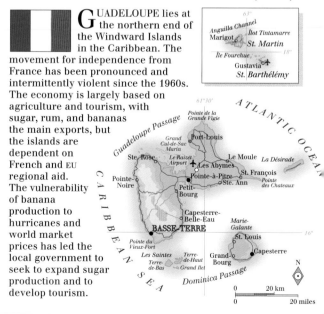

LAND HEIGHT   above Sea Level   200m/656ft   500m/1640ft   1000m/3281ft   1500m/4572ft   above 2000m/6562ft

GUERNSEY

STATUS: British Crown dependency **CLAIMED:** 1066
CAPITAL: St. Peter Port **POP.** : 58,681 **DENSITY:** 902/km² (2,336/mi²)

LYING 50 KM (30 miles) off the coast of France, Guernsey and its dependencies form the northwestern part of the Channel Islands, historically part of the Duchy of Normandy. English is the language most commonly used, but the Norman *patois* is spoken in some villages, and French is used in some formalities of the legislature. Some of the islands are too small for people to need cars, and life continues in an unhurried manner that has changed little through the centuries. The islanders guard this lifestyle with strict residential laws. Guernsey's mild climate has encouraged the development of tourism and market gardening as major industries. Tomatoes, mostly grown under glass, are produced mainly for the UK market. The flower trade is even more

valuable. The low tax system, independent of the UK, has led to a substantial and profitable financial services industry. Many international banks have Guernsey subsidiaries.

Tomato Packaging.
Tomatoes and flowers ripening early in Guernsey's mild climate, are despatched to mainland Britain.

GUAM

STATUS: Unincorporated territory of the USA **CLAIMED:** 1898
CAPITAL: Hagatna **POP.** : 149,249 **DENSITY:** 272/km² (704/mi²)

THE VOLCANIC island of Guam lies at the southern end of the Mariana Archipelago in the Pacific. Its tropical climate has encouraged tourism, although it lies in a region where typhoons are common. Guam's indigenous Chamorro people, who comprise just under half the population, dominate the island's political and social life. They are famous for a set of facial expressions, called "eyebrow," which virtually constitutes a language. Although English is the official language, Chamorro is commonly spoken, and in 1998 the spelling of the capital was changed from Agaña to Hagatna, the Chamorran version. The US military base, covering one-third of the island, has

made Guam strategically important to the USA. Military spending and tourism revenues have given islanders a high living standard. American culture has, however, threatened to upset Guam's social stability. Greater independence has been an issue since the early 1980s, with a series of referendums since 1982. In 1998 a draft Commonwealth Act was awaiting a full US Congress hearing.

ISLE OF MAN

STATUS: British Crown dependency **CLAIMED:** 1765
CAPITAL: Douglas **POP.** : 71,714 **DENSITY:** 125/km² (324/mi²)

LYING HALFWAY BETWEEN England and Northern Ireland in the Irish Sea, the Isle of Man has been inhabited for centuries by the Celtic Manx people. Established by the Vikings in the ninth century, the Manx parliament, the Tynwald, has autonomy from the UK in a number of matters, including taxation. The islanders have used this independence to establish a thriving financial and business sector, which has aided employment as the traditional industries of agriculture and fishing decline. There is still a shellfishing industry, specializing in scallops. Tourism is also important; there are more than 200,000 visitors each year. The Manx culture received a boost in 1993 when the local language, which was in danger of dying out,

once more began to be taught in the island's schools. The Calf of Man (a small island to the south of the main island), which is uninhabited, is administered as a nature reserve.

Isle of Man's TT motorbike race. Thousands of bikers come each year to see the island's famous Touring Trophy race. It is run on a 61-km circuit of the island.

JERSEY

STATUS: British Crown dependency   **CLAIMED:** 1066
CAPITAL: St. Helier   **POP.:** 85,150   **DENSITY:** 734/km² (1,896/mi²)

THE BAILIWICK OF JERSEY, the largest of the Channel Islands, lies some 20 km (12 miles) from the coast of Normandy in France. The official language (since 1960) is English, but French is still used in the courts. The island has a mild climate owing to the Gulf Stream, fine beaches, and more sunshine than anywhere in the British Isles. Jersey has its own legislative and taxation systems which are a blend of the French and British versions. It also has one of the oldest legislative bodies in the world, the Jersey States Assembly. Members stand as independents, rather than for political parties. The islanders have used their autonomy from the UK to develop the economy as an offshore tax haven.

Historically, agriculture has been Jersey's most important industry, with dairy cows its most famous export, closely followed by early potatoes, tomatoes, and flowers. Over the past 50 years, however, farming has been eclipsed by the rise of finance and tourism. The growth of these sectors, and rigid controls on the rights of residency, have ensured high living standards

for most of the inhabitants. Jersey also has a large Portuguese community whose members work in the island's tourist industry.

JOHNSTON ATOLL

STATUS: Unincorporated territory of the USA   **CLAIMED:** 1858
CAPITAL: *Not applicable*   **POP.:** 327   **DENSITY:** 109/km² (282/mi²)

JOHNSTON ATOLL LIES 1,150 km (714 miles) southwest of Hawaii. The atoll consists of a coral reef, two highly modified natural islands, Johnston and Sand, and two completely man-made islands, Akau and Hikina. Since 1971 the islands have been used by the US for nuclear weapons tests and storage and more recently for the destruction of chemical and biological weapons, including sarin nerve gas and the defoliant Agent Orange. Further contamination by plutonium was caused by a nuclear missile which failed to take off and exploded. The only inhabitants

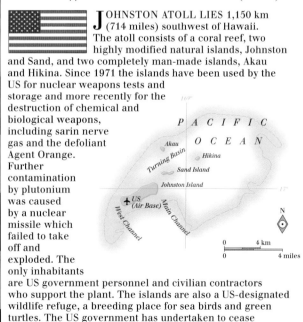

are US government personnel and civilian contractors who support the plant. The islands are also a US-designated wildlife refuge, a breeding place for sea birds and green turtles. The US government has undertaken to cease using the base in 2000, and to clean up the contamination over the following year.

MARTINIQUE

STATUS: French overseas department   **CLAIMED:** 1635
CAPITAL: Fort-de-France   **POP.:** 381,200   **DENSITY:** 342/km² (886/mi²)

CHRISTOPHER COLUMBUS called Martinique "The most beautiful country in the world." It lies in the eastern Caribbean and is dominated by the dormant volcano Montagne Pelée. The island is also situated in the Caribbean's hurricane belt, and suffers an average of one natural disaster every five years. Nearly 90% of the population are of African or mixed ethnicity. However, economic power remains in the hands of the *Bekes* (descendants of white colonial settlers), who own most of the agricultural land. In addition, the bureaucracy is largely staffed by expatriates. This situation has led to outbreaks of violence and increased popular demands for more autonomy. The French government has responded with some measures to increase the island's autonomy.

However, the islanders are aware that their high living standards, despite high unemployment rates, depend on French subsidies, which support a French-style social welfare system. The economy has traditionally relied on agriculture, particularly sugar cane and bananas, but recently tourism has become the biggest source of income and the largest provider of employment as EU subsidy reductions have forced the island to diversify its economy. Martinique has been successful in appealing to the upper end of the tourist market. Almost 80% of the half million annual visitors come from France. Despite lower productivity, wage levels have officially been linked to those in the rest of France; despite this, protests over low salaries in 1998 led to nearly 400 people at a holiday village being held hostage by staff. Unemployment and emigration have been high in the late 1980s and 1990s, with the result that over 30% of Martiniquais nationals are now resident in metropolitan France.

Martinique. *Tourists are attracted to the island's beaches, its mountainous interior and the historic towns of Fort-de-France and Saint Pierre.*

LAND HEIGHT   above Sea Level   200m/656ft   500m/1640ft   1000m/3281ft   1500m/4572ft   above 2000m/6562ft

MAYOTTE

STATUS: French territorial collectivity   CLAIMED: 1843
CAPITAL: Mamoudzou   POP.: 131,320   DENSITY: 351/km² (90/mi²)

PART OF THE COMOROS archipelago, Mayotte lies between Madagascar and the east African coast, and is about 8,000 km (4,960 miles) from France. In a 1974 referendum on independence for the whole archipelago, the vote was overwhelmingly in favor of independence, except on the island of Mayotte. The other islands declared unilateral independence in 1975, and claimed Mayotte. The Mahorais, however voted again in 1976 to maintain their links with France, despite widespread poverty, unemployment, and a cost of living twice that of France. The main political movement has demanded that Mayotte be given the status of a French *département*, hoping that this would bring more aid to develop their largely agricultural economy. The cost involved has led France to oppose the idea. It has, however, invested in an airport and port, but the tourism industry is being slow to develop. The economy is still largely agricultural, with rice, cassava, and maize grown for internal consumption, and ylang-ylang, vanilla, cinnamon, coconuts, and coffee exported, but large quantities of foodstuffs are also imported. Nevertheless, the relative prosperity of Mayotte has encouraged separatist movements on the two other small Comoros islands to seek to restore closer relations with France.

MIDWAY ISLANDS

STATUS: Unincorporated territory of the USA   CLAIMED: 1867
CAPITAL: *Not applicable*   POP.: 453   DENSITY: 91/km² (236/mi²)

NAMED BECAUSE OF its position between California and Japan, Midway is a coral atoll at the western end of the Hawaiian islands, and there have been moves to include it within Hawaii. The scene of a major World War II battle, the atoll comprises two larger islands, totaling over 4 square km (1.5 square miles), and several smaller ones. Midway functions as a naval air base and wildlife refuge. The population is limited to military personnel and civilian contractors, but some tourism is permitted, mainly connected with the wildlife.

MONTSERRAT

STATUS: British dependent territory   CLAIMED: 1632
CAPITAL: Plymouth   POP.: 2,850   DENSITY: 28/km² (73/mi²)

MONTSERRAT IS ONE of the Leeward Islands chain in the eastern Caribbean. In the 1980s its luxuriant flora and tropical climate made it a tourist destination for the rich, and tourism accounted for around one fifth of GDP. Data processing and the financial services industry were also growing, whereas the mountainous terrain held back agricultural development. Hurricane Hugo in 1989 caused a serious setback to the island's prosperity, and the issue of independence, which had dominated local politics, was further affected by a financial scandal. Volcanic eruptions from mid-1995 onwards, culminating in major explosions of the Soufrière Hills volcano in 1997 and 1998, proved devastating. Two-thirds of the island, including Plymouth, became uninhabitable, and mass evacuations reduced the population to a quarter of its former size. A bitter dispute with the UK over paying for resettlement and reconstruction was only partially resolved when the UK government promised a five-year program to develop the (relatively safer) north of the island.

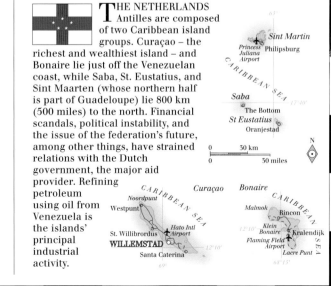

Monserrat. Known as the Caribbean's 'emerald isle' because of its luxuriant flora and Irish heritage.

NETHERLANDS ANTILLES

STATUS: Autonomous part of the Netherlands   CLAIMED: 1816
CAPITAL: Willemstad   POP.: 207,175   DENSITY: 259/km² (671/mi²)

THE NETHERLANDS Antilles are composed of two Caribbean island groups. Curaçao – the richest and wealthiest island – and Bonaire lie just off the Venezuelan coast, while Saba, St. Eustatius, and Sint Maarten (whose northern half is part of Guadeloupe) lie 800 km (500 miles) to the north. Financial scandals, political instability, and the issue of the federation's future, among other things, have strained relations with the Dutch government, the major aid provider. Refining petroleum using oil from Venezuela is the islands' principal industrial activity.

New Caledonia

Status: French overseas territory **Claimed:** 1853
Capital: Nouméa **Pop.**: 196,836 **Density:** 10/km² (26/mi²)

NEW CALEDONIA, or as the indigenous
Kanaks call it, Kanaky, is an island group
1,500 km (930 miles) off the northeast coast
of Australia. Tension over socioeconomic
inequalities and independence between the Melanesian
Kanaks, who form over half of the population, and the
Caldoches, the francophile expatriate population, who are
a large and influential minority, have resulted in a long
history of political violence. Under the 1988 Matignon
Accord, the French government imposed a year of direct
rule as the prelude to a new constitutional structure which
attempted to address Kanak grievances by providing greater
provincial autonomy. The Nouméa accord, signed in April
1998, allowed for greater autonomy and an eventual vote
on self-determination. Although
some racial violence
continued after 1988, it
has not again reached
the same level.

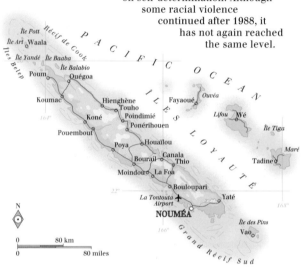

Nickel mining is the territory's most valuable export
industry, at over 90% of export income. New Caledonia has
30% of world reserves, and is the world's fourth largest
producer, but the industry employs relatively few people,
and is vulnerable to fluctuations in the world price. It was
seriously affected by the Asian financial crisis of 1998, when
300 jobs were lost. Tourism and agriculture are bigger
employers, although less than 1% of total land area is
cultivated. Maize, yams, sweet potatoes, and coconuts have
traditionally been the main crops, and in the 1990s large
numbers of melons have been exported to Japan. Fishing is
also important, the main products being tuna and shrimps,
most of which are exported to Japan. A project for the
production of giant clams started in 1996. Unemployment
nevertheless remains high among young Kanaks.

A nickel mine, New Caledonia. The importance of the nickel industry to the territory's economy has made the control of reserves a dominant issue in politics, and in negotiations over the island's independence from France.

Niue

Status: Territory in free association with New Zealand **Claimed:** 190
Capital: Alofi **Pop.**: 2,080 **Density:** 8/km² (21/mi²)

THE WORLD'S LARGEST coral island,
Niue lies 2,100 km (1,300 miles)
northeast of New Zealand.
The subsistence economy
produces tropical fruits, while tourism and
the sale of postage stamps provide foreign
currency. Despite the island's paradise
image, nearly 10,000 Niueans, frustrated
by the lack of job prospects, live in New
Zealand. In the hope of stopping further
emigration, New Zealand has invested
heavily in the economy. However,
cyclone damage and the inefficient
use of aid have held back growth.

Norfolk Island

Status: Australian external territory **Claimed:** 1774
Capital: Kingston **Pop.**: 2,181 **Density:** 62/km² (161/mi²)

INHABITED by
descendants of
the mutineers of
HMS *Bounty* and
more recent Australian migrants,
Norfolk Island lies 1,400 km (869
miles) east of Australia. The islanders
speak a hybrid language, mixing West
Country English, Gaelic, and ancient
Tahitian. They enjoy a fair degree of
autonomy, and in 1991 rejected a plan
to become part of the Australian federal
state. Tourists, attracted by the climate
and unique flora, have brought islanders
a relatively high standard of living.

Northern Mariana Is.

Status: Commonwealth territory of the USA **Claimed:** 1947
Capital: Saipan **Pop.**: 58,846 **Density:** 129/km² (334/mi²)

A FORMER UN trust
territory, the
Northern Marianas
preferred in 1987 to
retain links with the USA rather than opt for
independence. However, local politicians have
questioned their current status. US aid fueled
a boom during the 1980s, but it depended on
immigrant workers who by the early 1990s
outnumbered the local Chamorro population.
In addition, tourism has speeded the decline
of the traditional subsistence economy.

Rota, Northern Marianas. The limestone outcrop of Wedding Cake Mountain overlooks the small village of Songsong.

LAND HEIGHT above Sea Level 200m/656ft 500m/1640ft 1000m/3281ft 1500m/4572ft above 2000m/6562ft

PARACEL ISLANDS

STATUS: *Disputed* **CLAIMED:** *Not applicable*
CAPITAL: Woody Island **POPULATION:** *Unknown*

OCCUPIED BY CHINESE forces, but also claimed by Taiwan and Vietnam, the Paracel Islands are a small collection of coral atolls, situated some 400 km (248 miles) east of Vietnam, in the South China Sea. Subject to frequent typhoons and with a tropical climate, the Paracels are at the center of a regional dispute over the vast reserves of oil and natural gas which are believed to lie beneath their territorial waters. China has built port facilities and an airport on Woody Island to support its claim.

PITCAIRN ISLANDS

STATUS: British dependent territory **CLAIMED:** 1887
CAPITAL: Adamstown **POP.:** 55 **DENSITY:** 4/km² (10/mi²)

PITCAIRN, A GROUP of volcanic south Pacific islands, is Britain's most isolated dependency. Pitcairn Island provided the last refuge for the HMS *Bounty* mutineers. Emigration continues to be a major problem for the Pitcairners, who depend on regular airdrops from New Zealand and periodic visits by supply vessels. The economy operates by barter, fishing, and subsistence farming. Postage stamp sales provide foreign currency earnings. Mineral exploitation could boost the economy in future.

PUERTO RICO

STATUS: Commonwealth territory of the USA **CLAIMED:** 1898
CAPITAL: San Juan **POP.:** 3.8 million **DENSITY:** 424/km² (1,098/mi²)

PUERTO RICO, a US overseas territory since its invasion in 1898, is by far the world's most populous remaining non-independent territory. Situated in the Caribbean, the easternmost of the Greater Antilles, the island is split by a central mountain range. The population density, highest around the capital San Juan, is comparable with the Netherlands overall and is 14 times the US average. The tropical climate attracts growing numbers of tourists, 80% of them from mainland USA, and major efforts have been made in the 1990s to expand hotel and resort facilities. Puerto Rico was granted its current commonwealth status in 1952, giving the inhabitants US citizenship but only limited self-government. In three plebiscites, in 1967, 1993, and 1998, the islanders have endorsed continued commonwealth status rather than opting for US statehood or independence. The most recent of these votes was extremely close; the vote for the status quo was 50.2%, with only 2.5% favoring independence but 46.5% voting for statehood. The pro-statehood governor who called the 1993 and 1998 votes, Pedro Rossello, continues to pursue that option. Puerto Ricans, although poor in US terms, have one of the highest living standards in the region. Tax relief, cheap labor, and the

At night, the bright lights of Puerto Rico's well developed roads, settlements and busy ports are in sharp contrast to the rest of the Caribbean – notably the dark outline of Haiti, just to the west.

island's role as an export processing zone mainly for the US market brought many businesses to the island, especially in the clothing, electronics, petrochemical, and pharmaceuticals industries; Puerto Rico produces nearly all the tranquilizers consumed in the US. Growth has slowed in the last two decades; in 1996 the USA decided to phase out the tax exemptions for companies operating in Puerto Rico which reinvested their profits there. More emphasis is now being placed on the service sector, including health care and clinical testing, and on the biotechnology and other knowledge-based industries. Roads and bridges were damaged by hurricane Georges in 1998, but more money has been spent recently to upgrade neglected infrastructure, while key utilities have been privatized.

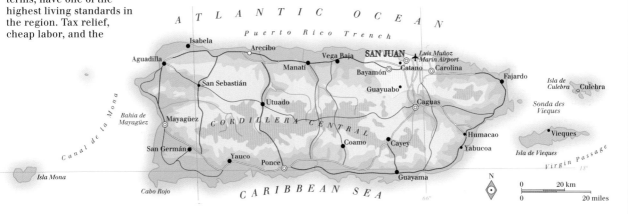

RÉUNION

STATUS: French overseas department **CLAIMED:** 1638
CAPITAL: Saint-Denis **POP.:** 697,600 **DENSITY:** 278/km² (720/mi²)

THE LARGE VOLCANIC island of Réunion, 800 km (497 miles) east of Madagascar, provides France with an important strategic presence – and a large military base – in the Indian Ocean. Its mountainous interior has forced the majority of the population to live along the coast. Socioeconomic differences between the poorer black community and the wealthier Indian and European groups have raised ethnic tensions, which were the cause of severe rioting in 1991. The French government responded with a series of measures, applicable to all overseas *départements*, to raise economic and social conditions to the level of those of France itself. Réunion's main crop is sugarcane.

ST. PIERRE & MIQUELON

STATUS: French territorial collectivity **CLAIMED:** 1604
CAPITAL: St. Pierre **POP.:** 6,600 **DENSITY:** 28/km² (73/mi²)

ST. PIERRE & Miquelon is a group of barren islands, just off the south coast of Newfoundland, Canada. The islands are surrounded by some of the world's richest fishing grounds. Their inhabitants have traditionally earned a living from fishing and from servicing foreign trawler fleets off the coast. A long-running and sometimes bitter dispute between Canada and France over fishing and mineral rights was settled in 1992. The ruling, which was generally deemed to be in Canada's favor, has led the French authorities to diversify the economy by developing port facilities and encouraging tourism.

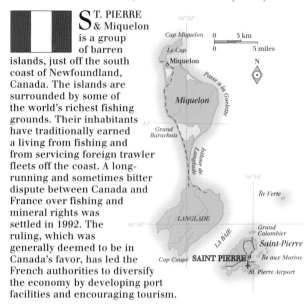

ST. HELENA & DEPENDENCIES

STATUS: British dependent territory **CLAIMED:** 1673
CAPITAL: Jamestown **POP.:** 6,472 **DENSITY:** 53/km² (137/mi²)

TOGETHER, the islands of St. Helena, Tristan da Cunha, and Ascension form the UK's main dependency in the south Atlantic. No resident population is allowed on Ascension Island, which operates as a military base and communications center, but civilian flights have been permitted since 1998. Tristan da Cunha, a volcanic island 2,000 km (1,240 miles) to the south of St. Helena, is inhabited by a small, closely knit farming community. St. Helena's main economic activities – fishing, livestock farming, and the sale of handicrafts – cannot support the population; as a result, underemployment is a major problem, and many St. Helenians have been forced to seek work on Ascension Island. The islanders' right to residence in the UK was removed in 1981. However, the constitutional position is again under review after a 1998 conference of dependent territories.

SPRATLY ISLANDS

STATUS: *Disputed* **CLAIMED:** *Not applicable*
CAPITAL: *Not applicable* **POPULATION:** *Unknown*

SCATTERED ACROSS a large area of the South China Sea, the reefs, islands, and atolls that make up the Spratly Islands have become one of southeast Asia's most serious security issues. Claimed, all or in part, by China, Taiwan, Vietnam, Brunei, Malaysia, and the Philippines, 44 of the larger islands now have garrisons from some of the claimant nations. The reasons for this interest, and the occasional skirmish, are twofold. Strategically, the islands command some of the world's most important shipping lanes. In addition, surveys suggest that some of the largest oil and gas reserves yet found lie in the Spratlys' territorial waters.

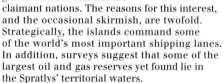

***The isolated Chinese** occupying force on one of the Spratly Islands.*

LAND HEIGHT above Sea Level 200m/656ft 500m/1640ft 1000m/3281ft 1500m/4572ft above 2000m/6562ft

SVALBARD

STATUS: Norwegian dependency **CLAIMED:** 1920
CAPITAL: Longyearbyen **POP.:** 3,231 **DENSITY:** 0.05/km² (0.15/mi²)

NINE ICE-COVERED ARCTIC islands, 650 km (400 miles) north of Norway, make up the territory of Svalbard. In accordance with the 1920 Spitsbergen Treaty, nationals of the treaty powers have equal rights to exploit Svalbard's coal deposits, subject to Norwegian regulation. The only companies still mining are Russian and Norwegian. There has been conflict with Iceland over fishing rights. Over half of the area of the islands are environmentally protected areas.

TOKELAU

STATUS: New Zealand dependent territory **CLAIMED:** 1926
CAPITAL: *Not applicable* **POP.:** 1,577 **DENSITY:** 156/km² (404/mi²)

ACCORDING TO a 1989 UN report, this south Pacific island will disappear under the sea in the 21st century unless global warming is halted. In 1990 a cyclone destroyed crops and wrecked Tokelau's infrastructure. A tuna cannery, the sale of fishing licenses, and the sale of postage stamps and coins make significant contributions to the economy, and a catamaran link between the atolls has increased tourist potential. However, its small size and continued economic weakness make independence unlikely, although in May 1996 it gained the right to enact internal legislation. Nearly 3,000 Tokelauans live in New Zealand.

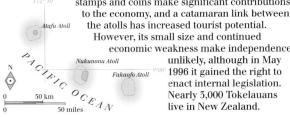

TURKS & CAICOS ISLANDS

STATUS: British dependent territory **CLAIMED:** 1766
CAPITAL: Cockburn Town **POP.:** 13,800 **DENSITY:** 32/km² (83/mi²)

SITUATED 40 KM (25 miles) south of the Bahamas, the Turks and Caicos Islands is a group of 30 low-lying islands, eight of which are inhabited. Services, particularly tourism and offshore banking, dominate the economy. There is a committee seeking political independence, and in 1996 local leaders demanded the replacement of the British governor.

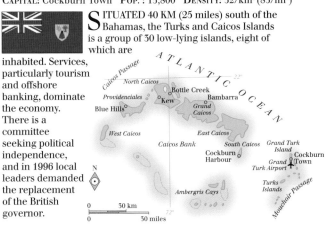

VIRGIN ISLANDS (US)

STATUS: Unincorporated territory of the USA **CLAIMED:** 1917
CAPITAL: Charlotte Amalie **POP.:** 101,809 **DENS.:** 293/km² (759/mi²)

THE US VIRGIN ISLANDS are a collection of 53 volcanic islands, just to the east of Puerto Rico. Most of the population – a mix of African and European ethnic groups – live on the main islands of St. John, St. Thomas, and St. Croix. Tourism is the principal activity, although St. Croix has also used federal aid to develop industry. It has one of the world's largest oil refineries.

St Thomas, US Virgin Islands, is a major stop-off for Caribbean cruise ships. Tourists are attracted by the island's duty-free shopping.

WAKE ISLAND

STATUS: Unincorporated territory of the USA **CLAIMED:** 1898
CAPITAL: Not applicable **POP.:** 302 **DENSITY:** 38/km² (98/mi²)

FORMED BY THE rim of an extinct underwater volcano, Wake Island, in the Pacific, is used as a stopover for cargo planes. A proposal in 1998 by a US company for a nuclear waste facility provoked condemnation by environmentalists and regional politicians.

WALLIS & FUTUNA

STATUS: French overseas territory **CLAIMED:** 1842
CAPITAL: Matá'Utu **POP.:** 15,000 **DENSITY:** 55/km² (143/mi²)

UNLIKE FRANCE'S other overseas territories in the south Pacific, the inhabitants of Wallis and Futuna have little desire for greater autonomy. The islands' subsistence economy produces a variety of tropical crops, while expatriate remittances and the sale of licenses to Japanese and Korean fishing fleets provide foreign exchange. Futuna was hit by an earthquake in 1993.

GLOSSARY OF GEOGRAPHICAL TERMS

THE GLOSSARY FOLLOWING lists all geographical terms occurring on the maps and in main-entry names in the Index~Gazetteer. These terms may precede, follow or be run together with the proper element of the name; where they precede it the term is reversed for indexing purposes - thus Poluostrov Yamal is indexed as Yamal, Poluostrov.

KEY
Geographical term *Language*, Term

A

Å *Danish, Norwegian*, River
Alpen *German*, Alps
Altiplanicie *Spanish*, Plateau
Älv(en) *Swedish*, River
Anse *French*, Bay
Archipiélago *Spanish*, Archipelago
Arcipelago *Italian*, Archipelago
Arquipélago *Portuguese*, Archipelago
Aukštuma *Lithuanian*, Upland

B

Bahía *Spanish*, Bay
Baía *Portuguese*, Bay
Baḥr *Arabic*, River
Baie *French*, Bay
Bandao *Chinese*, Peninsula
Banjaran *Malay*, Mountain range
Batang *Malay*, Stream
-berg *Afrikaans, Norwegian*, Mountain
Birket *Arabic*, Lake
Boğazı *Turkish*, Lake
Bucht *German*, Bay
Bugten *Danish*, Bay
Buḥayrat *Arabic*, Lake, reservoir
Buheiret *Arabic*, Lake
Bukit *Malay*, Mountain
-bukta *Norwegian*, Bay
bukten *Swedish*, Bay
Burnu *Turkish*, Cape, point
Buuraha *Somali*, Mountains

C

Cabo *Portuguese*, Cape
Cap *French*, Cape
Cascada *Portuguese*, Waterfall
Cerro *Spanish*, Mountain
Chaîne *French*, Mountain range
Chau *Cantonese*, Island
Chāy *Turkish*, River
Chhâk *Cambodian*, Bay
Chhu *Tibetan*, River
-chǒsuji *Korean*, Reservoir
Chott *Arabic*, Salt lake, depression
Ch'ün-tao *Chinese*, Island group
Chuôr Phnum *Cambodian*, Mountains
Cordillera *Spanish*, Mountain range
Costa *Spanish*, Coast
Côte *French*, Coast
Cuchilla *Spanish*, Mountains

D

Dağı *Azerbaijani, Turkish*, Mountain
Dağları *Azerbaijani, Turkish*, Mountains
-dake *Japanese*, Peak
Danau *Indonesian*, Lake
Đao *Vietnamese*, Island
Daryā *Persian*, River
Daryācheh *Persian*, Lake
Dasht *Persian*, Plain, desert
Dawḥat *Arabic*, Bay
Dere *Turkish*, Stream
Dili *Azerbaijani*, Spit
-do *Korean*, Island
Dooxo *Somali*, Valley
Düzü *Azerbaijani*, Steppe
-dwīp *Bengali*, Island

E

Embalse *Spanish*, Reservoir
Erg *Arabic*, Dunes
Estany *Catalan*, Lake
Estrecho *Spanish*, Strait
-ey *Icelandic*, Island
Ezero *Bulgarian, Macedonian*, Lake

F

Fjord *Danish*, Fjord
-fjorden *Norwegian*, Fjord
-fjørdhur *Faeroese*, Fjord
Fleuve *French*, River
Fliegu *Maltese*, Channel
-fljór *Icelandic*, River

G

-gang *Korean*, River
Ganga *Nepali, Sinhala*, River
Gaoyuan *Chinese*, Plateau
-gawa *Japanese*, River
Gebel *Arabic*, Mountain
-gebirge *German*, Mountains
Ghubbat *Arabic*, Bay
Gjiri *Albanian*, Bay
Gol *Mongolian*, River
Golfe *French*, Gulf
Golfo *Italian, Spanish*, Gulf
Gora *Russian, Serbian*, Mountain
Gory *Russian*, Mountains
Guba *Russian*, Bay
Gunung *Malay*, Mountain

H

Ḥadd *Arabic*, Spit
-haehyŏp *Korean*, Strait
Haff *German*, Lagoon
Hai *Chinese*, Sea, bay
Ḥammādat *Arabic*, Plateau
Hāmūn *Persian*, Lake

Hawr *Arabic*, Lake
Hāyk' *Amharic*, Lake
He *Chinese*, River
Helodrano *Malagasy*, Bay
-hegység *Hungarian*, Mountain range
Hka *Burmese*, River
-ho *Korean*, Lake
Hô *Korean*, Reservoir
Holot *Hebrew*, Dunes
Hora *Belorussian*, Mountain
Hrada *Belorussian*, Mountains, ridge
Hsi *Chinese*, River
Hu *Chinese*, Lake

I

Île(s) *French*, Island(s)
Ilha(s) *Portuguese*, Island(s)
Ilhéu(s) *Portuguese*, Islet(s)
Irmak *Turkish*, River
Isla(s) *Spanish*, Island(s)
Isola (Isole) *Italian*, Island(s)

J

Jabal *Arabic*, Mountain
Jāl *Arabic*, Ridge
-järvi *Finnish*, Lake
Jazīrat *Arabic*, Island
Jazīreh *Persian*, Island
Jebel *Arabic*, Mountain
Jezero *Serbo-Croatian*, Lake
Jiang *Chinese*, River
-joki *Finnish*, River
-jökull *Icelandic*, Glacier
Juzur *Arabic*, Islands

K

Kaikyō *Japanese*, Strait
-kaise *Lappish*, Mountain
Kali *Nepali*, River
Kalnas *Lithuanian*, Mountain
Kalns *Latvian*, Mountain
Kang *Chinese*, Harbour
Kangri *Tibetan*, Mountain(s)
Kaôh *Cambodian*, Island
Kapp *Norwegian*, Cape
Kavīr *Persian*, Desert
K'edi *Georgian*, Mountain range
Kediet *Arabic*, Mountain
Kepulauan *Indonesian, Malay*, Island group
Khalîg, Khalīj *Arabic*, Gulf
Khawr *Arabic*, Inlet
Khola *Nepali*, River
Khrebet *Russian*, Mountain range
Ko *Thai*, Island
Kolpos *Greek*, Bay
-kopf *German*, Peak
Körfäzi *Azerbaijani*, Bay
Körfezi *Turkish*, Bay

Kõrgustik *Estonian*, Upland
Koshi *Nepali*, River
Kowtal *Persian*, Pass
Kūh(hā) *Persian*, Mountain(s)
-kundo *Korean*, Island group
-kysten *Norwegian*, Coast
Kyun *Burmese*, Island

L

Laaq *Somali*, Watercourse
Lac *French*, Lake
Lacul *Romanian*, Lake
Lago *Italian, Portuguese, Spanish*, Lake
Laguna *Spanish*, Lagoon, Lake
Laht *Estonian*, Bay
Laut *Indonesian*, Sea
Lembalemba *Malagasy*, Plateau
Lerr *Armenian*, Mountain
Lerrnashght'a *Armenian*, Mountain range
Les *Czech*, Forest
Lich *Armenian*, Lake
Liqeni *Albanian*, Lake
Lumi *Albanian*, River
Lyman *Ukrainian*, Estuary

M

Mae Nam *Thai*, River
-mägi *Estonian*, Hill
Maja *Albanian*, Mountain
-man *Korean*, Bay
Marios *Lithuanian*, Lake
-meer *Dutch*, Lake
Melkosopochnik *Russian*, Plain
-meri *Estonian*, Sea
Mifraz *Hebrew*, Bay
Monkhafad *Arabic*, Depression
Mont(s) *French*, Mountain(s)
Monte *Italian, Portuguese*, Mountain
More *Russian*, Sea
Mörön *Mongolian*, River

N

Nagor'ye *Russian*, Upland
Nahal *Hebrew*, River
Nahr *Arabic*, River
Nam *Laotian*, River
Nehri *Turkish*, River
Nevado *Spanish*, Mountain (snow-capped)
Nisoi *Greek*, Islands
Nizmennost' *Russian*, Lowland, plain
Nosy *Malagasy*, Island
Nur *Mongolian*, Lake
Nuruu *Mongolian*, Mountains
Nuur *Mongolian*, Lake
Nyzovyna *Ukrainian*, Lowland, plain

O

Ostrov(a) *Russian*, Island(s)
Oued *Arabic*, Watercourse
-oy *Faeroese*, Island
-øy(a) *Norwegian*, Island
Oya *Sinhala*, River
Ozero *Russian, Ukrainian*, Lake

P

Passo *Italian*, Pass
Pegunungan *Indonesian, Malay*, Mountain range
Pelagos *Greek*, Sea
Penisola *Italian*, Peninsula
Peski *Russian*, Sands
Phanom *Thai*, Mountain
Phou *Laotian*, Mountain
Pi *Chinese*, Point
Pic *Catalan*, Peak
Pico *Portuguese, Spanish*, Peak
Pik *Russian*, Peak
Planalto *Portuguese*, Plateau
Planina, Planini *Bulgarian, Macedonian, Serbo-Croatian*, Mountain range
Ploskogor'ye *Russian*, Upland
Poluostrov *Russian*, Peninsula
Potamos *Greek*, River
Proliv *Russian*, Strait
Pulau *Indonesian, Malay*, Island
Pulu *Malay*, Island
Punta *Portuguese, Spanish*, Point

Q

Qā' *Arabic*, Depression
Qolleh *Persian*, Mountain

R

Raas *Somali*, Cape
-rags *Latvian*, Cape
Ramlat *Arabic*, Sands
Ra's *Arabic*, Cape, point, headland
Ravnina *Bulgarian, Russian*, Plain
Récif *French*, Reef
Represa (Rep.) *Spanish, Portuguese*, Reservoir
-rettō *Japanese*, Island chain
Riacho *Spanish*, Stream
Riban' *Malagasy*, Mountains
Rio *Portuguese*, River
Río *Spanish*, River
Riu *Catalan*, River
Rivier *Dutch*, River
Rivière *French*, River
Rowd *Pashtu*, River
Rūd *Persian*, River
Rudohorie *Slovak*, Mountains
Ruisseau *French*, Stream

S

Sabkhat *Arabic*, Salt marsh
Şahrā' *Arabic*, Desert
Samudra *Sinhala*, Reservoir
-san *Japanese, Korean*, Mountain
-sanchi *Japanese*, Mountains
-sanmaek *Korean*,
Sarīr *Arabic*, Desert
Sebkha, Sebkhet *Arabic*, Salt marsh, depression
See *German*, Lake
Selat *Indonesian*, Strait
-selkä *Finnish*, Ridge
Selseleh *Persian*, Mountain range
Serra *Portuguese*, Mountain
Serranía *Spanish*, Mountain
Sha'īb *Arabic*, Watercourse
Shamo *Chinese*, Desert
Shan *Chinese*, Mountain(s)

Shan-mo *Chinese*, Mountain range
Shaṭṭ *Arabic*, Distributary
-shima *Japanese*, Island
Shiqqat *Arabic*, Depression
Shui-tao *Chinese*, Channel
Sierra *Spanish*, Mountains
Sơn *Vietnamese*, Mountain
Sông *Vietnamese*, River
-spitze *German*, Peak
Štít *Slovak*, Peak
Stoeng *Cambodian*, River
Stretto *Italian*, Strait
Su Anbarı *Azerbaijani*, Reservoir
Sungai *Indonesian, Malay*, River
Suu *Turkish*, River

T

Tal *Mongolian*, Plain
Tandavan' *Malagasy*, Mountain range
Tangorombohitr' *Malagasy*, Mountain massif
Tao *Chinese*, Island
Tassili *Berber*, Plateau, mountain
Tau *Russian*, Mountain(s)
Taungdan *Burmese*, Mountain range
Teluk *Indonesian, Malay*, Bay
Terara *Amharic*, Mountain
Tog *Somali*, Valley
Tônlé *Cambodian*, Lake
Top *Dutch*, Peak
-tunturi *Finnish*, Mountain
Tur'at *Arabic*, Channel

V

Väin *Estonian*, Strait
-vatn *Icelandic*, Lake
-vesi *Finnish*, Lake
Vinh *Vietnamese*, Bay
Vodokhranilishche (Vdkhr.) *Russian*, Reservoir
Vodoskhovyshche (Vdskh.) *Ukrainian*, Reservoir
Volcán *Spanish*, Volcano
Vozvyshennost' *Russian*, Upland, plateau
Vrh *Macedonian*, Peak
Vysochyna *Ukrainian*, Upland
Vysočina *Czech*, Upland

W

Waadi *Somali*, Watercourse
Wādī *Arabic*, Watercourse
Wâhat, Wâhat *Arabic*, Oasis
Wald *German*, Forest
Wan *Chinese*, Bay
Wyżyna *Polish*, Upland

X

Xé *Laotian*, River

Y

Yarımadası *Azerbaijani*, Peninsula
Yazovir *Bulgarian*, Reservoir
Yoma *Burmese*, Mountains
Yü *Chinese*, Island

Z

Zaliv *Bulgarian, Russian*, Bay
Zatoka *Ukrainian*, Bay
Zemlya *Russian*, Bay

GLOSSARY OF ABBREVIATIONS

THIS GLOSSARY provides a comprehensive guide to the abbreviations used in this Atlas, and in the Index~Gazetteer.

A
abbrev. abbreviated
ABM anti-ballistic missile(s)
ACP African, Caribbean and Pacific countries
Afr. Afrikaans
Alb. Albanian
ALCM air-launched Cruise missile(s)
Amh. Amharic
ANC African National Congress
anc. ancient
APC armoured personnel carrier(s)
approx. approximately
Ar. Arabic
Arm. Armenian
ASSR Autonomous Soviet Socialist Republic
Aust. Australian
Az. Azerbaijani
Azerb. Azerbaijan

B
bbl billion barrels
Basq. Basque
BBC British Broadcasting Corporation
BCE Before Common Era
b/d barrels per day
Bel. Belorussian
Ben. Bengali
Ber. Berber
B-H Bosnia-Herzegovina
bn billion (one thousand million)
BP British Petroleum
Bret. Breton
Brig Brigadier
Brit. British
Bul. Bulgarian
Bur. Burmese

C
C central
C. Cape
°C degrees (Centigrade)
Cam. Cambodian
Cant. Cantonese
Capt Captain
CAR Central African Republic
Cast. Castilian
Cat. Catalan
CE Common Era
Chin. Chinese
CIA Central Intelligence Agency
cm centimetre(s)
Cmdr Commander
CNN Cable News Network
Col Colonel
Cro. Croat
Cz. Czech
Czech Rep. Czech Republic

D E
Dan. Danish
dept. department
dev. development
Dom. Rep. Dominican Republic
Dr Doctor
Dut. Dutch
dwt dead weight tonnage
E east
EEC/EC European Community
EEZ Exclusive Economic Zone
ECU European Currency Unit
EMS European Monetary System
Eng. English
est estimated
Est. Estonian
EU European Union

F G
°F degrees (Fahrenheit)
Faer. Faeroese
Fij. Fijian
Fin. Finnish
Fr Father
Fr. French
Franc Francophone – a loose association of French-speaking (mainly African) countries, plus France
Fris. Frisian
ft foot/feet
FYRM Former Yugoslav Republic of Macedonia
FZ Franc Zone
g gram(s)
Gael. Gaelic
Gal. Galician
GDP Gross Domestic Product (the total value of goods and services produced by a country excluding income from foreign countries)
Gen General
Geor. Georgian
Ger. German
Gk Greek
GNP Gross National Product (the total value of goods and services produced by a country)

H I
Heb. Hebrew
HEP hydroelectric power
HH His/Her Highness
Hind. Hindi
hist. historical
HM His/Her Majesty
HMS His/Her Majesty's ship
HRH His/Her Royal Highness
HSH His/Her Serene Highness
Hung. Hungarian
I. Island
ICBM intercontinental ballistic missile(s)
Icel. Icelandic
in inch(es)
In. Inuit (Eskimo)

Ind. Indonesian
Intl International
Ir. Irish
IRBM intermediate-range ballistic missile(s)
Is Islands
It. Italian

J K L
Jap. Japanese
Kaz. Kazakh
kg kilogram(s)
Kir. Kirghiz
km kilometre(s)
km² square kilometre (singular)
Kor. Korean
Kurd. Kurdish
kw kilowatt(s)
kwh kilowatt hour(s)
L. Lake
Lao. Laotian
Lapp. Lappish
Lat. Latin
Latv. Latvian
Liech. Liechtenstein
Lith. Lithuanian
LNG liquefied natural gas
Lt Lieutenant
Lusoph Lusophone – a loose association of Portugeuse-speaking countries, plus Portugal
Lux. Luxembourg

M N
m million/metre(s)
Mac. Macedonian
Maced. Macedonia
Maj Major
Mal. Malay
Malg. Malagasy
Malt. Maltese
mi. mile(s)
mi² square mile(s)
Mong. Mongolian
Mt. Mountain
Mts Mountains
N north
NASA National Aeronautics and Space Administration
Nep. Nepali
Neth. Netherlands
NGO Non-Governmental Organization
NIC Newly Industrialized Country
Nic. Nicaraguan
Nor. Norwegian
NZ New Zealand

P Q R
Pash. Pashtu
PC personal computer
Per. Persian
PLO Palestine Liberation Organization
PNG Papua New Guinea
Pol. Polish
Poly. Polynesian
Port. Portuguese
prev. previously

Rep. Represa (Spanish, Portuguese for reservoir)
Rep. Republic
Res. Reservoir
Rev Reverend
Rmsch. Romansch
Rom. Romanian
Rus. Russian
Russ. Fed. Russian Federation

S
S south
SALT Strategic Arms Limitation Treaty
SCr. Serbo-Croatian
Serb. Serbian
Sinh. Sinhala
SLBM submarine-launched ballistic missile(s)
Slvk. Slovak
Slvn. Slovene
Som. Somali
Sp. Spanish
sq. square
SSBN nuclear-fuelled ballistic-missile submarine(s)
SSM surface-to-surface missile(s)
St., St Saint
START Strategic Arms Reduction Treaty
Strs. Straits
Swa. Swahili
Swe. Swedish
Switz. Switzerland

T U
Taj. Tajik
Th. Thai
Thai. Thailand
Tib. Tibetan
Turk. Turkish
Turkm. Turkmenistan
TV television
UAE United Arab Emirates
Uigh. Uighur
UK United Kingdom
Ukr. Ukrainian
UN United Nations
Urd. Urdu
US/USA United States of America
USS United States ship
USSR Union of Soviet Socialist Republics
Uzb. Uzbek

V W X Y
var. variant
VCR video cassette recorder
Vdkhr. Vodokhranilishche (Russian for reservoir)
Vdskh. Vodoskhovyshche (Ukrainian for reservoir)
Vtn. Vietnamese
W west
Wel. Welsh
Yugo. Yugoslavia

GEOGRAPHICAL PLACENAMES

THE CHOICES confronting a map-maker when deciding which place-name style to use on a map are surprisingly varied. The criteria adopted may be affected by a range of factors: the existence of foreign and native language forms of a place name (London, Londres, Londra), variant spellings used within the country itself (Gent, Gand) and the existence of completely different language forms for international features (the English Channel, La Manche).

In addition to these, political expedience, simple clarity and the use to which the published map may be put are all factors that need consideration.

The revision of place-name forms and spellings, which is a continuin administrative activity worldwide, adds a further dimension of complexity to the subject. Since the collapse of Soviet communism, for instance, place names inn Russia have been altered to expunge traces of communist ideology (the most famous being the 1991 reversion of Leningrad to its pre-1914 name, St Petersburg). In many former Soviet republics, Russian names have been been replaced with native language forms (notably in Ukraine, Belarus, Georgia and Armenia).

Standardized Arabic names havebeen hindered by the persistent use of French forms in practice.

THE MAPS

The maps in the Nations of the World section of the Atlas have used the most up-to-date reference sources available to provide local name forms and spellings, that is to say those used within the country. In an age when international travel, on holidayor on business, is commonplace, this criterion seems the most appropriate.

English conventional forms have been used for all international features (such as sea areas between countries, and cross-border mountain ranges); for all country names (the Index-Gazetteer provides local forms and spellings, while commonly used alternative names, such as Burma/Myanmar are also made clear in the national A-Z entry) and for all capital cities. The Index-Gazatteer provides a fully cross-referenced system that will guide the reader the short distance from the English conventional 'Florence' to the local 'Firenze', as used on the maps.

English conventional forms also appear on all the maps in The World Today and Global Issues. These maps have not been indexed, as all contemporary places featured are most usefullyand accurately identified on the national maps.

THE INDEX GAZETTEER

The Index Gazetteer lists all names that appear on the maps in the Nations of the World section of the Atlas. Physical features are defined as such, as are countries and those administrative or regional names included on the maps; all other names are those of population centres. Location is given by page number, then country, and is narrowed down by positional reference as N(orth), S(outh), E(ast), W(est) or C(entral), or combinations of these as appropriate.

Following each main entry name are given: variant spelling s of the name most commonly found; its previos name or names; and such foreign-language forms of the name as are pertinent to modern history since 1940. This is the cut-off date generally adopted, permitting the inclusion of all place-name changes made during or after the Second World War. Exceptionally, name changes made in Russia and other countries of the former Soviet Union before 1940 are given, since many old names in these countries are now being restored.

INDEX

PAGE NUMBERS SHOWN IN ITALICS

Geographical Terms and Abbreviations on pages 654-657 / ❖ = *capital*

A

Aa *see* Gauja
Aabenraa *see* Åbenrå
Aachen *264 Fr.* Aix-la-Chapelle, *Dut.* Aken. W Germany
Aalborg *see* Ålborg
Aalesund *see* Ålesund
Aaley *364 var.* Ålayh, Aley. C Lebanon
Aalsmeer *429* W Netherlands
Aalst *127 Fr.* Alost. C Belgium
Aanaarjävri *see* Inarijärvi
Aanjar *364* C Lebanon
Aarau *546* N Switzerland
Aare *546 var.* Aar. River of W Switzerland
Aarhus *see* Århus
Aarlen *see* Arlon
Aarschot *127* C Belgium
Aassi, Nahr el *see* Orantes
Aba *440* S Nigeria
Abaco Island *112* island of N Bahamas
Ābādān *307* W Iran
Abai *see* Blue Nile
Abaiang *346* island of the Gilbert Is, W Kiribati
Abakan *485 prev.* Khakassk, Ust'-Abakanskoye. C Russia
Abancay *463* SE Peru
Abariringa *see* Kanton
Ābaya Hāyk' *243 It.* Abbaia, *Eng.* Lake Margherita. Lake of SW Ethiopia
Abay Wenz *see* Blue Nile
Abbeville *253* N France
'Abd al 'Azīz, Jabal *551* mountains of NE Syria
'Abdalī *354* S Kuwait
Abd-Al-Kuri *627* island of SE Yemen, off the Horn of Africa
Abéché *180 var.* Abécher. E Chad
Abemama *346* island of the Gilbert Is, W Kiribati
Abengourou *326* E Ivory Coast
Åbenrå *218 var.* Aabenraa, *Ger.* Apenrade. Jylland, SW Denmark
Abeokuta *440* SW Nigeria
Abercorn *see* Mbala
Aberdeen *593* NE Scotland, UK
Aberdeen *599* South Dakota, NC USA
Abergwaun *see* Fishguard
Abersee *see* Wolfgangsee
Abertawe *see* Swansea
Aberystwyth *593* W Wales, UK
Abhā *506* S Saudi Arabia
Abhe, Lake *222, 243 Amh.* Âbhē Bid Hāyk'. Lake of Djibouti and Ethiopia
Abidjan *326* S Ivory Coast
Åbo *see* Turku
Aboisso *326* SE Ivory Coast
Abo, Massif d' *180* mountain range of N Chad
Abomey *132* S Benin
Abong Mbang *168* SE Cameroon
Abou-Déïa *180* S Chad
Aboudouhour *see* Abū aḍ Ḍuhūr
Abou Kémal *see* Abū Kamāl
Aboumi *258* E Gabon
Abovyan *98 var.* Abovjan. C Armenia
Abra *466* river of Luzon, N Philippines
Abrād, Wādī *627* seasonal river of NW Yemen
Abraham Bay *see* Carlton, The
Abruzzese, Appennino *321* mountain range of C Italy
'Abs *627 var.* Sūq 'Abs. W Yemen
Abşeron Yarımadası *110 Rus.* Apsheronskiy Poluostrov. Oil-rich peninsula of E Azerbaijan
Abū aḍ Ḍuhūr *551 Fr.* Aboudouhour. NW Syria
Abū al Abyaḍ *590* island of N United Arab Emirates

Abū al Jirfān, Sha'īb *354 var.* Sh'ib Abu Jarfan. Dry watercourse of N Kuwait
Abū al Khaṣīb *310 var.* Abul Khasib. SE Iraq
Abu al Mawj, Ra's *115* cape of W Bahrain
Abu Dhabi *590 Ar.* Abū Ẓaby, *var.* Abū Ẓabī. ❖ of United Arab Emirates
Abuja *440* ❖ of Nigeria, C Nigeria
Abū Jarjūr, Ra's *115* cape of E Bahrain
Abū Kamāl *551 Fr.* Abou Kémal. E Syria
Abul Khasib *see* Abū al Khaṣīb
Abuná *136* river of Bolivia and Brazil
Abū Thaylah *479* NE Qatar
Abū Ẓabī *see* Abu Dhabi
Abū Ẓaby *see* Abu Dhabi
Abyaḍ, Baḥr al *see* White Nile
Åbybro *218* N Denmark
Abyssinia *see* Ethiopia
Acaill *see* Achill Island
Acajutla *235* W El Salvador
Acapulco *403 var.* Acapulco de Juárez. S Mexico
Acaraí, Serra *144 Eng.* Acarai Mountains. Mountain range of Brazil and Guyana
Acarigua *619* NW Venezuela
Achacachi *136* W Bolivia
Acharnés *273 prev.* Akharnaí. SE Greece
Acheloos *273 var.* Aspropotamos, *prev.* Akhelóös. River of W Greece
Achénouma *439* NE Niger
Achill Island *314 Ir.* Acaill. Island of W Ireland
Achna *see* Athna
Achorstock Point *652* headland of W Tristan da Cunha
Achwa *584 var.* Aswa. River of N Uganda
Acireale *321* Sicilia, S Italy
Acklins Island *112* island of S Bahamas
Aconcagua, Cerro *95* mountain of W Argentina
Açores *see* Azores
Açores, Arquipélago dos *see* Azores
A Coruña *530 Cast.* La Coruña. NW Spain
Acoua *649* NW Mayotte
Acquaviva *502* NW San Marino
Acre *see* 'Akko
Acurnam *236 var.* Acurenan, Akurenan. S Río Muni, Equatorial Guinea
Adalia *see* Antalya
Adalia, Gulf of *see* Antalya Körfezi
Adam *448* N Oman
Adama *see* Nazrēt
Adamaoua, Massif d' *168 Eng.* Adamawa. Plateau of West Africa
Adam-jo-Tando *see* Tando Ādam
Adam's Bridge *534* chain of shoals to the NW of Sri Lanka
Adamstown *651* ❖ of Pitcairn Islands, NE Pitcairn Island, Pitcairn Islands
'Adan *627 Eng.* Aden. SW Yemen
Adana *577 var.* Seyhan. S Turkey
Adapazarı *576 var.* Sakarya. NW Turkey
Aḍ Ḍab 'īyah *590* C United Arab Emirates
Aḍ Ḍafrah *590* desert region of W United Arab Emirates
Ad Dahnā' *506* N Saudi Arabia.
Ad Dakhla *414* W Western Sahara
Ad Dalanj *see* Dilling
Ad Dammām *506* desert region of NE Saudi Arabia

Ad Dawḥah *see* Doha
Ad Dibdibah *354* mountain of W Kuwait
Addīgrat *243* N Ethiopia
Ad Dirāz *115* NW Bahrain
Addis Ababa *243 Amh.* Ādīs Ābeba. ❖ of Ethiopia, C Ethiopia
Ad Dīwānīyah *310 var.* Diwaniya. C Iraq
Addu Atoll *390* atoll of S Maldives
Adelaide *101* S Australia
Adelphi *498* E St Vincent, St Vincent & the Grenadines
Adelsberg *see* Postojna
Aden *see* 'Adan
Aden, Gulf of *222, 524, 627 var.* Badyarada 'Adméd. Gulf connecting the Indian Ocean and Red Sea
Adh Dhayd *590 var.* Deira. NE United Arab Emirates
Adh Dhirā' *336* W Jordan
Ādī Ārk'ay *243 var.* Addi Arkay. N Ethiopia
Adige *321 Ger.* Etsch. River of N Italy
Adi Keyih *238 var.* Adi Keyah. SE Eritrea
Adi Kwala *238* S Eritrea
Ādīs Ābeba *see* Addis Ababa
Ādīs Zemen *243* NW Ethiopia
Adi Tekelezan *238* C Eritrea
Adıyaman *577* SE Turkey
Admiralty Islands *458* island group of N Papua New Guinea
Ado-Ekiti *440* SW Nigeria
Adola *see* Kibre Mengist
Ado-Odo *440 var.* Ado. SW Nigeria
Adour *253* river of SW France
Adrar des Ifôghas *392* mountainous region of C Sahara, NE Mali
Adriatic Sea *321, 630 It.* Mare Adriatico, *Slvn.* Jadransko Morje, *SCr.* Jadransko More, *Alb.* Deti Adriatik. Area of the Mediterranean Sea, between Italy and SE Europe
Adriatik, Deti *see* Adriatic Sea
Adventure Sound *645* bay of the South Atlantic Ocean, E Falkland Islands
Ādwa *243 var.* Adowa, *It.* Adua. N Ethiopia
Adygeya, Respublika *484* autonomous republic of SW Russia
Adzopé *326* SE Ivory Coast
Aeankan District *396* district of Majuro, SE Marshall Islands
Aegean Sea *273, 576 Gk* Aigaío Pélagos, *Turk.* Ege Denizi. Area of the Mediterranean Sea
Aeolian Islands *see* Eolie, Isole
Ærø *218 Ger.* Arrö. Island of S Denmark
Afadjado *270 var.* Afadjato, Afadjoto. Mountain of SE Ghana
'Afak *310* C Iraq
Afar Depression *see* Danakil Desert
Afghanistan *76-79* officially Islamic State of Afghanistan, *prev.* Republic of Afghanistan. Country of C Asia divided into 30 admin. units (velayats). ❖ Kābul
Afgooye *524 It.* Afgoi. S Somalia
Afikpo *440* S Nigeria
Afobaka *538* NE Suriname
'Afula *337* N Israel
Afyon *576 prev.* Afyonkarahisar. W Turkey
Agadez *439 prev.* Agadès. C Niger
Agadir *414* SW Morocco
Agaña *647* ❖ of Guam, NW Guam
Aga Point *647* headland on the S coast of Guam
Āgaro *243* W Ethiopia
Agat *647* W Guam
Agboville *326* SE Ivory Coast

Ağcabädi *110 Rus.* Agdzhabedi, *var.* Agdžabedi. C Azerbaijan
Agdam *110* SW Azerbaijan
Agedabia *see* Ajdābiyā
Agen *253* SW France
Agere Hiywet *see* Hägere Hiywet
Agia Napa *see* Ayia Napa
Agigialousa *see* Yenierenköy
Agios Ioannis *see* Ayios Ioannis
Agona Swedru *270 var.* Swedru. SE Ghana
Agordat *see* Akordat
Agou Gadzepe *567* SW Togo
Agou, Mont *567 prev.* Pic Baumann. Mountain of SW Togo
Āgra *296* N India
Agram *see* Zagreb
Agrigento *321 prev.* Girgenti. Sicilia, S Italy
Agrihan *650* island of N Northern Mariana Islands
Agrínio *273 prev.* Agrínion. W Greece
Aguachica *195* N Colombia
Aguadilla *651* NW Puerto Rico
Aguadulce *456* S Panama
Aguán *288* river of N Honduras
Aguarico *222* river of Ecuador and Peru
Aguascalientes *403* C Mexico
Aguijan *650* island of S Northern Mariana Islands
Agusan *466* river of Mindanao, S Philippines
Ahaggar *83 var.* Hoggar. Mountain range of SE Algeria
Ahja *240 var.* Ahja Jõgi. River of SE Estonia
Ahmadābād *296 var.* Ahmedabad. W India
Ahmadpur East *451* E Pakistan
Ahuachapán *235* W El Salvador
Ahvāz *307 var.* Ahwāz. W Iran
Ahvenanmaa *see* Åland
Aḥwar *627* SW Yemen
Aibak *see* Āybak
Aigaío Pélagos *see* Aegean Sea
Aiguá *607* S Uruguay
Ai-hun *see* Heihe
Ailigandí *456* E Panama
Ailinginae *396* island of NW Marshall Islands
Ailinglaplap *396 prev.* Ailinglapalap. Island of S Marshall Islands
Ailuk *396* island of NE Marshall Islands
'Aïn Ben Tili *398* N Mauritania
Aïn Oussera *83 var.* Aïn Wessara. N Algeria
Aintab *see* Gaziantep
Aïoun el Atroûss *see* 'Ayoûn el 'Atroûs
Aiquile *136* C Bolivia
Airai *455* C Palau
Airdrie *170* SW Canada
Airdrie *593* C Scotland, UK
Airlalang *see* Rokan
Aitape *458 var.* Eitape. NW Papua New Guinea
Aitos *see* Aytos
Aitutaki *644* island of Southern Cook Islands, S Cook Islands
Aitzu-Wakamatsu *330* Honshū, N Japan
Ajaccio *253* Corse, SE France
Ajdābiyā *371 var.* Ajdābiyah, Agedabia. NE Libya
Ajeltake District *396* district of Majuro, SE Marshall Islands
Ajjinena *see* Geneina
Ajka *290* W Hungary
Ajman *590 Ar.* 'Ajmān, *var.* 'Ujmān. NE United Arab Emirates
Ajtos *see* Aytos
Akaba *see* Al 'Aqabah

All Awash Island *198* island of E St Vincent & the Grenadines
Allenstein *see* Olsztyn
Allentown *599* Pennsylvania, NE USA
Al Liwā' *590* oasis region of SW United Arab Emirates
All Saints *92* C Antigua, Antigua & Barbuda
Al Lubnān *see* Lebanon
Al Luḥayyah *627* W Yemen
Al Ma'āmir *115* NE Bahrain
Alma-Ata *see* Almaty
Almada *474* W Portugal
Al Madīnah *506* *Eng.* Medina. W Saudi Arabia
Al Mafraq *336* *var.* Mafraq. N Jordan
Al Mahdīyah *see* Mahdia
Al Maḥmūdīyah *310* *var.* Mahmudiya. C Iraq
Al Mahrah *627* mountains of E Yemen
Al Majma'ah *506* C Saudi Arabia
Al Mālikīyah *115* W Bahrain
Al Mālikīyah *551* *var.* Dayrīk. NE Syria
Almalyk *see* Olmaliq
Al Mamlakah *see* Morocco
Al Manādir *590* *var.* Al Manadir. Desert region of Oman and United Arab Emirates
Al Manāmah *see* Manama
Al Manāṣif *551* mountains of E Syria
Al Manṣūrah *see* El Manṣūra
Al Maqta' *590* C United Arab Emirates
Al Marj *371* *var.* Barka, *It.* Barce. NE Libya
Al Marsá *see* La Marsa
Almaty *338* *var.* Alma-Ata. SE Kazakhstan
Al Mawṣil *310* *Eng.* Mosul. N Iraq
Al Mayādīn *551* *Fr.* Meyadine. E Syria
Al Mazra'ah *336* W Jordan
Almelo *429* E Netherlands
Almendra, Embalse de *531* reservoir of NW Spain
Almere *429* C Netherlands
Almería *531* S Spain
Al Mīnā' *see* El Mina
Al Minyā *see* El Minya
Al Miqdādīyah *see* Al Muqdādīyah
Almirante *456* W Panama
Al Mubarraz *506* NE Saudi Arabia
Al Mudawwarah *336* SW Jordan
Al Muḥammadīyah *115* *var.* Umm aş Şabbān. Island of NW Bahrain
Al Muḥarraq *115* *var.* Moharek, Muharraq, Jazirat al Muharraq. Bahrain
Al Mukallā *627* *var.* Mukalla. SE Yemen
Al Mukhā *627* *Eng.* Mocha. SW Yemen
Al Muknīn *see* Moknine
Al Munastīr *see* Monastir
Al Muqdādīyah *310* *var.* Al Miqdādīyah. C Iraq
Al Mussayyib *310* C Iraq
Al Obayyid *see* El Obeid
Alofi *650* ❖ of Niue, W Niue
Alofi, Île *653* ❖ of Île Futuna, N Wallis & Futuna
Alohungari *261* E Gambia
Alor, Kepulauan *302* island group of E Indonesia
Alor, Pulau *302* island of E Indonesia
Alor Setar *386* *var.* Alur Setar, Alor Star. NW Peninsular Malaysia
Alost *see* Aalst
Alotau *458* SE Papua New Guinea
Aloupos *215* *var.* Çiftlik Dere. River of NW Cyprus
Alpen *see* Alps
Alpes *see* Alps
Alphen aan de Rijn *429* W Netherlands
Alphonse Group *512* island group of C Seychelles
Alpi *see* Alps
Alps *106, 253, 320, 546* *It.* Alpi, *Fr.* Alpes, *Ger.* Alpen. Mountain range of C Europe
Al Qābil *448* *var.* Qabil. NW Oman
Al Qaḍārif *see* Gedaref
Al Qāhirah *see* Cairo
Al Qal'ah al Kubrá *see* Kalaa Kebira

Al Qāmishlī *551* *var.* Kamishli. NE Syria
Al Qaryah *115* NE Bahrain
Al Qaryāt *371* NW Libya
Al Qaṣr *336* W Jordan
Al-Qaṣrayn *see* Kasserine
Al Qayrawān *see* Kairouan
Al Qubayyāt *see* Qoubaïyât
Al Qubbah *371* NE Libya
Al Quds *see* Jerusalem
Al Qunayṭirah *551* *var.* El Quneitra, Kuneitra. SW Syria
Al Quṣayr *551* *var.* El Quseir, *Fr.* Kousseir. W Syria
Al Quṭayfah *551* *var.* Quṭayfah, Quteife, *Fr.* Kouteifé. SW Syria
Al Quwayrah *336* *var.* Makhfar al Quwayrah, El Quweira. SW Jordan
Als *218* *Ger.* Alsen. Island of S Denmark
Alsace *253* cultural region of NE France
Alsen *see* Als
Al Shahaniyah *see* Ash Shaḩanīyah
Alt *see* Olt
Alta *444* NE Norway
Altai Mountains *412* mountain range of C Asia
Altay *186* *Chin.* A-le-t'ai, *prev.* Ch'eng-hua, *var.* Chenghwa, *Mong.* Sharasume. Xinjiang Uygur Zizhiqu, NW China
Altay *412* W Mongolia
Alt de la Coma Pedrosa, Pic *86* mountain of NW Andorra
Altkanischa *see* Kanjiža
Alto Molócuè *419* C Mozambique
Alto Paraná *see* Paraná
Alt-Schwanenburg *see* Gulbene
Altsohl *see* Zvolen
Altun Shan *186* *var.* Altyn Tagh. Mountain range of Xinjiang Uygur Zizhiqu, NW China
Altyn Tagh *see* Altun Shan
Alu *see* Shortland Island
Al Ubayyiḍ *see* El Obeid
Al 'Udayd *590* *var.* Al Odaid. W United Arab Emirates
Alūksne *362* *Ger.* Marienburg. NE Latvia
Al 'Ulā *506* NW Saudi Arabia
Al 'Umarī *336* C Jordan
Al Uqṣur *see* Luxor
Al Wafrā' *354* SE Kuwait
Al Wāḥāt al Khārijah *see* El Wâhât el Khârga
Al Wajh *506* NW Saudi Arabia
Al Wakrah *479* *var.* Wakra. E Qatar
Al Wukayr *479* *var.* Al Wukair. E Qatar
Alyat *see* Älät
Alyaty-Pristan' *see* Älät
Alytus *376* *Pol.* Olita. S Lithuania
Al Zubair *see* Az Zubayr
Amadora *474* W Portugal
Amakusa-shotō *330* island group to the W of Kyūshū, SW Japan
Amala *342* river of SW Kenya
Amami-Ō-shima *330* island of Amami-shotō, SW Japan
Amami-shotō *330* island group of Nansei-shotō, SW Japan
Amara *see* Al 'Amārah
Amarapura *172* C Burma
Amasia *98* *Rus.* Amasiya, *var.* Amasija. NW Armenia
Amasya *577* N Turkey
Amatique, Bahía de, *278* bay of the Gulf of Honduras
Amaury *400* NE Mauritius
Amazon *145, 195, 463* *Sp.* Amazonas. River of South America
Amazonia *144* physical region of C South America
Ambalangoda *534* SW Sri Lanka
Ambalavao *382* S Madagascar
Ambam *168* S Cameroon
Ambanja *382* N Madagascar
Ambato *228* C Ecuador
Ambatondrazaka *382* E Madagascar
Ambergris Cay *130* island of NE Belize
Ambergris Cays *653* island group of S Turks and Caicos Islands

Ambilobe *382* N Madagascar
Amblève *127* river of E Belgium
Ambo *see* Hägere Hiywet
Amboasary *382* S Madagascar
Ambohidratrimo *382* C Madagascar
Ambon *302* *prev.* Amboina. Ambon, C Indonesia
Ambositra *382* C Madagascar
Ambre, Île d' *400* Island of NE Mauritius
Ambriz *88* NW Angola
Ambrym *615* *var.* Ambrim. Island of E Vanuatu
'Amd *627* C Yemen
Ameland *429* island of Waddeneilanden, N Netherlands
American Samoa *642* unincorporated territory of the USA, Pacific Ocean. ❖ Pago Pago
Amersfoort *429* C Netherlands
Amherst *see* Kyaikkami
Amiens *253* N France
Amilḥayt, Wādī *448* *var.* Wādī Umml Ḩayt. Seasonal watercourse of SW Oman
Amīndivi Islands *296* island group of Lakshadweep, SW India
Amioun *364* *var.* Amyūn. N Lebanon
Amirante Islands *512* *var.* Amirantes Group. Island of S Seychelles
Amlamé *567* C Togo
Amman *336* *Ar.* 'Ammān. ❖ of Jordan, NW Jordan
Ammassalik *646* *var.* Angmagssalik. SE Greenland
Ammochostos *see* Gazimağusa
Ammochostos Bay *see* Famagusta Bay
Amnok *see* Yalu
Āmol *307* *var.* Amul. N Iran
Amorgós *273* island of SE Greece
Amouli *642* *var.* Tau. Tau, E American Samoa
Amourj *398* SE Mauritania
Ampara *534* E Sri Lanka
Amphitrite Group *651* island group of N Paracel Islands
'Amrān *627* W Yemen
Amrāvati *296* *prev.* Amraoti. C India
Amritsar *296* N India
Amstelveen *429* W Netherlands
Amsterdam *429* ❖ of the Netherlands, C Netherlands
Amstetten *106* N Austria
Am Timan *180* SE Chad
Amu Darya *77, 558, 581, 610* *Turkm.* Amyderya, *Uzb.* Amudaryo. River of C Asia
Amudat *584* E Uganda
Amul *see* Āmol
Amund Ringnes Island *170* island of Sverdrup Islands, N Canada
Amundsen Gulf *170* gulf of the Beaufort Sea, on the NW coast of Canada
Amundsen-Scott *90* US research station at the South Pole, Greater Antarctica, Antarctica
Amundsen Sea *90* sea of the Pacific Ocean, off Antarctica
Amur *187, 485* *Chin.* Heilong Jiang. River of China and Russia
Amyderya *see* Amu Darya
Amyūn *see* Amioun
An Abhainn Mhór *see* Blackwater
Anaco *619* NE Venezuela
Anadolu Dağları *see* Doğu Karadeniz Dağlari
Anadyr' *485* NE Russia
Anadyr, Gulf of *see* Anadyrskiy Zaliv
Anadyrskiy Zaliv *485* *Eng.* Gulf of Anadyr. Gulf of Bering Sea, bordering NE Russia
Anáfi *273* island of SE Greece
Anaiza *see* 'Unayzah
Analalava *382* N Madagascar
Analamaitsa Plateau *382* plateau of NE Madagascar
Anambas, Kepulauan *302* island group to the NW of Borneo, W Indonesia
Anan *330* Shikoku, SW Japan
Anantapur *296* S India
Anápolis *145* S Brazil
Anarjokka *see* Inarijoki

Anatahan *650* island of C Northern Mariana Islands
Anatolia Plateau *576* plateau of C Turkey
Anatom *615* *var.* Aneityum, *prev.* Kéamu. Island of S Vanuatu
An Bhearú *see* Barrow
An Bhóinn *see* Boyne
Anchorage *598* Alaska, USA
Ancona *321* C Italy
Andalucia *530-531* autonomous community of S Spain
Andaman Islands *296* island group of SE India
Andaman Sea *159, 302, 563* sea of Indian Ocean, to the SW of Burma and Thailand
'Andām, Wadi *448* seasonal desert watercourse of E Oman
Andapa *382* NE Madagascar
Andaung Pech *see* Bâ Kêv
Andenne *127* SE Belgium
Andersen Air Force Base *647* NE Guam
Andes *95, 136, 183, 195, 463* mountain range of South America, running the entire length of the west coast
Andfjorden *444* fjord of NE Norway
Andijon *610* *Rus.* Andizhan. E Uzbekistan
Andizhan *see* Andijon
Andkhvoy *101* N Afghanistan
Andoany *382* *prev.* Hell-Ville. N Madagascar
Andong *350* *Jap.* Antō. E South Korea
Andong-ho *350* reservoir of E South Korea
Andorra *86-87* officially Principality of Andorra. Country of SW Europe divided into 7 admin. units (parishes). ❖ Andorra la Vella
Andorra la Vella *86* ❖ of Andorra, W Andorra
Andreas *647* N Isle of Man
Andreas, Cape *see* Apostolos Andreas, Cape
Andria *321* S Italy
Androna, Lembalemba Ambanin' *382* *var.* Plateau de l'Androna. Plateau of N Madagascar
Ándros *273* island of SE Greece
Andros Island *112* island of W Bahamas
Andros Town *112* Andros Island, Bahamas
Andújar *531* SW Spain
Anegada *643* island of NE British Virgin Islands
Aného *567* *var.* Anécho, *prev.* Petit-Popo. S Togo
Aneityum *see* Anatom
Änew *see* Annau
An Fheoir *see* Nore
Anfile Bay *238* bay of the Red Sea to the E of Eritrea
Angara *485* river of C Russia
Angarsk *485* C Russia
Angaur *455* island of S Palau
Änge *543* C Sweden
Angel *see* Úhlava
Ángel de la Guarda, Isla *403* island of NW Mexico
Angeles *466* Luzon, N Philippines
Angers *253* NW France
Anglesey *593* *Wel.* Môn. Island of NW Wales, UK
Angmagssalik *see* Ammassalik
Angoche *419* E Mozambique
Angola *88-89* officially Republic of Angola, *prev.* People's Republic of Angola. Country of Central Africa divided into 8 admin. units (provinces). ❖ Luanda
Angora *see* Ankara
Angoram *458* N Papua New Guinea
Angoulême *253* W France
Angra Pequena *see* Lüderitz
Angren *610* E Uzbekistan
Angtassom *see* Ăngk Tasaôm
Anguilla *642* British dependent territory of the Caribbean Sea. ❖ The Valley.
Anguilla Cays *112* islets of W Bahamas

Anguilla Channel *642, 646* channel of the Caribbean Sea between Anguilla and St-Martin
Anguilles, Rivière des *400* river of S Mauritius
Anguillita Island *642* island of S Anguilla
Angwa *636* river of Mozambique and Zimbabwe
Anhui *187 var.* Anhwei. Province of E China
Anhwei *see* Anhui
Anié *567* C Togo
Añisoc *236 var.* Añisok. NE Río Muni, Equatorial Guinea
Añisok *see* Añisoc
Aniwa *615* island of S Vanuatu
Anjou *252-253* cultural region of NW France
Anju *349* W North Korea
Ankara *577 prev.* Angora. ❖ of Turkey, C Turkey
Ankaratra, Tangorombohitr' *382 var.* Ankaratra Range. Mountains of C Madagascar
An Laoi *see* Lee
Ânlong Vêng *165* NW Cambodia
An Mhuir Cheilteach *see* Celtic Sea
Annaba *83 prev.* Bône. NE Algeria
An Nabk *551 var.* Nebk, El Nebk, *Fr.* Nébeck. SW Syria
An Nafūd *506* desert region of N Saudi Arabia
Annai *284* SW Guyana
An Najaf *310 var.* Najaf. C Iraq
Annam *see* Trung Phân
Annapolis *599* Maryland, E USA
Anna, Pulo *455* island of S Palau
Annapurna *427* mountain massif of C Nepal
An Nāqūrah *see* En Nâqaoûra
Ann Arbor *599* Michigan, NC USA
An Nás *see* Naas
An Naşīrīyah *310 var.* Nasiriya. SE Iraq
Annau *581 Turkm.* Änew. S Turkmenistan
Annecy *253* E France
An Nîl al Abyaḍ *see* White Nile
An Nîl al Azraq *see* Blue Nile
Annotto Bay *329* E Jamaica
An Nuwayḍirāt *115* NE Bahrain
Anşāb *see* Nişāb
Anse-à-Galets *286* Île de la Gonâve, Haiti
Anseba *238* seasonal river of W Eritrea
Anse Boileau *512* Mahé, Seychelles
Anse-d'Hainault *286* SW Haiti
Anse Étoile *512* Mahé, Seychelles
Anse Ger *497* SE St Lucia
Anse La Raye *497* NW St Lucia
Anse-Rouge *286* NW Haiti
Anse Royale *512 var.* Anse Royal. Mahé, Seychelles
Anshan *187 var.* An-shan. Liaoning, NE China
Anson Bay *650* bay of the South Pacific Ocean, NW Norfolk Island
Ansongo *392* E Mali
Antakya *577 var.* Hatay. S Turkey
Antalaha *382* NE Madagascar
Antalya *576 prev.* Adalia. SW Turkey
Antalya Körfezi *576 var.* Gulf of Adalia, *Eng.* Gulf of Antalya. Gulf of the Mediterranean Sea
Antananarivo *382 prev.* Tananarive. ❖ of Madagascar, C Madagascar
Antarctica *90-91* largely ice-covered continent centred on the South Pole. Though not internationally recognized, the following territorial claims have been made: Argentine Antarctica Sector, Australian Antarctic Territory, British Antarctic Territory, Chilean Antarctic Territory, Queen Maud Land (*Nor.*) Dronning Maud Land, Ross Dependency (*NZ*), Terre Adélie (*Fr.*)
Antequera *531* S Spain
Antibes *253* SE France
Antigua *see* Antigua Guatemala
Antigua *92* island of Lesser Antilles which, with Barbuda, forms Antigua & Barbuda

Antigua and Barbuda *92-93* island state of the West Indies, divided into 6 admin. units (parishes). ❖ St John's
Anti-Atlas *414* mountain range of SW Morocco
Antigua Guatemala *278 var.* Antigua. SW Guatemala
Antikýthira *273* island of S Greece
Anti-Lebanon Mountains *364, 551 Fr.* Anti-Liban, *Ar.* Al Jabal ash Sharqī, *var.* Jebel esh Sharqi. Mountain range of Lebanon and Syria
Anti-Liban *see* Anti-Lebanon
Antípsara *273* island of E Greece
Antivari *see* Bar
Antō *see* Andong
Antofagasta *183* N Chile
Antongila, Helodrano *382 var.* Baie d'Antongil, Antongil Bay. Bay to the NE of Madagascar
Antrim Mountains *382* mountain range of NE Northern Ireland, UK
Antseranana *see* Antsirañana
An tSionainn *see* Shannon
Antsirabe *382* C Madagascar
Antsirañana *382 var.* Antseranana, Antsirane, *prev.* Diégo-Suarez. N Madagascar
An tSiúir *see* Suir
Antsla *240 Ger.* Anzen. SE Estonia
An tSláine *see* Slaney
Antsohihy *382* N Madagascar
An-tung *see* Dandong
Antwerp *see* Antwerpen
Antwerpen *127 Eng.* Antwerp, *Fr.* Anvers. N Belgium
Anuradhapura *534* N Sri Lanka
Anuta *522 var.* Cherry I. Island of E Solomon Islands
Anvers *see* Antwerpen
Anyang *350* NW South Korea
Anzen *see* Antsla
Aoba *615 var.* Omba, Ambae. Island of C Vanuatu
Aola *522* NE Guadalcanal, Solomon Is
Aomori *330* Honshū, N Japan
Àʼopo *500* Sauaiʼi, Samoa
Aorangi *see* Mount Cook
Aosta *320* N Italy
Ao Thai *see* Thailand, Gulf of
Aouk *179, 180* river of Central African Republic and Chad
Aozou *180* N Chad
Apaporis *195* river of Brazil and Colombia
Aparan *98* C Armenia
Apartadó *195* NW Colombia
Apatity *484* NW Russia
Apatou *645* NW French Guiana
Ape *362* NE Latvia
Apeldoorn *429* C Netherlands
Apennines *320, 502 It.* Appennino. Mountain range of C Italy
Apenrade *see* Åbenrå
Apéyémé *see* Danyi-Apéyémé
Àpia *500* ❖ of Samoa, Upolu, Samoa
Apitiri, Monts *645* mountain range of S French Guiana
Apoera *538* NW Suriname
Apolima *500* Upolu, Samoa
Apolima Strait *500* strait between Savaiʼi and Upolu, Samoa
Apo, Mount *466* mountain of Mindanao, S Philippines
Apopa *235* C El Salvador
Apostolos Andreas, Cape *215 var.* Cape Andreas, Zafer Burnu. Cape of Cyprus
Apoteri *284* C Guyana
Appalachian Mountains *599* mountain range of E USA
Appennino *see* Apennines
Appikalo *538* S Suriname
Approuague, l' *645* river of E French Guiana
Apra Harbour *647* harbour of W Guam
Apra Heights *647* W Guam
Apsheronskiy Poluostrov *see* Abşeron Yarımadası
Apure *619* river of W Venezuela
Apurímac *463* river of S Peru

Aqaba *see* Al ʻAqabah
Aqaba, Gulf of *230, 317, 336 var.* Gulf of ʻAqabah, Gulf of Elat, *Ar.* Khalīj al ʻAqabah. Gulf of Red Sea between Egypt and Jordan
ʻAqabah, Gulf of *see* Aqaba, Gulf of
Āqchah *77 var.* Āqcheh. N Afghanistan
Aqmola *see* Akmola
Aqtaū *see* Aktau
Aqtöbe *see* Aktyubinsk
Aquila *see* L'Aquila
Aquila degli Abruzzi *see* L'Aquila
Aquin *286* SW Haiti
ʻArabah, Wādī al *317, 336 Heb.* Ha'Arava. Dry watercourse of Israel and Jordan
Arabian Gulf *see* Persian Gulf
Arabian Sea *448, 420-451* sea of the Indian Ocean between Arabia and India
ʻArab, Baḥr al *see* Arab, Bahr el
Arab, Bahr el *536 var.* Baḥr al ʻArab. River of S Sudan
ʻArabī, Khalīj al *see* Persian Gulf
Arab Sahara *see* Sahara
ʻArab, Shaṭṭ al *310 Per.* Arvand Rūd. River of Iran and Iraq
Aracaju *145* E Brazil
Árachthos *273 prev.* Árakhthos. River of W Greece
Arad *480* W Romania
ʻArad *317* S Israel
ʻArād *115* NE Bahrain
ʻArādah *590* SW United Arab Emirates
Aradhippou *215 var.* Aradippou. SE Cyprus
Arafura Sea *101, 302* sea of the Indian Ocean between Australia and New Guinea
Aragac *see* Aragats Lerr
Aragats Lerr *98 var.* Aragac. Mountain of W Armenia
Aragón *531* autonomous community of E Spain
Araguaia *145 var.* Araguaya. River of C Brazil
Araguaya *see* Araguaia
Aragvi *262* river of C Georgia
Arai *330* Honshū, C Japan
Arainn Mhór *see* Aran Island
Arāk *307* NW Iran
Arakan Yoma *159* mountain range of W Burma
Araks *see* Aras
Aral Sea *338, 610 Kaz.* Aral Tengizi, *Rus.* Aral'skoye More, *Uzb.* Orol Dengizi. Inland sea of Kazakhstan and Uzbekistan
Aral'sk *338 var.* Aral. SW Kazakhstan
Aral Tengizi *see* Aral Sea
Aran Island *314 Ir.* Arainn Mhór. Island of NW Ireland
Aran Islands *314* island group of W Ireland
Aranos *423* SE Namibia
Aranuka *346* island of the Gilbert Is, W Kiribati
Aranyosmarót *see* Zlaté Moravce
Arao *330* Kyūshū, SW Japan
Araouane *392* N Mali
Arapey Grande *607* river of N Uruguay
Ararat *98* S Armenia
Ararat, Mount *see* Büyükağrı Dağı
Aras *98, 110, 307, 577 Arm.* Arak's, *Per.* Rūd-e Aras, *Rus.* Araks, *Turk.* Aras Nehri. River of SW Asia
Arauca *195* NE Colombia
Arauca *619* river of Colombia and Venezuela
Arawa *458* Bougainville I, Papua New Guinea
Ārba Minch' *243* SW Ethiopia
Arbatax *320* Sardegna, W Italy
Arbīl *310 var.* Irbīl, Erbil, *Kurd.* Hawlêr. N Iraq
Arbon *546* NE Switzerland
Arcalis *86* NW Andorra
Archangel *see* Arkhangel'sk
Arctic Bay *170* N Canada

Arctic Ocean *170, 444, 485 Nor.* Nordishavet, *Rus.* Severnyy Ledovityy Okean. Ocean surrounding North Pole, between N America, N Europe and N Asia
Arctowski *90* Polish research station of South Shetland Islands, Antarctica
Arda *152* river of Bulgaria and Greece
Ardabīl *307 var.* Ardebil. NW Iran
Arḍ aş Şawwān *336 var.* Ardh es Suwwān. ain of C Jordan
Ardennes *127, 378* plateau of W Europe
Arecibo *651* N Puerto Rico
Arel *see* Arlon
Arenal, Laguna *206* lake of NW Costa Rica
Arenas *456* S Panama
Arendal *444* S Norway
Arensburg *see* Kuressaare
Arequipa *463* SE Peru
Arezzo *321* C Italy
Argentina *94-97* officially Argentine Republic. Country of S South America divided into 23 admin. units (22 provinces, 1 district). ❖ Buenos Aires
Arghandāb, Daryā-ye *77* river of S Afghanistan
Argirocastro *see* Gjirokastër
Argo *536* N Sudan
Argoub *414* W Western Sahara
Argun' *485* river of China and Russia
Argungu *440* NW Nigeria
Argyle, Lake *101* salt lake of NW Australia
Argyrokastron *see* Gjirokastër
Århus *218 var.* Aarhus. C Denmark
Ariamsvlei *423* S Namibia
Ariana *573 var.* Aryānah, L'Ariana. N Tunisia
Ari Atoll *390* atoll of C Maldives
Arica *183* N Chile
Aride, Île *512* island of the Inner Islands, NE Seychelles
Arīḥā *see* Jericho
Arima *570* N Trinidad, Trinidad & Tobago
Arinsal *86* NW Andorra
Arinsal, Riu d' *86* river of NW Andorra
Aripo, Mount *570 var.* El Cerro del Aripo. Mountain of N Trinidad & Tobago
Aripuanã *144* river of W Brazil
Arizona *598* state of SW USA
Arkalyk *338 Kaz.* Arqalyk. C Kazakhstan
Arkansas *599* river of SC USA
Arkansas *599* state of SC USA
Arkhangel'sk *484 Eng.* Archangel. NW Russia
Arklow *314 Ir.* Inbhear Mór. E Ireland
Arles *253* SE France
Arlon *127 Dut.* Aarlen, *Ger.* Arel. SE Belgium
Armagh *593* Northern Ireland, UK
Armathia *273* island of SE Greece
Armenia *195* W Colombia
Armenia *98-99* officially Republic of Armenia *prev.* Armenian Soviet Socialist Republic. Country of SW Asia divided into 39 admin. units (shrjaner). ❖ Yerevan
Armidale *101* E Australia
Arnaouti, Cape *215* cape of W Cyprus
Arnhem *429* SE Netherlands
Arnhem Land *101* region of N Australia
Arno *320* river C of Italy
Arno *396* island of SE Marshall Islands
Aroab *423* SE Namibia
Aroe Islands *see* Aru, Kepulauan
Arop Island *458 var.* Long I. Island of E Papua New Guinea
Arorae *346* island of the Gilbert Is, W Kiribati
Arp'a *98* river of Armenia and Azerbaijan
Arqalyk *see* Arkalyk
Ar Rahad *see* Er Rahad
Arraiján *456* C Panama
Arrak District *396* district of Majuro, SE Marshall Islands
Ar Ramādī *310* C Iraq

Banghiang 359 *var.* Bang Hieng. River of S Laos
Bangka, Pulau 302 island to the SE of Sumatra, W Indonesia
Bangkok 563 *Th.* Krung Thep. ❖ of Thailand, C Thailand
Bangladesh 116-119 officially People's Republic of Bangladesh, *prev.* East Pakistan. Country of S Asia divided into 4 admin. units (divisions). ❖ Dhaka
Bangor 593 Northern Ireland, UK
Bangor 593 N Wales, UK
Bangor 599 Maine, NE USA
Bangui 179 ❖ of Central African Republic, SW Central African Republic
Bangweulu, Lake 635 *var.* Lake Bengweulu. Lake of N Zambia
Banhã *see* Benha
Ban Hat Yai *see* Hat Yai
Ban Hin Heup 359 C Laos
Ban Houayxay 359 *var.* Ban Houei Sai. NW Sai Laos
Ban Hua Hin 563 C Thailand
Baní 226 S Dominican Republic
Bani 392 river of S Mali
Banias *see* Bāniyās
Banī Jamrah 115 NW Bahrain
Banikoara 132 N Benin
Banī Suwayf *see* Beni Suef
Banī Walīd 371 NW Libya
Bāniyās 551 *var.* Banias. W Syria
Banja Luka 140 NW Bosnia & Herzegovina
Banjarmasin 302 *prev.* Bandjarmasin. Borneo, C Indonesia
Banjës, Liqeni i 81 lake of C Albania
Banjul 261 *prev.* Bathurst. ❖ of Gambia, W Gambia
Ban Kenggnang 359 SE Laos
Ban Kengkabao 359 S Laos
Banket 636 N Zimbabwe
Banks, Îles *see* Banks Islands
Banks Island 170 island of NW Canada
Banks Islands 615 *Fr.* Îles Banks. Island group of N Vanuatu
Banks Peninsula 433 peninsula of E South Island, New Zealand
Ban Lakxao 359 *var.* Lak Sao. E Laos
Banmo *see* Bhamo
Ban Mun-Houamuang 359 SE Laos
Ban Nadou 359 S Laos
Ban Nakha 359 C Laos
Ban Na Kout 359 C Laos
Ban Na Môn 359 NE Laos
Ban Nanai 359 S Laos
Ban Nangeo 359 S Laos
Ban Napha 359 C Laos
Ban Nasi 359 E Laos
Ban Naxon 359 C Laos
Banningville *see* Bandundu
Ban Nongkeun 359 C Laos
Ban Nongsim 359 S Laos
Baños 228 C Ecuador
Bánovce nad Bebravou 519 *var.* Bánovce. W Slovakia
Ban Phon 359 *var.* Ban Phone. SE Laos
Ban Phone *see* Ban Phon
Ban Phou A Douk 359 E Laos
Ban Saka 359 C Laos
Bansang 261 E Gambia
Ban Set 359 S Laos
Banská Bystrica 519 *Ger.* Neusohl, *Hung.* Besztercebánya. C Slovakia
Ban Talak 359 E Laos
Bantè 132 W Benin
Ban Thabôk 359 C Laos
Bantry 314 SW Ireland
Bantry Bay 314 *Ir.* Bá Bheanntraí. Area of the Celtic Sea, SW Ireland
Ban Xot 359 S Laos
Banyak, Kepulauan 302 island group to the NW of Sumatra, W Indonesia
Banyo 168 N Cameroon
Banzart *see* Bizerte
Baoding 187 *var.* Pao-ting, *prev.* Tsingyuan. Hebei, NE China
Baoji 187 *var.* Pao-chi, Paoki. Shaanxi, C China
Baoro 179 W Central African Republic

Baoshan 186 *var.* Pao-shan. Yunnan, SW China
Baotou 187 *var.* Pao-t'ou, Paotow. Nei Mongol Zizhiqu, N China
Ba'qūbah 310 C Iraq
Bar 630 *It.* Antivari. S Montenegro, Yugoslavia
Baraawe 524 *It.* Brava. S Somalia
Baracaldo 531 N Spain
Baracoa 211 SE Cuba
Barahona 226 SW Dominican Republic
Baraka 238 seasonal river of Eritrea and Sudan
Barakī Barak 77 E Afghanistan
Baram 387 *var.* Barram. River of C Borneo, Malaysia
Barama 284 river of N Guyana
Baramanni 284 N Guyana
Baramita 284 NW Guyana
Baranavichy 122 *Rus.* Baranovichi, *Pol.* Baranowicze. W Belarus
Barbados 120-121 island state of the Lesser Antilles, Caribbean Sea divided into 11 admin. units (districts or parishes). ❖ Bridgetown
Bārbār 115 NW Bahrain
Barbuda 92 island of Lesser Antilles which, with Antigua, forms Antigua & Barbuda
Barce *see* Al Marj
Barcellona 321 Sicilia, S Italy
Barcelona 531 E Spain
Barcelona 619 NE Venezuela
Barclayville 368 SW Liberia
Barcoo *see* Cooper Creek
Bārda 110 C Azerbaijan
Bardaï 180 N Chad
Bardejov 519 *Hung.* Bártfa, *Ger.* Bartfeld. NE Slovakia
Bardera *see* Baardheere
Bardo 573 *var.* Bārdaw, Le Bardo. N Tunisia
Bareilly 296 *Hind.* Bareli. N India
Bareli *see* Bareilly
Barentsburg 653 Spitsbergen, W Svalbard
Barents Sea 444, 484 *Nor.* Barentshavet, *Rus.* Barentsevo More. Sea of Arctic Ocean bordering N Europe
Barentu 238 W Eritrea
Bargny 510 W Senegal
Bari 321 *var.* Bari delle Puglie. S Italy
Bari delle Puglie *see* Bari
Barika 83 N Algeria
Barīkowṭ 77 *var.* Barikot. NE Afghanistan
Barillas 278 NW Guatemala
Barīm 627 *Eng.* Perim. Island of SW Yemen
Barinas 619 N Venezuela
Baringo, Lake 342 lake of W Kenya
Barisāl 117 S Bangladesh
Barisan, Pegunungan 302 mountain range of Sumatra, W Indonesia
Barito 302 river of Borneo, C Indonesia
Barkā' 448 *var.* Birka. N Oman
Barka *see* Al Marj
Barkly Tableland 101 plateau of N Australia
Bârlad 480 E Romania
Barlavento, Ilhas de 176 northernmost of the two main island groups comprising Cape Verde
Bar-le-Duc 253 NE France
Barletta 321 S Italy
Barnaul 485 C Russia
Barnes Hill 92 N Antigua, Antigua & Barbuda
Barneveld 429 C Netherlands
Baroda *see* Vadodara
Barouk, Nahr el 364 river of C Lebanon
Baroul *see* Salisbury
Barqah 371 *Eng.* Cyrenaica. Cultural region of NE Libya
Barquisimeto 619 NW Venezuela
Barrage de Nzilo *see* Nzilo, Lac
Barrancabermeja 195 NW Colombia
Barranquilla 195 N Colombia

Barra Point 648 headland of Macao, NW Macao
Barreiro 474 W Portugal
Barrier Reef 130 coral reef E of Belize
Barrigada 647 C Guam
Barril 176 São Nicolau, N Cape Verde
Barrouallie 498 W St Vincent, St Vincent & the Grenadines
Barrow 314 *Ir.* An Bhearú. River of SE Ireland
Barrow-in-Furness 593 NW England, UK
Barr, Ra's al 115 cape of S Bahrain
Barsalogo 157 *var.* Barsalogho. N Burkina
Bartang 558 river of SE Tajikistan
Bártfa *see* Bardejov
Bartfeld *see* Bardejov
Bartica 284 NE Guyana
Bartolomé Masó 210 SE Cuba
Baruta 619 N Venezuela
Baruun-Urt 412 E Mongolia
Barú, Volcán 456 *var.* Volcán de Chiriquí. Volcanic peak of W Panama
Barxudarli 110 W Azerbaijan
Barysaw 122 *Rus.* Borisov. NE Belarus
Basäk 165 river of Cambodia and Vietnam
Basarabeasca 408 *Rus.* Bessarabka. SE Moldova
Basel 546 *Eng.* Basle, *Fr.* Bâle. NW Switzerland
Bashi Channel 555 *Chin.* Pa-shih Hai-hsia. Channel connecting the South China Sea and Pacific Ocean
Bashkend *see* Artsvashen
Bashkortostan, Respublika 484 autonomous republic of W Russia
Basilan Island 466 island of SW Philippines
Basilé, Pico de 236 *var.* Pico de Santa Isabel. Mountain of C Bioko, Equatorial Guinea
Basle *see* Basel
Basra *see* Al Baṣrah
Bassam *see* Grand-Bassam
Bassar 567 *var.* Bassari. NW Togo
Basse Santa Su 261 E Gambia
Bassein 159 *var.* Pathein. SW Burma
Basse-Terre 646 ❖ of Guadeloupe, SW Guadeloupe
Basseterre 494 ❖ of St Kitts & Nevis, S St Kitts
Bassikounou 398 SE Mauritania
Bassila 132 W Benin
Bass Strait 101 SE strait connecting South Pacific Ocean and Southern Ocean, between Australia and Tasmania
Bastia 253 Corse, SE France
Bastogne 127 SE Belgium
Basutoland *see* Lesotho
Bata 236 NW Río Muni, Equatorial Guinea
Batabanó, Golfo de 210 gulf of the Caribbean Sea, on the S coast of Cuba
Bataka 224 NE Dominica
Batak, Yazovir 152 reservoir of SW Bulgaria
Batangafo 179 NW Central African Republic
Batangas 466 Luzon, N Philippines
Batan Islands 466 island group of N Philippines
Batavia *see* Jakarta
Bătdâmbâng 165 *prev.* Battambang. W Cambodia
Batéké, Plateaux 200 plateau of Congo
Bates, Mount 650 mountain of N Norfolk Island
Bath 593 SW England, UK
Bath 329 E Jamaica
Bath 494 SW Nevis, St Kitts & Nevis
Batha 180 seasonal river of S Chad
Bathsheba 121 E Barbados
Bathurst 101 SE Australia
Bathurst *see* Banjul
Bathurst Island 101 island of N Australia

Bathurst Island 170 island of Parry Islands, N Canada
Bathyz *see* Badkhyz
Batī 243 NE Ethiopia
Batiki 246 *prev.* Mbatiki. Island to the E of Viti Levu, C Fiji
Bātin, Wādī al 354, 506 dry watercourse of SW Asia
Batjan *see* Bacan, Pulau
Batman 577 *var.* Īluh. SE Turkey
Batna 83 NE Algeria
Batoc *see* Batu, Kepulauan
Baton Rouge 599 Louisiana, SC USA
Batouri 168 E Cameroon
Batroûn 364 *var.* Al Batrūn. N Lebanon
Battambang *see* Bătdâmbâng
Batticaloa 534 E Sri Lanka
Battowia 498 island of C St Vincent & the Grenadines
Batu Gajah 386 W Peninsular Malaysia
Batu, Kepulauan 302 *prev.* Batoe. Island group to the W of Sumatra, W Indonesia
Bat'umi 262 W Georgia
Batu Pahat 386 *prev.* Bandar Penggaram. S Peninsular Malaysia
Bat Yam 317 C Israel
Bauchi 440 NE Nigeria
Baumann, Pic *see* Agou, Mont
Baures 136 river of NE Bolivia
Bauru 145 S Brazil
Bauska 362 *Ger.* Bauske. S Latvia
Bautzen 265 E Germany
Bavarian Alps 106, 265 *Ger.* Bayerische Alpen. Mountain range of Austria and Germany
Bawku 270 N Ghana
Baxoi 186 Xizang Zizhiqu, W China
Bayamo 210 SE Cuba
Bayamón 651 NE Puerto Rico
Bayanhongor 412 C Mongolia
Bayano, Lago 456 lake of E Panama
Baydhabo 524 *var.* Isha Baydhabo, *It.* Baidoa. SW Somalia
Bayerische Alpen *see* Bavarian Alps
Bâyir 336 *var.* Bā'ir. C Jordan
Bâyir, Wādī 336 *var.* Wādī Bā'ir. Dry watercourse of C Jordan
Baykal, Ozero 485 *Eng.* Lake Baikal. Lake of S Russia
Bay, Laguna de 466 lake of Luzon, N Philippines
Baynūnah 590 desert region of W United Arab Emirates
Bayonne 252 SW France
Bayram-Ali *see* Bayramaly
Bayramaly 581 *prev.* Bayram-Ali, *var.* Bajram-Ali. SE Turkmenistan
Bayrūt *see* Beirut
Baysun *see* Boysun
Bayt al Faqīh 627 W Yemen
Bayt Lahm *see* Bethlehem
Bayuda Desert 536 *var.* Baiyuda, Şaḩrā' Bayyūḍah. Desert NE Sudan
Bayy al Kabīr, Wādī 371 dry watercourse of NW Libya
Bayyūḍah, Şaḩrā' *see* Bayuda Desert
Bazardüzü Dağ 110 *Rus.* Gora Bazardyuzyu. Mountain of N Azerbaijan
Bazargic *see* Dobrich
Bazgrad 152 NE Bulgaria
Bazin *see* Pezinok
Bcharré 364 *var.* Bsharrī. NE Lebanon
Beagle Channel 183 channel connecting Pacific Ocean and Atlantic Ocean
Beata, Isla 226 island of SW Dominican Republic
Beatrice 636 NE Zimbabwe
Beau Bassin 400 W Mauritius
Beaufort Sea 170 sea of the Arctic Ocean to the N of North America
Beaufort West 527 *Afr.* Beaufort-Wes. Western Cape, SW South Africa
Beauvais 253 N France
Béchar 83 *prev.* Colomb-Béchar. W Algeria
Bécs *see* Vienna
Bedanda 282 S Guinea-Bissau

Colville Channel *433* channel linking the Bay of Plenty and Hauraki Gulf, N of North Island, New Zealand
Comarapa *136* C Bolivia
Comas *463* W Peru
Comayagua *288* W Honduras
Comendador *226 prev.* Elías Piña. W Dominican Republic
Comer *see* Como, Lago di
Comilla *117 Ben.* Kumillā. E Bangladesh
Commissioner's Point *643* headland of Ireland Island North, W Bermuda
Communism Peak *see* Garmo, Qullai
Como *320* N Italy
Comodoro Rivadavia *95* SE Argentina
Como, Lago di *320 var.* Lario, *Eng.* Lake Como, *Ger.* Comer See. Lake of N Italy
Comoros *198-199* officially Federal Islamic Republic of the Comoros. Island group of the Indian Ocean, between Madagascar and the African mainland, divided into 3 admin. units (districts). ❖ Moroni
Comrat *408 Rus.* Komrat. S Moldova
Conakry *281* ❖ of Guinea, SW Guinea
Concepción *136* E Bolivia
Concepción *183* C Chile
Concepción *460 var.* Villa Concepción. C Paraguay
Concepción *see* Riaba
Concepción de La Vega *see* La Vega
Conchos *403* river of NW Mexico
Concord *276* W Grenada island, Grenada
Concord *599* New Hampshire, NE USA
Concordia *95* E Argentina
Condado *210* C Cuba
Côn Dao *623 var.* Con Son. Island of S Vietnam
Condroz *127* physical region of SE Belgium
Congo *88, 200, 203 var.* Zaire, Kongo, Lualaba. River of C Africa
Congo *200-201* officially The Republic of the Congo. Country of C Africa divided into 9 admin. units (regions). ❖ Brazzaville
Congo Basin *203* drainage basin of C Africa
Congo, Democratic Republic of (Zaire) *202-205* officially Democratic Republic of Congo (Zaire), *prev.* Congo (Kinshasa), Belgian Congo, Zaire. Country of C Africa divided into 11 admin. units (10 provinces, 1 city). ❖ Kinshasa
Con, Loch *see* Conn, Lough
Connaught *314* province of W Ireland
Connecticut *599* state of NE USA
Conn, Lough *314 Ir.* Loch Con. Lake of NW Ireland
Consolación del Sur *210* W Cuba
Constance, Lake *106, 264, 546 Ger.* Bodensee. Lake of C Europe
Constanţa *480 Ger.* Konstantza, *Turk.* Köstence, *var.* Küstendje, *Eng.* Constanza. SE Romania
Constantine *83 Ar.* Qoussantína, *var.* Qacentina, NE Algeria
Constantine *276* SW Grenada island, Grenada
Constantinople *see* İstanbul
Constant Spring *329* SE Jamaica
Constanza *226* C Dominican Republic
Contagem *145* SE Brazil
Contuboel *282* NE Guinea-Bissau
Cook Islands *644* territory in free association with New Zealand, Pacific Ocean. ❖ Avarua.
Cook, Mount *433 prev.* Aorangi. Mountain of W South Island, New Zealand
Cook, Récif de *650* reef of the Pacific Ocean, N New Caledonia
Cook Strait *433 var.* Raukawa. Strait between North and South Islands of New Zealand, connecting the South Pacific Ocean and Tasman Sea
Cooktown *101* NE Australia
Cooper Creek *101 var.* Barcoo, Cooper's Creek. River of C Australia

Cooper Island *643* island of SE British Virgin Islands
Copacabana *136* W Bolivia
Copenhagen *218 Dan.* København. ❖ of Denmark, Sjælland, E Denmark
Copiapó *183* N Chile
Coppename *538 var.* Koppename. River of C Suriname
Coppermine *170 var.* Qurlurtuuq. NW Canada
Coquilhatville *see* Mbandaka
Coquimbo *183* N Chile
Corail *286* SW Haiti
Coral Harbour *171* Southampton Island, NE Canada
Coral Sea *101, 615, 458* sea of the Pacific Ocean between Australia and Papua New Guinea
Corantijn *284, 538 var.* Coeroeni, Corentyne, Courantyne. River of Guyana and Suriname
Córdoba *95* C Argentina
Córdoba *531 var.* Cordoba, *Eng.* Cordova. SW Spain
Cordova *598* Alaska, USA
Corentyne *see* Corantijin
Corfu *see* Kérkyra
Corinth *see* Kórinthos
Corinth *276* SE Grenada island, Grenada
Corinth, Gulf of *see* Korinthiakós Kólpos
Corinth, Isthmus of *see* Korínthou, Isthmós
Corinto *436* W Nicaragua
Coriole *see* Qoryooley
Corisco, Isla de *236* Island of SW Equatorial Guinea
Cork *314 Ir.* Corcaigh. S Ireland
Cork Hill *649* W Montserrat
Corleone *321* Sicilia, S Italy
Corner Brook *171* Newfoundland, E Canada
Corn Exchange *366* NW Lesotho
Corn Islands *see* Maíz, Islas
Cornwallis Island *170* island of Parry Islands, N Canada
Coro *619 var.* Santa Ana de Coro. NW Venezuela
Corocoro *136* W Bolivia
Coromandel Peninsula *433* peninsula of NE North Island, New Zealand
Coronel Bogado *460* S Paraguay
Coronel Oviedo *460* SE Paraguay
Çorovodë *81 var.* Çorovoda, Corovoda. SE Albania
Corozal *130* N Belize
Corrib, Lough *314 Ir.* Loch Corrib. Lake of W Ireland
Corrientes *95* NE Argentina
Corriverton *284* E Guyana
Corriza *see* Korçë
Corse *253 Eng.* Corsica. Island of SE France
Corsica *see* Corse
Cortés *206* SE Costa Rica
Corubal *282 var.* Cocoli, Rio Grande. River of W Africa
Çorum *577* N Turkey
Corvallis *598* Oregon, NW USA
Corvo *474 var.* Ilha do Corvo. Island of the Azores, Portugal
Cosenza *321* S Italy
Cosmolédo Atoll *512* atoll of the Aldabra Group, SW Seychelles
Cospicua *395* E Malta
Costa, Cordillera de la *619 var.* Cordillera de Venezuela. Mountain range of N Venezuela
Costa Rica *206-207* officially Republic of Costa Rica. Country of Central America divided into 7 admin. units (provinces). ❖ San José
Costermansville *see* Bukavu
Cotagaita *136* S Bolivia
Côtière, Chaîne *see* Coast Mountains
Cotonou *132 var.* Kotonu. S Benin
Cotopaxi *228* active volcano of N Ecuador
Cotswold Hills *593* hills of W England, UK
Cottbus *265 prev.* Kottbus. E Germany
Cottica *538* E Suriname

Cotton Ground *494* NW Nevis, St Kitts & Nevis
Cotuí *226* C Dominican Republic
Coulibistri *224* W Dominica
Coupe, Cap *652* cape of the Atlantic Ocean on the coast of Miquelon, S Saint Pierre and Miquelon
Courantyne *see* Corantijn
Courcelles *127* S Belgium
Courland *see* Kurzeme
Courtrai *see* Kortrijk
Couva *570* W Trinidad, Trinidad & Tobago
Cova Figueira *176* Fogo, S Cape Verde
Cove Bay *642* bay of the Caribbean Sea on the S coast of Anguilla
Coventry *593* C England, UK
Covilhã *474* E Portugal
Cox's Bāzār *117* S Bangladesh
Coyah *281* SW Guinea
Coyhaique *see* Coihaique
Cozumel, Isla de *403* island of SE Mexico
Cracow *see* Kraków
Cradock *527* Eastern Cape, S South Africa
Craiova *480* SW Romania
Cranbrook *170* SW Canada
Crane, The *121* SE Barbados
Crawley *593* SE England, UK
Créoles, River des *400* river of SE Mauritius
Cres *209 It.* Cherso. Island of W Croatia
Crescent Group *651* island group of C Paracel Islands
Crete *see* Kríti
Créteil *253* N France
Crete, Sea of *273 Gk* Kritikó Pélagos. Area of the Mediterranean Sea, SE Greece
Creuse *253* river of C France
Crikvenica *209 It.* Cirquenizza. NW Croatia
Crimea *see* Krym
Cristóbal *456* N Panama
Cristóbal Colón, Pico *195* peak of N Colombia
Crna Gora *see* Montenegro
Crna reka *381* river of S FYR Macedonia
Crni Drim *see* Drinit të Zi
Črnomelj *520 Ger.* Tschernembl. S Slovenia
Croatia *236 -209* officially Republic of Croatia, *SCr.* Hrvatska. Country of S Europe divided into 21 admin. units (provinces). ❖ Zagreb
Crochu *276* SE Grenada island, Grenada
Crocker, Banjaran *387 var.* Crocker Range. Mountain range of C Borneo, Malaysia
Crocodile *see* Limpopo
Crocus Bay *642* bay of the Caribbean Sea on the W coast of Anguilla
Croia *see* Krujë
Cromer *593* E England, UK
Crooked Island *112* island of the E Bahamas
Crooked Island Passage *112* passage of the Atlantic Ocean between Crooked Island and Long Island, Bahamas
Crooked Tree *130* NE Belize
Crosby *647* C Isle of Man
Cross *440* river of Cameroon and Nigeria
Crossroads *314* N Ireland
Crotone *321* S Italy
Crucero Contramaestre *210* S Cuba
Cruz Bay *653* Saint John, E Virgin Islands (US)
Cruz del Eje *95* C Argentina
Csaca *see* Čadca
Csakathurn *see* Čakovec
Csáktornya *see* Čakovec
Csíkszereda *see* Miercurea-Ciuc
Cuamba *419* N Mozambique
Cuan Dhun Dealgan *see* Dundalk Bay
Cuando *88, 635 var.* Kwando. River of southern Africa
Cuango *see* Kwango

Cuan na Gaillimhe *see* Galway Bay
Cuanza *88 var.* Kwanza. River of Angola
Cuareim *607 Port.* Quaraí. River of Brazil and Uruguay
Cuba *210-213* officially Republic of Cuba. Country of the West Indies divided into 15 admin. units (14 provinces and 1 special municipality). ❖ Havana
Cubal *88* W Angola
Cubango *88 var.* Kuvango, *Port.* Vila Artuur de Paiva, Vila da Ponte. C Angola
Cubango *88, 142, 423 var.* Kavango, Kavengo, Kubango, Okavango, Okavanggo. River of Southern Africa
Cúcuta *195 var.* San José de Cúcuta. N Colombia
Cuddapah *296* S India
Cudjoehead *649* NW Montserrat
Cuenca *228* S Ecuador
Cuenca *531* C Spain
Cueno *320* N Italy
Cuera *see* Chur
Cuernavaca *403* S Mexico
Cueto *210* SE Cuba
Cufra *see* Al Kufrah
Cuiabá *145 prev.* Cuyabá. SW Brazil
Cuilapa *278* S Guatemala
Cuito *88 var.* Kwito. River of Angola
Cuito Cuanquale *88* S Angola
Culebra *651* Isla de Culebra, NE Puerto Rico
Culebra, Isla de *651* island of NE Puerto Rico
Culiacán *403* W Mexico
Culion Island *466* island of Calamian Group, W Philippines
Cumaná *619* NE Venezuela
Cumberland *498* river of W St Vincent, St Vincent & the Grenadines
Cumberland Peninsula *171* peninsula of Baffin Island, NE Canada
Cumbrian Mountains *593 var.* Lake District. Mountain range of NW England, UK
Cunene *88, 423 var.* Kunene. River of Angola and Namibia
Cunnamulla *101* E Australia
Curaçao *619, 650* island of the Netherland Antilles, Caribbean Sea
Curanilahue *183* C Chile
Curaray *228* river of Ecuador and Peru
Curepe *570* NW Trinidad, Trinidad & Tobago
Curepipe *400* C Mauritius
Curicó *183* C Chile
Curitiba *145 prev.* Curytiba. S Brazil
Curral Velho *176* Boa Vista, Cape Verde
Current *112* Eleuthera Island, Bahamas
Curuguaty *460* E Paraguay
Curzola *see* Korčula
Cusco *463 var.* Cuzco. SE Peru
Čust *see* Chust
Cutch, Gulf of *see* Kachch, Gulf of
Cuttack *296* E India
Cutting Camp *366* SW Lesotho
Cuxhaven *264* NW Germany
Cuyabá *see* Cuiabá
Cuyo East Passage *466* passage of the Sulu Sea between Cuyo Islands and Panay, Philippines
Cuyo Islands *466* islands of C Philippines
Cuyo West Passage *466* passage of the Sulu Sea between Cuyo Islands and Palawan, Philippines
Cuyuni *284* river of Guyana and Venezuela
Cuzco *see* Cusco
Čvrsnica *140* mountain range of SW Bosnia & Herzegovina
Cyambwe, Lac *492* lake of E Rwanda
Cyangugu *492* SW Rwanda
Cyclades *see* Kyklades
Cymru *see* Wales
Cyohoha Sud, Lac *162, 492 var.* Cohoha, Lac Tshohoha Sud. Lake of Burundi and Rwanda

Cyprus *214-215* officially Republic of Cyprus, *Gk* Kypros, *Turk.* Kıbrıs, Kıbrıs Cumhuriyeti. Country of E Mediterranean divided into 5 admin. units (districts). ❖ Nicosia. Following Turkish invasion of 1974, northern sector became self-proclaimed state, officially Turkish Republic of Northern Cyprus (TRNC). ❖ Nicosia
Cyrenaica *see* Barqah
Czechoslovakia *see* Czech Republic and Slovakia
Czech Republic *216-217 Cz.* Česká Republika, *prev.* constituent republic of Czechoslovakia. Country of C Europe divided into 7 admin. units (regions). ❖ Prague
Czeglèd *see* Cegléd
Czernowitz *see* Chernivtsi
Częstochowa *471 Ger.* Tschenstochau. S Poland

D

Dabakala *326* NE Ivory Coast
Dabola *281* C Guinea
Dabou *326* S Ivory Coast
Dąbrowa Górnicza *471* S Poland
Dacca *see* Dhaka
Dachau *265* S Germany
Dadanawa *284* SW Guyana
Dadda 'to *222* N Ethiopia
Dadeldhura *427 var.* Dandeldhura. W Nepal
Dadnah *590 var.* Dhadnah. NE United Arab Emirates
Daegu *see* Taegu
Daga *134* S Bhutan
Dagana *510* N Senegal
Dagden *see* Hiiumaa
Dagestan, Respublika *484* autonomous republic of SW Russia
Dagö *see* Hiiumaa
Dagupan *466* Luzon, N Philippines
Dahar *573* physical region of S Tunisia
Da Hinggan Ling *187 Eng.* Great Khingan Range. Mountain range of Nei Mongol Zizhiqu, NE China
Dahlak Archipelago *238* island group of E Eritrea
Dahlak Island *238* island of Dahlak Archipelago, E Eritrea
Dahm, Ramlat *627* desert region of NW Yemen
Dahomey *see* Benin
Dahra *see* Dara
Dahūk *310 var.* Dohuk, *Kurd.* Dihōk. N Iraq
Dai Island *522* island of E Solomon Is
Dailekh *427* W Nepal
Daingin, Bá an *see* Dingle Bay
Dajabón *226* NW Dominican Republic
Dakar *510* ❖ of Senegal, W Senegal
Dakoro *439* SW Niger
Đakovica *630 var.* Djakovica, *Alb.* Gjakovë. S Serbia, Yugoslavia
Đakovo *209 var.* Djakovo, *Hung.* Diakovár. NE Croatia
Dakshin *see* Deccan
Dalaba *281* W Guinea
Dalai Nor *see* Hulun Nur
Dalälven *543* river of SE Sweden
Dalandzadgad *412* S Mongolia
Đa Lat *623* S Vietnam
Dali *see* Dhali
Dalian *187 var.* Jay Dairen, Ta-lien, *Rus.* Dalny. Liaoning, NE China
Dallas *599* Texas, SC USA
Dallol Bosso *439* seasonal watercourse of W Niger
Dalmā *590* island of W United Arab Emirates
Dalmacija *209 Eng.* Dalmatia. Cultural region of S Croatia
Dalmatia *see* Dalmacija
Dalny *see* Dalian
Daloa *326* C Ivory Coast
Dalvík *294* N Iceland
Damanhûr *230 var.* Damanhûr. N Egypt

Damar, Kepulauan *302 var.* Kepulauan Barat Daya. Island group to the E of Nusa Tenggara, C Indonesia
Damara *179* S Central African Republic
Damasak *441* NE Nigeria
Damascus *551 var.* Esh Sham, *Fr.* Damas, *Ar.* Dimashq. ❖ of Syria, SW Syria
Damâvand, Qolleh-ye *307* mountain of N Iran
Dambulla *534* C Sri Lanka
Dame-Marie *286* SW Haiti
Damêrdjôg *222* E Djibouti
Damietta *see* Dumyât
Damongo *270* NW Ghana
Damoûr *364 var.* Ad Dāmûr. W Lebanon
Damphu *134* S Bhutan
Damqawt *627 var.* Damqut. E Yemen
Dâmrei, Chuôr Phnum *165 Fr.* Chaîne de l'Éléphant. Mountain range of SW Cambodia
Danakil Desert *238, 243 var.* Danakil Plain, Afar Depression. Desert region of Eritrea and Ethiopia
Danané *326* W Ivory Coast
Đà Nẵng *623 prev.* Tourane. C Vietnam
Dandeldhura *see* Dadeldhura
Dandong *187 var.* Tan-tung, *prev.* An-tung. Liaoning, NE China
Daneborg *646 var.* Danborg. E Greenland
Dänew *see* Deynau
Dangal *238* SE Eritrea
Dangara *see* Danghara
Danger Island *643* island of W British Indian Ocean Territory
Danghara *558 Rus.* Dangara. W Tajikistan
Dängilä *243 var.* Dangila. NW Ethiopia
Dangme *134* river of S Bhutan
Dang Raek, Phanom *165, 563 var.* Phanom Dong Rak, *Cam.* Chuor Phmum Dângrêk, *Fr.* Chaîne des Dangrek. Mountain range of Cambodia and Thailand
Dangrak, Chaîne des *see* Dang Raek, Phanom
Dângrêk, Chuôr Phmun *see* Dang Raek, Phanom
Dangriga *130 var.* Stann Creek. SE Belize
Dank *448 var.* Dhank. NW Oman
Danlí *288* S Honduras
Danmark *see* Denmark
Danmark Havn *646* NE Greenland
Danmarksstraedet *see* Denmark Strait
Danube *106, 152, 209, 265, Bul.* Danav, *Hung.* Duna, *Cz.* Dunaj, *Ger.* Donau, *Rom.* Dunărea. River of C Europe
Danube, Mouths of the *480 Rom.* Delta Dunării. Delta of Romania and Ukraine
Danubian Plain *see* Dunavska Ravnina
Danyi-Apéyémé *567 prev.* Apéyémé. W Togo
Danzig *see* Gdańsk
Danzig, Gulf of *471 var.* Gulf of Gdańsk, *Gk* Danziger Bucht, *Pol.* Zatoka Gdańska, *Rus.* Gdan'skaya Bukhta. Gulf of the Baltic Sea, N Pola
Dapaong *567* N Togo
Dara *510 var.* Dahra. NW Senegal
Dar'ā *551 var.* Der'a, *Fr.* Déraa. SW Syria
Da Rang *623 var.* Ba. River of S Vietnam
Dardanelles *see* Canakkale Boğazi
Dar el Beida *see* Casablanca
Dar es Salaam *560* E Tanzania
Darfur *536 var.* Darfur Massif. Mountain range of W Sudan
Dargan-Ata *581 var.* Darganata. E Turkmenistan
Dargaville *433* NW North Island, New Zealand
Dargol *439* W Niger
Darhan *412* N Mongolia
Darien, Isthmus of *see* Panamá, Istmo de

Darién, Serranía del *456* mountain range of Colombia and Panama
Darjiling *297 prev.* Darjeeling. NE India
Darling *101* river of E Australia
Darling Range *100* mountain range of SW Australia
Darlington *593* N England, UK
Darmstadt *264* SW Germany
Darnah *371 var.* Derna. NE Libya
Daroot-Korgon *357 var.* Daraut-Kurgan. SW Kyrgyzstan
Darou Mousti *510* NW Senegal
Darrell Island *643* island of W Bermuda
Dartmoor *593* moorland of SW England, UK
Dartmouth *171* SE Canada
Daru *458* SW Papua New Guinea
Daru *514* SE Sierra Leone
Darvaza *581 Turkm.* Derweze. C Turkmenistan
Darvel Bay *see* Lahad Datu, Telukan
Darvel, Teluk *see* Lahad Datu, Telukan
Darvos, Qatorkûhi *558 Rus.* Darvazskiy Khrebet. Mountain range of C Tajikistan
Darwin *101* N Australia
Darwin, Isla *228* island of the NW Galapagos Is, Ecuador
Dashkhovuz *581 prev.* Tashauz, *var.* Tašauz, *Turkm.* Dashhowuz. N Turkmenistan
Dasht Kaur *450* river of SW Pakistan
Daska *451* NE Pakistan
Da, Sông *see* Black River
Dassa *132 var.* Dassa-Zoumé. S Benin
Datong *187 var.* Ta-t'ung. Shanxi, N China
Datu, Teluk *386* bay of the South China Sea, on the coast of Borneo, E Malaysia
Daua *342 Amh.* Dawa Wenz. River of E Africa
Daugava *see* Western Dvina
Daugavpils *362 Ger.* Dünaburg, *Rus.* Dvinsk. SE Latvia
Daule *228* W Ecuador
Daule *228* river of W Ecuador
Daurada, Costa *530 var.* Costa Dorada. Coastal region of E Spain
Davao *466* Mindanao, S Philippines
Davao Gulf *466* gulf of the Pacific Ocean
Davenport *599* Iowa, C USA
David *456* W Panama
Davis *90* Australian research station of Greater Antarctica, Antarctica
Davis Strait *171, 646* strait connecting the Atlantic Ocean and Baffin Bay, NE Canada between Baffin Island and Greenland
Davos *546* E Switzerland
Davyd-Haradok *122 Rus.* David Gorodok, *Pol.* Dawidgródek. S Belarus
Dawa Wenz *see* Daua
Dawei *see* Tavoy
Dawidgródek *see* Davyd-Haradok
Dawra *414* NW Western Sahara
Dawson *170* NW Canada
Dawwah *448 var.* Dauwa. E Oman
Dayrah *590 var.* Deira. NE United Arab Emirates
Dayr az Zawr *551 var.* Deir ez Zor. E Syria
Dayrîk *see* Al Mālikīyah
Dayton *599* Ohio, NE USA
De Aar *527* Northern Cape, C South Africa
Deadman's Bay *652* bay of the South Atlantic Ocean on the SW coast of Tristan da Cunha
Dead Sea *317, 318, 336 Ar.* Al Baḥr al Mayyit, Baḥrat Lūt, *Heb.* Yam HaMelaḥ Salt lake of SW Asia
Deadwood Plain *652* plain of N St Helena
Debar *381* W FYR Macedonia
Débo, Lac *392* lake of C Mali
Debre Birhan *243 var.* Debra Birhan. C Ethiopia

Debrecen *290 prev.* Debreczen, *Ger.* Debreczin. E Hungary
Debre Mark'os *243* NW Ethiopia
Debre Tabor *243* NW Ethiopia
Debre Zebit *243* N Ethiopia
Debre Zeyit *243 var.* Debre Zeyt, *prev.* Bishoftu, *It.* Biscoftù. C Ethiopia
Deccan *296 Hind.* Dakshin. Plateau of C India
Děčín *216 Ger.* Tetschen. NW Czech Republic
Dedeagach *see* Alexandroúpoli
Dededo *647* N Guam
Dedeağç *see* Alexandroúpoli
Dedoplistsqaro *262 Rus.* Dedoplis-Tskaro, *prev.* Tsiteli-Tskaro. SE Georgia
Dédougou *157* W Burkina
Deduru Oya *534* C Sri Lanka
Dedza *385* SW Malawi
Dee *593* river of NE Scotland, UK
Dee *593 Wel.* Dyfrdwy. River of N Wales, UK
Deep Bay *see* Chilumba
Deep Water Bay *see* Hau Hoi Wan
Değirmenlik *215 var.* Kythrea. N Cyprus
Dehiwala-Mount Lavinia *534* SW Sri Lanka
Deinze *127* W Belgium
Deira *see* Adh Dhayd
Deir el Balah *317, 318* C Gaza Strip
Deir el-Bahri *230* E Egypt
Deir ez Zo *see* Dayr az Zawr
Deirgeirt, Loch *see* Derg, Lough
Dej *480* NW Romania
Dekemhare *238* S Eritrea
Dékoa *179* C Central African Republic
Delagoa Bay *see* Maputo, Baía de
Delap District *396* district of Majuro, SE Marshall Islands
Delārām *77* SW Afghanistan
Delaware *599* state of E USA
Delčevo *381* NE FYR Macedonia
Delcommune, Lac *see* Nzilo, Lac
Delémont *546 Ger.* Delsberg. NW Switzerland
Delft *429* W Netherlands
Delft *534* island of NW Sri Lanka
Delfzijl *429* NE Netherlands
Delhi *296 Hind.* Dilli. N India
Délices *224* SE Dominica
Délices *645* C French Guiana
Delsberg *see* Delémont
Delvinë *81 var.* Delvina, *It.* Delvino. S Albania
Delvino *see* Delvinë
Demba *203* C Congo (Zaire)
Dembéni *649* E Mayotte
Dembéni *198* S Grande Comore, Comoros
Dembī Dolo *243 var.* Dembidollo. W Ethiopia
Demerara *284* river of N Guyana
Denau *see* Denow
Dender *127 Fr.* Dendre. River of W Belgium
Dendre *see* Dender
Den Haag *see* 's-Gravenhage
Den Helder *429* NW Netherlands
Denis, Île *512* island of the Inner Islands, NE Seychelles
Denizli *576* SW Turkey
Denmark *218-221* officially Kingdom of Denmark, *Dan.* Danmark. Country of N Europe, divided into 14 admin. units (counties). ❖ Copenhagen
Denmark Strait *294, 646 var.* Danmarksstraedet. Strait between Greenland and Iceland
Dennery *497* E St Lucia
Denow *610 Rus.* Denau. SE Uzbekistan
Denpasar *302 prev.* Paloe. Bali, C Indonesia
D'Entrecasteaux Islands *458* island group of SE Papua New Guinea
Denver *599* Colorado, SW USA
Der'a *see* Dar'ā
Deraa *see* Dar'ā
Dera Ghāzi Khān *451* C Pakistan
Dera Ismāīl Khān *451* N Pakistan*

Ejmiadzin 98 *Rus.* Echmiadzin, Ečmiadzin, Etchmiadzin. W Armenia
Ekaterinoslav *see* Dnipropetrovs'k
Ekerem *see* Okarem
Ekeren 127 N Belgium
Ekibastuz 338 NE Kazakhstan
El Alto 136 W Bolivia
El Araïche *see* Larache
El 'Arîsh 230 *var.* Al Arīsh. NE Egypt
El Asnam *see* Chlef
Elat 317 *var.* Elath, Eilat. S Israel
Elat, Gulf of *see* Aqaba, Gulf of,
Elato 406 atoll of C Micronesia
Elâzîg 577 *var.* Elâziz, Elâzîğ. E Turkey
Elba, Isola d' 320 island of C Italy
Elbasan 81 *var.* Elbasani. C Albania
Elbe 216, 265 *Cz.* Labe. River of Czech Republic and Germany
El Beqaa 364 *var.* Al Biqā', Bekaa Valley. Valley of E Lebanon
Elbing *see* Elblåg
Elbistan 577 S Turkey
Elblåg 471 *Ger.* Elbing. N Poland
El Boulaida *see* Blida
Elbow Bay 643 bay of the North Atlantic Ocean, C Bermuda
El Bur *see* Ceelbuur
Elburgon 342 W Kenya
Elburz Mountains *see* Alborz, Reshteh-ye Kuhhã-ye
El Carmen de Bolívar 195 NW Colombia
El Cayo *see* San Ignacio
El Cerro del Aripo *see* Aripo, Mount
Elche 531 *Cat.* Elx. SE Spain
El Congo 235 W El Salvador
El Copé 456 C Panama
Elda 531 SE Spain
El Dere *see* Ceeldheere
El Djazaïr *see* Algiers
El Djelfa *see* Djelfa
Eldoret 342 W Kenya
Eleja 362 C Latvia
Elemi Triangle 243, 342 disputed region of Kenya and Sudan
Éléphant, Chaîne de l' *see* Dâmrei, Chuŏr Phmun
Elephant Island 90 island of South Shetland Islands, Antarctica
Eleuthera Island 112 island of C Bahamas
El Faiyûm 230 *var.* Al Fayyūm. N Egypt
El Fasher 536 *var.* Al Fāshir. W Sudan
El Ferrol del Caudillo *see* Ferrol
El Gal *see* Ceel Gaal
El Gedaref *see* Gedaref
Elgin 593 NE Scotland, UK
El Gîza 230 *var.* Gîza, Al Jīzah. N Egypt
El Goléa 83 C Algeria
Elgon, Mount 584 mountain of E Uganda
El Hasaheisa 536 *var.* Al Ḩuşayḩişah, Al Hasahisa, Hasaheisa. C Sudan
El Haseke *see* Al Ḩasakah
Elías Piña *see* Comendador
Elimina 270 S Ghana
Élisabethville *see* Lubumbashi
El Iskandarîyah *see* Alexandria
Elizabeth 101 S Australia
El Jadida 414 *prev.* Mazagan. W Morocco
El Jafr *see* Qâ' al Jafr
El Jem 573 *var.* Al Djem, Al Jamm. NE Tunisia
El Kef *see* Le Kef
El Kelâa des Srarhna 414 C Morocco
El Khârga 230 *var.* Al Khārijah. C Egypt
El Khiyam 364 *var.* Khiam. S Lebanon
Elkhovo 152 *var.* Elhovo. SE Bulgaria
Ellás *see* Greece
Ellef Ringnes Island 170 island of Sverdrup Islands, N Canada
Ellerton 121 C Barbados
Ellesmere Island 170 island of Queen Elizabeth Islands, N Canada
Ellice Islands *see* Tuvalu
Ellsworth Land 90 physical region of Lesser Antarctica, Antarctica

El Mahalla el Kubra 230 *var.* Maḩallah al Kubrá. N Egypt
El Manşûra 230 *var.* Al Manşūrah. N Egypt
El Mediyya *see* Médéa
El Mina 364 *var.* Al Mīnā'. N Lebanon
El Minya 230 *var.* Al Minyā. C Egypt
El Mohammaïdia *see* Mohammadia
Elmshorn 264 N Germany
El Nebk *see* An Nabk
El Obeid 536 *var.* Al Ubayyiḏ, Al Obayyid. C Sudan
El Oued 83 *var.* El Ouâdi, El Wad. NE Algeria
Eloy Alfaro 228 *var.* Durán. SW Ecuador
El Palmar 136 E Bolivia
El Paraíso 288 S Honduras
el Pas de las Casa 86 E Andorra
El Paso 598 Texas, SC USA
Elpitiya 534 S Sri Lanka
El Porvenir 456 NE Panama
El Progreso 278 *var.* Guastatoya. C Guatemala
El Progreso 288 NW Honduras
El Qâhira *see* Cairo
Elqui 183 river of N Chile
El Quneitra *see* Al Qunayţirah
El Quseir *see* Al Quşur
El Quweira *see* Al Quwayrah
El Rama 436 SE Nicaragua
El Salvador 211 SE Cuba
El Salvador 234-235 officially Republic of El Salvador. Country of Central America divided into 14 admin. units (13 departments, 1 metropolitan area). ❖ San Salvador
El Seibo 226 *var.* Santa Cruz de El Seibo. E Dominican Republic
el Serrat 86 N Andorra
Elsinore *see* Helsingør
El Suweida *see* As Suwaydā'
el Tarter 86 NE Andorra
El Tigre 619 NE Venezuela
El Tigre de San Lorenzo 456 SW Panama
El Triunfo 235 SE El Salvador
Elva 240 *Ger.* Elwa. SE Estonia
Elvas 474 C Portugal
Elverum 444 S Norway
El Vigía 619 W Venezuela
El Wad *see* El Oued
El Wâhât el Khârga 230 *var.* Al Wāḩāt al Khārijah. S Egypt
Elx *see* Elche
Émaé 615 island of C Vanuatu
Emajõgi 240 *var.* Emajygi, Ema Jõgi. River of SE Estonia
Emao 615 island of C Vanuatu
Emba 338 W Kazakhstan
Emba 338 river of W Kazakhstan
Embangweni 385 *var.* Ephangweni. NW Malawi
Emborção, Represa da 145 reservoir of S Brazil
Embu 342 C Kenya
Emden 264 NW Germany
Emerald 101 E Australia
Emi Koussi 180 mountain of N Chad
Emlembe 540 mountain of South Africa and Swaziland
Emmen 429 NE Netherlands
Empada 282 SW Guinea-Bissau
Empty Quarter *see* Rub'al Khali
Ems 264, 429 *Dut.* Eems. River of Germany and Netherlands
Enareträsk *see* Inarijärvi
Encamp 86 C Andorra
Encarnación 460 S Paraguay
Enchi 270 SW Ghana
Endeavour 121 NW Barbados
Endelave 218 island of C Denmark
Enderbury Island 346 island of the Phoenix Is, C Kiribati
Enderby Land 90 physical region of Greater Antarctica, Antarctica
Enewetak 396 *var.* Eniwetok. Atoll of W Marshall Islands
Enghershatu 238 mountain of N Eritrea
England 593 national region of UK

English Channel 253, 593, 647 *var.* The Channel, *Fr.* La Manche. Channel connecting the North Sea and Atlantic Ocean between England and France
English Harbour Town 92 S Antigua, Antigua & Barbuda
Engordany 86 C Andorra
Engures Ezers 362 lake of NW Latvia
Enguri 262 *Rus.* Inguri. River of NW Georgia
Eniwetok *see* Enewetak
Enkeldoorn *see* Chivhu
Enkhuizen 429 NW Netherlands
Enna 321 Sicilia, S Italy
En Nâqaoûra 364 *var.* An Nāqūrah. SW Lebanon
Ennedi 180 plateau of E Chad
Ennis 314 *Ir.* Inis. W Ireland
Enniscorthy 314 E Ireland
Enniskillen 593 Northern Ireland, UK
Enns 106 river of C Austria
Enriquillo, Lago 226 lake of SW Dominican Republic
Enschede 429 E Netherlands
Ensenada 403 NW Mexico
Entebbe 584 S Uganda
Enugu 440 S Nigeria
Enu, Ilha de 282 island of SW Guinea-Bissau
Eolie, Isole 321 *var.* Isole Lipari, *Eng.* Lipari Islands, *var.* Aeolian Islands. Island group of S Italy
Epéna 200 NE Congo
Eperies *see* Prešov
Eperjes *see* Prešov
Ephangweni *see* Embangweni
Épi 615 island of C Vanuatu
Épinal 253 NE France
Epira 284 E Guyana
Episkopi 215 SW Cyprus
Episkopi Bay 215 bay of the Mediterranean Sea, on the SE coast of Cyprus
Epping Forest 276 S Grenada island, Grenada
Equatorial Channel 390 channel of the Indian Ocean between the atolls of Fuammulah and South Huvadhu Atoll, S Maldives
Equatorial Guinea 236-237 officially Republic of Equatorial Guinea. Country of W Africa divided into 7 admin. units (provinces). ❖ Malabo
Erbil *see* Arbīl
Erdenet 412 N Mongolia
Erdi Ma 180 desert region of NE Chad
Ereğli 577 S Turkey
Erenköy *see* Kokkina
Erenköy 215 W Cyprus
Erevan *see* Yerevan
Erfurt 265 C Germany
Erg Chech 83 desert region of SW Algeria
Erg du Djourab 180 desert region of C Chad
Erguig 180 river of SW Chad
Erhlin 555 *Jap.* Nirin. W Taiwan
Erie 599 Pennsylvania, NE USA
Erie, Lake 171, 599 *Fr.* Lac Érié. Lake of Canada and USA
Erigabo *see* Ceerigaabo
Erik Erikenstretet 653 strait of the Arctic Ocean, E Svalbard
Erikub 396 island of C Marshall Islands
Eritrea 238-239 officially State of Eritrea. Country of E Africa divided into 10 admin. units (regions). ❖ Asmara
Erivan *see* Yerevan
Erlangen 265 S Germany
Erlau *see* Eger
Ermak *see* Yermak
Ermelo 527 Eastern Transvaal, NE South Africa
Er Rachidia 414 E Morocco
Er Rahad 536 *var.* Ar Rahad. C Sudan
Er Rif *see* Rif
Erromango 615 island of S Vanuatu
Ersekë 81 *var.* Erseka, Kolonjë. SE Albania
Érsekújvár *see* Nové Zámky

Ertis *see* Irtysh
Erzenit 81 *var.* Erzen. River of C Albania
Erzgebirge 216, 265 *Cz.* Krušné Hory, *Eng.* Ore Mountains. Mountain range of Czech Republic and Germany
Erzincan 577 E Turkey
Erzurum 577 *prev.* Erzerum. NE Turkey
Esa'ala 458 Normanby I, Papua New Guinea
Esbjerg 218 Jylland, W Denmark
Esbo *see* Espoo
Escaut *see* Scheldt
Eschen 374 NW Liechtenstein
Esch-sur-Alzette 378 S Luxembourg
Escuintla 278 S Guatemala
Eséka 168 SW Cameroon
Esenguly *see* Gasan-Kuli
Esentepe 215 *var.* Ayios Amvrosios. N Cyprus
Eşfahān 307 *var.* Ispahan. W Iran
Esh Sham *see* Damascus
Esh Sharā *see* Ash Sharāh
Esigodini 636 *prev.* Essexvale. SW Zimbabwe
Esil *see* Ishim
Eski Dzhumaya *see* Turgovishte
Eskifjördhur 294 E Iceland
Eskije *see* Xánthi
Eskilstuna 543 S Sweden
Eskişehir 576 W Turkey
Esla, Embalse de 531 *var.* Embalse de Elsa. Reservoir of NW Spain
Esmeralda 210 E Cuba
Esmeraldas 228 N Ecuador
Esna *see* Isna
Esneux 127 E Belgium
España *see* Spain
Española, Isla 228 island of SE Galapagos Is, Ecuador
Esparta 288 NW Honduras
Esperance 100 W Australia
Esperanza 90 Argentinian research station of Antarctic Peninsula, Antarctica
Esperanza 226 N Dominican Republic
Espinal 195 C Colombia
Espinhaço, Serra do 145 mountain range of SE Brazil
Espiritu Santo 615 *var.* Santo. Island of C Vanuatu
Espoo 249 *Swe.* Esbo. SW Finland
Espungabera 419 SW Mozambique
Esquel 95 SW Argentina
Esquipulas 278 SE Guatemala
Êssalou 222 river of N Djibouti
Essaouira 414 *prev.* Mogador. W Morocco
Essau 261 W Gambia
Esseg *see* Osijek
Essen 264 W Germany
Essequibo 284 river of Guyana
Essequibo Islands 284 islands of N Guyana
Essexvale *see* Esigodini
Estados, Isla de los 95 *Eng.* Staten Island. Island to the E of Tierra del Fuego, Argentina
Estanyó, Pic de l' 86 mountain of N Andorra
Estcourt 527 Kwazulu Natal, E South Africa
Estelí 436 W Nicaragua
Estevan 170 S Canada
Est, Ile de l' 400 E Mauritius
Estonia 240-241 officially Republic of Estonia, *Est.* Eesti Vabariik, *prev.* Estonian SSR, *Rus.* Estonskaya SSR. Country of E Europe divided into 15 admin. units (counties). ❖ Tallinn
Estoril 474 W Portugal
Estrela 474 mountain of C Portugal
Estrela, Serra de 474 mountain range of C Portugal
Eszék *see* Osijek
Esztergom 290 *Ger.* Gran. N Hungary
Etchmiadzin *see* Ejmiadzin
Etembue 236 SW Río Muni, Equatorial Guinea

Ḥafar al Bāṭin *506* N Saudi Arabia
Hafnarfjördhur *294* W Iceland
Hafnarhreppur *294* S Iceland
Hafren *see* Severn
Hagar Nish Plateau *238* plateau of N Eritrea
Hagen *264* W Germany
Hāgere Hiywet *243* *var.* Agere Hiywet, Ambo. C Ethiopia
Hagi *330* Honshū, SW Japan
Ha Giang *623* NW Vietnam
Hago, Lac *492* lake of NE Rwanda
Hague, The *see* 's-Gravenhage
Haibak *see* Āybak
Haidarabad *see* Hyderābād
Hai Dương *623* N Vietnam
Haifa, Bay of *see* Mifraz Ḥefa
Haikou *187* *var.* Hoihow. Hainan, S China
Ḥā'il *506* N Saudi Arabia
Hailuoto *249* *Swe.* Karlö. Island of W Finland
Hainan *187* province of S China
Hainan Dao *187* island of S China
Hai Phong *623* *var.* Haiphong. N Vietnam
Haiti *286-287* officially Republic of Haiti. Country of the West Indies divided into 9 admin. units (departments). ❖ Port-au-Prince
Hajdarken *see* Khaydarkan
Hajdúböszörmény *290* NE Hungary
Ḥājī Ebrāhīm, Kūh-e *310* mountain of Iran and Iraq
Hajjah *627* W Yemen
Hakodate *330* Hokkaidō, N Japan
Hakupu *650* E Niue
Ḥalab *551* *Eng.* Aleppo, *Fr.* Alep. NW Syria
Ḥalabja *310* NE Iraq
Ḥalānīyāt, Juzur al *448* *var.* Jazā'iîBin Ghalfān, Jazā'ir Khurīyā Murīyā, *Eng.* Kuria Maria Islands. Island group of S Oman
Ḥalānīyāt, Khalīj al *448* *Eng.* Kuria Mur Bay. Bay of the Arabian Sea, S Oman
Halas *see* Kiskunhalas
Haldefjäll *see* Haltiatunturi
Halden *444* *prev.* Fredrikshald. S Norway
Halditjåkko *see* Haltiatunturi
Halfa el Gadida *536* *var.* New Halfa, Halfa Al Jadida. E Sudan
Halfmoon Bay *433* Stewart Island, SW New Zealand
Half Tree Hollow *652* N St Helena
Halifax *171* SE Canada
Halīl Rūd *307* river of SE Iran
Halla-san *350* *Jap.* Kanra-san. Mountain of Cheju-do, S South Korea
Halle *265* C Germany
Hallein *106* N Austria
Halley *90* UK research station of Greater Antarctica, Antarctica
Hall Islands *406* island group of C Micronesia
Hall Peninsula *171* peninsula of Baffin Island, NE Canada
Halls Creek *101* NW Australia
Halmahera *302* *prev.* Djailolo, Jailolo, Gilolo. Island of Maluku, E Indonesia
Halmahera, Laut *302* sea of the Pacific Ocean, E Indonesia
Halmstad *543* SW Sweden
Ḥalq al Wādī *see* La Goulette
Hälsingborg *see* Helsingborg
Haltiatunturi *249* *Swe.* Haldefjäll, *prev.* Halditjåkko, *Nor.* Reisduoddarhalde. Mountain of Finland and Norway
Ḥamad *see* Madīnat Ḥamad
Hamada *330* Honshū, W Japan
Hamadān *307* NW Iran
Hamada Town *see* Madīnat Ḥamad
Ḥamāh *551* W Syria
Hamamatsu *330* Honshū, C Japan
Hamar *444* S Norway
Hambantota *534* SE Sri Lanka
Hamburg *265* N Germany
Ḥamḍ, Wādī al *506* dry watercourse of W Saudi Arabia

Hämeenlinna *249* *Swe.* Tavastehus. SW Finland
Hamersley Range *100* mountain range to the W of Australia
Hamgyŏng-sanmaek *349* mountain range of N North Korea
Hamhŭng *349* C North Korea
Hami *186* *Uigh.* Kumul, *var.* Qomul. Xinjiang Uygur Zizhiqu. NW China
Hamilton *643* ❖ Bermuda, C Bermuda
Hamilton *171* S Canada
Hamilton *433* C North Island, New Zealand
Hamilton *593* C Scotland, UK
Ḥamīm, Wādī al *371* dry watercourse of NE Libya
Hamm *264* W Germany
Hammamet *573* *var.* Ḥammāmāt. N Tunisia
Hammamet, Golfe de *573* gulf of the Mediterranean Sea to the E of Tunisia
Hammam Lif *573* *var.* Ḥammâm al Anf. N Tunisia
Ḥammār, Hawr al *310* lake of SE Iraq
Hammerfest *444* NE Norway
Ḥamrīn, Jabal *310* mountain range of N Iraq
Hamriya *see* Al Ḥamrīyah
Ḥamrun *395* C Malta
Hāmūn, Daryācheh-ye *see* Sīstān, Daryācheh-ye
Han *350* *Jap.* Kan-kô. River of N South Korea
Hanábana *210* river of C Cuba
Hâncești *see* Hîncești
Handan *187* *var.* Han-tan. Hebei, NE China
Handeni *560* E Tanzania
Handréma, Baie de *649* *var.* Mandréma Bay. Bay of the Indian Ocean on the N coast of Mayotte
HaNegev *317* *Eng.* Negev. Desert of S Israel
Hanga Roa *183* Easter I, W Chile
Hangayn Nuruu *412* mountain range of W Mongolia
Hangzhou *187* *var.* Hangchow, Hang-chou. Zhejiang, E China
Hanka, Lake *see* Khanka, Lake
Hanko *249* *Swe.* Hangö. SW Finland
Hankow *see* Wuhan
Hannover *264* *Eng.* Hanover. NW Germany
Hanöbukten *543* bay of the Baltic Sea to the S of Sweden
Hanoi *623* *Vtn.* Ha Nôi. ❖ of Vietnam, N Vietnam
Hanover *see* Hannover
Hanstholm *218* Jylland, NW Denmark
Han-tan *see* Handan
Hantu, Pulau *517* island of SW Singapore
Hāora *297* *prev.* Howrah. E India
Haouach, Ouadi *180* dry watercourse of E Chad
Happy Valley-Goose Bay *171* *prev.* Goose Bay. E Canada
Hapsal *see* Haapsalu
Ḥaraḍ *506* *var.* Haradh. E Saudi Arabia
Ḥaraḍ *627* N Yemen
Hara Laht *240* bay of the Gulf of Finland, on the coast of N Estonia
Harare *636* *prev.* Salisbury. ❖ of Zimbabwe, NE Zimbabwe
Haraze-Mangueigne *180* SE Chad
Harbel *368* W Liberia
Harbin *187* *var.* Ha-erh-pin, *prev.* Pinkiang. Heilongjiang, NE China
Harbours, Bay of *645* bay of the South Atlantic Ocean, SE Falkland Islands
Harbour View *329* E Jamaica
Hardangerfjorden *444* fjord of SW Norway
Hardap Dam *423* dam of C Namibia
Haré Meron *317* Mountain of N Israel
Hārer *243* E Ethiopia
Hargeysa *524* NW Somalia

Ḥari *302* *var.* Batang Hari, *prev.* Djambi. River of Sumatra, W Indonesia
Ḥarīb *627* W Yemen
Hari Kurk *240* channel of Baltic Sea, between the island of Hiiumaa and Estonia mainland
Ḥārim *551* NW Syria
Ḥarīmā *336* N Jordan
Haringhat *117* river of SW Bangladesh
Harīrūd *77* river of C Asia
Harīrūd *see* Tedzhen
Harlingen *429* *Fris.* Harns. N Netherlands
Harmanli *see* Kharmanli
Harns *see* Harlingen
Harper *368* *var.* Cape Palmas. S Liberia
Ḥarrah *627* SE Yemen
Harrington Sound *643* bay of the North Atlantic Ocean, N Bermuda
Harris *649* E Montserrat
Harrisburg *599* Pennsylvania, NE USA
Harrismith *527* Orange Free State, E South Africa
Harstad *444* NE Norway
Hartford *368* SW Liberia
Hartford *599* Connecticut, NE USA
Hartley *see* Chegutu
Harz *265* *var.* Harz Mountains. Mountain range of C Germany
HaSharon *317* *Eng.* Plain of Sharon. Plain of C Israel
Haskovo *see* Khaskovo
Haspengouw *see* Hesbaye
Hasselt *127* NE Belgium
Hassetché *see* Al Ḥasakah
Hastings *121* SW Barbados
Hastings *433* SE North Island, New Zealand
Hastings *514* W Sierra Leone
Hastings *593* SE England, UK
Ḥatay *see* Antakya
Hātia *117* river and one of the main mouths of the Ganges, S Bangladesh
Hato Mayor *226* E Dominican Republic
Ḥattā *590* E United Arab Emirates
Hattiesburg *599* Mississippi, SE USA
Hattieville *130* E Belize
Hat Yai *563* *var.* Ban Hat Yai. S Thailand
Haud *243* *var.* Hawd. Plateau of Somalia and Ethiopia.
Haugesund *444* SW Norway
Haukeligrand *444* SW Norway
Haukivesi *249* lake of SE Finland
Hauraki Gulf *433* gulf on the N coast of North Island, New Zealand
Hau *623* river of SW Vietnam
Haut Atlas *414* *Eng.* High Atlas. Mountain range of C Morocco
Haute-Sangha *see* Mambéré-Kadéi
Hautes Fagnes *127* *Ger.* Hohes Venn. Mountain range of Belgium
Haute Sûre, Lac de la *378* reservoir of NW Luxembourg
Haut Plateau du Dra *see* Dra, Hamada du
Hauts Plateaux *83* plateau of NW Algeria
Havana *210* *var.* La Habana. ❖ of Cuba, NW Cuba
Havířov *216* E Czech Republic
Havlíčkův Brod *216* *prev.* Německý Brod, *Ger.* Deutsch-Brod. S CzecRepublic
Hawaii *598* island of Hawaiian group, Hawaii, USA, C Pacific
Hawaii *598* non-contiguous state of USA, C Pacific
Ḥawallī *354* E Kuwait
Hawash *see* Awash
Hawea, Lake *433* W South Island, New Zealand
Hawera *433* SW North Island, New Zealand
Hawick *593* S Scotland, UK
Hawke Bay *433* bay of the South Pacific Ocean, on the SE coast of North Island, New Zealand
Hawlēr *see* Arbīl
Ḥawmat as Sūq *see* Houmt Souk
Ḥawrā' *627* C Yemen

Ḥawrān, Wādī *310* dry watercourse of W Iraq
Hawwārah *336* *var.* Huwwāra. N Jordan
Hay River *170* W Canada
Ḥayyān, Ra's *115* *var.* Ra's Ḥayyān. Cape of E Bahrain
Hebei *187* *var.* Hopei. Province of NE China
Hebrides, Sea of the *593* sea of the Atlantic Ocean to the NW of UK
Hebron *317, 318* *Ar.* Al Khalil. S West Bank
Heerenveen *429* NE Netherlands
Heerlen *429* S Netherlands
Ḥefa *317* N Israel
Ḥefa, Mifraz *317* *Eng.* Bay of Haifa. Bay of the Mediterranean Sea
Hefei *187* *var.* Hofei, *hist.* Luchow. Anhui, E China
Heichin *see* P'ingchen
Heidelberg *264* SW Germany
Heihe *187* *prev.* Ai-hun. Heilongjiang, NE China
Hei-ho *see* Nagqu
Heilbronn *264* SW Germany
Heiligenkreuz *see* Žiar nad Hronom
Heilong Jiang *see* Amur
Heilongjiang *187* *var.* Heilungkiang, Hei-lung-chiang. Province of NE China
Heimaey Island *294* *var.* Heimaey, Heimaëy. Island of S Iceland
Heitō *see* P'ingtung
Helen *455* island of S Palau
Helena *598* Montana, NW USA
Helgoland *264* *Eng.* Heligoland. Island of NW Germany
Helgoländer Bucht *264* *var.* Helgoland Bay, Heligoland Bight. Bay of the North Sea
Hell-Ville *see* Andoany
Helmand, Daryā-ye *77* river of Afghanistan and Iran
Helmond *429* S Netherlands
Helsingborg *543* *prev.* Hälsingborg. S Sweden
Helsingør *218* *Eng.* Elsinore. Sjælland, E Denmark
Helsinki *249* *Swe.* Helsingfors. ❖ of Finland, S Finland
Helwân *230* *var.* Ḥulwân, Ḥilwân. N Egypt
Henan *187* *var.* Honan. Province of C China
Henderson Island *651* island of N Pitcairn Islands
Hendū Kosh *see* Hindu Kush
Hengduan Shan *186* mountain range of SW China
Hengelo *429* E Netherlands
Hengyang *187* Hunan, S China
Hentiesbaai *423* W Namibia
Henzada *159* SW Burma
Heradhsvötn *294* river of C Iceland
Herāt *77* W Afghanistan
Heredia *206* C Costa Rica
Hereford *593* C England, UK
Herisau *546* *Fr.* Hérisau. NE Switzerland
Héristal *see* Herstal
Herm *647* island of S Guernsey
Hermannstadt *see* Sibiu
Hermansverk *444* SW Norway
Hermel *364* *var.* Hirmil. NE Lebanon
Hermitage *276* C Grenada island, Grenada
Hermon, Mount *551* *Ar.* Jabal ash Shaykh. Mountain of SW Syria
Hermosillo *403* NW Mexico
Hernád *see* Hornád
Hernandarias *460* *prev.* Tacurupucú. SE Paraguay
Herne *264* W Germany
Herning *218* Jylland, W Denmark
Herstal *127* *Fr.* Héristal. E Belgium
Herzliyya *317* C Israel
Herzogenbusch *see* 's-Hertogenbosch
Hesbaye *127* *Dut.* Haspengouw. Physical region of C Belgium
Hesperange *378* SE Luxembourg
Hestur *644* island of C Faeroe Islands
Hetauda *427* C Nepal

Hida-sammyaku *330* mountain range of Honshū, C Japan
Hienghène *650* W New Caledonia
Hierro *531* *var.* Ferro. Island of Islas Canarias, SW Spain
High Atlas *see* Haut Atlas
Highgate *329* NE Jamaica
Highlands, The *92* highlands of Barbuda, Antigua & Barbuda
High Point *643* headland of W Bermuda
High Veld *see* Northern Karoo
Higüey *226* *var.* Salvaleon de Higüey. E Dominican Republic
Hiiumaa *240* *var.* Hiiuma, *Ger.* Dagden, *Swed.* Dagö. Island of W Estonia
Hikina *648* island, NE Johnston Atoll
Hildesheim *264* NW Germany
Hilla *see* Al Ḥillah
Hillaby, Mount *121* mountain of Barbados
Hillerød *218* Sjælland, E Denmark
Hillsborough *276* W Carriacou, Grenada
Hilo *598* Hawaii, USA
Hilversum *429* C Netherlands
Ḥilwan *see* Ḥelwân
Himachal Pradesh *296* state of N India
Himalayas *134, 186, 296, 427* mountain range of S Asia
Himeji *330* Honshū, C Japan
Himora *243* *var.* Humera. NW Ethiopia
Ḥimş *551* *var.* Homs. W Syria
Hîncești *408* *var.* Hânceşti, *prev.* Kotovsk. C Moldova
Hinche *286* C Haiti
Hindenburg *see* Zabrze
Hindiya *see* Al Hindīyah
Hindu Kush *77, 451* *Per.* Hendū Kosh. Mountain range of C Asia
Hingol *450* river of SW Pakistan
Hinson Island *643* island of W Bermuda
Hirmil *see* Hermel
Hirosaki *330* Honshū, N Japan
Hiroshima *330* Honshū, W Japan
Hirschberg in Riesengebirge *see* Jelenia Góra
Hirtshals *218* Jylland, N Denmark
Ḥisbān *336* NW Jordan
Ḥisb, Sha'īb *310* *var.* Sha'ib Hasb. Dry watercourse of S Iraq
Hisor *558* *Rus.* Gissar. W Tajikistan
Hitachi *330* Honshū, SE Japan
Hitra *444* *prev.* Hitteren. Island of W Norway
Hitteren *see* Hitra
Hiu *615* Torres Islands, N Vanuatu
Hjälmaren *543* *Eng.* Lake Hjalmar. Lake of S Sweden
Hjalmar, Lake *see* Hjälmaren
Hjørring *218* Jylland, N Denmark
Hkakabo Razi *159* mountain of Burma and China
Hlatikulu *540* *var.* Hlatikulu. S Swaziland
Hlohovec *519* *prev.* Frakštát, *Ger.* Freistadtl, *Hung.* Galgóc. W Slovakia
Hlotse *366* *var.* Leribe. NW Lesotho
Hlybokaye *122* *Rus.* Glubokoye. N Belarus
Ho *270* SE Ghana
Hoa Binh *623* N Vietnam
Hoang Liên Sơn *623* mountain range of China and Vietnam
Hoani *198* NW Mohéli, Comoros
Hobart *101* Tasmania, Australia
Hobro *218* Jylland, N Denmark
Hobyo *524* *It.* Obbia. E Somalia
Hô Chi Minh *623* *var.* Ho Chi Minh City, *prev.* Saigon. S Vietnam
Hodeida *see* Al Ḥudaydah
Hódmezővásárhely *290* SE Hungary
Hodonín *216* *Ger.* Göding. SE Czech Republic
Hoë Karoo *see* Northern Karoo
Hoeryŏng *349* NE North Korea
Höfdhakaupstadhur *see* Skagaströnd

Hofei *see* Hefei
Hofsá *294* river of E Iceland
Hofsjökull *294* glacier of C Iceland
Hofuf *see* Al Hufuf
Hõgen *see* Fengyüan
Hoggar *see* Ahaggar
Hogoley Islands *see* Chuuk Islands
Hohenems *106* W Austria
Hohes Venn *see* Hautes Fagnes
Hohe Tauern *106* mountain range of W Austria
Hohhot *187* *var.* Huhehot, *prev.* Kweisui. Nei Mongol Zizhiqu, N China
Hôi An *623* *prev.* Faifo. C Vietnam
Hoihow *see* Haikou
Hoima *584* W Uganda
Hojancha *206* W Costa Rica
Hokitika *433* W South Island, New Zealand
Hokkaidō *331, 335* island of N Japan
Hokkō *see* Peikang
Hokō *see* P'ohang
Hoktemberyan *98* *Rus.* Oktemberyan. SW Armenia
Holbæk *218* Sjælland, E Denmark
Holetown *121* *prev.* Jamestown. W Barbados
Holguín *210* SE Cuba
Holhol *222* SE Djibouti
Holland *see* Netherlands
Hollandia *see* Jayapura
Hólmavík *294* NW Iceland
Holmsland Klit *218* fjord of Jylland, W Denmark
Holon *317* C Israel
Holonga *568* Uta Vava'u, Tonga
Holot Ḥaluza *317* historic site of S Israel
Holstebro *218* Jylland, W Denmark
Holsteinsborg *see* Sisimiut
Holyhead *593* N Wales, UK
Homa Bay *342* W Kenya
Homāyūnshahr *see* Khomeynīshahr
Hombori Tondo *392* mountain of E Mali
Home Island *644* island of C Cocos Islands
Homenau *see* Humenné
Homonna *see* Humenné
Homs *see* Ḥimş
Homs *see* Al Khums
Homyel' *122* *Rus.* Gomel'. SE Belarus
Honan *see* Henan
Hondo *130, 403* river of Central America
Honduras *288-289* officially Republic of Honduras. Country of C America divided into 18 admin. units (departments).
❖ Tegucigalpa
Honduras, Gulf of *130, 278* gulf of the Caribbean Sea to the E of Central America
Hønefoss *444* S Norway
Hông Gai *623* *var.* Hongay. N Vietnam
Hong Kong *163* S China
Hongwŏn *349* E North Korea
Hongze Hu *187* *var.* Hung-tse Hu. Lake of E China
Honiara *522* ❖ of the Solomon Islands, N Guadalcanal, Solomon Islands
Honolulu *598* Oahu, Hawaii, USA
Honshū *330* island of C Japan
Honte *see* Westerschelde
Hoogeveen *429* NE Netherlands
Hoogezand *429* NE Netherlands
Hooker, Cape *527* cape of Marion Island, S South Africa
Hoorn *429* NW Netherlands
Hopei *see* Hebei
Hope Town *112* Great Abaco, Bahamas
Horgen *546* N Switzerland
Hōrin *see* Fenglin
Horki *122* *Rus.* Gorki. NE Belarus
Horlivka *586* *Rus.* Gorlovka. E Ukraine
Hormuz, Strait of *307, 448, 590* *var.* Strait of Ormuz, *Per.* Tangeh-ye Hormoz. Strait connecting the Persian Gulf and Arabian Sea

Hornád *519* *Ger.* Hernad, *Hung.* Hernád. River of Hungary and Slovakia
Horn, Cape *183* cape of S Chile
Horog *see* Khorog
Horoshiri-dake *331* mountain of Hokkaidō, N Japan
Horowupotana *534* NE Sri Lanka
Horqueta *460* C Paraguay
Horsburgh Atoll *390* atoll of N Maldives
Horsburgh Island *644* *var.* Pulu Luar. Island of C Cocos Islands
Horsens *218* Jylland, C Denmark
Horseshoe Bay *643* bay of the North Atlantic Ocean, W Bermuda
Horsham *101* SE Australia
Hørsholm *218* Sjælland, E Denmark
Hortabágny-Berettyó *290* river of E Hungary
Horten *444* S Norway
Horug *see* Khorugh
Hosa'ina *243* *var.* Hosseina, *It.* Hosanna. SW Ethiopia
Hose, Penunungan *386* *var.* Hose Mountains. Mountain range of Borneo, E Malaysia
Hotan *186* *var.* Khotan, *Chin.* Ho-t'ien. Xinjiang Uygur Zizhiqu. NW China
Hot Springs *599* Arkansas, SC USA
Hotte, Massif de la *286* highlands of SW Haiti
Houaïlou *650* C New Caledonia
Houmt Souk *573* *var.* Djerba, Ḥawmat as Sūd, Jerba. Île de Jerba, Tunisia
Houndé *157* SW Burkina
Houston *599* Texas, SC USA
Hovd *412* W Mongolia
Hoverla *586* *Rus.* Gora Goverla. Mountain of W Ukraine
Hövsgöl Nuur *412* lake of N Mongolia
Howe, Cape *101* cape on the SE coast of Australia
Howakil Bay *238* bay of the Red Sea to the E of Eritrea
Howrah *see* Hāora
Hōzan *see* Fengshan
Hradec Králové *216* *Ger.* Königgrätz. E Czech Republic
Hrazdan *98* *Rus.* Razdan. C Armenia
Hrazdan *98* *Rus.* Razdan, Zanga. River of C Armenia
Hrodna *122* *Rus.* Grodno. W Belarus
Hron *519* *Ger.* Gran, *Hung.* Garam. River of C Slovakia
Hsüeh Shan *555* mountain of N Taiwan
Hsi-an *see* Xi'an
Hsiang-t'an *see* Xiangtan
Hsi Chiang *see* Xi Jiang
Hsinchu *555* NW Taiwan
Hsinchuang *555* *var.* Sinchwang, *Jap.* Shinshō. N Taiwan
Hsing-K'ai Hu *see* Khanka, Lake
Hsi-ning *see* Xining
Hsinking *see* Changchun
Hsintien *555* *var.* Sintien, *Jap.* Shinten. N Taiwan
Hsin-yang *see* Xinyang
Hsinying *555* *var.* Sinying, *Jap.* Shinei. W Taiwan
Hsu-chou *see* Xuzhou
Hsüehshan Shanmo *555* mountain range of N Taiwan
Huacho *463* W Peru
Huainan *187* *var.* Hwainan. Anhui, E China
Hualien *555* *var.* Hwalien, *Jap.* Karen. E Taiwan
Huallaga *463* river of N Peru
Huambo *88* *Port.* Nova Lisboa. C Angola
Huancavelica *463* SW Peru
Huancayo *463* C Peru
Huang Hai *see* Yellow Sea
Huang He *187* *Eng.* Yellow River. River of C China
Huánuco *463* C Peru
Huanuni *136* W Bolivia
Huaral *463* W Peru
Huascarán, Nevado *463* mountain of W Peru
Huaraz *463* *var.* Huaráz. W Peru

Hubei *187* *var.* Hupei. Province of C China
Hubli *296* SW India
Huddersfield *593* N England, UK
Hudson *599* river of NE USA
Hudson Bay *171* bay of the Atlantic Ocean, NE Canada
Hudson Strait *171* strait connecting the Atlantic Ocean and Hudson Bay
Huê *623* C Vietnam
Huehuetenango *278* W Guatemala
Huelva *530* SW Spain
Huesca *531* NE Spain
Hughenden *101* NE Australia
Huhehot *see* Hohhot
Huizen *429* C Netherlands
Huksan-kundo *350* *var.* Huksan-chedo. Island group of SW South Korea
Hull *see* Kingston-upon-Hull
Hull *171* SE Canada
Hullo *240* Vormsi, Estonia
Hulun Nur *187* *Chin.* Hu-lun Ch'ih, *prev.* Dalai Nor. Lake of Nei Mongol Zizhiqu, NE China
Ḥulwan *see* Ḥelwân
Humacao *651* E Puerto Rico
Humaitá *460* S Paraguay
Humber *593* river of NE England, UK
Humenné *519* *Ger.* Homenau, *Hung.* Homonna. E Slovakia
Humera *see* Himora
Húnaflói *294* bay of the Norwegian Sea on the N coast of Iceland
Hunan *187* province of S China
Hundested *218* Sjælland, E Denmark
Hunga Ha'apai *568* island of the Nomuka Group, W Tonga
Hungary *290-293* officially Republic of Hungary, *Hung.* Magyarország, *prev.* Hungarian People's Republic. Country of C Europe divided into 19 admin. units (counties).
❖ Budapest
Hunga Tonga *568* island of the Nomuka Group, W Tonga
Hüngnam *349* E North Korea
Hung-tse Hu *see* Hongze Hu
Huntington *599* West Virginia, E USA
Huntsville *599* Alabama, SE USA
Hunyani *see* Manyame
Huon Gulf *458* gulf of the Solomon Sea, to the E of Papua New Guinea
Huo-shao Tao *see* Lan Yü
Hupei *see* Hubei
Hurghada *230* E Egypt
Huron, Lake *171, 599* lake of Canada and USA
Hurunui *433* river of NE South Island, New Zealand
Húsavík *644* Sandoy, C Faeroe Islands
Húsavík *294* NE Iceland
Ḥusayn, Dawḥat al *479* *var.* Dauhat al Husein. Inlet of the Gulf of Bahrain on the NW coast of Qatar
Hūth *627* NW Yemen
Huwār *479* island of SE Bahrain
Huwwāra *see* Hawwārah
Hvammstangi *294* N Iceland
Hvannadalshnúkur *294* mountain of S Iceland
Hvar *294* *It.* Lesina. Island of S Croatia
Hvítá *294* river of W Iceland
Hvolsvöllur *294* SW Iceland
Hwach'ŏn-chŏsuji *see* P'aro-ho
Hwainan *see* Huainan
Hwange *636* *prev.* Wankie. W Zimbabwe
Hwang-Hae *see* Yellow Sea
Hyargas Nuur *412* lake of W Mongolia
Hyderābād *296* *Hind.* Haydarābād. C India
Hyderābād *451* *var.* Haidarabad. S Pakistan
Hyères *253* SE France
Hyères, Îles d' *253* island group of SE France
Hyesan *349* NE North Korea

Hyvinge *see* Hyvinkää
Hyvinkää *249 Swe.* Hyvinge. S Finland

I

Ialomiţa *480* river of SE Romania
Ialpug *408 Rus.* Yalpug. River of S Moldova
Iaşi *480 Ger.* Jassy. NE Romania
Ibadan *440* SW Nigeria
Ibagué *195* C Colombia
Ibar *630* river of SW Serbia, Yugoslavia
Ibarra *228 var.* San Miguel de Ibarra. N Ecuador
Ibb *627* W Yemen
Ibbenbüren *264* NW Germany
Ibenga *200* river of N Congo
Ibérico, Sistema *531 var.* Cordillera Ibérica, *Eng.* Iberian Mountains. Mountains of NE Spain
Ibiza *see* Eivissa
Ibo *see* Sassandra
Iboundji *258* C Gabon
Ibrā *448* N Oman
Ibri *448* NW Oman
Irbil *see* Arbil
Ibusuki *330* Kyūshū, SW Japan
Içá *144* river of NW Brazil
Ica *463* SW Peru
Iceflavik *see* Keflavík
İçel *see* Mersin
Iceland *294-295* officially Republic of Iceland, *Icel.* Ísland. Country of the North Atlantic Ocean divided into 8 admin. units (regions). ❖ Reykjavík
Ichinomiya *330* Honshū, C Japan
Ichinoseki *330* Honshū, N Japan
Idah *440* S Nigeria
Idaho *598* state of NW USA
Idaho Falls *598* Idaho, NW USA
Idensalmi *see* Iisalmi
Idfu *230 var.* Idfū, Edfu. SE Egypt
Idi Amin, Lac *see* Edward, Lake
Idlib *551* NW Syria
Idrija *520 It.* Idria. W Slovenia
Idzhevan *see* Ijevan
Iecava *362* C Latvia
Ieper *127 Fr.* Ypres. W Belgium
Ifalik *406* atoll of C Micronesia
Ife *440* SW Nigeria
Iferouâne *439* N Niger
Iferten *see* Yverdon
Iganga *584* SE Uganda
Igarka *485* N Russia
Igatimí *see* Ygatimí
Iglau *see* Jihlava
Iglesias *320* Sardegna, W Italy
Igló *see* Spišská Nová Ves
Ignalina *376* E Lithuania
Iguaçu, Salto do *145 Sp.* Cataratas del Iguazú, *prev.* Victoria Falls. Waterfall of Argentina and Brazil
Iguetti, Sebkhet *398* salt lake of N Mauritania
Ihavandippolhu Atoll *390 var.* Ihavandiffulu Atoll. Atoll of N Maldives
Ihema, Lac *492* lake of Burundi and Rwanda
Ihosy *382* S Madagascar
Iida *330* Honshū, C Japan
Iijoki *249* river of C Finland
Irbil *see* Arbil
Iisalmi *249 Swe.* Idensalmi. C Finland
Ijebu-Ode *440* SW Nigeria
Ijevan *98 Rus.* Idzhevan, *var.* Idžhevan. N Armenia
IJssel *429 var.* Yssel. River of C Netherlands
IJsselmeer *429 prev.* Zuider Zee. Lake of N Netherlands
Ikare *440* SW Nigeria
Ikaría *273* island of SE Greece
Ikast *218* Jylland, W Denmark
Ikeja *440* SW Nigeria
Ikerre *440 var.* Ikerre-Ekiti. SW Nigeria
Iki *330* island to the NW of Kyūshū, SW Japan

Ikom *440* S Nigeria
Ikopa *382* river of N Madagascar
Ila *440* W Nigeria
Ilam *427* W Nepal
Ilan *555 Jap.* Giran. NE Taiwan
Ile *see* Ili
Ilebo *203 prev.* Port Francqui. W Congo (Zaire)
Ilesha *440* SW Nigeria
Ilha Solteira, Represa de *145* reservoir of S Brazil
Ili *338 Kaz.* Ile. River of China and Kazakhstan
Iligan *466* Mindanao, S Philippines
Ilirska Bistrica *520* SW Slovenia
Il'jaly *see* Yylanly
Illapel *183* C Chile
Illiassa *261* NW Gambia
Illinois *599* state of C USA
Ilobasco *235* C El Salvador
Ilobu *440* W Nigeria
Iloilo *466* Panay, C Philippines
Ilopango, Lago de *235* volcanic lake of C El Salvador
Ilorin *440* W Nigeria
Iluh *see* Batman
Ilulissat *646 Dan.* Jakobshavn. W Greenland
Il'yaly *see* Yylanly
Imatong Mountains *536* mountains of S Sudan
Imatra *249* SE Finland
Imeni 26 Bakinskikh Komissarov *see* Bakı Komissarı
Imilili *414* W Western Sahara
İmişli *110 Rus.* Imishli, Imišli. C Azerbaijan
Imja-do *350* island of SW South Korea
Imola *321* N Italy
Imperatriz *145* NE Brazil
Imperia *320* N Italy
Impfondo *200* NE Congo
Imphāl *297* E India
Ina *330* Honshū, C Japan
Inakona *522* S Guadalcanal, Solomon Is
In Aménas *83 var.* I-n-Amenas, In Amnas. E Algeria
Inárajan *647* SE Guam
Inarijärvi *249 Swe.* Enareträsk, *Lapp.* Aanaarjävri. Lake of N Finland
Inarijoki *249 Nor.* Anarjokka. River of Finland and Norway
Inawashiro-ko *330* lake of Honshū, N Japan
Inbhear Mór *see* Arklow
Inch'ŏn *350 prev.* Chemulpo, *Jap.* Jinsen. NW South Korea
Inchope *419* C Mozambique
Incles *86* river of NE Andorra
Independence *130* SE Belize
Inderagiri *see* Indragiri
India *296-301* officially Republic of India, *Hind.* Bharat. Country divided into 32 admin. units (25 states and 7 union territories). ❖ New Delhi
Indiana *599* state of C USA
Indianapolis *599* Indiana, C USA
Indian Desert *see* Thar Desert
Indian Ocean *90, 644* ocean bounded to the W by Africa, to the E by Australia and to the S by Antarctica
Indigirka *485* River of NE Russia
Indonesia *302-305* officially Republic of Indonesia, *Ind.* Republik Indonesia, *prev.* United States of Indonesia, Dutch East Indies, Netherlands East Indies. Country of SE Asia divided into 25 admin. units (24 provinces and 1 autonous district). ❖ Jakarta
Indonesian Borneo *see* Kalimantan
Indore *296* NW India
Indragiri *302 var.* Inderagiri. River of Sumatra, W Indonesia
Indre *253* river of C France
Indus *296, 451* river of S Asia
Indus, Mouths of the *451* river delta of S Pakistan
Infante Dom Henrique *505* SE Príncipe, Sao Tome & Principe
Ingolstadt *265* S Germany
Inguri *see* Enguri
Ingushetiya, Respublika *484* autonomous republic of SW Russia
Ingwavuma *see* Nggwavuma

Inhambane *419* S Mozambique
I-ning *see* Yining
Inírida *195* river of E Colombia
Inis *see* Ennis
Inland Sea *330 var.* Seto Naikai. Sea of the Pacific Ocean between Honshū and Shikoku, W Japan
Inn *106, 265* river of C Europe
Inner Channel *130 var.* Main Channel. Inlet of W Caribbean Sea
Inner Hebrides *593* island group of NW Scotland, UK
Inner Islands *512 var.* Central Group. Island group of NE Seychelles
Inner Mongolian Autonomous Region *see* Nei Mongol Zizhiqu
Innsbruck *106* W Austria
Inrin *see* Yüanlin
In Salah *83 var.* I-n-Salah. C Algeria
Insein *159* S Burma
Intelewa *538* S Suriname
Interlaken *546* SW Switzerland
Inthanon, Doi *563* mountain of NW Thailand
Intipucá *235* SE El Salvador
Inuvik *170* NW Canada
Invercargill *433* SW South Island, New Zealand
Inverness *593* N Scotland, UK
Inyanga *see* Nyanga
Inyangani *636* mountain of E Zimbabwe
Inyazura *see* Nyazura
Ioánnina *273 var.* Janina, Yannina. W Greece
Iolotan' *see* Yëloten
Ionian Islands *see* Iónioi Nísoi
Ionian Sea *81, 273, 321 Gk* Iónio Pélagos, *It.* Mar Ionio. Area of the Mediterranean Sea, between Italy and SE Europe
Ionio, Mar *see* Ionian Sea
Iónioi Nísoi *273 Eng.* Ionian Islands. Island group of W Greece
Iori *262* river of Azerbaijan and Georgia
Íos *273* island of SE Greece
Iowa *599* state of C USA
Ipel *see* Ipoly
Ipiales *195* SW Colombia
Ipoh *386* W Peninsular Malaysia
Ipoly *290, 519 Slvk. Ger.* Eipel. River of Hungary and Slovakia
Ippy *179* C Central African Republic
Ipswich *101* E Australia
Ipswich *593* E England, UK
Iqaluit *171 prev.* Frobisher Bay. Baffin Island, NE Canada
Iquique *183* N Chile
Iquitos *463* N Peru
Irákleio *273 Eng.* Candia, *prev.* Iráklion. Crete, S Greece
Iran *306-309* officially Islamic Republic of Iran, *prev.* Persia. Country of SW Asia divided into 24 admin. units (provinces). ❖ Tehrān
Iran, Pegunungan *387 var.* Iran Mountains. Mountain range of Borneo, Indonesia and Malaysia
Iran, Plateau of *307* plateau of C Iran
Irapuato *403* C Mexico
Iraq *310-313* officially Republic of Iraq, *Ar.* 'Irāq. Country of SW Asia divided into 18 admin. units (governorates). ❖ Baghdad
Irbe Strait *240 Est.* Kura Kurk, *prev.* Irbe Väin, *Latv.* Irbes Šaurums. Strait connecting the Baltic Sea and Gulf of Riga
Irbid *336* N Jordan
Ireland Island North *643* island of W Bermuda
Ireland Island South *643* island of W Bermuda
Ireland, Northern *see* Northern Ireland
Ireland, Republic of *314-315* officially Republic of Ireland, Éire. Country of W Europe divided into 26 admin. units (counties). ❖ Dublin
Ireng *284 var.* Maú. River of Brazil and Guyana
Irgalem *see* Yirga 'Alem

Iri *350 Jap.* Riri. W South Korea
Irian *see* New Guinea
Irian Jaya *302-303 Eng.* West Irian, *prev.* Dutch New Guinea. Province of W Indonesia
Iringa *560* C Tanzania
Iriomote-jima *330* island of Sakishima-shotō, SW Japan
Iriri *145* river of N Brazil
Irish Sea *314, 593, 647 Ir.* Muir Eireann. Sea of the Atlantic Ocean between Ireland and UK
Irkeshtam *357 var.* Irkeštam. SW Kyrgyzstan
Irkutsk *485* C Russia
Irmak *577* river of N Turkey
Iroise *252* area of the Atlantic Ocean to the NW of France
'Irqah *627* SW Yemen
Irrawaddy *159 var.* Ayeyarwady. River of C Burma
Irrawaddy, Mouths of the *159* delta area of SW Burma
Irrsee *106* lake of N Austria
Irtysh *338, 484 Kaz.* Ertis. River of Kazakhstan and Russia
Irun *531* N Spain
Iruñea *see* Pamplona
Isabela *651* NW Puerto Rico
Isabela, Isla *228* island of SW Galapagos Is, Ecuador
Isachsen *170* Ellef Ringnes Island, N Canada
Ísafdhardjúp *294* inlet of the Atlantic Ocean, NW Iceland
Isangel *615* Tanna, Vanuatu
Isa Town *see* Madīnat 'Īsá
Isalo, Tangorombohitr' *382* mountains of SW Madagascar
Ischia, Isola d' *321* island of S Italy
Ise *330* Honshū, C Japan
Isefjord *218* fjord of Sjælland, E Denmark
Isére *253* river of SE France
Iseyin *440* W Nigeria
Isfara *558* S Tajikistan
Ísfjördhur *294* NW Iceland
Isha Baydhabo *see* Baydhabo
Isherton *284* S Guyana
Ishigaki-jima *330* island of Sakishima-shotō, SW Japan
Ishikari *331* river of Hokkaidō, N Japan
Ishim *338 Kaz.* Esil. River of Kazakhstan and Russia
Ishinomaki *330* Honshū, N Japan
Ishkoshim *558 Rus.* Ishkashim. S Tajikistan
Ishurdi *117* W Bangladesh
Isidoro Noblia *607* NE Uruguay
Isiolo *342* C Kenya
Isiro *203* NE Congo (Zaire)
Iskeçe *see* Xánthi
İskele *215 var.* Trikomo. E Cyprus
İskenderun *577 Eng.* Alexandretta. S Turkey
İskenderun Körfezi *577 Eng.* Gulf of Alexandretta. Gulf of the Mediterranean Sea
Iskŭr *152* river of NW Bulgaria
Iskŭr, Yazovir *152* reservoir of W Bulgaria
Islāmābād *451* ❖ of Pakistan, NE Pakistan
Island Harbour *642* bay of the Caribbean Sea on the N coast of Anguilla
Islay *593* island of Inner Hebrides, W Scotland, UK
Isle *253* river of SW France
Ismâ'îlîya *230 var.* Al Ismā'īlīyah, *Eng.* Ismaila. N Egypt
Isna *230 var.* Isnā, Esna. SE Egypt
Isoka *635* NE Zambia
Isonzo *see* Soča.
Ispahan *see* Eşfahān
Isparta *577* SW Turkey
Israel *316-319* officially State of Israel, *Heb.* Yisra'el. Country of SW Asia divided into 6 admin. units (districts). ❖ Jerusalem
Issano *284* C Guyana

Issia *326* SW Ivory Coast
Issyk-Kul' *see* Balykchy
Issyk-Kul', Ozero *357 var.* Issiq Köl.
Lake of NE Kyrgyzstan
İstanbul *577 prev.* Constantinople,
Bul. Tsarigrad. NW Turkey
İstanbul Boğazı *577* Karadeniz
Boğazı, *Eng.* Bosporus. Strait
connecting rmara Denizi and
Black Sea
Istra *209 Eng.* Istria. Peninsula of
SE Europe
Istria *see* Istra
Itabuna *145* E Brazil
Itagüí *195* NW Colombia
Itaipú, Represa de *145, 460* reservoir
of Brazil and Paraguay
Italy *320-325* officially Italian
Republic, *It.* Italia, Repubblica
Italiana. Country of S Europe divided
into 20 admin. units (regions).
❖ Rome
Itany *see* Litani
Itassi *see* Vieille Case
Iténez *see* Guaporé
Itonamas *136* river of NE Bolivia
Itremo *382 var.* Massif de l'Itremo.
Mountain range of C Madagascar
Itsamia *198* S Mohéli, Comoros
Itsandra *198* W Grande Comore,
Comoros
Ittoqqortoormiit *646 Dan.*
Scoresbysund. E Greenland
Itu Aba Island *652* island of
W Spratly Islands
Ituni *284* C Guyana
Iturup *331* disputed island of Kurile
Islands, SE Russia
Ivakoany *382 var.* Massif de
l'Ivakoany. Mountain range of
SE Madagascar
Ivalojoki *249* river of N Finland
Ivano-Frankivs'k *586*
Rus. Ivano-Frankovsk,
prev. Stanislav, *Pol.* Stanisławów,
Ger. Stanislau. W Ukraine
Ivanovo *484* W Russia
Ivatsevichy *122* SW Belarus
Ivindo *258* river of C Africa
Iviza *see* Eivissa
Ivoire, Côte d' *see* Ivory Coast
Ivory Coast *326* Fr. Côte d'Ivoire.
Coastal region of S Ivory Coast
Ivory Coast *326-327* officially Republic
of the Ivory Coast, *Fr.* Côte d'Ivoire.
Country of W Africa divided into
54 admin. units (departments).
❖ Yamoussoukro
Ivujivik *171* NE Canada
Iwakuni *330* Honshū, W Japan
Iwaki *330* Honshū, N Japan
Iwŏn *349* E North Korea
Iwo *440* SW Nigeria
Ixcán *278* river of Guatemala
and Mexico
Izabal, Lago de *278 prev.* Golfo Dulce.
Lake of E Guatemala
Izhevsk *484 prev.* Ustinov. W Russia
Izki *448* N Oman
İzmir *577 prev.* Smyrna.
W Turkey
İzmit *577 var.* Kocaeli.
NW Turkey
Izuhara *330* Tsushima,
W Japan
Izumo *330* Honshū, W Japan
Izu-shotō *330* island group to the
SE of Honshū, SE Japan

J

Jabal aẓ Ẓannah *590 var.* Jebel
Dhanna, W United Arab Emirates
Jabāliya *317, 318* NE Gaza Strip
Jabalpur *296 prev.* Jubbulpore.
C India
Jabat *396 var.* Jabwot Island. island
of S Marshall Islands
Jabbul, Sabkhat al *551* salt-flat of
NW Syria
Jablah *551 var.* Jeble, *Fr.* Djéblé.
W Syria

Jablanica *81* mountain range of
E Albania
Jablonec nad Nisou *216*
Ger. Gablonz an der Neisse. N Czech
Republic
Jaboatão *145* E Brazil
Jabwot Island *see* Jabat
Jaceel *524 It.* Uadi Giahel. Seasonal
river of NE Somalia
Jackson *599* Mississippi, SE USA
Jacksonville *599* Florida, SE USA
Jacmel *286 var.* Jaquemel. S Haiti
Jacó *206* SW Costa Rica
Jacob *see* Nkayi
Jacobābād *451* SW Pakistan
Jadotville *see* Likasi
Jadransko More *see* Adriatic Sea
Jādū *371* NW Libya
Jaén *531* SW Spain
Jaffna *534* N Sri Lanka
Jaffna Lagoon *534* lagoon of
N Sri Lanka
Jafr, Qā' al *336 var.* El Jafr. Salt pan
of S Jordan
Jägala *240 var.* Jägala Jõgi. River of
N Estonia
Jägerndorf *see* Krnov
Jagodina *see* Svetozarevo
Jaguarão *see* Yaguarón
Jailolo *see* Halmahera
Jaipur *296 prev.* Jeypore. N India
Jaipur Hāt *117* NW Bangladesh
Jajce *140* W Bosnia & Herzegovina
Jakar *134* C Bhutan
Jakarta *302 prev.* Djakarta,
Dut. Batavia. ❖ of Indonesia, Java,
C Indonesia
Jakobshavn *see* Ilulissat
Jakobstad *see* Pietersaari.
W Finland
Jakobstadt *see* Jēkabpils
Jalal-Abad *see* Dzhalal-Abad
Jalālābād *77* E Afghanistan
Jalandhar *296 prev.* Jullundur. N India
Jalapa *403 var.* Jalapa Enríquez,
prev. Xalapa. SE Mexico
Jalapa *278* C Guatemala
Jalousie *497* SW St Lucia
Jālū *371* NW Libya
Jaluit *396* island of S Marshall Islands
Jamaame *524 It.* Giamame. S Somalia
Jamaare *440* river of NE Nigeria
Jamaica *328-329* island state of the
West Indies, divided into 14 admin.
units (parishes). ❖ Kingston
Jamaica Channel *286, 329* channel of
the Caribbean Sea between Haiti and
Jamaica
Jamālpur *117* N Bangladesh
Jambi *302 prev.* Djambi,
var. Telanaipura. Sumatra,
W Indonesia
Jambol *see* Yambol
Jamdena *see* Yamdena, Pulau
James Bay *171* inlet of Hudson Bay,
C Canada
Jamestown *652* ❖ of St Helena,
N St Helena
Jamestown *see* Holetown
Jammāl *see* Jemmel
Jammerbugten *218* bay to the
NW of Denmark
Jammu *296* N India
Jāmnagar *296 prev.* Navangar.
W India
Jämsä *249* S Finland
Jamshedpur *296* E India
Jamuna *117* lower course of the
Brahmaputra, N Bangladesh
Jamundá *see* Nhamundá
Janakpur *427* E Nepal
Janela *176* Santo Antão, N Cape Verde
Jangijul *see* Yangiyūl
Janīn *see* Jenin
Janina *see* Ioánnina
Janow *see* Jonava
Jantra *see* Yambol
Janzūr *371* NW Libya
Japan *330-335* country of E Asia, divid-
ed into 47 admin. units
(prefectures). ❖ Tokyo
Japan, Sea of *330, 349, 485, 350*
Rus. Yaponskoye More. Sea of Pacific
Ocean, between E Asia and Japan

Japurá *144 var.* Yapurá. River of Brazil
Jaquemel *see* Jacmel
Jarabacoa *226* C Dominican Republic
Jarābulus *551 var.* Jerablus,
Fr. Djérablous. N Syria
Jarash *336 var.* Jerash. NW Jordan
Jarbah, Jazīrat *see* Jerba, Île de
**Jardines de la Reina, Archipiélago
de los** *210* island group of S Cuba
Jarej District *396* district of Majuro,
SE Marshall Islands
Jari *145 var.* Jary. River of N Brazil
Jarīd, Shaṭṭ al *see* Jerid, Chott el
Jaromĕř *216* NE Czech Republic
Jarqŭrghon *610 Rus.* Dzharkurgan. SE
Uzbekistan
Jars, Plain of *see* Xiangkhoang,
Plateau de
Järvenpää *249 Swe.* Träskända.
S Finland
Jason Islands *645* island group of
NW Falkland Islands
Jassy *see* Iași
Jastrzębie Zdrój *471* S Poland
Jászberény *290* NE Hungary
Jauf *see* Al Jawf
Jaunpiebalga *362* NE Latvia
Java *302 var.* Jawa, *prev.* Djawa.
Island of C Indonesia
Javari *144 -145 var.* Yavarí. River
of Brazil and Peru
Java Sea *see* Jawa, Laut
Jawa *see* Java
Jawa, Laut *302 Eng.* Java Sea. Sea
of the Pacific Ocean, C Indonesia
Jawhar *524 var.* Jowhar, *It.* Giohar.
S Somalia
Jayapura *303 prev.* Sukarnapura,
Dut. Hollandia. Irian Jaya,
E Indonesia
Jaya, Puncak *303 prev.* Puntjak
Sukarno, Puntjak Carstensz.
Mountain of Irian Jaya, E Indonesia
Jazā'ir, Ra's al *115* cape of SW Bahrain
Jaz Murian, Hamun-e *307* lake of
SE Iran
Jazzīn *see* Jezzine
Jbaïl *364 var.* Jubayl. W Lebanon
Jdiriya *414* NE Western Sahara
Jebba *440* W Nigeria
Jebel *see* Dzhebel
Jebel, Bahr el *see* White Nile
Jebel Dhanna *see* Jabal aẓ Ẓannah
Jeble *see* Jablah
Jedda *see* Jiddah
Jeffara Plain *371, 573 var.* Gefara, Al
Jifārah. Plain of Libya and Tunisia
Jefferson City *599* Missouri, C USA
Jega *440* NW Nigeria
Jehegnadzor *see* Yeghegnadzor
Jēkabpils *362 Ger.* Jakobstadt.
SE Latvia
Jelenia Góra *471 Ger.* Hirschberg in
Riesengebirge. SW Poland
Jelgava *362 Ger.* Mitau. C Latvia
Jember *302 prev.* Djember. Java,
C Indonesia
Jemmel *573 var.* Jammāl. N Tunisia
Jemo *396* island of C Marshall Islands
Jena *265* C Germany
Jendouba *573 var.* Jundūbah.
NW Tunisia
Jenin *317, 318 var.* Janīn, *Ar.* Jinīn.
N West Bank
Jenné *see* Djenné
Jennings *92* W Antigua, Antigua
& Barbuda
Jenny *538* N Suriname
Jequitinhonha *145* river of E Brazil
Jerablus *see* Jarābulus
Jerada *414* NE Morocco
Jerash *see* Jarash
Jerba *see* Houmt Souk
Jerba, Île de *573 var.* Djerba, Jazīrat
Jarbah. Island of E Tunisia
Jérémie *286* SW Haiti
Jerevan *see* Yerevan
Jerez de la Frontera *530* SW Spain
Jericho *317, 318 Heb.* Yeriho,
Ar. Arīḥā. E West Bank
Jerid, Chott el *573 var.* Shaṭṭ al Jarīd.
Salt lake of SW Tunisia

Jermuk *98 Rus.* Dzhermuk.
SE Armenia
Jersey *252, 648* British Crown
dependency of the English Channel.
❖ St Helier.
Jerusalem *317, 318 Ar.* Al Quds,
Heb. Yerushalayim. ❖ of Israel, Israel
and West Bank
Jesenice *520 Ger.* Assling.
NW Slovenia
Jesselton *see* Kota Kinabalu
Jessore *117* W Bangladesh
Jesús Menéndez *210* SE Cuba
Jeta, Ilha de *282* island of
W Guinea-Bissau
Jevlah *see* Yevlax
Jeypore *see* Jaipur
Jezercës, Maja e *81 var.* Jezerce.
Mountain of N Albania
Jezzine *364 var.* Jazzīn. S Lebanon
Jhālakāti *117* S Bangladesh
Jhang *451 var.* Jhang Sadar, Jhang
Sadr. NE Pakistan
Jhelum *451* NE Pakistan
Jhelum *451* river of India and Pakistan
Jhenida *117* W Bangladesh
Jiamusi *187 var.* Chia-mu-ssu,
Kiamusze. Heilongjiang, NE China
Jiangsu *187 var.* Kiangsu, Chiang-su.
Province of E China
Jiangxi *187 var.* Kiangsi, Chiang-hsi.
Province of SE China
Jibuti *see* Djibouti
Jičín *216* N Czech Republic
Jiddah *506 Eng.* Jedda. W Saudi Arabia
Jiddah *115* island of NW Bahrain
Jidd Ḥafṣ *115 var.* Judd Ḥafṣ.
N Bahrain
Jiftlik Post *318* E West Bank
Jiguaní *210* SE Cuba
Jihlava *216 Ger.* Iglau. S Czech
Republic
Jijel *83 var.* Djidjel, *prev.* Djidjelli.
NE Algeria
Jijiga *524 It.* Giggiga. E Ethiopia
Jilf al Kabīr, Haḍabat al
see Gilf Kebir Plateau
Jilib *524 It.* Gelib. S Somalia
Jilin *187 var.* Kirin, Chi-lin,
prev. Yungki. Jilin, NE China
Jilin *187 var.* Kirin, Chi-lin. Province
of NE China
Jīma *243 var.* Jimma, Ft. Gimma.
SW Ethiopia
Jimaní *226* W Dominican Republic
Jinan *187 var.* Chinan, Tsinan.
Shandong, E China
Jinīn *see* Jenin
Jinja *584* S Uganda
Jinotega *436* C Nicaragua
Jinotepe *436* S Nicaragua
Jinsen *see* Inch'ŏn
Jintotlolo Channel *466* channel
connecting Mindoro Strait and
Visayan Sea
Jinzhou *187 var.* Chin-chou,
Chinchow, *prev.* Chinhsien. Liaoning,
NE China
Jipijapa *228* W Ecuador
Jiquilisco *235* S El Salvador
Jiquilisco, Bahia de *235* bay of the
Pacific Ocean to the S of El Salvador
Jirgatol *558 Rus.* Dzhirgatal'. C
Tajikistan
Jirriiban *524 prev.* Ceel Xamurre,
It. El Hamurre. E Somalia
Jisr ash Shughūr *551*
var. Djisr el Choghour. NW Syria
Jiu *480 Ger.* Schyl, *Hung.* Zsily. River
of S Romania
Jiulong *see* Kowloon
Jixi *187 var.* Chi-hsi. Heilongjiang,
NE China
Jīzān *506 var.* Qīzān. S Saudi Arabia
Jizuka *330* Kyūshū, SW Japan
Jiz', Wādī al *627* dry watercourse of
E Yemen
Jizzakh *610 Rus.* Dzhizak. SE
Uzbekistan
Jleeb, Shaqat Al *see* Qalib, Shiqqat al
Jleeb al Shuyoukh
see Qalīb ash Shuyūkh
Joal-Fadiout *510 prev.* Joal. W Senegal
João Barrosa *176* Boa Vista,
E Cape Verde

João Pessoa 145 prev. Paraíba. E Brazil
Jo-ch'iang see Ruoqiang
Joden Savanne 538 NE Suriname
Jodhpur 296 NW India
Joel's Drift 366 N Lesotho
Joensuu 249 SE Finland
Jõgeva 240 Ger. Laisholm. C Estonia
Jogjakarta see Yogyakarta
Johannesburg 527 Pretoria-Witwatersrand-Vereeniging, NE South Africa
John o'Groats 593 N Scotland, UK
Johnsons Point 92 SW Antigua, Antigua & Barbuda
Johnson, Rapides 203 rapids of Congo (Zaire) and Zambia
Johnston Atoll 648 unincorporated territory of the USA, Pacific Ocean
Johnston Island 648 island of S Johnston Atoll
Johor Bahru 386 SE Peninsular Malaysia
Johore Strait 517 strait connecting Strait of Malacca and South China Sea
Joinville 145 var. Joinvile. S Brazil
Jolo Group 466 island group of Sulu Archipelago, SW Philippines
Jolo Island 466 island of Jolo Group, SW Philippines
Jomsom 427 W Nepal
Jona 546 NE Switzerland
Jonava 376 Ger. Janow. C Lithuania
Jones Point 644 headland on the W coast of Christmas Island
Jonglei Canal 536 canal of S Sudan
Jönköping 543 S Sweden
Jonquière 171 SE Canada
Jordan 317, 318, 336 Ar. Urdunn, Heb. HaYarden. River of SW Asia
Jordan 336-337 officially Hashemite Kingdom of Jordan, Ar. Al Urdunn. Country of SW Asia divided into 8 admin. units (governorates). ❖ Amman
Jos 440 C Nigeria
José Batlle y Ordóñez 607 C Uruguay
José E. Bisanó 226 N Dominican Republic
José Pedro Varela 607 SE Uruguay
Joseph Bonaparte Gulf 101 gulf of Timor Sea on the coast of NW Australia
Jos Plateau 440 plateau of C Nigeria
Jos Sudarso see Yos Sudarso, Pulau
Jost Van Dyke 643 island of W British Virgin Islands
Jotunheimen 444 mountains of SW Norway
Joûnié 364 var. Jūniyah, Juniye. W Lebanon
Jovellanos 210 NW Cuba
Jozini Dam 540 reservoir of South Africa and Swaziland
Jsahaya 330 Kyūshū, SW Japan
Juan Fernández Islands 183 island group of W Chile
Juan L. Lacaze 607 prev. Sauce. SW Uruguay
Juarzon 368 var. Juazohn. SE Liberia
Juazeiro do Norte 145 E Brazil
Juazohn see Juarzon
Juba 243, 524 Som. Jubba, var. Ganaane, Amh. Genale Wenz, It. Guiba. River of Ethiopia and Somalia
Juba 536 var. Jūbā. S Sudan
Jubba see Juba
Jubbulpore see Jabalpur
Júcar 531 river of C Spain
Juclà, Estany de 86 lake of NE Andorra
Judd Ḥafṣ see Jidd Ḥafṣ
Judenburg 106 C Austria
Juigalpa 436 S Nicaragua
Juishui 555 E Taiwan
Juiz de Fora 145 SE Brazil
Jujuy see San Salvador de Jujuy
Juliaca 463 SE Peru
Julian Alps 520 Ger. Julische Alpen, It. Alpi Giulie, Slvn. Julijske Alpe. Mountains of NW Slovenia

Juliana Top 538 mountain of C Suriname
Julianehåb see Qaqortoq
Jullundur see Jalandhar
Jumayrah 590 var. Jumeirah. NE United Arab Emirates
Jumla 427 E Nepal
Jumna see Yamuna
Jundūbah see Jendouba
Juneau 598 Alaska, USA
Jungbunzlau see Mladá Boleslav
Junín 95 E Argentina
Junk Bay see Tseung Kwan O
Juntas 206 W Costa Rica
Junten see Sunch'ŏn
Juozapinės Kalnas 376 mountain of SE Lithuania
Jupiá, Represa de 145 reservoir of S Brazil
Jura 593 island of Inner Hebrides, W Scotland, UK
Jura 253, 546 var. Jura Mountains. Mountain range of France and Switzerland
Juraguá 210 C Cuba
Jura Mountains see Jura
Jurbarkas 376 Ger. Jurburg, var. Georgenburg. W Lithuania
Jūrmala 362 NW Latvia
Jurong Lake 517 lake of W Singapore
Jurong Town 517 W Singapore
Juruá 144 river of Brazil and Peru
Juruena 144 river of W Brazil
Jutiapa 278 S Guatemala
Juticalpa 288 C Honduras
Jutland see Jylland
Juventud, Isla de la 210 var. Isla de Pinos, Eng. Isle of Pines. Island of W Cuba
Južna Morava 630 river of SE Serbia, Yugoslavia
Jwaneng 142 S Botswana
Jylland 218 Eng. Jutland. Island of W Denmark
Jyrgalan see Dzhergalan
Jyväskylä 249 S Finland

K

K2 451 Eng. Mount Godwin Austen. Mountain of China and Pakistan
Kaabong 584 NE Uganda
Kaafu Atoll see Male' Atoll
Kaaimanston 538 NW Surinam
Kaakhka 581 var. Kaachka, Kaka. S Turkmenistan
Kaala see Caála
Kaapstad see Cape Town
Kaba 514 var. Little Scarcies. River of Guinea and Sierra Leone
Kabakama 261 E Gambia
Kabala 514 N Sierra Leone
Kabale 584 SW Uganda
Kabalega Falls see Murchison Falls
Kabara 246 prev. Kambara. Island of the Lau Group, E Fiji
Kabarnet 342 W Kenya
Kabarole 584 W Uganda
Kabaya 492 NW Rwanda
Kaberamaido 584 C Uganda
Kabinda 203 SE Congo (Zaire)
Kabinda see Cabinda
Kābol see Kābul
Kabompo 635 W Zambia
Kabompo 635 river of W Zambia
Kabou 567 N Togo
Kābul 77 Per. Kābol. ❖ of Afghanistan, E Afghanistan
Kabul 77, 451 river of Afghanistan and Pakistan
Kabwe 635 C Zambia
Kabye Plateau 567 plateau of E Togo
Kachch, Gulf of 296 var. Gulf of Cutch, Gulf of Kutch. Gulf of Arabian Sea to the W of India
Kachhi 451 lowland region of C Pakistan
Kadan Island 159 prev. King I. Island of S Burma

Kadavu 246 prev. Kandavu. Island to the S of Viti Levu, SW Fiji
Kadavu Passage 246 channel of the Pacific Ocean between Kadavu and Vitu Levu, Fiji
Kadeï 168, 179 river of Cameroon and Central African Republic
Kadoma 636 prev. Gatooma. C Zimbabwe
Kadugli 536 var. Kāduqlī. S Sudan
Kaduha 492 SW Rwanda
Kaduna 440 C Nigeria
Kaduna 440 river of N Nigeria
Kadzharan see K'ajaran
Kadzhi-Say 357 Kir. Kajisay. NE Kyrgyzstan
Kaédi 398 S Mauritania
Kaélé 168 N Cameroon
Kaesŏng 349 S North Korea
Kaewieng see Kavieng
Kafan see Kapan
Kāfar Jar Ghar 77 mountain range of C Afghanistan
Kaffrine 510 C Senegal
Kafr el Dauwâr 230 var. Kafr ad Dawwār. N Egypt
Kafr el Sheikh 230 var. Kafr ash Shaykh. N Egypt
Kafu 584 var. Kafo. River of W Uganda
Kafue 635 river of C Zambia
Kafue 635 SE Zambia
Kaga Bandoro 179 prev. Fort-Crampel. C Central African Republic
Kagan see Kogon
Kaganovichabad see Kolkhozobod
Kagera see Akagera
Kagi see Chiai
Kâgıthane 577 NW Turkey
Kagoshima 330 Kyūshū, SW Japan
Kagul see Cahul
Kahama 560 NW Tanzania
Kahayan 302 river of Borneo, C Indonesia
Kahnple 368 NE Liberia
Kahnwia 368 SE Liberia
Ká-Hó, Baía de 648 bay of the South China Sea, SE Macao
Kahramanmaraş 577 var. Marash, Maraş. S Turkey
Kaiaf 261 S Gambia
Kaieteur Falls 284 waterfall of C Guyana
Kaifeng 187 Henan, C China
Kai, Kepulauan 302 prev. Kei Islands. Island group of Maluku, E Indonesia
Kaikoura 433 NE South Island, New Zealand
Kailahun 514 E Sierra Leone
Kainan 330 Honshū, C Japan
Kainji Reservoir 440 reservoir of W Nigeria
Kaipara Harbour 433 harbour of NW North Island, New Zealand
Kairouan 573 var. Al Qayrawān. N Tunisia
Kaiserslautern 264 SW Germany
Kaitaia 433 NW North Island, New Zealand
Kajaani 249 Swe. Kajana. C Finland
Kajana see Kajaani
Kajang 386 W Peninsular Malaysia
K'ajaran 98 Rus. Kadzharan, var. Kadžaran. SE Armenia
Kajisay see Kadzhi-Say
Kaka see Kaakhaa
Kakamega 342 W Kenya
Kakata 368 C Liberia
Kakhovs'ke Vodokhovyshche 586 Rus. Kakhovskoye Vodokhranilische. Reservoir of SE Ukraine
Kakia see Khakhea
Kakogawa 330 Honshū, C Japan
Kakshaal-Too, Khrebet see Kokshaal-Tau
Kalaa Kebira 573 var. Al Qal'ah al Kubrá. N Tunisia
Kalabo 635 W Zambia
Kalahari Desert 142, 423, 527 desert region of southern Africa
Kalaikhum see Qal'aikhum
Kalai-Mor 581 Turkm. Galaymor. SE Turkmenistan

Kalamáki 273 prev. Kalmákion. SE Greece
Kalamariá 273 prev. Kalamaria. N Greece
Kalámata 273 prev. Kalámai. S Greece
Kalandula see Calandula
Kalang see Kallang
Kalanshiyū, Sarīr 371 var. Calanscio Sand Sea. Desert region of E Libya
Kalarash see Călăraşi
Kalasin 563 var. Muang Kalasin. NE Thailand
Kalāt 77 var. Qalāt. S Afghanistan
Kalāt 451 var. Kelat. W Pakistan
Kalbā 590 var. Kalba, NE United Arab Emirates
Kaldakvísl 294 river of C Iceland
Kalemie 203 prev. Albertville. SE Congo (Zaire)
Kalgan see Zhangjiakou
Kalgoorlie 100 SW Australia
Kali Gandaki 427 river of C Nepal
Kalima 203 E Congo (Zaire)
Kalimantan 302 Eng. Indonesian Borneo. Region of Borneo, administered by Indonesia
Kalinin 581 N Turkmenistan
Kalininabad see Kalininobod
Kaliningrad 484 W Russia
Kalinino see Tashir
Kalininobod 558 Rus. Kalininabad. SW Tajikistan
Kalinkavichy 122 Rus. Kalinkovichi. SE Belarus
Kaliro 584 SE Uganda
Kalisz 471 Ger. Kalisch. C Poland
Kalixälv 543 river of NE Sweden
Kalkandelen see Tetovo
Kalkfeld 423 NW Namibia
Kallang 517 var. Kalang. River of C Singapore
Kallaste 240 Ger. Krasnogor. E Estonia
Kallavesi 249 lake of SE Finland
Kalmar 543 S Sweden
Kalmykiya, Respublika 484 autonomous republic of SW Russia
Kalomo 635 S Zambia
Kalpeni Island 296 island of Lakshadweep, SW India
Kalsoy 644 var. Kalsø. Island of N Faeroe Islands
Kalu Ganga 534 river of S Sri Lanka
Kalulushi 635 C Zambia
Kalundborg 218 Sjælland, C Denmark
Kalungwishi 635 river of N Zambia
Kalutara 534 SW Sri Lanka
Kaluwawa see Fergusson Island
Kalyān 296 W India
Kálymnos 273 island of SE Greece
Kama 203 E Congo (Zaire)
Kamai 180 N Chad
Kamaishi 331 Honshū, N Japan
Kamakwie 514 NW Sierra Leone
Kamália 451 NE Pakistan
Kamanjab 423 NW Namibia
Kamarān 627 island of W Yemen
Kamarang 284 W Guyana
Kamativi 636 W Zimbabwe
Kambar 451 var. Qambar. SW Pakistan
Kambara see Kabara
Kamchatka, Poluostrov 485 Eng. Kamchatka Peninsula. Peninsula of NE Russia
Kamchiya 152 var. Kamčija. River of E Bulgaria
Kamenets-Podol'sk see Kam"yanets'-Podil's'kyy
Kamenets-Podol'skiy see Kam"yanets'-Podil's'kyy
Kamenica 381 NE FYR Macedonia
Kamenskoye see Dniprodzerzhyns'k
Kamina 203 S Congo (Zaire)
Kamishli see Al Qāmishlī
Kamloops 170 SW Canada
Kammersee see Attersee
Kamnik 520 Ger. Stein. C Slovenia
Kamo 98 C Armenia
Kamp 106 river of N Austria
Kampala 584 ❖ of Uganda, S Uganda
Kampar 386 W Peninsular Malaysia

Kayan *302* river of Borneo, C Indonesia
Kayan *159* S Burma
Kayangel Islands *455* island group of N Palau
Kayanza *162* N Burundi
Kayes *392* W Mali
Kayl *378* S Luxembourg
Kayogoro *162* S Burundi
Kayokwe *162* C Burundi
Kayrakkumskoye Vodokhranilishche *see* Qayrokkum, Obanbori
Kayseri *577* C Turkey
Kayts *534* island of N Sri Lanka
Kazakh *see* Qazax
Kazakhskiy Melkosopochnik *338 Eng.* Kazakh Uplands. Uplands of C Kazakhstan
Kazakhstan *338-341* officially Republic of Kazakhstan, *Kaz.* Qazaqstan, *prev.* Kazakh SSR. *Rus.* Kazakhskay SSR. Country of C Asia divided into 19 admin. units (provinces). ❖ Astana
Kazakh Uplands *see* Kazakhskiy Melkosopochnik
Kazan' *484* W Russia
Kazandzhik *see* Gazandzhyk
Kazanlŭk *152 var.* Kazanlăk, Kazanlik. C Bulgaria
Kazan-rettō *330 Eng.* Volcano Islands. Island group to the SE of Honshū, SE Japan
Kazarman *357* C Kyrgyzstan
Kazbek *262* mountain of N Georgia
Kazi Magomed *see* Qazimämmäd
Kazvin *see* Qazvin
Kéa *273* island of SE Greece
Kéamu *see* Anatom
Kebili *573 var.* Qibilī. C Tunisia
Kebnekaise *543* mountain of N Sweden
Kecskemét *290* C Hungary
Kédainiai *376* C Lithuania
Kediet ej Jill *398 var.* Kediet Ijill, Kédia d'Idjil. Mountain of NW Mauritania
Kediri *302* Java, C Indonesia
Kédougou *510* SE Senegal
Keeling Islands *see* Cocos Islands
Keelung *see* Chilung
Keetmanshoop *423* S Namibia
Kefallinía *273 Eng.* Cephalonia. Island of W Greece
Kefar Sava *317* C Israel
Kefar Tappuah *318* C West Bank
Keflavík *294 var.* Iceflavik. W Iceland
Kegalla *534 var.* Kegalle. C Sri Lanka
Kegel *see* Keila
Kei Islands *see* Kai, Kepulauan
Keijō *see* Seoul
Keila *240 Ger.* Kegel. NW Estonia
Keila *240 var.* Keila Jõgi. River of NW Estonia
Keishū *see* Kyŏngju
Kéita *180 var.* Doka. River of S Chad
Keïta *439* SW Niger
Keitele *249* lake of C Finland
Kék-Art *357 prev.* Alaykel'. SW Kyrgyzstan
Kékes *290* mountain of N Hungary
Kelang *386 var.* Klang, *prev.* Port Swettenham. W Peninsular Malaysia
Kelantan *386* river of N Peninsular Malaysia
Kelbia, Sebkhet *573 var.* Sabkhat Kalbīyah. Salt flat of NE Tunisia
Këlcyrë *81 var.* Këlcyra. S Albania
Kelifskiy Uzboy *581* region of SE Turkmenistan
Kéllé *200* W Congo
Kelmé *376* NW Lithuania
Kélo *180* SW Chad
Kelowna *170* SW Canada
Keluang *386 var.* Kluang. SE Peninsular Malaysia
Kembolcha *243 var.* Kombolcha. N Ethiopia
Kemerovo *485 prev.* Shcheglovsk. C Russia
Kemi *249* NW Finland
Kemijärvi *249* N Finland

Kemijoki *249* river of NW Finland
Kemin *357 prev.* Bystrovka. N Kyrgyzstan
Kemiö *see* Kimito
Kemmuna *395* island of NW Malta
Kemmunett *395* island of NW Malta
Kempen *127 Fr.* Campine, *Ger.* Kempenland. Heathland of NE Belgium
Kempten *265* S Germany
Kenema *514* SE Sierra Leone
Këneurgench *581 prev.* Kunya-Urgench, Kunja-Urgenč, *Turkm.* Köneür gench. N Turkmenistan
Kenitra *414 prev.* Port Lyautey. NW Morocco
Kenmare *314* SW Ireland
Kentau *338* S Kazakhstan
Kentucky *599* state of C USA
Kenya *342-345* officially Republic of Kenya. Country of E Africa divided into 7 admin. units (provinces). ❖ Nairobi
Kenya, Mount *see* Kirinyaga
Keppel Harbour *517* harbour, S Singapore
Keppel Island *see* Niuatoputapu
Kerava *249 Swe.* Kervo. S Finland
Kerch *586 Rus.* Kerch'. SE Ukraine
Kerema *458* S Papua New Guinea
Keren *238 var.* Cheren. C Eritrea
Kerewan *261* W Gambia
Kericho *342* W Kenya
Kerio *342* river of W Kenya
Kerkenah, Îles *573 var.* Kerkenna Islands, *Ar.* Juzur Qarqannah. Island group of E Tunisia
Kerki *581* SE Turkmenistan
Kerkrade *429* S Netherlands
Kérkyra *273 prev.* Kérkira, *Eng.* Corfu. Island of W Greece
Kérkyra *273 Eng.* Corfu, *prev.* Kérkira. W Greece
Kermān *307 var.* Kirman. SE Iran
Kermānshāh *see* Bākhtarān
Kerora *238* N Eritrea
Kérouané *281* SE Guinea
Kertel *see* Kärdla
Kerulen *412 var.* Herlen Gol. River of China and Mongolia
Kervo *see* Kerava
Keryneia *see* Girne
Kesen'-numa *331* Honshū, N Japan
Késmárk *see* Kežmarok
Kesra *573 var.* Kisrah. NW Tunisia
Keta *270* SE Ghana
Ketchikan *598* Alaska, USA
Kete-Krachi *270 var.* Kete Krakye. E Ghana
Kétou *132* SE Benin
Kettharin Island *see* Kanmaw Island
Keur Massène *398* SW Mauritania
Kévé *567* SW Togo
Kew *653* North Caicos, NW Turks and Caicos Islands
Kežmarok *319 Ger.* Käsmark, *Hung.* Késmárk. NE Slovakia
Khabarovsk *485* SE Russia
Khabura *see* Al Khaburah
Khachmas *see* Xaçmaz
Khairpur *451* S Pakistan
Khakasiya, Respublika *485* autonomous republic of C Russia
Khakassk *see* Abakan
Khakhea *142 var.* Kakia. S Botswana
Khalándrion *see* Chalándri
Khalkidhikí *see* Chalkidikí
Khalkís *see* Chalkída
Khalūf *448 var.* Al Khaluf. S Oman
Khambhat, Gulf of *296 Eng.* Gulf of Cambay. Gulf of Arabian Sea to the W of India
Khamir *627 var.* Khamr. W Yemen
Khamis Mushayt *506* S Saudi Arabia
Khānābād *77* NE Afghanistan
Khānaqīn *310* E Iraq
Khānewāl *451* NE Pakistan
Khanh Hung *see* Soc Trăng
Khanka, Lake *187, 485 var.* Lake Hanka, *Rus.* Ozero Khanka, *Chin.* Xingkai Hu, Hsing-K'ai Hu. Lake of China and Russia

Khanka, Ozero *see* Khanka, Lake
Khankendy *see* Xankändi
Khānpur *451* SE Pakistan
Khanty-Mansiysk *484 prev.* Ostyako-Voguls'k. C Russia
Khān Yūnis *317, 318 Ar.* Khan Yunus. Gaza Strip
Kharâb, Ghoubbet el *222* bay at the head of Golfe de Tadjoura, E of Djibouti
Kharanah *see* Al Kir'ānah
Khāriān *451* NE Pakistan
Kharît, Wādī el *230 var.* Wādī al Kharīţ. Dry watercoursef SE Egypt
Kharkiv *586 Rus.* Khar'kov. NE Ukraine
Kharmanli *152 var.* Harmanli. S Bulgaria
Khartoum *536 var.* Al Khurţūm. ❖ of Sudan, C Sudan
Khartoum North *536 var.* Al Khurţūm al Baḩrī. E Sudan
Khasab *see* Al Khaşab
Khāsh Rūd *77* river of W Afghanistan
Khashuri *262* C Georgia
Khaskovo *152 var.* Haskovo. S Bulgaria
Khatt *see* Al Khaţţ
Khawr al Bazm *590 var.* Khor al Bizm. Inlet of the Persian Gulf, on the coast of United Arab Emirates
Khawr al 'Udayd *479 var.* Khor al Udeid. Inlet of the Persian Gulf on the coast of Qatar
Duwayhin, Khawr *590* inlet of the Persian Gulf, on the coast of United Arab Emirates
Khawr Fakkān *590 var.* Khor Fakkan. NE United Arab Emirates
Khaydarkan *357 var.* Khaydarken, Hajdarken. SW Kyrgyzstan
Khazar, Baḩr-e *see* Caspian Sea
Khazar, Daryā-ye *see* Caspian Sea
Khenchela *83 var.* Khenchla. NE Algeria
Khénifra *414* C Morocco
Kherson *586 var.* Cherson. S Ukraine
Khezqazghan *see* Zhezkazgan
Khíos *see* Chíos
Khiwa *610 Uzb.* Khiwa. W Uzbekistan
Khmel 'nyts'kyy *586 Rus.* Khmel'nitskiy, *prev.* Proskurov. W Ukraine
Khodzhent *see* Khujand
Khodzheyli *see* Khujayli
Khoi *see* Khvoy
Khojend *see* Khujand
Kholm *77* N Afghanistan
Khomeynīshahr *307 prev.* Homāyūnshahr. W Iran
Khoms *see* Al Khums
Khong Sedone *see* Muang Khôngxédôn
Khon Kaen *563 var.* Muang Khon Kaen. N Thailand
Khor al Udeid *see* Khawr al 'Udayd
Khôr 'Angar *222* NE Djibouti
Khorixas *423* NW Namibia
Khorramābād *307* W Iran
Khorramshahr *307 prev.* Khūnīnshahr. W Iran
Khorugh *558 var.* Horug, *Rus.* Khorog. S Tajikistan
Khotan *see* Hotan
Khouribga *414* C Morocco
Khowst *77* E Afghanistan
Khoyniki *122* SE Belarus
Khrysokhou Bay *215 var.* Chrysochou Bay. Bay of the Mediterranean Sea, on the NW coast of Cyprus
Khujand *558 prev.* Leninabad, Khodzhent, Khojend. NW Tajikistan
Khujayli *610 Rus.* Khodzheyli. W Uzbekistan
Khulna *117* SW Bangladesh
Khūnīnshahr *see* Khorramshahr
Khurīyā Murīyā, Jazā'ir *see* İalānīyāt, Juzur al
Khurramshahr *see* Khorramshahr
Khushāb *451* NE Pakistan
Khvoy *307 var.* Khoi. NW Iran

Khyber Pass *77, 451* mountain pass connecting Afghanistan with Pakistan
Kia *522* SW Santa Isabel, Solomon Is
Kiamusze *see* Jiamusi
Kiangsi *see* Jiangxi
Kiangsu *see* Jiangsu
Kiayi *see* Chiai
Kibondo *560* NW Tanzania
Kibre Mengist *243 var.* Adola. S Ethiopia
Kibungo *492 var.* Kibungu. SE Rwanda
Kibuye *492* W Rwanda
Kičevo *381* W FYR Macedonia
Kidaho *492* NW Rwanda
Kiel *265* N Germany
Kiel Bay *218, 265 Ger.* Kieler Bucht. Bay of the Baltic Sea
Kielce *471* S Poland
Kieler Bucht *see* Kiel Bay
Kieta *458* Bougainville I, Papua New Guinea
Kiev *586 Ukr.* Kyyiv, *Rus.* Kiyev. ❖ of Ukraine, N Ukraine
Kiffa *398* S Mauritania
Kigali *492* ❖ of Rwanda, C Rwanda
Kigembe *492* S Rwanda
Kigoma *560* W Tanzania
Kigwena *162* SW Burundi
Kikila, Lac *653* lake of Île Uvea, S Wallis & Futuna
Kihnu *240* island of SW Estonia
Kikládhes *see* Kyklades
Kikori *458* river of C Papua New Guinea
Kikwit *203* W Congo(Zaire)
Kilchu *349* NE North Korea
Kili *396* island of S Marshall Islands
Kilien Mountains *see* Qilian Shan
Kilifi *342* SE Kenya
Kilimanjaro *560* mountain of NE Tanzania
Kilingi-Nõmme *240 Ger.* Kurkund. S Estonia
Kilinochchi *534* N Sri Lanka
Kilis *577* S Turkey
Kilkee *314* W Ireland
Kilkenny *314 Ir.* Cill Choinnigh. SE Ireland
Kilkís *273* N Greece
Kilkoch *314* E Ireland
Killarney *314 Ir.* Cill Airne. SW Ireland
Kilmarnock *593* W Scotland, UK
Kilosa *560* C Tanzania
Kilwa Masoko *560* SE Tanzania
Kimbe *458* New Britain, Papua New Guinea
Kimberley *527* Northern Cape, C South Africa
Kimberley Plateau *100* plateau of NW Australia
Kimch'aek *349 prev.* Sŏngjin. E North Korea
Kimch'ŏn *350* C South Korea
Kimhae *350* SE South Korea
Kimito *249 Swe.* Kemiö. Island of SW Finland
Kimje *350* SW South Korea
Kinabatangan *386* river of NE Borneo, Malaysia
Kinabalu, Gunung *386* mountain of N Borneo, Malaysia
Kindamba *200* S Congo
Kindia *281* SW Guinea
Kindu *203* C Congo (Zaire)
King George Bay *645* bay of the South Atlantic Ocean, W Falkland Islands
King George Land *90* island of South Shetland Islands, Antarctica
King Island *101* island of SE Australia
King Island *see* Kadan I
Kingissepp *see* Kuressaare
King's Lynn *593* E England, UK
King's Mills *647* SW Guernsey
Kingston *171* SE Canada
Kingston *329* ❖ of Jamaica, E Jamaica
Kingston *650* ❖ of Norfolk Island, S Norfolk Island
Kingston upon Hull *593 var.* Hull. NE England, UK
Kingstown *498* ❖ of St Vincent & the Grenadines, SW St Vincent

Mafa'a, Pointe *653* headland of Île Alofi, N Wallis & Futuna
Mafeteng *366* W Lesotho
Mafia *560* island of E Tanzania
Mafou *281* river of C Guinea
Mafraq *see* Al Mafraq
Mafraq *590* C United Arab Emirates
Mafungabusi Plateau *636* plateau of C Zimbabwe
Mafut *590* NE United Arab Emirates
Magadan *485* NE Russia
Magadi *342* SW Kenya
Magadi, Lake *342* lake of SW Kenya
Magallanes *see* Punta Arenas
Magallanes, Estrecho *see* Magellan, Strait of
Magangué *195* N Colombia
Magaria *439* S Niger
Magat *466* river of Luzon, N Philippines
Magburaka *514* C Sierra Leone
Magdalena *195* river of C Colombia
Magdalena *136* N Bolivia
Magdeburg *265* C Germany
Magelang *302* Java, C Indonesia
Magellan, Strait of *95, 183* *Sp.* Estrecho de Magallanes. Strait connecting the S Atlantic and S Pacific Oceans between Tierra del Fuego and mainland South America
Magerøya *444* *var.* Magerøy. Island of NE Norway
Maggiore, Lake *320, 546* *It.* Lago Maggiore. Lake of Italy and Switzerland
Magh Ealla *see* Mallow
Maglaj *140* N Bosnia & Herzegovina
Magnitogorsk *484* C Russia
Mago *246* *prev.* Mango. Island of the Lau Group, E Fiji
Magta' Lahjar *398* SW Mauritania
Magura *117* W Bangladesh
Magwe *159* *var.* Magway. W Burma
Magyarkanizsa *see* Kanjiža
Magyarország *see* Hungary
Magyaróvár *see* Mosonmagyaróvár
Mahafaly, Lembalemban' *382* *var.* Plateau Mahafaly. Plateau of SW Madagascar
Mahaicony Village *284* E Guyana
Mahajamba *382* seasonal river of N Madagascar
Mahajanga *382* *prev.* Majunga. N Madagascar
Mahajilo *382* seasonal river of C Madagascar
Mahakali *427* river of India and Nepal
Mahakam *302* *var.* Kutai, Koetai. River of Borneo, C Indonesia
Mahalapye *142* *var.* Mahalatswe. SE Botswana
Mahallah al Kubrá *see* El Mahalla el Kubra
Mahamba *540* SW Swaziland
Mahanādi *296* river of E India
Mahanoro *382* E Madagascar
Maha Sarakham *563* NE Thailand
Mahaut *224* W Dominica
Mahavavy *382* seasonal river of N Madagascar
Mahaweli Ganga *534* river of C SriLanka
Mahdia *573* *var.* Al Mahdīyah, Mehdia. NE Tunisia
Mahdia *284* C Guyana
Mahé *512* island of NE Seychelles
Mahebourg *400* SE Mauritius
Mahenge *560* SE Tanzania
Mahia Peninsula *433* peninsula of E North Island, New Zealand
Mahilyow *122* *Rus.* Mogilëv. E Belarus
Mahina *392* W Mali
Mahiyangana *534* E Sri Lanka
Mahmūd-e Rāqī *77* NE Afghanistan
Mahmudiya *see* Al Maḥmūdīyah
Mahou *392* S Mali
Mährisch-Ostrau *see* Ostrava
Mährisch-Schönberg *see* Šumperk
Maiana *346* island of the Gilbert Is, W Kiribati
Maicao *195* N Colombia
Mai Ceu *see* Maych'ew
Mai Chio *see* Maych'ew
Maiduguri *441* NE Nigeria

Mailand *see* Milano
Maimāna *see* Meymaneh
Main *264* river of C Germany
Main Camp *see* Banana
Main Channel *648* channel of the Pacific Ocean, S Johnston Atoll
Main Channel *see* Inner Channel
Mai-Ndombe, Lac *203* *prev.* Lac Léopold II. Lake of W Congo (Zaire)
Maine *599* state of NE USA
Maine *253* cultural region of NW France
Maïné-Soroa *439* SE Niger
Mainland *593* Shetland, NE UK
Mainland *593* Orkney, NE UK
Maintirano *382* W Madagascar
Mainz *264* *Fr.* Mayence. SW Germany
Maio *176* *var.* Vila de Maio. Maio, S Cape Verde
Maio *176* island of SE Cape Verde
Maiquetía *619* N Venezuela
Maissade *286* C Haiti
Maisur *see* Mysore
Maitland *101* E Australia
Maíz, Islas *436* *var.* Corn Islands. Island group of E Nicaragua
Maizuru *330* Honshū, C Japan
Majardah, Wādi *see* Mejerda, Oued
Majimbini, Réserve Forestière de *649* forest reserve of C Mayotte
Majorca *see* Mallorca
Majunga *see* Mahajanga
Majuro *396* atoll of SE Marshall Islands
Majuro District *396* district of Majuro, SE Marshall Islands
Makamba *162* S Burundi
Makarska *209* *It.* Macarsca. SE Croatia
Makasar *see* Ujungpandang
Makasar, Selat *302* *Eng.* Makassar Strait. Strait connecting the Celebes Sea and Laut Flores, C Indonesia
Makassar Strait *see* Makasar, Selat
Makay, Tangorombohitr' i *382* *var.* Massif du Makay. Mountains of SW Madagascar
Makebuko *162* C Burundi
Makeni *514* C Sierra Leone
Makgadikgadi *142* *var.* Makarikari Pans. Saltpans of NE Botswana
Makhachkala *484* *prev.* Petrovsk-Port. SW Russia
Makharadze *see* Ozurget'i
Makhfar al Quwayrah *see* Al Quwayrah
Makin *346* island of the Gilbert Is, W Kiribati
Makira *see* San Cristobal
Makiyivka *586* *Rus.* Makeyevka, *prev.* Dmitriyevsk. E Ukraine
Makkah *506* *Eng.* Mecca. W Saudi Arabia
Makō *see* MaKung
Makó *290* SE Hungary
Makogai *246* island to the NE of Viti Levu, C Fiji
Makokou *258* NE Gabon
Makona *281* river of S Guinea
Makoua *200* C Congo
Makran Coast *307* coastal region of SE Iran
MaKung *555* *Jap.* Makō. P'eng-hu Tao, W Taiwan
Makunudhoo Atoll *390* *var.* Makunudu Atoll. Atoll of N Maldives
Makurazaki *330* Kyūshū, SW Japan
Makurdi *440* C Nigeria
Makuti *636* N Zimbabwe
Makwate *142* SE Botswana
Mala *see* Malaita
Malabo *236* *prev.* Santa Isabel. ✤ of Equatorial Guinea, N Bioko
Malacca *see* Melaka
Malacca, Strait of *302* strait connecting the Andaman Sea and South China Sea between Malay Peninsula and Sumatra, SE Asia
Malacka *see* Malacky
Malacky *519* *Hung.* Malacka. W Slovakia
Maladzyechna *122* *Rus.* Molodechno, *Pol.* Molodeczno. NW Belarus
Málaga *531* S Spain

Malagasy Republic *see* Madagascar
Malaita *522* *var.* Mala, Island of C Solomon Islands
Malakal *536* *var.* Malakāl. S Sudan
Malambo *195* N Colombia
Malang *302* SE Java, Indonesia
Malange *see* Malanje
Malanje *88* *var.* Malange. NW Angola
Malanville *132* NE Benin
Mälaren *543* lake of SE Sweden
Malatya *576* SE Turkey
Malawi *384-385* officially Republic of Malawi, *prev.* Nyasaland, Nyasaland Protectorate. Country of S Africa divided into 3 admin. units (regions). ✤ Lilongwe
Malawi, Lake *see* Nyasa, Lake
Malaya *see* Peninsular Malaysia
Malāyer *307* NW Iran
Malay Peninsula *563* peninsula of Malaysia and Thailand
Malaysia *386-389* officially Republic of Maldives, *prev.* the separate territories of Federation of Malaya, Singapore (left 1965), Sarawak and Sabah (North Borneo). Country of SE Asia divided into 15 admin. units (13 states, 2 federal territories). ✤ Kuala Lumpur
Maldegem *127* NW Belgium
Malden Island *346* island of the Line Is, E Kiribati
Maldives *390-391* Officially Republic of Maldives, Maldivian Divehi. Country of the Indian Ocean divided into 19 admin. units (districts). ✤ Male'
Maldonado *607* S Uruguay
Male' *390* *var.* Male. ✤ of Maldives, Male' Atoll, C Maldives
Male *see* Male'
Male' Atoll *390* *var.* Kaafu Atoll. Atoll of C Maldives
Malebo Pool *see* Stanley Pool
Malékoula *see* Malekula
Malekula *615* *var.* Malakula, *prev.* Mallicolo. Island of W Vanuatu
Mali *392-393* officially Republic of Mali, *prev.* Sudanese Republic, French Sudan. Country divided into 8 admin. units (7 regions and 1 capital district). ✤ Bamako
Malibamatso *366* river of C Lesotho
Mali Hka *159* river of N Burma forming a headstream of the Irrawaddy river
Malindi *342* SE Kenya
Malines *see* Mechelen
Malinga *258* SE Gabon
Malin Head *314* headland on the N coast of Ireland
Mallāq, Wādī *see* Mellègue, Oued
Mallawi *230* *var.* Mallawī. C Egypt
Mallicolo *see* Malekula
Mallorca *531* *Eng.* Majorca. Island of the Islas Baleares, E Spain
Mallow *314* *Ir.* Magh Ealla. SW Ireland
Malmédy *127* E Belgium
Malmö *543* S Sweden
Malmok *650* headland of Bonaire, S Netherlands Antilles
Malo *615* island of W Vanuatu
Maloelap *396* island of E Marshall Islands
Malolo *246* island of the Mamanuca-i-ra Group, W Fiji
Malolos *466* Luzon, N Philippines
Maloma *540* S Swaziland
Malombe, Lake *385* lake of SE Malawi
Małopolska *471* plateau of S Poland
Maloti Mountains *see* Maluti
Malpasso *226* SW Dominican Republic
Mäls *374* S Liechtenstein
Malta *395* island of the Mediterranean Sea, with Gozo and Kemmuna forms the state of Malta
Malta *394-395* officially Republic of Malta. Country of the Mediterranean Sea. ✤ Valletta
Malta Channel *395* *It.* Canale di Malta. Strait of Mediterranean Sea between Malta and Sicily

Maltahöhe *423* S Namibia
Malta, Il-Fliegu ta' *395* *Eng.* South Comino Channel. Strait of Mediterranean Sea between Kemmuna and Malta islands, NW Malta
Maluku *302* *prev.* Spice Islands, *Eng.* Moluccas. Island group of E Indonesia
Maluku, Laut *302* *Eng.* Molucca Sea. Sea of the Pacific Ocean, E Indonesia
Malung *543* C Sweden
Maluti *366* *var.* Maluti Mountains, Maloti Mountains, Front Range. Mountain range of C Lesotho
Malvinas, Islas *see* Falkland Islands
Malyy Kavkaz *see* Lesser Caucasus
Mamanuca-i-ra Group *246* islands of W Fiji
Mamates *366* NW Lesotho
Mambéré *179* river of SW Central African Republic
Mambili *200* river of W Congo
Mamer *378* SW Luxembourg
Mamfe *168* W Cameroon
Mamiku *497* E St Lucia
Mamoré *136* river of Bolivia and Brazil
Mamou *281* W Guinea
Mamoudzou *649* ✤ of Mayotte, N Mayotte
Mampong *270* C Ghana
Mamțalah, Ra's al *see* Mummaţalah, Ra's al
Mamuno *142* W Botswana
Man *326* W Ivory Coast
Mana *645* NW French Guiana
Manado *302* *prev.* Menado. Celebes, C Indonesia
Managua *436* ✤ of Nicaragua, W Nicaragua
Managua, Lago de *436* *var.* Xolotlán. Lake of W Nicaragua
Manah *448* *var.* Bilād Manaḥ. N Oman
Manakara *382* SE Madagascar
Mana *645* river of C French Guiana
Manama *115* *Ar.* Al Manāmah. ✤ of Bahrain, NE Bahrain
Manambaho *382* seasonal river of NW Madagascar
Manambolo *382* river of W Madagascar
Mananjary *382* SE Madagascar
Manantali, Lac de *392* reservoir of W Mali
Manāqīsh *354* *var.* Manageesh. S Kuwait
Manas, Gora *610* mountain of NE Uzbekistan
Manatí *651* N Puerto Rico
Manaus *144* *prev.* Manáos. NW Brazil
Manbij *551* *Fr.* Membidj. N Syria
Manchester *593* N England, UK
Manchester *599* New Hampshire, NE USA
Man-chou-li *see* Manzhouli
Manda Island *342* island of SE Kenya
Mandal *444* SW Norway
Mandalay *159* N Burma
Mandalgovi *412* S Mongolia
Mandali *310* E Iraq
Mandaue *466* Cebu, C Philippines
Mandera *342* NE Kenya
Mandeville *329* SW Jamaica
Mandiana *281* E Guinea
Mandi Būrewāla *451* *var.* Būrewāla. E Pakistan
Mandidzudzure *see* Chimanimani
Mandié *419* NW Mozambique
Mandimba *419* N Mozambique
Mandji *258* C Gabon
Mandouri *567* N Togo
Manfredonia *321* S Italy
Manga *157* C Burkina
Mangai *203* W Congo (Zaire)
Mangaia *644* island of Southern Cook Islands, S Cook Islands
Mangalia *480* SE Romania
Mangalmé *180* SE Chad
Mangalore *296* SW India
Mangde *134* river of S Bhutan
Mange *514* NW Sierra Leone

Mango *see* Sansanné Mango
Mango *see* Mago
Mangoche *see* Mangochi
Mangochi *385 var.* Mangoche, *prev.* Fort Johnson. SE Malawi
Mangoky *382* river of SW Madagascar
Mangula *see* Mhangura
Mangyshlak *338* W Kazakhstan
Mania *382* river of C Madagascar
Manica *419 var.* Vila de Manica. W Mozambique
Manihiki *644* island of Northern Cook Islands, N Cook Islands
Maniitsoq *646 Dan.* Sukkertoppen. SW Greenland
Manikaraku *522* E Guadalcanal, Solomon Is
Manikganj *117* C Bangladesh
Manila *466 var.* Manila City.
❖ of the Philippines, Luzon, N Philippines
Manisa *576 prev.* Saruhan. W Turkey
Man, Isle of *593, 647* British Crown dependency of the Irish Sea. ❖ Douglas
Manitoba *170* province of S Canada
Manizales *195* W Colombia
Manjimup *100* SW Australia
Mankayane *540 var.* Mankaiana. W Swaziland
Mankono *326* C Ivory Coast
Mankulam *534* N Sri Lanka
Mannar *534 var.* Manar. NW Sri Lanka
Mannar, Gulf of *296, 534* gulf of Indian Ocean, to the S of India
Mannar Island *534* island to the N of Sri Lanka
Mannheim *264* SW Germany
Mano *514* SW Sierra Leone
Mano *514* river of Liberia and Sierra Leone
Manombo Atsimo *382 var.* Manombo. SW Madagascar
Manono *500* Upolu, Samoa
Manono *203* SE Congo (Zaire)
Manorhamilton *314* N Ireland
Manp'o *349 var.* Manp'ojin. NW North Korea
Manra *346 var.* Sydney I. Island of the Phoenix Is, C Kiribati
Mansa *635 prev.* Fort Rosebery. N Zambia
Mansabá *282* NW Guinea-Bissau
Mansajang Kunda *261* E Gambia
Mansa Konko *261* C Gambia
Mansion *494* NE St Kitts, St Kitts & Nevis
Mansôa *282* W Guinea-Bissau
Mansôa *282* river of W Guinea-Bissau
Manta *228* W Ecuador
Mantes-la-Jolie *253 prev.* Mantes-sur-Seine, Mantes-Gassicourt. N France
Mantova *320 Eng.* Mantua, *Fr.* Mantoue. N Italy
Mantsonyane *366* C Lesotho
Manuae *644* island of Southern Cook Islands, S Cook Islands
Manua Islands *642* island group of E American Samoa
Manukau Harbour *433* harbour of W North Island, New Zealand
Manurewa *433* N North Island, New Zealand
Manus Island *458 var.* Great Admiralty I. Island of NE Papua New Guinea
Manyame *636 var.* Panhame, *prev.* Hunyani. River of Mozambique and Zimbabwe
Manyame, Lake *636 prev.* Robertson, Lake. Reservoir of N Zimbabwe
Manyara, Lake *560* lake of NE Tanzania
Manyoni *560* C Tanzania
Manzanillo *210* SE Cuba
Manzhouli *187 var.* Man-chou-li. Nei Mongol Zizhiqu, NE China
Manzil Bū Ruqaybah *see* Menzel Bourguiba
Manzil Tamīm *see* Menzel Temime
Manzini *540 prev.* Bremersdorp. C Swaziland
Mao *180* W Chad
Mao *226* NW Dominican Republic

Maoke, Pegunungan *303 Dut.* Sneeuw-gebergte, *Eng.* Snow Mountains. Mountain range of Irian Jaya, E Indonesia
Mapoteng *366* NW Lesotho
Mapou *400* N Mauritius
Maputo *419 prev.* Lourenço Marques. ❖ of Mozambique, S Mozambique
Maputo, Baía de *419 var.* Baía de Lourenço Marques, *Eng.* Delagoa Bay. Bay on the coast of Mozambique
Mara *284* E Guyana
Marabá *145* NE Brazil
Maracaibo *619* NW Venezuela
Maracaibo, Lago de *619* inlet of Caribbean Sea, NW Venezuela
Maracay *619* N Venezuela
Marada *371* N Libya
Maradi *439* S Niger
Maragarazi *162, 560 var.* Muragarazi. River of Burundi and Tanzania
Marāgheh *307 var.* Maragha. NW Iran
Marahoué *see* Bandama Rouge
Marajó, Baía de *145* N Brazil
Marajó, Ilha de *145* island of N Brazil
Marakabei *366 var.* Marakabeis. C Lesotho
Marakei *346* island of the Gilbert Is, W Kiribati
Maralal *342* C Kenya
Maralik *98* W Armenia
Maramasike *522* island of E Solomon Is
Maramba *see* Livingstone
Marambio *90* Argentinian research station near Antarctic Peninsula, Antarctica
Maramvya *162* SW Burundi
Marandellas *see* Marondera
Marañón *463* river of N Peru
Marash *see* Kahramanmaraş
Maravovo *522* W Guadalcanal, Solomon Is
Marāwiḩ *590 var.* Merawwah. Island of W United Arab Emirates
Marbella *531* S Spain
Marburg *see* Maribor
Marburg an der Lahn *264* W Germany
Marcal *290* river of W Hungary
Marche *253* cultural region of C France
Marche-en-Famenne *127* SE Belgium
Marchena, Isla *228* island of N Galapagos Is, Ecuador
Marchfield *121* SE Barbados
Mar Chiquita, Lago *95* lake of C Argentina
Marcounda *see* Markounda
Marcovia *288* S Honduras
Mardān *451* N Pakistan
Mar del Plata *95* E Argentina
Mardin *577* SE Turkey
Maré *650* island, Îles Loyauté, E New Caledonia
Mareeq *524 var.* Mereeg, *It.* Meregh. E Somalia
Marek *see* Dupnitsa
Marfa Ridge *395* ridge of NW Malta
Margarita, Isla de *619* island of N Venezuela
Margate *527* Kwazulu Natal, SE South Africa
Margherita, Lake *see* Âbaya Hâyk'
Margherita Peak *584, 203* mountain of Uganda and Congo (Zaire)
Marghilon *610 var.* Margelan, *Rus.* Margilan. E Uzbekistan
Mārgow, Dasht-e- *77* desert of SW Afghanistan
Mari *215* S Cyprus
Marianao *210* NW Cuba
Marías, Islas *403* Island of W Mexico
Maria-Theresiopel *see* Subotica
Máriatölgyes *see* Dubnica nad Váhom
Mar'ib *627* W Yemen
Maribo *218* Lolland, S Denmark
Maribor *520 Ger.* Marburg. NE Slovenia
Marid *527* NE United Arab Emirates
Marie Byrd Land *90* physical region of Greater Antarctica, Antarctica
Marie-Galante *646* island of SE Guadeloupe

Mariehamn *249 var.* Maarianhamina. Aland, Finland
Mariel *210* NW Cuba
Marienburg *see* Alūksne
Mariental *423* S Namibia
Marigot *646* St. Martin, N Guadeloupe
Marigot *522* NE Dominica
Marigot de Baïla *510* river of SW Senegal
Mariguana *see* Mayaguana
Marijampolė *376 prev.* Kapsukas. S Lithuania
Marília *145* S Brazil
Marinduque Island *466* island of C Philippines
Maringá *145* S Brazil
Marins, Île aux *652* island of SE Saint Pierre and Miquelon
Marion Island *527* island of Prince Edward Islands, S South Africa
Ionio, Mar *see* Ionian Sea
Maripasoula *645* W French Guiana
Mariscal Estigarribia *460* NW Paraguay
Marisule Estate *497* N St Lucia
Maritsa *152, 273 var.* Marica, *Gk* Évros, *Turk.* Meriç. River of SE Europe
Mariupol' *586 prev.* Zhdanov. SE Ukraine
Mariy El, Respublika *484* autonomous republic of W Russia
Märjamaa *240 Ger.* Merjama. W Estonia
Marjayoun *364 var.* Marj 'Uyūn. S Lebanon
Marka *524 var.* Merca. S Somalia
Marka *385* S Malawi
Market Shop *494* SE Nevis, St Kitts & Nevis
Markounda *179 var.* Marcounda. NW Central African Republic
Marlánské Lázně *216* W Czech Republic
Marmara Denizi *576 Eng.* Sea of Marmara. Sea to the NW of Turkey
Marmaris *576* SW Turkey
Marne *253* river of NE France
Marneuli *262* S Georgia
Maro *180* S Chad
Maroantsetra *382* NE Madagascar
Maromokotro *382* mountain of N Madagascar
Marondera *636 var.* Marandellas. NE Zimbabwe
Maroni *538, 645 Dut.* Marowijne. River of French Guiana and Surinam
Maros *see* Mureş
Marosvásárhely *see* Târgu Mureş
Marotiri *646* island group of S French Polynesia
Maroua *168* N Cameroon
Marovoay *382* NW Madagascar
Marowijne *see* Maroni
Marqūbah *115* NE Bahrain
Marquises, Îles *646* island group of N French Polynesia
Marrakech *414 var.* Marakesh, *Eng.* Marrakesh, *prev.* Morocco. W Morocco
Marrupa *419* N Mozambique
Marsa *395* C Malta
Marsá al Burayqah *see* Al Burayqah
Marsabit *342* N Kenya
Marsala *321* Sicilia, S Italy
Marsaxlokk *395* SE Malta
Marsaxlokk Bay *395* inlet on the SW coast of Malta
Marseille *253 prev. Eng.* Marseilles. SE France
Marshall *368* W Liberia
Marshall Islands *396-397* officially Republic of the Marshall Islands. Country of the Pacific Ocean divided into 33 admin. units (districts). ❖ Majuro
Marsh Harbour *112* Great Abaco, Bahamas
Martaban *159* SE Burma
Martadi *427 var.* Bajura. W Nepal
Martigny *546* SW Switzerland
Martigues *253* SE France

Martin *519 prev.* Turčiansky Svätý Martin, *Ger.* Sankt Martin, *Hung.* Turócszentmárton. NW Slovakia
Martinique *649* French overseas department of the Caribbean Sea. ❖ Fort-de-France.
Martinique Passage *224 var.* Dominica Channel, Martinique Channel. Passage connecting the Atlantic Ocean and Caribbean Sea between Dominica and Martinique
Martuni *98* E Armenia
Marungu *203* mountain range of SE Congo (Zaire)
Mary *581 prev.* Merv. SE Turkmenistan
Maryborough *101* E Australia
Mary Island *see* Kanton
Maryland *599* state of E USA
Marzūq *see* Murzuq
Masai Steppe *560* grassland of NW Tanzania
Masaka *584* SW Uganda
Masâkin *see* M'saken
Masally *see* Massili
Masampo *see* Masan
Masan *350 prev.* Masampo. S South Korea
Masasi *560* SE Tanzania
Masatepe *436* SW Nicaragua
Masaya *436* S Nicaragua
Masbate *466* island of C Philippines
Mascara *83 var.* Mouaskar. NW Algeria
Maseru *366* ❖ of Lesotho, W Lesotho
Mas-ha *318* W West Bank
Mashava *636 prev.* Mashaba. SE Zimbabwe
Mashhad *307 var.* Meshed. NE Iran
Māshkel *307, 450 var.* Rūd-i Māshkel, Māshkīd. River of Iran and Pakistan
Māshkel, Hāmūn-i *450* salt marsh of Iran and Pakistan
Māshkīd *see* Māshkel
Mashtagi *see* Maştaği
Masīlah, Wādī al *627* dry watercourse of E Yemen
Masindi *584* W Uganda
Masinga Reservoir *342* reservoir of C Kenya
Masirah, Gulf of *see* Maşīrah, Khalīj
Maşīrah, Jazīrat *448 var.* Masirah, Masira. Island of E Oman
Maşīrah, Khalīj *448 var.* Gulf of Masirah. Bay of the Arabian Sea, E Oman
Masis *98* SW Armenia
Masjed Soleymān *307 var.* Masjed-e Soleymān, Masjid-i Sulaiman. W Iran
Maskall *130* NE Belize
Maskanah *551 var.* Meskene. N Syria
Maskin *448 var.* Miskin. N Oman
Mask, Lough *314 Ir.* Loch Measca. Lake of W Ireland
Ma *623* river of Laos and Vietnam
Massa *320* N Italy
Massachusetts *599* state of NE USA
Massacre *224* W Dominica
Massawa *238 Amh.* Mits'iwa. E Eritrea
Massawa Channel *238* channel of the Red Sea between Dahlak Archipelago and mainland Eritrea
Massenya *180* SW Chad
Massif Central *253* plateau region of C France
Massili *110 Rus.* Masally. S Azerbaijan
Massoukou *258 var.* Masuku, *prev.* Franceville. E Gabon
Maştağa *110 Rus.* Mastaga, *var.* Maštaga, Mashtagi. E Azerbaijan
Masterton *433* S North Island, New Zealand
Masuda *330* Honshū, W Japan
Masunga *142* NE Botswana
Masvingo *636 prev.* Nyanda, *prev.* Fort Victoria. SE Zimbabwe
Mât *652* river of NE Réunion
Matacawa Levu *246* island of the Yasawa Group, NW Fiji

Muğan Düzü *110 Rus.* Muganskaya Step'. Physical region of S Azerbaijan
Mugera *162* C Burundi
Mugesera, Lac *492* lake of E Rwanda
Mughsu *558 Rus.* Muksu. River of NE Tajikistan
Mugi *330* Shikoku, SW Japan
Mugla *576* SW Turkey
Muharraq *see* Al Muḥarraq
Muḩarraq, Jazīrat al *115* island of N Bahrain
Muhazi, Lac *492* lake of E Rwanda
Muhinga *see* Muyinga
Muh, Sabkhat al *551* salt-flat of S Syria
Muhu *240 Ger.* Mohn, Moon. Island of W Estonia
Muhu Väin *see* Väinameri
Muineachán *see* Monaghan
Muir Bhreatan *see* St. George's Channel
Muir Eireann *see* Irish Sea
Mukacheve *586* W Ukraine
Mukalla *see* Al Mukallā
Mukden *see* Shenyang
Muksu *558* river of NE Tajikistan
Mukungwa *492* river of NW Rwanda
Mulaku Atoll *390 var.* Meemu Atoll. Atoll of C Maldives
Mulanje *385 var.* Mlanje. S Malawi
Mulchén *183* C Chile
Mülheim *264 var.* Mulheim an der Ruhr. W Germany
Mulhouse *253 Ger.* Mülhausen. NE France
Mulifanua *500* Upolu, Samoa
Mulinu'ū, Cape *500* cape of Savai'i, Samoa
Mullaittivu *534 var.* Mullaitivu. NE Sri Lanka
Muller, Pegunungan *302 Dut.* Müller-gerbergte. Mountain range of Borneo, C Indonesia
Mullingar *314* C Ireland
Mull, Isle of *593* island of Inner Hebrides, W Scotland, UK
Multān *451* E Pakistan
Mumbai *see* Bombay
Mumbwa *635* C Zambia
Mummatalah, Ra's al *115 var.* Ra's al Mamtalah. Cape of SW Bahrain
Munamägi *see* Suur Munamägi
Muna, Pulau *302 prev.* Moena. Island to the SE of Celebes, C Indonesia
München *265, 269 Eng.* Munich, *It.* Monaco. S Germany
Munch'ŏn *349* SE North Korea
Munda *522* New Georgia, C Solomon Islands
Mundal Lagooon *534* lagoon of W Sri Lanka
Mu Nggava *see* Rennell
Mungla *117* S Bangladesh
Mungwi *635* NE Zambia
Munia *246* island of the Lau Group, E Fiji
Munich *see* München
Munini *492* SW Rwanda
Munshiganj *117* C Bangladesh
Munster *314* province of S Ireland
Münster *264 var.* Muenster. NW Germany
Muntinglupa *466* Luzon, N Philippines
Muong Sai *see* Muang Xay
Muonioälv *see* Muoniojoki
Muoniojoki *249, 543 Swe.* Muonioälv. River of Finland and Sweden
Muqdisho *see* Mogadishu
Mur *106, 520 SCr.* Mura. River of C Europe
Mura *see* Mur
Muragarazi *see* Maragarazi
Murai Reservoir *517* reservoir of NW Singapore
Murambi *492* C Rwanda
Muramvya *162* C Burundi
Murang'a *342 prev.* Fort Hall. SW Kenya
Murata *502* S San Marino
Murchison Falls *584 var.* Kabalega Falls. Waterfall of NW Uganda

Murcia *531* autonomous community of SE Spain
Mureş *480 var.* Mureşul, *Hung.* Maros, *Ger.* Muresch. River of Hungary and Romania
Murehwa *636 var.* Murewa. NE Zimbabwe
Muresch *see* Mureş
Murgab *581 prev.* Murgap. SE Turkmenistan
Murgab *581 var.* Murghab. River of SE Turkmenistan
Murgab *see* Murghob
Murghob *558 Rus.* Murgab. E Tajikistan
Muri *546 var.* Muri bei Bern. W Switzerland
Murilo *406* atoll of N Micronesia
Mūrītānīyah *see* Mauritania
Müritz *265 var.* Müritzee. Lake of NE Germany
Murmansk *484* NW Russia
Muroran *330* Hokkaidō, N Japan
Muroto *330* Shikoku, SW Japan
Murray *101* river of SE Australia
Murray, Lake *458* lake in swamp region of W Papua New Guinea
Murrumbidgee *101* river of SE Australia
Murska Sobota *520 Ger.* Olsnitz. NE Slovenia
Murua Island *458 var.* Woodlark I. Island of SE Papua New Guinea
Murupara *433* SE North Island, New Zealand
Mururoa Atoll *646 var.* Moruroa. Atoll of French Polynesia
Murzuq *371 var.* Marzūq, Murzuk. W Libya
Murzuq, Ḩammādāt *371* plateau of W Libya
Muş *577* E Turkey
Mūša *376* river of N Lithuania
Musaffah *590* C United Arab Emirates
Musā'id *371* NE Libya
Musala *152 prev.* Stalin Peak. Mountain of W Bulgaria
Musan *349* NE North Korea
Musandam Peninsula *448 Ar.* Ra's Musandam, *var.* Ras Masandam. Peninsular in N Oman
Musay'īd *479 var.* Umm Sa'īd. SE Qatar
Muscat *448 Ar.* Masqaţ. ❖ of Oman, N Oman
Muscat and Oman *see* Oman
Mushin *440* SW Nigeria
Musi *302 prev.* Moesi. River of Sumatra, W Indonesia
Musoma *560* N Tanzania
Mussau Island *458* island of NE Papua New Guinea
Mustafa-Pasha *see* Svilengrad
Mustique *498* island of C St Vincent & the Grenadines
Mustvee *240 Ger.* Tschorna. E Estonia
Mutalau *650* N Niue
Mu-tan-chiang *see* Mudanjiang
Mutare *636 prev.* Umtali. E Zimbabwe
Mutoko *636 prev.* Mtoko. NE Zimbabwe
Mutorashanga *636 prev.* Mtorashanga. N Zimbabwe
Muyaga *162* E Burundi
Muyinga *162 var.* Muhinga. NE Burundi
Muy Muy *436* C Nicaragua
Mŭynoq *610 Rus.* Muynak. NW Uzbekistan
Muyunkum, Peski *338* desert region of S Kazakhstan
Muzaffargarh *451* E Pakistan
Muzarabani *636* N Zimbabwe
Mvuma *636 prev.* Umvuma. C Zimbabwe
Mvurwi *636 prev.* Umvukwes. N Zimbabwe
Mwali *see* Mohéli
Mwanza *560* NW Tanzania
Mwanza *385* N Malawi
Mweka *203* C Congo (Zaire)
Mwenda *635* N Zambia
Mwene-Ditu *203* S Congo (Zaire)

Mwenezi *636* river of S Zimbabwe
Mwenezi *636 prev.* Nuanetsi. S Zimbabwe
Mweru, Lake *203, 635 Fr.* Lac Moero. Lake of Congo (Zaire) and Zambia
Mweru Wantipa, Lake *635* lake of N Zambia
Mwombezhi *635* river of W Zambia
Myanaung *159* SW Burma
Myanmar *see* Burma
Myaungmya *159* SW Burma
Myingyan *159* C Burma
Myitkyina *159* N Burma
Myitnge *159* river of NE Burma
Mykines *644* island of W Faeroe Islands
Mykolayiv *586 Rus.* Nikolayev. S Ukraine
Mýkonos *273* island of SE Greece
Mymensingh *117 prev.* Nasirābād. N Bangladesh
Mýrdalsjökull *294* glacier of S Iceland
Mysore *296 var.* Maisur. S India
My Tho *623* S Vietnam
Mytilíni *273* Lésvos, E Greece
Mývatn *294* lake of C Iceland
Mzimba *385* NW Malawi
Mzuzu *385* N Malawi

N

Naas *314 Ir.* Nás Na Riogh, An Nás. E Ireland
Nabatíyé *364 var.* Nabatiyet et Tahta, An Nabatīyah at Taḩtā. SW Lebanon
Nabavatu *246* Vanua Levu, N Fiji
Naberezhnyye Chelny *484 prev.* Brezhnev. W Russia
Nabeul *573 var.* Nābul. N Tunisia
Nabgha *590* NE United Arab Emirates
Nabih aş Şaliḩ, Jazīrat an *115 var.* Nabih Saleh, Nabīh Salīh. Island of NE Bahrain
Nabī Shu'ayb, Jabal an *627* mountain of W Yemen
Nablus *317, 318 Heb.* Shekhem. N West Bank
Nabouwalu *246* Vanua Levu, N Fiji
Nacala *419* NE Mozambique
Nacaome *288* S Honduras
Na-Chii *see* Nagqu
Nachingwea *560* SE Tanzania
Na Cruacha Dubha *see* Macgillicuddy's Reeks
Nacula *246 prev.* Nathula. Island of the Yasawa Group, NW Fiji
Nadi *246 prev.* Nandi. Viti Levu, W Fiji
Nador *414 prev.* Villa Nador. NE Morocco
Nadur *395* Gozo, Malta
Naduri *246 prev.* Nanduri. Vanua Levu, N Fiji
Nadym *484* N Russia
Næstved *218* Sjælland, SE Denmark
Nafūsah, Jabal *371* mountain range of NW Libya
Naga *466 prev.* Nueva Caceres. Luzon, N Philippines
Nagano *330* Honshū, C Japan
Nagaoka *330* Honshū, N Japan
Nagarote *436* SW Nicaragua
Nagasaki *330* Kyūshū, SW Japan
Nāgercoil *296* S India
Nagorno-Karabakh *110* former autonomous region of SW Azerbaijan
Nagoya *330* Honshū, C Japan
Nāgpur *296* C India
Nagqu *186 Chin.* Na-Ch'ii, *prev.* Hei-ho. Xizang Zizhiqu, W China
Nagua *226* N Dominican Republic
Nagybánya *see* Baia Mare
Nagybecskerek *see* Zrenjanin
Nagykanizsa *290 Ger.* Grosskanizsa. SW Hungary
Nagykőrös *290* C Hungary
Nagymihály *see* Michalovce

Nagysurány *see* Šurany
Nagyszeben *see* Sibiu
Nagyszombat *see* Trnava
Nagytapolcsány *see* Topoľčany
Nagyvárad *see* Oradea
Naha *330* Nansei-shotō, SW Japan
Naḥal Elisha *318* E West Bank
Nahariyya *317* N Israel
Nahiçevan' *see* Naxçivan
Nairai *246* island to the E of Viti Levu, C Fiji
Nairobi *342* ❖ of Kenya, S Kenya
Naitaba *246 prev.* Naitamba. Island of the Lau Group, E Fiji
Naitamba *see* Naitaba
Naivasha *342* SW Kenya
Naivasha, Lake *342* lake of SW Kenya
Najaf *see* An Najaf
Najafābād *307* W Iran
Najd *506 var.* Nejd. Region of C Saudi Arabia
Najin *349* NE North Korea
Najrān *506* S Saudi Arabia
Naju *see* Kumsong
Nakadōri-jima *330* island of Gotō-rettō, SW Japan
Nakamura *330* Shikoku, SW Japan
Nakasongola *584* W Uganda
Nakatsu *330* Kyūshū, SW Japan
Nakatsugawa *330* Honshū, C Japan
Nakfa *238* N Eritrea
Nakhichevan' *see* Naxcivan
Nakhodka *485* SE Russia
Nakhon Pathom *563* C Thailand
Nakhon Phanom *563* NE Thailand
Nakhon Ratchasima *563 var.* Korat. E Thailand
Nakhon Sawan *563 var.* Muang Nakhon Sawan. W Thailand
Nakhon Si Thammarat *563* S Thailand
Nakskov *218* Lolland, S Denmark
Naktong *350 var.* Nakdong, *Jap.* Rakutō-kō. River of South Korea
Nakuru *342* W Kenya
Nāl *451* river of W Pakistan
Nalayh *412* C Mongolia
Nal'chik *484* SW Russia
Nālūt *371* NW Libya
Nam *349* river of C North Korea
Nam *350* river of S South Korea
Namaacha *419* S Mozambique
Namacurra *419* E Mozambique
Namak, Daryācheh-ye *307* lake of W Iran
Namak, Kavīr-e *307* desert region of NE Iran
Namanga *342* S Kenya
Namangan *610* E Uzbekistan
Namatanai *458* New Ireland, Papua New Guinea
Nam Đinh *623* N Vietnam
Namen *see* Namur
Namhae-do *350 Jap.* Nankai-tō. Island of S South Korea
Namib Desert *423* coastal desert region of W Namibia
Namibe *88 Port.* Moçâmedes, *var.* Mossâmedes. SW Angola
Namibia *422-423* officially The Republic of Namibia, *prev.* South-West Africa, German Southwest Africa. Country of Southern Africa divided into 13 admin. units (districts). ❖ Windhoek
Namoluk *406* island of SE Micronesia
Namonuito *406* atoll of NW Micronesia
Namorik *396* island of S Marshall Islands
Nampa *598* Idaho, NW USA
Namp'o *349* SW North Korea
Nampula *419* NE Mozambique
Namsos *444* C Norway
Namu *396* island of C Marshall Islands
Namuka-i-lau *246* island of the Lau Group, E Fiji
Namunukula *534* SE Sri Lanka
Namur *127 Dut.* Namen. SE Belgium
Namutoni *423* N Namibia
Namwŏn *350 Jap.* Nangen. S South Korea

Namyit Island *652* island of S Spratly Islands
Nan *563* var. Muang Nan. N Thailand
Nanaimo *170* Vancouver Island, SW Canada
Nanao *330* Honshū, C Japan
Nanchang *187* Jiangxi, SE China
Nan-ching *see* Nanjing
Nancy *253* NE France
Nanda Devi *296* mountain of N India
Nandaime *436* S Nicaragua
Nandi *see* Nadi
Nanduri *see* Naduri
Nanga Eboko *168* C Cameroon
Nangbéto, Retenue de *567* reservoir of C Togo
Nangen *see* Namwŏn
Nan Hai *see* East China Sea and South China Sea
Nanhsi *555* SW Taiwan
Nanjing *187* var. Nanking, Nan-ching. Jiangsu, E China
Nankai-tō *see* Namhae-do
Nanning *187* prev. Yung-ning. Guangxi, S China
Nanortalik *646* S Greenland
Nansei-shotō *330* island group to the SW of Kyūshū, SW Japan
Nanshan Island *652* island of E Spratly Islands
Nansio *560* NW Tanzania
Nanterre *253* N France
Nantes *252* W France
Nanthi Kadal Lagoon *534* lagoon of N Sri Lanka
Nant'ou *555* W Taiwan
Nanuku Passage *246* channel of the Pacific Ocean between the Lau Group and Taveuni, NE Fiji
Nanumaga *583* prev. Nanumanga. Coral atoll of NW Tuvalu
Nanumea *583* coral atoll of NW Tuvalu
Nan Wan *555* bay of the South China Sea, S Taiwan
Nanyang *187* Henan, C China
Nanyuki *342* C Kenya
Naogaon *117* NW Bangladesh
Napier *433* SE North Island, New Zealand
Naples *see* Napoli
Napo *228, 463* river of Ecuador and Peru
Napoli *321* Eng. Naples, Ger. Neapel. S Italy
Nāra *451* irrigation canal of S Pakistan
Nara *330* Honshū, C Japan
Narathiwat *563* SW Thailand
Narayani *427* river of C Nepal
Narbada *see* Narmada
Narbonne *253* S France
Nare's Strait *646* strait of NW Greenland
Narew *471* river of E Poland
Narganá *456* NE Panama
Narikrik *396* prev. Knox Atoll. Atoll of SE Marshall Islands
Narmada *296* var. Narbada. River of C India
Narok *342* SW Kenya
Närpes *249* Swe. Närpiö. SW Finland
Narrows, The *494* channel connecting the Atlantic Ocean and Caribbean Sea, between Nevis and St Kitts
Narsaq Kujalleq *646* Dan. Frederiksdal. S Greenland
Narsingdi *117* C Bangladesh
Nartës, Gjol i *see* Nartës, Liqeni i
Nartës, Liqeni i *81* var. Gjol i Nartës. Lake of SW Albania
Naruto *330* Shikoku, SW Japan
Narva *240* prev. Narova. River of Estonia and Russia
Narva *240* NE Estonia
Narva Bay *240* Est. Narva Laht, Rus. Narviskiy Zaliv. Bay of the Gulf of Finland
Narva Reservoir *240* Est. Narva Veehoidla. Reservoir of Estonia and Russia
Narvik *444* NE Norway
Nar'yan-Mar *484* prev. Dzerzhinskiy, prev. Beloshchel'ye. NW Russia
Naryn *357* E Kyrgyzstan

Naryn *357* river of Kyrgyzstan and Uzbekistan
Nasau *246* Koro, C Fiji
Nāshik *296* prev. Nāsik. W India
Nasho, Lac *492* lake of E Rwanda
Nashville *599* Tennessee, SE USA
Näsijärvi *249* lake of SW Finland
Nasirābād *see* Mymensingh
Nâsir, Buheiret *230* var. Buḥayrat Nâṣir, Eng. Lake Nser. Lake of Egypt and Sudan
Nasiriya *see* An Nāṣirīyah
Nás Na Riogh *see* Naas
Nassau *112* ❖ of Bahamas, New Providence, Bahamas
Nassau *644* island of Northern Cook Islands, N Cook Islands
Nasser, Lake *see* Nâsir, Buheiret
Nata *142* N Botswana
Natal *145* E Brazil
Nathula *see* Nacula
Natitingou *132* NW Benin
Natl *336* var. Nitil. NW Jordan
Nator *117* W Bangladesh
Natron, Lake *560* lake of Kenya and Tanzania
Natuna Besar, Pulau *302* island of Kepulauan Natuna, W Indonesia
Natuna, Kepulauan *302* island group to the NW of Borneo, W Indonesia
Nau *see* Nov
Naujoji Akmenė *376* NW Lithuania
Nā'ūr *336* NW Jordan
Nauru *424-425* officially The Republic of Nauru, prev. Pleasant Island. Island country of the Pacific Ocean divided into 14 admin. units (districts)
Naushahra *see* Nowshera
Nausori *246* Viti Levu, Fiji
Navabad *see* Navobod
Navaga *246* W Koro, W Fiji
Navahrudak *122* Rus. Novogrudok, Pol. Nowogródek. W Belarus
Navangar *see* Jāmnagar
Navapolatsk *122* Rus. Novopolotsk. N Belarus
Navarra *531* autonomous community of N Spain
Naviti *246* island of the Yasawa Group, NW Fiji
Navoalevu *246* NE Vanua Levu, N Fiji
Navobod *558* Rus. Navabad. W Tajikistan
Navoi *see* Nawoiy
Navua *246* Viti Levu, W Fiji
Nawābganj *117* NW Bangladesh
Nawābshāh *451* S Pakistan
Nawmah, Ra's *115* var. Ra's Noma. Cape of SW Bahrain
Nawoiy *610* Rus. Navoi. S Uzbekistan
Naxçivan *110* Rus. Nakhichevan', var. Nahičevan'. SW Azerbaijan
Náxos *273* island of SE Greece
Nayau *246* island of the Lau Group, E Fiji
Nazareth *see* Naẓerat
Nazca *463* S Peru
Naze *330* Nansei-shotō, SW Japan
Naẓerat *317* Eng. Nazareth. N Israel
Naẓerat 'Illit *317* N Israel
Nazilli *576* SW Turkey
Nazran' *484* SW Russia
Nazrēt *243* var. Adama, Hadama. C Ethiopia
Nazwá *448* N Oman
Nchelenge *635* N Zambia
Ncheu *see* Ntcheu
Nchisi *see* Ntchisi
Ncue *236* N Río Muni, EquatorialGuinea
Ndaghamcha, Sebkra de *see* Te-n-Dghâmcha, Sebkhet
N'Dalatando *88* Port. Vila Salazar. NW Angola
Ndali *132* C Benin
Ndélé *179* N Central African Republic
Ndendé *258* S Gabon
Ndeni *see* Nendö
Ndindi *258* S Gabon
N'Djamena *180* var. Njamena, prev. Fort-Lamy. ❖ of Chad, W Chad
Ndjolé *258* C Gabon
Ndoki *200* river of N Congo
Ndola *635* C Zambia

Ndora *162* NW Burundi
Ndréméani *198* S Mohéli, Comoros
Ndrhamcha, Sebkha de *see* Te-n-Dghâmcha, Sebkhet
Nduindui *522* S Guadalcanal, Solomon Is
Nduke *see* Kolombangara
Neagh, Lough *593* lake of Northern Ireland, UK
Neapel *see* Napoli
Nébeck *see* An Nabk
Nebitdag *581* W Turkmenistan
Nebk *see* An Nabk
Neblina, Pico da *144* mountain of NW Brazil
Nebraska *599* state of C USA
Neckar *264* river of SW Germany
Necochea *95* E Argentina
Nederland *see* Netherlands
Neder-Rijn *429* Eng. Lower Rhine. River of C Netherlands
Nefasit *238* C Eritrea
Nefta *573* var. Naftah. W Tunisia
Neftezavodsk *see* Seydi
Negara Brunei Darussalam *see* Brunei
Negêlë *243* var. Negelli, It. Neghelli. S Ethiopia
Negev *see* HaNegev
Neghelli *see* Negêlë
Negomane *419* var. Negomano. N Mozambique
Negombo *534* SW Sri Lanka
Negotino *381* C FYR Macedonia
Negril *329* W Jamaica
Negro, Rio *144, 195* river of N South America
Negro, Río *see* Sico
Negro, Río *607* river of Brazil and Uruguay
Negro, Río *see* Chixoy
Negros *466* island of C Philippines
Neiafu *568* Uta Vava'u, Vava'u Group, Tonga
Neiba *226* SW Dominican Republic
Neiges, Piton des *652* mountain of C Réunion
Neily *206* SE Costa Rica
Nei Mongol Zizhiqu *187* Eng. Inner Mongolian Autonomous Region, prev. Nei Monggol Zizhiqu. Autonomous region of N China
Neiva *195* W Colombia
Nek'emtē *243* var. Nakamti, Lakamti, Lekemti. W Ethiopia
Nelson *170* river of C Canada
Nelson *433* S South Island, New Zealand
Nelson Island *643* island of N British Indian Ocean Territory
Nelspruit *527* Eastern Transvaal, NE South Africa
Néma *398* SE Mauritania
Neman *122, 376* Bel. Nyoman, Lith. Nemunas, Ger. Memel, Pol. Niemen. River of NE Europe
Německý Brod *see* Havlíčkův Brod
Nemunas *see* Neman
Nenagh *314* S Ireland
Nendeln *374* C Liechtenstein
Nendö *522* var. Ndeni. Santa Cruz Is, Solomon Islands
Nepal *426-427* officially Kingdom of Nepal. Country of Asia divided into 5 admin. units (regions). ❖ kathmandu
Nepalganj *427* W Nepal
Nepean Island *650* island of C Norfolk Island
Neretva *140* river of S Bosnia & Herzegovina
Neris *376* Bel. Viliya, Pol. Wilja. River of Belarus and Lithuania
Neskaupstadhur *294* E Iceland
Ness, Loch *593* lake of N Scotland, UK
Néstos *152, 273* Turk. Kara Su, Bul. Mesta. River of Bulgaria and Greece
Netanya *317* C Israel
Netherlands *430-431* officially Kingdom of the Netherlands, var. Holland, Dut. Nederland. Country of W Europe divided into 12 admin. units (provinces). ❖ Amsterdam, The Hague

Netherlands Antilles *619, 650* prev. Dutch West Indies. Autonomous part of the Netherlands, Caribbean Sea. ❖ Willemstad
Netherlands East Indies *see* Indonesia
Netrakona *117* N Bangladesh
Netze *see* Noteć
Neubrandenburg *265* NE Germany
Neuchâtel *546* Ger. Neuenburg. W Switzerland
Neuchâtel, Lac de *546* Ger. Neuenburger See. Lake of W Switzerland
Neuenburger See *see* Neuchâtel, Lac de
Neugradiska *see* Nova Gradiška
Neuhäusl *see* Nové Zámky
Neumarkt *see* Târgu Mures
Neumarktl *see* Tržič
Neumünster *265* N Germany
Neunkirchen *106* E Austria
Neuquén *95* SE Argentina
Neusatz *see* Novi Sad
Neusiedler See *106, 290* Hung. Fertő-tó. Lake of Austria and Hungary
Neusohl *see* Banská Bystrica
Neustadt *see* Baia Mare
Neustadtl *see* Novo Mesto
Neutra *see* Nitra
Neu-Ulm *265* S Germany
Nevada *598* state of W USA
Nevers *253* C France
Nevis *494* island of the Lesser Antilles which, with St Kitts, forms the independent state of St Kitts & Nevis
Nevis Peak *494* mountain peak of C Nevis, St Kitts & Nevis
Nevşehir *577* C Turkey
Newala *560* SE Tanzania
New Amsterdam *284* E Guyana
New Britain *458* island of E Papua New Guinea
New Brunswick *171* province of SE Canada
New Bussa *440* W Nigeria
New Caledonia *650* French overseas territory of the Pacific Ocean ❖ Nouméa
Newcastle *101* E Australia
Newcastle *494* N Nevis, St Kitts & Nevis
Newcastle upon Tyne *593* NE England, UK
New Delhi *296* ❖ of India, N India
Newfield *92* SE Antigua, Antigua & Barbuda
Newfoundland *171* Fr. Terre-Neuve. Island of S E Canada
Newfoundland *171* province of E Canada
New Georgia *522* island of the New Georgia Is, W Solomon Is
New Georgia Islands *522* island group of W Solomon Is
New Guinea *303, 458* Dut. Nieuw Guinea, Ind. Irian. Large island of W Pacific Ocean, divided administratively into the Indonesian state of Irian Jaya and the independent country of Papua New Guinea
New Halfa *see* Halfa el Gadida
New Hampshire *599* state of NE USA
New Haven *599* Connecticut, NE USA
New Hebrides *see* Vanuatu
New Ireland *458* island of NE Papua New Guinea
New Jersey *599* state of E USA
Newman *100* W Australia
New Mexico *598-599* state of SW USA
New Mirpur *451* prev. Mīrpur. NE Pakistan
New Orleans *599* Louisiana, SC USA
New Plymouth *433* SW North Island, New Zealand
Newport *593* S Wales, UK
Newport News *599* Virginia, E USA
New Providence *112* island of C Bahamas
New River *284* river of SE Guyana

Ogooué *200, 258* river of Congo and Gabon
Ogou *567* river of E Togo
Ogražden *381* mountain range of Bulgaria and FYR Macedonia
Ogre *362 Ger.* Oger. C Latvia
Ogulin *209* N Croatia
Ohau, Lake *433* W South Island, New Zealand
Ohio *599* river of NC USA
Ohio *599* state of NE USA
Ohobela *366* N Lesotho
'Ohonua *568* 'Eua, Tongatapu Group, Tonga
Ohře *216 Ger.* Eger. River of Czech Republic and Germany
Ohrid *381 var.* Ochrida. SW FYR Macedonia
Ohrid, Lake *81, 381 var.* Lake Ochrida, *Alb.* Liqeni i Ohrit, *Maced.* Ohridsko Ezero. Lake of Albania and Macedonia
Oiapoque *145, 645 var.* l'Oyapok. River of Brazil and French Guiana
Oil Islands *see* Chagos Archipelago
Oise *253* river of N France
Oistins *121* S Barbados
Ōita *330 Kyūshū,* SW Japan
Ojos del Salado, Nevado *183* mountain of N Chile
Okahandja *423* C Namibia
Okakarara *423* N Namibia
Ókanizsa *see* Kanjiža
Okāra *451* E Pakistan
Okarem *581 Turkm.* Ekerem. W Turkmenistan
Okavango *see* Cubango
Okavango Delta *142* large wetland area of N Botswana
Okaya *330 Honshū,* C Japan
Okayama *330 Honshū,* W Japan
Okazaki *330 Honshū,* C Japan
Okeechobee, Lake *599* lake of Florida, SE USA
Okhotsk, Sea of *485 Rus.* Okhotskoye More. Sea of Pacific Ocean, bordering E Russia
Oki *330* island to the N of Honshū, W Japan
Okinawa-shotō *330* island group of Nansei-shotō, SW Japan
Oklahoma *599* state of SC USA
Oklahoma City *599* Oklahoma, SC USA
Okondja *258* E Gabon
Okovanggo *see* Cubango
Okoyo *200* W Congo
Okpara *132* river of Benin and Nigeria
Oktemberyan *see* Hoktemberyan
Oktyabr'skoy Revolyutsii, Ostrov *485 Eng.* October Revolution Island. Island of Severnaya Zemlya, N Russia
Okushiri-tō *330* island to the W of Hokkaidō, N Japan
Ólafsfjördhur *294* N Iceland
Ólafsvík *294* W Iceland
Olaine *362* S Latvia
Olanchito *288* C Honduras
Öland *543* island of S Sweden
Olavarría *95* E Argentina
Olbia *320* Sardegna, W Italy
Oldenburg *264* NW Germany
Old Fort Point *649* headland on the S coast of Montserrat
Old Harbour *329* S Jamaica
Old Road *92* SW Antigua, Antigua & Barbuda
Old Road Town *494* W St Kitts, St Kitts & Nevis
Olëkminsk *485* C Russia
Oleksandriya *586 Rus.* Aleksandriya. C Ukraine
Olenëk *485 var.* Olenyok. N Russia
Oléron, Île d' *252* island of W France
Ölgiy *412* W Mongolia
Olhão *474* S Portugal
Olimarao *406* atoll of C Micronesia
Olimar Grande *607 var.* Olimar. River of E Uruguay
Ólimbos *see* Ólympos
Olinda *145* E Brazil
Olita *see* Alytus

Olmaliq *610 Rus.* Almalyk. E Uzbekistan
Olmütz *see* Olomouc
Olocuilta *235* SW El Salvador
Oloitokitok *342 var.* Laitokitok. S Kenya
Olomouc *216 Ger.* Olmütz. SE Czech Republic
Olongapo *466* Luzon, N Philippines
Olosega *642* island of Manua Islands, E American Samoa
Olsnitz *see* Murska Sobota
Olsztyn *471 Ger.* Allenstein. N Poland
Olt *480 Ger.* Alt. River of S Romania
Olten *546* NW Switzerland
O-luan Pi *555 var.* Cape Olwanpi. Cape on the S coast of Taiwan
O-luan-pi *555* S Taiwan
Olympia *598* Washington, NW USA
Ólympos *273 Eng.* Mount Olympus, *prev.* Ólimbos. Mountain of N Greece
Olympus, Mount *215 var.* Troodos, Olympos. Mountain of C Cyprus
Olympus, Mount *see* Ólympos
Omagh *593* Northern Ireland, UK
Omaha *599* Nebraska, C USA
Oman *448-449* officially Sultanate of Oman, *prev.* Muscat & Oman. Country of SW Asia divided into 3 admin. units (governorates). ❖ Muscat
Oman, Gulf of *307, 448, 590 Ar.* Khalīj 'Umān. Gulf of the Arabian Sea
Omaruru *423* C Namibia
Omba *see* Aoba
Omboué *258* W Gabon
Omdurman *536 var.* Umm Durmān. C Sudan
Ometepe, Isla de *436* island on Lago de Nicaragua, S Nicaragua
Om Hajer *238* SW Eritrea
Ōmiya *330* Honshū, SE Japan
Omo Wenz *243* river of SW Ethiopia
Omsk *484* C Russia
Ōmuta *330* Kyūshū, SW Japan
Ondangwa *423 var.* Ondangua. N Namibia
Ondava *519* river of NE Slovakia
Ondjiva *see* N'Giva
Ondo *440* SW Nigeria
Öndörhaan *412* E Mongolia
One and Half Degree Channel *390* channel of the Indian Ocean, S Maldives
Oneata *246* island of the Lau Group, E Fiji
Onega, Lake *see* Onezhskoye Ozero
Onezhskoye Ozero *484 Eng.* Lake Onega. Lake of NW Russia
Onga *258* E Gabon
Ongjin *349* SW North Korea
Oni *262* N Georgia
Onilahy *382* river of SW Madagascar
Onitsha *440* S Nigeria
Ono *246* island to the S of Viti Levu, SW Fiji
Ono-i-lau *246* island to the S of the Lau Group, SW Fiji
Onomichi *330* Honshū, W Japan
Ononte *see* Orantes
Onotoa *346* island of the Gilbert Is, W Kiribati
Onslow *100* W Australia
Onsŏng *349* NE North Korea
Ontario *170 -171* province of S Canada
Ontario, Lake *171, 599* lake of Canada and USA
Ontong Java Atoll *522 prev.* Lord Howe Island. Atoll of N Solomon Is
Onverwacht *538* N Suriname
Ooma *346* Banaba, W Kiribati
Oos-Londen *see* East London
Oostende *127 Fr.* Ostende, *Eng.* Ostend. NW Belgium
Oosterhout *429* SW Netherlands
Oosterschelde *429 Eng.* Eastern Scheldt. Inlet of the North Sea, on the coast of SW Netherlands
Opava *216 Ger.* Troppau. E Czech Republic
Opole *471 Ger.* Oppeln. SW Poland
Oporto *see* Porto

Oppdal *444* S Norway
Oppeln *see* Opole
Opuwo *423* NW Namibia
Oqtosh *610 Rus.* Aktash. S Uzbekistan
Oradea *480 prev.* Oradea Mare, *Ger.* Grosswardein, *Hung.* Nagyvárad. NW Romania
Oral *see* Ural'sk
Oran *83 var.* Ouahran, Wahran. NW Algeria
Orange *101* SE Australia
Orange Free State *see* Free State
Orange Mouth *see* Oranjemund
Orangemund *see* Oranjemund
Orange River *366, 423, 527 Afr.* Oranjerivier. River of southern Africa
Orange Walk *130* N Belize
Orango, Ilha de *282* island of Arquipélago dos Bijagós, SW Guinea-Bissau
Orangozinho, Ilha de *282* island of SW Guinea-Bissau
Oranjemund *423 var.* Orangemund, *Eng.* Orange Mouth. S Namibia
Oranjestad *650* St Eustatius, N Netherlands Antilles
Oranjestad *642* ❖ of Aruba, W Aruba
Orantes *364, 551 var.* Ononte, Orontes, *Ar.* Nahr al 'Āşī, *var.* Nahr al 'Āsī Oronte, Nr el Aassi. River of SW Asia
Orany *see* Varėna
Orapa *142* C Botswana
Orcadas *90* Argentinian research station of Greater Antarctica, Antarctica
Orchid Island *see* Lan Yü
Orchila, Isla le *619* island of N Venezuela
Ordino *86* NW Andorra
Ordu *577* N Turkey
Ordubad *110* SW Azerbaijan
Ordzhonikidze *see* Yenakiyeve
Ordzhonikidze *see* Vladikavkaz
Ordzhonikidzeabad *see* Kofarnihon
Orealla *284* E Guyana
Örebro *543* S Sweden
Oregon *598* state of NW USA
Orël *484* W Russia
Orem *598* Utah, SW USA
Orenburg *484 prev.* Chkalov. W Russia
Orense *see* Ourense
Orestiáda *273 prev.* Orestiás. NE Greece
Öresund *see* Sound, The
Øresund *see* Sound, The
Oreti *433* river of S South Island, New Zealand
Orgeyev *see* Orhei
Orhei *408 var.* Orheiu, *Rus.* Orgeyev. N Moldova
Orhon Gol *412* river of N Mongolia
Oriental, Cordillera *136* range of the Andes of C Bolivia
Oriental, Cordillera *195* range of the Andes of C Colombia
Oriental, Cordillera *463* range of the Andes of C Peru
Orikum *81 var.* Oriku. SW Albania
Orinoco *195, 619* river of Colombia and Venezuela
Oristano *320* Sardegna, W Italy
Orizaba, Volcán Pico de *403 var.* Citlaltépetl. Mountain of SE Mexico
Orkhanie *see* Botevgrad
Orkney *593* islands of NE UK
Orlau *see* Orlová
Orléanais *253* cultural region of N France
Orléans *253* N France
Orléansville *see* Chlef
Orlová *216 Ger.* Orlau, *Pol.* Orlowa. SE Czech Republic
Ormoc *466 var.* MacArthur. Leyte, E Philippines
Ormsö *see* Vormsi
Ormuz, Strait of *see* Hormuz, Strait of
Örnsköldsvik *543* NE Sweden
Oro *349* E North Korea
Orodara *157* SW Burkina
Orol Dengizi *see* Aral Sea
Oroluk *406* atoll of C Micronesia
Oron *440* S Nigeria
Orona *346 var.* Hull I. Island of the Phoenix Is, C Kiribati

Oronoque *284* river of SE Guyana
Orontes *see* Orantes
Orosháza *290* SE Hungary
Orotina *206* W Costa Rica
Orsha *122* NE Belarus
Orsk *484* C Russia
Ørsta *444* SW Norway
Ortoire *570* river of S Trinidad, Trinidad & Tobago
Orto-Tokoy *357 var.* Orto Tokoj. N Kyrgyzstan
Orūmīyeh *307 prev.* Rezāīyeh, Urmia. NW Iran
Orūmīyeh, Daryācheh-ye *307 prev.* Daryācheh-ye Rezā'īyeh, *Eng.* Lake Urmia. Lake of NW Iran
Oruro *136* W Bolivia
Orvieto *321* C Italy
Oryakhovo *152 var.* Orjahovo. NW Bulgaria
Oryokko *see* Yalu
Ōsaka *330, 335* Honshū, C Japan
Osa, Península de *206* peninsula of S Costa Rica
Ösel *see* Saaremaa
Osh *357 var.* Oš. SW Kyrgyzstan
Oshakati *423* N Namibia
Oshawa *171* SE Canada
Oshikango *423* N Namibia
Oshogbo *440* W Nigeria
Osijek *209 Hung.* Eszék, *Ger.* Esseg. NE Croatia
Osipenko *see* Berdyans'k
Osipovichi *see* Asipovichy
Öskemen *see* Ust'-Kamenogorsk
Ösling *378* physical region of N Luxembourg
Oslo *444 prev.* Christiania. ❖ of Norway, S Norway
Oslofjorden *444* fjord of S Norway
Osmaniye *577* S Turkey
Osnabrück *264* NW Germany
Osogovski Planini *381 var.* Osogovske Planine. Mountain range of Bulgaria and FYR Macedonia
Oss *429* S Netherlands
Ossa, Serra de *474* mountain range of SE Portugal
Ostee *see* Baltic Sea
Ostend *see* Oostende
Ostende *see* Oostende
Österbotten *see* Pohjanmaa
Östermyra *see* Seinäjoki
Österreich *see* Austria
Östersund *543* C Sweden
Ostfriesische Inseln *264 Eng.* East Frisian Islands. Island group of NW Germany
Ostrava *216 Ger.* Mährisch-Ostrau, *prev.* Moravská Ostrava. E Czech Republic
Ostrobothnia *see* Pohjanmaa
Ostrov *216* NW Czech Republic
Ostrowiec Świętokrzyski *471* E Poland
Ostyako-Voguls'k *see* Khanty-Mansiysk
Ōsumi-shotō *330* island group of Nansei-shotō, SW Japan
Osumit *81 var.* Osum. River of SE Albania
Otago Peninsula *433* peninsula of SE South Island, New Zealand
Otaru *330* Hokkaidō, N Japan
Otavalo *228* N Ecuador
Otavi *423* N Namibia
Otepää *240 Ger.* Odenpäh. SE Estonia
Oti *132, 270, 567* river of W Africa
Otjinene *423* NE Namibia
Otjiwarongo *423* N Namibia
Otra *444* river of SW Norway
Otranto, Strait of *81, 321 It.* Canale d'Otranto. Strait connecting the Adriatic Sea and Ionian Sea, between Albania and Italy
Otrokovice *216* SE Czech Republic
Ōtsu *330* Honshū, C Japan
Ottawa *171* ❖ of Canada, SE Canada
Ottawa *170 Fr.* Outaouais. River of SE Canada
Otterup *218* Fyn, C Denmark

Phetchaburi *563 var.* Phet Buri.
C Thailand
Philadelphia *599* Pennsylvania,
NE USA
Philip Island *650* island of S Norfolk
Island
Philippeville *see* Skikda
Philippines *466-469* officially Republic
of the Philippines. Country of SE Asia
divided into 14 admin. units
(regions). ❖ Manila
Philippine Sea *406, 466* sea of the
Pacific Ocean to the E of the
Philippines
Philipsburg *650* St Martin,
N Netherlands Antilles
Phillips *494* NE St Kitts, St Kitts
& Nevis
Phitsanulok *563 var.* Muang
Phitsanulok. N Thailand
Phlórina *see* Flórina
Phnom Penh *165 Cam.* Phnum Pénh.
❖ of Cambodia, S Cambodia
Phnum Aôral *165 var.* Phnom Aural.
Mountain of W Cambodia
Phoenix *598* Arizona, SW USA
Phoenix *400* C Mauritius
Phoenix Island *see* Rawaki
Phoenix Islands *346* island group of
C Kiribati
Phôngsali *359 var.* Phong Saly. N Laos
Phong Saly *see* Phôngsali
Phou Bia *359 var.* Pou Bia. Mountain
of C Laos
Phrae *563 var.* Muang Phrae.
N Thailand
Phra Nakhon Si Ayutthaya
see Ayutthaya
Phu Cuong *see* Thu Dâu Môt
Phuket *563 Mal.* Ujung Salang.
S Thailand
Phuket, Ko *563* island of S Thailand
Phumĭ Chhlong *165* S Cambodia
Phumĭ Chhuk *165* S Cambodia
Phumĭ Chŏăm *165* SW Cambodia
Phumĭ Kâmpóng Trâbêk *165*
prev. Phum Kompong Trabek.
C Cambodia
Phumĭ Koŭk Kdoŭch *165*
NW Cambodia
Phumĭ Krêk *165* SE Cambodia
Phumĭ Labăng Siêk *165* NE Cambodia
Phumĭ Mlu Prey *165* N Cambodia
Phumĭ Sâmraông *165 var.* Phumĭ
Sâmroŭng, *prev.* Phum Samrong.
NW Cambodia
Phumĭ Spoe Tbong *165* C Cambodia
Phumĭ Thmâ Pôk *165* NW Cambodia
Phumĭ Véal Rénh *165* SW Cambodia
Phuntsholing *134* SW Bhutan
Phu Quôc, Đao *623* island of
SW Vietnam
Piacenza *320 Fr.* Paisance. N Italy
Piatra-Neamţ *480* NE Romania
Piave *321* river of N Italy
Piaye *497* S St Lucia
Pibor *243* river of Ethiopia and Sudan
Picardie *253 Eng.* Picardy. Cultural
region of N France
Pichelin *224* S Dominica
Pico *474 var.* Ilha do Pico. Island of the
Azores, Portugal
Picton, Isla *183* island of S Chile
Pidjani *198* SE Grande Comore,
Comoros
Pidurutalagala *534* mountain of
S Sri Lanka
Piedras *463* river of E Peru
Pielinen *249 var.* Pielisjärvi. Lake of
E Finland
Pierre *599* South Dakota, NC USA
Piešťany *519 Ger.* Pistyan,
Hung. Pöstyén. W Slovakia
Pietermaritzburg *527* Kwazulu Natal,
E South Africa
Pietersaari *see* Jakobstad
Pietersburg *527* Northern Transvaal,
NE South Africa
Piet Retief *527* Eastern Transvaal,
E South Africa
Piggs Peak *540* NW Swaziland
Pigs, Bay of *210* bay of the
Caribbean Sea, on southern
coast of C Cuba

Pihkva Järv *see* Pskov, Lake
Pikelot *406* island of C Micronesia
Pikine *510* W Senegal
Pikounda *200* C Congo
Piła *471 Ger.* Schneidemühl.
NW Poland
Pilar *460 var.* Villa del Pilar.
S Paraguay
Pilas Group *466* island group of Sulu
Archipelago, SW Philippines
Pilcomayo *95, 136, 460* river of
C South America
Pilgrimkondre *538* NE Suriname
Pilis *290 var.* Philis. Mountain range of
N Hungary
Pillories, The *498* islands of
C St Vincent & the Grenadines
Pillsbury Sound *653* strait of the
Caribbean Sea, C Virgin Islands
Pilsen *see* Plzeň
Pimpri *296* W India
Pinang *see* George Town
Pinang, Pulau *386 prev.* Prince of
Wales Island. Island of NW
Peninsular Malaysia
Pinar del Río *210* W Cuba
Píndos *273 prev.* Píndhos, *Eng.* Pindus
Mountains, *var.* Píndhos Óros.
Mountain range of C Greece
Pine Bluff *599* Arkansas, SC USA
Pineiós *273 prev.* Piniós. River of
C Greece
Pines, Isle of *see* Juventud, Isla de la
Pinetown *527* Kwazulu Natal, E South
Africa
P'ingchen *555 Jap.* Heichin. N Taiwan
Pingelap *406* atoll of E Micronesia
P'ingtung *555 Jap.* Heitō. SW Taiwan
Pinkiang *see* Harbin
Pinos, Isla de *see* Juventud, Isla de la
Pins, Île des *650 var.* Kunyé. Island of
S New Caledonia
Pinsk *122 Pol.* Pińsk. SW Belarus
Pinta, Isla *228* island of N Galapagos
Is, Ecuador
Piracicaba *145* S Brazil
Pirada *282* NE Guinea-Bissau
Piran *520 It.* Pirano. SW Slovenia
Piriápolis *607* S Uruguay
Pirita *240* river of N Estonia
Pirna *265* E Germany
Pirojpur *117* SW Bangladesh
Pirot *630* SE Serbia, Yugoslavia
Pisa *320* N Italy
Pisco *463* SW Peru
Písek *216* SW Czech Republic
Pishchek *see* Bishkek
Pissila *157* C Burkina
Pistoia *320* N Italy
Pistyan *see* Piešťany
Pita *281* NW Guinea
Pitalito *195* SW Colombia
Pitcairn Island *651* island of S Pitcairn
Islands
Pitcairn Islands *651* British dependent
territory of the Pacific Ocean.
❖ Adamstown
Pitche *282* E Guinea-Bissau
Piteå *543* NE Sweden
Piteşti *480* S Romania
Pitseng *366* N Lesotho
Pitt Island *433* island of Chatham
Islands, New Zealand
Pittsburgh *599* Pennsylvania, NE USA
Pitt Strait *433* strait of Pacific Ocean,
between Chatham Island and Pitt
Island, New Zealand
Pituffik *646 prev.* Dundas. NW
Greenland
Piura *463* NW Peru
Piva *381 var.* Diva. River of
C Montenegro, Yugoslavia
Pivdennyy Buh *586 Rus.* Yuzhnyy Bug.
River of W and S Ukraine
Pivsko Jezero *630* lake of
NW Montenegro, Yugoslavia
Pjandž *see* Pyandzh
Placetas *210* C Cuba
Plačkovica *381* mountain range of
E FYR Macedonia
Plaisance *286* N Haiti
Plakenska Planina *381* mountain
range of SW FYR Macedonia

Plana Cays *112* islets of S Bahamas
Planken *374* C Liechtenstein
Plasencia *531* W Spain
Plate, Île *see* Flat Island
Platte *598-599* river of C USA
Platte, Île *512* Island of E Seychelles
Plattensee *see* Balaton
Plauer See *265* lake of NE Germany
Plây Cu *623 var.* Pleiku. S Vietnam
Pleasant Island *see* Nauru
Pleebo *see* Plibo
Pleiku *see* Plây Cu
Plenty, Bay of *433* inlet of the Pacific
Ocean, on the coast of NE North
Island, New Zealand
Pleskau *see* Pskov
Pleven *152 prev.* Plevna. N Bulgaria
Plezzo *see* Bovec
Plibo *368 var.* Pleebo. SE Liberia
Pljevlja *630 prev.* Plevlje. W Serbia,
Yugoslavia
Płock *471* C Poland
Plöcken *106 It.* Passo di Monte Croce
Carnico, *var.* Plöcken Pass,
Ger. Plöckenpass. Mountain pass of
SW Austria
Pločno *140* mountain of SW Bosnia &
Herzegovina
Ploieşti *480 prev.* Ploeşti. SE Romania
Plovdiv *152 prev.* Philippopolis, *anc.*
Eumolpias, *prev.* Eumolpias. SW Bulgaria
Plumtree *636* SW Zimbabwe
Plungė *376* NW Lithuania
Plyeshchanitsy *122* N Belarus
Plymouth *649* ❖ of Montserrat,
SW Montserrat
Plymouth *593* SW England, UK
Plymouth *570* SW Tobago, Trinidad
& Tobago
Plzeň *216 Ger.* Pilsen. W Czech
Republic
Po *321* river of N Italy
Pô *157* S Burkina
Poabil *368* E Liberia
Pobè *132 var.* Pobé. S Benin
Pobedy, Pik *357 var.* Pobeda Peak,
Chin. Tomur Feng. Mountain of
China and Kyrgyzstan
Pocatello *598* Idaho, NW USA
Pocrí *456* S Panama
Podgorica *630 prev.* Titograd.
S Montenegro, Yugoslavia
Podil's'ka Vysochyna *586* mountain
range of SW Ukraine
Podkamennaya Tunguska *485 Eng.*
Stony Tunguska. River of C Russia
Podravska Slatina *209 prev.* Slatina,
Hung. Szlatina. NE Croatia
Poeketi *538* E Suriname
Pogradec *81 var.* Pogradeci.
SE Albania
P'ohang *350 Jap.* Hokō. E South Korea
Pohjanlahti *see* Bothnia, Gulf of
Pohjanmaa *249 Swe.* Österbotten,
Eng. Ostrobothnia. Physical region of
W Finland
Pohnpei *406 prev.* Ascension, Ponape.
Island of E Micronesia
Pohnpei Islands *406* island group
E Micronesia
Poindimié *650* C New Caledonia
Point de Galle *see* Galle
Pointe-à-Pitre *646* C Guadeloupe
Pointe-à-Raquette *286* Île de la
Gonâve, Haiti
Pointe Michel *224 var.* La Pointe.
SW Dominica
Pointe-Noire *646* W Guadeloupe
Pointe-Noire *200* S Congo
Point Fortin *570* SW Trinidad,
Trinidad & Tobago
Poitiers *253* C France
Poitou *252-253* cultural region of
W France
Poivre Atoll *512* atoll of the Amirante
Islands, C Seychelles
Pokhara *427* C Nepal
Pokigron *538* C Suriname
Pokrovka *see* Kyzyl-Suu
Pola *see* Pula
Poland *470-473* officially Republic of
Poland, *Pol.* Polska. Country of
E Europe divided into 49 admin. units
(województwo). ❖ Warsaw

Polatli *576* C Turkey
Polatsk *122 Rus.* Polotsk. N Belarus
Pol-e Khomrī *77 var.* Pul-i-Khumri.
NE Afghanistan
Poliçan *81 var.* Poliçani. S Albania
Polillo Islands *466* island group of
N Philippines
Polis *215 var.* Poli. W Cyprus
Polochic *278* river of C Guatemala
Polonnaruwa *534* C Sri Lanka
Poltava *586* NE Ukraine
Poltoratsk *see* Ashgabat
Põltsamaa *240 Ger.* Oberpahlen.
C Estonia
Põltsamaa *240 var.* Pyltsamaa. River
of C Estonia
Põlva *240 Ger.* Pölwe.
SE Estonia
Pomeranian Bay *265, 471 Pol.* Zatoka
Pomorska, *Ger.* Pommersche Bucht.
Bay of the Baltic Sea, on the coasts of
Germany and Poland
Pomio *458* New Britain, Papua New
Guinea
Pommersche Bucht *see* Pomeranian
Bay
Pomona *130* E Belize
Pomorie *152 var.* Pomoriye.
E Bulgaria
Pomorska, Zatoka *see* Pomeranian
Bay
Ponape *see* Pohnpei
Ponce *651* S Puerto Rico
Pondicherry *296* S India
Ponérihouen *650* C New Caledonia
Ponferrada *531* NW Spain
Pongo *536* river of S Sudan
Ponta Delgada *474* São Miguel,
Azores, Portugal
Ponta Grossa *145* S Brazil
Pontevedra *531* NW Spain
Pontianak *302* Borneo, C Indonesia
Pontian Kechil *386 var.* Pontian Kecil,
Pontian Kecil. S Peninsular Malaysia
Pontoise *253* N France
Ponziane, Isole *321* island of C Italy
Pooh San *644* NE Christmas Island
Poole *593* S England, UK
Poona *see* Pune
Pooneryn *534* N Sri Lanka
Poopó, Lago *136 var.* Lago Pampa
Aullagas. Lake of W Bolivia
Popayán *195* SW Colombia
Popomanaseu, Mount *522* mountain
of S Guadalcanal, Solomon Islands
Popondetta *458* SE Papua New Guinea
Popovo *152* N Bulgaria
Poprad *519 Ger.* Deutschendorf,
Hung. Poprád. NE Slovakia
Poprad *519 Ger.* Popper, *Hung.*
Poprád. River of Poland and
Slovakia
Pori *249 Swe.* Björneborg.
SW Finland
Porirua *433* S North Island,
New Zealand
Porlamar *619* Isla de Margarita,
Venezuela
Porsangen *444* fjord of N Norway
Porsgrunn *444* S Norway
Portachuelo *136* C Bolivia
Portage la Prairie *170* S Canada
Portalegre *474* E Portugal
Port Alfred *527* Eastern Cape,
S South Africa
Port Antonio *329* E Jamaica
Port Augusta *101* S Australia
Port-au-Prince *286* ❖ of Haiti, S Haiti
Port Blair *296* S Andaman,
SE India
Port-Bouët *326* SE Ivory Coast
Port d'Envalira *86* zigzag pass of
E Andorra
Port-de-Paix *286* N Haiti
Port Dickson *386* SW Peninsular
Malaysia
Port Elizabeth *498* Bequia, St Vincent
& the Grenadines
Port Elizabeth *527* Eastern Cape,
S South Africa
Port Erin *647* SW Isle of Man
Port Étienne *see* Nouâdhibou
Port Florence *see* Kisumu

Rann of Kachch 296 *var.* Rann of Cutch, Rann of Kutch. Salt marsh of India and Pakistan
Ranongga 522 *var.* Ghanongga. New Georgia Is, Solomon Islands
Rantau, Puala *see* Tebingtinggi, Pulau
Rapallo 320 N Italy
Rapid City 599 South Dakota, NC USA
Räpina 240 *Ger.* Rappin. SE Estonia
Rapla 240 *Ger.* Rappel. NW Estonia
Rapperswil 546 NW Switzerland
Rappin *see* Räpina
Rarotonga 644 island of Southern Cook Islands, S Cook Islands
Ra's al 'Ayn 551 N Syria
Ras al Hadd *see* Al Ḩadd
Ras al Khaimah 590 NE United Arab Emirates
Ra's an Naqb 336 SW Jordan
Ras Dashen Terara 243 mountain of N Ethiopia
Rasdu Atoll 390 atoll of C Maldives
Raseiniai 376 W Lithuania
Rashîd 230 *Eng.* Rosetta. N Egypt
Rasht 307 *var.* Resht. NW Iran
Rashū *see* Kŭmsong
Raso, Ilhéu 176 island of NW Cape Verde
Rass Jebel 573 *var.* Ra's al Jabal. N Tunisia
Rastalt 264 SW Germany
Ras Tannūrah 506 E Saudi Arabia
Ratak Chain 396 island group of E Marshall Islands
Ratchaburi 563 *var.* Rat Buri. C Thailand
Rathkeale 314 SW Ireland
Rätische Alpen *see* Rhaetian Alps
Ratnapura 534 S Sri Lanka
Ratō *see* Lotung
Raub 386 C Peninsular Malaysia
Raufarhöfn 294 NE Iceland
Raukawa *see* Cook Strait
Rauma 249 *Swe.* Raumo. SW Finland
Rauna 362 NE Latvia
Răuţel 408 *var.* Reuţel. River of N Moldova
Ravenna 321 N Italy
Ravensthorpe 100 SW Australia
Rävi 451 river of India and Pakistan
Ravne na Koroškem 520 *Ger.* Gutenstein. N Slovenia
Rawaki 346 *var.* Phoenix Island. Island of Phoenix Islands, C Kiribati
Rāwalpindi 451 NE Pakistan
Rawson 95 SE Argentina
Rayak 364 *var.* Riyāq. E Lebanon
Rayong 563 C Thailand
Raysūt 448 SW Oman
Razāzah, Buḩayrat ar 310 *var.* Baḩr al Milḩ. Lake of C Iraq
Razdan *see* Hrazdan
Razim, Lacul 480 *prev.* Lacul Rezelm. Lagoon of E Romania
Reading 593 SE England, UK
Reăng Kései 165 W Cambodia
Rebun-tō 330 island to the NW of Hokkaidō, N Japan
Rechytsa 122 *Rus.* Rechitsa. SE Belarus
Recife 145 *prev.* Pernambuco. E Brazil
Recklinghausen 264 W Germany
Reconquista 95 NE Argentina
Redange 378 W Luxembourg
Redcliff 636 C Zimbabwe
Red Deer 170 S Canada
Redhead 570 NE Trinidad, Trinidad & Tobago
Redon 252 NW France
Red River 170 river of Canada and USA
Red River 599 river of SC USA
Red River 623 *var.* Sông Coi, *Chin.* Yuan Jiang. River of China and Vietnam
Red Sea 238, 627 sea of Indian Ocean, between the Arabian Peninsula and NE Africa
Red Sea Hills 536 hilly region of NE Sudan
Red Volta 157 *Fr.* Volta Rouge. River of Burkina and Ghana
Ree, Lough 314 *Ir.* Loch Ri. Lake of C Ireland

Reefton 133 N South Island, New Zealand
Regar *see* Tursunzode
Regensburg 265 SE Germany
Reggane 83 C Algeria
Reggio di Calabria 321 *var.* Reggio Calabria. S Italy
Reggio nell' Emilia 320 *var.* Reggio Emilia. N Italy
Reghin 480 N Romania
Regina 170 S Canada
Régina 645 E French Guiana
Rehoboth 423 C Namibia
Reḩovot 317 C Israel
Reichenberg *see* Liberec
Reifnitz *see* Ribnica
Ré, Île de 252 island of W France
Reims 253 *Eng.* Rheims. NE France
Reine-Charlotte, Îles de la *see* Queen Charlotte Islands
Reine-Élisabeth, Îles de la *see* Queen Elizabeth Islands
Reisduoddarhalde *see* Haltiatunturi
Reisui *see* Yōsu
Reka *see* Rijeka
Relizane 83 *var.* Ghilizane, Ghelîzâne. NW Algeria
Remel el Abiod 573 desert region of S Tunisia
Remich 378 SE Luxembourg
Remscheid 264 W Germany
Rendezvous Bay 642 bay of the Caribbean Sea on the S coast of Anguilla
Rendova 522 island of the New Georgia Is, W Solomon Is
Renens 546 SW Switzerland
Rengo 183 C Chile
Rennell 522 *var.* Mu Nggava. Island of S Solomon Islands
Rennes 252 *Bret.* Roazon. NW France
Reno 598 Nevada, W USA
Réo 157 W Burkina
Republiek 581 N Suriname
Rere 522 E Guadalcanal, Solomon Is
Resen 381 SW FYR Macedonia
Reservatório 648 reservoir of Coloane, SW Macao
Resistencia 95 NE Argentina
Reşiţa 480 *Hung.* Resicabánya, *Ger.* Reschiza. W Romania
Resolute 170 Cornwallis Island, N Canada
Resolution Island 433 island to the SW of South Island, New Zealand
Retalhuleu 278 SW Guatemala
Retan Laut, Pulau 517 island SW Singapore
Retiche, Alpi *see* Rhaetian Alps
Réunion 652 French overseas department of the Indian Ocean. ❖ St Denis
Reus 531 E Spain
Reutlingen 264 S Germany
Reval *see* Tallinn
Rewa 284 river of S Guyana
Rey 307 *var.* Shahr Rey. NW Iran
Reyes 136 NW Bolivia
Rey, Isla del 456 island of SE Panama
Reykjahlídh 294 NE Iceland
Reykjavík 294 ❖ of Iceland, W Iceland
Reynosa 403 N Mexico
Reza, Gora 581 *var.* Gora Riza. Mountain of SW Turkmenistan
Rezā 'īyeh *see* Orūmīyeh
Rezā'īyeh, Daryācheh-ye *see* Orūmīeh, Daryācheh-ye
Rēzekne 362 *Ger.* Rositten, *Rus.* Rezhitsa. E Latvia
Rezina 408 NE Moldova
Rēznas Ezers 362 lake of SE Latvia
Rhadames *see* Ghadames
Rhaetian Alps 546 *Ger.* Rätische Alpen, *Fr.* Alpes Rhétiques, *It.* Alpi Retiche. Mountain range of E Switzerland
Rheden 429 SE Netherlands
Rhein *see* Rhine
Rheine 264 NW Germany
Rheinisches Schiefergebirge 264 *Eng.* Rhenish Slate Mountains. Mountains of W Germany
Rhenish Slate Mountains *see* Rheinisches Schiefergebirge
Rhétiques, Alpes *see* Rhaetian Alps

Rhine 253, 264, 374, 546 *Ger.* Rhein, *Fr.* Rhin, *Dut.* Rijn. River of W Europe
Rhino Camp 584 NW Uganda
Rhode Island 599 state of NE USA
Rhodes *see* Rodos
Rhodesia *see* Zimbabwe
Rhodope Mountains 152, 273 *Gk* Orosirá Rodópis, *Bul.* Despoto Planina, *Turk.* Dospad Dagh. Mountain range of Bulgaria and Greece
Rhône 253, 546 river of France and Switzerland
Rhum 593 *var.* Rum. Island of Inner Hebrides, W Scotland, UK
Riaba 236 *prev.* Concepción. S Bioko, Equatorial Guinea
Riau, Kepulauan 302 *var.* Riau Archipelago, *Dut.* Riouw Archipel. Island group to the E of Sumatra, W Indonesia
Riban i Manamby 382 S Madagascar
Ribáuè 419 NE Mozambique
Ribble 593 river of NW England, UK
Ribe 218 Jylland, SW Denmark
Ribeira da Barça 176 Santiago, S Cape Verde
Ribeira Funda 176 São Nicolau, N Cape Verde
Ribeira Grande 176 Santo Antão, N Cape Verde
Ribeirão Preto 145 S Brazil
Riberalta 136 N Bolivia
Ribnica 520 *Ger.* Reifnitz. S Slovenia
Ribniţa 408 *var.* Râbniţa, *Rus.* Rybnitsa. NE Moldova
Richard's Bay 527 Kwazulu Natal, E South Africa
Richard Toll 510 N Senegal
Riche Fond 497 E St Lucia
Richmond 599 Virginia, E USA
Richmond Vale 498 NW St Vincent, St Vincent & the Grenadines
Ridā *see* Radāa
Ridderkerk 429 SW Netherlands
Rif 414 *var.* Riff, Er Rif. Mountain range of N Morocco
Rift Valley *see* Great Rift Valley
Riga 362 *Latv.* Rīga. ❖ of Latvia, C Latvia
Riga, Gulf of 240, 362 *Est.* Liivi Laht, *prev.* Riia Laht, *Rus.* Rizhskiy Zaliv, *Latv.* Rīgas Jūras Līci Gulf of the Baltic Sea, on the coasts of Estonia and Latvia
Rīgestān 77 *var.* Registan. Desert region of S Afghanistan
Riihimäki 249 SW Finland
Rijeka 209 *Slvn.* Reka, *Ger.* Sankt Veit am Flaum, *It.* Fiume. NW Croatia
Rijn *see* Rhine
Rijssel *see* Lille
Ri, Loch *see* Ree, Lough
Rimah, Wādī ar 506 dry watercourse of C Saudi Arabia
Rimaszombat *see* Rimavská Sobota
Rimavská Sobota 519 *Ger.* Gross-Steffelsdorf, *Hung.* Rimaszombat. SE Slovakia
Rimini 321 N Italy
Rincon 650 Bonaire, S Netherlands Antilles
Ringe 218 Fyn, S Denmark
Ringkøbing 218 Jylland, W Denmark
Ringkøbing Fjord 218 fjord of Jylland, W Denmark
Ringsted 218 Sjælland, SE Denmark
Ringvassøy 444 island of NE Norway
Riobamba 137 C Ecuador
Rio Branco 144 W Brazil
Río Branco 607 E Uruguay
Rio Claro 570 SE Trinidad, Trinidad & Tobago
Río Cuarto 95 C Argentina
Rio de Janeiro 145 SE Brazil
Río Gallegos 95 *var.* Puerto Gallegos, Gallegos. S Argentina
Rio Grande 145 *var.* São Pedro do Rio Grande do Sul. S Brazil
Ríohacha 195 N Colombia
Río Muni 236 mainland region of Equatorial Guinea

Río Negro, Embalse del 607 *var.* Lago Artificial de Rincón del Bonete. Reservoir of C Uruguay
Rioni 262 river of W Georgia
Río Sereno 457 NW Panama
Riouw Archipel *see* Riau, Kepulauan
Riri *see* Iri
Rîşcani 408 *var.* Râşcani. NW Moldova
Rishiri-tō 330 island to the NW of Hokkaidō, N Japan
Rishon Le Ziyyon 317 C Israel
Ritidian Point 647 headland on the N coast of Guam
Rivadavia 95 W Argentina
Rivas 436 S Nicaragua
Rivera 607 N Uruguay
Rivercess *see* Cess
River Sallee 276 NE Grenada island, Grenada
Rivière des Anguilles 400 S Mauritius
Rivière-Pilote 649 SE Martinique
Rivne 586 *Pol.* Równe, *Rus.* Rovno. NW Ukraine
Riyadh 506 *var.* Ar Riyāḑ. ❖ of Saudi Arabia, C Saudi Arabia
Riyāq *see* Rayak
Rize 577 NE Turkey
Rizhskiy Zaliv *see* Riga, Gulf of
Rizokarpaso *see* Dipkarpaz
Rkîz, Lac 398 lake of SW Mauritania
Road Bay 642 bay of the Caribbean Sea on the W coast of Anguilla
Road Town 643 ❖ of British Virgin Islands, Tortola, C British Virgin Islands
Roanne 253 E France
Roaring Creek 130 C Belize
Roatán 288 Islas de la Bahía, Honduras
Roazon *see* Rennes
Robertson, Lake *see* Manyame, Lake
Robertsport 368 W Liberia
Robinson Crusoe, Isla 183 island of Juan Fernández Islands, W Chile
Rocas, Atol das 145 island of E Brazil
Rocha 607 SE Uruguay
Rochambeau 645 NE French Guiana
Rochester 599 Minnesota, NC USA
Rochester 599 New York, NE USA
Rocheuses, Montagnes *see* Rocky Mountains
Rock, The 646 E Gibraltar
Rockford 599 Illinois, C USA
Rockhampton 101 E Australia
Rockies *see* Rocky Mountains
Rockingham 100 SW Australia
Rocklands 540 NW Swaziland
Rock Sound 112 Eleuthera I, Bahamas
Rock Springs 598 Wyoming, NW USA
Rockstone 284 E Guyana
Rocky Mountains 170, 598 *var.* Rockies, *Fr.* Montagnes Rocheuses. Mountain range of NW America
Rocky Point 644 headland on the N coast of Christmas Island
Rodez 253 S France
Ródhos *see* Rodos
Rodi *see* Rodos
Rodi Garganico 321 C Italy
Rodonit, Gjiri i 81 gulf of the Adriatic Sea, NW Albania
Rodópis, Orosirá *see* Rhodope Mountains
Rodos 273 *Eng.* Rhodes, *It.* Rodi, *prev.* Ródhos. Island of SE Greece
Ródos 273 *Eng.* Rhodes, *It.* Rodi, *prev.* Ródhos. Ródos, SE Greece
Rodosto *see* Tekirdağ
Rodrigues 400 *var.* Rodriquez. Island of E Mauritius
Roermond 429 S Netherlands
Roeselare 127 *Fr.* Roulers, *prev.* Rousselaere. W Belgium
Rogachëv *see* Rahachow
Rogaška Slatina 520 *prev.* Rogatec-Slatina, *Ger.* Rohitsch-Sauerbrunn. E Slovenia
Rogatec-Slatina *see* Rogaška Slatina
Roger 224 W Dominica
Rogozhina *see* Rrogozhinë
Rohitsch-Sauerbrunn *see* Rogaška Slatina
Roi Et 563 *var.* Muang Roi Et. NE Thailand

St. Catherine, Mt *276* mountain C Grenada island, Grenada
St. Catherine Point *643* headland of E Bermuda
Saint Catherines *171* SE Canada
St-Chamond *253* E France
Saint Croix *653* island of S Virgin Islands
St. David's *276* SE Grenada island, Grenada
St. David's Island *643* island of E Bermuda
St-Denis *652* ❖ of Réunion, N Réunion
Ste Anne *649* SE Martinique
Ste. Anne *646* E Guadeloupe
Saint-Élie *645* N French Guiana
Ste. Rose *646* W Guadeloupe
Saintes *253* W France
St-Étienne *253* E France
St Eustatius *650* island of C Netherlands Antilles
St. François *646* E Guadeloupe
Saint-Gall *see* Sankt Gallen
St-Georges *645* E French Guiana
St. George *643* St. George's Island, N Bermuda
St. George's *276* ❖ of Grenada, SW Grenada
St. George's Channel *314, 593* *Ir.* Muir Bhreatan. Channel connecting the Celtic Sea and Irish Sea
St. George's Harbour *643* bay of E Bermuda
St. George's Island *643* island of E Bermuda
St. Giles Islands *570* *prev.* Melville Islands. Islands to the NE of Tobago, Trinidad & Tobago
St Helena *652* British dependent territory of the South Atlantic Ocean ❖ Jamestown
St. Helena Bay *527* bay of Atlantic Ocean, of coast of W South Africa
St Helier *648* ❖ of Jersey, S Jersey
St John *648* N Jersey
St John *647* C Isle of Man
Saint John *171* SE Canada
St. John *368* river of Guinea and Liberia
Saint John Island *653* island of NE Virgin Islands
St John's *649* N Montserrat
Saint John's *171* Newfoundland, E Canada
St. John's *92* ❖ of Antigua & Barbuda, NW Antigua
St. John's Island *see* Sakijang Bendera, Pulau
St. Johnston Village *92* C Antigua, Antigua & Barbuda
St-Joseph *652* S Réunion
St Joseph *224* W Dominica
St. Joseph *570* SE Trinidad, Trinidad & Tobago
St Julian's *395* N Malta
St Kilda *593* island of NW Scotland, UK
Saint Kitts *494* island of the Lesser Antilles, which, with Nevis, forms the independent state of St Kitts & Nevis
Saint Kitts and Nevis *494-495* officially Federation of Saint Christopher and Nevis. Country of the West Indies. ❖ Basseterre
Saint-Laurent, Golfe du *see* Saint Lawrence, Gulf of
St-Laurent-du-Maroni *645* NW French Guiana
Saint Lawrence *171* *Fr.* Fleuve Saint-Laurent. River of SE Canada
Saint Lawrence, Gulf of *170* Gulf of the Atlantic Ocean, SE Canada
St-Lô *252* NW France
St-Louis *652* SW Réunion
St Louis *646* Marie-Galante, S Guadeloupe
St Louis *599* Missouri, C USA
Saint-Louis *510* NW Senegal
St-Louis-du-Nord *286* *var.* St-Luis du Nord. N Haiti
Saint Lucia *496-497* independent island state of the Caribbean. ❖ Castries

Saint Lucia Channel *497* channel connecting the Atlantic Ocean and Caribbean Sea
St. Lucia, Lake *527* lake of Kwazulu Natal, E South Africa
St-Malo *252* NW France
St-Malo, Golfe de *252* gulf of the English Channel to the NW of France
St-Marc *286* W Haiti
St-Marc, Canal de *286* channel of the Caribbean Sea between Île de la Gonâve and W Haiti
Sainte Marie, Nosy *382* *var.* Nosy Boraha. Island of NE Madagascar
Ste. Marie *649* NE Martinique
Ste-Marie *652* NE Réunion
St Martin *650* island of N Netherlands Antilles
St. Martin *646* island of N Guadeloupe
St. Martins *121* SE Barbados
St.Moritz *546* *Ger.* Sankt Mortiz, *Rmsch.* San Murezzan. SE Switzerland
St-Nazaire *252* W France
St-Nicolas *see* Sint-Niklaas
St. Patricks *121* S Barbados
St-Paul *652* NW Réunion
St Paul *599* Minnesota, NC USA
St. Paul *368* river of Guinea and Liberia
St. Paul's *494* NW St Kitts, St Kitts & Nevis
Saint Paul's Bay *see* San Pawl il Bahar
St Paul's Point *651* headland of Pitcairn Island, S Pitcairn Islands
St Peter Port *647* ❖ of Guernsey, C Guernsey
St Peters *494* SE St Kitts, St Kitts & Nevis
St Petersburg *599* Florida, SE USA
Saint Petersburg *484, 488* *var.* Sankt-Peterburg, *prev.* Leningrad, Petrograd. NW Russia
St. Philips *92* SE Antigua, Antigua & Barbuda
Saint-Pierre *652* ❖ of Saint Pierre and Miquelon, SE Saint Pierre
Saint Pierre *652* island of SE Saint Pierre and Miquelon
St-Pierre *652* SW Réunion
St Pierre *649* NW Martinique
St. Pierre *512* island of the Farquhar Group, Seychelles
Saint Pierre and Miquelon *652* French territorial collectivity of the Atlantic Ocean ❖ Saint-Pierre
St. Sampson *647* S Guernsey
Saint Sauveur *224* E Dominica
Saint Thomas Island *653* island of W Virgin Islands
Saint Thomas Island *see* São Tomé
St-Trond *see* Sint-Truiden
Saint Vincent *498* island of the Lesser Antilles which, with the Northern Grenadines forms the independent state of St Vincent & the Grenadines
Saint Vincent and the Grenadines *498-499* country of the West Indies. ❖ Kingstown
St Willibrordus *650* Curaçao, S Netherlands Antilles
Saipan *650* island of S Northern Mariana Islands
Saipan *650* ❖ of Northern Mariana Islands, Saipan, S Northern Mariana Islands
Saishū *see* Cheju
Sajama, Nevado *136* mountain of W Bolivia
Sakaide *330* Shikoku, SW Japan
Sakākah *506* N Saudi Arabia
Sakalua *583* islet of Nukufetau, Tuvalu
Sakanthit *see* Saganthit Island
Sakarya *see* Adapazari
Sakarya *576* river of NW Turkey
Sakata *330* Honshū, N Japan
Sakchu *349* W North Korea
Sakété *132* S Benin
Sakhalin, Ostrov *485* island of SE Russia
Sakha, Respublika *484* *var.* Respublika Yakutiya. Autonomous republic of E Russia

Şäki *110* *Rus.* Shcki, *var.* Šeki, *prev.* Nukha. NW Azerbaijan
Sakijang Bendera, Pulau *517* *prev.* St. John's Island S Singapore
Sakijang Pelepah, Pulau *517* *prev.* Lazarus Island S Singapore
Sakis-Adasi *see* Chíos
Sakishima-shotō *330* island group of Nansei-shotō, SW Japan
Sakon Nakhon *563* NE Thailand
Sakra, Pulau *517* island of SW Singapore
Sakskøbing *218* Lolland, SE Denmark
Sal *176* island of NE Cape Verde
Šafa *519* *Hung.* Sellye. SW Slovakia
Sala Ban Thin *359* C Laos
Salacgrīva *362* N Latvia
Salado *210* river of SE Cuba
Salaga *270* C Ghana
Sala'ilua *500* Savai'i, Samoa
Salala *368* C Liberia
Şalalah *448* SW Oman
Salamá *278* C Guatemala
Salamanca *403* C Mexico
Salamanca *530* NW Spain
Salamat *180* river of S Chad
Salamīyah *551* *var.* Selemia. W Syria
Salani *500* Upolu, Samoa
Salcedo *226* N Dominican Republic
Šalčininkai *376* SE Lithuania
Saldus *362* *Ger.* Frauenburg. W Latvia
Sale *101* SE Australia
Salé *414* NW Morocco
Sale'imou *500* Upolu, Samoa
Salekhard *484* *prev.* Obdorsk. N Russia
Salelologa *500* Savai'i, Samoa
Salem *649* W Montserrat
Salem *296* S India
Salem *540* S Swaziland
Salem *598* Oregon, NW USA
Salemy *see* As Salimi
Salentina, Penisola *321* peninsula of S Italy
Salerno *321* S Italy
Salerno, Golfo di *321* gulf of the Tyrrhenian Sea, on the W coast of Italy
Salgótarján *290* N Hungary
Salibea *570* NE Trinidad, Trinidad & Tobago
Salibia *224* NE Dominica
Salihorsk *122* *Rus.* Soligorsk. S Belarus
Salikene *261* W Gambia
Salima *385* C Malawi
Salinas *see* Chixoy
Salinas *228* W Ecuador
Saline Island *276* island to the S of Carriacou, Grenada
Salisbury *593* S England, UK
Salisbury *224* *var.* Baroui. W Dominica
Salisbury *see* Harare
Salisbury, Lake *see* Bisina, Lake
Salisbury Plain *593* plain of S England, UK
Salitje *540* S Swaziland
Saljani *see* Salyan
Salkhad *551* SW Syria
Salla *249* NE Finland
Sallūm, Khalīj as *see* Sollum, Gulf of
Sallyana *see* Salyan
Salomon Atoll *643* atoll of N British Indian Ocean Territory
Salona *see* Solin
Salon-de-Provence *253* SE France
Salonica *see* Thessaloníki
Saloum *510* river of C Senegal
Salpausselkä *249* physical region of S Finland
Sal Rei *176* *var.* Vila de Sal Rei. Boa Vista, E Cape Verde
Salt *see* As Salt
Salta *95* N Argentina
Saltholm *218* island of E Denmark
Saltibus *497* S St Lucia
Saltillo *403* N Mexico
Salt Island *643* island of SE British Virgin Islands

Salt Island Passage *643* passage of the Caribbean Sea between Peter Island and Salt Island, S British Virgin Islands
Salt Lake City *598* Utah, SW USA
Salto *607* NW Uruguay
Salto del Guairá *460* E Paraguay
Salto Grande, Embalse de *607* reservoir of Argentina and Uruguay
Saltpond *270* SE Ghana
Salvador *145* *prev.* São Salvador. E Brazil
Salvaleón de Higüey *see* Higüey
Salwa *see* As Salwá
Salwá, Dawḩat as *479* *var.* Dawḩat Salwah. Inlet of the Gulf of Bahrain on the coast of SW Qatar
Salwah *see* As Salwá
Salween *159, 186, 563* *Chin.* Nu Chiang, *var.* Nu Jiang, *Bur.* Thanlwin. River of SE Asia
Salyan *110* *Rus.* Sal'yany, *var.* Saljani. SE Azerbaijan
Salyan *427* *var.* Sallyana. W Nepal
Salzburg *106* N Austria
Salzburg Alps *106* *Ger.* Salzburger Kalkalpen. Mountain range of C Austria
Salzgitter *265* *prev.* Watenstedt-Salzgitter. C Germany
Samāḥij *115* Jazirat al Muharraq, Bahrain
Samā'il *448* *var.* Sumail. NE Oman
Samales Group *466* island group of Sulu Archipelago, SW Philippines
Samaná *226* NE Dominican Republic
Samana Cay *112* island of SE Bahamas
Samar *466* island of E Philippines
Samar *336* NW Jordan
Samara *484* *prev.* Kuybyshev. W Russia
Samarai *458* SE Papua New Guinea
Samarinda *302* Borneo, C Indonesia
Samarkandski *see* Temirtau
Samarqand *610* *Rus.* Samarkand. SE Uzbekistan
Sāmarrā' *310* C Iraq
Samawa *see* As Samāwah
Şamaxı *110* *Rus.* Shemakha. C Azerbaijan
Sambava *382* NE Madagascar
Sambre *127* river of Belgium and France
Samchi *134* SW Bhutan
Samch'ŏk *350* *Jap.* Sanchoku. NE South Korea
Samch'ŏnpŏ *350* *Jap.* Sansenhō. S South Korea
Samdrup Jongkhar *134* SE Bhutan
Same *560* NE Tanzania
Samfya *635* *var.* Samfya Mission. N Zambia
Sam Hall's Bay *643* bay of the North Atlantic Ocean, E Bermuda
Samina *374* river of Austria and Liechtenstein
Saminatal Valley *374* valley of Austria and Liechtenstein
Sam Neua *see* Xam Nua
Samoa *500-501* officially Independent State of Samoa, Sam. Samoa i Sisfo. Country of the Pacific Ocean divided into 11 admin. units (districts). ❖ Apia
Samobor *209* N Croatia
Samokov *152* W Bulgaria
Sámos *273* island of SE Greece
Samosch *see* Someş
Samothráki *273* *Eng.* Samothrace. Island of NE Greece
Samsø *218* island of C Denmark
Samsun *577* N Turkey
Samtredia *262* W Georgia
Samui, Ko *563* island of S Thailand
Samur *110* river of Azerbaijan and Russia
Samut Prakan *563* *var.* Muang Samut Prakan. C Thailand
Samut Sakhon *563* C Thailand
San *165* *var.* Se San. River of Cambodia and Vietnam
San *392* C Mali
San *471* river of SE Poland

São Marcos, Baía de *115* bay of the Atlantic Ocean, on the coast of N Brazil

São Miguel *474* island of the Azores, Portugal

Saona, Isla *226* island of SE Dominican Republic

Saône *253* river of E France

São Nicolau *176* island of N Cape Verde

São Paulo *145, 149* S Brazil

São Pedro *176* São Vincente, N Cape Verde

São Pedro do Rio Grande do Sul *see* Rio Grande

São Salvador *see* Salvador

São Salvador do Congo *see* M'Banza Congo

São Simão, Represa de *145* reservoir of S Brazil

São Tiago *see* Santiago

São Tomé *505* *Eng.* Saint Thomas. Island of S Sao Tome & Principe

São Tomé *505* ❖ of São Tome & Principe, NE São Tomé

Sao Tome & Principe *504-505* officially Democratic Republic of Sao Tome and Principe, *Port.* São Tomé e Príncipe. Country of W Africa divided into 7 admin. units (districts). ❖ São Tomé

São Tomé, Pico de *505* mountain of São Tomé, Sao Tome & Principe

São Vicente *145* S Brazil

São Vicente *176* island of N Cape Verde

Sapele *440* S Nigeria

Sapitwa *385* mountain of S Malawi

Saponé *157* C Burkina

Sappemeer *429* NE Netherlands

Sapporo *330* Hokkaidō, N Japan

Sapta Koshi *427* river of India and Nepal

Sār *115* NW Bahrain

Šara *381* mountain range of FYR Macedonia and Yugoslavia

Sara Buri *563* C Thailand

Saragossa *see* Zaragoza

Saragt *581* *prev.* Serakhs, *var.* Serahs. S Turkmenistan

Sarajevo *140* ❖ of Bosnia & Herzegovina, SE Bosnia & Herzegovina

Saran' *338* C Kazakhstan

Sarandë *81* *var.* Saranda, *It.* Porto Edda, *prev.* Santi Quaranta. S Albania

Sarandí del Yí *607* C Uruguay

Sarandí Grande *607* S Uruguay

Sarangani Islands *466* island group of SE Philippines

Saratov *484* W Russia

Saravan *359* *var.* Saravane. SE Laos

Sarbhang *134* S Bhutan

Sardegna *320* *Eng.* Sardinia. Island of W Italy

Sardinia *see* Sardegna

Sargodha *451* NE Pakistan

Sarh *180* *prev.* Fort-Archambault. S Chad

Sārī *307* N Iran

Sarigan *650* island of C Northern Mariana Islands

Sarikol Range *558* *Rus.* Sarykol'skiy Khrebet. Mountain range of China and Tajikistan

Sarimbun Reservoir *517* NW Singapore

Sariwŏn *349* SW North Korea

Sark *647* island of SE Guernsey

Sarpsborg *444* S Norway

Sarrebruck *see* Saarbrücken

Sarstoon *130, 278* *var.* Sarstún. River of Belize and Guatemala

Sarstún *see* Sarstoon

Sarthe *253* river of NW France

Saruhan *see* Manisa

Sarykol'skiy Khrebet *see* Sarikol Range

Sary-Tash *357* *var.* Sary-Ta#. SW Kyrgyzstan

Sasebo *330* Kyūshū, SW Japan

Saseno *see* Sazan

Saskatchewan *170* river of C Canada

Saskatchewan *170* province of C Canada

Saskatoon *170* SW Canada

Sasolburg *527* Orange Free State, C South Africa

Sassandra *326* S Ivory Coast

Sassandra *326* *var.* Ibo. River of S Ivory Coast

Sassari *320* Sardegna, W Italy

Sassnitz *265* NE Germany

Sasstown *368* SE Liberia

Sataua *500* Savai'i, Samoa

Satawal *406* island of C Micronesia

Satawan *406* atoll of C Micronesia

Sātkhira *117* SW Bangladesh

Satpura Range *296* mountains of C India

Satu Mare *480* *Hung.* Szatmárnémeti. NW Romania

Satunan-shotō *330* island group of Nansei-shotō, SW Japan

Sau *see* Sava

Sauce *see* Juan L. Lacaze

Saudhárkrókur *294* N Iceland

Saudi Arabia *506-509* officially Kingdom of Saudi Arabia. Country of SW Asia divided into 13 admin. units (provinces). ❖ Riyadh

Saül *645* C French Guiana

Saulkrasti *362* N Latvia

Sault Sainte Marie *171* S Canada

Sauma, Pointe *653* headland of Île Alofi, N Wallis & Futuna

Saûmâtre, Étang *286* lake of SE Haiti

Saurimo *88* *Port.* Vila Henrique de Carvalho. NE Angola

Sauteurs *276* N Grenada island, Grenada

Sava *140, 209, 520, 630* *Eng.* Save, *Hung.* Száva, *Ger.* Sau. River of SE Europe

Savai'i *500* island of NW Samoa

Savalou *132* S Benin

Savan Island *498* island of S St Vincent & the Grenadines

Savannah *599* Georgia, SE USA

Savannakhét *359* S Laos

Savanna-La-Mar *329* W Jamaica

Savave *583* islet of Nukufetau, Tuvalu

Save *419, 636* *var.* Sabi. River of Mozambique and Zimbabwe

Savè *132* SE Benin

Savissivik *646* NW Greenland

Savona *320* N Italy

Savonlinna *249* *Swe.* Nyslott. SE Finland

Savusavu *246* Vanua Levu, N Fiji

Savu Sea *see* Sawu, Laut

Savute *142* river of N Botswana

Sawdá', Jabal *506* mountain of SW Saudi Arabia

Sawdā, Jabal as *371* mountain range of C Libya

Sawdiri *see* Sodiri

Sawhaj *see* Sohâg

Şawqirah *448* SE Oman

Şawqirah, Ghubbat *see* Suqrah Bay

Sawu, Laut *302* *Eng.* Savu Sea. Sea of the Indian Ocean, C Indonesia

Say *439* SW Niger

Sayaboury *see* Muang Xaignabouri

Sayat *581* E Turkmenistan

Sayhūt *627* E Yemen

Saynshand *412* S Mongolia

Say 'ūn *627* *var.* Saywūn. C Yemen

Sazan *81* *It.* Saseno. Island of SW Albania

Scaldis *see* Scheldt

Scarborough *593* NE England, UK

Scarborough *570* S Tobago, Trinidad & Tobago

Scarborough *121* S Barbados

Scebeli *see* Shebeli

Schaan *374* W Liechtenstein

Schaanwald *374* NE Liechtenstein

Schaffhausen *546* N Switzerland

Schaulen *see* Šiauliai

Schefferville *171* E Canada

Scheldt *127* *Dut.* Schelde, *Fr.* Escaut. River of W Europe

Schellenberg *374* N Liechtenstein

Schiedam *429* SW Netherlands

Schiermonnikoog *429* island of Waddeneilanden, N Netherlands

Schifflange *378* S Luxembourg

Schneekoppe *see* Sněžka

Schneidemühl *see* Piła

Schœlcher *649* W Martinique

Schoten *127* N Belgium

Schouwen *429* island of SW Netherlands

Schwäbische Alb *264* *Eng.* Swabian Jura. Mountain range of SW Germany

Schwarzwald *see* Black Forest

Schwaz *106* W Austria

Schweizer Mittelland *see* Swiss Plateau

Schweizer Reneke *527* North West, N South Africa

Schwerin *265* N Germany

Schweriner See *264* lake of N Germany

Schwyz *546* C Switzerland

Schyl *see* Jiu

Sciacca *321* Sicilia, S Italy

Sciasciamana *see* Shashemenê

Scio *see* Chíos

Scoresbysund *see* Ittoqqortoormiit

Scotland *593, 597* national region of UK divided into 12 admin. units (9 regions, 3 island authorities)

Scott Base *90* New Zealand research station near Ross Shelf, Antarctica

Scott Island *90* island to the N of Ross Ice Shelf, Antarctica

Scotts Head Village *224* *var.* Cachacrou. S Dominica

Scrub Island *642* island of NE Anguilla

Scunthorpe *593* NE England, UK

Scutari *see* Shkodër

Scutari, Lake *81, 630* *Alb.* Liqeni i Shkodrës, *SCr.* Skadarsko Jezero. Lake of Albania and Yugoslavia

Seac Pai Van *648* bay of the South China Sea, SW Macao

Seal Island *642* island of NW Anguilla

Seatons *92* E Antigua, Antigua & Barbuda

Seattle *598, 603* Washington, NW USA

Sébaco *436* C Nicaragua

Sebaiera *414* C Western Sahara

Sebapala *366* SW Lesotho

Sebarok, Pulau *517* island S Singapore

Sebastián Vizcaíno, Bahía *403* bay of the Pacific Ocean, on the NW coast of Mexico

Sebastopol *see* Sevastopol'

Sebenico *see* Šibenik

Sébikhoutane *510* W Senegal

Sebou *414* river of N Morocco

Secos, Ilhéus *see* Rombo, Ilhéus de

Sedberat *238* W Eritrea

Sédhiou *510* SW Senegal

Seeheim Noord *423* S Namibia

Seeland *see* Sjælland

Sefadu *514* E Sierra Leone

Sefrou *414* N Morocco

Segamat *386* S of Peninsular Malaysia

Ségbana *132* NE Benin

Segewold *see* Sigulda

Segna *see* Senj

Ségou *392* *var.* Segu C Mali

Segovia *531* C Spain

Segovia *see* Coco

Segu *see* Ségou

Séguédine *439* NE Niger

Séguéla *326* W Ivory Coast

Séguénéga *157* NW Burkina

Segura *531* river of S Spain

Sehlabathebe *366* E Lesotho

Seinäjoki *249* *Swe.* Östermyra. SW Finland

Seine *253* river of N France

Seine, Baie de la *252-253* bay of the English Channel to the NW of France

Seiyū *see* Chŏngju

Sejerø *218* island of C Denmark

Šeki *see* Şäki

Sekoma *142* S Botswana

Sekondi-Takoradi *270* S Ghana

Selânik *see* Thessaloníki

Selemia *see* Salamīyah

Selenge *412* river of Mongolia and Russia

Seletar Reservoir *517* reservoir of C Singapore

Selfoss *294* SW Iceland

Seli *see* Rokel

Sélibabi *398* S Mauritania

Selibi Phikwe *142* E Botswana

Sélingué, Lac de *392* reservoir of S Mali

Selle, Massif de la *286* mountain range of S Haiti

Selle, Pic la *286* *var.* La Selle. Mountain of S Haiti

Sellore Island *see* Saganthit Island

Sellye *see* Skalica

Sellye *see* Šaľa

Sélouma *281* C Guinea

Selukwe *see* Shurugwi

Selvagens, Ilhas *474* island group of the Madeira Is, Portugal

Semakau, Pulau *517* island S Singapore

Semanit *81* *var.* Seman. River of W Albania

Semara *414* N Western Sahara

Semarang *302* Java, C Indonesia

Sembawang *517* area of N Singapore

Sembé *200* NW Congo

Sembehun *514* SW Sierra Leone

Semberong *386* river of SE Peninsular Malaysia

Semendria *see* Smederevo

Semipalatinsk *338* *Kaz.* Semey. E Kazakhstan

Semirara Islands *466* island group of C Philippines

Semliki *584* river of W Uganda

Sên *165* *var.* Sen. River of C Cambodia

Sena *see* Vila de Sena

Senafe *238* SE Eritrea

Senanayake Samudra *534* lake of E Sri Lanka

Senanga *635* SW Zambia

Senang, Pulau *517* island of S Singapore

Sendai *330* Kyūshū, SW Japan

Sendai *330* Honshū, N Japan

Senegal *510-511* officially Republic of Senegal. *Fr.* Sénégal. Country of West Africa divided into 10 admin. units (regions). ❖ Dakar

Senegal *398, 392, 510* *Fr.* Sénégal. River of W Africa

Senica *519* *Ger.* Senitz, *Hung.* Szenice. W Slovakia

Senigallia *321* C Italy

Senj *209* *Ger.* Zengg, *Ital.* Segna. NW Croatia

Senja *444* *prev.* Senjen. Island of NW Norway

Senkaku-shotō *330* island group of Nansei-shotō, SW Japan

Senmonorom *165* E Cambodia

Sennar *536* *var.* Sannâr. C Sudan

Senne *127* *Dut.* Zenne. River of C Belgium

Senqunyane *366* river of C Lesotho

Senshin-kō *see* Sŏmjin

Sensuntepeque *235* NE El Salvador

Sentery *203* SE Congo (Zaire)

Sentosa *517* island S Singapore

Senye *236* W Río Muni, Equatorial Guinea

Seongnam *see* Sŏngnam

Seoul *350* *Kor.* Sŏul, *prev.* Kyŏngsŏng, *Jap.* Keijō. ❖ of South Korea NW South Korea

Sepik *458* river of Indonesia and Papua New Guinea

Sepone *see* Muang Xéphôn

Sept-Îles *170* E Canada

Serahs *see* Saragt

Serahs *see* Saragt

Seraing *127* E Belgium

Serakhis *see* Serrakhis

Serakhs *see* Saragt

Seram *302* *var.* Serang, *Eng.* Ceram. Island of Maluku, E Indonesia

Seram, Laut *302* *Eng.* Ceram Sea. Sea of the Pacific Ocean, E Indonesia

Serang *302* Java, C Indonesia

Serangoon Harbour *517* harbour, E Singapore

Serasan, Selat *302, 386* strait of the South China Sea between Borneo and Kepulauan Natuna, W Indonesia

Seraya, Pulau *517* island of SW Singapore
Serbia *630 Serb.* Srbija. Republic of Yugoslavia
Sered *519 Hung.* Szered. SW Slovakia
Serekunda *261* W Gambia
Seremban *386* W Peninsular Malaysia
Serengeti Plain *560* plain of N Tanzania
Serenje *635* E Zambia
Sereth *see* Siret
Sérifos *273* island of SE Greece
Serov *484* C Russia
Serowe *142* SE Botswana
Serpa Pinto *see* Menongue
Serpent's Mouth, The *570*
  Sp. Boca de la Serpiente. Strait connecting the Colombus Channel and the Gulf of Paria
Serrakhis *215 var.* Serrachis, Serakhis. River of NW Cyprus
Serravalle *502* N San Marino
Sérres *273 prev.* Sérrai. NE Greece
Serule *142* E Botswana
Se San *see* Tônlé San
Sesana *see* Sežana
Sese Islands *584* island group of S Uganda
Sesvete *209* N Croatia
Seti *427* river of W Nepal
Sétif *83 var.* Stif. N Algeria
Settat *414* W Morocco
Setté Cama *258* SW Gabon
Settlement, The *643* Anegada, N British Virgin Islands
Setúbal *474* W Portugal
Setúbal, Baía de *474* bay of the Atlantic Ocean, to the SW of Portugal
Sevan *98* C Armenia
Sevana Lich *98 Eng.* Lake Sevan. Lake of E Armenia
Sevani Lerrnashght'a *see* Shakh-Dag
Sevan, Lake *see* Sevana Lich
Sévaré *392* C Mali
Sevastopol' *586 Eng.* Sebastopol. S Ukraine
Severn *593 Wel.* Hafren. River of England and Wales, UK
Severn *170* river of S Canada
Severnaya Dvina *484 Eng.* Northern Dvina. River of NW Russia
Severnaya Zemlya *485* island group of N Russia
Severnyy Ledovityy Okean *see* Arctic Ocean
Severodvinsk *484 prev.* Molotov, *prev.* Sudostroy. NW Russia
Severo Osetinskaya SSR *484* autonomous republic of SW Russia
Severo-Sibirskaya Nizmennost' *485 Eng.* North Siberian Lowland, *var.* North Siberian Plain. Lowland region of N Russia
Severskiy Donets *see* Donets
Sevilla *530 Eng.* Seville. SW Spain
Sevilla de Niefang *see* Niefang
Sevlievo *152* C Bulgaria
Sewa *514* river E Sierra Leone
Seychelles *512-513* officially Republic of the Seychelles. Country of the Indian Ocean divided into 25 admin. units (districts). ❖ Victoria
Seydhisfjördhur *294* E Iceland
Seydi *581 prev.* Neftezavodsk. E Turkmenistan
Seyhan *577* river of S Turkey
Seyhan *see* Adana
Sežana *520 It.* Sesana. SW Slovenia
Sfântu Gheorghe *480 prev.* Sfîntu Gheorghe. C Romania
Sfax *573 var.* Safāqis. E Tunisia
's-Gravenhage *429 var.* Den Haag, *Eng.* The Hague, *Fr.* La Haye. Seat of government, W Netherlands
Shaanxi *187 var.* Shensi, Shan-hsi. Province of C China
Shabani *see* Zvishavane
Shabeelle, Webi *see* Shebeli
Shaddādī *see* Ash Shadādah
Shah Alam *386* W Peninsular Malaysia
Shāhbāzpur *117* river of S Bangladesh
Shāhdādkot *451* SW Pakistan
Shaḥḥāt *371* NE Libya
Shahrikhon *610 Rus.* Shakhrikan. E Uzbekistan

Shahrisabz *610 Rus.* Shakhrisabz. SE Uzbekistan
Shahr Rey *see* Rey
Shahrtuz *558 Rus.* Shaartuz. W Tajikistan
Shahzadpur *117* W Bangladesh
Shakawe *142* NW Botswana
Shakh-Dag *98 Arm.* Sevani Lerrnashght'a, *Rus.* Shakhdagskiy Khrebet. Mountain range of Armenia and Azerbaijan
Shakhdagskiy Khrebet *see* Shakh-Dag
Shakhrisabz *see* Shahrisabz
Shakhtinsk *338* C Kazakhstan
Shaki *440* W Nigeria
Shām, Bādiyat ash *see* Syrian Desert
Shām, Jabal ash *448 var.* Jebel Sham. Mountain of N Oman
Shandī *see* Shendi
Shandong *187 var.* Shantung. Province of E China
Shandong Bandao *187 var.* Shantung Peninsula. Peninsula of E China
Shangani *636* river of W Zimbabwe
Shanghai *187, 190* city and municipality of E China
Shan-hsi *see* Shaanxi
Shan-hsi *see* Shanxi
Shanhua *555* SW Taiwan
Shannon *314 Ir.* An tSionainn. River of C Ireland
Shansi *see* Shanxi
Shantar Islands *see* Shantarskiye Ostrova
Shantarskiye Ostrova *485 Eng.* Shantar Islands. Island group of SE Russia
Shantou *187 var.* Swatow. Guangdong, SE China
Shantung *see* Shandong
Shantung Peninsula *see* Shandong Bandao
Shanxi *187 var.* Shansi, Shan-hsi. Province of NE China
Shaoguan *187 var.* Shao-kuan, *prev.* Ch'u-chiang, *Cant.* Kukong. Guangdong, SE China
Shao-kuan *see* Shaoguan
Shaqrā' *506* C Saudi Arabia
Shaqrā *see* Shuqrah
Sharasume *see* Altay
Shari *see* Chari
Sharīn Gol *412* N Mongolia
Sharjah *590* NE United Arab Emirates
Shark Bay *100* bay to the W of Australia
Sharon, Plain of *see* HaSharon
Sharqī, Jabal ash *see* Anti-Lebanon
Sharqī, Jazīrat ash *see* Chergui, Île
Sharqī, Jebel esh *see* Anti-Lebanon
Shashe *142, 636 var.* Shashi. River of Botswana and Zimbabwe
Shashemenē *243 var.* Shashemenne, Shashhamana, *It.* Sciasciamana. S Ethiopia
Shashi *187 var.* Sha-shih, Shasi. Hubei, C China
Shāṭi', Wādī ash *371* dry watercourse of W Libya
Shaykh, Jabal ash *see* Hermon, Mount
Shaykh 'Uthmān *627* SW Yemen
Shcheglovsk *see* Kemerovo
Shchuchinsk *338* N Kazakhstan
Shea *284* S Guyana
Shebeli *524 Som.* Webi Shabeelle, *Amh.* Shebele Wenz, *It.* Scebeli. River of Ethiopia and Somalia
Sheberghān *77 var.* Shibarghan. N Afghanistan
Shedadi *see* Ash Shadādah
Shefar'am *317* N Israel
Sheffield *593* N England, UK
Shekhem *see* Nablus
Shekhūpura *451* NE Pakistan
Sheki *see* Şäki
Shelikhova, Zaliv *485 Eng.* Shelekhov Gulf. Gulf of Sea of Okhotsk, bordering NE Russia
Shemakha *see* Şamaxı
Shemgang *154* C Bhutan
Shendi *536 var.* Shandī. NE Sudan
Shengking *see* Liaoning
Shensi *see* Shaanxi

Shenyang *187 prev.* Fengtien, *Eng.* Mukden. Liaoning, NE China
Shepherd Islands *615* islands to the C of Vanuatu
Shepparton *101* SE Australia
Sherbro Island *514* island of SW Sierra Leone
Sherbrooke *171* SE Canada
Sheridan *598* Wyoming, NW USA
Sherpur *117* N Bangladesh
's-Hertogenbosch *429 Ger.* Herzogenbusch, *Fr.* Bois-le-Duc. S Netherlands
Sherwood Ranch *142* SE Botswana
Shetland *593* islands of NE Scotland, UK
Shevchenko *see* Aktau
Shibām *627* C Yemen
Shibarghan *see* Sheberghān
Shibata *330* Honshū, N Japan
Shibh Jazīrat Sīnā' *see* Sinai
Shibîn el Kôm *230 var.* Shibîn al Kawm. N Egypt
Shihmen *see* Shijiazhuang
Shijak *81 var.* Shijaku. W Albania
Shijiazhuang *187 var.* Shihkiachwang, Shih-chia-chuang, *prev.* Shihmen. Hebei, NE China
Shikārpur *451* S Pakistan
Shikoku *330* island of SW Japan
Shiliguri *296 prev.* Siliguri. NE India
Shimbiris *524 var.* Shimbir Berris. Mountain of N Somalia
Shimizu *330* Honshū, SE Japan
Shimonoseki *330* Honshū, W Japan
Shimonoseki-kaikyō *330* strait connecting the Sea of Japan and Inland Sea, between Honshū and Kyūsh ū, W Japan
Shinano *330* river of Honshū, N Japan
Shināṣ *448* NW Oman
Shīndand *77* W Afghanistan
Shinei *see* Hsinying
Shinshō *see* Hsinchuang
Shinshū *see* Chinju
Shinten *see* Hsintien
Shinyanga *560* NW Tanzania
Shiogama *330* Honshū, N Japan
Shīrāz *307* SW Iran
Shire *385 Port.* Chire. River of Malawi and Mozambique
Shire Highlands *385* hilly region of S Malawi
Shirvanskaya Step' *see* Şirvan Düzü
Shirwa, Lake *see* Chilwa, Lake
Shizuoka *330* Honshū, SE Japan
Shkodër *81 var.* Shkodra, *It.* Scutari, *SCr.* Skadar. NW Albania
Shkodrës, Liqeni i *see* Scutari, Lake
Shkumbīn *81 var.* Shkumbî, Shkumbin. River of C Albania
Shoe Rock *649* headland on the S coast of Montserrat
Shōka *see* Changhua
Sholapur *see* Solāpur
Shorkot *451* NE Pakistan
Shortland Island *522 var.* Alu. Island of the Shortland Is, W Solomon Islands
Shortland Islands *522* island group of the W Solomon Islands
Shostka *586* N Ukraine
Shreveport *599* Louisiana, SC USA
Shrewsbury *593* C England, UK
Shū *see* Chu
Shu'aybah *354 var.* Shuaiba. E Kuwait
Shubrâ el Kheima *230 var.* Shubrâ al Khaymah. N Egypt
Shūlgareh *77* N Afghanistan
Shumen *152 var.* Šumen. E Bulgaria
Shunsen *see* Ch'unch'ŏn
Shuqrah *627 var.* Shaqrā. SW Yemen
Shurugwi *636 prev.* Selukwe. C Zimbabwe
Shwebo *159* N Burma
Shweli *159* river of Burma and China
Shymkent *338 prev.* Chimkent. S Kazakhstan
Shyashchytsy *122* C Belarus
Sīāhān Range *450* mountain range of W Pakistan
Sīāh Kūh *77* mountain range of W Afghanistan

Siālkot *451* NE Pakistan
Siam *see* Thailand
Siam, Gulf of *see* Thailand, Gulf of
Sian *see* Xi'an
Siangtan *see* Xiangtan
Siargao Island *466* island of E Philippines
Šiauliai *376 Ger.* Schaulen. NW Lithuania
Siazan' *see* Siyäzän
Šibenik *209 It.* Sebenico. S Croatia
Siberut, Pulau *302* island of Kepulauan Mentawai, W Indonesia
Sibi *451* C Pakistan
Sibiti *200* S Congo
Sibiu *480 Ger.* Hermannstadt, *Hung.* Nagyszeben. C Romania
Sibu *386* W Borneo, Malaysia
Sibut *179 prev.* Fort-Sibut. C Central African Republic
Sibutu Passage *386* passage connecting Celebes Sea and Sulu Sea
Sibuyan Island *466* island of C Philippines
Sibuyan Sea *466* sea of the Pacific Ocean
Sichuan *187 var.* Szechuan, Ssu-ch'uan. Province of SW China
Sicilia *321 Eng.* Sicily. Island of S Italy
Sicily *see* Sicilia
Sico *288 var.* Tinto, Río Negro. River of NE Honduras
Sicunusa *540* SW Swaziland
Siders *see* Sierre
Sidi Bel Abbès *83* NW Algeria
Sidi Bouzid *573 var.* Sīdī bū Zayd, Gammouda. C Tunisia
Sidi el Hani, Sebkhet de *573 var.* Sabkhat Sīd´ al Hāni'. Salt flat of NE Tunisia
Sidi Kacem *414 prev.* Petitjean. N Morocco
Sidra *see* Surt
Sidra, Gulf of *see* Surt, Khalīj
Sidvokodvo *540* C Swaziland
Siegen *264* W Germany
Sielo *368* N Liberia
Siĕmréab *165 prev.* Siem Reap. NW Cambodia
Siena *321 Fr.* Sienne. C Italy
Sienne *see* Siena
Sierra de Guadarrama *531* mountains of C Spain
Sierra Leone *514-515* officially Republic of Sierra Leone. Country of W Africa divided into 4 admin. units (provinces). ❖ Freetown
Sierra Madre *466* mountain range of Luzon, N Philippines
Sierra Madre *278, 403* mountain range of Guatemala and Mexico
Sierra Madre del Sur *403* mountain range of S Mexico
Sierra Madre Occidental *403 var.* Western Sierra Madre. Mountain range of NW Mexico
Sierra Madre Oriental *403 var.* Eastern Sierra Madre. Mountain range of N Mexico
Sierra Maestra *210* mountain range of SE Cuba
Sierra Morena *530-531* mountain range of SW Spain
Sierra Nevada *598* mountain range of W USA
Sierra Nevada de Mérida *see* Mérida, Cordillera de
Sierre *546 Ger.* Siders. SW Switzerland
Sigatoka *246 prev.* Singatoka. Viti Levu, W Fiji
Siġġiewi *395* S Malta
Sighisoara *480* C Romania
Siglufjördhur *294* N Iceland
Signy *90* UK research station of South Orkney Islands, Antarctica
Sigsig *228* S Ecuador
Siguatepeque *288* W Honduras
Siguiri *281* NE Guinea
Sigulda *362 Ger.* Segewold. NE Latvia
Sihanoukville *see* Kâmpóng Saôm
Siirt *577* SE Turkey
Sikasso *392* S Mali
Sikwane *142* S Botswana

Silay *466* Negros, C Philippines
Silesia *471* region of SW Poland
Silgadhi *427* var. Silgarhi. W Nepal
Silhouette *512* island of the Inner Islands, SE Seychelles
Siliana *573* var. Silyānah. NW Tunisia
Silicon Valley *602* business region of SW USA
Siliguri *see* Shiliguri
Silil *524* var. Silel. Seasonal river of NW Somalia
Silinhot *see* Xilinhot
Silisili, Mount *500* var. Mauga Silisili. Mountain of NW Samoa
Silistra *152* var. Silistria. NE Bulgaria
Silkeborg *218* Jylland, W Denmark
Sillamäe *240* Ger. Sillamäggi. NE Estonia
Sillein *see* Žilina
Šilutė *376* var. Šilute. W Lithuania
Silva Porto *see* Kuito
Silver City *644* NE Christmas Island
Silverek *577* SE Turkey
Sima *198* W Anjouan, Comoros
Simanggang *see* Bandar Sri Aman
Simbirsk *see* Ul'yanovsk
Simeto *321* river of Sicilia, S Italy
Simeulue, Pulau *321* island to the NW of Sumatra, W Indonesia
Simferopol *586* S Ukraine
Simikot *427* W Nepal
Siminiout *645* S French Guiana
Šimonovany *see* Partizánske
Simony *see* Partizánske
Simplon Pass *546* mountain pass of S Switzerland
Simplon Tunnel *546* tunnel of Italy and Switzerland
Simpson Desert *101* desert region of C Australia
Simunye *540* NE Swaziland
Sinai *230* Ar. Shibh Jazīrat Sīnā'. Desert region of NE Egypt
Sinazongwe *635* S Zambia
Sincelejo *195* NW Colombia
Sinchwang *see* Hsinchuang
Sin Cowe Island *652* island of SW Spratly Islands
Sindh *451* administrative region of SE Pakistan
Sindhulimadi *427* C Nepal
Sindi *240* SW Estonia
Sine *510* river of W Senegal
Sinendé *132* N Benin
Sines *474* S Portugal
Sinfra *326* C Ivory Coast
Singa *536* var. Sinjah, Sinja. E Sudan
Singapore *517* river of S Singapore
Singapore *516-517* officially Republic of Singapore. Country of SE Asia divided into 5 admin. units (districts). ❖ Singapore City
Singapore Strait *386, 517* var. Strait of Singapore. Strait connecting Strait of Malacca and South China Sea
Singatoka *see* Sigatoka
Sîngerei *408* var. Sângerei, prev. Lazovsk. N Moldova
Singida *560* C Tanzania
Singora *see* Songkhla
Sining *see* Xining
Sinj *209* SE Croatia
Sinjavina *630* var. Sinjajevina. Mountain range of N Montenegro, Yugoslavia
Sinkiang Uighur Autonomous Region *see* Xinjiang Uygur Zizhiqu
Sinnamary *645* N French Guiana
Sinnûris *230* var. Sinnūris. N Egypt
Sino *see* Greenville
Sinoe *see* Greenville
Sinoia *see* Chinhoyi
Sinoie, Lacul *480* prev. Lacul Sinoe. Lagoon of E Romania
Sinop *577* N Turkey
Sinp'o *349* N North Korea
Sintien *see* Hsintien
Sint-Niklaas *127* Fr. St.-Nicolas. N Belgium
Sintra *474* prev. Cintra. W Portugal
Sint-Truiden *127* Fr. St.-Trond. E Belgium

Sinŭiju *349* W North Korea
Sinyang *see* Xinyang
Sió *290* river of W Hungary
Sion *546* Ger. Sitten. SW Switzerland
Siorapaluk *646* NW Greenland
Sioux City *599* Iowa, C USA
Sioux Falls *599* South Dakota, NC USA
Sipaliwini *538* river of S Suriname
Siparia *570* SW Trinidad, Trinidad & Tobago
Siphofaneni *540* var. Sipofaneni. C Swaziland
Siping *187* var. Ssu-p'ing, Szeping, prev. Ssu-p'ing-chieh. Jilin, NE China
Siple *90* US research station of South Orkney Islands, Antarctica
Siput *386* var. Sungei Siput. NW Peninsular Malaysia
Siquirres *206* E Costa Rica
Siracusa *321* Eng. Syracuse. Sicilia, S Italy
Sirajganj *117* N Bangladesh
Şīr Banī Yās *590* island of W United Arab Emirates
Sirdaryo *see* Syr Darya
Sir Edward Pellew Group *101* island group of N Australia
Siret *480* var. Siretul, Ger. Sereth. River of Romania and Ukraine
Sir Francis Drake Channel *643* channel connecting the Atlantic Ocean and Caribbean Sea, C British Virgin Islands
Sirte *see* Surt
Sirte, Gulf of *see* Surt, Khalij
Şirvan Düzü *110* Rus. Shirvanskaya Step'. Mountain range of C Azerbaijan
Sirwan *see* Diyālá
Sisak *209* Hung. Sziszek, Ger. Sissek. N Croatia
Sisian *98* SE Armenia
Sisimiut *646* var. Holsteinsborg. SW Greenland
Sisŏphŏn *165* NW Cambodia
Sissek *see* Sisak
Sīstān, Daryācheh-ye *307* var. Hāmūṣāberī, Daryācheh-ye Hāmūn. Lake of E Iran
Sisters, The *276* islands N of Grenada island, Grenada
Siteki *540* var. Stegi. E Swaziland
Sithoniá *273* peninsula of NE Greece
Sitobela *540* S Swaziland
Sitona *238* SW Eritrea
Sitrah *115* var. Sitra. Island of NE Bahrain
Sittang *159* var. Sittoung. River of C Burma
Sittard *429* S Netherlands
Sitten *see* Sion
Sittwe *159* prev. Akyab. W Burma
Siuna *436* NE Nicaragua
Sivas *577* C Turkey
Sivers'kyy Donets' *see* Donets
Six Counties, the *see* Northern Ireland
Siyäzän *110* Rus. Siazan'. NE Azerbaijan
Sjælland *218* Ger. Seeland, Eng. Zealand. Island of E Denmark
Skadar *see* Shkodër
Skadarsko Jezero *see* Scutari, Lake
Skagaströnd *294* prev. Höfdhakaupstadhur. N Iceland
Skagen *218* Jylland, N Denmark
Skagerrak *218, 444, 543* var. Skagerak. Area of the Baltic Sea
Skalica *519* Hung. Sellye. W Slovakia
Skeleton Coast *423* coastal region of NW Namibia
Skellefteå *543* NE Sweden
Skellefteälv *543* river of N Sweden
Skien *444* S Norway
Skikda *83* prev. Philippeville. NE Algeria
Skive *218* Jylland, NW Denmark
Skjálfandafljót *294* river of C Iceland
Skjern *218* Jylland, W Denmark
Skjern Å *218* river of W Denmark
Skon *165* S Cambodia
Skopje *381* prev. Skoplje, Turk. Üsküb. ❖ of FYR Macedonia, N FYR Macedonia

Skoplje *see* Skopje
Skövde *543* S Sweden
Skrunda *362* W Latvia
Skúvoy *644* island of C Faeroe Islands
Skye, Isle of *593* island of W Scotland, UK
Skýros *273* island of E Greece
Slagelse *218* Sjælland, SE Denmark
Slaney *314* Ir. An tSláine. River of SE Ireland
Slatina *see* Podravska Slatina
Slatina *480* S Romania
Slave Coast *567* coastal region of W Africa, Atlantic Ocean
Slavonska Požega *209* prev. Požega, Hung. Pozsega. NE Croatia
Slavonski Brod *209* prev. Brod, Hung. Bród. E Croatia
Slavyansk *see* Slov"yans'k
Sléibhte Chill Mhantáin *see* Wicklow Mountains
Slēmānī *see* As Sulaymānīyah
Sliema *395* N Malta
Sligo *314* Ir. Sligeach. N Ireland
Sliven *152* var. Slivno. E Bulgaria
Slobozia *480* SE Romania
Slobozia *408* Rus. Slobodzeya. E Moldova
Slonim *122* Rus. Slonin. W Belarus
Slovakia *518-519* officially Slovak Republika, prev. constituent republic of Czechoslovakia. Country of C Europe divided into 4 admin. regions (kraj). ❖ Bratislava
Slovenia *520-521* officially Republic of Slovenia, Slvn. Slovenija. Country divided into 86 admin. units (občina). ❖ Ljubljana
Slovenské Rudohorie *519* Ger. Slowakisches Erzgebirge, var. Ungarisches Erzgebirge. Mountain range of C Slovakia
Slov'yans'k *586* Rus. Slavyansk. E Ukraine
Słupsk *471* Ger. Stolp. N Poland
Slutsk *122* C Belarus
Smallwood Reservoir *171* lake of S Canada
Smarhon' *122* NW Belarus
Smederevo *630* Ger. Semendria. N Serbia, Yugoslavia
Smila *586* C Ukraine
Smith's Island *643* island of E Bermuda
Smithson Bight *644* bay of the Indian Ocean on the S coast of Christmas Island
Smolensk *484* W Russia
Smolyan *152* var. Smoljan, prev. Pashmakli. SW Bulgaria
Smyrna *see* İzmir
Snaefell *647* mountain of C Isle of Man
Snake *598* river of NW USA
Sneeuw-gebergte *see* Maoke, Pegunungan
Snežka *216* Ger. Schneekoppe. Mountain of N Czech Republic
Snow Mountains *see* Maoke, Pegunungan
Snug Corner *276* SW Grenada island, Grenada
Snuŏl *165* E Cambodia
Soacha *195* C Colombia
Sobaek-sanmaek *350* mountain range of S South Korea
Sobat *536* river of Ethiopia and Sudan
Sobradinho, Represa de *145* var. Barragem de Sobradinho. Reservoir of E Brazil
Soča *321, 520* It. Isonzo. River of Italy and Slovenia
Socabaya *463* SE Peru
Sochi *484* SW Russia
Société, Archipel de la *646* island group of W French Polynesia
Socotra *see* Suquṭrá
Soc Trăng *623* var. Khanh, Hung. S Vietnam
Sodankylä *249* N Finland
Södertälje *543* SE Sweden
Sodiri *536* var. Sawdirī, Sodari. C Sudan
Sodo *243* var. Soddo, Soddu. SW Ethiopia
Soekaboemi *see* Sukabumi

Soela Väin *240* strait of Baltic Sea, between the islands of Hiiumaa and Saaremaa, W Estonia
Soembawa *see* Sumbawa
Soerabaja *see* Surabaya
Soerakarta *see* Surakarta
Sofala, Baía de *419* Bay of Indian Ocean, off Mozambique
Sofia *382* seasonal river of NW Madagascar
Sofia *152* var. Sofija, Bul. Sofiya. ❖ of Bulgaria, W Bulgaria
Sogamoso *195* C Colombia
Sognefjorden *444* fjord of SW Norway
Sohâg *230* var. Sawhaj. C Egypt
Sŏjosŏn-man *349* inlet of Korea Bay, on W coast of N Korea
Sokch'o *350* N South Korea
Söke *577* SW Turkey
Sokhumi *262* Rus. Sukhumi. NW Georgia
Sokodé *567* C Togo
Sokolov *216* NW Czech Republic
Sokoto *440* NW Nigeria
Sokoto *440* river of NW Nigeria
Sola *444* SW Norway
Solapur *296* var. Sholapur. SW India
Sol, Costa del *531* coastal region of S Spain
Soldeu *86* NE Andorra
Soledad *619* E Venezuela
Soledad *195* N Colombia
Soleure *see* Solothurn
Soligorsk *see* Salihorsk
Solimões *145* local name for a stretch of the Amazon river, NW Brazil
Solin *209* It. Salona. S Croatia
Solingen *264* W Germany
Sollum, Gulf of *230* Ar. Khalīj as Sallūm. Gulf of the Mediterranean Sea, NW Egypt
Sololá *278* W Guatemala
Solomon Islands *522-523* prev. British Solomon Islands Protectorate. Country of the South Pacific Ocean divided into 7 admin. units (provinces). ❖ Honiara
Solomon Sea *458, 522* sea of the Pacific Ocean, to the E of Papua New Guinea
Solothurn *546* Fr. Soleure. NW Switzerland
Solun *see* Thessaloníki
Solway Firth *593* arm of the Irish Sea, W UK
Solwezi *635* NW Zambia
Soma *261* C Gambia
Somalia *524-525* officially Somali Democratic Republic, prev. Somaliland Protectorate, Italian Somaliland. Country of E Africa divided into 16 admin. units (regions). ❖ Mogadishu
Sombor *630* Hung. Zombor. NW Serbia, Yugoslavia
Somerset *643* Somerset Island, W Bermuda
Somerset Island *643* island of W Bermuda
Somerset Island *170* island of N Canada
Somerset Nile *see* Victoria Nile
Someş *290, 480* Hung. Szamos, Ger. Samosch. River of Hungary and Romania
Sŏmjin *350* Jap. Senshin-kō. River of S South Korea
Somme *253* river of N France
Somosomo *246* Taveuni, N Fiji
Somotillo *436* W Nicaragua
Somoto *436* NW Nicaragua
Soná *456* SW Panama
Sonaco *282* NE Guinea-Bissau
Sonda des Vieques *651* bay of the Caribbean Sea, E Puerto Rico
Sønderborg *218* Ger. Sonderburg. Als, S Denmark
Søndre Strømfjord *see* Kangerlussuaq
Songea *560* S Tanzania
Songhua Jiang *see* Sungari
Sŏngjin *see* Kimch'aek
Songkhla *563* Mal. Singora. S Thailand

Sŏngnam *350 var.* Seongnam. NW South Korea
Songnim *349* SW North Korea
Songo *419* NW Mozambique
Sông Tiên Giang *see* Mekong
Songwe *385* river of Malawi and Tanzania
Sonmiāni Bay *451* bay of the Arabian Sea, on the S coast of Pakistan
Sonsonate *235* W El Salvador
Sonsorol Islands *455* island group of Palau
Soochow *see* Suzhou
Soomaaliya *see* Somalia
Soome Laht *see* Finland, Gulf of
Sop Hao *359* NE Laos
Sopron *290 Ger.* Ödenburg. NW Hungary
Sôp Xai *359* NE Laos
Sórd Choluim Chille *see* Swords
Soria *531* N Spain
Soriano *607* W Uruguay
Soro *see* Ghazal
Sorø *218* Sjælland, SE Denmark
Soroca *408 Rus.* Soroki. N Moldova
Sorocaba *145* S Brazil
Sorol *406* atoll of W Micronesia
Soroti *584* C Uganda
Sørøya *444 var.* Sørøy. Island of N Norway
Sŏsan *350 Jap.* Zuisan. W South Korea
Sosnowiec *471 Ger.* Sosnowitz. S Poland
Sota *132* river of NE Benin
Sotavento, Ilhas de *176* southernmost of the two main island groups comprising Cape Verde
Sotouboua *567* C Togo
Souanké *200* NW Congo
Soubré *326* S Ivory Coast
Soueida *see* As Suwaydā'
Soufrière *224* S Dominica
Soufrière *497* W St Lucia
Soufrière Hills *649* mountain range, E Montserrat
Souillac *400* S Mauritius
Souk Ahras *83* NE Algeria
Soukhné *see* As Sukhnah
Sŏul *see* Seoul
Sound, The *543 Swe.* Öresund, *Nor.* Øresund. Strait between Denmark and Sweden, connecting the Baltic Sea and Kattegat
Soûr *364 var.* Şūr. SW Lebanon
Sousse *573 var.* Sūsah. N Tunisia
South Africa *526-529* officially Republic of South Africa. Country of southern Africa, divided into 9 admin. units (provinces). ❖ Pretoria, Cape Town, Bloemfontein
Southampton *593* S England, UK
Southampton Island *171* island of N Canada
South Andaman *296* island of the Andaman Islands, SE India
South Australia *101* state of S Australia
South Bend *599* Indiana, C USA
South Caicos *653* island of C Turks and Caicos Islands
South Carolina *599* state of SE USA
South Carpathians *see* Carpaţii Meridionali
South China Sea *386, 466, 517, 555 Ind.* Laut Cina Selatan, *Chin.* Nan Hai, *Vtn.* Biên Đông. Sea of the Pacific Ocean
South Comino Channel *see* Malta, Il-Fliegu ta'
South Dakota *599* state of NC USA
South East China *190* region of SE China
Southeast Island *see* Tagula Island
South East Point *652* headland on the E coast of Ascension Island
Southend-on-Sea *593* SE England, UK
Southern Alps *433* mountains of N South Island, New Zealand
Southern Cook Islands *644* island group of S Cook Islands
Southern Uplands *593* mountain range of S Scotland, UK
South Hill Village *642* C Anguilla

South Huvadhu Atoll *390 var.* Gaafu Dhaalu Atoll. Atoll of S Maldives
South Island *644 var.* Pulu Atas. Island of SE Cocos Islands
South Island *433* southernmost of the two main islands that comprise New Zealand
South Island *342* NW Kenya
South Korea *350-353* officially Republic of South Korea, *Kor.* Taehan. Country of E Asia divided into 9 admin. units (provinces). ❖ Seoul
South Maalhosmadulu Atoll *390 var.* Baa Atoll. Atoll of N Maldives
South Miladummadulu Atoll *390* atoll of N Maldives
South Nilandhe Atoll *390 var.* Dhaalu Atoll. Atoll of C Maldives
South Orkney Islands *90* island group to the NE of Antarctic Peninsula, Antarctica
South Point *652* headland on the S coast of Ascension Island
South Point *644* headland on the S coast of Christmas Island
South Rukuru *385* river of NW Malawi
South Saskatchewan *170* river of SW Canada
South Shetland Islands *90* island group to the W of Antarctic Peninsula, Antarctica
South Sound *643* Virgin Gorda, E British Virgin Islands
South Taranaki Bight *433* area of the Tasman Sea, SW of North Island, New Zealand
South Town *644* Little Cayman, C Cayman Islands
South Uist *593* island of Outer Hebrides, NW Scotland, UK
South West Bay *652* bay of the South Atlantic Ocean on the SW coast of Ascension Island
Sowa *142 var.* Sua. NE Botswana
Soweto *527* Pretoria-Witwatersrand-Vereeniging, NE South Africa
Soyang-ho *350* reservoir of N South Korea
Sozh *122* river of NE Europe
Spain *530-533* officially Kingdom of Spain, *Sp.* España. Country of SW Europe divided into 18 admin. units (autonomous communities, comprised of 50 provinces). ❖ Madrid
Spalato *see* Split
Spaldings *329* C Jamaica
Spanish Point *92* S Barbuda, Antigua & Barbuda
Spanish Town *643* Virgin Gorda, E British Virgin Islands
Spanish Town *329* S Jamaica
Spanish Wells *112* Eleuthera I, Bahamas
Spartanburg *599* South Carolina, SE USA
Spárti *273 Eng.* Sparta. S Greece
Speedwell Island *645* island of S Falkland Islands
Speery Island *652* island of SW St Helena
Speightstown *121* N Barbados
Spence Bay *170* N Canada
Spencer Gulf *101* gulf of S Australia
Spey *593* river of NE Scotland, UK
Spice Islands *see* Maluku
Spiez *546* W Switzerland
Spijkenisse *429* SW Netherlands
Spīn Būldak *77* S Afghanistan
Spišská Nová Ves *519 Ger.* Zipser Neudorf, *Hung.* Igló. E Slovakia
Spitak *98* NW Armenia
Spitsbergen *653* island of NW Svalbard
Spittal an der Drau *106 var.* Spittal. S Austria
Split *209 It.* Spalato. S Croatia
Spokane *598* Washington, NW USA
Spot Bay *644* Cayman Brac, NE Cayman Islands
Spratly Island *652* island of Spratly Islands
Spratly Islands *652* Disputed island group of the South China Sea

Spree *265* river of E Germany
Springfield *599* Illinois, C USA
Springfield *599* Massachusetts, NE USA
Springfield *599* Missouri, C USA
Spring Garden *284* NE Guyana
Springs *527* Pretoria-Witwatersrand-Vereeniging, NE South Africa
Springs *276* SW Grenada island, Grenada
Srbija *see* Serbia, Yugoslavia
Srê Âmbêl *165* SW Cambodia
Srebrenica *140* E Bosnia & Herzegovina
Sredna Gora *152* mountain range of Bulgaria
Srednesibirskoye Ploskogor'ye *485 Eng.* Central Siberian Plateau, *var.* Central Siberian Uplands. Large upland area of C Russia
Sreng *165* river of NW Cambodia
Srêpôk *165* river of Cambodia and Vietnam
Sri Jayawardenapura *534 prev.* Kotte. Suburb of Colombo and admin. ❖ of Sri Lanka, W Sri Lanka
Sri Lanka *534-535* officially Democratic Socialist Republic of Sri Lanka, *prev.* Ceylon. Country of South Asia divided into 25 admin. units (districts). ❖ Colombo
Srimongal *117* E Bangladesh
Srīnagar *296* N India
Ssu-ch'uan *see* Sichuan
Ssu-p'ing *see* Siping
Ssu-p'ing-chieh *see* Siping
Stacklen *see* Strenči
Stadskanaal *429* NE Netherlands
Stäfa *546* N Switzerland
Stalin *see* Brașov
Stalin *see* Varna
Stalinabad *see* Dushanbe
Stalingrad *see* Volgograd
Stalino *see* Donets'k
Stalin Peak *see* Garmo, Qullai
Stalin Peak *see* Musala
Stalinsk *see* Novokuznetsk
Stampriet *423* S Namibia
Stamsund *444* NE Norway
Stange *444* S Norway
Stanislav *see* Ivano-Frankivs'k
Stanke Dimitrov *see* Dupnitsa
Stanley *645 var.* Port Stanley. ❖ of Falkland Islands, East Falkland, Falkland Islands
Stanley *see* Chek Chue
Stanley Pool *200, 203 var.* Pool Malebo. Expanded section of the Congo river between Congo and Congo (Zaire)
Stanleyville *see* Kisangani
Stann Creek *see* Dangriga
Stanovoye Nagor'ye *485* mountain range of E Russia
Staten Island *see* Estados, Isla de los
Station Hill *121* SW Barbados
Stavanger *444* SW Norway
Stavropol' *484 prev.* Voroshilovsk. SW Russia
Stavropol' *see* Tol'yatti
Stavropol'sky Kray *484* administrative region of SW Russia
Steels Point *650* headland of E Norfolk Island
Stefanie, Lake *342 see* Ch'ew Bahir
Steffisburg *546* W Switzerland
Stegi *see* Siteki
Stein *see* Kamnik
Steinamanger *see* Szombathely
Steinkjer *444* C Norway
Steirisch *106* mountain range of C Austria
Stendal *265* C Germany
Stende *362* NW Latvia
Stepanakert *see* Xankändi
Step'anavan *98* N Armenia
Sterlitamak *484* W Russia
Stettin *see* Szczecin
Stettiner Haff *see* Oderhaff

Stewart Island *433* island to the S of South Island, New Zealand
Steyr *106* N Austria
Stif *see* Sétif
Štip *381* E FYR Macedonia
Stirling *593* C Scotland, UK
Stjørdal *444* C Norway
Stockerau *106* NE Austria
Stockholm *543* ❖ of Sweden, SE Sweden
Stockton-on-Tees *593* NE England, UK
Stoelmanseiland *538* E Suriname
Stoke-on-Trent *593* C England, UK
Stolp *see* Słupsk
Stonyhill Point *652* headland on the S coast of Tristan da Cunha
Stony Tunguska *see* Podkamennaya Tunguska
Stóra Dímun *644* island of S Faeroe Islands
Storebælt *218 Eng.* Great Belt, *var.* Store Bælt. Channel between Fyn and Sjælland Denmark
Store Heddinge *218* Sjælland, E Denmark
Støren *444* C Norway
Storfjorden *653* area of the Greenland Sea, S Svalbard
Stornoway *593* Isle of Lewis, Outer Hebrides, NW Scotland, UK
Strakonice *216* SW Czech Republic
Stralsund *265* N Germany
Stranraer *593* SW Scotland, UK
Strasbourg *253 Ger.* Strassburg. NE France
Strǎşeni *408 var.* Strasheny. C Moldova
Strassburg *see* Strasbourg
Stratford-upon-Avon *593* C England, UK
Strenči *362 Ger.* Stacklen. NE Latvia
Streymoy *644 var.* Strømø. Island of N Faeroe Islands
Strickland *458* river of W Papua New Guinea
Strimón *273 Bul.* Struma. River of Bulgaria and Greece
Struer *218* Jylland, W Denmark
Struga *381* SW FYR Macedonia
Struma *152 Gk* Strimón. River of Bulgaria and Greece
Strumeshnitsa *see* Strumica
Strumica *381* E FYR Macedonia
Strumica *381 var.* Strumitsa, *Bul.* Strumeshnitsa. River of Bulgaria and FYR Macedonia
Strumitsa *see* Strumica
Stuart Peak *527* mountain of Central Marion Island, South Africa
Stubbs *498* SE St Vincent, St Vincent & the Grenadines
Studen Kladenets, Yazovir *152* reservoir of Bulgaria
Stuhlweissenburg *see* Székesfehérvár
Štúrovo *519 prev.* Parkan, *Hung.* Párkány. S Slovakia
Stuttgart *264, 269* SW Germany
Stykkishólmur *294* W Iceland
Sua *see* Sowa
Suao *555 Jap.* Suō. NE Taiwan
Subic Bay *466* bay of South China Sea, Luzon, N Philippines
Subotica *630 Hung.* Szabadka, *Ger.* Maria-Theresiopel. N Serbia, Yugoslavia
Suceava *480 Ger.* Suczawa. NE Romania
Suchow *see* Suzhou
Sucre *136* ❖ (judicial & legal) of Bolivia, S Bolivia
Suczawa *see* Suceava
Sudan *536-537* officially Republic of Sudan, *prev.* Anglo-Egyptian Sudan. Country of NE Africa divided into 9 admin. units (states). ❖ Khartoum
Sudan *157* physical region of C Africa, composed of desert region, plains and grassy steppes
Sudbury *171* S Canada
Sudd *536* swamp region of S Sudan
Suddie *284* NE Guyana
Sudeten *216, 471 var.* Sudetenland, Sudetes, Sudetic Mountains, *Cz./Pol.* Sudety. Mountain range of Czech Republic and Poland
Sudharam *see* Noākhāli

Sudhuroy *644 var.* Suderø. Island of S Faeroe Islands

Sudhuroyarfjørdhur *644* strait between Sudhuroy and Sandoy, C Faeroe Islands

Sudong, Pulau *517* island of SW Singapore

Sudostroy *see* Severodvinsk

Sue *536* river of S Sudan

Sue Wood Bay *643* bay of the North Atlantic Ocean, C Bermuda

Suez *230 Ar.* As Suways, *var.* El Suweis. NE Egypt

Suez Canal *230 Ar.* Qanāt as Suways. Canal of NE Egypt

Suez, Gulf of *230 Ar.* Khalīj al 'Aqabah. Gulf of the Red Sea, to the NE of Egypt

Sūf *336* NW Jordan

Sugar Loaf *276 var.* Levera Island. N of Grenada island, Grenada

Şuḩār *448 var.* Sohar. NW Oman

Sühbaatar *412* N Mongolia

Suigen *see* Suwŏn

Suir *314 Ir.* An tSiúir. River of S Ireland

Sukabumi *302 prev.* Soekaboemi. Java, C Indonesia

Sukagawa *330* Honshū, N Japan

Sukarnapura *see* Jayapura

Sukarno, Puntjak *see* Jaya, Puncak

Sukhne *see* As Sukhnah

Sukhumi *see* Sokhumi

Suki *536* E Sudan

Sukkertoppen *see* Maniitsoq

Sukkur *451* S Pakistan

Sukuta *261* W Gambia

Sulaimaniya *see* As Sulaymānīyah

Sulaimān Range *451* mountain range of C Pakistan

Sula, Kepulauan *302 prev.* Xulla Islands, Soela. Island group to the E of Celebes, E Indonesia

Sulawesi *see* Celebes

Sulawesi, Laut *see* Celebes Sea

Sulby *647* N Isle of Man

Sullana *463* NW Peru

Sullivan Island *see* Lanbi Island

Sultan Alonto, Lake *see* Lanao, Lake

Sulu Archipelago *466* island group of SW Philippines

Sulu Sea *387, 466* sea of the Pacific Ocean, to the NE of Borneo, Malaysia

Sulyukta *357 Kir.* Sülüktü. SW Kyrgyzstan

Sumatera *see* Sumatra

Sumatra *302 var.* Sumatera. Island of W Indonesia

Šumava *see* Bohemian Forest

Sumba *644* Sudhuroy, S Faeroe Islands

Sumba *302 prev.* Soemba, *Eng.* Sandalwood Island. Island of Nusa Tenggara, C Indonesia

Sumba, Selat *302* strait of the Indian Ocean between Sumba and Sumbawa, C Indonesia

Sumbawa *302 prev.* Soembawa. Island of Nusa Tenggara, C Indonesia

Sumbawanga *560* W Tanzania

Sumbe *88 Port.* Novo Redondo. W Angola

Sumbuya *514* S Sierra Leone

Šumen *see* Shumen

Sumisu-jima *330* island to the SE of Honshū, SE Japan

Šumperk *216 Ger.* Mährisch-Schönberg. E Czech Republic

Sumpul *235* river of Honduras and El Salvador

Sumqayıt *110 Rus.* Sumgait. E Azerbaijan

Sumy *586* NE Ukraine

Sunan *349* SW North Korea

Sunch'ŏn *349* SW North Korea

Sunch'ŏn *350 Jap.* Junten. S South Korea

Sunda, Selat *302* strait connecting Indian Ocean and Laut Jawa between Java and Sumatra, W Indonesia

Sunderland *593* NE England, UK

Sundsvall *543* C Sweden

Sungai Seletar Reservoir *517* reservoir of N Singapore

Sungari *187 Chin.* Songhua Jiang. River of NE China

Sun Koshi *427* river of E Nepal

Suntar-Khayata, Khrebet *485* mountain range of NE Russia

Sunyani *270* W Ghana

Sunzu *635* mountain NE Zambia

Suŏ *see* Suao

Suomenlahti *see* Finland, Gulf of

Suomenselkä *249* physical region of C Finland

Suŏng *165* SE Cambodia

Superior de Tristaina, Estany *86* lake of NW Andorra

Superior, Lake *171, 599 Fr.* Lac Supérieur. Lake of Canada and USA

Sup'ung-ho *349* reservoir of China and North Korea

Sūq 'Abs *see* 'Abs

Sūq ash Shuyūkh *310* SE Iraq

Suqrah Bay *448* Bay of the Arabian Sea, SE Oman

Suquṭrá *627 Eng.* Socotra. Island of SE Yemen, off the Horn of Africa

Şūr *448* NE Oman

Surabaya *302 prev.* Surabaja, Soerabaja. Java, C Indonesia

Surakarta *302 prev.* Soerakarta. Java, C Indonesia

Šurany *519 Hung.* Nagysurány. SW Slovakia

Sūrat *296* W India

Surat Thani *563* S Thailand

Sûre *378* river of W Europe

Sure, Lagh *342* dry watercourse of NE Kenya

Surin *563* E Thailand

Surinam *400* S Mauritius

Suriname *538-539* officially Republic of Surinam, *var.* Suriname. Country of Central America divided into 8 admin. units (provinces). ❖ Paramaribo

Surinam *121* E Barbados

Surkhet *see* Birendranagar

Surkhob *558* river of C Tajikistan

Şurmān *371* NW Libya

Surt *371 var.* Sidra, Sirte. N Libya

Surt, Khalīj *371 var.* Gulf of Sirte, Gulf of Sidra. Gulf of the Mediterranean Sea, off N coast of Libya

Sūsah *see* Sousse

Susana *282* W Guinea-Bissau

Susuman *485* Ostrov Sakhalin, E Russia

Sutlej *451* river of India and Pakistan

Suure-Jaani *240 Ger.* Gross-Sankt-Johannis. C Estonia

Suur Munamägi *240 var.* Munamägi. Mountain of SE Estonia

Suur Väin *240* strait of the Baltic Sea, between the mainland and the island of Muhu, W Estonia

Suva *246* ❖ of Fiji, Viti Levu, W Fiji

Suwa *238* SE Eritrea

Suwarrow *644* island of Northern Cook Islands, N Cook Islands

Suwayhān *590* E United Arab Emirates

Suways, Qanāt as *see* Suez Canal

Suwŏn *350 var.* Suweon, *Jap.* Suigen. NW South Korea

Suzhou *187 var.* Soochow, Su-chou, Suchow, *prev.* Wuhsien. Jiangsu, E China

Suzuka *330* Honshū, C Japan

Svalbard *653* Norwegian dependency of the Greenland Sea

Svätý Kríž nad Hronom *see* Žiar nad Hronom

Svay Chék *165* river of Cambodia and Thailand

Svay Riĕng *165* SE Cambodia

Svendborg *218* Fyn, S Denmark

Sverdlovsk *see* Yekaterinburg

Sverdrup Islands *170* island group of N Canada

Sveti Nikole *381 prev.* Sveti Nikola. C FYR Macedonia

Svetlogorsk *see* Svyetlahorsk

Svetozarevo *630 prev.* Jagodina. C Serbia, Yugoslavia

Svilengrad *152 prev.* Mustafa-Pasha. SE Bulgaria

Svínoy *644 var.* Svinø. Island of NE Faeroe Islands

Svishtov *152 var.* Svištov. N Bulgaria

Svitavy *216* E Czech Republic

Svyetlahorsk *122 Rus.* Svetlogorsk. SE Belarus

Swabian Jura *see* Schwäbische Alb

Swakopmund *423* W Namibia

Swallow Islands *522* small island group within Santa Cruz Is, E Solomon Is

Swan *100* river of SW Australia

Swansea *593 Wel.* Abertawe. S Wales, UK

Swatow *see* Shantou

Swaziland *540-541* officially Kingdom of Swaziland. Country of southern Africa divided into 4 admin. units (districts). ❖ Mbabane

Sweden *542-545* officially Kingdom of Sweden, *Swe.* Sverige. Country of Scandinavia divided into 24 admin. units (läns). ❖ Stockholm

Swedru *see* Agona Swedru

Swellendam *527* Western Cape, S South Africa

Swetes *92* S Antigua, Antigua & Barbuda

Swift Current *170* SW Canada

Swindon *593* C England, UK

Swiss Plateau *546 Ger.* Schweizer Mittelland. Plateau of W Switzerland

Switzerland *546-549* officially Swiss Confederation, *Ger.* Schweiz, *It.* Svizzera. Country of C Europe divided into 26 admin. units (cantons). ❖ Bern

Swords *314 Ir.* Sórd Choluim Chille. E Ireland

Syaphrubesi *427 var.* Syabrubensi. C Nepal

Sydney *101, 105* SE Australia

Sydney *171* Cape Breton Island, SE Canada

Sydney Island *see* Manra

Syktyvkar *484 prev.* Ust'-Sisol'sk. NW Russia

Sylhet *117* NE Bangladesh

Syowa *90* Japanese research station of Greater Antarctica, Antarctica

Syracuse *599* New York, NE USA

Syracuse *see* Siracusa

Syr Darya *338, 558, 610 Rus.* Syrdar'ya, *Kaz.* Syrdariya, *Uzb.* Sirdaryo. River of C Asia

Syrdar'ya *610* E Uzbekistan

Syria *550-553* officially Syrian Arab Republic, *Ar.* Suriyah. Country divided into 13 admin. units (governorates). ❖ Damascus

Syriam *159* S Burma

Syrian Desert *310, 336, 551 Ar.* Bādiyat ash Shām. Desert of SW Asia

Syvash, Zatoka *586* inlet of the Sea of Azov

Szabadka *see* Subotica

Szamos *see* Someş

Szatmárnémeti *see* Satu Mare

Szczecin *471 Ger.* Stettin. NW Poland

Szczeciński, Zalew *see* Oderhaff

Szechuan *see* Sichuan

Szeged *290 Ger.* Szegedin. SE Hungary

Székesfehérvár *290 Ger.* Stuhlweissenburg. W Hungary

Szekszárd *290* S Hungary

Szenice *see* Senica

Szentes *290* SE Hungary

Szeping *see* Siping

Szered *see* Sereď

Sziszek *see* Sisak

Szlatina *see* Podravska Slatina

Szolnok *290* C Hungary

Szombathely *290 Ger.* Steinamanger. W Hungary

Sztálinváros *see* Dunaújváros

T

Tabac, River *400* river of S Mauritius

Ṭabaqah *551* N Syria

Tabaquite *570* C Trinidad, Trinidad & Tobago

Tabarka *573 var.* Ṭabarqah. NW Tunisia

Tabasará, Serranía de *456* mountain range of W Panama

Tabasco *see* Grijalva

Tabernacle *494* NE St Kitts, St Kitts & Nevis

Tabiteuea *346* island of the Gilbert Is, W Kiribati

Tablas Island *466* island of C Philippines

Table Hill Gordon *92* SE Antigua, Antigua & Barbuda

Tabligbo *567* SE Togo

Tábor *216* SW Czech Republic

Tabora *560* W Tanzania

Tabou *326 var.* Tabu. S Ivory Coast

Tabrīz *307* NW Iran

Tabuaeran *346 var.* Fanning Island. Island of the Line Is, E Kiribati

Tabūk *506* NW Saudi Arabia

Tabwémasana *615* mountain of Espiritu Santo, W Vanuatu

Täby *543* SE Sweden

Tachia Hsi *555* river of W Taiwan

Tachoshui *555* E Taiwan

Tacloban *466* Leyte, E Philippines

Tacna *463* SE Peru

Tacoma *598* Washington, NW USA

Tacuarembó *607* N Uruguay

Tacuarembó *607* river of C Uruguay

Tacurupucú *see* Hernandarias

Tademaït, Plateau du *83* plateau of C Algeria

Tadine *650* Maré, Îles Loyauté, E New Caledonia

Tadjoura *222* E Djibouti

Tadjoura, Golfe de *222* inlet of the Gulf of Aden, E of Djibouti

T'aebaek-sanmaek *350* mountain range of South Korea

Taedong *349* river of C North Korea

Taegu *350 var.* Daegu, *Jap.* Taikyū. SE South Korea

Taehan-haehyŏp *see* Korea Strait

Taejŏn *350 Jap.* Taiden. C South Korea

Tafahi *568* island of N Tonga

Tafí Viejo *95* NW Argentina

Taftlund *218* Jylland, SW Denmark

Taga *500* Savai'i, Samoa

Taganrog, Gulf of *586 Ukr.* Tahanroz'ka Zatoka, *Rus.* Taganrogskiy Zaliv. Gulf of the Sea of Azov, SE Ukraine

Tagarzimat *414* W Western Sahara

Tagiura *see* Tājūrā'

Tagliamento *321* river of N Italy

Tagtabazar *see* Takhta-Bazar

Taguasco *210* C Cuba

Taguatinga *145* C Brazil

Tagula Island *458 prev.* Southeast I. Island of SE Papua New Guinea

Tagum *466* river of Mindanao, S Philippines

Tahanroz'ka Zatoka *see* Taganrog, Gulf of

Tahat *83* mountain of SE Algeria

Tahiti *646* island of W French Polynesia

Tahoua *439* W Niger

Taia *514* river of C Sierra Leone

Taiama *514* C Sierra Leone

T'aichung *555 Jap.* Taichū. W Taiwan

Taiden *see* Taejŏn

Taieri *433* river of S South Island, New Zealand

Taihoku *see* Taipei

T'aihsi *555* W Taiwan

Tai Hu *187* lake of E China

Taikyū *see* Taegu

T'ainan *555 Jap.* Tainan. SW Taiwan

Taipa *648* Taipa, C Macao

Taipa *648* island of C Macao

Taipa - Coloane Causeway *648* bridge between Taipa and Coloane islands, S Macao

Trou-du-Nord *286* N Haiti
Troumaka *498* NW St Vincent,
St Vincent & the Grenadines
Troyan *152 var.* Trojan.
NW Bulgaria
Troyes *253* NE France
Tršćanski Zaljev *see* Trieste, Gulf of
Trst *see* Trieste
Truc Giang *see* Bên Tre
Trucial Coast *590* coastal region
of the United Arab Emirates
Trucial States
see United Arab Emirates
Trujillo *288* N Honduras
Trujillo *463* NW Peru
Trujillo *619* NW Venezuela
Trung Phân *623 prev.* Annam. Cultural
region of Vietnam
Trunk Island *643* island of
C Bermuda
Truro *593* SW England, UK
Trutnov *216 Ger.* Trautenau.
NE Czech Republic
Tržaški Zaliv *see* Trieste, Gulf of
Tržič *520 Ger.* Neumarktl.
NW Slovenia
Trzynietz *see* Třinec
Tsabong *see* Tshabong
Tsaghkahovit *98* W Armenia
Tsamkong *see* Zhanjiang
Tsangpo *see* Brahmaputra
Tsaratanana, Tangorombohitr' i *382*
var. Massif du Tsaratanana.
Mountains of N Madagascar
Tsarigrad *see* İstanbul
Tsaritsyn *see* Volgograd
Tschakathurn *see* Čakovec
Tschenstochau *see* Częstochowa
Tschernembl *see* Črnomelj
Tschorna *see* Mustvee
Tselinograd *see* Akmola
Tsengwen Hsi *555* river of
SW Taiwan
Tsetserleg *412* W Mongolia
Tsévié *567* S Togo
Tshabong *142 var.* Tsabong.
SW Botswana
Tshane *142* C Botswana
Tshaneni *340* NE Swaziland
Tshangalele, Lac *see* Lufira,
Lac de Retenue de la
Tshela *203* W Congo (Zaire)
Tshikapa *203* SW Congo (Zaire)
Tshohoha Sud, Lac *see* Cyohoha
Sud, Lac
Tshuapa *203* river of C Congo (Zaire)
Tsinan *see* Jinan
Tsing Hai *see* Qinghai Hu
Tsinghai *see* Qinghai
Tsingtao *see* Qingdao
Tsingyuan *see* Baoding
Tsinkiang *see* Quanzhou
Tsiroanomandidy *382*
C Madagascar
Tsiteli-Tskaro *see* Dedoplistsqaro
Tsitsihar *see* Qiqihar
Tskhinvali *262* C Georgia
Tsna *122* river of S Belarus
Tsodilo Hills *142* mountain range
of NW Botswana
Tsoelike *366* SE Lesotho
Tsu *330* Honshū, C Japan
Tsuchiura *330* Honshū, SE Japan
Tsugaru-kaikyō *330* strait connecting
the Sea of Japan and Pacific Ocean,
between Hokkaidō and Honshū,
N Japan
Tsumeb *423* N Namibia
Tsumkwe *423* NE Namibia
Tsuruga *330* Honshū, C Japan
Tsuruoka *330* Honshū, N Japan
Tsushima *330* island group to the
W of Honshū, W Japan
Tsushima Strait *330 var.* Korea Strait.
Strait connecting the Sea of Japan
and East China Sea, between South
Korea and Japan
Tsuyama *330* Honshū, W Japan
Tuamotu, Îles *646* island group of
N French Polynesia
Tuasivi *500* Savai'i, Samoa
Tuban, Wādī *627* dry watercourse of
S Yemen
Tubmanburg *368* NW Liberia
Ṭubruq *371 Eng.* Tobruk, *It.* Tobruch.
NE Libya
Tucker's Town *643* E Bermuda

Tuckum *see* Tukums
Tucson *598* Arizona, SW USA
Tucumán *see* San Miguel de Tucumán
Tucupita *619* E Venezuela
Tucuruí, Represa de *145* reservoir
of N Brazil
Tudmur *551 var.* Tadmur,
Eng. Palmyra. C Syria
Tugalan *see* Kolkhozobod
Tuira *456* river of SE Panama
Tukangbesi, Kepulauan *302* island
group to the SE of Celebes,
C Indonesia
Tu-k'ou *see* Panzhihua
Ṭūkrah *371* NE Libya
Tukums *362 Ger.* Tuckum. W Latvia
Tukuyu *560* S Tanzania
Tula *642* Tutuila, W American Samoa
Tula *484* W Russia
Tulaghi *522* Florida I. Solomon Islands
Tulcán *228* N Ecuador
Tulcea *480* E Romania
Tuléar *see* Toliara
Tuli *see* Thuli
Tulkarm *317, 318* NW West Bank
Tulle *253* S France
Tulsa *599* Oklahoma, SC USA
Tulsipur *427* W Nepal
Tuluá *195* W Colombia
Tumaco *195* SW Colombia
Tumareng *284* NW Guyana
Tumba, Lac *see* Ntomba, Lac
Tumbes *463* NW Peru
Tumen *349 Rus.* Tumyntszyan. River of
China and North Korea
Tumpat *386* N Peninsular Malaysia
Tumuc-Humac Mountains *145*
Port. Serra Tumuc-Humac. Mountain
range of N South America
Tumuc-Humac, Serra *see*
Tumuc-Humac Mountains
Tunapuna *570* N Trinidad, Trinidad
& Tobago
Tunduru *560* S Tanzania
Tundzha *152 var.* Tundža. River of
Bulgaria and Turkey
Tungabhadra *296* river of S India
Tungaru *346 prev.* Gilbert Islands.
Island group of W Kiribati
Tungkang *555 var.* Tung-chiang, *Jap.*
Tōkō. SW Taiwa
Tungshih *555 Jap.* Tōsei. W Taiwan
Tung-t'ing Hu *see* Dongting Hu
Tunis *573 var.* Tūnis. of Tunisia,
NE Tunisia
Tunis, Golfe de *573* gulf of the
Mediterranean Sea on the NE coast
of Tunisia
Tunisia *572-575* officially Republic
of Tunisia. Country of North Africa
divided into 23 admin. units
(governorates). ❖ Tunis
Tunja *195* C Colombia
Tương Đương *623* NW Vietnam
Tupiza *136* S Bolivia
Turan Lowland *581, 610*
var. Turan Plain, *Rus.* Turanskaya
Nizmennost'. Plain of Turkmenistan
and Uzbekistan
Ṭurayf *506* N Saudi Arabia
Turbat *450* W Pakistan
Turčiansky Svätý Martin
see Martin
Turda *480* NW Romania
Turgel *see* Türi
Tŭrgovishte *152 var.* Tărgovište,
prev. Eski Dzhumaya.
NE Bulgaria
Turgutlu *576* W Turkey
Türi *240 Ger.* Turgel. C Estonia
Turin *see* Torino
Turkana, Lake *243, 342 Eng.* Lake
Rudolf. Lake of E Africa
Turkestan *338 Kaz.* Türkistan.
S Kazakhstan
Turkestan Range *558*
Rus. Turkestanskiy Khrebet.
Mountain range of NW Tajikistan
Turkestanskiy Khrebet
see Turkestan Range
Turkey *576-577* officially Republic
of Turkey, *Turk.* Türkiye
Cumhuriyeti. Country of W Asia
divided into 73 admin. units.
❖ Ankara

Turkish Republic of Northern Cyprus
see Cyprus
Turkmenbashi *581 prev.* Krasnovodsk.
W Turkmenistan
Turkmenistan *580-581* officially
Republic of Turkmenistan,
prev. Turkmenskaya Soviet Socialist
Republic. Country divided into
4 admin. units (oblasts).
❖ Ashgabat
Turkmenskiy Zaliv *581*
Turkm. Türkmen Aylagy. Inlet of
the Caspian Sea, on the W coast
of Turkmenistan
Turks and Caicos Islands *653*
British dependent territory of
the Atlantic Ocean
Turks Islands *653* island group of
SE Turks and Caicos Islands
Turku *249 Swe.* Åbo. SW Finland
Turkwel *342* seasonal river of
NW Kenya
Turmero *619* N Venezuela
Turneffe Islands *130* islands of
E Belize
Turnhout *127* NE Belgium
Turning Basin *648* undersea feature
of the Pacific Ocean,
NW Johnston Atoll
Turnov *216* N Czech Republic
Turnu Severin
see Drobeta-Turnu Severin
Turócszentmárton *see* Martin
Turquino, Pico *210* mountain of
SE Cuba
Turrialba *206* E Costa Rica
Tursunzode *558 prev.* Regar.
W Tajikistan
Tŭrtkŭl' *610*
prev. Petroaleksandrovsk,
Rus. Turtkul.
W Uzbekistan
Turtle Islands *514* island group of
SW Sierra Leone
Tuscaloosa *599* Alabama, SE USA
Tuscan Archipelago
see Toscano, Arcipelago
Tuscany *325.* region of Italy
Tuticorin *296* S India
Tutong *150* NW Brunei
Tutong *150* river of C Brunei
Tutrakan *152* N Bulgaria
Tutuila *642* island of
W American Samoa
Tutume *142* E Botswana
Tuvalu *582-583 prev.* The Ellice
Islands. Country of
the Pacific Ocean.
❖ Fongafale
Tuvana-i-colo *246* island to the
S of the Lau Group, SE Fiji
Tuvana-i-ra *246* island to the
S of the Lau Group, SE Fiji
Tuva, Respublika *484* autonomous
republic of C Russia
Tuvuca *246 prev.* Tuvutha. Island of
the Lau Group, E Fiji
Ṭuwayq, Jabal *506* mountain range
of C Saudi Arabia
Tuxtla Gutiérrez *403 var.* Tuxtla.
SE Mexico
Tuy Hoa *623* SE Vietnam
Tuz Gölü *577 Eng.* Lake Tuz.
Lake of C Turkey
Tuz Khurmātū *310* N Iraq
Tuzla *140* NE Bosnia & Herzegovina
Tver' *484* W Russia
Tvøroyri *644 var.* Tverå. Suðuroy,
S Faeroe Islands
Twante *159* S Burma
Tweed *593* river of
SE Scotland, UK
Twin Falls *598* Idaho,
NW USA
Twizel *433* C South Island,
New Zealand
Tychy *471 Ger.* Tichau. S Poland
Tynda *485* E Russia
Tyne *593* river of NE England, UK
Tyneside *569*
Tyrnau *see* Trnava
Tyrol *see* Tirol
Tyrrhenian Sea *321 It.* Mare Tirreno.
Area of the Mediterranean Sea
Tyumen' *484, 489* C Russia
Tyup *357 var.* Tjup. NE Kyrgyzstan
Tzekung *see* Zigong

U

Uaco Cungo *88 var.* Waku Kungo,
Port. Santa Comba. C Angola
UAE *see* United Arab Emirates
Uamba *see* Wamba
Uanle Uen *see* Wanlaweyn
Ubangi *179, 200, 203 Fr.* Oubangui.
River of C Africa
Ubarts' *122* river of Belarus
and Ukraine
Ubayyiḍ, Wādī al *310* dry
watercourse of SW Iraq
Ube *330* Honshū, W Japan
Uberaba *145* S Brazil
Uberlândia *145* S Brazil
Ubin, Pulau *517* island of
NE Singapore
Ubon Ratchathani *563* E Thailand
Ucar *110 Rus.* Udzhary.
C Azerbaijan
Ucayali *463* river of C Peru
Uchquduq *610 Rus.* Uchkuduk. C
Uzbekistan
Udine *321* N Italy
Udmurtiya *484* autonomous republic
of W Russia
Udon Thani *563* N Thailand
Udzhary *see* Ucar
Ueda *330* Honshū, C Japan
Uele *203 var.* Welle. River of N Congo
(Zaire)
Ufa *484* W Russia
Ugāle *362* NW Latvia
Uganda *584-585* officially Republic
of Uganda. Country of E Africa
divided into 39 admin. units
(districts). ❖ Kampala
Ugum *647* river, S Guam
Uherské Hradiště *216*
Ger. Ungarisch-Hradisch.
SE Czech Republic
Úhlava *216 Ger.* Angel. River of
W Czech Republic
Uíge *88 Port.* Vila Marechal Carmona,
Carmona. NW Angola
'Uiha *568 var.* Uiha. Island of the
Ha'apai Group, Tonga
Ŭijŏngbu *350 Jap.* Giseifu. NW South
Korea
Uis *423* NW Namibia
Uitenhage *527* Eastern Cape, S South
Africa
Ujae *396* island of W Marshall Islands
Ujelang *396* island of W Marshall
Islands
Újgradiska *see* Nova Gradiška
'Ujman *see* Ajman
Ujungpandang *302 prev.* Makasar,
Macassar. Celebes, C Indonesia
Ujung Salang *see* Phuket
Újvidék *see* Novi Sad
UK *see* United Kingdom
Ukerewe *560* island of
NW Tanzania, situated at the S of
Lake Victoria
Uki Island *522* island of E Solomon Is
Ukmergė *376* E Lithuania
Ukraine *586-589* officially Republic of
Ukraine, *Ukr.* Ukrayina,
Rus. Ukraína, *prev.* Ukrainian Soviet
Socialist Republic, Ukrainskaya S.S.R.
Country of E Europe divided into
25 admin. units (24 regions and 1
republic). ❖ Kiev
Uku-jima *330* island of Gotō-rettō,
SW Japan
Ula *122 Rus.* Ulla. River of N Belarus
Ulaangom *412* NW Mongolia
Ulan Bator *412 var.* Ulaanbaatar.
❖ of Mongolia, C Mongolia
Ulan-Ude *485 prev.* Verkhneudinsk.
C Russia
Ulawa Island *522* island of
E Solomon Is
Uleåborg *see* Oulu
Uleälv *see* Oulujoki
Uleträsk *see* Oulujärvi
Uli *338* NW Kazakhstan
Uliastay *412* W Mongolia
Ulithi *406* atoll of W Micronesia
Ulla *see* Ula
Ullapool *593* N Scotland, UK

ACKNOWLEDGEMENTS

DORLING KINDERSLEY would like to express their thanks to the following individuals, companies and institutions for their help in preparing this atlas:

ADDITIONAL CARTOGRAPHY
Advanced Illustration (Congleton, UK)
Andrew Bright
Cosmographics (Watford, UK)
Malcolm Porter
Swanston Publishing (Derby, UK)
Andrew Thompson

DESIGN
Boyd Annison, Icon Solutions (Chesham, UK) *for Macintosh consultancy and chart templates*
Bruno Maag, Dalton Maag (London, UK) *for font consultancy and production*

RESEARCH AND REFERENCE
Dr D Alkhateeb, Organization of Petroleum Exporting Countries (OPEC, Vienna, Austria)
Amnesty International (London, UK)
Caroline Blunden
CNN International (New York, USA)
DATAQUEST EUROPE SA (PARIS, FRANCE)
CSL Davies
Department of Trade and Industry Export Market Information Centre (London, UK)
The Flag Institute (Chester, UK)
Foreign and Commonwealth Office (London, UK)
Alexander Fyges-Walker
Christel Heideloff, Institute of Shipping Economics and Logistics (Bremen, Germany)
International Bank for Reconstruction and Development (World Bank, Washington, DC, USA)
International Committee of the Red Cross (ICRC, Geneva, Switzerland)
International Civil Aviation Organization (ICAO, Montreal, Canada)
International Criminal Police Organization (INTERPOL, Lyon, France)

International Institute for Strategic Studies, for information from *The Military Balance* (London, UK)
International Boundaries Research Unit, University of Durham
Institute of Latin American Studies, University of London (London, UK)
Intermediate Technology Development Group (Rugby, UK)
Chris Joseph, United States Travel and Tourism Administration (USTTA, London, UK)
Latin American Bureau (London, UK)
Patrick Mahaffey, Ohio European Office (Brussels, Belgium)
Peter Mansfield
Robert Minton-Taylor
National Meteorological Library and Archive (Bracknell, UK)
Oil and Gas Journal (Houston, Texas)
Organization for Economic Cooperation and Development (OECD, Paris, France)
Penal Reform International (London, UK)
Matt Ridley
Screen Digest (London, UK)
William Smith, Chicago Sun-Times (Chicago, USA)
Tourism Concern (London, UK)
United Nations Crime Prevention and Criminal Justice Branch (UNCPC, Vienna, Austria)
United Nations Development Programme (UNDP, New York, USA)
United Nations Environment Programme (UNEP, Nairobi, Kenya)
United Nations Food and Agriculture Organization (UNFAO, Rome, Italy)
United Nations International Labour Organization (UNILO, Geneva, Switzerland)
United Nations Population Fund (UNFPA, New York, USA)
Westminster Reference Library (London, UK)
World Conservation Monitoring Centre (Cambridge, UK)
World Health Organization (WHO, Geneva, Switzerland)
World Tourism Organization (Madrid, Spain)

The many embassies, High Commissions, airports, national information and tourist offices in London and around the world.

PICTURE CREDITS

t=top, b=below, a=above, l=left, r=right, c=centre

Ancient Art & Architecture Collection: 44bcr; 45bl; 45cr; 47tc; G Tortoli 45tcb; **Arcaid:** P Mauss Esto 598bc; **Aspect Picture Library:** 202tr; Brian Seed 418c; D Bayes 370bl; Fiona Nichols 302tr; **Associated Press AP:** 243bcr; 487bl; 618tr; 651bcl; AFP 415bcr; Fabrice Coffrini 547cr; Aaron Favila 467crl; Guilherme Venancio 475bcr; Hans Edinger 267br; Michel Spingler 254bcr; Humberto Pradera/Agencia Estado 149cb; Bullit Marquez 191bl; Jan Bauer 269cb; Alexander Zemlianichenko 488cb; **Bridgeman Art Library, London/New York:** Hermitage, St Petersburg 46bc; Lauros - Giraudon / Château de Malmaison 48bc; National Maritime Museum, London 47br; Private Collection 48bcl; **D Donne Bryant Stock Picture Agency:** 461tc; Byron Augustin 436tr; **Dale Buckton:** 594br; **Camera Press:** 657crr; A Pucciano 95cr; F Goodman 649bca; H Andrews 627bcr; S Smith 243bcl; T Charlier 607bl; **The J Allan Cash Photolibrary:** 55tl; 106c; 116bc; 146br; 149tl; 168tr; 171tr; 259tr; 289tc; 306tr; 518br; 357cr; 542bl; 583tc; 586c; 458bc; 440tr; 451bc; 474tr; 566bc; **Bruce Coleman Ltd:** 498bl; B&C Calhoun 174bc; Dr MP Kahl 94tr; F Prenzel 104tc; Gerald Cubitt 88tr; Gerald Cubitt 242bc; Gordon Langsbury 260bc; J Fry 511tc; J Jurka 542bc; K. Maj 470c; Kim Taylor 515tr; L Lee Rue 91tl; LC Marigo 279tc; M Berge 396tr; MPL Fogden 462ca; O Langrand 370tr; P Davey 214bc; S Prato 272bc; **Colorific:** J Polleross / JB Pictures 78br; M Kreiner 54cl; M Rogers 536tr; Sandro Tucci 159bl; **Comstock:** 194bc, 24tl, 535tc; Tor Eigeland 399tc; **Corbis UK Ltd:** AFP 587bcl; AFP 487bcl; Bettmann 555tcr; Bob Krist 642br; Francoise de Mulder 141bc; Jack Fields 648bl; Jack Fields 650bl; James L Amos 647tr; Miki Kratsman 486br; Wally McNamee 600br; Nik Wheeler 175tc; Franz-Marc Frei 259cb; Peter Wilson 325cb; Joseph Sohm 603bl; **James Davis Travel Photography:** 144bl; 145tl; 218c; 248bc; 528bc; 579tl; 390tr; 401tc; 411tl; 428bc; 432bc; 493tc; 494bl; 498b; 502tr; 550bc; 558tr; 586tr; 601tr; 626bl; 643cr; Prisma 86cla; Prisma / Schwarz 226tr; S Begawan 151tl; S Thingeyjar 295tc; World View - Fotootheek Amsterdam 177tc; **E.T. Archive:** 44bl; 49bl; 49cr; 511tcl; **Mary Evans Picture Library:** 47bl, 47brb; **Chris Fairclough Colour Library:** 51tcr; 575tl; 572br; **Robert Harding Picture Library:** 76tr; 180c; 225tl; 271tc; 280bl; 291tr; 510tr; 334bl; 356bc; 449tc; 466tr; 480tr; 484tr; 501tc; 513tc; A Woolfitt 114bc; C Martin 264bc; C Rennie 580ca; D Hughes 257bc; Explorer 377tc; Explorer / Roy 110tr; F Dubes 148bl; Frerck / Odyssey 402tr; G Hellier 217tr; G Hellier 518tr; G Roli 444tr; Gascoine 610bl; P Craven 252tr; Photri 222ca; R Rainford 593tl; Rosehaven Management Ltd 655ccr; Sassoon 134cb; Sassoon 262cl; **Paul Harris Photography:** Paul Harris Photography 491bl; **Hulton Getty:** 50bc; 51br; 53br; **Robert Hunt Library:** 55tc; **Hutchison Library:** 136bl; 369tc; 596bc; 636tr; Andrew Hill 634bc; Bernard Gérard 259bc; Christine Pemberton 210tr; J Henderson 284ca; JG Fuller 650bcr; L Taylor 484bl; M Macintyre 568ca; Robert Francis 560tr; Trevor Page 524ca; **Image Bank:** 594bl; A Rippy 186tr; G Jung 576tr; GA Rossi 646bl; M Beebe 209cl; ME Newman 522tr; P Trummer 250tr; T Madison 187br; **Images Colour Library:** 426bl; **Image Select:** Ann Ronan 42bc; **Impact Photos:** A le Garsmeur 412ca; Alain leGarsmeur 175bl; Ben Edwards 450tr; C Penn 584tr; G-J Norman 354tr; J Arthur 526tcr; Mark Henley 188tr; Robin Lubbock 254tr; Ben Edwards 301bl; Lionel Derimais 355bl; B Babarov/Vika 489bl; **David King Collection:** 55tcb **Magnum:** H Cartier-Bresson 55tcb; **Novosti:** 123bcr;

Panos Pictures: B Tobiasson 327bc; Chris Stowers 331bl; D Hulcher 358tr; Jeremy Hartley 156bc; Marc French 287tc; Morris Carpenter 365bc; Neil Cooper 130tc; R Giling 538tr; S Sprague 160tr; Sean Sprague 136c; Penny Tweedie 105tc; Michael Harvey 149cl; John Miles 190tr;.JC Tordai 518cl; 535tc; 488tr; 597cb; 602bl; **Pa News Photo Library:** 445cr; AFP 419cbl; AFP / M Clement 573tcr; AFP / M Shoraf 551br; **Popperfoto:** 51trb; 52br; 55bl; AFP / Armand 54br; Apichart Weerawong 563tr; David Mercado / Reuters 137crl; EPA Photo 137crl; Will Burgess / Reuters 105bl; Reuters 269cl; Sunil Malhorta / Reuters 301tc; Jeremy Piper / Reuters 102bcr; John Cobb / Reuters 343tr; Kamal Kishore / Reuters 298crb; Mohamed Hami / Reuters 231bcr; Official U.S. Air Force Photo 55cr; Oleg Popov / Reuters 153bcc; Shamil Zhumatov / Reuters 559bcr; **Reuters:** 125bcl, 146tcr; 507br; **Rex Features:** 116tcbr; 159bcl; 172bcr; 172crb; 188br; 249tr; 254crb; 273tcr; 273tr; 291bcl; 291bcr; 559bcl; 481cbr; 486bcr; 516bl; 526tr; 543tcl; 587tcr; 587tr; 594tca; 594tr; 611bc; 627bcl; Andy Hernandez 488cl, J Sutton Hibbert 597tc; Paul Brown 602tcr; David Hartley / F Stevens 211bcl; Farnood 307tcr; Francisco Arias 182tr; Gamma 107bcr; Ken McKay 551tr; Peter Broker 451tr; Peter Heimsath 481cr; Sipa-Press 303bcr; Sipa-Press 77tcr; Sipa-Press 85bcl; Sipa-Press 95cbr; Sipa-Press 127bcl; Sipa-Press 188bcr; Sipa-Press 511tc; Sipa-Press 316br; Sipa-Press 429tcl; Sipa-Press 445tc; Sipa-Press 508tcl; Sipa-Press 631bcr; Sipa-Press 645bl; Tony Kyriacou 351bcl; Torregano 419tcl; Viennareport 577trb;**Harry Smith Collection:** 46clb, **South American Pictures:** Jevan Berrange 206br; T Morrison 606tr; **Sovfoto/Eastfoto:** 652br; **Frank Spooner Pictures:** 53bl; 85bl; 322bc;543tcr; 543tr; 607bcl; A Denize 371tcr; A Sassaki 146car; A Sassaku 146tr; Alain Morvan 503bcl; Alain Morvan / Gamma 547c; Alexis Duclos 182tcr; Arnaud 153bcl; Bob Stern / Liason 241tr; C Angel 618tcr; C Hires 551bcr; C Poulet 647cr; Eric Vandeville 195tcr; Ferry - Liaison 463tcl; Tim Crosby / Gamma - Liaison 602ct; Gamma 195tcr; Gamma 254cb; Gamma 471tr; Gamma / B Iverson 251bcl; Gamma / CH Vioujard 415bcl; Gamma / E de Keerle 471tcr; Gamma / F Apesteguy 507bcr; Gamma / Iliona - Figaro Magazine 113tc; Gamma / JC Aunos 316bcr; Gamma / K Al Arab 573tcl; Gamma / K Kuukka 249tcr; Gamma / L Chaperon 266cbr; Gamma / Liason / Anderson 351bcr; Gamma / N Jallot 408tr; Gamma / Najer 387bcr; Gamma / R Gaillarder 475bcl; Gamma / Xinhua 188bcl; Georges Merillon 441bcl; KJ Eddy 107bcl; L Anticoli 322cbr; Liaison / B Asoto 467cr; Liason / Peterson 441bcr; Liason / Markel 637tcl; Loviny 165tcr; N Sagansky 205cr; P Perrin 311tcr; P Piel 266bcr; Patrick Piel 266bra; Photonews / Gamma 205bcl; Reglain 165tr; Stills / Ponopresse 172cbr; Victoria Brynner 451tcr; W Christopher 600bcr; **Tony Stone Images:** 179bc; 198tr; 352bl; 444br; A Cassidy 500br; Alan Kearney 182tr; Alan Smith 362c; C Waite 592bc; D Armand 172tr; D Hanson 562bl; D Schultz 50bl; Dennis Stone 542tr; G Allison 605bl; H Kurihara 268bc; J Pragen 616tr; Joe Cornish 315bc; Marcus Brooke 158tr; O Benn 93tc; 277tr; P Chesley 406ca; Penny Tweedie 584bc; R Evans 152tr; R. Everts 415tr; R Smith 102tr; R Smith 229tl; S Egan 550tr; S Egan 546tr; Steven Rothfeld 593tcc; **Sygma:** Baldev 348ca; R Reuter 502bl; **Telegraph Colour Library:** 100tr; Ford Motor Company Ltd 52clb; **Topham Picturepoint:** 153tc; 256tr; 358tl; 525cl; 571tr; 453cal; 478bc; 487tr; 504bc; 642c; Keystone 522cbl; Universal Pictorial Press 332cbl; **Trip:** 506bl; G Spenceley 580tr; T Goodman 283tc; V Shuba 122c; V Sidoropolev 358tr; **World Pictures:** 85cla; 520bl; 422ca; 554tr; **Zefa Picture Library:** 80bc; 120bl; 200ca; 526bl; 570bc; 618bl; Everts 630ca; F Lanting 142tr; Streichan 266bl.

729

NOTES

This book has its own website. For the very latest information, visit
www.dk.com/world-desk-reference

NOTES

This book has its own website. For the very latest information, visit
www.dk.com/world-desk-reference

NOTES

This book has its own website. For the very latest information, visit
www.dk.com/world-desk-reference

NOTES

NOTES

This book has its own website. For the very latest information, visit
www.dk.com/world-desk-reference

NOTES

This book has its own website. For the very latest information, visit
www.dk.com/world-desk-reference

NOTES

This book has its own website. For the very latest information, visit
www.dk.com/world-desk-reference